The Pocket Oxford Italian Dictionary

Edited by Lexus with

Debora Mazza

D0034088

Oxford   New York

OXFORD UNIVERSITY PRESS

1997

Oxford University Press, Great Clarendon Street, Oxford OX2 6DP

Oxford New York

*Athens Auckland Bangkok Bogota Bombay
Buenos Aires Calcutta Cape Town Dar es Salaam
Delhi Florence Hong Kong Istanbul Karachi
Kuala Lumpur Madras Madrid Melbourne
Mexico City Nairobi Paris Singapore
Taipei Tokyo Toronto
and associated companies in
Berlin Ibadan*

Oxford is a trade mark of Oxford University Press

© *Oxford University Press 1997*

First published 1997

*British Library Cataloguing in Publication Data
Data available*

*Library of Congress Cataloging in Publication Data
Data available*
ISBN 0–19–860008–9 (hardback edition)
ISBN 0–19–860007–0 (paperback edition)

*Printed in Great Britain by
Mackays plc
Chatham, Kent*

Contents/Indice

Preface/Prefazione ... iv

Introduction/Introduzione ... v

Pronunciation of Italian/Pronuncia italiana ... vi

Pronunciation of English/Pronuncia inglese ... vii

Abbreviations/Abbreviazioni ... viii - ix

Italian-English/Italiano-inglese ... 1 - 314

English-Italian/Inglese-italiano ... 1 - 373

Italian verb tables/Verbi italiani ... 375-378

English verb tables/Verbi inglesi ... 379-380

Editors/Redazione

Debora Mazza   Jane Goldie

Donatella Boi   Francesca Logi   Peter Terrell

Sonia Tinagli-Baxter   Carla Zipoli

Allan Cameron   Michela Masci   Ilaria Panuccio

Copy editors/Segreteria di redazione

Alice Grandison   Mary Rigby   Daphne Trotter

Project management by/A cura di

LEXUS

Preface

This new addition to the Oxford range of Italian dictionaries has been designed to meet the needs of students, tourists and all those who require quick and reliable answers to their translation questions. It provides clear guidance on selecting the most appropriate translation, illustrative examples to help with construction and usage, and precise information on grammar and style.

Focussing on everyday, idiomatic Italian and English, both spoken and written, this easy-to-use dictionary also offers generous treatment of business and computing vocabulary. Its up-to-the-minute coverage and wealth of accurate translations make it an ideal reference tool and study aid.

Prefazione

Questo nuovo dizionario, che viene ad aggiungersi alla serie dei dizionari inglese-italiano della Oxford, è stato creato per soddisfare le esigenze degli studenti, dei turisti e di tutti coloro che hanno bisogno di risposte rapide e sicure ai problemi di traduzione. Il lettore viene guidato con chiarezza nella scelta del termine più appropriato, con esempi di uso della lingua e con indicazioni precise di grammatica e di stile.

Basandosi sull'uso dell'inglese e dell'italiano contemporaneo, sia scritto che parlato, questo dizionario di facile consultazione dedica particolare attenzione al lessico dell'informatica e degli affari. Estremamente attuale e aggiornato, e grazie all'abbondante e precisa terminologia, rappresenta uno strumento di consultazione ideale e un valido sussidio didattico.

Introduction

Here is some basic information on the way the entries in this dictionary are organized.

A swung dash ~ is used to replace the headword within the entry.

Compounds are listed in alphabetical order. Remember this when looking for a word. The entry 'password', for example, is entered alphabetically – at some distance from the entry 'pass'. Likewise 'paintbrush' and 'paintpot' will have 'painter', 'pain threshold' and 'painting' entered in between.

Indicators are provided to guide the user to the best translation for a specific sense of a word. Types of indicator are:

field labels (see the list on pp viii-ix), which indicate a general area of usage (commercial, computing, photography etc);

sense indicators, eg: **bore** *n* ⟨*of gun*⟩ calibro *m*; ⟨*person*⟩ seccatore, -trice *mf*;

typical subjects of verbs, eg: **bond** *vt* ⟨*glue:*⟩ attaccare;

typical objects of verbs, placed after the translation of the verb, eg: **boost** *vt* stimolare ⟨*sales*⟩; sollevare ⟨*morale*⟩;

nouns that typically go together with certain adjectives, eg: **rich** *a* ricco; ⟨*food*⟩ pesante.

A solid black circle means that the same word is being translated as a different part of speech, eg. **partition** *n* ... ● *vt* ...

A solid black square is used to identify phrasal verbs, eg ■ **strip down** *vt* ... Phrasal verbs are listed in alphabetical order directly after the main verb. So 'strip down' comes after 'strip' and before 'strip cartoon'.

English pronunciation is given for the Italian user in the International Phonetic Alphabet (see p vii).

Italian stress is shown by a ' placed in front of the stressed syllable in a word.

Square brackets are used around parts of an expression which can be omitted without altering the sense.

Introduzione

Ecco le informazioni essenziali su come sono organizzate le voci nel dizionario.

Un trattino ondulato ~ è utilizzato al posto del lemma all'interno della voce.

I vocaboli composti sono in ordine alfabetico. È importante ricordarlo quando si cerca la parola che interessa. La voce 'password', ad esempio, essendo in ordine alfabetico, compare a una certa distanza dopo la voce 'pass'. Per la stessa ragione fra 'paintbrush' and 'paintpot' compaiono 'painter', 'pain threshold' e 'painting'.

Degli indicatori vengono forniti per indirizzare l'utente verso la traduzione corrispondente al senso voluto di una parola. I tipi di indicatori sono:

etichette semantiche (vedi la lista a pp viii-ix), indicanti l'ambito specifico in cui la parola viene generalmente usata in quel senso (commercio, informatica, fotografia ecc);

indicatori di significato, es.: **redazione** *nf* ⟨*ufficio*⟩ editorial office; ⟨*di testi*⟩ editing;

soggetti tipici di verbi, es.: **trovarsi** *vr* ⟨*luogo:*⟩ be;

complementi oggetti tipici di verbi, collocati dopo la traduzione dello stesso verbo, es: **superare** *vt* overtake ⟨*veicolo*⟩; pass ⟨*esame*⟩;

sostantivi che ricorrono tipicamente con certi aggettivi, es.: **solare** *a* ⟨*energia, raggi*⟩ solar; ⟨*crema*⟩ sun.

Un pallino nero indica che la stessa parola viene tradotta come una diversa parte del discorso, es. **calcolatore** *a* ... ● *nm* ...

Un quadratino nero viene utilizzato per indicare i phrasal verbs, ad esempio: ■ **strip down** *vt* ... I phrasal verbs si trovano in ordine alfabetico immediatamente dopo il verbo principale. Così 'strip down' viene subito dopo 'strip' e subito prima di 'strip cartoon'.

La pronuncia inglese è data usando l'Alfabetico Fonetico Internazionale (vedi p vii).

L'accento tonico nelle parole italiane è indicato dal segno ' collocato davanti alla sillaba accentata.

Delle parentesi quadre racchiudono parti di espressioni che possono essere omesse senza alterazioni di senso.

Pronunciation of Italian

Vowels:

a	is broad like *a* in *father*: **casa**.
e	has two sounds: closed like *ey* in *they*: **sera**; open like *e* in *egg*: **sette**.
i	is like *ee* in *feet*: **venire**.
o	has two sounds: closed like *o* in *show*: **bocca**; open like *o* in *dog*: **croma**.
u	is like *oo* in *moon*: **luna**.

When two or more vowels come together each vowel is pronounced separately: **buono**; **baia**.

Consonants:

b, **d**, **f**, **l**, **m**, **n**, **p**, **t**, **v** are pronounced as in English. When these are double they are sounded distinctly: **bello**.

c	before **a**, **o** or **u** and before consonants is like *k* in *king*: **cane**.
	before **e** or **i** is like *ch* in *church*: **cena**.
ch	is also like *k* in *king*: **chiesa**.
g	before **a**, **o**, or **u** is hard like *g* in *got*: **gufo**.
	before **e** or **i** is like *j* in *jelly*: **gentile**.
gh	is like *g* in *gun*: **ghiaccio**.
gl	when followed by **a**, **e**, **o**, **u** is like *gl* in *glass*: **gloria**.
gli	is like *lli* in *million*: **figlio**.
gn	is like *ni* in *onion*: **bagno**.
h	is silent.
ng	is like *ng* in *finger* (not *singer*): **ringraziare**.
r	is pronounced distinctly.
s	between two vowels is like *s* in *rose*: **riso**.
	at the beginning of a word it is like *s* in *soap*: **sapone**.
sc	before **e** or **i** is like *sh* in *shell*: **scienza**.
z	sounds like *ts* within a word: **fazione**; like *dz* at the beginning: **zoo**.

The stress is shown by the sign ' printed before the stressed syllable.

Pronuncia Inglese

SIMBOLI FONETICI

Vocali e dittonghi

æ bad	ʊ put	aʊ now
ɑ: ah	u: too	aʊə flour
e wet	ə ago	ɔɪ coin
ɪ sit	ɜ: work	ɪə here
i: see	eɪ made	eə hair
ɒ got	əʊ home	ʊə poor
ɔ: door	aɪ five	
ʌ cup	aɪə fire	

Consonanti

b boy	l leg	t ten
d day	m man	tʃ chip
dʒ page	n new	θ three
f foot	ŋ sing	ð this
g go	p pen	v verb
h he	r run	w wet
j yes	s speak	z his
k coat	ʃ ship	ʒ pleasure

Note: ' precede la sillaba accentata.
La vocale nasale in parole quali *nuance* è indicata nella trascrizione
fonetica come õ: njuːõs.

Abbreviations/Abbreviazioni

adjective	*a*	aggettivo
abbreviation	*abbr*	abbreviazione
administration	*Admin*	amministrazione
adverb	*adv*	avverbio
aeronautics	*Aeron*	aeronautica
American	*Am*	americano
anatomy	*Anat*	anatomia
archaeology	*Archaeol*	archeologia
architecture	*Archit*	architettura
attributive	*attrib*	attributo
astrology, astronomy	*Astr*	astrologia, astronomia
automobiles	*Auto*	automobile
auxiliary	*aux*	ausiliario
biology	*Biol*	biologia
botany	*Bot*	botanica
British English	*Br*	inglese britannico
Chemistry	*Chem*	chimica
commerce	*Comm*	commercio
computers	*Comput*	informatica
conjunction	*conj*	congiunzione
cooking	*Culin*	cucina
definite article	*def art*	articolo determinativo
	ecc	eccetera
economics	*Econ*	economia
electricity	*Electr*	elettricità
et cetera	*etc*	
feminine	*f*	femminile
familiar	*fam*	familiare
figurative	*fig*	figurato
finance	*Fin*	finanza
formal	*fml*	formale
geography	*Geog*	geografia
geology	*Geol*	geologia
grammar	*Gram*	grammatica
humorous	*hum*	umoristico
indefinite article	*indef art*	articolo indeterminativo
interjection	*int*	interiezione
interrogative	*inter*	interrogativo
invariable	*inv*	invariabile
(*no plural form*)		
journalism	*Journ*	giornalismo
law	*Jur*	legge/giuridico
literary	*liter*	letterario
masculine	*m*	maschile
mathematics	*Math*	matematica
mechanics	*Mech*	meccanica

medicine	*Med*	medicina
meteorology	*Metereol*	meteorologia
masculine or feminine	*mf*	maschile o femminile
military	*Mil*	militare
music	*Mus*	musica
noun	*n*	sostantivo
nautical	*Naut*	nautica
old use	*old*	antiquato
pejorative	*pej*	peggiorativo
personal	*pers*	personale
photography	*Phot*	fotografia
physics	*Phys*	fisica
plural	*pl*	plurale
politics	*Pol*	politica
possessive	*poss*	possessivo
past participle	*pp*	participio passato
prefix	*pref*	prefisso
preposition	*prep*	preposizione
present tense	*pres*	presente
pronoun	*pron*	pronome
psychology	*Psych*	psicologia
past tense	*pt*	tempo passato
	qcno	qualcuno
	qcsa	qualcosa
proprietary term	®	marca depositata
rail	*Rail*	ferrovia
reflexive	*refl*	riflessivo
religion	*Relig*	religione
relative pronoun	*rel pron*	pronome relativo
somebody	*sb*	
school	*Sch*	scuola
singular	*sg*	singolare
slang	*sl*	gergo
something	*sth*	
suffix	*suff*	suffisso
technical	*Techn*	tecnico
telephone	*Teleph*	telefono
theatrical	*Theat*	teatrale
television	*TV*	televisione
typography	*Typ*	tipografia
university	*Univ*	università
auxiliary verb	*v aux*	verbo ausiliare
intransitive verb	*vi*	verbo intransitivo
reflexive verb	*vr*	verbo riflessivo
transitive verb	*vt*	verbo transitivo
transitive and intransitive	*vt/i*	verbo transitivo e intransitivo
vulgar	*vulg*	volgare
cultural equivalent	≈	equivalenza culturale

Aa

a (*ad before vowel*) *prep* to; (*stato in luogo, tempo, età*) at; (*con mese, città*) in; (*mezzo, modo*) by; **dire qcsa a qcno** tell sb sth; **alle tre** at three o'clock; **a vent'anni** at the age of twenty; **a Natale** at Christmas; **a dicembre** in December; **ero al cinema** I was at the cinema; **vivo a Londra** I live in London; **a due a due** two by two; **a piedi** on *o* by foot; **maglia a maniche lunghe** long-sleeved sweater; **casa a tre piani** house with three floors; **giocare a tennis** play tennis; **50 km all'ora** 50 km an hour; **2 000 lire al chilo** 2,000 lire a kilo; **al mattino/alla sera** in the morning/evening; **a venti chilometri/due ore da qui** twenty kilometres/two hours away

'abaco *nm* abacus

a'bate *nm* abbot

abbacchia'mento *nm fam* dejection

abbacchi'ato *a fam* dejected, downhearted

ab'bacchio *nm* [young] lamb. **~ alla romana** spring lamb

abbaci'nare *vt* dazzle, blind; *fig* deceive

abbagli'ante *a* dazzling ● *nm* headlight; **mettere gli abbaglianti** put the headlights on full beam

abbagli'are *vt* dazzle

ab'baglio *nm* blunder; **prendere un ~** make a blunder

abbaia'mento *nm* barking

abbai'are *vi* bark

abba'ino *nm* dormer window; (*mansarda*) loft

abbando'nare *vt* abandon; leave (*luogo*); give up (*piani ecc*); **~ il campo** *Mil* desert in the face of the enemy

abbando'narsi *vr* let oneself go; **~ a** give oneself up to (*ricordi ecc*)

abbando'nato *a* abandoned

abban'dono *nm* abandoning; *fig* abandon; (*stato*) neglect

abbarbi'carsi *vr* **~ a** cling to

abbassa'mento *nm* (*di temperatura, acqua, prezzi*) drop

abbas'sare *vt* lower; turn down (*radio, TV*); **~ i fari** dip the headlights

abbas'sarsi *vr* stoop; (*sole ecc:*) sink; *fig* demean oneself

ab'basso *adv* below ● *int* down with

abba'stanza *adv* enough; (*alquanto*) quite; **~ nuovo** newish; **ne ho ~!** I've had enough!, I'm fed up!

ab'battere *vt* demolish; shoot down (*aereo*); put down (*animale*); topple (*regime*); (*fig: demoralizzare*) dishearten

ab'battersi *vr* (*cadere*) fall; *fig* be discouraged. **~ a terra/al suolo** fall down

abbatti'mento *nm* (*morale*) despondency

abbat'tuto *a* despondent, down-in-the-mouth

abba'zia *nf* abbey

abbelli'mento *nm* embellishment

abbel'lire *vt* embellish

abbel'lirsi *vr* adorn oneself

abbeve'rare *vt* water

abbevera'toio *nm* drinking trough

abbicci *nm inv fig* rudiments *pl*; **l'~ di** the ABC of

abbi'ente *a* well-to-do

abbi'etto *a* despicable, abject

abbiglia'mento *nm* clothes *pl*; (*industria*) clothing industry, rag trade. **~ da bambino** children's wear. **~ da donna** ladies' wear. **~ per uomo** menswear

abbigli'are *vt* dress

abbigli'arsi *vr* dress up

abbina'mento *nm* combining

abbi'nare *vt* combine; match (*colori*)

abbindo'lare *vt* cheat

abbocca'mento *nm* interview; (*conversazione*) talk

abboc'care *vi* bite; (*tubi:*) join; *fig* swallow the bait

abboc'cato *a* (*vino*) fairly sweet

abbof'farsi = **abbuffarsi**

abbona'mento *nm* subscription; (*ferroviario ecc*) season-ticket; **fare l'~** take out a subscription. **~ all'autobus** bus pass. **~ mensile** monthly ticket. **~ alla televisione** television licence

abbo'nare *vt* make a subscriber

abbo'narsi *vr* subscribe (**a** to); take out a season-ticket (**a** for) (*teatro, stadio*)

abbo'nato, -a *nmf* subscriber

abbon'dante *a* abundant; (*quantità*) copious; (*nevicata*) heavy; (*vestiario*) roomy; **~ di** abounding in

abbondante'mente *adv* (*mangiare*) copiously

abbon'danza *nf* abundance

abbon'dare *vi* abound

abbor'dabile *a* (*persona*) approachable; (*prezzo*) reasonable

abbor'daggio *nm Mil* boarding

abbor'dare *vt* board (*nave*); approach (*persona*); (*fam: attaccar bottone a*) chat up; tackle (*compito ecc*)

abbotto'nare *vt* button up

abbotto'nato *a fig* tight-lipped

abbottona'tura *nf* [row of] buttons; **con ~**

da donna/uomo ⟨*giacca*⟩ that buttons on the left/right

abboz'zare *vt* sketch [out]; **~ un sorriso** give a little smile ● *vi fam* (*rassegnarsi*) resign oneself

ab'bozzo *nm* sketch

abbracci'are *vt* embrace; hug, embrace ⟨*persona*⟩; take up ⟨*professione*⟩; *fig* include

ab'braccio *nm* hug

abbrevi'are *vt* shorten; (*ridurre*) curtail; abbreviate ⟨*parola*⟩

abbreviazi'one *nf* abbreviation

abbron'zante *nm* suntan lotion

abbron'zare *vt* bronze; tan ⟨*pelle*⟩

abbron'zarsi *vr* get a tan

abbron'zato *a* tanned

abbronza'tura *nf* [sun]tan

abbrusto'lire *vt* toast; roast ⟨*caffè ecc*⟩

abbruti'mento *nm* brutalization

abbru'tire *vt* brutalize; ⟨*lavoro:*⟩ stultify

abbru'tirsi *vr* become brutalized

abbuf'farsi *vr fam* stuff oneself

abbuf'fata *nf fam* blowout

abbuo'nare *vt* reduce; *fig* overlook ⟨*mancanza, errore*⟩

abbu'ono *nm* allowance; *Sport* handicap

abdi'care *vi* abdicate

abdicazi'one *nf* abdication

aber'rante *a* aberrant

aberrazi'one *nf* aberration

abe'taia *nf* wood of fir trees

a'bete *nm* fir

abi'etto *a* despicable

abiezi'one *nf* degradation

abige'ato *nm Jur* cattle-stealing, rustling

'abile *a* able; (*idoneo*) fit; (*astuto*) clever

abilità *nf inv* ability; (*idoneità*) fitness; (*astuzia*) cleverness

abili'tante *a* **corso ~** [officially recognized] training course

abili'tare *vt* qualify

abili'tato *a* qualified

abilitazi'one *nf* qualification; (*titolo*) diploma

abil'mente *adv* ably; (*con astuzia*) cleverly

abis'sale *a* abysmal

a'bisso *nm* abyss

abi'tabile *a* inhabitable

abitabilità *nf* fitness for human habitation; **licenza di ~** *document certifying that a building is fit for human habitation*

abi'tacolo *nm Auto* passenger compartment

abi'tante *nmf* inhabitant

abi'tare *vi* live

abi'tato *a* inhabited ● *nm* built-up area

abitazi'one *nf* house; **crisi delle abitazioni** housing problem

abi'tino *nm Relig* scapular

'abito *nm* (*da donna*) dress; (*da uomo*) suit; **abiti** *pl* clothes. **~ da ballo** ball dress. **~ da cerimonia** formal dress. **~ da cocktail** cocktail dress. **~ mentale** mentality. **'~ scuro'** (*su inviti*) 'black tie'. **~ da sera** evening dress. **~ talare** cassock. **~ da uomo** suit

abitu'ale *a* usual, habitual

abitual'mente *adv* usually

abitu'are *vt* accustom

abitu'arsi *vr* **~ a** get used to

abitu'ato *a* **~ a** used to

abitudi'nario, -a *a* of fixed habits ● *nmf* person of fixed habits

abi'tudine *nf* habit; **d'~** usually; **per ~** out of habit; **avere l'~ di fare qcsa** be in the habit of doing sth; **abitudini** *pl* customs

abiu'rare *vt* renounce

abla'tivo *nm* ablative

abluzi'oni *nfpl* **fare le ~** wash

abnegazi'one *nf* self-sacrifice

ab'norme *a* abnormal

abo'lire *vt* abolish; repeal ⟨*legge*⟩

abolizi'one *nf* abolition; (*di legge*) repeal

abolizio'nismo *nm* abolitionism

abolizio'nista *a & nmf* abolitionist

abomi'nevole *a* abominable

abo'rigeno, -a *a & nmf* aboriginal

abor'rire *vt* abhor

abor'tire *vi* miscarry; (*volontariamente*) have an abortion; *fig* fail

abor'tista *a* pro-choice

abor'tivo *a* abortive

a'borto *nm* miscarriage; (*volontario*) abortion

abrasi'one *nf* abrasion

abra'sivo *a & nm* abrasive

abro'gare *vt* repeal

abroga'tivo *a* **referendum ~** referendum to repeal a law

abrogazi'one *nf* repeal

abruz'zese *a* Abruzzi *attrib* ● *nmf* person from the Abruzzi ● *nm* Abruzzi dialect

'abside *nf* apse

abu'lia *nf* apathy

a'bulico *a* apathetic

abu'sare *vi* **~ di** abuse; over-indulge in ⟨*alcol*⟩; (*approfittare di*) take advantage of; (*violentare*) rape

abusi'vismo *nm* large-scale abuse; **~ edilizio** building without planning permission

abu'sivo *a* illegal

a'buso *nm* abuse; **'ogni ~ sarà punito'** 'penalty for misuse'. **~ di confidenza** breach of confidence

a.C. *abbr* (**avanti Cristo**) BC

a'cacia *nf* acacia

'acaro *nm Zool* mite

'acca *nf fam* **non ho capito un'~** I understood damn all

acca'demia *nf* academy. **A~ di Belle Arti** Academy of Fine Arts. **~ militare** military academy

acca'demico, -a *a* academic ● *nmf* academician

acca'dere *vi* happen; **accada quel che accada** come what may

acca'duto *nm* event

accalappia'cani *nm inv* dog-catcher

accalappi'are *vt* catch; *fig* allure

accal'care *vt* cram together

accal'carsi *vr* crowd

accal'darsi *vr* get overheated; (*per fatica*) get hot; *fig* get excited

accal'dato *a* overheated; (*per fatica*) hot; *fig* excited

accalo'rarsi *vr* get excited

accampa'mento *nm* camp

accam'pare *vt fig* put forth

accam'parsi *vr* camp

accani'mento *nm* tenacity; (*odio*) rage

acca'nirsi *vr* persist; (*infierire*) rage

accanita'mente *adv* ⟨*odiare*⟩ fiercely; ⟨*insistere*⟩ persistently; ⟨*lavorare*⟩ assiduously

acca'nito *a* persistent; ⟨*odio*⟩ fierce; ⟨*fumatore*⟩ inveterate; ⟨*lavoratore*⟩ assiduous

ac'canto *adv* near; ~ **a** *prep* next to; **la ragazza della porta** ~ the girl next door

accanto'nare *vt* set aside; *Mil* billet

accaparra'mento *nm* hoarding; *Comm* cornering

accapar'rare *vt* hoard

accapar'rarsi *vr* grab; corner ⟨*mercato*⟩

accaparra|'tore, -'trice *nmf* hoarder

accapigli'arsi *vr* scuffle; (*litigare*) squabble

accappa'toio *nm* bathrobe; (*per spiaggia*) beachrobe

accappo'nare *vt* fare ~ **la pelle a** qcno make sb's flesh creep

accarez'zare *vt* caress, stroke; *fig* cherish

accartocci'are *vt* scrunch up

accartocci'arsi *vr* curl up

acca'sarsi *vr* get married

accasci'arsi *vr* flop down; *fig* lose heart

accata'stare *vt* pile up

accatti'vante *a* beguiling

accatti'varsi *vr* ~ **le simpatie/la stima/ l'affetto di** qcno gain sb's sympathy/respect/affection

accatto'naggio *nm* begging

accat'tone, -a *nmf* beggar

accaval'lare *vt* cross ⟨*gambe*⟩

accaval'larsi *vr* pile up; *fig* overlap

acce'cante *a* ⟨*luce*⟩ blinding

acce'care *vt* blind ● *vi* go blind

ac'cedere *vi* access; ~ **a** enter; (*acconsentire*) comply with; *Comput* access

accele'rare *vi* accelerate ● *vt* speed up, accelerate; ~ **il passo** quicken one's pace

accele'rata *nf* sudden acceleration

accele'rato *a* rapid

accelera'tore *nm* accelerator. ~ **grafico** *Comput* graphics accelerator

accelerazi'one *nf* acceleration

ac'cendere *vt* light; turn on, switch on ⟨*luce, TV ecc*⟩; *fig* inflame; **ha da** ~**?** have you got a light?

ac'cendersi *vr* catch fire; (*illuminarsi*) light up; *fig* become inflamed; ⟨*tv, computer:*⟩ turn on, switch on

accendi'gas *nm inv* gas lighter; (*su cucina*) automatic ignition

accen'dino *nm* lighter

accendi'sigari *nm* cigar-lighter

accen'nare *vt* indicate; *hum* ⟨*melodia*⟩; give a hint of ⟨*sorriso*⟩ ● *vi* ~ **a** beckon to; *fig* hint at; (*far l'atto di*) make as if to; **accenna a piovere** it looks like rain

ac'cenno *nm* gesture; (*con il capo*) nod; *fig* hint

accensi'one *nf* lighting; (*di motore*) ignition

accen'tare *vt* accent; (*con accento tonico*) stress

accentazi'one *nf* accentuation

ac'cento *nm* accent; (*tonico*) stress. ~ **acuto** acute [accent]. ~ **circonflesso** circumflex [accent]. ~ **grave** grave [accent]

accentra'mento *nm* centralizing

accen'trare *vt* centralize

accentra'tore *a* ⟨*persona*⟩ who refuses to delegate; ⟨*politica*⟩ of centralization

accentu'are *vt* accentuate

accentu'arsi *vr* become more noticeable

accentu'ato *a* marked

accerchia'mento *nm* surrounding

accerchi'are *vt* surround

accerchi'ato *a* surrounded

accer'tabile *a* ascertainable

accerta'mento *nm* check; **accertamenti** *pl* [**medici**] tests

accer'tare *vt* ascertain; (*controllare*) check; assess ⟨*reddito*⟩

ac'ceso *a* lighted; ⟨*radio, TV ecc*⟩ on; ⟨*colore*⟩ bright

acces'sibile *a* accessible; ⟨*persona*⟩ approachable; ⟨*spesa*⟩ reasonable

ac'cesso *nm* access; (*Med: di rabbia*) fit; **'vietato l'~'** 'no entry'; **'~ riservato a...'** 'access restricted to...'. ~ **diretto** *Comput* direct access. ~ **multiplo** *Comput* multi-access. ~ **di pazzia** fit of madness. ~ **remoto** *Comput* remote access

accessori'ato *a* accessorized

acces'sorio *a* accessory; (*secondario*) of secondary importance ● *nm* accessory; **accessori** *pl* ⟨*rifiniture*⟩ fittings. **accessori** *pl* **per il bagno** bathroom fittings. **accessori** *pl* **moda** fashion accessories

ac'cetta *nf* hatchet

accet'tabile *a* acceptable

accet'tare *vt* accept; (*aderire a*) agree to

accettazi'one *nf* acceptance; (*luogo*) reception; [**banco**] ~ check-in [desk]. ~ [**bagagli**] check-in

ac'cetto *a* agreeable; **essere bene** ~ be very welcome

accezi'one *nf* meaning

acchiap'pare *vt* catch

+acchiotto *suff* **lupacchiotto** *nm* wolf cub; (*affettuoso*) baby wolf; **orsacchiotto** *nm* teddy bear; **fessacchiotto** *nm* nitwit

ac'chito *nm* **di primo** ~ at first

acciac'care *vt* crush; *fig* prostrate

acciac'cato, -a *a* **essere** ~ ache all over

acci'acco *nm* infirmity; **acciacchi** (*pl: afflizioni*) aches and pains

acciaie'ria nf steelworks

acci'aio nm steel; ~ **inossidabile** stainless steel

acciambel'larsi vr curl up

acciden'tale a accidental

acciden'talmente adv accidentally

acciden'tato a ⟨terreno⟩ uneven

acci'dente nm accident; Med stroke; **non capisce/non vede un ~** fam he doesn't understand/can't see a damn thing; **mandare un ~ a qcno** fam tell sb to go to hell

acci'denti int fam damn!; ~ **a te!** damn you!, blast you!

ac'cidia nf sloth

accigli'arsi vr frown

accigli'ato a frowning

ac'cingersi vr ~ **a** be about to

+accio suff **erbaccia** nf weed; **donnaccia** nf tart; **faticaccia** nf hard slog; **lavoraccio** nm ⟨lavoro faticoso⟩ helluva job fam; ⟨lavoro malfatto⟩ botched job; **parolaccia** nf swear word; **avaraccio** nm skinflint

acciotto'lato nm cobbled paving, cobblestones pl

acci'picchia int good Lord!

acciuf'fare vt catch

acci'uga nf anchovy

accla'mare vt applaud; ⟨eleggere⟩ acclaim

acclamazi'one nf applause

acclima'tare vt acclimatize

acclima'tarsi vr get acclimatized

acclimatazi'one nf acclimatization

ac'cludere vt enclose

ac'cluso a enclosed

accocco'larsi vr squat

acco'darsi vr tag along

accogli'ente a welcoming; ⟨confortevole⟩ cosy

accogli'enza nf welcome

ac'cogliere vt receive; ⟨conpiacere⟩ welcome; ⟨contenere⟩ hold

accol'lare vt ~ **qcsa a qcno** fig saddle sb with sth

accol'larsi vr take on ⟨responsabilità, debiti, doveri⟩

accol'lato a ⟨maglia⟩ high-necked

accoltel'lare vt knife

accoman'dante nmf Jur sleeping partner

accomanda'tario, -a nmf Jur general partner

accoman'dita nf Jur limited partnership. ~ **per azioni** limited partnership based on shares

accomia'tare vt dismiss

accomia'tarsi vr take one's leave (**da** of)

accomoda'mento nm arrangement

accomo'dante a accommodating

accomo'dare vt ⟨riparare⟩ mend; ⟨disporre⟩ arrange

accomo'darsi vr make oneself at home; **si accomodi!** come in!; ⟨si sieda⟩ take a seat!

accompagna'mento nm accompaniment; ⟨seguito⟩ retinue

accompa'gnare vt accompany; ~ **qcno a casa** see sb home; ~ **qcno alla porta** show sb to the door; ~ **qcno con lo sguardo** follow sb with one's eyes

accompa'gnarsi vr ⟨cibi, colori ecc.⟩ go [well] together; ~ **con** o **a qcno** accompany sb

accompagna|'tore, -'trice nmf companion; ⟨di comitiva⟩ escort; Mus accompanist. ~ **turistico** tour guide

accomu'nare vt pool

acconci'are vt arrange

acconci'arsi vr do one's hair

acconcia'tura nf hair-style; ⟨ornamento⟩ head-dress; **'acconciature'** 'ladies' hairdresser'

accondiscen'dente a too obliging

accondiscen'denza nf excessive desire to please

accondi'scendere vi ~ **a** condescend; comply with ⟨desiderio⟩; ⟨acconsentire⟩ consent to

acconsen'tire vi consent

acconten'tare vt satisfy

acconten'tarsi vr be content (**di** with)

ac'conto nm deposit; **in** ~ on account; **lasciare un** ~ leave a deposit. ~ **di dividendo** interim dividend

accop'pare vt fam bump off

accoppia'mento nm coupling; ⟨di animali⟩ mating

accoppi'are vt couple; mate ⟨animali⟩

accoppi'arsi vr pair off; ⟨animali:⟩ mate

accoppi'ata nf ⟨scommessa⟩ bet placed on two horses for first and second place; **sono una strana** ~ they make strange bedfellows; ~ **vincente** fig winning combination

accoppia'tore nm ~ **acustico** Comput acoustic coupler

acco'rato a sorrowful

accorci'are vt shorten

accorci'arsi vr get shorter

accor'dare vt concede; match ⟨colori ecc⟩; Mus tune

accor'darsi vr agree

accorda|'tore, -'trice nmf Mus tuner

ac'cordo nm agreement; Mus chord; ⟨armonia⟩ harmony; **andare d'~** get on well; **d'~!** agreed!; **essere d'~** agree; **in ~ con** in collusion with; **prendere accordi con qcno** make arrangements with sb. ~ **collettivo** joint agreement

ac'corgersi vr ~ **di** notice; ⟨capire⟩ realize

accorgi'mento nm shrewdness; ⟨espediente⟩ device

accorpa'mento nm amalgamation

accor'pare vt amalgamate

ac'correre vi hasten

accorta'mente adv astutely

accor'tezza nf ⟨previdenza⟩ forethought

ac'corto a shrewd; **mai** ~ incautious

accosta'mento nm ⟨di colori⟩ combination

acco'stare vt draw close to; approach ⟨persona⟩; put ajar ⟨porta ecc⟩

acco'starsi vr ~ **a** come near to

accovacci'arsi vr crouch, squat down

accovacci'ato *a* squatting

accoz'zaglia *nf* jumble; (*di persone*) mob

accoz'zare *vt* ~ **colori** mix colours that clash

accredi'tabile *a* reliable

accredita'mento *nm* credit. ~ **tramite bancogiro** Bank Giro Credit

accredi'tare *vt* confirm ⟨*notizia*⟩; *Comm* credit

accredi'tato *a* accredited; ⟨*notizia*⟩ reliable

ac'crescere *vt* increase

ac'crescersi *vr* grow larger

accresci'mento *nm* increase

accresci'tivo *a* augmentative

accucci'arsi *vr* ⟨*cane:*⟩ lie down; ⟨*persona:*⟩ crouch

accu'dire *vi* ~ **a** attend to

accumu'lare *vt* accumulate

accumu'larsi *vr* pile up, accumulate

accumula'tore *nm* accumulator; *Auto, Comput* battery

accumulazi'one *nf* accumulation

ac'cumulo *nm* (*di merce*) build-up

accurata'mente *adv* carefully

accura'tezza *nf* care

accu'rato *a* careful

ac'cusa *nf* accusation; *Jur* charge; **essere in stato di** ~ *Jur* have been charged; **mettere qcno sotto** ~ *Jur* charge sb; **la Pubblica A**~ *Jur* the public prosecutor

accu'sare *vt* accuse; *Jur* charge; complain of ⟨*dolore*⟩; ~ **ricevuta di** *Comm* acknowledge receipt of

accusa'tivo *nm Gram* accusative

accu'sato, -a *nmf* accused

accusa'tore *a* accusing ● *nm Jur* prosecutor

a'cerbo *a* sharp; (*non maturo*) unripe

'acero *nm* maple

a'cerrimo *a* implacable

ace'tato *nm* acetate

a'ceto *nm* vinegar

ace'tone *nm* nail polish remover

ace'tosa *nf Culin* [edible] sorrel

aceto'sella *nf Bot* sorrel

A.C.I. *nf abbr* (**Automobile Club d'Italia**) Italian Automobile Association

acidità *nf* acidity. ~ **di stomaco** acid stomach

'acido *a* acid; ⟨*persona*⟩ sour ● *nm* acid. ~ **cloridrico** hydrochloric acid

a'cidulo *a* slightly sour

'acino *nm* berry; (*chicco*) grape

'acme *nf* acme

'acne *nf* acne

'acqua *nf* water; **fare** ~ *Naut* leak; ~ **in bocca!** *fig* mum's the word!; **avere l'**~ **alla gola, essere con l'**~ **alla gola** *fig* be pushed for time; **ho fatto un buco nell'**~ *fig* I had no luck whatsoever; **in cattive acque** in deep water; **navigare in cattive acque** be in financial difficulties. ~ **calda** hot water. ~ **di Colonia** eau de Cologne. ~ **corrente** running water. ~ **dolce** fresh wa-

ter. ~ **minerale** mineral water. ~ **minerale gassata** fizzy mineral water. ~ **naturale** still mineral water. ~ **potabile** drinking water. ~ **del rubinetto** tap water. ~ **salata** salt water. ~ **saponata** suds. ~ **tonica** tonic water

acqua'forte *nf* etching

ac'quaio *nm* sink

acquama'rina *a* aquamarine

acqua'piano *nm* hydroplane

acqua'rello *nm* water-colour

a'cquario *nm* aquarium; *Astr* Aquarius

acquartie'rare *vt Mil* billet

acqua'santa *nf* holy water

acquasanti'era *nf* font

acqua'scooter *nm inv* water-scooter

a'cquata *nf fam* downpour

a'cquatico *a* aquatic; **sport** ~ water sport

acquat'tarsi *vr* crouch

acqua'vite *nf* brandy

acquaz'zone *nm* downpour

acque'dotto *nm* aqueduct

'acqueo *a* **vapore** ~ water vapour

acque'rello *nm* water-colour

acquicol'tura *nf* aquaculture

acquie'scente *a* acquiescent

acquie'tare *vt* appease; calm ⟨*dolore*⟩

acquie'tarsi *vr* calm down

acqui'rente *nmf* purchaser

acqui'sire *vt* acquire

acqui'sito *a* acquired

acquisizi'one *nf* attainment

acqui'stare *vt* purchase; (*ottenere*) acquire; ~ **in** ⟨*prestigio, bellezza*⟩ gain in

a'cquisto *nm* purchase; ~ **rateale** hire purchase, HP, installment plan *Am*; **uscire per acquisti** go shopping; **fare acquisti** shop; **ufficio acquisti** purchasing department. ~ **per impulso** impulse buy. ~ **a termine** *Fin* forward buying

acqui'trino *nm* marsh

acquo'lina *nf* **far venire l'**~ **in bocca a qcno** make sb's mouth water; **ho l'**~ **in bocca** my mouth is watering

a'cquoso *a* watery

'acre *a* acrid; (*al gusto*) sour; *fig* harsh

a'credine *nf* acridness; (*al gusto*) sourness; *fig* harshness

acre'mente *adv* acridly

a'crilico *nm* acrylic

a'critico *a* acritical

a'crobata *nmf* acrobat

acro'batico *a* acrobatic

acroba'zia *nf* acrobatics *pl*

acroba'zie *nfpl* acrobatics; **fare** ~ *fig* do acrobatics

a'cronimo *nm* acronym

a'cropoli *nf* acropolis

acu'ire *vt* sharpen

acu'irsi *vr* become more intense

a'culeo *nm* sting; *Bot* prickle

a'cume *nm* acumen

acumi'nato *a* pointed

a'custica *nf* acoustics *pl*

acustica'mente *adv* acoustically

a'custico *a* acoustic

acuta'mente *adv* shrewdly

acu'tezza *nf* acuteness; *fig* shrewdness; *(di suoni)* shrillness

acutiz'zare *vt* aggravate ⟨*dolore*⟩

acutiz'zarsi *vr* become worse

a'cuto *a* sharp; ⟨*suono*⟩ shrill; ⟨*freddo, odore*⟩ intense; *Gram, Math, Med* acute ● *nm Mus* high note

ad *(before vowel) prep* = **a**

A.D. *abbr Pol* (**Alleanza Democratica**) Democratic Alliance

adagi'are *vt* lay down

adagi'arsi *vr* lie down

a'dagio *adv* slowly ● *nm Mus* adagio; *(proverbio)* adage

ada'mitico *a* **in costume ~** in one's birthday suit, stark naked

adat'tabile *a* adaptable

adattabilità *nf* adaptability

adatta'mento *nm* adaptation; **avere spirito di ~** be adaptable. **~ cinematografico** film adaptation, adaptation for the cinema

adat'tare *vt* adapt; *(aggiustare)* fit

adat'tarsi *vr* adapt

adatta'tore *nm* adaptor

a'datto *a* suitable (**a** for); *(giusto)* right

addì *adv* **~ 15 settembre 1995** on 15th September 1995

addebita'mento *nm* debit. **~ diretto** direct debit

addebi'tare *vt* debit; *fig* ascribe ⟨*colpa*⟩

ad'debito *nm* charge

addensa'mento *nm* thickening; *(di persone)* gathering

adden'sare *vt* thicken

adden'sarsi *vr* thicken; *(affollarsi)* gather

adden'tare *vt* bite

adden'trarsi *vr* penetrate

ad'dentro *adv* deeply; **essere ~ in** be in on

addestra'mento *nm* training. **~ iniziale** basic training

adde'strare *vt* train

adde'strarsi *vr* train

addestra|'tore, -'trice *nmf* trainer

ad'detto, -a *a* assigned ● *nmf* employee; *(diplomatico)* attaché. **~ commerciale** salesman. **adetti** *pl* **ai lavori** persons involved in the work; **'vietato l'ingresso ai non addetti ai lavori'** 'staff only'. **~ culturale** cultural attaché. **~ stampa** information officer, press officer. **~ ai traslochi** removal man

addi'accio *nm* **dormire all'~** sleep in the open

addi'etro *adv* *(indietro)* back; *(nel passato)* before

ad'dio *nm & int* goodbye. **~ al celibato** stag night, stag party. **cena d'~** farewell dinner

addirit'tura *adv* *(perfino)* even; *(assolutamente)* absolutely; **~!** really!

ad'dirsi *vr* **~ a** suit

addi'tare *vt* point at; *(per identificare)* point out; *fig* point to

addi'tivo *a & nm* additive

addizio'nale *a* additional ● *nf (imposta)* surtax

addizional'mente *adv* additionally

addizio'nare *vt* add [up]

addiziona'trice *nf* adding machine

addizi'one *nf* addition

addob'bare *vt* decorate

ad'dobbo *nm* decoration

addol'cire *vt* sweeten; tone down ⟨*colore*⟩; *fig* soften

addol'cirsi *vr* *fig* mellow

addolo'rare *vt* grieve

addolo'rarsi *vr* be upset (**per** by)

addolo'rato *a* pained, distressed

ad'dome *nm* abdomen

addomesti'care *vt* tame

addomestica'tore *nm* tamer

addomi'nale *a* abdominal ● *nmpl* **addominali** abdominals

addormen'tare *vt* put to sleep

addormen'tarsi *vr* go to sleep

addormen'tato *a* asleep; *fig* slow

addos'sare *vt* **~ a** *(appoggiare)* lean against; *(attribuire)* lay on

addos'sarsi *vr* *(ammassarsi)* crowd; shoulder ⟨*responsabilità ecc*⟩

ad'dosso *adv* on; **~ a** *prep* on; *(molto vicino)* right next to; **andare/venire ~ qcno** run into sb; **mettere gli occhi ~ a qcno/qcsa** hanker after sb/sth; **non mettermi le mani ~!** keep your hands off me!; **stare ~ a qcno** *fig* be on sb's back; **farsela ~** *(fam: bisogni corporali)* dirty oneself; *(pipì)* wet oneself

ad'durre *vt* produce ⟨*prova, documento*⟩; give ⟨*pretesto, esempio*⟩

adegua'mento *nm* adjustment

adegu'are *vt* adjust

adegu'arsi *vr* conform

adeguata'mente *adv* suitably

adegua'tezza *nf* suitability

adegu'ato *a* suitable; **~ a** suited to, suitable for

a'dempiere *vt* fulfil

adempi'mento *nm* fulfilment

adem'pire *vt* fulfil

ade'noidi *nfpl* adenoids

a'depto, -a *nmf* adherent

ade'rente *a* adhesive; ⟨*vestito*⟩ tight ● *nmf* follower

ade'renza *nf* adhesion; **aderenze** *pl* connections

ade'rire *vi* **~ a** stick to, adhere to; support ⟨*sciopero, petizione*⟩; agree to ⟨*richiesta*⟩

adesca'mento *nm* *Jur* soliciting

ade'scare *vt* bait; *fig* entice

adesca'trice *nf* fille de joie

adesi'one *nf* adhesion; *fig* agreement

ade'sivo *a* adhesive ● *nm* sticker; *Auto* bumper sticker

a'desso *adv* now; *(poco fa)* just now; *(tra poco)* any moment now; **da ~ in poi** from now on; **per ~** for the moment; **fino ~** up till now

adia'cente *a* adjacent; **~ a** next to

adia'cenze *nfpl* adjacent areas

adi'bire *vt* **~ a** put to use as

'adipe *nm* adipose tissue

adi'poso *a* adipose

adi'rarsi *vr* get irate

adi'rato *a* irate

a'dire *vt* resort to; ~ **le vie legali** take legal proceedings. ~ **la successione** *Jur* take possession of an inheritance

'adito *nm* dare ~ **a** give rise to

adocchi'are *vt* eye; (*con desiderio*) covet

adole'scente *a* & *nmf* adolescent *attrib*

adole'scenza *nf* adolescence

adolescenzi'ale *a* adolescent

adombra'mento *nm* darkening

adom'brare *vt* darken; *fig* veil

adom'brarsi *vr* (*offendersi*) take offence

adope'rare *vt* use

adope'rarsi *vr* take trouble

ado'rabile *a* adorable

ado'rare *vt* adore

adorazi'one *nf* adoration; **in** ~ adoring

ador'nare *vt* adorn

a'dorno *a* adorned (**di** with)

adot'tare *vt* adopt

adot'tivo *a* adoptive

adozi'one *nf* adoption

adrena'lina *nf* adrenalin

adri'atico *a* Adriatic ● *nm* l'A~ the Adriatic

adu'lare *vt* flatter

adula|'tore, -'trice *nmf* flatterer

adula'torio *a* sycophantic

adulazi'one *nf* flattery

a'dultera *nf* adulteress

adulte'rare *vt* adulterate

adulte'rato *a* adulterated

adulte'rino *a* adulterous

adul'terio *nm* adultery

a'dultero *a* adulterous ● *nm* adulterer

a'dulto, -a *a* & *nmf* adult; (*maturo*) mature

adu'nanza *nf* assembly

adu'nare *vt* gather

adu'nata *nf* *Mil* parade

a'dunco *a* hooked

adunghi'are *vt* claw

ae'rare *vt* air ⟨*stanza*⟩

aera'tore *nm* ventilator

aerazi'one *nf* ventilation

a'ereo *a* aerial; (*dell'aviazione*) air ● *nm* aeroplane, plane; **andare in** ~ fly. ~ **da carico** cargo plane. ~ **da guerra** warplane. ~ **di linea** airliner. ~ **navetta** shuttle. ~ **a reazione** jet [plane]

ae'robica *nf* aerobics

ae'robico *a* aerobic

aerodi'namica *nf* aerodynamics *sg*

aerodi'namico *a* aerodynamic

aero'grafo *nm* airbrush

aero'gramma *nm* aerogram[me]

aero'linea *nf* airline

aero'mobile *nm* aircraft

aeromo'dello *nm* model aircraft

aero'nautica *nf* aeronautics; *Mil* Air Force

aero'nautico *a* aeronautical

aerona'vale *a* air and sea *attrib*

aero'plano *nm* aeroplane

aero'porto *nm* airport

aeroportu'ale *a* airport *attrib*

aero'scalo *nm* cargo and servicing area

aero'sol *nm inv* aerosol

aerospazi'ale *a* aerospace *attrib*

aero'statico *a* **pallone** ~ aerostat

ae'rostato *nm* aerostat

aerostazi'one *nf* air terminal

aerosti'ere *nm* balloonist

aero'via *nf* air-corridor

A.F. *abbr* (**alta frequenza**) HF

'afa *nf* sultriness

af'fabile *a* affable

affabilità *nf* affability

affaccen'darsi *vr* busy oneself (**a** with)

affacci'arsi *vr* show oneself; ~ **alla finestra** appear at the window

affacen'dato *a* busy

affa'mare *vt* starve [out]

affa'mato *a* starving

affan'nare *vt* leave breathless

affan'narsi *vr* busy oneself; (*agitarsi*) get worked up

affan'nato *a* breathless; **dal respiro** ~ wheezy

af'fanno *nm* breathlessness; *fig* worry; **essere in** ~ **per** be anxious about

affannosa'mente *adv* breathlessly

affan'noso *a* exhausting; **respiro** ~ heavy breathing

af'fare *nm* matter; (*occasione*) bargain; *Comm* transaction, deal; **pensa agli affari tuoi** mind your own business; **non sono affari tuoi** *fam* it's none of your business; **fare affari d'oro** have a field day; **af'fari** *pl* business; **d'affari** (*uomo, cena, viaggio*) business. **ministro degli affari esteri** Foreign Secretary *Br*, Secretary of State *Am*

affa'rismo *nm pej* wheeling and dealing

affa'rista *nmf* wheeler-dealer

affasci'nante *a* fascinating; ⟨*persona, sorriso*⟩ bewitching

affasci'nare *vt* bewitch; *fig* charm

affastel'lare *vt* tie up in bundles

affatica'mento *nm* fatigue

affati'care *vt* tire; (*sfinire*) exhaust

affati'carsi *vr* tire oneself out; (*affannarsi*) strive

affati'cato *a* fatigued, suffering from fatigue

af'fatto *adv* completely; **non...** ~ not... at all; **niente** ~! not at all!

affer'mare *vt* affirm; (*sostenere*) assert

affer'marsi *vr* establish oneself

affermativa'mente *adv* in the affirmative

afferma'tivo *a* affirmative

affer'mato *a* established

affermazi'one *nf* assertion; (*successo*) achievement

affer'rare *vt* seize; catch ⟨*oggetto*⟩; (*capire*) grasp; ~ **al volo** *fig* be quick on the uptake

affer'rarsi *vr* ~ **a** grasp at, clutch at

affet'tare *vt* slice; *(ostentare)* affect

affet'tato *a* sliced; *‹sorriso, maniere›* affected ● *nm* cold meat, sliced meat

affetta'trice *nf* bacon-slicer

affettazi'one *nf* affectation

affet'tivo *a* affective; **rapporto ~** emotional tie

af'fetto¹ *nm* affection; **con ~** affectionately; **gli affetti familiari** family ties

af'fetto² *a* ~ **da** suffering from

affettuosa'mente *adv* affectionately

affettuosità *nf inv (gesto)* affectionate gesture

affettu'oso *a* affectionate

affezio'narsi *vr* ~ **a** grow fond of

affezio'nato *a* devoted (**a** to)

affezi'one *nf* affection; *Med* ailment

affian'care *vt* put side by side; *Mil* flank; *fig* support

affian'carsi *vr* come side by side; *fig* stand together, stand shoulder to shoulder; **~ a qcno** *fig* help sb out

affiata'mento *nm* harmony

affia'tarsi *vr* get on well together

affia'tato *a* close-knit; **una coppia affiatata** a very close couple

affibbi'are *vt* ~ **qcsa a qcno** saddle sb with sth; **~ un pugno a qcno** let fly at sb

affi'dabile *a* reliable, dependable

affidabilità *nf* reliability, dependability

affida'mento *nm (Jur: dei minori)* custody; **fare ~ su qcno** rely on sb; **non dare ~ (a qcno)** not inspire confidence (in sb)

affi'dare *vt* entrust

affi'darsi *vr* ~ **a** rely on

affievoli'mento *nm* weakening

affievo'lirsi *vr* grow weak

af'figgere *vt* affix

affilacol'telli *nm inv* knife sharpener

affi'lare *vt* sharpen

affili'are *vt* affiliate

affili'arsi *vr* become affiliated

affiliazi'one *nf* affiliation

affi'nare *vt* sharpen; *(perfezionare)* refine

affinché *conj* so that, in order that

af'fine *a* similar

affinità *nf inv* affinity

affiora'mento *nm* emergence; *Naut* surfacing

affio'rare *vi* emerge; *fig* come to light

affissi'one *nf* bill-posting; **'divieto di ~'** 'stick no bills'

af'fisso *nm* bill; *Gram* affix

affitta'camere *nm inv* landlord ● *nf inv* landlady

affit'tare *vt (dare in affitto)* let; *(prendere in affitto)* rent. **af'fittasi** to let, for rent

af'fitto *nm* rent; **contratto d'~** lease; **dare in ~** let; **prendere in ~** rent

affittu'ario, -a *nmf Jur* lessee

af'fliggere *vt* distress

af'fliggersi *vr* distress oneself

af'flitto *a* distressed

afflizi'one *nf* distress; *fig* affliction

afflosci'are *vt* **la pioggia ha afflosciato**

le foglie the rain has made the leaves go all limp; **mi hai afflosciato il morale** you've demoralized me

afflosci'arsi *vr* become floppy; *(accasciarsi)* flop down; *‹morale:›* decline

afflu'ente *a & nm* tributary

afflu'enza *nf* flow; *(di gente)* crowd

afflu'ire *vi* flow; *fig* pour in

af'flusso *nm* influx

affoga'mento *nm* drowning

affo'gare *vt/i* drown; *Culin* poach; **~ in** *fig* be swamped with

affo'garsi *vr (suicidarsi)* drown oneself

affo'gato *a ‹persona›* drowned; *‹uova›* poached ● *nm* ~ **al caffè** ice cream with hot espresso poured over it

affolla'mento *nm* crowd

affol'lare *vt* crowd

affol'larsi *vr* crowd

affol'lato *a* crowded

affonda'mento *nm* sinking

affon'dare *vt/i* sink

affon'darsi *vr* sink

affossa'mento *nm (avvallamento)* pothole; *fig* burial

affran'care *vt* redeem *‹bene›*; stamp *‹lettera›*; free *‹schiavo›*

affran'carsi *vr* free oneself

affran'cato *a ‹lettera›* stamped; *‹schiavo›* freed; **già ~** *‹lettera›* prepaid

affranca'trice *nf* franking machine, franker

affranca'tura *nf* stamping; *(di spedizione)* postage. **~ per l'estero** postage abroad

af'franto *a* prostrate with grief, grief-stricken; *(esausto)* worn out

affre'scare *vt* paint a fresco on

af'fresco *nm* fresco

affret'tare *vt* speed up

affret'tarsi *vr* hurry

affrettata'mente *adv* hastily

affret'tato *a ‹passo›* fast; *‹decisione›* hasty; *‹lavoro›* rushed

affron'tare *vt* face; confront *‹nemico›*; meet *‹spese›*

affron'tarsi *vr* clash

af'fronto *nm* affront, insult; **fare un ~ a qcno** insult sb

affumi'care *vt* fill with smoke; *Culin* smoke

affumi'cato *a ‹prosciutto, formaggio›* smoked; *‹lenti, vetro›* tinted

affuso'lare *vt* taper [off]

affuso'lato *a* tapering

Af'ganistan *nm* Afghanistan

af'gano *a & nmf* Afghani, Afghan

AFI *nm abbr (Alfabeto Fonetico Internazionale)* IPA

aficio'nado, -a *nmf* aficionado

'afide *nm* aphid

'afono *a (senza voce)* unvoiced

afo'risma *nm* aphorism

a'foso *a* sultry

'Africa *nf* Africa. **~ orientale** East Africa. **~ nera** Black Africa. **~ del Nord** North Africa

afri'cano, -a *a & nmf* African

afri'kaans *nm* Afrikaans

afroameri'cano *a* Afro-American

afroasi'atico *a* Afro-Asian

afroca'ribico *a* Afro-Caribbean

afrocu'bano *a* Afro-Cuban

afrodi'siaco *a & nm* aphrodisiac

a'genda *nf* diary. **~ elettronica** personal organizer. **~ da tavolo** desk diary

agen'dina *nf* pocket-diary

a'gente *nm* agent; **agenti** *pl* **atmosferici** atmospheric agents. **~ di cambio** stockbroker. **~ di custodia** prison warder. **~ del fisco** assessor. **~ immobiliare** estate agent, realtor *Am*. **~ marittimo** shipping agent. **~ di polizia** police officer. **~ segreto** secret agent. **~ teatrale** theatrical agent; (*di compagnia*) impresario. **~ di viaggio** travel agent

agen'zia *nf* agency; (*filiale*) branch office; (*di banca*) branch. **~ di collocamento** employment exchange. **~ immobiliare** estate agency, realtor *Am*. **~ matrimoniale** dating agency. **~ pubblicitaria** advertising agency. **~ di recupero crediti** debt collection agency. **~ di stampa** news agency, press agency. **~ di viaggi** travel agency

agevo'lare *vt* facilitate

agevolazi'one *nf* facilitation. **agevolazioni** *pl* **fiscali** tax breaks **a'gevole** *a* easy; ⟨*strada*⟩ smooth

agevol'mente *adv* easily

agganci'are *vt* hook up; *Rail* couple

aggan'ciarsi *vr* ⟨*vestito:*⟩ hook up; **~ a** ⟨*maglia:*⟩ catch on; ⟨*rimorchio:*⟩ hook onto

ag'gancio *nm Aeron* docking

ag'geggio *nm* gadget

agget'tivo *nm* adjective

agghiacci'ante *a* terrifying

agghiacci'are *vt fig* **~ qcno** make sb's blood run cold

agghiacci'arsi *vr* freeze

agghin'dare *vt fam* dress up

agghin'darsi *vr fam* doll oneself up

agghin'dato *a* dressed up; ⟨*sala*⟩ decorated; ⟨*fig: stile*⟩ stilted

aggiornabilità *nf Comput* upgradability

aggiorna'mento *nm* update; (*azione*) updating; **corso di ~** refresher course

aggior'nare *vt* (*rinviare*) postpone; (*mettere a giorno*) bring up to date, update

aggior'narsi *vr* get up to date

aggior'nato *a* up-to-date; ⟨*versione*⟩ updated

aggio'taggio *nm Jur* manipulation of the market

aggira'mento *nm Mil* outflanking

aggi'rare *vt* surround; (*fig: ingannare*) trick

aggi'rarsi *vr* hang about; **~ su** ⟨*discorso ecc:*⟩ be about; ⟨*somma:*⟩ be around

aggiudi'care *vt* award; (*all'asta*) knock down

aggiudi'carsi *vr* win

aggi'ungere *vt* add

aggi'unta *nf* addition; **in ~** in addition

aggiun'tivo *a* supplementary

aggi'unto *a* added ● *a & nm* (*assistente*) assistant

aggiu'stare *vt* mend; (*sistemare*) settle; (*fam: mettere a posto*) fix; **ora l'aggiusto io** *fig* I'll sort him out

aggiu'starsi *vr* adapt; (*mettersi in ordine*) tidy oneself up; (*decidere*) sort things out; ⟨*tempo:*⟩ clear up

aggiusta'tina *nf* **dare un'~ a** neaten

agglomera'mento *nm* conglomeration

agglome'rante *nm* binder

agglome'rato *nm* built-up area

aggrap'pare *vt* grasp

aggrap'parsi *vr* **~ a** cling to

aggrava'mento *nm* worsening; (*di pena*) increase

aggra'vante *Jur nf* aggravation ● *a* aggravating; **circostanza ~** aggravation

aggra'vare *vt* (*peggiorare*) make worse; increase ⟨*pena*⟩; (*appesantire*) weigh down

aggra'varsi *vr* worsen

ag'gravio *nm* **~ fiscale** tax burden

aggrazi'ato *a* graceful

aggre'dire *vt* attack

aggre'gare *vt* add; (*associare a un gruppo ecc*) admit

aggre'garsi *vr* **~ a** join

aggre'gato *a* associated ● *nm* aggregate; (*di case*) block

aggregazi'one *nf* (*di persone*) gathering

aggressi'one *nf* aggression; (*atto*) attack. **~ a mano armata** armed assault

aggressività *nf* aggressiveness

aggres'sivo *a* aggressive

aggres'sore *nm* aggressor

aggrin'zare, aggrin'zire *vt* wrinkle

aggrin'zirsi *vr* wrinkle

aggrot'tare *vt* **~ le ciglia/la fronte** frown

aggrovigli'are *vt* tangle

aggrovigli'arsi *vr* get entangled; *fig* get complicated

aggrovigli'ato *a* entangled; *fig* confused

agguan'tare *vt* catch

agguan'tarsi *vr* **~ a** grasp

aggu'ato *nm* ambush; (*tranello*) trap; **stare in ~** lie in wait; **tendere un ~ a qcno** set an ambush for sb

agguer'rito *a* fierce

agiata'mente *adv* comfortably

agia'tezza *nf* comfort

agi'ato *a* ⟨*persona*⟩ well off; ⟨*vita*⟩ comfortable

a'gibile *a* ⟨*palazzo*⟩ fit for human habitation

agibilità *nf* fitness for human habitation

'agile *a* agile

agilità *nf* agility

agil'mente *adv* agilely

'agio *nm* ease; **mettersi a proprio ~** make oneself at home

a'gire *vi* act; (*comportarsi*) behave; (*funzionare*) work; **~ su** affect

agi'tare *vt* shake; wave ⟨*mano*⟩; (*fig: turbare*) trouble; **'~ prima dell'uso'** 'shake before using'

agi'tarsi *vr* toss about; *(essere inquieto)* be restless; *⟨mare:⟩* get rough

agi'tato *a* restless; *⟨mare⟩* rough

agita|'tore, -'trice *nmf (persona)* agitator

agitazi'one *nf* agitation; **mettere in ~ qcno** send sb into a flat spin

'agli = **a + gli**

'aglio *nm* garlic

a'gnello *nm* lamb

agno'lotti *nmpl* ravioli *sg*

a'gnostico, -a *a & nmf* agnostic

'ago *nm* needle; **a 9 aghi** *⟨stampante⟩* 9-pin. **~ di pino** pine-needle

ago'gnare *vt liter* yearn for, thirst for

ago'nia *nf* agony

ago'nismo *nm* competitiveness

ago'nistica *nf* competition

ago'nistico *a* competitive

agoniz'zante *a* in one's death throes

agoniz'zare *vi* be on one's deathbed

agopun|'tore, -'trice *nmf* acupuncturist

agopun'tura *nf* acupuncture

agorafo'bia *nf* agoraphobia

ago'rafobo, -a *nmf* agoraphobic

agostini'ano, -a *a & nmf* Augustinian

a'gosto *nm* August

a'graria *nf* agriculture

a'grario *a* agricultural ● *nm* landowner

a'greste *a* rustic

a'gricolo *a* agricultural

agricol'tore *nm* farmer

agricol'tura *nf* agriculture. **~ biologica** organic farming

agri'foglio *nm* holly

agrimen'sore *nm* land-surveyor

agritu'rismo *nm* farm holidays, agro-tourism

'agro[1] *a* sour; **all'~** *Culin* pickled

'agro[2] *nm countryside around a town*

agroalimen'tare *a* food *attrib*

agro'dolce *a* bitter-sweet; *Culin* sweet-and-sour; **in ~** sweet and sour

agrono'mia *nf* agronomy

a'gronomo, -a *nmf* agriculturalist

agropasto'rale *a* based on farming

a'grume *nm* citrus fruit; *(pianta)* citrus tree

agru'meto *nm* citrus plantation

aguz'zare *vt* sharpen; **~ le orecchie** prick up one's ears; **~ la vista** look hard

aguz'zino *nm* slave-driver; *(carceriere)* jailer

a'guzzo *a* pointed

ah *int* ah!; **ah, davvero?** oh really?

ahi *int* ow!

ahimè *int* alas!

'ai = **a + i**

'aia *nf* threshing-floor

'Aia *nf* **L'~** The Hague

Aids *nm* Aids

AIE *abbr* **(Associazione Italiana degli Editori)** *association of Italian publishers*

air bag *nm inv Auto* air bag

ai'rone *nm* heron

air terminal *nm inv* air terminal

ai'tante *a* sturdy

aiu'ola *nf* flower-bed

aiu'tante *nmf* assistant ● *nm Mil* adjutant. **~ di campo** aide-de-camp

aiu'tare *vt* help

ai'uto *nm* help, aid; *(assistente)* assistant; **dare un ~** lend a hand; **venire in ~ a qcno** come to sb's rescue; **~! help!. ~ chirurgo** assistant surgeon. **~ domestico** mother's help. **~ infermiere** nursing auxiliary. **~ in linea** *Comput* on-line help

aiz'zare *vt* incite; **~ contro** set on

al = **a + il**

'ala *nf* wing; **fare ~** make way; **avere le ali ai piedi** *fig* run like the wind; **tarpare le ali a qcno** *fig* clip sb's wings. **~ destra/sinistra** *(in calcio)* right/left wing

ala'bastro *nm* alabaster

'alacre *a* brisk

alam'bicco *nm* alembic

a'lano *nm* Great Dane

a'lare *nm* firedog; **apertura ~** wingspan

A'laska *nf* Alaska

'alba *nf* dawn

alba'nese *a & nmf* Albanian

Alba'nia *nf* Albania

'albatro *nm* albatross

albeggi'are *vi* dawn

albe'rare *vt* line with trees *⟨strada⟩*

albe'rato *a* wooded; *⟨viale⟩* tree-lined

albera'tura *nf Naut* masts *pl*

albe'rello *nm* sapling

alber'gare *vt ⟨edificio:⟩* accommodate ● *vi liter* lodge

alberga|'tore, -'trice *nmf* hotel-keeper

alberghi'ero *a* hotel *attrib*

al'bergo *nm* hotel; **~ diurno** *hotel where rooms are rented during the daytime*; **~ a 3 stelle** 3-star hotel

'albero *nm* tree; *Naut* mast; *Mech* shaft. **~ a camme** camshaft. **~ a foglie caduche** deciduous tree. **~ da frutto** fruit tree. **~ genealogico** family tree. **~ a gomiti** crankshaft. **~ maestro** *Naut* mainmast. **~ di Natale** Christmas tree. **~ di trasmissione** *Mech* transmission shaft, prop shaft

albi'cocca *nf* apricot

albi'cocco *nm* apricot-tree

al'bino *nm* albino

'albo *nm* register; *(libro ecc)* album; *(per avvisi)* notice board **'album** *nm inv* album. **~ da colorare** colouring book. **~ da disegno** sketch-book

al'bume *nm* albumen

albu'mina *nf* albumin

alca'lino *a* alkaline

'alce *nm* elk

alchi'mia *nf* alchemy

alchi'mista *nm* alchemist

'alcol *nm* alcohol; *Med* spirit; *(liquori forti)* spirits *pl*; **darsi all'~** take to drink. **~ denaturato** meths. **~ etilico** ethyl alcohol

alcolicità *nf* alcohol content

al'colico *a* alcoholic ● *nm* alcoholic drink

alco'lismo *nm* alcoholism

alco'lista *nmf* alcoholic

alcoliz'zato, -a *a & nmf* alcoholic

alco'test® *nm inv* Breathalyser *ℛ*
al'cova *nf* alcove
al'cun, al'cuno *a & pron* any; **non ha ~ amico** he hasn't any friends, he has no friends. **alcuni** *pl* some, a few; **~i suoi amici** some of his friends
aldilà *nm* next world, hereafter
alea'torio *a* unpredictable; *Jur* aleatory
aleggi'are *vi* ⟨*brezza:*⟩ blow gently; ⟨*profumo:*⟩ waft
a'letta *nf Mech* fin
alet'tone *nm Aeron* aileron; *Auto* stabilizer
'alfa *nf inv* alpha
alfa'betico *a* alphabetical
alfabetizzazi'one *nf* ~ **della popolazione** teaching people to read and write; **tasso di** ~ literacy rate
alfa'beto *nm* alphabet. **A~ Fonetico Internazionale** International Phonetic Alphabet. **~ Morse** Morse code
alfanu'merico *a* alphanumeric
alfi'ere *nm* ⟨*negli scacchi*⟩ bishop
al'fine *adv* eventually, in the end
'alga *nf* weed. **alghe** *pl* **marine** seaweed
'algebra *nf* algebra
Al'geri *nf* Algiers
Alge'ria *nf* Algeria
alge'rino, -a *a & nmf* Algerian
algocol'tura *nf* seaweed farming
algo'ritmo *nm* algorithm
ali'ante *nm* glider
'alibi *nm inv* alibi
a'lice *nf* anchovy
alie'nabile *a Jur* alienable
alie'nare *vt* alienate
alie'narsi *vr* become estranged; **~ le simpatie di qcno** lose sb's good will
ali'enato, -a *a* alienated ● *nmf* lunatic
alienazi'one *nf* alienation
a'lieno, -a *nmf* alien ● *a* **è ~ da invidia** envy is foreign *or* alien to him
alimen'tare *vt* feed; *fig* foment ● *a* food *attrib*; ⟨*abitudine*⟩ dietary ● *nm* **alimentari** *pl* food-stuffs
alimenta'tore *nm* power unit. **~ automatico di documenti** automatic paper feed
alimentazi'one *nf* feeding; ⟨*cibo*⟩ food; ⟨*elettrica, a gas ecc*⟩ supply
ali'mento *nm* food. **alimenti** *pl* food; *Jur* alimony
a'liquota *nf* share; ⟨*di imposta*⟩ rate. **~ minima** basic rate. **ad ~ zero** zero-rated
ali'scafo *nm* hydrofoil
'alito *nm* breath; **~ cattivo** bad breath
ali'tosi *nf inv* halitosis
all. *abbr* ⟨**allegato**⟩ encl
'alla = a + **la**
allaccia'mento *nm* connection
allacci'are *vt* fasten ⟨*cintura*⟩; lace up ⟨*scarpe*⟩; do up ⟨*vestito*⟩; ⟨*collegare*⟩ connect; form ⟨*amicizia*⟩
allacci'arsi *vr* do up, fasten ⟨*vestito, cintura*⟩
allaga'mento *nm* flooding
alla'gare *vt* flood

alla'garsi *vr* to become flooded
allampa'nato *a* lanky
allarga'mento *nm* ⟨*di strada, ricerche*⟩ widening
allar'gare *vt* widen; open ⟨*braccia, gambe*⟩; let out ⟨*vestito ecc*⟩; *fig* extend
allar'garsi *vr* to widen
allar'mante *a* alarming
allar'mare *vt* alarm
allar'mato *a* panicky
al'larme *nm* alarm; **dare l'~** raise the alarm; **mettere in ~ qcno** alarm sb; **far scattare il campanello d'~** set the alarm bells ringing; **falso ~** *fig* false alarm. **~ aereo** air-raid siren; ⟨*suono*⟩ air-raid warning. **~ antincendio** fire alarm
allar'mismo *nm* alarmism
allar'mista *nmf* alarmist
allatta'mento *nm* ⟨*di animale*⟩ suckling; ⟨*di neonato*⟩ feeding
allat'tare *vt* suckle ⟨*animale*⟩; feed ⟨*neonato*⟩; **~ artificialmente** bottle feed
'alle = a + **le**
alle'anza *nf* alliance. **A~ Democratica** *Pol* Democratic Alliance. **A~ Nazionale** *Pol* National Alliance
alle'are *vt* unite
alle'arsi *vr* form an alliance
alle'ato, -a *a* allied ● *nmf* ally
alle'gare[1] *vt Jur* allege
alle'gare[2] *vt* ⟨*accludere*⟩ enclose; set on edge ⟨*denti*⟩
alle'gato *a* enclosed ● *nm* enclosure; **in ~** attached, appended
allegazi'one *nf Jur* allegation
alleggeri'mento *nm* alleviation
allegge'rire *vt* lighten; *fig* alleviate
allegge'rirsi *vr* become lighter; ⟨*vestirsi leggero*⟩ put on lighter clothes
allego'ria *nf* allegory
alle'gorico *a* allegorical
allegra'mente *adv* breezily
alle'gria *nf* gaiety
al'legro *a* cheerful; ⟨*colore*⟩ bright; ⟨*brillo*⟩ tipsy ● *nm Mus* allegro
alle'luia *int* hallelujah
allena'mento *nm* training
alle'nare *vt* train
alle'narsi *vr* train
allena'tore, -'trice *nmf* trainer, coach
allen'tare *vt* loosen; *fig* relax
allen'tarsi *vr* become loose; *Mech* work loose
aller'gia *nf* allergy
al'lergico *a* allergic
aller'gologo, -a *nmf* allergist
al'lerta *nf* **stare ~** be alert, be on the alert; **essere in stato di ~** *Mil* be in a state of alert; **mettere in stato di ~** put on the alert
allesti'mento *nm* preparation; **in ~** in preparation; **~ scenico** *Theat* set
alle'stire *vt* prepare; stage ⟨*spettacolo*⟩; *Naut* fit out
allet'tante *a* alluring; **poco ~** unattractive
allet'tare *vt* entice

alleva'mento *nm* breeding; *(processo)* bringing up; *(luogo)* farm; *(per piante)* nursery; **pollo di** ~ battery chicken. ~ **in batteria** battery farming

alle'vare *vt* bring up *(bambini)*; breed *(animali)*; grow *(piante)*

alleva|'tore, -'trice *nmf* breeder

allevia'mento *nm* alleviation

allevi'are *vt* alleviate; *fig* lighten

alli'bito *a* astounded; **rimanere** ~ be astounded

allibra'tore *nm* bookmaker

allie'tare *vt* gladden

allie'tarsi *vr* rejoice

alli'evo, -a *nmf* pupil ● *nm Mil* cadet

alliga'tore *nm* alligator

allinea'mento *nm* alignment

alline'are *vt* line up; *Typ* align; *Fin* adjust

alline'arsi *vr* line up; *fig* fall into line; ~ **con qcno** *fig* align oneself with sb

alline'ato *a* lined up; **i paesi non allineati** the non-aligned states

'allo = **a** + **lo**

allo'care *vt* allocate

al'locco *nm* tawny owl

al'locco, -a *nmf fig* idiot

allocuzi'one *nf* speech

al'lodola *nf* [sky]lark

alloggi'are *vt* *(persona:)* put up; *(casa:)* provide accommodation for; *Mil* billet ● *vi* put up, stay; *Mil* be billeted

al'loggio *nm* *(appartamento)* flat, apartment *Am*; *Mil* billet. ~ **popolare** council flat

allontana'mento *nm* removal

allonta'nare *vt* move away; *(licenziare)* dismiss; avert *(pericolo)*

allonta'narsi *vr* go away

allopa'tia *nf Med* allopathy

al'lora *adv* then; *(in quel tempo)* at that time; *(in tal caso)* in that case; ~ ~ just then; **d'**~ **in poi** from then on; **e** ~**?** what now?; *(e con ciò?)* so what?; **fino** ~ until then

allorchè *conj* when, as soon as

al'loro *nm* laurel; *Culin* bay; **dormire sugli allori** rest on one's laurels

'alluce *nm* big toe

alluci'nante *a fam* incredible; **sostanza** ~ hallucinogen

alluci'nato, -a *nmf person who suffers from hallucinations*; *fam* space cadet

allucina'torio *a* hallucinatory

allucinazi'one *nf* hallucination

allucino'geno *a (sostanza)* hallucinatory

al'ludere *vi* ~ **a** allude to

allu'minio *nm* aluminium

allu'naggio *nm* moon-landing

allu'nare *vi* land on the moon

allun'gabile *a (tavolo)* extending

allun'gare *vt* lengthen; stretch out *(mano)*; stretch *(gamba)*; extend *(tavolo)*; *(diluire)* dilute; ~ **il collo** crane one's neck; ~ **il muso** pull a long face; ~ **il passo** quicken one's step; ~ **le mani su qcno** touch sb up; *(picchiare)* start fighting with sb; ~ **uno schiaffo a qcno** slap sb

allun'garsi *vr* grow longer; *(crescere)* grow taller; *(sdraiarsi)* lie down, stretch out

al'lungo *nm (nel calcio)* pass; *(nella corsa)* spurt; *(nel pugilato)* lunge

allusi'one *nf* allusion

allu'sivo *a* allusive

alluvio'nale *a* alluvial

alluvio'nato *a (popolazione)* flooded out; *(territorio)* flooded

alluvi'one *nf* flood

alma'nacco *nm* almanac. ~ **nobiliare** peerage

al'meno *adv* at least; **[se]** ~ **venisse il sole!** if only the sun would come out!

a'logena *nf* halogen lamp

a'logeno *nm* halogen ● *a* **lampada alogena** halogen lamp

a'lone *nm* halo

alo'pecia *nf Med* alopecia

al'paca *nm inv* alpaca

al'pestre *a* Alpine

'Alpi *nfpl* **le** ~ the Alps

alpi'nismo *nm* mountaineering

alpi'nista *nmf* mountaineer

alpi'nistico *a* mountaineering *attrib*

al'pino *a* Alpine ● *nm Mil* **gli alpini** the Alpine troops

al'quanto *a* a certain amount of ● *adv* rather

Al'sazia *nf* Alsace

alt *int* stop; **intimare l'**~ give the order to halt

alta'lena *nf* swing; *(tavola in bilico)* see-saw

altale'nare *vi fig* vacillate

alta'mente *adv* highly

al'tare *nm* altar

alta'rino *nm* **scoprire gli altarini di qcno** reveal sb's guilty secrets

alte'rabile *a* which can be changed, alterable

alte'rare *vt* alter; adulterate *(vino)*; *(falsificare)* falsify

alte'rarsi *vr* be altered; *(cibo:)* go bad; *(merci:)* deteriorate; *(arrabbiarsi)* get angry

alte'rato *a (suono)* distorted; *(viso)* careworn; *(cibo)* spoilt; *(vino)* adulterated; *(arrabbiato)* angry

alterazi'one *nf* alteration; *(di vino)* adulteration

al'terco *nm* altercation

alte'rigia *nf* haughtiness

alter'nanza *nf* alternation; *(in agricoltura)* rotation; *Pol* regular change in government

alter'nare *vt* alternate

alter'narsi *vr* alternate

alterna'tiva *nf* alternative

alterna'tivo *a* alternate; **medicina alternativa** alternative medicine

alter'nato *a* alternating

alterna'tore *nm Electr* alternator

al'terno *a* alternate; **a giorni alterni** every other day

al'tero *a* haughty

al'tezza *nf* height; *(profondità)* depth;

(*suono*) pitch; (*di tessuto*) width; (*titolo*) Highness; **essere all'~ di** be on a level with; *fig* be up to. **~ libera di passaggio** headroom

altezzosa'mente *adv* haughtily

altezzosità *nf* haughtiness

altez'zoso *a* haughty

al'ticcio *a* tipsy, merry

al'timetro *nm* altimeter

altipi'ano *nm* plateau

altiso'nante *a* high-sounding

alti'tudine *nf* altitude

'**alto** *a* high; (*di statura*) tall; (*profondo*) deep; (*suono*) high-pitched; (*tessuto*) wide; *Geog* northern; **a notte alta** in the middle of the night; **avere degli alti e bassi** have some ups and downs; **di ~ bordo** high-class; **di ~ rango** high-ranking; **ad alta definizione** high-definition; **ad alta fedeltà** high-fidelity; **ad ~ livello** high-level; **a voce alta, ad alta voce** in a loud voice; (*leggere*) aloud; **essere in ~ mare** be on the high seas; *fig* be all at sea. **alta borghesia** *nf* gentry. **~ commissariato** *nm* High Commission. **alta finanza** *nf* high finance. **alta frequenza** *nf* high frequency. **~ medioevo** *nm* Dark Ages. **alta moda** *nf* high fashion. **alta pressione** *nf* (*metereologica*) high pressure. **alta società** *nf* high society. **alta tensione** *nf* high voltage. **~ tradimento** *nm* high treason ● *adv* high; **in ~** (*essere*) at the top; (*guardare*) up; **mani in ~!** hands up!; **dall'~** from above; **guardare qcno dall'~ in basso** look down on sb

altoate'sino *a* South Tirolese

alto'forno *nm* blast-furnace

altolà *int* halt there!

altolo'cato *a* highly placed

altopar'lante *nm* loudspeaker

altopi'ano *nm* plateau

altret'tanto *a & pron* as much; (*pl*) as many ● *adv* likewise; **buona fortuna! – grazie, ~** good luck! – thank you, the same to you

altri'menti *adv* otherwise

'**altro** *a* other; **un ~, un'altra** another; **l'altr'anno** last year; **l'~ ieri** the day before yesterday; **domani l'~** the day after tomorrow; **l'ho visto l'~ giorno** I saw him the other day ● *pron* other [one]; **un ~, un'altra** another [one]; **ne vuoi dell'~?** would you like some more?; **l'un l'~** one another; **nessun ~** nobody else; **gli altri** (*la gente*) other people ● *nm* something else; **non fa ~ che lavorare** he does nothing but work; **desidera ~?** (*in negozio*) anything else?; **più che ~, sono stanco** I'm tired more than anything; **se non ~** at least; **senz'~** certainly; **tra l'~** what's more; **~ che!** absolutely!

altrochè *adv* absolutely!

altroi'eri *nm* **l'~** the day before yesterday

al'tronde: **d'~** *adv* on the other hand

al'trove *adv* elsewhere

al'trui *a* other people's ● *nm* other people's belongings *pl*

altru'ismo *nm* altruism

altruista *nmf* altruist

al'tura *nf* high ground; *Naut* deep sea

a'lunno, -a *nmf* pupil

alve'are *nm* hive

'**alveo** *nm* bed

alzabandi'era *nm inv* flag-raising

alzacri'stallo *nm Auto* window winder

al'zare *vt* lift, raise; (*costruire*) build; *Naut* hoist; **~ le spalle** shrug one's shoulders; **~ i tacchi** *fig* take to one's heels; **~ la voce** raise one's voice; **~ il volume** turn up the volume

al'zarsi *vr* (*in piedi*) stand up; (*da letto*) get up; (*vento, temperatura:*) rise

al'zata *nf* lifting; (*aumento*) rise; (*da letto*) getting up; *Archit* elevation. **~ di spalle** shrug of the shoulders

alza'taccia *nf fam* **fare un'~** get up at the crack of dawn

al'zato *a* up

A.M. *abbr* (**aeronautica militare**) Air Force

a'mabile *a* lovable; (*vino*) sweet

amabilità *nf* kindness

amabil'mente *adv* kindly

a'maca *nf* hammock

a'malgama *nm* amalgam

amalga'mare *vt* amalgamate

amalga'marsi *vr* amalgamate

ama'nita *nf Bot* amanita

a'mante *a* **~ di** fond of ● *nm* lover. **~ degli animali** animal lover ● *nf* mistress. **~ della lettura** book lover

amara'mente *adv* bitterly

ama'ranto *nm Bot* amarant[h]us; (*colore*) rich purple ● *a* rich purple

a'mare *vt* love; be fond of (*musica, sport ecc*)

amareggia'mento *nm* bitterness

amareggi'are *vt* embitter

amareggi'arsi *vr* become embittered

amareggi'ato *a* embittered

ama'rena *nf* sour black cherry

ama'retto *nm* macaroon

ama'rezza *nf* bitterness; (*dolore*) sorrow

a'maro *a* bitter ● *nm* bitterness; (*liquore*) bitters *pl*

ama'rognolo *a* rather bitter

a'mato, -a *a* loved ● *nmf* beloved

ama'|tore, -'trice *nmf* lover

a'mazzone *nf* (*in mitologia*) Amazon; **all'~** side saddle

Amaz'zonia *nf* Amazonia

amaz'zonico *a* Amazonian

ambasce'ria *nf* diplomatic mission

ambasci'ata *nf* embassy; (*messaggio*) message

ambascia'|tore, -'trice *nm* ambassador ● *nf* ambassadress

ambe'due *a & pron* both

ambi'destro *a* ambidextrous

ambien'tale *a* environmental

ambienta'lismo *nm* environmentalism

ambienta'lista *a & nmf* environmentalist

ambienta'mento *nm* acclimatization

ambien'tare *vt* acclimatize; set (*personaggio, film ecc*)

ambien'tarsi *vr* get acclimatized

ambi'ente *nm* environment; (*stanza*) room

ambiguità *nf inv* ambiguity; (*di persona*) shadiness

am'biguo *a* ambiguous; (*persona*) shady

am'bire *vi* ~ **a** aspire to

am'bito *a* (*lavoro, incarico*) much sought-after

'ambito *nm* sphere

ambiva'lente *a* ambivalent

ambiva'lenza *nf* ambivalence

ambizi'one *nf* ambition

ambizi'oso *a* ambitious

amblio'pia *nf* lazy eye

'ambo *a inv* both ● *nm* (*in tombola, lotto*) double

'ambra *nf* amber

am'brato *a* amber

ambu'lante *a* wandering; **venditore** ~ hawker

ambu'lanza *nf* ambulance

ambulatori'ale *a* **essere trattato con intervento** ~ have day surgery

ambula'torio *nm* (*di medico*) surgery; (*di ospedale*) out-patients' [department]. ~ **dentistico** dental clinic

Am'burgo *nf* Hamburg

a'meba *nf* amoeba

a'mebico *a* amoebic

'amen *int* amen; **e allora** ~! well, so be it!

amenità *nf inv* (*facezia*) pleasantry

a'meno *a* pleasant

amenor'rea *nf Med* amenorrhoea

A'merica *nf* America. ~ **centrale** Central America. ~ **Latina** Latin America. ~ **del nord/sud** North/South America

america'nata *nf* (*pej: film*) American rubbish

america'nismo *nm* Americanism; (*patriottismo*) flag-waving

americaniz'zarsi *vr* become Americanized

ameri'cano, -a *a* & *nmf* American

ame'rindio *a* a Native American

ame'tista *nf* amethyst

ami'anto *nm* asbestos

ami'chevole *a* friendly

ami'cizia *nf* friendship; **fare** ~ **con qcno** make friends with sb; **amicizie** *pl* (*amici*) friends

a'mico, -a *a* (*parola, persona*) friendly ● *nmf* friend; ~ **del cuore** bosom friend. ~ **d'infanzia** childhood friend. ~ **intimo** close friend. ~ **di penna** penfriend, penpal

'amido *nm* starch

ammac'care *vt* dent (*metallo*); bruise (*frutto*)

ammac'carsi *vr* (*metallo:*) get dented; (*frutto:*) bruise

ammac'cato *a* (*metallo*) dented; (*frutto*) bruised

ammacca'tura *nf* dent; (*livido*) bruise

ammaestra'mento *nm* training

ammae'strare *vt* (*istruire*) teach; train (*animale*)

ammae'strato *a* trained

ammaestra|'tore, -'trice *nmf* trainer

ammainabandi'era *nm inv* flag-lowering

ammai'nare *vt* lower (*bandiera*); furl (*vele*)

amma'larsi *vr* fall ill

amma'lato, -a *a* ill ● *nmf* sick person; (*paziente*) patient

ammali'are *vt* bewitch

ammali'ato *a* bewitched

ammalia|'tore, -'trice *a* bewitching ● *nm* enchanter ● *nf* enchantress

am'manco *nm* deficit

ammanet'tare *vt* handcuff

ammani'carsi *vr fig* acquire connections

ammani'cato *a* **essere** ~ have connections

ammanigli'arsi *vr fig* = **ammanicarsi**

ammanigli'ato *a fig* = **ammanicato**

amman'sire *vt* tame, domesticate (*animali*); *fig* pacify, placate

amman'sirsi *vr* (*animali:*) become tame; *fig* calm down

amman'tarsi *vr* (*persona:*) wrap oneself up in a cloak; ~ **di** *fig* feign (*virtù*)

amma'raggio *nm* splashdown

amma'rare *vi* put down on the sea; (*nave spaziale:*) splash down

ammassa'mento *nm Mil* build-up

ammas'sare *vt* amass

ammas'sarsi *vr* crowd together

am'masso *nm* mass; (*mucchio*) pile

ammat'tire *vi* go mad

ammazzacaffè *nm inv* liqueur

ammazza'fame *nm inv* stodge

ammaz'zare *vt* kill

ammaz'zarsi *vr* (*suicidarsi, fig*) kill oneself; (*rimanere ucciso*) be killed

am'menda *nf* amends *pl*; (*multa*) fine; **fare** ~ **di qcsa** make amends for sth

am'messo *pp di* **ammettere** ● *conj* ~ **che** supposing that

am'mettere *vt* admit; (*riconoscere*) acknowledge; (*supporre*) suppose; **ammettiamo che...** let's suppose [that]...

ammez'zato *nm* (*piano ammezzato*) mezzanine

ammic'care *vi* wink

ammini'strare *vt* administer; (*gestire*) run

ammini'strarsi *vr fig* manage one's finances

amministra'tivo *a* administrative

amministra|'tore, -'trice *nmf* administrator; (*di azienda*) manager; (*di società*) director; ~ **aggiunto** associate director. ~ **del condominio** property manger. ~ **delegato** managing director. ~ **unico** sole director

amministrazi'one *nf* administration; **fatti di ordinaria** ~ *fig* routine matters. ~ **aziendale** (*studi*) business studies. ~ **comunale** local council. ~ **controllata** receivership. ~ **pubblica** civil service. ~ **regionale** regional council

ammino'acido *nm* amino acid

ammi'rabile *a* admirable

ammi'raglia *nf* flag-ship

ammiragli'ato *nm* admiralty
ammi'raglio *nm* admiral
ammi'rare *vt* admire
ammi'rato *a* **restare/essere ~** be full of admiration
ammira|'tore, -'trice *nmf* admirer
ammirazi'one *nf* admiration
ammi'revole *a* admirable
ammis'sibile *a* admissible
ammissibilità *nf* acceptability
ammissi'one *nf* admission; (*approvazione*) acknowledgement
ammobili'are *vt* furnish
ammobili'ato *a* furnished; **stanza ammobiliata** furnished room
ammoderna'mento *nm* modernization
ammoder'nare *vt* modernize
ammoder'narsi *vr* move with the times
am'modo *a* proper ● *adv* properly
ammogli'are *vt* marry off
ammogli'arsi *vr* get married
ammogli'ato *a* married ● *nm* married man
am'mollo *nm* **in ~** soaking; **mettere in ~** pre-soak
ammo'niaca *nf* ammonia
ammoni'mento *nm* warning; (*di rimprovero*) admonishment
ammo'nire *vt* warn; (*rimproverare*) admonish
ammoni'tore *a* admonishing
ammonizi'one *nf* Sport warning; (*rimprovero*) admonishment
ammon'tare *vi* **~ a** amount to ● *nm* amount
ammonticchi'are *vt* heap up, pile up
ammonticchi'arsi *vr* pile up
ammor'bare *vt* (*con odore*) pollute; (*con malattie*) infect
ammorbi'dente *nm* (*per panni*) softener
ammorbi'dire *vt* soften
ammorbi'dirsi *vr* soften
ammorta'mento *nm* Comm amortization
ammor'tare *vt* pay off (*spesa*); Comm amortize (*debito*)
ammortiz'zare *vt* Comm = **ammortare**; Mech damp
ammortizza'tore *nm* shock-absorber
ammosci'are *vt* make flabby
ammosci'arsi *vi* get flabby
ammucchi'are *vt* pile up
ammucchi'arsi *vr* pile up
ammucchi'ata *nf* (*sl: orgia*) orgy; **un'~ di** (*fam: ammasso*) loads of
ammuf'fire *vi* go mouldy
ammuf'firsi *vr* go mouldy
ammuf'fito *a* mouldy; *fig* stuffy
ammutina'mento *nm* mutiny
ammuti'narsi *vr* mutiny
ammuti'nato *a* mutinous ● *nm* mutineer
ammuto'lire *vi* be struck dumb
ammuto'lirsi *vr* fall silent
amne'sia *nf* amnesia
amni'stia *nf* amnesty
amnisti'are *vt* amnesty
'amo *nm* hook; *fig* bait

amo'rale *a* amoral
amoralità *nf* amorality
a'more *nm* love; **d'~** (*canzone, film*) love; **fare l'~** make love; **per l'amor di Dio/del cielo!** for heaven's sake!; **andare d'~ e d'accordo** get on like a house on fire; **amor proprio** self-respect; **amor cortese** courtly love; **è un ~** (*persona:*) he's/she's a darling; **per ~ di** for the sake of; **amori** *pl* love affairs
amoreggi'are *vi* flirt
amo'revole *a* loving
amorevol'mente *adv* lovingly
a'morfo *a* shapeless; (*persona*) colourless, grey
amo'rino *nm* cherub
amorosa'mente *adv* lovingly
amo'roso *a* loving; (*sguardo ecc*) amorous; (*lettera, relazione*) love *attrib*
am'pere *nm inv* ampere; **da 15 ~** 15-amp
ampe'rometro *nm* ammeter
ampia'mente *adv* widely
ampi'ezza *nf* (*di esperienza*) breadth; (*di stanza*) spaciousness; (*di gonna*) fullness; (*importanza*) scale. **~ di vedute** broad-mindedness
'ampio *a* ample; (*esperienza*) wide; (*stanza*) spacious; (*vestito*) loose; (*gonna, descrizione*) full; (*pantaloni*) baggy; **~ di vedute** broadminded
am'plesso *nm* embrace
amplia'mento *nm* (*di casa, porto*) enlargement; (*di strada, conoscenze*) broadening
ampli'are *vt* broaden, widen (*strada, conoscenze*); enlarge (*casa*)
ampli'arsi *vr* broaden, grow wider
amplifi'care *vt* amplify; *fig* magnify
amplifica'tore *nm* amplifier
amplificazi'one *nf* amplification
am'polla *nf* cruet
ampol'loso *a* pompous
ampu'tare *vt* amputate
amputazi'one *nf* amputation
amu'leto *nm* amulet
A.N. *abbr* Pol (**Alleanza Nazionale**) National Alliance (*right-wing party*)
anabbagli'ante *a* Auto dipped ● *nm* **anabbaglianti** *pl* dipped headlights
anaboliz'zante *nm* anabolic steroid
ana'cardi *nmpl* cashew nuts
ana'cardio *nm* cashew
ana'conda *nf* Zool anaconda
anacro'nismo *nm* anachronism
anacro'nistico *a* anachronistic; **essere ~** be an anachronism
anae'robico *a* anaerobic
anafi'lattico *a* **shock ~** Med anaphylactic shock
a'nagrafe *nf* (*ufficio*) registry office; (*registro*) register of births, marriages and deaths
ana'grafico *a* **dati** *pl* **anagrafici** personal data
ana'gramma *nm* anagram
anal'colico *a* non-alcoholic ● *nm* soft drink, non-alcoholic drink

a'nale *a* anal

analfa'beta *a & nmf* illiterate

analfabe'tismo *nm* illiteracy

anal'gesico *nm* painkiller

a'nalisi *nf inv* analysis; *Med* test; **in ultima ~** in the final analysis. **~ grammaticale/ del periodo/logica** parsing. **~ di mercato** market research. **~ del percorso critico** critical path analysis. **~ del sangue** blood test

ana'lista *nmf* analyst. **~ economico** economic analyst. **~ finanziario** business analyst

ana'litico *a* analytical

analiz'zabile *a* analysable

analiz'zare *vt* analyse; *Med* test, analyse

anal'lergico *a* hypoallergenic

analoga'mente *adv* analogously

analo'gia *nf* analogy

ana'logico *a* analogue

analo'gismo *nm* reasoning by analogy

a'nalogo *a* analogous

anam'nesi *nf inv* medical history

'ananas *nm inv* pineapple

anar'chia *nf* anarchy

a'narchico, -a *a* anarchic ● *nmf* anarchist

anar'chismo *nm* anarchism

A.N.A.S. *nf abbr* (**Azienda Nazionale Autonoma delle Strade**) *national road maintenance authority*

ana'tema *nm* anathema

anato'mia *nf* anatomy

ana'tomico *a* anatomical; ⟨*sedia*⟩ contoured, ergonomic

'anatra *nf* duck. **~ selvatica** mallard

ana'troccolo *nm* duckling

'anca *nf* hip; (*di animale*) flank

ance'strale *a* ancestral

'anche *conj* also, too, as well; (*persino*) even; **parla ~ francese** he also speaks French, he speaks French too, he speaks French as well; **~ se** even if

ancheggi'are *vi* wiggle one's hips

anchilo'sarsi *vr fig* stiffen up

anchilo'sato *a fig* stiff

an'cora *adv* still; (*con negazione*) yet; (*di nuovo*) again; (*di più*) some more; **~ una volta** once more; **non ~** not yet; **~ esistente** extant; **~ più bello** even more beautiful; **~ una birra** another beer, one more beer

'ancora *nf* anchor; **gettare l'~** drop anchor. **~ di salvezza** last hope

anco'raggio *nm* anchorage

anco'rare *vt* anchor

anco'rarsi *vr* anchor, drop anchor; **~ a** *fig* cling to

Andalu'sia *nf* Andalusia

anda'luso, -a *a & nmf* Andalusian

anda'mento *nm* (*del mercato, degli affari*) trend

an'dante *a* (*corrente*) current; (*di poco valore*) cheap ● *nm Mus* andante

an'dare *vi* go; (*funzionare*) work; (*essere di moda*) be in; **~ via** (*partire*) leave; ⟨*macchia*⟩ come out; **~ a piedi** walk; **~ a sciare** go skiing; **~ [bene]** (*confarsi*) suit; ⟨*taglia*⟩ fit; **ti va bene alle tre?** does three o'clock suit you?; **non mi va di mangiare** I don't feel like eating; **~ di fretta** be in a hurry; **~ fiero di** be proud of; **~ di moda** be in fashion; **va per i 20 anni** he's nearly 20; **ma va'** [là]! come on!; **come va?** how are things?; **~ a male** go off; **~ a fuoco** go up in flames; **~ perduto** be lost; **va spedito [entro] stamattina** it must be sent this morning; **ne va del mio lavoro** my job is at stake; **come è andata a finire?** how did it turn out?; **cosa vai dicendo?** what are you talking about?; **andarsene** go away; (*morire*) pass away ● *nm* going; **~ e venire** (*andirivieni*) comings and goings *pl*; **a lungo ~** eventually; **a tutto ~** at full speed; **con l'~ del tempo** with the passing of time

an'data *nf* going; (*viaggio*) outward journey; **biglietto di sola ~/di ~ e ritorno** single/ return [ticket]

anda'tura *nf* walk; (*portamento*) bearing; *Naut* tack; *Sport* pace

an'dazzo *nm fam* turn of events; **prendere un brutto ~** turn nasty

'Ande *nfpl* **le ~** the Andes

an'dino *a* Andean

andirivi'eni *nm inv* comings and goings *pl*

'andito *nm* passage

An'dorra *nf* Andorra

an'drone *nm* entrance

andro'pausa *nf hum* male menopause

a'neddoto *nm* anecdote

ane'lare *vt* **~ a** long for

a'nelito *nm* longing

a'nello *nm* ring; (*di catena*) link. **~ di fidanzamento** engagement ring. **~ d'oro** gold ring

ane'mia *nf* anaemia

a'nemico *a* anaemic

a'nemone *nm* anemone

aneste'sia *nf* anaesthesia; (*sostanza*) anaesthetic. **~ epidurale** epidural

aneste'sista *nmf* anaesthetist

ane'stetico *a & nm* anaesthetic

anestetiz'zare *vt* anaesthetize

a'neto *nm* dill

anfeta'mina *nf* amphetamine

an'fibi *nmpl* (*stivali*) army boots

an'fibio *nm* amphibian ● *a* amphibious

anfite'atro *nm* amphitheatre

'anfora *nf* amphora

an'fratto *nm* ravine

an'gelico *a* angelic

'angelo *nm* angel. **~ custode** guardian angel

anghe'ria *nf* harassment

an'gina *nf inv* **~ [pectoris]** angina [pectoris]

angi'ologo, -a *nmf Med* angiologist

anglica'nesimo *nm Relig* Anglicanism

angli'cano, -a *a & nmf Relig* Anglican

angli'cismo *nm* Anglicism

angliciz'zare *vt* anglicize

anglo+ *pref* Anglo+

angloameri'cano, -a *nmf* Anglo-American

an'glofilo, -a *a & nmf* Anglophile

an'glofono, -a *nmf* English-speaker

anglofran'cese *a* Anglo-French

anglo'sassone *a & nmf* Anglo-Saxon

An'gola *nf* Angola

ango'lano, -a *a & nmf* Angolan

ango'lare *a* angular

angolazi'one *nf* angle shot; *fig* point of view

angoli'era *nf* (*mobile*) corner cupboard

'angolo *nm* corner; *Math* angle; **dietro l'~** round the corner; **fare ~ con** ‹*negozio, casa:*› be on the corner of. **~ acuto** acute angle. **~ [di] cottura** kitchenette. **~ retto** right angle

ango'loso *a* angular; ‹*carattere*› difficult to get on with

'angora *nf* [**lana d'**]**~** angora

an'goscia *nf* anguish

angosci'are *vt* torment

angosci'arsi *vr* (*preoccuparsi*) worry oneself sick, torment oneself

angosci'ato *a* agonized

angosci'oso *a* (*disperato*) anguished; (*che dà angoscia*) distressing

angu'illa *nf* eel

an'guria *nf* water-melon

an'gustia *nf* (*ansia*) anxiety; (*penuria*) poverty

angusti'are *vt* distress

angusti'arsi *vr* be distressed (**per** about)

angusti'ato *a* distressed

an'gusto *a* narrow

'anice *nm* anise; *Culin* aniseed; (*liquore*) anisette

ani'cino *nm* (*biscotto*) aniseed biscuit

ani'dride *nf* **~ carbonica** carbon dioxide. **~ solforosa** sulphur dioxide

'anima *nf* soul; **non c'era ~ viva** there was not a soul about; **all'~!** good grief!; **mi fa dannare l'~!** he'll be the death of me!; **l'~ della festa** the life and soul of the party; **un'~ in pena** a soul in torment; **volere un bene dell'~ a qcno** love sb to death; **la buon'~ della zia** my late aunt, God rest her soul. **~ gemella** soul mate

ani'male *a & nm* animal. **animali** *pl* **domestici** pets. **animali** *pl* **selvatici** wild animals

anima'lesco *a* animal

anima'lista *nmf* animal activist

ani'mare *vt* give life to; (*ravvivare*) enliven; (*incoraggiare*) encourage

ani'marsi *vr* come to life; (*accalorarsi*) become animated

ani'mato *a* animate; ‹*discussione*› animated; ‹*strada, paese*› lively

anima'tore, -'trice *nmf* leading spirit; *Cinema* animator

animazi'one *nf* animation; **con ~** animatedly

ani'melle *nfpl* (*di agnello, vitello*) sweetbread

'animo *nm* (*mente*) mind; (*indole*) disposition; (*cuore*) heart; **perdersi d'~** lose heart; **farsi ~** take heart

animosa'mente *adv* boldly

animosità *nf* animosity

ani'moso *a* brave; (*ostile*) hostile

ani'setta *nf* anisette

'anitra *nf* duck

annacqua'mento *nm fig* watering down, dilution

annac'quare *vt anche fig* water down

annac'quato *a* watered down; ‹*colore, resoconto*› insipid

annaffi'are *vt* water

annaffia'toio *nm* watering-can

an'nali *nmpl* annals; **restare negli ~** go down in history

anna'spare *vi* flounder

an'nata *nf* year; (*importo annuale*) annual amount; (*di vino*) vintage; **vino d'~** vintage wine

annebbia'mento *nm* fog build-up; *fig* clouding

annebbi'are *vt* cloud ‹*vista, mente*›

annebbi'arsi *vr* get misty; (*in città, su autostrada*) get foggy; ‹*vista, mente:*› grow dim

annega'mento *nm* drowning

anne'gare *vt/i* drown

anne'rire *vt/i* blacken

anne'rirsi *vr* become black

an'nessi *nmpl* (*costruzioni*) outbuildings; **tutti gli ~ e i connessi** all the appurtenances

annessi'one *nf* (*di nazione*) annexation

an'nesso *pp di annettere ● a* attached; ‹*Stato*› annexed

an'nettere *vt* add; (*accludere*) enclose; annex ‹*Stato*›

annichi'lire *vt* annihilate

anni'darsi *vr* nest

annienta'mento *nm* annihilation

annien'tare *vt* annihilate

annien'tarsi *vr* abase oneself

anniver'sario *a & nm* anniversary. **~ di matrimonio** wedding anniversary

'anno *nm* year; **Buon A~!** Happy New Year!; **quanti anni ha?** how old are you?; **Tommaso ha dieci anni** Thomas is ten [years old]; **gli anni '30** the '30s. **~ accademico** academic year. **~ bisestile** leap year. **~ civile** calendar year. **~ giudiziario** law year. **~ luce** light year. **~ nuovo** New Year. **~ sabbatico** *Univ* sabbatical. **anni** *pl* **verdi** salad days

anno'dare *vt* knot; do up ‹*cintura*›; *fig* form

anno'darsi *vr* become knotted

annoi'are *vt* bore; (*recare fastidio*) annoy

annoi'arsi *vr* get bored; (*condizione*) be bored

annoi'ato *a* bored

an'noso *a* ‹*questione*› age-old

anno'tare *vt* note down; annotate ‹*testo*›

annotazi'one *nf* note

annove'rare *vt* number

annu'ale *a* annual, yearly

annual'mente *adv* annually

annu'ario *nm* year-book

annu'ire *vi* nod; (*acconsentire*) agree

annulla'mento *nm* annulment; (*di appuntamento*) cancellation

annul'lare *vt* annul; cancel (*appuntamento*); (*togliere efficacia a*) undo; disallow (*gol*); (*distruggere*) destroy

annul'larsi *vr* cancel each other out

an'nullo *nm* (*timbro*) franking

annunci'are *vt* announce; (*preannunciare*) foretell

annuncia|'tore, -'trice *nmf* announcer

annunciazi'one *nf* Annunciation

an'nuncio *nm* announcement; (*pubblicitario*) advertisement; (*notizia*) news. **annunci** *pl* **economici** classified advertisements. **annunci** *pl* **mortuari** obituaries, death notices. **~ pubblicitario** advertisement

'annuo *a* annual, yearly

annu'sare *vt* sniff

annu'sata *nf* **dare un'~ a** have a sniff at

annuvola'mento *nm* clouding over

annuvo'lare *vt* cloud

annuvo'larsi *vr* cloud over

'ano *nm* anus

a'nodino *a* anodyne

'anodo *nm* anode

anoma'lia *nf* anomaly

a'nomalo *a* anomalous

a'nonima *nf* **A~ Alcolisti** Alcoholics Anonymous. **~ sequestri** *Italian criminal organization specializing in kidnapping*

anoni'mato *nm* **mantenere l'~** remain anonymous

anonimità *nf* anonymity

a'nonimo, -a *a* anonymous ● *nmf* unknown person; (*pittore, scrittore*) anonymous painter/writer

anores'sia *nf Med* anorexia

ano'ressico, -a *nmf* anorexic

anor'male *a* abnormal ● *nmf* deviant, abnormal person

anormalità *nf inv* abnormality

ANSA *nf abbr* (**Agenzia Nazionale Stampa Associata**) *Italian press agency*

'ansa *nf* handle; (*di fiume*) bend

an'sante *a* panting

an'sare *vi* pant

'ansia, ansietà *nf* anxiety; **stare/essere in ~ per** be anxious about

ansi'mante *a* breathless

ansi'mare *vi* gasp for breath

ansio'litico *nm* tranquillizer

ansi'oso *a* anxious

'anta *nf* (*di finestra*) shutter; (*di armadio*) door

antago'nismo *nm* antagonism

antago'nista *nmf* antagonist

antago'nistico *a* antagonistic

an'tartico *a & nm* Antarctic

An'tartide *nf* Antarctica

ante'bellico *a* pre-war

antece'dente *a* preceding ● *nm* precedent

ante'fatto *nm* prior event

ante'guerra *a* pre-war ● *nm* pre-war period

ante'nato, -a *nmf* ancestor

an'tenna *nf Radio, TV* aerial; (*di animale*) antenna; *Naut* yard; **rizzare le antenne** *fig* prick up one's ears. **~ parabolica** satellite dish. **~ radar** radar scanner

ante'porre *vt* put before

ante'prima *nf* preview; **vedere qcsa in ~** have a sneak preview of sth

anteri'ore *a* front *attrib*; (*nel tempo*) previous

anterior'mente *adv* (*nel tempo*) previously; (*nello spazio*) in front

antesi'gnano, -a *nmf fig* forerunner

anti+ *pref* anti+

antiabor'tista *nmf* antiabortionist ● *a* antiabortion *attrib*

anti'acido *nm* antacid

antiade'rente *a* (*padella*) nonstick

antia'ereo *a* anti-aircraft *attrib*

antial'lergico *a* hypoallergenic

antia'partheid *a inv* antiapartheid

antia'tomico *a* anti-nuclear; **rifugio ~** fall-out shelter

antibat'terico *a* antibacterial

antibi'otico *a & nm* antibiotic

antibloc'caggio *a inv* antilock *attrib*

anti'caglia *nf* (*oggetto*) piece of old junk

anti-cal'care *nm* softener

antica'mente *adv* in ancient times, long ago

anti'camera *nf* ante-room; **fare ~** be kept waiting

antichità *nf inv* antiquity; (*oggetto*) antique

antici'clone *nm* anticyclone

antici'clonico *a* (*area*) anti-cyclonic

antici'pare *vt* advance; *Comm* pay in advance; (*prevedere*) anticipate; (*prevenire*) forestall ● *vi* be early

anticipata'mente *adv* in advance

antici'pato *a* upfront; **pagamento ~** advance payment

anticipazi'one *nf* anticipation; (*notizia*) advance news

an'ticipo *nm* advance; (*caparra*) deposit; **in ~** early; (*nel lavoro*) ahead of schedule; **giocare d'~** *Sport, fig* anticipate the next move

an'tico *a* ancient; (*mobile ecc*) antique; (*vecchio*) old; **all'antica** old-fashioned ● *nm* **gli antichi** the ancients

anticomu'nista *a & nmf* anti-communist

anticoncezio'nale *a & nm* contraceptive

anticonfor'mismo *nm* unconventionality

anticonfor'mista *nmf* nonconformist

anticonfor'mistico *a* unconventional, nonconformist

anticonge'lante *a & nm* anti-freeze

anticonsu'mismo *nm* anti-consumerism

anti'corpo *nm* antibody

anticostituzio'nale *a* unconstitutional

anti'crimine *a inv* (*squadra*) crime *attrib*

antidemo'cratico *a* undemocratic

antidepres'sivo *nm* antidepressant

antidiluvi'ano *a fig* antediluvian

antidolo'rifico *nm* painkiller

anti'doping *nm inv Sport* dope test

an'tidoto *nm* antidote

anti'droga *a inv* ‹*campagna*› anti-drugs; ‹*squadra*› drug *attrib*

antie'stetico *a* ugly

antifa'scismo *nm* anti-fascism

antifa'scista *a & nmf* anti-fascist

an'tifona *nf fig* dull and repetitive speech; **capire l'~** take the hint; **sempre la stessa ~** always the same old story

anti'forfora *a inv* dandruff *attrib*

anti'fumo *a inv* anti-smoking

anti'furto *nm* anti-theft device; (*allarme*) alarm ●*a inv* ‹*sistema*› anti-theft

anti'gelo *a inv* anti-freeze ● *nm* antifreeze; (*parabrezza*) defroster

anti'gene *nm* antigen

antigi'enico *a* unhygienic

anti-inflazi'one *a inv* anti-inflation

An'tille *nfpl* **le ~** the West Indies

an'tilope *nf* antelope

anti'mafia *a inv* anti-Mafia

antimilita'rista *a inv* anti-militaristic ● *nmf* anti-militarist

antin'cendio *a inv* **allarme ~** fire alarm; **porta ~** fire door

anti'nebbia *a inv* [**faro**] **~** *Auto* foglamp, foglight

antine'vralgico *a* pain-killing ● *nm* pain-killer

antinfiamma'torio *a & nm* anti-inflammatory

antinflazio'nistico *a* anti-inflationary

antinquina'mento *a inv* anti-pollution

antinucle'are *a* anti-nuclear

antio'rario *a* anti-clockwise

antiparassi'tario *nm* insecticide

antiparlamen'tare *a* unparliamentary

antipasti'era *nf* hors d'oeuvre dish

anti'pasto *nm* hors d'oeuvre, starter. **antipasti** *pl* **caldi** hot starters. **antipasti** *pl* **freddi** cold starters. **antipasti** *pl* **misti** variety of starters

antipa'tia *nf* antipathy

anti'patico *a* unpleasant

an'tipodi *nmpl* Antipodes; **essere agli ~** *fig* be poles apart

anti'polio *nf inv* (*vaccino*) polio vaccine; **fare l'~** have a polio injection ● *a* ‹*siero, vaccino*› polio *attrib*

antipopo'lare *a* anti-working-class

antiprobizio'nismo *nm* anti-prohibitionism

antiproibizio'nista *a & nmf* anti-prohibitionist

antiproi'ettile *a inv* bullet-proof

antiquari'ato *nm* antique trade; **pezzo d'~** antique

anti'quario, -a *nmf* antique dealer

anti'quato *a* antiquated

antiraz'zismo *nm* antiracism

antireu'matico *a & nm* anti-rheumatic

antiri'flesso *a inv* antiglare

anti'ruggine *nm inv* rust-inhibitor ●*a* anti-rust

anti'rughe *a inv* anti-wrinkle *attrib*

anti'scasso *a inv* ‹*porta*› burglar-proof

antisci'opero *a inv* anti-strike

anti'scippo *a inv* theft-proof

anti'scivolo *a inv* nonskid

antise'mita *a* anti-Semitic

antisemi'tismo *nm* anti-Semitism

anti'settico *a & nm* antiseptic

antisinda'cale *a* ‹*comportamento*› anti-trade-union

anti'sismico *a* earthquake-proof

antisoci'ale *a* anti-social

antiso'lare *a & nm* suntan

antisommer'gibile *a inv* anti-submarine ● *nm* submarine hunter

antista'minico *nm* antihistamine

anti'stante *prep* **~ a** in front of

anti'tarlo *nm inv* woodworm treatment

anti'tarmico *a* mothproof

antiterro'rismo *nm* counter-terrorism

antiterro'rista *a* antiterrorist

antiterro'ristico *a* antiterrorist

an'titesi *nf inv* antithesis

antite'tanica *nf* tetanus injection

antite'tanico *a* tetanus *attrib*

anti'tetico *a* antithetical

anti'trust *a* antitrust

antitumo'rale *a* which stops the growth of tumours

anti'urto *a* shockproof

antivaio'losa *nf* smallpox injection

anti'vipera *a* **siero ~** snakebite antidote

antivi'rale *a* anti-viral

antolo'gia *nf* anthology

an'tonimo *nm* antonym

antono'masia: **per ~** *a* ‹*poeta*› quintessential

antra'cite *nf* anthracite; (*colore*) charcoal [grey]

'antro *nm* cavern

antro'pofago *a* man-eating, cannibalistic

antropolo'gia *nf* anthropology

antropo'logico *a* anthropological

antro'pologo, -a *nmf* anthropologist

anu'lare *nm* ring-finger

An'versa *nf* Antwerp

'anzi *conj* in fact; (*o meglio*) or better still; (*al contrario*) on the contrary

anzianità *nf* old age; (*di servizio*) seniority

anzi'ano, -a *a* old, elderly; (*di grado ecc*) senior ● *nmf* elderly person

anziché *conj* rather than

anzi'tempo *adv* prematurely

anzi'tutto *adv* first of all

a'orta *nf* aorta

A'pache *mf inv* Apache

apar'theid *nf* apartheid

apar'titico *a* unaligned

apa'tia *nf* apathy

a'patico *a* apathetic

'ape *nf* bee. **~ regina** queen bee

aperi'tivo *nm* aperitif

aperta'mente *adv* openly

a'perto *a* open; **all'aria aperta** in the open air; **all'~** ⟨*piscina, teatro*⟩ open-air. **~ a tutti** open to all comers. **rimanere a bocca aperta** be dumbfounded

aper'tura *nf* opening; (*inizio*) beginning; (*ampiezza*) spread; (*di arco*) span; *Pol* overtures *pl*; *Phot* aperture. **~ alare** wing span. **~ di credito** loan agreement. **~ mentale** openness

api'ario *nm* apiary

'apice *nm* apex; **l'~ di** the acme of

apicol'tore, -'trice *nmf* beekeeper

apicol'tura *nf* beekeeping

a'plomb *nm inv* (*di un abito*) hang; *fig* aplomb, self-assuredness

ap'nea *nf* **immersione in ~** free diving

Apoca'lisse *nf* **l'~** the Apocalypse

apoca'littico *a* apocalyptic

a'pocrifo *a* apocryphal

apo'geo *nm* apogee

a'polide *a* stateless ● *nmf* stateless person

apo'litico *a* apolitical

A'pollo *nm* Apollo

apolo'geta *nmf* apologist (**di** for)

apolo'gia *nf* apologia; (*celebrazione*) eulogy. **~ di reato** condoning of a criminal act

apoples'sia *nf* apoplexy

apo'plettico *a* apoplectic

a'postolo *nm* apostle

apostro'fare *vt* (*mettere un apostrofo a*) write with an apostrophe; reprimand ⟨*persona*⟩

a'postrofo *nm* apostrophe

apote'osi *nf* apotheosis

appaga'mento *nm* fulfilment

appa'gare *vt* satisfy

appa'garsi *vr* **~ di** be satisfied with

appa'gato *a* sated

appai'are *vt* pair; mate ⟨*animali*⟩

appallotto'lare *vt* roll into a ball

appallotto'larsi *vr* ⟨*gatto:*⟩ curl up in a ball; ⟨*farina:*⟩ become lumpy

appalta'tore *nm* contractor

ap'palto *nm* contract; **dare in ~** contract out; **gara di ~** call for tenders

appan'naggio *nm* (*in denaro*) annuity; *fig* prerogative

appan'nare *vt* mist ⟨*vetro*⟩; dim ⟨*vista*⟩

appan'narsi *vr* mist over; ⟨*vista:*⟩ grow dim

appa'rato *nm* apparatus; (*apparecchiamento*) array; (*pompa*) display. **~ digerente** digestive system. **~ scenico** set

apparecchi'are *vt* prepare ● *vi* lay the table *Br*, set the table

apparecchia'tura *nf* (*impianti*) equipment

appa'recchio *nm* apparatus; (*congegno*) device; (*radio, tv ecc*) set; (*aeroplano*) aircraft; (*telefono*) phone. **~ acustico** hearing aid

appa'rente *a* apparent

apparente'mente *adv* apparently

appa'renza *nf* appearance; **in ~** apparently

appa'rire *vi* appear; (*sembrare*) look

appari'scente *a* striking; *pej* gaudy

apparizi'one *nf* apparition

apparta'mento *nm* flat, apartment *Am*. **~ ammobiliato** furnished flat. **~ in multiproprietà** timeshare

appar'tarsi *vr* withdraw

appar'tato *a* secluded

apparte'nente *a* **~ a** belonging to

apparte'nenza *nf* membership

apparte'nere *vi* belong

appassio'nante *a* ⟨*storia, argomento*⟩ exciting

appassio'nare *vt* excite; (*commuovere*) move

appassio'narsi *vr* **~ a** become excited by

appassio'nato *a* passionate; **~ di** (*entusiastico*) fond of

appas'sire *vi* wither

appas'sirsi *vr* fade

appas'sito *a* faded

appel'larsi *vr* **~ a** appeal to

ap'pello *nm* appeal; (*chiamata per nome*) rollcall; (*esami*) exam session; **fare l'~** call the roll

ap'pena *adv* just; (*a fatica*) hardly ● *conj* [**non**] **~** as soon as, no sooner... than; **~ prima di** just before

ap'pendere *vt* hang [up]

appendi'abiti *nm inv* hat-stand, hallstand

appen'dice *nf* appendix; **romanzo d'~** novel serialized in a magazine or newspaper

appendi'cite *nf* appendicitis

Appen'nini *nmpl* **gli ~** the Apennines

appen'ninico *a* Apennine

appesan'tire *vt* weigh down

appesan'tirsi *vr* become heavy

ap'peso *pp di* **appendere** ● *a* hanging; (*impiccato*) hanged

appe'tito *nm* appetite; **aver ~** be hungry; **buon ~!** enjoy your meal!

appeti'toso *a* appetizing; *fig* tempting

appezza'mento *nm* plot of land

appia'nare *vt* level; *fig* smooth over

appia'narsi *vr* improve

appiat'tire *vt* flatten

appiat'tirsi *vr* flatten oneself; *fig* level out

appic'care *vt* **~ fuoco a** set fire to

appicci'care *vt* stick; **~ a** (*fig: appioppare*) palm off on ● *vi* be sticky

appicci'carsi *vr* stick; ⟨*cose:*⟩ stick together; **~ a qcno** *fig* stick to sb like glue

appiccica'ticcio *a* sticky; *fig* clingy

appicci'cato *a* **stare ~ a qcno** be all over sb

appicci'coso *a* sticky; *fig* clingy

appie'dato *a* **sono ~** I don't have the car; **sono rimasto ~** I was stranded

appi'eno *adv* fully

appigli'arsi *vr* **~ a** get hold of; *fig* stick to

ap'piglio *nm* fingerhold; (*per piedi*) foothold; *fig* pretext

appiop'pare *vt* **~ a** palm off on; (*fam: dare*) give; **~ un ceffone a qcno** slap sb

appiso'larsi *vr* doze off

applau'dire *vt/i* applaud

ap'plauso *nm* applause
appli'cabile *a* applicable
appli'care *vt* apply; enforce ‹*legge ecc*›
appli'carsi *vr* apply oneself
appli'cato *nmf* (*impiegato*) senior clerk ● *a* (*nel ricamo*) appliqué; **matematica applicata** applied mathematics
applica'tore *nm* applicator
applicazi'one *nf* application; (*di legge*) enforcement. **applicazioni** *pl* **tecniche** handicrafts
appoggi'are *vt* lean (**a** against); (*mettere*) put; (*sostenere*) back
appoggi'arsi *vr* ~ **a** lean against; *fig* rely on
appoggi'ato *a* leaning (**su** on; **contro**, **a** against)
ap'poggio *nm* support; **appoggi** *pl fig* influential contacts
appollai'arsi *vr fig* perch
ap'porre *vt* affix
appor'tare *vt* bring; (*causare*) cause; ~ **delle modifiche a qcsa** modify sth
ap'porto *nm* contribution
apposita'mente *adv* (*specialmente*) especially; **fatto** ~ purpose-made
ap'posito *a* proper
apposizi'one *nf* apposition
ap'posta *adv* on purpose; (*espressamente*) specially; **neanche a farlo** ~! what a coincidence!
apposta'mento *nm* ambush; (*caccia*) lying in wait
appo'stare *vt* post ‹*soldati*›
appo'starsi *vr* lie in wait
ap'prendere *vt* understand; (*imparare*) learn
apprendi'mento *nm* learning
appren'dista *nmf* apprentice
apprendi'stato *nm* apprenticeship
apprensi'one *nf* apprehension; **essere in** ~ **per** be anxious about
appren'sivo *a* apprehensive
ap'presso *adv* & *prep* (*vicino*) near; (*dietro*) behind; **come** ~ as follows
appre'stare *vt* prepare
appre'starsi *vr* get ready
apprez'zabile *a* appreciable
apprezza'mento *nm* appreciation; (*giudizio*) opinion
apprez'zare *vt* appreciate
apprez'zato *a* appreciated
ap'proccio *nm* approach
appro'dare *vi* land; ~ **a** *fig* come to; **non** ~ **a nulla** come to nothing
ap'prodo *nm* landing; (*luogo*) landing-stage
approfit'tare *vi* take advantage (**di** of), profit (**di** by)
approfitta'tore, -'trice *nmf* chancer
approfondi'mento *nm* deepening; **di** ~ ‹*corso*› advanced
approfon'dire *vt* broaden, widen ‹*indagine, conoscenze*›
approfon'dirsi *vr* ‹*divario:*› widen
approfon'dito *a* ‹*studio, ricerca*› in-depth

appron'tare *vt* get ready, prepare
appropri'arsi *vr* ~ **a** (*essere adatto a*) suit; ~ **di** take possession of; ~ **indebitamente di** embezzle, misappropriate
appropri'ato *a* appropriate
appropriazi'one *nf Jur* appropriation. ~ **indebita** *Jur* embezzlement
approssi'mare *vt* ~ **per eccesso/difetto** round up/down
approssi'marsi *vr* draw near
approssimativa'mente *adv* approximately
approssima'tivo *a* approximate
approssimazi'one *nf* approximation
appro'vare *vt* approve of; approve ‹*legge*›
approvazi'one *nf* approval
approvvigiona'mento *nm* supplying; **approvvigionamenti** *pl* provisions
approvvigio'nare *vt* supply
approvvigio'narsi *vr* stock up
appunta'mento *nm* appointment; *fam* date; **fissare un** ~, **prendere un** ~ make an appointment; **darsi** ~ decide to meet
appun'tare *vt* (*annotare*) take notes; (*fissare*) fix; (*con spillo*) pin; (*appuntire*) sharpen
appun'tarsi *vr* ~ **su** ‹*teoria:*› be based on
appun'tato *nm* (*carabiniere*) lowest rank in the carabinieri
appuntel'larsi *vr* (*sostenersi*) support oneself
appun'tino *adv* meticulously
appun'tire *vt* sharpen
appun'tito *a* ‹*matita*› sharp; ‹*mento*› pointed
ap'punto¹ *nm* note; (*piccola critica*) niggle
ap'punto² *adv* exactly; **per l'**~! exactly!; **stavo** ~ **dicendo...** I was just saying...
appura'mento *nm* verification
appu'rare *vt* verify
a'pribile *a* that can be opened; **tettuccio** ~ *Auto* sun roof
apribot'tiglie *nm inv* bottle-opener
a'prile *nm* April; **primo d'**~ April Fool's Day
aprio'ristico *a* a priori
a'prire *vt* open; turn on ‹*luce, acqua ecc*›; (*con chiave*) unlock; open up ‹*ferita ecc*›; ~ **le ostilità** *Mil* commence hostilities; **apriti cielo!** heavens above!
a'prirsi *vr* open; (*spaccarsi*) split; (*confidarsi*) confide (**con** in)
apri'scatole *nf inv* tin opener *Br*, can opener
APT *abbr* (**Azienda di Promozione Turistica**) Tourist Board
aqua'planing *nm* **andare in** ~ aquaplane
'aquila *nf* eagle; **non è un'** ~! *fig* he's no genius!
aqui'lino *a* aquiline
aqui'lone *nm* (*giocattolo*) kite
aqui'lotto *nm* (*piccolo dell'aquila*) eaglet
AR *abbr* (**andata e ritorno**) return [ticket];

abbr (**avviso di ricevimento**) return receipt for registered letters

ara'besco *nm* arabesque; *hum* scribble

A'rabia *nf* Arabia. **I'~ Saudita** Saudi Arabia

'arabo, -a *a* Arab; ⟨*lingua*⟩ Arabic ● *nmf* Arab ● *nm* (*lingua*) Arabic

arabo-israeli'ano *a* Arab-Israeli

a'rachide *nf* peanut

arago'nese *a* Aragonese

ara'gosta *nf* lobster

a'raldica *nf* heraldry

a'raldico *nm* herald ● *a* heraldic

aran'ceto *nm* orange grove

a'rancia *nf* orange; **succo d'~** orange juice

aranci'ata *nf* orangeade

a'rancio *nm* orange-tree; (*colore*) orange

aranci'one *a* & *nm* orange

a'rare *vt* plough

ara'tore *nm* ploughman

a'ratro *nm* plough

ara'tura *nf* ploughing

a'razzo *nm* tapestry

arbi'traggio *nm* Comm arbitrage; *Sport* refereeing; *Jur* arbitration

arbi'trare *vt* arbitrate in; *Sport* referee

arbitrarietà *nf* arbitrariness

arbi'trario *a* arbitrary

arbi'trato *nm* arbitration

ar'bitrio *nm* will; **è un ~** it's very high-handed

'arbitro *nm* arbiter; *Sport* referee; (*nel baseball*) umpire

arboricol'tura *nf* arboriculture

ar'busto *nm* shrub

'arca *nf* ark; (*cassa*) chest. **I'~ di Noè** Noah's Ark

ar'caico *a* archaic

arca'ismo *nm* archaism

ar'cangelo *nm* archangel

ar'cano *a* mysterious ● *nm* mystery

ar'cata *nf* arch; (*serie di archi*) arcade

archeolo'gia *nf* archaeology

archeo'logico *a* archaeological

arche'ologo, -a *nmf* archaeologist

ar'chetipo *nm* archetype

ar'chetto *nm* Mus bow

architet'tare *vt* fig devise; **cosa state architettando?** *fig* what are you plotting?

archi'tetto *nm* architect. **~ d'interni** interior designer

architet'tonico *a* architectural

architet'tura *nf* anche Comput architecture

archi'trave *nm* lintel

archivi'abile *a* that can be filed

archivi'are *vt* file; *Jur* close

archiviazi'one *nf* filing; (*Jur: di caso*) closing. **~ dati** data storage

ar'chivio *nm* archives *pl*; *Comput* file

archi'vista *nmf* filing clerk

archi'vistica *nf* rules governing the keeping of archives and records

ARCI *nf abbr* (**Associazione Ricreativa Culturale Italiana**) *Italian cultural and leisure association*

arci'duca *nm* archduke

arcidu'chessa *nf* archduchess

arci'ere *nm* archer

ar'cigno *a* grim

arci'one *nm* saddle

arci'pelago *nm* archipelago

arci'vescovo *nm* archbishop

'arco *nm* arch; *Math* arc; (*arma, Mus*) bow; **nell'~ di una giornata/due mesi** in the space of a day/two months. **~ rampante** flying buttress

arcoba'leno *nm* rainbow

arcu'are *vt* bend; **~ la schiena** ⟨*gatto:*⟩ arch its back

arcu'arsi *vr* bend

arcu'ato *a* bent; ⟨*schiena di gatto*⟩ arched

ar'dente *a* burning; *fig* ardent; **camera ~** chapel of rest

ardente'mente *adv* ardently

'ardere *vt/i* burn; **legna da ~** fire-wood

ar'desia *nf* slate

ardi'mento *nm* boldness

ar'dire *vi* dare ● *nm* (*coraggio*) daring, boldness; (*sfrontatezza*) impudence

ar'dito *a* daring; (*coraggioso*) bold; (*sfacciato*) impudent

ar'dore *nm* (*calore*) heat; *fig* ardour

'arduo *a* arduous; (*ripido*) steep

'area *nf* area; (*superficie*) surface. **~ fabbricabile** building land. **~ di rigore** (*in calcio*) penalty area, penalty box. **~ di servizio** service area

a'rena *nf* arena

are'naria *nf* sandstone

are'narsi *vr* run aground; ⟨*fig: trattative*⟩ reach deadlock; **mi sono arenato** I'm stuck

are'nile *nm* stretch of sand

areo'plano *nm* aeroplane

'argano *nm* winch

argen'tato *a* silver-plated

ar'genteo *a* silvery

argente'ria *nf* silver[ware]

argenti'ere *nm* silversmith

Argen'tina *nf* Argentina

argen'tina *nf* (*maglia*) round-necked pullover

argen'tino *a* silvery

argen'tino, -a *a* & *nmf* Argentinian

ar'gento *nm* silver; **d'~** silver. **~ vivo** Chem quicksilver

ar'gilla *nf* clay

argil'loso *a* ⟨*terreno*⟩ clayey; (*simile all'argilla*) clay-like

argi'nare *vt* embank; *fig* hold in check, contain

'argine *nm* embankment; (*diga*) dike; **fare ~ a** *fig* hold in check, contain

argomen'tare *vi* argue

argo'mento *nm* argument; (*motivo*) reason; (*soggetto*) subject

argu'ire *vt* deduce

arguta'mente *adv* (*con astuzia*) shrewdly; (*con facezia*) wittily

ar'guto *a* witty; (*astuto*) shrewd

ar'guzia *nf* wit; (*battuta*) witticism; (*astuzia*) shrewdness '**aria** *nf* air; (*aspetto*) appearance; *Mus* tune; **avere l'~...** look...; **corrente d'~** draught; **mandare all'~ qcsa** *fig* ruin sth; **andare all'~** *fig* fall through; **a tenuta d'~** draughtproof; **avere la testa per ~** *fig* be absent-minded, have one's head in the clouds; **che ~ tirava?** *fig* what was the atmosphere like?; **cambiare ~** *fig* have a change of scene; **cambia ~!** *hum* get out of here!. **~-~** *a inv Mil* air-to-air. **~ conditionata** air-conditioning. **~-terra** *a inv* air-to-ground

ari'ano *a* Aryan

arida'mente *adv* without emotion

aridità *nf* aridity

'**arido** *a* arid

arieggi'are *vt* air; **~ una stanza** give a room an airing

arieggi'ato *a* airy

ari'ete *nm* ram; (*strumento*) battering-ram; **A~** *Astr* Aries

ari'etta *nf* (*brezza*) breeze

a'ringa *nf* herring

ari'oso *a* ‹*locale*› light and airy

'**arista** *nf* chine of pork

aristo'cratico, -a *a* aristocratic ● *nmf* aristocrat

aristocra'zia *nf* aristocracy

arit'metica *nf* arithmetic

arit'metico *a* arithmetical

arlec'chino *nm* Harlequin; *fig* buffoon

'**arma** *nf* weapon; (*forze armate*) [armed] forces; **armi** *pl* arms; **chiamare alle armi** call up; **sotto le armi** in the army; **alle prime armi** *fig* inexperienced, fledg[e]ling; **prendere/deporre le armi** take up arms/ put down one's arms; **passare qcno per le armi** execute sb; **confrontarsi ad armi pari** compete on an equal footing. **~ bianca** knife. **~ a doppio taglio** *fig* double-edged sword. **~ da fuoco** firearm. **~ impropria** makeshift weapon. **armi** *pl* **nucleari** nuclear weapons

armadi'etto *nm* locker, cupboard; (*in aereo*) overhead locker. **~ del bagno** bathroom cabinet. **~ dei medicinali** medicine cabinet

arma'dillo *nm* armadillo

ar'madio *nm* cupboard; (*guardaroba*) wardrobe. **~ a muro** fitted cupboard

armamen'tario *nm* tools *pl*; *fig* paraphernalia

arma'mento *nm* armament; *Naut* fitting out

ar'mare *vt* arm; (*equipaggiare*) fit out; *Archit* reinforce

ar'marsi *vr* arm oneself (**di** with)

ar'mata *nf* army; (*flotta*) fleet

ar'mato *a* armed; **rapina a mano armata** armed robbery

arma'tore *nm* shipowner

arma'tura *nf* framework; (*impalcatura*) scaffolding; (*di guerriero*) armour

armeggi'are *vi* *fig* manoeuvre

Ar'menia *nf* Armenia

ar'meno, -a *a & nmf* Armenian

arme'ria *nf* *Mil* armoury

armi'stizio *nm* armistice

armo'nia *nf* harmony

ar'monica *nf* **~** [**a bocca**] mouth-organ

ar'monico *a* harmonic

armoniosa'mente *adv* harmoniously

armoni'oso *a* harmonious

armoniz'zare *vt* harmonize ● *vi* match

armoniz'zarsi *vr* ‹*colori:*› go together, match

ar'nese *nm* tool; (*oggetto*) thing; (*congegno*) gadget; **male in ~** in bad condition

'**arnia** *nf* beehive

a'roma *nm* aroma; **aromi** *pl* herbs; **aromi** *pl* **naturali/artificiali** natural/artificial flavourings

aromatera'pia *nf* aromatherapy

aro'matico *a* aromatic

aromatiz'zare *vt* flavour

'**arpa** *nf* harp

ar'peggio *nm* arpeggio

ar'pia *nf* harpy

arpi'one *nm* hook; (*pesca*) harpoon

ar'pista *nmf* harpist

arrabat'tarsi *vr* do all one can

arrabbi'arsi *vr* get angry

arrabbi'ato *a* angry

arrabbia'tura *nf* rage; **prendersi un'~** fly into a rage

arraf'fare *vt* grab

arraf'fone *nmf* *fam* thief

arrampi'carsi *vr* climb [up]; **~ sugli specchi** *fig* clutch at straws

arrampi'cata *nf* climb

arrampica|'tore, -'trice *nmf* climber. **~ sociale** social climber

arran'care *vi* limp, hobble; *fig* struggle, limp along

arrangia'mento *nm* arrangement

arrangi'are *vt* arrange

arrangi'arsi *vr* manage; **~ alla meglio** get by; **ar'rangiati!** get on with it!

arrangia|'tore, -'trice *nmf* *Mus* arranger

arra'parsi *vr* *vulg* get randy

arre'care *vt* bring; (*causare*) cause

arreda'mento *nm* interior decoration; (*l'arredare*) furnishing; (*mobili ecc*) furnishings *pl*

arre'dare *vt* furnish

arreda|'tore, -'trice *nmf* interior designer

ar'redo *nm* furnishings *pl*

arrem'baggio *nm* **buttarsi all'~** *fig* stampede

ar'rendersi *vr* surrender; **~ all'evidenza dei fatti** face facts

arren'devole *a* ‹*persona*› yielding

arrendevo'lezza *nf* softness

arre'stare *vt* arrest; (*fermare*) stop

arre'starsi *vr* halt

ar'resto *nm* stop; *Jur* arrest; **la dichiaro in** [**stato d'**]**~** you are under arrest; **mandato di ~** warrant. **~ cardiaco** heart failure, cardiac arrest. **arresti** *pl* **domiciliari** *Jur* house arrest

arretra'mento *nm* withdrawal

arre'trare *vt* withdraw; pull back ⟨*giocatore*⟩ ● *vi* withdraw

arre'trato *a* ⟨*paese ecc*⟩ backward; ⟨*Mil: posizione*⟩ rear; **numero ~** ⟨*di rivista*⟩ back number; **del lavoro ~** a backlog of work ● *nm* ⟨*di stipendio*⟩ back pay; **essere in ~** be behind schedule; **arretrati** *pl* arrears. **arretrati** *pl* **di paga** back pay

arricchi'mento *nm* enrichment

arric'chire *vt* enrich

arric'chirsi *vr* get rich

arric'chito, **-a** *nmf* nouveau riche

arriccia'pelli *nm inv* tongs

arricci'are *vt* curl; **~ il naso** turn up one's nose

ar'ridere *vi* **~ a qcno** ⟨*sorte:*⟩ smile on sb

ar'ringa *nf Jur* closing address

arrin'gare *vt* harangue

arrischi'arsi *vr* dare

arrischi'ato *a* risky; ⟨*imprudente*⟩ rash

arri'vare *vi* arrive; **~ a** ⟨*raggiungere*⟩ reach; ⟨*ridursi*⟩ be reduced to

arri'vato, **-a** *a* successful; **il primo/ secondo ~** ⟨*in gare*⟩; **ben ~!** welcome! ● *nmf* successful person

arrive'derci *int* goodbye; **~ a domani** see you tomorrow

arri'vismo *nm* social climbing; ⟨*nel lavoro*⟩ careerism

arri'vista *nmf* social climber; ⟨*nel lavoro*⟩ careerist

ar'rivo *nm* arrival; *Sport* finish; **~ previsto per le ore...** expected time of arrival...

arro'gante *a* arrogant

arro'ganza *nf* arrogance

arro'garsi *vr* **~ il diritto di fare qcsa** take it upon oneself to do sth; **~ il merito** take the credit

arrossa'mento *nm* reddening

arros'sare *vt* make red, redden ⟨*occhi*⟩

arros'sarsi *vr* go red

arros'sire *vi* blush, go red

arro'stire *vt* roast; toast ⟨*pane*⟩; ⟨*ai ferri*⟩ grill

arro'stirsi *vr fig* broil

ar'rosto *a* & *nm* roast; **molto fumo e niente ~** *fig* all show and no substance. **~ d'agnello** roast lamb

arro'tare *vt* sharpen; ⟨*fam: investire*⟩ run over

arro'tino *nm* knife-sharpener

arroto'lare *vt* roll up

arroton'dare *vt* round; *Math ecc* round off; **~ lo stipendio** supplement one's income

arroton'darsi *vr* become round; ⟨*persona:*⟩ get plump

arrovel'larsi *vr* **~ il cervello** rack one's brains

arroven'tare *vt* make red-hot

arroven'tarsi *vr* become red-hot

arroven'tato *a* red-hot; ⟨*fig: discorso*⟩ fiery

arruf'fare *vt* ruffle; *fig* confuse

arruf'farsi *vr* become ruffled

arruf'fato *a* ⟨*capelli*⟩ dishevelled

arruffia'narsi *vr* **~ [con] qcno** *fig* butter sb up

arruggi'nire *vt* rust

arruggi'nirsi *vr* go rusty; *fig* ⟨*fisicamente*⟩ stiffen up; ⟨*conoscenze:*⟩ go rusty

arruggi'nito *a* rusty

arruola'mento *nm* enlistment

arruo'lare *vt/i* enlist

arruo'larsi *vr* enlist

arse'nale *nm* arsenal; ⟨*cantiere*⟩ [naval] dockyard

ar'senico *nm* arsenic

'arso *pp di* ardere ● *a* burnt; ⟨*arido*⟩ dry

ar'sura *nf* burning heat; ⟨*sete*⟩ parching thirst

art déco *nf* art deco

'arte *nf* art; ⟨*abilità*⟩ craftsmanship; **senza ~ né parte** incapable; **nome d'~** professional name. **~ drammatica** dramatics. **le belle arti** *pl* the fine arts. **arti** *pl* **figurative** figurative arts. **arti** *pl* **dello spettacolo** performing arts

arte'fare *vt* adulterate ⟨*vino*⟩; disguise ⟨*voce*⟩

arte'fatto *a* fake; ⟨*vino*⟩ adulterated

ar'tefice *nm* craftsman; *fig* author ● *nf* craftswoman

ar'teria *nf* artery. **~ [stradale]** arterial road

arterio'sclerosi *nf* arteriosclerosis, hardening of the arteries

arterioscle'rotico *a* senile

arteri'oso *a* *Anat* arterial

'Artico *nm* **l'~** the Arctic

'artico *a* Arctic

artico'lare *a* articular ● *vt* articulate; ⟨*suddividere*⟩ divide

artico'larsi *vr fig* **~ in** consist of

artico'lato *a* *Auto* articulated; *fig* well-constructed

articolazi'one *nf* *Anat* articulation

ar'ticolo *nm* article. **articoli** *pl* **per la casa** household goods. **~ civetta** *Comm* loss leader. **articoli** *pl* **per la cucina** kitchenware. **~ determinativo** *Gram* definite article. **~ di fondo** leader, leading article. **~ indeterminativo** *Gram* indefinite article. **articoli** *pl* **di marca** brand name goods. **~ di prima pagina** *Journ* cover story. **articoli** *pl* **da regalo** gifts. **articoli** *pl* **da spiaggia** things for the beach. **articoli** *pl* **sportivi** sports gear; **negozio di ~ ~** sports shop

'Artide *nf* **l'~** the Arctic [region]

artifici'ale *a* artificial

artifici'ere *nm Mil* explosives expert, bomb disposal expert

arti'ficio *nm* artifice; ⟨*affettazione*⟩ affectation

artificiosità *nf* artificiality

artifici'oso *a* artful; ⟨*affettato*⟩ affected

artigi'ana *nf* craftswoman

artigia'nale *a* made by hand; *hum* amateurish

artigianal'mente *adv* with craftsmanship; *hum* amateurishly

artigia'nato *nm* craftsmanship; *(ceto)* craftsmen *pl*

artigi'ano *nm* craftsman

artigli'ato *a* with claws

artigli'ere *nm* artilleryman

artiglie'ria *nf* artillery. **~ antiaerea** flak

ar'tiglio *nm* claw; *fig* clutch; **sfoderare gli artigli** *fig* show one's claws

ar'tista *nmf* artist

artistica'mente *adv* artistically

ar'tistico *a* artistic

arti'stoide *a* arty

art nouveau *nf* art nouveau

'arto *nm* limb

ar'trite *nf* arthritis

ar'tritico, -a *nmf* arthritic

ar'trosi *nf* rheumatism

arzigogo'lato *a* fantastic, bizarre

ar'zillo *a* sprightly

a'scella *nf* armpit

ascen'dente *a* ascending ● *nm* *(antenato)* ancestor; *(influenza)* ascendancy; *Astr* ascendant

ascen'denza *nf* ancestry

a'scendere *vi* ascend

ascensi'one *nf* ascent; **l'A~** the Ascension

ascen'sore *nm* lift, elevator *Am*

a'scesa *nf* ascent; *(al trono)* accession; *(al potere)* rise

a'scesi *nf* asceticism

a'scesso *nm* abscess

a'sceta *nmf* ascetic

a'scetico *a* ascetic

'ascia *nf* axe

asciugabianche'ria *nm inv* *(stenditoio)* clothes horse; *(macchina)* tumble dryer

asciugaca'pelli *nm inv* hair dryer, hairdrier

asciuga'mano *nm* towel. **~ di carta** paper towel

asciu'gare *vt* dry; **~ le stoviglie** do the drying-up

asciu'garsi *vr* dry oneself; *(diventare asciutto)* dry up; **~ le mani** dry one's hands

asciuga'trice *nf* tumble dryer

asci'utto *a* dry; *(magro)* wiry; ⟨*risposta*⟩ curt; **essere all'~** *fig* be hard up

ascol'tare *vt* listen to ● *vi* listen

a'scolto *nm* listening; **dare ~ a** listen to; **essere in ~** *Radio* be listening; **mettersi in ~** *Radio* tune in; **prestare ~** listen

a'scrivere *vt* *(attribuire)* ascribe; **~ a** *(annoverare)* number among

asessu'ato *a* asexual

a'settico *a* aseptic

asfal'tare *vt* asphalt

asfal'tato *a* tarmac

a'sfalto *nm* asphalt

asfis'sia *nf* asphyxia

asfissi'ante *a* ⟨*caldo*⟩ oppressive; ⟨*fig: persona*⟩ annoying

asfissi'are *vt* asphyxiate; *fig* annoy

'Asia *nf* Asia. **~ Minore** Asia Minor

asi'ago *nm* full-fat white cheese

asi'atico, -a *a* & *nmf* Asian

a'silo *nm* shelter; *(d'infanzia)* nursery school. **~ infantile** day nursery. **~ nido** day nursery. **~ politico** political asylum

asim'metrico *a* asymmetric[al]

a'sincrono *a* asynchronous

'asino *nm* donkey; *(fig: persona stupida)* ass; *Sch* dunce; **qui casca l'~!** *fig* that's where it falls down!

'asma *nf* asthma

a'smatico *a* asthmatic

asoci'ale *a* asocial

'asola *nf* buttonhole

a'sparagi *nmpl* asparagus *sg*

aspara'gina *nf* *Bot* asparagus fern

a'sparago *nm* asparagus

a'spergere *vt* **~ con/di** sprinkle with

asperità *nf inv* harshness; *(di terreno)* roughness

asper'sorio *nm* aspergillum, holy-water sprinkler

aspet'tare *vt* wait for; *(prevedere)* expect; **~ un bambino** be expecting [a baby]; **fare ~ qcno** keep sb waiting ● *vi* wait

aspet'tarsi *vr* expect

aspetta'tiva *nf* expectation; *(nel lavoro)* leave of absence; **all'altezza delle aspettative** up to expectations; **inferiore alle aspettative** not up to expectations. **~ per malattia** sick leave. **~ per maternità** maternity leave

a'spetto¹ *nm* look; *(di problema)* aspect; **di bell'~** good-looking

a'spetto² *nm* **sala d'~** waiting room

aspi'rante *a* aspiring; ⟨*pompa*⟩ suction *attrib* ● *nmf* *(a un posto)* applicant; *(al trono)* aspirant; **gli aspiranti al titolo** the contenders for the title

aspira'polvere *nm inv* vacuum cleaner; **passare l'~** vacuum, hoover

aspi'rare *vt* inhale; *Mech* suck in; *(con elettrodomestici)* vacuum, hoover ● *vi* **~ a** aspire to

aspi'rato *a* aspirate

aspira'tore *nm* extractor fan

aspirazi'one *nf* inhalation; *Mech* suction; *(ambizione)* ambition

aspi'rina *nf* aspirin

aspor'tare *vt* take away

aspra'mente *adv* *(duramente)* severely

a'sprezza *nf* *(al gusto)* sourness; *(di clima)* severity; *(di carattere, parole, suono)* harshness; *(di odore)* pungency; *(di litigio)* bitterness

a'sprigno *a* slightly sour

'aspro *a* *(al gusto)* sour; ⟨*clima*⟩ severe; ⟨*suono, parole*⟩ harsh; ⟨*odore*⟩ pungent; ⟨*litigio*⟩ bitter

assaggi'are *vt* taste

assaggia'tore, -'trice *nmf* taster

assag'gini *nmpl* *Culin* samples

as'saggio *nm* tasting; *(piccola quantità)* taste; *(fig: campione)* sample

as'sai *adv* very; *(moltissimo)* very much; *(abbastanza)* enough

assa'lire *vt* attack

assali|'tore, -'trice *nmf* assailant

assal'tare *vt Mil* attack, charge; hold up ⟨*banca, treno*⟩

assalta'tore *nm* hold-up man

as'salto *nm* attack; **d'~** ⟨*giornalismo*⟩ aggressive; **prendere d'~** storm ⟨*città*⟩; *fig* mob ⟨*persona*⟩; hold up ⟨*banca*⟩

assapo'rare *vt* savour

assas'sina *nf* murderess

assassi'nare *vt* murder, assassinate; *fig* murder

assas'sinio *nm* murder, assassination

assas'sino *a* murderous ● *nm* murderer

'asse *nf* board ● *nm Techn* axle; *Math* axis. **~ da stiro** ironing board

assecon'dare *vt* satisfy; (*favorire*) support; **~ i capricci di qcno** indulge sb's every whim; **~ i desideri di qcno** comply with sb's wishes

assedi'are *vt* besiege

assedi'ato *a* besieged

as'sedio *nm* siege

assegna'mento *nm* allotment; **fare ~ su** rely on

asse'gnare *vt* allot; award ⟨*premio*⟩

assegna'tario, -a *nmf* recipient

assegnazi'one *nf* (*di alloggio, denaro, borsa di studio*) allocation; (*di premio*) award

as'segno *nm* allowance; (*bancario*) cheque; **contro ~** cash on delivery; **pagare con un ~** pay by cheque. **~ circolare** bank draft. **assegni** *pl* **familiari** family allowance, child benefit. **~ post-datato** post-dated cheque. **~ sbarrato** crossed cheque. **~ non trasferibile** cheque made out to "account payee only". **~ turistico** traveller's cheque. **~ a vuoto** bad cheque, dud cheque

assem'blaggio *nm* assemblage

assem'blare *vt* assemble

assem'blea *nf* assembly; (*adunanza*) gathering. **~ generale annuale** Annual General Meeting, AGM

assembra'mento *nm* gathering

assem'brare *vt* gather

assen'nato *a* sensible

as'senso *nm* assent

assen'tarsi *vr* go away; (*da stanza*) leave the room

as'sente *a* absent; (*distratto*) absent-minded ● *nmf* absentee

assente'ismo *nm* absenteeism

assente'ista *nmf* frequent absentee

assen'tire *vi* acquiesce (**a** in)

as'senza *nf* absence; (*mancanza*) lack. **~ di gravità** zero gravity

asse'rire *vt* assert

asserragli'arsi *vr* barricade oneself

asser'tivo *a* assertive

asser|'tore, -'trice *nmf* supporter

asservi'mento *nm* subservience

asser'vire *vt fig* enslave

asser'virsi *vr fig* be subservient

asserzi'one *nf* assertion

assesso'rato *nm* [council] department

asses'sore *nm* councillor

assesta'mento *nm* settlement

asse'stare *vt* arrange; **~ un colpo** deal a blow

asse'starsi *vr* settle oneself

asse'stato *a* **ben ~** well-judged

asse'tato *a* parched

as'setto *nm* order; *Naut, Aeron* trim; **in ~ di guerra** on a war footing; **cambiare l'~ territoriale dell'Europa** change the map of Europe

assi'cella *nf* lath

assicu'rabile *a* insurable

assicu'rare *vt* assure; *Comm* insure; register ⟨*posta*⟩; (*fissare*) secure; (*accertare*) ensure

assicu'rarsi *vr* (*con contratto*) insure oneself; (*legarsi*) fasten oneself; **~ che** make sure that

assicu'rata *nf* registered letter

assicura'tivo *a* insurance *attrib*

assicu'rato *a* insured; **lettera assicurata** registered letter

assicura|'tore, -'trice *nmf* insurance agent ● *a* insurance; **società assicuratrice** insurance company

assicurazi'one *nf* assurance; (*contratto*) insurance; **fare un'~** take out insurance. **~ multirischi** blanket cover. **~ sanitaria** medical insurance. **~ di viaggio** travel insurance

assidera'mento *nm* exposure

asside'rarsi *vr fam* be frozen; *Med* be suffering from exposure

asside'rato *a Med* suffering from exposure; *fam* frozen

assidua'mente *adv* assiduously

assiduità *nf* assiduity

as'siduo *a* assiduous; ⟨*cliente*⟩ regular

assi'eme *a* [together] with

assil'lante *a* ⟨*persona, pensiero*⟩ nagging

assil'lare *vt* pester

assil'larsi *vr* torment oneself

as'sillo *nm* worry

assimi'lare *vt* assimilate

assimilazi'one *nf* assimilation

assi'oma *nm* axiom

assio'matico *a* axiomatic

As'siria *nf* Assyria

as'sise *nfpl* assizes; **Corte d'A~** Court of Assize[s]

assi'stente *nmf* assistant. **~ sociale** social worker. **~ universitario** assistant lecturer. **~ di volo** flight attendant

assi'stenza *nf* assistance; (*presenza*) presence. **~ medica** medical care. **~ ospedaliera** hospital treatment. **~ sanitaria** health care. **~ sociale** social work

assistenzi'ale *a* welfare

assistenzia'lismo *nm* abuse of the welfare state

as'sistere *vt* assist; (*curare*) nurse ● *vi* **~ a** (*essere presente*) be present at; watch ⟨*spettacolo ecc*⟩

assi'stito *a* **~ da computer** computer-aided

'asso nm ace; **piantare in ~** leave in the lurch. **~ nella manica** trump card
associ'are vt join; (collegare) associate
associ'arsi vr join forces; Comm enter into partnership. **~ a** join; subscribe to ⟨giornale ecc⟩
associ'ato, -a a associate ● nmf partner
associazi'one nf association. **~ di categoria** trade-union. **~ per delinquere** criminal organization. **A~ Europea di Libero Scambio** European Free Trade Association. **~ in partecipazione** Comm joint venture
associazio'nismo nm Pol excessive tendency to form associations; Psych associationism
asso'dare vt ascertain ⟨verità⟩
assogget'tare vt subject
assogget'tarsi vr submit
asso'lato a sunny
assol'dare vt recruit
as'solo nm Mus solo
as'solto pp di assolvere
assoluta'mente adv absolutely
assolu'tismo nm absolutism
assolu'tista nmf absolutist
assolu'tistico a absolutist
asso'luto a absolute
assolu'torio a **formula assolutoria** acquittal
assoluzi'one nf acquittal; Relig absolution
as'solvere vt perform ⟨compito⟩; Jur acquit; Relig absolve
assolvi'mento nm performance
assomigli'are vi **~ a** be like, resemble
assomigli'arsi vr resemble each other
assom'marsi vr combine; **~ a qcsa** add to sth
asso'nanza nf assonance
asson'nato a drowsy
asso'pirsi vr doze off
assor'bente a & nm absorbent. **~ igienico** sanitary towel
assor'bire vt absorb
assor'dante a deafening
assor'dare vt deafen
assorti'mento nm assortment
assor'tire vt match ⟨colori⟩
assor'tito a assorted; ⟨colori, persone⟩ matched
as'sorto a engrossed
assottiglia'mento nm thinning; (aguzzamento) sharpening
assottigli'are vt make thin; (aguzzare) sharpen; (ridurre) reduce
assottigli'arsi vr grow thin; ⟨finanze:⟩ be whittled away
assue'fare vt accustom
assue'farsi vr **~ a** get used to
assue'fatto a (a caffè, aspirina) immune to the effects; (a droga) addicted
assuefazi'one nf (a caffè, aspirina) immunity to the effects; (a droga) addiction
as'sumere vt assume; take on ⟨impiegato⟩; **~ informazioni** make inquiries

as'sunto pp di assumere ● nm task
assunzi'one nf (di impiegato) employment; **l'A~** Assumption
assurdità nf inv absurdity; **dire delle ~** talk nonsense
as'surdo a absurd
'asta nf pole; Mech bar; Comm auction; **a mezz'~** at half-mast. **~ di livello [dell'olio]** Auto dip-stick
a'stemio a abstemious
aste'nersi vr abstain (**da** from)
astensi'one nf abstention
astensio'nismo nm persistent abstention
astensio'nista nmf persistent abstainer
astensio'nistico a **tendenza astensionistica** tendency to abstain
aste'nuto, -a nmf abstainer
aste'risco nm asterisk
aste'roide nm asteroid
'astice nm crayfish
asti'cella nf stick; (in salto in alto) bar
astig'matico a astigmatic
astigma'tismo nm astigmatism
asti'nenza nf abstinence; **crisi di ~** withdrawal symptoms
'astio nm rancour; **avere ~ contro qcno** bear sb a grudge
asti'oso a resentful
a'stragalo nm anklebone
'astrakan nm astrakhan
astrat'tezza nf abstractness
astrat'tismo nm abstractionism
a'stratto a abstract
astrin'gente a & nm astringent
'astro nm star
+astro suff **giovinastro** nm lout; **giallastro** a yellowish; **dolciastro** a sweetish; **fattaccio** nm hum foul deed
astro'fisica nf astrophysics
astro'fisico, -a a astrophysical ● nmf astrophysicist
astrolo'gia nf astrology
astro'logico a astrological
a'strologo, -a nmf astrologer
astro'nauta nmf astronaut
astro'nautica nf astronautics
astro'nave nf spaceship
astrono'mia nf astronomy
astro'nomico a (anche fig) astronomic, astronomical
a'stronomo nm astronomer
astrusità nf abstruseness
a'struso a abstruse
a'stuccio nm case
a'stuto a shrewd; (furbo) cunning
a'stuzia nf shrewdness; (azione) trick
a'tavico a atavistic
ate'ismo nm atheism
ate'lier nm inv (di alta moda) atelier; (di artista) [artist's] studio
A'tene nf Athens
ate'neo nm university
ateni'ese a & nmf Athenian
'ateo, -a a & nmf atheist
a'tipico a atypical

at'lante *nm* atlas; **i monti dell'A~** the Atlas Mountains

at'lantico *a* Atlantic; **l'[Oceano] A~** the Atlantic [Ocean]

at'leta *nmf* athlete

a'tletica *nf* athletics *sg.* **~ leggera** track and field events. **~ pesante** *weight-lifting, boxing, wrestling, etc*

a'tletico *a* athletic

atle'tismo *nm* athleticism

atmo'sfera *nf* atmosphere

atmo'sferico *a* atmospheric

a'tollo *nm* atoll

a'tomica *nf* atom bomb

a'tomico *a* atomic

atomiz'zare *vt* atomize

atomizza'tore *nm* atomizer

'atomo *nm* atom

'atono *a* unstressed

'atrio *nm* entrance hall, lobby

a'troce *a* atrocious; *(terrible)* dreadful

atroce'mente *adv* atrociously

atrocità *nf inv* atrocity

atro'fia *nf* atrophy

atrofiz'zare *vt* atrophy

atrofiz'zarsi *vr Med, fig* atrophy

attac'cabile *a* attachable

attaccabot'toni *nmf inv* [crashing] bore

attacca'brighe *nmf inv* troublemaker

attacca'mento *nm* attachment

attac'cante *a* attacking ● *nm Sport* forward

attacca'panni *nm inv* [coat-]hanger; *(a muro)* [clothes-]hook

attac'care *vt* attach; *(legare)* tie; *(appendere)* hang; *(cucire)* sew on; *(contagiare)* pass on; *(assalire)* attack; *(iniziare)* start ● *vi* stick; *(diffondersi)* catch on

attac'carsi *vr* cling; *(affezionarsi)* become attached; *(litigare)* quarrel

attacca'ticcio *a* sticky; *fig* clinging and tiresome

attac'cato *a* stuck

attacca'tura *nf* junction. **~ dei capelli** hairline

attac'chino *nm* billposter

at'tacco *nm* attack; *(punto d'unione)* junction; *(accesso)* fit. **~ cardiaco** heart attack. **~ epilettico** epileptic fit

attanagli'are *vt (fig: tormentare)* haunt

attar'darsi *vr* stay late; *(indugiare)* linger

attec'chire *vi* take; *(moda ecc:)* catch on

atteggia'mento *nm* attitude

atteggi'are *vt* assume

atteggi'arsi *vr* **~ a** pose as

attem'pato *a* elderly

atten'darsi *vr* camp, pitch camp

atten'dente *nm Mil* batman

at'tendere *vt* wait for ● *vi* **~ a** attend to

at'tendersi *vr* expect

atten'dibile *a* reliable

attendibilità *nf* reliability

atte'nersi *vr* **~ a** stick to

attenta'mente *adv* attentively

atten'tare *vi* **~ a** make an attempt on

atten'tato *nm* act of violence; *(contro politico ecc)* assassination attempt; **~ alla vita di** attempted murder of. **~ dinamitardo** bombing

attenta'tore, -'trice *nmf* attacker; *(a scopo politico)* terrorist

at'tento *a* attentive; *(accurato)* careful; **~!** look out!; **stare ~** pay attention; **'attenti al cane'** 'beware of the dog'

attenu'ante *nf* extenuating circumstance

attenu'are *vt* attenuate; *(minimizzare)* minimize; subdue *(colori ecc)*; calm *(dolore)*; soften *(colpo)*

attenu'arsi *vr* diminish

attenuazi'one *nf* lessening

attenzi'one *nf* attention; *(cura)* care; **fare ~** be careful; **~!** watch out!; **~, prego** your attention, please; **coprire di attenzioni** lavish attention on

atter'raggio *nm* landing. **~ di fortuna** emergency landing

atter'rare *vt* knock down ● *vi* land

atter'rire *vt* terrorize

atter'rirsi *vr* be terrified

at'tesa *nf* waiting; *(aspettativa)* expectation; **in ~ di** waiting for

at'teso *pp di* **attendere**

atte'stabile *a* certifiable

atte'stare *vt* state; *(certificare)* certify

atte'stato *nm* certificate

attestazi'one *nf* certificate; *(dichiarazione)* declaration

'Attica *nf* Attica

'attico¹ *nm (lingua)* Attic

'attico² *nm (appartamento)* penthouse

at'tiguo *a* adjacent

attil'lato *a (vestito)* close-fitting

'attimo *nm* second; **un ~!** just a sec!; **in un ~** in double-quick time; **non ho avuto un ~ di respiro** I haven't had time to draw breath

atti'nente *a* **~ a** pertaining to

at'tingere *vt* draw; *fig* obtain

atti'rare *vt* attract

atti'rarsi *vr* draw *(attenzione)*; incur *(odio)*

attitudi'nale *nm* test **~ aptitude test**

atti'tudine *nf (disposizione)* aptitude; *(atteggiamento)* attitude

atti'vare *vt* activate

attivazi'one *nf* setting in motion, turning on; *Phys, Chem* activation

atti'vismo *nm* activism

atti'vista *nmf* activist

attività *nf inv* activity; *Comm* assets *pl.* **~ pl fisse** fixed assets. **~ pl liquide** *Comm* liquid assets

at'tivo *a* active; *Comm* productive ● *nm* assets *pl*

attiz'zare *vt* poke; *fig* stir up

attizza'toio *nm* poker

'atto *nm* act; *(azione)* action; *Comm, Jur* deed; *(certificato)* certificate; **fare ~ di presenza** put in an appearance; **mettere in ~** put into action; **atti** *pl (di società ecc)* proceedings. **atti** *pl* **di libidine violenta** inde-

cent assault. **atti** *pl* **osceni** gross indecency.
~ di vendita bill of sale
+attolo *suff* **vermiciattolo** *nm* slimy individual
at'tonito *a* astonished
attorcigli'are *vt* twist
attorcigli'arsi *vr* get twisted
at'tore *nm* actor
attorni'are *vt* surround
attorni'arsi *vr* ~ **di** surround oneself with
at'torno *adv* around, about ●*prep* ~ **a** around, about
attrac'care *vt/i* dock
attra'ente *a* attractive
at'trarre *vt* attract
at'trarsi *vr* be attracted to each other
attrat'tiva *nf* charm, attraction
attraversa'mento *nm* (*di strada*) crossing. ~ **pedonale** pedestrian crossing, crosswalk *Am*
attraver'sare *vt* cross; (*passare*) go through
attra'verso *prep* through; (*obliquamente*) across
attrazi'one *nf* attraction. **attrazioni** *pl* **turistiche** tourist attractions
attrez'zare *vt* equip; *Naut* rig
attrez'zarsi *vr* kit oneself out
attrezza'tura *nf* equipment; *Naut* rigging. ~ **da campeggio** camping equipment
at'trezzo *nm* tool. **at'trezzi** *pl* equipment; *Sport* appliances *pl*
attribu'ibile *a* attributable
attribu'ire *vt* attribute
attribu'irsi *vr* ascribe to oneself; ~ **il merito di** claim credit for
attri'buto *nm* attribute
attribuzi'one *nf* attribution
at'trice *nf* actress
at'trito *nm* friction
attrup'pare *vt* assemble
attrup'parsi *vr* gather
attu'abile *a* feasible
attuabilità *nf* viability
attu'ale *a* present; (*di attualità*) topical; (*effettivo*) actual
attualità *nf inv* topicality; (*avvenimento*) news; **programma di** ~ current affairs programme
attualiz'zare *vt* update
attual'mente *adv* at present
attu'are *vt* carry out
attu'ario, -a *nmf* actuary
attu'arsi *vr* be realized
attua'tore *nm* Techn actuator
attuazi'one *nf* carrying out
attuti'mento *nm* (*di colpo*) softening; (*di suoni*) muffling
attu'tire *vt* deaden; ~ **il colpo** soften the blow
au'dace *a* daring, bold; (*insolente*) audacious
au'dacia *nf* daring, boldness; (*insolenza*) audacity
audiapprendi'mento *nm* audio-based learning

'**audience** *nf inv* (*telespettatori*) audience
'**audio** *nm* audio
audiocas'setta *nf* audio cassette
audio'leso *a* hearing-impaired
audio'libro *nm* audiobook
audio'metrico *a Med* aural
audiovi'sivo *a* audiovisual
'**auditing** *nm* auditing
audi'torio *nm* auditorium
audizi'one *nf* audition; *Jur* hearing
'**auge** *nm* height; **essere in** ~ be popular
augu'rare *vt* wish
augu'rarsi *vr* hope
au'gurio *nm* wish; (*presagio*) omen; **auguri!** all the best!; (*a Natale*) Happy Christmas!; **tanti auguri** best wishes
au'gusto *a* august
'**aula** *nf* classroom; *Univ* lecture-hall; (*sala*) hall; **silenzio in ~!** silence in court!. ~ **bunker** (*in tribunale*) secure courtroom. ~ **magna** *Univ* great hall. ~ **del tribunale** courtroom
aumen'tare *vt/i* increase; ~ **di peso** gain weight
au'mento *nm* increase; (*di stipendio*) [pay] rise. ~ **di prezzo** price increase
'**aureo** *a* golden
au'reola *nf* halo
au'rora *nf* dawn. ~ **boreale** aurora borealis, Northern Lights
auscul'tare *vt Med* auscultate
ausili'are *a* & *nmf* auxiliary
auspi'cabile *a* è ~ **che...** it is to be hoped that...
auspi'care *vt* hope for
au'spicio *nm* omen; **auspici** *pl* (*protezione*) auspices; **è di buon** ~ it is a good omen
austerità *nf* austerity
au'stero *a* austere
Austra'lasia *nf* Australasia
au'strale *a* southern
Au'stralia *nf* Australia
australi'ano, -a *a* & *nmf* Australian
'**Austria** *nf* Austria
au'striaco, -a *a* & *nmf* Austrian
austroun'garico *a* Austro-Hungarian
autar'chia *nf* autarchy
au'tarchico *a* autarchic
aut aut *nm inv* either-or [choice]
autenti'care *vt* authenticate
autenticità *nf* authenticity
au'tentico *a* authentic; (*vero*) true
au'tismo *nm* autism
au'tista *nm* driver
au'tistico *a* autistic
'**auto** *nf inv* car; **viaggiare in** ~ travel by car. ~ **blindata** armour-plated car. ~ **a quattro ruote motrici** four-wheel drive car. ~ **sportiva** sports car. ~ **a trazione anteriore** front-wheel drive car. ~ **usata** second-hand car
auto+ *pref* self+
autoabbron'zante *nm* self-tan ●*a* self-

tanning

autoaccesso'rista *nmf* car accessory supplier

autoade'sivo *a* self-adhesive ● *nm* sticker

autoaffermazi'one *nf* self-assertion

autoambu'lanza *nf* ambulance

autoa'nalisi *nf* self-analysis

autoartico'lato *nm* articulated lorry

autobiogra'fia *nf* autobiography

autobio'grafico *a* autobiographical

auto'blinda *nf* armoured car

auto'bomba *nf* car-bomb

auto'botte *nf* tanker

'autobus *nm inv* bus

auto'carro *nm* lorry

autocertificazi'one *nf* self-certification

autoci'sterna *nf* tanker

auto'clave *nf* (*contenitore ad alta pressione*) autoclave; (*idraulica*) surge tank

autocombusti'one *nf* spontaneous combustion

autocommiserazi'one *nf* self-pity

autocompiaci'mento *nm* smugness, self-satisfaction

autocompiaci'uto *a* smug, self-satisfied

autoconcessio'nario *nm* car dealer

autocon'trollo *nm* self-control

au'tocrate *nm* autocrat

auto'cratico *a* autocratic

auto'critica *nf* self-criticism

au'toctono *a* native, aboriginal

autodemolizi'one *nf* self-destruction

autode'nuncia *nf* spontaneous confession

autodeterminazi'one *nf* self-determination

autodi'datta *a* self-taught ● *nmf* self-educated person, autodidact

autodi'fesa *nf* self-defence

autodisci'plina *nf* self-discipline

autodi'struggersi *vr* self-destruct

autoferrotranvi'ario *a* public-transport *attrib*

autoferrotranvi'eri *nmpl* public-transport workers

autoffi'cina *nf* garage

autofinanzia'mento *nm* self-financing

autofinanzi'arsi *vr* be self-financing; (*persona:*) use one's own finance

autogesti'one *nf* self-management

autoge'stirsi *vr* (*operai, studenti*) be self-managing; **mio figlio si autogestisce** my son can cope by himself

autoge'stito *a* self-managed

auto'gol *nm inv Sport* own goal

au'tografo *a & nm* autograph

auto'grill *nm inv* motorway café

autogrù *nf inv* breakdown truck

autogui'dato *a* homing *attrib*

autoim'mune *a* autoimmune

autoiro'nia *nf* self-mockery

autola'vaggio *nm* car wash

autolesi'one *nf* self-inflicted wound

autolesio'nismo *nm fig* self-destruction

autolesio'nistico *a* self-destructive

auto'linea *nf* bus line

au'toma *nm* robot

automatica'mente *adv* automatically

auto'matico *a* automatic; **auto con il cambio** ~ automatic ● *nm* (*bottone*) press-stud; (*fucile*) automatic

automatiz'zare *vt* automate

automatizzazi'one *nf* automation

automazi'one *nf* automation

auto'mezzo *nm* motor vehicle; **uscita automezzi** motor vehicles exit

auto'mobile *nf* [motor] car. ~ **da corsa** racing car

automobi'lina *nf* toy car

automobi'lismo *nm* motoring

automobi'lista *nmf* motorist

automobi'listico *a* (*industria*) automobile *attrib*

automodel'lismo *nm* model car making; (*collezione*) model car collecting

autono'leggio *nm* car rental

autonoma'mente *adv* autonomously

autono'mia *nf* autonomy; *Auto* range; (*di laptop, cellulare*) battery life

au'tonomo *a* autonomous

auto'parco *nm* (*insieme di auto*) fleet of cars

autopat'tuglia *nf* patrol car

auto'pista *nf* [fairground] race track

auto'pompa *nf* fire engine

auto'psia *nf* autopsy

autopunizi'one *nf* self-punishment

auto'radio *nf inv* car radio; (*veicolo*) radio car

au|'tore, -'trice *nmf* author; (*di pitture*) painter; (*di furto ecc*) perpetrator; **quadro d'~** genuine master

autoregolamentazi'one *nf* self-regulation

autore'parto *nm Mil* mechanized unit

auto'revole *a* authoritative; (*che ha influenza*) influential

autorevo'lezza *nf* authority

autoriduzi'one *nf* protest which takes the form of paying less than the requisite amount

autori'messa *nf* garage

autoriparazi'oni *nfpl* '~' 'car repairs', 'auto repairs'

autorità *nf inv* authority

autori'tario *a* autocratic

autorita'rismo *nm* authoritarianism

autori'tratto *nm* self-portrait

autoriz'zare *vt* authorize

autorizzazi'one *nf* authorization

auto'scatto *nm Phot* automatic shutter release

auto'scontro *nm inv* bumper car

autoscu'ola *nf* driving school

autosno'dato *nm* articulated bus

autosoc'corso *nm* breakdown service; (*veicolo*) breakdown van, breakdown truck

auto'starter *nm inv Auto* self-starter

auto'stop *nm* hitch-hiking, hitching; **fare l'~** hitch-hike, hitch

autostop'pista *nmf* hitch-hiker

auto'strada *nf* motorway, highway *Am.* **A~ del Sole** Highway of the Sun (*connecting Milan and Reggio Calabria*)

autostra'dale *a* motorway *attrib*, highway *attrib Am*

autosuffici'ente *a* self-sufficient

autosuffici'enza *nf* self-sufficiency

autosuggesti'one *nf* autosuggestion

autotrasporta|'tore, -'trice *nmf* haulier, carrier

autotra'sporto *nm* road haulage

auto'treno *nm* articulated lorry, roadtrain

autove'icolo *nm* motor vehicle

auto'velox *nm inv* speed camera

autovet'tura *nf* motor vehicle

autun'nale *a* autumnal; ⟨*giornata, vestiti*⟩ autumn *attrib*

au'tunno *nm* autumn

aval'lare *vt* endorse, back ⟨*cambiale*⟩; *fig* endorse

a'vallo *nm* endorsement

avam'braccio *nm* forearm

avam'posto *nm Mil* forward position

A'vana *nf* Havana

a'vana *nm inv* (*sigaro*) Havana [cigar]; (*colore*) tobacco, dark brown ● *a inv* ⟨*colore*⟩ tobacco-coloured, dark brown

avangu'ardia *nf* vanguard; *fig* avant-garde; **essere all'~** be in the forefront; *Techn* be at the leading edge; **d'~** avant-garde

avansco'perta *nf* reconnaissance; **andare in ~** reconnoitre

avanspet'tacolo *nm* **da ~** in poor taste

a'vanti *adv* (*in avanti*) forward; (*davanti*) in front; (*prima*) before; **~!** (*entrate*) come in!; (*suvvia*) come on!; **'~'** (*su semaforo*) 'cross now', 'walk' *Am*; **~ diritto** straight ahead; **più ~** further on; **va' ~!** go ahead!; **andare ~** (*precedere*) go ahead; ⟨*orologio:*⟩ be fast; **~ e indietro** backwards and forwards ● *a* (*precedente*) before ● *prep* **~ a** before; (*in presenza di*) in the presence of

avanti'eri *adv* the day before yesterday

avan'treno *nm* front axle assembly

avanza'mento *nm* progress; (*promozione*) promotion

avan'zare *vi* advance; (*progredire*) progress; (*essere d'avanzo*) be left [over] ● *vt* advance; (*superare*) surpass; (*promuovere*) promote

avan'zarsi *vr* advance; (*avvicinarsi*) approach

avan'zata *nf* advance

avan'zato *a* advanced; (*nella notte*) late; **in età avanzata** elderly

a'vanzo *nm* remainder; *Comm* surplus; **avanzi** *pl* (*rovine*) remains; (*di cibo*) leftovers. **~ di galera** jailbird

ava'raccio *nm* Scrooge

ava'ria *nf* (*di motore*) engine failure

avari'arsi *vr* spoil

avari'ato *a* ⟨*frutta, verdura*⟩ rotten; ⟨*carne*⟩ tainted

ava'rizia *nf* avarice

a'varo, -a *a* stingy ● *nmf* miser

a'vena *nf* oats *pl*

a'vere *vt* have; (*ottenere*) get; (*indossare*) wear; (*provare*) feel; **ho trent'anni** I'm thirty; **ha avuto il posto** he got the job; **~ fame/freddo** be hungry/cold; **ho mal di denti** I've got toothache; **cos'ha a che fare con lui?** what has it got to do with him?; **~ da fare** be busy; **~ luogo** take place; **che hai?** what's the matter with you?; **nei hai per molto?** will you be long?; **quanti ne abbiamo oggi?** what date is it today?; **avercela con qcno** have it in for sb ● *v aux* have; **non l'ho visto** I haven't seen him; **lo hai visto?** have you seen him?; **l'ho visto ieri** I saw him yesterday ● *nm* **averi** *pl* wealth *sg*

avia|'tore, -'trice *nmf* aviator

aviazi'one *nf* aviation; *Mil* Air Force

avicol'tura *nm* poultry farming

avida'mente *adv* avidly

avidità *nf* avidness

'avido *a* avid

avi'ere *nm* aircraft[s]man

avio'getto *nm* jet [plane]

avio'linea *nf* airline

aviotraspor'tato *a* airborne

avitami'nosi *nf* vitamin deficiency

a'vito *a* ancestral

'avo, -a *nmf* ancestor

avo'cado *nm inv* avocado

a'vorio *nm* ivory

a'vulso *a* **~ dal contesto** *fig* taken out of context

Avv. *abbr* **avvocato**

avva'lersi *vr* avail oneself (**of** di)

avvalla'mento *nm* depression

avvalo'rare *vt* bear out ⟨*tesi*⟩; endorse ⟨*documento*⟩; (*accrescere*) enhance

avvam'pare *vi* flare up; (*arrossire*) blush

avvantaggi'are *vt* favour

avvantaggi'arsi *vr* **~ di** benefit from; (*approfittare*) take advantage of

avve'dersi *vr* (*accorgersi*) notice; (*capire*) realize

avve'duto *a* shrewd

avvelena'mento *nm* poisoning

avvele'nare *vt* poison

avvele'narsi *vr* poison oneself

avvele'nato *a* poisoned

avve'nente *a* attractive

avve'nenza *nf* attraction, charm

avveni'mento *nm* event

avve'nire *vi* happen; (*aver luogo*) take place ● *nm* future

avveni'rismo *nm* excessive confidence in the future

avveni'ristico *a* futuristic

avven'tarsi *vr* fling oneself

avventata'mente *adv* recklessly

avven'tato *a* ⟨*decisione*⟩ rash

avven'tizio *a* (*personale*) temporary; (*guadagno*) casual

av'vento *nm* advent; *Relig* Advent

avven'tore *nm* regular customer

avven'tura *nf* adventure; (*amorosa*) affair; **d'~** ⟨*film*⟩ adventure *attrib*

avventu'rarsi *vr* venture

avventuri'ero, -a *nm* adventurer ● *nf* adventuress

avventu'rismo *nm* adventurism

avventu'ristico *a* adventurist

avventu'roso *a* adventurous

avve'rabile *a* ‹*previsione*› that may come true

avve'rarsi *vr* come true

av'verbio *nm* adverb

avver'sare *vt* oppose

avver'sario, -a *a* opposing ● *nmf* opponent

avversi'one *nf* aversion

avversità *nf inv* adversity

av'verso *a* ‹*sfavorevole*› adverse; (*contrario*) averse

avver'tenza *nf* (*cura*) care; (*avvertimento*) warning; (*avviso*) notice; (*premessa*) foreword; **avvertenze** *pl* (*istruzioni*) instructions

avver'tibile *a* (*disagio*) perceptible

avverti'mento *nm* warning

avver'tire *vt* warn; (*informare*) inform; (*sentire*) feel

avvertita'mente *adv* deliberately

avvez'zare *vt* accustom

avvez'zarsi *vr* accustom oneself

av'vezzo *a* ~ **a** used to

avvia'mento *nm* starting; *Comm* goodwill

avvi'are *vt* start

avvi'arsi *vr* set out

avvi'ato *a* under way; **bene** ~ thriving

avvicenda'mento *nm* (*in agricoltura*) rotation; (*nel lavoro*) replacement; (*delle stagioni*) change

avvicen'dare *vt* rotate

avvicen'darsi *vr* take turns, alternate

avvicina'mento *nm* approach

avvici'nare *vt* bring near; approach ‹*persona*›

avvici'narsi *vr* come nearer, approach; **avvicinarsi a** come nearer to, approach

avvi'lente *a* demoralizing; (*umiliante*) humiliating

avvili'mento *nm* despondency; (*degradazione*) degradation

avvi'lire *vt* dishearten; (*degradare*) degrade

avvi'lirsi *vr* lose heart; (*degradarsi*) degrade oneself

avvi'lito *a* disheartened; (*degradato*) degraded

avvilup'pare *vt* envelop

avvilup'parsi *vr* wrap oneself up; (*aggrovigliarsi*) get entangled

avvinaz'zato *a* drunk

avvin'cente *a* ‹*libro ecc*› enthralling

av'vincere *vt* enthral

avvinghi'are *vt* clutch

avvinghi'arsi *vr* cling

av'vio *nm* start-up; **dare l'**~ **a qcsa** get sth under way; **prendere l'**~ get under way

avvi'saglia *nf* (*di malattia*) first sign

avvi'sare *vt* inform; (*mettere in guardia*) warn

av'viso *nm* notice; (*annuncio*) announcement; (*avvertimento*) warning; (*pubblicitario*) advertisement; **a mio** ~ in my opinion. ~ **di garanzia** *Jur* notification that one is to be the subject of a legal enquiry

avvista'mento *nm* sighting

avvi'stare *vt* catch sight of; ~ **terra** make landfall

avvi'tare *vt* screw in; screw down ‹*coperchio*›

avvi'tarsi *vr* ‹*aereo:*› go into a spin

avvi'tata *nf* (*di aereo*) spin

avviz'zire *vi* wither

avviz'zito *a* withered

avvo'cato *nm* lawyer; *fig* advocate. ~ **del diavolo** devil's advocate

avvoca'tura *nf* legal profession; (*insieme di avvocati*) lawyers

av'volgere *vt* wrap [up]

av'volgersi *vr* wrap oneself up

avvol'gibile *nm* roller blind

avvolgi'mento *nm* winding

av'volto *a* ~ **in** wrapped in

avvol'toio *nm* vulture

aza'lea *nf* azalea

Azerbaigi'an *nm* Azerbaijan

azerbaigi'ano, -a *a & nmf* Azerbaijani

azi'enda *nf* business, firm. ~ **agricola** farm. ~ **elettrica** electricity board. ~ **a partecipazioni statali** enterprise in which the government has a shareholding. ~ **di soggiorno** tourist bureau

azien'dale *a* ‹*politica, dirigente*› company *attrib*; ‹*giornale*› in-house

azienda'listico *a* company *attrib*

azio'nabile *a* which can be operated

aziona'mento *nm* operation

azio'nare *vt* operate

azio'nario *a* share *attrib*; **mercato** ~ share market

azi'one *nf* action; *Fin* share; **d'**~ ‹*romanzo, film*› action[-packed]; **ad** ~ **ritardata** delayed action. ~ **sindacale** industrial action

azio'nista *nmf* shareholder

a'zoto *nm* nitrogen

az'teco, -a *a & nmf* Aztec

azzan'nare *vt* seize with its teeth; sink its teeth into ‹*gamba*›

azzar'dare *vt* risk

azzar'darsi *vr* dare

azzar'dato *a* risky; (*precipitoso*) rash

az'zardo *nm* hazard; **gioco d'**~ game of chance

azzec'care *vt* hit; (*fig: indovinare*) guess

azzera'mento *nm* setting to zero; *fig* **corso di** ~ remedial classes *pl*

azze'rare *vt* reset

azzi'mato *a* dapper

'azzimo *a* unleavened

azzit'tirsi *vr* go quiet, fall silent

azzit'tire *vt* silence, hush

azzop'pare *vt* lame

Az'zorre *nfpl* **le** ~ the Azores

azzuf'farsi *vr* come to blows

azzur'rato *a* ‹*lenti*› blue-tinted

az'zurro *a & nm* blue; **principe** ~ Prince Charming; **gli azzurri** *the Italian national team*

azzur'rognolo *a* bluish

Bb

babà *nm inv* ~ **al rum** rum baba
bab'beo *a* foolish ● *nm* idiot
'**babbo** *nm fam* dad, daddy. **B~ Natale** Father Christmas
bab'buccia *nf* slipper
babbu'ino *nm* baboon
ba'bordo *nm Naut* port side
baby boom *nm* baby boom
baby'sitter *nmf inv* baby-sitter; **fare il/la ~** babysit, do baby-sitting
ba'cato *a* wormeaten; **avere il cervello ~** have a slate loose
'**bacca** *nf* berry
baccalà *nm inv* dried salted cod
bac'cano *nm* din
bac'cello *nm* pod
bac'chetta *nf* rod; (*magica*) wand; (*di direttore d'orchestra*) baton; (*di tamburo*) drumstick
ba'checa *nf* showcase; (*in ufficio*) notice board. **~ elettronica** *Comput* bulletin board
bacia'mano *nm* kiss on the hand; **fare il ~ a qcno** kiss sb's hand
baci'are *vt* kiss
baci'arsi *vr* kiss [each other]
ba'cillo *nm* bacillus
baci'nella *nf* basin; (*contenuto*) basinful
ba'cino *nm* basin; *Anat* pelvis; (*di porto*) dock; (*di minerali*) field. **~ d'utenza** catchment area
'**bacio** *nm* kiss; **~ sulla bocca** kiss on the lips
backgammon *nm* backgammon
'**baco** *nm* worm. **~ da seta** silkworm
'**bacon** *nm* bacon
ba'cucco *a* **un vecchio ~** a senile old man
'**bada** *nf* **tenere qcno a ~** keep sb at bay
ba'dare *vi* take care (**a** of); (*fare attenzione*) look out; **bada ai fatti tuoi!** mind your own business!
ba'dia *nf* abbey
ba'dile *nm* shovel
'**badminton** *nm* badminton
'**baffi** *nmpl* moustache *sg*; (*di animale*) whiskers; **mi fa un baffo** I don't give a damn; **ridere sotto i ~** laugh up one's sleeve
baf'futo *a* moustached
ba'gagli *nmpl* luggage, baggage; **ritiro bagagli** baggage claim
bagagli'aio *nm Rail* luggage van, baggage car *Am*; *Auto* boot
ba'gaglio *nm* luggage, baggage; *Mil* kit; **un ~** a piece of luggage. **~ a mano** hand-luggage, hand-baggage. **~ in eccesso, ~ eccedente** excess baggage
baga'rino *nm* ticket tout
baga'tella *nf* trifle; *Mus* bagatelle
baggia'nata *nf* piece of nonsense; **non dire baggianate** don't talk nonsense
Bagh'dad *nf* Baghdad
bagli'ore *nm* glare; (*improvviso*) flash; (*fig: di speranza*) glimmer
bagna'cauda *nf* vegetables (*especially raw*) in an oil, garlic and anchovy sauce
ba'gnante *nmf* bather
ba'gnare *vt* wet; (*inzuppare*) soak; (*immergere*) dip; (*innaffiare*) water; (*mare, lago:*) wash; (*fiume:*) flow through
ba'gnarsi *vr* get wet; (*al mare ecc*) swim, bathe; '**vietato ~**' 'no bathing'
bagnasci'uga *nm inv* edge of the water, waterline
ba'gnato *a* wet; **~ fradicio** soaked
ba'gnino, -a *nmf* life guard
'**bagno** *nm* bath; (*stanza*) bathroom; (*gabinetto*) toilet; (*al mare*) swim, bathe; **bagni** *pl* (*stabilimento*) lido; **fare il ~** have a bath; (*nel mare ecc*) [have a] swim, bathe; **andare in ~** go to the bathroom, go to the toilet; **mettere a ~** soak; **con ~** (*camera*) en suite. **~ oculare** eyebath. **~ rivelatore** *Phot* developing bath. **~ di sangue** bloodbath. **~ di sviluppo** *Phot* developing bath. **~ turco** Turkish bath
bagnoma'ria *nm* **cuocere a ~** cook in a double saucepan
bagnoschi'uma *nm inv* bubble bath
ba'guette *nf inv* French loaf, baguette
Ba'hamas *nfpl* **le ~** the Bahamas
Bah'rain *nm* Bahrain, Bahrein
'**baia** *nf* bay
baio'netta *nf* bayonet
'**baita** *nf* mountain chalet
bala'ustra, balau'strata *nf* balustrade
balbet'tare *vt/i* stammer; (*bambino:*) babble
balbet'tio *nm* stammering; (*di bambino*) babble
bal'buzie *nf* stutter
balbuzi'ente *a* stuttering ● *nmf* stutterer
Bal'cani *nmpl* Balkans
bal'canico *a* Balkan
balco'nata *nf Theat* balcony, dress circle
balcon'cino *nm* **reggiseno a ~** underwired bra
bal'cone *nm* balcony
baldac'chino *nm* canopy; **letto a ~** four-poster bed

bal'danza nf boldness

baldan'zoso a bold

bal'doria nf revelry; **far ~** have a riotous time

Bale'ari nfpl **le [isole] ~** the Balearics, the Balearic Islands

ba'lena nf whale

bale'nare vi lighten; fig flash; **mi è balenata un'idea** I've just had an idea

bale'niera nf whaler

ba'leno nm **in un ~** in a flash

balenot'tera nf **~ azzurra** blue whale

ba'lera nf dance hall

ba'lestra nf crossbow

'balia nf wetnurse

ba'lìa nf **in ~ di** at the mercy of

ba'listico a ballistic; **perito ~** ballistics expert

'balla nf bale; (fam: frottola) tall story

bal'labile a essere **~** be good for dancing to

bal'lare vi dance; **andare a ~** go dancing

bal'lata nf ballad

balla'toio nm (nelle scale) landing

balle'rino, -a nmf dancer; (classico) ballet dancer ● nf nf (classica) ballet dancer, ballerina

bal'letto nm ballet

bal'lista nmf fam bull-shitter

'ballo nm dance; (il ballare) dancing; **sala da ~** ballroom; **essere in ~** ‹lavoro, vita:› be at stake; ‹persona:› be committed; **tirare qcno in ~** involve sb. **~ liscio** ballroom dancing. **~ in maschera** masked ball

ballonzo'lare vi skip about

ballot'taggio nm second count [of votes]

balne'are a bathing attrib; **stagione ~** swimming season; **stazione ~** seaside resort

balneazi'one nf **'divieto di ~'** 'no bathing'

ba'lordo a foolish; (stordito) stunned; **tempo ~** nasty weather

bal'samico a ‹aria› balmy

'balsamo nm balsam; (per capelli) conditioner; (lenimento) remedy

'baltico a Baltic. **il [mar] B~** The Baltic [Sea]

balu'ardo nm bulwark

'balza nf crag; (di abito) flounce

bal'zano a (idea) weird

bal'zare vi bounce; (saltare) jump; **~ in piedi** leap to one's feet

'balzo nm bounce; (salto) jump; **prendere la palla al ~** fig seize an opportunity

bam'bagia nf cotton wool; **vivere nella ~** fig be in clover

bam'bina nf little girl; (piccola) baby; **ha avuto una ~** she had a [baby] girl

bambi'naia nf nursemaid, nanny

bambi'nata nf childish thing to do/say

bam'bino nm child; (appena nato) baby; **avere un ~** have a baby; (maschio) have a [baby] boy; **bambini** pl children, kids; (piccoli) babies. **~ prodigio** child prodigy

bambi'none, -a nmf pej big or overgrown child

bam'boccio nm chubby child; (sciocco) simpleton; (fantoccio) rag doll

'bambola nf doll

bambo'lotto nm male doll

bambù nm bamboo

ba'nale a banal

banalità nf inv banality

banaliz'zare vt trivialize

ba'nana nf banana

ba'nano nm banana-tree

'banca nf bank. **~ d'affari** merchant bank, investment bank. **~ [di] dati** databank. **B~ Europea per la Ricostruzione e lo Sviluppo** European Bank for Reconstruction and Development. **~ degli occhi** eye bank. **~ del sangue** blood bank. **~ dello sperma** sperm bank

banca'rella nf stall

bancarel'lista nmf stallholder

ban'cario, -a a banking attrib; **trasferimento ~** bank transfer ● nmf bank employee

banca'rotta nf bankruptcy; **fare ~** go bankrupt

banchet'tare vi banquet

ban'chetto nm banquet

banchi'ere nm banker

ban'china nf Naut quay; (in stazione) platform; (di strada) path. **~ spartitraffico** central reservation, median strip Am. **~ non transitabile** soft verge

ban'chisa nf floe

'banco nm (di scuola) desk; (di negozio) counter; (di officina) bench; (di gioco, banca) bank; (di mercato) stall; (degli imputati) dock; **sotto ~** under the counter; **medicinale da ~** over the counter medicines. **~ dei formaggi** (in supermercato) cheese counter; (in mercato) cheese stall. **~ di ghiaccio** ice floe. **~ informazioni** information desk. **~ di nebbia** fog bank. **~ di sabbia** sandbank

'bancomat® nm inv autobank, cashpoint; (carta) bank card, cash card

ban'cone nm counter; (in bar) bar

banco'nota nf banknote, bill Am; **banco'note** pl paper currency

'banda nf band; (di delinquenti) gang. **~ d'atterraggio** Aeron landing strip. **~ passante** bandwidth. **~ rumorosa** rumble strip

banderu'ola nf weathercock; Naut pennant

bandi'era nf flag; **cambiare ~** change sides, switch allegiances

bandie'rina nf (nel calcio) corner flag

bandie'rine nfpl bunting

ban'dire vt banish; (pubblicare) publish; fig dispense with ‹formalità, complimenti›

ban'dista nmf bandsman

bandi'tismo nm banditry

ban'dito nm bandit

bandi'tore nm (di aste) auctioneer

'bando nm proclamation; **~ di concorso** job advertisement (published in an official gazette for a job for which a competitive examination has to be sat)

bang *nm inv* wham. ~ **sonico** sonic boom
Bangla'desh *nm* Bangladesh
bar *nm inv* bar
'**bara** *nf* coffin
ba'racca *nf* hut; (*catapecchia*) hovel;
mandare avanti la ~ keep the ship afloat
barac'cato, -a *a* living in a shanty town
● *nmf* shanty town dweller
barac'chino *nm* (*di gelati, giornali*) kiosk;
Radio CB radio
barac'cone *nm* (*roulotte*) circus caravan;
(*in luna park*) booth; (*fig: organizzazione*)
lumbering great dinosaur of an organization
barac'copoli *nf inv* shanty town
bara'onda *nf* chaos; **non fare** ~ don't make
a mess
ba'rare *vi* cheat
'**baratro** *nm* chasm
barat'tare *vt* barter
ba'ratto *nm* barter
ba'rattolo *nm* jar; (*di latta*) tin
'**barba** *nf* beard; (*fam: noia*) bore; **farsi la** ~
shave; **in** ~ **a** in spite of; **è una** ~ (*noia*) it's
boring
barbabi'etola *nf* beetroot; **barbabietole** *pl*
beetroot. ~ **da zucchero** sugar-beet
Bar'bados *nfpl* **le** ~ Barbados
barbagi'anni *nm inv* barn owl
bar'barico *a* barbaric
bar'barie *nf inv* barbarity
barba'rismo *nm* barbarism
'**barbaro** *a* barbarous ● *nm* barbarian
'**barbecue** *nm inv* barbecue
bar'betta *nf Naut* painter
barbi'ere *nm* barber; (*negozio*) barber's
bar'biglio *nm* barb
barbi'turico *nm* barbiturate
bar'bone, -a *nm* (*vagabondo*) vagrant;
(*cane*) poodle ● *nf* bag lady
bar'boso *a fam* boring
barbu'gliare *vi* mumble
bar'buto *a* bearded
'**barca** *nf* boat; **una** ~ **di** *fig* a lot of. ~ **a**
motore motorboat. ~ **da pesca** fishing
boat. ~ **a remi** rowing boat, rowboat *Am*. ~
di salvataggio lifeboat. ~ **a vela** sailing
boat, sailboat *Am*
barcai'olo *nm* boatman
barcame'narsi *vr* manage
barca'rola *nf Mus* barcarolle
Barcel'lona *nf* Barcelona
barcol'lare *vi* stagger
barcol'loni *adv* **camminare** ~ stagger
bar'cone *nm* barge; (*di ponte*) pontoon
bar'dare *vt* harness
bar'darsi *vr hum* dress up
barda'tura *nf* (*per cavallo*) harness
ba'rella *nf* stretcher
barelli'ere *nm* stretcher-bearer
'**Barents: mare di** ~ Barents Sea
ba'rese *a* from Bari
bari'centro *nm* centre of gravity
ba'rile *nm* barrel
ba'rilotto *nm fig* tub of lard
ba'rista *nm* barman ● *nf* barmaid

ba'ritono *nm* baritone
bar'lume *nm* glimmer; **un** ~ **di speranza** a
glimmer of hope
'**barman** *nm inv* barman
'**baro** *nm* cardsharper
ba'rocco *a & nm* baroque
ba'rometro *nm* barometer
baro'nale *a* baronial
ba'rone *nm* baron; **i baroni** *fig* the top brass
baro'nessa *nf* baroness
'**barra** *nf* bar; (*lineetta*) oblique; *Naut* tiller. ~
retroversa backslash. ~ **di rimorchio** tow
bar. ~ **spazio** space bar. ~ **di stato** *Comput*
status bar. ~ **strumenti** *Comput* tool bar
bar'rage *nm inv Sport* jump-off
bar'rare *vt* block off ‹*strada*›
barri'care *vt* barricade
barri'cata *nf* barricade
barri'era *nf* barrier; (*stradale*) road-block;
Geol reef. ~ **corallina** coral reef. ~
linguistica language barrier. ~ **razziale** colour bar. ~ **del suono** sound barrier
bar'rire *vi* trumpet
bar'rito *nm* trumpeting
ba'ruffa *nf* scuffle. **far** ~ quarrel
barzel'letta *nf* joke; ~ **sporca** *o* **spinta**
dirty joke
basa'mento *nm* base; *Geol* bedrock
ba'sare *vt* base
ba'sarsi *vr* ~ **su** be based on; **mi baso su**
ciò che ho visto I'm going on [the basis of]
what I saw
'**basco, -a** *a & nmf* Basque ● *nm* (*copricapo*)
beret
'**base** *nf* basis; (*fondamento*) foundation; *Mil*
base; *Pol* rank and file; **a** ~ **di** containing; **in**
~ **a** on the basis of. ~ **di controllo** ground
control. ~ **[di] dati** database. ~ **d'intesa**
common ground. ~ **logica** logical basis. ~
navale naval base
'**baseball** *nm* baseball
ba'setta *nf* sideburn
basi'lare *a* basic
ba'silica *nf* basilica
Basili'cata *nf* Basilicata
ba'silico *nm* basil
ba'sista *nm* grass roots politician; (*di un*
crimine) mastermind
'**basket** *nm* basketball
bas'sezza *nf* lowness; (*di statura*) shortness; (*viltà*) vileness
bas'sista *nmf* bassist
'**basso** *a* low; (*di statura*) short; ‹*acqua*› shallow; ‹*televisione*› quiet; (*vile*) despicable;
parlare a bassa voce speak quietly, speak
in a low voice. **la bassa Italia** southern Italy
● *nm* lower part; *Mus* bass; **guardare in** ~
look down
basso'fondo *nm* (*pl* **bassifondi**) shallows;
bassifondi *pl* (*quartieri poveri*) slums
bassorili'evo *nm* bas-relief
bas'sotto *nm* dachshund
ba'stardo, -a *a* bastard; (*di animale*) mongrel ● *nmf* bastard; (*animale*) mongrel
ba'stare *vi* be enough; (*durare*) last; **basta!**

that's enough!, that'll do!; **basta che**
(*purchè*) provided that; **basta così** that's
enough; **basta così?** is that enough?, will
that do?; (*in negozio*) will there be anything
else?; **basta andare alla posta** you only
have to go to the post office; **basta che tu lo
faccia bene** make sure you do it well

Basti'an con'trario *nm* contrary old so-
and-so

basti'mento *nm* ship; (*carico*) cargo

basti'one *nm* bastion

basto'nare *vt* beat

basto'nata *nf* **dare una ~ a** beat with a
stick

baston'cino *nm* (*da sci*) ski pole. **~ di
pesce** fish finger, fish stick *Am*

ba'stone *nm* stick; (*da golf*) club; (*da
passeggio*) walking stick. **~ da hockey**
hockey stick

ba'tosta *nf* blow

bat'tage *nm inv* **~ pubblicitario** media
hype

bat'taglia *nf* battle; (*lotta*) fight

battagli'are *vi* battle; *fig* fight

bat'taglio *nm* (*di campana*) clapper; (*di
porta*) knocker

battagli'one *nm* battalion

bat'tello *nm* boat; (*motonave*) steamer

bat'tente *nm* (*di porta*) wing; (*di finestra*)
shutter; (*battaglio*) knocker

'battere *vt* beat; hit, knock ‹*testa, spalla*›;
(*percorrere*) scour; thresh ‹*grano*›; break
‹*record*› ● *vi* (*bussare, urtare*) knock; ‹*cuore:*›
beat; ‹*ali ecc:*› flap; *Tennis* serve; **~ a
macchina** type; **~ gli occhi** blink; **~ il
piede** tap one's foot; **~ le mani** clap [one's
hands]; **~ le ore** strike the hours

bat'teri *nmpl* bacteria

batte'ria *nf* battery; *Mus* drums *pl*; (*Sport:
eliminatoria*) heat

bat'terico *a* bacterial

bat'terio *nm* bacterium

batteriolo'gia *nf* bacteriology

batterio'logico *a* bacteriological

batte'rista *nmf* drummer

'battersi *vr* fight

bat'tesimo *nm* baptism, christening

battez'zare *vt* baptize, christen

battiba'leno *nm* **in un ~** in a flash

batti'becco *nm* squabble

batticu'ore *nm* palpitation; **mi venne il ~** I
was scared

bat'tigia *nf* water's edge

batti'mano *nm* applause

batti'panni *nm inv* carpetbeater

batti'scopa *nm inv* skirting board

batti'stero *nm* baptistery

batti'strada *nm inv* outrider; (*di
pneumatico*) tread; *Sport* pacesetter

battitap'peto *nm inv* carpet sweeper

'battito *nm* (*alle tempie*) throbbing; (*di
orologio*) ticking; (*della pioggia*) beating. **~
cardiaco** heartbeat

batti|'tore, -'trice *nmf Sport* batsman

bat'tuta *nf* beat; (*colpo*) knock; (*spirito-

saggine) wisecrack; (*osservazione*) remark;
Mus bar; *Tennis* service; *Theat* cue; (*dattilografia*) stroke. **~ d'arresto** setback

ba'tuffolo *nm* flock

ba'ule *nm* trunk

bau'xite *nf* bauxite

'bava *nf* dribble; (*di cane ecc*) slobber; **aver la
~ alla bocca** foam at the mouth

bava'glino *nm* bib

ba'vaglio *nm* gag

bava'rese *nf* ice-cream cake with milk, eggs
and cream

'bavero *nm* collar

ba'zar *nm inv* bazaar

ba'zooka *nm inv* bazooka

baz'zecola *nf* trifle

bazzi'care *vt/i* haunt

baz'zotto *a* softboiled

be'arsi *vr* delight (**di** in)

beata'mente *adv* blissfully

beatifi'care *vt* beatify

beati'tudine *nf* bliss

be'ato *a* blissful; *Relig* blessed; **~ te!** lucky
you!

beauty-'case *nm inv* toilet bag

bebè *nm inv* baby

bec'caccia *nf* woodcock

bec'care *vt* peck; *fig* catch

bec'carsi *vr* (*litigare*) quarrel

bec'cata *nf* beakful; (*colpo*) peck

beccheggi'are *vi* pitch

bec'chime *nm* birdseed

bec'chino *nm* grave-digger

'becco *nm* beak; (*di caffettiera ecc*) spout;
chiudi il ~ *fam* shut your trap; **non ha il ~
di un quattrino** *fam* he's skint; **restare a ~
asciutto** *fam* end up with nothing. **~
Bunsen** Bunsen [burner]. **~ a gas** gas
burner

bec'cuccio *nm* spout

'beeper *nm inv* beeper

be'fana *nf* legendary old woman who brings
presents to children on Twelfth Night; (*giorno*)
Twelfth Night; (*donna brutta*) old witch

'beffa *nf* hoax; **farsi beffe di qcno** mock sb

bef'fardo *a* derisory; ‹*persona*› mocking

bef'fare *vt* mock

bef'farsi *vr* **~ di** make fun of

beffeggi'are *vt* taunt

'bega *nf* quarrel; **è una bella ~** it's really
annoying

be'gonia *nf* begonia

beh *int* well

'beige *a & nm* beige

Bei'rut *nf* Beirut

be'lare *vi* bleat

be'lato *nm* bleating

'belga *a & nmf* Belgian

'Belgio *nm* Belgium

Bel'grado *nf* Belgrade

Be'lize *nm* Belize

'bella *nf* (*in carte, Sport*) decider;
(*innamorata*) sweetheart. **~ di giorno** *Bot*
morning glory. **~ di notte** *fig* lady of the
night

bel'lezza *nf* beauty; **che ~!** how lovely!; **per ~** (*per decorazione*) for decoration; **chiudere/finire in ~** end on a high note; **la ~ di tre mesi/200 000 lire** all of three months/200,000 lire

belli'cismo *nm* warmongering

belli'cistico *a* warmongering

'bellico *a* war *attrib*; **periodo ~** wartime

bellicosità *nf* belligerence

belli'coso *a* warlike

bellige'rante *a* & *nmf* belligerent

bellige'ranza *nf* belligerence

bellim'busto *nm* dandy

'bello *a* nice; (*di aspetto*) beautiful; ⟨*uomo*⟩ handsome; (*moralmente*) good; **cosa fai di ~ stasera?** what are you up to tonight?; **oggi fa ~** it's a nice day; **una bella cifra** a lot; **un bel piatto di pasta** a big plate of pasta; **nel bel mezzo** right in the middle; **un bel niente** absolutely nothing; **bell'e fatto** over and done with; **bell'amico!** fine friend he is/you are!; **questa è bella!** that's a good one!; **bel voto** good mark; **il bel mondo** the beautiful people; **le belle arti** the fine arts; **bella lì!** *sl* hi!; (*arrivederci*) bye!, see you! ● *nm* (*bellezza*) beauty; (*innamorato*) sweetheart; **sul più ~** at the crucial moment; **il ~ è che...** the funny thing is that...

beltà *nf liter* beauty

'belva *nf* wild beast

be'molle *nm Mus* flat

ben *vedi* **bene**

benché *conj* though, although

'benda *nf* bandage; (*per occhi*) blindfold

ben'dare *vt* bandage; blindfold ⟨*occhi*⟩

bendi'sposto *a* **essere ~ verso** be well-disposed towards

'bene *adv* well; **ben ~** thoroughly; **~!** good!; **star ~** (*di salute*) be well; ⟨*vestito, stile:*⟩ suit; (*finanziariamente*) be well off; **non sta ~** (*non è educato*) it's not nice; **sta/va ~!** all right!; **ti sta ~!** [it] serves you right!; **ti auguro ~** I wish you well; **voler ~ a** love; **di ~ in meglio** better and better; **fare ~** (*aver ragione*) do the right thing; **fare ~ a** ⟨*cibo:*⟩ be good for; **una persona per ~** a good person; **per ~** ⟨*fare*⟩ properly; **è ben difficile** it's very difficult; **ben cotto** well done; **come tu ben sai** as you well know; **lo credo ~!** I can well believe it! ● *nm* good; **per il tuo ~** for your own good. **beni** *pl* (*averi*) property *sg*; **un ~ di famiglia** a family heirloom. **beni** *pl* **ambientali** environment. **beni** *pl* **di consumo** consumer products, consumer goods. **beni** *pl* **culturali** cultural heritage. **beni** *pl* **immobili** real estate, realty *Am*. **beni** *pl* **mobili** movables

benedet'tino *a* & *nm* Benedictine

bene'detto *a* blessed

bene'dire *vt* bless; **mandare qcno a farsi ~** *fam* tell sb to get lost

benedizi'one *nf* blessing

benedu'cato *a* well-mannered

benefat'tore, -'trice *nmf* benefactor; benefactress

benefi'care *vt* help

benefi'cenza *nf* charity

benefici'are *vi* **~ di** profit by

benefici'ario, -a *a* & *nmf* beneficiary

bene'ficio *nm* benefit; **con ~ di inventario** with reservations. **~ accessorio** perquisite

be'nefico *a* beneficial; (*di beneficenza*) charitable

'Benelux *nm* Benelux

beneme'renza *nf* benevolence

bene'merito *a* worthy

bene'placito *nm* consent, approval

be'nessere *nm* well-being

bene'stante *a* well off ● *nmf* well-off person

bene'stare *nm* consent

benevo'lenza *nf* benevolence

be'nevolo *a* benevolent

ben'fatto *a* well-made

Ben'gala *nm* Bengal

ben'godi *nm* **il paese di ~** a land of plenty

'beni *nmpl* property *sg*; *Fin* assets; **~ di consumo** consumer goods

benia'mino *nm* favourite

be'nigno *a* kindly; *Med* benign

Be'nin *nm* Benin

beninfor'mato *a* well-informed ● *npl* **i beninformati** those in the know

benintenzio'nato, -a *a* well-meaning ● *nmf* well-meaning person

benin'teso *adv* needless to say, of course; **~ che...** of course,... ◀

be'nissimo *int* fine

benpen'sante *a* & *nmf* self-righteous

benser'vito *nm* **dare il ~ a qcno** give sb the sack

bensì *conj* but rather

benve'nuto *a* & *nm* welcome; **benvenuta!** welcome!

ben'visto *a* **essere ~** (*da qcno*) go down well (with sb)

benvo'lere *vt* **farsi ~ da qcno** win sb's affection; **prendere qcno in ~** take a liking to sb; **essere benvoluto da tutti** be well-liked by everyone

benvo'luto *a* well-liked

ben'zene *nm* benzene

ben'zina *nf* petrol, gas *Am*; **far ~** get petrol. **~ avio** aviation fuel. **~ senza piombo** leadfree petrol. **~ super** four-star petrol, premium gas *Am*. **~ verde** unleaded petrol

benzi'naio, -a *nmf* petrol station attendant, gas station attendant *Am*

be'one, -a *nmf fam* boozer

'berbero, -a *a* & *nmf* Berber

'bere *vt* drink; (*assorbire*) absorb; *fig* swallow; **~ una tazza di tè** have a cup of tea ● *nm* drinking; **da ~ e da mangiare** food and drink

berga'motto *nm* bergamot

'Bering *nm* **il mare di ~** the Bering Sea; **lo stretto di ~** the Bering Straits

ber'lina *nf Auto* saloon; **mettere alla ~ qcno** ridicule sb

berli'nese *nmf* Berliner ● *a* Berlin *attrib*

Ber'lino *nm* Berlin. **~ Est** East Berlin
Ber'muda *nfpl* **le ~** the Bermudas
ber'muda *nfpl* (*pantaloni*) Bermuda shorts
'Berna *nf* Berne
ber'noccolo *nm* bump; (*disposizione*) flair
ber'retto *nm* beret, cap. **~ a pompon** bobble hat
bersagli'are *vt fig* bombard
ber'saglio *nm* target
bescia'mella *nf* béchamel, white sauce
be'stemmia *nf* swear-word; (*maledizione*) oath; (*sproposito*) blasphemy
bestemmi'are *vi* swear
'bestia *nf* animal; (*persona brutale*) beast; (*persona sciocca*) fool; **andare in ~** *fam* blow one's top; **lavorare come una ~** slave away
besti'ale *a* bestial; (*espressione, violenza*) brutal; ⟨*fam: freddo, fame*⟩ terrible; **fa un caldo/freddo ~** it's dreadfully hot/cold
bestialità *nf inv* bestiality; *fig* nonsense
besti'ame *nm* livestock
betabloc'cante *nm* betablocker
Be'tlemme *nf* Bethlehem
betoni'era *nf* concrete mixer
'bettola *nf fig* dive
be'tulla *nf* birch
be'vanda *nf* drink. **~ alcolica** alcoholic drink
bevi'tore, -'trice *nmf* drinker
be'vuta *nf* drink
be'vuto *pp di* **bere**
Bhu'tan *nm* Bhutan
bi+ *pref* bi+
bi'ada *nf* fodder
bianche'ria *nf* linen. **~ per la casa** white goods, household linen. **~ intima** underwear; (*da donna*) lingerie. **~ da letto** bed linen
bian'chetto *nm* whitener
bi'anco, -a *a* white; ⟨*foglio*⟩ blank; **voce bianca** treble voice ● *nmf* white ● *nm* white; **mangiare in ~** eat bland food; **andare in ~** *fam* not score; **in ~ e nero** ⟨*film, fotografia*⟩ black and white, monochrome; **passare una notte in ~** have a sleepless night. **~ sporco** off white. **~ d'uovo** egg white
biancomangi'are *nm* blancmange
bian'core *nm* (*bianchezza*) whiteness
bianco'segno *nm* *Jur* blank document bearing a signature
bianco'spino *nm* hawthorn
biasci'care *vt* (*mangiare*) eat noisily; (*parlare*) mumble
biasi'mare *vt* blame
biasi'mevole *a* blameworthy
bi'asimo *nm* blame
'Bibbia *nf* Bible
bibe'ron *nm inv* [baby's] bottle
'bibita *nf* [soft] drink. **~ gasata** fizzy drink
'biblico *a* biblical
bibliogra'fia *nf* bibliography
biblio'grafico *a* bibliographical
biblio'teca *nf* library; (*mobile*) bookcase
bibliote'cario, -a *nmf* librarian

bicame'rale *a* two-chamber *attrib*, bicameral
bicarbo'nato *nm* bicarbonate. **~ di sodio** bicarbonate of soda
bicchie'rata *nf* glassful
bicchi'ere *nm* glass
bicchie'rino *nm fam* tipple
bicente'nario *nm* bicentenary
bici'cletta *nf* bicycle, bike; **andare in ~** cycle, go by bike; (*sapere*) ride a bicycle. **~ da corsa** racer
bi'cipite *nm* biceps
bi'cocca *nf* hovel
bico'lore *a* two-coloured
bidè *nm inv* bidet
bi'dello, -a *nmf* janitor, [school] caretaker
bidirezio'nale *a* bidirectional
bido'nare *vt* con, swindle; **farsi ~** be conned
bido'nata *nf fam* swindle
bi'done *nm* bin; (*fam: truffa*) swindle; **fare un ~ a qcno** *fam* stand sb up. **~ dell'immondizia, ~ della spazzatura** rubbish bin, trash can *Am*
bidon'ville *nf inv* shantytown
bi'eco *a* callous
bi'ella *nf* connecting rod
Bielo'russia *nf* Belarus
bielo'russo, -a *a & nmf* Belorussian
bien'nale *a* biennial
bi'ennio *nm* two-year period
bi'erre *nfpl* (*Brigate Rosse*) Red Brigades
bi'etola *nf* beet
bifo'cale *a* bifocal
bi'folco, -a *nmf fig* boor
bifor'carsi *vr* fork
biforcazi'one *nf* fork
bifor'cuto *a* forked
biga'mia *nf* bigamy
'bigamo, -a *a* bigamous ● *nmf* bigamist
big bang *nm* big bang
bighello'nare *vi* loaf around
bighel'lone *nm* loafer
bigiotte'ria *nf* costume jewellery; (*negozio*) jeweller's
bigliet'taio *nm* booking clerk; (*sui treni*) ticket-collector
bigliette'ria *nf* ticket-office; *Theat* box-office. **~ automatica** ticket vending machine
bigli'etto *nm* ticket; (*lettera breve*) note; (*cartoncino*) card; (*di banca*) banknote. **~ di sola andata** single [ticket]. **~ di andata e ritorno** return [ticket]. **~ di auguri** card. **~ chilometrico** *ticket allowing travel up to a maximum specified distance.* **~ collettivo** group ticket. **~ giornaliero** day pass. **~ d'ingresso** entrance ticket. **~ della lotteria** lottery ticket. **~ da visita** business card
bigliet'tone *nm* (*fam: soldi*) big one
bignè *nm inv* puff. **~ alla crema** cream puff
bigo'dino *nm* roller
bi'gotto *nm* bigot
bi'kini *nm inv* bikini
bi'lancia *nf* scales *pl*; (*di orologio, Comm*) balance; **B~** *Astr* Libra. **~ commerciale** balance of trade. **~ da cucina** kitchen scales.

~ dei pagamenti balance of payments. **~ pesapersone** scales

bilanci'are vt balance; fig weigh

bilancia'tura nf **~ gomme** wheel-balancing

bilanci'ere nm (in sollevamento pesi) barbell; (di orologio) balance wheel

bi'lancio nm budget; Comm balance [sheet]; **fare il ~** balance the books; fig take stock; **chiudere il ~ in attivo/passivo** to end the financial year in profit/with a loss. **~ preventivo** budget

bilate'rale a bilateral

'bile nf bile; fig rage

bili'ardo nm billiards sg

'bilico nm equilibrium; **in ~** in the balance

bi'lingue a bilingual

bilingu'ismo nm bilingualism

bili'one nm billion

bili'oso a bilious

bilo'cale a two-room ● nm two-room flat

'bimbo, -a nmf child. **~ in fasce** babe in arms

bimen'sile a fortnightly Br, twice-monthly

bime'strale a bimonthly

bi'mestre nm two months

bi'nario nm track; (piattaforma) platform

bi'nocolo nm binoculars pl

bi'nomio nm binomial

bio+ pref bio+

bioagricol'tore nm organic farmer

bioagricol'tura nf organic farming

bio'chimica nf biochemistry

bio'chimico, -a nmf biochemist ● a biochemical

biodegra'dabile a biodegradable

biodiversità nf biodiversity

bio'etica nf bioethics

bio'fisica nf biophysics

biogra'fia nf biography

bio'grafico a biographical

bi'ografo, -a nmf biographer

bioingegne'ria nf bioengineering

biolo'gia nf biology

biologica'mente adv biologically

bio'logico a biological

bi'ologo, -a nmf biologist

bi'onda nf blonde. **~ ossigenata** peroxide blonde

bi'ondo a blond ● nm fair colour; (uomo) fair-haired man. **~ cenere** ash blond. **~ platino** platinum blonde

bi'onico a bionic

bio'psia nf biopsy

bio'ritmo nm biorhythm

bio'sfera nf biosphere

bi'ossido nm dioxide. **~ di carbonio** carbon dioxide

biotecnolo'gia nf biotechnology

bip nm inv blip

bipar'titico a bipartisan

biparti'tismo nm two-party system

bipar'tito a bipartite, two-party attrib ● nm two-party coalition

bipartizi'one nf division into two parts

bipo'lare a Electr bipolar; Pol dominated by two large parties

bipola'rismo nm Pol system in which the numerous parties line up behind two main parties

bipolarizzazi'one nf Pol tendency towards 'bipolarismo'

bi'posto a inv & nm inv two-seater

'birba nf, **bir'bante** nm rascal, rogue

birbo'nata nf trick

bir'bone a wicked

birdie nm inv (golf) birdie

biri'chino, -a a naughty ● nmf little devil

bi'rillo nm skittle

Bir'mania nf Burma

bir'mano, -a a & nmf Burmese

'birra nf beer; **a tutta ~** fig flat out. **~ chiara** lager. **~ grande** ≈ pint. **~ piccola** ≈ half-pint. **~ scura** dark beer, brown ale Br

birre'ria nf beer-house; (fabbrica) brewery

bis nm inv encore

bi'saccia nf haversack

bi'sbetica nf shrew

bi'sbetico a bad-tempered

bisbigli'are vt/i whisper

bi'sbiglio nm whisper

bi'sboccia nf **fare ~** make merry

'bisca nf gambling-house

Bi'scaglia nf **il golfo di ~** the Bay of Biscay

'biscia nf snake

biscotti'era nf biscuit barrel, biscuit tin

bi'scotto nm biscuit. **~ per cani** dog-biscuit

bisessu'ale a & nmf bisexual

bise'stile a **anno ~** leap year

bisettima'nale a twice-weekly

biset'trice nf bisector

bisezi'one nf bisection

bisil'labico a two-syllable attrib, bisyllabic

bi'slacco a peculiar

bi'slungo a oblong

bi'snonno, -a nm great-grandfather ● nf great-grandmother

biso'gnare vi **bisogna agire subito** we must act at once; **bisogna farlo** it is necessary to do it; **non bisogna venire** you don't have to come

bi'sogno nm need; (povertà) poverty; **aver ~ di** need

biso'gnoso a needy; (povero) poor; **~ di** in need of

bi'sonte nm bison

bi'stecca nf steak. **~ di cavallo** horsemeat steak. **~ ai ferri** grilled steak. **~ alla fiorentina** large grilled beef steak

bi'sticci nmpl bickering

bisticci'are vi quarrel

bi'sticcio nm quarrel; (gioco di parole) pun

bistrat'tare vt mistreat

bistrò nm inv bistro

'bisturi nm inv scalpel

bi'sunto a very greasy

bit nm inv bit

bito'nale a two-tone

bi'torzolo nm lump

'bitter *nm inv* bitter aperitif
bi'tume *nm* bitumen
bivac'care *vi* bivouac
bi'vacco *nm* bivouac
'bivio *nm* crossroads; *(di strada)* fork
bizan'tino *a* Byzantine
'bizza *nf* tantrum; **fare le bizze** *(bambini:)* play up
bizzar'ria *nf* eccentricity
biz'zarro *a* bizarre
biz'zeffe *adv* **a ~** galore
'blackjack *nm* blackjack
blan'dire *vt* soothe; *(allettare)* flatter
'blando *a* mild
bla'sfemo *a* blasphemous
bla'sone *nm* coat of arms
blate'rare *vi* blether, blather; **~ di qcsa** burble on about sth
'blatta *nf* cockroach
'bleso *a* lisping
blin'dare *vt* armour-plate
blin'dato *a* armoured
'blinker *nm inv* blinker
'blister *nm inv* blister pack
blitz *nm inv* blitz
bloc'care *vt* block; *(isolare)* cut off; *Mil* blockade; *Comm* freeze; stop *(assegno)*; **~ l'accesso a** seal off
bloc'carsi *vr Mech* jam
blocca'sterzo *nm* steering lock
bloc'cato *a* blocked
bloc'chetto *nm* **~ per appunti** memo pad. **~ di biglietti** book of tickets
'blocco *nm* block; *Mil* blockade; *(dei fitti)* restriction; *(di carta)* pad; *(unione)* coalition; **in ~** *Comm* in bulk. **~ per appunti** notepad. **~ psicologico** mental block. **~ stradale** roadblock
block-notes *nm inv* memo pad
blu *a & nm* blue
blu'astro *a* bluish
blue chip *nf inv Fin* blue chip
blue-'jeans *nmpl* jeans
bluff *nm inv (carte, fig)* bluff
bluf'fare *vi (carte, fig)* bluff
'blusa *nf* blouse
'boa *nm* boa [constrictor]; *(sciarpa)* [feather] boa ● *nf Naut* buoy
bo'ato *nm* rumbling
bo'bina *nf* spool; *(di film)* reel; *Electr* coil
bobi'nare *vt* spool
'bocca *nf* mouth; **a ~ aperta** *fig* dumbfounded; **in ~ al lupo!** *fam* break a leg!; **fare la respirazione ~ a ~ a qcno** give sb mouth to mouth resuscitation, give sb the kiss of life; **essere di ~ buona** eat anything; *fig* be easily satisfied; **essere sulla ~ di tutti** be the talk of the town. **~ del camino** chimneybreast. **~ di leone** snapdragon
boccac'cesco *a* licentious
boc'caccia *nf* grimace; **far boccacce** make faces
boc'caglio *nm* nozzle
boc'cale *nm* jug; *(da birra)* mug
bocca'porto *nm Naut* hatch

bocca'scena *nm inv* proscenium
boc'cata *nf (di fumo)* puff; **prendere una ~ d'aria** get a breath of fresh air
boc'cetta *nf* small bottle
boccheggi'are *vi* gasp
boc'chino *nm* cigarette holder; *(di pipa, Mus)* mouthpiece
'boccia *nf (palla)* bowl; **bocce** *pl (gioco)* bowls *sg*; **giocare a bocce** play bowls
bocci'are *vt (agli esami)* fail; *(respingere)* reject; *(alle bocce)* hit; **essere bocciato** fail; *(ripetere)* repeat a year
boccia'tura *nf* failure
bocci'olo *nm* bud
'boccolo *nm* ringlet
boccon'cino *nm* morsel
boc'cone *nm* mouthful; *(piccolo pasto)* snack
boc'coni *adv* face down[wards]
Bo'emia *nf* Bohemia
bo'emo, -a *a & nmf* Bohemian
bo'ero, -a *nmf* Afrikaner
bofonchi'are *vi* grumble
boh *int* dunno
'boia *nm* executioner; **fa un freddo ~** *fam* it's brass-monkey weather; **ho un sonno ~** *fam* I can't keep my eyes open
boi'ata *nf fam* rubbish
boicot'taggio *nm* boycotting
boicot'tare *vt* boycott
bo'lero *nm* bolero
'bolgia *nf (caos)* bedlam
'bolide *nm* meteor; **passare come un ~** shoot past [like a rocket]
Bo'livia *nf* Bolivia
bolivi'ano, -a *a & nmf* Bolivian
'bolla *nf* bubble; *(vescica, in tappezzeria)* blister; **finire in una ~ di sapone** go up in smoke. **~ di accompagnamento** packing list. **~ d'aria** *(in acqua)* air bubble. **~ di consegna** packing list
bol'lare *vt* stamp; *fig* brand
bol'lato *a fig* branded; **carta bollata** paper with stamp showing payment of duty
bol'lente *a* boiling [hot]
bol'letta *nf* bill; **essere in ~** be hard up
bollet'tino *nm* bulletin; *Comm* list. **~ d'informazione** fact sheet. **~ meteorologico** weather report. **~ ufficiale** gazette
bolli'latte *nm* milk pan
bol'lino *nm* coupon
bol'lire *vt/i* boil
bol'lito *nm* boiled meat
bolli'tore *nm* boiler; *(per l'acqua)* kettle
bolli'tura *nf* boiling
'bollo *nm* stamp; *Auto* tax disc
bol'lore *nm* boil; *(caldo)* intense heat; *fig* ardour
Bo'logna *nf* Bologna
bolo'gnese *nmf* person from Bologna; **spaghetti alla ~** spaghetti bolognese
'bomba *nf* bomb; **a prova di ~** bomb-proof; **tornare a ~** get back to the point. **~ atomica** nuclear bomb. **~ a mano** hand gre-

nade. ~ **molotov** petrol bomb. ~ **ad orologeria** time bomb

bombarda'mento *nm* shelling; *(con aerei)* bombing; *fig* bombardment. ~ **aereo** air raid

bombar'dare *vt* shell; *(con aerei)* bomb; *fig* bombard

bombardi'ere *nm* bomber

bom'bato *a* domed

'bomber *nm inv* bomber jacket

bom'betta *nf* bowler [hat]

'bombo *nm* bumblebee

'bombola *nf* cylinder. ~ **di gas** gas bottle, gas cylinder

bcmbo'lone *nm* doughnut

bomboni'era *nf* wedding keep-sake

bo'naccia *nf Naut* calm

bonacci'one, -a *nmf* good-natured person ● *a* good-natured

bo'nario *a* kindly

bo'nifica *nf* land reclamation

bonifi'care *vt* reclaim

bo'nifico *nm Comm* discount; ~ **[bancario] [credit] transfer**

bontà *nf* goodness; *(gentilezza)* kindness

'bonus-'malus *nm inv Auto* car-insurance policy with no claims bonus clause

'boogie *nm* boogie

'bookmaker *nm inv* bookmaker

'boomerang *nm inv* boomerang

boot *nm Comput* boot-up; **eseguire il ~** boot up

'bora *nf cold north-east wind in the upper Adriatic*

borbot'tare *vi* mumble; *⟨stomaco:⟩* rumble

borbot'tio *nm* mumbling; *(di stomaco)* rumbling

'borchia *nf* stud

borchi'ato *a* studded

bor'dare *vt* border

bor'data *nf Naut* broadside

borda'tura *nf* border

bor'deaux *nm inv (vino)* claret, Bordeaux ● *a inv (colore)* claret

bor'dello *nm* brothel; *fig* bedlam; *(disordine)* mess

bor'dino *nm* narrow border

'bordo *nm* border; *(estremità)* edge; **a ~** *Aeron, Naut* on board; **d'alto ~** *⟨prostituta⟩* high-class. ~ **d'attacco** *Aeron* leading edge

bor'dura *nf* border

bor'gata *nf* hamlet

bor'ghese *a* bourgeois; *⟨abito⟩* civilian; **in ~** in civilian dress; *⟨poliziotto⟩* in plain clothes

borghe'sia *nf* middle classes *pl*

'borgo *nm* village; *(quartiere)* district

'boria *nf* conceit

bori'oso *a* conceited

bor'lotto *nm* **[fagiolo] ~** borlotto bean

'Borneo *nm* Borneo

boro'talco *nm* talcum powder

bor'raccia *nf* flask

'Borsa *nf* ~ **[valori]** Stock Exchange

'borsa *nf* bag; *(borsetta)* handbag. ~ **dell'acqua calda** hot-water bottle. ~ **frigo**

cool-box. ~ **della spesa** shopping bag. ~ **di studio** scholarship. ~ **termica** cool bag. ~ **da viaggio** travel bag

borsai'olo *nm* pickpocket

bor'seggio *nm* pickpocketing

borsel'lino *nm* purse

bor'sello *nm (portamonete)* purse; *(borsetto)* man's handbag

bor'setta *nf* handbag

bor'setto *nm* man's handbag

bor'sino *nm Fin* dealing room

bor'sista *nmf Fin* speculator; *Sch* scholarship holder

bo'scaglia *nf* woodlands *pl*

boscai'olo *nm* woodman; *(guardaboschi)* forester

bo'schetto *nm* grove

'bosco *nm* wood

bo'scoso *a* wooded

'Bosnia *nf* Bosnia

bos'niaco, -a *a & nmf* Bosnian

Bosnia-Erzego'vina *nf* Bosnia-Herzegovina

boss *nm inv* ~ **mafioso** Mafia boss

'bosso *nm* boxwood

'bossolo *nm* cartridge case

Bot *nm abbr* **(Buoni Ordinari Del Tesoro)** T-bills

bo'tanica *nf* botany

bo'tanico *a* botanical ● *nm* botanist

'botola *nf* trapdoor

Bot'swana *nm* Botswana

'botta *nf* blow; *(rumore)* bang; **fare a botte** come to blows. ~ **e risposta** *fig* thrust and counter-thrust

botta'trice *nf* monkfish

'botte *nf* barrel

bot'tega *nf* shop; *(di artigiano)* workshop

botte'gaio, -a *nmf* shopkeeper

botte'ghino *nm Theatr* box-office; *(del lotto)* lottery-shop

bot'tiglia *nf* bottle; **in ~** bottled

bottiglie'ria *nf* wine shop

bot'tino *nm* loot; *Mil* booty

'botto *nm* bang. **di ~** all of a sudden

bot'tone *nm* button; *Bot* bud. ~ **di carica** winder

botu'lismo *nm* botulism

'bourbon *nm inv* bourbon

bo'vini *nmpl* cattle

bo'vino *a* bovine

'bowling *nm* bowling

box *nm inv (per cavalli)* loosebox; *(recinto per bambini)* play-pen

'boxe *nf* boxing

'bozza *nf* draft; *Typ* proof; *(bernoccolo)* bump; ~ **in colonna** galley [proof]. ~ **definitiva** page proof. ~ **impaginata** page proof. ~ **di stampa** page proofs

boz'zetto *nm* sketch

'bozzolo *nm* cocoon

BR *nfpl abbr* **(Brigate Rosse)** Red Brigades

brac'care *vt* hunt

brac'cetto *nm* **a ~** arm in arm

bracci'ale *nm* bracelet; *(fascia)* armband

braccia'letto *nm* bracelet; (*di orologio*) watch-strap

bracci'ante *nm* day labourer

bracci'ata *nf* (*nel nuoto*) stroke

'braccio *nm* (*pl* *nf* **braccia**) arm; (*di fiume*, *pl* **bracci**) arm. ~ **di ferro** arm wrestling

bracci'olo *nm* (*di sedia*) arm[rest]; (*da nuoto*) armband

'bracco *nm* hound

bracconi'ere *nm* poacher

'brace *nf* embers *pl*; **alla** ~ char-grilled

'brache *nfpl* (*fam: pantaloni*) britches; **calare le** ~ *fig* chicken out

braci'ere *nm* brazier

braci'ola *nf* chop. ~ **di maiale** pork chop

'brado *a* **allo stato** ~ in the wild

braille *nm* Braille

brain-'storming *nm inv* brainstorming

'brama *nf* longing

bra'mare *vt* long for

bra'mino *nm* Brahmin

bramo'sia *nf* yearning

'branca *nf* branch

'branchia *nf* gill

'branco *nm* (*di cani*) pack; (*pej: di persone*) gang

branco'lare *vi* grope

'branda *nf* camp-bed

bran'dello *nm* scrap; **a brandelli** in tatters

bran'dina *nf* cot

bran'dire *vt* brandish

'brandy *nm inv* brandy

'brano *nm* piece; (*di libro*) passage

bran'zino *nm* sea bass

bra'sare *vt* braise

bra'sato *nm* braised beef with herbs

Bra'sile *nm* Brazil

brasili'ano, -a *a & nmf* Brazilian

bra'vata *nf* bragging

'bravo *a* good; (*abile*) clever; (*coraggioso*) brave; ~! well done!

bra'vura *nf* skill

'breccia *nf* breach; **sulla** ~ *fig* very successful, at the top

brecci'ame *nm* loose chippings *pl*

bre'saola *nf* dried, salted beef sliced thinly and eaten cold

Bre'tagna *nf* Brittany

bre'tella *nf* shoulder-strap; *Mech* brace; **bretelle** *pl* (*di calzoni*) braces, suspenders *Am*

'bretone *a & nmf* Breton

'breve *a* brief, short; **in** ~ briefly; **tra** ~ shortly

brevet'tare *vt* patent

bre'vetto *nm* patent; (*attestato*) licence

brevità *nf* shortness

'brezza *nf* breeze

'bricco *nm* jug. ~ **del latte** milk jug

bricco'nata *nf* dirty trick

bric'cone *nm* blackguard; *hum* rascal

'briciola *nf* crumb; *fig* grain

'briciolo *nm* fragment; **non hai un** ~ **di cervello!** you don't have an ounce of common sense!

bridge *nm inv* (*carte*) bridge

'briga *nf* (*fastidio*) trouble; (*lite*) quarrel; **attaccar** ~ pick a quarrel; **prendersi la** ~ **di fare qcsa** go to the trouble of doing sth

brigadi'ere *nm* (*dei carabinieri*) sergeant

brigan'taggio *nm* highway robbery

bri'gante *nm* bandit; *hum* rogue

bri'gare *vi* to intrigue

bri'gata *nf* brigade; (*gruppo*) group

briga'tista *nmf Pol* member of the Red Brigades

'briglia *nf* rein; **a** ~ **sciolta** at full gallop; *fig* at breakneck speed

bril'lante *a* brilliant; (*scintillante*) sparkling ● *nm* diamond

brillan'tina *nf* brilliantine

bril'lare *vi* shine; ⟨*metallo:*⟩ glitter; (*scintillare*) sparkle

'brillo *a* tipsy

'brina *nf* hoar-frost

brin'dare *vi* toast; ~ **a qcno** drink a toast to sb

'brindisi *nm inv* toast

'brio *nm* vivacity

bri'oche *nf inv* croissant

bri'oso *a* vivacious

'briscola *nf* (*seme*) trumps

bri'tannico *a* British

'brivido *nm* shiver; (*di paura ecc*) shudder; (*di emozione*) thrill; **avere i brividi** have the shivers; **dare i brividi a qcno** give sb the shivers

brizzo'lato *a* ⟨*capelli, barba*⟩ greying

'brocca *nf* jug

broc'cato *nm* brocade

'broccoli *nmpl* broccoli

bro'daglia *nf pej* dishwater

'brodo *nm* broth; (*per cucinare*) stock. ~ **di manzo** beef tea. ~ **di pollo** chicken broth; (*per cucinare*) chicken stock. ~ **ristretto** consommé. ~ **vegetale** clear broth; (*per cucinare*) vegetable stock

'broglio *nm* ~ **elettorale** gerrymandering

'broker *nmf inv* broker; ~ **d'assicurazioni** insurance broker

'bromo *nm Chem* bromine

bro'muro *nm* bromide

bronchi'ale *a* bronchial

bron'chite *nf* bronchitis

bron'chitico *a* chesty

'broncio *nm* sulk; **fare il** ~ sulk

bronto'lare *vi* grumble; ⟨*tuono ecc:*⟩ rumble; ~ **contro qcno/qcsa** grumble *or* grouch about sb/sth

bronto'lio *nm* grumbling; (*di tuono, stomaco*) rumbling

bronto'lone, -a *nmf* grumbler

'bronzo *nm* bronze; **una faccia di** ~ *fam* a brass neck

bros'sura *nf* **edizione in** ~ paperback

bru'care *vt* ⟨*pecora:*⟩ graze

bruciacchi'are *vt* scorch

bruci'ante *a* burning

brucia'pelo *adv* **a** ~ point-blank

bruci'are vt burn; (scottare) scald; (incendiare) set fire to ● vi burn; (scottare) scald
bruci'arsi vr burn oneself
bruci'ato a burnt; fig burnt-out
brucia'tore nm burner
brucia'tura nf burn
bruci'ore nm burning sensation
'bruco nm grub
'brufolo nm spot
brughi'era nf heath
bruli'care vi swarm
bruli'chio nm swarming
'brullo a bare
'bruma nf mist
Bru'nei nm Brunei
'bruno a brown; ⟨occhi, capelli⟩ dark
brusca'mente adv (di colpo) suddenly
bru'schetta nf toasted bread rubbed with garlic and sprinkled with olive oil
'brusco a sharp; ⟨persona⟩ brusque, abrupt; (improvviso) sudden
bru'sio nm buzzing
bru'tale a brutal
brutalità nf brutality
brutaliz'zare vt brutalize
'bruto a & nm brute
brut'tezza nf ugliness
'brutto a ugly; ⟨tempo, tipo, situazione, affare⟩ nasty; (cattivo) bad. **brutta copia** nf rough copy. ~ **tiro** nm dirty trick
brut'tura nf ugly thing
bub'bone nm Med swelling
'buca nf hole; (avvallamento) hollow. ~ **delle lettere** letter-box
buca'neve nm inv snowdrop
bucani'ere nm buccaneer
bu'care vt make a hole in; (pungere) prick; punch ⟨biglietti⟩ ● vi have a puncture
'Bucarest nf Bucharest
bu'carsi vr prick oneself; (con droga) shoot up
buca'tini nmpl pasta similar to spaghetti but thicker and hollow
bu'cato nm washing; **fare il** ~ do the washing
'buccia nf peel, skin; **bucce** pl (di frutta) parings. ~ **di banana** banana skin
bucherel'lare vt riddle
bucherel'lato a pitted
'buco nm hole. ~ **della serratura** keyhole
bu'colica nf bucolic
bu'colico a bucolic
'Budda nm Buddha
bud'dista nmf Buddhist
bu'dello nm (pl nf **budella**) bowel
'budget nm inv budget; ~ **provvisorio** minibudget
budge'tario a budgetary
bu'dino nm pudding
'bue nm (pl **buoi**) ox; **carne di** ~ beef
'bufalo nm buffalo
bu'fera nf storm; (di neve) blizzard
bufferiz'zato a Comput buffered
buf'fet nm inv snack bar; (mobile) sideboard; (pasto) buffet
buf'fetto nm cuff

'buffo a funny; Theat comic ● nm funny thing
buffo'nata nf (scherzo) joke
buf'fone nm buffoon; **fare il** ~ play the fool
bu'gia nf lie; ~ **pietosa** white lie
bugi'ardo, -a a lying ● nmf liar
bugi'gattolo nm cubby-hole
'buio a dark ● nm darkness; **al** ~ in the dark; ~ **pesto** pitch dark
'bulbo nm bulb; (dell'occhio) eyeball
Bulga'ria nf Bulgaria
'bulgaro, -a a & nmf Bulgarian
buli'mia nf bulimia
bu'limico nmf bulimic
'bullo nm bully
bul'lone nm bolt
'bunker nm inv bunker
buona'fede nf good faith
buo'nanima nf **quella** ~ **di mio zio** my late uncle, God rest his soul
buona'notte int good night
buona'sera int good evening
buonco'stume nf Vice Squad
buondì int good day!
buon'giorno int good morning; (di pomeriggio) good afternoon
buon'grado nm **di** ~ willingly
buongu'staio, -a nmf gourmet
buon'gusto nm good taste
bu'ono a good; ⟨momento⟩ right; **dar** ~ (convalidare) accept; **alla buona** easy-going; ⟨cena⟩ informal; **buona fortuna!** good luck!; **buona notte/sera** good night/evening; **buon compleanno/Natale!** happy birthday/merry Christmas!; **buon viaggio!** have a good trip!; **buon appetito!** enjoy your meal!; ~ **senso** common sense; **di buon'ora** early; **a buon mercato** cheap; **una buona volta** once and for all; **buona parte di** the best part of; **tre ore buone** three good hours ● nm good; (in film) goody; (tagliando) voucher; (titolo) bond; **con le buone** gently. ~ **acquisto** gift token. ~ **sconto** money-off coupon ● nmf **buono, -a a nulla** dead loss
buontem'pone, -a nmf happy-go-lucky person
buonu'more nm good temper
buonu'scita nf retirement bonus; (di dirigente) golden handshake
buratti'naio nm puppeteer
burat'tino nm puppet
'burbero a surly; (nei modi) rough
bu'rino, -a nmf hick
'burla nf joke; **fare una** ~ **a** play a trick on; **per** ~ for fun
bur'lare vt make a fool of
bur'larsi vr ~ **di** make fun of
buro'crate nm bureaucrat
burocra'tese nm gobbledygook
buro'cratico a bureaucratic
burocra'zia nf bureaucracy
bu'rotica nf office automation
bur'rasca nf storm
burra'scoso a stormy
'burro nm butter. ~ **di arachidi** peanut butter

bur'rone *nm* ravine
Bu'rundi *nm* Burundi
bus *nm inv Comput* bus. **~ locale** local bus
bu'scare *vt* catch; **buscarle** *fam* get a hiding
bu'scarsi *vr* catch
bus'sare *vt* knock
'bussola *nf* compass; **perdere la ~** lose one's bearings
'busta *nf* envelope; (*astuccio*) case. **~ affrancata** business reply envelope. **~ a finestra** window envelope. **~ imbottita** Jiffy bag®, padded envelope. **~ paga** pay packet
busta'rella *nf* bribe

bu'stina *nf* (*di tè*) tea bag; (*per medicine*) sachet
'busto *nm* bust; (*indumento*) girdle; **a mezzo ~** half-length
bu'tano *nm* Calor gas®
buttafu'ori *nm inv* bouncer
but'tare *vt* throw; **~ giù** (*demolire*) knock down; (*inghiottire*) gulp down; scribble down ‹*scritto*›; *fam* put on ‹*pasta*›; (*scoraggiare*) dishearten; **~ via** throw away
but'tarsi *vr* throw oneself; (*saltare*) jump
butte'rato *a* pitted
buz'zurro *nm fam* yokel
byte *nm inv Comput* byte

Cc

ca. *abbr* (**circa**) c.
caba'ret *nm inv* cabaret
cabaret'tisco *a* cabaret *attrib*
ca'bina *nf Naut, Aeron* cabin; (*al mare*) beach hut; (*di funivia*) [cable] car. **~ elettorale** polling booth. **~ di pilotaggio** cockpit; (*di aereo di linea*) flight deck. **~ di prova** fitting room. **~ telefonica** telephone box *Br*, phone booth
cabi'nato *nm* cabin cruiser
ca'blaggio *nm Electr* wiring
ca'blato *a* ‹*messaggio*› cable *attrib*
cablo'gramma *nm* cablegram
cabo'taggio *nm Naut* coastal navigation
cabrio'let *nm inv Auto* convertible
ca'cao *nm* cocoa
ca'care *vi vulg* have a crap
caca'toa *nm inv* cockatoo
'cacca *nf fam* poo, number two
'cacchio *nm fam* hell; **ma che ~ fai/dici?** *fam* what the hell are you doing/saying?
'caccia *nf* hunt; (*con fucile*) shooting; (*inseguimento*) chase; (*selvaggina*) game ● *nm inv Aeron* fighter; *Naut* destroyer; **andare a ~** go hunting. **~ grossa** big game. **~ all'uomo** man-hunt
cacciabombardi'ere *nm Aeron* fighter-bomber
cacciagi'one *nf* game
cacci'are *vt* hunt; (*mandar via*) chase away; (*scacciare*) drive out; (*ficcare*) shove; **caccia** [**fuori**] **i soldi!** *fam* out with the money!; **~ un urlo** *fam* let out a yell ● *vi* go hunting
cacci'arsi *vr* (*nascondersi*) hide; (*andare a finire*) get to; **~ nei guai** get into trouble
caccia'tora: alla ~ *a Culin* chasseur
caccia'tore, -'trice *nmf* hunter. **~ di dote** gold digger. **~ di frodo** poacher. **~ di taglie** bounty hunter. **~ di teste** *Comm* head-hunter

cacciatorpedini'ere *nm inv* destroyer
caccia'vite *nm inv* screwdriver
cacci'ucco *nm* **~ alla livornese** soup of seafood, tomato and wine served with bread
cache-'sexe *nm inv* thong
ca'chet *nm inv Med* capsule; (*colorante*) colour rinse; (*stile*) cachet
'cachi *nm inv* persimmon ● *a inv* (*colore*) khaki
'cacio *nm* (*formaggio*) cheese
caci'otta *nf* creamy, fairly soft cheese
'caco *nm fam* persimmon
cacofo'nia *nf* cacophony
'cactus *nm inv* cactus
cada'uno *a* each
ca'davere *nm* corpse
cada'verico *a fig* deathly pale
ca'dente *a* falling; ‹*casa*› crumbling
ca'denza *nf* cadence; (*ritmo*) rhythm; *Mus* cadenza
caden'zare *vt* give rhythm to
caden'zato *a* measured
ca'dere *vi* fall; ‹*capelli ecc:*› fall out; (*capitombolare*) tumble; ‹*vestito ecc:*› hang; **far ~** (*di mano*) drop; **~ dal sonno** feel very sleepy; **lasciar ~** drop; **~ dalle nuvole** *fig* be taken aback; **~ dalla finestra** fall out of the window
ca'detto *nm* cadet
ca'duta *nf* fall; *fig* downfall. **~ dei capelli** hair loss. **~ libera** freefall. **~ massi** falling rocks
ca'duto *nm* **i caduti** the dead; **monumento ai caduti** war memorial
caffè *nm inv* coffee; (*locale*) café. **~ corretto** espresso with a dash of liqueur. **~ lungo** weak black coffee. **~ macchiato** coffee with a dash of milk. **~ ristretto** extra-strong espresso coffee. **~ solubile** instant coffee

caffe'ina *nf* caffeine
caffel'latte *nm inv* white coffee
caffette'ria *nf* coffee bar
caffetti'era *nf* coffee-pot
cafo'naggine *nf* boorishness
cafo'nata *nf* boorishness
ca'fone, -a *nmf* boor
cafone'ria *nf* (*comportamento*) boorishness;
 è stata una ~ it was boorish
ca'gare *vi vulg* crap; **va' a ~!** go and get
 stuffed!
cagio'nare *vt* cause
cagio'nevole *a* delicate
cagli'are *vi* curdle
cagli'arsi *vr* curdle
cagli'ata *nf* curd cheese
caglia'tura *nf* curdling
'cagna *nf* bitch
ca'gnara *nf fam* din
ca'gnesco *a* **guardare qcno in ~** scowl at
 sb
ca'gnetto *nm* lapdog
C.A.I. *nm abbr* (**Club Alpino Italiano**) *Italian mountain sports association*
cai'mano *nm* cayman
'caio *nm* so-and-so
'Cairo *nm* **il ~** Cairo
'cala *nf* creek
cala'brese *a & nmf* Calabrian
Ca'labria *nf* Calabria
cala'brone *nm* hornet
Cala'hari *nm* **il ~** the Kalahari [Desert]
cala'maio *nm* inkpot
calama'retto *nm* small squid
cala'mari *nmpl* squid *sg*
cala'maro *nm* squid
cala'mita *nf* magnet
calamità *nf inv* calamity. **~ pl naturali**
 natural disasters
calami'tare *vt* draw ⟨*attenzione*⟩
ca'lante *a* waning
ca'lare *vi* come down; ⟨*vento:*⟩ drop;
 (*diminuire*) fall; (*tramontare*) set; **~ di peso**
 lose weight; **~ di tono** *fig* drag ● *vt*
 (*abbassare*) lower; (*nei lavori a maglia*) decrease ● *nm* (*di luna*) waning
ca'larsi *vr* lower oneself
ca'lata *nf* (*invasione*) invasion
'calca *nf* throng
cal'cagno *nm* (*pl f* **calcagna**) heel; **stare
 alle calcagna di qcno** *fig* follow sb around
cal'care[1] *nm* limestone
cal'care[2] *vt* tread; (*premere*) press [down]; **~
 la mano** *fig* exaggerate; **~ le orme di qcno**
 fig follow in sb's footsteps; **~ le scene** *fig*
 tread the boards
'calce[1] *nf* lime. **~ viva** quicklime
'calce[2] *nm* **in ~** at the foot of the page
calce'struzzo *nm* concrete
cal'cetto *nm Sport* five-a-side [football]; (*da
 tavolo*) table football
calci'are *vt* kick
calcia'tore *nm* footballer
calcifi'carsi *vr* calcify
calcificazi'one *nf* calcification

cal'cina *nf* mortar
calci'naccio *nm* (*pezzo di intonaco*) flake of
 plaster; (*pezzo di muro*) piece of rubble
'calcio[1] *nm* kick; *Sport* football; (*di arma da
 fuoco*) butt; **dare un ~ a** a kick; **giocare a ~**
 play football. **~ d'angolo** corner [kick]. **~ di
 punizione** free kick. **~ di rigore** penalty
 [kick]
'calcio[2] *nm Chem* calcium
calcio-mer'cato *nm inv* transfer market
'calco *nm* (*con carta*) tracing; (*arte*) cast
calco'lare *vt* calculate; (*considerare*) consider
calco'lato *a* calculated
calcola'tore *a* calculating ● *nm* calculator;
 (*macchina elettronica*) computer. **~ digitale**
 (*calcolatrice*) calculator
calcola'trice *nf* calculating machine
'calcolo *nm* calculation; *Med* stone; **per ~**
 fig out of self-interest; **mi sono fatto i
 calcoli** *fig* I've weighed up the pros and
 cons. **~ approssimativo** guesstimate. **~
 biliare** gallstone. **~ renale** kidney stone
cal'daia *nf* boiler
caldar'rosta *nf* roast chestnut
caldeggi'are *vt* support
'caldo *a* warm; (*molto caldo*) hot; ⟨*situazione,
 zona*⟩ dangerous; ⟨*notizie*⟩ latest; **non gli fa
 né ~ né freddo** *fig* he doesn't give a damn;
 ondata di ~ heatwave; **tavola calda** snack
 bar ● *nm* heat; **avere ~** be warm, be hot; **fa
 ~** it's warm, it's hot
caleido'scopio *nm* kaleidoscope
calen'dario *nm* calendar. **~ sportivo** sporting calendar
ca'lesse *nm* gig
cali'brare *vt* calibrate
cali'brato *a* calibrated; *fig* balanced; **taglie
 pl calibrate** clothes for non-standard sizes
'calibro *nm* calibre; (*strumento*) callipers *pl*;
 di grosso ~ ⟨*persona*⟩ top *attrib*
'calice *nm* goblet; *Relig* chalice
californi'ano, -a *a & nmf* Californian
ca'ligine *nm* fog; (*industriale*) smog
call-girl *nf inv* call girl
calligra'fia *nf* handwriting; (*cinese*) calligraphy
calli'grafico *a* **perizia calligrafica** handwriting analysis
cal'ligrafo, -a *nmf* calligrapher
cal'lista *nmf* chiropodist
'callo *nm* corn; **fare il ~ a** become hardened
 to
cal'loso *a* callous
'calma *nf* calm; **mantenere la ~** keep calm;
 prendersela con ~ *fig* take it easy; **fare
 qcsa con ~** take one's time doing sth
cal'mante *a* calming ● *nm* sedative
cal'mare *vt* calm [down]; (*lenire*) soothe
cal'marsi *vr* calm down; ⟨*vento:*⟩ drop;
 ⟨*dolore:*⟩ die down
calmie'rare *vt* control the prices of
calmi'ere *nm* price control

'**calmo** *a* calm

'**calo** *nm Comm* fall; (*di volume*) shrinkage; (*di peso*) loss; **in ~** dwindling

ca'**lore** *nm* heat; (*moderato*) warmth; **in ~** (*di animale*) on heat

calo'**ria** *nf* calorie

ca'**lorico** *a* calorific

calo'**rifero** *nm* radiator

calorosa'**mente** *adv* warmly

caloro**sità** *nf fig* warmth

calo'**roso** *a* warm

ca'**lotta** *nf* **~ cranica** skullcap. **~ glaciale** icecap. **~ polare** polar icecap

calpe'**stare** *vt* trample [down]; *fig* trample on ⟨*diritti, sentimenti*⟩; **'vietato ~ l'erba'** 'keep off the grass'

calpe'**stio** *nm* (*passi*) footsteps *pl*; (*rumore*) stamping

ca'**lunnia** *nf* slander

calunni'**are** *vt* slander

calunni'**oso** *a* slanderous

ca'**lura** *nf* heat

cal'**vario** *nm* Calvary; *fig* trial

calvi'**nismo** *nm* Calvinism

calvi'**nista** *nmf* Calvinist

cal'**vizie** *nf* baldness

'**calvo** *a* bald

'**calza** *nf* (*da reggicalze*) stocking; (*da uomo*) sock. **~ della befana** ≈ Christmas stocking

calza'**maglia** *nf* tights *pl*; (*per danza*) leotard

cal'**zante** *a fig* fitting

cal'**zare** *vt* (*indossare*) wear; (*mettersi*) put on ● *vi* fit; **~ a pennello** ⟨*indumenti:*⟩ fit like a glove

calza'**scarpe** *nm inv* shoehorn

calza'**tura** *nf* footwear; **calzature** *pl* footwear *sg*

calzaturi'**ficio** *nm* shoe factory

cal'**zetta** *nf* ankle sock; **è una mezza ~** *fig* he's no use

calzet'**tone** *nm* knee-length woollen sock

cal'**zino** *nm* sock

calzo'**laio** *nm* shoe mender

calzole'**ria** *nf* (*negozio*) shoe shop

calzon'**cini** *nmpl* shorts. **~ da bagno** swimming trunks

cal'**zone** *nm Culin* folded pizza with tomato, mozzarella etc inside

cal'**zoni** *nmpl* trousers, pants *Am*. **~ alla cavallerizza** jodhpurs

camale'**onte** *nm* chameleon

cambi'**ale** *nf Comm* bill of exchange

cambia'**mento** *nm* change

cambi'**are** *vt* change; move ⟨*casa*⟩; (*fare cambio di*) exchange; **~ canale** *TV* switch over; **~ rotta** *Naut* alter course; **~ l'aria in una stanza** air a room ● *vi* change; (*fare cambio*) exchange

cambi'**arsi** *vr* change

cambiava'**lute** *nm* bureau de change

'**cambio** *nm* change; (*Comm, scambio*) exchange; *Mech* gear; **dare il ~ a qcno** relieve sb; **in ~ di** in exchange for. **~ della guardia** changeover. **~ dell'olio** oil change

Cam'**bogia** *nf* Cambodia

cambogi'**ano** *a & nmf* Cambodian

cam'**busa** *nf* pantry

ca'**melia** *nf* camellia

'**camera** *nf* room; (*mobili*) [bedroom] suite; *Phot* camera; **C~** *Pol, Comm* Chamber. **~ ammobiliata** bedsit. **~ ardente** chapel of rest. **~ d'aria** inner tube. **~ blindata** strong room. **C~ di Commercio** Chamber of Commerce. **C~ dei Comuni** House of Commons. **C~ dei Deputati** *Pol* ≈ House of Commons. **~ doppia** double room. **~ a gas** gas chamber. **~ da letto** bedroom. **~ a due letti** twin room. **~ matrimoniale** double room. **~ oscura** darkroom. **~ degli ospiti** guest room. **~ singola** single room

came'**rata**¹ *nf* (*dormitorio*) dormitory; *Mil* barrack room

came'**rata**² *nmf* mate

camera'**tesco** *a* comradely

camera'**tismo** *nm* comradeship

cameri'**era** *nf* maid; (*di ristorante*) waitress; (*in albergo*) chamber-maid

cameri'**ere** *nm* manservant; (*di ristorante*) waiter

came'**rino** *nm* dressing-room

came'**ristico** *a Mus* chamber

'**Camerun** *nm* il **~** Cameroon

'**camice** *nm* overall

camice'**ria** *nf* shirt shop

cami'**cetta** *nf* blouse

ca'**micia** *nf* shirt; **essere nato con la ~** *fig* be born lucky; **uovo in ~** poached egg. **~ di forza** strait-jacket. **~ nera** Blackshirt. **~ da notte** nightdress; (*da uomo*) nightshirt

camici'**aio** *nm* (*venditore*) shirtseller; (*sarto*) shirtmaker

camici'**ola** *nf* vest

cami'**netto** *nm* fireplace

ca'**mino** *nm* chimney; (*focolare*) fireplace, hearth

'**camion** *nm inv* lorry *Br*, truck

camion'**cino** *nm* van

camio'**netta** *nf* jeep

camio'**nista** *nmf* lorry driver *Br*, truck driver

'**camma** *nf* cam; **albero a camme** *Auto* camshaft

cam'**mello** *nm* camel; (*tessuto*) camel-hair ● *a inv* (*colore*) camel

cam'**meo** *nm* cameo

cammi'**nare** *vi* walk; ⟨*auto, orologio:*⟩ go; **~ avanti e indietro** pace up and down

cammi'**nata** *nf* walk; **fare una ~** go for a walk

cam'**mino** *nm* way; **essere in ~** be on the way; **mettersi in ~** set out; **cammin facendo** on the way

camo'**milla** *nf* camomile; (*bevanda*) camomile tea

camo'**millarsi** *vr sl* **camomillati!** don't get your knickers in a twist!, cool it!

Ca'**morra** *nf* local mafia

camor'**rista** *nmf* member of the 'Camorra'

ca'**moscio** *nm* chamois; (*pelle*) suede

cam'pagna *nf* country; (*paesaggio*) countryside; *Comm, Mil* campaign; **in ~** in the country. **~ elettorale** election campaign. **~ promozionale** promotional campaign, marketing campaign. **~ pubblicitaria** publicity campaign

campa'gnola *nf Auto* cross-country vehicle

campa'gnolo, -a *a* rustic ● *nm* countryman ● *nf* countrywoman

cam'pale *a* field *attrib*; **giornata ~** *fig* strenuous day

cam'pana *nf* bell; (*di vetro*) belljar; **a ~** bell-shaped; **essere sordo come una ~** be as deaf as a doorpost; **sentire anche l'altra ~** *fig* hear the other side of the story; **vivere sotto una ~ di vetro** *fig* be mollycoddled. **campane** *pl* **a morto** death knell

campa'naccio *nm* cowbell

campa'naro *nm* bell-ringer

campa'nella *nf* (*di tenda*) curtain ring

campa'nello *nm* door-bell; (*cicalino*) buzzer

Cam'pania *nf* Campania

campa'nile *nm* bell tower

campani'lismo *nm* parochialism

campani'lista *nmf* person with a parochial outlook

campani'listico *a* parochial

cam'panula *nf Bot* campanula

cam'pare *vi* live; (*a stento*) get by; **tirare a ~** *fig* live from day to day

cam'pato *a* **~ in aria** unfounded

campeggi'are *vi* camp; (*spiccare*) stand out; **'vietato ~'** 'no camping'

campeggia|'tore, -'trice *nmf* camper

cam'peggio *nm* camping; (*terreno*) campsite; **andare in ~** go camping; **fare ~ libero** camp in the wild. **~ per roulotte** caravan site

cam'pestre *a* rural

Campi'doglio *nm* Capitol

'camping *nm inv* campsite

campiona'mento *nm* sampling

campio'nario *nm* [set of] samples ● *a* **fiera campionaria** trade fair

campio'nato *nm* championship. **C~ Mondiale di Calcio** World Cup

campiona'tura *nf* (*di merce*) range of samples; (*in statistica*) sampling. **~ casuale** random sample

campi'one *nm* champion; *Comm* sample; (*esemplare*) specimen; **indagine ~** (*in statistica*) sample. **~ gratuito** free sample. **'~ senza valore'** 'sample, no commercial value'

campio'nessa *nf* ladies' champion

'campo *nm* field; (*accampamento*) camp; *Mil* encampment; **abbandonare il ~** *Mil* desert in the face of the enemy; *fig* throw in the towel; **a tutto ~** *fig* wide-ranging; **avere ~ libero** *fig* have a free hand; **giocare a tutto ~** *Sport* cover the entire pitch. **~ base** base camp. **~ da battaglia** battlefield. **~ da calcio** football pitch. **~ di concentramento** concentration camp. **~ da golf** golf course. **~ di grano** cornfield. **~ da hockey** hockey field. **~ di mais** cornfield. **~ sportivo** sports ground. **~ di sterminio** death camp. **~ da tennis** tennis court

campo'santo *nm* cemetery

'campus *nm inv* (*di università*) campus

camuf'fare *vt* disguise

camuf'farsi *vr* disguise oneself

ca'muso *a* **naso ~** snub nose

'Canada *nm* Canada

cana'dese *a* & *nmf* Canadian

ca'naglia *nf* scoundrel; (*plebaglia*) rabble

ca'nale *nm* channel; (*artificiale*) canal. **Canal Grande** Gran Canal. **~ della Manica** English Channel. **~ di scolo** dyke

canaliz'zare *vt* channel (*acque, energie*)

canalizzazi'one *nf* channelling; (*rete*) pipes *pl*

'canapa *nf* hemp. **~ indiana** (*droga*) cannabis

Ca'narie *nfpl* **le ~** the Canaries

cana'rino *nm* canary

ca'nasta *nf* (*gioco*) canasta

cancel'labile *a* erasable; (*impegno, incontro*) which can be cancelled

cancel'lare *vt* cross out; (*con la gomma*) rub out; *fig* wipe out; (*annullare*) cancel; *Comput* delete, erase

cancel'larsi *vr* be erased, be wiped out

cancel'lata *nf* railings *pl*

cancel'lato *a* cancelled

cancella'tura *nf* erasure

cancellazi'one *nf* cancellation; *Comput* deletion

cancelle'ria *nf* chancellery; (*articoli per scrivere*) stationery

cancelli'ere *nm* chancellor; (*di tribunale*) clerk

cancel'lino *nm* duster

can'cello *nm* gate

cance'rogeno *nm* carcinogen ● *a* carcinogenic

cance'roso *a* cancerous

can'crena *nf* gangrene; **andare in ~** become gangrenous

cancre'noso *a* gangrenous

'cancro *nm* cancer. **C~** *Astr* Cancer; **tropico del C~** Tropic of Cancer

candeggi'are *vt* bleach

candeg'gina *nf* bleach

can'deggio *nm* bleaching

can'dela *nf* candle; *Auto* spark plug; **a lume di ~** by candle-light; (*cena*) candlelit; **tenere la ~** *fig* play gooseberry; **il gioco non vale la ~** the game is not worth the candle

cande'labro *nm* candelabra

cande'letta *nf Med* pessary

candeli'ere *nm* candlestick

cande'line *nfpl* candles

cande'lotto *nm* (*di dinamite*) stick. **~ lacrimogeno** tear gas grenade

candida'mente *adv* innocently

candi'dare *vt* put forward as a candidate

candi'darsi *vr* stand as a candidate

candi'dato, -a *nmf* candidate

candida'tura *nf Pol* candidacy; (*per lavoro*) application

'candido *a* snow-white; (*sincero*) candid; (*puro*) pure

can'dito *a* candied ● *nm* piece of candied fruit

can'dore *nm* whiteness; *fig* innocence

'cane *nm* dog; (*di arma da fuoco*) cock; **un tempo da cani** foul weather; **fa un freddo ~** it's bitterly cold; **non c'era un ~** *fig* there wasn't a soul about; **solo come un ~** *fig* all on one's own; **essere come ~ e gatto** *fig* fight like cat and dog; **essere un ~** ‹*attore, cantante*› be appalling, be a dog *sl*; **fatto da cani** *fig* ‹*lavoro*› botched; **mangiare da cani** *fig* eat very badly; **figlio di un ~** *fam* son of a bitch. **~ da caccia** hunting dog. **~ per ciechi** guide-dog. **~ da corsa** greyhound. **~ da guardia** guard-dog. **~ lupo** alsatian. **~ poliziotto** police dog. **~ da salotto** lapdog. **~ sciolto** *fig* maverick

ca'nestro *nm* basket; **fare ~** score a basket

'canfora *nf* camphor

cangi'ante *a* iridescent; **seta ~** shot silk

can'guro *nm* kangaroo

ca'nicola *nf* scorching heat

ca'nile *nm* kennel; (*di allevamento*) kennels *pl*. **~ municipale** dog pound

ca'nino *a & nm* canine

ca'nizie *nm* white hair

'canna *nf* reed; (*da zucchero*) cane; (*di fucile*) barrel; (*bastone*) stick; (*di bicicletta*) crossbar; (*asta*) rod; (*fam: hascish*) joint; **povero in ~** destitute. **~ fumaria** flue. **~ da pesca** fishing-rod

'cannabis *nm inv* cannabis

can'nella *nf* cinnamon

cannel'loni *nmpl* **~ al forno** *rolls of pasta stuffed with meat and baked in the oven*

can'neto *nm* bed of reeds

can'nibale *nm* cannibal

canniba'lismo *nm* cannibalism

cannocchi'ale *nm* telescope

can'noli *nmpl* **~ alla siciliana** *cylindrical pastries filled with ricotta and candied fruit*

canno'nata *nf* cannon shot; **è una ~** *fig* it's brilliant

cannon'cino *nm* (*dolce*) cream horn

can'none *nm* cannon; *fig* ace

cannoneggia'mento *nm* cannonade

cannoni'era *nf* gunboat

cannoni'ere *nm* (*soldato*) gunner; (*calciatore*) top goal scorer

can'nuccia *nf* [drinking] straw; (*di pipa*) stem

ca'noa *nf* canoe

'canone *nm* canon; (*affitto*) rent; **equo ~** rent set by law

ca'nonica *nf* manse

ca'nonico *nm* canon

canoniz'zare *vt* canonize

canonizzazi'one *nf* canonization

ca'noro *a* melodious

ca'notta *nf* (*estiva*) vest top

canot'taggio *nm* canoeing; (*voga*) rowing

canotti'era *nf* vest

canotti'ere *nm* oarsman

ca'notto *nm* [rubber] dinghy

cano'vaccio *nm* (*trama*) plot; (*straccio*) duster; (*per ricamo*) canvas

can'tante *nmf* singer. **~ lirico** opera-singer

can'tare *vt/i* sing; **~ vittoria** *fig* crow; **fare ~ qcno** *sl* make sb talk; **me le ha cantate** *fam* he told me off

canta'storie *nmf inv* story-teller

can'tata *nf Mus* cantata

can'tato *a* sung

cantau|'tore, -'trice *nmf* singer-songwriter

canticchi'are *vt* sing softly; (*a bocca chiusa*) hum

'cantico *nm* hymn

canti'ere *nm* yard; *Naut* shipyard; (*di edificio*) construction site. **~ navale** naval dockyard; (*per piccole imbarcazioni*) boatyard

canti'eristica *nf* construction

canti'lena *nf* singsong; (*ninna-nanna*) lullaby

can'tina *nf* cellar; (*osteria*) wine shop

'canto[1] *nm* singing; (*canzone*) song; *Relig* chant; (*poesia*) poem. **~ di Natale, ~ natalizio** Christmas carol. **~ degli uccelli** birdsong

'canto[2] *nm* (*angolo*) corner; (*lato*) side; **dal ~ mio** for my part; **d'altro ~** on the other hand

canto'nale *a* cantonal

canto'nata *nf* **prendere una ~** *fig* be sadly mistaken

can'tone *nm* canton; (*angolo*) corner

can'tore *nm* chorister

can'tuccio *nm* nook; **stare in un ~** *fig* hold oneself aloof

ca'nuto *a liter* whitehaired

canzo'nare *vt* tease

canzona'torio *a* teasing

canzona'tura *nf* teasing

can'zone *nf* song. **~ d'amore** love song

canzo'netta *nf fam* pop song

canzoni'ere *nm* songbook

'caos *nm* chaos

ca'otico *a* chaotic

C.A.P. *nm abbr* (**Codice di Avviamento Postale**) zip code *Am*

cap. *abbr* (**capitolo**) chap

ca'pace *a* able; (*esperto*) skilled; ‹*stadio, contenitore*› big; **~ di** (*disposto a*) capable of; **è ~ a cantare?** can he sing?

capacità *nf inv* ability; (*attitudine*) skill; (*capienza*) capacity. **~ d'assorbimento** absorbency. **~ di credito** creditworthiness. **~ di memorizzazione** retentiveness. **~ produttiva** production capacity. **~ di resistenza** staying power

capaci'tarsi *vr* **~ di** (*rendersi conto*) understand; (*accorgersi*) realize

ca'panna *nf* hut

capan'nello *nm* knot of people; **fare ~ intorno a qcno/qcsa** gather round sb/sth

ca'panno *nm* **~ degli attrezzi** garden shed. **~ da spiaggia** beach hut, cabana

capan'none *nm* shed; *Aeron* hangar

caparbietà nf obstinacy

ca'parbio a obstinate

ca'parra nf deposit

capa'tina nf short visit; **fare una ~ in città/da qcno** pop into town/in on sb

ca'pello nm hair; **non torcere un ~ a qcno** fig not lay a finger on sb; **capelli** pl (capigliatura) hair sg; **asciugarsi/lavarsi i capelli** dry/wash one's hair; **avere i capelli a spazzola** have a crew-cut; **spaccare il ~ in quattro** split hairs; **averne fin sopra i capelli** fig be fed up to the back teeth; **mettersi le mani nei capelli** fig tear one's hair out. **capelli** pl **d'angelo** vermicelli

capel'lone nm long-haired type, hippie

capel'luto a hairy; **cuoio ~** scalp

ca'pestro nm noose; **contratto ~** strait-jacket of a contract

capez'zale nm bolster; fig bedside

ca'pezzolo nm nipple

capi'ente a capacious

capi'enza nf capacity

capiglia'tura nf hair

capil'lare a capillary

ca'pire vt understand; **non capisco** I don't understand; **~ male** misunderstand; **si capisce!** naturally!; **sì, ho capito** yes, I see

capi'tale a Jur capital; (principale) main ● nf (città) capital ● nm Comm capital. **~ di avviamento** start-up capital. **~ azionario** Fin equity capital, share capital. **~ di investimento** investment capital. **~ di rischio** venture capital. **~ sociale** Fin share capital

capita'lismo nm capitalism

capita'lista nmf capitalist

capita'listico a capitalist

capitaliz'zare vt capitalize

capitalizzazi'one nf capitalization

capita'nare vt lead ⟨rivolta⟩; Sport captain

capitane'ria nf **~ di porto** port authorities pl

capi'tano nm captain. **~ di lungo corso** Naut captain

capi'tare vi (giungere per caso) come; (accadere) happen

'capite: pro ~ adv per capita

capi'tello nm Archit capital

capito'lare vi capitulate

capitolazi'one nf capitulation

ca'pitolo nm chapter

capi'tombolo nm headlong fall; **fare un ~** tumble down

'capo nm head; (chi comanda) boss fam; (di vestiario) item; Geog cape; (in tribù) chief; (parte estrema) top; **a ~** (in dettato) new paragraph; **da ~** over again; **giramento di ~** dizziness; **mal di ~** headache; **in ~ a un mese** within a month; **non ha né ~ né coda** ⟨discorso, ragionamento:⟩ I can't make head nor tail of it. **~ d'abbigliamento** item of clothing. **~ d'accusa** Jur charge, count. **~ di bestiame** head of cattle. **C~ di Buona Speranza** Cape of Good Hope. **~ reparto** head of department. **il C~ Verde** Cape Verde

capo'banda nm Mus band-master; (di delinquenti) ringleader

capocameri'ere, -a nm head waiter ● nf head waitress

ca'pocchia nf **~ di spillo** pinhead

ca'poccia nf (fam: testa) nut

capocci'one, -a nm/f fam brainbox

capo'classe nmf ≈ form captain

capocor'data nmf (alpinista) leader

capocu'oco, -a nmf headcook

capo'danno nm New Year's Day

capofa'miglia nm head of the family

capo'fitto nm **a ~** headlong

capo'giro nm giddiness

capo'gruppo nm group leader

capola'voro nm masterpiece

capo'linea nm terminus

capo'lino nm **fare ~** peep in

capo'lista nmf Sport league leaders pl; Pol candidate whose name appears first on the list

capolu'ogo nm main town

capo'mafia nm Mafia boss

capo'mastro nm master builder

capo'rale nm lance-corporal

capore'parto nmf department head, head of department

capo'sala nf inv Med ward sister

capo'saldo nm stronghold

capo'scalo nm airline manager

capo'squadra nm inv foreman; Sport team captain

capostazi'one nm inv stationmaster

capo'stipite nmf (di famiglia) progenitor; (di esemplare) archetype

capo'tavola nmf (persona) head of the table; **sedere a ~** sit at the head of the table

capo'treno nm guard

ca'potta nf top

capot'tare vi somersault

capouf'ficio nmf department head

capo'verso nm first line; Jur paragraph

capo'volgere vt overturn; fig reverse

capo'volgersi vr overturn; ⟨barca:⟩ capsize; fig be reversed

capovolgi'mento nm turnaround

capo'volto pp di **capovolgere** ● a upside-down

'cappa nf cloak; (di camino) cowl; (di cucina) hood

cappa'santa nf Culin scallop

cap'pella nf chapel. **la C~ Sistina** the Sistine Chapel

cappel'lano nm chaplain

cappel'letti nmpl small filled pasta parcels

cappelli'era nf hatbox

cappel'lino nm **~ di carta** party hat

cap'pello nm hat; **tanto di ~!** I take my hat off to you!. **~ a cilindro** top hat. **~ da cow boy** stetson, cowboy hat. **~ di feltro** homburg. **~ di paglia** straw hat. **~ da sole** sun hat

'cappero nm caper; **capperi!** fam gosh!

'cappio nm noose; **avere il ~ al collo** fig have a millstone round one's neck; ⟨marito:⟩ be henpecked cap'pone *nm* capon

cap'potto *nm* [over]coat

cappuc'cino *nm* (*frate*) Capuchin [friar]; (*bevanda*) white coffee

cap'puccio *nm* hood; (*di penna stilografica*) cap

'capra *nf* goat; **salvare ~ e cavoli** *fig* run with the hare and hunt with the hounds

ca'pretto *nm* kid

ca'priccio *nm* whim; (*bizzarria*) freak; **fare i capricci** have tantrums

capricci'oso *a* capricious; (*bambino*) naughty

Capri'corno *nm Astr* Capricorn

capri'foglio *nm* honeysuckle

ca'prino *nm* goat's cheese

capri'ola *nf* somersault

capri'olo *nm* roe-deer

'capro *nm* [billy-]goat. **~ espiatorio** scapegoat

ca'prone *nm* [billy-]goat

'capsula *nf* capsule; (*di proiettile*) cap; (*di dente*) crown

cap'tare *vt Radio, TV* pick up; catch (*attenzione*)

C.A.R. *nm abbr* (**Centro Addestramento Reclute**) basic training camp

cara'bina *nf* carbine

carabini'ere *nm* carabiniere; **carabini'eri** *pl Italian police force (which is a branch of the army)*

ca'raffa *nf* carafe

Ca'raibi *nmpl* (*zona*) Caribbean *sg*; (*isole*) Caribbean Islands; **il mar dei ~** the Caribbean [Sea]

cara'ibico *a* Caribbean

cara'mella *nf* sweet. **~ alla menta** mint

cara'mello *nm* caramel

ca'rato *nm* carat

ca'rattere *nm* character; (*caratteristica*) characteristic; **di buon ~** good-natured; **in ~ con** (*intonato*) in keeping with; **è una persona di ~** (*deciso*) he's got character. **~ jolly** *Comput* wild card. **~ tipografico** typeface

caratte'rino *nm* difficult nature

caratte'rista *nm* character actor ● *nf* character actress

caratte'ristico, -a *a* characteristic; (*pittoresco*) quaint ● *nf* characteristic

caratteriz'zare *vt* characterize

caratterizzazi'one *nf* characterization

cara'tura *nf* carats; *Comm* part-ownership

'caravan *nm inv* caravan

carboi'drato *nm* carbohydrate

car'bonchio *nm* anthrax

carbon'cino *nm* (*per disegno*) charcoal

car'bone *nm* coal; **stare sui carboni ardenti** *fig* be on tenterhooks. **~ fossile** anthracite

carbo'nifero *a* carboniferous

car'bonio *nm* carbon. **~ 14** carbon-14

carboniz'zare *vt* burn to a cinder, burn to a crisp; **è morto carbonizzato** he was burned to death

carbu'rante *nm* fuel

carbu'rare *vt* carburize ● *vi fig* be firing on all four cylinders; **il motore carbura male** the mixture is wrong

carbura'tore *nm* carburettor

carburazi'one *nf* carburation

car'cassa *nf* carcass; *fig* old wreck

carce'rario *a* prison *attrib*

carce'rato, -a *nmf* prisoner

carcerazi'one *nf* imprisonment. **~ preventiva** preventive detention

'carcere *nm* prison; (*punizione*) imprisonment. **~ di massima sicurezza** maximum-security prison

carceri'ere, -a *nmf* gaoler

carci'noma *nm* carcinoma

carcio'fino *nm* baby artichoke

carci'ofo *nm* artichoke

cardel'lino *nm* goldfinch

car'diaco *a* cardiac; **disturbo ~** heart disease

'cardigan *nm inv* cardigan

cardi'nale *a & nm* cardinal

'cardine *nm* hinge

cardiochi'rurgo *nm* heart surgeon

cardiolo'gia *nf* cardiology

cardi'ologo *nm* heart specialist

cardio'patico *nmf* person suffering from a heart complaint

cardio'tonico *nm* heart stimulant

cardiovasco'lare *a* cardiovascular

'cardo *nm* thistle

ca'rena *nf Naut* bottom

care'naggio *nm* **bacino di ~** dry dock

ca'rente *a* **~ di** lacking in

ca'renza *nf* lack; (*scarsità*) scarcity

care'stia *nf* famine; (*mancanza*) dearth

ca'rezza *nf* stroke; (*di madre, amante*) caress; **fare una ~ a** stroke; (*madre, amante:*) caress

carez'zare *vt* stroke; (*madre, amante:*) caress

carez'zevole *a fig* sweet

'cargo *nm inv* (*nave*) cargo boat, freighter; (*aereo*) cargo plane, freight plane

cari'are *vt* decay

cari'arsi *vi* decay

cari'ato *a* decayed

'carica *nf* office; *Mil, Electr* charge; *fig* drive; **dotato di una forte ~ di simpatia** really likeable. **~ esplosiva** payload

caricabatte'ria *nm inv* battery charger

cari'care *vt* load (*camion, software*); *Mil, Electr* charge; wind up (*orologio*)

cari'carsi *vr Electr* charge [up]; **~ di lavoro** take on too much work

cari'cato *a fig* affected

carica'tore *nm* (*per proiettile*) magazine; (*per diapositive*) carousel

carica'tura *nf* caricature

caricatu'rale *a* grotesque

caricatu'rista *nmf* caricaturist

'carico *a* loaded (**di** with); (*colore*) strong; (*orologio*) wound [up]; (*batteria*) charged ● *nm* load; (*di nave*) cargo; (*il caricare*) loading; **avere un ~ di lavoro** have a heavy workload; **testimone a ~** *Jur* witness for the prosecution; **a ~ di** *Comm* to be charged to; ⟨*persona*⟩ dependent on. **~ utile** payload

'**carie** *nf* [tooth] decay

caril'lon *nm inv* musical box

ca'rino *a* pretty; (*piacevole*) agreeable

ca'risma *nm* charisma

cari'smatico *a* charismatic

carità *nf* charity; **per ~!** (*come rifiuto*) God forbid!

carita'tevole *a* charitable

car'linga *nf* fuselage

car'lino *nm* pug

carnagi'one *nf* complexion

car'naio *nm fig* shambles

car'nale *a* carnal; **cugino ~** first cousin

'**carne** *nf* flesh; (*alimento*) meat; **di ~** meaty. **~ macinata** mince, ground beef *Am*. **~ di maiale** pork. **~ di manzo** beef. **~ di vitello** veal

car'nefice *nm* executioner

carnefi'cina *nf* slaughter

carne'vale *nm* carnival

carneva'lesco *a* carnival

car'nivoro *nm* carnivore ● *a* carnivorous

car'noso *a* fleshy

'**caro, -a** *a* dear; **cari saluti** kind regards ● *nmf fam* darling, dear; **i miei cari** my nearest and dearest

ca'rogna *nf* carcass; *fig* bastard

caro'sello *nm* merry-go-round

ca'rota *nf* carrot

caro'vana *nf* caravan; (*di veicoli*) convoy

caro'vita *nm* high cost of living

'**carpa** *nf* carp

car'paccio *nm* finely sliced raw beef with oil, lemon and grated Parmesan

Car'pazi *nmpl* **i ~** the Carpathians

carpenti'ere *nm* carpenter

car'pire *vt* seize; (*con difficoltà*) extort

car'pone, car'poni *adv* on all fours; **camminare ~** crawl

car'rabile *a* suitable for vehicles; **passo ~ = passo carraio**

car'raio *a* **passo ~** entrance to driveway, garage etc where parking is forbidden

carreggi'ata *nf* roadway; **doppia ~** dual carriageway, divided highway *Am*; **rimettersi in ~** *fig* straighten oneself out

carrel'lata *nf* TV pan; (*fig: di notizie*) round-up

car'rello *nm* trolley; (*di macchina da scrivere*) carriage; *Aeron* undercarriage; *Cinema, TV* dolly. **~ d'atterraggio** *Aeron* landing gear. **~ dei dolci** dessert trolley. **~ portabagagli** luggage trolley, baggage cart *Am*

car'retta *nf* (*veicolo vecchio*) old banger; **tirare la ~** *fig* plod along

car'retto *nm* cart

carri'era *nf* career; **di gran ~** at full speed; **fare ~** get on

carrie'rismo *nm* careerism

carrie'rista *nmf* **è un ~** his career is all that matters

carri'ola *nf* wheelbarrow

'**carro** *nm* cart. **~ armato** tank. **~ attrezzi** breakdown vehicle, wrecker *Am*. **~ funebre** hearse. **~ merci** truck

car'rozza *nf* carriage; *Rail* coach, car. **~ bagagliaio** *Rail* guard's van. **~ belvedere** *Rail* observation car. **~ cuccette** sleeping car. **~ fumatori** *Rail* smoker. **~ letti** *Rail* sleeping car. **~ ristorante** *Rail* restaurant car, buffet car

carroz'zella *nf* (*per bambini*) pram; (*per invalidi*) wheelchair

carrozze'ria *nf* bodywork; (*officina*) bodyshop

carrozzi'ere *nm* panel beater

carroz'zina *nf* pram; (*pieghevole*) pushchair, stroller *Am*

carroz'zone *nm* (*di circo*) caravan; (*fig: organizzazione*) slow-moving great monster of an organization

car'ruba *nf* carob

car'rubo *nm* carob

car'rucola *nf* pulley

'**carta** *nf* paper; (*da gioco*) card; (*statuto*) charter; *Geog* map. **~ di addebito** charge card, debit card. **~ d'argento** senior citizens' railcard. **~ assegni** cheque card. **~ assorbente** blotting-paper. **~ carbone** carbon paper. **~ di credito** credit card. **~ crespata** crepe paper. **~ geografica** map. **~ d'identità** identity card. **~ igienica** toilet-paper. **~ d'imbarco** boarding pass, boarding card. **~ intelligente** smart card. **~ da lettere** writing-paper. **~ millimetrata** graph paper. **~ da pacchi** wrapping paper. **~ da regali** giftwrap. **~ di riso** rice paper. **~ smerigliata** emery paper. **~ stagnola** silver paper; *Culin* aluminium foil. **~ straccia** waste paper. **~ stradale** road map. **~ termica** thermal paper. **~ topografica** ≈ Ordnance Survey Map. **~ velina** tissue-paper. **~ verde** *Auto* green card. **~ vetrata** sandpaper. **~ dei vini** wine-list

cartacar'bone *nf* carbon paper

car'taccia *nf* waste paper

car'taceo *a* paper

carta'modello *nm* pattern

cartamo'neta *nf* paper money

carta'pecora *nf* vellum

carta'pesta *nf* papier mâché

carta'straccia *nf* waste paper

cartave'trare *vt* sand [down]

car'teggio *nm* correspondence

car'tella *nf* (*per documenti ecc*) briefcase; (*di cartone*) folder; (*di scolaro*) satchel. **~ clinica** medical record

cartel'lina *nf* document wallet, folder

cartel'lino *nm* (*etichetta*) label; (*dei prezzi*) price-tag; (*di presenza*) time-card; **timbrare il ~** clock in; (*all'uscita*) clock out

car'tello *nm* sign; (*pubblicitario*) poster; (*stradale*) road sign; (*di protesta*) placard; (*Comm, di droga*) cartel

cartel'lone *nm* poster; *Theat* bill. **~ pubblicitario** billboard

cartello'nista *nmf* poster designer
cartello'nistica *nf* poster designing
carti'era *nf* paper-mill
carti'lagine *nf* cartilage
car'tina *nf* map. ~ **di tornasole** litmus paper
car'toccio *nm* paper bag; **al** ~ *Culin* baked in foil
cartogra'fia *nf* cartography
car'tografo *nm* cartographer
carto'laio, -a *nmf* stationer
cartole'ria *nf* stationer's [shop]
cartolibre'ria *nf* stationer's and book shop
carto'lina *nf* postcard. ~ **postale** postcard. ~ **[precetto]** call-up papers
carto'mante *nmf* fortune-teller
carton'cino *nm* (*materiale*) card; (*biglietto*) card
car'tone *nm* cardboard; (*arte*) cartoon. ~ **animato** [animated] cartoon. ~ **ondulato** corrugated cardboard. ~ **di uova** egg box
car'tuccia *nf* cartridge; **mezza** ~ *fig* weakling. ~ **d'inchiostro** ink cartridge
'casa *nf* house; (*abitazione propria*) home; (*ditta*) firm; **amico di** ~ family friend; **andare a** ~ go home; **uscire di** ~ leave the house; **essere di** ~ be like one of the family; **fatto in** ~ home-made. ~ **di correzione** ≈ reform school. ~ **di cura** nursing home. ~ **del custode** gatehouse. ~ **madre** *Comm* parent company. ~ **di moda** fashion house. ~ **in multiproprietà** timeshare. ~ **popolare** council house. ~ **di riposo** old people's home. ~ **di sartoria** fashion house. ~ **dello studente** hall of residence. ~ **per le vacanze** holiday home
ca'sacca *nf* military coat; (*giacca*) jacket
ca'saccio *adv* **a** ~ at random; **sparare a** ~ **su** qcno/qcsa take a potshot at sb/sth
ca'sale *nm* (*gruppo di case*) hamlet; (*casolare*) farmhouse
casa'linga *nf* housewife
casa'lingo *a* domestic; (*fatto in casa*) home-made; (*amante della casa*) home-loving; (*semplice*) homely ● *nm* **casalinghi** *pl* household goods
casa'nova *nm inv* (*donnaiolo*) Casanova
ca'sata *nf* family
ca'sato *nm* family name
ca'scante *a* falling; (*floscio*) flabby
ca'scare *vi* fall [down]
ca'scata *nf* (*di acqua*) waterfall
casca|'tore, -'trice *nm* stuntman ● *nf* stuntwoman
cas'chetto *nm* [capelli a] ~ bob
ca'scina *nf* farm building
casci'nale *nf* farmhouse
'casco *nm* crash-helmet; (*asciuga-capelli*) [hair-]drier. ~ **di banane** bunch of bananas. **Caschi** *pl* **blu** *Mil* Blue Helmets, Blue Berets
caseggi'ato *nm* block of flats *Br*, apartment block
casei'ficio *nm* dairy
ca'sella *nf* pigeon-hole. ~ **postale** post-office box, PO box; (*elettronica*) mailbox

casel'lante *nmf* (*per treni*) signalman; (*in autostrada*) toll collector
casel'lario *nm* (*mobile*) filing cabinet; (*di documenti*) file. ~ **giudiziario** record of convictions; **avere il** ~ **giudiziario vuoto** have no criminal record
ca'sello *nm* (*di autostrada*) [motorway] toll booth
case'reccio *a* home-made
ca'serma *nf* barracks *pl*; (*dei carabinieri*) [police] station; **da** ~ ‹*linguaggio*› barrack room *attrib*. ~ **dei carabinieri** military police station. ~ **dei pompieri, ~ dei vigili del fuoco** fire station
caser'mone *nm pej* barracks *pl*
cash and carry *nm inv* cash-and-carry
casi'nista *nmf fam* muddler
ca'sino *nm fam* (*bordello*) brothel; (*fig sl: confusione*) racket; (*disordine*) mess; **un** ~ **di** loads of; **è un** ~ (*complicato*) it's too complicated
casinò *nm inv* casino
ca'sistica *nf* (*classificazione*) record of occurrences
'caso *nm* chance; (*fatto, circostanza, Med, Gram*) case; **a** ~ at random; **~ mai** if need be; **far** ~ **a** pay attention to; **non far** ~ **a** take no account of; **per** ~ by chance. ~ **[giudiziario]** [legal] case. ~ **urgente** *Med* emergency case
caso'lare *nm* farmhouse
'caspita *int* good gracious
'cassa *nf* till; (*di legno*) crate; *Comm* cash; (*luogo di pagamento*) cash desk; (*mobile*) chest; (*istituto bancario*) bank. ~ **automatica prelievi** cash dispenser, automatic teller. ~ **comune** kitty ~ **continua** autobank. ~ **da morto** coffin. ~ **di risparmio** savings bank. ~ **toracica** ribcage
cassa'forte *nf* safe
cassa'panca *nf* linen chest
cas'sata *nf* ice-cream cake
cas'sero *nm Naut* quarterdeck
casseru'ola *nf* saucepan
cas'setta *nf* case; (*per registratore*) cassette. **far buona** ~ *Theatr* be good box-office. ~ **degli attrezzi** toolbox. ~ **delle lettere** postbox, letterbox. ~ **delle offerte** charity box. ~ **portapane** breadbin. ~ **portavalori** cash box. ~ **del pronto soccorso** first-aid kit. ~ **di sicurezza** strong-box
cas'setto *nm* drawer; (*di fotocopiatrice ecc*) tray. ~ **di inserimento** [dei] **fogli** paper feed tray
casset'tone *nm* chest of drawers
cassi'ere, -a *nmf* cashier; (*di supermercato*) checkout assistant, checkout operator; (*di banca*) teller
cassinte'grato *nmf* person who has been laid off
cas'sone *nm* (*cassa*) chest; (*per acqua*) cofferdam
casso'netto *nm* rubbish bin, trash can *Am*
'casta *nf* caste
ca'stagna *nf* chestnut; **prendere qcno in**

~ *fig* catch sb in the act. ~ **d'India** horse chestnut

casta'gnaccio *nm tart from Tuscany made with chestnut flour*

casta'gneto *nm* chestnut grove

ca'stagno *nm* chestnut[-tree]

casta'gnola *nf* (*petardo*) firecracker

ca'stano *a* chestnut; ⟨*occhi, capelli*⟩ brown

ca'stello *nm* castle; (*impalcatura*) scaffold. ~ **incantato** enchanted castle. ~ **di sabbia** sandcastle

casti'gare *vt* punish

casti'gato *a* (*casto*) chaste; ⟨*abito, atteggiamento*⟩ prim and proper

ca'stigo *nm* punishment

castità *nf* chastity

'casto *a* chaste

ca'storo *nm* beaver

ca'strante *a fig* frustrating

ca'strare *vt* castrate

ca'strato *a* castrated; (*inibito*) inhibited; (*cantante*) castrato

castrazi'one *nf* gelding

ca'strone *nm* gelding

castrone'ria *nf fam* rubbish

'casual *nm inv* casual wear

casu'ale *a* chance *attrib*

casual'mente *adv* by chance

ca'supola *nf* little house

cata'clisma *nm fig* upheaval

cata'comba *nf* catacomb

cata'falco *nm* catafalque

cata'fascio *nm* **andare a ~** go to rack and ruin

cata'litico *a* **marmitta catalitica** *Auto* catalytic converter

cataliz'zare *vt fig* heighten

cataliz'zato *a Auto* fitted with a catalytic converter

catalizza'tore *a Phys* catalysing; **centro ~** *fig* catalyst ● *nm Auto* catalytic converter; *fig* catalyst

catalo'gabile *a* which can be listed

catalo'gare *vt* catalogue

catalogazi'one *nf* cataloguing

cata'logna *nf type of chicory with large leaves*

ca'talogo *nm* catalogue

catama'rano *nm* (*da diporto*) catamaran

cata'pecchia *nf* hovel; *fam* dump

cata'pulta *nf* catapult

catapul'tare *vt* (*scaraventare fuori*) eject

catapul'tarsi *vr* (*precipitarsi*) dive

catarifran'gente *nm* reflector

ca'tarro *nm* catarrh

catar'roso *a* (*voce*) catarrhal

ca'tarsi *nf inv* catharsis

ca'tartico *a* cathartic

ca'tasta *nf* pile

cata'stale *a* **registro ~** land registry; **rendita ~** revenue from landed property

ca'tasto *nm* land register

ca'tastrofe *nf* catastrophe

cata'strofico *a* catastrophic

catastro'fismo *nm* catastrophe theory

catch *nm* all-in wrestling

cate'chismo *nm* catechism

catego'ria *nf* category

cate'gorico *a* categorical

ca'tena *nf* chain. ~ **montuosa** mountain range. **catene** *pl* **da neve** [snow] chains

cate'naccio *nm* bolt

cate'nella *nf* (*collana*) chain; (*di orologio*) watch chain; **tirare la ~** (*del gabinetto*) flush, pull the plug

cate'nina *nf* chain

cate'ratta *nf* cataract

ca'terva *nf* **una ~ di** heaps of, loads of

ca'tetere *nm* catheter

'catgut *nm inv* catgut

cati'nella *nf* basin; **piovere a catinelle** bucket down

ca'tino *nm* basin

ca'todico *a* cathode; **raggi catodici** cathode rays

ca'torcio *nm fam* old wreck

catra'mare *vt* tar

ca'trame *nm* tar

'cattedra *nf* (*tavolo di insegnante*) desk; (*di università*) chair

catte'drale *nf* cathedral

catte'dratico, -a *nmf* professor ● *a* ⟨*pedante*⟩ pedantic; ⟨*insegnamento*⟩ university *attrib*

catti'veria *nf* wickedness; (*azione*) wicked action; **fare una ~ a qcno** be nasty to sb

cattività *nf* captivity

cat'tivo *a* bad; ⟨*bambino*⟩ naughty

cattocomu'nista *nmf* Catholic-communist

cattoli'cesimo *nm* Catholicism

cat'tolico, -a *a* & *nmf* [Roman] Catholic

cat'tura *nf* capture

cattu'rare *vt* capture

cau'casico, -a *nmf* Caucasian

'Caucaso *nm* **il ~** the Caucasus

caucciù *nm* rubber

'causa *nf* cause; *Jur* lawsuit; **far ~ a qcno** sue sb; ~ **di forza maggiore** circumstances beyond one's control; (*in assicurazione*) act of God

cau'sale *a* causal

cau'sare *vt* cause

'caustico *a* caustic

cauta'mente *adv* cautiously

cau'tela *nf* caution

caute'lare *vt* protect

caute'larsi *vr* take precautions

cauteriz'zare *vt* cauterize

cauterizzazi'one *nf* cauterization

'cauto *a* cautious

cauzi'one *nf* security; (*per libertà provvisoria*) bail; (*deposito*) deposit

cav. *abbr* (**cavaliere**) Kt, Knight

'cava *nf* quarry; *fig* mine

caval'care *vt* ride; (*stare a cavalcioni*) sit astride

caval'cata *nf* ride; (*corteo*) cavalcade

cavalca'via *nm* flyover

cavalci'oni: a ~ *adv* astride

cavali'ere *nm* rider; (*titolo*) knight; (*accompagnatore*) escort; (*al ballo*) partner

cavalle'resco *a* chivalrous

cavalle'ria *nf* chivalry; *Mil* cavalry

cavalle'rizzo, -a *nm* horseman ● *nf* horsewoman

caval'letta *nf* grasshopper

caval'letto *nm* trestle; (*di macchina fotografica*) tripod; (*di pittore*) easel

caval'lina *nf* (*ginnastica*) horse; (*gioco*) leapfrog; **correre la ~** *fig* pursue a life of pleasure

caval'lino *a* equine

ca'vallo *nm* horse; (*misura di potenza*) horsepower; (*scacchi*) knight; (*dei pantaloni*) crotch; **a ~** on horseback; **andare a ~** go horse-riding. **~ di battaglia** war horse. **~ a dondolo** rocking-horse. **~ da tiro** carthorse. **~ di Troia** Trojan horse

caval'lona *nf pej* ungainly female

caval'lone *nm* (*ondata*) roller

caval'luccio *nm* **~ marino** sea horse

ca'vare *vt* take out; (*di dosso*) take off; **cavarsela** get away with it; **se la cava bene** he's/she's doing all right

cavasti'vali *nm inv* bootjack

cava'tappi *nm inv* corkscrew

ca'veau *nm inv* (*di banca*) vault

ca'verna *nf* cave

caver'nicolo, -a *nmf* cave dweller

caver'noso *a* (*voce*) deep

ca'vetto *nm Electr* lead

ca'vezza *nf* halter; **mettere la ~ al collo a qcno** put sb on a tight rein

'cavia *nf* guinea-pig

cavi'ale *nm* caviar

ca'viglia *nf* ankle

cavil'lare *vi* quibble

ca'villo *nm* quibble

cavil'loso *a* pettifogging

cavità *nf inv* cavity

'cavo *a* hollow ● *nm* cavity; (*di metallo*) cable; *Naut* rope; **televisione via ~** cable TV. **~ di collegamento** [connecting] cable. **~ seriale** serial cable. **~ di spiegamento** ripcord

cavo'lata *nf fam* rubbish; **non dire cavolate** *fam* don't talk rubbish; **non fare cavolate** *fam* don't act like an idiot

cavo'letto *nm* **~ di Bruxelles** Brussels sprout

cavolfi'ore *nm* cauliflower

'cavolo *nm* cabbage; **~!** *fam* sugar!; **non ho capito un ~** *fam* I understood bugger-all; **che ~ succede?** what the heck is going on?. **~ cappuccio** spring cabbage

caz'zata *nf vulg* shit; **non dire cazzate** don't talk shit; **non fare cazzate** don't fuck things up

'cazzo *vulg nm* prick ● *int* fuck!; **non capisce un ~** he doesn't understand a fucking thing; **non me ne importa un ~!** I don't give a fuck!; **sono cazzi miei!** it's my fucking business!

caz'zotto *nm* punch; **prendere qcno a cazzotti** beat sb up

cazzu'ola *nf* trowel

CB *nf abbr* (**banda cittadina**) CB

cc *abbr* (**centimetri cubi**) cc

c/c *abbr* (**conto corrente**) c/a

CCT *nm abbr* (**Certificato di Credito del Tesoro**) T-bill

CD *nm inv* CD

CD-ROM *nm inv* CD-Rom

ce *pers pron* (*a noi*) us; **ce lo ha dato** he gave it to us ● *adv* there; **ce ne sono molti** there are many; **ce ne vuole!** it takes some doing!

cec'chino *nm* sniper; *Pol* MP who votes against his own party

'cece *nm* chick-pea

cecità *nf* blindness

ceco, -a *a & nmf* Czech; **la Repubblica Ceca** the Czech Republic

Cecoslo'vacchia *nf* Czechoslovakia

cecoslo'vacco, -a *a & nmf* Czechoslovak

'cedere *vi* (*arrendersi*) surrender; (*concedere*) yield; (*sprofondare*) subside ● *vt* give up; make over (*proprietà ecc*)

ce'devole *a* (*terreno ecc*) soft; *fig* yielding

ce'diglia *nf* cedilla

cedi'mento *nm* (*di terreno*) subsidence

'cedola *nf* coupon

'cedro *nm* (*albero*) cedar; (*frutto*) citron

C.E.E. *nf abbr* (**Comunità Economica Europea**) E[E]C

cefa'lea *nf* headache

ce'falo *nm* mullet

'ceffo *nm* (*muso*) snout; (*pej: persona*) mug

cef'fone *nm* slap

ce'lare *vt* conceal

ce'larsi *vr* conceal oneself

ce'lato *a* concealed

cele'brare *vt* celebrate, observe (*festività*)

celebra'tivo *a* celebratory

celebrazi'one *nf* celebration

'celebre *a* famous

celebrità *nf inv* celebrity

'celere *a* swift; **corso ~** crash course ● *nf* (*polizia*) flying squad

celerità *nf* speed; **con ~** speedily

ce'leste *a* (*divino*) heavenly ● *a & nm* (*colore*) pale blue

celesti'ale *a* celestial

celi'bato *nm* celibacy

'celibe *a* single ● *nm* bachelor

'cella *nf* cell. **~ frigorifera** cold store. **~ di isolamento** solitary confinement

+cello *suff* **monticello** *nm* mound; **praticello** *nm* small meadow

'cellofan *nm inv* cellophane; *Culin* cling film

cellofa'nare *vt* wrap in cling film

'cellula *nf* cell. **~ fotoelettrica** electronic eye

cellu'lare *nm* (*telefono*) cellular [phone] ● *a* **furgone ~** police van; **telefono ~** cellular [phone]

cellu'lite *nf* cellulite

cellu'litico *a* full of cellulite

cellu'loide *a* celluloid; **il mondo della ~** *fig* the celluloid world

cellu'losa *nf* cellulose

'Celsius *a inv* Celsius

'celta *nm* Celt

'celtico *a* Celtic

'cembalo *nm Mus* cembalo, harpsichord

cemen'tare *vt* cement

cementifi'care *vt* turn into a cement jungle

cementificazi'one *nf* turning into a cement jungle

cementi'ficio *nm* cement factory

ce'mento *nm* cement. **~ armato** reinforced concrete

'cena *nf* dinner; (*leggera*) supper; (*festa*) dinner party

ce'nacolo *nm* circle

ce'nare *vi* have dinner; **~ fuori** eat out

'cencio *nm* rag; (*per spolverare*) duster; **bianco come un ~** white as a sheet

cenci'oso *a* in rags

'cenere *nf* ash; (*di carbone ecc*) cinders *pl*; **Ceneri** *pl* Ash Wednesday

Cene'rentola *nf* Cinderella

ce'netta *nf* (*cena semplice*) informal dinner; (*cena intima*) romantic dinner

'cenno *nm* sign; (*col capo*)·nod; (*con la mano*) wave; (*allusione*) hint; (*breve resoconto*) mention; **far ~ di sì** nod

ce'none *nm* **il ~ di Capodanno/Natale** *special New Year's Eve/Christmas Eve dinner*

ceno'tafio *nm* cenotaph

censi'mento *nm* census

cen'sire *vt* take a census of

CENSIS *nm abbr* (**Centro Studi Investimenti Sociali**) *national opinion research institute*

cen'sore *nm* censor

cen'sura *nf* censorship

censu'rare *vt* censor

centelli'nare *vt* sip; *fig* measure out carefully

cente'nario, -a *a & nmf* centenarian ● *nm* (*commemorazione*) centenary

centen'nale *a* centennial

cen'tesimo *a* hundredth ● *nm* hundredth; (*di dollaro*) cent; **non avere un ~** be penniless

cen'tigrado *a* centigrade

cen'tilitro *nm* centilitre

cen'timetro *nm* centimetre

centi'naia *nfpl* hundreds

centi'naio *nm* hundred

'cento *a & nm* *a or* one hundred; **per ~** per cent

centodi'eci *nm* *a or* one hundred and ten; **~ e lode** *Univ* ≈ first class honours

centome'trista *nmf Sport* one hundred metres runner

cento'mila *nm* *a or* one hundred thousand

cen'trale *a* central ● *nf* (*di società ecc*) head office. **~ atomica** atomic power station. **~ elettrica** power station. **~ idroelettrica** hydroelectric power station. **~ nucleare** nuclear power station. **~ operativa** (*di polizia*) operations room. **~ telefonica** [telephone] exchange

centra'lina *nf Teleph* switchboard; (*apparecchiatura*) junction box

centrali'nista *nmf* [switchboard] operator

centra'lino *nm Teleph* exchange; (*di albergo ecc*) switchboard

centra'lismo *nm* centralism

centraliz'zare *vt* centralize

cen'trare *vt* **~ qcsa** hit sth in the centre; (*fissare nel centro*) centre; *fig* hit on the head (*idea*)

cen'trato *a* (*tiro, colpo*) well-aimed; (*fig: osservazione*) right on target

centrat'tacco *nm Sport* centre forward

centra'vanti *nm Sport* centre forward

cen'trifuga *nf* spin-drier. **~ [asciugaverdure]** shaker. **~ elettrica** juice extractor

centrifu'gare *vt Techn* centrifuge; (*lavatrice:*) spin

cen'trino *nm* doily

cen'trismo *nm Pol* centrism

cen'trista *a Pol* centrist

'centro *nm* centre; **in ~** (*essere*) in town; (*andare*) into town. **~ di accoglienza** reception centre. **~ di attrazione** focal point. **~ città** city centre. **~ commerciale** shopping centre, mall. **~ di costi** *Comm* cost centre. **~ culturale** arts centre. **~ di gravità** centre of gravity. **~ di informazioni turistiche** tourist information office. **~ operativo** *Mil* operations room. **~ di riabilitazione** halfway house. **~ sociale** community centre. **~ sportivo** leisure centre. **~ storico** old town

centrocam'pista *nm Sport* midfield player, midfielder

centro'campo *nm* midfield

centro'destra *nm inv Pol* centre right

centromedi'ano *nm Sport* centre half

centrosi'nistra *nm inv Pol* centre left

centro'tavola *nm inv* centre-piece

centupli'care *vt fig* multiply

'ceppo *nm* (*di albero*) stump; (*da ardere*) log; (*fig: gruppo*) stock

'cera *nf* wax; (*aspetto*) look. **~ d'api** beeswax. **~ per auto** car wax. **~ per il pavimento** floor-polish

cera'lacca *nf* sealing-wax

ce'ramica *nf* (*arte*) ceramics; (*materia*) pottery; (*oggetto*) piece of pottery

cera'mista *nmf* ceramicist

ce'rato *a* (*tela*) waxed

cerbi'atto *nm* fawn

cerbot'tana *nf* blowpipe

'cerca *nf* **andare in ~ di** look for

cercaper'sone *nm inv* beeper; **chiamare con il ~** beep

cer'care *vt* look for ● *vi* **~ di** try to

cerca|'tore, -'trice *nmf* **~ d'oro** gold seeker

'cerchia *nf* circle. **~ familiare** family circle

cerchi'are *vt* circle, draw a circle around (*parola*)

cerchi'ato *a* (*occhi*) black-ringed

cerchi'etto *nm* (*per capelli*) hairband
'cerchio *nm* circle; (*giocattolo*) hoop
cerchi'one *nm* alloy wheel
cere'ale *nm* cereal
cerea'licolo *a* grain *attrib*, cereal *attrib*
cere'brale *a* cerebral
'cereo *a* waxen
ce'retta *nf* depilatory wax; **fare la ~** wax
cer'foglio *nm* chervil
ceri'monia *nf* ceremony. **~ inaugurale** induction ceremony. **~ nuziale** marriage ceremony. **~ di premiazione** awards ceremony
cerimoni'ale *nm* ceremonial
cerimoni'ere *nm* master of ceremonies
cerimoni'oso *a* ceremonious
ce'rino *nm* [wax] match
cerni'era *nf* hinge; (*di borsa*) clasp. **~ lampo** zip[-fastener], zipper *Am*
'cernita *nf* selection
'cero *nm* candle
ce'rone *nm* greasepaint
ce'rotto *nm* [sticking] plaster. **~ callifugo** corn plaster
certa'mente *adv* certainly
cer'tezza *nf* certainty
certifi'care *vt* certify
certifi'cato *nm* certificate. **~ medico** doctor's note. **~ di morte** death certificate
certificazi'one *nf* certification. **~ di bilancio** *Fin* auditors' report
'certo *a* certain; (*notizia*) definite; (*indeterminativo*) some; **sono ~ di riuscire** I am certain to succeed; **a una certa età** at a certain age; **certi giorni** some days; **un ~ signor Giardini** a Mr Giardini; **una certa Anna** somebody called Anna; **certa gente** *pej* some people; **ho certi dolori!** I'm in such pain!. **certi** *pron pl* some; (*alcune persone*) some people ● *adv* of course; **sapere per ~** know for certain, know for sure; **di ~** surely; **~ che...** surely...
cer'tosa *nf* Carthusian monastery
certo'sino *nm* Carthusian [monk]; **pazienza certosina** exceptional patience
cer'tuni *pron* some
ce'rume *nm* earwax
cer'vello *nm* brain; **avere un ~ da gallina** be a bird-brain
cervel'lone, -a *nmf hum* brainbox
cervel'lotico *a* (*macchinoso*) over-elaborate
cervi'cale *a* cervical
'cervice *nf* cervix
'cervo *nm* deer
ce'sareo *a* *Med* Caesarean; **parto ~** Caesarean
cesel'lare *vt* chisel
cesel'lato *a* chiselled
cesella'tura *nf* chiselling
ce'sello *nm* chisel
ce'soie *nfpl* shears
'cespite *nm* source of income
ce'spuglio *nm* bush
cespugli'oso *a* (*terreno*) bushy
ces'sare *vi* stop, cease ● *vt* stop
ces'sate *nm* **~ il fuoco** ceasefire

ces'sato *a* **~ allarme/pericolo** all clear
cessazi'one *nf* cessation. **~ d'esercizio** closing down
cessi'one *nf* handover
'cesso *nm* *sl* (*gabinetto*) bog, john *Am*; (*fig: locale, luogo*) dump
'cesta *nf* [large] basket
ce'stello *nm* (*per lavatrice*) drum
cesti'nare *vt* throw away; bin (*lettera*); turn down (*proposta*)
ce'stino *nm* [small] basket; (*per la carta straccia*) waste-paper basket
'cesto *nm* basket. **~ della biancheria** linen basket
ce'sura *nf* caesura
ce'taceo *nm* cetacean
'ceto *nm* [social] class
'cetra *nf* lyre
cetrio'lino *nm* gherkin
cetri'olo *nm* cucumber
cfr *abbr* (**confronta**) cf
C.G.I.L. *nf abbr* (**Confederazione Generale Italiana del Lavoro**) *trades union organization*
cha'let *nm inv* chalet
cham'pagne *nm inv* champagne
'chance *nf inv* chance
char'lotte *nf* ice-cream cake with fresh cream, biscuits and fruit
'charter *nm inv* charter plane; **volo ~** charter flight
che *rel pron* (*persona: soggetto*) who; (*persona: oggetto*) whom; (*cosa, animale*) which; **questa è la casa ~ ho comprato** this is the house [that] I've bought; **il ~ mi sorprende** which surprises me; **dal ~ deduco che...** from which I gather that...; **avere di ~ vivere** have enough to live on; **grazie! – non c'è di che!** thank you – don't mention it; **il giorno ~ ti ho visto** *fam* the day I saw you ● *inter a* what; (*esclamativo: con aggettivo*) how; (*con nome*) what a; **~ macchina prendiamo, la tua o la mia?** which car are we taking, yours or mine?; **~ bello!** how nice!; **~ idea!** what an idea!; **~ bella giornata!** what a lovely day! ● *inter pron* what; **a ~ pensi?** what are you thinking about? ● *conj* that; (*con comparazioni*) than; **credo ~ abbia ragione** I think [that] he is right; **era così commosso ~ non riusciva a parlare** he was so moved, [that] he couldn't speak; **aspetto ~ telefoni** I'm waiting for him to phone; **è da un po' ~ non lo vedo** it's been a while since I saw him; **mi piace più Roma ~ Milano** I like Rome better than Milan; **~ ti piaccia o no** whether you like it or not; **~ io sappia** as far as I know
'checca *nf fam* queen
checché *pron* whatever
check-'in *nm inv* check-in; **fare il ~** check in
check-'up *nm inv* *Med* check-up; **fare un ~** have a check-up
cheese'burger *nm inv* cheeseburger
'chef *nm inv* chef

'**chela** nf nipper

chemiotera'pia nf chemotherapy. chemo fam

chemisi'er nm inv chemise

chero'sene nm paraffin

cheru'bino nm cherub

che'tare vt quieten

che'tarsi vr quieten down

cheti'chella: **alla ~** adv silently

'**cheto** a quiet

chi rel pron whoever; (coloro che) people who; **ho trovato ~ ti può aiutare** I found somebody who can help you; **c'è ~ dice che...** some people say that...; **senti ~ parla!** listen to who's talking! ● inter pron (soggetto) who; (oggetto, con preposizione) whom; (possessivo) **di ~** whose; **~ sei?** who are you?; **~ hai incontrato?** who did you meet?, whom did you meet? fml; **di ~ sono questi libri?** whose books are these?; **con ~ parli?** who are you talking to?, to whom are you talking? fml; **a ~ lo dici!** tell me about it!

chi'acchiera nf chat; (pettegolezzo) gossip; **chiacchiere** pl chitchat; **far quattro chiacchiere** have a chat

chiacchie'rare vi chat; (far pettegolezzi) gossip

chiacchie'rato a **essere ~** (persona:) be the subject of gossip

chi'acchiere nfpl (dolci) sweet pastries fried and sprinkled with fine sugar

chiacchie'rone, -a a talkative ● nmf chatterer

chia'mare vt call; (far venire) send for; **come ti chiami?** what's your name?; **mi chiamo Roberto** my name is Robert; **~ alle armi** call up; **mandare a ~** send for; **~ a rapporto** debrief

chia'marsi vr be called

chia'mata nf call; Mil call-up. **~ a carico del destinatario** reverse charge call. **~ interurbana** long-distance call. **~ in teleselezione** direct dialling. **~ urbana** local call

chi'appa nf fam cheek

chiara'mente adv clearly

chia'rezza nf clarity; (limpidezza) clearness

chiarifi'care vt clarify

chiarifica'tore a clarificatory

chiarificazi'one nf clarification

chiari'mento nm clarification

chia'rire vt make clear; (spiegare) clear up

chia'rirsi vr become clear

chi'aro a clear; (luminoso) bright; (colore) light

chia'rore nm glimmer

chiaro'scuro nm (tecnica) chiaroscuro

chiaroveg'gente a clear-sighted ● nmf clairvoyant

chi'asso nm din

chiassosa'mente adv (rumorosamente) rowdily; (vistosamente) gaudily

chias'soso a (rumoroso) rowdy; (vistoso) gaudy

chi'atta nf canal boat, canal barge

chi'ave nf key; **chiudere a ~** lock. **~ dell'accensione** ignition key. **~ di basso** Mus bass clef. **~ inglese** monkey-wrench. **~ [inglese] a rullino** adjustable spanner

chia'vetta nf (in tubi) key

chiavi'stello nm latch

chi'azza nf stain. **~ di petrolio** oil-slick

chiaz'zare vt stain

chiaz'zato a dappled

chic a inv chic

chicches'sia pron anybody

chicchirichì nm inv cock-a-doodle-doo

'**chicco** nm grain; (di caffè) bean; (d'uva) grape. **~ di caffè** coffee bean. **~ di grandine** hailstone. **~ d'orzo** barleycorn

chi'edere vt ask; (per avere) ask for; (esigere) demand; **~ notizie di** ask after

chi'edersi vr wonder

chieri'chetto nm altar boy

chi'erico nm cleric

chi'esa nf church

chi'esto pp di chiedere

chif'fon nm chiffon

'**chiglia** nf keel

chi'gnon nm inv bun

'**chilo** nm kilo

chilo'grammo nm kilogram[me]

chilo'hertz nm inv kilohertz

chilo'metrico a in kilometres; fig endless

chi'lometro nm kilometre

'**chilowatt** nm inv kilowatt

chilowat'tora nm inv kilowatt hour

chi'mera nf fig illusion

'**chimica** nf chemistry. **~ organica** organic chemistry

'**chimico, -a** a chemical ● nmf chemist

chi'mono nm kimono

'**china** nf (declivio) slope; **inchiostro di ~** Indian ink

chi'nare vt lower

chi'narsi vr stoop

chincaglie'rie nfpl knick-knacks

chinesitera'pia nf physiotherapy

chi'nino nm quinine

'**chino** a bent

chi'notto nm sparkling soft drink

chintz nm chintz

chi'occia nf sitting hen

chi'occiola nf snail; **scala a ~** spiral staircase

chio'dato a **pneumatici chiodati** snow tyres; **scarpe chiodate** shoes with crampons

chi'odo nm nail; (idea fissa) obsession. **~ di garofano** clove

chi'oma nf [head of] hair; (fogliame) foliage

chi'osco nm kiosk; (per giornali) newsstand

chi'ostro nm cloister

chip nm inv **~ [di silicio]** chip

'**chipset** nm inv chipset

chiro'mante nmf fortune teller, palmist

chiroman'zia nf palmistry

chirur'gia *nf* surgery. ~ **estetica** cosmetic surgery

chirurgica'mente *adv* surgically

chi'rurgico *a* surgical

chi'rurgo *nm* surgeon

chissà *adv* who knows; ~ **quando arriverà** I wonder when he will arrive

chi'tarra *nf* guitar. ~ **acustica** acoustic guitar

chitar'rista *nmf* guitarist

chi'udere *vt* shut, close; (*con chiave*) lock; turn off, switch off ‹*luce ecc*›; turn off ‹*acqua*›; (*per sempre*) close down ‹*negozio, fabbrica ecc*›; (*recingere*) enclose; **chiudi il becco!** shut up! ● *vi* shut, close; (*con chiave*) lock up

chi'udersi *vr* shut; ‹*tempo:*› cloud over; ‹*ferita:*› heal over; *fig* withdraw into oneself

chi'unque *pron* anyone, anybody ● *rel pron* whoever

chi'usa *nf* enclosure; (*di canale*) lock; (*conclusione*) close

chi'uso *pp di* **chiudere** ● *a* closed, shut; ‹*tempo*› overcast; ‹*persona*› reserved; **'~ per turno'** 'closing day'

chiu'sura *nf* closing; (*sistema*) lock; (*allacciatura*) fastener; **'~ settimanale il lunedì'** 'closed on Mondays'. ~ **centralizzata** *Auto* central locking. ~ **lampo** zip, zipper *Am*

ci *pron* (*personale*) us; (*riflessivo*) ourselves; (*reciproco*) each other; (*a ciò, di ciò ecc*) about it; **non ci disturbare** don't disturb us; **aspettateci** wait for us; **ci ha detto tutto** he told us everything; **ci consideriamo...** we consider ourselves...; **ci laviamo le mani** we wash our hands; **ci odiamo** we hate each other; **non ci penso mai** I never think about it; **pensaci!** think about it! ● *adv* (*qui*) here; (*lì*) there; (*moto per luogo*) through it; **ci siamo** here we are; **ci siete?** are you there?; **ci siamo passati tutti** we all went through it; **c'è** there is; **ci vuole pazienza** it takes patience; **non ci vedo/sento** I can't see/hear

C.ia *abbr* (**compagnia**) Co.

cia'batta *nf* slipper

ciabat'tare *vi* shuffle

ciabat'tino *nm* cobbler

ci'ac *nm inv Cinema* ~ **si gira!** action!

ci'alda *nf* wafer

cial'trone *nm* (*mascalzone*) scoundrel; (*fannullone*) wastrel

ciam'bella *nf Culin* ring-shaped cake; (*salvagente*) lifebelt; (*gonfiabile*) rubber ring

ci'ance *nfpl* yapping

cianci'are *vi* gossip

cianfru'saglie *nfpl* knick-knacks

cia'notico *a* ‹*viso*› puce

cia'nuro *nm* cyanide

ci'ao *int fam* (*all'arrivo*) hello!, hi!; (*alla partenza*) bye-bye!, cheerio!

ciar'lare *vi* chat

ciarla'tano *nm* charlatan

ciarli'ero *a* (*loquace*) talkative

cia'scuno *a* each ● *pron* everyone, everybody; (*distributivo*) each [one]; **per ~** each

ci'bare *vt* feed

ci'barie *nfpl* provisions

ci'barsi *vr* eat; ~ **di** live on

ciber'netica *nf* cybernetics

ciber'netico *a* cybernetic

ciber'spazio *nm* cyberspace

'cibo *nm* food; **non toccare ~** leave one's food untouched; **non ha toccato ~ da ieri** he hasn't had a bite to eat since yesterday. **cibi** *pl* **precotti** ready meals

ci'cala *nf* cicada

cica'lino *nm* buzzer

cica'trice *nf* scar

cicatriz'zante *nm* ointment

cicatriz'zare *vi* heal [up]

cicatriz'zarsi *vr* heal [up]

cicatrizzazi'one *nf* healing

'cicca *nf* cigarette end; (*fam: sigaretta*) fag; (*fam: gomma*) [chewing] gum

cic'chetto *nm fam* (*bicchierino*) nip; (*rimprovero*) telling-off

'ciccia *nf fam* fat, flab

cicci'one, -a *nmf fam* fatty, fatso

cice'rone *nm* guide

cicla'mino *nm* cyclamen

ciclica'mente *adv* cyclically

'ciclico *a* cyclical

ci'clismo *nm* cycling

ci'clista *nmf* cyclist

'ciclo *nm* cycle; (*di malattia*) course. ~ **economico** business cycle

ciclo'cross *nm inv* cyclo-cross

ciclomo'tore *nm* moped

ci'clone *nm* cyclone

ci'clonico *a* cyclonic

ciclosti'lare *vt* duplicate

ciclosti'lato *nm* duplicate [copy] ● *a* duplicate

ci'cogna *nf* stork

ci'coria *nf* chicory

ci'cuta *nf* hemlock

ci'eco, -a *a* blind ● *nmf* blind man; blind woman; **i parzialmente ciechi** the partially sighted

ciel'lino *nmf Pol* member of the Comunione e Liberazione movement

ci'elo *nm* sky; *Relig* heaven; **al settimo ~** in seventh heaven; **santo ~!** good heavens!

'cifra *nf* figure; (*somma*) sum; (*monogramma*) monogram; (*codice*) code; **una ~** *sl* like crazy

ci'frare *vt* embroider with a monogram; (*codificare*) code

ci'frato *a* monogrammed; (*codificato*) coded

'ciglio *nm* (*bordo*) edge; (*degli occhi*) eyelash; **ciglia** *pl* eyelashes

'cigno *nm* swan

cigo'lante *a* squeaky

cigo'lare *vt* squeak

cigo'lio *nm* squeak

'Cile *nm* Chile

ci'lecca *nf* **far ~** miss

ci'leno, -a *a & nmf* Chilean

cili'egia *nf* cherry

cili'egio *nm* cherry[-tree]

cilin'drata *nf* cubic capacity, c.c.; **macchina di alta** ~ highpowered car

ci'lindro *nm* cylinder; *(cappello)* top hat, topper

'**cima** *nf* top; *(fig: persona)* genius; **in** ~ **a** at the top of; **da** ~ **a fondo** from top to bottom. ~ **alla genovese** *baked veal stuffed with chicken and chopped vegetables, served cold.* **cime** *pl* **di rapa** turnip greens

ci'melio *nm* relic; **cimeli** *pl* memorabilia

cimen'tare *vt* put to the test

cimen'tarsi *vr (provare)* try one's hand; ~ **in** *(arrischiarsi)* venture into

'**cimice** *nf* bug; *(puntina)* drawing pin, thumbtack *Am*

cimini'era *nf* chimney; *Naut* funnel

cimi'tero *nm* cemetery. ~ **delle macchine** breaker's yard

ci'mosa *nf* selvage, selvedge

ci'murro *nm* distemper

'**Cina** *nf* China

cincial'legra *nf* great tit

cincia'rella *nf* blue tit

cincillà *nm inv* chinchilla

cin cin *int* cheers!

cincischi'are *vi* fiddle

cincischi'arsi *vr* mess around

'**cine** *nm fam* cinema

cine'asta *nmf* film maker

Cinecittà *nf (stabilimento) film complex in the suburbs of Rome*

cine'club *nm inv* film club

ci'nefilo, -a *nmf* cinemagoer

cinegior'nale *nm* newsreel

'**cinema** *nm inv* cinema. ~ **d'essai** arts cinema

cine'matica *nf* kinematics

cinematogra'fare *vt* film

cinematogra'fia *nf* cinematography

cinemato'grafico *a* film *attrib*

cinema'tografo *nm* cinema

cine'presa *nf* cine-camera

ci'nereo *a* ashen

ci'nese *a & nmf* Chinese

cinese'rie *nfpl* chinoiserie

cine'teca *nf (raccolta)* film collection

ci'netico *a* kinetic

'**cingere** *vt (circondare)* surround

'**cinghia** *nf* strap; *(cintura)* belt. ~ **del ventilatore** fanbelt. ~ **della ventola** fanbelt

cinghi'ale *nm* wild boar; **pelle di** ~ pigskin

cinghi'ata *nf* lash

cingo'lato *a* ‹*mezzi*› caterpillar *attrib* ● *nm* caterpillar

'**cingolo** *nm Mech* belt

cinguet'tare *vi* twitter

cinguet'tio *nm* twittering

cinica'mente *adv* cynically

'**cinico** *a* cynical

ci'niglia *nf (tessuto)* chenille

ci'nismo *nm* cynicism

ci'nofilo *a* ‹*unità*› dog-loving

cin'quanta *a & nm* fifty

cinquanten'nale *nm* fiftieth anniversary

cinquan'tenne *a & nmf* fifty-year-old

cinquan'tesimo *a & nm* fiftieth

cinquan'tina *nf* **una** ~ **di** about fifty

'**cinque** *a & nm* five

cinquecen'tesco *a* sixteenth-century

cinque'cento *a* five hundred ● *nm* **il C**~ the sixteenth century

cinque'mila *a & nm* five thousand

cin'quina *nf (in tombola)* five in a row

'**cinta** *nf (di pantaloni)* belt; **muro di** ~ [boundary] wall

cin'tare *vt* enclose

'**cintola** *nf (di pantaloni)* belt

cin'tura *nf* belt. ~ **nera** black belt. ~ **di salvataggio** lifebelt. ~ **di sicurezza** *Aeron, Auto* seat belt

cintu'rato *nm Auto* radial tyre

cintu'rino *nm* ~ [**dell'orologio**] watchstrap; *(di metallo)* bracelet

ciò *pron* this; that; ~ **che** what; ~ **nondimeno** nevertheless

ci'occa *nf* lock

ciocco'lata *nf* chocolate; *(bevanda)* [hot] chocolate. ~ **in polvere** drinking chocolate

ciocco'la'tino *nm* chocolate

ciocco'lato *nm* chocolate. ~ **fondente** plain chocolate, dark chocolate. ~ **al latte** milk chocolate. ~ **da pasticceria** cooking chocolate

cioè *adv* that is

ciondo'lare *vi* dangle

ciondo'lio *nm* dangling

ci'ondolo *nm* pendant

ciondo'loni *adv fig* hanging about

cionono'stante *adv* nonetheless

ci'otola *nf* bowl

ci'ottolo *nm* pebble; **ciottoli** *pl (in spiaggia)* shingle

ci'piglio *nm* frown; **con** ~ with a frown

ci'polla *nf* onion; *(bulbo)* bulb

ci'presso *nm* cypress

'**cipria** *nf* [face] powder

cipri'ota *a & nmf* Cypriot

'**Cipro** *nm* Cyprus

'**circa** *adv & prep* about

cir'cense *a* circus *attrib*

'**circo** *nm* circus

circo'lare *a* circular ● *nf* circular; *(di metropolitana)* circle line ● *vi* circulate

circola'torio *a Med* circulatory

circolazi'one *nf* circulation; *(traffico)* traffic

'**circolo** *nm* circle; *(società)* club. ~ **del golf** golf-club. **C**~ **polare antartico** Antarctic Circle. **C**~ **polare artico** Arctic Circle

circon'cidere *vt* circumcise

circoncisi'one *nf* circumcision

circon'dare *vt* surround

circon'dario *nm (amministrativo)* administrative district; *(vicinato)* neighbourhood

circon'darsi *vr* ~ **di** surround oneself with

circonfe'renza *nf* circumference. ~ **del**

collo collar size. **~ dei fianchi** hip measurement. **~ [della] vita** waist measurement

circon'flesso *a* e con l'accento **~** circumflex e

circonvallazi'one *nf* ring road

circo'scritto *pp di* **circoscrivere ●** *a* limited

circo'scrivere *vt* circumscribe

circoscrizio'nale *a* area

circoscrizi'one *nf* area. **~ elettorale** constituency

circo'spetto *a* wary

circospezi'one *nf* con **~** warily

circo'stante *a* surrounding

circo'stanza *nf* circumstance; *(occasione)* occasion

circostanzi'ato *a* circumstantial

circu'ire *vt (ingannare)* trick

circuite'ria *nf* circuitry

cir'cuito *nm* circuit

circumnavi'gare *vt* circumnavigate

circumnavigazi'one *nf* circumnavigation

ci'rillico *a* Cyrillic

cir'ripede *nm* barnacle

cir'rosi *nf* cirrhosis

Cisgior'dania *nf* West Bank

C.I.S.L. *nf abbr* (**Confederazione Italiana Sindacati Lavoratori**) *trades union organization*

C.I.S.N.A.L. *nf abbr* (**Confederazione Italiana Sindacati Nazionali dei Lavoratori**) *trades union organization*

'cispa *nf (nell'occhio)* sleep

ci'sposo *a* bleary-eyed

'ciste *nf inv* cyst

ci'sterna *nf* cistern; *(serbatoio)* tank

'cisti *nf* cyst

cisti'fellea *nf* gall bladder

ci'stite *nf* cystitis

C.I.T. *nm abbr* (**Compagnia Italiana Turismo**) *Italian tourist organization*

ci'tare *vt (riportare brani ecc)* quote; *(come esempio)* cite; *Jur* summons

citazi'one *nf* quotation; *Jur* summons *sg*

citofo'nare *vt* buzz

ci'tofono *nm* entry phone; *(in ufficio, su aereo ecc)* intercom

cito'logico *a* cytological

'citrico *a* citric

ci'trullo *nmf fam* dimwit

città *nf inv* town; *(grande)* city. **C~ del Capo** Cape Town. **~ fantasma** ghost town. **~ giardino** garden city. **C~ del Vaticano** Vatican City

citta'della *nf* citadel

citta'dina *nf* town

cittadi'nanza *nf* citizenship; *(popolazione)* citizens *pl*

citta'dino, -a *nmf* citizen; *(abitante di città)* city dweller

ciucci'are *vt fam* suck

ci'uccio *nm fam* dummy

ci'uco *nm* ass

ci'uffo *nm* tuft

ci'urma *nf Naut* crew

ciur'maglia *nf (gentaglia)* rabble

ci'vetta *nf* owl; *(fig: donna)* flirt; **[auto] ~** unmarked police car

civet'tare *vi* flirt

civette'ria *nf* flirtatiousness, coquettishness

civettu'olo *a* flirtatious, coquettish

'civico *a* civic

ci'vile *a* civil **●** *nm* civilian

civi'lista *nmf (avvocato)* specialist in civil law

civiliz'zare *vt* civilize

civiliz'zarsi *vr* become civilized

civiliz'zato *a (paese)* civilized

civilizzazi'one *nf* civilization

civil'mente *adv* civilly

civiltà *nf* civilization; *(cortesia)* civility

ci'vismo *nm* public spirit

CL *nf abbr* (**Comunione e Liberazione**) *young Catholics association*

cl *abbr* (**centilitri**) centilitre(s)

'clacson *nm inv* horn

clacso'nare *vi* beep the horn, hoot

cla'more *nm* clamour; **fare ~** cause a sensation

clamorosa'mente *adv (sbagliare)* sensationally

clamo'roso *a* noisy; *(sbaglio)* sensational

clan *nm inv* clan; *fig* clique

clandestina'mente *adv* secretly

clandestinità *nf* secrecy; **vivere nella ~** live underground

clande'stino *a* clandestine; **movimento ~** underground movement; **passeggero ~** stowaway

claque *nf inv* claque

clarinet'tista *nmf* clarinettist

clari'netto *nm* clarinet

'classe *nf* class; *(aula)* classroom; **di prima ~** first-class. **~ economica** economy class. **~ operaia** working class. **~ turistica** tourist class

classicheggi'ante *a* classical

classi'cismo *nm* classicism

classi'cista *nmf* classicist

'classico *a* classical; *(tipico)* classic **●** *nm* classic

clas'sifica *nf* classification; *Sport* results *pl*

classifi'cabile *a* classifiable

classifi'care *vt* classify

classifi'carsi *vr* be placed

classifica'tore *nm (cartella)* folder; *(mobile)* filing cabinet

classificazi'one *nf* classification

clas'sista *a* class-conscious **●** *nmf* class-conscious person

claudi'cante *a* lame

'clausola *nf* clause. **~ penale** *Jur, Comm* penalty clause. **~ di recesso** *Jur, Comm* escape clause

claustrofo'bia *nf* claustrophobia

claustro'fobico *a* claustrophobic

clau'sura nf Relig cloistered life; **di ~** ⟨suora⟩ cloistered; **essere in ~** fig shut oneself up; **vivere in ~** fig live like a hermit

'clava nf club

clavicemba'lista nmf harpsichord player

clavi'cembalo nm harpsichord

cla'vicola nf collar-bone

clavi'cordo nm clavichord

cle'mente a merciful; ⟨tempo⟩ mild

cle'menza nf mercy, clemency

clep'tomane nmf kleptomaniac

cleptoma'nia nf kleptomania

cleri'cale a clerical

'clero nm clergy

cles'sidra nf hourglass

clic nm inv Comput click; **fare ~ su** click on

clic'care vi Comput click; **~ su** click on

cliché nm inv cliché

click = **clic**

cli'ente nmf client; (di negozio) customer

clien'tela nf customers pl, clientèle; (di avvocato) clientèle

cliente'lare a Pol nepotistic

cliente'lismo nm nepotism

'clima nm climate

clima'terio nm climacteric

climatica'mente adv climatically

cli'matico a climatic; **stazione climatica** health resort

climatizza'tore nm air conditioner

climatizzazi'one nf air conditioning

'clinica nf clinic. **~ odontoiatrica** dental clinic. **~ ostetrica** maternity hospital. **~ psichiatrica** mental hospital

'clinico a clinical ● nm clinician

clip nf inv paper-clip; (di orecchino) clip

cli'stere nm Med enema

clo'aca nf sewer

cloche nf inv cloche hat

clo'nare vt clone

'clone nm clone

clo'rato a chlorate

'cloro nm chlorine

cloro'filla nf chlorophyll

clorofluorocar'buro nm chlorofluorocarbon, CFC

cloro'formio nm chloroform

clou a inv **momenti ~** highlights

club-'sandwich nm inv club sandwich

cm abbr (**centimetro**) cm

CNR nm abbr (**Consiglio Nazionale delle Ricerche**) national research council

Co. abbr (**compagnia**) Co

coabi'tare vi live together

coabitazi'one nf (di razze) coexistence

coadiu'tore, -'trice nmf (in ufficio) assistant

coadiu'vare vt cooperate with

coagu'lante nm coagulant

coagu'lare vt coagulate

coagu'larsi vr coagulate

coagulazi'one nf coagulation

coalizi'one nf coalition

coaliz'zare vt fig unite

coaliz'zarsi vr unite

co'atto a Jur compulsory

co'balto nm cobalt; (colore) cobalt blue

COBAS nmpl abbr (**Comitati di Base**) independent trade unions

'cobra nm inv cobra

'Coca® nf Coke®

Coca 'cola® nf Coca Cola

coca'ina nf cocaine

cocai'nomane nmf cocaine addict

coc'carda nf rosette

cocchi'ere nm coachman

coc'chio nm coach

'coccige nm coccyx

cocci'nella nf ladybird

'coccio nm earthenware; (frammento) fragment

cocciu'taggine nf stubbornness

cocciuta'mente adv stubbornly

cocci'uto a stubborn

'cocco nm coconut palm; fam love; **noce di ~** coconut

coccodè nm inv cluck

cocco'drillo nm crocodile

cocco'lare vt cuddle

co'cente a ⟨sole⟩ burning; ⟨lacrime, delusione⟩ bitter

'cocker nm inv **~ [spaniel]** cocker spaniel

'cocktail nm inv (ricevimento) cocktail party

co'comero nm watermelon

co'cuzzolo nm top; (di testa, cappello) crown

'coda nf tail; (di abito) train; (fila) queue; (di traffico) tailback; **fare la ~** queue [up], stand in line Am. **~ di cavallo** (acconciatura) pony tail. **~ dell'occhio** corner of one's eye. **~ di paglia** guilty conscience

co'dardo, -a a cowardly ● nmf coward

co'dazzo nm train

code'ina nf codeine

co'desto a that

'codice nm code; **in ~** ⟨messaggio⟩ coded, in code; **mettere in ~** encode. **~ di avviamento postale** postal code, zip code Am. **~ a barre** bar-code. **~ civile** civil code. **~ fiscale** tax code. **~ penale** penal code. **~ segreto** (di carta di credito) PIN. **~ della strada** highway code

codi'cillo nm codicil

co'difica nf coding

codifi'care vt encode; codify ⟨legge⟩

codifica'tore, -'trice nmf Comput encoder

codificazi'one nf encoding; (di legge) codification

co'dini nmpl bunches

coeffici'ente nm coefficient

coercizi'one nf coercion

coe'rente a consistent

coe'renza nf consistency

coesi'one nf cohesion

coe'sistere vi coexist

coe'sivo a cohesive

coe'taneo, -a a & nmf contemporary

cofa'netto nm casket

'cofano nm (forziere) chest; Auto bonnet, hood Am

cofirma'tario, -a nmf cosignatory

coge'stire vt co-manage

cogi'tare vi ponder

'cogliere vt pick; (sorprendere) catch; (afferrare) seize; (colpire) hit; **~ la palla al balzo** seize the opportunity; **~ di sorpresa** take by surprise

co'glione nm vulg ball; (sciocco) dickhead; **rompere i coglioni a qcno** get on sb's tits

'Cognac nm cognac

co'gnato, -a nm brother-in-law ● nf sister-in-law

cognizi'one nf knowledge; **con ~ di causa** on an informed basis

co'gnome nm surname. **~ da ragazza/da nubile** maiden name

cogu'aro nm cougar

'coi = con + i

coi'bente a insulating

coinci'denza nf coincidence; (di treno ecc) connection

coin'cidere vi coincide

coinqui'lino nm flatmate

coin'volgere vt involve

coinvolgi'mento nm involvement

coin'volto a involved

'coito nm coitus

col = con + il

colà adv there

cola'brodo nm inv strainer; **ridotto a un ~** fam full of holes

cola'pasta nm inv colander

co'lare vt strain; (versare lentamente) drip ● vi (gocciolare) drip; (perdere) leak; **~ a picco** Naut sink

co'lata nf (di metallo) casting; (di lava) flow

colazi'one nf (del mattino) breakfast; (di mezzogiorno) lunch; **prima ~** breakfast; **far ~** have breakfast/lunch. **~ di lavoro** working lunch. **~ al sacco** packed lunch

col'bacco nm fur hat

co'lei pron f the one

co'lera nm cholera

coleste'rolo nm cholesterol

colf nf abbr (collaboratrice familiare) home help

colibrì nm inv humming-bird

'colica nf colic

co'lino nm [tea] strainer

'colla nf glue; (di farina) paste. **~ di pesce** gelatine

collabo'rare vi collaborate; **~ con** ⟨polizia⟩ co-operate with; **~ a** ⟨rivista⟩ contribute to

collabora|'tore, -'trice nmf collaborator; (di rivista) contributor. **~ familiare** domestic help

collaborazi'one nf collaboration; (con polizia) co-operation

collaborazio'nista nmf collaborator

col'lage nm inv collage

col'lana nf necklace; (serie) series. **~ di perle** pearl necklace

col'lant nmpl tights. **~ velati** sheer tights

col'lante a adhesive

col'lare nm collar

colla'rino nm dog collar

col'lasso nm collapse. **~ cardiaco** syncope. **~ renale** kidney failure

collate'rale a collateral

collau'dare vt test

collauda|'tore, -'trice nmf tester

col'laudo nm test

collazio'nare vt collate

'colle nm hill; (passo) pass

col'lega nmf colleague

colle'gabile a compatible (**a** with)

collega'mento nm connection; Mil liaison; Radio ecc link. **~ dati** data link. **~ in rete** networking

colle'gare vt connect

colle'garsi vr TV, Radio link up (**a** with); (Comput: a una rete ecc) go on line (**a** to)

collegi'ale nmf boarder ● a ⟨responsabilità, decisione⟩ collective

col'legio nm (convitto) boarding-school. **~ elettorale** constituency

'collera nf anger; **andare in ~** get angry

col'lerico a irascible

col'letta nf collection

collettività nf inv community

collet'tivo a collective; ⟨interesse⟩ general; **biglietto ~** group ticket ● nm (studentesco, femminista) collective

col'letto nm collar

collet'tore nm (di fognatura) main sewer. **~ delle imposte** collector of taxes

collezio'nare vt collect

collezi'one nf collection. **~ invernale** winter collection

collezio'nismo nm collecting

collezio'nista nmf collector. **~ di franco-bolli** stamp collector

colli'mare vi coincide

col'lina nf hill

colli'nare a hill attrib

colli'netta nf knoll

colli'noso a ⟨terreno⟩ hilly

col'lirio nm eyewash

collisi'one nf collision

'collo nm neck; (pacco) package; **a ~ alto** high-necked; **a rotta di ~** breakneck. **~ del piede** instep

colloca'mento nm placing; (impiego) employment

collo'care vt place

collo'carsi vr take one's place

collocazi'one nf placing

colloqui'ale a ⟨termine⟩ colloquial; ⟨tono⟩ informal

col'loquio nm conversation; (udienza ecc) interview; (esame) oral [exam]

col'loso a glutinous

col'lottola nf nape

collusi'one nf collusion

colluttazi'one nf scuffle

col'mare vt fill; bridge ⟨divario⟩; **~ qcno di gentilezze** overwhelm sb with kindness

'colmo _a_ full ● _nm_ top; _fig_ height; **al ~ della disperazione** in the depths of despair; **questo è il ~!** (_con indignazione_) this is the last straw!; (_con stupore_) I don't believe it!; **per ~ di sfortuna** to crown it all

+colo _suff_ **poetucolo** second rate poet

co'lomba _nf_ dove. **~ pasquale** dove-shaped cake with candied fruit eaten at Easter

colom'baccio _nm_ wood pigeon

colom'baia _nf_ dovecote

Co'lombia _nf_ Colombia

colombi'ano _a & nmf_ Colombian

co'lombo _nm_ pigeon; **colombi** _pl_ (_innamorati_) lovebirds

Co'lonia _nf_ Cologne; [**acqua di**] **c~** [eau de] Cologne

co'lonia _nf_ colony; (_per bambini_) holiday camp

coloni'ale _a_ colonial

co'lonico _a_ ⟨_terreno, casa_⟩ farm _attrib_

coloniz'zare _vt_ colonize

colonizza'|tore, -'trice _nmf_ colonizer

co'lonna _nf_ column; (_di auto_) tailback. **~ sonora** sound-track. **~ vertebrale** spine

colon'nato _nm_ colonnade

colon'nello _nm_ colonel

colon'nina _nf_ (_distributore_) petrol pump, gas pump _Am_

co'lono _nm_ tenant farmer

colo'rante _nm_ colouring. **~ alimentare** food colouring

colo'rare _vt_ colour; colour in ⟨_disegno_⟩

co'lore _nm_ colour; (_carte_) suit; **a colori** in colour; **di ~** coloured; **farne di tutti i colori** get up to all sorts of mischief; **passarne di tutti i colori** go through hell. **diventare di tutti i colori** _fig_ turn scarlet. **~ a olio** oil paint

colori'ficio _nm_ paint and dyes shop

colo'rito _a_ coloured; ⟨_viso_⟩ rosy; ⟨_racconto, linguaggio_⟩ colourful ● _nm_ complexion

co'loro _pron pl_ the ones

colos'sale _a_ colossal

Colos'seo _nm_ Coliseum

co'losso _nm_ colossus

'colpa _nf_ fault; (_biasimo_) blame; (_colpevolezza_) guilt; (_peccato_) sin; **dare la ~ a** blame; **essere in ~** be at fault; **per ~ di** because of; **è ~ mia** it's my fault

col'pevole _a_ guilty ● _nmf_ culprit

col'pire _vt_ hit, strike; _fig_ strike; **~ nel segno** hit the nail on the head

'colpo _nm_ blow; (_di arma da fuoco_) shot; (_urto_) knock; (_emozione_) shock; _Med, Sport_ stroke; (_furto_) robbery; **di ~** suddenly; **far ~** make a strong impression; **far venire un ~ a qcno** _fig_ give sb a fright; **perdere colpi** ⟨_motore:_⟩ keep missing; **a ~ d'occhio** at a glance; **a ~ sicuro** for certain. **~ d'aria** chill. **~ basso** blow below the belt. **~ di frusta** _Med_ whiplash injury. **~ di grazia** kiss of death. **~ da maestro** masterstroke. **~ di scena** sensational development. **~ di sole** sunstroke. **colpi** _pl_ **di sole** (_su capelli_) highlights. **~ di Stato** coup [d'état]. **~ di**

telefono ring, call; **dare un ~ di telefono a qn** give sb a ring _or_ call. **~ di testa** [sudden] impulse. **~ di vento** gust of wind

col'poso _a_ **omicidio ~** manslaughter

coltel'lata _nf_ stab

coltelle'ria _nf_ cutlery shop

col'tello _nm_ knife; **avere il ~ dalla parte del manico** have the upper hand. **~ per il pane** breadknife. **~ a serramanico** jack-knife

colti'vare _vt_ cultivate

coltiva'|tore, -'trice _nmf_ farmer

coltivazi'one _nf_ farming; (_di piante_) growing. **~ intensiva** intensive farming

'colto _pp di_ **cogliere** ● _a_ cultured

'coltre _nf_ blanket

col'tura _nf_ cultivation. **~ alternata** crop rotation

co'lui _pron m_ the one

'colza _nf Bot_ rape

'coma _nm inv_ coma; **in ~** in a coma; **in ~ irreversibile** brain dead

comanda'mento _nm_ commandment

coman'dante _nm_ commander; _Naut, Aeron_ captain

coman'dare _vt_ command; _Mech_ control; **~ a qcno di fare qcsa** order sb to do sth ● _vi_ be in charge

co'mando _nm_ command; (_di macchina_) control

co'mare _nf_ (_pettegola_) gossip

coma'toso _a Med_ comatose

combaci'are _vi_ fit together; ⟨_testimonianze:_⟩ concur

combat'tente _a_ fighting ● _nm_ combatant. **ex ~** ex-serviceman

com'battere _vt/i_ fight

combatti'mento _nm_ fight; _Mil_ battle; **fuori ~** ⟨_pugilato_⟩ knocked out

combat'tuto _a_ ⟨_gara_⟩ hard fought; (_tormentato_) torn; ⟨_discussione_⟩ heated

combi'nare _vt/i_ arrange; (_mettere insieme_) combine; (_fam: fare_) do; **cosa stai combinando?** what are you doing?

combi'narsi _vr_ combine; (_mettersi d'accordo_) come to an agreement

combinazi'one _nf_ combination; (_caso_) coincidence; **per ~** by chance

com'briccola _nf_ gang

combu'stibile _a_ combustible ● _nm_ fuel

combusti'one _nf_ combustion

com'butta _nf_ gang; **in ~** in league

'come _adv_ like; (_in qualità di_) as; (_interrogativo, esclamativo_) how; **questo vestito è ~ il tuo** this dress is like yours; **~?** pardon?; **~ stai?** how are you?; **~ va?** how are things?; **~ mai?** how come?; **~?** what?; **non sa ~ fare** he doesn't know what to do; **~ sta bene!** how well he looks!; **~ no!** that will be right!; **~ tu sai** as you know; **fa ~ vuoi** do as you like; **~ se** as if ● _conj_ (_non appena_) as soon as

come'done _nm_ blackhead

co'meta *nf* comet

'comfort *nm inv* comfort; **con tutti i ~** with all mod cons

'comico *a* comical; ⟨*teatro, attore*⟩ comic ● *nm* funny side; (*attore*) comic actor, comedian ● *nf* comedienne; (*attrice*) comic actress, comedienne; (*a torte in faccia*) slapstick sketch

co'mignolo *nm* chimney-pot

cominci'are *vt/i* begin, start; **a ~ da oggi** from today; **per ~** to begin with; **cominciamo bene!** we're off to a fine start!

comi'tato *nm* committee. **~ consultivo** advisory committee. **~ direttivo** steering committee. **~ esecutivo** executive committee. **~ di gestione** management committee

comi'tiva *nf* party, group

co'mizio *nm* meeting. **~ elettorale** election rally

'comma *nm* (*capoverso*) paragraph

com'mando *nm inv* commando

com'media *nf* comedy; (*opera teatrale*) play; *fig* sham. **~ musicale** musical

commedi'ante *nm* comic actor; *fig pej* phoney ● *nf* comic actress; *fig pej* phoney

commedi'ografo, -a *nmf* playwright

commemo'rare *vt* commemorate

commemorazi'one *nf* commemoration. **~ dei defunti** (2 novembre) All Souls' Day

commenda'tore *nm* commander

commen'sale *nmf* fellow diner

commen'tare *vt* comment on; (*annotare*) annotate

commen'tario *nm* commentary

commenta|'tore, -'trice *nmf* commentator

com'mento *nm* comment; *TV, Radio* commentary. **~ musicale** music

commerci'ale *a* commercial; ⟨*relazioni, trattative*⟩ trade; ⟨*attività*⟩ business; **centro ~** shopping centre

commercia'lista *nmf* business consultant; (*contabile*) accountant

commercializ'zare *vt* market; *pej* commercialize

commercializzazi'one *nf* marketing; *pej* commercialization

commerci'ante *nmf* trader, merchant; (*negoziante*) shopkeeper. **~ all'ingrosso** wholesaler. **~ di oggetti d'arte** art dealer

commerci'are *vi* **~ in** deal in

com'mercio *nm* commerce; (*internazionale*) trade; (*affari*) business; **in ~** ⟨*prodotto*⟩ on sale. **~ all'ingrosso** wholesale trade. **~ al minuto** retail trade

com'messo, -a *pp di* **commettere** ● *nmf* shop assistant; **commessi** *pl* counter staff. **~ viaggiatore** commercial traveller ● *nf* (*ordine*) order

comme'stibile *a* edible ● *nm* **commestibili** *pl* groceries

com'mettere *vt* commit; make ⟨*sbaglio*⟩; **~ un reato** commit an offence

commi'ato *nm* leave; **prendere ~ da** take leave of

commise'rare *vt* commiserate

commise'rarsi *vr* feel sorry for oneself

commissari'ato *nm* (*di polizia*) police station

commis'sario *nm* ≈ [police] superintendent; (*membro di commissione*) commissioner; *Sport* steward; *Comm* commission agent. **~ di bordo** purser. **~ capo** chief superintendent. **~ d'esame** examiner. **~ di gara** race official, steward. **~ tecnico** (*della nazionale*) national team manager

commissi'one *nf* (*incarico*) errand; (*comitato, percentuale*) commission; (*Comm: di merce*) order; **commissioni** *pl* (*acquisti*) **fare commissioni** go shopping. **~ d'esame** board of examiners. **C~ Europea** European Commission. **~ d'inchiesta** court of inquiry

commit'tente *nmf* purchaser

com'mosso *pp di* **commuovere** ● *a* moved

commo'vente *a* moving

commozi'one *nf* emotion. **~ cerebrale** concussion

commu'overe *vt* touch, move

commu'oversi *vr* be touched

commu'tare *vt* change; *Jur* commute

commuta'tore *nm Electr* commutator

commutazi'one *nf* (*di pena*) commutation

comò *nm inv* chest of drawers

comoda'mente *adv* comfortably

como'dino *nm* bedside table

comodità *nf inv* comfort; (*convenienza*) convenience

'comodo *a* comfortable; (*conveniente*) convenient; (*spazioso*) roomy; (*facile*) easy; **stia comodo!** don't get up!; **far ~** be useful ● *nm* comfort; **fare il proprio ~** do as one pleases; **prendila con ~!** take it easy!

'compact disc *nm inv* compact disc

compae'sano, -a *nm* fellow countryman ● *nf* fellow countrywoman

com'pagine *nf* (*squadra*) team

compa'gnia *nf* company; (*gruppo*) party; **fare ~ a qcno** keep sb company; **essere di ~** be sociable. **~ aerea** airline. **~ di bandiera** (*aerea*) national airline

com'pagno, -a *nmf* companion; (*Comm, Sport, in coppia*) partner; *Pol* comrade. **~ di classe** classmate. **~ di scuola** schoolmate. **~ di squadra** team-mate. **~ di viaggio** fellow traveller

compa'rabile *a* comparable

compa'rare *vt* compare

compara'tivo *a & nm* comparative

comparazi'one *nf* comparison

com'pare *nm* sidekick

compa'rire *vi* appear; (*spiccare*) stand out. **~ in giudizio** appear in court

com'parso, -a *pp di* **comparire** ● *nf* appearance; *Cinema* extra; *Theat* walk-on

compartecipazi'one *nf* sharing; (*quota*) share

comparti'mento *nm* compartment; (*amministrativo*) department

compas'sato *a* calm and collected

compassi'one *nf* compassion; **aver ~ per** feel pity for; **far ~** arouse pity

compassio'nevole *a* compassionate

com'passo *nm* [pair of] compasses *pl*

compa'tibile *a* (*conciliabile*) compatible; (*scusabile*) excusable

compatibilità *nf* compatibility

compatibil'mente *adv* **~ con i miei impegni** if my commitments allow

compati'mento *nm* **un'aria di ~** air of condescension

compa'tire *vt* pity; (*scusare*) make allowances for

compatri'ota *nmf* compatriot

compat'tezza *nf* (*di materia*) compactness; (*fig: di partito*) solidarity

com'patto *a* compact; (*denso*) dense; (*solido*) solid; *fig* united

compendi'are *vt* (*fare un sunto*) summarize

com'pendio *nm* outline; (*sunto*) synopsis; (*libro*) compendium

compene'trare *vt* pervade

compen'sare *vt* compensate; (*supplire*) make up for

compen'sarsi *vr* balance each other out

compen'sato *nm* (*legno*) plywood

compensazi'one *nf* compensation

com'penso *nm* compensation; (*retribuzione*) remuneration; **in compenso** (*in cambio*) in return; (*d'altra parte*) on the other hand; (*invece*) instead

'compera *nf* purchase; **far compere** do some shopping

compe'rare *vt* buy

compe'tente *a* competent; (*ufficio*) appropriate

compe'tenza *nf* competence; (*responsabilità*) responsibility; **competenze** *pl* (*onorari*) fees

com'petere *vi* compete; **~ a** (*compito:*) be the responsibility of

competitività *nf* competitiveness

competi'tivo *a* (*prezzo, carattere*) competitive

competi|'tore, -'trice *nmf* competitor

competizi'one *nf* competition

compia'cente *a* obliging

compia'cenza *nf* obligingness; **avere la ~ di...** be so obliging as to...

compia'cere *vt/i* please

compia'cersi *vr* (*congratularsi*) congratulate; **~ di** (*degnarsi*) condescend to

compiaci'mento *nm* satisfaction; *pej* smugness

compiaci'uto *a* satisfied; (*aria, sorriso*) smug

compi'angere *vt* pity; (*per lutto ecc*) sympathize with

'compiere *vt* (*concludere*) complete; commit (*delitto*); **~ gli anni** have one's birthday

'compiersi *vr* end; (*avverarsi*) come true

compi'lare *vt* compile; fill in (*modulo*)

compila|'tore, -'trice *nmf* compiler

compilazi'one *nf* compilation

compi'mento *nm* completion; **portare a ~ qcsa** conclude sth

com'pire *vt* = **compiere**

compi'tare *vt* spell

'compito¹ *nm* task; (*dovere*) duty; *Sch* homework; **fare i compiti** do one's homework

com'pito² *a* polite

compiu'tezza *nf* completeness

compi'uto *a* **avere 30 anni compiuti** be over 30

comple'anno *nm* birthday

complemen'tare *a* complementary; (*secondario*) subsidiary

comple'mento *nm* complement; *Mil* draft. **~ oggetto** *Gram* direct object

comples'sato *a* hung-up

complessità *nf* complexity

complessiva'mente *adv* on the whole; (*in totale*) altogether

comples'sivo *a* comprehensive; (*totale*) total

com'plesso *a* complex; (*difficile*) complicated ● *nm* complex, hang up *fam*; *Psych* complex; (*di cantanti ecc*) group; (*di circostanze, fattori*) combination; **in ~** on the whole; (*in totale*) altogether. **~ di inferiorità** inferiority complex

completa'mente *adv* completely

completa'mento *nm* completion

comple'tare *vt* complete

comple'tezza *nf* completeness

com'pleto *a* complete; (*pieno*) full [up]; **al ~** (*teatro:*) sold out; (*albergo*) full; **'~'** 'no vacancies'; **la famiglia al ~** the whole family ● *nm* (*vestito*) suit; (*insieme di cose*) set

compli'care *vt* complicate

compli'carsi *vr* become complicated

compli'cato complicated

complicazi'one *nf* complication; **salvo complicazioni** all being well

'complice *nmf* accomplice ● *a* (*sguardo*) knowing

complicità *nf* complicity

complimen'tare *nm* compliment ● *vt* compliment

complimen'tarsi *vr* **~ con** congratulate

compli'mento *nm* compliment. **complimenti** *pl* (*ossequi*) regards; (*congratulazioni*) congratulations; **far complimenti** stand on ceremony

complot'tare *vi* plot

com'plotto *nm* plot

compo'nente *a & nm* component ● *nmf* member

componen'tistica *nf* (*per auto, elettronica*) accessories *pl*

compo'nibile *a* (*cucina*) fitted; (*mobili*) modular

componi'mento *nm* composition; (*letterario*) work

com'porre *vt* compose; (*sistemare*) put in order; *Typ* set; lay out (*salma*); settle (*lite*)

com'porsi *vr* **~ di** be made up of

comportamen'tale *a* behavioural

comporta'mento *nm* behaviour
compor'tare *vt* (*implicare*) involve
compor'tarsi *vr* behave
com'posito *a* *Chem, Phot* composite
composi'tore, -'trice *nmf* composer; *Typ* compositor
composizi'one *nf* composition. **~ floreale** flower arrangement
com'posta *nf* stewed fruit; (*concime*) compost
compo'stezza *nf* composure
com'posto *pp di* **comporre ●** *a* (*parola*) compound; **essere ~ da** consist of, comprise; **stai ~!** sit properly! **●** *nm* *Chem* compound; *Culin* mixture
com'prare *vt* buy; (*fig: corrompere*) buy off, bribe
compra|'tore, -'trice *nmf* buyer
compra'vendita *nf* buying and selling; **atto di ~** deed of sale
com'prendere *vt* understand; (*includere*) comprise
compren'donio *nm* **essere duro di ~** be slow on the uptake
compren'sibile *a* understandable
comprensibil'mente *adv* understandably
comprensi'one *nf* understanding
compren'sivo *a* understanding; (*che include*) inclusive
com'preso *pp di* **comprendere ●** *a* included; **tutto ~** (*prezzo*) all-in; **da lunedì a venerdì ~** Monday to Friday inclusive
com'pressa *nf* compress; (*pastiglia*) tablet
compressi'one *nf* compression. **~ dati** *Comput* data compression
com'presso *pp di* **comprimere ●** *a* compressed
compres'sore *nm* (*rullo*) steamroller
compri'mario *nm* *Theat* supporting actor **●** *nf* supporting actress
com'primere *vt* press; (*reprimere*) repress
compro'messo *pp di* **compromettere ●** *nm* compromise; (*contratto*) preliminary *but binding agreement*
compromet'tente *a* compromising
compro'mettere *vt* compromise
comproprietà *nf* multiple ownership
comproprie'tario, -a *nmf* joint owner
compro'vare *vt* prove
com'punto *a* contrite
compunzi'one *nf* compunction
compu'tare *vt* calculate; (*addebitare*) estimate
com'puter *nm inv* computer. **~ da casa** home computer
computeriz'zare *vt* computerize
computeriz'zato *a* computerized
computerizzazi'one *nf* computerization
computiste'ria *nf* book-keeping
'computo *nm* calculation
comu'nale *a* municipal
co'mune *a* common; (*parti*) communal,

common; (*amico*) mutual; (*ordinario*) ordinary **●** *nm* municipality; **fuori del ~** out of the ordinary; **avere qcsa in ~** have sth in common **●** *nf* collective farm
comu'nella *nf* **fare ~** form a clique
comune'mente *adv* commonly
comuni'cante *a* interconnecting
comuni'care *vt* communicate; pass on (*malattia*); *Relig* administer Communion to
comuni'carsi *vr* receive Communion
comunica'tiva *nf* communicativeness
comunica'tivo *a* communicative
comuni'cato *nm* communiqué. **~ commerciale** *Radio* commercial. **~ stampa** press release
comunicazi'one *nf* communication; *Teleph* [phone] call; **avere la ~** get through; **dare la ~ a qcno** put sb through. **~ dati** *Comput* data communications
comuni'one *nf* communion; *Relig* [Holy] Communion
comu'nismo *nm* communism
comu'nista *a & nmf* communist
comunità *nf inv* community. **C~ [Economica] Europea** European [Economic] Community. **C~ degli Stati Indipendenti** Commonwealth of Independent States. **~ terapeutica** residential therapy group
co'munque *conj* however **●** *adv* anyhow
con *prep* with; (*mezzo*) by; **~ facilità** easily; **~ mia grande gioia** to my great delight; **è gentile ~ tutti** he is kind to everyone; **col treno** by train; **~ questo tempo** in this weather
co'nato *nm* **~ di vomito** retching
'conca *nf* basin; (*valle*) dell
concate'nare *vt* link together
concate'narsi *vr* (*idee:*) be connected
concatenazi'one *nf* connection
'concavo *a* concave
con'cedere *vt* grant; award (*premio*); (*ammettere*) admit
con'cedersi *vr* allow oneself (*pausa*); treat oneself to (*lusso, vacanza*)
concentra'mento *nm* concentration
concen'trare *vt* concentrate
concen'trarsi *vr* concentrate
concen'trato *a* concentrated **●** *nm* concentrate. **~ di pomodoro** tomato purée
concentrazi'one *nf* concentration
con'centrico *a* concentric
concepi'mento *nm* conception
conce'pire *vt* conceive (*bambino*); (*capire*) understand; (*figurarsi*) conceive of; devise (*piano ecc*)
con'cernere *vt* concern
concer'tare *vt* *Mus* harmonize; (*organizzare*) arrange
concer'tarsi *vr* agree
concer'tista *nmf* concert performer
con'certo *nm* concert; (*composizione*) concerto. **~ rock** rock concert
concessio'nario *nm* agent
concessi'one *nf* concession

con'cesso *pp di* **concedere**

con'cetto *nm* concept; (*opinione*) opinion

concet'toso *a* cerebral

concezi'one *nf* conception; (*idea*) concept

con'chiglia *nf* [sea] shell. ~ **del pellegrino, ~ di san Giacomo** scallop shell

'**concia** *nf* tanning; (*di tabacco*) curing

conci'are *vt* tan; cure ⟨*tabacco*⟩; ~ **qcno per le feste** give sb a good hiding

conci'arsi *vr* (*sporcarsi*) get dirty; (*vestirsi male*) dress badly

conci'ato *a* ⟨*pelle, cuoio*⟩ tanned; **essere ~ come un barbone** look like something the cat dragged in

concili'abile *a* compatible

concili'abolo *nm* private meeting

concili'ante *a* conciliatory

concili'are *vt* reconcile; pay ⟨*contravvenzione*⟩; (*favorire*) induce

concili'arsi *vr* go together; (*mettersi d'accordo*) become reconciled

conciliazi'one *nf* reconciliation; *Jur* settlement

con'cilio *nm Relig* council; (*riunione*) assembly

conci'maia *nf* dunghill

conci'mare *vt* feed ⟨*pianta*⟩

con'cime *nm* manure; (*chimico*) fertilizer

concisi'one *nf* conciseness

con'ciso *a* concise

conci'tato *a* excited

concitta'dino, -a *nmf* fellow citizen

concla'mato *a Med* full blown

con'clave *nm* conclave

con'cludere *vt* conclude; (*finire con successo*) successfully complete

con'cludersi *vr* come to an end

conclusi'one *nf* conclusion; **in ~** (*insomma*) in short

conclu'sivo *a* conclusive

con'cluso *pp di* **concludere**

concomi'tante *a* contributory

concomi'tanza *nf* (*di circostanze, fatti*) combination; **in ~ con** combined with, in conjunction with

concor'danza *nf* agreement

concor'dare *vt* agree [on]; *Gram* make agree ● *vi* (*sul prezzo*) agree

concor'dato *nm* agreement; *Jur, Comm* composition

con'corde *a* in agreement; (*unanime*) unanimous

con'cordia *nf* concord

concor'rente *a* concurrent; (*rivale*) competing ● *nmf Comm, Sport* competitor; (*candidato*) candidate; (*a quiz, concorso di bellezza*) contestant

concor'renza *nf* competition. ~ **sleale** unfair competition

concorrenzi'ale *a* competitive

con'correre *vi* (*contribuire*) combine; (*andare insieme*) go together; (*competere*) compete

con'corso *pp di* **concorrere** ● *nm* competition; **fuori ~** not in the official competition.

~ **di bellezza** beauty contest. ~ **di circostanze** combination of circumstances. ~ **di colpa** contributory negligence. ~ **ippico** showjumping event. ~ **a premi** prizewinning competition. ~ **in reato** *Jur* complicity. ~ **per titoli** *competition in which exam results are not the sole criterion*

concreta'mente *adv* concretely

concre'tare, concretiz'zare *vt* put into concrete form

con'creto *a* concrete; **in ~** in concrete terms

concu'bina *nf* concubine

concussi'one *nf* acceptance of a bribe

con'danna *nf* sentence; **pronunziare una ~** hand down a sentence. ~ **a morte** death sentence. ~ **penale** prison sentence

condan'nare *vt* (*disapprovare*) condemn; *Jur* sentence

condan'nato, -a *a* (*destinato*) forced ● *nmf* prisoner

con'densa *nf* condensation

conden'sare *vt* condense

conden'sarsi *vr* condense

condensa'tore *nm Electr* condenser

condensazi'one *nf* condensation

condi'mento *nm* seasoning; (*salsa*) dressing. ~ **per insalata** salad dressing

con'dire *vt* flavour; dress ⟨*insalata*⟩

condiscen'dente *a* indulgent; *pej* condescending; (*arrendevole*) compliant

condiscen'denza *nf* indulgence; *pej* condescension; (*arrendevolezza*) compliance

con'dito *a Culin* seasoned

condi'videre *vt* share

condizio'nale *a & nm* conditional ● *nf Jur* suspended sentence

condiziona'mento *nm Psych* conditioning

condizio'nare *vt* condition

condizionata'mente *adv* conditionally

condizio'nato *a* conditional (**da** on); **aria condizionata** air-conditioning

condiziona'tore *nm* air conditioner

condizi'one *nf* condition; **a ~ che** on condition that. **condizioni** *pl* **di credito** credit terms. ~ **imprescindibile** precondition

condogli'anze *nfpl* condolences; **fare le ~ a** offer one's condolences to

'**condom** *nm inv* condom

condomini'ale *a* ⟨*spese*⟩ common; ⟨*riunione*⟩ tenants' *attrib*

condo'minio *nm* joint ownership; (*edificio*) condominium

condo'mino, -a *nmf* joint owner

condo'nare *vt* remit

con'dono *nm* remission

con'dotta *nf* conduct, (*circoscrizione di medico*) country practice; (*di gara ecc*) management; (*tubazione*) pipe

con'dotto *pp di* **condurre** ● *a* **medico ~** country doctor ● *nm* pipe; *Anat* duct. ~ **dell'aria** air duct. ~ **sotterraneo** culvert

condu'cente *nm* driver. ~ **di autobus** bus driver

con'durre vt lead; drive ⟨veicoli⟩; (accompagnare) take; conduct ⟨gas, elettricità ecc⟩; (gestire) run; ~ **a termine** complete; ~ **delle indagini** carry out an investigation

con'dursi vr behave

condut'tore a **filo** ~ leitmotif

condut'|tore, -'trice nmf TV presenter; (di veicolo) ● nm Electr conductor

condut'tura nf duct. ~ **del gas** gas main

conduzi'one nf conduction

confabu'lare vi have a confab

confa'cente a suitable

con'farsi vr **confarsi a** suit

confederazi'one nf confederation. **C~ elvetica** Swiss Confederation

confe'renza nf (discorso) lecture; (congresso) conference. ~ **stampa** press conference, news conference

conferenzi'ere, -a nmf lecturer, speaker

confe'rire vt (donare) confer ● vi (consultarsi) confer

con'ferma nf confirmation; **dare** ~ confirm

confer'mare vt confirm

confes'sare vt confess

confes'sarsi vr confess

confessio'nale a ⟨segreto⟩ of the confession ● nm confessional

confessi'one nf confession

confes'sore nm confessor

con'fetto nm (di mandorla) sugared almond

confet'tura nf jam

confezio'nare vt manufacture; make ⟨abiti⟩; package ⟨merci⟩

confezio'nato a ⟨vestiti⟩ off-the-peg; ⟨gelato⟩ wrapped

confezi'one nf manufacture; (di abiti) making; (di pacchi) packaging; **di** ~ ⟨abiti⟩ off-the-peg; **confezioni** pl clothes. ~ **economica** economy pack, economy size. ~ **famiglia** family size. ~ **regalo** gift set. ~ **da sei** (di bottiglie, lattine) six-pack

confic'care vt thrust

confic'carsi vr lodge

confic'cato a ~ **in** lodged in, embedded in

confi'dare vt confide ● vi ~ **in** trust

confi'darsi vr ~ **con** confide in

confi'dente a confident ● nmf confidant; (informatore) informer

confi'denza nf confidence; (familiarità) familiarity; **prendersi delle confidenze** take liberties

confidenzi'ale a confidential; ⟨tono⟩ familiar; **in via** ~ confidentially

configu'rare vt Comput configure

configurazi'one nf configuration

confi'nante a neighbouring

confi'nare vt (relegare) confine ● vi ~ **con** border on

confi'narsi vr (ritirarsi) withdraw

confi'nato a confined ● nm prisoner

con'fine nm border; (tra terreni) boundary

con'fino nm political exile

con'fisca nf (di proprietà) confiscation

confi'scare vt confiscate

conflagrazi'one nf conflagration

con'flitto nm conflict

conflittu'ale a adversarial

conflittualità nf adversarial nature

conflu'enza nf confluence; (di strade) junction

conflu'ire vi ⟨fiumi:⟩ flow together; ⟨strade:⟩ meet

con'fondere vt confuse; (imbarazzare) embarrass

con'fondersi vr (mescolarsi) mingle; (sbagliarsi) be mistaken

confor'mare vt standardize (**a** in line with)

confor'marsi vr conform

conformazi'one nf conformity (**a** with); (del terreno) nature

con'forme a standard

conforme'mente adv accordingly

confor'mismo nm conformity

confor'mista nmf conformist

conformità nf (a norma) conformity (**a** with); **in** ~ **a** in accordance with, in conformity with

confor'tante a comforting

confor'tare vt comfort

confor'tevole a (comodo) comfortable

con'forto nm comfort; **a** ~ **di** ⟨una tesi⟩ in support of; **conforti** pl **religiosi** last rites

confra'telli nmpl brethren

confra'ternita nf brotherhood

confron'tare vt compare

con'fronto nm comparison; **in** ~ **a** by comparison with; **nei tuoi confronti** towards you; **senza** ~ far and away, by far. ~ **diretto** head to head

confusio'nario a ⟨persona⟩ muddle-headed

confusi'one nf confusion; (baccano) racket; (disordine) mess; (imbarazzo) embarrassment

con'fuso pp di **confondere** ● a confused; (indistinto) indistinct; (imbarazzato) embarrassed

confu'tare vt confute

conge'dare vt dismiss; Mil discharge

conge'darsi vr take one's leave

con'gedo nm leave; **essere in** ~ be on leave. ~ **malattia** sick leave. ~ **[di] maternità** maternity leave. ~ **[di] paternità** paternity leave

conge'gnare vt devise; (mettere insieme) assemble

con'gegno nm device

congela'mento nm freezing; Med frostbite

conge'lare vt freeze

conge'lato a ⟨cibo⟩ deep-frozen

congela'tore nm freezer

congeni'ale a congenial

con'genito a congenital

congestio'nare vt congest

congestio'nato a ⟨traffico⟩ congested; ⟨viso⟩ flushed

congesti'one nf congestion

conget'tura *nf* conjecture

congi'ungere *vt* join, connect; join ⟨*mani*⟩; combine ⟨*sforzi*⟩

congi'ungersi *vr* join, connect

congiunti'vite *nf* conjunctivitis

congiun'tivo *nm* subjunctive

congi'unto *pp di* **congiungere** ● *a* joined; ⟨*azione*⟩ joint; ⟨*forze, sforzo*⟩ combined ● *nm* relative

congiun'tura *nf* junction; (*situazione*) situation

congiuntu'rale *a* economic

congiunzi'one *nf Gram* conjunction

congi'ura *nf* conspiracy

congiu'rare *vi* conspire

conglome'rato *nm* conglomerate; *fig* conglomeration; (*da costruzione*) concrete

'Congo *nm* Congo

congo'lese *a & nmf* Congolese

congratu'larsi *vr* ~ **con qcno per** congratulate sb on

congratulazi'oni *nfpl* congratulations

con'grega *nf* band

congre'gare *vt* gather

congre'garsi *vr* congregate

congregazi'one *nf* congregation

congres'sista *nmf* convention participant

con'gresso *nm* congress, convention; (*americano*) Congress. **C~ Nazionale Africano** African National Congress

'congrua *nf* stipend

'congruo *a* proper; (*giusto*) fair

conguagli'are *vt* balance

congu'aglio *nm* balance

coni'are *vt* coin

conia'tura *nf* coinage

coniazi'one *nf* coinage

'conico *a* conical

co'nifera *nf* conifer

co'niglia *nf* female rabbit, doe

conigli'era *nf* rabbit hutch

conigli'etta *nf* bunny girl

conigli'etto *nm* bunny

co'niglio *nm* rabbit

coniu'gale *a* marital; ⟨*vita*⟩ married

coniu'gare *vt* conjugate

coniu'garsi *vr* get married; *Gram* conjugate

coniu'gato *a* ⟨*sposato*⟩ married

coniugazi'one *nf* conjugation

'coniuge *nmf* spouse

connazio'nale *nmf* compatriot

connessi'one *nf* connection

con'nesso *pp di* **connettere**

con'nettere *vt* connect ● *vi* think rationally

con'nettersi *vr* (*Comput: a bacheca elettronica*) log on (**a** to)

connet'tore *nm* connector

conni'vente *a* conniving

conno'tare *vt* connote

conno'tato *nm* distinguishing feature; **connotati** *pl* description; **rispondere ai connotati** fit the description; **cambiare i connotati a qcno** *hum* re-arrange sb's face

con'nubio *nm fig* union

'cono *nm* cone

cono'scente *nmf* acquaintance

cono'scenza *nf* knowledge; (*persona*) acquaintance; (*sensi*) consciousness; **perdere** ~ lose consciousness; **riprendere** ~ regain consciousness, come to. ~ **di lavoro** business contact

co'noscere *vt* know; (*essere a conoscenza di*) be acquainted with; (*fare la conoscenza di*) meet; ~ **qcsa a fondo** know sth inside out

conosci'tore, -'trice *nmf* connoisseur

conosci'uto *pp di* **conoscere** ● *a* well-known

con'quista *nf* conquest

conqui'stare *vt* conquer; *fig* win

conquista'tore *nm* conqueror; *fig* lady-killer

consa'crare *vt* consecrate; ordain ⟨*sacerdote*⟩; (*dedicare*) dedicate

consa'crarsi *vr* devote oneself

consa'crato *a* ⟨*suolo*⟩ hallowed

consacrazi'one *nf* consecration

consangu'ineo, -a *nmf* blood-relation

consa'pevole *a* conscious

consapevo'lezza *nf* consciousness

consapevol'mente *adv* consciously

conscia'mente *adv* consciously

'conscio *a* conscious

consecu'tivo *a* consecutive; (*seguente*) next

con'segna *nf* delivery; (*merce*) consignment; (*custodia*) care; (*di prigioniero*) handover; (*Mil: ordine*) orders *pl*; (*Mil: punizione*) confinement to barracks; **pagamento alla** ~ cash on delivery. ~ **della posta** mail delivery

conse'gnare *vt* deliver; *Mil* confine to barracks; hand over ⟨*prigioniero, chiavi*⟩

consegna'tario *nm* consignee

consegu'ente *a* consequent

consegu'enza *nf* consequence; **di** ~ (*perciò*) consequently; ⟨*agire, comportarsi*⟩ accordingly

consegui'mento *nm* achievement

consegu'ire *vt* achieve ● *vi* follow

con'senso *nm* consent; (*della popolazione*) consensus

consensu'ale *a* consensus-based

consen'tire *vi* consent ● *vt* allow

consenzi'ente *a* consenting

con'serto *a* **a braccia conserte** with one's arms folded

con'serva *nf* preserve; (*di frutta*) jam; (*di agrumi*) marmalade. ~ **di pomodoro** tomato sauce

conser'vare *vt* preserve; (*mantenere*) keep; ~ **in frigo** keep refrigerated; ~ **in luogo asciutto** keep dry

conser'varsi *vr* keep; ~ **in salute** keep well

conserva'tore, -'trice *a & nmf Pol* conservative; **partito** ~ Conservative Party, Tory Party *Br*

conserva'torio *nm* conservatory, school of music

conservato'rismo nm conservatism

conservazi'one nf preservation; **a lunga ~** long-life

con'sesso nm assembly

conside'rare vt consider; (stimare) regard

conside'rato a (stimato) esteemed

considerazi'one nf consideration; (osservazione, riflessione) remark; (stima) respect

conside'revole a considerable

consigli'abile a advisable

consigli'are vt advise; (raccomandare) recommend

consigli'arsi vr **~ con qcno** ask sb's advice

consigli'ere, -a nmf adviser; (membro di un consiglio) councillor. **~ d'amministrazione** board member. **~ delegato** managing director

con'siglio nm advice; (ente) council; **un ~** a piece of advice. **~ d'amministrazione** board of directors. **~ di guerra** war cabinet. **~ d'istituto** parent-teacher association. **~ dei ministri** Cabinet. **~ scolastico** education committee. **C~ di Sicurezza** (dell'ONU) Security Council. **C~ Superiore della Magistratura** body responsible for ensuring the independence of the judiciary

con'simile a similar

consi'stente a substantial; (spesso) thick; (fig: argomento) solid

consi'stenza nf consistency; (spessore) thickness; (fig: di argomento) solidity

consi'stere vi **~ in** consist of

consoci'arsi vr go into partnership

consoci'ata nf (azienda) subsidiary

consociati'vismo nm excessive tendency to form associations

consoci'ato nm associate

con'socio, -a nmf fellow-member

conso'lante a consoling

conso'lare[1] a consular

conso'lare[2] vt console

conso'larsi vr console oneself

conso'lato nm consulate

consolazi'one nf consolation

'console nm consul

con'sole nf inv (tastiera) console

consolida'mento nm consolidation

consoli'dare vt consolidate

consoli'darsi vr consolidate

consommé nm inv consommé

conso'nante nf consonant

conso'nanza nf consonance

'consono a appropriate (**a** to), suitable (**a** for)

con'sorte nmf consort

con'sorzio nm consortium

con'stare vi **~ di** consist of; (risultare) appear; **a quanto mi consta** as far as I know; **mi consta che...** seemingly,...

consta'tare vt ascertain

constatazi'one nf statement of fact

consu'eto a usual ● nm **più del ~** more than usual

consuetudi'nario a (diritto) common; (persona) set in one's ways

consue'tudine nf habit; (usanza) custom

consu'lente nmf consultant. **~ aziendale** management consultant; (azienda) management consultancy. **~ matrimoniale** marriage guidance counsellor

consu'lenza nf consultancy

consul'tare vt consult

consul'tarsi vr **~ con** consult with

consultazi'one nf consultation

consul'tivo a consultative

con'sulto nm consultation

consul'torio nm free clinic providing treatment for sexual problems and advice

consu'mare vt (usare) consume; wear out (abito, scarpe); consummate (matrimonio); commit (delitto)

consu'marsi vr consume; (abito, scarpe:) wear out; (struggersi) pine; **'da ~ preferibilmente entro il...'** 'best before...'

consu'mato a (politico) consummate; (scarpe, tappeto) worn [out]

consuma'tore, -'trice nmf consumer

consumazi'one nf consumption; (bibita) drink; (spuntino) snack; (di matrimonio) consummation; (di delitto) commission

consu'mismo nm consumerism

consu'mista nmf consumerist

con'sumo nm consumption; (uso) use; **generi di ~** consumer goods. **~ [di carburante]** [fuel] consumption

consun'tivo nm **bilancio ~** balance sheet; **fare il ~ di** fig take stock of

con'sunto a well-worn

conta'balle nmf fam storyteller

con'tabile a book-keeping ● nmf accountant

contabilità nf inv accounting; (ufficio) accounts department; **tenere la ~** keep the accounts. **~ di gestione** management accounts. **~ in partita doppia** double entry book-keeping

contachi'lometri nm inv mileometer, odometer Am

conta'dino, -a nmf farm-worker, agricultural labourer; (proprietario) farmer; (medievale) peasant

contagi'are vt infect; **la sua allegria contagia tutti** his cheerfulness is very contagious

contagi'ato a infected

con'tagio nm contagion

contagi'oso a contagious

conta'giri nm inv rev counter

conta'gocce nm inv dropper; **dare qcsa col ~** fig dole sth out in dribs and drabs

contami'nare vt contaminate

contaminazi'one nf contamination

contami'nuti nm inv timer

con'tante nm cash; **pagare in contanti** pay cash

con'tare vt count; (tenere conto di) take into

account; **devi ~ un'ora per il viaggio** you have to allow for the hour for the journey ● *vi* count; **~ di fare qcsa** plan to do sth

conta'scatti *nm inv Teleph* time-unit counter

con'tato *a* ⟨*giorni, ore*⟩ numbered

conta'tore *nm* meter. **~ del gas** gas meter

contat'tare *vt* contact

con'tatto *nm* contact; **essere in ~ con** be in touch *or* contact with; **mettersi in ~ con** contact, get in touch with

'**conte** *nm* count, earl *Br*

con'tea *nf* county

conteggi'are *vt* include ● *vi* calculate

con'teggio *nm* calculation. **~ alla rovescia** countdown

con'tegno *nm* behaviour; (*atteggiamento*) attitude; **darsi un ~** pull oneself together

conte'gnoso *a* dignified

contem'plare *vt* contemplate; (*fissare*) gaze at

contempla'tivo *a* contemplative

contemplazi'one *nf* contemplation

con'tempo *nm* **nel ~** in the meantime

contemporanea'mente *adv* at the same time

contempo'raneo, -a *a* & *nmf* contemporary

conten'dente *nmf* competitor

con'tendere *vi* compete; (*litigare*) quarrel ● *vt* dispute

con'tendersi *vr* **~ qcsa** compete for sth

conte'nere *vt* contain; (*reprimere*) repress

conte'nersi *vr* contain oneself

conteni'tore *nm* container

conten'tabile *a* **facilmente ~** easy to please

conten'tare *vt* please

conten'tarsi *vr* **~ di** be content with

conten'tezza *nf* happiness

conten'tino *nm* placebo

con'tento *a* glad; (*soddisfatto*) happy

conte'nuto *nm* contents *pl*; (*di libro, testo*) content

contenzi'oso *a* contentious ● *nm* dispute; (*ufficio*) legal department

con'tesa *nf* disagreement; *Sport* contest

con'teso *pp di* **contendere** ● *a* contested

con'tessa *nf* countess

conte'stare *vt* contest; *Jur* give notification of ⟨*contravvenzione*⟩; **~ un reato a qcno** charge sb with an offence

contesta|'tore, -'trice *nmf person who is anti-authority* ● *a* anti-authority

contestazi'one *nf* (*disputa*) dispute; (*protesta*) protest; (*di contravvenzione*) notification

con'testo *nm* context

con'tiguo *a* adjacent

continen'tale *a* continental

conti'nente *nm* continent

conti'nenza *nf* continence

contin'gente *nm* contingent; (*quota*) quota

contin'genza *nf* contingency

continua'mente *adv* (*senza interruzione*) continuously; (*frequentemente*) continually

continu'are *vt/i* continue; (*riprendere*) resume; **~ gli studi** stay on at school

continua'tivo *a* on-going, continuous

continuazi'one *nf* continuation

continuità *nf* continuity

con'tinuo *a* continuous; (*molto frequente*) continual; **di ~** continuously; (*frequentemente*) continually; **corrente continua** direct current

con'tinuum *nm inv* continuum

'**conto** *nm* calculation; (*in banca, negozio*) account; (*di ristorante ecc*) bill; (*stima*) consideration; **a conti fatti** all things considered; **ad ogni buon ~** in any case; **di poco/nessun ~** of little/no importance; **in fin dei conti** when all's said and done; **per ~ di** on behalf of; **per ~ mio** (*a mio parere*) in my opinion; (*da solo*) on my own; **per ~ terzi** for a third party; **sul ~ di qcno** ⟨*voci, informazioni*⟩ about sb; **far ~ di** (*supporre*) suppose; (*proporsi*) intend; **far ~ su** rely on; **fare i propri conti** do one's accounts; **fare i conti con qcno** *fig* sort sb out; **fare i conti in tasca a qcno** estimate how much sb is worth; **fare i conti senza l'oste** forget the most important thing; **render ~ a qcno di qcsa** be accountable to sb for sth; **rendersi ~ di qcsa** realize sth; **starsene per ~ proprio** be on one's own; **tener ~ di qcsa** take sth into account; **tenere da ~ qcsa** look after sth. **~ in banca** bank account. **~ congiunto** joint account. **~ corrente** current account, checking account *Am*. **~** [**corrente**] **comune** joint account. **~ corrente postale** Giro account. **~ profitti e perdite** profit and loss account. **~ alla rovescia** countdown. **~ spese** expense account

con'torcere *vt* twist

con'torcersi *vr* twist about

contor'nare *vt* surround

con'torno *nm* contour; *Culin* vegetables *pl*

contorsi'one *nf* contortion

contorsio'nista *nmf* contortionist

con'torto *pp di* **contorcere** ● *a* twisted

contrabban'dare *vt* smuggle

contrabbandi'ere, -a *nmf* smuggler

contrab'bando *nm* contraband

contrabbas'sista *nmf* double bass player

contrab'basso *nm* double bass

contraccambi'are *vt* return

contrac'cambio *nm* return

contraccet'tivo *nm* contraceptive

contraccezi'one *nf* contraception

contrac'colpo *nm* rebound; (*di arma da fuoco*) recoil; *fig* repercussion

con'trada *nf* (*rione*) district

contrad'detto *pp di* **contraddire**

contrad'dire *vt* contradict

contraddi'stinguere *vt* differentiate, distinguish

contraddi'stinto *pp di* **distinguere** ● *a* ~ **da** distinguished by

contraddit'torio *a* contradictory

contraddizi'one *nf* contradiction

contra'ente *nmf* contracting party

contra'ereo *a* anti-aircraft

contraf'fare *vt* disguise

contraf'fatto *pp di* **contraffare** ● *a* disguised

contraffazi'one *nf* disguising

contraf'forte *nm* buttress

con'tralto *nm* countertenor ● *nf* contralto

contrap'peso *nm* counterbalance

contrap'porre *vt* (*confrontare*) compare; ~ **A a B** counter B with A

contrap'porsi *vr* be in opposition; ~ **a** contrast with; (*opporsi a*) be opposed to

contrap'punto *nm Mus* counterpoint

contraria'mente *adv* ~ **a** contrary to; ~ **a me** unlike me

contrari'are *vt* oppose; (*infastidire*) annoy

contrari'arsi *vr* get annoyed

contrarietà *nf* adversity; (*ostacolo*) setback

con'trario *a* contrary, opposite; (*direzione*) opposite; (*esito, vento*) unfavourable ● *nm* contrary, opposite; **al** ~ on the contrary

con'trarre *vt* contract

contrasse'gnare *vt* mark

contras'segno *nm* mark; [**in**] ~ (*spedizione*) cash on delivery, COD. ~ **IVA** VAT receipt

contra'stante *a* contrasting

contra'stare *vt* oppose; (*contestare*) contest ● *vi* contrast; (*colori:*) clash

con'trasto *nm* contrast; (*di colori*) clash; (*litigio*) dispute

contrattac'care *vt* counter-attack

contrat'tacco *nm* counter-attack

contrat'tare *vt/i* negotiate; (*mercanteggiare*) bargain

contrattazi'one *nf* contravention; (*multa*) fine; (*salariale*) bargaining. ~ **di azioni** share dealing

contrat'tempo *nm* hitch

con'tratto *pp di* **contrarre** ● *nm* contract. ~ **di lavoro** employment contract. ~ **a termine** fixed-term contract. **contratti** *pl* **a termine** *Fin* futures

contrattu'ale *a* contractual

contravve'nire *vi* contravene a law

contrazi'one *nf* contraction; (*di prezzi*) reduction

contribu'ente *nmf* contributor; (*del fisco*) taxpayer

contribu'ire *vi* contribute

contribu'tivo *a* contributory

contri'buto *nm* contribution. **contributi** *pl* **pensionistici** pension contributions

con'trito *a* contrite

'**contro** *prep* against; ~ **di me** against me ● *nm* **il pro e il** ~ the pros and cons *pl*

contro'battere *vt* counter

controbilanci'are *vt* counterbalance

controcor'rente *a* (*idee, persona*) non-conformist ● *adv* upriver; *fig* upstream; **andare** ~ *fig* swim against the tide

controcul'tura *nf* counterculture

contro'curva *nf* second bend

contro'esodo *nm massive return from holiday*

controfa'gotto *nm* double bassoon

controffen'siva *nf* counter-offensive

controfi'gura *nf* stand-in

controfi'letto *nm* sirloin

controfir'mare *vt* countersign

controindicazi'one *nf Med* contra-indication

controinterroga'torio *nm* cross-examination

control'labile *a* (*emozione*) controllable; *Tech* which can be monitored

control'lare *vt* control; (*verificare*) check

control'larsi *vr* control oneself

control'lato *a* controlled

con'troller *nm inv Fin* controller

con'trollo *nm* control; (*verifica*) check; *Med* check-up; **perdere il** ~ **di** lose control of. ~ **degli armamenti** arms control. ~ **automatico della velocità** automatic speed check. ~ **bagagli** baggage control. ~ **biglietti** ticket inspection. ~ **dei cambi** exchange control. ~ **del credito** credit control. ~ **medico** check-up. ~ **delle nascite** birth control. ~ **passaporti** passport control. ~ [**di**] **qualità** quality control. ~ **radar della velocità** radar speed check

control'lore *nm* controller; (*sui treni ecc*) [ticket] inspector. ~ **di volo** air-traffic controller

contro'luce *nf* **in** ~ against the light

contro'mano *adv* in the wrong direction

contromi'sura *nf* countermeasure

contropar'tita *nf* compensation; **in** ~ in return

contropi'ede *nm Sport* breakaway; **prendere in** ~ *fig* catch off guard

controprodu'cente *a* counter-productive

contro'prova *nf* cross-check; **fare la** ~ **di qcsa** cross-check sth

con'trordine *nm* counter order; **salvo contrordini** unless I/you hear to the contrary

contro'senso *nm* contradiction in terms

controspio'naggio *nm* counterespionage

controten'denza *nf* countertrend

controva'lore *nm* equivalent

contro'vento *adv* against the wind

contro'versia *nf* controversy; *Jur* dispute

contro'verso *a* controversial

contro'voglia *adv* unwillingly

contu'mace *a Jur* in default, absent

contu'macia *nf* default; **in** ~ in one's absence

contun'dente *a* (*corpo, arma*) blunt

contur'bante *a* perturbing

contur'bare *vt* perturb

contusi'one *nf* bruise

con'tuso *nm person suffering from cuts and bruises*

convale'scente *a & nmf* convalescent

convale'scenza *nf* convalescence; **essere in ~** be convalescing

con'valida *nf* ratification; (*di nomina*) confirmation; (*di biglietto*) validation

convali'dare *vt* ratify; confirm ‹*nomina*›; validate ‹*atto, biglietto*›

con'vegno *nm* meeting; (*congresso*) convention, congress

conve'nevole *a* suitable

conve'nevoli *nmpl* pleasantries

conveni'ente *a* convenient; (*vantaggioso*) advantageous; ‹*prezzo*› attractive

conveni'enza *nf* convenience; (*interesse*) advantage; (*di prezzo*) attractiveness

conve'nire *vi* agree; (*riunirsi*) gather; (*essere opportuno*) be convenient; **ci conviene andare** it's better to go; **non mi conviene stancarmi** I'd better not tire myself out ● *vt* agree [on]

conven'ticola *nf* clique

con'vento *nm* (*di suore*) convent; (*di frati*) monastery

conve'nuto *a* agreed

convenzio'nale *a* conventional

convenzio'nato *a* ‹*prezzo*› controlled

convenzi'one *nf* convention

conver'gente *a* converging

conver'genza *nf* convergence

con'vergere *vi* converge

con'versa *nf* lay sister

conver'sare *vi* converse

conversa|'tore, -'trice *nmf* conversationalist

conversazi'one *nf* conversation

conversi'one *nf* conversion

con'verso *pp di* **convergere**

conver'tibile *nf Auto* convertible

conver'tire *vt* convert

conver'tirsi *vr* convert

conver'tito, -a *a* converted ● *nmf* convert

converti'tore *nm* converter

con'vesso *a* convex

convezi'one *nf* convection

convin'cente *a* convincing

con'vincere *vt* convince

con'vinto *a* convinced

convinzi'one *nf* conviction

convi'tato *nm* guest

con'vitto *nm* boarding school

convi'vente *nm* common-law husband ● *nf* common-law wife

convi'venza *nf* cohabitation

con'vivere *vi* live together

convivi'ale *a* convivial

convo'care *vt* summon; *Jur* summons; convene ‹*riunione*›

convocazi'one *nf* summoning; *Jur* summonsing; (*atto*) summons; (*riunione*) meeting

convogli'are *vt* convey; ‹*navi:*› convoy

con'voglio *nm* convoy; (*ferroviario*) train

convo'lare *vi* **~ a giuste nozze** *hum* tie the knot

convulsa'mente *adv* convulsively

convulsi'one *nf* convulsion; *fig* fit

convul'sivo *a Med* convulsive; ‹*riso*› hysterical

coope'rare *vi* co-operate

coopera'tiva *a* co-operative

cooperazi'one *nf* co-operation

coordina'mento *nm* co-ordination

coordi'nare *vt* co-ordinate

coordi'nata *nf Math* co-ordinate; **coordinate** *pl* (*su mappa*) grid reference. **coordinate** *pl* **bancarie** [bank] sort code

coordi'nato *a* co-ordinated

coordina|'tore, -'trice *nmf* co-ordinator

coordinazi'one *nf* co-ordination

co'perchio *nm* lid; (*copertura*) cover

co'perta *nf* blanket; (*copertura*) cover; *Naut* deck. **~ elettrica** electric blanket

coper'tina *nf* cover; (*di libro*) dust-jacket

co'perto *pp di* **coprire** ● *a* covered; (*vestito*) wrapped up; ‹*cielo*› overcast; ‹*piscina*› indoor ● *nm* (*a tavola*) place; (*prezzo del coperto*) cover charge; **al ~** under cover

coper'tone *nm* tarpaulin; (*gomma*) tyre

coper'tura *nf* cover; (*azione*) covering; (*di strada*) surfacing; (*di malefatta*) cover-up. **~ globale** blanket coverage

'copia *nf* copy; **bella/brutta ~** fair/rough copy; **essere la ~ spiccicata di qcno** be the spitting image of sb. **~ su carta** hardcopy. **~ pirata** pirate copy. **~ di riserva** *Comput* backup copy

copi'are *vt* copy

copia'trice *nf* copier

copi'lota *nmf* co-pilot; (*di auto*) co-driver

copi'one *nm Cinema, TV* script

copi'oso *a* copious

'coppa *nf* (*calice*) goblet; (*bicchiere*) glass; (*per gelato ecc*) dish; *Sport* cup. **~ [di] gelato** ice-cream (*served in a dish*). **~ del mondo** World Cup

cop'petta *nf* (*di ceramica, vetro*) bowl; (*di gelato*) small tub

'coppia *nf* couple; (*in carte, voga*) pair

co'prente *a* (*cipria, vernice*) thick; ‹*collant*› opaque

copri'capo *nm* head covering

coprifu'oco *nm* curfew

copri'letto *nm* bedspread

copri'mozzo *nm* hub-cap

copripiu'mino *nm* duvet cover

co'prire *vt* cover; drown [out] ‹*suono*›; hold ‹*carica*›

co'prirsi *vr* (*vestirsi*) cover oneself up; (*vestirsi pesante*) dress warmly; *fig* cover up; (*proteggersi*) cover oneself; ‹*cielo:*› become overcast

copritei'era *nm* tea cosy

co-protago'nista *nmf Cinema* co-star

'coque: alla ~ *a* ‹*uovo*› soft-boiled

co'raggio *nm* bravery, courage; (*sfacciataggine*) nerve; **~!** chin up!

coraggiosa'mente *adv* bravely, courageously

coraggi'oso *a* brave, courageous

co'rale *a* choral

co'rallo nm coral

co'rano nm Koran

co'razza nf armour; (di animali) shell

coraz'zata nf battleship

coraz'zato a ⟨nave⟩ armour-plated

corazza'tura nf armour plate, armour plating

corazzi'ere nm cuirassier

corbelle'ria nf piece of nonsense; **dire corbellerie** talk nonsense

'corda nf cord; (spago, Mus) string; (fune) rope; (cavo) cable; **essere giù di ~** be down; **dare ~ a qcno** encourage sb; **tagliare la ~** cut and run; **tenere qcno sulla ~** keep sb on tenterhooks. **corde** pl **vocali** vocal cords

cor'data nf roped party

cordi'ale a cordial ● nm (bevanda) cordial; **cordiali saluti** best wishes

cordialità nf cordiality; **~** pl (saluti) best wishes

cor'doglio nm grief; (lutto) mourning

cor'done nm cord; (schieramento) cordon. **~ ombelicale** umbilical cord. **~ sanitario** cordon sanitaire

Co'rea nf Korea

core'ano, -a a & nmf Korean

coreogra'fia nf choreography; **fare la ~ di** choreograph

core'ografo, -a nmf choreographer

Corfù nf Corfu

cori'aceo a tough

cori'andoli nmpl (di carta) confetti sg

cori'andolo nm (spezia) coriander

cori'care vt put to bed

cori'carsi vr go to bed

Co'rinto nf Corinth

co'rista nmf choir member

'corna vedi **corno**

cor'nacchia nf crow

corna'musa nf bagpipes pl

'cornea nf cornea

'corner nm inv corner; **salvarsi in ~** fig have a lucky escape

cor'netta nf Mus cornet; (del telefono) receiver

cor'netto nm (brioche) croissant. **~ acustico** ear trumpet

cor'nice nf frame

cornici'one nm cornice

cornifi'care vt fam cheat on

'corno nm (pl f **corna**) horn; **fare le corna a qcno** fam cheat on sb; **fare le corna** (per scongiuro) ≈ touch wood; **un ~!** you must be joking!; (per niente) nonsense!. **~ da caccia** French horn

Corno'vaglia nf Cornwall

cornu'copia nf cornucopia

cor'nuto a horned ● nm (fam: marito tradito) cuckold; (insulto) bastard

'coro nm chorus; Relig choir

co'rolla nf corolla

corol'lario nm corollary

co'rona nf crown; (di fiori) wreath; (rosario) rosary

corona'mento nm (di sogno) fulfilment; (di carriera) crowning achievement

coro'nare vt fulfil ⟨sogno⟩

coro'nario a ⟨arteria⟩ coronary

cor'petto nm bodice

'corpo nm body; (Mil, diplomatico) corps inv; **[a] ~ a ~** Mil hand to hand; **lottare [a] ~ a ~** have a punch-up, slug it out; **dare ~ a qcsa** give substance to sth; **buttarsi a ~ morto in qcsa** throw oneself desperately into sth; **andare di ~** move one's bowels. **~ di ballo** corps de ballet. **~ insegnante** teaching staff. **~ del reato** incriminating piece of evidence

corpo'rale a corporal

corporati'vismo nm corporatism

corpora'tura nf build

corporazi'one nf corporation

cor'poreo a bodily

cor'poso a full-bodied

corpu'lento a stout

'corpus nm inv corpus

cor'puscolo nm corpuscle

corre'dare vt (di note) supply (di with); **corredato di curriculum** accompanied by a CV

corre'dino nm (per neonato) layette

cor'redo nm (nuziale) trousseau; (di informazioni ecc) set

cor'reggere vt correct; lace ⟨bevanda⟩

corre'lare vt correlate

cor'rente a running; (in vigore) current; (frequente) everyday; ⟨inglese ecc⟩ fluent ● nf current; (d'aria) draught; **essere al ~ di qcsa** be aware of sth; **tenersi al ~** keep up to date (di with). **~ continua** direct current. **~ trasversale** cross current

corrente'mente adv ⟨parlare⟩ fluently; (comunemente) commonly

'correre vi run; (affrettarsi) hurry; Sport race; ⟨notizie:⟩ circulate; **lascia ~!** let it go!; **~ dietro a** run after; **tra loro non corre buon sangue** there is bad blood between them ● vt run; **~ un pericolo** run a risk; **corre voce che...** there's a rumour that...

correspon'sabile nmf person jointly responsible

corresponsi'one nf payment

corretta'mente adv correctly; ⟨sedersi, mangiare⟩ properly; ⟨trattare, fare qcsa⟩ right

corret'tivo nm corrective

cor'retto pp di **correggere** ● a correct; ⟨caffè⟩ with a drop of alcohol

corret|'tore, -'trice nmf **~ di bozze** proof-reader ● nm **~ grammaticale** Comput grammar checker. **~ ortografico** Comput spellcheck[er]

correzi'one nf correction. **~ di bozze** proof-reading. **~ errori** Comput error correction

cor'rida nf bullfight

corri'doio nm corridor; Aeron aisle

corri'dore, -'trice *nmf* (*automobilistico*) driver; (*ciclista*) cyclist; (*a piedi*) runner

corri'era *nf* coach, bus

corri'ere *nm* courier; (*posta*) mail; (*spedizioniere*) carrier

corri'mano *nm* banister

corrispet'tivo *nm* amount due

corrispon'dente *a* corresponding ● *nmf* correspondent

corrispon'denza *nf* correspondence; **tenersi in ~ con** correspond with; **per ~** ⟨*fare un corso*⟩ by correspondence; **corso per ~** correspondence course; **vendite per ~** mail-order [shopping]

corri'spondere *vi* correspond; ⟨*stanza:*⟩ communicate; **~ a** (*contraccambiare*) return

corri'sposto *a* ⟨*amore*⟩ reciprocated

corrobo'rare *vt* strengthen; *fig* corroborate

cor'rodere *vt* corrode

cor'rodersi *vr* corrode

cor'rompere *vt* corrupt; (*con denaro*) bribe

corrosi'one *nf* corrosion

corro'sivo *a* corrosive

cor'roso *pp di* **corrodere**

cor'rotto *pp di* **corrompere** ● *a* corrupt

corrucci'arsi *vr* be vexed

corrucci'ato *a* vexed

corru'gare *vt* wrinkle; **~ la fronte** knit one's brows

corrut'tela *nf* depravity

corruzi'one *nf* corruption; (*con denaro*) bribery

'corsa *nf* running; (*rapida*) dash; *Sport* race; (*di treno ecc*) journey; **di ~** at a run; **di gran ~** in a great hurry; **fare una ~** (*sbrigarsi*) run, hurry. **~ agli armamenti** arms race. **~ ciclistica** cycle race. **~ a ostacoli** obstacle race. **~ piana** flat racing. **~ semplice** one way [ticket]

cor'sia *nf* gangway; (*di ospedale*) ward; *Auto* lane; (*di supermercato*) aisle. **~ autobus** bus lane. **~ d'emergenza** *Auto* hard shoulder. **~ di sorpasso** fast lane, outside lane

'Corsica *nf* Corsica

cor'sivo *nm* italics *pl*; **in ~** in italics

'corso *pp di* **correre** ● *nm* course; (*strada*) main street; *Comm* circulation; (*in borsa*) price, quotation; **essere in ~** be underway; **lavori in ~** work in progress; **nel ~ di** during; **avere ~ legale** be legal tender. **~ d'acqua** waterway. **~ per corrispondenza** correspondence course; **~ di formazione professionale** training course. **~ del giorno** current daily price. **~ di laurea** degree course. **~ serale** evening class

'corso, -a *a & nmf* (*della Corsica*) Corsican

'corte *nf* [court]yard; (*Jur, regale*) court; **fare la ~ a qcno** court sb. **~ d'appello** court of appeal. **~ d'assise** ≈ crown court. **C~ di cassazione** supreme court of appeal. **C~ dei conti** ≈ National Audit Office. **C~ europea per i diritti dell'uomo** European Court of Human Rights. **C~ europea di giustizia** European Court of Justice. **~ di giustizia** court of law

cor'teccia *nf* bark

corteggia'mento *nm* courtship

corteggi'are *vt* court

corteggia'tore *nm* admirer

cor'teo *nm* procession. **~ di auto** motorcade. **~ funebre** funeral cortège. **~ nuziale** bridal party

cor'tese *a* courteous

corte'sia *nf* courtesy; **per ~** please

cortigi'ano, -a *nmf* courtier ● *nf* courtesan

cor'tile *nm* courtyard

cor'tina *nf* curtain; (*schermo*) screen

'corto *a* short; **per farla corta** to cut a long story short; **a ~ di** short of, hard up for. **~ circuito** *nm* short [circuit]

cortome'traggio *nm Cinema* short

cor'vino *a* jet-black

'corvo *nm* raven

'cosa *nf* thing; (*faccenda*) matter; *inter, rel* what; [*che*] **~** what; **nessuna ~** nothing; **ogni ~** everything; **per prima ~** first of all; **tante cose** [so] many things; (*augurio*) all the best; **~?** what?; **~ hai detto?** what did you say?; **le cose le vanno bene** she's doing all right

'cosca *nf* clan

'coscia *nf* thigh; *Culin* leg; **cosce** *pl* **di rana** frogs' legs

cosci'ente *a* conscious

cosci'enza *nf* conscience; (*consapevolezza*) consciousness; **mettersi la ~ a posto** salve one's conscience

coscienziosa'mente *adv* conscientiously

coscienzi'oso *a* conscientious

cosci'otto *nm* leg

co'scritto *nm* conscript

coscrizi'one *nf* conscription

cosi *adv* so; (*in questo modo*) like this, like that; (*perciò*) therefore; **le cose stanno ~** that's how things stand; **fermo ~!** hold it; **proprio ~!** exactly!; **basta ~!** that will do!; **ah, è ~?** it's like that, is it?; **~ so-so**; **e ~ via** and so on; **per ~ dire** so to speak; **più di ~** any more; **una ~ cara ragazza!** such a nice girl!; **è stato ~ generoso da aiutarti** he was kind enough to help you ● *conj* (*allora*) so ● *a inv* (*tale*) like that, such; **una ragazza ~** a girl like that, such a girl

cosicché *conj* and so

cosid'detto *a* so-called

co'smesi *nf* beauty treatment

co'smetico *a* cosmetic ● *nm* **cosmetici** *pl* cosmetics; (*trucchi*) make-up

'cosmico *a* cosmic

'cosmo *nm* cosmos

cosmo'nauta *nmf* cosmonaut

cosmopo'lita *a* cosmopolitan

co'spargere *vt* sprinkle; (*disseminare*) scatter; **~ il pavimento di cera** spread wax on the floor

co'spetto *nm* **al ~ di** in the presence of

co'spicuo *a* conspicuous; ⟨*somma ecc*⟩ considerable

cospi'rare *vi* conspire, plot

cospira|'tore, -'trice *nmf* conspirator, plotter

cospirazi'one *nf* conspiracy, plot

'costa *nf* coast, coastline; *Anat* rib; **sotto ~** inshore. **C~ d'Avorio** Ivory Coast. **C~ Azzurra** Côte d'Azur. **C~ Smeralda** Emerald coast (*in Sardinia*)

costà *adv* there

co'stante *a* & *nf* constant

co'stanza *nf* constancy

co'stare *vi* cost; **quanto costa?** how much is it?; **costi quel che costi** whatever the cost

co'stata *nf* chop. **~ [di manzo]** rib steak

co'stato *nm* ribs *pl*

costeggi'are *vt* (*per mare*) coast; (*per terra*) skirt

co'stei *pers pron* (*soggetto*) she; (*complemento*) her

costellazi'one *nf* constellation

coster'nato *a* dismayed

costernazi'one *nf* consternation

costi'era *nf* stretch of coast

costi'ero *a* coastal

co'stine *nfpl* (*di maiale*) spare ribs

'costing *nm inv* costing

costi'pato *a* constipated; **essere ~** (*raffreddato*) have a bad cold

costipazi'one *nf* constipation; (*raffreddore*) bad cold

costitu'ire *vt* constitute; (*essere*) be; (*formare*) form; (*nominare*) appoint

costitu'irsi *vr* (*criminale:*) give oneself up

costituzio'nale *a* constitutional

costituzional'mente *adv Pol* constitutionally

costituzi'one *nf* constitution; (*formazione*) formation

'costo *nm* cost; **a nessun ~** on no account; **a ~ di perdere la salute** at the cost of one's health; **sotto ~** at less than cost price. **~ del denaro** *Fin* cost of money. **costi** *pl* **di gestione** administration costs. **costi** *pl* **di spedizione** freight charges. **~ unitario** unit cost. **~ della vita** cost of living

'costola *nf* rib; (*di libro*) spine; **stare alle costole di qcno** follow sb around

costo'letta *nf* cutlet

co'storo *pron* (*soggetto*) they; (*complemento*) them

co'stoso *a* costly

co'stretto *pp di* **costringere**

co'stringere *vt* force, compel

costrit'tivo *a* coercive

costrizi'one *nf* compulsion

costru'ire *vt* build, construct

costrut'tivo *a* constructive

costruzi'one *nf* building, construction; (*edificio*) building

co'stui *pers pron* (*soggetto*) he; (*complemento*) him

co'stume *nm* (*usanza*) custom; (*indumento*) costume; **buon ~** vice squad; **costumi** *pl* (*morale*) morals. **~ da bagno** swim-suit; (*da uomo*) swimming trunks. **~ tradizionale** traditional costume

costu'mista *nmf* wardrobe assistant

cote'chino *nm* spiced pork sausage

co'tenna *nf* pigskin; (*della pancetta*) rind. **~ arrostita** crackling

co'togna *nf* quince

coto'letta *nf* cutlet. **~ alla milanese** veal cutlet in breadcrumbs

coto'nato *a* (*capelli*) back-combed

co'tone *nm* cotton. **~ idrofilo** cotton wool, absorbent cotton *Am*

cotoni'ficio *nm* cotton mill

'cotta *nf Relig* surplice; (*fam: innamoramento*) crush; **prendere una ~ per qcno** *fam* have a crush on sb

'cottimo *nm* piece-work

'cotto *pp di* **cuocere** ●*a* done; (*fam: innamorato*) in love; (*sbronzo*) drunk; **ben ~** well cooked; (*carne*) well done; **poco ~** undercooked; (*carne*) underdone; **troppo ~** overcooked; (*carne*) overdone

'cotton fi'oc® *nm inv* cotton bud

cot'tura *nf* cooking

'country *nm inv* country and western

cou'pon *nm inv* coupon

cou'scous *nm inv* couscous

co'vare *vt* hatch; sicken for (*malattia*); harbour (*rancore*)

co'vata *nf* brood

'covo *nm* den

co'vone *nm* sheaf

cow'boy *nm inv* cowboy

'cozza *nf* mussel. **cozze** *pl* **alla marinara** moules marinière

coz'zare *vi* **~ contro** bump into

'cozzo *nm fig* clash

C.P. *abbr* (**Casella Postale**) PO Box

crac *nm inv* crack; (*di tessuto*) rip

crack *nm* (*droga*) crack

Cra'covia *nf* Cracow

'crafen *nm inv* cream doughnut

'crampo *nm* cramp

'cranio *nm* skull

cra'tere *nm* crater

cra'vatta *nf* tie; (*a farfalla*) bow-tie

cre'anza *nf* manners; **mala ~** bad manners

cre'are *vt* create; **~ assuefazione** be habit-forming

creatività *nf* creativity

crea'tivo *a* creative

cre'ato *nm* creation

crea|'tore, -'trice *nmf* creator; **andare al ~** go to meet one's maker

crea'tura *nf* creature; (*bambino*) baby; **povera ~!** poor thing!

creazi'one *nf* creation

cre'dente *nmf* believer

cre'denza *nf* belief; *Comm* credit; (*mobile*) sideboard

credenzi'ali *nfpl* credentials

'credere *vt* believe; (*pensare*) think ●*vi* **~ in** believe in; **credo di sì** I think so; **non ti credo** I don't believe you; **non posso crederci!** I can't believe it!

'credersi vr think oneself to be; **si crede uno scrittore** he flatters himself he is a writer

cre'dibile a credible, believable

credibilità nf credibility

credi'tizio a credit attrib

'credito nm credit; (stima) esteem; **comprare a ~** buy on credit; **dare ~ a qcsa** give credence to sth; **fare ~** give credit. **~ all'esportazione** export credit. **~ inesigibile** bad debt

credi|'tore, -'trice nmf creditor

'credo nm inv credo

credulità nf credulity

'credulo a credulous

credu'lone, -a nmf simpleton

'crema nf cream; (di uova e latte) custard. **~ base per il trucco** vanishing cream. **~ depilatoria** depilatory [cream]. **~ detergente** cleansing cream. **~ idratante** moisturizer. **~ per le mani** hand cream. **~ pasticciera** confectioner's custard. **~ per la pelle** skin cream. **~ protettiva** barrier cream. **~ solare** suntan lotion. **~ per il viso** face cream

cremagli'era nf ratchet

cre'mare vt cremate

crema'torio nm crematorium

cremazi'one nf cremation

crème cara'mel nf crème caramel

creme'ria nf dairy (also selling ice cream and cakes)

Crem'lino nm Kremlin

cre'moso a creamy

cren nm horseradish

'crepa nf crack

cre'paccio nm cleft; (di ghiacciaio) crevasse

crepacu'ore nm heart-break

crepa'pelle: a ~ adv fit to burst

cre'pare vi crack; (fam: morire) kick the bucket; **~ dal ridere** laugh fit to burst

crepa'tura nf crevice

crêpe nf inv pancake

crepi'tare vi crackle

crepi'tio nm crackling

cre'puscolo nm twilight

cre'scendo nm crescendo

cre'scenza nf creamy white cheese

'crescere vi grow; (aumentare) increase, grow ● vt (allevare) bring up; (aumentare) increase

cresci'one nm watercress

'crescita nf growth; (aumento) increase, growth

cresci'uto pp di **crescere**

'cresima nf confirmation

cresi'mare vt confirm

cre'spato a crinkly

cre'spella nf pancake

'crespo a (capelli) frizzy ● nm crêpe

'cresta nf crest; (cima) peak; **abbassare la ~** become less cocky; **alzare la ~** become cocky; **sulla ~ dell'onda** on the crest of a wave

'creta nf clay

'Creta nf Crete

cre'tese a & nmf Cretan

creti'nata nf something stupid; **dire cretinate** talk nonsense

cre'tino, -a a stupid ● nmf idiot

C.R.I. abbr (**Croce Rossa Italiana**) Italian Red Cross

'cribbio int gosh!, golly!

cric nm inv jack

'cricca nf gang

'cricco nm jack

cri'ceto nm hamster

'cricket nm cricket

crimi'nale a & nmf criminal

criminalità nf crime. **~ organizzata** organized crime

'crimine nm crime

criminolo'gia nf criminology

crimi'nologo, -a nmf criminologist

crimi'noso a criminal

'crine nm horsehair

crini'era nf mane

crino'lina nf crinoline

'cripta nf crypt

crisan'temo nm chrysanthemum

'crisi nf inv crisis; Med fit; **essere in ~ di astinenza** be having withdrawal symptoms, be cold turkey fam. **~ di nervi** hysterics. **~ del settimo anno** seven-year itch

cristal'lino a crystal clear ● nm crystalline lens

cristalliz'zare vt crystallize

cristalliz'zarsi vr crystallize; (fig: parola, espressione) become part of the language

cri'stallo nm crystal

Cristia'nesimo nm Christianity

cristianità nf Christendom

cristi'ano, -a a & nmf Christian

'Cristo nm Christ; **avanti ~** BC; **dopo ~** AD; **un povero c~** a poor beggar

cri'terio nm criterion; (buon senso) [common] sense

'critica nf criticism; (recensione) review; **fare la ~ di** review (film, libro)

criti'care vt criticize

'critico a critical ● nm critic. **~ letterario** literary critic

criti'cone, -a nmf fault finder

crittazi'one nf **~ [dei] dati** Comput data encryption

crivel'lare vt riddle (**di** with)

cri'vello nm sieve

cro'ato, -a a & nmf Croatian, Croat

Cro'azia nf Croatia

croc'cante a crisp ● nm type of crunchy nut biscuit

croc'chetta nf croquette

'crocchia nf bun

'crocchio nm cluster

'croce nf cross; **a occhio e ~** roughly; **fare testa e ~** toss a coin; **fare o mettere una ~ sopra qcsa** fig forget about sth; **mettere in ~** (criticare) crucify; (tormentare) nag nonstop. **C~ Rossa** Red Cross

crocero'ssina nf Red Cross nurse

croce'via nm inv crossroads sg

croci'ata nf crusade

croci'ato *a* cruciform ● *nm* crusader
cro'cicchio *nm* crossroads *sg*
croci'era *nf* cruise; **velocità di ~** cruising speed
croci'figgere *vt* crucify
crocifissi'one *nf* crucifixion
croci'fisso *pp di* **crocifiggere** ● *a* crucified ● *nm* crucifix
crogi'olo *nm* crucible; *fig* melting pot
crogio'larsi *vr* bask
crogiu'olo *nm* = **crogiolo**
crois'sant *nm inv* croissant
crol'lare *vi* collapse; ⟨*prezzi:*⟩ slump
'crollo *nm* collapse; (*dei prezzi*) slump
'croma *nf* quaver
cro'mato *a* chromium-plated
'cromo *nm* chrome
cromo'soma *nm* chromosome
'cronaca *nf* chronicle; (*di giornale*) news; *TV, Radio* commentary; **fatto di ~** news item. **~ mondana** gossip column. **~ nera** crime news
'cronico *a* chronic
cro'nista *nmf* reporter; (*di partita*) commentator
croni'storia *nf* chronicle
cro'nografo *nm* chronograph
cronolo'gia *nf* chronology
cronologica'mente *adv* chronologically
crono'logico *a* chronological
cronome'traggio *nm* timing
cronome'trare *vt* time
cronome'trista *nmf Sport* timekeeper
cro'nometro *nm* chronometer; *Sport* stopwatch
cross *nm* (*corsa campestre*) cross-country; (*motocross*) motocross
cros'sista *nmf* scrambler; (*a piedi*) cross-country runner
'crosta *nf* crust; (*di formaggio*) rind; (*di ferita*) scab; (*quadro*) daub
cro'staceo *nm* shellfish
cro'stata *nf* tart. **~ di frutta** fruit tart. **~ di mele** apple pie
cro'stino *nm* croûton; **crostini** *pl* pieces of toasted bread served as a starter
croupi'er *nmf inv* croupier
crucci'are *vt* torment
crucci'arsi *vr* torment oneself
'cruccio *nm* torment
cruci'ale *a* crucial
cruci'verba *nm inv* crossword [puzzle]
cru'dele *a* cruel
crudel'mente *adv* cruelly
crudeltà *nf* cruelty
'crudo *a* raw; ⟨*linguaggio*⟩ crude
cru'ento *a* bloody
cru'miro *nm* blackleg, scab
'crusca *nf* bran
cru'scotto *nm* dashboard
C.S.I. *nf abbr* (**Comunità degli Stati Indipendenti**) CIS
'Cuba *nf* Cuba
cu'bano, -a *a & nmf* Cuban
cu'betto *nm* **~ di ghiaccio** ice cube
'cubico *a* cubic

cu'bismo *nm* cubism
cu'bista *a & nmf* cubist
cubi'tale *a* **a caratteri cubitali** in enormous letters
'cubo *nm* cube
cuc'cagna *nf* abundance; (*baldoria*) merry-making; **paese della ~** land of plenty
cuc'cetta *nf* (*su un treno*) couchette; *Naut* berth
cucchiai'ata *nf* spoonful
cucchia'ino *nm* teaspoon; (*contenuto*) teaspoon[ful]
cucchi'aio *nm* spoon; **un ~** a spoon[ful] (**di** of); **al ~** ⟨*dolce*⟩ creamy. **~ di legno** wooden spoon. **~ da minestra** soup-spoon. **~ tavola** tablespoon; (*contenuto*) tablespoon[ful]
cucchiai'one *nm* serving spoon
'cuccia *nf* basket; (*in giardino*) kennel; **[fa' la] ~!** down!
cuccio'lata *nf* litter
'cucciolo *nm* puppy
cu'cina *nf* kitchen; (*il cucinare*) cooking; (*cibo*) food; (*apparecchio*) cooker; **far da ~** cook; **libro di ~** cook[ery] book. **~ a gas** gas cooker. **~ componibile** fitted kitchen. **~ economica** cooker
cuci'nare *vt* cook
cuci'nino *nm* kitchenette
cu'cire *vt* sew; **macchina per ~** sewing-machine; **cucilo a macchina** do it on the machine
cu'cito *nm* sewing
cuci'tura *nf* seam
cucù *nm inv* cuckoo; **~!** peekaboo!
'cuculo *nm* cuckoo
'cuffia *nf* bonnet; (*ricevitore*) headphones *pl*. **~ da bagno** bathing cap
cu'gino, -a *nmf* cousin
'cui *pron rel* (*persona: con prep*) who[m]; (*cose, animali: con prep*) which; (*tra articolo e nome*) whose; **la persona con ~ ho parlato** the person I spoke to, the person to whom I spoke *fml*; **la ditta per ~ lavoro** the company I work for, the company for which I work; **l'amico il ~ libro è stato pubblicato** the friend whose book was published; **in ~** (*dove*) where; (*quando*) that; **per ~** (*perciò*) so; **la città in ~ vivo** the city I live in, the city where I live; **il giorno in ~ l'ho visto** the day [that] I saw him
cu'latta *nf* breech
culi'naria *nf* cookery
culi'nario *a* culinary
'culla *nf* cradle
cul'lare *vt* rock; *fig* cherish ⟨*sogno, speranza*⟩
cul'larsi *vr* **~ nella speranza di** *liter* cherish the fond hope that
culmi'nante *a* culminating
culmi'nare *vi* culminate
'culmine *nm* peak
'culo *nm vulg* arse; (*fortuna*) luck; **prendere qcno per il ~** take the piss out of sb
'culto *nm* cult; *Relig* religion; (*adorazione*) worship

cul'tura *nf* culture. **~ generale** general knowledge. **~ di massa** mass culture
cultu'rale *a* cultural
cultu'rismo *nm* body-building
cultu'rista *nmf* body-builder
cu'mino *nm* **~ nero** cumin
cumula'tivo *a* cumulative; ⟨*prezzo*⟩ all-in, all-inclusive; **biglietto ~** group ticket
'cumulo *nm* pile; (*mucchio*) heap; (*nuvola*) cumulus
'cuneo *nm* wedge
cu'netta *nf* gutter
cu'nicolo *nm* tunnel
cu'ocere *vt* cook; fire ⟨*ceramica*⟩ ● *vi* cook; ⟨*ceramica*⟩ fire
cu'oco, -a *nmf* cook
cu'oia *nfpl* **tirare le ~** *fam* kick the bucket
cu'oio *nm* leather. **~ capelluto** scalp
cu'ore *nm* heart; **cuori** *pl* (*carte*) hearts; **di [buon] ~** ⟨*persona*⟩ kind-hearted; **di tutto ~** wholeheartedly; **ti ringrazio di tutto ~** many thanks; **nel profondo del ~** in one's heart of hearts; **nel ~ della notte** in the middle of the night; **senza ~** heartless; **mettersi il ~ in pace** come to terms with it; **parlare a ~ aperto** have a heart-to-heart (**con** with); **stare a ~ a qcno** be very important to sb. **~ tenero** (*persona*) softy
cupa'mente *adv* darkly
cupi'digia *nf* greed
Cu'pido *nm* Cupid
'cupo *a* gloomy; (*voce*) deep
'cupola *nf* dome; **a ~** domed
'cura *nf* care; (*amministrazione*) management; *Med* treatment; **aver ~ di** look after; **a ~ di** ⟨*libro*⟩ edited by; **in ~** under treatment; **fare delle cure termali** take the waters. **~ dimagrante** diet
cu'rabile *a* curable
cu'rante *a* **medico ~** GP, doctor
cu'rare *vt* take care of, look after; *Med* treat; (*guarire*) cure; edit ⟨*testo*⟩
cu'rarsi *vr* take care of oneself, look after oneself; **~ dei fatti propri** mind one's own business

cu'rato *nm* parish priest
cura‖**tore, -'trice** *nmf* trustee; (*di testo*) editor. **~ fallimentare** official receiver
'curcuma *nf* turmeric
curcu'mina *nf* turmeric
'curdo, -a *nmf* Kurd ● *a* Kurdish
'curia *nf* curia
curio'saggine *nf* nosiness
curio'sare *vi* be curious; (*mettere il naso*) pry (**in** into); (*nei negozi*) look around
curiosità *nf inv* curiosity
curi'oso *a* curious; (*strano*) odd, curious ● *nm* busybody
'curling *nm inv* *Sport* curling
cur'ricolo *nm* curriculum
cur'riculum *nm inv* curriculum
'curry *nm inv* curry. **~ in polvere** curry powder
cur'sore *nm* *Comput* cursor
'curva *nf* curve; (*stradale*) bend. **~ a gomito** dogleg. **~ di apprendimento** learning curve
cur'vare *vt/i* bend, curve
cur'varsi *vr* bend, curve
'curvo *a* curved; (*piegato*) bent
cusci'netto *nm* pad; *Mech* bearing. **~ puntaspilli** pincushion. **~ a sfere** ball bearing
cu'scino *nm* cushion; (*guanciale*) pillow. **~ gonfiabile** air cushion
cu'scus *nm inv* couscous
'cuspide *nf* spire
cu'stode *nm* caretaker; (*di abitazione*) concierge; (*di fabbrica*) guard; (*di museo*) custodian. **~ giudiziario** official receiver
cu'stodia *nf* care; *Jur* custody; (*astuccio*) case; **ottenere la ~ di** get custody of. **~ cautelare** remand
custo'dire *vt* keep; (*badare*) look after
cu'taneo *a* skin *attrib*
'cute *nf* skin
cu'ticola *nf* cuticle
'cutter *nm inv* cutter
CV *abbr* (**cavallo vapore**) hp
cyber'spazio *nm* cyberspace
cy'clette® *nf inv* exercise bicycle

....

Dd

....

da *prep* from; (*con verbo passivo*) by; (*moto a luogo*) to; (*moto per luogo*) through; (*stato in luogo*) at; (*temporale*) since; (*continuativo*) for; (*causale*) with; (*in qualità di*) as; (*con caratteristica*) with; (*come*) like; **da Roma a Milano** from Rome to Milan; **staccare un quadro dalla parete** take a picture off the wall; **i bambini dai 5 ai 10 anni** children between 5 and 10; **vedere qcsa da vicino/lontano** see sth from up close/from a dis-

tance; **amato da tutti** loved by everybody; **scritto da** written by; **andare dal panettiere** go to the baker's; **passo da te più tardi** I'll come over to your place later; **passiamo da qui** let's go this way; **un appuntamento dal dentista** an appointment at the dentist's; **il treno passa da Venezia** the train goes through Venice; **dall'anno scorso** since last year; **vivo qui da due anni** I've been living here for two years; **da domani** from tomorrow; **piangere dal dolore** cry with pain; **ho molto da fare** I have a lot to do; **occhiali da sole** sunglasses; **qualcosa da mangiare** something to eat; **un uomo dai capelli scuri** a man with dark hair; **è un oggetto da poco** it's not worth much; **da solo** alone; **l'ho fatto da solo** I did it by myself; **si è fatto da sé** he is a self-made man; **vive da re** he lives like a king; **non è da lui** it's not like him

dab'bene *a* honest

dac'capo *adv* again; (*dall'inizio*) from the beginning

dacché *conj* since

dada'ismo *nm* (*arte*) Dadaism

dada'ista *a & nmf* Dadaist

'dado *nm* dice; *Culin* stock cube; *Techn* nut. ~ **ad alette** wing nut

daf'fare *nm* work

'dagli = da + gli

'dai¹ = da + i

'dai² *int* come on!; ~, **non fare così!** come on, don't be like that!; ~, **sbrigati!** come on, get a move on!

'daino *nm* deer; (*pelle*) buckskin

dal = da + il

'dalla = da + la

'dalle = da + le

'dallo = da + lo

'dalia *nf* dahlia

'dalmata *nmf* (*cane*) Dalmatian

Dal'mazia *nf* Dalmatia

dal'tonico *a* colour-blind

'dama *nf* lady; (*nei balli*) partner; (*gioco*) draughts. ~ **di compagnia** lady's companion. ~ **di corte** lady-in-waiting

dama'scato *a* damask

da'masco *nm* (*tessuto*) damask

dame'rino *nm* (*bellimbusto*) dandy

dami'gella *nf* (*di sposa*) bridesmaid

damigi'ana *nf* demijohn

dam'meno *adv* **non essere** ~ be no less good (**di** than)

DAMS *nm abbr* (**Discipline delle Arti, della Musica e dello Spettacolo**) (*corso di laurea*) degree in fine art, music and drama

da'naro *nm* = denaro

dana'roso *a* (*fam: ricco*) loaded

da'nese *a* Danish ● *nmf* Dane ● *nm* (*lingua*) Danish

Dani'marca *nf* Denmark

dan'nare *vt* damn; **far** ~ **qcno** drive sb mad

dan'narsi *vr fig* wear oneself out; ~ **l'anima** (**a fare qcsa**) wear oneself out (doing sth)

dan'nato, -a *a* damned, damn *fam* ● *nmf* damned person; **lavorare/studiare come un** ~ *fig* work/study like mad

dannazi'one *nf* damnation

danneggia'mento *nm* damage

danneggi'are *vt* damage; (*nuocere*) harm

danneggi'ato *a* *Jur* injured

'danno *nm* damage; (*a persona*) harm; **danni** *pl* damage

dan'noso *a* harmful

dan'tesco *a* Dantean, Dantesque

danubi'ano *a* Danubian

Da'nubio *nm* Danube

'danza *nf* dance; (*il danzare*) dancing. ~ **folcloristica** country dancing

dan'zante *a* **serata** ~ dance

dan'zare *vi* dance

danza'tore, -'trice *nmf* dancer. **danzatrice del ventre** belly dancer

dapper'tutto *adv* everywhere

dap'poco *a* worthless

dap'prima *adv* at first

Darda'nelli *nmpl* **i** ~ the Dardanelles

'dardo *nm* dart

'dare *vt* give; sit (*esame*); have (*festa*); ~ **qcsa a qcno** give sb sth; ~ **da mangiare a qcno** give sb something to eat; ~ **fuoco a qcsa** set fire to sth; ~ **il benvenuto a qcno** welcome sb; ~ **la buonanotte a qcno** say good night to sb; ~ **del tu/del lei a qcno** address sb as "tu"/"lei"; ~ **del cretino a qcno** call sb an idiot; ~ **qcsa per scontato** take sth for granted; ~ **fastidio a** annoy; ~ **cosa danno alla TV stasera?** what's on TV tonight?; **darle a qcno** (*picchiare*) give sb a walloping ● *vi* ~ **nell'occhio** be conspicuous; ~ **alla testa** go to one's head; ~ **su** (*finestra, casa:*) look on to; ~ **sui** *o* **ai nervi a qcno** get on sb's nerves ● *nm Comm* debit

'darsena *nf* dock

'darsi *vr* (*scambiarsi*) give each other; ~ **da fare** get down to it; **si è dato tanto da fare** he went to so much trouble!; ~ **a** (*cominciare*) take up; ~ **al bere** take to drink; ~ **per** (*malato*) pretend to be; ~ **per vinto** give up; **può** ~ maybe

darvini'ano *a* Darwinian

darvi'nista *nmf* Darwinist

'data *nf* date; **di lunga** ~ old-established. ~ **di emissione** date of issue. ~ **di nascita** date of birth. ~ **di scadenza** expiry date; (*su cibo*) best before date

data'base *nm inv* database. ~ **relazionale** relational database

da'tabile *a* dateable

da'tare *vt* date; **a** ~ **da** as from

da'tario *nm* (*su orologio*) calendar

da'tato *a* dated

da'tivo *nm* dative

'dato *a* given; (*dedito*) addicted; ~ **che** seeing that, given that ● *nm* datum; **dati** *pl* data. ~ **di fatto** well established fact

da'tore *nm* giver. ~ **di lavoro** employer

'dattero *nm* date

dattilogra'fare *vt/i* type; ~ **a tastiera cieca** touch-type

dattilogra'fia *nf* typing. ~ **a tastiera cieca** touch-typing

datti'lografo, -a *nmf* typist

dattilo'scritto *a* (*copia*) typewritten, typed

dat'torno *adv* **togliersi** ~ clear off

da'vanti *adv* before; (*dirimpetto*) opposite; (*di fronte*) in front ● *a inv* front ● *nm* front; ~ **di dietro** (*maglia*) back-to-front · ~ **a** *prep* before, in front of; **passare** ~ **a** pass, go past

davan'zale *nm* window sill

da'vanzo *adv* **ce n'è ~** there is more than enough

dav'vero *adv* really; **per ~** in earnest; **dici ~?** honestly?

dazi'ario *a* excise

'dazio *nm* duty; (*ufficio*) customs *pl.* **dazi** *pl* **doganali** customs duties. **~ d'importazione** import duty

D.C. *nf abbr* (**Democrazia Cristiana**) Christian Democratic Party

d.C. *abbr* (**dopo Cristo**) AD

D.D.T. *nm* (*insetticida*) DDT

'dea *nf* goddess

deambula'torio *a* ambulatory

debel'lare *vt* defeat

debili'tante *a* weakening

debili'tare *vt* weaken

debili'tarsi *vr* become debilitated

debilitazi'one *nf* debilitation

debita'mente *adv* duly

'debito *a* due; **a tempo ~** in due course ● *nm* debt. **~ pubblico** national debt

debi'|tore, -'trice *nmf* debtor

'debole *a* weak; (*luce*) dim; (*suono*) faint ● *nm* weak point; **avere un ~ per qcno** have a soft spot for sb; **avere un ~ per qcsa** have a weakness for sth

debo'lezza *nf* weakness

debor'dare *vi* overflow

debosci'ato *a* debauched

debrai'ata *nf Auto* declutching

debut'tante *a* beginner ● *nmf* beginner; (*attore*) actor/actress making his/her début

debut'tare *vi* make one's début

de'butto *nm* début

'decade *nf* period of ten days

deca'dente *a* decadent

decaden'tismo *nm* decadence

deca'denza *nf* decline; *Jur* loss

deca'dere *vi* lapse

decadi'mento *nm* (*delle arti*) decline

deca'duto *a* (*persona*) impoverished; (*decreto, norma*) no longer in force

decaffei'nato *a* decaffeinated ● *nm* decaffeinated coffee, decaf *fam*

deca'grammo *nm* decagram

decal'care *vt* trace

decalcifi'carsi *vr* become brittle

decalcificazi'one *nf* (*condizione*) brittle bones

decalcoma'nia *nf* transfer

de'calitro *nm* decalitre

de'calogo *nm fig* rule book

de'cametro *nm* decametre

de'cano *nm* dean

decan'tare *vt* (*lodare*) praise

decapi'tare *vt* decapitate; behead (*condannato*)

decapitazi'one *nf* decapitation; beheading

decappot'tabile *a* convertible

decappot'tare *vt* take down the hood of

'decathlon *nm inv* decathlon

de'cedere *vi* (*morire*) die

dece'duto *a* deceased

dece'lerare *vt/i* slow down, decelerate

decelerazi'one *nf* deceleration

decen'nale *a* ten-yearly ● *nm* (*anniversario*) tenth anniversary

de'cenne *a* (*bambino*) ten-year-old

de'cennio *nm* decade

de'cente *a* decent

decente'mente *adv* decently

decentraliz'zare *vt* decentralize

decentra'mento *nm* decentralization

decen'trare *vt* decentralize

de'cenza *nf* decency

de'cesso *nm* death, decease *fml*; **atto di ~** death certificate

'decibel *nm inv* decibel

de'cidere *vt* decide; settle (*questione*)

de'cidersi *vr* make up one's mind

deci'frabile *a* decipherable

deci'frare *vt* decipher; (*documenti cifrati*) decode

decifrazi'one *nf* deciphering

de'cigrado *nm* tenth of a degree

deci'grammo *nm* decigram[me]

de'cilitro *nm* decilitre

deci'male *a* decimal

deci'mare *vt* decimate

de'cimetro *nm* decimetre

'decimo *a & nm* tenth

de'cina *nf Math* ten; **una ~ di** (*circa dieci*) about ten

decisa'mente *adv* definitely, decidedly

decisio'nale *a* decision-making

decisi'one *nf* decision; **prendere una ~** make *or* take a decision; **con ~** decisively

decisio'nismo *nm* tendency to make decisions without consulting others

decisio'nista *nmf* person who does not consult others before making decisions

deci'sivo *a* decisive

de'ciso *pp di* **decidere** ● *a* decided

decla'mare *vt/i* declaim

declama'torio *a* (*stile*) declamatory

declas'sare *vt* downgrade

decli'nabile *a Gram* declinable; (*offerta*) that can be refused

decli'nare *vt* decline; turn down, refuse (*invito*); **~ ogni responsabilità** disclaim all responsibility ● *vi* go down; (*tramontare*) set

declinazi'one *nf Gram* declension

de'clino *nm* decline; **in ~** (*popolarità*) on the decline

de'clivio *nm* downward slope

dé'co *a inv* Art Deco

deco'difica *nf* decoding

decodifi'care *vt* decode

decodifica'tore *nm TV* descrambler

decodificazi'one *nf* decoding

decol'lare *vi* take off

décolle'té *a inv* low cut ● *nm inv* low neckline

de'collo *nm* take-off

decolonizzazi'one *nf* decolonization

decolo'rante *nm* bleach

decolo'rare *vt* bleach

decolorazi'one *nf* bleaching

decom'porre *vt* decompose

decom'porsi *vr* decompose
decomposizi'one *nf* decomposition
decompressi'one *nf* decompression
deconcen'trarsi *vr* become distracted
deconge'lare *vt* defrost
decongestio'nare *vt Med, fig* relieve congestion in
decontami'nare *vt Techn* decontaminate
decontaminazi'one *nf* decontamination
decontrazi'one *nf* relaxation
deco'rare *vt* decorate
decora'tivo *a* decorative
deco'rato *a* (ornato) decorated
decora|'tore, -'trice *nmf* decorator
decorazi'one *nf* decoration. **~ floreale** flower arranging
de'coro *nm* decorum
decorosa'mente *adv* decorously
deco'roso *a* dignified
decor'renza *nf* **~ dal…** with effect from…, effective…
de'correre *vi* pass; **a ~ da** with effect from
de'corso *pp di* **decorrere** ● *nm* passing; *Med* course
decre'mento *nm* decrease
de'crepito *a* decrepit
decre'scente *a* decreasing
de'crescere *vi* decrease; ⟨prezzi:⟩ go down; ⟨acque:⟩ subside
decre'tare *vt* decree; **~ lo stato d'emergenza** declare a state of emergency
de'creto *nm* decree. **~ ingiuntivo** decree. **~ legge** decree which has the force of law. **~ legislativo** decree requiring the approval of Parliament
decre'tone *nm Pol* portmanteau bill
de'cubito *nm* **piaghe da ~** bedsores
decur'tare *vt* reduce
decurtazi'one *nf* reduction
'dedalo *nm* maze
'dedica *nf* dedication
dedi'care *vt* dedicate
dedi'carsi *vr* dedicate oneself
'dedito *a* **~ a** given to; (assorto) engrossed in; addicted to ⟨vizi⟩
dedizi'one *nf* dedication
de'dotto *pp di* **dedurre** ● *a* deduced
dedu'cibile *a* ⟨tassa⟩ allowable
de'durre *vt* deduce; (sottrarre) deduct
dedut'tivo *a* deductive
deduzi'one *nf* deduction
défail'lance *nf inv* (cedimento) collapse
defal'care *vt* deduct
defalcazi'one *nf* deduction
defe'care *vi* defecate
defecazi'one *nf* defecation
defene'strare *vt fig* remove from office
defe'rente *a* deferential
defe'renza *nf* deference
deferi'mento *nm* referral
defe'rire *vt Jur* remit
defezio'nare *vi* (abbandonare) defect
defezi'one *nf* defection
defezio'nista *nmf* defector
defici'ente *a* (mancante) deficient; *Med*

mentally deficient ● *nmf* mental defective; *pej* half-wit
defici'enza *nf* deficiency; (lacuna) gap; *Med* mental deficiency
'deficit *nm inv* deficit, shortfall; **essere in ~** be in deficit
defici'tario *a* ⟨bilancio⟩ deficit *attrib*; ⟨sviluppo⟩ insufficient
defi'larsi *vr* (scomparire) slip away; **~ da qcsa** sneak away from sth
défi'lé *nm inv* fashion show
defi'nibile *a* definable; **~ dall'utente** *Comput* user-definable
defi'nire *vt* define; (risolvere) settle
definitiva'mente *adv* for good
defini'tivo *a* definitive
defi'nito *a* definite
definizi'one *nf* definition; (soluzione) settlement
defiscaliz'zare *vt* abolish the tax on
defiscalizzazi'one *nf* abolition of tax
defla'grare *vt* (esplodere) explode
deflagrazi'one *nf* (esplosione) explosion
deflazio'nare *vt* deflate
deflazi'one *nf* deflation
deflazio'nistico *a* deflationary
deflet'tore *nm Auto* quarterlight
deflu'ire *vi* ⟨liquidi:⟩ flow away; ⟨persone:⟩ stream out
de'flusso *nm* (di marea) ebb
defogli'ante *a* defoliating ● *nm* defoliant
deforestazi'one *nf* deforestation
defor'mante *a* **artrite ~** acute arthritis
defor'mare *vt* deform ⟨arto⟩; *fig* distort
defor'marsi *vr* lose its shape
defor'mato *a* warped
deformazi'one *nf* (di fatti) distortion; **è una ~ professionale** put it down to the job
de'forme *a* deformed
deformità *nf inv* deformity
defrau'dare *vt* defraud
de'funto, -a *a & nmf* deceased
degene'rare *vi* degenerate
degene'rativo *a* ⟨processo⟩ degenerative
degene'rato *a* degenerate
degenerazi'one *nf* degeneration
de'genere *a* degenerate
de'gente *a* bedridden ● *nmf* patient
de'genza *nf* confinement. **~ ospedaliera** stay in hospital
'degli = di + gli
deglu'tire *vt* swallow
deglutizi'one *nf* swallowing
de'gnare *vt* **~ qcno/qcsa di uno sguardo** deign *or* condescend to look at sb/sth
de'gnarsi *vr* deign, condescend
'degno *a* worthy; (meritevole) deserving. **~ di lode** praiseworthy. **~ di nota** noteworthy
degrada'mento *nm* degradation
degra'dante *a* demeaning
degra'dare *vt* degrade
degra'darsi *vr* lower oneself; ⟨città:⟩ fall into a state of disrepair
degradazi'one *nf* degradation
de'grado *nm* deterioration; **~ ambientale**

environmental damage. ~ **urbano** urban blight, urban decay

degu'stare vt taste

degustazi'one nf tasting. ~ **di vini** wine tasting

'dei = **di** + **i**

deindiciz'zare vt deindex

déjà vu nm inv déjà vu

del = **di** + **il**

dela'tore, -'trice nmf [police] informer

delazi'one nf informing

'delega nf proxy; **legge** ~ law that does not require Parliamentary approval

dele'gante nmf Jur representative

dele'gare vt delegate

dele'gato nm delegate

delegazi'one nf delegation

dele'terio a harmful

del'fino nm dolphin; (stile di nuoto) butterfly [stroke]; **nuotare a** ~ do the butterfly

de'libera nf bylaw

delibe'rante a (organo) decision making

delibe'rare vt/i deliberate; ~ **su/in** rule on/ in

deliberata'mente adv deliberately

delibe'rato a (intenzionale) deliberate

delicata'mente adv delicately

delica'tezza nf delicacy; (fragilità) frailty; (tatto) tact

deli'cato a delicate; (salute) frail; (suono, colore) soft

deligitti'mare vt delegitimize

delimi'tare vt define

delimita'tivo a defining

delimitazi'one nf definition

deline'are vt outline

deline'arsi vr be outlined; fig take shape

deline'ato a outlined

delineazi'one nf outline

delinqu'ente nmf delinquent. ~ **mino-renne** young offender

delinqu'enza nf delinquency. ~ **minorile** juvenile crime

delinquenzi'ale a criminal

de'linquere vi commit a criminal act; **associazione per** ~ conspiracy [to commit a crime]; **istigazione a** ~ incitement to crime

de'liquio nm **cadere in** ~ swoon

deli'rante a Med delirious; (assurdo) insane; (sfrenato) frenzied

deli'rare vi be delirious

de'lirio nm delirium; fig frenzy; **mandare/andare in** ~ fig send/go into a frenzy

de'litto nm crime. ~ **passionale** crime of passion

delittu'oso a criminal

de'lizia nf delight

delizi'are vt delight

delizi'arsi vr ~ **di** delight in

delizi'oso a delightful; (cibo) delicious

'della = **di** + **la**

'delle = **di** + **le**

'dello = **di** + **lo**

'delta nm inv delta

delta'plano nm hang-glider; **fare** ~ go hang-gliding

deluci'dare vt fig clarify

delucidazi'one nf clarification

delu'dente a disappointing

de'ludere vt disappoint

delusi'one nf disappointment

de'luso a disappointed; **essere** ~ **di qcsa/qcno** be disillusioned with sth/sb

dema'gogico a popularity-seeking, demagogic

dema'gogo nm demagogue

deman'dare vt entrust

demani'ale a (proprietà) government attrib

de'manio nm government property

demar'care vt demarcate

demarcazi'one nf demarcation; **linea di** ~ demarcation line

de'mente a demented

de'menza nf dementia. ~ **senile** senile dementia

demenzi'ale a (assurdo) zany

de'merito nm **nota di** ~ demerit mark

demilitariz'zare vt demilitarize

demilitarizzazi'one nf demilitarization

demistifi'care vt debunk

demistifica'tore, -'trice nmf debunker

demistifica'torio a debunking

demistificazi'one nf debunking

demitiz'zare vt demythologize

demitizzazi'one nf demythologization

democratica'mente adv democratically

demo'cratico a democratic

democratiz'zare vt democratize

democra'zia nf democracy

democristi'ano, -a a & nmf Christian Democrat

'demodisk nm inv Comput demo disk

demogra'fia nf demography

demo'grafico a demographic; **incremento** ~ increase in population

demo'lire vt demolish

demo'lito a demolished

demolizi'one nf demolition

'demone nm demon

demo'niaco a demonic

de'monio nm demon

demoniz'zare vt demonize

demonizzazi'one nf demonization

demoraliz'zante a demoralizing

demoraliz'zare vt demoralize

demoraliz'zarsi vr become demoralized

demoraliz'zato a demoralized

de'mordere vi give up

demoti'vare vt demotivate

demoti'varsi vr become demotivated

demoti'vato a demotivated

demotivazi'one nf demotivation

de'nari nmpl (nelle carte) diamonds

de'naro nm money

denatu'rato a **alcol** ~ methylated spirits

denazionaliz'zare vt denationalize

deni'grare vt denigrate

denigra'tore, -'trice a denigrating ● nmf denigrator

denigra'torio *a* denigratory
denigrazi'one *nf* denigration
denomi'nare *vt* name
denomi'narsi *vr* be named
denomina'tivo *a* denominative
denomina'tore *nm* denominator
denominazi'one *nf* denomination. **~ di origine controllata** *mark guaranteeing the quality of a wine*
deno'tare *vt* denote
denotazi'one *nf* denotation
densa'mente *adv* densely
densità *nf* density. **ad alta/bassa ~ di popolazione** densely/sparsely populated
'denso *a* thick, dense
den'tale *a* dental
den'tario *a* dental
den'tata *nf* bite
den'tato *a* ‹*lama*› serrated
denta'tura *nf* teeth *pl*; *Techn* serration
'dente *nm* tooth; (*di forchetta*) prong; (*di montagna*) jagged peak; **al ~** *Culin* just slightly firm; **lavarsi i denti** brush one's teeth. **~ del giudizio** wisdom tooth. **~ di latte** milk tooth. **~ di leone** *Bot* dandelion
'dentice *nm* dentex (*type of sea bream*)
denti'era *nf* dentures *pl*, false teeth *pl*; **mettersi la ~** put one's false teeth in
denti'fricio *nm* toothpaste
den'tista *nmf* dentist
'dentro *adv* in, inside; (*in casa*) indoors; **da ~** from within; **qui ~** in here; **metter ~** (*fam: in prigione*) lock up, put inside ● *prep* in, inside; (*di tempo*) within, by ● *nm* inside
denucleariz'zare *vt* denuclearize
denuclEariz'zato *a* nuclear-free, denuclearized
denuclearizzazi'one *nf* denuclearization
denu'dare *vt* bare
denu'darsi *vr* strip
de'nuncia *nf* denunciation; (*alla polizia*) reporting; **fare una ~** draw up a report. **~ dei redditi** income tax return
denunci'are *vt* denounce; (*accusare*) report
de'nunzia = **denuncia**
denu'trito *a* underfed
denutrizi'one *nf* malnutrition
deodo'rante *a* & *nm* deodorant. **~ antitraspirante** antiperspirant. **~ a sfera** roll-on
deodo'rare *vt* deodorize
deontolo'gia *nf* (*etica professionale*) code of conduct
depenaliz'zare *vt* decriminalize
depenalizzazi'one *nf* decriminalization
dépen'dance *nf inv* outbuilding
depe'ribile *a* perishable
deperi'mento *nm* wasting away; (*di merci*) deterioration
depe'rire *vi* waste away
depe'rito *a* wasted
depi'lare *vt* depilate
depi'larsi *vr* shave ‹*gambe*›; pluck ‹*sopracciglia*›

depila'tore *a* depilatory ● *nm* (*apparecchio*) hair remover
depila'torio *nm* depilatory
depilazi'one *nf* hair removal. **~ diatermica** electrolysis
depi'staggio *nm fig* diversionary manoeuvre
depi'stare *vt fig* throw off the track
dépli'ant *nm inv* brochure, leaflet
deplo'rabile *a* deplorable
deplo'rare *vt* deplore; (*dolersi di*) grieve over
deplo'revole *a* deplorable
depoliticiz'zare *vt* depoliticize
de'porre *vt* put down; lay down ‹*armi*›; lay ‹*uova*›; (*togliere da una carica*) depose; (*testimoniare*) testify
depor'tare *vt* deport
depor'tato, -a *nmf* deportee
deportazi'one *nf* deportation
deposi'tante *nmf Fin* depositor
deposi'tare *vt* deposit; (*lasciare in custodia*) leave; (*in magazzino*) store
deposi'tario, -a *nmf* (*di segreto*) repository
deposi'tarsi *vr* settle
de'posito *nm* deposit; (*luogo*) warehouse; *Mil* depot. **~ d'armi** arms dump. **~ bagagli** left-luggage office, baggage checkroom *Am*. **~ bancario** deposit account. **~ bancario vincolato** fixed term deposit account
deposizi'one *nf* deposition; (*da una carica*) removal
de'posto *a* deposed
depotenzi'are *vt* weaken
depra'vare *vt* deprave
depra'vato *a* depraved
depravazi'one *nf* depravity
depre'cabile *a* appalling
depre'care *vt* deprecate
depre'dare *vt* plunder
depressio'nario *a* **area depressionaria** *Meteorol* area of low pressure
depressi'one *nf* depression; **area di ~** *Meteorol* area of low pressure; *Econ* depressed area
depres'sivo *a* depressive
de'presso *pp di* **deprimere** ● *a* depressed
depressuriz'zare *vt* depressurize
depressurizzazi'one *nf* depressurization
deprezza'mento *nm* depreciation
deprez'zare *vt* depreciate
deprez'zarsi *vr* depreciate
depri'mente *a* depressing
de'primere *vt* depress
de'primersi *vr* get depressed
deprivazi'one *nf* deprivation
depu'rare *vt* purify
depu'rarsi *vr* be purified
depura'tore *nm* purifier
depurazi'one *nf* purification; (*di detriti*) effluent
depu'tare *vt* delegate
depu'tato, -a *nmf* ≈ Member of Parliament, MP
deputazi'one *nf* deputation

dequalifi'care vt disqualify

dequalifi'carsi vr disqualify oneself

dequalificazi'one nf disqualification

deraglia'mento nm derailment

deragli'are vi go off the lines; **far ~** derail

deraglia'tore nm derailleur gears pl

dera'pare vi Auto skid; ‹sciatore:› sideslip

derattiz'zare vt clear of rats

derattizzazi'one nf rodent control

'derby nm inv Sport local Derby

deregolamen'tare vt Comm deregulate

deregolamentazi'one nf deregulation

dere'litto a derelict

deresponsabiliz'zare vt deprive of responsibility

deresponsabiliz'zarsi vr abdicate responsibility

deresponsabilizzazi'one nf depriving of responsibility

dere'tano nm backside, bottom

de'ridere vt deride

derisi'one nf derision

deri'sorio a derisory

de'riva nf drift; **andare alla ~** drift

deri'vabile a derivable

deri'vare vi **~ da** (provenire) derive from ● vt derive; (sviare) divert

deri'vata nf Math derivative

deri'vato a derived ● nm by-product

derivazi'one nf derivation; (di fiume) diversion

derma'tite nf dermatitis

dermatolo'gia nf dermatology

dermato'logico a dermatological

derma'tologo, -a nmf dermatologist

derma'tosi nf dermatosis

dermoprotet'tivo a ‹crema› skin attrib; ‹azione› protective

'deroga nf dispensation

dero'gare vi **~ a** depart from

deroga'torio a derogatory

der'rata nf merchandise. **derrate** pl **alimentari** foodstuffs

deru'bare vt rob

deru'bato a robbed

desaliniz'zare vt desalinate

desalinizzazi'one nf desalination

desapare'cido nmf (pl ~s) disappeared man/woman, desaparecido

descolarizzazi'one nf deschooling

descrit'tivo a descriptive

de'scritto pp di **descrivere**

de'scrivere vt describe

descri'vibile a describable

descrizi'one nf description

desensibiliz'zare vt desensitize

desensibilizzazi'one nf desensitization

de'sertico a desert

de'serto a uninhabited ● nm desert

deside'rabile a desirable

deside'rare vt wish; (volere) want; (intensamente) long for; (bramare) desire; **desidera?** what would you like?, can I help you?; **lasciare a ~** leave a lot to be desired

deside'rato a intended

desi'derio nm wish; (brama) desire; (intenso) longing

deside'roso a desirous; (bramoso) longing

desi'gnare vt appoint, designate; (fissare) fix

desi'gnato a designate attrib

designazi'one nf appointment

de'signer nmf inv designer

desi'nare vi dine ● nm dinner

desi'nenza nf ending

de'sistere vi **~ da** desist from

'desktop 'publishing nm inv desktop publishing, DTP

deso'lante a distressing

deso'lare vt distress

deso'lato a desolate; (spiacente) sorry; **siamo desolati di dovervi comunicare che...** (in lettere) we are sorry to have to inform you that...

desolazi'one nf desolation

'despota nm despot

desqua'marsi vr flake off

desquamazi'one nf flaking off

destabiliz'zante a destabilizing

destabiliz'zare vt destabilize

destabilizzazi'one nf destabilization

de'stare vt waken; fig awaken

de'starsi vr waken; fig awaken

desti'nare vt destine; (nominare) appoint; (assegnare) assign; (indirizzare) address

destina'tario nm (di lettera, pacco) addressee

desti'nato a **essere ~ a fare qcsa** be destined or fated to do sth

destinazi'one nf destination; fig purpose; **con ~ Parigi** ‹aereo, treno› destined for Paris

de'stino nm destiny; (fato) fate

destitu'ire vt dismiss

destitu'ito a **~ di** devoid of

destituzi'one nf dismissal

'desto a liter awake

'destra nf (parte) right; (mano) right hand; **prendere a ~** turn right; **a ~** (essere) on the right; ‹andare› to the right; **la prima a ~** the first on the right; **di ~** Pol right wing; **la ~** Pol the Right

destreggi'are vi manoeuvre

destreggi'arsi vr manoeuvre

de'strezza nf dexterity; (abilità) skill

'destro a right; (abile) skilful

de'stroide a Pol right-wing

destruttu'rato a (incoerente) unstructured

desu'eto a obsolete

de'sumere vt (congetturare) infer; (ricavare) obtain

desu'mibile a inferable

detas'sare vt abolish the tax on

detassazi'one nf abolition of tax

detei'nato a tannin free

dete'nere vt hold; ‹polizia:› detain

deten'tivo a **pena detentiva** custodial sentence

deten|'tore, -'trice nmf holder. **~ del titolo** title-holder

dete'nuto, -a nmf prisoner

detenzi'one *nf* detention

deter'gente *a* cleaning; ⟨*latte, crema*⟩ cleansing ●*nm* detergent; (*per la pelle*) cleanser

deteriora'mento *nm* deterioration

deterio'rare *vt* cause to deteriorate ⟨*cibo, relazione*⟩

deterio'rarsi *vr* deteriorate

determi'nabile *a* determinable

determinabilità *nf* determinability

determi'nante *a* decisive

determi'nare *vt* determine

determi'narsi *vr* ~ **a** resolve to

determina'tezza *nf* determination

determina'tivo *a* ⟨*articolo*⟩ definite; **pronome** ~ determiner

determi'nato *a* (*risoluto*) determined; (*particolare*) specific; (*stabilito*) certain

determinazi'one *nf* determination; (*decisione*) decision

determi'nismo *nm* determinism

deter'rente *a* & *nm* deterrent

deter'sivo *nm* detergent. ~ **biologico** biological powder. ~ **per bucato** washing powder. ~ **per i piatti** washing-up liquid, dishwashing liquid *Am*

dete'stare *vt* detest, hate

dete'starsi *vr* hate oneself

deto'nare *vi* detonate

detona'tore *nm* detonator

detonazi'one *nf* detonation

detra'ibile *a* deductible

de'trarre *vt* deduct (**da** from)

de'tratto *pp di* **detrarre** ●*a* deducted

detrat|'tore, -'trice *nmf* detractor

detrazi'one *nf* deduction; (*da tasse*) tax allowance

detri'mento *nm* detriment; **a** ~ **di** to the detriment of

de'trito *nm* debris; **detriti** *pl* (*di fiume*) detritus. ~ **di falda** scree

detroniz'zare *vt* dethrone

'detta *nf* **a** ~ **di** according to

dettagli'ante *nmf Comm* retailer

dettagli'are *vt* detail

dettagliata'mente *adv* in detail

det'taglio *nm* detail; **al** ~ *Comm* retail

det'tame *nm* dictate; **i dettami della moda** the dictates of fashion

det'tare *vt* dictate; ~ **legge** *fig* lay down the law

det'tato *nm Sch* dictation

detta'tura *nf* dictation

'detto *a* said; (*chiamato*) called; (*soprannominato*) nicknamed; ~ **fatto** no sooner said than done ●*nm* ~ [*popolare*] saying

detur'pare *vt* disfigure

deturpazi'one *nf* disfigurement

deumidifi'care *vt* dehumidify

deumidifica'tore *nm* dehumidifier

deumidificazi'one *nf* dehumidification

devalutazi'one *nf* devaluation

deva'stante *a* devastating

deva'stare *vt* devastate

deva'stato *a* devastated

devasta|'tore, -'trice *a* destructive; *fig* devastating ●*nmf* destroyer

devastazi'one *nf* devastation; *fig* ravages *pl*

devi'ante *a* deviant

devi'anza *nf* deviance

devi'are *vi* deviate ●*vt* divert

devi'ato *a* ⟨*mente*⟩ warped

deviazi'one *nf* deviation; (*stradale*) diversion; **fare una** ~ *Auto* make a detour

devitaliz'zare *vt* kill the nerve of, devitalize *fml*

devitalizzazi'one *nf* killing of the nerve, devitalization *fml*

devo'luto *pp di* **devolvere** ●*a* devolved

devoluzi'one *nf* devolution

de'volvere *vt* devolve; ~ **qcsa in beneficenza** give sth to charity

devota'mente *adv* devoutly

de'voto *a* devout; (*affezionato*) devoted

devozi'one *nf* devotion

dg *abbr* (**decigrammi**) decigrams

di *prep* of; (*partitivo*) some; (*scritto da*) by; ⟨*parlare, pensare ecc*⟩ about; (*con causa, mezzo*) with; (*con provenienza*) from; (*in comparazioni*) than; (*con infinito*) to; **la casa di mio padre/dei miei genitori** my father's house/my parents' house; **compra del pane** buy some bread; **hai del pane?** do you have any bread?; **un film di guerra** a war film; **piangere di dolore** cry with pain; **coperto di neve** covered with snow; **sono di Genova** I'm from Genoa; **uscire di casa** leave one's house; **mi è uscito di mente** it slipped my mind; **più alto di te** taller than you; **è ora di partire** it's time to go; **crede di aver ragione** he thinks he's right; **dire di sì** say yes; **di domenica** on Sundays; **di sera** in the evening; **una pausa di un'ora** an hour's break; **un corso di due mesi** a two-month course

dia'bete *nm* diabetes

dia'betico, -a *a* & *nmf* diabetic

diabolica'mente *adv* devilishly

dia'bolico *a* diabolic[al]

di'acono *nm* deacon

dia'critico *a* diacritic

dia'dema *nm* diadem; (*di donna*) tiara

di'afano *a* diaphanous

dia'framma *nm* diaphragm; (*divisione*) screen

di'agnosi *nf inv* diagnosis

dia'gnostica *nf Med* diagnostics

diagnosti'care *vt* diagnose

dia'gnostici *nmpl Comput* diagnostics

dia'gnostico *a* diagnostic

diago'nale *a* & *nf* diagonal

diagonal'mente *adv* diagonally

dia'gramma *nm* diagram. ~ **a barre** bar chart. ~ **di flusso** flowchart

dialet'tale *a* dialect *attrib*; **poesia** ~ poetry in dialect

dialettaleggi'ante *a* dialect *attrib*

dia'lettica *nf* dialectics

dia'lettico *a* dialectic

dia'letto *nm* dialect

di'alisi *nf* dialysis

dialo'gante *a* **unità ~** *Comput* interactive terminal

dialo'gare *vt* write the dialogue for ‹scena› ● *vi* **~ con** converse with

dialo'gato *a* in dialogue

dialo'ghista *nmf* (*scrittore*) dialogue writer

di'alogo *nm* dialogue

dia'mante *nm* diamond

diaman'tifero *a* diamond bearing

diametral'mente *adv* diametrically

di'ametro *nm* diameter

di'amine *int* **che ~...** what on earth...

di'apason *nm inv* (*per accordartura*) tuning fork

diaposi'tiva *nf* slide

di'aria *nf* daily allowance

di'ario *nm* diary. **~ di bordo** logbook. **~ di classe** class register

dia'rista *nmf* (*scrittore*) diarist

diar'rea *nf* diarrhoea

di'aspora *nf* Diaspora

dia'triba *nf* diatribe

diavole'ria *nf* (*azione*) devilment; (*marchingegno*) weird contraption

diavo'letto *nm* imp; (*hum: bambino*) little devil

di'avolo *nm* devil; **va' al ~!** *fam* go to hell!; **che ~ fai?** *fam* what the hell are you doing?

di'battere *vt* debate

di'battersi *vr* struggle

dibattimen'tale *a* *Jur* of the hearing

dibatti'mento *nm* (*discussione*) debate; *Jur* hearing

di'battito *nm* debate; (*meno formale*) discussion

dica'stero *nm* office

di'cembre *nm* December

dice'ria *nf* rumour

dichia'rare *vt* state; (*ufficialmente*) declare; **~ colpevole** *Jur* convict; **niente da ~?** anything to declare?

dichia'rarsi *vr* (*in amore*) declare one's love; **~ soddisfatto** declare oneself satisfied; **si dichiara innocente** he says he's innocent; **~ a favore di qcsa** declare oneself in favour of sth; **si dichiara che...** (*in documenti*) it is hereby declared that...; **~ vinto** acknowledge defeat

dichia'rato *a* avowed

dichiarazi'one *nf* statement; (*documento, di guerra, d'amore*) declaration; **fare una ~** (*ufficialmente*) make a statement. **~ dei diritti** *Pol* bill of rights. **~ doganale** customs declaration. **~ dei redditi** [income] tax return

dician'nove *a & nm* nineteen

dicianno'venne *a & nmf* nineteen-year-old

dicianno'vesimo *a & nm* nineteenth

dicias'sette *a & nm* seventeen

diciasset'tenne *a & nmf* seventeen-year-old

diciasset'tesimo *a & nm* seventeenth

diciot'tenne *a & nmf* eighteen-year-old

diciot'tesimo *a & nm* eighteenth

dici'otto *a & nm* eighteen

dici'tura *nf* wording

dicoto'mia *nf* dichotomy

didasca'lia *nf* (*di film*) subtitle; (*di illustrazione*) caption; *Theat* stage direction

dida'scalico *a* ‹letteratura› didactic

di'dattica *nf* didactics

didattica'mente *adv* didactically

di'dattico *a* didactic; ‹televisione› educational

di'dentro *adv* inside

didi'etro *adv* behind ● *nm* *hum* hindquarters *pl*

di'eci *a & nm* ten

dieci'mila *a & nm* ten thousand

die'cina = **decina**

di'eresi *nf* diaeresis

'diesel *a & nm inv* diesel

di'esis *nm inv* sharp

di'eta *nf* diet; **a ~** on a diet

die'tetica *nf* dietetics

die'tetico *a* diet

die'tista *nmf* dietician

die'tologo *nmf* dietician

di'etro *adv* behind ● *prep* behind; (*dopo*) after ● *a* back; (*di zampe*) hind ● *nm* back; **le stanze di ~** the back rooms; **le zampe di ~** the hind legs

dietro'front *nm inv* about-turn; *fig* U-turn; **~!** about turn!

dietrolo'gia *nf* investigative journalism

di'fatti *adv* in fact

di'fendere *vt* defend

di'fendersi *vr* defend oneself; (*fam: cavarsela*) get by

difen'dibile *a* defendable, defensible

difen'siva *nf* **stare sulla ~** be on the defensive

difen'sivo *a* defensive

difen'sore *a* **avvocato ~** defence counsel ● *nm* defender. **~ civico** ombudsman

di'fesa *nf* defence; **prendere le difese di qcno** come to sb's defence. **~ civile** Civil Defence

di'feso *pp di* **difendere** ● *a* defended; ‹luogo› sheltered

difet'tare *vi* be defective; **~ di** lack

difet'tivo *a* defective

di'fetto *nm* defect; (*morale*) fault, flaw; (*mancanza*) lack; (*in tessuto, abito*) flaw; **essere in ~** be at fault; **far ~** be lacking

difet'toso *a* defective; ‹abito› flawed

diffa'mare *vt* (*con parole*) slander; (*per iscritto*) libel

diffama|'tore, -'trice *nmf* slanderer; (*per iscritto*) libeller

diffama'torio *a* slanderous; (*per iscritto*) libellous

diffamazi'one *nf* slander; (*scritta*) libel

diffe'rente *a* different

differente'mente *adv* differently

diffe'renza *nf* difference; **a ~ di** unlike; **non fare ~** make no distinction (**fra** between)

differenzi'abile *a* differentiable

differenzi'ale *a* & *nm* differential

differenzi'are *vt* differentiate

differenzi'arsi *vr* **~ da** differ from

differenzi'ato *a* differentiated

differenziazi'one *nf* differentiation

diffe'ribile *a* postponable

diffe'rire *vt* postpone ● *vi* be different

diffe'rita *nf* **in ~** *TV* prerecorded

dif'ficile *a* difficult; (*duro*) hard; (*improbabile*) unlikely ● *nm* difficulty

diffici'mente *adv* with difficulty

difficoltà *nf* difficulty; **trovarsi in ~** be in trouble; **mettere qcno in ~** put sb on the spot

dif'fida *nf* warning

diffi'dare *vi* **~ di** distrust ● *vt* warn

diffi'dente *a* mistrustful

diffi'denza *nf* mistrust

dif'fondere *vt* spread; diffuse (*calore, luce ecc*)

dif'fondersi *vr* spread

difformità *nf inv* deformation; (*di opinioni*) difference of opinion

diffusa'mente *adv* at length

diffusi'one *nf* diffusion; (*di giornale*) circulation

dif'fuso *pp di* **diffondere** ● *a* common; (*malattia*) widespread; (*luce*) diffuse

diffu'sore *nm* (*per asciugacapelli*) diffuser

difi'lato *adv* straight; (*subito*) straightaway

di'fronte *a inv* & *adv* opposite; **~ all'ingresso** in front of the entrance; (*dall'altro lato della strada*) opposite the entrance

difte'rite *nf* diphtheria

'diga *nf* dam; (*argine*) dike

dige'rente *a* alimentary

dige'ribile *a* digestible

digeribilità *nf* digestibility

dige'rire *vt* digest; *fam* stomach

digesti'one *nf* digestion

dige'stivo *a* digestive ● *nm* digestive; (*dopo cena*) liqueur

Digi'one *nf* Dijon

digi'tale *a* digital; (*delle dita*) finger *attrib* ● *nf* (*fiore*) foxglove

digitalizzazi'one *nf* digitalizing

digi'tare *vt* key in (*dati*)

digiu'nare *vi* fast

digi'uno *a* **essere ~** have an empty stomach ● *nm* fast; **a ~** (*bere ecc*) on an empty stomach

dignità *nf* dignity

digni'tario *nm* dignitary

dignitosa'mente *adv* with dignity

digni'toso *a* dignified

DIGOS *nf abbr* (**Divisione Investigazioni Generali e Operazioni Speciali**) ≈ riot police

digressi'one *nf* digression

digri'gnare *vi* **~ i denti** grind one's teeth

digros'sare *vt fig* impart basic concepts to

dik'tat *nm inv* (*trattato*) diktat

dila'gare *vi* flood; *fig* spread

dilani'are *vt* tear to pieces

dilapi'dare *vt* squander

dilapidazi'one *nf* squandering

dila'tare *vt* dilate

dila'tarsi *vr* dilate; (*legno:*) swell; (*metallo, gas:*) expand

dila'tato *a* dilated; (*legno*) swollen; (*metallo, gas*) expanded

dilatazi'one *nf* dilation; (*di legno*) swelling; (*di metallo, gas*) expansion

dilazio'nabile *a* postponable

dilazio'nare *vt* delay

dilazi'one *nf* delay

dileggi'are *vt* mock

dilegu'are *vt* disperse

dilegu'arsi *vr* disappear

di'lemma *nm* dilemma

dilet'tante *nmf* amateur

dilettan'tesco *a* amateurish

dilettan'tismo *nm* amateurism

dilettan'tistico *a* amateurish

dilet'tare *vt* delight

dilet'tarsi *vr* **~ di** delight in

dilet'tevole *a* delightful

di'letto, -a *a* beloved ● *nm* (*piacere*) delight ● *nmf* (*persona*) beloved

dili'gente *a* diligent; (*lavoro*) accurate

dili'genza *nf* diligence

dilu'ente *nm* diluent

dilu'ire *vt* dilute

diluizi'one *nf* dilution

dilun'gare *vt* prolong

dilun'garsi *vr* **~ su** dwell on (*argomento*)

diluvi'are *vi* pour [down]

di'luvio *nm* downpour; *fig* flood. **il ~ universale** the Flood

dima'grante *a* slimming, diet

dimagri'mento *nm* loss of weight

dima'grire *vi* lose weight

dima'grirsi *vr* lose weight

dime'nare *vt* wave; wag (*coda*)

dime'narsi *vr* be agitated

dimensio'nare *vt fig* get into proportion

dimensi'one *nf* dimension; (*misura*) size

dimenti'canza *nf* forgetfulness; (*svista*) oversight; **per ~** accidentally

dimenti'care *vt* forget; **l'ho dimenticato a casa** I left it at home

dimenti'carsi *vr* **~ [di]** forget

dimentica'toio *nm* **andare/finire nel ~** *hum* fall into oblivion

di'mentico *a* **~ di** (*che non ricorda*) forgetful of; (*non curante*) oblivious of

dimessa'mente *adv* modestly

di'messo *pp di* **dimettere** ● *a* humble; (*trasandato*) shabby; (*voce*) low

dimesti'chezza *nf* familiarity

di'mettere *vt* dismiss; (*da ospedale ecc*) discharge

di'mettersi *vr* resign

dimez'zare *vt* halve

diminu'ire *vt/i* diminish; (*in maglia*) decrease

diminu'ito *a Mus* diminished

diminu'tivo *a & nm* diminutive

diminuzi'one *nf* decrease; (*riduzione*) reduction; **in ~** dwindling

dimissio'nario *a* outgoing ● *nmf* outgoing chairman/president etc

dimissi'oni *nfpl* resignation *sg*; **dare le ~** resign

di'mora *nf* residence

dimo'rare *vi* reside

dimo'strabile *a* demonstrable

dimostrabilità *nf* demonstrability

dimo'strante *nmf* demonstrator

dimo'strare *vt* demonstrate; (*provare*) prove; (*mostrare*) show

dimo'strarsi *vr* prove [to be]

dimostra'tivo *a* demonstrative

dimostrazi'one *nf* demonstration; *Math* proof

di'namica *nf* dynamics; **~ dei fatti** sequence of events

di'namico *a* dynamic

dina'mismo *nm* dynamism

dinami'tardo *a* **attentato ~** bomb attack ● *nmf* bomber

dina'mite *nf* dynamite

'dinamo *nf inv* dynamo

di'nanzi *adv* in front ● *prep* **~ a** in front of

'dinaro *nm* (*moneta*) dinar

dina'stia *nf* dynasty

di'nastico *a* dynastic

din'don *nm inv* dingdong

'dingo *nm* (*cane*) dingo

dini'ego *nm* denial

dinocco'lato *a* lanky

dino'sauro *nm* dinosaur

din'torni *nmpl* outskirts; **nei ~ di** in the vicinity of

din'torno *adv* around

'dio *nm* (*pl* **'dei**) god; **D~** God; **D~ mio!** my God!

dioce'sano *a* diocesan

di'ocesi *nf inv* diocese

dioni'siaco *a* Dionysian

dios'sina *nf* dioxin

diot'tria *nf* dioptre

dipa'nare *vt* wind into a ball; *fig* unravel

diparti'mento *nm* department

dipen'dente *a* depending ● *nmf* employee

dipen'denza *nf* dependence; (*edificio*) annexe

di'pendere *vi* **~ da** depend on; (*provenire*) derive from; **dipende** it depends

di'pingere *vt* paint; (*descrivere*) describe

di'pinto *pp di* dipingere ● *a* painted ● *nm* painting

di'ploma *nm* diploma

diplo'mare *vt* graduate

diplo'marsi *vr* graduate

diplomatica'mente *adv* diplomatically

diplo'matico *a* diplomatic ● *nm* diplomat; (*pasticcino*) millefeuille (*with alcohol*)

diplo'mato *nmf* person with school qualification ● *a* qualified

diploma'zia *nf* diplomacy

di'porto *nm* **imbarcazione da ~** pleasure craft

dirada'mento *nf* thinning out

dira'dare *vt* thin out; make less frequent ⟨*visite*⟩

dira'darsi *vr* thin out; ⟨*nebbia:*⟩ clear

dira'mare *vt* issue

dira'marsi *vr* branch out

diramazi'one *nf* (*di strada, fiume*) fork; (*di albero, impresa*) branch; (*di ordine*) issuing

'dire *vt* say; (*raccontare, riferire*) tell; **~ quello che si pensa** speak one's mind; **voler ~** mean; **volevo ben ~!** I wondered!; **~ di sì/no** say yes/no; **si dice che...** rumour has it that...; **come si dice "casa" in inglese?** what's the English for "casa"?; **questo nome mi dice qualcosa** the name rings a bell; **che ne dici di...?** how about...?; **non c'è che ~** there's no disputing that; **e ~ che...** to think that...; **a dir poco/tanto** at least/most ● *vi* **~ bene/male di** speak highly/ill of sb; **dica pure** (*in negozio*) how can I help you?; **dici sul serio?** are you serious?; **per modo di ~** as it were

di'retta *nf TV* live broadcast; **in ~** live

diretta'mente *adv* directly

diret'tissima *nf* (*strada*) main route; **per ~** *Jur* ⟨*processare*⟩ without going through the normal procedures

diret'tissimo *nm* fast train

diret'tiva *nf* directive; **direttive** *pl* (*indicazioni*) guidelines

diret'tivo *a* (*dirigente*) management *attrib*, managerial ● *nm Pol* executive

di'retto *pp di* dirigere ● *a* direct; **il mio ~ superiore** my immediate superior; **~ a** (*inteso*) meant for; **essere ~ a** be heading for; **in diretta** ⟨*trasmissione*⟩ live ● *nm* (*treno*) through train

diret'tore *nm* manager; (*più in alto nella gerarchia*) director; (*di scuola*) headmaster. **~ amministrativo** company secretary. **~ artistico** artistic director. **~ del carcere** prison governor. **~ di filiale** branch manager. **~ di gara** referee. **~ generale** managing director, chief executive officer. **~ di giornale** newspaper editor. **~ d'istituto** *Univ* department head. **~ d'orchestra** conductor. **~ del personale** personnel manager/director. **~ di produzione** production manager/director. **~ spirituale** spiritual advisor. **~ sportivo** team manager. **~ tecnico** *Sport* manager. **~ di zona** area manager; regional director

diret'trice *nf* manageress; (*di scuola*) headmistress; (*indirizzo*) guiding principle

direzio'nale *a* directional

direzio'nare *vt* direct

direzi'one *nf* direction; (*di società*) management; *Sch* headmaster's/headmistress's office (*primary school*); **in ~ nord** (*traffico*) northbound; **'tutte le direzioni'** *Auto* 'all routes'

diri'gente *a* ruling ● *nmf* executive. **~ di partito** *Pol* party leader

diri'genza *nf* management; *Pol* leadership. ~ **aziendale** business management

dirigenzi'ale *a* management *attrib*, managerial

di'rigere *vt* direct; conduct ‹*orchestra*›; run ‹*impresa*›

di'rigersi *vr* ~ **verso** head for

diri'gibile *nm* airship

dirim'petto *adv* opposite ● *prep* ~ **a** facing

di'ritto¹ *a* straight; (*destro*) right ● *adv* straight; **andare** ~ go straight on; **sempre** ~ straight ahead, straight on ● *nm* right side; *Tennis* forehand; **fare un** ~ (*a maglia*) knit one

di'ritto² *nm* right; *Jur* law. **diritti** *pl* **d'autore** royalties. ~ **civile** civil law. **diritti** *pl* **civili** civil rights. ~ **commerciale** commercial law. ~ **penale** criminal law. **diritti** *pl* **di prelievo** *Fin* drawing rights. **diritti** *pl* **umani** human rights. ~ **di voto** right to vote, suffrage

dirit'tura *nf* straight line; *fig* honesty. ~ **d'arrivo** *Sport, fig* home straight

diroc'cato *a* tumbledown

dirom'pente *a anche fig* explosive

dirotta'mento *nm* hijacking

dirot'tare *vt* reroute ‹*treno, aereo*›; (*illegalmente*) hijack; divert ‹*traffico*› ● *vi* alter course

dirotta'|tore, -'trice *nmf* hijacker

di'rotto *a* ‹*pioggia*› pouring; ‹*pianto*› uncontrollable; **piovere a** ~ rain heavily

di'rupo *nm* precipice

di'sabile *a* disabled ● *nmf* disabled person

disabili'tare *vt* disable

disabi'tato *a* uninhabited

disabitu'arsi *vr* ~ **a** get out of the habit of

disac'cordo *nm* disagreement

disadatta'mento *nm* maladjustment

disadat'tato, -a *a* maladjusted ● *nmf* misfit

disa'dorno *a* unadorned

disaffezi'one *nf* disaffection

disa'gevole *a* (*scomodo*) uncomfortable; (*difficile*) inconvenient

disagi'ato *a* poor; ‹*vita*› hard; (*scomodo*) uncomfortable

di'sagio *nm* discomfort; (*difficoltà*) inconvenience; (*imbarazzo*) embarrassment; **sentirsi a** ~ feel uncomfortable; **disagi** *pl* (*privazioni*) hardships

di'samina *nf* close examination

disamora'mento *nm* estrangement

disanco'rare *vt Fin* de-link

disappro'vare *vt* disapprove of

disapprovazi'one *nf* disapproval

disap'punto *nm* disappointment; **con suo grande** ~ [much] to his chagrin

disarcio'nare *vt* unseat

disar'mante *a fig* disarming

disar'mare *vt/i* disarm

disar'mato *a* disarmed; *fig* defenceless

di'sarmo *nm* disarmament

disartico'lato *a fig* disjointed

disa'strato, -a *a* devastated ● *nmf* victim (*of flood, earthquake ecc*)

di'sastro *nm* disaster; (*fam: grande confusione*) mess; (*fam: persona*) disaster area

disastrosa'mente *adv* disastrously

disa'stroso *a* disastrous

disat'tento *a* inattentive

disattenzi'one *nf* inattention; (*svista*) oversight

disatti'vare *vt* de-activate

disa'vanzo *nm* deficit

disavve'duto *a* thoughtless

disavven'tura *nf* misadventure

disavver'tenza *nf* inadvertence

di'sbrigo *nm* dispatch

di'scapito *nm* **a** ~ **di** to the detriment of

di'scarica *nf* scrap-yard

di'scarico *nm* (*di merce*) unloading; **prova a** ~ evidence for the defence; **testimone a** ~ witness for the defence

discen'dente *a* descending ● *nmf* descendant

discen'denza *nf* descent; (*discendenti*) descendants *pl*

di'scendere *vi* (*dal treno*) get off; (*da cavallo*) dismount; (*sbarcare*) land. ~ **da** (*trarre origine da*) be a descendant of ● *vt* descend

discen'sore *nm* (*attrezzo*) karabiner

di'scepolo, -a *nmf* disciple

di'scernere *vt* discern

discerni'mento *nm* discernment

di'scesa *nf* descent; (*pendio*) slope; ~ **in picchiata** (*di aereo*) nosedive; **essere in** ~ ‹*strada:*› go downhill. ~ **libera** (*in sci*) downhill race

disce'sista *nmf* (*sciatore*) downhill skier

di'sceso *pp di* **discendere**

di'schetto *nm Comput* diskette

dischi'udere *vt* open; (*svelare*) disclose

dischi'udersi *vr* open up

di'scinto *a* scantily dressed

disci'ogliere *vt* dissolve; thaw ‹*neve*›; (*fondere*) melt

disci'ogliersi *vr* dissolve; ‹*neve:*› thaw; (*fondersi*) melt

disci'olto *pp di* **disciogliere**

disci'plina *nf* discipline

discipli'nare *a* disciplinary ● *vt* discipline

discipli'nato *a* disciplined

disc-'jockey *nm inv* disc jockey, DJ

'disco *nm* disc; *Sport* discus; *Mus* record; **ernia del** ~ slipped disc. ~ **a 33 giri** LP. ~ **a 45 giri** single. ~ **fisso** *Comput* fixed disk, hard disk. ~ **dei freni** brake disc. ~ **master** *Comput* master disk. ~ **rigido** *Comput* hard disk. ~ **volante** flying saucer

discogra'fia *nf* (*insieme di incisioni*) discography; (*industria*) record industry

disco'grafico *a* ‹*industria*› record *attrib*, recording; ‹*mercato, raccolta*› record *attrib*; **casa discografica** record company, recording company ● *nmf* record producer

'discolo *nmf* rascal ● *a* unruly

di'scolpa *nf* clearing; **a sua ~ si deve dire che...** in his defence it must be said that...
discol'pare *vt* clear
discol'parsi *vr* clear oneself
disco'noscere *vt* deny; disown ⟨*figlio*⟩
discontinuità *nf inv* (*nel lavoro*) irregularity; (*di stile*) unevenness
discon'tinuo *a* intermittent; ⟨*fig: impegno, rendimento*⟩ uneven
discopa'tia *nf* disc problems *pl*
discor'dante *a* discordant
discor'danza *nf* discordance; **essere in ~** clash
discor'dare *vi* ⟨*opinioni:*⟩ conflict
di'scorde *a* clashing
di'scordia *nf* discord; (*dissenso*) dissension
di'scorrere *vi* talk (**di** about)
discor'sivo *a* colloquial
di'scorso *pp di* **discorrere** ● *nm* speech; (*conversazione*) talk. **~ di ringraziamento** vote of thanks
di'scosto *a* distant ● *adv* far away; **stare ~** stand apart
disco'teca *nf* disco; (*raccolta*) record library
discote'caro *nmf pej* disco freak
di'scount *nm inv* discount store
discredi'tare *vt* discredit
di'scredito *nm* discredit
discre'pante *a* contradictory
discre'panza *nf* discrepancy
di'screto *a* discreet; (*moderato*) moderate; (*abbastanza buono*) fairly good
discrezionalità *nf* discretion
discrezi'one *nf* discretion; (*giudizio*) judgement; **a ~ di** at the discretion of
discrimi'nante *a* extenuating ● *nf Jur* extenuating circumstances *pl*
discrimi'nare *vt* discriminate
discrimina'tivo *a* ⟨*provvedimento*⟩ discriminatory
discrimina'torio *a* ⟨*atteggiamento*⟩ discriminatory
discriminazi'one *nf* discrimination
discussi'one *nf* discussion; (*alterco*) argument; **messa in ~** questioning
di'scusso *pp di* **discutere** ● *a* controversial
di'scutere *vt* discuss; (*formale*) debate; (*litigare*) argue ● *vi* **~ su qcsa** discuss sth
discu'tibile *a* debatable; ⟨*gusto*⟩ questionable
disde'gnare *vt* disdain
di'sdegno *nm* disdain
disde'gnoso *a* disdainful
di'sdetta *nf* retraction; (*sfortuna*) bad luck; *Comm* cancellation
di'sdetto *pp di* **disdire**
disdi'cevole *a* unbecoming
di'sdire *vt* retract; (*annullare*) cancel
disedu'care *vt* have a bad effect on
diseduca'tivo *a* bad for children
dise'gnare *vt* draw; (*progettare*) design
disegna|'tore, -'trice *nmf* designer. **~ di moda** fashion designer

di'segno *nm* drawing; (*progetto, linea*) design. **~ di legge** bill
diser'bante *nm* herbicide, weed-killer ● *a* herbicidal, weed-killing
diser'bare *vt* weed
disere'dare *vt* disinherit
disere'dato *a* dispossessed ● *nmf* **i diseredati** the dispossessed
diser'tare *vt/i* desert; **~ la scuola** stay away from school
diser'tore *nm* deserter
diserzi'one *nf* desertion
disfaci'mento *nm* decay; *fig* decline; **in ~** decaying; *fig* in decline
di'sfare *vt* undo; strip ⟨*letto*⟩; (*smantellare*) take down; (*annientare*) defeat; **~ le valigie** unpack [one's bags]
di'sfarsi *vr* fall to pieces; (*sciogliersi*) melt; **~ di** (*liberarsi di*) get rid of; **~ in lacrime** dissolve into tears
di'sfatta *nf* defeat
disfat'tismo *nm* defeatism
disfat'tista *a & nmf* defeatist
di'sfatto *a fig* worn out
disfunzi'one *nf* disorder
disge'lare *vt/i* thaw
disge'larsi *vr* thaw
di'sgelo *nm* thaw
disgi'ungere *vt* disconnect
disgi'unto *a* ⟨*firme*⟩ separate
di'sgrazia *nf* misfortune; (*incidente*) accident; (*sfavore*) disgrace
disgraziata'mente *adv* unfortunately
disgrazi'ato, -a *a* unfortunate ● *nmf* wretch
disgrega'mento *nm* disintegration
disgre'gare *vt* break up
disgre'garsi *vr* disintegrate
disgrega'tivo *a* disintegrating
disgrega'tore *a* disintegrating
disgregazi'one *nf* (*di società*) break-up
disgu'ido *nm* **~ postale** mistake in delivery
disgu'stare *vt* disgust
disgu'starsi *vr* **~ di** be disgusted by
di'sgusto *nm* disgust
disgustosa'mente *adv* disgustingly; **~ dolce** nauseatingly sweet
disgu'stoso *a* disgusting
disidra'tante *a* dehydrating
disidra'tare *vt* dehydrate
disidra'tarsi *vr* become dehydrated
disidra'tato *a* dehydrated
disidratazi'one *nf* dehydration
disil'ludere *vt* disenchant, disillusion
disil'ludersi *vr* become disenchanted, become disillusioned
disillusi'one *nf* disenchantment, disillusionment
disil'luso *a* disenchanted, disillusioned
disimbal'laggio *nm* unpacking
disimbal'lare *vt* unpack
disimpa'rare *vt* forget
disimpe'gnare *vt* release; (*compiere*) fulfil; redeem ⟨*oggetto dato in pegno*⟩

disimpe'gnarsi vr disengage oneself; (cavarsela) manage

disim'pegno nm (locale) vestibule; (disinteresse) lack of interest

disimpi'ego nm re-allocation; (di truppe) re-assignment

disincagli'are vt Naut refloat

disincagli'arsi vr Naut float off

disincan'tato a (disilluso) disillusioned

disincar'nato a disembodied

disincenti'vante a demotivating

disincenti'vare vt demotivate

disincen'tivo nm disincentive

disincroci'are vt uncross

disinfe'stare vt disinfest

disinfestazi'one nf disinfestation

disinfet'tante a & nm disinfectant

disinfet'tare vt disinfect

disinfezi'one nf disinfection

disinfiam'marsi vr become less inflamed

disinflazio'nare vt disinflate

disinflazi'one nf disinflation

disinflazio'nistico a disinflationary

disinfor'mato a uninformed

disinformazi'one nf lack of information; (informazione erronea) misinformation

disingan'nare vt disabuse

disin'ganno nm disillusion

disini'birsi vr lose one's inhibitions

disini'bito a uninhibited

disinne'scare vt defuse

disin'nesco nm (di bomba) bomb disposal

disinne'stare vt disengage

disinne'starsi vr disengage

disin'nesto nm disengagement

disinquina'mento nm cleaning up

disinqui'nare vt clean up

disinse'rire vt disconnect

disinse'rito a disconnected

disinte'grare vt disintegrate

disinte'grarsi vr disintegrate

disintegrazi'one nf disintegration

disinteressa'mento nm lack of interest

disinteres'sarsi vr ~ **di** take no interest in

disinteressata'mente adv without interest; (senza secondo fine) disinterestedly

disinteres'sato a uninterested; (senza secondo fine) disinterested

disinte'resse nm indifference; (oggettività) disinterestedness

disintossi'care vt detoxify

disintossi'carsi vr come off drugs; ‹alcolizzato:› dry out

disintossicazi'one nf giving up alcohol/drugs; **programma di** ~ detox programme

disinvolta'mente adv in a relaxed way

disin'volto a relaxed

disinvol'tura nf confidence

disi'stima nf lack of respect

disles'sia nf dyslexia

di'slessico a dyslexic

disli'vello nm difference in height; fig inequality

disloca'mento nm Mil posting

dislo'care vt Mil post

dismenor'rea nf dysmenorrhoea

dismi'sura nf excess; **a** ~ excessively

disobbedi'ente a disobedient

disobbe'dire vt disobey

disoccu'pato, -a a unemployed ● nmf unemployed person

disoccupazi'one nf unemployment

disonestà nf dishonesty

diso'nesto a dishonest

disono'rare vt dishonour

disono'rato a dishonoured

diso'nore nm dishonour

di'sopra adv above ● a upper ● nm top

disordi'nare vt disarrange

disordinata'mente adv untidily

disordi'nato a untidy; (sregolato) immoderate

di'sordine nm disorder, untidiness; (sregolatezza) debauchery

disores'sia nf eating disorder

disor'ganico a inconsistent

disorganiz'zare vt disorganize

disorganiz'zato a disorganized

disorganizzazi'one nf disorganization

disorienta'mento nm disorientation

disorien'tare vt disorientate

disorien'tarsi vr lose one's bearings

disorien'tato a fig bewildered

disos'sare vt bone

disos'sato a boned

di'sotto adv below ● a lower ● nm bottom

di'spaccio nm dispatch

dispa'rato a disparate

'dispari a odd, uneven

dispa'rire vi disappear

disparità nf inv disparity

di'sparte adv in ~ apart; **stare in** ~ stand aside

di'spendio nm expenditure; pej waste

dispendiosa'mente adv extravagantly

dispendi'oso a expensive

di'spensa nf pantry; (distribuzione) distribution; (mobile) cupboard; Jur exemption; Relig dispensation; (pubblicazione periodica) number

dispen'sare vt distribute; (esentare) exonerate

dispen'sario nm dispensary

di'spenser nm inv display rack; (confezione) dispenser

dispe'rare vi despair (**di** of)

dispe'rarsi vr despair

disperata'mente adv ‹piangere› desperately; ‹studiare› like mad

dispe'rato a desperate

disperazi'one nf despair

di'sperdere vt scatter, disperse

di'sperdersi vr scatter, disperse

dispersi'one nf dispersion; (di truppe) dispersal

disper'sivo a disorganized

di'sperso pp di disperdere ● a scattered; (smarrito) lost ● nm missing soldier

di'spetto nm spite; **a** ~ **di** in spite of; **fare un** ~ **a qcno** spite sb

dispet'toso *a* spiteful

dispia'cere *nm* upset; (*rammarico*) regret; (*dolore*) sorrow; (*preoccupazione*) worry ● *vi* **mi dispiace** I'm sorry; **non mi dispiace** I don't dislike it; **se non ti dispiace** if you don't mind

dispiaci'uto *a* sorry

dispie'gare *vt* unfold

dispie'garsi *vr* unfurl

dispo'nibile *a* available; (*gentile*) helpful

disponibilità *nf* availability; (*gentilezza*) helpfulness. **~** *pl* **correnti** *Fin* current assets

di'sporre *vt* arrange ● *vi* dispose; (*stabilire*) order; **~ di** have at one's disposal

di'sporsi *vr* (*in fila*) line up

disposi'tivo *nm* device. **~ di emergenza** emergency button/handle. **~ di puntamento** *Comput* pointing device

disposizi'one *nf* disposition; (*ordine*) order; (*libera disponibilità*) disposal

di'sposto *pp di* **disporre** ● *a* ready; (*incline*) disposed; **essere ben disposto verso** be favourably disposed towards

dispotica'mente *adv* despotically

di'spotico *a* despotic

dispo'tismo *nm* despotism

dispregia'tivo *a* disparaging

disprez'zabile *a* despicable

disprez'zare *vt* despise

di'sprezzo *nm* contempt

'disputa *nf* dispute

dispu'tare *vi* dispute; (*gareggiare*) compete

dispu'tarsi *vr* **~ qcsa** contend for sth

disqui'sire *vi* discourse

disquisizi'one *nf* disquisition

dissa'crante *a* debunking

dissa'crare *vt* debunk

dissacra|'tore, -'trice *nmf* debunker

dissacra'torio *a* debunking

dissacrazi'one *nf* debunking

dissangua'mento *nm* loss of blood; *fig* impoverishment

dissangu'are *vt* bleed; *fig* bleed dry

dissangu'arsi *vr* bleed; *fig* become impoverished

dissangu'ato *a* bloodless; *fig* impoverished

dissa'pore *nm* disagreement

dissec'care *vt* dry up

dissec'carsi *vr* dry up

dissemi'nare *vt* disseminate; (*notizie*) spread

dissen'nato *a* (*politica*) senseless

dis'senso *nm* dissent; (*disaccordo*) disagreement

dissente'ria *nf* dysentery

dissen'tire *vi* disagree (**da** with)

dissepelli'mento *nm* exhumation

dissepel'lire *vt* exhume (*cadavere*); disinter (*rovine*); *fig* unearth

dissertazi'one *nf* dissertation

disser'vizio *nm* poor service

disse'stare *vt* upset; *Comm* damage

disse'stato *a* (*strada*) uneven; (*azienda*) shaky

dis'sesto *nm* ruin

disse'tante *a* thirst-quenching

disse'tare *vt* **~ qcno** quench sb's thirst

disse'tarsi *vr* quench one's thirst

dissezio'nare *vr* dissect

dissezi'one *nf* dissection

dissi'dente *a & nmf* dissident

dissi'denza *nf* dissidence

dis'sidio *nm* disagreement

dis'simile *a* unlike, dissimilar

dissimu'lare *vt* conceal

dissimu'lato *a* concealed

dissimula|'tore, -'trice *nmf* dissembler

dissimulazi'one *nf* concealment

dissi'pare *vt* dissipate; (*sperperare*) squander

dissi'parsi *vr* (*nebbia:*) clear; (*dubbio:*) disappear

dissipa'tezza *nf* dissipation

dissi'pato *a* dissipated

dissipa'tore *nm* **~ termico** heat sink

dissipazi'one *nf* squandering

dissoci'abile *a* separable

dissoci'are *vt* dissociate

dissoci'arsi *vr* dissociate oneself

dissoci'ato, -a *a Pol* dissenting ● *nmf Pol* dissenter

dissociazi'one *nf Pol* dissociation

dissoda'mento *nm* tillage

disso'dare *vt* till

dis'solto *pp di* **dissolvere**

disso'lubile *a* dissoluble

dissolu'tezza *nf* dissoluteness

dissolu'tivo *a* divisive

disso'luto *a* dissolute

dissol'venza *nf* (*di immagine*) fade-out, dissolve

dis'solvere *vt* dissolve; (*disperdere*) dispel

dis'solversi *vr* dissolve; (*disperdersi*) clear

disso'nante *a* dissonant

disso'nanza *nf* dissonance

dissotterra'mento *nm* disinterment

dissotter'rare *vt* disinter (*bara*); *fig* resurrect (*rancore*)

dissua'dere *vt* dissuade

dissuasi'one *nf* dissuasion

dissua'sivo *a* dissuasive

distacca'mento *nm Mil* detachment

distac'care *vt* detach; *Sport* leave behind

distac'carsi *vr* be detached

distac'cato *a* (*tono, voce*) expressionless

di'stacco *nm* detachment; (*separazione*) separation; *Sport* lead

di'stante *a* far away; (*fig: person*) detached ● *adv* far away

di'stanza *nf* distance

distanzia'mento *nm* spacing [out]; *Sport* outdistancing

distanzi'are *vt* space out; *Sport* outdistance

di'stare *vi* be distant; **quanto dista?** how far is it?; **Roma dista 20 chilometri da qui** Rome is 20 kilometres away, Rome is 20 kilometres from here

di'stendere *vt* stretch out ⟨*parte del corpo*⟩; (*spiegare*) spread; (*deporre*) lay

di'stendersi *vr* stretch; (*sdraiarsi*) lie down; (*rilassarsi*) relax

distensi'one *nf* stretching; (*rilassamento*) relaxation; *Pol* détente

disten'sivo *a* relaxing

di'stesa *nf* expanse

di'steso *pp di* distendere

distil'lare *vt/i* distil

distil'lato *a* distilled ● *nm* distillate

distillazi'one *nf* distillation

distille'ria *nf* distillery

di'stinguere *vt* distinguish

di'stinguersi *vr* (*per bravura ecc*) distinguish oneself; **si distingue dagli altri per...** it is distinguished from the others by...

distin'guibile *a* distinguishable

di'stinguo *nm inv* distinction

di'stinta *nf Comm* list. **~ di pagamento** receipt. **~ di versamento** paying-in slip

distinta'mente *adv* (*separatamente*) individually, separately; (*chiaramente*) clearly; (*in modo elegante*) in a distinguished way; **vi saluto ~** yours truly

distin'tivo *a* distinctive ● *nm* badge

di'stinto *pp di* distinguere ● *a* distinct; (*signorile*) distinguished; **distinti saluti** Yours faithfully

distinzi'one *nf* distinction

di'stogliere *vt* **~ da** (*allontanare*) remove from; (*dissuadere*) dissuade from

di'stolto *pp di* distogliere

di'storcere *vt* twist; distort ⟨*suono*⟩

di'storcersi *vr* sprain ⟨*la caviglia*⟩

distorsi'one *nf Med* sprain; (*alterazione*) distortion

di'storto *a* warped; ⟨*suono*⟩ distorted

di'strarre *vt* distract; (*divertire*) amuse

di'strarsi *vr* (*deconcentrarsi*) be distracted; (*svagarsi*) amuse oneself; **non ti distrarre!** pay attention!

distratta'mente *adv* absently

di'stratto *pp di* distrarre ● *a* absent-minded; (*disattento*) inattentive

distrazi'one *nf* absent-mindedness; (*errore*) inattention; (*svago*) amusement; **errore di ~** absent-minded mistake

di'stretto *nm* district

distrettu'ale *a* district *attrib*

distribu'ire *vt* distribute; (*disporre*) arrange; deal ⟨*carte*⟩

distribu'tore *nm* distributor; (*di benzina*) petrol pump, gas pump *Am*; (*automatico*) slot-machine. **~ automatico di biglietti** ticket machine. **~ di bevande** drinks dispenser. **~ di monete** change machine

distribuzi'one *nf* distribution

distri'care *vt* disentangle

distri'carsi *vr fig* get out of it

distro'fia *nf* **~ muscolare** muscular dystrophy

di'strofico *a* dystrophic

di'struggere *vt* destroy

di'struggersi *vr* **si distrugge col bere** he is destroying himself with drink; **la macchina si è distrutta** the car has been written off

distruttività *nf* destructiveness

distrut'tivo *a* destructive; ⟨*critica*⟩ negative

di'strutto *pp di* distruggere ● *a* destroyed; **un uomo ~** a broken man

distrut'tore *nm* **~ di documenti** paper shredder

distruzi'one *nf* destruction

distur'bare *vt* disturb; (*sconvolgere*) upset

distur'barsi *vr* trouble oneself; **non si disturbi** please don't trouble yourself

distur'bato *a* ⟨*Med: mente*⟩ disordered; ⟨*intestino*⟩ upset

di'sturbo *nm* bother; (*indisposizione*) trouble; *Med* problem; *Radio, TV* interference; **disturbi** *pl Radio, TV* static. **disturbi** *pl di* **stomaco** stomach trouble

disubbidi'ente *a* disobedient

disubbidi'enza *nf* disobedience

disubbi'dire *vi* **~ a** disobey

disuguagli'anza *nf* disparity; (*eterogeneità*) irregularity

disugu'ale *a* unequal; (*eterogeneo*) irregular

disumanità *nf* inhumanity

disu'mano *a* inhuman

disuni'one *nf* disunity

disu'nire *vt* divide

di'suso *nm* **cadere in ~** fall into disuse

di'tale *nm* thimble

di'tata *nf* poke; (*impronta*) finger-mark

'dito *nm* (*pl nf* **dita**) finger; (*di vino, acqua*) finger. **~ del piede** toe

'ditta *nf* firm. **~ di vendita per corrispondenza** mail order firm

dit'tafono *nm* dictaphone

ditta'tore *nm* dictator

dittatori'ale *a* dictatorial

ditta'tura *nf* dictatorship

dit'tongo *nm* diphthong

diu'retico *a* diuretic

di'urno *a* daytime; **spettacolo ~** matinée

'diva *nf* diva

diva'gare *vi* digress

divagazi'one *nf* digression. **~ sul tema** digression

divam'pare *vi* burst into flames; *fig* spread like wildfire

di'vano *nm* settee, sofa. **~ letto** sofa bed

divari'care *vt* open

divari'carsi *vr* splay

divari'cata *nf* splits *pl*

divari'cato *a* ⟨*gambe, braccia*⟩ splayed

di'vario *nm* discrepancy; **un ~ di opinioni** a difference of opinion

di'vellere *vt* (*sradicare*) uproot

di'velto *pp di* divellere

dive'nire *vi* = divenire

diven'tare *vi* become; (*lentamente*) grow; (*rapidamente*) turn

dive'nuto *pp di* divenire

di'verbio *nm* squabble

diver'gente *a* divergent

diver'genza *nf* divergence; **~ di opinioni** difference of opinion

di'vergere *vi* diverge

diversa'mente *adv* (*altrimenti*) otherwise; (*in modo diverso*) differently

di'versi *a & pron* (*parecchi*) several

diversifi'care *vt* diversify

diversifi'carsi *vr* differ, be different

diversifi'cato *a* broad-based

diversificazi'one *nf* diversification

diversi'one *nf* diversion

diversità *nf inv* diversity; **ci sono molte ~** there are many differences

diver'sivo *a* diversionary ● *nm* diversion

di'verso *a* different ● *nm* (*omosessuale*) deviant

diver'tente *a* amusing

diver'ticolo *nm* digression

diverti'mento *nm* fun, amusement; **buon ~!** enjoy yourself!, have fun!

diver'tire *vt* amuse

diver'tirsi *vr* enjoy oneself, have fun

diver'tito *a* amused

divi'dendo *nm* dividend

di'videre *vt* divide; (*condividere*) share

di'vidersi *vr* (*separarsi*) separate

divi'eto *nm* prohibition; **'~ di pesca'** 'fishing prohibited'; **'~ di sosta'** 'no parking'

divina'mente *adv* divinely

divinco'larsi *vr* wriggle

divinità *nf inv* divinity

di'vino *a* divine

di'visa *nf* uniform; *Comm* currency

divi'sibile *a* divisible

divisi'one *nf* division

divisio'nismo *nm* (*in arte*) pointillism

di'vismo *nm* worship; (*atteggiamento*) superstar mentality

di'viso *pp di* **dividere** ● *a* divided

divi'sore *nm* divisor

divi'sorio *a* dividing; **muro ~** partition wall

'divo, -a *nmf* star

divo'rare *vt* devour

divo'rarsi *vr* **~ da** be consumed with

divorzi'are *vi* divorce

divorzi'ato, -a *nmf* divorcee

di'vorzio *nm* divorce

divul'gare *vt* divulge; (*rendere popolare*) popularize

divul'garsi *vr* spread

divulga'tivo *a* popular

divulgazi'one *nf* spread; (*di cultura, scienza*) popularization

dizio'nario *nm* dictionary. **~ dei sinonimi** thesaurus

dizi'one *nf* diction

DJ *nm inv* DJ

DNA *nm inv* DNA

do *nm Mus* (*chiave, nota*) C

'doccia *nf* shower; (*grondaia*) gutter; **fare la ~** have a shower, shower

doccia'tura *nf Med* douche

D.O.C. *abbr* (**Denominazione di Origine Controllata**) *mark guaranteeing the quality of a wine*

do'cente *a* teaching ● *nmf* teacher; (*di università*) lecturer

do'cenza *nf* university teacher's qualification

D.O.C.G. *abbr* (**Denominazione di Origine Controllata e Garantita**) *mark guaranteeing the high quality of a wine*

'docile *a* docile

docilità *nf* docility

documen'tare *vt* document

documen'tario *a & nm* documentary

documen'tarsi *vr* gather information (**su** about)

documen'tato *a* well-documented; (*persona*) well-informed

documentazi'one *nf* documentation

docu'mento *nm* document; **documenti** *pl* papers. **~ d'identità** ID

dodeca'fonico *a Mus* dodecaphonic

Dodecan'neso *nm* **il ~** the Dodecanese

dodi'cenne *a & nmf* twelve-year-old

dodi'cesimo *a & nm* twelfth

'dodici *a & nm* twelve

do'gana *nf* customs *pl*; (*dazio*) duty. **~ merci** customs for freight. **~ passeggeri** passenger customs

doga'nale *a* customs *attrib*

dogani'ere *nm* customs officer

'doglie *nfpl* labour pains

'dogma *nm* dogma

dog'matico *a* dogmatic

dogma'tismo *nm* dogmatism

'dolce *a* sweet; (*clima*) mild; (*voce, consonante*) soft; (*acqua*) fresh ● *nm* (*portata*) dessert; (*torta*) cake; **non mangio dolci** I don't eat sweet things; **dolci** *pl* **della casa** (*in menu*) home-made cakes

dolce'mente *adv* sweetly

dolce'vita *a inv* (*maglione*) rollneck

dol'cezza *nf* sweetness; (*di clima*) mildness

dolci'ario *a* confectionery

dolci'astro *a* sweetish

dolcifi'cante *nm* sweetener ● *a* sweetening

dolcifica'tore *nm* (*per acqua*) softener

dolci'umi *nmpl* sweets

do'lente *a* painful; (*spiacente*) sorry; **punto ~** sore point

do'lere *vi* ache, hurt; (*dispiacere*) regret

do'lersi *vr* regret; (*protestare*) complain; **~ di** be sorry for

'dollaro *nm* dollar

'dolly *nm inv Cinema, TV* dolly

'dolmen *nm inv* dolmen

'dolo *nm Jur* malice; (*truffa*) fraud

Dolo'miti *nfpl* **le ~** the Dolomites

dolo'mitico *a* Dolomite, of the Dolomites

dolo'rante *a* aching

do'lore *nm* pain; (*morale*) sorrow; **avere dei dolori** be in pain. **dolori** *pl* post-partum after-pains

dolorosa'mente *adv* painfully

dolo'roso *a* painful

do'loso *a* malicious

do'manda *nf* question; (*richiesta*) request; (*scritta*) application; *Comm* demand; **~ e offerta** supply and demand; **fare una ~** (a **qcno**) ask (sb) a question. **~ di impiego** job application. **~ riconvenzionale** counter-claim

doman'dare *vt* ask; (*esigere*) demand; **~ qcsa a qcno** ask sb for sth

doman'darsi *vr* wonder

do'mani *adv* tomorrow; **~ sera** tomorrow evening; **a ~** see you tomorrow ● *nm* **il ~** the future

do'mare *vt* tame; *fig* control ‹*emozioni*›

doma|'tore, -'trice *nmf* tamer. **~ di cavalli** horsebreaker

domat'tina *adv* tomorrow morning

doma'tura *nf* (*di cavallo*) breaking

do'menica *nf* Sunday; **di ~** on Sundays. **~ delle palme** Palm Sunday

domeni'cale *a* Sunday *attrib*

domeni'cano *a* Dominican

do'mestico, -a *a* domestic; **le pareti domestiche** one's own four walls ● *nm* servant ● *nf* maid

domicili'are *a* **arresti domiciliari** *Jur* house arrest; **perquisizione ~** *Jur* house search

domicili'arsi *vr* settle

domi'cilio *nm* domicile; (*abitazione*) home; **recapitiamo a ~** we do home deliveries

domi'nante *a* ‹*nazione, colore*› dominant; ‹*caratteri*› chief; ‹*opinione*› prevailing; ‹*motivo*› main

domi'nanza *nf Biol, Zool* dominance

domi'nare *vt* dominate; (*controllare*) control ● *vi* rule over; (*prevalere*) be dominant

domi'narsi *vr* control oneself

domina|'tore, -'trice *a* domineering ● *nmf* ruler

dominazi'one *nf* domination

domini'cano *a* **la Repubblica Domini-cana** the Dominican Republic

do'minio *nm* control; *Pol* dominion; (*ambito*) field; **di ~ pubblico** common knowledge

'domino *nm* (*gioco*) dominoes

don *nm inv* (*ecclesiastico*) Father

do'nare *vt* give; donate ‹*sangue, organo*› ● *vi* **~ a** (*giovare esteticamente*) suit

do'narsi *vr* dedicate oneself

dona|'tore, -'trice *nmf* donor. **~ di organi** organ donor

donazi'one *nf* donation

dondo'lare *vt* swing; (*cullare*) rock ● *vi* sway

dondo'larsi *vr* swing

dondo'lio *nm* rocking

'dondolo *nm* swing; **cavallo/sedia a ~** rocking-horse/chair

dongio'vanni *nm inv* Romeo, Don Juan

'donna *nf* woman; **fare la prima ~** act like a prima donna; **'donne'** 'ladies'. **~ d'affari** businesswoman. **~ delle pulizie** cleaner. **~ di servizio** domestic help. **~ di vita** (*prostituta*) lady of the night

don'naccia *nf pej* hussy

donnai'olo *nm* womanizer

donnicci'ola *nf fig* old woman

'donnola *nf* weasel

'dono *nm* gift

'doping *nm inv Sport* drug-taking; **fa uso di ~** he takes drugs

'dopo *prep* after; (*a partire da*) since ● *adv* after, afterwards; (*più tardi*) later; (*in seguito*) later on; **~ di me** after me

dopo'barba *nm inv* aftershave

dopo'cena *nm inv* evening

dopodiché *adv* after which

dopodo'mani *adv* the day after tomorrow

dopogu'erra *nm inv* post-war period

dopola'voro *nm inv* working man's club

dopo'pranzo *nm inv* afternoon

dopo'sci *a & nm inv* après-ski

doposcu'ola *nm inv* after-school activities *pl*

dopo-'shampoo *nm inv* conditioner ● *a inv* conditioning

dopo'sole *nm inv* aftersun cream ● *a inv* aftersun

dopo'tutto *adv* after all

doppi'aggio *nm* dubbing

doppia'mente *adv* (*in misura doppia*) doubly

doppi'are *vt Naut* double; *Sport* lap; *Cinema* dub

doppia|'tore, -'trice *nmf* dubber

doppi'etta *nf* (*fucile*) double-barrelled shotgun; *Auto* double-declutch; (*in calcio*) two goals; (*in pugilato*) one-two

doppi'ezza *nf* duplicity

'doppio *a & adv* double. **~ clic** *Comput* double click; **fare un ~ ~ su** double-click on. **~ fallo** *nm Tennis* double fault. **~ gioco** *nm* double-dealing. **~ mento** *nm* double chin. **~ senso** *nm* double entendre. **doppi vetri** *nmpl* double glazing ● *nm* double, twice the quantity; *Tennis* doubles *pl.* **~ misto** *Tennis* mixed doubles

doppio'fondo *nm Naut* double hull; (*in valigia*) false bottom

doppiogio'chista *nmf* double-dealer

doppi'one *nm* duplicate

doppio'petto *a* double-breasted

dop'pista *nmf Tennis* doubles player

do'rare *vt* gild; *Culin* brown

do'rato *a* gilt; (*color oro*) golden

dora'tura *nf* gilding

'dorico *a Archit* Doric

do'rifora *nf* Colorado beetle

dormicchi'are *vi* doze

dormigli'one, -a *nmf* sleepyhead; *fig* lazybones

dor'mire *vi* sleep; (*essere addormentato*) be asleep; *fig* be asleep; **andare a ~** go to bed; **~ come un ghiro** sleep like a log; **~ in piedi** *fig* be half asleep; (*essere stanco*) be dead tired; **dormirci sopra** sleep on it

dor'mita *nf* good sleep; **fare una bella ~** have a good sleep

dormi'tina *nf* nap

dormi'torio *nm* dormitory. **~ pubblico** night shelter

dormi'veglia *nm* **essere nel ~** be half asleep

dor'sale *a* dorsal ● *nf* (*di monte*) ridge

dor'sista *nmf* backstroke swimmer

'dorso *nm* back; (*di libro*) spine; (*di monte*) crest; (*nel nuoto*) backstroke; **a ~ di cavallo** on horseback

do'saggio *nm* dosage; *fig* weighing; **sbagliare il ~** get the amount wrong

do'sare *vt* dose; *fig* measure; **~ le parole** weigh one's words

do'sato *a* measured

dosa'tore *nm* measuring jug

'dose *nf* dose; **~ eccessiva** overdose; **in buona ~** *fig* in good measure

dos'sier *nm inv* (*raccolta di dati, fascicolo*) file

'dosso *nm* (*dorso*) back; **levarsi di ~ gli abiti** take off one's clothes

do'tare *vt* endow; (*di accessori*) equip

do'tato *a* (*persona*) gifted; (*fornito*) equipped

dotazi'one *nf* (*attrezzatura*) equipment; (*mezzi finanziari*) endowment; **avere qcsa in ~** be equipped with sth

'dote *nf* dowry; (*qualità*) gift

dott. *abbr* (**dottore**) Dr.

'dotto *a* learned ● *nm* scholar; *Anat* duct

dotto'rale *a* doctoral; *pej* pedantic

dotto'rando, -a *nmf* postgraduate student

dotto'rato *nm* doctorate

dot'tor|e, ~'essa *nmf* doctor

dot'trina *nf* doctrine

dott.ssa *abbr* (**dottoressa**) Dr.

'dove *adv* where; **di ~ sei?** where do you come from; **fin ~?** how far?; **per ~?** which way?

do'vere *vi* (*obbligo*) have to, must; **devo andare** I have to go, I must go; **devo venire anch'io?** do I have to come too?; **avresti dovuto dirmelo** you should have told me, you ought to have told me; **devo sedermi un attimo** I must sit down for a minute, I need to sit down for a minute; **dev'essere successo qualcosa** something must have happened; **come si deve** properly ● *vt* (*essere debitore di, derivare*) owe; **essere dovuto a** be due to ● *nm* duty; **per ~** out of duty; **rivolgersi a chi di ~** apply to the appropriate authorities

dove'roso *a* right and proper, only right

do'vizia *nf* **con ~ di particolari** in great detail

do'vunque *adv* (*dappertutto*) everywhere; (*in qualsiasi luogo*) anywhere ● *conj* wherever

dovuta'mente *adv* duly

do'vuto *a* due; (*debito*) proper; **essere ~ a** be attributable to; **ha fatto più del ~** he did more than he had to

Down: sindrome di ~ *Med* Down's syndrome

doz'zina *nf* **una ~ di uova** a dozen eggs; **mezza ~ di uova** half a dozen eggs

dozzi'nale *a* cheap

'draga *nf* (*scavatrice*) dredger

draga'mine *nf* minesweeper

dra'gare *vt* dredge

'drago *nm* dragon

'dramma *nm* drama; **fare un ~ di qcsa** *fig* make a drama out of sth

drammatica'mente *adv* dramatically

drammaticità *nf* dramatic force

dram'matico *a* dramatic

drammatiz'zare *vt* dramatize

drammatizzazi'one *nf* dramatization

drammatur'gia *nf* (*genere*) drama

dramma'turgo *nm* playwright

dram'mone *nm* (*film*) tear-jerker, weepy

drappeggi'are *vt* drape

drap'peggio *nm* drapery

drap'pello *nm Mil* squad; (*gruppo*) band

'drappo *nm* (*tessuto*) cloth

drastica'mente *adv* drastically

'drastico *a* drastic

dre'naggio *nm* drainage. **~ di capitali** transfer of capital. **~ fiscale** fiscal drag

dre'nare *vt* drain

'Dresda *nf* Dresden

dres'sage *nm inv* (*gara*) dressage

drib'blare *vt* (*in calcio*) dribble; *fig* dodge

'dribbling *nm inv* (*in calcio*) dribble

'dritta *nf* (*mano destra*) right hand; *Naut* starboard; (*informazione*) pointer, tip; **a ~ e a manca** (*dappertutto*) left, right and centre

dritta'mente *adv* (*furbescamente*) craftily

'dritto *a* = **diritto**[1] ● *nmf fam* crafty so-and-so

drive *nm inv Comput* drive

drive-in *nm inv* drive-in

driz'zare *vt* straighten; (*rizzare*) prick up

driz'zarsi *vr* straighten [up]; (*alzarsi*) raise; **mi sono drizzati i capelli** *fig* my hair stood on end

'droga *nf* drug. **~ leggera** soft drug. **~ pesante** hard drug

dro'gare *vt* drug

dro'garsi *vr* take drugs

dro'gato, -a *nmf* drug addict

droghe'ria *nf* grocery

droghi'ere, -a *nmf* grocer

drome'dario *nm* dromedary

'druso *nmf* Druse

dua'lismo *nm* dualism; (*contrasto*) conflict

'dubbio *a* doubtful; (*ambiguo*) dubious ● *nm* doubt; (*sospetto*) suspicion; **mettere in ~** doubt; **essere fuori ~** be beyond doubt; **essere in ~** be doubtful

dubbiosa'mente *adv* doubtfully

dubbi'oso, dubi'tante *a* doubtful

dubi'tare *vi* doubt; **~ di** doubt; (*diffidare*) mistrust; **dubito che venga** I doubt whether he'll come

dubita'tivo *a* (*ambiguo*) ambiguous

duble-'face *a inv* reversible

Du'blino *nf* Dublin

'duca *nm* duke

du'cale *a* ducal

'duce *nm* (*capo del fascismo*) Duce

du'chessa *nf* duchess

'due *a* & *nm* two

duecen'tesco *a* thirteenth-century

duecen'tesimo two hundredth

due'cento *a* & *nm* two hundred

duel'lante *nmf* dueller

duel'lare *vi* duel

du'ello *nm* duel

due'mila *a* & *nm* two thousand

due'pezzi *nm inv* (*bikini*) bikini; (*vestito*) two-piece suit

du'etto *nm* duo; *Mus* duet

'dumping *nm inv Fin* dumping

'duna *nf* dune

dune 'buggy *nm inv* beach buggy

'dunque *conj* therefore; (*allora*) well [then]; **arrivare al ~** get down to the nitty-gritty

'duo *nm inv* duo; *Mus* duet

duodeci'male *a* duodecimal

duode'nale *a* **ulcera ~** duodenal ulcer

duo'deno *nm* duodenum

du'omo *nm* cathedral

'duplex *nm Teleph* party line

dupli'care *vt* duplicate

dupli'cato *nm* duplicate

duplicazi'one *nf* duplication

'duplice *a* double; **in ~** in duplicate

duplicità *nf* duplicity

dura'mente *adv* (*lavorare*) hard; (*rimproverare*) harshly

du'rante *prep* during

du'rare *vi* last; (*cibo:*) keep; (*resistere*) hold out; **così non può ~** this can't go on any longer; **~ in carica** remain in office; **finché dura** as long as it lasts ● *vt* **~ fatica** sweat blood

du'rata *nf* duration. **~ del collegamento** on-line time. **~ di conservazione** shelflife. **~ della vita** life span

dura'turo *a* lasting

du'revole *a* (*pace*) lasting, enduring

du'rezza *nf* hardness; (*di carne*) toughness; (*di voce, padre*) harshness

'duro, -a *a* hard; (*persona, carne*) tough; (*voce*) harsh; (*pane*) stale; **tieni ~!** (*resistere*) hang in there!; **~ d'orecchio** hard of hearing ● *nmf* (*persona*) tough person, toughie *fam*

du'rone *nm* hardened skin

'duttile *a* (*materiale*) ductile; (*carattere, persona*) malleable

duttilità *nf* (*di materiale*) ductility; (*di individuo*) malleability

'duty free *nm inv* duty-free shop

Ee

---

e *conj* and

eba'nista *nmf* cabinet-maker

'ebano *nm* ebony

eb'bene *conj* well [then]

eb'brezza *nf* inebriation; (*euforia*) elation; **guida in stato di ~** drink-driving; **l'~ della velocità** the thrill of speed

'ebbro *a* inebriated; **~ di gioia** delirious with joy

'ebete *a* stupid

ebollizi'one *nf* boiling

e'braico *a* & *nm* Hebrew

ebra'ismo *nm* Judaism

e'breo, -a *a* Jewish ● *nm* Jew ● *nf* Jewess

'Ebridi *nfpl* **le ~** the Hebrides

eca'tombe *nf* **fare un'~** wreak havoc

ecc *abbr* (**eccetera**) etc

ecce'dente *a* (*peso, bagaglio*) excess

ecce'denza *nf* excess; (*d'avanzo*) surplus; **avere qcsa in ~** have an excess of sth; **bagagli in ~** excess baggage. **~ di cassa** surplus. **~ di peso** excess weight

ec'cedere *vt* exceed ● *vi* go too far; **~ nel bere** drink to excess; **~ nel mangiare** overeat

eccel'lente *a* excellent

eccel'lenza *nf* excellence; (*titolo*) Excellency; **per ~** par excellence

ec'cellere *vi* excel (**in** at)

eccentricità *nf* eccentricity

ec'centrico, -a *a* & *nmf* eccentric

ecce'pire *vt* object to

eccessiva'mente *adv* excessively

ecces'sivo *a* excessive

ec'cesso *nm* excess; **andare agli eccessi** go to extremes; **dare in eccessi** fly into a temper; **all'~** to excess. **~ di personale** overmanning. **~ di peso** excess weight. **~ di velocità** speeding

ec'cetera *adv* et cetera

ec'cetto *prep* except; **~ che** (*a meno che*) unless

eccettu'are *vt* except

eccezio'nale *a* exceptional; **in via [del tutto] ~** as an exception

eccezional'mente *adv* exceptionally; (*contrariamente alla regola*) as an exception

eccezi'one *nf* exception; *Jur* objection; **a ~ di** with the exception of; **d'~** exceptional

ec'chimosi *nf inv* bruising

eccì *int* atishoo

ec'cidio *nm* massacre

ecci'tabile *a* (*persona, carattere*) excitable

eccita'mento *nm* excitement

ecci'tante *a* exciting; (*sostanza*) stimulant ● *nm* stimulant

ecci'tare *vt* excite; (*sessualmente*) excite, arouse

ecci'tarsi *vr* get excited; (*sessualmente*) become aroused *or* excited

ecci'tato *a* excited; (*sessualmente*) excited, aroused; ~ **da** flushed with

eccitazi'one *nf* excitement; (*sessuale*) arousal, excitement

ecclesi'astico *a* ecclesiastical ● *nm* priest

'**ecco** *adv* (*qui*) here; (*là*) there; ~! (*con approvazione*) that's right!; ~ **qua!** (*dando qcsa*) here you are!; ~ **la tua borsa** here is your bag; ~ **mio figlio** there is my son; **eccomi** here I am; ~ **fatto** there we are; ~ **perché** this is why; ~ **tutto** that is all

ec'come *adv* & *int* and how!

ECG *abbr* (**elettrocardiogramma**) ECG

echeggi'are *vi* echo

e'clettico *a* eclectic

eclet'tismo *nm* eclecticism

eclis'sare *vt fig* eclipse

eclis'sarsi *vr* (*sparire*) disappear

e'clissi *nf inv* eclipse

'**eco** *nmf* (*pl m* **echi**) echo; **ha suscitato una vasta** ~ it caused a great stir

eco+ *pref* eco+

ecogra'fia *nf* scan

ecolo'gia *nf* ecology

eco'logico *a* ecological; (*prodotto*) environmentally friendly, eco-friendly

e'cologo, -a *nmf* ecologist

e commerci'ale *nf* ampersand

econo'mia *nf* economy; (*scienza*) economics; **fare** ~ economize (**di** on); [**fatto**] **in** ~ [done] on the cheap; **senza** ~ unstintingly; **fare qcsa senza** ~ spare no expense doing sth. ~ **aziendale** business administration. ~ **domestica** *Sch* home economics. ~ **di mercato** market economy. ~ **mista** mixed economy. ~ **sommersa** black economy

economicità *nf* economy

eco'nomico *a* economic; (*a buon prezzo*) cheap; (*con pochi costi*) economical; **difficoltà economiche** financial difficulties; **classe economica** economy class; **edizione economica** paperback

econo'mie *nfpl* (*risparmi*) savings

econo'mista *nmf* economist

economiz'zare *vt* save (*tempo, denaro*) ● *vi* economize (**su** on)

economizza'tore *nm Auto* fuel economizer

e'conomo, -a *a* thrifty ● *nmf* (*di collegio*) bursar

ecosi'stema *nm* ecosystem

é'cru *a inv* fawn

'**Ecu** *nm inv* ECU, ecu

Ecua'dor *nm* Ecuador

ecuadori'ano, -a *a* & *nmf* Ecuadorian

ecu'menico *a* ecumenical

ec'zema *nm* eczema

ed *conj vedi* **e**

e'dema *nm* oedema

'**Eden** *nm* Eden

'**edera** *nf* ivy

e'dicola *nf* [newspaper] kiosk

edifi'cabile *a* (*area, terreno*) classified as suitable for development

edifi'cante *a* edifying

edifi'care *vt* build; (*indurre al bene*) edify

edi'ficio *nm* building; *fig* structure

e'dile *a* building *attrib* ● *nm* **edili** *pl* construction workers

edi'lizia *nf* building trade

edi'lizio *a* building *attrib*

Edim'burgo *nf* Edinburgh

E'dipo *nm* Oedipus; **complesso di** ~ Oedipus complex

edi'tare *vt* edit

'**editing** *nm* editing

'**edito** *a* published

edi'|tore, -'trice *a* publishing ● *nmf* publisher; (*curatore*) editor

edito'ria *nf* publishing. ~ **elettronica** desktop publishing. ~ **telematica** online publishing

editori'ale *a* publishing ● *nm* (*articolo*) editorial, leader

e'ditto *nm* edict

edizi'one *nf* edition; (*di manifestazione*) performance; **in** ~ **italiana** (*film*) dubbed into Italian. ~ **ridotta** abridgement, abridged version. ~ **della sera** (*di telegiornale*) evening news

edo'nismo *nm* hedonism

edo'nistico *a* hedonistic

educagi'oco *nm* edutainment

edu'canda *nf* [convent school] boarder; *fig* prim and proper girl

edu'care *vt* educate; (*allevare*) bring up

educa'tivo *a* educational

edu'cato *a* polite

educa'|tore, -'trice *nmf* educator

educazi'one *nf* education; (*di bambini*) upbringing; (*buone maniere*) [good] manners *pl*; **bella** ~! what manners!. ~ **fisica** physical education

edulco'rare *vt* ~ **la pillola** sweeten the pill

e'felide *nf* freckle

effemi'nato *a* effeminate

effe'rato *a* brutal

efferve'scente *a* effervescent; (*frizzante*) fizzy; (*aspirina*) soluble

effettiva'mente *adv* **è troppo tardi** – ~ it's too late – so it is

effet'tivo *a* actual; (*efficace*) effective; (*personale*) permanent; *Mil* regular ● *nm* (*somma totale*) sum total

ef'fetto *nm* effect; (*impressione*) impression; (*cambiale*) bill; **fare** ~ (*medicina:*) take effect; **fare** ~ **su** have an effect on, affect; **in effetti** in fact; **a tutti gli effetti** to all intents and purposes; **ad effetto** (*frase*) catchy; **la vista del sangue mi fa** ~ I can't stand the sight of blood; **tiro con** ~ spin. ~ **boomerang** boomerang effect. ~ **di luce** trick of the light. **effetti** *pl* **personali** personal belongings, personal effects *fml*. ~ **ritardato** delayed effect. ~ **serra** greenhouse effect. ~

sonoro sound effect. **~ speciale** *Cinema, TV* special effect

effettu'are *vt* effect; carry out ⟨*controllo, sondaggio*⟩

effettu'arsi *vr* take place; **'si effettua dal... al...'** 'this service is available from... till...'

effi'cace *a* effective

effi'cacia *nf* effectiveness

effici'ente *a* efficient

effici'enza *nf* efficiency; **in piena ~** in full swing

ef'figie *nf* effigy

ef'fimero *a* ephemeral

ef'flusso *nm* outflow

ef'fluvio *nm* stink

ef'fondersi *vr* **~ in ringraziamenti** be profusive in one's thanks

effrazi'one *nf* **~ con scasso** *Jur* breaking and entering

effusi'one *nf* effusion

'Egadi *nfpl* **le [isole] ~** the Egadi Islands

egemo'nia *nf* hegemony

E'geo *nm* **l'~** the Aegean [Sea]

e'gida *nf* **sotto l'~ di** under the aegis of

E'gitto *nm* Egypt

egizi'ano, -a *a & nmf* Egyptian

e'gizio, -a *a & nmf* Ancient Egyptian

'egli *pers pron* he; **~ stesso** he himself

ego'centrico, -a *a* egocentric ● *nmf* egocentric person

egocen'trismo *nm* egocentricity

ego'ismo *nm* selfishness

ego'ista *a* selfish ● *nmf* selfish person

egoistica'mente *adv* selfishly

ego'istico *a* selfish

Egr. *abbr* **(egregio) ~ Sig.** (*su busta*) Mr.

e'gregio *a* distinguished; **E~ Signore** Dear Sir

eguali'tario *a & nm* egalitarian

eh *int* huh!

'ehi *int* hey!

ehilà *int* hi!

ehm *int* um

eiacu'lare *vi* ejaculate

eiaculazi'one *nf* ejaculation

eiet'tabile *a* ⟨*sedile*⟩ ejector

eiezi'one *nf Aeron* ejection

'Eire *nf* Eire

elabo'rare *vt* elaborate; process ⟨*dati*⟩

elabo'rato *a* elaborate ● *nm* (*tabulato*) pre-printed form

elabora'tore *nm* **~ [di testi]** word processor

elaborazi'one *nf* elaboration; (*di dati*) processing. **~ [dei] dati** data processing. **~ sequenziale** *Comput* batch processing. **~ [di] testi** word processing

elar'gire *vt* lavish

elasticità *nf* elasticity. **~ mentale** mental agility. **~ di movimento** litheness

elasticiz'zato *a* ⟨*stoffa*⟩ elasticated

e'lastico *a* elastic; ⟨*tessuto*⟩ stretch; ⟨*passo*⟩ springy; ⟨*orario, mente*⟩ flexible; ⟨*persona*⟩ easy-going; ⟨*morale*⟩ lax; **collant** *pl* **elastici**

support tights ● *nm* elastic; (*fascia*) rubber band

'Elba *nf* Elba

eldo'rado *nm* eldorado

ele'fante *nm* elephant; **avere una memoria da ~** have a memory like an elephant; **fare passi da ~** thump about. **~ marino** sea-elephant

elefan'tesco *a* elephantine

elefan'tessa *nf* cow[-elephant]

elefan'tiaco *a* (*enorme*) elephantine

ele'gante *a* elegant

elegante'mente *adv* elegantly

ele'ganza *nf* elegance

e'leggere *vt* elect

eleg'gibile *a* eligible

ele'gia *nf* elegy

elemen'tare *a* elementary; **scuola ~** primary school

ele'mento *nm* element; (*componente*) part; **trovarsi nel proprio ~** be in one's element; **elementi** *pl* (*fatti*) data; (*rudimenti*) elements

ele'mosina *nf* charity; **chiedere l'~** beg. **vivere d'~** live on charity; **fare l'~** give money to beggars

elemosi'nare *vt/i* beg

elen'care *vt* list

e'lenco *nm* list. **~ [degli] abbonati** *Teleph* telephone directory. **~ telefonico** telephone directory

elet'tivo *a* ⟨*carica*⟩ elective

e'letto, -a *pp di* **eleggere** ● *a* chosen ● *nmf* (*nominato*) elected member; **per pochi eletti** *fig* for the chosen few

eletto'rale *a* electoral

elettora'lismo *nm* electioneering

eletto'rato *nm* electorate

elet'|tore, -'trice *nmf* voter

elet'trauto *nm* electrics garage

elettri'cista *nm* electrician

elettricità *nf* electricity; **togliere l'~** cut the electricity off; **è mancata l'~** there was a power cut

e'lettrico *a* electric

elettriz'zante *a* ⟨*notizia, gara*⟩ electrifying

elettriz'zare *vt fig* electrify

elettriz'zato *a fig* electrified

elettro+ *pref* electro+

elettrocardio'gramma *nm* electrocardiogram, ECG

elettrocuzi'one *nf* electrocution

e'lettrodo *nm* electrode

elettrodo'mestico *nm* [electrical] household appliance

elettroencefalo'gramma *nm* electroencephalogram

elettroesecuzi'one *nf* electrocution

elet'trogeno *a* **gruppo ~** generator

elet'trolisi *nf* electrolysis

elettromo'tore *nm* electric motor

elettromo'trice *nf* electric train

elet'trone *nm* electron

elet'tronico, -a *a* electronic ● *nf* electronics

elettroshocktera'pia *nf* electroshock therapy, electroshock treatment, EST

elettro'tecnica *nf* electrical engineering

elettro'tecnico *nm* electrical engineer

elettro'treno *nm* electric train

ele'vare *vt* raise; *(promuovere)* promote; *(erigere)* erect; *(fig: migliorare)* better; **~ al quadrato/cubo** square/cube

ele'varsi *vr* rise; *(edificio:)* stand

ele'vato *a* high; *(fig: sentimento)* lofty; **~ al cubo/al quadrato** cubed/squared; **~ a dieci** raised to the power of ten

eleva'tore *nm* fork-lift truck

elevazi'one *nf* elevation

elezi'one *nf* election. **elezioni** *pl* **amministrative** local council elections. **elezioni** *pl* **politiche** general election

eliambu'lanza *nf* air ambulance

'elica *nf Naut* screw, propeller; *Aeron* propeller; *(del ventilatore)* blade

eli'cottero *nm* helicopter

elimi'nabile *a* which can be eliminated

elimi'nare *vt* eliminate

elimina'toria *nf Sport* [preliminary] heat

eliminazi'one *nf* elimination

'elio *nm (gas)* helium

eli'porto *nm* heliport

elisabetti'ano *a & nmf* Elizabethan

é'lite *nf inv* élite

eli'tista *a* élitist

'ella *pers pron liter* she; **~ stessa** she herself

el'lenico *a* Hellenic

elle'nistico *a* Hellenistic

ellepì *nm inv* LP

+ellino *suff* **campanellino** *nm* [small] bell; **fiorellino** *nm* [little] flower; **gonnellina** *nf* short skirt

el'lisse *nf* ellipse

el'lissi *nf inv* ellipsis

el'littico *a* elliptical

+ello *suff* **finestrella** *nf* little window; **pecorella** *nf* woolly sheep; **saltello** *nm* skip

el'metto *nm* helmet

elogi'are *vt* praise

elogia'tivo *a* laudatory

e'logio *nm* praise; *(discorso, scritto)* eulogy; **degno di ~** laudable, praiseworthy; **ti faccio i miei elogi per** congratulations on. **~ funebre** funeral oration

elo'quente *a* eloquent; *fig* tell-tale

elo'quenza *nf* eloquence

El Salva'dor *nm* El Salvador; **nel Salvador** in El Salvador

e'ludere *vt* elude; evade *(sorveglianza, controllo)*

elusi'one *nf* **~ fiscale** tax avoidance

elu'sivo *a* elusive

el'vetico *a* Swiss; **Confederazione Elvetica** Swiss Confederation

emaci'ato *a* emaciated

'E-mail *nf* e-mail; **mandare per ~** e-mail, send by e-mail

ema'nare *vt* give off; pass *(legge)* ● *vi* emanate

emanazi'one *nf* giving off; *(di legge)* enactment

emanci'pare *vt* emancipate

emanci'parsi *vr* become emancipated

emanci'pato *a* emancipated

emancipazi'one *nf* emancipation

emargi'nato *nm* marginalized person

emarginazi'one *nf* marginalization

ema'toma *nm* haematoma

em'bargo *nm* embargo

em'blema *nm* emblem

emble'matico *a* emblematic

embo'lia *nf* embolism

'embolo *nm* embolus

embrio'nale *a Biol, fig* embryonic; **allo stato ~** *(progetto, idea)* embryonic

embri'one *nm* embryo

emenda'mento *nm* amendment

emen'dare *vt* amend

emen'darsi *vr* reform

emer'gente *a* emergent

emer'genza *nf* emergency; **in caso di ~** in an emergency; **di ~** *(di riserva)* stand-by; **uscita d'~** emergency exit. **~ sanitaria** ambulance

e'mergere *vi* emerge; *(sottomarino:)* surface; *(distinguersi)* stand out

e'merito *a (professore)* emeritus; **un ~ imbecille** a prize idiot

e'merso *pp di* **emergere**

e'messo *pp di* **emettere**

e'metico *a* emetic

e'mettere *vt* emit; give out *(luce, suono)*; let out *(grido)*; *(mettere in circolazione)* issue

emi'crania *nf* migraine

emi'grare *vi* emigrate

emi'grato, -a *nmf* immigrant

emigrazi'one *nf* emigration

emi'nente *a* eminent

emi'nenza *nf* eminence; **Sua E~** His/Your Eminence. **~ grigia** éminence grise

emi'rato *nm* emirate; **Emirati** *pl* **Arabi Uniti** United Arab Emirates

e'miro *nm* emir

emi'sfero *nm* hemisphere

emis'sario *nm* emissary; *(fiume)* effluent

emissi'one *nf* emission; *(di denaro, francobolli)* issue; *(trasmissione)* broadcast; **'~ del biglietto'** 'take your ticket here'

emit'tente *a* issuing; *(trasmittente)* broadcasting ● *nf Radio* transmitter

'emmental *nm* Emmenthal

emofi'lia *nf* haemophilia

emofi'liaco, -a *nmf* haemophiliac

emoglo'bina *nf* haemoglobin

emorra'gia *nf* haemorrhage; **avere un'~** haemorrhage

emor'roidi *nfpl* haemorrhoids, piles

emo'statico *a* haemostatic

emotività *nf* emotional make-up

emo'tivo *a* emotional

emozio'nante *a* exciting; *(commovente)* moving

emozio'nare *vt* excite; *(commuovere)* move

emozio'narsi *vr* become excited; (*commuoversi*) be moved

emozio'nato *a* excited; (*commosso*) moved

emozi'one *nf* emotion; (*agitazione*) excitement

empietà *nf* impiety

'empio *a* impious; (*spietato*) pitiless; (*malvagio*) wicked

em'pirico *a* empirical

empi'rismo *nm* empiricism

empi'rista *nmf* empiricist

em'porio *nm* emporium; (*negozio*) general store

emù *nm inv* emu

emu'lare *vt* emulate

emulazi'one *nf* emulation. **~ di terminale** terminal emulation

emulsio'nare *vt* emulsify

emulsio'narsi *vr* emulsify

emulsi'one *nf* emulsion

ena'lotto *nm* weekly lottery

encefa'lite *nf* **~ bovina spongiforme** Bovine Spongiform Encephalopathy, BSE

encefalo'gramma *nm* encephalogram

en'ciclica *nf* encyclical

enciclope'dia *nf* encyclopaedia

enciclo'pedico *a* ‹*mente, cultura, dizionario*› encyclopaedic

encomi'are *vt* commend

en'comio *nm* commendation

ende'mia *nf* (*situazione*) endemic

en'demico *a* endemic

en'divia *nf* Belgian endive

endocrinolo'gia *nf* endocrinology

endo'vena *nf* intravenous injection ● *adv* intravenously

endove'noso *a* intravenous; **per via endovenosa** intravenously

ener'getico *a* ‹*risorse, crisi*› energy *attrib*; ‹*alimento*› energy-giving

ener'gia *nf* energy; **pieno di ~** full of energy. **~ atomica** atomic energy. **~ elettrica** electricity. **~ eolica** wind power. **~ nucleare** nuclear energy, nuclear power. **~ solare** solar energy, solar power

energica'mente *adv* energetically

e'nergico *a* energetic; (*efficace*) strong

ener'gumeno *nm* Neanderthal

'enfasi *nf* emphasis

en'fatico *a* emphatic

enfatiz'zare *vt* emphasize

enfi'sema *nm* emphysema

e'nigma *nm* enigma

enig'matico *a* enigmatic

enig'mistica *nf* puzzles *pl*

E.N.I.T. *nm abbr* (**Ente Nazionale Italiano per il Turismo**) Italian State Tourist Office

en'nesimo *a* Math nth; *fam* umpteenth; **all'ennesima potenza** Math, *fig* to the nth power/degree

eno'logico *a* wine *attrib*

e'norme *a* enormous; **è un'ingiustizia ~** it's enormously unfair

enorme'mente *adv* massively

enormità *nf inv* enormity; (*assurdità*) absurdity

eno'teca *nf* wine-tasting shop

eno'tera *nf* evening primrose

en pas'sant *adv* in passing

'ente *nm* board; (*società*) company; (*in filosofia*) being

ente'rite *nf* enteritis

entero'clisma *nm* Med enema

entità *nf inv* (*filosofia*) entity; (*gravità*) seriousness; (*dimensione*) extent

entomolo'gia *nf* entomology

entou'rage *nm inv* entourage

en'trambi *a* & *pron* both

en'trare *vi* go in, enter; **~ in** go into; (*stare in, trovar posto in*) fit into; (*arruolarsi*) join; **entrarci** (*avere a che fare*) have to do with; **tu che c'entri?** what has it got to do with you?; **da che parte si entra?** how do you get in?; **fallo ~** (*in ufficio, dal medico ecc*) show him in; **'vietato ~'** 'no entry'

en'trata *nf* entry, entrance; **~ libera** admission free; **en'trate** *pl* Comm takings; (*reddito*) income *sg*

entre'côte *nf* beef entrecote

'entro *prep* (*tempo*) within; **~ oggi** by the end of today

entro'bordo *nm* (*motore*) inboard motor; (*motoscafo*) speedboat

entro'terra *nm inv* hinterland

entusia'smante *a* fascinating, exciting

entusia'smare *vt* arouse enthusiasm in

entusia'smarsi *vr* be enthusiastic (**per** about)

entusi'asmo *nm* enthusiasm

entusi'asta *a* enthusiastic ● *nmf* enthusiast

entusi'astico *a* enthusiastic

enucle'are *vt* define

enume'rare *vt* enumerate

enumerazi'one *nf* enumeration

enunci'are *vt* enunciate

enunciazi'one *nf* enunciation

E'olie *nfpl* **le ~** the Aeolian Islands

epa'tite *nf* hepatitis

epi'centro *nm* epicentre

'epico *a* epic

epide'mia *nf* epidemic

epi'dermide *nf* epidermis

epidu'rale *a* (*Med: anestesia*) epidural

Epifa'nia *nf* Epiphany

epi'gramma *nm* epigram

epiles'sia *nf* epilepsy

epi'lettico, -a *a* & *nmf* epileptic

e'pilogo *nm* epilogue

episco'pato *nm* episcopacy

epi'sodico *a* episodic; **caso ~** one-off case

epi'sodio *nm* episode

e'pistola *nf* epistle

episto'lare *a* epistolary

episto'lario *nm* correspondence, letters *pl*

epi'taffio *nm* epitaph

e'piteto *nm* epithet

'epoca *nf* age; (*periodo*) period; **a quell'~** in those days; **un avvenimento che ha fatto**

~ an epoch-making event; **auto d'~** vintage car; **mobile d'~** period furniture

e'ponimo *a* eponymous

epo'pea *nf* epic

ep'pure *conj* [and] yet

E.P.T. *abbr* (**Ente Provinciale per il Turismo**) *Italian local tourist board*

epu'rare *vt* purge; purify ⟨*acqua*⟩

epura'tore *nm* water purifier

epurazi'one *nf* purging; (*di acqua*) purification. **~ etnica** ethnic cleansing

equalizza'tore *nm* equalizer

e'quanime *a* level-headed; (*imparziale*) impartial

equa'tore *nm* equator

equatori'ale *a* equatorial

equazi'one *nf* equation

e'questre *a* equestrian; **circo ~** circus

equidi'stante *a* equidistant

equi'latero *a* equilateral

equili'brare *vt* balance

equili'brato *a* ⟨*persona*⟩ well-balanced

equi'librio *nm* balance; (*buon senso*) common sense; (*di bilancia*) equilibrium

equili'brismo *nm* **fare ~** do a balancing act

equili'brista *nmf* tightrope walker

e'quino *a* horse *attrib*

equi'nozio *nm* equinox

equipaggia'mento *nm* equipment

equipaggi'are *vt* equip; (*di persone*) man

equi'paggio *nm* crew; *Aeron* cabin crew. **~ di volo** aircrew

equipa'rare *vt* make equal

equipa'rato *a* equal

é'quipe *nf inv* team

equità *nf* equity

equitazi'one *nf* riding

equiva'lente *a & nm* equivalent

equiva'lenza *nf* equivalence

equiva'lere *vi* **~ a** be equivalent to

equivo'care *vi* misunderstand

e'quivoco *a* equivocal; (*sospetto*) suspicious; **un tipo ~** a shady character ● *nm* misunderstanding; **a scanso di equivoci** to avoid any misunderstandings; **giocare sull'~** equivocate

'equo *a* fair, just

'era *nf* era. **~ glaciale** Ice Age

'erba *nf* grass; (*aromatica, medicinale*) herb; **in ~** ⟨*atleta, attore*⟩ budding. **~ cipollina** chives

er'baccia *nf* weed

er'baceo *a* herbaceous

erbi'cida *nm* weed-killer

erbi'voro *a* herbivorous ● *nm* herbivore

erbo'rista *nmf* herbalist

erboriste'ria *nf* herbalist's shop

er'boso *a* grassy

Erco'lano *nf* Herculaneum

'Ercole *nm* Hercules

er'culeo *a* ⟨*forza*⟩ herculean

e'rede *nm* heir ● *nf* heiress

eredità *nf inv* inheritance; *Biol* heredity

eredi'tare *vt* inherit

ereditarietà *nf* heredity

eredi'tario *a* hereditary

erediti'era *nf* heiress

+erello *suff* **furterello** *nm* petty theft; **pioggerella** *nf* drizzle

ere'mita *nm* hermit

'eremo *nm* isolated place; *fig* retreat

ere'sia *nf* heresy

e'retico, -a *a* heretical ● *nmf* heretic

e'retto *pp di* **erigere** ● *a* erect

erezi'one *nf* erection; (*costruzione*) building

ergasto'lano, -a *nmf* prisoner serving a life sentence, lifer *fam*

er'gastolo *nm* life sentence; (*luogo*) prison

ergono'mia *nf* ergonomics

ergo'nomico *a* ergonomic

ergotera'pia *nf* occupational therapy

ergotera'pista *nmf* occupational therapist

'erica *nf* heather

e'rigere *vt* erect; (*fig: fondare*) found

eri'tema *nm* (*cutaneo*) inflammation; (*solare*) sunburn; **~ da pannolini** nappy rash

Eri'trea *nf* Eritrea

eri'treo, -a *a & nmf* Eritrean

ermafro'dito *a & nm* hermaphrodite

ermel'lino *nm* ermine

ermetica'mente *adv* hermetically

er'metico *a* hermetic; (*a tenuta d'aria*) airtight

'ernia *nf* hernia

e'rodere *vi* erode

e'roe *nm* hero

ero'gare *vt* distribute; (*fornire*) supply

erogazi'one *nf* supply

e'rogeno *a* erogenous

eroica'mente *adv* heroically

e'roico *a* heroic

ero'ina *nf* heroine; (*droga*) heroin

ero'ismo *nm* heroism

'eros *nm* Eros

erosi'one *nf* erosion

e'rotico *a* erotic

ero'tismo *nm* eroticism

'erpice *nm* harrow

er'rante *a* wandering

er'rare *vi* (*vagare*) wander; (*sbagliare*) be mistaken

er'rato *a* (*sbagliato*) mistaken; **se non vado ~** if I'm not mistaken

'erre *nf* **~ moscia** burr

erronea'mente *adv* mistakenly

er'rore *nm* error, mistake; (*di stampa*) misprint; **essere in ~** be wrong. **~ giudiziario** miscarriage of justice. **~ di stampa** printing error, typo

'erta *nf* **stare all'~** be on the alert

eru'dirsi *vr* get educated

eru'dito *a* learned

erut'tare *vt* ⟨*vulcano:*⟩ erupt ● *vi* (*ruttare*) belch

eruzi'one *nf* eruption; *Med* rash

Es *nm Psych* **l'~** the id

es. *abbr* (**esempio**) eg.

esacer'bare *vt* exacerbate

esage'rare *vt* exaggerate; **~ le cose** exaggerate things, go over the top ● *vi* exaggerate; (*nel comportamento*) go over the top; ~ **nel mangiare** eat too much

esagerata'mente *adv* excessively

esage'rato *a* exaggerated; (*prezzo*) exorbitant ● *nm* **è un** ~ he exaggerates

esagerazi'one *nf* exaggeration; **è costato un'**~ it cost the earth; **senza** ~ with no exaggeration

esago'nale *a* hexagonal

e'sagono *nm* hexagon

esa'lare *vt* give off; ~ **l'ultimo respiro** breathe one's last ● *vi* emanate

esalazi'one *nf* emission; **esalazioni** *pl* fumes

esal'tare *vt* exalt; (*entusiasmare*) elate

esal'tarsi *vr* (*entusiasmarsi*) get excited (**per** about)

esal'tato *a* (*fanatico*) fanatical ● *nm* fanatic

esaltazi'one *nf* exaltation; (*in discorso*) fervour

e'same *nm* examination, exam; **dare un** ~ take *or* sit an exam; **prendere in** ~ examine. ~ **di ammissione** *Sch* entrance examination. ~ **di coscienza** soul-searching. ~ **di guida** driving test. **esami** *pl* **di maturità** ≈ A-levels. ~ **orale** *Sch, Univ* viva. ~ **del sangue** blood test. ~ **della vista** eye test

esami'nando, -a *nmf* examinee

esami'nare *vt* examine

esamina|'tore, -'trice *nmf* examiner

e'sangue *a* bloodless

e'sanime *a* lifeless

esaspe'rante *a* exasperating

esaspe'rare *vt* exasperate

esaspe'rarsi *vr* get exasperated

esasperazi'one *nf* exasperation

esatta'mente *adv* exactly

esat'tezza *nf* exactness; (*precisione*) precision; (*di risposta, risultato*) accuracy

e'satto *pp di* **esigere** ● *a* exact; (*risposta, risultato*) correct; (*orologio*) right; **hai l'ora** ~? do you have the right time?; **sono le due esatte** it's two o'clock exactly

esat'tore *nm* collector. ~ **dei crediti** *Fin* debt collector. ~ **delle imposte** tax collector, tax man

esau'dire *vt* grant; fulfil (*speranze*)

esauri'ente *a* exhaustive

esauri'mento *nm* exhaustion; **'fino ad** ~ **delle scorte'** 'subject to availability'. ~ **nervoso** nervous breakdown

esau'rire *vt* exhaust

esau'rirsi *vr* exhaust oneself; (*merci ecc:*) run out

esau'rito *a* exhausted; (*merci*) sold out; (*libro*) out of print; **fare il tutto** ~ (*spettacolo:*) play to a full house

esazi'one *nf* collection; ~ **crediti** debt collection

'esca *nf* bait

escande'scenza *nf* outburst; **dare in escandescenze** lose one's temper

escava'tore *nm* excavator

escava'trice *nf* excavator

escla'mare *vi* exclaim

esclama'tivo *a* exclamatory

esclamazi'one *nf* exclamation

e'scludere *vt* exclude; rule out (*possibilità, ipotesi*)

esclusi'one *nf* exclusion; **senza** ~ **di colpi** (*attacco*) all-out

esclu'siva *nf* exclusive right, sole right; **in** ~ exclusive

esclusiva'mente *adv* exclusively

esclusi'vista *nmf* exclusive agent

esclu'sivo *a* exclusive

e'scluso *pp di* **escludere** ● *a* non è ~ **che ci sia** it's not out of the question that he'll be there; **esclusi i presenti** with the exception of those present; **esclusi sabati e festivi** except Saturdays and Sundays/holidays ● *nm* outcast

escogi'tare *vt* contrive

escoriazi'one *nf* graze

escre'mento *nm* excrement; **escrementi** *pl* excrement

escursi'one *nf* excursion; (*scorreria*) raid; ~ **termica** difference between the lowest and the highest temperature in a 24 hours period

ese'crabile *a* abominable

ese'crare *vt* abhor

esecu'tivo *a* & *nm* executive

esecu|'tore, -'trice *nmf* executor; *Mus* performer

esecuzi'one *nf* execution; *Mus* performance. ~ **capitale** capital punishment

esegu'ibile *nm* *Comput* executable file

esegu'ire *vt* carry out; *Jur* execute; *Mus* perform

e'sempio *nm* example; **ad** *o* **per** ~ for example; **dare l'**~ **a qcno** set sb an example; **fare un** ~ give an example

esem'plare *a* examplary ● *nm* specimen; (*di libro*) copy

esemplifi'care *vt* exemplify

esen'tare *vt* exempt

esen'tare *vr* free oneself

esen'tasse *a* tax-free

e'sente *a* exempt. ~ **da imposta** duty-free. ~ **da IVA** VAT exempt

e'sequie *nfpl* funeral rites

eser'cente *nmf* shopkeeper

eserci'tare *vt* exercise; (*addestrare*) train; (*fare uso di*) exert; (*professione*) practise

eserci'tarsi *vr* practise; ~ **nella danza** practise dancing

eserci'tato *a* (*occhio*) practised; **tenere la memoria esercitata** give one's memory some exercise

esercitazi'one *nf* exercise; *Mil* drill; (*di musica, chimica*) practical class

e'sercito *nm* army. **E**~ **della Salvezza** Salvation Army

eser'cizio *nm* exercise; (*pratica*) practice; *Comm* financial year; (*azienda*) business; **essere fuori** ~ be out of practice; **nell'**~ **delle proprie funzioni** in the line of duty. ~

finanziario financial year. **~ fiscale** fiscal year, tax year. **esercizi** *pl* **a terra** floor exercises. **~ tributario** fiscal year, tax year

esi'bire *vt* show off; produce ⟨*documenti*⟩

esi'birsi *vr Theat* perform; *fig* show off

esibizi'one *nf Theat* performance; ⟨*di documenti*⟩ production

esibizio'nismo *nm* showing off

esibizio'nista *nmf* exhibitionist

esi'gente *a* exacting; ⟨*pignolo*⟩ fastidious

esi'genza *nf* demand; ⟨*bisogno*⟩ need

e'sigere *vt* demand; ⟨*riscuotere*⟩ collect

e'siguo *a* meagre

esila'rante *a* exhilarating

esila'rare *vt* exhilarate

'esile *a* slender; ⟨*voce*⟩ thin

esili'are *vt* exile

esili'arsi *vr* go into exile

esili'ato, -a *a* exiled ● *nmf* exile

e'silio *nm* exile

e'simere *vt* release

e'simersi *vr* **~ da** get out of

e'simio *a* distinguished

esi'stente *a* existing

esi'stenza *nf* existence

esistenzi'ale *a* existential

esistenzia'lismo *nm* existentialism

e'sistere *vi* exist

esi'tante *a* hesitating; ⟨*voce*⟩ faltering

esi'tare *vi* hesitate

esitazi'one *nf* hesitation

'esito *nm* result; **avere buon ~** be a success

'esodo *nm* exodus

e'sofago *nm* oesophagus

esone'rare *vt* exempt

e'sonero *nm* exemption

esorbi'tante *a* exorbitant

esorbi'tare *vi* **~ da** exceed

esor'cismo *nm* exorcism

esor'cista *nmf* exorcist

esorciz'zare *vt* exorcize

esordi'ente *nmf* person making his/her début

e'sordio *nm* opening; ⟨*di attore*⟩ début

esor'dire *vi* début

esor'tare *vt* ⟨*pregare*⟩ beg; ⟨*incitare*⟩ urge

eso'terico *a* esoteric

e'sotico *a* exotic

espa'drillas *nfpl* espadrilles

e'spandere *vt* expand

e'spandersi *vr* expand; ⟨*diffondersi*⟩ extend

espan'dibile *a Comput* upgradeable

espandibilità *nf inv Comput* upgradeability

espansi'one *nf* expansion; **in ~** expanding

espansio'nista *nmf* expansionist

espansio'nistico *a* expansionist

espan'sivo *a* expansive; ⟨*persona*⟩ friendly

espatri'are *vi* leave one's country

espatri'ato, -a *nmf* expatriate, expat *fam*

e'spatrio *nm* expatriation

espedi'ente *nm* expedient; **vivere di espedienti** live by one's wits

e'spellere *vt* expel; send off ⟨*calciatore*⟩

esperi'enza *nf* experience; **per ~** ⟨*sapere,*

parlare⟩ from experience; **non ha ~** he doesn't have any experience

esperi'mento *nm* experiment

e'sperto, -a *a* & *nmf* expert. **~ di computer** computer expert

espi'are *vt* atone for

espia'torio *a* expiatory

espi'rare *vt/i* breathe out

espirazi'one *nf* exhalation; ⟨*scadenza*⟩ expiry

espli'care *vt* carry on

esplicita'mente *adv* explicitly

e'splicito *a* explicit

e'splodere *vi* explode ● *vt* ⟨*arma:*⟩ fire

esplo'rare *vt* explore

esplora|'tore, -'trice *nmf* explorer; **giovane ~** boy scout; **giovane esploratrice** girl guide

esplorazi'one *nf* exploration

esplosi'one *nf* explosion

esplo'sivo *a* & *nm* explosive

espo'nente *nm* exponent; **2 all'~** superscript 2

esponenzi'ale *a* exponential

e'sporre *vt* expose; display ⟨*merci*⟩; ⟨*spiegare*⟩ expound; exhibit ⟨*quadri ecc*⟩

e'sporsi *vr* ⟨*compromettersi*⟩ compromise oneself; ⟨*al sole*⟩ expose oneself; ⟨*alle critiche*⟩ lay oneself open

espor'tare *vt Comm, Comput* export

esporta|'tore, -'trice *nmf* exporter

esportazi'one *nf* export

espo'simetro *nm* light meter

esposi|'tore, -'trice *nmf* exhibitor ● *nm* display rack

esposizi'one *nf* ⟨*mostra*⟩ exhibition; ⟨*in vetrina*⟩ display; ⟨*spiegazione ecc*⟩ exposition; ⟨*posizione, fotografia*⟩ exposure; **con ~ a nord/sud** north-/south-facing

e'sposto *pp di* **esporre** ● *a* exposed; ⟨*merce*⟩ on show; ⟨*spiegato*⟩ set out; **~ a nord/sud** north-/south-facing ● *nm* submission

espressa'mente *adv* expressly; **non l'ha detto ~** he didn't put it in so many words

espressi'one *nf* expression

espressio'nismo *nm* expressionism

espressio'nista *a* & *nmf* expressionist

espressio'nistico *a* expressionistic

espres'sivo *a* expressive

e'spresso *pp di* **esprimere** ● *a* express ● *nm* ⟨*lettera*⟩ special delivery; ⟨*treno*⟩ express train; ⟨*caffè*⟩ espresso; **per ~** ⟨*spedire*⟩ [by] express [post]; **piatto ~** meal made to order

e'sprimere *vt* express

e'sprimersi *vr* express oneself

espropri'are *vt* dispossess

espropriazi'one *nf Jur* expropriation

e'sproprio *nm* expropriation

espulsi'one *nf* expulsion

e'spulso *pp di* **espellere**

esqui'mese *a* & *nmf* Eskimo

es'senza *nf* essence

essenzi'ale *a* essential ● *nm* important thing; **l'~** (*di teoria ecc*) the bare bones; **l'~ è...** (*la cosa più importante*) the main thing is...

essenzial'mente *a* essentially

'essere *vi* be; **c'è** there is; **ci sono** there are; **ci sono!** (*ho capito*) I've got it!; **ci siamo!** (*siamo arrivati*) here we are at last!; **non ce n'è più** there's none left; **c'è di che essere contenti** there's a lot to be happy about; **che ora è? – sono le dieci** what time is it? – it's ten o'clock; **chi è? – sono io** who is it? – it's me; **è stato detto che** it has been said that; **siamo in due** there are two of us; **questa camicia è da lavare** this shirt is to be washed; **non è da te** it's not like you; **~ di** belong to; (*provenire da*) be from; **~ per** (*favorevole*) be in favour of; **se fossi in te,...** if I were you,...; **sarà!** if you say so!; **come sarebbe a dire?** what are you getting at? ● *v aux* have; (*in passivi*) be; **siamo arrivati** we have arrived; **ci sono stato ieri** I was there yesterday; **sono nato a Torino** I was born in Turin; **è riconosciuto come...** he is recognized as... ● *nm* being. **~ umano** human being; **~ vivente** living creature

essic'care *vt* dry

essic'cato *a* dried; ‹*noce di cocco*› desiccated

'esso, -a *pers pron* he, she; (*cosa, animale*) it

est *nm* east; **l'E~ europeo** Eastern Europe

'estasi *nf* ecstasy; **andare in ~ per** go into raptures over

estasi'are *vt* enrapture

estasi'arsi *vr* go into raptures

e'state *nf* summer

e'statico *a* ecstatic

estempo'raneo *a* impromptu

e'stendere *vt* extend

e'stendersi *vr* spread; (*allungarsi*) stretch

estensi'one *nf* extension; (*ampiezza*) expanse; *Mus* range

esten'sivo *a* extensive

estenu'ante *a* exhausting

estenu'are *vt* exhaust

estenu'arsi *vr* exhaust oneself

'estere *nm* ester

esteri'ore *a* & *nm* exterior

esteriorità *nf inv* outward appearance; **badare all'~** judge by appearances

esterioriz'zare *vt* externalize

esterior'mente *adv* externally; (*di persone*) outwardly

esterna'mente *adv* on the outside

ester'nare *vt* express, show

e'sterno, -a *a* external; (*scala*) outside; **per uso ~** for external use only ● *nm Archit* exterior; (*in film*) location shot ● *nmf* day-pupil

'estero *a* foreign ● *nm* foreign countries *pl*; **all'~** abroad; **ministero degli esteri** ≈ Foreign Office *Br*, State Department *Am*

esterofi'lia *nf* xenophilia

este'rofilo *a* xenophile

esterre'fatto *a* horrified

e'steso *pp di* **estendere** ● *a* extensive; (*diffuso*) widespread; **per ~** ‹*scrivere*› in full

e'steta *nmf* aesthete

e'stetica *nf* aesthetics

estetica'mente *adv* aesthetically

esteticità *nf* aestheticism

e'stetico *a* aesthetic; ‹*chirurgia, chirurgo*› plastic

este'tismo *nm* (*dottrina, carattere*) aestheticism

este'tista *nmf* beautician

estima'tore, -'trice *nmf* fan

'estimo *nm* estimate

e'stinguere *vt* extinguish; close ‹*conto*›

e'stinguersi *vr* die out

e'stinto, -a *pp di* **estinguere** ● *nmf* deceased

estin'tore *nm* [fire] extinguisher

estinzi'one *nf* extinction; (*di incendio*) putting out

estir'pare *vt* uproot; extract ‹*dente*›; *fig* eradicate ‹*crimine, malattia*›

estirpazi'one *nf* eradication; (*di dente*) extraction

e'stivo *a* summer *attrib*

e'stone *a* & *nm* Estonian

E'stonia *nf* Estonia

e'storcere *vt* extort

estorsi'one *nf* extortion

e'storto *pp di* **estorcere**

estradizi'one *nf* extradition

estra'gone *nm* tarragon

estra'ibile *a* removeable

e'straneo, -a *a* extraneous; (*straniero*) foreign ● *nmf* stranger

estrani'are *vt* estrange

estrani'arsi *vr* become estranged

estrapo'lare *vt* extrapolate

e'strarre *vt* extract; (*sorteggiare*) draw

e'stratto *pp di* **estrarre** ● *nm* extract; (*brano*) excerpt; (*documento*) abstract. **~ conto** statement [of account], bank statement

estrazi'one *nf* extraction; (*a sorte*) draw

estrema'mente *adv* extremely

estre'mismo *nm* extremism

estre'mista *nmf* extremist

estremità *nf inv* extremity; (*di una corda*) end; **~** *pl Anat* extremities

e'stremo *a* extreme; (*ultimo*) last; **misure estreme** drastic measures; **fare un ~ tentativo** make one last try; **l'E~ Oriente** the Far East; **~ saluto** *Mil* military funeral; **l'estrema unzione** last rites ● *nm* (*limite*) extreme; **all'~** in the extreme; **passare da un ~ all'altro** go from one extreme to the other; **estremi** *pl* (*di documento*) main points; (*di reato*) essential elements; **essere agli estremi** be at the end of one's tether; **andare agli estremi** go to extremes; **essere all'~ delle forze** have no strength left

'estro *nm* (*disposizione artistica*) talent; (*ispirazione*) inspiration; (*capriccio*) whim

e'strogeno *nm* oestrogen

estro'mettere *vt* expel

estromissi'one *nf* ejection

e'stroso *a* talented; (*capriccioso*) unpredictable

estro'verso *a* extroverted ● *nm* extrovert
estu'ario *nm* estuary
esube'rante *a* exuberant
esube'ranza *nf* exuberance
e'subero *nm* ~ **cassa integrazione** voluntary redundancy
esu'lare *vt* ~ **da** be beyond the scope of
'esule *nmf* exile
esul'tante *a* exultant
esul'tanza *nf* exultation
esul'tare *vi* rejoice
esu'mare *vt* exhume
età *nf* age; **raggiungere la maggiore** ~ come of age; **un uomo di mezz'**~ a middle-aged man; **avere la stessa** ~ be the same age; **che** ~ **gli daresti?** how old would you say he was?; **fin dalla più tenera** ~ from his/her etc earliest years; **in** ~ **avanzata** of advanced years; **è senza** ~ it's hard to tell his age. ~ **del Bronzo** Bronze Age. ~ **della pensione** retirement age
e'tano *nm* ethane
eta'nolo *nm* ethanol
'etere *nm* ether. ~ **etilico** ether
e'tereo *a* ethereal
eterna'mente *adv* eternally
eternità *nf* eternity; **è un'**~ **che non la vedo** I haven't seen her for ages
e'terno *a* eternal; ⟨*questione, problema*⟩ age-old; ⟨*fig: dicorso, conferenza*⟩ never-ending; **in** ~ *fam* for ever; **giurare** ~ **amore** swear undying love; **un** ~ **bambino** a child
etero'geneo *a* diverse, heterogeneous
eterosessu'ale *a & nmf* heterosexual
eterosessualità *nf* heterosexuality
'etica *nf* ethics
eti'chetta[1] *nf* label; (con il prezzo) price-tag
eti'chetta[2] *nf* (*cerimoniale*) etiquette
etichet'tare *vt* label
etichetta'trice *nf* labelling machine
etichetta'tura *nf* (*operazione*) labelling
'etico *a* ethical
eti'lometro *nm* Breathalyzer®
etimolo'gia *nf* etymology
e'tiope *a & nmf* Ethiopian
Eti'opia *nf* Ethiopia
eti'opico *a* Ethiopian
'Etna *nm* Etna
et'nia *nf* ethnic group
'etnico *a* ethnic
etnolo'gia *nf* ethnology
e'trusco *a & nmf* Etruscan
'ettaro *nm* hectare
+ettino *suff* **cosettina** *nf* small thing; **è una cosettina da niente** it's nothing
'etto, etto'grammo *nm* hundred grams, quarter pound
+etto *suff* **cameretta** *nf* little bedroom; **scherzetto** *nf* prank; **piccoletto** *nm pej* shorty
et'tolitro *nm* hectolitre
euca'lipto *nm* eucalyptus
eucari'stia *nf* Eucharist
eufe'mismo *nm* euphemism
eufe'mistico *a* euphemistic

eufo'ria *nf* elation; *Med* euphoria
eu'forico *a* elated; *Med* euphoric
euge'netica *nf* eugenics
eu'nuco *nm* eunuch
Eur'asia *nf* Eurasia
eurasi'atico *a* Eurasian
'EURATOM *nf abbr* (**Comunità Europea dell'Energia Atomica**) EURATOM
euro+ *pref* Euro+
eurobbligazi'one *nf* Eurobond
euro'cheque *nm inv* Eurocheque
Euro'city *nm inv Rail* international Intercity
eurodepu'tato *nm* Euro MP, MEP
eurodi'visa *nf* Eurocurrency
euro'dollaro *nm* Eurodollar
Eu'ropa *nf* Europe
europe'ismo *nm* Europeanism
euro'peo, -a *a & nmf* European
euro'scettico *nm* eurosceptic
eutana'sia *nf* euthanasia
evacu'are *vt* evacuate
evacuazi'one *nf* evacuation
e'vadere *vt* evade; (*sbrigare*) deal with ● *vi* ~ **da** escape from
evane'scente *a* vanishing
evan'gelico *a* evangelical
evange'lista *nm* evangelist
evan'gelo *nm* = **vangelo**
evapo'rare *vi* evaporate
evaporazi'one *nf* evaporation
evasi'one *nf* escape; (*fiscale*) evasion; *fig* escapism
evasiva'mente *adv* evasively
eva'sivo *a* evasive
e'vaso, -a *pp di* **evadere** ● *nmf* fugitive
eva'sore *nm* ~ **fiscale** tax evader
eveni'enza *nf* eventuality; **in ogni** ~ if need be
e'vento *nm* event
eventu'ale *a* possible
eventualità *nf inv* eventuality; **in ogni** ~ at all events; **nell'**~ **che** in the event that
eventual'mente *adv* if necessary
ever'sivo *a* subversive
evi'dente *a* evident
evidente'mente *adv* evidently
evi'denza *nf* evidence; **mettere in** ~ emphasize; **mettersi in** ~ make oneself conspicuous; **arrendersi all'**~ face the facts
evidenzi'are *vt* highlight
evidenzia'tore *nm* (*penna*) highlighter
evi'rare *vt* emasculate
evi'tare *vt* avoid; (*risparmiare*) spare
'evo *nm* age
evo'care *vt* evoke
evolu'tivo *a* evolutionary
evo'luto *pp di* **evolvere** ● *a* evolved; (*progredito*) progressive; ⟨*civiltà, nazione*⟩ advanced; **una donna evoluta** a modern woman
evoluzi'one *nf* evolution; (*di ginnasta, aereo*) circle
e'volvere *vt* develop
e'volversi *vr* evolve
ev'viva *int* hurray; ~ **il Papa!** long live the

Pope!; **gridare** ~ cheer; ~ **la modestia!** what modesty!

ex *prep* ex, former; **ex moglie** ex-wife

ex 'aequo *adv* **arrivare** ~ ~ come in joint first

ex-Jugo'slavia *nf* ex-Yugoslavia

ex-jugo'slavo *a & nmf* ex-Yugoslav

ex 'libris *nm inv* bookplate

ex'ploit *nm inv* feat, exploit

'extra *a inv* extra; ⟨qualità⟩ first-class ● *nm*

inv extra

extracomuni'tario *a* non-EC, non-EU

extraconiu'gale *a* extramarital

extraeuro'peo *a* non-European

extraparlamen'tare *a* extraparliamentary

extrasco'lastico *a* extra-curricular

extrasensori'ale *a* extrasensory

extrater'restre *nmf* extra-terrestrial

extrauniversi'tario *a* extramural

ex 'voto *nm inv* ex voto

Ff

fa¹ *nm inv* Mus ⟨chiave, nota⟩ F

fa² *adv* ago; **due mesi** ~ two months ago

fabbi'sogno *nm* requirements *pl*, needs *pl*. ~ **dello Stato** government spending estimates

'fabbrica *nf* factory

fabbri'cabile *a* ⟨area, terreno⟩ that can be built on

fabbri'cante *nm* manufacturer. ~ **d'armi** arms manufacturer

fabbri'care *vt* build; ⟨produrre⟩ manufacture; ⟨fig: inventare⟩ fabricate

fabbri'cato *nm* building

fabbricazi'one *nf* manufacturing; ⟨costruzione⟩ building

'fabbro *nm* blacksmith

fac'cenda *nf* matter; **faccende** *pl* **domestiche** housework *sg*

faccendi'ere *nm* wheeler-dealer

fac'chino *nm* porter

'faccia *nf* face; ⟨di foglio⟩ side; ~ **a** ~ face to face; ~ **tosta** cheek; **voltar** ~ change sides; **di** ~ ⟨palazzo⟩ opposite; **alla** ~ **di** ⟨fam: a dispetto di⟩ in spite of; **alla** ~**!** ⟨stupore⟩ bloody hell!

facci'ata *nf* façade; ⟨di foglio⟩ side; ⟨fig: esteriorità⟩ outward appearance

fa'cente *nmf* ~ **funzioni** deputy

fa'ceto *a* facetious; **tra il serio e il** ~ half joking

fa'cezia *nf* ⟨battuta⟩ witticism

fa'chiro *nm* fakir

'facile *a* easy; ⟨affabile⟩ easy-going; **essere** ~ **alle critiche** be quick to criticize; **essere** ~ **al riso** laugh a lot; ~ **a farsi** easy to do; **è** ~ **che piova** it's likely to rain

facilità *nf inv* ease; ⟨disposizione⟩ aptitude; **avere** ~ **di parola** express oneself well. ~ **d'uso** ease of use, user-friendliness

facili'tare *vt* facilitate

facilitazi'one *nf* facility; **facilitazioni** *pl* Fin special terms; **facilitazioni** *pl* **di pagamento** Fin easy terms

facil'mente *adv* ⟨con facilità⟩ easily; ⟨probabilmente⟩ probably

faci'lone *a* slapdash

facilone'ria *nf* slapdash attitude

facino'roso *a* violent

facoltà *nf inv* faculty; ⟨potere⟩ power; **essere nel pieno possesso delle proprie** ~ be compos mentis

facolta'tivo *a* optional; **fermata facoltativa** request stop

facol'toso *a* wealthy

fac'simile *nm* facsimile

fac'totum *nm inv* man Friday ● *nf inv* girl Friday

'faggio *nm* beech

fagi'ano *nm* pheasant

fagio'lino *nm* French bean

fagi'olo *nm* bean; **a** ~ ⟨arrivare, capitare⟩ at the right time. ~ **borlotto** borlotti bean. ~ **di Spagna** runner bean, string bean

fagoci'tare *vt* gobble up ⟨società⟩

fa'gotto *nm* bundle; *Mus* bassoon

Fahren'heit *a* Fahrenheit

'faida *nf* feud

fai da te *nm* do-it-yourself, DIY

fa'ina *nf* weasel

fa'lange *nf* ⟨dito, Mil⟩ phalanx

fal'cata *nf* stride

'falce *nf* scythe; ~ **e martello** ⟨simbolo⟩ the hammer and sickle

fal'cetto *nm* sickle

falci'are *vt* cut; *fig* mow down

falci'ata *nf* ⟨quantità d'erba⟩ swathe

falcia'trice *nf* [lawn-]mower

'falco *nm* hawk

fal'cone *nm* falcon

'falda *nf* stratum; ⟨di neve⟩ flake; ⟨di cappello⟩ brim; ⟨di cappotto, frac⟩ coat-tails; ⟨pendio⟩ slope. ~ **freatica** water table

fale'gname *nm* carpenter

falegname'ria *nf* carpentry

fa'lena *nf* moth

'Falkland *nfpl* le [isole] ~ the Falklands

'falla *nf* leak

fal'lace *a* deceptive

'fallico *a* phallic**

fallimen'tare *a* disastrous; *Jur* bankruptcy

falli'mento *nm Comm* bankruptcy; *fig* failure

fal'lire *vi Comm* go bankrupt; *fig* fail ● *vt* miss ⟨*colpo*⟩

fal'lito *a* unsuccessful ● *a & nm* bankrupt

'**fallo** *nm* fault; (*errore*) mistake; *Sport* foul; (*imperfezione*) flaw; **senza ~** without fail; **cogliere in ~** catch red-handed; **mettere un piede in ~** slip. **~ di mano** (*in calcio*) handball

falò *nm inv* bonfire

fal'sare *vt* alter; (*falsificare*) falsify

falsa'riga *nf* **sulla ~ di** along the same lines as

fal'sario, -a *nmf* forger; (*di documenti*) counterfeiter

fal'setto *nm* falsetto

falsifi'care *vt* fake; (*contraffare*) forge

falsificazi'one *nf* (*di documento*) falsification

falsità *nf* falseness

'**falso** *a* false; (*sbagliato*) wrong; ⟨*opera d'arte ecc*⟩ fake; ⟨*gioielli, oro*⟩ imitation; **essere un ~ magro** be fatter than one looks ● *nm* forgery; **giurare il ~** commit perjury. **~ in atto pubblico** forgery of a legal document

'**fama** *nf* fame; (*reputazione*) reputation

'**fame** *nf* hunger; **aver ~** be hungry; **fare la ~** barely scrape a living; **da ~** ⟨*stipendio*⟩ miserly; **avere una ~ da lupo** be ravenous

fa'melico *a* ravenous

famige'rato *a* infamous

fa'miglia *nf* family

famili'are *a* family *attrib*; (*ben noto*) familiar; (*senza cerimonie*) informal ● *nm* relative, relation

familiarità *nf* familiarity; (*informalità*) informality

familiariz'zarsi *vr* familiarize oneself

fa'moso *a* famous

fa'nale *nm* lamp; *Auto ecc* light. **fanali** *pl* **posteriori** *Auto* rear lights

fana'lino *nm* **~ di coda** *Auto* tail light; **essere il ~ di coda** *fig* bring up the rear, be the back marker

fa'natico, -a *a* fanatical; **essere ~ di calcio/cinema** be a football/cinema fanatic ● *nmf* fanatic

fana'tismo *nm* fanaticism

fanciul'lezza *nf* childhood

fanci'ullo, -a *nmf* young boy; young girl

fan'donia *nf* lie; **fandonie!** nonsense!

fan'fara *nf* fanfare; (*complesso*) brass band

fanfaro'nata *nf* brag; **fanfaronate** *pl* bragging

fanfa'rone, -a *nmf* braggart

fan'ghiglia *nf* mud

'**fango** *nm* mud

fan'goso *a* muddy

fannul'lone, -a *nmf* idler

fantasci'enza *nf* science fiction

fanta'sia *nf* fantasy; (*immaginazione*) imagination; (*capriccio*) fancy; (*di tessuto*) pattern; **fantasie** *pl* (*sciocchezze*) moonshine

fantasi'oso *a* ⟨*stilista, ragazzo*⟩ imaginative; ⟨*resoconto*⟩ improbable, fanciful

fan'tasma *nm* ghost; **essere il ~ di se stesso** be a shadow of one's former self; **città ~** ghost town; **governo ~** shadow cabinet

fantasti'care *vi* day-dream, fantasize

fantasti'cheria *nf* day-dream, fantasy

fan'tastico *a* fantastic; ⟨*racconto*⟩ fantasy *attrib*

'**fante** *nm* infantryman; (*nelle carte*) jack

fante'ria *nf* infantry

fan'tino *nm* jockey

fan'toccio *nm* puppet

fanto'matico *a* (*inafferrabile*) phantom *attrib*; (*immaginario*) mythical

fara'butto *nm* trickster

fara'ona *nf* (*uccello*) guinea-fowl

'**farcia** *nf* stuffing; ⟨*di torta*⟩ filling

far'cire *vt* stuff; fill ⟨*torta*⟩

far'cito *a* stuffed; ⟨*dolce*⟩ filled

fard *nm inv* blusher

far'dello *nm* bundle; *fig* burden

'**fare** *vt* do; make ⟨*dolce, letto, ecc*⟩; (*recitare la parte di*) play; (*trascorrere*) spend; **~ una pausa/un sogno** have a break/a dream; **~ colpo su** impress; **~ paura a** frighten; **~ piacere a** please; **farla finita** put an end to it; **~ l'insegnante** be a teacher; **~ lo scemo** play the idiot; **~ una settimana al mare** spend a week at the seaside; **3 più 3 fa 6** 3 and 3 makes 6; **quanto fa? – fanno 10 000 lire** how much is it? – it's 10,000 lire; **far ~ qcsa a qcno** get sb to do sth; (*costringere*) make sb do sth; **~ vedere** show; **fammi parlare** let me speak; **niente a che ~ con** nothing to do with; **non c'è niente da ~** (*per problema*) there is nothing we/you etc can do; **fa caldo/ buio** it's warm/dark; **non fa niente** it doesn't matter; **strada facendo** on the way. **farcela** (*riuscire*) manage ● *vi* **fai in modo di venire** try and come; **~ da** act as; **~ per** make as if to; **~ presto** be quick; **non fa per me** it's not for me ● *nm* (*comportamento*) manner; **sul far del giorno** at daybreak

fa'retto *nm* spot[light]

far'falla *nf* butterfly

farfal'lino *nm* (*cravatta*) bow tie

farfugli'are *vt* mutter

fa'rina *nf* flour. **~ di ceci** chickpea flour, gram flour. **~ gialla** maize flour. **~ integrale** wholemeal flour. **~ lattea** powdered milk for babies. **~ d'ossa** bonemeal

fari'nacei *nmpl* starchy food *sg*

fa'ringe *nf* pharynx

farin'gite *nf* pharyngitis

fari'noso *a* ⟨*neve*⟩ powdery; ⟨*mela*⟩ soft; ⟨*patata*⟩ floury

farma'ceutico *a* pharmaceutical; **industria farmaceutica** pharmaceuticals industry

farma'cia *nf* pharmacy; (*negozio*) chemist's [shop]. **~ di turno** duty pharmacy

farma'cista *nmf* chemist, pharmacist

'**farmaco** *nm* drug; **essere sotto farmaci** be on medication

'**faro** *nm Auto* headlight; *Aeron* beacon; (*costruzione*) lighthouse; **abbassare i fari** dip one's headlights; **accendere i fari** switch on one's lights. **fari** *pl* **antinebbia** fog lamps. **fari** *pl* **posteriori** rear lights

farragi'noso *a* confused

'**farsa** *nf* farce

far'sesco *a* farcical

'**farsi** *vr* (*diventare*) get; (*sl: drogarsi*) shoot up; **~ avanti** come forward; **~ i fatti propri** mind one's own business; **~ la barba** shave; **~ la villa** *fam* buy a villa; **~ il ragazzo** *fam* find a boyfriend; **~ due risate** have a laugh; **~ male** hurt oneself; **~ un nome** make a name for oneself; **farsela sotto** *fam* wet oneself

Far 'west *nm* Wild West

fa'scetta *nf* strip; (*per capelli*) hair band; (*di giornale*) wrapper

'**fascia** *nf* band; (*zona*) area; (*ufficiale*) sash; (*benda*) bandage; (*di smoking*) cummerbund; (*in statistica*) bracket. **~ per capelli** hair band. **~ elastica** crepe bandage; (*ventriera*) girdle. **~ d'età** age bracket, age group. **~ d'ozono** ozone layer. **~ di reddito** income bracket

fasci'are *vt* bandage; cling to ⟨*fianchi*⟩

fasci'arsi *vr* bandage; **~ la testa prima di rompersela** worry about something that might never happen

fascia'tura *nf* dressing; (*azione*) bandaging

fascicola|'tore, -'trice *nmf* sorter

fa'scicolo *nm* file; (*di rivista*) issue; (*libretto*) booklet

fa'scina *nf* faggot

'**fascino** *nm* fascination

fasci'noso *a* charming

'**fascio** *nm* bundle; (*di fiori*) bunch. **~ di luce** beam of light

fa'scismo *nm* fascism

fa'scista *a* & *nmf* fascist

'**fase** *nf* phase; **il motore è fuori ~** the timing is wrong; **sono fuori ~** I'm not firing on all four cylinders; **essere in ~ di miglioramento** be on the mend, be recovering; **essere in ~ di espansione** be expanding

fast 'food *nm inv* fast food; (*ristorante*) fast food restaurant

fa'stidio *nm* nuisance; (*scomodo*) inconvenience. **~** *pl* (*preoccupazioni*) worries; (*disturbi*) troubles; **dar ~ a qcno** bother sb

fastidi'oso *a* tiresome

'**fasto** *nm* pomp

fa'stoso *a* sumptuous

fa'sullo *a* bogus

'**fata** *nf* fairy

fa'tale *a* fatal; (*inevitabile*) fated; **donna ~** femme fatale

fata'lismo *nm* fatalism

fata'lista *nmf* fatalist ● *a* fatalistic

fatalità *nf inv* fate; (*caso sfortunato*) misfortune

fatal'mente *adv* inevitably

fa'tato *a* ⟨*anello, bacchetta*⟩ magic

fa'tica *nf* effort; (*lavoro faticoso*) hard work; (*stanchezza, di metalli*) fatigue; **a ~** with great difficulty; **è ~ sprecata** it's a waste of time; **fare ~ a fare qcsa** find it difficult to do sth; **senza [nessuna] ~** without [any] effort; **fare ~ a finire qcsa** struggle to finish sth; **uomo di ~** odd-job man

fati'caccia *nf* pain

fati'care *vi* toil; **~ a** (*stentare*) find it difficult to

fati'cata *nf* effort; (*sfacchinata*) grind

fati'coso *a* tiring; (*difficile*) difficult

fati'scente *a* crumbling

'**fato** *nm* fate

fat'taccio *nm hum* foul deed

fat'tezze *nfpl* features

fat'tibile *a* feasible

fatti'specie *nf* **nella ~** in this case

'**fatto** *pp di* **fare; ormai è fatta!** what's done is done ● *a* made; **~ a mano/in casa** hand-made/home-made; **essere ben ~** ⟨*persona*⟩ have a nice figure; **un uomo ~** a grown man ● *nm* fact; (*azione*) action; (*avvenimento*) event; (*faccenda*) business, matter; **sa il ~ suo** he knows his business; **le ho detto il ~ suo** I told her what I thought of him; **di ~** in fact; **in ~ di** as regards; **~ sta che** the fact remains that; **mettere di fronte al ~ compiuto** present with a fait accompli

fat'tore *nm* (*causa, Math*) factor; (*di fattoria*) farm manager

fatto'ria *nf* farm; (*casa*) farmhouse

fatto'rino *nm* messenger [boy]. **~ d'albergo** bellboy

fattucchi'era *nf* witch

fat'tura *nf* (*stile*) cut; (*lavorazione*) workmanship; *Comm* invoice. **~ di acquisto** purchase invoice. **~ pro-forma** pro forma [invoice]. **~ di vendita** sales invoice

fattu'rare *vt* invoice; (*adulterare*) adulterate

fattu'rato *nm* turnover, sales *pl*

fatturazi'one *nf* invoicing, billing

'**fatuo** *a* fatuous

'**fauci** *nfpl* (*di leone*) maw *sg*

'**fauna** *nf* fauna

'**fausto** *a* propitious

fau'tore *nm* supporter

'**fava** *nf* broad bean

fa'vella *nf* speech

fa'villa *nf* spark

'**favo** *nm* honeycomb

'**favola** *nf* fable; (*fiaba*) story; (*oggetto di pettegolezzi*) laughing-stock; **è una ~!** (*meraviglia*) it's divine!

favo'loso *a* fabulous

fa'vore *nm* favour; **essere a ~ di** be in favour of; **per ~** please; **di ~** ⟨*condizioni, trattamento*⟩ preferential; **col ~ delle tenebre** under cover of darkness

favoreggia'mento *nm Jur* aiding and abetting

favo'revole *a* favourable

favorevol'mente *adv* favourably

favo'rire *vt* favour; (*promuovere*) promote;
vuol ~? (*a cena, pranzo*) will you have some?;
(*entrare*) will you come in?; **favorisca alla
cassa** please pay at the cash-desk; **favorisca
i documenti** your papers please
favo'rito, -a *a* & *nmf* favourite
fax *nm inv* fax; **inviare via ~** fax, send by
fax. **~ a carta comune** plain paper fax
fa'xare *vt* fax
fazi'one *nf* faction
faziosità *nf* bias
fazi'oso *nm* sectarian
fazzolet'tino *nm* **~ [di carta]** [paper] tissue
fazzo'letto *nm* handkerchief; (*da testa*)
headscarf
feb'braio *nm* February
'febbre *nf* fever; **avere la ~** have *o* run a
temperature; **~ da fieno** hay fever
febbrici'tante *a* fevered
feb'brile *a* feverish
febbril'mente *adv* feverishly
'feccia *nf* dregs *pl*
'fecola *nf* potato flour
fecon'dare *vt* fertilize
feconda'tore *nm* fertilizer
fecondazi'one *nf* fertilization; **~ artificiale** artificial insemination. **~ in vitro** in
vitro fertilization, IVF
fe'condo *a* fertile
'fede *nf* faith; (*fiducia*) trust; (*anello*) wedding ring; **in buona/mala ~** in good/bad
faith; **prestar ~ a** believe; **tener ~ alla
parola** keep one's word; **aver ~ in qcno**
have faith in sb, believe in sb; **degno di ~** reliable; **in ~** Yours faithfully
fe'dele *a* faithful ● *nmf* believer; (*seguace*)
follower; **i fedeli** the faithful
fedel'mente *adv* faithfully
fedeltà *nf* faithfulness; **alta ~** high fidelity
'federa *nf* pillowcase
fede'rale *a* federal
federa'lismo *nm* federalism
federa'lista *nm* federalist
fede'rato *a* federate
federazi'one *nf* federation
fe'difrago, -a *a* faithless; *hum* two-timing
● *nm* faithless wretch; *hum* two-timer
fe'dina *nf* **avere la ~ penale sporca/
pulita** have a/no criminal record
fega'telli *nmpl* (*di maiale*) pork liver
fega'tino *nm* **fegatini** *pl* **di pollo** chicken
livers
'fegato *nm* liver; *fig* guts *pl*; **mangiarsi il ~,
rodersi il ~** be consumed with rage
'felce *nf* fern
fe'lice *a* happy; (*fortunato*) lucky; **~ come
una Pasqua** blissfully happy
felice'mente *adv* happily; (*con successo*)
successfully
felicità *nf* happiness
felici'tarsi *vr* **~ con** congratulate
felicitazi'oni *nfpl* congratulations
fe'lino *a* feline
'felpa *nf* (*indumento*) sweatshirt; (*stoffa*) felt

fel'pato *a* brushed; (*passo*) stealthy
'feltro *nm* felt; (*cappello*) felt hat
'femmina *nf* female
femmi'nile *a* feminine; (*rivista, abbigliamento*) women's; (*sesso*) female ● *nm* feminine
femminilità *nf* femininity
femmi'nismo *nm* feminism
'femore *nm* femur
'fendere *vt* split
fendi'nebbia *nm inv* fog lamp
fendi'tura *nf* split; (*in roccia*) crack
fe'nice *nf* phoenix
feni'cottero *nm* flamingo
fenome'nale *a* phenomenal
fe'nomeno *nm* phenomenon
'feretro *nm* coffin
feri'ale *a* weekday; **giorno ~** weekday
'ferie *nfpl* holidays; (*di università, tribunale
ecc*) vacation *sg*; **andare in ~** go on holiday;
prendere le ~ go on holiday; **prendere
delle ~** take time off; **prendere un giorno
di ~** take a day off
feri'mento *nm* wounding
fe'rire *vt* wound; (*in incidente*) injure; *fig*
hurt
fe'rirsi *vr* injure oneself
fe'rita *nf* wound
fe'rito *a* wounded ● *nm* wounded person; *Mil*
casualty; **~ grave** seriously injured person
feri'toia *nf* loophole; **feritoie** *pl* **per le
schede di espansione** *Comput* expansion
slots
'ferma *nf Mil* period of service
fermacal'zoni *nm inv* cycle clip
fermaca'pelli *nm inv* hair slide
ferma'carte *nm inv* paperweight
fermacra'vatta *nm inv* tiepin
ferma'fogli *nm inv* bulldog clip
fer'maglio *nm* clasp; (*spilla*) brooch; (*per
capelli*) hair slide
ferma'mente *adv* firmly
ferma'porta *nm inv* doorstop
fer'mare *vt* stop; (*fissare*) fix; *Jur* detain ● *vi*
stop
fer'marsi *vr* stop
fer'mata *nf* stop; **'~ prenotata'** 'bus stopping'; **senza fermate** (*tragitto*) non-stop. **~
dell'autobus** bus stop. **~ obbligatoria** compulsory stop. **~ a richiesta** request stop
fermen'tare *vi* ferment
fermentazi'one *nf* fermentation
fer'mento *nm* ferment; (*lievito*) yeast;
essere in ~ be in/get into a tizzy
fer'mezza *nf* firmness
'fermo *a* still; (*veicolo*) stationary; (*stabile*)
steady; (*orologio*) not working; **~!** don't
move!; **~ restando che...** it being understood that...; **'~ per manutenzione'** 'closed
for repairs' ● *nm Jur* detention; *Mech* catch;
in stato di ~ in custody. **~ immagine** *TV*
freeze frame. **~ posta** poste restante, general
delivery *Am*

fer'net® *nm inv* bitter digestive liqueur

fe'roce *a* fierce, ferocious; ‹*bestia*› wild; ‹*freddo, dolore*› unbearable

feroce'mente *adv* fiercely, ferociously

fe'rocia *nf* ferocity

fer'raglia *nf* scrap iron

ferra'gosto *nm* 15 August (*bank holiday in Italy*); (*periodo*) August holidays *pl*

ferra'menta *nfpl* ironmongery *sg*; **negozio di ~** ironmonger's

fer'rare *vt* shoe ‹*cavallo*›

fer'rato *a* **~ in** (*preparato in*) well up in

'ferreo *a* iron

'ferro *nm* iron; (*attrezzo*) tool; (*di chirurgo*) instrument; **di ~** ‹*memoria*› excellent; ‹*alibi*› cast-iron; **salute di ~** iron constitution; **ai ferri** ‹*bistecca*› grilled; **essere ai ferri corti** be at daggers drawn; **mettere il paese a ~ e fuoco** put a country to the sword; **i ferri del mestiere** the tools of the trade. **~ battuto** wrought iron. **~ da calza** knitting needle. **~ di cavallo** horseshoe. **~ da stiro** iron. **~ a vapore** steam iron

fer'roso *a* ferrous

ferro'vecchio *nm* scrap merchant

ferro'via *nf* railway, railroad *Am*; **Ferrovie** *pl* **dello Stato** Italian State Railways

ferrovi'ario *a* railway *attrib*, railroad *Am attrib*

ferrovi'ere *nm* railwayman, railroad worker *Am*

'fertile *a* fertile

fertilità *nf* fertility

fertiliz'zante *nm* fertilizer

fertilizzazi'one *nf* fertilization

fer'vente *a* blazing; *fig* fervent

fervente'mente *adv* fervently

'fervere *vi* ‹*preparativi:*› be well under way

fervida'mente *adv* fervently

'fervido *a* fervent; **fervidi auguri** best wishes

fer'vore *nm* fervour; (*di discussione*) heat

'fesa *nf* (*carne*) rump

fesse'ria *nf* **dire/fare una ~** *fam* say/do something stupid

'fesso *pp* **di fendere** ● *a* cracked; (*fam: sciocco*) foolish ● *nm* (*fam: idiota*) fool; **far ~ qcno** *fam* con sb

fes'sura *nf* crack; (*per gettone ecc*) slot. **~ [per la scheda] di espansione** *Comput* expansion slot

'festa *nf* feast; (*giorno festivo*) holiday; (*compleanno*) birthday; (*ricevimento*) party; *fig* joy; **fare ~ a qcno** welcome sb; **essere in ~** be on holiday; **far ~** celebrate; **della ~** ‹*vestito, tovaglia*› best; **conciare qcno per le feste** give sb a sound thrashing; **le feste** (*Natale, Capodanno ecc*) the holidays. **~ di compleanno** birthday party. **~ della mamma** Mother's Day, Mothering Sunday. **~ nazionale** public holiday. **~ del papà** Father's Day

festai'olo *a* festive

festeggia'mento *nm* celebration; (*mani-*

festazione) festivity; **festeggiamenti** *pl* celebrations

festeggi'are *vt* celebrate; (*accogliere festosamente*) give a hearty welcome to

fe'stino *nm* party

festività *nfpl* festivities

fe'stivo *a* holiday; (*lieto*) festive; **festivi** *pl* public holidays

fe'stone *nm* (*nel cucito*) scallop, scollop; (*di carta*) paper chain

fe'stoso *a* merry

fe'tente *a* evil smelling; *fig* revolting ● *nmf fam* bastard

fe'ticcio *nm* fetish

'feto *nm* foetus

fe'tore *nm* stench

'fetta *nf* slice; **a fette** sliced. **~ biscottata** slices of crispy toast-like bread

fet'tina *nf* thin slice

fet'tuccia *nf* tape; (*con nome*) name tape

fettuc'cine *nfpl* ribbon-shaped pasta

feu'dale *a* feudal

'feudo *nm* feud

fez *nm inv* fez

FFSS *abbr* (**Ferrovie dello Stato**) Italian State Railways

fi'aba *nf* fairy-tale

fia'besco *a* fairy-tale *attrib*

fi'acca *nf* weariness; (*indolenza*) laziness; **battere la ~** be sluggish

fiac'care *vt* weaken

fi'acco *a* weak; (*indolente*) slack; (*stanco*) weary; (*partita*) dull

fi'accola *nf* torch

fiacco'lata *nf* torchlight procession

fi'ala *nf* phial

fia'letta *nf* phial; **~ puzzolente** stink bomb

fi'amma *nf* flame; *Naut* pennant; **in fiamme** in flames; **andare in fiamme** go up in flames; **dare alle fiamme** commit to the flames; **alla ~** *Culin* flambé. **le Fiamme Gialle** body responsible for border control and investigating fraud. **~ ossidrica** blowtorch

fiam'mante *a* flaming; **nuovo ~** brand new

fiam'mata *nf* blaze

fiammeggi'are *vi* blaze ● *vt* singe ‹*pollo*›

fiam'mifero *nm* match

fiam'mingo, -a *a & nm* Flemish ● *nmf* Fleming

fian'cata *nf* wing

fiancheggi'are *vt* border; *fig* support

fi'anco *nm* side; (*di persona*) hip; (*di animale*) flank; *Mil* wing; **al mio ~** by my side; **~ a ~** ‹*lavorare*› side by side

Fi'andre *nfpl* **le ~** Flanders

fia'schetta *nf* hip flask

fiaschet'teria *nf* wine shop

fi'asco *nm* flask; *fig* fiasco; **fare ~** be a fiasco

fia'tare *vi* breathe; (*parlare*) breathe a word

fi'ato *nm* breath; (*vigore*) stamina; **strumenti a ~** wind instruments; **avere il ~ corto** be short of breath; **senza ~** breathlessly; **tutto d'un ~** ‹*bere, leggere*› all in one go

'fibbia *nf* buckle

'fibra *nf* fibre; **fibre** *pl* (*alimentari*) roughage. **fibre** *pl* **artificiali** man-made fibres. ~ **ottica** optical fibre; **a fibre ottiche** ‹*cavo*› fibre optic. ~ **sintetica** man-made fibre, synthetic. ~ **di vetro** fibreglass

fi'broma *nm* fibroid

fi'broso *a* fibrous

ficca'naso *nmf* nosey parker

fic'care *vt* thrust; drive ‹*chiodo ecc*›; (*fam: mettere*) shove

fic'carsi *vr* thrust oneself; (*nascondersi*) hide; ~ **nei guai** get oneself into trouble

'fiche *nf inv* (*gettone*) chip

'fico *nm* (*albero*) fig-tree; (*frutto*) fig. ~ **d'India** prickly pear; **non me ne importa un ~** [**secco**] *fam* I don't give a damn; **non capisce un ~** [**secco**] *fam* he doesn't understand a bloody thing; **non vale un ~** [**secco**] *fam* it's totally worthless

'fico, -a *fam nmf* cool sort ● *a* cool

fidanza'mento *nm* engagement; **rompere il ~** break off one's engagement, break it off

fidan'zarsi *vr* get engaged

fidan'zata *nf* (*ufficiale*) fiancée; (*innamorata*) girlfriend

fidan'zato *nm* (*ufficiale*) fiancé; (*innamorato*) boyfriend

fi'darsi *vr* ~ **di** trust

fi'dato *a* trustworthy

'fido *a* ‹*compagno*› loyal ● *nm* devoted follower; *Comm* credit

fi'ducia *nf* confidence; **degno di ~** trustworthy; **persona di ~** reliable person; **di ~** ‹*fornitore, banca*› regular, usual; **avere ~ in se stessi** believe in oneself; **incarico di ~** important job

fiduci'ario, -a *a* ‹*rapporto, transazione*› based on trust ● *nmf* trustee

fiduci'oso *a* hopeful

fi'ele *nm* bile; *fig* bitterness; **amaro come il ~** bitter

fienagi'one *nf* haymaking

fie'nile *nm* barn

fi'eno *nm* hay

fi'era *nf* fair. ~ **commerciale** trade fair. ~ **del libro** book fair

fie'rezza *nf* (*dignità*) pride

fi'ero *a* proud

fi'evole *a* faint; ‹*luce*› dim

'fifa *nf fam* jitters; **aver ~** have the jitters

fi'fone, -a *nmf fam* chicken, yellowbelly

FIGC *nf abbr* (**Federazione Italiana Gioco Calcio**) Italian Football Association

'figli *nmpl* children

'figlia *nf* daughter; ~ **unica** only child

figli'are *vi* ‹*animale:*› calve

figli'astra *nf* stepdaughter

figli'astro *nm* stepson

'figlio *nm* son; (*generico*) child; **è ~ d'arte** he was born in a trunk. ~ **adottivo** adopted child. ~ **di papà** spoilt brat. ~ **di puttana** *vulg* son of a bitch. ~ **unico** only child

figli'occia *nf* goddaughter

figli'occio *nm* godson

figli'ola *nf* girl

figlio'lanza *nf* offspring

figli'olo *nm* boy; **figlioli** *pl* children

'figo, -a *a vedi* **fico, -a**

fi'gura *nf* figure; (*aspetto esteriore*) shape; (*illustrazione*) illustration; **far bella/brutta ~** make a good/bad impression; **mi hai fatto fare una brutta ~** you made me look a fool; **che ~!** how embarrassing!. ~ **paterna** father figure. ~ **retorica** figure of speech

figu'raccia *nf* bad impression

figu'rare *vt* represent; (*simboleggiare*) symbolize; (*immaginare*) imagine ● *vi* (*far figura*) cut a fine figure; (*in lista*) appear, figure; ~ **in testa al cartellone** *Theat* get top billing

figu'rarsi *vr* (*immaginarsi*) imagine; **figurati!** imagine that!; **posso? – [ma] figurati!** may I? – of course!

figura'tivo *a* figurative

figu'rina *nf* (*da raccolta*) cigarette card; (*statuetta*) figurine

figuri'nista *nmf* dress designer

figu'rino *nm* fashion sketch

figu'rone *nm* **fare un ~** make an excellent impression

fi'guro *nm* **un losco ~** a shady character

fil *nm* ~ **di ferro** wire

'fila *nf* line; (*di soldati ecc*) file; (*di oggetti*) row; (*coda*) queue; **di ~** in succession; **fare la ~** queue [up], stand in line *Am*; **in ~ indiana** single file

fila'mento *nm* filament

fi'lanca® *nf* type of synthetic stretch fabric

fi'lante *a* ‹*formaggio*› stringy; **stella ~** (*di carta*) streamer

filantro'pia *nf* philanthropy

filan'tropico *a* philanthropic

fi'lantropo, -a *nmf* philanthropist

fi'lare *vt* spin; *Naut* pay out ● *vi* (*andarsene*) run away; (*liquido:*) trickle; **fila!** *fam* scram!; ~ **con** (*fam: amoreggiare*) go out with; ~ **dritto** toe the line ● *vi* ‹*ragionamento:*› hang together ● *nm* (*di viti, di alberi*) row

filar'monica *nf* (*orchestra*) orchestra

filar'monico *a* philharmonic

fila'strocca *nf* rigmarole; (*per bambini*) nursery rhyme

fila'telia *nf* philately, stamp collecting

fila'telico, -a *nmf* philatelist

fi'lato *a* spun; (*ininterrotto*) running; (*continuato*) uninterrupted; **di ~** (*subito*) immediately; **andare dritto ~ a** go straight to ● *nm* yarn

fila|'tore, -'trice *nmf* spinner

fila'tura *nf* spinning; (*filanda*) spinning mill

file *nm inv Comput* file

filetta'tura *nf* (*di vite*) thread

fi'letto *nm* (*bordo*) border; (*di vite*) thread; *Culin* fillet. ~ **ai ferri** grilled fillet of beef

fili'ale *a* filial ● *nf Comm* branch

filibusti'ere *nm* rascal

fili'forme *a* stringy

fili'grana *nf* filigree; (*su carta*) watermark

fi'lippica *nf* invective

Filip'pine *nfpl* **le ~** the Philippines

filip'pino, -a *a & nmf* Filipino

film *nm inv* film. **~ comico** comedy. **~ drammatico** drama. **~ di fantascienza** science fiction film. **~ giallo** thriller. **~ a lungo metraggio** feature film. **~ dell'orrore** horror film. **~ poliziesco** detective film

fil'mare *vt* film

fil'mato *a* filmed ● *nm* short film

fil'mina *nf* film strip

fil'mino *nm* cine film

'filo *nm* thread; (*tessile*) yarn; (*metallico*) wire; (*di lama*) edge; (*venatura*) grain; (*di perle*) string; (*d'erba*) blade; (*di luce*) ray; **un ~ di** (*poco*) a drop of; **con un ~ di voce** in a whisper; **per ~ e per segno** in detail; **fare il ~ a qcno** fancy sb; **perdere il ~** lose the thread; **essere appeso a un ~** be hanging by a thread; **essere sul ~ del rasoio** be on a knife-edge; **un ~ d'aria** a breath of air; **un ~ di speranza** a glimmer of hope. **~ interdentale** dental floss. **~ a piombo** plumb-line. **~ spinato** barbed wire

filo+ *pref* philo+

filoameri'cano *a* pro-American

'filobus *nm inv* trolleybus

filocomu'nista *a* pro-communist

filodiffusi'one *nf* rediffusion

filodram'matica *nf* amateur dramatic society

filolo'gia *nf* philology

filo'logico *a* philological

fi'lologo, -a *nmf* philologist

filon'cino *nm* ≈ French stick

fi'lone *nm* vein; (*di pane*) long loaf, Vienna loaf

fi'loso *a* stringy

filoso'fia *nf* philosophy

fi'losofo, -a *nmf* philosopher

fil'traggio *nm* filtering

fil'trare *vt* filter

'filtro *nm* filter. **~ dell'olio** oil filter

'filza *nf* string

fin *vedi* **fine, fino¹**

fi'nale *a* final ● *nm* end ● *nf* Sport final

fina'lista *nmf* finalist

finalità *nf inv* finality; (*scopo*) aim

final'mente *adv* at last; (*in ultimo*) finally

fi'nanza *nf* finance

finanzia'mento *nm* funding

finanzi'are *vt* fund, finance

finanzi'aria *nf* investment company; (*holding*) holding company; Jur finance bill

finanzi'ario *a* financial

finanzia|'tore, -'trice *nmf* backer

finanzi'ere *nm* financier; (*guardia di finanza*) customs officer

finché *conj* until; (*per tutto il tempo che*) as long as

'fine *a* fine; (*sottile*) thin; ‹*udito, vista*› keen; (*raffinato*) refined ● *nf* end; **alla ~** in the end; **alla fin ~** after all; **in fin dei conti** when all's said and done; **andare a buon ~** be successful; **te lo dico a fin di bene** I'm telling you for your own good; **che ~ ha fatto Anna?** what became of Anna?; **che ~**

hanno fatto le chiavi? where have the keys got to?; **senza ~** endless ● *nm* aim. **~ settimana** weekend

fi'nestra *nf* window. **~ a battenti** casement window

fine'strella *nf* **~ di aiuto** *Comput* help window. **~ di dialogo** *Comput* dialog box

fine'strino *nm Rail, Auto* window

fi'nezza *nf* fineness; (*sottigliezza*) thinness; (*raffinatezza*) refinement

'fingere *vt* pretend; feign ‹*affetto ecc*›

'fingersi *vr* pretend to be

fini'menti *nmpl* finishing touches; (*per cavallo*) harness *sg*

fini'mondo *nm* end of the world; *fig* pandemonium

fi'nire *vt/i* finish, end; (*smettere*) stop; (*diventare, andare a finire*) end up; **finiscila!** stop it!

fi'nito *a* finished; (*abile*) accomplished

fini'tura *nf* finish

finlan'dese *a* Finnish ● *nmf* Finn ● *nm* (*lingua*) Finnish

Fin'landia *nf* Finland

'fino¹ *prep* **~ a** till, until; (*spazio*) as far as; **~ all'ultimo** to the last; **~ alla nausea** ‹*ripetere, leggere*› ad nauseam; **fin da** (*tempo*) since; (*spazio*) from; **fin dall'inizio** from the beginning; **fin qui** as far as here; **fin troppo** too much; **~ a che punto** how far

'fino² *a* fine; (*acuto*) subtle; (*puro*) pure

fi'nocchio *nm* fennel; (*fam: omosessuale*) poof

fi'nora *adv* so far, up till now

'finta *nf* pretence, sham; *Sport* feint; **far ~ di** pretend to; **far ~ di niente** act as if nothing had happened; **per ~** (*per scherzo*) for a laugh

'finto, -a *pp di* **fingere** ● *a* false; (*artificiale*) artificial; **finta pelle** fake leather; **fare il ~ tonto** act dumb

finzi'one *nf* pretence

fi'occo *nm* bow; (*di neve*) flake; (*nappa*) tassel; *Naut* jib; **coi fiocchi** *fig* excellent; **fiocchi** *pl* **di avena** oatmeal; (*cotti*) porridge; **fiocchi** *pl* **di granoturco** cornflakes. **fiocchi** *pl* **di latte** cottage cheese. **~ di neve** snowflake

fi'ocina *nf* harpoon

fi'oco *a* weak; ‹*luce*› dim

fi'onda *nf* catapult

fio'raio, -a *nmf* florist

fiorda'liso *nm* cornflower

fi'ordo *nm* fiord

fi'ore *nm* flower; (*parte scelta*) cream; **a fior d'acqua** on the surface of the water; **a fiori** flowery; **in ~** flowering; **fior di** (*abbondanza*) a lot of; **il fior ~ di** the cream of; **ha i nervi a fior di pelle** his nerves are on edge; **nel ~ degli anni** in one's prime; **è il suo ~ all'occhiello** that's a feather in his cap; **suo figlio è il suo ~ all'occhiello** his son is his pride and joy. **fiori** *pl* **d'arancio** orange blossom. **~ di campo** wild flower. **fior di latte** (*formaggio*) soft cheese. **~ selvatico** wild flower. **fiori** *pl* **di zucca fritti** fried pumpkin flowers

fio'rente *a* ⟨*industria*⟩ booming

fioren'tina *nf* (*bistecca*) T-bone steak

fioren'tino *a* Florentine

fio'retto *nm* (*scherma*) foil; *Relig* act of mortification

fi'ori *nmpl* (*nelle carte*) clubs

fiori'era *nf* container

fio'rino *nm* ~ **olandese** guilder

fio'rire *vi* flower; ⟨*albero:*⟩ blossom; *fig* flourish

fio'rista *nmf* florist; (*negozio*) florist's

fiori'tura *nf* flowering; (*di albero*) blossoming; (*insieme di fiori*) flowers *pl*

fio'rone *nm* (*fico*) early fig

fi'otto *nm* (*di sangue*) spurt; **scorrere a fiotti** pour out; **piove a fiotti** the rain is pouring down

Fi'renze *nf* Florence

'firma *nf* signature; (*nome*) name

firma'mento *nm* firmament

fir'mare *vt* sign

firma'tario, -a *nmf* signatory

fir'mato *a* ⟨*quadro, lettera*⟩ signed; ⟨*abito, borsa*⟩ designer *attrib*

fisar'monica *nf* accordion

fi'scale *a* fiscal

fisca'lista *nmf* tax consultant

fiscaliz'zare *vt* finance with government funds

fischi'are *vi* whistle ● *vt* whistle; (*in segno di disapprovazione*) boo; **mi fischiano le orecchie** I've got a ringing noise in my ears; *fig* my ears are burning

fischi'ata *nf* whistle

fischiet'tare *vt* whistle

fischiet'tio *nm* whistling

fischi'etto *nm* whistle

'fischio *nm* whistle; **fischi** *pl Theat* booing; **prendere fischi per fiaschi** get hold of the wrong end of the stick

'fisco *nm* treasury; (*tasse*) taxation; **il** ~ the taxman

fisica'mente *adv* physically

'fisico, -a *a* physical ● *nmf* physicist. ~ **nucleare** atomic scientist ● *nm* physique ● *nf* physics. ~ **nucleare** nuclear physics

'fisima *nf* whim

fisiolo'gia *nf* physiology

fisio'logico *a* physiological

fisi'ologo, -a *nmf* physiologist

fisiono'mia *nf* features *pl*, face; (*di paesaggio*) appearance

fisiotera'pia *nf* physiotherapy

fisiotera'pista *nmf* physiotherapist, physio *fam*

fissa'mente *adv* fixedly; (*permanentemente*) steadily

fis'sare *vt* fix, fasten; (*guardare fissamente*) stare at; arrange ⟨*appuntamento, ora*⟩

fis'sarsi *vr* (*stabilirsi*) settle; (*fissare lo sguardo*) stare; ~ **su** (*ostinarsi*) set one's mind on; ~ **di fare qcsa** become obsessed with doing sth

fissa'tivo *nm Phot* fixative

fis'sato, -a *a* (*al muro*) fixed; ⟨*prezzo*⟩ agreed ● *nm* (*persona*) person with an obsession

fissa'tore *nm* hair spray

fissazi'one *nf* fixation; (*ossessione*) obsession

'fisso *a* fixed; **un lavoro** ~ a regular job; **senza fissa dimora** of no fixed abode; **avere una ragazza fissa** have a steady girlfriend ● *adv* fixedly; **guardare** ~ **negli occhi** qcno stare at sb; ⟨*innamorato:*⟩ gaze into sb's eyes

fitotera'pia *nf* herbalism; (*per piante*) plant health

'fitta *nf* sharp pain

fit'tavolo *nm* tenant

fit'tizio *a* fictitious

'fitto[1] *a* thick; ~ **di** full of ● *nm* depth

fitto[2] *nm* (*affitto*) rent; **dare a** ~ let; **prendere a** ~ rent; (*noleggiare*) hire

fiu'mana *nf* swollen river; *fig* stream

fi'ume *nm* river; *fig* stream ● *a inv* ⟨*discussione*⟩ endless, never-ending; **romanzo** ~ roman-fleuve

fiu'tare *vt* smell; ⟨*animale:*⟩ scent; snort ⟨*cocaina*⟩

fi'uto *nm* [sense of] smell; *fig* nose

'flaccido *a* flabby

fla'cone *nm* bottle

flagel'lare *vt* flog

flagellazi'one *nf* flagellation

fla'gello *nm* scourge

fla'grante *a* flagrant; **in** ~ in the act

fla'menco *nm* flamenco

flan *nm inv* baked custard

fla'nella *nf* flannel

'flangia *nf* (*su ruota*) flange

flash *nm inv Journ* newsflash

flau'tista *nmf* flautist

'flauto *nm* flute. ~ **diritto** recorder. ~ **traverso** flute

'flebile *a* feeble

fle'bite *nf* phlebitis

flebo'clisi *nf* drip

'flemma *nf* calm; *Med* phlegm

flem'matico *a* phlegmatic

fles'sibile *a* flexible

flessibilità *nf* flexibility

flessi'one *nf* (*del busto in avanti*) forward bend; (*a terra*) sit-up; (*delle ginocchia*) knee-bend; (*di vendite, produzione*) drop, fall

fles'sivo *a Gram* inflected

'flesso *pp di* **flettere** ● *a Gram* inflected

flessu'oso *a* supple

'flettere *vt* bend

flip-'flop *nm inv* flip flop

flir'tare *vi* flirt

F.lli *abbr* (**fratelli**) Bros.

'floppy disk *nm inv* floppy disk

'flora *nf* flora

'florido *a* flourishing

floroviva'istica *nf* ⟨*attività*⟩ growing under glass

'floscio *a* limp; (*flaccido*) flabby

'**flotta** *nf* fleet
flot'tiglia *nf* flotilla
flu'ente *a* fluent
fluidità *nf* fluidity; (*nel parlare*) fluency
flu'ido *nm* fluid
flu'ire *vi* flow
fluore'scente *a* fluorescent
fluore'scenza *nf* fluorescence
fluo'oro *nm* fluorine
fluo'ruro *nm* fluoride
'**flusso** *nm* flow; *Med* flux; (*del mare*) flood-tide; **~ e riflusso** ebb and flow. **~ di cassa** cash flow
'**flutti** *nmpl* billows
fluttu'ante *a* fluctuating
fluttu'are *vi* ⟨*prezzi:*⟩ fluctuate; ⟨*moneta:*⟩ float
fluttuazi'one *nf* fluctuation; (*di moneta*) floating
fluvi'ale *a* river
fo'bia *nf* phobia
'**fobico** *a* phobic
'**foca** *nf* seal
fo'caccia *nf* (*pane*) flat bread; (*dolce*) ≈ raisin bread
fo'cale *a* ⟨*distanza, punto*⟩ focal
focaliz'zare *vt* get into focus ⟨*fotografia*⟩; focus ⟨*attenzione*⟩; define ⟨*problema*⟩
'**foce** *nf* mouth
fo'chista *nm* stoker
foco'laio *nm Med* focus; *fig* centre
foco'lare *nm* hearth; (*caminetto*) fireplace; *Techn* furnace
fo'coso *a* fiery
'**fodera** *nf* lining; (*di libro*) dust-jacket; (*di poltrona ecc*) loose cover
fode'rare *vt* line; cover ⟨*libro*⟩
fode'rato *a* lined; ⟨*libro*⟩ covered
'**foga** *nf* impetuosity
'**foggia** *nf* fashion; (*maniera*) manner; (*forma*) shape
foggi'are *vt* mould
'**foglia** *nf* leaf; (*di metallo*) foil; **mangiare la ~** catch on. **~ d'alloro** bay leaf
fogli'ame *nm* foliage
fogli'etto *nm* **~ igienico** (*per pannolini*) nappy liner
fogli'etto *nm* (*pezzetto di carta*) piece of paper
'**foglio** *nm* sheet; (*pagina*) leaf; (*di domanda, di iscrizione*) form. **~ di carta** sheet of paper. **~ elettronico** *Comput* spreadsheet. **~ illustrativo** instruction leaflet. **~ protocollo** foolscap. **~ rosa** provisional driving licence. **~ di via** expulsion order
'**fogna** *nf* sewer
fogna'tura *nf* sewerage
fohn *nm inv* hair dryer
fo'lata *nf* gust
fol'clore *nm* folklore
folclo'ristico *a* folk; (*bizzarro*) weird
folgo'rante *a* ⟨*idea*⟩ brilliant
folgo'rare *vi* (*splendere*) shine ● *vt* (*con un fulmine*) strike

folgo'rato *a fig* thunderstruck
folgorazi'one *nf* (*da fulmine, elettrica*) electrocution; (*fig: idea*) brainwave
'**folgore** *nf* thunderbolt
'**folio**: **in ~** *a* folio
'**folla** *nf* crowd
'**folle** *a* mad; ⟨*velocità*⟩ breakneck; **in ~** *Auto* in neutral; **andare in ~** *Auto* coast
folleggi'are *vi* paint the town red
folle'mente *adv* madly
fol'letto *nm* elf
fol'lia *nf* madness; **alla ~** ⟨*amare*⟩ to distraction; **costare una ~** cost the earth; **fare una ~** go mad; **farei follie per lei** I'd do anything for her
'**folto** *a* thick
fomen'tare *vt* stir up
fond'ale *nm Theat* backcloth. **~ marino** sea bed
fonda'menta *nfpl* foundations
fondamen'tale *a* fundamental
fondamenta'lismo *nm* fundamentalism
fondamenta'lista *nmf* fundamentalist
fonda'mento *nm* (*di principio, teoria*) foundation; **privo di ~** groundless, without foundation
fon'dant *nm inv* fondant
fon'dare *vt* establish; base ⟨*ragionamento, accusa*⟩
fon'darsi *vr* be based (**su** on)
fon'dato *a* ⟨*ragionamento*⟩ well-founded; **~ su** based on
fondazi'one *nf* establishment; **fondazioni** *pl* (*di edificio*) foundations
fon'delli *nmpl* **prendere qcno per i ~** *fam* pull sb's leg
fon'dente *a* ⟨*cioccolato*⟩ dark
'**fondere** *vt* melt; fuse ⟨*metallo*⟩ ● *vi* melt; ⟨*metallo:*⟩ fuse; ⟨*colori:*⟩ blend
fonde'ria *nf* foundry
'**fondersi** *vr* melt; *Comm* merge
'**fondo** *a* deep; **è notte fonda** it's the middle of the night ● *nm* bottom; (*fine*) end; (*sfondo*) background; (*indole*) nature; (*somma di denaro*) fund; (*feccia*) dregs *pl*; (*terreno*) land; [**sci di**] **~** cross-country skiing; **andare a ~** ⟨*nave:*⟩ sink; **in ~** after all; **in ~ a** at the end/bottom of; **in ~ in ~** deep down; **fino in ~** right to the end; ⟨*capire*⟩ thoroughly; **andare fino in ~ a qcsa** get to the bottom of sth; **dar ~ a** use up; **a doppio ~** false bottomed; **toccare il ~** touch bottom; *fig* hit rock bottom; **senza ~** bottomless; **articolo di ~** (*in giornale*) editorial; **fondi** *pl* (*denaro*) funds; (*di caffè*) grounds. **~ fiduciario** trust fund. **~ [comune] di investimento** investment trust. **fondi** *pl* **di magazzino** old stock. **F~ Monetario Internazionale** International Monetary Fund. **fondi** *pl* **neri** slush fund. **~ pensione** pension fund. **~ per la ricostruzione** disaster fund. **~ sopravvenienze passive** contingency fund. **~ stradale** road surface
fondo'tinta *nm inv* foundation [cream]
fon'due *nf* (*di formaggio*) fondue

fon'duta *nf* fondue

fo'nema *nm* phoneme

fo'netica *nf* phonetics

fo'netico *a* phonetic

fonolo'gia *nf* phonology

fon'tana *nf* fountain; *(di farina)* well

fonta'nella *nf* drinking fountain; *Anat* fontanelle

'fonte *nf* spring; *fig* source ● *nm* font

fon'tina *nf* soft, mature cheese often used in cooking

'football *nm* ~ **americano** American football

foraggi'are *vt* fodder

fo'raggio *nm* forage

fo'rare *vt* pierce; punch *(biglietto)* ● *vi* puncture

fo'rarsi *vr* *(gomma, pallone:)* go soft

fora'tura *nf* puncture

'forbici *nfpl* scissors; **un paio di** ~ a pair of scissors. ~ **da siepe** garden shears. ~ **a zigzag** pinking shears, pinking scissors

forbi'cina *nf* earwig; **forbicine** *pl* *(per le unghie)* nail scissors

for'bito *a* erudite

'forca *nf* fork; *(patibolo)* gallows *pl*

for'cella *nf* fork; *(per capelli)* hairpin

for'chetta *nf* fork; **essere una buona** ~ enjoy one's food

forchet'tata *nf* *(quantità)* forkful

forchet'tone *nm* carving fork

for'cina *nf* hairpin

'forcipe *nm* forceps *pl*

for'cone *nm* pitchfork

fo'rense *a* forensic

fo'resta *nf* forest. ~ **equatoriale** rain forest. **F~ Nera** Black Forest

fore'stale *a* forest *attrib*; **la F~** branch of the police with responsibility for national forests

foreste'ria *nf* guest rooms *pl*

foresti'ero, -a *a* foreign ● *nmf* foreigner.

for'fait *nm* *inv* fixed price; **dare** ~ *(abbandonare)* give up; **prezzo [a]** ~ all-in price; **contratto [a]** ~ lump-sum contract

forfe'tario *a* flat rate

'forfora *nf* dandruff

'forgia *nf* forge

forgi'are *vt* forge

'forma *nf* form; *(sagoma)* shape; *Culin* mould; *(per scarpe)* shoe tree; *(di calzolaio)* last; **essere in** ~ be in good form; **in (gran)** ~ (very) fit, on (top) form; **a** ~ **di** in the shape of; **sotto** ~ **di** in the form of; **forme** *pl* *(del corpo)* curves; *(convenzioni)* appearances

formag'gera *nf* [covered] cheese board

formag'gino *nm* processed cheese

for'maggio *nm* cheese

for'male *a* formal

forma'lina *nf* formalin

forma'lismo *nm* formalism

forma'lista *nmf* formalist

formalità *nf inv* formality

formaliz'zare *vt* formalize

formaliz'zarsi *vr* stand on ceremony, be formal

formal'mente *adv* formally

'forma 'mentis *nf inv* way of thinking, mindset

for'mare *vt* form; dial *(numero di telefono)*

for'marsi *vr* form; *(svilupparsi)* develop

for'mato *nm* size; *(di libro, dischetto)* format; ~ **famiglia** economy pack, economy size; ~ **tessera** *(fotografia)* passport-size

format'tare *vt* format

formattazi'one *nf* formatting

formazi'one *nf* formation; *Sport* line-up; **in** ~ in the process of being formed. ~ **professionale** vocational training

for'mella *nf* tile

for'mica *nf* ant

'formica® *nf* Formica

formi'caio *nm* anthill

formichi'ere *nm* anteater

formico'lare *vi* *(braccio ecc:)* tingle; ~ **di** be swarming with; **mi formicola la mano** I have pins and needles in my hand

formico'lio *nm* swarming; *(di braccio ecc)* pins and needles *pl*

formi'dabile *a* *(tremendo)* formidable; *(eccezionale)* tremendous

for'mina *nf* mould

for'moso *a* curvy

'formula *nf* formula; **assolvere con** ~ **piena** acquit. ~ **di cortesia** polite form of address

formu'lare *vt* formulate; *(esprimere)* express

formulazi'one *nf* formulation

for'nace *nf* furnace; *(per laterizi)* kiln

for'naio, -a *nmf* baker; *(negozio)* bakery

fornel'letto *nm* ~ **da campeggio** camping stove. ~ **a gas** gas stove

for'nello *nm* stove; *(di pipa)* bowl. ~ **da campeggio** camping stove

fornicazi'one *nf* fornication

for'nire *vt* supply (**di** with); ~ **qcsa a qcno** supply sb with sth

for'nirsi *vr* ~ **di** provide oneself with

forni'tore *nm* supplier. ~ **di servizi** service provider

forni'tura *nf* supply; **forniture** *pl* **per ufficio** office supplies

'forno *nm* oven; *(panetteria)* bakery; **al** ~ roast; **da** ~ *(stoviglie)* ovenproof. ~ **crematorio** cremator. ~ **elettrico** electric oven. ~ **a gas** gas oven. ~ **a microonde** microwave [oven]

'foro *nm* hole; *(romano)* forum; *(tribunale)* [law] court

'forse *adv* perhaps, maybe; **essere in** ~ be in doubt

forsen'nato, -a *a* mad ● *nmf* madman; madwoman

'forte *a* strong; *(colore)* bright; *(suono)* loud; *(resistente)* tough; *(spesa)* considerable; *(dolore)* severe; *(pioggia)* heavy; *(fam: simpatico)* great; *(taglia)* large; **essere** ~ **in qcsa**

be good at sth ● *adv* strongly; ⟨*parlare*⟩ loudly; ⟨*velocemente*⟩ fast; ⟨*piovere*⟩ heavily ● *nm* (*fortezza*) fort; (*specialità*) strong point

for'tezza *nf* fortress; (*forza morale*) fortitude

fortifi'care *vt* fortify

fortifi'cato *a* ⟨*città*⟩ walled

for'tino *nm* Mil blockhouse

for'tissimo *a* ⟨*caffè, liquore*⟩ extra-strong

for'tuito *a* fortuitous; **incontro** ~ chance encounter

for'tuna *nf* fortune; (*successo*) success; (*buona sorte*) luck; **atterraggio di** ~ forced landing; **aver** ~ be lucky; **buona** ~**!** good luck!; **di** ~ makeshift; **per** ~ luckily; **hai una** ~ **sfacciata!** *fam* you lucky blighter!

fortu'nale *nm* storm

fortunata'mente *adv* fortunately

fortu'nato *a* lucky, fortunate; ⟨*impresa*⟩ successful

fortu'noso *a* ⟨*giornata*⟩ eventful

fo'runcolo *nm* pimple; (*grosso*) boil

forunco'loso *a* spotty

'forza *nf* strength; (*potenza*) power; (*fisica*) force; **di** ~ by force; **a** ~ **di** by dint of; **con** ~ hard; ~**!** come on!; **in** ~ **di** under, in accordance with; ~ **maggiore** circumstances beyond one's control; **la** ~ **pubblica** the police; **le forze armate** the armed forces; **per** ~ against one's will; (*naturalmente*) of course; **farsi** ~ bear up; **mare** ~ **8** force 8 gale; **bella** ~**!** *fam* big deal!; **che** ~**!** (*che simpatico, divertente*) cool eh?. ~ **di gravità** [force of] gravity. ~ **lavoro** workforce. **forze** *pl* **di mercato** market forces. ~ **di volontà** willpower

for'zare *vt* force; (*scassare*) break open; (*sforzare*) strain

for'zato *a* forced; ⟨*sorriso*⟩ strained ● *nm* convict

forza'tura *nf* (*di cassaforte*) forcing; **sostenere che... è una** ~ to maintain that... is forcing things

forzi'ere *nm* coffer

for'zuto *a* strong

fo'schia *nf* haze

'fosco *a* dark

fo'sfato *nm* phosphate

'fosforo *nm* phosphorus

'fossa *nf* pit; (*tomba*) grave. ~ **biologica** cesspool. ~ **comune** mass grave. ~ **dell'orchestra** orchestra pit

fos'sato *nm* (*di fortificazione*) moat

fos'setta *nf* (*di guancia*) dimple

'fossile *nm* fossil

'fosso *nm* ditch; Mil trench

'foto *nf inv fam* photo; **fare delle** ~ take some photos

foto'cellula *nf* photocell

fotocomposi|'tore, -'trice *nmf* filmsetter

fotocomposizi'one *nf* filmsetting, photocomposition

foto'copia *nf* photocopy

fotocopi'are *vt* photocopy

fotocopia'trice *nf* photocopier

foto'finish *nm inv* photo finish

foto'genico *a* photogenic

fotogiorna'lista *nmf* photojournalist

fotogra'fare *vt* photograph

fotogra'fia *nf* (*arte*) photography; (*immagine*) photograph; **fare fotografie** take photographs

foto'grafico *a* photographic; **macchina fotografica** camera

fo'tografo, -a *nmf* photographer; (*negozio*) photographer's

foto'gramma *nm* frame

fotoincisi'one *nf* photoengraving

fotomo'dello, -a *nmf* [photographer's] model

fotomon'taggio *nm* photomontage

foto'ottica *nf* camera shop and optician's

fotorepor'tage *nm inv* photo essay

fotore'porter *nmf inv* newspaper photographer; (*di rivista*) magazine photographer

fotori'tocco *nm* retouching

foto'romanzo *nm* photo story

foto'sintesi *nf* photosynthesis

'fottere *vt* (*sl: rubare*) nick; (*sl: imbrogliare*) screw; *vulg* fuck, screw

'fottersene *vr vulg* not give a fuck; **va' a farti** ~**!** *vulg* fuck off!

fot'tuto *a* (*sl: maledetto*) bloody

fou'lard *nm inv* scarf

'foxhound *nm inv* foxhound

fox-'terrier *nm inv* fox terrier

fo'yer *nm inv* foyer

fra *prep* (*in mezzo a due*) between; (*in un insieme*) among; (*tempo, distanza*) in; **detto** ~ **noi** between you and me; ~ **sé e sé** to oneself; ~ **l'altro** what's more; ~ **breve** soon; ~ **quindici giorni** in two weeks' time; ~ **tutti, siamo in venti** there are twenty of us altogether

fracas'sare *vt* smash

fracas'sarsi *vr* shatter

fracas'sato *a* smashed

fra'casso *nm* din; (*di cose che cadono*) crash

fracas'sone, -a *nmf* clumsy person

'fradicio *a* (*bagnato*) soaked; **ubriaco** ~ blind drunk

'fragile *a* fragile; *fig* frail

fragilità *nf* fragility; *fig* frailty

'fragola *nf* strawberry

fra'gore *nm* uproar; (*di cose rotte*) clatter; (*di tuono*) rumble

frago'roso *a* uproarious; ⟨*tuono*⟩ rumbling; ⟨*suono*⟩ clanging

fra'grante *a* fragrant

fra'granza *nf* fragrance

frain'tendere *vt* misunderstand

frain'tendersi *vr* be at cross-purposes

frain'teso *pp di* **fraintendere**

frammen'tario *a* fragmentary

fram'mento *nm* fragment

fram'misto *a* ~ **di** interspersed with

'frana *nf* landslide; (*fam: persona*) walking disaster area

fra'nare *vi* slide down

franca'mente adv frankly

france'scano a & nm Franciscan

fran'cese a French ● nm Frenchman; (lingua) French ● nf Frenchwoman

france'sina nf (scarpa) brogue

fran'chezza nf frankness; **in tutta ~** in all honesty

fran'chigia nf **~ bagaglio** (per aereo) baggage allowance

'Francia nf France

'franco¹ a frank; Comm free; **farla franca** get away with sth; **parlare ~** speak frankly. **~ a bordo** free on board. **~ domicilio** delivered free of charge. **~ fabbrica** ex-works; **~ di porto** carriage free, carriage paid

'franco² nm (moneta) franc

franco'bollo nm stamp

franco-cana'dese a & nmf French Canadian

fran'cofono a Francophone

Franco'forte nf Frankfurt

fran'gente nm (onda) breaker; (scoglio) reef; (fig: momento difficile) crisis; **in quel ~** in the circumstances

fran'getta nf fringe

'frangia nf fringe

frangi'flutti nm inv bulwark

frangi'vento nm windbreak

fra'noso a subject to landslides

fran'toio nm olive-press

frantu'mare vt shatter

frantu'marsi vr shatter

fran'tumi nmpl splinters; **in ~** smashed; **andare in ~** be smashed to smithereens

frappé nm inv milkshake

frap'porre vt interpose

frap'porsi vr intervene

fra'sario nm vocabulary; (libro) phrase book

'frasca nf [leafy] branch; **saltare di palo in ~** jump from subject to subject

'frase nf sentence; (espressione) phrase. **~ fatta** cliché

fraseolo'gia nf phrases pl

'frassino nm ash[-tree]

frastagli'are vt make jagged

frastagli'ato a jagged

frastor'nare vt daze

frastor'nato a dazed

frastu'ono nm racket

'frate nm friar; (monaco) monk

fratel'lanza nf brotherhood

fratel'lastro nm half-brother

fratel'lino nm little brother

fra'tello nm brother; **fratelli** pl (fratello e sorella) brother and sister; Relig brethren. **~ gemello** twin brother. **~ di sangue** blood brother

fraternità nf brotherhood

fraterniz'zare vi fraternize

fra'terno a brotherly

fratri'cida a fratricidal ● nm fratricide

frat'taglie nfpl (di pollo ecc) giblets

frat'tanto adv in the meantime

frat'tura nf fracture

frattu'rare vt break

frattu'rarsi vr break

fraudo'lento a fraudulent

frazi'one nf fraction; (borgata) hamlet; (paese) administrative division of a municipality

'freccia nf arrow; Auto indicator

frecci'ata nf (osservazione pungente) cutting remark

fredda'mente adv coldly

fred'dare vt cool; (fig: con sguardo, battuta) cut down; (uccidere) kill

fred'dezza nf coldness

'freddo a & nm cold; **aver ~** be cold; **fa ~** it's cold; **a ~** (sparare) in cold blood; (lavare) in cold water

freddo'loso a sensitive to cold, chilly

fred'dura nf pun

fre'gare vt rub; (fam: truffare) cheat; (fam: rubare) swipe; **fregarsene** fam not give a damn; **me ne frego!** I don't give a damn!; **chi se ne frega!** what the heck!

fre'garsi vr rub (occhi, mani)

fre'gata nf rub; (nave) frigate

frega'tura nf fam (truffa) swindle; (delusione) letdown

'fregio nm Archit frieze; (ornamento) decoration

'fregola nf rutting; **avere la ~ di fare qcsa** fam have a craze for doing sth

fre'mente a quivering

'fremere vi quiver

'fremito nm quiver

fre'nare vt brake; fig restrain; hold back (lacrime, impazienza) ● vi brake

fre'narsi vr check oneself

fre'nata nf **fare una ~ brusca** hit the brakes

frene'sia nf frenzy; (desiderio smodato) craze

frenetica'mente adv frantically

fre'netico a frantic

'freno nm brake; fig check; **togliere il ~** release the brake; **usare il ~** apply the brake; **tenere a ~** restrain; **tenere a ~ la lingua** hold one's tongue; **porre un ~ a** fig rein in. **freni** pl **a disco** disc brakes. **~ a mano** handbrake. **~ a pedale** footbrake

frequen'tare vt frequent; attend (scuola ecc); mix with (persone); **non ci frequentiamo più** we don't see each other any more

fre'quente a frequent; **di ~** frequently

fre'quenza nf frequency; (assiduità) attendance

'fresa nf mill

fre'sare vt mill

fre'schezza nf freshness; (di temperatura) coolness

'fresco a fresh; (temperatura) cool; **~ di studi** fresh out of school; **stai ~!** fam you're for it!; **se ti vede, stai ~** fam you're done for if he sees you ● nm coolness; **far ~** be cool; **mettere/tenere in ~** put/keep in a cool place; **al ~** (fam: in prigione) inside

fre'scura nf cool

'fresia nf freesia

'fretta nf hurry, haste; **aver ~** be in a hurry; **far ~ a qcno** hurry sb; **in ~ e furia** in a great hurry; **andarsene in** ~ rush away; **senza [nessuna]** ~ at your/his etc leisure

frettolosa'mente *adv* hurriedly

fretto'loso *a* ⟨*persona*⟩ hasty; ⟨*lavoro*⟩ rushed, hurried

fri'abile *a* crumbly

fricas'sea *nf* stewed meat served with an egg and lemon sauce

'**friggere** *vt* fry; **vai a farti** ~**!** get lost! ● *vi* sizzle; ~ **di impazienza** be on tenterhooks

friggi'trice *nf* electric chip pan

frigidità *nf* frigidity

'**frigido** *a* frigid

fri'gnare *vi* whine

fri'gnone, -a *nmf* whiner

'**frigo** *nm inv* fridge

frigo'bar *nm inv* minibar

frigo'rifero *a* refrigerating; ⟨*camion*⟩ refrigerated ● *nm* refrigerator

fringu'ello *nm* chaffinch

'**frisbee**® *nm inv* frisbee

frit'tata *nf* omelette

frit'tella *nf* fritter; (*fam: macchia d'unto*) grease stain

'**fritto** *pp di* **friggere** ● *a* fried; **essere** ~ be done for ● *nm* fried food. ~ **misto** mixed fried fish/vegetables

frit'tura *nf* (*pietanza*) fried dish. ~ **di pesce** variety of fried fish

frivo'lezza *nf* frivolity

'**frivolo** *a* frivolous

frizio'nare *vt* rub

frizi'one *nf* friction; *Mech* clutch; (*di pelle*) rub

friz'zante *a* fizzy; ⟨*vino*⟩ sparkling; ⟨*aria*⟩ bracing

'**frizzo** *nm* gibe

fro'dare *vt* defraud

'**frode** *nf* fraud. ~ **fiscale** tax evasion; **con la** ~ *Jur* under false pretences

frol'lino *nm* (*biscotto*) ≈ shortbread biscuit

'**frollo** *a* tender; ⟨*selvaggina*⟩ high; ⟨*persona*⟩ spineless; **pasta frolla** short[crust] pastry

'**fronda** *nf* [leafy] branch; *fig* rebellion

fron'doso *a* leafy

fron'tale *a* frontal; ⟨*scontro*⟩ head-on

'**fronte** *nf* forehead; (*di edificio*) front ● *nm Mil, Pol* front; **di** ~ opposite; **di** ~ **a** opposite, facing; (*a paragone*) compared with; **far** ~ **a** face

fronteggi'are *vt* face

fronte'spizio *nm* title page

fronti'era *nf* frontier, border

fron'tone *nm* pediment

'**fronzolo** *nm* frill

'**frotta** *nf* swarm; (*di animali*) flock

'**frottola** *nf* fib; **frottole** *pl* nonsense *sg*

fru'gale *a* frugal

fru'gare *vi* rummage ● *vt* search

fru'ire *vi* ~ **di** make use of, take advantage of

frul'lare *vt Culin* whisk ● *vi* ⟨*ali:*⟩ whirr

frul'lato *nm* ~ **di frutta** *fruit drink with milk and crushed ice*

frulla'tore *nm* [electric] mixer

frul'lino *nm* whisk

fru'mento *nm* wheat

frusci'are *vi* rustle

fru'scio *nm* rustle; (*radio, giradischi*) ground noise; (*di acque*) murmur

'**frusta** *nf* whip; (*frullino*) whisk

fru'stare *vt* whip

fru'stata *nf* lash

fru'stino *nm* riding crop

fru'strare *vt* frustrate

fru'strato *a* frustrated

frustrazi'one *nf* frustration

'**frutta** *nf* fruit; **negozio di** ~ **e verdura** greengrocer's. ~ **esotica** exotic fruit, tropical fruit. ~ **fresca di stagione** seasonal fruit. ~ **secca** nuts *pl*

frut'tare *vi* bear fruit; *Comm* give a return ● *vt* yield

frut'teto *nm* orchard

frutticol'tore *nm* fruit farmer

frutticol'tura *nf* fruit farming, fruit growing

frutti'era *nf* fruit bowl

frut'tifero *a* ⟨*albero*⟩ fruit-bearing; ⟨*Fin: deposito*⟩ interest-bearing

frutti'vendolo, -a *nmf* greengrocer

'**frutto** *nm anche fig* fruit; *Fin* yield. **frutti** *pl* **di bosco** fruits of the forest. **frutti** *pl* **di mare** seafood *sg*. ~ **della passione** passion fruit

fruttu'oso *a* profitable

FS *abbr* (**Ferrovie dello Stato**) Italian State Railways

f.to *abbr* (**firmato**) signed

fu *a* (*defunto*) late; **il fu signor Rossi** the late Mr Rossi

fuci'lare *vt* shoot, execute by firing squad

fucilazi'one *nf* execution [by firing squad]

fu'cile *nm* rifle. ~ **ad aria compressa** air rifle

fucil'lata *nf* shot

fu'cina *nf* forge

'**fuco** *nm* kelp

'**fucsia** *nf* fuchsia

'**fuga** *nf* escape; (*perdita*) leak; (*di ciclisti*) breakaway; *Mus* fugue; **darsi alla** ~ take to flight; **mettere qcno in** ~ put sb to flight. ~ **di cervelli** brain drain. ~ **di gradini** flight of steps. ~ **di notizie** leak. ~ **romantica** elopement

fu'gace *a* fleeting

fug'gevole *a* short-lived

fuggi'asco, -a *nmf* fugitive

fuggi'fuggi *nm* stampede

fug'gire *vi* flee; ⟨*innamorati:*⟩ elope; *fig* fly

fuggi'tivo, -a *nmf* fugitive

'**fulcro** *nm* fulcrum

ful'gore *nm* splendour

fu'liggine *nf* soot

fuliggi'noso *a* sooty

full *nm inv* (*nel poker*) full house

fulmi'nante *a* (*sguardo*) withering; **è morto di leucemia** ~ he died very soon after contracting leukaemia

fulmi'nare *vt* strike by lightning; (*con sguardo*) look daggers at; (*con scarica elettrica*) electrocute

fulmi'narsi *vr* burn out

fulmi'nato *a* **rimanere ~** electrocute oneself

'**fulmine** *nm* lightning; **colpo di ~** *fig* love at first sight; **un ~ a ciel sereno** a bolt from the blue

ful'mineo *a* rapid; ⟨*sguardo*⟩ withering

'**fulvo** *a* tawny

fumai'olo *nm* funnel; (*di casa*) chimney

fu'mante *a* ⟨*minestra, tazza*⟩ steaming

fu'mare *vt/i* smoke; (*in ebollizione*) steam; '**vietato ~**' 'no smoking'

fu'mario *a* (*canna*) flue

fu'mata *nf* (*segnale*) smoke signal

fuma|'tore, -'trice *nmf* smoker; **non fumatori** ⟨*Rail: scompartimento*⟩ non-smoker, non-smoking

fu'metto *nm* comic strip; **fumetti** *pl* comics

'**fumo** *nm* smoke; (*vapore*) steam; *fig* hot air; **andare in ~** vanish; **vendere ~** put on an act; **cercava di vendere ~** it was all hot air; **fumi** *pl* (*industriali*) fumes; **sotto i fumi dell'alcol** under the influence of alcohol. **~ passivo** passive smoking

fu'mogeno *a* **cortina fumogena** smoke screen

fu'moso *a* ⟨*ambiente*⟩ smoky; ⟨*discorso*⟩ vague

funambo'lesco *a* acrobatic

fu'nambolo, -a *nmf* tightrope walker

'**fune** *nf* rope; (*cavo*) cable

'**funebre** *a* funeral; (*cupa*) gloomy

fune'rale *nm* funeral

fu'nereo *a* ⟨*aria*⟩ funereal

fu'nesto *a* sad

fu'ngere *vi* **~ da** act as

'**fungo** *nm* mushroom; *Bot, Med* fungus; **funghi** *pl Bot* fungi. **~ atomico** mushroom cloud. **~ commestibile** edible mushroom

funico'lare *nf* funicular [railway]

funi'via *nf* cableway

funzio'nale *a* functional

funzionalità *nf* functionality

funziona'mento *nm* functioning

funzio'nare *vi* work, function; **~ da** (*fungere da*) act as

funzio'nario *nm* official. **~ statale** civil servant

funzi'one *nf* function; (*carica*) office; *Relig* service; **entrare in ~** take up office; **mettere in ~** ⟨*motore*⟩ start up; **vivere in ~ di** live for

fu'oco *nm* fire; (*fisica, fotografia*) focus; **far ~** fire; **dar ~ a** set fire to; **andare a ~** go up in flames; **prendere ~** catch fire; **a ~ vivo** ⟨*cuocere*⟩ on a high heat; **a ~ lento** ⟨*cuocere*⟩ on a low heat; '**vietato accendere fuochi**' 'no campfires'. **fuochi** *pl* **d'artificio** fireworks. **~ di paglia** nine-days' wonder. **fuochi** *pl* **pirotecnici** pyrotechnics

fuorché *prep* except

fu'ori *adv* out; (*all'esterno*) outside; (*all'aperto*) outdoors; **~!** *fam* get out!; **~ i soldi!** fork up!; **andare di ~** (*traboccare*)

spill over; **essere ~ di sé** be beside oneself; **essere in ~** (*sporgere*) stick out; **far ~** *fam* get rid of; **~ commercio** not for sale; **~ luogo** (*inopportuno*) out of place; **~ mano** out of the way; **~ moda** old-fashioned; **~ pasto** between meals; **~ pericolo** out of danger; **~ programma** unscheduled; **~ questione** out of the question; **~ uso** out of use ● *nm* outside

fuori'bordo *nm* speedboat (*with outboard motor*)

fuori'campo *a inv* ⟨*Cinema: voce*⟩ off-screen

fuori'classe *nmf inv* champion

fuoricombatti'mento *nm* knockout

fuorigi'oco *nm & adv* offside

fuori'legge *nmf* outlaw

fuori'pista *nm inv* (*sci*) off-piste skiing

fuori'serie *a* custom-made ● *nf Auto* custom-built model

fuori'strada *nm inv* off-road vehicle

fuoriu'scita *nf* (*perdita*) leak

fuoriu'scito, -a *nmf* exile

fuorvi'are *vt* lead astray ● *vi* go astray

furbacchi'one *nm* crafty old devil

fur'bastro, -a *nmf* crafty devil

furbe'ria *nf* cunning

fur'besco *a* sly, cunning

fur'bizia *nf* cunning

'**furbo** *a* sly, cunning; (*intelligente*) clever; (*astuto*) shrewd; **bravo ~!** nice one!; **fare il ~** try to be clever

fu'rente *a* furious

fur'fante *nm* scoundrel

furgon'cino *nm* delivery van

fur'gone *nm* van. **~ postale** mail van

'**furia** *nf* fury; (*fretta*) haste; **a ~ di** by dint of; **andare su tutte le furie** fly into a rage

furi'bondo *a* furious

furi'ere *nm Mil* quartermaster

furiosa'mente *adv* furiously

furi'oso *a* furious; ⟨*litigio*⟩ violent

fu'rore *nm* fury; (*veemenza*) frenzy; **far ~** be all the rage

furoreggi'are *vi* be a great success

furtiva'mente *adv* covertly

fur'tivo *a* furtive

'**furto** *nm* theft; **commettere un ~** steal; **è un ~!** *fig* it's daylight robbery!. **~ con scasso** burglary

'**fusa** *nfpl* **fare le ~** purr

fu'scello *nm* (*di legno*) twig; (*di paglia*) straw; **sei un ~** you're as light as a feather

fu'seaux *mpl* leggings

fu'sibile *nm* fuse

fu'silli *nmpl* pasta twirls

fusi'one *nf* fusion; *Comm* merger

'**fuso** *pp di* **fondere** ● *a* melted ● *nm* spindle; **a ~** spindle-shaped. **~ orario** time zone

fusoli'era *nf* fuselage

fu'stagno *nm* corduroy

fu'stella *nf* (*talloncino*) part of packaging on prescribed medicine returned by the pharmacist to claim a refund

fusti'gare *vt* flog; *fig* castigate

fu'stino *nm* (*di detersivo*) box

'**fusto** *nm* stem; (*tronco*) trunk; (*recipiente di metallo*) drum; (*di legno*) barrel. **~ del letto** bedstead
'**futile** *a* futile
futilità *nf* futility

futu'rismo *nm* futurism
futu'rista *nmf* futurist
fu'turo *a* & *nm* future; **predire il ~** tell fortunes, foretell. **~ anteriore** *Gram* future perfect

Gg

gabar'dine *nf* (*tessuto*) gabardine
gab'bare *vt* cheat
gab'barsi *vr* **~ di** make fun of
'**gabbia** *nf* cage; (*da imballaggio*) crate. **~ dell'ascensore** lift cage. **~ degli imputati** dock. **~ toracica** rib cage
gabbi'ano *nm* [sea]gull. **~ comune** common gull
gabi'netto *nm* (*di medico*) consulting room; *Pol* cabinet; (*toletta*) toilet; (*laboratorio*) laboratory; **andare al ~** go to the toilet. **gabinetti** *pl* **pubblici** public convenience
'**Gabon** *nm* Gabon
ga'elico *nm* Gaelic
'**gaffa** *nf* boathook
'**gaffe** *nf inv* blunder
gagli'ardo *a* vigorous
gai'ezza *nf* gaiety
'**gaio** *a* cheerful
'**gala** *nf* gala
ga'lante *a* gallant
galante'ria *nf* gallantry
galantu'omo *nm* (*pl* **galantuomini**) gentleman
ga'lassia *nf* galaxy
gala'teo *nm* [good] manners *pl*; (*trattato*) book of etiquette
gale'otto *nm* (*rematore*) galley-slave; (*condannato*) convict
ga'lera *nf* (*nave*) galley; *fam* slammer
'**galla** *nf Bot* gall; **a ~** afloat; **venire a ~** surface
galleggi'ante *a* floating ● *nm* craft; (*boa*) float
galleggi'are *vi* float
galle'ria *nf* (*traforo*) tunnel; (*d'arte*) gallery; *Theat* circle; (*arcata*) arcade; **prima ~** dress circle. **~ aerodinamica** wind tunnel. **~ d'arte** art gallery
'**Galles** *nm* Wales
gal'lese *a* Welsh ● *nm* Welshman; (*lingua*) Welsh ● *nf* Welshwoman
gal'letta *nf* cracker
gal'letto *nm* cockerel; **fare il ~** show off, impress the girls
'**gallico** *a* Gallic
gal'lina *nf* hen
galli'nella *nf* **~ d'acqua** moorhen
gal'lismo *nm* machismo
'**gallo** *nm* cock. **~ cedrone** capercaillie

gal'lone *nm* stripe; (*misura*) gallon
galop'pante *a* galloping
galop'pare *vi* gallop
galop'pino *nm* **fare da ~ a qcno** *fam* be sb's gopher
ga'loppo *nm* gallop; **al ~** at a gallop
galvaniz'zare *vt* galvanize
'**gamba** *nf* leg; (*di lettera*) stem; **a quattro gambe** on all fours; **darsela a gambe** take to one's heels; **essere in ~** (*essere forte*) be strong; (*capace*) be smart
gam'bale *nm* leg; **gambali** *pl* (*calzamaglia*) leggings
gamba'letto *nm* pop sock
gambe'retti *nmpl* shrimps. **~ in salsa rosa** prawn cocktail
'**gambero** *nm* prawn; (*di fiume*) crayfish
gambe'roni *nmpl* king prawns
'**Gambia** *nf* the Gambia
gambiz'zare *vt* kneecap
'**gambo** *nm* stem; (*di pianta*) stalk
ga'mella *nf* billy
game point *nm inv* game point
ga'mete *nm* gamete
'**gamma** *nf Mus* scale; *fig* range. **~ d'onda** waveband. **~ di prezzi** price range. **~ di prodotti** product range
ga'nascia *nf* jaw; **ganasce** *pl* **del freno** brake shoes
'**gancio** *nm* hook
'**Gange** *nm* Ganges
'**ganghero** *nm* **uscire dai gangheri** *fig* get into a temper
'**gangster** *nm inv* gangster
'**gara** *nf* competition; (*di velocità*) race; **fare a ~** compete. **~ d'appalto** call for tenders. **~ a cronometro** time-trial
ga'rage *nm inv* garage
gara'gista *nmf* garage owner
ga'rante *nmf* guarantor
garan'tire *vt* guarantee; (*rendersi garante*) vouch for; (*assicurare*) assure
garan'tirsi *vr* **~ contro, ~ da** guard against, insure against
garan'tismo *nm* protection of civil liberties
garan'tito *a* guaranteed
garan'zia *nf* guarantee; **in ~** under guarantee. **~ collaterale** collateral. **~ di rimborso** money-back guarantee. **~ a vita** lifetime guarantee

gar'bare _vi_ like; **non mi garba** I don't like it

gar'bato _a_ courteous

'garbo _nm_ courtesy; (_grazia_) grace; **con ~** graciously

gar'buglio _nm_ muddle

gar'denia _nf_ gardenia

gareggi'are _vi_ compete

garga'nella _nf_ **a ~** from the bottle

garga'rismo _nm_ gargle; **fare i gargarismi** gargle

ga'ritta _nf_ sentry box

ga'rofano _nm_ carnation; **chiodo di ~** clove

gar'retto _nm_ shank

gar'rire _vi_ chirp

gar'rotta _nf_ garrotte

'garrulo _a_ garrulous

'garza _nf_ gauze

gar'zone _nm_ boy. **~ di stalla** stable-boy

gas _nm inv_ gas; **dare ~** _Auto_ accelerate; **a ~** gas-fired; **a tutto ~** flat out. **~ asfissiante** poisonous gas. **~ esilarante** laughing gas. **~ lacrimogeno** tear gas. **~ nobile** inert gas. **~ propellente** propellant. **~ pl di scarico** exhaust fumes

gas'dotto _nm_ natural gas pipeline

ga'solio _nm_ diesel oil. **~ invernale** diesel containing anti-freeze

ga'sometro _nm_ gasometer

gas'sare _vt_ aerate; (_uccidere col gas_) gas

gas'sato _a_ gassy

gas'soso, -a _a_ gassy; ‹_bevanda_› fizzy ●_nf_ lemonade

'gastrico _a_ gastric

ga'strite _nf_ gastritis

gastroente'rite _nf_ gastro-enteritis

gastrono'mia _nf_ gastronomy

gastro'nomico _a_ gastronomic[al]

ga'stronomo, -a _nmf_ gourmet

'gatta _nf_ **una ~ da pelare** a headache

gatta'buia _nf_ _hum_ clink

gatta'iola _nf_ catflap

gat'tino, -a _nmf_ kitten

'gatto, -a _nmf_ cat; **c'erano solo quattro gatti** there weren't many. **~ delle nevi** snowmobile. **~ a nove code** cat-o'-nine-tails. **~ selvatico** wildcat

gat'toni _adv_ on all fours

gat'tuccio _nm_ dogfish

gau'dente _a_ pleasure-loving

'gaudio _nm_ joy

ga'vetta _nf_ mess tin; **fare la ~** rise through the ranks

gay _a inv_ gay

ga'zebo _nm inv_ gazebo

'gazza _nf_ magpie

gaz'zarra _nf_ racket; **fare ~** make a racket

gaz'zella _nf_ gazelle; _Auto_ police car

gaz'zetta _nf_ gazette. **G~ Ufficiale** official journal

gazzet'tino _nm_ (_titolo_) title page; (_rubrica_) page

gaz'zosa _nf_ clear lemonade

GB _abbr_ (**Gran Bretagna**) GB

'geco _nm_ gecko

ge'lare _vt/i_ freeze; **far ~ il sangue** make sb's blood run cold

ge'lata _nf_ frost

gela'taio, -a _nmf_ ice-cream seller ●_nm_ (_negozio_) ice-cream shop

gelate'ria _nf_ ice-cream parlour

gelati'era _nf_ ice-cream maker

gela'tina _nf_ gelatine; (_dolce_) jelly. **~ di frutta** fruit jelly

gelati'noso _a_ gelatinous

ge'lato _a_ frozen ●_nm_ ice-cream. **~ alla vaniglia** vanilla ice-cream

'gelido _a_ freezing

'gelo _nm_ (_freddo intenso_) freezing cold; (_brina_) frost; _fig_ chill

ge'lone _nm_ chilblain

gelosa'mente _adv_ jealously

gelo'sia _nf_ jealousy

ge'loso _a_ jealous

'gelso _nm_ mulberry[-tree]

gelso'mino _nm_ jasmine

gemel'laggio _nm_ twinning

gemel'lare _vt_ twin ●_a_ twin

ge'mello, -a _a_ & _nmf_ twin; **gemelli** _pl_ (_di polsino_) cuff-link; **Gemelli** _pl Astr_ Gemini _sg_

'gemere _vi_ groan

'gemito _nm_ groan

'gemma _nf_ gem; _Bot_ bud

gemmolo'gia _nf_ gemology

gen'darme _nm_ gendarme

'gene _nm_ gene

genealo'gia _nf_ genealogy

genea'logico _a_ genealogical

gene'rale[1] _a_ general; **in ~** (_tutto sommato_) in general, on the whole; **parlando in ~** generally speaking

gene'rale[2] _nm Mil_ general. **~ di divisione** major-general

generalità _nf inv_ (_qualità_) generality, general nature; (_maggior parte_) majority; **~ pl** (_dati_) particulars _pl_

generaliz'zare _vt_ generalize

generalizzazi'one _nf_ generalization

general'mente _adv_ generally

gene'rare _vt_ give birth to; (_causare_) breed; _Techn_ generate

genera'tore _nm Techn_ generator

generazio'nale _a_ generation

generazi'one _nf_ generation; **di ~ in ~** from generation to generation

'genere _nm_ kind; _Biol_ genus; _Gram_ gender; (_letterario, artistico_) genre; (_prodotto_) product; **cose del ~** such things; **il ~ umano** mankind; **in ~** generally. **generi** _pl_ **alimentari** provisions. **generi** _pl_ **di prima necessità** essentials

generica'mente _adv_ generically

ge'nerico _a_ generic; **medico ~** general practitioner

'genero _nm_ son-in-law

generosa'mente _adv_ generously

generosità _nf_ generosity

gene'roso _a_ generous

'genesi _nf_ genesis

genetica'mente *adv* genetically

ge'netico, -a *a* genetic ● *nf* genetics

gene'tista *nmf* geneticist

gen'giva *nf* gum

geni'ale *a* ingenious; (*congeniale*) congenial

geni'ere *nm* Mil sapper

'genio *nm* genius; **andare a ~** be to one's taste. **~ civile** civil engineering. **~ incompreso** misunderstood genius. **~ [militare]** Engineers

geni'tale *a* genital ● *nm* **genitali** *pl* genitals

geni'tore *nm* parent

gen'naio *nm* January

geno'cidio *nm* genocide

'Genova *nf* Genoa

geno'vese *a* Genoese

gen'taglia *nf* rabble

'gente *nf* people *pl*

gen'tile *a* kind; **G~ Signore** (*in lettere*) Dear Sir

genti'lezza *nf* kindness; **per ~** (*per favore*) please

gentil'mente *adv* kindly

gentilu'omo (*pl* **gentilu'omini**) *nm* gentleman

genu'flettersi *vr* kneel down

genuina'mente *adv* genuinely

genu'ino *a* genuine; ⟨*cibo, prodotto*⟩ natural

genzi'ana *nf* gentian

geo'fisica *nf* geophysics

geo'fisico, -a *nmf* geophysician

geogra'fia *nf* geography

geo'grafico *a* geographical

ge'ografo, -a *nmf* geographer

geolo'gia *nf* geology

geo'logico *a* geological

ge'ologo, -a *nmf* geologist

ge'ometra *nmf* surveyor

geome'tria *nf* geometry

geometrica'mente *adv* geometrically

geo'metrico *a* geometric[al]

geopo'litico *a* geopolitical

geo'termico *a* geothermal, geothermic

ge'ranio *nm* geranium

gerar'chia *nf* hierarchy

gerarchica'mente *adv* hierarchically

ge'rarchico *a* hierarchic[al]

ger'billo *nm* gerbil

ge'rente *nm* manager ● *nf* manageress

'gergo *nm* jargon; (*dei giovani*) slang. **~ burocratico** bureaucratic jargon

geri'atra *nmf* geriatrician

geria'tria *nf* geriatrics

geri'atrico *a* geriatric

'gerla *nf* wicker basket

Ger'mania *nf* Germany. **~ [dell']Est** East Germany. **~ [dell']Ovest** West Germany

ger'manico *a* Germanic

'germe *nm* germ; (*fig: principio*) seed. **~ di grano** seedcorn

germogli'are *vi* sprout

ger'moglio *nm* sprout; **in ~** *Bot* sprouting. **germogli** *pl* **di soia** beansprouts

gero'glifico *nm* hieroglyph

geron'tologo, -a *nmf* gerontologist

ge'rundio *nm* gerund

Gerusa'lemme *nf* Jerusalem

ges'setto *nm* chalk

'gesso *nm* chalk; (*Med, scultura*) plaster

ge'staccio *nm* V-sign

gestazi'one *nf* gestation

gestico'lare *vi* gesticulate

gestio'nale *a* management *attrib*

gesti'one *nf* management. **~ aziendale** business management. **~ dei dati** *Comput* data management. **~ disco** *Comput* disk management. **~ dell'energia** energy resource management. **~ del flusso di cassa** cashflow management. **~ patrimoniale** financial mangement

ge'stire *vi* manage; **~ male** mishandle

ge'stirsi *vr* budget one's time and money

'gesto *nm* gesture; (*azione: pl f* **gesta**) deed

ge'store *nm* manager

Gesù *nm* Jesus. **~ bambino** baby Jesus

gesu'ita *nm* Jesuit

gesu'itico *a* Jesuit *attrib*

get'tare *vt* throw; (*scagliare*) fling; (*emettere*) spout; *Techn, fig* cast; **~ via** throw away

get'tarsi *vr* throw oneself; **~ in** ⟨*fiume:*⟩ flow into

get'tata *nf* throw; *Techn* casting

'gettito *nm* **~ fiscale** tax revenue

'getto *nm* throw; (*di liquidi, gas*) jet; **a ~ continuo** in a continuous stream; **di ~** straight off

getto'nato *a* ⟨*canzone*⟩ popular

get'tone *nm* token; (*per giochi*) counter

gettoni'era *nf* coin box

'geyser *nm inv* geyser

'Ghana *nm* Ghana

ghe'pardo *nm* cheetah

'gheppio *nm* kestrel

gher'mire *vt* grasp

'ghette *nfpl* (*per neonato*) leggings

ghettiz'zare *vt* ghettoize

'ghetto *nm* ghetto

ghiacci'aia *nf* glacier

ghiacci'aio *nm* glacier

ghiacci'are *vt/i* freeze

ghiacci'ato *a* frozen; (*freddissimo*) ice-cold

ghi'accio *nm* ice; *Auto* black ice. **~ secco** dry ice

ghiacci'olo *nm* icicle; (*gelato*) ice lolly

ghi'aia *nf* gravel

ghiai'oso *a* gritty

ghi'anda *nf* acorn

ghi'andola *nf* gland. **~ pituitaria** pituitary gland. **~ sudoripara** sweat gland. **~ surrenale** adrenal gland

ghiglio't tina *nf* guillotine

ghi'gnare *vi* sneer

'ghigno *nm* sneer

ghi'otto *a* greedy, gluttonous; (*appetitoso*) appetizing

ghiot'tone, -a *nmf* glutton

ghiottone'ria *nf* (*caratteristica*) gluttony; (*cibo*) tasty morsel

ghiri'goro *nm* flourish

ghir'landa nf (corona) wreath; (di fiori) garland

'ghiro nm dormouse; **dormire come un ~** sleep like a log

'ghisa nf cast iron

già adv already; (un tempo) formerly; **~!** indeed!; **~ da ieri** since yesterday

gi'acca nf jacket. **~ a vento** wind-cheater

giacché conj since

giac'cone nm jacket

gia'cenza nf **giacenze** pl **di magazzino** unsold stock

gia'cere vi lie

giaci'mento nm deposit. **~ di petrolio** oil deposit

gia'cinto nm hyacinth

gi'ada nf jade

giaggi'olo nm iris

giagu'aro nm jaguar

gial'lastro a yellowish

gi'allo a & nm yellow; [libro] **~** crime novel; [film] **~** thriller. **~ dell'uovo** egg yolk

Gia'maica nf Jamaica

giamai'cano, -a a & nmf Jamaican

Giap'pone nm Japan

giappo'nese a & nmf Japanese

gi'ara nf jar

giardi'naggio nm gardening

giardini'era nf **~ di verdure** diced, mixed vegetables, cooked and pickled

giardini'ere, -a nmf gardener ● nf Auto estate car; (sottaceti) pickles pl

giar'dino nm garden. **~ d'infanzia** kindergarten. **~ pensile** roof-garden. **giardini** pl **pubblici** park. **~ zoologico** zoo

giarretti'era nf garter

giavel'lotto nm javelin

gi'gante nm giant

gigan'tesco a gigantic

gigantogra'fia nf blow-up

'giglio nm lily

gilè nm inv waistcoat

gin nm inv gin

gin'cana nf gymkhana

ginecolo'gia nf gynaecology

gineco'logico a gynaecological

gine'cologo, -a nmf gynaecologist

gi'nepro nm juniper

gi'nestra nf broom

Gi'nevra nf Geneva

gingil'larsi vr fiddle; (perder tempo) potter

gin'gillo nm plaything; (ninnolo) knick-knack

gin'nasio nm (scuola) grammar school

gin'nasta nmf gymnast

gin'nastica nf gymnastics; (esercizi) exercises pl. **~ ritmica** eurhythmics

ginocchi'ata nf **prendere una ~** bang one's knee

ginocchi'era nf knee-pad

gi'nocchio nm (pl m **ginocchi** o f **ginocchia**) knee; **in ~** on one's knees, kneeling; **mettersi in ~** kneel down; (per supplicare) go down on one's knees; **al ~** (gonna) knee-length

ginocchi'oni adv kneeling

gio'care vt/i play; (giocherellare) toy; (d'azzardo) gamble; (puntare) stake; (ingannare) trick; **~ a calcio/a pallavolo** play football/volleyball; **~ d'astuzia** be crafty; **~ d'azzardo** gamble; **~ in Borsa** speculate on the Stock Exchange; **~ in casa** Sport, fig play on one's home ground, play at home

gio'carsi vr **~ la carriera** throw one's career away

gioca|'tore, -'trice nmf player; (d'azzardo) gambler

gio'cattolo nm toy

giocherel'lare vi toy; (nervosamente) fiddle

giocherel'lone a skittish

gi'oco nm game; (di bambini, Techn) play; (d'azzardo) gambling; (scherzo) joke; (insieme di pezzi ecc) set; **essere in ~** be at stake; **fare il doppio ~ con qcno** double-cross sb; **è un ~ da ragazzi** fam it's a cinch. **~ elettronico** computer game. **giochi** pl **della gioventù** nation-wide sports tournament for children. **~ dell'oca** snakes and ladders. **Giochi** pl **Olimpici** Olympic Games. **~ di parole** play on words. **~ di pazienza** game of manual skill. **~ di prestigio** conjuring trick. **~ di società** board game

giocoli'ere nm juggler

gio'coso a playful

gi'ogo nm yoke

gi'oia nf joy; (gioiello) jewel; (appellativo) sweetie

gioiel'leria nf jeweller's [shop]

gioi'elli nmpl jewellery

gioielli'ere, -a nmf jeweller; (negozio) jeweller's

gioi'ello nm jewel

gioiosa'mente adv joyfully

gioi'oso a joyful

gio'ire vi **~ per** rejoice at

Gior'dania nf Jordan

gior'dano, -a a & nmf Jordanian

giorna'laio, -a nmf newsagent, newsdealer

gior'nale nm [news]paper; (diario) journal. **~ di bordo** logbook. **~ gratuito** freebie. **~ del mattino** morning paper. **~ radio** radio news. **~ della sera** evening paper

giornali'ero a daily ● nm (per sciare) day pass

giorna'lino nm comic

giorna'lismo nm journalism

giorna'lista nmf journalist

giornal'mente adv daily

gior'nata nf day; **buona ~!** have a good day!; **in ~** today; **a ~** (essere pagato) on a day-to-day basis; **vivere alla ~** live from day to day. **~ lavorativa** working day

gi'orno nm day; **al ~** per day; **al ~ d'oggi** nowadays; **di ~** by day; **in pieno ~** in broad daylight; **un ~ si, un ~ no** every other day; **~ per ~** day by day. **~ di chiusura** closing day. **~ fatidico** (importante) D-day. **~ feriale** weekday. **~ festivo** public holiday. **~ del giudizio** Judgement Day

gi'ostra *nf* merry-go-round

gio'strarsi *vr* manage

giova'mento *nm* **trarre ~ da** derive benefit from

gi'ovane *a* young; (*giovanile*) youthful ● *nm* youth, young man ● *nf* girl, young woman; **giovani** *pl* young people

giova'nile *a* youthful; ‹*scritto*› early

giova'notto *nm* young man

gio'vare *vi* **~ a** be useful to; (*far bene a*) be good for

gio'varsi *vr* **~ di** avail oneself of

giovedì *nm inv* Thursday; **di ~** on Thursdays. **~ grasso** *last Thursday before Lent.* **~ santo** Maundy Thursday

Gi'ove *nm* Jupiter, Jove

gioventù *nf* youth; (*i giovani*) young people *pl.* **~ bruciata** young drop-outs *pl*

giovi'ale *a* jovial

giovi'nezza *nf* youth

gi'rabile *a* ‹*assegno*› endorsable

gira'dischi *nm inv* record-player

gi'raffa *nf* giraffe; *Cinema* boom

gira'mondo *nmf inv* globetrotter; **da ~** globetrotting

gi'randola *nf* (*fuoco d'artificio*) Catherine wheel; (*giocattolo*) windmill; (*banderuola*) weathercock

gi'rare *vt* turn; (*andare intorno, visitare*) go round; *Comm* endorse; *Cinema* shoot ● *vi* turn; ‹*aerei, uccelli:*› circle; (*andare in giro*) wander; **~ sotto...** *Comput* run under...; **mi gira la testa** I feel dizzy; **far ~ la testa a qcno** make sb's head spin; **far ~ le scatole a qcno** *fam* drive sb round the twist; **~ al largo** steer clear

girar'rosto *nm* spit

gi'rarsi *vr* turn [round]

gira'sole *nm* sunflower

gi'rata *nf* turn; *Comm* endorsement; (*in macchina ecc*) ride; **fare una ~** (*a piedi*) go for a walk; (*in macchina*) go for a ride

gira'volta *nf* spin; *fig* U-turn

gi'rello *nm* (*per bambini*) babywalker; *Culin* topside

gi'revole *a* revolving; **ponte ~** swing bridge

gi'rino *nm* tadpole

'giro *nm* turn; (*circolo*) circle; (*percorso*) round; (*viaggio*) tour; (*passeggiata*) short walk; (*in macchina*) drive; (*in bicicletta*) ride; (*circolazione di denaro*) circulation; **andare a fare un ~** (*a piedi*) go for a stroll; (*in macchina*) go for a drive; (*in bicicletta*) go for a cycle ride; **fare il ~ di** go round; **nel ~ di un mese/anno** within a month/year; **prendere in ~ qcno** pull sb's leg; **sentir dire in ~ qcsa** hear sth on the grapevine; **a ~ di posta** by return mail. **~ d'affari** *Comm* turnover. **~ in barca** boat trip. **~ guidato** guided tour. **~ [della] manica** armhole. **giri** *pl* **al minuto** revs per minute, rpm. **~ d'onore** lap of honour. **giri** *pl* **di parole** beating about the bush. **~ di pista** lap. **~ di prova** trial lap. **~ turistico** sightseeing tour. **~ vita** waist measurement

giro'collo *nm* choker; **a ~** roundneck

gi'rone *nm* round. **~ di andata** first half of the season. **~ di ritorno** second half of the season

gironzo'lare *vi* wander about

giro'tondo *nm* ring-a-ring-o'-roses

girova'gare *vi* wander about

gi'rovago *nm* wanderer

'gita *nf* trip; **andare in ~** go on a trip. **~ organizzata** package tour. **~ in pullman** coach trip. **~ scolastica** school trip

gi'tano, -a *nmf* gipsy

gi'tante *nmf* tripper

giù *adv* down; (*sotto*) below; (*dabbasso*) downstairs; **a testa in ~** (*a capofitto*) headlong; **essere ~** (*di morale*) be down, be depressed; (*di salute*) be run down; **~ di corda** down; **~ di lì, su per ~** more or less; **non andare ~ a qcno** stick in sb's craw

gi'ubba *nf* jacket; *Mil* tunic

giub'botto *nm* bomber jacket, jerkin. **~ antiproiettile** bulletproof vest. **~ di pelle** leather jacket. **~ di salvataggio** lifejacket

gi'ubilo *nm* rejoicing

giudi'care *vt* judge; (*ritenere*) consider

gi'udice *nm* judge. **~ conciliatore** justice of the peace. **~ di gara** umpire. **~ di linea** linesman

giudizi'ario *a* legal, judicial

giu'dizio *nm* judg[e]ment; (*opinione*) opinion; (*senno*) wisdom; (*processo*) trial; (*sentenza*) sentence; **mettere ~** become wise. **~ universale** Last Judgement

giudizi'oso *a* sensible

gi'ugno *nm* June

giugu'lare *nf* jugular

giul'lare *nm* jester

giu'menta *nf* mare

giun'chiglia *nf* jonquil

gi'unco *nm* reed

gi'ungere *vi* arrive; **~ a** (*riuscire*) succeed in; **mi giunge nuovo** it's news to me ● *vt* (*unire*) join

gi'ungla *nf* jungle. **~ d'asfalto** concrete jungle

gi'unta *nf* addition; *Mil* junta; **per ~** in addition. **~ comunale** district council. **~ [militare]** [military] junta

gi'unto *pp di* **giungere** ● *nm Mech* joint. **~ sferico** ball-and-socket joint

giun'tura *nf* joint

giuo'care, giu'oco = **giocare, gioco**

giura'mento *nm* oath; **sotto ~** under oath; **prestare ~** take the oath. **~ d'Ippocrate** Hippocratic oath

giu'rare *vt/i* swear

giu'rato, -a *a* sworn ● *nmf* juror

giu'ria *nf* jury

giu'ridico *a* legal

giurisdizi'one *nf* jurisdiction

giurispru'denza *nf* jurisprudence

giu'rista *nmf* jurist

giu'stezza *nf* justness

giustifi'care *vt* justify

giustifi'carsi *vr* justify oneself; ~ **di** *o* **per qcsa** give an explanation for sth

giustificazi'one *nf* justification

giu'stizia *nf* justice; **farsi ~ da sé** take the law into one's own hands

giustizi'are *vt* execute

giustizi'ere *nm* executioner

gi'usto *a* just, fair; (*adatto*) right; (*esatto*) exact ● *nm* (*uomo retto*) just man; (*cosa giusta*) right ● *adv* exactly; ~ **ora** just now

glaci'ale *a* glacial

gladia'tore *nm* gladiator

gla'diolo *nm* gladiolus

'glassa *nf Culin* icing

glau'coma *nm* glaucoma

gli *def art m pl* the; (*a lui*) [to] him; (*a esso*) [to] it; (*a loro*) [to] them; **non ~ credo** I don't believe him/them

glice'mia *nf* glycaemia

glice'rina *nf* glycerine

'glicine *nm* wisteria

gli'elo *pron* (*a lui*) to him; (*a lei*) to her; (*a loro*) to them; (*a Lei, forma di cortesia*) to you; ~ **prestai** I lent it to him/her etc; **gliel'ho chiesto** I've asked him/her etc

glie'ne *pron* (*di ciò*) of it; ~ **ho dato un po'** I gave him/her/them/you some [of it]; ~ **ho parlato** I've talked to him/her etc about it

glis'sare *vi* avoid the issue; ~ **su qcsa** skate over sth

glo'bale *a* global; *fig* overall

global'mente *adv* globally

'globo *nm* globe. ~ **oculare** eyeball. ~ **terrestre** globe

'globulo *nm* globule; *Med* corpuscle. ~ **bianco** white cell, white corpuscle. ~ **rosso** red cell, red corpuscle

'gloria *nf* glory

glori'arsi *vr* ~ **di** be proud of

glorifi'care *vt* glorify

gloriosa'mente *adv* gloriously

glori'oso *a* glorious

'glossa *nf* gloss

glos'sario *nm* glossary

glottolo'gia *nf* linguistics

glu'cosio *nm* glucose

glutam'mato *nm* ~ **di sodio** monosodium glutamate

'gluteo *nm* buttock

'gnocchi *nmpl small flour and potato dumplings*

'gnomo *nm* gnome

'gnorri *nm* **fare lo ~** play dumb

goal *nm inv* goal; **fare un ~** score *or* get a goal

'gobba *nf* hump

'gobbo, -a *a* hunchbacked ● *nmf* hunchback

goc'cetto *nm* pick-me-up

'goccia *nf* drop; (*di sudore*) bead; **è stata l'ultima ~** it was the last straw. ~ **di pioggia** raindrop. ~ **di rugiada** dewdrop

goccio'lare *vi* drip

goccio'lio *nm* dripping

go'dere *vi* (*sl: sessualmente*) come; ~ **di qcsa** enjoy sth, make the most of sth

go'dersi *vr* ~ **qcsa** enjoy sth; **godersela** have a good time

godi'mento *nm* enjoyment

goffaggine *nf* awkwardness

goffa'mente *adv* awkwardly

'goffo *a* awkward

go-'kart *nm inv* go-kart

'gola *nf* throat; (*ingordigia*) gluttony; *Geog* gorge; (*di camino*) flue; **avere mal di ~** have a sore throat; **far ~ a qcno** tempt sb

go'letta *nf* schooner

golf *nm inv* jersey; *Sport* golf

gol'fino *nm* jumper

'golfo *nm* gulf

goli'ardico *a* student *attrib*

golosità *nf inv* greediness; (*cibo*) tasty morsel

go'loso *a* greedy

'golpe *nm inv* coup

go'mena *nf* painter

gomi'tata *nf* nudge; **dare una ~ a qcno** elbow sb

'gomito *nm* elbow; **alzare il ~** (*fam: bere*) raise one's elbow; ~ **a** (*lavorare*) side by side

go'mitolo *nm* ball

'gomma *nf* rubber; (*colla, da masticare*) gum; (*pneumatico*) tyre; **avere una ~ a terra** have a flat. ~ **arabica** gum arabic. ~ **da masticare** chewing gum. ~ **di scorta** spare tyre

gommapi'uma® *nf* foam rubber

gom'mino *nm* rubber tip

gom'mista *nm* tyre specialist

gom'mone *nm* [rubber] dinghy

gom'moso *a* chewy

'gondola *nf* gondola

gondoli'ere *nm* gondolier

gonfa'lone *nm* banner

gonfi'abile *a* inflatable

gonfi'are *vi* swell ● *vt* blow up; pump up (*pneumatico*); (*esagerare*) exaggerate

gonfi'arsi *vr* swell; (*acque:*) rise

'gonfio *a* swollen; (*pneumatico*) inflated

gonfi'ore *nm* swelling

gongo'lante *a* overjoyed

gongo'lare *vi* be overjoyed

goni'ometro *nm* protractor

'gonna *nf* skirt. ~ **pantalone** culottes *pl*. ~ **a pieghe** pleated skirt. ~ **a portafoglio** wrapover skirt

gonor'rea *nf* gonorrh[o]ea

'gonzo *nm* simpleton

gorgheggi'are *vi* warble

gor'gheggio *nm* warble

'gorgo *nm* whirlpool

gorgogli'ante *a* burbling, gurgling

gorgogli'are *vi* gurgle

gor'goglio *nm* burble

gorgon'zola *nf* strong, soft blue cheese

go'rilla *nm inv* gorilla; (*guardia del corpo*) bodyguard, minder

'gota *nf* cheek

'gotico *a & nm* Gothic

'gotta *nf* gout

gover'nante *nf* housekeeper

gover'nare *vt* govern; (*dominare*) rule; (*dirigere*) manage; (*curare*) look after

governa'tivo *a* government

governa'tore *nm* governor

go'verno *nm* government; (*dominio*) rule; **al ~ in** power. **~ ombra** shadow government

'gozzo *nm* (*di animale*) crop; *Med* goitre; *fam* throat

gozzovigli'are *vi* eat, drink and be merry

gracchi'are *vi* caw; ⟨*fig: persona:*⟩ screech

'gracchio *nm* caw

graci'dare *vi* croak

'gracile *a* delicate

gra'dasso *nm* braggart

gradata'mente *adv* gradually

gradazi'one *nf* gradation. **~ alcoolica** alcohol[ic] content

gra'devole *a* agreeable

gradevol'mente *adv* pleasantly, agreeably

gradi'ente *nm* gradient

gradi'mento *nm* liking; **indice di ~** *Radio*, *TV* popularity rating; **non è di mio ~** it's not to my liking

gradi'nata *nf* flight of steps; (*di stadio*, *teatro*) tiers *pl*

gra'dino *nm* step

gra'dire *vt* like; (*desiderare*) wish

gra'dito *a* pleasant; (*bene accetto*) welcome

'grado *nm* degree; (*rango*) rank; **di buon ~** willingly; **essere in ~ di fare qcsa** be in a position to do sth; (*essere capace a*) be able to do sth; **per gradi** ⟨*procedere*⟩ by degrees

gradu'ale *a* gradual

gradual'mente *adv* gradually

gradu'are *vt* graduate

gradu'ato *a* graded; (*provvisto di scala graduata*) graduated ● *nm Mil* noncommissioned officer

gradua'toria *nf* list

graduazi'one *nf* graduation

'graffa *nf* clip; (*segno grafico*) brace

graf'fetta *nf* staple

graffi'are *vt* scratch

graffia'tura *nf* scratch

'graffio *nm* scratch

gra'fia *nf* [hand]writing; (*ortografia*) spelling

'grafica *nf* graphics; (*disciplina*) graphics, graphic design. **~ pubblicitaria** commercial art

grafica'mente *adv* in graphics, graphically

'grafico *a* graphic ● *nm* graph; (*persona*) graphic designer. **~ a torta** pie chart

gra'fite *nf* graphite

gra'fologo, -a *nmf* graphologist

gra'migna *nf* weed

gram'matica *nf* grammar

grammati'cale *a* grammatical

grammatical'mente *adv* grammatically

gram'matico *nm* grammarian

'grammo *nm* gram[me]

gram'mofono *nm* gramophone

gran *vedi* **grande**

'grana *nf* grain; (*formaggio*) parmesan; (*fam: seccatura*) trouble; (*fam: soldi*) readies *pl*

gra'naio *nm* barn

gra'nata *nf Mil* grenade; (*frutto*) pomegranate

granati'ere *nm Mil* grenadier

gra'nato *nm* garnet

Gran Bre'tagna *nf* Great Britain

gran'cassa *nf* bass drum

gran'cevola *nf* spiny spider crab

'granchio *nm* crab; (*fig: errore*) blunder; **prendere un ~** make a blunder

grandango'lare *nm* wide-angle lens

gran'dangolo *nm* wide-angle lens

'grande (*a volte* **gran**) *a* (*ampio*) large; (*grosso*) big; (*alto*) tall; (*largo*) wide; (*fig: senso morale*) great; (*grandioso*) grand; (*adulto*) grown-up; **~ e grosso** beefy; **ho una gran fame** I'm very hungry; **fa un gran caldo** it is very hot; **in ~** on a large scale; **in gran parte** to a great extent; **non è un gran che** it is nothing much; **di gran carriera** hotfoot; **un gran ballo** a grand ball; **alla ~** *sl* in a big way ● *nmf* (*persona adulta*) grown-up; (*persona eminente*) great man/woman

grandeggi'are *vi* **~ su** tower over; (*darsi arie*) show off

gran'dezza *nf* greatness; (*ampiezza*) largeness; (*larghezza*) width, breadth; (*dimensione*) size; (*fasto*) grandeur; (*prodigalità*) lavishness; **a ~ naturale** life-size

grandi'nare *vi* hail; **grandina** it's hailing

'grandine *nf* hail

grandiosità *nf* grandeur

grandi'oso *a* grand

gran'duca *nm* grand duke

grandu'cato *nm* grand duchy

grandu'chessa *nf* grand duchess

gra'nello *nm* grain; (*di frutta*) pip

gra'nita *nf* crushed ice drink

gra'nito *nm* granite

'grano *nm* grain; (*frumento*) wheat. **~ di pepe** peppercorn. **~ saraceno** buckwheat

gran[o]'turco *nm* corn

'granulo *nm* granule

'grappa *nf* very strong, clear spirit distilled from grapes; (*morsa*) cramp

'grappolo *nm* bunch. **~ d'uva** bunch of grapes

gras'setto *nm* bold [type]

gras'sezza *nf* fatness; (*untuosità*) greasiness

'grasso *a* fat; ⟨*cibo*⟩ fatty; (*unto*) greasy; ⟨*terreno*⟩ rich; (*grossolano*) coarse ● *nm* fat; (*sostanza*) grease; **a basso contenuto di grassi** low-fat; **senza grassi** nonfat, fat-free

gras'soccio *a* plump

gras'sone, -a *nmf* dumpling

'grata *nf* grating

gra'tella *nf Culin* grill

gra'ticcio *nm* (*per piante*) trellis; (*stuoia*) rush matting

gra'ticola *nf Culin* grill

gra'tifica *nf* bonus

gratificazi'one *nf* satisfaction

gra'tin *nm inv* gratin. ~ **di patate** *potatoes with grated cheese*

grati'nare *vt* cook au gratin

grati'nato *a* au gratin

'gratis *adv* free

grati'tudine *nf* gratitude

'grato *a* grateful; (*gradito*) pleasant

gratta'capo *nm* trouble

grattaci'elo *nm* skyscraper

grat'tare *vt* scratch; (*raschiare*) scrape; (*grattugiare*) grate; (*fam: rubare*) pinch ● *vi* grate

grat'tarsi *vr* scratch oneself

grat'tugia *nf* grater

grattugi'are *vt* grate

gratuita'mente *adv* free [of charge]

gra'tuito *a* free [of charge]; (*ingiustificato*) gratuitous

gra'vare *vt* burden ● *vi* ~ **su** weigh on

'grave *a* (*pesante*) heavy; (*serio*) serious; (*difficile*) hard; ⟨*voce, suono*⟩ low; (*fonetica*) grave; **essere** ~ (*gravemente ammalato*) be seriously ill

grave'mente *adv* seriously, gravely

gravi'danza *nf* pregnancy. ~ **extrauterina** ectopic pregnancy. ~ **indesiderata** unwanted pregnancy

'gravido *a* pregnant

gravità *nf* seriousness; *Phys* gravity

gravi'tare *vi* gravitate

gra'voso *a* onerous

'grazia *nf* grace; (*favore*) favour; *Jur* pardon; **entrare nelle grazie di qcno** get into sb's good books; **ministero di** ~ **e giustizia** Ministry of Justice

grazi'are *vt* pardon

'grazie *int* thank you!, thanks!; ~ **mille!** many thanks!, thanks a lot!; ~ **a Dio/al cielo!** thank God/goodness!; ~ **a** thanks to

grazi'oso *a* charming; (*carino*) pretty

'Grecia *nf* Greece

'greco, -a *a & nmf* Greek; ~ **antico** (*lingua*) classical Greek

gre'gario *a* gregarious ● *nm* (*ciclismo*) supporting rider

'gregge *nm* flock

'greggio *a* raw ● *nm* (*petrolio*) crude [oil]

grembi'ale, grembi'ule *nm* apron

'grembo *nm* lap; (*utero*) womb; *fig* bosom

gre'mire *vt* pack

gre'mirsi *vr* become crowded (**di** with)

gre'mito *a* packed

'gretto *a* stingy; (*di vedute ristrette*) narrow-minded

'greve *a* heavy

'grezzo *a* = **greggio**

gri'dare *vi* shout; (*di dolore*) scream; ⟨*animale:*⟩ cry ● *vt* shout; ~ **qcsa ai quattro venti** shout sth from the rooftops

'grido *nm* (*pl m* **gridi** *o pl f* **grida**) shout, cry; (*di animale*) cry; **all'ultimo** ~ the latest fashion; **scrittore di** ~ celebrated writer. ~ **d'aiuto** cry for help. ~ **di battaglia** battle cry

'grigio *a & nm* grey. ~ **perla** pearl grey

'griglia *nf* grill; **alla** ~ grilled; **cuocere alla** ~ grill

grigli'ata *nf* barbecue. ~ **mista** mixed grill. ~ **di pesce** grilled fish

gril'letto *nm* trigger

'grillo *nm* cricket; (*fig: capriccio*) whim

grimal'dello *nm* picklock

'grinfia *nf fig* clutch

'grinta *nf* grit

grin'toso *a* determined

'grinza *nf* wrinkle; (*di stoffa*) crease; **non fare una** ~ ⟨*fig: ragionamento:*⟩ be flawless

grip'pare *vi Mech* seize up

gri'sou *nm* firedamp

gris'sino *nm* bread-stick

'grizzly *nm inv* grizzly

groenlan'dese *a* of Greenland ● *nmf* Greenlander

Groen'landia *nf* Greenland

'groggy *a inv* punch-drunk

'gronda *nf* eaves *pl*

gron'daia *nf* gutter

gron'dare *vi* pour; (*essere bagnato fradicio*) be dripping wet

'groppa *nf* back

'groppo *nm* knot; **avere un** ~ **alla gola** have a lump in one's throat

gros'sezza *nf* size; (*spessore*) thickness

gros'sista *nmf* wholesaler

'grosso *a* big, large; (*spesso*) thick; (*grossolano*) coarse; (*grave*) serious ● *nm* big part; (*massa*) bulk; **farla grossa** do a stupid thing

grossolanità *nf inv* (*qualità*) coarseness; (*di errore*) grossness; (*gesto*) boorishness

grosso'lano *a* coarse; ⟨*errore*⟩ gross; ⟨*comportamento*⟩ boorish

grosso'modo *adv* roughly

'grotta *nf* cave, grotto

grot'tesco *a & nm* grotesque

grovi'era *nmf* Gruyère

gro'viglio *nm* tangle; *fig* muddle

gru *nf inv* (*uccello, edilizia*) crane

'gruccia *nf* (*stampella*) crutch; (*per vestito*) hanger

gru'gnire *vi* grunt

gru'gnito *nm* grunt

'grugno *nm* snout

'grullo *a* silly

'grumo *nm* clot; (*di farina ecc*) lump

gru'moso *a* lumpy

grunge *nm inv* grunge

'gruppo *nm* group; (*comitiva*) party. ~ **pop** pop group. ~ **sanguigno** blood group

gruvi'era *nmf* = **groviera**

'gruzzolo *nm* nest-egg

guada'gnare *vt* earn; gain ⟨*tempo, forza ecc*⟩

guada'gnarsi *vr* ~ **da vivere** earn a living

gua'dagno *nm* gain; (*profitto*) profit; (*entrate*) earnings *pl*. **guadagni** *pl* **illeciti** ill-gotten gains

gu'ado *nm* ford; **passare a** ~ ford

gua'ina *nf* sheath; (*busto*) girdle

gu'aio *nm* trouble; **che** ~**!** that's just brilliant!; **essere nei guai** be in a fix; **guai a te se lo tocchi!** don't you dare touch it!

gua'ire *vi* yelp

gua'ito *nm* yelp; **guaiti** *pl* yelping

gu'ancia *nf* cheek

guanci'ale *nm* pillow

gu'anto *nm* glove. ~ **da forno** oven glove. ~ **di spugna** face cloth

guan'tone *nm* mitt. **guantoni** *pl* [**da boxe**] boxing gloves

guarda'boschi *nm inv* forester

guarda'caccia *nm inv* gamekeeper

guarda'coste *nm inv* coastguard

guarda'linee *nm inv Sport* linesman

guarda'macchine *nmf* car-park attendant

guarda'parco *nm inv* park ranger

guar'dare *vt* look at; (*osservare*) watch; (*badare a*) look after; ‹*finestra:*› look out on; ~ **la televisione** watch television ● *vi* look; (*essere orientato verso*) face; ~ **in su** look up

guarda'roba *nm inv* wardrobe; (*di locale pubblico*) cloakroom

guardarobi'ere, -a *nmf* cloakroom attendant

guar'darsi *vr* look at oneself; ~ **da** beware of; (*astenersi*) refrain from

gu'ardia *nf* guard; (*poliziotto*) policeman; (*vigilanza*) watch; **essere di** ~ be on guard; ‹*medico:*› be on duty; **fare la** ~ **a** keep guard over; **mettere in** ~ **qcno** warn sb; **stare in** ~ be on one's guard. ~ **carceraria** prison warder. ~ **del corpo** bodyguard, minder. ~ **di finanza** *body responsible for border control and for investigating fraud.* ~ **forestale** forest ranger. ~ **medica** duty doctor

guardi'ano, -a *nmf* caretaker. ~ **notturno** night watchman

guar'dingo *a* cautious

guardi'ola *nf* gatekeeper's lodge

guarigi'one *nf* recovery

gua'rire *vt* cure ● *vi* recover; ‹*ferita:*› heal [up]

gua'rito *a* cured

guari'tore, -'trice *nmf* healer

guarnigi'one *nf* garrison

guar'nire *vt* trim; *Culin* garnish

guarnizi'one *nf* trimming; *Culin* garnish; *Mech* gasket. ~ **del freno** brake lining

guasta'feste *nmf inv* spoilsport

gua'stare *vt* spoil; (*rovinare*) ruin; break (*meccanismo*)

gua'starsi *vr* spoil; (*andare a male*) go bad; ‹*tempo:*› change for the worse; ‹*meccanismo:*› break down

gu'asto *a* broken; ‹*ascensore, telefono*› out of order; (*auto*) broken down; ‹*cibo, dente*› bad ● *nm* breakdown; (*danno*) damage; **ho un** ~ **alla macchina** my car's not working. ~ **al motore** engine failure

guazza'buglio *nm* muddle

guaz'zare *vi* wallow

gu'ercio *a* cross-eyed

gu'erra *nf* war; (*tecnica bellica*) warfare. ~ **batteriologica** germ warfare. ~ **biologica** biological warfare. ~ **civile** civil war. ~ **fredda** Cold War. ~ **del Golfo** Gulf War. ~ **lampo** blitzkrieg. ~ **mondiale** world war. ~ **dei prezzi** price war. ~ **di secessione** American Civil War

guerrafon'daio, -a *nmf* warmonger

guerreggi'are *vi* wage war

guer'resco *a* (*di guerra*) war; (*bellicoso*) warlike

guerri'ero *nm* warrior

guer'riglia *nf* guerrilla warfare

guerrigli'ero, -a *nmf* guerrilla

'gufo *nm* owl

'guglia *nf* spire

gu'ida *nf* guide; (*direzione*) guidance; (*comando*) leadership; (*elenco*) directory; *Auto* driving; (*tappeto*) runner; **chi era alla** ~? who was driving?; **essere alla** ~ **di** *fig* be the head of; **fare da** ~ be a guide (**a** to). ~ **commerciale** trade directory. ~ **a destra** right-hand drive. ~ **a sinistra** left-hand drive. ~ **telefonica** phone book, telephone directory. ~ **turistica** tourist guide

gui'dare *vt* guide; *Auto* drive; steer ‹*nave*›; ~ **a passo d'uomo** drive at walking speed

guida'tore, -'trice *nmf* driver. ~ **della domenica** Sunday driver

guin'zaglio *nm* leash

gu'isa *nf* **a** ~ **di** like

guiz'zare *vi* dart; ‹*luce:*› flash

gu'izzo *nm* dart; (*di luce*) flash

gulag *nm inv* Gulag

'gulasch *nm inv* goulash

'guru *nm inv* high priest

'guscio *nm* shell

gu'stare *vt* taste ● *vi* like

'gusto *nm* taste; (*piacere*) liking; **mangiare di** ~ eat heartily; **prenderci** ~ come to enjoy it, develop a taste for it; **al** ~ **di pistacchio** pistachio flavoured. **buon** ~ good taste

gu'stoso *a* tasty; *fig* delightful

guttu'rale *a* guttural

'habitat nm inv habitat
habitué nmf inv regular [customer]
'hacker nmf inv Comput hacker
Ha'iti nf Haiti
haiti'ano, -a a & nmf Haitian
hall nf inv foyer; (di stazione) concourse
ham'burger nm inv hamburger
'handicap nm inv handicap
handicap'pare vt handicap
handicap'pato, -a a disabled ● nmf disabled person. **~ mentale** mentally handicapped person
'hangar nm inv hangar
hard[-core] a hard core
hard disk nm inv hard disk
hard rock nm hard rock
'hardware nm inv Comput hardware
'harem nm inv harem
'hascisc nm hashish
hawai'ano, -a a & nmf Hawaiian

Ha'waii nfpl le **~** Hawaii
'heavy 'metal nm Mus heavy metal
henné nm henna
'herpes nm inv herpes; (su labbra) cold sore. **~ zoster** shingles
hi-fi nm inv hi-fi
high tech nf high tech
Hima'laia nm Himalayas pl
'hinterland nm inv hinterland
'hippy a & nmf hippy
'hit parade nf hit parade, charts pl
HIV nm HIV
'hockey nm hockey. **~ su ghiaccio** ice hockey. **~ su prato** field hockey
'holding nf inv holding company
hollywoodi'ano a Hollywood
Hong Kong nf Hong Kong
'hostess nf inv stewardess
hot dog nm inv hot dog
ho'tel nm inv hotel
'humus nm humus

i def art mpl the; vedi **il**
i'ato nm hiatus
i'berico a Iberian
iber'nare vi hibernate
ibernazi'one nf hibernation
i'bisco nm hibiscus
ibri'dare vt interbreed
ibridazi'one nf interbreeding
'ibrido a & nm hybrid
'iceberg nm inv iceberg; **la punta dell'~** fig the tip of the iceberg
i'cona nf icon
icono'clasta a & nmf iconoclast
icono'clastico a iconoclastic
Id'dio nm God
i'dea nf idea; (opinione) opinion; (ideale) ideal; (indizio) inkling; (piccola quantità) hint; (intenzione) intention; **cambiare ~** change one's mind; **neanche per ~!** not on your life!; **chiarirsi le idee** get one's ideas straight; **dare l'~ di…** give the impression that…; **essere dell'~ che…** be of the opinion that…; **non ne ho ~!** I've no idea!. **~ fissa** obsession
ide'ale a & nm ideal

idea'lista nmf idealist
idealiz'zare vt idealize
ide'are vt conceive
idea|'tore, -'trice nmf originator
'idem adv the same
identica'mente adv identically
i'dentico a identical
identifi'cabile a identifiable
identifi'care vt identify
identificazi'one nf identification
identi'kit[R] nm inv identikit
identità nf inv identity
ideo'gramma nm ideogram
ideolo'gia nf ideology
ideologica'mente adv ideologically
ideo'logico a ideological
idillica'mente adv idyllically
i'dillico a idyllic
i'dillio nm idyll
idi'oma nm language
idio'matico a idiomatic; **espressione idiomatica** idiom, idiomatic expression
idiosincra'sia nf fig aversion; Med allergy
idi'ota a idiotic ● nmf idiot
idio'zia nf idiocy; **dire/fare un'~** do/say

something stupid; **dire idiozie** talk nonsense; **non fare idiozie!** don't act daft!
idola'trare *vt* worship
idoleggi'are *vt* idolize
'idolo *nm* idol
idoneità *nf* suitability; *Mil* fitness; **esame di** ~ qualifying examination
i'doneo *a* ~ **a** suitable for; *Mil* fit for
i'drante *nm* hydrant; (*tubo*) hose
idra'tante *a* (*crema*) moisturizing
idra'tare *vt* hydrate; (*cosmetico:*) moisturize
idratazi'one *nf* moisturizing
i'draulico *a* hydraulic ● *nm* plumber
'idrico *a* water *attrib*
idrocar'buro *nm* hydrocarbon
idroelettricità *nf* hydroelectricity
idroe'lettrico *a* hydroelectric
i'drofilo *a* **cotone** ~ cotton wool, absorbent cotton *Am*
idrofo'bia *nf* rabies *sg*
i'drofobo *a* rabid; *fig* furious
i'drofugo *a* water-repellent
i'drogeno *nm* hydrogen
idrogra'fia *nf* hydrography
i'drolisi *nf* hydrolysis
idromas'saggio *nm* (*sistema*) whirlpool bath
idro'mele *nm* mead
idrorepel'lente *a* & *nm* water-repellent
idroso'lubile *a* water-soluble
idrotera'pia *nf* hydrotherapy
idrovo'lante *nm* seaplane
i'druro *nm* hydride
i'ella *nf fam* bad luck; **portare** ~ be bad luck
iel'lato *a fam* jinxed, plagued by bad luck
i'ena *nf* hyena
i'eri *adv* yesterday; ~ **l'altro, l'altro** ~ the day before yesterday; **il giornale di** ~ yesterday's paper; ~ **mattina** yesterday morning; ~ **notte** last night; ~ **pomeriggio** yesterday afternoon; ~ **sera** yesterday evening
ietta|**'tore, -'trice** *nmf* jinx
ietta'tura *nf* (*sfortuna*) bad luck
igi'ene *nf* hygiene; **ufficio d'**~ ≈ Public Health Service. ~ **mentale** mental health. ~ **personale** personal hygiene. ~ **pubblica** public health
igienica'mente *adv* hygienically
igi'enico *a* hygienic
igie'nista *nmf* hygienist
ig'loo *nm inv* igloo
i'gname *nm* yam
i'gnaro *a* unaware
i'gnifugo *a* flame-retardant
i'gnobile *a* despicable
ignobil'mente *adv* despicably
igno'minia *nf* disgrace
igno'rante *a* ignorant ● *nmf* ignoramus
igno'ranza *nf* ignorance; ~ **crassa** crass ignorance
igno'rare *vt* (*non sapere*) be unaware of; (*trascurare*) ignore; **essere ignorato** go unheeded
i'gnoto *a* unknown
i'guana *nf* iguana

il *def art m* the; **il latte fa bene** milk is good for you; **il signor Magnetti** Mr Magnetti; **il dottor Piazza** Doctor Piazza; **ha il naso grosso** he's got a big nose; **ha gli occhi azzurri** he's got blue eyes; **mettiti il cappello** put your hat on; **il lunedì** on Mondays; **il 1986** 1986; **5 000 lire il chilo** it costs 5,000 lire a kilo
'ilare *a* merry
ilarità *nf* hilarity
i'leo *nm* hipbone
illangui'dire *vi* grow weak
illazi'one *nf* inference
illecita'mente *adv* illicitly
il'lecito *a* illicit
ille'gale *a* illegal
illegalità *nf* illegality
illegal'mente *adv* illegally
illeg'gibile *a* illegible; (*libro*) unreadable
illegittimità *nf* illegitimacy
ille'gittimo *a* illegitimate
il'leso *a* unhurt
illette'rato, -a *a* & *nmf* illiterate
illi'bato *a* chaste
illimitata'mente *adv* indefinitely
illimi'tato *a* unlimited
illivi'dire *vt* bruise ● *vi* (*per rabbia*) turn livid
illogica'mente *adv* illogically
il'logico *a* illogical
il'ludere *vt* deceive
il'ludersi *vr* deceive oneself
illumi'nare *vt* light up; *fig* enlighten; ~ **a giorno** floodlight
illumi'narsi *vr* light up
illuminazi'one *nf* lighting; *fig* enlightenment. ~ **a gas** gas lighting
Illumi'nismo *nm* Enlightenment
illusi'one *nf* illusion; **farsi illusioni** delude oneself. ~ **ottica** optical illusion
illusio'nismo *nm* conjuring
illusio'nista *nmf* conjurer
il'luso, -a *pp di* **illudere** ● *a* deluded ● *nmf* day-dreamer
illu'sorio *a* illusory
illu'strare *vt* illustrate
illustra'tivo *a* illustrative
illustra|**'tore, -'trice** *nmf* illustrator
illustrazi'one *nf* illustration. ~ **a colori/in bianco e nero** colour/black and white illustration
il'lustre *a* distinguished
imbacuc'care *vt* wrap up
imbacuc'carsi *vr* wrap up
imbacuc'cato *a* wrapped up
imbal'laggio *nm* packing
imbal'lare *vt* pack; *Auto* race
imballa|**'tore, -'trice** *nmf* packer
imbalsa'mare *vt* embalm; stuff (*animale*)
imbalsa'mato *a* embalmed; (*animale*) stuffed
imbambo'lato *a* vacant
imban'dito *a* (*tavolo*) covered with food

imbaraz'zante *a* embarrassing

imbaraz'zare *vt* embarrass; (*ostacolare*) encumber

imbaraz'zato *a* embarrassed

imba'razzo *nm* embarrassment; (*ostacolo*) hindrance; **trarre qcno d'~** help sb out of a difficulty; **avere l'~ della scelta** be spoilt for choice. **~ di stomaco** indigestion.

imbarba'rire *vt* barbarize

imbarba'rirsi *vr* become barbarized

imbarca'dero *nm* landing-stage

imbar'care *vt* embark; (*fam: rimorchiare*) score; **~ acqua** ship water

imbar'carsi *vr* go on board; *fig* embark (**in** on)

imbarcazi'one *nf* boat. **~ da pesca** fishing boat. **~ di salvataggio** lifeboat

im'barco *nm* boarding; (*banchina*) landing-stage. **'~ immediato'** 'now boarding'

imbastar'dire *vt* debase

imbastar'dirsi *vr* become debased

imba'stire *vt* tack, baste; *fig* sketch

imbasti'tura *nf* tacking, basting

im'battersi *vr* **~ in** run into

imbat'tibile *a* unbeatable

imbat'tuto *a* unbeaten

imbavagli'are *vt* gag

imbec'cata *nf* *Theat* prompt

imbe'cille *a* stupid ● *nmf* *Med* imbecile

imbellet'tarsi *vr* *hum* doll oneself up

imbel'lire *vt* embellish

im'berbe *a* beardless; *fig* inexperienced

imbestia'lire *vi* fly into a rage; **far ~ qcno** drive sb crazy

imbestia'lirsi *vr* fly into a rage

imbestia'lito *a* enraged

im'bevere *vt* imbue (**di** with)

im'beversi *vr* absorb

imbe'vibile *a* undrinkable

imbe'vuto *a* **~ di** (*acqua*) soaked in; (*nozioni*) imbued with

imbian'care *vt* whiten ● *vi* turn white

imbian'chino *nm* [house] painter

imbion'dire *vt* bleach ● *vi* become bleached

imbion'dirsi *vr* become bleached

imbizzar'rire *vi* become restless; (*arrabbiarsi*) become angry

imbizzar'rirsi *vr* become restless; (*arrabbiarsi*) become angry

imboc'care *vt* feed; (*entrare*) enter; *fig* prompt

imbocca'tura *nf* opening; (*ingresso*) entrance; (*Mus: di strumento*) mouthpiece

im'bocco *nm* entrance

imboni'mento *nm* spiel

imboni'tore *nm* clever talker

imborghe'sire *vi* become middle class

imborghe'sirsi *vr* become middle class

imbo'scare *vt* hide

imbo'scarsi *vr* *Mil* shirk military service

imbo'scata *nf* ambush

imbo'scato *nm* draft dodger

imbottiglia'mento *nm* traffic jam

imbottigli'are *vt* bottle

imbottigli'arsi *vr* get snarled up in a traffic jam

imbottigli'ato *a* (*vino, acqua*) bottled; (*auto*) stuck in a traffic jam, snarled up; **nave imbottigliata** ship in a bottle

imbot'tire *vt* stuff; pad (*giacca*); *Culin* fill

imbot'tirsi *vr* **~ di** (*fig: di pasticche*) stuff oneself with

imbot'tita *nf* quilt

imbot'tito *a* (*spalle*) padded; (*cuscino*) stuffed; (*panino*) filled

imbotti'tura *nf* stuffing; (*di giacca*) padding; *Culin* filling

imbraca'tura *nf* harness

imbracci'are *vt* shoulder (*fucile*); grasp (*scudo*)

imbra'nato *a* clumsy

imbrat'tare *vt* mark

imbrat'tarsi *vr* dirty oneself

imbrigli'are *vt* bridle (*cavallo*); dam (*acque*)

imbroc'care *vt* hit; **imbroccarla giusta** hit the nail on the head

imbrogli'are *vt* muddle; (*raggirare*) cheat. **~ le carte** *fig* confuse the issue

imbrogli'arsi *vr* get tangled; (*confondersi*) get confused

im'broglio *nm* tangle; (*pasticcio*) mess; (*inganno*) trick

imbrogli'one, -a *nmf* cheat

imbronci'are *vi* sulk

imbronci'arsi *vr* sulk

imbronci'ato *a* sulky

imbru'nire *vi* get dark; **all'~** at dusk

imbrut'tire *vt* make ugly ● *vi* become ugly

imbu'care *vt* post, mail; (*nel biliardo*) pot

imbu'cato *a fam* **è ~** he only got the job because of who he knows

imbufa'lirsi *vr* hit the roof

imbur'rare *vt* butter

im'buto *nm* funnel

i'mene *nm* hymen

imi'tare *vt* imitate

imita|'tore, -'trice *nmf* imitator, impersonator

imitazi'one *nf* imitation; **'diffidare delle imitazioni'** 'beware of imitations'

immaco'lato *a* spotless, immaculate; **l'Immacolata Concezione** the Immaculate Conception

immagazzi'nare *vt* store

immagi'nare *vt* imagine; (*supporre*) suppose; **s'immagini!** imagine that!

immagi'nario *a* imaginary

immaginazi'one *nf* imagination; **è frutto della tua ~** it's a figment of your imagination

im'magine *nf* image; (*rappresentazione, idea*) picture. **~ aziendale** corporate image. **~ della marca** brand image. **~ speculare** mirror image

immagi'noso *a* full of imagery

immalinco'nire *vt* sadden

immalinco'nirsi *vr* grow melancholy

imman'cabile *a* unfailing

immancabil'mente *adv* without fail

im'mane *a* huge; (*orribile*) terrible

imma'nente *a* immanent

immangi'abile *a* inedible

immatrico'lare *vt* register

immatrico'larsi *vr* ‹*studente:*› matriculate

immatricolazi'one *nf* registration; (*di studente*) matriculation

immaturità *nf* immaturity

imma'turo *a* unripe; ‹*persona*› immature; (*precoce*) premature

immedesi'marsi *vr* ~ **in** identify oneself with

immedesimazi'one *nf* identification

immediata'mente *adv* immediately

immedia'tezza *nf* immediacy

immedi'ato *a* immediate; **nell'**~ **futuro** in the immediate future

immemo'rabile *a* immemorial

im'memore *a* oblivious

immensa'mente *adv* enormously

immensità *nf* immensity

im'menso *a* immense

immensu'rabile *a* immeasurable

im'mergere *vt* immerse

im'mergersi *vr* plunge; ‹*sommergibile:*› dive; ~ **in** immerse oneself in

immeritata'mente *adv* undeservedly

immeri'tato *a* undeserved

immeri'tevole *a* undeserving

immersi'one *nf* immersion; (*di sommergibile, palombaro*) dive. ~ **[subacquea]** skin diving, scuba diving

im'merso *pp di* **immergere**

im'mettere *vt* introduce

im'mettersi *vr* introduce oneself

immi'grante *a & nmf* immigrant

immi'grare *vi* immigrate

immi'grato, -a *nmf* immigrant

immigrazi'one *nf* immigration. ~ **interna** migration

immi'nente *a* imminent

immi'nenza *nf* imminence

immischi'are *vt* involve

immischi'arsi *vr* ~ **in** meddle in

immi'scibile *a* immiscible

immis'sario *nm* tributary

immissi'one *nf* insertion; *Techn* intake; (*introduzione*) introduction. ~ **[di] dati** data entry

im'mobile *a* motionless

im'mobili *nmpl* real estate

immobili'are *a* **società** ~ building society, savings and loan *Am*

immobilità *nf* immobility

immobiliz'zare *vt* immobilize; *Comm* tie up

immobiliz'zato *a* immobilized. ~ **a letto** confined to bed

immobilizzazi'one *nf* immobilization; *Fin* fixed asset; **spese d'**~ capital expenditure

immoderata'mente *adv* immoderately

immode'rato *a* immoderate

immo'destia *nf* immodesty

immo'desto *a* immodest

immo'lare *vt* sacrifice

immo'larsi *vr* sacrifice oneself

immondez'zaio *nm* rubbish tip

immon'dizia *nf* filth; (*spazzatura*) rubbish

im'mondo *a* filthy

immo'rale *a* immoral

immoral'mente *adv* immorally

immorta'lare *vt* immortalize

immor'tale *a* immortal

immortalità *nf* immortality

immoti'vato *a* unjustified

im'moto *a* motionless

im'mune *a* exempt; *Med* immune

immunità *nf* immunity. ~ **diplomatica** diplomatic immunity. ~ **parlamentare** parliamentary privilege

immuniz'zare *vt* immunize

immunizzazi'one *nf* immunization

immunodefici'enza *nf* immunodeficiency

immunolo'gia *nf* immunology

immuno'logico *a* immunological

immuso'nirsi *vr* sulk

immuso'nito *a* sulky

immu'tabile *a* unchangeable

immu'tato *a* unchanging

impacchet'tare *vt* wrap up

impacci'are *vt* hamper; (*disturbare*) inconvenience; (*imbarazzare*) embarrass

impacciata'mente *adv* awkwardly

impacci'ato *a* embarrassed; (*goffo*) awkward

im'paccio *nm* embarrassment; (*ostacolo*) hindrance; (*situazione difficile*) awkward situation; **trarsi d'**~ get out of an awkward situation

im'pacco *nm* compress

impadro'nirsi *vr* ~ **di** take possession of; (*fig: imparare*) master

impa'gabile *a* priceless

impagi'nare *vt* paginate

impaginazi'one *nf* pagination

impagli'are *vt* stuff ‹*animale*›

impa'lare *vt* impale

impa'lato *a fig* stiff

impalca'tura *nf* scaffolding; *fig* structure

impal'lare *vt* snooker

impalli'dire *vi* turn pale; (*fig: perdere d'importanza*) pale into insignificance

impalli'nare *vt* riddle with bullets

impal'pabile *a* impalpable; ‹*tessuto*› gossamer-like

impa'nare *vt Culin* bread

impa'nato *a* breaded

impanta'narsi *vr* get bogged down

impape'rarsi *vr* falter, stammer

impappi'narsi *vr* falter, stammer

impa'rare *vt* learn; ~ **a propie spese** learn to one's cost

impara'ticcio *nm* half-baked

impareggi'abile *a* incomparable

imparen'tarsi *vr* ~ **con** become related to

imparen'tato *a* related

'impari *a* unequal; (*dispari*) odd

impar'tire *vt* impart

imparzi'ale *a* impartial

imparzialità *nf* impartiality
im'passe *nf inv* impasse
impas'sibile *a* impassive; **con aria ~** impassively
impa'stare *vt Culin* knead; blend ‹colori›
impasta'tura *nf* kneading
impastic'carsi *vr* pop pills
impasticci'are *vt* make a mess of
im'pasto *nm Culin* dough; (miscuglio) mixture
im'patto *nm* impact. **~ ambientale** environmental impact
impau'rire *vt* frighten
impau'rirsi *vr* get frightened
im'pavido *a* fearless
impazi'ente *a* impatient; **~ di fare qcsa** eager to do sth
impazien'tirsi *vr* lose patience
impazi'enza *nf* impatience
impaz'zata *nf* **all'~** at breakneck speed
impaz'zire *vi* go mad; ‹maionese:› separate; **far ~ qcno** drive sb mad; **~ per** be crazy about; **da ~** ‹mal di testa› blinding
impaz'zito *a* crazed
impec'cabile *a* impeccable
impeccabil'mente *adv* impeccably
impedi'mento *nm* hindrance; (ostacolo) obstacle
impe'dire *vt* (impacciare) hinder; (ostruire) obstruct; **~ di** prevent from; **~ a qcno di fare qcsa** prevent sb [from] doing sth
impe'gnare *vt* (dare in pegno) pawn; (vincolare) bind; (prenotare) reserve; (assorbire) take up
impe'gnarsi *vr* apply oneself; **~ a fare qcsa** commit oneself to doing sth
impegna'tiva *nf* referral
impegna'tivo *a* binding; ‹lavoro› demanding
impe'gnato *a* politically committed
im'pegno *nm* engagement; *Comm* commitment; (zelo) care; **con ~** with dedication; **ho un ~** I'm doing something
impego'larsi *vr* **~ in** become enmeshed in
impel'lente *a* pressing
impene'trabile *a* impenetrable
impen'narsi *vr* ‹cavallo:› rear; *fig* bristle
impen'nata *nf* (di prezzi) sharp rise; (di cavallo) rearing; (di moto) wheelie; (di aereo) climb
impen'sabile *a* unthinkable
impen'sato *a* unexpected
impensie'rire *vt* worry
impensie'rirsi *vr* worry
impe'rante *a* prevailing
impe'rare *vi* reign
impera'tivo *a & nm* imperative
impera|'tore, -'trice *nm* emperor ● *nf* empress
impercet'tibile *a* imperceptible
impercettibil'mente *adv* imperceptibly
imperdo'nabile *a* unforgivable
imperfetta'mente *adv* imperfectly
imper'fetto *a & nm* imperfect
imperfezi'one *nf* imperfection

imperi'ale *a* imperial
imperia'lismo *nm* imperialism
imperia'lista *a & nmf* imperialist
imperia'listico *a* imperialistic
imperi'oso *a* imperious; (impellente) urgent
imperi'turo *a* immortal
impe'rizia *nf* lack of skill
imper'lare *vt* bead
imperma'lire *vt* offend
imperma'lirsi *vr* take offence
imperme'abile *a* ‹orologio› waterproof; ‹terreno› impermeable ● *nm* raincoat
imperni'are *vt* pivot; (fondare) base
imperni'arsi *vr* **~ su** be based on
im'pero *nm* empire; (potere) rule; **stile ~** empire style
imperscru'tabile *a* inscrutable
imperso'nale *a* impersonal
imperso'nare *vt* personify; (interpretare) act [the part of]
imper'territo *a* undaunted
imperti'nente *a* impertinent
imperti'nenza *nf* impertinence
impertur'babile *a* imperturbable
impertur'bato *a* unperturbed
imperver'sare *vi* rage
im'pervio *a* inaccessible
'impeto *nm* impetus; (impulso) impulse; (slancio) transport
impet'tito *a* stiff
impetuosa'mente *adv* impetuously
impetu'oso *a* impetuous; (vento) blustering
impiallacci'are *vt* veneer
impiallacci'ato *a* veneered
impian'tare *vt* install; set up ‹azienda›
impi'anto *nm* plant; (sistema) system; (operazione) installation. **~ di amplificazione** public address system, PA system. **~ audio** sound system. **~ elettrico** electrical system. **impianti** *pl* **fissi** fixtures and fittings. **~ radio** *Auto* car stereo system. **~ di riscaldamento** heating system. **~ stereo** hi-fi
impia'strare *vt* plaster; (sporcare) dirty
impia'strarsi *vr* get dirty; **~ le mani** get one's hands dirty
impi'astro *nm* poultice; (persona noiosa) bore; (pasticcione) cack-handed person
impiccagi'one *nf* hanging
impic'care *vt* hang
impic'carsi *vr* hang oneself
impic'cato, -a *nm* hanged man ● *nf* hanged woman
impicci'arsi *vr* meddle
im'piccio *nm* hindrance; (seccatura) bother
impicci'one, -a *nmf* nosey parker
impie'gare *vt* employ; (usare) use; spend ‹tempo, denaro›; *Fin* invest; **l'autobus ha impiegato un'ora** it took the bus an hour
impie'garsi *vr* get [oneself] a job
impie'ga'tizio *a* clerical
impie'gato, -a *nmf* employee; (di ufficio) office worker. **~ di banca** bank clerk. **~ di concetto** administrative employee. **~ in prova** probationer. **~ statale** civil servant
impi'ego *nm* employment; (posto) job; *Fin*

investment; **pubblico** ~ public sector. ~
fisso permanent job. **impieghi** *pl* **saltuari**
odd jobs, casual employment. ~ **tempo-
raneo** temporary job
impieto'sire *vt* move to pity
impieto'sirsi *vr* be moved to pity
impie'toso *a* pitiless
impie'trito *a* petrified
impigli'are *vt* entangle
impigli'arsi *vr* get entangled
impi'grire *vt* make lazy
impi'grirsi *vr* get lazy
impi'lare *vt* stack
impingu'are *vt fig* fill
impiom'bare *vt* seal ‹*cassa, porta*›
impla'cabile *a* implacable
implemen'tare *vt* implement
impli'care *vt* implicate; (*sottintendere*) imply
impli'carsi *vr* become involved
implicazi'one *nf* implication
implicita'mente *adv* implicitly
im'plicito *a* implicit
implo'rante *a* imploring
implo'rare *vt* implore
implorazi'one *nf* entreaty
implosi'one *nf* implosion
impolli'nare *vt* pollinate
impollinazi'one *nf* pollination
impoltro'nire *vt* make lazy
impoltro'nirsi *vr* become lazy
impolve'rare *vt* cover with dust
impolve'rarsi *vr* get covered with dust
impolve'rato *a* dusty
impoma'tare *vt* put brilliantine on
impoma'tarsi *vr* put brilliantine on
‹*capelli*›
imponde'rabile *a* imponderable; ‹*causa,
evento*› unpredictable
impo'nente *a* imposing
impo'nenza *nf* impressiveness
impo'nibile *a* taxable ● *nm* taxable income
impopo'lare *a* unpopular
impopolarità *nf* unpopularity
imporpo'rarsi *vr* turn red
im'porre *vt* impose; (*ordinare*) order
im'porsi *vr* assert oneself; (*aver successo*) be
successful; ~ **di** (*prefiggersi di*) set oneself the
task of
impor'tante *a* important ● *nm* important
thing
impor'tanza *nf* importance; **di vitale** ~
crucially important
impor'tare *vt* *Comm, Comput* import;
(*comportare*) cause ● *vi* matter; (*essere
necessario*) be necessary. **non importa!** it
doesn't matter!; **non me ne importa niente!**
I couldn't care less!
importa|'tore, -'trice *a* importing ● *nmf*
importer
importazi'one *nf* importation; (*merce
importata*) import
import-'export *nm inv* import-export
im'porto *nm* amount
importu'nare *vt* pester; ~ **qcno per qcsa**
pester sb for sth

impor'tuno *a* troublesome; (*inopportuno*)
untimely
imposizi'one *nf* imposition; (*imposta*) tax
imposses'sarsi *vr* ~ **di** seize
impos'sibile *a* impossible ● *nm* **fare l'**~ do
absolutely all one can
impossibilità *nf* impossibility
im'posta[1] *nf* tax. ~ **fondiaria** land tax. ~
patrimoniale property tax. ~ **sul reddito**
income tax. ~ **sui redditi di capitale** capital gains tax. ~ **sulle società** corporation
tax. ~ **supplementare** surtax. ~ **sul valore
aggiunto** value added tax
im'posta[2] *nf* (*di finestra*) shutter
impo'stare *vt* (*progettare*) plan; (*basare*)
base; *Mus* pitch; (*imbucare*) post, mail; set out
‹*domanda, problema*›
impostazi'one *nf* planning; (*di voce*) pitch-
ing
im'posto *pp di* **imporre**
impo'store, -a *nmf* impostor
impo'stura *nf* imposture
impo'tente *a* powerless; *Med* impotent
impo'tenza *nf* powerlessness; *Med* impotence
impoveri'mento *nm* impoverishment
impove'rire *vt* impoverish
impove'rirsi *vr* become poor; ‹*risorse:*› become depleted; ‹*linguaggio:*› become impoverished
imprati'cabile *a* impracticable; ‹*strada*›
impassable
impraticabilità *nf* **per** ~ **del terreno/
delle strade** because of the state of the
pitch/roads
imprati'chire *vt* train
imprati'chirsi *vr* ~ **in** *o* **a** get practice in
impre'care *vi* curse
imprecazi'one *nf* curse
impreci'sabile *a* indeterminable
impreci'sato *a* indeterminate
imprecisi'one *nf* inaccuracy
impre'ciso *a* inaccurate
impre'gnare *vt* impregnate; (*imbevere*)
soak; *fig* imbue
impre'gnarsi *vr* become impregnated with
imprendi|'tore, -'trice *nmf* entrepreneur
imprenditori'ale *a* entrepreneurial
imprepa'rato *a* unprepared
im'presa *nf* undertaking; (*gesta*) exploit;
(*azienda*) firm. ~ **edile** property developer.
~ **familiare** family business. ~ **di pompe
funebri** undertakers, funeral directors. ~
pubblica state-owned company. ~ **di
traslochi** furniture remover
impre'sario *nm* impresario; (*appaltatore*)
contractor. ~ **di pompe funebri** undertaker,
funeral director, mortician *Am*. ~ **teatrale**
theatre manager
imprescin'dibile *a* inescapable
impressio'nabile *a* impressionable
impressio'nante *a* impressive; (*spaventoso*) frightening
impressio'nare *vt* impress; (*spaventare*)
frighten; expose ‹*foto*›

impressio'narsi *vr* be affected; (*spaventarsi*) be frightened
impressi'one *nf* impression; (*sensazione*) sensation; (*impronta*) mark; **far ~ a qcno** upset sb; **dare l'~ di essere...** give the impression of being...
impressio'nismo *nm* impressionism
impressio'nista *a & nmf* impressionist
impressio'nistico *a* impressionistic
im'presso *pp di* **imprimere ●** *a* printed
impre'stare *vt* lend
impreve'dibile *a* unforeseeable; (*persona*) unpredictable
imprevedibil'mente *adv* unexpectedly
imprevi'dente *a* improvident
impre'visto *a* unforeseen ● *nm* unforeseen event; **salvo imprevisti** all being well
imprigiona'mento *nm* imprisonment
imprigio'nare *vt* imprison
im'primere *vt* impress; (*stampare*) print; (*comunicare*) impart; **rimanere impresso a qcno** stick in sb's mind
impro'babile *a* unlikely, improbable; **è ~ che ci sia** he is unlikely to be there
improbabilità *nf* improbability
improdut'tivo *a* unproductive
im'pronta *nf* impression; *fig* mark. **~ digitale** fingerprint. **impronte** *pl* **genetiche** genetic fingerprinting. **~ del piede** footprint
impron'tato *a* **~ all'ironia** tinged with irony
impronunci'abile *a* unpronounceable
impro'perio *nm* insult; **improperi** *pl* abuse *sg*
impropo'nibile *a* unrealistic
im'proprio *a* improper
improro'gabile *a* which cannot be extended
improvvisa'mente *adv* suddenly
improvvi'sare *vt/i* improvise
improvvi'sarsi *vr* turn oneself into a
improvvi'sata *nf* surprise
improvvi'sato *a* (*discorso*) unrehearsed
improvvisazi'one *nf* improvisation
improv'viso *a* unexpected, sudden; **all'~** unexpectedly, suddenly
impru'dente *a* imprudent
imprudente'mente *adv* imprudently
impru'denza *nf* imprudence
impu'dente *a* impudent
impudente'mente *adv* impudently
impu'denza *nf* impudence
impu'dico *a* immodest
impu'gnare *vt* grasp; *Jur* contest
impugna'tura *nf* grip; (*manico*) handle. **~ a due mani** two-handed grip
impulsiva'mente *adv* impulsively
impulsività *nf* impulsiveness
impul'sivo *a* impulsive
im'pulso *nm* impulse; **agire d'~** act on impulse
impune'mente *adv* with impunity
impunità *nf* impunity
impu'nito *a* unpunished
impun'tarsi *vr fig* dig one's heels in

impun'tura *nf* stitching
impuntu'rare *vt* backstitch
impurità *nf inv* impurity
im'puro *a* impure
impu'tabile *a* attributable (**a** to); *Jur* indictable
impu'tare *vt* attribute; *Jur* charge
impu'tato, -a *nmf* accused
imputazi'one *nf* charge. **~ di omicidio** murder charge
imputri'dire *vi* putrefy
imputri'dito *a* putrefied
in *prep* in; (*moto a luogo*) to; (*su*) on; (*dentro*) within; (*mezzo*) by; (*con materiale*) made of; **essere in casa/ufficio** be at home/at the office; **in mano/tasca** in one's hand/pocket; **in fondo alla strada/borsa** at the bottom of the street/bag; **andare in Francia/campagna** go to France/the country; **salire in treno** get on the train; **versa la birra nel bicchiere** pour the beer into the glass; **in alto** up there; **in giornata** within the day; **nel 1997** in 1997; **una borsa in pelle** a bag made of leather, a leather bag; **alzarsi in piedi** stand up; **in macchina** (*viaggiare, venire*) by car; **in contanti** [in] cash; **in vacanza** on holiday; **di giorno in giorno** from day to day; **se fossi in te** if I were you; **siamo in sette** there are seven of us
inabbor'dabile *a* unapproachable
i'nabile *a* incapable; (*fisicamente*) unfit
inabilità *nf* incapacity
inabi'tabile *a* uninhabitable
inacces'sibile *a* inaccessible; (*persona*) unapproachable
inaccet'tabile *a* unacceptable
inaccettabilità *nf* unacceptability
inacer'barsi *vr* grow bitter
inacer'bire *vt* embitter; exacerbate (*rapporto*)
inaci'dire *vt* turn sour
inaci'dirsi *vr* go sour; (*persona:*) become embittered
ina'datto *a* unsuitable
inadegua'tezza *nf* inadequacy
inadegu'ato *a* inadequate
inadempi'ente *nmf* defaulter
inadempi'enza *nf* nonfulfilment (**a** of). **~ contrattuale** breach of contract
inadempi'mento *nm* nonfulfilment
inaffer'rabile *a* elusive
inaffon'dabile *a* unsinkable
ina'lare *vt* inhale
inala'tore *nm* inhaler
inalazi'one *nf* inhalation
inalbe'rare *vt* hoist
inalbe'rarsi *vr* (*cavallo:*) rear [up]; (*adirarsi*) lose one's temper
inalie'nabile *a* inalienable
inalte'rabile *a* unchanging; (*colore*) fast
inalte'rato *a* unchanged
inami'dare *vt* starch
inami'dato *a* starched
inammis'sibile *a* inadmissible
inamovi'bile *a* (*disco ecc*) non-removable

inanel'lato *a* bejewelled

inani'mato *a* inanimate; (*senza vita*) lifeless

inappa'gabile *a* unsatisfiable

inappaga'mento *nm* nonfulfilment

inappa'gato *a* unfulfilled

inappel'labile *a* final

inappe'tenza *nf* lack of appetite

inappli'cabile *a* inapplicable

inappropri'ato *a* inapt

inappun'tabile *a* faultless

inar'care *vt* arch; raise ⟨*sopracciglia*⟩

inar'carsi *vr* ⟨*legno:*⟩ warp; ⟨*ripiano:*⟩ sag; ⟨*linea:*⟩ curve

inari'dire *vt* parch; empty of feelings ⟨*persona*⟩

inari'dirsi *vr* dry up; ⟨*persona:*⟩ become empty of feelings

inarre'stabile *a* unstoppable

inartico'lato *a* inarticulate

inascol'tato *a* unheard

inaspettata'mente *adv* unexpectedly

inaspet'tato *a* unexpected

inaspri'mento *nm* (*di carattere*) embitterment; (*di conflitto*) worsening

ina'sprire *vt* embitter

ina'sprirsi *vr* become embittered

inattac'cabile *a* unassailable; (*irreprensibile*) irreproachable

inatten'dibile *a* unreliable

inat'teso *a* unexpected

inattività *nf* inactivity

inat'tivo *a* inactive

inattu'abile *a* impracticable

inau'dito *a* unheard of

inaugu'rale *a* inaugural; **cerimonia** ~ official opening; **viaggio** ~ maiden voyage

inaugu'rare *vt* inaugurate; open ⟨*mostra*⟩; unveil ⟨*statua*⟩; christen ⟨*lavastoviglie ecc*⟩

inaugurazi'one *nf* inauguration; (*di mostra*) opening; (*di statua*) unveiling

inavve'duto *a* inadvertent; (*sbadato*) careless

inavver'tenza *nf* inadvertence

inavvertita'mente *adv* inadvertently

inavvici'nabile *a* unapproachable

in'breeding *nm inv* inbreeding

incagli'are *vi* ground ● *vt* hinder

incagli'arsi *vr* run aground

in'caglio *nm* running aground; *fig* obstacle

'inca *a & nmf* (*pl* **inca** *o* **incas**) Inca

incalco'labile *a* incalculable

incal'lirsi *vr* grow callous; (*abituarsi*) become hardened

incal'lito *a* callous; (*abituato*) hardened

incal'zante *a* ⟨*ritmo*⟩ driving; ⟨*richiesta*⟩ urgent; ⟨*crisi*⟩ imminent

incal'zare *vt* pursue; *fig* press

iname'rare *vt* appropriate

incammi'nare *vt* get going; (*fig: guidare*) set off

incammi'narsi *vr* set out

incanala'mento *nm* canalization; *fig* channelling

incana'lare *vt* canalize; *fig* channel

incana'larsi *vr* converge on

incancel'labile *a* indelible

incande'scente *a* incandescent; ⟨*discussione*⟩ burning

incande'scenza *nf* incandescence

incan'tare *vt* enchant

incan'tarsi *vr* stand spellbound; (*inceparsi*) jam

incanta|'tore, -'trice *nmf* enchanter; enchantress. ~ **di serpenti** snake charmer

incan'tesimo *nm* spell

incan'tevole *a* enchanting

in'canto *nm* spell; *fig* delight; (*asta*) auction; **come per** ~ as if by magic

incanu'tire *vt* turn white

incanu'tito *a* white

inca'pace *a* incapable; ~ **d'intendere e di volere** *Jur* unfit to plead

incapacità *nf* incapability

incapo'nirsi *vr* be set

incap'pare *vi* ~ **in** run into

incappucci'arsi *vr* wrap up

incapretta'mento *nm* method of trussing up a victim by the ankles

incapricci'arsi *vr* ~ **di** take a fancy to

incapsu'lare *vt* seal; crown ⟨*dente*⟩

incar'care *vt* imprison

incarcerazi'one *nf* imprisonment

incari'care *vt* charge

incari'carsi *vr* take upon oneself; **me ne incarico io** I will see to it

incari'cato, -a *a* in charge ● *nmf* representative. ~ **d'affari** chargé d'affaires

in'carico *nm* charge; **per** ~ **di** on behalf of

incar'nare *vt* embody

incar'narsi *vr* become incarnate

incarnazi'one *nf* incarnation

incarta'mento *nm* documents *pl*

incartapeco'rito *a* shrivelled up

incar'tare *vt* wrap [in paper]

incasel'lare *vt* pigeonhole

incasi'nato *a fam* ⟨*vita*⟩ screwed up; ⟨*stanza*⟩ messed up

incas'sare *vt* pack; *Mech* embed; (*incastonare*) set; (*riscuotere*) cash; take ⟨*colpo*⟩

incas'sato *a* set; ⟨*fiume*⟩ deeply embanked

in'casso *nm* collection; (*introito*) takings *pl*

incasto'nare *vt* set

incasto'nato *a* embedded; ⟨*anello*⟩ inset (**di** with)

incastona'tura *nf* setting

inca'strare *vt* fit in; (*fam: in situazione*) corner

inca'strarsi *vr* fit

in'castro *nm* joint; **a** ~ ⟨*pezzi*⟩ interlocking. ~ **a coda di rondine** dovetail joint

incate'nare *vt* chain

incatra'mare *vt* tar

incatti'vire *vt* turn nasty

incauta'mente *adv* imprudently

in'cauto *a* imprudent

inca'vare *vt* hollow out

inca'vato *a* hollow

incava'tura *nf* hollow

in'cavo *nm* hollow; (*scanalatura*) groove

incavo'larsi *vr fam* get shirty

incavo'lato *a fam* shirty

in'cedere *fml vi* advance solemnly ● *nm* solemn gait

incendi'are *vt* set fire to; *fig* inflame

incendi'ario, -a *a* incendiary; ⟨*fig: discorso*⟩ inflammatory; ⟨*fig: bellezza*⟩ sultry ● *nmf* arsonist

incendi'arsi *vr* catch fire

in'cendio *nm* fire. ~ **doloso** arson; **incendi pl dolosi** cases of arson

inceneri'mento *nm* incineration; (*cremazione*) cremation

incene'rire *vt* burn to ashes; (*cremare*) cremate

incene'rirsi *vr* be burnt to ashes

inceneri'tore *nm* incinerator

in'censo *nm* incense

incensu'rabile *a* irreproachable

incensu'rato *a* blameless; **essere ~** *Jur* have a clean record

incenti'vare *vt* motivate

incen'tivo *nm* incentive. ~ **fiscale** tax incentive

incen'trarsi *vr* ~ **su** centre on

incep'pare *vt* block; *fig* hamper

incep'parsi *vr* jam

ince'rata *nf* oilcloth

incerot'tato *a* with a plaster on

incer'tezza *nf* uncertainty

in'certo *a* uncertain ● *nm* uncertainty; **sono gli incerti del mestiere** that's the way it goes in this business

incespi'care *vi* (*inciampare*) stumble

inces'sante *a* unceasing

incessante'mente *adv* incessantly

in'cesto *nm* incest

incestu'oso *a* incestuous

in'cetta *nf* buying up; **fare ~ di** stockpile

inchi'esta *nf* investigation; **fare un'~** conduct an inquiry. ~ **giudiziaria** criminal investigation. ~ **parlamentare** parliamentary inquiry

inchi'nare *vt* bow

inchi'narsi *vr* bow

in'chino *nm* bow; (*di donna*) curtsy

inchio'dare *vt* nail; nail down ⟨*coperchio*⟩; ~ **a letto** ⟨*malattia:*⟩ confine to bed

inchi'ostro *nm* ink. ~ **di china** Indian ink. ~ **simpatico** invisible ink. ~ **di stampa** newsprint

inciam'pare *vi* stumble; ~ **in** trip over; (*imbattersi*) run into

inci'ampo *nm* hindrance

inciden'tale *a* incidental

inci'dente *nm* (*episodio*) incident; (*infortunio*) accident. ~ **aereo** plane crash. ~ **d'auto** car accident. ~ **sul lavoro** industrial accident. ~ **stradale** road accident

inci'denza *nf* incidence

in'cidere *vt* cut; (*arte*) engrave; (*registrare*) record ● *vi* ~ **su** (*gravare*) weigh upon

in'cinta *a* pregnant

incipi'ente *a* incipient

incipri'are *vt* powder

incipri'arsi *vr* powder one's face

in'circa *adv* **all'~** more or less

incisi'one *nf* incision; (*arte*) engraving; (*acquaforte*) etching; (*registrazione*) recording

inci'sivo *a* incisive ● *nm* (*dente*) incisor

in'ciso *nm* **per ~** incidentally

inci'sore *nm* engraver

incita'mento *nm* incitement

inci'tare *vt* incite

inci'vile *a* uncivilized; (*maleducato*) impolite

inciviltà *nf* barbarism; (*maleducazione*) rudeness

inclassifi'cabile *adv* unclassifiable

incle'mente *a* harsh

incle'menza *nf* harshness

incli'nabile *a* reclining

incli'nare *vt* tilt ● *vi* ~ **a** be inclined to

incli'narsi *vr* list

incli'nato *a* tilted; ⟨*terreno*⟩ sloping

inclinazi'one *nf* slope, inclination

in'cline *a* inclined

in'cludere *vt* include; (*allegare*) enclose

inclusi'one *nf* inclusion

inclu'sivo *a* inclusive

in'cluso *pp di* **includere** ● *a* included; (*compreso*) inclusive; (*allegato*) enclosed

incoe'rente *a* (*contraddittorio*) inconsistent

incoerente'mente *adv* inconsistently

incoe'renza *nf* inconsistency

in'cognita *nf* unknown quantity

in'cognito *a* unknown ● *nm* **in ~** incognito

incol'lare *vt* stick; (*con colla liquida*) glue; *Comput* paste

incol'larsi *vr* stick to; ~ **a qcno** stick close to sb

incolla'tura *nf* (*nell'ippica*) neck

incolle'rirsi *vr* lose one's temper

incolle'rito *a* enraged

incol'mabile *a* ⟨*differenza*⟩ unbridgeable; ⟨*vuoto*⟩ unfillable

incolon'nare *vt* line up

inco'lore *a* colourless

incol'pare *vt* blame

in'colto *a* uncultivated; ⟨*persona*⟩ uneducated

in'colume *a* unhurt

incom'bente *a* impending

incom'benza *nf* task

in'combere *vi* ~ **su** hang over; ~ **a** (*spettare*) be incumbent on

incombu'stibile *a* noncombustible

incominci'are *vt/i* begin, start

incommensu'rabile *a* immeasurable

incomo'dare *vt* inconvenience

incomo'darsi *vr* trouble

in'comodo *a* uncomfortable; (*inopportuno*) inconvenient ● *nm* inconvenience; **fare il terzo ~** play gooseberry

incompa'rabile *a* incomparable

incompa'tibile *a* incompatible

incompatibilità *nf inv* incompatibility. ~ **di carattere** incompatibility

incompe'tente *a* incompetent
incompe'tenza *nf* incompetence
incompi'uto *a* unfinished
incom'pleto *a* incomplete
incompren'sibile *a* incomprehensible
incomprensibil'mente *adv* incomprehensibly
incomprensi'one *nf* lack of understanding; (*malinteso*) misunderstanding
incom'preso *a* misunderstood
inconce'pibile *a* inconceivable
inconcili'abile *a* irreconcilable
inconclu'dente *a* inconclusive; ⟨*persona*⟩ ineffectual
incondizionata'mente *adv* unconditionally
incondizio'nato *a* unconditional
inconfes'sabile *a* unmentionable
inconfon'dibile *a* unmistakable
inconfondibil'mente *adv* unmistakably
inconfu'tabile *a* irrefutable
inconfutabil'mente *adv* irrefutably
incongru'ente *a* inconsistent
incongru'enza *nf* incongruity
in'congruo *a* inadequate
inconsa'pevole *a* unaware; (*inconscio*) unconscious
inconsapevol'mente *adv* unwittingly
inconscia'mente *adv* unconsciously
in'conscio *a & nm Psych* unconscious
inconsegu'ente *a* **essere** ~ be a non sequitur
inconside'rabile *a* negligible
inconside'rato *a* inconsiderate
inconsi'stente *a* insubstantial; ⟨*notizia ecc*⟩ unfounded
inconsi'stenza *nf* (*di ragionamento, prove*) flimsiness
inconso'labile *a* inconsolable
inconsu'eto *a* unusual
incon'sulto *a* rash
incontami'nato *a* uncontaminated
inconte'nibile *a* irrepressible
inconten'tabile *a* insatiable; (*esigente*) hard to please
inconte'stabile *a* indisputable
inconte'stato *a* unchallenged
inconti'nente *a* incontinent
inconti'nenza *nf* incontinence
incon'trare *vt* meet; encounter, meet with ⟨*difficoltà*⟩
incon'trario: all'~ *adv* the other way around; (*in modo sbagliato*) the wrong way around
incon'trarsi *vr* meet (**con qcno** sb)
incontra'stabile *a* incontrovertible
incontra'stato *a* undisputed
in'contro *nm* meeting; (*casuale*) encounter; (*di calcio, rugby*) match; (*di tennis*) game; (*di pugilato*) bout. ~ **al vertice** summit meeting ● *prep* ~ **a** towards; **andare** ~ **a qcno** go to meet sb; *fig* meet sb half way
incontrol'labile *a* uncontrollable
incontrollata'mente *adv* uncontrollably
inconveni'ente *nm* drawback

incoraggia'mento *nm* encouragement
incoraggi'ante *a* encouraging
incoraggi'are *vt* encourage
incor'nare *vt* gore
incornici'are *vt* frame
incornicia'tura *nf* framing
incoro'nare *vt* crown
incoronazi'one *nf* coronation
incorpo'rare *vt* incorporate; (*mescolare*) blend
incorpo'rarsi *vr* blend; ⟨*territori:*⟩ merge
incorreg'gibile *a* incorrigible
in'correre *vt* ~ **in** incur; ~ **nel pericolo di...** run the risk of...
incorrut'tibile *a* incorruptible
incosci'ente *a* unconscious; (*irresponsabile*) reckless ● *nmf* irresponsible person
incosci'enza *nf* unconsciousness; (*irresponsabilità*) recklessness
inco'stante *a* changeable; ⟨*persona*⟩ fickle
inco'stanza *nf* changeableness; (*di persona*) fickleness
incostituzio'nale *a* unconstitutional
incostituzionalità *nf* unconstitutionality
incre'dibile *a* incredible, unbelievable
incredibil'mente *adv* incredibly, unbelievably
incredulità *nf* incredulity
in'credulo *a* incredulous
incremen'tale *a Comput, Math* incremental
incremen'tare *vt* increase; (*intensificare*) step up
incre'mento *nm* increase. ~ **demografico** population growth. ~ **produttivo** increase in production
incresci'oso *a* regrettable
incre'spare *vt* ruffle; wrinkle ⟨*tessuto*⟩; make frizzy ⟨*capelli*⟩; ~ **la fronte** frown
incre'sparsi *vr* ⟨*acqua:*⟩ ripple; ⟨*tessuto:*⟩ wrinkle; ⟨*capelli:*⟩ go frizzy
incrimi'nabile *a* indictable
incrimi'nare *vt* indict; *fig* incriminate
incriminazi'one *nf* indictment
incri'nare *vt* crack; *fig* affect ⟨*amicizia*⟩
incri'narsi *vr* crack; ⟨*amicizia:*⟩ be affected
incrina'tura *nf* crack
incroci'are *vt* cross ● *vi Naut, Aeron* cruise
incroci'arsi *vr* cross; ⟨*razze:*⟩ interbreed
incroci'ato *a* crossover
incrocia'tore *nm* cruiser
in'crocio *nm* crossing; (*di strade*) crossroads *sg*
incrol'labile *a* indestructible
incro'stare *vt* encrust
incrostazi'one *nf* encrustation
incuba'trice *nf* incubator
incubazi'one *nf* incubation
'incubo *nm* nightmare; **da** ~ nightmarish
in'cudine *nf* anvil
incul'care *vt* inculcate
incune'are *vt* wedge
incune'arsi *vr* slot in
incune'ato *a Med* impacted
incu'pirsi *vr fig* darken

incu'rabile *a* incurable
incu'rante *a* careless
in'curia *nf* negligence
incurio'sire *vt* make curious
incurio'sirsi *vr* become curious
incursi'one *nf* raid. **~ aerea** air raid
incurva'mento *nm* bending
incur'vare *vt* bend
incur'varsi *vr* bend
incurva'tura *nf* bending
in'cusso *pp di* incutere
incusto'dito *a* unguarded
in'cutere *vt* arouse; **~ spavento a qcno** strike fear into sb
'indaco *nm* indigo
indaffa'rato *a* busy
inda'gare *vt/i* investigate
in'dagine *nf* research; (*giudiziaria*) investigation. **~ demoscopica** public opinion poll. **~ di mercato** market survey
indebi'tare *vt* get into debt
indebi'tarsi *vr* get into debt
in'debito *a* undue
indeboli'mento *nm* weakening
indebo'lire *vt* weaken
indebo'lirsi *vr* weaken
inde'cente *a* indecent
indecente'mente *adv* indecently
inde'cenza *nf* indecency; (*vergogna*) disgrace
indeci'frabile *a* indecipherable
indecisi'one *nf* indecision
inde'ciso *a* undecided
indecli'nabile *a* indeclinable
indeco'roso *a* indecorous
inde'fesso *a* tireless
indefi'nibile *a* indefinable
indefi'nito *a* indefinite
indefor'mabile *a* crushproof
in'degno *a* unworthy
inde'lebile *a* indelible
indelebil'mente *adv* indelibly
indelicata'mente *adv* indiscreetly
indelica'tezza *nf* indelicacy; (*azione*) tactless act
indeli'cato *a* indiscreet; (*grossolano*) indelicate
indemagli'abile *a* ladderproof
indemoni'ato *a* possessed
in'denne *a* uninjured; (*da malattia*) unaffected
inden'nità *nf inv* allowance; (*per danni*) compensation. **~ di accompagnamento** mobility allowance. **~ di contingenza** cost-of-living allowance. **~ di fine rapporto** severance payment. **~ parlamentare** MP's salary. **~ di trasferimento** relocation allowance. **~ di trasferta** travel allowance
indenniz'zare *vt* compensate
inden'nizzo *nm* compensation
indepen'denza *nf* independence
indero'gabile *a* binding
indescri'vibile *a* indescribable
indescrivibil'mente *adv* indescribably
indeside'rabile *a* undesirable

indeside'rato *a* ⟨*figlio, ospite*⟩ unwanted
indetermi'nabile *a* indeterminable
indetermina'tezza *nf* vagueness
indetermina'tivo *a* indefinite
indetermi'nato *a* indeterminate
'India *nf* India
indi'ano, -a *a* & *nmf* Indian; **in fila indiana** in single file. **~ d'America** American Indian
indiavo'lato *a* possessed; (*vivace*) wild
indi'care *vt* show, indicate; (*col dito*) point at; (*far notare*) point out; (*consigliare*) advise
indicativa'mente *adv* as an idea; **può dirmi quanto costa ~?** can you give me an idea of the price?
indica'tivo *a* indicative; ⟨*prezzo, cifra*⟩ rough ● *nm* Gram indicative
indica'tore *nm* indicator; *Techn* gauge; (*prontuario*) directory. **~ di direzione** indicator light. **~ economico** economic indicator. **~ [del livello] dell'olio** oil gauge. **~ di velocità** speedometer
indicazi'one *nf* indication; (*istruzione*) direction. **~ stradale** road sign
'indice *nm* (*dito*) forefinger; (*lancetta*) pointer; (*di libro, statistica*) index; (*fig: segno*) sign. **~ di ascolto** audience rating. **~ azionario** share index. **~ di gradimento** popularity rating. **~ di mortalità** death rate. **~ di natalità** birth rate
indi'cibile *a* inexpressible
indiciz'zare *vt* index-link
indiciz'zato *a* index-linked
indicizzazi'one *nf* indexing
indietreggi'are *vi* draw back; *Mil* withdraw
indi'etro *adv* back, behind; **all'~** backwards; **essere ~** be behind; (*mentalmente*) be backward; (*con pagamenti*) be in arrears; (*di orologio*) be slow; **fare marcia ~** reverse; **rimandare ~** send back; **rimanere ~** be left behind; **torna ~!** come back!
indifen'dibile *a* indefensible
indi'feso *a* undefended; (*inerme*) helpless
indiffe'rente *a* indifferent; **mi è ~** it's all the same to me
indifferente'mente *adv* (*senza fare distinzioni*) without distinction; (*con indifferenza*) indifferently; **funziona ~ con i due programmi** it works equally well with either program
indiffe'renza *nf* indifference
in'digeno, -a *a* indigenous ● *nmf* native
indi'gente *a* needy
indi'genza *nf* poverty
indigesti'one *nf* indigestion
indi'gesto *a* indigestible
indi'gnare *vt* make indignant
indi'gnarsi *vr* be indignant
indi'gnato *a* indignant
indignazi'one *nf* indignation
indimenti'cabile *a* unforgettable
'indio, -a *a* Indian ● *nmf* (*mpl* indii *o* indios) Indian
indipen'dente *a* independent; (*economicamente*) self-supporting

indipendente'mente *adv* independently; ~ **da** regardless of

in'dire *vt* announce

indiretta'mente *adv* indirectly

indi'retto *a* indirect

indiriz'zare *vt* address; *(mandare)* send; *(dirigere)* direct

indiriz'zario *nm* mailing list

indiriz'zarsi *vr* direct one's steps

indi'rizzo *nm* address; *(direzione)* direction. ~ **di consegna** delivery address. '~ **del destinatario'** 'addressee'. ~ **di memoria** *Comput* memory address. '~ **del mittente'** 'sender's address'. ~ **di posta elettronica** e-mail address

indisci'plina *nf* lack of discipline

indiscipli'nato *a* undisciplined

indi'screto *a* indiscreet; **in modo** ~ indiscreetly

indiscrezi'one *nf* indiscretion

indiscriminata'mente *adv* indiscriminately

indiscrimi'nato *a* indiscriminate

indi'scusso *a* unquestioned

indiscu'tibile *a* unquestionable

indiscutibil'mente *adv* unquestionably

indispen'sabile *a* essential; *‹persona›* indispensable

indispet'tire *vt* irritate

indispet'tirsi *vr* get irritated

indi'sporre *vt* anger

indisposizi'one *nf* indisposition

indi'sposto *pp di* **indisporre** ● *a* indisposed

indisso'lubile *a* indissoluble

indissolubil'mente *adv* indissolubly

indistin'guibile *a* indiscernible

indistinta'mente *adv* without exception

indi'stinto *a* indistinct

indistrut'tibile *a* indestructible

indistur'bato *a* undisturbed

in'divia *nf* endive

individu'abile *a* detectable

individu'ale *a* individual

individua'lista *nmf* individualist

individua'listico *a* individualistic

individualità *nf* individuality

individu'are *vt* individualize; *(localizzare)* locate; *(riconoscere)* single out

indi'viduo *nm* individual

indivi'sibile *a* indivisible

indivisibilità *nf* indivisibility

indi'viso *a* undivided

indizi'are *vt* throw suspicion on

indizi'ario *a* circumstantial

indizi'ato, -a *a* suspected ● *nmf* suspect

in'dizio *nm* sign; *Jur* circumstantial evidence

Indo'cina *nf* Indochina

indoeuro'peo *a* Indo-European

'indole *nf* nature

indo'lente *a* indolent

indo'lenza *nf* indolence

indolenzi'mento *nm* stiffness, ache

indolen'zire *vt* stiffen up

indolen'zirsi *vr* stiffen up, go stiff

indolen'zito *a* stiff

indo'lore *a* painless

indo'mabile *a* untameable

indo'mani *nm* l'~ the following day

in'domito *a* untamed

Indo'nesia *nf* Indonesia

indonesi'ano, -a *a & nmf* Indonesian

indo'rare *vt* gild; ~ **la pillola** sugar the pill

indos'sare *vt* wear; *(mettere addosso)* put on

indossa'|tore, -'trice *nm* [male] model ● *nf* model

in'dotto *pp di* **indurre**

indottri'nare *vt* indoctrinate

indovi'nare *vt* guess; *(predire)* foretell

indovi'nato *a* successful; *(scelta)* well-chosen

indovi'nello *nm* riddle

indo'vino, -a *nmf* fortune-teller

indù *a inv & nmf inv* Hindu

indubbia'mente *adv* undoubtedly

in'dubbio *a* undoubted

indubi'tabile *a* indubitable

indubitabil'mente *adv* indubitably

indugi'are *vi* linger

indugi'arsi *vr* linger

in'dugio *nm* delay

indu'ismo *nm* Hinduism

indul'gente *a* indulgent

indul'genza *nf* indulgence

in'dulgere *vi* ~ **a** indulge in

in'dulto *pp di* **indulgere** ● *nm Jur* pardon

indu'mento *nm* garment; **indumenti** *pl* clothes. **indumenti** *pl* **intimi** underwear

induri'mento *nm* hardening

indu'rire *vt* harden

indu'rirsi *vr* harden

in'durre *vt* induce; ~ **qcno a fare** induce sb to do; ~ **in tentazione** lead into temptation

in'dustria *nf* industry. ~ **dell'ab-bigliamento** clothing industry, rag trade *fam.* ~ **leggera** light industry. ~ **pesante** heavy industry. ~ **dello spettacolo** show business, showbiz *fam.* ~ **terziaria** service industry. ~ **tessile** textile industry, textiles

industri'ale *a* industrial; **zona** ~ industrial estate ● *nmf* industrialist

industrializ'zare *vt* industrialize

industrializ'zato *a* industrialized

industrializzazi'one *nf* industrialization

industrial'mente *adv* industrially

industri'arsi *vr* ~ **per guadagnare qualcosa** set to and earn some money

industriosa'mente *adv* industriously

industri'oso *a* industrious

indut'tivo *a* inductive

indut'tore *nm* inductor

induzi'one *nf* induction

inebe'tire *vt* daze

inebe'tito *a* stunned

inebri'ante *a* intoxicating, exciting

inebri'are *vt* intoxicate

inebri'arsi *vr* become inebriated

inecce'pibile *a* unexceptionable

i'nedia *nf* starvation

i'nedito a unpublished
inedu'cato a impolite
inef'fabile a inexpressible
ineffi'cace a ineffective
ineffici'ente a inefficient
ineffici'enza nf inefficiency
ineguagli'abile a incomparable
ineguagli'ato a unequalled
inegu'ale a unequal; ⟨superficie⟩ uneven
inelut'tabile a inescapable
inenar'rabile a indescribable
inequivo'cabile a unequivocal
inequivocabil'mente adv unequivocally
ine'rente a ~ a inherent in
inerente'mente adv ~ a concerning
i'nerme a unarmed; fig defenceless
inerpi'carsi vr ~ su clamber up
i'nerte a inactive; Phys inert
i'nerzia nf inactivity; Phys inertia
inesat'tezza nf inaccuracy
ine'satto a inaccurate; ⟨erroneo⟩ incorrect; ⟨non riscosso⟩ uncollected
inesau'ribile a inexhaustible
inesi'stente a non-existent
inesi'stenza nf non-existence
ineso'rabile a inexorable
inesorabil'mente adv inexorably
inesperi'enza nf inexperience
ine'sperto a inexperienced
inespli'cabile a inexplicable
inesplicabil'mente adv inexplicably
inesplo'rato a undiscovered
ine'sploso a unexploded
inespres'sivo a expressionless
inespri'mibile a inexpressible
inespu'gnabile a impregnable
ineste'tismo nm blemish
inesti'mabile a inestimable
inestin'guibile a ⟨sete⟩ insatiable; ⟨odio⟩ undying
inestir'pabile a impossible to eradicate
inestri'cabile a inextricable
inestricabil'mente adv inextricably
inetti'tudine nf ineptitude
i'netto a inept. ~ a unsuited to
ine'vaso a ⟨pratiche, corrispondenza⟩ pending
inevi'tabile a inevitable
inevitabil'mente adv inevitably
in ex'tremis adv ⟨segnare un gol⟩ in the nick of time; ⟨prima di morire⟩ in extremis
i'nezia nf trifle
infagot'tare vt wrap up
infagot'tarsi vr wrap [oneself] up
infal'libile a infallible
infa'mante a defamatory
infa'mare vt defame
infama'torio a defamatory
in'fame a infamous; ⟨fam: orrendo⟩ awful, shocking
in'famia nf infamy
infan'gare vt cover with mud; fig sully
infan'garsi vr get muddy
infanti'cida nmf infanticide
infanti'cidio nm infanticide

infan'tile a ⟨letteratura, abbigliamento⟩ children's attrib; ⟨ingenuità⟩ childlike; pej childish
in'fanzia nf childhood; ⟨bambini⟩ children pl; **prima ~** infancy
infar'cire vt stuff (di with)
infari'nare vt flour; **~ di** sprinkle with
infarina'tura nf fig smattering
in'farto nm coronary
infasti'dire vt irritate
infasti'dirsi vr get irritated
infati'cabile a untiring
infaticabil'mente adv tirelessly
in'fatti conj as a matter of fact; ⟨veramente⟩ indeed
infatu'arsi vr ~ di become infatuated with
infatu'ato a infatuated
infatuazi'one nf infatuation
in'fausto a ill-omened
infecondità nf infertility
infe'condo a infertile
infe'dele a unfaithful
infedeltà nf unfaithfulness
infe'lice a unhappy; ⟨inappropriato⟩ unfortunate; ⟨cattivo⟩ bad
infelicità nf unhappiness
infel'trire vi matt
infel'trirsi vr matt
infel'trito a matted
inferi'ore a ⟨più basso⟩ lower; ⟨qualità⟩ inferior ● nmf inferior
inferiorità nf inferiority
infe'rire vt infer; strike ⟨colpo⟩
inferme'ria nf infirmary; ⟨di nave⟩ sick-bay
infermi'ere, -a nm [male] nurse ● nf nurse
infermità nf sickness. **~ mentale** mental illness
in'fermo, -a a sick ● nmf invalid
infer'nale a infernal; ⟨spaventoso⟩ hellish
in'ferno nm hell; **va' all'~!** I go to hell!
infero'cirsi vr become fierce
inferri'ata nf grating
infervo'rare vt arouse enthusiasm in
infervo'rarsi vr get excited
infe'stare vt infest
infestazi'one nf infestation
infet'tare vt infect
infet'tarsi vr become infected
infet'tivo a infectious
in'fetto a infected
infezi'one nf infection
infiac'chire vt/i weaken
infiac'chirsi vr weaken
infiam'mabile a [in]flammable
infiam'mare vt set on fire; Med, fig inflame
infiam'marsi vr catch fire; Med become inflamed
infiammazi'one nf Med inflammation
infia'scare vt bottle
infici'are vt Jur invalidate
in'fido a treacherous
infie'rire vi ⟨imperversare⟩ rage; **~ su** attack furiously
in'figgere vt drive
in'figgersi vr ~ in penetrate

infi'lare *vt* thread; (*mettere*) insert; (*indossare*) put on

infi'larsi *vr* slip on ‹*vestito*›; **~ in** (*introdursi*) slip into

infil'trarsi *vr* infiltrate

infil'trato, -a *nmf* infiltrator

infiltrazi'one *nf* infiltration; (*d'acqua*) seepage; (*Med: iniezione*) injection

infil'zare *vt* pierce; (*infilare*) string; (*conficcare*) stick

'infimo *a* lowest

in'fine *adv* finally; (*insomma*) in short

infin'gardo *a* slothful

infinità *nf* infinity; **un'~ di** masses of

infinita'mente *adv* infinitely

infinitesi'male *a* infinitesimal

infi'nito *a* infinite; *Gram* infinitive ● *nm* infinite; *Gram* infinitive; *Math* infinity; **all'~** endlessly

infinocchi'are *vt fam* hoodwink

infiocchet'tare *vt* tie up with ribbons

infiore'scenza *nf* inflorescence

infischi'arsi *vr* **~ di** not care about; **me ne infischio** *fam* I couldn't care less

in'fisso *pp di* **infiggere** ● *nm* fixture; (*di porta, finestra*) frame

infit'tire *vt/i* thicken

infit'tirsi *vr* thicken

inflazi'one *nf* inflation. **~ galoppante** galloping inflation. **~ strisciante** creeping inflation

inflazio'nistico *a* inflationary

infles'sibile *a* inflexible

inflessibilità *nf* inflexibility

inflessi'one *nf* inflection, inflexion

in'fliggere *vt* inflict

in'flitto *pp di* **infliggere**

influ'ente *a* influential

influ'enza *nf* influence; *Med* influenza; **prendere l'~** catch the flu. **~ gastro-intestinale** gastric flu

influen'zabile *a* ‹*mente, opinione*› impressionable

influen'zare *vt* influence

influen'zato *a* **essere ~** (*con febbre*) have the flu

influ'ire *vi* **~ su** influence

in'flusso *nm* influence

info'carsi *vr* catch fire; ‹*viso:*› go red; ‹*discussione:*› become heated

info'gnarsi *vr fam* get into a mess

infol'tire *vt/i* thicken

infon'dato *a* unfounded

in'fondere *vt* instil

infor'care *vt* fork ‹*fieno*›; get on ‹*bici*›; put on ‹*occhiali*›

inforca'tura *nf* crotch

infor'male *a* informal

infor'mare *vt* inform

infor'marsi *vr* inquire (**di** about)

infor'matica *nf* information technology, IT

infor'matico *a* computer *attrib*

informa'tivo *a* informative

infor'mato *a* informed; **male ~** ill-informed

informa|'tore, -'trice *nmf* (*di polizia*) in-former. **~ medico scientifico** representa-tive of a pharmaceutical company

informazi'one *nf* information; **un'~** a piece of information; **informazioni** *pl* infor-mation; **servizio informazioni** enquiries. **~ genetica** genetic code. **~ riservata** confi-dential information. **informazioni** *pl* **sbagliate** misinformation

in'forme *a* shapeless

infor'nare *vt* put into the oven

infortu'narsi *vr* have an accident

infortu'nato, -a *a* injured ● *nmf* injured person; **gli infortunati** the injured

infor'tunio *nm* accident. **~ sul lavoro** in-dustrial accident

infortu'nistica *nf* study of industrial acci-dents

infos'sarsi *vr* sink; ‹*guance, occhi:*› become hollow

infos'sato *a* sunken, hollow

infradici'are *vt* drench

infradici'arsi *vr* get drenched; (*diventare marcio*) rot

infra'dito *nmpl* (*scarpe*) flip-flops

in'frangere *vt* break; (*in mille pezzi*) shatter

in'frangersi *vr* break; (*in mille pezzi*) shat-ter

infran'gibile *a* unbreakable

in'franto *pp di* **infrangere** ● *a* shattered; ‹*fig: cuore*› broken

infra'rosso *a* infra-red

infrasettima'nale *a* midweek

infrastrut'tura *nf* infrastructure

infrazi'one *nf* offence. **~ al codice della strada** traffic offence

infredda'tura *nf* cold

infreddo'lirsi *vr* feel cold

infreddo'lito *a* cold

infre'quente *a* infrequent

infruttu'oso *a* fruitless

infuo'care *vt* make red-hot

infuo'cato *a* burning

infu'ori *adv* **all'~** outwards; **all'~ di** except; **denti ~** buck teeth

infuri'are *vi* rage

infuri'arsi *vr* fly into a rage

infuri'ato *a* blustering

infusi'one *nf* infusion

in'fuso *pp di* **infondere** ● *nm* infusion

Ing. *abbr* **ingegnere**

ingabbi'are *vt* cage; (*fig: mettere in prigione*) jail

ingaggi'are *vt* engage; sign up ‹*calciatori ecc*›; begin ‹*lotta, battaglia*›

in'gaggio *nm* engagement; (*di calciatore*) signing [up]

ingan'nare *vt* deceive; (*essere infedele a*) be unfaithful to; **~ l'attesa** kill time

ingan'narsi *vr* deceive oneself; **se non m'inganno** if I am not mistaken

ingan'nevole *a* deceptive

in'ganno *nm* deceit; (*frode*) fraud; **trarre in ~** deceive

ingarbugli'are *vt* entangle; (*confondere*) confuse

ingarbugli'arsi *vr* get entangled; (*confondersi*) become confused

ingarbu'gliato *a* confused

inge'gnarsi *vr* do one's best; **~ per vivere** try to scrape a living

inge'gnere *nm* engineer. **~ aeronautico** aeronautical engineer. **~ civile** civil engineer. **~ edile** structural engineer. **~ meccanico** mechanical engineer. **~ minerario** mining engineer. **~ navale** marine engineer

ingegne'ria *nf* engineering. **~ aeronautica** aeronautical engineering. **~ civile** civil engineering. **~ edile** structural engineering. **~ genetica** genetic engineering. **~ meccanica** mechanical engineering

in'gegno *nm* brains *pl*; (*genio*) genius; (*abilità*) ingenuity

ingegnosa'mente *adv* ingeniously

ingegnosità *nf* ingenuity

inge'gnoso *a* ingenious

ingelo'sire *vt* make jealous

ingelo'sirsi *vr* become jealous

in'gente *a* huge

ingenua'mente *adv* artlessly

ingenuità *nf* ingenuousness

in'genuo *a* ingenuous; (*credulone*) naïve

inge'renza *nf* interference

inge'rire *vt* swallow

inges'sare *vt* put in plaster

ingessa'tura *nf* plaster

Inghil'terra *nf* England

inghiot'tire *vt* swallow

in'ghippo *nm* trick

ingial'lire *vi* turn yellow

ingial'lirsi *vr* turn yellow

ingial'lito *a* yellowed

ingigan'tire *vt* magnify; blow up out of proportion (*problema*) ● *vi* take on gigantic proportions

ingigan'tirsi *vr* take on gigantic proportions

inginocchi'arsi *vr* kneel [down]

inginocchi'ato *a* kneeling

inginocchia'toio *nm* prie-dieu

ingioiel'larsi *vr* put on one's jewels

ingioiel'lato *a* bejewelled

ingiù *adv* down; **all'~** downwards; **a testa ~** head downwards

ingi'ungere *vt* order

ingiunzi'one *nf* injunction, court order. **~ di pagamento** final demand

ingi'uria *nf* insult; (*torto*) wrong; (*danno*) damage

ingiuri'are *vt* insult; (*fare un torto a*) wrong

ingiuri'oso *a* insulting

ingiusta'mente *adv* unjustly

ingiustifi'cabile *a* unjustifiable; (*comportamento*) indefensible

ingiustifi'cato *a* unjustified

ingiu'stizia *nf* unjustice

ingi'usto *a* unjust

in'glese *a* English ● *nm* Englishman; (*lingua*) English; **gli inglesi** the English ● *nf* Englishwoman

inglori'oso *a* inglorious

ingob'bire *vi* become stooped

ingoi'are *vt* swallow

ingol'fare *vt* flood (*motore*)

ingol'farsi *vr* *fig* get involved; (*motore:*) flood

ingol'lare *vt* gulp down

ingom'brante *a* cumbersome

ingom'brare *vt* clutter up; *fig* cram (*mente*)

in'gombro *nm* encumbrance; **essere d'~** be in the way

ingor'digia *nf* greed

in'gordo *a* greedy

ingor'gare *vt* block

ingor'garsi *vr* be blocked [up]

in'gorgo *nm* blockage; (*del traffico*) jam

ingoz'zare *vt* gobble up; (*nutrire eccessivamente*) stuff; fatten (*animali*)

ingoz'zarsi *vr* stuff oneself (**di** with)

ingra'naggio *nm* gear; *fig* mechanism

ingra'nare *vt* engage ● *vi* be in gear

ingrandi'mento *nm* enlargement

ingran'dire *vt* enlarge; (*esagerare*) magnify

ingran'dirsi *vr* become larger; (*aumentare*) increase

ingrandi'tore *nm* *Phot* enlarger

ingras'saggio *nm* greasing, lubrication

ingras'sare *vt* fatten [up]; *Mech* lubricate, grease ● *vi* put on weight

ingras'sarsi *vr* put on weight

in'grasso *nm* **mettere all'~** force-feed

ingrati'tudine *nf* ingratitude

in'grato *a* ungrateful; (*sgradevole*) thankless

ingrazi'arsi *vr* ingratiate oneself with

ingredi'ente *nm* ingredient

in'gresso *nm* entrance; (*accesso*) admittance; (*sala*) hall; *Comput* input **~ gratuito** o **libero** admission free; **'vietato l'~'** 'no entry; no admittance'. **~ degli artisti** stage door. **~ principale** main entrance. **~ di servizio** tradesmen's entrance. **~/uscita** *Comput* input/output. **~ video** *Techn* video input

ingros'sare *vt* make big; (*gonfiare*) swell ● *vi* grow big; (*gonfiare*) swell

ingros'sarsi *vr* grow big; (*gonfiare*) swell

in'grosso: **all'~** *adv* wholesale; (*pressappoco*) roughly

inguai'arsi *vr* get into trouble

ingua'nare *vt* sheathe

ingual'cibile *a* crease-resistant

ingua'ribile *a* incurable

inguaribil'mente *adv* incurably

'inguine *nm* groin

ingurgi'tare *vt* gulp down

ini'bire *vt* inhibit; (*vietare*) forbid

ini'bito *a* inhibited

inibi'tore *nm* suppressant

inibizi'one *nf* inhibition; (*divieto*) prohibition

iniet'tare *vt* inject

iniet'tarsi *vr* **~ di sangue** (*occhi:*) become bloodshot

iniezi'one *nf* injection. **~ endovenosa** intravenous injection. **~ intramuscolare** intramuscular injection

inimic'arsi *vr* ~ **qcno** make an enemy of sb
inimi'cizia *nf* enmity
inimi'tabile *a* inimitable
inimmagi'nabile *a* unimaginable
infiam'mabile *a* nonflammable
inintelli'gibile *a* unintelligible
ininterrotta'mente *adv* continuously
ininter'rotto *a* continuous
iniquità *nf inv* iniquity
i'niquo *a* iniquitous
inizi'ale *a & nf* initial
inizial'mente *adv* initially
inizi'are *vt* begin; (*avviare*) open; ~ **a fare qcsa** begin doing sth; ~ **qcno a qcsa** initiate sb in sth ● *vi* begin
inizia'tiva *nf* initiative; **prendere l'**~ take the initiative. ~ **privata** private enterprise
inizi'ato, -a *nmf* initiated
inizia|'tore, -'trice *nmf* initiator
iniziazi'one *nf* initiation
i'nizio *nm* beginning; **dare** ~ **a** start; **avere** ~ get under way
innaffi'are *vt* water
innaffia'toio *nm* watering-can
innal'zare *vt* raise; (*erigere*) erect
innal'zarsi *vr* rise
innamo'rarsi *vr* fall in love (**di** with)
innamo'rato *a* in love ● *nm* boyfriend
in'nanzi *adv* (*stato in luogo*) in front; (*di tempo*) ahead; (*avanti*) forward; (*prima*) before; **d'ora** ~ from now on ● *prep* (*prima*) before; ~ **a** in front of; ~ **tutto** = **innanzitutto**
innanzi'tutto *adv* (*soprattutto*) above all; (*per prima cosa*) first of all
in'nato *a* innate
innatu'rale *a* unnatural
inne'gabile *a* undeniable
innegabil'mente *adv* undeniably
inneggi'are *vi* praise
innervo'sire *vt* make nervous
innervo'sirsi *vr* get irritated
inne'scare *vt* prime
in'nesco *nm* primer
inne'stare *vt* graft; *Mech* engage; (*inserire*) insert
in'nesto *nm* graft; *Mech* clutch; *Electr* connection
inneva'mento *nm* snowfall. ~ **artificiale** snow-making
inne'vato *a* covered in snow
'inno *nm* hymn. ~ **nazionale** national anthem
inno'cente *a* innocent; *Jur* not guilty
innocente'mente *adv* innocently
inno'cenza *nf* innocence
in'nocuo *a* innocuous
inno'vare *vt* update
innova'tivo *a* innovative
innova'tore *a* trail-blazing
innovazi'one *nf* innovation
innume'revole *a* innumerable
+ino *suff* **fratellino** *nm* little brother; **sorellina** *nf* little sister; **freddino** (*piuttosto freddo*) chilly; **bellino** *a* (*abbastanza bello*) pretty; **benino** *adv* (*così così*) not bad;

pochino *a* (*troppo poco*) not enough; **un pochino** a little bit
inocu'lare *vt* inoculate
ino'doro *a* odourless
inoffen'sivo *a* inoffensive, harmless; (*animale*) harmless
inol'trare *vt* forward
inol'trarsi *vr* advance
inol'trato *a* late
i'noltre *adv* besides
i'noltro *nm* forwarding
inon'dare *vt* flood
inondazi'one *nf* flood
inope'roso *a* idle
inopi'nabile *a* unimaginable
inoppor'tuno *a* untimely
inor'ganico *a* inorganic
inorgo'glire *vt* make proud
inorgo'glirsi *vr* become proud
inorri'dire *vt* horrify ● *vi* be horrified
inospi'tale *a* inhospitable
inosser'vato *a* unobserved; (*non rispettato*) disregarded; **passare** ~ go unobserved
inossi'dabile *a* stainless
'inox *a inv* (*acciaio*) stainless; (*pentole*) stainless steel
'input *nm inv* ~ **dati** data input
inqua'drare *vt* frame; *fig* set
inqua'drarsi *vr* ~ **in** fit into
inquadra'tura *nf* framing
inqualifi'cabile *a* unspeakable
inquie'tante *a* unnerving
inquie'tare *vt* worry
inquie'tarsi *vr* get worried; (*impazientirsi*) get cross
inqui'eto *a* restless; (*preoccupato*) worried
inquie'tudine *nf* anxiety
inqui'lino, -a *nmf* tenant
inquina'mento *nm* pollution. ~ **acustico** noise pollution. ~ **atmosferico** air pollution. ~ **delle prove** *Jur* tampering with the evidence
inqui'nare *vt* pollute
inqui'nato *a* polluted
inqui'rente *a Jur* (*magistrato*) examining; (*commissione*) of investigation
inqui'sire *vt/i* investigate
inqui'sito *a* under investigation ● *nm* person under investigation
inquisi|'tore, -'trice *a* inquiring ● *nmf* inquisitor
inquisi'torio *a* questioning
inquisizi'one *nf* inquisition
insabbi'are *vt* bury
insabbi'arsi *vr* run aground
insa'lata *nf* salad. ~ **belga** Belgian endive. ~ **di mare** seafood salad. ~ **mista** mixed salad. ~ **di riso** rice salad. ~ **russa** Russian salad
insalati'era *nf* salad bowl
insa'lubre *a* unhealthy
insa'nabile *a* incurable
insangui'nare *vt* stain with blood
insangui'nato *a* blood-stained
insapo'nare *vt* soap

insapo'narsi *vr* soap oneself
insapo'nata *nf* soaping
insa'pore *a* tasteless
insapo'rire *vt* flavour
insa'puta *nf* **all'~ di** unknown to
in'saturo *a* unsaturated
insazi'abile *a* insatiable
inscato'lare *vt* can
inscatola'trice *nf* canning machine
insce'nare *vt* stage
inscin'dibile *a* inseparable
in'scrivere *vt Math* inscribe
insec'chire *vt/i* wither
insedia'mento *nm* installation
insedi'are *vt* install
insedi'arsi *vr* install oneself
in'segna *nf* sign; (*bandiera*) flag; (*decorazione*) decoration; (*emblema*) insignia *pl*; (*stemma*) symbol. **~ luminosa** neon sign
insegna'mento *nm* teaching
inse'gnante *a* teaching ● *nmf* teacher. **~ di matematica** maths teacher. **~ di sostegno** tutor
inse'gnare *vt/i* teach; **~ qcsa a qcno** teach sb sth
insegui'mento *nmf* pursuit
insegu'ire *vt* pursue
insegui'|tore, -'trice *nmf* pursuer
inselvati'chire *vt* make wild ● *vi* grow wild
inselvati'chirsi *vr* grow wild
insemi'nare *vt* inseminate
inseminazi'one *nf* insemination. **~ artificiale** artificial insemination
insena'tura *nf* inlet
insensata'mente *adv* senselessly
insen'sato *a* senseless; (*folle*) crazy
insen'sibile *a fig* insensitive; **avere le gambe insensibili** have no feeling in one's legs
insensibilità *nf* lack of feeling; *fig* insensitivity
insepa'rabile *a* inseparable
inseri'mento *nm* insertion
inse'rire *vt* insert; place ⟨*annuncio*⟩; *Electr* connect
inse'rirsi *vr* **~ in** get into
inseri'tore *nm inv* **~ fogli (singoli)** (single) sheetfeed
in'serto *nm* file; (*in un film ecc*) insert
inservi'ente *nmf* attendant
inserzi'one *nf* insertion; (*avviso*) advertisement; **inserzioni** *pl* classified ads
inserzio'nista *nmf* advertiser
insetti'cida *nm* insecticide
insetti'fugo *nm* insect repellent
in'setto *nm* insect
insicu'rezza *nf* insecurity
insi'curo *a* insecure
in'sidia *nf* trick; (*tranello*) snare
insidi'are *vt/i* lay a trap for
insidi'oso *a* insidious
insi'eme *adv* together; (*contemporaneamente*) at the same time ● *prep* **~ a** [together] with ● *nm* whole; (*completo*) outfit; *Theat* en-

semble; *Math* set; **nell'~** as a whole; **tutto ~** (*in una volta*) at one go
insie'mistica *nf* set theory
in'signe *a* renowned
insignifi'cante *a* insignificant
insi'gnire *vt* decorate
insin'cero *a* insincere
insinda'cabile *a* final
insinu'ante *a* insinuating
insinu'are *vt* insinuate
insinu'arsi *vr* penetrate; **~ in** *fig* creep into
insinuazi'one *nf* insinuation
in'sipido *a* insipid
insi'stente *a* insistent
insistente'mente *adv* repeatedly
insi'stenza *nf* insistence
in'sistere *vi* insist; (*perseverare*) persevere
'insito *a* inherent
insoddisfa'cente *a* unsatisfactory
insoddi'sfatto *a* unsatisfied; (*scontento*) dissatisfied
insoddisfazi'one *nf* dissatisfaction
insoffe'rente *a* intolerant
insoffe'renza *nf* intolerance
insolazi'one *nf* sunstroke
inso'lente *a* rude, insolent
insolente'mente *adv* insolently
inso'lenza *nf* rudeness, insolence; (*commento*) insolent remark
insolita'mente *adv* unusually
in'solito *a* unusual
inso'lubile *a* insoluble
inso'luto *a* unsolved; (*non pagato*) unpaid
insol'vente *a Jur* insolvent
insol'venza *nf* insolvency
insol'vibile *a* insolvent
in'somma *adv* in short; **~!** well!
inson'dabile *a* unfathomable
in'sonne *a* sleepless
in'sonnia *nf* insomnia
insonno'lito *a* sleepy
insonoriz'zare *vt* soundproof
insonoriz'zato *a* soundproofed
insoppor'tabile *a* unbearable
insoppri'mibile *a* unsuppressible
insor'genza *nf* onset
in'sorgere *vi* revolt, rise up; ⟨*problema*⟩ arise
insormon'tabile *a* ⟨*ostacolo, difficoltà*⟩ insurmountable
in'sorto *pp di* **insorgere** ● *a* rebellious ● *nm* rebel
insospet'tabile *a* unsuspected
insospet'tire *vt* make suspicious ● *vi* become suspicious
insospet'tirsi *vr* become suspicious
insoste'nibile *a* untenable; (*insopportabile*) unbearable
insostitu'ibile *a* irreplaceable
insoz'zare *vt* dirty
inspe'rabile *a* hopeless; (*insperato*) unhoped-for
inspe'rato *a* unhoped-for
inspie'gabile *a* inexplicable
inspiegabil'mente *adv* inexplicably

inspi'rare *vt* breathe in

in'stabile *a* unstable; (*variabile*) unsettled

instabilità *nf* instability; (*di tempo*) change-ability

instal'lare *vt* install

instal'larsi *vr* (*in casa, lavoro*) settle in

installa|'tore, -'trice *nmf* fitter

installazi'one *nf* installation. **installa-zioni** *pl* **di bordo** on-board equipment

instan'cabile *a* untiring

instancabil'mente *adv* tirelessly

instau'rare *vt* found

instau'rarsi *vr* become established

instaurazi'one *nf* foundation

instra'dare *vt* direct

insù: **all'~** *adv* upwards; **naso all'~** turned-up nose

insubordi'nato *a* insubordinate

insubordinazi'one *nf* insubordination

insuc'cesso *nm* failure

insudici'are *vt* dirty

insudici'arsi *vr* get dirty

insuffici'ente *a* insufficient; (*inadeguato*) inadequate ● *nf Sch* fail

insufficiente'mente *adv* insufficiently

insuffici'enza *nf* insufficiency; (*inadeguatezza*) inadequacy; *Sch* fail. **~ cardiaca** cardiac insufficiency. **~ di prove** lack of evidence

insu'lare *a* insular

insu'lina *nf* insulin

in'sulso *a* insipid; (*sciocco*) silly

insul'tare *vt* insult

in'sulto *nm* insult; **coprire qcno di insulti** heap abuse on sb

insupe'rabile *a* insuperable; (*eccezionale*) incomparable

insurrezi'one *nf* insurrection

insussi'stente *a* groundless

intac'cabile *a* subject to corrosion; *fig* open to criticism

intac'care *vt* nick; (*corrodere*) corrode; draw on ‹*capitale*›; (*danneggiare*) damage

intagli'are *vt* carve

in'taglio *nm* carving

intan'gibile *a* untouchable

in'tanto *adv* meanwhile; (*per ora*) for the moment; (*avversativo*) but; **~ che** while

intarsi'are *vt* inlay

intarsi'ato *a* **~ di** inset with

in'tarsio *nm* inlay

intasa'mento *nm* (*ostruzione*) blockage; (*ingorgo*) traffic jam

inta'sare *vt* block, clog

inta'sarsi *vr* become blocked

inta'sato *a* blocked

inta'scare *vt* pocket

in'tatto *a* intact

intavo'lare *vt* start

inte'gerrimo *a* of integrity

inte'grale *a* whole; **edizione ~** unabridged edition; **pane ~** wholemeal bread; **versione ~** (*di film*) uncut version; (*di romanzo*) unabridged version

integra'lista *nmf* fundamentalist

integral'mente *adv* fully

inte'grante *a* integral

inte'grare *vt* integrate; (*aggiungere*) supplement

inte'grarsi *vr* integrate

integra'tivo *a* supplementary, additional; **esame ~** test taken by pupil wishing to tranfer from arts to a scientific stream etc

integra'tore *nm* **~ alimentare** dietary supplement

integrazi'one *nf* integration

integrità *nf* integrity

'integro *a* complete; (*retto*) upright

intelaia'tura *nf* framework

intellet'tivo *a* intellectual

intel'letto *nm* intellect

intellettu'ale *a & nmf* intellectual

intellettual'mente *adv* intellectually

intelli'gente *a* intelligent

intelligente'mente *adv* intelligently

intelli'genza *nf* intelligence. **~ artificiale** artificial intelligence

intelli'ghenzia *nf* intelligentsia

intelli'gibile *a* intelligible

intelligibil'mente *adv* intelligibly

intelligi'oco *nm* computer game

intempe'rante *a* intemperate

intempe'ranza *nf* intemperance; **intemperanze** *pl* excesses

intem'perie *nfpl* bad weather

intempe'stivo *a* untimely

inten'dente *nm* superintendent

inten'denza *nf* **~ di finanza** inland revenue office

in'tendere *vt* (*comprendere*) understand; (*udire*) hear; (*avere intenzione*) intend; (*significare*) mean; [**siamo**] **intesi?** is that clear?

in'tendersi *vr* (*capirsi*) understand each other; **~ di** (*essere esperto in*) have a good knowledge of; **intendersela con** (*fam: avere una relazione con*) have it off with

intendi'mento *nm* understanding; (*intenzione*) intention

intendi|'tore, -'trice *nmf* connoisseur; **intenditori** *pl* cognoscenti

intene'rire *vt* soften; (*commuovere*) touch

intene'rirsi *vr* be touched

intensa'mente *adv* intensely

intensifi'care *vt* intensify

intensifi'carsi *vr* intensify

intensità *nf* intensity

intensiva'mente *adv* intensively

inten'sivo *a* intensive

in'tenso *a* intense

inten'tare *vt* start up; **~ causa contro qcno** bring *o* institute proceedings against sb

inten'tato *a* **non lasciare nulla di ~** try everything

in'tento *a* engrossed (**a** in) ● *nm* purpose

intenzio'nale *a* intentional

intenzio'nato *a* **essere ~ a fare qcsa** have the intention of doing sth

intenzi'one *nf* intention; **senza ~** unintentionally; **avere ~ di fare qcsa** intend to do sth, have the intention of doing sth

intera'gire *vi* interact

intera'mente *adv* completely, entirely

interat'tivo *a* interactive

interazi'one *nf* interaction

interca'lare *nm* stock phrase ● *vt* insert ‹*esclamazione*›

intercambi'abile *a* interchangeable

interca'pedine *nf* cavity

inter'cedere *vi* intercede

intercessi'one *nf* intercession

intercet'tare *vt* intercept; tap ‹*telefono*›

intercettazi'one *nf* interception. **~ telefonica** telephone tapping

inter'city *nm inv* inter-city

intercomuni'cante *a* [inter]communicating

interconfessio'nale *a* interdenominational

intercon'nettere *vt* interconnect

intercontinen'tale *a* intercontinental

inter'correre *vi* ‹*tempo:*› elapse; ‹*esistere*› exist

interco'stale *a* intercostal; **dolori intercostali** *fam* growing pains

interden'tale *a* between the teeth; **filo ~** dental floss

inter'detto *pp di* **interdire** ● *a* astonished; ‹*proibito*› forbidden; **rimanere ~** be taken aback; **lasciare qcno ~** astonish sb, dumbfound sb ● *nm Relig* interdict

interdipartimen'tale *a* interdepartmental

interdipen'dente *a* interdependent

interdipen'denza *nf* interdependence

inter'dire *vt* ban; ‹*nel calcio*› intercept; *Jur* deprive of civil rights; *Relig* interdict; **~ a qcno di fare qcsa** forbid sb to do sth

interdiscipli'nare *a* interdisciplinary

interdizi'one *nf* ban; ‹*nel calcio*› interception; *Relig* interdict. **~ giudiziale** *appointment of a legal guardian to a minor of unsound mind*. **~ legale** *legally imposed ban*. **~ dai pubblici uffici** *ban on taking public office*

interessa'mento *nm* interest

interes'sante *a* interesting; **essere in stato ~** be pregnant

interes'sare *vt* interest; ‹*riguardare*› concern ● *vi* **~ a** interest; **non mi interessa** I'm not interested; ‹*non mi importa*› I don't care, it doesn't matter to me

interes'sarsi *vr* **~ a** take an interest in; **~ di** take care of

interes'sato *a* ‹*attento*› interested; *pej* self-interested; **diretto ~** person concerned

inte'resse *nm* interest; **fare qcsa per ~** do sth out of self-interest; **essere nell'~ di qcno** be in sb's interest; **un ~ del 4%** 4% interest. **~ attivo** interest charge. **~ maturato** accrued interest. **~ privato in atti di ufficio** abuse of public office. **~ a tasso variabile** floating rate interest

interes'senza *nf Econ* profit-sharing

inter'faccia *nf* interface. **~ uomo/macchina** man/machine interface. **~ utente** user interface

interfacci'are *vt* interface

interfacci'arsi *vr* interface

interfe'renza *nf* interference

interfe'rire *vi* interfere

inter'fono *nm* intercom

interga'lattico *a* intergalactic

interiet'tivo *a* interjectory

interiezi'one *nf* interjection

'interim *nm inv* ‹*incarico*› temporary appointment; ‹*periodo*› interim; **ad ~** on a temporary basis; ‹*presidente*› acting

interi'ora *nfpl* entrails

interi'ore *a* inner

interioriz'zare *vt* internalize

interior'mente *adv* ‹*nella parte interiore*› internally; ‹*emotivamente*› inwardly

inter'linea *nf* line spacing; *Typ* leading. **~ doppia** double spacing

interline'are *vt* space out ● *a* line *attrib*

interlocu'|tore, -'trice *nmf* speaker, interlocutor *fml*; **il mio ~** the person I am/was speaking to

inter'ludio *nm* interlude

intermedi'ario, -a *a & nmf* intermediary; *Econ* middleman

intermediazi'one *nf* ‹*intervento*› mediation

inter'medio *a* in-between

inter'mezzo *nm Theat, Mus* intermezzo

intermi'nabile *a* interminable

interministeri'ale *a* interdepartmental

intermissi'one *nf* intermission

intermit'tente *a* intermittent; ‹*vulcano*› dormant

intermit'tenza *nf* **a ~** intermittent

interna'mente *adv* internally

interna'mento *nm* internment; ‹*in manicomio*› committal

inter'nare *vt* intern; ‹*in manicomio*› commit [to a mental institution]

inter'nato, -a *a* interned ● *nmf* internee ● *nm* boarding school

internazio'nale *a* international

internazional'mente *adv* internationally

'Internet *nm* Internet; **in ~** on the Internet; **via ~** through the Internet

inter'nista *nmf* internist

in'terno *a* internal; *Geog* inland; ‹*interiore*› inner; ‹*politica*› national; **alunno ~** boarder ● *nm* interior; ‹*di condominio*› flat; *Teleph* extension; *Cinema* interior shot; **all'~** inside; **ministero degli interni** Ministry of the Interior, ≈ Home Office

in'tero *a* whole, entire; *Math* whole; ‹*intatto*› intact; ‹*completo*› complete; **per ~** in full ● *nm* ‹*totalità*› whole

interparlamen'tare *a* interparliamentary

interpel'lanza *nf* parliamentary question

interpel'lare *vt* consult

interpel'lato, -a *nmf* person being questioned

interperso'nale *a* interpersonal
interplane'tario *a* interplanetary
interpo'lare *vt* interpolate
inter'porre *vt* interpose; use ⟨*influenza*⟩; **~ ostacoli a** put obstacles in the way of
inter'porsi *vr* intervene; **~ tra** come between
inter'posto *a* **per interposta persona** through a third party
interpre'tare *vt* interpret; *Mus* perform; **~ male** misinterpret
interpretari'ato *nm* interpreting
interpretazi'one *nf* interpretation; *Mus* performance
in'terprete *nmf* interpreter; *Mus* performer
interpunzi'one *nf* punctuation
inter'rare *vt* (*seppellire*) bury; (*riempire*) fill in; lay underground ⟨*cavo, tubo*⟩; plant ⟨*pianta, seme*⟩
inter'rato *nm* basement
interregio'nale *nm* *long-distance train, stopping at all stations*
interro'gante *nmf* questioner
interro'gare *vt* question; *Sch* examine
interrogativa'mente *adv* ⟨*guardare*⟩ inquiringly
interroga'tivo *a* interrogative; (*sguardo*) questioning ● *nm* question
interro'gato *a* ⟨*studente*⟩ examinee; *Jur* person questioned
interroga'torio *a & nm* questioning
interrogazi'one *nf* question; *Sch* oral [test]. **~ ciclica** polling. **~ parlamentare** parliamentary question
inter'rompere *vt* interrupt; (*sospendere*) stop; cut off ⟨*collegamento*⟩
inter'rompersi *vr* break off
interrut'tore *nm* switch. **~ a reostato** dimmer
interruzi'one *nf* interruption; **senza ~** non-stop. **~ della corrente** power cut. **~ di gravidanza** termination of pregnancy
interscambi'abile *a* interchangeable
inter'scambio *nm* import-export trade
interse'care *vt* intersect
interse'carsi *vr* intersect
intersezi'one *nf* intersection
inter'stizio *nm* interstice
interur'bana *nf* long-distance call
interur'bano *a* inter-city; **telefonata interurbana** long-distance call
interval'lare *vt* space out
inter'vallo *nm* interval; (*spazio*) space; (*in ufficio*) tea/coffee break; *TV, Sch* break; **fare un ~** have a break; **a intervalli regolari** at regular intervals. **~ del pranzo** lunch hour, lunch break. **~ pubblicitario** commercial break
interve'nire *vi* intervene; (*Med: operare*) operate; **~ a** take part in
inter'vento *nm* intervention; (*presenza*) presence; (*chirurgico*) operation; **pronto ~** emergency services. **un ~ a cuore aperto** open-heart surgery
inter'vista *nf* interview. **~ esclusiva** exclusive interview

intervi'stare *vt* interview
intervi'stato, -a *nmf* interviewee
intervista|'tore, -'trice *nmf* interviewer
in'tesa *nf* understanding; **d'~** ⟨*cenno*⟩ of acknowledgment
in'teso, -a *pp di* **intendere** ● *a* **resta ~ che...** needless to say,...; **~ a** meant to; [**siamo**] **intesi!** agreed! ● *nf* understanding
in'tessere *vt* weave together
inte'stare *vt* head; write one's name and address at the top of ⟨*lettera*⟩; *Comm* register
inte'starsi *vr* **~ a fare qcsa** take it into one's head to do sth
intesta'tario, -a *nmf* holder
intestazi'one *nf* heading; (*su carta da lettere*) letterhead
intesti'nale *a* intestinal
inte'stino *a* ⟨*lotte*⟩ internal ● *nm* intestine. **~ crasso** large intestine. **~ tenue** small intestine
intiepi'dire *vt* (*scaldare*) warm; cool ⟨*passione, desiderio*⟩
intiepi'dirsi *vr* cool [down]; (*scaldarsi*) warm [up]; ⟨*fede:*⟩ wane
intima'mente *adv* ⟨*conoscere*⟩ intimately
inti'mare *vt* order; **~ l'alt** give the order to halt; **~ l'alt a qcno** order sb to stop
intimazi'one *nf* order. **~ di sfratto** eviction notice
intimida'torio *a* threatening
intimidazi'one *nf* intimidation
intimi'dire *vt* intimidate
intimi'dirsi *vr* be overwhelmed with shyness
intimità *nf* cosiness
'intimo *a* intimate; (*interno*) innermost; ⟨*amico*⟩ close ● *nm* (*amico*) close friend; (*dell'animo*) heart
intimo'rire *vt* frighten
intimo'rirsi *vr* get frightened
intimo'rito *a* frightened
in'tingere *vt* dip
in'tingolo *nm* sauce; (*pietanza*) stew
intiriz'zire *vt* numb
intiriz'zirsi *vr* grow numb
intiriz'zito *a* **essere ~** (*dal freddo*) be perished
intito'lare *vt* entitle; (*dedicare*) dedicate
intito'larsi *vr* be called
intolle'rabile *a* intolerable
intolle'rante *a* intolerant
intona'care *vt* plaster
intonaca'tore *nm* plasterer
in'tonaco *nm* plaster. **~ a pinocchino** pebbledash
into'nare *vt* start to sing; tune ⟨*strumento*⟩; (*accordare*) match
into'narsi *vr* match
into'nato *a* ⟨*persona*⟩ able to sing in tune; ⟨*voce, strumento*⟩ in tune; ⟨*colore*⟩ matching
intonazi'one *nf* (*inflessione*) intonation; ⟨*ironica*⟩ tone; (*cantando*) ability to sing in tune
in'tonso *a* ⟨*libro*⟩ untouched
inton'tire *vt* ⟨*botta:*⟩ stun, daze; ⟨*gas:*⟩ make dizzy; *fig* stun ● *vi* go ga-ga

inton'tito *a* dazed; *fig* stunned; *(con l'età)* ga-ga

intop'pare *vi* ~ **in** run into

in'toppo *nm* **c'è un** ~ something's come up

in'torno *adv* around ● *prep* ~ **a** around; *(circa)* about

intorpi'dire *vt* numb

intorpi'dirsi *vr* become numb

intorpi'dito *a* torpid

intossi'care *vt* poison

intossi'carsi *vr* be poisoned

intossicazi'one *nf* poisoning. ~ **alimentare** food poisoning

intra-azien'dale *a* in-house

intradu'cibile *a* untranslatable

intralci'are *vt* hamper

in'tralcio *nm* hitch; **essere d'**~ **(a qcno/ qcsa)** be a hindrance (to sb/sth)

intrallaz'zare *vi* intrigue

intral'lazzo *nm* racket

intramon'tabile *a* timeless

intramusco'lare *a* intramuscular

intransi'gente *a* intransigent, uncompromising

intransi'genza *nf* intransigence

intransi'tivo *a* intransitive

intrappolato *a* **rimanere** ~ be trapped

intrapren'dente *a* enterprising

intrapren'denza *nf* initiative

intra'prendere *vt* undertake

intrat'tabile *a* very difficult

intratte'nere *vt* entertain

intratte'nersi *vr* linger

intratteni'mento *nm* entertainment

intrave'dere *vt* catch a glimpse of; *(presagire)* foresee

intrecci'are *vt* interweave; plait ‹*capelli, corda*›; ~ **le mani** clasp one's hands

intrecci'are *vt* interweave

intrecci'arsi *vr* intertwine; *(aggrovigliarsi)* become tangled

in'treccio *nm* *(trama)* plot; *(di nastri, strade)* tangle

in'trepido *a* intrepid

intri'cato *a* tangled

intri'gante *a* intriguing ● *nmf* schemer

intri'gare *vt* entangle; *(incuriosire)* intrigue ● *vi* be intriguing

intri'garsi *vr* become entangled; *(immischiarsi)* meddle

in'trigo *nm* plot; **intrighi** *pl* plotting; *(di corte)* intrigues

intrinseca'mente *adv* intrinsically

in'trinseco *a* intrinsic

in'triso *a* ~ **di** soaked with; *fig* imbued with

intri'stire *vt* sadden

intri'stirsi *vr* grow sad

intro'durre *vt* introduce; *(inserire)* insert; ~ **a** *(iniziare a)* introduce to

intro'dursi *vr* get in; ~ **in** get into

introdut'tivo *a* ‹*pagine, discorso*› introductory

introduzi'one *nf* introduction

in'troito *nm* income, revenue; *(incasso)* takings *pl*

intro'mettere *vt* introduce

intro'mettersi *vr* interfere; *(interporsi)* intervene

intromissi'one *nf* intervention

introspet'tivo *a* introspective

intro'vabile *a* unobtainable

intro'verso, -a *a* introverted ● *nmf* introvert

intrufo'larsi *vr* sneak in

in'truglio *nm* concoction

intrusi'one *nf* intrusion

in'truso, -a *nmf* intruder

intu'ibile *a* deducible

intu'ire *vt* perceive

intuitiva'mente *adv* intuitively

intui'tivo *a* intuitive

in'tuito *nm* intuition

intuizi'one *nf* intuition

inuguagli'anza *nf* inequality

inu'mano *a* inhuman

inu'mare *vt* inter

inumi'dire *vt* dampen; moisten ‹*labbra*›

inumi'dirsi *vr* become damp

i'nutile *a* useless; *(superfluo)* unnecessary

inutilità *nf* uselessness

inutiliz'zabile *a* unusable

inutiliz'zato *a* unused

inutil'mente *adv* fruitlessly

inva'dente *a* intrusive

in'vadere *vt* invade; *(affollare)* overrun

inva'ghirsi *vr* ~ **di** take a fancy to

invali'cabile *a* impassable; **'limite** ~**'** *Mil* 'no access beyond this point'

invali'dare *vt* invalidate

invalidità *nf* disability; *Jur* invalidity

in'valido, -a *a* invalid; *(handicappato)* disabled ● *nmf* disabled person; **gli invalidi** the handicapped. ~ **di guerra** disabled ex-serviceman. ~ **del lavoro** industrial accident victim

in'vano *adv* in vain

invari'abile *a* invariable

invariabil'mente *adv* invariably

invari'ato *a* unchanged

invasi'one *nf* invasion

in'vaso *pp di* **invadere**

inva'sore *a* invading ● *nm* invader

invecchia'mento *nm* *(di vino)* maturation

invecchi'are *vt/i* age

in'vece *adv* instead; *(anzi)* but; ~ **di** instead of

inve'ire *vi* ~ **contro** inveigh against

invele'nito *a* embittered

inven'dibile *a* unsaleable

inven'duto *a* unsold

inven'tare *vt* invent

inventari'are *vt* make an inventory of

inven'tario *nm* inventory

inven'tato *a* made-up

inven'tiva *nf* inventiveness

inven'tivo *a* inventive

inven|'tore, -'trice *nmf* inventor

invenzi'one *nf* invention

inver'nale *a* wintry; **sport** *pl* **invernali** winter sports

in'verno *nm* winter
invero'simile *a* improbable
inverosimil'mente *adv* incredibly
inversa'mente *adv* inversely; ~ **proporzionale** in inverse proportion
inversi'one *nf* inversion; *Mech* reversal; **fare un'~ a U** do a U-turn. ~ **di fondo** *Comput* reverse video. ~ **di tendenza** turnaround
in'verso *a* inverse; (*opposto*) opposite ● *nm* opposite
inverte'brato *a & nm* invertebrate
inver'tire *vt* reverse; (*capovolgere*) turn upside-down
inver'tito, -a *nmf* homosexual
investi'gare *vt* investigate
investiga'tore, -'trice *nmf* investigator. ~ **privato** private investigator
investigazi'one *nf* investigation
investi'mento *nm* investment; (*incidente*) crash
inve'stire *vt* invest; (*urtare*) collide with; (*travolgere*) run over; ~ **qcno di** invest sb with
investi'tura *nf* investiture
invete'rato *a* inveterate
invet'tiva *nf* invective
invi'are *vt* send
invi'ato, -a *nmf* envoy; (*di giornale*) correspondent. ~ **di pace** peace envoy
in'vidia *nf* envy
invidi'are *vt* envy
invidi'oso *a* envious
invigo'rire *vt* invigorate
invigo'rirsi *vr* become strong
invin'cibile *a* invincible
in'vio *nm* dispatch; *Comput* enter
invio'labile *a* inviolable
invipe'rirsi *vr* get nasty
invipe'rito *a* furious
invischi'arsi *vr* get involved (**in** in)
invi'sibile *a* invisible
invisibilità *nf* invisibility
invi'tante *a* ⟨*piatto, profumo*⟩ enticing
invi'tare *vt* invite
invi'tato, -a *nmf* guest
in'vito *nm* invitation
invo'care *vt* invoke; (*implorare*) beg
invocazi'one *nf* invocation
invogli'are *vt* tempt; (*indurre*) induce
invogli'arsi *vr* ~ **di** take a fancy to
involga'rire *vt* vulgarize
involontaria'mente *adv* involuntarily
involon'tario *a* involuntary
invol'tini *nmpl* stuffed rolls (*of meat, pastry*)
in'volto *nm* parcel; (*fagotto*) bundle
in'volucro *nm* wrapping
invo'luto *a* involved
invulne'rabile *a* invulnerable
inzacche'rare *vt* splash with mud
inzup'pare *vt* soak; (*intingere*) dip
inzup'parsi *vr* get soaked
'io *pers pron* I; **sono io** it's me; **l'ho fatto io [stesso]** I did it myself ● *nm* **l'io** the ego
i'odio *nm* iodine

i'one *nm* ion
i'onico *a* Ionic
l'onio *nm* **lo ~** the Ionian [Sea]
iono'sfera *nf* ionosphere
i'osa: a iosa *adv* in abundance
iperattività *nf* hyperactivity
iperat'tivo *a* hyperactive
i'perbole *nf* hyperbole
iper'critico *a* hypercritical
ipermer'cato *nm* hypermarket
iper'metrope *a* long-sighted
ipersen'sibile *a* hypersensitive
ipertensi'one *nf* high blood pressure
iper'testo *nm Comput* hypertext
iperventi'lare *vi* hyperventilate
ip'nosi *nf* hypnosis
ipnotera'pia *nf* hypnotherapy
ip'notico *a* hypnotic
ipno'tismo *nm* hypnotism
ipnotiz'zare *vt* hypnotize
ipoaller'genico *a* hypoallergenic
ipoca'lorica *a* low-calorie
ipo'centro *nm* focus
ipocon'dria *nf* hypochondria
ipocon'driaco, -a *a & nmf* hypochondriac
ipocri'sia *nf* hypocrisy
i'pocrita *a* hypocritical ● *nmf* hypocrite
ipocrita'mente *adv* hypocritically
ipo'dermico *a* hypodermic
i'pofisi *nf inv* pituitary gland
ipo'teca *nf* mortgage
ipote'cabile *a* mortgageable
ipote'care *vt* mortgage
ipote'cario *a* mortgage *attrib*
ipote'nusa *nf* hypotenuse
ipo'termia *nf* hypothermia
i'potesi *nf inv* hypothesis; (*caso, eventualità*) eventuality; **nella migliore delle ~** at best; **nella peggiore delle ~** if the worst comes to the worst
ipo'tetico *a* hypothetical
ipotiz'zare *vt* hypothesize
'ippico, -a *a* horse *attrib* ● *nf* riding
ippoca'stano *nm* horse-chestnut
ip'podromo *nm* racecourse
ippo'potamo *nm* hippopotamus
'ipsilon *nf inv* [the letter] y
'ira *nf* anger
ira'scibile *a* irascible
i'rato *a* irate
'iride *nf Anat* iris; (*arcobaleno*) rainbow
'iris *nm inv Bot* iris
Ir'landa *nf* Ireland. ~ **del Nord** Northern Ireland
irlan'dese *a* Irish ● *nm* Irishman; (*lingua*) Irish ● *nf* Irishwoman
iro'nia *nf* irony
i'ronico *a* ironic[al]
irradi'are *vt/i* radiate
irradiazi'one *nf* radiation
irraggiun'gibile *a* unattainable
irragio'nevole *a* unreasonable; ⟨*speranza, timore*⟩ irrational; (*assurdo*) absurd
irranci'dire *vi* go rancid
irrazio'nale *a* irrational

irrazionalità *a* irrationality
irrazional'mente *adv* irrationally
irre'ale *a* unreal
irrea'listico *a* unrealistic
irrealiz'zabile *a* unattainable
irrealtà *nf* unreality
irrecupe'rabile *a* irrecoverable
irrecu'sabile *a* incontrovertible
irredi'mibile *a* irredeemable
irrefre'nabile *a* uncontrollable
irrefu'tabile *a* irrefutable
irrego'lare *a* irregular
irregolarità *nf inv* irregularity; (*di terreno*) unevenness; *Sport* foul
irregolar'mente *adv* (*frequentare*) irregularly; (*comportarsi*) erratically; (*disporre*) unevenly
irremo'vibile *a fig* adamant
irrepa'rabile *a* irreparable
irrepe'ribile *a* (*persona*) not to be found; **sarò irreperibile** I'm not going to be contactable
irrepren'sibile *a* irreproachable
irrepri'mibile *a* irrepressible
irrequi'eto *a* restless
irresi'stibile *a* irresistible
irresistibil'mente *adv* irresistibly
irreso'luto *a* irresolute
irrespon'sabile *a* irresponsible
irresponsabilità *nf* irresponsibility
irrestrin'gibile *a* preshrunk
irre'tire *vt* seduce
irrever'sibile *a* irreversible
irreversibil'mente *adv* irreversibly
irrevo'cabile *a* irrevocable
irrevocabil'mente *adv* irrevocably
irricono'scibile *a* unrecognizable
irridu'cibile *a* irreducible
irri'gare *vt* irrigate; (*fiume:*) flow through
irrigazi'one *nf* irrigation
irrigidi'mento *nm* (*di muscoli*) stiffening; (*di disciplina*) tightening
irrigi'dire *vt* stiffen up
irrigi'dirsi *vr* stiffen up
irrile'vante *a* unimportant
irrimedi'abile *a* irreparable
irrimediabil'mente *adv* irreparably
irripe'tibile *a* unrepeatable
irri'solto *a* unresolved
irri'sorio *a* derisive; (*insignificante*) derisory
irri'tabile *a* irritable
irri'tante *a* aggravating
irri'tare *vt* irritate
irri'tarsi *vr* get annoyed
irri'tato *a* irritated; (*gola*) sore
irritazi'one *nf* irritation
irrive'renza *nf* (*qualità*) irreverence; (*azione*) irreverent action
irrobu'stire *vt* fortify
irrobu'stirsi *vr* get stronger
ir'rompere *vi* burst (**in** into)
irro'rare *vt* sprinkle
irrorazi'one *nf* (*di piante*) crop spraying
irru'ente *a* impetuous

irruvi'dire *vt* roughen
irruvi'dirsi *vr* become rough
irruzi'one *nf* raid; *fig* eruption; **fare ~ in** burst into
ir'suto *a* shaggy
'irto *a* bristly
i'scritto, -a *pp di* **iscrivere** ● *a* registered ● *nmf* member; **per ~** in writing
i'scrivere *vt* register
i'scriversi *vr* **~ a** register at, enrol at (*scuola*); join (*circolo ecc*)
iscrizi'one *nf* registration; (*epigrafe*) inscription
i'slamico *a* Islamic
isla'mismo *nm* Islam
I'slanda *nf* Iceland
islan'dese *a* Icelandic ● *nmf* Icelander
'ismi *nmpl* isms
i'sobara *nf* isobar
'isola *nf* island. **le isole britanniche** the British Isles. **~ deserta** desert island. **~ pedonale** traffic island. **~ spartitraffico** traffic island
iso'lano, -a *a* insular ● *nmf* islander
iso'lante *a* insulating ● *nm* insulator
iso'lare *vt* isolate; *Mech, Electr* insulate; (*acusticamente*) soundproof
iso'lato *a* isolated ● *nm* (*di appartamenti*) block
isolazio'nismo *nm* isolationism
iso'metrico *a* isometric
i'soscele *a* isosceles
is'panico *a* Hispanic
ispessi'mento *nm* thickening
ispes'sire *vt* thicken
ispes'sirsi *vr* thicken
ispetto'rato *nm* inspectorate
ispet'tore *nm* inspector. **~ capo** chief inspector. **~ di polizia** police inspector. **~ scolastico** inspector of schools. **~ di zona** *Comm* area manager
ispezio'nare *vt* inspect
ispezi'one *nf* inspection; (*di nave*) boarding
'ispido *a* bristly
ispi'rare *vt* inspire; suggest (*idea, soluzione*)
ispi'rarsi *vr* **~ a** be based on
ispi'rato *a* inspired
ispirazi'one *nf* inspiration; (*idea*) idea
Isra'ele *nm* Israel
israeli'ano, -a *a* & *nmf* Israeli
is'sare *vt* hoist
ist. *abbr* (**istituto**) dept
istan'taneo, -a *a* instantaneous ● *nf* snapshot
i'stante *nm* instant; **all'~** instantly
i'stanza *nf* petition. **~ di divorzio** petition for divorce
isterecto'mia *nf* hysterectomy
i'sterico *a* hysterical; **attacco ~** hysterics *pl*
iste'rismo *nm* hysteria. **~ di massa** mass hysteria
isti'gare *vt* instigate; **~ qcno al male** incite sb to evil
istiga|'tore, -'trice *nmf* instigator

istigazi'one *nf* instigation. **~ a delinquere** incitement to crime
istintiva'mente *adv* instinctively
istin'tivo *a* instinctive
i'stinto *nm* instinct; **d'~** instinctively. **~ di conservazione** instinct of self-preservation. **~ materno** maternal instinct
istitu'ire *vt* institute; (*fondare*) found; initiate ‹*manifestazione*›
isti'tuto *nm* institute; *Sch* secondary school; *Univ* department. **~ di bellezza** beauty salon. **~ commerciale** business college. **~ di credito** bank. **~ per l'infanzia** children's home
istitu|'tore, -'trice *nmf* (*insegnante*) tutor; (*fondatore*) founder
istituzio'nale *a* institutional
istituzionaliz'zare *vt* institutionalize
istituzionaliz'zarsi *vr* become an institution
istituzionalizzazi'one *nf* institutionalization
istituzi'one *nf* institution; **le istituzioni** state institutions
'istmo *nm* isthmus
isto'gramma *nm* bar chart
istolo'gia *nf* histology
istra'dare *vt* divert; *fig* guide (**a** towards)

'istrice *nm* porcupine
istri'one *nm* clown; *Theat sl* ham
istru'ire *vt* instruct; (*addestrare*) train; (*informare*) inform; *Jur* prepare
istru'ito *a* well-educated
istrut'tivo *a* instructive
istrut|'tore, -'trice *nmf* instructor; **giudice ~** examining magistrate. **~ di guida** driving instructor. **~ di nuoto** swimming instructor
istrut'toria *nf Jur* investigation
istruzi'one *nf* instruction; *Sch* education; **ministero della pubblica ~** Department of Education. **istruzioni** *pl* **per l'uso** instructions for use
istupi'dire *vt* stupefy
l'talia *nf* Italy
itali'ano, -a *a & nmf* Italian
itine'rante *a* wandering
itine'rario *nm* route, itinerary. **~ turistico** tourist route
itte'rizia *nf* jaundice
'ittico *a* fishing *attrib*
i'uta *nf* jute
I.V.A. *nf abbr* (**imposta sul valore aggiunto**) VAT; **~ compresa** inclusive of VAT, VAT inclusive
'ivi *adv* (*linguaggio burocratico*) therein

Jj

ja'bot *nm inv* jabot
jack *nm inv* jack
jac'quard *a inv* (*nella maglia*) jacquard
'jais *nm* jet
'jam-session *nf inv* jam-session
jazz *nm* jazz
jaz'zista *nmf* jazz player
jeep *nf inv* jeep
'jersey *nm* jersey
jet *nm inv* jet. **~ privato** private jet
jet-'set *nm* jet set
'jingle *nm inv* jingle
'jodel *nm inv* yodel

'jogging *nm* jogging
joint venture *nf inv Comm* joint venture
'jolly *nm inv* (*carta da gioco*) joker ● *a Comput* **carattere ~** wildcard [character]
'joystick *nm inv* joystick
Jugo'slavia *nf* Yugoslavia
jugo'slavo, -a *a & nmf* Yugoslav[ian]
juke box *nm inv* juke box
jumbo-'jet *nm inv* jumbo jet
junghi'ano, -a *a & nmf* Jungian
'junior *a inv* junior ● *nm* (*pl* **juniores**) junior
'juta *nf* jute

Kk

kafki'ano *a* Kafkan, Kafkaesque
ka'jal *nm inv* kohl
'kaki *a inv* khaki ● *nm inv* persimmon
ka'pok *nm* kapok
ka'putt *a inv* kaput
kara'kiri *nm* **fare ~** commit hara-kiri
kara'oke *nm inv* karaoke
kara'te *nm* karate
kart *nm inv* go-kart
kar'tismo *nm* go-karting; **fare del ~** go-karting
'kasher *a inv* kosher
Kashmir *nm* Kashmir
ka'yak *nm inv* kayak
KB *Comput abbr* (**kilobyte**) K, KB
Kbyte *Comput abbr* (**kilobyte**) kbyte
ker'messe *nf inv* fair; *fig* rowdy celebration
kero'sene *nm* paraffin
'ketchup *nm* ketchup
kg *abbr* (**chilogrammo**) kg

kib'butz *nm inv* kibbutz
'killer *mf inv* assassin, hit man
'kilo *nm* kilo
kilt *nm inv* kilt
ki'mono *nm inv* kimono
kinesitera'pia *nf* physiotherapy
kit *nm inv* **~ di aggiornamento** upgrade kit. **~ multimediale** multimedia kit
kitsch *a inv* kitschy
'kleenex® *nm inv* Kleenex
km *abbr* (**chilometro**) km
km/h *abbr* (**chilometri all'ora**) kph
kmq *abbr* (**chilometro quadrato**) km^2
ko'ala *nm inv* koala
'krapfen *nm inv* doughnut
'kripton *nm* krypton
'Kurdistan *nm* Kurdistan
kuwaiti'ano *nm* Kuwaiti
kW *abbr* (**kilowatt**) kW
K-'way® *nm inv* cagoule
kWh *abbr* (**kilowatt all'ora**) kWh

Ll

l' *def art mf* (*before vowel*) the; *vedi* **il**
la *def art f* the; *vedi* **il** ● *pron* (*oggetto, riferito a persona*) her; (*riferito a cosa, animale*) it; (*forma di cortesia*) you ● *nm inv Mus* (*chiave, nota*) A
là *adv* there; **di là** (*in quel luogo*) in there; (*da quella parte*) that way; **eccolo là!** there he is!; **farsi più in là** (*far largo*) make way; **là dentro** in there; **là fuori** out there; **[ma] va là!** come off it!; **più in là** (*nel tempo*) later on; (*nello spazio*) further on
'labbro *nm* (*pl nf* **labbra**) lip; **pendere dalle labbra di qcno** hang on sb's every word. **~ leporino** harelip
labi'ale *a & nf* labial
'labile *a* fleeting
labiolet'tura *nf* lip-reading
labi'rinto *nm* labyrinth; (*di sentieri ecc*) maze
labora'torio *nm* laboratory; (*di negozio, officina ecc*) workshop. **~ linguistico** language lab
laboriosa'mente *adv* laboriously
labori'oso *a* (*operoso*) industrious; (*faticoso*) laborious

labra'dor *nm inv* labrador
labu'rista *a* Labour ● *nmf* member of the Labour Party
'lacca *nf* lacquer; (*per capelli*) hairspray
lac'care *vt* lacquer
lacchè *nm inv* lackey
'laccio *nm* noose; (*lazo*) lasso; (*trappola*) snare; (*stringa*) lace. **~ emostatico** tourniquet
lace'rante *a* ⟨*grido*⟩ earsplitting
lace'rare *vt* tear; lacerate ⟨*carne*⟩
lace'rarsi *vr* tear
lacerazi'one *nf* laceration
'lacero *a* torn; (*cencioso*) ragged
la'conico *a* laconic
'lacrima *nf* tear; (*goccia*) drop
lacri'male *a* ⟨*condotto, ghiandola*⟩ tear *attrib*
lacri'mare *vi* weep
lacri'mevole *a* tear-jerking
lacri'mogeno *a* gas **~** tear gas
lacri'moso *a* tearful
la'cuna *nf* gap
lacu'noso *a* ⟨*preparazione, resoconto*⟩ incomplete

la'custre *a* lake *attrib*

lad'dove *conj* whereas

'ladro, -a *a* thieving ● *nmf* thief; al ~! stop thief!

ladro'cinio *nm* theft

la'druncolo *nm* petty thief

'lager *nm inv* concentration camp

laggiù *adv* down there; (*lontano*) over there

'lagna *nf* (*fam: persona*) moaning Minnie; (*film*) bore

la'gnanza *nf* complaint

la'gnarsi *vr* moan; (*protestare*) complain (di about)

la'gnoso *a* (*persona*) moaning; (*film*) weepy

'lago *nm* lake. ~ di Garda Lake Garda. ~ di sangue pool of blood

la'guna *nf* lagoon

lagu'nare *a* lagoon *attrib*

laiciz'zare *vt* laicize

'laico, -a *a* lay; (*vita*) secular ● *nm* layman ● *nf* laywoman

'lama *nf* blade; a doppia ~ (*rasoio*) twin-blade ● *nm inv* (*animale*) llama

lambic'carsi *vr* ~ il cervello rack one's brains

lam'bire *vt* lap

lamé *nm inv* lamé

la'mella *nf* (*di fungo*) lamella; (*di metallo, plastica*) sheet

lamen'tare *vt* lament

lamen'tarsi *vr* moan; ~ di (*lagnarsi*) complain about

lamen'tela *nf* complaint

lamen'tevole *a* mournful; (*pietoso*) pitiful

la'mento *nm* moan

la'metta *nf* ~ [da barba] razor blade

lami'era *nf* sheet metal. ~ ondulata corrugated iron

'lamina *nf* foil. ~ d'oro gold leaf

lami'nare *vt* laminate

lami'naria *nf* kelp

lami'nato *a* laminated ● *nm* laminate; (*tessuto*) lamé

'lampada *nf* lamp. ~ abbronzante sunlamp. ~ alogena halogen lamp. ~ da comodino bedside lamp. ~ a gas gas lamp. ~ a olio oil lamp. ~ a pila torch. ~ da soffitto overhead light. ~ da tavolo table lamp

lampa'dario *nm* chandelier

lampa'dato *nm sl* sun-bed freak

lampa'dina *nf* light bulb

lam'pante *a* clear

lam'para *nf* light used when fishing at night

lampeggi'are *vi* flash

lampeggia'tore *nm* Auto indicator

lampi'one *nm* street lamp

'lampo *nm* flash of lightning; (*luce*) flash; lampi *pl* lightning *sg*; cerniera ~ zip [fastener], zipper *Am*. ~ di genio stroke of genius. ~ al magnesio magnesium flash

lam'pone *nm* raspberry

'lana *nf* wool; di ~ woollen. ~ d'acciaio steel wool. ~ grossa double knitting [wool]. ~ merino botany wool. ~ vergine new wool. ~ di vetro glass wool

lan'cetta *nf* pointer; (*di orologio*) hand. ~ dei minuti minute hand. ~ delle ore hour hand. ~ dei secondi second hand

'lancia *nf* (*arma*) spear, lance; *Naut* launch. ~ di salvataggio lifeboat

lanciafi'amme *nm inv* flamethrower

lancia'missili *nm inv* missile launcher

lancia'palle *a inv* macchina ~ ball launcher for tennis practice

lancia'razzi *a inv* pistola ~ Very pistol ● *nm inv* rocket launcher

lanci'are *vt* throw; (*da un aereo*) drop; launch (*missile, prodotto, attacco*); give (*grido*); *Comput* run (*file*); ~ uno sguardo a glance at; ~ in alto throw up

lanci'arsi *vr* fling oneself; (*intraprendere*) launch out

lanci'nante *a* piercing

'lancio *nm* throwing; (*da aereo*) drop; (*di missile, prodotto*) launch; (*Comput: di file*) running. ~ del disco discus [throwing]. ~ del giavellotto javelin [throwing]. ~ con paracadute airdrop. ~ del peso putting the shot

'landa *nf* moor

languida'mente *adv* languidly

'languido *a* languid; (*debole*) feeble

langu'ore *nm* languor; (*spossatezza*) listlessness; ~ di stomaco hunger pangs *pl*

lani'ero *a* wool; industria laniera wool industry

lani'ficio *nm* woollen mill

lano'lina *nf* lanolin

la'noso *a* woolly

lan'terna *nf* lantern; (*faro*) lighthouse

la'nugine *nf* down

lapalissi'ano *a* obvious

laparosco'pia *nf* laparoscopy

lapi'dare *vt* stone; *fig* demolish

lapi'dario *a* (*conciso*) terse; arte lapidaria stone carving

'lapide *nf* tombstone; (*commemorativa*) memorial tablet

'lapis *nm inv* pencil

lapi'slazzuli *nm inv* lapis lazuli

'lappa *nf Bot* burr

Lap'ponia *nf* Lapland

'lapsus *nm inv* lapse, error. ~ freudiano Freudian slip

'laptop *nm inv* laptop

lardel'lare *vt Culin* lard

'lardo *nm* lard

larga'mente *adv* (*ampiamente*) widely

largheggi'are *vi* ~ in be free with

lar'ghezza *nf* width; (*di spalle*) breadth; *fig* liberality. ~ di vedute broad-mindedness

'largo *a* wide; (*ampio*) broad; (*abito*) loose; (*liberale*) liberal; (*abbondante*) generous; stare alla larga keep away; ~ di manica *fig* generous; ~ di spalle/vedute broad-shouldered/-minded; a gambe larghe with one's legs wide apart; di larghe vedute broad-minded ● *nm* width; andare al ~ *Naut* go out to sea; fare ~ make room; farsi ~ make one's way; al ~ di off the coast of

'**larice** *nm* larch
la'**ringe** *nf* larynx
larin'**gite** *nf* laryngitis
'**larva** *nf* larva; (*persona emaciata*) shadow. ~ **di pidocchio** nit
la'**sagne** *nfpl* lasagna
'**lasca** *nf* roach
lasciapas'**sare** *nm inv* pass
lasci'**are** *vt* leave; (*rinunciare*) give up; (*rimetterci*) lose; (*smettere di tenere*) let go [of]; (*concedere*) let; ~ **a desiderare** leave a lot to be desired; ~ **di fare qcsa** (*smettere*) stop doing sth; **lascia perdere!** forget it!; **lascialo venire, lascia che venga** let him come
lasci'**arsi** *vr* (*reciproco*) leave each other, split up; ~ **andare** let oneself go
'**lascito** *nm* legacy
la'**scivo** *a* lascivious
'**laser** *a & nm inv* [raggio] ~ laser [beam]
lassa'**tivo** *a & nm* laxative
las'**sismo** *nm* laxity
'**lasso** *nm* ~ **di tempo** period of time
lassù *adv* up there
'**lastra** *nf* slab; (*di ghiaccio*) sheet; (*di metallo, Phot*) plate; (*radiografia*) X-ray [plate]. ~ **di pietra** paving slab, paving stone
lastri'**care** *vt* pave
lastri'**cato** *nm* pavement
'**lastrico** *nm* paving; **sul** ~ on one's beam-ends
la'**tente** *a* latent
late'**rale** *a* side *attrib*; *Med, Techn ecc* lateral; **via** ~ side street
lateral'**mente** *adv* sideways
late'**rizi** *nmpl* bricks
'**latice** *nm* latex
latifon'**dista** *nm* big landowner
lati'**fondo** *nm* large estate
lati'**nismo** *nm* Latinism
la'**tino** *a & nm* Latin
latino-ameri'**cano, -a** *a & nmf* Latin American
lati'**tante** *a* in hiding ● *nmf* fugitive [from justice]
lati'**tanza** *nf* **darsi alla** ~ go into hiding
lati'**tudine** *nf* latitude
'**lato** *a* (*ampio*) broad; **in senso** ~ broadly speaking ● *nm* side; (*aspetto*) aspect; **a** ~ **di** beside; **dal** ~ **mio** (*punto di vista*) for my part; **d'altro** ~ *fig* on the other hand. ~ **B** B side
la'|**tore, -'trice** *nmf Comm* bearer
la'**trare** *vi* bark
la'**trato** *nm* barking
la'**trina** *nf* latrine
'**latta** *nf* tin, can
lat'**taio, -a** *nm* milkman ● *nf* milkwoman
lat'**tante** *a* breast-fed ● *nmf* suckling
'**latte** *nm* milk. ~ **acido** sour milk. ~ **condensato** condensed milk. ~ **detergente** cleansing milk. ~ **di gallina** eggnog. ~ **intero** whole milk. ~ **a lunga conservazione** long-life milk. ~ **materno** mother's milk, breast milk. ~ **parzialmente scremato** semi-skimmed milk. ~ **in pol-**

vere powdered milk. ~ **scremato** skimmed milk. ~ **di soia** soya milk
lat'**teo** *a* milky; **dieta lattea** milk diet. **la Via Lattea** the Milky Way
latte'**ria** *nf* dairy
'**lattice** *nm* latex
latti'**cello** *nm* buttermilk
latti'**cini** *nmpl* dairy products
latti'**era** *nf* milk jug
lattigi'**noso** *a* milky
lat'**tina** *nf* can
lat'**tosio** *nm* lactose
lat'**tuga** *nf* lettuce. ~ **romana** cos lettuce
'**laudano** *nm* laudanum
'**laurea** *nf* degree; **prendere la** ~ graduate. ~ **breve** *degree that takes less than the standard period of time.* ~ **in Lettere** arts degree
laure'**ando, -a** *nmf* final-year student
laure'**are** *vt* confer a degree on
laure'**arsi** *vr* graduate
laure'**ato, -a** *a & nmf* graduate
'**lauro** *nm* laurel
'**lauto** *a* lavish; ~ **guadagno** handsome profit
'**lava** *nf* lava
la'**vabile** *a* washable
la'**vabo** *nm* wash-basin
lavacri'**stallo** *nm* windscreen wiper
la'**vaggio** *nm* washing. ~ **automatico** (*per auto*) carwash. ~ **del cervello** brainwashing. ~ **a secco** dry-cleaning
la'**vagna** *nf* slate; *Sch* blackboard. ~ **a fogli mobili** flipchart. ~ **luminosa** overhead projector
lava'**macchine** *nmf inv* car washer
la'**vanda** *nf* wash; *Bot* lavender; **gli hanno fatto la** ~ **gastrica** he had his stomach pumped
lavan'**daia** *nf* washerwoman
lavande'**ria** *nf* laundry. ~ **automatica** launderette
lavan'**dino** *nm* sink; (*hum: persona*) bottomless pit
lavapi'**atti** *nmf inv* dishwasher
la'**vare** *vt* wash; ~ **i piatti** wash up; ~ **a secco** dry-clean; ~ **a mano** wash by hand; ~ **i panni** do the washing
la'**varsi** *vr* wash, have a wash; ~ **i denti** brush one's teeth; ~ **le mani/il viso** wash one's hands/face; ~ **la testa** *o* **i capelli** wash one's hair
lava'**secco** *nmf inv* dry-cleaner's
lavasto'**viglie** *nf inv* dishwasher
la'**vata** *nf* wash; **darsi una** ~ have a wash; ~ **di capo** *fig* scolding
lava'**tivo, -a** *nmf* idler
lava'**trice** *nf* washing-machine
lava'**vetri** *nm inv* squeegee
la'**vello** *nm* kitchen sink
'**lavico** *a* formed by lava
la'**vina** *nf* snowslide
lavo'**rante** *nmf* worker

lavo'rare _vi_ work; ~ **di fantasia** (_sognare_) day-dream ● _vt_ work; knead (_pasta ecc_); till (_la terra_); ~ **a maglia** knit; ~ **troppo** overwork

lavora'tivo _a_ working; **giorno** ~ workday; **settimana lavorativa** working week

lavo'rato _a_ (_pietra, legno_) carved; (_cuoio_) tooled; (_metallo_) wrought; (_golf_) patterned; (_terra_) cultivated

lavora'tore, -'trice _nmf_ worker. ~ **a domicilio** outworker, homeworker ● _a_ working

lavorazi'one _nf_ manufacture; (_di terra_) working; (_del terreno_) cultivation. ~ [_artigianale_] workmanship. ~ **del metallo** metalwork. ~ **in serie** mass production

lavo'rio _nm_ intense activity

la'voro _nm_ work; (_faticoso, sociale_) labour; (_impiego_) job; (_Theat_ play; **andare al** ~ go to work; **essere senza** ~ be out of work; **mettersi al** ~ (**su qcsa**) set to work (on sth); **ministero del** ~ Department of Employment; **ministero dei lavori pubblici** Department of Public Works. **lavori** _pl_ **di casa** housework. **lavori** _pl_ **in corso** roadworks. **lavori** _pl_ **forzati** hard labour _sg_. ~ **di gruppo** _Sch_ working in groups, group work. ~ **a maglia** knitting. ~ **nero** moonlighting. ~ **part time** part-time job. **lavori** _pl_ **stradali** roadworks. ~ **straordinario** overtime. ~ **teatrale** play. ~ **a tempo pieno** full-time job

lazza'rone _nm_ rascal

le _def art fpl_ the; _vedi_ **il** ● _pers pron_ (_oggetto_) them; (_a lei_) her; (_forma di cortesia_) you

'leader _nm inv_ leader. ~ **della marca** brand leader ● _a inv_ leading; **prodotto** ~ market leader

le'ale _a_ loyal

leal'mente _adv_ loyally

lealtà _nf_ loyalty

'leasing _nm inv_ lease-purchase

'lebbra _nf_ leprosy

lecca 'lecca _nm inv_ lollipop

leccapi'edi _nmf inv pej_ bootlicker

lec'care _vt_ lick; _fig_ suck up to

lec'carsi _vr_ lick; (_fig: agghindarsi_) doll oneself up; **da** ~ **i baffi** mouth-watering

lec'cata _nf_ lick

lec'cato _a_ (_persona_) dressed to kill

'leccio _nm_ holm oak

leccor'nia _nf_ delicacy

lecita'mente _adv_ lawfully

'lecito _a_ lawful; (_permesso_) permissible

'ledere _vt_ damage; _Med_ injure

'lega _nf_ league; (_di metalli_) alloy; **far** ~ **con qcno** take up with sb. ~ **doganale** customs union

le'gaccio _nm_ string; (_delle scarpe_) shoelace

le'gale _a_ legal ● _nm_ lawyer

legalità _nf_ legality

legaliz'zare _vt_ authenticate; (_rendere legale_) legalize

legalizzazi'one _nf_ legalization

legal'mente _adv_ legally

le'game _nm_ tie; (_amoroso_) liaison; (_connes-_

sione) link. ~ **di parentela** family relationship. ~ **di sangue** blood relationship. ~ **sentimentale** emotional relationship

lega'mento _nm Med_ ligament

le'gare _vt_ tie; tie up (_persona_); tie together (_due cose_); (_unire, rilegare_) bind; alloy (_metalli_); (_connettere_) connect; **legarsela al dito** _fig_ bear a grudge ● _vi_ (_far lega_) get on well

le'garsi _vr_ bind oneself; ~ **a qcno** become attached to sb

lega'tario, -a _nmf_ legatee

le'gato _nm_ legacy; _Relig_ legate

lega'tura _nf_ tying; (_di libro_) binding

legazi'one _nf_ legation

'legge _nf_ law; (_parlamentare_) act; **a norma di** ~ by law. ~ **marziale** martial law

leg'genda _nf_ legend; (_didascalia_) caption

leggen'dario _a_ legendary

'leggere _vt/i_ read; ~ **male** (_sbagliato_) misread

legge'rezza _nf_ lightness; (_frivolezza_) frivolity; (_incostanza_) fickleness

legger'mente _adv_ slightly

leg'gero _a_ light; (_bevanda_) weak; (_lieve_) slight; (_frivolo_) frivolous; (_incostante_) fickle; ~ **come una piuma** [as] light as a feather; **alla leggera** lightly

leggi'adro _a_ liter graceful

leg'gibile _a_ (_scrittura_) legible; (_stile_) readable

leg'gio _nm_ lectern; _Mus_ music stand

legife'rare _vi_ legislate

legio'nario _nm_ legionary

legi'one _nf_ legion

legisla'tivo _a_ legislative

legisla'tore _nm_ legislator

legisla'tura _nf_ legislature

legislazi'one _nf_ legislation

legittima'mente _adv_ legitimately

legittimità _nf_ legitimacy

le'gittimo _a_ legitimate; (_giusto_) proper; **legittima difesa** self-defence

'legna _nf_ firewood

le'gnaia _nf_ woodshed

le'gname _nm_ timber

le'gnata _nf_ blow with a stick

'legno _nm_ wood; **di** ~ wooden; **legni** _pl Mus_ woodwind. ~ **compensato** plywood

le'gnoso _a_ woody; (_di legno_) wooden; (_gambe_) stiff; (_movimento_) wooden

le'gume _nm_ pod

'lei _pers pron_ (_soggetto_) she; (_oggetto, con prep_) her; (_forma di cortesia_) you; **lo ha fatto** ~ **stessa** she did it herself

'lembo _nm_ edge; (_di terra_) strip

'lemma _nm_ headword

'lemming _nm inv_ lemming

'lena _nf_ vigour

'lendine _nm_ nit

le'nire _vt_ soothe

lenta'mente _adv_ slowly

'lente _nf_ lens. ~ **a contatto** contact lens; **mettersi le lenti a contatto** put in one's contact lenses. **~ a contatto morbida** soft lens. **~ a contatto rigida** hard lens. **~ d'ingrandimento** magnifying glass. **~ semi-rigida** gas-permeable lens

len'tezza nf slowness

len'ticchia nf lentil

len'tiggine nf freckle

'lento a slow; (allentato) slack; ‹abito› loose

'lenza nf fishing-line

len'zuolo nm sheet; **le lenzuola** the sheets. **~ con gli angoli** fitted sheet. **~ funebre** shroud

leon'cino nm lion cub

le'one nm lion; Astr Leo. **~ marino** sea lion

leo'nessa nf lioness

leo'pardo nm leopard

lepo'rino a **labbro ~** hare-lip

'lepre nf hare

le'protto nm leveret

'lercio a filthy

lerci'ume nm filth

'lesbica nf lesbian

'lesbico a lesbian

lesi'nare vt grudge ● vi be stingy

lesio'nare vt damage

lesi'one nf lesion; (danno) damage. **~ cerebrale** brain damage. **~ interna** internal injury. **lesioni** pl **personali** grievous bodily harm, GBH

'leso pp di **ledere** ● a injured; **lesa maestà** high treason

les'sare vt boil

lessi'cale a lexical

'lessico nm vocabulary

lessicogra'fia nf lexicography

lessi'cografo, -a nmf lexicographer

'lesso a boiled ● nm boiled meat

'lesto a quick; ‹mente› sharp. **~ di mano** light-fingered

le'tale a lethal

leta'maio nm dunghill; fig pigsty

le'tame nm dung

le'targico a lethargic

le'targo nm lethargy; (di animali) hibernation

le'tizia nf joy

'lettera nf letter; **alla ~** literally; **eseguire qcsa alla ~** carry out sth to the letter; **lettere** pl (letteratura) literature sg; Univ Arts; **dottore in lettere** BA, Bachelor of Arts. **~ d'accompagnamento** covering letter. **~ d'amore** love letter. **~ assicurata** registered letter. **~ di cambio** bill of exchange. **~ di credito** letter of credit. **~ maiuscola** capital [letter]. **~ minuscola** small letter. **~ di presentazione** letter of introduction. **~ raccomandata** recorded delivery letter. **~ di scuse** letter of apology. **~ di trasporto aereo** air waybill

lette'rale a literal

letteral'mente adv literally

lette'rario a literary

lette'rato a well-read ● nm scholar; **letterati** pl literati

lettera'tura nf literature

letti'era nf (per gatto) litter

let'tiga nf stretcher

let'tino nm cot; Med couch. **~ [pieghevole]** camp bed

'letto nm bed; **andare a ~** go to bed; **[ri]fare il ~** make the bed. **~ a castello** bunkbed. **~ di fiume** river bed. **letti** pl **gemelli** twin beds. **~ matrimoniale** double bed. **~ a una piazza** single bed. **~ a due piazze** double bed. **~ singolo** single bed

Let'tonia nf Latvia

letto'rato nm (corso) tutorial

let'tore, -'trice nmf reader; Univ language assistant ● nm Comput disk drive. **~ di CD** CD player, CD system. **~ [di] CD-ROM** CD-Rom drive. **~ di codice a barre** barcode reader, scanner. **~ di compact disc** compact disc player. **~ di disco** disk drive. **~ di floppy** floppy [disk] drive

let'tura nf reading

leuce'mia nf leukaemia

'leva nf lever; Mil call-up; **nuove leve** pl new blood, young blood; **far ~** lever. **~ del cambio** gear lever. **~ di comando** control lever

le'vante nm East; (vento) east wind

leva'punti nm inv staple remover

le'vare vt (alzare) raise; (togliere) take away; (rimuovere) take off; (estrarre) pull out; lift, abolish ‹divieto, tassa›; **~ di mezzo** qcsa get sth out of the way

le'varsi vr move (da away from); ‹vento:› get up; ‹sole:› rise; **~ di mezzo** get out of the way

le'vata nf rising; (di posta) collection

leva'taccia nf **fare una ~** get up at the crack of dawn

leva'toio a **ponte ~** drawbridge

leva'trice nf midwife

leva'tura nf intelligence

levi'gare vt smooth; (con carta vetro) rub down

levi'gato a ‹superficie› polished; ‹pelle› smooth

leviga'trice nf sander

levi'tare vi levitate

levitazi'one nf levitation

Le'vitico nm Leviticus

levri'ero nm greyhound. **~ afgano** Afghan hound

lezi'one nf lesson; Univ lecture; (rimprovero) rebuke. **~ di guida** driving lesson. **~ di italiano** Italian lesson, Italian class

lezi'oso a ‹stile, modi› affected

'lezzo nm stench

li pers pron mpl them

lì adv there; **fin lì** as far as there; **giù di lì** thereabouts; **lì per lì** there and then; **la cosa è finita lì** that was the end of it

li'ana nf liana

liba'nese a & nmf Lebanese

Li'bano nm Lebanon

'libbra nf (peso) pound

li'beccio nm south-west wind

li'bello nm libel

li'bellula nf dragon-fly

libe'rale a liberal; (generoso) generous ● nmf liberal

libera'lismo nm ~ [economico] economic liberalism

liberalità nf generosity

liberal'mente adv liberally

libe'rare vt free; release ⟨prigioniero⟩; vacate ⟨stanza⟩; (salvare) rescue

libe'rarsi vr ⟨stanza:⟩ become vacant; Teleph become free; (da impegno) get out of it; ~ **di** get rid of

libera'tore, -'trice a liberating ● nmf liberator

libera'torio a liberating; **pagamento ~** full and final payment

liberazi'one nf liberation; **la** L~ (ricorrenza) Liberation Day. ~ **della donna** women's liberation, women's lib

libe'rismo nm free trade

'libero a free; ⟨strada⟩ clear; ~ **come l'aria** free as a bird. ~ **arbitrio** nm free will. ~ **docente** nm qualified university lecturer. ~ **professionista** nm self-employed person

libertà nf freedom; (di prigioniero) release; ~ pl (confidenze) liberties; **prendersi la ~ di fare qcsa** take the liberty of doing sth. ~ **di espressione** freedom of speech. ~ **di pensiero** freedom of thought. ~ **provvisoria** Jur bail. ~ **di stampa** freedom of the press. ~ **vigilata** probation

liber'tino, -a a dissolute, libertine ● nmf libertine

'liberty nm & a inv Art Nouveau

'Libia nf Libya

'libico, -a a & nmf Libyan

li'bidine nf lust

libidi'noso a lustful

li'bido nf libido

libra'io nm bookseller

libre'ria nf (biblioteca) library; (negozio) bookshop; (mobile) bookcase

li'bretto nm booklet; Mus libretto. ~ **degli assegni** cheque book. ~ **di circolazione** logbook. ~ **d'istruzioni** instruction booklet. ~ **di risparmio** savings account; (documento) passbook, savings book. ~ **universitario** book held by students which records details of their exam performances

'libro nm book. ~ **bianco** White Paper. ~ **dei canti** hymn-book. ~ **contabile** account book. ~ **di esercizi** workbook. ~ **di fumetti** comic book. ~ **giallo** crime novel. ~ **mastro** Comm ledger. ~ **paga** payroll. ~ **di ricette** cookbook, recipe book. **libri** pl **sociali** company's books. ~ **tascabile** paperback. ~ **di testo** course book

li'cantropo nm werewolf

lice'ale nmf secondary-school student ● a secondary-school attrib

li'cenza nf licence; (permesso) permission; Mil leave; Sch school-leaving certificate; **essere in ~** be on leave. ~ **di caccia** hunting licence. ~ **di esportazione** export licence. ~ **matrimoniale** marriage licence. ~

di pesca fishing licence. ~ **poetica** poetic licence. ~ **di porto d'armi** gun licence

licenzia'mento nm dismissal

licenzi'are vt dismiss, sack fam; (conferire un diploma) grant a school-leaving certificate to

licenzi'arsi vr (da un impiego) resign; (accomiatarsi) take one's leave

licenzi'oso a licentious

li'ceo nm secondary school, high school. ~ **classico** secondary school with an emphasis on humanities. ~ **scientifico** secondary school with an emphasis on sciences

li'chene nm lichen

'lido nm beach

'Liechtenstein nm Liechtenstein

lieta'mente adv happily

li'eto a glad; ⟨evento⟩ happy; **molto ~!** pleased to meet you!

li'eve a light; (debole) faint; (trascurabile) slight

lievi'tare vi rise ● vt leaven

li'evito nm yeast. ~ **in polvere** baking powder

lift nm inv liftboy

'lifting nm inv face-lift

'ligio a essere ~ **al dovere** have a sense of duty

li'gnaggio nm lineage

'ligneo a wooden

'lilla nf Bot lilac ● nm (colore) lilac

'lima nf file

limacci'oso a slimy

li'manda nf dab

li'mare vt file

lima'tura nf (atto) filing; (residui) filings pl

'limbo nm limbo

li'metta nf ~ **[da unghie]** nail file; (di carta) emery board

limi'tare nm threshold ● vt limit

limi'tarsi vr ~ **a fare qcsa** restrict oneself to doing sth; ~ **in qcsa** cut down on sth

limitata'mente adv to a limited extent

limita'tivo a limiting

limi'tato a limited

limitazi'one nf limitation

'limite a ⟨caso⟩ extreme ● nm limit; (confine) boundary; **entro certi limiti** within certain limits. ~ **di credito** credit limit, credit ceiling. ~ **di sopportazione** breaking point. '~ **di sosta** 'restricted parking'. ~ **di tempo** time limit. ~ **di velocità** speed limit; **rispettare il ~** ~ ~ keep to the speed limit

li'mitrofo a neighbouring

'limo nm slime

limo'nata nf (bibita) lemonade; (succo) lemon juice. ~ **amara** bitter lemon

li'mone nm lemon; (albero) lemon tree

'limpido a clear; ⟨occhi⟩ limpid

'lince nf lynx

linci'are vt lynch

'lindo a neat; (pulito) clean

'linea nf line; (di autobus, aereo) route; (di metro) line; (di abito) cut; (di auto, mobile) design; (fisico) figure; **in ~ d'aria** as the crow flies; **è caduta la ~** I've been cut off; **in ~ di massima** as a rule; **a grandi linee** in outline; **mantenere la ~** keep one's figure; **in ~** *Comput* on-line; **in prima ~** in the front line; **mettersi in ~** line up; **nave di ~** liner; **volo di ~** scheduled flight. **~ aerea** airline. **~ d'arrivo** *Sport* finishing line. **~ commutata** *Teleph* switched line. **~ di confine** boundary. **~ continua** unbroken line. **~ dedicata** dedicated line. **~ di demarcazione** border line. **~ ferroviaria** railway line. **~ di fondo** baseline. **~ d'immersione** water line. **~ laterale** *Sport* touch line. **linee** *pl* **della mano** lines of the hand. **~ di marea** tidemark. **~ mediana** *Sport* halfway line. **~ di partenza** *Sport* starting line. **~ principale** *Rail* main line. **~ punteggiata** dotted line. **~ secondaria** *Rail* branch line. **~ di tiro** line of fire. **~ tratteggiata** broken line

linea'menti *nmpl* features

line'are *a* linear; ⟨*discorso*⟩ to the point; ⟨*ragionamento*⟩ consistent

line'etta *nf* (*tratto lungo*) dash; (*d'unione*) hyphen

'linfa *nf Anat* lymph; *Bot* sap. **~ vitale** *fig* life blood

lin'fatico *a Anat* lymphatic

linfoghi'andola *nf* lymph gland

linfo'nodo *nm* lymph node

linge'rie *nf* lingerie

lin'gotto *nm* ingot

'lingua *nf* tongue; (*linguaggio*) language; **avere la ~ lunga** *fig* have a big mouth. **~ moderna** modern language. **~ morta** dead language. **~ straniera** foreign language

lingu'accia *nf* (*persona*) backbiter; **fare le linguacce** put one's tongue out (**a** at)

lingu'aggio *nm* language. **~ infantile** babytalk. **~ dei segni** sign language

lingu'etta *nf* (*di scarpa*) tongue; (*di strumento*) reed; (*di busta*) flap; *Mus* reed; (*per tirare*) tab

lingu'ista *nmf* linguist

lingu'istica *nf* linguistics

lingu'istico *a* linguistic

'lino *nm Bot* (*tessuto*) linen

li'noleum *nm* linoleum

liofiliz'zare *vt* freeze-dry

liofiliz'zato *a* freeze dried

li'pide *nm* lipid

liposuzi'one *nf* liposuction

li'quame *nm* slurry

lique'fare *vt* liquefy; (*sciogliere*) melt

lique'farsi *vr* liquefy; (*sciogliersi*) melt

liqui'dare *vt* liquidate; settle ⟨*conto*⟩; pay off ⟨*debiti*⟩; clear ⟨*merce*⟩; (*fam: uccidere*) get rid of

liquida'tore *nm* liquidator

liquidazi'one *nf* liquidation; (*di conti*) settling; (*di merce*) clearance sale. **~ totale** [**per cessata attività**] closing-down sale

'liquido *a & nm* liquid. **~ dei freni** brake fluid. **~ scongelante** *Auto* de-icer. **~ tergicristallo** screen wash

liqui'gas® *nm inv* Calor gas®

liqui'rizia *nf* liquorice

li'quore *nm* liqueur; **liquori** *pl* (*bevande alcooliche*) liquors

'lira *nf* lira; *Mus* lyre. **~ sterlina** pound sterling

'lirico, -a *a* lyrical; ⟨*poesia*⟩ lyric; ⟨*cantante, musica*⟩ opera *attrib* ● *nf* lyric poetry; *Mus* opera

li'rismo *nm* lyricism

'lisca *nf* fishbone; **avere la ~** (*fam: nel parlare*) have a lisp

lisci'are *vt* smooth; (*accarezzare*) stroke

'liscio *a* smooth; ⟨*capelli*⟩ straight; ⟨*liquore*⟩ neat, straight; ⟨*acqua minerale*⟩ still; **passarla liscia** get away with it

li'seuse *nf inv* bed jacket, liseuse

'liso *a* worn [out]

'lista *nf* list; (*striscia*) strip; **fare una ~** make out a list. **~ di attesa** waiting list; **in ~ ~** on the waiting list; *Aeron* on stand-by. **~ elettorale** list of candidates. **~ degli invitati** guest list. **~ nera** blacklist. **~ di nozze** wedding list. **~ della spesa** shopping list. **~ dei vini** wine list

li'stare *vt* edge; *Comput* list

li'stino *nm* list. **~ di borsa** Stock-Exchange list. **~ dei cambi** exchange rates *pl*. **~ [dei] prezzi** price list

Lit. *abbr* (**lire italiane**) Italian lire

lita'nia *nf* litany

'litchi *nm inv* lychee

'lite *nf* quarrel; (*baruffa*) row; *Jur* lawsuit

liti'gante *nmf Jur* litigant

liti'gare *vi* quarrel; *Jur* litigate

li'tigio *nm* quarrel

litigi'oso *a* quarrelsome

'litio *nm* lithium

litogra'fia *nf* (*procedimento*) lithography; (*stampa*) lithograph

li'tografo, -a *nmf* lithographer

lito'rale *a* coastal ● *nm* coast

lito'raneo *a* coastal

'litro *nm* litre

Litu'ania *nf* Lithuania

litu'ano, -a *a & nmf* Lithuanian

litur'gia *nf* liturgy

li'turgico *a* liturgical

li'uto *nm* lute

li'vella *nf* level. **~ a bolla d'aria** spirit level

livella'mento *nm* levelling out, levelling off

livel'lare *vt* level

livel'larsi *vr* level out

livella'tore *a* levelling

livella'trice *nf* bulldozer

li'vello *nm* level; **passaggio a ~** level crossing; **sotto/sul ~ del mare** below/above sea level; **ad alto ~** ⟨*conferenza, trattative*⟩ toplevel, high-level; **a più livelli** multilevel. **~ di guardia** danger level. **~ di magazzino** stock level. **~ occupazionale** level of employment

'livido *a* livid; (*per il freddo*) blue; (*per una botta*) black and blue; **~ di rabbia** livid ● *nm* bruise

li'vore *nm* spite

Li'vorno *nf* Leghorn

li'vrea *nf* livery

'lizza *nf* lists *pl*; **essere in ~ per qcsa** be in the running for sth

lo *def art m* (*before s + consonant, gn, ps, z*) the; *vedi* **il ●** *pron* (*riferito a persona*) him; (*riferito a cosa*) it; **non lo so** I don't know

'lobbia *nf* Homburg [hat]

lob'bista *nmf* lobbyist

'lobby *nf inv* lobby

lo'belia *nf* lobelia

'lobo *nm* lobe

loboto'mia *nf* lobotomy

lo'cale *a* local **●** *nm* (*stanza*) room; (*treno*) local train; **locali** *pl* (*edifici*) premises. **~ notturno** night-club

località *nf* locality. **~ balneare** seaside resort. **~ turistica** tourist resort. **~ di villeggiatura** holiday resort

localiz'zare *vt* localize; (*reperire*) locate

localiz'zarsi *vr* **~ in** be located in

localiz'zato *a* localized

localizzazi'one *nf* localization; (*reperimento*) location

local'mente *adv* locally

lo'canda *nf* inn

locandi'ere, -a *nmf* innkeeper

locan'dina *nf* bill, poster

loca'tario, -a *nmf* tenant. **~ residente** sitting tenant

loca'tivo *a Gram* locative; *Jur* rental

loca|'tore, -'trice *nm* landlord **●** *nf* landlady

locazi'one *nf* tenancy

locomo'tiva *nf* locomotive. **~ a vapore** steam engine

locomo'tore *nm* locomotive, engine

locomozi'one *nf* locomotion; **mezzi di ~** means of transport

'loculo *nm* burial niche

lo'custa *nf* locust

locuzi'one *nf* expression

lo'dare *vt* praise

'lode *nf* praise; **degno di ~** praiseworthy; **laurea con ~** first-class degree

'loden *nm inv* (*cappotto*) loden [coat]; (*stoffa*) loden

lo'devole *a* praiseworthy

'lodola *nf* lark

loga'ritmo *nm* logarithm

'loggia *nf* loggia; (*massonica*) lodge

loggi'one *nm* gallery, gods *pl*

'logica *nf* logic

logica'mente *adv* (*in modo logico*) logically; (*ovviamente*) of course

logicità *nf* logic

'logico *a* logical

lo'gistica *nf* logistics

lo'gistico *a* logistic[al]

'logo *nm inv* logo

logope'dia *nf* speech therapy

logope'dista *nmf* speech therapist

logo'rante *a* (*attesa, esperienza*) wearing

logo'rare *vt* wear out; (*sciupare*) waste

logo'rarsi *vr* wear out; (*persona:*) wear oneself out

logo'rio *nm* wear and tear; (*stress*) stress

'logoro *a* worn-out

logor'roico *a* loquacious

lom'baggine *nf* lumbago

Lombar'dia *nf* Lombardy

lom'bardo *a* Lombardy *attrib*

lom'bare *a* lumbar

lom'bata *nf* loin. **~ di manzo** sirloin

'lombo *nm Anat* loin

lom'brico *nm* earthworm

londi'nese *a* London *attrib* **●** *nmf* Londoner

'Londra *nf* London

long-'drink *nm inv* long drink

longevità *nf* longevity

lon'gevo *a* long-lived

longhe'rone *nm* strut

longi'lineo *a* rangy

longitudi'nale *a* lengthwise

longitudinal'mente *adv* lengthwise

longi'tudine *nf* longitude

long 'playing *nm inv* LP, long-playing record

lontana'mente *adv* distantly; (*vagamente*) vaguely; **neanche ~** not for a moment

lonta'nanza *nf* distance; (*separazione*) separation; **in ~** in the distance

lon'tano *a* far; (*distante*) distant; (*nel tempo*) far-off, distant; (*parente*) distant; (*vago*) vague; (*assente*) absent; **più ~** further; **è ~ un paio di chilometri** it is a couple of kilometres away **●** *adv* far [away]; **da ~** from a distance; **tenersi ~ da** keep away from; **andare ~** (*allontanarsi*) go away; (*avere successo*) go far

'lontra *nf* otter

'lonza *nf* (*lombata*) loin

lo'quace *a* talkative

'lordo *a* dirty; (*somma, peso*) gross; **al ~ di imposte** pre-tax

'loro[1] *pers pron pl* (*soggetto*) they; (*oggetto*) them; (*forma di cortesia*) you; **sta a ~** it is up to them

'loro[2] (**il ~** *m*, **la ~** *f*, **i ~** *mpl*, **le ~** *fpl*) *poss a* their; (*forma di cortesia*) your; **un ~ amico** a friend of theirs; (*forma di cortesia*) a friend of yours **●** *poss pron* theirs; (*forma di cortesia*) yours; **i ~** (*famiglia*) their folk

lo'sanga *nf* lozenge; **a losanghe** diamond-shaped

losca'mente *adv* suspiciously

'losco *a* suspicious

'loto *nm* lotus

'lotta *nf* fight, struggle; (*contrasto*) conflict; *Sport* wrestling. **~ di classe** class struggle. **~ libera** all-in wrestling

lot'tare *vi* fight, struggle; *Sport, fig* wrestle

lotta|'tore, -'trice *nmf* wrestler

lotte'ria *nf* lottery

lottiz'zare *vt* divide up (*terreno*); *fig* parcel out

lottizzazi'one *nf* (*di terreno*) division into lots; *fig* parcelling out

'lotto *nm* [state] lottery; (*porzione*) lot; (*di terreno*) plot

lozi'one *nf* lotion. **~ idratante** moisturizer. **~ solare** suntan lotion

lubrifi'cante *a* lubricating ● *nm* lubricant
lubrifi'care *vt* lubricate
luc'chetto *nm* padlock
lucci'cante *a* sparkling
lucci'care *vi* sparkle
lucci'chio *nm* sparkle
lucci'cone *nm* **far venire i lucciconi** bring tears to the eyes
'luccio *nm* pike
'lucciola *nf* glow-worm; ⟨*prostituta*⟩ lady of the night
'luce *nf* light; *Auto* highlight; **accendere/ spegnere la ~** switch the light on/off; **far ~ su** *fig* shed light on; **dare alla ~** give birth to; **venire alla ~** come to light. **luci** *pl* **di arresto** *Auto* stop lights. **luci** *pl* **d'atterraggio** landing lights. **luci** *pl* **d'emergenza** *Auto* hazard [warning] lights, hazards. **~ della luna** moonlight. **luci** *pl* **di posizione** *Auto* sidelights. **luci** *pl* **posteriori** *Auto* rear-lights. **luci** *pl* **di retromarcia** *Auto* reversing lights. **~ del sole** sunlight. **~ stroboscopica** strobe
lu'cente *a* shining
lucen'tezza *nf* shine
lucer'nario *nm* skylight
lu'certola *nf* lizard
lucida'labbra *nm inv* lip gloss
luci'dare *vt* polish
lucida'trice *nf* [floor-]polisher
'lucido *a* shiny; ⟨*pavimento, scarpe*⟩ polished; ⟨*chiaro*⟩ clear; ⟨*persona, mente*⟩ lucid; ⟨*occhi*⟩ watery ● *nm* shine. **~ [da scarpe]** [shoe] polish
lucra'tivo *a* lucrative
'lucro *nm* lucre; **senza fini di ~** non-profit-making, not-for-profit *Am*
luculli'ano *a* ⟨*pranzo*⟩ lavish
ludo'teca *nf* playroom
'luglio *nm* July
'lugubre *a* gloomy
'lui *pers pron* ⟨*soggetto*⟩ he; ⟨*oggetto, con prep*⟩ him; **lo ha fatto ~ stesso** he did it himself
lu'maca *nf* ⟨*mollusco*⟩ snail; *fig* slowcoach
'lume *nm* lamp; ⟨*luce*⟩ light; **a ~ di candela** by candlelight; **perdere il ~ della ragione** be beside oneself with rage
lumi'nare *nmf* luminary
lumi'narie *nfpl* illuminations
lumine'scente *a* luminescent
lumine'scenza *nf* luminescence
lu'mino *nm* **~ da notte** nightlight
luminosa'mente *adv* luminously
luminosità *nf* brightness
lumi'noso *a* luminous; ⟨*stanza, cielo ecc*⟩ bright; **idea luminosa** brain wave
'luna *nf* moon; **chiaro di ~** moonlight; **avere la ~ storta** be in a bad mood. **~ di miele** honeymoon. **~ piena** full moon
'luna park *nm inv* fairground
lu'nare *a* lunar
lu'naria *nf* moonstone
lu'nario *nm* almanac; **sbarcare il ~** make

[both] ends meet
lu'natico *a* moody
lunedì *nm inv* Monday; **di ~** on Mondays
lu'netta *nf* half-moon [shape]
lun'gaggine *nf* slowness
lunga'mente *adv* at great length
lun'ghezza *nf* length; **di ~ media** medium-length. **~ d'onda** wavelength
'lungi *adv* ero [ben] **~ dall'immaginare che...** I never dreamt for a moment that...
lungimi'rante *a* far-seeing
lungimi'ranza *nf* far-sightedness
'lungo *a* long; ⟨*diluito*⟩ weak; ⟨*lento*⟩ slow; **a ~ andare** in the long run; **saperla lunga** be shrewd ● *nm* length; **andare per le lunghe** drag on; **di gran lunga** by far ● *prep* ⟨*durante*⟩ throughout; ⟨*per la lunghezza di*⟩ along
lungofi'ume *nm* riverside
lungo'lago *nm* lakeside
lungo'mare *nm inv* sea front
lungome'traggio *nm* feature film
lu'notto *nm* rear window. **~ termico** heated rear window
'lunula *nf* half-moon
lu'ogo *nm* place; ⟨*punto preciso*⟩ spot; ⟨*passo d'autore*⟩ passage; **aver ~** take place; **dar ~ a** give rise to; **fuori ~** out of place; **del ~** ⟨*usanze*⟩ local. **~ comune** cliché. **~ di nascita** birth-place. **~ natale** birthplace. **~ pubblico** public place. **~ di villeggiatura** holiday resort
luogote'nente *nm Mil* lieutenant
'lupa *nf* she-wolf
lu'para *nf* sawn-off shotgun
lu'petto *nm* Cub [Scout]
'lupo *nm* wolf. **~ mannaro** werewolf
'luppolo *nm* hop
'lurido *a* filthy
luri'dume *nm* filth
lu'singa *nf* flattery
lusin'gare *vt* flatter
lusin'garsi *vr* flatter oneself; ⟨*illudersi*⟩ fool oneself
lusinghi'ero *a* flattering
lus'sare *vt* dislocate
lus'sarsi *vr* dislocate
lussazi'one *nf* dislocation
Lussem'burgo *nm* Luxembourg
'lusso *nm* luxury; **di ~** luxury *attrib*
lussuosa'mente *adv* luxuriously
lussu'oso *a* luxurious
lussureggi'ante *a* luxuriant
lus'suria *nf* lust
lussuri'oso *a* dissolute
lu'strare *vt* polish
lu'strino *nm* sequin
'lustro *a* shiny ● *nm* sheen; *fig* prestige; ⟨*quinquennio*⟩ five-year period
lute'rano *a & nmf* Lutheran
'lutto *nm* mourning; **parato a ~** draped in black; **~ stretto** deep mourning
luttu'oso *a* mournful

Mm

m *abbr* ⟨**metro**⟩ m
ma *conj* but; ⟨*eppure*⟩ yet; **ma!** ⟨*dubbio*⟩ I don't know; ⟨*indignazione*⟩ really!; **ma davvero?** really?; **ma va?** really?; **ma sì!** why not!; ⟨*certo che sì*⟩ of course!
'**macabro** *a* macabre
macché *int* of course not!
macche'roni *nmpl* macaroni *sg*
macche'ronico *a* ⟨*italiano*⟩ broken
'**macchia**[1] *nf* stain; ⟨*di diverso colore*⟩ spot; ⟨*piccola*⟩ speck; **senza ~** spotless; **spargersi a ~ d'olio** spread rapidly. **~ di colore** splash of colour. **~ d'inchiostro** ink stain. **~ di sangue** bloodstain
'**macchia**[2] *nf* ⟨*boscaglia*⟩ scrub; **darsi alla ~** take to the woods
macchi'are *vt* stain
macchi'arsi *vr* stain
macchi'ato *a* ⟨*caffè*⟩ with a dash of milk; ⟨*pelo*⟩ spotted; **~ di** ⟨*sporco*⟩ stained with; **~ d'inchiostro** ink-stained, inky. ● *nm* ⟨*caffè*⟩ espresso with a dash of milk
macchi'etta *nf* spot
'**macchina** *nf* machine; ⟨*motore*⟩ engine; ⟨*automobile*⟩ car; **in ~** by car; **giro in ~** drive; **cimitero delle macchine** scrapyard. **~ del caffè** coffee-maker. **~ da cucire** sewing machine. **~ per l'espresso** coffee machine. **~ fotografica** camera. **~ obliteratrice** ticket-stamping machine. **~ da presa** cine camera. **~ da scrivere** typewriter. **~ sverniciante** paint stripper. **~ utensile** machine tool. **~ della verità** lie detector
macchinal'mente *adv* mechanically
macchi'nare *vt* plot
macchi'nario *nm* machinery
macchinazi'oni *nfpl* machinations, scheming
macchi'netta *nf* ⟨*per i denti*⟩ brace; ⟨*per il caffè*⟩ espresso coffee maker; ⟨*accendino*⟩ lighter
macchi'nista *nm Rail* engine driver; *Naut* engineer; *Theat* stagehand
macchi'noso *a* complicated
Mace'donia *nf* Macedonia
mace'donia *nf* fruit salad
macel'laio *nm* butcher
macel'lare *vt* slaughter
macellazi'one *nf* slaughtering
macelle'ria *nf* butcher's [shop]
ma'cello *nm* ⟨*mattatoio*⟩ slaughterhouse; *fig* shambles *sg*; **andare al ~** *fig* go to the slaughter; **mandare al ~** *fig* send to his/her death
mace'rare *vt* macerate; *fig* distress

mace'rarsi *vr* be consumed
macerazi'one *nf* maceration
ma'cerie *nfpl* rubble *sg*; ⟨*rottami*⟩ debris *sg*
'**macero** *nm* pulping; ⟨*stabilimento*⟩ pulping mill
Mach *nm inv* Mach
ma'chete *nm inv* machete
machia'vellico *a* Machiavellian
ma'chismo *nm* machismo
'**macho** *a* macho
ma'cigno *nm* boulder
maci'lento *a* emaciated
'**macina** *nf* millstone
macinacaffè *nm inv* coffee mill
macina'pepe *nm inv* pepper mill
maci'nare *vt* mill
maci'nato *a* ground ● *nm* ⟨*carne*⟩ mince
maci'nino *nm* mill; ⟨*hum: macchina*⟩ old banger
maciul'lare *vt* ⟨*stritolare*⟩ crush
'**macro** *nf inv Comput* macro
macrobi'otica *nf* **negozio di ~** health-food shop
macrobi'otico *a* macrobiotic
macro'clima *nm* macroclimate
macro'cosmo *nm* macrocosm
macrofotogra'fia *nf* macrophotography
macro'scopico *a* macroscopic
macu'lato *a* spotted
Madaga'scar *nm* Madagascar
madami'gella *nf* young lady
'**madia** *nf* cupboard with a covered trough on top for making bread
'**madido** *a* **~ di** damp with ⟨*sudore*⟩
Ma'donna *nf* Our Lady
'**madre** *nf* mother
madre'lingua *a inv* **inglese ~** English native speaker
madre'patria *nf* native land
madre'perla *nf* mother-of-pearl
ma'drepora *nf* madrepore
madri'gale *nm* madrigal
ma'drina *nf* godmother
maestà *nf* majesty
maestosa'mente *adv* majestically
maestosità *nf* majesty
mae'stoso *a* majestic
ma'estra *nf* teacher; *Sch* primary school teacher. **~ d'asilo** kindergarten teacher. **~ di canto** singing teacher. **~ di piano** piano teacher. **~ di sci** ski instructor
mae'strale *nm* northwest wind
mae'stranza *nf* workers *pl*
mae'stria *nf* mastery

ma'estro *nm* teacher; *Sch* primary school teacher; *Mus* maestro; (*esperto*) master. **colpo da ~** masterstroke. **~ d'asilo** kindergarten teacher. **~ di canto** singing teacher. **~ di cerimonie** master of ceremonies. **~ di piano** piano teacher. **~ di sci** ski instructor ● *a* (*principale*) main; (*di grande abilità*) skilful

'mafia *nf* Mafia

mafi'oso *a* of the Mafia ● *nm* member of the Mafia, Mafioso

'maga *nf* sorceress, magician

ma'gagna *nf* fault

ma'gari *adv* (*forse*) maybe ● *int* I wish! ● *conj* (*per esprimere desiderio*) if only; (*anche se*) even if

magazzini'ere *nm* storeman, warehouseman

magaz'zino *nm* warehouse; (*emporio*) shop; **grande ~** department store. **magazzini** *pl* **portuali** naval stores

Magg. *abbr* (**maggiore**) Maj

mag'gese *nm* field lying fallow

'maggio *nm* May

maggio'lino *nm* May bug

maggio'rana *nf* marjoram

maggio'ranza *nf* majority

maggio'rare *vt* increase

maggior'domo *nm* butler

maggi'ore *a* (*di dimensioni, numero*) bigger, larger; (*superlativo*) biggest, largest; (*di età*) older; (*superlativo*) oldest; (*di importanza, Mus*) major; (*superlativo*) greatest; **la maggior parte di** most; **la maggior parte del tempo** most of the time ● *pron* (*di dimensioni*) the bigger, the larger; (*superlativo*) the biggest, the largest; (*di età*) the older; (*superlativo*) the oldest; (*di importanza*) the major; (*superlativo*) the greatest ● *nm Mil* major; *Aeron* squadron leader

maggio'renne *a* of age ● *nmf* adult

maggiori'tario *a* (*della maggioranza*) majority; ⟨*sistema*⟩ first-past-the-post *attrib*

maggior'mente *adv* [all] the more; (*più di tutto*) most

'Magi *nmpl* **i re ~** the Magi

ma'gia *nf* magic; (*trucco*) magic trick

magica'mente *adv* magically

'magico *a* magic

magi'stero *nm* (*insegnamento*) teaching; (*maestria*) skill; **facoltà di ~** arts faculty

magi'strale *a* masterly; **istituto ~** teacher-training college

magistral'mente *adv* in a masterly fashion

magi'strato *nm* magistrate

magistra'tura *nf* magistrature. **la ~** the Bench

'maglia *nf* stitch; (*lavoro ai ferri*) knitting; (*tessuto*) jersey; (*di rete*) mesh; (*di catena*) link; (*indumento*) vest; **fare la ~** knit. **~ diritta** knit. **~ rosa** (*ciclismo*) ≈ yellow jersey. **~ rovescia** purl

magli'aia *nf* knitter

maglie'ria *nf* knitwear

magli'etta *nf* **~** [**a maniche corte**] tee-shirt

magli'ficio *nm* knitwear factory

ma'glina *nf* (*tessuto*) jersey

'maglio *nm* mallet

magli'one *nm* sweater, jumper. **~ dolcevita** polo neck [jumper]. **~ a girocollo** crew neck [sweater]. **~ a V** V-neck [sweater]

'magma *nm* magma

ma'gnaccia *nm inv fam* pimp

ma'gnanimo *a* magnanimous

ma'gnate *nm* magnate

ma'gnesia *nf* magnesia

ma'gnesio *nm* magnesium

ma'gnete *nm* magnet

magnetica'mente *adv* magnetically

ma'gnetico *a* magnetic

magne'tismo *nm* magnetism

magne'tofono *nm* tape recorder

magnifica'mente *adv* magnificently

magnifi'cenza *nf* magnificence; (*generosità*) munificence

ma'gnifico *a* magnificent; (*generoso*) munificent

magni'tudine *nf Astr* magnitude

'magno *a* **aula magna** main hall

ma'gnolia *nf* magnolia

'magnum *nm inv* (*bottiglia*) magnum ● *nf inv* (*pistola*) magnum

'mago *nm* magician

ma'gone *nm* **avere il ~** be down; **mi è venuto il ~** I've got a lump in my throat

'magra *nf* low water

ma'grezza *nf* thinness

'magro *a* thin; ⟨*carne*⟩ lean; (*scarso*) meagre; **magra consolazione** cold comfort

'mai *adv* never; (*inter, talvolta*) ever; **caso ~** if anything; **caso ~ tornasse** in case he comes back; **come ~?** why?; **cosa ~?** what on earth?; **~ più** never again; **più che ~** more than ever; **quando ~?** whenever?; **quasi ~** hardly ever

mai'ale *nm* pig; (*carne*) pork. **~ arrosto** roast pork

maia'lino *nm* piglet

mai'olica *nf* majolica

maio'nese *nf* mayonnaise

'mais *nm* maize

mai'uscola *nf* capital [letter]

mai'uscolo *a* capital

mai'zena[R] *nf* cornflour

mal *vedi* **male**

'mala *nf sl* **la ~** the underworld

malac'corto *a* unwise

mala'fede *nf* bad faith

malaf'fare *nm* **gente di ~** shady characters *pl*

mala'lingua *nf* backbiter

mala'mente *adv* ⟨*ridotto*⟩ badly; ⟨*rispondere*⟩ rudely

malan'dato *a* in bad shape; (*di salute*) in poor health

ma'lanimo *nm* ill will

ma'lanno *nm* misfortune; (*malattia*) illness; **prendersi un ~** catch something

mala'pena *adv* **a ~** hardly
ma'laria *nf* malaria
mala'ticcio *a* sickly
ma'lato, -a *a* ill, sick; ⟨*pianta*⟩ diseased ● *nmf* sick person. **~ di mente** mentally ill person
malat'tia *nf* disease, illness; **ho preso due giorni di ~** I had two days off sick; **essere in ~** be on sick leave. **~ nervosa** nervous disease. **~ venerea** venereal disease, VD
malaugurata'mente *adv* unfortunately
malaugu'rato *a* ill-omened
malau'gurio *nm* bad *o* ill omen
mala'vita *nf* underworld
malavi'toso, -a *nmf* gangster
mala'voglia *nf* unwillingness; **di ~** unwillingly
malcapi'tato *a* wretched
malce'lato *a* ill-concealed
mal'concio *a* battered
malcon'tento *nm* discontent
malco'stume *nm* immorality
mal'destro *a* awkward; (*inesperto*) inexperienced
maldi'cente *a* slanderous
maldi'cenza *nf* slander
maldi'sposto *a* ill-disposed
'male *adv* badly; **funzionare ~** not work properly; **star ~** be ill; **star ~ a qcno** ⟨*vestito ecc.*⟩ not suit sb; **rimanerci ~** be hurt; **ho dormito ~** I didn't sleep well; **non c'è ~!** not bad at all! ● *nm* evil; (*dolore*) pain, ache; (*malattia*) illness; (*danno*) harm. **distinguere il bene dal ~** know right from wrong; **andare a ~** go off; **aver ~ a** have a pain in; **dove hai ~?** where does it hurt?, where is the pain?; **far ~ a qcno** (*provocare dolore*) hurt sb; ⟨*cibo:*⟩ be bad for sb; **le cipolle mi fanno ~** onions don't agree with me; **mi fa ~ la schiena** my back is hurting; **farsi ~ alla schiena** hurt one's back. **mal d'aereo** airsickness. **mal d'aria** airsickness; **soffrire il ~ ~** be airsick. **mal d'auto** carsickness. **mal di denti** toothache. **mal di gola** sore throat. **mal di mare** seasickness; **avere il ~ ~ ~** be seasick. **mal d'orecchi** earache. **mal di pancia** stomach-ache. **mal di testa** headache
maledetta'mente *adv* flipping
male'detto *a* cursed; (*orribile*) awful
male'dire *vt* curse
maledizi'one *nf* curse; **~!** damn!
maleducata'mente *adv* rudely
maledu'cato *a* ill-mannered
maleducazi'one *nf* rudeness
male'fatta *nf* misdeed
male'ficio *nm* witchcraft
ma'lefico *a* ⟨*azione*⟩ evil; (*nocivo*) harmful
maleodo'rante *a* foul-smelling
ma'lese *a & nmf* Malaysian
Ma'lesia *nf* Malaysia
ma'lessere *nm* indisposition; *fig* uneasiness
ma'levolo *a* malevolent
malfa'mato *a* of ill repute

mal'fatto *a* badly done; (*malformato*) ill-shaped
malfat'tore *nm* wrongdoer
mal'fermo *a* unsteady; ⟨*salute*⟩ poor
malfor'mato *a* misshapen
malformazi'one *nf* malformation
mal'gascio, -a *a & nmf* Malagasy
malgo'verno *nm* misgovernment
mal'grado *prep* in spite of ● *conj* although
'Mali *nm* Mali
ma'lia *nf* spell
maligna'mente *adv* maliciously
mali'gnare *vi* malign
malignità *nf* malice; *Med* malignancy
ma'ligno *a* malicious; (*perfido*) evil; *Med* malignant
malinco'nia *nf* melancholy
malinconica'mente *adv* melancholically
malin'conico *a* melancholy
malincu'ore: a ~ *adv* unwillingly, reluctantly
malinfor'mato *a* misinformed
malintenzio'nato, -a *nmf* miscreant
malin'teso *a* mistaken ● *nm* misunderstanding
ma'lizia *nf* malice; (*astuzia*) cunning; (*espediente*) trick
maliziosa'mente *adv* mischievously, naughtily
maliziosità *nf* naughtiness
malizi'oso *a* (*birichino*) mischievous, naughty
malle'abile *a* malleable
mal'leolo *nm Anat* malleolus
malleva'dore *nm* guarantor
'mallo *nm* husk
mal'loppo *nm fam* loot
malme'nare *vt* ill-treat
mal'messo *a* (*vestito male*) shabbily dressed; (*casa*) poorly furnished; (*fig: senza soldi*) hard up
malnu'trito *a* undernourished
malnutrizi'one *nf* malnutrition
'malo *a* **in ~ modo** badly
ma'locchio *nm* evil eye
ma'lora *nf* ruin; **della ~** awful; **andare in ~** go to ruin
ma'lore *nm* illness; **essere colto da ~** be suddenly taken ill
malri'dotto *a* ⟨*persona*⟩ in a sorry state; ⟨*auto, casa*⟩ dilapidated, in a sorry state
mal'sano *a* unhealthy
malsi'curo *a* unsafe; (*incerto*) uncertain
'malta *nf* mortar
mal'tempo *nm* bad weather
mal'tese *a & nmf* Maltese
'malto *nm* malt
mal'tosio *nm* maltose
maltratta'mento *nm* ill-treatment
maltrat'tare *vt* ill-treat
malu'more *nm* bad mood; **di ~** in a bad mood
'malva *a inv* mauve
mal'vagio *a* wicked
malvagità *nf* wickedness

malva'sia *nf* type of dessert wine

malversazi'one *nf* embezzlement

mal'visto *a* unpopular (**da** with)

malvi'vente *nm* criminal

malvolenti'eri *adv* unwillingly

malvo'lere *vt* **farsi ~** make oneself unpopular; **prendere qcno a ~** take a dislike to sb

'mamma *nf* mummy, mum; **~ mia!** good gracious!

mam'mario *a* mammary

mam'mella *nf* breast

mam'mifero *nm* mammal

mam'mismo *nm* (*del figlio*) dependency on the mother figure; (*della madre*) excessive motherliness

mammogra'fia *nf* mammograph

'mammola *nf* violet

mammo'letta *nf* shrinking violet

mam'mone *nm* mummy's boy

mam'mut *nm inv* mammoth

ma'nata *nf* handful; (*colpo*) slap

'manca *nf* vedi **manco**

manca'mento *nm* **avere un ~** faint

man'cante *a* missing

man'canza *nf* lack; (*assenza*) absence; (*insufficienza*) shortage; (*fallo*) fault; (*imperfezione*) defect; **in ~ d'altro** failing all else; **sento la sua ~** I miss him. **~ di tatto** lack of tact, indelicacy

man'care *vi* be lacking; (*essere assente*) be missing; (*venir meno*) fail; (*morire*) pass away; **~ di** be lacking in; **~ a** fail to keep (*promessa*); **mi manca casa** I miss home; **mi manchi** I miss you; **mi è mancato il tempo** I didn't have [the] time; **mi mancano 1000 lire** I'm 1,000 lire short; **quanto manca alla partenza?** how long before we leave?; **è mancata la corrente** there was a power failure; **sentirsi ~** feel faint; **sentirsi ~ il respiro** be unable to breathe [properly] ● *vt* miss (*bersaglio*); **è mancato poco che cadesse** he nearly fell

man'cato *a* (*appuntamento*) missed; (*tentativo*) unsuccessful; (*occasione*) wasted

'manche *nf inv* heat

man'chevole *a* defective

'mancia *nf* tip. **~ competente** reward

manci'ata *nf* handful

man'cino *a* left-handed

'manco, -a *a* left ● *nf* left hand ● *adv* (*nemmeno*) not even

man'dante *nmf* (*di delitto*) instigator; *Jur* principal

manda'rancio *nm* clementine

man'dare *vt* send; (*emettere*) give off; utter (*suono*); **~ a chiamare** send for; **~ avanti la casa** run the house; **~ giù** (*ingoiare*) swallow

manda'rino *nm Bot* mandarin

man'data *nf* consignment; (*di serratura*) turn; **chiudere a doppia ~** double lock

manda'tario *nm Jur* agent

man'dato *nm* (*incarico*) mandate; *Jur* warrant; (*di pagamento*) money order. **~ di comparizione** [**in giudizio**] subpoena. **~ di**

pagamento money order. **~ di perquisizione** search warrant

man'dibola *nf* jaw

mando'lino *nm* mandolin

'mandorla *nf* almond; **a ~** (*occhi*) almond-shaped. **~ amara** bitter almond

mandor'lato *nm* nut brittle (*type of nougat*)

'mandorlo *nm* almond[-tree]

man'dragola *nf* mandrake

'mandria *nf* herd

mandri'ano *nm* cowherd

man'drillo *nm* (*scimmia*) mandrill; (*attrezzo*) mandrel; *fig fam* goat

maneg'gevole *a* easy to handle

maneggi'are *vt* handle

ma'neggio *nm* handling; (*intrigo*) plot; (*scuola di equitazione*) riding school

ma'nesco *a* quick to hit out

ma'netta *nf* lever; **a tutta ~** flat out; **manette** *pl* handcuffs

man'forte *nm* **dare ~ a qcno** support sb

manga'nello *nm* truncheon

manga'nese *nm* manganese

mange'reccio *a* edible

mangiacas'sette *nm inv* cassette player

mangia'dischiᴿ *nm inv* portable record player

mangia'fumo *a inv* **candela ~** air-purifying candle

mangia'nastri *nm inv* cassette player

mangi'are *vt/i* eat; (*consumare*) eat up; (*corrodere*) eat away; take (*scacchi, carte ecc*) ● *nm* eating; (*cibo*) food; (*pasto*) meal; **dar da ~ al gatto/cane** feed the cat/dog

mangi'arsi *vr* **~ le parole** mumble; **~ le unghie** bite one's nails

mangia'soldi *a inv* **macchinetta ~** one-armed bandit

mangi'ata *nf* big meal; **farsi una bella ~ di...** feast on...

mangia'toia *nf* manger

mangia|'tore, -'trice *nmf* eater. **~ di fuoco** fire-eater. **mangiatrice di uomini** man-eater

man'gime *nm* fodder. **~ per i polli** chicken feed

mangi'one, -a *nmf fam* glutton

mangiucchi'are *vt* nibble

'mango *nm* mango

man'grovia *nf* mangrove

man'gusta *nf* mongoose

ma'nia *nf* mania. **~ di grandezza** delusions of grandeur. **~ di persecuzione** persecution complex

mania'cale *a* manic

ma'niaco, -a *a* maniacal ● *nmf* maniac. **~ sessuale** sex maniac

ma'niaco-depres'sivo *a & nmf* manic-depressive

'Manica *nf* **la ~** the [English] Channel

'manica *nf* sleeve; (*fam: gruppo*) band; **a maniche lunghe** long-sleeved; **senza maniche** sleeveless; **essere in maniche di camicia** be in shirt sleeves; **essere di ~ larga** be generous; **essere di ~ stretta** be strict. **~ a vento** wind sock

manica'retto *nm* tasty dish

maniche'ismo *nm* Manicheism

mani'chetta *nf* hose

mani'chino *nm* (*da sarto, vetrina*) dummy

'manico *nm* handle; *Mus* neck. **~ di scopa** broom handle

mani'comio *nm* mental home; (*fam: confusione*) tip

mani'cotto *nm* muff; *Mech* sleeve

mani'cure *nf* manicure ● *nmf inv* (*persona*) manicurist

mani'era *nf* manner; **in ~ che** so that

manie'rato *a* affected; (*stile*) mannered

manie'rismo *nm* mannerism

mani'ero *nm* manor

manifat'tura *nf* manufacture; (*fabbrica*) factory

manifatturi'ero *a* manufacturing

manifesta'mente *adv* demonstrably, manifestly

manife'stante *nmf* demonstrator

manife'stare *vt* show; (*esprimere*) express ● *vi* demonstrate

manifes'tarsi *vr* show oneself

manifestazi'one *nf* show; (*espressione*) expression; (*sintomo*) manifestation; (*dimostrazione pubblica*) demonstration

mani'festo *a* evident ● *nm* poster; (*dichiarazione pubblica*) manifesto

ma'niglia *nf* handle; (*sostegno, in autobus ecc*) strap

manipo'lare *vt* handle; (*massaggiare*) massage; (*alterare*) adulterate; *fig* manipulate

manipola'tore, -'trice *nmf* manipulator

manipolazi'one *nf* handling; (*massaggio*) massage; (*alterazione*) adulteration; *fig* manipulation

mani'scalco *nm* smith

'manna *nf* **~ dal cielo** manna from heaven

man'naia *nf* (*scure*) axe; (*da macellaio*) cleaver

man'naro *a* **lupo ~** werewolf

'mano *nf* hand; (*strato di vernice ecc*) coat; **alla ~** informal; **fuori ~** out of the way; **man ~** little by little; **man ~ che** as; **sotto ~** to hand; **di seconda ~** secondhand; **a mani vuote** empty-handed; **a ~** (*scritto, ricamato, fatto*) by hand; (*trapano ecc*) hand[-held]; **dare una ~ a qcno** give *or* lend sb a hand; **ha le mani di pastafrolla** he is a butterfingers

mano'dopera *nf* labour

ma'nometro *nm* manometer, pressure gauge

mano'mettere *vt* tamper with; (*violare*) violate

ma'nopola *nf* (*di apparecchio*) knob; (*guanto*) mitten; (*su pullman*) handle

mano'scritto *a* handwritten ● *nm* manuscript

mano'vale *nm* labourer

mano'vella *nf* handle; *Techn* crank. **~ alzacristalli** winder

ma'novra *nf* manoeuvre; *Rail* shunting;

fare le manovre *Auto* manoeuvre. **manovre** *pl* **di corridoio** lobbying

mano'vrabile *a* manoeuvrable; (*fig: persona*) easy to manipulate

mano'vrare *vt* (*azionare*) operate; *fig* manipulate (*persona*) ● *vi* manoeuvre

manro'vescio *nm* slap

man'sarda *nf* attic

mansio'nario *nm* job description

mansi'one *nf* task; (*dovere*) duty

mansu'eto *a* meek; (*animale*) docile

'manta *nf* *Zool* manta

mante'cato *nm* soft ice cream ● *a* creamy

man'tella *nf* cape

man'tello *nm* cloak; (*soprabito, di animale*) coat; (*di neve*) mantle

mante'nere *vt* (*conservare*) keep; (*in buono stato, sostentare*) maintain

mante'nersi *vr* **~ in forma** keep fit

manteni'mento *nm* maintenance. **~ della pace** *Mil, Pol* peacekeeping

mante'nuta *nf* kept woman

'mantice *nm* bellows *pl*; (*di automobile*) hood, top

'mantide *nf* mantis

man'tiglia *nf* mantilla

'manto *nm* cloak; (*coltre*) mantle

'Mantova *nf* Mantua

manto'vana *nf* (*di tende*) pelmet

manu'ale *a* & *nm* manual. **~ di conversazione** phrasebook. **~ d'uso** user manual

manual'mente *adv* manually

ma'nubrio *nm* handle; (*di bicicletta*) handlebars *pl*; (*per ginnastica*) dumb-bell

manu'fatto *a* manufactured

manutenzi'one *nf* maintenance

'manzo *nm* steer; (*carne*) beef

maomet'tano *a* & *nm* Muslim

ma'ori *a inv* & *nm* Maori

'mappa *nf* map

mappa'mondo *nm* globe

mar *vedi* **mare**

mara'chella *nf* prank

maragià *nm inv* maharajah

maran'tacea *nf* *Bot* arrowroot

mara'schino *nm* maraschino, *sweet liqueur*

ma'rasma *nm* *fig* decline

mara'tona *nf* marathon

marato'neta *nmf* marathon runner

'marca *nf* mark; *Comm* brand; (*fabbricazione*) make; (*scontrino*) ticket. **~ da bollo** stamp showing that the necessary duties have been paid

mar'care *vt* mark; *Sport* score

marcata'mente *adv* markedly

mar'cato *a* (*tratto, accento*) strong, marked

marca'tore *nm* (*nel calcio*) scorer; (*chi marca un avversario*) marker; (*pennarello*) marker pen

'Marche *nfpl* Marches

mar'chese, -a *nm* marquis ● *nf* marchioness

mar'chetta *nf* (*assicurativa*) National Insurance stamp; **fare marchette** *fam* be on the game

marchi'are *vt* brand

'**marchio** *nm* brand; (*caratteristica*) mark. **~ deposito** registered trademark. **~ di fabbrica** trademark. **~ registrato** registered trademark

'**marcia** *nf* march; *Auto* gear; *Sport* walk; **mettere in ~** put into gear; **mettersi in ~** start off; **cambiare ~** change gear; **~ a senso unico alternato** temporary one way system in operation. **~ forzata** forced march. **~ funebre** funeral march. **~ indietro** reverse gear; **fare ~ ~** reverse; *fig* back-pedal. **~ nuziale** wedding march

marcia'longa *nf* (*di sci*) cross-country skiing race; (*a piedi*) long-distance race

marciapi'ede *nm* pavement, sidewalk *Am*; (*di stazione*) platform

marci'are *vi* march; (*funzionare*) go, work

marcia'|tore, -'trice *nmf* walker

'**marcio** *a* rotten ●*nm* rotten part; *fig* corruption

mar'cire *vi* go bad, rot

mar'cita *nf* water meadow

'**marco** *nm* (*moneta*) mark

marco'nista *nmf* radio operator

'**mare** *nm* sea; (*luogo di mare*) seaside; **sul ~** (*casa*) at the seaside; (*città*) on the sea; **andare al ~** go to the sea; **in alto ~** on the high seas; **d'alto ~** ocean-going; **essere in alto ~** *fig* not know which way to turn. **~ Adriatico** Adriatic Sea. **mar Cinese** China Sea. **mar Ionio** Ionian Sea. **mar Mediterraneo** Mediterranean. **mar Morto** Dead Sea. **mar Nero** Black Sea. **~ del Nord** North Sea. **mar Tirreno** Tyrrhenian Sea

ma'rea *nf* tide; **una ~ di** hundreds of; **alta/ bassa ~** high/low tide. **~ montante** flood tide

mareggi'ata *nf* [sea] storm

mare'moto *nm* tidal wave, seaquake

maresci'allo *nm* (*ufficiale*) marshal; (*sottufficiale*) warrant-officer

ma'retta *nf* choppiness; *fig* tension

marga'rina *nf* margarine

marghe'rita *nf* marguerite. **~ settembrina** Michaelmas daisy

margheri'tina *nf* daisy

margi'nale *a* marginal

marginal'mente *adv* marginally

'**margine** *nm* margin; (*orlo*) brink; (*bordo*) border. **~ di errore** margin of error. **~ di sicurezza** safety margin. **~ di vendita** mark-up

mari'ano *a Relig* Marian

ma'rina *nf* navy; (*costa*) seashore; (*quadro*) seascape. **~ mercantile** merchant navy. **~ militare** navy

mari'naio *nm* sailor. **~ d'acqua dolce** landlubber

mari'nare *vt* marinate; **~ la scuola** play truant

mari'naro *a* seafaring

mari'nata *nf* marinade

mari'nato *a Culin* marinated

ma'rino *a* sea *attrib*, marine

mario'netta *nf* puppet

mari'tare *vt* marry

mari'tarsi *vr* get married

ma'rito *nm* husband

mari'tozzo *nm* currant bun

ma'rittimo *a* maritime

mar'maglia *nf* rabble

marmel'lata *nf* jam; (*di agrumi*) marmalade

mar'mitta *nf* pot; *Auto* silencer. **~ catalitica** catalytic converter

'**marmo** *nm* marble

mar'mocchio *nm fam* brat

mar'moreo *a* marble

marmoriz'zato *a* marbled

mar'motta *nf* marmot

maroc'chino *a & nmf* Moroccan

Ma'rocco *nm* Morocco

ma'roso *nm* breaker

mar'rone *a* brown ●*nm* brown; (*castagna*) chestnut. **marroni** *pl* **canditi** marrons glacés

mar'sina *nf* tails *pl*

marsupi'ale *nm* marsupial

mar'supio *nm* (*borsa*) bumbag

martedì *nm* Tuesday; **di ~** on Tuesdays. **~ grasso** Shrove Tuesday

martel'lante *a* (*mal di testa*) pounding; **hanno fatto una pubblicità ~** they hyped the product, they bombarded the market with publicity

martel'lare *vt* hammer ●*vi* throb

martel'lata *nf* hammer blow

martel'letto *nm* (*di giudice*) gavel; (*di pianoforte*) hammer; (*di medico*) percussion hammer

martel'lio *nm* hammering

mar'tello *nm* hammer; (*di battente*) knocker. **~ pneumatico** pneumatic drill

marti'netto *nm Mech* jack

mar'tin pesca'tore *nm inv* kingfisher

'**martire** *nmf* martyr

mar'tirio *nm* martyrdom

'**martora** *nf* marten

martori'are *vt* torment

mar'xismo *nm* Marxism

mar'xista *a & nmf* Marxist

marza'pane *nm* marzipan

marzi'ale *a* martial

marzi'ano, -a *a & nmf* Martian

'**marzo** *nm* March

mascal'zone *nm* rascal

ma'scara *nm inv* mascara

mascar'pone *nm full-fat cream cheese often used for desserts*

ma'scella *nf* jaw

'**maschera** *nf* mask; (*costume*) fancy dress; *Cinema, Theat* usher *m*, usherette *f*; (*nella commedia dell'arte*) stock character. **~ antigas** gas mask. **~ di bellezza** face pack. **~ mortuaria** death mask. **~ ad ossigeno** oxygen mask

maschera'mento *nm* masking; *Mil* camouflage

masche'rare *vt* mask; *fig* camouflage

masche'rarsi *vr* put on a mask; **~ da** dress up as

masche'rata *nf* masquerade

maschi'accio *nm* (*ragazza*) tomboy

ma'schile *a* masculine; (*sesso*) male ● *nm* masculine [gender]

maschi'lista *a* sexist

'maschio *a* male; (*virile*) manly ● *nm* male; (*figlio*) son

masco'lino *a* masculine

ma'scotte *nf inv* mascot

maso'chismo *nm* masochism

maso'chista *a & nmf* masochist

'massa *nf* mass; *Electr* earth, ground *Am*; **communicazioni di ~** mass media; **una ~ [di gente]** a crowd [of people]

massa'crante *a* gruelling

massa'crare *vt* massacre

mas'sacro *nm* massacre; *fig* mess

massaggi'are *vt* massage

massaggia|'tore, -'trice *nm* masseur ● *nf* masseuse

mas'saggio *nm* massage. **~ cardiaco** heart massage

mas'saia *nf* housewife

mas'sello *nm* (*metallo*) ingot ● *a* (*legno*) solid

masse'rizie *nfpl* household effects

massiccia'mente *adv* on a big scale

massicci'ata *nf* hard core

mas'siccio *a* massive; (*oro ecc*) solid; (*corporatura*) heavy ● *nm* massif

massifi'care *vt* de-individualize (*società*)

massificazi'one *nf* de-individualization

'massima *nf* maxim; (*temperatura*) maximum

massi'male *nm* (*assicurazione*) limit of indemnity

massimizzazi'one *nf* maximization

'massimo *a* greatest; (*quantità*) maximum, greatest ● *nm* **il ~** the maximum; **al ~** at [the] most, as a maximum. **~ storico** all-time high

'masso *nm* rock

mas'sone *nm* [Free]mason

massone'ria *nf* Freemasonry

mastecto'mia *nf* mastectomy

ma'stello *nm* wooden box for the grape or olive harvest

masti'care *vt* chew; (*borbottare*) mumble

'mastice *nm* mastic; (*per vetri*) putty

ma'stino *nm* mastiff

masto'dontico *a* gigantic

ma'stoide *nm* mastoid

'mastro *nm* master; **libro ~** ledger

mastur'barsi *vr* masturbate

masturbazi'one *nf* masturbation

ma'tassa *nf* skein

match 'point *nm inv Tennis* match point

matelassé *nm inv* quilting

mate'matica *nf* mathematics, maths, math *Am*. **~ pura** pure mathematics

mate'matico, -a *a* mathematical ● *nmf* mathematician

materas'sino *nm* small mattress. **~ gonfiabile** air bed, lilo[R]

mate'rasso *nm* mattress. **~ ad acqua** water bed. **~ di gommapiuma** foam mattress. **~ a molle** spring mattress

ma'teria *nf* matter; (*materiale*) material; (*di studio*) subject. **~ grigia** grey matter. **~ prima** raw material

materi'ale *a* material; (*grossolano*) coarse ● *nm* material. **~ da costruzione** building material. **~ pubblicitario** publicity material. **~ di scarto** waste material

materia'lismo *nm* materialism

materia'lista *a* materialistic; **non ~** unworldly ● *nmf* materialist

materializ'zarsi *vr* materialize

material'mente *adv* physically

materna'mente *adv* maternally

maternità *nf* motherhood; **è alla prima ~** it's her first baby; **ospedale di ~** maternity hospital

ma'terno *a* maternal; **lingua materna** mother tongue

ma'tita *nf* pencil. **matite pl colorate** colour[ed] pencils. **~ emostatica** styptic pencil. **~ per gli occhi** eyeliner pencil

matriar'cale *a* matriarchal

ma'trice *nf* matrix; (*origini*) roots *pl*; *Comm* counterfoil. **~ attiva** *Comput* active matrix. **~ passiva** *Comput* passive matrix

ma'tricola *nf* (*registro*) register; *Univ* fresher; **numero di ~** (*di studente*) matriculation number

ma'trigna *nf* stepmother

matrimoni'ale *a* matrimonial; **vita ~** married life

matri'monio *nm* marriage; (*cerimonia*) wedding. **~ in bianco** white wedding. **~ civile** civil wedding. **~ di convenienza** marriage of convenience

ma'trona *nf* matron

'matta *nf* (*nelle carte*) joker

mattacchi'one, -a *nmf* rascal

mat'tanza *nf* (*di tonni*) tuna fishing; *fig* killings *pl*

matta'toio *nm* slaughterhouse

matta'tore *nm* (*artista*) star performer

matte'rello *nm* rolling-pin

mat'tina *nf* morning; **la ~, alla ~** in the morning; **domani ~** tomorrow morning; **ieri ~** yesterday morning

matti'nata *nf* morning; *Theat* matinée

mattini'ero *a* **essere ~** be an early riser

mat'tino *nm* morning

'matto, -a *a* mad, crazy; *Med* insane; (*falso*) false; (*opaco*) matt; **~ da legare** barking mad; **avere una voglia matta di…** be dying for… ● *nm* madman ● *nf* madwoman

mat'tone *nm* brick; (*libro*) bore

matto'nella *nf* tile

mattu'tino *a* morning *attrib*

matu'rare *vt* ripen; *Fin* mature

maturazi'one *nf* ripening; *Fin* maturity;

(*fig: di idea ecc*) gestation; **arrivare a ~** ⟨*frutta:*⟩ ripen; ⟨*polizza:*⟩ mature

maturità *nf* maturity; *Sch* school-leaving certificate

ma'turo *a* mature; ⟨*frutto*⟩ ripe

ma'tusa *nm* old fogey

Mau'rizio *nf* [**isola di**] ~ Mauritius

mauso'leo *nm* mausoleum

maxi+ *pref* maxi+

'**mayday** *nm inv Radio* Mayday

'**mazza** *nf* club; (*martello*) hammer; (*da baseball, cricket*) bat. ~ **da golf** golf-club

maz'zata *nf* blow

maz'zetta *nf* (*di banconote*) bundle; (*tangente*) bribe

'**mazzo** *nm* bunch; (*carte da gioco*) pack

Mb *nm abbr* (**megabyte**) *Comput* Mb

me *pers pron* me; **me lo ha dato** he gave it to me; **secondo me** in my opinion; **fai come me** do as I do; **è più veloce di me** he is faster than me *o* faster than I am

me'andro *nm* meander

M.E.C. *nm abbr* (**Mercato Comune Europeo**) EEC

'**Mecca** *nf* **La** ~ Mecca

mec'canica *nf* mechanics. ~ **quantistica** quantum mechanics

meccanica'mente *adv* mechanically

mec'canico *a* mechanical ● *nm* mechanic. ~ **laser** laser engine

mecca'nismo *nm* mechanism

meccanogra'fia *nf* data processing

meccano'grafico *a* data processing *attrib*

mece'nate *nmf* patron

mèche *nfpl* highlights; [**farsi**] **fare le** ~ have highlights put in, have one's hair streaked

me'daglia *nf* medal. ~ **al valore** medal for valour

medagli'ere *nm* medal collection

medagli'one *nm* medallion; (*gioiello*) locket. **medaglioni** *pl* **di vitello** *Culin* medallions of veal

me'desimo *a* same

'**media** *nf* average; *Sch* average mark; *Math* mean; **essere nella** ~ be in the mid-range

medi'ano *a* middle ● *nm* (*calcio*) half-back. ~ **di mischia** scrum half

medi'ante *prep* by

medi'are *vt* act as intermediary in

media|'tore, -'trice *nmf* mediator; *Comm* middleman. ~ **d'affari** business agent

mediazi'one *nf* mediation

medica'mento *nm* medicine

medi'care *vt* treat; dress ⟨*ferita*⟩

medi'cato *a* ⟨*shampoo*⟩ medicated

medicazi'one *nf* medication; (*di ferita*) dressing

me'diceo *a* from the period of the Medici, Medicean

medi'cina *nf* medicine. ~ **alternativa** alternative medicine. ~ **del lavoro** occupational health. ~ **legale** forensic medicine. ~ **popolare** folk medicine

medici'nale *a* medicinal ● *nm* medicine

'**medico** *a* medical ● *nm* doctor. ~ **di base** general practitioner, GP. ~ **di famiglia** family doctor. ~ **generico** general practitioner, GP. ~ **legale** forensic scientist. ~ **di turno** duty doctor

medie'vale *a* medieval

'**medio** *a* average; ⟨*punto*⟩ middle; ⟨*statura*⟩ medium; **scuola media** secondary school ● *nm* (*dito*) middle finger. **M~ Oriente** Middle East

medi'ocre *a* mediocre; (*scadente*) poor

mediocre'mente *adv* indifferently

medio'evo *nm* Middle Ages *pl*

medita'bondo *a* meditative

medi'tare *vt* meditate; (*progettare*) plan; (*considerare attentamente*) think over ● *vi* meditate

medita'tivo *a* meditative

meditazi'one *nf* meditation

mediter'raneo *a* Mediterranean; **il** [**mar**] **M~** the Mediterranean [Sea]

me'dusa *nf* jellyfish

'**megabyte** *nm inv Comput* megabyte

me'gafono *nm* megaphone

megaga'lattico *a* gigantic

mega'lite *nm* megalith

mega'lomane *nmf* megalomaniac

me'gera *nf* hag

'**meglio** *adv* better; **tanto** ~, ~ **così** so much the better ● *a* better; (*superlativo*) best ● *nmf* best ● *nf* **avere la** ~ **su** have the better of; **fare qcsa alla** [**bell'e**] ~ do sth as best one can ● *nm* **fare del proprio** ~ do one's best; **fare qcsa il** ~ **possibile** make an excellent job of sth; **al** ~ to the best of one's ability; **per il** ~ for the best

'**mela** *nf* apple; **succo di** ~ apple juice. ~ **cotogna** quince

mela'grana *nf* pomegranate

mé'lange *nm inv* flecked wool ● *a inv* ⟨*lana*⟩ flecked

mela'nina *nf* melanin

melan'zana *nf* aubergine, eggplant *Am*. **melanzane** *pl* **alla parmigiana** baked layers of aubergine, tomato and cheese

me'lassa *nf* molasses *sg*

me'lenso *a* ⟨*persona, film*⟩ dull

me'leto *nm* apple orchard

mel'lifluo *a* ⟨*parole*⟩ honeyed; ⟨*voce*⟩ sugary

'**melma** *nf* slime

mel'moso *a* slimy

'**melo** *nm* apple[-tree]

melo'dia *nf* melody

me'lodico *a* melodic

melodi'oso *a* melodious

melo'dramma *nm* melodrama

melodrammatica'mente *adv* melodramatically

melodram'matico *a* melodramatic

melo'grano *nm* pomegranate tree

me'lone *nm* melon

mem'brana *nf* membrane

'**membro** *nm* member; (*pl nf* **membra** *Anat*) limb

memo'rabile *a* memorable

'**memore** *a* mindful; (*riconoscente*) grateful

me'**moria** *nf* memory; (*oggetto ricordo*) souvenir; **imparare a** ~ learn by heart; **memorie** *pl* (*biografiche*) memoirs. ~ **cache** *Comput* cache memory. ~ **collettiva** folk memory. ~ **dinamica** *Comput* RAM. ~ **di massa** *Comput* mass storage. ~ **permanente** *Comput* non-volatile memory; ~ **di sola lettura** *Comput* read-only memory, ROM. ~ **a tampone** *Comput* buffer [memory]. ~ **volatile** *Comput* volatile memory

memori'**ale** *nm* memorial

memoriz'**zare** *vt* memorize; *Comput* save, store

mena'**dito**: **a** ~ *adv* perfectly

me'**nare** *vt* lead; (*fam: picchiare*) hit; ~ **la coda** (*cane:*) wag its tail; ~ **qcno per il naso** pull sb's leg

mendi'**cante** *nmf* beggar

mendi'**care** *vt/i* beg

menefre'**ghista** *a* devil-may-care

mene'**strello** *nm* minstrel

me'**ningi** *nfpl* **spremersi le** ~ rack one's brains

menin'**gite** *nf* meningitis

me'**nisco** *nm* meniscus

'**meno** *adv* less; (*superlativo*) least; (*in operazioni, con temperatura*) minus; ~ **di** less than; **di** ~ less; ~ **moderno** less modern; **il** ~ **moderno di tutti** the least modern of all; **far qcsa alla** ~ **peggio** do sth as best one can; **fare a** ~ **di qcsa** do without sth; **non posso fare a** ~ **di ridere** I can't help laughing; ~ **male!** thank goodness!; **sempre** ~ less and less; **venir** ~ (*svenire*) faint; **venir** ~ **a qcno** (*coraggio:*) fail sb; **sono le tre** ~ **un quarto** it's a quarter to three; **che tu venga o** ~ whether you're coming or not; **quanto** ~ at least ● *a inv* less; (*con nomi plurali*) fewer ● *nm* least; *Math* minus sign; **il** ~ **possibile** as little as possible; **per lo** ~ at least ● *prep* except [for] ● *conj* **a** ~ **che** unless

meno'**mare** *vt* (*incidente:*) maim

meno'**mato** *a* disabled ● *nmf* disabled person

meno'**pausa** *nf* menopause

'**mensa** *nf* table; *Mil* mess; *Sch, Univ* refectory

men'**sile** *a* monthly ● *nm* (*stipendio*) [monthly] salary; (*rivista*) monthly

mensilità *nf inv* monthly salary

mensil'**mente** *adv* monthly

'**mensola** *nf* bracket; (*scaffale*) shelf

'**menta** *nf* mint; **al gusto di** ~ mint-flavoured. ~ **peperita** peppermint. ~ **verde** spearmint

men'**tale** *a* mental

mentalità *nf inv* mentality

'**mente** *nf* mind; **a** ~ **fredda** in cold blood; **cosa ti è saltato in** ~? what possessed you?; **venire in** ~ **a qcno** occur to sb

men'**tina** *nf* mint

men'**tire** *vi* lie

'**mento** *nm* chin

men'**tolo** *nm* menthol; **al** ~ mentholated

'**mentre** *conj* (*temporale*) while; (*invece*) whereas

me'**nu** *nm inv* menu. ~ **a discesa** *Comput* pull-down menu. ~ **fisso** set menu. ~ **a tendina** *Comput* pull-down menu. ~ **turistico** tourist menu

menzio'**nare** *vt* mention

menzi'**one** *nf* mention. ~ **speciale** special mention

men'**zogna** *nf* lie

mera'**viglia** *nf* wonder; **a** ~ marvellously; **che** ~! how wonderful!; **con mia grande** ~ much to my amazement; **mi fa** ~ **che...** I am surprised that...

meravigli'**are** *vt* surprise

meravigli'**arsi** *vr* ~ **di** be surprised at

meravigliosa'**mente** *adv* marvellously

meravigli'**oso** *a* marvellous, wonderful

mer'**cante** *nm* merchant. ~ **d'arte** art dealer. ~ **di schiavi** slave trader

mercanteggi'**are** *vi* trade; (*sul prezzo*) bargain

mercan'**tile** *a* mercantile ● *nm* merchant ship

mercan'**zia** *nf* merchandise, goods *pl*

merca'**tino** *nm* (*di quartiere*) local street market; *Fin* unlisted securities market

mer'**cato** *nm* market; *Fin* market[place]. **a buon** ~ (*comprare*) cheap[ly]; (*articolo*) cheap. ~ **aperto** *Econ* open market. ~ **azionario** *Fin* equity market, share market. ~ **dei cambi** foreign exchange market. **M**~ **Comune** [**Europeo**] [European] Common Market. ~ **coperto** covered market, indoor market. ~ **dell'eurovaluta** eurocurrency market. ~ **immobiliare** property market. ~ **libero** free market. ~ **di massa** mass market. ~ **nero** black market. ~ **di prova** test market. ~ **al rialzo** *Fin* bull market. ~ **al ribasso** *Fin* bear market. ~ **specializzato** niche market. ~ **unico** Single Market

'**merce** *nf* goods *pl*, merchandise; **la** ~ **venduta non si cambia senza lo scontrino** goods will not be exchanged without a receipt. ~ **in conto vendita** sale or return goods. ~ **deperibile** perishable goods

mercé *nf* **alla** ~ **di** at the mercy of

merce'**nario** *a & nm* mercenary

merceolo'**gia** *nf* study of commodities

merce'**ria** *nf* haberdashery; (*negozio*) haberdasher's

mercifi'**care** *vt* commercialize

mercificazi'**one** *nf* commercialization

mercoledì *nm inv* Wednesday; **di** ~ on Wednesdays. ~ **delle Ceneri** Ash Wednesday

mer'**curio** *nm* mercury

me'**renda** *nf* afternoon snack; **far** ~ have an afternoon snack

meridi'**ana** *nf* sundial

meridi'**ano** *a* midday ● *nm* meridian

meridio'**nale** *a* southern ● *nmf* southerner

meridi'**one** *nm* south

me'**ringa** *nf* meringue

merin'**gata** *nf* meringue pie

meri'**tare** *vt* deserve

meri'tato *a* deserved
meri'tevole *a* deserving
'merito *nm* merit; (*valore*) worth; **in ~ a** as to; **per ~ di** thanks to
merito'cratico *a* meritocratic
meri'torio *a* meritorious
merla'tura *nf* battlements *pl*
merlet'taia *nf* lacemaker
mer'letto *nm* lace
'merlo *nm* blackbird; **bravo ~!** you fool!
mer'luzzo *nm* cod
'mero *a* mere
mesca'lina *nf* mescaline
'mescere *vt* pour out
meschine'ria *nf* meanness
me'schino *a* wretched; (*gretto*) mean ● *nm* wretch
'mescita *nf* wine shop
mescola'mento *nm* mixing
mesco'lanza *nf* mixture
mesco'lare *vt* mix; shuffle ⟨*carte*⟩; (*confondere*) mix up; blend ⟨*tè, tabacco ecc*⟩
mesco'larsi *vr* mix; (*immischiarsi*) meddle
mesco'lata *nf* (*a carte*) shuffle; *Culin* stir
'mese *nm* month. **~ civile** calendar month
me'setto *nm* **un ~** about a month, a month or so
'messa¹ *nf* Mass. **~ nera** black mass. **~ da requiem** requiem mass. **~ solenne** High Mass
'messa² *nf* (*il mettere*) putting. **~ in moto** *Auto* starting. **~ in piega** (*di capelli*) set; **farsi fare la ~ ~ ~** have one's hair set. **~ a punto** adjustment. **~ in scena** production; *fig* production number. **~ a terra** earthing, grounding *Am*
messag'gero *nm* messenger
mes'saggio *nm* message. **~ di errore** *Comput* error message
mes'sale *nm* missal
'messe *nf* harvest
Mes'sia *nm* Messiah
messi'cano, -a *a & nmf* Mexican
'Messico *nm* Mexico
messin'scena *nf* staging; *fig* act
'messo *pp di* **mettere** ● *nm* messenger
mesti'ere *nm* trade; (*lavoro*) job; **essere del ~** be an expert, know one's trade
'mesto *a* sad
'mestola *nf* (*di cuoco*) ladle; (*di muratore*) trowel
mestru'ale *a* menstrual
mestruazi'one *nf* menstruation; **me-struazioni** *pl* period
'meta *nf* destination; *fig* aim
metà *nf inv* half; (*centro*) middle; **~ prezzo** half price; **a ~ strada** half-way; **a ~ serata** half-way through the evening; **fare a ~ con qcno** go halves with sb, go fifty-fifty with sb; **fare [a] ~ e ~** go fifty-fifty, go halves
metabo'lismo *nm* metabolism
meta'carpo *nm* metacarpus
meta'done *nm* methadone
meta'fisica *n* metaphysics
meta'fisico *a* metaphysical

me'tafora *nf* metaphor
metafori ca'mente *adv* metaphorically
meta'forico *a* metaphorical
me'tallico *a* metallic
metalliz'zato *a* ⟨*grigio*⟩ metallic
me'tallo *nm* metal. **~ vile** base metal
metal'loide *nm* metalloid
metallur'gia *nf* metallurgy
metal'lurgico *a* metallurgical
metalmec'canico *a* engineering ● *nm* engineering worker
meta'morfosi *nf* metamorphosis
me'tano *nm* methane
metano'dotto *nm* methane pipeline
meta'nolo *nm* methanol
me'tastasi *nf inv* metastasis
meta'tarso *nm* metatarsus
me'teora *nf* meteor
meteo'rite *nm* meteorite
meteorolo'gia *nf* meteorology
meteoro'logico *a* meteorological
meteo'rologo *nm* meteorologist
me'ticcio, -a *nmf* half-caste
meticolosa'mente *adv* meticulously
metico'loso *a* meticulous
me'tile *nm* methyl
me'todico *a* methodical
meto'dista *a & nmf* Methodist
'metodo *nm* method
metodolo'gia *nf* methodology
metodo'logico *a* methodological
me'traggio *nm* length (*in metres*); **vendere a ~** sell by the metre
'metrico, -a *a* metric; (*in poesia*) metrical ● *nf* metrics
'metro *nm* metre; (*nastro*) tape measure. **~ cubo** cubic metre. **~ quadrato** square metre
'metro *nf inv fam* underground, subway *Am*
me'tronomo *nm* metronome
metro'notte *nmf inv* night security guard
me'tropoli *nf inv* metropolis
metropoli'tana *nf* underground, subway *Am*
metropoli'tano *a* metropolitan
'mettere *vt* put; (*indossare*) put on; (*fam: installare*) put in; **~ al mondo** bring into the world; **~ da parte** set aside; **~ fiducia** inspire trust; **~ qcsa in chiaro** make sth clear; **~ in mostra** display; **~ a posto** tidy up; **~ in vendita** put up for sale; **~ su** set up ⟨*casa, azienda*⟩; **metter su famiglia** start a family; **ci ho messo un'ora** it took me an hour; **mettiamo che...** let's suppose that...
'mettersi *vr* (*indossare*) put on; (*diventare*) turn out; **~ a** start to; **~ con qcno** (*fam: formare una coppia*) start to go out with sb; **~ a letto** go to bed; **~ a sedere** sit down; **~ in viaggio** set out
metti'foglio *nm* feeder
'mezza *nf* **è la ~** it's half past twelve; **sono le quattro e ~** it's half past four
mez'zadria *nf* sharecropping
mezza'luna *nf* half moon; (*simbolo islamico*) crescent; (*coltello*) two-handled chopping knife; **a ~** half-moon

mezza'manica nf **a ~** ⟨maglia⟩ short-sleeved; **mezzemaniche** pl pej lowest grade of clerks, pen-pushers

mezza'nino nm mezzanine

mez'zano, -a a middle

mezza'notte nf midnight; **aspettare la ~** see in the New Year

mezz'asta: a ~ at half mast

mezze'ria nf centre line

'mezzo a half; **di mezza età** middle aged; **~ bicchiere** a glass; **una mezza idea** a vague idea; **siamo mezzi morti** we're half dead; **sono le quattro e ~** it's half past four. **mezza cartuccia** nf runt. **mezza dozzina** nf half-dozen. **mezza età** nf midlife. **mezza giornata** nf half day. **~ guanto** nm mitt. **~ litro** nm half a litre. **mezz'ora** nf half an hour. **mezza pensione** nf half board. **mezza stagione** nf **una giacca di ~ ~** a spring/autumn jacket. **mezza verità** nf half-truth ● adv (a metà) half; **~ addormentato** half asleep; **~ morto** half-dead; **~ morto di paura** petrified; **~ e ~** (così così) so so ● nm (metà) half; (centro) middle; (per raggiungere un fine) means sg; **uno e ~** one and a half; **tre anni e ~** three and a half years; **in ~ a** in the middle of; **il giusto ~** the happy medium; **levare di ~** clear away; **per ~ di** by means of; **a ~ posta** by mail; **via di ~** fig halfway house; (soluzione) middle way; **mezzi** pl (denaro) means pl. **mezzi** pl **di comunicazione di massa** mass media. **mezzi** pl **pubblici** public transport. **mezzi** pl **di trasporto** [means of] transport

mezzo'busto nm (statua) bust; TV talking head; **a ~** ⟨foto, ritratto⟩ half-length

mezzo'fondo nm middle-distance running

mezzogi'orno nm midday, noon; (sud) South. **il M~** Southern Italy. **~ in punto** high noon

mezzo'sangue nmf crossbreed

mezzo'servizio nm **lavorare a ~** do part-time cleaning work

mi pers pron me; (refl) myself; **mi ha dato un libro** he gave me a book; **mi lavo le mani** I wash my hands; **eccomi** here I am ● nm Mus (chiave, nota) E

mia vedi mio

miago'lare vi miaow

miago'lio nm miaowing

mi'ao nm miaow

'mica[1] nf mica

'mica[2] adv fam (per caso) by any chance; **hai ~ visto Paolo?** have you seen Paul, by any chance?; **non è ~ bello** it is not at all nice; **~ male** not bad

'miccia nf fuse

micidi'ale a deadly

'micio nm pussy-cat

mi'cosi nf athlete's foot

mi'cotico a fungal

microbiolo'gia nf microbiology

'microbo nm microbe

microchirur'gia nf microsurgery

micro'clima nm microclimate

microcom'puter nm inv microcomputer

micro'cosmo nm microcosm

micro'fiche nf inv microfiche

micro'film nm inv microfilm

micro'fisica nf microphysics

mi'crofono nm microphone. **~ con la clip** clip-on microphone. **~ spia** bugging device, bug. **~ a stelo** boom microphone

microfotogra'fia nf Phot micrograph; (tecnica) micrography

microinfor'matica nf microcomputing

micro'onda nf microwave

microorga'nismo nm microorganism

microproces'sore nm microprocessor

micro'scheda nf microfiche

micro'scopico a microscopic

micro'scopio nm microscope; **passare qcsa al ~** fig examine sth in microscopic detail

microse'condo nm microsecond

micro'solco nm (disco) long-playing record

micro'spia nf bug

mi'dollo nm (pl nf **midolla**, Anat) marrow; **fino al ~** ⟨bagnato⟩ through and through; ⟨corrotto⟩ to the core. **~ osseo** bone marrow. **~ spinale** spinal cord

'mie vedi mio

mi'ei vedi mio

mi'ele nm honey. **~ d'acacia** acacia honey

mi'etere vt reap

mietitrebbia'trice nf combine harvester

mieti'trice nf harvester

mieti'tura nf harvest

migli'aia nfpl thousands

migli'aio nm (pl nf **migliaia**) thousand. **a migliaia** in thousands

'miglio nm Bot millet; (misura: pl f **miglia**) mile. **~ nautico** nautical mile. **miglia** pl **all'ora** miles per hour, mph. **~ terrestre** mile

migliora'mento nm improvement

miglio'rare vt/i improve

migli'ore a better; (superlativo) the best; **~ amico** best friend; **i migliori auguri** best wishes ● nmf **il/la ~** the best

miglio'ria nf improvement

mi'gnatta nf leech

'mignolo nm little finger, pinkie fam; (del piede) little toe

mi'gnon a inv (bottiglie) miniature

mi'grare vi migrate

migra'tore a migratory

migra'torio a migratory

migrazi'one nf migration

'mila vedi mille

mila'nese a & nmf Milanese

Mi'lano nf Milan

miliar'dario, -a nm millionaire; (plurimiliardario) billionaire ● nf millionairess; billionairess

mili'ardo nm billion

mili'are a **pietra ~** milestone

milio'nario, -a nm millionaire ● nf millionairess

mili'one nm million

milio'nesimo *a & nm* millionth

mili'tante *a & nmf* militant

mili'tanza *nf* militancy

mili'tare *vi* ~ **in** be a member of ⟨*un partito ecc*⟩ ● *a* military ● *nm* soldier; **fare il** ~ do one's military service. ~ **di carriera** regular [soldier]. ~ **di leva** National Serviceman

milita'rismo *nm* militarism

milita'rista *a* militaristic

militariz'zare *vt* militarize

militas'solto *a* having done National Service

'milite *nm* soldier

milite'sente *a* exempt from National Service

mil'izia *nf* militia

millanta|'tore, -'trice *nmf* boaster

'mille *a & nm (pl* **mila)** *a o* one thousand; **due/tre mila** two/three thousand; ~ **grazie!** thanks a lot!; **millenovecentonovanta-quattro** *nm* nineteen ninety-four

mille'foglie *nm inv* Culin vanilla slice

mil'lennio *nm* millennium

millepi'edi *nm inv* centipede

mil'lesimo *a & nm* thousandth

milli'bar *nm inv* millibar

milli'grammo *nm* milligram

milli'litro *nm* millilitre

mil'limetro *nm* millimetre

'milza *nf* spleen

mi'mare *vt* mimic ⟨*persona*⟩ ● *vi* mime

mi'metico *a* tuta *f* mimetica camouflage; **animale** ~ animal which has the ability to camouflage itself; **vernice mimetica** camouflage paint

mime'tismo *nm* ability to camouflage itself; ~ **politico** chameleon-like political traits

mimetiz'zare *vt* camouflage

mimetiz'zarsi *vr* camouflage oneself

'mimica *nf* mime. ~ **facciale** facial expressions *pl*

'mimico *a* mimic

'mimo *nm* mime

mi'mosa *nf* mimosa

'mina *nf* mine; (*di matita*) lead

mi'naccia *nf* threat. **avere una** ~ **di aborto** come close to having a miscarriage. ~ **di morte** death threat

minacci'are *vt* threaten

minacciosa'mente *adv* threateningly, menacingly

minacci'oso *a* threatening; ⟨*onde*⟩ menacing

mi'nare *vt* mine; *fig* undermine

mina'reto *nm* minaret

mina'tore *nm* miner

mina'torio *a* threatening

mine'rale *a & nm* mineral

mineralo'gia *nf* mineralogy

mine'rario *a* mining *attrib*

mi'nestra *nf* soup. ~ **in brodo** noodle soup. ~ **di verdure** vegetable soup

mine'strone *nm* minestrone (*vegetable soup*); (*fam: insieme confuso*) hotchpotch

mingher'lino *a* skinny

'mini *nf inv* (*gonna*) mini ● *a inv* mini

mini+ *pref* mini+

miniapparta'mento *nm* studio flat *Br*, studio apartment

minia'tura *nf* miniature

miniaturiz'zato *a* miniaturized

mini'bus *nm inv* minibus

mini'disco *nm* minidiskette

mini'era *nf* mine; **una** ~ **di notizie** a mine of information; **è una** ~ **di idee** he's full of ideas. ~ **a cielo aperto** opencast mine. ~ **d'oro** gold-mine

mini'golf *nm* minigolf, miniature golf

mini'gonna *nf* miniskirt, mini

'minima *nf* (*atmosferica*) minimum temperature; *Med* minimum blood-pressure level; *Mus* minim

minima'lista *nmf* minimalist

minima'mente *adv* minimally

mini'market *nm inv* minimarket

minimiz'zare *vt* minimize

'minimo *a* least, slightest; (*il più basso*) lowest; (*salario, quantità ecc*) minimum ● *nm* minimum; **girare al** ~ *Auto* idle; **toccare il** ~ **storico** be at an all-time low; **come** ~ at least, as a minimum

'minio *nm* red lead

ministeri'ale *a* (*di ministero*) ministerial; (*di governo*) government

mini'stero *nm* ministry; (*governo*) government. ~ **degli [affari] esteri** Foreign Office, State Department *Am*. ~ **della difesa** Department of Defence. ~ **della pubblica istruzione** Department of Education. ~ **della sanità** Department of Health

mi'nistro *nm* minister. ~ **della difesa** Defence Minister, Defense Secretary *Am*. ~ **degli esteri** Foreign Secretary, Secretary of State *Am*. ~ **di grazia e giustizia** ≈ Attorney General. ~ **dell'interno** Home Secretary, Secretary of the Interior *Am*. ~ **del lavoro** Employment Minister, Employment Secretary. ~ **del tesoro** Chancellor of the Exchequer, Secretary of the Treasury *Am*

mini'tower *nm* Comput minitower

mino'ranza *nf* minority

mino'rato, -a *a* disabled ● *nmf* disabled person

Mi'norca *nf* Menorca

mi'nore *a* ⟨*gruppo, numero*⟩ smaller; (*superlativo*) smallest; ⟨*distanza*⟩ shorter; (*superlativo*) shortest; ⟨*prezzo*⟩ lower; (*superlativo*) lowest; (*di età*) younger; (*superlativo*) youngest; (*di importanza*) minor; (*superlativo*) least important ● *nmf* younger; (*superlativo*) youngest; *Jur* minor; **il** ~ **dei mali** the lesser of two evils; **i minori di 14 anni** children under 14

mino'renne *a* under age ● *nmf* minor

minori'tario *a* minority *attrib*

minu'etto *nm* minuet

mi'nuscolo, -a *a* tiny ● *nf* small letter

mi'nuta *nf* rough copy

minuta'mente *adv* ‹*esaminato*› in minute detail, minutely; ‹*lavorato, tritato*› finely

mi'nuto¹ *a* minute; ‹*persona*› delicate; ‹*ricerca*› detailed; ‹*pioggia, neve*› fine; **al ~** *Comm* retail

mi'nuto² *nm* (*di tempo*) minute; **spaccare il ~** be dead on time. **minuti** *pl* **di recupero** *Sport* injury time

mi'nuzia *nf* trifle; **minuzie** *pl* minutiae

minuziosa'mente *adv* minutely

minuzi'oso *a* minute, detailed; ‹*persona*› meticulous

'mio (**il mio** *m*, **la mia** *f*, **i miei** *mpl*, **le mie** *fpl*) *poss a* my; **questa macchina è mia** this car is mine; **~ padre** my father; **un ~ amico** a friend of mine ● *poss pron* mine; **i miei** (*genitori ecc*) my folks

'miope *a* short-sighted

mio'pia *nf* short-sightedness

'mira *nf* aim; (*bersaglio*) target; **prendere la ~** take aim; **prendere di ~ qcno** *fig* have it in for sb

mi'rabile *a* admirable

miraco'lato *a* ‹*malato*› miraculously cured

mi'racolo *nm* miracle

miracolosa'mente *adv* miraculously

miraco'loso *a* miraculous

mi'raggio *nm* mirage

mi'rare *vi* [take] aim; **~ alto** aim high

mi'rarsi *vr* (*guardarsi*) look at oneself

mi'riade *nf* myriad

mi'rino *nm* sight; *Phot* view-finder

'mirra *nf* myrrh

mir'tillo *nm* blueberry

'mirto *nm* myrtle

mi'santropo, -a *nmf* misanthropist

mi'scela *nf* mixture; (*di caffè, tabacco ecc*) blend

misce'lare *vt* mix

miscela'tore *nm* (*apparecchio*) blender; (*di acqua*) mixer tap

miscel'lanea *nf* miscellany

'mischia *nf* scuffle; (*nel rugby*) scrum

mischi'are *vt* mix; shuffle ‹*carte da gioco*›

mischi'arsi *vr* mix; (*immischiarsi*) interfere

misco'noscere *vt* not appreciate

miscre'dente *nmf* heretic

mi'scuglio *nm* mixture; *fig* medley

mise'rabile *a* wretched

misera'mente *adv* ‹*finire*› miserably; ‹*vivere*› in abject poverty; ‹*vestito*› shabbily

mi'seria *nf* poverty; (*infelicità*) misery; **guadagnare una ~** earn a pittance; **miserie** *pl* (*disgrazie*) misfortunes; **porca ~!** *fam* hell!

miseri'cordia *nf* mercy

misericordi'oso *a* merciful

'misero *a* (*miserabile*) wretched; (*povero*) poor; (*scarso*) paltry

mi'sfatto *nm* misdeed

mi'sogino *nm* misogynist

mis'saggio *nm* vision mixer

'missile *nm* missile. **~ cruise** cruise missile. **~ terra-aria** surface-to-air missile

missi'listico *a* missile *attrib*

missio'nario, -a *nmf* missionary

missi'one *nf* mission. **~ di pace** peace mission

misteriosa'mente *adv* mysteriously

misteri'oso *a* mysterious

mi'stero *nm* mystery

'mistica *nf* mysticism

misti'cismo *nm* mysticism

'mistico *a* mystic[al] ● *nm* mystic

mistifi'care *vt* distort ‹*verità*›

mistificazi'one *nf* (*della verità*) distortion

'misto *a* mixed; **scuola mista** mixed *o* co-educational school ● *nm* mixture; (*di oggetti*) miscellany. **~ lana** wool mixture; **~ lana/cotone** wool/cotton mix

mi'sura *nf* measure; (*dimensione*) measurement; (*taglia*) size; (*limite*) limit; **su ~** ‹*abiti*› made to measure; ‹*mobile*› custom-made; **a ~** ‹*andare, calzare*› perfectly; **a ~ che** as; **nella ~ in cui** insofar as. **~ di sicurezza** safety measure. **~ di capacità** unit of capacity. **~ di lunghezza** unit of length. **~ profilattica** prophylactic

misu'rare *vt* measure; try on ‹*indumenti*›; (*limitare*) limit

misu'rarsi *vr* **~ con** (*gareggiare*) compete with

misu'rato *a* measured

misu'rino *nm* measuring spoon

'mite *a* mild; ‹*prezzo*› moderate

'mitico *a* mythical

miti'gare *vt* mitigate

miti'garsi *vr* calm down; ‹*clima:*› become mild

'mitilo *nm* mussel

mitiz'zare *vt* mythicize

'mito *nm* myth

mitolo'gia *nf* mythology

mito'logico *a* mythological

mi'tomane *nmf* compulsive liar

'mitra *nf* *Relig* mitre ● *nm inv* *Mil* machine-gun

mitragli'are *vt* machine-gun; **~ di domande** fire questions at

mitraglia'trice *nf* machine-gun

mitt. *abbr* (*mittente*) sender

mitteleuro'peo *a* Central European

mit'tente *nmf* sender

'mixer *nm inv* mixer

mne'monico *a* mnemonic; **frase mnemonica** mnemonic

mo' *nm* **a mo' di** by way of ‹*esempio, consolazione*›

'mobile¹ *a* mobile; (*volubile*) fickle; (*che si può muovere*) movable; **beni** *pl* **mobili** moveable personal estate; **squadra ~** flying squad

'mobile² *nm* piece of furniture; **mobili** *pl* furniture *sg*. **~ bar** drinks cabinet. **mobili** *pl* **da giardino** garden furniture. **mobili** *pl* **in stile** reproduction furniture

mo'bilia *nf* furniture

mobili'are *a* ‹*capitale*› movable; ‹*credito*› medium-term; ‹*mercato*› share *attrib*; **patrimonio ~** non-property assets

mobili'ere *nm* furniture dealer

mobili'ficio *nm* furniture factory

mo'bilio *nm* furniture

mobilità *nf* mobility

mobili'tare *vt* mobilize

mobilitazi'one *nf* mobilization

'moca *nm inv* mocha

mocas'sino *nm* moccasin

mocci'coso, -a *a* snotty ● *nmf* snotty-nosed kid, brat

'moccolo *nm* (*di candela*) candle-end; (*moccio*) snot

'moda *nf* fashion; **di ~** in fashion; **andare di ~** be in fashion; **alla ~** ⟨*musica, vestiti*⟩ up-to-date; **fuori ~** unfashionable

mo'dale *a* ⟨*verbo*⟩ modal

modalità *nf inv* formality; **~ d'uso** instruction

modana'tura *nf* moulding

mo'della *nf* model

model'lare *vt* model

model'lino *nm* model

model'lismo *nm* model-making; (*collezionismo*) collecting models

model'lista *nmf* model-maker; (*moda*) [fashion] designer

mo'dello *nm* model; (*stampo*) mould; (*di carta*) pattern; (*modulo*) form; (*moda*) male model. **~ in scala** scale model

'modem *nm inv* modem; **mandare per ~** modem, send by modem

'modem-fax *nm* fax-modem

mode'rare *vt* moderate; (*diminuire*) reduce

mode'rarsi *vr* control oneself

moderata'mente *adv* moderately

mode'rato *a* moderate

modera'|tore, -'trice *nmf* (*in tavola rotonda*) moderator ● *a* moderating

moderazi'one *nf* moderation

moderna'mente *adv* (*in modo moderno*) in a modern style

modernari'ato *nm* collecting 20th-century art and products

moder'nismo *nm* modernism

modernità *nf* modernity

moderniz'zare *vt* modernize

modernizzazi'one *nf* modernization

mo'derno *a* modern

mo'destia *nf* modesty

mo'desto *a* modest

'modico *a* reasonable

mo'difica *nf* modification

modifi'care *vt* modify

modifica'tore *nm* modifier

modificazi'one *nf* modification

mo'dista *nf* milliner

'modo *nm* way; (*garbo*) manners *pl*; (*occasione*) chance; *Gram* mood; **ad ogni ~** anyhow; **di ~ che** so that; **fare in ~ di** try to; **in che ~** (*inter*) how; **in qualche ~** somehow; **in questo ~** like this; **~ di dire** idiom; **per ~ di dire** so to speak; **in ~ ottimistico/pessimistico/anormale** optimistically/pessimistically/abnormally

modu'lare *vt* modulate

modula'tore *nm* modulator. **~ di frequenza** frequency modulator

modulazi'one *nf* modulation. **~ di frequenza** frequency modulation

'modulo *nm* form; (*lunare, di comando*) module. **~ continuo** continuous paper. **~ di domanda** application form. **~ di iscrizione** enrolment form. **~ di ordinazione** order form

'modus ope'randi *nm inv* modus operandi

'modus vi'vendi *nm inv* modus vivendi

mof'fetta *nf* skunk

'mogano *nm* mahogany

'mogio *a* dejected

'moglie *nf* wife

moi'cano *a* **taglio [di capelli] alla moicana** mohican [haircut]

mo'ine *nfpl* **fare le ~** behave in an affected way

'mola *nf* millstone; *Mech* grindstone

mo'lare *nm* molar

mo'lato *a* ⟨*vetro*⟩ cut

mola'trice *nf Mech* grinder

'mole *nf* mass; (*dimensione*) size

mo'lecola *nf* molecule

moleco'lare *a* molecular

mole'stare *vt* bother; (*più forte*) molest

molesta'|tore, -'trice *nmf* molester

mo'lestia *nf* nuisance. **molestie** *pl* **sessuali** sexual harassment *sg*

mo'lesto *a* bothersome

Mo'lise *nm* Molise

'molla *nf* spring; **molle** *pl* tongs; **prendere qcno con le molle** handle sb with kid gloves

mol'lare *vt* let go; (*fam: lasciare*) leave; *fam* give ⟨*ceffone*⟩; *Naut* cast off ● *vi* cease; **mollala!** *fam* stop that!

'molle *a* soft; (*bagnato*) wet

molleggi'are *vi* be springy ● *vt* spring

molleggi'arsi *vr* bend at the knees

molleggi'ato *a* bouncy

mol'leggio *nm* (*di auto*) suspension; (*di letto*) springs *pl*; (*esercizio*) knee-bends *pl*

mol'letta *nf* (*per capelli*) hairgrip, barrette *Am*; (*per bucato*) clothes-peg; **mollette** *pl* (*per ghiaccio ecc*) tongs. **~ da bucato** clothes peg

mollet'tone *nm* (*per tavolo*) padded table cloth

mol'lezza *nf* softness; **mollezze** *pl fig* luxury

mol'lica *nf* crumb

mol'liccio *a* squidgy

mol'lusco *nm* mollusc

'molo *nm* pier; (*banchina*) dock

'molotov *a inv* **bottiglia ~** Molotov cocktail

mol'teplice *a* manifold; (*numeroso*) numerous

molteplicità *nf* multiplicity

mol'tiplica *nf* (*di bicicletta*) gear ratio

moltipli'care *vt* multiply

moltipli'carsi *vr* multiply

moltiplica'tore *nm* multiplier

moltiplica'trice *nf* calculating machine

moltiplicazi'one *nf* multiplication

molti'tudine *nf* multitude

'molto *a* a lot of; (*con negazione e interrogazione*) much, a lot of; (*con nomi plurali*) many, a lot of; **non ~ tempo** not much time, not a lot of time; **molte grazie** thank you very much ● *adv* very; (*con verbi*) a lot; (*con avverbi*) much; **~ stupido** very stupid; **~ bene, grazie** very well, thank you; **mangiare ~** eat a lot; **~ più veloce** much faster; **non mangiare ~** not eat a lot, not eat much ● *pron* a lot; (*molto tempo*) a lot of time; (*con negazione e interrogazione*) much, a lot; (*plurale*) many; **non ne ho ~** I don't have much, I don't have a lot; **non ne ho molti** I don't have many, I don't have a lot; **non ci metterò ~** I won't be long; **fra non ~** before long; **molti** (*persone*) a lot of people; **eravamo in molti** there were a lot of us

momentanea'mente *adv* momentarily; **è ~ assente** he's not here at the moment

momen'taneo *a* momentary

mo'mento *nm* moment; **a momenti** (*a volte*) sometimes; (*fra un momento*) in a moment; **dal ~ che** since; **per il ~** for the time being; **al ~** at the moment; **da un ~ all'altro** ‹*cambiare idea ecc*› from one moment to the next; ‹*aspettare qcno ecc*› at any moment

'monaca *nf* nun

'Monaco *nm* Monaco ● *nf* (*di Baviera*) Munich

'monaco *nm* monk

mo'narca *nm* monarch

monar'chia *nf* monarchy

mo'narchico, -a *a* monarchic ● *nmf* monarchist

mona'stero *nm* (*di monaci*) monastery; (*di monache*) convent

mo'nastico *a* monastic

monche'rino *nm* stump

'monco *a* maimed; (*fig: troncato*) truncated; **~ di un braccio** one-armed

mon'dana *nf* lady of the night

mondanità *nf* (*gente*) beau monde; **~** *pl* pleasures of the world

mon'dano *a* worldly; **vita mondana** social life

mon'dare *vt* (*sbucciare*) peel; shell ‹*piselli*›; (*pulire*) clean

mondi'ale *a* world *attrib*; ‹*scala*› worldwide; (*fam: fantastico*) fantastic; **di fama ~** world-famous

mondi'ali *nmpl* World Cup

mondial'mente *adv* ‹*operare*› worldwide; **~ noto** world-famous

mon'dina *nf* seasonal worker in the rice fields

'mondo *nm* world; **il bel ~** fashionable society; **un ~** (*molto*) a lot. **non è la fine del ~** it's not the end of the world; **è la fine del ~** (*fam: fantastico*) it's out of this world; **~ cane!** *fam* damn!. **~ accademico** academia. **~ del lavoro** world of work. **~ dei sogni** never-never land. **~ dello spettacolo** show biz

mondovisi'one *nf* **in ~** transmitted worldwide

monelle'ria *nf* prank

mo'nello, -a *nmf* urchin

mo'neta *nf* coin; (*denaro*) money; (*denaro spicciolo*) [small] change. **~ estera** foreign currency. **~ [a corso] legale** legal tender. **~ unica** single currency

mone'tario *a* monetary

mongolfi'era *nf* hot air balloon

'mongolo *a* Mongol; *Med* mongol

mo'nile *nm* jewel

'monito *nm* warning

'monitor *nm inv* monitor

monito'raggio *nm* monitoring

moni'tore *nm* monitor

mono'albero *a inv* single-camshaft *attrib*

mono'blocco *nm Auto* cylinder block ● *a inv* ‹*cucina*› fitted

mo'nocolo *nm* monocle

monoco'lore *a Pol* one-party

monocro'matico *a* monochrome

mono'dose *a inv* individually packaged

monoga'mia *nf* monogamy

mo'nogamo *a* monogamous

monogra'fia *nf* monograph

mono'gramma *nm* monogram

mono'kini *nm inv* monokini

mono'lingue *a* monolingual

mono'lito *nm* monolith

monolo'cale *nm* studio flat *Br*, studio apartment

mo'nologo *nm* monologue

monoma'nia *nf* monomania

mononucle'osi *nf inv* **~ infettiva** glandular fever

mono'pattino *nm* [child's] scooter

mono'petto *a* single-breasted

mono'plano *nm* monoplane

mono'polio *nm* monopoly. **~ di Stato** state monopoly

monopoliz'zare *vt* monopolize

mono'posto *nm* single-seater

mono'reddito *a* single-income *attrib*

monosac'caride *nm* monosaccharide

mono'sci *nm inv* monoski

monosil'labico *a* monosyllabic

mono'sillabo *nm* monosyllable ● *a* monosyllabic

mo'nossido *nm* **~ di carbonio** carbon monoxide

monote'istico *a* monotheistic

monotona'mente *adv* monotonously

monoto'nia *nf* monotony

mo'notono *a* monotonous

mono'uso *a* disposable

monou'tente *a inv* single-user *attrib*

monsi'gnore *nm* monsignor

mon'sone *nm* monsoon

'monta *nf Zool* covering; (*modo di cavalcare*) riding style; **stallone da ~** stud horse

monta'carichi *nm inv* hoist

mon'taggio *nm Mech* assembly; *Cinema* editing; **scatola di ~** assembly kit; **catena di ~** production line

mon'tagna *nf* mountain; (*zona*) mountains *pl*; **montagne** *pl* **russe** roller coaster, big dipper

monta'gnoso *a* mountainous

monta'naro, -a *nmf* highlander

mon'tano *a* mountain *attrib*

mon'tante *nm* (*di finestra, porta*) upright; *Fin* total amount; (*nel pugilato*) upper cut

mon'tare *vt/i* mount; get on (*veicolo*); (*aumentare*) rise; *Mech* assemble; frame (*quadro*); *Culin* whip; edit (*film*); (*a cavallo*) ride; *fig* blow up

mon'tarsi *vr* ~ **la testa** get big-headed

mon'tato, -a *nmf fam* poser

monta'|tore, -'trice *nmf* assembler

monta'tura *nf Mech* assembling; (*di occhiali*) frame; (*di gioiello*) mounting; *fig* exaggeration

'monte *nm anche fig* mountain; **a ~** upstream; **andare a ~** be ruined; **mandare a ~ qcsa** ruin sth. **M~ Bianco** Mont Blanc. **~ di pietà** pawnshop

monte'premi *nm inv* jackpot

mont'gomery *nm inv* duffle coat

mon'tone *nm* ram; **carne di ~** mutton

montu'oso *a* mountainous

monumen'tale *a* monumental

monu'mento *nm* monument. **~ ai caduti** war memorial. **~ commemorativo** memorial. **~ nazionale** national monument

mo'plen[®] *nm* moulded plastic

mo'quette *nf* (*tappeto*) fitted carpet

'mora *nf* (*del gelso*) mulberry; (*del rovo*) blackberry

mo'rale *a* moral ● *nf* morals *pl*; (*di storia*) moral ● *nm* morale

mora'lista *nmf* moralist

mora'listico *a* moralistic

moralità *nf inv* morality; (*condotta*) morals *pl*

moraliz'zare *vt/i* moralize

moral'mente *adv* morally

mora'toria *nf* moratorium

morbida'mente *adv* softly

morbi'dezza *nf* softness

'morbido *a* soft

mor'billo *nm* measles *sg*

'morbo *nm* disease. **~ della mucca pazza** mad cow disease

morbosa'mente *adv* morbidly

morbosità *nf* (*qualità*) morbidity

mor'boso *a* morbid

'morchia *nf* sludge

mor'dace *a* cutting

mor'dente *a* biting

'mordere *vt* bite; (*corrodere*) bite into

mordicchi'are *vt* gnaw

mo'rello *nm* black horse ● *a* blackish

mo'rena *nf* moraine

mo'rente *a* dying

mo'resco *a* Moorish

mor'fina *nf* morphine

morfi'nomane *nmf* morphine addict

morfolo'gia *nf* morphology

morfo'logico *a* morphological

mori'bondo *a* dying; (*istituzione*) moribund

morige'rato *a* moderate

mo'rire *vi* die; *fig* die out; **fa un freddo da ~** it's freezing cold, it's perishing; **~ di noia** be bored to death; **c'era da ~ dal ridere** it was hilariously funny; **morir di fame** starve to death; *fig* starve

mor'mone *nmf* Mormon

mormo'rare *vt/i* murmur; (*brontolare*) mutter

mormo'rio *nm* murmuring; (*lamentela*) grumbling

'moro *a* dark ● *nm* Moor; (*negro*) black

mo'roso *a* in arrears

'morra *nf* game for two players where each shouts a number at the same time as showing a number of fingers

'morsa *nf* vice; *fig* grip

'morse *a* alfabeto ~ Morse code

mor'setto *nm* clamp; (*stringinaso*) nose clip. **~ per batteria** battery lead connection

morsi'care *vt* bite

morsica'tura *nf* [snake] bite

'morso *nm* bite; (*di cibo, briglia*) bit; **i morsi della fame** hunger pangs

morta'della *nf* mortadella (*type of salted pork*)

mor'taio *nm* mortar

mor'tale *a* mortal; (*simile a morte*) deadly; **di una noia ~** deadly

mortalità *nf* mortality

mortal'mente *adv* (*ferito*) fatally; (*offeso*) mortally; (*annoiato*) to death. **~ stanco** *fam* dead tired

morta'retto *nm* firecracker

'morte *nf* death; **non è la ~ di nessuno** it's not the end of the world; **lo odia a ~** *fam* she can't stand the sight of him; **annoiarsi a ~** *fam* be bored to death. **~ cerebrale** brain death

mortifi'cante *a* mortifying

mortifi'care *vt* mortify

mortifi'carsi *vr* be mortified

mortifi'cato *a* mortified

mortificazi'one *nf* mortification

'morto, -a *pp di* **morire** ● *a* dead; **~ di freddo** frozen to death; **stanco ~** dead tired ● *nm* dead man ● *nf* dead woman

mor'torio *nm* funeral

mo'saico *nm* mosaic

'Mosca *nf* Moscow

'mosca *nf* fly; (*barba*) goatee; **cadere come le mosche** be dropping like flies; **essere una ~ bianca** be a rarity; **non si sentiva volare una ~** you could have heard a pin drop. **~ cieca** blindman's buff

mo'scato *a* muscat. **noce moscata** nutmeg ● *nm* muscatel

mosce'rino *nm* midge; (*fam: persona*) midget

mo'schea *nf* mosque

moschetti'ere *nm* musketeer

mo'schetto *nm* musket

moschet'tone *nm* (*in alpinismo*) snaplink; (*gancio*) spring clip

moschi'cida *a inv* **carta ~** flypaper; **liquido ~** fly spray

'moscio *a* limp; **avere l'erre moscia** not be able to say one's r's properly

mo'scone *nm* bluebottle; ⟨*barca*⟩ pedalo

Mosè *nm* Moses

'mossa *nf* movement; ⟨*passo*⟩ move

'mosso *pp di* **muovere** ● *a* ⟨*mare*⟩ rough; ⟨*capelli*⟩ wavy; ⟨*fotografia*⟩ blurred

mo'starda *nf* mustard. **~ di Cremona** *preserve made from candied fruit in grape must or sugar with mustard*

'mostra *nf* show; ⟨*d'arte*⟩ exhibition; **far ~ di** pretend; **in ~** on show; **mettersi in ~** make oneself conspicuous; **far ~ di sé** show off; **far bella ~ di sé** look impressive

'mostra-mer'cato *nf* trade fair

mo'strare *vt* show; ⟨*indicare*⟩ point out; ⟨*spiegare*⟩ explain; **~ di** ⟨*sembrare*⟩ seem; ⟨*fingere*⟩ pretend

mos'trarsi *vr* show oneself; ⟨*apparire*⟩ appear

mo'strina *nf* flash

'mostro *nm* monster; ⟨*fig: persona*⟩ genius; **~ sacro** *fig* sacred cow

mostruosa'mente *adv* tremendously

mostru'oso *a* monstrous; ⟨*incredibile*⟩ enormous

mo'tel *nm inv* motel

moti'vare *vt* cause; *Jur* justify

moti'vato *a* ⟨*persona*⟩ motivated; ⟨*azione*⟩ justified

motivazi'one *nf* motivation; ⟨*giustificazione*⟩ justification

mo'tivo *nm* reason; ⟨*movente*⟩ motive; ⟨*in musica, letteratura*⟩ theme; ⟨*disegno*⟩ pattern, motif; **senza ~** for no reason; ⟨*senza giustificazione*⟩ unjustifiably. **~ a scacchi** chequered pattern

'moto *nm* motion; ⟨*esercizio*⟩ exercise; ⟨*gesto*⟩ movement; ⟨*sommossa*⟩ rising. **~ ondoso** swell. **~ perpetuo** perpetual motion ● *nf inv* ⟨*motocicletta*⟩ motor bike; **mettere in ~** start ⟨*motore*⟩

moto'carro *nm* three-wheeler

motoci'cletta *nf* motor cycle. **~ da corsa** racing motorbike, racer

motoci'clismo *nm* motorcycling

motoci'clista *nmf* motorcyclist

moto'cross *nm* motocross

motocros'sista *nmf* scrambler

moto'lancia *nf* motor launch

moto'nautica *nf* speedboat racing

moto'nave *nf* motor vessel

mo'tore *a* motor *attrib* ● *nm* motor, engine; **con ~ turbo** turbocharged. . **~ diesel** diesel engine. **~ a iniezione** fuel injection engine. **~ raffreddato ad aria** air-cooled engine. **~ a reazione** jet [engine]. **~ a scoppio** internal combustion engine

moto'retta *nf* motor scooter

moto'rino *nm* moped. **~ d'avviamento** starter motor

mo'torio *a* motor *attrib*

moto'rista *mf* **~ di bordo** flight engineer

motoriz'zare *vt* motorize

motoriz'zato *a Mil* motorized

motorizzazi'one *nf* ⟨*ufficio*⟩ vehicle licensing office

moto'scafo *nm* motorboat

moto'sega *nf* chain saw

motove'detta *nf* patrol vessel

mo'trice *nf* engine

'motto *nm* motto; ⟨*facezia*⟩ witticism; ⟨*massima*⟩ saying

'mountain bike *nf inv* mountain bike

mouse *nm inv* Comput mouse

mousse *nf inv* Culin mousse. **~ al cioccolato** chocolate mousse

mo'vente *nm* motive

mo'venze *nfpl* movements

movimen'tare *vt* enliven

movimen'tato *a* lively

movi'mento *nm* movement; **essere sempre in ~** be always on the go. **~ passeggeri e merci** passenger and freight traffic

mozi'one *nf* motion. **~ d'ordine** point of order

mozzafi'ato *a inv* nail-biting

moz'zare *vt* cut off; dock ⟨*coda*⟩; **~ il fiato a qcno** take sb's breath away

mozza'rella *nf* mozzarella ⟨*mild, white cheese*⟩

mozzi'cone *nm* ⟨*di sigaretta*⟩ stub

'mozzo *nm* Mech hub; *Naut* ship's boy ● *a* ⟨*coda*⟩ truncated; ⟨*testa*⟩ severed

ms *abbr* ⟨**manoscritto**⟩ MS

'mucca *nf* cow; **morbo della ~ pazza** mad cow disease

'mucchio *nm* heap, pile; **un ~ di** *fig* lots of

mucil'lagine *nf Bot* mucilage

'muco *nm* mucus

'muffa *nf* mould; **fare la ~** go mouldy

muf'fire *vi* go mouldy

muf'fola *nf* mitt

mu'flone *nm* Zool mouflon

mugghi'are *vi* ⟨*vento, mare:*⟩ roar

mug'gire *vi* ⟨*mucca:*⟩ moo, low; ⟨*toro:*⟩ bellow

mug'gito *nm* moo; ⟨*di toro*⟩ bellow; ⟨*azione*⟩ mooing; bellowing

mu'ghetto *nm* lily of the valley

mugo'lare *vi* whine; ⟨*persona:*⟩ moan

mugo'lio *nm* whining

mugu'gnare *vt fam* mumble

mulatti'era *nf* mule track

mu'latto, -a *nmf* mulatto

mu'leta *nf inv* muleta

muli'ebre *a* liter feminine

muli'nare *vi* spin

muli'nello *nm* ⟨*d'acqua*⟩ whirlpool; ⟨*di vento*⟩ eddy; ⟨*giocattolo*⟩ windmill

mu'lino *nm* mill. **~ a vento** windmill

'mulo *nm* mule

'multa *nf* fine. **~ per divieto di sosta** parking ticket

mul'tare *vt* fine

multico'lore *a* multicoloured

multicultu'rale *a* multicultural

multifunzio'nale *a* multifunction[al]
multilate'rale *a* multilateral
multi'lingue *a* multilingual
multi'media *mpl* multimedia
multimedi'ale *a* multimedia *attrib*
multimedialità *nf* multimedia
multimiliar'dario, -a *nmf* multi-million-aire
multinazio'nale *a & nf* multinational
'multiplo *a & nm* multiple
multiproprietà *nf inv* time-share; **una casa in ~** a time-share
multi'sale *a inv* **cinema ~** multiplex [cinema]
multi'tasking *nm Comput* multitasking
multi'uso *a ‹utensile›* all-purpose
'mummia *nf* mummy; *(fig: persona)* old fogey
mummifi'care *vt* mummify
'mungere *vt* milk
mungi'tura *nf* milking
munici'pale *a* municipal
municipalità *nf inv* town council
muni'cipio *nm* town hall
munifi'cenza *nf* munificence, bounty
mu'nifico *a* munificent
mu'nire *vt* fortify; **~ di** *(provvedere)* supply with; **munitevi di un carrello/cestino** please take a trolley/basket
munizi'oni *nfpl* ammunition *sg*
'munto *pp di* **mungere**
mu'overe *vt* move; *(suscitare)* arouse
mu'oversi *vr* move; **muoviti!** hurry up!, come on!
'mura *nfpl (cinta di città)* walls
mu'raglia *nf* wall
mu'rale *a* mural; *‹pittura›* wall *attrib*
mur'are *vt* wall up
mu'rario *a* masonry *attrib*; **cinta muraria** walls *pl*; **opera muraria** masonry
mura'tore *nm* bricklayer; *(con pietre)* mason; *(operaio edile)* builder
mura'tura *nf (di pietra)* masonry, stonework; *(di mattoni)* brickwork
mu'rena *nf* moray eel
'muro *nm* wall; *(di nebbia)* bank; **a ~** *‹armadio›* built-in. **~ divisorio** partition wall. **~ di gomma** *fig* wall of indifference. **~ a intercapedine** cavity wall. **M~ del pianto** Wailing Wall. **~ portante** load-bearing wall. **~ del suono** sound barrier
'musa *nf anche fig* muse
muschi'ato *a* musky
'muschio *nm Bot* moss

musco'lare *a* muscular
muscola'tura *nf* muscles *pl*
'muscolo *nm* muscle
musco'loso *a* muscular
mu'seo *nm* museum
museru'ola *nf* muzzle
'musica *nf* music
musica folk *nf* folk [music]
'musical *nm inv* musical
musi'cale *a* musical
musi'care *vt* set to music
musicas'setta *nf* cassette
musi'cista *nmf* musician
musicolo'gia *nf* musicology
'muso *nm* muzzle; *(pej: di persona)* mug; *(di aeroplano)* nose; **fare il ~** sulk
mu'sone, -a *nmf* sulker
'mussola *nf* muslin
mussul'mano, -a *a & nmf* Muslim, Moslem
'muta *nf (cambio)* change; *(di penne)* moult; *(di cani)* pack; *(per immersione subacquea)* wetsuit
muta'mento *nm* change
mu'tande *nfpl* pants
mutan'dine *nfpl* panties; **~ da bagno** bathing trunks; *(da donna)* bikini bottom
mutan'doni *nmpl (da uomo)* long johns; *(da donna)* bloomers
mu'tante *nmf* mutant
mu'tare *vt* change
mutazi'one *nf* mutation
mu'tevole *a* changeable
muti'lare *vt* mutilate
muti'lato, -a *a* crippled ● *nmf* disabled person. **~ di guerra** disabled ex-serviceman. **~ del lavoro** person disabled at work
mutilazi'one *nf* mutilation
mu'tismo *nm* dumbness; *fig* obstinate silence
'muto *a* dumb; *(silenzioso)* silent; *(fonetica)* mute
'mutua *nf* **[cassa] ~** sickness benefit fund
mutu'abile *a ‹farmaco›* prescribable on the NHS
mutu'are *vt* borrow *‹teoria, parola›*
mutu'atario, -a *nmf Fin* borrower
mutu'ato, -a *nmf* ≈ NHS patient
'mutuo[1] *a* mutual
'mutuo[2] *nm* loan; *(per la casa)* mortgage; **fare un ~** take out a mortgage; **società di ~ soccorso** friendly society. **~ per la casa** home loan. **~ ipotecario** mortgage

Nn

na'babbo *nm* nabob; **vivere come un ~** live in the lap of luxury

'nacchera *nf* castanet

na'dir *nm* nadir

'nafta *nf* naphtha; (*per motori*) diesel oil; **a ~** ‹*bruciatore*› oil-burning

'naia *nf* cobra; (*sl: servizio militare*) national service

'nailon *nm* nylon

Na'mibia *nf* Namibia

na'nismo *nm* dwarfism

'nanna *nf* (*sl: infantile*) byebyes; **andare a ~** go byebyes; **fare la ~** sleep

'nano, -a *a & nmf* dwarf

'napalm *nm* napalm

napole'tana *nf* (*caffettiera*) Neapolitan coffee maker

napole'tano, -a *a & nmf* Neapolitan

'Napoli *nf* Naples

'nappa *nf* tassel; (*pelle*) soft leather

narci'sismo *nm* narcissism

narci'sista *a & nmf* narcissist

nar'ciso *nm* narcissus

nar'cosi *nf* general anaesthesia

nar'cotici *nf* Drug Squad

nar'cotico *a & nm* narcotic

na'rice *nf* nostril

nar'rare *vt* tell

narra'tivo, -a *a* narrative ● *nf* fiction

narra|'tore, -'trice *nmf* narrator

narrazi'one *nf* narration; (*racconto*) story

na'sale *a* nasal

na'scente *a* budding

'nascere *vi* (*venire al mondo*) be born; (*germogliare*) sprout; (*sorgere*) rise; **~ da** *fig* arise from

'nascita *nf* birth

nasci'turo *nm* unborn child

na'scondere *vt* hide

na'scondersi *vr* hide

nascon'diglio *nm* hiding-place

nascon'dino *nm* hide-and-seek

na'scosto *pp di* **nascondere** ● *a* hidden; **di ~** secretly

na'sello *nm* (*pesce*) hake

'naso *nm* nose

na'sone *nm* big nose, hooter *fam*

'nassa *nf* lobster pot

'nastro *nm* ribbon; (*di registratore ecc*) tape. **~ adesivo** adhesive tape. **~ isolante** insulating tape. **~ magnetico** magnetic tape, mag tape *fam*. **~ trasportatore** conveyor belt

Na'tale *nm* Christmas

na'tale *a* (*giorno, paese*) of one's birth

na'tali *nmpl* parentage

natalità *nf* [number of] births, birthrate

nata'lizio *a* (*del Natale*) Christmas *attrib*; (*di nascita*) of one's birth

na'tante *a* floating ● *nm* craft

'natica *nf* buttock

na'tio *a* native

Natività *nf* Nativity

na'tivo, -a *a & nmf* native

NATO *nf* Nato, NATO

'nato *pp di* **nascere** ● *a* born; **uno scrittore ~** a born writer; **nata Rossi** née Rossi

na'tura *nf* nature; **pagare in ~** pay in kind; **di ~ politica** of a political nature. **~ morta** still life

natu'rale *a* natural; **al ~** ‹*alimento*› plain, natural; **~!** naturally, of course

natura'lezza *nf* naturalness

naturaliz'zare *vt* naturalize

natural'mente *adv* (*ovviamente*) naturally, of course

natu'rista *nmf* naturalist

natu'ristico *a* naturist

naufra'gare *vi* be wrecked; ‹*persona:*› be shipwrecked

nau'fragio *nm* shipwreck; *fig* wreck

'naufrago, -a *nmf* survivor

'nausea *nf* nausea; **avere la ~** feel sick

nausea'bondo *a* nauseating

nause'ante *a* nauseating

nause'are *vt* nauseate

'nautica *nf* navigation

'nautico *a* nautical

na'vale *a* naval

na'vata *nf* (*centrale*) nave; (*laterale*) aisle

'nave *nf* ship. **~ ammiraglia** flagship. **~ da carico** cargo boat. **~ cisterna** tanker. **~ da crociera** cruise liner. **~ fattoria** factory ship. **~ da guerra** warship. **~ di linea** liner. **~ passeggeri** passenger ship. **~ porta-container** container ship. **~ spaziale** spaceship. **~ traghetto** ferry

na'vetta *nf* shuttle

navi'cella *nf* **~ spaziale** nose cone

navi'gabile *a* navigable

navi'gare *vi* sail; **~ in Internet** surf the Net

naviga|'tore, -'trice *mf* navigator; (*in Internet*) surfer; **~ solitario** lone yachtsman. **~ spaziale** spaceman

navigazi'one *nf* navigation; **della ~** navigational

na'viglio *nm* fleet; (*canale*) canal

nazifa'scismo *nm* Nazi fascism

nazifa'scista *nmf* Nazi fascist

nazio'nale *a* national ● *nf* *Sport* national team

naziona'lismo *nm* nationalism
naziona'lista *nmf* nationalist
nazionalità *nf inv* nationality
nazionaliz'zare *vt* nationalize
nazi'one *nf* nation. **Nazioni** *pl* **Unite** United Nations
na'zista *a & nmf* Nazi
N.B. *abbr* (**nota bene**) NB
n.d.r. *abbr* (**nota del redattore**) editor's note
'n'drangheta *nf* Calabrian Mafia
n.d.t. *abbr* (**nota del traduttore**) translator's note
NE *abbr* (**nord-est**) NE
ne *pron* (*di lui*) about him; (*di lei*) about her; (*di loro*) about them; (*di ciò*) about it; (*da ciò*) from that; (*di un insieme*) of it; (*di un gruppo*) of them; **ne sono contento** I'm happy about it; **non ne conosco nessuno** I don't know any of them; **ne ho** I have some; **non ne ho più** I don't have any left ● *adv* from there; **ne vengo ora** I've just come from there; **me ne vado** I'm off; **ne va della mia reputazione** my reputation is at stake
né *conj* **né... né...** neither... nor...; **non ne ho il tempo né la voglia** I don't have either the time or the inclination; **né tu né io vogliamo andare** neither you nor I want to go; **né l'uno né l'altro** neither [of them/us]
ne'anche *adv* (*neppure*) not even; (*senza neppure*) without even ● *conj* (*e neppure*) neither... nor; **non parlo inglese, e lui ~** I don't speak English, neither does he *o* and he doesn't either
'nebbia *nf* mist; (*in città, autostrada*) fog
nebbi'oso *a* misty; (*in città, autostrada*) foggy
nebuliz'zare *vt* atomize
nebulizza'tore *nm* atomizer; (*per il naso*) nasal spray
nebulizzazi'one *nf* atomizing; **fare delle nebulizzazioni** take nasal sprays
nebulosità *nf* vagueness
nebu'loso *a* hazy; (*teoria*) nebulous; (*discorso*) woolly
necessaria'mente *adv* necessarily
neces'sario *a* necessary ● *nm* **fare il ~** do the necessary, do the needful
necessità *nf inv* necessity; (*bisogno*) need
necessi'tare *vi* **~ di** need; (*essere necessario*) be necessary
necro'logio *nm* obituary
ne'cropoli *nf inv* necropolis
ne'crosi *nf* necrosis
ne'fando *a* wicked
ne'fasto *a* ill-omened
ne'frite *nf* nephritis
nefrolo'gia *nf* nephrology
ne'frologo, -a *nmf* nephrologist
ne'gabile *a* deniable
ne'gare *vt* deny; (*rifiutare*) refuse; **essere negato per qcsa** be no good at sth
nega'tiva *nf* negative
nega'tivo *a* negative

negazi'one *nf* negation; (*diniego*) denial; *Gram* negative; **essere la ~ per** know nothing about
ne'gletto *a* neglected
'negli = **in** + **gli**
negli'gente *a* negligent
negli'genza *nf* negligence
negozi'abile *a* negotiable
negozi'ante *nmf* dealer; (*bottegaio*) shopkeeper
negozi'are *vt* negotiate ● *vi* **~ in** trade in, deal in
negozi'ati *nmpl* negotiations
ne'gozio *nm* shop. **~ di abbigliamento** fashion boutique. **~ di alimentari** grocer's. **~ di antiquariato** antique shop. **~ duty free** duty-free shop. **~ giuridico** legal transaction
'negro, -a *a* Negro, black ● *nmf* Negro, black; (*scrittore*) ghost writer; **come un ~** (*lavorare*) like a slave
negro'mante *nmf* necromancer
'nei = **in** + **i**
nel = **in** + **il**
'nella = **in** + **la**
'nelle = **in** + **le**
'nello = **in** + **lo**
'nembo *nm* nimbus
ne'mesi *nf* nemesis
ne'mico, -a *a* hostile ● *nmf* enemy
nem'meno *conj* not even
'nenia *nf* dirge; (*per bambini*) lullaby; (*piagnucolio*) wail
'neo *nm* mole; (*applicato*) beauty spot
neo+ *pref* neo+
neo'classico *a* neoclassical
neocolonia'lismo *nm* neocolonialism
neofa'scismo *nm* neofascism
neola'tino *a* Romance
neolaure'ato, -a *nmf* recent graduate
neo'litico *a* Neolithic
neolo'gismo *nm* neologism
'neon *nm* neon
neo'nato, -a *a* newborn ● *nmf* newborn baby
neona'zismo *nm* Neonazism
neona'zista *a & nmf* Neonazi
neozelan'dese *a* New Zealand *attrib* ● *nmf* New Zealander
nep'pure *conj* not even
ne'rastro *a* blackish
'nerbo *nm* (*forza*) strength; *fig* backbone; **senza ~** effete
nerbo'ruto *a* brawny
ne'retto *nm* *Typ* bold [type]
'nero *a* black; (*fam: arrabbiato*) fuming ● *nm* black; **l'ho visto ~ su bianco** I've seen it in black and white; **mettere ~ su bianco** put in writing. **~ pieno** *Typ* solid. **~ di seppia** sepia
nerva'tura *nf* nerves *pl*; *Bot* veining; (*di libro*) band
ner'vetti *nmpl* chopped beef and veal with onions
ner'vino *a* (*gas*) nerve *attrib*

'**nervo** nm nerve; Bot vein; **avere i nervi** be bad-tempered; **dare ai nervi a qcno** get on sb's nerves

nervo'**sismo** nm nerviness

ner'**voso** a nervous; (irritabile) bad-tempered; **avere il ~** be irritable; **esaurimento ~** nervous breakdown

'**nespola** nf medlar

'**nespolo** nm medlar[-tree]

'**nesso** nm link, connection

nes'**suno** a no, not... any; (qualche) any; **non ho nessun problema** I don't have any problems, I have no problems; **non ha nessun valore** it hasn't any value, it has no value; **da nessuna parte** nowhere; **non lo trovo da nessuna parte** I can't find it anywhere; **in nessun modo** on no account; **per nessun motivo** for no reason; **nessuna notizia?** any news? ● pron nobody, no one, not ... anybody, not... anyone; (qualcuno) anybody, anyone; **hai delle domande? – nessuna** do you have any questions? – none; **~ di voi** none of you; **~ dei due** (di voi due) neither of you; **non ho visto ~ dei tuoi amici** I haven't seen any of your friends; **c'è ~?** is anybody there?

'**nesting** nm inv Comput nesting

net nm inv Tennis net cord

'**nettare** nm nectar

net'**tare** vt clean

net'**tezza** nf cleanliness. **~ urbana** cleansing department

'**netto** a clean; (chiaro) clear; Comm net; **di ~** just like that

Net'tuno nm Neptune

nettur'**bino** nm dustman

'**neuro** nf neurological clinic

neuro+ pref neuro+

neurochirur'**gia** nf brain surgery

neurochi'**rurgo** nm brain surgeon

neurolo'**gia** nf neurology

neuro'**logico** a neurological

neuropsichi'**atra** nm neuropsychiatry

neuropsichia'**tria** nf neuropsychiatrist

neu'**trale** a & nm neutral

neutralità nf neutrality

neutraliz'**zare** vt neutralize

'**neutro** a neutral; Gram neuter ● nm Gram neuter

neu'**trone** nm neutron

ne'**vaio** nm snow-field

'**neve** nf snow

nevi'**care** vi snow; **nevica** it is snowing

nevi'**cata** nf snowfall

ne'**vischio** nm sleet

ne'**voso** a snowy

nevral'**gia** nf neuralgia

ne'**vralgico** a neuralgic; **punto ~** nerve centre; (di questione ecc) crucial point

nevraste'**nia** nf neurasthenia

nevra'**stenico** a neurasthenic; (irritabile) hot tempered

ne'**vrite** nf neuritis

ne'**vrosi** nf inv neurosis

ne'**vrotico** a neurotic

'**nibbio** nm kite

Nica'**ragua** nm Nicaragua

nicara'**guense** a & nmf Nicaraguan

'**nicchia** nf niche

nicchi'**are** vi shilly-shally

'**nichel** nm nickel

nichi'**lista** nmf nihilist ● a nihilistic

nico'**tina** nf nicotine

nidi'**ace** nm nestling

nidi'**ata** nf brood

nidifi'**care** vi nest

nidifi'**cato** a Comput nested

nidificazi'**one** nf Zool nesting

'**nido** nm nest; (giardino d'infanzia) crèche; **a ~ d'ape** (tessuto) honeycomb. **~ di uccello** bird's nest. **~ di vipere** fig nest of vipers

ni'**ente** pron nothing, not... anything; (qualcosa) anything; **non ho fatto ~ di male** I didn't do anything wrong, I did nothing wrong; **nient'altro?** anything else?; **grazie! – di ~!** thank you! – don't mention it!; **non serve a ~** it is no use; **vuoi ~?** do you want anything?; **dal ~** (venire su) from nothing; **da ~** (poco importante) minor; (di poco valore) worthless ● a inv fam **~ pesci oggi** no fish today; **non ho ~ fame** I'm not the slightest bit hungry ● adv **non fa ~** (non importa) it doesn't matter; **per ~** at all; (litigare) over nothing; **~ affatto!** no way! ● nm **un bel ~** absolutely nothing, damn-all fam; **basta un ~ per spaventarlo** it doesn't take much to scare him

nientedi'**meno**, niente'**meno** adv **~ che** no less than ● int fancy that!

night nm inv night club

'**Nilo** nm Nile

'**ninfa** nf nymph

nin'**fea** nf water-lily

nin'**fomane** nf nymphomaniac; **da ~** nymphomaniac

ninna'**nanna** nf lullaby

'**ninnolo** nm plaything; (fronzolo) knickknack

ni'**pote** nm (di zii) nephew; (di nonni) grandson, grandchild; **nipoti** pl grandchildren, nephews and nieces ● nf (di zii) niece; (di nonni) granddaughter, grandchild

nip'**ponico** a Japanese

'**nisba** pron (sl: niente) zilch

'**nitido** a neat; (chiaro) clear

ni'**trato** nm nitrate

'**nitrico** a nitric

ni'**trire** vi neigh

ni'**trito** nm (di cavallo) neigh; Chem nitrite

nitro+ pref nitro+

nitroglice'**rina** nf nitroglycerine

'**niveo** a snow-white

N.N. abbr (numeri) Nos

NO abbr (nord-ovest) NW

N° abbr (numero) No.

no adv no; **credo di no** I don't think so; **perché no?** why not?; **io no not me; sì o no?** yes or no?; **ha detto così, no?** he said so, didn't he?; **fa freddo, no?** it's cold, isn't it?; **se no** otherwise ● nm no; (nelle votazioni) nay

nobil'**donna** nf noblewoman

'**nobile** *a* noble; **metallo ~** noble metal; **di animo ~** noble-minded ● *nm* noble, nobleman ● *nf* noble, noblewoman

nobili'are *a* noble

nobiltà *nf* nobility

nobilu'omo *nm* nobleman

'**nocca** *nf* knuckle

nocci'ola *nf* hazelnut

noccio'line [americane] *nfpl* peanuts

nocci'olo *nm* (*albero*) hazel

'**nocciolo** *nm* stone; *Phys* core; *fig* heart; **il ~ della questione** the heart of the matter

'**noce** *nf* walnut. **~ moscata** nutmeg. **~ pecan** pecan. **~ di vitello** veal with mushrooms ● *nm* (*legno*) walnut; (*albero*) walnut [tree]

noce'pesca *nf* nectarine

no'cino *nm* walnut liqueur

no'civo *a* harmful

no'dino *nm* veal chop

'**nodo** *nm* knot; *fig* lump; *Comput* node; **fare il ~ della cravatta** do up one's tie. **~ alla gola** lump in the throat; **~ della questione** crux of the matter. **~ ferroviario** railway junction. **~ piano** reef knot. **~ scorsoio** slipknot

no'doso *a* knotty

'**nodulo** *nm* nodule

Noè *nm* Noah

'**noi** *pers pron* (*soggetto*) we; (*oggetto, con prep*) us; **chi è? – siamo ~** who is it? – it's us; **noi due** the two of us

'**noia** *nf* boredom; (*fastidio*) bother; (*persona*) bore; **dar ~** annoy

noi'altri *pers pron* we

noi'oso *a* boring; (*fastidioso*) tiresome

noleggi'are *vt* hire; (*dare a noleggio*) hire out; charter (*nave, aereo*)

no'leggio *nm* hire; (*di nave, aereo*) charter. **~ barche/biciclette/sci** boat/cycle/ski hire

'**nolo** *nm* hire; *Naut* freight; **a ~** for hire

'**nomade** *a* nomadic ● *nmf* nomad

'**nome** *nm* name; *Gram* noun; **a ~ di** (*da parte di*) on behalf of; **di ~** by name; **farsi un ~** make a name for oneself; **nel ~ di...** in the name of.... **~ d'arte** professional name. **~ di battaglia** nom de guerre. **~ di battesimo** first name, Christian name. **~ depositato** trade-name. **~ di famiglia** surname, family name. **~ proprio** proper name, proper noun. **~ da ragazza** maiden name. **~ da sposata** married name

no'mea *nf* reputation

nomencla'tura *nf* nomenclature

no'mignolo *nm* nickname

'**nomina** *nf* appointment; **di prima ~** newly appointed

nomi'nale *a* nominal; *Gram* noun *attrib*

nomi'nare *vt* name; (*menzionare*) mention; (*eleggere*) appoint

nomina'tivo *a* nominative; *Comm* registered ● *nm* nominative; (*nome*) name; **caso ~** nominative case

non *adv* not; **~ ti amo** I do not *o* don't love you; **~ c'è di che** not at all; **~ più** no longer

nonché *conj* (*tanto meno*) let alone; (*e anche*) as well as

nonconfor'mista *a* & *nmf* *inv* nonconformist

nonconformità *nf* noncompliance

noncu'rante *a* nonchalant; (*negligente*) indifferent

noncu'ranza *nf* nonchalance; (*negligenza*) indifference

nondi'meno *conj* nevertheless

'**nonna** *nf* grandmother, grandma *fam*, gran *fam*

'**nonno** *nm* grandfather, grandpa *fam*; **nonni** *pl* grandparents

non'nulla *nm inv* trifle

'**nono** *a* & *nm* ninth

nono'stante *prep* in spite of ● *conj* although

non stop *a inv* & *adv* nonstop

nontiscordardimé *nm inv* forget-me-not

nonvio'lento *a* nonviolent

nonvio'lenza *nf* nonviolence

nor'cino *nm* pig butcher

nord *nm* north; **del ~** northern

nord-'est *nm* northeast; **a ~** northeasterly; **del ~** northeastern; **vento di ~** northeasterly [wind]

'**nordico** *a* northern

nor'dista *a* & *nmf* Yankee

nordocciden'tale *a* northwestern

nordorien'tale *a* northeastern

nord-'ovest *nm* northwest; **a ~** northwesterly; **del ~** northwestern **vento di ~** northwesterly [wind]

'**norma** *nf* norm; (*regola*) rule; (*per l'uso*) instruction; **a ~ di legge** according to law; **è buona ~** it's advisable; **di ~** as a rule, normally

nor'male *a* normal ● *nm* **fuori del ~** out of the ordinary; **superiore al ~** above average

normalità *nf* normality; **rientrare nella ~** be quite normal

normaliz'zare *vt* normalize

normal'mente *adv* normally

Norman'dia *nf* Normandy

nor'manno *a* from Normandy; (*storico*) Norman

norma'tivo *a* normative, prescriptive

nor'mografo *nm* stencil

nor'reno *a* Norse

norve'gese *a* & *nmf* Norwegian

Nor'vegia *nf* Norway

noso'comio *nm fml* hospital

nossi'gnore *adv* (*assolutamente no*) no way

nostal'gia *nf* (*di casa, patria*) homesickness; (*del passato*) nostalgia; **aver ~** be homesick; **aver ~ di qcno** miss sb

no'stalgico, -a *a* nostalgic ● *nmf* reactionary

nostra *vedi* **nostro**

no'strale *a* local

no'strano *a* local; (*fatto in casa*) home-made

'**nostre** *vedi* **nostro**

'**nostri** *vedi* **nostro**

'**nostro** (**il nostro** *m*, **la nostra** *f*, **i nostri** *mpl,* **le nostre** *fpl*) *poss a* our; **quella macchina è nostra** that car is ours; **~ padre** our father; **un ~ amico** a friend of ours ● *poss pron* ours

no'stromo *nm* bo's'n, boatswain

'**nota** *nf* (*segno*) sign; (*comunicazione, commento, Mus*) note; (*conto*) bill; (*lista*) list; **degno di ~** noteworthy; **prendere ~** take note; **una ~ di colore** a touch of colour; **mettere in ~ qcsa** add sth to the list. **~ di accredito** *Comm* credit note. **note** *pl* **caratteristiche** distinguishing marks. **~ spese** expense account

no'tabile *a & nm* notable

no'taio *nm* notary

no'tare *vt* (*segnare*) mark; (*annotare*) note down; (*osservare*) notice; **far ~ qcsa** point sth out; **farsi ~** get oneself noticed; **nota bene che...** please note that...

notazi'one *nf* marking; (*annotazione*) notation

'**notebook** *nm inv Comput* notebook

'**notes** *nm inv* notepad

no'tevole *a* (*degno di nota*) remarkable; (*grande*) considerable

no'tifica *nf* notification

notifi'care *vt* notify; *Comm* advise; **~ un ordine di comparizione [in giudizio]** subpoena

notificazi'one *nf* notification

no'tizia *nf* **una ~** a piece of news, some news; (*informazione*) a piece of information, some information; **le notizie** the news *sg*; **per avere ~ di** (*telefonare*) for news of; **non ha più dato notizie di sé** he hasn't been in touch since. **~ di attualità** news item

notizi'ario *nm* news *sg*

'**noto** *a* [well-]known; **rendere ~** (*far sapere*) announce

notori'età *nf* fame; **raggiungere la ~** become famous

no'torio *a* well-known; *pej* notorious

not'tambulo *nm* night-bird

not'tata *nf* night; **far ~** stay up all night

'**notte** *nf* night; **di ~** at night; **a ~ fatta** when night had fallen; **la ~** (*durante la notte*) at night; **buona ~** good night; **fermarsi per la ~** stay overnight; **peggio che andar di ~** worse than ever; **prima ~ di nozze** wedding night. **~ bianca** sleepless night

notte'tempo *adv* at night[time]

not'turno *a* nocturnal; ‹*servizio ecc*› night *attrib*; **in notturna** ‹*partita*› under floodlights

'**notula** *nf* (*conto*) fee note

no'vanta *a & nm* ninety

novan'tenne *a & nmf* ninety year old

novan'tesimo *a & nm* ninetieth

novan'tina *nf* about ninety

'**nove** *a & nm* nine; **prova del nove** *Math* casting out nines

nove'cento *a & nm* nine hundred. **il N~** the twentieth century; **stile ~** twentieth-century

no'vella *nf* short story

novelli'ere *nm* short-story writer

novel'lino, -a *a* inexperienced ● *nmf* novice, beginner

no'vello *a* new

no'vembre *nm* November

nove'mila *a & nm* nine thousand

no'vena *nf* novena

novi'lunio *nm* new moon

novità *nf inv* novelty; (*notizie*) news *sg*; **l'ultima ~** (*moda*) the latest fashion

novizi'ato *nm Relig* novitiate; (*tirocinio*) apprenticeship

nozi'one *nf* notion; **perdere la ~ del tempo** lose track of time; **non avere la ~ del tempo** have no sense of time; **nozioni** *pl* rudiments; **poche nozioni di inglese** very basic English

nozio'nismo *nm* accumulation of facts

'**nozze** *nfpl* marriage *sg*; (*cerimonia*) wedding *sg*; **andare a ~** (*godersela*) have a field day. **~ d'argento** silver wedding [anniversary]. **~ di diamante** diamond wedding [anniversary]. **~ d'oro** golden wedding [anniversary]

'**nube** *nf* cloud. **~ di mistero** shroud of mystery. **~ tossica** toxic cloud

nubi'fragio *nm* cloudburst

'**nubile** *a* unmarried ● *nf* unmarried woman

'**nuca** *nf* nape

nucle'are *a* nuclear

'**nucleo** *nm* nucleus; (*unità*) unit

nu'dismo *nm* nudism

nu'dista *nmf* nudist

nudità *nf* nudity, nakedness

'**nudo** *a* naked; (*spoglio, terra*) bare; **a occhio ~** to the naked eye; **verità nuda e cruda** naked truth; **a piedi nudi** bare-foot

'**nugolo** *nm* large number

'**nulla** *pron* = **niente**; **da ~** worthless; **per ~** for nothing

nulla'osta *nm inv* permit

nullate'nente *nm* **i nullatenenti** the have-nots

nullità *nf inv* (*persona*) nonentity

'**nullo** *a Jur* null and void

'**nume** *nm* numen

nume'rabile *a* countable

nume'rale *a & nm* numeral

nume'rare *vt* number

numera'tore *nm Math* numerator

numerazi'one *nf* numbering

nu'merico *a* numerical

'**numero** *nm* number; (*romano, arabo*) numeral; (*di scarpe ecc*) size; **fare** *o* **comporre il ~** dial [the number]; **dare i numeri** *fam* be off one's head; **avere tutti i numeri per** have what it takes to. **~ arretrato** back issue. **~ cardinale** cardinal [number]. **~ di conto** account number. **~ decimale** decimal. **~ intero** whole number. **~ ordinale** ordinal [number]. **~ d'ordine** *Comm* order number. **~ di previdenza sociale** ≈ National Insurance number. **~ di protocollo** reference number. **~ di scarpa** shoe size. **~ di telefono** phone number. **~ uno** number one. **~ verde** ≈ Freephone number, toll-free number *Am*. **~ di volo** flight number

nume'roso *a* numerous
numi'smatico *a* numismatic
'nunzio *nm* nuncio
nu'ocere *vi* ~ **a** harm
nu'ora *nf* daughter-in-law
nuo'tare *vi* swim; *fig* wallow; ~ **come un pesce** swim like a fish; ~ **nell'oro** be stinking rich, be rolling in it
nuo'tata *nf* swim; **fare una** ~ have a swim
nuota'|tore, -'trice *nmf* swimmer
nu'oto *nm* swimming; **stili** *mpl* **del** ~ swimming strokes
nu'ova *nf* piece of news; **buone nuove** good news; **nessuna** ~, **buona** ~ no news is good news
Nu'ova Cale'donia *nf* New Caledonia
Nu'ova Gui'nea *nf* New Guinea
nuova'mente *adv* again
Nu'ova Ze'landa *nf* New Zealand
nu'ovo *a* new; **di** ~ again; **uscire di nuovo** go/come back out, go/come out again; **mi risulta** ~ that's news to me; ~ **di pacca** *o*

zecca brand new; **rimettere a** ~ give a new lease of life to; ~ **del mestiere** new to the job; **il** ~ **anno** [the] New Year. **nuova linfa** *nf* new blood. ~ **stile** *nm* new look. **N~ Testamento** *nm* New Testament
'nursery *nf* nursery
nutri'ente *a* nourishing
nutri'mento *nm* nourishment
nu'trire *vt* feed ⟨*animale, malato, pianta*⟩; harbour ⟨*sentimenti*⟩; cherish ⟨*sogno*⟩ ● *vi* (*essere nutriente*) be nourishing
nu'trirsi *vr* eat; ~ **di** *fig* live on
nutri'tivo *a* nourishing, nutritional
nutrizi'one *nf* nutrition
'nuvola *nf* cloud; **avere la testa fra le nuvole** have one's head in the clouds; **vivere fra le nuvole** live in cloud cuckoo land; **cadere dalle nuvole** be astounded
nuvo'loso *a* cloudy
nuzi'ale *a* nuptial; ⟨*vestito, anello ecc*⟩ wedding *attrib*; **pranzo** ~ wedding breakfast

Oo

O *abbr* (**ovest**) W
o *conj* or; ~ **l'uno** ~ **l'altro** one or the other, either; **o... o...** either... or...
'oasi *nf inv* oasis
obbedi'ente = **ubbidiente**
obbedi'enza = **ubbidienza**
obbe'dire = **ubbidire**
obbli'gare *vt* force, oblige
obbli'garsi *vr* ~ **a** undertake to
obbli'gato *a* obliged
obbligatoria'mente *adv* **fare qcsa** ~ be obliged to do sth; **bisogna** ~ **farlo** you absolutely have to do it
obbliga'torio *a* compulsory
obbligazi'one *nf* obligation; *Comm* bond
'obbligo *nm* obligation; (*dovere*) duty; **avere obblighi verso** be under an obligation to; **d'**~ obligatory
ob'brobrio *nm* disgrace
obbrobri'oso *a* disgraceful
obe'lisco *nm* obelisk
obe'rare *vt* overburden
obesità *nf* obesity
o'beso *a* obese
obiet'tare *vt/i* object; ~ **su** object to
obiettiva'mente *adv* objectively
obiettività *nf* objectivity
obiet'tivo *a* objective ● *nm* objective; (*scopo*) object
obiet'tore *nm* objector. ~ **di coscienza** conscientious objector
obiezi'one *nf* objection; **fare** ~ **di coscienza** be a conscientious objector

obi'torio *nm* mortuary
o'blio *nm* oblivion
o'bliquo *a* oblique; *fig* underhand
oblite'rare *vt* obliterate
oblò *nm inv* porthole
ob'lungo *a* oblong
'oboe *nm* oboe
obsole'scenza *nf* obsolescence
obso'leto *a* obsolete
'oca *nf* (*pl* **oche**) goose; (*donna*) silly girl
occasio'nale *a* occasional
occasional'mente *adv* occasionally
occasi'one *nf* occasion; (*buon affare*) bargain; (*motivo*) cause; (*opportunità*) chance; **d'**~ secondhand
occhi'aia *nf* eye socket; **occhiaie** *pl* shadows under the eyes
occhi'ali *nmpl* glasses, spectacles. ~ **scuri** dark glasses. ~ **da sole** sunglasses. ~ **da vista** glasses, spectacles
occhia'luto *a* wearing glasses
occhi'ata *nf* look; **dare un'**~ **a** have a look at
occheggi'are *vt* ogle ● *vi* (*far capolino*) peep
occhi'ello *nm* buttonhole; (*asola*) eyelet
'occhio *nm* eye; ~! watch out!; ~ **ai falsi** beware of imitations; **a quattr'occhi** in private; **abbassare gli occhi** look down, lower one's eyes; **sollevare gli occhi** look up, raise one's eyes; **tenere d'**~ **qcno** keep an eye on sb; **perdere d'**~ lose sight of; **a** ~ **[e croce]** roughly; **chiudere un'**~ **(su qcsa)** turn a

blind eye (to sth); **dare nell'~** attract attention; **pagare** *o* **spendere un ~** [**della testa**] pay an arm and a leg; **saltare agli occhi** be blindingly obvious. **~ di falco** eagle eye. **~ nero** (*pesto*) black eye. **~ di pernice** (*callo*) corn

occhio'lino *nm* fare l'~ a qcno wink at sb, give sb a wink

occiden'tale *a* western ● *nmf* westerner

occi'dente *nm* west; (*paesi capitalisti*) West

oc'cludere *vt* obstruct

occlusi'one *nf* occlusion

occor'rente *a* necessary ● *nm* the necessary

occor'renza *nf* need; **all'~** if need be

oc'correre *vi* be necessary; **non occorre farlo** there is no need to do it

occulta'mento *nm* ~ di prove concealment of evidence

occul'tare *vt* hide

occul'tismo *nm* occult

oc'culto *a* hidden; (*magico*) occult

occu'pante *nmf* occupier; (*abusivo*) squatter

occu'pare *vt* occupy; spend ‹*tempo*›; take up ‹*spazio*›; (*dar lavoro a*) employ

occu'parsi *vr* occupy oneself; (*trovare lavoro*) find a job; **~ di** (*badare*) look after; **occupati dei fatti tuoi!** mind your own business!

occu'pato *a* engaged; ‹*persona*› busy; ‹*posto*› taken; **casa occupata** (*alloggio abusivo*) squat

occupazi'one *nf* occupation; *Comm* employment; (*passatempo*) pastime; **trovarsi un'~** (*interesse*) find oneself something to do

o'ceano *nm* ocean. **~ Atlantico** Atlantic [Ocean]. **~ Indiano** Indian Ocean. **~ Pacifico** Pacific [Ocean]

'ocra *nf* ochre

OCSE *nf abbr* (**Organizzazione per la Cooperazione el lo Sviluppo Economico**) OECD

ocu'lare *a* ocular; ‹*testimone, bagno*› eye *attrib*

ocula'tezza *nf* care

ocu'lato *a* ‹*scelta, persona*› prudent

ocu'lista *nmf* optician; (*per malattie*) ophthalmologist

od *conj* (*davanti alla vocale o*) or

'ode *nf* ode

odi'are *vt* hate; **~ a morte** not be able to stand

odi'erno *a* of today; (*attuale*) present

'odio *nm* hatred; **avere in ~** hate

odi'oso *a* hateful

odis'sea *nf* odyssey

o'dometro *nm Auto* mileometer, odometer *Am*

odo'rare *vt* smell; (*profumare*) perfume ● *vi* **~ di** smell of

odo'rato *nm* sense of smell

o'dore *nm* smell; (*profumo*) scent; **c'è ~ di...** there's a smell of...; **avere un buon/cattivo ~** smell nice/awful; **sentire ~ di** smell; **odori** *pl Culin* herbs

odo'roso *a* fragrant

of'fendere *vt* offend; (*ferire*) injure

of'fendersi *vr* take offence

offen'siva *nf Mil, fig* offensive

offen'sivo *a* offensive

offen'sore *nm* offender

offe'rente *nmf* offerer; (*in aste*) bidder; **il miglior ~** the highest bidder

of'ferta *nf* offer; (*donazione*) donation; *Comm* supply; (*nelle aste*) bid; (*di appalto*) tender; **in ~ speciale** on special offer; **"offerte d'impiego"** "situations vacant". **~ pubblica di acquisto** takeover bid

of'ferto *pp di* offrire

offer'torio *nm* offertory

of'fesa *nf* offence

of'feso *pp di* offendere ● *a* offended

offi'ciare *vt* officiate

offi'cina *nf* workshop; **~ [meccanica]** garage; **capo [di] ~** foreman

of'frire *vt* offer

of'frirsi *vr* offer oneself; ‹*occasione:*› present itself; **~ di fare qcsa** offer to do sth

off'set *nm inv* offset printing

off'shore *nm inv* (*motoscafo*) speedboat

offu'scare *vt* darken; *fig* dull ‹*memoria, bellezza*›; blur ‹*vista*›

offu'scarsi *vr* darken; ‹*fig: memoria, bellezza:*› fade away; ‹*vista:*› become blurred

of'talmico *a* ophthalmic

ogget'tistica *nf manufacture and selling of household and gift items*; (*oggetti*) household and gift items; **negozio di ~** gift shop

oggettività *nf* objectivity

ogget'tivo *a* objective

og'getto *nm* object; (*argomento*) subject; **oggetti** *pl* **smarriti** lost property, lost and found *Am*

'oggi *adv & nm* today; (*al giorno d'oggi*) nowadays; **da ~ in poi** from today on; **~ [a] otto** a week today; **dall'~ al domani** overnight; **il giornale di ~** today's paper; **al giorno d'~** these days, nowadays

oggi'giorno *adv* nowadays

o'giva *nf Mil* warhead

'ogni *a inv* every; (*qualsiasi*) any; **~ tre giorni** every three days; **ad ~ costo** at any cost; **ad ~ modo** anyway; **~ ben di Dio** all sorts of good things; **~ cosa** everything; **~ tanto** now and then; **~ volta che** every time, whenever

o'gnuno *pron* everyone, everybody; **~ di voi** each of you

ohibò *int* oh dear!

ohimè *int* oh dear!

o'kay *nm* dare l'~ a qcno/qcsa give sb/sth the OK

'ola *nf inv* Mexican wave

O'landa *nf* Holland

olan'dese *a* Dutch ● *nm* Dutchman; (*lingua*) Dutch; (*formaggio*) Edam ● *nf* Dutchwoman

ole'andro *nm* oleander

ole'ato *a* oiled; **carta oleata** grease-proof paper

oleo'dotto *nm* oil pipeline

ole'oso *a* oily

ol'fatto *nm* sense of smell

oli'are *vt* oil

olia'tore *nm* oilcan

oli'era *nf* cruet

olim'piadi *nfpl* Olympic games, Olympics

o'limpico *a* Olympic

olim'pionico *a* ⟨*primato, squadra*⟩ Olympic; **costume** ~ Olympic swimming costume

+olino *suff* **bestiolina** *nf* ⟨*affettuoso*⟩ little creature; **macchiolina** *nf* spot; **pesciolino** *nm* little fish; **risolino** *nm* giggle; **sassolino** *nm* pebble; **strisciolina** *nf* thin strip; **magrolino** *a* skinny

'olio *nm* oil; **sott'**~ in oil; **colori a** ~ oils; **quadro a** ~ oil painting. ~ **di fegato di merluzzo** cod-liver oil. ~ **di gomito** elbow grease. ~ **lubrificante** lubricating oil. ~ **di mais** corn oil. ~ **minerale** mineral oil. ~ **[del] motore** engine oil. ~ **d'oliva** olive oil. ~ **di semi** vegetable oil. ~ **[di semi] di lino** linseed oil. ~ **solare** suntan oil

o'liva *nf* olive

oli'vastro *a* olive

oli'veto *nm* olive grove

oli'vetta *nf* toggle

o'livo *nm* olive tree

'olmo *nm* elm

olo'causto *nm* holocaust; **l'O**~ the Holocaust

o'lografo *a* holograph

olo'gramma *nm* hologram

oltraggi'are *vt* offend

ol'traggio *nm* offence. ~ **al pudore** *Jur* gross indecency

oltraggi'oso *a* offensive

ol'tranza *nf* **ad** ~ to the bitter end

'oltre *adv* ⟨*di luogo*⟩ further; ⟨*di tempo*⟩ longer ● *prep* ⟨*nello spazio*⟩ beyond; ⟨*di tempo*⟩ later than; ⟨*più di*⟩ more than; ⟨*in aggiunta*⟩ besides; ~ **a** ⟨*eccetto*⟩ except, apart from; **per** ~ **due settimane** for more than two weeks; **una settimana e** ~ a week and more

oltrecon'fine *a* cross-border

oltre'mare *adv* overseas

oltre'modo *adv* extremely

oltrepas'sare *vt* go beyond; ⟨*eccedere*⟩ exceed; **oltrepassi il semaforo** go past the traffic lights; ~ **il limite di velocità** break the speed limit; **'non** ~**'** 'no trespassing'

OM *abbr Radio* (**onde medie**) MW

omacci'one *nm* bruiser

o'maggi *nmpl* ⟨*saluti*⟩ respects

o'maggio *nm* homage; ⟨*dono*⟩ gift; **in** ~ **con** free with

ombeli'cale *a* umbilical; **cordone** ~ umbilical cord

ombe'lico *nm* navel

'ombra *nf* ⟨*zona*⟩ shade; ⟨*immagine oscura*⟩ shadow; **all'**~ in the shade

ombreggi'are *vt* shade

ombreggia'ture *nfpl* shading

om'brello *nm* umbrella

ombrel'lone *nm* beach umbrella

om'bretto *nm* eye-shadow

om'broso *a* shady; ⟨*cavallo*⟩ skittish; ⟨*persona*⟩ touchy

ome'lette *nf inv* omelette

ome'lia *nf Relig* sermon

omeopa'tia *nf* homoeopathy

omeo'patico *a* homoeopathic ● *nm* homoeopath

omertà *nf inv* conspiracy of silence

o'messo *pp di* **omettere**

o'mettere *vt* omit

omi'cida *a* murderous ● *nmf* murderer

omi'cidio *nm* murder. ~ **colposo** manslaughter. ~ **di massa** mass murder. ~ **volontario** *Jur* culpable homicide

omissi'one *nf* omission

'omnibus *nm inv* omnibus

omofo'bia *nf* homophobia

omogeneiz'zare *vt* homogenize

omogeneiz'zato *a* homogenized

omo'geneo *a* homogeneous

o'mografo *nm* homograph

omolo'gare *vt* approve; **fare** ~ **un testamento** prove a will

omologazi'one *nf* probate

o'monimo, -a *nmf* namesake ● *nm* ⟨*parola*⟩ homonym ● *a* of the same name

omosessu'ale *a & nmf* homosexual

omosessualità *nf* homosexuality

On. *abbr* (**onorevole**) MP

'oncia *nf* ounce. ~ **fluida** fluid ounce

'onda *nf* wave; **andare in** ~ *TV, Radio* go on the air; **seguire l'**~ go with the crowd. **onde** *pl* **corte** short wave. **onde** *pl* **lunghe** long wave. ~ **di maremoto** tidal wave. **onde** *pl* **medie** medium wave. **onde** *pl* **radio** radio waves. ~ **d'urto** shock wave

on'data *nf* wave; **a ondate** in waves. ~ **di freddo** cold snap

'onde *conj fml* so that

ondeggi'are *vi* wave; ⟨*barca:*⟩ roll

ondu'lato *a* wavy

ondula'torio *a* undulating

ondulazi'one *nf* undulation; ⟨*di capelli*⟩ wave

+one *suff* **cucchiaione** *nm* big spoon; **gattone** *nm* fat cat; **bacione** *nm* smacker; **bacioni** *pl* ⟨*in lettera*⟩ love and kisses; **omone** *nm* big guy; **nasone** *nm* big nose; **nebbione** *nm* dense fog, peasouper *fam*; **simpaticone** *nm* very friendly person; **lumacone** *nm* slowcoach; **testone** *nm* mule; **facilone** *nm pej* over-casual sort of person; **grassone** *nm pej* fat slob; **pigrone** *nm* lazybones *sg*; **chiacchierone** *nm* chatterbox; **criticone** *nm* nit-picker; **pasticcione** *nm* bungler

'onere *nm* burden

oner'oso *a* onerous

onestà *nf* honesty; ⟨*rettitudine*⟩ integrity, honesty

o'nesto *a* honest; (*giusto*) just

'onice *nf* onyx

o'nirico *a* dream *attrib*

o'nisco *nm* slater

onnipo'tente *a* omnipotent

onnipre'sente *a* ubiquitous; *Rel* omnipresent

onnisci'ente *a* omniscient

ono'mastico *nm* name-day

onomato'pea *nf* onomatopoeia

onomato'peico *a* onomatopoeic

ono'rabile *a* honourable

ono'rare *vt* (*fare onore a*) be a credit to; honour (*promessa*)

ono'rario *a* honorary ● *nm* fee

ono'rarsi *vr* ~ **di** be proud of

ono'rato *a* (*famiglia, professione*) respectable; **considerarsi** ~ **da qcsa** consider oneself honoured by sth. **l'onorata società** *nf* the Mafia

o'nore *nm* honour; **in** ~ **di** (*festa, ricevimento*) in honour of; **fare** ~ **a** do justice to (*pranzo*); **farsi** ~ **in** excel in; **a onor del vero** to tell the truth; **fare gli onori di casa** do the honours

ono'revole *a* honourable ● *nmf* Member of Parliament

onorifi'cenza *nf* honour; (*decorazione*) decoration

ono'rifico *a* honorary

'onta *nf* shame

on'tano *nm* alder

O.N.U. *nf abbr* (**Organizzazione delle Nazioni Unite**) UN

opacità *nf* opaqueness, opacity

o'paco *a* opaque; (*colori ecc*) dull; (*fotografia, rossetto*) matt

o'pale *nf* opal

OPEC *nf inv* Opec, OPEC

'opera *nf* (*lavoro*) work; (*azione*) deed; *Mus* opera; (*teatro*) opera house; (*ente*) institution; **mettere in** ~ put into effect; **mettersi all'**~ get to work. ~ **d'arte** work of art. ~ **lirica** opera. **opere** *pl* **pubbliche** public works

ope'rabile *a* operable

ope'raio, -a *a* working ● *nmf* worker. ~ **edile** building worker. ~ **specializzato** skilled worker

ope'rare *vt Med* operate on; ~ **qcno al cuore** operate on sb's heart; **farsi** ~ have an operation ● *vi* operate; (*agire*) work

opera'tivo, opera'torio *a* operating *attrib*

opera|'tore, -'trice *nmf* operator; *TV* cameraman. ~ **ecologico** refuse collector. ~ **sanitario** health worker. ~ **turistico** tour operator

operazi'one *nf* operation; *Comm* transaction. ~ **antidroga** anti-drug operation. **operazioni** *pl* **di soccorso** rescue operations. ~ **d'urgenza** emergency operation

ope'retta *nf* operetta

ope'roso *a* industrious

opini'one *nf* opinion; **rimanere della propria** ~ still feel the same way. ~ **pubblica** public opinion, vox pop

oplà *int* oops

o'possum *nm inv* possum

'oppio *nm* opium

oppo'nente *a* opposing ● *nmf* opponent

op'porre *vt* oppose; (*obiettare*) object; ~ **resistenza** offer resistance

op'porsi *vr* ~ **a** oppose

opportu'nismo *nm* expediency

opportu'nista *nmf* opportunist

opportunità *nf inv* opportunity; (*l'essere opportuno*) timeliness; **avere il senso dell'**~ have a sense of what is appropriate

oppor'tuno *a* opportune; (*adeguato*) appropriate; **ritenere** ~ **fare qcsa** think it appropriate to do sth; **il momento** ~ the right moment

opposi'tore *nm* opposer

opposizi'one *nf* opposition; **d'**~ (*giornale, partito*) opposition *attrib*; **in** ~ in opposition

op'posto *pp di* **opporre** ● *a* opposite; (*opinioni*) opposing ● *nm* opposite; **all'**~ on the contrary

oppressi'one *nf* oppression

oppres'sivo *a* oppressive

op'presso *pp di* **opprimere** ● *a* oppressed

oppres'sore *nm* oppressor

oppri'mente *a* oppressive

op'primere *vt* oppress; (*gravare*) weigh down

op'pure *conj* otherwise, or [else]; **lunedì** ~ **martedì** Monday or Tuesday

ops *int* oops

op'tare *vi* ~ **per** opt for

'optional *nm inv* optional extra

opu'lento *a* opulent

opu'lenza *nf* opulence

o'puscolo *nm* booklet; (*pubblicitario*) brochure

opzio'nale *a* optional

opzi'one *nf* option

'ora[1] *nf* time; (*unità*) hour; **di buon'**~ early; **che** ~ **è?, che ore sono?** what time is it?; **a che** ~? at what time?; **mezz'**~ half an hour; **a ore** (*lavorare, pagare*) by the hour; **50 km all'**~ 50 km an hour; **è** ~ **di finirla!** that's enough now!; **a un'**~ **di macchina** one hour by car; **non vedo l'**~ **di vederti** I can't wait to see you; **fare le ore piccole** stay up until the small hours. ~ **d'arrivo** arrival time. ~ **di cena** dinnertime. **l'**~ **esatta** *Teleph* speaking clock. ~ **legale** daylight saving time. ~ **locale** local time. ~ **di pranzo** dinnertime. ~ **di punta, ore** *pl* **di punta** peak time; (*per il traffico*) rush hour. ~ **solare** Greenwich Mean Time, GMT. ~ **zero** *Mil, fig* zero hour

'ora[2] *adv* now; (*tra poco*) presently; ~ **come** ~ just now, at the moment; **d'**~ **in poi** from now on; **per** ~ for the time being, for now; ● *conj* (*dunque*) now [then]; ~ **che ci penso,...** now that I [come to] think about it...

o'racolo *nm* oracle

'orafo *nm* goldsmith

o'rale *a & nm* oral; **per via ~** by mouth

ora'mai *adv* = **ormai**

o'rario *a* ‹*tariffa*› hourly; ‹*segnale*› time *attrib*; ‹*velocità*› per hour; **in senso ~** clockwise ● *nm* time; ‹*tabella dell'orario*› timetable, schedule *Am*; **essere in ~** be on time; **partire in ~** leave on time; **lavorare fuori ~** work outside normal hours. **~ di apertura** opening hours *pl*. **~ di chiusura** closing time. **~ estivo** summer timetable. **~ ferroviario** railway timetable, railroad schedule *Am*. **~ flessibile** flexitime. **~ invernale** winter timetable. **~ di lavoro** working hours *pl*. **~ degli spettacoli** performance times *pl*. **~ di sportello** banking hours *pl*. **~ d'ufficio** business hours *pl*. **~ di visita** visiting hours *pl*, visiting time; ‹*del medico*› consulting hours *pl*. **~ di volo** flight time

o'rata *nf* gilthead

ora|'tore, -'trice *nmf* orator; ‹*conferenziere*› speaker

ora'torio, -a *a* oratorical ● *nm Mus* oratorio ● *nmf* oratory

orazi'one *nf Relig* prayer

'orbita *nf* orbit; *Anat* [eye-]socket

'Orcadi *nfpl* Orkneys

or'chestra *nf* orchestra; ‹*parte del teatro*› pit. **~ da camera** chamber orchestra

orche'strale *a* orchestral ● *nmf* member of an/the orchestra

orche'strare *vt* orchestrate

orchi'dea *nf* orchid

'orco *nm* ogre

'orda *nf* horde

or'digno *nm* device; ‹*arnese*› tool. **~ esplosivo** explosive device. **~ incendiario** incendiary device

ordi'nale *a & nm* ordinal

ordina'mento *nm* order; ‹*leggi*› rules *pl*

ordi'nanza *nf* ‹*del sindaco*› bylaw; **d'~** ‹*soldato*› on duty

ordi'nare *vt* ‹*sistemare*› arrange; ‹*comandare*› order; ‹*prescrivere*› prescribe; *Relig* ordain

ordi'nario *a* ordinary; ‹*grossolano*› common; ‹*professore*› with a permanent position; **di ordinaria amministrazione** routine ● *nm* ordinary; *Univ* professor; **fuori dell'~** out of the ordinary

ordi'nato *a* ‹*in ordine*› tidy

ordinazi'one *nf* order; **fare un'~** place an order

'ordine *nm* order; ‹*di avvocati, medici*› association; **mettere in ~** put in order; tidy up ‹*appartamento ecc*›; **di prim'~** first-class; **di terz'~** ‹*film, albergo*› third-rate; **di ~ pratico/economico** ‹*problema*› of a practical/economic nature; **fino a nuovo ~** until further notice; **parola d'~** password. **~ di acquisto** *Comm* purchase order. **~ del giorno** agenda. **~ di pagamento** banker's order. **~ permanente** *Fin* standing order.

ordini *pl* sacri Holy Orders

or'dire *vt* ‹*tramare*› plot

orecchi'ette *nfpl* small pasta shells

orec'chino *nm* ear-ring. **orecchini** *pl* **con le clip** clip-ons

o'recchio *nm* ‹*pl nf* **orecchie**› ear; **avere ~** have a good ear; **esser duro d'~** be hard of hearing; **mi è giunto all'~ che...** I've heard that...; **parlare all'~ a** qcn whisper in sb's ear; **suonare a ~** play by ear

orecchi'oni *nmpl Med* mumps *sg*

o'refice *nm* jeweller

orefice'ria *nf* ‹*arte*› goldsmith's art; ‹*negozio*› goldsmith's [shop]

'orfano, -a *a* orphan ● *nmf* orphan

orfano'trofio *nm* orphanage

orga'netto *nm* barrel-organ; ‹*a bocca*› mouth-organ; ‹*fisarmonica*› accordion

or'ganico *a* organic ● *nm* personnel

orga'nino *nm* hurdy-gurdy

orga'nismo *nm* organism; ‹*corpo umano*› body

orga'nista *nmf* organist

organiz'zare *vt* organize

organiz'zarsi *vr* get organized

organizza'tivo *a* organizational

organizza|'tore, -'trice *nmf* organizer

organizzazi'one *nf* organization. **~ dei soccorsi** relief organization

'organo *nm* organ

or'gasmo *nm* orgasm; *fig* agitation

'orgia *nf* orgy

or'goglio *nm* pride

orgogli'oso *a* proud

orien'tale *a* eastern; ‹*cinese ecc*› oriental

orienta'mento *nm* orientation; **perdere l'~** lose one's bearings; **senso dell'~** sense of direction. **~ professionale** careers guidance. **~ scolastico** educational guidance

orien'tare *vt* orientate

orien'tarsi *vr* find one's bearings; ‹*tendere*› tend

ori'ente *nm* east. **l'Estremo O~** the Far East. **il Medio O~** the Middle East

orien'teering *nm inv* orienteering

o'rigano *nm* oregano

origi'nale *a* original; ‹*eccentrico*› odd ● *nm* original

originalità *nf* originality

origi'nare *vt/i* originate

origi'nario *a* ‹*nativo*› native

o'rigine *nf* origin; **in ~** originally; **aver ~ da** originate from; **dare ~ a** give rise to

origli'are *vi* eavesdrop

o'rina *nf* urine

ori'nale *nm* chamber-pot

ori'nare *vi* urinate

ori'undo *a* native

orizzon'tale *a* horizontal

orizzon'tare *vt* = **orientare**

oriz'zonte *nm* horizon

or'lare *vt* hem

orla'tura *nf* hem

'orlo *nm* edge; ‹*di vestito ecc*› hem

'orma *nf* track; ‹*di piede*› footprint; ‹*impronta*› mark

or'mai *adv* by now; (*passato*) by then; (*quasi*) almost

ormegg'iare *vt* moor

or'meggio *nm* mooring

ormo'nale *a* hormonal

or'mone *nm* hormone

ornamen'tale *a* ornamental

orna'mento *nm* ornament; **d'~** ⟨*oggetto*⟩ ornamental

or'nare *vt* decorate

or'narsi *vr* deck oneself

or'nato *a* ⟨*stile*⟩ ornate

ornitolo'gia *nf* ornithology

orni'tologo, -a *nmf* ornithologist

ornito'rinco *nm* platypus

'oro *nm* gold; **d'~** gold; *fig* golden; **una persona d'~** a wonderful person. **~ nero** black gold

orologe'ria *nf* watchmaker

orologi'aio, -a *nmf* clockmaker, watchmaker

oro'logio *nm* (*portatile*) watch; (*da tavolo, muro ecc*) clock. **~ biologico** biological clock. **~ a carica automatica** self-winding watch. **~ a cucù** cuckoo clock. **~ digitale** digital clock. **~ a pendolo** grandfather clock. **~ da polso** wrist-watch. **~ al quarzo** quartz watch. **~ a sveglia** alarm clock

o'roscopo *nm* horoscope

or'rendo *a* awful, dreadful

or'ribile *a* horrible

orribil'mente *adv* horribly

orripi'lante *a* horrifying

or'rore *nm* horror; **avere qcsa in ~** hate sth; **~!** heck!; **film/romanzo dell'~** horror film/story

orsacchi'otto *nm* teddy bear

or'setto *nm* **~ lavatore** raccoon

'orso *nm* bear; (*persona scontrosa*) hermit. **~ bianco** polar bear. **~ bruno** brown bear

orsù *int* come now!

or'taggio *nm* vegetable

or'tensia *nf* hydrangea

or'tica *nf* nettle; **buttare qcsa alle ortiche** *fig fam* chuck in

orti'caria *nf* nettle-rash

orticol'tura *nf* horticulture

'orto *nm* vegetable plot

orto'dontico *a* orthodontic

ortodon'zia *nf* orthodontics

ortodos'sia *nf* conformity

orto'dosso *a* orthodox

ortofrut'ticolo *a* **mercato ~** fruit and vegetable market

ortofrutticol'tore *nm* market gardener, truck farmer *Am*

ortogo'nale *a* perpendicular

ortogra'fia *nf* spelling

orto'grafico *a* spelling *attrib*

orto'lano *nm* market gardener, truck farmer *Am*; (*negozio*) greengrocer's

ortope'dia *nf* orthopaedics

orto'pedico *a* orthopaedic ● *nm* orthopaedic specialist

orzai'olo *nm* sty

or'zata *nf* barley-water

'orzo *nm* barley. **~ perlato** pearl barley

osan'nato *a* (*esaltato*) praised to the skies

o'sare *vt/i* dare; (*avere audacia*) be daring

oscenità *nf inv* obscenity

o'sceno *a* obscene

oscil'lare *vi* swing; ⟨*prezzi ecc*⟩ fluctuate; *Tech* oscillate; (*fig: essere indeciso*) vacillate

oscillazi'one *nf* swinging; (*di prezzi*) fluctuation; *Tech* oscillation

oscura'mento *nm* darkening; (*fig: di vista, mente*) dimming; (*totale*) black-out

oscu'rare *vt* darken; *fig* obscure

oscu'rarsi *vr* get dark

oscurità *nf* darkness; (*incomprensibilità*) obscurity; **uscire dall'~** *fig* emerge from obscurity; **morire nell'~** *fig* die in obscurity

o'scuro *a* dark; (*triste*) gloomy; (*incomprensibile*) obscure

o'smosi *nf inv* osmosis

ospe'dale *nm* hospital

ospedali'ero *a* hospital *attrib*

ospi'tale *a* hospitable

ospitalità *nf* hospitality; **non voglio abusare della tua ~** I don't want to outstay my welcome

ospi'tare *vt* give hospitality to

'ospite *nm* (*chi ospita*) host; (*chi viene ospitato*) guest ● *nf* hostess; guest

o'spizio *nm* (*per vecchi*) [old people's] home

ossa'tura *nf* bone structure; (*di romanzo*) structure, framework

'osseo *a* bone *attrib*

osse'quente *a* deferential; **~ alla legge** law-abiding

ossequi'are *vt* pay one's respects to

os'sequio *nm* homage; **ossequi** *pl* respects

ossequi'oso *a* obsequious

osser'vabile *a* observable

osser'vante *a* ⟨*cattolico*⟩ practising

osser'vanza *nf* observance

osser'vare *vt* observe; (*notare*) notice; keep ⟨*ordine, silenzio*⟩

osserva'|tore, -'trice *nmf* observer

osserva'torio *nm* *Astr* observatory; *Mil* observation post

osservazi'one *nf* observation; (*rimprovero*) reproach

ossessio'nante *a* haunting; ⟨*persona*⟩ nagging

ossessio'nare *vt* obsess; (*infastidire*) nag

ossessi'one *nf* obsession; (*assillo*) pain in the neck

osses'sivo *a* obsessive; ⟨*paura*⟩ neurotic

os'sesso *a* obsessed

os'sia *conj* that is

ossi'dabile *a* liable to tarnish

ossi'dante *a* tarnishing

ossi'dare *vt* oxidize

ossi'darsi *vr* oxidize

'ossido *nm* oxide. **~ di carbonio** carbon monoxide. **~ di zinco** zinc oxide

os'sidrico *a* **fiamma ossidrica** blowlamp

ossige'nare *vt* oxygenate; (*decolorare*) bleach

ossige'narsi *vr* put back on its feet ‹*azienda*›; ~ **i capelli** dye one's hair blonde

os'sigeno *nm* oxygen

'osso *nm* (*Anat pl nf* **ossa**) bone; (*di frutto*) stone; **senz'~** boneless. ~ **mascellare** jaw-bone

osso'buco *nm* marrowbone

os'suto *a* bony

ostaco'lare *vt* hinder, obstruct

ostaco'lista *nmf* hurdler

o'stacolo *nm* obstacle; *Sport* hurdle

o'staggio *nm* hostage; **prendere in ~** take hostage

o'stello *nm* ~ **della gioventù** youth hostel

osten'tare *vt* show off; ~ **indifferenza** pretend to be indifferent

ostentata'mente *adv* ostentatiously

ostentazi'one *nf* ostentation

osteopo'rosi *nf inv* osteoporosis

oste'ria *nf* inn

oste'tricia *nf* obstetrics

o'stetrico, -a *a* obstetric ● *nmf* obstetrician

'ostia *nf* host; (*cialda*) wafer

'ostico *a* tough

o'stile *a* hostile

ostilità *nf inv* hostility

osti'narsi *vr* ~ persist (**a** in)

osti'nato *a* obstinate

ostinazi'one *nf* obstinacy

ostra'cismo *nm* ostracism

'ostrica *nf* oyster

ostro'goto *nm* **parlare ~** talk double Dutch

ostru'ire *vt* obstruct

ostruzi'one *nf* obstruction

ostruzio'nismo *nm* obstructionism; *Sport* obstruction. ~ **sindacale** work-to-rule

oto'rino *nm* ear, nose and throat *attrib*

otorinolaringoi'atra *nmf* ear, nose and throat specialist

'otre *nm* leather bottle

ottago'nale *a* octagonal

ot'tagono *nm* octagon

ot'tanta *a & nm* eighty

ottan'tenne *a & nmf* eighty-year-old

ottant'tesimo *a & nm* eightieth

ottant'tina *nf* about eighty

ot'tava *nf* octave

ot'tavo *a & nm* eighth

otte'nere *vt* obtain; (*più comune*) get; (*conseguire*) achieve

ot'tetto *nm* *Mus* octet

'ottico, -a *a* optic[al] ● *nmf* optician ● *nf* (*scienza*) optics *sg*; (*di lenti ecc*) optics *pl*

otti'male *a* optimum

ottima'mente *adv* very well

otti'mismo *nm* optimism

otti'mista *nmf* optimist

otti'mistico *a* optimistic

ottimiz'zare *vt* optimize

'ottimo *a* very good ● *nm* optimum; **essere all'~ della forma** be on top form

'otto *a & nm* eight

+otto *suff* **bassotto** (*piuttosto basso*) quite short; **contadinotto** *nm pej* (*semplicciotto*) country bumpkin; **paesotto** *nm* hamlet; **leprotto** *nm* leveret; (*affettuoso*) baby hare; **pienotto** *a* ‹*viso*› chubby

ot'tobre *nm* October

otto'cento *a & nm* eight hundred; **l'O~** the nineteenth century

ot'tone *nm* brass; **gli ottoni** *Mus* the brass

ottuage'nario, -a *a & nmf* octogenarian

ot'tundere *vt* blunt

ottu'rare *vt* block; fill ‹*dente*›

ottu'rarsi *vr* clog

ottura'tore *nm* *Phot* shutter

otturazi'one *nf* stopping; (*di dente*) filling

ot'tuso *pp di* **ottundere** ● *a* obtuse

ouver'ture *nf inv* overture

o'vaia *nf* ovary

o'vale *a & nm* oval

o'vatta *nf* cotton wool, absorbent cotton *Am*

ovat'tato *a* ‹*suono, passi*› muffled

ovazi'one *nf* ovation

'ove *adv liter* where

over'dose *nf inv* overdose

'overdrive *nm inv* *Auto* overdrive

'ovest *nm* west

o'vile *nm* sheep-fold, pen

o'vino *a* sheep *attrib*

ovoi'dale *a* egg-shaped

ovo'via *nf* two-seater cable car

ovulazi'one *nf* ovulation

o'vunque *adv* = **dovunque**

ov'vero *conj* or; (*cioè*) that is

ovvia'mente *adv* obviously

ovvi'are *vi* ~ **a qcsa** counter sth

'ovvio *a* obvious

ozi'are *vi* laze around

'ozio *nm* idleness; **stare in ~** idle about

ozi'oso *a* idle; ‹*questione*› pointless

o'zono *nm* ozone; **buco nell'~** hole in the ozone layer

Pp

pa'care *vt* calm
paca'tezza *nf* calm[ness]
pa'cato *a* calm
'pacca *nf* slap
pac'chetto *nm* packet; (*postale*) parcel, package; (*di sigarette*) pack, packet. **~ integrato** *Comput* integrated package; **~ software** software package
'pacchia *nf* (*fam: situazione*) bed of roses
pacchia'nata *nf* è una **~** it's so garish
pacchi'ano *a* garish
'pacco *nm* parcel; (*involto*) bundle; **disfare un ~** unwrap a parcel; **fare un ~** make up a parcel. **pacchi** *pl* **postali** parcels, packages. **~ regalo** gift-wrapped package; **le faccio un ~ ~?** would you like it gift-wrapped?
paccot'tiglia *nf* (*roba scadente*) junk, rubbish
'pace *nf* peace; **darsi ~** forget it; **fare ~ con qcno** make it up with sb; **lasciare in ~ qcno** leave sb in peace; **mettere ~ fra** pacify, make [the] peace between; **andate in ~** *Relig* peace be with you; **in tempo di ~** in peacetime; **del tempo di ~** peacetime; **di ~** (*milizia*) peacekeeping; **firmare la ~** sign a peace treaty; **per amor di ~** for a quiet life
pace-'maker *nm* (*apparecchio*) pacemaker
pachi'derma *nm* (*animale*) pachyderm; *fig* thick-skinned person
pachi'stano, -a *nmf* & *a* Pakistani
paci'ere *nm* peacemaker
pacifi'care *vt* reconcile; (*mettere pace*) pacify
pacificazi'one *nf* reconciliation
pa'cifico *a* pacific; (*calmo*) peaceful; **è ~ che...** (*comunemente accettato*) it is clear that... ● *nm* **il P~** the Pacific
paci'fismo *nm* pacifism
paci'fista *a* & *nmf* pacifist
pacioc'cone, -a *nmf fam* chubby-chops
paci'ugo *nm* (*poltiglia*) mush
pa'dano *a* **pianura padana** Po Valley
pa'della *nf* frying-pan; (*per malati*) bedpan; **cuocere in ~** fry; **dalla ~ alla brace** out of the frying pan into the fire
padel'lata *nf* **una ~ di** a frying-panful of
padigli'one *nm* pavilion. **~ auricolare** auricle
'Padova *nf* Padua
'padre *nm* father; **padri** *pl* (*antenati*) forefathers; **i padri della chiesa** the Church Fathers; **di ~ in figlio** from father to son. **~ adottivo** (*marito della madre*) stepfather. **~ di famiglia** father, paterfamilias; **sono ~ ~**

~ I have a family to look after. **~ spirituale** spiritual father
padre'nostro *nm* **il ~** the Lord's Prayer
padre'terno *nm* God Almighty
pa'drino *nm* godfather; **~ e madrina** godparents
padro'nale *a* principal
padro'nanza *nf* mastery. **~ di sé** self-control
pa'drone, -a *nmf* master; mistress; (*datore di lavoro*) boss; (*proprietario*) owner. **~ di casa** (*di inquilini*) landlord; landlady; (*in ricevimento*) master of the house; lady of the house
padroneggi'are *vt* master
padro'nesco *a* domineering
padro'nissimo *a* **essere ~ di fare qcsa** be quite at liberty to do sth
pae'saggio *nm* scenery; (*pittura*) landscape. **~ marino** seascape. **~ montano** mountain landscape
paesag'gista *nmf* landscape architect
paesag'gistico *a* landscape *attrib*
pae'sano, -a *a* country *attrib* ● *nmf* villager
pa'ese *nm* (*nazione*) country; (*territorio*) land; (*villaggio*) village; **il Bel Paese** Italy; **va' a quel ~!** get lost!; **il mio ~ natio** where I was born; **Paesi** *pl* **Bassi** Netherlands. **paesi** *pl* **dell'est** Eastern Bloc countries
paf'futo *a* plump
pag. *abbr* (**pagina**) p.
'paga *nf* pay, wages *pl*
pa'gabile *a* payable
pa'gaia *nf* paddle
paga'mento *nm* payment; **a ~** (*parcheggio*) which you have to pay to use. **~ anticipato** *Comm* advance payment. **~ alla consegna** cash on delivery, COD. **~ pedaggio** toll
paga'nesimo *nm* paganism
pa'gano, -a *a* & *nmf* pagan
pa'gante *nmf* payer
pa'gare *vt/i* pay; **~ da bere a qcno** buy sb a drink; **pagato in anticipo** prepaid, paid in advance; **te la faccio ~** you'll pay for this; **quanto pagherei per poter venire!** what I wouldn't give to be able to come!
pa'gella *nf* [school] report
pagg. *abbr* (**pagine**) pp.
'pagina *nf* page; **prima ~** *Journ* front page; **~ economica** financial news, financial pages; **pagine** *pl* **gialle** Yellow Pages. **~ mastra** master page. **~ web** *Comput* web page
pagi'none *nm* centre-fold

'**paglia** *nf* straw; ~ **e fieno** *Culin mixture of ordinary and green tagliatelle*
pagliac'cesco *a* farcical
pagliac'cetto *nm* (*per bambini*) rompers *pl*; (*da donna*) camiknickers
pagliac'ciata *nf* farce
pagli'accio *nm* clown; **fare il** ~ act *or* play the clown
pagli'aio *nm* haystack
paglie'riccio *nm* straw mattress
pagli'etta *nf* (*cappello*) boater; (*per pentole*) steel wool
pagli'uzza *nf* wisp of straw; (*di metallo*) particle
pa'gnotta *nf* [round] loaf
'**pago** *a* satisfied
pa'goda *nf* pagoda
pa'guro *nm* hermit crab
pail'lard *nf inv* slice of grilled veal
pail'lette *nf inv* sequin
'**paio** *nm* (*pl nf* **paia**) pair; **un** ~ (*circa due*) a couple; **un** ~ **di** ‹*scarpe, forbici*› a pair of; **è un altro** ~ **di maniche** *fig* that's a different kettle of fish
pai'olo *nm* copper pot
'**Pakistan** *nm* Pakistan
paki'stano, -a *a* & *nmf* Pakistani
'**pala** *nf* shovel; (*di remo, elica*) blade; (*di ruota*) paddle; (*di mulino*) blade, vane. ~ **d'altare** altar piece. ~ **da fornaio** shovel. ~ **meccanica** mechanical digger
pala'dino *nm* paladin; *fig* champion
pala'fitta *nf* pile-dwelling
palan'drana *nf* (*abito largo*) big long coat
pala'sport *nm inv* indoor sports arena
pa'late *nfpl* **a** ~ ‹*fare soldi*› hand over fist
pa'lato *nm* palate
palaz'zetto *nm* ~ **dello sport** indoor sports arena
palaz'zina *nf* villa
pa'lazzo *nm* palace; (*edificio*) building. ~ **comunale** town hall. **P~ Ducale** Doge's Palace. ~ **delle esposizioni** exhibition centre. ~ **di giustizia** law courts *pl*, courthouse. ~ **dello sport** indoor sports arena
'**palco** *nm* (*pedana*) platform; *Theat* box; (*palcoscenico*) stage
palco'scenico *nm* stage
paleogra'fia *nf* palaeography
paleo'grafico *a* palaeographical
pale'ografo, -a *nmf* palaeographer
paleo'litico *a* palaeolithic
pale'sare *vt* disclose
pale'sarsi *vr* reveal oneself
pa'lese *a* evident
Pale'stina *nf* Palestine
palesti'nese *a* & *nmf* Palestinian
pa'lestra *nf* gymnasium, gym; (*ginnastica*) gymnastics *pl*
pa'letta *nf* spade; (*per focolare*) shovel. ~ [**della spazzatura**] dustpan
palet'tata *nf* shovelful
pa'letto *nm* peg

palin'sesto *nm* (*documento*) palimpsest; *TV* programme schedule
'**palio** *nm* (*premio*) prize. **il P~** *horse-race held at Siena*
palis'sandro *nm* rosewood
paliz'zata *nf* fence
'**palla** *nf* ball; (*proiettile*) bullet; (*fam: bugia*) porkie; **prendere la** ~ **al balzo** seize an opportunity; **essere una** ~ *sl* be a drag; **che palle!** *vulg* this is a pain in the arse!, what a drag!. ~ **da biliardo** billiard ball. ~ **medica** medicine ball. ~ **di neve** snowball. ~ **al piede** *fig* millstone round one's neck
pallaca'nestro *nf* basketball
palla'mano *nf* handball
pallanuo'tista *nmf* water polo player
pallanu'oto *nf* water polo
palla-'goal *nf* **hanno avuto molte palle-goal** they had a lot of goal-scoring opportunities
pallavo'lista *nmf* volleyball player
palla'volo *nf* volleyball
palleggi'are *vi* (*calcio*) practise ball control; *Tennis* knock up
pal'leggio *nm Sport* warm-up
'**pallet** *nm inv* pallet
pallet'toni *nmpl* buckshot
pallia'tivo *nm* palliative
'**pallido** *a* pale; **non ne ho la più pallida idea** I don't have the faintest *or* foggiest idea
pal'lina *nf* (*di vetro*) marble
pal'lino *nm* **avere il** ~ **del calcio** be crazy about football, be football crazy
pallon'cino *nm* balloon; (*lanterna*) Chinese lantern; (*fam: etilometro*) Breathalyzer[R]
pal'lone *nm* ball; (*calcio*) football; (*aerostato*) balloon; **essere/andare nel** ~ be/become confused. ~ **da calcio** football. ~ **gonfiato: è un** ~ ~ he's so puffed-up. ~ **sonda** weather balloon
pallo'netto *nm* lob
pal'lore *nm* pallor
pal'loso *a sl* boring
pal'lottola *nf* pellet; (*proiettile*) bullet. ~ **dum-dum** dumdum bullet
pallottoli'ere *nm* abacus
'**palma** *nf Bot* palm. ~ **da cocco** coconut palm. ~ **da datteri** date palm
palmarès *nm inv* (*di festival*) award winners *pl*; (*fig: i migliori*) top names *pl*
pal'mato *a* ‹*piede*› webbed
pal'mento *nm* **mangiava a quattro palmenti** he was really tucking in
pal'meto *nm* palm grove
palmi'pede *nm* web-footed animal
'**palmo** *nm Anat* palm; (*misura*) hand's-breadth; **restare con un** ~ **di naso** feel disappointed
'**palo** *nm* pole; (*di sostegno*) stake; (*in calcio*) goalpost; **fare il** ~ ‹*ladro*› keep a lookout. ~ **d'arrivo** (*in ippica*) finishing post ~ **della luce** lamppost. ~ **di partenza** (*in ippica*) starting post
palom'baro *nm* diver

pa'lombo *nm* dogfish

pal'pare *vt* feel

pal'pata *nf* **dare una ~ a qcsa** give sth a feel

'palpebra *nf* eyelid

palpeggi'are *vt* feel

palpi'tare *vi* throb; (*fremere*) quiver

palpitazi'one *nf* palpitation; **avere le palpitazioni** have palpitations

'palpito *nm* throb; (*del cuore*) beat

paltò *nm inv* overcoat

pa'lude *nf* marsh, swamp

palu'doso *a* marshy

pa'lustre *a* marshy; ⟨*piante, uccelli*⟩ marsh *attrib*

'pampas *nfpl* pampas

'pamphlet *nm inv* pamphlet

pamphlet'tista *nmf* pamphleteer

'pampino *nm* vine leaf

pan *nm vedi* **pane**

pana'cea *nf* panacea

pa'nache *nm inv* **far ~** (*in ippica*) fall

'panca *nf* bench; (*in chiesa*) pew

pancarré *nm* sliced bread

pan'cetta *nf* Culin bacon; (*di una certa età*) paunch. **~ affumicata** smoked bacon

pan'chetto *nm* [foot]stool

pan'china *nf* garden seat; (*in calcio*) bench

'pancia *nf* belly, tummy *fam*; (*di bottiglia, vaso*) body; **mal di ~** stomach-ache; **a ~ piena/vuota** on a full/empty stomach; **metter su ~** develop a paunch; **a ~ in giù** lying face down

panci'ata *nf* **prendere una ~** (*in tuffo*) do a belly flop

panci'era *nf* corset

panci'olle: stare in ~ lounge about

panci'one *nm* (*persona*) pot belly

panci'otto *nm* waistcoat

panci'uto *a* potbellied

'pancreas *nm inv* pancreas

pancre'atico *a* pancreatic

'panda *a* panda

pande'monio *nm* pandemonium

pan'dolce *nm* *Christmas cake similar to panettone*

pan'doro *nm* *kind of sponge cake traditionally eaten at Christmas time*

'pane *nm* bread; (*pagnotta*) loaf; (*di burro*) block. **~ casereccio** home-made bread. **~ a cassetta** sliced bread. **pan grattato** breadcrumbs *pl*. **~ integrale** wholemeal bread. **~ nero** blackbread. **~ di segale** rye bread. **pan di Spagna** sponge cake. **~ tostato** toast

'panel *nm inv* (*gruppo*) panel

panette'ria *nf* bakery; (*negozio*) baker's [shop]

panetti'ere, -a *nmf* baker

panet'tone *nf* *dome-shaped cake with sultanas and candied fruit eaten at Christmas*

'panfilo *nm* yacht

pan'forte *nm* *nougat-like spicy delicacy from Siena*

'panico *nm* panic; **lasciarsi prendere dal ~** panic

pani'ere *nm* basket; (*cesta*) hamper

pani'ficio *nm* bakery; (*negozio*) baker's [shop]

pani'naro *nm sl* preppie

pa'nino *nm* [bread] roll. **~ imbottito** filled roll. **~ al prosciutto** ham roll

panino'teca *nf* sandwich bar

'panna *nf* cream. **~ cotta** *kind of creme caramel*. **~ da cucina** [single] cream. **~ montata** whipped cream

'panne *nf* Mech **in ~** broken down; **restare in ~** break down

panneggi'ato *a* draped

pan'neggio *nm* drapery

pan'nello *nm* panel. **~ comandi** control panel. **~ solare** solar panel

'panno *nm* cloth; (*di tavolo da gioco e da biliardo*) baize; **panni** *pl* (*abiti*) clothes; **mettersi nei panni di qcno** *fig* put oneself in sb's shoes

pan'nocchia *nf* (*di granoturco*) cob

panno'lenci[K] *nm inv* brightly coloured felt

panno'lino *nm* (*per bambini*) nappy; (*da donna*) sanitary towel

pano'rama *nm* panorama; *fig* overview

pano'ramica *nf* (*rassegna*) overview

pano'ramico *a* panoramic

panpe'pato *nm* type of gingerbread

pantacol'lant *nmpl* leggings

pantagru'elico *a* ⟨*pranzo*⟩ gargantuan

pantalon'cini *nmpl* shorts. **~ da ciclista** cycling shorts. **~ corti** shorts

panta'loni *nmpl* trousers, pants *Am*. **~ da sci** ski pants. **~ a tubo** drain-pipe trousers. **~ a zampa d'elefante** bell-bottoms

pan'tano *nm* bog

panta'noso *a* marshy

pan'tera *nf* panther; (*auto della polizia*) high-speed police car. **~ nera** black panther

pan'tofola *nf* slipper

pantofo'laio, -a *nmf fig* stay-at-home

panto'mima *nf* pantomime; *fig* act

pan'zana *nf* fib

'panzer *nm inv* Mil tank

pao'nazzo *a* purple

'papa *nm* Pope; **a ogni morte di ~** *fig* once in a blue moon

papà *nm inv* dad[dy]

pa'paia *nf* papaw, papaya

pa'pale *a* papal

papa'lina *nf* skull-cap

papa'razzo *nm* paparazzo

pa'pato *nm* papacy

pa'pavero *nm* poppy

'papera *nf* (*errore*) slip of the tongue

'papero *nm* gosling

pa'pilla *nf* **~ gustativa** taste bud

papil'lon *nm inv* bow tie

pa'piro *nm* papyrus

'pappa *nf* (*per bambini*) baby food; **trovare la ~ pronta** *fig* have everything ready and waiting

pappagal'lino *nm* budgerigar, budgie

pappa'gallo *nm* parrot
pappa'gorgia *nf* double chin
pappa'molle *nmf* wimp
pap'parsi *vr fam* tuck away
pappar'delle *nfpl* strips of pasta with a meat sauce
pap'pone *nm sl* (*mangione*) pig; (*sfruttatore*) pimp
'paprica *nf* paprika
Pap test *nm inv* smear test
'para *nf* **suole di** ~ crêpe soles
parà *nm inv* para
pa'rabola *nf* parable; (*curva*) parabola
para'bolico *a* parabolic
para'brezza *nm inv* windscreen, windshield *Am*
paracadu'tare *vt* parachute
paracadu'tarsi *vr* parachute
paraca'dute *nm inv* parachute
paracadu'tismo *nm* parachuting. ~ **ascensionale** parascending
paracadu'tista *nmf* parachutist
para'carro *nm* roadside post
para'digma *nm Gram* paradigm
paradi'siaco *a* heavenly
para'diso *nm* paradise. ~ **fiscale** tax haven. ~ **terrestre** Eden, earthly paradise
parados'sale *a* paradoxical
para'dosso *nm* paradox
para'fango *nm* mudguard
paraf'fina *nf* paraffin
parafra'sare *vt* paraphrase
pa'rafrasi *nf inv* paraphrase
para'fulmine *nm* lightning-conductor
para'fuoco *nm* fire-screen
pa'raggi *nmpl* neighbourhood *sg*
parago'nabile *a* comparable (**a** to)
parago'nare *vt* compare
parago'narsi *vr* compare oneself
para'gone *nm* comparison; **a** ~ **di** in comparison with; **non c'è** ~**!** there's no comparison!
paragra'fare *vt* paragraph
pa'ragrafo *nm* paragraph
paraguai'ano, -a *a & nmf* Paraguyan
Paragu'ay *nm* Paraguay
pa'ralisi *nf inv* paralysis
para'litico, -a *a & nmf* paralytic
paraliz'zante *a* crippling
paraliz'zare *vt* paralyse
paraliz'zato *a* (*dalla paura*) transfixed
paral'lela *nf* parallel line; **è una** ~ **di...** (*strada:*) it runs parallel to...; **parallele** *pl* parallel bars
parallela'mente *adv* in parallel
paralle'lismo *nm* parallelism
paral'lelo *a & nm* parallel; **fare un** ~ **tra** draw a parallel between
parallelo'gramma *nm* parallelogram
para'lume *nm* lampshade
para'medico *nm* paramedic
para'mento *nm* hangings *pl*
pa'rametro *nm* parameter
paramili'tare *a* paramilitary
pa'ranco *nm* block and tackle

para'noia *nf* paranoia
para'noico, -a *a & nmf* paranoid
paranor'male *a & nm* paranormal
para'occhi *nmpl* blinkers
parao'recchie *nm* earmuffs
parapen'dio *nm* paragliding
para'petto *nm* parapet
para'piglia *nm* turmoil
para'plegico, -a *a & nmf* paraplegic
pa'rare *vt* (*addobbare*) adorn; (*riparare*) shield; save (*tiro, pallone*); ward off, parry (*schiaffo, pugno*) ● *vi* (*mirare*) lead up to
pa'rarsi *vr* (*abbigliarsi*) dress up; (*da pioggia, pugni*) protect oneself; ~ **dinanzi a qcno** appear in front of sb
parasco'lastico *a* (*attività*) extracurricular
para'sole *nm inv* parasol
paras'sita *a* parasitic ● *nm* parasite
parassi'tario *a anche fig* parasitic
parassi'tismo *nm* parasitism
parasta'tale *a* government-controlled
para'stinchi *nm inv* shin-guard
pa'rata *nf* parade; (*in calcio*) save; (*in scherma, pugilato*) parry. ~ **aerea** flypast
para'tia *nf* bulkhead
parauniversi'tario *a* at university level
para'urti *nm inv Auto* bumper, fender *Am*
para'vento *nm* screen
par'boiled *a* **riso** ~ parboiled rice
par'cella *nf* bill
parcheggi'are *vt anche fig* park; ~ **in doppia fila** double-park
parcheggia'|tore, -'trice *nmf* parking attendant. ~ **abusivo** person who illegally earns money by looking after parked cars
par'cheggio *nm* parking; (*posteggio*) carpark, parking lot *Am*. ~ **carta** *Comput* paper park. ~ **custodito** car park with attendant. ~ **incustodito** unattended car park. ~ **a pagamento** paying car-park. ~ **sotterraneo** underground car park, underground parking garage *Am*
par'chimetro *nm* parking meter
'parco[1] *a* sparing; (*moderato*) moderate; **essere** ~ **nel mangiare** eat sparingly
'parco[2] *nm* park. ~ **di divertimenti** fun-fair. ~ **giochi** playground. ~ **macchine** *Auto* fleet of cars. ~ **naturale** wildlife park. ~ **nazionale** national park. ~ **regionale** [regional] wildlife park
pa'recchio *a* quite a lot of; **parecchi** *pl* several, quite a lot of ● *pron* quite a lot; **parecchi** *pl* several, quite a lot ● *adv* rather; (*parecchio tempo*) quite a time
pareggi'are *vt* level; (*eguagliare*) equal; *Comm* balance; ~ **il bilancio** balance the scales ● *vi* draw
pa'reggio *nm Comm* balance; *Sport* draw
paren'tado *nm* relatives *pl*; (*vincolo di sangue*) relationship
pa'rente *nmf* relative, relation. ~ **acquisito** relation by marriage. ~ **alla lontana** distant relation. ~ **stretto** close relation
paren'tela *nf* relatives *pl*; (*vincolo di*

sangue) relationship; **grado di ~** degree of kinship

pa'rentesi nf inv parenthesis; (segno grafico) bracket; (fig: pausa) break; **aprire una ~** fig digress. **~ pl graffe** curly brackets. **~ quadre** square brackets. **~ tonde** round brackets; **fra ~,...** (tra l'altro) in parenthesis

pa'reo nm (copricostume) sarong; **a ~** (gonna) wrap-around

pa'rere¹ nm opinion; **a mio ~** in my opinion; **essere del ~ che** be of the opinion that

pa'rere² vi seem; (pensare) think; **che te ne pare?** what do you think of it?; **pare di sì** it seems so; **mi pare che...** I think that...; **non mi par vero** I can't believe it; **mi pareva bene!** I thought as much!

pa'rete nf wall; (in alpinismo) face. **~ divisoria** partition wall

'pargolo nf liter child

'pari a inv equal; (numero) even; **andare di ~ passo** keep pace; **essere ~** be even o quits; **arrivare ~** draw; **~ ~** (copiare, ripetere) word for word; **fare ~ o dispari** toss a coin ● nmf inv equal, peer; **ragazza alla ~** au pair [girl]; **lavorare alla ~** work [as an] au pair; **mettersi in ~ con qcsa** catch up with sth ● nm (titolo nobiliare) peer

'paria nm inv pariah

parifi'cato a (scuola) state-recognized

Pa'rigi nf Paris

pari'gino, -a a & nmf Parisian

pa'riglia nf pair; **rendere la ~ a qcno** give sb tit for tat

parità nf equality; Tennis deuce; **a ~ di condizioni/voti** if all circumstances/the votes are equal; **finire in ~** (partita:) end in a draw. **~ dei diritti** equal rights. **~ monetaria** monetary parity. **~ dei sessi** sexual equality, equality of the sexes

pari'tario a parity attrib

'parka nm inv parka

parlamen'tare a parliamentary ● nmf Member of Parliament ● vi discuss

parla'mento nm Parliament. **il P~ europeo** the European Parliament

parlan'tina nf avere la **~** be a chatterbox

par'lare vt/i speak, talk; speak (inglese, italiano); (confessare) talk; **~ bene/male di qcno** speak well/ill of somebody; **~ da solo** speak to oneself; **chi parla?** Teleph who's speaking?; **senti chi parla!** look who's talking!; **non parliamone più** let's forget about it; **non se ne parla nemmeno!** don't even mention it!; **~ a braccio** speak off the top of one's head; **far ~ qcno** make sb talk

par'lato a (lingua) spoken

parla'tore, -'trice nmf speaker

parla'torio nm parlour; (in prigione) visiting room

parlot'tare vi mutter

parlot'tio nm muttering

parlucchi'are vt speak a little, have a smattering of (lingua)

parmigi'ano nm Parmesan

paro'dia nf parody; **fare la ~ di** parody

parodi'are vt parody

paro'distico a (tono) parodying; **programma ~** parody

pa'rola nf word; (facoltà) speech; **è una ~!** it is easier said than done!; **parole** pl (di canzone) words, lyrics; **rivolgere la ~ a** address; **passare ~** spread the word; **non fare ~ di qcsa con nessuno** not breathe a word of sth to anybody; **ti credo sulla ~** I'll take your word for it; **togliere la ~ di bocca a qcno** take the words [right] out of sb's mouth; **voler sempre l'ultima ~** always want to have the last word; **dire due parole a qcno** have a word o chat with sb; **di poche parole** (persona) of few words; **dare a qcno la propria ~** give sb one's word; **~ per ~** word-for-word; **in parole povere** crudely speaking. **~ chiave** inv keyword. **parole incrociate** crossword [puzzle]. **~ di moda** buzzword. **~ d'onore** word of honour. **~ d'ordine** password

paro'laccia nf swear-word

paro'lina nf dire due paroline a qcno have a word o chat with sb

paro'loni nmpl mumbo jumbo

paros'sismo nm paroxysm

paros'sistico a Med paroxysmal

par'quet nm inv (pavimento) parquet flooring

parri'cida nmf parricide

parri'cidio nm parricide

par'rocchia nf parish

parrocchi'ale a parish attrib

parrocchi'ano, -a nmf parishioner

'parroco nm parish priest

par'rucca nf wig

parrucchi'ere, -a nmf hairdresser

parruc'chino nm toupée, hairpiece

parsi'monia nf thrift

parsimoni'oso a thrifty

'parso pp di **parere**

'parte nf part; (lato) side; (partito) party; (porzione) share; (fazione) group; **a ~** apart from; **in ~** in part; **la maggior ~ di** the majority of; **d'altra ~** on the other hand; **da ~** aside; (in disparte) to one side; **farsi da ~** stand aside; **da ~ di** from; (per conto di) on behalf of; **è gentile da ~ tua** it is kind of you; **fare una brutta ~ a qcno** behave badly towards sb; **da che ~ è...?** whereabouts is...?; **da una parte..., dall'altra...** on the one hand..., on the other hand...; **dall'altra ~ di** on the other side of; **da nessuna ~** nowhere; **da qualche ~** somewhere; **da qualche altra ~** somewhere else, elsewhere; **da tutte le parti** (essere) everywhere; **da questa ~** (in questa direzione) this way; **da queste parti** hereabouts; **da un anno a questa ~** for about a year now; **mettere qcsa da ~** put sth aside; **essere dalla ~ di qcno** be on sb's side; **prendere le parti di qcno** take sb's side; **dalla ~ della ragione/del torto** in the right/the wrong; **essere ~ in causa** be involved; **fare ~ di** (appartenere *a)* be a member of; **fare la propria ~** do one's share *o* bit; **far ~ di qcsa a qcno** inform sb of sth; **rendere ~ a** take part in; **prendere ~ a qcsa** take part in sth. **~ civile** plaintiff. **~ del discorso** part of speech

parteci'pante *nmf* participant

parteci'pare *vi* **~ a** participate in, take part in; *(condividere)* share in

partecipazi'one *nf* participation; *(annuncio)* announcement; *Fin* shareholding; *(presenza)* presence; **con la ~ [straordinaria] di...** featuring... **~ statale** *(quota)* state interest

par'tecipe *a* participating

parteggi'are *vi* **~ per** side with

par'tenza *nf* departure; *Sport* start; **in ~ per** leaving for; **falsa ~** false start

parti'cella *nf* particle

parti'cina *nf* bit part

parti'cipio *nm* participle. **~ passato** past participle. **~ presente** present participle

partico'lare *a* particular; *(privato)* private; *(speciale)* special, particular ● *nm* detail, particular; **fin nei minimi particolari** down to the smallest detail; **in ~** *(particolarmente)* in particular

particolareggi'ato *a* detailed

particolarità *nf inv* particularity; *(dettaglio)* detail

particolar'mente *adv* particularly

partigi'ano, -a *a & nmf* partisan

par'tire *vi* leave; *(aver inizio)* start; *(fam: rompersi)* break. **a ~ da** [beginning] from; **~ molto bene** get off to a flying start; **~ in quarta** go off at half cock; **è partito** *(fam: ubriaco)* he's away

par'tita *nf* game; *(incontro)* match; *Comm* lot; *(contabilità)* entry; **dare ~ vinta a qcno** *fig* give in to sb. **~ amichevole** friendly [match]. **~ di calcio** football match. **~ a carte** game of cards. **~ doppia** *Comm* double-entry book keeping. **~ di ritorno** *Sport* return match, rematch. **~ semplice** *Comm* single-entry book keeping

parti'tario *nm Comm* ledger. **~ vendite** sales ledger

par'tito *nm* party; *(scelta)* choice; *(occasione di matrimonio)* match; **per ~ preso** out of sheer pig-headedness. **~ di governo** governing party. **~ di maggioranza** majority party. **~ politico** political party

partitocra'zia *nf* concentration of power in the hands of political parties to the detriment of parliamentary democracy

partizi'one *nf (divisione)* division; *(Comput: di disco)* partition

'partner *nmf inv (in affari, coppia)* partner

'parto *nm* childbirth; **un ~ facile** an easy birth *o* labour; **dolori pl del ~** labour pains; **morire di ~** die in childbirth. **~ cesareo** Caesarian section. **~ indolore** natural childbirth. **~ indotto** induction, induced labour. **~ prematuro** premature birth

partori'ente *nf* woman in labour

parto'rire *vt anche fig* give birth to

part-'time *a* part-time ● *nm* **chiedere il ~** ask to work part-time

pa'rure *nf inv (di gioielli)* set of jewellery; *(di biancheria intima)* set of matching lingerie

par'venza *nf* appearance

parzi'ale *a* partial

parzialità *nf* partiality; **fare ~ per qcno** be biased towards sb

parzial'mente *adv* partially; *(con parzialità)* with bias; **~ cieco** partially sighted; **~ scremato** semi-skimmed

'pascere *vi* ⟨mucche:⟩ graze ● *vt* graze on ⟨erba⟩

pasci'uto *a* **ben ~** plump

pasco'lare *vt* graze

'pascolo *nm* pasture

'Pasqua *nf* Easter

pa'squale *a* Easter *attrib*; **l'isola di P~** Easter Island

pa'squetta *nf (lunedì di Pasqua)* Easter Monday

'passa: e ~ *adv (e oltre)* plus

pas'sabile *a* passable

pas'saggio *nm* passage; *(traversata)* crossing; *Sport* pass; *(su veicolo)* lift, ride; **essere di ~** be passing through; **è stato un ~ obbligato** *fig* it was something essential, it had to be done. **~ a livello** level crossing, grade crossing *Am*. **~ pedonale** pedestrian crossing, crosswalk *Am*. **~ di proprietà** transfer of ownership

passamane'ria *nf* braid

passamon'tagna *nm inv* balaclava

pas'sante *nmf* passer-by ● *nm (di cintura)* loop ● *a Tennis* passing

passa'porto *nm anche fig* passport. **~ europeo** European passport, Europassport

pas'sare *vi* pass; *(attraversare)* pass through; *(far visita)* call; *(andare)* go; *(essere approvato)* be passed; **~ davanti a qcno** go in front of sb; **~ alla storia** go down in history; **~ di moda** go out of fashion; **mi è passato di mente** it slipped my mind; **~ sopra a qcsa** pass over sth; **~ per un genio/idiota** be taken for a genius/an idiot; **farsi ~ per qcno** pass oneself off as sb; **passo!** *(nelle carte)* pass!; *(per radio)* over! ● *vt (far scorrere)* pass over; *(sopportare)* go through; *(al telefono)* put through; *Culin* strain; *(pass ⟨esame, visita⟩; **~ in rivista** review; **~ qcsa a qcno** pass sth to sb; **le passo il signor Rossi** *Teleph* I'll put you through to Mr Rossi; **~ qcsa su qcsa** ⟨crema, cera ecc⟩ give sth a coat of sth ; **~ il limite** go over the limit; **passarsela bene** be well off; **come te la passi?** how are you doing? ● *nm* **col ~ del tempo** with the passing *or* passage of time

pas'sata *nf (di vernice)* coat; *(spolverata)* dusting; *(occhiata)* look

passa'tempo *nm* pastime

pas'sato *a* past; **l'anno ~** last year; **sono le tre passate** it's past *o* after three o'clock ● *nm* past; *Culin* purée; *Gram* past tense; **in ~** in the past. **~ di moda** old-fashioned. **~**

prossimo *Gram* present perfect. **~ remoto** *Gram* [simple] past. **~ di verdure** cream of vegetable soup

passaver'dure *nm inv* food mill

passavi'vande *nm inv* serving hatch

passeg'gero, -a *a* passing ● *nmf* passenger. **~ in transito** transit passenger

passeggi'are *vi* walk, stroll

passeg'giata *nf* walk, stroll; (*luogo*) public walk; (*in bicicletta*) ride; **fare una ~** go for a walk

passeggia'trice *nf* streetwalker

passeg'gino *nm* pushchair, stroller *Am*

pas'seggio *nm* walk; (*luogo*) promenade; **andare a ~** go for a walk; **scarpe da ~** walking shoes

passe-par'tout *nm inv* master-key

passe'rella *nf* gangway; *Aeron* boarding bridge; (*per sfilate*) catwalk

'passero *nm* sparrow

passe'rotto *nm* (*passero*) sparrow

pas'sibile *a* **~ di** liable to

passio'nale *a* passionate; **delitto ~** crime of passion

passi'one *nf* passion; **avere la ~ del gioco** have a passion for gambling

passiva'mente *adv* passively

passività *nf* (*inerzia*) passiveness, passivity; *Fin* liabilities *pl*. **~ pl correnti** current liabilities

pas'sivo *a* passive ● *nm* passive; *Fin* liabilities *pl*; **in ~** ‹*azienda*› in deficit; ‹*bilancio*› debit, in deficit

'passo *nm* step; (*orma*) footprint; (*andatura*) pace, step; (*di libro*) passage; (*valico*) pass; **a due passi da qui** a stone's throw away; **a ~ d'uomo** at walking pace; **di buon ~** at a spanking pace, at a cracking pace; **a passi felpati** stealthily; **di questo ~** at this rate; **~ ~** step by step; **fare due passi** go for a stroll; **allungare il ~** quicken one's pace, step out; **tornare sui propri passi** retrace one's steps; **fare un ~ avanti** *anche fig* take a step forward; **fare un ~ falso** *fig* make a wrong move; **di pari ~** *fig* hand in hand; **stare al ~ con i tempi** keep up with the times, keep abreast of the times; **tenere il ~** keep up. **~ carrabile, ~ carraio** driveway. **~ dell'oca** goose-step

'pasta *nf* (*impasto per pane ecc*) dough; (*per dolci, pasticcino*) pastry; (*pastasciutta*) pasta; (*massa molle*) paste; *fig* nature; **sono fatti della stessa ~** they're birds of a feather. **~ e fagioli** very thick soup with blended borlotti beans and small pasta. **~ al forno** pasta baked in white sauce with grated cheese. **~ frolla** shortcrust pastry. **~ al ragù** pasta with Bolognese sauce

pastasci'utta *nf* pasta

pa'stella *nf* batter

pa'stello *nm* pastel

pa'sticca *nf* pastille; (*fam: pastiglia*) pill

pasticce'ria *nf* cake shop, patisserie; (*pasticcini*) pastries *pl*; (*arte*) confectionery

pasticci'are *vi* make a mess ● *vt* make a mess of

pasticci'ere, -a *nmf* confectioner

pastic'cino *nm* little cake

pa'sticcio *nm* *Culin* pie; (*lavoro disordinato*) mess; **mettersi nei pasticci** get into trouble

pasticci'one, -a *nmf* bungler ● *a* bungling

pasti'ficio *nm* pasta factory

pa'stiglia *nf* *Med* pill, tablet; (*di menta*) sweet. **~ dei freni** brake pad. **~ per la gola** throat pastille. **~ per la tosse** cough sweet

pa'stina *nf* small pasta shape. **~ in brodo** noodle soup

'pasto *nm* meal; **fuori ~** between meals; **dare qcsa in ~ a** *fig* serve sth up on a platter to ‹*pubblico, stampa*›

pa'stora *nf* shepherdess

pasto'rale *a* pastoral

pa'store *nm* shepherd; *Relig* pastor, vicar. **~ scozzese** collie. **~ tedesco** German shepherd, Alsatian

pasto'rizio *a* sheep farming *attrib*

pastoriz'zare *vt* pasteurize

pastoriz'zato *a* pasteurized

pastorizzazi'one *nf* pasteurization

pa'stoso *a* doughy; *fig* mellow

pa'strocchio *nm* mess

pa'stura *nf* pasture; (*per pesci*) bait

pa'tacca *nf* (*macchia*) stain; (*fig: oggetto senza valore*) piece of junk

pa'tata *nf* potato. **patate** *pl* **arrosto** roast potatoes. **patate** *pl* **al cartoccio** jacket potatoes. **patate** *pl* **fritte** chips *Br*, French fries. **patate** *pl* **in insalata** potato salad. **patate** *pl* **lesse** boiled potatoes

pata'tine *nfpl* [potato] crisps, chips *Am*

pata'trac *nm inv* (*crollo*) crash

patch'work *nm inv* patchwork

pâté *nm inv* pâté. **~ di fegato** liver pâté

pa'tella *nf* limpet

pa'tema *nm* anxiety

pa'tente *nf* licence; **prendere la ~** get one's driving licence. **~ di guida** driving licence, driver's license *Am*

pater'nale *nf* scolding

paterna'lismo *nm* paternalism

paterna'lista *nm* paternalist

paterna'listico *a* paternalistic

paternità *nf inv* paternity

pa'terno *a* paternal; ‹*affetto ecc*› fatherly

pa'tetico *a* pathetic; **cadere nel ~** become over-sentimental

'pathos *nm* pathos

pa'tibolo *nm* gallows *sg*

pati'mento *nm* suffering

'patina *nf* patina; (*sulla lingua*) coating

'patio *nm* patio garden

pa'tire *vt/i* suffer

pa'tito, -a *a* suffering ● *nmf* fanatic. **~ della musica** music lover

patolo'gia *nf* pathology

pato'logico *a* pathological

pa'tologo, -a *nmf* pathologist

'**patria** *nf* native land; **amor di** ~ love of one's country
patri'arca *nm* patriarch
patriar'cale *a* patriarchal
patriar'cato *nm* patriarchy
pa'trigno *nm* stepfather
patrimoni'ale *a* property *attrib*
patri'monio *nm* estate
patri'ota *nmf* patriot
patri'ottico *a* patriotic
patriot'tismo *nm* patriotism
pa'trizio, -a *a & nmf* patrician
patroci'nante *a* sponsoring
patroci'nare *vt* support
patro'cinio *nm* support; **sotto il** ~ **di** under the sponsorship of; *Jur* defended by. ~ **gratuito** legal aid
patro'nato *nm* patronage
pa'trono *nm Relig* patron saint; *Jur* counsel
'**patta**[1] *nf* (*di tasca*) flap
'**patta**[2] *nf* (*pareggio*) draw
patteggia'mento *nm* bargaining
patteggi'are *vt/i* negotiate
patti'naggio *nm* skating. ~ **artistico** figure skating. ~ **su ghiaccio** ice skating. ~ **a rotelle** roller skating
patti'nare *vi* skate; ⟨*auto:*⟩ skid
pattina|'tore, -'trice *nmf* skater
'**pattino** *nm* skate; *Aeron* skid. ~ **da ghiaccio** ice skate. ~ **a rotelle** roller skate
'**patto** *nm* deal; *Pol* pact; **a** ~ **che** on condition that; **scendere a patti, venire a patti** reach a compromise
pat'tuglia *nf* patrol; **essere di** ~ be on patrol. ~ **stradale** highway patrol *Am*, ≈ patrol car; police motorbike
pattu'ire *vt* negotiate
pat'tume *nm* rubbish
pattumi'era *nf* dustbin, trashcan *Am*
pa'ura *nf* fear; (*spavento*) fright; **aver** ~ be afraid; **mettere** ~ **a** frighten; **per** ~ **di** for fear of; **da** ~ ⟨*sl: libro, film*⟩ brilliant
pau'roso *a* (*che fa paura*) frightening; (*che ha paura*) fearful; (*fam: enorme*) awesome
'**pausa** *nf* pause; (*nel lavoro*) break; **fare una** ~ pause; (*nel lavoro*) have a break. ~ **per il caffè** coffee break. ~ **del pranzo** lunch break, lunch hour
pavida'mente *adv* timidly
'**pavido** *a* cowardly ● *nm* coward
pavimen'tare *vt* pave ⟨*strada*⟩
pavimentazi'one *nf* paving
pavi'mento *nm* floor
pa'vone *nm* peacock
pavoneggi'arsi *vr* strut
pay tv *nf inv* pay TV
pazien'tare *vi* be patient
pazi'ente *a & nmf* patient
paziente'mente *adv* patiently
pazi'enza *nf* patience; ~! never mind!; **perdere la** ~ lose one's patience
'**pazza** *nf* madwoman
pazza'mente *adv* madly
pazzerel'lone, -a *nmf* madcap
paz'zesco *a* foolish; (*esagerato*) crazy

paz'zia *nf* madness; (*azione*) [act of] folly
'**pazzo** *a* mad; *fig* crazy; **sei** ~**?** you must be crazy!, are you crazy? ● *nm* madman; **essere** ~ **di/per** be crazy about; ~ **di gioia** mad with joy; **da pazzi** *fam* crackpot; **darsi alla pazza gioia** live it up
paz'zoide *a fam* whacky
P.C.I. *nm abbr* (**Partito Comunista Italiano**) Italian Communist Party
'**pecan** *nm inv* pecan
'**pecca** *nf* fault; **senza** ~ flawless
peccami'noso *a* sinful
pec'care *vi* sin; ~ **di** be guilty of ⟨*ingratitudine*⟩
pec'cato *nm* sin; ~ **che...** it's a pity that...; [**che**] ~**!** [what a] pity!. ~ **di gioventù** youthful folly
pecca|'tore, -'trice *nmf* sinner
'**pece** *nf* pitch; **nero come la** ~ black as pitch
pechi'nese *nm* Pekin[g]ese
Pe'chino *nf* Peking
'**pecora** *nf* sheep. ~ **nera** black sheep
peco'raio *nm* shepherd
peco'rella *nf* **cielo a pecorelle** sky full of fluffy white clouds. ~ **smarrita** lost sheep
peco'rino *nm* (*formaggio*) sheep's milk cheese
peculi'are *a* ~ **di** peculiar to
peculiarità *nf inv* peculiarity
pecuni'ario *a* money *attrib*
pe'daggio *nm* toll
pedago'gia *nf* pedagogy
peda'gogico *a* pedagogical
peda'gogo, -a *nmf* pedagogue
peda'lare *vi* pedal
peda'lata *nf* push on the pedals
pe'dale *nm* pedal. ~ **del freno** brake pedal
pedalò *nm inv* pedalo
pe'dana *nf* footrest; *Sport* springboard
pe'dante *a* pedantic
pedante'ria *nf* pedantry
pedan'tesco *a* pedantic
pe'data *nf* (*in calcio*) kick; (*impronta*) footprint
pede'rasta *nm* pederast
pe'destre *a* pedestrian
pedi'atra *nmf* paediatrician
pedia'tria *nf* paediatrics
pedi'atrico *a* paediatric
pedi'cure *nmf inv* chiropodist, podiatrist *Am* ● *nm* (*cura dei piedi*) pedicure
pedi'gree *nm inv* pedigree
pedi'luvio *nm* footbath
pe'dina *nf* (*alla dama*) piece; *fig* pawn
pedina'mento *nm* shadowing
pedi'nare *vt* shadow
pedofi'lia *nf* paedophilia
pe'dofilo, -a *nmf* paedophile
pedo'nale *a* pedestrian
pe'done, -a *nmf* pedestrian
'**pedula** *nf* desert boot
'**peeling** *nm inv* exfoliation treatment
'**peggio** *adv* worse; ~ **per te!** too bad!, tough!; ~ **di così** any worse; **la persona** ~

vestita the worst dressed person ● *a* worse; **niente di ~** nothing worse; **stare ~ di** be worse off than ● *nm* **il ~ è che...** the worst of it is that...; **pensare al ~** think the worst ● *nf* **alla ~** at worst; **avere la ~** get the worst of it; **alla meno ~** as best I can

peggiora'mento *nm* worsening

peggiora'rare *vt* make worse, worsen ● *vi* get worse, worsen

peggiora'tivo *a* pejorative

peggi'ore *a* worse; (*superlativo*) worst; **nella ~ delle ipotesi** if the worst comes to the worst; **tanto ~** too bad ● *nmf* **il/la ~** the worst

'**pegno** *nm* pledge; (*nei giochi di società*) forfeit; *fig* token; **dare qcsa in ~** pawn sth; **in ~ d'amicizia** as a token of friendship

pelan'drone *nm* slob

pe'lare *vt* (*spennare*) pluck; (*spellare*) skin; (*sbucciare*) peel; (*fam: spillare denaro*) fleece

pe'larsi *vr fam* lose one's hair

pe'lati *nmpl* (*pomodori*) peeled tomatoes

pe'lato *a* (*calvo*) bald

pel'lame *nm* skins *pl*

'**pelle** *nf* skin; (*cuoio*) leather; (*buccia*) peel; **avere la ~ d'oca** have goose-flesh; **non stare più nella ~** be beside oneself; **salvare la ~** save one's skin; **lasciarci la ~** buy it; **essere ~ e ossa** be all skin and bones; **avere la ~ dura** be tough; **borsa di ~** leather bag. **~ scamosciata** suede

pellegri'naggio *nm* pilgrimage

pelle'grino, -a *nmf* pilgrim

pelle'rossa *nmf* Red Indian, Redskin

pellette'ria *nf* leather goods *pl*

pelli'cano *nm* pelican

pellicce'ria *nf* furrier's [shop]

pel'liccia *nf* fur; (*indumento*) fur [coat]

pellicci'aio, -a *nmf* furrier

pel'licola *nf Phot, Cinema* film. **~ a colori** colour film. **~ trasparente** *Culin* cling film

'**pelo** *nm* hair; (*di animale*) coat; (*di lana*) pile; **per un ~** by the skin of one's teeth; **cavarsela per un ~** have a narrow escape; **cercare il ~ nell'uovo** nitpick

pe'loso *a* hairy

'**peltro** *nm* pewter

pe'luche *nm inv* **giocattolo di ~** soft toy; **orsetto di ~** teddy bear

pe'luria *nf* down

'**pelvico** *a* pelvic

'**pena** *nf* (*punizione*) punishment; (*sofferenza*) pain; (*dispiacere*) sorrow; (*disturbo*) trouble; **a mala ~** hardly; **mi fa ~** I pity him; **vale la ~ andare** it is worth [while] going. **pene** *pl* **dell'inferno** hellfire. **~ di morte** death sentence

pe'nale *a* criminal; **diritto ~** criminal law

pena'lista *nmf* criminal lawyer

penalità *nf inv* penalty

penaliz'zare *vt* penalize

penalizzazi'one *nf* (*penalità*) penalty

pe'nare *vi* suffer; (*faticare*) find it difficult

pen'daglio *nm* pendant

pen'dant *nm inv* **fare ~** [**con**] match

pen'dente *a* hanging; *Comm* outstanding ● *nm* (*ciondolo*) pendant; **pendenti** *pl* drop earrings

pen'denza *nf* slope; *Comm* outstanding account

'**pendere** *vi* hang; (*superficie:*) slope; (*essere inclinato*) lean

pen'dio *nm* slope: **in ~** sloping

'**pendola** *nf* clock

pendo'lare *a* pendulum ● *nmf* commuter

pendo'lino *nm* (*treno*) special, first class only, fast train

'**pendolo** *nm* pendulum; **orologio a ~** pendulum clock

'**pene** *nm* penis

pene'trante *a* penetrating; (*freddo*) biting

pene'trare *vt/i* penetrate; (*trafiggere*) pierce ● *vt* (*odore:*) get into ● *vi* (*entrare furtivamente*) steal in

penetrazi'one *nf* penetration

penicil'lina *nf* penicillin

pe'nisola *nf* peninsula

peni'tente *a* & *nmf* penitent

peni'tenza *nf* penitence; (*punizione*) penance; (*in gioco*) forfeit

penitenzi'ario *nm* penitentiary

'**penna** *nf* (*da scrivere*) pen; (*di uccello*) feather. **~ a feltro** felt-tip[ped pen]. **~ ottica** light pen. **~ a sfera** ball-point [pen]. **~ stilografica** fountain-pen

pen'nacchio *nm* plume

penna'rello *nm* felt-tip[ped pen]

'**penne** *nfpl* pasta quills

pennel'lare *vt* paint

pennel'lata *nf* brushstroke

pen'nello *nm* brush; **a ~** (*a perfezione*) perfectly. **~ da barba** shaving brush

pen'nino *nm* nib

pen'none *nm* (*di bandiera*) flagpole

pen'nuto *a* feathered

pe'nombra *nf* half-light

pe'noso *a* (*fam: pessimo*) painful

pen'sabile *a* **non è ~** it's unthinkable

pen'sare *vi* think; **penso di sì** I think so; **~ a** think of; remember to (*chiudere il gas ecc*); **pensa ai fatti tuoi!** mind your own business!; **ci penso io** I'll take care of it; **~ di fare qcsa** think of doing sth; **a pensarci bene** on second thoughts; **~ tra sé e sé** think to oneself; **pensarci su** think over ● *vt* think

pen'sata *nf* idea

pensa'|tore, -'trice *nmf* thinker

pensi'ero *nm* thought; (*mente*) mind; (*preoccupazione*) worry; **stare in ~ per** be anxious about; **levarsi il ~** to get something out of the way

pensie'roso *a* pensive

'**pensile** *a* hanging; **giardino ~** roof-garden ● *nm* (*mobile*) wall unit

pensi'lina *nf* (*di fermata d'autobus*) bus shelter

pensio'nante *nmf* boarder; (*ospite pagante*) lodger

pensio'nato, -a *nmf* pensioner ● *nm* (*per*

anziani) [old folks'] home; (*per studenti*) hostel

pensi'one *nf* pension; (*albergo*) boarding-house; (*vitto e alloggio*) board and lodging; **andare in ~** retire; **essere in ~** be retired; **mezza ~** half board. **~ di anzianità** old-age pension. **~ completa** full board. **~ di invalidità** disability pension

pen'soso *a* pensive

pen'tagono *nm* pentagon; **il P~** the Pentagon

pen'tathlon *nm inv* pentathlon

Pente'coste *nf* Whitsun

penti'mento *nm* repentance

pen'tirsi *vr* **~ di** repent of; (*rammaricarsi*) regret

penti'tismo *nm* turning informant

pen'tito *nm* Mafioso turned informant

'pentola *nf* saucepan; (*contenuto*) potful. **~ a pressione** pressure cooker

pento'lino *nf* saucepan

pe'nultimo *a* last but one, penultimate

pe'nuria *nf* shortage

penzo'lare *vi* dangle

penzo'loni *adv* dangling

pe'onia *nf* peony

pepai'ola *nf* pepper pot

pe'pare *vt* pepper

pe'pato *a* peppery

'pepe *nm* pepper; **grano di ~** peppercorn. **~ di Caienna** cayenne pepper. **~ in grani** whole peppercorns. **~ macinato** ground pepper. **~ nero** black pepper

pepero'nata *nf* dish of green peppers and tomatoes

peperon'cino *nm* chilli pepper

pepe'rone *nm* [sweet] pepper; **rosso come un ~** red as a beetroot; **peperoni** *pl* **ripieni** stuffed peppers. **~ verde** green pepper

pepi'era *nf* pepper pot; (*macinino*) pepper mill

pe'pita *nf* nugget

'peptico *a* peptic

'per *prep* for; (*attraverso*) through; (*stato in luogo*) in, on; (*distributivo*) per; (*mezzo, entro*) by; (*causa*) with; (*in qualità di*) as; **mi è passato per la mente** it crossed my mind; **~ strada** on the street; **~ la fine del mese** by the end of the month; **in fila ~ due** in double file; **l'ho sentito ~ telefono** I spoke to him on the phone; **~ iscritto** in writing; **~ caso** by chance; **~ esempio** for example; **ho aspettato ~ ore** I've been waiting for hours; **~ tutta la durata del viaggio** for the entire journey; **~ tempo** in time; **~ sempre** forever; **~ scherzo** as a joke; **gridare ~ il dolore** scream with pain; **vendere ~ 10 milioni** sell for 10 million; **uno ~ volta** one at a time; **uno ~ uno** one by one; **venti ~ cento** twenty per cent; **~ fare qcsa** [in order to] do sth; **stare ~** be about to; **è troppo bello ~ essere vero** it's too good to be true

'pera *nf* pear; **farsi una ~** (*sl: di eroina*) shoot up

perbe'nismo *nm* prissiness

perbe'nista *a inv* prissy

per'calle *nm* gingham

per'cento *adv* per cent

percentu'ale *nf* percentage

perce'pibile *a* perceivable; (*somma*) payable

perce'pire *vt* perceive; (*riscuotere*) cash

percet'tibile *a* perceptible

percettibil'mente *adv* perceptibly

percezi'one *nf* perception

perché *conj* (*in interrogazioni*) why; (*per il fatto che*) because; (*affinché*) so that; **~ non vieni?** why don't you come?; **dimmi ~** tell me why; **~ no/sì!** because!; **la ragione ~ l'ho fatto** the reason [that] I did it, the reason why I did it; **è troppo difficile ~ lo possa capire** it's too difficult for me to understand ● *nm inv* reason [why]; **senza un ~** without any reason

perciò *conj* so

per'correre *vt* cover (*distanza*); (*viaggiare*) travel

percor'ribile *a* (*strada*) driveable, passable

percorribilità *nf* **~ delle strade** road conditions *pl*

per'corso *pp di* percorrere ● *nm* (*tragitto*) course, route; (*distanza*) distance; (*viaggio*) journey. **~ ecologico** nature trail. **~ di guerra** assault course. **~ a ostacoli** obstacle course

per'cossa *nf* blow; **percosse** *pl Jur* assault and battery

per'cosso *pp di* percuotere

percu'otere *vt* strike

percussi'one *nf* percussion; **strumenti a ~** percussion instruments

percussio'nista *nmf* percussionist

per'dente *nmf* loser

'perdere *vt* lose; (*sprecare*) waste; (*non prendere*) miss; (*fig: vizio:*) ruin; **~ tempo** waste time; **lascia ~!** forget it!; **~ di vista** lose touch [with each other] ● *vi* lose; (*recipiente:*) leak; **a ~** (*vuoto*) nonreturnable; **non avere niente da ~** have nothing to lose

'perdersi *vr* get lost; (*reciproco*) lose touch

perdi'fiato: a ~ *adv* (*gridare*) at the top of one's voice

perdigi'orno *nmf inv* idler

'perdita *nf* loss; (*spreco*) waste; (*falla*) leak; **a ~ d'occhio** as far as the eye can see; **chiudere in ~** (*azienda:*) show a loss. **~ di gas** gas leak. **~ di sangue** loss of blood, bleeding. **~ di tempo** waste of time

perdi'tempo *nm* waste of time

perdizi'one *nf* perdition

perdo'nare *vt* forgive; (*scusare*) excuse; **mi perdoni se interrompo** sorry to interrupt, excuse me for interrupting; **per farsi ~** as an apology ● *vi* **~ a qcno** forgive sb; **un male che non perdona** an incurable disease

per'dono *nm* forgiveness; *Jur* pardon; **chiedere ~** ask for forgiveness; (*scusarsi*) apologize

perdu'rare *vi* last; (*perseverare*) persist

perduta'mente *adv* hopelessly

per'duto *pp di* **perdere** ● *a* lost; (*rovinato*) ruined

pe'renne *a* everlasting; *Bot* perennial; **nevi perenni** perpetual snow

perenne'mente *adv* perpetually

peren'torio *a* peremptory

per'fetto *a* perfect ● *nm Gram* perfect [tense]

perfezio'nare *vt* perfect; (*migliorare*) improve

perfezio'narsi *vr* improve oneself; (*specializzarsi*) specialize

perfezi'one *nf* perfection; **alla ~** to perfection

perfezio'nismo *nm* perfectionism

perfezio'nista *nmf* perfectionist

per'fidia *nf* wickedness; (*atto*) wicked act

'perfido *a* treacherous; (*malvagio*) perverse

per'fino *adv* even

perfo'rare *vt* pierce; punch (*schede*); *Mech* drill

perfora'tore *nm* (*apparecchio*) punch. **~ di schede** card punch

perfora|'tore, -'trice *nmf* punch-card operator

perforazi'one *nf* perforation; (*di schede*) punching

per'formance *nf inv Theat* performance

perga'mena *nf* parchment

'pergola *nf* pergola

pergo'lato *nm* bower

periar'trite *nf* rheumatoid arthritis

perico'lante *a* precarious; (*azienda*) shaky

pe'ricolo *nm* danger; (*rischio*) risk; **mettere in ~** endanger; **essere fuori ~** be out of danger. **~ pubblico** danger to society. **~ di valanghe** danger of avalanches

pericolosa'mente *adv* dangerously

pericolosità *nf* danger

perico'loso *a* dangerous

peridu'rale *nf* epidural

perife'ria *nf* periphery; (*di città*) outskirts *pl*; *fig* fringes *pl*

peri'ferica *nf* peripheral; (*strada*) ring road. **~ di input** *Comput* input device

peri'ferico *a* peripheral; (*quartiere*) outlying

pe'rifrasi *nf inv* circumlocution

perime'trale *a* (*muro*) perimeter *attrib*

pe'rimetro *nm* perimeter

peri'odico *nm* periodical ● *a* periodical; (*vento, mal di testa, Math*) recurring

pe'riodo *nm* period; *Gram* sentence. **~ nero** bad patch. **~ di prova** trial period. **~ di ripensamento** cooling-off period. **~ di riposo** breathing space. **~ di transizione** transitional period, interim. **~ di validità** period of validity

peripe'zie *nfpl* misadventures

pe'rire *vi* perish

peri'scopio *nm* periscope

pe'rito, -a *a* skilled ● *nmf* expert. **~ agrario** agriculturalist. **~ di assicurazione** *Comm* loss adjuster. **~ edile** chartered surveyor. **~ elettronico** electronics engineer

perito'nite *nf* peritonitis

pe'rizia *nf* skill; (*valutazione*) survey

peri'zoma *nm inv* loincloth

'perla *nf* pearl. **~ coltivata** cultured pearl

per'lina *nf* bead

perli'nato *nm* matchboard

perlo'meno *adv* at least

perlu'strare *vt* patrol

perlustrazi'one *nf* patrol; **andare in ~** go on patrol

perma'loso *a* touchy

perma'nente *a* permanent ● *nf* perm; **farsi [fare] la ~** have a perm

perma'nenza *nf* permanence; (*soggiorno*) stay; **in ~** permanently. **~ in carica** tenure

perma'nere *vi* remain

perme'are *vt* permeate

perme'ato *a* **~ di** *fig* permeated with

per'messo *pp di* **permettere** ● *nm* permission; (*autorizzazione*) permit, licence; *Mil* leave; [è] **~?, con ~** (*posso entrare?*) may I come in?; (*posso passare?*) excuse me. **~ di lavoro** work permit. **~ di soggiorno** residence permit

per'mettere *vt* allow, permit; **potersi ~ qcsa** (*finanziariamente*) be able to afford sth

per'mettersi *vr* **~ di fare qcsa** allow oneself to do sth; **come si permette?** how dare you?

permis'sivo *a* permissive

permutazi'one *nf* exchange; *Math* permutation

per'nacchia *nf* (*sl: con la bocca*) raspberry *sl*

per'nice *nf* partridge

pernici'oso *a* pernicious

'perno *nm* pivot

pernot'tare *vi* stay overnight

'pero *nm* pear-tree

però *conj* but; (*tuttavia*) however

pe'rone *nm Anat* fibula

pero'rare *vt* plead

perpendico'lare *a & nf* perpendicular

perpe'trare *vt* perpetrate

per'petua *nf* (*di prete*) priest's housekeeper

perpetu'are *vt* perpetuate

per'petuo *a* perpetual

perplessità *nf inv* perplexity; (*dubbio*) doubt

per'plesso *a* perplexed

perqui'sire *vt* search

perquisizi'one *nf* search. **~ domiciliare** search of the premises

persecu|'tore, -'trice *nmf* persecutor

persecuzi'one *nf* persecution

persegu'ire *vt* pursue

persegui'tare *vt* persecute

persegui'tato, -a *nmf* victim of persecution

perseve'rante *a* persevering

perseve'ranza *nf* perseverance

perseve'rare *vi* persevere

'Persia *nf* Persia

persi'ana *nf* shutter. **~ avvolgibile** roller shutter

persi'ano, -a a & nmf Persian
'persico a Persian
per'sino adv = **perfino**
persi'stente a persistent; ⟨dubbio⟩ nagging
persi'stenza nf persistence
per'sistere vi persist; ~ **nel fare qcsa** persist in doing sth
'perso pp di **perdere** ● a lost; **a tempo** ~ in one's spare time
per'sona nf person; ⟨un tale⟩ somebody; **di ~, in** ~ in person, personally; **per** ~ per person, a head; **per interposta** ~ through an intermediary; **curare la propria** ~ look after oneself, look after number one; **persone** pl people. ~ **a carico** dependant. ~ **di colore** nonwhite, coloured person. ~ **giuridica** legal person. ~ **di servizio** domestic
perso'naggio nm ⟨persona di riguardo⟩ personality; Theat ecc character
perso'nale a personal ● nm staff; ⟨aspetto⟩ build. ~ **di terra** ground crew
personalità nf inv personality
personaliz'zare vt customize ⟨auto ecc⟩; personalize ⟨penna ecc⟩
personifi'care vt personify
personificazi'one nf personification
perspi'cace a shrewd
perspi'cacia nf shrewdness
persua'dere vt convince; impress ⟨critici⟩; ~ **qcno a fare qcsa** persuade sb to do sth
persuasi'one nf persuasion; **fare opera di** ~ **su qcno** try to persuade sb
persuasività nf persuasiveness
persua'sivo a persuasive
persu'aso pp di **persuadere**
persua'sore nm persuader
per'tanto conj therefore
'pertica nf pole
perti'nace a pertinacious
perti'nente a relevant
per'tosse nf whooping cough
per'tugio nm opening
pertur'bare vt perturb
perturbazi'one nf disturbance. ~ **atmosferica** atmospheric disturbance
Perù nm Peru
peruvi'ano, -a a & nmf Peruvian
per'vadere vt pervade
perva'sivo a pervasive
per'vaso pp di **pervadere**
perven'ire vi reach; **far** ~ **qcsa a qcno** send sth to sb
perversa'mente adv perversely
perversi'one nf perversion
perversità nf perversity
per'verso a perverse
perver'tire vt pervert
perver'tirsi vr ⟨gusti, costumi:⟩ become debased
perver'tito a perverted ● nm pervert
pervi'cace a obstinate
pervicace'mente adv obstinately
pervi'cacia nf obstinacy
per'vinca nm ⟨colore⟩ blue with a touch of purple

per'vinca nf Bot periwinkle
p. es. abbr (**per esempio**) e.g.
'pesa nf weighing; ⟨bilancia⟩ weighing machine; ⟨per veicoli⟩ weighbridge
pe'sante a heavy; ⟨stomaco⟩ overfull; ⟨accusa, ingiuria⟩ serious; ⟨noioso⟩ boring; **andarci** ~ **con qcno** be heavy-handed with sb ● adv ⟨vestirsi⟩ warmly
pesante'mente adv ⟨cadere⟩ heavily; ⟨insultare⟩ seriously
pesan'tezza nf heaviness
pesaper'sone nm inv scales
pe'sare vt weigh; ~ **le parole** weigh one's words ● vi weigh; ⟨essere pesante⟩ be heavy; ~ **su** fig lie heavy on
pe'sarsi vr weigh oneself
'pesca[1] nf ⟨frutto⟩ peach
'pesca[2] nf fishing; **andare a** ~ go fishing. ~ **di beneficenza** lucky dip. ~ **con la lenza** angling. ~ **subacquea** underwater fishing
pe'scare vt ⟨andare a pesca di⟩ fish for; ⟨prendere⟩ catch; ⟨fam: trovare⟩ dig up, find; **guai se ti pesco!** there will be trouble if I catch you!
pesca'tore nm fisherman. ~ **di frodo** poacher. ~ **di perle** pearl diver
'pesce nm fish; **non sapere che pesci pigliare** fig not know which way to turn; **prendere qcno a pesci in faccia** fig treat sb like dirt; **sentirsi un** ~ **fuor d'acqua** feel like a fish out of water. ~ **d'aprile!** April Fool!. ~ **in carpione** soused fish. ~ **al cartoccio** fish baked in foil. ~ **gatto** catfish. ~ **grosso** fig big fish. ~ **persico** perch. ~ **piccolo** fig small fry. ~ **rosso** goldfish. ~ **spada** swordfish
pesce'cane nm shark
pesche'reccio nm fishing boat
pesche'ria nf fishmonger's [shop]
peschi'era nf fish-pond
'Pesci nmpl Astr Pisces
pescio'lino nm ~ **d'acqua dolce** minnow
pesci'vendolo nm fishmonger
'pesco nm peach tree
pe'scoso a teeming with fish
pe'seta nf peseta
pe'sista nm ⟨in sollevamento pesi⟩ weight-lifter; ⟨in lancio del peso⟩ shotputter
'peso nm weight; **essere di** ~ **per qcno** be a burden to sb; **alzare di** ~ lift up in one go; **avere un** ~ **sullo stomaco** have a lead weight on one's stomach; **di poco** ~ ⟨senza importanza⟩ not very important; **non dare** ~ **a qcsa** not attach any importance to sth. ~ **massimo** ⟨nel pugilato⟩ heavy weight. ~ **medio** ⟨nel pugilato⟩ middleweight. ~ **morto** dead weight. ~ **netto** net weight. ~ **piuma** ⟨nel pugilato⟩ featherweight ~ **specifico** specific gravity
pessi'mismo nm pessimism
pessi'mista nmf pessimist ● a pessimistic
pessimistica'mente adv pessimistically
'pessimo a very bad
pe'staggio nm beating-up

pe'stare *vt* tread on; (*picchiare*) beat; crush (*aglio, prezzemolo, uva*); ~ **i piedi [per terra]** stamp one's feet [on the ground]; ~ **un piede a qcno** tread on sb's foot

pe'stata *nf* bash; **dare una ~ a un piede a qcno** tread on sb's foot

'peste *nf* plague; (*persona*) pest; **dire ~ e corna di qcno** tear sb to bits. ~ **bubbonica** bubonic plague

pe'stello *nm* pestle

pesti'cida *nm* pesticide

pe'stifero *a* (*fastidioso*) pestilential

pesti'lenza *nf* pestilence; (*fetore*) stench, stink

pestilenzi'ale *a* (*odore, aria*) noxious

'pesto *a* ground; **occhio ~** black eye ● *nm* basil and garlic sauce

'petalo *nm* petal

pe'tardo *nm* banger

petizi'one *nf* petition; **fare una ~** draw up a petition

petrol'chimico *a* petrochemical

petrol'dollaro *nm* petrodollar

petroli'era *nf* [oil] tanker

petroli'ere *nm* oilman

petro'lifero *a* oil-bearing

pe'trolio *nm* oil

pettego'lare *vi* gossip

pettego'lezzo *nm* piece of gossip; **pettegolezzi** *pl* gossip *sg*; **far pettegolezzi** gossip

pet'tegolo, -a *a* gossipy ● *nmf* gossip

petti'nare *vt* comb

petti'narsi *vr* comb one's hair

pettina'tura *nf* combing; (*acconciatura*) hairstyle. ~ **a caschetto** bob

'pettine *nm* comb

'petting *nm* petting

petti'nino *nm* (*fermaglio*) comb

petti'rosso *nm* robin [redbreast]

'petto *nm* chest; (*seno*) breast; **a doppio ~** double-breasted; **prendere qcsa/qcno di ~** face up to sth/sb. ~ *pl* **di pollo** chicken breasts

petto'rale *nm Sport* number ● *a* pectoral

petto'rina *nf* (*di salopette*) bib

petto'ruto *a* (*donna*) full-breasted; (*uomo*) broad-chested

petu'lante *a* impertinent

petu'lanza *nf* impertinence

pe'tunia *nf* petunia

'pezza *nf* cloth; (*toppa*) patch; (*rotolo di tessuto*) roll; **trattare qcno come una ~ da piedi** walk all over sb. ~ **d'appoggio** voucher. ~ **giustificativa** voucher

pez'zato *a* (*cavallo, mucca*) piebald

pez'zente *nmf* tramp; (*avaro*) miser

'pezzo *nm* piece; (*parte*) part; *Mus* piece. **un bel ~ d'uomo** a fine figure of a man; **un ~** (*di tempo*) some time; (*di spazio*) a long way; **al ~** (*costare*) each; **essere a pezzi** (*stanco*) be shattered; **fare a pezzi** tear to shreds; **andare in mille pezzi** break into a thousand pieces; **cadere a pezzi** fall to pieces, fall to bits. ~ **forte** centre-piece. **pezzi** *pl* **grossi**

top brass. ~ **grosso** bigwig, big shot. ~ **di imbecille** stupid idiot. ~ **di ricambio** spare [part]

pezzu'ola *nf* scrap of material

photo'fit [R] *nm inv* Photofit

pia'cente *a* attractive

pia'cere *nm* pleasure; (*favore*) favour; **a ~** as much as one likes; **per ~!** please!; ~ **[di conoscerla]!** (*nelle presentazioni*) pleased to meet you!; **con ~** with pleasure; **fare un ~ a qcno** do sb a favour ● *vi* **la Scozia mi piace** I like Scotland; **mi piacciono i dolci** I like sweets; **mi piacerebbe venire** I'd like to come; **faccio come mi pare e piace** I do as I please; **ti piace?** do you like it?; **lo spettacolo è piaciuto** the show was a success

pia'cevole *a* pleasant

piacevol'mente *adv* agreeably

piaci'mento *nm* **a ~** as much as you like

pia'dina *nf* unleavened focaccia bread

pi'aga *nf* sore; *fig* scourge; (*fig: persona noiosa*) pain; (*fig: ricordo doloroso*) wound

pia'gato *a* covered with sores

piagni'steo *nm* whining

piagnuco'lare *vi* whimper

piagnuco'lio *nm* whimpering

piagnuco'loso *a* maudlin

pi'alla *nf* plane

pial'lare *vt* plane

pialla'tura *nf* planing

pi'ana *nf* (*pianura*) plane

pianeggi'ante *a* level

piane'rottolo *nm* landing

pia'neta *nm* planet

pi'angere *vi* cry; (*disperatamente*) weep; **mi piange il cuore** my heart bleeds; **mettersi a ~ come una fontana** turn the waterworks on; ~ **sul latte versato** cry over spilt milk ● *vt* (*lamentare*) lament; (*per un lutto*) mourn; ~ **la morte di qcno** mourn sb's death

pianifi'care *vt* plan

pianificazi'one *nf* planning. ~ **aziendale** corporate planning. ~ **familiare** family planning

pia'nista *nmf Mus* pianist

pi'ano *a* flat; (*a livello*) flush; (*regolare*) smooth; (*facile*) easy; **i 400 metri piani** the 400 metres flat race ● *adv* slowly; (*con cautela*) gently; (*sottovoce*) quietly; **andarci ~** go carefully ● *nm* plain; (*di edificio*) floor, storey; (*livello*) plane; (*progetto*) plan; *Mus* piano; **di primo ~** first-rate; **primo ~** *Phot* close-up; **in ~ piano** in the foreground; **essere/mettersi in ~ piano** *fig* take/occupy centre-stage; **secondo ~** middle distance. ~ **d'emergenza** contingency plan. ~ **di lavoro** work surface; (*programma*) work schedule. ~ **di pensionamento** pension plan, pension scheme. ~ **regolatore** town plan. ~ **di sopra** upstairs. ~ **di sotto** downstairs. ~ **di studi** syllabus. ~ **superiore** upper floor

piano'forte *nm* piano. ~ **bar** piano bar. ~ **a**

coda grand [piano]. ~ **verticale** upright [piano]

pia'nolaᴷ *nf* pianola

piano'terra *nm inv* ground floor, first floor *Am*

pi'anta *nf* plant; (*del piede*) sole; (*disegno*) plan; (*di città*) map; **di sana ~** (*totalmente*) entirely; **in ~ stabile** permanently. ~ **da appartamento** house-plant. ~ **stradale** road map

piantagi'one *nf* plantation

pianta'grane *nmf fam* **è un/una ~** he's/she's bolshy

pian'tare *vt* plant; (*conficcare*) drive; pitch ⟨tenda⟩; (*fam: abbandonare*) dump; **piantala!** *fam* stop it!; **piantato in** ⟨spina, chiodo⟩ embedded in; ~ **baracca** e **burattini** drop everything; (*per sempre*) chuck everything in

pian'tarsi *vr* plant oneself; (*fam: lasciarsi*) leave each other

pianta|'tore, -'trice *nmf* planter

pianter'reno *nm* ground floor, first floor *Am*

pi'anto *pp di* **piangere** ● *nm* crying; (*disperato*) weeping; (*lacrime*) tears *pl*

pianto'nare *vt* guard

pian'tone *nm* guard; **stare di ~** stand guard; **mettere di ~** put on guard. ~ **dello sterzo** *Auto* steering column

pia'nura *nf* plain. ~ **padana** Po valley

pi'astra *nf* plate; (*lastra*) slab; *Culin* griddle. ~ **elettronica** circuit board. ~ **madre** *Comput* motherboard. ~ **di registrazione** cassette deck

pia'strella *nf* tile

pia'strina *nf Mil* identity disc; *Med* platelet; *Comput* chip. ~ **di riconoscimento** identity tag. ~ **di silicio** silicon chip

piatta'forma *nf* platform. ~ **di lancio** launch pad. ~ **petrolifera** oil platform, offshore rig. ~ **rivendicativa** *o* **sindacale** union claims *pl*

piat'tino *nm* saucer

pi'atto *a* flat; (*monotono*) dull ● *nm* plate; (*da portata, vivanda*) dish; (*portata*) course; (*parte piatta*) flat; (*di giradischi*) turntable; (*di bilancia*) pan. **piatti** *pl Mus* cymbals; **lavare i piatti** do the dishes, do the washing-up. **piatti** *pl* **caldi** hot dishes. **piatti** *pl* **carne** meat dishes. ~ **fondo** soup plate. ~ **del giorno** dish of the day. ~ **piano** [ordinary] plate. ~ **di portata** serving dish, server. ~ **unico** cold sliced meat with pickles

pi'azza *nf* square; *Comm* market; **letto a una ~** single bed; **letto a due piazze** double bed; **far ~ pulita** make a clean sweep; **mettere qcsa in ~** *fig* make sth public; **scendere in ~** *fig* take to the streets. ~ **d'armi** parade ground. ~ **del mercato** market square. **P~ San Pietro** St Peter's Square

piazza'forte *nf* stronghold

piaz'zale *nm* large square

piazza'mento *nm* (*in classifica*) placing

piaz'zare *vt* place

piaz'zarsi *vr Sport* be placed; ~ **secondo** come second, be placed second

piaz'zato *a* ⟨cavallo⟩ placed; **ben ~** (*robusto*) well-built

piaz'zista *nm* salesman ● *nf* saleswoman

piaz'z[u]ola *nf* ~ **di partenza** (*nel golf*) tee. ~ **di sosta** pull-in

pic'cante *a* hot; (*pungente*) sharp; (*salace*) spicy

pic'carsi *vr* (*risentirsi*) take offence; ~ **di** (*vantarsi di*) claim to

pic'cata *nf* veal in sour lemon sauce

'picche *nfpl* (*in carte*) spades

picchet'taggio *nm* picketing

picchet'tare *vt* stake; (*scioperanti:*) picket

pic'chetto *nm* picket

picchi'are *vt* hit; ~ **la testa** (**contro qcsa**) bang *o* hit one's head (against sth) ● *vi* (*bussare*) knock; *Aeron* nosedive; ~ **in testa** ⟨motore:⟩ knock

picchi'arsi *vr* ~ **il petto** beat one's breast

picchi'ata *nf* beating; *Aeron* nosedive; **scendere in ~** nosedive

picchi'ato *a* (*matto*) touched

picchia'tore *nm* goon

picchiet'tare *vt* tap; (*punteggiare*) spot

picchiet'tato *a* spotted

picchiet'tìo *nm* tapping

'picchio *nm* woodpecker

pic'cino *a* tiny; (*gretto*) mean; (*di poca importanza*) petty ● *nm* little one, child

piccion'cini *nmpl fam* lovebirds; **fare i ~** get all lovey-dovey

picci'one *nm* pigeon; **prendere due piccioni con una fava** kill two birds with one stone. ~ **viaggiatore** carrier pigeon

'picco *nm* peak; **a ~** vertically; **colare a ~** sink

pico'lezza *nf* (*di persona, ambiente*) smallness; (*grettezza*) meanness; (*inezia*) trifle

'piccolo, -a *a* small, little; (*vacanza, pausa*) little, short; (*di statura*) short; (*gretto*) petty ● *nmf* child, little one; **da ~** as a child; **in ~** in miniature; **nel mio ~** in my own small way

pic'cone *nm* pickaxe. ~ **da ghiaccio** ice pick

pic'cozza *nf* ice axe

pic'nic *nm inv* picnic

pi'docchio *nm* louse

pidocchi'oso *a* flea-bitten; (*fam: avaro*) stingy ● *nm fam* miser

piè *nm inv* **a ~ di pagina** at the foot of the page; **saltare a ~ pari** skip; **ad ogni ~ sospinto** all the time, endlessly

pi'ede *nm* foot; (*di armadio, letto*) leg; **a piedi** on foot; **andare a piedi** walk; **a piedi nudi** barefoot; **avere i piedi piatti** have flat feet, be flat-footed; **a ~ libero** free; **in piedi** standing; **alzarsi in piedi** stand up; **in punta di piedi** on tiptoe; **ai piedi di** ⟨montagna⟩ at the foot of; **avere qcno ai propri piedi** have sb at one's feet; **essere sul ~ di guerra** be ready for action; ⟨nazione:⟩ be on war footing; **prendere ~** *fig* gain ground; ⟨moda:⟩ catch on; **partire col ~ sbagliato** get off on the wrong foot; **mettere in piedi** (*allestire*) set up; **togliti dai piedi!** get out of the way!. **~ di insalata** head of lettuce. **~ di porco** (*strumento*) jemmy

pie'dino *nm* **fare ~ a qcno** *fam* play footsie with sb

piedi'stallo *nm* pedestal

pi'ega *nf* (*piegatura*) fold; (*di gonna*) pleat; (*di pantaloni*) crease; (*grinza*) wrinkle; (*andamento*) turn; **a pieghe** with pleats, pleated; **non fare una ~** (*ragionamento:*) be flawless; (*persona:*) not bat an eyelid; **prendere una brutta ~** get into bad ways

pie'gare *vt* fold; (*flettere*) bend ● *vi* bend

pie'garsi *vr* bend; **~ a** *fig* yield to

piega'tura *nf* folding; (*piega*) fold

pieghet'tare *vt* pleat

pieghet'tato *a* pleated

pie'ghevole *a* pliable; (*tavolo*) folding ● *nm* leaflet

Pie'monte *nm* Piedmont

piemon'tese *a & nmf* Piedmontese

pi'ena *nf* (*di fiume*) flood; (*folla*) crowd

pi'eno *a* full; (*massiccio*) solid; **in piena estate** in the middle of summer; **a pieni voti** (*diplomarsi*) ≈ with A-grades, with first class honours ● *nm* (*colmo*) height; (*carico*) full load; **in ~** (*completamente*) fully; **fare il ~** (*di benzina*) fill up; **nel ~ delle forze** in top physical form

pie'none *nm* **c'era il ~** the place was packed

pietà *nf* pity; (*misericordia*) mercy; **senza ~** (*persona*) pitiless; (*spietatamente*) pitilessly; **avere ~ di qcno** take pity on sb; **far ~** (*far pena*) be pitiful; (*fam: essere orrendo*) be useless

pie'tanza *nf* dish

pie'toso *a* pitiful, merciful; (*fam: pessimo*) terrible

pi'etra *nf* stone. **~ dura** semiprecious stone. **~ preziosa** precious stone. **~ dello scandalo** cause of the scandal

pie'traia *nf* scree

pie'trame *nm* stones *pl*

pietrifi'care *vt* petrify

pie'trina *nf* (*di accendino*) flint

pie'troso *a* stony

'piffero *nm* fife

pigi'ama *nm* pyjamas *pl*, pajamas *Am*

'pigia 'pigia *nm inv* crowd, crush

pigi'are *vt* press

pigia'trice *nf* winepress

pigi'one *nf* rent; **dare a ~** let, rent out; **prendere a ~** rent

pigli'are *vt* (*fam: afferrare*) catch

'piglio *nm* air

pig'mento *nm* pigment

pig'meo, -a *a & nmf* pygmy

'pigna *nf* cone. **~ di abete** fir cone

pi'gnolo *a* pedantic

pignora'mento *nm Jur* distraint

pigno'rare *vt Jur* distrain upon

pigo'lare *vi* chirp

pigo'lio *nm* chirping

pigra'mente *adv* lazily

pi'grizia *nf* laziness

'pigro *a* lazy; (*intelletto*) slow

PIL *abbr* (**prodotto interno lordo**) GDP

'pila *nf* pile; *Electr* battery; (*fam: lampadina tascabile*) torch; (*vasca*) basin; **a pile** battery operated, battery powered

pi'lastro *nm* pillar

'pillola *nf* pill; **prendere la ~** be on the pill. **~ del giorno dopo** morning-after pill

pi'lone *nm* pylon; (*di ponte*) pier

pi'lota *nmf* pilot. **~ automatico** automatic pilot. **~ di caccia** fighter pilot ● *nm Auto* driver ● *a inv* **progetto ~** pilot project

pilo'taggio *nm* flying; **cabina di ~** flight deck

pilo'tare *vt* pilot; drive (*auto*)

pinaco'teca *nf* art gallery

'Pinco Pal'lino *nm* so-and-so

pi'neta *nf* pine-wood

ping-'pong *nm* table tennis, ping-pong *fam*

'pingue *a* fat

pingu'edine *nf* fatness

pingu'ino *nm* penguin; (*gelato*) choc ice on a stick

'pinna *nf* fin; (*per nuotare*) flipper

pin'nacolo *nm* pinnacle

'pino *nm* pine[-tree]. **~ marittimo** cluster pine, maritime pine

pi'nolo *nm* pine kernel

'pinta *nf* pint

pin-'up *nf inv* pin-up [girl]

'pinza *nf* pliers *pl*; *Med* forceps *pl*; **prendere qcsa con le pinze** *fig* treat sth cautiously

pin'zare *vt* (*con pinzatrice*) staple

pinza'trice *nf* stapler

pin'zette *nfpl* tweezers

pinzi'monio *nm* sauce for crudités

'pio *a* pious; (*benefico*) charitable

piogge'rella *nf* drizzle

pi'oggia *nf* rain; (*fig: di pietre, insulti*) hail, shower; **sotto la ~** in the rain. **~ acida** acid rain. **~ radioattiva** radioactive fallout

pi'olo *nm* (*di scala*) rung

piom'bare *vi* fall heavily; **~ su** fall upon; **~ all'improvviso nella stanza** suddenly burst into the room ● *vt* **~ qcno nella disperazione** plunge sb into despair

piom'bino *nm* (*sigillo*) [lead] seal; (*da pesca*) sinker; (*in gonne*) weight

pi'ombo *nm* lead; (*sigillo*) [lead] seal; **a ~** plumb; **senza ~** (*benzina*) lead-free; **avere un sonno di ~** be a very heavy sleeper; **andare con i piedi di ~** tread carefully; **anni di ~** *years when terrorism was at its height*

pioni'ere, -a *nmf* pioneer

pi'oppo *nm* poplar

pior'rea *nf* pyorrhoea

pio'vano *a* **acqua piovana** rainwater

pi'overe *vi* rain; **~ it's raining; ~ addosso a qcno** (*guai, debiti:*) rain down on sb; **non ci piove [sopra]** *fam* that's for sure

pioviggi'nare *vi* drizzle

pio'voso *a* rainy

pi'ovra *nf* octopus

pio'vuto *a* ~ **dal cielo** fallen into one's lap

'pipa *nf* pipe

pipe'rito *a* **menta piperita** peppermint

pipì *nf* **fare [la]** ~ pee, piddle; **andare a fare [la]** ~ go for a pee

pipi'strello *nm* bat

piqué *nm inv* piqué

'pira *nf* pyre

pi'ramide *nf* pyramid

pi'ranha *nf* piranha

pi'rata *nm* pirate. ~ **della strada** hit-and-run driver; (*prepotente*) road-hog ● *a inv* pirate

pirate'ria *nf* piracy. ~ **informatica** hacking

pi'rite *nf* pyrite

piro'etta *nf* pirouette

pi'rofila *nf* (*tegame*) oven-proof dish

pi'rofilo *a* heat-resistant

pi'romane *nmf* pyromaniac

piroma'nia *nf* pyromania

pi'roscafo *nm* steamer. ~ **di linea** liner

'piscia *nf vulg* piss

pisci'are *vi vulg* piss

pisci'ata *nf vulg* piss

pi'scina *nf* [swimming] pool. ~ **coperta** indoor [swimming] pool. ~ **gonfiabile** [inflatable] paddling pool. ~ **olimpionica** Olympic [swimming] pool. ~ **scoperta** outdoor [swimming] pool, lido

pi'sello *nm* pea; (*fam: pene*) willie. **piselli** *pl* odorosi sweetpeas

piso'lino *nm* nap; **fare un** ~ have a nap

'pista *nf* track; *Aeron* runway, tarmac; (*orma*) footprint; (*sci*) slope, piste. ~ **d'atterraggio** runway. ~ **da ballo** dance floor. ~ **ciclabile** cycle track. ~ **da fondo** cross-country ski track. ~ **da pattinaggio** ice rink. ~ **per principianti** nursery slope. ~ **da sci** ski slope, ski run, piste. ~ **per slitte** toboggan run

pi'stacchio *nm* pistachio

pi'stola *nf* pistol; (*per spruzzare*) spray-gun. ~ **a capsule** cap gun. ~ **a spruzzo** paint spray. ~ **a tamburo** revolver

pisto'lero *nm* gunslinger

pi'stone *nm* piston

pi'tocco *nm* miser

pi'tone *nm* python

pitto'gramma *nm* pictogram

pit'tore, -'trice *nmf* painter

pitto'resco *a* picturesque

pit'torico *a* pictorial

pit'tura *nf* painting. **pitture** *pl* **di guerra** warpaint. ~ **rupestre** cave painting

pittu'rare *vt* paint

pitui'tario *a* pituitary

più *adv* more; (*superlativo*) most; *Math* plus; ~ **importante** more important; **il** ~ **importante** the most important; ~ **caro/grande** dearer/bigger; **il** ~ **caro/grande** the dearest/biggest; **di** ~ more; **una coperta in** ~ an extra blanket; **non ho** ~ **soldi** I don't have any more money; **non vive** ~ **a Milano**

he no longer lives in Milan; ~ **o meno** more or less; **il** ~ **lentamente possibile** as slow as possible; **al** ~ **presto** as soon as possible; **per di** ~ what's more; **mai** ~**!** never again!; ~ **di** more than; **sempre** ~ more and more ● *a* more; (*superlativo*) most; ~ **tempo** more time; **la classe con** ~ **alunni** the class with most pupils; ~ **volte** several times ● *nm* most; *Math* plus; **il** ~ **è fatto** the worst is over; **parlare del** ~ **e del meno** make small talk; **i** ~ the majority

piuccheper'fetto *nm* pluperfect

pi'uma *nf* feather

piu'maggio *nm* plumage

piu'mato *a* plumed

piu'mino *nm* (*di cigni*) down; (*copriletto*) eiderdown; (*per cipria*) powder-puff; (*per spolverare*) feather duster; (*giacca*) down jacket

piu'mone® *nm* duvet, continental quilt

piut'tosto *adv* rather; (*invece*) instead

'piva *nf* **con le pive nel sacco** empty-handed

pi'vello *nm fam* greenhorn

'pivot *nm inv* (*in pallacanestro*) centre

'pizza *nf* pizza; *Cinema* reel; (*fam: noia*) bore. ~ **margherita** tomato and mozzarella pizza. ~ **marinara** pizza with tomato, oregano, garlic and anchovies. ~ **napoletana** pizza with tomato, mozzarella and anchovies. ~ **quattro stagioni** pizza with tomato, mozzarella, ham, mushrooms and baby artichokes

pizzai'ola: **alla** ~ with tomatoes, garlic and oregano

pizze'ria *nf* pizza restaurant, pizzeria

piz'zetta *nf* small pizza

pizzi'care *vt* pinch; (*pungere*) sting; (*di sapore*) taste sharp; (*fam: sorprendere*) catch; *Mus* pluck ● *vi* scratch; (*cibo:*) be spicy

'pizzico, **pizzi'cotto** *nm* pinch

'pizzo *nm* lace; (*di montagna*) peak

pla'care *vt* placate; assuage (*fame, dolore*)

pla'carsi *vr* calm down

'placca *nf* plate; (*commemorativa, dentale*) plaque; *Med* patch. ~ **batterica** plaque

plac'care *vt* plate

plac'cato *a* ~ **d'argento** silver-plated. ~ **d'oro** gold-plated

placca'tura *nf* plating

pla'cebo *nm inv* placebo; **effetto** ~ placebo effect

pla'centa *nf* placenta, afterbirth

'placido *a* placid

pla'fond *nm inv* Comm ceiling

plafoni'era *nf* ceiling light

plagi'are *vt* plagiarize; pressure (*persona*)

'plagio *nm* plagiarism

plaid *nm inv* tartan rug

pla'nare *vi* glide

'plancia *nf* Naut bridge; (*passerella*) gangplank

'plancton *nm* plankton

plane'tario *a* planetary ● *nm* planetarium

pla'smare *vt* mould

'plastica *nf* (*materia*) plastic; *Med* plastic

surgery; (arte) plastic art; **sacchetto di ~** plastic bag

'**plastico** a plastic; ⟨rappresentazione⟩ three-dimensional ● nm plastic model

'**platano** nm plane tree

pla'tea nf stalls pl; (pubblico) audience

'**platino** nm platinum

pla'tonico a platonic

plau'sibile a plausible; **poco ~** implausible

plausibilità nf plausibility

'**plauso** nm (consenso) approval

play'back nm **cantare in ~** mime

play'boy nm inv playboy

play'maker nm inv Sport playmaker

p.le abbr (**piazzale**) Sq.

ple'baglia nf pej mob

'**plebe** nf common people

ple'beo, -a a & nmf plebeian

plebi'scito nm plebiscite

ple'nario a plenary

pleni'lunio nm full moon

'**plettro** nm plectrum

pleu'rite nf pleurisy

'**plico** nm packet; **in ~ a parte** under separate cover

plissé a inv plissé; ⟨gonna⟩ accordeon pleated

plop nm inv plop; **fare ~** plop

plo'tone nm platoon; (di ciclisti) group. **~ d'esecuzione** firing squad

'**plotter** nm inv Comput plotter. **~ da tavolo** flatbed plotter

'**plumbeo** a leaden

plum-'cake nm inv fruit cake

plu'rale a & nm plural; **al ~** in the plural

pluralità nf (maggioranza) majority

pluridiscipli'nare a multidisciplinary

plurien'nale a **~ esperienza** many years' experience

plurigemel'lare a ⟨parto⟩ multiple

pluripar'titico a Pol multi-party

plu'tonio nm plutonium

pluvi'ale a rain attrib

pluvi'ometro nm rain gauge

pneu'matico a pneumatic ● nm tyre. **~ radiale** radial [tyre]

pneu'monia nf pneumonia

PNL abbr (**prodotto nazionale lordo**) GNP

Po nm Po

po' vedi poco

po'chette nf inv clutch bag

po'chino nm **un ~** a little bit

'**poco** a little; ⟨tempo⟩ short; (con nomi plurali) few ● pron little; (poco tempo) a short time; (plurale) few ● nm little; **un po'** a little [bit]; **un po' di** a little, some; (con nomi plurali) a few; **a ~ a ~** little by little; **fra ~** soon; **per ~** (a poco prezzo) cheap; (quasi) nearly; **~ fa** a little while ago; **sono arrivato da ~** I have just arrived; **un bel po'** quite a lot; **un bel po' di più/meno** quite a lot more/less; **un ~ di buono** a shady character ● adv (con verbi) not much; (con avverbi, aggettivi) not very; **parla ~** he doesn't speak much; **lo conosco ~** I don't know him very well; **~ spesso** not very often

po'dere nm farm

pode'roso a powerful

'**podio** nm dais; Mus podium

po'dismo nm walking

po'dista nmf walker

po'ema nm poem. **~ epico** epic [poem]. **~ sinfonico** symphonic poem

poe'sia nf poetry; (componimento) poem

po'eta nm poet

poe'tessa nf poetess

po'etico a poetic

poggiapi'edi nm inv footrest

poggi'are vt lean; (posare) place ● vi **~ su** be based on

poggia'testa nm inv head-rest

'**poggio** nm hillock

poggi'olo nm balcony

'**poi** adv (dopo) then; (più tardi) later [on]; (finalmente) finally. **d'ora in ~** from now on; **questa ~!** well! ● nm **pensare al ~** think of the future

poiché conj since

pois nm inv **a ~** polka-dot

'**poker** nm poker

po'lacco, -a a Polish ● nmf Pole ● nm (lingua) Polish

po'lare a polar

polarità nf inv polarity

polariz'zare vt polarize

'**polca** nf polka

po'lemica nf controversy

polemica'mente adv controversially

polemiciz'zare vi engage in controversy

po'lemico a controversial

po'lenta nf cornmeal porridge

poli'clinico nm general hospital

policro'mia nf polychromy

po'licromo a polychrome

poli'estere nm polyester

polieti'lene nm polyethylene

poliga'mia nf polygamy

poli'gamico a polygamous

po'ligamo a polygamous

poli'glotta nmf polyglot

po'ligono nm polygon; (di tiro) rifle range

po'limero nm polymer

Poli'nesia nf Polynesia

polinesi'ano a & nmf Polynesian

'**polio[mie'lite]** nf polio[myelitis]

'**polipo** nm polyp

polisti'rolo nm polystyrene

poli'tecnico nm polytechnic

po'litica nf politics sg; (linea di condotta) policy; **fare ~** be in politics; **darsi alla ~** go into politics. **~ estera** foreign policy. **~ monetaria** monetary policy

politica'mente adv politically; **~ corretto** politically correct, pc

politi'chese nm political jargon

politiciz'zare vt politicize

po'litico, -a a political ● nmf politician

poliva'lente *a* all-purpose
poli'zia *nf* police. ~ **giudiziaria** ≈ Criminal Investigation Department, CID. ~ **stradale** traffic police
polizi'esco *a* police *attrib*; ‹*romanzo, film*› detective *attrib*
polizi'otto *nm* policeman. ~ **in borghese** plain clothes policeman. ~ **privato** private detective ● *a* police *attrib*
'polizza *nf* policy. ~ **di assicurazione** insurance policy
pol'laio *nm* chicken run; (*fam: luogo chiassoso*) mad house
pol'lame *nm* poultry
polla'strella *nf* spring chicken; *fig fam* bird
polla'strello *nm* spring chicken
pol'lastro *nm* cockerel
polle'ria *nf* poultry butcher, poulterer
'pollice *nm* thumb; (*unità di misura*) inch
'polline *nm* pollen; **allergia al** ~ hay fever
polli'vendolo, -a *nmf* poulterer
'pollo *nm* chicken; (*fam: semplicione*) simpleton; **far ridere i polli** be ridiculous. ~ **arrosto** roast chicken. ~ **alla cacciatora** chicken chasseur
polmo'nare *a* pulmonary
pol'mone *nm* lung. ~ **d'acciaio** iron lung
polmo'nite *nf* pneumonia
'polo *nm* pole; *Sport* polo; (*maglietta*) polo top; *Pol* party; (*conservatori*) Italian Conservatives. ~ **magnetico** magnetic pole. ~ **nord** North Pole. ~ **sud** South Pole
Po'lonia *nf* Poland
'polpa *nf* pulp
pol'paccio *nm* calf
polpa'strello *nm* fingertip
pol'petta *nf* meatball. ~ **di carne** meatball
polpet'tone *nm* meatloaf. ~ **sentimentale** *fam* hokum
'polpo *nm* octopus
pol'poso *a* fleshy
pol'sino *nm* cuff
'polso *nm* pulse; *Anat* wrist; *fig* authority; **avere** ~ be strict; **essere privo di** ~ be soft
pol'tiglia *nf* mush
pol'trire *vi* lie around
pol'trona *nf* armchair; *Theat* seat in the stalls
pol'trone *a* lazy
'polvere *nf* dust; (*sostanza polverizzata*) powder; **in** ~ powdered; **sapone in** ~ soap powder. ~ **da sparo** gun powder
polveri'era *nf* gunpowder magazine; *fig* tinderbox
polve'rina *nf* (*medicina*) powder
polveriz'zare *vt* pulverize; (*nebulizzare*) atomize; smash, shatter ‹*record*›; ~ **qcno** pulverize sb
polve'rone *nm* cloud of dust
polve'roso *a* dusty
po'mata *nf* ointment, cream. ~ **cicatrizzante** healing cream for cuts
pomel'lato *a* dappled
po'mello *nm* knob; (*guancia*) cheek
pomeridi'ano *a* afternoon *attrib*; **alle tre**

pomeridiane at three in the afternoon, at three pm
pome'riggio *nm* afternoon; **buon** ~**!** have a good afternoon!; **oggi** ~ this afternoon; **questo** ~ this afternoon
'pomice *nf* pumice
pomici'are *vi fam* snog, neck
pomici'ata *nf fam* snogging, necking
'pomo *nm* (*oggetto*) knob. ~ **d'Adamo** Adam's apple
pomo'doro *nm* tomato
'pompa *nf* pump; (*sfarzo*) pomp. ~ **della benzina** petrol pump, gas pump *Am*. **pompe** *pl* **funebri** (*funzione*) funeral
pom'pare *vt* pump; (*gonfiare d'aria*) pump up; (*fig: esagerare*) exaggerate; ~ **fuori** pump out
pompei'ano, -a *a & nmf* Pompeian
pom'pelmo *nm* grapefruit
pompi'ere *nm* fireman; **i pompieri** the fire brigade
pom'pon *nm inv* pompom
pom'poso *a* pompous
'poncho *nm inv* poncho
ponde'rare *vt* ponder
ponde'roso *a* ponderous
po'nente *nm* west
'ponte *nm* bridge; *Naut* deck; (*impalcatura*) scaffolding; **fare il** ~ *fig* make a long weekend of it; **legge** ~ interim *or* bridging law; **governo** ~ interim government. ~ **aereo** airlift. ~ **di coperta** main deck. ~ **levatoio** drawbridge. ~ **radio** radio link. ~ **dei Sospiri** Bridge of Sighs. ~ **di volo** flight deck
pon'tefice *nm* pontiff
pontifi'care *vi* pontificate
pontifi'cato *nm* pontificate
ponti'ficio *a* papal
pon'tile *nm* jetty
'pony *nm inv* pony. ~ **express** express delivery service
pool *nm inv* *Comm* consortium; (*di giornalisti*) team; (*di esperti*) pool, team. ~ **genico** gene pool
pop'corn *nm inv* popcorn
'popelin *nm* poplin
popò *nm inv fam* bottie, bum
popò *nf inv fam* pooh
popo'lano *a* of the [common] people
popo'lare *a* popular; (*comune*) common ● *vt* populate; **essere popolato da** (*pieno di*) be full by
popolarità *nf* popularity
popo'larsi *vr* get crowded
popolazi'one *nf* population
'popolo *nm* people
popo'loso *a* populous
'poppa *nf Naut* stern; (*mammella*) breast; **a** ~ astern
pop'pare *vt* suck
pop'pata *nf* (*pasto*) feed
poppa'toio *nm* [feeding-]bottle
popu'lista *nmf* populist
por'caio *nf anche fig* pigsty; **fare un** ~ *fam* make a mess

por'cata *nf* load of rubbish; **porcate** *pl* (*fam: cibo*) junk food; **fare una ~ a qcno** play a dirty trick on sb

porcel'lana *nf* porcelain, china. **~ fine** bone china

porcel'lino *nm* piglet. **~ d'India** guinea-pig

porche'ria *nf* dirt; (*fig: cosa orrenda*) piece of filth; (*fam: robaccia*) rubbish

por'chetta *nf* roast sucking pig

por'cile *nm* pigsty

por'cino *a* pig *attrib* ● *nm* (*fungo*) cep (*edible mushroom*)

'porco *nm* pig; (*carne*) pork

porco'spino *nm* porcupine

'porfido *nm* porphyry

'porgere *vt* give; (*offrire*) offer; **~ orecchio** lend an ear; **porgo distinti saluti** (*in lettera*) I remain, yours sincerely

'porno *a inv* porn

pornogra'fia *nf* pornography

porno'grafico *a* pornographic

'poro *nm* pore

po'roso *a* porous

'porpora *nf* purple

'porre *vt* put; (*collocare*) place; (*supporre*) suppose; ask ‹*domanda*›; present ‹*candidatura*›; **~ una domanda a qcno** ask sb a question; **poniamo [il caso] che...** let us suppose that...; **~ fine** *o* **termine a** put an end to

'porro *nm* Bot leek; (*verruca*) wart

'porsi *vr* put oneself; **~ a sedere** sit down; **~ in cammino** set out

'porta *nf* door; *Sport* goal; (*di città*) gate; *Comput* port. **~ a ~** door-to-door; **mettere alla ~** show sb the door; **a porte chiuse** ‹*riunione, processo*› behind closed doors, in camera; **essere alle porte** (*vicino*) be on the doorstep. **~ a due battenti** double door[s]. **~ d'ingresso** front door. **~ parallela** *Comput* parallel port. **~ seriale** *Comput* serial port. **~ di servizio** tradesman's entrance. **~ di sicurezza** emergency exit. **~ per la stampante** *Comput* printer port. **~ a vento** swing-door

portaba'gagli *nm inv* (*facchino*) porter; (*di treno ecc*) luggage-rack; *Auto* boot, trunk *Am*; (*sul tetto di un'auto*) roof-rack

portabandi'era *nmf inv* standard-bearer

portabici'clette *nm inv* cycle rack

portabot'tiglie *nm inv* bottle rack, wine rack

porta'burro *nm inv* butter dish

porta'cenere *nm inv* ashtray

portachi'avi *nm inv* keyring

porta'cipria *nm inv* compact

portacon'tainers *nm inv* container truck

portadocu'menti *nm inv* document wallet

porta'erei *nf inv* aircraft carrier

portafi'nestra *nf* French window

porta'foglio *nm* wallet; (*per documenti*) portfolio; (*ministero*) ministry

portafor'tuna *nm inv* lucky charm ● *a inv* lucky

portagi'oie *nm inv* jewellery box

por'tale *nm* door

portama'tite *nm inv* pencil case

porta'mento *nm* carriage; (*condotta*) behaviour

porta'mina *nm inv* propelling pencil

portamo'nete *nm inv* purse

por'tante *a* bearing *attrib*

portan'tina *nf* sedan-chair

portaom'brelli *nm inv* umbrella stand

porta'pacchi *nm inv* roof rack; (*su bicicletta*) luggage rack

porta'penne *nm inv* pencil case

por'tare *vt* (*verso chi parla*) bring; (*lontano da chi parla*) take; (*sorreggere, Math*) carry; (*condurre*) lead; (*indossare*) wear; (*avere*) bear; **~ a spasso il cane** take the dog for a walk; **~ a termine** bring to a close; **~ avanti** carry on; **~ ~ bene/male** bring good/bad luck; **~ fortuna** be lucky; **~ rancore** bear a grudge; **~ via** take away

portari'viste *nm inv* magazine rack

por'tarsi *vr* (*trasferirsi*) move; (*comportarsi*) behave; **~ bene/male gli anni** look young/old for one's age

porta'sci *nm inv* ski rack

portasciuga'mano *nm* towel rail

portasiga'rette *nm inv* cigarette-case

porta'spilli *nm inv* pin-cushion

por'tata *nf* (*di pranzo*) course; *Auto* carrying capacity; (*di arma*) range; (*fig: abilità*) capability; **a ~ di mano** within reach; **alla ~ di tutti** accessible to all; (*finanziariamente*) within everybody's reach; **di grande ~** ‹*scoperta*› with far-reaching consequences

por'tatile *a & nm* portable

por'tato *a* ‹*indumento*› worn; (*dotato*) gifted; **essere ~ per qcsa** have a gift for sth; **essere ~ a** (*tendere a*) be inclined to

porta'tore, -'trice *nmf* bearer; **al ~** to the bearer. **~ di handicap** disabled person

portatovagli'olo *nm* napkin ring

portau'ovo *nm inv* egg-cup

porta'voce *nm inv* spokesman ● *nf inv* spokeswoman

por'tello *nm* hatch. **~ di sicurezza** escape hatch

por'tento *nm* marvel; (*persona dotata*) prodigy

porten'toso *a* wonderful

port'folio *nm inv* (*di fotografie ecc*) portfolio

porti'cato *nm* portico

'portico *nm* portico

porti'era *nf* door; (*tendaggio*) door curtain

porti'ere *nm* porter, doorman; *Sport* goalkeeper. **~ di notte** night porter

porti'naio, -a *nmf* caretaker, concierge

portine'ria *nf* concierge's room; (*di ospedale*) porter's lodge

'porto *pp di* **porgere** ● *nm* harbour; (*complesso*) port; (*vino*) port [wine]; (*spesa di trasporto*) carriage; **andare in ~** succeed. **~ d'armi** gun licence. **~ container** container port. **~ fluviale** river port. **~ franco** free port. **~ marittimo** seaport

Porto'gallo *nm* Portugal

porto'ghese *a* & *nmf* Portuguese
por'tone *nm* main door
portori'cano, -a *a* & *nmf* Puerto Rican
Porto'rico *nf* Puerto Rico
portu'ale *nm* dockworker, docker
porzi'one *nf* portion
'posa *nf* laying; (*riposo*) rest; *Phot* exposure; (*atteggiamento*) pose; **mettersi in ~** pose; **senza ~** without rest
po'sare *vt* put; (*giù*) put [down] ● *vi* (*poggiare*) rest; (*per un ritratto*) pose
po'sarsi *vr* alight; (*sostare*) rest; *Aeron* land
po'sata *nf* piece of cutlery; **posate** *pl* cutlery *sg*, flatware *sg Am*
po'sato *a* sedate
po'scritto *nm* postscript
posi'tivo *a* positive
posizio'nare *vt* position
posizi'one *nf* position; **farsi una ~** get ahead; **prendere ~** take a stand
posolo'gia *nf* dosage
po'sporre *vt* place after; (*posticipare*) postpone
po'sposto *pp di* posporre
posse'dere *vt* possess, own
possedi'mento *nm* possession
posses'sivo *a* possessive
pos'sesso *nm* possession, ownership; (*bene*) possession; **entrare in ~ di** come into possession of; **essere in ~ di** be in possession of; **prendere ~ di** take possession of
posses'sore *nm* owner
pos'sibile *a* possible; **il più presto ~** as soon as possible ● *nm* **fare [tutto] il ~** do one's best
possibilità *nf inv* possibility; (*occasione*) chance; **avere la ~ di fare qcsa** have the chance *o* opportunity to do sth ● *nfpl* (*mezzi*) means
possi'dente *nmf* land-owner
'posso *vedi* potere
'posta *nf* post, mail; (*ufficio postale*) post office; (*al gioco*) stake; **spese di ~** postage; **per ~** by post, by mail; **la ~ in gioco è... ** *fig* what's at stake is...; **a bella ~** on purpose; **Poste e Telecomunicazioni** [Italian] Post Office. **~ aerea** airmail. **~ centrale** main post office, central post office. **~ del cuore** agony column. **~ elettronica** electronic mail, e-mail; **spedire via ~** ~ e-mail. **~ elettronica vocale** voicemail
posta'giro *nm* postal giro
po'stale *a* postal
postazi'one *nf* position; *Mil* emplacement
post'bellico *a* postwar
postda'tare *vt* postdate (*assegno*)
posteggi'are *vt/i* park
posteggia'tore, -'trice *nmf* parking attendant
po'steggio *nm* car-park, parking lot *Am*; (*di taxi*) taxi-rank
'posteri *nmpl* descendants
posteri'ore *a* back *attrib*, rear *attrib*; (*nel tempo*) later ● *nm fam* posterior, behind
posterità *nf* posterity

po'sticcio *a* artificial; (*baffi, barba*) false ● *nm* hair-piece
postici'pare *vt* postpone
po'stilla *nf* note; *Jur* rider
po'stino *nm* postman, mailman *Am*
'posto *pp di* **porre** ● *nm* place; (*spazio*) room; (*impiego*) job; *Mil* post; (*sedile*) seat; **a/fuori ~** in/out of place; **prendere ~** take up room; **sul ~** on-site; **essere a ~** (*casa, libri*) be tidy; **non grazie, sono a ~** no thanks, I'm all right; **mettere a ~** tidy (*stanza*); **fare ~ a** make room for; **al ~ di** (*invece di*) in place of, instead of. **~ di blocco** checkpoint. **~ di guardia** guard post. **~ di guida** driving seat. **~ di lavoro** job; *Comput* workstation. **posti** *pl* **in piedi** standing room. **~ di polizia** police station. **posti** *pl* **a sedere** seating, seats
post-'partum *a* post-natal
'postumo *a* posthumous ● *nm* after-effect; **postumi** *pl* **della sbornia** hangover
po'tabile *a* drinkable; **acqua ~** drinking water; **non ~** undrinkable
po'tare *vt* prune
po'tassa *nf* potash
po'tassio *nm* potassium
po'tente *a* powerful; (*efficace*) potent
po'tenza *nf* power; (*efficacia*) potency. **~ nucleare** nuclear power
potenzi'ale *a* & *nm* potential
po'tere *nm* power; **al ~** in power. **~ d'acquisto** purchasing power. **il quarto ~** the fourth estate ● *vi* can, be able to; **posso entrare?** can I come in?; (*formale*) may I come in?; **mi spiace, non posso venire alla festa** I'm sorry, I can't come to the party *or* I won't be able to come to the party; **posso fare qualche cosa?** can I do something?; **che tu possa essere felice!** may you be happy!; **non ne posso più** (*sono stanco*) I can't go on; (*sono stufo*) I can't take any more; **può darsi** perhaps; **può darsi che sia vero** perhaps it's true; **potrebbe aver ragione** he could be right, he might be right; **avresti potuto telefonare** you could have phoned, you might have phoned; **spero di poter venire** I hope to be able to come; **senza poter telefonare** without being able to phone; **spero che potremo incontrarci presto** I hope we can meet soon
potestà *nf* power
pot-pour'ri *nm inv* medley
'povero, -a *a* poor; (*semplice*) plain; **~ di** (*paese, terreno*) lacking in; **in parole povere** in a few words ● *nf* poor woman ● *nm* poor man; **i poveri** the poor
povertà *nf* poverty
pozi'one *nf* potion
'pozza *nf* pool
poz'zanghera *nf* puddle
'pozzo *nm* well; (*minerario*) pit. **~ petrolifero** oil well. **~ di petrolio** oil well. **~ di ventilazione** air shaft
pp. (*pagine*) *abbr* pp
PP.TT. *abbr* (**Poste e Telecomunicazioni**) [Italian] Post Office

PR *nfpl abbr* PR

'Praga *nf* Prague

prag'matico *a* pragmatic

prali'nato *a* ⟨*mandorla, gelato*⟩ praline-coated

pram'matica *nf* **essere di** ~ be customary

pranotera'pia *nf* laying on of hands

pran'zare *vi* dine; (*a mezzogiorno*) lunch

'pranzo *nm* dinner; (*a mezzogiorno*) lunch. ~ **di lavoro** business lunch, working lunch. ~ **di nozze** wedding breakfast

'prassi *nf* standard procedure

prate'ria *nf* grassland

'pratica *nf* practice; (*esperienza*) experience; (*documentazione*) file; **avere** ~ **di qcsa** be familiar with sth, have experience of sth; **mettere qcsa in** ~ put sth into practice; **far** ~ gain experience; **fare le pratiche per** gather the necessary papers for

prati'cabile *a* practicable; ⟨*strada*⟩ passable

pratica'mente *adv* practically

prati'cante *nmf* apprentice; *Relig* [regular] church-goer

prati'care *vt* practise; (*frequentare*) associate with; (*fare*) make

praticità *nf* practicality

'pratico *a* practical; (*esperto*) experienced, knowledgeable; ⟨*comodo*⟩ convenient; **essere** ~ **di qcsa** know about sth; **all'atto** ~ in practice

'prato *nm* meadow; (*di giardino*) lawn. ~ **all'inglese** lawn

preaccensi'one *nf Auto* pre-ignition

pre'ambolo *nm* preamble

preannunci'are *vt* give advance notice of

prean'nuncio *nm* advance notice

preavvi'sare *vt* forewarn

preav'viso *nm* warning

precari'cato *a* preloaded

precarietà *nf inv* frailty

pre'cario *a* precarious

precauzi'one *nf* precaution; (*cautela*) care

prece'dente *a* previous ● *nm* precedent; **avere dei precedenti penali** have a police record; **senza precedenti** ⟨*successo*⟩ unprecedented

precedente'mente *adv* previously

prece'denza *nf* precedence; (*di veicoli*) right of way; **dare la** ~ **a** give priority to; *Auto* give way to; **avere la** ~ have priority; *Auto* have right of way; ~ **assoluta** top priority

pre'cedere *vt* precede

pre'cetto *nm* precept

precet'tore, -'trice *nmf* tutor

precipi'tare *vt* ~ **le cose** precipitate events; ~ **qcno nella disperazione** cast sb into a state of despair ● *vi* fall headlong; ⟨*situazione, eventi:*⟩ come to a head

precipi'tarsi *vr* (*gettarsi*) throw oneself; (*affrettarsi*) rush; ~ **a fare qcsa** rush to do sth

precipitazi'one *nf* (*fretta*) haste; (*atmosferica*) precipitation

precipi'toso *a* hasty; (*avventato*) reckless; ⟨*caduta*⟩ headlong

preci'pizio *nm* precipice; **a** ~ headlong

preci'sabile *a* specifiable

precisa'mente *adv* precisely

preci'sare *vt* specify; (*spiegare*) clarify; **ci tengo a** ~ **che...** I want to make the point that...

precisazi'one *nf* clarification

precisi'one *nf* precision

pre'ciso *a* precise; ⟨*calcolo, risposta*⟩ accurate; ⟨*ore*⟩ sharp; (*identico*) identical

pre'cludere *vt* preclude

pre'cludersi *vr* ~ **ogni possibilità** preclude every possibility

pre'cluso *pp di* **precludere**

pre'coce *a* precocious; (*prematuro*) premature

precocità *nf* precociousness

precon'cetto *a* preconceived ● *nm* prejudice

preconfezio'nato *a* pre-packed

preconfigu'rato *a* preconfigured

pre'correre *vt* (*anticipare*) anticipate; ~ **i tempi** be ahead of one's time

precorri'tore, -'trice *nmf* precursor, forerunner

precur'sore *nm* forerunner, precursor

'preda *nf* prey; (*bottino*) booty; **essere in** ~ **al panico** be panic-stricken; **in** ~ **alle fiamme** engulfed in flames

pre'dare *vt* plunder

preda'tore *nm* predator

predeces'sore *nmf* predecessor

pre'della *nf* platform

predel'lino *nm* step

predesti'nare *vt* predestine

predesti'nato *a* predestined, preordained

predestinazi'one *nf* predestination

predetermi'nare *vt* predetermine

predetermi'nato *a* predetermined, preordained

pre'detto *pp di* **predire**

'predica *nf* sermon; *fig* lecture

predi'care *vt* preach

predi'cato *nm* predicate

predige'rito *a* predigested

predi'letto, -a *pp di* **prediligere** ● *a* favourite ● *nmf* pet

predilezi'one *nf* predilection; **avere una** ~ **per** have a predilection for, be partial to

predi'ligere *vt* prefer

prediposizi'one *nf* predisposition; (*al disegno ecc*) bent (**a** for)

pre'dire *vt* foretell

predi'sporre *vt* arrange; ~ **qcno a qcsa** *Med* predispose sb to sth; (*preparare*) prepare sb for sth

predi'sporsi *vr* ~ **a** prepare oneself for

predi'sposto *pp di* **predisporre**

predizi'one *nf* prediction

predomi'nante *a* predominant

predomi'nare *vi* predominate

predo'minio *nm* predominance

pre'done *nm* robber

prefabbri'cato *a* prefabricated ● *nm* prefabricated building

prefazi'one *nf* preface

prefe'renza *nf* preference; **di ~** preferably

preferenzi'ale *a* preferential; **corsia ~** bus and taxi lane

prefe'ribile *a* preferable

preferibil'mente *adv* preferably

prefe'rire *vt* prefer

prefe'rito, -a *a & nmf* favourite

pre'fetto *nm* prefect

prefet'tura *nf* prefecture

pre'figgere *vt* decide in advance, pre-arrange ⟨*termine*⟩

pre'figgersi *vr* **~ uno scopo** set oneself an objective

prefigu'rare *vt* ⟨*anticipare*⟩ foreshadow

prefinanzia'mento *nm* bridging loan

prefis'sare *vt* pre-arrange ⟨*data, appuntamento*⟩

pre'fisso *pp di* **prefiggere** ● *nm* prefix; *Teleph* [dialling] code

pre'gare *vi Relig* pray ● *vt Relig* pray to; ⟨*supplicare*⟩ beg; **farsi ~** need persuading; **~ qcno di fare qcsa** ask sb to do sth; **si prega di...** please...; **si pregai di non...** please do not...; **si prega di non fumare** please refrain from smoking

pre'gevole *a* valuable

preghi'era *nf* prayer; ⟨*richiesta*⟩ request

pregi'arsi *vr* **si pregia di non essere mai in ritardo** he prides himself on never being late

pre'giato *a* esteemed; ⟨*prezioso*⟩ valuable

'**pregio** *nm* esteem; ⟨*valore*⟩ value; ⟨*di persona*⟩ good point; **di ~** valuable

pregiudi'care *vt* prejudice; ⟨*danneggiare*⟩ harm

pregiudi'cato *a* prejudiced ● *nm Jur* previous offender

pregiu'dizio *nm* prejudice; ⟨*danno*⟩ detriment

pre'gnante *a* ⟨*parola*⟩ pregnant, pregnant with meaning

'**pregno** *a* ⟨*parola*⟩ pregnant; ⟨*pieno*⟩ full; **~ di** ⟨*umidità*⟩ saturated with; ⟨*significato*⟩ pregnant with

'**prego** *int* ⟨*non c'è di che*⟩ don't mention it!; ⟨*per favore*⟩ please; **~?** I beg your pardon?; **posso? -** ~ may I? - please do

pregu'stare *vt* look forward to

preinstal'lato *a* preinstalled

prei'storia *nf* prehistory

prei'storico *a* prehistoric

pre'lato *nm* prelate

prela'vaggio *nm* prewash

preleva'mento *nm* withdrawal

prele'vare *vt* withdraw ⟨*denaro*⟩; collect ⟨*merci*⟩; *Med* take

preli'evo *nm* ⟨*di soldi*⟩ withdrawal. **~ di sangue** blood sample

prelimi'nare *a* preliminary ● *nm* **preliminari** *pl* preliminaries

pre'ludere *vi* **~ a** herald

pre'ludio *nm* prelude

prema'man *nm inv* maternity dress ● *a* maternity *attrib*

prematrimoni'ale *a* premarital

prematura'mente *adv* prematurely

prema'turo, -a *a* premature ● *nmf* premature baby

premedi'tare *vt* premeditate

premeditazi'one *nf* premeditation; **con ~** ⟨*omicidio*⟩ premeditated

'**premere** *vt* press; *Comput* hit ⟨*tasto*⟩ ● *vi* **~ a** ⟨*importare*⟩ matter to; **mi preme sapere** I need to know; **~ su** press on; push ⟨*pulsante*⟩; ⟨*fig: fare pressione su*⟩ put pressure on, pressure; **~ per ottenere qcsa** push for sth

pre'messa *nf* introduction; **senza tante premesse** without further ado

pre'messo *pp di* **premettere**; **~ che** bearing in mind that

pre'mettere *vt* ⟨*mettere prima*⟩ put before; **premetto che...** I want to make it clear first that...; **~ un'introduzione a un libro** put an introduction at the beginning of a book

premi'are *vt* give a prize to; ⟨*ricompensare*⟩ reward

premi'ato *a* award-winning

premiazi'one *nf* prize giving

premi'nente *a* pre-eminent

premi'nenza *nf* pre-eminence

'**premio** *nm* prize; ⟨*ricompensa*⟩ reward; ⟨*di produzione ecc*⟩ bonus; *Fin* premium. **~ di assicurazione** insurance premium. **~ di consolazione** consolation prize; ⟨*ridicolo*⟩ booby prize. **~ di ingaggio** *Sport* signing fee. **~ di produzione** productivity bonus

premoni'tore *a* ⟨*sogno, segno*⟩ premonitory

premonizi'one *nf* premonition

premu'nire *vt* fortify

premu'nirsi *vr* take protective measures; **~ di** provide oneself with; **~ contro** protect oneself against

pre'mura *nf* ⟨*fretta*⟩ hurry; ⟨*cura*⟩ care; **far ~ a qcno** hurry sb up

premu'roso *a* thoughtful

prena'tale *a* antenatal

'**prendere** *vt* take; ⟨*afferrare*⟩ seize; catch ⟨*treno, malattia, ladro, pesce*⟩; have ⟨*cibo, bevanda*⟩; ⟨*far pagare*⟩ charge; ⟨*assumere*⟩ take on; ⟨*ottenere*⟩ get; ⟨*occupare*⟩ take up; ⟨*guadagnare*⟩ earn; **~ informazioni** make inquiries; **~ qcno in giro** pull sb's leg; **~ a calci/pugni** kick/punch; **che ti prende?** what's got into you?; **quanto prende?** what do you charge?; **~ una persona per un'altra** mistake a person for somebody else; **passare a ~ qcno** collect sb, pick sb up ● *vi* ⟨*voltare*⟩ turn; ⟨*attecchire*⟩ take root; ⟨*rapprendersi*⟩ set; ⟨*fuoco:*⟩ catch, take; **~ a destra/sinistra** turn right/left; **~ a fare qcsa** start doing sth; **la colla non ha preso** the glue didn't take

'**prendersi** *vr* **~ a pugni** come to blows; **~ cura di** take care of ⟨*ammalato*⟩; **prendersela** take it to heart; **si prende troppo sul serio** he takes himself too seriously

prendi'sole *nm* sundress

preno'tare *vt* book, reserve

preno'tarsi *vr* ~ **per** put one's name down for

preno'tato *a* booked, reserved

prenotazi'one *nf* booking, reservation

'prensile *a* prehensile

preoccu'pante *a* alarming

preoccu'pare *vt* worry

preoccu'parsi *vr* ~ worry (**di** about); ~ **di fare qcsa** take the trouble to do sth

preoccu'pato *a* (*ansioso*) worried

preoccupazi'one *nf* worry; (*apprensione*) concern

preopera'torio *a* preoperative

prepa'rare *vt* prepare; study for (*esame*); ~ **da mangiare** prepare a meal

prepa'rarsi *vr* get ready

prepara'tivi *nmpl* preparations

prepa'rato *nm* (*prodotto*) preparation

prepara'torio *a* preparatory

preparazi'one *nf* preparation; (*competenza*) knowledge

prepensiona'mento *nm* early retirement

preponde'rante *a* predominant, preponderant

preponde'ranza *nf* preponderance, prevalence

pre'porre *vt* place before

preposizi'one *nf* preposition

pre'posto *pp di* **preporre** ● *a* ~ **a** (*addetto a*) in charge of

prepo'tente *a* overbearing ● *nmf* bully; **fare il** ~ **con qcno** bully sb

prepo'tenza *nf* high-handedness

preprogram'mato *a* *Comput* preprogrammed

pre'puzio *nm* foreskin, prepuce

preroga'tiva *nf* prerogative

'presa *nf* taking; (*conquista*) capture; (*stretta*) hold; (*di cemento ecc*) setting; *Electr* socket; (*di gas, acqua*) inlet, connection; (*pizzico*) pinch; **essere alle prese con** be struggling *o* grappling with; **macchina da** ~ cine camera; **a** ~ **rapida** (*cemento, colla*) quick-setting; **fare** ~ **su qcno** influence sb. ~ **d'aria** air vent. ~ **in giro** leg-pull. ~ **multipla** adaptor

pre'sagio *nm* omen

presa'gire *vt* foretell

presa'lario *nm* maintenance grant

'presbite *a* long-sighted

presbiteri'ano, -a *a & nmf* Presbyterian

presbi'terio *nm* presbytery

pre'scelto *a* selected

pre'scindere *vi* ~ **da** leave aside; **a** ~ **da** apart from

presco'lare *a* pre-school; **in età** ~ pre-school

pre'scritto *pp di* **prescrivere**

pre'scrivere *vt* prescribe

prescrizi'one *nf* prescription; (*norma*) rule; **cadere in** ~ cease to be valid as a result of the statute of limitations

preselezi'one *nf* preliminary selection; (*per il traffico*) advance lane markings; *Sport* [qualifying] heats *pl*

presen'tare *vt* present; (*far conoscere*) introduce; show (*documento*); (*inoltrare*) submit

presen'tarsi *vr* present oneself; (*farsi conoscere*) introduce oneself; (*a ufficio*) attend; (*alla polizia ecc*) report; (*come candidato*) stand, run (**a** for); (*occasione:*) occur; ~ **bene/male** (*persona:*) make a good/bad impression; (*situazione:*) look good/bad

presenta'tore, -'trice *nmf* presenter; (*di notizie*) announcer

presentazi'one *nf* presentation; (*per conoscersi*) introduction; **fare le presentazioni** do the introductions; **dietro** ~ **di ricetta medica** on doctor's prescription only

pre'sente *a* present; (*attuale*) current; (*questo*) this; **aver** ~ remember ● *nm* present; **i presenti** those present ● *nf* **allegato alla** ~ (*in lettera*) enclosed

presenti'mento *nm* foreboding

pre'senza *nf* presence; (*aspetto*) appearance; **in** ~ **di, alla** ~ **di** in the presence of; **di bella** ~ personable. ~ **di spirito** presence of mind

presenzi'are *vi* ~ **a** attend

pre'sepe *nm*, **pre'sepio** *nm* crib

preser'vare *vt* preserve; (*proteggere*) protect (**da** from)

preserva'tivo *nm* condom

preservazi'one *nf* preservation

'preside *nm* headmaster; *Univ* dean ● *nf* headmistress; *Univ* dean

presi'dente *nm* chairman; *Pol* president ● *nf* chairwoman; *Pol* president. ~ **del consiglio [dei ministri]** Prime Minister. ~ **della repubblica** President of the Republic

presiden'tessa *nf* chairwoman

presi'denza *nf* presidency; (*di assemblea*) chairmanship

presidenzi'ale *a* presidential

presidi'are *vt* garrison

pre'sidio *nm* garrison

presi'edere *vt* preside over

'preso *pp di* **prendere**

'pressa *nf Mech* press

press-'agent *mf inv* publicist, press agent

pres'sante *a* urgent

pressap'poco *adv* about

pres'sare *vt* press

pressi'one *nf* pressure; **far** ~ **su** put pressure on; **essere sotto** ~ *fig* be under pressure; **esercitare pressioni su qcno** put pressure on sb; **a/di alta** ~ high pressure. ~ **fiscale** tax burden. ~ **gomme** tyre pressure. ~ **del sangue** blood pressure

'presso *prep* near; (*a casa di*) with; (*negli indirizzi*) care of, c/o; (*lavorare*) for; **richiedere qcsa** ~ **una società** request sth from a company ● *nmpl* **pressi: nei pressi di...** in the neighbourhood *or* vicinity of...

pressoché *adv* almost

pressuriz'zare *vt* pressurize

pressuriz'zato *a* pressurized

prestabi'lire *vt* arrange in advance

prestabi'lito *a* agreed, predetermined

prestam'pato *a* printed ●*nm (modulo)* form

pre'stante *a* good-looking

pre'stanza *nf* good looks *pl*

pre'stare *vt* lend; **~ attenzione** pay attention; **~ aiuto** lend a hand; **~ ascolto** lend an ear; **~ fede** a give credence to; **~ giuramento** take the oath; **farsi ~** borrow *(da from)*

pre'starsi *vr ⟨frase:⟩* lend itself; *⟨persona:⟩* offer

prestazi'one *nf* performance; **prestazioni** *pl (servizi)* services

prestigia|'tore, -'trice *nmf* conjurer

pre'stigio *nm* prestige; **gioco di ~** conjuring trick

prestigi'oso *nm* prestigious

'prestito *nm* loan; **dare in ~** lend; **prendere in ~** borrow. **~ bancario** bank loan. **~ con garanzia collaterale** collateral loan

'presto *adv* soon; *(di buon'ora)* early; *(in fretta)* quickly; **a ~** see you soon; **al più ~** as soon as possible; **~ o tardi** sooner or later; **far ~** be quick

pre'sumere *vt* presume; *(credere)* think

presu'mibile *a* è **~ che...** presumably,...

pre'sunto *a ⟨colpevole⟩* presumed

presuntu'oso *a* presumptuous ●*nmf* presumptuous person

presunzi'one *nf* presumption

presup'porre *vt* suppose; *(richiedere)* presuppose

presupposizi'one *nf* presupposition

presup'posto *nm* essential requirement

prêt-à-por'ter *nm* ready-to-wear clothing

'prete *nm* priest

preten'dente *nmf* pretender ●*nm (corteggiatore)* suitor

pre'tendere *vt (sostenere)* claim; *(esigere)* demand ●*vi* **~ a** a claim to; **~ di** *(esigere)* demand to

pretensi'one *nf* pretension

pretenzi'oso *a* pretentious

preterintenzio'nale *a* **omicidio ~** manslaughter

pre'terito *nm* preterite

pre'tesa *nf* pretension; *(esigenza)* claim; **senza pretese** unpretentious

pre'teso *pp di* **pretendere**

pre'testo *nm* pretext

pre'tore *nm* magistrate

pretta'mente *adv* decidedly

'pretto *a* pure

pre'tura *nf* magistrate's court

preva'lente *a* prevalent

prevalente'mente *adv* primarily

preva'lenza *nf* prevalence

preva'lere *vi* prevail

pre'valso *pp di* **prevalere**

preve'dere *vt* foresee; forecast *⟨tempo⟩*; *⟨legge ecc.:⟩* provide for

preve'nire *vt* precede; *(evitare)* prevent; *(avvertire)* forewarn

preventi'vare *vt* estimate; *(aspettarsi)* budget for

preven'tivo *a* preventive; **bilancio ~** budget ●*nm Comm* estimate

preve'nuto *a* forewarned; *(mal disposto)* prejudiced

prevenzi'one *nf* prevention; *(preconcetto)* prejudice

previ'dente *a* provident

previ'denza *nf* foresight. **~ integrativa** supplementary social security, supplementary welfare *Am*. **~ sociale** social security, welfare *Am*

previdenzi'ale *a* provident

'previo *a* **~ pagamento** on payment

previsi'one *nf* forecast; **in ~ di** in anticipation of. **previsioni** *pl* **del tempo** weather forecast

pre'visto *pp di* **prevedere** ●*a* foreseen ●*nm* **più/meno/prima del ~** more/less/earlier than expected

prezi'oso *a* precious

prez'zemolo *nm* parsley

'prezzo *nm* price; **[a] metà ~** half price; **a ~ ribassato** at a reduced price; **non aver ~** *fig* be priceless. **~ d'acquisto** purchase price. **~ di costo** cost price. **~ al dettaglio** retail price. **~ di fabbrica** factory price. **~ di favore** special price. **~ all'ingrosso** wholesale price. **~ intero** full price. **~ di mercato** market price. **~ al minuto** retail price. **~ d'offerta** offer price. **~ politico** subsidized price. **~ di riferimento** benchmark price. **~ sorvegliato** controlled price. **~ stracciato** slashed price, drastically reduced price. **~ trattabile** price negotiable. **~ unitario** unit price. **~ di vendita** selling price

prigi'one *nf* prison; *(pena)* imprisonment; **mettere in ~** imprison, put in prison

prigio'nia *nf* imprisonment

prigioni'ero, -a *a* imprisoned ●*nmf* prisoner; **tenere ~ qcno** keep sb prisoner. **~ di guerra** prisoner of war, POW

'prima *adv* before; *(più presto)* earlier; *(in anticipo)* beforehand; *(in primo luogo)* first; **~, finiamo questo** let's finish this first; **puoi venire ~?** *(di giorni)* can't you come any sooner?; *(di ore)* can't you come any earlier?; **~ o poi** sooner or later; **quanto ~** as soon as possible ●*prep* **~ di** before; **~ di mangiare** before eating; **~ d'ora** before now ●*conj* **~ che** before; **~ che posso** as soon as I can ●*nf* first class; *Theat* first night; *Auto* first [gear]

pri'mario *a* primary; *(principale)* principal

pri'mate *nm* primate

pri'mato *nm* supremacy; *Sport* record

prima'vera *nf* spring

primave'rile *a* spring *attrib*

primeggi'are *vi* excel

primi'tivo *a* primitive; *(originario)* original

pri'mizie *nfpl* early produce *sg*

'primo *a* first; *(fondamentale)* principal; *(in*

importanza) main; (*precedente di due*) former; (*iniziale*) early; (*migliore*) best ● *nm* first; **il ~ d'aprile** April the first, April Fools' Day; **primi** *pl* (*i primi giorni*) the beginning; **in un ~ tempo** at first. **prima colazione** *nf* breakfast. **prima copia** *nf* master copy. **prima linea** *nf Mil* front line. **prima serata** *nf* prime time; **in ~ ~ trasmetteremo...** in the early evening slot we're bringing you...

primo'genito, -a *a* & *nmf* first-born

primogeni'tura *nf* primogeniture; **vendere la ~** sell one's birthright

primordi'ale *a* primordial

'primula *nf* primrose

princi'pale *a* main ● *nm* head, boss *fam*

princi'pato *nm* principality

'principe *nm* prince; **da ~** princely. **~ ereditario** crown prince. **~ del foro** famous lawyer

princi'pesco *a* princely

princi'pessa *nf* princess

principi'ante *nmf* beginner

principi'are *vt/i* begin, start

prin'cipio *nm* beginning; (*concetto*) principle; (*causa*) cause; **per ~** on principle; **una questione di ~** a matter of principle. **~ attivo** active ingredient

pri'ore *nm* prior

pri'ori: a ~ *adv* ‹*decidere*› a priori; **farsi ~ ~ un'opinione di** prejudge ● *a* a priori

priorità *nf inv* priority

priori'tario *a* having priority; ‹*obiettivo*› priority *attrib*; **la nostra scelta prioritaria** our decision, which must take priority

'prisma *nm* prism

'privacy *nf* privacy

pri'vare *vt* deprive

pri'varsi *vr* deprive oneself

privatiz'zare *vt* privatize

privatizzazi'one *nf* privatization

pri'vato, -a *a* private ● *nmf* private citizen; **in ~** in private; **ritirarsi a vita privata** withdraw from public life

privazi'one *nf* deprivation

privilegi'are *vt* privilege; (*considerare più importante*) favour

privi'legio *nm* privilege; **avere il ~ di** have the privilege of; **questo dizionario ha il ~ della chiarezza** this dictionary has the merit of clarity

'privo *a* **~ di** devoid of; (*mancante*) lacking in

pro *prep* for ● *nm* advantage; **a che ~?** what's the point?; **il ~ e il contro** the pros and cons

pro'babile *a* probable

probabilità *nf inv* probability; **avere buone ~** have a fighting chance; **~ di riuscita** chances of success

probabil'mente *adv* probably

pro'bante *a* convincing

probità *nf* probity

pro'blema *nm* problem; **non c'è ~** no problem

proble'matico *a* problematic

pro'boscide *nf* trunk

procacci'are *vt* obtain

procacci'arsi *vr* obtain

pro'cace *a* ‹*ragazza*› provocative

pro'cedere *vi* (*in percorso, discorso*) go on, proceed *fml*; (*iniziare*) start; **il lavoro procede bene** the work is going well; **~ contro** *Jur* start legal proceedings against

procedi'mento *nm* process; *Jur* proceedings *pl*

proce'dura *nf* procedure. **~ civile** civil proceedings *pl*. **~ fallimentare** bankruptcy proceedings *pl*

procedu'rale *a* procedural

proces'sare *vt Jur* try

processi'one *nf* procession

pro'cesso *nm* process; *Jur* trial; **essere sotto ~** be on trial; **mettere sotto ~** put on trial

proces'sore *nm Comput* processor

processu'ale *a* trial *attrib*

pro'cinto *nm* **essere in ~ di** be about to

proci'one *nm* raccoon

pro'clama *nm* proclamation

procla'mare *vt* proclaim

proclamazi'one *nf* proclamation

procrasti'nare *vt liter* postpone

procre'are *vt* procreate

procreazi'one *nf* procreation

pro'cura *nf* power of attorney; **per ~** by proxy. **P~ [della Repubblica]** Public Prosecutor's office

procu'rare *vt/i* procure; (*causare*) cause; (*cercare*) try

procura'tore *nm* attorney. **P~ Generale** Attorney General. **~ legale** ≈ lawyer. **~ della repubblica** public prosecutor

'prode *a* brave

pro'dezza *nf* bravery

prodi'gare *vt* lavish

prodi'garsi *vr* do one's best

pro'digio *nm* prodigy

prodigi'oso *a* prodigious

'prodigo *a* prodigal

prodi'torio *a* treasonable

pro'dotto *pp di* **produrre** ● *nm* product. **prodotti** *pl* **agricoli** farm produce *sg*. **~ artigianalmente** *a* made by craftsmen. **prodotti** *pl* **di bellezza** cosmetics. **~ derivato** by-product. **~ di fabbrica** *a* factory-made. **~ finito** end product, finished product. **~ interno lordo** gross domestic product. **~ nazionale lordo** gross national product

pro'durre *vt* produce

pro'dursi *vr* ‹*attore:*› play; (*accadere*) happen, occur

produttività *nf* productivity

produt'tivo *a* productive

produt'tore, -'trice *a* producing; **~ di petrolio** oil-producing ● *nmf* producer

produzi'one *nf* production. **~ in serie** mass production

Prof. *abbr* (**professore**) Prof.

profa'nare *vt* desecrate

profanazi'one *nf* desecration

pro'fano *a* profane ● *nm* **i profani** *pl* the uninitiated

profe'rire *vt* utter

Prof.essa *abbr* (**Professoressa**) Prof.

profes'sare *vt* profess; practise ⟨*professione*⟩

professio'nale *a* professional; **istituto ~** training college

professionalità *nf* professionalism

professi'one *nf* profession; **libera ~** profession

professio'nismo *nm* professionalism

professio'nista *nmf* professional

professo'rale *a* professorial

profes'sor|e, -'essa *nmf Sch* teacher; *Univ* lecturer; (*titolare di cattedra*) professor

pro'feta *nm* prophet

pro'fetico *a* prophetic

profetiz'zare *vt* prophesy

profe'zia *nf* prophecy

pro'ficuo *a* profitable

profi'lare *vt* outline; (*ornare*) border; *Aeron* streamline

profi'larsi *vr* stand out

profi'lattico *a* prophylactic ● *nm* condom

pro'filo *nm* profile; (*breve studio*) outline; **di ~** in profile

profite'roles *nmpl* profiteroles

profit'tare *vi* **~ di** (*avvantaggiarsi*) profit by; (*approfittare*) take advantage of

pro'fitto *nm* profit; (*vantaggio*) advantage; **mettere qcsa a ~** turn sth to one's advantage; **trarre ~ da** (*vantaggio*) derive benefit from

profonda'mente *adv* deeply, profoundly

profondità *nf inv* depth; (*del pensiero ecc*) depth, profundity; **in ~** in depth; **passaggio in ~** *Sport* deep pass [down the field]. **~ di campo** *Phot* depth of field

pro'fondo *a* deep; ⟨*pensiero ecc*⟩ profound; ⟨*cultura*⟩ great

pro 'forma *a* routine; **fattura ~ ~** pro forma [invoice] ● *adv* as a formality ● *nm* formality

'profugo, -a *nmf* refugee

profu'mare *vt* perfume

profu'marsi *vr* put on perfume

profumata'mente *adv* **pagare ~** pay through the nose

profu'mato *a* ⟨*fiore*⟩ fragrant; ⟨*fazzoletto ecc*⟩ scented

profume'ria *nf* perfumery

pro'fumo *nm* perfume, scent

profusi'one *nf* profusion; **a ~** in profusion

pro'fuso *pp di* **profondere** ● *a* profuse

pro'genie *nf* progeny

progeni|'tore, -'trice *nmf* ancestor

proget'tare *vt* plan; plan, design ⟨*costruzione*⟩

progettazione *nf* planning, design. **~ assistita da computer** computer-aided design, CAD

proget'tista *nmf* designer

pro'getto *nm* plan; (*di lavoro importante*) project. **~ di legge** bill

prog'nosi *nf inv* prognosis; **in ~ riservata** on the danger list

pro'gramma *nm* programme; *Comput* program; **avere qcsa in ~** have sth planned, have sth on. **~ di antivirus** *Comput* antivirus program. **~ assemblatore** *Comput* assembler. **~ aziendale** business plan. **~ per la gestione dei file** *Comput* file manager. **~ di grafico** *Comput* graphics program. **~ politico** manifesto. **~ scolastico** syllabus. **~ di setup** *Comput* setup program. **~ di utilità** *Comput* utility

program'mare *vt* programme; *Comput* program

program'mato *a* ⟨*sviluppo*⟩ planned

programma|'tore, -'trice *nmf* [computer] programmer

programmazi'one *nf* programming

progre'dire *vi* [make] progress

progres'sione *nf* progression

progres'sista *nmf* progressive

progres'sivo *a* progressive

pro'gresso *nm* progress; **fare progressi** make progress

proi'bire *vt* forbid

proibi'tivo *a* prohibitive

proibito *a* forbidden; **è ~ fumare qui** it's no smoking here

proibizi'one *nf* prohibition

proibizio'nismo *nm* prohibition

proiet'tare *vt* project; show ⟨*film*⟩

proi'ettile *nm* bullet

proiet'tore *nm* projector; *Auto* headlight

proiezi'one *nf* projection

'prole *nf* offspring

proletari'ato *nm* proletariat

prole'tario *a & nm* proletarian

prolife'rare *vi* proliferate

pro'lifico *a* prolific

prolissità *nf* prolixity, diffuseness

pro'lisso *a* verbose, prolix

pro 'loco *nf* tourist office (*in small places*)

'prologo *nm* prologue

pro'lunga *nf Electr* extension

prolunga'mento *nm* extension

prolun'gare *vt* extend ⟨*contratto, scadenza, strada*⟩; prolong ⟨*vita*⟩; lengthen ⟨*vita, strada*⟩

prolun'garsi *vr* continue, go on; **~ su** (*dilungarsi*) dwell upon

prome'moria *nm* memo; (*per se stessi*) reminder, note; (*formale*) memorandum

pro'messa *nf* promise; **era già una ~ del...** he was already a promising new talent in...

pro'messo *pp di* promettere ● *a* ⟨*terra*⟩ promised. **promessa sposa** *nf* betrothed. **~ sposo** *nm* betrothed

promet'tente *a* promising

pro'mettere *vt/i* promise

promi'nente *a* prominent

promi'nenza *nf* prominence

promiscuità *nf* promiscuity

pro'miscuo *a* promiscuous

promon'torio *nm* promontory

pro'mosso *pp di* **promuovere** ● *a Sch* who has gone up a year; *Univ* who has passed an exam

promo|'tore, -'trice *nmf* promoter

promozio'nale *a* promotional; **vendita ~** special offer

promozi'one *nf* promotion

promul'gare *vt* promulgate

promulgazi'one *nf* promulgation

promu'overe *vt* promote; *Sch* move up a class; **essere promosso** *Sch, Univ* pass one's exams

proni'pote *nm* (*di bisnonno*) great-grandson; (*di prozio*) great-nephew; **pronipoti** *pl* great-grandchildren ● *nf* (*di bisnonno*) great-granddaughter; (*di prozio*) great-niece

pro'nome *nm* pronoun

pronomi'nale *a* pronominal

pronosti'care *vt* forecast, predict

pronostica|'tore, -trice *nmf* forecaster

pro'nostico *nm* forecast

pron'tezza *nf* readiness; (*rapidità*) quickness; **~ di riflessi** quick reflexes *pl*; **con ~ di spirito** quick-wittedly

'pronto *a* ready; (*rapido*) quick; **~!** *Teleph* hello!; **tenersi ~** (**per qcsa**) be ready (*for sth*); **pronti, via!** (*in gare*) ready! steady! go!; **a pronta cassa** cash on delivery. **~ intervento** *nm* emergency service. **~ soccorso** *nm* first aid; (*in ospedale*) accident and emergency, A&E

prontu'ario *nm* handbook

pro'nuncia *nf* pronunciation

pronunci'are *vt* pronounce; (*dire*) utter; deliver ‹*discorso*›

pronunci'arsi *vr* (*su un argomento*) give one's opinion; **~ a favore/contro qcsa** pronounce oneself in favour of/against sth

pronunci'ato *a* pronounced; (*prominente*) prominent

pro'nunzia = **pronuncia**

pronunzi'are = **pronunciare**

propa'ganda *nf* propaganda. **~ elettorale** electioneering. **~ di partito** party political propaganda

propa'gare *vt* propagate

propa'garsi *vr* spread

propagazi'one *nf* propagation

prope'deutico *a* introductory

propel'lente *nm* propellant

pro'pendere *vi* **~ per** be in favour of

propensi'one *nf* inclination, propensity

pro'penso *pp di* **propendere** ● *a* **essere ~ a fare qcsa** be inclined to do sth

propi'nare *vt* administer

pro'pizio *a* favourable

proponi'mento *nm* resolution

pro'porre *vt* propose; (*suggerire*) suggest

pro'porsi *vr* set oneself ‹*obiettivo, meta*›; **~ di** intend to

proporzio'nale *a* proportional

proporzio'nare *vt* proportion

proporzio'nato *a* proportioned

proporzi'one *nf* proportion

pro'posito *nm* intention; **ho fatto il ~ di...** I have made the decision to...; **a ~** by the way; **a ~ di** with regard to; **di ~** (*apposta*) on purpose; **capitare a ~**, **giungere a ~** come at just the right time. **propositi** *pl* **per l'anno nuovo** New Year's resolutions

proposizi'one *nf* clause; (*frase*) sentence

pro'posta *nf* proposal, suggestion. **~ di legge** bill. **~ di matrimonio** [marriage] proposal

pro'posto *pp di* **proporre**

propriamente *adv* **~ detto** in the strict sense of the word

proprietà *nf inv* property; (*diritto*) ownership; (*correttezza*) propriety; **essere di ~ di qcno** be sb's property. **~ collettiva** collective ownership. **~ immobiliare** property. **~ di linguaggio** correct use of language. **~ privata** private property

proprie'taria *nf* owner; (*di casa affittata*) landlady

proprie'tario *nm* owner; (*di casa affittata*) landlord

'proprio *a* one's [own]; (*caratteristico*) typical; (*appropriato*) proper ● *adv* just; (*veramente*) really; **non ~** not really, not exactly; (*affatto*) not... at all ● *pron* one's own ● *nm* one's own; **lavorare in ~** be one's own boss; **mettersi in ~** set up on one's own

propu'gnare *vt* support

propulsi'one *nf* propulsion; **a ~ atomica** atomic[-powered]. **~ a getto** jet propulsion

propul'sore *nm* propeller

'prora *nf Naut* prow

'proroga *nf* extension

proro'gabile *a* extendable

proro'gare *vt* extend

pro'rompere *vi* burst out

'prosa *nf* prose

pro'saico *a* prosaic

pro'sciogliere *vt* release; *Jur* acquit

prosciogli'mento *nm* release

pro'sciolto *pp di* **prosciogliere**

prosciu'gare *vt* dry up; (*bonificare*) reclaim

prosciu'garsi *vr* dry up

prosci'utto *nm* ham. **~ cotto** cooked ham. **~ crudo** type of dry-cured ham, Parma ham

pro'scritto, -a *pp di* **proscrivere** ● *nmf* exile

pro'scrivere *vt* exile, banish

proscrizi'one *nf* exile, banishment

prosecuzi'one *nf* continuation

prosegui'mento *nm* continuation; **buon ~!** (*viaggio*) have a good journey!; (*festa*) enjoy the rest of the party!

prosegu'ire *vt* continue ● *vi* go on, continue

pro'selito *nm* convert

prospe'rare *vi* prosper

prosperità *nf* prosperity

'prospero *a* prosperous; (*favorevole*) favourable

prospe'roso *a* flourishing; ‹*ragazza*› buxom

prospet'tare *vt* show

prospet'tarsi *vr* seem
prospet'tiva *nf* perspective; (*panorama*) view; *fig* prospect
pro'spetto *nm* (*vista*) view; (*facciata*) façade; (*tabella*) table
prospici'ente *a* facing
prossima'mente *adv* soon
prossimità *nf* proximity; **in ~ di** near
'prossimo, -a *a* near; (*seguente*) next; (*molto vicino*) close; **l'anno ~** next year; **~ venturo** next; **essere ~ a fare qcsa** be about to do sth ● *nmf* neighbour
'prostata *nf* prostate
prostitu'irsi *vr* prostitute oneself
prosti'tuta *nf* prostitute
prostituzi'one *nf* prostitution
pro'strare *vt* prostrate
pro'strarsi *vr* prostrate oneself
pro'strato *a* prostrate
protago'nista *nmf* protagonist
pro'teggere *vt* protect; (*favorire*) favour
pro'teico *a* protein *attrib*; **molto ~** rich in protein
prote'ina *nf* protein
pro'tendere *vt* stretch out
pro'tendersi *vr* (*in avanti*) lean out
pro'teso *pp di* **protendere**
pro'testa *nf* protest; (*dichiarazione*) protestation
prote'stante *a & nmf* Protestant
prote'stare *vt/i* protest
prote'starsi *vr* **~ innocente** protest one's innocence
protet'tivo *a* protective
pro'tetto *pp di* **proteggere**
protetto'rato *nm* protectorate
protet|'tore, -'trice *nmf* protector; (*sostenitore*) patron ● *nm* (*di prostituta*) pimp
protezi'one *nf* protection. **~ civile** civil defence. **~ della natura** nature conservancy
protocol'lare *a* ⟨*visita*⟩ protocol ● *vt* register
proto'collo *nm* protocol; (*registro*) register; **carta ~** official stamped paper
pro'totipo *nm* prototype
pro'trarre *vt* protract; (*differire*) postpone
pro'trarsi *vr* go on, continue
pro'tratto *pp di* **protrarre**
protube'rante *a* protuberant
protube'ranza *nf* protuberance
'prova *nf* test; (*dimostrazione*) proof; (*tentativo*) try, attempt; (*di abito*) fitting; *Sport* heat; *Theat* rehearsal; (*bozza*) proof; **prove** *pl* evidence; **fino a ~ contraria** until I'm told otherwise; **in ~** (*assumere*) for a trial period; **mettere alla ~** put to the test; **a ~ di bomba** bombproof; **a ~ di ladro** burglarproof. **~ del fuoco** acid test. **~ generale** dress rehearsal
pro'vare *vt* test; (*dimostrare*) prove; (*tentare*) try; try on ⟨*abiti ecc*⟩; (*sentire*) feel; *Theat* rehearse; **prova!** just try!
pro'varsi *vr* try
proveni'enza *nf* origin
prove'nire *vi* **~ da** come from

pro'vento *nm* proceeds *pl*
prove'nuto *pp di* **provenire**
pro'verbio *nm* proverb
pro'vetta *nf* test-tube; **bambino in ~** test-tube baby
pro'vetto *a* skilled
pro'vincia *nf* province; (*strada*) B road, secondary road
provinci'ale *a* provincial; **strada ~** B road, secondary road
pro'vino *nm* specimen; *Cinema* screen test
provo'cante *a* provocative
provo'care *vt* provoke; (*causare*) cause
provoca|'tore, -'trice *nmf* trouble-maker
provoca'torio *a* provocative
provocazi'one *nf* provocation
provo'lone *nm* type of cheese with a slightly smoked flavour
provve'dere *vi* **~ a** provide for
provvedi'mento *nm* measure; (*previdenza*) precaution. **~ disciplinare** disciplinary measure
provvedito'rato *nm* **~ agli studi** education department
provvedi'tore *nm* **~ agli studi** director of education
provvi'denza *nf* providence
provvidenzi'ale *a* providential
provvigi'one *nf* *Comm* commission; **lavorare a ~** work on commission
provvi'sorio *a* provisional; **in via provisoria** provisionally, for the time being
prov'vista *nf* supply
pro'zia *nf* great-aunt
pro'zio *nm* great-uncle
'prua *nf* *Naut* prow
pru'dente *a* prudent
pru'denza *nf* prudence; **per ~** as a precaution
prudenzi'ale *a* prudential
'prudere *vi* itch
'prugna *nf* plum. **~ secca** prune. **~ selvatica** damson
'prugno *nm* plum[-tree]
'prugnolo *nm* sloe
pruri'ginoso *a* itchy
pru'rito *nm* itch
P.S. *abbr* (**Pubblica Sicurezza**) police
pseu'donimo *nm* pseudonym
psica'nalisi *nf* psychoanalysis
psicana'lista *nmf* psychoanalyst
psicanaliz'zare *vt* psychoanalyse
'psiche *nf* psyche
psiche'delico *a* psychedelic
psichi'atra *nmf* psychiatrist
psichia'tria *nf* psychiatry
psichi'atrico *a* psychiatric
'psichico *a* mental
psico'farmaco *nm* drug that affects the mind
psicolo'gia *nf* psychology
psico'logico *a* psychological
psi'cologo, -a *nmf* psychologist
psico'patico, -a *a* psychopathic ● *nmf* psychopath

psicopedago'gia *nf* educational psychology

psi'cosi *nf inv* psychosis

psicoso'matico *a* psychosomatic

psicotera'peuta *nmf* psychotherapist

psicotera'pista *nmf* psychotherapist

psi'cotico, -a *a & nmf* psychotic

PT *abbr* (**Posta e Telegrafi**) PO

puàh *int* yuck!

pub *nm* pub

pubbli'care *vt* publish

pubblicazi'one *nf* publication. **pubblicazioni** *pl* (*di matrimonio*) banns. ~ **periodica** periodical

pubbli'cista *nmf Journ* correspondent

pubblicità *nf inv* publicity, advertising; (*annuncio*) advertisement, advert; **fare ~ a qcsa** advertise sth; **piccola ~** small advertisements

pubblici'tario *a* advertising

'pubblico *a* public; **scuola pubblica** state school ● *nm* public; (*spettatori*) audience; **in ~** in public; **grande ~** general public. **Pubblica Sicurezza** police. ~ **ministero** public prosecutor. ~ **ufficiale** civil servant

'pube *nm* pubis

pubertà *nf* puberty

pu'dico *a* modest

pu'dore *nm* modesty

pue'rile *a* children's; *pej* childish

'puerpera *nf* new mother

puerpe'rale *a* of childbirth, puerperal *fml*; (*depressione*) postnatal

puer'perio *nm* postnatal period

pugi'lato *nm* boxing

'pugile *nm* boxer

'Puglia *nf* Apulia

pugli'ese *a & nmf* Apulian

pugna'lare *vt* stab

pugna'lata *nf* stab

pu'gnale *nm* dagger

'pugno *nm* fist; (*colpo*) punch; (*manciata*) fistful; (*fig: numero limitato*) handful; **dare un ~ a** punch; **di proprio ~** (*scrivere*) in one's own hand; **fare a pugni** (*colori:*) clash; **tenere in ~** (*situazione*) have under control; have in the palm of one's hand (*persona*); **un ~ in un occhio** *fig* an eyesore. ~ **di ferro** iron fist

'pula *nf sl* **la ~** the fuzz

'pulce *nf* flea; (*microfono*) bug; **mettere la ~ nell'orecchio a qcno** sow a doubt in sb's mind

pul'cino *nm* chick; (*nel calcio*) junior

pu'ledra *nf* filly

pu'ledro *nm* foal, colt

pu'leggia *nf* pulley

pu'lire *vt* clean. ~ **a secco** dry-clean; **far ~ qcsa** have sth cleaned

puliscipi'edi *nm inv* boot scraper

pu'lito *a* clean

puli'tura *nf* cleaning

puli'zia *nf* (*il pulire*) cleaning; (*l'essere pulito*) cleanliness; **pulizie** *pl* housework;

fare le pulizie do the cleaning. ~ **personale** personal hygiene

'pullman *nm inv* coach, bus; (*urbano*) bus; **gita in ~** coach trip

pull'over *nm* pullover

pul'mino *nm* minibus

'pulpito *nm* pulpit

pul'sante *nm* button; *Electr* [push-]button. ~ **di accensione** on/off switch. ~ **di alimentazione** power switch

pul'sare *vi* pulsate

pulsazi'one *nf* pulsation

pul'viscolo *nm* dust

'puma *nm inv* puma

pun'gente *a* prickly; (*insetto*) stinging; (*odore ecc*) sharp

'pungere *vt* prick; (*insetto:*) sting; ~ **qcno sul vivo** cut sb to the quick

pungersi *vr* prick oneself; ~ **un dito** prick one's finger

pungigli'one *nm* sting

pungo'lare *vt* goad

pu'nire *vt* punish

puni'tivo *a* punitive

punizi'one *nf* punishment; *Sport* penalty; (*in calcio*) free kick. ~ **corporale** corporal punishment

'punta *nf* point; (*estremità*) tip; (*di monte*) peak, top; (*un po'*) pinch; *Sport* forward; **doppie punte** (*di capelli*) split ends; **di ~** (*ore*) peak; (*personaggio*) leading

pun'tare *vt* point; (*spingere con forza*) push; (*scommettere*) bet; (*fam: appuntare*) fasten ● *vi* ~ **su** *fig* rely on; (*scommettere*) bet on; ~ **verso** (*dirigersi*) head for; ~ **a** aspire to; **punta e clicca** *Comput* point and click

punta'spilli *nm inv* pincushion

pun'tata *nf* (*di una storia*) instalment; (*televisiva*) episode; (*al gioco*) stake, bet; (*breve visita*) flying visit; **a puntate** serialized, in instalments; **fare una ~ a/in** pop over to (*luogo*)

punteggia'tura *nf* punctuation

pun'teggio *nm* score

puntel'lare *vt* prop

pun'tello *nm* prop

punteru'olo *nm* awl

pun'tiglio *nm* spite; (*ostinazione*) obstinacy

puntigli'oso *a* punctilious, pernickety *pej*

pun'tina *nf* (*da disegno*) drawing pin, thumb tack *Am*; (*di giradischi*) stylus. ~ **da disegno** drawing pin, thumb tack *Am*

pun'tine *nfpl* points

pun'tino *nm* dot; **a ~** perfectly; (*cotto*) to a T. **puntini** *pl* [**di sospensione**] suspension points

'punto *nm* point; (*in cucito, Med*) stitch; (*in punteggiatura*) full stop; **in che ~?** where, exactly?; **di ~ in bianco** all of a sudden; **essere sul ~ di fare qcsa** be on the point of doing sth, be about to do sth; **in ~** sharp; **mettere a ~** put right; *fig* fine-tune; tune up (*motore*); **messa a ~** fine tuning; **due punti** colon. **punti** *pl* **cardinali** points of the compass. ~ **cieco** blind spot. ~ **di congela-**

mento freezing point. **~ croce** cross-stitch. **~ debole** blind spot. **~ di domanda** question mark. **~ di ebollizione** boiling point. **~ esclamativo** exclamation mark. **~ di fuga** vanishing point. **~ di fusione** melting point. **~ d'incontro** meeting-point. **~ di infiammabilità** flashpoint. **~ interrogativo** question mark. **~ nero** *Med* blackhead. **~ di pareggio** *Fin* breakeven point. **~ di partenza** starting point. **~ di riferimento** landmark; *(per la qualità)* benchmark. **~ di rottura** breaking point. **~ a smerlo** blanket stitch. **~ di vendita** point of sale, outlet; **pubblicità al ~ ~ ~** point-of-sale publicity. **~ e virgola** semicolon. **~ di vista** point of view

puntu'ale *a* punctual; **essere ~** be punctual, be on time

puntualità *nf* punctuality

puntualiz'zare *vt* make clear, clarify

puntual'mente *adv* punctually, on time; *(come al solito)* as usual

pun'tura *nf (di insetto)* sting; *(di ago ecc)* prick; *Med* puncture; *(iniezione)* injection; *(fitta)* stabbing pain. **~ d'ape** bee sting. **~ d'insetto** insect bite. **~ di spillo** pinprick. **~ di zanzara** mosquito bite

punzecchi'are *vt* prick; *fig* tease

punzo'nare *vt Techn* punch, stamp

pun'zone *nm* punch

può *vedi* **potere**; **~ darsi** maybe, perhaps

'pupa *nf* doll

pu'pazzo *nm* puppet. **~ di neve** snowman

pup'illa *nf Anat* pupil

pu'pillo, -a *nmf Jur* ward; *(di professore)* favourite

purché *conj* provided

'pure *adv* too, also; *(concessivo)* **fate ~!** please do! ● *conj (tuttavia)* yet; *(anche se)* even if; **pur di** just to; **io ~** me too; **è venuto ~ lui** he came too, he also came

purè *nm inv* purée. **~ di patate** mashed potatoes, creamed potatoes

pu'rezza *nf* purity

'purga *nf* purge

pur'gante *nm* laxative

pur'gare *vt* purge

purga'torio *nm* purgatory

purifi'care *vt* purify

purificazi'one *nf* purification

pu'rista *nmf* purist

puri'tano, -a *a & nmf* Puritan

'puro *a* pure; *(vino ecc)* undiluted; **per ~ caso** by sheer chance, purely by chance. **~ cotone** *nm* pure cotton, 100% cotton. **pura lana vergine** *nf* pure new wool. **pura seta** *nf* pure silk

puro'sangue *a & nm* thoroughbred

pur'troppo *adv* unfortunately

'pus *nm* pus

'pustola *nf* pimple

puti'ferio *nm* uproar

putre'fare *vi* putrefy

putre'farsi *vr* putrefy

putre'fatto *a* rotten

putrefazi'one *nf* putrefaction

'putrido *a* putrid

putt *nm inv* putt

put'tana *nf vulg* whore

'puzza *nf* stink; **avere la ~ sotto il naso** be sniffy

puz'zare *vi anche fig* stink; **~ di bruciato** *fig* smell fishy; **~ d'imbroglio** stink; **~ di corruzione** stink of corruption; **questa storia mi puzza** the story stinks

'puzzo *nm* stink

'puzzola *nf* polecat

puzzo'lente *a* stinking

puz'zone *nm fam* bastard

p.zza *abbr* (**piazza**) Sq.

Qq

QI *abbr* (**quoziente di intelligenza**) IQ

qua *adv* here; **da un anno in ~** for the last year; **da quando in ~?** since when?; **di ~ this way; **di ~ di** on this side of; **~ dentro** in here; **~ sotto** under here; **~ vicino** near here; **~ e là** here and there

'quacchero, -a *nmf* Quaker

qua'derno *nm* exercise book; *(per appunti)* notebook. **~ a quadretti** maths exercise book. **~ a righe** lined exercise book

quadrango'lare *a (forma)* quadrangular; **incontro ~** *Sport* four-sided tournament

qua'drangolo *nm* quadrangle

qua'drante *nm* quadrant; *(di orologio)* dial

qua'drare *vt* square; *(contabilità)* balance ● *vi* fit in

qua'drato *a* square; *(equilibrato)* level-headed ● *nm* square; *(nel pugilato)* ring; **al ~** squared

quadra'tura *nf Math* squaring; *(di bilancio)* balancing

quadret'tare *vt* divide into small squares

quadret'tato *a* squared; *(carta)* graph *attrib; (tessuto)* check, checked

qua'dretto *nm* square; *(piccolo quadro)* small picture; **a quadretti** *(tessuto)* check

quadrico'mia *nf* four-colour printing

quadrien'nale *a (che dura quattro anni)* four-year; *(ogni quattro anni)* four-yearly

quadri'foglio *nm* four-leaf clover
qua'driglia *nf* square dance
quadri'latero *nm* quadrilateral
quadri'mestre *nm* (*periodo*) four-month period; *Sch* term
quadrimo'tore *nm* four-engined plane
quadri'nomio *nm Math* quadrinomial
quadripar'tito *a* four-party ● *nm* (*politica*) four-party government
quadri'plegico *a* quadriplegic
'quadro *nm* picture, painting; (*quadrato*) square; (*fig: scena*) sight; (*tabella*) table; *Theat* scene; (*dirigente*) executive; **fare il ~ della situazione** outline the situation; **fuori ~** *Cinema, TV* out of shot; **quadri** *pl* (*carte*) diamonds; **a quadri** (*tessuto, giacca, motivo*) check, checked. **~ clinico** case history. **~ di comando** control panel. **quadri** *pl* **direttivi** senior management. **~ di distribuzione** *Electr* switchboard. **quadri** *pl* **intermedi** middle management. **~ degli interruttori** switch panel
qua'drupede *nm* quadruped
quadrupli'care *vt* quadruple
quadrupli'carsi *vr* quadruple
qua'druplice *a* quadruple
'quadruplo *a & nm* quadruple
quaggiù *adv* down here
'quaglia *nf* quail
'qualche *a* (*alcuni*) a few, some; (*un certo*) some; (*in interrogazioni*) any; **ho ~ problema** I have a few problems, I have some problems; **~ tempo fa** some time ago; **hai ~ libro italiano?** have you any Italian books?; **posso prendere ~ libro?** can I take some books?; **in ~ modo** somehow; **in ~ posto** somewhere; **~ volta** sometimes; **~ cosa =** qualcosa
qualche'duno *pron* somebody, someone
qual'cosa *pron* something; (*in interrogazioni*) anything; **qualcos'altro** something else; **vuoi qualcos'altro?** would you like anything else?; **~ di strano** something strange; **vuoi ~ da mangiare?** would you like something to eat?; **vuoi ~ da bere?** would you like a drink?, would you like something to drink?
qual'cuno *pron* someone, somebody; (*in interrogazioni*) anyone, anybody; (*alcuni*) some; (*in interrogazioni*) any; **c'è ~?** is anybody in?; **qualcun altro** someone else, somebody else; **c'è qualcun altro che aspetta?** is anybody else waiting?; **ho letto ~ dei suoi libri** I've read some of his books; **conosci ~ dei suoi amici?** do you know any of his friends?
'quale *a* which; (*indeterminato*) what; (*come*) as, like; **~ macchina è la tua?** which car is yours?; **~ motivo avrà di parlare così?** what reason would he have to speak like that?; **~ onore!** what an honour!; **città quali Venezia** towns like Venice; **~ che sia la tua opinione** whatever you may think ● *pron inter* which [one]; **~ preferisci?** which [one] do you prefer? ● *pron rel* **il/la ~** (*persona*)

who; (*animale, cosa*) that, which; (*oggetto: con prep*) whom; (*oggetto: animale, cosa*) which; **ho incontrato tua madre, la ~ mi ha detto...** I met your mother who told me...; **l'ufficio nel ~ lavoro** the office in which I work; **l'uomo con il ~ parlavo** the man to whom I was speaking ● *adv* (*come*) as
qua'lifica *nf* qualification; (*titolo*) title
qualifi'cabile *a* qualifiable
qualifi'care *vt* qualify; (*definire*) define
qualifi'carsi *vr* be placed
qualifica'tivo *a* qualifying
qualifi'cato *a* (*operaio*) semi-skilled
qualificazi'one *nf* qualification
qualità *nf inv* quality; (*specie*) kind; **in ~ di** in one's capacity as; **di prima ~** high quality; **di ottima/cattiva ~** top/poor quality
qualitativa'mente *adv* qualitatively
qualita'tivo *a* qualitative
qua'lora *conj* in case
qual'siasi, qua'lunque *a* any; (*non importa quale*) whatever; (*ordinario*) ordinary; **dammi una penna ~** give me any pen [whatsoever]; **farei ~ cosa** I would do anything; **~ cosa io faccia** whatever I do; **~ persona** anyone, anybody; **in ~ caso** in any case; **uno ~** any one, whichever; **l'uomo qualunque** the man in the street; **vivo in una casa ~** I live in an ordinary house
qualunqu'ismo *nm* lack of political views
qualunqu'ista *nmf* (*menefreghista*) person with no political views
'quando *conj & adv* when; **da ~ ti ho visto** since I saw you; **da ~ esci con lui?** how long have you been going out with him?; **da ~ in qua?** since when?; **~... ~...** sometimes..., sometimes...; **continua ad insistere ~ sa di avere torto** he keeps on insisting even when he knows he's wrong
quantifi'cabile *a* quantifiable
quantifi'care *vt* quantify
quantità *nf inv* quantity; **una ~ di** (*gran numero*) a great deal of
quantitativa'mente *adv* quantitatively
quantita'tivo *nm* amount ● *a* quantitative
'quanto *a inter* how much; (*con nomi plurali*) how many; (*in esclamazione*) what a lot of; (*tempo*) how long; **quanti anni hai?** how old are you? ● *a rel* as much... as; (*tempo*) as long as; (*con nomi plurali*) as many... as; **prendi ~ denaro ti serve** take as much money as you need; **prendi quanti libri vuoi** take as many books as you like ● *pron inter* how much; (*quanto tempo*) how long; (*plurale*) how many; **quanti ne abbiamo oggi?** what date is it today? ● *pron rel* as much as; (*quanto tempo*) as long as; (*plurale*) as many as; **prendine ~/quanti ne vuoi** take as much/as many as you like; **stai ~ vuoi** stay as long as you like; **questo è ~** that's it ● *adv inter* how much; (*quanto tempo*) how long; **~ sei alto?** how tall are you?; **~ hai aspettato?** how long did you wait for?; **~ costa?** how much is it?; **~ mi dispiace!** I'm so sorry!; **~ è bello!** how nice! ● *adv rel* as much as; **lavoro ~ posso** I

work as much as I can; **è tanto intelligente ~ bello** he's as intelligent as he's good-looking; **in ~** (*in qualità di*) as; (*poiché*) since; **~ a** as for; **in ~ a me** as far as I'm concerned; **per ~** however; **per ~ ne sappia** as far as I know; **per ~ mi riguarda** as far as I'm concerned; **per ~ mi sia simpatico** much as I like him; **~ prima** (*al più presto*) as soon as possible

quan'tunque *conj* although

qua'ranta *a & nm* forty

quaran'tena *nf* quarantine

quaran'tenne *a* forty-year-old; (*sulla quarantina*) in his/her forties ● *nmf* forty-year-old; (*sulla quarantina*) person in his/her forties

quaran'tennio *nm* period of forty years

quaran'tesimo *a & nm* fortieth

quaran'tina *nf* **una ~** about forty

qua'resima *nf* Lent

quar'tetto *nm* quartet

quarti'ere *nm* district, area; *Mil* quarters *pl.* **quartieri** *pl* **alti** smart districts. **quartieri** *pl* **bassi** poor areas. **~ cinese** Chinatown. **~ dormitorio** dormitory town. **~ generale** headquarters. **~ residenziale** residential area

quar'tino *nm* (*strumento musicale*) instrument similar to a clarinet; *Typ* quarto; (*di vino*) quarter litre

'quarto *a* fourth ● *nm* fourth; (*quarta parte*) quarter; **le sette e un ~** [a] quarter past seven, [a] quarter after seven *Am*; **a tre quarti** (*giacca, maniche*) three-quarter length. **quarti** *pl* **di finale** quarter-finals. **~ d'ora** quarter of an hour ● *nf*(*marcia*) fourth [gear]

quarto'genito, -a *nmf* fourth child

quar'tultimo, -a *a & nmf* fourth last

'quarzo *nm* quartz; **al ~** quartz. **~ rosa** rose quartz

'quasi *adv* almost, nearly; **~ mai** hardly ever ● *conj* (*come se*) as if; **~ ~ sto a casa** I'm tempted to stay home

quassù *adv* up here

qua'terna *nf* (*lotto, tombola*) set of four winning numbers

quater'nario *nm* (*era*) Quaternary

'quatto *a* crouching; (*silenzioso*) silent; **starsene ~ ~** keep very quiet

quattordi'cenne *a & nmf* fourteen-year-old

quattordi'cesimo *a & nm* fourteenth

quat'tordici *a & nm* fourteen

quat'trini *nmpl* money *sg*, dosh *sg fam*

'quattro *a & nm* four; **dirne ~ a qcno** give sb a piece of one's mind; **farsi in ~** (**per qcno/per fare qcsa**) go to a lot of trouble (*for sb/to do sth*); **in ~ e quattr'otto** in a flash. **~ per ~** *nm inv Auto* four-wheel drive [vehicle]; **a ~ tempi** *Auto* four-stroke

quat'trocchi *adv* **a ~ in** private

quattrocen'tesco *a* fifteenth-century

quattro'cento *a & nm* four hundred; **il Q~** the fifteenth century

quattro'mila *a & nm* four thousand

Qué'bec *nm* Quebec

'quello *a* that (*pl* those); **quell'albero** that tree; **quegli alberi** those trees; **quel cane** that dog; **quei cani** those dogs ● *pron* that [one] (*pl* those [ones]); **~ li** that one over there; **~ che** the one that; (*ciò che*) what; **quelli che** the ones that, those that; **~ a destra** the one on the right

'quercia *nf* oak; **di ~** oak

que'rela *nf* [legal] action

quere'lante *nmf* plaintiff

quere'lare *vt* bring an action against

quere'lato, -a *nmf* defendant

que'sito *nm* question

questio'nare *vi* dispute

questio'nario *nm* questionnaire

quest'ione *nf* question; (*faccenda*) matter; (*litigio*) quarrel; **in ~** in doubt; **è fuori ~** it's out of the question; **è ~ di vita o di morte** it's a matter of life and death; **mettere qcsa in ~** cast doubt on sth; **una ~ personale** a personal matter

'questo *a* this (*pl* these) ● *pron* this [one] (*pl* these [ones]); **~ qui, ~ qua** this one here; **~ è quello che a detto** that's what he said; **per ~** for this *or* that reason; **quest'oggi** today

que'store *nm* chief of police

'questua *nf* collection

que'stura *nf* police headquarters

qui *adv* here; **da ~ in poi, da ~ in avanti** from now on; **di ~ a una settimana** in a week's time; **fin ~** (*di tempo*) up till now, until now; **~ dentro** in here; **~ sotto** under here; **qui vicino** *adv* near here ● *nm* **~ pro quo** misunderstanding

quie'scenza *nf* (*di vulcano*) dormancy; (*pensione*) retirement; **trattamento di ~** retirement package

quie'tanza *nf* receipt

quie'tare *vt* calm

quie'tarsi *vr* calm down

qui'ete *nf* quiet; **disturbo della ~ pubblica** breach of the peace; **stato di ~** *Phys* state of rest

qui'eto *a* quiet

'quindi *adv* then ● *conj* therefore

quindi'cenne *a & nmf* fifteen-year-old

quindi'cesimo *a & nm* fifteenth

'quindici *a & nm* fifteen; **~ giorni** a fortnight *Br*, two weeks *pl*

quindi'cina *nf* **una ~** about fifteen; **una ~ di giorni** a fortnight *Br*, two weeks *pl*

quindici'nale *a* fortnightly *Br*, twice-monthly ● *nm* fortnightly magazine *Br*, twice-monthly magazine

quinquen'nale *a* (*che dura cinque anni*) five-year; (*ogni cinque anni*) five-yearly

quin'quennio *nm* [period of] five years

'quinta *nf Auto* fifth [gear], overdrive

quin'tale *nm* a hundred kilograms

'quinte *nfpl Theat* wings

quintes'senza *nf* quintessence

quin'tetto *nm* quintet

'quinto *a & nm* fifth

quintupli'care *vt* quintuple

quin'tuplo *a* quintuple

qui'squiglia *nf* trifle; **perdersi in quisquiglie** get bogged down in details

quiz *nm inv* **[gioco a]** ~ quiz game. ~ **radiofonico** radio quiz

'quota *nf* quota; (*rata*) instalment; (*altitudine*) height; *Aeron* altitude, height; (*ippica*) odds *pl*; **perdere/prendere** ~ lose/ gain altitude *o* height; **da alta** ~ high-flying. ~ **fissa** fixed amount. ~ **non imponibile** personal allowance. ~ **di iscrizione** entry

fee; (*di club*) membership fee. ~ **di mercato** market share. ~ **zero** sea level

quo'tare *vt Comm* quote

quo'tato *a* quoted; **essere** ~ **in Borsa** be quoted on the Stock Exchange

quotazi'one *nf* quotation. ~ **d'acquisto** buying rate. ~ **ufficiale** (*in Borsa*) official quotation. ~ **di vendita** selling rate

quotidiana'mente *adv* daily

quotidi'ano *a* daily; (*ordinario*) everyday ● *nm* daily [paper]

'quoto *nm Math* quotient

quozi'ente *nm* quotient. ~ **d'intelligenza** intelligence quotient, IQ. ~ **di purezza** purity

....

Rr

....

ra'barbaro *nm* rhubarb

'rabbia *nf* rage; (*ira*) anger; *Med* rabies *sg*; **che** ~! what a nuisance!; **mi fa** ~ it makes me angry

'rabbico *a* ⟨*virus*⟩ rabies *attrib*

rab'bino *nm* rabbi

rabbiosa'mente *adv* furiously

rabbi'oso *a* hot-tempered; *Med* rabid; (*violento*) violent

rabboc'care *vt* top up ⟨*fiasco*⟩

rabbo'nire *vt* pacify

rabbo'nirsi *vr* calm down

rabbrivi'dire *vi* shudder; (*di freddo*) shiver

rabbuf'fare *vt* reprimand; ruffle ⟨*capelli*⟩

rab'buffo *nm* reprimand

rabbui'arsi *vr* get dark; ⟨*viso:*⟩ darken

rabdo'mante *nmf* water diviner

rabdoman'zia *nf* water divining

raccapez'zare *vt* put together

raccapez'zarsi *vr* see one's way ahead

raccapricci'ante *a* horrifying

raccatta'palle *nm inv* ball boy ● *nf inv* ball girl

raccat'tare *vt* pick up

rac'chetta *nf* racket. ~ **da neve** snowshoe. ~ **da ping pong** table-tennis bat. ~ **da sci** ski stick, ski pole. ~ **da tennis** tennis racket

'racchio *a fam* ugly

racchi'udere *vt* contain

rac'cogliere *vt* pick; (*da terra*) pick up; (*mietere*) harvest; (*collezionare*) collect; (*radunare*) gather; win ⟨*voti ecc*⟩; (*dare asilo a*) take in

rac'cogliersi *vr* gather; (*concentrarsi*) collect one's thoughts

raccogli'mento *nm* concentration

raccogli|'tore, -'trice *nmf* collector ● *nm* ~ **[a fogli mobili]** ring-binder

rac'colta *nf* collection; (*di scritti*) compilation; (*del grano ecc*) harvesting; (*adunata*)

gathering; **chiamare a** ~ call *o* gather together. ~ **differenziata** *collection of items for recycling.* ~ **di fondi** fund-raising

rac'colto, -a *pp di* **raccogliere** ● *a* (*rannicchiato*) hunched; (*intimo*) cosy; (*concentrato*) engrossed ● *nm* (*mietitura*) harvest

raccoman'dabile *a* advisable; **poco** ~ ⟨*persona*⟩ shady

raccoman'dare *vt* recommend; (*affidare*) entrust

raccoman'darsi *vr* (*implorare*) beg

raccoman'data *nf* letter sent by recorded delivery; **per** ~ by recorded delivery. ~ **con ricevuta di ritorno** *letter sent by recorded delivery with acknowledgement of receipt*

raccoman'data-e'spresso *nf express recorded delivery service*

raccomandazi'one *nf* recommendation

raccomo'dare *vt* repair

raccon'tare *vt* tell

rac'conto *nm* story

raccorci'are *vt* shorten

raccorci'arsi *vr* become shorter; ⟨*giorni:*⟩ draw in

raccor'dare *vt* join

rac'cordo *nm* connection; (*stradale*) feeder. ~ **anulare** ring road. ~ **autostradale** motorway junction *Br*, intersection. ~ **ferroviario** siding. ~ **a gomito** elbow

ra'chitico *a* rickety; (*poco sviluppato*) stunted

racimo'lare *vt* scrape together

'racket *nm inv* racket

'rada *nf Naut* roads *pl*

'radar *nm* radar; **uomo** ~ air traffic controller

radden'sare *vt* thicken

radden'sarsi *vr* thicken

raddob'bare *vt* refit

rad'dobbo *nm* refit

raddol'cire vt sweeten; fig soften

raddol'cirsi vr become milder; ⟨carattere:⟩ mellow

raddoppia'mento nm doubling

raddoppi'are vt double

rad'doppio nm doubling; (equitazione) gallop; (biliardo) double

raddriz'zabile a which can be straightened

raddriz'zare vt straighten

raddrizza'tore nm (di corrente) rectifier

ra'dente a grazing, shaving; **tiro ~** Mil grazing fire; Sport low shot just skimming the surface; **volo ~** Aeron hedge-hopping

'radere vt shave; graze ⟨muro⟩; **~ al suolo** raze [to the ground]

'radersi vr shave

radi'ale a radial

radi'ante a radiant ● nm Math radian

radi'are vt strike off; **~ dall'albo** strike off ⟨medico⟩; debar ⟨avvocato⟩

radia'tore nm radiator

radiazi'one nf radiation. **~ nucleare** nuclear radiation

'radica nf briar

radi'cale a radical ● nm Gram root; Pol radical

radical'mente adv radically

radi'carsi vr **~ in** be rooted in

radi'cato a deep-seated

ra'dicchio nm chicory

ra'dice nf root; **mettere [le] radici** ⟨pianta:⟩ take root; fig put down roots. **~ quadrata** square root

'radio nf inv radio; **via ~** by radio; **contatto ~** radio contact; **ponte ~** radio link. **~ pirata** pirate radio. **~ portatile** portable radio. **~ ricevente** receiver. **~ [a] transistor** transistor radio. **~ trasmittente** transmitter ● nm Chem radium

radioama|'tore, -'trice nmf radio ham

radioascolta|'tore, -'trice nmf listener

radioassi'stito a radio-assisted

radioattività nf radioactivity

radioat'tivo a radioactive

radiobiolo'gia nf radiobiology

radio'bussola nf radio compass

radiocoman'dare vt operate by remote control

radiocoman'dato a remote-controlled, radio-controlled

radio'cronaca nf radio commentary; **fare la ~ di** commentate on

radiocro'nista nmf radio reporter

radiodiffusi'one nf broadcasting

radio'faro nm radio beacon

radio'fonico a radio attrib

radiofre'quenza nf radio frequency

radiogo'niometro nm direction finder, radiogoniometer

radiogra'fare vt X-ray

radiogra'fia nf X-ray [photograph]; (radiologia) radiography; **fare una ~** ⟨paziente:⟩ have an X-ray; ⟨dottore:⟩ take an X-ray

radio'lina nf transistor

radiolocaliz'zare vt locate by radar

radi'ologo, -a nmf radiologist

radio'onda nf radio wave

radioregistra'tore nm **~ portatile** portable radio cassette recorder

radiosco'pia nf Med radioscopy

radio'scopico a radioscopic

radi'oso a radiant

radio'spia nf bug

radio'sveglia nf radio alarm, clock radio

radio'taxi nm inv radio taxi

radiote'lefono nm radio-telephone; (privato) cordless [phone]

radiotelevi'sivo a broadcasting attrib

radiotera'pia nf radiotherapy

radiotra'smettere vt radio

radiotrasmetti'tore nm radio

radiotrasmit'tente nf radio station

'rado a sparse; (non frequente) rare; **di ~** seldom

radu'nare vt gather [together]

radu'narsi vr gather [together]

radu'nata nf gathering. **~ sediziosa** seditious assembly

ra'duno nm meeting; Sport rally

ra'dura nf clearing

'rafano nm horseradish

raffazzo'nato a ⟨discorso, lavoro⟩ botched

raf'fermo a stale

'raffica nf gust; (di armi da fuoco) burst; (di domande, insulti) barrage

raffigu'rare vt represent

raffigurazi'one nf representation

raffi'nare vt refine

raffinata'mente adv elegantly

raffina'tezza nf refinement

raffi'nato a refined

raffine'ria nf refinery. **~ di petrolio** oil refinery

rafforza'mento nm reinforcement; (di muscolatura, carattere) strengthening

raffor'zare vt reinforce

rafforza'tivo a Gram intensifying ● nm Gram intensifier

raffredda'mento nm (processo) cooling; **di ~** cooling. **~ ad acqua** water-cooling. **~ ad aria** air-cooling

raffred'dare vt cool

raffred'darsi vr get cold; (prendere un raffreddore) catch a cold; ⟨sentimento, passione:⟩ cool [off]

raffred'dato a **essere ~** ⟨persona⟩ have a cold

raffred'dore nm cold; **avere il ~** have a cold. **~ da fieno** hay fever

raf'fronto nm comparison

'rafia nf raffia

Rag. abbr **ragioniere**

ra'gazza nf girl; (fidanzata) girlfriend; **nome da ~** maiden name. **~ copertina** cover girl. **~ madre** unmarried mother. **~ alla pari** au pair [girl]. **~ squillo** call girl

ragaz'zata nf prank

ra'gazzo *nm* boy; (*fidanzato*) boyfriend; **da ~** (*da giovane*) as a boy. **~ padre** unmarried father. **~ di strada** guttersnipe. **~ di vita** rent boy

ragge'lare *vt fig* freeze

ragge'larsi *vr fig* turn to ice

raggi'ante *a* radiant; **~ di successo** flushed with success

raggi'era *nf* **a ~** with a pattern like spokes radiating from a centre

raggi'era *nf* (*di ruota*) spokes *pl*

'raggio *nm* ray; *Math* radius; (*di ruota*) spoke; **a raggi infrarossi** infrared. **~ d'azione** range. **~ laser** laser beam. **~ di luna** moonbeam. **~ di sole** ray of sunshine, sunbeam. **~ di speranza** ray of hope. **~ ultravioletto** ultraviolet ray. **raggi** *pl* **X** X-rays

raggi'rare *vt* trick

rag'giro *nm* trick

raggi'ungere *vt* reach; (*conseguire*) achieve

raggiun'gibile *a* (*luogo*) within reach

raggiungi'mento *nm* attainment

raggomito'lare *vt* wind

raggomito'larsi *vr* curl up

raggranel'lare *vt* scrape together

raggrin'zire *vt* wrinkle

raggrin'zirsi *vr* wrinkle

raggru'mare *vt* curdle (*latte*)

raggru'marsi *vr* (*latte:*) curdle

raggruppa'mento *nm* (*gruppo*) group; (*azione*) grouping; *Comm* groupage

raggrup'pare *vt* group together

ragguagli'are *vt* compare; (*informare*) inform

raggu'aglio *nm* comparison; (*informazione*) information

ragguar'devole *a* considerable

'ragia *nf* resin; **acqua ~** turpentine

ragià *nm inv* rajah

ragiona'mento *nm* reasoning; (*discussione*) discussion. **~ per assurdo** reductio ad absurdum

ragio'nare *vi* reason; (*discutere*) discuss

ragio'nato *a* (*argomento*) reasoned; (*cruciverba*) cryptic

ragi'one *nf* reason; (*ciò che è giusto*) right; **a ~ o a torto** rightly or wrongly; **aver ~** be right; **perdere la ~** go out of one's mind; **a ragion veduta** after due consideration; **prenderle/darle di santa ~** get/give a good walloping. **ragion d'essere** raison d'être. **~ di scambio** terms of trade. **~ sociale** company name. **ragion di Stato** reasons of State

ragione'ria *nf* accountancy; (*scuola*) secondary school which provides training in accountancy

ragio'nevole *a* reasonable

ragionevol'mente *adv* reasonably

ragioni'ere, -a *nmf* accountant

ra'glan *a inv* (*manica*) raglan

ragli'are *vi* bray

'raglio *nm* bray

ragna'tela *nf* cobweb

'ragno *nm* spider

ragù *nm inv* meat sauce

RAI *nf abbr* (**Radio Audizioni Italiane**) Italian public broadcasting company

'raid *nm inv* raid

'raionᴿ *nm* rayonᴿ

ra'lenti *nm* **al ~** in slow motion

rallegra'menti *nmpl* congratulations

ralle'grare *vt* gladden

ralle'grarsi *vr* rejoice; **~ con qcno** congratulate sb

rallenta'mento *nm* slowing down

rallen'tare *vt/i* slow down; (*allentare*) slacken

rallen'tarsi *vr* slow down

rallenta'tore *nm* (*su strada*) speed bump; **al ~** in slow motion

'rally *nm inv* rally

RAM *nf inv* RAM

ramai'olo *nm* ladle

raman'zina *nf* reprimand

ra'mare *vt* stake (*pianta*)

ra'marro *nm* (*animale*) type of lizard

ra'mato *a* (*capelli*) copper[-coloured], coppery

'rame *nm* copper; **color ~** copper-coloured

ramifi'care *vi* (*pianta:*) put out branches

ramifi'carsi *vr* (*pianta:*) put out branches; (*strada, fiume, matematica ecc:*) branch; (*teoria:*) ramify, branch

ramificazi'one *nf* ramification

ra'mino *nm* rummy

rammari'carsi *vr* **~ di** regret; (*lamentarsi*) complain (**di** about)

ram'marico *nm* regret

rammen'dare *vt* darn

ram'mendo *nm* darning

rammen'tare *vt* remember; **~ qcsa a qcno** (*richiamare alla memoria*) remind sb of sth

rammen'tarsi *vr* remember

rammol'lire *vt* soften

rammol'lirsi *vr* go soft

rammol'lito, -a *nmf* wimp

'ramo *nm* branch

ramo'scello *nm* twig

'rampa *nf* (*di scale*) flight. **~ d'accesso** slip road. **~ di carico** loading ramp. **~ di lancio** launch[ing] pad

ram'pante *a* (*leone, cavallo*) rampant; **giovane ~** yuppie

rampi'cante *a* climbing ● *nm Bot* creeper

ram'pino *nm* hook; *fig* pretext

ram'pollo *nm hum* brat; (*discendente*) descendant

ram'pone *nm* harpoon; (*per scarpe*) crampon

'rana *nf* frog; (*nel nuoto*) breaststroke; **uomo ~** frogman

ranch *nm inv* ranch

'rancido *a* rancid

'rancio *nm* rations *pl*

ran'core *nm* rancour, resentment; **serbare ~ verso qcno** bear sb a grudge

'randa *nf* mainsail

ran'dagio *a* stray

randel'lata *nf* blow with a club

ran'dello *nm* club

'rango *nm* rank

rannicchi'arsi *vr* huddle up

rannuvola'mento *nm* clouding over

rannuvo'larsi *vr* cloud over

ra'nocchio *nm* frog

ranto'lare *vi* wheeze

'rantolo *nm* wheeze; (*di moribondo*) death-rattle

ra'nuncolo *nm* buttercup

'rapa *nf* turnip

ra'pace *a* rapacious; ‹*uccello*› predatory

rapa'nello *nm* radish

ra'pare *vt* crop

ra'parsi *vr fam* have one's head shaved

'rapida *nf* rapids *pl*

rapida'mente *adv* quickly, rapidly

rapidità *nf* speed

'rapido *a* fast, quick; ‹*guarigione, sviluppo*› rapid ● *nm* (*treno*) express [train]

rapi'mento *nm* (*crimine*) kidnapping

ra'pina *nf* robbery, hold-up *fam;* ~ **a mano armata** armed robbery. ~ **in banca** bank robbery

rapi'nare *vt* rob

rapina'tore *nm* robber. ~ **di banca** bank robber

ra'pire *vt* abduct; (*per riscatto*) kidnap; (*fig: estasiare*) ravish

ra'pito, -a *a* abducted; (*per riscatto*) kidnapped; (*estasiato*) rapt ● *nmf* kidnap victim

rapi|'tore, -'trice *nmf* kidnapper

rappacifi'care *vt* pacify

rappacifi'carsi *vr* be reconciled, make it up

rappacificazi'one *nf* reconciliation

'rapper *nmf inv Mus* rapper

rappez'zare *vt* patch up

rappor'tare *vt* reproduce ‹*disegno*›; (*confrontare*) compare

rap'porto *nm* report; (*connessione*) relation; (*legame*) relationship; *Math, Techn* ratio; **rapporti** *pl* relations, relationship; **essere in buoni rapporti** be on good terms. **rapporti** *pl* **d'affari** business relations. ~ **di amicizia** friendship; **avere un** ~ ~ ~ **con qcno** be friends with sb. ~ **di lavoro** working relationship. ~ **di parentela** family relationship; **aver un** ~ ~ ~ **con qcno** be related to sb. **rapporti** *pl* **prematrimoniali** premarital sex. ~ **prezzo-prestazioni** price/performance ratio. ~ **prezzo-qualità** value for money. **rapporti** *pl* **sessuali** sexual intercourse. ~ **di trasmissione** *Auto* gear

rap'prendersi *vr* set; ‹*latte:*› curdle

rappre'saglia *nf* reprisal

rappresen'tante *nmf* representative. ~ **di classe** class representative. ~ **di commercio** sales representative, [sales] rep *fam.* ~ **sindacale** trade union representative

rappresen'tanza *nf* delegation; *Comm* agency; **spese di** ~ entertainment expenses; **di** ~ ‹*appartamento, macchina*› company

attrib. ~ **esclusiva** sole agency. ~ **legale** legal representation. ~ **proporzionale** proportional representation, PR

rappresen'tare *vt* represent; *Theat* perform

rappresentativa *nf* representatives *pl*

rappresenta'tivo *a* representative

rappresentazi'one *nf* representation; (*spettacolo*) performance

rap'preso *pp di* **rapprendersi**

rapso'dia *nf* rhapsody

'raptus *nm inv* fit of madness

rara'mente *adv* rarely, seldom

rare'fare *vt* rarefy

rare'farsi *vr* rarefy

rare'fatto *a* rarefied

rarità *nf inv* rarity

'raro *a* rare

ra'sare *vt* shave; trim ‹*siepe ecc*›

ra'sarsi *vr* shave

ra'sato *a* shaved

rasa'tura *nf* shaving

raschia'mento *nm Med* curettage

raschi'are *vt* scrape; (*togliere*) scrape off

raschi'arsi *vr* ~ **la gola** clear one's throat

rasen'tare *vt* go close to

ra'sente *prep* very close to

'raso *pp di* **radere** ● *a* smooth; (*colmo*) full to the brim; ‹*barba*› close-cropped; ~ **terra** close to the ground; **un cucchiaio** ~ a level spoonful ● *nm* satin

ra'soio *nm* razor. ~ **elettrico** electric shaver. ~ **a mano libera** cut-throat razor

'raspa *nf* rasp

'raspo *nm* (*di uva*) small bunch

ras'segna *nf* review; (*mostra*) exhibition; (*musicale, cinematografica*) festival; **passare in** ~ review; *Mil* inspect

rasse'gnare *vt* present

rasse'gnarsi *vr* resign oneself

rassegnata'mente *adv* with resignation

rasse'gnato *a* ‹*persona, aria, tono*› resigned

rassegnazi'one *nf* resignation

rassere'nare *vt* clear; *fig* cheer up

rassere'narsi *vr* become clear; *fig* cheer up

rasset'tare *vt* tidy up; (*riparare*) mend

rassicu'rante *a* ‹*persona, parole, presenza*› reassuring

rassicu'rare *vt* reassure

rassicurazi'one *nf* reassurance

rasso'dare *vt* harden; *fig* strengthen

rassomigli'ante *a* similar

rassomigli'anza *nf* resemblance

rassomigli'are *vi* ~ **a** resemble

rastrella'mento *nm* (*di fieno*) raking; (*perlustrazione*) combing

rastrel'lare *vt* rake; (*perlustrare*) comb

rastrelli'era *nf* rack; (*per biciclette*) bicycle rack; (*scolapiatti*) [plate] rack

ra'strello *nm* rake

'rata *nf* instalment; (*di mutuo*) mortgage repayment; **pagare a rate** pay by instalments; **comprare qcsa a rate** buy sth on hire purchase, buy sth on the installment plan *Am*

rate'ale *a* by instalments; **pagamento ~** payment by instalments; **vendita ~** hire purchase

rate'are, rateiz'zare *vt* divide into instalments

ra'tifica *nf Jur* ratification

ratifi'care *vt Jur* ratify

'ratto¹ *nm* (*rapimento*) abduction

'ratto² *nm* (*roditore*) rat. **~ comune** black rat

rattop'pare *vt* patch

rat'toppo *nm* patch

rattrap'pire *vt* make stiff

rattrap'pirsi *vr* become stiff

rattri'stare *vt* sadden

rattri'starsi *vr* become sad

rau'cedine *nf* hoarseness

'rauco *a* hoarse

rava'nello *nm* radish

ravi'oli *nmpl* ravioli *sg*

ravve'dersi *vr* mend one's ways

ravvi'are *vt* tidy ⟨*capelli, stanza*⟩

ravvicina'mento *nm* (*tra persone*) reconciliation; *Pol* rapprochement

ravvici'nare *vt* bring closer; (*riconciliare*) reconcile

ravvici'narsi *vr* be reconciled

ravvi'sare *vt* recognize

ravvi'vare *vt* revive; *fig* brighten up

ravvi'varsi *vr* revive

rav'volgere *vt* roll up

rav'volgersi *vr* wrap oneself up

'rayon *nm* rayon

razio'cinio *nm* rational thought; (*buon senso*) common sense

razio'nale *a* rational

razionalità *nf* (*raziocinio*) rationality; (*di ambiente*) functional nature

razionaliz'zare *vt* rationalize ⟨*programmi, metodi, spazio*⟩

razional'mente *adv* (*con raziocinio*) rationally

raziona'mento *nm* rationing

razio'nare *vt* ration

razi'one *nf* ration

'razza *nf* race; (*di cani ecc*) breed; (*genere*) kind; **che ~ di idiota!** *fam* what an idiot!

raz'zia *nf* raid

razzi'ale *a* racial

raz'zismo *nm* racism

raz'zista *a & nmf* racist

'razzo *nm* rocket. **~ da segnalazione** flare

razzo'lare *vi* ⟨*polli:*⟩ scratch about

re *nm inv* king; (*Mus: chiave, nota*) D. **Re** *pl* **Magi** Wise Men

rea'gente *a & nm* reactant

rea'gire *vi* react

re'ale *a* real; (*di re*) royal

rea'lismo *nm* realism

rea'lista *nmf* realist; (*fautore del re*) royalist

realistica'mente *adv* realistically

rea'listico *a* realistic

realiz'zabile *a* feasible

realiz'zare *vt* (*attuare*) carry out, realize; *Comm* make; score ⟨*gol, canestro*⟩; (*rendersi conto di*) realize

realiz'zarsi *vr* come true; (*nel lavoro ecc*) fulfil oneself

realiz'zato *a* ⟨*persona*⟩ fulfilled

realizzazi'one *nf* realization; (*di sogno, persona*) fulfilment. **~ scenica** production

rea'lizzo *nm* (*vendita*) proceeds *pl*; (*riscossione*) yield

real'mente *adv* really

realtà *nf inv* reality; **in ~** in reality; (*a dire il vero*) actually. **~ virtuale** virtual reality

re'ame *nm* realm

re'ato *nm* crime, criminal offence. **~ minore** minor offence

reattività *nf* reactivity; (*a farmaco*) reaction

reat'tivo *a* reactive

reat'tore *nm* reactor; *Aeron* jet [aircraft]. **~ nucleare** atomic reactor

reazio'nario, -a *a & nmf* reactionary

reazi'one *nf* reaction; **a ~** ⟨*motore, aereo*⟩ jet. **~ a catena** chain reaction. **~ chimica** chemical reaction

'rebus *nm inv* rebus; (*enigma*) puzzle

recapi'tare *vt* deliver

re'capito *nm* address; (*consegna*) delivery; **in caso di mancato ~...** if undelivered.... **~ a domicilio** home delivery. **~ telefonico** contact telephone number

re'care *vt* bear; (*produrre*) cause

re'carsi *vr* go

re'cedere *vi* recede; *fig* give up

recensi'one *nf* review

recen'sire *vt* review

recen'sore *nm* reviewer

re'cente *a* recent; **di ~** recently

recente'mente *adv* recently

re'ception *nf inv* reception [desk]

re'ceptionist *nmf* receptionist

recessi'one *nf* recession

reces'sivo *a* *Biol* recessive; *Econ* recessionary

re'cesso *nm* recess

re'cidere *vt* cut off

reci'diva *nf Jur* recidivism; *Med* relapse; **furto con ~** repeat offence of theft

recidività *nf inv* recidivism

reci'divo, -a *a Med* recurrent ● *nmf* repeat offender, recidivist *fml*; **è ~** *fig* he's lapsed back into his old ways

recin'tare *vt* close off

re'cinto *nm* enclosure; (*per animali*) pen; (*per bambini*) play-pen. **~ delle grida** *Fin* [trading] floor. **~ del peso** (*ippica*) weigh-in room

recinzi'one *nf* (*azione*) enclosure; (*muro*) wall; (*rete*) wire fence; (*cancellata*) railings *pl*

recipi'ente *nm* container

reci'proco *a* reciprocal

re'ciso *pp di* **recidere** ● *a* (*risoluto*) definite

'recita *nf* performance. **~ scolastica** school play

re'cital *nm inv* recital

reci'tare *vt* recite; *Theat* act; play ⟨*ruolo*⟩ ● *vi* act; ~ **a soggetto** improvise

recitazi'one *nf* recitation; *Theat* acting; **scuola di** ~ drama school

recla'mare *vi* protest ● *vt* claim

ré'clame *nf inv* advertising; (*avviso pubblicitario*) advertisement

reclamiz'zare *vt* advertise

re'clamo *nm* complaint; **ufficio reclami** complaints department

recli'nabile *a* reclining; **sedile** ~ reclining seat

recli'nare *vt* tilt ⟨*sedile*⟩; lean ⟨*capo*⟩

reclusi'one *nf* imprisonment

re'cluso, -a *a* secluded ● *nmf* prisoner

'recluta *nf* recruit

recluta'mento *nm* recruitment

reclu'tare *vt* recruit

re'condito *a* secluded; (*intimo*) secret

'record *nm inv* record; **a tempo di** ~ in record time ● *a inv* ⟨*cifra*⟩ record *attrib*

recrimi'nare *vi* recriminate

recriminazi'one *nf* recrimination

recrude'scenza *nf Med* fresh outbreak; *fig* (*di violenza*) renewed outbreak; (*di criminalità*) upsurge

recupe'rare *vt* recover; rehabilitate ⟨*tossicodipendente*⟩; make up ⟨*ore di assenza*⟩; ~ **il tempo perduto** make up for lost time ● *vi* catch up

re'cupero *nm* recovery; (*di tossicodipendenti*) rehabilitation; (*salvataggio*) rescue; **corso di** ~ additional classes *pl*; **materiali di** ~ recycled material; (*che possono essere recuperati*) recyclable material; [**minuti di**] ~ *Sport* injury time; **partita di** ~ rematch. ~ **crediti** debt collection. ~ [**dei**] **dati** data recovery

redargu'ire *vt* rebuke

re'datto *pp di* **redigere**

redat|'tore, -'trice *nmf* editor; (*di testo*) writer. ~ **capo** editor in chief

redazi'one *nf* (*ufficio*) editorial office; (*di testi*) editing

redditività *nf* earning power

reddi'tizio *a* profitable

'reddito *nm* income; **imposta sul** ~ income tax. ~ **complessivo** gross income. ~ **imponibile** taxable income. ~ **non imponibile** non-taxable income. ~ **da lavoro** earned income. **redditi** *pl* **occasionali** casual earnings. ~ **pubblico** government revenue

re'dento *pp di* **redimere**

reden'tore *nm* redeemer

redenzi'one *nf* redemption

re'digere *vt* write; draw up ⟨*documento*⟩

re'dimere *vt* redeem

re'dimersi *vr* redeem oneself

redi'mibile *a* ⟨*titoli*⟩ redeemable

'redine *nf* rein

redin'gote *nf inv* frock-coat; **abito a** ~ fitted button-through dress

'redini *nfpl* reins

redi'vivo *a* restored to life

'reduce *a* ~ **da** back from ● *nmf* survivor

refe'rendum *nm inv* referendum

refe'renza *nf* reference

referenzi'ato *a* with references

re'ferto *nm* report. ~ **medico** medical report

refet'torio *nm* refectory

reflazio'nare *vt Econ* reflate

reflazi'one *nf Econ* reflation

'reflex *nm inv* reflex camera

'refluo *nm* effluent

refrat'tario *a* refractory; **essere** ~ **a** *fig* be insensitive to ⟨*sentimenti*⟩; **sono** ~ **alla matematica** maths are a closed book to me

refrige'rante *a* cooling *attrib*

refrige'rare *vt* refrigerate

refrigerazi'one *nf* refrigeration

refur'tiva *nf* stolen goods *pl*

re'fuso *nm Typ* literal, typo

rega'lare *vt* give

re'gale *a* regal

re'galo *nm* present, gift; **articoli da** ~ gifts ● *a* **confezione** ~ gift set

re'gata *nf* regatta

'reggae *nm inv Mus* reggae

reg'gente *nmf* regent

reg'genza *nf* regency

'reggere *vt* ⟨*sorreggere*⟩ bear; (*tenere in mano*) hold; (*dirigere*) run; (*governare*) govern; *Gram* take ● *vi* (*resistere*) hold out; (*durare*) last; *fig* stand

'reggersi *vr* stand

'reggia *nf* royal palace

reggi'calze *nm inv* suspender belt

reggi'mento *nm* regiment; (*fig: molte persone*) army

re'gia *nf Cinema* direction; *Theat* production

re'gime *nm* regime; (*dieta*) diet; (*di fiume*) rate of flow; **a** ~ **torrentizio** in spate; **a pieno** ~ ⟨*funzionare*⟩ at full speed. ~ **alimentare** diet. ~ **fiscale** tax system. ~ **di giri** (*di motore*) revs per minute, rpm. ~ **militare** military regime. ~ **monetario aureo** gold standard. ~ **di vita** lifestyle

re'gina *nf* queen; **ape** ~ queen bee. ~ **madre** queen mother

'regio *a* royal

regio'nale *a* regional

regiona'lismo *nm* (*parola*) regionalism

regional'mente *adv* regionally

regi'one *nf* region

re'gista *nmf Cinema*, *TV* director; *Theat* producer

regi'strare *vt* register; *Comm* enter; (*incidere su nastro*) tape, record; (*su disco*) record

registra'tore *nm* recorder; (*magnetofono*) tape-recorder. ~ **di cassa** cash register. ~ **a cassette** tape recorder, cassette recorder. ~ **di volo** flight recorder

registrazi'one *nf* registration; *Comm* entry; (*di programma*) recording; **sala di** ~ recording studio. ~ [**dei**] **dati** data capture

re'gistro *nm* register; (*ufficio*) registry. ~ **di**

bordo log. ~ **di cassa** ledger. ~ **di classe** class register. ~ **linguistico** register

re'gnare *vi* reign

'**regno** *nm* kingdom; (*sovranità*) reign. ~ **animale** animal kingdom. **R~ Unito** United Kingdom. ~ **vegetale** plant kingdom

'**regola** *nf* rule; **essere in** ~ be in order; (*persona:*) have one's papers in order; **a ~ d'arte** in a workmanlike fashion

rego'labile *a* (*velocità, luminosità*) adjustable

regola'mento *nm* regulation; *Comm* settlement. ~ **di conti** settling of scores

rego'lare *a* regular ● *vt* regulate; (*ridurre, moderare*) limit; (*sistemare*) settle

regolarità *nf inv* regularity

regolariz'zare *vt* settle (*debito*); regularize (*situazione*)

rego'larsi *vr* (*agire*) act; (*moderarsi*) control oneself

rego'lata *nf* **darsi una** ~ pull oneself together

regola'tore, -'trice *a* **piano** ~ urban development plan ● *nmf* regulator

'**regolo** *nm* ruler. ~ **calcolatore** slide-rule

regre'dire *vi* *Biol, Psych* regress

regressi'one *nf* regression

regres'sivo *a* regressive

re'gresso *nm* decline

reincar'narsi *vr* ~ **in...** be reincarnated as...

reincarnazi'one *nf* reincarnation

reinseri'mento *nm* (*di persona*) reintegration

reinser'irsi *vr* (*in ambiente*) reintegrate

reinte'grare *vt* restore

reinven'tare *vt* reinvent

reinvesti'mento *nm* reinvestment

reinve'stire *vt* reinvest (*soldi*)

reite'rare *vt* reiterate

reiterazi'one *nf* reiteration

re'lais *nm inv* relay

relativa'mente *adv* relatively; ~ **a** as regards

relatività *nf* relativity

rela'tivo *a* relative

rela|'tore, -'trice *nmf* (*in una conferenza*) speaker; (*di tesi*) supervisor

re'lax *nm* relaxation

relazi'one *nf* relation; (*di lavoro ecc*) relationship; (*rapporto amoroso*) [love] affair; (*resoconto*) report; **pubbliche relazioni** *pl* public relations. ~ **extraconiugale** extramarital relationship

rele'gare *vt* relegate

relegazi'one *nf* relegation

religi'one *nf* religion

religi'oso, -a *a* religious ● *nm* monk ● *nf* nun

re'liquia *nf* relic

reliqui'ario *nm* reliquary

re'litto *nm* wreck

re'mainder *nm inv* (*libro*) remainder

re'make *nm inv* remake

re'mare *vi* row

rema|'tore, -'trice *nmf* rower

remini'scenza *nf* reminiscence

remissi'one *nf* remission; (*sottomissione*) submissiveness. ~ **del debito** remission of debt. ~ **di querela** withdrawal of an action

remissiva'mente *adv* submissively

remis'sivo *a* submissive

re'mix *nm inv* *Mus* remix

'**remo** *nm* oar

'**remora** *nf* **senza remore** without hesitation

re'moto *a* remote

remo'vibile *a* removeable

remune'rare *vt* remunerate

remunera'tivo *a* remunerative

remunerazi'one *nf* remuneration

re'nale *a* renal

'**rendere** *vt* (*restituire*) return; (*esprimere*) render; (*fruttare*) yield; (*far diventare*) make

'**rendersi** *vr* become; ~ **conto di qcsa** realize sth; ~ **utile** make oneself useful

rendi'conto *nm* report

rendi'mento *nm* rendering; (*produzione*) yield

'**rendita** *nf* income; (*dello Stato*) revenue; **vivere di** ~ *fig* rest on one's laurels. ~ **vitalizia** life annuity

'**rene** *nm* kidney. ~ **artificiale** kidney machine

'**reni** *nfpl* (*schiena*) back

reni'tente *a* **essere** ~ **a** (*consigli di qcno*) be loth to accept; refuse to obey (*legge*) ● *nm* ~ **alla leva** person who fails to report for military service after being called up

'**renna** *nf* reindeer (*pl inv*); (*pelle*) buckskin

'**Reno** *nm* Rhine

'**reo, -a** *a* guilty ● *nmf* criminal. ~ **confesso** self-confessed criminal

Rep. *abbr* (**repubblica**) Rep.

re'parto *nm* department; *Mil* unit. **reparti** *pl* **d'assalto** *Mil* assault troops. ~ **d'attacco** *Sport* attack. ~ **difensivo** *Sport* defence. ~ **grandi ustionati** *Med* burns unit. ~ **maternità** obstetrics [department]

repel'lente *a* repulsive

repen'taglio *nm* **mettere a** ~ risk

repentina'mente *adv* suddenly

repen'tino *a* sudden

reper'ibile *a* available; **non è** ~ (*perduto*) it's not to be found

reperibilità *nf* availability

repe'rire *vt* trace (*fondi*)

re'perto *nm* ~ **archeologico** find. ~ **giudiziario** exhibit

reper'torio *nm* repertory; (*elenco*) index; **immagini** *pl* **di** ~ archive footage

re'play *nm inv* [instant] replay

'**replica** *nf* reply; (*obiezione*) objection; (*copia*) replica; *Theat* repeat performance

repli'care *vt* reply; *Theat* repeat

repor'tage *nm inv* report

repressi'one *nf* repression

repres'sivo *a* repressive

re'presso *pp di* **reprimere**

re'primere *vt* repress

re'pubblica *nf* republic. **R~ Ceca** Czech Republic. **R~ Dominicana** Dominican Republic. **R~ Federale Tedesca** Federal Republic of Germany. **R~ d'Irlanda** Republic of Ireland. **~ parlamentare** parliamentary republic. **~ Popolare cinese** People's Republic of China. **~ presidenziale** presidential-style republic. **R~ Slovacca** Slovakia

repubbli'cano, -a *a a & nmf* republican

repu'tare *vt* consider

repu'tarsi *vr* consider oneself

reputazi'one *nf* reputation

'requiem *nm inv* requiem

requi'sire *vt* requisition

requi'sito *nm* requirement

requisi'toria *nf (arringa)* closing speech

requisizi'one *nf* requisition

'resa *nf* surrender; *Comm* rendering. **~ dei conti** rendering of accounts. **~ incondizionata** unconditional surrender

re'scindere *vt* cancel

'residence *nm inv* residential hotel

resi'dente *a & nmf* resident

resi'denza *nf* residence; *(soggiorno)* stay

residenzi'ale *a* residential; **zona ~** residential district

re'siduo *a* residual ● *nm* remainder. **residui** *pl* **industriali** industrial waste

'resina *nf* resin

resi'stente *a* resistant; **~ all'acqua** water resistant

resi'stenza *nf* resistance; *(fisica)* stamina; *Electr* resistor; **la ~** the Resistance. **~ passiva** passive resistance. **~ a pubblico ufficiale** resisting arrest

re'sistere *vi* **~ [a]** resist; *(a colpi, scosse)* stand up to; **~ alla pioggia/al vento** be rain-/wind-resistant

'reso *pp di* **rendere**

reso'conto *nm* report

respin'gente *nm* *Rail* buffer

re'spingere *vt* repel; *(rifiutare)* reject; *(bocciare)* fail

re'spinto *pp di* **respingere**

respi'rare *vt/i* breathe

respira'tore *nm* respirator; **~ [a tubo]** snorkel

respira'torio *a* respiratory

respirazi'one *nf* breathing; *Med* respiration. **~ artificiale** artificial respiration. **~ bocca a bocca** mouth-to-mouth resuscitation, kiss of life

re'spiro *nm* breath; *(il respirare)* breathing; *fig* respite. **~ di sollievo** sigh of relief

respon'sabile *a* responsible (**di** for); *Jur* liable ● *nmf* person responsible. **~ della produzione** production manager

responsabilità *nf inv* responsibility; *Jur* liability. **~ civile** *Jur* civil liability. **~ limitata** limited liability. **~ penale** criminal liability

responsabiliz'zare *vt* give responsibility to *(dipendente)*; give a sense of responsibility to *(gente)*

responsabil'mente *adv* responsibly

re'sponso *nm* response

'ressa *nf* crowd

re'stante *a* remaining ● *nm* remainder

re'stare *vi* = **rimanere**

restau'rare *vt* restore

restaura|'tore, -'trice *nmf* restorer

restaurazi'one *nf* restoration

re'stauro *nm (riparazione)* repair

re'stio *a* restive; **~ a** reluctant to

restitu'ibile *a* returnable

restitu'ire *vt* return; *(reintegrare)* restore

restituzi'one *nf* return; *Jur* restitution

'resto *nm* rest, remainder; *(saldo)* balance; *(denaro)* change; **resti** *pl (avanzi)* remains; **del ~** besides

re'stringere *vt* contract; take in *(vestiti)*; *(limitare)* restrict; shrink *(stoffa)*

re'stringersi *vr* contract; *(farsi più vicini)* close up; *(stoffa:)* shrink

restringi'mento *nm (di tessuto)* shrinkage

restrit'tivo *a* restrictive

restrizi'one *nf* restriction

resurrezi'one *nf* resurrection

resusci'tare *vt* revive; resuscitate *(moribondo)* ● *vi (Cristo:)* rise again; *fig* revive

re'taggio *nm* hangover

re'tata *nf* round-up

'rete *nf* net; *(sistema)* network; *(televisiva)* channel; *(in calcio, hockey)* goal; *fig* trap; *(per la spesa)* string bag. **~ commutata pubblica** *Teleph* switched public network. **~ di distribuzione** *Comm* distribution network. **~ locale** *Comput* local [area] network, LAN. **~ di protezione** *(per acrobata)* safety net. **~ stradale** road network. **~ telematica** communications network. **~ televisiva** television channel

reti'cente *a* reticent

reti'cenza *nf* reticence

retico'lato *nm* grid; *(rete metallica)* wire netting

re'ticolo *nm* network. **~ geografico** grid

re'tina *nf (per capelli)* hair net

'retina *nf Anat* retina

re'tino *nm* net

retorica'mente *adv* rhetorically

re'torico, -a *a* rhetorical; **domanda retorica** rhetorical question; **figura retorica** figure of speech ● *nf* rhetoric

re'trattile *a (punta:)* retractable

retribu'ire *vt* remunerate

retribu'tivo *a* salary *attrib*

retribuzi'one *nf* remuneration

'retro *adv* behind; **vedi ~** see over ● *nm inv* back. **~ di copertina** outside back cover

retroat'tivo *a* retroactive

retrobot'tega *nm inv* back shop

retro'cedere *vi* retreat ● *vt Mil* demote; *Sport* relegate

retrocessi'one *nf Sport* relegation

retroda'tare *vt* backdate

retro'fit *nm inv Auto* retrofitted catalytic converter

re'trogrado *a* retrograde; *fig* old-fashioned; *Pol* reactionary

retrogu'ardia *nf Mil* rearguard

retro'gusto *nm* after-taste

retro'marcia *nf* reverse [gear]

retro'scena *nm inv Theat* backstage; **i ~** *fig* the real story

retrospettiva'mente *adv* retrospectively

retrospet'tivo *a* retrospective

retro'stante *a* **il palazzo ~** the building behind

retro'via *nf Mil* area behind the front lines

retro'virus *nm inv* retrovirus

retrovi'sore *nm* rear-view mirror

'retta¹ *nf Math* straight line; (*di collegio, pensionato*) fee

'retta² *nf* **dar ~ a qcno** take sb's advice

rettango'lare *a* rectangular

ret'tangolo *a* right-angled ● *nm* rectangle

retti'fica *nf* rectification

rettifi'care *vt* rectify

'rettile *nm* reptile

retti'lineo *a* rectilinear; (*retto*) upright ● *nm Sport* back straight

retti'tudine *nf* rectitude

'retto *pp di* **reggere** ● *a* straight; *fig* upright; (*giusto*) correct; **angolo ~** right angle

'retto *nm* rectum

ret'tore *nm Relig* rector; *Univ* chancellor

reu'matico *a* rheumatic

reuma'tismi *nmpl* rheumatism

reve'rendo *a* reverend

rever'sibile *a* reversible

revisio'nare *vt* revise; *Comm* audit; *Auto* overhaul

revisi'one *nf* revision; *Comm* audit; *Auto* overhaul. **~ di bilancio** audit. **~ di bozze** proof-reading. **~ dello stipendio** salary review

revisio'nismo *nm Pol* revisionism

revisio'nista *a* ⟨*politica*⟩ revisionist

revi'sore *nm* (*di conti*) auditor; (*di bozze*) proof-reader; (*di traduzioni*) revisor. **~ di bozze** proof-reader. **~ dei conti** auditor

re'vival *nm inv* revival

'revoca *nf* repeal

revo'care *vt* repeal

revolve'rata *nf* revolver shot

rhythm and blues *nm* rhythm and blues, R & B

riabbas'sare *vt* lower again

riabbas'sarsi *vr* ⟨*acque:*⟩ recede; ⟨*temperatura:*⟩ fall again

riabbotto'nare *vt* button up again

riabbracci'are *vt* (*abbracciare di nuovo*) embrace again; (*fig: rivedere*) see again

riabili'tare *vt* rehabilitate

riabilitazi'one *nf* rehabilitation; **centro di ~** rehabilitation centre

riabitu'are *vt* **~ qcno a qcsa** reaccustom sb to sth, get sb used to sth again

riabitu'arsi *vr* **~ a qcsa** get used to sth again, reaccustom oneself to sth

riac'cendere *vt* switch on again ⟨*luce, tv*⟩;

rekindle, revive ⟨*interesse, passione*⟩; rekindle ⟨*fuoco*⟩

riac'cendersi *vr* ⟨*luce:*⟩ come back on; ⟨*interesse, passione:*⟩ rekindle, revive

riaccensi'one *nf* **la continua ~** continual switching on and off

riaccer'tare *vt* reassess

riacqui'stare *vt* buy back; regain ⟨*libertà, prestigio*⟩; recover ⟨*vista, udito*⟩

riacutiz'zarsi *vr* get worse again

riadatta'mento *nm* readjustment

riadat'tare *vt* convert ⟨*stanza*⟩; alter ⟨*indumento*⟩

riadat'tarsi *vr* readjust

riaddormen'tare *vt* get [back] to sleep again

riaddormen'tarsi *vr* fall asleep again

riadope'rare *vt* reuse

riaffacci'arsi *vr* (*alla finestra*) appear again; ⟨*idea:*⟩ surface again

riaffer'mare *vt* reaffirm

riaffon'dare *vi* sink again

riaffron'tare *vt* deal with again ⟨*situazione*⟩; take up again ⟨*argomento*⟩

riagganci'are *vt* replace ⟨*ricevitore*⟩; **~ la cornetta** hang up ● *vi* hang up

riaggre'garsi *vr* regroup

riallac'ciare *vt* refasten; reconnect ⟨*corrente*⟩; renew ⟨*amicizia*⟩

riallar'gare *vt* widen again ⟨*tunnel, strada*⟩

riallinea'mento *nm* realignment

rialline'are *vt* realign

rialloggi'are *vt* rehouse

rial'zare *vt* raise ● *vi* rise

rial'zarsi *vr* get up again

rial'zato *a* **piano ~** mezzanine

ri'alzo *nm* rise; **al ~** *Fin* bullish

ria'mare *vt* **~ qcno** reciprocate sb's love, love sb back

riamma'larsi *vr* fall ill again

riam'mettere *vt* readmit ⟨*socio, studente*⟩

rian'dare *vi* return

riani'mare *vt Med* resuscitate; (*ridare forza a*) revive; (*ridare coraggio a*) cheer up

riani'marsi *vr* regain consciousness; (*riprendere forza*) revive; (*riprendere coraggio*) cheer up

rianimazi'one *nf* intensive care [unit]; **centro di ~** intensive care unit

rianno'dare *vt* retie ⟨*filo*⟩; renew ⟨*rapporti*⟩

riaper'tura *nf* reopening

riappa'rire *vi* reappear

riap'pendere *vt* replace ⟨*cornetta*⟩; **mi ha riappeso il telefono in faccia** he hung up on me, he slammed the phone down on me

riappiso'larsi *vr* doze off again

riappropri'arsi *vr* **~ di** take back

ria'prire *vt* reopen

ria'prirsi *vr* reopen

ri'armo *nm* rearmament

riascol'tare *vt* listen to again

riasse'gnare *vt* reallocate

riassicu'rare *vt* reinsure

riassicurazi'one *nf* reinsurance

riassorbi'mento *nm* reabsorption

riassor'bire *vt* reabsorb

rias'sumere *vt* re-employ, take on again ⟨*impiegato*⟩; ⟨*ricapitolare*⟩ resume

riassu'mibile *a* ⟨*riepilogabile*⟩ which can be summarized, summarizable

riassun'tivo *a* summarizing

rias'sunto *pp di* **riassumere** ● *nm* summary

riattac'care *vt* ~ **il telefono** hang up ● *vi* ⟨*al telefono*⟩ hang up

riatti'vare *vt* reactivate ⟨*processo*⟩; reintroduce, bring back ⟨*servizio*⟩; start up again, restart ⟨*congegno*⟩; stimulate ⟨*circolazione sanguigna*⟩

ria'vere *vt* get back; regain ⟨*salute, vista*⟩

ria'versi *vr* recover

riavvicina'mento *nm* ⟨*tra persone*⟩ reconciliation; ⟨*tra paesi*⟩ rapprochement

riavvici'nare *vt fig* reconcile ⟨*paesi, persone*⟩

riavvici'narsi *vr* ⟨*riconciliarsi*⟩ be reconciled, make it up *fam*

riav'volgere *vt* rewind

riba'dire *vt* ⟨*confermare*⟩ reaffirm

ri'balta *nf* flap; *Theat* footlights *pl*; *fig* limelight

ribal'tabile *a* tip-up

ribal'tare *vt/i* tip over; *Naut* capsize

ribal'tarsi *vr* tip over; *Naut* capsize

ribas'sare *vt* lower ● *vi* fall

ribas'sato *a* reduced

ri'basso *nm* fall; ⟨*sconto*⟩ discount

ri'battere *vt* ⟨*a macchina*⟩ retype; ⟨*controbattere*⟩ deny ● *vi* answer back

ribattez'zare *vt* rename

ribel'larsi *vr* rebel

ri'belle *a* rebellious ● *nmf* rebel

ribelli'one *nf* rebellion

'ribes *nm inv* ⟨*rosso*⟩ redcurrant; ⟨*nero*⟩ blackcurrant

ribol'lire *vi* ⟨*fermentare*⟩ ferment; *fig* seethe

ri'brezzo *nm* disgust; **far** ~ **a** disgust

ribut'tante *a* repugnant

ribut'tare *vt* ⟨*buttare di nuovo*⟩ throw back

rica'dere *vi* fall back; ⟨*nel peccato ecc*⟩ lapse; ⟨*pendere*⟩ hang [down]; ~ **su** ⟨*riversarsi*⟩ fall on

rica'duta *nf* relapse; **avere una** ~ to have a relapse

rical'care *vt* trace

ricalci'trante *a* recalcitrant

ricalco'lare *vt* recalculate

rica'mare *vt* embroider

rica'mato *a* embroidered

ri'cambi *nmpl* spare parts

ricambi'are *vt* return; reciprocate ⟨*sentimento*⟩; ~ **qcsa a qcno** repay sb for sth

ri'cambio *nm* replacement; *Biol* metabolism; **pezzo di** ~ spare [part]

ri'camo *nm* embroidery

ricandi'dare *vt* ⟨*a elezioni*⟩ put forward as a candidate again

ricandi'darsi *vr* ⟨*a elezioni*⟩ stand again

ricapito'lare *vt* sum up; **ricapitoliamo** let's recap

ricapitolazi'one *nf* summary, recap *fam*

ri'carica *nf* ⟨*di sveglia*⟩ winder; ⟨*di batteria*⟩ recharging; ⟨*di penna*⟩ refill; ⟨*di fucile*⟩ reloading

ricari'care *vt* reload ⟨*macchina fotografica, fucile, camion*⟩; recharge ⟨*batteria*⟩; *Comput* reboot; rewind ⟨*orologio*⟩

ricat'tare *vt* blackmail

ricatta|'tore, -'trice *nmf* blackmailer

ricatta'torio *a* blackmail *attrib*

ri'catto *nm* blackmail. ~ **morale** moral blackmail, emotional blackmail

rica'vare *vt* get; ⟨*ottenere*⟩ obtain; ⟨*dedurre*⟩ draw

rica'vato *nm* proceeds *pl*

ri'cavo *nm* proceeds *pl*

'ricca *nf* rich woman

ricca'mente *adv* lavishly

ric'chezza *nf* wealth; *fig* richness; **ricchezze** *pl* riches

'riccio *a* curly ● *nm* curl; ⟨*animale*⟩ hedgehog. ~ **di mare** sea-urchin

'ricciolo *nm* curl

riccio'luto *a* curly

'ricco *a* rich. ~ **sfondato** *fam* filthy rich ● *nm* rich man

ri'cerca *nf* search; ⟨*indagine*⟩ investigation; ⟨*scientifica*⟩ research; *Sch* project. ~ **sul campo** field work. ~ **di mercato** market research. ~ **operativa** operational research. ~ **scientifica** scientific research

ricer'care *vt* search for; ⟨*fare ricerche su*⟩ research

ricer'cata *nf* wanted woman

ricercata'mente *adv* ⟨*vestire*⟩ with refinement; ⟨*parlare*⟩ in a refined way

ricerca'tezza *nf* refinement

ricer'cato *a* sought-after; ⟨*raffinato*⟩ refined ● *nm* ⟨*dalla polizia*⟩ wanted man

ricerca|'tore, -'trice *nmf* researcher

ricetrasmit'tente *nf* transceiver

ri'cetta *nf Culin* recipe; *Med* prescription

ricet'tacolo *nm* receptacle

ricet'tario *nm* ⟨*di cucina*⟩ recipe book; ⟨*di medico*⟩ prescription pad

ricetta|'tore, -'trice *nmf* receiver of stolen goods, fence *fam*

ricettazi'one *nf* receiving [stolen goods]

rice'vente *a* ⟨*apparecchio, stazione*⟩ receiving ● *nmf* receiver

ri'cevere *vt* receive; ⟨*dare il benvenuto*⟩ welcome; ⟨*di albergo*⟩ accommodate

ricevi'mento *nm* receiving; ⟨*accoglienza*⟩ welcome; ⟨*trattenimento*⟩ reception

ricevi'tore *nm* receiver. ~ **delle imposte** tax man. ~ **del lotto** lottery ticket agent

ricevito'ria *nf* ~ **delle imposte** ≈ Inland Revenue. ~ **del lotto** *agency authorized to sell lottery tickets*

rice'vuta *nf* receipt. ~ **doganale** docket. ~ **fiscale** tax receipt. ~ **di ritorno** acknowledgement of receipt. ~ **di versamento** receipt ⟨*given for bills etc paid at the Post Office*⟩

rice'vuto *int* roger

ricezi'one *nf Radio, TV* reception

richia'mare *vt* (*al telefono*) call back; (*far tornare*) recall; (*rimproverare*) rebuke; (*attirare*) draw; **~ alla mente** call to mind

richi'amo *nm* recall; (*attrazione*) call

richie'dente *nmf* applicant

richi'edere *vt* ask for; (*di nuovo*) ask again for; **~ a qcno di fare qcsa** ask *o* request sb to do sth

richi'esta *nf* request; *Comm* demand. **~ di indennizzo** claim for damages

richi'esto *a* sought-after

ri'chiudere *vt* shut again, close again

ri'chiudersi *vr* ⟨*ferita:*⟩ heal; ⟨*porta:*⟩ shut again, close again

rici'clabile *a* recyclable

rici'claggio *nm* recycling; (*di denaro*) laundering

rici'clare *vt* recycle

rici'clarsi *vr* retrain; (*cambiare lavoro*) change one's line of work

'ricino *nm* **olio di ~** castor oil

ricogni'tore *nm* reconnaissance plane

ricognizi'one *nf Mil* reconnaissance

ricolle'gare *vt* (*collegare di nuovo*) reconnect

ricolle'garsi *vr* **~ a** ⟨*evento, fatto:*⟩ relate to, tie up with

ricol'mare *vt* fill to the brim

ri'colmo *a* full

ricominci'are *vt/i* start again; **~ da capo** start all over again

ricompa'rire *vi* reappear

ricom'parsa *nf* reappearance

ricom'pensa *nf* reward

ricompen'sare *vt* reward

ricom'porre *vt* (*riscrivere*) rewrite; (*ricostruire*) reform; *Typ* reset

ricom'porsi *vr* regain one's composure

riconcili'are *vt* reconcile

riconcili'arsi *vr* be reconciled

riconciliazi'one *nf* reconciliation

riconfer'mare *vt* reappoint

ricongi'ungere *vt* reunite

ricongi'ungersi *vr* become reunited

ricono'scente *a* grateful

ricono'scenza *nf* gratitude

rico'noscere *vt* recognize; (*ammettere*) acknowledge

riconosci'mento *nm* recognition; (*ammissione*) acknowledgement; (*per la polizia*) identification

riconosci'uto *a* recognized

ricon'quista *nf* reconquest

riconqui'stare *vt Mil* reconquer

ricon'segna *nf* return

riconse'gnare *vt* return

riconside'rare *vt* rethink

ricontrol'lare *vt* double-check

riconversi'one *nf Econ* restructuring

ricopi'are *vt* copy again

rico'prire *vt* re-cover; (*rivestire*) coat; (*di insulti*) shower (**di** with); hold ⟨*carica*⟩; **~ qcno di attenzioni** lavish attention on sb

ricor'dare *vt* remember; (*richiamare alla memoria*) recall; (*far ricordare*) remind; (*rassomigliare*) look like

ricor'darsi *vr* **~ [di]** remember; **~ di fare qcsa** remember to do sth

ri'cordo *nm* memory; (*oggetto*) memento; (*di viaggio*) souvenir; **ricordi** *pl* (*memorie*) memoirs. **~ di famiglia** family heirloom

ricor'reggere *vt* correct again

ricor'rente *a* recurrent

ricor'renza *nf* recurrence; (*anniversario*) anniversary

ri'correre *vi* recur; (*accadere*) occur; ⟨*data:*⟩ fall; **~ a** have recourse to; (*rivolgersi a*) turn to

ri'corso *pp di* **ricorrere** ● *nm* recourse; *Jur* appeal

ricostitu'ente *nm* tonic

ricostitu'ire *vt* re-establish

ricostru'ire *vt* reconstruct

ricostruzi'one *nf* reconstruction

ricove'rare *vt* give shelter to; **~ in ospedale** admit to hospital, hospitalize

ricove'rato, -a *nmf* hospital patient

ri'covero *nm* shelter; (*ospizio*) home

ricre'are *vt* re-create; (*ristorare*) restore

ricre'arsi *vr* amuse oneself

ricrea'tivo *a* recreational

ricreazi'one *nf* recreation; *Sch* break

ri'credersi *vr* change one's mind

ri'crescere *vi* grow again

ricu'cire *vt* sew up; stitch up ⟨*ferita*⟩

ricupe'rare, ri'cupero = **recuperare, recupero**

ri'curvo *a* bent

ricu'sare *vt* refuse

ridacchi'are *vi* giggle

ri'dare *vt* give back, return

rida'rella *nf* giggles *pl*

ridefi'nire *vt* redefine

ri'dente *a* (*piacevole*) pleasant

'ridere *vi* laugh; **~ di** (*deridere*) laugh at

ride'stare *vt* reawaken ⟨*ricordo, sentimento*⟩

ri'detto *pp di* **ridire**

ridicoliz'zare *vt* ridicule

ri'dicolo *a* ridiculous

ridimensiona'mento *nm* restructuring

ridimensio'nare *vt* restructure ⟨*azienda*⟩; *fig* get into perspective

ridi'pingere *vt* repaint

ri'dire *vt* repeat; **trova sempre da ~** he's always finding fault; **hai qualcosa da ~?** do you have something to say?; **se non hai niente da ~,...** if you've no objection...

ridi'scendere *vi* go back down

ridistribu'ire *vt* redistribute

ridistribuzi'one *nf* redistribution

ridon'dante *a* redundant

ri'dosso: a ~ di *adv* behind

ri'dotto *pp di* **ridurre** ● *a* **essere ~ a uno straccio** be worn out ● *nm Theat* foyer ● *a* reduced

ri'durre *vt* reduce

ri'dursi vr diminish; **~ a fare qcsa** be reduced to doing sth; **~ a** ⟨problema:⟩ come down to

ridut'tivo a reductive

ridut'tore nm Electr adaptor

riduzi'one nf reduction; ⟨per cinema, teatro⟩ adaptation. **~ cinematografica** film adaptation. **~ della pena** reduced sentence. **~ teatrale** adaptation for the theatre

riedifi'care vt rebuild

rieducazi'one nf ⟨di malato⟩ rehabilitation

rie'leggere vt re-elect

rielezi'one nf re-election

rie'mergere vi resurface

riem'pire vt fill [up]; fill in ⟨moduli ecc⟩

riem'pirsi vr fill [up]

riempi'tivo a filling ● nm filler

rien'tranza nf recess

rien'trare vi go/come back in; ⟨tornare⟩ return; ⟨piegare indentro⟩ recede; **~ in** ⟨far parte⟩ fall within

ri'entro nm return; ⟨di astronave⟩ re-entry

riepilo'gare vt recapitulate

rie'pilogo nm summing-up

rie'same nm reassessment

riesami'nare vt reappraise

ri'essere vi **ci risiamo!** here we go again!

riesu'mare vt exhume

rievo'care vt ⟨commemorare⟩ commemorate; recall ⟨passato⟩

rievocazi'one nf ⟨commemorazione⟩ commemoration; ⟨ricordo⟩ recollection

rifaci'mento nm remake

ri'fare vt do again; ⟨creare⟩ make again; ⟨riparare⟩ repair; ⟨imitare⟩ imitate; make ⟨letto⟩

ri'farsi vr ⟨rimettersi⟩ recover; ⟨vendicarsi⟩ get even; **~ una vita/carriera** make a new life/career for oneself; **~ il trucco** touch up one's makeup; **~ di** make up for

ri'fatto pp di **rifare**

riferi'mento nm reference

rife'rire vt report; **~ a** attribute to ● vi make a report

rife'rirsi vr **~ a** refer to

rifi'lare vt ⟨tagliare a filo⟩ trim; ⟨fam: affibbiare⟩ saddle

rifi'nire vt finish off

rifini'tura nf finish

rifio'rire vi blossom again; fig flourish again

rifiu'tare vt refuse; **~ di fare qcsa** refuse to do sth

rifi'uto nm refusal; **acque** pl **di ~** waste water; **rifiuti** pl ⟨immondizie⟩ rubbish. **rifiuti** pl **industriali** industrial waste. **rifiuti** pl **urbani** urban waste

riflessi'one nf reflection; ⟨osservazione⟩ remark

rifles'sivo a thoughtful; Gram reflexive

ri'flesso pp di **riflettere** ● nm ⟨luce⟩ reflection; Med reflex; **per ~** indirectly

ri'flettere vt reflect ● vi think ⟨su about⟩

ri'flettersi vr be reflected

riflet'tore nm reflector; ⟨proiettore⟩ searchlight

ri'flusso nm ebb

rifocil'lare vt restore

rifocil'larsi vr liter, hum take some refreshment

rifondazi'one nf refounding; **R~ Comunista** diehard Communist party

ri'fondere vt ⟨rimborsare⟩ refund

ri'forma nf reform; Relig reformation; Mil exemption on medical grounds

rifor'mare vt re-form; ⟨migliorare⟩ reform; Mil declare unfit for military service

rifor'mato a ⟨chiesa⟩ Reformed; ⟨recluta, soldato⟩ unfit for military service

riforma'tore, -'trice nmf reformer

riforma'torio nm reformatory

riformat'tare vt Comput reformat

rifor'mista a & nmf reformist

riformu'lare vt recast

riforni'mento nm supply; ⟨scorta⟩ stock; ⟨di combustibile⟩ refuelling; **stazione di ~** petrol station

rifor'nire vt restock; **~ di** provide with

rifor'nirsi vr restock, stock up ⟨**di** with⟩

ri'frangere vt refract

ri'fratto pp di **rifrangere**

rifrazi'one nf refraction

rifug'gire vt shun ⟨gloria, celebrità⟩ ● vi escape again; **~ da** fig shun

rifugi'arsi vr take refuge

rifugi'ato, -a nmf refugee

ri'fugio nm shelter; ⟨nascondiglio⟩ hideaway. **~ antiaereo** bomb shelter. **~ antiatomico** fallout shelter

'riga nf line; ⟨fila⟩ row; ⟨striscia⟩ stripe; ⟨scriminatura⟩ parting; ⟨regolo⟩ rule; **a righe** ⟨stoffa⟩ striped; ⟨quaderno⟩ ruled; **mettersi in ~** line up

ri'gaglie nfpl ⟨interiora⟩ giblets

ri'gagnolo nm rivulet

ri'gare vt rule ⟨foglio⟩ ● vi **~ dritto** behave well

riga'toni nmpl small ridged pasta tubes

rigatti'ere nm junk dealer

rigene'rante a regenerative

rigene'rare vt regenerate

riget'tare vt ⟨gettare indietro⟩ throw back; ⟨respingere⟩ reject; ⟨vomitare⟩ throw up

ri'getto nm rejection

ri'ghello nm ruler

rigida'mente adv rigidly

rigidità nf rigidity; ⟨di clima⟩ severity; ⟨severità⟩ strictness. **~ cadaverica** rigor mortis

'rigido a rigid; ⟨freddo⟩ severe; ⟨severo⟩ strict

rigi'rare vt turn again; ⟨ripercorrere⟩ go round; fig twist ⟨argomentazione⟩ ● vi walk about

rigi'rarsi vr turn round; ⟨nel letto⟩ turn over

ri'giro nm ⟨imbroglio⟩ trick

'rigo nm line; Mus staff

ri'goglio nm bloom

rigogliosa'mente adv luxuriantly

rigogli'oso a luxuriant

rigonfia'mento nm swelling

rigonfi'are vt reinflate

ri'gonfio a swollen

ri'gore nm rigours pl; **a rigor di logica** strictly speaking; **calcio di ~** penalty [kick]; **area di ~** penalty area; **essere di ~** be compulsory

rigorosa'mente adv ⟨giudicare⟩ severely; ⟨seguire istruzioni⟩ exactly; **vestito ~ in giacca e cravatta** wearing the obligatory jacket and tie

rigo'roso a ⟨severo⟩ strict; ⟨scrupoloso⟩ rigorous

rigover'nare vt wash up

riguada'gnare vt regain, win back ⟨stima⟩; win more ⟨tempo, punti⟩

riguar'dare vt look at again; ⟨considerare⟩ regard; ⟨concernere⟩ concern; **per quanto riguarda...** with regard to...

riguar'darsi vr take care of oneself

rigu'ardo nm care; ⟨considerazione⟩ consideration; **nei riguardi di** towards; **~ a** with regard to

rigurgi'tante a **~ di** swarming with

rigurgi'tare vt regurgitate ● vi **~ di** fig be swarming with

ri'gurgito nm regurgitation; ⟨di rabbia⟩ fit; ⟨di razzismo⟩ resurgence

rilanci'are vt throw back ⟨palla⟩; ⟨di nuovo⟩ throw again; increase ⟨offerta⟩; revive ⟨moda⟩; relaunch ⟨prodotto⟩ ● vi ⟨a carte⟩ raise the stakes; **rilancio di dieci** I'll raise you ten

ri'lancio nm ⟨di offerta⟩ increase; ⟨di prodotto⟩ re-launch

rilasci'are vt ⟨concedere⟩ grant; ⟨liberare⟩ release; issue ⟨documento⟩

rilasci'arsi vr relax

ri'lascio nm release; ⟨di documento⟩ issue

rilassa'mento nm relaxation. **~ cutaneo** sagging of the skin

rilas'sare vt relax

rilas'sarsi vr relax

rilas'sato a relaxed

rile'gare vt bind ⟨libro⟩

rile'gato a bound

rilega'tore, -'trice nmf bookbinder

rilega'tura nf binding

ri'leggere vt reread

ri'lento: a ~ adv slowly

rileva'mento nm survey; Comm buyout. **~ dirigenti** management buyout, MBO

rile'vante a considerable

rile'vanza nf significance

rile'vare vt ⟨trarre⟩ get; ⟨mettere in evidenza⟩ point out; ⟨notare⟩ notice; ⟨topografia⟩ survey; Comm take over; Mil relieve

rilevazi'one nf ⟨statistica⟩ survey

rili'evo nm relief; Geog elevation; ⟨topografia⟩ survey; ⟨importanza⟩ importance; ⟨osservazione⟩ remark; **mettere in ~ qcsa** point sth out

rilut'tante a reluctant

rilut'tanza nf reluctance

'rima nf rhyme; **far ~ con qcsa** rhyme with sth; **rispondere a qcno per le rime** give sb

as good as one gets. **~ alternata** alternate rhyme. **~ baciata** rhyming couplet

riman'dare vt ⟨posporre⟩ postpone; ⟨mandare indietro⟩ send back; ⟨mandare di nuovo⟩ send again; ⟨far ridare un esame⟩ make resit an examination

ri'mando nm return; ⟨in un libro⟩ cross-reference

rimaneggia'mento nm rejig

rimaneggi'are vt rejig, recast

rima'nente a remaining ● nm remainder

rima'nenza nf remainder; **rimanenze** pl remnants. **rimanenze** pl **di magazzino** unsold stock

rima'nere vi stay, remain; ⟨essere d'avanzo⟩ be left; ⟨venirsi a trovare⟩ be; ⟨restare stupito⟩ be astonished; ⟨restare d'accordo⟩ agree; **~ senza parole** be speechless

rimangi'are vt ⟨mangiare di nuovo⟩ have again, eat again

rimangi'arsi vr **~ la parola** break one's promise

rimar'care vt remark

rimar'chevole a remarkable

ri'mare vt/i rhyme

rimargi'nare vt heal

rimargi'narsi vr heal

ri'masto pp di **rimanere**

rima'sugli nmpl ⟨di cibo⟩ leftovers

rimbal'zare vi rebound; ⟨proiettile:⟩ ricochet; **far ~** bounce

rim'balzo nm rebound; ⟨di proiettile⟩ ricochet

rimbam'bire vi be in one's dotage ● vt stun

rimbam'bito a in one's dotage

rimbec'care vi retort

rimbecil'lire vt make brain-dead

rimbecil'lito a ⟨stupido⟩ brain-dead; ⟨frastornato⟩ stunned

rimboc'care vt turn up; roll up ⟨maniche⟩; tuck in ⟨coperte⟩; **~ le coperte a qcno** tuck sb into bed

rimboc'carsi vr **~ le maniche** roll up one's sleeves

rimbom'bare vi boom, resound

rim'bombo nm boom

rimbor'sare vt reimburse, repay

rim'borso nm reimbursement, repayment. **~ d'imposta** tax rebate. **~ spese** reimbursement of expenses

rimboschi'mento nm reafforestation Br, reforestation

rim'brotto nm reproach

rimedi'abile a ⟨errore⟩ which can be remedied

rimedi'are vi **~ a** remedy; make up for ⟨errore⟩; ⟨procurare⟩ scrape up

ri'medio nm remedy

rimesco'lare vt mix [up]; shuffle ⟨carte⟩; ⟨rivangare⟩ rake up; **mi fa ~ il sangue** it makes my blood boil

rimesco'lio nm ⟨turbamento⟩ shock

ri'messa nf ⟨locale per veicoli⟩ garage; ⟨per aerei⟩ hangar; ⟨per autobus⟩ depot; ⟨di denaro⟩

remittance; (*di merci*) consignment. **~ laterale** *Sport* throw-in

ri'messo *pp di* **rimettere**

rime'stare *vt* stir well

ri'mettere *vt* (*a posto*) put back; (*restituire*) return; (*affidare*) entrust; (*perdonare*) remit; (*rimandare*) put off; (*vomitare*) bring up; **~ in gioco** (*nel calcio*) throw in; **rimetterci** (*fam: perdere*) lose [out]

ri'mettersi *vr* (*ristabilirsi*) recover; ‹*tempo:*› clear up; **~ a** start again

'rimmel[R] *nm inv* mascara

rimoder'nare *vt* modernize

ri'monta *nf Sport* recovery

rimon'tare *vt* (*risalire*) go up; *Mech* reassemble ● *vi* remount; **~ a** (*risalire*) go back to

rimorchi'are *vt* tow; *fam* pick up ‹*ragazza*›

rimorchia'tore *nm* tug[boat]

ri'morchio *nm* tow; (*veicolo*) trailer

ri'mordere *vt* **mi rimorde la coscienza** *fig* it's preying on my conscience

ri'morso *nm* remorse

rimo'stranza *nf* complaint

rimo'vibile *a* removable

rimozi'one *nf* removal; (*da un incarico*) dismissal. **~ forzata** *illegally parked vehicles removed at owner's expense*

rimpagi'nare *vt* regret

rim'pallo *nm* bounce

rim'pasto *nm Pol* reshuffle

rimpatri'are *vt* repatriate ● *vi* return home

rimpatri'ata *nf* reunion

rim'patrio *nm* repatriation

rim'piangere *vt* regret

rimpiangi'mento *pp di* **rimpiangere** ● *nm* regret

rimpiat'tino *nm* hide-and-seek

rimpiaz'zare *vt* replace

rimpi'azzo *nm* replacement

rimpiccioli'mento *nm* shrinkage

rimpiccio'lire *vt* make smaller ● *vi* become smaller

rimpinz'are *vt* **~ di** stuff with

rimpin'zarsi *vr* stuff oneself

rimpol'pare *vt* (*ingrassare*) fatten up; *fig* pad out ‹*scritto*›

rimprove'rare *vt* reproach; **~ qcsa a qcno** reproach sb for sth

rim'provero *nm* reproach

rimugi'nare *vt* rummage; *fig* **~ su** brood over

rimune'rare *vt* remunerate

rimunera'tivo *a* remunerative

rimunerazi'one *nf* remuneration

ri'muovere *vt* remove

ri'nascere *vi* be reborn, be born again

rinascimen'tale *a* Renaissance

Rinasci'mento *nm* Renaissance

ri'nascita *nf* rebirth

rincal'zare *vt* (*sostenere*) support; (*rimboccare*) tuck in

rin'calzo *nm* support; **rincalzi** *pl Mil* reserves

rincantucci'arsi *vr* hide oneself away in a corner

rinca'rare *vt* increase the price of ● *vi* become more expensive

rin'caro *nm* price increase

rincar'tare *vt* rewrap

rinca'sare *vi* return home

rinchi'udere *vt* shut up

rinchi'udersi *vr* shut oneself up

rincon'trare *vt* meet again

rincon'trarsi *vr* meet [each other] again

rin'correre *vt* run after

rin'corsa *nf* run-up

rin'corso *pp di* **rincorrere**

rin'crescere *vi* **mi rincresce di non...** I'm sorry *o* I regret that I can't...; **se non ti rincresce** if you don't mind; **rincresce vedere...** it's sad to see...

rincresci'mento *nm* regret

rincresci'uto *pp di* **rincrescere**

rincreti'nire *vt* make brain-dead ● *vi* go brain-dead

rincu'lare *vi* ‹*arma:*› recoil; ‹*cavallo:*› shy

rin'culo *nm* recoil

rincuo'rare *vt* encourage

rincuo'rarsi *vr* take heart

rinfacci'are *vt* **~ qcsa a qcno** throw sth in sb's face

rinfode'rare *vt* sheathe

rinfor'zare *vt* strengthen; (*rendere più saldo*) reinforce

rinfor'zarsi *vr* become stronger

rin'forzo *nm* reinforcement; *fig* support; **rinforzi** *pl Mil* reinforcements

rinfran'care *vt* reassure

rinfre'scante *a* cooling

rinfre'scare *vt* cool; (*rinnovare*) freshen up ● *vi* get cooler

rinfre'scarsi *vr* freshen [oneself] up

rin'fresco *nm* light refreshment; (*ricevimento*) party

rin'fusa *nf* **alla ~** at random

ringalluz'zire *vt* make cocky ● *vi* get cocky

ringhi'are *vi* snarl

ringhi'era *nf* railing; (*di scala*) banisters *pl*

ringhi'oso *a* snarling

ringiova'nire *vt* rejuvenate ‹*pelle, persona*›; ‹*vestito:*› make look younger ● *vi* become young again; (*sembrare*) look young again

ringrazia'mento *nm* thanks *pl*

ringrazi'are *vt* thank

rinne'gare *vt* disown

rinne'gato, -a *nmf* renegade

rinno'vabile *a* renewable

rinnova'mento *nm* renewal; (*di edifici*) renovation

rinno'vare *vt* renew; renovate ‹*edifici*›

rinno'varsi *vr* be renewed; (*ripetersi*) recur, happen again

rin'novo *nm* renewal

rinoce'ronte *nm* rhinoceros

rino'mato *a* renowned

rinsal'dare *vt* consolidate

rinsa'vire *vi* come to one's senses

rinsec'chire *vi* shrivel up

rinsec'chito *a* shrivelled up

rinta'narsi *vr* hide oneself away; ⟨*animale:*⟩ retreat into its den

rintoc'care *vi* ⟨*campana:*⟩ toll; ⟨*orologio:*⟩ strike

rin'tocco *nm* toll; (*di orologio*) stroke

rinton'tire *vt anche fig* stun

rinton'tito *a* (*stordito*) dazed

rintracci'are *vt* trace

rintro'nare *vt* stun ● *vi* boom

rintuz'zare *vt* blunt; (*ribattere*) retort; (*reprimere*) repress

ri'nuncia *nf* renunciation

rinunci'are *vi* ~ **a** renounce, give up

rinuncia'tario *a* defeatist

ri'nunzia, rinunzi'are = **rinuncia, rinunciare**

rinveni'mento *nm* (*di reperti*) discovery; (*di refurtiva*) recovery

rinve'nire *vt* find ● *vi* (*riprendere i sensi*) come round; (*ridiventare fresco*) revive

rinvi'are *vt* put off; (*mandare indietro*) return; (*in libro*) refer; ~ **a giudizio** indict

rinvigo'rire *vt* strengthen

rin'vio *nm Sport* goal kick; (*in libro*) cross-reference; (*di appuntamento*) postponement; (*di merce*) return. ~ **a giudizio** indictment

rioccu'pare *vt* reoccupy

rio'nale *a* local

ri'one *nm* district

riordina'mento *nm* reorganization

riordi'nare *vt* tidy [up]; (*ordinare di nuovo*) reorder

riorganiz'zare *vt* reorganize

riorganizzazi'one *nf* reorganization

R.I.P. *abbr* (**riposi in pace**) RIP

ripa'gare *vt* repay

ripa'rare *vt* (*proteggere*) shelter, protect; (*aggiustare*) repair; (*porre rimedio*) remedy ● *vi* ~ **a** make up for

ripa'rarsi *vr* take shelter

ripa'rato *a* ⟨*luogo*⟩ sheltered

riparazi'one *nf* repair; *fig* reparation

ripar'lare *vi* **ne riparliamo stasera** we'll talk about it again tonight

ri'paro *nm* shelter; (*rimedio*) remedy

ripar'tire *vt* (*dividere*) divide ● *vi* leave again

ripartizi'one *nf* division

ripas'sare *vt* recross; (*rivedere*) revise ● *vi* pass again

ripas'sata *nf* (*spolverata*) quick dust; (*stirata*) quick iron; (*di vernice*) second coat; (*fam: rimprovero*) telling-off; **dar una ~ a** ⟨*lezione*⟩ revise

ri'passo *nm* (*di lezione*) revision

ripensa'mento *nm* second thoughts *pl*

ripen'sare *vi* ~ **a** think back to; **ripensarci** (*cambiare idea*) change one's mind; **ripensaci!** think again!

riper'correre *vt* (*con la memoria*) go back over; trace ⟨*storia*⟩; ~ **la strada fatta** go back the way one came

riper'cosso *pp di* **ripercuotere**

ripercu'otere *vt* strike again

ripercu'otersi *vr* ⟨*suono:*⟩ reverberate; ~ **su qcsa** (*fig: avere conseguenze*) impact on sth

ripercussi'one *nf* repercussion

ripe'scare *vt* (*recuperare*) fish out; (*ritrovare*) find again

ripe'tente *nmf* student who is repeating a year

ri'petere *vt* repeat

ri'petersi *vr* ⟨*evento:*⟩ recur; ⟨*persona:*⟩ repeat oneself

ripeti'tore *nm* TV relay

ripetizi'one *nf* repetition; (*di lezione*) revision; (*lezione privata*) private lesson

ripetuta'mente *adv* repeatedly

ri'piano *nm* (*di scaffale*) shelf; (*terreno pianeggiante*) terrace

ri'picca *nf* spite; **fare qcsa per** ~ do sth out of spite

ri'picco = **ripicca**

ripida'mente *adv* steeply

'ripido *a* steep

ripie'gare *vt* refold; (*abbassare*) lower ● *vi* (*indietreggiare*) retreat

ripie'garsi *vr* bend; ⟨*sedile:*⟩ fold

ripi'ego *nm* expedient; (*via d'uscita*) way out

ripi'eno *a* full; *Culin* stuffed ● *nm* filling; *Culin* stuffing

ripiom'bare *vi* (*per terra*) fall down again; (*fig: tornare*) turn up on the doorstep again; (*nello sconforto*) sink back

ripopo'lare *vt* repopulate

ripopo'larsi *vr* be repopulated

ri'porre *vt* put back; (*mettere da parte*) put away; (*collocare*) place; repeat ⟨*domanda*⟩

ripor'tare *vt* (*restituire*) bring/take back; (*riferire*) report; (*subire*) suffer; *Math* carry; win ⟨*vittoria*⟩; transfer ⟨*disegno*⟩

ripor'tarsi *vr* go back; (*riferirsi*) refer

ri'porto *nm* (*su abito, scarpa*) appliqué; ~ **di 4** *Math* carry 4; **cane da** ~ gun dog, retriever; **nascondere la calvizie con un** ~ comb one's hair over a bald spot

ripo'sante *a* restful

ripo'sare *vi* rest ● *vt* put back

ripo'sarsi *vr* rest

ripo'sato *a* ⟨*mente*⟩ fresh; ⟨*viso*⟩ rested

ri'poso *nm* rest; **andare a** ~ retire; ~**!** *Mil* at ease!; **giorno di** ~ day off

ripo'stiglio *nm* cupboard

ri'posto *pp di* **riporre**

ri'prendere *vt* take again; (*prendere indietro*) take back; (*riconquistare*) recapture; (*ricuperare*) recover; (*ricominciare*) resume; (*rimproverare*) reprimand; take in ⟨*cucitura*⟩; *Cinema* shoot

ri'prendersi *vr* recover; (*correggersi*) correct oneself

ri'presa *nf* resumption; (*ricupero*) recovery; *Theat* revival; *Cinema* shot; *Auto* acceleration; *Mus* repeat; ~ **aerea** bird's-eye view

ripresen'tare *vt* resubmit ⟨*domanda, certificato*⟩; reintroduce ⟨*problema, persona*⟩

ripresen'tarsi *vr* (*a ufficio*) go/come back again; (*come candidato*) stand again, run again; (*occasione:*) arise again; (*problema:*) come up again, reappear; (*a esame*) resit

ri'preso *pp di* **riprendere**

ripristi'nare *vt* restore

ripro'dotto *pp di* **riprodurre**

ripro'durre *vt* reproduce

ripro'dursi *vr* Biol reproduce; (*fenomeno:*) happen again, recur

riprodut'tivo *a* reproductive

riproduzi'one *nf* reproduction. **'~ vietata'** 'copyright'

ripro'mettersi *vr* (*intendere*) intend

ripro'porre *vt* put forward again

ripro'porsi *vr* ~ **di fare qcsa** intend to do sth; (*come candidato*) stand again; (*problema:*) come up again, reappear

ri'prova *nf* confirmation; **a ~ di** as confirmation of

ripro'vare *vt/i* Comput retry

riprovazi'one *nf* ~ **generale** outcry

riprove'vole *a* reprehensible

ripubbli'care *vt* republish

ripudi'are *vt* repudiate

ripu'gnante *a* repugnant

ripu'gnanza *nf* disgust

ripu'gnare *vi* ~ **a** disgust

ripu'lire *vt* clean [up]; *fig* polish

ripu'lita *nf* quick clean; **darsi una ~** have a wash and brushup

ripulsi'one *nf* repulsion

ripul'sivo *a* repulsive

ri'quadro *nm* square; (*pannello*) panel

ri'sacca *nf* undertow

ri'saia *nf* rice field, paddy field

risa'lire *vt* go back up ● *vi* ~ **a** (*nel tempo*) go back to; (*essere datato a*) date back to, go back to

risa'lita *nf* ascent; **impianto di ~** ski lift

risal'tare *vi* (*emergere*) stand out

ri'salto *nm* prominence; (*rilievo*) relief

risana'mento *nm* improvement

risa'nare *vt* heal; (*bonificare*) reclaim

risa'puto *a* well-known

risar'cibile *a* indemnifiable

risarci'mento *nm* compensation

risar'cire *vt* indemnify; **mi hanno risarcito i danni** they compensated me for the damage

ri'sata *nf* laugh

riscalda'mento *nm* heating. **~ autonomo** central heating (*for one flat*). **~ centralizzato** *central heating system for whole block of flats*

riscal'dare *vt* heat; warm (*persona*)

riscal'darsi *vr* warm up

riscat'tabile *a* redeemable

riscat'tare *vt* ransom

riscat'tarsi *vr* redeem oneself

ri'scatto *nm* ransom; (*morale*) redemption

rischia'rare *vt* light up; brighten (*colore*)

rischia'rarsi *vr* light up; (*cielo:*) clear up

rischi'are *vt* risk ● *vi* run the risk; **~ inutilmente** take needless risks

'rischio *nm* risk

rischi'oso *a* risky

risciac'quare *vt* rinse

risci'acquo *nm* rinse

risciò *nm inv* rickshaw

riscon'trare *vt* (*confrontare*) compare; (*verificare*) verify; (*rilevare*) find

ri'scontro *nm* comparison; (*verifica*) verification; (*Comm: risposta*) reply

risco'prire *vt* rediscover

ri'scossa *nf* revolt; (*riconquista*) recovery

riscossi'one *nf* collection

ri'scosso *pp di* **riscuotere**

ri'scrivere *vt* (*scrivere di nuovo*) rewrite; (*rispondere*) write back

riscu'otere *vt* shake; (*percepire*) draw; (*ottenere*) gain; cash (*assegno*)

riscu'otersi *vr* rouse oneself

risen'tire *vt* hear again; (*provare*) feel ● *vi* ~ **di** feel the effect of

risen'tirsi *vr* (*offendersi*) take offence

risentita'mente *adv* resentfully

risen'tito *a* resentful

ri'serbo *nm* reserve; **mantenere il ~** remain tight-lipped

ri'serva *nf* reserve; (*di caccia, pesca*) preserve; *Sport* substitute, reserve; **di ~** spare. **~ di caccia** game reserve. **~ indiana** Indian reservation. **~ naturale** wildlife reserve

riser'vare *vt* reserve; (*prenotare*) book; (*per occasione*) keep

riser'varsi (*ripromettersi*) plan for oneself (*cambiamento*); **mi riservo la sorpresa** I want it to be a surprise

riserva'tezza *nf* reserve

riser'vato *a* reserved; **'~ ai clienti dell'albergo'** 'for hotel guests only'; **'~ carico'** 'loading only'

ri'sguardo *nm* endpaper

ri'siedere *vi* ~ **a** reside in

'risma *nf* ream; *fig* kind

'riso¹ *pp di* **ridere** ● *nm* (*pl nf* **risa**) laughter; (*singolo*) laugh

'riso² *nm* (*cereale*) rice. **~ integrale** brown rice

riso'lino *nm* giggle

risolle'vare *vt* raise again; raise (*il morale*); raise again, bring up again (*problema, questione*); increase, improve (*le sorti*)

risolle'varsi *vr* (*da terra*) rise again; *fig* pick up

ri'solto *pp di* **risolvere**

risoluta'mente *adv* energetically

risolu'tezza *nf* determination

risolu'tivo *a* (*determinante*) decisive; **scelta risolutiva** solution

riso'luto *a* resolute, determined

risoluzi'one *nf* resolution

ri'solvere *vt* resolve; *Math* solve

ri'solversi *vr* (*decidersi*) decide; **~ in** turn into

riso'nanza *nf* resonance; **aver ~** *fig* arouse great interest. **~ magnetica** magnetic resonance

riso'nare *vi* resound; (*rimbombare*) echo

ri'sorgere *vi* rise again

risorgi'mento *nm* revival; **il R~** *(storico)* the Risorgimento

ri'sorsa *nf* resource; *(espediente)* resort. **risorse** *pl* **energetiche** energy resources. **risorse** *pl* **naturali** natural resources. **risorse** *pl* **umane** human resources

ri'sorto *pp di* **risorgere**

ri'sotto *nm* risotto. **~ alla marinara** seafood risotto. **~ alla milanese** risotto with saffron

ri'sparmi *nmpl* *(soldi)* savings

risparmi'are *vt* save; *(salvare)* spare

risparmia|'tore, -'trice *nmf* saver

ri'sparmio *nm* saving. **~ energetico** energy saving

rispecchi'are *vt* reflect

rispe'dire *vr* send back, return

rispet'tabile *a* respectable

rispettabilità *nf* respectability

rispet'tare *vt* respect; **farsi ~** command respect

rispet'tivo *a* respective

ri'spetto *nm* respect; **~ a** as regards; *(in paragone a)* compared to

rispettosa'mente *adv* respectfully

rispet'toso *a* respectful

risplen'dente *a* shining

ri'splendere *vi* shine

rispon'dente *a* **~ a** in keeping with

rispon'denza *nf* correspondence

ri'spondere *vi* answer; *(rimbeccare)* answer back; *(obbedire)* respond; **~ a** reply to; **~ di** *(rendersi responsabile)* answer for

rispo'sare *vt* remarry

rispo'sarsi *vr* remarry

ri'sposta *nf* answer, reply; *(reazione)* response

ri'sposto *pp di* **rispondere**

rispun'tare *vi* *(persona, sole:)* reappear

'rissa *nf* brawl

ris'soso *a* pugnacious

ristabi'lire *vt* re-establish

ristabi'lirsi *vr* *(in salute)* recover

rista'gnare *vi* stagnate; *(sangue:)* coagulate

ri'stagno *nm* stagnation

ri'stampa *nf* reprint; *(azione)* reprinting

ristam'pare *vt* reprint

risto'rante *nm* restaurant

risto'rare *vt* refresh

risto'rarsi *vr* liter take some refreshment; *(riposarsi)* take a rest

ristora|'tore, -'trice *nmf* *(proprietario di ristorante)* restaurateur; *(fornitore)* caterer ● *a* refreshing

ri'storo *nm* refreshment; *(sollievo)* relief; **servizio di ~** refreshments *pl*

ristret'tezza *nf* narrowness; *(povertà)* poverty; **vivere in ristrettezze** live in straitened circumstances

ri'stretto *pp di* **restringere** ● *a* narrow; *(condensato)* condensed; *(limitato)* restricted; **di idee ristrette** narrow-minded

ristruttu'rante *a* *(cosmetico)* conditioning

ristruttu'rare *vt* Comm restructure; renovate *(casa)*; repair *(capelli)*

ristrutturazi'one *nf* Comm restructuring; *(di casa)* renovation

risucchi'are *vt* suck in

ri'succhio *nm* whirlpool; *(di corrente)* undertow

risul'tare *vi* result; *(riuscire)* turn out

risul'tato *nm* result. **risultati** *pl* **parziali** *(di elezioni)* preliminary results; *(di partite)* half-time results

risuo'nare *vt* play again *(pezzo musicale)*; ring again *(campanello)* ● *vi* *(grida, parola:)* echo; Phys resonate

risurrezi'one, risusci'tare = **resurrezione, resuscitare**

risvegli'are *vt* reawaken *(interesse)*

risvegli'arsi *vr* wake up; *(natura:)* awake; *(desiderio:)* be aroused

ri'sveglio *nm* waking up; *(dell'interesse)* revival; *(del desiderio)* arousal

ri'svolto *nm* *(di giacca)* lapel; *(di pantaloni)* turn-up, cuff *Am*; *(di manica)* cuff; *(di tasca)* flap; *(di libro)* inside flap

ritagli'are *vt* cut out

ri'taglio *nm* cutting; *(di stoffa)* scrap

ritar'dare *vi* be late; *(orologio:)* be slow ● *vt* delay; slow down *(progresso)*; *(differire)* postpone

ritarda'tario, -a *nmf* latecomer

ritar'dato *a* Psych retarded

ri'tardo *nm* delay; **essere in ~** be late; *(volo:)* be delayed

ri'tegno *nm* reserve

ritem'prare *vt* restore

rite'nere *vt* retain; deduct *(somma)*; *(credere)* believe

riten'tare *vt* try again

rite'nuta *nf* *(sul salario)* deduction. **~ d'acconto** tax deducted in advance from payments made to self-employed people. **~ diretta** taxation at source. **~ alla fonte** taxation at source, deduction at source

ritenzi'one *nf* Med retention

riti'rare *vt* throw back *(palla)*; *(prelevare)* withdraw; *(riscuotere)* draw; collect *(pacco)*

riti'rarsi *vr* withdraw; *(stoffa:)* shrink; *(da attività)* retire; *(marea:)* recede

riti'rata *nf* retreat; *(WC)* toilet

ri'tiro *nm* withdrawal; Relig retreat; *(da attività)* retirement; **~ bagagli** baggage reclaim

'ritmica *nf* rhythmic gymnastics

ritmica'mente *adv* rhythmically

'ritmico *a* rhythmic[al]

'ritmo *nm* rhythm; **a ~ serrato** at a cracking pace

'rito *nm* rite; **di ~** customary. **~ funebre** funeral service

ritoc'care *vt* *(correggere)* touch up

ri'tocco *nm* alteration; **ritocchi** *pl* Phot retouching

ri'torcersi *vr* **~ contro qcno** boomerang on sb

ritor'nare *vi* return; *(andare/venire indietro)* go/come back; *(ricorrere)* recur; *(ridiventare)* become again

ritor'nello *nm* refrain

ri'torno *nm* return

ritorsi'one *nf* retaliation

ritra'durre *vt* (*tradurre di nuovo*) re-translate

ri'trarre *vt* (*ritirare*) withdraw; (*distogliere*) turn away; (*rappresentare*) portray

ritra'smettere *vt TV* show again, re-broadcast

ritrat'tabile *a* ‹*accuso*› which can be withdrawn

ritrat'tare *vt* retract, withdraw ‹*dichiarazione*›

ritrattazi'one *nf* withdrawal, retraction

ritrat'tista *nmf* portrait painter

ri'tratto *pp di* ritrarre ● *nm* portrait

ritrazi'one *nf* retraction

ritrosa'mente *adv* shyly

ritro'sia *nf* shyness

ri'troso *a* (*timido*) shy; **a ~** backwards; **~ a** reluctant to

ritrova'mento *nm* (*azione*) finding; (*cosa*) find

ritro'vare *vt* find [again]; regain ‹*salute*›

ritro'varsi *vr* meet; (*di nuovo*) meet again; (*capitare*) find oneself; (*raccapezzarsi*) see one's way

ritro'vato *nm* discovery

ri'trovo *nm* meeting-place. **~ notturno** night club

'ritto *a* upright; (*diritto*) straight

ritu'ale *a & nm* ritual

ritual'mente *adv* ritually

riunifi'care *vt* reunify

riunifi'carsi *vr* be reunited

riunificazi'one *nf* reunification

riuni'one *nf* meeting; (*dopo separazione*) reunion

riu'nire *vt* (*unire*) join together; (*radunare*) gather

riu'nirsi *vr* be reunited; (*adunarsi*) meet

riu'sare *vt* reuse

riusc'ire *vi* (*aver successo*) succeed; (*in matematica ecc*) be good (**in** at); (*aver esito*) turn out; **le è riuscito simpatico** she found him likeable

riu'scita *nf* (*esito*) result; (*successo*) success

ri'uso *nm* reuse

riutiliz'zare *vt* reuse

'riva *nf* (*di mare, lago*) shore; (*di fiume*) bank

rivacci'nare *vt* revaccinate

ri'vale *nmf* rival

rivaleggi'are *vi* compete (**con** with)

rivalità *nf inv* rivalry

ri'valsa *nf* revenge; **prendersi una ~ su qcno** take revenge on sb

rivalu'tare *vt* reappraise

rivalutazi'one *nf* revaluation

rivan'gare *vt* dig up again

rive'dere *vt* see again; revise ‹*lezione*›; review ‹*accordo*›; (*verificare*) check

rive'dibile *a* ‹*accordo*› reviewable; ‹*recluta*› temporarily unfit

rive'lare *vt* reveal

rive'larsi *vr* (*dimostrarsi*) turn out

rivela'tore *a* revealing ● *nm Techn* detector. **~ di mine** mine detector

rivelazi'one *nf* revelation

ri'vendere *vt* resell

rivendi'care *vt* claim

rivendicazi'one *nf* claim

ri'vendita *nf* (*negozio*) shop. **~ autorizzata** authorized retailer

rivendi'tore, -'trice *nmf* retailer. **~ autorizzato** authorized retailer

riverbe'rare *vt* reflect ‹*luce*›

ri'verbero *nm* reverberation; (*bagliore*) glare

rive'renza *nf* reverence; (*inchino*) curtsy; (*di uomo*) bow

rive'rire *vt* respect; (*ossequiare*) pay one's respects to

rivernici'are *vt* repaint; (*con flatting*) revarnish

river'sare *vt* pour

river'sarsi *vr* ‹*fiume:*› flow

river'sibile *a* reversible

rivesti'mento *nm* covering

rive'stire *vt* (*rifornire di abiti*) clothe; (*ricoprire*) cover; (*internamente*) line; hold ‹*carica*›

rive'stirsi *vr* get dressed again; (*per una festa*) dress up

rive'stito *a* **~ di** covered with

rivi'era *nf* coast; **la ~ ligure** the Italian Riviera

ri'vincita *nf Sport* return match; (*vendetta*) revenge

rivis'suto *pp di* rivivere

ri'vista *nf* review; (*pubblicazione*) magazine; *Theat* revue; **passare in ~** review

rivitaliz'zare *vt* revitalize

rivitalizzazi'one *nf* revitalization

ri'vivere *vi* come to life again; (*riprendere le forze*) revive ● *vt* relive

'rivo *nm* stream

rivo'lere *vt* (*volere di nuovo*) want again; (*volere indietro*) want back

ri'volgere *vt* turn; (*indirizzare*) address; **~ da** (*distogliere*) turn away from

ri'volgersi *vr* turn round; **~ a** (*indirizzarsi*) turn to

rivolgi'mento *nm* upheaval

ri'volta *nf* revolt

rivol'tante *a* revolting, disgusting

rivol'tare *vt* turn [over]; (*mettendo l'interno verso l'esterno*) turn inside out; (*sconvolgere*) upset

rivol'tarsi *vr* (*ribellarsi*) revolt

rivol'tella *nf* revolver

ri'volto *pp di* rivolgere

rivol'toso, -a *nmf* rebel, insurgent

rivoluzio'nare *vt* revolutionize

rivoluzio'nario, -a *a & nmf* revolutionary

rivoluzi'one *nf* revolution; (*fig: disordine*) chaos. **~ francese** French Revolution. **~ industriale** Industrial Revolution

riz'zare *vt* raise; (*innalzare*) erect; prick up ‹*orecchie*›

riz'zarsi *vr* stand up; ‹*capelli:*› stand on end; ‹*orecchie:*› prick up '**roast-beef** *nm inv* thin slices of roast beef served cold with lemon

'**roba** *nf* stuff; (*personale*) belongings *pl*, stuff; (*faccenda*) thing; (*sl: droga*) drugs *pl*; **~ da matti!** absolute madness!. **~ da bere** drink. **~ da lavare** washing. **~ da mangiare** food, things to eat. **~ da stirare** ironing

ro'**baccia** *nf* rubbish

robi'**vecchi** *nm inv* second-hand dealer

ro'**bot** *nm inv* robot; (*da cucina*) food processor

ro'**botica** *nf* robotics

ro'**botico** *a* robotic

robotiz'**zato** *a* robotic, robotized

robu'**stezza** *nf* sturdiness, robustness; (*forza*) strength

ro'**busto** *a* sturdy, robust; (*forte*) strong

rocambo'**lesco** *a* incredible

'**rocca** *nf* fortress

rocca'**forte** *nf* stronghold

rocchetti'**era** *nf* winder

roc'**chetto** *nm* reel

'**roccia** *nf* rock; (*sport*) rock-climbing

rock *nm* rock [music]. **~ acrobatico** rock 'n' roll

'**roco** *a* throaty

ro'**daggio** *nm* running in

'**Rodano** *nm* Rhone

ro'**dare** *vt* run in

ro'**deo** *nm* rodeo

'**rodere** *vt* gnaw; (*corrodere*) corrode

'**rodersi** *vr* **~ da** (*logorarsi*) be consumed with

rodi'**tore** *nm* rodent

rodo'**dendro** *nm* rhododendron

'**rogito** *nm Jur* deed

'**rogna** *nf* scabies *sg*; *fig* nuisance

ro'**gnone** *nm Culin* kidney

ro'**gnoso** *a* scabby

'**rogo** *nm* (*supplizio*) stake; (*per cadaveri*) pyre

rol'**lare** *vt* roll (*sigaretta*) ● *vi* (*aereo, nave:*) roll

ROM *nf inv Comput* ROM

'**Roma** *nf* Rome

Roma'**nia** *nf* Romania

ro'**manico** *a* Romanesque

ro'**mano, -a** *a & nmf* Roman

romantica'**mente** *adv* romantically

romanti'**cismo** *nm* romanticism

ro'**mantico** *a* romantic

ro'**manza** *nf* romance

roman'**zato** *a* romanticized

roman'**zesco** *a* fictional; (*stravagante*) wild, unrealistic

roman'**zetto** *nm* **~ rosa** novelette

romanzi'**ere** *nm* novelist

ro'**manzo** *a* Romance ● *nm* novel; (*storia incredibile romantica*) romance. **~ d'appendice** serial story. **~ giallo** thriller. **~ sceneggiato** novel adapted for television/radio

rom'**bare** *vi* rumble

'**rombo** *nm* rumble; *Math* rhombus; (*pesce*) turbot

romboi'**dale** *a* rhomboid, diamond-shaped

'**rompere** *vt* break; break off (*relazione*); **non ~ [le scatole]!** (*fam: seccare*) don't be a pain [in the neck]!

'**rompersi** *vr* break; **~ una gamba** break one's leg

rompi'**capo** *nm* nuisance; (*indovinello*) puzzle

rompi'**collo** *nm* daredevil; **a ~** at breakneck speed

rompighi'**accio** *nm* ice-breaker

rompi'**mento** *nm fam* pain

rompi'**scatole** *nmf inv fam* pain

'**ronda** *nf* rounds *pl*

ron'**della** *nf Mech* washer

'**rondine** *nf* swallow

ron'**done** *nm* swift

ron'**fare** *vi* (*russare*) snore; (*fare le fusa*) purr

ron'**zare** *vi* buzz; **~ attorno a qcno** *fig* hang about sb

ron'**zino** *nm* jade

ron'**zio** *nm* buzz

'**rosa** *nf* rose. **~ rampicante** rambler, rambling rose. **~ selvatica** wild rose. **~ dei venti** wind rose ● *a & nm* (*colore*) pink

ro'**saio** *nm* rosebush

ro'**sario** *nm* rosary

ro'**sato** *a* rosy ● *nm* (*vino*) rosé

'**rosbif** = **roast-beef**

rosé *nm inv* rosé

'**roseo** *a* pink

ro'**seto** *nm* rose garden

ro'**setta** *nf* (*coccarda*) rosette; *Mech* washer

rosicchi'**are** *vt* nibble; (*rodere*) gnaw

rosma'**rino** *nm* rosemary

'**roso** *pp di* **rodere**

roso'**lare** *vt* brown

roso'**lato** *a* sauté

roso'**lia** *nf* German measles *sg*

ro'**sone** *nm* rosette; (*apertura*) rose window

'**rospo** *nm* toad

ros'**setto** *nm* (*per labbra*) lipstick

'**rosso** *a & nm* red; **diventare ~** go red; **passare col ~** go through a red light, jump a red light. **~ carota** *a* (*capelli*) ginger. **~ mattone** *a* brick red. **~ sangue** *a* blood red. **~ scarlatto** *a* scarlet. **~ d'uovo** [egg] yolk. **~ vermiglio** *a* vermilion

ros'**sore** *nm* redness; (*della pelle*) flush

rosticce'**ria** *nf* shop selling cooked meat and other prepared food

'**rostro** *nm* rostrum; (*becco*) bill

ro'**tabile** *a* strada **~** carriageway

ro'**taia** *nf* rail; (*solco*) rut

ro'**tante** *a* rotating

ro'**tare** *vt/i* rotate

rota'**tiva** *nf* rotary press

rota'**torio** *a* rotary

rotazi'**one** *nf* rotation; (*di personale*) turnover. **~ delle colture** crop rotation

rote'**are** *vt/i* roll

ro'**tella** *nf* small wheel; (*di mobile*) castor

roto'calco *nm* (*sistema*) rotogravure; (*rivista*) illustrated magazine

roto'lare *vt/i* roll

roto'larsi *vr* roll [about]

roto'lio *nm* rolling

'rotolo *nm* roll; **andare a rotoli** go to rack and ruin. **~ di carta igienica** toilet roll

roto'loni *adv* **cadere ~** tumble

ro'tonda *nf* roundabout, traffic circle *Am*

rotondità *nf* (*qualità*) roundness; **~** *pl* (*curve femminili*) curves *pl*, curvaceousness

ro'tondo, -a *a* round ● *nf* (*spiazzo*) terrace

ro'tore *nm* rotor

'rotta¹ *nf* *Naut, Aeron* course; **far ~ per** set a course for; **fuori ~** off course; **in ~ di collisione** on a collision course

'rotta² *nf* **a ~ di collo** at breakneck speed; **essere in ~ con** be on bad terms with

rotta'maio *nm* junkyard

rot'tame *nm* scrap; *fig* wreck

'rotto *pp di* **rompere** ● *a* broken; (*stracciato*) torn

rot'tura *nf* break; **che ~ di scatole!** *fam* what a pain!

'rotula *nf* kneecap

rou'lette *nf inv* roulette. **~ russa** Russian roulette

rou'lotte *nf inv* caravan, trailer *Am*

rou'tine *nf inv* routine; **di ~** (*operazioni, controlli*) routine

ro'vente *a* scorching

'rovere *nm* (*legno*) oak

rovescia'mento *nm* overthrow

rovesci'are *vt* (*buttare a terra*) knock over; (*sottosopra*) turn upside down; (*rivoltare*) turn inside out; spill (*liquido*); overthrow (*governo*); reverse (*situazione*)

rovesci'arsi *vr* (*capovolgersi*) overturn; (*riversarsi*) pour

ro'vescio *a* (*contrario*) reverse; **alla rovescia** (*capovolto*) upside down; (*con l'interno all'esterno*) inside out ● *nm* reverse; (*nella maglia*) purl; (*di pioggia*) downpour; *Tennis* backhand

ro'vina *nf* ruin; (*crollo*) collapse; **in ~** in ruins

rovi'nare *vt* ruin; (*guastare*) spoil ● *vi* crash

rovi'narsi *vr* be ruined; (*persona:*) ruin oneself

rovi'nato *a* ruined

ro'vine *nfpl* ruins

rovi'noso *a* ruinous

rovi'stare *vt* ransack

'rovo *nm* bramble

rozza'mente *adv* crudely

roz'zezza *nf* indelicacy

'rozzo *a* rough

R.R. *abbr* (**ricevuta di ritorno**) acknowledgment of receipt

R.U. *abbr* (**Regno Unito**) UK

'ruba *nf* **andare a ~** sell like hot cakes

rubacchi'are *vt* pilfer

rubacu'ori *nm inv* heart-throb

ru'bare *vt* steal

rubi'condo *a* ruddy

rubi'netto *nm* tap, faucet *Am*

ru'bino *nm* ruby

ru'bizzo *a* spry

'rublo *nm* rouble

ru'brica *nf* (*in giornale*) column; (*in programma televisivo*) TV report; (*quaderno con indice*) address book. **~ sportiva** sports column. **~ telefonica** telephone and address book

'rucola *nf* rocket

'rude *a* rough

'rudere *nm* ruin

ru'dezza *nf* bluntness

rudimen'tale *a* rudimentary

rudi'menti *nmpl* rudiments

ruffi'ana *nf* procuress

ruffi'ano *nm* pimp; (*adulatore*) bootlicker

'ruga *nf* wrinkle

'ruggine *nf* rust; **fare la ~** go rusty

ruggi'noso *a* rusty

rug'gire *vi* roar

rug'gito *nm* roar

rugi'ada *nf* dew

ru'goso *a* wrinkled

rul'lare *vi* roll; *Aeron* taxi

rul'lino *nm* film

rul'lio *nm* rolling; *Aeron* taxiing

'rullo *nm* roll; *Techn* roller

rum *nm inv* rum

ru'meno, -a *a* & *nmf* Romanian

rumi'nante *nm* ruminant

rumi'nare *vt* ruminate

ru'more *nm* noise; *fig* rumour

rumoreggi'are *vi* rumble

rumorosa'mente *adv* noisily

rumo'roso *a* noisy; (*sonoro*) loud

ru'olo *nm* roll; *Theat* role; **di ~** on the staff. **~ delle imposte** tax notice. **~ primario/ secondario** major/minor role

ru'ota *nf* wheel; **andare a ~ libera** free-wheel; **fare la ~** do a cartwheel. **~ dentata** cogwheel. **~ di scorta** spare wheel. **~ di stampa** (*di stampante*) print wheel. **~ del timone** helm

'rupe *nf* cliff

ru'pestre *a* (*pittura*) rock *attrib*

ru'pia *nf* rupee

ru'rale *a* rural

ru'scello *nm* stream

'ruspa *nf* bulldozer

ru'spante *a* free-range

rus'sare *vi* snore

'Russia *nf* Russia

'russo, -a *a* & *nmf* Russian ● *nm* (*lingua*) Russian

'rustico *a* rural; (*carattere*) rough

'ruta *nf* *Bot* rue

rut'tare *vi* belch, burp

rut'tino *nm* (*di bambino*) burp

'rutto *nm* belch, burp

'ruvido *a* coarse

ruzzo'lare *vi* tumble down

ruzzo'lone *nm* tumble; **cadere ruzzoloni** tumble down, tumble [helter-skelter]

Ss

S. *abbr* (**santo, santa**) St.; *abbr* (**sud**) south

'**sabato** *nm* Saturday; **di ~** on Saturdays

sab'batico *a* sabbatical; **anno ~** sabbatical [year]

'**sabbia** *nf* sand. **sabbie** *pl* **mobili** quicksand

sabbi'are *vt* sandblast

sabbia'tura *nf* (*di vetro, metallo*) sandblasting; (*terapeutica*) sand-bath

sabbi'oso *a* sandy

sabo'taggio *nm* sabotage

sabo'tare *vt* sabotage

sabota|'tore, -'trice *nmf* saboteur

'**sacca** *nf* bag. **~ di resistenza** pocket of resistance. **~ da viaggio** travel[ling]-bag

sacca'rina *nf* saccharin

sac'cente *a* conceited ● *nmf* know-all, know-it-all *Am*

saccente'ria *nf* conceit

sacceggi'are *vt* sack; *hum* plunder ⟨*frigo*⟩

saccheggia|'tore, -'trice *nmf* plunderer

sac'cheggio *nm* sack

sac'chetto *nm* bag. **~ di plastica** plastic bag. **~ per la spazzatura** bin liner

'**sacco** *nm* sack; *Anat* sac; (*sl: biglietto da mille lire*) thousand lire note; (*contenuto*) sack[ful]; **mettere nel ~** *fig* swindle; **un ~** (*moltissimo*) a lot; **un ~ di** (*gran quantità*) lots of. **~ a pelo** sleeping-bag. **~ postale** mail-bag

saccope'lista *nmf* backpacker

sacer'dote *nm* priest

sacer'dozio *nm* priesthood

sacra'mento *nm* sacrament

sacrifi'cale *a* sacrificial

sacrifi'care *vt* sacrifice

sacrifi'carsi *vr* sacrifice oneself

sacrifi'cato *a* sacrificed; (*non valorizzato*) wasted

sacri'ficio *nm* sacrifice

sacri'legio *nm* sacrilege

sa'crilego *a* sacrilegious

'**sacro** *a* sacred ● *nm Anat* sacrum

sacro'santo *a* sacrosanct; ⟨*verità*⟩ gospel; ⟨*diritto*⟩ sacred

'**sadico, -a** *a* sadistic ● *nmf* sadist

sa'dismo *nm* sadism

sa'etta *nf* arrow; (*fulmine*) thunderbolt; **correre come una ~** run like the wind

sa'fari *nm inv* safari

'**saga** *nf* saga

sa'gace *a* shrewd

sa'gacia *nf* sagacity

sag'gezza *nf* wisdom

saggia'mente *adv* sagely

saggi'are *vt* test

'**saggio**[1] *nm* (*scritto*) essay; (*prova*) proof; (*di metallo*) assay; (*campione*) sample; (*esempio*) example

'**saggio**[2] *a* wise ● *nm* (*persona*) sage

sag'gista *nmf* essayist

sag'gistica *nf* non-fiction

Sagit'tario *nm Astr* Sagittarius

'**sago** = **sagù**

'**sagoma** *nf* shape; (*profilo*) outline; (*in falegnameria*) template; **che ~!** *fam* what a character!

sago'mare *vt* make according to a template

'**sagra** *nf* festival

sa'grato *nm* churchyard

sagre'stano *nm* sacristan

sagre'stia *nf* sacristy

sagù *nm inv* sago

Sa'hara *nm* Sahara

'**sala** *nf* hall; (*salotto*) living room; (*per riunioni ecc*) room; (*di cinema*) cinema. **~ arrivi** arrivals lounge. **~ d'aspetto** waiting room. **~ d'attesa** waiting room. **~ da ballo** ballroom. **~ di comando** control room. **~ conferenze** conference hall. **~ giochi** amusement arcade. **~ d'imbarco** departure lounge. **~ di lettura** reading room. **~ macchine** engine room. **~ operatoria** operating theatre *Br*, operating room *Am*. **~ parto** delivery room. **~ da pranzo** dining room. **~ professori** staff room, common room. **~ di regia** *Radio, TV* control room. **~ di ricevimento** function room. **~ riunioni** conference room. **~ da tè** tea shop

sa'lace *a* salacious

sa'lame *nm* salami

salame'lecchi *nmpl* **fare ~** bow and scrape; **prendi quello che vuoi senza tanti ~** don't stand on ceremony, take what you want

sala'moia *nf* brine

sa'lare *vt* salt

salari'ato *nm* wage earner

sa'lario *nm* wages *pl*

salas'sare *vt Med* bleed; *fig* bleed dry

sa'lasso *nm* bleeding; **essere un ~** *fig* cost a fortune

sala'tini *nmpl* savouries (*eaten with aperitifs*)

sa'lato *a* salty; (*costoso*) dear; **acqua salata** salt water

sal'ciccia *nf* = **salsiccia**

sal'dare *vt* weld; set ⟨*osso*⟩; pay off ⟨*debito*⟩; settle ⟨*conto*⟩; **~ a stagno** solder

sal'darsi *vr* ⟨*osso:*⟩ knit; ⟨*ferita:*⟩ heal

saldat'rice *nf* soldering iron

salda'tura *nf* soldering; (*giunzione*) join

'saldo *a* firm; (*resistente*) strong; **~ come una roccia** solid as a rock; **essere ~ nei propri principi** stick to one's principles ● *nm* (*pagamento*) settlement; *Comm* balance; (*di conto corrente*) bank balance; **saldi** *pl* sale; **i ~ di fine stagione** the end of season sales; **in ~** ⟨*essere*⟩ on sale; ⟨*comprato*⟩ in a sale. **~ iniziale** opening balance

'sale *nm* salt; **non ha ~ in zucca** *fam* he hasn't got an ounce of common sense; **restare di ~** be struck dumb [with astonishment]; **sali** *pl* *Med* smelling salts. **sali** *pl* **da bagno** bath salts. **~ da cucina** cooking salt. **~ fino** table salt. **~ grosso** cooking salt. **sali** *pl* **e tabacchi** (*negozio*) tobacconist's shop

'salice *nm* willow. **~ piangente** weeping willow

sali'ente *a* outstanding; **i punti salienti** the main points, the highlights

sali'era *nf* salt-cellar

sa'lina *nf* salt-works *sg*

salinità *nf* saltiness

sa'lino *a* saline

sa'lire *vi* go/come up; (*levarsi*) rise; (*su treno ecc*) get on; (*in macchina*) get in ● *vt* go/come up ⟨*scale*⟩

sa'lita *nf* climb; (*aumento*) rise; **in ~** uphill

sa'liva *nf* saliva

sali'vare *vt* salivate ● *a* ⟨*ghiandola*⟩ salivary

'salma *nf* corpse

sal'mastro *a* brackish ● *nm* salt air

salmi *nm* **in ~** marinated and slowly cooked in the marinade

salmi'strare *vt* *Culin* cure

'salmo *nm* psalm

sal'mone *nm* & *a* *inv* salmon. **~ affumicato** smoked salmon

salmo'nella *nf* salmonella

sa'lone *nm* (*salotto*) living room; (*di parrucchiere*) salon. **~ dell'automobile** motor show. **~ di bellezza** beauty parlour. **~ del libro** book fair

salo'pette *nf* *inv* dungarees *pl*

salotti'ero *a* *pej* mundane; **discorso ~** small talk

salot'tino *nm* bower

sa'lotto *nm* drawing room; (*soggiorno*) sitting room; (*mobili*) [three-piece] suite; **fare ~** chat. **~ letterario** literary salon

sal'pare *vi* sail ● *vt* **~ l'ancora** weigh anchor

'salsa *nf* sauce; *Mus* salsa. **~ di pomodoro** tomato sauce. **~ di soia** soy sauce. **~ tartara** tartar sauce

sal'sedine *nf* saltiness

sal'siccia *nf* sausage

salsi'era *nf* sauce-boat

sal'tare *vi* jump; (*venir via*) come off; (*balzare*) leap; (*esplodere*) blow up; **saltar fuori** spring from nowhere; ⟨*oggetto cercato:*⟩ turn up; **è saltato fuori che...** it emerged

that...; **~ fuori con...** come out with...; **salta agli occhi** (*è evidente*) it hits you; **~ in aria** blow up; **~ in mente** spring to mind ● *vt* jump [over]; skip ⟨*pasti, lezioni*⟩; *Culin* sauté

sal'tato *a* *Culin* sautéed

saltel'lare *vi* hop; (*di gioia*) skip

saltim'banco *nm* acrobat

saltim'bocca *nm inv* slice of veal rolled with ham and sage and fried

'salto *nm* jump; (*balzo*) leap; (*dislivello*) drop; (*fig: omissione, lacuna*) gap; **fare un ~ da** (*visitare*) drop in on; **in un ~** *fig* in a jiffy; **fare i salti mortali** *fig* go to great lengths; **fare quattro salti** *fam* go dancing; **fare un ~ nel buio** *fig* take a leap in the dark. **~ in alto** high jump. **~ con l'asta** pole-vault. **~ della corda** skipping. **~ in lungo** long jump. **~ pagina** *Comput* page down. **~ di qualità** quality leap

saltuaria'mente *adv* occasionally, from time to time

saltu'ario *a* desultory; **lavoro ~** casual work

sa'lubre *a* healthy

salume'ria *nf* delicatessen

sa'lumi *nmpl* cold cuts

salumi'ere *nm* person who sells cold meat

salu'tare *vt* greet; (*congedandosi*) say goodbye to; (*portare i saluti a*) give one's regards to; *Mil* salute; **ti saluto!** *fam* cheerio! ● *a* healthy

salu'tarsi *vr* (*all'arrivo*) greet each other; (*in partenza*) say goodbye to each other

sa'lute *nf* health; **godere di ottima ~** be in the best of health, enjoy excellent health; **in ~** in good health; **~!** (*dopo uno starnuto*) bless you!; (*a un brindisi*) cheers!. **~ di ferro** iron constitution

salu'tista *nmf* health fanatic; (*dell'Esercito della Salvezza*) Salvationist

sa'luto *nm* greeting; (*di addio*) goodbye; *Mil* salute; **saluti** *pl* (*ossequi*) regards

'salva *nf* salvo; **sparare a salve** shoot blanks; **a salve** ⟨*pistola*⟩ loaded with blank cartridges

salvacon'dotto *nm* safe conduct

salvada'naio *nm* money box

salva'gente *nm* lifebelt; (*a giubbotto*) lifejacket; (*ciambella*) rubber ring; (*spartitraffico*) traffic island

salvaguar'dare *vt* protect, safeguard

salvaguar'darsi *vr* protect oneself

salvagu'ardia *nf* safeguard

sal'vare *vt* save; (*proteggere*) protect; **~ la faccia** save face; **~ la pelle** save one's skin

sal'varsi *vr* save oneself

salva'schermo *nm* *Comput* screen saver

salva'slip *nm inv* panty-liner

salva'taggio *nm* rescue; *Naut* salvage; *Comput* saving; **battello di ~** lifeboat

salva|'tore, -'trice *nmf* saviour

'salve *vedi* **salva**

sal'vezza *nf* safety; *Relig* salvation; **ancora di ~** *fig* salvation

'salvia *nf* sage

salvi'etta *nf* serviette

'salvo *a* safe ● *nm* **trarre in ~** rescue ● *prep* except [for] ● *conj* **~ che** (*a meno che*) unless; (*eccetto che*) except that

samari'tano, -a *a & nmf* Samaritan

'samba *nf* samba

sam'buca *nf* sambuca

sam'buco *nm* elder

san *nm* (*before proper names starting with a consonant*) saint; *vedi* **santo**

sa'nabile *a* curable

sa'nare *vt* heal; (*bonificare*) reclaim; **~ il bilancio** balance the books

sana'toria *nf decree legitimizing a situation which is in principle illegal*

sana'torio *nm* sanatorium

san'cire *vt* sanction

'sandalo *nm* sandal; *Bot* sandalwood

sandi'nista *a & nmf* Sandinista

'sandwich *nm inv* sandwich; **uomo ~** sandwich-man

san'gallo *nm* (*tessuto*) broderie anglaise

san'gria *nf* sangria

'sangue *nm* blood; **a ~ freddo** in cold blood; **al ~** *Culin* rare; **appena al ~** *Culin* medium-rare; **farsi cattivo ~ per** worry about; **iniettato di ~** (*occhio*) bloodshot; **all'ultimo ~** (*lotta*) to the death; **di ~ blu** blue-blooded; **sudare ~** sweat blood. **~ freddo** composure. **~ da naso** nose bleed

sangue'misto *nm* half-caste

sangu'igno *a* blood *attrib*

sangui'naccio *nm Culin* black pudding

sangui'nante *a* bleeding

sangui'nare *vi* bleed

sangui'nario *a* bloodthirsty

sangui'noso *a* bloody

sangui'suga *nf* leech

sanità *nf* soundness; (*salute*) health; **ministero della ~** Department of Health. **~ di costumi** morality. **~ mentale** sanity, mental health

sani'tario *a* sanitary; **servizio ~** health service ● *nm* doctor

San Ma'rino *nm* San Marino

'sano *a* sound; (*salutare*) healthy; **~ di mente** sane; **~ come un pesce** as fit as a fiddle

'sansa *nf* husk

San Sil'vestro *nm* New Year's Eve

santifi'care *vt* sanctify

santità *nf* sainthood

'santo, -a *a* holy; (*con nome proprio*) saint; **Sant'Antonio** St Anthony; **San Francesco d'Assisi** St Francis of Assisi; **di santa ragione** in no uncertain terms ● *nmf* saint. **~ patrono, -a** patron saint

san'tone *nm* guru

santo'reggia *nf Bot* savory

santu'ario *nm* sanctuary

san Valen'tino *nm* St Valentine's Day; **giorno di ~ ~** Valentine's Day

sanzio'nare *vt* sanction

sanzi'one *nf* sanction. **~ amministrativa** administrative sanction. **~ penale** legal sanction

sa'pere *vt* know; (*essere capace di*) be able to; (*venire a sapere*) hear; **saperla lunga** know a thing or two; **non lo so** I don't know; **non so che farci** there's nothing I can do about it; **~ a memoria** know by heart; **~ il fatto proprio** know what one is talking about; **per quanto ne sappia** insofar as I know ● *vi* **~ di** know about; (*aver sapore di*) taste of; (*aver odore di*) smell of; **saperci fare** know how to go about it; **saperci fare con i bambini** be good with children ● *nm* knowledge

sapi'ente *a* wise; (*esperto*) expert ● *nm* sage

sapiente'mente *adv* wisely; (*abilmente*) skilfully

sapien'tone *nm* smart alec[k]

sapi'enza *nf* wisdom

sa'pone *nm* soap; **bolla di ~** soap bubble; **finire in una bolla di ~** *fig* come to nothing. **~ da barba** shaving soap. **~ da bucato** washing soap

sapo'netta *nf* bar of soap

sapo'noso *a* soapy

sa'pore *nm* taste; **sentire ~ di** detect a hint of

saporita'mente *adv* (*condire*) skilfully; (*mangiare*) appreciatively; (*dormire*) soundly

sapo'rito *a* tasty

sapu'tello, -a *a & nm sl* know-all, know-it-all *Am*

sara'banda *nf fig* uproar

sara'ceno, -a *a & nmf* Saracen; **grano ~** buckwheat

saraci'nesca *nf* roller shutter; (*di chiusa*) sluice gate

'sarago *nm* white bream

sar'casmo *nm* sarcasm

sarcastica'mente *adv* sarcastically

sar'castico *a* sarcastic

sar'cofago *nm* sarcophagus

Sar'degna *nf* Sardinia

sar'dina *nf* sardine

'sardo, -a *a & nmf* Sardinian

sar'donico *a* sardonic

sarti'ame *nm* rigging

'sarto, -a *nm* tailor ● *nf* dressmaker

sarto'ria *nf* (*da uomo*) tailor's; (*da donna*) dressmaker's; (*arte*) couture

s.a.s. *abbr* **società in accomandita semplice**

sas'saia *nf* stony ground

sassai'ola *nf* hail of stones

sas'sata *nf* blow with a stone; **una ~ ha rotto il vetro** a stone broke the window; **prendere a sassate** throw stones at, stone

'sasso *nm* stone; (*ciottolo*) pebble; **sono rimasto di ~** I was struck dumb [with astonishment]

sassofo'nista *nmf* saxophonist

sas'sofono *nm* saxophone

'sassone *nmf* Saxon; **genitivo ~** Saxon genitive

sas'soso *a* stony

'Satana *nm* Satan
sa'tanico *a* satanic
sa'tellite *a inv & nm* satellite; **città ~** satellite town
sati'nare *vt* glaze; polish ‹*metallo*›
sati'nato *a* glazed; ‹*metallo*› polished
'satira *nf* satire
sa'tirico *a* satirical
satol'lare *vt hum* stuff
sa'tollo *a hum* replete, full
satu'rare *vt* saturate
saturazi'one *nf* saturation
satur'nismo *nm* lead poisoning
Sa'turno *nm* Saturn
'saturo *a* saturated; (*pieno*) full
S.A.U.B. *nf abbr* (**Struttura Amministrativa Unificata di Base**) *Italian national health service*
'sauna *nf* sauna
sa'vana *nf* savannah
savoi'ardo *nm* (*biscotto*) sponge finger
savoir-'faire *nm inv* expertise, know-how
sazi'are *vt* satiate
sazi'arsi *vr ~ di fig* weary of, grow tired of
sazietà *nf* **mangiare a ~** eat one's fill
'sazio *a* satiated
sbaciucchi'are *vt* smother with kisses
sbaciucchi'arsi *vr* kiss and cuddle
sbada'taggine *nf* carelessness; **è stata una ~** it was careless
sbadata'mente *adv* carelessly
sba'dato *a* careless
sbadigli'are *vi* yawn
sba'diglio *nm* yawn
sba'fare *vt* sponge
sba'fata *nf fam* nosh; **farsi una ~** *fam* have a nosh-up
'sbaffo *nm* smear
'sbafo *nm* sponging; **a ~** (*gratis*) without paying
sbagli'are *vi* make a mistake; (*aver torto*) be wrong ● *vt* make a mistake in; **~ strada** go the wrong way; **~ numero** get the number wrong; *Teleph* dial a wrong number; **sbagliando s'impara** practice makes perfect
sbagli'arsi *vr* make a mistake; **ti sbagli** you're mistaken, you're wrong; **~ di grosso** be totally wrong
sbagli'ato *a* wrong
'sbaglio *nm* mistake; **per ~** by mistake
sbale'strare *vt fig* disconcert
sbale'strato *a* disconcerted
sbal'lare *vt* unpack; *fam* screw up ‹*conti*› ● *vi fam* go crazy
sbal'lato *a* (*squilibrato*) unbalanced
'sballo *nm fam* scream; (*per droga*) trip; **da ~** *sl* terrific
sballot'tare *vt* toss about
sbalordi'mento *nm* amazement
sbalor'dire *vt* stun ● *vi* be stunned
sbalordi'tivo *a* amazing
sbalor'dito *a* stunned; **restare ~** be stunned

sbal'zare *vt* throw; (*da una carica*) dismiss ● *vi* bounce; (*saltare*) leap
'sbalzo *nm* bounce; (*sussulto*) jolt; (*di temperatura*) sudden change; **a sbalzi** in spurts; **a ~** (*a rilievo*) embossed
sban'care *vt* bankrupt; excavate ‹*terreno*›; **~ il banco** break the bank
sbanda'mento *nm Auto* skid; *Naut* list; *fig* going off the rails
sban'dare *vi Auto* skid; *Naut* list
sban'darsi *vr* (*disperdersi*) disperse
sban'data *nf* skid; *Naut* list; **prendere una ~ per** get a crush on
sban'dato, -a *a* mixed-up ● *nmf* mixed-up person
sbandie'rare *vt* wave; *fig* display
sbarac'care *vt/i* clear up
sbaragli'are *vt* rout
sba'raglio *nm* rout; **mettere allo ~** rout
sbaraz'zare *vt* clear
sbaraz'zarsi *vr ~ di* get rid of
sbaraz'zino, -a *a* mischievous ● *nmf* scamp
sbar'bare *vt* shave
sbar'barsi *vr* shave
sbarba'tello, -a *a & nmf* novice
sbar'care *vt/i* disembark; **~ il lunario** make ends meet
'sbarco *nm* landing; (*di merci*) unloading
'sbarra *nf* bar; (*di passaggio a livello*) barrier. **~ spaziatrice** space bar
sbarra'mento *nm* barricade
sbar'rare *vt* bar; (*ostruire*) block; cross ‹*assegno*›; (*spalancare*) open wide
sbar'retta *nf* oblique
sbatacchi'are *vt/i sl* bang, slam
'sbattere *vt* bang; slam, bang ‹*porta*›; (*urtare*) knock; *Culin* beat; flap ‹*ali*›; shake ‹*tappeto*›; **~ le palpebre** blink ● *vi* bang; ‹*porta:*› slam, bang; **~ contro** knock against; **andare a ~ contro** run into
sbat'tersi *vr sl* rush around; **sbattersene di qcsa** not give a toss about sth
sbat'tuto *a* tossed; *Culin* beaten; *fig* run down
sba'vare *vi* dribble; ‹*colore:*› smear
sbava'tura *nf* smear; **senza sbavature** *fig* faultless
sbeccucci'are *vt* chip
sbeccucci'ato *a* chipped
sbeffeggi'are *vt* mock
sbelli'carsi *vr* **~ dalle risa** split one's sides [with laughter]
sben'dare *vt* unbandage
'sberla *nf* slap
sbevaz'zare *vi fam* tipple
sbia'dire *vt/i* fade
sbia'dirsi *vr* fade
sbia'dito *a* faded; *fig* colourless
sbian'cante *nm* whitener
sbian'care *vt/i* whiten
sbian'carsi *vr* whiten
sbi'eco *a* slanting; **di ~** on the slant;

⟨guardare⟩ sidelong; **guardare qcno di ~** look askance at sb; **tagliare di ~** cut on the bias

sbigot'tire vt dismay ● vi be dismayed

sbigot'tirsi vr be dismayed

sbigot'tito a dismayed

sbilanci'are vt unbalance ● vi ⟨perdere l'equilibrio⟩ overbalance

sbilanci'arsi vr lose one's balance

sbi'lancio nm lack of balance; Comm deficit

sbirci'are vt cast sidelong glances at

sbirci'ata nf furtive glance

sbircia'tina nf **dare una ~ a** sneak a glance at

'**sbirro** nm pej cop

sbizzar'rirsi vr satisfy one's whims

sbloc'care vt unblock; Mech release; decontrol ⟨prezzi⟩

'**sbobba** nf fam pigswill

sboc'care vi **~ in** ⟨fiume:⟩ flow into; ⟨strada:⟩ lead to; ⟨folla:⟩ pour into

sboc'cato a foul-mouthed

sbocci'are vi blossom

'**sbocco** nm flowing; ⟨foce⟩ mouth; Comm outlet

sbolo'gnare vt fam get rid of

'**sbornia** nf **prendere una ~** get drunk; **smaltire la ~** sober up

sbor'sare vt pay out

sbot'tare vi burst out

sbotto'nare vt unbutton

sbotto'narsi vr ⟨fam: confidarsi⟩ open up; **~ la camicia** unbutton one's shirt

sboz'zare vt draft; sketch out ⟨dipinto⟩

sbra'carsi vr put on something more comfortable; **~ dalle risate** fam kill oneself laughing

sbracci'arsi vr wave one's arms

sbracci'ato a bare-armed; ⟨abito⟩ sleeveless

sbrai'tare vi bawl

sbra'nare vt tear to shreds or pieces

sbra'narsi vr tear each other to shreds

sbrat'tare vt clean up

sbrec'cato a chipped

sbricio'lare vt crumble

sbricio'larsi vr crumble

sbri'gare vt expedite; ⟨occuparsi di⟩ attend to

sbri'garsi vr hurry up, be quick

sbriga'tivo a hurried, quick

sbrigli'ato a ⟨fantasia⟩ unbridled

sbri'nare vt defrost; Auto de-ice

sbrina'tore nm Auto de-icer; ⟨di frigo⟩ defrost button

sbrindel'lare vt tear to shreds

sbrindel'lato a in rags

sbrodo'lare vt stain

sbrodo'lone, -a nmf messy eater

sbrogli'are vt disentangle

'**sbronza** nf fam **prendersi una ~** get drunk

sbron'zarsi vr get drunk

'**sbronzo** a ⟨ubriaco⟩ drunk

sbruffo'nata nf boast

sbruf'fone, -a nmf boaster

sbu'care vi come out

sbucci'are vt peel; shell ⟨piselli⟩

sbucci'arsi vr graze oneself

sbuccia'tore nm parer

sbuccia'tura nf graze

sbudel'lare vt gut ⟨pesce⟩; draw ⟨pollo⟩; disembowel ⟨persona⟩

sbudel'larsi vr **~ dal ridere** die laughing

sbuf'fare vi snort; ⟨per impazienza⟩ fume

'**sbuffo** nm puff; **a ~** ⟨maniche⟩ puff attrib

sbugiar'dare vt show to be a liar

sbuz'zare vt gut ⟨pesce⟩; draw ⟨pollo⟩; disembowel ⟨persona⟩

'**scabbia** nf scabies sg

'**scabro** a rough; ⟨terreno⟩ uneven; ⟨stile⟩ bald

sca'broso a rough; ⟨terreno⟩ uneven; ⟨fig: questione⟩ difficult; ⟨scena⟩ offensive

scacchi'era nf chess-board

scacciapensi'eri nm inv Mus Jew's harp

scacci'are vt chase away

'**scacco** nm check; **scacchi** pl ⟨gioco⟩ chess; ⟨pezzi⟩ chessmen; **dare ~ matto a** checkmate; **a scacchi** ⟨tessuto⟩ checked; **subire uno ~** fig suffer a humiliating defeat

sca'dente a shoddy

sca'denza nf ⟨di contratto⟩ expiry; ⟨di progetto, candidatura⟩ deadline; Comm maturity; **a breve/lunga ~** short-/long-term

scaden'zario nm schedule

sca'dere vi expire; ⟨valore:⟩ decline; ⟨debito:⟩ be due

sca'duto a ⟨biglietto⟩ out-of-date

sca'fandro nm diving suit; ⟨di astronauta⟩ spacesuit

scaffala'tura nf shelves pl, shelving

scaf'fale nm shelf; ⟨libreria⟩ bookshelf

'**scafo** nm hull

scagion'are vt exonerate

'**scaglia** nf scale; ⟨di sapone⟩ flake; ⟨scheggia⟩ chip

scagli'are vt fling

scagli'arsi vr fling oneself; **~ contro** fig rail against

scaglio'nare vt space out

scagli'one nm group; **a scaglioni** in groups. **~ di reddito** tax bracket

sca'gnozzo nm henchman

'**scala** nf staircase; ⟨portatile⟩ ladder; ⟨Mus, misura⟩ scale; **scale** pl stairs; **in ~** to scale; **modello in ~** scale model; **su larga ~** large-scale attrib. **~ allungabile** extension ladder. **~ antincendio** fire escape. **~ Beaufort** Beaufort scale. **~ a chiocciola** spiral staircase. **~ mobile** escalator; ⟨dei salari⟩ cost of living index. **~ Richter** Richter scale. **~ di servizio** backstairs. **~ di sicurezza** fire escape. **~ di valori** scale of values

sca'lare a scalar ● vt climb; layer ⟨capelli⟩; ⟨detrarre⟩ deduct

sca'lata nf climb; ⟨dell'Everest ecc⟩ ascent; **fare delle scalate** go climbing

scala|'tore, -'trice nmf climber

scalca'gnato a down at heel

scalci'are *vi* kick
scalci'nato *a* shabby
scalda'bagno *nm* water heater
scalda'muscoli *nm inv* legwarmer
scal'dare *vt* heat
scal'darsi *vr* warm up; (*eccitarsi*) get excited
sca'leno *a* scalene
sca'leo *nm* step-ladder
scal'fire *vt* scratch
scalfit'tura *nf* scratch
scali'nata *nf* flight of steps. ~ **di piazza di Spagna** Spanish Steps
sca'lino *nm* step; (*di scala a pioli*) rung
scalma'narsi *vr* rush about; (*nel parlare*) get worked up
scalma'nato *a* worked up; **è** ~ (*vivace*) he can't sit still
'scalmo *nm* rowlock
'scalo *nm* slipway; *Naut* port of call; **fare** ~ **a** a call at; *Aeron* land at; **senza** ~ nonstop. ~ **merci** freight depot, goods yard. ~ **passeggeri** stopover
sca'logna *nf fam* bad luck
scalo'gnato *a fam* unlucky
sca'logno *nm Bot* scallion
scalop'pina *nf* escalope
scal'pare *vt* scalp
scalpel'lare *vt* chisel
scalpel'lino *nm* stone-cutter
scal'pello *nm* chisel
scalpi'tare *vi* paw the ground; *fig* champ at the bit
scalpi'tio *nm* pawing of the ground
'scalpo *nm* scalp
scal'pore *nm* noise; **far** ~ *fig* cause a sensation
scal'trezza *nf* shrewdness
scal'trirsi *vr* get shrewder
'scaltro *a* shrewd
scal'zare *vt* bare the roots of (*albero*); *fig* undermine; (*da una carica*) oust
'scalzo *a & adv* barefoot
scambi'are *vt* exchange; ~ **qcno per qualcun altro** mistake sb for somebody else
scambi'arsi *vr* exchange; ~ **i saluti** exchange greetings
scambi'evole *a* reciprocal
'scambio *nm* exchange; *Comm* trade; **libero** ~ free trade. ~ **di persona** mistaken identity
scamici'ato *nf* pinafore [dress]
sca'morza *nf* soft cheese
scamosci'ato *a* suede
scampa'gnata *nf* trip to the country
scampa'nato *a* (*gonna*) flared
scampanel'lata *nf* [loud] ring
scampanel'lio *nm* ringing
scampan'io *nm* peal[ing]
scam'pare *vt* save; (*evitare*) escape; **scamparla bella** have a lucky escape
scam'pato *a* **lo** ~ **pericolo** the escape from danger ● *nmf* survivor

'scampi *nmpl* (*crostaceo*) scampi
'scampo *nm* escape; **non c'è** ~ there's no way out
'scampolo *nm* remnant
scanala'tura *nf* groove
scandagli'are *vt* sound
scanda'lismo *nm* muckraking
scanda'listico *a* sensational; (*giornale*) sensationalist
scandaliz'zare *vt* scandalize
scandaliz'zarsi *vr* be scandalized
'scandalo *nm* scandal
scanda'loso *a* scandalous; (*somma ecc*) scandalous; (*fortuna*) outrageous
Scandi'navia *nf* Scandinavia
scan'dinavo, -a *a & nmf* Scandinavian
scan'dire *vt* scan (*verso*); pronounce clearly (*parole*); ~ **il tempo** beat time
scandi'tore *nm* ~ **ottico** *Comput* optical scanner
scan'nare *vt* slaughter
scan'nello *nm* lectern
'scanner *nm inv* scanner. ~ **manuale** *Comput* handheld scanner
scanneriz'zare *vt Comput* scan
scansafa'tiche *nmf inv* lazybones *sg*
scan'sare *vt* shift; (*evitare*) avoid
scan'sarsi *vr* get out of the way
scan'sia *nf* shelves *pl*
scansi'one *nf Comput* scanning
'scanso *nm* **a** ~ **di** in order to avoid; **a** ~ **di equivoci** to avoid any misunderstanding
scanti'nato *nm* basement
scanto'nare *vi* turn the corner; (*svignarsela*) sneak off
scanzo'nato *a* easy-going
scapacci'one *nm* smack
scape'strato *a* dissolute
scapigli'ato *a* dishevelled
'scapito *nm* loss; **a** ~ **di** to the detriment of
'scapola *nf* shoulder-blade
'scapolo *nm* bachelor
scappa'mento *nm Auto* exhaust
scap'pare *vi* escape; (*andarsene*) dash [off]; (*sfuggire*) slip; **mi scappa da ridere!** I want to burst out laughing; **mi scappa la pipì** I'm bursting, I need a pee; **mi ha fatto** ~ **la pazienza** he tried my patience a bit too far; **lasciarsi** ~ **l'occasione** let the opportunity slip; **scappar via** run off or away
scap'pata *nf fam* short visit
scappa'tella *nf* escapade; (*infedeltà*) fling
scappa'toia *nf* way out
scappel'lotto *nm* cuff
scara'beo¹ *nm* scarab beetle
scara'beo²[R] *nm* Scrabble[R]
scarabocchi'are *vt* scribble
scara'bocchio *nm* scribble
scara'faggio *nm* cockroach
scara'mantico *a* (*gesto*) to ward off the evil eye
scaraman'zia *nf* superstition
scara'mazzo *a* (*perla*) baroque
scara'muccia *nf* skirmish
scaraven'tare *vt* hurl

scarcas'sato *a* ⟨*fam: macchina*⟩ beat-up

scarce'rare *vt* release [from prison]

scardi'nare *vt* unhinge

'scarica *nf* discharge; ⟨*di arma da fuoco*⟩ volley; *fig* shower; **una ~ di botte** a hail of blows

scaricaba'rili *nm* **fare a ~** blame each other

scari'care *vt* discharge; unload ⟨*arma, merci, auto*⟩; *fig* unburden

scari'carsi *vr* ⟨*fiume:*⟩ flow; ⟨*orologio, batteria:*⟩ run down; *fig* unwind

scarica'tore *nm* loader; ⟨*di porto*⟩ docker

'scarico *a* unloaded; ⟨*vuoto*⟩ empty; ⟨*orologio*⟩ run-down; ⟨*batteria*⟩ flat; *fig* untroubled ● *nm* unloading; ⟨*di rifiuti*⟩ dumping; ⟨*di acqua*⟩ draining; ⟨*di sostanze inquinanti*⟩ discharge; ⟨*luogo*⟩ [rubbish] dump; *Auto* exhaust; ⟨*idraulico*⟩ drain; ⟨*tubo*⟩ waste pipe; **'divieto di ~'** 'no dumping'; **tubo di ~** waste pipe

scarlat'tina *nf* scarlet fever

scar'latto *a* scarlet

scarmigli'ato *a* ruffled

sca'rnire *vt fig* simplify

'scarno *a* thin; ⟨*fig: stile*⟩ bare

sca'rogna, scaro'gnato = **scalogna, scalognato**

sca'rola *nf* curly endive

'scarpa *nf* shoe; ⟨*fam: persona*⟩ dead loss; **fare le scarpe a qcno** *fig* double-cross sb. **scarpe** *pl* **basse** flat shoes, flats. **scarpe** *pl* **da danza** ballet shoes. **scarpe** *pl* **da ginnastica** trainers. **scarpe** *pl* **col tacco** high heels. **scarpe** *pl* **col tacco a spillo** stilettos. **scarpe** *pl* **con la zeppa** platform shoes

scar'pata *nf* slope; ⟨*burrone*⟩ escarpment

scarpi'era *nf* shoe rack

scarpi'nare *vi* hike

scar'pone *nm* boot. **~ da alpinismo** climbing boot. **scarponi** *pl* **da sci** ski boots. **scarponi** *pl* **da trekking** walking boots

scarroz'zare *vt/i* drive around

scarroz'zata *nf fam* trip

scarruf'fato *a* ruffled

scarseggi'are *vi* be scarce; **~ di** ⟨*mancare*⟩ be short of

scar'sezza *nf* scarcity, shortage

scarsità *nf* shortage

'scarso *a* scarce; ⟨*manchevole*⟩ short

scartabel'lare *vt* skim through

scarta'mento *nm* *Rail* gauge. **~ ridotto** narrow gauge

scar'tare *vt* discard; unwrap ⟨*pacco*⟩; ⟨*respingere*⟩ reject ● *vi* ⟨*deviare*⟩ swerve

scartave'trare *vt* sand

'scarto *nm* scrap; ⟨*in carte*⟩ discard; ⟨*deviazione*⟩ swerve; ⟨*distacco*⟩ gap

scartocci'are *vt* unwrap

scar'toffie *nfpl* bumf, bumph

scas'sare *vt* break

scas'sato *a fam* clapped out

scassi'nare *vt* force open

scassina'|tore, -'trice *nmf* burglar

'scasso *nm* ⟨*furto*⟩ house-breaking

scata'fascio = **catafascio**

scate'nare *vt fig* stir up ⟨*folla*⟩; arouse ⟨*sentimenti*⟩

scate'narsi *vr* break out; ⟨*fig: temporale:*⟩ break; ⟨*fam: darsi alla pazza gioia*⟩ go crazy, go wild; ⟨*fam: infiammarsi*⟩ get excited

scate'nato *a* crazy, wild; **pazzo ~** *fam* off his head

'scatola *nf* box; ⟨*di latta*⟩ can, tin *Br*; **in ~** ⟨*cibo*⟩ canned, tinned *Br*; **rompere le scatole a qcno** *fam* get on sb's nerves; **a ~ chiusa** ⟨*comprare*⟩ sight unseen. **~ del cambio** gearbox. **~ nera** *Aeron* black box

scato'lame *nm* ⟨*cibo*⟩ canned food

scato'letta *nf* small box

scato'logico *a* scatological

scat'tante *a* zippy

scat'tare *vi* go off; ⟨*balzare*⟩ spring up; ⟨*adirarsi*⟩ lose one's temper; take ⟨*foto*⟩

'scatto *nm* ⟨*balzo*⟩ spring; ⟨*d'ira*⟩ outburst; ⟨*di telefono*⟩ unit; ⟨*dispositivo*⟩ release; **a scatti** jerkily; **di ~** suddenly

scatu'rire *vi* spring

scaval'care *vt* jump over ⟨*muretto*⟩; climb over ⟨*muro*⟩; ⟨*fig: superare*⟩ overtake

sca'vare *vt* dig ⟨*buca*⟩; dig up ⟨*tesoro*⟩; excavate ⟨*città sepolta*⟩

scava'trice *nf* excavator

scavezza'collo *nm* daredevil

'scavo *nm* excavation

scazzot'tare *vt fam* beat up

scazzot'tata *nf fam* punch-up; **prendersi una ~** get beaten up

'scegliere *vt* choose, select

sce'icco *nm* sheikh

scelle'rato *a* wicked

'scelta *nf* choice; ⟨*di articoli*⟩ range; **...a ~** ⟨*in menù*⟩ choice of...; **prendine uno a ~** take your choice o pick; **di prima ~** top-grade, choice; ⟨*albergo*⟩ first-rate; **di seconda ~** second grade; *pej* second-rate

'scelto *pp di* **scegliere** ● *a* select; ⟨*merce ecc*⟩ choice; **tiratore ~** marksman

sce'mare *vt/i* diminish

sce'menza *nf* silliness; ⟨*azione*⟩ silly thing to do/say; **non diciamo scemenze!** let's not be silly!

'scemo *a* idiotic ● *nm* idiot

scempi'aggine *nf* foolish thing to do/say

'scempio *nm* havoc; ⟨*fig: di paesaggio*⟩ ruination; **fare ~ di** play havoc with

'scena *nf* scene; ⟨*palcoscenico*⟩ stage; **entrare in ~** *Theat* go/come on [stage]; *fig* come on the scene; **fare ~** put on an act; **fare una ~** make a scene; **fare scene** make a fuss; **andare in ~** ⟨*Theat: spettacolo:*⟩ be staged, be put on; **fare ~ muta** not open one's mouth; **scomparire dalla ~** *fig* vanish from the scene; **mettere in ~** produce, stage; **messa in ~** production, staging; *fig* set-up

sce'nario *nm* scenery

sce'nata *nf* row, scene

'scendere *vi* go/come down; ⟨*da treno, autobus*⟩ get off; ⟨*da macchina*⟩ get out;

⟨*strada:*⟩ slope; ⟨*notte, prezzi:*⟩ fall ● *vt* go/come down ⟨*scale*⟩

scendi'letto *nm* bedside rug

scenegi'are *vt* dramatize

scenegi'ato *nm* television serial

sceneggia'tura *nf* screenplay

'**scenico** *a* scenic

scenogra'fia *nf* set design

sce'nografo, -a *nmf* set designer

sce'riffo *nm* sheriff

scervel'larsi *vr* rack one's brains

scervel'lato *a* brainless

'**sceso** *pp di* **scendere**

scetti'cismo *nm* scepticism

'**scettico, -a** *a* sceptical ● *nmf* sceptic

'**scettro** *nm* sceptre

'**scheda** *nf* card. ~ **audio** *Comput* sound card. ~ **elettorale** ballot-paper. ~ **di espansione** *Comput* expansion card. ~ **grafica** *Comput* graphics card. ~ **madre** *Comput* motherboard. ~ **magnetica** card key. ~ **perforata** punch card. ~ **di rete** *Comput* network card. ~ **sonora** *Comput* sound card. ~ **telefonica** phonecard. ~ **video** *Comput* video card

sche'dare *vt* file

sche'dario *nm* file; ⟨*mobile*⟩ filing cabinet

sche'dato, -a *a* with a police record ● *nmf* person with a police record

sche'dina *nf* ≈ pools coupon; **giocare la ~** ≈ do the pools

'**scheggia** *nf* fragment; ⟨*di legno*⟩ splinter

scheggi'are *vt* splinter

scheggi'arsi *vr* chip; ⟨*legno:*⟩ splinter

sche'letrico *a* skeletal

'**scheletro** *nm* skeleton; **essere ridotto ad uno ~** be all skin and bones

'**schema** *nm* diagram; ⟨*abbozzo*⟩ outline; **uscire dagli schemi** break with tradition

schematica'mente *adv* schematically

sche'matico *a* schematic

schematiz'zare *vt* present schematically

'**scherma** *nf* fencing

scher'maglia *nf* skirmish

scher'mirsi *vr* protect oneself

'**schermo** *nm* screen; **grande ~** big screen; **farsi ~ con** shield oneself with. ~ **panoramico** wide screen. ~ **a sfioramento** *Comput* touch-sensitive screen

scher'nire *vt* mock

'**scherno** *nm* mockery

scher'zare *vi* joke; ⟨*giocare*⟩ play; **c'è poco da ~!** it's nothing to laugh about!

'**scherzo** *nm* joke; ⟨*trucco*⟩ trick; ⟨*effetto*⟩ play; *Mus* scherzo; **fare uno ~ a qcno** play a joke on sb; **giocare brutti scherzi (a qcno)** ⟨*memoria, vista:*⟩ play tricks (on sb); **per ~** for fun; **scherzi a parte** joking apart, seriously; **stare allo ~** take a joke. ~ **di natura** freak of nature

scher'zoso *a* playful

schiaccia'noci *nm inv* nutcrackers *pl*

schiacci'ante *a* damning; ⟨*vittoria*⟩ crushing

schiacci'are *vt* crush; ⟨*in tennis ecc*⟩ smash; press ⟨*pulsante*⟩; crack ⟨*noce*⟩; ~ **un pisolino** grab forty winks

schiacci'arsi *vr* get crushed

schiaccia'sassi *nf inv* steamroller

schiaf'fare *vt fam* shove

schiaffeggi'are *vt* slap

schi'affo *nm* slap; **dare uno ~ a** slap. ~ **morale** slap in the face; **avere una faccia da schiaffi** have the kind of face you'd love to take a swipe at

schiamaz'zare *vi* make a racket; ⟨*galline:*⟩ cackle

schia'mazzo *nm* din. **schiamazzi** *pl* **notturni** disturbing the peace

schian'tare *vt* break

schian'tarsi *vr* crash ● *vi* **schianto dalla fatica** I'm wiped out

'**schianto** *nm* crash; *fam* knock-out; ⟨*divertente*⟩ scream

schia'rire *vt* clear; ⟨*sbiadire*⟩ fade ● *vi* brighten up

schia'rirsi *vr* brighten up; ~ **la gola** clear one's throat; ~ **le idee** get things clear in one's head; ⟨*dopo aver bevuto*⟩ clear one's head

schia'rita *nf* sunny interval

schiat'tare *vi* burst; ~ **di invidia** be green with envy

schia'vista *nmf* slave-driver

schiavitù *nf* slavery

schi'avo, -a *nmf* slave

schi'ena *nf* back; **mal di ~** backache

schie'nale *nm* ⟨*di sedia*⟩ back

schi'era *nf Mil* rank; ⟨*moltitudine*⟩ crowd

schiera'mento *nm* lining up; *Mil* battle line. ~ **di forze** rallying of the troops

schie'rare *vt* draw up; rally ⟨*forze*⟩

schie'rarsi *vr* draw up; ⟨*forze:*⟩ rally; ~ **dalla parte di qcno**, ~ **con qcno** rally [in support] to sb; ~ **contro qcno** rally in opposition to sb

schiet'tezza *nf* frankness

schi'etto *a* frank; ⟨*puro*⟩ pure

schi'fezza *nf* **è una ~** it's disgusting; ⟨*film, libro:*⟩ it's rubbish

schifil'toso *a* fussy

'**schifo** *nm* disgust; **fare ~** be disgusting; **è uno ~!** it's disgusting!

schi'foso *a* disgusting; ⟨*di cattiva qualità*⟩ rubbishy

schioc'care *vt* crack ⟨*frusta*⟩; snap, click ⟨*dita*⟩; click ⟨*lingua*⟩ ● *vi* crack

schi'occo *nm* ⟨*di frusta*⟩ crack; ⟨*di bacio*⟩ smack; ⟨*di dita, lingua*⟩ click

schioppet'tata *nf* shot

schi'oppo *nm fam* rifle; **a un tiro di ~** *fig* a stone's throw away

schiri'bizzo *nm fam* fancy; **se mi salta lo ~...** if it takes my fancy...

schi'udere *vt* open

schi'udersi *vr* open

schi'uma *nf* foam; ⟨*di sapone*⟩ lather; ⟨*di bucato*⟩ suds; ⟨*feccia*⟩ scum. ~ **da barba** shaving foam

schiu'mare *vt* skim ● *vi* foam

schiuma'rola nf Culin skimmer
schiu'mogeno a foaming
schiu'moso a ⟨birra, crema⟩ frothy, foamy; ⟨liquido⟩ scummy
schi'uso pp di **schiudere**
schi'vare vt avoid
'schivo a bashful
schizofre'nia nf schizophrenia
schizo'frenico, -a a & nmf schizophrenic
schiz'zare vt squirt; (inzaccherare) splash; (abbozzare) sketch; ~ **qcno/qcsa di qcsa** splatter sb/sth with sth ● vi spurt ~ **via** fig scurry away
schiz'zato, -a a & nmf fam loony
schizzi'noso a squeamish
'schizzo nm squirt; (di fango) splash; (abbozzo) sketch
sci nm inv ski; (sport) skiing. ~ **d'acqua,** ~ **acquatico** water-skiing. ~ **acrobatico** hot dogging. ~ **di fondo** cross-country skiing
'scia nf wake; (di fumo ecc) trail; **sulla ~ di qcno** following in sb's footsteps
sci'abola nf sabre
sciabor'dare vt/i lap
sciabor'dio nm lapping
sciacal'laggio nm profiteering
scia'callo nm jackal; fig profiteer
sciac'quare vt rinse
sciac'quarsi vr rinse oneself
sci'acquo nm mouthwash
scia'gura nf disaster
sciagu'rato a unfortunate; (scellerato) wicked
scialac'quare vt squander
scialacqua'tore, -'trice nmf squanderer
scia'lare vi spend money like water
sci'albo a pale; fig dull
sci'alle nm shawl
scia'luppa nf dinghy. ~ **di salvataggio** lifeboat
sciaman'nato a good-for-nothing
scia'mano n shaman
scia'mare vi swarm
sci'ame nm swarm; **a sciami** in swarms
sci'ampo nm shampoo
scian'cato a lame
sci'are vi ski; **andare a ~** go skiing
sci'arpa nf scarf
sci'atica nf Med sciatica
scia'tore, -'trice nmf skier
sciatte'ria nf slovenliness
sci'atto a slovenly; ⟨stile⟩ careless
sciat'tone, -a nmf slovenly person
'scibile nm knowledge; **lo ~ umano** the sum of human knowledge
scic'coso a fam snazzy
scienti'fico a scientific
sci'enza nf science; (sapere) knowledge; **avere la ~ infusa** be naturally talented
scienzi'ato, -a nmf scientist
sci'ita a & nmf Shiite
scilin'guagnolo nm fig **avere lo ~** be a chatterbox
'scimmia nf monkey

scimmiot'tare vt ape
scimpanzé nm inv chimpanzee, chimp
scimu'nito a idiotic
'scindere vt separate; ~ **in** break down into
'scindersi vr divide; ~ **in** divide into
scin'tilla nf spark
scintil'lante a sparkling
scintil'lare vi sparkle
scintil'lio nm sparkle
sciò int shoo!
scioc'cante a shocking
scioc'care vt shock
scioc'chezza nf foolishness; (assurdità) foolish thing; **sciocchezze!** nonsense!
sci'occo a foolish
sci'ogliere vt untie; undo, untie ⟨nodo⟩; (liberare) release; (liquefare) melt; dissolve ⟨contratto, qcsa nell'acqua⟩; loosen up ⟨muscoli⟩
sci'ogliersi vr ⟨nodo:⟩ come undone; (liquefarsi) melt; ⟨contratto:⟩ be dissolved; ⟨pastiglia:⟩ dissolve
sciogli'lingua nm inv tongue-twister
scio'lina nf ski wax
sciol'tezza nf agility; (disinvoltura) ease
sci'olto pp di **sciogliere** ● a loose; (agile) agile; (disinvolto) easy; **versi** pl **sciolti** blank verse
sciope'rante nmf striker
sciope'rare vi go on strike, strike
sci'opero nm strike; **in ~** on strike. ~ **bianco** work-to-rule. ~ **generale** general strike. ~ **a singhiozzo** on-off strike
sciori'nare vt fig show off
sciovi'nismo nm chauvinism
sciovi'nista nmf Pol chauvinist
sciovi'nistico a Pol chauvinistic
sci'pito a insipid
scip'pare vt fam snatch; ~ **qcno** snatch sb's bag/bracelet etc
scippa'tore, -'trice nmf bag-snatcher
'scippo nm bag-snatching
sci'rocco nm sirocco
scirop'pato a ⟨frutta⟩ in syrup
sci'roppo nm syrup
scirop'poso a syrupy
'scisma nm schism
scissi'one nf division
scissio'nista a breakaway attrib
'scisso pp di **scindere**
sciupacchi'are vt spoil
sciupacchi'ato a spoilt
sciu'pare vt spoil; (sperperare) waste
sciu'parsi vr get spoiled; (deperire) wear oneself out
sciu'pio nm waste
scivo'lare vi slide; (involontariamente) slip
'scivolo nm slide; Techn chute
scivo'lone nm fall; (fig: errore) blunder
scivo'loso a slippery
scle'rosi nf sclerosis. ~ **multipla,** ~ **a placche** multiple sclerosis, MS
scoc'care vt fire ⟨freccia⟩; strike ⟨ore⟩ ● vi ⟨scintilla:⟩ shoot out; **sono scoccate le cinque** five o'clock has just struck

scocci'are *vt fam* (*dare noia a*) bother

scocci'arsi *vr fam* be bored; **mi sono scocciato di aspettare** I'm fed up waiting

scocci'ato *a fam* fed up

scoccia'tore, -'trice *nmf* nuisance

scoccia'tura *nf fam* nuisance

sco'della *nf* bowl

scodel'lare *vt* dish out, dish up

scodinzo'lare *vi* wag its tail

scogli'era *nf* cliff; (*a fior d'acqua*) reef

'scoglio *nm* rock; (*fig: ostacolo*) stumbling block

scoglio'nato *a vulg* pissed off

scoi'attolo *nm* squirrel

scola'pasta *nm inv* colander

scolapi'atti *nm inv* dish drainer

sco'lara *nf* schoolgirl

sco'lare[1] *vt* drain; strain (*pasta, verdura*) ● *vi* drip

sco'lare[2] *a* school *attrib*; **in età ~** (*bambino*) school-age

scola'resca *nf* pupils *pl*

sco'laro *nm* schoolboy

sco'lastico *a* school *attrib*; **gita scolastica** school trip

scoli'osi *nf* curvature of the spine

scollacci'ato *a* low-cut

scol'lare *vt* cut away the neck of (*abito*); (*staccare*) unstick

scol'lato *a* (*abito*) low-necked

scolla'tura *nf* neckline; **~ profonda** plunging neckline

scolle'gare *vt* disconnect

'scollo *nm* neckline

'scolo *nm* drainage

scolo'rare *vt* fade

scolori'mento *nm* fading

scolo'rire *vt* fade

scolo'rirsi *vr* fade

scolo'rito *a* faded

scol'pire *vt* carve; (*imprimere*) engrave

scombi'nare *vt* upset

scombus'solare *vt* muddle up

scom'messa *nf* bet

scom'messo *pp di* **scommettere**

scom'mettere *vt* bet; **ci puoi ~!** you bet!

scomo'dare *vt* trouble

scomo'darsi *vr* trouble

scomodità *nf inv* discomfort

'scomodo *a* uncomfortable ● *nm* **essere di ~ a qcno** be a trouble to sb

scompagin'are *vt* mess up

scompa'gnare *vt* split

scompa'gnato *a* odd

scompa'rire *vi* disappear; (*morire*) pass away

scom'parsa *nf* disappearance; (*morte*) death, passing

scom'parso, -a *pp di* **scomparire** ● *a* departed ● *nmf* departed

scomparti'mento *nm* compartment

scom'parto *nf* compartment

scompen'sare *vt* throw off balance

scom'penso *nm* imbalance. **~ cardiaco** cardiac insufficiency

scompigli'are *vt* disarrange

scom'piglio *nm* confusion

scompisci'arsi *vr fam* **~ [dalle risa]** wet oneself, split one's sides laughing

scom'porre *vt* break down; ruffle (*capelli*); (*fig: turbare*) upset

scom'porsi *vr* lose one's composure

scomposizi'one *nf* breaking down

scom'posto *pp di* **scomporre** ● *a* (*sguaiato*) unseemly; (*disordinato*) untidy

sco'munica *nf* excommunication

scomuni'care *vt* excommunicate

sconcer'tante *a* disconcerting; (*che rende perplesso*) bewildering

sconcer'tare *vt* disconcert; (*rendere perplesso*) bewilder

sconcer'tato *a* disconcerted; (*perplesso*) bewildered

scon'cezza *nf* indecency

'sconcio *a* indecent ● *nm* **è uno ~ che...** it's a disgrace that...

sconclusio'nato *a* incoherent

scon'dito *a* unseasoned; (*insalata*) with no dressing

sconfes'sare *vt* disown

scon'figgere *vt* defeat

sconfi'nare *vi* cross the border; (*in proprietà privata*) trespass

sconfi'nato *a* unlimited

scon'fitta *nf* defeat; **subire una ~** be defeated, suffer defeat

scon'fitto *pp di* **sconfiggere**

sconfor'tante *a* disheartening, discouraging

scon'forto *nm* discouragement; **farsi prendere dallo ~** get discouraged, get disheartened

sconge'lare *vt* thaw out (*cibo*); defrost (*frigo*)

scongiu'rare *vt* beseech; (*evitare*) avert

scongi'uro *nm* **fare gli scongiuri** ≈ touch wood, knock on wood *Am*

scon'nesso *pp di* **sconnettere** ● *a fig* incoherent

scon'nettere *vt* disconnect

sconosci'uto, -a *a* unknown ● *nmf* stranger

sconquas'sare *vt* smash; (*sconvolgere*) upset

sconsa'crare *vt* deconsecrate

sconsiderata'mente *adv* inconsiderately

sconsidera'tezza *nf* lack of consideration, thoughtlessness

sconside'rato *a* inconsiderate, thoughtless

sconsigli'abile *a* not advisable

sconsigli'are *vt* advise against

sconso'lato *a* disconsolate

scon'tare *vt* discount; (*dedurre*) deduct; (*pagare*) pay off; serve (*pena*); **~ la propria colpa** pay for one's sins

scon'tato *a* discounted; (*ovvio*) expected; **~ del 10%** with 10% discount; **era ~** it was to be expected; **dare qcsa per ~** take sth for granted scon'tento *a* displeased ● *nm* discontent

'sconto *nm* discount; **fare uno ~** give a discount. **~ commerciale** trade discount

scon'trarsi *vr* clash; ⟨*urtare*⟩ collide

scon'trino *nm* ticket; ⟨*di cassa*⟩ receipt; **'munirsi dello ~ alla cassa'** sign reminding customers that payment must be made at the cash desk beforehand

'scontro *nm* clash; ⟨*urto*⟩ collision. **~ frontale** head-on collision. **~ a fuoco** shoot-out

scontrosità *nf* blackness

scon'troso *a* disagreeable

sconveni'ente *a* unprofitable; ⟨*scorretto*⟩ unseemly

sconvol'gente *a* mind-blowing

scon'volgere *vt* upset; ⟨*mettere in disordine*⟩ disarrange

sconvolgi'mento *nm* upheaval

scon'volto *pp di* **sconvolgere** ● *a* distraught

'scooter *nm inv* scooter

'scopa *nf* broom; ⟨*gioco di carte*⟩ type of card game

sco'pare *vt* sweep; *vulg* shag

sco'pata *nf* sweep; *vulg* shag; **dare una ~ per terra** give the floor a sweep

scoperchi'are *vt* take the lid off ⟨*pentola*⟩; take the roof off ⟨*casa*⟩

sco'perta *nf* discovery

sco'perto *pp di* **scoprire** ● *a* uncovered; ⟨*senza riparo*⟩ exposed; ⟨*conto*⟩ overdrawn; ⟨*spoglio*⟩ bare

'scopo *nm* aim; **a ~ di** for the sake of; **allo ~ di** in order to

sco'pone *nm* ⟨*gioco di carte*⟩ type of card game

scoppi'are *vi* burst; *fig* break out

scoppiet'tare *vi* crackle

'scoppio *nm* burst; ⟨*di guerra*⟩ outbreak; ⟨*esplosione*⟩ explosion; **a ~ ritardato** ⟨*bomba*⟩ delayed action; **ha reagito a ~ ritardato** he did a double take

sco'prire *vt* discover; ⟨*togliere la copertura a*⟩ uncover; unveil ⟨*statua*⟩; **~ gli altarini** *fam* reveal his/her etc guilty secrets

scoraggia'mento *nm* discouragement

scoraggi'ante *a* discouraging

scoraggi'are *vt* discourage

scoraggi'arsi *vr* lose heart

scor'butico *a Med* suffering from scurvy; ⟨*fig: scontroso*⟩ disagreeable

scor'buto *nm Med* scurvy

scorci'are *vt* shorten

scorcia'toia *nf* short cut

'scorcio *nm* ⟨*di cielo*⟩ patch; ⟨*in arte*⟩ foreshortening; **di ~** ⟨*vedere*⟩ from an angle. **~ panoramico** panoramic view. **~ del secolo** end of the century

scor'dare *vt* forget; **~ qcsa a casa** leave sth at home

scor'darsi *vr* forget; **~ di qcsa** forget sth

scor'dato *a Mus* out of tune

scorda'tura *nf Mus* going out of tune

sco'reggia *nf fam* fart

scoreggi'are *vi fam* fart

'scorfano *nm* scorpion fish

'scorgere *vt* make out; ⟨*notare*⟩ notice

'scoria *nf* waste; ⟨*di carbone*⟩ slag

scor'nare *vt fig* humiliate

scor'narsi *vr fig* come a cropper

scor'nato *a fig* hangdog

'scorno *nm* humiliation

scorpacci'ata *nf* bellyful; **fare una ~ di** stuff oneself with

scorpi'one *nm* scorpion; *Astr* Scorpio

scorraz'zare *vi* run about

'scorrere *vt* ⟨*dare un'occhiata*⟩ glance through ● *vi* run; ⟨*scivolare*⟩ slide; ⟨*fluire*⟩ flow; *Comput* scroll; ⟨*attorno a un oggetto*⟩ wrap

scorre'ria *nf* raid

scorret'tezza *nf* ⟨*mancanza di educazione*⟩ bad manners *pl*

scor'retto *a* incorrect; ⟨*sconveniente*⟩ improper

scor'revole *a* **porta ~** sliding door

scorri'banda *nf* raid; *fig* excursion

scorri'mento *nm Comput* scrolling; ⟨*attorno a un oggetto*⟩ wrapping

'scorsa *nf* glance; **dare una ~ a** glance through

'scorso *pp di* **scorrere** ● *a* last; **l'anno ~** last year

scor'soio *a* **nodo ~** noose

'scorta *nf* escort; ⟨*provvista*⟩ supply

scor'tare *vt* escort

scortecci'are *vt* debark ⟨*albero*⟩; strip ⟨*muro*⟩

scor'tese *a* rude

scorte'sia *nf* rudeness

scorti'care *vt* skin

scortica'tura *nf* graze

'scorto *pp di* **scorgere**

'scorza *nf* peel; ⟨*crosta*⟩ crust; ⟨*corteccia*⟩ bark; *fig* exterior. **~ d'arancia** orange peel

scorzo'nera *nf* salsify

sco'sceso *a* steep

'scossa *nf* shake; *Electr*, *fig* shock; **prendere la ~** get an electric shock. **~ elettrica** electric shock. **~ sismica** earth tremor

'scosso *pp di* **scuotere** ● *a* shaken; ⟨*sconvolto*⟩ upset

scos'sone *nm* jolt

sco'stante *a* off-putting

sco'stare *vt* push away

sco'starsi *vr* stand aside

scostu'mato *a* dissolute; ⟨*maleducato*⟩ ill-mannered

scoten'nare *vt* skin ⟨*maiale*⟩; scalp ⟨*persona*⟩

scot'tante *a* ⟨*argomento*⟩ burning; ⟨*fig: notizia*⟩ sensational

scot'tare *vt* burn; ⟨*con liquido, vapore*⟩ scald; *Culin* blanch ● *vi* ⟨*bevanda, cibo:*⟩ be too hot; ⟨*sole, pentola:*⟩ be very hot

scot'tarsi *vr* burn oneself; ⟨*con liquido, vapore*⟩ scald oneself; ⟨*al sole*⟩ get sunburnt; *fig* get one's fingers burnt

scot'tato *a Culin* blanched

scotta'tura nf burn; (da liquido) scald; fig painful experience; **~ solare** sunburn

'Scottex[R] nm paper towel

'scotto[1] a overcooked

'scotto[2] nm score; **pagare lo ~ di qcsa** pay for sth

scout a inv scout attrib ● nmf inv scout

scou'tismo nm scout movement

sco'vare vt (scoprire) discover

scovo'lino nm bottle brush; (per pipa) pipe cleaner

'Scozia nf Scotland

scoz'zese a Scottish ● nmf Scot

'scrambler nm inv Radio, Teleph scrambler

screan'zato a rude

scredi'tare vt discredit

scre'mare vt skim

screpo'lare vt chap

screpo'larsi vr get chapped; ⟨intonaco:⟩ crack

screpo'lato a chapped; ⟨intonaco⟩ cracked

screpola'tura nf crack

screzi'ato a speckled

'screzio nm disagreement

scribacchi'are vt scribble

scribac'chino, -a nmf scribbler; (impiegato) penpusher

scricchio'lante a creaky

scricchio'lare vi creak

scricchio'lio nm creaking

'scricciolo nm wren; fig delicate-looking creature

'scrigno nm casket

scrimina'tura nf parting

scriteri'ato a empty-headed

'scritta nf writing; (su muro) graffiti

'scritto pp di **scrivere** ● a written; **~ col computer** word-processed; **~ a macchina** typed; **~ a mano** handwritten ● nm writing; (lettera) letter

scrit'toio nm writing-desk

scrit|'tore, -'trice nmf writer

scrit'tura nf writing; Relig scripture; (calligrafia) handwriting. **scritture** pl **contabili** account books. **~ privata** Jur legal document drawn up by an individual

scrittu'rare vt engage

scriva'nia nf desk

scri'vente nmf writer

'scrivere vt write; (descrivere) write about; **~ a macchina** type

scroc'care vt fam **~ a** sponge off

scrocchi'are vi crack

'scrocco[1] nm fam **a ~** without paying; **vivere a ~** sponge off other people

'scrocco[2] nm **coltello a ~** pocket knife; **serratura a ~** spring lock

scroc'cone, -a nmf fam sponger

'scrofa nf sow

scrol'lare vt shake; **~ le spalle** shrug one's shoulders; **~ la testa** shake one's head

scrol'larsi vr shake oneself; **~ qcsa di dosso** shake sth off

'scrolling nm Comput scrolling

scrosci'ante a pouring; ⟨applausi⟩ thunderous

scrosci'are vi roar; ⟨pioggia:⟩ pelt down

'scroscio nm roar; (di pioggia) pelting; **uno ~ di applausi** thunderous applause; **piovere a ~** lash down

scro'stare vt scrape

scro'starsi vr flake

scro'stato a flaky

'scroto nm scrotum

'scrupolo nm scruple; (diligenza) care; **senza scrupoli** unscrupulous, without scruples; **farsi scrupoli per qcsa** have scruples about sth

scrupo'loso a scrupulous

scru'tare vt scan; (indagare) search

scruta'tore nm (di voti) returning officer

scruti'nare vt scrutinize

scru'tinio nm (di voti) poll; Sch assessment of progress; **scrutini** pl Sch meeting of teachers to discuss pupils' work and assign marks. **~ segreto** secret ballot

scu'cire vt unstitch; **scuci i soldi!** fig fam cough up [the money]!

scu'cirsi vr come unstitched; (fig: parlare) talk; **non si scuce** he won't talk

scuci'tura nf unstitching

scude'ria nf stable; **scuderie** pl mews

scu'detto nm Sport championship shield; (campionato) national championship

scudi'ero nm squire

scudisci'ata nf whipping

'scudo nm shield; **farsi ~ con qcsa** shield oneself with sth

scuffi'are vi capsize

scu'gnizzo nm street urchin

sculacci'are vt spank

sculacci'ata nf spanking; **prendere a sculacciate** spank

sculacci'one nm spanking

sculet'tare vi wiggle one's hips

scul|'tore, -'trice nm sculptor ● nf sculptress

scul'tura nf sculpture

scu'ola nf school. **~ allievi ufficiali** cadet school. **~ elementare** primary school. **~ guida** driving school. **~ materna** day nursery. **~ media** secondary school. **~ media inferiore** secondary school (10-13). **~ media superiore** secondary school (13-18). **~ dell'obbligo** compulsory education. **~ privata** private school, public school Br. **~ di sci** ski school. **~ serale** evening school. **~ statale** state school. **~ superiore** high school

scu'otere vt shake

scu'otersi vr (destarsi) rouse oneself; **~ qcsa di dosso** fig shake sth off

'scure nf axe

scu'rire vt/i darken

'scuro a dark ● nm darkness; (imposta) shutter

scur'rile a scurrilous

'scusa nf excuse; (giustificazione) apology;

scusare | segare

(*pretesto*) pretext; **chiedere** ~ apologize; [**chiedo**] ~! [I'm] sorry!

scu'sare *vt* excuse

scu'sarsi *vr* apologize (**di** for); [**mi**] **scusi!** excuse me!; (*chiedendo perdono*) [I'm] sorry!

'sdarsi *vr fam* lose interest

sdebi'tarsi *vr* repay the kindness

sde'gnare *vt* despise; (*fare arrabbiare*) enrage

sde'gnarsi *vr* become angry

sde'gnato *a* indignant

'sdegno *nm* disdain; (*ira*) indignation

sde'gnoso *a* disdainful

sden'tato *a* toothless

sdipa'nare *vt* wind

sdogana'mento *nm* customs clearance

sdoga'nare *vt* clear through customs

sdolci'nato *a* sentimental, schmaltzy

sdoppia'mento *nm* splitting. ~ **della personalità** split personality

sdoppi'are *vt* halve

sdrai'arsi *vr* lie down

'sdraio *nm* [**sedia a**] ~ deckchair

sdrammatiz'zare *vt* take the heat out of ● *vi* take the heat out of the situation

sdruccio'lare *vi* slither

sdruccio'levole *a* slippery

sdruccio'lone *nm* slip

SE *abbr* (**sud-est**) SE

se *conj* if; (*interrogativo*) whether, if; **se mai** (*caso mai*) if need be; **se mai telefonasse,...** should he call,..., if he calls,...; **se no** otherwise, or else; **se non altro** at least, if nothing else; **se pure** (*sebbene*) even though; (*anche se*) even if; **non so se sia vero** I don't know whether it's true, I don't know if it's true; **come se** as if; **se lo avessi saputo prima!** if only I had known before!; **e se andassimo fuori a cena?** how about going out for dinner? ● *nm inv* if; **non voglio né se né ma** I don't want any ifs or buts

sé *pers pron* oneself; (*lui*) himself; (*lei*) herself; (*esso, essa*) itself; (*loro*) themselves; **l'ha fatto da sé** he did it himself; **ha preso i soldi con sé** he took the money with him; **si sono tenuti le notizie per sé** they kept the news to themselves

se'baceo *a* sebaceous

seb'bene *conj* although

'sebo *nm* sebum

sec. *abbr* (**secolo**) c.

'secca *nf* shallows *pl*; **in** ~ ⟨*nave*⟩ grounded

sec'cante *a* annoying

sec'care *vt* dry; (*importunare*) annoy ● *vi* dry up

sec'carsi *vr* dry up; (*irritarsi*) get annoyed

secca'tura *nf* bother; **dare una** ~ **a** qcno trouble sb, bother sb; **non voglio seccare!** I don't want the bother!

secchi'ata *nf* bucketful

secchi'ello *nm* bucket. ~ **del ghiaccio** ice bucket

'secchio *nm* bucket. ~ **della spazzatura** rubbish bin, trash can *Am*

'secco, -a *a* dry; (*disseccato*) dried; (*magro*) thin; (*brusco*) curt; (*preciso*) sharp; **restare a** ~ be left penniless; **restarci** ~ ⟨*fam: morire di colpo*⟩ be killed on the spot; **frutta secca** nuts *pl* ● *nm* (*siccità*) drought; **lavare a** ~ dry-clean

secessi'one *nf* secession; **guerra di** ~ War of Secession

seco'lare *a* age-old; (*laico*) secular

'secolo *nm* century; (*epoca*) age; **è un** ~ **che non lo vedo** *fam* I haven't seen him for ages *o* yonks

se'conda *nf Sch, Rail* second class; *Auto* second [gear] ● *prep* **a** ~ **di** according to

secon'dario *a Jur* collateral; **effetto** ~ side effect

se'condo *a* second ● *nm* second, sec *fam*; (*secondo piatto*) main course; **un** ~! just a sec[ond]! ● *prep* according to; ~ **me** in my opinion

secondo'genito, -a *a & nm* second-born

secrezi'one *nf* secretion

'sedano *nm* celery. ~ **rapa** celeriac

se'dare *vt* put down, suppress ⟨*rivolta*⟩; *fig* soothe

seda'tivo *a & nm* sedative; **somministrare sedativi a** sedate

'sede *nf* seat; (*centro*) centre; *Relig* see; *Comm* head office; **in** ~ **di esami** during the exams; **in separata** ~ in private. ~ **centrale** head office. ~ **sociale** registered office

seden'tario *a* sedentary

se'dere *vi* sit

se'dersi *vr* sit down ● *nm* (*deretano*) bottom

'sedia *nf* chair. ~ **a dondolo** rocking chair. ~ **elettrica** electric chair. ~ **da giardino** garden seat. ~ **a rotelle** wheelchair. ~ **a sdraio** deckchair

sedi'cenne *a & nmf* sixteen-year-old

sedi'cente *a* self-styled

sedi'cesimo, -a *a & nm* sixteenth

'sedici *a & nm* sixteen

se'dile *nm* seat

sedimen'tare *vi* leave a sediment

sedi'mento *nm* sediment

sedizi'one *nf* sedition

sedizi'oso *a* seditious

se'dotto *pp di* sedurre

sedu'cente *a* seductive; (*allettante*) enticing

se'durre *vt* seduce

se'duta *nf* session; (*di posa*) sitting. ~ **stante** *adv* here and now

se'duto *a* sitting

sedut|'tore, -'trice *nm* charmer ● *nf* temptress

seduzi'one *nf* seduction

seg. *abbr* (**seguente**) foll.

'sega *nf* saw; *vulg* wank; **mezza** ~ *vulg* tosser; **non capire una** ~ understand damn all. ~ **circolare** circular saw. ~ **a mano** handsaw. ~ **a nastro** band saw

'segale *nf* rye; **pane di** ~ rye bread

sega'ligno *a* wiry

se'gare *vt* saw

sega'trice *nf* saw. ~ **a nastro** band saw
sega'tura *nf* sawdust
'seggio *nm* seat. ~ **elettorale** polling station
seg'giola *nf* chair
seggio'lino *nm* seat; (*da bambino*) child's seat; ~ **regolabile** adjustable seat
seggio'lone *nm* (*per bambini*) high chair
seggio'via *nf* chair lift
seghe'ria *nf* sawmill
se'ghetto *nm* hacksaw
segmen'tare *vt* segment
seg'mento *nm* segment
segna'carte *nm* bookmark
segna'lare *vt* signal; (*annunciare*) announce; (*indicare*) point out
segna'larsi *vr* distinguish oneself
segnalazi'one *nf* signals *pl*; (*di candidato*) recommendation. ~ **stradale** road signs *pl*
se'gnale *nm* signal; (*stradale*) sign. ~ **acustico** beep. ~ **d'allarme** alarm; (*in treno*) communication cord *Br*, emergency brake; *fig* danger signal. ~ **digitale** *Comput* digital signal. ~ **di libero** *Teleph* dialling tone. ~ **orario** time signal
segna'letica *nf* signals *pl*; '~ **in rifacimento**' 'road signs being repainted'. ~ **orizzontale** painted road markings *pl*. ~ **stradale** road signs *pl*
segna'letico *a* **dati segnaletici** description; **foto segnaletica** *photograph used for identification purposes*
segna'libro *nm* bookmark
segna'punti *nm inv* pegboard
se'gnare *vt* mark; (*prendere nota*) note; (*indicare*) indicate; *Sport* score; ~ **la fine di qcsa** sound the death knell for sth; ~ **il passo** mark time
se'gnarsi *vr* cross oneself
se'gnato *a* marked
'segno *nm* sign; (*traccia, limite*) mark; (*bersaglio*) target; **far** ~ (*col capo*) nod; (*con la mano*) beckon; **fare** ~ **di no** (*con la testa*) shake one's head; **fare** ~ **di sì** (*con la testa*) nod [one's head]; **lasciare il** ~ leave a mark; **non dare segni di vita** give no sign of life; **oltrepassare il** ~ *fig* overstep the mark. ~ **della croce** sign of the cross. ~ **premonitore** early warning. ~ **zodiacale** sign of the Zodiac, birth sign
segre'gare *vt* segregate
segre'garsi *vr* cut oneself off
segre'gato *a* in isolation
segregazi'one *nf* segregation
segretari'ato *nm* secretariat
segre'tario, -a *nmf* secretary; **fare da ~ a qcno** be sb's secretary. ~ **bilingue** bilingual secretary. ~ **comunale** town clerk. ~ **di direzione** executive secretary. ~ **personale** personal assistant, PA. **S~ di Stato** Secretary of State. **segretaria tuttofare** girl Friday
segrete'ria *nf* (*ufficio*) administrative office; (*segretariato*) secretariat. ~ **telefonica** answering machine, answerphone

segre'tezza *nf* secrecy
se'greto *a & nm* secret; **in** ~ in secret
segu'ace *nmf* follower; **avere molti seguaci** have a large following
segu'ente *a* following, next
se'gugio *nm* bloodhound
segu'ire *vt/i* follow; (*continuare*) continue; ~ **con lo sguardo** follow with one's eyes; ~ **le orme di qcno** follow in sb's footsteps; ~ **un corso** take a course
segui'tare *vt/i* continue
'seguito *nm* retinue; (*sequela*) series; (*continuazione*) continuation; **di** ~ in succession; **in** ~ later on; **in** ~ **a** following; **al** ~ in his/her wake; (*a causa di*) owing to; **fare** ~ **a** *Comm* follow up; **di** ~ one after the other
'sei *a & nm* six
sei'cento *a & nm* six hundred; **il S~** the seventeenth century
sei'mila *a & nm* six thousand
'selce *nf* flint
sel'ciato *nm* paving
se'lenio *nm* selenium
selettività *nf* selectivity
selet'tivo *a* selective; **memoria selettiva** selective memory
selet'tore *nm* selector
selezio'nare *vt* select; '~ **il numero**' 'dial [the number]'
selezi'one *nf* selection. ~ **naturale** natural selection
self-con'trol *nm* self-control
self-'service *a & nm inv* self-service
'sella *nf* saddle
sel'lare *vt* saddle
seltz *nm inv* soda water
'selva *nf* forest; (*fig: di errori, capelli*) mass; (*di ammiratori*) horde
selvag'gina *nf* game
sel'vaggio, -a *a* wild; (*primitivo*) savage
● *nmf* savage
sel'vatico *a* wild
selvicol'tura *nf* forestry
se'maforo *nm* traffic lights *pl*
se'mantica *nf* semantics
se'mantico *a* semantic
sembi'anza *nf* semblance; **sembianze** *pl* (*di persona*) appearance
sem'brare *vi* seem; (*assomigliare*) look like; **che te ne sembra?** what do you think?; **mi sembra che...** I think...; **sembra che vada bene** it's fine, seemingly *or* apparently
'seme *nm* seed; (*di mela*) pip; (*di carte*) suit; (*sperma*) semen. ~ **della discordia** seeds *pl* of discord
se'mente *nf* seed
seme'strale *a* (*corso*) six-month; (*pagamento*) six-monthly, half-yearly
se'mestre *nm* six months; *Univ* term, semester *Am*
semia'perto *a* half-open
semi'asse *nm* axle
semiauto'matico *a* semiautomatic
semi'breve *nf Mus* semibreve
semi'cerchio *nm* semicircle

semicircolare | separazione

semicirco'lare *a* semicircular
semiconfe'renza *nf* semicircle
semicondut'tore *a & nm* semiconductor
semicon'vitto *nm* **scuola a ~** school for dayboarders
semicosci'ente *a* semi-conscious, half-conscious
semi'croma *nf Mus* semiquaver
semifi'nale *nf* semifinal
semi'freddo *nm* cold dessert resembling ice cream
semilavo'rato *a* semi-finished ● *nm* **semilavorati** *pl* semi-finished goods
semi'minima *nf Mus* crotchet
'semina *nf* sowing
semi'nare *vt* sow; *fam* shake off ⟨inseguitori⟩; **seminar zizzania** cause trouble
semi'nario *nm* seminar; *Relig* seminary
semina'rista *nm* seminarist
seminfermità *nf* partial disability. **~ mentale** diminished responsibility
seminter'rato *nm* basement
semi'nudo *a* half-naked
semioscurità *nf* semi-darkness
semiprezi'oso *a* semiprecious
semi'secco *a* medium-dry
semi'serio *a* semi-serious
se'mitico *a* Semitic
semi'tono *nm Mus* semitone
sem'mai *conj* in case ● *adv* **è lui, ~, che...** if anyone, it's him who...
'semola *nf* bran
semo'lato *a* ⟨zucchero⟩ caster *attrib*
semo'lino *nm* semolina
'semplice *a* simple; **in parole semplici** in plain words
semplice'mente *adv* simply
semplici'otto, -a *nmf* simpleton
sempli'cistico *a* simplistic
semplicità *nf* simplicity
semplifi'care *vt* simplify
'sempre *adv* always; ⟨ancora⟩ still; **per ~** for ever; **~ più** more and more; **pur ~** still, nevertheless
sempre'verde *a & nm* evergreen
'senape *nf* mustard
se'nato *nm* senate
sena|'tore, -'trice *nmf* senator
se'nile *a* senile
senilità *nf* senility
'senior *a* senior ● *nmf* (*pl* **seniores**) *Sport* senior
'senno *nm* sense; **giudicare col ~ del poi** use hindsight
sennò *adv* otherwise, or else
sennonché *conj* but, except that; (*fuorché*) but, except
'seno *nm* (*petto*) breast; *Math* sine; **in ~ a** in the bosom of
sen'sale *nm* broker
sen'sato *a* sensible
sensazio'nale *a* sensational
sensazi'one *nf* sensation; **fare ~** ⟨notizia, scoperta:⟩ cause a sensation
sen'sibile *a* sensitive; (*percepibile*) percepti-

ble; (*notevole*) considerable; **mondo ~** tangible world
sensibilità *nf* sensitivity
sensibiliz'zare *vt* make more aware (**a** of)
sensibil'mente *adv* appreciably
sensi'tivo *a* sensory ● *nmf* sensitive person; (*medium*) medium
'senso *nm* sense; (*significato*) meaning; (*direzione*) direction; **far ~ a qcno** make sb shudder; **in ~ orario/antiorario** clockwise/anticlockwise; **ai sensi della legge** in accordance with the law; **non ha ~** it doesn't make sense; **avere il ~ degli affari** have good business sense; **di buon ~** ⟨persona⟩ sensible; **senza ~** meaningless; **in un certo ~...** in a sense o way...; **perdere i sensi** lose consciousness; **a ~** ⟨ripetere, tradurre⟩ in general terms; **in ~ opposto** in the opposite direction; **a ~ unico** ⟨strada⟩ one-way; **a doppio ~** [di marcia] ⟨strada⟩ two-way; **a doppio ~** ⟨parola, espressione⟩ with a double meaning. **~ dell'umorismo** sense of humour. **'~ vietato'** 'no entry'
sen'sore *nm* sensor
sensu'ale *a* sensual
sensualità *nf* sensuality
sen'tenza *nf* sentence; (*massima*) saying; **pronunciare una ~** hand down a sentence; **pronunciare la ~** pronounce sentence
sentenzi'are *vi* pass judgment
senti'ero *nm* path. **~ luminoso di avvicinamento** *Aeron* approach lights
sentimen'tale *a* sentimental
sentimenta'lista *nmf* sentimentalist
sentimental'mente *adv* sentimentally
senti'mento *nm* feeling; **essere fuori di ~** be out of one's mind
sen'tina *nf Naut* bilge
senti'nella *nf* sentry; **essere di ~** be on guard
sen'tire *vt* feel; (*udire*) hear; (*ascoltare*) listen to; (*gustare*) taste; (*odorare*) smell ● *vi* feel; (*udire*) hear; **~ caldo/freddo** feel hot/cold
sen'tirsi *vr* feel; **~ di fare qcsa** feel like doing sth; **~ bene/male** feel well/ill; **sen'tirsela di fare qcsa** feel up to doing sth
sen'tito *a* (*sincero*) sincere; **per ~ dire** by hearsay
sen'tore *nm* inkling
'senza *prep* without; **~ ombrello** without an umbrella; **~ correre** without running; **senz'altro** certainly; **~ un soldo** penniless; **'~ conservanti'** 'no preservatives'; **fare ~** do without
senza'tetto *nm inv* **i ~** the homeless
'sepalo *nm* sepal
sepa'rare *vt* separate
sepa'rarsi *vr* separate; ⟨prendere commiato⟩ part; **~ da** be separated from
separata'mente *adv* separately
separa'tista *nmf* separatist
sepa'rato *a* separate
separazi'one *nf* separation. **~ consensuale** separation by mutual consent. **~ legale** legal separation

sepol'crale *a liter* sepulchral
se'polcro *nm* sepulchre
se'polto *pp di* **seppellire** ● *a* buried; **morto e ~** *fig* dead and buried
sepol'tura *nf* burial; **dare ~ a qcno** bury sb
seppel'lire *vt* bury
seppel'lirsi *vr fig* cut oneself off
'seppia *nf* cuttle fish ● *a inv* sepia
sep'pure *conj* even if
se'quela *nf* series, succession; (*di insulti*) string
se'quenza *nf* sequence
sequenzi'ale *a* sequential
seque'strare *vt* (*rapire*) kidnap; (*confiscare*) confiscate; *Jur* impound
sequestra|'tore, -'trice *nmf* kidnapper
se'questro *nm Jur* impounding; (*di persona*) kidnap[ping]
se'quoia *nf* sequoia
'sera *nf* evening, night; **di ~, la ~** in the evening; **da ~** ⟨*abito*⟩ evening *attrib*; **alle 8 di ~** at 8 o'clock in the evening, at 8 o'clock at night; **buona ~!** good evening!; **dalla mattina alla ~** from morning to night; **ieri ~** yesterday evening, last night; **questa ~** this evening, tonight
se'rale *a* evening *attrib*
seral'mente *adv* every evening, every night
se'rata *nf* evening; (*ricevimento*) party. **~ danzante** dance. **~ di gala** gala night
ser'bare *vt* keep; harbour ⟨*odio*⟩; cherish ⟨*speranza*⟩
serba'toio *nm* tank. **~ d'acqua** water tank; (*per una città*) reservoir. **~ della benzina** petrol tank, gas tank *Am*
'Serbia *nf* Serbia
'serbo, -a *a & nmf* Serbian ● *nm* (*lingua*) Serbian
'serbo *nm* **mettere in ~** put aside
serbo-cro'ato *nmf* Serbo-Croat[ian]
sere'nata *nf* serenade
serenità *nf* serenity
se'reno *a* serene; ⟨*cielo*⟩ clear; **un fulmine a ciel ~** *fam* bolt from the blue
ser'gente *nm* sergeant
'serial *nm* **~ [televisivo]** television serial
seri'ale *a* serial
seria'mente *adv* seriously
'serico *a* silk
'serie *nf inv* series; (*complesso*) set; *Sport* division; **~ A** (*di calcio*) ≈ Premier League; **~ B** (*di calcio*) ≈ First Division; **di ~ B** *fig* second-rate; **fuori ~** custom-built; **produzione in ~** mass production. **~ numerica** numerical series
serietà *nf* seriousness
'serio *a* serious; (*degno di fiducia*) reliable; **sul ~** seriously; (*davvero*) really
ser'mone *nm* sermon
'serpe *nf liter* viper
serpeggi'ante *a* ⟨*strada*⟩ twisting, winding
serpeggi'are *vi* ⟨*strada:*⟩ twist, wind; (*fig: diffondersi*) spread

ser'pente *nm* snake. **~ a sonagli** rattlesnake. **~ velenoso** poisonous snake
serpen'tina *nf* **a ~** twisting and turning, winding; **fare una ~** weave
'serra *nf* greenhouse; **effetto ~** greenhouse effect
ser'raglio *nm* harem
ser'randa *nf* shutter
ser'rare *vt* shut; (*stringere*) tighten; (*incalzare*) press on
ser'rata *nf* lockout
serra'tura *nf* lock
ser'vibile *a* usable
ser'vile *a* servile
servi'lismo *nm* servility
ser'vire *vt* serve; (*al ristorante*) wait on ● *vi* serve; (*essere utile*) be of use; **non serve** it's no good; '**~ freddo**' 'serve chilled'
ser'virsi *vr* (*di cibo*) help oneself; **~ da** buy from; **~ di** use
servi|'tore, -'trice *nmf* retainer ● *nm Comput* server
servitù *nf* servitude; (*personale di servizio*) servants *pl*
servizi'evole *a* obliging
ser'vizio *nm* service; (*da caffè ecc*) set; (*di cronaca, sportivo*) report; (*in tennis*) serve. **servizi** *pl* bathroom; **donna di ~** maid; **essere di ~** be on duty; **fare ~** ⟨*autobus ecc:*⟩ run; **fuori ~** ⟨*bus*⟩ not in service; ⟨*ascensore*⟩ out of order; **~ compreso** service charge included; **~ escluso** not including service charge; **area di ~** service station; **servizi** *pl* (*terziario*) services. **~ bancario a domicilio** home banking. **~ in camera** room service. **~ civile** civilian duties done instead of national service. **~ filmato** film report. **servizi** *pl* **igienici** toilet block. **~ di linea** passenger service. **~ militare** military service. **servizi** *pl* **di pronto intervento** emergency services. **~ pubblico** utility company. **servizi** *pl* **pubblici** (*bagni*) public toilets. **servizi** *pl* **sociali** welfare services. **~ al tavolo** waiter service. **~ traghetto** passenger ferry
'servo, -a *nmf* servant
servo'freno *nm* servo brake
servo'sterzo *nm* power steering
'sesamo *nm* sesame
ses'santa *a & nm* sixty
sessan'tenne *a & nmf* sixty-year-old
sessan'tesimo *a & nm* sixtieth
sessan'tina *nf* **una ~ di** about sixty
Sessan'totto *nm* protest movement of 1968
sessi'one *nf* session
ses'sista *a* sexist
'sesso *nm* sex; **fare ~** *sl* have sex. **~ forte** stronger sex. **gentil ~** fair sex. **~ sicuro** safe sex
sessu'ale *a* sexual
sessualità *nf* sexuality
'sesto¹ *a & nm* sixth
'sesto² *nm* **rimettere in ~** put back on its feet ⟨*azienda*⟩; restore ⟨*vestito*⟩; recondition ⟨*motore, auto*⟩

set | sfociare

set *nm inv* set

'seta *nf* silk; **di ~** silk *attrib*

setacci'are *vt* sieve

se'taccio *nm* sieve; **passare qcsa al ~** *fig* go through sth with a fine-tooth comb

'sete *nf* thirst; **avere ~** be thirsty. **~ di sangue** blood lust

'setola *nf* bristle

'setta *nf* sect

set'tanta *a & nm* seventy

settan'tenne *a & nmf* seventy-year-old

settan'tesimo *a & nm* seventieth

settan'tina *nf* **una ~ di** about seventy

set'tario *a* sectarian

'sette *a & nm* seven

sette'cento *a & nm* seven hundred; **il S~** the eighteenth century

set'tembre *nm* September

settentrio'nale *a* northern ●*nmf* northerner

settentri'one *nm* north

'setter *nm inv* setter

'settico *a* septic

setti'mana *nf* week; **alla ~** per week; **a metà ~** midweek, half-way through the week. **~ corta** five-day week. **~ lavorativa** working week

settima'nale *a & nm* weekly

setti'mino, -a *a* born two months premature ●*nmf* baby born two months premature

'settimo *a & nm* seventh

set'tore *nm* sector

settori'ale *a* sector-based

severità *nf* severity

se'vero *a* severe; (*rigoroso*) strict

se'vizia *nf* torture; **se'vizie** *pl* torture *sg*

sevizi'are *vt* torture

sezio'nare *vt* divide; *Med* dissect

sezi'one *nf* section; (*reparto*) department; *Med* dissection

sfaccen'dare *vi* bustle about

sfaccen'dato *a* idle

sfaccet'tare *vt* cut

sfaccet'tato *a* cut; *fig* many-sided, multi-faceted

sfaccetta'tura *nf* cutting; *fig* facet

sfacchi'nare *vi* toil

sfacchi'nata *nf* drudgery

sfaccia'taggine *nf* cheek

sfacciata'mente *adv* cheekily

sfacci'ato *a* cheeky, fresh *Am*

sfa'celo *nm* ruin; **in ~** in ruins

sfagio'lare *vi fam* **non mi sfagiola** it's/ he's/she's not my cup of tea

sfal'darsi *vr* flake off

sfal'sare *vt* stagger; **~ il tiro** shoot wide

sfa'mare *vt* feed

sfa'marsi *vr* satisfy one's hunger, eat one's fill

sfarfal'lio *nm* (*di schermo, luce*) flicker

'sfarzo *nm* pomp

sfar'zoso *a* sumptuous

sfa'sato *a fam* confused; (*motore*) which needs tuning; **sentirsi ~** *fam* be out of sync[h]

sfasci'are *vt* unbandage; (*fracassare*) smash

sfasci'arsi *vr* fall to pieces

sfasci'ato *a* beat-up

'sfascio *nm* ruin; **andare allo ~** go to rack and ruin

sfa'tare *vt* explode

sfati'cato *a* lazy

'sfatto *a* unmade

sfavil'lante *a* sparkling

sfavil'lare *vi* sparkle

sfavo'revole *a* unfavourable

sfavo'rire *vt* disadvantage, put at a disadvantage

sfeb'brare *vi* **comincia a ~** his temperature is starting to come down

'sfera *nf* sphere. **~ affettiva** area of feelings and emotions. **~ celeste** celestial sphere. **~ di cristallo** crystal ball. **~ di influenza** sphere of influence

'sferico *a* spherical

sfer'rare *vt* unshoe (*cavallo*); give (*calcio, pugno*)

sferruz'zare *vi* knit

sfer'zare *vt* whip

sfer'zata *nf* whip; *fig* telling-off

sfian'cante *a* wearing

sfian'care *vt* wear out

sfian'carsi *vr* wear oneself out

sfiata'toio *nm* blowhole

sfi'brare *vt* exhaust

sfi'brato *a* exhausted

'sfida *nf* challenge

sfi'dare *vt* challenge

sfi'ducia *nf* mistrust

sfiduci'ato *a* discouraged

'sfiga *nf sl* bloody bad luck; **avere ~** be bloody unlucky

sfi'gato, -a *sl a* a bloody unlucky ●*nmf* unlucky beggar

sfigu'rare *vt* disfigure ●*vi* (*far cattiva figura*) look out of place

sfilacci'are *vt* fray

sfilacci'arsi *vr* fray

sfi'lare *vt* unthread; (*togliere di dosso*) take off ●*vi* (*truppe:*) march past; (*in parata*) parade

sfi'larsi *vr* come unthreaded; (*collant:*) ladder; take off (*pantaloni*)

sfi'lata *nf* parade; (*sfilza*) series. **~ di moda** fashion show

sfila'tino *nm* long, thin loaf

'sfilza *nf* string

'sfinge *nf* sphinx

sfi'nirsi *vr* wear oneself out

sfi'nito *a* worn out

sfio'rare *vt* skim; touch on (*argomento*)

sfio'rire *vi* wither; (*bellezza:*) fade

sfis'sare *vt* cancel

'sfitto *a* vacant

'sfizio *nm* whim, fancy; **togliersi uno ~** satisfy a whim

sfizi'oso *a* nifty

sfo'cato *a* out of focus

sfoci'are *vi* **~ in** flow into

sfode'rare vt draw ⟨pistola, spada⟩; fig show off ⟨cultura⟩; **~ un sorriso** smile insincerely

sfode'rato a ⟨giacca⟩ unlined

sfo'gare vt vent

sfo'garsi vr give vent to one's feelings

sfoggi'are vt/i show off

'sfoggio nm show, display; **fare ~ di** show off

'sfoglia nf sheet of pastry; **pasta ~** puff pastry

sfogli'are vt leaf through

sfogli'ata[1] nf flaky pastry with filling

sfogli'ata[2] nf **dare una ~ a** ⟨libro, giornale⟩ flick through

'sfogo nm outlet; fig outburst; Med rash; **dare ~ a** give vent to

sfolgo'rante a blazing

sfolgo'rare vi blaze

sfolla'gente nm truncheon, billy Am

sfol'lare vt clear ● vi Mil be evacuated

sfol'lato, -a nmf evacuee

sfol'tire vt thin [out]; **farsi ~ i capelli** have one's hair thinned

sfon'dare vt break down ● vi ⟨aver successo⟩ make a name for oneself

'sfondo nm background

sfon'done nm fam blunder

sfor'mare vt pull out of shape ⟨tasche⟩

sfor'marsi vi lose its shape; ⟨persona:⟩ lose one's figure

sfor'mato nm Culin flan

sfor'nito a **~ di** ⟨negozio⟩ out of

sfor'tuna nf bad luck

sfortunata'mente adv unfortunately

sfortu'nato a unlucky

sfor'zare vt force

sfor'zarsi vr try hard

sfor'zato a forced

'sforzo nm effort; ⟨tensione⟩ stress

'sfottere vt sl tease

sfracel'larsi vr smash; **~ al suolo** crash to the ground

sfrangi'ato a fringed

sfrat'tare vt evict

'sfratto nm eviction

sfrecci'are vi flash past

sfrega'mento nm crackling

sfre'gare vt rub

sfregi'are vt slash

sfregi'ato, -a a scarred ● nmf scarface

'sfregio nm slash

sfre'narsi vr run wild

sfre'nato a wild

sfrigo'lio nm crackling

sfron'dare vt prune

sfron'tato a shameless

sfrutta'mento nm exploitation

sfrut'tare vt exploit; take advantage of, make the most of ⟨occasione⟩

sfug'gente a elusive; ⟨mento⟩ receding

sfug'gire vi escape; **~ a** escape [from]; **mi sfugge** it escapes me; **mi è sfuggito [di mente]** it [completely] slipped my mind; **mi è sfuggito di mano** I lost hold of it;

lasciarsi ~ un'occasione let an opportunity slip; **mi è sfuggito un rutto** I just came out with a belch; **gli è sfuggito un colpo dal fucile** the rifle just went off in his hands ● vt avoid

sfug'gita nf **di ~** in passing

sfu'mare vi ⟨svanire⟩ vanish; ⟨colore:⟩ shade off ● vt soften ⟨colore⟩

sfuma'tura nf shade

sfuri'ata nf outburst [of anger]

sga'bello nm stool

sgabuz'zino nm cupboard

sgam'bato a ⟨costume da bagno⟩ high-cut

sgambet'tare vi kick one's legs; ⟨camminare⟩ trot

sgam'betto nm **fare lo ~ a qcno** trip sb up

sganasci'arsi vr **~ dalle risa** roar with laughter

sganci'are vt unhook; Rail uncouple; drop ⟨bombe⟩; fam cough up ⟨denaro⟩

sganci'arsi vr become unhooked; fig get away

sganghe'rato a ramshackle

sgar'bato a rude

'sgarbo nm discourtesy; **fare uno ~ a qcno** be rude to sb; **ricevere uno ~** be treated rudely

sgargi'ante a garish

sgar'rare vi be wrong; ⟨da regola⟩ stray from the straight and narrow

'sgarro nm mistake, slip

sga'sato a flat

sgattaio'lare vi sneak away; **~ via** decamp

sge'lare vt/i thaw

'sghembo a slanting; **a ~** obliquely

sghiacci'are vt defrost; thaw out ⟨carne⟩

sghignaz'zare vi laugh scornfully

sghiri'bizzo nm whim, fancy

sgob'bare vi slog; ⟨fam: studente:⟩ swot

sgob'bone, -a nmf slogger; ⟨fam: studente⟩ swot

sgoccio'lare vi drip

'sgocciolo nm dripping

sgo'larsi vr shout oneself hoarse

sgomb[e]'rare vt clear [out]

'sgombro a clear ● nm ⟨trasloco⟩ removal; ⟨pesce⟩ mackerel

sgomen'tare vt dismay

sgomen'tarsi vr be dismayed

sgo'mento nm dismay

sgomi'nare vt defeat

sgom'mare vi make the tyres screech

sgom'mata nf screech of tyres

sgonfi'are vt deflate

sgonfi'arsi vr go down

'sgonfio a flat

'sgorbio nm scrawl; ⟨fig: vista sgradevole⟩ sight

sgor'gare vi gush [out] ● vt flush out, unblock ⟨lavandino⟩

sgoz'zare vt **~ qcno** cut sb's throat

sgra'devole a disagreeable

sgra'dito a unwelcome

sgraffi'are vt scratch

'sgraffio nm scratch

sgrammaticata'mente *adv* ungram-matically

sgrammati'cato *a* ungrammatical

sgra'nare *vt* shell ⟨*piselli*⟩; open wide ⟨*occhi*⟩

sgra'nato *a* grainy; ⟨*fagioli*⟩ shelled; ⟨*occhi*⟩ wide-open

sgran'chire *vt* stretch

sgran'chirsi *vr* stretch

sgranocchi'are *vt* munch

sgras'sare *vt* remove the grease from

'sgravio *nm* relief. **~ fiscale** tax relief

sgrazi'ato *a* ungainly

sgreto'lare *vt* crumble

sgreto'larsi *vr* crumble

sgri'dare *vt* scold

sgri'data *nf* scolding

sgron'dare *vt* drain

sgros'sare *vt* rough-hew ⟨*marmo*⟩; *fig* polish

sguai'ato *a* coarse

sgual'cire *vt* crumple

sgual'drina *nf* slut

sgu'ardo *nm* look; (*breve*) glance; **dare uno ~ a** glance at ⟨*giornale, testo*⟩. **~ di insieme** overview

sguar'nito *a* unadorned; (*privo di difesa*) undefended

'sguattero, -a *nmf* skivvy

sguaz'zare *vi* splash; (*nel fango*) wallow

'sguincio *nm* sidelong glance

sguinzagli'are *vt* unleash

sgusci'are *vt* shell ● *vi* (*sfuggire*) slip away; **~ fuori** slip out

'shaker *nm inv* shaker

shake'rare *vt* shake

'shampoo *nm inv* shampoo; **~ e messa in piega** shampoo and set

'shopper *nm inv* carrier bag

'shuttle *nm inv* [space] shuttle

si *pers pron* (*riflessivo*) oneself; (*lui*) himself; (*lei*) herself; (*esso, essa*) itself; (*loro*) themselves; (*reciproco*) each other; (*tra più di due*) one another; (*impersonale*) you, one *fml*; **lavarsi** wash [oneself]; **si è lavata** she washed [herself]; **lavarsi le mani** wash one's hands; **si è lavata le mani** she washed her hands; **si è mangiato un pollo intero** he ate an entire chicken by himself; **incontrarsi** meet each other; **la gente si aiuta a vicenda** people help one another; **si potrebbe pensare che…** you might think that…, one might think that… *fml*; **non si sa mai** you never know, one never knows; **queste cose si dimenticano facilmente** these things are easily forgotten

si *nm Mus* (*chiave, nota*) B

si *adv yes*; **credo di sì** I believe so; **penso di sì** I think so; **ha detto di sì** she said yes; **sì?** really?; **sì che mi piace!** yes I do like it!

'sia¹ *vedi* essere

'sia² *conj* **~…~…** (*entrambi*) both…and…; (*o l'uno o l'altro*) either…or…**~ che venga, ~ che non venga** whether he comes or not; **scegli ~ questo ~ quello** choose either

this one or that one; **voglio ~ questo che quello** I want both this one and that one; **verranno ~ Giuseppe ~ Giacomo** both Giuseppe and Giacomo are coming

sia'mese *a* Siamese

sibi'lare *vi* hiss

sibil'lino *a* sibylline

'sibilo *nm* hiss

si'cario *nm* hired killer

sicché *conj* (*perciò*) so [that]; (*allora*) then

siccità *nf* drought

sic'come *conj* as

Si'cilia *nf* Sicily

sicili'ano, -a *a & nmf* Sicilian

sico'moro *nm* sycamore

si'cura *nf* safety catch; (*di portiera*) child-proof lock

sicura'mente *adv* definitely; **~, sarà arrivato** he must have arrived by now

sicu'rezza *nf* (*certezza*) certainty; (*salvezza*) safety; **di ~** ⟨*dispositivo*⟩ safety *attrib*; **uscita di ~** emergency exit; **di massima** ~ top security

si'curo *a* (*non pericoloso*) safe; (*certo*) sure; ⟨*saldo*⟩ steady; *Comm* sound ● *adv* certainly ● *nm* safety; **al ~** safe; **andare sul ~** play [it] safe; **di ~** definitely; **di ~, sarà arrivato** he must have arrived; **~!** sure!

'sidecar *nm inv* sidecar

siderur'gia *nf* iron and steel industry

side'rurgico *a* iron and steel *attrib*

'sidro *nm* cider

si'epe *nf* hedge

si'ero *nm* serum

sieroposi'tivo, -a *a* HIV positive ● *nmf* person who is HIV positive

Si'erra Le'one *nf* Sierra Leone

si'esta *nf* afternoon nap, siesta; **fare la ~** have an afternoon nap

si'fone *nm* siphon

Sig. *abbr* (*signore*) Mr

Sig.a *abbr* (*signora*) Mrs, Ms

siga'retta *nf* cigarette; **pantaloni** *pl* **a ~** drainpipes

'sigaro *nm* cigar

Sigg. *abbr* (*signori*) Messrs

sigil'lare *vt* seal

si'gillo *nm* seal

'sigla *nf* initials *pl*. **~ musicale** signature tune

si'glare *vt* initial

Sig.na *abbr* (*signorina*) Miss, Ms

signifi'care *vt* mean

significa'tivo *a* significant

signifi'cato *nm* meaning

si'gnora *nf* lady; (*davanti a nome proprio*) Mrs; (*non sposata*) Miss; (*in lettere ufficiali*) Dear Madam; **la ~ Rossi** Mrs Rossi; **il signor Vené e ~** Mr and Mrs Vené

si'gnore *nm* gentleman; *Relig* lord; (*davanti a nome proprio*) Mr; **il signor Rossi** Mr Rossi

signo'rile *a* gentlemanly; (*di lusso*) luxury

signo'rina *nf* young lady; (*seguito da nome proprio*) Miss; **la ~ Rossi** Miss Rossi

silenzia'tore *nm* silencer

si'lenzio *nm* silence. **~ di tomba** deathly hush

silenzi'oso *a* silent

'silfide *nf* sylph

silhou'ette *nf inv* silhouette, outline; **che ~!** you're so slim!

si'licio *nm* **piastrina di ~** silicon chip

sili'cone *nm* silicone

'sillaba *nf* syllable

silla'bario *nm* primer

sillaba'tore *nm Comput* hyphenation program

sillo'gismo *nm* syllogism

silu'rare *vt* torpedo

si'luro *nm* torpedo

simbi'osi *nf* symbiosis; **vivere in ~** need each other, have a symbiotic relationship

simboleggi'are *vt* symbolize

sim'bolico *a* symbolic[al]

simbo'lismo *nm* symbolism

simbo'lista *nmf* symbolist

'simbolo *nm* symbol

similarità *nf inv* similarity

'simile *a* similar; (*tale*) such; **è ~ a...** it's like..., it's similar to...; **qualcosa di ~** something similar ● *nm* (*il prossimo*) fellow human being, fellow man

simili'tudine *nf Gram* simile

simil'mente *adv* similarly

simil'pelle *nf* Leatherette®

simme'tria *nf* symmetry

sim'metrico *a* symmetric[al]

simpa'tia *nf* liking; (*compenetrazione*) sympathy; **prendere qcno in ~** take a liking to sb; **provare ~ per** like

sim'patico *a* nice; **inchiostro ~** invisible ink

simpatiz'zante *nmf* well-wisher

simpatiz'zare *vi* **~ con** take a liking to; **~ per qcsa/qcno** lean towards sth/sb

sim'posio *nm* symposium

simu'lare *vt* simulate; feign ⟨*amicizia, interesse*⟩

simula'tore *nm* simulator

simulazi'one *nf* simulation. **~ di reato** *Jur* making of false accusations

simul'tanea *nf* **in ~** simultaneously

simul'taneo *a* simultaneous

sina'goga *nf* synagogue

since'ramente *adv* sincerely; (*a dire il vero*) honestly

since'rarsi *vr* make sure

sincerità *nf* sincerity

sin'cero *a* sincere

'sincope *nf* syncopation; *Med* fainting fit

sincron'ia *nf* sync[h]

sincro'nismo *nm* synchronism

sincroniz'zare *vt* synchronize

sincroniz'zato *a* synchronized; **essere ben ~ con** be in sync[h]

sincronizzazi'one *nf* synchronization

'sincrono *a* synchronous

sinda'cabile *a* arguable

sinda'cale *a* [trade] union *attrib*, [labor] union *Am*

sindaca'lista *nmf* trade unionist, labor union member *Am*

sinda'care *vt* inspect

sinda'cato *nm* [trade] union, [labor] union *Am*; (*associazione*) syndicate. **~ di categoria** trade union

'sindaco *nm* mayor

'sindrome *nf* syndrome. **~ di Down** Down's syndrome. **~ premestruale** premenstrual syndrome, PMS

sinfo'nia *nf* symphony

sin'fonico *a* symphonic

singhioz'zare *vi* (*di pianto*) sob

singhi'ozzo *nm* hiccup; (*di pianto*) sob; **avere il ~** have the hiccups

'single *nmf inv* single

singo'lare *a* singular; (*strano*) peculiar ● *nm Gram* singular

singolar'mente *adv* individually; (*stranamente*) peculiarly

'singolo *a* single ● *nm* individual; *Tennis* singles *pl*

si'nistra *nf* left; **a ~** on the left; **girare a ~** turn to the left; **la seconda a ~** the second on the left; **con la guida a ~** ⟨*auto*⟩ with left-hand drive; **la ~** *Pol* the left; **di ~** *Pol* left wing

sini'strare *vt* injure; damage ⟨*casa*⟩

sini'strato *a* injured; ⟨*casa*⟩ damaged

si'nistro *a* left[-hand]; (*avverso*) sinister ● *nm* accident

sini'strorso, -a *nmf pej* leftie

'sino *prep* = **fino**

si'nonimo *a* synonymous ● *nm* synonym

sin'tassi *nf* syntax

sin'tattico *a* syntactic[al]

'sintesi *nf* synthesis; (*riassunto*) summary

sin'tetico *a* synthetic; (*conciso*) summary

sintetiz'zare *vt* summarize

sintetizza'tore *nm* synthesizer

sinto'matico *a* symptomatic

'sintomo *nm* symptom

sinto'nia *nf* tuning; **in ~** on the same wavelength; **in ~ con** in harmony with, in tune with

sintonizza'tore *nm* tuner

sinu'oso *a* ⟨*strada*⟩ winding

sinu'site *nf* sinusitis

sio'nismo *nm* Zionism

sio'nista *a* & *nmf* Zionist

si'pario *nm* curtain

si'rena *nf* siren; (*di nave*) hooter

'Siria *nf* Syria

siri'ano, -a *a* & *nmf* Syrian

si'ringa *nf* syringe

'sismico *a* seismic

si'smografo *nm* seismograph

sismolo'gia *nf* seismology

si'stema *nm* system; **non è il ~!** that's no way to behave!. **~ di gestione banca dati** database management system, DBMS. **~ immunitario** immune system. **S~ Monetario Europeo** European Monetary System. **~**

nervoso nervous system. **~ operativo** *Comput* operating system. **~ solare** solar system. **~ di vita** way of life

siste'mare *vt* (*mettere*) put; tidy up ⟨*casa, camera*⟩; (*risolvere*) sort out; (*procurare lavoro a*) fix up with a job; (*trovare alloggio a*) find accommodation for; (*sposare*) marry off; (*fam: punire*) sort out

siste'marsi *vr* settle down; (*trovare un lavoro*) find a job; (*trovare alloggio*) find accommodation; (*sposarsi*) marry

sistematica'mente *adv* systematically

siste'matico *a* systematic

sistemazi'one *nf* arrangement; (*di questione*) settlement; (*lavoro*) job; (*alloggio*) accommodation; (*matrimonio*) marriage

siste'mista *nmf Comput* systems engineer

'sistole *nf* systole

'sit-in *nm inv* sit-in

'sito *nm* site. **~ web** *Comput* web site

situ'are *vt* place

situazi'one *nf* situation; **essere all'altezza della ~** be equal to the situation, be up to the situation

'skai *nm* Leatherette®

'skateboard *nm inv* skateboard

sketch *nm inv* sketch

ski-'lift *nm* ski tow

'skipper *nmf inv* skipper

slab'brare *vt* stretch out of shape ⟨*maglia, tasca*⟩

slab'brato *a* ⟨*maglia, tasca*⟩ shapeless

slacci'are *vt* unfasten

'slalom *nm inv* slalom; **a ~** slalom *attrib*

slanci'arsi *vr* hurl oneself

slanci'ato *a* slender

'slancio *nm* impetus; (*impulso*) impulse; **agire di ~** act on impulse

sla'vato *a* ⟨*carnagione, capelli*⟩ fair

'slavo *a* Slav[onic]

sle'ale *a* disloyal; **concorrenza ~** unfair competition

slealtà *nf* disloyalty

sle'gare *vt* untie

sle'garsi *vr* untie oneself

slip *nmpl* underpants

'slitta *nf* sledge; (*trainata*) sleigh

slitta'mento *nm* (*di macchina*) skid; (*fig: di riunione*) postponement

slit'tare *vi Auto* skid; ⟨*riunione:*⟩ be put off

slit'tata *nf* skid

slit'tino *nm* toboggan

'slogan *nm inv* slogan

slo'gare *vt* dislocate

slo'garsi *vr* **~ una caviglia** sprain one's ankle

slo'gato *a* sprained

sloga'tura *nf* sprain

sloggi'are *vt* dislodge ● *vi* move out

slot *nm* **~ di espansione** *Comput* expansion slot

slot-ma'chine *nf inv* slot-machine, one-armed bandit

Slo'vacchia *nf* Slovakia

slo'vacco, -a *a & nmf* Slovak

Slo'venia *nf* Slovenia

smacchi'are *vt* clean

smacchia'tore *nm* stain remover

'smacco *nm* humiliating defeat

smache'rarsi *vr* (*tradirsi*) give oneself away

smagli'ante *a* dazzling

smagli'arsi *vr* ⟨*calza:*⟩ ladder *Br*, run

smaglia'tura *nf* ladder *Br*, run

smagnetiz'zare *vt* demagnetize

smagnetiz'zatore *nm* demagnetizer

sma'grito *a* thinner

smalizi'ato *a* cunning

smal'tare *vt* enamel; glaze ⟨*ceramica*⟩; varnish ⟨*unghie*⟩

smal'tato *a* enamelled; ⟨*ceramica*⟩ glazed; ⟨*unghie*⟩ varnished

smalta'tura *nf* enamelling; (*di ceramica*) glazing

smalti'mento *nm* disposal; (*di merce*) selling off. **~ rifiuti** waste disposal; (*di grassi*) burning off

smal'tire *vt* burn off; (*merce*) sell off; *fig* get through ⟨*corrispondenza*⟩; **~ la sbornia** sober up

'smalto *nm* enamel; (*di ceramica*) glaze; (*per le unghie*) nail varnish, nail polish

smance'ria *nf* **fare smancerie** be overpolite

smance'roso *a* simpering

'smania *nf* fidgets *pl*; (*desiderio*) longing; **avere la ~ di** have a craving for

smani'are *vi* have the fidgets; **~ per** long for

smani'oso *a* restless

smantella'mento *nm* dismantling

smantel'lare *vt* dismantle

smarri'mento *nm* loss; (*psicologico*) bewilderment

smar'rire *vt* lose; (*temporaneamente*) mislay

smar'rirsi *vr* get lost; (*turbarsi*) be bewildered

smar'rito *a* lost; ⟨*sguardo*⟩ bewildered, lost

smasche'rare *vt* unmask

smasche'rarsi *vr fig* reveal oneself

SME *nm abbr* (**Sistema Monetario Europeo**) EMS

smem'brare *vt* dismember

smemo'rato, -a *a* forgetful ● *nmf* scatterbrain

smen'tire *vt* deny

smen'tita *nf* denial

sme'raldo *nm & a* emerald

smerci'are *vt* sell off

'smercio *nm* sale

smerigli'ato *a* emery; **vetro ~** frosted glass

sme'riglio *nm* emery

smer'lare *vt* scallop

'smerlo *nm* scallop

'smesso *pp di* **smettere** ● *a* ⟨*abiti*⟩ cast-off

'smettere *vt* stop; stop wearing ⟨*abiti*⟩; **smettila!** stop it!

smidol'lato *a* spineless

smilitariz'zare *vt* demilitarize

'smilzo *a* thin

sminu'ire *vt* diminish

sminu'irsi *vr fig* belittle oneself

sminuz'zare *vt* crumble; (*fig: analizzare*) analyse in detail

smista'mento *nm* clearing; (*postale*) sorting; **stazione di ~** shunting yard, marshalling yard. **~ rifiuti** sorting of waste

smi'stare *vt* sort; *Mil* post; *Rail* marshall

smisu'rato *a* boundless; (*esorbitante*) excessive

smitiz'zare *vt* demythologize

smobili'tare *vt* demobilize

smobilitazi'one *nf* demobilization

smo'dato *a* immoderate

smog *nm* smog

'smoking *nm inv* dinner jacket, tuxedo *Am*

smon'tabile *a* jointed

smon'taggio *nm* disassembly

smon'tare *vt* take to pieces; (*scoraggiare*) dishearten; take down (*tenda*) ● *vi* (*da veicolo*) get off; (*da cavallo*) dismount; (*dal servizio*) go off duty

smon'tarsi *vr* lose heart

'smorfia *nf* grimace; (*moina*) simper; **fare smorfie** make faces

smorfi'oso *a* affected

'smorto *a* pale; (*colore*) dull

smor'zare *vt* dim (*luce*); tone down (*colori*); deaden (*suoni*); quench (*sete*)

smor'zata *nf Sport* drop shot

'smosso *pp di* **smuovere**

smotta'mento *nm* landslide

'smunto *a* emaciated

smu'overe *vt* shift; (*commuovere*) move

smu'oversi *vr* move; (*commuoversi*) be moved

smus'sare *vt* round off; (*fig: attenuare*) tone down

smus'sarsi *vr* go blunt

smussa'tura *nf* bevel

snack bar *nm inv* snack bar

snatu'rato *a* inhuman

snazionaliz'zare *vt* denationalize

S.N.C. *abbr* **società in nome collettivo**

snel'lire *vt* slim down

snel'lirsi *vr* slim [down]

'snello *a* slim

sner'vante *a* enervating

sner'vare *vt* enervate

sner'varsi *vr* get exhausted

sni'dare *vt* drive out

snif'fare *vt* snort

snob'bare *vt* snub

sno'bismo *nm* snobbery

snoccio'lare *vt* stone; *fig* blurt out

snoccio'lato *a* (*olive*) pitted, with the stones removed

sno'dabile *a* jointed

sno'dare *vt* untie; (*sciogliere*) loosen

sno'darsi *vr* come untied; (*strada:*) wind

sno'dato *a* (*persona*) double-jointed; (*dita*) flexible

'snodo *nm* coupling. **~ ferroviario** coupling

SO *abbr* (**sud-ovest**) SW

soap 'opera *nf inv* soap [opera]

so'ave *a* gentle

sobbal'zare *vi* jerk; (*trasalire*) start

sob'balzo *nm* jerk; (*trasalimento*) start

sobbar'carsi *vr* **~ a** undertake

sobbol'lire *vi* simmer

sob'borgo *nm* suburb

sobil'lare *vt* stir up

sobilla|'tore, -'trice *nm* instigator

sobrietà *nf inv* sobriety

'sobrio *a* sober

soc'chiudere *vt* half-close

socchi'uso *pp di* **socchiudere** ● *a* (*occhi*) half-closed; (*porta*) ajar

soc'combere *vi* succumb

soc'correre *vt* assist

soc'corso *pp di* **soccorrere** ● *nm* assistance, help; **venire in ~** come to help, come to the rescue; **venire in ~ a qcno** come to sb's rescue; **soccorsi** *pl* help; (*persone*) rescuers; (*dopo disastro*) relief workers. **~ alpino** mountain rescue. **~ stradale** breakdown service, wrecking service *Am*

socialdemo'cratico, -a *a* Social Democratic ● *nmf* Social Democrat

socialdemocra'zia *nf* Social Democracy

soci'ale *a* social

socia'lismo *nm* Socialism

socia'lista *a & nmf* Socialist

socializ'zare *vi* socialize

società *nf inv* society; *Comm* company. **~ in accomandita semplice** limited partnership. **~ per azioni** public limited company, plc. **~ dei consumi** consumer society. **~ in nome collettivo** commercial partnership. **~ a responsabilità limitata** limited liability company

soci'evole *a* sociable

'socio, -a *nmf* member; *Comm* partner

socioeco'nomico *a* socio-economic

soci'ologa *nf* sociologist

sociolo'gia *nf* sociology

socio'logico *a* sociological

soci'ologo *nm* sociologist

'soda *nf* soda. **~ da bucato** washing soda

soda'lizio *nf* association, society

soddisfa'cente *a* satisfactory

soddi'sfare *vt/i* satisfy; meet (*richiesta*); make amends for (*offesa*)

soddi'sfatto *pp di* **soddisfare** ● *a* satisfied

soddisfazi'one *nf* satisfaction

'sodo *a* hard; *fig* firm; (*sodo*) hard-boiled ● *adv* hard; **dormire ~** sleep soundly ● *nm* **venire al ~** get to the point

sofà *nm inv* sofa

soffe'rente *a* (*malato*) ill

soffe'renza *nf* suffering

soffer'marsi *vr* pause; **~ su** dwell on

sof'ferto *pp di* **soffrire**

soffi'are *vt* blow; reveal (*segreto*); (*rubare*) pinch *fam* ● *vi* blow

soffi'ata *nf* **datti una ~ al naso** blow your nose; **fare una ~ a qcno** *fig sl* tip sb off, give sb a tip-off

'soffice *a* soft
soffi'etto *nm* bellows; **a ~** ‹*borsa*› expanding. **~ editoriale** blurb
'soffio *nm* puff; *Med* murmur
sof'fitta *nf* attic
sof'fitto *nm* ceiling
soffoca'mento *nm* suffocation
soffo'cante *a* suffocating
soffo'care *vt/i* choke; *fig* stifle
sof'friggere *vt* fry lightly
sof'frire *vt/i* suffer; (*sopportare*) bear; **~ di** suffer from; **~ di [mal di] cuore** suffer from *o* have a heart condition
sof'fritto *pp di* **soffriggere ●** *nm* fried ingredients *pl*
sof'fuso *a* ‹*luce*› soft, suffused
sofisti'care *vt* (*adulterare*) adulterate **●** *vi* (*sottilizzare*) quibble
sofisti'cato *a* sophisticated
soft *a* soft
'softcopy *nf Comput* soft copy
'soft-core *nm* softcore, soft porn **●** *a inv* **pornografia ~** soft porn
'software *nm inv* software; **dei ~** software packages. **~ di accesso** access software. **~ applicativo** application software. **~ di autoapprendimento** tutorial package, tutorial software. **~ di comunicazione** communications software, comms software. **~ didattico** educational software. **~ di gestione errori** error correction software. **~ di OCR** OCR software. **~ di sistema** system software
softwa'rista *nm Comput* software engineer
soggettiva'mente *adv* subjectively
sogget'tivo *a* subjective
sog'getto *nm* subject; **cattivo ~** bad sort **●** *a* subject; **essere ~ a** be subject to
soggezi'one *nf* subjection; (*rispetto*) awe
sogghi'gnare *vi* sneer
sog'ghigno *nm* sneer
soggio'gare *vt* subdue
soggior'nare *vi* stay
soggi'orno *nm* stay; (*stanza*) living room; **permesso di ~** residence permit
soggi'ungere *vt* add
'soglia *nf* threshold; **alle soglie di qcsa** on the threshold of sth. **~ del dolore** pain threshold
'sogliola *nf* sole. **~ limanda** lemon sole
so'gnare *vt/i* dream; **~ a occhi aperti** daydream; **non te lo sogni neppure!** forget it!, don't even think of it!
so'gnarsi *vr* dream
sogna|'tore, -'trice *nmf* dreamer
'sogno *nm* dream; **fare un ~** have a dream; **neanche per ~!** not on your life!; **essere un ~** (*bellissimo*) be a dream; **il mio ~ nel cassetto** my secret dream
'soia *nf* soya
sol *nm Mus* (*chiave, nota*) G
so'laio *nm* attic
sola'mente *adv* only
so'lare *a* ‹*energia, raggi*› solar; ‹*crema*› sun *attrib*

so'larium *nm inv* solarium
sol'care *vt* plough
'solco *nm* furrow; (*di ruota*) track; (*di nave*) wake; (*di disco*) groove
sol'dato *nm* soldier. **~ semplice** private
'soldo *nm* **non ha un ~** he hasn't got a penny to his name; **senza un ~** penniless; **al ~ di** in the pay of; **soldi** *pl* (*denaro*) money *sg*; **fare [i] soldi** make money; **prelevare dei soldi** withdraw money; **da quattro soldi** cheapo, nickel-and-dime *Am*
'sole *nm* sun; (*luce del sole*) sun[light]; **al ~** in the sun; **prendere il ~** sunbathe
sole'cismo *nm* solecism
soleggi'ato *a* sunny
so'lenne *a* solemn
solennità *nf* solemnity
so'lere *vi* be in the habit of; **come si suol dire** as they say
so'letta *nf* insole
sol'fato *nm* sulphate
sol'feggio *nm* solfa
'solfuro *nm* sulphur
soli'dale *a* in agreement
solidarietà *nf* solidarity
solidifi'care *vt/i* solidify
solidifi'carsi *vr* solidify
solidità *nf* solidity; (*di colori*) fastness
'solido *a* solid; (*robusto*) sturdy; ‹*colore*› fast; **in ~** *Jur* jointly and severally **●** *nm* solid
soli'loquio *nm* soliloquy
so'lista *a* solo **●** *nmf* soloist
solita'mente *adv* usually
soli'tario *a* solitary; (*isolato*) lonely **●** *nm* (*brillante*) solitaire; (*gioco di carte*) patience, solitaire
'solito *a* usual; **essere ~ fare qcsa** be in the habit of doing sth **●** *nm* the usual; **di ~** usually
soli'tudine *nf* solitude
solleci'tare *vt* speed up; urge ‹*persona*›
sollecitazi'one *nf* (*richiesta*) request; (*preghiera*) entreaty
sol'lecito *a* prompt **●** *nm* reminder
solleci'tudine *nf* promptness; (*interessamento*) concern; **con la massima ~** *Comm* as soon as possible
solle'one *nm* noonday sun; (*periodo*) dog days of summer
solleti'care *vt* tickle
sol'letico *nm* tickling; **fare il ~ a qcno** tickle sb; **soffrire il ~** be ticklish
solleva'mento *nm* **~ pesi** weightlifting
solle'vare *vt* lift; (*elevare*) raise; (*confortare*) comfort; **~ una questione** raise a question; **~ qcno da un incarico** relieve sb of a responsibility
solle'varsi *vr* rise; (*riaversi*) recover
solle'vato *a* relieved
solli'evo *nm* relief; **che ~!** what a relief!
'solo, -a *a* alone; (*isolato*) lonely; (*unico*) only; *Mus* solo; **da ~** by myself/yourself/himself etc **●** *nmf* **il ~, la sola** the only one **●** *nm Mus* solo **●** *adv* only; **~ il sabato/la**

domenica Saturdays/Sundays only, only on Saturdays/Sundays

sol'stizio nm solstice

sol'tanto adv only

so'lubile a soluble; ⟨caffè⟩ instant

soluzi'one nf solution; Comm payment; **senza ~ di continuità** without interruption; **in unica ~** Comm as a lump sum. **~ salina per lenti** soaking solution

sol'vente nm solvent. **~ per lo smalto** nail varnish remover. **~ per unghie** nail polish remover ● a solvent; **reparto ~** pay ward

solvibilità nf Fin solvency

'soma nf load; **bestia da ~** beast of burden

'somalo, -a a & nmf Somali

so'maro nm ass, donkey; Sch dunce

so'matico a somatic; **tratti somatici** physical features

somatiz'zare vt react psychosomatically to

som'brero nm sombrero

somigli'ante a similar

somigli'anza nf resemblance

somigli'are vi **~ a** look like, resemble; **chi si somiglia si piglia** birds of a feather flock together

somigli'arsi vr be alike

'somma nf sum; Math addition

som'mare vt add; ⟨totalizzare⟩ add up

sommaria'mente adv summarily

som'mario a & nm summary

som'mato a **tutto ~** all things considered

somme'lier nm inv wine waiter

som'mergere vt submerge

sommer'gibile nm submarine

som'merso pp di **sommergere** ● nm Econ black economy

som'messo a soft

sommini'strare vt administer

somministrazi'one nf administration; **~ per via orale** to be taken orally

sommità nf inv summit

'sommo a highest; fig supreme ● nm summit

som'mossa nf rising

sommozza'tore nm frogman

so'naglio nm bell

'sonar nm sonar

so'nata nf sonata; fig fam beating

'sonda nf Mech drill; ⟨spaziale, Med⟩ probe

son'daggio nm drilling; ⟨spaziale, Med⟩ probe; ⟨indagine⟩ survey. **~ d'opinioni** opinion poll

son'dare vt sound; ⟨investigare⟩ probe

so'netto nm sonnet

sonnambu'lismo nm sleepwalking

son'nambulo, -a nmf sleepwalker

sonnecchi'are vi doze

son'nifero nm sleeping-pill

'sonno nm sleep; **aver ~** be sleepy; **morire di ~** be dead tired, be dead on one's feet; **morto di ~** (fam: stupido) zombie; **perdere il ~** anche fig lose sleep. **~ eterno** Relig eternal rest

sonno'lenza nf sleepiness

'sono vedi **essere**

sonoriz'zare vt add a soundtrack to

so'noro a resonant; ⟨rumoroso⟩ loud; ⟨onde, scheda⟩ sound attrib ● nm (Tech: di film) soundtrack

sontu'oso a sumptuous

sopo'rifero a soporific

sop'palco nm platform

soppe'rire vi **~ a qcsa** provide for sth

soppe'sare vt weigh up ⟨situazione⟩

soppi'atto: di ~ adv furtively

soppor'tare vt support; ⟨tollerare⟩ stand; bear ⟨dolore⟩

sopportazi'one nf patience

soppressi'one nf removal; ⟨di legge⟩ abolition; ⟨di diritti, pubblicazione⟩ suppression; ⟨annullamento⟩ cancellation

sop'presso pp di **sopprimere**

sop'primere vt get rid of; abolish ⟨legge⟩; suppress ⟨diritti, pubblicazione⟩; ⟨annullare⟩ cancel

'sopra adv on top; ⟨più in alto⟩ higher [up]; ⟨al piano superiore⟩ upstairs; ⟨in testo⟩ above; **mettilo lì ~** put it up there; **di ~** upstairs; **dormirci ~** fig sleep on it; **pensarci ~** think about it; **vedi ~** see above ● prep **~ [a]** on; ⟨senza contatto, oltre⟩ over; ⟨riguardo a⟩ about; **è ~ al tavolo, è ~ il tavolo** it's on the table; **il quadro è appeso ~ al camino** the picture is hanging over the fireplace; **il ponte passa ~ all'autostrada** the bridge crosses over the motorway; **è caduto ~ il tetto** it fell on the roof; **l'uno sopra l'altro** one on top of the other; ⟨senza contatto⟩ one above the other; **abita ~ di me** he lives upstairs from me; **i bambini ~ i dieci anni** children over ten; **20° ~ lo zero** 20° above zero; **~ il livello del mare** above sea level; **rifletti ~ quello che è successo** think about what happened; **prendere ~ di sé la responsabilità di qcsa** assume responsibility for sth; **scaricare la colpa ~ qcno** put the blame on sb; **non ha nessuno ~ di sé** he has nobody above him; **al di ~ di** over; **al di ~ di ogni sospetto** beyond suspicion ● nm **il [di] ~** the top

so'prabito nm overcoat

soprac'ciglio nm (pl nf **sopracciglia**) eyebrow

sopracco'perta nf ⟨di letto⟩ bedspread; ⟨di libro⟩ [dust-]jacket

sopraccoper'tina nf book jacket

soprad'detto a above-mentioned

sopraele'vare vt raise

sopraele'vata nf elevated railway

sopraele'vato a raised

sopraf'fare vt overwhelm

sopraf'fatto pp di **sopraffare**

sopraffazi'one nf abuse of power

sopraf'fino a excellent; ⟨gusto, udito⟩ highly refined

sopraggi'ungere vi ⟨persona:⟩ turn up; ⟨accadere⟩ happen; **è sopraggiunta la pioggia** and then it started to rain

soprallu'ogo nm inspection

sopram'mobile nm ornament

soprannatu'rale *a* & *nm* supernatural
sopran'nome *nm* nickname
soprannomi'nare *vt* nickname
sopran'numero *adv* **sono in ~** there are too many of them; **ce ne sono 15 in ~** there are 15 too many of them, there are 15 of them too many
so'prano *nmf* soprano
soprappensi'ero *adv* lost in thought
sopras'salto *nm* **di ~** with a start
soprasse'dere *vi* **~ a** postpone
soprat'tassa *nf* surtax. **~ postale** excess postage
soprat'tenda *nm* fly sheet
soprat'tetto *nm* fly sheet
soprat'tutto *adv* above all
sopravvalu'tare *vt* overvalue; overestimate ⟨*forze*⟩
sopravvalutazi'one *nf* overvaluation; (*di forze*) overestimation
sopravve'nire *vi* turn up; (*accadere*) happen
soprav'vento *nm fig* upper hand; **prendere il ~** take the upper hand
sopravvis'suto, -a *pp di* **sopravvivere** ● *nmf* survivor
sopravvi'venza *nf* survival
soprav'vivere *vi* survive; **~ a** outlive ⟨*persona*⟩
soprinten'dente *nmf* supervisor; (*di museo ecc*) keeper
soprinten'denza *nf* supervision; (*ente*) board
so'pruso *nm* abuse of power
soq'quadro *nm* **mettere a ~** turn upside down
sor'betto *nm* sorbet
sor'bire *vt* sip; *fig* put up with
'sorcio *nm* mouse; **far vedere i sorci verdi a qcno** give sb a rough time
'sordido *a* sordid; (*avaro*) stingy
sor'dina *nf* mute; **in ~** *fig* on the quiet
sordità *nf* deafness
'sordo, -a *a* deaf; ⟨*rumore, dolore*⟩ dull ● *nmf* deaf person
sordo'muto, -a *a* deaf-and-dumb ● *nmf* deaf mute
so'rella *nf* sister. **~ gemella** twin sister
sorel'lastra *nf* stepsister
sor'gente *nf* spring; (*fonte*) source; **programma ~** *Comput* source program
'sorgere *vi* rise; *fig* arise
sormon'tare *vt* surmount
sorni'one *a* sly
sorpas'sare *vt* surpass; (*eccedere*) exceed, overtake, pass *Am* ⟨*veicolo*⟩
sorpas'sato *a* old-fashioned
sor'passo *nm* overtaking, passing *Am*
sorpren'dente *a* surprising; (*straordinario*) remarkable
sorprendente'mente *adv* surprisingly
sor'prendere *vt* surprise; (*cogliere in flagrante*) catch
sor'prendersi *vr* be surprised; **~ a fare qcsa** catch oneself doing sth; **non c'è da ~** it's hardly surprising
sor'presa *nf* surprise; **di ~** by surprise; **provare ~** feel surprised
sor'preso *pp di* **sorprendere**
sor'reggere *vt* support; (*tenere*) hold up
sor'reggersi *vr* support oneself
sor'retto *pp di* **sorreggere**
sorri'dente *a* smiling
sor'ridere *vi* smile; **la fortuna mi ha sorriso** fortune smiled on me
sor'riso *pp di* **sorridere** ● *nm* smile
sorseggi'are *vt* sip
'sorso *nm* sip; (*piccola quantità*) drop
'sorta *nf* sort; **di ~** whatever; **ogni ~ di** all sorts of
'sorte *nf* fate; (*caso imprevisto*) chance; **tirare a ~** draw lots; **per buona ~** *liter* by good fortune
sorteggi'are *vt* draw lots for
sor'teggio *nm* draw
sorti'legio *nm* witchcraft
sor'tire *vi* come out ● *vt* bring about ⟨*effetto*⟩
sor'tita *nf Mil* sortie; (*battuta*) witticism
'sorto *pp di* **sorgere**
sorvegli'ante *nmf* keeper; (*controllore*) overseer
sorvegli'anza *nf* watch; *Mil ecc* surveillance
sorvegli'are *vt* watch over; (*controllare*) oversee; ⟨*polizia:*⟩ watch, keep under surveillance
sorvegli'ato, -a *a* under surveillance ● *nmf* **~ speciale** person kept under special surveillance
sorvo'lare *vt* fly over; *fig* skip
SOS *nm* SOS
'sosia *nm inv* double
so'spendere *vt* hang; (*interrompere*) stop; (*privare di una carica*) suspend
sospensi'one *nf* suspension
sospen'sorio *nm Sport* jockstrap
so'speso *pp di* **sospendere** ● *a* ⟨*impiegato, alunno*⟩ suspended; **~ a** hanging from; **~ a un filo** *fig* hanging by a thread ● *nm* **in ~** pending; (*emozionato*) in suspense
sospet'tare *vt* suspect
so'spetto *a* suspicious ● *nm* suspicion; (*persona*) suspect; **al di sopra di ogni ~** above suspicion
sospet'toso *a* suspicious
so'spingere *vt* drive
so'spinto *pp di* **sospingere**
sospi'rare *vi* sigh ● *vt* long for
so'spiro *nm* sigh
'sosta *nf* stop; (*pausa*) pause; **senza ~** nonstop; **'divieto di ~'** 'no parking'; **'~ autorizzata...'** 'parking permitted for...'
sostan'tivo *nm* noun
so'stanza *nf* substance; **sostanze** *pl* (*patrimonio*) property *sg*; **in ~** to sum up; **la ~ della questione** the nub of the matter
sostanzi'oso *a* substantial; ⟨*cibo*⟩ nourishing; **poco ~** insubstantial
so'stare *vi* stop; (*fare una pausa*) pause

so'stegno *nm* support. **~ morale** moral support

soste'nere *vt* support; (*sopportare*) bear; (*resistere*) withstand; (*affermare*) maintain; (*nutrire*) sustain; sit (*esame*); **~ le spese** meet the costs; **~ delle spese** incur expenditure; **~ una carica** hold a position; **~ una parte** play a role

soste'nersi *vr* support oneself

soste'nitore, -'trice *nmf* supporter

sostenta'mento *nm* maintenance

soste'nuto *a* (*stile*) formal; (*velocità*) high; (*mercato, prezzi*) steady ● *nm* **fare il ~** be stand-offish

sostitu'ire *vt* substitute (**a** for), replace (**con** with)

sostitu'irsi *vr* **~ a** replace

sosti'tuto, -a *nmf* replacement, stand-in ● *nm* (*surrogato*) substitute

sostituzi'one *nf* substitution

sotta'ceto *a* pickled; **sottaceti** *pl* pickles

sot'tacqua *adv* underwater

sot'tana *nf* petticoat; (*di prete*) cassock

sotter'fugio *nm* subterfuge; **di ~** secretly

sotter'raneo *a* underground ● *nm* cellar

sotter'rare *vt* bury

sottigli'ezza *nf* slimness; *fig* subtlety

sot'tile *a* thin; (*udito, odorato*) keen; (*osservazione, distinzione*) subtle

sotti'letta[R] *nf* cheese slice

sottiliz'zare *vi* split hairs

sottin'tendere *vt* imply

sottin'teso *pp di* **sottintendere** ● *nm* allusion; **senza sottintesi** openly ● *a* implied

'sotto *adv* below; (*più in basso*) lower [down]; (*al di sotto*) underneath; (*al piano di sotto*) downstairs; **è lì ~** it's underneath; **~ ~** deep down; (*di nascosto*) on the quiet; **di ~** downstairs; **mettersi ~** *fig* get down to it; **mettere ~** (*fam: investire*) knock down; **fatti ~!** *fam* get stuck in! ● *prep* **~** [**a**] under; (*al di sotto di*) under[neath]; **il fiume passa ~ un ponte** the river passes under[neath] a bridge; **è ~ il tavolo**, **è ~ al tavolo** it's under[neath] the table; **abita ~ di me** he lives downstairs from me; **i bambini ~ i dieci anni** children under ten; **20° ~ zero** 20° below zero; **~ il livello del mare** below sea level; **~ la pioggia** in the rain; **~ Elisabetta I** under Elizabeth I; **~ calmante** under sedation; **~ chiave** under lock and key; **~ condizione che...** on condition that...; **~ giuramento** under oath; **~ sorveglianza** under surveillance; **~ Natale/gli esami** around Christmas/exam time; **al di ~ di** under; **andare ~ i 50 all'ora** do less than 50km an hour ● *nm* **il [di] ~** the bottom

sotto'banco *adv* (*vendere, comprare*) under the counter

sottobicchi'ere *nm* coaster

sotto'bosco *nm* undergrowth

sotto'braccio *adv* arm in arm

sottoccu'pato *a* underemployed

sottochi'ave *adv* under lock and key

sotto'costo *a & adv* at less than cost price

sottodi'rectory *nf Comput* subdirectory

sottoe'sporre *vt* underexpose

sotto'fondo *nm* background

sotto'gamba *adv* **prendere qcsa ~** take sth lightly

sotto'gonna *nf* underskirt

sottoindi'cato *a* undermentioned

sottoinsi'eme *nm Math* subset

sottoline'are *vt* underline; *fig* underline (*importanza*); emphasize (*forma degli occhi ecc*)

sot'tolio *adv* in oil

sotto'mano *adv* within reach

sottoma'rino *a & nm* submarine

sotto'messo *pp di* **sottomettere** ● *a* (*remissivo*) submissive

sotto'mettere *vt* submit; subdue (*popolo*)

sotto'mettersi *vr* submit

sottomissi'one *nf* submission

sottopa'gare *vt* underpay

sottopas'saggio *nm* underpass; (*pedonale*) subway

sottopi'atto *nm* place mat

sotto'porre *vt* submit; (*costringere*) subject

sotto'porsi *vr* submit oneself; **~ a** undergo

sotto'posto *pp di* **sottoporre**

sottoproletari'ato *nm* underclass

sotto'scala *nm* cupboard under the stairs

sotto'scritto *pp di* **sottoscrivere** ● *nm* undersigned

sotto'scrivere *vt* sign; (*approvare*) sanction, subscribe to

sottoscrizi'one *nf* (*petizione*) petition; (*approvazione*) sanction; (*raccolta di denaro*) appeal

sottosegre'tario *nm* undersecretary

sotto'sopra *adv* upside-down

sotto'stante *a* **la strada ~** the road below

sottosu'olo *nm* subsoil

sottosvilup'pato *a* underdeveloped

sottosvi'luppo *nm* underdevelopment

sottote'nente *nm* second lieutenant; *Naut* sub-lieutenant

sotto'terra *adv* underground

sotto'titolo *nm* subtitle

sottovalu'tare *vt* underestimate

sotto'vento *adv* downwind

sotto'veste *nf* slip

sotto'voce *adv* in a low voice

sottovu'oto *a* vacuum-packed

sotto'zero *a inv* subzero

sot'trarre *vt* remove; embezzle (*fondi*); *Math* subtract

sot'trarsi *vr* **~ a** escape from; avoid (*responsabilità*)

sot'tratto *pp di* **sottrarre**

sottrazi'one *nf* removal; (*di fondi*) embezzlement; *Math* subtraction

sottuffici'ale *nm* non-commissioned officer; *Naut* petty officer

sou'brette *nf* showgirl

souf'flé *nm inv* soufflé

souve'nir *nm inv* souvenir; **negozio di ~** souvenir shop

so'vente *adv* liter often

soverchie'ria *nf* bullying; **fare sover-chierie a** bully

so'vietico, -a *a & nmf* Soviet

sovrabbon'danza *nf* overabundance

sovraccari'care *vt* overload

sovrac'carico *a* overloaded (**di** with) ● *nm* overload

sovraffati'carsi *vr* overexert oneself

sovraffolla'mento *nm* overcrowding

sovralimen'tare *vt* overfeed

sovrannatu'rale *a & nm* = **soprannaturale**

sovrannazio'nale *a* supranational

so'vrano, -a *a* sovereign; *fig* supreme ● *nmf* sovereign

sovrappopo'lato *a* overpopulated

sovrap'porre *vt* superimpose

sovrap'porsi *vr* overlap

sovrapposizi'one *nf* superimposition

sovrapro'fitto *nm* excess profits

sovra'stare *vt* dominate; ⟨fig: pericolo:⟩ hang over

sovrastrut'tura *nf* superstructure

sovratensi'one *nf Electr* overload, overtension

sovrecci'tarsi *vr* get overexcited

sovrecci'tato *a* overexcited

sovresposizi'one *nf Phot* overexposure

sovrimpressi'one *nf Phot* double exposure

sovrinten'dente, sovrinten'denza = **soprintendente, soprintendenza**

sovru'mano *a* superhuman

sovvenzio'nare *vt* subsidize

sovvenzi'one *nf* subsidy

sovver'sivo, -a *a & nmf* subversive

sovver'tire *vt* subvert

'sozzo *a* filthy

SP *nf abbr* (**strada provinciale**) secondary road

S.p.A. *abbr* (**società per azioni**) plc

spac'care *vt* split; chop ⟨legna⟩; ~ **il minuto** keep perfect time; ~ **il muso a qcno** *sl* smash sb's face in; **o la va o la spacca** it's all or nothing; **un sole che spacca le pietre** a sun hot enough to fry an egg

spac'carsi *vr* split

spacca'tura *nf* split

spacci'are *vt* deal in, push ⟨droga⟩; ~ **qcsa per qcsa** pass sth off as sth; **essere spacciato** be done for, be a goner

spacci'arsi *vr* ~ **per** pass oneself off as

spaccia|'tore, -'trice *nmf* ⟨di droga⟩ pusher; ⟨di denaro falso⟩ distributor of forged bank notes

'spaccio *nm* ⟨di droga⟩ dealer, pusher; (negozio) shop

'spacco *nm* split

spacco'nate *nfpl* blustering

spac'cone, -a *nmf* boaster

'spada *nf* sword

spadac'cino *nm* swordsman

spadroneggi'are *vi* act the boss

spae'sato *a* disorientated

spa'ghetti *nmpl* spaghetti *sg.* ~ **in bianco** spaghetti with butter, oil and cheese. ~ **alla carbonara** spaghetti with egg, cheese and diced bacon. ~ **al sugo** spaghetti with a sauce

spa'ghetto *nm* (fam: spavento) fright

'Spagna *nf* Spain

spagno'letta *nf* spool

spa'gnolo, -a *a* Spanish ● *nmf* Spaniard ● *nm* (lingua) Spanish

'spago *nm* string; (fam: spavento) fright; **dare ~ a qcno** encourage sb

spai'ato *a* odd

spalan'care *vt* open wide

spalan'carsi *vr* open wide

spalan'cato *a* wide open

spa'lare *vt* shovel

'spalla *nf* shoulder; ⟨di comico⟩ straight man; **spalle** *pl* (schiena) back; **alzata di spalle** shrug [of the shoulders]; **alle spalle di** behind; **alle spalle di qcno** ⟨ridere⟩ behind sb's back; **avere qnco/qcsa alle spalle** have sb/sth behind one; **di ~** ⟨violino ecc⟩ second; **vivere alle spalle di qcno** live off sb; **con le spalle al muro** anche fig with one's back to the wall; **voltare le spalle** turn one's back

spal'lata *nf* push with the shoulder; (alzata di spalle) shrug [of the shoulders]

spalleggi'are *vt* back up

spal'letta *nf* parapet

spalli'era *nf* back; (di letto) headboard; (ginnastica) wall bars *pl*

spal'lina *nf* strap; (imbottitura) shoulder pad; **senza spalline** strapless

spal'mare *vt* spread

spal'marsi *vr* cover oneself

spa'nato *a* ⟨vite⟩ threadless

spanci'ata *nf* belly flop

'spandere *vt* spread; (versare) spill; **spendere e ~** spend and spend

'spandersi *vr* spread

spandighi'aia *nm inv* gritter

'spaniel *nm inv* spaniel

spappo'lare *vt* crush

spa'rare *vt/i* shoot; **spararle grosse** talk big; ~ **fandonie** talk nonsense

spa'rarsi *vr* shoot oneself; **si è sparato un colpo di pistola alla tempia** he shot himself in the temple

spa'rata *nf fam* tall story

spa'rato *nm* (della camicia) dicky

spara'toria *nf* shooting

sparecchi'are *vt* clear

spa'reggio *nm Comm* deficit; *Sport* play-off

'spargere *vt* scatter; (diffondere) spread; shed ⟨lacrime, sangue⟩

'spargersi *vr* spread

spargi'mento *nm* scattering; (di lacrime, sangue) shedding; ~ **di sangue** bloodshed

spa'rire *vi* disappear; **sparisci!** get lost!, scram!

sparizi'one *nf* disappearance

spar'lare *vi* ~ **di** run down

'sparo *nm* shot

sparpagli'are *vt* scatter

sparpagli'arsi *vr* scatter

sparpagli'ato *a* far-flung

'sparso *pp di* **spargere** ● *a* scattered; (*sciolto*) loose

sparti'neve *nm inv* snowplough

spar'tire *vt* share out; (*separare*) separate

spar'tirsi *vr* share

spar'tito *nm Mus* score

sparti'traffico *nm inv* traffic island; (*di autostrada*) central reservation, median strip *Am*

spartizi'one *nf* division

spa'ruto *a* gaunt; ⟨*gruppo*⟩ small; ⟨*peli, capelli*⟩ sparse

sparvi'ero *nm* sparrow-hawk

spasi'mante *nm hum* admirer

spasi'mare *vi* suffer agonies; **~ per** be madly in love with

'spasimo *nm* spasm

spa'smodico *a* spasmodic

spas'sarsi *vr* amuse oneself; **spas'sarsela** have a good time

spassio'nato *a* ⟨*osservatore*⟩ dispassionate, impartial

'spasso *nm* fun; **essere uno ~** be hilarious; **andare a ~** go for a walk; **essere a ~** be out of work

spas'soso *a* hilarious

'spastico *a* spastic

'spatola *nf* spatula

spau'racchio *nm* scarecrow; *fig* bugbear

spau'rire *vt* frighten

spa'valdo *a* defiant

spaventa'passeri *nm inv* scarecrow

spaven'tare *vt* frighten, scare

spaven'tarsi *vr* be frightened, be scared

spa'vento *nm* fright; **brutto da fare ~** incredibly ugly

spaven'toso *a* frightening; (*fam: enorme*) incredible

spazi'ale *a* spatial; (*cosmico*) space *attrib*

spazi'are *vt* space out ● *vi* range

spazien'tirsi *vr* lose [one's] patience

'spazio *nm* space. **~ aereo** airspace. **~ indietro** *Comput* backspace. **~ di tempo** period of time. **~ vitale** elbowroom

spazi'oso *a* spacious

spazio-tempo'rale *a* spatiotemporal

spazzaca'mino *nm* chimney sweep

spazza'neve *nm inv* (*anche sci*) snowplough

spaz'zare *vt* sweep; **~ via** sweep away; (*fam: mangiare*) devour

spazza'trice *nf* sweeper

spazza'tura *nf* (*immondizia*) rubbish

spaz'zino *nm* road sweeper; (*netturbino*) dustman

'spazzola *nf* brush; (*di tergicristallo*) blade; **capelli a ~** crew cut

spazzo'lare *vt* brush

spazzo'larsi *vr* **~ i capelli** brush one's hair

spazzo'lino *nm* small brush. **~ da denti** toothbrush. **~ per le unghie** nailbrush

spazzo'lone *nm* scrubbing brush

'speaker *nm inv* Radio, TV announcer

specchi'arsi *vr* look at oneself in a/the mirror; (*riflettersi*) be mirrored; **~ in qcno** model oneself on sb

specchi'ato *a* **di specchiata onestà** of spotless integrity

specchi'etto *nm* small mirror. **~ laterale** wing mirror. **~ retrovisore** driving mirror, rear-view mirror

'specchio *nm* mirror

speci'ale *a* special ● *nm* TV special [programme]

specia'lista *nmf* specialist

specialità *nf inv* speciality, specialty

specializ'zare *vt* specialize

specializ'zarsi *vr* specialize

specializ'zato *a* ⟨*operaio*⟩ skilled; **siamo specializzati in...** we specialize in...

special'mente *adv* especially

'specie *nf* (*scientifico*) species; (*tipo*) kind; **fare ~ a** surprise; **in ~** especially

specifi'care *vt* specify

specificata'mente *adv* specifically

spe'cifico *a* specific

speci'oso *a* specious

specu'lare *vi* speculate; **~ su** (*indagare*) speculate on; *Fin* speculate in

specu'lare *a* mirror *attrib*

specula'tivo *a* speculative

specula'tore *nm* speculator

speculazi'one *nf* speculation

spe'dire *vt* send; **~ per posta** mail, post *Br*; **~ qcno all'altro mondo** send sb to meet his/her maker

spe'dito *pp di* **spedire** ● *a* quick; ⟨*parlata*⟩ fluent

spedizi'one *nf* (*di lettere ecc*) dispatch; *Comm* consignment, shipment; (*scientifica*) expedition

spedizioni'ere *nm Comm* freight forwarder

'spegnere *vt* put out; turn off, switch off ⟨*motore, luce, televisione*⟩; turn off ⟨*gas*⟩; quench, slake ⟨*sete*⟩

'spegnersi *vr* go out; (*morire*) pass away

spegni'mento *nm* standby

spelacchi'ato *a* ⟨*tappeto*⟩ threadbare; ⟨*cane*⟩ mangy

spe'lare *vt* remove the fur of ⟨*coniglio*⟩

spe'larsi *vr* ⟨*cane, tappeto:*⟩ moult; ⟨*persona:*⟩ peel

speleolo'gia *nf* potholing, speleology

spel'lare *vt* skin; *fig* fleece

spel'larsi *vr* ⟨*serpente:*⟩ shed its skin; (*per il sole*) peel; **mi sono spellato un ginocchio** I grazed *or* skinned my knee

spe'lonca *nf* cave; *fig* dingy hole

spendacci'one, -a *nmf* spendthrift

'spendere *vt* spend; **~ fiato** waste one's breath

spen'nare *vt* pluck; *fam* fleece ⟨*cliente*⟩

spennel'lare *vt* brush ● *vi* paint

spensierata'mente *adv* blithely

spensiera'tezza *nf* lightheartedness

spensie'rato *a* lighthearted, carefree

'spento *pp di* **spegnere** ● *a* off; ⟨*gas*⟩ out; (*smorto*) dull; ⟨*vulcano*⟩ extinct

spenzo'lare vt dangle

spe'ranza nf hope; **pieno di ~** hopeful; **senza ~** hopeless

spe'rare vt hope for; (aspettarsi) expect ● vi **~ in** trust in; **spero di sì** I hope so

'sperdersi vr get lost

sper'duto a lost; (isolato) secluded

spergiu'rare vi commit perjury

spergi'uro, -a nmf perjurer ● nm perjury

sperico'lato a swashbuckling

sperimen'tale a experimental

sperimen'tare vt experiment with; test ⟨resistenza, capacità, teoria⟩

sperimen'tato a ⟨metodo⟩ tried and tested

sperimentazi'one nf experimentation; **~ sugli animali** animal testing

'sperma nm sperm

spermi'cida a spermicidal ● nm spermicide

spero'nare vt ram

spe'rone nm spur

sperpe'rare vt squander

'sperpero nm waste, squandering

spersonaliz'zare vt depersonalize

spersonaliz'zarsi vr become depersonalized

spersonalizzazi'one nf depersonalization

'spesa nf expense; (acquisto) purchase; **andare a far spese** go shopping; **fare la ~** do the shopping; **fare le spese di** pay for; **a proprie spese** at one's own expense. **spese** pl **bancarie** bank charges. **spese** pl **di capitale** capital expenditure. **spese** pl **a carico del destinatario** carriage forward. **spese** pl **di esercizio** business expenses. **spese** pl **extra** out-of-pocket expenses. **spese** pl **di gestione** operating costs. **spese** pl **di spedizione** shipping costs. **spese** pl **di viaggio** travel expenses

spe'sare vt pay expenses for; **spesato della ditta** paid for by the company, on the company

spe'sato a all-expenses-paid

'speso pp di **spendere**

'spesso[1] a thick

'spesso[2] adv often

spes'sore nm thickness; (fig: consistenza) substance

spet'tabile a (Comm abbr **Spett.**) **S~ ditta Rossi** Messrs Rossi

spettaco'lare a spectacular

spet'tacolo nm spectacle; (rappresentazione) show; **dare ~ di sé** make a spectacle o an exhibition of oneself; **il mondo dello ~** show business. **~ di burattini** Punch-and-Judy show

spettaco'loso a spectacular

spet'tanza nf concern

spet'tare vi **~ a** be up to; ⟨diritto:⟩ be due to

spetta|'tore, -'trice nmf spectator; **spettatori** pl (di cinema ecc) audience sg

spettego'lare vi gossip

spetti'nare vt **~ qcno** ruffle sb's hair

spetti'narsi vr ruffle one's hair

spet'trale a ghostly

'spettro nm ghost; (fig: della fame) spectre; Phys spectrum; **ad ampio ~** ⟨medicina⟩ broad-spectrum

spezi'are vt add spices to, spice

spezi'ato a spicy

'spezie nfpl spices

spez'zare vt break

spez'zarsi vr break

spezza'tino nm stew

spez'zato a broken ● nm coordinated jacket and trousers

spezzet'tare vt break into small pieces

spez'zone nm Cinema clip, footage no pl; (bomba) cluster bomb

'spia nf spy; (della polizia) informer; (di porta) peep-hole; **fare la ~** sneak. **~ di accensione** power-on light. **~ di attività dell'hard disk** Comput hard disk activity light. **~ della benzina** petrol gauge. **~ [luminosa]** light. **~ dell'olio** oil [warning] light

spiacci'care vt squash

spia'cente a sorry

spia'cevole a unpleasant

spi'aggia nf beach

spia'nare vt level; (rendere liscio) smooth; roll out ⟨pasta⟩; raze to the ground ⟨edificio⟩

spia'nata nf flat ground

spi'ano nm **a tutto ~** flat out

spian'tato a fig penniless

spi'are vt spy on; wait for ⟨occasione ecc⟩

spiattel'lare vt blurt out; shove ⟨oggetto⟩

spiaz'zare vt wrong-foot

spi'azzo nm (radura) clearing

spic'care vt **~ un salto** jump; **~ il volo** take flight ● vi stand out

spic'cato a marked

'spicchio nm (di agrumi) segment; (di aglio) clove

spicci'arsi vr hurry up

spiccia'tivo a speedy

'spiccio a no-nonsense

'spiccioli nmpl change

'spicciolo a (comune) banal; ⟨denaro, 10 000 lire⟩ in change

'spicco nm relief; **fare ~** stand out; **di ~** high-profile

'spider nmf inv open-top sports car

spie'dino nm kebab

spi'edo nm spit; **allo ~** on a spit, spit-roasted

spiega'mento nm deployment

spie'gare vt explain; open out ⟨cartina⟩; unfurl ⟨vele⟩

spie'garsi vr explain oneself; ⟨vele, bandiere:⟩ unfurl; **non so se mi spiego** need I say more?; **mi sono spiegato?** (minaccia) do I make myself clear?; **non riesco a spiegarmi come...** I can't understand how...

spie'gato a ⟨ale⟩ outspread; **a sirene spiegate** with sirens blaring; **a voce spiegata** at the top of one's voice; **a vele spiegate** under full sail, with all sails in the wind

spiegazi'one *nf* explanation; **venire a una ~ con qcno** sort things out with sb
spiegaz'zare *vt* crumple
spiegaz'zato *a* crumpled
spieta'tezza *nf* ruthlessness
spie'tato *a* ruthless
spiffe'rare *vt* blurt out ● *vi* ⟨*vento:*⟩ whistle
'spiffero *nm* ⟨*corrente d'aria*⟩ draught
'spiga *nf* spike; *Bot* ear
spi'gato *a* herringbone
spigli'ato *a* self-possessed
'spigola *nf* sea bass
spigo'lare *vt* glean
'spigolo *nm* edge; ⟨*angolo*⟩ corner
'spilla *nf* ⟨*gioiello*⟩ brooch. **~ da balia** safety pin. **~ di sicurezza** safety pin
spil'lare *vt* tap
'spillo *nm* pin. **~ di sicurezza** safety pin; ⟨*in arma*⟩ safety catch
spil'lone *nm* hatpin
spilluzzi'care *vt* pick at
spi'lorcio, -a *a* stingy ● *nm* miser, skinflint
spilun'gone, -a *nmf* beanpole
'spina *nf* thorn; ⟨*di pesce*⟩ bone; *Electr* plug; **a ~ di pesce** ⟨*tessuto, disegno*⟩ herringbone; ⟨*parcheggio*⟩ in two angled rows; **stare sulle spine** be on tenterhooks. **~ dorsale** spine; **essere una ~ nel fianco** thorn in one's side
spi'naci *nmpl* spinach
spi'nale *a* spinal
spi'nato *a* ⟨*filo*⟩ barbed; ⟨*pianta*⟩ thorny ● *nm* herringbone
spi'nello *nm* ⟨*fam: droga*⟩ joint
'spingere *vt* push; *fig* drive
'spingersi *vr* ⟨*andare*⟩ proceed
'spinnaker *nm* spinnaker
spi'noso *a* thorny
spi'notto *nm* *Electr* plug
'spinta *nf* push; ⟨*violenta*⟩ thrust; *fig* spur; **dare una ~ a qcsa/qcno** give sb/sth a push; **farsi largo a spinte** push one's way through
'spinto *pp di* **spingere**
spio'naggio *nm* espionage, spying
spi'one, -a *nmf* tell-tale
spio'vente *a* ⟨*tetto*⟩ sloping ● *nm* slope
spi'overe *vi liter* stop raining; ⟨*ricadere*⟩ fall; ⟨*scorrere*⟩ flow down
'spira *nf* coil
spi'raglio *nm* small opening; ⟨*soffio d'aria*⟩ breath of air; ⟨*raggio di luce*⟩ gleam of light
spi'rale *a* spiral ● *nm* spiral; ⟨*negli orologi*⟩ hairspring; ⟨*anticoncezionale*⟩ coil; **a ~** spiral-shaped
spi'rare *vi* ⟨*soffiare*⟩ blow; ⟨*morire*⟩ pass away
spiri'tato *a* possessed; ⟨*espressione*⟩ wild
spiri'tismo *nm* spiritualism
spiri'tista *nmf* spiritualist
spiri'tistico *a* spiritualist
'spirito *nm* spirit; ⟨*arguzia*⟩ wit; ⟨*intelletto*⟩ mind; **fare dello ~** be witty; **persona di ~** witty person; **sotto ~** in brandy. **~ civico** community spirit. **~ di contraddizione** contrariness. **S~ Santo** Holy Spirit, Holy Ghost
spirito'saggine *nf* witticism

spiri'toso *a* witty
spiritu'ale *a* spiritual
spiritual'mente *adv* spiritually
splen'dente *a* shining
'splendere *vi* shine
'splendido *a* splendid
splen'dore *nm* splendour
'spocchia *nf* conceit
spocchi'oso *a* conceited
spode'stare *vt* dispossess; depose ⟨*re*⟩
spoetiz'zare *vt* disenchant
'spoglia *nf* ⟨*di animale*⟩ skin; **spoglie** *pl* ⟨*salma*⟩ mortal remains; ⟨*bottino*⟩ spoils; **sotto false spoglie** under false pretences
spogli'are *vt* strip; ⟨*svestire*⟩ undress; ⟨*fare lo spoglio di*⟩ go through; **~ qcno di un diritto** divest sb of a right
spoglia'rello *nm* strip-tease
spogliarel'lista *nf* strip-tease artist, stripper
spogli'arsi *vr* strip, undress
spoglia'toio *nm* dressing room; *Sport* changing room; ⟨*guardaroba*⟩ cloakroom, checkroom *Am*
'spoglio *a* undressed; ⟨*albero, muro*⟩ bare. **~ di** ⟨*privo*⟩ stripped of ● *nm* ⟨*scrutinio*⟩ perusal
'spoiler *nm inv Auto* spoiler
'spola *nf* shuttle; **fare la ~** shuttle
spo'letta *nf* spool
spolmo'narsi *vr* shout oneself hoarse
spol'pare *vt* take the flesh off; *fig* fleece
spolve'rare *vt* dust; *fam* devour ⟨*cibo*⟩
'sponda *nf* ⟨*di mare, lago*⟩ shore; ⟨*di fiume*⟩ bank; ⟨*bordo*⟩ edge
sponsoriz'zare *vt* sponsor
sponsorizzazi'one *nf* sponsorship
spontaneità *nf* spontaneity
spon'taneo *a* spontaneous
'spooling *nm Comput* spooling
spopo'lare *vt* depopulate ● *vi* ⟨*avere successo*⟩ draw the crowds
spopo'larsi *vr* become depopulated
'spora *nf* spore
sporadica'mente *adv* sporadically
spo'radico *a* sporadic
sporcacci'one, -a *nmf* dirty pig
spor'care *vt* dirty; ⟨*macchiare*⟩ soil
spor'carsi *vr* get dirty
spor'cizia *nf* dirt
'sporco *a* dirty; **avere la coscienza sporca** have a guilty conscience ● *nm* dirt
spor'gente *a* jutting
spor'genza *nf* projection
'sporgere *vt* stretch out; **~ querela contro** take legal action against ● *vi* jut out
'sporgersi *vr* lean out
sport *nm inv* sport; **fare qcsa per ~** do sth for fun. **~ invernali** *pl* winter sports
'sporta *nf* shopping basket
spor'tello *nm* door; ⟨*di banca ecc*⟩ window. **~ automatico** cash dispenser, cash point. **~ pacchi** parcels counter
spor'tivo, -a *a* sports *attrib*; ⟨*persona*⟩ sporty ● *nm* sportsman ● *nf* sportswoman
'sporto *pp di* **sporgere**

'sposa *nf* bride; **dare in ~** give in marriage, give away; **prendere in ~** marry

sposa'lizio *nm* wedding

spo'sare *vt* marry; *fig* espouse

spo'sarsi *vr* get married; ⟨*vino:*⟩ go (**con** with)

spo'sato *a* married

spo'sini *nmpl* newly-weds

'sposo *nm* bridegroom; **sposi** *pl* [**novelli**] newlyweds

spossa'tezza *nf* exhaustion

spos'sato *a* exhausted, worn out

sposses'sato *a* dispossessed

sposta'mento *nm* displacement. **~ d'aria** airflow

spo'stare *vt* move; (*differire*) postpone; (*cambiare*) change

spo'starsi *vr* move

spo'stato, -a *a* ill-adjusted ● *nmf* (*disadattato*) misfit

spot *nm inv* **~** [**pubblicitario**] commercial

'spranga *nf* bar

spran'gare *vt* bar

'sprazzo *nm* (*di colore*) splash; (*di luce*) flash; *fig* glimmer

spre'care *vt* waste

'spreco *nm* waste

spre'cone *a* spendthrift

spre'gevole *a* despicable

spregia'tivo *a* pejorative

'spregio *nm* contempt; **fare uno ~ a qcno** offend sb

spregiudi'cato *a* unprejudiced; *pej* unscrupulous

'spremere *vt* squeeze

'spremersi *vr* **~ le meningi** rack one's brains

spremi'aglio *nm inv* garlic press

spremia'grumi *nm inv* lemon squeezer

spremili'moni *nm inv* lemon squeezer

spre'muta *nf* juice. **~ d'arancia** fresh orange [juice], freshly squeezed orange juice

spre'tato *nm* former priest

sprez'zante *a* contemptuous

sprigio'nare *vt* emit

sprigio'narsi *vr* burst out

sprint *nm* sprint; **fare uno ~** put on a spurt

spriz'zare *vt/i* spurt; be bursting with ⟨*salute, gioia*⟩

sprofon'dare *vi* sink; (*crollare*) collapse

sprofon'darsi *vr* **~ in** sink into; *fig* be engrossed in

spron *nm vedi* **sprone**

spro'nare *vt* spur on

'sprone *nm* spur; (*sartoria*) yoke; **a spron battuto** instantly; **andare a spron battuto** go hell-for-leather

sproporzio'nato *a* disproportionate

sproporzi'one *nf* disproportion

spropositato *a* full of blunders; (*enorme*) huge

spro'posito *nm* blunder; (*eccesso*) excessive amount; **a ~** inopportunely

sprovve'duto *a* unprepared; **~ di** lacking in

sprov'visto *a* **~ di** out of; lacking in ⟨*fantasia, pazienza*⟩; **alla sprovvista** unexpectedly

spruz'zare *vt* sprinkle; (*vaporizzare*) spray; (*inzaccherare*) spatter

spruzza'tore *nm* spray

'spruzzo *nm* spray; (*di fango*) splash

spudorata'mente *adv* shamelessly

spudora'tezza *nf* shamelessness

spudo'rato *a* shameless

'spugna *nf* sponge; (*tessuto*) towelling

spu'gnoso *a* spongy

'spuma *nf* foam; (*schiuma*) froth; *Culin* mousse

spu'mante *nm* sparkling wine, spumante

spumeggi'ante *a* bubbly; ⟨*mare*⟩ foaming

spumeggi'are *vi* ⟨*champagne:*⟩ bubble; ⟨*birra:*⟩ foam

spun'tare *vt* (*rompere la punta di*) break the point of; trim ⟨*capelli*⟩; **spuntarla** *fig* win ● *vi* ⟨*pianta:*⟩ sprout; ⟨*capelli:*⟩ begin to grow; (*sorgere*) rise; (*apparire*) appear

spun'tarsi *vr* get blunt

spun'tata *nf* trim

spun'tino *nm* snack

'spunto *nm* cue; *fig* starting point; **dare ~ a** give rise to

spur'gare *vt* purge

spur'garsi *vr Med* expectorate

'spurio *a* spurious

spu'tacchio *nm* spittle

spu'tare *vt/i* spit; spit out ⟨*cibo*⟩; **~ sentenze** pass judgment; **~ l'osso** *sl* spit it out

'sputo *nm* spit

'squadra *nf* (*gruppo*) team, squad; (*di polizia ecc*) squad; (*da disegno*) square; **lavoro di ~** teamwork. **~ del buoncostume** Vice Squad. **~ mobile** Flying Squad. **~ narcotici** Drug Squad. **~ soccorso** rescue team

squa'drare *vt* square; (*guardare*) look up and down

squa'driglia *nf*, **squadrigli'one** *nm* squadron

squa'drone *nm* squadron

squagli'are *vt* melt

squagli'arsi *vr* melt; **squagliarsela** (*fam:* *svignarsela*) steal out

squa'lifica *nf* disqualification

squalifi'care *vt* disqualify

'squallido *a* squalid

squal'lore *nm* squalor

'squalo *nm* shark

'squama *nf* scale; (*di pelle*) flake

squa'mare *vt* scale

squa'marsi *vr* ⟨*pelle:*⟩ flake off

squa'moso *a* scaly; ⟨*pelle*⟩ flaky

squarcia'gola: a ~ *adv* at the top of one's voice

squarci'are *vt* rip

'squarcio *nm* rip; (*di ferita, in nave*) gash; (*di cielo*) patch

squar'tare *vt* quarter; dismember ⟨*animale*⟩

squarta'tore *nm* **Jack lo ~** Jack the Ripper

squash *nm inv* squash
squas'sare *vt* shake
squattri'nato *a* penniless
squaw *nf inv* squaw
squilib'rare *vt* unbalance
squili'brato, -a *a* unbalanced ● *nmf* lunatic
squi'librio *nm* imbalance
squil'lante *a* shrill
squil'lare *vi* ⟨campana:⟩ peal; ⟨tromba:⟩ blare; ⟨telefono:⟩ ring
'**squillo** *nm* blare; *Teleph* ring; ⟨ragazza⟩ call girl
squinter'nato *a anche fig* crazy
squisi'tezza *nf* refinement
squi'sito *a* exquisite
squit'tire *vi* ⟨pappagallo, fig:⟩ squawk; ⟨topo:⟩ squeak
sradi'care *vt* uproot; eradicate ⟨vizio, male⟩
sragio'nare *vi* rave
sregola'tezza *nf* dissipation
srego'lato *a* inordinate; ⟨dissoluto⟩ dissolute
s.r.l. *abbr* (**società a responsabilità limitata**) Ltd
sroto'lare *vt* uncoil
SS *abbr* (**strada statale**) national road; *abbr* (**Santissimo**) Most Holy
ss *abbr* (**seguenti**) following
sst *int* sh!
'**stabile** *a* stable; ⟨permanente⟩ lasting; ⟨saldo⟩ steady; **compagnia ~** *Theat* repertory company ● *nm* ⟨edificio⟩ building
stabili'mento *nm* factory; ⟨industriale⟩ plant; ⟨edificio⟩ establishment. **~ balneare** lido
stabi'lire *vt* establish; ⟨decidere⟩ decide
stabi'lirsi *vr* settle
stabilità *nf* stability
stabi'lito *a* established
stabiliz'zare *vt* stabilize
stabiliz'zarsi *vr* stabilize
stabilizza'tore *nm* stabilizer
stacano'vista *nmf* workaholic
stac'care *vt* detach; pronounce clearly ⟨parole⟩; ⟨separare⟩ separate; turn off ⟨corrente⟩; **~ gli occhi da** take one's eyes off ● *vi* ⟨fam: finire di lavorare⟩ knock off
stac'carsi *vr* come off; **~ da** break away from ⟨partito, famiglia⟩; **si stacca alle cinque** knocking off time is five o'clock
staccata'mente *adv* staccato
stac'cato *a Mus* staccato
staccio'nata *nf* fence
'**stacco** *nm* gap
'**stadio** *nm* stadium
'**staffa** *nf* stirrup; **perdere le staffe** *fig* fly off the handle
staf'fetta *nf* dispatch rider
staffet'tista *nmf Sport* anchorman
stagio'nale *a* seasonal
stagio'nare *vt* season ⟨legno⟩; mature ⟨formaggio⟩
stagio'nato *a* ⟨legno⟩ seasoned; ⟨formaggio⟩ matured

stagiona'tura *nf* ⟨di legno⟩ seasoning; ⟨di formaggio⟩ maturation, maturing
stagi'one *nf* season; **alta/bassa ~** high/low season; **di ~** in season; **fuori ~** out of season. **~ lirica** opera season
stagli'arsi *vr* stand out
sta'gnante *a* stagnant
sta'gnare *vt* ⟨saldare⟩ solder; ⟨chiudere ermeticamente⟩ seal ● *vi* ⟨acqua:⟩ stagnate
'**stagno** *a* ⟨a tenuta d'acqua⟩ watertight ● *nm* ⟨acqua ferma⟩ pond; ⟨metallo⟩ tin
sta'gnola *nf* tinfoil
stalag'mite *nf* stalagmite
stalat'tite *nf* stalactite
'**stalla** *nf* stable; ⟨per buoi⟩ cowshed
stalli'ere *nm* groom
stal'lone *nm* stallion
sta'mani, stamat'tina *adv* this morning
stam'becco *nm* ibex
stam'berga *nf* hovel
'**stampa** *nf Typ* printing; ⟨giornali, giornalisti⟩ press; ⟨riproduzione⟩ print. **stampe** ⟨postale⟩ printed matter. **~ fronte retro** two-sided printing, duplex printing. **~ scandalistica** gutter press, tabloid press
stam'pante *nf* printer. **~ ad aghi** dot matrix [printer]. **~ a getto d'inchiostro** inkjet [printer]. **~ laser** laser [printer]. **~ a matrice di punti** dot matrix [printer]. **~ seriale** serial printer. **~ termica** thermal printer
stam'pare *vt* print
stampa'tello *nm* block letters *pl*, block capitals *pl*
stam'pato *a* printed ● *nm* leaflet; *Comput* hard copy, printout; ⟨modulo⟩ print; **stampati** ⟨pubblicità⟩ promotional literature
stam'pella *nf* crutch
stampigli'are *vt* stamp
stampiglia'tura *nf* stamping; ⟨dicitura⟩ stamp
stam'pino *nm* stencil
'**stampo** *nm* mould; **di vecchio ~** ⟨persona⟩ of the old school
sta'nare *vt* drive out
stan'care *vt* tire; ⟨annoiare⟩ bore
stan'carsi *vr* get tired
stan'chezza *nf* tiredness
'**stanco** *a* tired; **~ di** ⟨stufo⟩ fed up with. **~ morto** dead tired, knackered *fam*
stand *nm inv* stand
'**standard** *a & nm inv* standard
standardiz'zare *vt* standardize
standardizzazi'one *nf* standardization
'**stand-by** *a inv* stand-by
'**stanga** *nf* bar; ⟨persona⟩ beanpole
stan'gare *vt fam* fail ⟨studente⟩; ⟨con le tasse ecc⟩ clobber
stan'gata *nf fig* blow; ⟨fam: nel calcio⟩ big kick; **prendere una ~** ⟨fam: agli esami, economica⟩ come a cropper
stan'ghetta *nf* ⟨di occhiali⟩ leg
sta'notte *nf* tonight; ⟨la notte scorsa⟩ last night
'**stante** *prep* on account of; **a sé ~** separate

stan'tio *a* stale

stan'tuffo *nm* piston

'**stanza** *nf* room; (*metrica*) stanza. ~ **dei giochi** games room. ~ **da pranzo** dining room

stanzia'mento *nm* appropriation

stanzi'are *vt* allocate

stan'zino *nm* walk-in

stap'pare *vt* uncork

star *nf inv* Cinema star

'**stare** *vi* (*rimanere*) stay; (*abitare*) live; (*con gerundio*) be; **sto solo cinque minuti** I'll stay only five minutes; **sto in piazza Peyron** I live in Peyron Square; **sta dormendo** he's sleeping; ~ **a** (*attenersi*) keep to; (*spettare*) be up to; ~ **bene** (*economicamente*) be well off; (*di salute*) be well; (*addirsi*) suit; **sta bene!** that's fine!; ~ **dietro a** (*seguire*) follow; (*sorvegliare*) keep an eye on; (*corteggiare*) run after; ~ **in piedi** stand; ~ **per** be about to; ~ **sempre a fare qcsa** be always doing sth; **ben ti sta!** it serves you right!; **come stai/sta?** how are you?; **lasciar** ~ leave alone; **starci** (*essere contenuto*) go into; (*essere d'accordo*) agree; **il 3 nel 12 ci sta 4 volte** 3 into 12 goes 4; **non sa** ~ **agli scherzi** he can't take a joke; ~ **su** (*con la schiena*) sit up straight; ~ **sulle proprie** keep oneself to oneself

'**starna** *nf* partridge

starnaz'zare *vi* quack; *fig* shriek

starnu'tire *vi* sneeze

star'nuto *nm* sneeze

'**starsene** *vr* (*rimanere*) stay

'**starter** *nm inv* choke

sta'sera *adv* this evening, tonight

'**stasi** *nm* stasis

sta'tale *a* state *attrib* ● *nmf* state employee, civil servant ● *nf* (*strada*) main road, trunk road

'**statico** *a* static

sta'tista *nm* statesman

sta'tistica *nf* statistics *sg*

sta'tistico *a* statistical

'**Stati 'Uniti [d'America]** *nmpl* **gli** ~ ~ the United States [of America]

'**stato** *pp di* **essere**, **stare** ● *nm* state; (*posizione sociale*) position; *Jur* status; **lo S~** *Pol* the state. ~ **d'animo** frame of mind. ~ **di attesa** *Comput* wait state. ~ **civile** marital status. ~ **cuscinetto** buffer state. **S~ Maggiore** *Mil* General Staff. ~ **di salute** state of health

stato-nazi'one *nm* nation-state

'**statua** *nf* statue

statu'ario *a* statuesque

statuni'tense *a* United States *attrib*, US *attrib* ● *nmf* citizen of the United States, US citizen

sta'tura *nf* height; **di alta** ~ **tall**; **di bassa** ~ short; **di media** ~ of average height. ~ **morale** moral stature

sta'tuto *nm* statute

stazio'nario *a* stationary

stazi'one *nf* station; (*città*) resort. ~ **degli autobus** bus station. ~ **balneare** seaside resort. ~ **climatica** health resort. ~ **delle corriere** coach station *Br*; bus station. ~ **ferroviaria** railway station *Br*, train station. ~ **marittima** ferry terminal. ~ **master** *Comput* master station. ~ **multimediale** *Comput* multimedia station. ~ **dei pullman** coach station *Br*, bus station. ~ **di servizio** petrol station *Br*, service station. ~ **slave** *Comput* slave station ~ **termale** spa, health resort

'**stecca** *nf* stick; (*di ombrello*) rib; (*da biliardo*) cue; *Med* splint; (*di sigarette*) carton; (*di reggiseno*) stiffener; **fare una** ~ *Mus* fluff a note

stec'cato *nm* fence

stec'chino *nm* cocktail stick

stec'chito *a* skinny; (*rigido*) stiff; (*morto*) stone cold dead

'**stele** *nf* stele

'**stella** *nf* star; **salire alle stelle** ⟨*prezzi:*⟩ rise sky-high, rocket. ~ **alpina** edelweiss. ~ **cadente** shooting star. ~ **del cinema** movie star. ~ **cometa** comet. ~ **filante** streamer. ~ **di mare** starfish. ~ **polare** Pole Star, North Star

stel'lare *a* star *attrib*; ⟨*grandezza*⟩ stellar

stel'lato *a* starry

stel'lina *nf* starlet

'**stelo** *nm* stem; **lampada a** ~ standard lamp *Br*, floor lamp

'**stemma** *nm* coat of arms

stempe'rare *vt* dilute

stempi'ato *a* bald at the temples

sten'dardo *nm* standard

'**stendere** *vt* spread out; (*appendere*) hang out; (*distendere*) stretch [out]; (*scrivere*) write down

'**stendersi** *vr* stretch out

stendibianche'ria *nm inv* clothes horse

stendi'toio *nm* clothes horse

stenodattilogra'fia *nf* shorthand typing

stenodatti'lografo, -a *nmf* shorthand typist

stenogra'fare *vt* take down in shorthand

stenogra'fia *nf* shorthand

sten'tare *vi* ~ **a** find it hard to

sten'tato *a* laboured

'**stento** *nm* (*fatica*) effort; **a** ~ with difficulty; **stenti** *pl* hardships, privations

'**steppa** *nf* steppe

'**sterco** *nm* dung

'**stereo['fonico]** *a* stereo[phonic]

stereo'scopico *a* stereoscopic

stereoti'pato *a* stereotyped; ⟨*sorriso*⟩ insincere

stere'otipo *nm* stereotype

'**sterile** *a* sterile; ⟨*terreno*⟩ barren

sterilità *nf* sterility

steriliz'zare *vt* sterilize

sterilizzazi'one *nf* sterilization

ster'lina *nf* pound; **lira** ~ [pound] sterling

stermi'nare *vt* exterminate

stermi'nato *a* immense

ster'minio *nm* extermination

'sterno *nm* breastbone

sternu'tire, ster'nuto = **starnutire, starnuto**

ste'roide *nm* steroid

ster'paglia *nf* brushwood

ster'rare *vt* excavate; dig up ⟨*strada*⟩

ster'rato *a* ⟨*strada*⟩ dug up ● *nm* excavation; (*di strada*) digging up

ster'zare *vi* steer

'sterzo *nm* steering; (*volante*) steering wheel

'steso *pp di* **stendere**

'stesso *a* same; **io ~** myself; **tu ~** yourself; **me ~** myself; **se ~** himself; **in quel momento ~** at that very moment; **è stato ricevuto dalla stessa regina** (*in persona*) he was received by the Queen herself; **tuo fratello ~ dice che hai torto** even your brother says you're wrong; **l'ho visto coi miei stessi occhi** I saw it with my own eyes; **con le mie stesse mani** with my own hands ● *pron* **lo ~** the same one; (*la stessa cosa*) the same; **fa lo ~** it's all the same; **ci vado lo ~** I'll go just the same; **è venuto il giorno ~** he came the same day, he came that very day; **lo farò oggi ~** I'll do it straight away today

ste'sura *nf* drawing up; (*documento*) draft

steto'scopio *nm* stethoscope

'steward *nm inv* steward

stick *nm inv* **colla a ~** glue stick; **deodorante a ~** stick deodorant

stiepi'dire *vt* warm

'stigma *nm* stigma

'stigmate *nfpl* stigmata

sti'lare *vt* draw up

'stile *nm* style; **in grande ~** in style; **essere nello ~ di qcno** be typical of sb, be just like sb. **~ libero** (*nel nuoto*) freestyle, crawl. **~ di vita** life style

sti'lista *nmf* [fashion] designer; (*parrucchiere*) stylist

stiliz'zato *a* stylized

'stilla *nf* drop

stil'lare *vi* ooze

stilo'grafica *nf* fountain pen

stilo'grafico *a* **penna stilografica** fountain pen

'stima *nf* esteem; (*valutazione*) estimate

sti'mare *vt* esteem; (*valutare*) estimate; (*ritenere*) consider

sti'marsi *vr* consider oneself

sti'mato *a* well-thought-of

stimo'lante *a* stimulating ● *nm* stimulant

stimo'lare *vt* stimulate; (*incitare*) incite

'stimolo *nm* stimulus; (*fitta*) pang

'stinco *nm* shin; **non è uno ~ di santo** *fam* he's no saint

'stingere *vt/i* fade

'stingersi *vr* fade

'stinto *pp di* **stingere**

sti'pare *vt* cram

sti'parsi *vr* crowd together

stipendi'are *vt* pay a salary to

stipendi'ato *a* salaried ● *nm* salaried worker

sti'pendio *nm* salary. **~ base** basic salary. **~ iniziale** starting salary

'stipite *nm* doorpost

stipu'lare *vt* stipulate

stipulazi'one *nf* stipulation; (*accordo*) agreement

stira'mento *nm* sprain

sti'rare *vt* iron; (*distendere*) stretch

sti'rarsi *vr* (*distendersi*) stretch; pull ⟨*muscolo*⟩

stira'tura *nf* ironing

'stiro *nm* **ferro da ~** iron

'stirpe *nf* stock

stiti'chezza *nf* constipation

'stitico *a* constipated

'stiva *nf Naut* hold

sti'vale *nm* boot; **lo S~** (*Italia*) Italy. **stivali** *pl* **di gomma** Wellington boots, Wellingtons; **poeta dei miei stivali!** *fam* poet my eye!, poet my foot!

stiva'letto *nm* ankle boot

stiva'lone *nm* high boot; **stivaloni** *pl* **da caccia** hunting boots; **stivaloni** *pl* **di gomma** waders

sti'vare *vt* load

'stizza *nf* anger

stiz'zire *vt* irritate

stiz'zirsi *vr* become irritated

stiz'zito *a* irritated

stiz'zoso *a* peevish

stocca'fisso *nm* stockfish

stoc'cata *nf* stab; (*battuta pungente*) gibe

stock *nm Comm* stock

'stock-car *nm inv* stock car

'stoffa *nf* material; *fig* stuff; **avere ~** have what it takes

stoi'cismo *nm* stoicism

'stoico *a & nm* stoic

sto'ino *nm* doormat

'stola *nf* stole

'stolido *a* stolid

'stolto *a* foolish

stoma'chevole *a* revolting

'stomaco *nm* stomach; **mal di ~** stomachache

stoma'tite *nf* stomatitis

sto'nare *vt/i* sing/play out of tune ● *vi* (*non intonarsi*) clash

sto'nato *a* out of tune; (*discordante*) clashing; (*confuso*) bewildered

stona'tura *nf* false note; (*discordanza*) clash

stop *nm inv* (*segnale stradale*) stop sign; (*in telegramma*) stop

stop'pare *vt* stop

'stopper *nm Sport* fullback

'stoppia *nf* stubble

stop'pino *nm* wick

stop'poso *a* tough

'storcere *vt* twist

'storcersi *vr* twist

stor'dire *vt* stun; (*intontire*) daze

stor'dirsi *vr* dull one's senses

stor'dito *a* stunned; (*intontito*) dazed; (*sventato*) heedless

'storia *nf* history; (*racconto, bugia*) story;

(*pretesto*) excuse; **senza storie!** no fuss!; **fare [delle] storie** make a fuss. **~ d'amore** love story

'**storico** *a* historical; (*di importanza storica*) historic ● *nm* historian

stori'ella *nf fam* little story

storiogra'fia *nf* historiography

stori'ografo *nm* historiographer

stori'one *nm* sturgeon

'stormo *nm* flock

stor'nare *vt* avert; transfer ⟨*somma*⟩

'storno *nm* starling

storpi'are *vt* cripple; mangle ⟨*parole*⟩

storpia'tura *nf* deformation

'storpio, -a *a* crippled ● *nmf* cripple

'storta *nf* (*distorsione*) sprain; **prendere una ~ alla caviglia** sprain one's ankle

'storto *pp di* storcere ● *a* crooked; (*ritorto*) twisted; (*gambe*) bandy; *fig* wrong

stor'tura *nf* deformity; **~ mentale** twisted way of thinking

sto'viglie *nfpl* crockery *sg*, flatware *Am*

'strabico *a* cross-eyed; **essere ~** be cross-eyed, [have a] squint

strabili'ante *a* astonishing

strabili'are *vt* astonish

stra'bismo *nm* squint

straboc'care *vi* overflow

strabuz'zare *vt* **~ gli occhi** goggle; **ha strabuzzato gli occhi** his eyes popped out of his head

straca'narsi *vr fam* work like a slave, slave away

stra'carico *a* overloaded

strac'chino *nm* soft cheese from Lombardy

stracci'are *vt* tear; (*fam: vincere*) thrash

straccia'tella *nf* vanilla ice cream with chocolate chips

stracci'ato *a* torn; ⟨*persona*⟩ in rags; (*prezzi*) slashed; **a un prezzo ~** at a knock-down price, dirt cheap

'straccio *a* torn ● *nm* rag; (*strofinaccio*) cloth; **essere ridotto ad uno ~** feel like a wet rag

stracci'one *nm* tramp

stracci'vendolo *nm* ragman

stracol'larsi *vr* sprain

stra'cotto *a* overdone; (*fam: innamorato*) head over heels ● *nm* stew

'strada *nf* road; (*di città*) street; (*fig: cammino*) way; **essere fuori ~** be on the wrong track; **fare ~** lead the way; **tener la macchina in ~** keep the car on the road; (*parcheggiare*) keep the car on the street; **su ~** ⟨*trasportare*⟩ by road; **farsi ~** (*aver successo*) make one's way [in the world]. **~ d'accesso** approach road. **~ camionabile** road for heavy vehicles. **~ maestra** main road. **~ pedonale** pedestrianized street. **~ principale** main road. **~ privata** private road. **~ secondaria** secondary road. **~ a senso unico** one-way street. **~ senza uscita** dead end, cul-de-sac. **~ di terra battuta** dirt track

stra'dale *a* road *attrib* traffic police ● *nm* **la S~** *fam* traffice police

stra'dina *nf* little street; (*in campagna*) little road

strafalci'one *nm* blunder

stra'fare *vi* overdo it, overdo things

stra'foro: **di ~** *adv* on the sly

strafot'tente *a* arrogant

strafot'tenza *nf* arrogance

'strage *nf* slaughter

stra'grande *a* vast

stralci'are *vt* remove

'stralcio *nm* removal; (*parte*) extract

stralu'nare *vt* **~ gli occhi** open one's eyes wide

stralu'nato *a* ⟨*occhi*⟩ staring; ⟨*persona*⟩ distraught

stramaz'zare *vi* fall heavily; **~ al suolo** crash to the ground

strambe'ria *nf* oddity

'strambo *a* strange

strampa'lato *a* odd

stra'nezza *nf* strangeness

strango'lare *vt* strangle

strangugli'one *nm* tonsillitis

strani'ero, -a *a* foreign ● *nmf* foreigner

'strano *a* strange; **~ ma vero** surprisingly enough, funnily enough

straordinaria'mente *adv* extraordinarily

straordi'nario *a* extraordinary; (*notevole*) remarkable; (*edizione*) special; **lavoro ~** overtime; **treno ~** special [train]

strapaz'zare *vt* ill-treat; scramble ⟨*uova*⟩

strapaz'zarsi *vr* tire oneself out

stra'pazzo *nm* strain; **da ~** *fig* worthless

strapi'eno *a* overflowing

strapi'ombo *nm* projection; **a ~** sheer

strapo'tere *nm* overwhelming power

strappa'lacrime *a inv* weepy

strap'pare *vt* tear; (*per distruggere*) tear up; pull out ⟨*dente, capelli*⟩; (*sradicare*) pull up; (*estorcere*) wring

strap'parsi *vr* get torn; (*allontanarsi*) tear oneself away; **~ i capelli** *fig* be tearing one's hair out

'strappo *nm* tear; (*strattone*) jerk; (*fam: passaggio*) lift; **fare uno ~ alla regola** make an exception to the rule. **~ muscolare** muscle strain

strapun'tino *nm* folding seat

strari'pare *vi* flood

strasci'care *vt* trail; shuffle ⟨*piedi*⟩; drawl ⟨*parole*⟩

'strascico *nm* train; *fig* after-effect

strasci'coni: **a ~** *adv* dragging one's feet

straseco'lare *vi* be amazed

strass *nm inv* rhinestone

strata'gemma *nm* stratagem

stra'tega *nmf* strategist

strate'gia *nf* strategy

stra'tegico *a* strategic; **mossa strategica** strategic move

stratifi'care *vt* stratify

stratigra'fia *nf Geol* stratigraphy

'strato *nm* layer; (*di vernice ecc*) coat, layer; (*roccioso, sociale*) stratum. **~ di nuvole** cloud layer

strato'sfera *nf* stratosphere

strato'sferico *a* stratospheric; *fig* sky-high

stravac'carsi *vr fam* slouch

stravac'cato *a fam* slouching

strava'gante *a* extravagant; (*eccentrico*) eccentric

strava'ganza *nf* extravagance; (*eccentricità*) eccentricity

stra'vecchio *a* ancient

strave'dere *vt* ~ **per** worship

stravizi'are *vi* indulge oneself

stra'vizio *nm* excess

stra'volgere *vt* twist; (*turbare*) upset

stravolgi'mento *nm* twisting

stra'volto *a* distraught; (*fam: stanco*) done in

strazi'ante *a* heartrending; ⟨*dolore*⟩ agonizing

strazi'are *vt* grate on ⟨*orecchie*⟩; break ⟨*cuore*⟩

'strazio *nm* agony; **essere uno** ~ be agony; **che** ~! *fam* it's awful!; **fare** ~ **di qcsa** ⟨*fam: attore, cantante:*⟩ murder sth

'streamer *nm inv Comput* streamer

'strega *nf* witch

stre'gare *vt* bewitch

stre'gone *nm* wizard

stregone'ria *nf* witchcraft

'stregua *nf* **alla** ~ **di** in the same way as; **alla stessa** ~ ⟨*giudicare*⟩ by the same yardstick; **a questa** ~ at this rate

stre'mare *vt* exhaust

stre'mato *a* exhausted

'stremo *a* extreme ● *nm* **ridotto allo** ~ at the end of one's tether

'strenna *nf* present

'strenuo *a* strenuous

strepi'tare *vi* make a din

strepi'tio *nm* din, uproar

strepi'toso *a* noisy; *fig* resounding

strepto'cocco *nm Med* streptococcus

streptomi'cina *nf Med* streptomycin

stress *nm* stress

stres'sante *a* ⟨*lavoro, situazione*⟩ stressful

stres'sare *vt* put under stress, be stressful for

stres'sarsi *vr* get stressed

stres'sato *a* stressed [out]

'stretta *nf* grasp; (*dolore*) pang; **essere alle strette** be in dire straits; **mettere alle strette qcno** have sb's back up against the wall; **provare una** ~ **al cuore** feel a pang. ~ **di mano** handshake

stret'tezza *nf* narrowness; **stret'tezze** *pl* (*difficoltà finanziarie*) financial difficulties

'stretto *pp di* **stringere** ● *a* narrow; (*serrato*) tight; (*vicino*) close; ⟨*dialetto*⟩ broad; (*rigoroso*) strict; **lo** ~ **necessario** the bare minimum ● *nm Geog* strait. ~ **di Messina** Straits of Messina

stret'toia *nf* bottleneck; (*fam: difficoltà*) tight spot

stri'ato *a* striped

stria'tura *nf* streak

stri'dente *a* strident

'stridere *vi* squeak; *fig* clash

stri'dore *nm* screech

'stridulo *a* shrill

strigli'are *vt* groom

strigli'ata *nf* grooming; *fig* dressing down

stril'lare *vi/t* scream

'strillo *nm* scream

stril'lone *nm* newspaper seller

strimin'zito *a* skimpy; (*magro*) skinny

strimpel'lare *vt* strum

stri'nare *vt* singe, scorch

'stringa *nf* lace; *Comput* string

strin'gato *a fig* terse

'stringere *vt* press; (*serrare*) squeeze; (*tenere stretto*) hold tight; take in ⟨*abito*⟩; (*comprimere*) be tight; (*restringere*) tighten; ~ **la mano a** shake hands with ● *vi* (*premere*) press

'stringersi *vr* (*accostarsi*) draw close (**a** to); (*avvicinarsi*) squeeze up

strip'pata *nf fam* nosh-up; **farsi una** ~ have a nosh-up

strip-'tease *nm* striptease

'striscia *nf* strip; (*riga*) stripe; **a strisce** striped. **strisce** *pl* **di mezzeria** *Auto* lane markings. **strisce** *pl* [**pedonali**] zebra crossing *sg*, crosswalk *Am*

strisci'are *vi* crawl; (*sfiorare*) graze ● *vt* drag ⟨*piedi*⟩

strisci'arsi *vr* ~ **a** rub against

strisci'ata *nf* scratch

'striscio *nm* graze; *Med* smear; **colpire di** ~ graze

strisci'one *nm* banner

strito'lare *vt* grind

strizzacer'velli *nmf sl* shrink

striz'zare *vt* squeeze; (*torcere*) wring [out]; ~ **l'occhio** wink

'strofa *nf* strophe

strofi'naccio *nm* cloth; (*per spolverare*) duster. ~ **da cucina** tea towel

strofi'nare *vt* rub

strofi'nio *nm* rubbing

strom'bare *vt* splay

strombaz'zare *vt* boast about ● *vi* hoot

strombaz'zata *nf* (*di clacson*) hoot

stron'care *vt* cut off; (*reprimere*) crush; (*criticare*) tear to shreds

stron'zate *nfpl vulg* crap

'stronzo *nm vulg* shit

stropicci'are *vt* rub; crumple ⟨*vestito*⟩

stropicci'ata *nf* rub

stro'piccio *nm* rubbing

stroppi'are *vt* **il troppo stroppia** enough is as good as a feast

stroz'zare *vt* strangle

strozza'tura *nf* strangling; (*di strada*) narrowing

strozzi'naggio *nm* loan-sharking

stroz'zino *nm pej* usurer; (*truffatore*) shark

struc'cante *nm* make-up remover

struc'carsi *vr* remove one's make-up

strug'gente *a* all-consuming

'struggersi *vr liter* pine [away]; ~ **di invidia/desiderio** be consumed with envy/desire

struggi'mento nm yearning
strumen'tale a instrumental
strumentaliz'zare vt make use of
strumen'tario nm instruments pl
strumentazi'one nf instrumentation
strumen'tista nm instrumentalist
stru'mento nm instrument; (arnese) tool. ~ a corda/fiato string/wind instrument. ~ musicale musical instrument. ~ a percussione percussion instrument
strusci'are vt rub
strusci'arsi vr ‹gatto:› rub itself; ‹due innamorati:› caress each other; ~ intorno a qcno fam suck up to sb
'**strutto** nm lard
strut'tura nf structure
struttu'rale a structural
struttura'lismo nm structuralism
struttural'mente adv structurally
struttu'rare vt structure
strutturazi'one nf structuring
'**struzzo** nm ostrich
stuc'care vt plaster; (per decorazione) stucco; put putty in ‹vetri›
stucca'tore nm plasterer; (decorativo) stucco worker
stucca'tura nf plastering; (decorativo) stucco work
stuc'chevole a nauseating
'**stucco** nm plaster; (decorativo) stucco; (per vetro) putty; **rimanere di ~** be thunderstruck
stu'dente, studen'tessa nmf student; (di scuola) schoolboy; schoolgirl
studen'tesco a student; (di scolaro) school attrib
studi'are vt study
studi'arsi vr ~ di try to
'**studio** nm studying; (stanza, ricerca) study; (di artista, TV ecc) studio; (di professionista) office. ~ **dentistico** dental surgery
studi'oso, -a a studious ● nmf scholar
'**stufa** nf stove. ~ **elettrica** electric fire. ~ a gas fire. ~ a legna wood[-burning] stove
stu'fare vt Culin stew; (dare fastidio) bore
stu'farsi vr get bored
stu'fato nm stew
'**stufo** a bored; **essere ~ di** be bored with, be fed up with
stu'oia nf mat
stu'olo nm crowd
stupefa'cente a amazing ● nm drug
stupe'fare vt stun
stu'pendo a stupendous; ~! brilliant!
stupi'daggine nf (azione) stupid thing; (cosa da poco) nothing; **non dire stupidaggini!** don't talk stupid!
stupi'data nf stupid thing
stupidità nf stupidity
'**stupido** a stupid
stu'pire vt astonish ● vi be astonished
stu'pirsi vr be astonished
stu'pore nm amazement
stu'prare vt rape
stupra'tore nm rapist

'**stupro** nm rape
sturabot'tiglie nm inv corkscrew
sturalavan'dini nm inv plunger
stu'rare vt uncork; unblock ‹lavandino›
stuzzica'denti nm inv toothpick
stuzzi'care vt prod [at]; pick ‹denti›; poke ‹fuoco›; (molestare) tease; whet ‹appetito›
stuzzi'chino nm Culin appetizer
su prep on; (senza contatto) over; (riguardo a) about; (circa, intorno a) about, around; **le chiavi sono sul tavolo** the keys are on the table; **il quadro è appeso sul camino** the picture is hanging over the fireplace; **un libro sull'antico Egitto** a book on o about Ancient Egypt; **sarò lì sulle cinque** I'll be there about five, I'll be there around five; **è durato sulle tre ore** it lasted for about three hours; **costa sulle 50 000 lire** it costs about 50,000 lire; **decidere sul momento** decide at the time; **su commissione** on commission; **su due piedi** on the spot; **su misura** made to measure; **uno su dieci** one out of ten; **stare sulle proprie** keep oneself to oneself; **sul mare** ‹casa› by the sea ● adv (sopra) up; (al piano di sopra) upstairs; (addosso) on; **andare su** go up; (al piano di sopra) go upstairs; **ho su il cappotto** I've got my coat on; **in su** ‹guardare› up; **dalla vita in su** from the waist up; **su!** come on!
sua'dente a persuasive
sub nmf inv skin-diver
sub+ pref sub+
su'bacqueo, -a a underwater ● nmf skindiver
subaffit'tare vt sublet
subaf'fitto nm sublet; **in ~** sublet
suba'gente nm subagent
subal'terno a & nm subordinate
subappal'tare vt subcontract
subappalta'|tore, -'trice nmf subcontractor
subap'palto nm subcontract; **in ~** subcontracted; **dare in ~** subcontract; **prendere in ~** take on a subcontract basis
sub'buglio nm turmoil
sub'conscio a & nm subconscious
subconti'nente nm subcontinent
subcosci'ente a & nm subconscious
subdi'rectory nf Comput subdirectory
subdola'mente adv deviously
'**subdolo** a devious, underhand
suben'trare vi ‹circostanze:› come up; ~ a take the place of
su'bentro nm changeover
subequatori'ale a subequatorial
su'bire vt undergo; (patire) suffer
subis'sare vt fig ~ **di** overwhelm with
subi'taneo a sudden
'**subito** adv at once, immediately; ~ **dopo** straight after; **vengo ~** I'll be right there
subli'mare vt sublimate
su'blime a sublime
sublimi'nale a subliminal
sublingu'ale a sublingual
sublo'care vt sublease

subloca'tario *nm* sublessor
sublocazi'one *nf* sublease
subnor'male *a* subnormal
subodo'rare *vt* suspect
subordi'nare *vt* subordinate
subordi'nato, -a *a & nmf* subordinate
su'bordine *nm* in ~ second in order of importance
subrou'tine *nf Comput* subroutine
subsi'denza *nf Geol* subsidence
sub'strato *nm* substratum, substrate
subto'tale *nm* subtotal
subtropi'cale *a* subtropical
subu'mano *a* subhuman
subur'bano *a* suburban
suc'cedere *vi (accadere)* happen; ~ **a** succeed; *(venire dopo)* follow; ~ **al trono** succeed to the throne
suc'cedersi *vr* happen one after the other; **si sono succeduti molti...** there was a series of...
successi'one *nf* succession; **in** ~ in succession
successiva'mente *adv* subsequently
succes'sivo *a* successive; ⟨*mese, giorno*⟩ following
suc'cesso *pp di* **succedere** ● *nm* success; *(esito)* outcome; *(disco ecc)* hit
succes'sone *nm* huge success
succes'sore *nm* successor
succhi'are *vt* suck [up]; ~ **il sangue a qcno** *fig* bleed sb dry
succhi'ello *nm* gimlet
succinta'mente *adv* succinctly
suc'cinto *a (conciso)* concise; ⟨*abito*⟩ scanty
'succo *nm* juice; *fig* essence. ~ **d'arancia** orange juice. ~ **di frutta** fruit juice. ~ **di limone** lemon juice
suc'coso *a* juicy
'succube *nm* **essere** ~ **di qcno** be totally dominated by sb
succu'lento *a* succulent
succur'sale *nf* branch [office]
sud *nm* south; **del** ~ southern; **a** ~ **di** [to the] south of
Sud 'Africa *nm* South Africa
sudafri'cano *a & nmf* South African
Suda'merica *nf* South America
sudameri'cano, -a *a & nmf* South American
Su'dan *nm* **il** ~ the Sudan
suda'nese *a & nmf* Sudanese
su'dare *vi* sweat, perspire; *(faticare)* sweat blood; ~ **freddo** be in a cold sweat; ~ **sangue** sweat blood; **mi fa** ~ **freddo** it brings me out in a cold sweat; ~ **sette camicie** sweat blood
su'data *nf anche fig* sweat
suda'ticcio *a* sweaty
su'dato *a* sweaty; ⟨*vittoria*⟩ hard-won; ⟨*pane*⟩ hard-earned
sud'detto *a* above-mentioned
'suddito, -a *nmf* subject
suddi'videre *vt* subdivide
suddivisi'one *nf* subdivision

su'd-est *nm* southeast
'sudicio *a* dirty, filthy
sudici'ume *nm* dirt, filth
sudocciden'tale *a* southwestern
sudorazi'one *nf* perspiring
su'dore *nm* sweat, perspiration; *fig* sweat; **in un bagno di** ~ bathed in sweat. ~ **freddo** cold sweat; **con il** ~ **della fronte** *fig* by the sweat of one's brow
sudo'riparo *a* sweat *attrib*
su'd-ovest *nm* southwest
'sue *vedi* **suo**
suffici'ente *a* sufficient; *(presuntuoso)* conceited ● *nm* bare essentials *pl; Sch* pass mark
suffici'enza *nf* sufficiency; *(presunzione)* conceit; *Sch* pass; **a** ~ enough; **prendere la** ~ get the pass-mark
suf'fisso *nm* suffix
sufflè *nm Culin* soufflé
suffra'getta *nf* suffragette
suf'fragio *nm (voto)* vote; **in** ~ **di qcno** in homage to. ~ **universale** universal suffrage
suffu'migio *nm* inhalation
suggel'lare *vt* seal
suggeri'mento *nm* suggestion
sugge'rire *vt* suggest; *Theat* prompt
suggeri|'tore, -'trice *nmf Theat* prompter
suggestio'nabile *a* suggestible
suggestio'nare *vt* influence
suggestio'nato *a* influenced
suggesti'one *nf* influence
sugge'stivo *a* suggestive; ⟨*musica ecc*⟩ evocative
'sughero *nm* cork
'sugli = **su + gli**
'sugo *nm (di frutta)* juice; *(di carne)* gravy; *(salsa)* sauce; *(sostanza)* substance
'sui = **su + i**
sui'cida *a* suicidal ● *nmf* suicide
suici'darsi *vr* commit suicide
sui'cidio *nm anche fig* suicide; **commettere** ~ commit suicide; **tentato** ~ attempted suicide
su'ino *a* **carne suina** pork ● *nm* swine
suite *nf* suite
sul = **su + il**
sulfa'midico *nm* sulphonamide/sulpha drug
sul'fureo *a* sulphuric
'sulla = **su + la**
'sulle = **su + le**
'sullo = **su + lo**
sul'tana *nf (persona)* sultana
sulta'nina *a* **uva** ~ sultana
sul'tano *nm* sultan
'sunto *nm* summary
'suo, -a *poss a* **il** ~, **i suoi** his; *(di cosa, animale)* its; *(forma di cortesia)* your; **la sua, le sue** her; *(di cosa, animale)* its; *(forma di cortesia)* your; **questa macchina è sua** this car is his/hers; ~ **padre** his/her/your father; **un** ~ **amico** a friend of his/hers/yours ● *poss pron* **il** ~, **i suoi** his; *(di cosa, animale)* its;

(*forma di cortesia*) yours; **la sua, le sue** hers; (*di cosa animale*) its; (*forma di cortesia*) yours; **i suoi** his/her folk[s]

su'ocera *nf* mother-in-law

su'ocero *nm* father-in-law

su'oi *vedi* **suo**

su'ola *nf* sole. **suole** *pl* **di para** crepe soles

su'olo *nm* ground; (*terreno*) soil; **~ pubblico** public land

suo'nare *vt Mus* play; ring ‹*campanello*›; sound ‹*allarme, clacson*›; ‹*orologio:*› strike; **~ il clacson** sound the horn, hoot the horn; (*fam: imbrogliare*) do ● *vi* ‹*campanello, telefono, sveglia:*› ring; ‹*clacson:*› hoot; ‹*sirena:*› go [off]; ‹*giradischi:*› play

suo'nato *a fam* bonkers

suona'tore, -'trice *nmf* player

suone'ria *nf* alarm

su'ono *nm* sound

su'ora *nf* nun; **Suor Maria** Sister Maria

'super *nf* 4-star [petrol], premium [gas] *Am*

super+ *pref* super+

supe'rabile *a* surmountable

superal'colico *nm* spirit ● *a* **bevande superalcoliche** spirits

supera'mento *nm* (*di timidezza*) overcoming; (*di esame*) success (**di** in)

supe'rare *vt* surpass; (*eccedere*) exceed; (*vincere*) overcome; overtake, pass *Am* ‹*veicolo*›; pass ‹*esame*›; **~ la barriera del suono** break the sound barrier; **~ se stessi** surpass oneself; **ha superato la trentina** he's over thirty

su'perbia *nf* haughtiness

su'perbo *a* haughty; (*magnifico*) superb

super'donna *nf* superwoman

superdo'tato *a* highly gifted, super-talented

superfici'ale *a* superficial ● *nmf* superficial person

superficialità *nf* superficiality

super'ficie *nf* surface; (*area*) area; **in ~** on the surface; ‹*fig: esaminare*› superficially

su'perfluo *a* superfluous

superi'ora *nf* superior; *Relig* mother superior

superi'ore *a* superior; (*di grado*) senior; (*più elevato*) higher; (*sovrastante*) upper; (*al di sopra*) above ● *nm* superior

superiorità *nf* superiority

Super-'Io *nm Psych* superego

superla'tivo *a & nm* superlative

supermer'cato *nm* supermarket

supermo'della *nf* supermodel

super'nova *nf Astr* supernova

superpetroli'era *nf Naut* supertanker

superpo'tenza *nf* superpower

super'sonico *a* supersonic

su'perstite *a* surviving ● *nmf* survivor

superstizi'one *nf* superstition

superstizi'oso *a* superstitious

super'strada *nf* toll-free motorway. **~ dell'informatica** information superhighway

superu'omo *nm* superman

supervalu'tare *vt* overvalue

supervalutazi'one *nf* overvaluation

supervisi'one *nf* supervision

supervi'sore *nm* supervisor

su'pino *a* supine

suppel'lettili *nfpl* furnishings

suppergiù *adv* about

supplemen'tare *a* additional, supplementary

supple'mento *nm* supplement. **~ illustrato** colour supplement. **~ rapido** express train supplement

sup'plente *a* temporary ● *nmf Sch* supply teacher

sup'plenza *nf* temporary post

'supplica *nf* plea; (*domanda*) petition

suppli'care *vt* beg

suppli'chevole *a* imploring

sup'plire *vt* replace ● *vi* **~ a** (*compensare*) make up for

sup'plizio *nm* torture

sup'porre *vt* suppose

suppor'tare *vt Comput* support

sup'porto *nm* support. **~ di sistema** *Comput* system support

supposizi'one *nf* supposition

sup'posta *nf* suppository

sup'posto *pp di* **supporre**

suppu'rare *vi* fester

suppurazi'one *nf* suppuration; **andare in ~** fester

suprema'zia *nf* supremacy

su'premo *a* supreme

surclas'sare *vt* outclass

surf *nm* surfboard; (*sport*) surfboarding

sur'fare *vi* **~ in Internet** surf the Net

sur'fista *nmf Sport, Comput* surfer

surge'lare *vt* deep-freeze

surge'lato *a* frozen ● *nm* **surgelati** *pl* frozen food *sg*

'surplus *nm* surplus

surre'ale *a* surreal

surrea'lismo *nm* surrealism

surrea'lista *nmf* surrealist

surrea'listico *a* surrealist

surre'nale *a* adrenal

surriscal'dare *vt* overheat

surriscal'darsi *vr* overheat

surro'gato *nm* substitute

suscet'tibile *a* touchy

suscettibilità *nf* touchiness

susci'tare *vt* stir up; arouse ‹*ammirazione ecc*›

su'sina *nf* plum. **~ selvatica** damson

su'sino *nm* plumtree

su'spense *nf* suspense

sussegu'ente *a* subsequent

sussegu'irsi *vr* follow one after the other

sussidi'are *vt* subsidize

sussidi'ario *a* subsidiary

sus'sidio *nm* subsidy; (*aiuto*) aid. **~ di disoccupazione** unemployment benefit. **~ di malattia** sickness benefit

sus'siego *nm* haughtiness; **con ~** haughtily

sussi'stenza *nf* subsistence

sus'sistere *vi* subsist; (*essere valido*) hold good

sussul'tare *vi* start; **far ~ qcno** give sb a start

sus'sulto *nm* start

sussur'rare *vt/i* whisper; **si sussurra che...** it is rumoured that...

sussur'rio *nm* murmur

sus'surro *nm* whisper

su'tura *nf* suture

sutu'rare *vt* suture

suv'via *int* come on!

sva'gare *vt* amuse

sva'garsi *vr* amuse oneself

'svago *nm* relaxation; (*divertimento*) amusement; **prendersi un po' di ~** have a break

svaligi'are *vt* rob; burgle ‹*casa*›

svalu'tare *vt* devalue; *fig* underestimate

svalu'tarsi *vr* lose value

svalutazi'one *nf* devaluation

svam'pito *a* absent-minded

sva'nire *vi* vanish

sva'nito, -a *a* ‹*persona*› absent-minded; ‹*sapore, sogno*› faded ● *nmf* absent-minded person

svantaggi'ato *a* at a disadvantage; ‹*bambino, paese*› disadvantaged

svan'taggio *nm* disadvantage; **essere in ~** *Sport* be losing; **in ~ di tre punti** three points down; **in ~ rispetto a qcno** at a disadvantage compared with sb

svantaggi'oso *a* disadvantageous

svapo'rare *vi* evaporate

svari'ato *a* varied

svari'one *nm* blunder

sva'sare *vt* splay; flare ‹*gonna*›

sva'sato *a* ‹*gonna*› flared

svasa'tura *nf* flare

'svastica *nf* swastika

sve'dese *a & nm* (*lingua*) Swedish ● *nmf* Swede

'sveglia *nf* (*orologio*) alarm [clock]; **~!** get up!; **mettere la ~** set the alarm [clock]. **~ automatica** alarm call. **~ telefonica** wake-up call

svegli'are *vt* wake up; *fig* awaken; **~ l'appetito a qcno** whet sb's appetite

svegli'arsi *vr* wake up

'sveglio *a* awake; (*di mente*) alert, sharp

sve'lare *vt* reveal

svel'tezza *nf* speed; *fig* quick-wittedness

svel'tire *vt* quicken

svel'tirsi *vr* ‹*persona:*› liven up

'svelto *a* quick; (*slanciato*) svelte; **alla svelta** quickly; **a passo ~** quickly

sve'narsi *vr* slash one's wrists; *fig* reduce oneself to poverty

'svendere *vt* undersell

'svendita *nf* [clearance] sale

sve'nevole *a* sentimental

sveni'mento *nm* fainting fit

sve'nire *vi* faint; **da ~** incredibly

sven'tare *vt* foil

sven'tato *a* thoughtless ● *nmf* thoughtless person

'sventola *nf* slap; **orecchie a ~** protruding ears, jug-handle ears *fam*

svento'lare *vt/i* wave

svento'larsi *vr* fan oneself

svento'lio *nm* flutter

sventra'mento *nm* disembowelment; (*di pollo*) gutting; (*fig: di edificio*) demolition ‹*edificio*›

sven'trare *vt* disembowel; gut ‹*pollo*›; *fig* demolish ‹*edificio*›

sven'tura *nf* misfortune

sventu'rato *a* unfortunate

sve'nuto *pp di* svenire

svergi'nare *vt* deflower

svergo'gnato *a* shameless

sver'nare *vi* winter

svernici'ante *nm* paint stripper

svernici'are *vt* strip

sve'stire *vt* undress

sve'stirsi *vr* undress, get undressed

svet'tare *vi* ‹*albero, torre:*› stand out; **~ verso il cielo** stretch skywards

'Svezia *nf* Sweden

svezza'mento *nm* weaning

svez'zare *vt* wean

svi'are *vt* divert; (*corrompere*) lead astray

svi'arsi *vr fig* go astray

svico'lare *vi* turn down a side street; (*fig: dalla questione ecc*) evade the issue; (*fig: da una persona*) dodge out of the way

svi'gnarsela *vr* slip away

svigo'rire *vt* emasculate

svili'mento *nm* debasement

svi'lire *vt* debase

svilup'pare *vt* develop

svilup'parsi *vr* develop

svilup'pa|tore, -'trice *nmf* developer

svi'luppo *nm* development; **paese in via di ~** developing country

svinco'lare *vt* release; clear ‹*merce*›; redeem ‹*deposito*›

svinco'larsi *vr* free oneself

'svincolo *nm* clearance; (*di autostrada*) exit; **~ di un deposito cauzionale** redemption of a deposit

svioli'nata *nf* fawning

svisce'rare *vt* gut; *fig* dissect

svisce'rato *a* ‹*amore*› passionate; (*ossequioso*) obsequious

'svista *nf* oversight

svi'tare *vt* unscrew

svi'tato *a* (*fam: matto*) cracked, nutty

'Svizzera *nf* Switzerland

'svizzera *nf* hamburger

'svizzero, -a *a & nmf* Swiss

svoglia'taggine *nf* laziness; (*riluttanza*) unwillingness

svoglia'tamente *adv* half-heartedly; (*senza energia*) listlessly

svoglia'tezza *nf* half-heartedness; (*mancanza di energia*) listlessness

svogli'ato *a* half-hearted; (*senza energia*) listless

svolaz'zante *a* ‹*capelli*› wind-swept

svolaz'zare *vi* flutter

svolaz'zio *nm* flutter

'svolgere *vt* unwind; unwrap *(pacco)*; *(risolvere)* solve; *(portare a termine)* carry out; *(sviluppare)* develop

'svolgersi *vr (accadere)* take place

svolgi'mento *nm* course; *(sviluppo)* development

'svolta *nf* turning; *fig* turning-point

svol'tare *vi* turn

'svolto *pp di* **svolgere**

svuo'tare *vt* empty [out]; *(fig: di significato)* deprive

swing *nm Mus* swing

switch *nm Comput* switch

Tt

T *abbr* (**tabaccheria**) tobacconist

tabac'caio, -a *nmf* tobacconist

tabacche'ria *nf* tobacconist's *(which also sells stamps, postcards etc)*

ta'bacco *nm* tobacco; **tabacchi** *pl* cigarettes and tobacco

taba'gismo *nm* nicotine addiction

ta'bella *nf* table; *(lista)* list. **~ di conversione** conversion table. **~ di marcia** *fig* schedule. **~ dei prezzi** price list. **~ retributiva** salary scale

tabel'lina *nf Math* multiplication table

tabel'lone *nm* wall chart. **~ degli arrivi** arrivals board. **~ del canestro** backboard. **~ delle partenze** departures board. **~ segnapunti** scoreboard

taber'nacolo *nm* tabernacle

tabù *a & nm inv* taboo

tabu'lare *vt* tabulate

tabu'lato *nm Comput* [data] printout

tabula'tore *nm* tabulator

tabulazi'one *nf* tabulation

'tacca *nf* notch; **di mezza ~** *(attore, giornalista)* second-rate

taccagne'ria *nf* penny-pinching

tac'cagno *a fam* stingy

taccheggia|'tore, -'trice *nmf* shoplifter

tac'cheggio *nm* shoplifting

tac'chetto *nm Sport* stud

tac'chino *nm* turkey

tacci'are *vt* **~ qcno di qcsa** accuse sb of sth

'tacco *nm* heel; **alzare i tacchi** take to one's heels; **scarpe senza ~** flat shoes, flats; **colpo di ~** backheel; **tacchi** *pl* **a spillo** stiletto heels, stilettos

taccu'ino *nm* notebook

ta'cere *vi* be silent ● *vt* say nothing about; **mettere a ~ qcsa** *(scandalo)* hush sth up; **mettere a ~ qcno** silence sb

tachicar'dia *nf* tachycardia

ta'chigrafo *nm* tachograph

ta'chimetro *nm* speedometer

tacita'mente *adv* tacitly; *(in silenzio)* silently

'tacito *a* tacit; *(silenzioso)* silent

taci'turno *a* taciturn

ta'fano *nm* horsefly

taffe'ruglio *nm* scuffle

taffettà *nm* taffeta

'taglia *nf (riscatto)* ransom; *(ricompensa)* reward; *(statura)* height; *(di abiti)* size; **per taglie forti** outsize, OS. **~ unica** one size

taglia'carte *nm inv* paperknife

taglia'erba *nm inv* lawn-mower

tagliafu'oco *a inv* **porta ~** fire door; **striscia ~** fire break ● *nm (in bosco)* fire break

tagli'ando *nm* coupon; **fare il ~** ≈ put one's car in for its MOT. **~ di controllo** manufacturer's sticker; *(da raccogliere)* token. **~ controllo bagaglio** baggage claim sticker. **~ di garanzia** warranty

taglia'pasta *a* **rotella ~** pastry cutter ● *nm inv* pastry cutter

tagliapa'tate *nm inv* potato peeler

tagli'are *vt* cut; *(attraversare)* cut across; cut off *(telefono, elettricità)*; carve *(carne)*; mow *(erba)*; **farsi ~ i capelli** have a haircut, have one's hair cut; **~ i viveri a qcno** stop sb's allowance ● *vi* cut

tagli'arsi *vr* cut oneself; **~ i capelli** have a haircut, have one's hair cut

taglia'sigari *nm inv* cigar cutter

tagli'ata *nf finely-cut beef fillet;* **dare una ~ a qcsa** give sth a cut, cut sth

tagli'ato *a (a pezzi)* jointed; **essere ~ per qcsa** *fig* be cut out for sth

taglia'unghie *nm inv* nail clippers *pl*

tagleggi'are *vt* extort money from

tagli'ente *a* sharp ● *nm* cutting edge

tagli'ere *nm* chopping board. **~ per il pane** breadboard

taglie'rina *nf (per carta)* guillotine; *(per foto)* trimmer; *(per metallo, vetro)* cutter

'taglio *nm* cut; *(di stoffa)* length; *(di capelli)* [hair-]cut; *(parte tagliente)* cutting edge; **di ~** edgeways; **a doppio ~** *fig* double-edged; **~ e cucito** dressmaking; **dacci un ~!** *fam* put a sock in it!. **~ di carne** cut of meat. **~ cesareo** Caesarean section. **~ di personale** personnel cut. **~ dei prezzi** price cutting

tagli'ola *nf* trap

taglio'lini *nmpl* thin soup noodles

tagli'one *nm* **legge del ~** an eye for an eye and a tooth for a tooth, law of talion

tagliuz'zare *vt* cut into small pieces

tail'leur *nm inv* [lady's] suit

ta'lare *a* **prendere la veste ~** take holy orders

talassotera'pia *nf therapy based on seawater*

'**talco** *nm* talcum powder, talc

'**tale** *a* such a; (*con nomi plurali*) such; **c'è un ~ disordine** there is such a mess; **non accetto tali scuse** I won't accept such excuses; **è un ~ bugiardo!** he's such a liar!; **il rumore era ~ che non si sentiva nulla** there was so much noise you couldn't hear yourself think; **il ~ giorno** on such and such a day; **quel tal signore** that gentleman; **~ padre ~ figlio** like father like son; **~ quale** just like ● *pron* **un ~** someone; **quel ~** that man; **il tal dei tali** such and such a person

ta'lea *nf* cutting

ta'lento *nm* talent

'**talent scout** *nmf inv* talent scout

tali'smano *nm* talisman

tallo'nare *vt* be hot on the heels of

tallon'cino *nm* coupon. **~ del prezzo** price tag

tal'lone *nm* heel. **~ di Achille** *fig* Achilles' heel. **~ aureo** *Econ* gold standard

tal'mente *adv* so

ta'lora *adv* = **talvolta**

'**talpa** *nf* mole

tal'volta *adv* sometimes

tamburel'lare *vi* (*con le dita*) drum; ⟨*pioggia:*⟩ beat, drum

tambu'rello *nm* tambourine

tambu'rino *nm* drummer

tam'buro *nm* drum. **~ del freno** brake drum

tame'rice *nf* tamarisk

'**tamia** *nm inv* chipmunk

Ta'migi *nm* Thames

tampona'mento *nm Auto* collision; (*di ferita*) dressing; (*di falla*) plugging. **~ a catena** pile-up

tampo'nare *vt* (*urtare*) crash into; plug ⟨*falla*⟩; dress ⟨*ferita*⟩

tam'pone *nm* swab; (*per timbri*) pad; (*per mestruazioni*) tampon; (*per treni, Comput*) buffer

tam'tam *nm inv* bush telegraph

'**tana** *nf* den

'**tandem** *nm inv* tandem; **in ~** ⟨*lavorare*⟩ in tandem

'**tanfo** *nm* stench

'**tanga** *nm inv* tanga

tan'gente *a* tangent ● *nf* tangent; (*somma*) bribe

tangen'topoli *nf widespread corruption in Italy in the early 90s*

tangenzi'ale *nf* orbital road

tan'gibile *a* tangible

tangibil'mente *adv* tangibly

'**tango** *nm inv* tango

'**tanica** *nf* (*contenitore*) jerry can; (*serbatoio di nave*) tank

tan'nino *nm* tannin

tan'tino: un ~ *adv* a little [bit]

'**tanto** *a* [so] much; (*con nomi plurali*) [so] many, [such] a lot of; **~ tempo** [such] a long time; **non ha tanta pazienza** he doesn't have much patience; **~ tempo quanto ti serve** as much time as you need; **non è ~ intelligente quanto suo padre** he's not as intelligent as his father; **tanti amici quanti parenti** as many friends as relatives ● *pron* much; (*plurale*) many; (*tanto tempo*) much time; **è un uomo come tanti** he's just an ordinary man; **tanti** (*molte persone*) many people; **non ci vuole così ~** it doesn't take that long; **~ quanto** as much as; **tanti quanti** as many as ● *conj* (*comunque*) anyway, in any case ● *adv* (*così*) so; (*con verbi*) so much; **è ~ debole che non sta in piedi** he's so weak that he can't stand; **è ~ ingenuo da crederle** he's naive enough to believe her; **di ~ in ~** every now and then; **~ l'uno come l'altro** both; **~ quanto** as much as; **tre volte ~** three times as much; **una volta ~** once in a while; **~ meglio così!** so much the better!; **tant'è** so much so; **~ vale che andiamo a casa** we might as well go home; **~ per cambiare** for a change

tapi'oca *nf* tapioca

ta'piro *nm* tapir

ta'pis rou'lant *nm inv* conveyor belt

'**tappa** *nf* (*parte di viaggio*) stage; **fare ~** a break one's journey in

tappa'buchi *nm inv* stopgap

tap'pare *vt* plug; cork ⟨*bottiglia*⟩; **~ la bocca a qcno** *fam* shut sb up

tappa'rella *nf fam* roller blind; **tirar su la ~** pull the blind up

tap'parsi *vr* **~ gli occhi** cover one's eyes; **~ il naso** hold one's nose; **~ le orecchie** put one's fingers in one's ears

tappe'tino *nm* mat; *Comput* mouse mat. **~ antiscivolo** [anti-slip] safety bathmat. **~ da bagno** bathmat

tap'peto *nm* carpet; (*piccolo*) rug; **andare al ~** ⟨*pugilato:*⟩ hit the canvas; **mandare qcno al ~** knock sb down; **bombardamento a ~** carpet bombing. **~ erboso** lawn. **~ persiano** Persian carpet. **~ stradale** road surface. **~ verde** (*tavolo*) card table. **~ volante** magic carpet

tappez'zare *vt* paper ⟨*pareti*⟩; (*con manifesti*) cover

tappez'zeria *nf* tapestry; (*di carta*) wallpaper; (*arte*) upholstery; **fare da ~** *fig* be a wallflower

tappezzi'ere *nm* upholsterer; (*imbianchino*) decorator

'**tappo** *nm* plug; (*di sughero*) cork; (*di metallo, per penna*) top; (*fam: persona piccola*) dwarf. **~ di bottiglia** bottle top. **~ a corona** crown cap. **tappi** *pl* **per le orecchie** earplugs. **~ salvagocce** anti-drip top. **~ di scarico** [della coppa] sump drain plug. **~ a strappo** ring-pull. **~ di sughero** cork. **~ a vite** screw top '**tara** *nf* (*difetto*) flaw; (*ereditaria*) hereditary defect; (*peso*) tare

taran'tella *nf* tarantella

ta'rantola *nf* tarantula

ta'rare *vt Techn* calibrate; *Comm* discount

ta'rato *a Comm* discounted; *Techn* calibrated; *Med* with a hereditary defect; *fam* crazy

tarchi'ato *a* stocky

tar'dare *vi* be late ● *vt* delay

'**tardi** *adv* late; **al più ~** at the latest; **più ~** later [on]; **sul ~** late in the day; **far ~** (*essere in ritardo*) be late; (*con gli amici*) stay up late; **a più ~** see you later; **svegliarsi troppo ~** oversleep

tardiva'mente *adv* late

tar'divo *a* late; ⟨*bambino*⟩ retarded

'**tardo** *a* slow; ⟨*pomeriggio, mattinata*⟩ late

'**targa** *nf* plate; *Auto* numberplate

tar'gato *a* **un'auto targata...** a car with the registration number...

targ'hetta *nf* (*su porta*) nameplate; (*sulla valigia*) name tag. **~ di circolazione** numberplate. **~ commemorativa** memorial plaque. **~ stradale** street sign

ta'riffa *nf* rate, tariff; **a ~ ridotta** *Teleph* off-peak. **~ doganale** customs tariff. **~ ferroviaria** [rail] fares. **~ interna** inland postage. **~ professionale** [professional] fee. **~ telefonica** telephone charges. **~ unica** flat rate

tarif'fario *a* tariff *attrib* ● *nm* price list

tar'larsi *vr* get worm-eaten

tar'lato *a* worm-eaten

'**tarlo** *nm* woodworm

'**tarma** *nf* moth

tar'marsi *vr* get moth-eaten

tarmi'cida *nm* ≈ moth-repellent

ta'rocco *nm* tarot; **tarocchi** *pl* tarot

tar'pare *vt* clip

tartagli'are *vi* stutter

'**tartaro** *a & nm* tartar; **salsa tartara** tartar[e] sauce

tarta'ruga *nf* tortoise; (*di mare*) turtle; (*per pettine ecc*) tortoiseshell

tartas'sare *vt* (*angariare*) harass

tar'tina *nf* canapé

tar'tufo *nm* truffle

'**tasca** *nf* pocket; (*in borsa*) compartment; *Culin* icing bag; **da ~** pocket *attrib*; **avere le tasche piene di qcsa** *fam* have had a bellyful of sth; **se ne è stato con le mani in ~** *fig* he didn't lift a finger [to help]. **~ a battente** flap pocket. **~ del nero** (*di polpo, seppia*) ink sac. **~ da pasticciere** icing bag. **~ tagliata** slit pocket. **~ a toppa** patch-pocket

ta'scabile *a* pocket *attrib* ● *nm* paperback

tasca'pane *nm inv* haversack

ta'schino *nm* breast pocket

'**tassa** *nf* tax; (*d'iscrizione ecc*) fee; (*doganale*) duty. **~ di circolazione** road tax. **~ di esportazione** export duty. **~ d'iscrizione** registration fee. **~ di soggiorno** tourist tax, visitors' tax

tas'sabile *a* taxable

tas'sametro *nm* meter

tas'sare *vt* tax

tassativa'mente *adv* without fail

tassa'tivo *a* strict

tassazi'one *nf* taxation

tas'sello *nm* wedge; (*di stoffa*) gusset

tassì *nm inv* taxi

tas'sista *nmf* taxi driver

'**tasso**[1] *nm Bot* yew; (*animale*) badger

'**tasso**[2] *Comm* rate. **~ agevolato** cut rate; **prestito a ~ agevolato** soft loan. **~ base** base rate. **~ base di interesse** base lending rate. **~ di cambio** exchange rate. **~ di crescita** growth rate. **~ inquinamento** pollution level. **~ di interesse** interest rate. **~ di mortalità** death rate. **~ di sconto** discount rate

ta'stare *vt* feel; **~ il terreno** *fig* test the water *or* ground

tasti'era *nf* keyboard. **~ numerica** *Comput* numeric keypad

tastie'rino *nm* key. **~ numerico** numeric keypad

tastie'rista *nmf* keyboarder

'**tasto** *nm* key; (*tatto*) touch. **~ di controllo** *Comput* control key. **~ cursore** *Comput* cursor key. **~ delicato** *fig* touchy subject. **~ funzione** *Comput* function key. **~ numerico** *Comput* numeric[al] key. **~ di ritorno a margine** return key. **~ tabulatore** tab [key]

ta'stoni: a ~ *adv* gropingly; **camminare a ~** grope around; **cercare qcsa a ~** grope for sth

'**tattica** *nf* tactics *pl*

'**tattico** *a* tactical

'**tattile** *a* tactile

'**tatto** *nm* (*senso*) touch; (*accortezza*) tact; **aver ~** be tactful

tatu'aggio *nm* tattoo

tatu'are *vt* tattoo

tautolo'gia *nf* tautology

tauto'logico *a* tautological

'**tavola** *nf* table; (*illustrazione*) plate; (*asse*) plank; **saper stare a ~** have good table manners; **calmo come una ~** ⟨*mare*⟩ like a mill pond. **~ calda** snackbar. **~ fredda** salad bar. **~ periodica degli elementi** periodic table. **~ pitagorica** multiplication table. **~ rotonda** *fig* round table. **~ a vela** sailboard; **fare ~ ~ ~** sailboard, windsurf

tavo'lato *nm* (*pavimento*) wooden flooring

tavo'letta *nf* bar; (*medicinale*) tablet; **andare a ~** *Auto* drive flat out. **~ di cioccolata** chocolate bar. **~ grafica** *Comput* digitizer

tavo'lino *nm* [small] table; (*da salotto*) occasional table

'**tavolo** *nm* table. **~ anatomico** mortuary table, slab *fam*. **~ da cucina** kitchen table. **~ da gioco** card table. **~ operatorio** *Med* operating table. **~ da pranzo** dining-table

tavo'lozza *nf* palette

'**tazza** *nf* cup; (*del water*) bowl. **~ da caffè/tè** coffee-cup/teacup

taz'zina *nf* ~ **da caffè** espresso coffee cup
TBC *abbr* (**tubercolosi**) TB
T.C.I. *abbr* (**Touring Club Italiano**) *association promoting tourism nationally and internationally*
te *pers pron* you; **te l'ho dato** I gave it to you
tè *nm inv* tea. **tè al latte** tea with milk. **tè al limone** lemon tea
tea'trale *a* theatre *attrib*; (*affettato*) theatrical
te'atro *nm* theatre. ~ **all'aperto** open-air theatre. ~ **lirico** opera [house]. ~ **neorealista** kitchen sink drama. ~ **di posa** *Cinema* set. ~ **tenda** *marquee for theatre performances*
'tecnico, -a *a* technical ● *nmf* technician. ~ **elettronico** electronics engineer. ~ **informatico** computer engineer. ~ **delle luci** *Cinema, TV* gaffer. ~ **del suono** sound technician ● *nf* technique
tec'nigrafo *nm* drawing board
tec'nocrate *nmf* technocrat
tecnolo'gia *nf* technology
tecno'logico *a* technological
te'desco, -a *a & nmf* German. ~ **dell'est** East German
'tedio *nm* tedium
tedi'oso *a* tedious
TEE *nm abbr* (**treno espresso trans-europeo**) Trans-Europe-Express [train]
te'game *nm* saucepan; **uova al** ~ fried eggs
'teglia *nf* baking tin
'tegola *nf* tile; *fig* blow
tei'era *nf* teapot
te'ina *nf* theine
tek *nm* teak
tel. *abbr* (**telefono**) tel.
'tela *nf* cloth; (*per quadri, vele*) canvas; *Theat* curtain. ~ **cerata** oilcloth. ~ **indiana** cheesecloth. ~ **di iuta** hessian. ~ **di lino** linen. ~ **rigida** buckram
te'laio *nm* (*di bicicletta, finestra*) frame; *Auto* chassis; (*per tessere*) loom
'tele *nf fam* telly, TV
tele'camera *nf* television camera
telecoman'dato *a* remote-controlled, remote control *attrib*
teleco'mando *nm* remote control
'Telecom I'talia *nf* Italian State telephone company
telecomunicazi'oni *nfpl* telecommunications, telecomms
teleconfe'renza *nf* teleconference
tele'cronaca *nf* [television] commentary; **fare la** ~ **di** commentate on. ~ **diretta** live [television] coverage. ~ **registrata** recording
telecro'nista *nmf* television commentator
tele'ferica *nf* cableway
tele'film *nm inv* film [made] for television; ~ **a episodi** series
telefo'nare *vt/i* [tele]phone, ring
telefo'nata *nf* call, [tele]phone call; **fare una** ~ make a phone call. ~ **anonima** nuisance call. ~ **a carico del destinatario** re-

verse charge [phone] call; **fare una** ~ **a carico** [**del destinatario**] reverse the charges. ~ **interurbana** long-distance call. ~ **di lavoro** business call. ~ **in teleselezione** ≈ STD call. ~ **urbana** local call
telefonica'mente *adv* by [tele]phone
tele'fonico *a* [tele]phone *attrib*
telefo'nino *nm* mobile [phone]
telefo'nista *nmf* operator
te'lefono *nm* [tele]phone; **numero di** ~ [tele]phone number. ~ **azzurro** children in need help line. ~ **cellulare** cellular [tele]phone, cellular. ~ **senza filo** cordless [phone]. ~ **a gettoni** pay phone. ~ **interno** intercom. ~ **a monete** pay phone. ~ **pubblico** public telephone. ~ **rosso** *Mil, Pol* hotline. ~ **a scatti** *telephone with call charges based on time-units*. ~ **a schede** cardphone. ~ **a tastiera** push-button phone
tele'genico *a* telegenic
telegior'nale *nm* television news
telegra'fare *vt* telegraph
telegra'fia *nf* telegraphy
telegrafica'mente *adv* (*con telegrafo*) by telegram
tele'grafico *a* telegraphic; ‹*risposta*› monosyllabic; **sii** ~ keep it brief
te'legrafo *nm* telegraph
tele'gramma *nm* telegram
tele'matica *nf* data communications, telematics
teleno'vela *nf* soap opera
teleobiet'tivo *nm* telephoto lens
telepa'tia *nf* telepathy
tele'patico *a* telepathic
tele'quiz *nm inv* TV quiz programme
teleradiotra'smettere *vt* simulcast
telero'manzo *nm* television serial
tele'schermo *nm* television screen
tele'scopio *nm* telescope
telescri'vente *nf* telex [machine]
teleselet'tivo *a* direct dialling
teleselezi'one *nf* subscriber trunk dialling, STD; **chiamare in** ~ call direct, dial direct. ~ **internazionale** international direct dialling
telespetta|'tore, -'trice *nmf* viewer; **i telespettatori** the viewing public
tele'text[®] *nm* Teletext
'telethon *nm inv* telethon
tele'video *nm* videophone
televisi'one *nf* television; **guardare la** ~ watch television; **alla** ~ on television. ~ **in bianco e nero** black and white television. ~ **via cavo** cable TV. ~ **a circuito chiuso** closed-circuit television, CCT. ~ **a colori** colour television
televi'sivo *a* television, TV *attrib*; **operatore** ~ television cameraman; **apparecchio** ~ television set
televi'sore *nm* television [set], TV [set]. ~ **portatile** portable [TV], portable [television set]
'telex *nm inv* telex ● *a inv* telex *attrib*

tel'lurico a telluric

'telo nm [piece of] cloth; **~ da bagno** beach towel. **~ di salvataggio** rescue blanket

'tema nm theme; Sch essay

te'matica nf main theme

teme'rario a reckless

te'mere vt be afraid of ● vi be afraid

tem'paccio nm filthy weather

'tempera nf tempera; (pittura) painting in tempera

temperama'tite nm inv pencil-sharpener

tempera'mento nm temperament

tempe'rare vt temper; sharpen ‹matita›

tempe'rato a temperate

tempera'tura nf temperature. **~ ambiente** room temperature

tempe'rino nm penknife

tem'pesta nf storm. **~ magnetica** magnetic storm. **~ di neve** snowstorm. **~ di sabbia** sandstorm

tempe'stare vt **~ qcno di colpi** rain blows on sb; **~ qcno di domande** bombard sb with questions

tempe'stato a ‹anello, diadema› encrusted (**di** with)

tempestiva'mente adv quickly, in a short space of time

tempe'stivo a timely

tempe'stoso a stormy

'tempia nf Anat temple

'tempio nm Relig temple

tem'pismo nm timing

'tempo nm time; (atmosferico) weather; Mus tempo; Gram tense; (di film) part; (di partita) half; **a suo ~** in due course; **~ fa** some time ago; **per molto ~**, **per tanto ~** for a long time; **tanto ~ fa** a long time ago; **un ~** once; **ha fatto il suo ~** it's out of date; **a ~ indeterminato** ‹contratto› permanent; **primo ~** (di film, partita) first half. **~ di accesso** Comput access time. **~ di cottura** cooking time. **~ di esposizione** Phot exposure time. **~ libero** free time, leisure time. **~ limite di accettazione** latest check-in time. **~ di pace** peacetime. **~ reale** Comput real time; **in ~ ~** real-time attrib. **~ supplementare** extra time; Sport extra time, overtime Am; **andare ai tempi supplementari** Sport go into extra time

tempo'rale a temporal ● nm [thunder]storm

temporanea'mente adv temporarily

tempo'raneo a temporary

temporeggi'are vi play for time

tem'prare vt form

te'nace a tenacious

tenace'mente adv tenaciously

te'nacia nf tenacity

te'naglia nf pincers pl

'tenda nf curtain; (per campeggio) tent; (tendone) awning; **tirare le tende** draw the curtains. **~ della doccia** shower curtain. **~ a ossigeno** oxygen tent

ten'denza nf tendency. **~ al rialzo/ribasso** Fin bull/bear market

tendenzial'mente adv by nature

tendenzi'oso a tendentious

'tendere vt (allargare) stretch [out]; (tirare) tighten; (porgere) hold out; fig lay ‹trappola› ● vi **~ a** aim at; (essere portato a) tend to

'tendersi vr tauten

'tendine nm tendon. **~ d'Achille** Achilles tendon. **~ del garretto** hamstring. **~ del ginocchio** hamstring

ten'done nm awning; (di circo) tent. **~ del circo** big top

ten'dopoli nf inv tent city

'tenebre nfpl darkness

tene'broso a gloomy ● nm bel **~** dark and handsome man

te'nente nm lieutenant. **~ colonnello** wing commander

tenera'mente adv tenderly

te'nere vt hold; (mantenere) keep; (gestire) run; (prendere) take; (seguire) follow; (considerare) consider ● vi hold; **~ stretto** hold tight; **~ a qcsa** (oggetto) be fond of sth; **tengo alla sua presenza** I very much want him to be there; **~ per** ‹squadra› support

tene'rezza nf tenderness

'tenero a tender

tene'rone, -a nmf softie

te'nersi vr hold on (**a** to); (in una condizione) keep oneself; **~ indietro** stand back

'tenia nf tapeworm

'tennis nm tennis. **~ da tavolo** table tennis

ten'nista nmf tennis player

te'nore nm standard; Mus tenor; **a ~ di legge** by law. **~ di vita** standard of living

tensi'one nf tension; Electr voltage; **mettere sotto ~** energize; **in ~** under stress. **alta ~** high voltage. **~ premestruale** premenstrual tension, PMT

ten'tacolo nm tentacle

ten'tare vt attempt; (sperimentare) try; (indurre in tentazione) tempt; **~ la strada di** make a foray or venture into

tenta'tivo nm attempt

ten'tato a **~ suicidio** suicide attempt

tentazi'one nf temptation

tentenna'mento nm wavering; **ha avuto dei tentennamenti** he wavered a bit

tenten'nare vi waver

ten'toni adv **cercare qcsa a ~** grope for sth

'tenue a fine; (debole) weak; (esiguo) small; (leggero) slight

te'nuta nf (capacità) capacity; (Sport: resistenza) stamina; (possedimento) estate; (divisa) uniform; (abbigliamento) clothes pl; **a ~ d'aria** airtight. **~ di strada** road holding

teolo'gia nf theology

teo'logico a theological

te'ologo nm theologian

teo'rema nm theorem

teo'ria nf theory

teorica'mente adv theoretically

te'orico a theoretical

te'pore nm warmth

'**teppa** *nf* mob

tep'pismo *nm* hooliganism

tep'pista *nm* hooligan

te'quila *nf inv* tequila

tera'peutico *a* therapeutic

tera'pia *nf* therapy; **in ~** in therapy. **~ di gruppo** group therapy. **~ d'urto** shock treatment

tergicri'stallo *nm* windscreen wiper, windshield wiper *Am*

tergilu'notto *nm* rear windscreen wiper

tergiver'sante *a* equivocating, pussyfooting *fam*

tergiver'sare *vi* equivocate, pussyfoot around *fam*

'**tergo** *nm* **a ~** behind; **segue a ~** please turn over, PTO

teri'lene® *nm* Terylene®

'**terital**® *nm* Terylene®

ter'male *a* thermal; **stazione ~** spa

'**terme** *nfpl* thermal baths

'**termico** *a* thermal; **borsa termica** cool bag

'**terminal** *nm inv* air terminal

termi'nale *a & nm* terminal; **malato ~** terminally ill person

termina'lista *nmf* computer operator

termi'nare *vt/i* end, finish

terminazi'one *nf* (*fine*) termination; *Gram* ending. **~ nervosa** nerve ending

'**termine** *nm* (*limite*) limit; (*fine*) end; (*condizione, parola*) term; (*scadenza*) deadline; **ai termini della legge...** under the terms of act...; **contratto a ~** fixed-term contract. **~ di paragone** *Gram* term of comparison. **~ ultimo** final deadline

terminolo'gia *nf* terminology

'**termite** *nf* termite

termoco'perta *nf* electric blanket

ter'mometro *nm* thermometer

'**termos** *nm inv* thermos®

termosi'fone *nm* radiator; (*sistema*) central heating

ter'mostato *nm* thermostat

termotera'pia *nf Med* heat treatment

termoventila'tore *nm* fan heater

'**terra** *nf* earth; (*regione*) land; (*terreno*) ground; (*argilla*) clay; (*cosmetico*) bronzing powder; **a ~** (*sulla costa*) ashore; (*installazioni*) onshore; **essere a ~** (*gomma:*) be flat; *fig* be at rock bottom; **per ~** on the ground; (*su pavimento*) on the floor; **sotto ~** underground; **far ~ bruciata** carry out a scorched earth policy. **~ promessa** Promised Land. **~ di Siena** sienna

terra'cotta *nf* terracotta; **vasellame di ~** earthenware

terra'ferma *nf* dry land

Terra'nova *nf* Newfoundland

terrapi'eno *nm* embankment

ter'razza *nf*, **ter'razzo** *nm* balcony

terremo'tato, -a *a* (*zona*) affected by an earthquake ● *nmf* earthquake victim

terre'moto *nm* earthquake

ter'reno *a* earthly ● *nm* ground; (*suolo*) soil; (*proprietà terriera*) land; **perdere/guadagnare ~** lose/gain ground. **~ alluvionale** alluvial soil. **~ di bonifica** reclaimed land. **~ edificabile** building land. **~ di gioco** playing field. **~ di scontro** battlefield

ter'restre *a* terrestrial; ⟨*superficie, diametro*⟩ of the earth; **esercito ~** land forces *pl*

ter'ribile *a* terrible

terribil'mente *adv* terribly

ter'riccio *nm* potting compost

'**terrier** *nm inv* terrier

terri'ero *a* ⟨*proprietario*⟩ land *attrib*; ⟨*aristocrazia*⟩ landed; **proprietà** *pl* **terriere** landed property

terrifi'cante *a* terrifying

territori'ale *a* territorial; **acque territoriali** territorial waters

terri'torio *nm* territory

ter'rone, -a *nmf pej* bloody Southerner

ter'rore *nm* terror

terro'rismo *nm* terrorism

terro'rista *nmf* terrorist

terroriz'zare *vt* terrorize

'**terso** *a* clear

'**terza** *nf* (*marcia*) third [gear]

ter'zetto *nm* trio

terzi'ario *a* tertiary ● *nm* service sector, tertiary sector. **~ avanzato** high technology, hi-tech sector

'**terzo** *a* third; **di terz'ordine** ⟨*locale, servizio*⟩ third-rate; **fare il ~ grado a qcno** give sb the third degree; **la terza età** the third age; **il ~ mondo** the Third World ● *nm* third; **terzi** *pl Jur* third party

terzo'genito, -a *nmf* third-born

ter'zultimo, -a *a & n* third from last

'**tesa** *nf* brim

'**teschio** *nm* skull

'**tesi** *nf inv* thesis

'**teso** *pp di* **tendere** ● *a* taut; *fig* tense

tesore'ria *nf* treasury

tesori'ere *nm* treasurer

te'soro *nm* treasure; (*tesoreria*) treasury; **ministro del T~** Finance Minister, ≈ Chancellor of the Exchequer *Br*

'**tessera** *nf* card; (*abbonamento all'autobus*) season ticket; (*di club*) membership card

'**tessere** *vt* weave; hatch ⟨*complotto*⟩; **~ le lodi di qcsa** sing the praises of sth

tesse'rino *nm* travel card

'**tessile** *a* textile ● *nm* **tessili** *pl* textiles; (*operai*) textile workers

tessi'tore, -'trice *nmf* weaver

tessi'tura *nf* weaving

tes'suto *pp di* **tessere** ● *a* woven; **~ a mano** hand-woven ● *nm* fabric, material; *Anat* tissue. **~ sintetico** synthetic material

'**testa** *nf* head; (*cervello*) brain; **essere in ~ a** be ahead of; **in ~** *Sport* in the lead; **~ o croce?** heads or tails?; **fare ~ o croce** spin a coin, toss a coin; **andare a ~ alta** hold one's head up. **~ di rapa** *fam* pinhead. **~ di sbarco** beachhead. **~ di serie** (*squadra*) seeded team. **~ del treno** front of the train

testa-'coda *nm inv* fare un ~ spin right round

testa'mento *nm* will. **Antico T~** *Relig* Old Testament. **Nuovo T~** *Relig* New Testament

testar'daggine *nf* stubbornness

testarda'mente *adv* stubbornly

te'stardo *a* stubborn

te'stata *nf* head; *(intestazione)* heading; *(colpo)* [head]butt. ~ **nucleare** nuclear warhead

'teste *nmf* witness

'tester *nm inv* tester

te'sticolo *nm* testicle

testi'mone *nmf* witness; **essere** ~ **di qcsa** witness sth. ~ **di Geova** Jehovah's Witness. ~ **oculare** eye witness

testi'monial *nmf inv* celebrity who promotes a brand of cosmetics

testimoni'anza *nf* testimony; **falsa** ~ *Jur* perjury

testimoni'are *vt* testify to ● *vi* testify, give evidence

te'stina *nf* head; *(di stampante)* printhead. ~ **di cancellazione** *Comput* erase head. ~ **di lettura** *Comput* read head. ~ **rotante** *(di macchina da scrivere)* golf-ball. ~ **di vitello** *Culin* calf's head

'testo *nm* text; **far** ~ be authoritative; **con** ~ **a fronte** *(traduzione)* with the original text on the opposite page

te'stone, -a *nmf* blockhead

testoste'rone *nm* testosterone

testu'ale *a* textual

'tetano *nm* tetanus

te'traggine *nf* bleakness

tetra'pak® *nm inv* tetrapak

'tetro *a* bleak

tetta'rella *nf* teat

'tetto *nm* roof; **abbandono del** ~ **coniugale** *Jur* desertion. ~ **apribile** *(di auto)* sun[shine] roof. ~ **a terrazza** flat roof

tet'toia *nf* roofing

tet'tuccio *nm* ~ **apribile** sun-roof

teu'tonico *a* Teutonic

'Tevere *nm* Tiber

ti *pers pron* you; *(riflessivo)* yourself; **ti ha dato un libro** he gave you a book; **lavati le mani** wash your hands; **eccoti!** here you are!; **sbrigati!** hurry up!

ti'ara *nf* tiara

tic *nm inv* tic

ticchet'tare *vi* tick

ticchet'tio *nm* ticking

'ticchio *nm* tic; *(ghiribizzo)* whim

'ticket *nm inv* *(per farmaco, esame)* amount paid by National Health patients

tie-break *nm inv* tie break[er]

tiepida'mente *adv* half-heartedly

ti'epido *a* lukewarm; *fig* half-hearted

ti'fare *vi* ~ **per** shout for

'tifo *nm* *Med* typhus; **far il** ~ **per** *fig* be a fan of

tifoi'dea *nf* typhoid

ti'fone *nm* typhoon

ti'foso, -a *nmf* fan

tight *nm inv* morning dress

'tiglio *nm* lime

'tigna *nf* ringworm

ti'grato *a* gatto ~ tabby [cat]

'tigre *nf* tiger

'tilde *nmf* tilde

tim'ballo *nm* *Culin* pie

tim'brare *vt* stamp; ~ **il cartellino** *(all'entrata)* clock in; *(all'uscita)* clock out

'timbro *nm* stamp; *(di voce)* tone. ~ **a secco** embossing stamp

time out *nm inv* *Sport* time-out

'timer *nm inv* timer

timida'mente *adv* timidly, shyly

timi'dezza *nf* timidity, shyness

'timido *a* timid, shy

'timo *nm* thyme

ti'mone *nm* rudder. ~ **di direzione** *(di aereo)* rudder. ~ **di quota** *(di aereo)* elevator

timoni'ere *nm* helmsman

timo'rato *a* ~ **di Dio** God-fearing

ti'more *nm* fear; *(soggezione)* awe

timo'roso *a* timorous

'timpano *nm* eardrum; *Mus* kettledrum; **timpani** *pl Mus* timpani, kettledrums; **rompere i timpani a qcno** *fig* shatter sb's eardrums

ti'nello *nm* dining-room

'tingere *vt* dye; *(macchiare)* stain

'tingersi *vr* *(viso, cielo:)* be tinged **(di** with); ~ **i capelli** have one's hair dyed; *(da solo)* dye one's hair

'tino *nm*, **ti'nozza** *nf* tub

'tinta *nf* dye; *(colore)* colour; **in** ~ **unita** plain, self-coloured

tinta'rella *nf fam* suntan

tintin'nare *vi* tinkle

'tinto *pp di* **tingere**

tinto'ria *nf* *(negozio)* cleaner's

tin'tura *nf* dyeing; *(colorante)* dye. ~ **di iodio** iodine

tipica'mente *adv* typically

'tipico *a* typical

'tipo *nm* type; *(fam: individuo)* chap, guy

tipogra'fia *nf* printer's; *(arte)* typography

tipo'grafico *a* typographic[al]

ti'pografo *nm* printer

tip tap *nm* tap dancing

ti'raggio *nm* draught

tiranneggi'are *vt* tyrannize

tiran'nia *nf* tyranny

ti'ranno, -a *a* tyrannical ● *nmf* tyrant

tiranno'sauro *nm* tyrannosaurus

ti'rante *nm* rope

tirapi'edi *nm inv pej* hanger-on

tira'pugni *nm inv* knuckle-duster

ti'rare *vt* pull; *(gettare)* throw; *(nel calcio)* kick; *(tracciare)* draw; *(stampare)* print; *fam* land *(calci, pugni)* ● *vi* pull; *(vento:)* blow; *(abito:)* be tight; *(sparare)* fire; ~ **avanti** *fig* get by; ~ **su** bring up *(figli)*; *(da terra)* pick up; **tirar su [col naso]** sniffle

ti'rarsi *vr* ~ **indietro** *fig* back out, pull out

tiras'segno *nm* target shooting; *(alla fiera)* rifle range

ti'rata *nf* (*strattone*) pull, tug; **in una ~** in one go; **dare a qcno una ~ d'orecchi** *fig* give sb a telling off

tira'tore *nm* shot. **~ scelto** marksman

tira'tura *nf* printing; (*di giornali*) circulation; (*di libri*) [print]run

tirchie'ria *nf* meanness

'tirchio *a* mean

tiri'tera *nf* spiel

'tiro *nm* (*lancio*) throw; (*azione*) throwing; (*sparo*) shot; (*azione*) shooting; (*scherzo*) trick; **cavallo da ~** draught horse. **~ con l'arco** archery. **~ al bersaglio** target practice. **~ alla fune** tug-of-war. **~ al piattello** clay pigeon shooting. **~ in porta** shot at goal. **~ a segno** rifle-range

tiroci'nante *nmf* trainee

tiro'cinio *nm* training

ti'roide *nf* thyroid

Tir'reno *nm* **il [mar] ~** the Tyrrhenian Sea

ti'sana *nf* herb[al] tea

'tisi *nf* consumption

ti'tanio *nm* titanium

tito'lare *a* permanent ● *nmf* (*proprietario*) owner; (*calcio*) regular player; (*Jur: di diritto*) holder

'titolo *nm* title; (*accademico*) qualification; *Comm* security; **a ~ di** as; **a ~ di favore** as a favour; **titoli** *pl* (*di giornale, telegiornale*) headlines. **titoli** *pl* **di coda** closing credits. **~ di credito** credit instrument. **~ mondiale** world title. **~ obbligazionario** bond. **titoli** *pl* **delle principali notizie** news headlines. **~ in sovrimpressione** superimposed title. **~ di Stato** government security. **titoli** *pl* **di studio** qualifications. **titoli** *pl* **di testa** *Cinema, TV* opening credits. **~ a tutta pagina** banner headline

titu'bante *a* hesitant

titu'banza *nf* hesitation

titu'bare *vi* hesitate

tivù *nf inv fam* TV, telly

'tizio, -a *nm* so-and-so; **un ~** some man ● *nf* **una tizia** some woman

tiz'zone *nm* brand

toc'cante *a* touching

toc'care *vt* touch; touch on (*argomento*); (*tastare*) feel; (*riguardare*) concern ● *vi* **~ a** (*capitare*) happen to; **mi tocca aspettare** I'll have to wait; **tocca a te** it's your turn; (*da pagare da bere*) it's your round; **'non ~'** 'please do not touch'

tocca'sana *nm inv* panacea

toc'cato *a* (*fam: matto*) touched

'tocco *nm* touch; (*di pennello, orologio*) stroke; (*di pane ecc*) chunk; **il ~ finale** the finishing touches ● *a fam* crazy, touched

toc 'toc *nm inv* knock, knock

'toga *nf* toga; (*accademica, di magistrato*) gown

'togliere *vt* take off (*coperta*); (*Math, da scuola*) take away; quench (*sete*); take out, remove (*tonsille, dente ecc*); **~ qcsa di mano a qcno** take sth away from sb; **~ qcno dei guai** get sb out of trouble; **ciò non toglie**

che... nevertheless..., the fact remains that...; **farsi ~ le tonsille** have one's tonsils [taken] out

'togliersi *vr* take off (*abito*); **~ la vita** take one's [own] life; **~ di mezzo** get out of the way; **togliti dai piedi!** get out of the way!

toi'lette *nf inv* toilet; (*mobile*) dressing table

to'letta *nf* toilet; (*mobile*) dressing table

tolle'rante *a* tolerant

tolle'ranza *nf* tolerance; **casa di ~** brothel

tolle'rare *vt* tolerate

'tolto *pp di* **togliere**

to'maia *nf* upper

'tomba *nf* grave

tom'bino *nm* manhole cover

'tombola *nf* bingo; (*caduta*) tumble

to'mino *nm* goat cheese

'tomo *nm* tome

tomogra'fia *nf Med* tomography. **~ assiale computerizzata** computerized axial tomography, CAT

'tonaca *nf* habit

to'nale *a* tonal

tonalità *nf inv Mus* tonality

to'nante *a* booming

'tondo *a* (*cifra*) round ● *nm* circle

'toner *nm inv* toner

'tonfo *nm* thud; (*in acqua*) splash

'tonica *nf Mus* keynote

'tonico *a* (*sillaba*) stressed; (*muscoli*) well toned ● *nm* tonic

tonifi'care *vt* tone up (*muscoli*)

ton'nara *nf* tuna-fishing net

ton'nato *a* **vitello ~** veal with a tuna and mayonnaise sauce

tonnel'laggio *nm* tonnage

tonnel'lata *nf* ton. **~ corta americana** short ton, net ton

'tonno *nm* tuna [fish]

'tono *nm* tone

ton'sille *nfpl* tonsils

tonsil'lite *nf* tonsillitis

'tonto *a fam* thick

top *nm inv* (*indumento*) sun-top

to'pazio *nm* topaz

'topless *nm inv* **in ~** topless

top 'model *nf inv* supermodel, top model

'topo *nm* mouse. **~ di albergo/ appartamento** thief in a hotel/block of flats. **~ di biblioteca** bookworm. **~ domestico** domestic mouse

topogra'fia *nf* topography

topo'grafico *a* topographic[al]

to'ponimo *nm* place name

topo'ragno *nm* shrew

'toppa *nf* (*rattoppo*) patch; (*serratura*) keyhole

to'race *nm* chest

to'racico *a* thoracic; **gabbia toracica** rib cage

'torba *nf* peat

'torbido *a* cloudy; *fig* troubled

'torcere *vt* twist; wring [out] (*biancheria*)

'torcersi *vr* twist

'torchio *nm* press

'**torcia** nf torch. ~ **elettrica** torch
torci'collo nm stiff neck
'**tordo** nm thrush
to'rero nm bullfighter
To'rino nf Turin
tor'menta nf snowstorm
tormen'tare vt torment
tormen'tato a tormented
tor'mento nm torment
torna'conto nm benefit
tor'nado nm tornado
tor'nante nm hairpin bend
tor'nare vi return, go/come back; (ridiventare) become again; ‹conto:› add up; ~ **a sorridere** smile again; ~ **su** go back up
tor'neo nm tournament
'**tornio** nm lathe
'**torno** nm **togliersi di** ~ get out of the way
'**toro** nm bull; Astr Taurus
tor'pedine nf torpedo
torpedini'era nf torpedo boat
tor'pore nm torpor
'**torre** nf tower; (scacchi) castle. ~ **d'avorio** ivory tower. ~ **di controllo** control tower. ~ **di osservazione** observation tower. ~ **pendente**, ~ **di Pisa** Leaning Tower of Pisa
torrefazi'one nf roasting; (negozio) coffee retailer
tor'rente nm torrent, mountain stream; (fig: di lacrime) flood; (fig: di parole) torrent
torrenzi'ale a torrential; **in regime** ~ **in** spate
tor'retta nf turret
'**torrido** a torrid
torri'one nm keep
tor'rone nm nougat
torsi'one nf twisting; (in ginnastica) twist
'**torso** nm torso; (di mela, pera) core; **a** ~ **nudo** bare-chested
'**torsolo** nm core
'**torta** nf cake; (crostata) tart. ~ **di compleanno** birthday cake. ~ **di mele** apple tart. ~ **nuziale** wedding cake. ~ **pasqualina** spinach pie
torti'era nf cake tin
tor'tino nm pie
'**torto** pp di **torcere** ● a twisted ● nm wrong; (colpa) fault; **aver** ~ be wrong; **a** ~ wrongly; **far** ~ **a qcno** wrong sb; fig not do sb justice; **non hai tutti i torti** you're not altogether wrong
tor'tora nf turtle-dove
tortuosa'mente adv tortuously
tortu'oso a winding; (ambiguo) tortuous
tor'tura nf torture
tortu'rare vt torture
'**torvo** a ‹sguardo› menacing
tosa'erba nm inv lawnmower
to'sare vt shear
tosasi'epi nm inv hedge trimmer
tosa'tura nf shearing
To'scana nf Tuscany
to'scano, -a a & nmf Tuscan
'**tosse** nf cough
'**tossico** a toxic ● nm poison

tossicodipen'denza nf drug addiction
tossi'comane nmf drug addict, drug user
tos'sire vi cough
tosta'pane nm inv toaster. ~ **a espulsione automatica** pop-up toaster
to'stare vt toast ‹pane›; roast ‹caffè›
'**tosto** adv (subito) soon ● a fam cool; **faccia tosta** cheek
tot a inv **una cifra** ~ such and such a figure ● nm **un** ~ so much
to'tale a & nm total. ~ **parziale** subtotal
totalità nf entirety; **la** ~ **dei presenti** all those present
totali'tario a totalitarian
totaliz'zare vt total; score ‹punti›
totalizza'tore nm (per scommesse) totalizer, tote
total'mente adv totally
'**totano** nm squid
'**totem** nm inv totem pole
toto'calcio nm ≈ [football] pools pl
touche nf inv touch line
tou'pet nm inv toupee
tournée nf inv tour
to'vaglia nf tablecloth
tovagli'etta nf ~ [**all'americana**] place mat
tovagli'olo nm napkin. ~ **di carta** paper napkin
'**tozzo** a squat ● nm ~ **di pane** stale piece of bread
tra = **fra**
trabal'lante a staggering; ‹sedia› rickety, wonky
trabal'lare vi stagger; ‹veicolo:› jolt
tra'biccolo nm fam contraption; (auto) jalopy
traboc'care vi overflow
traboc'chetto nm trap
traca'gnotto a dumpy
tracan'nare vt gulp down
'**traccia** nf track; (orma) footstep; (striscia) trail; (residuo) trace; fig sign
tracci'are vt trace; sketch out ‹schema›; draw ‹linea›
tracci'ato nm (schema) layout. ~ **di gara** circuit
tra'chea nf windpipe, trachea
tra'colla nf shoulder-strap; **borsa a** ~ shoulder-bag
tra'collo nm collapse
tradi'mento nm betrayal; Pol treason; **alto** ~ high treason
tra'dire vt betray; be unfaithful to ‹moglie, marito›
tradi|'tore, -'trice nmf traitor
tradizio'nale a traditional
tradiziona'lista nmf traditionalist
tradizional'mente adv traditionally
tradizi'one nf tradition
tra'dotto pp di **tradurre**
tra'durre vt translate
tradut|'tore, -'trice nmf translator. ~ **elettronico** electronic phrasebook
traduzi'one nf translation. ~ **consecutiva**

consecutive interpreting. ~ **simultanea** simultaneous interpreting

tra'ente *nmf Comm* drawer

trafe'lato *a* breathless

traffi'cante *nmf* dealer. ~ **d'armi** arms dealer. ~ **di droga** drug dealer

traffi'care *vi* (*affaccendarsi*) busy oneself; ~ **in** *pej* traffic in

'traffico *nm* traffic; *Comm* trade. ~ **aereo** air traffic. ~ **della droga** drug trafficking. ~ **ferroviario** rail traffic. ~ **di stupefacenti** drug trafficking

traffi'cone, -a *nmf fam* wheeler dealer

tra'figgere *vt* penetrate, pierce; *fig* pierce

tra'fila *nf fig* rigmarole

trafi'letto *nm* minor news item

trafo'rare *vt* bore, drill

tra'foro *nm* boring, drilling; (*galleria*) tunnel; **lavoro di** ~ fretwork

trafu'gare *vt* steal

tra'gedia *nf* tragedy

traghet'tare *vt* ferry

tra'ghetto *nm* ferrying; (*nave*) ferry

tragica'mente *adv* tragically

'tragico *a* tragic ● *nm* (*autore*) tragedian

tra'gitto *nm* journey; (*per mare*) crossing

tragu'ardo *nm* finishing post; (*meta*) goal

traiet'toria *nf* trajectory

trai'nare *vt* drag; (*rimorchiare*) tow

tralasci'are *vt* interrupt; (*omettere*) leave out; ~ **di fare qcsa** fail to do sth, omit to do sth

'tralcio *nm Bot* shoot

tra'liccio *nm* (*tela*) ticking; (*graticcio*) trellis

tra'lice: **in** ~ *adv* ⟨*tagliare*⟩ on the slant; ⟨*guardare*⟩ sideways

tralu'cente *a* shining

tram *nm inv* tram, streetcar *Am*

'trama *nf* weft; (*di film ecc*) plot

traman'dare *vt* hand down

tra'mare *vt* weave; (*macchinare*) plot

tram'busto *nm* turmoil

trame'stio *nm* bustle

tramez'zino *nm* sandwich

tra'mezzo *nm* partition

'tramite *prep* through ● *nm* link; **con il** ~ **di** by means of; **fare da** ~ act as go-between

tramon'tana *nf* north wind

tramon'tare *vi* set; (*declinare*) decline

tra'monto *nm* sunset; (*declino*) decline

tramor'tire *vt* stun ● *vi* faint

trampoli'ere *nm* wader

trampo'lino *nm* springboard; (*per lo sci*) ski-jump. ~ **di lancio** *fig* launch pad

'trampolo *nm* stilt

tramu'tare *vt* transform

trance *nf inv* trance; **essere in** ~ be in a trance

'trancia *nf* shears *pl*; (*fetta*) slice

tra'nello *nm* trap

trangugi'are *vt* gulp down

'tranne *prep* except

tranquilla'mente *adv* peacefully

tranquil'lante *nm* tranquillizer

tranquillità *nf* calm; (*di spirito*) tranquillity

tranquilliz'zare *vt* reassure

tran'quillo *a* quiet; (*pacifico*) peaceful; (*coscienza*) easy; **stai** ~! (*non preoccuparti*) don't worry!

transa'tlantico *a* transatlantic ● *nm* ocean liner

tran'satto *pp di* **transigere**

transazi'one *nf Comm* transaction; *Jur* settlement

tran'senna *nf* (*barriera*) barrier

transessu'ale *nmf* transsexual

tran'setto *nm* transept

'transfert *nm inv Psych* transference

tran'sigere *vi Jur* reach a settlement; (*cedere*) compromise

tran'sistor *nm inv fam* transistor [radio]

transi'tabile *a* passable

transi'tare *vi* pass

transi'tivo *a* transitive

'transito *nm* transit; '**divieto di** ~' 'no thoroughfare'; **diritto di** ~ right of way; '~ **alterno**' 'temporary one-way system'

transi'torio *a* transitory

transizi'one *nf* transition; **di** ~ transitional

tran'tran *nm fam* routine

tranvi'ere *nm* tram driver, streetcar driver *Am*

'trapano *nm* drill. ~ **elettrico** electric drill

trapas'sare *vt* pierce, penetrate ● *vi* (*morire*) pass away

trapas'sato *nm* pluperfect

tra'passo *nm* passage

trape'lare *vi anche fig* leak out

tra'pezio *nm* trapeze; *Math* trapezium

trapian'tare *vt* transplant

trapi'anto *nm* transplant. ~ **di cuore** heart transplant

'trappola *nf* trap

tra'punta *nf* quilt

'trarre *vt* draw; (*ricavare*) obtain; ~ **in inganno** deceive

trasa'lire *vi* start

trasan'dato *a* shabby

trasbor'dare *vt* transfer; *Naut* tran[s]ship ● *vi* change

tra'sbordo *nm* trans[s]hipment

trascenden'tale *a* transcendental

tra'scendere *vt* transcend ● *vi* (*eccedere*) go too far

trasci'nare *vt* drag; ⟨*fig: entusiasmo:*⟩ carry away

trasci'narsi *vr* drag oneself; (*camminare piano*) dawdle

tra'scorrere *vt* spend ● *vi* pass

tra'scritto *pp di* **trascrivere**

tra'scrivere *vt* transcribe

trascrizi'one *nf* transcription

trascu'rabile *a* negligible

trascu'rare *vt* neglect; (*non tenere conto di*) disregard

trascurata'mente *adv* carelessly

trascura'tezza *nf* negligence

trascu'rato *a* negligent; (*curato male*) neglected; (*nel vestire*) slovenly

traseco'lato *a* amazed

trasferi'mento *nm* transfer; (*trasloco*) move. **~ automatico** direct debit. **~ bancario** bank transfer

trasfe'rire *vt* transfer

trasfe'rirsi *vr* move

tra'sferta *nf* transfer; (*indennità*) subsistence allowance; *Sport* away match; **in ~** ⟨*impiegato*⟩ on secondment; **giocare in ~** play away

trasfigu'rare *vt* transfigure

trasfor'mare *vt* transform; (*in rugby*) convert

trasfor'marsi *vr* be transformed; **~ in** turn into

trasforma'tore *nm* transformer

trasformazi'one *nf* transformation; (*in rugby*) conversion

trasfor'mista *nmf* (*artista*) quick-change artist

trasfusi'one *nf* transfusion

trasgre'dire *vt* disobey; *Jur* infringe

trasgredi'trice *nf* transgressor

trasgressi'one *nf* infringement; (*di ordine*) failure to obey

trasgres'sivo *a* intended to shock

trasgres'sore *nm* transgressor

tra'slato *a* metaphorical

traslitte'rare *vt* transliterate

traslo'care *vt* move ● *vi* move [house]

traslo'carsi *vr* move [house]

tra'sloco *nm* move; **compagnia di ~** removal company

tra'smesso *pp di* **trasmettere**

tra'smettere *vt* pass on; *TV, Radio* broadcast; *Techn, Med* transmit

trasmetti'tore *nm* transmitter

trasmis'sibile *a* transmissible

trasmissi'one *nf* transmission; *TV, Radio* programme. **~ dati** data transmission. **~ via fax** fax transmission. **~ radiofonica** radio programme. **~ remota** remote transmission. **~ televisiva** television programme

trasmit'tente *nm* transmitter ● *nf* broadcasting station

traso'gnare *vi* day-dream

traso'gnato *a* dreamy

traspa'rente *a* transparent

traspa'renza *nf* transparency; **in ~** against the light

traspa'rire *vi* show [through]

traspi'rare *vi* perspire; *fig* transpire

traspirazi'one *nf* perspiration

tra'sporre *vt* transpose

traspor'tare *vt* transport; **lasciarsi ~ da** get carried away by; **~ con ponte aereo** airlift

traspor'tato *a* transported; **~ dall'aria** airborne

trasporta'tore *nm* conveyor; (*società*) transport company, road haulier

tra'sporto *nm* transport; (*fig: passione*) passion; **ministro dei trasporti** Ministry of Transport. **~ aereo** air freight. **~ ferroviario** rail transport. **~ pesante** heavy goods transport. **trasporti** *pl* **pubblici** public transport. **~ stradale** road transport, road haulage

trastul'lare *vt* amuse

trastul'larsi *vr* amuse oneself; (*perdere tempo*) fool around

trasu'dare *vt* ooze [with] ● *vi* ooze

trasver'sale *a* transverse; **strada ~** cross street

trasversal'mente *adv* widthways

trasvo'lare *vt* fly over ● *vi* **~ su** *fig* skim over

trasvo'lata *nf* crossing [by air]

'tratta *nf* (*traffico illegale*) trade; *Comm* draft. **~ bancaria** *Fin* banker's draft. **~ delle bianche** white slave trade. **~ documentaria** documentary bill

trat'tabile *a* or nearest offer, o.n.o.

tratta'mento *nm* treatment. **~ automatico delle informazioni** electronic data processing, EDP. **~ di bellezza** beauty treatment. **~ di fine rapporto** severance pay. **~ di riguardo** special treatment

trat'tante *a* conditioning

trat'tare *vt* treat; (*commerciare in*) deal in; (*negoziare*) negotiate ● *vi* **~ di** deal with

trat'tario *nm* Comm drawee

trat'tarsi *vr* **di che si tratta?** what's it about?; **si tratta di...** it's about...

tratta'tive *nfpl* negotiations; **il tavolo delle ~** the negotiating table

trat'tato *nm* treaty; (*opera scritta*) treatise. **~ di pace** peace treaty

tratteggi'are *vt* outline; (*descrivere*) sketch

tratte'nere *vt* (*far restare*) keep; hold ⟨*respiro, in questura*⟩; hold back ⟨*lacrime, riso*⟩; (*frenare*) restrain; (*da paga*) withhold; **sono stato trattenuto** (*ritardato*) I got held up

tratte'nersi *vr* restrain oneself; (*fermarsi*) stay; **~ su** (*indugiare*) dwell on

tratteni'mento *nm* entertainment; (*ricevimento*) party

tratte'nuta *nf* deduction

trat'tino *nm* dash; (*in parole composte*) hyphen

'tratto *pp di* **trarre** ● *nm* (*di spazio, tempo*) stretch; (*di penna*) stroke; (*linea*) line; (*brano*) passage; **'tratti** *pl* (*lineamenti*) features; **a tratti** at intervals; **ad un ~** suddenly

trat'tore *nm* tractor

tratto'ria *nf* restaurant

'trauma *nm* trauma

trau'matico *a* traumatic

traumatiz'zante *a* traumatic

traumatiz'zare *vt* traumatize

tra'vaglio *nm* labour; (*angoscia*) anguish

trava'sare *vt* decant

tra'vaso *nm* decanting

trava'tura *nf* beams *pl*

'trave *nf* beam. **~ a sbalzo** cantilever

tra'veggole *nfpl* **avere le ~** be seeing things

'travellers cheque *nm inv* traveller's cheque

tra'versa *nf* (*nel calcio*) crossbar; **è una ~ di via Roma** it's off via Roma, it crosses via Roma

traver'sare *vt* cross

traver'sata *nf* crossing

traver'sie *nfpl* misfortunes

traver'sina *nf Rail* sleeper

tra'verso *a* crosswise ● *adv* **di ~** crossways; **andare di ~** ⟨*cibo:*⟩ go down the wrong way; **camminare di ~** not walk in a straight line; **guardare qcno di ~** look askance at sb; **sapere per vie traverse** *fam* find out indirectly

traver'sone *nm* (*in calcio*) cross

travesti'mento *nm* disguise

trave'stire *vt* disguise

trave'stirsi *vr* disguise oneself

travesti'tismo *nm* transvestism, cross-dressing

trave'stito *a* disguised ● *nm* transvestite

travi'are *vt* lead astray

travisa'mento *nm* distortion

travi'sare *vt* distort

travol'gente *a* overwhelming

tra'volgere *vt* sweep away; (*sopraffare*) overwhelm

tra'volto *pp di* **travolgere**

trazi'one *nf* traction. **~ anteriore/posteriore** front-/rear-wheel drive

tre *a & nm* three

tre'alberi *nm inv* three-masted ship, three-master

trebbi'are *vt* thresh

trebbia'trice *nf* threshing machine

'treccia *nf* plait, braid; (*in maglia*) cable; **a trecce** cable *attrib*

tre'cento *a & nm* three hundred; **il T~** the fourteenth century

tredi'cesima *nf extra month's salary paid as a Christmas bonus*

tredi'cesimo, -a *a & nm* thirteenth

'tredici *a & nm* thirteen

'tregua *nf* truce; *fig* respite

'trekking *nm* trekking

tre'mante *a* trembling, quivering; (*per il freddo*) shivering

tre'mare *vi* tremble, quiver; (*di freddo*) shiver

trema'rella *nf fam* jitters *pl*

tremenda'mente *adv* terribly, tremendously

tre'mendo *a* terrible, tremendous; **ho una fame tremenda** I'm terribly hungry

tremen'tina *nf* turpentine

tre'mila *a & nm* three thousand

'tremito *nm* tremble, quiver; (*per il freddo*) shiver

tremo'lare *vi* shake; ⟨*luce:*⟩ flicker

tre'more *nm* trembling

'tremulo *a* tremulous

tre'nino *nm* miniature railway

'treno *nm* train. **~ merci** freight train, goods train. **~ navetta** shuttle. **~ passeggeri** passenger train. **~ postale** mail train. **~ straordinario** special train

'trenta *a & nm* thirty; **~ e lode** *Univ* ≈ first-class honours

trentatré 'giri *nm inv* LP

tren'tenne *a & nmf* thirty-year-old

tren'tesimo *a & nm* thirtieth

tren'tina *nf* **una ~ di** about thirty

trepi'dare *vi* be anxious

'trepido *a* anxious

treppi'ede *nm* tripod

'tresca *nf* intrigue; (*amorosa*) affair

'trespolo *nm* perch

triango'lare *a* triangular

tri'angolo *nm* triangle. **~ delle Bermude** Bermuda Triangle. **~ equilatero** equilateral triangle. **~ isoscele** isosceles triangle. **~ rettangolo** right-angled triangle

tri'bale *a* tribal

tribo'lare *vi* (*soffrire*) suffer; (*fare fatica*) go to a lot of trouble

tribolazi'one *nf* suffering

tri'bordo *nm* starboard

tribù *nf inv* tribe

tri'buna *nf* podium, dais; (*per uditori*) gallery; *Sport* stand. **~ coperta** stand. **~ riservata al pubblico** public gallery. **~ della stampa** press gallery

tribu'nale *nm* court. **~ fallimentare** bankruptcy court. **~ minorile** juvenile court

tribu'tare *vt* bestow, confer

tribu'tario *a* tax *attrib*

tri'buto *nm* tribute; (*tassa*) tax

tri'checo *nm* walrus

tri'ciclo *nm* tricycle

trico'lore *a* three-coloured ● *nm* (*bandiera*) Italian flag

tri'dente *nm* trident

tridimensio'nale *a* three-dimensional

trien'nale *a* (*ogni tre anni*) three-yearly; (*lungo tre anni*) three-year

tri'ennio *nm* three-year period

tri'fase *a* three-phase

tri'foglio *nm* clover

trifo'lato *a* sliced thinly and cooked with olive oil, parsley and garlic

tri'gemino *a* **parto ~** birth of triplets

'triglia *nf* mullet

trigonome'tria *nf* trigonometry, trig *fam*

tri'lingue *a* trilingual

tril'lare *vi* trill

'trillo *nm* trill

trilo'gia *nf* trilogy

trime'strale *a* quarterly

tri'mestre *nm* quarter

'trina *nf* lace

trin'cea *nf* trench

trince'rare *vt* entrench

trincia'pollo *nm inv* poultry shears *pl*

trinci'are *vt* cut up

trincia'trice *nf* **~ di documenti** document shredder

Trinità *nf* Trinity

'trio *nm* trio

trion'fale *a* triumphal

trionfal'mente *adv* triumphantly

trion'fante *a* triumphant

trion'fare *vi* triumph (**su** over)

tri'onfo *nm* triumph

tri'pletta *nf Sport* hat trick

tripli'care *vt* triple

'triplice *a* triple; **in ~ [copia]** in triplicate

'triplo *a* treble, triple; **una somma tripla del previsto** an amount three times as much as forecast ● *nm* **il ~ (di)** three times as much (as)

'trippa *nf* tripe; (*fam: pancia*) belly

tripudi'are *vi* rejoice

tri'pudio *nm* jubilation

tris *nm* (*gioco*) noughts and crosses, tick-tack-toe *Am*

'triste *a* sad; ⟨*luogo*⟩ gloomy

tri'stezza *nf* sadness; (*di luogo*) gloominess

'tristo *a* nasty

trita'carne *nm inv* mincer

tritaghi'accio *nm inv* ice-crusher

tri'tare *vt* mince

trita'tutto *nm inv* (*elettrico*) [food] processor

'trito *a* **~ e ritrito** well-worn, trite

tri'tolo *nm* TNT

tri'tone *nm* (*mitologia*) Triton; *Zool* newt

'trittico *nm* triptych

trit'tongo *nm* triphthong

tritu'rare *vt* chop finely

triumvi'rato *nm* triumvirate

tri'vella *nf* drill

trivel'lare *vt* drill

trivi'ale *a* vulgar

tro'feo *nm* trophy

troglo'dita *nmf* (*preistoria*) cave-dweller; *fig* Neanderthal

'trogolo *nm* (*per maiali*) trough

'troia *nf* sow; *vulg* bitch; (*sessuale*) whore

'tromba *nf* trumpet; *Auto* horn; (*delle scale*) well; **partire in ~** dive in head first. **~ d'aria** whirlwind. **~ di Eustachio** Eustachian tube. **~ di Falloppio** Fallopian tube. **~ delle scale** stairwell

trom'bare *vt vulg* bonk; (*fam: in esame*) fail ● *vi vulg* bonk

trom'betta *nm* toy trumpet

trombetti'ere *nm* bugler

trombet'tista *nmf* trumpet-player

trom'bone *nm* trombone

trom'bosi *nf* thrombosis. **~ coronarica** coronary thrombosis

tron'care *vt* sever; truncate ⟨*parola*⟩

tron'chese *nm* wire cutters *pl*

tronche'sino *nm* (*per le unghie*) nail clippers *pl*

tron'chetto *nm* **~ natalizio** Yule log

'tronco *a* truncated; **licenziare in ~** fire on the spot ● *nm* trunk; (*di strada*) section. **~ d'albero** tree trunk. **~ di cono** truncated cone

tron'cone *nm* stump

troneggi'are *vi* **~ su** tower over

'trono *nm* throne

tropi'cale *a* tropical

'tropici *nmpl* Tropics

'tropico *nm* tropic. **~ del Cancro** Tropic of Cancer. **~ del Capricorno** Tropic of Capricorn

'troppo *a* too much; (*con nomi plurali*) too many ● *pron* too much; (*plurale*) too many; (*troppo tempo*) too long; **troppi** (*troppa gente*) too many people; **me ne hai dato ~** you gave me too much ● *adv* too; (*con verbi*) too much; **~ stanco** too tired; **ho mangiato ~** I ate too much; **hai fame? – non ~** are you hungry? – not very; **sentirsi di ~** feel unwanted

'trota *nf* trout. **~ di mare** sea trout. **~ salmonata** salmon trout

trot'tare *vi* trot

trotterel'lare *vi* trot along; ⟨*bambino:*⟩ toddle

'trotto *nm* trot; **andare al ~** trot

'trottola *nf* [spinning] top; (*movimento*) spin

troupe *nf inv* **~ televisiva** camera crew

trousse *nf inv* (*per trucco*) make-up bag

tro'vare *vt* find; (*scoprire*) find out; (*incontrare*) meet; (*ritenere*) think; **andare a ~** go to see

trova'robe *nmf* (*persona*) props *sg*

tro'varsi *vr* find oneself; ⟨*luogo:*⟩ be; (*sentirsi*) feel

tro'vata *nf* bright idea. **~ pubblicitaria** advertising gimmick

trova'tello, -a *nmf* foundling

truc'care *vt* make up; cook ⟨*libri contabili*⟩; soup up ⟨*motore*⟩; rig ⟨*partita, elezioni*⟩

truc'carsi *vr* put one's make-up on

truc'cato *a* made-up; ⟨*libri contabili*⟩ cooked; ⟨*partita, elezioni*⟩ rigged; ⟨*motore*⟩ souped up

trucca|'tore, -'trice *nmf* make-up artist

'trucco *nm* (*cosmetici*) make-up; (*imbroglio*) trick; **trucchi pl del mestiere** tricks of the trade

'truce *a* fierce; ⟨*delitto*⟩ savage

truci'dare *vt* slay

trucio'lato *nm* chipboard

'truciolo *nm* shaving

trucu'lento *a* ⟨*delitto*⟩ savage; ⟨*film*⟩ violent

'truffa *nf* fraud

truf'fare *vt* defraud

truffa|'tore, -'trice *nmf* fraudster

'trullo *nm* traditional house with a conical roof found in Apulia

'truppa *nf* troops *pl*; (*gruppo*) group; **truppe pl d'assalto** assault troops

T-shirt *nf inv* tee-shirt, T-shirt

tu *pers pron* you; **sei tu?** is that you?; **l'hai fatto tu?** did you do it yourself?; **a tu per tu** in private; **darsi del tu** use the familiar *tu* to each other

'tua *vedi* **tuo**

'tuba *nf Mus* tuba; (*cappello*) top hat

tu'bare *vi* coo; ⟨*innamorati:*⟩ bill and coo

tuba'tura *nf* piping

tubazi'one *nf* piping; **tubazioni pl** piping *sg*, pipes

tuberco'lina *nf* tuberculin

tuberco'losi *nf* tuberculosis

'tubero *nm* tuber

tube'rosa *nf* tuberose

tu'betto *nm* tube. **~ di colore** tube of paint

tu'bino *nm* (*vestito*) shift; (*cappello*) bowler, derby *Am*

'tubo *nm* pipe; *Anat* canal; **non ho capito un ~** *fam* I understood zilch. **~ digerente** alimentary canal. **~ a raggi catodici** cathode-ray tube. **~ di scappamento** exhaust [pipe]. **~ di scarico** waste pipe

tubo'lare *a* tubular

'tue *vedi* **tuo**

tuf'fare *vt* plunge

tuf'farsi *vr* dive; **'vietato ~'** 'no diving'

'tuffo *nm* dive; (*bagno*) dip; **ho avuto un ~ al cuore** my heart leapt into my mouth. **~ di testa** dive

'tufo *nm* tufa

tu'gurio *nm* hovel

tuli'pano *nm* tulip

'tulle *nm* tulle

tume'fatto *a* swollen

tumefazi'one *nf* swelling

'tumido *a* swollen

tu'more *nm* tumour. **~ benigno** benign tumour. **~ maligno** malignant tumour

tumulazi'one *nf* burial

'tumulo *nm* (*di pietre*) cairn

tu'multo *nm* turmoil; (*sommossa*) riot

tumultu'oso *a* tumultuous

tung'steno *nm* tungsten

'tunica *nf* tunic

Tuni'sia *nf* Tunisia

tuni'sino *a* & *nmf* Tunisian

'tunnel *nm inv* tunnel. **~ sotto la Manica** Channel Tunnel

'tuo (**il ~** *m*, **la tua** *f*, **i tuoi** *mpl*, **le tue** *fpl*) *poss a* your; **è tua questa macchina?** is this car yours?; **un ~ amico** a friend of yours; **~ padre** your father ● *poss pron* yours; **i tuoi** your folk

tu'oi *vedi* **tuo**

tuo'nare *vi* thunder

tu'ono *nm* thunder

tu'orlo *nm* yolk

tu'racciolo *nm* stopper; (*di sughero*) cork

tu'rarsi *vr* become blocked; **~ le orecchie** stick one's fingers in one's ears; **~ il naso** hold one's nose

'turba *nf* (*folla*) rabble. **~ psichica** mental illness

turba'mento *nm* disturbance; (*sconvolgimento*) upsetting. **~ della quiete pubblica** breach of the peace

tur'bante *nm* turban

tur'bare *vt* upset

tur'barsi *vr* get upset

tur'bato *a* upset

tur'bina *nf* turbine

turbi'nare *vi* whirl

'turbine *nm* whirl. **~ di polvere** dust storm. **~ di vento** whirlwind

'turbo *nm inv* turbo

turbocompres'sore *nm* *Tech* turbocharger

turbo'lento *a* turbulent

turbo'lenza *nf* turbulence

turboreat'tore *nm* turbo-jet

tur'chese *a* & *nmf* turquoise

Tur'chia *nf* Turkey

tur'chino *a* & *nm* deep blue

'turco, -a *a* Turkish ● *nmf* Turk; **fumare come un ~** smoke like a chimney; **bestemmiare come un ~** swear like a trooper ● *nm* (*lingua*) Turkish; *fig* double Dutch

'turgido *a* turgid

tu'rismo *nm* tourism

tu'rista *nmf* tourist

tu'ristico *a* tourist *attrib*

tur'nista *nmf* shift-worker

'turno *nm* turn; **a ~** in turn; **fare a ~** take turns; **fare i turni** work shifts; **di ~** on duty. **~ eliminatorio** heat. **~ di giorno** day shift. **~ di guardia** guard duty. **~ di lavoro** shift. **~ di notte** night shift; **del ~ ~ ~** night shift *attrib*; **fare il ~ ~ ~** be on night shift

'turpe *a* base

turpi'loquio *nm* foul language

'tuta *nf* overalls *pl*; *Sport* tracksuit. **~ da ginnastica** tracksuit. **~ da lavoro** overalls *pl*. **~ mimetica** camouflage. **~ spaziale** spacesuit. **~ subacquea** wetsuit

tu'tela *nf* *Jur* guardianship; (*protezione*) protection. **~ dell'ambiente** environmental protection

tute'lare *vt* protect

tu'tina *nf* sleepsuit; (*da danza*) leotard

tu'tore, -'trice *nmf* guardian

'tutta *nf* **mettercela ~ per fare qcsa** go flat out for sth

'tutto *a* whole; (*con nomi plurali*) all; (*ogni*) every; **tutta la classe** the whole class, all the class; **tutti gli alunni** all the pupils; **a tutta velocità** at full speed; **ho aspettato ~ il giorno** I waited all day [long]; **vestito di ~ punto** all kitted out; **in ~ il mondo** all over the world; **noi tutti** all of us; **era tutta contenta** she was delighted; **tutti e due** both; **tutti e tre** all three ● *pron* all; (*tutta la gente*) everybody; (*tutte le cose*) everything; (*qualunque cosa*) anything; **c'è ancora del dolce? – no, l'ho mangiato ~** is there still some cake? – no, I ate it all; **le finestre sono pulite, le ho lavate tutte** the windows are clean, I washed them all; **raccontami ~** tell me everything; **lo sanno tutti** everybody knows; **è capace di ~** he's capable of anything; **~ compreso** all in; **del ~** quite; **in ~** altogether ● *adv* completely; **tutt'a un tratto** all at once; **tutt'altro** not at all; **tutt'altro che** anything but ● *nm* whole; **tentare il ~ per ~** go for broke; **~ compreso** all-inclusive. **~ esaurito** *Theat* full house

tutto'fare *a inv* & *nmf* [**impiegato**] **~** general handyman

tut'tora *adv* still

tutù *nm inv* tutu; (*lungo*) ballet dress

tv *nf inv* TV. **tv interattiva** interactive TV. **tv via cavo** cable TV

tweed *nm inv* tweed

Uu

ubbidi'ente *a* obedient
ubbidiente'mente *adv* obediently
ubbidi'enza *nf* obedience
ubbi'dire *vi* ~ (a) obey
ubi'cato *a* located
ubicazi'one *nf* location
ubiquità *nf* **non ho il dono dell'**~ I can't be in two places at once
ubria'care *vt* get drunk
ubria'carsi *vr* get drunk; ~ **di** *fig* become intoxicated with
ubria'chezza *nf* drunkenness; **in stato di** ~ inebriated; **in stato di** ~ **molesta** drunk and disorderly
ubri'aco, -a *a* drunk; ~ **fradicio** dead *o* blind drunk ● *nmf* drunk
ubria'cone *nm* drunkard ● *a* **un marito** ~ a drunkard of a husband
uccelli'era *nf* aviary
uccel'lino *nm* baby bird
uc'cello *nm* bird; (*vulg: pene*) cock. ~ **acquatico** water fowl. ~ **da cacciagione** game bird. ~ **del malaugurio** bird of ill omen. ~ **notturno** night *o* nocturnal bird. ~ **del paradiso** bird of paradise. ~ **di passo** bird of passage. ~ **rapace** bird of prey
uc'cidere *vt* kill
uc'cidersi *vr* kill oneself; (*morire*) be killed
+uccio *suff* **boccuccia** *nf* pretty little mouth; **calduccio** *nm* cosy warmth; **c'è un bel calduccio** it's nice and cosy; **tesoruccio** *nm* sweetie; **avvocatuccio** *nm pej* small town lawyer; **cosuccia** *nf* trifle; **è una cosuccia da niente** it's nothing; **doloruccio** *nm* twinge; **vestituccio** *nm pej* skimpy little dress
uccisi'one *nf* killing
uc'ciso *pp di* **uccidere**
ucci'sore *nm* killer
U'craina *nf* **l'**~ the Ukraine
u'craino, -a *a & nmf* Ukrainian
u'dente *a* **i non udenti** the hearing-impaired
u'dibile *a* audible
udi'enza *nf* audience; (*colloquio*) interview; *Jur* hearing. ~ **a porte chiuse** hearing in camera
u'dire *vt* hear
udi'tivo *a* auditory
u'dito *nm* hearing
udi'tore, -'trice *nmf* listener; *Sch* unregistered student (*allowed to sit in on lectures*)
udi'torio *nm* audience
UE *abbr* (**Unione Europea**) EU
'uffa *int* (*con impazienza*) come on!; (*con tono seccato*) damn!

uffici'ale *a* official ● *nm* officer; (*funzionario*) official; **pubblico** ~ public official. ~ **dell'esercito** army officer. ~ **giudiziario** clerk of the court. ~ **sanitario** health officer. ~ **dello Stato civile** registrar
ufficialità *nf* official status
ufficializ'zare *vt* make official, officialize
ufficial'mente *adv* officially
uf'ficio *nm* office; (*dovere*) duty; (*reparto*) department; **andare in** ~ go to the office; **grazie a suoi buoni uffici** thanks to his kind offices. ~ **acquisti** purchasing department. ~ **cambi** bureau de change, exchange bureau. ~ **di collocamento** employment office, jobcentre *Br*. **U**~ **Dazi e Dogana** Customs and Excise. ~ **funebre** *Relig* funeral service. ~ **informazioni** information office. ~ **di informazioni turistiche** tourist information office *o* centre. ~ **oggetti smarriti** lost property office, lost and found *Am*. ~ **del personale** personnel department. ~ **postale** post office. ~ **prenotazioni** advance booking office. ~ **della redazione** newspaper office. ~ **del turismo** tourist office. ~ **turistico** tourist office
ufficiosa'mente *adv* unofficially
uffici'oso *a* unofficial
uff *int* phew!
'ufo[1] *nm inv* ufo
'ufo[2]: **a** ~ *adv* without paying
ufolo'gia *nf* ufology
U'ganda *nf* Uganda
ugan'dese *a & nmf* Ugandan
uggiosità *nf* dullness
uggi'oso *a* boring
uguagli'anza *nf* equality
uguagli'are *vt* make equal; (*essere uguale*) equal; (*livellare*) level
uguagli'arsi *vr* ~ **a** compare oneself to
ugu'ale *a* equal; (*lo stesso*) the same; (*simile*) like; **due più due è** ~ **a quattro** two plus two equals four ● *nm Math* equals sign; **che non ha** ~ unequalled
ugual'mente *adv* equally; (*malgrado tutto*) all the same
'ulcera *nf* ulcer. ~ **gastrica** gastric ulcer. ~ **peptica** peptic ulcer
u'liva *nf vedi* **oliva**
uli'veto *nm* olive grove
u'livo *nm* olive[-tree]
'ulna *nf Anat* ulna
ulteri'ore *a* further
ulterior'mente *adv* further
ultima'mente *adv* lately
ulti'mare *vt* complete

ulti'matum *nm inv* ultimatum

ulti'missime *nfpl Journ* stop press, latest news *sg*

'**ultimo** *a* last; (*notizie ecc*) latest; (*più lontano*) farthest; *fig* ultimate; (*prezzo*) rock-bottom ● *nm* last; **fino all'** ~ to the last; **per** ~ at the end; **l'~ piano** the top floor

ultimo'genito, -a *nmf* last-born

ultrà *nmf inv Sport* fanatical supporter

ultramo'derno *a* ultra-modern

ultrapi'atto *a* ultra-thin

ultrapo'tente *a* extra-strong

ultra'rapido *a* extra-fast

ultraresi'stente *a* extra-strong

ultrasen'sibile *a* ultrasensitive

ultra'sonico *a* ultrasonic

ultrasu'ono *nm* ultrasound

ultrater'reno *a* (*vita*) after death

ultravio'letto *a* ultraviolet

ulu'lare *vi* howl

ulu'lato *nm* howling; **gli ululati** the howls, the howling

umana'mente *adv* (*trattare*) humanely; ~ **impossibile** not humanly possible

uma'nesimo *nm* humanism

uma'nista *nmf* humanist

umanità *nf* humanity

umani'tario *a* humanitarian

u'mano *a* human; (*benevolo*) humane

'**Umbria** *nf* Umbria

'**umbro, -a** *a & nmf* Umbrian

umet'tare *vt* moisten

umidifica'tore *nm* humidifier

umidità *nf* dampness; (*di clima*) humidity

'**umido** *a* damp; (*clima*) humid; (*mani, occhi*) moist ● *nm* dampness; **in** ~ *Culin* stewed

'**umile** *a* humble

umili'ante *a* humiliating

umili'are *vt* humiliate

umili'arsi *vr* humble oneself

umiliazi'one *nf* humiliation

umil'mente *adv* humbly

umiltà *nf* humility

u'more *nm* humour; (*stato d'animo*) mood; **di cattivo/buon** ~ in a bad/good mood

umo'rismo *nm* humour

umo'rista *nmf* humorist

umoristica'mente *adv* humorously

umo'ristico *a* humorous

un *vedi* **uno**

un' *vedi* **uno**

'**una** *vedi* **uno**

u'nanime *a* unanimous

unanime'mente *adv* unanimously

unanimità *nf* unanimity; **all'~** unanimously

unci'nare *vt* hook

unci'nato *a* hooked; (*parentesi*) angle *attrib*

unci'netto *nm* crochet hook

un'cino *nm* hook

undi'cenne *a & nmf* eleven-year-old

undi'cesimo *a & nm* eleventh

'**undici** *a & nm* eleven

'**ungere** *vt* grease; (*sporcare*) get greasy; *Relig* anoint; (*blandire*) flatter

'**ungersi** *vr* (*con olio solare*) oil oneself; ~ **le mani** get one's hands greasy

unghe'rese *a & nmf* Hungarian ● *nm* (*lingua*) Hungarian

Unghe'ria *nf* Hungary

'**unghia** *nf* nail; (*di animale*) claw; **cadere sotto le unghie di qcno** fall into sb's clutches. ~ **fessa** cloven hoof

unghi'ata *nf* (*graffio*) scratch

ungu'ento *nm* ointment

unica'mente *adv* only

unicellu'lare *a* single-cell, unicellular

unicità *nf* uniqueness

'**unico** *a* only; (*singolo*) single; (*incomparabile*) unique

uni'corno *nm* unicorn

unidimensio'nale *a* one-dimensional

unidirezio'nale *a* unidirectional

unifamili'are *a* one-family

unifi'care *vt* unify

unificazi'one *nf* unification

unifor'mare *vt* level

unifor'marsi *vr* conform (**a** to)

uni'forme *a* uniform ● *nf* uniform. ~ **di gala** *Mil* mess dress

uniformità *nf* uniformity

unilate'rale *a* unilateral

unilateral'mente *adv* unilaterally

uninomi'nale *a Pol* single-candidate

uni'one *nf* union; (*armonia*) unity. **U~ economica e monetaria** Economic and Monetary Union. **U~ Europea** European Union. **U~ Monetaria Europea** European Monetary Union. ~ **sindacale** trade union, labor union *Am*. **U~ Sovietica** Soviet Union

u'nire *vt* unite; (*collegare*) join; blend (*colori ecc*)

u'nirsi *vr* unite; (*collegarsi*) join

'**unisex** *a inv* unisex

u'nisono *nm* **all'~** in unison

unità *nf inv* unity; (*Math, Mil, reparto ecc*) unit; *Comput* drive. ~ **di backup a nastro** *Comput* tape backup drive. ~ **centrale di elaborazione** *Comput* central processing unit, CPU. ~ **floppy disk** *Comput* floppy disk drive. ~ **di inizializzazione** *Comput* boot drive. ~ **di memoria di massa** *Comput* mass storage device. ~ **di misura** unit of measurement. ~ **a nastro magnetico** *Comput* tapedrive. ~ **periferica** *Comput* peripheral. ~ **di produzione** factory unit. ~ **socio-sanitaria locale** local health centre. ~ **di visualizzazione** *Comput* visual display unit, VDU

uni'tario *a* unitary; **prezzo** ~ unit price

u'nito *a* united; (*tinta*) plain; (*comunità*) tight-knit

univer'sale *a* universal

universaliz'zare *vt* universalize

universal'mente *adv* universally

università *nf inv* university

universi'tario, -a *a* university *attrib* ● *nmf* (*insegnante*) university lecturer; (*studente*) undergraduate

uni'verso *nm* universe

u'nivoco *a* unambiguous

'unto *pp di* ungere ● *a* greasy ● *nm* grease

untu'oso *a* greasy

uno, -a *art indef* a; (*davanti a vocale o h muta*) an; **un esempio** an example; ● *pron* one; **a ~ a ~** one by one; **~ alla volta** one at a time; **l'~ e l'altro** both [of them]; **né l'~ né l'altro** neither [of them]; **~ di noi** one of us; **~ fa quello che può** you do what you can ● *a* a, one ● *nm* (*numerale*) one; (*un tale*) some man ● *nf* some woman

unzi'one *nf* **l'Estrema U~** Extreme Unction, last rites

u'omo *nm* (*pl* **uomini**) man; **'uomini'** (*bagni*) 'gents', 'men's room'. **~ d'affari** business man. **~ di colore** black man. **~ di fiducia** right-hand man. **~ di mondo** man of the world. **~-oggetto** toy boy. **~ delle pulizie** cleaner. **~ sandwich** sandwich-man. **~ di Stato** statesman. **~ della strada** man on the street

u'ovo *nm* (*pl f* **uova**) egg. **uova** *pl* **al bacon** bacon and eggs. **~ barzotto** *o* **bazzotto** soft-boiled egg. **~ in camicia** poached egg. **~ di Colombo** obvious simple solution. **~ alla coque** boiled egg. **~ all'occhio di bue** fried egg. **~ all'ostrica** raw egg. **~ di Pasqua** Easter egg. **uova** *pl* **al prosciutto** ham and eggs. **~ sodo** hard-boiled egg. **~ strapazzato** scrambled egg. **~ al tegamino** fried egg

upgra'dabile *a* upgradeable

'upupa *nf* hoopoe

ura'gano *nm* hurricane

u'ranio *nm* uranium

urba'nesimo *nm* urbanization

urba'nista *nmf* town planner

urba'nistica *nf* town planning

urba'nistico *a* urban

urbaniz'zare *vt* urbanize

urbanizzazi'one *nf* urbanization

ur'bano *a* urban; (*cortese*) urbane

u'rea *nf* urea

u'retra *nf Anat* urethra

ur'gente *a* urgent

urgente'mente *adv* urgently

ur'genza *nf* urgency; **in caso d'~** in an emergency; **d'~** (*misura, chiamata*) emergency *attrib*; **operare d'~** perform an emergency operation on

'urgere *vi* be urgent

u'rina *nf* urine

uri'nare *vi* urinate

ur'lare *vi* shout, yell; (*cane, vento:*) howl

'urlo *nm* (*pl m* **urli**, *pl f* **urla**) shout; (*di cane, vento*) howling

'urna *nf* urn; (*elettorale*) ballot box; **andare alle urne** go to the polls

urrà *int* hurrah!

URSS *nf abbr* (**Unione delle Repubbliche Socialiste Sovietiche**) USSR

ur'tare *vt* knock against; (*scontrarsi*) bump into; *fig* irritate

ur'tarsi *vr* collide; *fig* clash

'urto *nm* knock; (*scontro*) crash; (*contrasto*) conflict; *fig* clash; **d'~** (*misure, terapia*) shock

U.S.A. *nmpl* US[A] *sg*

usa e getta *a inv* (*rasoio, siringa*) throw-away, disposable

u'sanza *nf* custom; (*moda*) fashion

u'sare *vt* use; (*impiegare*) employ; (*esercitare*) exercise; **~ fare qcsa** be in the habit of doing sth ● *vi* (*essere di moda*) be fashionable; **non si usa più** it is out of fashion; (*attrezzatura, espressione:*) it's not used any more

u'sato *a* used; (*non nuovo*) second-hand ● *nm* second-hand goods *pl*; **dell'~** second-hand; **fuori dell'~** unusual

u'sbeco, -a *a & nmf* Uzbekistani

u'scente *a* (*presidente*) outgoing

usci'ere *nm* usher

'uscio *nm* door

u'scire *vi* come out; (*andare fuori*) go out; (*sfuggire*) get out; (*essere sorteggiato*) come up; (*giornale:*) come out; **~ da** *Comput* exit from, quit; **~ di strada** leave the road

u'scita *nf* exit, way out; (*spesa*) outlay; (*di autostrada*) junction; (*battuta*) witty remark; (*in ginnastica artistica*) dismount; **uscite** *pl Fin* outgoings; **essere in libera ~** be off duty. **~ di servizio** back door. **~ di sicurezza** emergency exit

usi'gnolo *nm* nightingale

'uso *nm* use; (*abitudine*) custom; (*usanza*) usage; **fuori ~** out of use; **per ~ esterno** (*medicina*) for external use only; **~ e dosi** use and dosage

us'saro *nm* hussar

U.S.S.L. *nf abbr* (**Unità Socio-Sanitaria Locale**) local health centre

ustio'narsi *vr* burn oneself

ustio'nato, -a *nmf* burns case ● *a* burnt

usti'one *nf* burn; **ustioni di primo grado** first-degree burns

usu'ale *a* usual

usual'mente *adv* usually

usucapi'one *nf Jur* usucaption

usufru'ire *vi* **~ di** take advantage of, make use of

usufruttu'ario, -a *nmf* user, usufructuary *fml*

usu'frutto *nm Jur* use, usufruct *fml*

u'sura *nf* usury

usu'raio *nm* usurer

usur'pare *vt* usurp

usurpa'tore, -'trice *nmf* usurper

u'tensile *nm* tool; *Culin* utensil; **cassetta degli utensili** tool box; **utensili** *pl* **da cucina** kitchen utensils

u'tente *nmf* user. **~ finale** end user. **utenti** *pl* **della strada** road users

u'tenza *nf* use; (*utenti*) users *pl*; **~ finale** end users *pl*

ute'rino *a* uterine

'utero *nm* womb

'utile *a* useful ● *nm Comm* profit; **unire l'~ al dilettevole** combine business with pleas-

ure. **~ su cambi** foreign exchange gain. **~ sul capitale investito** return on investment
utilità *nf* usefulness, utility; *Comput* utility
utili'tario, -a *a* utilitarian ● *nf Auto* small car
utilita'ristico *a* utilitarian
u'tility *nm* utility
utiliz'zare *vt* utilize
utilizzazi'one *nf* utilization
uti'lizzo *nm* use
util'mente *adv* usefully
Uto'pia *nf* Utopia

uto'pista *nmf* Utopian
uto'pistico *a* Utopian
UVA *nmpl abbr* (**ultravioletto prossimo**) UV
'uva *nf* grapes *pl*; **chicco d'~** grape. **~ bianca** white grapes. **~ nera** black grapes. **~ passa** raisins *pl*. **~ sultanina** currants *pl*. **~ da tavola** [eating] grapes. **~ da vino** wine grapes
u'vetta *nf* raisins *pl*
uxori'cida *nm* wife-killer, uxoricide *fml* ● *nf* husband-killer
Uzbeki'stan *nm* Uzbekistan

....

Vv

....

va' *vedi* **andare**
va'cante *a* vacant
va'canza *nf* holiday, vacation *Am*; [**giorno di**] **~** holiday; (*posto vacante*) vacancy; **vacanze** *pl* holidays, vacation *Am*; *Univ* vacation, vac *fam*. **essere in ~** be on holiday/vacation; **prendersi una ~** take a holiday/vacation; **andare in ~** go on holiday/vacation; **è ~** it's a holiday. **vacanze** *pl* **estive** summer holidays/vacation. **vacanze** *pl* **di Natale** Christmas holidays/vacation. **vacanze** *pl* **di Pasqua** Easter holidays/vacation. **vacanze** *pl* **scolastiche** school holidays/vacation
'vacca *nf* cow. **~ da latte** dairy cow
vac'caro m, -a *nf* cowherd
vacci'nare *vt* vaccinate; **farsi ~** get vaccinated
vaccinazi'one *nf* vaccination
vac'cino *nm* vaccine
vacil'lante *a* tottering; ⟨*oggetto*⟩ wobbly; ⟨*luce*⟩ flickering; *fig* wavering
vacil'lare *vi* totter; ⟨*oggetto:*⟩ wobble; ⟨*luce:*⟩ flicker; *fig* waver
'vacuo *a* (*vano*) vain; *fig* empty ● *nm* vacuum
'vado *vedi* **andare**
vaffan'culo *int vulg* fuck off!
vagabon'daggio *nm Jur* vagrancy
vagabon'dare *vi* wander
vaga'bondo *a* ⟨*cane*⟩ stray; **gente** *pl* **vagabonda** tramps ● *nmf* tramp
vaga'mente *adv* vaguely
va'gante *a* wandering; **mina ~** floating mine; **proiettile ~** stray bullet
va'gare *vi* wander
vagheggi'are *vt* long for
va'ghezza *nf* vagueness
va'gina *nf* vagina
vagi'nale *a* vaginal
va'gire *vi* whimper
va'gito *nm* whimper

'vaglia *nm inv* money order. **~ bancario** bank draft. **~ cambiario** promissory note. **~ internazionale** international money order. **~ postale** postal order
vagli'are *vt* sift; *fig* weigh
'vaglio *nm* sieve
'vago *a* vague
vagon'cino *nm* (*di funivia*) car. **~ a piattaforma** flat[bed] wagon
va'gone *nm* (*per passeggeri*) carriage, car; (*per merci*) truck, wagon. **~ bagagliaio** luggage van, baggage car *Am*. **~ frigorifero** refrigerator van. **~ letto** sleeper. **~ postale** mail coach. **~ ristorante** restaurant car, dining car
vai'olo *nm* smallpox
va'langa *nf* avalanche
val'chiria *nf* Valkyrie
val'dese *a & nmf* Waldensian
va'lente *a* skilful
va'lenza *nf Chem* valency; (*fig: valore*) value
va'lere *vi* be worth; (*contare*) count; ⟨*regola:*⟩ apply (**per** to); (*essere valido*) be valid; **far ~ i propri diritti** assert one's rights; **farsi ~** assert oneself; **non vale!** that's not fair!; **tanto vale che me ne vada** I might as well go ● *vt* **~ qcsa a qcno** (*procurare*) earn sb sth; **valerne la pena** be worth it; **vale la pena di vederlo** it's worth seeing; **valersi di** avail oneself of
valeri'ana *nf* valerian
va'levole *a* valid
'valgo *a* **alluce ~** hallux valgus; **ginocchia** *pl* **valghe** knock knees
vali'care *vt* cross
'valico *nm* pass
valida'mente *adv* validly; (*efficacemente*) efficiently; ⟨*contribuire*⟩ effectively
validità *nf inv* validity; **con ~ illimitata** valid indefinitely
'valido *a* valid; (*efficace*) efficient; ⟨*contributo*⟩ valuable

valige'ria nf (fabbrica) leather factory; (negozio) leather goods shop

vali'getta nf small case; (per attrezzi) box. ~ **del pronto soccorso** first aid kit. ~ **ventiquattrore** overnight bag

va'ligia nf suitcase; **fare le valigie** pack; fig pack one's bags. ~ **diplomatica** diplomatic bag

val'lata nf valley

'valle nf valley; **a ~** downstream

val'letta nf TV assistant

val'letto nm valet; TV assistant

'vallo nm wall; **il ~ Adriano** Hadrian's Wall

val'lone nm (valle) deep valley

val'lone, -a a & nmf Walloon

va'lore nm value, worth; (merito) merit; (coraggio) valour; **valori** pl Comm securities; **di ~** (oggetto) valuable; **oggetti di ~** valuables; **di grande ~** of great value; (medico, scienziato) top attrib; **senza ~** worthless; **a ~ aggiunto** value-added. ~ **bollato** revenue stamp. ~ **contabile** book value. ~ **effettivo** real value. ~ **di mercato** market value. ~ **mobiliare** security. ~ **nominale** nominal value. ~ **di realizzo** break-up value. ~ **di riscatto** surrender value

valoriz'zare vt (mettere in valore) use to advantage; (aumentare di valore) increase the value of; (migliorare l'aspetto di) enhance

valoriz'zarsi vr **il paese ha bisogno di ~ migliorando…** the country needs to enhance the value of its assets by improving…

valorosa'mente adv courageously

valo'roso a courageous

'valso pp di **valere**

va'luta nf currency. ~ **a corso legale** legal tender. ~ **estera** foreign currency

valu'tare vt value; weigh up (situazione)

valu'tario a (mercato, norme) currency attrib

valu'tativo a for evaluation, evaluative

valutazi'one nf valuation

'valva nf valve

'valvola nf valve; Electr fuse. ~ **a farfalla** butterfly valve. ~ **pneumatica** air valve. ~ **di sicurezza** anche fig safety valve

'valzer nm inv waltz

vamp nf inv vamp

vam'pata nf blaze; (di calore) blast; (al viso) flush

vam'piro nm vampire; fig blood-sucker

va'nadio nm vanadium

vanaglori'oso a vainglorious

vana'mente adv (inutilmente) in vain; (con vanità) vainly

van'dalico a **atto ~** act of vandalism

vanda'lismo nm vandalism

vandalizzare vt vandalize

vandalizzazione nf vandalizing

'vandalo, -a nmf vandal

vaneggia'mento nm delirium

vaneggi'are vi rave

va'nesio a conceited

'vanga nf spade

van'gare vt dig

van'gata nf (quantità) spadeful; (azione) blow with a spade

van'gelo nm Gospel; (fam: verità) gospel [truth]

vanifi'care vt nullify

va'niglia nf vanilla

vanigli'ato a (zucchero) vanilla

vanil'lina nf vanillin

vanità nf vanity

vanitosa'mente adv vainly

vani'toso a vain

'vano a vain ● nm (stanza) room; (spazio vuoto) hollow. ~ **doccia** shower room. ~ **portabagagli** Auto boot, trunk Am

van'taggio nm advantage; Sport lead; Tennis advantage; **trarre ~ da qcsa** derive benefit from sth

vantaggiosa'mente adv advantageously

vantaggi'oso a advantageous

van'tare vt praise; (possedere) boast

van'tarsi vr boast

vante'ria nf boasting; **vanterie** pl boasting

'vanto nm boast

'vanvera nf **a ~** at random; **parlare a ~** talk nonsense

va'pore nm steam; (di benzina, cascata) vapour; **a ~** steam attrib; **al ~** Culin steamed; **battello a ~** steamboat. ~ **acqueo** steam, water vapour

vapo'retto nm ferry

vapori'era nf steam engine

vaporiz'zare vt vaporize

vaporizza'tore nm spray

vapo'roso a (vestito) filmy; **capelli** pl **vaporosi** big hair

va'rano nm monitor [lizard]

va'rare vt launch

var'care vt cross

'varco nm passage; **aspettare al ~** lie in wait

vare'china nf bleach

vari'abile a changeable, variable ● nf Math variable

variabilità nf changeableness, variability

varia'mente adv variously

vari'ante nf variant

vari'are vt/i vary; ~ **di umore** change one's mood

vari'ato a varied

variazi'one nf variation

va'rice nf varicose vein

vari'cella nf chickenpox

vari'coso a varicose

varie'gato a variegated

varietà nf inv variety ● nm inv variety show

'vario a varied; (al pl, parecchi) various; **varie** pl (molti) several; **varie ed eventuali** any other business

vario'pinto a multicoloured

'varo nm launch

Var'savia Warsaw

vas'aio nm potter

'vasca nf tub; (piscina) pool; (lunghezza)

length. **~ da bagno** bath. **~ di sviluppo** *Phot* developing tank

va'scello *nm* vessel; **capitano di ~** captain

va'schetta *nf* tub; *Phot* tray. **~ per il ghiaccio** ice-tray

vasco'lare *a Anat, Bot* vascular

vasecto'mia *nf* vasectomy

vase'lina *nf* Vaseline®

vasel'lame *nm* china. **~ d'oro/d'argento** gold/silver plate

va'setto *nm* small pot; (*per marmellata*) jam jar

'vaso *nm* pot; (*da fiori*) vase; *Anat* vessel; (*per cibi*) jar. **~ da notte** chamberpot. **~ sanguigno** blood vessel

vasocostrit'tore *a* vasoconstrictor

vasodilata'tore *a* vasodilator

vas'sallo *nm* vassal

vas'soio *nm* tray

vastità *nf* vastness

'vasto *a* vast; **di vaste vedute** broadminded

Vati'cano *nm* Vatican

vati'cinio *nm* prophecy

vattela'pesca *adv fam* God knows

'vattene! go away!; *vedi* andarsene

VCR *abbr* (*videoregistratore*) VCR

ve *pers pron* you; **ve l'ho dato** I gave it to you

'vecchia *nf* old woman

vecchi'aia *nf* old age

'vecchio, -a *a* old ● *nmf* old man; old woman; **i vecchi** old people; **~ mio** old man

'veccia *nf* vetch

'vece *nf in* **~ di** in place of; **fare le veci di qcno** take sb's place

ve'dente *a* **i non ~** the visually handicapped

ve'dere *vt* see; see, watch (*film, partita*); **far ~** show; **farsi ~** show one's face; **non si vede** (*macchia, imperfezione:*) it doesn't show; **non veder l'ora di fare qcsa** be raring to go; **non poter ~ qcno** not be able to stand the sight of sb; **vederci doppio** have double vision; **ne ho viste di tutti i colori** *fig* I've really seen life; **da ~** (*film, spettacolo*) not to be missed; **questo è da ~!** that remains to be seen!; **chi si vede!** *fam* look who it is! ● *vi* see

ve'dersi *vr* see oneself; (*reciproco*) see each other; **vedersela brutta** have a narrow escape

ve'detta *nf* (*luogo*) lookout; *Naut* patrol vessel

'vedova *nf* widow. **~ nera** *Zool* black widow [spider]

'vedovo *nm* widower

ve'duta *nf* view

vee'mente *a* vehement

vege'tale *a & nm* vegetable

vegetali'ano *a & nmf* vegan

vege'tare *vi* vegetate

vegetari'ano, -a *a & nmf* vegetarian

vegeta'tivo *a* vegetative

vegetazi'one *nf* vegetation

'vegeto *a vedi* vivo

veg'gente *nmf* clairvoyant

'veglia *nf* watch; **fare la ~** keep watch. **~ funebre** vigil

vegli'are *vi* be awake; **~ su** watch over

vegli'one *nm* **~ di capodanno** New Year's Eve celebration

veico'lare *vt* carry (*malattia*) ● *a* (*traffico*) vehicular

ve'icolo *nm* vehicle. **~ pesante** heavy goods vehicle, HGV. **~ spaziale** spacecraft

'vela *nf* sail; *Sport* sailing; **andare a gonfie vele** *fig* go beautifully; (*affari:*) be booming; **far ~** set sail. **~ di taglio** mainsail

ve'lare *vt* veil; (*fig: nascondere*) hide

ve'larsi *vr* (*vista:*) mist over; (*voce:*) go husky

velata'mente *adv* indirectly

ve'lato *a* veiled; (*occhi*) misty; (*collant*) sheer

vela'tura *nf* sails *pl*

'velcro® *nm* velcro

veleggi'are *vi* sail

ve'leno *nm* poison

velenosa'mente *adv* (*rispondere*) venomously

vele'noso *a* poisonous; (*frase*) venomous

ve'letta *nf* (*di cappello*) veil

ve'lico *a* (*circolo*) sailing *attrib*; **superficie velica** sail area

veli'ero *nm* sailing ship

ve'lina *nf* (*carta*) **~** tissue paper; (*copia*) carbon copy

ve'lista *nm* yachtsman ● *nf* yachtswoman

ve'livolo *nm* aircraft

velleità *nf inv* foolish ambition

vellei'tario *a* unrealistic

'vello *nm* fleece

vellu'tato *a* velvety

vel'luto *nm* velvet. **~ a coste** corduroy

'velo *nm* veil; (*di zucchero, cipria*) dusting; (*tessuto*) voile

ve'loce *a* fast

veloce'mente *adv* quickly

velo'cipede *nm* penny-farthing

velo'cista *nmf Sport* sprinter

velocità *nf inv* speed; (*Auto: marcia*) gear. **~ di clock** *Comput* clock speed. **~ di crociera** cruising speed. **~ di stampa** print speed

velociz'zare *vt* speed up

ve'lodromo *nm* cycle track

'vena *nf* vein; **essere in ~ di** be in the mood for. **~ poetica** poetic mood

ve'nale *a* venal; (*persona*) mercenary, venal

ve'nato *a* grainy

vena'torio *a* hunting *attrib*

vena'tura *nf* (*di legno*) grain; (*di foglia, marmo*) vein

ven'demmia *nf* grape harvest

vendemmi'are *vt* harvest

vendemmia|'tore, -'trice *nmf* grapepicker

'vendere *vt* sell

'vendersi *vr* sell oneself; **vendesi** for sale

ven'detta *nf* revenge. **~ trasversale** vendetta

vendi'care *vt* avenge

vendi'carsi *vr* take revenge, get one's revenge; **~ di qcno** take one's vengeance on sb; **~ di qcsa** take revenge for sth

vendicativa'mente *adv* vindictively

vendica'tivo *a* vindictive

vendica'|tore, -'trice *nmf* avenger

'vendita *nf* sale; **in ~** on sale. **~ all'asta** sale by auction. **~ di beneficenza** bring and buy sale. **~ per corrispondenza** mail-order; **azienda di ~ ~ ~** mail-order company; **catalogo di ~ ~ ~** mail-order catalogue. **~ al dettaglio** retailing. **~ all'ingrosso** wholesaling. **~ al minuto** retailing. **~ porta a porta** door-to-door selling. **~ a rate** hire purchase, installment plan *Am*

vendi'|tore, -'trice *nmf* seller. **~ ambulante** hawker, pedlar. **~ al dettaglio** retailer. **~ all'ingrosso** wholesaler. **~ al mercato** market trader. **~ al minuto** retailer

ven'duto *a* ⟨*merce*⟩ sold; ⟨*fig: arbitro*⟩ bent; **arbitro ~!** whose side are you on, ref!

vene'rabile, vene'rando *a* venerable

vene'rare *vt* revere

venerazi'one *nf* reverence

venerdì *nm inv* Friday; **di ~** on Fridays. **V~ Santo** Good Friday

'Venere *nf* Venus

ve'nereo *a* venereal

'Veneto *nm* Veneto

'veneto *a* from the Veneto

Ve'nezia *nf* Venice

venezi'ano, -a *a & nmf* Venetian ● *nf* ⟨*persiana*⟩ Venetian blind; *Culin* sweet bun

Vene'zuela *nm* Venezuela

venezue'lano, -a *a & nmf* Venezuelan

'vengo *vedi* **venire**

veni'ale *a* venial

ve'nire *vi* come; ⟨*riuscire*⟩ turn out; ⟨*costare*⟩ cost; ⟨*in passivi*⟩ be; **quanto viene?** how much is it?; **viene prodotto in serie** it's mass-produced; **~ a sapere** learn; **~ in mente** occur; **mi è venuto un dubbio** I've just had a doubt; **gli è venuta la febbre** he's got a temperature; **~ meno** ⟨*svenire*⟩ faint; **~ meno a un contratto** go back on a contract, renege on a contract; **~ via** come away; ⟨*staccarsi*⟩ come off; **mi viene da piangere** I feel like crying; **vieni a prendermi** come and pick me up; **vieni a trovarmi** come and see me; **nei giorni a ~** in [the] days to come

ve'noso *a* venous

ven'taglio *nm* fan

ven'tata *nf* gust [of wind]; *fig* breath

ven'tenne *a & nmf* twenty-year-old

ven'tesimo *a & nm* twentieth

'venti *a & nm* twenty

venti'lare *vt* ventilate, air; **~ un'idea** give an idea an airing; **poco ventilato** ⟨*stanza*⟩ airless

ventila'tore *nm* fan

ventilazi'one *nf* ventilation

ven'tina *nf* **una ~** ⟨*circa venti*⟩ about twenty

ventiquat'trore *nf inv* ⟨*valigia*⟩ overnight case ● *adv* **~ su ventiquattro** ⟨*lavorare*⟩ round-the-clock; ⟨*aperto*⟩ 24 hours

'vento *nm* wind; **c'è molto ~** it's very windy; **farsi ~** fan oneself. **~ contrario** headwind. **~ di prua** headwind. **~ di traverso** crosswind

'ventola *nf* fan

vento'lina *nf* fan. **~ di raffeddamento** *Comput* cooling fan

ven'tosa *nf* sucker

ven'toso *a* windy

'ventre *nm* stomach; ⟨*fig: di terra*⟩ bowels *pl*; **basso ~** lower abdomen

ventrico'lare *a Med* ventricular

ven'tricolo *nm* ventricle

ven'triloquo *nm* ventriloquist

ventu'nesimo *a & nm* twenty-first

ven'tuno *a & nm* twenty-one

ven'tura *nf* fortune; **andare alla ~** trust to luck

ven'turo *a* next

ve'nuta *nf* coming. **~ meno a** breaking

'vera *nf* ⟨*anello*⟩ wedding ring

vera'mente *adv* really

ve'randa *nf* veranda

ver'bale *a* verbal ● *nm* ⟨*di riunione*⟩ minutes *pl*. **~ di contravvenzione** fine

verbal'mente *adv* verbally

ver'bena *nf* verbena

'verbo *nm* verb; **il V~** *Relig* the Word. **~ ausiliare** auxiliary [verb]. **~ modale** modal auxiliary

ver'boso *a* verbose

ver'dastro *a* greenish

'verde *a* green; **~ d'invidia** green with envy ● *nm* green; ⟨*vegetazione*⟩ greenery; ⟨*semaforo*⟩ green light; **essere al ~** be broke. **~ bottiglia** bottle green. **~ oliva** olive green. **~ pisello** pea green. **~ pubblico** public parks *pl*

verdeggi'ante *a liter* verdant

verde'mare *a & nm inv* sea-green

verde'rame *nm* verdigris

ver'detto *nm* verdict. **~ di assoluzione** not guilty verdict. **~ di condanna** guilty verdict

ver'done *nm* greenfinch

ver'dura *nf* vegetables *pl*; **una ~** a vegetable; **verdure** *pl* **miste** mixed vegetables

'verga *nf* rod

ver'gato *a* lined

vergi'nale *a* virginal

'vergine *nf* virgin; *Astr* Virgo ● *a* virgin; ⟨*cassetta*⟩ blank

verginità *nf* virginity

ver'gogna *nf* shame; ⟨*timidezza*⟩ shyness

vergo'gnarsi *vr* feel ashamed; ⟨*essere timido*⟩ feel shy

vergognosa'mente *adv* shamefully

vergo'gnoso *a* ashamed; ⟨*timido*⟩ shy; ⟨*disonorevole*⟩ shameful

veridicità *nf* veracity

ve'rifica *nf* check. **~ dei bilanci** audit. **~ di cassa** cash check

verifi'cabile *a* verifiable

verifi'care *vt* check; verify ⟨*teoria*⟩

verifi'carsi *vr* come true

verifica'|tore, -'trice *nmf* checker

ve'rismo *nm* realism
verità *nf inv* truth
veriti'ero *a* truthful
'verme *nm* worm. **~ solitario** tapeworm
vermi'celli *nmpl* vermicelli *sg* (*pasta thinner than spaghetti*)
ver'mifugo *a* vermifugal ● *nm* vermifuge
ver'miglio *a & nm* vermilion
'vermut *nm inv* vermouth
ver'nacolo *nm* vernacular
ver'nice *nf* paint; (*trasparente*) varnish; (*pelle*) patent leather; *fig* veneer; **'~ fresca'** wet paint. **~ a spirito** spirit varnish
vernici'are *vt* paint; (*con vernice trasparente*) varnish
vernici'atura *nf* painting; (*con vernice trasparente*) varnishing; (*strato*) paintwork; *fig* veneer
vernis'sage *nm inv* vernissage
'vero *a* true; (*autentico*) real; (*perfetto*) perfect; **è ~?** is that so?; **~ e proprio** full-blown; **sei stanca, ~?** you're tired, aren't you; **non ti piace, ~?** you don't like it, do you?. **~ cuoio** real leather ● *nm* truth; (*realità*) life
verosimigli'anza *nf* plausibility
vero'simile *a* probable, likely
verosimil'mente *adv* probably
ver'ruca *nf* wart; (*sotto la pianta del piede*) verruca
versa'mento *nm* (*pagamento*) payment; (*in banca*) deposit
ver'sante *nm* slope
ver'sare *vt* pour; (*spargere*) shed; (*rovesciare*) spill; pay (*denaro*); (*in banca*) pay in ● *vi* (*trovarsi*) be
ver'sarsi *vr* spill; (*sfociare*) flow
ver'satile *a* versatile
versatilità *nf* versatility
ver'sato *a* (*pratico*) versed
ver'setto *nm* verse
versifica|'tore, -'trice *nmf* versifier
versi'one *nf* version; (*traduzione*) translation; **'~ integrale** 'unabridged version'; **~ originale** original version. **'~ ridotta'** 'abridged version'. **~ teatrale** dramatization
'verso[1] *nm* verse; (*grido*) cry; (*gesto*) gesture; (*senso*) direction; (*modo*) manner; **fare il ~ a qcno** ape sb; **non c'è ~ di** there is no way of. **versi** *pl* **sciolti** blank verse
'verso[2] *prep* towards; (*nei pressi di*) round about; **~ dove?** which way?
'vertebra *nf* vertebra
verte'brale *a* vertebral
verte'brato *nm* vertebrate
ver'tenza *nf* dispute. **~ sindacale** industrial dispute
'vertere *vi* **~ su** focus on
verti'cale *a* vertical; (*in parole crociate*) down ● *nm* vertical ● *nf* handstand; **fare la ~** do a handstand
vertical'mente *adv* vertically
'vertice *nm* summit; *Math* vertex; **conferenza al ~** summit conference; **incontro al ~** summit meeting
ver'tigine *nf* dizziness; *Med* vertigo; **ver-**

tigini *pl* giddy spells; **aver le vertigini** feel dizzy
vertiginosa'mente *adv* dizzily
vertigi'noso *a* dizzy; (*velocità*) breakneck; (*prezzi*) sky-high; (*scollatura*) plunging
'vescia *nf* puffball
ve'scica *nf* bladder; (*sulla pelle*) blister
'vescovo *nm* bishop
'vespa *nf* wasp
vespasi'ano *nm* urinal
'vespro *nm* vespers *pl*
ves'sare *vt fml* oppress
ves'sillo *nm* standard
ve'staglia *nf* dressing gown, robe *Am*
'veste *nf* dress; (*rivestimento*) covering; **in ~ di** in the capacity of; **in ~ ufficiale** in an official capacity. **~ da camera** dressing gown, robe *Am*. **~ editoriale** layout. **~ tipografica** typographical design
vesti'ario *nm* clothing
ve'stibolo *nm* hall
ve'stigio *nm* (*pl m* **vestigi**, *pl f* **vestigia**) trace
ve'stire *vt* dress
ve'stirsi *vr* get dressed; **~ da** dress up as a
ve'stito *a* dressed ● *nm* (*da uomo*) suit; (*da donna*) dress; **vestiti** *pl* clothes. **~ da sposa** wedding dress. **~ da uomo** suit
vete'rano, -a *a & nmf* veteran
veteri'nario, -a *a* veterinary ● *nm* veterinary surgeon ● *nf* veterinary science
'veto *nm inv* veto
ve'traio *nm* glazier
ve'trato, -a *a* glazed ● *nf* big window; (*in chiesa*) stained-glass window; (*porta*) glass door
vetre'ria *nf* glass works
ve'trina *nf* [shop-]window; (*mobile*) display cabinet
vetri'nista *nmf* window dresser
ve'trino *nm* (*di microscopio*) slide
vetri'olo *nm* vitriol
'vetro *nm* glass; (*di finestra, porta*) pane. **~ di sicurezza** safety glass
vetro'resina *nf* fibreglass
ve'troso *a* vitreous
'vetta *nf* peak
vet'tore *nm* vector
vetto'vaglie *nfpl* provisions
vet'tura *nf* coach; (*ferroviaria*) coach, carriage; *Auto* car. **~ d'epoca** vintage car
vettu'rino *nm* coachman
vezzeggi'are *vt* fondle
vezzeggia'tivo *nm* pet name
'vezzo *nm* habit; (*attrattiva*) charm; **vezzi** *pl* (*moine*) affectation
vez'zoso *a* charming; *pej* affected
VF *abbr* (*Vigili del Fuoco*) fire brigade, fire department *Am*
vi *pers pron* you; (*riflessivo*) yourselves; (*reciproco*) each other; (*tra più persone*) one another; **vi ho dato un libro** I gave you a book; **lavatevi le mani** wash your hands; **eccovi!** here you are! ● *adv* = **ci**
'via[1] *nf* street, road; *fig* way; *Anat* tract; **in ~**

di in the course of; **per ~ di** on account of; **per ~ aerea** by airmail. **V~ Lattea** *Astr* Milky Way. **~ di mezzo** halfway house. **~ respiratoria** *Anat* airway. **~ d'uscita** let-out

'via² *adv* away; (*fuori*) out; **andar ~** go away; ‹*macchia:*› come off, come out; **e così ~** and so on; **e ~ dicendo** and whatnot; **~ ~ che** as ● *int* **~!** go away!; *Sport* go!; (*andiamo*) come on!; **~, non ci credo** come off it *or* come on, I don't believe it ● *nm* starting signal

viabilità *nf* road conditions *pl*; (*rete*) road network; (*norme*) road and traffic laws *pl*

via'card *nf* motorway card

vi'ado *nm* (*pl* **viados**) rent boy

via'dotto *nm* viaduct

viaggi'are *vi* travel; **il treno viaggia con 20 minuti di ritardo** the train is 20 minutes late

viaggia|'tore, -'trice *nmf* traveller

vi'aggio *nm* journey; (*breve*) trip; **buon ~!** safe journey!, have a good trip!; **fare un ~** go on a journey; **essere in ~** be underway; **mettersi in ~** get underway. **~ d'affari** business trip. **~ di lavoro** working trip ● **di nozze** honeymoon. **~ organizzato** package tour

vi'ale *nm* avenue; (*privato*) drive

via'letto *nm* path

via'vai *nm* coming and going

vi'brante *a* vibrant

vi'brare *vi* vibrate; (*fremere*) quiver

vibra'tore *nm* vibrator

vibra'torio *a* vibratory

vibrazi'one *nf* vibration

vi'cario *nm* vicar

'vice *nmf* deputy

vice+ *pref* vice+

vicecoman'dante *nm* *Mil* second in command

vicediret|'tore, -'trice *nm* assistant manager ● *nf* assistant manageress

vi'cenda *nf* event; **a ~** (*fra due*) each other; (*a turno*) in turn[s]

vicendevol'mente *adv* each other

vice'preside *nmf* vice-principal

vicepresi'dente *nm* vice-president; *Comm* vice-chairman, vice-president *Am*

vicepresi'denza *nf* vice-presidency; *Sch* deputy head's office

vicerè *nm inv* viceroy

viceret'tore *nm* vice-chancellor

vice'versa *adv* vice versa

vi'chingo, -a *a & nmf* Viking

vi'cina *nf* neighbour

vici'nanza *nf* nearness; **vicinanze** (*pl: paraggi*) neighbourhood

vici'nato *nm* neighbourhood; (*vicini*) neighbours *pl*

vi'cino, -a *a* near; (*accanto*) next ● *adv* near, close ● *prep* **~ a** near [to] ● *nmf* neighbour. **~ di casa** nextdoor neighbour

vicissi'tudine *nf* vicissitude

'vicolo *nm* alley. **~ cieco** *anche fig* blind alley

'video *nm* (*musicale*) video; (*schermo*) screen. **~ interattivo** interactive video

video'camera *nf* camcorder

videocas'setta *nf* video, video cassette

videoci'tofono *nm* video entry phone

video'clip *nm inv* video clip

videoconfe'renza *nf* videoconference

videogi'oco *nm* video game

video'leso, -a *a* visually handicapped ● *nmf* visually handicapped person

videoregistra'tore *nm* videorecorder

videoscrit'tura *nf* word processing

videosorvegli'anza *nf* video surveillance

video'teca *nf* video library

video'telᴿ *nm* ≈ Videotexᴿ

videote'lefono *nm* view phone

videotermi'nale *nm* visual display unit, VDU

vidi'mare *vt* authenticate

vi'eni *vedi* **venire**

Vi'enna *nf* Vienna

vien'nese *a & nmf* Viennese

vie'tare *vt* forbid; **~ qcsa a qcno** forbid sb sth

vie'tato *a* forbidden; **sosta vietata** no parking; **~ fumare** no smoking; **~ ai minori di 18 anni** prohibited to children under the age of 18

Vi'etnam *nm* Vietnam

vietna'mita *a & nmf* Vietnamese

vi'gente *a* in force

'vigere *vi* be in force

vigi'lante *a* vigilant

vigi'lanza *nf* vigilance; (*sorveglianza*) (*a scuola*) supervision; (*di polizia*) surveillance. **~ notturna** night security guards *pl*. **~ urbana** traffic police (*in towns*)

vigi'lare *vt* keep an eye on ● *vi* keep watch

vigi'lato, -a *a* under surveillance ● *nmf* person under police surveillance. **~ speciale** person under special police surveillance

'vigile *a* watchful ● *nm* **~ [urbano]** traffic policeman. **~ del fuoco** fireman. **vigili** *pl* **del fuoco** firemen, fire brigade. **vigili** *pl* **urbani** traffic police (*in towns*)

vi'gilia *nf* eve; *Relig* fast. **~ di Natale** Christmas Eve

vigliacca'mente *adv* in a cowardly way

vigliacche'ria *nf* cowardice

vigli'acco, -a *a* cowardly ● *nmf* coward

'vigna *nf*, **vi'gneto** *nm* vineyard

vi'gnetta *nf* cartoon

vignet'tista *nm* cartoonist

vi'gogna *nf* (*tessuto*) vicuña

vi'gore *nm* vigour; **entrare in ~** come into force; **essere in ~** be in force

vigorosa'mente *adv* energetically

vigo'roso *a* vigorous

'vile *a* cowardly; (*abietto*) vile

vili'pendio *nm* scorn, contempt

'villa *nf* villa

vil'laggio *nm* village. **~ olimpico** Olympic village. **~ residenziale** commuter town. **~ satellite** satellite village. **~ turistico** holiday village

villa'nia *nf* rudeness
vil'lano *a* rude ● *nm* boor; (*contadino*) peasant
villeggi'ante *nmf* holiday-maker
villeggi'are *vi* spend one's holidays
villeggia'tura *nf* holiday[s] [*pl*], vacation *Am*
vil'letta *nf* small detached house. **~ bifamiliare** semi-detached house. **villette** *pl* **a schiera** terraced houses
vil'lino *nm* detached house
vil'loso *a* hairy
vil'mente *adv* in a cowardly way; (*in modo spreggevole*) contemptibly
viltà *nf* cowardice
'**vimine** *nm* wicker; **sedia di vimini** wicker chair
vi'naio, -a *nmf* wine merchant
'**vincere** *vt* win; (*sconfiggere*) beat; (*superare*) overcome
'**vincita** *nf* win; (*somma vinta*) winnings *pl*
vinci'tore, -'trice *nmf* winner; (*di battaglia*) victor, winner ● *a* winning, victorious
vinco'lante *a* binding
vinco'lare *vt* bind; *Comm* tie up
vinco'lato *a Fin* nonredeemable; **deposito ~** fixed deposit, term deposit
'**vincolo** *nm* bond
vi'nicolo *a* wine *attrib*
vi'nile *nm* vinyl
vi'nilico *a* vinyl
vinil'pelle[R] *nm* Leatherette[R]
'**vino** *nm* wine. **~ d'annata** vintage wine. **~ bianco** white wine. **~ brûlé** mulled wine. **~ della casa** house wine. **~ da dessert** dessert wine. **~ nuovo** new wine. **~ rosato** rosé [wine]. **~ rosé** rosé [wine]. **~ rosso** red wine. **~ spumante** sparkling wine. **~ da taglio** blending wine. **~ da tavola** table wine
vin'santo *nm dessert wine from Tuscany*
'**vinto** *pp di* **vincere**
vi'ola *nf Bot* violet; *Mus* viola. **~ del pensiero** *Bot* pansy
vio'laceo *a* purplish; (*labbra*) blue
vio'lare *vt* violate
violazi'one *nf* violation. **~ di contratto** breach of contract. **~ di domicilio** breaking and entering
violen'tare *vt* rape
violente'mente *adv* violently
vio'lento *a* violent
vio'lenza *nf* violence. **~ carnale** rape
vio'letto, -a *a & nm* (*colore*) violet ● *nf* violet
violi'nista *nmf* violinist
vio'lino *nm* violin
violon'cello *nm* cello
vi'ottolo *nm* path
'**vipera** *nf* viper
vi'raggio *nm Phot* toning; *Naut, Aeron* turn
vi'rale *a* viral
vi'rare *vi* turn; (*nave:*) put about; **~ di bordo** change course

vi'rata *nf* (*di aereo*) turning; (*di nave*) coming about; (*nel nuoto*) turn; *fig* change of direction
'**virgola** *nf* comma; *Math* [decimal] point; **punto e ~** semicolon; **quattro ~ due (4,2)** (*decimali*) four point two (4.2)
virgo'lette *nfpl* inverted commas, quotation marks
vi'rile *a* virile; (*da uomo*) manly
virilità *nf* virility; manliness
viril'mente *adv* in a manly way
vi'rologo *nm* virologist
virtù *nf inv* virtue; **in ~ di** (*legge*) under
virtu'ale *a* virtual
virtual'mente *adv* virtually
virtuo'sismo *nm* bravura
virtu'oso *a* virtuous ● *nm* virtuoso
viru'lento *a* virulent
'**virus** *nm* virus
visa'gista *nmf* beautician
visce'rale *a* visceral; (*odio*) deep-seated; (*reazione*) gut
'**viscere** *nm* internal organ ● *nfpl* guts
'**vischio** *nm* mistletoe
vischi'oso *a* viscous; (*appiccicoso*) sticky
'**viscido** *a* slimy
vi'sconte *nm* viscount
viscon'tessa *nf* viscountess
vi'scoso *a* viscous
vi'sibile *a* visible
visi'bilio *nm* profusion; **andare in ~** go into ecstasies
visibilità *nf* visibility; **scarsa ~** poor visibility
visi'era *nf* (*di elmo*) visor; (*di berretto*) peak
visio'nare *vt* examine; *Cinema* screen
visio'nario, -a *a & nmf* visionary
visi'one *nf* vision; **prima ~** *Cinema* first showing; **seconda ~** re-release, second showing. **~ notturna** night vision
'**visita** *nf* visit; (*breve*) call; *Med* examination; **fare ~ a qcno** pay sb a visit. **~ di controllo** *Med* checkup. **~ di convenienza** courtesy visit. **~ doganale** customs inspection. **~ a domicilio** home visit, call-out. **~ fiscale** tax inspection. **~ guidata** guided tour. **~ lampo** flying visit. **~ di leva** medical examination
visi'tare *vt* visit; (*brevemente*) call on; *Med* examine
visita'tore, -'trice *nmf* visitor
visiva'mente *adv* visually
vi'sivo *a* visual
'**viso** *nm* face. **~ pallido** paleface
vi'sone *nm* mink
'**vispo** *a* lively
vis'suto *pp di* **vivere** ● *a* experienced
'**vista** *nf* sight; (*veduta*) view; **a ~ d'occhio** (*crescere*) visibly; (*estendersi*) as far as the eye can see; **in ~ di** in view of; **perdere di ~ qcno** lose sight of sb; *fig* lose touch with sb; **a prima ~** at first sight
'**visto** *pp di* **vedere** ● *nm* visa. **~ di entrata** *o* **di ingresso** entry visa, entry permit. **~ d'uscita** exit visa ● *conj* **~ che...** seeing that...

vistosa'mente *adv* conspicuously
vi'stoso *a* showy; (*notevole*) considerable
visu'ale *a* visual
visualiz'zare *vt* visualize; *Comput* display
visualizza'tore *nm Comput* display, VDU.
~ **a cristalli liquidi** *Comput* liquid crystal display
visualizzazi'one *nf Comput* display
'**vita** *nf* life; (*durata della vita*) lifetime; *Anat* waist; **a ~** for life; **essere in fin di ~** be at death's door; **essere in ~** be alive; **fare la bella ~** lead the good life; **costo della ~** cost of living. ~ **eterna** eternal life. ~ **media** *Biol* life expectancy. ~ **mondana** high life; **fare ~ ~** lead the high life. ~ **notturna** night life. ~ **terrena** *Relig* life on earth
vi'taccia *nf* slog
vi'tale *a* vital
vitalità *nf* vitality
vita'lizio *a* life *attrib* ● *nm* [life] annuity
vita'mina *nf* vitamin
vita'minico *a* vitamin-enriched
vitaminiz'zato *a* vitamin-enriched
'**vite** *nf Mech* screw; *Bot* vine; **giro di ~** *fig* turn of the screw. ~ **canadese** Virginia creeper. ~ **di coda** *Aeron* tailspin. ~ **perpetua** endless screw
vi'tella *nf* (*animale*) calf; (*carne*) veal
vi'tello *nm* calf; (*carne*) veal; (*pelle*) calfskin. ~ **di latte** milk-fed veal. ~ **tonnato** *sliced veal with tuna, anchovy, oil and lemon sauce*
vi'ticcio *nm* tendril
viticol'tore *nm* wine grower
viticol'tura *nf* wine growing
vi'tino *nm* narrow waist; ~ **di vespa** slender little waist
'**vitreo** *a* vitreous; (*sguardo*) glassy
'**vittima** *nf* victim
'**vitto** *nm* food; (*pasti*) board. ~ **e alloggio** board and lodging
vit'toria *nf* victory
vittori'ano *a* Victorian
vittoriosa'mente *adv* victoriously, triumphantly
vittori'oso *a* victorious
vitupe'rare *vt* vituperate
vitu'perio *nm* insult
vi'uzza *nf* narrow lane
'**viva** *int* hurrah!; ~ **la Regina!** long live the Queen!
vi'vace *a* vivacious; (*mente*) lively; (*colore*) bright
vivace'mente *adv* vivaciously
vivacità *nf* vivacity; (*di mente*) liveliness; (*di colore*) brightness
vivaciz'zare *vt* liven up
vi'vaio *nm* nursery; (*per pesci*) pond; *fig* breeding ground
viva'mente *adv* (*ringraziare*) warmly
vi'vanda *nf* food; (*piatto*) dish
vi'vente *a* living ● *nmpl* **i viventi** the living
'**vivere** *vi* live; ~ **di** live on; **vive** *Typ* stet ● *vt* (*passare*) go through ● *nm* life; **modo di ~** way of life
'**viveri** *nmpl* provisions

vivida'mente *adv* vividly
'**vivido** *a* vivid
vivi'paro *a* viviparous
vivisezio'nare *vt* vivisect
vivisezi'one *nf* vivisection
'**vivo** *a* alive; (*vivente*) living; (*vivace*) lively; (*colore*) bright; ~ **e vegeto** alive and kicking; **farsi ~** keep in touch; (*arrivare*) turn up ● *nm* **colpire qcno sul ~** cut sb to the quick; **dal ~** (*trasmissione*) live; (*disegnare*) from life; **i vivi** the living
vizi'are *vt* spoil (*bambino ecc*); (*guastare*) vitiate
vizi'ato *a* spoilt; (*aria*) stale
'**vizio** *nm* vice; (*cattiva abitudine*) bad habit; (*difetto*) flaw. ~ **capitale** deadly sin. ~ **di forma** legal technicality. ~ **procedurale** procedural error
vizi'oso *a* dissolute; (*difettoso*) faulty; **circolo ~** vicious circle
'**vizzo** *a* (*pelle*) wrinked; (*pianta*) withered
V.le *abbr* (**viale**) Ave
vocabo'lario *nm* dictionary; (*lessico*) vocabulary
vo'cabolo *nm* word
vo'cale *a* vocal ● *nf* vowel
vo'calico *a* (*corde*) vocal; (*suono*) vowel *attrib*
vocazi'one *nf* vocation
'**voce** *nf* voice; (*diceria*) rumour; (*di bilancio, dizionario*) entry. ~ **bianca** *Mus* treble voice. ~ **fuori campo** voiceover
voci'are *vi* (*spettegolare*) gossip ● *nm* buzz of conversation
vocife'rare *vi* shout; **si vocifera che...** it is rumoured that...
'**vodka** *nf inv* vodka
'**voga** *nf* rowing; (*lena*) enthusiasm; (*moda*) vogue; **essere in ~** be in vogue
vo'gare *vi* row. ~ **a bratto** scull. ~ **di coppia** scull
voga'tore *nm* oarsman; (*attrezzo*) rowing machine
'**voglia** *nf* desire; (*volontà*) will; (*della pelle*) birthmark; **aver ~ di fare qcsa** feel like doing sth; **morire dalla ~ di qcsa** be dying for sth; **di buona ~** willingly
'**voglio** *vedi* **volere**
vogli'oso *a* (*occhi, persona*) covetous; **essere ~ di qcsa** want sth
'**voi** *pers pron* you; **siete ~?** is that you?; **l'avete fatto ~?** did you do it yourself?
voia'ltri *pers pron* you
vo'lano *nm* shuttlecock; *Mech* flywheel
vo'lant *nm inv* valance
vo'lante *a* flying; (*foglio*) loose ● *nm* steering-wheel
volanti'nare *vi* hand out leaflets
volan'tino *nm* leaflet
vo'lare *vi* fly
vo'lata *nf Sport* final sprint; **di ~** in a rush
vo'latile *a* (*liquido*) volatile ● *nm* bird
volatiliz'zarsi *vr* vanish
vol-au-'vent *nm inv* vol-au-vent
vo'lée *nf inv Tennis* volley

vo'lente *a* ~ **o nolente** whether you like it or not

volente'roso *a* willing

volenti'eri *adv* willingly; ~! with pleasure!

vo'lere *vt* want; (*chiedere di*) ask for; (*aver bisogno di*) need; **non voglio** I don't want to; **vuole che lo faccia io** he wants me to do it; **fai come vuoi** do as you like; **se tuo padre vuole, ti porto al cinema** if your father agrees, I'll take you to the cinema; **questa pianta vuole molte cure** this plant needs a lot of care; **vorrei un caffè** I'd like a coffee; **la leggenda vuole che...** legend has it that...; **la vuoi smettere?** will you stop that!; **senza** ~ without meaning to; **voler bene/male a qcno** love/have something against sb; **voler dire** mean; **ci vuole il latte** we need milk; **ci vuole tempo/pazienza** it takes time/patience; **volerne a** have a grudge against; **vuoi... vuoi...** either... or... ● *nm* will; **voleri** *pl* wishes

vol'gare *a* vulgar; (*popolare*) common

volgarità *nf* vulgarity; **dire** ~ use vulgar language, be vulgar

volgariz'zare *vt* popularize

volgarizzazi'one *nf* popularization

volgar'mente *adv* (*grossolanamente*) vulgarly; (*comunemente*) commonly, popularly

'volgere *vt/i* turn

'volgersi *vr* turn [round]; ~ **a** (*dedicarsi*) take up

'volgo *nm* common people

voli'era *nf* aviary

voli'tivo *a* strong-minded

'volo *nm* flight; **al** ~ ⟨*fare qcsa*⟩ quickly; ⟨*prendere qcsa*⟩ in mid-air; **alzarsi in** ~ ⟨*uccello:*⟩ take off; **in** ~ airborne. ~ **di andata** outward flight. ~ **charter** charter flight. ~ **diretto** direct flight. ~ **di linea** scheduled flight. ~ **nazionale** domestic flight. ~ **di ritorno** return flight. ~ **strumentale** flying on instruments. ~ **a vela** gliding

volontà *nf inv* will; (*desiderio*) wish; **a** ~ ⟨*mangiare*⟩ as much as you like

volontaria'mente *adv* voluntarily

volon'tario *a* voluntary ● *nm* volunteer

volonte'roso *a* willing

'volpe *nf* fox

vol'pino *a* ⟨*astuzia*⟩ fox-like ● *nm* ⟨*cane*⟩ Pomeranian

volt *nm inv* volt

'volta *nf* time; (*turno*) turn; (*curva*) bend; *Archit* vault; **4 volte 4** 4 times 4; **a volte, qualche** ~ sometimes; **c'era una** ~... once upon a time, there was...; **una** ~ once; **due volte** twice; **tre/quattro volte** three/four times; **una** ~ **per tutte** once and for all; **una** ~ **ogni tanto** every so often; **uno alla** ~ one at a time; **alla** ~ **di** in the direction of. ~ **a botte** barrel vault. ~ **celeste** vault of heaven. ~ **cranica** cranial vault. ~ **a crociera** groin vault. ~ **a vela** ribbed vault. ~ **a ventaglio** fan vault

volta'faccia *nm inv* volte-face

voltagab'bana *mf inv* turncoat

vol'taggio *nm* voltage

vol'tare *vt/i* turn; (*rigirare*) turn round; (*rivoltare*) turn over; ~ **pagina** *fig* start with a clean sheet

vol'tarsi *vr* turn [round]

volta'stomaco *nm* nausea; *fig* disgust

volteggi'are *vi* circle; (*ginnastica*) vault

'volto *pp di* **volgere** ● *nm* face; **mi ha mostrato il suo vero** ~ he revealed his true colours

vol'tura *nf* (*catastale*) transfer of property. ~ **di contratto** transfer of contract

vo'lubile *a* fickle

volubil'mente *adv* in a fickle way, inconstantly

vo'lume *nm* volume. ~ **di gioco** *Sport* possession

volumi'noso *a* voluminous

vo'luta *nf* (*spirale*) spiral; (*di capitello*) volute

voluta'mente *adv* deliberately

vo'luto *a* deliberate, intended

voluttà *nf* voluptuousness

voluttu'ario *a* non-essential; **beni** *pl* **voluttuari** non-essentials

voluttu'oso *a* voluptuous

vomi'tare *vt* vomit, be sick

vomi'tevole *a* nauseating

'vomito *nm* vomit

'vongola *nf* clam

vo'race *a* voracious

vorace'mente *adv* voraciously

vo'ragine *nf* abyss

vor'rei *vedi* **volere**

'vortice *nm* whirl; (*gorgo*) whirlpool; (*di vento*) whirlwind

vorticosa'mente *adv* in whirls

'vostro (**il** ~ *m*, **la vostra** *f*, **i vostri** *mpl*, **le vostre** *fpl*) *poss a* your; **è vostra questa macchina?** is this car yours?; **un** ~ **amico** a friend of yours; ~ **padre** your father ● *poss pron* yours; **i vostri** your folk

vo'tante *nmf* voter

vo'tare *vi* vote

votazi'one *nf* voting; *Sch* marks *pl*. ~ **di fiducia** *Pol*, *fig* vote of confidence. ~ **a scrutinio segreto** secret ballot

'voto *nm* vote; *Sch* mark; *Relig* vow. ~ **decisivo** casting vote

vs. *abbr Comm* (**vostro**) yours

'vudu *nm inv* voodoo

vul'canico *a* volcanic

vul'cano *nm* volcano. ~ **intermittente** dormant volcano. ~ **spento** extinct volcano

vulne'rabile *a* vulnerable

vulnerabilità *nf* vulnerability

'vulva *nf* vulva

vuo'tare *vt* empty

vuo'tarsi *vr* empty

vu'oto *a* empty; (*non occupato*) vacant; ~ **di** (*sprovvisto*) devoid of ● *nm* empty space; *Phys* vacuum; *fig* void; **assegno a** ~ dud cheque; **sotto** ~ ⟨*prodotto*⟩ vacuum-packed. ~ **d'aria** air pocket. ~ **a perdere** no deposit. ~ **a rendere** ⟨*bottiglia*⟩ returnable

Ww

W *abbr* (**viva**) long live
'wafer *nm inv* (*biscotto*) wafer
wagon-'lit *nm inv* sleeping car
walkie-'talkie *nm inv* walkie-talkie
'water *nm inv* toilet, loo *fam*
watt *nm inv* watt
wat'tora *nm inv Phys* watt-hour

WC *nm* WC
week'end *nm inv* weekend
'welter *a & nm inv* (*in pugilato*) welterweight
'western *a inv* cowboy *attrib* ● *nm inv Cinema* western
'whisky *nm inv* whisky. **~ di malto** malt [whisky]

Xx

xenofo'bia *nf* xenophobia
xe'nofobo, -a *a* xenophobic ● *nmf* xenophobe
xe'res *nm inv* sherry
xero'copia *nf* xerox

xerocopi'are *vt* photocopy
xerocopia'trice *nf* photocopier
xilofo'nista *nmf* xylophone player
xi'lofono *nm* xylophone

Yy

yacht *nm inv* yacht
yak *nm inv Zool* yak
'yankee *nmf inv* Yank
'Yemen *nm* Yemen
yeme'nita *nmf* Yemeni
yen *nm inv* yen
'yeti *nm* yeti

'yiddish *a inv & nm* Yiddish
'yoga *nm* yoga ● *a inv* yoga *attrib*
'yogurt *nm inv* yoghurt
yogurti'era *nf* yoghurt-maker
'yorkshire *nm inv* (*cane*) Yorkshire terrier
yo-'yo[R] *nm inv* yoyo
yup'pismo *nm* yuppiedom

Zz

zaba[gl]i'one *nm* zabaglione (*dessert made from eggs, wine or marsala and sugar*)

'zacchera *nf* (*schizzo*) splash of mud

zaf'fata *nf* whiff; (*di fumo*) cloud

zaffe'rano *nm* saffron

zaf'firo *nm* sapphire

'zagara *nf* orange-blossom

'zaino *nm* rucksack

'zampa *nf* leg; **a quattro zampe** (*animale*) four-legged; (*carponi*) on all fours. **zampe pl di gallina** *fig* crow's feet

zam'pata *nf* paw; **dare una ~ a** hit with its paw

zampet'tare *vi* scamper

zam'petto *nm* Culin knuckle

zampil'lante *a* spurting

zampil'lare *vi* spurt

zam'pillo *nm* spurt

zam'pino *nm* paw; **mettere lo ~ in** *fig* have a hand in

zam'pogna *nf* bagpipe

zampo'gnaro *nm* piper

zam'pone *nfpl* stuffed pig's trotter with lentils

'zanna *nf* fang; (*di elefante*) tusk

zan'zara *nf* mosquito

zanzari'era *nf* (*velo*) mosquito net; (*su finestra*) insect screen

'zappa *nf* hoe; **darsi la ~ sui piedi** *fig* shoot oneself in the foot

zap'pare *vt* hoe

zap'pata *nf* **dare una ~ a** hit with a hoe

zappet'tare *vt* hoe

zar *nm inv* tzar

za'rina *nf* tzarina

za'rista *a & nmf* tzarist

'zattera *nf* raft

zatte'roni *nmpl* (*scarpe*) wedge shoes

za'vorra *nf* ballast; *fig* dead wood

zavor'rare *vt* load with ballast

'zazzera *nf* mop of hair

'zebra *nf* zebra; **zebre pl** (*passaggio pedonale*) zebra crossing, crosswalk *Am*

ze'brato *a* (*tessuto*) with black and white stripes

'zecca[1] *nf* mint; **nuovo di ~** brand-new

'zecca[2] *nf* (*parassita*) tick

zec'chino *nm* sequin; **oro ~** pure gold

ze'lante *a* zealous

'zelo *nm* zeal

'zenit *nm* zenith

'zenzero *nm* ginger

'zeppa *nf* wedge

'zeppo *a* packed full; **pieno ~ di** crammed *o* packed with

zer'bino *nm* doormat

'zero *nm* zero, nought; (*in calcio*) nil; *Tennis* love; **due a ~** (*in partite*) two nil; **ricominciare da ~** *fig* start again from scratch; **sparare a ~ su qcno** *fig* lay into sb; **avere il morale sotto ~** *fig* be down in the dumps

'zeta *nf* zed, zee *Am*

'zia *nf* aunt

zibel'lino *nm* sable

zi'gano, -a *a & nmf* gypsy

'zigolo *nm* Zool bunting

'zigomo *nm* cheek-bone

zigri'nato *a* (*pelle*) grained; (*metallo*) milled

zig'zag *nm inv* zigzag; **andare a ~** zigzag

Zim'babwe *nm* Zimbabwe

zim'bello *nm* decoy; (*oggetto di scherno*) laughing-stock

'zinco *nm* zinc

zinga'resco *a* gypsy *attrib*

'zingaro, -a *nmf* gypsy

'zio *nm* uncle

'zippo *nm sl* lighter

zi'tella *nf* spinster; *pej* old maid

zitel'lona *nf pej* old maid

zit'tire *vi* fall silent ● *vt* silence

'zitto *a* silent; **sta' ~!** keep quiet!

ziz'zania *nf* (*discordia*) discord; **seminare ~** cause trouble

'zoccola *nf vulg* whore

'zoccolo *nm* clog; (*di cavallo*) hoof; (*di terra*) clump; (*di parete*) skirting board, baseboard *Am*; (*di colonna*) base. **~ duro** *Pol* hard core. **~ fesso** cloven foot, cloven hoof

zodia'cale *a* of the zodiac; **segno ~** sign of the zodiac, birth sign

zo'diaco *nm* zodiac

zolfa'nello *nm* match

'zolfo *nm* sulphur

'zolla *nf* clod; (*di zucchero*) lump

zol'letta *nf* sugar cube, sugar lump

'zombi *nmf inv fig* zombi

zom'pare *vi sl* bonk

'zona *nf* zone; (*area*) area. **~ denuclearizzata** nuclear-free zone. **~ di depressione** area of low pressure. **~ disastrata** disaster area. **~ disco** area for parking discs only. **~ erogena** erogenous zone. **~ giorno** living area. **~ industriale** industrial estate. **~ notte** sleeping area. **~ pedonale** pedestrian precinct. **~ a traffico limitato** restricted traffic area. **~ verde** green belt

zonizzazi'one *nf* zoning

'zonzo: andare a ~ stroll about

zoo *nm inv* zoo

zoolo'gia *nf* zoology

zoo'logico *a* zoological

zo'ologo, -a *nmf* zoologist

zoosa'fari *nm inv* safari park

zootec'nia *nf* animal husbandry
zoo'tecnico *a* ⟨*progresso*⟩ in animal husbandry; **patrimonio ~** livestock
zoppi'cante *a* limping; *fig* shaky
zoppi'care *vi* limp; (*essere debole*) be shaky
'zoppo, -a *a* lame ● *nmf* cripple
'zotico *a* uncouth
zoti'cone *nm* boor
zu'ava *nf* **calzoni** *pl* **alla ~** plus-fours
'zucca *nf* marrow; (*fam: testa*) head; (*fam: persona*) thickie; **cos'hai in quella ~?** haven't you got anything between your ears?
zuc'cata *nf* **prendere una ~** *fam* hit one's head
zucche'rare *vt* sugar
zuccherato *a* sugared; **non ~** ⟨*succo d'arancia ecc*⟩ unsweetened
zuccheri'era *nf* sugar bowl
zuccheri'ficio *nm* sugar refinery
zucche'rino *a* sugary ● *nm* sugar cube,

sugar lump; *fig* sweetener; **essere uno ~** *fig* ⟨*persona:*⟩ be a softy; ⟨*cosa:*⟩ be a cinch
'zucchero *nm* sugar. **~ di canna** cane sugar. **~ greggio** brown sugar. **~ vanigliato** vanilla sugar. **~ a velo** icing sugar, confectioners' sugar *Am*
zucche'roso *a fig* honeyed
zuc'china *nf* courgette, zucchini *Am*
zuc'chino *nm* courgette, zucchini *Am*
zuc'cone *nm fam* blockhead
zuc'cotto *nm* dessert made with sponge, cream, chocolate and candied fruit
'zuffa *nf* scuffle
zufo'lare *vt/i* whistle
'zufolo *nm* penny whistle
zu'mare *vi* zoom
zu'mata *nf* zoom
'zuppa *nf* soup. **~ inglese** trifle
zup'petta *nf* **fare ~** [**con**] dunk
zuppi'era *nf* soup tureen
'zuppo *a* soaked

Aa

a, A /eɪ/ (*letter*) a, A *f inv*; *Mus* la *m inv*

a /ə/, *accentato* /eɪ/ (*davanti a una vocale* **an**) *indef art* un *m*, una *f*; (*before s + consonant, gn, ps, z*) uno; (*before nf starting with vowel*) un'; (*each*) a; **I am a lawyer** sono avvocato; **a tiger is a feline** la tigre è un felino; **a knife and fork** un coltello e una forchetta; **a Mr Smith is looking for you** un certo signor Smith ti sta cercando; **£2 a kilo/a head** due sterline al chilo/a testa ● *n Mus* la *m inv*

A4 *a* A4

AA *n Br abbr* (**Automobile Association**) ≈ A.C.I. *f; abbr* **Alcoholics Anonymous**

aback /ə'bæk/ *adv* **be taken ~** essere preso in contropiede

abacus /'æbəkəs/ *n* (*pl* **-cuses**) abaco *m*

abandon /ə'bændən/ *vt* abbandonare; (*give up*) rinunciare a ● *n* abbandono *m*

abandoned /ə'bændnd/ *a* abbandonato; ‹*behaviour*› dissoluto

abandonment /ə'bændnmənt/ *n* (*of strike, plan etc*) rinuncia *f*

abashed /ə'bæʃt/ *a* imbarazzato

abate /ə'beɪt/ *vi* calmarsi

abattoir /'æbətwɑ:(r)/ *n* mattatoio *m*

abbess /'æbes/ *n* badessa *f*

abbey /'æbɪ/ *n* abbazia *f*

abbot /'æbət/ *n* abate *m*

abbreviate /ə'bri:vɪeɪt/ *vt* abbreviare

abbreviation /əbri:vɪ'eɪʃn/ *n* abbreviazione *f*

ABC *n* (*alphabet*) alfabeto *m*; **the ~ of** (*basics*) l'ABC *m inv* di ● *n abbr* (**American Broadcasting Company**) *rete f televisiva americana*

abdicate /'æbdɪkeɪt/ *vi* abdicare ● *vt* rinunciare a

abdication /æbdɪ'keɪʃn/ *n* abdicazione *f*

abdomen /'æbdəmən/ *n* addome *m*

abdominal /æb'dɒmɪnl/ *a* addominale

abduct /əb'dʌkt/ *vt* rapire

abduction /əb'dʌkʃn/ *n* rapimento *m*

abductor /əb'dʌktə(r)/ *n* rapitore, -trice *mf*

aberrant /ə'berənt/ *a* ‹*behaviour, nature*› aberrante

aberration /æbə'reɪʃn/ *n* aberrazione *f*

abet /ə'bet/ *vt* (*pt/pp* **abetted**) **aid and ~** *Jur* essere complice di

abeyance /ə'beɪəns/ *n* **in ~** in sospeso; **fall into ~** cadere in disuso

abhor /əb'hɔ:(r)/ *vt* (*pt/pp* **abhorred**) aborrire

abhorrence /əb'hɒrəns/ *n* orrore *m*

abhorrent /əb'hɒrənt/ *a* ripugnante

abide /ə'baɪd/ *vt* (*pt/pp* **abided**) (*tolerate*) sopportare. ● **abide by** *vi* rispettare

abiding /ə'baɪdɪŋ/ *a* perpetuo

ability /ə'bɪlətɪ/ *n* capacità *f inv*

abject /'æbdʒekt/ *a* ‹*poverty*› degradante; ‹*apology*› umile; ‹*coward*› abietto

ablative /'æblətɪv/ *n* ablativo *m*

ablaze /ə'bleɪz/ *a* in fiamme; **be ~ with light** risplendere di luci

able /'eɪbl/ *a* capace, abile; **be ~ to do sth** poter fare qcsa; **were you ~ to...?** sei riuscito a...?

able-bodied /-'bɒdɪd/ *a* robusto; *Mil* abile

able seaman *n* marinaio *m* scelto

ably /'eɪblɪ/ *adv* abilmente

abnegation /æbnɪ'geɪʃn/ *n* (*of rights, privileges*) rinuncia *f*; (*self-abnegation*) abnegazione *f*

abnormal /æb'nɔ:ml/ *a* anormale

abnormality /æbnɔ:'mælətɪ/ *n* anormalità *f inv*

abnormally /æb'nɔ:məlɪ/ *adv* in modo anormale

aboard /ə'bɔ:d/ *adv & prep* a bordo

abode /ə'bəʊd/ *n* dimora *f*

abolish /ə'bɒlɪʃ/ *vt* abolire

abolition /æbə'lɪʃn/ *n* abolizione *f*

abominable /ə'bɒmɪnəbl/ *a* abominevole

abominably /ə'bɒmɪnəblɪ/ *adv* disgustosamente

abominate /ə'bɒmɪneɪt/ *vt* abominare

aboriginal /æbə'rɪdʒɪnl/ *a & n* (*native*) aborigeno, -a *mf*, indigeno, -a *mf*

Aborigine /æbə'rɪdʒəni:/ *n* aborigeno, -a *mf* d'Australia

abort /ə'bɔ:t/ *vt* fare abortire; *fig* annullare

abortion /ə'bɔ:ʃn/ *n* aborto *m*; **have an ~** abortire

abortionist /ə'bɔ:ʃnɪst/ *n* persona *f* che pratica aborti, specialmente clandestini

abortive /ə'bɔ:tɪv/ *a* ‹*attempt*› infruttuoso

abound /ə'baʊnd/ *vi* abbondare (**in** di)

about /ə'baʊt/ *adv* (*here and there*) [di] qua e [di] là; (*approximately*) circa; **be ~** ‹*illness, tourists*:› essere in giro; **be up and ~** essere alzato; **leave sth lying ~** lasciare in giro qcsa ● *prep* (*concerning*) su; (*in the region of*) intorno a; (*here and there in*) per; **what is the book/the film ~?** di cosa parla il libro/il film?; **he wants to see you – what ~?** ti vuole vedere – a che proposito?; **talk/know ~** parlare/sapere di; **I know nothing ~ it** non ne so niente; **~ 5 o'clock** intorno alle 5; **travel ~ the world** viaggiare per il mondo; **be ~ to do sth** stare per fare qcsa; **how ~ going to the cinema?** e se andassimo al cinema?

about-face *n*, **about-turn** *n* dietro front *m inv*

above /ə'bʌv/ adv & prep sopra; ~ **all** soprattutto

above: above-board a onesto. **above-ground** adv in superficie. **above-mentioned** /-'menʃnd/ a suddetto. **above-named** /-neimd/ a suddetto

abrasion /ə'breiʒn/ n (injury) abrasione f

abrasive /ə'breisiv/ a abrasivo; ‹remark› caustico ● n abrasivo m

abreast /ə'brest/ adv fianco a fianco; **come** ~ **of** allinearsi con; **keep** ~ **of** tenersi al corrente di

abridged /ə'bridʒd/ a ridotto

abridg[e]ment /ə'bridʒmnt/ n (version) edizione f ridotta

abroad /ə'brɔːd/ adv all'estero

abrupt /ə'brʌpt/ a brusco

abruptly /ə'brʌptlı/ adv bruscamente

ABS n abbr (**anti-lock braking system**) ABS m inv

abscess /'æbsis/ n ascesso m

abscond /əb'skɒnd/ vi fuggire

absence /'æbsəns/ n assenza f; (lack) mancanza f

absent¹ /'æbsənt/ a assente

absent² /æb'sent/ vt ~ **oneself** essere assente

absentee /æbsən'tiː/ n assente mf

absenteeism /æbsən'tiːɪzm/ n assenteismo m

absentee landlord n proprietario m che affitta una casa in cui non abita

absently /'æbsəntlı/ adv ‹say, look› distrattamente

absent-minded /-'maındıd/ a distratto

absent-mindedly /-'maındıdlı/ adv distrattamente

absent-mindedness /-'maındıdnıs/ n distrazione f

absolute /'æbsəluːt/ a assoluto; **an** ~ **idiot** un perfetto idiota

absolutely /'æbsəluːtlı/ adv assolutamente; (fam: indicating agreement) esattamente; ~ **not** assolutamente no

absolution /æbsə'luːʃn/ n assoluzione f

absolve /əb'zɒlv/ vt assolvere

absorb /əb'sɔːb/ vt assorbire; ~**ed in** assorto in

absorbency /əb'sɔːbənsı/ n capacità f d'assorbimento

absorbent /əb'sɔːbənt/ a assorbente

absorbent cotton n Am cotone m idrofilo, ovatta f

absorbing /əb'sɔːbıŋ/ a avvincente

absorption /əb'sɔːpʃn/ n assorbimento m; (in activity) concentrazione f

abstain /əb'steın/ vi astenersi (**from** da)

abstemious /əb'stiːmıəs/ a moderato

abstention /əb'stenʃn/ n Pol astensione f

abstinence /'æbstınəns/ n astinenza f

abstract /'æbstrækt/ a astratto ● n astratto m; (summary) estratto m

abstraction /əb'strækʃn/ n **an air of** ~ un'aria distratta

absurd /əb'sɜːd/ a assurdo

absurdity /əb'sɜːdətı/ n assurdità f inv

absurdly /əb'sɜːdlı/ adv assurdamente

abundance /ə'bʌndəns/ n abbondanza f

abundant /ə'bʌndənt/ a abbondante

abundantly /ə'bʌndəntlı/ adv ~ **clear** più che chiaro

abuse¹ /ə'bjuːz/ vt (misuse) abusare di; (insult) insultare; (ill-treat) maltrattare

abuse² /ə'bjuːs/ n abuso m; (verbal) insulti mpl; (ill-treatment) maltrattamento m; ~ **of power** sopraffazione f

abusive /ə'bjuːsıv/ a offensivo

abut /ə'bʌt/ vi (pt/pp **abutted**) confinare (**onto** con)

abysmal /ə'bızml/ a fam pessimo; ‹ignorance› abissale

abyss /ə'bıs/ n abisso m

a/c abbr (**account**) c/c

academia /ækə'diːmıə/ n mondo m accademico

academic /ækə'demık/ a teorico; ‹qualifications, system› scolastico; **be** ~ ‹person:› avere predisposizione allo studio ● n docente mf universitario, -a

academically /ækə'demıklı/ adv ‹gifted› accademicamente

academician /əkædə'mıʃn/ n accademico, -a mf

academy /ə'kædəmı/ n accademia f; (of music) conservatorio m

ACAS /'eıkæs/ n Br abbr (**Advisory Conciliation and Arbitration Service**) organismo m pubblico di mediazione tra i lavoratori e i datori di lavoro

accede /ək'siːd/ vi ~ **to** accedere a ‹request›; salire a ‹throne›

accelerate /ək'seləreıt/ vt/i accelerare

acceleration /əkselə'reıʃn/ n accelerazione f

accelerator /ək'seləreıtə(r)/ n Auto, Comput acceleratore m

accent¹ /'æksənt/ n accento m

accent² /æk'sent/ vt accentare

accented /'æksəntıd/ a ‹speech› con accento marcato

accentuate /ək'sentjueıt/ vt accentuare

accept /ək'sept/ vt accettare

acceptability /ækseptə'bılıtı/ n ammissibilità f

acceptable /ək'septəbl/ a accettabile

acceptance /ək'septəns/ n accettazione f

access /'ækses/ n accesso m ● vt Comput accedere a

accessible /ək'sesəbl/ a accessibile

accession /ək'seʃn/ n (to throne) ascesa f al trono

accessory /ək'sesərı/ n accessorio m; Jur complice mf

accident /'æksıdənt/ n incidente m; (chance) caso m; **by** ~ per caso; (unintentionally) senza volere; **I'm sorry, it was an** ~ mi dispiace, non l'ho fatto apposta

accidental /æksı'dentl/ a ‹meeting› casuale; ‹death› incidentale; (unintentional) involontario

accidentally /æksɪ'dentəlɪ/ *adv* per caso; (*unintentionally*) inavvertitamente

acclaim /ə'kleɪm/ *n* acclamazione *f* ● *vt* acclamare (**as** come)

acclimatization /əklaɪmətaɪ'zeɪʃn/ *n* acclimatazione *f*

acclimatize /ə'klaɪmətaɪz/ *vt* **become ~d** acclimatarsi

accolade /'ækəleɪd/ *n* riconoscimento *m*

accommodate /ə'kɒmədeɪt/ *vt* ospitare; (*oblige*) favorire

accommodating /ə'kɒmədeɪtɪŋ/ *a* accomodante

accommodation /əkɒmə'deɪʃn/ *n* (*place to stay*) sistemazione *f*; **look for ~** cercare una sistemazione

accompaniment /ə'kʌmpənɪmənt/ *n* accompagnamento *m*

accompanist /ə'kʌmpənɪst/ *n Mus* accompagnatore, -trice *mf*

accompany /ə'kʌmpənɪ/ *vt* (*pt/pp* **-ied**) accompagnare

accomplice /ə'kʌmplɪs/ *n* complice *mf*

accomplish /ə'kʌmplɪʃ/ *vt* (*achieve*) concludere; realizzare ⟨*aim*⟩

accomplished /ə'kʌmplɪʃt/ *a* dotato; ⟨*fact*⟩ compiuto

accomplishment /ə'kʌmplɪʃmənt/ *n* realizzazione *f*; (*achievement*) risultato *m*; (*talent*) talento *m*

accord /ə'kɔːd/ *n* (*treaty*) accordo *m*; **with one ~** tutti d'accordo; **of his own ~** di sua spontanea volontà ● *vt* accordare

accordance /ə'kɔːdəns/ *n* **in ~ with** in conformità di *o* a

according /ə'kɔːdɪŋ/ *adv* **~ to** secondo

accordingly /ə'kɔːdɪŋlɪ/ *adv* di conseguenza

accordion /ə'kɔːdɪən/ *n* fisarmonica *f*

accost /ə'kɒst/ *vt* abbordare

account /ə'kaʊnt/ *n* conto *m*; (*report*) descrizione *f*; (*of eyewitness*) resoconto *m*; **~s** *pl Comm* conti *mpl*; **on ~ of** a causa di; **on no ~** per nessun motivo; **on this ~** per questo motivo; **on my ~** per causa mia; **of no ~** di nessuna importanza; **take into ~** tener conto di

■ **account for** *vt* (*explain*) spiegare; ⟨*person:*⟩ render conto di; (*constitute*) costituire; (*destroy*) distruggere

accountability /əkaʊntə'bɪlətɪ/ *n* responsabilità *f*

accountable /ə'kaʊntəbl/ *a* responsabile (**for** di)

accountant /ə'kaʊntənt/ *n* (*book-keeper*) contabile *mf*; (*consultant*) commercialista *mf*

account: account book *n* libro *m* contabile. **account director** *n* account director *mf inv*. **account holder** /ə'kaʊnthəʊldə(r)/ *n* (*with bank, credit company*) titolare *mf* del conto

accounting /ə'kaʊntɪŋ/ *n* (*field*) ragioneria *f*; (*auditing*) contabilità *f*

accounting period *n* periodo *m* contabile

account number *n* numero *m* di conto

accounts: accounts department *n* [uffi-cio *m*] contabilità *f*. **accounts payable** *npl* conto *m* creditori diversi. **accounts receivable** *npl* conto *m* debitori diversi

accoutrements /ə'kuːtrəmənts/ *npl* equipaggiamento *msg*

accredited /ə'kredɪtɪd/ *a* accreditato

accretion /ə'kriːʃn/ *n* accrescimento *m*

accrue /ə'kruː/ *vi* ⟨*interest:*⟩ maturare

accumulate /ə'kjuːmjʊleɪt/ *vt* accumulare ● *vi* accumularsi

accumulation /əkjuːmjʊ'leɪʃn/ *n* accumulazione *f*

accumulator /ə'kjuːmjʊleɪtə(r)/ *n Electr* accumulatore *m*

accuracy /'ækjʊrəsɪ/ *n* precisione *f*

accurate /'ækjʊrət/ *a* preciso

accurately /'ækjʊrətlɪ/ *adv* con precisione

accusation /ækjʊ'zeɪʃn/ *n* accusa *f*

accusative /ə'kjuːzətɪv/ *a & n* **~** [**case**] *Gram* accusativo *m*

accuse /ə'kjuːz/ *vt* accusare; **~ sb of doing sth** accusare qcno di fare qcsa

accused /ə'kjuːzd/ *n* **the ~** l'accusato *m*, l'accusata *f*

accuser /ə'kjuːzə(r)/ *n* accusatore, -trice *mf*

accusing /ə'kjuːzɪŋ/ *a* accusatore

accusingly /ə'kjuːzɪŋlɪ/ *adv* ⟨*say, point*⟩ in modo accusatorio

accustom /ə'kʌstəm/ *vt* abituare (**to** a)

accustomed /ə'kʌstəmd/ *a* abituato; **grow** *or* **get ~ to** abituarsi a

ace /eɪs/ *n* (*in cards*) asso *m*; *Tennis* ace *m inv*

acerbic /ə'sɜːbɪk/ *a* acido

acetate /'æsɪteɪt/ *n* acetato *m*

ache /eɪk/ *n* dolore *m* ● *vi* dolere, far male; **~ all over** essere tutto indolenzito

achieve /ə'tʃiːv/ *vt* ottenere ⟨*success*⟩; realizzare ⟨*goal, ambition*⟩

achievement /ə'tʃiːvmənt/ *n* (*feat*) successo *m*

achiever /ə'tʃiːvə(r)/ *n* persona *f* di successo

Achilles' heel /əkɪliːz'hiːl/ *n* tallone *m* di Achille

aching /'eɪkɪŋ/ *a* ⟨*body, limbs*⟩ dolorante; **an ~ void** un vuoto incolmabile

acid /'æsɪd/ *a* acido ● *n* acido *m*

acid drop *n* caramella *f* agli agrumi

acidic /ə'sɪdɪk/ *a* acido

acidity /ə'sɪdətɪ/ *n* acidità *f*

acid: acid rain *n* pioggia *f* acida. **acid stomach** *n Med* acidità *f* di stomaco. **acid test** *n fig* prova *f* del fuoco

acknowledge /ək'nɒlɪdʒ/ *vt* riconoscere; rispondere a ⟨*greeting*⟩; far cenno di aver notato ⟨*sb's presence*⟩; **~ receipt of** accusare ricevuta di ; **~ defeat** dichiararsi vinto

acknowledgement /ək'nɒlɪdʒmənt/ *n* riconoscimento *m*; **send an ~ of a letter** confermare il ricevimento di una lettera

acme /'ækmɪ/ *n* **the ~ of** l'apice *m* di

acne /'æknɪ/ *n* acne *f*

acorn /'eɪkɔːn/ *n* ghianda *f*

acoustic /ə'kuːstɪk/ *a* acustico

acoustically /ə'kuːstɪklɪ/ *adv* acusticamente

acoustic guitar *n* chitarra *f* acustica

acoustics /ə'kuːstɪks/ *npl* acustica *fsg*

acquaint /ə'kweɪnt/ *vt* ~ **sb with** metter qcno al corrente di; **be ~ed with** conoscere ‹*person*›; essere a conoscenza di ‹*fact*›

acquaintance /ə'kweɪntəns/ *n* (*person*) conoscente *mf*; **make sb's** ~ fare la conoscenza di qcno

acquiesce /ækwɪ'es/ *vi* acconsentire (**to, in** a)

acquiescence /ækwɪ'esəns/ *n* acquiescenza *f*

acquiescent /ækwɪ'esənt/ *a* arrendevole

acquire /ə'kwaɪə(r)/ *vt* acquisire

acquired /ə'kwaɪəd/ *a* ‹*characteristic*› acquisito; **it's an** ~ **taste** è una cosa che si impara ad apprezzare

acquisition /ækwɪ'zɪʃn/ *n* acquisizione *f*

acquisitive /ə'kwɪzətɪv/ *a* avido

acquit /ə'kwɪt/ *vt* (*pt/pp* **acquitted**) assolvere; ~ **oneself well** cavarsela bene

acquittal /ə'kwɪtəl/ *n* assoluzione *f*

acre /'eɪkə(r)/ *n* acro *m* (= 4 047 *m²*)

acreage /'eɪkərɪdʒ/ *n* superficie *f* in acri

acrid /'ækrɪd/ *a* acre

acrimonious /ækrɪ'məʊnɪəs/ *a* aspro

acrimony /'ækrɪmənɪ/ *n* asprezza *f*

acrobat /'ækrəbæt/ *n* acrobata *mf*

acrobatic /ækrə'bætɪk/ *a* acrobatico

acrobatics /ækrə'bætɪks/ *npl* acrobazie *fpl*

acronym /'ækrənɪm/ *n* acronimo *m*

across /ə'krɒs/ *adv* dall'altra parte; (*wide*) in larghezza; (*not lengthwise*) attraverso; (*in crossword*) orizzontale; **come** ~ **sth** imbattersi in qcsa; **go** ~ attraversare ● *prep* (*crosswise*) di traverso su; (*on the other side of*) dall'altra parte di

across-the-board *a* generale ● *adv* in generale

acrylic /ə'krɪlɪk/ *n* acrilico *m* ● *attrib* ‹*garment*› acrilico

act /ækt/ *n* atto *m*; (*in variety show*) numero *m*; **put on an** ~ *fam* fare scena ● *vi* agire; (*behave*) comportarsi; *Theat* recitare; (*pretend*) fingere; ~ **as** fare da ● *vt* recitare ‹*role*›
  ■ **act for** *vi* agire per conto di
  ■ **act up** *vi* ‹*child, photocopier:*› fare i capricci

acting /'æktɪŋ/ *a* ‹*deputy*› provvisorio ● *n* *Theat* recitazione *f*; (*profession*) teatro *m*; ~ **profession** professione *f* dell'attore

action /'ækʃn/ *n* azione *f*; *Mil* combattimento *m*; *Jur* azione *f* legale; **out of** ~ ‹*machine:*› fuori uso; **take** ~ agire; ~ ! *Cinema* ciac si gira!

action: action-packed *a* ‹*film*› d'azione. **action painting** *n* pittura *f* d'azione. **action replay** *n* replay *m inv*

activate /'æktɪveɪt/ *vt* attivare; (*Chem, Phys*) rendere attivo

active /'æktɪv/ *a* attivo

active duty, active service *n* *Mil* **be on** ~ ~ prestare servizio in zona di operazioni

actively /'æktɪvlɪ/ *adv* attivamente

activist /'æktɪvɪst/ *n* attivista *mf*

activity /æk'tɪvətɪ/ *n* attività *f inv*

activity holiday *n* *Br* vacanza *f* con attività ricreative

act of God *n* causa *f* di forza maggiore

actor /'æktə(r)/ *n* attore *m*

actress /'æktrəs/ *n* attrice *f*

actual /'æktʃʊəl/ *a* ‹*real*› reale

actually /'æktʃʊəlɪ/ *adv* in realtà

actuary /'æktʃʊərɪ/ *n* attuario, -a *mf*

acumen /'ækjʊmən/ *n* acume *m*

acupuncture /'ækjʊpʌŋktʃə(r)/ *n* agopuntura *f*

acupuncturist /ækjʊ'pʌŋktʃərɪst/ *n* agopuntore, -trice *mf*

acute /ə'kjuːt/ *a* acuto; ‹*shortage, hardship*› estremo

acute accent *n* accento *m* acuto

acute angle *n* angolo *m* acuto

acutely /ə'kjuːtlɪ/ *adv* acutamente; ‹*embarrassed, aware*› estremamente

AD *abbr* (**Anno Domini**) d.C.

ad /æd/ *n* pubblicità *f inv*; (*in paper*) inserzione *f*, annuncio *m*

adage /'ædɪdʒ/ *n* detto *m*, adagio *m*

adamant /'ædəmənt/ *a* categorico (**that** sul fatto che)

Adam's apple /'ædəmz/ *n* pomo *m* di Adamo

adapt /ə'dæpt/ *vt* adattare ‹*play*› ● *vi* adattarsi

adaptability /ədæptə'bɪlətɪ/ *n* adattabilità *f*

adaptable /ə'dæptəbl/ *a* adattabile

adaptation /ædæp'teɪʃn/ *n* *Theat* adattamento *m*

adapter, adaptor /ə'dæptə(r)/ *n* adattatore *m*; (*two-way*) presa *f* multipla

add /æd/ *vt* aggiungere; *Math* addizionare ● *vi* addizionare. ~ **to** *vi* (*fig: increase*) aggravare
  ■ **add in** *vt* (*include*) includere
  ■ **add on** *vt* aggiungere
  ■ **add up** *vt* addizionare ‹*figures*› ● *vi* addizionare; **it doesn't** ~ **up** *fig* non quadra; ~ **up to** ammontare a

added /'ædɪd/ *a* maggiore

adder /'ædə(r)/ *n* vipera *f*

addict /'ædɪkt/ *n* tossicodipendente *mf*; *fig* fanatico, -a *mf*

addicted /ə'dɪktɪd/ *a* assuefatto (**to** a); ~ **to drugs** tossicodipendente; **he's** ~ **to television** è videodipendente

addiction /ə'dɪkʃn/ *n* dipendenza *f*; (*to drugs*) tossicodipendenza *f*

addictive /ə'dɪktɪv/ *a* **be** ~ dare assuefazione

addition /ə'dɪʃn/ *n* *Math* addizione *f*; (*thing added*) aggiunta *f*; **in** ~ in aggiunta

additional /ə'dɪʃnəl/ *a* supplementare

additionally /ə'dɪʃnəlɪ/ *adv* in più

additive /'ædɪtɪv/ *n* additivo *m*

addled /'ædld/ *a* ‹*thinking*› confuso

add-on *a* accessorio

address /ə'dres/ *n* indirizzo *m*; (*speech*) discorso *m*; **form of** ~ formula *f* di cortesia

● *vt* indirizzare; (*speak to*) rivolgersi a ‹*person*›; tenere un discorso a ‹*meeting*›

address book *n* rubrica *f*

addressee /ædre'si:/ *n* destinatario, -a *mf*

adenoids /'ædənɔɪdz/ *npl* adenoidi *fpl*

adept /'ædept/ *a* esperto, -a *mf* (**at** in)

adequate /'ædɪkwət/ *a* adeguato

adequately /'ædɪkwətlɪ/ *adv* adeguatamente

adhere /əd'hɪə(r)/ *vi* aderire; **~ to** attenersi a ‹*principles, rules*›

adherence /əd'hɪərəns/ *n* fedeltà *f*

adherent /əd'hɪərənt/ *n* (*of doctrine*) adepto, -a *mf*; (*of policy*) sostenitore, -trice *mf*; (*of cult*) seguace *mf*

adhesion /əd'hi:ʒn/ *n* adesione *f*

adhesive /əd'hi:sɪv/ *a* adesivo ● *n* adesivo *m*

ad hoc /æd'hɒk/ *a* ‹*alliance, arrangement*› ad hoc; ‹*committee, legislation*› apposito; **on an ~ ~ basis** secondo le esigenze del momento

adieu /ə'dju:/ *n* **bid sb ~** dire addio a qcno

ad infinitum /ædɪnfɪ'naɪtəm/ *adv* ‹*continue*› all'infinito

adjacent /ə'dʒeɪsənt/ *a* adiacente

adjective /'ædʒɪktɪv/ *n* aggettivo *m*

adjoin /ə'dʒɔɪn/ *vt* essere adiacente a

adjoining /ə'dʒɔɪnɪŋ/ *a* adiacente

adjourn /ə'dʒɜːn/ *vt/i* aggiornare (**until** a)

adjournment /ə'dʒɜːnmənt/ *n* aggiornamento *m*

adjudge /ə'dʒʌdʒ/ *vt Jur* (*decree*) giudicare; aggiudicare ‹*costs, damages*›

adjudicate /ə'dʒuːdɪkeɪt/ *vi* decidere; (*in competition*) giudicare

adjudicator /ə'dʒuːdɪkeɪtə(r)/ *n* giudice *m*, arbitro *m*

adjunct /'ædʒʌŋkt/ *n* aggiunta *f*; (*hum: person*) appendice *f*

adjust /ə'dʒʌst/ *vt* modificare; regolare ‹*focus, sound etc*› ● *vi* adattarsi

adjustable /ə'dʒʌstəbl/ *a* regolabile

adjustable spanner *n* chiave *f* [inglese] a rullino

adjustment /ə'dʒʌstmənt/ *n* adattamento *m*; *Techn* regolamento *m*

adjutant /'ædʒʊtənt/ *n Mil* aiutante *mf*

ad lib /æd'lɪb/ *a* improvvisato ● *adv* a piacere ● *vi* (*pt/pp* **ad libbed**) *fam* improvvisare

adman /'ædmæn/ *n fam* pubblicitario *m*

admin /'ædmɪn/ *n Br fam* amministrazione *f*

administer /əd'mɪnɪstə(r)/ *vt* amministrare; somministrare ‹*medicine*›

administration /ədmɪnɪ'streɪʃn/ *n* amministrazione *f*; *Pol* governo *m*

administration costs *n* costi *mpl* di gestione

administrative /əd'mɪnɪstrətɪv/ *a* amministrativo

administrator /əd'mɪnɪstreɪtə(r)/ *n* amministratore, -trice *mf*

admirable /'ædmərəbl/ *a* ammirevole

admiral /'ædmərəl/ *n* ammiraglio *m*

admiralty /'ædmɪrəltɪ/ *n Br ministero m della marina militare britannica*

admiration /ædmə'reɪʃn/ *n* ammirazione *f*

admire /əd'maɪə(r)/ *vt* ammirare

admirer /əd'maɪrə(r)/ *n* ammiratore, -trice *mf*

admiring /əd'maɪrɪŋ/ *a* ‹*person*› pieno d'ammirazione; ‹*look*› ammirativo

admiringly /əd'maɪrɪŋlɪ/ *adv* ‹*look, say*› con ammirazione

admissible /əd'mɪsəbl/ *a* ammissibile

admission /əd'mɪʃn/ *n* ammissione *f*; (*to hospital*) ricovero *m*; (*entry*) ingresso *m*

admit /əd'mɪt/ *vt* (*pt/pp* **admitted**) (*let in*) far entrare; (*to hospital*) ricoverare; (*acknowledge*) ammettere ● *vi* **~ to sth** ammettere qcsa

admittance /əd'mɪtəns/ *n* ammissione *f*; **'no ~'** 'vietato l'ingresso'

admittedly /əd'mɪtɪdlɪ/ *adv* bisogna riconoscerlo

admonish /əd'mɒnɪʃ/ *vt* ammonire

admonition /ædmə'nɪʃn/ *n* ammonimento *m*

ad nauseam /æd'nɔːzɪæm/ *adv* ‹*discuss, repeat*› fino alla nausea

ado /ə'du:/ *n* **without more ~** senza ulteriori indugi

adolescence /ædə'lesns/ *n* adolescenza *f*

adolescent /ædə'lesnt/ *a & n* adolescente *mf*

adopt /ə'dɒpt/ *vt* adottare; *Pol* scegliere ‹*candidate*›

adopted /ə'dɒptɪd/ *a* ‹*son, daughter*› adottivo

adoption /əd'ɒpʃn/ *n* adozione *f*

adoption agency *n* agenzia *f* di adozioni

adoptive /ə'dɒptɪv/ *a* adottivo

adorable /ə'dɔːrəbl/ *a* adorabile

adoration /ædə'reɪʃn/ *n* adorazione *f*

adore /ə'dɔː(r)/ *vt* adorare

adoring /ə'dɔːrɪŋ/ *a* ‹*fan*› in adorazione; **she has an ~ husband** ha un marito che la adora

adoringly /ə'dɔːrɪŋlɪ/ *adv* con adorazione

adorn /ə'dɔːn/ *vt* ornare

adornment /ə'dɔːnmənt/ *n* ornamento *m*

adrenalin /ə'drenəlɪn/ *n* adrenalina *f*

Adriatic /eɪdrɪ'ætɪk/ *a & n* **the ~** [**Sea**] il mare Adriatico, l'Adriatico *m*

adrift /ə'drɪft/ *a* alla deriva; **be ~** andare alla deriva; **come ~** staccarsi

adroit /ə'drɔɪt/ *a* abile

adroitly /ə'drɔɪtlɪ/ *adv* abilmente

adulation /ædjʊ'leɪʃn/ *n* adulazione *f*

adult /'ædʌlt/ *n* adulto, -a *mf*

Adult Education *n Br* ≈ corsi *mpl* serali

adulterate /ə'dʌltəreɪt/ *vt* adulterare ‹*wine*›

adulterated /ə'dʌltəreɪtɪd/ *a* ‹*wine*› adulterato

adulterous /ə'dʌltərəs/ *a* ‹*relationship*› adulterino; ‹*person*› adultero

adultery /ə'dʌltərɪ/ *n* adulterio *m*

adulthood /'ædʌlthʊd/ *n* età *f* adulta

adult literacy classes *n Br* lezioni *fpl* di alfabetizzazione per adulti

advance /əd'vɑːns/ *n* avanzamento *m*; *Mil*

avanzata *f*; (*payment*) anticipo *m*; **in ~** in anticipo ● *vi* avanzare: (*make progress*) fare progressi ● *vt* promuovere ‹*cause*›; avanzare ‹*theory*›; anticipare ‹*money*›

advance booking *n* prenotazione *f* [in anticipo]

advance booking office *n* ufficio *m* prenotazioni

advanced /əd'vɑːnst/ *a* avanzato

Advanced Level *n Br Sch* = **A-Level**

advancement /əd'vɑːnsmənt/ *n* promozione *f*

advance: advance notice *n* preannuncio *m*. **advance party** *n Mil* avanguardia *f*. **advance payment** *n Comm* pagamento *m* anticipato. **advance warning** *n* preavviso *m*

advantage /əd'vɑːntɪdʒ/ *n* vantaggio *m*; **take ~ of** approfittare di

advantageous /ædvən'teɪdʒəs/ *a* vantaggioso

advent /'ædvent/ *n* avvento *m*; **A~** *Relig* Avvento *m*

adventure /əd'ventʃə(r)/ *n* avventura *f*

adventure playground *n Br* parco *m* giochi

adventurer /əd'ventʃərə(r)/ *n* avventuriero, -a *mf*

adventuress /əd'ventʃərɪs/ *n* avventuriera *f*

adventurous /əd'ventʃərəs/ *a* avventuroso

adverb /'ædvɜːb/ *n* avverbio *m*

adversary /'ædvəsərɪ/ *n* avversario, -a *mf*

adverse /'ædvɜːs/ *a* avverso

adversity /əd'vɜːsətɪ/ *n* avversità *f*

advert /'ædvɜːt/ *n fam* = **advertisement**

advertise /'ædvətaɪz/ *vt* reclamizzare; mettere un annuncio per ‹*job, flat*› ● *vi* fare pubblicità; (*for job, flat*) mettere un annuncio

advertisement /əd'vɜːtɪsmənt/ *n* pubblicità *f inv*; (*in paper*) inserzione *f*, annuncio *m*

advertiser /'ædvətaɪzə(r)/ *n* (*in newspaper*) inserzionista *mf*

advertising /'ædvətaɪzɪŋ/ *n* pubblicità *f* ● *attrib* pubblicitario

advertising: advertising agency *n* agenzia *f* di pubblicità. **advertising campaign** *n* campagna *f* pubblicitaria. **advertising executive** *n* dirigente *mf* pubblicitario, -a. **advertising industry** *n* settore *m* pubblicitario. **Advertising Standards Authority** *n Br organo m di controllo sulla pubblicità*

advice /əd'vaɪs/ *n* consigli *mpl*; **piece of ~** consiglio *m*

advice note *n* avviso *m*

advisability /ədvaɪzə'bɪlətɪ/ *n* opportunità *f*

advisable /əd'vaɪzəbl/ *a* consigliabile

advise /əd'vaɪz/ *vt* consigliare; (*inform*) avvisare; **~ sb to do sth** consigliare a qcno di fare qcsa; **~ sb against sth** sconsigliare qcsa a qcno

advisedly /əd'vaɪzɪdlɪ/ *adv* ‹*say*› deliberatamente

adviser /əd'vaɪzə(r)/ *n* consulente *mf*

advisory /əd'vaɪzərɪ/ *a* consultivo

advisory committee *n* comitato *m* consultivo

advocacy /'ædvəkəsɪ/ *n* appoggio *m*

advocate¹ /'ædvəkət/ *n* (*supporter*) fautore, -trice *mf*

advocate² /'ædvəkeɪt/ *vt* propugnare

Aegean /ɪ'dʒiːən/ *n* **the ~** l'Egeo *m*

aegis /'iːdʒɪs/ *n* **under the ~ of** sotto l'egida di

aeon /'iːən/ *n* **~s ago** milioni *mpl* e milioni di anni fa

aerate /'eəreɪt/ *vt* aerare; addizionare anidride carbonica a ‹*water*›

aerial /'eərɪəl/ *a* aereo ● *n* antenna *f*

aerial camera *n* macchina *f* fotografica per fotografie aeree

aerial warfare *n* guerra *f* aerea

aerie /'eərɪ/ *n Am* (*eyrie*) nido *m* [d'aquila]

aerobatics /eərə'bætɪks/ *npl* (*manoeuvres*) acrobazie *fpl* aeree

aerobics /eə'rəʊbɪks/ *n* aerobica *fsg*

aerodrome /'eərədrəʊm/ *n* aerodromo *m*

aerodynamic /eərəʊdaɪ'næmɪk/ *a* aerodinamico

aerodynamics /eərəʊdaɪ'næmɪks/ *n* aerodinamica *f*

aerogram[me] /'eərəʊgræm/ *n* aerogramma *m*

aeronautic[al] /eərə'nɔːtɪk[əl]/ *a* aeronautico

aeronautic[al] engineer *n* ingegnere *m* aeronautico

aeronautic[al] engineering *n* ingegneria *f* aeronautica

aeronautics /eərə'nɔːtɪks/ *n* aeronautica *f*

aeroplane /'eərəpleɪn/ *n* aeroplano *m*

aerosol /'eərəsɒl/ *n* bomboletta *f* spray

aerospace /'eərəspeɪs/ *n* (*industry*) industria *f* aerospaziale ● *attrib* ‹*engineer, company*› aerospaziale

aesthete /'iːsθiːt/ *n* esteta *mf*

aesthetic /iːs'θetɪk/ *a* estetico

aesthetically /iːs'θetɪklɪ/ *adv* ‹*restore*› con gusto; ‹*satisfying*› esteticamente

aestheticism /iːs'θetɪsɪzm/ *n* (*taste*) esteticità *f*; (*doctrine, quality*) estetismo *m*

aesthetics /iːs'θetɪks/ *n* estetica *f*

afar /ə'fɑː(r)/ *adv* **from ~** da lontano

affable /'æfəbl/ *a* affabile

affably /'æfəblɪ/ *adv* affabilmente

affair /ə'feə(r)/ *n* affare *m*; (*scandal*) caso *m*; (*sexual*) relazione *f*

affect /ə'fekt/ *vt* influire su; (*emotionally*) colpire; (*concern*) riguardare; (*pretend*) affettare

affectation /æfek'teɪʃn/ *n* affettazione *f*

affected /ə'fektɪd/ *a* affettato

affectedly /ə'fektɪdlɪ/ *adv* ‹*talk*› con affettazione

affection /ə'fekʃn/ *n* affetto *m*

affectionate /ə'fekʃnət/ *a* affettuoso

affectionately /ə'fekʃnətlɪ/ *adv* affettuosamente

affidavit /æfɪ'deɪvɪt/ *n* affidavit *m inv* (*di-*

chiarazione scritta e giurata davanti a un pubblico ufficiale)
affiliated /ə'fɪlieɪtɪd/ *a* affiliato
affiliation /əfɪlɪ'eɪʃn/ *n* (*process, state*) affiliazione *f*; (*link*) legame *m*
affinity /ə'fɪnəti/ *n* affinità *f inv*
affirm /ə'fɜːm/ *vt* affermare; *Jur* dichiarare solennemente
affirmative /ə'fɜːmətɪv/ *a* affermativo ● *n* **in the ~** affermativamente
affix /ə'fɪks/ *vt* affiggere; apporre (*signature*)
afflict /ə'flɪkt/ *vt* affliggere
affliction /ə'flɪkʃn/ *n* afflizione *f*
affluence /'æfluəns/ *n* agiatezza *f*
affluent /'æfluənt/ *a* agiato
afford /ə'fɔːd/ *vt* (*provide*) fornire; **be able to ~ sth** potersi permettere qcsa
affordable /ə'fɔːdəbl/ *a* abbordabile
affray /ə'freɪ/ *n* rissa *f*
affront /ə'frʌnt/ *n* affronto *m* ● *vt* fare un affronto a
Afghan /'æfgæn/ *n* (*person*) afgano, -a *mf*; (*language*) afgano *m*; (*coat*) pellicciotto *m* afgano
Afghan hound *n* levriero *m* afgano
Afghanistan /æf'gænɪstæn/ *n* Afganistan *m*
aficionado /æfɪsjə'nɑːdəʊ/ *n* aficionado, -a *mf*
afield /ə'fiːld/ *adv* **further ~** più lontano
aflame /ə'fleɪm/ *a & adv liter* in fiamme, sfolgorante; **be ~** (*cheek:*) essere in fiamme; **be ~ with desire** ardere dal desiderio
afloat /ə'fləʊt/ *a* a galla
afoot /ə'fʊt/ *a* **there's something ~** si sta preparando qualcosa
aforesaid /ə'fɔːsed/ *a Jur* suddetto
afraid /ə'freɪd/ *a* **be ~** aver paura; **I'm ~ not** purtroppo no; **I'm ~ so** temo di sì; **I'm ~ I can't help you** mi dispiace, ma non posso esserle d'aiuto
afresh /ə'freʃ/ *adv* da capo
Africa /'æfrɪkə/ *n* Africa *f*
African /'æfrɪkən/ *a & n* africano, -a *mf*
Afrikaans /æfrɪ'kɑːns/ *n* afrikaans *m*
Afrikaner /æfrɪ'kɑːnə(r)/ *n* boero, -a *mf*
Afro-American /æfrəʊə'merɪkən/ *a & n* afroamericano, -a *mf*
Afro-Caribbean /æfrəʊkærə'bɪən/ *a & n* afrocaraibico, -a *mf*
aft /ɑːft/ *adv Naut* a poppa; (*towards the stern*) verso poppa
after /'ɑːftə(r)/ *adv* dopo; **the day ~** il giorno dopo; **be ~** cercare ● *prep* dopo; **~ all** dopotutto; **the day ~ tomorrow** dopodomani ● *conj* dopo che
after: after-birth *n* residui *mpl* di placenta. **after-care** *n Med* ospedalizzazione *f* domiciliare. **after-dinner speaker** *n* persona *f* invitata a tenere un discorso dopo una cena o un ricevimento. **after-effect** *n* conseguenza *f*. **after-life** *n* vita *f* nell'aldilà
aftermath /'ɑːftəmɑːθ/ *n* conseguenze *fpl*; **the ~ of war** il dopoguerra; **in the ~ of** nel periodo successivo a

after: afternoon *n* pomeriggio *m*; **good ~!** buon giorno!. **afternoon tea** *n* merenda *f*. **after-pains** *npl* dolori *mpl* post-partum. **after-sales service** *n* servizio *m* assistenza clienti. **aftershave** *n* [lozione *f*] dopobarba *m inv*. **after-shock** *n fig* effetti *mpl*. **aftersun** *n & a* doposole *m inv*. **after-taste** *n* retrogusto *m*. **after-tax** *a* (*profits, earnings*) al netto. **afterthought** *n* **added as an ~** aggiunto in un secondo momento; **as an ~, why not...?** ripensandoci bene, perché non...?
afterwards /'ɑːftəwədz/ *adv* in seguito
again /ə'geɪn/ *adv* di nuovo; [then] **~** (*besides*) inoltre; (*on the other hand*) d'altra parte; **~ and ~** continuamente
against /ə'geɪnst/ *prep* contro
age /eɪdʒ/ *n* età *f inv*; (*era*) era *f*; **~s** *fam* secoli; **~s ago** *fam* secoli fa; **what ~ are you?** quanti anni hai?; **be under ~** non avere l'età richiesta; **he's two years of ~** ha due anni ● *vt/i* (*pres p* **ageing**) invecchiare
age bracket, age group *n* fascia *f* d'età
aged[1] /eɪdʒd/ *a* **~ two** di due anni
aged[2] /'eɪdʒɪd/ *a* anziano ● *n* **the ~** *pl* gli anziani
aged debt *n Fin* somma *f* in scadenza
ageing /'eɪdʒɪŋ/ *n* invecchiamento *m* ● *a* (*person, population*) che sta invecchiando
ageism /'eɪdʒɪzm/ *n* discriminazione *f* contro chi non è più giovane
ageless /'eɪdʒlɪs/ *a* senza età
agency /'eɪdʒənsi/ *n* agenzia *f*; **have the ~ for** essere un concessionario di
agency-fee *n* commissione *f*
agency-nurse *n* infermiere, -a *mf* privato, -a
agenda /ə'dʒendə/ *n* ordine *m* del giorno; **on the ~** all'ordine del giorno; *fig* in programma
agent /'eɪdʒənt/ *n* agente *mf*
age-old *a* secolare
age range *n* fascia *f* d'età
aggravate /'ægrəveɪt/ *vt* aggravare; (*annoy*) esasperare
aggravating /'ægrəveɪtɪŋ/ *a Jur* aggravante; (*fam: irritating*) irritante
aggravation /ægrə'veɪʃn/ *n* aggravamento *m*; (*annoyance*) esasperazione *f*
aggregate /'ægrɪgət/ *a* totale ● *n* totale *m*; **on ~** nel complesso
aggression /ə'greʃn/ *n* aggressione *f*
aggressive /ə'gresɪv/ *a* aggressivo
aggressively /ə'gresɪvlɪ/ *adv* aggressivamente
aggressiveness /ə'gresɪvnɪs/ *n* aggressività *f*
aggressor /ə'gresə(r)/ *n* aggressore *m*
aggrieved /ə'griːvd/ *a* risentito
aggro /'ægrəʊ/ *n fam* aggressività *f*; (*problems*) grane *fpl*
aghast /ə'gɑːst/ *a* inorridito
agile /'ædʒaɪl/ *a* agile
agility /ə'dʒɪlətɪ/ *n* agilità *f*
agitate /'ædʒɪteɪt/ *vt* mettere in agitazione;

(*shake*) agitare ● *vi fig* ~ **for** creare delle agitazioni per

agitated /'adʒɪteɪtɪd/ *a* agitato

agitation /adʒɪ'teɪʃn/ *n* agitazione *f*

agitator /'adʒɪteɪtə(r)/ *n* agitatore, -trice *mf*

AGM *n abbr* (**annual general meeting**) assemblea *f* generale annuale

agnostic /æg'nɒstɪk/ *a & n* agnostico, -a *mf*

ago /ə'gəʊ/ *adv* fa; **a long time/a month** ~ molto tempo/un mese fa; **how long** ~ **was it?** quanto tempo fa è successo?

agog /ə'gɒg/ *a* eccitato

agonize /'ægənaɪz/ *vi* angosciarsi (**over** per)

agonized /'ægənaɪzd/ *a* (*expression, cry*) angosciato

agonizing /'ægənaɪzɪŋ/ *a* angosciante

agony /'ægənɪ/ *n* agonia *f*; (*mental*) angoscia *f*; **be in** ~ avere dei dolori atroci

agony aunt *n persona f* chi tiene la posta del cuore in una rivista

agoraphobia /ægərə'fəʊbɪə/ *n* agorafobia *f*

agoraphobic /ægərə'fəʊbɪk/ *a* agorafobo, -a *mf*

agree /ə'gri:/ *vt* accordarsi su; ~ **to do sth** accettare di fare qcsa; ~ **that** essere d'accordo [sul fatto] che ● *vi* essere d'accordo; (*figures:*) concordare; (*reach agreement*) mettersi d'accordo; (*get on*) andare d'accordo; (*consent*) acconsentire (**to** a); **it doesn't** ~ **with me** mi fa male; ~ **with sth** (*approve of*) approvare qcsa

agreeable /ə'gri:əbl/ *a* gradevole; (*willing*) d'accordo

agreeably /ə'gri:əblɪ/ *adv* (*pleasantly*) piacevolmente; (*amicably*) in modo amichevole

agreed /ə'gri:d/ *a* convenuto

agreement /ə'gri:mənt/ *n* accordo *m*; **in** ~ d'accordo; **reach** ~ arrivare a un accordo

agricultural /ægrɪ'kʌltʃərəl/ *a* agricolo

agriculturalist /ægrɪ'kʌltʃərəlɪst/ *n* agronomo, -a *mf*

agricultural show *n* fiera *f* agricola

agriculture /'ægrɪkʌltʃə(r)/ *n* agricoltura *f*

agronomy /ə'grɒnəmɪ/ *n* agronomia *f*

aground /ə'graʊnd/ *adv* **run** ~ (*ship:*) arenarsi

ah /ɑ:/ *int* ~ **well!** (*resignedly*) va be'!

ahead /ə'hed/ *adv* avanti; **be** ~ **of** essere davanti a; *fig* essere avanti rispetto a; **draw** ~ passare davanti (**of** a); **go on** ~ cominciare ad andare; **get** ~ (*in life*) riuscire; **go** ~! fai pure!; **look** ~ pensare all'avvenire; **plan** ~ fare progetti per l'avvenire

AI *n abbr* (**artificial intelligence**) I.A. *f*

aid /eɪd/ *n* aiuto *m*; **in** ~ **of** a favore di ● *vt* aiutare

aide /eɪd/ *n* assistente *mf*

Aids /eɪdz/ *n* AIDS *m*

ailing /'eɪlɪŋ/ *a* malato

ailment /'eɪlmənt/ *n* disturbo *m*

aim /eɪm/ *n* mira *f*; *fig* scopo *m*; **take** ~ prendere la mira ● *vt* puntare (*gun*) (**at** su) ● *vi* mirare; ~ **to do sth** aspirare a fare qcsa

aimless /'eɪmlɪs/ *a* senza scopo

aimlessly /'eɪmlɪslɪ/ *adv* senza scopo

ain't /eɪnt/ *fam* = **am not; is not; are not; have not; has not**

air /eə(r)/ *n* aria *f*; **be on the** ~ (*programme:*) essere in onda; **put on** ~**s** darsi delle arie; **by** ~ in aereo; (*airmail*) per via aerea ● *vt* arieggiare; far conoscere (*views*); *pej* sfoggiare (*knowledge*)

air: air ambulance *n* aereo *m* ambulanza; (*helicopter*) eliambulanza *f*. **air bag** *n* Auto air bag *m inv*. **air-bed** *n* materassino *m* [gonfiabile]

airborne /'eəbɔ:n/ *a* (*plane*) in volo; (*troops*) aerotrasportato

air: airbrush *n* aerografo *m*. **airbubble** *n* (*in liquid, plastic, wallpaper*) bolla *f* d'aria. **air-conditioned** *a* con aria condizionata. **air conditioner** *n* condizionatore *m*. **air-conditioning** *n* aria *f* condizionata. **air-cooled** *a* (*engine*) raffreddato ad aria. **aircraft** *n* aereo *m*. **aircraft carrier** *n* portaerei *f inv*. **aircraft[s]man** *n Br* aviere *m*. **aircrew** *n* equipaggio *m* di volo. **air cushion** *n* (*inflatable cushion*) cuscino *m* gonfiabile; (*of hovercraft*) cuscino *m* d'aria. **air disaster** *n* disastro *m* aereo. **airdrop** *n* lancio *m* con paracadute. **air duct** *n* condotto *m* dell'aria. **airfare** *n* tariffa *f* aerea. **airfield** *n* campo *m* d'aviazione. **airflow** *n* spostamento *m* d'aria. **air force** *n* aviazione *f*. **airfreight** *n* (*goods*) merce *f* spedita via aerea; (*method of transport*) trasporto *m* aereo; (*charge*) costo *m* per trasporto aereo. **air freshener** *n* deodorante *m* per l'ambiente. **airgun** *n* fucile *m* pneumatico. **airhead** *n pej fam* idiota *mf*. **air hole** *n* sfiatatoio *m*. **air hostess** *n* hostess *f inv*

airing /'eərɪŋ/ *n* **give a room an** ~ arieggiare una stanza; **give an idea an** ~ *fig* ventilare un'idea

airing cupboard *n Br* sgabuzzino *m* del boiler dove viene riposta la biancheria ad asciugare

airless /'eəlɪs/ *a* (*evening*) senza vento; (*room*) poco ventilato

air: air letter *n* aerogramma *m*. **airlift** *vt* trasportare con ponte aereo ● *n* ponte *m* aereo. **airline** *n* compagnia *f* aerea. **airliner** *n* aereo *m* di linea. **airlock** *n* bolla *f* d'aria. **airmail** *n* posta *f* aerea. **air marshal** *n Br* maresciallo *m* d'aviazione. **airplane** *n Am* aereo *m*. **air pocket** *n* vuoto *m* d'aria. **airport** *n* aeroporto *m*. **air power** *n* potenza *f* aerea. **air-raid** *n* incursione *f* aerea. **air-raid shelter** *n* rifugio *m* antiaereo. **air-raid siren** *n* allarme *m* aereo. **air-raid warning** *n* allarme *m* aereo. **air rifle** *n* fucile *m* ad aria compressa. **air-sea rescue** *n* salvataggio *m* dal mare con impiego di mezzi aerei. **air shaft** *n* (*in mine*) pozzo *m* di ventilazione. **airship** *n* dirigibile *m*. **air show** *n* (*trade exhibition*) salone *m* dell'aviazione; (*flying show*) manifestazione *f* aerea. **airsickness** *n* mal *m* d'aereo. **air sock** *n* manica *f* a vento. **airspeed** *n* velocità *f* relativa all'aria. **airspeed indicator** *n* indicatore *m* di velocità (*su un aereo*). **airstream** *n* corren-

te *f* d'aria. **airstrip** *n* pista *f* d'atterraggio. **air terminal** *n* (*in town, terminus*) [air-]terminal *m inv.* **airtight** *a* ermetico. **airtime** *n Radio, TV* spazio *m* radiofonico/televisivo. **air-to-air** *a* ⟨*missile*⟩ aria-aria; ⟨*refuelling*⟩ in volo. **air traffic** *n* traffico *m* aereo. **air-traffic controller** *n* controllore *m* di volo. **air valve** *n* valvola *f* pneumatica. **air vent** *n* presa *f* d'aria. **air vice-marshal** *n Br* vice-maresciallo *m* dell'aviazione. **airwaves** *npl Radio, TV* onde *fpl* radio. **airway** *n* (*route*) rotta *f* aerea; (*airline*) compagnia *f* aerea; *Anat* via *f* respiratoria; (*ventilating passage*) pozzo *m* di ventilazione. **air waybill** *n* polizza *f* di carico aerea. **airworthiness** *n* idoneità *f* di volo. **airworthy** *a* idoneo al volo
airy /'eərɪ/ *a* (**-ier, -iest**) arieggiato; ⟨*manner*⟩ noncurante
airy-fairy /eərɪ'feərɪ/ *a Br fam* ⟨*plan, person*⟩ fuori dalla realtà
aisle /aɪl/ *n* corridoio *m*; (*in supermarket*) corsia *f*; (*in church*) navata *f*
ajar /ə'dʒɑ:(r)/ *a* socchiuso
aka *abbr* (**also known as**) alias
akin /ə'kɪn/ *a* **~ to** simile a
alabaster /'æləbɑ:stə(r)/ *n* alabastro *m*
alacrity /ə'lækrətɪ/ *n* alacrità *f inv*
alarm /ə'lɑ:m/ *n* allarme *m*; **set the ~** (*of alarm clock*) mettere la sveglia; **in ~** in stato di allarme ● *vt* allarmare; **don't be ~ed!** non si allarmi!
alarm: alarm bell *n* campanello *m* d'allarme; **set the ~ ~s ringing** *n Br fig* far scattare il campanello d'allarme. **alarm call** *n Teleph* sveglia *f* automatica. **alarm clock** *n* sveglia *f*
alarming /ə'lɑ:mɪŋ/ *a* allarmante, preoccupante
alarmist /ə'lɑ:mɪst/ *a & n* allarmista *mf*
alas /ə'læs/ *int* ahimè
Albania /æl'beɪnɪə/ *n* Albania *f*
Albanian /æl'beɪnɪən/ *n* (*person*) albanese *mf*; (*language*) albanese *m* ● *a* albanese
albatross /'ælbətrɒs/ *n* (*also in golf*) albatro *m*
albeit /ɔ:l'bi:ɪt/ *adv & conj* benché
albino /æl'bi:nəʊ/ *a & n* albino, -a *mf*
album /'ælbəm/ *n* album *m inv*
albumen /'ælbjʊmɪn/ *n Biol, Bot* albume *m*
alchemist /'ælkɪmɪʃt/ *n* alchimista *m*
alchemy /'ælkɪmɪ/ *n Chem, fig* alchimia *f*
alcohol /'ælkəhɒl/ *n* alcool *m*
alcoholic /ælkə'hɒlɪk/ *a* alcolico ● *n* alcolizzato, -a *mf*
Alcoholics Anonymous *n* Anonima *f* Alcolisti
alcoholism /'ælkəhɒlɪzm/ *n* alcolismo *m*
alcove /'ælkəʊv/ *n* alcova *f*
alder /ɔ:ldə(r)/ *n* (*tree, wood*) ontano *m*
ale /eɪl/ *n* birra *f*
alert /ə'lɜ:t/ *a* attento; (*watchful*) vigile ● *n* segnale *m* d'allarme; **be on the ~** stare allerta ● *vt* allertare
alertness /ə'lɜ:tnɪs/ *n* (*attentiveness*) attenzione *f*; (*liveliness*) vivacità *f*

A-level *n Br Sch* **~s** ≈ esami *mpl* di maturità; **he got an ~ in history** ha portato storia alla maturità
Alexandria /ælɪg'zændrɪə/ *n* Alessandria *f* [d'Egitto]
alfalfa /æl'fælfə/ *n* erba *f* medicinale
alfresco /æl'freskəʊ/ *a & adv* all'aperto
algae /'ældʒi:/ *npl* alghe *fpl*
algebra /'ældʒɪbrə/ *n* algebra *f*
Algeria /æl'dʒɪərɪə/ *n* Algeria *f*
Algerian /æl'dʒɪərɪən/ *a & n* algerino, -a *mf*
Algiers /æl'dʒɪəz/ *n* Algeri *f*
algorithm /'ælgərɪðm/ *n* algoritmo *m*
alias /'eɪlɪəs/ *n* pseudonimo *m* ● *adv* alias
alibi /'ælɪbaɪ/ *n* alibi *m inv*
alien /'eɪlɪən/ *a* straniero; *fig* estraneo ● *n* straniero, -a *mf*; (*from space*) alieno, -a *mf*
alienate /'eɪlɪəneɪt/ *vt* alienare
alienation /eɪlɪə'neɪʃn/ *n* alienazione *f*
alight¹ /ə'laɪt/ *vi* scendere; ⟨*bird:*⟩ posarsi
alight² *a* **be ~** essere in fiamme; **set ~** dar fuoco a
align /ə'laɪn/ *vt* allineare
alignment /ə'laɪnmənt/ *n* allineamento *m*; **out of ~** non allineato
alike /ə'laɪk/ *a* simile; **be ~** rassomigliarsi ● *adv* in modo simile; **look ~** rassomigliarsi; **summer and winter ~** sia d'estate che d'inverno
alimentary /ælɪ'mentərɪ/ *a* ⟨*system*⟩ digerente; ⟨*process*⟩ digestivo
alimentary canal *n* tubo *m* digerente
alimony /'ælɪmənɪ/ *n* alimenti *mpl*
alive /ə'laɪv/ *a* vivo; **~ with** brulicante di; **~ to** sensibile a; **~ and kicking** vivo e vegeto
alkali /'ælkəlaɪ/ *n* alcali *m*
alkaline /'ælkəlaɪn/ *a* alcalino
all /ɔ:l/ *a* tutto; **~ the children, ~ children** tutti i bambini; **~ day** tutto il giorno; **he refused ~ help** ha rifiutato qualsiasi aiuto; **for ~ that** (*nevertheless*) perciò; **in ~ sincerity** in tutta sincerità; **be ~ for** essere favorevole a ● *pron* tutto; **~ of you/them** tutti voi/loro; **~ of it** tutto; **~ of the town** tutta la città; **~ but one** tutti tranne uno; **in ~** in tutto; **~ in ~** tutto sommato; **most of ~** più di ogni altra cosa; **once and for ~** una volta per tutte; **~ being well** salvo complicazioni ● *adv* completamente; **~ but** quasi; **~ at once** (*at the same time*) tutto in una volta; **~ at once, ~ of a sudden** all'improvviso; **~ too soon** troppo presto; **~ the same** (*nevertheless*) ciononostante; **~ the better** meglio ancora; **she's not ~ that good an actress** non è poi così brava come attrice; **~ in** in tutto; *fam* esausto; **thirty/three ~** (*in sport*) trenta/tre pari; **~ over** (*finished*) tutto finito; (*everywhere*) dappertutto; **it's ~ right** (*I don't mind*) non fa niente; **I'm ~ right** (*not hurt*) non ho niente; **~ right!** va bene!
all-American *a* ⟨*record, champion*⟩ americano; ⟨*girl, boy, hero*⟩ tipicamente americano
all-around *a* ⟨*improvement*⟩ generale
allay /ə'leɪ/ *vt* placare ⟨*suspicions, anger*⟩
all-clear *n Mil* cessato *m* allarme/pericolo;

(*from doctor*) autorizzazione *f*; **give sb the ~ ~** *fig* dare il via libera a qcno

all-consuming *a* ⟨*passion*⟩ sfrenato; ⟨*ambition*⟩ smisurato

all-day *a* ⟨*event*⟩ che dura tutto il giorno

allegation /ælɪˈgeɪʃn/ *n* accusa *f*

allege /əˈledʒ/ *vt* dichiarare

alleged /əˈledʒd/ *a* presunto

allegedly /əˈledʒɪdlɪ/ *adv* a quanto si dice

allegiance /əˈliːdʒəns/ *n* fedeltà *f*

allegorical /ælɪˈgɒrɪkl/ *a* allegorico

allegory /ˈælɪgərɪ/ *n* allegoria *f*

all-embracing /-əmˈbreɪsɪŋ/ *a* globale

allergic /əˈlɜːdʒɪk/ *a* allergico

allergist /ˈælədʒɪst/ *n* allergologo, -a *mf*

allergy /ˈælədʒɪ/ *n* allergia *f*

alleviate /əˈliːvɪeɪt/ *vt* alleviare

alleviation /əliːvɪˈeɪʃn/ *n* alleviamento *m*, alleggerimento *m*

alley /ˈælɪ/ *n* vicolo *m*; (*for bowling*) corsia *f*

alley-way /ˈælɪweɪ/ *n* vicolo *m*

all-found *a* £200 ~ 200 sterline inclusi vitto e alloggio

alliance /əˈlaɪəns/ *n* alleanza *f*

allied /ˈælaɪd/ *a* alleato; (*fig: related*) connesso (**to** a)

alligator /ˈælɪgeɪtə(r)/ *n* alligatore *m*

all-important *a* essenziale

all in *a* (*Br fam: exhausted*) distrutto; ⟨*fee, price*⟩ tutto compreso

all-inclusive *a* ⟨*fee, price*⟩ tutto compreso

all-in-one *a* ⟨*garment*⟩ in un pezzo solo

all-in wrestling *n* Sport catch *m*

all-night *a* ⟨*party, meeting*⟩ che dura tutta la notte; ⟨*radio station*⟩ che trasmette tutta la notte; ⟨*service*⟩ notturno

allocate /ˈæləkeɪt/ *vt* assegnare; distribuire ⟨*resources*⟩

allocation /æləˈkeɪʃn/ *n* assegnazione *f*; (*of resources*) distribuzione *f*

all-or-nothing *a* ⟨*approach, policy*⟩ senza vie di mezzo

allot /əˈlɒt/ *vt* (*pt/pp* **allotted**) distribuire

allotment /əˈlɒtmənt/ *n* distribuzione *f*; (*share*) parte *f*; (*land*) piccolo lotto *m* di terreno

all-out *a* ⟨*effort*⟩ estremo; ⟨*attack*⟩ senza esclusione di colpi ● *adv* **go all out to do sth/for sth** mettercela tutta per fare qcsa/per qcsa

all-over *a* ⟨*tan*⟩ integrale

all over *prep* ~ ~ **China** in/per tutta la Cina; **the news is ~ ~ the village** lo sanno tutti in paese; **be ~ ~ sb** (*fawning over*) stare appiccicato a qcno ● *adv* **be trembling ~ ~** tremare tutto; **that's Mary ~ ~!** è proprio da Mary! ● *a* **when it's ~ ~** (*finished*) quando è tutto finito

allow /əˈlaʊ/ *vt* permettere; (*grant*) accordare; (*reckon on*) contare; (*agree*) ammettere; **~ for** tener conto di; **~ sb to do sth** permettere a qcno di fare qcsa; **you are not ~ed to...** è vietato...; **how much are you ~ed?** qual è il limite?

allowable /əˈlaʊəbl/ *a* permissibile; *Jur* lecito; ⟨*tax*⟩ deducibile

allowance /əˈlaʊəns/ *n* sussidio *m*; (*Am: pocket money*) paghetta *f*; (*for petrol etc*) indennità *f inv*; (*of luggage, duty free*) limite *m*; (*for tax purposes*) deduzione *f*; **make ~s for** essere indulgente verso ⟨*sb*⟩; tener conto di ⟨*sth*⟩

alloy /ˈælɔɪ/ *n* lega *f*

alloy steel *n* lega *f* d'acciaio

alloy wheel *n* cerchione *m* in lega d'acciaio

all points bulletin *n Am* allarme *m* generale

all-powerful *a* onnipotente

all-purpose *a* ⟨*building*⟩ polivalente; ⟨*utensil*⟩ multiuso

all right *a* **is it ~ ~ if...?** va bene se...?; **is that ~ ~ with you?** ti va bene?; **sounds ~ ~ to me** per me va bene; **that's [quite] ~ ~** (*it doesn't matter*) non c'è problema; **is my hair ~ ~?** sono a posto i miei capelli?; **it's ~ ~ for you!** è facile per te!; **she's ~ ~** (*competent*) è abbastanza brava; (*attractive*) non è niente male; (*pleasant*) è piuttosto simpatica; **will you be ~ ~?** (*able to manage*) te la caverai?; **feel ~ ~** (*well*) sentirsi bene ● *adv* ⟨*function, see*⟩ bene; (*not brilliantly*) così così; **can I? – ~ ~** posso? – d'accordo; **she's doing ~ ~** (*in life*) le cose le vanno bene; (*in health*) sta bene; (*in activity*) se la cava bene; **she knows ~ ~!** (*without doubt*) lei lo sa di sicuro!; **~ ~, ~ ~!** va bene, va bene!

all-risk *a* ⟨*policy, cover*⟩ multirischi

all-round *a* ⟨*improvement*⟩ generale; ⟨*athlete*⟩ completo

all-rounder /-ˈraʊndə(r)/ *n* **be a good ~** essere versatile

allspice /ˈɔːlspaɪs/ *n* pepe *m* della Giamaica

all square *a* **be ~ ~** ⟨*people:*⟩ essere pari; ⟨*accounts:*⟩ quadrare

all-time *a* ⟨*record*⟩ assoluto, senza precedenti; **the ~ greats** (*people*) i grandi; **~ high** massimo *m* storico; **be at an ~ low** ⟨*person, morale:*⟩ essere a terra; ⟨*figures, shares:*⟩ toccare il minimo storico

all told *adv* tutto sommato

allude /əˈluːd/ *vi* alludere

allure /æˈljʊə(r)/ *n* attrattiva *f*

alluring /əˈljʊrɪŋ/ *a* allettante, affascinante

allusion /əˈluːʒn/ *n* allusione *f*

ally[1] /ˈælaɪ/ *n* alleato, -a *mf*

ally[2] /əˈlaɪ/ *vt* (*pt/pp* **-ied**) alleare; **~ oneself with** allearsi con

almighty /ɔːlˈmaɪtɪ/ *a* (*fam: big*) mega *inv* ● *n* **the A ~** l'Onnipotente *m*

almond /ˈɑːmənd/ *n* mandorla *f*; (*tree*) mandorlo *m*

almost /ˈɔːlməʊst/ *adv* quasi

alms /ɑːmz/ *npl* (*liter*) elemosina *f sg*

aloft /əˈlɒft/ *adv* in alto; *Naut* sull'alberatura; **from ~** dall'alto

alone /əˈləʊn/ *a* solo; **leave me ~!** lasciami in pace!; **let ~** (*not to mention*) figurarsi ● *adv* da solo

along /ə'lɒŋ/ *prep* lungo ● *adv* ~ **with** assieme a; **all** ~ tutto il tempo; **come** ~! (*hurry up*) vieni qui!; **I'll bring it** ~ lo porto lì; **I'll be** ~ **in a minute** arrivo tra un attimo; **move** ~ spostarsi; **move** ~! circolare!

alongside /əlɒŋ'saɪd/ *adv* lungo bordo ● *prep* lungo; **work** ~ **sb** lavorare fianco a fianco con qcno

aloof /ə'lu:f/ *a* distante

aloud /ə'laʊd/ *adv* ad alta voce

alpaca /æl'pækə/ *n* alpaca *m inv*

alpha /'ælfə/ *n* (*letter*) alfa *f inv*; *Br Univ* ≈ trenta *m inv* e lòde

alphabet /'ælfəbet/ *n* alfabeto *m*

alphabetical /ælfə'betɪkl/ *a* alfabetico

alphabetically /ælfə'betɪklɪ/ *adv* in ordine alfabetico

alpine /'ælpaɪn/ *a* alpino

Alps /ælps/ *npl* Alpi *fpl*

already /ɔ:l'redɪ/ *adv* già

alright /ɔ:l'raɪt/ = **all right**

Alsace /æl'zæs/ *n* Alsazia *f*

Alsatian /æl'seɪʃn/ *n* (*dog*) pastore *m* tedesco

also /'ɔ:lsəʊ/ *adv* anche; ~, **I need...** inoltre, ho bisogno di...

altar /'ɔ:ltə(r)/ *n* altare *m*

altar: **altar boy** *n* chierichetto *m*. **altar cloth** *n* tovaglia *f* da altare. **altar piece** *n* pala *f* d'altare

alter /'ɔ:ltə(r)/ *vt* cambiare; aggiustare ⟨*clothes*⟩ ● *vi* cambiare

alteration /ɔ:ltə'reɪʃn/ *n* modifica *f*

altercation /ɔ:ltə'keɪʃn/ *n* alterco *m*

alternate[1] /'ɔ:ltəneɪt/ *vi* alternarsi ● *vt* alternare

alternate[2] /ɔ:l'tɜ:nət/ *a* alterno; **on** ~ **days** a giorni alterni

alternately /ɔ:l'tɜ:nətlɪ/ *adv* in modo alterno; (*Am: alternatively*) alternativamente

alternating current /'ɔ:ltəneɪtɪŋ/ *n* corrente *f* alternata

alternation /ɔ:ltə'reɪʃn/ *n* alternanza *f*

alternative /ɔ:l'tɜ:nətɪv/ *a* alternativo ● *n* alternativa *f*

alternatively /ɔ:l'tɜ:nətɪvlɪ/ *adv* alternativamente

alternative medicine *n* medicina *f* alternativa

alternative technology *n* tecnologia *f* alternativa

alternator /'ɔ:ltəneɪtə(r)/ *n Electr* alternatore *m*

although /ɔ:l'ðəʊ/ *conj* benché, sebbene

altimeter /'æltɪmi:tə(r)/ *n* altimetro *m*

altitude /'æltɪtju:d/ *n* altitudine *f*

alto /'æltəʊ/ *n* contralto *m*

altogether /ɔ:ltə'geðə(r)/ *adv* (*in all*) in tutto; (*completely*) completamente; **I'm not** ~ **sure** non sono del tutto sicuro

altruism /'æltruɪzm/ *n* altruismo *m*

altruistic /æltru'ɪstɪk/ *a* altruistico

aluminium /æljʊ'mɪnɪəm/ *n*, *Am* **aluminum** /ə'lu:mɪnəm/ *n* alluminio *m*

aluminium foil *n* carta *f* stagnola

alumna /ə'lʌmnə/ *n Am Sch, Univ* ex allieva *f*

alumnus /ə'lʌmnəs/ *n Am Sch, Univ* ex allievo *m*

always /'ɔ:lweɪz/ *adv* sempre

am /æm/ *see* **be**

a.m. *abbr* (**ante meridiem**) del mattino

amalgam /ə'mælgəm/ *n* amalgama *m*

amalgamate /ə'mælgəmeɪt/ *vt* fondere ● *vi* fondersi

amalgamation /əmælgə'meɪʃn/ *n* fusione *f*; (*of styles*) amalgama *m*

amass /ə'mæs/ *vt* accumulare

amateur /'æmətə(r)/ *n* non professionista *mf*; *pej* dilettante *mf* ● *attrib* dilettante; ~ **dramatics** filodrammatica *f*

amateurish /'æmətərɪʃ/ *a* dilettantesco

amaze /ə'meɪz/ *vt* stupire

amazed /ə'meɪzd/ *a* stupito

amazement /ə'meɪzmənt/ *n* stupore *m*; **to her** ~ con suo grande stupore; **in** ~ stupito

amazing /ə'meɪzɪŋ/ *a* incredibile

amazingly /ə'meɪzɪŋlɪ/ *adv* incredibilmente

Amazon /'æməzən/ *n* (*in myths*) Amazzone *f*; (*fig: strong woman*) amazzone *f*; (*river*) Rio *m* delle Amazzoni ● *attrib* ⟨*basin, forest, tribe*⟩ amazzonico

ambassador /æm'bæsədə(r)/ *n* ambasciatore, -trice *mf*

ambassador-at-large *n Am* ambasciatore, -trice *mf* a disposizione

amber /'æmbə(r)/ *n* ambra *f* ● *a* (*colour*) ambra *inv*

ambidextrous /æmbɪ'dekstrəs/ *a* ambidestro

ambience /'æmbɪəns/ *n* atmosfera *f*

ambient /'æmbɪənt/ *a* ⟨*temperature*⟩ ambiente *inv*; ⟨*noise*⟩ circostante

ambiguity /æmbɪ'gju:ətɪ/ *n* ambiguità *f inv*

ambiguous /æm'bɪgjʊəs/ *a* ambiguo

ambiguously /æm'bɪgjʊəslɪ/ *adv* in modo ambiguo

ambition /æm'bɪʃn/ *n* ambizione *f*; (*aim*) aspirazione *f*

ambitious /æm'bɪʃəs/ *a* ambizioso

ambivalence /æm'bɪvələns/ *n* ambivalenza *f*

ambivalent /æm'bɪvələnt/ *a* ambivalente

amble /'æmb(ə)l/ *vi* camminare senza fretta

ambulance /'æmbjʊləns/ *n* ambulanza *f*

ambulance man *n* guidatore *m* di ambulanze

ambush /'æmbʊʃ/ *n* imboscata *f* ● *vt* tendere un'imboscata a

ameba /ə'mi:bə/ *n Am* ameba *f*

amen /ɑ:'men/ *int* amen

amenability /əmi:nə'bɪlɪtɪ/ *n* arrendevolezza *f*

amenable /ə'mi:nəbl/ *a* conciliante; ~ **to** sensibile a

amend /ə'mend/ *vt* modificare ● *npl* **make** ~**s** fare ammenda (**for** di, per)

amendment /ə'mendmənt/ *n* modifica *f*

amenities /ə'mi:nətɪz/ *npl* comodità *fpl*

America /ə'merɪkə/ n America f
American /ə'merɪkən/ a & n americano, -a mf
American: American Civil War n guerra f di secessione [americana]. **American English** n inglese m americano. **American Indian** n indiano, -a mf d'America
Americanism /ə'merɪkənɪzm/ n americanismo m
amethyst /'æməθɪst/ n (gem) ametista f
Amex /'æmeks/ n abbr (**American Stock Exchange**) Borsa f valori americana; abbr **American Express**
amiable /'eɪmɪəbl/ a amabile
amicable /'æmɪkəbl/ a amichevole
amicably /'æmɪkəblɪ/ adv amichevolmente
amid[st] /ə'mɪd[st]/ prep in mezzo a
amino acid /ə'mi:nəʊ/ n amminoacido m
amiss /ə'mɪs/ a **there's something ~** c'è qualcosa che non va ● adv **take sth ~** prendersela [a male]; **it won't come ~** non sarebbe sgradito
ammo /'æməʊ/ n abbr (**ammunition**) munizioni fpl
ammonia /ə'məʊnɪə/ n ammoniaca f
ammunition /æmjʊ'nɪʃn/ n munizioni fpl
amnesia /æm'ni:zɪə/ n amnesia f
amnesty /'æmnəstɪ/ n amnistia f
amoeba /ə'mi:bə/ n ameba f
amoebic /ə'mi:bɪk/ a (dysentry etc) amebico
amok /ə'mɒk/ adv **run ~** essere in preda a furore; (imagination:) scatenarsi
among[st] /ə'mʌŋ[st]/ prep tra, fra; **talk ~ yourselves** parlate tra [di] voi
amoral /eɪ'mɒrəl/ a amorale
amorality /eɪmə'rælətɪ/ n amoralità f
amorous /'æmərəs/ a amoroso
amorphous /ə'mɔ:fəs/ a Chem amorfo; (ideas, plans) confuso; (shape, collection) informe
amount /ə'maʊnt/ n quantità f inv; (sum of money) montante m ● vi **~ to** ammontare a; fig equivalere a
amp /æmp/ n ampère m inv
ampere /'æmpeə(r)/ n ampere m inv
ampersand /'æmpəsænd/ n e f inv commerciale
amphetamine /æm'fetəmi:n/ n anfetamina f
amphibian /æm'fɪbɪən/ n anfibio m
amphibious /æm'fɪbɪəs/ a anfibio
amphitheatre /'æmfɪθi:ətə(r)/ n anfiteatro m
ample /'æmpl/ a (large) grande; (proportions) ampio; (enough) largamente sufficiente
amplifier /'æmplɪfaɪə(r)/ n amplificatore m
amplify /'æmplɪfaɪ/ vt (pt/pp -ied) amplificare (sound)
amply /'æmplɪ/ adv largamente
amputate /'æmpjuteɪt/ vt amputare
amputation /æmpjʊ'teɪʃn/ n amputazione f
amputee /æmpjʊ'ti:/ n mutilato, -a mf (in seguito ad amputazione)
amuse /ə'mju:z/ vt divertire

amused /ə'mju:zd/ a divertito
amusement /ə'mju:zmənt/ n divertimento m
amusement arcade n sala f giochi
amusement park n luna park m inv
amusing /ə'mju:zɪŋ/ a divertente
an /ən/, accentato /æn/ see **a**
anabolic steroid /ænə'bɒlɪk/ n anabolizzante m
anachronism /ə'nækrənɪzm/ n **be an ~** (object, custom etc:) essere anacronistico
anaemia /ə'ni:mɪə/ n anemia f
anaemic /ə'ni:mɪk/ a anemico
anaerobic /æneə'rəʊbɪk/ a anaerobico
anaesthesia /ænəs'θi:zɪə/ n anestesia f
anaesthetic /ænəs'θetɪk/ n anestesia f; **give sb an ~** somministrare a qcno l'anestesia
anaesthetist /ə'ni:sθətɪst/ n anestesista mf
anaesthetize /ə'ni:sθətaɪz/ vt anestetizzare
anagram /'ænəgræm/ n anagramma m
analgesic /ænəl'dʒi:zɪk/ a & n analgesico m
analogous /ə'næləgəs/ a analogo
analog[ue] /'ænəlɒg/ a analogico
analogy /ə'nælədʒɪ/ n analogia f
analyse /'ænəlaɪz/ vt analizzare
analysis /ə'næləsɪs/ n analisi f inv
analyst /'ænəlɪst/ n analista mf
analytical /ænə'lɪtɪkl/ a analitico
anarchic[al] /ə'nɑ:kɪk[l]/ a anarchico
anarchist /'ænəkɪst/ n anarchico, -a mf
anarchy /'ænəkɪ/ n anarchia f
anathema /ə'næθəmə/ n eresia f
anatomical /ænə'tɒmɪkl/ a anatomico
anatomically /ænə'tɒmɪklɪ/ adv anatomicamente
anatomy /ə'nætəmɪ/ n anatomia f
ANC n abbr (**African National Congress**) Congresso m Nazionale Africano
ancestor /'ænsestə(r)/ n antenato, -a mf
ancestral /æn'sestrəl/ a ancestrale; (home) avito
ancestry /'ænsestrɪ/ n antenati mpl
anchor /'æŋkə(r)/ n ancora f ● vi gettar l'ancora ● vt ancorare
anchorage /'æŋkərɪdʒ/ n ancoraggio m
anchorman /'æŋkəmæn/ n Radio, TV anchor man m inv; Sport staffettista m dell'ultima frazione
anchorwoman /'æŋkəwʊmən/ n Radio TV anchor woman f inv
anchovy /'æntʃəvɪ/ n acciuga f
ancient /'eɪnʃənt/ a antico; fam vecchio; **~ Rome** l'antica Roma f
ancillary /æn'sɪlərɪ/ a ausiliario
and /ənd/, accentato /ænd/ conj e; **~ so on** e così via; **two ~ two** due più due; **six hundred ~ two** seicentodue; **more ~ more** sempre più; **nice ~ warm** bello caldo; **try ~ come** cerca di venire; **go ~ get** vai a prendere
Andean /'ændɪən/ a andino
Andes /'ændi:z/ npl **the ~** le Ande
Andorra /æn'dɔ:rə/ n Andorra f
anecdote /'ænɪkdəʊt/ n aneddoto m

anemone /ə'nemənɪ/ n Bot anemone m

anew /ə'njuː/ adv di nuovo

angel /'eɪndʒl/ n angelo m

angel cake n dolce m di pan di Spagna

angelfish /'eɪndʒlfɪʃ/ n angelo m di mare

angelic /æn'dʒelɪk/ a angelico

anger /'æŋgə(r)/ n rabbia f ● vt far arrabbiare

angina (pectoris) /æn'dʒaɪnə('pektərɪs)/ n angina f pectoris

angle[1] /'æŋgl/ n angolo m; fig angolazione f; **at an ~** storto

angle[2] vi pescare con la lenza; **~ for** fig cercare di ottenere

angle bracket n Techn parentesi f inv uncinata

Anglepoise [lamp] /'æŋglpɔɪz/ n lampada f a braccio estensibile

angler /'æŋglə(r)/ n pescatore, -trice mf

Anglican /'æŋglɪkən/ a & n anglicano, -a mf

anglicism /'æŋglɪsɪzm/ n anglicismo m

anglicize /'æŋglɪsaɪz/ vt anglicizzare

angling /'æŋglɪŋ/ n pesca f con la lenza

Anglo+ /'æŋgləʊ/ pref anglo+

Anglo-American a & n angloamericano, -a mf

Anglophone /'æŋgləfəʊn/ a & n anglofono, -a mf

Anglo-Saxon /æŋgləʊ'sæksn/ a & n anglo-sassone mf

Angola /æŋ'gəʊlə/ n Angola f

angora /æŋ'gɔːrə/ n lana f d'angora

angrily /'æŋgrɪlɪ/ adv rabbiosamente

angry /'æŋgrɪ/ a (**-ier, -iest**) arrabbiato; **get ~** arrabbiarsi; **~ with** or **at sb** arrabbiato con qcno; **~ at** or **about sth** arrabbiato per qcsa

anguish /'æŋgwɪʃ/ n angoscia f; **in ~** in preda all'angoscia

anguished /'æŋgwɪʃt/ a (suffering) straziante; ⟨person⟩ angosciato

angular /'æŋgjʊlə(r)/ a angolare

animal /'ænɪml/ a & n animale m

animal: animal activist n animalista mf. **animal experiment** n esperimento m sugli animali. **animal husbandry** n allevamento m. **animal kingdom** n regno m animale. **animal lover** n amante mf degli animali. **animal product** n prodotto m di origine animale. **animal sanctuary** n rifugio m per animali. **animal testing** n sperimentazione f sugli animali

animate[1] /'ænɪmət/ a animato

animate[2] /'ænɪmeɪt/ vt animare

animated /'ænɪmeɪtɪd/ a animato; ⟨person⟩ vivace

animation /ænɪ'meɪʃn/ n animazione f

animator /'ænɪmeɪtə(r)/ n (film cartoonist) animatore, -trice mf; (director) regista mf di film d'animazione

animosity /ænɪ'mɒsətɪ/ n animosità f inv

aniseed /'ænɪsiːd/ n anice f

ankle /'æŋk(ə)l/ n caviglia f

ankle: anklebone n astragalo m. **ankle-deep** a **be ~ in mud** a essere nel fan-

go fino alle caviglie. **ankle-length** a ⟨dress⟩ alla caviglia. **ankle sock** n calzino m

annals /'ænəlz/ npl **go down in the ~** [**of history**] passare agli annali

annex /ə'neks/ vt annettere

annexation /ænek'seɪʃn/ n (action) annessione f; (land annexed) territorio m annesso

annex[e] /'æneks/ n annesso m

annihilate /ə'naɪəleɪt/ vt annientare

annihilation /ənaɪə'leɪʃn/ n annientamento m

anniversary /ænɪ'vɜːsərɪ/ n anniversario m

Anno Domini /ænəʊ'dɒmɪnaɪ/ adv dopo Cristo

annotate /'ænəteɪt/ vt annotare

announce /ə'naʊns/ vt annunciare

announcement /ə'naʊnsmənt/ n annuncio m

announcer /ə'naʊnsə(r)/ n annunciatore, -trice mf

annoy /ə'nɔɪ/ vt dare fastidio a; **get ~ed** essere infastidito

annoyance /ə'nɔɪəns/ n seccatura f; (anger) irritazione f

annoying /ə'nɔɪɪŋ/ a fastidioso

annual /'ænjʊəl/ a annuale; ⟨income⟩ annuo ● n Bot pianta f annua; (children's book) almanacco m

Annual General Meeting n assemblea f generale annuale

annually /'ænjʊəlɪ/ adv annualmente; **she earns £50,000 ~** guadagna 50 000 sterline all'anno

annuity /ə'njuːətɪ/ n annualità f inv

annul /ə'nʌl/ vt (pt/pp annulled) annullare

Annunciation /ənʌnsɪ'eɪʃn/ n Annunciazione f

anode /'ænəʊd/ n anodo m

anodyne /'ænədaɪn/ a liter (bland) anodino; (inoffensive) innocuo

anoint /ə'nɔɪnt/ vt ungere

anomalous /ə'nɒmələs/ a anomalo

anomaly /ə'nɒməlɪ/ n anomalia f

anon /ə'nɒn/ abbr (**anonymous**) anonimo

anonymity /ænə'nɪmətɪ/ n anonimità f

anonymous /ə'nɒnɪməs/ a anonimo; **remain ~** mantenere l'anonimato

anonymously /ə'nɒnɪməslɪ/ adv anonimamente

anorak /'ænəræk/ n giacca f a vento

anorexia /ænə'reksɪə/ n anoressia f

anorexic /ænə'reksɪk/ a & n anoressico, -a mf

another /ə'nʌðə(r)/ a & pron; **~ [one]** un altro, un'altra; **~ day** un altro giorno; **in ~ way** diversamente; **~ time** un'altra volta; **one ~** l'un l'altro

answer /'ɑːnsə(r)/ n risposta f; (solution) soluzione f ● vt rispondere a ⟨person, question, letter⟩; esaudire ⟨prayer⟩; **~ the door** aprire la porta; **~ the telephone** rispondere al telefono ● vi rispondere

■ **answer back** vi ribattere

■ **answer for** vt rispondere di

answerable /'ɑːnsərəbl/ *a* responsabile; **be ~ to sb** rispondere a qcno

answering machine *n Teleph* segreteria *f* telefonica

answering service *n* servizio *m* di segreteria telefonica

answerphone /'ɑːnsəfəʊn/ *n* segreteria *f* telefonica

ant /ænt/ *n* formica *f*

antacid /ænt'æsɪd/ *a* & *n* antiacido *m*

antagonism /æn'tægənɪzm/ *n* antagonismo *m*

antagonistic /æntægə'nɪstɪk/ *a* antagonistico

antagonize /æn'tægənaɪz/ *vt* provocare l'ostilità di

Antarctic /æn'tɑːktɪk/ *n* Antartico *m* ●*a* antartico

Antarctica /æn'tɑːktɪkə/ *n* Antartide *f*

Antarctic Circle *n* Circolo *m* polare antartico

Antarctic Ocean *n* mare *m* antartico

anteater /'ænti:tə(r)/ *n* formichiere *m*

antecedent /æntɪ'siːdənt/ *n* (*precedent*) antecedente *m*; (*ancestor*) antenato, -a *mf*

antedate /æntɪ'deɪt/ *vt* (*put earlier date on*) retrodatare; (*predate*) precedere

antediluvian /æntɪdɪ'luːvɪən/ *a* antidiluviano

antelope /'æntɪləʊp/ *n* antilope *m*

antenatal /æntɪ'neɪtl/ *a* prenatale

antenatal class *n* corso *m* di preparazione al parto

antenatal clinic *n Br* assistenza *f* medica prenatale

antenna /æn'tenə/ *n* antenna *f*

anterior /æn'tɪərɪə/ *a* anteriore

ante-room /'æntɪ-/ *n* anticamera *f*

antheap /'ænthiːp/ = **anthill**

anthem /'ænθəm/ *n* inno *m*

anthill /'ænthɪl/ *n* formicaio *m*

anthology /æn'θɒlədʒɪ/ *n* antologia *f*

anthracite /'ænθrəsaɪt/ *n* antracite *f*

anthrax /'ænθræks/ *n* (*disease*) carbonchio *m*; (*pustule*) pustola *f* di carbonchio

anthropological /ænθrəpə'lɒdʒɪkl/ *a* antropologico

anthropologist /ænθrə'pɒlədʒɪst/ *n* antropologo, -a *mf*

anthropology /ænθrə'pɒlədʒɪ/ *n* antropologia *f*

anti /'æntɪ/ *pref* anti- ●*prep* **be ~** essere contro

anti-abortion *a* antiabortista

anti-abortionist *n* antiabortista *mf*

anti-aircraft *a* antiaereo

anti-apartheid *a* antiapartheid *inv*

antibacterial /æntɪbæk'tɪərɪəl/ *a* antibatterico

antiballistic missile /æntɪbəlɪstɪk-'mɪsaɪl/ *n* missile *m* antimissile

antibiotic /æntɪbaɪ'ɒtɪk/ *n* antibiotico *m*

antibody /'æntɪbɒdɪ/ *n* anticorpo *m*

anticipate /æn'tɪsɪpeɪt/ *vt* prevedere; (*forestall*) anticipare

anticipation /æntɪsɪ'peɪʃn/ *n* anticipo *m*; (*excitement*) attesa *f*; **in ~ of** in previsione di

anticlimax /æntɪ'klaɪmæks/ *n* delusione *f*

anticlockwise /æntɪ'klɒkwaɪz/ *a* & *adv* in senso antiorario

antics /'æntɪks/ *npl* gesti *mpl* buffi

anticyclone /æntɪ'saɪkləʊn/ *n* anticiclone *m*

antidepressant /æntɪdɪ'pres(ə)nt/ *a* & *n* antidepressivo *m*

antidote /'æntɪdəʊt/ *n* antidoto *m*

anti-establishment *a* contestatario

antifreeze /'æntɪfriːz/ *n* antigelo *m*

antiglare /æntɪ'gleə(r)/ *a* (*screen*) antirifleso *inv*

antihistamine /æntɪ'hɪstəmiːn/ *n* antistaminico *m*

anti-inflammatory /-ɪn'flæmətrɪ/ *a* & *n* antinfiammatorio *m*

anti-inflation *a* anti-inflazione *inv*

anti-inflationary /-ɪn'fleɪʃnərɪ/ *a* antinflazionistico

anti-lock *a* antibloccaggio *inv*

antipathy /æn'tɪpəθɪ/ *n* antipatia *f*

antiperspirant /æntɪ'pɜːspɪrənt/ *n* deodorante *m* antitraspirante

antipodean /æntɪpə'diːən/ *a* & *n* australiano, -a e/o neozelandese *mf*

Antipodes /æn'tɪpədiːz/ *npl Br* **the ~** gli antipodi

antiquarian /æntɪ'kweərɪən/ *a* antiquario; **~ bookshop** negozio *m* di libri antichi

antiquated /'æntɪkweɪtɪd/ *a* antiquato

antique /æn'tiːk/ *a* antico ●*n* antichità *f inv*

antique: antiques fair *n* fiera *f* dell'antiquariato. **antique dealer** *n* antiquario, -a *mf*. **antique shop** *n* negozio *m* d'antiquariato. **antiques trade** *n* antiquariato *m*

antiquity /æn'tɪkwətɪ/ *n* antichità *f*

anti-racism *n* antirazzismo *m*

anti-riot *a* (*police*) antisommossa *inv*

anti-rust *a* antiruggine *inv*

anti-Semitic /æntɪsɪ'mɪtɪk/ *a* antisemita

anti-Semitism /æntɪ'semɪtɪzm/ *n* antisemitismo *m*

antiseptic /æntɪ'septɪk/ *a* & *n* antisettico *m*

anti-skid *a* antiscivolo *inv*

anti-smoking *a* contro il fumo, antifumo

antisocial /æntɪ'səʊʃəl/ *a* (*behaviour*) antisociale; (*person*) asociale

anti-terrorist *a* antiterrorista

anti-theft *a* (*lock, device*) antifurto *inv*; (*camera*) di sorveglianza; **~ steering lock** bloccasterzo *m*

antithesis /æn'tɪθəsɪs/ *n* antitesi *f*

antitrust /æntɪ'trʌst/ *a* antitrust *inv*

antivirus /æntɪ'vaɪrəs/ **program** *n Comput* programma *m* antivirus

antivivisectionist /æntɪvɪvɪ'sekʃənɪst/ *n* antivivisezionista *mf* ●*a* antivivisezionistico

antlers /'æntləz/ *npl* corna *fpl*

antonym /'æntənɪm/ *n* antonimo *m*

Antwerp /'æntwɜːp/ *n* Anversa *f*

anus /'eɪnəs/ *n* ano *m*

anvil /'ænvɪl/ *n* incudine *f*

anxiety /æŋ'zaɪətɪ/ n ansia f

anxious /'æŋkʃəs/ a ansioso

anxiously /'æŋkʃəslɪ/ adv con ansia

any /'enɪ/ a (no matter which) qualsiasi, qualunque; **have we ~ wine/biscuits?** abbiamo del vino/dei biscotti?; **have we ~ jam/apples?** abbiamo della marmellata/delle mele?; **~ colour/number you like** qualsiasi colore/numero ti piaccia; **we don't have ~ wine/biscuits** non abbiamo vino/biscotti; **I don't have ~ reason to lie** non ho nessun motivo per mentire; **for ~ reason** per qualsiasi ragione ● pron (some) ne; (no matter which) uno qualsiasi; **I don't want ~ [of it]** non ne voglio [nessuno]; **there aren't ~** non ce ne sono; **have we ~?** ne abbiamo?; **have you read ~ of her books?** hai letto qualcuno dei suoi libri? ● adv **I can't go ~ quicker** non posso andare più in fretta; **is it ~ better?** va un po' meglio?; **would you like ~ more?** ne vuoi ancora?; **I can't eat ~ more** non posso mangiare più niente

anybody /'enɪbʌdɪ/ pron chiunque; (after negative) nessuno; **~ can do that** chiunque può farlo; **I haven't seen ~** non ho visto nessuno

anyhow /'enɪhaʊ/ adv ad ogni modo, comunque; (badly) non importa come

anyone /'enɪwʌn/ pron = **anybody**

anyplace /'enɪpleɪs/ adv Am = **anywhere**

anything /'enɪθɪŋ/ pron qualche cosa, qualcosa; (no matter what) qualsiasi cosa; (after negative) niente; **take/buy ~ you like** prendi/compra quello che vuoi; **I don't remember ~** non mi ricordo niente; **he's ~ but stupid** è tutto, ma non stupido; **I'll do ~ but that** farò qualsiasi cosa, tranne quello

anytime /'enɪtaɪm/ adv **if at ~ you feel lonely...** se mai ti dovessi sentire solo...; **he could arrive ~ now** potrebbe arrivare da un momento all'altro; **~ after 2 pm** a qualsiasi ora dopo le due; **at ~ of the day or night** a qualsiasi ora del giorno o della notte; **~ you like** quando vuoi

anyway /'enɪweɪ/ adv ad ogni modo, comunque

anywhere /'enɪweə(r)/ adv dovunque; (after negative) da nessuna parte; **put it ~** mettilo dove vuoi; **I can't find it ~** non lo trovo da nessuna parte; **~ else** da qualch'altra parte; (after negative) da nessun'altra parte; **I don't want to go ~ else** non voglio andare da nessun'altra parte

aorta /eɪ'ɔːtə/ n aorta f

Aosta /æ'ɒstə/ n Aosta f

apace /ə'peɪs/ adv liter rapidamente

apart /ə'pɑːt/ adv lontano; **live ~** vivere separati; **100 miles ~** lontani 100 miglia; **born 20 minutes ~** nati a distanza di 20 minuti; **~ from** a parte; **you can't tell them ~** non si possono distinguere; **joking ~** scherzi a parte

apartheid /ə'pɑːthaɪt/ n apartheid f

apartment /ə'pɑːtmənt/ n (Am: flat) appartamento m; **in my ~** a casa mia

apartment block n stabile m

apartment house n stabile m

apathetic /æpə'θetɪk/ a (by nature) apatico; **~ about sth/towards sb** (from illness, depression) indifferente a qcsa/nei confronti di qcno

apathy /'æpəθɪ/ n apatia f

ape /eɪp/ n scimmia f ● vt scimmiottare

Apennines /'æpənaɪnz/ npl **the ~** gli Appennini

aperitif /ə'perɪtiːf/ n aperitivo m

aperture /'æpətʃə(r)/ n apertura f

apex /'eɪpeks/ n vertice m

aphid /'eɪfɪd/ n afide m

aphrodisiac /æfrə'dɪzɪæk/ a & n afrodisiaco m

apiary /'eɪpɪərɪ/ n apiario m

apiece /ə'piːs/ adv ciascuno

aplenty /ə'plentɪ/ adv **there were goals ~** c'è stata una valanga di gol

apocalypse /ə'pɒkəlɪps/ n Apocalisse f; (disaster, destruction) apocalisse f

apocalyptic /əpɒkə'lɪptɪk/ a apocalittico

apocryphal /ə'pɒkrɪfəl/ a apocrifo

apogee /'æpədʒiː/ n apogeo m

apolitical /eɪpə'lɪtɪkl/ a apolitico

Apollo /ə'pɒləʊ/ n also fig Apollo m

apologetic /əpɒlə'dʒetɪk/ a ⟨air, remark⟩ di scusa; **be ~** essere spiacente

apologetically /əpɒlə'dʒetɪklɪ/ adv per scusarsi

apologist /ə'pɒlədʒɪst/ n apologeta mf (**for** di)

apologize /ə'pɒlədʒaɪz/ vi scusarsi (**for** per)

apology /ə'pɒlədʒɪ/ n scusa f; fig **an ~ for a dinner** una sottospecie di cena

apoplectic /æpə'plektɪk/ a (furious) furibondo; ⟨fit, attack⟩ apoplettico

apoplexy /'æpəpleksɪ/ n Med apoplessia f; (rage) rabbia f

apostle /ə'pɒsl/ n apostolo m

apostrophe /ə'pɒstrəfɪ/ n apostrofo m

apotheosis /əpɒθɪ'əʊsɪs/ n apoteosi f inv

appal /ə'pɔːl/ vt (pt/pp **appalled**) sconvolgere

Appalachians /æpə'leɪtʃnz/ npl **the ~** gli Appalachi

appalling /ə'pɔːlɪŋ/ a sconvolgente; **he's an ~ teacher** fig è un disastro come professore

appallingly /ə'pɔːlɪŋlɪ/ adv ⟨behave, treat⟩ orribilmente; **unemployment figures are ~ high** il tasso di disoccupazione è spaventosamente alto; **furnished in ~ bad taste** arredato con pessimo gusto

apparatus /æpə'reɪtəs/ n apparato m

apparel /ə'pærəl/ n abbigliamento m

apparent /ə'pærənt/ a evidente; (seeming) apparente

apparently /ə'pærəntlɪ/ adv apparentemente

apparition /æpə'rɪʃn/ n apparizione f

appeal /ə'piːl/ n appello m; (attraction) attrattiva f ● vi fare appello; **~ to** (be attractive to) attrarre

appeal[s] court n corte f d'appello

appeal fund *n* raccolta *f* di fondi
appealing /ə'pi:lɪŋ/ *a* attraente
appealingly /ə'pi:lɪŋlɪ/ *adv* (*beseechingly*) in modo supplichevole; (*attractively*) in modo attraente
appear /ə'pɪə(r)/ *vi* apparire; (*seem*) sembrare; (*publication:*) uscire; *Theat* esibirsi; **he finally ~ed at...** *fam* si è fatto finalmente vedere alle...; **~ in court** comparire in giudizio
appearance /ə'pɪərəns/ *n* apparizione *f*; (*look*) aspetto *m*; **to all ~s** a giudicare dalle apparenze; **keep up ~s** salvare le apparenze
appease /ə'pi:z/ *vt* placare
appeasement /ə'pi:zmənt/ *n* **a policy of ~** una politica troppo conciliante
append /ə'pend/ *vt* apporre (*signature*) (**to** a)
appendage /ə'pendɪdʒ/ *n* appendice *f*
appendicitis /əpendɪ'saɪtɪs/ *n* appendicite *f*
Appenine /'æpənaɪn/ *a* appenninico
Appenines /'æpənaɪnz/ *npl* Appennini *mpl*
appendix /ə'pendɪks/ *n* (*pl* **-ices** /-ɪsi:z/) (*of book*) appendice *f*; (*pl* **-es**) *Anat* appendice *f*
appertain /æpə'teɪn/ *vi* **~ to** essere pertinente a
appetite /'æpɪtaɪt/ *n* appetito *m*
appetite suppressant *n* pillola *f* antifame
appetizer /'æpɪtaɪzə(r)/ *n* (*drink*) aperitivo *m*; (*starter*) antipasto *m*; (*biscuit, olive etc*) stuzzichino *m*
appetizing /'æpɪtaɪzɪŋ/ *a* appetitoso
applaud /ə'plɔ:d/ *vt/i* applaudire
applause /ə'plɔ:z/ *n* applauso *m*
apple /'æpl/ *n* mela *f*; **she's the ~ of his eye** è la luce dei suoi occhi
apple: apple core *n* torsolo *m* di mela. **apple orchard** *n* meleto *m*. **apple tree** *n* melo *m*
appliance /ə'plaɪəns/ *n* attrezzo *m*; [**electrical**] **~** elettrodomestico *m*
applicable /'æplɪkəbl/ *a* **be ~ to** essere valido per; **not ~** (*on form*) non applicabile
applicant /'æplɪkənt/ *n* candidato, -a *mf*
application /æplɪ'keɪʃn/ *n* applicazione *f*; (*request*) domanda *f*; (*for job*) candidatura *f*; **on ~** su richiesta
application form *n* modulo *m* di domanda
applicator /'æplɪkeɪtə(r)/ *n* applicatore *m*
applied /ə'plaɪd/ *a* applicato
appliqué /ə'pli:keɪ/ *n* applicazione *f* ● *attrib* (*motif, decoration*) applicato
apply /ə'plaɪ/ *vt* (*pt/pp* **-ied**) applicare; **~ oneself** applicarsi; **~ the brakes** frenare ● *vi* applicarsi; (*law:*) essere applicabile; **~ to** (*ask*) rivolgersi a; **~ for** fare domanda per (*job etc*)
appoint /ə'pɔɪnt/ *vt* nominare; fissare (*time*); **well ~ed** ben equipaggiato
appointee /əpɔɪn'ti:/ *n* incaricato, -a *mf*
appointment /ə'pɔɪntmənt/ *n* appuntamento *m*; (*to job*) nomina *f*; (*job*) posto *m*
apportion /ə'pɔ:ʃn/ *vt* ripartire, attribuire
apposite /'æpəzɪt/ *a* appropriato
apposition /æpə'zɪʃn/ *n* apposizione *f*

appraisal /ə'preɪzəl/ *n* valutazione *f*; **make an ~ of sth** valutare qcsa
appraise /ə'preɪz/ *vt* valutare
appreciable /ə'pri:ʃəbl/ *a* sensibile
appreciably /ə'pri:ʃəblɪ/ *adv* sensibilmente
appreciate /ə'pri:ʃɪeɪt/ *vt* apprezzare; (*understand*) comprendere ● *vi* (*increase in value*) aumentare di valore
appreciation /əpri:ʃɪ'eɪʃn/ *n* (*gratitude*) riconoscenza *f*; (*enjoyment*) apprezzamento *m*; (*understanding*) comprensione *f*; (*in value*) aumento *m*; **in ~** come segno di riconoscenza (**of** per)
appreciative /ə'pri:ʃətɪv/ *a* riconoscente
apprehend /æprɪ'hend/ *vt* arrestare
apprehension /æprɪ'henʃn/ *n* arresto *m*; (*fear*) apprensione *f*
apprehensive /æprɪ'hensɪv/ *a* apprensivo
apprehensively /æprɪ'hensɪvlɪ/ *adv* con apprensione
apprentice /ə'prentɪs/ *n* apprendista *mf*
apprenticeship /ə'prentɪsʃɪp/ *n* apprendistato *m*
apprise /ə'praɪz/ *vt fml* informare (**of** di)
approach /ə'prəʊtʃ/ *n* avvicinamento *m*; (*to problem*) approccio *m*; (*access*) accesso *m*; **make ~es to** fare degli approcci con ● *vi* avvicinarsi ● *vt* avvicinarsi a; (*with request*) rivolgersi a; affrontare (*problem*)
approachable /ə'prəʊtʃəbl/ *a* accessibile
approach: approach lights *npl* *Aeron* sentiero *m* luminoso di avvicinamento. **approach path** *n* *Aeron* rotta *f* di avvicinamento. **approach road** *n* strada *f* d'accesso
approbation /æprə'beɪʃn/ *n* approvazione *f*
appropriate[1] /ə'prəʊprɪət/ *a* appropriato
appropriate[2] /ə'prəʊprɪeɪt/ *vt* appropriarsi di
appropriately /ə'prəʊprɪətlɪ/ *adv* (*suitably*) in modo appropriato; (*sited*) convenientemente; (*designed, chosen, behave*) adeguatamente
appropriation /əprəʊprɪ'eɪʃn/ *n* *Am Comm* stanziamento *m*; (*Jur: removal*) appropriazione *f*
approval /ə'pru:vl/ *n* approvazione *f*; **on ~** in prova
approve /ə'pru:v/ *vt* approvare ● *vi* **~ of** approvare (*sth*); avere una buona opinione di (*sb*)
approving /ə'pru:vɪŋ/ *a* (*smile, nod*) d'approvazione
approvingly /ə'pru:vɪŋlɪ/ *adv* con approvazione
approximate[1] /ə'prɒksɪmeɪt/ *vi* **~ to** avvicinarsi a
approximate[2] /ə'prɒksɪmət/ *a* approssimativo
approximately /ə'prɒksɪmətlɪ/ *adv* approssimativamente
approximation /əprɒksɪ'meɪʃn/ *n* approssimazione *f*
APR *n abbr* (**annual percentage rate**) tasso *m* percentuale annuo

apricot /'eɪprɪkɒt/ n albicocca f; ~ **tree** albicocco m

April /'eɪprəl/ n aprile m; **make an ~ Fool of sb** fare un pesce d'aprile a qcno; ~ **Fool's Day** il primo d'aprile

apron /'eɪprən/ n grembiule m

apropos /'æprəpəʊ/ adv ~ [**of**] a proposito [di]

apse /æps/ n abside f

apt /æpt/ a appropriato; ⟨pupil⟩ dotato; **be ~ to do sth** avere tendenza a fare qcsa

aptitude /'æptɪtjuːd/ n disposizione f

aptitude test n test m inv attitudinale

aptly /'æptlɪ/ adv appropriatamente

Apulia /ə'pjuːlɪə/ n Puglia f

aqualung /'ækwəlʌŋ/ n autorespiratore m

aquamarine /ækwəmə'riːn/ a & n acquamarina f

aquaplane /'ækwəpleɪn/ vi Sport praticare l'acquaplano; Br Auto andare in aquaplaning

aquarium /ə'kweərɪəm/ n acquario m

Aquarius /ə'kweərɪəs/ n Astr Acquario m; **be ~** essere dell'Acquario

aquatic /ə'kwætɪk/ a acquatico

aqueduct /'ækwədʌkt/ n acquedotto m

aquiline /'ækwɪlaɪn/ a ⟨nose, features⟩ aquilino

Arab /'ærəb/ a & n arabo, -a mf

Arabia /ə'reɪbɪə/ n Arabia f

Arabian /ə'reɪbɪən/ a arabo

Arabic /'ærəbɪk/ a arabo; ~ **numerals** numeri mpl arabici ● n arabo m

Arab-Israeli a arabo-israeliano

arable /'ærəbl/ a coltivabile

arbiter /'ɑːbɪtə(r)/ n arbitro m

arbitrarily /ɑːbɪ'treɪlɪ/ adv arbitrariamente

arbitrary /'ɑːbɪtrərɪ/ a arbitrario

arbitrate /'ɑːbɪtreɪt/ vi arbitrare

arbitration /ɑːbɪ'treɪʃn/ n arbitraggio m

arbitrator /'ɑːbɪtreɪtə(r)/ n arbitro m

arbour /'ɑːbə(r)/ n pergolato m

arc /ɑːk/ n arco m

arcade /ɑː'keɪd/ n portico m; ⟨shops⟩ galleria f

arcane /ɑː'keɪn/ a arcano

arch /ɑːtʃ/ n arco m; ⟨of foot⟩ dorso m del piede ● vt **the cat ~ed its back** il gatto ha arcuato la schiena

archaeological /ɑːkɪə'lɒdʒɪkl/ a archeologico

archaeologist /ɑːkɪ'ɒlədʒɪst/ n archeologo, -a mf

archaeology /ɑːkɪ'ɒlədʒɪ/ n archeologia f

archaic /ɑː'keɪɪk/ a arcaico

archbishop /ɑːtʃ'bɪʃəp/ n arcivescovo m

arched /ɑːtʃt/ a ⟨eyebrows⟩ arcuato

arch-enemy n acerrimo nemico m

archer /'ɑːtʃə(r)/ n arciere m

archery /'ɑːtʃərɪ/ n tiro m con l'arco

archetypal /ɑːkɪ'taɪpl/ a **the ~ hero** il prototipo dell'eroe

archetype /'ɑːkɪtaɪp/ n archetipo m

archipelago /ɑːkɪ'peləgəʊ/ n arcipelago m

architect /'ɑːkɪtekt/ n architetto m

architectural /ɑːkɪ'tektʃərəl/ a architettonico

architecturally /ɑːkɪ'tektʃərəlɪ/ adv architettonicamente

architecture /'ɑːkɪtektʃə(r)/ n architettura f

archives /'ɑːkaɪvz/ npl archivi mpl

archiving /'ɑːkaɪvɪŋ/ n Comput archiviazione f

archway /'ɑːtʃweɪ/ n arco m

Arctic /'ɑːktɪk/ a artico ● **the ~** l'Artico

Arctic Circle n Circolo m polare artico

Arctic Ocean n mare m artico

ardent /'ɑːdənt/ a ardente

ardently /'ɑːdəntlɪ/ adv ardentemente

ardour /'ɑːdə(r)/ n ardore m

arduous /'ɑːdjʊəs/ a arduo

arduously /'ɑːdjʊəslɪ/ adv con fatica, con difficoltà

are /ɑː(r)/ see **be**

area /'eərɪə/ n area f; ⟨region⟩ zona f; ⟨fig: field⟩ campo m

area code n prefisso m [telefonico]

area manager n direttore, -trice mf di zona

aren't /ɑːnt/ = **are not** see **be**

arena /ə'riːnə/ n arena f

Argentina /ɑːdʒən'tiːnə/ n Argentina f

Argentine /'ɑːdʒəntaɪn/ a argentino

Argentinian /ɑːdʒən'tɪnɪən/ a & n argentino, -a mf

arguable /'ɑːgjʊəbl/ a **it's ~ that...** si può sostenere che...

arguably /'ɑːgjʊəblɪ/ adv **he is ~...** è probabilmente...

argue /'ɑːgjuː/ vi litigare (**about** su); ⟨debate⟩ dibattere; **don't ~!** non discutere! ● vt ⟨debate⟩ dibattere; ⟨reason⟩ ~ **that** sostenere che

argument /'ɑːgjʊmənt/ n argomento m; ⟨reasoning⟩ ragionamento m; **have an ~** litigare

argumentative /ɑːgjʊ'mentətɪv/ a polemico

aria /'ɑːrɪə/ n aria f

arid /'ærɪd/ a arido

aridity /ə'rɪdətɪ/ n also fig aridità f

Aries /'eəriːz/ n Astr Ariete m; **be ~** essere dell'Ariete

arise /ə'raɪz/ vi (pt **arose**, pp **arisen**) ⟨opportunity, need, problem:⟩ presentarsi; ⟨result⟩ derivare

aristocracy /ærɪ'stɒkrəsɪ/ n aristocrazia f

aristocrat /'ærɪstəkræt/ n aristocratico, -a mf

aristocratic /ærɪstə'krætɪk/ a aristocratico

arithmetic /ə'rɪθmətɪk/ n aritmetica f

arithmetical /ærɪθ'metɪkl/ a aritmetico

ark /ɑːk/ n **Noah's A ~** l'Arca f di Noè

arm /ɑːm/ n braccio m; ⟨of chair⟩ bracciolo m; ~**s** pl ⟨weapons⟩ armi fpl; ~ **in ~** a braccetto; **up in ~s** fam furioso (**about** per); fig **with open ~s** a braccia aperte ● vt armare

armadillo /ɑːmə'dɪləʊ/ n armadillo m

armaments /'ɑːməmənts/ npl armamenti mpl

armband /'ɑːmbænd/ n ⟨for swimmer⟩ bracciolo *m* ⟨*per nuotare*⟩; ⟨*for mourner*⟩ fascia *f* al braccio

armchair /'ɑ:mtʃeə(r)/ *n* poltrona *f*

armchair traveller *n persona f che si interessa di viaggi senza viaggiare*

armed /ɑ:md/ *a* armato

armed forces /'fɔ:sɪz/ *npl* forze *fpl* armate

armed robbery *n* rapina *f* a mano armata

Armenia /ɑ:'mi:nɪə/ *n* Armenia *f*

Armenian /ɑ:'mi:nɪən/ *a* & *n* ⟨*person*⟩ armeno, -a *mf*; ⟨*language*⟩ armeno *m*

armful /'ɑ:mfʊl/ *n* bracciata *f*

armhole /'ɑ:mhəʊl/ *n* giro *m* manica *inv*

armistice /'ɑ:mɪstɪs/ *n* armistizio *m*

Armistice Day *n* l'Anniversario *m* dell'Armistizio ⟨*1 nov. 1918*⟩

armour /'ɑ:mə(r)/ *n* armatura *f*

armour-clad /-'klæd/ *a* ⟨*vehicle*⟩ blindato; ⟨*ship*⟩ corazzato

armoured /'ɑ:məd/ *a* ⟨*vehicle*⟩ blindato

armoured car *n* autoblinda[ta] *f*

armour plate, armour plating /'pleɪtɪŋ/ *n* corazzatura *f*

armour-plated /-'pleɪtɪd/ *a* corazzato

armoury /'ɑ:mərɪ/ *n* ⟨*factory*⟩ fabbrica *f* d'armi; ⟨*store*⟩ arsenale *m*, armeria *f*

armpit /'ɑ:mpɪt/ *n* ascella *f*

armrest /'ɑ:mrest/ *n* bracciolo *m* ⟨*di sedia*⟩

arms: arms control *n* controllo *m* degli armamenti. **arms dealer** *n* trafficante *mf* d'armi. **arms dump** *n* deposito *m* d'armi. **arms factory** *n* fabbrica *f* d'armi. **arms limitation** *n* controllo *m* degli armamenti. **arms manufacturer** *n* fabbricante *mf* d'armi. **arms race** *n* corsa *f* agli armamenti. **arms treaty** *n* trattato *m* sul controllo degli armamenti

arm-twisting /'ɑ:mtwɪstɪŋ/ *n* pressioni *fpl*

arm-wrestling *n* braccio *m* di ferro

army /'ɑ:mɪ/ *n* esercito *m*; **join the ~** arruolarsi

A road *n Br* ⟨strada *f*⟩ statale *f*

aroma /ə'rəʊmə/ *n* aroma *f*

aromatherapy /ərəʊmə'θerəpɪ/ *n* aromaterapia *f*

aromatic /ærə'mætɪk/ *a* aromatico

arose /ə'rəʊz/ *see* **arise**

around /ə'raʊnd/ *adv* intorno; **all ~** tutt'intorno; **I'm not from ~ here** non sono di qui; **he's not ~** non c'è ● *prep* intorno a; in giro per ⟨*room, shops, world*⟩

arousal /ə'raʊzl/ *n* eccitazione *f*

arouse /ə'raʊz/ *vt* svegliare; ⟨*sexually*⟩ eccitare

arpeggio /ɑ:'pedʒɪəʊ/ *n* arpeggio *m*

arrange /ə'reɪndʒ/ *vt* sistemare ⟨*furniture, books*⟩; organizzare ⟨*meeting*⟩; fissare ⟨*date, time*⟩; **~ to do sth** combinare di fare qcsa

arrangement /ə'reɪndʒmənt/ *n* ⟨*of furniture*⟩ sistemazione *f*; *Mus* arrangiamento *m*; ⟨*agreement*⟩ accordo; ⟨*of flowers*⟩ composizione *f*; **make ~s** prendere disposizioni; **I've made other ~s** ho preso altri impegni

array /ə'reɪ/ *n* ⟨*clothes*⟩ abbigliamento *m*; ⟨*of troops, people*⟩ schieramento *m*; ⟨*of numbers*⟩

tabella *f*; ⟨*of weaponry*⟩ apparato *m*; ⟨*of goods, products*⟩ assortimento *m*; *Comput* matrice *f* ● *vt* **~ed in ceremonial robes** abbigliato da gran cerimonia

arrears /ə'rɪəz/ *npl* arretrati *mpl*; **be in ~** essere in arretrato; **paid in ~** pagato a lavoro eseguito

arrest /ə'rest/ *n* arresto *m*; **under ~** in stato d'arresto ● *vt* arrestare

arresting /ə'restɪŋ/ *a* ⟨*striking*⟩ che colpisce

arrival /ə'raɪvl/ *n* arrivo *m*; **new ~s** *pl* nuovi arrivati *mpl*

arrival: arrival lounge *n* sala *f* arrivi. **arrivals board** *n* tabellone *m* degli arrivi. **arrival time** *n* ora *f* d'arrivo

arrive /ə'raɪv/ *vi* arrivare; **~ at** *fig* raggiungere

arrogance /'ærəg(ə)ns/ *n* arroganza *f*

arrogant /'ærəg(ə)nt/ *a* arrogante

arrogantly /'ærəg(ə)ntlɪ/ *adv* con arroganza

arrow /'ærəʊ/ *n* freccia *f*

arrowhead /'ærəʊhed/ *n* punta *f* di freccia

arse /ɑ:s/ *n vulg* culo *m*

■ **arse about, arse around** *vi vulg* coglioneggiare

arsenal /'ɑ:sən(ə)l/ *n* arsenale *m*

arsenic /'ɑ:sənɪk/ *n* arsenico *m*

arson /'ɑ:sən/ *n* incendio *m* doloso

arsonist /'ɑ:sənɪst/ *n* incendiario, -a *mf*

art /ɑ:t/ *n* arte *f*; **work of ~** opera *f* d'arte; **~s and crafts** *pl* artigianato *m*; **the A~s** *pl* l'arte *f*; **A~s degree** *Univ* laurea *f* in Lettere

art: art collection *n* collezione *f* d'arte. **art collector** *n* collezionista *mf* d'arte. **art college** *n* ≈ accademia *f* di belle arti. **art dealer** *n* commerciante *mf* di oggetti d'arte. **art deco** *n* art déco *f*

artefact /'ɑ:tɪfækt/ *n* manufatto *m*

arterial /ɑ:'tɪərɪəl/ *a Anat* arterioso

arterial road *n* arteria *f* [stradale]

artery /'ɑ:tərɪ/ *n* arteria *f*

art exhibition *n* mostra *f* d'arte. **art form** *n* forma *f* d'arte

artful /'ɑ:tfl/ *a* scaltro

artfully /'ɑ:tfʊlɪ/ *adv* astutamente

art gallery *n* galleria *f* d'arte

arthritic /ɑ:'θrɪtɪk/ *a* & *n* artritico, -a *mf*

arthritis /ɑ:'θraɪtɪs/ *n* artrite *f*

artichoke /'ɑ:tɪtʃəʊk/ *n* carciofo *m*

article /'ɑ:tɪkl/ *n* articolo *m*; **~ of clothing** capo *m* d'abbigliamento

articulate[1] /ɑ:'tɪkjʊlət/ *a* ⟨*speech*⟩ chiaro; **be ~** esprimersi bene

articulate[2] /ɑ:'tɪkjʊleɪt/ *vt* scandire ⟨*words*⟩

articulated lorry /ɑ:'tɪkjʊleɪtɪd/ *n* autotreno *m*

articulately /ɑ:'tɪkjʊlətlɪ/ *adv* chiaramente

articulation /ɑ:tɪkjʊ'leɪʃn/ *n* ⟨*pronunciation, Anat*⟩ articolazione *f*; ⟨*expression*⟩ espressione *f*

artifice /'ɑ:tɪfɪs/ *n* artificio *m*

artificial /ɑ:tɪ'fɪʃl/ *a* artificiale

artificial insemination *n* inseminazione *f* artificiale

artificial intelligence *n* intelligenza *f* artificiale

artificiality /ɑ:tɪfɪʃɪ'ælətɪ/ *n* artificiosità *f*

artificial limb *n* arto *m* artificiale

artificially /ɑ:tɪ'fɪʃəlɪ/ *adv* artificialmente; *‹smile›* artificiosamente

artificial respiration *n* respirazione *f* artificiale

artillery /ɑ:'tɪlərɪ/ *n* artiglieria *f*

artisan /ɑ:tɪ'zæn/ *n* artigiano, -a *mf*

artist /'ɑ:tɪst/ *n* artista *mf*

artiste /ɑ:'ti:st/ *n* Theat artista *mf*

artistic /ɑ:'tɪstɪk/ *a* artistico

artistically /ɑ:'tɪstɪklɪ/ *adv* artisticamente

artistry /'ɑ:tɪstrɪ/ *n* arte *f*, talento *m*

artless /'ɑ:tlɪs/ *a* spontaneo

artlessly /'ɑ:tlɪslɪ/ *adv ‹smile›* ingenuamente

art nouveau /ɑ:nu:'vəʊ/ *a & n* liberty *m*

art school *n* ≈ accademia *f* di belle arti

arts: arts degree *n* laurea *f* in Lettere. **arts funding** *n* sovvenzioni *fpl* alle belle arti. **arts student** *n* studente, -essa *mf* di Lettere

art student *n* studente, -essa *mf* di belle arti

artwork /'ɑ:twɜ:k/ *n* illustrazioni *fpl*

arty /'ɑ:tɪ/ *a fam ‹person›* intellettualoide; *‹district›* degli intellettuali

Aryan /'eərɪən/ *a & n* ariano, -a *mf*

as /æz/ *conj* come; *(since)* siccome; *(while)* mentre; **as he grew older** diventando vecchio; **as you get to know her** conoscendola meglio; **young as she is** per quanto sia giovane ● *prep* come; **as a friend** come amico; **as a child** da bambino; **as a foreigner** in quanto straniero; **disguised as** travestito da ● *adv* **as well** *(also)* anche; **as soon as I get home** [non] appena arrivo a casa; **as quick as you** veloce quanto te; **as quick as you can** più veloce che puoi; **as far as** *(distance)* fino a; **as far as I'm concerned** per quanto mi riguarda; **as long as** finché; *(provided that)* purché

asbestos /æz'bestɒs/ *n* amianto *m*

ascend /ə'send/ *vi* salire ● *vt* salire a *‹throne›*

ascendancy /ə'ʃend(ə)nsɪ/ *n* **gain the ~ over sb** acquisire una posizione dominante su qcno

ascendant /ə'send(ə)nt/ *n* **be in the ~** *Astr* essere in ascendente; *‹fig: person›* essere in auge

Ascension /ə'senʃn/ *n Relig* Ascensione *f*

ascent /ə'sent/ *n* ascesa *f*

ascertain /æsə'teɪn/ *vt* accertare

ascetic /ə'setɪk/ *a & n* ascetico, -a *mf*

asceticism /ə'setɪsɪzm/ *n* ascesi *f*

ascribable /ə'skraɪbəbl/ *a* attribuibile

ascribe /ə'skraɪb/ *vt* attribuire

aseptic /eɪ'septɪk/ *a* asettico

asexual /eɪ'seksjʊəl/ *a* asessuale, asessuato

ash[1] /æʃ/ *n (tree)* frassino *m*

ash[2] *n* cenere *f*

ashamed /ə'ʃeɪmd/ *a* **be/feel ~** vergognarsi

ash blond *a* biondo cenere

ashen /'æʃ(ə)n/ *a ‹complexion›* cinereo

ashore /ə'ʃɔ:(r)/ *adv* a terra; **go ~** sbarcare

ash: ashtray *n* portacenere *m*. **ash tree** *n* frassino *m*. **Ash Wednesday** *n* mercoledì *m inv* delle Ceneri

Asia /'eɪʒə/ *n* Asia *f*

Asia Minor *n* Asia *f* Minore

Asian /'eɪʒ(ə)n/ *a & n* asiatico, -a *mf*; *(Br: Indian, Pakistani)* indiano, -a *mf*

Asiatic /eɪʒɪ'ætɪk/ *a* asiatico

aside /ə'saɪd/ *adv* **take sb ~** prendere qcno a parte; **put sth ~** mettere qcsa da parte; **~ from you** *Am* a parte te; **~ from his injuries** *Am* a parte le sue ferite ● **n in an ~** tra parentesi

asinine /'æsɪnaɪn/ *a* sciocco

ask /ɑ:sk/ *vt* fare *‹question›*; *(invite)* invitare; **~ sb sth** domandare *or* chiedere qcsa a qcno; **~ sb to do sth** domandare *or* chiedere a qcno di fare qcsa ● *vi* **~ about sth** informarsi su qcsa; **~ after** chiedere [notizie] di; **~ for** chiedere *‹sth›*; chiedere di *‹sb›*; **~ for trouble** *fam* andare in cerca di guai

■ **ask in** *vt* **~ sb in** invitare qcno ad entrare

■ **ask out** *vt* **~ sb out** chiedere a qcno di uscire

askance /ə'skɑ:ns/ *adv* **look ~ at sb/sth** guardare qcno/qcsa di traverso

askew /ə'skju:/ *a & adv* di traverso

asking price /ɑ:skɪŋ/ *n* prezzo *m* trattabile

asleep /ə'sli:p/ *a* **be ~** dormire; **fall ~** addormentarsi

asparagus /ə'spærəgəs/ *n* asparagi *mpl*

aspect /'æspekt/ *n* aspetto *m*

aspen /'æspən/ *n* pioppo *m* tremulo

aspersions /ə'spɜ:ʃnz/ *npl* **cast ~ on** diffamare

asphalt /'æsfælt/ *n* asfalto *m*

asphyxia /əs'fɪksɪə/ *n* asfissia *f*

asphyxiate /əs'fɪksɪeɪt/ *vt* asfissiare

asphyxiation /əsfɪksɪ'eɪʃn/ *n* asfissia *f*

aspirate[1] /'æspəreɪt/ *vt* aspirare

aspirate[2] /'æspɪrət/ *a* aspirato

aspirations /æspə'reɪʃnz/ *npl* aspirazioni *fpl*

aspire /ə'spaɪə(r)/ *vi* **~ to** aspirare a

aspiring /ə'spaɪərɪŋ/ *a* **~ authors/journalists** aspiranti scrittori/giornalisti

ass /æs/ *n* asino *m*

assailant /ə'seɪlənt/ *n* assalitore, -trice *mf*

assassin /ə'sæsɪn/ *n* assassino, -a *mf*

assassinate /ə'sæsɪneɪt/ *vt* assassinare

assassination /əsæsɪ'neɪʃn/ *n* assassinio *m*

assault /ə'sɔ:lt/ *n Mil* assalto *m*; *Jur* aggressione *f* ● *vt* aggredire

assault and battery *n Jur* lesioni *fpl* personali

assault course *n Mil* percorso *m* di guerra

assemblage /ə'semblɪdʒ/ *n* assemblaggio *m*

assemble /ə'sembl/ *vi* radunarsi ● *vt* radunare; *Techn* montare

assembler /ə'semblə(r)/ *n (in factory)*

montatore, -trice *mf*; *Comput* [programma *m*] assemblatore *m*

assembly /ə'semblɪ/ *n* assemblea *f*; *Sch assemblea f giornaliera di alunni e professori di una scuola*; *Techn* montaggio *m*

assembly line *n* catena *f* di montaggio

assent /ə'sent/ *n* assenso *m* ● *vi* acconsentire

assert /ə'sɜːt/ *vt* asserire; far valere ⟨*one's rights*⟩; ~ **oneself** farsi valere

assertion /ə'sɜːʃn/ *n* asserzione *f*

assertive /ə'sɜːtɪv/ *a* be ~ farsi valere

assertiveness /ə'sɜːtɪvnɪs/ *n* capacità *f* di farsi valere; **lack of** ~ scarsa sicurezza *f* di sé

assess /ə'ses/ *vt* valutare; (*for tax purposes*) stabilire l'imponibile di

assessment /ə'sesmənt/ *n* valutazione *f*; (*of tax*) accertamento *m*

assessor /ə'sesə(r)/ *n* (*Jur, in insurance*) perito *m*; (*tax*) agente *m* del fisco

asset /'æset/ *n* (*advantage*) vantaggio *m*; (*person*) elemento *m* prezioso. ~**s** *pl* beni *mpl*; (*on balance sheet*) attivo *msg*

asset stripping /'æsetstrɪpɪŋ/ *n* rilevamento *m* di un'azienda per rivenderne le singole attività fisse

assiduity /æsɪ'djuːətɪ/ *n* assiduità *f*

assiduous /ə'sɪdjʊəs/ *a* assiduo

assign /ə'saɪn/ *vt* assegnare

assignation /æsɪg'neɪʃn/ *n* *hum* appuntamento *m* galante

assignment /ə'saɪnmənt/ *n* (*task*) incarico *m*

assimilate /ə'sɪmɪleɪt/ *vt* assimilare; integrare ⟨*person*⟩

assimilation /əsɪmɪ'leɪʃn/ *n* assimilazione *f*

assist /ə'sɪst/ *vt/i* assistere; ~ **sb to do sth** assistere qcno nel fare qcsa

assistance /ə'sɪstəns/ *n* assistenza *f*

assistant /ə'sɪstənt/ *n* assistente *mf*; (*in shop*) commesso, -a *mf*

assistant manager *n* vicedirettore, -trice *mf*

assistant professor *n* *Am Univ* docente *mf* universitario, -a del grado più basso

associate¹ /ə'səʊʃɪeɪt/ *vt* associare (**with** a); **be ~d with sth** (*involved in*) essere coinvolto in qcsa ● *vi* ~ **with** frequentare

associate² /ə'səʊʃət/ *a* associato ● *n* collega *mf*; (*member*) socio, -a *mf*

associate: **associate company** *n* consociata *f*. **associate director** *n* *Comm* amministratore *m* aggiunto. **associate editor** *n* coredattore, -trice *mf*. **associate member** *n* membro *m* associato

association /əsəʊsɪ'eɪʃn/ *n* associazione *f*

Association Football *n* [gioco *m* del] calcio *m*

assorted /ə'sɔːtɪd/ *a* assortito

assortment /ə'sɔːtmənt/ *n* assortimento *m*

assuage /ə'sweɪdʒ/ *vt* *liter* alleviare

assume /ə'sjuːm/ *vt* presumere; assumere ⟨*control*⟩; ~ **office** entrare in carica; **assuming that you're right,...** ammettendo che tu abbia ragione,...

assumption /ə'sʌmpʃn/ *n* supposizione *f*; **on the** ~ **that** partendo dal presupposto che; **the A~** *Relig* l'Assunzione *f*

assurance /ə'ʃʊərəns/ *n* assicurazione *f*; (*confidence*) sicurezza *f*

assure /ə'ʃʊə(r)/ *vt* assicurare; **he ~d me of his innocence** mi ha assicurato di essere innocente

assured /ə'ʃʊəd/ *a* sicuro

Assyria /ə'sɪrɪə/ *n* Assiria *f*

asterisk /'æstərɪsk/ *n* asterisco *m*

astern /ə'stɜːn/ *adv* a poppa

asteroid /'æstərɔɪd/ *n* asteroide *m*

asthma /'æsmə/ *n* asma *f*

asthmatic /æs'mætɪk/ *a* asmatico

astigmatism /ə'stɪgmətɪzm/ *n* astigmatismo *m*

astonish /ə'stɒnɪʃ/ *vt* stupire

astonished /ə'stɒnɪʃt/ *a* sorpreso

astonishing /ə'stɒnɪʃɪŋ/ *a* stupefacente

astonishingly /ə'stɒnɪʃɪŋlɪ/ *adv* sorprendentemente

astonishment /ə'stɒnɪʃmənt/ *n* stupore *m*

astound /ə'staʊnd/ *vt* stupire

astounding /ə'staʊndɪŋ/ *a* incredibile

astrakhan /æstrə'kæn/ *n* astrakan *m*

astray /ə'streɪ/ *adv* **go** ~ smarrirsi; (*morally*) uscire dalla retta via; **lead** ~ traviare

astride /ə'straɪd/ *adv* [a] cavalcioni ● *prep* a cavalcioni di

astringent /ə'strɪndʒənt/ *a* astringente; *fig* austero ● *n* astringente *m*

astrologer /ə'strɒlədʒə(r)/ *n* astrologo, -a *mf*

astrological /æstrə'lɒdʒɪkl/ *a* astrologico

astrology /ə'strɒlədʒɪ/ *n* astrologia *f*

astronaut /'æstrənɔːt/ *n* astronauta *mf*

astronomer /ə'strɒnəmə(r)/ *n* astronomo, -a *mf*

astronomic /æstrə'nɒmɪk/ *a* *fig* astronomico

astronomical /æstrə'nɒmɪkl/ *a* *also fig* astronomico

astronomically /æstrə'nɒmɪklɪ/ *adv* ~ **expensive** dal prezzo astronomico; **prices are** ~ **high** i prezzi sono astronomici

astronomy /ə'strɒnəmɪ/ *n* astronomia *f*

astrophysicist /æstrəʊ'fɪzɪsɪst/ *n* astrofisico, -a *mf*

astrophysics /æstrəʊ'fɪzɪks/ *n* astrofisica *f*

astute /ə'stjuːt/ *a* astuto

astutely /ə'stjuːtlɪ/ *adv* con astuzia

astuteness /ə'stjuːtnɪs/ *n* astuzia *f*

asylum /ə'saɪləm/ *n* [**political**] ~ asilo *m* politico; [**lunatic**] ~ manicomio *m*

asylum-seeker /ə'saɪləmsiːkə(r)/ *n* persona *f* che chiede asilo politico

asymmetric[al] /æsɪ'metrɪk, æsɪ'metrɪkl/ *a* asimmetrico

at /ət/, *accentato* /æt/ *prep* a; **at the station/the market** alla stazione/al mercato; **at the office/the bank** in ufficio/banca; **at the beginning** all'inizio; **at John's** da John; **at the hairdresser's** dal parrucchiere; **at home** a casa; **at work** al lavoro; **at**

21

school a scuola; **at a party/wedding** a una festa/un matrimonio; **at one o'clock** all'una; **at 50 km an hour** ai 50 all'ora; **at Christmas/Easter** a Natale/Pasqua; **at times** talvolta; **two at a time** due alla volta; **good at languages** bravo nelle lingue; **at sb's request** su richiesta di qcno; **are you at all worried?** sei preoccupato?

atavistic /ætə'vɪstɪk/ a atavico

ate /et/ see **eat**

atheism /'eɪθɪɪzm/ n ateismo m

atheist /'eɪθɪɪst/ n ateo, -a mf

atheistic /eɪθɪ'ɪstɪk/ a ⟨principle⟩ ateistico; ⟨person⟩ ateo

Athenian /ə'θiːnɪən/ a & n ateniese mf

Athens /'æθənz/ n Atene f

athlete-/'æθliːt/ n atleta mf

athlete's foot n micosi f

athletic /æθ'letɪk/ a atletico

athletics /æθ'letɪks/ n atletica fsg

Atlantic /ət'læntɪk/ a & n **the ~** [**Ocean**] l'[Oceano m] Atlantico m

atlas /'ætləs/ n atlante m

Atlas Mountains npl Monti mpl dell'Atlante

ATM n abbr (**automatic teller machine**) cassa f continua di prelevamento

atmosphere /'ætməsfɪə(r)/ n atmosfera f

atmospheric /ætməs'ferɪk/ a atmosferico

atom /'ætəm/ n atomo m

atom bomb n bomba f atomica

atomic /ə'tɒmɪk/ a atomico

atomic: atomic power station n centrale f atomica. **atomic reactor** n reattore m nucleare. **atomic scientist** n fisico, -a mf nucleare

atomize /'ætəmaɪz/ vt atomizzare

atomizer /'ætəmaɪzə(r)/ n atomizzatore m

atone /ə'təʊn/ vi **~ for** pagare per

atonement /ə'təʊnmənt/ n espiazione f

atrocious /ə'trəʊʃəs/ a atroce; ⟨fam: meal, weather⟩ abominevole

atrociously /ə'trəʊʃəslɪ/ adv atrocemente; ⟨rude etc⟩ terribilmente

atrocity /ə'trɒsətɪ/ n atrocità f inv

atrophy /'ætrəfɪ/ n Med atrofia f ● vi Med, fig atrofizzarsi

attach /ə'tætʃ/ vt attaccare; attribuire ⟨importance⟩; **be ~ed to** fig essere attaccato a

attaché /ə'tæʃeɪ/ n addetto m

attaché case n ventiquattrore f inv

attachment /ə'tætʃmənt/ n ⟨affection⟩ attaccamento m; ⟨accessory⟩ accessorio m

attack /ə'tæk/ n attacco m; ⟨physical⟩ aggressione f ● vt attaccare; ⟨physically⟩ aggredire

attacker /ə'tækə(r)/ n assalitore, -trice mf; ⟨critic⟩ detrattore, -trice mf

attain /ə'teɪn/ vt realizzare ⟨ambition⟩; raggiungere ⟨success, age, goal⟩

attainable /ə'teɪnəbl/ a ⟨ambition⟩ realizzabile; ⟨success⟩ raggiungibile

attainment /ə'teɪnmənt/ n ⟨of knowledge⟩ acquisizione f; ⟨of goal⟩ realizzazione f, raggiungimento m; ⟨success⟩ risultato m

attempt /ə'tempt/ n tentativo m ● vt tentare

attend /ə'tend/ vt essere presente a; ⟨go regularly to⟩ frequentare; ⟨accompany⟩ accompagnare; ⟨doctor:⟩ avere in cura ● vi essere presente; ⟨pay attention⟩ prestare attenzione

■ **attend to** vt occuparsi di; ⟨in shop⟩ servire

attendance /ə'tendəns/ n presenza f

attendance record n ⟨of MP, committee member, schoolchild⟩ tasso m di presenza

attendance register n Sch registro m

attendant /ə'tendənt/ n guardiano, -a mf

attention /ə'tenʃn/ n attenzione f; **~!** Mil attenti!; **pay ~** prestare attenzione; **need ~** aver bisogno di attenzioni; ⟨skin, hair, plant:⟩ dover essere curato; ⟨car, tyres:⟩ dover essere riparato; **for the ~ of** all'attenzione di

attention-seeking /ə'tenʃnsiːkɪŋ/ n bisogno m di attirare l'attenzione ● a ⟨person⟩ che cerca di attirare l'attenzione.

attention span n he has a very short ~ ~ non è capace di mantenere a lungo la concentrazione

attentive /ə'tentɪv/ a ⟨pupil, audience⟩ attento; ⟨son⟩ premuroso

attentively /ə'tentɪvlɪ/ adv attentamente

attentiveness /ə'tentɪvnɪs/ n ⟨concentration⟩ attenzione f; ⟨solicitude⟩ sollecitudine f

attenuate /ə'tenjʊeɪt/ vt attenuare

attest /ə'test/ vt/i attestare

attic /'ætɪk/ n soffitta f

attic room n mansarda f

attic window n lucernario m

attire /ə'taɪə(r)/ n abiti mpl ● vt vestire (**in con**)

attitude /'ætɪtjuːd/ n atteggiamento m

attorney /ə'tɜːnɪ/ n ⟨Am: lawyer⟩ avvocato m; **power of ~** delega f

Attorney General n Br ≈ Procuratore m Generale; Am ≈ Ministro m di Grazia e Giustizia

attract /ə'trækt/ vt attirare

attraction /ə'trækʃn/ n attrazione f; ⟨feature⟩ attrattiva f

attractive /ə'træktɪv/ a ⟨person⟩ attraente; ⟨proposal, price⟩ allettante

attractiveness /ə'træktɪvnɪs/ n ⟨of person, place⟩ fascino m; ⟨of proposal⟩ carattere m allettante; ⟨of investment⟩ convenienza f

attributable /ə'trɪbjʊtəbl/ a ⟨error, fall, loss etc⟩ attribuibile; **be ~ to** ⟨change, profit, success etc:⟩ essere dovuto a

attribute¹ /'ætrɪbjuːt/ n attributo m

attribute² /ə'trɪbjuːt/ vt attribuire

attribution /ætrɪ'bjuːʃn/ n attribuzione f

attributive /ə'trɪbjʊtɪv/ a attributivo

attrition /ə'trɪʃn/ n **war of ~** guerra f di logoramento

attune /ə'tjuːn/ vt **be ~d to** ⟨in harmony with⟩ essere sintonizzato con; ⟨accustomed to⟩ essere abituato a

aubergine /'əʊbəʒiːn/ n melanzana f

auburn /'ɔːbən/ a castano ramato

auction /'ɔːkʃn/ n asta f ● vt vendere all'asta

auctioneer /ɔːkʃə'nɪə(r)/ n banditore m

auction rooms npl sala f d'aste

auction sale n vendita f all'asta

audacious /ɔː'deɪʃəs/ a sfacciato; (*daring*) audace

audaciously /ɔː'deɪʃəslɪ/ adv sfacciatamente; (*daringly*) con audacia

audacity /ɔː'dæsətɪ/ n sfacciataggine f; (*daring*) audacia f

audible /'ɔːdəbl/ a udibile

audience /'ɔːdɪəns/ n Theat pubblico m; TV telespettatori mpl; (*Radio*) ascoltatori mpl; (*meeting*) udienza f

audience: audience participation n partecipazione f del pubblico. **audience ratings** npl indici mpl di ascolto. **audience research** n sondaggio m tra il pubblico

audio /'ɔːdɪəʊ/: **audiobook** n audiolibro m. **audio cassette** n audiocassetta f. **audio system** n impianto m stereo. **audiotape** n audiocassetta f. **audiotyping** n trascrizione f da audiocassetta. **audio typist** n dattilografo, -a mf (*che trascrive registrazioni*). **audiovisual** a audiovisivo

audit /'ɔːdɪt/ n verifica f del bilancio ● vt verificare

auditing /'ɔːdɪtɪŋ/ n auditing m inv

audition /ɔː'dɪʃn/ n audizione f ● vi fare un'audizione

auditor /'ɔːdɪtə(r)/ n revisore m di conti

auditorium /ɔːdɪ'tɔːrɪəm/ n sala f

auditory /'ɔːdɪt(ə)rɪ/ a acustico, uditivo

augment /ɔːg'ment/ vt aumentare

augur /'ɔːgə(r)/ vi ~ **well**/**ill** essere di buon/cattivo augurio

August /'ɔːgəst/ n agosto m

august /ɔː'gʌst/ a augusto

Augustinian /ɔːgə'stɪnɪən/ a agostiniano

aunt /ɑːnt/ n zia f

auntie, aunty /'ɑːntɪ/ n fam zietta f

au pair /əʊ'peə(r)/ n ~ **[girl]** ragazza f alla pari

aura /'ɔːrə/ n aura f

aural /'ɔːrəlɪ/ a uditivo; ‹Sch: comprehension, test› orale; ‹Med: test› audiometrico ● n Sch esercizio m di comprensione ed espressione orale; Mus ≈ dettato m musicale

aurora australis/borealis /ɔː'rɔːrəʊ-'strɑːlɪs/bɒrɪ'ɑːlɪs/ n aurora f australe/boreale

auspices /'ɔːspɪsɪz/ npl **under the ~ of** sotto l'egida di

auspicious /ɔː'spɪʃəs/ a di buon augurio

Aussie /'ɒzɪ/ a & n fam australiano, -a mf

austere /ɒ'stɪə(r)/ a austero

austerity /ɒ'sterətɪ/ n austerità f

Australasia /ɒstrə'leɪʒə/ n Australasia f

Australia /ɒ'streɪlɪə/ n Australia f

Australian /ɒ'streɪlɪən/ a & n australiano, -a mf

Austria /'ɒstrɪə/ n Austria f

Austrian /'ɒstrɪən/ a & n austriaco, -a mf

Austro-Hungarian /ɒstrəʊhʌŋ'geərɪən/ a austroungarico

autarchy /'ɔːtɑːkɪ/ n autarchia f

authentic /ɔː'θentɪk/ a autentico

authenticate /ɔː'θentɪkeɪt/ vt autenticare

authenticity /ɔːθen'tɪsətɪ/ n autenticità f

author /'ɔːθə(r)/ n autore m

authoritarian /ɔːθɒrɪ'teərɪən/ a autoritario

authoritative /ɔː'θɒrɪtətɪv/ a autorevole; ‹manner› autoritario

authority /ɔː'θɒrətɪ/ n autorità f; (*permission*) autorizzazione f; **who's in ~ here?** chi è il responsabile qui?; **be in ~ over** avere autorità su; **be an ~ on** essere un'autorità in materia di

authorization /ɔːθəraɪ'zeɪʃn/ n autorizzazione f

authorize /'ɔːθəraɪz/ vt autorizzare

authorized dealer /ɔːθəraɪzd/ rivenditore m autorizzato

autism /'ɔːtɪzm/ n autismo m

autistic /ɔː'tɪstɪk/ a autistico

auto /'ɔːtəʊ/ n Am fam auto f ● attrib ‹industry› automobilistico; ‹workers› dell'industria automobilistica

autobiographical /ɔːtəbaɪə'græfɪkl/ a autobiografico

autobiography /ɔːtəbaɪ'ɒgrəfɪ/ n autobiografia f

autocrat /'ɔːtəkræt/ n autocrate m

autocratic /ɔːtə'krætɪk/ a autocratico

autocue /'ɔːtəʊkjuː/ n TV gobbo m

autograph /'ɔːtəgrɑːf/ n autografo m ● vt autografare

autoimmune /ɔːtəʊ'mjuːn/ a ‹disease, system› autoimmune

automate /'ɔːtəmeɪt/ vt automatizzare

automatic /ɔːtə'mætɪk/ a automatico ● n (*car*) macchina f col cambio automatico; (*washing machine*) lavatrice f automatica

automatically /ɔːtə'mætɪklɪ/ adv automaticamente

automatic pilot n (*device*) pilota m automatico; **be on ~ ~** also fig viaggiare con il pilota automatico inserito

automatic teller machine /'telə/ n cassa f continua di prelevamento

automation /ɔːtə'meɪʃn/ n automazione f

automaton /ɔː'tɒmətən/ n automa m

automobile /'ɔːtəməbiːl/ n automobile f

automotive /ɔːtə'məʊtɪv/ a (*self-propelling*) autopropulso; ‹design, industry› automobilistico

autonomous /ɔː'tɒnəməs/ a autonomo

autonomously /ɔː'tɒnəməslɪ/ adv autonomamente

autonomy /ɔː'tɒnəmɪ/ n autonomia f

autopilot /'ɔːtəʊpaɪlət/ n Aeron, fig pilota m automatico

autopsy /'ɔːtɒpsɪ/ n autopsia f

auto-suggestion /ɔːtəʊsə'dʒestʃən/ n autosuggestione f

autumn /'ɔːtəm/ n autunno m

autumnal /ɔː'tʌmnl/ a autunnale

auxiliary /ɔːg'zɪlɪərɪ/ a ausiliario ● n ausiliare m

auxiliary nurse n infermiere, -a mf ausiliario, -a

auxiliary verb n ausiliare m

avail /əˈveɪl/ *n* **to no ~** invano ● *vi* ~ **oneself of** approfittare di

availability /əveɪləˈbɪlətɪ/ *n* (*of option, service*) disponibilità *f*; (*of drugs*) reperibilità *f*, disponibilità *f*; **subject to ~** fino ad esaurimento

available /əˈveɪləbl/ *a* disponibile; ‹*book, record etc*› in vendita

avalanche /ˈævəlɑːnʃ/ *n* valanga *f*

avant-garde /ævɒˈɡɑːd/ *n* avanguardia *f* ● *a* d'avanguardia

avarice /ˈævərɪs/ *n* avidità *f*

avaricious /ævəˈrɪʃəs/ *a* avido

Ave *abbr* (**Avenue**) V.le

avenge /əˈvendʒ/ *vt* vendicare

avenger /əˈvendʒə(r)/ *n* vendicatore, -trice *mf*

avenging /əˈvendʒɪŋ/ *a* vendicatore

avenue /ˈævənjuː/ *n* viale *m*; *fig* strada *f*

average /ˈævərɪdʒ/ *a* medio; (*mediocre*) mediocre ● *n* media *f*; **on ~** in media; **above ~** superiore al normale ● *vt* ‹*sales, attendance etc*›› raggiungere una media di

■ **average out at** *vt* risultare in media

averse /əˈvɜːs/ *a* **not be ~ to sth** non essere contro qcsa

aversion /əˈvɜːʃn/ *n* avversione *f* (**to** per)

avert /əˈvɜːt/ *vt* evitare ‹*crisis*›; distogliere ‹*eyes*›

aviary /ˈeɪvɪərɪ/ *n* uccelliera *f*

aviation /eɪvɪˈeɪʃn/ *n* aviazione *f*

aviation fuel *n* benzina *f* avio

aviation industry *n* industria *f* aeronautica

aviator /ˈeɪvɪeɪtə(r)/ *n* aviatore, -trice *mf*

avid /ˈævɪd/ *a* avido (**for** di); ‹*reader*› appassionato

avidity /əˈvɪdətɪ/ *n* avidità

avidly /ˈævɪdlɪ/ *adv* ‹*read, collect*› avidamente; ‹*support*› con entusiasmo

avocado /ævəˈkɑːdəʊ/ *n* avocado *m*

avoid /əˈvɔɪd/ *vt* evitare

avoidable /əˈvɔɪdəbl/ *a* evitabile

avoidance /əˈvɔɪdəns/ *n* ~ **of one's duty** astensione *f* dal proprio dovere

avowed /əˈvaʊd/ *a* dichiarato

avuncular /əˈvʌŋkʊlə(r)/ *a* benevolo

await /əˈweɪt/ *vt* attendere

awake /əˈweɪk/ *a* sveglio; **wide ~** completamente sveglio ● *vi* (*pt* **awoke**, *pp* **awoken**) svegliarsi

awaken /əˈweɪkn/ *vt* svegliare ● *vi* svegliarsi

awakening /əˈweɪknɪŋ/ *n* risveglio *m*

award /əˈwɔːd/ *n* premio *m*; (*medal*) riconoscimento *m*; (*of prize*) assegnazione *f* ● *vt* assegnare; (*hand over*) consegnare

award: award ceremony *n* cerimonia *f* di premiazione. **award winner** *n* vincitore, -trice *mf* di un premio. **award-winning** *a* ‹*book, film, design*› premiato

aware /əˈweə(r)/ *a* **be ~ of** (*sense*) percepire; (*know*) essere conscio di; **become ~ of** accorgersi di; (*learn*) venire a sapere di; **be ~ that** rendersi conto che

awareness /əˈweənɪs/ *n* percezione *f*; (*knowledge*) consapevolezza *f*

awash /əˈwɒʃ/ *a* inondato (**with** di)

away /əˈweɪ/ *adv* via; **go/stay ~** andare/stare via; **he's ~ from his desk/the office** non è alla sua scrivania/in ufficio; **far ~** lontano; **four kilometres ~** a quattro chilometri; **play ~** *Sport* giocare fuori casa

away game *n* partita *f* fuori casa

awe /ɔː/ *n* soggezione *f*; **stand in ~ of sb** avere soggezione di qcno

awe-inspiring *a* maestoso

awesome /ˈɔːsəm/ *a* imponente

awful /ˈɔːf(ə)l/ *a* terribile; **that's an ~ pity** è un gran peccato ● *adv fam* estremamente

awfully /ˈɔːf(ʊ)lɪ/ *adv* terribilmente; ‹*pretty*› estremamente; **that's ~ nice of you** è veramente gentile da parte tua; **thanks ~** grazie mille

awhile /əˈwaɪl/ *adv* per un po'

awkward /ˈɔːkwəd/ *a* ‹*movement*› goffo; ‹*moment, situation*› imbarazzante; ‹*time*› scomodo

awkwardly /ˈɔːkwədlɪ/ *adv* ‹*move*› goffamente; ‹*say*› con imbarazzo; **the meeting is ~ timed** la riunione è ad un orario scomodo

awkwardness /ˈɔːkwədnɪs/ *n* (*clumsiness*) goffaggine *f*; (*inconvenience*) scomodità *f*; (*embarrassment*) imbarazzo *m*; (*delicacy of situation*) delicatezza *f*

awl /ɔːl/ *n* (*for wood etc*) punteruolo *m*

awning /ˈɔːnɪŋ/ *n* tendone *m*

awoke(n) /əˈwəʊk(ən)/ *see* **awake**

AWOL /ˈeɪwɒl/ *a* & *adv abbr* (**absent without leave**) **be/go ~** *Mil* assentarsi senza permesso; *hum* volatilizzarsi

awry /əˈraɪ/ *adv* storto

axe /æks/ *n* scure *f*; **have an ~ to grind** *fig* avere il proprio tornaconto ● *vt* (*pres p* **axing**) fare dei tagli a (*budget*›; sopprimere ‹*jobs*›; annullare ‹*project*›

axiom /ˈæksɪəm/ *n* assioma *m*

axiomatic /æksɪəˈmætɪk/ *a* **it is ~ that...** è indiscutibile che...

axis /ˈæksɪs/ *n* (*pl* **axes** /-siːz/) asse *m*

axle /ˈæksl/ *n Techn* asse *m*

ay[e] /aɪ/ *adv* sì ● *n* sì *m invar*

Azerbaijan /æzəbaɪˈdʒɑːn/ *n* Azerbaigian *m*

Azerbaijani /æzəbaɪˈdʒɑːnɪ/ *a* & *n* (*person*) azerbaigiano, -a *mf*; (*language*) azerbaigiano *m*

Azores /əˈzɔːz/ *npl* **the ~** le Azzorre

Aztec /ˈæztek/ *a* & *n* (*person*) azteco, -a *mf*; (*language*) azteco *m*

azure /ˈeɪʒə(r)/ *a* & *n* azzurro *m*

Bb

b, B /biː/ *n* (*letter*) b, B *f inv*; *Mus* si *m inv*
b *abbr* **born**
BA *abbr* **Bachelor of Arts**
BAA *n abbr* (**British Airports Authority**) ente *m* che gestisce gli aeroporti britannici
baa /baː/ *vi* belare ● *int* bee
b. & b. *abbr* **bed and breakfast**
babble /ˈbæbl/ *vi* farfugliare; ⟨*stream*:⟩ gorgogliare
babe /beɪb/ *n liter* bimbo, -a *mf*; (*fam*: *woman*) ragazza *f*; (*fam*: *form of address*) bella *f*; **a ~ in arms** un bimbo in fasce; *fig* uno sprovveduto
baboon /bəˈbuːn/ *n* babbuino *m*
baby /ˈbeɪbɪ/ *n* bambino, -a *mf*; (*fam*: *darling*) tesoro *m*
baby: baby bird *n* uccellino *m*. **baby boom** *n* baby boom *m inv*. **baby boomer** *n persona f* nata durante il baby boom. **baby buggy** *n Br* carrozzina *f*. **baby carriage** *n Am* carrozzina *f*. **baby carrier** *n* zaino *m* portabimbo *inv*. **baby-faced** *a* ⟨*person*⟩ con la faccia da bambino
babyish /ˈbeɪbɪʃ/ *a* bambinesco
baby: baby-sit *vi* fare da baby-sitter. **baby-sitter** *n* baby-sitter *mf*. **baby-sitting** *n* do ~ fare il/la baby-sitter. **baby talk** *n* linguaggio *m* infantile. **baby tooth** *n* dente *m* di latte. **baby walker** *n* girello *m*. **babywear** *n* abbigliamento *m* per bambini
bachelor /ˈbætʃələ(r)/ *n* scapolo *m*; **B~ of Arts/Science** laureato, -a *mf* in lettere/in scienze
bachelor apartment, bachelor flat *Br n* appartamento *m* da scapolo
bachelorhood /ˈbætʃələhʊd/ *n* celibato *m*
bacillus /bəˈsɪləs/ *n* (*pl* **-lli**) bacillo *m*
back /bæk/ *n* schiena *f*; (*of horse, hand*) dorso *m*; (*of chair*) schienale *m*; (*of house, cheque, page*) retro *m*; (*in football*) difesa *f*; **at the ~** in fondo; **in the ~** *Auto* dietro; **stand ~ to ~** stare in piedi schiena contro schiena. **~ to front** ⟨*sweater*⟩ il davanti di dietro; **you've got it all ~ to front** *fig* hai capito tutto all'incontrario; **at the ~ of beyond** in un posto sperduto ● *a* posteriore; ⟨*taxes, payments*⟩ arretrato ● *adv* indietro; (*returned*) di ritorno; **turn/move ~** tornare/spostarsi indietro; **put it ~ here/there** rimettilo qui/là; **~ at home** di ritorno a casa; **I'll be ~ in five minutes** torno fra cinque minuti; **I'm just ~** sono appena tornato; **when do you want the book ~?** quando rivuoi il libro?; **pay ~** ripagare ⟨*sb*⟩; restituire ⟨*money*⟩; **~ in power** di nuovo al potere ● *vt* (*support*) sostenere; (*with money*) finanziare; puntare su ⟨*horse*⟩;

(*cover the back of*) rivestire il retro di ● *vi Auto* fare retromarcia
■ **back away** *vi* tirarsi indietro
■ **back down** *vi* battere in ritirata
■ **back in** *vi Auto* entrare in retromarcia; ⟨*person*:⟩ entrare camminando all'indietro
■ **back out** *vi Auto* uscire in retromarcia; ⟨*person*:⟩ uscire camminando all'indietro; *fig* tirarsi indietro (**of** da)
■ **back up** *vt* sostenere; confermare ⟨*person's alibi*⟩; *Comput* fare una copia di salvataggio di; **be ~ed up** ⟨*traffic*:⟩ essere congestionato ● *vi Auto* fare retromarcia
back: backache *n* mal *m* di schiena. **backbench** *n Br Pol* scanni mpl del Parlamento dove siedono i parlamentari ordinari. **backbencher** *n Br Pol* parlamentare *mf* ordinario, -a. **backbiting** *n* maldicenza *f*. **backboard** *n* (*in basketball*) tabellone *m*. **back boiler** *n* caldaia *f* (*posta dietro un caminetto*). **backbone** *n* spina *f* dorsale. **back-breaking** *a* massacrante. **back burner** *n* **put sth on the ~ ~** rimandare qcsa. **backchat** *n* risposta *f* impertinente. **backcloth** *n Theat* fondale *m*; *fig* sfondo *m*. **back comb** *vt* cotonare. **back copy** *n* numero *m* arretrato. **back cover** *n* retro *m* di copertina. **backdate** *vt* retrodatare ⟨*cheque*⟩; **~d to** valido a partire da. **back door** *n* porta *f* di servizio. **backdrop** *n Theat* fondale *m*; *fig* sfondo *m*. **back-end** *n* (*rear*) fondo *m*
backer /ˈbækə(r)/ *n* sostenitore, -trice *mf*; (*with money*) finanziatore, -trice *mf*
back: backfire *vi Auto* avere un ritorno di fiamma; ⟨*fig*: *plan*⟩ fallire; **the joke ~d on him** lo scherzo si è ritorto contro di lui. **backgammon** *n* backgammon *m*. **background** *n* sfondo *m*; (*environment*) ambiente *m*. **background noise** *n* rumore *m* di sottofondo. **background reading** *n* letture *fpl* generali. **backhand** *n Tennis* rovescio *m*. **backhanded** *a* ⟨*compliment*⟩ implicito. **backhander** *n* (*fam*: *bribe*) bustarella *f*
backing /ˈbækɪŋ/ *n* (*support*) supporto *m*; (*material used*) fondo *m*; *Mus* accompagnamento *m*
backing group *n* gruppo *m* d'accompagnamento
back issue *n* numero *m* arretrato
backlash /ˈbæklæʃ/ *n fig* reazione *f* opposta
backless /ˈbæklɪs/ *a* ⟨*dress*⟩ scollato dietro
back: backlist *n* opere *fpl* pubblicate. **backlog** *n* **~ of work** lavoro *m* arretrato. **back marker** *n Sport* ultimo, -a *mf*. **back number** *n* numero *m* arretrato. **backpack** *n* zaino *m*. **backpacker** *n* saccopelista *mf*.

backpacking *n* go ~ viaggiare con zaino e sacco a pelo. **back passage** *n Anat* retto *m*. **back pay** *n* arretrato *m* di stipendio. **backpedal** *vi* pedalare all'indietro; *fig* fare marcia indietro. **back pocket** *n* tasca *f* di dietro. **backrest** *n* schienale *m*. **back room** *n* stanza *f* sul retro. **back room boys** *npl esperti mpl che lavorano dietro le quinte*. **backscratcher** *n* manina *f* grattaschiena *inv*. **back seat** *n* sedile *m* posteriore. **back-seat driver** *n persona f che dà consigli non richiesti*. **backside** *n fam* fondoschiena *m inv*. **backslash** *n Typ* barra *f* retroversa. **backspace** *n Comput* spazio *m* indietro. **backstage** *a & adv* dietro le quinte. **backstairs** *npl* scala *f* di servizio. **backstitch** *n* impuntura *f ● vi* impunturare. **backstop** *n Sport* ricevitore *m*. **back straight** *n Sport* rettilineo *m*. **backstreet** *n* vicolo *m ● attrib* ⟨abortionist⟩ clandestino. **backstroke** *n* dorso *m*. **backtalk** *n Am* = **backchat**. **backtrack** *vi* tornare indietro; *fig* fare marcia indietro. **back translation** *n* traduzione *f* di una traduzione. **backup** *n* rinforzi *mpl*; *Comput* riserva *f*, backup *m inv*; **do a** ~ realizzare un backup. **backup copy** *n* copia *f* di riserva. **backup light** *n Am* luce *f* della retromarcia

backward /'bækwəd/ *a* ⟨step⟩ indietro; ⟨child⟩ lento nell'apprendimento; ⟨country⟩ arretrato

backward-looking /'bækwədlʊkɪŋ/ *a* retrogrado

backwards /'bækwədz/ *adv* (also *Am:* **backward**) indietro; ⟨fall, walk⟩ all'indietro; ~ **and forwards** avanti e indietro

backwater /'bækwɔːtə(r)/ *n fig* luogo *m* allo scarto

backyard /bæk'jɑːd/ *n* cortile *m*; **not in my** ~ **yard** *fam* non a casa propria

bacon /'beɪk(ə)n/ *n* ≈ pancetta *f*

bacon-slicer /'beɪkənslaɪsə(r)/ *n* affettatrice *f*

bacteria /bæk'tɪərɪə/ *npl* batteri *mpl*

bacterial /bæk'tɪərɪəl/ *a* batterico

bacteriology /bæktɪərɪ'ɒlədʒɪ/ *n* batteriologia *f*

bad /bæd/ *a* (**worse, worst**) cattivo; ⟨weather, habit, news, accident⟩ brutto; ⟨apple etc⟩ marcio; **the light is** ~ non c'è una buona luce; **my eyesight is** ~ non ho una buona vista; **use** ~ **language** dire delle parolacce; **she's going through a** ~ **patch** sta attraversando un brutto periodo; **feel** ~ sentirsi male; ⟨feel guilty⟩ sentirsi in colpa; **have a** ~ **back** avere dei problemi alla schiena; **smoking is** ~ **for you** fumare fa male; **go** ~ andare a male; **that's just too** ~! pazienza!; **not** ~ niente male; **things have gone from** ~ **to worse** le cose sono andate di male in peggio

bad: bad blood *n* **there is** ~ ~ **between them** tra loro non corre buon sangue. **bad boy** *n* ragazzaccio *m*. **bad breath** *n* alito *m* cattivo. **bad cheque** *n* assegno *m* a vuoto

bad debt *n* credito *m* inesigibile

baddie, baddy /'bædɪ/ *n fam* cattivo, -a *mf*

bade /bæd/ *see* **bid**

bad faith *n* malafede *f*

badge /bædʒ/ *n* distintivo *m*

badger /'bædʒə(r)/ *n* tasso *m ● vt* tormentare

badly /'bædlɪ/ *adv* male; ⟨hurt⟩ gravemente; ~ **off** povero; ~ **behaved** maleducato; **need** ~ aver estremamente bisogno di

bad-mannered /-'mænəd/ *a* maleducato

badminton /'bædmɪntən/ *n* badminton *m*

bad-tempered /-'tempəd/ *a* irascibile

baffle /'bæfl/ *vt* confondere

baffling /'bæflɪŋ/ *a* sconcertante

bag /bæg/ *n* borsa *f*; ⟨of paper⟩ sacchetto *m*; **old** ~ *sl* megera *f*; ~**s under the eyes** occhiaie *fpl*; ~**s of** *fam* un sacco di; **it's in the** ~ *fig* è fatta *● vt* ⟨pt/pp **bagged**⟩ ⟨fam: take⟩ accaparrarsi; ~ **sb a seat** tenere un posto a qcno

bagel /'beɪgəl/ *n panino m a forma di ciambella*

baggage /'bægɪdʒ/ *n* bagagli *mpl*

baggage: baggage allowance *n* franchigia *f* bagaglio. **baggage car** *n Rail* bagagliaio *m*. **baggage carousel** *n* nastro *m* trasportatore per ritiro bagagli. **baggage check** *n* controllo *m* bagagli. **baggage handler** *n* addetto, -a *mf* ai bagagli. **baggage locker** *n* armadietto *m* per deposito bagagli. **baggage reclaim** *n* ritiro *m* bagagli

baggy /'bægɪ/ *a* ⟨clothes⟩ ampio

Baghdad /bæg'dæd/ *n* Baghdad *f*

bag: bag lady *n fam* barbona *f*. **bag person** *n fam* barbone, -a *mf*. **bagpipes** *npl* cornamusa *f sg*. **bag snatcher** *n* scippatore, -trice *mf*

Bahamas /bə'hɑːməz/ *npl* **the** ~ le Bahamas

Bahrain, Bahrein /bɑː'reɪn/ *n* Bahrein *m*

bail /beɪl/ *n* cauzione *f*; **on** ~ su cauzione

■ **bail out** *vt Naut* aggottare; ~ **sb out** *Jur* pagare la cauzione per qcno; *fig* trarre qcno d'impaccio *● vi Aeron* paracadutarsi

bail bond *n Am Jur* cauzione *f*

bailiff /'beɪlɪf/ *n* ufficiale *m* giudiziario; ⟨of estate⟩ fattore *m*

bait /beɪt/ *n* esca *f*; **rise to the** ~ abboccare [all'amo] *● vt* innescare; ⟨fig: torment⟩ tormentare

baize /beɪz/ *n* panno *m* ⟨di tavolo da gioco e da biliardo⟩

bake /beɪk/ *vt* cuocere al forno; ⟨make⟩ fare *● vi* cuocersi al forno

baked beans /beɪkt'biːnz/ *n Culin* fagioli *mpl* al pomodoro

baked potato *n* patata *f* cotta al forno ⟨con la buccia⟩

baker /'beɪkə(r)/ *n* fornaio, -a *mf*, panettiere, -a *mf*

baker's [shop] /'beɪkəz/ *n* panetteria *f*

bakery /'beɪkərɪ/ *n* panificio *m*, forno *m*

baking /'beɪkɪŋ/ *n* cottura *f* al forno

baking: baking powder *n* lievito *m* in pol-

vere. **baking soda** n Culin bicarbonato m di
sodio. **baking tin** n teglia f
balaclava /ˈbæləˈklɑːvə/ n passamontagna
m inv
balance /ˈbæləns/ n (equilibrium) equilibrio m; Comm bilancio m; (outstanding sum)
saldo m; [**bank**] ~ saldo m; **be** or **hang in the**
~ fig essere in sospeso; **on** ~ tutto sommato
● vt bilanciare; equilibrare ⟨budget⟩; Comm
fare il bilancio di ⟨books⟩ ● vi bilanciarsi;
Comm essere in pareggio
balanced /ˈbælənst/ a equilibrato
balance: balance of payments n bilancia
f dei pagamenti. **balance of power** n Pol
equilibrio m delle forze. **balance sheet** n bilancio m [d'esercizio]. **balance of trade** n
bilancia f commerciale
balancing act /ˈbælənsɪŋ/ n fig **do a** ~ ~
fare equilibrismo
balcony /ˈbælkənɪ/ n balcone m
bald /bɔːld/ a ⟨person⟩ calvo; ⟨tyre⟩ liscio;
⟨statement⟩ nudo e crudo; **go** ~ perdere i capelli
balderdash /ˈbɔːldədæʃ/ n sciocchezze fpl
balding /ˈbɔːldɪŋ/ a **be** ~ stare perdendo i capelli
baldly /ˈbɔːldlɪ/ adv ⟨state⟩ in modo nudo e
crudo
baldness /ˈbɔːldnɪs/ n calvizie f
bale /beɪl/ n balla f
Balearic Islands /bælɪˈærɪk/ npl isole fpl
Baleari
baleful /ˈbeɪlfl/ a malvagio; (sad) triste
balefully /ˈbeɪlfʊlɪ/ adv con malvagità
balk /bɔːlk/ vt ostacolare ● vi ~ **at** ⟨horse:⟩
impennarsi davanti a; fig tirarsi indietro davanti a
Balkans /ˈbɔːlknz/ npl Balcani mpl
ball[1] /bɔːl/ n palla f; (football) pallone m; (of
yarn) gomitolo m; **on the** ~ fam sveglio
ball[2] n (dance) ballo m
ballad /ˈbæləd/ n ballata f
ball and chain n palla f al piede
ball-and-socket joint n giunto m sferico
ballast /ˈbæləst/ n zavorra f
ball: ball-bearing n cuscinetto m a sfera.
ballboy n Tennis raccattapalle m inv.
ballcock n Techn galleggiante m (in serbatoio). **ball control** n controllo m della palla.
ball dress n abito m da sera
ballerina /bæləˈriːnə/ n ballerina f [classica]
ballet /ˈbæleɪ/ n balletto m; (art form) danza f
ballet: ballet dancer n ballerino, -a mf
[classico, -a]. **ballet dress** n tutù m inv.
ballet shoes scarpe fpl da danza
ball: ballgame n gioco m con la palla; Am
partita f di baseball; **that's a whole**
different ~ fig è tutto un altro paio di maniche. **ballgirl** n Tennis raccattapalle f inv. **ball**
gown n abito m da sera
ballistic /bəˈlɪstɪk/ a balistico
ballistics n balistica fsg
balloon /bəˈluːn/ n pallone m; Aeron
mongolfiera f
balloonist /bəˈluːnɪst/ n aeronauta mf

ballot /ˈbælət/ n votazione f
ballot box n urna f
ballot paper n scheda f di votazione
ball: ballpark n Am stadio m di baseball.
ballpark figure n fam cifra f approssimativa.
ball-point [pen] n penna f a sfera. **ballroom**
n sala f da ballo. **ballroom dancing** n ballo m
liscio
■ **balls up** vulg vi incasinarsi ● vt
incasinare
ballyhoo /bælɪˈhuː/ n (publicity) battage m
inv pubblicitario; (uproar) baccano m
balm /bɑːm/ n balsamo m
balmy /ˈbɑːmɪ/ a (-ier, -iest) mite; (fam:
crazy) strampalato
balsam /ˈbɒlsəm/ n (oily) balsamo m
Baltic /ˈbɔːltɪk/ a & n **the** ~ [Sea] il [mar]
Baltico
balustrade /bæləˈstreɪd/ n balaustra f
bamboo /bæmˈbuː/ n bambù m
bamboozle /bæmˈbuːzl/ vt (fam: mystify)
confondere
ban /bæn/ n proibizione f ● vt (pt/pp
banned) proibire; ~ **from** espellere da
⟨club⟩; **she was** ~**ned from driving** le hanno ritirato la patente
banal /bəˈnɑːl/ a banale
banality /bəˈnælɪtɪ/ n banalità f inv
banana /bəˈnɑːnə/ n banana f
banana republic n pej repubblica f delle
banane
banana skin n buccia f di banana
band /bænd/ n banda f; (stripe) nastro m;
(Mus: pop group) complesso m; (Mus: brass ~)
banda f; Mil fanfara f
■ **band together** vi riunirsi
bandage /ˈbændɪdʒ/ n benda f ● vt fasciare
■ **bandage up** vt fasciare
Band-Aid n Med cerotto m
bandit /ˈbændɪt/ n bandito m
band: band leader n leader mf di un complesso. **bandmaster** n capobanda m (di banda musicale). **band saw** n segatrice f a nastro. **bandsman** n bandista m. **bandstand** n
palco m coperto [dell'orchestra]. **band-**
wagon n **jump on the** ~ fig seguire la corrente
bandy[1] /ˈbændɪ/ vt (pt/pp -ied) scambiarsi
⟨words⟩
■ **bandy about** vt far circolare
bandy[2] a (-ier, -iest) **be** ~ avere le gambe
storte
bandy-legged /-ˈlegd/ a con le gambe storte
bane /beɪn/ n **she/it is the** ~ **of my life!** è la
mia rovina!
bang /bæŋ/ n (noise) fragore m; (of gun,
firework) scoppio m; (blow) colpo m; **go with**
a ~ fam essere una cannonata ● adv ~ **in the**
middle of fam proprio nel mezzo di; **go** ~
⟨gun:⟩ sparare; ⟨balloon:⟩ esplodere ● int
bum! ● vt battere ⟨fist⟩; battere su ⟨table⟩;
sbattere ⟨door, head⟩ ● vi scoppiare; ⟨door:⟩
sbattere

■ **bang about, bang around** *vi* far rumore

■ **bang into** *vt* sbattere contro

banger /'bæŋə(r)/ *n* (*firework*) petardo *m*; (*fam: sausage*) salsiccia *f*; **old** ~ (*fam: car*) macinino *m*

Bangladesh /bæŋglə'deʃ/ *n* Bangladesh *m*

bangle /'bæŋgl/ *n* braccialetto *m*

banish /'bænɪʃ/ *vt* bandire

banishment /'bænɪʃmənt/ *n* bando *m*

banisters /'bænɪstəz/ *npl* ringhiera *fsg*

banjo /'bændʒəʊ/ *n* banjo *m inv*

bank¹ /bæŋk/ *n* (*of river*) sponda *f*; (*slope*) scarpata *f* ● *vi* Aeron inclinarsi in virata

bank² *n* banca *f* ● *vt* depositare in banca ● *vi* ~ **with** avere un conto [bancario] presso

■ **bank on** *vt* contare su

bank: bank account *n* conto *m* in banca. **bank balance** *n* saldo *m*. **bank-book** *n* libretto *m* di risparmio. **bank borrowings** *npl* prestiti *mpl* bancari. **bank card** *n* carta *f* assegni. **bank charges** *npl* spese *fpl* bancarie, commissioni *fpl*. **bank clerk** *n* bancario, -a *mf*

banker /'bæŋkə(r)/ *n* banchiere *m*

banker's draft *n* tratta *f* bancaria

banker's order *n* ordine *m* di pagamento

Bank Giro Credit *n Br* accreditamento *m* tramite bancogiro

bank holiday *n* giorno *m* festivo

banking /'bæŋkɪŋ/ *n* banca *m*

banking hours *npl* orario *m* di sportello (*in banca*)

bank: bank manager *n* direttore, -trice *mf* di banca. **banknote** *n* banconota *f*. **bank raid** *n* rapina *f* in banca. **bank robber** *n* rapinatore, -trice *mf* di banca. **bank robbery** *n* rapina *f* in banca. **bankroll** *n* finanziamento *m* ● *vt* finanziare ⟨*person, party*⟩

bankrupt /'bæŋkrʌpt/ *a* fallito; **go** ~ fallire ● *n* persona *f* che ha fatto fallimento ● *vt* far fallire

bankruptcy /'bæŋkrʌptsɪ/ *n* bancarotta *f*

bankruptcy court *n* tribunale *m* fallimentare

bankruptcy proceedings *npl* procedura *f* fallimentare

bank statement *n* estratto *m* conto

bank transfer *n* bonifico *m* bancario

banner /'bænə(r)/ *n* stendardo *m*; (*of demonstrators*) striscione *m*

banner headline *n* titolo *m* a tutta pagina

banns /bænz/ *npl* Relig pubblicazioni *fpl* [di matrimonio]

banquet /'bæŋkwɪt/ *n* banchetto *m*

bantam /'bæntəm/ *n* gallo *m* bantam

banter /'bæntə(r)/ *n* battute *fpl* di spirito

baptism /'bæptɪzm/ *n* battesimo *m*; ~ **of fire** *fig* battesimo *m* del fuoco

Baptist /'bæptɪst/ *a & n* battista *mf*

baptize /bæp'taɪz/ *vt* battezzare

bar /bɑ:(r)/ *n* sbarra *f*; Jur ordine *m* degli avvocati; (*of chocolate*) tavoletta *f*; (*café*) bar *m inv*; (*counter*) banco *m*; Mus battuta *f*; (*fig: obstacle*) ostacolo *m*; ~ **of soap/gold** sapo-

netta *f* /lingotto *m*; **be called to the** ~ *Jur* entrare a far parte dell'ordine degli avvocati; **behind** ~**s** *fam* dietro le sbarre ● *vt* ⟨*pt/pp* **barred**⟩ sbarrare ⟨*way*⟩; sprangare ⟨*door*⟩; escludere ⟨*person*⟩ ● *prep* tranne; ~ **none** in assoluto

barb /bɑ:b/ *n* barbiglio *m*; (*fig: remark*) frecciata *f*

Barbados /bɑ:'beɪdɒs/ *n* Barbados *fsg*

barbarian /bɑ:'beərɪən/ *n* barbaro, -a *mf*

barbaric /bɑ:'bærɪk/ *a* barbarico

barbarism /'bɑ:bərɪzm/ *n* (*brutality, primitiveness*) barbarie *f inv*; (*error of style*) barbarismo *m*

barbarity /bɑ:'bærətɪ/ *n* barbarie *f inv*

barbarous /'bɑ:bərəs/ *a* barbaro

barbecue /'bɑ:bɪkju:/ *n* barbecue *m inv*; (*party*) grigliata *f*, barbecue *m inv* ● *vt* arrostire sul barbecue

barbed /bɑ:bd/ *a* ~ **wire** filo *m* spinato

barber /'bɑ:bə(r)/ *n* barbiere *m*

barber's shop *n* barbiere *m*

barbiturate /bɑ:'bɪtjʊrət/ *n* barbiturico *m*

bar: bar chart *n* istogramma *m*. **bar code** *n* codice *m* a barre. **bar-coded** *a* con codice a barre. **bar code reader** *n* lettore *m* di codice a barre

bard /bɑ:d/ *n liter* bardo *m*

bare /beə(r)/ *a* nudo; ⟨*tree, room*⟩ spoglio; ⟨*floor*⟩ senza moquette; **the** ~ **bones** l'essenziale *m* ● *vt* scoprire; mostrare ⟨*teeth*⟩

bare: bareback *adv* senza sella. **barefaced** *a* sfacciato. **barefoot** *adv* scalzo. **bareheaded** *a* a capo scoperto

barely /'beəlɪ/ *adv* appena

bareness /'beənɪs/ *n* nudità *f*

bargain /'bɑ:gɪn/ *n* (*agreement*) patto *m*; (*good buy*) affare *m*; **into the** ~ per di più ● *vi* contrattare; (*haggle*) trattare

■ **bargain for** *vt* (*expect*) aspettarsi

bargain basement *n* reparto *m* occasioni

bargaining /'bɑ:gɪnɪŋ/ *n* (*over pay*) contrattazione *f* ● *attrib* ⟨*power, rights*⟩ contrattuale; ⟨*position*⟩ di negoziato

barge /bɑ:dʒ/ *n* barcone *m*

■ **barge in** *vi fam* (*to room*) piombare dentro; (*into conversation*) interrompere bruscamente; ~ **into** piombare dentro a ⟨*room*⟩; venire addosso a ⟨*person*⟩

bargepole /'bɑ:dʒpəʊl/ *n* **I wouldn't touch him/it with a** ~ non lo toccherei nemmeno con un dito

baritone /'bærɪtəʊn/ *n* baritono *m*

bark¹ /bɑ:k/ *n* (*of tree*) corteccia *f*

bark² *n* abbaiamento *m* ● *vi* abbaiare

barking /'bɑ:kɪŋ/ *n* abbaiamento *m* ● *a* ⟨*dog*⟩ che abbaia; ⟨*cough, laugh*⟩ convulso ● *adv* **be** ~ **mad** *Br fam* essere matto da legare

barley /'bɑ:lɪ/ *n* orzo *m*

barley: barleycorn *n* orzo *m*; (*grain*) chicco *m* d'orzo. **barley sugar** *n* caramella *f* d'orzo. **barley water** *n Br* orzata *f*. **barley wine** *n Br* birra *f* molto forte

barmaid /'bɑ:meɪd/ *n* barista *f*

barman /'bɑ:mən/ *n* barista *m*

barmy /'bɑːmɪ/ *a fam* strampalato

barn /bɑːn/ *n* granaio *m*

barnacle /'bɑːnəkl/ *n* cirripede *m*

barn: barn dance *n ballo m tradizionale statunitense*; (*social gathering*) *festa f negli USA in cui si fanno balli tradizionali*. **barn owl** *n* barbagianni *m inv*. **barnstorming** *a* sensazionale. **barnyard** *n* aia *f*

barometer /bə'rɒmɪtə(r)/ *n* barometro *m*

baron /'bærən/ *n* barone *m*

baroness /'bærənɪs/ *n* baronessa *f*

baronial /bə'rəʊnɪəl/ *a* baronale

baroque /bə'rɒk/ *a & n* barocco *m*

barracking /'bærəkɪŋ/ *n* fischi *mpl* e insulti *mpl*

barrack room *n* camerata *f* ● *attrib pej* (*language*) da caserma

barracks /'bærəks/ *npl* caserma *fsg*

barrage /'bærɑːʒ/ *n* (*in river*) [opera *f* di] sbarramento *m*; *Mil* sbarramento *m*; (*fig: of criticism, abuse*) sfilza *f*

barrage balloon *n* pallone *m* di sbarramento

barrel /'bærəl/ *n* barile *m*, botte *f*; (*of gun*) canna *f*

barrel organ *n* organetto *m* [a cilindro]

barren /'bærən/ *a* sterile; (*landscape*) brullo

barrette /bæ'ret/ *n Am* (*for hair*) molletta *f*

barricade /'bærɪkeɪd/ *n* barricata *f* ● *vt* barricare

barrier /'bærɪə(r)/ *n* barriera *f*; *Rail* cancello *m*; *fig* ostacolo *m*

barrier: barrier cream *n* crema *f* protettiva. **barrier method** *n Med* metodo *m* anticoncezionale meccanico. **barrier reef** *n* barriera *f* corallina

barring /'bɑːrɪŋ/ *prep* ~ **accidents** tranne imprevisti

barrister /'bærɪstə(r)/ *n* avvocato *m*

barrow /'bærəʊ/ *n* carretto *m*; (*wheel*~) carriola *f*

bar stool *n* sgabello *m* da bar

bartender /'bɑːtendə(r)/ *n* barista *mf*

barter /'bɑːtə(r)/ *vi* barattare (**for** con)

base /beɪs/ *n* base *f* ● *a* vile ● *vt* basare; **be ~d on** basarsi su

baseball /'beɪsbɔːl/ *n* baseball *m*

baseball cap *n* berretto *m* da baseball

base: base camp *n* campo *m* base *inv*. **base form** *n* (*of verb*) forma *f* non coniugata di un verbo. **base lending rate** *n* tasso *m* base *inv* di interesse

baseless /'beɪslɪs/ *a* infondato

baseline /'beɪslaɪn/ *n Tennis* linea *f* di fondo; *fig* riferimento *m*

basement /'beɪsmənt/ *n* seminterrato *m*

basement flat *n* appartamento *m* nel seminterrato

base metal *n* metallo *m* vile *inv*

base rate *n* tasso *m* base *inv*

bash /bæʃ/ *n* colpo *m* violento; **have a** ~! *fam* provaci! ● *vt* colpire [violentemente]; (*dent*) ammaccare; **~ed in** ammaccato

■ **bash down** *vt* sfondare (*door*)

bashful /'bæʃfl/ *a* timido

bashfully /'bæʃfʊlɪ/ *adv* timidamente

bashing /'bæʃɪŋ/ *n fam* (*beating*) pestaggio *m*; (*criticism*) critica *f* feroce; (*defeat*) batosta *f*; **take a** ~ prendere una batosta

basic /'beɪsɪk/ *a* di base; (*condition, requirement*) basilare; (*living conditions*) povero; **my Italian is pretty** ~ il mio italiano è abbastanza rudimentale; **the ~s** (*of language, science*) i rudimenti; (*essentials*) l'essenziale *m*

basically /'beɪsɪklɪ/ *adv* fondamentalmente

basic rate *n* tariffa *f* minima; (*in tax*) aliquota *f* minima

basil /'bæzɪl/ *n* basilico *m*

basilica /bə'zɪlɪkə/ *n* basilica *f*

basin /'beɪsn/ *n* bacinella *f*; (*wash-hand* ~) lavabo *m*; (*for food*) recipiente *m*; *Geog* bacino *m*

basinful /'beɪsɪnfʊl/ *n* bacinella *f* (*contenuto*)

basis /'beɪsɪs/ *n* (*pl* **-ses** /'beɪsiːz/) base *f*

bask /bɑːsk/ *vi* crogiolarsi

basket /'bɑːskɪt/ *n* cestino *m*

basket: basketball *n* pallacanestro *f*. **basket chair** *n* sedia *f* di vimini. **basketwork** *n* (*objects*) oggetti *mpl* in vimini; (*craft*) lavoro *m* artigianale di oggetti in vimini

Basle /bɑːl/ *n* Basilea *f*

Basque /bæsk/ *a & n* (*person*) basco, -a *mf*; (*language*) basco *m*

bass /beɪs/ *a* basso; ~ **voice** voce *f* di basso ● *n* basso *m*

bass: bass-baritone *n* baritono *m* basso. **bass clef** *n* chiave *f* di basso. **bass drum** *n* grancassa *f*

basset hound /'bæsɪt/ *n* basset hound *m inv*

bassist /'beɪsɪst/ *n* bassista *mf*

bassoon /bə'suːn/ *n* fagotto *m*

bastard /'bɑːstəd/ *n* (*illegitimate child*) bastardo, -a *mf*; *sl* figlio *m* di puttana

baste¹ /beɪst/ *vt* (*sew*) imbastire

baste² *vt Culin* ungere con grasso

bastion /'bæstɪən/ *n* bastione *m*

bat¹ /bæt/ *n* mazza *f*; (*for table tennis*) racchetta *f*; **off one's own** ~ *fam* tutto da solo ● *vt* (*pt/pp* **batted**) battere; **she didn't** ~ **an eyelid** *fig* non ha battuto ciglio

bat² *n Zool* pipistrello *m*

batch /bætʃ/ *n* gruppo *m*; (*of goods*) partita *f*; (*of bread*) infornata *f*

batch file *n Comput* batch file *m inv*

batch processing /'prəʊsesɪŋ/ *n Comput* elaborazione *f* a gruppi

bated /'beɪtɪd/ *a* **with** ~ **breath** col fiato sospeso

bath /bɑːθ/ *n* (*pl* **~s** /bɑːðz/) bagno *m*; (*tub*) vasca *f* da bagno; **~s** *pl* piscina *f*; **have a** ~ fare un bagno ● *vt* fare il bagno a ● *vi* fare il bagno

bathe /beɪð/ *n* bagno *m* ● *vi* fare il bagno ● *vt* lavare (*wound*)

bather /'beɪðə(r)/ *n* bagnante *mf*

bathing /'beɪðɪŋ/ *n* bagni *mpl*

bathing: bathing cap *n* cuffia *f*. **bathing**

costume *n* costume *m* da bagno. **bathing hut** *n* cabina *f* (*al mare*). **bathing suit** *n* costume *m* da bagno. **bathing trunks** *n* calzoncini *mpl* da bagno

bath mat *n* tappetino *m* da bagno

bathrobe /'bæθrəʊb/ *n* accappatoio *m*

bathroom /'bæθru:m/ *n* (*also: toilet*) bagno *m*

bathroom: bathroom cabinet *n* armadietto *m* del bagno. **bathroom fittings** *npl* accessori *mpl* per il bagno. **bathroom scales** *npl* bilancia *f* pesapersone

bath: bath salts *npl* sali *mpl* da bagno. **bath-towel** *n* asciugamano *m* da bagno. **bathtub** *n* vasca *f* da bagno

baton /'bæt(ə)n/ *n Mus* bacchetta *f*

baton charge *n Br* carica *f* con lo sfollagente

baton round *n Br* proiettile *m* di gomma

batsman /'bætsmən/ *n Sport* battitore *m*

battalion /bə'tælɪən/ *n* battaglione *m*

batten /'bætn/ *n* assicella *f*

batter /'bætə(r)/ *n Culin* pastella *f*

battered /'bætəd/ *a* ⟨*car*⟩ malandato; ⟨*wife, baby*⟩ maltrattato

battering /'bæt(ə)rɪŋ/ *n* **take a ~** (*from bombs, storm, waves*) essere colpito; (*from other team*) prendersi una batosta; (*from other boxer*) prendersele

battering ram *n* ariete *m*

battery /'bætərɪ/ *n* batteria *f*; (*of torch, radio*) pila *f*

battery: battery charger *n* caricabatterie *m inv*. **battery chicken** *n* pollo *m* di allevamento in batteria. **battery controlled** *a* a pile. **battery farming** *n* allevamento *m* in batteria. **battery hen** *n* gallina *f* d'allevamento in batteria. **battery life** *n* autonomia *f*. **battery operated, battery powered** *a* a pile

battle /'bæt(ə)l/ *n* battaglia *f*; *fig* lotta *f* • *vi* lottare

battle: battleaxe *n fam* virago *f inv*. **battle cry** *n also fig* grido *m* di battaglia. **battle dress** *n* uniforme *f* da combattimento. **battlefield** *n*, **battleground** *n* campo *m* di battaglia; *fig* terreno *m* di scontro. **battle lines** *npl Mil* schieramenti *mpl*

battlements /'bætlmənts/ *npl* bordo *m* merlato; (*crenellations*) merlatura *f*

battle: battle order *n also fig* ordine *m* di battaglia. **battle-scarred** *a* agguerrito; *fig* segnato dalla vita. **battleship** *n* corazzata *f*

batty /'bætɪ/ *a fam* strampalato

bauble /'bɔːb(ə)l/ *n* (*ornament*) gingillo *m*; (*jewellery*) ninnolo *m*

bawdiness /'bɔːdɪnɪs/ *n* oscenità *f*

bawdy /'bɔːdɪ/ *a* (*-ier, -iest*) piccante

bawl /bɔːl/ *vt/i* urlare

■ **bawl out** *vt fam* urlare ⟨*name, order*⟩; fare una sfuriata a ⟨*sb*⟩

bay¹ /beɪ/ *n Geog* baia *f*

bay² *n* **keep at ~** tenere a bada

bay³ *n Bot* alloro *m*

bay⁴ *n* (*horse*) baio *m*

bay leaf *n* foglia *f* d'alloro

bayonet /'beɪənet/ *n* baionetta *f*

bay window *n* bay window *f inv* (*grande finestra sporgente*)

bazaar /bə'zɑː(r)/ *n* bazar *m inv*

bazooka /bə'zuːkə/ *n* bazooka *m inv*

BBC *n abbr* (**British Broadcasting Corporation**) BBC *f*

BC *abbr* (**before Christ**) a.C.

BE *abbr* (**bill of exchange**) cambiale *f*

be /biː/ *vi* (*pres* **am, are, is, are**; *pt* **was, were**; *pp* **been**) essere; **he is a teacher** è insegnante, fa l'insegnante; **what do you want to be?** cosa vuoi fare?; **be quiet!** sta' zitto!; **I am cold/hot** ho freddo/caldo; **it's cold/hot, isn't it?** fa freddo/caldo, vero?; **how are you?** come stai?; **I am well** sto bene; **there is c'è**; **there are** ci sono; **I have been to Venice** sono stato a Venezia; **has the postman been?** è passato il postino?; **you're coming too, aren't you?** vieni anche tu, no?; **it's yours, is it?** è tuo, vero?; **was John there? – yes, he was** c'era John? – sì; **John wasn't there – yes he was!** John non c'era – sì che c'era!; **three and three are six** tre più tre fanno sei; **he is five** ha cinque anni; **that will be £10, please** fanno 10 sterline, per favore; **how much is it?** quanto costa?; **that's £5 you owe me** mi devi 5 sterline • *v aux* **I am coming/reading** sto venendo/leggendo; **I'm staying** (*not leaving*) resto; **I am being lazy** sono pigro; **I was thinking of you** stavo pensando a te; **you are not to tell him** non devi dirgielo; **you are to do that immediately** devi farlo subito • *passive* essere; **I have been robbed** sono stato derubato

beach /biːtʃ/ *n* spiaggia *f*

beach: beach ball *n* pallone *m* da spiaggia. **beach buggy** *n* dune buggy *f inv*. **beachcomber** *n* persona *f* che vive rivendendo gli oggetti trovati sulla spiaggia. **beachhead** *n* testa *f* di sbarco. **beach hut** *n* cabina *f* [da spiaggia]. **beachrobe** *n* accappatoio *m*. **beachwear** *n* abbigliamento *m* da spiaggia

beacon /'biːk(ə)n/ *n* faro *m*; *Naut, Aeron* fanale *m*

bead /biːd/ *n* perlina *f*

beady-eyed /biːdɪ'aɪd/ *a* (*sharp-eyed*) a cui non sfugge niente

beagle /'biːg(ə)l/ *n* beagle *m inv*, bracchetto *m*

beak /biːk/ *n* becco *m*

beaker /'biːkə(r)/ *n* coppa *f*; (*in laboratory*) becher *m inv*

beam /biːm/ *n* trave *f*; (*of light*) raggio *m* • *vi* irradiare; ⟨*person*⟩ essere raggiante; **~ at sb** fare un gran sorriso a qcno

beaming /'biːmɪŋ/ *a* raggiante

bean /biːn/ *n* fagiolo *m*; (*of coffee*) chicco *m*; **spill the ~s** *fam* spiattellare tutto

bean: bean bag *n* (*seat*) poltrona *f* imbottita di pallini di polistirolo. **beanfeast** *n fam* festa *f*. **beanpole** *n* (*fig fam: tall thin person*) spilungone, -a *mf.* **beansprout** *n* germoglio *m* di soia

bear¹ /beə(r)/ *n* orso *m*

bear² *v* (*pt* **bore**, *pp* **borne**) ● *vt* (*endure*) sopportare; mettere al mondo ⟨*child*⟩; (*carry*) portare; **~ in mind** tenere presente; **~ fruit** ⟨*tree:*⟩ produrre; *fig* dare frutto ● *vi* **~ left/right** andare a sinistra/a destra

■ **bear out** *vt* confermare ⟨*story, statement*⟩

■ **bear with** *vt* aver pazienza con

bearable /'beərəbl/ *a* sopportabile

bear cub *n* cucciolo *m* di orso

beard /bɪəd/ *n* barba *f*; **have a ~** avere la barba

bearded /'bɪədɪd/ *a* barbuto

bearer /'beərə(r)/ *n* portatore, -trice *mf*; (*of passport*) titolare *mf*

bearing /'beərɪŋ/ *n* portamento *m*; *Techn* cuscinetto *m* [a sfera]; **have a ~ on** avere attinenza con; **get one's ~s** orientarsi; **lose one's ~s** perdere l'orientamento

bear market *n Fin* mercato *m* al ribasso

bearskin *n* (*pelt*) pelle *f* d'orso; (*hat*) colbacco *m* militare

beast /bi:st/ *n* bestia *f*; (*fam: person*) animale *m*

beastly /'bi:stlɪ/ *a* (**-ier, -iest**) *fam* orribile

beat /bi:t/ *n* battito *m*; (*rhythm*) battuta *f*; (*of policeman*) giro *m* d'ispezione ● *v* (*pt* **beat**, *pp* **beaten**) ● *vt* battere; picchiare ⟨*person*⟩; **~ a retreat** *Mil* battere in ritirata; **~ it!** *fam* darsela a gambe!; **it ~s me why...** *fam* non capisco proprio perché...

■ **beat down** *vt* buttare giù ⟨*door*⟩ ● *vi* ⟨*sun:*⟩ battere a picco

■ **beat off** *vt* respingere ⟨*attacker*⟩

■ **beat out** *vt* domare ⟨*flames*⟩

■ **beat up** *vt* picchiare

beaten /'bi:tn/ *a* **off the ~ track** fuori mano

beatify /bɪ'ætɪfaɪ/ *vt* beatificare

beating /'bi:tɪŋ/ *n* bastonata *f*; **get a ~** (*with fists*) essere preso a pugni; ⟨*team, player:*⟩ prendere una batosta

beating-up *n fam* pestaggio *m*

beat-up *a* ⟨*fam: car*⟩ sfasciato

beau /bəʊ/ *n liter, hum* spasimante *m*

Beaufort scale /'bəʊfət/ *n* scala *f* Beaufort

beautician /bju:'tɪʃn/ *n* estetista *mf*

beautiful /'bju:tɪfl/ *a* bello; **the ~ people** il bel mondo

beautifully /'bju:tɪfʊlɪ/ *adv* splendidamente

beautify /'bju:tɪfaɪ/ *vt* (*pt/pp* **-ied**) abbellire

beauty /'bju:tɪ/ *n* bellezza *f*

beauty: beauty contest *n* concorso *m* di bellezza. **beauty editor** *n* redattore, -trice *mf* di articoli di bellezza. **beauty parlour** *n* istituto *m* di bellezza. **beauty queen** *n* reginetta *f* di bellezza. **beauty salon** *n* istituto *m* di bellezza. **beauty sleep** *n hum* **need one's ~ ~** aver bisogno delle proprie ore di sonno. **beauty spot** *n* neo *m*; (*place*) luogo *m* pittoresco

beaver /'bi:və(r)/ *n* castoro *m*

■ **beaver away** *vi* (*fam: work hard*) sgobbare

becalmed /bɪ'kɑ:md/ *a* in bonaccia

became /bɪ'keɪm/ *see* **become**

because /bɪ'kɒz/ *conj* perché; (*at start of sentence*) poiché ● *adv* **~ of** a causa di

beck /bek/ *n* **be at sb's ~ and call** dover essere a completa disposizione di qcno

beckon /'bekn/ *vt/i* ~ [**to**] chiamare con un cenno

become /bɪ'kʌm/ *v* (*pt* **became**, *pp* **become**) ● *vt* diventare ● *vi* diventare; **what has ~ of her?** che ne è di lei?

becoming /bɪ'kʌmɪŋ/ *a* ⟨*clothes*⟩ bello

bed /bed/ *n* letto *m*; (*of sea, lake*) fondo *m*; (*layer*) strato *m*; (*of flowers*) aiuola *f*; **in ~** a letto; **go to ~** andare a letto; **~ and breakfast** pensione *f* familiare in cui il prezzo della camera comprende anche la prima colazione

■ **bed down** *vi* coricarsi

BEd *n abbr* (**Bachelor of Education**) ≈ laurea *f* in magistero

bed: bed and board *n* vitto e alloggio *m*. **bed base** *n* fondo *m* del letto. **bed bath** *n* **give sb a ~ ~** lavare qcno a letto. **bedbug** *n* cimice *f*. **bedchamber** *n* camera *f* da letto. **bedclothes** *npl* lenzuola e coperte *fpl*

bedding /'bedɪŋ/ *n* biancheria *f* per il letto, materasso e guanciali

bedeck /bɪ'dek/ *vt* ornare

bedevil /bɪ'devəl/ *vt* tormentare ⟨*person*⟩; intralciare ⟨*plans*⟩

bed: bedfellow *n* **make strange ~s** *fig* fare una strana coppia. **bedhead** *n* testata *f* del letto. **bed jacket** *n* liseuse *f inv*

bedlam /'bedləm/ *n* baraonda *f*

bed linen *n* biancheria *f* per il letto

bedpan /'bedpæn/ *n* padella *f*

bedraggled /bɪ'drægld/ *a* inzaccherato

bedridden /'bedrɪdən/ *a* costretto a letto

bedrock /'bedrɒk/ *n* basamento *m*; *fig* fondamento *m*

bedroom /'bedru:m/ *n* camera *f* da letto

bedroom: bedroom farce *n Theat* pochade *f inv*. **bedroom slipper** *n* pantofola *f*. **bedroom suburb** *n Am* città *f inv* dormitorio

bed-settee *n* divano *m* letto

bedside /'bedsaɪd/ *n* **at his ~** al suo capezzale

bedside: bedside lamp *n* abat-jour *m inv*. **bedside manner** *n* modo *m* di trattare i pazienti; **have a good ~ ~** saperci fare con i pazienti. **bedside rug** *n* scendiletto *m*. **bedside table** *n* comodino *m*

bed: bed-sit *n*, **bed-sitter** *n*, **bed-sitting-room** *n* camera *f* ammobiliata [fornita di cucina]. **bedsock** *n* calzino *m* da notte. **bedsore** *n* piaga *f* da decubito. **bedspread** *n* copriletto *m*. **bedstead** *n* fusto *m* del letto. **bedtime** *n* l'ora *f* di andare a letto. **bedwetting** *n* il bagnare il letto

bee /bi:/ *n* ape *f*

beech /bi:tʃ/ *n* faggio *m*

beef /biːf/ n manzo m

beef: beefburger n hamburger m inv.
beefeater n guardia f della Torre di Londra.
beefsteak n bistecca f. **beefsteak tomato**
n grosso pomodoro m. **beef stew** n stufato m
di manzo. **beef tea** n brodo m di manzo

beefy /'biːfɪ/ a ⟨flavour⟩ di manzo; ⟨fam:
man⟩ grande e grosso

beehive /'biːhaɪv/ n alveare m

bee: bee-keeper n apicoltore, -trice mf.
bee-keeping n apicoltura f. **bee-line** n
make a ~ for fam precipitarsi verso

been /biːn/ see **be**

beep /biːp/ n ⟨of car⟩ suono m di clacson; ⟨of
telephone⟩ segnale m acustico; ⟨of electronic
device, radio⟩ bip m inv ● vi ⟨car, driver:⟩
clacsonare; ⟨device:⟩ fare bip ● vt ⟨with
beeper⟩ chiamare con il cercapersone; **~ the
horn** clacsonare

beeper /'biːpə(r)/ n cercapersone m inv

beer /bɪə(r)/ n birra f

beer: beer belly n pancia f da beone. **beer
bottle** n bottiglia f da birra. **beer garden** n
giardino m di un pub. **beer mat** n sottobicchiere m. **beerswilling** a pej ubriacone

bee sting n puntura f d'ape

beeswax /'biːzwæks/ n cera f d'api

beet /biːt/ n ⟨Am: beetroot⟩ barbabietola f;
[**sugar**] **~** barbabietola f da zucchero

beetle /'biːtl/ n scarafaggio m

■ **beetle off** vi ⟨fam: hurry away⟩ scappere

beetroot /'biːtruːt/ n barbabietola f

befall /bɪ'fɔːl/ vt liter accadere a

befit /bɪ'fɪt/ vt liter addirsi a

befitting /bɪ'fɪtɪŋ/ a ⟨modesty, honesty⟩ opportuno

before /bɪ'fɔː(r)/ prep prima di; **the day ~
yesterday** ieri l'altro; **~ long** fra poco ● adv
prima; **never ~ have I seen...** non ho mai
visto prima...; **~ that** prima; **~ going** prima
di andare ● conj ⟨time⟩ prima che; **~ you go**
prima che tu vada

beforehand /bɪ'fɔːhænd/ adv in anticipo

before tax a ⟨profit, income⟩ lordo, al lordo
di imposte

befriend /bɪ'frend/ vt trattare da amico

befuddle /bɪ'fʌdl/ vt confondere ⟨mind⟩

beg /beg/ v ⟨pt/pp **begged**⟩ ● vi mendicare
● vt pregare; chiedere ⟨favour, forgiveness⟩

began /bɪ'gæn/ see **begin**

beggar /'begə(r)/ n mendicante mf; **you
lucky ~!** che fortuna sfacciata!; **poor ~!** povero cristo!; **you little ~!** monellaccio!

beggarly /'begəlɪ/ a ⟨existence, meal⟩ miserabile; ⟨wage⟩ da fame

begging bowl /'begɪŋ/ n ciotola f del mendicante

begging letter n lettera f che sollecita offerte in denaro

begin /bɪ'gɪn/ vt/i ⟨pt **began**, pp **begun**, pres
p **beginning**⟩ cominciare; **well, to ~ with**
dunque, per cominciare

beginner /bɪ'gɪnə(r)/ n principiante mf

beginning /bɪ'gɪnɪŋ/ n principio m

begonia /bɪ'gəʊnɪə/ n begonia f

begrudge /bɪ'grʌdʒ/ vt ⟨envy⟩ essere invidioso di; dare malvolentieri ⟨money⟩

beguile /bɪ'gaɪl/ vt ⟨charm⟩ affascinare;
⟨cheat⟩ ingannare

beguiling /bɪ'gaɪlɪŋ/ a accattivante

begun /bɪ'gʌn/ see **begin**

behalf /bɪ'hɑːf/ n **on ~ of** a nome di; **on my
~** a nome mio; **say hello on my ~** salutalo
da parte mia

behave /bɪ'heɪv/ vi comportarsi; **~
[oneself]** comportarsi bene

behaviour /bɪ'heɪvjə(r)/ n comportamento
m; ⟨of prisoner, soldier⟩ condotta f

behavioural /bɪ'heɪvjərəl/ a comportamentale

behaviourist /bɪ'heɪvjərɪst/ a & n compor-
tamentista mf

behaviour pattern n modello m comportamentale

behead /bɪ'hed/ vt decapitare

beheld /bɪ'held/ see **behold**

behind /bɪ'haɪnd/ prep dietro; ⟨with pronoun⟩
dietro di; **be ~ sth** fig stare dietro qcsa ● adv
dietro, indietro; ⟨late⟩ in ritardo; **a long way
~** molto indietro; **in the car ~** nella macchina dietro ● n fam didietro m

behindhand /bɪ'haɪndhænd/ adv indietro

behold /bɪ'həʊld/ vt ⟨pt/pp **beheld**⟩ liter vedere

beholden /bɪ'həʊldn/ a obbligato (**to** verso)

beholder /bɪ'həʊldə(r)/ n **beauty is in the
eye of the ~** è bello ciò che piace

beige /beɪʒ/ a & n beige m inv

Beijing /beɪ'dʒɪŋ/ n Pechino f

being /'biːɪŋ/ n essere m; **come into ~** nascere

Beirut /beɪ'ruːt/ n Beirut f

bejewelled /bɪ'dʒuːəld/ a ingioiellato

belated /bɪ'leɪtɪd/ a tardivo

belatedly /bɪ'leɪtɪdlɪ/ adv tardi

belch /beltʃ/ vi ruttare ● vt **~ [out]** eruttare
⟨smoke⟩

beleaguered /bɪ'liːgəd/ a ⟨city⟩ assediato;
⟨troops⟩ accerchiato; ⟨fig: person⟩ tormentato;
⟨fig: company⟩ in difficoltà

Belfast /bel'fɑːst/ n Belfast f

belfry /'belfrɪ/ n campanile m

Belgian /'beldʒən/ a & n belga mf

Belgium /'beldʒəm/ n Belgio m

Belgrade /bel'greɪd/ n Belgrado f

belie /bɪ'laɪ/ vt ⟨give false impression of⟩ dissimulare; ⟨disprove⟩ smentire

belief /bɪ'liːf/ n fede f; ⟨opinion⟩ convinzione f

believable /bɪ'liːvəbl/ a credibile

believe /bɪ'liːv/ vt/i credere

■ **believe in** vt avere fiducia in ⟨person⟩; credere a ⟨ghosts⟩

believer /bɪ'liːvə(r)/ n Relig credente mf; **be
a great ~ in** credere fermamente in

belittle /bɪ'lɪtl/ vt sminuire ⟨person,
achievements⟩

belittling /bɪ'lɪtlɪŋ/ a ⟨comment⟩ che sminui-
sce

Belize /be'liːz/ n Belize m

bell /bel/ n campana f; (on door) campanello m; **that rings a ~** fig mi dice qualcosa

bell-bottoms npl pantaloni mpl a zampa d'elefante

bellboy /'belbɔɪ/ n Am fattorino m d'albergo

belle /bel/ n bella f

bellhop /'belhɒp/ n Am fattorino m d'albergo

belligerence /bɪ'lɪdʒərəns/ n bellicosità f; Pol belligeranza f

belligerent /bɪ'lɪdʒərənt/ a belligerante; (aggressive) bellicoso

bell-jar n campana f di vetro

bellow /'beləʊ/ vi gridare a squarciagola; ⟨animal:⟩ muggire
■ **bellow out** vt urlare ⟨name, order⟩

bellows /'beləʊz/ npl (for fire) soffietto m

bell: bell-pull n (rope) cordone m di campanello. **bell-push** n pulsante m di campanello. **bell-ringer** n campanaro m. **bell-shaped** a a campana. **bell tower** n campanile m

belly /'beli/ n pancia f

belly: bellyache n fam mal m di pancia ● vi fam lamentarsi. **belly button** n fam ombelico m. **belly dancer** n danzatrice f del ventre. **belly flop** n (in swimming) spanciata f

bellyful /'belifʊl/ n fam **have had a ~ of sth** avere le tasche piene di qcsa

belong /bɪ'lɒŋ/ vi appartenere (**to** a); (be member) essere socio (**to** di)

belongings /bɪ'lɒŋɪŋz/ npl cose fpl

beloved /bɪ'lʌvɪd/ a & n amato, -a mf

below /bɪ'ləʊ/ prep sotto; (with numbers) al di sotto di ● adv sotto, di sotto; Naut sotto coperta; **see ~** guardare qui di seguito

belt /belt/ n cintura f; (area) zona f; Techn cinghia f ● vi (fam: rush) **~ along** filare velocemente ● vt (fam: hit) picchiare
■ **belt up** vi (in car) mettersi la cintura [di sicurezza]; **~ up!** (sl: be quiet) stai zitto!

bemoan /bɪ'məʊn/ vt lamentare

bemused /bɪ'mju:zd/ a confuso

bench /bentʃ/ n panchina f; (work~) piano m da lavoro; **the B~** Jur la magistratura

benchmark /'bentʃmɑ:k/ n punto m di riferimento; Comput paragone m con un campione; (fin: price) prezzo m di riferimento

bend /bend/ n curva f; (of river) ansa f; **round the ~** fam fuori di testa ● v (pt/pp bent) ● vt piegare ● vi piegarsi; ⟨road:⟩ curvare; **~ [down]** chinarsi
■ **bend over** vi inchinarsi

beneath /bɪ'ni:θ/ prep sotto, al di sotto di; **he thinks it's ~ him** fig pensa che sia sotto al suo livello; **~ contempt** indegno ● adv giù

Benedictine /benɪ'dɪkti:n/ a & n Relig benedettino m

benediction /benɪ'dɪkʃn/ n Relig benedizione f

benefactor /'benɪfæktə(r)/ n benefattore, -trice mf

beneficial /benɪ'fɪʃl/ a benefico

beneficiary /benɪ'fɪʃərɪ/ n beneficiario, -a mf

benefit /'benɪfɪt/ n vantaggio m; (allowance) indennità f inv ● v (pt/pp **-fited,** pres p **-fiting**) ● vt giovare a ● vi trarre vantaggio (**from** da)

Benelux /'benɪlʌks/ n Benelux m ● attrib ⟨countries, organization⟩ del Benelux

benevolence /bɪ'nevələns/ n benevolenza f

benevolent /bɪ'nevələnt/ a benevolo

benevolently /bɪ'nevələntlɪ/ adv con benevolenza

Bengal /beŋ'gɔ:l/ n Bengala m

benign /bɪ'naɪn/ a benevolo; Med benigno

benignly /bɪ'naɪnlɪ/ adv con benevolenza

Benin /be'ni:n/ n Benin m

bent /bent/ see bend ● a ⟨person⟩ ricurvo; (distorted) curvato; (fam: dishonest) corrotto; **be ~ on doing sth** essere ben deciso a fare qcsa ● n predisposizione f

benzene /'benzi:n/ n benzene m

benzine /'benzi:n/ n benzina f

bequeath /bɪ'kwi:ð/ vt lasciare in eredità

bequest /bɪ'kwest/ n lascito m

berate /bɪ'reɪt/ vt fml redarguire

bereaved /bɪ'ri:vd/ n **the ~** pl i familiari del defunto

bereavement /bɪ'ri:vmənt/ n lutto m

bereft /bɪ'reft/ a **~ of** privo di

beret /'bereɪ/ n berretto m

Berlin /bɜ:'lɪn/ n Berlino f

Berliner /bɜ:'lɪnə(r)/ n berlinese mf

Bermuda /bə'mju:də/ n le Bermuda.
Bermuda shorts npl bermuda m inv

Berne /bɜ:n/ n Berna f

berry /'berɪ/ n bacca f

berserk /bə'sɜ:k/ a **go ~** diventare una belva

berth /bɜ:θ/ n (bed) cuccetta f; (anchorage) ormeggio m; **give a wide ~ to** fam stare alla larga da ● vi ormeggiare

beseech /bɪ'si:tʃ/ vt (pt/pp **beseeched** or **besought**) supplicare

beseeching /bɪ'si:tʃɪŋ/ a implorante

beset /bɪ'set/ a **a country ~ by strikes** un paese vessato dagli scioperi

beside /bɪ'saɪd/ prep accanto a; **~ oneself** fuori di sé

besides /bɪ'saɪdz/ prep oltre a ● adv inoltre

besiege /bɪ'si:dʒ/ vt assediare

besotted /bɪ'sɒtɪd/ a infatuato (**with** di)

besought /bɪ'sɔ:t/ see beseech

bespatter /bɪ'spætə(r)/ vt schizzare

bespectacled /bɪ'spektək(ə)ld/ a con gli occhiali

bespoke /bɪ'spəʊk/ a ⟨suit⟩ su misura; ⟨tailor⟩ che lavora su ordinazione

best /best/ a migliore; **the ~ part of a year** la maggior parte dell'anno; **~ before** Comm preferibilmente prima di; **~ wishes** migliori auguri ● n **the ~** il meglio; (person) il/la migliore; **at ~** tutt'al più; **all the ~!** tanti auguri!; **do one's ~** fare del proprio meglio; **to the ~ of my knowledge** per quel che ne so; **make the ~ of it** cogliere il lato buono della cosa ● adv meglio, nel modo migliore; **as ~ I could** meglio che potevo; **like ~** preferire

best before date n data f di scadenza

best friend n migliore amico, -a mf
bestial /'bestɪəl/ a also fig bestiale
bestiality /bestɪ'ælətɪ/ n bestialità f
best man n testimone m
bestow /bɪ'stəʊ/ vt conferire (on a)
best-seller /-'selə(r)/ n bestseller m inv
best-selling /-'selɪŋ/ a ‹novelist› più venduto
bet /bet/ n scommessa f ● vt/i (pt/pp **bet** or **betted**) scommettere
beta blocker /'bi:təblɒkə(r)/ n betabloccante m
Bethlehem /'beθlɪhem/ n Betlemme f
betray /bɪ'treɪ/ vt tradire
betrayal /bɪ'treɪəl/ n tradimento m
betrothal /bɪ'trəʊðəl/ n fidanzamento m
betrothed /bɪ'trəʊðd/ n liter, hum promesso sposo m; promessa sposa f; **be ~** essere fidanzato
better /'betə(r)/ a migliore, meglio; **get ~** migliorare; (after illness) rimettersi; **I waited the ~ part of a week** ho aspettato buona parte della settimana ● adv meglio; **~ off** meglio; (wealthier) più ricco; **all the ~** tanto meglio; **the sooner the ~** prima è, meglio è; **I've thought ~ of it** ci ho ripensato; **you'd ~ stay** faresti meglio a restare; **I'd ~ not** è meglio che non lo faccia ● vt migliorare; **~ oneself** migliorare le proprie condizioni
betting /'betɪŋ/ n (activity) scommesse fpl; **what's the ~ that...?** quanto scommettiamo che...?
betting shop n ricevitoria f (dell'allibratore)
between /bɪ'twi:n/ prep fra, tra; **~ you and me** detto fra di noi; **~ us** (together) tra me e te ● adv [**in**] **~** in mezzo; (time) frattempo
betwixt /bɪ'twɪkst/ adv **be ~ and between** essere una via di mezzo
bevel /'bevl/ n (edge) spigolo m smussato; (tool) squadra f falsa ● vt smussare ‹mirror, edge›
beverage /'bevərɪdʒ/ n bevanda f
bevy /'bevɪ/ n frotta f
beware /bɪ'weə(r)/ vi guardarsi (of da); **~ of the dog!** attenti al cane!
bewilder /bɪ'wɪldə(r)/ vt disorientare
bewildered /bɪ'wɪldəd/ a ‹look, person› perplesso, sconcertato
bewildering /bɪ'wɪldərɪŋ/ a sconcertante
bewilderment /bɪ'wɪldəmənt/ n perplessità f
bewitch /bɪ'wɪtʃ/ vt stregare; fig affascinare completamente
beyond /bɪ'jɒnd/ prep oltre; **~ reach** irraggiungibile; **~ doubt** senza alcun dubbio; **~ belief** da non credere; **it's ~ me** fam non riesco proprio a capire ● adv più in là
B film n film m inv di serie B
bias /'baɪəs/ n (preference) preferenza f; pej pregiudizio m ● vt (pt/pp **biased**) (influence) influenzare
bias binding, bias tape /'baɪndɪŋ/ n (in sewing) fettuccia f in sbieco

biased /'baɪəst/ a parziale
bib /bɪb/ n bavaglino m
Bible /'baɪbl/ n Bibbia f
Bible Belt n zona f del sud degli USA, dove predomina il fondamentalismo protestante
biblical /'bɪblɪkl/ a biblico
bibliographic[al] /bɪblɪə'græfɪk[l]/ a bibliografico
bibliography /bɪblɪ'ɒgrəfɪ/ n bibliografia f
bicarbonate /baɪ'kɑ:bəneɪt/ n **~ of soda** bicarbonato m di sodio
bicentenary /baɪsen'ti:nərɪ/ n bicentenario m ● attrib ‹celebration, year› bicentenario
biceps /'baɪseps/ n bicipite m
bicker /'bɪkə(r)/ vi litigare
bickering /'bɪkərɪŋ/ n bisticci mpl
bicycle /'baɪsɪkl/ n bicicletta f ● vi andare in bicicletta
bicycle: bicycle clip n molletta f (per pantaloni). **bicycle lane** n pista f ciclabile. **bicycle rack** n (in yard) rastrelliera f per biciclette; (on car) portabiciclette m inv
bid[1] /bɪd/ n offerta f; (attempt) tentativo m ● vt/i (pt/pp **bid**, pres p **bidding**) offrire; (in cards) dichiarare
bid[2] vt (pt **bade** or **bid**, pp **bidden** or **bid**, pres p **bidding**) liter (command) comandare; **~ sb welcome** dare il benvenuto a qcno
bidder /'bɪdə(r)/ n offerente mf
bide /baɪd/ vt **~ one's time** aspettare il momento buono
bidet /'bi:deɪ/ n bidè m inv
biennial /baɪ'enɪəl/ a biennale
bier /bɪə(r)/ n catafalco m
bifocals /baɪ'fəʊklz/ npl occhiali mpl bifocali
big /bɪg/ a (**bigger, biggest**) grande; ‹brother, sister› più grande; (fam: generous) generoso; **make ~ money** fare i soldi ● adv **talk ~** fam sparerle grosse
bigamist /'bɪgəmɪst/ n bigamo, -a mf
bigamous /'bɪgəməs/ a bigamo
bigamy /'bɪgəmɪ/ n bigamia f
big: big bang n (in astronomy) big bang m. **big business** n le grandi imprese; **be ~** essere un grosso affare. **big cat** n grosso felino m. **big deal** n fam **~ ~!** bella forza!. **big dipper** n (Br: at fair) montagne fpl russe. **big game hunting** n caccia f grossa. **bighead** n fam montato, -a mf, gasato, -a mf. **big-headed** a fam montato, gasato. **big-hearted** a generoso. **bigmouth** n fam pej chiacchierone, -a mf; **he's such a ~!** (indiscreet) ha una lingua lunga!. **big name** n (in film, art) grosso nome m. **big noise** n fam pezzo m grosso
bigot /'bɪgət/ n fanatico, -a mf
bigoted /'bɪgətɪd/ a di mentalità ristretta
big: big screen n grande schermo m. **big shot** n fam pezzo m grosso. **Big Smoke** n Br hum Londra f. **big time** n **make** or **hit the ~ ~** n fam raggiungere il successo ● attrib
big-time ‹crook› di alto livello. **big toe** n alluce m. **big top** n (tent) tendone m del circo; (fig: circus) circo m. **bigwig** n fam pezzo m grosso

bike /baɪk/ *n fam* bici *f inv*
biker['s] jacket /ˈbaɪkə(z)dʒækɪt/ *n fam* giubbotto *m* di pelle
bikini /bɪˈkiːnɪ/ *n* bikini *m inv*
bilateral /baɪˈlætrəl/ *a* bilaterale
bilberry /ˈbɪlbərɪ/ *n* mirtillo *m*
bile /baɪl/ *n* bile *f*
bilge /bɪldʒ/ *n Naut* (*place*) carena *f*; (*substance*) sentina *f*; (*fam: nonsense*) idiozie *fpl*
bilingual /baɪˈlɪŋgwəl/ *a* bilingue
bilingual secretary *n* segretario, -a *mf* bilingue
bilious /ˈbɪljəs/ *a Med* ~ **attack** attacco *m* di bile
bill¹ /bɪl/ *n* fattura *f*; (*in restaurant etc*) conto *m*; (*poster*) manifesto *m*; *Pol* progetto *m* di legge; (*Am: note*) biglietto *m* di banca; *Theat* **be top of the** ~ essere in testa al cartellone ● *vt* fatturare
bill² *n* (*beak*) becco *m*
billboard /ˈbɪlbɔːd/ *n* cartellone *m* pubblicitario
billet /ˈbɪlɪt/ *n Mil* alloggio *m* ● *vt* (*pt/pp* **billeted**) alloggiare (**on** presso)
bill: bill of exchange *n* cambiale *f*. **bill of fare** *n* menù *m inv*. **billfold** *n Am* portafoglio *m*. **bill of rights** *n* dichiarazione *f* dei diritti. **bill of sale** *n* atto *m* di vendita
billiard ball *n* palla *f* da biliardo
billiards /ˈbɪljədz/ *n* biliardo *m*
billiard table /ˈbɪljəd/ *n* tavolo *m* da biliardo
billing /ˈbɪlɪŋ/ *n Comm* fatturazione *f*; **get top** ~ *Theat* comparire in testa al cartellone
billion /ˈbɪljən/ *n* (*thousand million*) miliardo *m*; (*old-fashioned Br: million million*) mille miliardi *mpl*
billionaire /bɪljəˈneə(r)/ *n* miliardario, -a *mf*
billow /ˈbɪləʊ/ *n* (*of smoke*) nube *f* ● *vi* alzarsi in volute
billposter /ˈbɪlpəʊstə(r)/ *n* attacchino *m*
billy /ˈbɪlɪ/ *n* (*Am: truncheon*) sfollagente *m inv*
billycan /ˈbɪlɪkæn/ *n* gamella *f*
billy goat *n* caprone *m*
bimbo /ˈbɪmbəʊ/ *n pej fam* bambolona *f*; **his latest** ~ la sua ultima amichetta
bin /bɪn/ *n* bidone *m*
binary /ˈbaɪnərɪ/ *a* binario
bind /baɪnd/ *vt* (*pt/pp* **bound**) legare (**to** a); (*bandage*) fasciare; *Jur* obbligare
binder /ˈbaɪndə(r)/ *n* (*for papers*) raccoglitore *m*; (*for cement, paint*) agglomerante *m*
binding /ˈbaɪndɪŋ/ *a* (*promise, contract*) vincolante ● *n* (*of book*) rilegatura *f*; (*on ski*) attacco *m*
binge /bɪndʒ/ *n fam* **have a** ~ fare baldoria; (*eat a lot*) abbuffarsi ● *vi* abbuffarsi (**on** di)
bingo /ˈbɪŋgəʊ/ *n* ≈ tombola *f*
bin liner *n Br* sacchetto *m* per la spazzatura
binoculars /bɪˈnɒkjʊləz/ *npl* [**pair of**] ~ binocolo *msg*
biochemist /baɪəʊˈkemɪst/ *n* biochimico, -a *mf*

biochemistry /baɪəʊˈkemɪstrɪ/ *n* biochimica *f*
biodegradable /baɪəʊdɪˈgreɪdəbl/ *a* biodegradabile
biodiversity /baɪəʊdaɪˈvɜːsətɪ/ *n* biodiversità *f*
bioengineering /baɪəʊendʒɪˈnɪərɪŋ/ *n* bioingegneria *f*
biographer /baɪˈɒgrəfə(r)/ *n* biografo, -a *mf*
biographical /baɪəˈgræfɪkl/ *a* biografico
biography /baɪˈɒgrəfɪ/ *n* biografia *f*
biological /baɪəˈlɒdʒɪkl/ *a* biologico
biological clock *n* orologio *m* biologico
biologically /baɪəˈlɒdʒɪklɪ/ *adv* biologicamente
biological powder *n* detersivo *m* biologico
biological warfare *n* guerra *f* biologica
biologist /baɪˈɒlədʒɪst/ *n* biologo, -a *mf*
biology /baɪˈɒlədʒɪ/ *n* biologia *f*
bionic /baɪˈɒnɪk/ *a* bionico
biopic /ˈbaɪəʊpɪk/ *n Cin film m* basato *su una biografia*
biopsy /ˈbaɪɒpsɪ/ *n* biopsia *f*
biorhythm /ˈbaɪəʊrɪðəm/ *n* bioritmo *m*
biotechnology /baɪəʊtekˈnɒlədʒɪ/ *n* biotecnologia *f*
bipartisan /baɪpɑːtɪˈzæn/ *a Pol* bipartitico
bipartite /baɪˈpɑːtaɪt/ *a* bipartito
birch /bɜːtʃ/ *n* (*tree*) betulla *f*
bird /bɜːd/ *n* uccello *m*; (*fam: girl*) ragazza *f*; **kill two** ~**s with one stone** prendere due piccioni con una fava
birdbrain /ˈbɜːdbreɪn/ *n fam* **he's such a** ~ ha un cervello da gallina
bird call *n* cinguettio *m*
birdie /ˈbɜːdɪ/ *n* (*in golf*) birdie *m*
birdlike /ˈbɜːdlaɪk/ *a* come un uccello
bird: bird of paradise *n* uccello *m* del paradiso. **bird of prey** *n* [uccello *m*] rapace *m*. **bird sanctuary** *n* riserva *f* per uccelli. **birdseed** *n* becchime *m*. **bird's eye view** *n* veduta *f* panoramica dall'alto. **bird's nest** *n* nido *m* di uccello. **bird's nest soup** *n* zuppa *f* di nidi di rondine. **birdsong** *n* canto *m* degli uccelli. **birdwatcher** *n* persona *f* che pratica il bird-watching. **bird-watching** *n* **go** ~ fare del bird-watching
Biro® /ˈbaɪrəʊ/ *n* biro® *f inv*
birth /bɜːθ/ *n* nascita *f*; **give** ~ partorire; **give** ~ **to** partorire
birth: birth certificate *n* certificato *m* di nascita. **birth-control** *n* controllo *m* delle nascite. **birthday** *n* compleanno *m*. **birthday party** *n* festa *f* di compleanno. **birthmark** *n* voglia *f*. **birthplace** *n* luogo *m* di nascita. **birth-rate** *n* natalità *f*. **birthright** *n* diritto *m* di nascita. **births column** *n* annunci *mpl* delle nascite (*nel giornale*). **birth sign** *n* segno *m* zodiacale. **births, marriages, and deaths** *npl* annunci *mpl* di nascite, di matrimonio, mortuari (*nel giornale*)
biscuit /ˈbɪskɪt/ *n* biscotto *m*
biscuit barrel, biscuit tin *n* biscottiera *f*

bisect /bar'sekt/ *vt* dividere in due [parti]
bisexual /bar'seksjʊəl/ *a & n* bisessuale *mf*
bishop /'bɪʃəp/ *n* vescovo *m*; *Chess* alfiere *m*
bistro /'bi:strəʊ/ *n* bistrò *m inv*
bit[1] /bɪt/ *n* pezzo *m*; (*smaller*) pezzetto *m*; (*for horse*) morso *m*; *Comput* bit *m inv*; **a ∼ of** un pezzo di (*cheese, paper*); un po' di (*time, rain, silence*); **∼ by ∼** poco a poco; **do one's ∼** fare la propria parte
bit[2] *see* **bite**
bitch /bɪtʃ/ *n* cagna *f*; *sl* arpia *f*
bitchy /'bɪtʃɪ/ *a* velenoso
bite /baɪt/ *n* morso *m*; (*insect* ∼) puntura *f*; (*mouthful*) boccone *m* ● *vt* (*pt* **bit**, *pp* **bitten**) mordere; (*insect:*) pungere; **∼ one's nails** mangiarsi le unghie ● *vi* mordere; (*insect:*) pungere
■ **bite off** *vt* staccare (*con un morso*)
biting /'baɪtɪŋ/ *a* (*wind, criticism*) pungente; (*remark*) mordace
bit part *n Theat* particina *f*
bitter /'bɪtə(r)/ *a* amaro ● *n Br* birra *f* amara
bitter almond *n* mandorla *f* amara
bitter lemon *n* limonata *f* amara
bitterly /'bɪtəlɪ/ *adv* amaramente; **it's ∼ cold** c'è un freddo pungente
bitterness /'bɪtənɪs/ *n* amarezza *f*
bittersweet /'bɪtə'swi:t/ *a liter* agrodolce
bitty /'bɪtɪ/ *a Br fam* frammentario
bitumen /'bɪtjʊmɪn/ *n* bitume *m*
bivouac /'bɪvʊæk/ *n* bivacco *m* ● *vi* bivaccare
bizarre /bɪ'zɑ:(r)/ *a* bizzarro
blab /blæb/ *vi* (*pt/pp* **blabbed**) cianciare
black /blæk/ *a* nero; **be ∼ and blue** essere coperto di lividi ● *n* nero *m* ● *vt* boicottare (*goods*)
■ **black out** *vt* cancellare ● *vi* (*lose consciousness*) perdere coscienza
black: Black Africa *n* Africa *f* nera. **Black American** *n* negro, -a americano, -a *mf*. **black and white** *n* bianco e nero. **blackball** *vt* dare voto contrario a. **black belt** *n* cintura *f* nera. **blackberry** *n* mora *f*. **blackberry bush** *n* rovo *m*. **blackbird** *n* merlo *m*. **blackboard** *n Sch* lavagna *f*. **black box** *n Aeron* scatola *f* nera. **black bread** *n* pane *m* nero. **blackcurrant** *n* ribes *m inv* nero
blacken /'blækən/ *vt* annerire
black: black eye *n* occhio *m* nero. **Black Forest gateau** *n* dolce *m* a base di cioccolato, panna e ciliegie. **black gold** *n fam* oro *m* nero
blackguard /'blægəd/ *n hum* brigante *m*
black: blackhead *n Med* punto *m* nero. **black-headed gull** *n* gabbiano *m* comune. **black humour** umorismo *m* nero. **black ice** *n* ghiaccio *m* (*sulla strada*)
blacking /'blækɪŋ/ *n* (*Br: boycotting*) boicottaggio *m*; (*polish*) lucido *m* nero (*per scarpe*)
blackish /'blækɪʃ/ *a* nerastro
black: blackjack *n* blackjack *m*. **blackleg** *n Br* crumiro *m*. **blacklist** *vt* mettere sulla lista nera. **blackmail** *n* ricatto *m* ● *vt* ricattare. **blackmailer** *n* ricattatore, -trice *mf*. **black mark** *n fig* neo *m*. **black market** *n* borsa *f*

nera. **black marketeer** *n* borsanerista *mf*. **black mass** *n* messa *f* nera
blackness /'blæknɪs/ *n* nero *m*; (*evilness*) cattiveria *f*; (*of moods*) scontrosità *f*
black: black-out *n* blackout *m inv*; **have a ∼** *Med* perdere coscienza. **black pepper** *n* pepe *m* nero. **black pudding** *n* ≈ sanguinaccio *m*. **Black Sea** *n* Mar *m* Nero. **Blackshirt** *n* camicia *f* nera. **blacksmith** *n* fabbro *m*. **black sheep** *n fig* pecora *f* nera. **black spot** *n fig luogo m* conosciuto per gli *incidenti stradali*. **black swan** *n* cigno *m* nero. **black tie** (*on invitation*) abito scuro. **black widow [spider]** *n* vedova *f* nera
bladder /'blædə(r)/ *n Anat* vescica *f*
blade /bleɪd/ *n* lama *f*; (*of grass*) filo *m*
blame /bleɪm/ *n* colpa *f* ● *vt* dare la colpa a; **∼ sb for doing sth** dare la colpa a qcno per aver fatto qcsa; **no one is to ∼** non è colpa di nessuno
blameless /'bleɪmlɪs/ *a* innocente
blameworthy /'bleɪmwɜ:ðɪ/ *a* biasimevole
blanch /blɑːntʃ/ *vi* sbiancare ● *vt Culin* sbollentare
blancmange /blə'mɒnʒ/ *n* biancomangiare *m*
bland /blænd/ *a* (*food*) insipido; (*person*) insulso
blandly /'blændlɪ/ *adv* (*say*) in modo piatto
blank /blæŋk/ *a* bianco; (*look*) vuoto ● *n* spazio *m* vuoto; (*cartridge*) cartuccia *f* a salve
blank cheque *n* assegno *m* in bianco
blanket /'blæŋkɪt/ *n* coperta *f*; **wet ∼** *fam* guastafeste *mf inv*
blanket: blanket box, blanket chest *n Br* cassapanca *f*. **blanket cover** *n* (*in insurance*) assicurazione *f* che copre tutti i rischi. **blanket stitch** *n* punto *m* di rinforzo
blankly /'blæŋklɪ/ *adv* (*uncomprehendingly*) con espressione attonita; (*without expression*) senza espressione
blank verse *n* versi *mpl* sciolti
blare /bleə(r)/ *vi* suonare a tutto volume
■ **blare out** *vt* strombazzare rumorosamente
blarney /'blɑːnɪ/ *n fam* lusinga *f*
blasé /'blɑːzeɪ/ *a* blasé *inv*
blaspheme /blæs'fi:m/ *vi* bestemmiare
blasphemous /'blæsfəməs/ *a* blasfemo
blasphemy /'blæsfəmɪ/ *n* bestemmia *f*
blast /blɑːst/ *n* (*gust*) raffica *f*; (*sound*) scoppio *m* ● *vt* (*with explosive*) far saltare ● *int sl* maledizione!
blasted /'blɑːstɪd/ *a sl* maledetto
blast furnace *n* altoforno *m*
blasting /'blɑːstɪŋ/ *n* brillamento *m*
blast-off *n* (*of missile*) lancio *m*
blatant /'bleɪtənt/ *a* sfacciato
blatantly /'bleɪtəntlɪ/ *adv* (*copy, disregard*) sfacciatamente; **it's ∼ obvious** è lampante
blather /'blæðə(r)/ *vi fam* blaterare
blaze /bleɪz/ *n* incendio *m*; **a ∼ of colour** un'esplosione *f* di colori ● *vi* ardere
■ **blaze down** *vi* (*sun:*) essere cocente
blazer /'bleɪzə(r)/ *n* blazer *m inv*

bleach /bli:tʃ/ n decolorante m; (for cleaning) candeggina f, varechina f ● vt sbiancare; ossigenare ⟨hair⟩

bleak /bli:k/ a desolato; ⟨fig: prospects, future⟩ tetro

bleakly /'bli:klɪ/ adv ⟨stare, say⟩ in modo tetro

bleakness /'bli:knɪs/ n (of weather) tetraggine f; (of surroundings, future) desolazione f

bleary-eyed /blɪərɪ'aɪd/ a **be ~** avere gli occhi gonfi

bleat /bli:t/ vi belare ● n belato m

bleed /bli:d/ v (pt/pp **bled**) ● vi sanguinare ● vt spurgare ⟨brakes, radiator⟩

bleeding /'bli:dɪŋ/ n perdita di sangue f; (heavy) emorragia f; (deliberate) salasso m ● a ⟨wound, hand⟩ sanguinante; sl = **bloody**

bleeding heart n fig pej cuore m troppo tenero

bleep /bli:p/ n bip m ● vi suonare ● vt chiamare col cercapersone

bleeper /'bli:pə(r)/ n cercapersone m inv

blemish /'blemɪʃ/ n macchia f

blend /blend/ n (of tea, coffee, whisky) miscela f; (of colours) insieme m ● vt mescolare ● vi ⟨colours, sounds:⟩ fondersi (**with** con)

blender /'blendə(r)/ n Culin frullatore m

blending /'blendɪŋ/ n (of coffees, whiskies) miscela f

bless /bles/ vt benedire

blessed /'blesɪd/ a also sl benedetto

blessing /'blesɪŋ/ n benedizione f

blew /blu:/ see **blow²**

blight /blaɪt/ n Bot ruggine f ● vt far avvizzire ⟨plants⟩

blighter /'blaɪtə(r)/ (Br fam: annoying person) idiota mf; **you lucky ~** hai una fortuna sfacciata!; **poor ~** povero diavolo m

blimey /'blaɪmɪ/ int Br fam accidenti!

blind /blaɪnd/ a cieco; **~ man/woman** cieco/cieca ● npl **the ~** i ciechi ● vt accecare ● n [roller] **~** avvolgibile m; [**Venetian**] **~** veneziana f

blind: blind alley n vicolo m cieco. **blind date** n appuntamento m galante con una persona sconosciuta. **blind drunk** a ubriaco fradicio. **blindfold** adv con gli occhi bendati ● a **be ~** avere gli occhi bendati ● n benda f ● vt bendare gli occhi a

blinding /'blaɪndɪŋ/ a ⟨light⟩ accecante; ⟨headache⟩ da impazzire, tremendo

blindingly /'blaɪndɪŋlɪ/ adv ⟨shine⟩ in modo accecante; **be ~ obvious** essere così lampante

blindly /'blaɪndlɪ/ adv ciecamente

blind-man's buff n moscacieca f

blindness /'blaɪndnɪs/ n cecità f

blind spot n (in car, on hill) punto m privo di visibilità; (in eye) punto m cieco; (fig: point of ignorance) punto m debole

blink /blɪŋk/ vi sbattere le palpebre; ⟨light:⟩ tremolare

blinkered /'blɪŋkəd/ a ⟨fig: attitude, approach⟩ ottuso; **be ~** avere i paraocchi

blinkers /'blɪŋkəz/ npl paraocchi mpl

blinking /'blɪŋkɪŋ/ n (of light) intermittenza f; (of eye) battere m

blip /blɪp/ n (on screen) segnale m luminoso a intermittenza; (on graph, line) piccola irregolarità f; (sound) ticchettio m; (hitch) intoppo m

bliss /blɪs/ n Rel beatitudine f; (happiness) felicità f

blissful /'blɪsfʊl/ a beato; (happy) meraviglioso

blissfully /'blɪsfəlɪ/ adv beatamente; **~ ignorant** beatamente ignaro

blister /'blɪstə(r)/ n Med vescica f; (in paint) bolla f ● vi ⟨paint:⟩ formare una bolla/delle bolle

blistering /'blɪst(ə)rɪŋ/ n (of skin) vescica f; (of paint) bolle fpl ● a ⟨sun⟩ scottante; ⟨heat⟩ soffocante; ⟨attack, criticism⟩ feroce

blister pack n blister m inv

blithe /blaɪð/ a (cheerful) gioioso; (nonchalant) spensierato

blithely /'blaɪðlɪ/ adv (nonchalantly) spensieratamente

blitz /blɪts/ n bombardamento m aereo; **have a ~ on sth** fig darci sotto con qcsa

blitzkrieg /'blɪtskri:g/ n guerra f lampo

blizzard /'blɪzəd/ n tormenta f

bloated /'bləʊtɪd/ a gonfio

blob /blɒb/ n goccia f

bloc /blɒk/ n Pol blocco m

block /blɒk/ n blocco m; (building) isolato m; (building ~) cubo m (per giochi di costruzione); **~ of flats** palazzo m ● vt bloccare

■ **block up** vt bloccare

blockade /blɒ'keɪd/ n blocco m ● vt bloccare

blockage /'blɒkɪdʒ/ n ostruzione f

block: block and tackle n paranco m. **block book** vt prenotare in blocco. **block booking** n prenotazione f in blocco. **blockbuster** n (fam: book, film) successone m; Mil bomba f potente. **block capital** n **in ~ ~s** in stampatello. **blockhead** n fam testone, -a mf. **blockhouse** n Mil fortino m. **block letters** npl stampatello m. **block vote** n voto m per delega. **block voting** n votazione f per delega

bloke /bləʊk/ n fam tizio m

blonde /blɒnd/ a biondo ● n bionda f

blood /blʌd/ n sangue m

blood: blood-and-thunder a ⟨novel, film⟩ pieno di sangue. **blood bank** n banca f del sangue. **blood bath** n bagno m di sangue. **blood blister** n vescica f di sangue. **blood brother** n fratello m di sangue. **blood cell, blood corpuscle** n globulo m. **blood count** n esame m emocromocitometrico. **blood-curdling** a raccapricciante. **blood donor** n donatore, -trice mf di sangue. **blood group** n gruppo m sanguigno. **bloodhound** n segugio m

bloodless /'blʌdlɪs/ a (pale) esangue; ⟨revolution, coup⟩ senza spargimento di sangue

blood: blood-letting n Med salasso m; (killing) spargimento m di sangue. **blood lust** n sete f di sangue. **blood money** n compenso versato ad un killer o delatore. **blood**

orange *n* arancia *f* sanguigna. **blood poisoning** *n* setticemia *f*. **blood pressure** *n* pressione *f* del sangue. **blood-red** *a* rosso sangue *inv*. **blood relative** *n* parente *mf* consanguineo, -a. **bloodshed** *n* spargimento *m* di sangue. **bloodshot** *a* iniettato di sangue. **blood sports** *npl* sport *mpl* cruenti. **bloodstained** *a* macchiato di sangue. **bloodstream** *n* sangue *m*. **bloodsucker** *n* also fig sanguisuga *f*. **blood test** *n* analisi *f* del sangue. **bloodthirsty** *a* assetato di sangue. **blood transfusion** *n* trasfusione *f* del sangue. **blood type** *n* gruppo *m* sanguigno. **blood vessel** *n* vaso *m* sanguigno

bloody /'blʌdɪ/ *a* (**-ier, -iest**) insanguinato; *sl* maledetto ● *adv sl* ~ **easy/difficult** facile/difficile da matti; ~ **tired/funny** stanco/divertente da morire; **you** ~ **well will!** e, accidenti, lo farai!

bloody-minded /blʌdɪ'maɪndɪd/ *a* scorbutico

bloom /bluːm/ *n* fiore *m*; **in** ~ (*of flower*) sbocciato; (*of tree*) in fiore ● *vi* fiorire; *fig* essere in forma smagliante

bloomer /'bluːmə(r)/ *n fam* papera *f*

bloomers /'bluːməz/ *npl* mutandoni *mpl* da donna

blooming /'bluːmɪŋ/ *a fam* maledetto

blossom /'blɒsəm/ *n* fiori *mpl* (*d'albero*); (*single one*) fiore *m* ● *vi* sbocciare

■ **blossom out** *vi fig* trasformarsi

blot /blɒt/ *n also fig* macchia *f*

■ **blot out** *vt* (*pt/pp* **blotted**) *fig* cancellare

blotch /blɒtʃ/ *n* macchia *f*

blotchy /'blɒtʃɪ/ *a* chiazzato

blotter /'blɒtə(r)/ *n* tampone *m* di carta assorbente; (*Am: police*) registro *m* di polizia

blotting paper /'blɒtɪŋ/ *n* carta *f* assorbente

blotto /'blɒtəʊ/ *a fam* ubriaco fradicio

blouse /blaʊz/ *n* camicetta *f*

blow¹ /bləʊ/ *n* colpo *m*

blow² *v* (*pt* **blew**, *pp* **blown**) ● *vi* (*wind:*) soffiare; (*fuse:*) saltare ● *vt* (*fam: squander*) sperperare; ~ **one's nose** soffiarsi il naso; ~ **one's top** *fam* andare in bestia

■ **blow away** *vt* far volar via (*papers*) ● *vi* (*papers:*) volare via

■ **blow down** *vt* abbattere ● *vi* abbattersi al suolo

■ **blow off** *vt* (*wind:*) portar via ● *vi* (*hat, roof:*) volare via

■ **blow out** *vt* (*extinguish*) soffiare ● *vi* (*candle:*) spegnersi

■ **blow over** *vt* (*wind:*) buttare giù ● *vi* (*storm:*) passare; (*fig: fuss, trouble:*) dissiparsi

■ **blow up** *vt* (*inflate*) gonfiare; (*enlarge*) ingrandire (*photograph*); (*shatter by explosion*) far esplodere ● *vi* esplodere

blow: blow-by-blow *a* (*account*) particolareggiato. **blow-dry** *vt* asciugare con l'asciugacapelli. **blowfly** *n* moscone *m* (*della carne*). **blowhole** *n* (*of whale*) sfiatatoio *m*. **blowlamp** *n* fiamma *f* ossidrica

blown /bləʊn/ *see* **blow²**

blow: blowout *n Elec* corto circuito *m*; (*in oil or gas well*) fuga *f*; (*of tyre*) scoppio *m*; (*fam: meal*) abbuffata *f*. **blowpipe** *n* cerbottana *f*. **blowtorch** *n* cannello *m* ossidrico. **blow-up** *n Phot* ingrandimento *m* ● *a* (*doll, toy, dinghy*) gonfiabile

blowy /'bləʊɪ/ *a* ventoso

blowzy /'blaʊzɪ/ *a pej* (*woman*) volgarmente appariscente

blubber /'blʌbə(r)/ *n* (*of whale*) grasso *m* di balena; (*fam: of person*) ciccia *f* ● *vi fam* piagnucolare

bludgeon /'blʌdʒən/ *vt* manganellare

blue /bluː/ *a* (*pale*) celeste; (*navy*) blu *inv*; (*royal*) azzurro; **feel** ~ essere giù di corda; ~ **with cold** livido per il freddo; **once in a** ~ **moon** una volta ogni morte di papa ● *n* blu *m inv*; **have the** ~**s** essere giù di corda; **out of the** ~ inaspettatamente; **a bolt from the** ~ un fulmine a ciel sereno

blue: bluebell *n* giacinto *m* di bosco. **Blue Berets** *npl Mil* Caschi blu *mpl*. **blueberry** *n* mirtillo *m*. **blue blood** *n* sangue *m* blu. **blue-blooded** *a* di sangue blu. **bluebottle** *n* moscone *m*. **blue chip** *a* (*company*) di altissimo livello; (*investment*) sicuro. **blue-collar job** *n* lavoro *m* manuale. **blue-collar worker** *n* operaio *m*. **blue-eyed** *a* con gli occhi azzurri. **blue-eyed boy** *n Br fig fam* prediletto *m*. **blue film** *n* film *m* a luci rosse. **blue jeans** *npl* bluejeans *mpl inv*. **blue light** *n* (*on emergency vehicles*) luce *f* della sirena della macchina della polizia

blueness /'bluːnɪs/ *n* azzurro *m*

blue: blue pencil *n* **go through sth with the** ~ ~ (*censor*) censurare qcsa; (*edit*) fare una revisione di qcsa. **blueprint** *n fig* progetto *m*. **blue rinse** *n* **she's had a** ~ ~ si è tinta i capelli color grigio argentato. **bluestocking** *n pej* [donna] intellettualoide *f*. **blue tit** *n* cinciarella *f*. **blue whale** *n* balenottera *f* azzurra

bluff /blʌf/ *n* bluff *m inv* ● *vi* bluffare

bluish /'bluːɪʃ/ *a* bluastro, azzurrognolo

blunder /'blʌndə(r)/ *n* gaffe *f inv* ● *vi* fare una/delle gaffe

blundering /'blʌnd(ə)rɪŋ/ *a* ~ **idiot** rimbecillito *m*

blunt /blʌnt/ *a* spuntato; (*person*) reciso

bluntly /'blʌntlɪ/ *adv* schiettamente

bluntness /'blʌntnɪs/ *n* (*of manner*) rudezza *f*; (*of person*) brutale schiettezza *f*

blur /blɜː(r)/ *n* **it's all a** ~ *fig* è tutto confuso ● *vt* (*pt/pp* **blurred**) rendere confuso

blurb /blɜːb/ *n* soffietto *m* editoriale

blurred /blɜːd/ *a* (*vision, photo*) sfocato

■ **blurt out** /blɜːt/ *vt* spifferare

blush /blʌʃ/ *n* rossore *m* ● *vi* arrossire

blusher /'blʌʃə(r)/ *n* fard *m inv*

bluster /'blʌstə(r)/ *n* (*showing off*) sbruffonata *f*

blustering /'blʌst(ə)rɪŋ/ *n* (*rage*) sfuriata *f*; (*boasting*) spacconata *f* ● *a* (*angry*) infuriato; (*boastful*) sbruffone

blustery /'blʌst(ə)rɪ/ a ⟨wind⟩ furioso; ⟨day, weather⟩ molto ventoso

B movie n film m inv di serie B

BO n fam puzza f di sudore

boa /'bəʊə/ n boa m inv

boa constrictor /kən'strɪktə(r)/ boa m inv

boar /bɔ:(r)/ n cinghiale m

board /bɔ:d/ n tavola f; (for notices) tabellone m; (committee) assemblea f; (of directors) consiglio m; ~ **of directors** consiglio m di amministrazione; **full** ~ Br pensione f completa; **half** ~ Br mezza pensione f; ~ **and lodging** vitto e alloggio m; **go by the** ~ fam andare a monte ● vt Naut, Aeron salire a bordo di ● vi ⟨passengers:⟩ salire a bordo; ~ **with** stare a pensione da

■ **board up** vt sbarrare con delle assi

boarder /'bɔ:də(r)/ n pensionante mf; Sch convittore, -trice mf

board game n gioco m da tavolo

boarding /'bɔ:dɪŋ/ n Aeron, Naut imbarco m; (by customs officer) ispezione f; Mil abbordaggio m

boarding: boarding card n carta f di imbarco. **boarding house** n pensione f. **boarding party** n squadra f d'ispezione. **boarding school** n collegio m

board: board meeting n riunione f del consiglio di amministrazione. **boardroom** n sala f consiglio, sala f riunioni del consiglio di amministrazione. **boardwalk** n Am (by sea) lungomare m

boast /bəʊst/ vi vantarsi **(about** di) ● vt vantare

boaster /'bəʊstɪə(r)/ n sbruffone, -a mf

boastful /'bəʊstfʊl/ a vanaglorioso

boat /bəʊt/ n barca f; (ship) nave f

boater /'bəʊtə(r)/ n (hat) paglietta f

boat-hook n gaffa f

boathouse /'bəʊthaʊs/ n rimessa f [per imbarcazioni]

boating /'bəʊtɪŋ/ n canottaggio m ● a ⟨accident⟩ di navigazione

boating trip n traversata f per mare

boat: boatload n carico m; ~**s of tourists** navi fpl cariche di turisti. **boatswain** /'bəʊs(ə)n/ n nostromo m. **boatyard** n cantiere m per imbarcazioni

bob /bɒb/ n (hairstyle) caschetto m ● vi (pt/pp bobbed) (also ~ **up and down**) andare su e giù

bobbin /'bɒbɪn/ n bobina f

bobble hat /'bɒblhæt/ n berretto m a pompon

bobby /'bɒbɪ/ n Br fam poliziotto m

bobcat /'bɒbkæt/ n lince f

bobsleigh /'bɒbsleɪ/ n bob m inv ● vi andare sul bob

bode /bəʊd/ vi ~ **well/ill** essere di buono/cattivo augurio

bodge /bɒdʒ/ Br = **botch**

bodice /'bɒdɪs/ n corpetto m

bodily /'bɒdɪlɪ/ a fisico ● adv (forcibly) fisicamente

body /'bɒdɪ/ n corpo m; (organization) ente m; (amount: of poems etc) quantità f; **over my dead** ~! fam devi passare prima sul mio corpo!

body: body blow n deal a ~ ~ **to** fig assestare un duro colpo a. **bodybuilder** n culturista mf. **body-building** n culturismo m. **bodyguard** n guardia f del corpo. **body heat** n calore m del corpo. **body language** n linguaggio m del corpo. **body odour** n fam puzza f di sudore. **body politic** n corpo m sociale. **body shop** n autocarrozzeria f. **body snatching** n furto m dei cadaveri. **body stocking, body suit** n body m inv. **body warmer** n gilet m inv imbottito. **bodywork** n Auto auto-carrozzeria f

boffin /'bɒfɪn/ n Br fam scienziato m

bog /bɒg/ n palude f

■ **bog down** vt (pt/pp bogged) **get** ~**ged down** impantanarsi

bogey /'bəʊgɪ/ n (evil spirit) spirito m malvagio; (to frighten people) spauracchio m

boggle /'bɒg(ə)l/ vi **the mind** ~**s** non posso neanche immaginarlo

boggy /'bɒgɪ/ a (swampy) paludoso; (muddy) fangoso

bogus /'bəʊgəs/ a falso

bohemian /bəʊ'hi:mɪən/ a ⟨lifestyle, person⟩ bohémien

boil¹ /bɔɪl/ n Med foruncolo m

boil² n **bring/come to the** ~ portare/arrivare ad ebollizione ● vt [far] bollire ● vi bollire; (fig: with anger) ribollire; **the water or kettle's** ~**ing** l'acqua bolle

■ **boil away** vi ⟨water:⟩ evaporare

■ **boil down to** vi fig ridursi a

■ **boil over** vi straboccare (bollendo)

■ **boil up** vt far bollire

boiler /'bɔɪlə(r)/ n caldaia f

boiler: boiler house n caldaia f. **boiler room** n locale m per la caldaia. **boiler suit** n tuta f

boiling /'bɔɪlɪŋ/ a ⟨water⟩ bollente; **it's** ~ **in here!** qui si bolle!

boiling hot a fam ⟨liquid⟩ bollente; ⟨day⟩ torrido

boiling point n punto m di ebollizione

boisterous /'bɔɪstərəs/ a chiassoso

bold /bəʊld/ a audace ● n Typ neretto m

boldly /'bəʊldlɪ/ adv audacemente

boldness /'bəʊldnɪs/ n audacia f

Bolivia /bə'lɪvɪə/ n Bolivia f

bollard /'bɒlɑ:d/ n colonnina m di sbarramento al traffico

Bolognese /bɒlə'neɪz/ n sugo m al ragù

boloney /bə'ləʊnɪ/ n fam idiozie fpl

bolshy /'bɒlʃɪ/ a Br fam (on one occasion) brontolone; **he's/she's** ~ (by temperament) è un/una piantagrane; **get** ~ fare [delle] storie

bolster /'bəʊlstə(r)/ n cuscino m (lungo e rotondo) ● vt ~ **[up]** sostenere

bolt /bəʊlt/ n (for door) catenaccio m; (for fixing) bullone m ● vt fissare [con bulloni] **(to** a); chiudere col chiavistello ⟨door⟩; ingurgitare ⟨food⟩ ● vi svignarsela; ⟨horse:⟩ scappar via ● adv ~ **upright** diritto come un fuso

bolt-hole *n Br* rifugio *m*
bomb /bɒm/ *n* bomba *f* ● *vt* bombardare
■ **bomb along** *vi* (*fam: move quickly*) sfrecciare
bombard /bɒmˈbɑːd/ *vt also fig* bombardare
bombardment /bɒmˈbɑːdmənt/ *n* bombardamento *m*
bombastic /bɒmˈbæstɪk/ *a* ampolloso
bomb: bomb attack *n* bombardamento *m*.
bomb blast *n* esplosione *f*. **bomb disposal** *n* disinnesco *m*. **bomb disposal expert** *n* artificiere *m*. **bomb disposal squad** *n* squadra *f* artificieri
bomber /ˈbɒmə(r)/ *n Aviat* bombardiere *m*; (*person*) dinamitardo *m*
bomber jacket *n* bomber *m inv*
bombing /ˈbɒmɪŋ/ *n Mil* bombardamento *m*; (*by terrorists*) attentato *m* dinamitardo
bomb: bombproof *a* a prova di bomba.
bombscare *n* stato *m* di allarme per la presunta presenza di una bomba. **bombshell** *n* (*fig: news*) bomba *f*; **blonde ~** bionda *f* esplosiva. **bomb shelter** *n* rifugio *m* antiaereo. **bombsite** *n* zona *f* bombardata; (*fig: mess*) campo *f* di battaglia. **Bomb Squad** *n* squadra *f* artificieri
bona fide /bəʊnəˈfaɪd/ *a* (*member, refugee*) autentico; (*attempt*) genuino; (*offer*) serio
bonanza /bəˈnænzə/ *n* (*windfall*) momento *m* di prosperità; (*in mining*) filone *m* d'oro/d'argento
bond /bɒnd/ *n fig* legame *m*; *Comm* obbligazione *f* ● *vt* (*glue:*) attaccare
bondage /ˈbɒndɪdʒ/ *n* schiavitù *f*
bonded warehouse /ˈbɒndɪd/ *n* magazzino *m* doganale
bonding /ˈbɒndɪŋ/ *n* (*between mother and baby*) legame *m* madre-figlio; **male ~** solidarietà *f* maschile
bone /bəʊn/ *n* osso *m*; (*of fish*) spina *f* ● *vt* disossare (*meat*); togliere le spine da (*fish*)
bone china *n* porcellana *f* fine
boned /bəʊnd/ *a* (*joint, leg, chicken*) disossato; (*fish*) senza lische; (*corset, bodice*) con le stecche
bone: bone-dry *a* secco. **bonehead** *n fam* cretino, -a *mf*. **bone idle** *a fam* fannullone
boneless /ˈbəʊnlɪs/ *a* (*chicken*) disossato; (*chicken breast*) senz'osso; (*fish*) senza lische
bone: bone marrow *n* midollo *m* osseo.
bone-marrow transplant *n* trapianto *m* di midollo osseo. **bonemeal** *n* farina *f* d'ossa
bonfire /ˈbɒnfaɪə(r)/ *n* falò *m inv*
Bonfire Night *n Br* sera *f* del 5 novembre *festeggiata con falò e fuochi d'artificio*
bonk /bɒŋk/ *vt sl* zompare
bonkers /ˈbɒŋkəz/ *a fam* suonato
bonnet /ˈbɒnɪt/ *n* cuffia *f*; (*of car*) cofano *m*
bonus /ˈbəʊnəs/ *n* (*individual*) gratifica *f*; (*production ~*) premio *m*; (*life insurance*) dividendo *m*; **a ~** *fig* qualcosa in più
bonus point *n* **five ~ ~s** un bonus di cinque punti
bony /ˈbəʊnɪ/ *a* (**-ier, -iest**) ossuto; (*fish*) pieno di spine

boo /buː/ *interj* (*to surprise or frighten*) bu!
● *vt/i* fischiare
boob /buːb/ *n* (*fam: mistake*) gaffe *f inv*; (*breast*) tetta *f* ● *vi fam* fare una gaffe
booboo /ˈbuːbuː/ *n fam* gaffe *f inv*
booby prize /ˈbuːbɪ/ *n* premio *m* di consolazione per il peggior contendente
booby trap *n Mil* ordigno *m* che esplode al contatto; (*joke*) trabocchetto *m* ● *vt Mil* mettere un ordigno esplosivo in
boogie /ˈbuːgɪ/ *n fam* boogie *m*
booing /ˈbuːɪŋ/ *n* fischi *mpl*
book /bʊk/ *n* libro *m*; (*of tickets*) blocchetto *m*; **keep the ~s** *Comm* tenere la contabilità; **be in sb's bad/good ~s** essere nel libro nero/nelle grazie di qcno; **do sth by the ~** seguire strettamente le regole ● *vt* (*reserve*) prenotare; (*for offence*) multare ● *vi* (*reserve*) prenotare
bookable /ˈbʊkəbl/ *a* (*event, ticket*) che si può prenotare; (*offence*) che può essere multato
book: bookbinder *n* rilegatore, -trice *mf*.
bookbinding *n* rilegatura *f*. **bookcase** *n* libreria *f*. **book club** *n* club *m inv* del libro.
book-ends *npl* reggilibri *mpl*. **book fair** *n* fiera *f* del libro
bookie /ˈbʊkɪ/ *n fam* bookmaker *m inv*, allibratore *m*
booking /ˈbʊkɪŋ/ *n* (*Br: reservation*) prenotazione *f*; **make a ~** fare una prenotazione; **get a ~** (*Br: from referee*) ricevere un'ammonizione
booking: booking clerk *n Br* impiegato, -a *mf* in un ufficio prenotazioni. **booking form** *n Br* modulo *m* di prenotazione. **booking office** *n* biglietteria *f*
bookish /ˈbʊkɪʃ/ *a* (*person*) secchione
book: book jacket *n* sopraccoperta *f*.
bookkeeper *n* contabile *mf*. **bookkeeping** *n* contabilità *f*
booklet /ˈbʊklɪt/ *n* opuscolo *m*
book: book lover *n* amante *mf* della lettura.
bookmaker *n* allibratore *m*. **bookmark** *n* segnalibro *m*. **bookplate** *n* ex libris *m inv*.
bookrest *n* leggio *m*. **bookseller** *n* libraio, -a *mf*. **bookshelf** *n* (*single*) scaffale *f*; (*bookcase*) libreria *f*. **bookshop** *n* libreria *f*.
bookstall *n* edicola *f*. **bookstore** *n Am* libreria *f*. **book token** *n Br* buono *m* acquisto per libri. **bookworm** *n* topo *m* di biblioteca
boom /buːm/ *n Comm* boom *m inv*; (*upturn*) impennata *f*; (*of thunder, gun*) rimbombo *m* ● *vi* (*thunder, gun:*) rimbombare; *fig* prosperare
boomerang /ˈbuːməræŋ/ *n* boomerang *m inv* ● *vi* **~ on sb** (*plan:*) ritorcersi contro qcno
boomerang effect *n* effetto *m* boomerang
booming /ˈbuːmɪŋ/ *a* (*sound*) sonoro; (*voice*) tonante; (*economy*) fiorente; (*demand, exports, sales*) in crescita
boom microphone *n* microfono *m* a stelo
boon /buːn/ *n* benedizione *f*
boor /bʊə(r)/ *n* zoticone *m*

boorish /'buərɪʃ/ a maleducato

boost /bu:st/ n spinta f ● vt stimolare ⟨sales⟩; sollevare ⟨morale⟩; far crescere ⟨hopes⟩

booster /'bu:stə(r)/ n Med dose f supplementare

boot /bu:t/ n stivale m; (up to ankle) stivaletto m; (football) scarpetta f; (climbing) scarpone m; Auto portabagagli m inv ● vt Comput mettere in funzione

■ **boot out** vt fam cacciare

■ **boot up** Comput vi caricarsi ● vt caricare

boot black n lustrascarpe mf inv

boot drive n Comput unità f inv di inizializzazione

bootee /bu:'ti:/ n (knitted) babbuccia f di lana; (leather) stivaletto m

booth /bu:ð/ n (for phoning, voting) cabina f; (at market) bancarella f

boot: bootlace n laccio m, stringa f. **bootlegger** n Am contrabbandiere m di alcolici. **bootlicker** n leccapiedi mf inv. **bootmaker** n calzolaio m. **boot polish** n lucido m da scarpe. **boot scraper** n puliscipiedi m inv. **bootstrap** n (on boot) linguetta f calzastivali; Comput lancio m; **pull oneself up by one's ~s** riuscire con le proprie forze. **boot-up** n Comput boot m inv

booty /'bu:tɪ/ n bottino m

booze /bu:z/ n fam alcolici mpl

boozer /'bu:zə(r)/ n fam (person) beone, -a mf; (Br: pub) bar m inv

booze-up n bella bevuta f

boozy /'bu:zɪ/ a fam ⟨laughter⟩ da ubriaco; ⟨meal⟩ in cui si beve molto

bop /bɒp/ fam n (blow) colpo m ● vt dare un colpo a ● vi Br (dance) ballare

border /'bɔ:də(r)/ n bordo m; (frontier) frontiera f; (in garden) bordura f ● vi ~ **on** confinare con; fig essere ai confini di

border: border dispute n (fight) conflitto m al confine; (disagreement) contesa f sul confine. **border guard** n guardia f di frontiera. **borderline** n linea f di demarcazione; ~ **case** caso m dubbio. **border raid** n incursione f

bore[1] /bɔ:(r)/ see **bear**[2]

bore[2] vt Techn forare

bore[3] n (of gun) calibro m; (person) seccatore, -trice mf; (thing) seccatura f ● vt annoiare

bored /bɔ:d/ a annoiato, stufo; **be ~ (to tears** or **to death)** annoiarsi (da morire)

boredom /'bɔ:dəm/ n noia f

boring /'bɔ:rɪŋ/ a noioso

born /bɔ:n/ pp **be ~** nascere; **I was ~ in 1963** sono nato nel 1963 ● a nato; **a ~ liar/actor** un bugiardo/un attore nato

born-again a convertito alla chiesa evangelica

borne /bɔ:n/ see **bear**[2]

Borneo /'bɔ:nɪəʊ/ n Borneo m

borough /'bʌrə/ n municipalità f inv

borough council n Br ≈ comune m

borrow /'bɒrəʊ/ vt prendere a prestito (**from** da); **can i ~ your pen?** mi presti la tua penna?

borrower /'bɒrəʊə(r)/ n debitore, -trice mf

borrowing /'bɒrəʊɪŋ/ n prestito m; **increase in ~** Fin aumento m dell'indebitamento

borrowing costs n Fin costo m del denaro

borstal /'bɔ:stəl/ n Br riformatorio m

Bosnia /'bɒznɪə/ n Bosnia f

Bosnia-Herzegovina /-hɜ:tsəgəʊ'vi:nə/ n Bosnia-Erzegovina f

Bosnian /'bɒznɪən/ a & n bosniaco, -a mf

bosom /'bʊzm/ n seno m

bosom buddy, bosom friend n fam amico, -a mf del cuore

boss /bɒs/ n direttore, -trice mf ● vt (also ~ **about**) comandare a bacchetta

bossy /'bɒsɪ/ a autoritario

bosun /'bəʊsən/ n nostromo m

botanical /bə'tænɪkl/ a botanico

botanist /'bɒtənɪst/ n botanico, -a mf

botany /'bɒtənɪ/ n botanica f

botch /bɒtʃ/ vt fare un pasticcio con

both /bəʊθ/ a & pron tutti e due, entrambi ● adv ~ **men and women** entrambi uomini e donne; ~ [**of**] **the children** tutti e due i bambini; **they are ~ dead** sono morti entrambi; ~ **of them** tutti e due

bother /'bɒðə(r)/ n preoccupazione f; (minor trouble) fastidio m; **it's no ~** non c'è problema ● int fam che seccatura! ● vt (annoy) dare fastidio a; (disturb) disturbare ● vi preoccuparsi (**about** di); **don't ~** lascia perdere

Botswana /bɒt'swɑ:nə/ n Botswana m

bottle /'bɒt(ə)l/ n bottiglia f; (baby's) biberon m inv ● vt imbottigliare

■ **bottle up** vt fig reprimere

bottle: bottle bank n contenitore m per la raccolta del vetro. **bottle-feed** vt allattare col biberon. **bottle-feeding** n allattamento m col biberon. **bottle green** a & n verde m bottiglia inv. **bottleneck** n fig ingorgo m. **bottle-opener** n apribottiglie m inv. **bottle top** n tappo m di bottiglia. **bottle-washer** n hum **chief cook and ~** tuttofare mf inv

bottom /'bɒtm/ a ultimo; **the ~ shelf** l'ultimo scaffale m basso ● n (of container) fondo m; (of river) fondale m; (of hill) piedi mpl; (buttocks) sedere m; **at the ~** in fondo; **at the ~ of the page** in fondo alla pagina; **get to the ~ of** fig vedere cosa c'è sotto

■ **bottom out** vi ⟨inflation, unemployment etc.⟩ assestarsi

bottom drawer n fig corredo m

bottom gear n Br Auto prima f

bottomless /'bɒtəmlɪs/ a senza fondo

bottom line n Fin utile m; **that's the ~ ~** (decisive factor) la questione è tutta qui

botulism /'bɒtjʊlɪzm/ n botulismo m

bouffant /'bu:fɒ̃/ a ⟨hair, hairstyle⟩ cotonato; ⟨sleeve⟩ a sbuffo

bough /baʊ/ n ramoscello m

bought /bɔ:t/ see **buy**

boulder /'bəʊldə(r)/ n masso m

bounce /baʊns/ vi rimbalzare; ⟨fam: cheque:⟩ essere respinto ● vt far rimbalzare ⟨ball⟩

bounce back *vi fig* riprendersi

bouncer /'baʊnsə(r)/ *n fam* buttafuori *m inv*

bouncy /'baʊnsɪ/ *a* ⟨*ball*⟩ che rimbalza bene; ⟨*mattress, walk*⟩ molleggiato; ⟨*fig: person*⟩ esuberante

bound¹ /baʊnd/ *n* balzo *m* ● *vi* balzare

bound² *see* **bind** ● *a* ~ **for** ⟨*ship*⟩ diretto a; **be** ~ **to do** ⟨*likely*⟩ dovere fare per forza; ⟨*obliged*⟩ essere costretto a fare

boundary /'baʊndrɪ/ *n* limite *m*

boundless /'baʊndlɪs/ *a* illimitato

bounds /baʊndz/ *npl fig* limiti *mpl*; **out of** ~ fuori dai limiti

bounty /'baʊntɪ/ *n* ⟨*gift*⟩ dono *m*; ⟨*generosity*⟩ munificenza *f*

bounty hunter *n* cacciatore *m* di taglie

bouquet /bʊ'keɪ/ *n* mazzo *m* di fiori; ⟨*of wine*⟩ bouquet *m*

bourbon /'bʊəbən/ *n* bourbon *m inv*

bourgeois /'bʊəʒwɑ:/ *a pej* borghese

bourgeoisie /bʊəʒwɑ:'zi:/ *n* borghesia *f*

bout /baʊt/ *n Med* attacco *m*; *Sport* incontro *m*

boutique /bu:'ti:k/ *n* negozio *m*; **fashion** ~ negozio *m* di abbigliamento

bovine /'bəʊvaɪn/ *a* bovino

bow¹ /bəʊ/ *n* ⟨*weapon*⟩ arco *m*; *Mus* archetto *m*; ⟨*knot*⟩ nodo *m*

bow² /baʊ/ *n* inchino *m* ● *vi* inchinarsi ● *vt* piegare ⟨*head*⟩

bow³ /baʊ/ *n Naut* prua *f*

■ **bow out** *vi* ⟨*withdraw*⟩ ritirarsi ⟨*of* da⟩

bowel /'baʊəl/ *n* intestino *m*; **have a** ~ **movement** andare di corpo; ~**s** *pl* intestini *mpl*

bower /'baʊə(r)/ *n* ⟨*in garden*⟩ pergolato *m*; ⟨*liter: chamber*⟩ salottino *m*

bowl¹ /bəʊl/ *n* ⟨*for soup, cereal*⟩ scodella *f*; ⟨*of pipe*⟩ fornello *m*

bowl² *n* ⟨*ball*⟩ boccia *f* ● *vt* lanciare ● *vi* *Cricket* servire; ⟨*in bowls*⟩ lanciare

■ **bowl along** *vi* ⟨*in car etc*⟩ andare spedito

■ **bowl over** *vt* buttar giù; ⟨*fig: leave speechless*⟩ lasciar senza parole

bow-legged /bəʊ'legd/ *a* dalle gambe storte

bowler¹ /'bəʊlə(r)/ *n Cricket* lanciatore *m*; *Bowls* giocatore *m* di bocce

bowler² *n* ~ [**hat**] bombetta *f*

bowling /'bəʊlɪŋ/ *n* gioco *m* delle bocce

bowling alley /'bəʊlɪŋælɪ/ *n* pista *f* da bowling

bowling green *n* prato *m* da bocce

bowls /bəʊlz/ *n* gioco *m* delle bocce

bow /bəʊ/: **bowstring** *n* corda *f* d'arco. **bow tie** *n* cravatta *f* a farfalla. **bow window** *n* bow window *f inv*

box¹ /bɒks/ *n* scatola *f*; *Theat* palco *m*

box² *vi Sport* fare il pugile ● *vt* ~ **sb's ears** dare uno scapaccione a qcno

boxer /'bɒksə(r)/ *n* pugile *m*

boxer shorts *npl* boxer *mpl*

boxing /'bɒksɪŋ/ *n* pugilato *m*

Boxing Day *n Br* [giorno *m* di] Santo Stefano *m*

box: box number *n* casella *f*. **box office** *n*

Theat botteghino *m*. **boxroom** *n Br* sgabuzzino *m*. **boxwood** *n* bosso *m*

boy /bɔɪ/ *n* ragazzo *m*; ⟨*younger*⟩ bambino *m*

boycott /'bɔɪkɒt/ *n* boicottaggio *m* ● *vt* boicottare

boyfriend /'bɔɪfrend/ *n* ragazzo *m*

boyhood /'bɔɪhʊd/ *n* ⟨*childhood*⟩ infanzia *f*; ⟨*adolescence*⟩ adolescenza *f*

boyish /'bɔɪʃ/ *a* da ragazzino

boy scout *n* boy scout *m inv*

BR *abbr* (**British Rail**) ente *m* ferroviario britannico, ≈ FS

bra /brɑ:/ *n* reggiseno *m*

brace /breɪs/ *n* sostegno *m*; ⟨*dental*⟩ apparecchio *m* ● *vt* ~ **oneself** *fig* farsi forza (**for** per affrontare)

bracelet /'breɪslɪt/ *n* braccialetto *m*

braces /'breɪsɪz/ *npl* bretelle *fpl*

bracing /'breɪsɪŋ/ *a* tonificante

bracken /'brækn/ *n* felce *f*

bracket /'brækɪt/ *n* mensola *f*; ⟨*group*⟩ categoria *f*; *Typ* parentesi *f inv* ● *vt* mettere fra parentesi

brackish /'brækɪʃ/ *a* salmastro

bradawl /'brædɔ:l/ *n* punteruolo *m*

brag /bræg/ *vi* (*pt/pp* **bragged**) vantarsi ⟨**about** di⟩

bragging /'brægɪŋ/ *n* vanterie *fpl*

Brahmin /'brɑ:mɪn/ *n Relig* bramino *m*

braid /breɪd/ *n* ⟨*edging*⟩ passamano *m*

braille /breɪl/ *n* braille *m*

brain /breɪn/ *n* cervello *m*; ~**s** *pl fig* testa *fsg*

brain: brainbox *n fam* capoccione *m*. **brainchild** *n* invenzione *f* personale. **brain damage** *n* lesione *f* cerebrale. **brain-dead** *a Med* cerebralmente morto; *fig* senza cervello. **brain death** *n* morte *f* cerebrale. **brain drain** *n* fuga *f* di cervelli

brainless /'breɪnlɪs/ *a* senza cervello

brain: brain scan *n* scan *m inv* del cervello. **brain scanner** *n* scanner *m inv* (*per il cervello*). **brainstorm** *n Med, fig* accesso *m* di pazzia; ⟨*Am: brainwave*⟩ lampo *m* di genio. **brainstorming session** *n* brain-storming *m inv*. **brains trust** *n* brains-trust *m inv*, gruppo *m* di esperti. **brain surgeon** *n* neurochirurgo *m*. **brain surgery** *n* chirurgia *f* cerebrale. **brain teaser** *n fam* rompicapo *m*. **brainwash** *vt* fare il lavaggio del cervello a. **brainwashing** *n* lavaggio *m* del cervello. **brainwave** *n* lampo *m* di genio

brainy /'breɪnɪ/ *a* (**-ier, -iest**) intelligente

braise /breɪz/ *vt* brasare

brake /breɪk/ *n* freno *m* ● *vi* frenare

brake: brake block *n* pastiglia *f*. **brake disc** *n* disco *m* dei freni. **brake drum** *n* tamburo *m* del freno. **brake fluid** *n* liquido *m* dei freni. **brake-light** *n* stop *m inv*. **brake lining** *n* guarnizione *f* del freno. **brake pad** *n* ganascia *f* del freno. **brake pedal** *n* pedale *m* del freno

bramble /'bræmb(ə)l/ *n* rovo *m*; ⟨*fruit*⟩ mora *f*

bran /bræn/ *n* crusca *f*

branch /brɑ:ntʃ/ *n also fig* ramo *m*; *Comm*

succursale *f*, filiale *f*; (*of bank*) agenzia *f*; **our Oxford St ~** (*of store*) il negozio di Oxford St ● *vi* ⟨*road*⟩ biforcarsi

■ **branch off** *vi* biforcarsi

■ **branch out** *vi* **~ out into** allargare le proprie attività nel ramo di

branch: branch line *n* linea *f* secondaria. **branch manager** *n* (*of bank*) direttore, -trice *mf* di agenzia; (*of company*) direttore, -trice *mf* di filiale; (*of shop*) direttore, -trice *mf* di succursale. **branch office** *n* filiale *f*; (*of bank*) agenzia *f*

brand /brænd/ *n* marca *f*; (*on animal*) marchio *m* ● *vt* marcare ⟨*animal*⟩; *fig* tacciare (**as** di)

brand image *n* immagine *f* della marca

brandish /ˈbrændɪʃ/ *vt* brandire

brand: brand leader *n* marca *f* leader *inv*. **brand name** *n* marca *f*. **brand-new** *a* nuovo fiammante

brandy /ˈbrændɪ/ *n* brandy *m inv*

brash /bræʃ/ *a* sfrontato

brass /brɑːs/ *n* ottone *m*; **the ~** *Mus* gli ottoni *mpl*; **top ~** *fam* pezzi *mpl* grossi

brass band *n* banda *f* (*di soli ottoni*)

brassiere /ˈbræzɪə(r)/ *n fml, Am* reggipetto *m*

brass: brass instrument *n Mus* ottone *m*. **brass neck** *n Br fam* faccia *f* tosta. **brass rubbing** *n* ricalco *m* di iscrizione tombale o commemorativa

brassy /ˈbrɑːsɪ/ *a* (**-ier, -iest**) *fam* volgare

brat /bræt/ *n pej* marmocchio, -a *mf*

bravado /brəˈvɑːdəʊ/ *n* bravata *f*

brave /breɪv/ *a* coraggioso ● *vt* affrontare

bravely /ˈbreɪvlɪ/ *adv* con coraggio

bravery /ˈbreɪvərɪ/ *n* coraggio *m*

bravo /ˌbrɑːˈvəʊ/ *int* bravo!

bravura /brəˈvjʊərə/ *n* virtuosismo *m*

brawl /brɔːl/ *n* rissa *f* ● *vi* azzuffarsi

brawn /brɔːn/ *n Culin* ≈ soppressata *f*

brawny /ˈbrɔːnɪ/ *a* muscoloso

brazen /ˈbreɪzn/ *a* sfrontato

brazier /ˈbreɪzɪə(r)/ *n* braciere *m*

Brazil /brəˈzɪl/ *n* Brasile *m*

Brazilian /brəˈzɪlɪən/ *a & n* brasiliano, -a *mf*

Brazil [nut] *n* noce *f* del Brasile

breach /briːtʃ/ *n* (*of law*) violazione *f*; (*gap*) breccia *f*; (*fig: in party*) frattura *f* ● *vt* recedere ⟨*contract*⟩

breach: breach of contract *n Jur* inadempienza *f* contrattuale. **breach of promise** *n Jur* inadempienza *f* a una promessa di matrimonio. **breach of the peace** *n Jur* violazione *f* dell'ordine pubblico. **breach of trust** *n Jur* abuso *m* di fiducia

bread /bred/ *n* pane *m*; **a slice of ~ and butter** una fetta di pane imburrato

bread: breadbasket *n* cestino *m* per il pane; *fig* granaio *m*. **breadbin** *n Br* cassetta *f* portapane *inv*. **breadboard** *n* tagliere *m* per il pane. **breadcrumbs** *npl* briciole *fpl*; *Culin* pangrattato *m*. **breadfruit** *n* frutto *m* dell'albero del pane. **breadknife** *n* coltello *m* per il pane. **breadline** *n* **be on the ~** essere povero

in canna. **bread roll** *n* panino *m*. **breadstick** *n* filoncino *m*

breadth /bredθ/ *n* larghezza *f*

breadwinner /ˈbredwɪnə(r)/ *n* quello, -a *mf* che porta il soldi a casa

break /breɪk/ *n* rottura *f*; (*interval*) intervallo *m*; (*interruption*) interruzione *f*; (*fam: chance*) opportunità *f inv* ● *v* (*pt* **broke**, *pp* **broken**) ● *vt* rompere; (*interrupt*) interrompere; **~ one's arm** rompersi un braccio ● *vi* rompersi; ⟨*day:*⟩ spuntare; ⟨*storm:*⟩ scoppiare; ⟨*news:*⟩ diffondersi; ⟨*boy's voice:*⟩ cambiare

■ **break away** *vi* scappare; *fig* chiudere (**from** con)

■ **break down** *vi* ⟨*machine, car:*⟩ guastarsi; ⟨*negotiations:*⟩ interrompersi; (*in tears*) scoppiare in lacrime ● *vt* sfondare ⟨*door*⟩; ripartire ⟨*figures*⟩

■ **break in** *vi* ⟨*burglar:*⟩ introdursi

■ **break into** *vt* introdursi con la forza in; forzare ⟨*car*⟩

■ **break off** *vt* rompere ⟨*engagement*⟩ ● *vi* ⟨*part of whole:*⟩ rompersi; (*when speaking*) interrompersi

■ **break out** *vi* ⟨*argument, war:*⟩ scoppiare

■ **break through** *vi* ⟨*sun:*⟩ spuntare

■ **break up** *vt* far cessare ⟨*fight*⟩; disperdere ⟨*crowd*⟩ ● *vi* ⟨*crowd:*⟩ disperdersi; ⟨*marriage:*⟩ naufragare; ⟨*couple:*⟩ separarsi; *Sch* iniziare le vacanze

breakable /ˈbreɪkəbl/ *a* fragile

breakage /ˈbreɪkɪdʒ/ *n* rottura *f*

breakaway /ˈbreɪkəweɪ/ *n* (*from person*) separazione *f*, allontanamento *m*; (*from organization*) scissione *f*; *Sport* contropiede *m* ● *attrib* ⟨*faction, group, state*⟩ separatista

breakdown /ˈbreɪkdaʊn/ *n* (*of car, machine*) guasto *m*; *Med* esaurimento *m* nervoso; (*of figures*) analisi *f inv*

breaker /ˈbreɪkə(r)/ *n* (*wave*) frangente *m*

breaker's yard *n Auto* cimitero *m* delle macchine

break-even *n* pareggio *m*

break-even point *n* punto *m* di pareggio, punto *m* di equilibrio

breakfast /ˈbrekfəst/ *n* [prima] colazione *f*

breakfast: breakfast bar *n* tavolo *m* a penisola. **breakfast bowl** *n* scodella *f* per i cereali. **breakfast cereals** *npl* cereali *mpl* per la colazione. **breakfast television** *n* programmi *mpl* televisivi del mattino

break-in *n* irruzione *f*

breaking /ˈbreɪkɪŋ/ *n* (*of glass, seal, contract*) rottura *f*; (*of bone*) frattura *f*; (*of law, treaty*) violazione *f*; (*of voice*) cambiamento *m*; (*of promise*) venuta *f* meno; (*of horse*) domatura *f*; (*of link, sequence, tie*) interruzione *f*

breaking and entering /breɪkɪŋənd ˈentərɪŋ/ *n Jur* effrazione *f* con scasso

breaking point *n Techn* punto *m* di rottura; *fig* limite *m* di sopportazione

break: breakneck *a* ⟨*pace, speed*⟩ a rotta di collo. **break-out** *n* (*from prison*) evasione *f*. **breakpoint** *n Tennis* breakpoint *m inv*.

breakthrough *n* (*discovery*) scoperta *f*; (*in negotiations*) passo *m* avanti. **break-up** *n* (*of family, company*) disgregazione *f*; (*of alliance, relationship*) rottura *f*; (*of marriage*) dissoluzione *f*. **breakwater** *n* frangiflutti *m inv*

breast /brest/ *n* seno *m*

breast: breastbone *n* sterno *m*. **breast-feed** *vt* allattare al seno. **breast pocket** *n* taschino *m*. **breast-stroke** *n* nuoto *m* a rana

breath /breθ/ *n* respiro *m*, fiato *m*; **out of** ~ senza fiato; **under one's** ~ sottovoce; **a** ~ **of air** un filo d'aria

breathalyse /'breθəlaɪz/ *vt* sottoporre alla prova del palloncino

breathalyser® /'breθəlaɪzə(r)/ *n Br* alcoltest *m inv*

breathe /briːð/ *vt/i* respirare; ~ **a sigh of relief** tirare un sospiro di sollievo

■ **breathe in** *vi* inspirare ● *vt* respirare ⟨*scent, air*⟩

■ **breathe out** *vt/i* espirare

breather /'briːðə(r)/ *n* pausa *f*

breathing /'briːðɪŋ/ *n* respirazione *f*

breathing apparatus *n* respiratore *m*

breathing space *n* (*respite*) tregua *f*; **give oneself a** ~ ~ riprendere fiato

breathless /'breθlɪs/ *a* senza fiato

breathlessly /'breθlɪslɪ/ *adv* senza fiato

breathtaking /'breθteɪkɪŋ/ *a* mozzafiato

breathtakingly /'breθteɪkɪŋlɪ/ *adv* ~ **audacious** di un'audacia stupefacente; ~ **beautiful** di una bellezza mozzafiato

breath test *n* prova *f* del palloncino

bred /bred/ *see* **breed**

breech /briːtʃ/ *n Med* natiche *fpl*; (*of gun*) culatta *f*

breed /briːd/ *n* razza *f* ● *v* (*pt/pp* **bred**) ● *vt* allevare; (*give rise to*) generare ● *vi* riprodursi

breeder /'briːdə(r)/ *n* allevatore, -trice *mf*

breeding /'briːdɪŋ/ *n* allevamento *m*; *fig* educazione *f*

breeding ground *n* zona *f* di riproduzione; *fig* terreno *m* fertile

breeding period, breeding season *n* stagione *f* di riproduzione

breeze /briːz/ *n* brezza *f*

breeze block *n Br* mattone *m* fatto con scorie di coke

breezily /'briːzɪlɪ/ *adv* (*confidently*) con sicurezza; (*casually*) con disinvoltura; (*cheerfully*) allegramente

breezy /'briːzɪ/ *a* ventoso

brevity /'brevətɪ/ *n* brevità *f*

brew /bruː/ *n* infuso *m* ● *vt* mettere in infusione ⟨*tea*⟩; produrre ⟨*beer*⟩ ● *vi fig* ⟨*trouble:*⟩ essere nell'aria

brewer /'bruːə(r)/ *n* birraio *m*

brewery /'bruərɪ/ *n* fabbrica *f* di birra

brew-up *n Br fam* tè *m inv*

briar /'braɪə(r)/ *n* rosa *f* selvatica; (*heather*) erica *f*; (*thorns*) rovo *m*; (*pipe*) pipa *f* in radica

bribe /braɪb/ *n* (*money*) bustarella *f*; (*large sum of money*) tangente *f* ● *vt* corrompere

bribery /'braɪbərɪ/ *n* corruzione *f*

brick /brɪk/ *n* mattone *m*

■ **brick up** *vt* murare

brick: brickbat *n fig* critica *f* spietata. **brick-built** *a* di mattoni. **bricklayer** *n* muratore *m*. **bricklaying** *n* muratura *f*. **brick red** *a* rosso mattone *inv*. **brickwork** *n* muratura *f* di mattoni. **brickworks** *n* fabbrica *f* di mattoni

bridal /'braɪdl/ *a* nuziale

bridal: bridal party *n* corteo *m* nuziale. **bridal suite** *n* camera *f* nuziale. **bridal wear** *n* confezioni *fpl* da sposa

bride /braɪd/ *n* sposa *f*

bridegroom /'braɪdgruːm/ *n* sposo *m*

bridesmaid /'braɪdzmeɪd/ *n* damigella *f* d'onore

bridge¹ /brɪdʒ/ *n* ponte *m*; (*of nose*) setto *m* nasale; (*of spectacles*) ponticello *m* ● *vt fig* colmare ⟨*gap*⟩

bridge² *n Cards* bridge *m*

bridge-building *n* costruzione *f* di ponti provvisori; *fig* mediazione *f*

bridging loan /'brɪdʒɪŋ/ *n Br Fin* prefinanziamento *m*, credito *m* provvisorio

bridle /'braɪd(ə)l/ *n* briglia *f*

bridle track, bridleway /'braɪd(ə)lweɪ/ *n* sentiero *m* per cavalli

brief¹ /briːf/ *a* breve; **in** ~ in breve

brief² *n* istruzioni *fpl*; (*Jur: case*) causa *f* ● *vt* dare istruzioni a; *Jur* affidare la causa a

briefcase /'briːfkeɪs/ *n* cartella *f*

briefing /'briːfɪŋ/ *n* briefing *m inv*

briefly /'briːflɪ/ *adv* brevemente; **briefly,...** in breve,...

briefness /'briːfnɪs/ *n* brevità *f*

briefs /briːfs/ *npl* slip *m inv*

brigade /brɪ'geɪd/ *n* brigata *f*

brigadier /brɪgə'dɪə(r)/ *n* generale *m* di brigata

bright /braɪt/ *a* ⟨*metal, idea*⟩ brillante; ⟨*day, room, future*⟩ luminoso; (*clever*) intelligente; ~ **red** rosso *m* acceso

brighten /'braɪt(ə)n/ *v* ~ [**up**] ● *vt* ravvivare; rallegrare ⟨*person*⟩ ● *vi* ⟨*weather:*⟩ schiarirsi; ⟨*face:*⟩ illuminarsi; ⟨*person:*⟩ rallegrarsi

brightly /'braɪtlɪ/ *adv* ⟨*shine*⟩ intensamente; ⟨*smile*⟩ allegramente

brightness /'braɪtnɪs/ *n* luminosità *f*; (*intelligence*) intelligenza *f*

bright spark *n Br fam* genio *m*

bright young things *npl Br* i giovani di belle speranze

brill /brɪl/ *n Zool* rombo *m* liscio ● *a Br fam* fantastico

brilliance /'brɪljəns/ *n* luminosità *f*; (*of person*) genialità *f*

brilliant /'brɪljənt/ *a* (*very good*) eccezionale; (*very intelligent*) brillante; ⟨*sunshine*⟩ splendente

brilliantly /'brɪljəntlɪ/ *adv* ⟨*shine*⟩ intensamente; ⟨*perform*⟩ in modo eccezionale

Brillo pad® /'brɪləʊ/ *n* paglietta *f* d'acciaio

brim /brɪm/ *n* bordo *m*; (*of hat*) tesa *f*

■ **brim over** *vi* (*pt/pp* **brimmed**) traboccare

brine /braɪn/ n salamoia f

bring /brɪŋ/ vt (pt/pp **brought**) portare ⟨person, object⟩

■ **bring about** vt causare

■ **bring along** vt portare [con sé]

■ **bring back** vt restituire ⟨sth borrowed⟩; reintrodurre ⟨hanging⟩; fare ritornare in mente ⟨memories⟩

■ **bring down** vt portare giù; fare cadere ⟨government⟩; fare abbassare ⟨price⟩

■ **bring in** vt introdurre ⟨legislation⟩; **his job ~s in £30,000 a year** guadagna 30 000 sterline all'anno

■ **bring off** vt ~ **sth off** riuscire a fare qcsa

■ **bring on** vt ⟨cause⟩ provocare

■ **bring out** vt ⟨emphasize⟩ mettere in evidenza; pubblicare ⟨book⟩

■ **bring round** vt portare; ⟨persuade⟩ convincere; far rinvenire ⟨unconscious person⟩

■ **bring up** vt ⟨vomit⟩ rimettere; allevare ⟨children⟩; tirare fuori ⟨question, subject⟩

bring and buy sale n Br vendita f di beneficenza

brink /brɪŋk/ n orlo m; **on the ~ of disaster** sull'orlo del disastro

brinkmanship /'brɪŋkmənʃɪp/ n strategia f del rischio calcolato

brisk /brɪsk/ a svelto; ⟨person⟩ sbrigativo; ⟨trade, business⟩ redditizio; ⟨walk⟩ a passo spedito

brisket /'brɪskɪt/ n Culin punta f di petto

briskly /'brɪsklɪ/ adv velocemente; ⟨say⟩ frettolosamente; ⟨walk⟩ di buon passo

bristle /'brɪsl/ n setola f ● vi bristling with pieno di

bristly /'brɪslɪ/ a ⟨chin⟩ ispido

Britain /'brɪtn/ n Gran Bretagna f

British /'brɪtɪʃ/ a britannico; ⟨ambassador⟩ della Gran Bretagna ● npl the ~ il popolo britannico

British: British Airports Authority n ente m che gestisce gli aeroporti britannici. **British Broadcasting Corporation** n ente m radiotelevisivo nazionale britannico. **British Columbia** n Columbia f Britannica

Britisher /'brɪtɪʃə(r)/ n Am britannico, -a mf

British: British Gas n Br società f del gas britannica. **British Isles** npl Isole fpl Britanniche. **British Rail** n ente m ferroviario britannico. **British Telecom** n Br società f britannica di telecomunicazioni

Briton /'brɪtən/ n cittadino, -a britannico, -a mf

Brittany /'brɪtənɪ/ n Bretagna f

brittle /'brɪtl/ a fragile

brittle-bone disease n decalcificazione f ossea, osteoporosi f

broach /brəʊtʃ/ vt toccare ⟨subject⟩

B road n Br ≈ strada f provinciale

broad /brɔːd/ a ampio; ⟨hint⟩ chiaro; ⟨accent⟩ marcato. **two metres ~** largo due metri; **in ~ daylight** in pieno giorno

broad-based /-'beɪst/ a ⟨coalition, education⟩ diversificato; ⟨approach, campaign⟩ su larga scala; ⟨consensus⟩ generale

broad bean n fava f

broadcast /'brɔːdkæst/ n trasmissione f ● vt/i (pt/pp **-cast**) trasmettere

broadcaster /'brɔːdkæstə(r)/ n giornalista mf radiotelevisivo, -a

broadcasting /'brɔːdkæstɪŋ/ n diffusione f radiotelevisiva; **be in ~** lavorare per la televisione/radio

broad-chested a con il torace robusto

broaden /'brɔːdn/ vt allargare; **~ one's horizons** allargare i propri orizzonti ● vi allargarsi

broadly /'brɔːdlɪ/ adv largamente; **~ [speaking]** generalmente

broad-minded /-'maɪndɪd/ a di larghe vedute

broadness /'brɔːdnɪs/ n larghezza f

broad: broadsheet n quotidiano m di grande formato. **broad-shouldered** a con le spalle larghe. **broadside** n (Naut: of ship) fiancata f; (enemy fire) bordata f; n (criticism) attacco m; **deliver a ~** lanciare un attacco ● adv di fianco

brocade /brə'keɪd/ n broccato m

broccoli /'brɒkəlɪ/ n inv broccoli mpl

brochure /'brəʊʃə(r)/ n opuscolo m; (travel ~) dépliant m inv

brogue /brəʊg/ n (shoe) scarpa m da passeggio; (accent) cadenza f dialettale

broil /brɔɪl/ vt Culin cuocere alla griglia ⟨meat⟩ ● vi cuocere alla griglia; fig arrostire

broiler /'brɔɪlə(r)/ n (chicken) pollastro m; (Am: grill) griglia f

broke /brəʊk/ see **break** ● a fam al verde

broken /'brəʊk(ə)n/ see **break** ● a rotto; **~ English** inglese m stentato

broken: broken-down a ⟨machine⟩ guasto; ⟨wall⟩ pericolante. **broken heart** n cuore m infranto; **die of a ~ ~** essere distrutto da una delusione amorosa. **broken-hearted** /-'hɑːtɪd/ a affranto. **broken home n he comes from a ~ ~** i suoi sono divisi. **broken marriage** n matrimonio m fallito

broker /'brəʊkə(r)/ n broker m inv

brokerage /'brəʊkərɪdʒ/ n (fee, business) intermediazione f

broking /'brəʊkɪŋ/ n attività f di intermediazione

brolly /'brɒlɪ/ n fam ombrello m

bromide /'brəʊmaɪd/ n (in pharmacy, printing) bromuro m; (fig: comment) banalità f inv

bronchial /'brɒŋkɪəl/ a ⟨infection⟩ bronchiale; ⟨wheeze, cough⟩ di petto

bronchitis /brɒŋ'kaɪtɪs/ n bronchite f

bronze /brɒnz/ n bronzo m ● attrib di bronzo

Bronze Age n età f del Bronzo

brooch /brəʊtʃ/ n spilla f

brood /bruːd/ n covata f; (hum: children) prole f ● vi covare; fig rimuginare

brooding /'bruːdɪŋ/ a ⟨person, face⟩ pensieroso; ⟨landscape⟩ sinistro

broody /'bruːdɪ/ a ⟨depressed⟩ pensieroso; **feel ~** ⟨Br fam: woman:⟩ desiderare un figlio

broody hen n chioccia f

brook¹ /brʊk/ n ruscello m

brook² vt sopportare

broom /bru:m/ n scopa f; Bot ginestra f

broom: broom cupboard n ripostiglio m. **broom handle** n Br manico m di scopa. **broomstick** n manico m di scopa

Bros. abbr (**brothers**) F.lli

broth /brɒθ/ n brodo m

brothel /ˈbrɒθ(ə)l/ n bordello m

brother /ˈbrʌðə(r)/ n fratello m

brotherhood /ˈbrʌðəhʊd/ n (bond) fratellanza f; (of monks) confraternita f

brother-in-law n (pl **-s-in-law**) cognato m

brotherly /ˈbrʌðəlɪ/ a fraterno

brought /brɔ:t/ see bring

brow /braʊ/ n fronte f; (eye~) sopracciglio m; (of hill) cima f

browbeat /ˈbraʊbi:t/ vt (pt **-beat**, pp **-beaten**) intimidire

brown /braʊn/ a marrone; castano ⟨hair⟩ ● n marrone m ● vt rosolare ⟨meat⟩ ● vi ⟨meat:⟩ rosolarsi

brown: brown ale n Br birra f scura. **brown bear** n orso m bruno. **brown bread** n pane m integrale

browned-off /braʊnd'ɒf/ a Br fam stufo (with di)

brown envelope n busta f di carta da pacchi

Brownie /ˈbraʊnɪ/ n coccinella f (negli scout)

brownie point n fam punto m di merito

brownish /ˈbraʊnɪʃ/ a sul marrone

brown: brownout n Am oscuramento m parziale. **brown owl** n allocco m. **brown paper** n carta f da pacchi. **brown rice** n riso m integrale. **brown-skinned** /-'skɪnd/ a scuro di pelle. **brownstone** n (Am: house) palazzo m in arenaria. **brown sugar** n Culin zucchero m greggio

browse /braʊz/ vi (read) leggicchiare; (in shop) curiosare

bruise /bru:z/ n livido m; (on fruit) ammaccatura f ● vt ammaccare ⟨fruit⟩; ~ one's arm farsi un livido sul braccio

bruised /bru:zd/ a (physically) contuso; ⟨eye⟩ pesto; ⟨fruit⟩ ammaccato; ⟨ego, spirit⟩ ferito

bruiser /ˈbru:zə(r)/ n fam omaccione m

bruising /ˈbru:zɪŋ/ n livido m, contusione f ● a ⟨game⟩ violento; (emotionally) ⟨remark⟩ pesante; ⟨campaign, encounter⟩ traumatizzante; ⟨defeat⟩ cocente

brunch /brʌntʃ/ n brunch m inv

Brunei /bru:'naɪ/ n Brunei m

brunette /bru:'net/ n bruna f

brunt /brʌnt/ n bear the ~ of sth subire maggiormente qcsa

brush /brʌʃ/ n spazzola f; (with long handle) spazzolone m; (for paint) pennello m; (bushes) boscaglia f; (fig: conflict) breve scontro m ● vt spazzolare ⟨hair⟩; lavarsi ⟨teeth⟩; scopare ⟨stairs, floor⟩

■ **brush against** vt sfiorare

■ **brush aside** vt fig ignorare

■ **brush off** vt spazzolare; (with hands) togliere; ignorare ⟨criticism⟩

■ **brush up** vt/i fig ~ up [on] rinfrescare

brush: brush-off n fam give sb the ~ mandare qcno a quel paese. **brushstroke** n pennellata f. **brushup** n Br have a [wash and] brushup darsi una ripulita. **brushwork** n tocco m

brusque /brʊsk/ a brusco

brusquely /ˈbrʊsklɪ/ adv bruscamente

Brussels /ˈbrʌsəlz/ n Bruxelles f

Brussels sprouts npl cavoletti mpl di Bruxelles

brutal /ˈbru:t(ə)l/ a brutale

brutality /bru:'tælətɪ/ n brutalità f inv

brutalize /ˈbru:təlaɪz/ vt brutalizzare

brutally /ˈbru:təlɪ/ adv brutalmente

brute /bru:t/ n bruto m; ~ force n forza f bruta

brutish /ˈbru:tɪʃ/ a da bruto

BSc abbr **Bachelor of Science**

BSE n abbr (**bovine spongiform encephalitis**) encefalite f bovina spongiforme

B side n (of record) lato m B

BST abbr (**British Summer Time**) ora f legale in Gran Bretagna

bubble /ˈbʌbl/ n bolla f; (in drink) bollicina f

bubble: bubble bath n bagnoschiuma m inv. **bubble car** n Br fam auto f monoposto a tre ruote. **bubblegum** n gomma f da masticare. **bubble pack** n Br (for pills) blister m inv; (for small item) involucro m di plastica. **bubble wrap** n plastica f a bolle

bubbling /ˈbʌblɪŋ/ n (sound) gorgoglio m ● a che ribolle

bubbly /ˈbʌblɪ/ n fam champagne m inv, spumante m ● a ⟨liquid⟩ effervescente; ⟨personality⟩ spumeggiante

bubonic plague /bjʊbɒnɪk'pleɪg/ n peste f bubbonica

buccaneer /bʌkə'nɪə(r)/ n bucaniere m

Bucharest /bju:kə'rest/ n Bucarest f

buck¹ /bʌk/ n maschio m del cervo; (rabbit) maschio m del coniglio ● vi ⟨horse:⟩ saltare a quattro zampe

buck² n Am fam dollaro m

buck³ n pass the ~ scaricare la responsabilità

■ **buck up** vi fam tirarsi su; (hurry) sbrigarsi ● vt you'll have to ~ your ideas up fam dovresti darti una regolata

bucket /ˈbʌkɪt/ n secchio m; kick the ~ (fam: die) crepare ● vi it's ~ing down fam piove a catinelle

bucketful /ˈbʌkɪtfʊl/ n secchio m

bucket seat n Auto, Aeron sedile m anatomico

bucket shop n Br fam agenzia f di viaggi che vende biglietti a prezzi scontati

bucking bronco /bʌkɪŋ'brɒŋkəʊ/ n cavallo m da rodeo

buckle /ˈbʌkl/ n fibbia f ● vt allacciare ● vi ⟨shelf:⟩ piegarsi; ⟨wheel:⟩ storcersi

■ **buckle down** vi (to work) mettersi sotto

■ **buckle in** vt legare

buck: buckram *n* tela *f* rigida. **buckshot** *n* pallettoni *mpl*. **buckskin** *n* pelle *f* di daino. **buck teeth** denti *mpl* da coniglio. **buckwheat** *n* grano *m* saraceno

bucolic /bjʊˈkɒlɪk/ *a & n* bucolico *m*

bud /bʌd/ *n* bocciolo *m*

Buddha /ˈbʊdə/ *n* Budda *m inv*

Buddhism /ˈbʊdɪzm/ *n* buddismo *m*

Buddhist /ˈbʊdɪst/ *a & n* buddista *mf*

budding /ˈbʌdɪŋ/ *a Bot (into leaf)* in germoglio; *(into flower)* in boccio; ‹*athlete, champion, artist*› in erba; ‹*talent, romance*› nascente; ‹*career*› promettente

buddy /ˈbʌdɪ/ *n fam* amico, -a *mf*

budge /bʌdʒ/ *vt* spostare ● *vi* spostarsi

budgerigar /ˈbʌdʒərɪɡɑː(r)/ *n* cocorita *f*

budget /ˈbʌdʒɪt/ *n* bilancio *m*; *(allotted to specific activity)* budget *m inv*; **I'm on a ~** cerco di limitare le spese ● *vi (pt/pp* **budgeted)** prevedere le spese; **~ for sth** includere qcsa nelle spese previste

budgetary /ˈbʌdʒɪt(ə)rɪ/ *a* budgetario; **~ year** esercizio *m* finanziario

budget day *n Br Pol* giorno *m* della presentazione del bilancio dello Stato

budgie /ˈbʌdʒɪ/ *n fam* = **budgerigar**

buff /bʌf/ *a (colour)* [color] camoscio ● *n* [color *m*] camoscio *m*; *fam* fanatico, -a *mf* ● *vt* lucidare

buffalo /ˈbʌfələʊ/ *n (inv or pl* **-es)** bufalo *m*

buffer /ˈbʌfə(r)/ *n Rail* respingente *m*; *Comput* buffer *m inv*; **old ~** *fam* vecchio bacucco *m*

buffer state *n* stato *m* cuscinetto *inv*

buffer zone *n* zona *f* cuscinetto *inv*

buffet¹ /ˈbʊfeɪ/ *n (meal, in station)* buffet *m inv*

buffet² /ˈbʌfɪt/ *vt (pt/pp* **buffeted)** sferzare

buffet car *n Br Rail* carrozza *f* ristorante

buffoon /bəˈfuːn/ *n* buffone, -a *mf*

bug /bʌɡ/ *n (insect)* insetto *m*; *Comput* bug *m inv*; *(fam: device)* cimice *f* ● *vt (pt/pp* **bugged)** *fam* installare delle microspie in ‹*room*›; mettere sotto controllo ‹*telephone*›; *(fam: annoy)* scocciare

bugbear /ˈbʌɡbeə(r)/ *n (problem, annoyance)* spauracchio *m*

bugger /ˈbʌɡə(r)/ *fam n* bastardo *m* ● *int* merda!

■ **bugger about, bugger around** *fam vi (behave stupidly)* fare il cretino ● *vt* **~ sb about** creare problemi a qcno

■ **bugger off** *vi (fam: go away)* andarsene; **~ off!** vai a farti friggere!

bugging device *n* microfono *m* spia

buggy /ˈbʌɡɪ/ *n (baby)* **~** passeggino *m*

bugle /ˈbjuːɡ(ə)l/ *n* tromba *f*

bugler /ˈbjuːɡlə(r)/ *n* trombettiere *m*

build /bɪld/ *n (of person)* corporatura *f* ● *vt/i (pt/pp* **built)** costruire

■ **build on** *vt* aggiungere ‹*extra storey*›; sviluppare ‹*previous work*›

■ **build up** *vt* **~ up one's strength** rimettersi in forza ● *vi* ‹*pressure, traffic:*› aumentare; ‹*excitement, tension:*› crescere

builder /ˈbɪldə(r)/ *n (company)* costruttore *m*; *(worker)* muratore *m*

builder's labourer *n* muratore *m*

builder's merchant *n* fornitore *m* di materiale da costruzione

building /ˈbɪldɪŋ/ *n* edificio *m*

building: building block *n (child's toy)* pezzo *m* delle costruzioni; *(basic element)* componente *m*. **building contractor** *n* imprenditore *m* edile. **building land** *n* terreno *m* edificabile. **building materials** *npl* materiali *mpl* da costruzione. **building permit** *n* permesso *m* per edificare. **building plot** *n* terreno *m* edificabile. **building site** *n* cantiere *m* [di costruzione]. **building society** *n* istituto *m* di credito immobiliare. **building trade** *n* edilizia *f*. **building worker** *n Br* muratore *m*

build-up *n (increase)* aumento *m*; *(in tension, of gas, in weapons)* accumulo *m*; *(publicity)* battage *m inv* pubblicitario; **give sth a good ~** *(publicity)* fare buona pubblicità a qcsa

built /bɪlt/ *see* **build**

built-in *a* ‹*unit*› a muro; ‹*fig: feature*› incorporato

built-up area *n Auto* centro *m* abitato

bulb /bʌlb/ *n* bulbo *m*; *Electr* lampadina *f*

bulbous /ˈbʌlbəs/ *a* grassoccio

Bulgaria /bʌlˈɡeərɪə/ *n* Bulgaria *f*

bulge /bʌldʒ/ *n* rigonfiamento *m*; **it shows all my ~s** mette in evidenza tutti i miei cuscinetti [di grasso] ● *vi* esser gonfio **(with** di); ‹*stomach, wall:*› sporgere; ‹*eyes, with surprise:*› uscire dalle orbite

bulging /ˈbʌldʒɪŋ/ *a* gonfio; ‹*eyes*› sporgente

bulimia (nervosa) /bʊˈlɪmɪə(nɜːˈvəʊsə)/ *n* bulimia *f*

bulimic /bʊˈlɪmɪk/ *a & n* bulimico, -a *mf*

bulk /bʌlk/ *n* volume *m*; *(greater part)* grosso *m*; **in ~** in grande quantità; *(loose)* sfuso

bulk: bulk-buy *vt/i* comprare in grandi quantità. **bulk-buying** *n* acquisto *m* in grande quantità. **bulk carrier** *n* mezzo *m* per il trasporto di rinfuse. **bulkhead** *n Naut, Aeron* paratia *f*

bulky /ˈbʌlkɪ/ *a* voluminoso

bull /bʊl/ *n* toro *m*; **take the ~ by the horns** *fig* prendere il toro per le corna

bull: bulldog *n* bulldog *m inv*. **bulldog clip** *n* fermagli *m inv*. **bulldoze** *vt (knock down)* demolire [con bulldozer]; *(clear)* spianare [con bulldozer]; *(fig: force)* costringere. **bulldozer** /ˈbʊldəʊzə(r)/ *n* bulldozer *m inv*

bullet /ˈbʊlɪt/ *n* pallottola *f*

bulletin /ˈbʊlɪtɪn/ *n* bollettino *m*

bulletin board *n Comput* bacheca *f* elettronica

bulletproof /ˈbʊlɪtpruːf/ *a* antiproiettile *inv*; ‹*vehicle*› blindato

bulletproof vest *n* giubbotto *m* antiproiettile

bullfight /ˈbʊlfaɪt/ *n* corrida *f*

bullfighter /ˈbʊlfaɪtə(r)/ *n* torero *m*

bullion /ˈbʊlɪən/ *n* **gold ~** oro *m* in lingotti

bullish /ˈbʊlɪʃ/ *a (optimistic)* ottimistico; ‹*market, shares, stocks*› al rialzo

bull market n Fin mercato m al rialzo

bullock /'bʊlək/ n manzo m

bullring /'bʊlrɪŋ/ n arena f

bull's-eye /'bʊlzaɪ/ n centro m del bersaglio; **score a ~** fare centro

bully /'bʊlɪ/ n prepotente mf ● vt fare il/la prepotente con

bullying /'bʊlɪŋ/ n prepotenze fpl

bulrush /'bʊlrʌʃ/ n giunco m di palude

bulwark /'bʊlwək/ n Mil, fig baluardo m; Naut parapetto m; (breakwater) frangiflutti m inv

bum¹ /bʌm/ n sl sedere m

bum² n Am fam vagabondo, -a mf

■ **bum around** vi fam vagabondare

bumbag /'bʌmbæg/ n Br fam marsupio m

bumble-bee /'bʌmblbi:/ n calabrone m

bumbling /'bʌmblɪŋ/ a (attempt) maldestro; (person) inconcludente

bumf /bʌmf/ n (Br: toilet paper) carta f igienica; (fam: documents) scartoffie f pl

bump /bʌmp/ n botta f; (swelling) bozzo m, gonfiore m; (in road) protuberanza f ● vt sbattere

■ **bump into** vt sbattere contro; (meet) imbattersi in

■ **bump off** vt fam far fuori

■ **bump up** vt fam [far] aumentare (prices, salaries)

bumper /'bʌmpə(r)/ n Auto paraurti m inv ● a abbondante

bumper car n autoscontro m

bumph /bʌmf/ n = bumf

bumpkin /'bʌmpkɪn/ n **country ~** zoticone, -a mf

bumptious /'bʌmpʃəs/ a presuntuoso

bumpy /'bʌmpɪ/ a (road) accidentato; (flight) turbolento

bun /bʌn/ n focaccina f (dolce); (hair) chignon m inv

bunch /bʌntʃ/ n (of flowers, keys) mazzo m; (of bananas) casco m; (of people) gruppo m; **~ of grapes** grappolo m d'uva

bundle /'bʌndl/ n fascio m; (of money) mazzetta f; **a ~ of nerves** fam un fascio di nervi ● vt **~ [up]** affastellare

bung /bʌŋ/ vt fam (throw) buttare

■ **bung up** vt (block) otturare

bungalow /'bʌŋɡələʊ/ n bungalow m inv

bungee jumping /'bʌndʒɪdʒʌmpɪŋ/ n salto m da ponti, grattacieli, ecc. con un cavo elastico attaccato alla caviglia

bungle /'bʌŋɡl/ vt fare un pasticcio di

bunion /'bʌnjən/ n Med callo m all'alluce

bunk /bʌŋk/ n cuccetta f; **do a ~** fam svignarsela ● vi **~ off school** fam marinare la scuola

bunk beds npl letti mpl a castello

bunker /'bʌŋkə(r)/ n (for coal) carbonaia f; (golf) ostacolo m; Mil bunker m inv

bunkum /'bʌŋkəm/ n fandonie fpl

bunny /'bʌnɪ/ n fam coniglietto m

Bunsen [**burner**] /'bʌnsən[bɜːnə(r)]/ n becco m Bunsen

bunting /'bʌntɪŋ/ n (flags on ship) gran pavese m; Zool zigolo m

buoy /bɔɪ/ n boa f

■ **buoy up** vt fig sostenere (prices); tirare su (person)

buoyancy /'bɔɪənsɪ/ n galleggiabilità f

buoyancy aid n salvagente m

buoyant /'bɔɪənt/ a (boat) galleggiante; (water) che aiuta a galleggiare; (fig: person) allegro; (prices) in aumento

burble /'bɜːb(ə)l/ n (of stream) gorgoglio m; (of voices) borbottio m ● vi (stream:) gorgogliare; **~ on about sth** (person:) blaterare di qcsa

burbling /'bɜːblɪŋ/ n (of stream) gorgoglio m; (rambling talk) borbottio m ● a (stream) gorgogliante; (voice) che borbotta

burden /'bɜːdn/ n carico m ● vt caricare

burdensome /'bɜːdnsəm/ a gravoso

bureau /'bjʊərəʊ/ n (pl **-x** /'bjʊərəʊz/ or **~s**) (desk) scrivania f; (office) ufficio m

bureaucracy /bjʊə'rɒkrəsɪ/ n burocrazia f

bureaucrat /'bjʊərəkræt/ n burocrate mf

bureaucratic /bjʊərə'krætɪk/ a burocratico

burgeon /'bɜːdʒən/ vi (plant:) germogliare; (fig: flourish) fiorire; (fig: multiply) moltiplicarsi rapidamente, crescere rapidamente

burger /'bɜːɡə(r)/ n hamburger m inv

burger bar n fast-food m inv

burglar /'bɜːɡlə(r)/ n svaligiatore, -trice mf

burglar alarm n antifurto m inv

burglarize /'bɜːɡləraɪz/ vt Am svaligiare

burglar-proof a a prova di ladro

burglary /'bɜːɡlərɪ/ n furto m con scasso

burgle /'bɜːɡl/ vt svaligiare; **they have been ~d** sono stati svaligiati

Burgundy /'bɜːɡəndɪ/ n Borgogna f; **b~** (wine) borgogna m inv ● a (colour) rosso scuro

burial /'berɪəl/ n sepoltura f

burial ground n cimitero m

burlesque /bɜː'lesk/ n parodia f

burly /'bɜːlɪ/ a (-ier, -iest) corpulento

Burma /'bɜːmə/ n Birmania f

Burmese /bɜː'mi:z/ a & n birmano, -a mf

burn /bɜːn/ n bruciatura f ● v (pt/pp **burnt** or **burned**) ● vt bruciare; **~ one's boats** or **bridges** fig tagliarsi i ponti alle spalle ● vi bruciare

■ **burn down** vt/i bruciare

■ **burn out** vi fig esaurirsi

burned-out a = burnt-out

burner /'bɜːnə(r)/ n (on stove) bruciatore m

burning /'bɜːnɪŋ/ n (setting on fire) incendio m; **I can smell ~!** sento odore di bruciato! ● a (ember, coal) acceso; (on fire) in fiamme; (fig: fever, desire) bruciante; **a ~ sensation** una sensazione di bruciore; **a ~ question** una questione scottante

burnish /'bɜːnɪʃ/ vt lucidare

burns unit n Med reparto m grandi ustionati

burnt /bɜːnt/ see **burn**

burnt-out a (building, car) distrutto dalle fiamme; (fig: person) sfinito

burp /bɜːp/ n fam rutto m ● vi fam ruttare
burr /bɜː(r)/ n Bot lappa f; (in language) erre f moscia
burrow /ˈbʌrəʊ/ n tana f ● vt scavare ‹hole›
bursar /ˈbɜːsə(r)/ n economo, -a mf
bursary /ˈbɜːsərɪ/ n borsa f di studio
burst /bɜːst/ n (of gunfire, energy, laughter) scoppio m; (of speed) scatto m ● v (pt/pp **burst**) ● vt far scoppiare; ~ **its banks** ‹river:› rompere gli argini ● vi scoppiare; ~ **into tears** scoppiare in lacrime; ~ **into flames** andare in fiamme; **she ~ into the room** ha fatto irruzione nella stanza; **be ~ing at the seams** ‹room:› scoppiare
■ **burst in** vi (enter suddenly) fare irruzione
■ **burst out** vi ~ **out laughing/crying** scoppiare a ridere/piangere
Burundi /bʊˈrʊndɪ/ n Burundi m
bury /ˈberɪ/ vt (pt/pp **-ied**) seppellire; (hide) nascondere
bus /bʌs/ n autobus m inv, pullman m inv; (long distance) pullman m inv, corriera f ● vt (pt/pp **bussed**) trasportare in autobus
busby /ˈbʌzbɪ/ n colbacco m militare
bus: bus conductor n ≈ bigliettaio m. **bus conductress** n ≈ bigliettaia f. **bus driver** n conducente mf di autobus
bush /bʊʃ/ n cespuglio m; (land) boscaglia f
bushed /bʊʃt/ a (fam: tired) distrutto
bushel /ˈbʊʃ(ə)l/ n **hide one's light under a ~** essere troppo modesto; Am fam **~s of** un sacco di
bush: bushfighting n Mil guerriglia f. **bushfire** n incendio m in aperta campagna. **bush telegraph** n fig hum tamtam m inv
bushy /ˈbʊʃɪ/ a (**-ier, -iest**) folto
busily /ˈbɪzɪlɪ/ adv con grande impegno
business /ˈbɪznɪs/ n affare m; Comm affari mpl; (establishment) attività f di commercio; **on ~** per affari; **he has no ~ to** non ha alcun diritto di; **mind one's own ~** farsi gli affari propri; **that's none of your ~** non sono affari tuoi
business: business activity n attività f inv economica; (of single company) attività f inv aziendale. **business analyst** n analista mf finanziario, -a. **business associate** n socio, -a mf. **business call** n (phone call) telefonata f di lavoro; (visit) appuntamento m di lavoro. **business card** n biglietto m da visita. **business centre** n centro m affari. **business class** n Aeron business class f inv. **business college** n scuola f di amministrazione aziendale. **business contact** n contatto m di lavoro. **business cycle** n ciclo m economico. **business deal** n operazione f commerciale. **business expenses** npl spese fpl di lavoro. **business failures** npl chiusura f di aziende. **business hours** npl (in office) orario m d'ufficio; (of shop) orario m d'apertura. **business-like** a efficiente. **business lunch** n pranzo m di lavoro or d'affari
businessman /ˈbɪznɪsmən/ n uomo m d'affari
business: business management n am-

ministrazione f aziendale. **business park** n centro m affari. **business plan** n piano m economico; (of single company) programma m aziendale. **business premises** npl sede f di un'azienda. **business proposition** n proposta f d'affari. **business reply envelope** n busta f affrancata. **business school** n scuola f di amministrazione aziendale. **business software** n software m per l'ufficio. **business studies** npl economia f e commercio. **business suit** n (for man) abito m scuro. **business trip** n viaggio m di lavoro
businesswoman /ˈbɪznɪswʊmən/ n donna f d'affari
busk /bʌsk/ vi Br ‹singer:› cantare per strada; ‹musician:› suonare per strada
busker /ˈbʌskə(r)/ n suonatore, -trice mf ambulante
bus lane n corsia f autobus
busload /ˈbʌsləʊd/ n **a ~ of tourists** una comitiva di turisti; **by the ~** in massa
busman's holiday /bʌsmənzˈhɒlɪdeɪ/ n Br vacanze fpl passate a fare quello che si fa normalmente
bus: bus pass n abbonamento m all'autobus. **bus route** n percorso m dell'autobus. **bus shelter** n pensilina f alla fermata dell'autobus. **bus station** n stazione f degli autobus. **bus stop** n fermata f d'autobus
bust¹ /bʌst/ n busto m; (chest) petto m
bust² a fam rotto; **go ~** fallire ● v (pt/pp **busted** or **bust**) fam ● vt far scoppiare ● vi scoppiare
bustle /ˈbʌsl/ n (activity) trambusto m
■ **bustle about** vi affannarsi
bustling /ˈbʌslɪŋ/ a animato
bust size n circonferenza f del torace
bust-up n fam lite f
busy /ˈbɪzɪ/ a (**-ier, -iest**) occupato; ‹day, time› intenso; ‹street› affollato; (with traffic) pieno di traffico; **be ~ doing** essere occupato a fare ● vt ~ **oneself** darsi da fare
busybody /ˈbɪzɪbɒdɪ/ n ficcanaso mf inv
but /bʌt/, /bət/ conj ma ● prep eccetto, tranne; **nobody ~ you** nessuno tranne te; ~ **for** (without) se non fosse stato per; **the last ~ one** il penultimo; **the next ~ one** il secondo ● adv soltanto; **there were ~ two** ce n'erano soltanto due
butane /ˈbjuːteɪn/ n butano m
butch /bʊtʃ/ a fam ‹man› macho inv; ‹woman› mascolino
butcher /ˈbʊtʃə(r)/ n macellaio m ● vt macellare; fig massacrare
butcher's [shop] /ˈbʊtʃəz[ʃɒp]/ n macelleria f
butchery /ˈbʊtʃərɪ/ n (trade) macelleria f; (slaughter) massacro m
butler /ˈbʌtlə(r)/ n maggiordomo m
butt /bʌt/ n (of gun) calcio m; (of cigarette) mozzicone m; (for water) barile m; (fig: target) bersaglio m ● vt dare una testata a; ‹goat:› dare una cornata a
■ **butt in** vi interrompere
butter /ˈbʌtə(r)/ n burro m ● vt imburrare

■ **butter up** *vt fam* arruffianarsi

butter: butter-bean *n* fagiolo *m* bianco. **buttercup** *n* ranuncolo *m*. **butter dish** *n* portaburro *m inv*. **butter-fingered** *a* con le mani di pasta frolla. **butter-fingers** *n fam* mani *fpl* di pasta frolla

butterfly /'bʌtəflaɪ/ *n* farfalla *f*

butterfly: butterfly net *n* retino *m* per farfalle. **butterfly nut** *n* dado *m* ad alette. **butterfly stroke** *n* nuoto *m* a farfalla

buttermilk /'bʌtəmɪlk/ *n* latticello *m*

butterscotch /'bʌtəskɒtʃ/ *n* caramella *f* dura a base di burro e zucchero

buttocks /'bʌtəks/ *npl* natiche *fpl*

button /'bʌtn/ *n* bottone *m*; (*on mouse, of status bar*) pulsante *m* ● *vt* ~ [up] abbottonare ● *vi* ~ [up] abbottonarsi

button: button-down *a* ⟨collar⟩ button down, coi bottoni; ⟨shirt⟩ con il colletto coi bottoni, button down. **buttonhole** *n* occhiello *m*, asola *f*. **buttonhook** *n* asola *f*, occhiello *m*. **button mushroom** *n* piccolo champignon *m inv*

buttress /'bʌtrɪs/ *n* contrafforte *m* ● *vt fig* sostenere

buxom /'bʌksəm/ *a* formosa

buy /baɪ/ *n* **good/bad** ~ buon/cattivo acquisto *m* ● *vt* (*pt/pp* bought) comprare; ~ **sb a drink** pagare da bere a qcno; **I'll** ~ **this one** (*drink*) questo, lo offro io

■ **buy off** *vt* (*bribe*) comprare

■ **buy out** *vt* rilevare la quota di ⟨one's partner⟩

■ **buy up** *vt* (*buy all of*) accaparrarsi

buyer /'baɪə(r)/ *n* compratore, -trice *mf*

buyout /'baɪaʊt/ *n Comm* rilevamento *m*

buzz /bʌz/ *n* ronzio *m*; **give sb a** ~ *fam* (*on phone*) dare un colpo di telefono a qcno; (*excite*) mettere in fermento qcno ● *vi* ronzare ● *vt* ~ **sb** chiamare qcno col cicalino

■ **buzz off** *vi fam* levarsi di torno

buzzard /'bʌzəd/ *n* poiana *f*

buzzer /'bʌzə(r)/ *n* cicalino *m*

buzzing /'bʌzɪŋ/ *n* (*of buzzer*) trillo *m*; (*of insects*) ronzio *m* ● *a* ⟨party, atmosphere, town⟩ molto animato

buzzword /'bʌzwɜːd/ *n fam* parola *f* di moda

by /baɪ/ *prep* (*near, next to*) vicino a; (*at the latest*) per; **by Mozart** di Mozart; **he was run over by a bus** è stato investito da un autobus; **by oneself** da solo; **by the sea** al mare; **by sea** via mare; **by car/bus** in macchina/ autobus; **by day/night** di giorno/notte; **by the hour/metre** a ore/metri; **six metres by four** sei metri per quattro; **he won by six metres** ha vinto di sei metri; **I missed the train by a minute** ho perso il treno per un minuto; **I'll be home by six** sarò a casa per le sei; **by this time next week** a quest'ora tra una settimana; **he rushed by me** mi è passato accanto di corsa ● *adv* **she'll be here by and by** sarà qui fra poco; **by and by the police arrived** poco dopo, la polizia è arrivata; **by and large** in complesso; **put by** mettere da parte; **go/pass by** passare

bye-bye /baɪ'baɪ/ *int fam* ciao, arrivederci; **go** ~**s** *Br* (*baby talk*) andare a fare la nanna

by-election *n* elezione *f* straordinaria indetta per coprire una carica rimasta vacante in Parlamento

Byelorussia /bjeləʊ'rʌʃə/ *n* Bielorussia *f*

Byelorussian /bjeləʊ'rʌʃn/ *a & n* bielorusso

by: bygone *a* passato. **by-law** *n* legge *f* locale. **by-line** *n* (*in newspaper*) nome *m* dell'autore; *Sport* linea *f* laterale. **bypass** *n* circonvallazione *f*; *Med* by-pass *m inv* ● *vt* evitare. **by-product** *n* sottoprodotto *m*. **by-road** *n* strada *f* secondaria. **bystander** *n* spettatore, -trice *mf*

byte /baɪt/ *n Comput* byte *m inv*

by: byway *n* strada *f* secondaria. **byword** *n* **be a** ~ **for** essere sinonimo di. **by-your-leave** *n* **without so much as a** ~ senza neanche chiedere il permesso

Byzantine /bɪ'zæntaɪn/ *a* bizantino

Cc

c, C /siː/ *n* (*letter*) c, C *f inv*; (*Br Sch: grade*) voto *m* scolastico corrispondente alla sufficienza; *Mus* do *m inv*

c, C *abbr* (**Celsius, centigrade**) C; *abbr* (**cent(s)**) c; *abbr* (**circa**) ca

CA *Br abbr* (**Chartered Accountant**) [dottore *m*] commercialista *m*; *Am abbr* (**California**) Cal; *abbr* (**Central America**) America *f* centrale

CAA *n Br abbr* (**Civil Aviation Authority**) organismo *m* di controllo dell'aviazione civile

CAB *n Br abbr* (**Citizens' Advice Bureau**) ufficio *m* di consulenza legale gratuita per i cittadini

cab /kæb/ *n* taxi *m inv*; (*of lorry, train*) cabina *f*

cabana /kə'bɑːnə/ *n* (*Am: hut*) cabina *f* da spiaggia

cabaret /'kæbəreɪ/ *n* cabaret *m inv*

cabbage /'kæbɪdʒ/ *n* cavolo *m*

cabby /'kæbɪ/ *n fam* tassista *mf*

cab driver *n* tassista *mf*

cabin /'kæbɪn/ *n* (*of plane, ship*) cabina *f*; (*hut*) capanna *f*

cabin: cabin boy *n* mozzo *m*. **cabin crew** *n* Aeron equipaggio *m*. **cabin cruiser** *n* cabinato *m*

cabinet /'kæbɪnɪt/ *n* armadietto *m*; [**display**] ~ vetrina *f*; **C**~ *Pol* consiglio *m* dei ministri

cabinet: cabinet-maker *n* ebanista *mf*. **cabinet meeting** *n Br* riunione *f* del governo. **cabinet minister** *n Br* ministro *m*. **cabinet reshuffle** *n Br* rimpasto *m* del governo

cable /'keɪb(ə)l/ *n* cavo *m*

cable: cable car *n* cabina *f* (*della funivia*). **cablegram** *n* cablogramma *m*. **cable-knit** (*sweater*) a trecce. **cable railway** *n* funicolare *f*. **cable television** *n* televisione *f* via cavo. **cable TV** *n* TV *f inv* via cavo. **cableway** *n* (*for people*) funivia *f*

caboodle /kə'buːdl/ *n fam* **the whole** ~ baracca e burattini

cab rank, cab stand *n* posteggio *m* dei taxi

cache /kæʃ/ *n* nascondiglio *m*; ~ **of arms** deposito *m* segreto di armi

cache memory *n Comput* memoria *f* cache

cachet /'kæʃeɪ/ *n* prestigio *m*

cackle /'kækl/ *vi* ridacchiare

cacophony /kə'kɒfənɪ/ *n* cacofonia *f*

cactus /'kæktəs/ *n* (*pl* **-ti** /'kæktaɪ/ *or* **-tuses**) cactus *m inv*

CAD /kæd/ *n abbr* (**computer-aided design**) CAD *m inv*

cadaver /kə'dɑːvə(r)/ *n* cadavere *m*

cadaverous /kə'dævərəs/ *a* cadaverico

CADCAM /'kædkæm/ *n abbr* (**computer-aided design and computer-aided manufacture**) CADCAM *m inv*

caddie /'kædɪ/ *n* portabastoni *m inv*

caddy /'kædɪ/ *n* [**tea-**]~ barattolo *m* del tè

cadence /'keɪdəns/ *n* cadenza *f*

cadet /kə'det/ *n* cadetto *m*

cadet corps *n Mil* corpo *m* dei cadetti

cadet school *n* scuola *f* allievi ufficiali

cadge /kædʒ/ *vt/i fam* scroccare

cadre /'kɑːdr(ə)/ *n Admin, Pol* quadri *mpl*

CAE *n abbr* (**computer-aided engineering**) CAE *m inv*

Caesarean /sɪ'zeərɪən/ *n* parto *m* cesareo

café /'kæfeɪ/ *n* caffè *m inv*

cafeteria /kæfə'tɪərɪə/ *n* tavola *f* calda

caffeine /'kæfiːn/ *n* caffeina *f*

cage /keɪdʒ/ *n* gabbia *f*

cage bird *n* uccello *m* da gabbia

cagey /'keɪdʒɪ/ *a fam* riservato (**about** su)

cagoule /kə'guːl/ *n Br* K-way™ *m inv*

cahoots /kə'huːts/ *npl fam* **be in** ~ essere in combutta

cairn /keən/ *n* (*of stones*) tumulo *m* di pietre

Cairo /'kaɪrəʊ/ *n* il Cairo

cajole /kə'dʒəʊl/ *vt* persuadere con le lusinghe

cake /keɪk/ *n* torta *f*; (*small*) pasticcino *m*; ~ **of soap** saponetta *f*; **it was a piece of** ~ *fam* è stato un gioco da ragazzi; **you can't have your** ~ **and eat it** *fig* non si può avere

la botte piena e la moglie ubriaca; **sell like hot** ~**s** andare a ruba

caked /keɪkt/ *a* incrostato (**with** di)

cake: cake mix *n* miscela *f* per torte. **cake shop** *n* pasticceria *f*. **cake tin** *n* (*for baking*) tortiera *f*; (*for storing*) scatola *f* di latta (*per torte*)

Calabria /kə'læbrɪə/ *n* Calabria *f*

Calabrian /kə'læbrɪən/ *a & n* calabrese

calamine lotion /'kæləmaɪn/ *n* lozione *f* alla calamina

calamitous /kə'læmɪtəs/ *a* disastroso

calamity /kə'læmətɪ/ *n* calamità *f inv*

calcify /'kælsɪfaɪ/ *vi* calcificarsi

calcium /'kælsɪəm/ *n* calcio *m*

calculate /'kælkjʊleɪt/ *vt* calcolare

calculated /'kælkjʊleɪtɪd/ *a* (*risk, insult, decision*) calcolato; (*crime*) premeditato

calculating /'kælkjʊleɪtɪŋ/ *a fig* calcolatore

calculating machine *n* calcolatrice *f*

calculation /kælkjʊ'leɪʃn/ *n* calcolo *m*

calculator /'kælkjʊleɪtə(r)/ *n* calcolatrice *f*

calculus /'kælkjʊləs/ *n Math, Med* calcolo *m*

calendar /'kælɪndə(r)/ *n* calendario *m*

calendar month *n* mese *m* civile

calendar year *n* anno *m* civile

calf¹ /kɑːf/ *n* (*pl* **calves**) vitello *m*

calf² *n* (*pl* **calves**) *Anat* polpaccio *m*

calfskin /'kɑːfskɪn/ *n* [pelle *f* di] vitello *m*

calibrate /'kælɪbreɪt/ *vt* calibrare (*instrument*); tarare (*scales*)

calibre /'kælɪbə(r)/ *n* calibro *m*

calico /'kælɪkəʊ/ *n* cotone *m* grezzo

California /kælɪ'fɔːnɪə/ *n* California *f*

Californian /kælɪ'fɔːnɪən/ *a & n* californiano, -a *mf*

CALL *n abbr* (**computer-assisted language learning**) CALL *m inv*

call /kɔːl/ *n* grido *m*; *Teleph* telefonata *f*; (*visit*) visita *f*; **be on** ~ (*doctor:*) essere di guardia ● *vt* chiamare; indire (*strike*); **be** ~**ed** chiamarsi ● *vi* chiamare; ~ [**in** *or* **round**] passare

■ **call back** *vt/i* richiamare

■ **call by** *vi* (*make brief visit*) passare

■ **call for** *vt* (*ask for*) chiedere; (*require*) richiedere; (*fetch*) passare a prendere

■ **call off** *vt* richiamare (*dog*); disdire (*meeting*); revocare (*strike*)

■ **call on** *vt* chiamare; (*appeal to*) fare un appello a; (*visit*) visitare

■ **call out** *vt* chiamare ad alta voce (*names*) ● *vi* chiamare ad alta voce

■ **call together** *vt* riunire

■ **call up** *vt Mil* chiamare alle armi; *Teleph* chiamare

callback facility /'kɔːlbæk/ *n Teleph* servizio *m* telefonico che permette di individuare il numero che ha chiamato

call box *n* cabina *f* telefonica

caller /'kɔːlə(r)/ *n* visitatore, -trice *mf*; *Teleph* persona *f* che telefona

call-girl *n* call-girl *f inv*, [ragazza *f*] squillo *f inv*

calligrapher /kə'lɪɡrəfə(r)/ n calligrafo, -a mf

calligraphy /kə'lɪɡrəfɪ/ n calligrafia f

calling /'kɔ:lɪŋ/ n vocazione f

calliper /'kælɪpə(r)/ (for measuring) calibro m; (leg support) tutore m

callisthenics /kælɪs'θenɪks/ n ginnastica f

callous /'kæləs/ a insensibile

callousness /'kæləsnɪs/ n insensibilità f

call-out n (doctor) visita f a domicilio; (plumber, electrician) chiamata f

call-out charge n costo m della chiamata

callow /'kæləʊ/ a immaturo

call: call sign n Radio segnale m di chiamata. **call-up** n Mil chiamata f alle armi. **call-up papers** npl cartolina f precetto

calm /kɑ:m/ a calmo ● n calma f

■ **calm down** vt calmare ● vi calmarsi

calmly /'kɑ:mlɪ/ adv con calma

calmness /'kɑ:mnɪs/ n calma f

Calor gas® /'kælə/ n Br liquigas* m inv

calorie /'kælərɪ/ n caloria f

calorific /kælə'rɪfɪk/ a calorico

calve /kɑ:v/ vi figliare

calves /kɑ:vz/ npl see **calf¹** & ²

cam /kæm/ n Techn camma f

camaraderie /kæmə'rædərɪ/ n cameratismo m

camber /'kæmbə(r)/ n curvatura f

Cambodia /kæm'bəʊdɪə/ n Cambogia f

Cambodian /kæm'bəʊdɪən/ a & n cambogiano, -a mf

camcorder /'kæmkɔ:də(r)/ n videocamera f

came /keɪm/ see **come**

camel /'kæml/ n cammello m

camel hair n cammello m

camellia /kə'mi:lɪə/ n camelia f

cameo /'kæmɪəʊ/ n cammeo m

cameo role n Theat, Cinema breve apparizione f

camera /'kæmərə/ n macchina f fotografica; TV telecamera f

camera crew n troupe f inv televisiva

cameraman /'kæmərəmæn/ n operatore m [televisivo], cameraman m inv

Cameroon /kæməru:n/ n il Camerun

camisole /'kæmɪsəʊl/ n canottiera f

camomile /'kæməmaɪl/ n camomilla f

camouflage /'kæmə'flɑ:ʒ/ n mimetizzazione f ● vt mimetizzare

camp¹ /kæmp/ n campeggio f; Mil campo m ● vi campeggiare; Mil accamparsi

camp² a (affected) affettato

campaign /kæm'peɪn/ n campagna f ● vi fare una campagna

campaign trail n be on the ~ ~ fare la campagna elettorale

campaign worker n Br Pol membro m dello staff di una campagna elettorale

camp bed n letto m da campo

camper /'kæmpə(r)/ n campeggiatore, -trice mf; Auto camper m inv

campfire /'kæmpfaɪə(r)/ n fuoco m di bivacco

camphor /'kæmfə(r)/ n canfora f

camping /'kæmpɪŋ/ n campeggio m

camping: camping equipment n attrezzatura f da campeggio. **camping gas** n gas m inv da campeggio. **camping holiday** n vacanza f in tenda. **camping site** n campeggio m. **camping stool** n Br sgabello m pieghevole. **camping stove** n fornello m da campeggio

campsite /'kæmpsaɪt/ n campeggio m

campus /'kæmpəs/ n (pl **-puses**) Univ città f universitaria, campus m inv

camshaft /'kæmʃɑ:ft/ n albero m a camme

can¹ /kæn/ n (for petrol) latta f; (tin) scatola f; ~ **of beer** lattina f di birra ● vt mettere in scatola

can² /kæn/, atono /kən/ v aux (pres **can**; pt **could**) (be able to) potere; (know how to) sapere; **I cannot** or **can't go** non posso andare; **he could not** or **couldn't go** non poteva andare; **she can't swim** non sa nuotare; **I ~ smell something burning** sento odor di bruciato

Canada /'kænədə/ n Canada m

Canadian /kə'neɪdɪən/ a & n canadese mf

canal /kə'næl/ n canale m

canal boat, canal barge n chiatta f

canapé /'kænəpeɪ/ n canapè m inv

Canaries /kə'neərɪz/ npl Canarie fpl

canary /kə'neərɪ/ n canarino m

cancel /'kænsl/ v (pt/pp **cancelled**) ● vt disdire ‹meeting, newspaper›; revocare ‹contract, order›; annullare ‹reservation, appointment, stamp› ● vi ‹guest, host:› annullare

cancellation /kænsə'leɪʃn/ n (of meeting, contract) revoca f; (in hotel, restaurant, for flight) cancellazione f

cancer /'kænsə(r)/ n cancro m; **C~** Astr Cancro m

cancerous /'kænsərəs/ a canceroso

cancer research n ricerca f sul cancro

candelabra /kændə'lɑ:brə/ n candelabro m

candid /'kændɪd/ a franco

candidacy /'kændɪdəsɪ/ n Pol candidatura f

candidate /'kændɪdət/ n candidato, -a mf

candidly /'kændɪdlɪ/ adv francamente

candied /'kændɪd/ a candito

candle /'kændl/ n candela f

candlelight /'kænd(ə)llaɪt/ n **by ~** a lume di candela

candlelit dinner /'kænd(ə)llɪt/ n cena f a lume di candela

candlestick /'kænd(ə)lstɪk/ n portacandele m inv

candlewick bedspread /'kænd(ə)lwɪk/ n copriletto m inv di ciniglia

candour /'kændə(r)/ n franchezza f

candy /'kændɪ/ n Am caramella f; **a [piece of]** ~ una caramella

candyfloss /'kændɪflɒs/ n zucchero m filato

candy-striped /straɪpt/ a (blue) a righe bianche e celesti; (pink) a righe bianche e rosa

cane /keɪn/ n (stick) bastone m; Sch bacchetta f ● vt prendere a bacchettate ‹pupil›

cane sugar n zucchero m di canna

canine /'kemaɪn/ *a* canino

canine tooth *n* canino *m*

canister /'kænɪstə(r)/ *n* barattolo *m*

cannabis /'kænəbɪs/ *n* cannabis *f*

canned /kænd/ *a* in scatola; ~ **music** *fam* musica *f* registrata

cannibal /'kænɪbl/ *n* cannibale *mf*

cannibalism /'kænɪbəlɪzm/ *n* cannibalismo *m*

cannibalize /'kænɪbəlaɪz/ *vt* riciclare parti di

cannon /'kænən/ *n inv* cannone *m*

cannon ball *n* palla *f* di cannone

cannon fodder *n* carne *f* da cannone, carne *f* da macello

cannot /'kænɒt/ *see* **can²**

canny /'kænɪ/ *a* astuto

canoe /kə'nu:/ *n* canoa *f* ● *vi* andare in canoa

canon /'kænən/ *n* (*rule*) canone *m*; (*person*) canonico *m*

canonization /kænənaɪ'zeɪʃn/ *n* canonizzazione *f*

canonize /'kænənaɪz/ *vt* canonizzare

canoodle /kə'nu:dl/ *vi fam* sbaciucchiarsi

can-opener *n* apriscatole *m inv*

canopy /'kænəpɪ/ *n* baldacchino *f*; (*of parachute*) calotta *f*

cant /kænt/ *n* (*hypocrisy*) ipocrisia *f*; (*jargon*) gergo *m*

can't /kɑ:nt/ = **cannot** *see* **can²**

cantankerous /kæn'tæŋkərəs/ *a* stizzoso

cantata /kæn'tɑːtə/ *n Mus* cantata *f*

canteen /kæn'ti:n/ *n* mensa *f*; ~ **of cutlery** servizio *m* di posate

canter /'kæntə(r)/ *n* piccolo galoppo *m* ● *vi* andare a piccolo galoppo

cantilever /'kæntɪli:və(r)/ *n* cantilever *m inv*, trave *f* a sbalzo

cantonal /'kæntənəl/ *a* cantonale

canvas /'kænvəs/ *n* tela *f*; (*painting*) dipinto *m* su tela

canvass /'kænvəs/ *vi Pol* fare propaganda elettorale

canvassing /'kænvəsɪŋ/ *n* (*door to door for votes*) propaganda *f* porta a porta; (*door to door for sales*) vendita *f* porta a porta

canyon /'kænjən/ *n* canyon *m inv*

cap /kæp/ *n* berretto *m*; (*nurse's*) cuffia *f*; (*top, lid*) tappo *m* ● *vt* (*pt/pp* **capped**) (*fig: do better than*) superare

capability /keɪpə'bɪlətɪ/ *n* capacità *f*

capable /'keɪpəbl/ *a* capace; (*skilful*) abile; **be ~ of doing sth** essere capace di fare qcsa

capably /'keɪpəblɪ/ *adv* con abilità

capacious /kə'peɪʃəs/ *a* (*pocket, car boot*) capace

capacity /kə'pæsətɪ/ *n* capacità *f*; (*function*) qualità *f*; **in my ~ as** in qualità di

cape¹ /keɪp/ *n* (*cloak*) cappa *f*

cape² *n Geog* capo *m*

Cape of Good Hope *n* Capo *m* di Buona Speranza

caper¹ /'keɪpə(r)/ *vi* saltellare ● *n fam* birichinata *f*

caper² *n Culin* cappero *m*

Cape Town *n* Città *f* del Capo

capful /'kæpfʊl/ *n* tappo *m*

cap gun *n* pistola *f* a capsule

capillary /kə'pɪlərɪ/ *a & n* capillare *m*

capital /'kæpɪtl/ *n* (*town*) capitale *f*; (*money*) capitale *m*; (*letter*) lettera *f* maiuscola

capital: capital allowances *npl* detrazioni *mpl* per ammortamento. **capital city** *n* capitale *f*. **capital expenditure** *n* spese *fpl* in conto capitale; (*personal*) spese *fpl* di capitale. **capital gains tax** *n* imposta *f* sui redditi di capitale. **capital goods** *npl* beni *mpl* strumentali. **capital-intensive** *a* ad uso intensivo di capitale. **capital investment** *n* investimento *m* di capitale

capitalism /'kæpɪtəlɪzm/ *n* capitalismo *m*

capitalist /'kæpɪtəlɪst/ *a & n* capitalista *mf*

capitalize /'kæpɪtəlaɪz/ *vi* ~ **on** *fig* trarre vantaggio da

capital: capital letter *n* lettera *f* maiuscola. **capital punishment** *n* pena *f* capitale. **capital spending** *n* spese *fpl* in conto capitale. **capital transfer tax** *n* imposta *f* sui trasferimenti di capitale

capitulate /kə'pɪtjʊleɪt/ *vi* capitolare

capitulation /kəpɪtjʊ'leɪʃn/ *n* capitolazione *f*

capon /'keɪpɒn/ *n* cappone *m*

caprice /kə'pri:s/ *n* (*whim*) capriccio *m*

capricious /kə'prɪʃəs/ *a* capriccioso

Capricorn /'kæprɪkɔ:n/ *n Astr* Capricorno *m*

capsicum /'kæpsɪkəm/ *n* peperone *m*

capsize /kæp'saɪz/ *vi* capovolgersi ● *vt* capovolgere

caps lock *n Comput* bloccamaiuscole *m inv*

capstan /'kæpstən/ *n* argano *m*

capsule /'kæpsju:l/ *n* capsula *f*

captain /'kæptɪn/ *n* capitano *m* ● *vt* comandare (*team*)

caption /'kæpʃn/ *n* intestazione *f*; (*of illustration*) didascalia *f*

captious /'kæpʃəs/ *a* (*remark*) ipercritico

captivate /'kæptɪveɪt/ *vt* incantare

captive /'kæptɪv/ *a* prigioniero; **hold/take ~** tenere/fare prigioniero ● *n* prigioniero, -a *mf*

captivity /kæp'tɪvətɪ/ *n* prigionia *f*; (*animals*) cattività *f*

captor /'kæptə(r)/ *n* (*of person*) persona *f* che tiene prigioniero qcno; (*of person for ransom*) rapitore, -trice *mf*

capture /'kæptʃə(r)/ *n* cattura *f* ● *vt* catturare; attirare (*attention*)

car /kɑ:(r)/ *n* macchina *f*; **by ~** in macchina

carafe /kə'ræf/ *n* caraffa *f*

caramel /'kærəml/ *n* (*sweet*) caramella *f* al mou; *Culin* caramello *m*

carat /'kærət/ *n* carato *m*

caravan /'kærəvæn/ *n* roulotte *f inv*; (*horse-drawn*) carovana *f*

caraway /'kærəweɪ/ *n* (*plant*) cumino *m* dei prati

carbohydrate /kɑ:bə'haɪdreɪt/ *n* carboidrato *m*

carbolic /kɑ:'bɒlɪk/ *a* (*soap*) al fenolo

car bomb *n* autobomba *f*

carbon /ˈkɑːbən/ *n* carbonio *m*; (*paper*) carta *f* carbone; (*copy*) copia *f* in carta carbone

carbon: carbon copy *n* copia *f* in carta carbone; (*fig: person*) ritratto *m*. **carbon-date** *vt* datare con il carbonio 14. **carbon dating** *n* datazione *f* con il carbonio 14. **carbon dioxide** *n* anidride *f* carbonica. **carbon filter** *n* filtro *m* al carbone. **carbon monoxide** *n* monossido *m* di carbonio. **carbon paper** *n* carta *f* carbone

car boot sale *n Br* mercatino *m* di oggetti usati, esposti nei bagagliai delle macchine

carbuncle /ˈkɑːbʌŋk(ə)l/ *n Med* foruncolo *m*

carburettor /kɑːbjʊˈretə(r)/ *n* carburatore *m*

carcass /ˈkɑːkəs/ *n* carcassa *f*

carcinogen /kɑːˈsɪnədʒən/ *n* cancerogeno *m*

carcinogenic /kɑːsɪnəˈdʒenɪk/ *a* cancerogeno

card /kɑːd/ *n* (*for birthday, Christmas etc*) biglietto *m* di auguri; (*playing ~*) carta *f* [da gioco]; (*membership ~*) tessera *f*; (*business ~*) biglietto *m* da visita; (*credit ~*) carta *f* di credito; *Comput* scheda *f*

cardboard /ˈkɑːdbɔːd/ *n* cartone *m*

cardboard box *n* scatola *f* di cartone; (*large*) scatolone *m*

card game *n* gioco *m* di carte

cardiac /ˈkɑːdɪæk/ *a* cardiaco

cardigan /ˈkɑːdɪgən/ *n* cardigan *m inv*

cardinal /ˈkɑːdɪnl/ *a* cardinale; **~ number** numero *m* cardinale ● *n Relig* cardinale *m*

card index *n* schedario *m*

cardiologist /kɑːdɪˈɒlədʒɪst/ *n* cardiologo, -a *mf*

cardiology /kɑːdɪˈɒlədʒɪ/ *n* cardiologia *f*

cardiovascular /kɑːdɪəˈvæskjʊlə(r)/ *a* cardiovascolare

card: card key *n* scheda *f* magnetica. **card table** *n* tappeto *m* verde. **card trick** *n* trucco *m* con le carte

care /keə(r)/ *n* cura *f*; (*caution*) attenzione *f*; (*worry*) preoccupazione *f*; **~ of** (*on letter abbr* **c/o**) presso; **take ~** (*be cautious*) fare attenzione; **bye, take ~** ciao, stammi bene; **take ~ of** occuparsi di; **be taken into ~** essere preso in custodia da un ente assistenziale; **'[handle] with ~'** 'fragile' ● *vi* **~ about** interessarsi di; **~ for** (*feel affection for*) volere bene a; (*look after*) aver cura di; **I don't ~ for chocolate** non mi piace il cioccolato; **I don't ~** non me ne importa; **who ~s?** chi se ne frega?; **for all I ~** per quello che me ne importa

care assistant *n Br Med* assistente *mf* a domicilio

career /kəˈrɪə(r)/ *n* carriera *f*; (*profession*) professione *f*. **~ woman** *n* donna in carriera ● *vi* andare a tutta velocità

career: career break *n* pausa *f* nella carriera. **career move** *n* passo *m* utile per un avanzamento di carriera. **careers adviser** *n* consulente *mf* di orientamento professionale. **careers office** *n* centro *m* di orientamento

professionale. **careers service** *n* servizio *m* di orientamento professionale

carefree /ˈkeəfriː/ *a* spensierato

careful /ˈkeəfʊl/ *a* attento; (*driver*) prudente

carefully /ˈkeəfʊlɪ/ *adv* con attenzione

careless /ˈkeəlɪs/ *a* irresponsabile; (*in work*) trascurato; (*work*) fatto con poca cura; (*driver*) distratto

carelessly /ˈkeəlɪslɪ/ *adv* negligentemente

carelessness /ˈkeəlɪsnɪs/ *n* trascuratezza *f*

carer /ˈkeərə(r)/ *n Br* (*relative*) familiare *m* che assiste un anziano o un handicappato; (*professional*) assistente *mf* a domicilio

caress /kəˈres/ *n* carezza *f* ● *vt* accarezzare

caretaker /ˈkeəteɪkə(r)/ *n* custode *mf*; (*in school*) bidello *m*

careworn /ˈkeəwɔːn/ *a* (*face*) segnato dalle preoccupazioni

car ferry *n* traghetto *m* (*per il trasporto di auto*)

cargo /ˈkɑːgəʊ/ *n* (*pl* -es) carico *m*

cargo plane *n* aereo *m* da carico

cargo ship *n* nave *f* da carico

car hire *n* autonoleggio *m*

Caribbean /kærɪˈbiːən/ *n* **the ~** (*sea*) il Mar *m* dei Caraibi ● *a* caraibico

caricature /ˈkærɪkətjʊə(r)/ *n* caricatura *f* ● *vt* fare una caricatura di

caricaturist /ˈkærɪkətjʊərɪst/ *n* caricaturista *mf*

caring /ˈkeərɪŋ/ *a* (*parent*) premuroso; (*attitude*) altruista; **the ~ professions** le attività assistenziali

carjacking /ˈkɑːdʒækɪŋ/ *n* furto *m* d'auto con aggressione al conducente

carload /ˈkɑːləʊd/ *n* **a ~ of people** un'automobile *f* piena di persone

carnage /ˈkɑːnɪdʒ/ *n* carneficina *f*

carnal /ˈkɑːn(ə)l/ *a* carnale

carnation /kɑːˈneɪʃn/ *n* garofano *m*

carnival /ˈkɑːnɪvl/ *n* carnevale *m*

carnivore /ˈkɑːnɪvɔː(r)/ *n* carnivoro *m*

carnivorous /kɑːˈnɪvərəs/ *a* carnivoro

carob /ˈkærəb/ *n* (*pod*) carruba *f*; (*tree*) carrubo *m*

carol /ˈkærəl/ *n* [**Christmas**] **~** canzone *f* natalizia; **~ concert** concerto *m* natalizio; **go ~ singing** andare a cantare le canzoni natalizie per le strade

carousel /kærʊˈsel/ *n* (*merry-go-round*) giostra *f*; (*for luggage*) nastro *m* trasportatore; (*for slides*) caricatore *m* circolare

carp[1] /kɑːp/ *n inv* carpa *f*

carp[2] *vi* lamentarsi; **~ at** trovare da ridire su

car park *n* parcheggio *m*

carpenter /ˈkɑːpəntə(r)/ *n* falegname *m*

carpentry /ˈkɑːpəntrɪ/ *n* falegnameria *f*

carpet /ˈkɑːpɪt/ *n* tappeto *m*; (*wall-to-wall*) moquette *f inv*; **be on the ~** *fig* essere ammonito ● *vt* mettere la moquette in (*room*)

carpet: carpet fitter *n* artigiano *m* che mette in opera la moquette. **carpet slipper** *n* pantofola *f*. **carpet sweeper** *n* battitappeto *m inv*. **carpet tile** *n* riquadro *m* di moquette

car phone *n* telefono *m* in macchina

car radio *n* autoradio *f inv*

carriage /'kærɪdʒ/ *n* carrozza *f*; (*of typewriter*) carrello *m*; (*of goods*) trasporto *m*; (*cost*) spese *fpl* di trasporto; (*bearing*) portamento *m*; **~ paid** *Comm* franco di porto

carriage clock *n* orologio *m* da tavolo

carriageway /'kærɪdʒweɪ/ *n* strada *f* carrozzabile; **north-bound ~** carreggiata *f* nord

carrier /'kærɪə(r)/ *n* (*company*) impresa *f* di trasporti; *Aeron* compagnia *f* di trasporto aereo; (*of disease*) portatore *m*

carrier [bag] *n* borsa *f* [per la spesa]

carrier pigeon *n* piccione *m* viaggiatore

carrot /'kærət/ *n* carota *f*

carry /'kærɪ/ *v* (*pt/pp* **-ied**) ● *vt* portare; (*transport*) trasportare; *Math* riportare; **get carried away** *fam* lasciarsi prender la mano ● *vi* ⟨*sound:*⟩ trasmettersi

■ **carry off** *vt* portare via; vincere ⟨*prize*⟩

■ **carry on** *vi* continuare; (*fam: make scene*) fare delle storie; **~ on with sth** continuare qcsa; **~ on with sb** *fam* intendersela con qcno ● *vt* mantenere ⟨*business*⟩; **~ on doing sth** continuare a fare qcsa

■ **carry out** *vt* portare fuori; eseguire ⟨*instructions, task*⟩; mettere in atto ⟨*threat*⟩; effettuare ⟨*experiment, survey*⟩

carrycot /'kærɪkɒt/ *n* porte-enfant *m inv*

carry-on *n fam* (*complicated procedure*) impresa *f*; (*bad behaviour*) storie *fpl*

carsick /'kɑ:sɪk/ *a* **be ~** avere il mal d'auto

cart /kɑ:t/ *n* carretto *m*; **put the ~ before the horse** *fig* mettere il carro davanti ai buoi ● *vt* (*fam: carry*) portare

cartel /kɑ:'tel/ *n* cartello *m*

carthorse /'kɑ:thɔ:s/ *n* cavallo *m* da tiro

cartilage /'kɑ:tɪlɪdʒ/ *n Anat* cartilagine *f*

cartographer /kɑ:'tɒɡrəfə(r)/ *n* cartografo, -a *mf*

cartography /kɑ:'tɒɡrəfɪ/ *n* cartografia *f*

carton /'kɑ:t(ə)n/ *n* scatola *f* di cartone; (*for drink*) cartone *m*; (*of cream, yoghurt*) vasetto *m*; (*of cigarettes*) stecca *f*

cartoon /kɑ:'tu:n/ *n* vignetta *f*; (*strip*) vignette *fpl*; (*film*) cartone *m* animato; (*in art*) bozzetto *m*

cartoonist /kɑ:'tu:nɪst/ *n* vignettista *mf*; (*for films*) disegnatore, -trice *mf* di cartoni animati

cartridge /'kɑ:trɪdʒ/ *n* cartuccia *f*; (*for film*) bobina *f*; (*of record player*) testina *f*

cartwheel /'kɑ:twi:l/ *n* (*of cart*) ruota *f* di carro; (*in gymnastics*) ruota *f*; **do a ~** (*in gymnastics*) fare la ruota

carve /kɑ:v/ *vt* scolpire; tagliare ⟨*meat*⟩

carving /'kɑ:vɪŋ/ *n* scultura *f*

carving knife *n* trinciante *m*

car wash *n* autolavaggio *m inv*

car worker *n* operaio, -a *mf* dell'industria automobilistica

Casanova /'kæsənəʊvə/ *n* casanova *m inv*

cascade /kæs'keɪd/ *vi* scendere a cascata ● *n* cascata *f*

case¹ /keɪs/ *n* caso *m*; **in any ~** in ogni caso;

in that ~ in questo caso; **just in ~** per sicurezza; **in ~ he comes** nel caso in cui venisse; **in ~ of emergency** in caso d'emergenza

case² *n* (*container*) scatola *f*; (*crate*) cassa *f*; (*for spectacles*) astuccio *m*; (*suitcase*) valigia *f*; (*for display*) vetrina *f*

case history *n Med* cartella *f* clinica

casement window /'keɪsmənt/ *n* finestra *f* a battenti

case: casenotes *npl* pratica *f*. **case study** *n* analisi *f inv*. **casework** *n* **do ~** occuparsi di assistenza sociale

cash /kæʃ/ *n* denaro *m* contante; (*fam: money*) contanti *mpl*; **pay [in] ~** pagare in contanti; **~ on delivery** pagamento alla consegna ● *vt* incassare ⟨*cheque*⟩

■ **cash in on** *vt fam* approfittarsi di

cash: cash-and-carry *n* cash and carry *m inv*. **cash box** *n* cassetta *f* portavalori. **cash card** *n* bancomat® *m inv*. **cash desk** *n* cassa *f*. **cash dispenser** *n* sportello *m* automatico, cassa *f* automatica

cashew /kə'ʃu:/ *n* anacardio *m*

cash flow *n* flusso *m* di cassa; **~ difficulties** difficoltà *fpl* di flusso di cassa; **~ management** gestione *f* del flusso di cassa

cashier /kæ'ʃɪə(r)/ *n* cassiere, -a *mf*

cashmere /'kæʃmɪə(r)/ *n* cachemire *m inv*

cash: cash on delivery *n* pagamento *m* alla consegna. **cashpoint** *n* sportello *m* automatico. **cash register** *n* registratore *m* di cassa

casing /'keɪsɪŋ/ *n* (*of machinery*) rivestimento *m*; (*of gearbox*) scatola *f*; (*of tyre*) copertone *m*

casino /kə'si:nəʊ/ *n* casinò *m inv*

cask /kɑ:sk/ *n* barile *m*

casket /'kɑ:skɪt/ *n* scrigno *m*; (*Am: coffin*) bara *f*

casserole /'kæsərəʊl/ *n* casseruola *f*; (*stew*) stufato *m*

cassette /kə'set/ *n* cassetta *f*

cassette: cassette deck *n* piastra *f* di registrazione. **cassette player** *n* mangiacassette *m inv*. **cassette recorder** *n* registratore *m* (*a cassette*). **cassette tape** *n* cassetta *f*

cassock /'kæsək/ *n* tonaca *f*

cast /kɑ:st/ *n* (*throw*) lancio *m*; (*mould*) forma *f*; *Theat* cast *m inv*; [**plaster**] **~** *Med* ingessatura *f* ● *vt* (*pt/pp* **cast**) dare ⟨*vote*⟩; *Theat* assegnare le parti di ⟨*play*⟩; fondere ⟨*metal*⟩; (*throw*) gettare; (*shed*) sbarazzarsi di; **~ an actor as** dare ad un attore il ruolo di; **~ a glance at** lanciare uno sguardo a

■ **cast off** *vi Naut* sganciare gli ormeggi ● *vt* (*in knitting*) diminuire

■ **cast on** *vt* (*in knitting*) avviare

castanets /kæstə'nets/ *npl* nacchere *fpl*

castaway /'kɑ:stəweɪ/ *n* naufrago, -a *mf*

caste /kɑ:st/ *n* casta *f*

caster /'kɑ:stə(r)/ *n* (*wheel*) rotella *f*

caster sugar *n* zucchero *m* raffinato

casting director /'kɑ:stɪŋ/ *n* direttore *m* del casting

casting vote *n* voto *m* decisivo

cast iron *n* ghisa *f* ● *a* **cast-iron** di ghisa; *fig* solido

castle /'kɑ:sl/ *n* castello *m*; (*in chess*) torre *f*

cast-offs *npl* abiti *mpl* smessi

castor /'kɑ:stə(r)/ *n* (*wheel*) rotella *f*

castor oil *n* olio *m* di ricino

castor sugar *n* zucchero *m* raffinato

castrate /kæ'streɪt/ *vt* castrare

castration /kæ'streɪʃn/ *n* castrazione *f*

castrato /kæs'trɑ:təʊ/ *n* castrato *m*

casual /'kæʒʊəl/ *a* (*chance*) casuale; (*remark*) senza importanza; (*glance*) di sfuggita; (*attitude, approach*) disinvolto; (*chat*) informale; (*clothes*) casual *inv*; (*work*) saltuario; **~ wear** abbigliamento *m* casual

casually /'kæʒʊəlɪ/ *adv* (*dress*) casual; (*meet*) casualmente

casualty /'kæʒʊəltɪ/ *n* (*injured person*) ferito *m*; (*killed*) vittima *f*

casualty [**department**] *n* pronto soccorso *m*

cat /kæt/ *n* gatto *m*; *pej* arpia *f*

catacombs /'kætəku:mz/ *npl* catacombe *fpl*

catalogue /'kætəlɒg/ *n* catalogo *m* ● *vt* catalogare

catalyst /'kætəlɪst/ *n* *Chem* & *fig* catalizzatore *m*

catalytic converter /kætə'lɪtɪk/ *n* *Auto* marmitta *f* catalitica

catamaran /kætəmə'ræn/ *n* catamarano *m*

catapult /'kætəpʌlt/ *n* catapulta *f*; (*child's*) fionda *f* ● *vt fig* catapultare

cataract /'kætərækt/ *n* *Med* cataratta *f*

catarrh /kə'tɑ:(r)/ *n* catarro *m*

catastrophe /kə'tæstrəfɪ/ *n* catastrofe *f*

catastrophic /kætə'strɒfɪk/ *a* catastrofico

cat burglar *n* *Br* scassinatore, -trice *mf* acrobata

catch /kætʃ/ *n* (*of fish*) pesca *f*; (*fastener*) fermaglio *m*; (*on door*) fermo *m*; (*on window*) gancio *m*; (*fam: snag*) tranello *m* ● *v* (*pt/pp* **caught**) ● *vt* acchiappare (*ball*); (*grab*) afferrare; prendere (*illness, fugitive, train*); **~ a cold** prendersi un raffreddore; **~ sight of** scorgere; **I caught him stealing** l'ho sorpreso mentre rubava; **~ one's finger in the door** chiudersi il dito nella porta; **~ sb's eye** *or* **attention** attirare l'attenzione di qcno ● *vi* (*fire:*) prendere; (*get stuck*) impigliarsi

■ **catch on** *vi fam* (*understand*) afferrare; (*become popular*) diventare popolare

■ **catch out** *vt* (*show to be wrong*) prendere in castagna

■ **catch up** *vt* raggiungere ● *vi* recuperare; (*runner:*) riguadagnare terreno; **~ up with** raggiungere (*sb*); mettersi in pari con (*work*)

catch-22 situation *n* situazione *f* senza uscita

catch-all *a* (*term*) polivalente; (*clause*) che comprende tutte le possibilità

catching /'kætʃɪŋ/ *a* contagioso

catchment area /'kætʃmənt/ *n* bacino *m* d'utenza

catchphrase /'kætʃfreɪz/ *n* tormentone *m*

catchword /'kætʃwɜːd/ *n* slogan *m inv*

catchy /'kætʃɪ/ *a* (**-ier, -iest**) orecchiabile

catechism /'kætɪkɪzm/ *n* catechismo *m*

categorical /kætɪ'gɒrɪkl/ *a* categorico

categorically /kætə'gɒrɪlkɪ/ *adv* categoricamente

category /'kætɪgərɪ/ *n* categoria *f*

cater /'keɪtə(r)/ *vi* **~ for** provvedere a (*needs*); *fig* venire incontro alle esigenze di ● *vt* occuparsi del rinfresco di (*party*)

caterer /'keɪtərə(r)/ *n* persona *f* che si occupa di ristorazione

catering /'keɪtərɪŋ/ *n* (*trade*) ristorazione *f*; (*food*) rinfresco *m*

caterpillar /'kætəpɪlə(r)/ *n* bruco *m*

caterwaul /'kætəwɔːl/ *vi* miagolare

cat: **catfish** *n* pesce *m* gatto. **catflap** *n* gattaiola *f*. **catgut** *n* catgut *m inv*

cathedral /kə'θiːdrl/ *n* cattedrale *f*

Catherine wheel /'kæθ(ə)rɪn/ *n* girandola *f*

catheter /'kæθɪtə(r)/ *n* catetere *m*

cathode-ray tube /kæθəʊd'reɪ/ *n* tubo *m* a raggi catodici

Catholic /'kæθəlɪk/ *a* & *n* cattolico, -a *mf*

Catholicism /kə'θɒlɪsɪzm/ *n* cattolicesimo *m*

catkin /'kætkɪn/ *n* *Bot* amento *m*

cat: **cat litter** *n* lettiera *f* del gatto. **catnap** *vi* fare un pisolino ● *n* pisolino *m*. **cat-o'-nine-tails** *n* gatto *m* a nove code. **cat's-eye** *n* *Br* catarifrangente *m* (*inserito nell'asfalto*). **catsuit** *n* tuta *f*

cattery /'kætərɪ/ *n* pensione *f* per gatti

cattle /'kæt(ə)l/ *npl* bestiame *msg*

cattle: **cattle grid** *n* recinto *m* metallico che impedisce al bestiame di accedere a una strada. **cattle market** *n* mercato *m* del bestiame; (*fig fam: for sexual encounters*) locale *m* dove la gente va per rimorchiare. **cattle shed** *n* stalla *f*

catty /'kætɪ/ *a* (**-ier, -iest**) dispettoso

catwalk /'kætwɔːk/ *n* passerella *f*

Caucasian /kɔ:'keɪʒ(ə)n/ *n* (*Geog: inhabitant*) caucasico, -a *mf*; (*white person*) bianco, -a *mf* ● *a* *Geog* caucasico; (*race, man*) bianco

caught /kɔːt/ *see* **catch**

cauldron /'kɔːldrən/ *n* calderone *m*

cauliflower /'kɒlɪflaʊə(r)/ *n* cavolfiore *m*

cauliflower cheese *n* cavolfiori *mpl* gratinati

causal /'kɔːzəl/ *a* causale

cause /kɔːz/ *n* causa *f*; (*reason*) motivo *m*; **good ~** buona causa ● *vt* causare; **~ sb to do sth** far fare qcsa a qcno

causeway /'kɔːzweɪ/ *n* strada *f* sopraelevata

caustic /'kɔːstɪk/ *a* caustico

cauterize /'kɔːtəraɪz/ *vt* cauterizzare

caution /'kɔːʃn/ *n* cautela *f*; (*warning*) ammonizione *f* ● *vt* mettere in guardia; *Jur* ammonire

cautious /'kɔːʃəs/ *a* cauto

cautiously /'kɔːʃəslɪ/ *adv* cautamente

cavalcade /kævəl'keɪd/ *n* sfilata *f*

cavalier /kævə'lɪə(r)/ *a* noncurante ● *n* **C~**

sostenitore, -trice mf di Carlo I durante la guerra civile inglese

cavalry /'kævəlrı/ *n* cavalleria *f*

cave /keɪv/ *n* caverna *f*

■ **cave in** *vi* ⟨*roof:*⟩ crollare; (*fig: give in*) capitolare

caveat /'kævɪæt/ *n* avvertimento *m*

cave: cave dweller *n* cavernicolo, -a *mf.* **caveman** *n* cavernicolo *m.* **cave painting** *n* pittura *f* rupestre

caver /'keɪvə(r)/ *n* speleologo, -a *mf*

cavern /'kævən/ *n* caverna *f*

caviare /'kævɪɑ:(r)/ *n* caviale *m*

caving /'keɪvɪŋ/ *n* speleologia *f*

cavity /'kævətɪ/ *n* cavità *f inv*; (*in tooth*) carie *f inv*

cavity wall insulation *n* isolamento *m* per muri a intercapedine

cavort /kə'vɔːt/ *vi* saltellare

caw /kɔː/ *n* (*noise*) gracchio *m* ● *vi* gracchiare

cayenne pepper /'kaɪen/ *n* pepe *m* di Caienna

cayman /'keɪmən/ *n* caimano *m*

CB *n abbr* (**Citizens' Band**) CB *f inv* ● *attrib* ⟨*equipment, radio, wavelength*⟩ CB

cc *n abbr* (**cubic centimetres**) cc *m inv*

CCTV *abbr* (**closed-circuit television**) televisione *f* a circuito chiuso

CD *n abbr* (**Civil Defence**) difesa *f* civile; *abbr* (**compact disc**) CD *m inv*; *Am abbr* (**Congressional District**) circoscrizione *f* del Congresso; *abbr* (**corps diplomatique**) CD *m inv*

CD player *n* lettore *m* [di] compact, lettore *m* di CD

CD-Rom /si:di:'rɒm/ *n* CD-Rom *m inv*

CD-Rom drive *n* lettore *m* CD-Rom

cease /si:s/ *n* **without** ~ incessantemente ● *vt/i* cessare

ceasefire /'si:sfaɪə(r)/ *n* cessate il fuoco *m inv*

ceaseless /'si:slɪs/ *a* incessante

ceaselessly /'si:slɪslɪ/ *adv* incessantemente

cedar /'si:də(r)/ *n* cedro *m*

cede /si:d/ *vt* cedere

ceiling /'si:lɪŋ/ *n* soffitto *m*; *fig* tetto *m* [massimo]

celebrate /'selɪbreɪt/ *vt* festeggiare ⟨*birthday, victory*⟩ ● *vi* far festa

celebrated /'selɪbreɪtɪd/ *a* celebre (**for** per)

celebration /selɪ'breɪʃn/ *n* celebrazione *f*

celebrity /sɪ'lebrətɪ/ *n* celebrità *f inv*

celeriac /sɪ'lerɪæk/ *n* sedano *m* rapa

celery /'selərɪ/ *n* sedano *m*

celestial /sɪ'lestɪəl/ *a* celestiale

celibacy /'selɪbəsɪ/ *n* celibato *m*

celibate /'selɪbət/ *a* ⟨*man*⟩ celibe; ⟨*woman*⟩ nubile

cell /sel/ *n* cella *f*; *Biol* cellula *f*

cellar /'selə(r)/ *n* scantinato *m*; (*for wine*) cantina *f*

cellist /'tʃelɪst/ *n* violoncellista *mf*

cello /'tʃeləʊ/ *n* violoncello *m*

Cellophane® /'seləfeɪn/ *n* cellofan* *m inv*

cellphone /'selfəʊn/ *n* [telefono *m*] cellulare *m*

cellular phone /seljʊlə'fəʊn/ *n* [telefono *m*] cellulare *m*

cellulite /'seljʊlaɪt/ *n* cellulite *f*

celluloid /'seljʊlɔɪd/ *n* celluloide *f*

Celsius /'selsɪəs/ *a* Celsius

Celt /kelt/ *n* celta *mf*

Celtic /'keltɪk/ *a* celtico

cement /sɪ'ment/ *n* cemento *m*; (*adhesive*) mastice *m* ● *vt* cementare; (*stick*) attaccare col mastice; *fig* consolidare

cement mixer *n* betoniera *f*

cemetery /'semətrɪ/ *n* cimitero *m*

cenotaph /'senətæf/ *n* cenotafio *m*

censor /'sensə(r)/ *n* censore *m* ● *vt* censurare

censorship /'sensəʃɪp/ *n* censura *f*

censure /'senʃə(r)/ *n* biasimo *m* ● *vt* biasimare

census /'sensəs/ *n* censimento *m*

cent /sent/ *n* (*coin*) centesimo *m*

centenary /sen'ti:nərɪ/ *n*, *Am* **centennial** /sen'tenɪəl/ *n* centenario *m*

center /'sentə(r)/ *n Am* = **centre**

centigrade /'sentɪgreɪd/ *a* centigrado

centilitre /'sentɪli:tə(r)/ *n* centilitro *m*

centimetre /'sentɪmi:tə(r)/ *n* centimetro *m*

centipede /'sentɪpi:d/ *n* centopiedi *m inv*

central /'sentrəl/ *a* centrale

central heating *n* riscaldamento *m* autonomo

centralize /'sentrəlaɪz/ *vt* centralizzare

central locking *n* *Auto* chiusura *f* centralizzata

centrally /'sentrəlɪ/ *adv* al centro; ~ **heated** con riscaldamento autonomo

central: central nervous system *n* sistema *m* nervoso centrale. **central processing unit** *n* *Comput* unità *f inv* centrale di elaborazione. **central reservation** *n* *Auto* banchina *f* spartitraffico *inv*

centre /'sentə(r)/ *n* centro *m* ● *v* (*pt/pp* **centred**) ● *vt* centrare ● *vi* ~ **on** *fig* incentrarsi su

centre: centrefold *n* (*pin-up picture*) paginone *m*; (*model*) pin-up *f inv.* **centre forward** *n* centravanti *m inv.* **centre half** *n* *Sport* centromediano *m.* **centre of gravity** *n* centro *m* di gravità. **centrepiece** *n* (*of table*) centrotavola *m*; (*fig: of exhibition*) pezzo *m* forte. **centre spread** *n* paginone *m.* **centre stage** *n* *Theat* centro *m* della scena; **stand** ~ ~ tenersi al centro della scena; **take/occupy** ~ ~ *fig* essere/mettersi in primo piano

centrifugal /sentrɪ'fjʊgl/ *a* ~ **force** forza *f* centrifuga

century /'sentʃərɪ/ *n* secolo *m*

CEO *n abbr* (**Chief Executive Officer**) *n* direttore, -trice *mf* generale

ceramic /sɪ'ræmɪk/ *a* ceramico

ceramics /sɪ'ræmɪks/ *n* (*art*) ceramica *fsg*; (*objects*) ceramiche *fpl*

cereal /'sɪərɪəl/ *n* cereale *m*

cerebral /'serɪbrl/ *a* cerebrale
cerebral palsy /'pɔ:lzɪ/ *n* paralisi *f* cerebrale
ceremonial /serɪ'məʊnɪəl/ *a* da cerimonia ● *n* cerimoniale *m*
ceremonially /serɪ'məʊnɪəlɪ/ *adv* secondo il rituale
ceremonious /serɪ'məʊnɪəs/ *a* cerimonioso
ceremoniously /serɪ'məʊnɪəslɪ/ *adv* in modo cerimonioso
ceremony /'serɪmənɪ/ *n* cerimonia *f*; **without ~** senza cerimonie
cert /sɜ:t/ *n Br fam* **it's a [dead] ~!** ci puoi scommettere!
certain /'sɜ:tn/ *a* certo; **for ~** di sicuro; **make ~** accertarsi ; **he is ~ to win** è certo di vincere; **it's not ~ whether he'll come** non è sicuro che venga
certainly /'sɜ:tnlɪ/ *adv* certamente; **~ not!** no di certo!
certainty /'sɜ:tntɪ/ *n* certezza *f*; **it's a ~** è una cosa certa
certifiable /'sɜ:tɪfaɪəbl/ *a* ‹verifiable statement, evidence› dimostrabile; (*mad*) pazzo
certificate /sə'tɪfɪkət/ *n* certificato *m*
certify /'sɜ:tɪfaɪ/ *vt* (*pt/pp* -**ied**) certificare; (*declare insane*) dichiarare malato di mente
certitude /'sɜ:tɪtju:d/ *n* certezza *f*
cervical /'sɜ:vɪkl/ *a* cervicale
cervix /'sɜ:vɪks/ *n* cervice *f* uterina, collo *m* dell'utero
cessation /se'seɪʃn/ *n* cessazione *f*
cesspool /'sespu:l/ *n* pozzo *m* nero
cf. *abbr* (**compare**) cf, cfr
CFC *n abbr* (**chlorofluorocarbon**) CFC *m inv*
CFE *abbr* **College of Further Education**
chafe /tʃeɪf/ *vt* irritare
chaff /tʃɑ:f/ *n* pula *f*
chaffinch /'tʃæfɪntʃ/ *n* fringuello *m*
chagrin /'ʃægrɪn/ *n* **much to his ~** con suo grande dispiacere
chain /tʃeɪn/ *n* catena *f* ● *vt* incatenare ‹prisoner›; attaccare con la catena ‹dog› (**to** a)
■ **chain up** *vt* legare alla catena ‹dog›
chain: **chain gang** *n* gruppo *m* di prigionieri incatenati. **chain letter** *n* lettera *f* della catena di Sant'Antonio. **chain mail** *n* cotta *f* di maglia. **chain reaction** *n* reazione *f* a catena. **chain saw** *n* motosega *f*. **chain-smoke** *vi* fumare una sigaretta dopo l'altra. **chain-smoker** *n* fumatore, -trice *mf* accanito, -a. **chain store** *n* negozio *m* appartenente a una catena
chair /tʃeə(r)/ *n* sedia *f*; *Univ* cattedra *f* ● *vt* presiedere
chairlift /'tʃeəlɪft/ *n* seggiovia *f*
chairman /'tʃeəmən/ *n* presidente *m*; **~ and managing director** presidente *m* direttore generale
chairperson /'tʃeəpɜ:s(ə)n/ *n* presidente *m*, -essa *f*
chairwoman /'tʃeəwʊmən/ *n* presidentessa *f*

chalet /'ʃæleɪ/ *n* chalet *m inv*; (*in holiday camp*) bungalow *m inv*
chalice /'tʃælɪs/ *n Relig* calice *m*
chalk /tʃɔ:k/ *n* gesso *m*
chalky /'tʃɔ:kɪ/ *a* gessoso
challenge /'tʃælɪndʒ/ *n* sfida *f*; *Mil* intimazione *f* ● *vt* sfidare; *Mil* intimare il chi va là a; *fig* mettere in dubbio ‹statement›
challenger /'tʃælɪndʒə(r)/ *n* sfidante *mf*
challenging /'tʃælɪndʒɪŋ/ *a* ‹job› impegnativo
chamber /'tʃeɪmbə(r)/ *n* **C~ of Commerce** camera *f* di commercio
chamber: **chambermaid** *n* cameriera *f* [d'albergo]. **chamber music** *n* musica *f* da camera. **Chamber of Commerce** *n* Camera *f* di Commercio. **chamber orchestra** *n* orchestra *f* da camera. **chamber pot** *n* vaso *m* da notte
chambers /'tʃeɪmbəz/ *n pl Jur* studio *m* [legale]
chameleon /kə'mi:lɪən/ *n also fig* camaleonte *m*
chamois[1] /'ʃæmwɑ:/ *n inv* (*animal*) camoscio *m*
chamois[2] /'ʃæmɪ/ *n* **~[-leather]** [pelle *f* di] camoscio *m*
champagne /ʃæm'peɪn/ *n* champagne *m inv*
champion /'tʃæmpɪən/ *n Sport* campione *m*; (*of cause*) difensore *m*, difenditrice *f* ● *vt* (*defend*) difendere; (*fight for*) lottare per
championship /'tʃæmpɪənʃɪp/ *n Sport* campionato *m*
chance /tʃɑ:ns/ *n* caso *m*; (*possibility*) possibilità *f inv*; (*opportunity*) occasione *f*; **by ~** per caso; **take a ~** provarci; **give sb a second ~** dare un'altra possibilità a qcno ● *attrib* fortuito ● *vt* **if you ~ to see him** se ti capita di vederlo; **I'll ~ it** *fam* corro il rischio
chancel /'tʃɑ:nsəl/ *n Archit* coro *m*
chancellor /'tʃɑ:nsələ(r)/ *n* cancelliere *m*; *Univ* rettore *m*; **C~ of the Exchequer** ≈ ministro *m* del tesoro
chancy /'tʃɑ:nsɪ/ *a* rischioso
chandelier /ʃændə'lɪə(r)/ *n* lampadario *m*
chandler /'tʃɑ:ndlə(r)/ *n* fornitore *m* navale
change /tʃeɪndʒ/ *n* cambiamento *m*; (*money*) resto *m*; (*small coins*) spiccioli *mpl*; **for a ~** tanto per cambiare; **have a ~ of heart** cambiare idea; **a ~ of clothes** un cambio di vestiti; **~ of address** cambiamento *m* d'indirizzo; **a ~ of scene** *also fig* un cambiamento di scena; **the ~ [of life]** la menopausa ● *vt* cambiare; (*substitute*) scambiare (**for** con); **~ one's clothes** cambiarsi [i vestiti]; **~ trains** cambiare treno ● *vi* cambiare; (~ *clothes*) cambiarsi; **all ~!** stazione terminale!
■ **change down** *vi Auto* passare alla marcia inferiore
■ **change up** *vi Auto* passare alla marcia superiore
changeability /tʃeɪndʒə'bɪlɪtɪ/ *n* (*of weather*) instabilità *f*

changeable /'tʃeɪndʒəbl/ *a* mutevole; ⟨*weather*⟩ variabile

changeless /'tʃeɪndʒlɪs/ *a* ⟨*appearance*⟩ inalterabile; ⟨*character*⟩ costante; ⟨*law, routine*⟩ immutabile

change machine *n* distributore *m* di monete

changeover /'tʃeɪndʒəʊvə(r)/ *n* (*time period*) periodo *m* di transizione; (*transition*) passaggio *m*; (*of leaders*) subentro *m*; (*of employees, guards*) cambio *m*; (*Sport: in relay*) passaggio *m* del testimone; (*Sport: of ends*) cambiamento *m*

changing-room *n* camerino *m*; (*for sports*) spogliatoio *m*

channel /'tʃænl/ *n* canale *m*; **the** [**English**] **C∼** la Manica ● *vt* (*pt/pp* **channelled**) ∼ **one's energies into sth** convogliare le proprie energie in qcsa

channel: channel ferry *n* traghetto *m* attraverso la Manica. **Channel Islands** *npl* Isole *fpl* del Canale. **Channel Tunnel** *n* tunnel *m* *inv* sotto la Manica

chant /tʃɑ:nt/ *n* cantilena *f*; (*of demonstrators*) slogan *m inv* di protesta ● *vt* cantare; ⟨*demonstrators*⟩ gridare ● *vi* ⟨*demonstrators*⟩ gridare slogan di protesta

chaos /'keɪɒs/ *n* caos *m*

chaotic /keɪ'ɒtɪk/ *a* caotico

chap /tʃæp/ *n fam* tipo *m*

chapel /'tʃæpl/ *n* cappella *f*

chaperon /'ʃæpərəʊn/ *n* chaperon *f inv* ● *vt* fare da chaperon a ⟨*sb*⟩

chaplain /'tʃæplɪn/ *n* cappellano *m*

chapped /tʃæpt/ *a* ⟨*skin, lips*⟩ screpolato

chapter /'tʃæptə(r)/ *n* capitolo *m*

char¹ /tʃɑ:(r)/ *n fam* donna *f* delle pulizie

char² *vt* (*pt/pp* **charred**) (*burn*) carbonizzare

character /'kærɪktə(r)/ *n* carattere *m*; (*in novel, play*) personaggio *m*; **that's out of ∼** non è da te/lui; **quite a ∼** *fam* un tipo particolare

character actor *n* caratterista *mf*

character assassination *n* denigrazione *f*

characteristic /kærəktə'rɪstɪk/ *a* caratteristico ● *n* caratteristica *f*

characteristically /kærəktə'rɪstɪlkɪ/ *adv* tipicamente

characterization /kærɪktəraɪ'zeɪʃn/ *n* caratterizzazione *f*

characterize /'kærɪktəraɪz/ *vt* caratterizzare

character reference *n* referenze *fpl* (*relative al carattere*)

charade /ʃə'rɑ:d/ *n* farsa *f*; ∼**s** sciarada *fsg*

charcoal /'tʃɑ:kəʊl/ *n* carbonella *f*

charge /tʃɑ:dʒ/ *n* (*cost*) prezzo *m*; *Electr, Mil* carica *f*; *Jur* accusa *f*; **free of ∼** gratuito; **be in ∼** essere responsabile (**of** di); **take ∼** assumersi la responsabilità; **take ∼ of** occuparsi di ● *vt* far pagare ⟨*fee*⟩; far pagare a ⟨*person*⟩; *Electr, Mil* caricare; *Jur* accusare (**with** di); ∼ **sb for sth** far pagare qcsa a qcno; **what do you ∼?** quanto prende?; ∼ **it to my account** lo addebiti sul mio conto ● *vi* (*attack*) caricare

charge card *n* (*credit card*) carta *f* di addebito; (*store card*) carta *f* di credito [di un negozio]

charged /tʃɑ:dʒd/ *a Phys* carico; **emotionally ∼** ⟨*atmosphere*⟩ carico di emozione

chargé d'affaires /ʃɑ:ʒeɪdæ'feə(r)/ *n* incaricato *m* d'affari

charge hand *n* caposquadra *mf*

charge nurse *n* caposala *mf*

char-grilled /-'grɪld/ *a* alla brace

chariot /'tʃærɪət/ *n* cocchio *m*

charisma /kə'rɪzmə/ *n* carisma *m*

charismatic /kærɪz'mætɪk/ *a* carismatico

charitable /'tʃærɪtəbl/ *a* caritatevole; (*kind*) indulgente

charity /'tʃærɪtɪ/ *n* carità *f*; (*organization*) associazione *f* di beneficenza; **concert given for ∼** concerto *m* di beneficenza; **live on ∼** vivere di elemosina

charity: charity box *n* (*in church*) cassetta *f* delle offerte. **charity shop** *n* negozio *m* dell'usato a scopo di beneficenza. **charity work** *n* lavoro *m* volontario (*per beneficenza*)

charlady /'tʃɑ:leɪdɪ/ *n Br* donna *f* delle pulizie

charlatan /'ʃɑ:lətən/ *n* ciarlatano, -a *mf*

charm /tʃɑ:m/ *n* fascino *m*; (*object*) ciondolo *m* ● *vt* affascinare

charmer /'tʃɑ:mə(r)/ *n* **he's a real ∼** è un vero seduttore

charming /'tʃɑ:mɪŋ/ *a* affascinante

charmingly /'tʃɑ:mɪŋlɪ/ *adv* in modo affascinante

chart /tʃɑ:t/ *n* carta *f* nautica; (*table*) tabella *f*

charter /'tʃɑ:tə(r)/ *n* ∼ [**flight**] [volo *m*] charter *m inv* ● *vt* noleggiare

chartered: chartered accountant *n* commercialista *mf*. **chartered flight** *n Br* volo *m* charter *inv*. **chartered surveyor** *n Br* perito *m* edile

charter plane *n Br* charter *m inv*

charwoman /'tʃɑ:wʊmən/ *n* donna *f* delle pulizie

chase /tʃeɪs/ *n* inseguimento *m*; **give ∼** mettersi all'inseguimento ● *vt* inseguire

■ **chase away, chase off** *vt* cacciare via

■ **chase up** *vt fam* cercare

chaser /'tʃeɪsə(r)/ *n* (*fam: drink*) liquore *m* bevuto dopo la birra

chasm /'kæz(ə)m/ *n* abisso *m*

chassis /'ʃæsɪ/ *n* (*pl* **chassis** /'ʃæsɪz/) telaio *m*

chaste /tʃeɪst/ *a* casto

chasten /'tʃeɪs(ə)n/ *vt* castigare; **they looked suitably ∼ed** avevano l'aria mortificata

chastise /tʃæ'staɪz/ *vt* castigare

chastity /'tʃæstɪtɪ/ *n* castità *f*

chat /tʃæt/ *n* chiacchierata *f*; **have a ∼ with** fare quattro chiacchere con ● *vi* (*pt/pp* **chatted**) chiacchierare

■ **chat up** *vt* abbordare

chat show *n* talk show *m inv*

chattel /'tʃæt(ə)l/ *n Jur* **goods and ~s** beni *mpl* mobili

chatter /'tʃætə(r)/ *n* chiacchiere *fpl* ● *vi* chiacchierare; ‹teeth:› battere

chatterbox /'tʃætəbɒks/ *n fam* chiacchierone, -a *mf*

chatty /'tʃætɪ/ *a* (**-ier**, **-iest**) chiacchierone; ‹style› familiare

chauffeur /'ʃəʊfə(r)/ *n* autista *mf*

chauvinism /'ʃəʊvɪnɪzm/ *n* sciovinismo *m*

chauvinist /'ʃəʊvɪnɪst/ *n* sciovinista *mf*. **male ~** *fam* maschilista *m*

cheap /tʃiːp/ *a* a buon mercato; ‹rate› economico; ‹vulgar› grossolano; (of poor quality) scadente ● *adv* a buon mercato

cheapen /'tʃiːp(ə)n/ *vt* **~ oneself** screditarsi

cheaply /'tʃiːplɪ/ *adv* a buon mercato

cheap rate *a & adv Teleph* a tariffa ridotta

cheat /tʃiːt/ *n* imbroglione, -a *mf*; (at cards) baro *m* ● *vt* imbrogliare; **~ sb out of sth** sottrarre qcsa a qcno con l'inganno ● *vi* imbrogliare; (at cards) barare

■ **cheat on** *vt fam* tradire ‹wife›

check¹ /tʃek/ *a* ‹pattern› a quadri ● *n* disegno *m* a quadri

check² *n* verifica *f*; (of tickets) controllo *m*; (in chess) scacco *m*; (Am: bill) conto *m*; (Am: cheque) assegno *m*; (Am: tick) segnetto *m*; **keep a ~ on** controllare; **keep in ~** tenere sotto controllo ● *vt* verificare; controllare ‹tickets›; (restrain) contenere; (stop) bloccare ● *vi* controllare; **~ on sth** controllare qcsa

■ **check in** *vi* registrarsi all'arrivo (in albergo); *Aeron* fare il check-in ● *vt* registrare all'arrivo (in albergo)

■ **check out** *vi* (of hotel) saldare il conto ● *vt* (fam: investigate) controllare

■ **check up** *vi* accertarsi

■ **check up on** *vt* prendere informazioni su

checked /tʃekt/ *a* a quadri

checkers /'tʃekəz/ *n Am* dama *f*

check-in *n* accettazione *f*, check-in *m inv*

check-in desk *n* banco *m* dell'accettazione, banco *m* del check-in

check-in time *n* check-in *m inv*

checking account /'tʃekɪŋ/ *n Am* conto *m* corrente

check: checklist *n* lista *f* di controllo. **check mark** *n Am* segnetto *m*. **checkmate** *int* scacco matto!. **checkout** *n* (in supermarket) cassa *f*. **checkout assistant, checkout operator** *n Br* cassiere, -a *mf*. **checkpoint** *n* posto *m* di blocco. **checkroom** *n Am* deposito *m* bagagli. **check-up** *n Med* visita *f* di controllo, check-up *m inv*

cheddar /'tʃedə(r)/ *n formaggio m semistagionato*

cheek /tʃiːk/ *n* guancia *f*; (impudence) sfacciataggine *f*

cheekbone /'tʃiːkbəʊn/ *n* zigomo *m*

cheekily /'tʃiːkɪlɪ/ *adv* sfacciatamente

cheeky /'tʃiːkɪ/ *a* sfacciato

cheep /tʃiːp/ *vi* pigolare

cheer /tʃɪə(r)/ *n* evviva *m inv*; **three ~s** tre

urrà; **~s!** salute!; (goodbye) arrivederci!; (thanks) grazie! ● *vt/i* acclamare

■ **cheer up** *vt* tirare su [di morale] ● *vi* tirarsi su [di morale]; **~ up!** su con la vita!

cheerful /'tʃɪəfʊl/ *a* allegro

cheerfully /'tʃɪəfʊlɪ/ *adv* allegramente; **I could ~ strangle him!** lo strangolerei volentieri!

cheerfulness /'tʃɪəfʊlnɪs/ *n* allegria *f*

cheerily /'tʃɪərɪlɪ/ *adv* allegramente

cheering /'tʃɪərɪŋ/ *n* acclamazione *f*

cheerio /tʃɪərɪ'əʊ/ *int fam* arrivederci

cheerleader /'tʃɪəliːdə(r)/ *n* leader *mf* dei tifosi

cheerless /'tʃɪəlɪs/ *a* triste, tetro

cheery /'tʃɪərɪ/ *a* allegro

cheese /tʃiːz/ *n* formaggio *m*

■ **cheese off** *vt fam* **be ~d off with one's job** essere stufo del proprio lavoro; **I'm really ~d off about it** ne ho le scatole piene

cheese: cheeseboard *n* (object) vassoio *m* dei formaggi; (selection) piatto *m* di formaggi. **cheeseburger** *n* cheeseburger *m inv*. **cheesecake** *n* dolce al formaggio. **cheesecloth** *n* mussola *f*, tela *f* indiana. **cheese counter** *n* banco *m* dei formaggi

cheesy /'tʃiːzɪ/ *a* ‹smell› di formaggio; ‹grin› smagliante

cheetah /'tʃiːtə/ *n* ghepardo *m*

chef /ʃef/ *n* cuoco, -a *mf*, chef *mf inv*

chemical /'kemɪk/ *a* chimico ● *n* prodotto *m* chimico

chemically /'kemɪklɪ/ *adv* chimicamente

chemise /ʃə'miːz/ *n* (undergarment) sottoveste *f inv*; (dress) chemisier *m inv*

chemist /'kemɪst/ *n* (pharmacist) farmacista *mf*; (scientist) chimico, -a *mf*

chemistry /'kemɪstrɪ/ *n* chimica *f*

chemist's [**shop**] *n* farmacia *f*

chemotherapy /kiːməʊ'θerəpɪ/ *n* chemioterapia *f*

cheque /tʃek/ *n* assegno *m*

chequebook /'tʃekbʊk/ *n* libretto *m* degli assegni

cheque card *n* carta *f* assegni

chequer /'tʃekə(r)/ *n* (square) scacco *m*; (pattern) motivo *m* a scacchi; (in game) pedina *f*

chequered /'tʃekəd/ *a* (patterned) a scacchi; ‹fig: career, history› movimentato

chequers /'tʃekəz/ *n* dama *f*

cherish /'tʃerɪʃ/ *vt* curare teneramente; (love) avere caro; nutrire ‹hope›

cherry /'tʃerɪ/ *n* ciliegia *f*; (tree) ciliegio *m*

cherry brandy *n* cherry-brandy *m inv*

cherry tree *n* ciliegio *m*

cherub /'tʃerəb/ *n* cherubino *m*

chervil /'tʃɜːvɪl/ *n* cerfoglio *m*

chess /tʃes/ *n* scacchi *mpl*

chess: chessboard *n* scacchiera *f*. **chessman** *n* pezzo *m* degli scacchi. **chessplayer** *n* scacchista *mf*. **chess set** *n* scacchi *mpl*

chest /tʃest/ *n* petto *m*; (box) cassapanca *f*; **get sth off one's ~** *fig* levarsi un peso [dallo stomaco]

chest freezer *n* freezer *m inv* orizzontale, congelatore *m* orizzontale

chestnut /'tʃesnʌt/ *n* castagna *f*; *(tree)* castagno *m*

chest of drawers *n* cassettone *m*, comò *m inv*

chesty /'tʃestɪ/ *a* ‹person› che soffre di bronchite; ‹cough› bronchitico

chew /tʃuː/ *vt* masticare

■ **chew over** *vt (fam: think about carefully)* rimuginare su

chewing gum /'tʃuːɪŋ/ *n* gomma *f* da masticare

chewy /'tʃuːɪ/ *a* ‹meat› legnoso; ‹toffee› gommoso

chic /ʃiːk/ *a* chic *inv*

chick /tʃɪk/ *n* pulcino *m*; *(fam: girl)* ragazza *f*

chicken /'tʃɪkn/ *n* pollo *m* ● *attrib* ‹soup, casserole› di pollo ● *a fam* fifone

■ **chicken out** *vi fam* he ~ed out gli è venuta fifa

chicken: chicken breast *n* petto *m* di pollo. **chicken curry** *n* pollo *m* al curry. **chicken feed** *n* mangime *m* per i polli; *(fam: paltry sum)* miseria *f*. **chicken livers** *npl* fegatini *mpl* di pollo. **chicken noodle soup** *n* vermicelli *mpl* in brodo di pollo. **chickenpox** *n* varicella *f*. **chicken wire** *n* rete *f* metallica *(a maglia esagonale)*

chickpea /'tʃɪkpiː/ *n* cece *m*

chicory /'tʃɪkərɪ/ *n* cicoria *f*

chief /tʃiːf/ *a* principale ● *n* capo *m*

chief executive officer *n* direttore, -trice *mf* generale

chief inspector *n (Br: of police)* ispettore *m* capo

chiefly /'tʃiːflɪ/ *adv* principalmente

chief superintendent *n (Br: of police)* commissario *m* capo

chiffon /'ʃɪfɒn/ *n* chiffon *m* ● *a* ‹dress, scarf› di chiffon

chilblain /'tʃɪlbleɪn/ *n* gelone *m*

child /tʃaɪld/ *n (pl* ~ren*)* bambino, -a *mf*; *(son/daughter)* figlio, -a *mf*

child: child abuse *n* violenza *f* sui minori; *(sexual)* violenza *f* sessuale sui minori. **childbearing** *n* gravidanza *f*; **of ~ age** in età feconda. **child benefit** *n Br* assegni *mpl* familiari. **childbirth** *n* parto *m*. **childcare** *n (bringing up children)* educazione *f* dei bambini; *(nurseries etc)* strutture *fpl* di assistenza ai bambini

childhood /'tʃaɪldhʊd/ *n* infanzia *f*

childish /'tʃaɪldɪʃ/ *a* infantile

childishness /'tʃaɪldɪʃnɪs/ *n* puerilità *f*

childless /'tʃaɪldlɪs/ *a* senza figli

childlike /'tʃaɪldlaɪk/ *a* ingenuo

child: child-minder *n* baby-sitter *mf inv*. **child molester** *n* molestatore, -trice *mf* di bambini. **child prodigy** *n* bambino prodigio. **child-proof** *a (container)* a prova di bambino; **~ lock** sicura *f* a prova di bambino

children /'tʃɪldrən/ *npl see* **child**

children's home *n* istituto *m* per l'infanzia

Chile /'tʃɪlɪ/ *n* Cile *m*

Chilean /'tʃɪlɪən/ *a & n* cileno, -a *mf*

chill /tʃɪl/ *n* freddo *m*; *(illness)* infreddatura *f* ● *vt* raffreddare

chilli /'tʃɪlɪ/ *n (pl* -es*)* ~ [**pepper**] peperoncino *m*

chilly /'tʃɪlɪ/ *a* freddo

chime /tʃaɪm/ *vi* suonare

chimera /kɪ'mɪərə/ *n (beast, idea)* chimera *f*

chimney /'tʃɪmnɪ/ *n* camino *m*

chimney: chimneybreast *n* bocca *f* del camino. **chimney-pot** *n* comignolo *m*. **chimney-sweep** *n* spazzacamino *m*

chimp /tʃɪmp/ *n fam* scimpanzé *m*

chimpanzee /tʃɪmpæn'ziː/ *n* scimpanzé *m inv*

chin /tʃɪn/ *n* mento *m*

China /'tʃaɪnə/ *n* Cina *f*

china *n* porcellana *f*

China: China Sea *n* Mar *m* Cinese. **China tea** *n* tè *m inv* cinese. **Chinatown** *n* quartiere *m* cinese

Chinese /tʃaɪ'niːz/ *a & n* cinese *mf*; *(language)* cinese *m*; **the ~** *pl* i cinesi

Chinese lantern *n* lanterna *f* cinese

chink[1] /tʃɪŋk/ *n (slit)* fessura *f*

chink[2] *n (noise)* tintinnio *m* ● *vi* tintinnare

chinos /'tʃiːnəʊz/ *npl* pantaloni *mpl* cachi di cotone

chintz /tʃɪnts/ *n* chintz *m inv*

chip /tʃɪp/ *n (fragment)* scheggia *f*; *(in china, paintwork)* scheggiatura *f*; *Comput* chip *m inv*; *(in gambling)* fiche *f inv*; ~**s** *pl Br Culin* patatine *fpl* fritte; *Am Culin* patatine *fpl*; **have a ~ on one's shoulder** avere un complesso di inferiorità ● *vt (pt/pp* **chipped***) (damage)* scheggiare

■ **chip in** *fam vi* intromettersi; *(with money)* contribuire

chipboard /'tʃɪpbɔːd/ *n* truciolato *m*

chipmunk /'tʃɪpmʌŋk/ *n* tamia *m inv*

chip pan *n* friggitrice *f*

chipped /tʃɪpt/ *a (damaged)* scheggiato

chippings /'tʃɪpɪŋz/ *npl (on road)* breccia *f*; **'loose ~'** 'attenzione: breccia'

chippy /'tʃɪpɪ/ *n (Br fam: chip shop)* negozio *m* di fish and chips

chip shop *n Br* negozio *m* di fish and chips

chiropodist /kɪ'rɒpədɪst/ *n* podiatra *mf inv*

chiropody /kɪ'rɒpədɪ/ *n* podiatria *f*

chirp /tʃɜːp/ *vi* cinguettare; ‹cricket:› fare cri cri

chirpy /'tʃɜːpɪ/ *a fam* pimpante

chisel /'tʃɪzl/ *n* scalpello *m* ● *vt (pt/pp* **chiselled***)* scalpellare

chit /tʃɪt/ *n* bigliettino *m*

chitchat /'tʃɪt(t)tʃæt/ *n fam* chiacchiere *fpl*; **spend one's time in idle ~** *fam* perdere tempo in chiacchiere

chivalrous /'ʃɪvlrəs/ *a* cavalleresco

chivalrously /'ʃɪvlrəslɪ/ *adv* con cavalleria

chivalry /'ʃɪvlrɪ/ *n* cavalleria *f*

chives /tʃaɪvz/ *npl* erba *f* cipollina

chlorine /'klɔːriːn/ *n* cloro *m*

chlorofluorocarbon /klɔːrəʊflʊərəʊˈkɑː-b(ə)n/ n clorofluorocarburo m

chloroform /ˈklɒrəfɔːm/ n cloroformio m

chlorophyll /ˈklɒrəfɪl/ n clorofilla f

choc ice n Br gelato m ricoperto di cioccolato

chock /tʃɒk/ n zeppa f

chock-a-block /tʃɒkəˈblɒk/, **chock-full** /tʃɒkˈfʊl/ a pieno zeppo

chocolate /ˈtʃɒkələt/ n cioccolato m; (drink) cioccolata f; **a ~** un cioccolatino

choice /tʃɔɪs/ n scelta f ● a scelto

choir /ˈkwaɪə(r)/ n coro m

choirboy /ˈkwaɪəbɔɪ/ n corista m

choirgirl /ˈkwaɪəgɜːl/ n corista f

choke /tʃəʊk/ n Auto aria f ● vt/i soffocare; **~d on a fishbone** mi è rimasta in gola una lisca

choker /ˈtʃəʊkə(r)/ n girocollo m

cholera /ˈkɒlərə/ n colera m

cholesterol /kəˈlestərɒl/ n colesterolo m

■ **chomp on** /tʃɒmp/ vi fam masticare rumorosamente

choose /tʃuːz/ vt/i (pt chose, pp chosen) scegliere; **~ to do sth** scegliere di fare qcsa; **as you ~** come vuoi

choos[e]y /ˈtʃuːzɪ/ a fam difficile

chop /tʃɒp/ n (blow) colpo m (d'ascia); Culin costata f; **get the ~** ⟨fam: employee⟩ essere licenziato; ⟨project:⟩ essere bocciato ● vt (pt/pp chopped) tagliare

■ **chop down** vt abbattere ⟨tree⟩

■ **chop off** vt spaccare

chopper /ˈtʃɒpə(r)/ n accetta f; fam elicottero m

chopping: chopping block n ceppo m; **put one's head on the ~** ~ fig esporsi a rischi. **chopping board** n tagliere m. **chopping knife** n coltello m

choppy /ˈtʃɒpɪ/ a increspato

chopsticks /ˈtʃɒpstɪks/ npl bastoncini mpl cinesi

choral /ˈkɔːrəl/ a corale; **~ society** coro m

chord /kɔːd/ n Mus corda f

chore /tʃɔː(r)/ n corvé f inv; [household] **~s** faccende fpl domestiche

choreographer /kɒrɪˈɒgrəfə(r)/ n coreografo, -a mf

choreography /kɒrɪˈɒgrəfɪ/ n coreografia f

chorister /ˈkɒrɪstə(r)/ n corista mf

chortle /ˈtʃɔːtl/ vi ridacchiare

chorus /ˈkɔːrəs/ n coro m; (of song) ritornello m

chorus girl n ballerina f di varietà

chose, chosen /tʃəʊz, ˈtʃəʊzn/ see **choose**

chowder /ˈtʃaʊdə(r)/ n zuppa m di pesce

chow mein /tʃaʊˈmeɪn/ n piatto m cinese di spaghetti fritti con gamberetti, ecc. e verdure

Christ /kraɪst/ n Cristo m; **~ Almighty!** fam porca miseria!

christen /ˈkrɪs(ə)n/ vt battezzare

christening /ˈkrɪsnɪŋ/ n battesimo m

Christian /ˈkrɪstʃən/ a & n cristiano, -a mf

Christianity /krɪstɪˈænətɪ/ n cristianesimo m

Christian name n nome m di battesimo

Christmas /ˈkrɪsməs/ n Natale m ● attrib di Natale

Christmas: Christmas box n Br mancia f natalizia. **Christmas card** n biglietto m d'auguri di Natale. **Christmas carol** n canto m natalizio, canto m di Natale. **Christmas cracker** n tubo m di cartone colorato contente una sorpresa. **Christmas Day** n il giorno di Natale. **Christmas Eve** n la vigilia di Natale. **Christmas present** n regalo m di Natale. **Christmas stocking** n calza f (per i doni di Babbo Natale). **Christmas tree** n albero m di Natale

chrome /krəʊm/ n, **chromium** /ˈkrəʊmɪəm/ n cromo m

chromium-plated /-ˈpleɪtɪd/ a cromato

chromosome /ˈkrəʊməsəʊm/ n cromosoma m

chronic /ˈkrɒnɪk/ a cronico

chronicle /ˈkrɒnɪk/ n cronaca f

chronological /krɒnəˈlɒdʒɪk/ a cronologico

chronologically /krɒnəˈlɒdʒɪlkɪ/ adv ⟨ordered⟩ in ordine cronologico

chrysalis /ˈkrɪsəlɪs/ n crisalide f

chrysanthemum /krɪˈsænθəməm/ n crisantemo m

chubby /ˈtʃʌbɪ/ a (-ier, -iest) paffuto

chuck /tʃʌk/ vt fam buttare

■ **chuck in** vt fam mollare ⟨job, boyfriend⟩

■ **chuck out** vt fam buttare via ⟨object⟩; buttare fuori ⟨person⟩

■ **chuck up** vt fam = **chuck in**

chuckle /ˈtʃʌk(ə)l/ vi ridacchiare

chuffed /tʃʌft/ a fam felice come una Pasqua

chug /tʃʌg/ vi **the train ~ged into/out of the station** il treno è entrato nella/uscito dalla stazione sbuffando

chum /tʃʌm/ n fam amico, -a mf

chummy /ˈtʃʌmɪ/ a fam **be ~ with** essere amico di

chump /tʃʌmp/ n fam zuccone m, -a f; Culin braciola f

chunk /tʃʌŋk/ n grosso pezzo m

chunky /ˈtʃʌŋkɪ/ a ⟨sweater⟩ di lana grossa; ⟨jewellery⟩ massiccio; ⟨fam: person⟩ tarchiato

Chunnel /ˈtʃʌnl/ n Br fam tunnel m inv sotto la Manica

church /tʃɜːtʃ/ n chiesa f

church hall n sala f parrocchiale

churchyard /ˈtʃɜːtʃjɑːd/ n cimitero m

churlish /ˈtʃɜːlɪʃ/ a sgarbato

churn /tʃɜːn/ n zangola f; (for milk) bidone m

● vt churn out sfornare

chute /ʃuːt/ n scivolo m; (for rubbish) canale m di scarico

chutney /ˈtʃʌtnɪ/ n salsa f piccante a base di frutti e spezie

CID abbr **Criminal Investigation Department**

cider /ˈsaɪdə(r)/ n sidro m

cigar /sɪˈgɑː(r)/ n sigaro m

cigarette /sɪgəˈret/ n sigaretta f

cigarette: cigarette butt, cigarette end

n cicca *f*, mozzicone *m* di sigaretta. **cigarette lighter** *n* accendino *m*

cinch /sɪntʃ/ *n fam* **it's a ~** è un gioco da ragazzi

cinder /'sɪndə(r)/ *n* (*glowing*) brace *f*; **burn sth to a ~** carbonizzare qcsa

Cinderella /sɪndə'relə/ *n* cenerentola *f*

cinder track *n* pista *f* di cenere

cine-camera /'sɪnɪ-/ *n* cinepresa *f*

cine-film *n* filmino *m* a passo ridotto

cinema /'sɪnɪmə/ *n* cinema *m inv*

cinema complex *n* cinema *m inv* multisale

cinemagoer /'sɪnɪməgəʊə(r)/ *n* (*spectator*) spettatore, -trice *mf*; (*regular*) cinefilo, -a *mf*

cinematography /sɪnəmə'tɒgrəfɪ/ *n* cinematografia *f*

cinnamon /'sɪnəmən/ *n* cannella *f*

cipher /'saɪfə(r)/ *n* (*code*) cifre *fpl*; *fig* nullità *f inv*

circa /'sɜːkə/ *prep* circa

circle /'sɜːkl/ *n* cerchio *m*; *Theat* galleria *f*; **in a ~** in cerchio ● *vt* girare intorno a; cerchiare ⟨*mistake*⟩ ● *vi* descrivere dei cerchi

circuit /'sɜːkɪt/ *n* circuito *m*; (*lap*) giro *m*

circuit board *n* circuito *m* stampato

circuitous /sə'kjuːɪtəs/ *a* **~ route** percorso *m* lungo e indiretto

circular /'sɜːkjʊlə(r)/ *a* & *n* circolare *f*

circular letter *n* circolare *f*

circular saw *n* sega *f* circolare

circulate /'sɜːkjʊleɪt/ *vt* far circolare ● *vi* circolare

circulation /sɜːkjʊ'leɪʃn/ *n* circolazione *f*; (*of newspaper*) tiratura *f*

circulatory /sɜːkjʊ'leɪtərɪ/ *a Med* circolatorio

circumcise /'sɜːkəmsaɪz/ *vt* circoncidere

circumcision /sɜːkəm'sɪʒn/ *n* circoncisione *f*

circumference /ʃə'kʌmfərəns/ *n* conconferenza *f*

circumflex /'sɜːkəmfleks/ *n* accento *m* circonflesso

circumnavigate /sɜːkəm'nævɪgeɪt/ *vt* doppiare ⟨*cape*⟩; circumnavigare ⟨*world*⟩

circumnavigation /sɜːkəmnævɪ'geɪʃn/ *n* circumnavigazione *f*

circumspect /'sɜːkəmspekt/ *a* circospetto

circumspectly /'sɜːkəmspektlɪ/ *adv* in modo circospetto

circumstance /'sɜːkəmstəns/ *n* circostanza *f*; **~s** *pl* (*financial*) condizioni *fpl* finanziarie

circumstantial /sɜːkəm'stænʃl/ *a* ⟨*Jur: evidence*⟩ indiziario; (*detailed*) circostanziato

circus /'sɜːkəs/ *n* circo *m*

cirrhosis /sɪ'rəʊsɪs/ *n* cirrosi *f inv*

CIS *abbr* (**Commonwealth of Independent States**) CSI *f*

cistern /'sɪstən/ *n* (*tank*) cisterna *f*; (*of WC*) serbatoio *m*

citadel /'sɪtədəl/ *n* cittadella *f*

cite /saɪt/ *vt* citare

citizen /'sɪtɪzn/ *n* cittadino, -a *mf*; (*of town*) abitante *mf*

citizen: Citizens' Advice Bureau *n* ufficio *m* di consulenza legale gratuita per i cittadini. **citizen's arrest** *n* arresto *m* effettuato da un privato cittadino. **citizens' band** *n Radio* banda *f* cittadina

citizenship /'sɪtɪznʃɪp/ *n* cittadinanza *f*

citric acid /sɪtrɪk'æsɪd/ acido *m* citrico

citrus /'sɪtrəs/ *n* **~** [**fruit**] agrume *m*

city /'sɪtɪ/ *n* città *f inv*; **the C~** la City [di Londra]

city centre *n Br* centro *m* [della città]

city slicker *n fam* cittadino *m* sofisticato

civic /'sɪvɪk/ *a* civico ● **~s** *npl* educazione *fsg* civica

civic centre *n* centro *m* municipale

civil /'ʃɪvl/ *a* civile

civil engineer *n* ingeniere *m* civile

civil engineering *n* ingegneria *f* civile

civilian /sɪ'vɪljən/ *a* civile; **in ~ clothes** in borghese ● *n* civile *mf*

civility /sɪ'vɪlətɪ/ *n* cortesia *f*

civilization /sɪvɪlaɪ'zeɪʃn/ *n* civiltà *f inv*

civilize /'sɪvɪlaɪz/ *vt* civilizzare

civilized /'sɪvɪlaɪzd/ *a* ⟨*country*⟩ civilizzato; ⟨*person, behaviour*⟩ civile; **become ~** civilizzarsi

civil: civil law *n* diritto *m* civile. **civil liability** *n Jur* responsabilità *f inv* civile. **civil liberty** *n* libertà *f inv* civile

civilly /'sɪvɪlɪ/ *adv* civilmente

civil: civil rights *npl* diritti *mpl* civili ● *attrib* ⟨*march, activist*⟩ per i diritti civili. **civil servant** *n* impiegato, -a *mf* statale. **Civil Service** *n* pubblica amministrazione *f*. **civil war** *n* guerra *f* civile. **civil wedding** *n* matrimonio *m* civile

civvies /'sɪvɪz/ *npl fam* **in ~** in borghese

cl *abbr* (**centilitre(s)**) cl

clad /klæd/ *a* vestito (**in** di)

cladding /'klædɪŋ/ *n* rivestimento *m*

claim /kleɪm/ *n* richiesta *f*; (*right*) diritto *m*; (*assertion*) dichiarazione *f*; **lay ~ to sth** rivendicare qcsa ● *vt* richiedere; reclamare ⟨*lost property*⟩; rivendicare ⟨*ownership*⟩; **~ that** sostenere che

■ **claim back** *vt* reclamare ⟨*money*⟩

claimant /'kleɪmənt/ *n* richiedente *mf*; (*to throne*) pretendente *mf*

clairvoyant /kleə'vɔɪənt/ *n* chiaroveggente *mf*

clam /klæm/ *n Culin* vongola *f*

■ **clam up** *vi* zittirsi

clamber /'klæmbə(r)/ *vi* arrampicarsi

clammy /'klæmɪ/ *a* (**-ier, -iest**) appiccicaticcio

clamour /'klæmə(r)/ *n* (*noise*) clamore *m*; (*protest*) rimostranza *f* ● *vi* **~ for** chiedere a gran voce

clamp /klæmp/ *n* morsa *f* ● *vt* ammorsare; *Auto* mettere i ceppi bloccaruote a

■ **clamp down** *vi fam* essere duro

■ **clamp down on** *vt* reprimere

clan /klæn/ *n* clan *m inv*

clandestine /klæn'destɪn/ *a* clandestino
clang /klæŋ/ *n* suono *m* metallico
clanger /'klæŋə(r)/ *n fam* gaffe *f inv*
clank /klæŋk/ *n* rumore *m* metallico ● *vi* fare un rumore metallico
clannish /'klænɪʃ/ *a* ⟨*pej: family, profession*⟩ chiuso
clap /klæp/ *n* **give sb a ~** applaudire qcno; **~ of thunder** tuono *m* ● *vt/i* (*pt/pp* **clapped**) applaudire; **~ one's hands** applaudire
clapboard /'klæpbɔ:d/ *n Am* rivestimento *m* di legno ● *attrib Am* rivestito di legno
clapped out /klæpt/ *a fam* (*past it*) sfinito; (*exhausted*) stanco morto; ⟨*car, machine*⟩ scassato
clapping /'klæpɪŋ/ *n* applausi *mpl*
claptrap /'klæptræp/ *n fam* sciocchezze *fpl*
claret /'klærət/ *n* claret *m inv*
clarification /klærɪfɪ'keɪʃn/ *n* chiarimento *m*
clarify /'klærɪfaɪ/ *vt/i* (*pt/pp* **-ied**) chiarire
clarinet /klærɪ'net/ *n* clarinetto *m*
clarinettist /klærɪ'netɪst/ *n* clarinettista *mf*
clarity /'klærətɪ/ *n* chiarezza *f*
clash /klæʃ/ *n* scontro *m*; (*noise*) fragore *m* ● *vi* scontrarsi; ⟨*colours:*⟩ stonare; ⟨*events:*⟩ coincidere
clasp /klɑ:sp/ *n* chiusura *f* ● *vt* agganciare; (*hold*) stringere
class /klɑ:s/ *n* classe *f*; (*lesson*) corso *m* ● *vt* classificare
class-conscious *a* classista
class-consciousness *n* classismo *m*
classic /'klæsɪk/ *a* classico ● *n* classico *m*; **~s** *pl Univ* lettere *fpl* classiche
classical /'klæsɪk(ə)l/ *a* classico
classification /klæsɪfɪ'keɪʃn/ *n* classificazione *f*
classified ad /klæsɪfaɪd'æd/ *n* annuncio *m*
classified section *n* pagina *f* degli annunci
classify /'klæsɪfaɪ/ *vt* (*pt/pp* **-ied**) classificare
class: classmate *n* compagno, -a *mf* di classe. **classroom** *n* aula *f*. **class system** *n* sistema *m* classista
classy /'klɑ:sɪ/ *a* (**-ier, -iest**) *fam* d'alta classe
clatter /'klætə(r)/ *n* fracasso *m* ● *vi* far fracasso
clause /klɔ:z/ *n* clausola *f*; *Gram* proposizione *f*
claustrophobia /klɒstrə'fəʊbɪə/ *n* claustrofobia *f*
claustrophobic /klɒstrə'fəʊbɪk/ *a* claustrofobico
clavichord /'klævɪkɔ:d/ *n* clavicordo *m*
clavicle /'klævɪkl/ *n* clavicola *f*
claw /klɔ:/ *n* artiglio *m*; (*of crab, lobster & Techn*) tenaglia *f* ● *vt* ⟨*cat:*⟩ graffiare
clay /kleɪ/ *n* argilla *f*
clayey /'kleɪɪ/ *a* ⟨*soil*⟩ argilloso
clay pigeon shooting *n* tiro *m* al piattello
clean /kli:n/ *a* pulito, lindo ● *adv* completa-

mente ● *vt* pulire ⟨*shoes, windows*⟩; **~ one's teeth** lavarsi i denti; **have a coat ~ed** portare un cappotto in lavanderia
■ **clean out** *vt* ripulire ⟨*room*⟩; **be ~ed out** (*fig: have no money*) essere senza un soldo
■ **clean up** *vt* pulire ● *vi* far pulizia
clean-cut *a* ⟨*image, person*⟩ rispettabile
cleaner /'kli:nə(r)/ *n* uomo *m*/donna *f* delle pulizie; (*substance*) detersivo *m*; [**dry**] **~'s** lavanderia *f*, tintoria *f*
cleaning /'kli:nɪŋ/ *n* pulizia *f*; **do the ~** fare le pulizie
cleaning lady *n* donna *f* delle pulizie
cleaning product *n* detergente *m*
cleanliness /'klenlɪnɪs/ *n* pulizia *f*
clean-living /-'lɪvɪŋ/ *n* vita *f* integra ● *a* ⟨*person*⟩ integro
cleanse /klenz/ *vt* pulire
cleanser /'klenzə(r)/ *n* detergente *m*
clean-shaven /-'ʃeɪvən/ *a* sbarbato
clean sheet *n* **start with a ~ ~** *fig* voltare pagina
cleansing cream /'klenzɪŋ/ *n* latte *m* detergente
clear /klɪə(r)/ *a* chiaro; ⟨*conscience*⟩ pulito; ⟨*road*⟩ libero; ⟨*profit, advantage, majority*⟩ netto; ⟨*sky*⟩ sereno; ⟨*water*⟩ limpido; ⟨*glass*⟩ trasparente; **make sth ~** mettere qcsa in chiaro; **have I made myself ~?** mi sono fatto capire?; **I'm not ~ about what I have to do** non mi è ben chiaro quello che devo fare; **five ~ days** cinque giorni buoni; **be in the ~** essere a posto ● *adv* **stand ~ of** allontanarsi da; **keep ~ of** tenersi alla larga da ● *vt* sgombrare ⟨*room, street*⟩; sparecchiare ⟨*table*⟩; (*acquit*) scagionare; (*authorize*) autorizzare; scavalcare senza toccare ⟨*fence, wall*⟩; guadagnare ⟨*sum of money*⟩; passare ⟨*Customs*⟩; **~ one's throat** schiarirsi la gola ● *vi* ⟨*face, sky:*⟩ rasserenarsi; ⟨*fog:*⟩ dissiparsi
■ **clear away** *vt* metter via
■ **clear off** *vi fam* filar via
■ **clear out** *vt* sgombrare ● *vi fam* filar via
■ **clear up** *vt* (*tidy*) mettere a posto; chiarire ⟨*mystery*⟩ ● *vi* ⟨*weather:*⟩ schiarirsi
clearance /'klɪərəns/ *n* (*space*) spazio *m* libero; (*authorization*) autorizzazione *f*; (*Customs*) sdoganamento *m*
clearance sale *n* liquidazione *f*
clear-cut *a* ⟨*plan, division*⟩ ben definito; ⟨*problem, rule*⟩ chiaro; ⟨*difference, outline*⟩ netto; **the matter is not so ~** la faccenda non è così semplice
clear-headed /-'hedɪd/ *a* lucido
clearing /'klɪərɪŋ/ *n* radura *f*
clearly /'klɪəlɪ/ *adv* chiaramente
clear-sighted /-'saɪtɪd/ *a* perspicace
clearway /'klɪəweɪ/ *n Auto* strada *f* con divieto di sosta
cleavage /'kli:vɪdʒ/ *n* (*woman's*) décolleté *m inv*
cleave /kli:v/ *vt* spaccare
cleaver /'kli:və(r)/ *n* mannaia *f*
clef /klef/ *n Mus* chiave *f*
cleft /kleft/ *n* fenditura *f*

clemency /'klemənsɪ/ *n* clemenza *f*

clement /'klemənt/ *a* clemente

clench /klentʃ/ *vt* serrare

clergy /'klɜːdʒɪ/ *npl* clero *m*

clergyman /'klɜːdʒɪmən/ *n* ecclesiastico *m*

cleric /'klerɪk/ *n* ecclesiastico *m*

clerical /'klerɪlk/ *a* impiegatizio; *Relig* clericale

clerical assistant *n* impiegato, -a *mf*

clerk /klɑːk/, *Am* /klɜːk/ *n* impiegato, -a *mf*; (*Am: shop assistant*) commesso, -a *mf*

clever /'klevə(r)/ *a* intelligente; (*skilful*) abile

cleverly /'klevəlɪ/ *adv* intelligentemente; (*skilfully*) abilmente

cliché /'kliːʃeɪ/ *n* cliché *m inv*

clichéd /'kliːʃeɪd/ *a* ‹*idea, technique*› convenzionale; ‹*art, music*› stereotipato; **~ expression** frase *f* fatta

click /klɪk/ *vi* scattare; (*Comput: with mouse*) cliccare ● *n* (*Comput: with mouse*) click *m inv*

■ **click on** *vt Comput* cliccare su

client /'klaɪənt/ *n* cliente *mf*

clientele /kliːɒn'tel/ *n* clientela *f*

cliff /klɪf/ *n* scogliera *f*

cliffhanger /'klɪfhæŋə(r)/ *n* **it was a real ~** ci ha lasciato in sospeso

climate /'klaɪmət/ *n* clima *f*

climatic /klaɪ'mætɪk/ *a* climatico

climax /'klaɪmæks/ *n* punto *m* culminante

climb /klaɪm/ *n* salita *f* ● *vt* scalare ‹*mountain*›; arrampicarsi su ‹*ladder, tree*› ● *vi* arrampicarsi; (*rise*) salire; ‹*road:*› salire

■ **climb down** *vi* scendere; (*from ladder, tree*) scendere; *fig* tornare sui propri passi

■ **climb over** *vt* scavalcare ‹*fence, wall*›

■ **climb up** *vt* salire su ‹*hill*›

climber /'klaɪmə(r)/ *n* alpinista *mf*; (*plant*) rampicante *m*

climbing: climbing boot *n* scarpone *m* da alpinismo. **climbing expedition** *n* scalata *f*. **climbing frame** *n* struttura *f* su cui possono arrampicarsi i bambini

clinch /klɪntʃ/ *vt fam* concludere ‹*deal*› ● *n* (*in boxing*) clinch *m inv*

clincher /'klɪntʃə(r)/ *n* (*fam: act, remark*) fattore *m* decisivo; (*argument*) argomento *m* decisivo

cling /klɪŋ/ *vi* (*pt/pp* clung) aggrapparsi; (*stick*) aderire

cling film *n* pellicola *f* trasparente

clingy /'klɪŋɪ/ *a* ‹*dress*› attillato; ‹*person*› appiccicoso

clinic /'klɪnɪk/ *n* ambulatorio *m*

clinical /'klɪnɪkl/ *a* clinico

clinically /'klɪnɪklɪ/ *adv* clinicamente

clink /klɪŋk/ *n* tintinnio *m*; (*fam: prison*) galera *f* ● *vi* tintinnare

clip¹ /klɪp/ *n* fermaglio *m*; (*jewellery*) spilla *f* ● *vt* (*pt/pp* clipped) attaccare

clip² *n* (*extract*) taglio *m* ● *vt* obliterare ‹*ticket*›

clip: clipboard *n* fermablocco *m*. **clip-clop** *n* rumore *m* fatto dagli zoccoli dei cavalli. **clip-on** *a* ‹*bow tie*› con la clip. **clip-on**

microphone *n* microfono *m* con la clip. **clip-ons** *npl* (*earrings*) orecchini *mpl* con le clip

clippers /'klɪpəz/ *npl* (*for hair*) rasoio *m*; (*for hedge*) tosasiepi *m inv*; (*for nails*) tronchesina *f*

clipping /'klɪpɪŋ/ *n* (*from newspaper*) ritaglio *m*

clique /kliːk/ *n* cricca *f*

cliquey, cliquish /'kliːkɪ, 'kliːkɪʃ/ *a* ‹*atmosphere*› esclusivo; ‹*profession, group*› chiuso

cloak /kləʊk/ *n* mantello *m*

cloak: cloak-and-dagger *a* ‹*film*› d'avventura; (*surreptitious*) clandestino. **cloakroom** *n* guardaroba *m inv*; (*toilet*) bagno *m*. **cloakroom attendant** *n* (*Br: at toilets*) addetto, -a *mf* ai bagni; (*in hotel*) guardarobiere, -a *mf*. **cloakroom ticket** *n* scontrino *m* del guardaroba

clobber /'klɒbə(r)/ *n fam* armamentario *m* ● *vt* (*fam: hit*) colpire; (*defeat*) stracciare

cloche /klɒʃ/ *n* (*in garden*) campana *f* di vetro

cloche hat *n* cloche *f inv*

clock /klɒk/ *n* orologio *m*; (*fam: speedometer*) tachimetro *m*

■ **clock in** *vi* attaccare

■ **clock out** *vi* staccare

clock: clock face *n* quadrante *m*. **clockmaker** *n* orologiaio, -a *mf*. **clock radio** *n* radiosveglia *f*. **clock speed** *n Comput* velocità *f* di clock. **clock tower** *n* torre *f* dell'orologio. **clock-watch** *vi* guardare continuamente l'orologio. **clockwise** *a & adv* in senso orario. **clockwork** *n* meccanismo *m*; **like ~** *fam* alla perfezione ● *attrib* a molla

clod /klɒd/ *n* zolla *f*

clog /klɒg/ *n* zoccolo *m* ● *vt* (*pt/pp* clogged) **~** [**up**] intasare ‹*drain*›; inceppare ‹*mechanism*› ● *vi* ‹*drain:*› intasarsi

cloister /'klɔɪstə(r)/ *n* chiostro *m*

clone /kləʊn/ *n Biol, Comput, fig* clone *m* ● *vt* clonare

close¹ /kləʊs/ *a* vicino; ‹*friend*› intimo; ‹*weather*› afoso; **have a ~ shave** *fam* scamparla bella; **be ~ to sb** essere unito a qcno ● *adv* vicino; **~ by** vicino; **it's ~ on five o'clock** sono quasi le cinque

close² /kləʊz/ *n* fine *f*; **draw to a ~** concludere ● *vt* chiudere ● *vi* chiudersi; ‹*shop:*› chiudere

■ **close down** *vt* chiudere ● *vi* ‹*TV station:*› interrompere la trasmissione; ‹*factory:*› chiudere

■ **close in** *vi* ‹*mist:*› calare; ‹*enemy:*› avvicinarsi da ogni lato

■ **close up** *vi* (*come closer together*) stringersi; ‹*shop:*› chiudere ● *vt* (*bring closer together*) avvicinare; chiudere ‹*shop*›

close combat *n* corpo a corpo *m inv*

close-cropped /-'krɒpt/ *a* ‹*hair*› rasato

closed-circuit television /kləʊzdsɜːkɪttelɪ'vɪʒən/ *n* televisione *f* a circuito chiuso

closed shop /kləʊzd'ʃɒp/ *n* azienda *f* che as-

sume solo personale aderente ad un dato sindacato

close-fitting /kləʊsˈfɪtɪŋ/ *a ⟨garment⟩* attillato

close-knit /kləʊsˈnɪt/ *a fig ⟨family, group⟩* affiatato

closely /ˈkləʊslɪ/ *adv* da vicino; *⟨watch, listen⟩* attentamente

close season /kləʊs/ *n stagione f di chiusura della caccia e della pesca*

closet /ˈklɒzɪt/ *n Am* armadio *m*

close-up /ˈkləʊs-/ *n* primo piano *m*

closing: closing date *n* data *f* di scadenza. **closing-down sale** *n* liquidazione *f* totale [per cessata attività]. **closing time** *n* orario *m* di chiusura

closure /ˈkləʊʒə(r)/ *n* chiusura *f*

clot /klɒt/ *n* grumo *m*; *(fam: idiot)* tonto, -a *mf* ● *vi (pt/pp* **clotted**) *⟨blood:⟩* coagularsi

cloth /klɒθ/ *n (fabric)* tessuto *m*; *(duster etc)* straccio *m*

clothe /kləʊð/ *vt* vestire

clothes /kləʊðz/ *npl* vestiti *mpl*, abiti *mpl*

clothes: clothes-brush *n* spazzola *f* per abiti. **clothes horse** *n* stendibiancheria *m inv*. **clothes-line** *n* corda *f* stendibiancheria

clothing /ˈkləʊðɪŋ/ *n* abbigliamento *m*

clotted cream *n Br* panna *f* rappresa *(ottenuta scaldando il latte)*

cloud /klaʊd/ *n* nuvola *f*

■ **cloud over** *vi* rannuvolarsi

cloudburst /ˈklaʊdbɜːst/ *n* acquazzone *m*

cloudy /ˈklaʊdɪ/ *a* (**-ier, -iest**) nuvoloso; *⟨liquid⟩* torbido

clout /klaʊt/ *n fam* colpo *m*; *(influence)* impatto *m* (**with** su) ● *vt fam* colpire

clove /kləʊv/ *n* chiodo *m* di garofano; ~ **of garlic** spicchio *m* d'aglio

cloven foot, cloven hoof /ˈkləʊvən/ *n (of animal)* zoccolo *m* fesso; *(of devil)* piede *m* biforcuto

clover /ˈkləʊvə(r)/ *n* trifoglio *m*

clover leaf *n* raccordo *m* di due autostrade

clown /klaʊn/ *n* pagliaccio *m* ● *vi* ~ (**about**) fare il pagliaccio

club /klʌb/ *n* club *m inv*; *(weapon)* clava *f*; *Sport* mazza *f*; ~**s** *pl (Cards)* fiori *mpl* ● *v (pt/pp* **clubbed**) *vt* bastonare

■ **club together** *vi* unirsi

club: club foot *n* piede *m* deformato. **clubhouse** *n (for socializing)* circolo *m*; *(Am: for changing)* spogliatoio *m*. **club sandwich** *n* club-sandwich *m inv*

cluck /klʌk/ *vi* chiocciare

clue /kluː/ *n* indizio *m*; *(in crossword)* definizione *f*; **I haven't a** ~ *fam* non ne ho idea

clued-up /kluːdˈʌp/ *a Br fam* ben informato

clueless /ˈkluːlɪs/ *a Br fam* incapace

clump /klʌmp/ *n* gruppo *m*

clump about, clump around *vi (walk noisily)* camminare con passo pesante

clumsily /ˈklʌmzɪlɪ/ *adv* in modo maldestro; *⟨remark⟩* senza tatto

clumsiness /ˈklʌmzɪnɪs/ *n* goffaggine *f*

clumsy /ˈklʌmzɪ/ *a* (**-ier, -iest**) maldestro; *⟨tool⟩* scomodo; *⟨remark⟩* senza tatto

clung /klʌŋ/ *see* **cling**

cluster /ˈklʌstə(r)/ *n* gruppo *m* ● *vi* raggrupparsi (**round** intorno a)

clutch /klʌtʃ/ *n* stretta *f*; *Auto* frizione *f*; **be in sb's** ~**es** essere in balia di qcno ● *vt* stringere; *(grab)* afferrare ● *vi* ~ **at** afferrare

clutch bag *n* pochette *f inv*

clutch cable *n* cavo *m* della frizione

clutter /ˈklʌtə(r)/ *n* caos *m* ● *vt* ~ [**up**] ingombrare

cm *abbr* (**centimetre**) cm

CND *n abbr* (**Campaign for Nuclear Disarmament**) campagna *f* per il disarmo nucleare

Co. *abbr* (**company**) C., C.ia; **and** ~ *hum* e compagnia; *abbr* (**county**) contea *f*

c/o *abbr* (**care of**) c/o, presso

coach /kəʊtʃ/ *n* pullman *m inv*; *Rail* vagone *m*; *(horse-drawn)* carrozza *f*; *Sport* allenatore, -trice *mf* ● *vt* fare esercitare; *Sport* allenare

coach: coach party *n Br* gruppo *m* di gitanti *(in pullman)*. **coach station** *n Br* stazione *f* dei pullman. **coach trip** *n* viaggio *m* in pullman. **coachwork** *n Br* carrozzeria *f*

coagulate /kəʊˈægjʊleɪt/ *vi* coagularsi

coagulation /kəʊægjʊˈleɪʃn/ *n* coagulazione *f*

coal /kəʊl/ *n* carbone *m*

coalition /kəʊəˈlɪʃn/ *n* coalizione *f*

coal: coal-mine *n* miniera *f* di carbone. **coal scuttle** *n* secchio *m* del carbone. **coal seam** *n* giacimento *m* di carbone

coarse /kɔːs/ *a* grossolano; *⟨joke⟩* spinto

coarse-grained /-ˈɡreɪnd/ *a ⟨texture⟩* a grana grossa

coarsely /ˈkɔːslɪ/ *adv ⟨ground⟩* grossolanamente; *⟨joke⟩* in modo spinto

coast /kəʊst/ *n* costa *f* ● *vi (freewheel)* scendere a ruota libera; *Auto* scendere in folle

coastal /ˈkəʊstəl/ *a* costiero

coastguard /ˈkəʊs(t)ɡɑːd/ *n* guardia *f* costiera

coaster /ˈkəʊstə(r)/ *n (mat)* sottobicchiere *m inv*

coastline /ˈkəʊstlaɪm/ *n* litorale *m*

coat /kəʊt/ *n* cappotto *m*; *(of animal)* manto *m*; *(of paint)* mano *f*; ~ **of arms** stemma *f* ● *vt* coprire; *(with paint)* ricoprire

coat-hanger *n* gruccia *f*

coat-hook *n* gancio *m* [appendiabiti]

coating /ˈkəʊtɪŋ/ *n* rivestimento *m*; *(of paint)* stato *m*

coat-tails *npl* falde *fpl*; **be always hanging on sb's** ~ attaccarsi sempre alle falde di qcno

coax /kəʊks/ *vt* convincere con le moine

cob /kɒb/ *n (of corn)* pannocchia *f*

cobble /ˈkɒbl/ *vt* ~ **together** raffazzonare

cobbler /ˈkɒblə(r)/ *n* ciabattino *m*

cobblestones /ˈkɒbəlstəʊnz/ *npl* ciottolato *msg*

cobra /ˈkəʊbrə/ *n* cobra *m inv*

cobweb /ˈkɒbweb/ *n* ragnatela *f*

cocaine /kə'keɪn/ n cocaina f

coccyx /'kɒksɪks/ n coccige m

cock /kɒk/ n gallo m; (any male bird) maschio m; vulg cazzo m ● vt sollevare il grilletto di (gun); ~ **its ears** (animal) drizzare le orecchie

■**cock up** fam vt incasinare ● vi incasinarsi

cock-a-doodle-doo /kɒkədu:d(ə)l'du:/ int chicchirichì

cock-a-hoop a fam al settimo cielo

cock-and-bull story n fam panzana f

cockatoo /kɒkə'tu:/ n cacatoa m inv

cockcrow /'kɒkkrəʊ/ n at ~ al primo canto del gallo

cocked hat /kɒkt'hæt/ n fam **knock sb/sth into a ~** ~ schiacciare qcno/qcsa

cockerel /'kɒkərəl/ n galletto m

cocker spaniel /'kɒkə(r)/ n cocker m inv [spaniel]

cock-eyed /-'aɪd/ a fam storto; (absurd) assurdo

cockfighting /'kɒkfaɪtɪŋ/ n combattimenti mpl di galli

cockle /'kɒkl/ n cardio m

cockney /'kɒknɪ/ n (dialect) dialetto m londinese; (person) abitante mf dell'est di Londra

cockpit /'kɒkpɪt/ n Aeron cabina f

cockroach /'kɒkrəʊtʃ/ n scarafaggio m

cocksure /kɒk'ʃʊə(r)/ a (person, manner, attitude) presuntuoso

cocktail /'kɒkteɪl/ n cocktail m inv

cocktail: cocktail bar n [cocktail] bar m inv. **cocktail dress** n abito m da cocktail. **cocktail-party** m inv. **cocktail party** n cocktail m inv. **cocktail shaker** n shaker m inv. **cocktail stick** n stecchino m

cock-up n sl **make a ~** fare un casino (of con)

cocky /'kɒkɪ/ a (-ier, -iest) fam presuntuoso

cocoa /'kəʊkəʊ/ n cacao m

coconut /'kəʊkənʌt/ n noce f di cocco

coconut palm n palma f di cocco

coconut shy n Br tiro m al bersaglio in cui si devono abbattere noci di cocco

cocoon /kə'ku:n/ n bozzolo m

COD abbr (**cash on delivery**) pagamento m alla consegna

cod /kɒd/ n inv merluzzo m

coddle /'kɒd(ə)l/ vt coccolare

code /kəʊd/ n codice m

coded /'kəʊdɪd/ a codificato

codeine /'kəʊdi:n/ n codeina f

coding /'kəʊdɪŋ/ n Comput codifica f

cod-liver oil n olio m di fegato di merluzzo

coeducational /kəʊedjʊ'keɪʃənəl/ a misto

coefficient /kəʊɪ'fɪʃənt/ n coefficiente m

coerce /kəʊ'ɜ:s/ vt costringere

coercion /kəʊ'ɜ:ʃn/ n coercizione f

coexist /kəʊɪg'zɪst/ vi coesistere

coexistence /kəʊɪg'zɪstəns/ n coesistenza f

coffee /'kɒfɪ/ n caffè m inv

coffee: coffee bar n caffè m inv, bar m inv. **coffee bean** n chicco m di caffè. **coffee bre-**

ak n pausa f per il caffè. **coffee grinder** n macinacaffè m inv. **coffee machine** n (in café) macchina f per l'espresso. **coffee-maker** n (on stove) caffettiera f; (electric) macchina f per il caffè (con il filtro). **coffee morning** n Br riunione m mattutina in cui viene servito il caffè. **coffee percolator** n (on stove) caffettiera f; (electric) macchina f per il caffè (con il filtro). **coffee-pot** n caffettiera f. **coffee shop** n torrefazione f; (café) caffè m inv, bar m inv. **coffee table** n tavolino m

coffer /'kɒfə(r)/ n forziere m

coffin /'kɒfɪn/ n bara f

cog /kɒg/ n Techn dente m

cogent /'kəʊdʒənt/ a convincente

cogitate /'kɒdʒɪteɪt/ vi cogitare

cognac /'kɒnjæk/ n Cognac m

cognoscenti /kɒnə'ʃentɪ/ npl intenditori mpl

cogwheel /'kɒgwi:l/ n ruota f dentata

cohabit /kəʊ'hæbɪt/ vi Jur convivere

coherent /kəʊ'hɪərənt/ a coerente; (when speaking) logico

cohesion /kəʊ'hi:ʒən/ n coesione f

cohort /'kəʊhɔ:t/ n fig seguito m

coil /kɔɪl/ n rotolo m; Electr bobina f; ~s pl spire fpl ● vt ~[up] avvolgere

coin /kɔɪn/ n moneta f ● vt coniare (word)

coinage /'kɔɪnɪdʒ/ n (of coins, currency) coniatura f; (word, phrase) neologismo m

coin box n (pay phone) telefono m a monete; (on pay phone, in laundromat) gettoniera f

coincide /kəʊɪn'saɪd/ vi coincidere

coincidence /kəʊ'ɪnsɪdəns/ n coincidenza f

coincidental /kəʊɪnsɪ'dentl/ a casuale

coincidentally /kəʊɪnsɪ'dentlɪ/ adv casualmente

Coke® /kəʊk/ n Coca® f

coke n [carbone m] coke m

colander /'kʌləndə(r)/ n Culin colapasta m inv

cold /kəʊld/ a freddo; **I'm ~** ho freddo; **get ~ feet** farsi prendere dalla fifa; **give sb the ~ shoulder** trattare qcno freddamente ● n freddo m; Med raffreddore m

cold: cold-blooded /-'blʌdɪd/ a spietato. **cold calling** n Comm visita f senza preavviso. **cold comfort** n magra consolazione f. **cold frame** n telaio m coperto di vetro per proteggere le piante dal gelo. **cold-hearted** /-'hɑ:tɪd/ a insensibile

coldly /'kəʊldlɪ/ adv fig freddamente

cold meat n salumi mpl

coldness /'kəʊldnɪs/ n freddezza f

cold: cold shoulder n **give sb the ~** ~ snobbare qcno ● **cold-shoulder** vt trattare freddamente. **cold snap** n ondata f di freddo. **cold sore** n herpes m inv. **cold store** n cella f frigorifera. **cold sweat** n sudore m freddo; **bring sb out in a ~** ~ far sudare freddo qcno. **cold turkey** n (reaction) crisi f inv di astinenza; **be ~** ~ avere una crisi di astinenza; **quit ~** ~ smettere di colpo di drogarsi.

Cold War n guerra f fredda

coleslaw /'kəʊlslɔ:/ n insalata f di cavolo crudo, cipolle e carote in maionese

colic /'kɒlɪk/ n colica f

collaborate /kə'læbəreɪt/ vi collaborare; ~ **on sth** collaborare in qcsa

collaboration /kəlæbə'reɪʃn/ n collaborazione f; (with enemy) collaborazionismo m

collaborator /kə'læbəreɪtə(r)/ n collaboratore, -trice mf; (with enemy) collaborazionista mf

collage /kɒ'lɑ:ʒ/ n collage m inv; (film) montaggio m

collapse /kə'læps/ n crollo m ● vi ⟨person:⟩ svenire; ⟨roof, building:⟩ crollare

collapsible /kə'læpsəbl/ a pieghevole

collar /'kɒlə(r)/ n colletto m; (for animal) collare m

collarbone /'kɒləbəʊn/ n clavicola f

collar size n taglia f di camicia

collate /kə'leɪt/ vt collazionare

collateral /kɒ'lætərəl/ n garanzia f collaterale; **put up** ~ offrire una garanzia collaterale

collateral loan a Fin prestito m con garanzia collaterale

colleague /'kɒli:g/ n collega mf

collect /kə'lekt/ vt andare a prendere ⟨person⟩; ritirare ⟨parcel, tickets⟩; riscuotere ⟨taxes⟩; raccogliere ⟨rubbish⟩; (as hobby) collezionare ● vi riunirsi ● adv **call** ~ Am telefonare a carico del destinatario

collected /kə'lektɪd/ a controllato

collection /kə'lekʃn/ n collezione f; (in church) questua f; (of rubbish) raccolta f; (of post) levata f

collective /kə'lektɪv/ a collettivo

collective: collective bargaining n contrattazione f collettiva. **collective farm** n comune f. **collective noun** n nome m collettivo. **collective ownership** n comproprietà f

collector /kə'lektə(r)/ n (of stamps etc) collezionista mf

collector's item n pezzo m da collezionista

college /'kɒlɪdʒ/ n istituto m parauniversitario; **C~ of...** Scuola f di...

college of education n Br ≈ facoltà f inv di magistero

college of further education n Br istituto m parauniversitario

collide /kə'laɪd/ vi scontrarsi

collie /'kɒli/ n pastore m scozzese, collie m inv

colliery /'kɒlɪərɪ/ n miniera f di carbone

collision /kə'lɪʒn/ n scontro m; **be on a ~ course** essere in rotta di collisione

colloquial /kə'ləʊkwɪəl/ a colloquiale

colloquialism /kə'ləʊkwɪəlɪzm/ n espressione f colloquiale

colloquially /kə'ləʊkwɪəlɪ/ adv colloquialmente

colloquium /kə'ləʊkwɪəm/ n colloquio m

collude /kə'l(j)u:d/ vi complottare

collusion /kə'l(j)u:ʒn/ n collusione f; **in ~ with** in accordo con

cologne /kə'ləʊn/ n colonia f

Colombia /kə'lɒmbɪə/ n Colombia f

Colombian /kə'lɒmbɪən/ a & n colombiano, -a mf

colon /'kəʊlən/ n due punti mpl; Anat colon m inv

colonel /'kɜ:nl/ n colonnello m

colonial /kə'ləʊnɪəl/ a coloniale

colonize /'kɒlənaɪz/ vt colonizzare

colonnade /kɒlə'neɪd/ n colonnato m

colony /'kɒlənɪ/ n colonia f

Colorado beetle /kɒlə'rɑ:dəʊ/ n dorifora f

colossal /kə'lɒsl/ a colossale

colour /'kʌlə(r)/ n colore m; (complexion) colorito m; **~s** pl (flag) bandiera fsg; **show one's true ~s** fig buttare giù la maschera; **in ~** a colori; **off ~** fam giù di tono ● vt colorare; ~ **[in]** colorare ● vi (blush) arrossire

colour: colour bar n discriminazione f razziale. **colour-blind** a daltonico. **colour code** vt distinguere per mezzo di colori diversi

coloured /'kʌləd/ a colorato; ⟨person⟩ di colore ● n (person) persona f di colore

colour fast a dai colori resistenti

colour film n film m inv a colori

colourful /'kʌləfʊl/ a pieno di colore

colouring /'kʌlərɪŋ/ n (of plant, animal) colorazione f; (complexion) colorito m; (dye: for hair) tinta f; (for food) colorante m

colouring book n album m inv da colorare

colourless /'kʌləlɪs/ a incolore

colour: colour photo[graph] n fotografia f a colori. **colour scheme** n [combinazione f di] colori mpl. **colour sense** n senso m del colore. **colour supplement** n supplemento m illustrato a colori. **colour television** n televisione f a colori

colt /kəʊlt/ n puledro m

column /'kɒləm/ n colonna f

columnist /'kɒləmnɪst/ n giornalista mf che cura una rubrica

coma /'kəʊmə/ n coma m inv

comatose /'kəʊmətəʊz/ a Med in stato comatoso

comb /kəʊm/ n pettine m; (for wearing) pettinino m ● vt pettinare; (fig: search) setacciare; ~ **one's hair** pettinarsi i capelli ■ **comb through** vt setacciare ⟨files, desk⟩

combat /'kɒmbæt/ n combattimento m ● vt (pt/pp **combated**) combattere

combat jacket n giubba f da combattimento

combination /kɒmbɪ'neɪʃn/ n combinazione f

combine[1] /kəm'baɪn/ vt unire; ~ **a job with being a mother** conciliare il lavoro con il ruolo di madre ● vi ⟨chemical elements:⟩ combinarsi

combine[2] /'kɒmbaɪn/ n Comm associazione f

combine [harvester] n mietitrebbia f

combustible /kəm'bʌstəbl/ a combustibile

combustion /kəm'bʌstʃn/ n combustione f

come /kʌm/ vi (pt **came**, pp **come**) venire; **after coming all this way** dopo tutta questa strada; **where do you ~ from?** da dove vieni?; ~ **to** (*reach*) arrivare a; **that ~s to £10** fanno 10 sterline; **I've ~ to appreciate her** ho finito per apprezzarla; **I don't know what the world is coming to** mi chiedo dove andremo a finire; ~ **into money** ricevere dei soldi; **that's what comes of being ...** ecco cosa significa essere ...; ~ **true/open** verificarsi/aprirsi; ~ **first** arrivare primo; *fig* venire prima di tutto; ~ **in two sizes** esistere in due misure; **the years to ~** gli anni a venire; **how ~?** *fam* come mai?

■ **come about** *vi* succedere

■ **come across** *vi* ~ **across as being** *fam* dare l'impressione di essere ● *vt* (*find*) imbattersi in

■ **come after** *vt* (*follow*) venire dopo; (*chase, pursue*) inseguire

■ **come along** *vi* venire; ⟨*job, opportunity:*⟩ presentarsi; (*progress*) andare bene

■ **come apart** *vi* smontarsi; (*break*) rompersi

■ **come at** *vt* (*attack*) avventarsi su

■ **come away** *vi* venir via; ⟨*button, fastener:*⟩ staccarsi

■ **come back** *vi* ritornare

■ **come before** *vt* (*precede*) precedere; (*be more important than*) venire prima di

■ **come by** *vi* passare ● *vt* (*obtain*) avere

■ **come down** *vi* scendere; ~ **down to** (*reach*) arrivare a; **the situation comes down to...** la situazione si riduce a...; **don't ~ down too hard on her** vacci piano con lei; ~ **down with flu** prendersi l'influenza

■ **come forward** *vi* farsi avanti

■ **come in** *vi* entrare; (*in race*) arrivare; ⟨*tide:*⟩ salire; ~ **in with sb** (*in an undertaking*) associarsi a qcno

■ **come in for** *vt* ~ **in for criticism** essere criticato

■ **come off** *vi* staccarsi; (*take place*) esserci; (*succeed*) riuscire; ~ **off it!** non farmi ridere!

■ **come on** *vi* (*make progress*) migliorare; ~ **on!** (*hurry*) dai!; (*indicating disbelief*) ma va là!

■ **come out** *vi* venir fuori; ⟨*book, sun:*⟩ uscire; ⟨*stain:*⟩ andar via; ⟨*homosexual:*⟩ rivelare la propria omosessualità; ~ **out [on strike]** scioperare

■ **come out with** *vt* venir fuori con ⟨*joke, suggestion*⟩

■ **come over** *vi* venire; **what's ~ over you?** cosa ti prende?

■ **come round** *vi* venire; (*after fainting*) riaversi; (*change one's mind*) farsi convincere

■ **come through** *vi* ⟨*news:*⟩ arrivare ● *vt* attraversare ⟨*operation*⟩

■ **come to** *vi* (*after fainting*) riaversi.

■ **come under** *vi* trovarsi sotto

■ **come up** *vi* salire; ⟨*sun:*⟩ sorgere; ⟨*plant:*⟩ crescere; ⟨*name, subject:*⟩ venir fuori; ⟨*job, opportunity:*⟩ presentarsi; **something came up** (*I was prevented*) ho avuto un imprevisto

■ **come up against** *vt* incontrare

■ **come up to** *vt* (*reach*) arrivare a; essere all'altezza di ⟨*expectations*⟩

■ **come up with** *vt* tirar fuori

come-back *n* ritorno *m*

comedian /kə'miːdɪən/ *n* [attore *m*] comico *m*

comedienne /kəmiːdɪ'ren/ *n* attrice *f* comica

come-down *n* passo *m* indietro

comedy /'kɒmədɪ/ *n* commedia *f*

comer /'kʌmə(r)/ *n* **open to all ~s** aperto a tutti; **take on all ~s** battersi contro tutti gli sfidanti

comet /'kɒmɪt/ *n* cometa *f*

come-uppance /kʌm'ʌpəns/ *n* **get one's ~** *fam* avere quel che si merita

comfort /'kʌmfət/ *n* benessere *m*; (*consolation*) conforto *m*; **all the ~s** tutti i comfort ● *vt* confortare

comfortable /'kʌmfətəbl/ *a* comodo; **be ~** ⟨*person:*⟩ stare comodo; (*fig: in situation*) essere a proprio agio; (*financially*) star bene

comfortably /'kʌmfətəblɪ/ *adv* comodamente

comforting /'kʌmfətɪŋ/ *a* confortante

comfort station *n Am* bagno *m* pubblico

comfy /'kʌmfɪ/ *a fam* comodo

comic /'kɒmɪk/ *a* comico ● *n* comico, -a *mf*; (*periodical*) fumetto *m*

comical /'kɒmɪk(ə)l/ *a* comico

comically /'kɒmɪk(ə)lɪ/ *adv* comicamente

comic: **comic book** *n* giornalino *m* [a fumetti]. **comic relief** *n Theat* **provide some ~** ~ fare una parentesi comica; *fig* sdrammatizzare. **comic strip** *n* striscia *f* di fumetti

coming /'kʌmɪŋ/ *a* promettente ● *n* venuta *f*; **~s and goings** viavai *m*

comma /'kɒmə/ *n* virgola *f*

command /kə'mɑːnd/ *n also Comput* comando *m*; (*order*) ordine *m*; (*mastery*) padronanza *f*; **in ~** al comando ● *vt* ordinare; comandare ⟨*army*⟩

commandant /'kɒməndænt/ *n Mil* comandante *m*

commandeer /kɒmən'dɪə(r)/ *vt* requisire

commander /kə'mɑːndə(r)/ *n* comandante *m*

commanding /kə'mɑːndɪŋ/ *a* ⟨*view*⟩ imponente; ⟨*lead*⟩ dominante

commanding officer *n* comandante *m*

commandment /kə'mɑːndmənt/ *n* comandamento *m*

commando /kə'mɑːndəʊ/ *n* commando *m* *inv*

command performance *n Br Theat* serata *f* di gala (su richiesta del capo di stato)

commemorate /kə'meməreɪt/ *vt* commemorare

commemoration /kəmemə'reɪʃn/ *n* commemorazione *f*

commemorative /kə'memərətɪv/ *a* commemorativo

commence /kə'mens/ *vt/i* cominciare

commencement /kə'mensmənt/ n inizio m

commend /kə'mend/ vt complimentarsi con (**on** per); (recommend) raccomandare (**to** a)

commendable /kə'mendəbl/ a lodevole

commendation /kɒmen'deɪʃn/ n elogio m; (for bravery) riconoscimento m

commensurate /kə'menʃərət/ a proporzionato (**with** a)

comment /'kɒment/ n commento m; **no ~!** no comment! ● vi fare commenti (**on** su)

commentary /'kɒməntrɪ/ n commento m; [running] ~ (on radio, TV) cronaca f diretta

commentate /'kɒmənteɪt/ vt ~ **on** TV, Radio fare la cronaca di

■ **commentate on** vt fare la radiocronaca/ telecronaca di (sporting event)

commentator /'kɒmənteɪtə(r)/ n cronista mf

commerce /'kɒmɜːs/ n commercio m

commercial /kə'mɜːʃl/ a commerciale ● n TV pubblicità f inv

commercial break n spot m inv [pubblicitario], interruzione f pubblicitaria

commercialism /kə'mɜːʃ(ə)lɪzm/ n pej affarismo m

commercialize /kə'mɜːʃ(ə)laɪz/ vt commercializzare

commercial law n diritto m commerciale

commercially /kə'mɜːʃ(ə)lɪ/ adv commercialmente

commiserate /kə'mɪzəreɪt/ vi esprimere il proprio rincrescimento (**with** a)

commissar /kɒmɪ'sɑː(r)/ n commissario m

commission /kə'mɪʃn/ n commissione f; **receive one's ~** Mil essere promosso ufficiale; **out of ~** fuori uso ● vt commissionare; Mil promuovere ufficiale; **~ a painting from sb, ~ sb to do a painting** commissionare un dipinto a qcno

commissionaire /kəmɪʃə'neə(r)/ n portiere m

commissioner /kə'mɪʃənə(r)/ n commissario m; **C~ for Oaths** ≈ notaio m

commit /kə'mɪt/ vt (pt/pp committed) commettere; (to prison, hospital) affidare (**to** a); impegnare (funds); **~ oneself** impegnarsi; **~ sth to memory** imparare qcsa a memoria

commitment /kə'mɪtmənt/ n impegno m; (involvement) compromissione f

committed /kə'mɪtɪd/ a impegnato

committee /kə'mɪtɪ/ n comitato m

commodity /kə'mɒdətɪ/ n prodotto m

commodore /'kɒmədɔː(r)/ n commodoro m

common /'kɒmən/ a comune; (vulgar) volgare ● n prato m pubblico; **have in ~** avere in comune; **House of C~s** Camera f dei Comuni

common cold n raffreddore m

commoner /'kɒmənə(r)/ n persona f non nobile

common: common ground n fig terreno m d'intesa. **common law** n diritto m consuetudinario. **common-law husband** n convivente m (more uxorio). **common-law wife** n convivente f (more uxorio)

commonly /'kɒmənlɪ/ adv comunemente

common: Common Market n Mercato m Comune. **common-or-garden** a ordinario. **commonplace** a banale. **common-room** n sala f dei professori/degli studenti. **common sense** n buon senso m. **Commonwealth** n Br Commonwealth m inv ● attrib (country, Games) del Commonwealth

commotion /kə'məʊʃn/ n confusione f

communal /'kɒmjʊnl/ a comune

commune /'kɒmjuːn/ n comune f ● /kə'mjuːn/ vi ~ **with** essere in comunione con (nature); comunicare con (person)

communicable /kə'mjuːnɪkəbl/ a (disease) trasmissibile

communicate /kə'mjuːnɪkeɪt/ vt/i comunicare

communication /kəmjuːnɪ'keɪʃn/ n comunicazione f; (of disease) trasmissione f; **be in ~ with sb** essere in contatto con qcno; **~s** pl (technology) telecomunicazioni fpl

communication cord n fermata f d'emergenza

communications satellite n satellite m per telecomunicazioni

communications software n software m di comunicazione

communication studies /'stʌdɪz/ n studi mpl di comunicazione

communicative /kə'mjuːnɪkətɪv/ a comunicativo

Communion /kə'mjuːnɪən/ n [Holy] ~ comunione f

communiqué /kə'mjuːnɪkeɪ/ n comunicato m stampa

Communism /'kɒmjʊnɪzm/ n comunismo m

Communist /'kɒmjʊnɪst/ a & n comunista mf

Communist Party n partito m communista

community /kə'mjuːnətɪ/ n comunità f

community: community care n cura f fuori dell'ambito ospedaliero. **community centre** n centro m sociale. **community policing** n polizia f di quartiere. **community service** n servizio m civile (in sostituzione di pene per reati minori). **community spirit** n spirito m civico

commute /kə'mjuːt/ vi fare il pendolare ● vt Jur commutare

commuter /kə'mjuːtə(r)/ n pendolare mf

commuter belt n zona f suburbana abitata dai pendolari

commuter train n treno m dei pendolari

compact¹ /kəm'pækt/ a compatto

compact² /'kɒmpækt/ n portacipria m inv

compact disc n compact disc m inv

compact disc player n lettore m di compact disc

companion /kəm'pænjən/ n compagno, -a mf

companionable /kəm'pænjənəbl/ *a* ⟨*person*⟩ socievole; ⟨*silence*⟩ non pesante

companionship /kəm'pænjən∫ɪp/ *n* compagnia *f*

company /'kʌmpənɪ/ *n* compagnia *f*; (*guests*) ospiti *mpl*; **I didn't know you had ~** pensavo che fossi solo

company: company brochure *n* opuscolo *m* dell'azienda. **company car** *n* macchina *f* della ditta. **company letterhead** *n* carta *f* intestata dell'azienda. **company pension scheme** *n* piano *m* di pensionamento aziendale. **company policy** *n* politica *f* aziendale. **company secretary** *n* direttore, -trice *mf* amministrativo, -a

comparable /'kɒmpərəbl/ *a* paragonabile

comparative /kəm'pærətɪv/ *a* comparativo; (*relative*) relativo ● *n Gram* comparativo *m*

comparatively /kəm'pærətɪvlɪ/ *adv* relativamente

compare /kəm'peə(r)/ *vt* paragonare (**with/ to** a) ● *vi* **it can't ~** non ha paragoni

comparison /kəm'pærɪsn/ *n* paragone *m*

compartment /kəm'pɑːtmənt/ *n* compartimento *m*; *Rail* scompartimento *m*

compass /'kʌmpəs/ *n* bussola *f*

compasses /'kʌmpəsɪz/ *npl* **pair of ~** compasso *msg*

compassion /kəm'pæ∫n/ *n* compassione *f*

compassionate /kəm'pæ∫ənət/ *a* compassionevole

compatible /kəm'pætəbl/ *a* compatibile; **be ~** ⟨*people:*⟩ avere caratteri compatibili

compatriot /kəm'pætrɪət/ *n* compatriota *mf*

compel /kəm'pel/ *vt* (*pt/pp* **compelled**) costringere

compelling /kəm'pelɪŋ/ *a* ⟨*reason, argument*⟩ convincente; ⟨*performance, film, speaker*⟩ avvincente

compendium /kəm'pendɪəm/ *n* (*handbook*) compendio *m*; (*Br: box of games*) scatola *f* di giochi

compensate /'kɒmpənseɪt/ *vt* risarcire ● *vi* **~ for** *fig* compensare di

compensation /kɒmpən'seɪ∫n/ *n* risarcimento *m*; (*fig: comfort*) consolazione *f*

compère /'kɒmpeə(r)/ *n* presentatore, -trice *mf*

compete /kəm'piːt/ *vi* competere; (*take part*) gareggiare

competence /'kɒmpɪtəns/ *n* competenza *f*

competent /'kɒmpɪtənt/ *a* competente

competition /kɒmpə'tɪ∫n/ *n* concorrenza *f*; (*contest*) gara *f*

competitive /kəm'petɪtɪv/ *a* competitivo; **~ prices** prezzi *mpl* concorrenziali

competitor /kəm'petɪtə(r)/ *n* concorrente *mf*

compilation /kɒmpɪ'leɪ∫n/ *n* compilazione *f*; (*collection*) raccolta *f*

compile /kəm'paɪl/ *vt* compilare

complacency /kəm'pleɪsənsɪ/ *n* compiacimento *m*

complacent /kəm'pleɪsənt/ *a* compiaciuto

complacently /kəm'pleɪsəntlɪ/ *adv* con compiacimento

complain /kəm'pleɪn/ *vi* lamentarsi (**about** di); (*formally*) reclamare; **~ of** *Med* accusare

complaint /kəm'pleɪnt/ *n* lamentela *f*; (*formal*) reclamo *m*; *Med* disturbo *m*

complement[1] /'kɒmplɪmənt/ *n* complemento *m*; **with a full ~ of 25** con un effettivo al completo di 25

complement[2] /'kɒmplɪmənt/ *vt* complementare; **~ each other** complementarsi a vicenda

complementary /kɒmplɪ'mentərɪ/ *a* complementare

complete /kəm'pliːt/ *a* completo; (*utter*) finito ● *vt* completare; compilare ⟨*form*⟩

completely /kəm'pliːtlɪ/ *adv* completamente

completion /kəm'pliː∫n/ *n* fine *f*

complex /'kɒmpleks/ *a* & *n* complesso *m*

complexion /kəm'plek∫n/ *n* carnagione *f*; **that puts a different ~ on the matter** questo mette la questione in una luce nuova

complexity /kəm'pleksətɪ/ *n* complessità *f inv*

compliance /kəm'plaɪəns/ *n* accettazione *f*; (*with rules*) osservanza *f*; **in ~ with** in osservanza a ⟨*law*⟩; conformemente a ⟨*request*⟩

complicate /'kɒmplɪkeɪt/ *vt* complicare

complicated /'kɒmplɪkeɪtɪd/ *a* complicato

complication /kɒmplɪ'keɪ∫n/ *n* complicazione *f*

complicity /kəm'plɪsətɪ/ *n* complicità *f*

compliment /'kɒmplɪmənt/ *n* complimento *m*; **~s** *pl* omaggi *mpl* ● *vt* complimentare

complimentary /kɒmplɪ'mentərɪ/ *a* complimentoso; (*given free*) in omaggio

comply /kəm'plaɪ/ *vi* (*pt/pp* **-ied**) **~ with** conformarsi a

component /kəm'pəʊnənt/ *a* & *n* **~ [part]** componente *m*

compose /kəm'pəʊz/ *vt* comporre; **~ oneself** ricomporsi; **be ~d of** essere composto da

composed /kəm'pəʊzd/ *a* (*calm*) composto

composer /kəm'pəʊzə(r)/ *n* compositore, -trice *mf*

composite /'kɒmpəzɪt/ *a* composto; ⟨*style*⟩ composito

composition /kɒmpə'zɪ∫n/ *n* composizione *f*; (*essay*) tema *m*

compos mentis /kɒmpɒs'mentɪs/ *a* nel pieno possesso delle proprie facoltà

compost /'kɒmpɒst/ *n* composta *f*

composure /kəm'pəʊʒə(r)/ *n* calma *f*

compound[1] /kəm'paʊnd/ *vt* (*make worse*) aggravare

compound[2] /'kɒmpaʊnd/ *a* composto ● *n Chem* composto *m*; *Gram* parola *f* composta; (*enclosure*) recinto *m*

compound fracture *n* frattura *f* esposta

compound interest *n* interesse *m* composto

comprehend /kɒmprɪ'hend/ *vt* comprendere

comprehensible /kɒmprɪ'hensəbl/ *a* comprensible

comprehensibly /kɒmprɪ'hensəblɪ/ *adv* comprensibilmente

comprehension /kɒmprɪ'henʃn/ *n* comprensione *f*

comprehensive /kɒmprɪ'hensɪv/ *a* & *n* comprensivo; ~ [**school**] *scuola f media in cui gli allievi hanno capacità d'apprendimento diverse*

comprehensive insurance *n* Auto polizza *f* casco

compress[1] /'kɒmpres/ *n* compressa *f*

compress[2] /kəm'pres/ *vt* comprimere

compressed air /kəm'prest/ *n* aria *f* compressa

compression /kəm'preʃn/ *n* compressione *f*

comprise /kəm'praɪz/ *vt* comprendere; (*form*) costituire

compromise /'kɒmprəmaɪz/ *n* compromesso *m* ● *vt* compromettere ● *vi* fare un compromesso

compulsion /kəm'pʌlʃn/ *n* desiderio *m* irresistibile

compulsive /kəm'pʌlsɪv/ *a* Psych patologico; ~ **eating** voglia *f* ossessiva di mangiare

compulsory /kəm'pʌlsərɪ/ *a* obbligatorio; ~ **subject** materia *f* obbligatoria

compulsory purchase *n* Br espropriazione *f* (*per pubblica utilità*)

compunction /kəm'pʌŋkʃn/ *n* liter scrupolo *m*

computation /kɒmpjʊ'teɪʃn/ *n* calcolo *m*

computer /kəm'pju:tə(r)/ *n* computer *m* inv

computer: computer-aided *a* assistito da computer. **computer-aided design** *n* progettazione *f* assistita da computer. **computer-assisted language learning** *n* apprendimento *m* della lingua assistito da computer. **computer dating service** *n* agenzia *f* matrimoniale computerizzata. **computer engineer** *n* tecnico *m* informatico. **computer error** *n* errore *m* informatico. **computer game** *n* gioco *m* su computer; ~ ~**s** intelligiochi *mpl*. **computer graphics** *n* grafica *f* su computer. **computer hacker** *n* pirata *m* informatico

computerization /kəmpju:tərər'zeɪʃn/ *n* computerizzazione *f*

computerize /kəm'pju:təraɪz/ *vt* computerizzare

computer: computer-literate *a* che sa usare il computer. **computer operator** *n* terminalista *mf*. **computer program** *n* programma *m* [di computer]. **computer programmer** *n* programmatore, -trice *mf* di computer. **computer virus** *n* virus *m* inv [su computer]

computing /kəm'pju:tɪŋ/ *n* informatica *f*

comrade /'kɒmreɪd/ *n* camerata *m*; Pol compagno, -a *mf*

comradeship /'kɒmreɪdʃɪp/ *n* cameratismo *m*

con[1] /kɒn/ *see* **pro**

con[2] *n* fam fregatura *f* ● *vt* (*pt/pp* **conned**) *fam* fregare

concave /'kɒnkeɪv/ *a* concavo

conceal /kən'si:l/ *vt* nascondere

concealment /kən'si:lmənt/ *n* dissimulazione *f*

concede /kən'si:d/ *vt* (*admit*) ammettere; (*give up*) rinunciare a; lasciar fare ⟨*goal*⟩

conceit /kən'si:t/ *n* presunzione *f*

conceited /kən'si:tɪd/ *a* presuntuoso

conceivable /kən'si:vəbl/ *a* concepibile

conceive /kən'si:v/ *vt* Biol concepire ● *vi* aver figli; ~ **of** *fig* concepire

concentrate /'kɒnsəntreɪt/ *vt* concentrare ● *vi* concentrarsi ● *n* concentrato *m*

concentration /kɒnsən'treɪʃn/ *n* concentrazione *f*

concentration camp *n* campo *m* di concentramento

concentric /kən'sentrɪk/ *a* concentrico

concept /'kɒnsept/ *n* concetto *m*

conception /kən'sepʃn/ *n* concezione *f*; (*idea*) idea *f*

conceptual /kən'septjʊəl/ *a* concettuale

concern /kən'sɜ:n/ *n* preoccupazione *f*; Comm attività *f* inv ● *vt* (*be about, affect*) riguardare; (*worry*) preoccupare; **be** ~**ed about** essere preoccupato per; ~ **oneself with** preoccuparsi di; **as far as I am** ~**ed** per quanto mi riguarda

concerning /kən'sɜ:nɪŋ/ *prep* riguardo a

concert /'kɒnsət/ *n* concerto *m*

concerted /kən'sɜ:tɪd/ *a* collettivo

concert hall *n* sala *f* da concerti

concertina /kɒnsə'ti:nə/ *n* piccola fisarmonica *f*

concert master *n* Am primo violino *m*

concerto /kən'tʃeətəʊ/ *n* concerto *m*

concession /kən'seʃn/ *n* concessione *f*; (*reduction*) sconto *m*

concessionary /kən'seʃənrɪ/ *a* (*reduced*) scontato

conciliate /kən'sɪlɪeɪt/ *vt* blandire

conciliation /kənsɪlɪ'eɪʃn/ *n* conciliazione *f*

conciliator /kən'sɪlɪeɪtə(r)/ *n* mediatore, -trice *mf*

concise /kən'saɪs/ *a* conciso

concisely /kən'saɪslɪ/ *adv* in modo conciso

conciseness /kən'saɪsnɪs/ *n* concisione *f*

conclude /kən'klu:d/ *vt* concludere ● *vi* concludersi

concluding /kən'klu:dɪŋ/ *a* finale, conclusivo

conclusion /kən'klu:ʒn/ *n* conclusione *f*; **in** ~ per concludere

conclusive /kən'klu:sɪv/ *a* definitivo

conclusively /kən'klu:sɪvlɪ/ *adv* in modo definitivo

concoct /kən'kɒkt/ *vt* confezionare; *fig* inventare

concoction /kən'kɒkʃn/ *n* mistura *f*; (*drink*) intruglio *m*

concord /'kɒnkɔ:d/ *n* concordia *f*

concordance /kən'kɔ:dəns/ *n* accordo *m*;

(*index*) concordanze *fpl*; **be in ~ with** essere in accordo con

concourse /'kɒŋkɔːs/ *n* atrio *m*

concrete /'kɒŋkriːt/ *a* concreto ● *n* calcestruzzo *m* ● *vt* ricoprire di calcestruzzo

concrete jungle *n* giungla *f* d'asfalto

concrete mixer *n* betoniera *f*

concur /kən'kɜː(r)/ *vi* (*pt/pp* **concurred**) essere d'accordo

concurrently /kən'kʌrəntlɪ/ *adv* contemporaneamente

concussion /kən'kʌʃn/ *n* commozione *f* cerebrale

condemn /kən'dem/ *vt* condannare; dichiarare inagibile ‹*building*›

condemnation /kɒndem'neɪʃn/ *n* condanna *f*

condensation /kɒnden'seɪʃn/ *n* condensazione *f*

condense /kən'dens/ *vt* condensare; *Phys* condensare ● *vi* condensarsi

condensed milk /kəndenst'mɪlk/ *n* latte *m* condensato

condescend /kɒndɪ'send/ *vi* degnarsi

condescending /kɒndɪ'sendɪŋ/ *a* condiscendente

condescendingly /kɒndɪ'sendɪŋlɪ/ *adv* in modo condiscendente

condiment /'kɒndɪmənt/ *n* condimento *m*

condition /kən'dɪʃn/ *n* condizione *f*; **on ~ that** a condizione che ● *vt Psych* condizionare

conditional /kən'dɪʃənəl/ *a* ‹*acceptance*› condizionato; *Gram* condizionale; **be ~ on** essere condizionato da ● *n Gram* condizionale

conditionally /kən'dɪʃənəlɪ/ *adv* condizionatamente

conditioner /kən'dɪʃənə(r)/ *n* balsamo *m*; (*for fabrics*) ammorbidente *m*

conditioning /kən'dɪʃənɪŋ/ *n* (*of hair*) balsamo *m*; *Psych* condizionamento *m* ● *a* ‹*shampoo, lotion etc*› trattante

condole /kən'dəʊl/ *vi* fare le condoglianze (**with** a)

condolences /kən'dəʊlənsɪz/ *npl* condoglianze *fpl*

condom /'kɒndəm/ *n* preservativo *m*

condo[minium] /'kɒndəʊ, kɒndə'mɪnɪəm/ *n Am* condominio *m*

condone /kən'dəʊn/ *vt* passare sopra a

conducive /kən'djuːsɪv/ *a* **be ~ to** contribuire a

conduct¹ /'kɒndʌkt/ *n* condotta *f*

conduct² /kən'dʌkt/ *vt* condurre; dirigere ‹*orchestra*›

conduction /kən'dʌkʃn/ *n* conduzione *f*

conductor /kən'dʌktə(r)/ *n* direttore *m* d'orchestra; (*of bus*) bigliettaio *m*; *Phys* conduttore *m*

conductress /kən'dʌktrɪs/ *n* bigliettaia *f*

cone /kəʊn/ *n* cono *m*; *Bot* pigna *f*; *Auto* birillo *m*

■ **cone off** *vt* **be ~d off** *Auto* essere chiuso da birilli

confection /kən'fekʃn/ *n* (*cake, dessert*) dolce *m*; **a ~ of** (*combination*) una combinazione di

confectioner /kən'fekʃənə(r)/ *n* pasticciere, -a *mf*

confectionery /kən'fekʃənərɪ/ *n* pasticceria *f*

confederation /kənfedə'reɪʃn/ *n* confederazione *f*

confer /kən'fɜː(r)/ *v* (*pt/pp* **conferred**) ● *vt* conferire (**on** a) ● *vi* (*discuss*) conferire

conference /'kɒnfərəns/ *n* conferenza *f*

conference room *n* sala *f* riunioni

confess /kən'fes/ *vt* confessare ● *vi* confessare; *Relig* confessarsi

confession /kən'feʃn/ *n* confessione *f*

confessional /kən'feʃənəl/ *n* confessionale *m*

confessor /kən'fesə(r)/ *n* confessore *m*

confetti /kən'fetɪ/ *n* coriandoli *mpl*

confide /kən'faɪd/ *vt* confidare

■ **confide in** *vt* **~ in sb** fidarsi di

confidence /'kɒnfɪdəns/ *n* (*trust*) fiducia *f*; (*self-assurance*) sicurezza *f* di sé; (*secret*) confidenza *f*; **in ~** in confidenza

confidence trick *n* truffa *f*

confidence trickster /'kɒnfɪdəns-trɪkstə(r)/ *n* imbroglione, -a *mf*

confident /'kɒnfɪdənt/ *a* fiducioso; (*self-assured*) sicuro di sé

confidential /kɒnfɪ'denʃl/ *a* confidenziale

confidentiality /kɒnfɪdenʃɪ'ælətɪ/ *n* riservatezza *f*

confidentially /kɒnfɪ'denʃəlɪ/ *adv* confidenzialmente

confidently /'kɒnfɪdəntlɪ/ *adv* con aria fiduciosa; **we ~ expect to win** siamo fiduciosi nella vittoria

confine /kən'faɪn/ *vt* rinchiudere; (*limit*) limitare; **be ~d to bed** essere confinato a letto

confined /kən'faɪnd/ *a* ‹*space*› limitato

confinement /kən'faɪnmənt/ *n* detenzione *f*; *Med* parto *m*

confines /'kɒnfaɪnz/ *npl* confini *mpl*

confirm /kən'fɜːm/ *vt* confermare; *Relig* cresimare

confirmation /kɒnfə'meɪʃn/ *n* conferma *f*; *Relig* cresima *f*

confirmed /kən'fɜːmd/ *a* incallito; **~ bachelor** scapolo *m* impenitente

confiscate /'kɒnfɪskeɪt/ *vt* confiscare

confiscation /kɒnfɪs'keɪʃn/ *n* confisca *f*

conflagration /kɒnflə'greɪʃn/ *n* conflagrazione *f*

conflate /kən'fleɪt/ *vt* fondere

conflict¹ /'kɒnflɪkt/ *n* conflitto *m*

conflict² /kən'flɪkt/ *vi* essere in contraddizione

conflicting /kən'flɪktɪŋ/ *a* contraddittorio

confluence /'kɒnfluəns/ *n* (*of rivers*) confluenza *f*; *fig* convergenza *f*

conform /kən'fɔːm/ *vi* ‹*person*:› conformarsi; ‹*thing*:› essere conforme (**to** a)

conformist /kən'fɔːmɪst/ *n* conformista *mf*

conformity /kən'fɔːmətɪ/ n conformità f; Relig ortodossia f; **in ~ with** in conformità a

confound /kən'faʊnd/ vt (perplex) confondere; (show to be wrong) confutare

confounded /kən'faʊndɪd/ a fam maledetto

confront /kən'frʌnt/ vt affrontare; **the problems ~ing us** i problemi che dobbiamo affrontare

confrontation /kɒnfrʌn'teɪʃn/ n confronto m

confuse /kən'fjuːz/ vt confondere

confused /kən'fjuːzd/ a (presentation, idea) ingarbugliato

confusing /kən'fjuːzɪŋ/ a che confonde

confusion /kən'fjuːʒn/ n confusione f

congeal /kən'dʒiːl/ vi (blood:) coagularsi

congenial /kən'dʒiːnɪəl/ a congeniale

congenital /kən'dʒenɪtl/ a congenito

congested /kən'dʒestɪd/ a congestionato

congestion /kən'dʒestʃn/ n congestione f

conglomerate /kən'glɒmərət/ n conglomerato m

Congo /'kɒŋgəʊ/ n Congo m

Congolese /kɒŋgəli:z/ a & n congolese mf

congratulate /kən'grætjʊleɪt/ vt congratularsi con (**on** per)

congratulations /kəngrætjʊ'leɪʃnz/ npl congratulazioni fpl

congregate /'kɒŋgrɪgeɪt/ vi radunarsi

congregation /kɒŋgrɪ'geɪʃn/ n Relig assemblea f

congress /'kɒŋgres/ n congresso m

congressman /'kɒŋgresmən/ n Am Pol membro m del congresso

conical /'kɒnɪkl/ a conico

conifer /'kɒnɪfə(r)/ n conifera f

conjecture /kən'dʒektʃə(r)/ n congettura f ● vt congetturare ● vi fare congetture

conjugal /'kɒndʒʊgl/ a coniugale

conjugate /'kɒndʒʊgeɪt/ vt coniugare

conjugation /kɒndʒʊ'geɪʃn/ n coniugazione f

conjunction /kən'dʒʌŋkʃn/ n congiunzione f; **in ~ with** insieme a

conjunctivitis /kəndʒʌŋktɪ'vaɪtɪs/ n congiuntivite f

■ **conjure up** /'kʌndʒə(r)/ vt evocare (image); tirar fuori dal nulla (meal)

conjuring /'kʌndʒərɪŋ/ n giochi mpl di prestigio

conjuring trick /'kʌndʒərɪŋ/ n gioco m di prestigio

conjuror /'kʌndʒərə(r)/ n prestigiatore, -trice mf

conk /kɒŋk/ vi **~ out** fam (machine:) guastarsi; (person:) crollare

conker /'kɒŋkə(r)/ n fam castagna f (d'ippocastano)

conman /'kɒnmæn/ n fam truffatore m

connect /kə'nekt/ vt collegare; **be ~ed with** avere legami con; (be related to) essere imparentato con; **be well ~ed** aver conoscenze influenti ● vi essere collegato (**with** a); (train:) fare coincidenza

connecting /kə'nektɪŋ/ a (room) di comunicazione

connecting flight n coincidenza f

connection /kə'nekʃn/ n (between ideas) nesso m; (in travel) coincidenza f; Electr, Comput collegamento m; **in ~ with** con riferimento a; **~s** pl (people) conoscenze fpl

connector /kə'nektə(r)/ n Comput connettore m

connivance /kə'naɪvəns/ n connivenza f

connive /kə'naɪv/ vi **~ at** essere connivente a

connoisseur /kɒnə'sɜː(r)/ n intenditore, -trice mf

connotation /kɒnə'teɪʃn/ n connotazione f

connote /kə'nəʊt/ vt evocare; (in linguistics) connotare

conquer /'kɒŋkə(r)/ vt conquistare; fig superare (fear)

conqueror /'kɒŋkərə(r)/ n conquistatore m

conquest /'kɒŋkwest/ n conquista f

conscience /'kɒnʃəns/ n coscienza f

conscientious /kɒnʃɪ'enʃəs/ a coscienzioso

conscientiously /kɒnsɪ'enʃəslɪ/ adv coscienziosamente

conscientious objector /əb'dʒektə(r)/ n obiettore m di coscienza

conscious /'kɒnʃəs/ a conscio; (decision) meditato; [fully] ~ cosciente; **be/become ~ of sth** rendersi conto di qcsa

consciously /'kɒnʃəslɪ/ adv consapevolmente

consciousness /'kɒnʃəsnɪs/ n consapevolezza f; Med conoscenza f

conscript¹ /'kɒnskrɪpt/ n coscritto m

conscript² /kən'skrɪpt/ vt Mil chiamare alle armi; **~ sb to do sth** fig reclutare qcno per fare qcsa

conscription /kən'skrɪpʃn/ n coscrizione f, leva f

consecrate /'kɒnsɪkreɪt/ vt consacrare

consecration /kɒnsɪ'kreɪʃn/ n consacrazione f

consecutive /kən'sekjʊtɪv/ a consecutivo

consecutively /kən'sekjʊtɪvlɪ/ adv consecutivamente

consensus /kən'sensəs/ n consenso m

consent /kən'sent/ n consenso m ● vi acconsentire

consequence /'kɒnsɪkwəns/ n conseguenza f; (importance) importanza f

consequent /'kɒnsɪkwənt/ a conseguente

consequently /'kɒnsɪkwəntlɪ/ adv di conseguenza

conservation /kɒnsə'veɪʃn/ n conservazione f

conservationist /kɒnsə'veɪʃənɪst/ n fautore, -trice mf della tutela ambientale

conservatism /kən'sɜːvətɪzm/ n conservatorismo m

conservative /kən'sɜːvətɪv/ a conservativo; (estimate) ottimistico; **C~** Pol a conservatore ● n conservatore, -trice mf

conservatory /kən'sɜːvətrɪ/ n spazio m chiuso da vetrate adiacente alla casa

conserve /kən'sɜːv/ vt conservare

consider /kən'sɪdə(r)/ vt considerare; ~ **doing sth** considerare la possibilità di fare qcsa

considerable /kən'sɪdərəbl/ a considerevole

considerably /kən'sɪdərəblɪ/ adv considerevolmente

considerate /kən'sɪdərət/ a pieno di riguardo

considerately /kən'sɪdərətlɪ/ adv con riguardo

consideration /kənsɪdə'reɪʃn/ n considerazione f; (thoughtfulness) attenzione f; (respect) riguardo m; (payment) compenso m; **take into ~** prendere in considerazione

considering /kən'sɪdərɪŋ/ prep considerando; ~ **that** considerando che

consign /kən'saɪn/ vt affidare

consignment /kən'saɪnmənt/ n consegna f

consist /kən'sɪst/ vi ~ **of** consistere di

consistency /kən'sɪstənsɪ/ n coerenza f; (density) consistenza f

consistent /kən'sɪstənt/ a coerente; (loyalty) costante; **be ~ with** far pensare a

consistently /kən'sɪstəntlɪ/ adv coerentemente; (late, loyal) costantemente

consolation /kɒnsə'leɪʃn/ n consolazione f

consolation prize n premio m di consolazione

console /kən'səʊl/ vt consolare

consolidate /kən'sɒlɪdeɪt/ vt consolidare

consolidation /kənsɒlɪ'deɪʃn/ n (of knowledge, position) consolidamento m

consoling /kən'səʊlɪŋ/ a consolante

consonant /'kɒnsənənt/ n consonante f

consort¹ /'kɒnsɔːt/ n consorte mf

consort² /kən'sɔːt/ vi ~ **with** frequentare

consortium /kən'sɔːtɪəm/ n consorzio m

conspicuous /kən'spɪkjʊəs/ a facilmente distinguibile; **be ~ by one's absence** brillare per la propria assenza

conspicuously /kən'spɪkjʊəslɪ/ adv (dressed) vistosamente; (placed) in evidenza; (silent, empty) in modo evidente

conspiracy /kən'spɪrəsɪ/ n cospirazione f

conspirator /kən'spɪrətə(r)/ n cospiratore, -trice mf

conspire /kən'spaɪə(r)/ vi cospirare

constable /'kʌnstəbl/ n agente m [di polizia]

constabulary /kən'stæbjʊlərɪ/ n Br polizia f

constancy /'kɒnstənsɪ/ n costanza f

constant /'kɒnstənt/ a costante

constantly /'kɒnstəntlɪ/ adv costantemente

constellation /kɒnstə'leɪʃn/ n costellazione f

consternation /kɒnstə'neɪʃn/ n costernazione f

constipated /'kɒnstɪpeɪtɪd/ a stitico

constipation /kɒnstɪ'peɪʃn/ n stitichezza f

constituency /kən'stɪtjʊənsɪ/ n area f elettorale di un deputato nel Regno Unito

constituent /kən'stɪtjʊənt/ n costituente m; Pol elettore, -trice mf

constitute /'kɒnstɪtjuːt/ vt costituire

constitution /kɒnstɪ'tjuːʃn/ n costituzione f

constitutional /kɒnstɪ'tjuːʃnl/ a costituzionale ● n passeggiata f salutare

constitutionally /kɒnstɪ'tjuːʃnəlɪ/ adv Pol costituzionalmente; (innately) di costituzione

constrain /kən'streɪn/ vt costringere

constraint /kən'streɪnt/ n costrizione f; (restriction) restrizione f; (strained manner) disagio m

constrict /kən'strɪkt/ vt (tight jacket:) stringere

constriction /kən'strɪkʃn/ n (of chest, throat) senso m di oppressione; (constraint) costrizione f; (of blood vessel) restrizione f

construct /kən'strʌkt/ vt costruire

construction /kən'strʌkʃn/ n costruzione f; (interpretation) interpretazione f; **under ~** in costruzione

construction: construction engineer n ingegnere m edile. **construction site** n cantiere m. **construction worker** n [operaio m] edile m

constructive /kən'strʌktɪv/ a costruttivo

constructively /kən'strʌktɪvlɪ/ adv in modo costruttivo

construe /kən'struː/ vt interpretare

consul /'kɒnsl/ n console m

consular /'kɒnsjʊlə(r)/ a consolare

consulate /'kɒnsjʊlət/ n consolato m

consult /kən'sʌlt/ vt consultare

consultancy /kən'sʌltənsɪ/ n (advice) consulenza f; (firm) ufficio m di consulenza; Br Med posto m di specialista; **do ~** fare il/la consulente ● attrib (fees, service, work) di consulenza

consultant /kən'sʌltənt/ n consulente mf; Med specialista mf

consultation /kɒnsl'teɪʃn/ n consultazione f; Med consulto m

consultative /kən'sʌltətɪv/ a di consulenza

consulting hours /kən'sʌltɪŋ/ npl Med orario m di visita

consulting room n Med ambulatorio m

consumable /kən'sjuːməbl/ n bene m di consumo

consume /kən'sjuːm/ vt consumare

consumer /kən'sjuːmə(r)/ n consumatore, -trice mf

consumer: consumer advice n consigli mpl ai consumatori. **consumer confidence** n fiducia f del consumatore. **consumer goods** npl beni mpl di consumo

consumerism /kən'sjuːmərɪzm/ n consumismo m

consumer: consumer organization n organizzazione f per la tutela dei consumatori. **consumer products** npl beni mpl di consumo. **consumer protection** n tutela f dei con-

75

consumer society | contradict

sumatori. **consumer society** *n* società *f inv*
consumista, società *f inv* dei consumi
consuming /kən'sju:mɪŋ/ *a* ⟨*passion*⟩ struggente; ⟨*urge*⟩ pressante; ⟨*hatred*⟩ insaziabile
consummate /'kɒnsjʊmeɪt/ *vt* consumare
consummation /kɒnsjʊ'meɪʃn/ *n* consu-
mazione *f*
consumption /kən'sʌmpʃn/ *n* consumo *m*
contact /'kɒntækt/ *n* contatto *m*; (*person*)
conoscenza *f* ● *vt* mettersi in contatto con
contactable /'kɒntæktəbl/ *a* ⟨*person*⟩ repe-
ribile
contact lenses *npl* lenti *fpl* a contatto
contagious /kən'teɪdʒəs/ *a* contagioso
contain /kən'teɪn/ *vt* contenere; ~ **oneself**
controllarsi
container /kən'teɪnə(r)/ *n* recipiente *m*; (*for
transport*) container *m inv*
container: container port *n* porto *m*
container. **container ship** *n* [nave *f*] portacontainers *f inv*. **container truck** *n* [autocar-
ro *m*] portacontainers *m inv*
contaminate /kən'tæmɪneɪt/ *vt* contaminare
contamination /kəntæmɪ'neɪʃn/ *n* conta-
minazione *f*
contd *abbr* (**continued**) segue
contemplate /'kɒntəmpleɪt/ *vt* contempla-
re; (*consider*) considerare; ~ **doing sth** considerare di fare qcsa
contemplation /kɒntəm'pleɪʃn/ *n* contem-
plazione *f*
contemplative /kən'templətɪv/ *a* contem-
plativo
contemporaneous /kəntempə'reɪnɪəs/ *a*
contemporaneo (**with** a)
contemporaneously /kəntempə'reɪnɪəslɪ/
adv contemporaneamente (**with** a)
contemporary /kən'tempərərɪ/ *a & n* contemporaneo, -a *mf*
contempt /kən'tempt/ *n* disprezzo *m*;
beneath ~ più che vergognoso; ~ **of court**
oltraggio *m* alla Corte
contemptible /kən'tem(p)təbl/ *a* spregevo-
le
contemptuous /kən'tem(p)tjʊəs/ *a* sprezzante
contemptuously /kən'tem(p)tjʊəslɪ/ *adv*
sprezzantemente
contend /kən'tend/ *vi* ~ **with** occuparsi di
● *vt* (*assert*) sostenere
contender /kən'tendə(r)/ *n* concorrente *mf*
content¹ /'kɒntent/ *n* contenuto *m*
content² /kən'tent/ *a* soddisfatto ● *n* **to
one's heart's** ~ finché se ne ha voglia ● *vt* ~
oneself accontentarsi (**with** di)
contented /kən'tentɪd/ *a* soddisfatto
contentedly /kən'tentɪdlɪ/ *adv* con aria
soddisfatta
contention /kən'tenʃn/ *n* (*assertion*) opinione *f*
contentious /kən'tenʃəs/ *a* ⟨*subject*⟩ controverso; ⟨*view*⟩ discutibile; ⟨*person, group*⟩
polemico

contentment /kən'tentmənt/ *n* soddisfazione *f*
contents /'kɒntents/ *npl* contenuto *m*
contest¹ /'kɒntest/ *n* gara *f*
contest² /kən'test/ *vt* contestare ⟨*statement*⟩; impugnare ⟨*will*⟩; Pol ⟨*candidates:*⟩
contendersi; ⟨*one candidate:*⟩ aspirare a
contestant /kən'testənt/ *n* concorrente *mf*
context /'kɒntekst/ *n* contesto *m*
continent /'kɒntɪnənt/ *n* continente *m*; **the
C~** l'Europa *f* continentale
continental /kɒntɪ'nentl/ *a* continentale
continental breakfast *n* prima colazione *f* a base di pane, burro, marmellata,
croissant ecc
continental quilt *n* piumone *m*
contingency /kən'tɪndʒənsɪ/ *n* eventualità
f inv
contingency fund *n* fondo *m* sopravvenienze passive
contingency plan *n* piano *m* d'emergenza
contingent /kən'tɪndʒənt/ *a* **be** ~ **on** dipendere da ● *n* Mil contingente *m*
continual /kən'tɪnjʊəl/ *a* continuo
continually /kən'tɪnjʊəlɪ/ *adv* continuamente
continuation /kəntɪnjʊ'eɪʃn/ *n* continuazione *f*
continue /kən'tɪnju:/ *vt* continuare; ~
doing *or* **to do sth** continuare a fare qcsa; **to
be** ~**d** continua ● *vi* continuare
continued /kən'tɪnju:d/ *a* continuo
continuity /kɒntɪ'nju:ətɪ/ *n* continuità *f*
continuity announcer *n* annunciatore,
-trice *mf*
continuity girl *n* segretaria *f* di produzione
continuous /kən'tɪnjʊəs/ *a* continuo
continuously /kən'tɪnjʊəslɪ/ *adv* continuamente
continuum /kən'tɪnjʊəm/ *n* continuum *m
inv*
contort /kən'tɔ:t/ *vt* contorcere
contortion /kən'tɔ:ʃn/ *n* contorsione *f*
contortionist /kən'tɔ:ʃənɪst/ *n* contorsioni-
sta *mf*
contour /'kɒntʊə(r)/ *n* contorno *m*; (*line*)
curva *f* di livello
contraband /'kɒntrəbænd/ *n* contrabbando *m*
contraception /kɒntrə'sepʃn/ *n* contraccezione *f*; **use** ~ ricorrere alla contraccezione
contraceptive /kɒntrə'septɪv/ *a & n* con-
traccettivo *m*
contract¹ /'kɒntrækt/ *n* contratto *m*
contract² /kən'trækt/ *vi* (*get smaller*) contrarsi ● *vt* contrarre ⟨*illness*⟩
contraction /kən'trækʃn/ *n* contrazione *f*
contract killer *n* sicario *m*
contractor /kən'træktə(r)/ *n* imprenditore,
-trice *mf*
contractual /kən'træktjʊəl/ *a* contrattuale
contract work *n* lavoro *m* su commissione
contract worker *n* lavoratore, -trice *mf*
con contratto a termine
contradict /kɒntrə'dɪkt/ *vt* contraddire

contradiction /kɒntrə'dɪkʃn/ *n* contraddizione *f*

contradictory /kɒntrə'dɪktəri/ *a* contradditorio

contraflow /'kɒntrəfləʊ/ *n utilizzazione f di una corsia nei due sensi di marcia durante lavori stradali*

contraindication /kɒntrəɪndɪ'keɪʃn/ *n* controindicazione *f*

contralto /kən'træltəʊ/ *n* contralto *m*

contraption /kən'træpʃn/ *n fam* aggeggio *m*

contrariness /kən'treərɪnɪs/ *n* spirito *m* di contraddizione

contrariwise /kən'treərɪwaɪz/ *adv* ⟨*conversely*⟩ d'altra parte, d'altro canto; ⟨*in the opposite direction*⟩ in direzione opposta

contrary¹ /'kɒntrəri/ *a* contrario ● *adv* ~ **to** contrariamente a ● *n* contrario *m*; **on the ~** al contrario

contrary² /kən'treəri/ *a* disobbediente

contrast¹ /'kɒntrɑːst/ *n* contrasto *m*

contrast² /kən'trɑːst/ *vt* confrontare ● *vi* contrastare

contrasting /kən'trɑːstɪŋ/ *a* contrastante

contravene /kɒntrə'viːn/ *vt* trasgredire

contravention /kɒntrə'venʃn/ *n* trasgressione *f*

contribute /kən'trɪbjuːt/ *vt/i* contribuire

contribution /kɒntrɪ'bjuːʃn/ *n* contribuzione *f*; ⟨*what is contributed*⟩ contributo *m*

contributor /kən'trɪbjʊtə(r)/ *n* contributore, -trice *mf*

contributory /kən'trɪbjʊtəri/ *a* ⟨*factor*⟩ concomitante; **be ~ to** contribuire a

contrite /kən'traɪt/ *a* contrito

contrive /kən'traɪv/ *vt* escogitare; **~ to do sth** riuscire a fare qcsa

contrived /kən'traɪvd/ *a* ⟨*style, effect*⟩ artificioso; ⟨*plot, ending*⟩ forzato; ⟨*incident, meeting*⟩ non fortuito

control /kən'trəʊl/ *n* controllo *m*; **~s** *pl* ⟨*of car, plane*⟩ comandi *mpl*; **get out of ~** sfuggire al controllo ● *vt* ⟨*pt/pp* **controlled**⟩ controllare; **~ oneself** controllarsi

control column *n* Aeron cloche *f inv*

control key *n* Comput tasto *m* di controllo

controlled /kən'trəʊld/ *a* ⟨*explosion, performance, person*⟩ controllato; **Labour-~** dominato dai laburisti

controller /kən'trəʊlə(r)/ *n* controllore *m*; *Fin* controllore *m* [della gestione]; *Radio, TV* direttore, -trice *mf*

control: control panel *n* ⟨*on machine*⟩ quadro *m* dei comandi; ⟨*for plane*⟩ quadro *m* di comando. **control room** *n* sala *f* di comando; *Radio, TV* sala *f* di regia. **control tower** *n* torre *f* di controllo

controversial /kɒntrə'vɜːʃl/ *a* controverso

controversy /'kɒntrəvɜːsi/ *n* controversia *f*

conundrum /kə'nʌndrəm/ *n* enigma *m*

conurbation /kɒnɜː'beɪʃn/ *n* conurbazione *f*

convalesce /kɒnvə'les/ *vi* essere in convalescenza

convalescence /kɒnvə'lesəns/ *n* convalescenza *f*

convalescent /kɒnvə'lesənt/ *a* convalescente

convalescent home *n* convalescenziario *m*

convection /kən'vekʃn/ *n* convezione *f*

convector /kən'vektə(r)/ *n* ~ [**heater**] convettore *m*

convene /kən'viːn/ *vt* convocare ● *vi* riunirsi

convener /kən'viːnə(r)/ *n* ⟨*organizer*⟩ organizzatore, -trice *mf*; ⟨*chair*⟩ presidente *m*

convenience /kən'viːnɪəns/ *n* convenienza *f*; [**public**] ~ gabinetti *mpl* pubblici; **with all modern ~s** con tutti i comfort

convenience foods *npl* cibi *mpl* precotti

convenience store *n* negozio *m* aperto fino a tardi

convenient /kən'viːnɪənt/ *a* comodo; **be ~ for sb** andar bene per qcno; **if it is ~ [for you]** se ti va bene

conveniently /kən'viːnɪəntli/ *adv* comodamente; **~ located** in una posizione comoda

convent /'kɒnvənt/ *n* convento *m*

convention /kən'venʃn/ *n* convenzione *f*; ⟨*assembly*⟩ convegno *m*

conventional /kən'venʃnəl/ *a* convenzionale

conventionally /kən'venʃnəli/ *adv* convenzionalmente

convention centre *n* palazzo *m* dei congressi

convent school *n* scuola *f* retta da religiose

converge /kən'vɜːdʒ/ *vi* convergere

conversant /kən'vɜːsənt/ *a* ~ **with** pratico di

conversation /kɒnvə'seɪʃn/ *n* conversazione *f*

conversational /kɒnvə'seɪʃnəl/ *a* di conversazione

conversationalist /kɒnvə'seɪʃnəlɪst/ *n* conversatore, -trice *mf*

converse¹ /kən'vɜːs/ *vi* conversare

converse² /'kɒnvɜːs/ *n* inverso *m*

conversely /'kɒnvɜːsli/ *adv* viceversa

conversion /kən'vɜːʃn/ *n* conversione *f*

conversion rate *n* [tasso *m* di] cambio *m*

conversion table *n* tabella *f* di conversione

convert¹ /'kɒnvɜːt/ *n* convertito, -a *mf*

convert² /kən'vɜːt/ *vt* convertire (**into** in); sconsacrare ⟨*church*⟩

converter /kən'vɜːtə(r)/ *n* Electr convertitore *m*

convertible /kən'vɜːtəbl/ *a* convertibile ● *n* Auto macchina *f* decappottabile

convex /'kɒnveks/ *a* convesso

convey /kən'veɪ/ *vt* portare; trasmettere ⟨*idea, message*⟩

conveyance /kən'veɪəns/ *n* trasporto *m*; ⟨*vehicle*⟩ mezzo *m* di trasporto

conveyor /kən'veɪə(r)/ *n* ⟨*of goods, persons*⟩ trasportatore *m*

conveyor belt *n* nastro *m* trasportatore

convict¹ /'kɒnvɪkt/ *n* condannato, -a *mf*

convict² /kən'vɪkt/ vt giudicare colpevole

conviction /kən'vɪkʃn/ n condanna f; (belief) convinzione f; **previous ~** precedente m penale

convince /kən'vɪns/ vt convincere

convincing /kən'vɪnsɪŋ/ a convincente

convincingly /kən'vɪnsɪŋlɪ/ adv in modo convincente

convivial /kən'vɪvɪəl/ a conviviale

convoluted /'kɒnvəlu:tɪd/ a contorto

convoy /'kɒnvɔɪ/ n convoglio m

convulse /kən'vʌls/ vt sconvolgere; **be ~d with laughter** contorcersi dalle risa

convulsion /kən'vʌlʃn/ n convulsione f

convulsive /kən'vʌlsɪv/ a convulso; Med convulsivo

convulsively /kən'vʌsɪvlɪ/ adv convulsamente

coo /ku:/ vi tubare

cooing /'ku:ɪŋ/ n (of bird, lovers) tubare m inv

cook /kʊk/ n cuoco, -a mf ● vt cucinare; **is it ~ed?** è cotto? **~ the books** fam truccare i libri contabili ● vi ⟨food:⟩ cuocere; ⟨person:⟩ cucinare

▪ **cook up** vt (fam) inventare ⟨excuse, story etc⟩

cookbook /'kʊkbʊk/ n libro m di cucina

cooked meats /kʊkt'mi:ts/ npl salumi mpl

cooker /'kʊkə(r)/ n cucina f; (apple) mela f da cuocere

cookery /'kʊkərɪ/ n cucina f

cookery book n libro m di cucina

cookie /'kʊkɪ/ n Am biscotto m

cooking /'kʊkɪŋ/ n cucina f; **be good at ~** saper cucinare bene; **do the ~** cucinare

cooking: cooking apple n mela f da cuocere. **cooking chocolate** n cioccolato m da pasticceria. **cooking foil** n carta f stagnola. **cooking salt** n sale m da cucina. **cooking time** n tempo m di cottura

cool /ku:l/ a fresco; (calm) calmo; (unfriendly) freddo ● n fresco m; **keep/lose one's ~** mantenere/perdere la calma ● vt rinfrescare ● vi rinfrescarsi

▪ **cool down** vi ⟨soup, tea etc:⟩ raffreddarsi; (fig: become calm) calmarsi ● vt raffreddare ⟨soup, tea etc⟩; (fig) calmare

cool: cool bag n Br borsa f frigo. **cool-box** n borsa f termica. **cool-headed** a equilibrato

cooling /'ku:lɪŋ/ n raffreddamento m ● a ⟨agent⟩ refrigerante; ⟨system, tower⟩ di raffreddamento; ⟨drink, swim⟩ rinfrescante

cooling-off period n (in industrial relations) periodo m di tregua [sindacale]; Comm fase f di riflessione

coolly /'ku:llɪ/ adv freddamente

coolness /'ku:lnɪs/ n freddezza f

coop /ku:p/ n stia f ● vt ~ **up** rinchiudere

co-op /'kəʊɒp/ n abbr (**cooperative**) cooperativa f

cooperate /kəʊ'ɒpəreɪt/ vi cooperare

cooperation /kəʊɒpə'reɪʃn/ n cooperazione f

cooperative /kəʊ'ɒpərətɪv/ a & n cooperativa f

co-opt /kəʊ'ɒpt/ vt eleggere

coordinate /kəʊ'ɔ:dɪneɪt/ vt coordinare

coordinated /kəʊ'ɔ:dɪneɪtɪd/ a coordinato

coordination /kəʊɔ:dɪ'neɪʃn/ n coordinazione f

coordinator /kəʊ'ɔ:dɪneɪtə(r)/ n coordinatore, -trice mf

co-owner /kəʊ'əʊnə(r)/ n comproprietario, -a mf

cop /kɒp/ n fam poliziotto m

cope /kəʊp/ vi fam farcela; **can she ~ by herself?** ce la fa da sola?; **~ with** farcela con; **I couldn't ~ with five kids** non ce la farei con cinque bambini

Copenhagen /kəʊpən'heɪgən/ n Copenhagen f

copier /'kɒpɪə(r)/ n fotocopiatrice f

co-pilot /'kəʊpaɪlət/ n copilota m

copious /'kəʊpɪəs/ a abbondante

copiously /'kəʊpɪəslɪ/ adv abbondantemente

cop-out n fam (evasive act) bidone m; (excuse) scappatoia f

copper¹ /'kɒpə(r)/ n rame m; **~s** pl monete fpl da uno o due pence ● attrib di rame

copper² n fam poliziotto m

copper: copper beech n faggio m rosso. **copper-coloured** a [color] rame inv; ⟨hair⟩ ramato. **copperplate** n calligrafia f ornata

coppice /'kɒpɪs/ n, **copse** /kɒps/ n boschetto m

co-property /'kəʊprɒpətɪ/ n comproprietà f inv

copulate /'kɒpjʊleɪt/ vi accoppiarsi

copulation /kɒpjʊ'leɪʃn/ n copulazione f

copy /'kɒpɪ/ n copia f ● vt (pt/pp -ied) copiare

▪ **copy down** vt = copy

▪ **copy out** vt = copy

copy: copybook n blot one's **~** rovinarsi la reputazione. **copycat** n pej fam copione, -a mf ● a ⟨crime, murder⟩ ispirato da un altro. **copy editor** n segretario, -a mf di redazione. **copyright** n diritti mpl d'autore. **copytypist** n dattilografo, -a mf. **copywriter** n copywriter mf inv

coquetry /'kɒkɪtrɪ/ n civetteria f

coquettish /kɒ'ketɪʃ/ a civettuolo

coral /'kɒrəl/ n corallo m

coral: coral island n isola f di corallo. **coral pink** a & n rosa m inv corallo. **coral reef** n barriera f corallina

cord /kɔ:d/ n corda f; (thinner) cordoncino m; (fabric) velluto m a coste; **~s** pl pantaloni mpl di velluto a coste

cordial /'kɔ:dɪəl/ a cordiale ● n analcolico m

cordially /'kɔ:dɪəlɪ/ adv con tutto il cuore

cordless telephone /'kɔ:dlɪs/ a telefono m senza fili

cordon /'kɔ:dn/ n cordone m (di persone)

▪ **cordon off** vt bloccare

corduroy /'kɔ:dərɔɪ/ n velluto m a coste

core /kɔ:(r)/ n (of apple, pear) torsolo m; (fig:

of organization) cuore *m*; (*of problem, theory*) nocciolo *m*

co-respondent /kəʊrɪ'spɒndənt/ *n Jur* correo, -a *mf* in adulterio

Corfu /kɔː'fuː/ *n* Corfù *f*

coriander /kɒrɪ'ændə(r)/ *n* coriandolo *m*

cork /kɔːk/ *n* sughero *m*; (*for bottle*) turacciolo *m*

corkage /'kɔːkɪdʒ/ *n* somma *f* pagata a un ristorante per servire una bottiglia di vino portata da fuori

corker /'kɔːkə(r)/ *n Br fam* (*story*) storia *f* strabiliante; (*stroke, shot*) tiro *m* da maestro

corkscrew /'kɔːkskruː/ *n* cavatappi *m inv*

corkscrew curls *npl* boccoli *mpl*

corn¹ /kɔːn/ *n* grano *m*; (*Am: maize*) granturco *m*

corn² *n Med* callo *m*

corncob /'kɔːnkɒb/ *n* pannocchia *f* [di mais]

cornea /'kɔːnɪə/ *n* cornea *f*

corned beef /kɔːnd'biːf/ *n* manzo *m* sotto sale

corner /'kɔːnə(r)/ *n* angolo *m*; (*football*) calcio *m* d'angolo, corner *m inv* ● *vt fig* bloccare; *Comm* accaparrarsi ⟨*market*⟩

corner shop *n* negozio *m* di quartiere

cornerstone /'kɔːnəstəʊn/ *n* pietra *f* angolare

cornet /'kɔːnɪt/ *n Mus* cornetta *f*; (*for icecream*) cono *m*

cornfield /'kɔːnfiːld/ *n* campo *m* di grano; (*sweetcorn*) campo *m* di mais

cornflour /'kɔːnflaʊə(r)/ *n* farina *f* finissima di mais

cornflower /'kɔːnflaʊə(r)/ *n* fiordaliso *m*

cornice /'kɔːnɪs/ *n* (*inside*) cornice *f*; (*outside*) cornicione *m*

Cornish pasty /kɔːnɪʃ'pæstɪ/ *n* fagottino *m* di pasta sfoglia ripieno di carne e verdura

corn: corn oil *n* olio *m* di mais. **corn on the cob** *n* pannocchia *f* cotta. **corn plaster** *n* [cerotto *m*] callifugo *m*. **cornstarch** *n Am* farina *f* di granturco

cornucopia /kɔːnjʊ'kəʊpɪə/ *n* cornucopia *f*; *fig* abbondanza *f*

Cornwall /'kɔːnwɔːl/ *n* Cornovaglia *f*

corny /'kɔːnɪ/ *a* (-ier, -iest) ⟨*fam: joke, film*⟩ scontato; ⟨*person*⟩ banale; (*sentimental*) sdolcinato

corollary /kə'rɒlərɪ/ *n* corollario *m*

coronary /'kɒrənərɪ/ *a* coronario ● *n* ~ [**thrombosis**] trombosi *f* coronarica

coronation /kɒrə'neɪʃn/ *n* incoronazione *f*

coroner /'kɒrənə(r)/ *n* coroner *m inv* (*nel diritto britannico, ufficiale incaricato delle indagini su morti sospette*)

coronet /'kɒrənet/ *n* coroncina *f*

corporal¹ /'kɔːpərəl/ *n Mil* caporale *m*

corporal² *a* corporale; **~ punishment** punizione *f* corporale

corporate /'kɔːpərət/ *a* ⟨*decision, policy, image*⟩ aziendale; **~ life** la vita in un'azienda

corporate: corporate image *n* immagine *f* aziendale. **corporate lawyer** *n* legale *mf* specializzato, -a in diritto aziendale.

corporate planning *n* pianificazione *f* aziendale

corporation /kɔːpə'reɪʃn/ *n* ente *m*; (*of town*) ≈ consiglio *m* comunale

corporation tax *n Br* imposta *f* sul reddito delle aziende

corps /kɔː(r)/ *n* (*pl* **corps** /kɔːz/) corpo *m*

corps de ballet /kɔːdə'bæleɪ/ *n* corpo *m* di ballo

corpse /kɔːps/ *n* cadavere *m*

corpulent /'kɔːpjʊlənt/ *a* corpulento

corpus /'kɔːpəs/ *n* (*of words*) corpus *m inv*

corpuscle /'kɔːpʌsl/ *n* globulo *m*

correct /kə'rekt/ *a* corretto; **be ~** ⟨*person:*⟩ aver ragione; **~!** esatto! ● *vt* correggere

correcting fluid *n* bianchetto *m*

correction /kə'rekʃn/ *n* correzione *f*

corrective /kə'rektɪv/ *n* correttivo *m*

correctly /kə'rektlɪ/ *adv* correttamente

correlate /'kɒrəleɪt/ *vt* correlare ● *vi* essere correlato

correlation /kɒrə'leɪʃn/ *n* correlazione *f*

correspond /kɒrɪ'spɒnd/ *vi* corrispondere (**to** a); ⟨*two things:*⟩ corrispondere; (*write*) scriversi

correspondence /kɒrɪ'spɒndəns/ *n* corrispondenza *f*

correspondence course *n* corso *m* per corrispondenza

correspondent /kɒrɪ'spɒndənt/ *n* corrispondente *mf*

corresponding /kɒrɪ'spɒndɪŋ/ *a* corrispondente

correspondingly /kɒrɪ'spɒndɪŋlɪ/ *adv* in modo corrispondente

corridor /'kɒrɪdɔː(r)/ *n* corridoio *m*

corroborate /kə'rɒbəreɪt/ *vt* corroborare

corrode /kə'rəʊd/ *vt* corrodere ● *vi* corrodersi

corrosion /kə'rəʊʒn/ *n* corrosione *f*

corrugated /'kɒrəgeɪtɪd/ *a* ondulato

corrugated iron *n* lamiera *f* ondulata

corrupt /kə'rʌpt/ *a* corrotto ● *vt* corrompere

corruption /kə'rʌpʃn/ *n* corruzione *f*

corset /'kɔːsɪt/ *n* & **-s** *pl* busto *m*

Corsica /'kɔːsɪkə/ *n* Corsica *f*

Corsican /'kɔːsɪkən/ *a* & *n* corso, -a *mf*

cortège /kɔː'teɪʒ/ *n* [**funeral**] **~** corteo *m* funebre

cosh /kɒʃ/ *n* randello *m*

co-signatory /kəʊ'sɪgnətrɪ/ *n* cofirmatario, -a *mf*

cosily /'kəʊzɪlɪ/ *adv* ⟨*sit, lie*⟩ in modo confortevole

cosiness /'kəʊzɪnɪs/ *n* (*of room*) comodità *f*; (*intimacy*) intimità *f*

cos lettuce /kɒs/ *n* lattuga *f* romana

cosmetic /kɒz'metɪk/ *a* cosmetico ● *n* **~s** *pl* cosmetici *mpl*

cosmetic surgery *n* chirurgia *f* estetica

cosmic /'kɒzmɪk/ *a* cosmico

cosmonaut /'kɒzmənɔːt/ *n* cosmonauta *mf*

cosmopolitan /kɒzmə'pɒlɪtən/ *a* cosmopolita

cosmos /'kɒzmɒs/ *n* cosmo *m*

Cossack /'kɒsæk/ *a & n* cosacco, -a *mf*

cosset /'kɒsɪt/ *vt* coccolare

cost /kɒst/ *n* costo *m*; **~s** *pl Jur* spese *fpl* processuali; **at all ~s** a tutti i costi; **I learnt to my ~** ho imparato a mie spese ● *vt* (*pt/pp* **cost**) costare; **it ~ me £20** mi è costato 20 sterline ● *vt* (*pt/pp* **costed**) **~** [**out**] stabilire il prezzo di

co-star /'kəʊstɑː/ *n Cinema, Theat* co-protagonista *mf* ● **film ~ring X and Y** un film con X e Y come protagonisti

cost: **cost centre** *n* centro *m* di costi. **cost-cutting** *n* tagli *mpl* sulle spese; **as a ~ exercise** [come misura] per ridurre le spese. **cost-effective** *a* conveniente. **cost-effectiveness** *n* convenienza *f*

costing /'kɒstɪŋ/ *n* (*process*) determinazione *f* dei costi; (*discipline*) costing *m inv*

costly /'kɒstlɪ/ *a* (**-ier, -iest**) costoso

cost of living *n* costo *m* della vita

cost-of-living index *n* indice *m* del costo della vita

cost price *n* prezzo *m* di costo

costume /'kɒstjuːm/ *n* costume *m*

costume drama *n* dramma *m* storico

costume jewellery *n* bigiotteria *f*

cosy /'kəʊzɪ/ *a* (**-ier, -iest**) (*pub, chat*) intimo; **it's nice and ~ in here** si sta bene qui ● *n* tea **~** copriteiera *m inv*

cot /kɒt/ *n* lettino *m*; (*Am: camp bed*) branda *f*

cot death *n Br* morte *f* inspiegabile di un neonato nel sonno

Côte d'Azur /kəʊtdæ'zʊə(r)/ *n* Costa *f* Azzurra

cottage /'kɒtɪdʒ/ *n* casetta *f*

cottage: **cottage cheese** *n* fiocchi *mpl* di latte. **cottage hospital** *n Br* piccolo ospedale *m* (*in zona rurale*). **cottage industry** *n* attività *f inv* artigianale basata sul lavoro a domicilio. **cottage loaf** *n* pagnotta *f* casereccia. **cottage pie** *n Br* pasticcio *m* di patate *e* carne macinata

cotton /'kɒtn/ *n* cotone *m* ● *attrib* di cotone

■ **cotton on** *vi fam* capire

cotton: **cotton bud** *n* cotton fioc® *m inv*. **cotton mill** *n* cotonificio *m*. **cotton reel** *n* rocchetto *m*, spagnoletta *f*. **cotton wool** *n Br* cotone *m* idrofilo

couch /kaʊtʃ/ *n* divano *m*

couchette /kuː'ʃet/ *n* cuccetta *f*

couch potato *n* pantofolaio, -a *mf*

cougar /'kuːgə(r)/ *n* coguaro *m*

cough /kɒf/ *n* tosse *f* ● *vi* tossire

■ **cough up** *vt/i* sputare; (*fam: pay*) sborsare

cough mixture *n* sciroppo *m* per la tosse

could /kʊd/, *atono* /kəd/ *v aux* (*see also* **can**²) **~ I have a glass of water?** potrei avere un bicchier d'acqua?; **I ~n't do it even if I wanted to** non potrei farlo nemmeno se lo volessi; **I ~n't care less** non potrebbe importarmene di meno; **he ~n't have done it without help** non avrebbe potuto farlo senza aiuto; **you ~ have phoned** avresti potuto telefonare

council /'kaʊnsl/ *n* consiglio *m*

council: **council estate** *n Br* complesso *m* di case popolari. **council house** *n* casa *f* popolare. **council housing** *n Br* case *fpl* popolari

councillor /'kaʊnsələ(r)/ *n* consigliere, -a *mf*

council tax *n* imposta *f* locale sugli immobili

counsel /'kaʊnsl/ *n* consigli *mpl*; *Jur* avvocato *m* ● *vt* (*pt/pp* **counselled**) consigliare a (*person*)

counselling, *Am* **counseling** /'kaʊnsəlɪŋ/ *n* (*psychological*) terapia *f* [psichiatrica]; *Sch* orientamento *m* scolastico; **careers ~** orientamento *m* professionale ● *attrib* (*group, centre, service*) di assistenza

counsellor /'kaʊnsələ(r)/ *n* consigliere, -a *mf*

count¹ /kaʊnt/ *n* (*nobleman*) conte *m*

count² *n* conto *m*; **keep ~** tenere il conto ● *vt/i* contare

■ **count against** *vt* (*inexperience, police record:*) deporre a sfavore di

■ **count among** *vt* **~ sb among one's friends** annoverare qcno tra i propri amici

■ **count in** *vt* (*include*) includere; **~ me in!** io ci sto!

■ **count on** *vt* contare su

■ **count out** *vt* contare (*money*); **~ me out!** fate senza di me!

■ **count up** *vt* contare ● *vi* **~ to ten** contare fino a dieci

countable /'kaʊntəbl/ *a* (*noun*) numerabile

countdown /'kaʊntdaʊn/ *n* conto *m* alla rovescia

countenance /'kaʊntənəns/ *n* espressione *f* ● *vt* approvare

counter¹ /'kaʊntə(r)/ *n* banco *m*; (*in games*) gettone *m*

counter² *adv* **~ to** contro, in contrasto a; **go ~ to sth** andare contro qcsa ● *vt/i* opporre (*measure, effect*); parare (*blow*)

counteract /kaʊntər'ækt/ *vt* neutralizzare

counter-attack *n* contrattacco *m*

counterbalance /'kaʊntəbæləns/ *n* contrappeso *m* ● *vt* controbilanciare

counter-claim *n* replica *f*

counter-culture /'kaʊntəkʌltʃə(r)/ *n* controcultura *f*

counter-espionage *n* controspionaggio *m*

counterfeit /'kaʊntəfɪt/ *a* contraffatto ● *n* contraffazione *f* ● *vt* contraffare

counterfoil /'kaʊntəfɔɪl/ *n* matrice *f*

counter-inflationary /-ɪn'fleɪʃənərɪ/ *a* antinflazionistico

counter-insurgency /-ɪn'sɜːdʒənsɪ/ *attrib* per reprimere un'insurrezione

counter-intelligence *n* controspionaggio *m*

countermeasure /'kaʊntəmeʒə(r)/ *n* contromisura *f*

counter-offensive *n* controffensiva *f*

counterpane /'kaʊntəpeɪn/ *n* copriletto *m*

counterpart /'kaʊntəpɑːt/ *n* equivalente *mf*

counterpoint /ˈkaʊntəpɔɪnt/ n contrappunto mf
counter-productive a controproduttivo
countersign /ˈkaʊntəsaɪn/ vt controfirmare
counter staff n commessi mpl
counter-terrorism n antiterrorismo m
countess /ˈkaʊntɪs/ n contessa f
countless /ˈkaʊntlɪs/ a innumerevole
countrified /ˈkʌntrɪfaɪd/ a ⟨person⟩ campagnolo
country /ˈkʌntrɪ/ n nazione f, paese m; (native land) patria f; (countryside) campagna f; **in the ~** in campagna; **go to the ~** andare in campagna; Pol indire le elezioni politiche
country: country and western n country m inv. **country bumpkin** n pej buzzurro , -a mf. **country club** n club m inv sportivo e ricreativo in campagna. **country cousin** n pej provinciale mf. **country dancing** n danza f folcloristica. **country house** n villa f di campagna. **countryman** n uomo m di campagna; (fellow ~man) compatriota m. **country music** n country m inv. **countryside** n campagna f. **countrywide** a & adv in tutto il paese
county /ˈkaʊntɪ/ n contea f (unità amministrativa britannica)
county council n Br Pol consiglio m di contea
county court n Br Jur tribunale m di contea
coup /kuː/ n Pol colpo m di stato
couple /ˈkʌpl/ n coppia f; **a ~ of** un paio di
coupon /ˈkuːpɒn/ n tagliando m; (for discount) buono m sconto
courage /ˈkʌrɪdʒ/ n coraggio m
courageous /kəˈreɪdʒəs/ a coraggioso
courageously /kəˈreɪdʒəslɪ/ adv coraggiosamente
courgette /kʊəˈʒet/ n zucchino m
courier /ˈkʊrɪə(r)/ n corriere m; (for tourists) guida f
course /kɔːs/ n Sch corso m; Naut rotta f; Culin portata f; (for golf) campo m; **~ of treatment** Med serie f inv di cure; **of ~** naturalmente; **in the ~ of** durante; **in due ~** a tempo debito; **~ of action** linea f d'azione
course book n libro m di testo
coursework /ˈkɔːswɜːk/ n Sch, Univ esercitazioni fpl scritte che contano per la media
court /kɔːt/ n tribunale m; Sport campo m; **take sb to ~** citare qcno in giudizio ● vt fare la corte a ⟨woman⟩; sfidare ⟨danger⟩; **~ing couples** coppiette fpl
court circular n bollettino quotidiano f di corte
courteous /ˈkɜːtɪəs/ a cortese
courteously /ˈkɜːtɪəslɪ/ adv cortesemente
courtesy /ˈkɜːtəsɪ/ n cortesia f
courthouse /ˈkɔːthaʊs/ n Jur palazzo m di giustizia, tribunale m
courtier /ˈkɔːtɪə(r)/ n cortigiano, -a mf
court: court martial n (pl ~s martial) corte f marziale ●**court-martial** vt (pt ~-martialled) portare davanti alla corte marziale. **court of inquiry** n commissione f d'inchiesta. **court of law** n Jur corte f di giustizia. **court order** n Jur ingiunzione f.
courtroom n Jur aula f [di tribunale]
courtship /ˈkɔːtʃɪp/ n corteggiamento m
courtyard /ˈkɔːtjɑːd/ n cortile m
cousin /ˈkʌzn/ n cugino, -a mf
cove /kəʊv/ n insenatura f
covenant /ˈkʌvənənt/ n (agreement) accordo m; (payment agreement) impegno m scritto a pagare
cover /ˈkʌvə(r)/ n copertura f; (of cushion, to protect sth) fodera f; (of book, magazine) copertina f; **take ~** mettersi al riparo; **under separate ~** a parte ● vt coprire; foderare ⟨cushion⟩; Journ fare un servizio su
■ **cover for** vt (replace) sostituire ⟨sb⟩
■ **cover up** vt coprire; fig soffocare ⟨scandal⟩
■ **cover up for** vt fare da copertura a ⟨sb⟩
coverage /ˈkʌvərɪdʒ/ n Journ **it got a lot of ~** i media gli hanno dedicato molto spazio
cover charge n coperto m
covered market n mercato m coperto
covered wagon n carro m coperto
cover girl n ragazza f copertina
covering /ˈkʌv(ə)rɪŋ/ n copertura f; (for floor) rivestimento m; **~ of snow** strato m di neve
covering fire n fuoco m di copertura
covering letter n lettera f d'accompagnamento
cover note n (from insurance company) polizza f provvisoria
cover story n (in paper) articolo m di prima pagina
covert /ˈkəʊvɜːt/ a ⟨threat⟩ velato; ⟨operation⟩ segreto; ⟨glance⟩ furtivo
covertly /ˈkəʊvɜːtlɪ/ adv furtivamente; ⟨operate⟩ in segreto
cover-up n messa f a tacere
cover version n Mus versione f non originale
covet /ˈkʌvɪt/ vt bramare
covetous /ˈkʌvətəs/ a avido
covetously /ˈkʌvətəslɪ/ adv avidamente
cow /kaʊ/ n vacca f, mucca f
coward /ˈkaʊəd/ n vigliacco, -a mf
cowardice /ˈkaʊədɪs/ n vigliaccheria f
cowardly /ˈkaʊədlɪ/ a da vigliacco
cowbell /ˈkaʊbel/ n campanaccio m
cowboy /ˈkaʊbɔɪ/ n cowboy m inv; fig fam buffone m
cower /ˈkaʊə(r)/ vi acquattarsi
cowherd /ˈkaʊhɜːd/ n vaccaro m
cowhide /ˈkaʊhaɪd/ n (leather) pelle f di mucca
cowl /kaʊl/ n cappuccio m
cowlick /ˈkaʊlɪk/ n fam ciocca f ribelle
cowl neck n collo m ad anello
cowpat /ˈkaʊpæt/ n sterco m di vacca
cowshed /ˈkaʊʃed/ n stalla f
cox /kɒks/ n, **coxswain** /ˈkɒks(ə)n/ n timoniere, -a mf

coy /kɔɪ/ *a* falsamente timido; (*flirtatiously*) civettuolo; **be ~ about sth** essere evasivo su qcsa

coyly /'kɔɪlɪ/ *adv* con falsa modestia; ⟨*flirtatiously*⟩ con civetteria

CPU *n abbr* (**central processing unit**) CPU *f inv*

crab /kræb/ *n* granchio *m*

crab apple *n* mela *f* selvatica

crack /kræk/ *n* (*in wall*) crepa *f*; (*in china, glass, bone*) incrinatura *f*; (*noise*) scoppio *m*; (*fam: joke*) battuta *f*; **have a ~** (*try*) fare un tentativo ● *a* (*fam: best*) di prim'ordine ● *vt* incrinare ⟨*china, glass*⟩; schiacciare ⟨*nut*⟩; decifrare ⟨*code*⟩; *fam* risolvere ⟨*problem*⟩; **~ a joke** *fam* fare una battuta ● *vi* ⟨*china, glass:*⟩ incrinarsi; ⟨*whip:*⟩ schioccare

■ **crack down** *vi fam* prendere seri provvedimenti

■ **crack down on** *vt fam* prendere seri provvedimenti contro

■ **crack up** *vi* crollare

crackdown /'krækdaʊn/ *n* misure *fpl* (**on** contro)

cracked /krækt/ *a* ⟨*plaster*⟩ crepato; ⟨*skin*⟩ screpolato; ⟨*rib*⟩ incrinato; (*fam: crazy*) svitato

cracker /'krækə(r)/ *n* (*biscuit*) cracker *m inv*; (*firework*) petardo *m*; [**Christmas**] **~** cilindro *m* di cartone contenente una sorpresa che produce una piccola esplosione quando viene aperto

crackers /'krækəz/ *a fam* matto

cracking /'krækɪŋ/ *a Br fam* eccellente; **at a ~ pace** a ritmo incalzante

crackle /'krækl/ *vi* crepitare

crackling /'kræklɪŋ/ *n* (*on radio*) disturbo *m*; (*of foil, cellophane*) sfregamento *m*; (*of fire*) crepitio *m*; (*crisp pork*) cotenna *f* arrostita

crackpot /'krækpɒt/ *fam n* pazzo, -a *mf* ● *a* da pazzi

cradle /'kreɪdl/ *n* culla *f*

cradle-snatcher *n fam* **he's/she's a ~** se la intende con i ragazzini/le ragazzine

craft[1] /krɑːft/ *n inv* (*boat*) imbarcazione *f*

craft[2] *n* mestiere *m*; (*technique*) arte *f*

craftily /'krɑːftɪlɪ/ *adv* con astuzia

craftsman /'krɑːftsmən/ *n* artigiano *m*

craftsmanship /'krɑːftsmənʃɪp/ *n* maestria *f*

crafty /'krɑːftɪ/ *a* (**-ier, -iest**) astuto

crag /kræg/ *n* rupe *f*

craggy /'krægɪ/ *a* scosceso; ⟨*face*⟩ dai lineamenti marcati

cram /kræm/ *v* (*pt/pp* **crammed**) ● *vt* stipare (**into** in) ● *vi* (*for exams*) sgobbare

crammer /'kræmə(r)/ *n* (*Br fam: school*) ≈ istituto *m* di recupero

cramp /kræmp/ *n* crampo *m*

cramped /kræmpt/ *a* ⟨*room*⟩ stretto; ⟨*handwriting*⟩ appiccicato; **it's a bit ~ed in here** si sta un po' stretti qui

crampon /'kræmpən/ *n* rampone *m*

cranberry /'krænbərɪ/ *n Culin* mirtillo *m* rosso

crane /kreɪn/ *n* (*at docks, bird*) gru *f inv* ● *vt* **~ one's neck** allungare il collo

cranium /'kreɪnɪəm/ *n* cranio *m*

crank[1] /kræŋk/ *n* tipo, -a *mf* strampalato, -a

crank[2] *n Techn* manovella *f*

crankshaft /'kræŋkʃɑːft/ *n* albero *m* a gomiti

cranky /'kræŋkɪ/ *a* strampalato; (*Am: irritable*) irritabile

cranny /'krænɪ/ *n* fessura *f*

crap /kræp/ *n sl* (*faeces*) merda *f*; (*film, book etc*) schifezza *f*; (*nonsense*) stronzate *fpl*; **have a ~** cacare

crappy /'kræpɪ/ *a sl* di merda

crash /kræʃ/ *n* (*noise*) fragore *m*; *Auto, Aeron* incidente *m*; *Comm* crollo *m*; *Comput* crash *m inv* ● *vi* schiantarsi (**into** contro); ⟨*plane:*⟩ precipitare ● *vt* schiantare ⟨*car*⟩

■ **crash out** *vi* (*sl: go to sleep*) crollare; (*on sofa etc*) dormire

crash: crash barrier *n* guardrail *m inv*. **crash course** *n* corso *m* intensivo. **crash diet** *n* dieta *f* drastica. **crash-helmet** *n* casco *m*. **crash-land** *vi* fare un atterraggio di fortuna. **crash-landing** *n* atterraggio *m* di fortuna.

crass /kræs/ *a* ⟨*ignorance*⟩ crasso

crate /kreɪt/ *n* (*for packing*) cassa *f*

crater /'kreɪtə(r)/ *n* cratere *m*

cravat /krə'væt/ *n* foulard *m inv*

crave /kreɪv/ *vt* morire dalla voglia di

craving /'kreɪvɪŋ/ *n* voglia *f* smodata

crawl /krɔːl/ *n* (*swimming*) stile *m* libero; **do the ~** nuotare a stile libero; **at a ~** a passo di lumaca ● *vi* andare carponi; **~ with** brulicare di

crawler lane /'krɔːlə/ *n Auto* corsia *f* riservata al traffico lento

crayfish /'kreɪfɪʃ/ *n* gambero *m* d'acqua dolce

crayon /'kreɪən/ *n* pastello *m* a cera; (*pencil*) matita *f* colorata

craze /kreɪz/ *n* mania *f*

crazed /kreɪzd/ *a* ⟨*china, glaze*⟩ screpolato; ⟨*animal, person*⟩ impazzito; **power-~** ubriaco di potere

crazy /'kreɪzɪ/ *a* (**-ier, -iest**) matto; **be ~ about** andar matto per

crazy golf *n Br* minigolf *m inv*

crazy paving *n Br* pavimentazione *f* a mosaico irregolare

creak /kriːk/ *n* scricchiolio *m* ● *vi* scricchiolare

creaky /'kriːkɪ/ *a* ⟨*leather*⟩ che cigola; ⟨*door, hinge*⟩ cigolante; ⟨*joint, bone, floorboard*⟩ scricchiolante; ⟨*fig fam: alibi, policy*⟩ traballante

cream /kriːm/ *n* crema *f*; (*fresh*) panna *f* ● *a* (*colour*) [bianco] panna *inv* ● *vt Culin* sbattere

■ **cream off** *vt* accaparrarsi ⟨*top pupils, scientists etc*⟩

cream: cream cheese *n* formaggio *m* cremoso. **cream cracker** *n Br* cracker *m inv*. **cream puff** *n* sfogliatina *f* alla panna *inv*. **cream soda** *n* soda *f* aromatizzata alla vaniglia. **cream tea** *n Br* tè *m inv* servito con pasticcini da mangiare con marmellata e panna

creamy /'kri:mɪ/ *a* (**-ier, iest**) cremoso

crease /kri:s/ *n* piega *f* ● *vt* stropicciare ● *vi* stropicciarsi

crease-resistant *a* che non si stropiccia

create /kri:'eɪt/ *vt* creare

creation /kri:'eɪʃn/ *n* creazione *f*

creative /kri:'eɪtɪv/ *a* creativo

creative director *n* direttore, -trice *mf* creativo, -a

creative writing *n* (*school subject*) composizione *f*

creativity /kri:eɪ'tɪvɪtɪ/ *n* creatività *f*

creator /kri:'eɪtə(r)/ *n* creatore, -trice *mf*

creature /'kri:tʃə(r)/ *n* creatura *f*

creature comforts *npl* comodità *fpl*; **like one's ~ ~** amare le proprie comodità

crèche /kreʃ/ *n* asilo *m* nido *inv*

credence /'kri:dəns/ *n* credito *m*; **give ~ to sth** (*believe*) dare credito a qcsa

credentials /krɪ'denʃlz/ *npl* credenziali *fpl*

credibility /kredə'bɪlətɪ/ *n* credibilità *f*

credible /'kredəbl/ *a* credibile

credit /'kredɪt/ *n* credito *m*; (*honour*) merito *m*; **take the ~ for** prendersi il merito di ● *vt* accreditare; **~ sb with sth** *Comm* accreditare qcsa a qcno; *fig* attribuire qcsa a qcno

creditable /'kredɪtəbl/ *a* lodevole

credit: credit balance *n* saldo *m* attivo. **credit card** *n* carta *f* di credito. **credit control** *n* controllo *m* del credito. **credit limit** *n* limite *m* di credito. **credit note** *n Comm* nota *f* di accredito

creditor /'kredɪtə(r)/ *n* creditore, -trice *mf*

credit: credit side *n* **on the ~ ~** tra i lati positivi. **credit squeeze** *n* stretta *f* creditizia. **credit terms** *npl* condizioni *fpl* di credito. **credit transfer** *n* bonifico *m*

creditworthiness /'kredɪ(t)wɜ:ðɪnɪs/ *n* capacità *f* di credito

creditworthy /'kredɪ(t)wɜ:ðɪ/ *a* meritevole di credito

credulity /krɪ'dju:lətɪ/ *n* credulità *f*; **strain sb's ~** essere ai limiti della credibilità

credulous /'kredjʊləs/ *a* credulo

creed /kri:d/ *n* credo *m inv*

creek /kri:k/ *n* insenatura *f*; (*Am: stream*) torrente *m*; **up the ~** (*fam: in trouble*) nei guai

creep /kri:p/ *vi* (*pt/pp* **crept**) muoversi furtivamente ● *n fam* tipo *m* viscido; **it gives me the ~s** mi fa venire i brividi

creeper /'kri:pə(r)/ *n* pianta *f* rampicante

creepy /'kri:pɪ/ *a* che fa venire i brividi

creepy-crawly /-'krɔ:lɪ/ *n fam* insetto

cremate /krɪ'meɪt/ *vt* cremare

cremation /krɪ'meɪʃn/ *n* cremazione *f*

crematorium /kremə'tɔ:rɪəm/ *n* crematorio *m*

crepe /kreɪp/ *n* (*fabric*) crespo *m*

crepe: crepe bandage *n* fascia *f* elastica. **crepe paper** *n* carta *f* crespata. **crepe soles** *npl* suole *fpl* di para

crept /krept/ *see* **creep**

crescendo /krɪ'ʃendəʊ/ *n Mus* crescendo *m*; **reach a ~** *fig* (*noise, protests:*) raggiungere il picco; (*campaign:*) raggiungere il culmine

crescent /'kresənt/ *n* mezzaluna *f*

crescent moon *n* mezzaluna *f*

cress /kres/ *n* crescione *m*

crest /krest/ *n* cresta *f*; (*coat of arms*) cimiero *m*; **be on the ~ of a wave** essere sulla cresta dell'onda

crestfallen /'krestfɔ:lən/ *a* mogio

Crete /kri:t/ *n* Creta *f*

crevasse /krɪ'væs/ *n* crepaccio *m*

crevice /'krevɪs/ *n* crepa *f*

crew /kru:/ *n* equipaggio *m*; (*gang*) équipe *f inv*

crew cut *n* capelli *mpl* a spazzola

crew neck *n* girocollo *m*

crew neck sweater *n* maglione *m* a girocollo

crib¹ /krɪb/ *n* (*for baby*) culla *f*

crib² *vt/i* (*pt/pp* **cribbed**) *fam* copiare

cribbage /'krɪbɪdʒ/ *n* gioco *m* di carte

crick /krɪk/ *n* **~ in the neck** torcicollo *m*

cricket¹ /'krɪkɪt/ *n* (*insect*) grillo *m*

cricket² *n* cricket *m*

cricketer /'krɪkɪtə(r)/ *n* giocatore *m* di cricket

crime /kraɪm/ *n* crimine *m*; (*criminality*) criminalità *f*; **it's a ~** *fig* è un delitto

crime of passion *n* delitto *m* passionale

crime prevention *n* prevenzione *f* della criminalità

criminal /'krɪmɪnl/ *a* criminale; (*law, court*) penale ● *n* criminale *mf*

criminal: criminal charges *npl* **face ~ ~** essere imputato. **criminal investigation** *n* inchiesta *f* giudiziaria. **Criminal Investigation Department** *n Br* ≈ polizia *f* giudiziaria. **criminal justice** *n* sistema *m* penale. **criminal law** *n* diritto *m* penale.

criminally insane /'krɪmɪnəlɪ/ *a* pazzo criminale

criminal offence *n* reato *m*

criminal record *n* **have a/no ~ ~** avere la fedina penale sporca/pulita

criminology /krɪmɪ'nɒlədʒɪ/ *n* criminologia *f*

crimp /krɪmp/ *vt* pieghettare (*fabric*); increspare (*pastry*); arricciare (*hair*)

crimson /'krɪmz(ə)n/ *a* cremisi *inv*

cringe /krɪndʒ/ *vi* (*cower*) acquattarsi; (*at bad joke etc*) fare una smorfia

crinkle /'krɪŋk(ə)l/ *vt* spiegazzare ● *vi* spiegazzarsi

crinkly /'krɪŋklɪ/ *a* (*paper, material*) crespato; (*hair*) crespo

cripple /'krɪpl/ *n* storpio, -a *mf* ● *vt* storpiare; *fig* danneggiare

crippled /'krɪpld/ *a* (*person*) storpio; (*ship*) danneggiato

crippling /'krɪplɪŋ/ *a* (*taxes, debts*) esorbitante; (*disease*) devastante; (*strike, effect*) paralizzante

crisis /'kraɪsɪs/ n (pl -ses /'kraɪsi:z/) crisi f inv

crisp /krɪsp/ a croccante; ⟨air⟩ frizzante; ⟨style⟩ incisivo

crispbread /'krɪs(p)bred/ n crostini mpl di pane

crisps /krɪsps/ npl patatine fpl

crispy /'krɪspɪ/ a croccante

criss-cross /'krɪs-/ a a linee incrociate

criterion /kraɪ'tɪərɪən/ n (pl -ria /kraɪ'tɪərɪə/) criterio m

critic /'krɪtɪk/ n critico, -a mf

critical /'krɪtɪkl/ a critico

critically /'krɪtɪklɪ/ adv in modo critico; ~ ill gravemente malato

critical path analysis n analisi f inv del percorso critico

criticism /'krɪtɪsɪzm/ n critica f; **he doesn't like** ~ non ama le critiche

criticize /'krɪtɪsaɪz/ vt criticare

croak /krəʊk/ vi gracchiare; ⟨frog:⟩ gracidare

Croatia /krəʊ'eɪʃə/ n Croazia f

crochet /'krəʊʃeɪ/ n lavoro m all'uncinetto ● vt fare all'uncinetto

crochet-hook n uncinetto m

crock /krɒk/ n fam old ~ ⟨person⟩ rudere m; ⟨car⟩ macinino m

crockery /'krɒkərɪ/ n terrecotte fpl

crocodile /'krɒkədaɪl/ n coccodrillo m

crocodile tears npl lacrime fpl di coccodrillo

crocus /'krəʊkəs/ n (pl -es) croco m

croft /krɒft/ n piccola fattoria f

crone /krəʊn/ n pej vecchiaccia f

crony /'krəʊnɪ/ n compare m

crook /krʊk/ n ⟨fam: criminal⟩ truffatore, -trice mf

crooked /'krʊkɪd/ a storto; ⟨limb⟩ storpiato; ⟨fam: dishonest⟩ disonesto; ~ **deal** fregatura f

croon /kru:n/ vt/i canticchiare

crop /krɒp/ n raccolto m; fig quantità f inv ● v (pt/pp cropped) ● vt coltivare

■ **crop up** vi fam presentarsi

crop rotation n rotazione f delle colture

crop spraying /'krɒpspreɪɪŋ/ n irrorazione f

croquet /'krəʊkeɪ/ n croquet m

croquette /krəʊ'ket/ n crocchetta f

cross /krɒs/ a ⟨annoyed⟩ arrabbiato; **talk at** ~ **purposes** fraintendersi ● n croce f; Bot, Zool incrocio m ● vt sbarrare ⟨cheque⟩; incrociare ⟨road, animals⟩; ~ **oneself** farsi il segno della croce; ~ **one's arms** incrociare le braccia; ~ **one's legs** accavallare le gambe; **keep one's fingers ~ed for sb** tenere le dita incrociate per qcno; **it ~ed my mind** mi è venuto in mente ● vi ⟨go across⟩ attraversare; ⟨lines:⟩ incrociarsi

■ **cross off** vt ⟨from list⟩ depennare

■ **cross out** vt sbarrare; ⟨from list⟩ depennare

cross: crossbar n ⟨of goal⟩ traversa f; ⟨on bicycle⟩ canna f. **cross-border** a oltreconfine. **crossbow** n balestra f. **crossbred** a ibrido. **crossbreed** vt ibridare, incrociare ⟨animals, plants⟩ ● n ⟨animal⟩ incrocio m, ibrido m. **cross-Channel** a attraverso la Manica; ⟨ferry⟩ che attraversa la Manica. **cross-check** n controprova f ● vt fare la controprova di. **cross-country** n Sport corsa f campestre. **cross-country skiing** n sci m di fondo. **cross-court** a ⟨shot, volley⟩ diagonale. **cross-cultural** a multiculturale. **crosscurrent** n corrente f trasversale. **cross-dressing** n travestitismo m. **cross-examination** n controinterrogatorio m. **cross-examine** vt sottoporre a controinterrogatorio. **cross-eyed** /'krɒsaɪd/ a strabico. **crossfire** n fuoco m incrociato

crossing /'krɒsɪŋ/ n ⟨for pedestrians⟩ passaggio m pedonale; ⟨sea journey⟩ traversata f

cross-legged /krɒs'legd/ a & adv con le gambe incrociate

crossly /'krɒslɪ/ adv con rabbia

cross: crossover a ⟨straps⟩ incrociato. **cross-purposes** npl **we are at** ~ non ci siamo capiti. **cross-question** vt interrogare ⟨person⟩. **cross-reference** n rimando m. **crossroads** n incrocio m; **reach a** ~ fig arrivare a un bivio. **cross-section** n sezione f; ⟨of community⟩ campione m. **cross-stitch** n punto m croce. **crosswalk** n Am attraversamento m pedonale. **crosswind** n vento m di traverso. **crosswise** adv in diagonale. **crossword** n ~ **[puzzle]** parole fpl crociate

crotch /krɒtʃ/ n Anat inforcatura f; ⟨in trousers⟩ cavallo m

crotchet /'krɒtʃɪt/ n Mus semiminima f

crotchety /'krɒtʃətɪ/ a irritabile

crouch /kraʊtʃ/ vi accovacciarsi

croupier /'kru:pɪə(r)/ n croupier m inv

crouton /'kru:tɒn/ n crostino m

crow /krəʊ/ n corvo m; **as the** ~ **flies** in linea d'aria ● vi cantare

crowbar /'krəʊbɑ:/ n piede m di porco

crowd /kraʊd/ n folla f ● vt affollare ● vi affollarsi

crowd control n controllo m della folla

crowded /'kraʊdɪd/ a affollato

crowd-puller /'kraʊdpʊlə(r)/ n ⟨event⟩ grande attrazione f

crowd scene n Cinema, Theat scena f di massa

crown /kraʊn/ n corona f ● vt incoronare; incapsulare ⟨tooth⟩

Crown court n Br Jur ≈ corte f d'assise

crowning glory /'kraʊnɪŋ/ n culmine m; **her hair is her** ~ ~ i capelli sono il suo punto forte

crown jewels npl gioielli mpl della corona

crown prince n principe m ereditario

crow's feet /krəʊz'fi:t/ npl ⟨on face⟩ zampe fpl di gallina

crow's nest /krəʊz'nest/ n coffa f

crucial /'kru:ʃl/ a cruciale

crucially /'kru:ʃəlɪ/ adv ~ **important** di vitale importanza

crucifix /'kru:sɪfɪks/ n crocifisso m

crucifixion /kru:sɪ'fɪkʃn/ n crocifissione f

crucify /'kru:sɪfaɪ/ vt (pt/pp -ied) crocifiggere

crude /kru:d/ a ⟨oil⟩ greggio; ⟨language⟩ crudo; ⟨person⟩ rozzo

crudely /'kru:dlɪ/ adv (vulgarly) in modo crudo; (simply) schematicamente; (roughly: assembled) sommariamente; ⟨painted, made⟩ rozzamente; ~ **speaking** in parole povere

crudity /'kru:dətɪ/ n (vulgarity) volgarità f

cruel /'kru:əl/ a (-ler, -lest) crudele (**to** verso)

cruelly /'kru:əlɪ/ adv con crudeltà

cruelty /'kru:əltɪ/ n crudeltà f

cruise /kru:z/ n crociera f ● vi fare una crociera; ⟨car:⟩ andare a velocità di crociera

cruise liner n nave f da crociera

cruise missile n missile m cruise inv

cruiser /'kru:zə(r)/ n Mil incrociatore m; (motor boat) motoscafo m

cruising speed /'kru:zɪŋ/ n velocità m inv di crociera

crumb /krʌm/ n briciola f

crumble /'krʌmbl/ vt sbriciolare ● vi sbriciolarsi; ⟨building, society:⟩ sgretolarsi

crumbling /'krʌmblɪŋ/ a fatiscente

crumbly /'krʌmblɪ/ a friabile

crummy /'krʌmɪ/ a fam (substandard) scadente; (Am: unwell) malato

crumpet /'krʌmpɪt/ n Culin focaccina f da tostare e mangiare con burro e marmellata

crumple /'krʌmpl/ vt spiegazzare ● vi spiegazzarsi

crunch /krʌntʃ/ n fam **when it comes to the** ~ quando si viene al dunque ● vt sgranocchiare ● vi ⟨snow:⟩ scricchiolare

crunchy /'krʌntʃɪ/ a ⟨vegetables, biscuits⟩ croccante

crusade /kru:'seɪd/ n crociata f

crusader /kru:'seɪdə(r)/ n crociato m

crush /krʌʃ/ n (crowd) calca f; **have a** ~ **on sb** essersi preso una cotta per qcno ● vt schiacciare; sgualcire ⟨clothes⟩

crushed ice /krʌʃt'aɪs/ n ghiaccio m frantumato

crushed velvet n velluto m stazzonato

crust /krʌst/ n crosta f

crustacean /krʌ'steɪʃn/ n crostaceo m

crusty /'krʌstɪ/ a ⟨bread⟩ croccante; (irritable) scontroso

crutch /krʌtʃ/ n gruccia f; Anat inforcatura f

crux /krʌks/ n fig punto m cruciale; ~ **of the matter** nodo m della questione

cry /kraɪ/ n grido m; ~ **for help** grido d'aiuto; **have a** ~ farsi un pianto; **a far** ~ **from** fig tutta un'altra cosa rispetto a ● vi (pt/pp **cried**) (weep) piangere; (call) gridare

■ **cry out** vi (shout) urlare

crypt /krɪpt/ n cripta f

cryptic /'krɪptɪk/ a criptico

cryptically /'krɪptɪklɪ/ adv ⟨say, speak⟩ in modo enigmatico; ~ **worded** espresso in maniera sibillina

crystal /'krɪstl/ n cristallo m; (glassware) cristalli mpl

crystal ball n sfera f di cristallo

crystal clear a ⟨water, sound⟩ cristallino; **let me make it** ~ ~ lasciatemelo spiegare chiaramente

crystal-gazing /'krɪstlgeɪzɪŋ/ n predizione f del futuro (con la sfera di cristallo)

crystallize /'krɪstəlaɪz/ vi (become clear) concretizzarsi

CS gas n Br gas m inv lacrimogeno

cub /kʌb/ n (animal) cucciolo m; **C~** [Scout] lupetto m

Cuba /'kju:bə/ n Cuba f

Cuban /'kju:bən/ a & n cubano -a, mf

cubby-hole /'kʌbɪ-/ n (compartment) scomparto m; (room) ripostiglio m

cube /kju:b/ n cubo m

cubic /'kju:bɪk/ a cubico

cubicle /'kju:bɪkl/ n cabina f

cubism /'kju:bɪzm/ n cubismo m

cubist /'kju:bɪst/ a & n cubista mf

cub reporter n cronista mf alle prime armi

cuckoo /'kʊku:/ n cuculo m

cuckoo clock n orologio m a cucù

cucumber /'kju:kʌmbə(r)/ n cetriolo m

cud /kʌd/ n also fig **chew the** ~ ruminare

cuddle /'kʌd(ə)l/ vt coccolare ● vi ~ **up to** starsene accoccolato insieme a ● n **have a** ~ ⟨child:⟩ farsi coccolare; ⟨lovers:⟩ abbracciarsi

cuddly /'kʌd(ə)lɪ/ a tenerone; (wanting cuddles) coccolone

cuddly toy n peluche m inv

cudgel /'kʌdʒl/ n randello m

cue¹ /kju:/ n segnale m; Theat battuta f d'entrata

cue² n (in billiards) stecca f

cue ball n pallino m

cuff /kʌf/ n polsino m; (Am: turn-up) orlo m; (blow) scapaccione m; **off the** ~ improvvisando ● vt dare una pacca a

cuff link n gemello m

cuisine /kwɪ'zi:n/ n cúcina f; **haute** ~ /əʊt/ haute cuisine f

cul-de-sac /'kʌldəsæk/ n vicolo m cieco

culinary /'kʌlɪnərɪ/ a culinario

cull /kʌl/ vt scegliere ⟨flowers⟩; (kill) selezionare e uccidere

culminate /'kʌlmɪneɪt/ vi culminare

culmination /kʌlmɪ'neɪʃn/ n culmine m

culottes /kju:'lɒts/ npl gonna f sg pantalone

culpable /'kʌlpəbl/ a colpevole

culpable homicide n Jur omicidio m colposo

culprit /'kʌlprɪt/ n colpevole mf

cult /kʌlt/ n culto m

cultivate /'kʌltɪveɪt/ vt coltivare; fig coltivarsi ⟨person⟩

cultivated /'kʌltɪveɪtɪd/ a ⟨soil⟩ lavorato; ⟨person⟩ colto

cultural /'kʌltʃərəl/ a culturale

cultural attaché n addetto m culturale

culture /'kʌltʃə(r)/ n cultura f

cultured /'kʌltʃəd/ a colto

cultured pearl n perla f coltivata

culture shock n shock m inv culturale

culture vulture *n fam* fanatico, -a *mf* di cultura
culvert /'kʌlvət/ *n* condotto *m* sotterraneo
cumbersome /'kʌmbəsəm/ *a* ingombrante
cumin /'kjuːmɪn/ *n* cumino *m* nero
cummerbund /'kʌməbʌnd/ *n* fascia *f* (*dello smoking*)
cumulative /'kjuːmjʊlətɪv/ *a* cumulativo
cunning /'kʌnɪŋ/ *a* astuto ● *n* astuzia *f*
cup /kʌp/ *n* tazza *f*; (*prize, of bra*) coppa *f*
cupboard /'kʌbəd/ *n* armadio *m*
cupboard love *n Br hum* amore *m* interessato
cupboard space *n* spazio *m* negli armadi
Cup Final *n* finale *f* di coppa
cupful /'kʌpfʊl/ *n* tazza *f* (*contenuto*)
Cupid /'kjuːpɪd/ *n* Cupido *m*
cupola /'kjuːpələ/ *n Archit* cupola *f*
cup tie *n Br* partita *f* eliminatoria
cur /kɜː(r)/ *n* (*pej: dog*) cagnaccio *m*
curable /'kjʊərəbl/ *a* curabile
curate /'kjʊərət/ *n* curato *m*
curator /kjʊə'reɪtə(r)/ *n* direttore, -trice *mf* (*di museo*)
curb /kɜːb/ *vt* tenere a freno
curd cheese /kɜːd/ *n* cagliata *f*
curdle /'kɜːdl/ *vi* coagularsi
cure /kjʊə(r)/ *n* cura *f* ● *vt* curare; (*salt*) mettere sotto sale; (*smoke*) affumicare
cure-all *n* toccasana *m inv*, panacea *f*
curfew /'kɜːfjuː/ *n* coprifuoco *m*
curio /'kjʊərɪəʊ/ *n* curiosità *f inv*
curiosity /kjʊərɪ'ɒsətɪ/ *n* curiosità *f*
curious /'kjʊərɪəs/ *a* curioso
curiously /'kjʊərɪəslɪ/ *adv* curiosamente
curl /kɜːl/ *n* ricciolo *m* ● *vt* arricciare ● *vi* arricciarsi
■ **curl up** *vi* raggomitolarsi
curler /'kɜːlə(r)/ *n* bigodino *m*
curling /'kɜːlɪŋ/ *n Sport* curling *m*
curly /'kɜːlɪ/ *a* (**-ier, -iest**) riccio
curly-haired, curly-headed /-'heəd, -'hedɪd/ *a* (*tight curls*) dai capelli crespi; (*loose curls*) riccio
currant /'kʌrənt/ *n* (*dried*) uvetta *f*
currency /'kʌrənsɪ/ *n* valuta *f*; (*of word*) ricorrenza *f*; **foreign ~** valuta *f* estera
current /'kʌrənt/ *a* corrente ● *n* corrente *f*. **~ affairs** *or* **events** *npl* attualità *fsg*
current: current account *n Br* conto *m* corrente. **current assets** *n Fin* disponibilità *fpl* correnti. **current liabilities** *npl Fin* passività *fpl* correnti
currently /'kʌrəntlɪ/ *adv* attualmente
curriculum /kə'rɪkjʊləm/ *n* programma *m* di studi
curriculum vitae /'viːtaɪ/ *n* curriculum vitae *m inv*
curry /'kʌrɪ/ *n* curry *m inv*; (*meal*) piatto *m* cucinato nel curry ● *vt* (*pt/pp* **-ied**) **~ favour with sb** cercare d'ingraziarsi qcno
curry powder *n* curry *m* in polvere
curse /kɜːs/ *n* maledizione *f*; (*oath*) imprecazione *f* ● *vt* maledire ● *vi* imprecare

cursor /'kɜːsə(r)/ *n* cursore *m*
cursor keys *npl* tasti *mpl* cursore
cursory /'kɜːsərɪ/ *a* sbrigativo
curt /kɜːt/ *a* brusco
curtail /kə'teɪl/ *vt* ridurre
curtailment /kə'teɪlmənt/ *n* (*of rights, freedom*) limitazione *f*; (*of expenditure, service*) riduzione *f*; (*of holiday*) interruzione *f*
curtain /'kɜːtn/ *n* tenda *f*; *Theat* sipario *m*
■ **curtain off** *vt* separare con una tenda
curtain call *n Theat* chiamata *f* alla ribalta
curtly /'kɜːtlɪ/ *adv* bruscamente
curtsy /'kɜːtsɪ/ *n* inchino *m* ● *vi* (*pt/pp* **-ied**) fare l'inchino
curvaceous /kɜː'veɪʃəs/ *a* formoso
curve /kɜːv/ *n* curva *f* ● *vi* curvare; **~ to the right/left** curvare a destra/sinistra
curved /kɜːvd/ *a* curvo
curvy /'kɜːvɪ/ *a* (**-ier, iest**) ⟨*woman*⟩ formoso
cushion /'kʊʃn/ *n* cuscino *m* ● *vt* attutire; (*protect*) proteggere
cushy /'kʊʃɪ/ *a* (**-ier, -iest**) *fam* facile
custard /'kʌstəd/ *n* (*liquid*) crema *f* pasticciera
custard: custard cream *n Br* biscotto *m* farcito alla crema. **custard pie** *n* torta *f* alla crema (*nei film comici*). **custard tart** *n* torta *f* alla crema
custodial sentence /kʌ'stəʊdɪəl/ *n* condanna *f* a una pena detentiva
custodian /kʌ'stəʊdɪən/ *n* custode *mf*
custody /'kʌstədɪ/ *n* (*of child*) custodia *f*; (*imprisonment*) detenzione *f* preventiva
custom /'kʌstəm/ *n* usanza *f*; *Jur* consuetudine *f*; *Comm* clientela *f*
customary /'kʌstəmərɪ/ *a* (*habitual*) abituale; **it's ~ to...** è consuetudine...
custom-built /-'bɪlt/ *a* ⟨*house*⟩ ad hoc
custom car *n* vettura *f* personalizzata
customer /'kʌstəmə(r)/ *n* cliente *mf*
customer: customer feedback *n* feedback *m inv* dai clienti. **customer relations** *npl* rapporto *m* con i clienti. **customer service** *n* assistenza *f* ai clienti
customize /'kʌstəmaɪz/ *vt* personalizzare
custom-made /-'meɪd/ *a* su misura
customs /'kʌstəmz/ *npl* dogana *f*
customs: Customs and Excise *n Br* Ufficio *m* Dazi e Dogana. **customs clearance** *n* sdoganamento *m*. **customs declaration** *n* dichiarazione *f* doganale. **customs duties** *npl* dazi *mpl* doganali. **customs hall** *n* dogana *f*. **customs officer** *n* doganiere *m*, guardia *f* di finanza
cut /kʌt/ *n* (*with knife etc, of clothes*) taglio *m*; (*reduction*) riduzione *f*; (*in public spending*) taglio *m* ● *vt/i* (*pt/pp* **cut**, *pres p* **cutting**) tagliare; (*reduce*) ridurre; **~ one's finger** tagliarsi il dito; **~ sb's hair** tagliare i capelli a qcno ● *vi* (*with cards*) alzare
■ **cut away** *vt* tagliar via
■ **cut back** *vt* tagliare ⟨*hair*⟩; potare ⟨*hedge*⟩; (*reduce*) ridurre

■ **cut back on** *vt* (*reduce*) ridurre

■ **cut down** *vt* abbattere ‹tree›; (*reduce*) ridurre

■ **cut in** *vi Auto* tagliare la strada; (*into conversation*) interrompere ● *vt* ~ **sb in on a deal** dare una percentuale a qcno

■ **cut off** *vt* tagliar via; (*disconnect*) interrompere; *fig* isolare; **I was ~ off** *Teleph* la linea è caduta

■ **cut out** *vt* ritagliare; (*delete*) eliminare; **be ~ out for** *fam* essere tagliato per; ~ **it out!** *fam* dacci un taglio!

■ **cut up** *vt* (*slice*) tagliare a pezzi

cut-and-dried *a* ‹answer, solution› ovvio; **I like everything to be ~** mi piace che tutto sia ben chiaro e definito

cut and thrust *n* **the ~ ~ ~ of debate** gli scambi *mpl* animati del dibattito

cutback /'kʌtbæk/ *n* riduzione *f*; (*in government spending*) taglio *m*

cute /kju:t/ *a fam* (*in appearance*) carino; (*clever*) acuto

cut glass *n* vetro *m* intagliato

cuticle /'kju:tɪkl/ *n* cuticola *f*

cutlery /'kʌtlərɪ/ *n* posate *fpl*

cutlet /'kʌtlɪt/ *n* cotoletta *f*

cut-off *n* (*upper limit*) limite *m* [massimo]

cut-off date *n* data *f* di scadenza

cut-off point *n* limite *m*; *Comm* data *f* di scadenza

cut-offs *npl* (*jeans*) jeans *mpl* tagliati

cut-out *n* (*outline*) ritaglio *m*

cut-price *a* a prezzo ridotto; ‹shop› che fa prezzi ridotti

cutter /'kʌtə(r)/ *n* (*ship*) cutter *m inv*; (*on ship*) lancia *f*; (*for metal, glass*) taglierina *f*

cut-throat *n* assassino, -a *mf* ● *a* ‹competition› spietato

cut-throat razor *n Br* rasoio *m* da barbiere

cutting /'kʌtɪŋ/ *a* ‹remark› tagliente ● *n* (*from newspaper*) ritaglio *m*; (*of plant*) talea *f*

cutting edge *n* (*blade*) filo *m*; **be at the ~ ~** *fig* essere all'avanguardia

cuttingly /'kʌtɪŋlɪ/ *adv* ‹speak› in maniera tagliente

cutting room *n Cinema* **end up on the ~ ~ floor** essere tagliato in fase di montaggio

CV *abbr of* **curriculum vitae**

cwt *abbr* (**hundredweight**) ≈ 50 kg, *Am* ≈ 45 kg

cyanide /'saɪənaɪd/ *n* cianuro *m*

cybernetics /saɪbə'netɪks/ *n* cibernetica *f*

cyberspace /'saɪbəspeɪs/ *n* ciberspazio *m*

cyclamen /'sɪkləmən/ *n* ciclamino *m*

cycle /'saɪk(ə)l/ *n* ciclo *m*; (*bicycle*) bicicletta *f*, *fam* bici *f inv* ● *vi* andare in bicicletta

cycle: cycle clip *n* fermacalzoni *m inv*. **cycle lane** *n* pista *f* ciclabile. **cycle race** *n* corsa *f* ciclistica. **cycle rack** *n* portabiciclette *m inv*. **cycle track** *n* pista *f* ciclabile

cyclical /'saɪklɪkl/ *a* ciclico

cycling /'saɪklɪŋ/ *n* ciclismo *m*

cycling holiday *n Br* vacanza *f* in bicicletta; **go on a ~ ~** fare una vacanza in bicicletta

cycling shorts *npl* pantaloncini *mpl* da ciclista

cyclist /'saɪklɪst/ *n* ciclista *mf*

cyclo-cross /'saɪkləʊ-/ *n* ciclocross *m inv*

cyclone /'saɪkləʊn/ *n* ciclone *m*

cygnet /'sɪgnɪt/ *n* cigno *m* giovane

cylinder /'sɪlɪndə(r)/ *n* cilindro *m*

cylindrical /sɪl'lɪndrɪkl/ *a* cilindrico

cymbals /'sɪmblz/ *npl Mus* piatti *mpl*

cynic /'sɪnɪk/ *n* cinico, -a *mf*

cynical /'sɪnɪk(ə)l/ *a* cinico

cynically /'sɪnɪklɪ/ *adv* cinicamente

cynicism /'sɪnɪsɪzm/ *n* cinismo *m*

cypress /'saɪprəs/ *n* cipresso *m*

Cypriot /'sɪprɪət/ *a & n* cipriota *mf*

Cyprus /'saɪprəs/ *n* Cipro *m*

Cyrillic /sɪ'rɪlɪk/ *a* cirillico

cyst /sɪst/ *n* ciste *f*

cystitis /sɪ'staɪtɪs/ *n* cistite *f*

Czar, czar /zɑ:(r)/ *n* zar *m inv*

Czech /tʃek/ *a & n* ceco, -a *mf*

Czechoslovak /tʃekə'sləʊvæk/ *a* cecoslovacco

Czechoslovakia /tʃekəslə'vækɪə/ *n* Cecoslovacchia *f*

Czech Republic *n* Repubblica *f* Ceca

Dd

d, D /di:/ n (*letter*) d, D f *inv*; *Mus* re m *inv*
d *abbr* (**died**) morto
dab /dæb/ n colpetto m; **a ~ of** un pochino di
● vt (*pt/pp* **dabbed**) toccare leggermente
⟨*eyes*⟩
■ **dab on** vt mettere un po' di ⟨*paint etc*⟩
dabble /'dæbl/ vi **~ in sth** *fig* occuparsi di
qcsa a tempo perso
dachshund /'dækshʊnd/ n bassotto m
dad[dy] /'dæd[ɪ]/ n *fam* papà m *inv*, babbo m
daddy-long-legs n zanzarone m [dei bo-
schi]; (*Am: spider*) ragno m
daffodil /'dæfədɪl/ n giunchiglia f
daft /dɑːft/ a sciocco
dagger /'dægə(r)/ n stiletto m; *Typ* croce f;
be at ~s drawn *fam* essere ai ferri corti
dahlia /'deɪlɪə/ n dalia f
daily /'deɪlɪ/ a giornaliero ● adv giornalmen-
te ● n (*newspaper*) quotidiano m; (*fam:
cleaner*) donna f delle pulizie
daintily /'deɪntɪlɪ/ adv delicatamente
dainty /'deɪntɪ/ a (**-ier, -iest**) grazioso;
⟨*movement*⟩ delicato
dairy /'deərɪ/ n caseificio m; (*shop*) latteria f
dairy cow n mucca f da latte
dairyman /'deərɪmən/ n (*on farm*) operaio
m addetto all'allevamento di mucche [da lat-
te]; (*Am: farmer*) allevatore m
dairy products npl latticini mpl
dais /'deɪɪs/ n pedana f
daisy /'deɪzɪ/ n margheritina f; (*larger*) margherita f
dale /deɪl/ n *liter* valle f
dally /'dælɪ/ vi (*pt/pp* **-ied**) stare a gingillarsi
dam /dæm/ n diga f ● vt (*pt/pp* **dammed**) costruire una diga su
damage /'dæmɪdʒ/ n danno m (**to** a); **~s** pl
Jur risarcimento *msg* ● vt danneggiare; *fig*
nuocere a
damaging /'dæmɪdʒɪŋ/ a dannoso
damask /'dæməsk/ n damasco m
dame /deɪm/ n *liter* dama f; *Am sl* donna f
dammit /'dæmɪt/ *int Br fam* accidenti
damn /dæm/ c *fam* maledetto ● adv ⟨*lucky,
late*⟩ maledettamente ● n **I don't care** *or*
give a ~ *fam* non me ne frega un accidente
● vt dannare
damnation /dæm'neɪʃn/ n dannazione f
● *int fam* accidenti!
damnedest /'dæmdɪst/ n **do one's ~** (**to
do**) (*fam: hardest*) fare del proprio meglio
(per fare) ● **a it was the ~ thing**
(*surprising*) era la cosa più straordinaria
damning /'dæmɪŋ/ a schiacciante
damp /dæmp/ a umido ● n umidità f ● vt =
dampen

dampen /'dæmpən/ vt inumidire; *fig* raffreddare ⟨*enthusiasm*⟩
damper /'dæmpə(r)/ n **the news put a ~
on the evening** *fam* la notizia ha raggelato
l'atmosfera della serata
dampness /'dæmpnɪs/ n umidità f
damson /'dæmzən/ n (*fruit*) susina f selvatica, prugna f selvatica
dance /dɑːns/ n ballo m ● vt/i ballare
dance hall n sala f da ballo
dance music n musica f da ballo
dancer /'dɑːnsə(r)/ n ballerino, -a mf
dandelion /'dændɪlaɪən/ n dente m di leone
dandruff /'dændrʌf/ n forfora f
Dane /deɪn/ n danese mf; **Great ~** danese m
danger /'deɪndʒə(r)/ n pericolo m; **in/out of
~** in/fuori pericolo
danger level n livello m di guardia
danger list n **on the ~ ~** in prognosi riservata; **off the ~ ~** fuori pericolo
danger money n indennità f di rischio
dangerous /'deɪndʒərəs/ a pericoloso
dangerously /'deɪndʒərəslɪ/ adv pericolosamente; **~ ill** in pericolo di vita
danger signal n *also fig* segnale m di pericolo
dangle /'dæŋgl/ vi penzolare; *fig* **leave sb
dangling** lasciare qcno in sospeso ● vt far
penzolare
Danish /'deɪnɪʃ/ a danese ● n (*language*) danese m
Danish pastry n dolce m di pasta sfoglia
contenente pasta di mandorle, mele ecc.
dank /dæŋk/ a umido e freddo
Danube /'dænjuːb/ n Danubio m
dapper /'dæpə(r)/ a azzimato
dappled /'dæp(ə)ld/ a ⟨*grey, horse*⟩
pomellato; ⟨*sky*⟩ screziato; ⟨*shade, surface*⟩
chiazzato
dare /deə(r)/ vt/i osare; (*challenge*) sfidare
(**to** a); **~** [**to**] **do sth** osare fare qcsa; **I ~ say!**
molto probabilmente ● n sfida f
daredevil /'deədevl/ n spericolato, -a mf
daring /'deərɪŋ/ a audace ● n audacia f
dark /dɑːk/ a buio; **~ blue/brown** blu/mar-
rone scuro; **it's getting ~** sta cominciando a
fare buio; **~ horse** *fig* (*in race, contest*) vincitore m imprevisto; (*not much known about*)
misterioso m; **keep sth ~** *fig* tenere qcsa nascosto ● n **after ~** col buio; **in the ~** al buio;
keep sb in the ~ *fig* tenere qcno all'oscuro
Dark Ages n alto Medioevo m
dark chocolate n cioccolato m fondente
darken /'dɑːkn/ vt oscurare ● vi oscurarsi
dark-eyed /-'aɪd/ a ⟨*person*⟩ dagli occhi scuri

dark glasses *npl* occhiali *mpl* scuri

darkly /'dɑːklɪ/ *adv* ‹*mutter, hint*› cupamente

darkness /'dɑːknɪs/ *n* buio *m*

darkroom /'dɑːkruːm/ *n* camera *f* oscura

dark-skinned *a* ‹*person*› dalla pelle scura

darling /'dɑːlɪŋ/ *a* adorabile; **my ~ Joan** carissima Joan ● *n* tesoro *m*; **be a ~ and... sii** gentile e...

darn /dɑːn/ *vt* rammendare

darning needle /'dɑːnɪŋ/ *n* ago *m* da rammendo

dart /dɑːt/ *n* dardo *m*; (*in sewing*) pince *f inv*; **~s** *sg* (*game*) freccette *fpl* ● *vi* lanciarsi

dartboard /'dɑːtbɔːd/ *n* bersaglio *m* [per freccette]

dash /dæʃ/ *n* Typ trattino *m*; (*in Morse*) linea *f*; **a ~ of milk** un goccio di latte; **make a ~ for** lanciarsi verso ● *vi* **I must ~** devo scappare ● *vt* far svanire ‹*hopes*›; (*hurl*) gettare
■ **dash off** *vi* scappar via ● *vt* (*write quickly*) buttare giù
■ **dash out** *vi* uscire di corsa

dashboard /'dæʃbɔːd/ *n* cruscotto *m*

dashing /'dæʃɪŋ/ *a* (*bold*) ardito; (*in appearance*) affascinante

DAT *abbr* (**digital audio tape**) DAT *f inv*

data /'deɪtə/ *npl* & *sg* dati *mpl*

data: databank *n* banca *f* di dati. **database** *n* banca *f* dati, database *m inv*. **database management system** *n* sistema *m* di gestione di data base

data: data capture *n* registrazione *f* di dati. **data communications** *npl* comunicazione *f* dati, telematica *f*. **data compression** *n* compressione *f* dati. **data disk** *n* dischetto *m* di dati. **data entry** *n* immissione *f* [di] dati. **data file** *n* file *m inv* dati. **data handling** *n* manipolazione *f* [di] dati. **data input** *n* input *m* dati. **data link** *n* collegamento *m* dati. **data processing** *n* elaborazione *f* [di] dati. **data protection** *n* protezione *f* dati. **data protection act** *n* Jur legge *f* britannica per la salvaguardia delle informazioni personali. **data retrieval** *n* recupero *m* dati. **data security** *n* sicurezza *f* dei dati. **data storage** *n* archiviazione *f* dati. **data transmission** *n* trasmissione *f* dati

date¹ /deɪt/ *n* (*fruit*) dattero *m*

date² *n* data *f*; (*meeting*) appuntamento *m*; **to ~ fino ad oggi; out of ~** (*not fashionable*) fuori moda; (*expired*) scaduto; (*information*) non aggiornato; **make a ~ with sb** dare un appuntamento a qcno; **be up to ~** essere aggiornato ● *vt/i* datare; (*go out with*) uscire con
■ **date back to** *vi* risalire a

dated /'deɪtɪd/ *a* fuori moda; ‹*language*› antiquato

date line *n* linea *f* [del cambiamento] di data

date of issue *n* data *f* di emissione

date stamp *n* (*mark*) timbro *m* con la data

dating agency /'deɪtɪŋ/ *n* agenzia *f* matrimoniale

dative /'deɪtɪv/ *n* dativo *m*

daub /dɔːb/ *vt* imbrattare ‹*walls*›

daughter /'dɔːtə(r)/ *n* figlia *f*

daughter-in-law *n* (*pl* **~s-in-law**) nuora *f*

daunt /dɔːnt/ *vt* scoraggiare; **nothing ~ed** per niente scoraggiato

daunting /'dɔːntɪŋ/ *a* ‹*task, prospect*› poco allettante; ‹*person*› che intimidisce; **I'm faced with a ~ amount of work** mi aspetta una quantità di lavoro preoccupante; **it can be** (**quite**) **~** può essere (piuttosto) allarmante

dauntless /'dɔːntlɪs/ *a* intrepido

dawdle /'dɔːdl/ *vi* bighellonare; (*over work*) cincischiarsi

dawn /dɔːn/ *n* alba *f*; **at ~** all'alba ● *vi* albeggiare; **it ~ed on me** *fig* mi è apparso chiaro

dawn raid *n* (*police*) raid *m* della polizia all'alba; (*stock market*) dawn raid *m inv*

day /deɪ/ *n* giorno *m*; (*whole day*) giornata *f*; (*period*) epoca *f*; **~ by ~** giorno per giorno; **~ after ~** giorno dopo giorno; **these ~s** oggigiorno; **in those ~s** a quei tempi; **it's had its ~** *fam* ha fatto il suo tempo

day: day-boy *n* Br Sch alunno *m* esterno. **daybreak** *n* **at ~** allo spuntar del giorno. **day-care** *n* (*for young children*) scuola *f* materna. **day centre** *n* centro *m* di accoglienza. **day-dream** *n* sogno *m* ad occhi aperti ● *vi* sognare ad occhi aperti. **day-girl** *n* Sch alunna *f* esterna. **daylight** *n* luce del giorno *f*. **daylight robbery** *n* fam **it's ~ ~** è un furto!. **daylight saving time** *n* ora *f* legale. **day nursery** *n* (*0-3 years*) asilo *m* nido; (*3-6 years*) scuola *f* materna. **day off** *n* giorno *m* di riposo

day pass *n* biglietto *m* giornaliero. **day release** *n* giorno *m* di congedo settimanale dal lavoro da dedicare a corsi di formazione. **day return** *n* (*ticket*) biglietto *m* di andata e ritorno con validità giornaliera. **day school** *n* scuola *f* che non fornisce alloggio. **daytime** *n* giorno *m*; **in the ~** di giorno. **day-to-day** *a* quotidiano; **on a ~ basis** giorno per giorno. **day trip** *n* gita *f* (*di un giorno*). **day tripper** *n* gitante *mf*

daze /deɪz/ *n* **in a ~** stordito; *fig* sbalordito

dazed /deɪzd/ *a* stordito; *fig* sbalordito

dazzle /'dæzl/ *vt* abbagliare

DBMS *n abbr* (**database management system**) DBMS *m*

D-day *n* Mil D-day *m inv*; (*important day*) giorno *m* fatidico

deacon /'diːk(ə)n/ *n* diacono *m*

dead /ded/ *a* morto; (*numb*) intorpidito; **~ and buried** morto e sepolto; **~ body** morto *m*; **~ centre** pieno centro *m* ● *adv* **~ tired** stanco morto; **~ slow/easy** lentissimo/facilissimo; **you're ~ right** hai perfettamente ragione; **stop ~** fermarsi di colpo; **be ~ on time** essere in perfetto orario ● *n* **the ~** *pl* i morti; **in the ~ of night** nel cuore della notte

deaden /'ded(ə)n/ *vt* attutire ‹*sound*›; calmare ‹*pain*›

dead: dead end *n* vicolo *m* cieco ● *attrib* **dead-end** ‹*job*› senza prospettive. **dead heat** *n* **it was a ~ ~** è finita a pari merito.

deadline n scadenza f. **deadlock** n reach ~ fig giungere a un punto morto. **dead loss** n fam (person) buono, -a mf a nulla; (thing) oggetto m inutile

deadly /'dedlɪ/ a (**-ier, -iest**) mortale; (fam: dreary) barboso; ~ **sins** peccati mpl capitali

dead: dead on arrival a Med deceduto durante il trasporto. **deadpan** a impassibile; ⟨humour⟩ all'inglese. **dead ringer** n fam be a ~ ~ **for sb** essere la copia spiccicata di qualcuno. **Dead Sea** n Mar m Morto. **dead weight** n (fig: burden) peso m morto. **dead wood** n Br fig zavorra f

deaf /def/ a sordo; ~ **and dumb** sordomuto

deaf aid n apparecchio m acustico

deafen /'def(ə)n/ vt assordare; (permanently) render sordo

deafening /'defənɪŋ/ a assordante

deaf mute a & n sordomuto, -a mf

deafness /'defnɪs/ n sordità f

deal /diːl/ n (agreement) patto m; (in business) accordo m; **who's ~?** (Cards) a chi tocca dare le carte?; **a good** or **great** ~ molto; **get a raw** ~ fam ricevere un trattamento ingiusto ● v (pt/pp **dealt** /delt/) ● vt (in cards) dare; ~ **sb a blow** dare un colpo a qcno

■ **deal in** vt trattare in

■ **deal out** vt ⟨hand out⟩ distribuire

■ **deal with** vt ⟨handle⟩ occuparsi di; trattare con ⟨company⟩; (be about) trattare di; **that's been ~t with** è stato risolto

dealer /'diːlə(r)/ n commerciante mf; (in drugs) spacciatore, -trice mf

dealership /'diːlaʃɪp/ n Comm concessione f

dealing room /'diːlɪŋ/ n Fin borsino m

dealings /'diːlɪŋz/ npl have ~ **with** avere a che fare con

dean /diːn/ n decano m; Univ preside mf di facoltà

dear /dɪə(r)/ a caro; (in letter) Caro; (formal) Gentile ● n caro, -a mf ● int **oh** ~! Dio mio!

dearly /'dɪəlɪ/ adv ⟨love⟩ profondamente; ⟨pay⟩ profumatamente

dearth /dɜːθ/ n penuria f

death /deθ/ n morte f

death: deathbed n letto m di morte. **death camp** n campo m di sterminio. **death certificate** n certificato m di morte. **death duty** n tassa f di successione. **death knell** n campane fpl a morto; fig tramonto m. **death list** n lista f dei bersagli (di un assassino)

deathly /'deθlɪ/ a ~ **silence** silenzio m di tomba ● adv ~ **pale** di un pallore cadaverico

death: death mask n maschera f mortuaria. **death penalty** n pena f di morte. **death rate** n tasso m di mortalità. **death ray** n raggio m mortale. **death row** n Am braccio m della morte. **death sentence** n also fig condanna f a morte. **death's head** n teschio m. **death threat** n minaccia f di morte. **death throes** npl also fig agonia f. **death toll** n bilancio m delle vittime. **death trap** n trappola f mortale. **death warrant** n ordine m di esecuzione di una condanna a morte. **death wish** n desiderio m di morire

debacle /deɪ'bɑːk(ə)l/ n sfacelo m

debar /dɪ'bɑː(r)/ vt (pt/pp **debarred**) escludere

debase /dɪ'beɪs/ vt degradare

debatable /dɪ'beɪtəbl/ a discutibile

debate /dɪ'beɪt/ n dibattito m ● vt discutere; (in formal debate) dibattere ● vi ~ **whether to...** considerare se

debauchery /dɪ'bɔːtʃərɪ/ n dissolutezza f

debenture bond /dɪ'bentʃə(r)/ n obbligazione f non garantita

debilitating /dɪ'bɪlɪteɪtɪŋ/ a ⟨disease⟩ debilitante

debility /dɪ'bɪlətɪ/ n debilitazione f

debit /'debɪt/ n debito m ● vt (pt/pp **debited**) Comm addebitare ⟨sum, account⟩

debonair /debə'neə(r)/ a ⟨person⟩ elegante e cortese

debrief /diː'briːf/ vt chiamare a rapporto; be ~ed ⟨defector, freed hostage:⟩ essere interrogato; ⟨diplomat, agent:⟩ essere chiamato a rapporto

debriefing /diː'briːfɪŋ/ n (of hostage, defector) interrogatorio m

debris /'debriː/ n macerie fpl

debt /det/ n debito m; **be in** ~ avere dei debiti

debt collection n esazione f crediti

debt collection agency n agenzia f di recupero crediti

debt collector n esattore m dei crediti

debtor /'detə(r)/ n debitore, -trice mf

debug /diː'bʌg/ vt (pt/pp **debugged**) Comput correggere gli errori di; togliere i microfoni spia da ⟨room⟩

debunk /dɪ'bʌŋk/ vt ridicolizzare ⟨theory, myth⟩

début /'deɪbuː/ n debutto m

decade /'dekeɪd/ n decennio m

decadence /'dekədəns/ n decadenza f

decadent /'dekədənt/ a decadente

decaffeinated /diː'kæfɪneɪtɪd/ a decaffeinato

decalitre /'dekəliːtə(r)/ n decalitro m

decametre /'dekəmiːtə(r)/ n decametro m

decamp /dɪ'kæmp/ vi sgattaiolare via; ~ **with sth** (steal) squagliarsela con qcsa

decant /dɪ'kænt/ vt travasare

decanter /dɪ'kæntə(r)/ n caraffa f (di cristallo)

decapitate /dɪ'kæpɪteɪt/ vt decapitare

decathlon /dɪ'kæθlɒn/ n decathlon m inv

decay /dɪ'keɪ/ n (also fig) decadenza f; (rot) decomposizione f; (of tooth) carie f inv ● vi imputridire; (rot) decomporsi; ⟨tooth:⟩ cariarsi

deceased /dɪ'siːst/ a defunto ● n the ~ il defunto; la defunta

deceit /dɪ'siːt/ n inganno m

deceitful /dɪ'siːtfʊl/ a falso

deceitfully /dɪ'siːtfʊlɪ/ adv falsamente

deceive /dɪ'siːv/ vt ingannare

decelerate /diː'seləreɪt/ vi decelerare

deceleration /diːselə'reɪʃn/ n decelerazione f

December /dɪˈsembə(r)/ n dicembre m

decency /ˈdiːsənsɪ/ n decenza f

decent /ˈdiːsənt/ a decente; (respectable) rispettabile; **very ~ of you** molto gentile da parte tua

decently /ˈdiːsəntlɪ/ adv decentemente; (kindly) gentilmente

decentralization /diːsentrəlaɪˈzeɪʃn/ n decentramento m

decentralize /diːˈsentrəlaɪz/ vt decentrare

deception /dɪˈsepʃn/ n inganno m

deceptive /dɪˈseptɪv/ a ingannevole

deceptively /dɪˈseptɪvlɪ/ adv ingannevolmente; **it looks ~ easy** sembra facile, ma non lo è

decibel /ˈdesɪbel/ n decibel m inv

decide /dɪˈsaɪd/ vt decidere; **that's ~d then** siamo d'accordo, allora ● vi decidere (**on** di)

decided /dɪˈsaɪdɪd/ a risoluto

decidedly /dɪˈsaɪdɪdlɪ/ adv risolutamente; (without doubt) senza dubbio

decider /dɪˈsaɪdə(r)/ n (point) punto m decisivo; (goal) goal m inv decisivo; (game) spareggio m

deciduous /dɪˈsɪdjʊəs/ a a foglie decidue

decigram[me] /ˈdesɪɡræm/ n decigrammo m

decilitre /ˈdesɪliːtə(r)/ n decilitro m

decimal /ˈdesɪml/ a decimale ● n numero m decimale

decimal point n virgola f

decimal system n sistema m decimale

decimate /ˈdesɪmeɪt/ vt decimare

decimetre /ˈdesɪmiːtə(r)/ n decimetro m

decipher /dɪˈsaɪfə(r)/ vt decifrare

decision /dɪˈsɪʒn/ n decisione f

decision-maker /dɪˈsɪʒnmeɪkə(r)/ n persona f che ama o ha il potere di prendere decisioni

decision-making /dɪˈsɪʒnmeɪkɪŋ/ n **be good/bad at ~** saper/non saper prendere decisioni; **~ process** n processo m decisionale

decisive /dɪˈsaɪsɪv/ a decisivo

decisively /dɪˈsaɪsɪvlɪ/ adv con decisione

deck[1] /dek/ vt abbigliare

deck[2] n Naut ponte m; **on ~** in coperta; **top ~** (of bus) piano m di sopra; **~ of cards** mazzo m

deckchair /ˈdektʃeə(r)/ n (sedia f a) sdraio f inv

declaration /dekləˈreɪʃn/ n dichiarazione f

declare /dɪˈkleə(r)/ vt dichiarare; **anything to ~?** niente da dichiarare?; **~ one's love** dichiararsi

declassify /diːˈklæsɪfaɪ/ vt rimuovere dai vincoli di segretezza (document, information)

declension /dɪˈklenʃn/ n declinazione f

decline /dɪˈklaɪn/ n declino m ● vt also Gram declinare ● vi (decrease) diminuire; (health:) deperire; (say no) rifiutare

declutch /diːˈklʌtʃ/ vi Br lasciare la frizione

decode /diːˈkəʊd/ vt decifrare; Comput decodificare

decoding /diːˈkəʊdɪŋ/ n decodifica f, decodificazione f

décolleté /deɪˈkɒlteɪ/ a décolleté inv, scollato

decompose /diːkəmˈpəʊz/ vi decomporsi

decomposition /diːkɒmpəˈzɪʃn/ n scomposizione f

decompression /diːkəmˈpreʃn/ n decompressione f

decontaminate /diːkənˈtæmɪneɪt/ vt decontaminare

décor /ˈdeɪkɔː(r)/ n decorazione f; (including furniture) arredamento m

decorate /ˈdekəreɪt/ vt decorare; (paint) pitturare; (wallpaper) tappezzare

decoration /dekəˈreɪʃn/ n decorazione f

decorative /ˈdekərətɪv/ a decorativo

decorator /ˈdekəreɪtə(r)/ n **painter and ~** imbianchino m

decorous /ˈdekərəs/ a decoroso

decorously /ˈdekərəslɪ/ adv decorosamente

decorum /dɪˈkɔːrəm/ n decoro m

decoy[1] /ˈdiːkɔɪ/ n esca f

decoy[2] /dɪˈkɔɪ/ vt adescare

decrease[1] /ˈdiːkriːs/ n diminuzione f; **be on the ~** essere in diminuzione

decrease[2] /dɪˈkriːs/ vt/i diminuire

decreasingly /dɪˈkriːsɪŋlɪ/ adv sempre meno

decree /dɪˈkriː/ n decreto m ● vt decretare

decrepit /dɪˈkrepɪt/ a decrepito

decriminalization /diːkrɪmɪnəlaɪˈzeɪʃn/ n depenalizzazione f

decriminalize /diːˈkrɪmɪnəlaɪz/ vt depenalizzare

dedicate /ˈdedɪkeɪt/ vt dedicare

dedicated /ˈdedɪkeɪtɪd/ a (person) scrupoloso

dedication /dedɪˈkeɪʃn/ n dedizione f; (in book) dedica f

deduce /dɪˈdjuːs/ vt dedurre (**from** da)

deduct /dɪˈdʌkt/ vt dedurre

deduction /dɪˈdʌkʃn/ n deduzione f

deed /diːd/ n azione f; Jur atto m di proprietà

deed of covenant n Jur accordo m accessorio ad un contratto immobiliare

deed poll n **change one's name by ~ ~** cambiare nome con un atto unilaterale

deem /diːm/ vt ritenere

deep /diːp/ a profondo; **go off the ~ end** fam arrabbiarsi

deepen /ˈdiːpn/ vt approfondire; scavare più profondamente (trench) ● vi approfondirsi; (fig: mystery:) infittirsi

deep: deep-fat-fryer n friggitrice f. **deep-felt** a profondo. **deep-freeze** n congelatore m. **deep-fried** a fritto (in molto olio). **deep-frozen** a surgelato. **deep-fry** vt friggere (in molto olio)

deeply adv profondamente

deep: deep-rooted a (habit, prejudice) radicato. **deep-sea** a (exploration, diving) in profondità; (fisherman, fishing) d'alto mare. **deep-sea diver** n palombaro m. **deep-seated** a radicato. **deep-set** a (eyes) infossato. **deep South** n Am il profondo Sud

deer /dɪə(r)/ n inv cervo m

deface /dɪ'feɪs/ *vt* sfigurare ⟨*picture*⟩; deturpare ⟨*monument*⟩

defamation /defə'meɪʃn/ *n* diffamazione *f*

defamatory /dɪ'fæmətərɪ/ *a* diffamatorio

default /dɪ'fɔːlt/ *n* (*Jur*: *non-payment*) morosità *f*; (*failure to appear*) contumacia *f*; **win by ~** *Sport* vincere per abbandono dell'avversario; **in ~ of** per mancanza di ● **a ~ drive** *Comput* lettore *m* di default ● *vi* (*not pay*) venir meno a un pagamento

defeat /dɪ'fiːt/ *n* sconfitta *f* ● *vt* sconfiggere; (*frustrate*) vanificare ⟨*attempts*⟩; **that ~s the object** questo fa fallire l'obiettivo

defeatist /dɪ'fiːtɪst/ *a & n* disfattista *mf*

defecate /'defəkeɪt/ *vi* defecare

defect[1] /dɪ'fekt/ *vi* *Pol* fare defezione

defect[2] /'diːfekt/ *n* difetto *m*

defective /dɪ'fektɪv/ *a* difettoso

defector /dɪ'fektə(r)/ *n* (*from party*) defezionista *mf*; (*from country*) fuor[i]uscito, -a *mf*

defence /dɪ'fens/ *n* difesa *f*

defenceless /dɪ'fenslɪs/ *a* indifeso

Defence Minister *n* ministro *m* della difesa

defend /dɪ'fend/ *vt* difendere; (*justify*) giustificare

defendant /dɪ'fendənt/ *n* *Jur* imputato, -a *mf*

defender /dɪ'fendə(r)/ *n* difensore *m*, -ditrice *f*

defensive /dɪ'fensɪv/ *a* difensivo ● *n* difensiva *f*; **on the ~** sulla difensiva

defer /dɪ'fɜː(r)/ *vt* (*pt/pp* **deferred**) (*postpone*) rinviare ● *vi* **~ to sb** rimettersi a qcno

deference /'defərəns/ *n* deferenza *f*

deferential /defə'renʃl/ *a* deferente

deferentially /defə'renʃəlɪ/ *adv* con deferenza

deferment, deferral /dɪ'fɜːmənt, dɪ'fɜːrəl/ *n* (*postponement*) rinvio *m*

defiance /dɪ'faɪəns/ *n* sfida *f*; **in ~ of** sfidando

defiant /dɪ'faɪənt/ *a* ⟨*person*⟩ ribelle; ⟨*gesture, attitude*⟩ di sfida

defiantly /dɪ'faɪəntlɪ/ *adv* con aria di sfida

deficiency /dɪ'fɪʃənsɪ/ *n* insufficienza *f*

deficient /dɪ'fɪʃənt/ *a* insufficiente; **be ~ in** mancare di

deficit /'defɪsɪt/ *n* deficit *m* *inv*

defile /dɪ'faɪl/ *vt* *fig* contaminare

define /dɪ'faɪn/ *vt* definire

defined *a* ⟨*role*⟩ definito

definite /'defɪnɪt/ *a* definito; (*certain*) ⟨*answer, yes*⟩ definitivo; ⟨*improvement, difference*⟩ netto; **he was ~ about it** è stato chiaro in proposito

definite article *n* (*grammatical*) articolo *m* determinativo

definitely /'defɪnɪtlɪ/ *adv* sicuramente

definition /defɪ'nɪʃn/ *n* definizione *f*

definitive /dɪ'fɪnətɪv/ *a* definitivo

deflate /dɪ'fleɪt/ *vt* sgonfiare

deflation /dɪfl'eɪʃn/ *n* *Comm* deflazione *f*

deflationary /dɪ'fleɪʃənrɪ/ *a* deflazionistico

deflect /dɪ'flekt/ *vt* deflettere

deformed /dɪ'fɔːmd/ *a* deforme

deformity /dɪ'fɔːmətɪ/ *n* deformità *f* *inv*

defraud /dɪ'frɔːd/ *vt* defraudare

defray /dɪ'freɪ/ *vt* *fml* sostenere

defrost /diː'frɒst/ *vt* sbrinare ⟨*fridge*⟩; scongelare ⟨*food*⟩

deft /deft/ *a* abile

deftly /'deftlɪ/ *adv* con destrezza

deftness /'deftnɪs/ *n* destrezza *f*

defunct /dɪ'fʌŋkt/ *a* morto e sepolto; ⟨*law*⟩ caduto in disuso

defuse /diː'fjuːz/ *vt* disinnescare; calmare ⟨*situation*⟩

defy /dɪ'faɪ/ *vt* (*pt/pp* **-ied**) (*challenge*) sfidare; resistere a ⟨*attempt*⟩; (*not obey*) disobbedire a

degenerate[1] /dɪ'dʒenəreɪt/ *vi* degenerare; **~ into** *fig* degenerare in

degenerate[2] /dɪ'dʒenərət/ *a* degenerato

degeneration /dɪdʒenə'reɪʃn/ *n* degenerazione *f*

degenerative /dɪ'dʒenərətɪv/ *a* degenerativo

degradation /degrə'deɪʃn/ *n* (*debasement*) degradazione *f*; (*of culture*) deterioramento *m*; (*squalor*) desolazione *f*

degrade /dɪ'greɪd/ *vt* (*humiliate*) degradare ⟨*person*⟩; (*damage*) deteriorare ⟨*environment*⟩

degrading /dɪ'greɪdɪŋ/ *a* degradante

degree /dɪ'griː/ *n* grado *m*; *Univ* laurea *f*; **20 ~s** 20 gradi; **not to the same ~** non allo stesso livello

degree ceremony *n* *Br Univ* cerimonia *f* di consegna delle lauree

degree course *n* *Br Univ* corso *m* di laurea

dehydrate /diːhaɪ'dreɪt/ *vt* disidratare

dehydrated /diːhaɪ'dreɪtɪd/ *a* disidratato

dehydration /diːhaɪ'dreɪʃn/ *n* disidratazione *f*

de-ice /diː'aɪs/ *vt* togliere il ghiaccio da

de-icer /diː'aɪsə(r)/ *n* (*mechanical*) sbrinatore *m*; (*chemical*) liquido *m* scongelante

deign /deɪn/ *vi* **~ to do sth** degnarsi di fare qcsa

deity /'diːətɪ/ *n* divinità *f* *inv*

déjà vu /deɪʒɑː'vuː/ *n* déjà vu *m* *inv*

dejected /dɪ'dʒektɪd/ *a* demoralizzato

dejectedly /dɪ'dʒektɪdlɪ/ *adv* con aria demoralizzata

dejection /dɪ'dʒekʃn/ *n* abbacchiamento *m*

delay /dɪ'leɪ/ *n* ritardo *m* **without ~** senza indugio ● *vt* ritardare **be ~ed** ⟨*person*:⟩ essere trattenuto; ⟨*train, aircraft*:⟩ essere in ritardo ● *vi* indugiare

delayed action /dɪ'leɪd/ *a* ad azione ritardata; ⟨*bomb*⟩ a scoppio ritardato

delegate[1] /'delɪgət/ *n* delegato, -a *mf*

delegate[2] /'delɪgeɪt/ *vt* delegare

delegation /delɪ'geɪʃn/ *n* delegazione *f*

delete /dɪ'liːt/ *vt* cancellare

deletion /dɪ'liːʃn/ *n* cancellatura *f*

deliberate[1] /dɪ'lɪbərət/ *a* deliberato; (*slow*) posato

deliberate² /dɪˈlɪbəreɪt/ *vt/i* deliberare
deliberately /dɪˈlɪbərətlɪ/ *adv* deliberatamente; *(slowly)* in modo posato
deliberation /dɪlɪbəˈreɪʃn/ *n* deliberazione *f*; **with ~** in modo posato
delicacy /ˈdelɪkəsɪ/ *n* delicatezza *f*; *(food)* prelibatezza *f*
delicate /ˈdelɪkət/ *a* delicato
delicately /ˈdelɪkətlɪ/ *adv* ⟨*handle, phrase*⟩ con delicatezza; ⟨*crafted, flavoured*⟩ con raffinatezza
delicatessen /delɪkəˈtesn/ *n* negozio *m* di specialità gastronomiche
delicious /dɪˈlɪʃəs/ *a* delizioso
delight /dɪˈlaɪt/ *n* piacere *m* ● *vt* deliziare ● *vi* **~ in** dilettarsi con
delighted /dɪˈlaɪtɪd/ *a* lieto
delightful /dɪˈlaɪtfʊl/ *a* delizioso
delineate /dɪˈlɪnɪeɪt/ *vt also fig* delineare
delineation /dɪlɪnɪˈeɪʃn/ *n* delineazione *f*
delinquency /dɪˈlɪŋkwənsɪ/ *n* delinquenza *f*
delinquent /dɪˈlɪŋkwənt/ *a* delinquente ● *n* delinquente *mf*
delirious /dɪˈlɪrɪəs/ *a* **be ~** delirare; *(fig: very happy)* essere pazzo di gioia
delirium /dɪˈlɪrɪəm/ *n* delirio *m*
deliver /dɪˈlɪvə(r)/ *vt* consegnare; recapitare ⟨*post, newspaper*⟩; tenere ⟨*speech*⟩; dare ⟨*message*⟩; tirare ⟨*blow*⟩; *(set free)* liberare; **~ a baby** far nascere un bambino
deliverance /dɪˈlɪv(ə)rəns/ *n* liberazione *f*
delivery /dɪˈlɪvərɪ/ *n* consegna *f*; *(of post)* distribuzione *f*; *Med* parto *m*; **cash on ~** pagamento *m* alla consegna
delivery: delivery address *n* indirizzo *m* del destinatario. **delivery man** *n* fattorino *m*. **delivery room** *n Med* sala *f* parto
delta /ˈdeltə/ *n* delta *m inv*
delude /dɪˈluːd/ *vt* ingannare; **~ oneself** illudersi
deluge /ˈdeljuːdʒ/ *n* diluvio *m* ● *vt* *(fig: with requests etc)* inondare
delusion /dɪˈluːʒn/ *n* illusione; **~s of grandeur** mania *f* di grandezza
de luxe /dəˈlʌks/ *a* di lusso
delve /delv/ *vi* **~ into** *(into pocket etc)* frugare in; *(into notes, the past)* fare ricerche in
demagnetize /diːˈmægnətaɪz/ *vt* smagnetizzare
demand /dɪˈmɑːnd/ *n* richiesta *f*; *Comm* domanda *f*; **in ~** richiesto; **on ~** a richiesta ● *vt* esigere (**of/from** da)
demanding /dɪˈmɑːndɪŋ/ *a* esigente
demanning /diːˈmænɪŋ/ *n Br* taglio *m* di personale
demarcation /diːmɑːˈkeɪʃn/ *n* demarcazione *f*
demean /dɪˈmiːn/ *vt* **~ oneself** abbassarsi (**to** a)
demeaning /dɪˈmiːnɪŋ/ *a* degradante
demeanour /dɪˈmiːnə(r)/ *n* comportamento *m*
demented /dɪˈmentɪd/ *a* demente
dementia /dɪˈmenʃə/ *n* demenza *f*

demerara [**sugar**] /deməˈreərə/ *n* zucchero *m* grezzo di canna
demilitarization /diːmɪlɪtəraɪˈzeɪʃn/ *n* demilitarizzazione *f*
demilitarize /diːˈmɪlɪtəraɪz/ *vt* smilitarizzare
demise /dɪˈmaɪz/ *n* decesso *m*
demister /diːˈmɪstə(r)/ *n Auto* sbrinatore *m*
demo /ˈdeməʊ/ *n* *(pl* **~s**) *fam* manifestazione *f*
demobilize /diːˈməʊbəlaɪz/ *vt Mil* smobilitare
democracy /dɪˈmɒkrəsɪ/ *n* democrazia *f*
democrat /ˈdeməkræt/ *n* democratico, -a *mf*
democratic /deməˈkrætɪk/ *a* democratico
democratically /deməˈkrætɪklɪ/ *adv* democraticamente
demo disk *n Comput* demodisk *m inv*
demographic /deməˈgræfɪk/ *a* demografico
demolish /dɪˈmɒlɪʃ/ *vt* demolire
demolition /deməˈlɪʃn/ *n* demolizione *f*
demon /ˈdiːmən/ *n* demonio *m*
demonic /dɪˈmɒnɪk/ *a* ⟨*aspect, power*⟩ demoniaco
demonize /ˈdiːmənaɪz/ *vt* demonizzare
demonstrable /ˈdemənstrəbl/ *a* dimostrabile
demonstrably /ˈdemənstrəblɪ/ *adv* ⟨*false, untrue*⟩ manifestamente
demonstrate /ˈdemənstreɪt/ *vt* dimostrare; fare una dimostrazione sull'uso di ⟨*appliance*⟩ ● *vi Pol* manifestare
demonstration /demənˈstreɪʃn/ *n* dimostrazione *f*; *Pol* manifestazione *f*
demonstrative /dɪˈmɒnstrətɪv/ *a Gram* dimostrativo; **be ~** essere espansivo
demonstrator /ˈdemənstreɪtə(r)/ *n Pol* manifestante *mf*; *(for product)* dimostratore, -trice *mf*
demoralize /dɪˈmɒrəlaɪz/ *vt* demoralizzare
demoralizing /dɪˈmɒrəlaɪzɪŋ/ *a* demoralizzante, avvilente
demote /dɪˈməʊt/ *vt* retrocedere di grado; *Mil* degradare
demur /dɪˈmɜː/ *vi* *(pt/pp* **demurred**) *(complain)* protestare; *(disagree)* obiettare ● *n* **without ~** senza obiezioni
demure /dɪˈmjʊə(r)/ *a* schivo
demurely /dɪˈmjʊəlɪ/ *adv* in modo schivo
den /den/ *n* tana *f*; *(room)* rifugio *m*
denationalize /diːˈnæʃ(ə)nəlaɪz/ *vt* denazionalizzare
denial /dɪˈnaɪəl/ *n* smentita *f*
denier /ˈdenɪə(r)/ *n* denaro *m*
denigrate /ˈdenɪgreɪt/ *vt* denigrare
denigrating /ˈdenɪgreɪtɪŋ/ *a* denigratore
denim /ˈdenɪm/ *n* [tessuto *m*] jeans *m*; **~s** *pl* [blue]jeans *mpl*
Denmark /ˈdenmɑːk/ *n* Danimarca *f*
denomination /dɪnɒmɪˈneɪʃn/ *n Relig* confessione *f*; *(money)* valore *f*
denote /dɪˈnəʊt/ *vt* denotare
denounce /dɪˈnaʊns/ *vt* denunciare

dense /dens/ a denso; ⟨crowd, forest⟩ fitto; (stupid) ottuso

densely /'dɛnslɪ/ adv ⟨populated⟩ densamente; **~ wooded** fittamente ricoperto di alberi

density /'dɛnsətɪ/ n densità f inv; (of forest) fittezza f

dent /dɛnt/ n ammaccatura f ● vt ammaccare

dental /'dɛntl/ a dei denti; ⟨treatment⟩ dentistico; ⟨hygiene⟩ dentale

dental: dental appointment n appuntamento m dal dentista. **dental clinic** n (hospital) clinica f odontoiatrica; (part of hospital) reparto m odontoiatrico. **dental floss** n filo m interdentale. **dental plate** n dentiera f. **dental surgeon** n odontoiatra mf, medico m dentista. **dental surgery** n Br (premises) studio m dentistico; (treatment) visita f dentistica

dented /'dɛntɪd/ a ammaccato; **~ pride** orgoglio m ferito

dentist /'dɛntɪst/ n dentista mf

dentistry /'dɛntɪstrɪ/ n odontoiatria f

dentures /'dɛntʃəz/ npl dentiera fsg

denude /dɪ'njuːd/ vt denudare

denunciation /dɪnʌnsɪ'eɪʃn/ n denuncia f

deny /dɪ'naɪ/ vt (pt/pp -ied) negare; (officially) smentire; **~ sb sth** negare qcsa a qcno; **I can't ~ it** non posso negarlo

deodorant /diː'əʊdərənt/ n deodorante m

deodorize /diː'əʊdəraɪz/ vt deodorare

depart /dɪ'pɑːt/ vi ⟨plane, train:⟩ partire; ⟨liter: person⟩ andare via; (deviate) allontanarsi (from da)

departed /dɪ'pɑːtɪd/ a (euph: dead) scomparso

department /dɪ'pɑːtmənt/ n reparto m; Pol ministero m; (of company) sezione f; Univ dipartimento m

departmental /diːpɑː'tmɛntl/ a ⟨Pol: colleague, meeting⟩ di sezione; (in business) di reparto

department: Department of Defense n Am ministero m della difesa. **Department of Energy** n Am ≈ Ministero m dell'Industria. **Department of the Environment** n Br Ministero m dell'Ambiente. **department head** n caporeparto mf; Univ direttore, -trice mf d'istituto. **Department of Health** n ministero m della sanità. **department manager** n (of business) direttore, -trice mf di reparto; (of store) caporeparto mf inv. **Department of Social Security** n Br ≈ Istituto m Nazionale della Previdenza Sociale. **department store** n grande magazzino m. **Department of Trade and Industry** n Br Ministero m del Commercio e dell'Industria

departure /dɪ'pɑːtʃə(r)/ n partenza f; (from rule) allontanamento m; **new ~** svolta f

departure: departure gate n (at airport) uscita f. **departure lounge** n (at airport) sala f d'attesa. **departure platform** n Rail binario m. **departures board** n tabellone m delle partenze

depend /dɪ'pɛnd/ vi dipendere (**on** da); (rely) contare (**on** su); **it all ~s** dipende; **~ing on what he says** a seconda di quello che dice

dependability /dɪpɛndə'bɪlətɪ/ n affidabilità f

dependable /dɪ'pɛndəbl/ a fidato

dependant /dɪ'pɛndənt/ n persona f a carico

dependence /dɪ'pɛndəns/ n dipendenza f

dependent /dɪ'pɛndənt/ a dipendente (**on** da)

depict /dɪ'pɪkt/ vt (in writing) dipingere; (with picture) rappresentare

depiction /dɪ'pɪkʃn/ n rappresentazione f

depilatory /dɪ'pɪlətərɪ/ n (cream) crema f depilatoria

deplete /dɪ'pliːt/ vt ridurre; **totally ~d** completamente esaurito

depletion /dɪ'pliːʃn/ n (of resources, funds) impoverimento m

deplorable /dɪ'plɔːrəbl/ a deplorevole

deplore /dɪ'plɔː(r)/ vt deplorare

deploy /dɪ'plɔɪ/ vt Mil spiegare ● vi schierarsi

deployment /dɪ'plɔɪmənt/ n schieramento m

depoliticize /diːpə'lɪtɪsaɪz/ vt depoliticizzare

depopulate /diː'pɒpjʊleɪt/ vt spopolare

deport /dɪ'pɔːt/ vt deportare

deportation /diːpɔː'teɪʃn/ n deportazione f

deportee /diːpɔː'tiː/ n deportato, -a mf

deportment /dɪ'pɔːtmənt/ n portamento m

depose /dɪ'pəʊz/ vt deporre

deposit /dɪ'pɒzɪt/ n deposito m; (against damage) cauzione f; (first instalment) acconto m ● vt depositare

deposit account n libretto m di risparmio; (without instant access) conto m vincolato

depositor /dɪ'pɒzɪtə(r)/ n Fin depositante mf

deposit slip n (in bank) distinta f di versamento

depot /'dɛpəʊ/ n deposito m; Am Rail stazione f ferroviaria

deprave /dɪ'preɪv/ vt depravare

depraved /dɪ'preɪvd/ a depravato

depravity /dɪ'prævətɪ/ n depravazione f

deprecate /'dɛprəkeɪt/ vt disapprovare

deprecatory /dɛprɪ'keɪtərɪ/ a (disapproving) di disapprovazione; (apologetic) di scusa

depreciate /dɪ'priːʃeɪt/ vi deprezzarsi

depreciation /dɪpriːsɪ'eɪʃn/ n deprezzamento m

depress /dɪ'prɛs/ vt deprimere; (press down) premere

depressed /dɪ'prɛst/ a depresso; **~ area** zona f depressa

depressing /dɪ'prɛsɪŋ/ a deprimente

depression /dɪ'prɛʃn/ n depressione f

depressive /dɪ'prɛsɪv/ a depressivo ● n depresso, -a mf

depressurize /diː'prɛʃəraɪz/ vi depressurizzare

deprivation /dɛprɪ'veɪʃn/ n privazione f

deprive /dɪˈpraɪv/ *vt* ~ **sb of sth** privare qcno di qcsa

deprived /dɪˈpraɪvd/ *a* ‹area, childhood› disagiato

dept *abbr* **department**

depth /depθ/ *n* profondità *f inv*; **in** ~ ‹study, analyse› in modo approfondito; **in the** ~**s of winter** in pieno inverno; **in the** ~**s of despair** nella più profonda disperazione; **be out of one's** ~ (*in water*) non toccare il fondo; *fig* sentirsi in alto mare

deputation /depjʊˈteɪʃn/ *n* deputazione *f*

deputize /ˈdepjʊtaɪz/ *vi* ~ **for** fare le veci di

deputy /ˈdepjʊtɪ/ *n* vice *mf*; (*temporary*) sostituto, -a *mf* ● *attrib* ~ **leader** ≈ vicesegretario, -a *mf*; ~ **chairman** vicepresidente *mf*

deputy: deputy chairman *n* vicepresidente *m*. **deputy leader** *n Br Pol* sottosegretario *m*. **deputy premier**, **deputy prime minister** *n Pol* vice primo ministro *m*. **deputy president** *n* vicepresidente *mf*

derail /dɪˈreɪl/ *vt* **be** ~**ed** ‹train:› essere deragliato

derailleur gears /dɪˈreɪljə/ *npl* deragliatore *msg*

derailment /dɪˈreɪlmənt/ *n* deragliamento *m*

deranged /dɪˈreɪndʒd/ *a* squilibrato

deregulate /diːˈregjʊleɪt/ *vt* deregolamentare ‹market›

deregulation /diːregjʊˈleɪʃn/ *n* deregolamentazione *f*

derelict /ˈderəlɪkt/ *a* abbandonato

deride /dɪˈraɪd/ *vt* deridere

derision /dɪˈrɪʒn/ *n* derisione *f*

derisive /dɪˈraɪsɪv/ *a* derisorio

derisory /dɪˈraɪsərɪ/ *a* ‹laughter› derisorio; ‹offer› irrisorio

derivation /derɪˈveɪʃn/ *n* derivazione *f*

derivative /dɪˈrɪvətɪv/ *a* derivato ● *n* derivato *m*

derive /dɪˈraɪv/ *vt* (*obtain*) derivare; **be** ~**d from** ‹word:› derivare da ● *vi* ~ **from** derivare da

dermatitis /dɜːməˈtaɪtɪs/ *n* dermatite *f*

dermatologist /dɜːməˈtɒlədʒɪst/ *n* dermatologo, -a *mf*

derogatory /dɪˈrɒɡətrɪ/ *a* ‹comments› peggiorativo

derrick /ˈderɪk/ *n* derrick *m inv*

derv /dɜːv/ *n Br* gasolio *m*

descaler /diːˈskeɪlə(r)/ *n Br* disincrostante *m*

descend /dɪˈsend/ *vi* scendere; **be** ~**ed from** discendere da ● *vt* scendere da

■ **descend on** *vt* (*attack*) piombare su; (*visit*) capitare [all'improvviso]

descendant /dɪˈsendənt/ *n* discendente *mf*

descent /dɪˈsent/ *n* discesa *f*; (*lineage*) origine *f*

descrambler /diːˈskræmblə(r)/ *n Teleph, TV* decodificatore *m*

describe /dɪˈskraɪb/ *vt* descrivere

description /dɪˈskrɪpʃn/ *n* descrizione *f*;

they had no help of any ~ non hanno avuto proprio nessun aiuto

descriptive /dɪˈskrɪptɪv/ *a* descrittivo; (*vivid*) vivido

desecrate /ˈdesɪkreɪt/ *vt* profanare

desecration /desɪˈkreɪʃn/ *n* profanazione *f*

desegregate /diːˈsegrɪgeɪt/ *vt* abolire la segregazione razziale in ‹school›

deselect /diːsɪˈlekt/ *vt Br* **be** ~**ed** *non avere riconferma della candidatura alle elezioni da parte del proprio partito*

desensitize /diːˈsensɪtaɪz/ *vt* desensibilizzare

desert¹ /ˈdezət/ *n* deserto *m* ● *a* deserto; ~ **island** isola *f* deserta

desert² /dɪˈzɜːt/ *vt* abbandonare ● *vi* disertare

deserted /dɪˈzɜːtɪd/ *a* deserto

deserter /dɪˈzɜːtə(r)/ *n Mil* disertore *m*

desertion /dɪˈzɜːʃn/ *n Mil* diserzione *f*; (*of family*) abbandono *m*

deserts /dɪˈzɜːts/ *npl* **get one's just** ~ ottenere ciò che ci si merita

deserve /dɪˈzɜːv/ *vt* meritare

deservedly /dɪˈzɜːvədlɪ/ *adv* meritatamente

deserving /dɪˈzɜːvɪŋ/ *a* meritevole; ~ **cause** opera *f* meritoria

desiccated /ˈdesɪkeɪtɪd/ *a* essiccato; (*pej: dried up*) secco

design /dɪˈzaɪn/ *n* progettazione *f*; (*fashion* ~, *appearance*) design *m inv*; (*pattern*) modello *m*; (*aim*) proposito *m*; **have** ~**s on** aver mire su ● *vt* progettare; disegnare ‹clothes, furniture, models›; **be** ~**ed for** essere fatto per

designate /ˈdezɪɡneɪt/ *vt* designare

designation /dezɪɡˈneɪʃn/ *n* designazione *f*

design consultant *n* progettista *mf*

designer /dɪˈzaɪnə(r)/ *n* progettista *mf*; (*of clothes*) stilista *mf*; (*Theat: of set*) scenografo, -a *mf*

design fault *n* difetto *m* di concezione

design feature *n* prestazione *f*

designing /dɪˈzaɪnɪŋ/ *a pej* calcolatore

desirable /dɪˈzaɪərəbl/ *a* desiderabile

desire /dɪˈzaɪə(r)/ *n* desiderio *m* ● *vt* desiderare

desist /dɪˈzɪst/ *vi* desistere (**from** da)

desk /desk/ *n* scrivania *f*; (*in school*) banco *m*; (*in hotel*) reception *f inv*; (*cash* ~) cassa *f*; (*check-in* ~) check-in *m inv*

desk: deskbound *a* ‹job› sedentario. **desk diary** *n* agenda da tavolo. **desk pad** *n* (*blotter*) tampone *m*; (*notebook*) block-notes *m inv*. **desktop** *n* piano *m* della scrivania; (*computer*) [computer *m inv*] desktop *m inv*. **desktop publishing** *n* desktop publishing *m inv*, editoria *f* da tavolo

desolate /ˈdesələt/ *a* desolato

desolation /desəˈleɪʃn/ *n* desolazione *f*

despair /dɪˈspeə(r)/ *n* disperazione *f*; **in** ~ disperato; ‹say› per disperazione ● *vi* **I** ~ **of that boy** quel ragazzo mi fa disperare

desperate /ˈdespərət/ *a* disperato; **be** ~ ‹criminal:› essere un disperato; **be** ~ **for sth** morire dalla voglia di

desperately /'despərətlɪ/ *adv* disperatamente; **he said ~** ha detto, disperato

desperation /despə'reɪʃn/ *n* disperazione *f*; **in ~** per disperazione

despicable /dɪ'spɪkəbl/ *a* disprezzevole

despise /dɪ'spaɪz/ *vt* disprezzare

despite /dɪ'spaɪt/ *prep* malgrado

despondency /dɪ'spɒndənsɪ/ *n* abbattimento *m*

despondent /dɪ'spɒndənt/ *a* abbattuto

despot /'despɒt/ *n* despota *m*

despotism /'despətɪzm/ *n* dispotismo *m*

des res /dez'rez/ *n abbr fam* (**desirable residence**) abitazione *f* desiderabile

dessert /dɪ'zɜːt/ *n* dolce *m*

dessert spoon *n* cucchiaio *m* da dolce

dessert wine *n* vino *m* da dessert

destabilize /diː'steɪbɪlaɪz/ *vt* destabilizzare

destination /destɪ'neɪʃn/ *n* destinazione *f*

destine /'destɪn/ *vt* destinare; **be ~d for sth** essere destinato a qcsa; **~d for each other** fatti l'uno per l'altra

destined /'destɪnd/ *a* ~ **for Paris** ⟨*train, package*⟩ a destinazione di Parigi; **it was ~ to happen** era destino che succedesse

destiny /'destɪnɪ/ *n* destino *m*

destitute /'destɪtjuːt/ *a* bisognoso

destitution /destɪ'tjuːʃn/ *n* indigenza *f*

destroy /dɪ'strɔɪ/ *vt* distruggere

destroyer /dɪ'strɔɪə(r)/ *n Naut* cacciatorpediniere *m*

destruct /dɪ'strʌkt/ *vi* distruggersi

destruction /dɪ'strʌkʃn/ *n* distruzione *f*

destructive /dɪ'strʌktɪv/ *a* distruttivo; ⟨*fig: criticism*⟩ negativo

destructiveness /dɪ'strʌktɪvnɪs/ *n* distruttività *f*

desultory /'desəltrɪ/ *a* ⟨*conversation*⟩ sconnesso; ⟨*friendship*⟩ incostante; ⟨*attempt*⟩ poco convinto

detach /dɪ'tætʃ/ *vt* staccare

detachable /dɪ'tætʃəbl/ *a* separabile

detached /dɪ'tætʃt/ *a fig* distaccato; **~ house** villetta *f*

detached retina *n Med* retina *f* distaccata

detachment /dɪ'tætʃmənt/ *n* distacco *m*; *Mil* distaccamento *m*

detail /'diːteɪl/ *n* particolare *m*, dettaglio *m*; **in ~** particolareggiatamente ● *vt* esporre con tutti i particolari; *Mil* assegnare

detail drawing *n* disegno *m* dettagliato

detailed /'diːteɪld/ *a* particolareggiato, dettagliato

detain /dɪ'teɪn/ *vt* ⟨*police:*⟩ trattenere; (*delay*) far ritardare

detainee /diːteɪ'niː/ *n* detenuto, -a *mf*

detect /dɪ'tekt/ *vt* individuare; (*perceive*) percepire

detectable /dɪ'tektəbl/ *a* individuabile

detection /dɪ'tekʃn/ *n* scoperta *f*

detective /dɪ'tektɪv/ *n* investigatore, -trice *mf*

detective: detective constable *n Br* agente *mf* della polizia giudiziaria. **detective inspector** *n Br* ispettore, -trice *mf* della polizia giudiziaria. **detective story** *n* racconto *m* poliziesco. **detective work** *n* indagini *fpl*

detector /dɪ'tektə(r)/ *n* (*for metal*) cercametalli *m inv*, metal detector *m inv*

detention /dɪ'tenʃn/ *n* detenzione *f*; *Sch* punizione *f*

deter /dɪ'tɜː(r)/ *vt* (*pt/pp* **deterred**) impedire; **~ sb from doing sth** impedire a qcno di fare qcsa

detergent /dɪ'tɜːdʒənt/ *n* detersivo *m*

deteriorate /dɪ'tɪərɪəreɪt/ *vi* deteriorarsi

deterioration /dɪtɪərɪə'reɪʃn/ *n* deterioramento *m*

determination /dɪtɜːmɪ'neɪʃn/ *n* determinazione *f*

determine /dɪ'tɜːmɪn/ *vt* (*ascertain*) determinare; **~ to** (*resolve*) decidere di

determined /dɪ'tɜːmɪnd/ *a* deciso

determining /dɪ'tɜːmɪnɪŋ/ *a* determinante

deterrent /dɪ'terənt/ *n* deterrente *m*

detest /dɪ'test/ *vt* detestare

detestable /dɪ'testəbl/ *a* detestabile

detonate /'detəneɪt/ *vt* far detonare ● *vi* detonare

detonation /detə'neɪʃn/ *n* detonazione *f*

detonator /'detəneɪtə(r)/ *n* detonatore *m*

detour /'diːtʊə(r)/ *n* deviazione *f*

detoxify /diː'tɒksɪfaɪ/ *vt* disintossicare

detract /dɪ'trækt/ *vi* ~ **from** sminuire ⟨*merit*⟩; rovinare ⟨*pleasure, beauty*⟩

detractor /dɪ'træktə(r)/ *n* detrattore, -trice *mf*

detriment /'detrɪmənt/ *n* **to the ~ of** a danno di

detrimental /detrɪ'mentl/ *a* dannoso

detritus /dɪ'traɪtəs/ *n* detriti *mpl*

deuce /djuːs/ *n Tennis* deuce *m inv*

devaluation /diːvæljuː'eɪʃn/ *n* svalutazione *f*

devalue /diː'væljuː/ *vt* svalutare ⟨*currency*⟩

devastate /'devəsteɪt/ *vt* devastare

devastated /'devəsteɪtɪd/ *a fam* sconvolto

devastating /'devəsteɪtɪŋ/ *a* devastante; ⟨*news*⟩ sconvolgente

devastation /devə'steɪʃn/ *n* devastazione *f*

develop /dɪ'veləp/ *vt* sviluppare; contrarre ⟨*illness*⟩; (*add to value of*) valorizzare ⟨*area*⟩ ● *vi* svilupparsi; **~ into** divenire

developer /dɪ'veləpə(r)/ *n* [**property**] ~ imprenditore, -trice *mf* edile

developing /dɪ'veləpɪŋ/: **developing bath** *n Phot* bagno *m* di sviluppo, bagno *m* rivelatore. **developing country** *n* paese *m* in via di sviluppo. **developing tank** *n Phot* vasca *f* di sviluppo

development /dɪ'veləpmənt/ *n* sviluppo *m*; (*of vaccine etc*) messa *f* a punto

development company *n* (*for property*) impresa *f* edile

deviant /'diːvɪənt/ *a* deviato

deviate /'diːvɪeɪt/ *vi* deviare

deviation /diːvɪ'eɪʃn/ *n* deviazione *f*

device /dɪ'vaɪs/ *n* dispositivo *m*; **leave sb to his own ~s** lasciare qcno per conto suo

devil /'devl/ *n* diavolo *m*

devilish /'dev(ə)lɪʃ/ a diabolico

devilishly /'dev(ə)lɪʃlɪ/ adv fig fam terribilmente

devil-may-care a menefreghista

devilment /'dev(ə)lmənt/ n Br cattiveria f

devil's advocate n avvocato m del diavolo

devil worship n culto m demoniaco

devious /'di:vɪəs/ a ⟨person⟩ subdolo; ⟨route⟩ tortuoso

deviously /'di:vɪəslɪ/ adv subdolamente

devise /dɪ'vaɪz/ vt escogitare

devoid /dɪ'vɔɪd/ a ~ **of** privo di

devolution /di:və'lu:ʃn/ n (of power) decentramento m

devote /dɪ'vəʊt/ vt dedicare

devoted /dɪ'vəʊtɪd/ a ⟨daughter etc⟩ affezionato; **be ~ to sth** consacrarsi a qcsa

devotedly /dɪ'vəʊtɪdlɪ/ adv con dedizione

devotee /devə'ti:/ n appassionato, -a mf

devotion /dɪ'vəʊʃn/ n dedizione f; **~s** pl Relig devozione fsg

devour /dɪ'vaʊə(r)/ vt divorare

devout /dɪ'vaʊt/ a devoto

devoutly /dɪ'vaʊtlɪ/ adv Relig devotamente; ⟨sincerely⟩ fervidamente

dew /dju:/ n rugiada f

dewy /'dju:ɪ/ a rugiadoso

dewy-eyed /-'aɪd/ a ⟨moved⟩ con gli occhi lucidi; ⟨naive⟩ ingenuo

dexterity /dek'sterətɪ/ n destrezza f

dexterous /'dekstrəs/ a ⟨person, movement⟩ agile, destro; ⟨hand⟩ abile; ⟨mind⟩ acuto

dexterously /'dekstrəslɪ/ adv ⟨move⟩ agilmente; ⟨manage⟩ abilmente

dg abbr (**decigram**) dg m

diabetes /daɪə'bi:ti:z/ n diabete m

diabetic /daɪə'betɪk/ a & n diabetico, -a mf

diabolical /daɪə'bɒlɪkl/ a diabolico

diabolically /daɪə'bɒlɪklɪ/ adv ⟨wickedly⟩ diabolicamente; ⟨fam: badly⟩ orribilmente

diacritic /daɪə'krɪtrɪk/ a ⟨accent, mark⟩ diacritico

diaeresis /daɪ'erɪsɪs/ n dieresi f inv

diagnose /daɪəg'nəʊz/ vt diagnosticare

diagnosis /daɪəg'nəʊsɪs/ n (pl **-oses** /daɪəg'nəʊsi:z/) diagnosi f inv

diagnostic /daɪəg'nɒstɪk/ a diagnostico

diagnostics /daɪəg'nɒstɪks/ n Med diagnostica f

diagonal /daɪ'ægənl/ a & n diagonale f

diagonally /daɪ'ægənlɪ/ adv diagonalmente

diagram /'daɪəgræm/ n diagramma m

dial /'daɪəl/ n (of clock, machine) quadrante m; Teleph disco m combinatore ● v (pt/pp **dialled**) ● vi Teleph fare il numero; ~ **direct** chiamare in teleselezione ● vt fare ⟨number⟩

dialect /'daɪəlekt/ n dialetto m

dialectic /daɪə'lektɪk/ n dialettica f ● a dialettico

dialectics /daɪə'lektɪks/ n dialettica f

dialling code /'daɪəlɪŋ/ n prefisso m

dialling tone n segnale m di linea libera

dialogue /'daɪəlɒɡ/ n dialogo m

dial tone n Am Teleph segnale m di linea libera

dial-up a ⟨network⟩ collegato telefonicamente

dialysis /daɪ'ælɪsɪs/ n dialisi f

dialysis machine n rene m artificiale

diameter /daɪ'æmɪtə(r)/ n diametro m

diametrically /daɪə'metrɪklɪ/ adv ~ **opposed** diametralmente opposto

diamond /'daɪəmənd/ n diamante m, brillante m; (shape) losanga f; ~**s** pl (in cards) quadri mpl

diamond: diamond jubilee n sessantesimo anniversario m. **diamond-shaped** a romboidale. **diamond wedding** [**anniversary**] n nozze fpl di diamante

diaper /'daɪəpə(r)/ n Am pannolino m

diaphanous /daɪ'æfənəs/ a diafano

diaphragm /'daɪəfræm/ n diaframma m

diarist /'daɪərɪst/ n ⟨author⟩ diarista mf; ⟨journalist⟩ giornalista mf di piccola cronaca

diarrhoea /daɪə'ri:ə/ n diarrea f

diary /'daɪərɪ/ n (for appointments) agenda f; (for writing in) diario m

diatribe /'daɪətraɪb/ n diatriba f

dice /daɪs/ n inv dadi mpl ● vt Culin tagliare a dadini

dicey /'daɪsɪ/ a fam rischioso

dichotomy /daɪ'kɒtəmɪ/ n dicotomia f

dicky /'dɪkɪ/ n (shirt front) pettino m, sparato m ● a ⟨Br fam: heart⟩ malandato

dictate /dɪk'teɪt/ vt/i dettare

dictation /dɪk'teɪʃn/ n dettato m

dictator /dɪk'teɪtə(r)/ n dittatore m

dictatorial /dɪktə'tɔ:rɪəl/ a dittatoriale

dictatorship /dɪk'teɪtəʃɪp/ n dittatura f

diction /'dɪkʃn/ n dizione f

dictionary /'dɪkʃənrɪ/ n dizionario m

dictum /'dɪktəm/ n (maxim) massima f; (statement) affermazione f

did /dɪd/ see **do**

didactic /dɪ'dæktɪk/ a didattico

diddle /'dɪdl/ vt fam gabbare

didn't /'dɪdnt/ = **did not**

die[1] /daɪ/ n Techn (metal mould) stampo m; (for cutting) matrice f

die[2] vi (pres p **dying**) morire (**of** di); **be dying to do sth** fam morire dalla voglia di fare qcsa; **be dying for a drink** fam morire dalla voglia di bere qualcosa

■ **die away** vi ⟨noise, applause:⟩ smorzarsi

■ **die down** vi calmarsi; ⟨fire, flames:⟩ spegnersi

■ **die off** vi morire uno dopo l'altro

■ **die out** vi estinguersi; ⟨custom:⟩ morire

diehard /'daɪhɑ:d/ n (pol: in party) fanatico, -a mf; (stubborn person) ultraconservatore mf

diesel /'di:zl/ n diesel m. ~ **engine** n motore m diesel

diesel train n treno m con locomotiva diesel

diet /'daɪət/ n regime m alimentare; (restricted) dieta f; **be on a** ~ essere a dieta ● vi essere a dieta

dietary /'daɪətrɪ/ a ⟨habit⟩ alimentare

dietary fibre n fibre fpl alimentari

dietary supplement *n* integratore *m* dietetico

dietician /daɪəˈtɪʃn/ *n* dietologo, -a *mf*

differ /ˈdɪfə(r)/ *vi* differire; (*disagree*) non essere d'accordo

difference /ˈdɪfrəns/ *n* differenza *f*; (*disagreement*) divergenza *f*

different /ˈdɪfrənt/ *a* diverso, differente; (*various*) diversi; **be ~ from** essere diverso da

differential /dɪfəˈrenʃl/ *a* differenziale ● *n* differenziale *m*

differentiate /dɪfəˈrenʃɪeɪt/ *vt* distinguere (**between** fra); (*discriminate*) discriminare (**between** fra); (*make different*) differenziare

differentiation /dɪfərenʃɪˈeɪʃn/ *n* differenziazione *f*

differently /ˈdɪfrəntlɪ/ *adv* in modo diverso; **~ from** diversamente da

difficult /ˈdɪfɪkəlt/ *a* difficile

difficulty /ˈdɪfɪkəltɪ/ *n* difficoltà *f inv*; **with ~** con difficoltà

diffidence /ˈdɪfɪdəns/ *n* mancanza *f* di sicurezza

diffident /ˈdɪfɪdənt/ *a* senza fiducia in se stesso

diffidently /ˈdɪfɪdəntlɪ/ *adv* senza fiducia in se stesso

diffuse[1] /dɪˈfjuːs/ *a* diffuso; (*wordy*) prolisso

diffuse[2] /dɪˈfjuːz/ *vt Phys* diffondere

diffuseness /dɪˈfjuːsnɪs/ *n* (*of organization*) estensione *f*; (*of argument*) prolissità *f*

dig /dɪg/ *n* (*poke*) spinta *f*; (*remark*) frecciata *f*; *Archaeol* scavo *m*; **~s** *pl fam* camera *f sg* ammobiliata ● *vt/i* (*pt/pp* **dug**, *pres p* **digging**) scavare ⟨*hole*⟩; vangare ⟨*garden*⟩; (*thrust*) conficcare; **~ sb in the ribs** dare una gomitata a qcno

■ **dig out** *vt fig* tirar fuori

■ **dig up** *vt* scavare ⟨*garden, street, object*⟩; sradicare ⟨*tree, plant*⟩; (*fig: find*) scovare

digest[1] /ˈdaɪdʒest/ *n* compendio *m*

digest[2] /daɪˈdʒest/ *vt* digerire

digestible /daɪˈdʒestəbl/ *a* digeribile

digestion /daɪˈdʒestʃn/ *n* digestione *f*

digestive /daɪˈdʒestɪv/ *a* digestivo

digestive: digestive [**biscuit**] *n Br* biscotto *m* di farina integrale. **digestive system** *n* apparato *m* digerente. **digestive tract** *n* apparato *m* digerente

digger /ˈdɪgə(r)/ *n Techn* scavatrice *f*

diggings /ˈdɪgɪŋz/ *npl* (*in archaeology*) scavi *mpl*

digit /ˈdɪdʒɪt/ *n* cifra *f*; (*finger*) dito *m*

digital /ˈdɪdʒɪtl/ *a* digitale

digital: digital audio tape *n* audiocassetta *f* digitale. **digital clock** *n* orologio *m* digitale. **digital computer** *n* computer *m* digitale

digitizer /ˈdɪdʒɪtaɪzə(r)/ *n Comput* tavoletta *f* grafica

dignified /ˈdɪgnɪfaɪd/ *a* dignitoso

dignify /ˈdɪgnɪfaɪ/ *vt* nobilitare ⟨*occasion, building*⟩

dignitary /ˈdɪgnɪtərɪ/ *n* dignitario *m*

dignity /ˈdɪgnətɪ/ *n* dignità *f*

digress /daɪˈgres/ *vi* divagare

digression /daɪˈgreʃn/ *n* digressione *f*

dike /daɪk/ *n* diga *f*

dilapidated /dɪˈlæpɪdeɪtɪd/ *a* cadente

dilapidation /dɪlæpɪˈdeɪʃn/ *n* rovina *f*

dilate /daɪˈleɪt/ *vt* dilatare ● *vi* dilatarsi

dilation /daɪˈleɪʃn/ *n* dilatazione *f*

dilatory /ˈdɪlətərɪ/ *a* dilatorio

dilemma /dɪˈlemə/ *n* dilemma *m*

dilettante /dɪlɪˈtæntɪ/ *n* dilettante *mf*

diligence /ˈdɪlɪdʒəns/ *n* diligenza *f*

diligent /ˈdɪlɪdʒənt/ *a* diligente

dill /dɪl/ *n* aneto *m*

dilly-dally /ˈdɪlɪdælɪ/ *vi* (*pt/pp* **-ied**) *fam* tentennare

dilute /daɪˈljuːt/ *vt* diluire

dilution /daɪˈljuːʃn/ *n also fig* diluizione *f*

dim /dɪm/ *a* (**dimmer, dimmest**) debole ⟨*light*⟩; (*dark*) scuro; ⟨*prospect, chance*⟩ scarso; (*indistinct*) impreciso; (*fam: stupid*) tonto ● *vt/i* (*pt/pp* **dimmed**) affievolire

dime /daɪm/ *n Am* moneta *f* da dieci centesimi

dimension /daɪˈmenʃn/ *n* dimensione *f*

dime store *n Am grande magazzino m con prezzi molto bassi*

diminish /dɪˈmɪnɪʃ/ *vt/i* diminuire

diminished /dɪˈmɪnɪʃt/ *a* ridotto; *Mus* diminuito; **on grounds of ~ responsibility** *Jur* per seminfermità mentale

diminutive /dɪˈmɪnjʊtɪv/ *a* & *n* diminutivo *m*

dimly /ˈdɪmlɪ/ *adv* (*see, remember*) indistintamente; ⟨*shine*⟩ debolmente

dimmer /ˈdɪmə(r)/ *n* interruttore *m* a reostato

dimple /ˈdɪmpl/ *n* fossetta *f*

dimwit /ˈdɪmwɪt/ *n fam* stupido *m*

dim-witted /-ˈwɪtɪd/ *a fam* stupido

din /dɪn/ *n* baccano *m*

■ **din into** *vt* **~ sth into sb** ficcare qcsa in testa a qcno

dine /daɪn/ *vi* pranzare

diner /ˈdaɪnə(r)/ *n* (*Am: restaurant*) tavola *f* calda; **the last ~ in the restaurant** l'ultimo cliente nel ristorante

dingdong /ˈdɪŋdɒŋ/ *n* dindon *m*

dingdong battle *n Br* battibecco *m*

dinghy /ˈdɪŋgɪ/ *n* dinghy *m*; (*inflatable*) canotto *m* pneumatico

dingy /ˈdɪndʒɪ/ *a* (**-ier, -iest**) squallido e tetro

dining /ˈdaɪnɪŋ/: **dining car** *n* carrozza *f* ristorante. **dining hall** *n* refettorio *m*. **dining room** *n* sala *f* da pranzo. **dining table** *n* tavolo *m* da pranzo

dinky /ˈdɪŋkɪ/ *a Br fam* carino

dinner /ˈdɪnə(r)/ *n* cena *f*; (*at midday*) pranzo *m*

dinner: dinner dance *n* cena *f* danzante. **dinner fork** *n* forchetta *f*. **dinner hour** *n Br Sch* pausa *f* del pranzo. **dinner jacket** *n* smoking *m inv*. **dinner knife** *n* coltello *m*. **dinner money** *n Br Sch* soldi *mpl* dati dai genitori agli scolari per il pranzo. **dinner party** *n* cena *f* (*con invitati*). **dinner plate** *n* piatto *m* piano. **dinner service, dinner set** *n* servizio *m* da tavola. **dinner time** *n* (*evening*) ora *f* di cena; (*midday*) ora *f* di pranzo

dinnerware /'dɪnəweə(r)/ *n* servizio *m* da tavola

dinosaur /'daɪnəsɔ:(r)/ *n* dinosauro *m*

dint /dɪnt/ *n* **by ~ of** a forza di

diocese /'daɪəsɪs/ *n* diocesi *f inv*

diode /'daɪəʊd/ *n* diodo *m*

dioxide /daɪ'ɒksaɪd/ *n* biossido *m*

dip /dɪp/ *n* (*in ground*) inclinazione *f*; *Culin* salsina *f*; **go for a ~** andare a fare una nuotata ● *v* (*pt/pp* **dipped**) ● *vt* (*in liquid*) immergere; abbassare ⟨*head, headlights*⟩ ● *vi* ⟨*land*⟩ formare un avvallamento

■ dip into *vt* scorrere ⟨*book*⟩

diphtheria /dɪf'θɪərɪə/ *n* difterite *f*

diphthong /'dɪfθɒŋ/ *n* dittongo *m*

diploma /dɪ'pləʊmə/ *n* diploma *m*

diplomacy /dɪ'pləʊməsɪ/ *n* diplomazia *f*

diplomat /'dɪpləmæt/ *n* diplomatico, -a *mf*

diplomatic /dɪplə'mætɪk/ *a* diplomatico

diplomatically /dɪplə'mætɪklɪ/ *adv* con diplomazia

diplomatic bag *n* valigia *f* diplomatica

diplomatic immunity *n* immunità *f* diplomatica

dippy /'dɪpɪ/ *a* (*fam: crazy, weird*) pazzo

dipstick /'dɪpstɪk/ *n Auto* astina *f* dell'olio

dire /'daɪə(r)/ *a* ⟨*situation, consequences*⟩ terribile

direct /daɪ'rekt/ *a* diretto ● *adv* direttamente ● *vt* (*aim*) rivolgere ⟨*attention, criticism*⟩; (*control*) dirigere; fare la regia di ⟨*film, play*⟩; **~ sb** (*show the way*) indicare la strada a qcno; **~ sb to do sth** ordinare a qcno di fare qcsa

direct: direct access *n Comput* accesso *m* diretto. **direct current** *n* corrente *m* continua. **direct debit** *n* addebitamento *m* diretto. **direct dialling** *n* teleselezione *f*. **direct hit** *n* *Mil* colpo *m* diretto

direction /dɪ'rekʃn/ *n* direzione *f*; (*of play, film*) regia *f*; **~s** *pl* indicazioni *fpl*; **~s for use** istruzioni *fpl* per l'uso

directional /daɪ'rekʃənəl/ *a* direzionale

directive /daɪ'rektɪv/ *n* direttiva *f*

directly /daɪ'rektlɪ/ *adv* direttamente; (*at once*) immediatamente ● *conj* [non] appena

directness /daɪ'rektnɪs/ *n* (*of person, attitude*) franchezza *f*; (*of play, work, writing*) chiarezza *f*

direct object *n* complemento *m* oggetto

director /dɪ'rektə(r)/ *n* *Comm* direttore, -trice *mf*; (*of play, film*) regista *mf*

directorate /dɪ'rektərət/ *n* (*board*) consiglio *m* d'amministrazione

director general *n* presidente *mf*

Director of Public Prosecutions *n Br* ≈ Procuratore *m* della Repubblica

directorship /dɪ'rektəʃɪp/ *n* posto *m* di direttore

directory /dɪ'rektərɪ/ *n* elenco *m*; *Teleph* elenco *m* [telefonico]; (*of streets*) stradario *m*

directory assistance *n Am* servizio *m* informazioni abbonati

directory enquiries *npl Br* servizio *m* informazioni abbonati

direct: direct rule *n Pol* sottomissione *f* al governo centrale. **direct speech** *n* discorso *m* diretto. **direct transfer** *n* trasferimento *m* automatico

dirt /dɜ:t/ *n* sporco *m*; **~ cheap** *fam* a [un] prezzo stracciato

dirtiness /'dɜ:tɪnɪs/ *n* (*of person etc*) sporcizia *f*

dirt track *n* (*road*) strada *f* sterrata; *Sport* pista *f* sterrata

dirty /'dɜ:tɪ/ *a* (**-ier, -iest**) sporco ● *vt* sporcare

dirty: dirty-minded /-'maɪndɪd/ *a* fissato sul sesso. **dirty trick** *n* brutto scherzo *m*. **dirty tricks** *npl Pol* faccende *fpl* sporche. **dirty weekend** *n fam* weekend *m inv* clandestino con l'amante. **dirty word** *n* parolaccia *f*

disability /dɪsə'bɪlətɪ/ *n* infermità *f inv*

disable /dɪ'seɪbl/ *vt* (*make useless*) mettere fuori uso ⟨*machine*⟩; (*in accident*) rendere invalido; *Comput* disabilitare; **be ~d by arthritis** essere menomato dall'artrite

disabled /dɪ'seɪbld/ *a* invalido

disabled: disabled access *n* (*to public building etc*) accesso *m* per gli invalidi. **disabled driver** *n* guidatore, -trice *mf* invalido, -a. **disabled person** *n* invalido, -a *mf*

disabuse /dɪsə'bju:z/ *vt* disingannare

disadvantage /dɪsəd'vɑ:ntɪdʒ/ *n* svantaggio *m*; **at a ~** in una posizione di svantaggio

disadvantaged /dɪsəd'vɑ:ntɪdʒd/ *a* svantaggiato

disadvantageous /dɪsædvən'teɪdʒəs/ *a* svantaggioso

disaffected /dɪsə'fektɪd/ *a* disilluso

disagree /dɪsə'gri:/ *vi* non essere d'accordo; **~ with** ⟨*food*⟩ far male a

disagreeable /dɪsə'gri:əbl/ *a* sgradevole

disagreement /dɪsə'gri:mənt/ *n* disaccordo *m*; (*quarrel*) dissidio *m*

disallow /dɪsə'laʊ/ *vt* respingere; *Sport* annullare

disappear /dɪsə'pɪə(r)/ *vi* scomparire

disappearance /dɪsə'pɪərəns/ *n* scomparsa *f*

disappoint /dɪsə'pɔɪnt/ *vt* deludere

disappointed /dɪsə'pɔɪntɪd/ *a* deluso; **I am ~ in you** mi hai deluso

disappointing /dɪsə'pɔɪntɪŋ/ *a* deludente

disappointment /dɪsə'pɔɪntmənt/ *n* delusione *f*

disapproval /dɪsə'pru:vəl/ *n* disapprovazione *f*

disapprove /dɪsə'pru:v/ *vi* disapprovare; **~ of sb/sth** disapprovare qcno/qcsa

disapproving /dɪsə'pru:vɪŋ/ *a* ⟨*look, gesture*⟩ di disapprovazione

disarm /dɪs'ɑ:m/ *vt* disarmare ● *vi Mil* disarmarsi

disarmament /dɪs'ɑ:məmənt/ *n* disarmo *m*

disarming /dɪs'ɑ:mɪŋ/ *a* ⟨*frankness etc*⟩ disarmante

disarrange /dɪsə'reɪndʒ/ *vt* scompigliare

disarray /dɪsəˈreɪ/ n **in ~** in disordine
disaster /dɪˈzɑːstə(r)/ n disastro m
disaster: disaster area n zona f disastrata; (fig: person) disastro m. **disaster fund** n fondi mpl a favore dei disastrati. **disaster victim** n disastrato, -a mf
disastrous /dɪˈzɑːstrəs/ a disastroso
disastrously /dɪˈzɑːstrəslɪ/ adv ⟨fail⟩ disastrosamente; ⟨end, turn out⟩ in modo catastrofico; **go ~ wrong** essere un disastro
disband /dɪsˈbænd/ vt scogliere; smobilitare ⟨troops⟩ ● vi scogliersi; ⟨regiment:⟩ essere smobilitato
disbelief /dɪsbɪˈliːf/ n incredulità f; **in ~** con incredulità
disbelieve /dɪsbɪˈliːv/ vt non credere
disc /dɪsk/ n disco m; (CD) compact disc m inv
discard /dɪˈskɑːd/ vt scartare; ⟨throw away⟩ eliminare; scaricare ⟨boyfriend⟩
disc brakes npl Auto freni mpl a disco
discern /dɪˈsɜːn/ vt discernere
discernible /dɪˈsɜːnəbl/ a discernibile
discerning /dɪˈsɜːnɪŋ/ a perspicace
discharge¹ /ˈdɪstʃɑːdʒ/ n Electr scarica f; (dismissal) licenziamento m; Mil congedo m; (Med: of blood) emissione f; (of cargo) scarico m
discharge² /dɪsˈtʃɑːdʒ/ vt scaricare ⟨battery, cargo⟩; (dismiss) licenziare; Mil congedare; Jur assolvere ⟨accused⟩; dimettere ⟨patient⟩; **~ one's duty** esaurire il proprio compito ● vi Electr scaricarsi
disciple /dɪˈsaɪpl/ n discepolo m
disciplinarian /dɪsɪplɪˈneərɪən/ n persona f autoritaria
disciplinary /ˈdɪsɪplɪnərɪ/ a disciplinare
discipline /ˈdɪsɪplɪn/ n disciplina f ● vt disciplinare; (punish) punire
disciplined /ˈdɪsɪplɪnd/ a ⟨person, approach⟩ sistematico
disc jockey n disc jockey m inv
disclaim /dɪsˈkleɪm/ vt negare
disclaimer /dɪsˈkleɪmə(r)/ n rifiuto m
disclose /dɪsˈkləʊz/ vt svelare
disclosure /dɪsˈkləʊʒə(r)/ n rivelazione f
disco /ˈdɪskəʊ/ n discoteca f
discoloration /dɪskʌləˈreɪʃn/ n (process) scolorimento m; (spot) macchia f scolorita
discolour /dɪsˈkʌlə(r)/ vt scolorire ● vi scolorirsi
discomfort /dɪsˈkʌmfət/ n scomodità f, fig disagio m
disconcert /dɪskənˈsɜːt/ vt sconcertare
disconcerting /dɪskənˈsɜːtɪŋ/ a sconcertante
disconnect /dɪskəˈnekt/ vt disconnettere
disconsolate /dɪsˈkɒnsələt/ a sconsolato
discontent /dɪskənˈtent/ n scontentezza f
discontented /dɪskənˈtentɪd/ a scontento
discontinue /dɪskənˈtɪnjuː/ vt cessare, smettere; Comm sospendere la produzione di; **~d line** fine f serie
discontinuity /dɪskɒntɪˈnjuːɪtɪ/ n discontinuità f

discord /ˈdɪskɔːd/ n discordia f; Mus dissonanza f
discordant /dɪsˈkɔːdənt/ a **~ note** nota f discordante
discothèque /ˈdɪskətek/ n discoteca f
discount¹ /ˈdɪskaʊnt/ n sconto m
discount² /dɪsˈkaʊnt/ vt (not believe) non credere a; (leave out of consideration) non tener conto di
discount flight n volo m a prezzo ridotto
discount store n discount m inv
discourage /dɪsˈkʌrɪdʒ/ vt scoraggiare; (dissuade) dissuadere
discouragement /dɪsˈkʌrɪdʒmənt/ n (despondency) scoraggiamento m; (disincentive) disincentivo m
discourse /ˈdɪskɔːs/ n discorso m
discourteous /dɪsˈkɜːtɪəs/ a scortese
discourteously /dɪsˈkɜːtɪəslɪ/ adv scortesemente
discover /dɪˈskʌvə(r)/ vt scoprire
discovery /dɪsˈkʌvərɪ/ n scoperta f
discredit /dɪsˈkredɪt/ n discredito m ● vt screditare
discreet /dɪˈskriːt/ a discreto
discreetly /dɪˈskriːtlɪ/ adv discretamente
discrepancy /dɪˈskrepənsɪ/ n discrepanza f
discretion /dɪˈskreʃn/ n discrezione f
discriminate /dɪˈskrɪmɪneɪt/ vi discriminare (**against** contro); **~ between** distinguere tra
discriminating /dɪˈskrɪmɪneɪtɪŋ/ a esigente
discrimination /dɪskrɪmɪˈneɪʃn/ n discriminazione f; (quality) discernimento m
discriminatory /dɪsˈkrɪmɪnətərɪ/ a discriminatorio, discriminativo
discus /ˈdɪskəs/ n disco m
discuss /dɪˈskʌs/ vt discutere; (examine critically) esaminare
discussion /dɪˈskʌʃn/ n discussione f
discussion document, discussion paper n documento m in abbozzo
disdain /dɪsˈdeɪn/ n sdegno f ● vt sdegnare
disdainful /dɪsˈdeɪnfʊl/ a sdegnoso
disease /dɪˈziːz/ n malattia f
diseased /dɪˈziːzd/ a malato
disembark /dɪsemˈbɑːk/ vi sbarcare
disembodied /dɪsemˈbɒdɪd/ a ⟨voices⟩ evanescente; ⟨head⟩ senza corpo; ⟨soul⟩ disincarnato
disenchant /dɪsenˈtʃɑːnt/ vt disincantare
disenchantment /dɪsenˈtʃɑːntmənt/ n disincanto m
disenfranchise /dɪsenˈfræntʃaɪz/ vt privare del diritto di voto
disengage /dɪsenˈgeɪdʒ/ vt disimpegnare; disinnestare ⟨clutch⟩
disentangle /dɪsenˈtæŋgəl/ vt districare
disfavour /dɪsˈfeɪvə(r)/ n sfavore m; **fall into ~** perdere il favore
disfigure /dɪsˈfɪgə(r)/ vt deformare
disgorge /dɪsˈgɔːdʒ/ vt rigettare
disgrace /dɪzˈgreɪs/ n vergogna f; **fall into ~** cadere in disgrazia; **I am in ~** sono caduto

in disgrazia; **it's a ~** è una vergogna ● *vt* disonorare

disgraceful /dɪz'greɪsfʊl/ *a* vergognoso

disgruntled /dɪs'grʌntld/ *a* malcontento

disguise /dɪs'gaɪz/ *n* travestimento *m*; **in ~** travestito ● *vt* contraffare ⟨*voice*⟩; dissimulare ⟨*emotions*⟩; **~d as** travestito da

disgust /dɪs'gʌst/ *n* disgusto *m*; **in ~** con aria disgustata ● *vt* disgustare

disgusting /dɪs'gʌstɪŋ/ *a* disgustoso

dish /dɪʃ/ *n* piatto *m*; **do the ~es** lavare i piatti

■ **dish out** *vt* ⟨*serve*⟩ servire; ⟨*distribute*⟩ distribuire

■ **dish up** *vt* servire

dishcloth /'dɪʃklɒθ/ *n* strofinaccio *m*

dishearten /dɪs'hɑːt(ə)n/ *vt* scoraggiare

disheartening /dɪs'hɑːt(ə)nɪŋ/ *a* scoraggiante

dishevelled /dɪ'ʃevld/ *a* scompigliato

dishonest /dɪs'ɒnɪst/ *a* disonesto

dishonestly /dɪs'ɒnɪstlɪ/ *adv* disonestamente

dishonesty /dɪs'ɒnɪstɪ/ *n* disonestà *f*

dishonour /dɪs'ɒnə(r)/ *n* disonore *m* ● *vt* disonorare ⟨*family*⟩; non onorare ⟨*cheque*⟩

dishonourable /dɪs'ɒnərəbl/ *a* disonorevole

dishonourably /dɪs'ɒnərəblɪ/ *adv* in modo disonorevole

dishwasher /'dɪʃwɒʃə(r)/ *n* lavapiatti *f inv*

dishy /'dɪʃɪ/ *a* (**-ier, est**) ⟨*Br fam*: *man, woman*⟩ fico, figo

disillusion /dɪsɪ'luːʒn/ *vt* disilludere

disillusioned /dɪsɪ'luːʒnd/ *a* deluso (**with** di)

disillusionment /dɪsɪ'luːʒnmənt/ *n* disillusione *f*

disincentive /dɪsɪn'sentɪv/ *n* disincentivo *m*

disinclined /dɪsɪn'klaɪnd/ *a* riluttante

disinfect /dɪsɪn'fekt/ *vt* disinfettare

disinfectant /dɪsɪn'fektənt/ *n* disinfettante *m*

disingenuous /dɪsɪn'dʒenjʊəs/ *a* ⟨*comment*⟩ insincero; ⟨*smile*⟩ falso

disinherit /dɪsɪn'herɪt/ *vt* diseredare

disintegrate /dɪs'ɪntɪgreɪt/ *vi* disintegrarsi

disintegration /dɪsɪntɪ'greɪʃn/ *n* disgregazione *f*

disinterested /dɪs'ɪntərestɪd/ *a* disinteressato

disjointed /dɪs'dʒɔɪntɪd/ *a* sconnesso

disk /dɪsk/ *n* ⟨*Comput*⟩ disco *m*; ⟨*diskette*⟩ dischetto *m*

disk drive *n* lettore *m* [di disco]

disk operating system /'dɪskɒpəreɪtɪŋ/ *n* sistema *m* operativo su disco

dislike /dɪs'laɪk/ *n* avversione *f*; **your likes and ~s** i tuoi gusti ● *vt* **I ~ him/it** non mi piace; **I don't ~ him/it** non mi dispiace

dislocate /'dɪsləkeɪt/ *vt* slogare; **~ one's shoulder** slogarsi una spalla

dislocation /dɪslə'keɪʃn/ *n* ⟨*of hip, knee*⟩ lussazione *f*

dislodge /dɪs'lɒdʒ/ *vt* sloggiare

disloyal /dɪs'lɔɪəl/ *a* sleale

disloyally /dɪs'lɔɪəlɪ/ *adv* slealmente

disloyalty /dɪs'lɔɪəltɪ/ *n* slealtà *f*

dismal /'dɪzməl/ *a* ⟨*person*⟩ abbacchiato; ⟨*news, weather*⟩ deprimente; ⟨*performance*⟩ mediocre

dismantle /dɪs'mæntl/ *vt* smontare ⟨*tent, machine*⟩; *fig* smantellare

dismay /dɪs'meɪ/ *n* sgomento *m*; **much to my ~** con mio grande sgomento

dismayed /dɪs'meɪd/ *a* sgomento

dismember /dɪs'membə(r)/ *vt* *also fig* smembrare

dismiss /dɪs'mɪs/ *vt* licenziare ⟨*employee*⟩; ⟨*reject*⟩ scartare ⟨*idea, suggestion*⟩

dismissal /dɪs'mɪsəl/ *n* licenziamento *m*

dismissive /dɪs'mɪsɪv/ *a* ⟨*person, attitude*⟩ sprezzante; **be ~ of** essere sprezzante verso

dismount /dɪs'maʊnt/ *vi* smontare

disobedience /dɪsə'biːdɪəns/ *n* disubbidienza *f*

disobedient /dɪsə'biːdɪənt/ *a* disubbidiente

disobey /dɪsə'beɪ/ *vt* disubbidire a ⟨*rule*⟩ ● *vi* disubbidire

disorder /dɪs'ɔːdə(r)/ *n* disordine *m*; *Med* disturbo *m*

disordered /dɪs'ɔːdəd/ *a* ⟨*life*⟩ disordinato; ⟨*mind*⟩ disturbato

disorderly /dɪs'ɔːdəlɪ/ *a* disordinato; ⟨*crowd*⟩ turbolento; **~ conduct** turbamento *m* della quiete pubblica

disorganization /dɪsɔːgənar'zeɪʃn/ *n* disorganizzazione *f*

disorganized /dɪs'ɔːgənaɪzd/ *a* disorganizzato

disorientate /dɪs'ɔːrɪənteɪt/ *vt* disorientare

disorientation /dɪsɔːrɪen'teɪʃn/ *n* disorientamento *m*

disown /dɪs'əʊn/ *vt* disconoscere; **I'll ~ you** *fam* faccio finta di non conoscerti

disparaging /dɪ'spærɪdʒɪŋ/ *a* sprezzante

disparagingly /dɪ'spærɪdʒɪŋlɪ/ *adv* sprezzantemente

disparate /'dɪspərət/ *a* ⟨*different*⟩ eterogeneo; ⟨*incompatible*⟩ disparato

disparity /dɪ'spærətɪ/ *n* disparità *f inv*

dispassionate /dɪ'spæʃənət/ *a* spassionato

dispassionately /dɪs'pæʃənətlɪ/ *adv* spassionatamente

dispatch /dɪ'spætʃ/ *n* *Comm* spedizione *f*; ⟨*Mil, report*⟩ dispaccio *m*; **with ~** con prontezza ● *vt* spedire; ⟨*kill*⟩ spedire al creatore

dipatch: Dispatch Box *n Br Pol* postazione *f* da cui parlano i ministri nel Parlamento britannico. **dispatch box** *n* valigia *f* diplomatica. **dispatch rider** *n* staffetta *f*

dispel /dɪ'spel/ *vt* ⟨*pt/pp* **dispelled**⟩ dissipare

dispensable /dɪ'spensəbl/ *a* dispensabile

dispensary /dɪ'spensərɪ/ *n* farmacia *f*

dispense /dɪ'spens/ *vt* distribuire; **~ with** fare a meno di

dispenser /dɪ'spensə(r)/ *n* ⟨*device*⟩ distributore *m*

dispensing chemist /dɪˈspensɪŋ/ n farmacista mf; (shop) farmacia f

dispensing optician n Br ottico m

dispersal /dɪˈspɜːsl/ n dispersione f

disperse /dɪˈspɜːs/ vt disperdere ● vi dispersi

dispersion /dɪˈspɜːʃn/ n dispersione f

dispirited /dɪˈspɪrɪtɪd/ a scoraggiato

displace /dɪsˈpleɪs/ vt spostare

displaced person n profugo, -a mf

displacement /dɪsˈpleɪsmənt/ n spostamento m

display /dɪˈspleɪ/ n mostra f; Comm esposizione f; (of feelings) manifestazione f; pej ostentazione f; Comput display m inv ● vt mostrare; esporre ⟨goods⟩; manifestare ⟨feelings⟩; Comput visualizzare

display: display advertisement n annuncio m pubblicitario di grande formato.
display cabinet, display case n vetrina f.
display rack n espositore m. **display window** n vetrina f

displease /dɪsˈpliːz/ vt non piacere a; **be ~d with** essere scontento di

displeasure /dɪsˈpleʒə(r)/ n malcontento m; **incur sb's ~** scontentare qcno

disposable /dɪˈspəʊzəbl/ a ⟨throwaway⟩ usa e getta; ⟨income⟩ disponibile

disposal /dɪˈspəʊzl/ n (getting rid of) eliminazione f; **be at sb's ~** essere a disposizione di qcno

dispose /dɪˈspəʊz/ vi ~ **of** (get rid of) disfarsi di; **be well ~d** essere ben disposto (**to** verso)

disposition /dɪspəˈzɪʃn/ n disposizione f; (nature) indole f

dispossessed /dɪspəˈzest/ a ⟨family⟩ spossessato; ⟨son⟩ diseredato

disproportionate /dɪsprəˈpɔːʃənət/ a sproporzionato

disproportionately /dɪsprəˈpɔːʃənətlɪ/ adv in modo sproporzionato

disprove /dɪsˈpruːv/ vt confutare

dispute /dɪˈspjuːt/ n disputa f; (industrial) contestazione f ● vt contestare ⟨statement⟩

disqualification /dɪskwɒlɪfɪˈkeɪʃn/ n squalifica f; (from driving) ritiro m della patente

disqualify /dɪsˈkwɒlɪfaɪ/ vt escludere; Sport squalificare; **~ sb from driving** ritirare la patente a qcno

disquiet /dɪsˈkwaɪət/ n inquietudine f

disquieting /dɪsˈkwaɪətɪŋ/ a allarmante

disregard /dɪsrɪˈɡɑːd/ n mancanza f di considerazione ● vt ignorare

disrepair /dɪsrɪˈpeə(r)/ n **fall into ~** deteriorarsi; **in a state of ~** in cattivo stato

disreputable /dɪsˈrepjʊtəbl/ a malfamato

disrepute /dɪsrɪˈpjuːt/ n discredito m; **bring sb into ~** rovinare la reputazione a qcno

disrespect /dɪsrɪˈspekt/ n mancanza f di rispetto

disrespectful /dɪsrɪˈspektfʊl/ a irrispettoso

disrespectfully /dɪsrɪˈspektfʊlɪ/ adv irrispettosamente

disrupt /dɪsˈrʌpt/ vt creare scompiglio in; sconvolgere ⟨plans⟩

disruption /dɪsˈrʌpʃn/ n scompiglio m; (of plans) sconvolgimento m

disruptive /dɪsˈrʌptɪv/ a ⟨person, behaviour⟩ indisciplinato

dissatisfaction /dɪ(s)sætɪsˈfækʃn/ n malcontento m

dissatisfied /dɪ(s)ˈsætɪsfaɪd/ a scontento

dissect /dɪˈsekt/ vt sezionare

dissection /dɪˈsekʃn/ n dissezione f

disseminate /dɪˈsemɪneɪt/ vt divulgare

dissemination /dɪsemɪˈneɪʃn/ n divulgazione f

dissension /dɪˈsenʃn/ n (discord) dissenso m

dissent /dɪˈsent/ n dissenso m ● vi dissentire

dissertation /dɪsəˈteɪʃn/ n tesi f inv

disservice /dɪ(s)ˈsɜːvɪs/ n **do sb/oneself a ~** rendere un cattivo servizio a qcno/se stesso

dissidence /ˈdɪsɪdəns/ n dissidenza f

dissident /ˈdɪsɪdənt/ n dissidente mf

dissimilar /dɪ(s)ˈsɪmɪlə(r)/ a dissimile (**to** da)

dissimilarity /dɪs(s)ɪmɪˈlærətɪ/ n diversità f inv

dissipate /ˈdɪsɪpeɪt/ vt dissipare ⟨hope, enthusiasm⟩

dissipated /ˈdɪsɪpeɪtɪd/ a dissipato

dissipation n dissipatezza f, sregolatezza f

dissociate /dɪˈsəʊʃɪeɪt/ vt dissociare; **~ oneself from** dissociarsi da

dissolute /ˈdɪsəluːt/ a dissoluto

dissolution /dɪsəˈluːʃn/ n scioglimento m

dissolve /dɪˈzɒlv/ vt dissolvere ● vi dissolversi

dissonance /ˈdɪsənəns/ n dissonanza f

dissonant /ˈdɪsənənt/ a Mus dissonante

dissuade /dɪˈsweɪd/ vt dissuadere

distance /ˈdɪstəns/ n distanza f; **it's a short ~ from here to the station** la stazione non è lontana da qui; **in the ~** in lontananza; **from a ~** da lontano

distant /ˈdɪstənt/ a distante; ⟨relative⟩ lontano

distantly /ˈdɪstəntlɪ/ adv ⟨reply⟩ con distacco

distaste /dɪsˈteɪst/ n avversione f

distasteful /dɪsˈteɪstfʊl/ a spiacevole

distemper /dɪˈstempə(r)/ n (paint) tempera f; (in horses, dogs) cimurro m

distend /dɪˈstend/ vi dilatarsi

distil /dɪˈstɪl/ vt (pt/pp distilled) distillare

distillation /dɪstɪˈleɪʃn/ n distillazione f

distillery /dɪˈstɪlərɪ/ n distilleria f

distinct /dɪˈstɪŋkt/ a chiaro; (different) distinto

distinction /dɪˈstɪŋkʃn/ n distinzione f; Sch massimo m dei voti

distinctive /dɪˈstɪŋktɪv/ a caratteristico

distinctly /dɪˈstɪŋktlɪ/ adv chiaramente

distinguish /dɪˈstɪŋgwɪʃ/ vt/i distinguere; **~ oneself** distinguersi

distinguishable /dɪˈstɪŋgwɪʃəbl/ a distinguibile

distinguished /dɪˈstɪŋgwɪʃt/ a rinomato; ‹appearance› distinto; ‹career› brillante

distort /dɪˈstɔːt/ vt distorcere

distortion /dɪˈstɔːʃn/ n distorsione f

distract /dɪˈstrækt/ vt distrarre

distracted /dɪˈstræktɪd/ a assente; (fam: worried) preoccupato

distracting /dɪˈstræktɪŋ/ a che distrae; **I found the noise too ~** il rumore mi disturbava troppo

distraction /dɪˈstrækʃn/ n distrazione f; (despair) disperazione f; **drive sb to ~** portare qcno alla disperazione

distraught /dɪˈstrɔːt/ a sconvolto

distress /dɪˈstres/ n angoscia f; (pain) sofferenza f; (danger) difficoltà f ● vt sconvolgere; (sadden) affliggere

distressed /dɪˈstrest/ a (upset) turbato; (stronger) afflitto

distressing /dɪˈstresɪŋ/ a penoso; (shocking) sconvolgente

distress signal n segnale m di richiesta di soccorso

distribute /dɪˈstrɪbjuːt/ vt distribuire

distribution /ˌdɪstrɪˈbjuːʃn/ n distribuzione f

distribution network n rete f di distribuzione

distributor /dɪˈstrɪbjʊtə(r)/ n distributore m

district /ˈdɪstrɪkt/ n regione f; Admin distretto m

district: district council n Br consiglio m distrettuale. **district court** n Am corte f distrettuale federale. **district manager** n direttore, -trice mf di zona. **district nurse** n infermiere, -a mf che fa visite a domicilio

distrust /dɪsˈtrʌst/ n sfiducia f ● vt non fidarsi di

distrustful /dɪsˈtrʌstfʊl/ a diffidente

disturb /dɪˈstɜːb/ vt disturbare; (emotionally) turbare; spostare ‹papers›

disturbance /dɪˈstɜːbəns/ n disturbo m; **~s** pl (rioting etc) disordini mpl

disturbed /dɪˈstɜːbd/ a turbato; [**mentally**] **~** malato di mente

disturbing /dɪˈstɜːbɪŋ/ a inquietante

disuse /dɪsˈjuːs/ n **fall into ~** cadere in disuso

disused /dɪsˈjuːzd/ a non utilizzato

ditch /dɪtʃ/ n fosso m ● vt (fam: abandon) abbandonare ‹plan, car›; piantare ‹lover›

ditchwater /ˈdɪtʃwɔːtə(r)/ n **as dull as ~** una barba

dither /ˈdɪðə(r)/ vi titubare

ditto /ˈdɪtəʊ/ adv idem; (in list) idem come sopra

ditto marks npl virgolette fpl

divan /dɪˈvæn/ n divano m

dive /daɪv/ n tuffo m; Aeron picchiata f; (fam: place) bettola f ● vi tuffarsi; (when in water) immergersi; Aeron scendere in picchiata; (fam: rush) precipitarsi

dive-bomb vt Mil bombardare in picchiata

diver /ˈdaɪvə(r)/ n (from board) tuffatore,

-trice mf; (scuba) sommozzatore, -trice mf; (deep sea) palombaro m

diverge /daɪˈvɜːdʒ/ vi divergere

divergent /daɪˈvɜːdʒənt/ a divergente

diverse /daɪˈvɜːs/ a vario

diversify /daɪˈvɜːsɪfaɪ/ vt/i (pt/pp -ied) diversificare; Comm diversificare

diversion /daɪˈvɜːʃn/ n deviazione f; (distraction) diversivo m

diversionary /daɪˈvɜːʃənərɪ/ a ‹tactic, attack› diversivo

diversity /daɪˈvɜːsətɪ/ n varietà f

divert /daɪˈvɜːt/ vt deviare ‹traffic›; distogliere ‹attention›

divest /daɪˈvest/ vt privare (**of** di)

divide /dɪˈvaɪd/ vt dividere (**by** per); **six ~d by two** sei diviso due ● vi dividersi
■ **divide out** vt = **divide**
■ **divide up** vt = **divide**

dividend /ˈdɪvɪdend/ n dividendo m; **pay ~s** fig ripagare

divider /dɪˈvaɪdə(r)/ n (in room) divisorio m; (in file) cartoncino m separatore

dividers /dɪˈvaɪdəz/ npl compasso m a punte fisse

dividing /dɪˈvaɪdɪŋ/ a ‹wall, fence› divisorio

dividing line n linea f di demarcazione

divine /dɪˈvaɪn/ a divino

divinely /dɪˈvaɪnlɪ/ adv also fam divinamente

diving /ˈdaɪvɪŋ/ n (from board) tuffi mpl; (scuba) immersione f

diving: diving board n trampolino m. **diving mask** n maschera f [subacquea]. **diving suit** n muta f; (deep sea) scafandro m

divinity /dɪˈvɪnətɪ/ n divinità f inv; (subject) teologia f; (at school) religione f

divisible /dɪˈvɪzəbl/ a divisibile (**by** per)

division /dɪˈvɪʒn/ n divisione f; (in sports league) serie f

divisional /dɪˈvɪʒənəl/ a ‹commander, officer› di divisione

divisive /dɪˈvaɪsɪv/ a ‹policy› che crea discordia; **be socially ~** creare delle divisioni sociali

divorce /dɪˈvɔːs/ n divorzio m ● vt divorziare da

divorced /dɪˈvɔːst/ a divorziato; **get ~** divorziare

divorcee /dɪvɔːˈsiː/ n divorziato, -a mf

divulge /daɪˈvʌldʒ/ vt rendere pubblico
■ **divvy up** vt fam = **divide up**

DIY abbr **do-it-yourself**

dizziness /ˈdɪzɪnɪs/ n giramenti mpl di testa

dizzy /ˈdɪzɪ/ a (-ier, -iest) vertiginoso; **I feel ~** mi gira la testa

DJ n abbr (**disc jockey**) DJ m inv; Br abbr (**dinner jacket**) smoking m inv

DNA n abbr (**deoxyribonucleic acid**) DNA m inv ● attrib ‹testing› del DNA

do /duː/ n (pl **dos** or **do's**) fam festa f ● v (3 sg pres tense **does**; pt **did**; pp **done**) ● vt fare; (fam: cheat) fregare; **do sb out of sth** (money) fregare qcsa a qcno; (opportunity) defraudare qcno di qcsa; **be done** Culin essere cotto; **well done** bravo; *Culin* ben cotto; **do the flowers** sistemare i fiori; **do the washing up** lavare i piatti; **do one's hair** farsi i capelli ● *vi* (*be suitable*) andare; (*be enough*) bastare; **this will do** questo va bene; **that will do!** basta così!; **do well/badly** cavarsela bene/male; **how is he doing?** come sta? ● *v aux* **do you speak Italian?** parli italiano?; **you don't like him, do you?** non ti piace, vero?; (*expressing astonishment*) non dirmi che ti piace!; **yes, I do** sì; (*emphatic*) invece sì; **no, I don't** no; **I don't smoke** non fumo; **don't you/doesn't he?** vero?; **so do I** anch'io; **do come in, John** entra, John; **how do you do?** piacere

■ **do away with** *vt* abolire ‹*rule*›

■ **do for** *vt* (*ruin*) rovinare

■ **do in** *vt* (*fam: kill*) uccidere; farsi male a ‹*back*›; **done in** *fam* esausto

■ **do up** *vt* (*fasten*) abbottonare; (*renovate*) rimettere a nuovo; (*wrap*) avvolgere

■ **do with** *vt* **I could do with a spanner** mi ci vorrebbe una chiave inglese

■ **do without** *vt* fare a meno di

d.o.b. *abbr* (**date of birth**) data *f* di nascita

docile /'dəʊsaɪl/ *a* docile

dock¹ /dɒk/ *n Jur* banco *m* degli imputati

dock² *n Naut* bacino *m* ● *vi* entrare in porto; ‹*spaceship:*› congiungersi

docker /'dɒkə(r)/ *n* portuale *m*

docket /'dɒkɪt/ *n* (*Comm: label*) etichetta *f*; (*customs certificate*) ricevuta *f* doganale ● *vt Comm* etichettare ‹*parcel, package*›

docking /'dɒkɪŋ/ *n Naut* ormeggio *m*; (*of spaceshuttle*) aggancio *m*

docks /dɒks/ *npl* porto *m*

dockworker /'dɒkwɜːkə(r)/ *n* portuale *m*

dockyard /'dɒkjɑːd/ *n* cantiere *m* navale

doctor /'dɒktə(r)/ *n* dottore *m*, dottoressa *f* ● *vt* alterare ‹*drink*›; castrare ‹*cat*›

doctorate /'dɒktərət/ *n* dottorato *m*

Doctor of Philosophy *n* titolare *mf* di un dottorato di ricerca

doctor's note /'dɒktəz/ *n* certificato *m* medico

doctrine /'dɒktrɪn/ *n* dottrina *f*

document /'dɒkjʊmənt/ *n* documento *m*

documentary /dɒkjʊ'mentərɪ/ *a* & *n* documentario *m*

documentation /dɒkjʊmen'teɪʃn/ *n* documentazione *f*

document holder *n* (*for keyboarder*) leggio *m*

document wallet *n* (*folder*) cartellina *f*

doddery /'dɒdərɪ/ *a fam* barcollante

doddle /'dɒd(ə)l/ *n Br fam* **it's a ~** è un gioco da ragazzi

dodge /dɒdʒ/ *n fam* trucco *m* ● *vt* schivare ‹*blow*›; evitare ‹*person*› ● *vi* scansarsi; **~ out of the way** scansarsi

dodgems /'dɒdʒəmz/ *npl* autoscontro *msg*

dodgy /'dɒdʒɪ/ *a* (**-ier, -iest**) (*fam: dubious*) sospetto

DOE *n Br abbr* (**Department of the Environment**) ministero *m* dell'ambiente; *Am*

abbr (**Department of Energy**) ≈ ministero *m* dell'industria

doe /dəʊ/ *n* femmina *f* (*di daino, renna, lepre*); (*rabbit*) coniglia *f*

does /dʌz/ *see* **do**

doesn't /'dʌznt/ = **does not**

dog /dɒg/ *n* cane *m* ● *vt* (*pt/pp* **dogged**) ‹*illness, bad luck:*› perseguitare

dog: dog biscuit *n* biscotto *m* per cani. **dog breeder** *n* allevatore, -trice *mf* di cani. **dog collar** *n* collare *m* (*per cani*); *Relig fam* collare *m* del prete. **dog-eared** /-ɪəd/ *a* con le orrechie. **dog-end** *n fam* cicca *f*. **dogfight** *n* combattimento *m* di cani; *Aeron* combattimento *m* aereo

dogged /'dɒgɪd/ *a* ostinato

doggedly /'dɒgɪdlɪ/ *adv* ostinatamente

doggy bag /'dɒgɪ/ *n* sacchetto *m* per portarsi a casa gli avanzi di un pasto al ristorante

doggy-paddle *n fam* nuoto *m* a cagnolino

dog handler *n* addestratore, -trice *mf* di cani

doghouse /'dɒghaʊs/ *n Am* canile *m*; **in the ~** *Br & Am fam* in disgrazia

dogma /'dɒgmə/ *n* dogma *m*

dogmatic /dɒg'mætɪk/ *a* dogmatico

do-gooder /duː'gʊdə(r)/ *n pej* pseudo benefattore, -trice *mf*

dog: dog-paddle *n* nuoto *m* a cagnolino. **dogsbody** *n fam* tirapiedi *mf inv*. **dog tag** *n Am Mil fam* piastrina *f* di riconoscimento

doh /dəʊ/ *n Mus* do *m*

doily /'dɔɪlɪ/ *n* centrino *m*

doing /'duːɪŋ/ *n* **it's none of my ~** non sono stato io; **this is her ~** questa è opera sua; **it takes some ~!** ce ne vuole!

do-it-yourself /duːɪtjə'self/ *n* fai da te *m*, bricolage *m*

do-it-yourself shop *n* negozio *m* di bricolage

doldrums /'dɒldrəmz/ *npl* **be in the ~** essere giù di corda; ‹*business:*› essere in fase di stasi

dole /dəʊl/ *n* sussidio *m* di disoccupazione; **be on the ~** essere disoccupato

■ **dole out** *vt* distribuire

doleful /'dəʊlfl/ *a* triste

dolefully /'dəʊlfʊlɪ/ *adv* tristemente

dole queue *n Br* coda *f* per riscuotere il sussidio di disoccupazione; (*fig: number of unemployed*) numero *m* dei disoccupati

doll /dɒl/ *n* bambola *f*

■ **doll up** *vt fam* **~ oneself up** mettersi in ghingheri

dollar /'dɒlə(r)/ *n* dollaro *m*

dollar: dollar bill *n* banconota *f* da un dollaro. **dollar diplomacy** *n politica f di investimenti all'estero*. **dollar sign** *n* simbolo *m* del dollaro

dollop /'dɒləp/ *n fam* cucchiaiata *f*

dolly /'dɒlɪ/ *n* (*fam: doll*) bambola *f*; *Cinema, TV* dolly *m inv*

Dolomites /'dɒləmaɪts/ *npl* Dolomiti *mpl*

dolphin /'dɒlfɪn/ *n* delfino *m*

domain /də'meɪn/ *n* dominio *m*

dome /dəʊm/ n cupola f

domed /dəʊmd/ a ⟨skyline, city⟩ ricco di cupole; ⟨roof, ceiling⟩ a cupola; ⟨forehead, helmet⟩ bombato

domestic /də'mestɪk/ a domestico; Pol interno; Comm nazionale.

domestic animal n animale m domestico

domestic appliance n elettrodomestico m

domesticated /də'mestɪkeɪtɪd/ a ⟨animal⟩ addomesticato

domestic flight n volo m nazionale

domestic help n collaboratore, -trice mf familiare

domesticity /dɒme'stɪsəti/ n ⟨home life⟩ vita f di famiglia; ⟨household duties⟩ faccende fpl domestiche

domestic servant n domestico, -a mf

domiciliary /dɒmɪ'sɪlɪəri/ a ⟨visit, care⟩ a domicilio

dominance /'dɒmɪnəns/ n Biol, Zool dominanza f; ⟨domination⟩ predominio m; ⟨numerical strength⟩ preponderanza f

dominant /'dɒmɪnənt/ a dominante

dominate /'dɒmɪneɪt/ vt/i dominare

domination /dɒmɪ'neɪʃn/ n dominio m

domineering /dɒmɪ'nɪərɪŋ/ a autoritario

Dominican Republic /də'mɪnɪkən/ n Repubblica f Dominicana

dominion /də'mɪnjən/ n Br Pol dominion m inv

domino /'dɒmɪnəʊ/ n ⟨pl -es⟩ tessera f del domino; ~es sg ⟨game⟩ domino m

don¹ /dɒn/ vt ⟨pt/pp donned⟩ liter indossare

don² n docente mf universitario, -a

donate /dəʊ'neɪt/ vt donare

donation /dəʊ'neɪʃn/ n donazione f

done /dʌn/ see do

donkey /'dɒŋki/ n asino m

donkey: donkey jacket n giacca f pesante. **donkey's years** fam not for ~ ~ non da secoli. **donkey-work** n sgobbata f

donor /'dəʊnə(r)/ n donatore, -trice mf

donor card n tessera f del donatore di organi

don't /dəʊnt/ = **do not**

doodle /'du:dl/ vi scarabocchiare

doom /du:m/ n fato m; ⟨ruin⟩ rovina f ● vt be ~ed to failure essere destinato al fallimento

doomed /du:md/ a ⟨vessel⟩ destinato ad affondare

doomsday /'du:mzdeɪ/ n giorno m del giudizio

doomwatch /'du:mwɒtʃ/ n catastrofismo m

door /dɔ:(r)/ n porta f; ⟨of car⟩ portiera f; **out of ~s** all'aperto

door: door bell n campanello m. **doorman** n portiere m. **doormat** n zerbino m. **door plate** n ⟨of doctor etc⟩ targa f. **doorstep** n gradino m della porta. **doorstop** n fermaporta m inv. **door-to-door** a ⟨canvassing, selling⟩ porta a porta ● adv ⟨sell⟩ porta a porta. **doorway** n vano m della porta

dope /dəʊp/ n fam ⟨drug⟩ droga f leggera;

⟨information⟩ indiscrezioni fpl; ⟨idiot⟩ idiota mf ● vt drogare; Sport dopare

dope test n Sport antidoping m inv

dopey /'dəʊpɪ/ a fam addormentato

dormant /'dɔ:mənt/ a latente; ⟨volcano⟩ inattivo

dormer /'dɔ:mə(r)/ n ~ [**window**] abbaino m

dormitory /'dɔ:mɪtərɪ/ n dormitorio m

dormouse /'dɔ:maʊs/ n ⟨pl **dormice** /'dɔ:maɪs/⟩ ghiro m

dosage /'dəʊsɪdʒ/ n dosaggio m

dose /dəʊs/ n dose f

doss /dɒs/ vi sl accamparsi

■ **doss down** vi sistemarsi [a dormire]

dosser /'dɒsə(r)/ n barbone, -a mf

doss-house n dormitorio m pubblico

dot /dɒt/ n punto m; **at 8 o'clock on the ~** alle 8 in punto

dotage /'dəʊtɪdʒ/ n **be in one's ~** essere un vecchio rimbambito

dote /dəʊt/ vi ~ **on** stravedere per

dot matrix [**printer**] n stampante f a matrice di punti

dotted /'dɒtɪd/ a ~ **line** linea f punteggiata; **sign on the ~ line** firmare nell'apposito spazio; **be ~ with** essere punteggiato di

dotty /'dɒtɪ/ a (-ier, -iest) fam tocco; ⟨idea⟩ folle

double /'dʌbl/ a doppio ● adv **cost ~** costare il doppio; **see ~** vedere doppio; **~ the amount** la quantità doppia ● n doppio m; ⟨person⟩ sosia m inv; **~s** pl Tennis doppio m; **at the ~** di corsa ● vt raddoppiare; ⟨fold⟩ piegare in due ● vi raddoppiare

■ **double back** vi ⟨go back⟩ fare dietro front

■ **double up** vi ⟨bend over⟩ piegarsi in due ⟨with per⟩; ⟨share⟩ dividere una stanza

double: double act n Theat, fig numero m eseguito da due attori. **double-barrelled** /-'bærəld/ a ⟨gun⟩ a doppia canna. **double-barrelled surname** n cognome m doppio. **double-bass** n contrabbasso m. **double bed** n letto m matrimoniale. **double bend** n Auto doppia curva f. **double bill** n Theat rappresentazione f di due spettacoli. **double bluff** n atto m del dire la verità facendola sembrare una menzogna. **double-book** vi ⟨hotel, airline, company:⟩ fare prenotazioni doppie ● vt ~ **a room/seat etc** riservare la stessa camera/lo stesso posto a due persone. **double-breasted** a a doppio petto. **double-check** vt/i ricontrollare ● n **double check** ulteriore controllo m. **double chin** n doppio mento m. **double cream** n Br ≈ panna f densa. **double-cross** vt ingannare. **double cuff** n polsino m con risvolto. **double-dealing** n doppio gioco m ● a doppio. **double-decker** n autobus m inv a due piani. **double door[s]** n[pl] porta f a due battenti. **double Dutch** n fam ostrogoto m. **double-edged** /-'edʒd/ a also fig a doppio taglio. **double entendre** /du:blɒ'tɒdr(ə)/ n doppio senso m. **double entry book-keeping** n contabilità f in partita doppia. **double exposure** n Phot sovrimpressione f. **double fault** n Tennis doppio fallo *m.* **double feature** *n* Cinema proiezione *f* di due film con biglietto unico. **double-fronted** /-'frʌntɪd/ *a* ⟨house⟩ con due finestre ai lati della porta principale. **double glazing** *n* doppiovetro *m.* **double-jointed** *a* ⟨person, limb⟩ snodato. **double knitting** [**wool**] *n* lana *f* grossa. **double lock** *vt* chiudere a doppia mandata. **double-park** *vt/i* parcheggiare in doppia fila. **double-quick** *adv* rapidissimamente ● *a* **in ~ time** in un baleno. **double room** *n* camera *f* doppia. **double saucepan** *n Br* bagnomaria *m inv.* **double spacing** *n Typ* interlinea *f* doppia. **double spread** *n Journ* articolo *m*/pubblicità *f* su due pagine. **double standard** *n* **have ~ ~s** usare metri diversi. **double take** *n* **do a ~ ~** reagire a scoppio ritardato. **double talk** *n pej* discorso *m* ambiguo. **double time** *n Am Mil* marcia *f* forzata; **be paid ~ ~** ricevere doppia paga per lo straordinario. **double vision** *n* **have ~ ~** vederci doppio. **double whammy** *n* (*fam: two bits of bad luck*) sfortuna *f* doppia. **double yellow line**[**s**] *n[pl] Br Aut* due linee *fpl* gialle continue indicanti divieto di fermata e di sosta

doubly /'dʌblɪ/ *adv* doppiamente

doubt /daʊt/ *n* dubbio *m* ● *vt* dubitare di

doubtful /'daʊtfʊl/ *a* dubbio; (*having doubts*) in dubbio

doubtfully /'daʊtfʊlɪ/ *adv* con aria dubbiosa

doubtless /'daʊtlɪs/ *adv* indubbiamente

douche /duːʃ/ *n* (*Med: vaginal*) irrigazione *f*

dough /dəʊ/ *n* pasta *f*; ⟨*for bread*⟩ impasto *m*; (*fam: money*) quattrini *mpl*

doughnut /'dəʊnʌt/ *n* bombolone *m*, krapfen *m inv*

dour /'dʊə(r)/ *a* ⟨mood, landscape⟩ cupo; ⟨person, expression⟩ arcigno; ⟨building⟩ austero

douse /daʊs/ *vt* spegnere

dove /dʌv/ *n* colomba *f*

dovecot[**e**] /'dʌvkɒt/ *n* colombaia *f*

dovetail /'dʌvteɪl/ *n Techn* incastro *m* a coda di rondine

dowdy /'daʊdɪ/ *a* (**-ier, -iest**) trasandato

down¹ /daʊn/ *n* (*feathers*) piumino *m*

down² *adv* giù; **go**/**come ~** scendere; **~ there** laggiù; **sales are ~** le vendite sono diminuite; **£50 ~** 50 sterline d'acconto; **~ 10%** ridotto del 10%; **~ with...!** abbasso...! ● *prep* **walk ~ the road** camminare per strada; **~ the stairs** giù per le scale; **fall ~ the stairs** cadere giù dalle scale; **get that ~ you!** *fam* butta giù!; **be ~ the pub** *fam* essere al pub ● *vt* bere tutto d'un fiato ⟨drink⟩; **~ tools** staccare; (*in protest*) interrompere il lavoro per protestare

down: down-and-out *n* spiantato, -a *mf.* **downbeat** *a* (*pessimistic*) pessimistico; (*laidback*) distaccato. **downcast** *a* abbattuto. **downfall** *n* caduta *f*; (*of person*) rovina *f.* **downgrade** *vt* (*in seniority*) degradare. **down-hearted** /-'hɑːtɪd/ *a* scoraggiato. **downhill** *adv* in discesa; **go ~** *fig* essere in declino. **downhill skiing** *n* sci *m* di fondo.

down-in-the-mouth *a fam* abbattuto. **download** *vt Comput* scaricare. **downmarket** *a* ⟨newspaper, programme⟩ rivolto al pubblico delle fasce basse; ⟨products⟩ dozzinale; ⟨area⟩ popolare; ⟨hotel, restaurant⟩ economico. **down payment** *n* deposito *m.* **downpipe** *n Br* tubo *m* di scolo. **downpour** *n* acquazzone *m.* **downright** *a* ⟨absolute⟩ totale; ⟨lie⟩ bell'e buono; ⟨idiot⟩ perfetto ● *adv* (*completely*) completamente

downs /daʊnz/ *npl Br* ⟨hills⟩ colline *fpl* di gesso nell'Inghilterra meridionale

downside /'daʊnsaɪd/ *n* svantaggio *m*

downside up *a* & *adv Am* sottosopra

Down's syndrome /'daʊnz/ *n* sindrome *f* di Down

down: downstairs *adv* al piano di sotto ● *a* del piano di sotto. **downstream** *adv* a valle. **down-to-earth** *a* ⟨person⟩ con i piedi per terra. **downtown** *adv Am* in centro. **downtrodden** /'daʊntrɒd(ə)n/ *a* oppresso. **downturn** *n* (*in economy*) fase *f* discendente; (*in career*) svolta *f* negativa. **down under** *adv fam* in Australia e/o Nuova Zelanda

downward[**s**] /'daʊnwəd[z]/ *a* verso il basso; ⟨slope⟩ in discesa ● *adv* verso il basso

downwind /daʊn'wɪnd/ *adv* sottovento

downy /'daʊnɪ/ *a* (**-ier, -iest**) coperto di peluria

dowry /'daʊrɪ/ *n* dote *f*

doz *abbr* (**dozen**) dozzina *f*

doze /dəʊz/ *n* sonnellino *m* ● *vi* sonnecchiare

■ **doze off** *vi* assopirsi

dozen /'dʌzn/ *n* dozzina *f*; **~s of books** libri a dozzine

DPhil *n abbr* (**Doctor of Philosophy**) titolare *mf* di un dottorato di ricerca

DPP *n Br abbr* (**Director of Public Prosecutions**) ≈ Procuratore *m* della Repubblica

Dr *abbr* (**doctor**) Dott. *m*, Dott.essa *f*; *abbr* (**drive**) ≈ via *f*

drab /dræb/ *a* ⟨colour⟩ spento; ⟨building⟩ tetro; ⟨life⟩ scialbo

draft¹ /drɑːft/ *n* abbozzo *m*; *Comm* cambiale *f*; *Am Mil* leva *f* ● *vt* abbozzare; *Am Mil* arruolare

draft² *n Am* = **draught**

drag /dræg/ *n fam* scocciatura *f*; **in ~** *fam* ⟨man⟩ travestito da donna ● *vt* (*pt/pp* **dragged**) trascinare; dragare ⟨river⟩

■ **drag on** *vi* ⟨time, meeting:⟩ trascinarsi

■ **drag out** *vt* tirare per le lunghe ⟨discussion⟩; **~ sth out of sb** tirar fuori qcsa a qcno con le pinze

■ **drag up** *vt* (*mention unnecessarily*) tirare in ballo

dragon /'drægən/ *n* drago *m*

dragonfly /'drægənflaɪ/ *n* libellula *f*

drag show *n* spettacolo *m* di travestiti

drain /dreɪn/ *n* tubo *m* di scarico; ⟨grid⟩ tombino *m*; **the ~s** le fognature; **be a ~ on sb's finances** prosciugare le finanze di qcno ● *vt* drenare ⟨land, wound⟩; scolare ⟨liquid, vegetables⟩; svuotare ⟨tank, glass, person⟩

● *vi* ~ [*away*] andar via; **leave sth to** ~ lasciare qcsa a scolare

drainage /'dreɪnɪdʒ/ *n* (*system*) drenaggio *m*; (*of land*) scolo *m*

draining board /'dreɪnɪŋ/ *n* scolapiatti *m inv*

drainpipe /'dreɪmpaɪp/ *n* tubo *m* di scarico

drainpipe trousers *npl* pantaloni *mpl* a tubo

drake /dreɪk/ *n* maschio *m* dell'anatra

drama /'drɑːmə/ *n* arte *f* drammatica; (*play*) opera *f* teatrale; (*event*) dramma *m*

dramatic /drə'mætɪk/ *a* drammatico

dramatically /drə'mætɪklɪ/ *adv* in modo drammatico

dramatics /drə'mætɪks/ *npl* arte *f* drammatica; *pej* atteggiamento *m* teatrale

dramatist /'dræmətɪst/ *n* drammaturgo, -a *mf*

dramatization /dræmətaɪ'zeɪʃn/ *n* (*for cinema*) adattamento *m* cinematografico; (*for stage*) adattamento *m* teatrale; (*for TV*) adattamento *m* televisivo; (*exaggeration*) drammatizzazione *f*

dramatize /'dræmətaɪz/ *vt* adattare per il teatro; *fig* drammatizzare

drank /dræŋk/ *see* **drink**

drape /dreɪp/ *n Am* tenda *f* ● *vt* appoggiare (**over** su)

drastic /'dræstɪk/ *a* drastico

drastically /'dræstɪklɪ/ *adv* drasticamente

draught /drɑːft/ *n* corrente *f* [d'aria]

draught beer *n* birra *f* alla spina

draught-proof *a* a tenuta d'aria ● *vt* tappare le fessure di

draughts /drɑːfts/ *n sg* (*game*) [gioco *m* della] dama *fsg*

draughtsman /'drɑːftsmən/ *n* disegnatore, -trice *mf*

draughty /'drɑːftɪ/ *a* pieno di correnti d'aria; **it's** ~ c'è corrente

draw /drɔː/ *n* (*attraction*) attrazione *f*; *Sport* pareggio *m*; (*in lottery*) sorteggio *m* ● *v* (*pt* **drew**, *pp* **drawn**) ● *vt* tirare; (*attract*) attirare; disegnare (*picture*); tracciare (*line*); ritirare (*money*); attingere (*water*); ~ **lots** tirare a sorte ● *vi* (*tea:*) essere in infusione; *Sport* pareggiare; ~ **near** avvicinarsi

■ **draw back** *vt* tirare indietro; ritirare (*hand*); tirare (*curtains*) ● *vi* (*recoil*) tirarsi indietro

■ **draw in** *vt* ritrarre (*claws etc*) ● *vi* (*train:*) arrivare; (*days:*) accorciarsi

■ **draw on** *vt* attingere a (*savings, sb's experience*)

■ **draw out** *vt* (*pull out*) tirar fuori; ritirare (*money*) ● *vi* (*train:*) partire; (*days:*) allungarsi

■ **draw up** *vt* redigere (*document*); accostare (*chair*); ~ **oneself up** [**to one's full height**] drizzarsi ● *vi* (*stop*) fermarsi

drawback /'drɔːbæk/ *n* inconveniente *m*

drawbridge /'drɔːbrɪdʒ/ *n* ponte *m* levatoio

drawee *n* trattario *m*

drawer /drɔː(r)/ *n* cassetto *m*; *Fin* traente *mf*

drawing /'drɔːɪŋ/ *n* disegno *m*

drawing: drawing board *n* tavolo *m* da disegno; *fig* **go back to the** ~ ~ ricominciare da capo. **drawing pin** *n* puntina *f*. **drawing rights** *npl Fin* diritti *mf* di prelievo. **drawing room** *n* salotto *m*

drawl /drɔːl/ *n* pronuncia *f* strascicata

drawn /drɔːn/ *see* **draw**

dread /dred/ *n* terrore *m* ● *vt* aver il terrore di

dreadful /'dredfʊl/ *a* terribile

dreadfully /'dredfʊlɪ/ *adv* terribilmente

dream /driːm/ *n* sogno *m* ● *attrib* di sogno ● *vt*/*i* (*pt*/*pp* **dreamt** /dremt/ *or* **dreamed**) sognare (**about/of** di)

dreamer /'driːmə(r)/ *n* (*idealist*) sognatore, -trice *mf*; (*inattentive*) persona *f* con la testa fra le nuvole

dream-world *n* **live in a** ~ vivere tra le nuvole

dreamy /'driːmɪ/ *a fam* (*house etc*) di sogno; (*person*) che è un sogno; (*distracted*) distratto; (*sound, music*) dolce

dreary /'drɪərɪ/ *a* (-**ier**, -**iest**) tetro; (*boring*) monotono

dredge /dredʒ/ *vt*/*i* dragare

■ **dredge up** *vt* riesumare (*the past*)

dredger /'dredʒə(r)/ *n* draga *f*

dregs /dregz/ *npl* feccia *fsg*

drench /drentʃ/ *vt* **get** ~**ed** inzupparsi

drenched /drentʃt/ *a* zuppo

dress /dres/ *n* (*woman's*) vestito *m*; (*clothing*) abbigliamento *m* ● *vt* vestire; (*decorate*) adornare; *Culin* condire; *Med* fasciare; ~ **oneself, get** ~**ed** vestirsi ● *vi* vestirsi

■ **dress up** *vi* mettersi elegante; (*in disguise*) travestirsi (**as** da)

dress: dress circle *n Theat* prima galleria *f*. **dress designer** *n* stilista *mf*

dresser /'dresə(r)/ *n* (*furniture*) credenza *f*; (*Am: dressing table*) toilette *f inv*

dressing /'dresɪŋ/ *n Culin* condimento *m*; *Med* fasciatura *f*

dressing: dressing down *n fam* sgridata *f*. **dressing gown** *n* vestaglia *f*. **dressing room** *n* (*in gym*) spogliatoio *m*; *Theat* camerino *m*. **dressing table** *n* toilette *f inv*

dress: dressmaker *n* sarta *f*. **dressmaking** *n* confezioni *fpl* (*per donna*). **dress rehearsal** *n* prova *f* generale. **dress sense** *n* **have** ~ ~ saper abbinare i capi d'abbigliamento

dressy /'dresɪ/ *a* (-**ier**, -**iest**) elegante

drew /druː/ *see* **draw**

dribble /'drɪbl/ *vi* gocciolare; (*baby:*) sbavare; *Sport* dribblare

dribs and drabs /'drɪbzən'dræbz/ *npl* **in** ~ alla spicciolata

dried /draɪd/ *a* (*food*) essiccato

drier /'draɪə(r)/ *n* asciugabiancheria *m inv*

drift /drɪft/ *n* movimento *m* lento; (*of snow*) cumulo *m*; (*meaning*) senso *m* ● *vi* (*off course*) andare alla deriva; (*snow:*) accumularsi; (*fig: person:*) procedere senza meta

■ **drift apart** *vi* ⟨*people:*⟩ allontanarsi l'uno dall'altro

drifter /'drɪftə(r)/ *n* persona *f* senza meta

driftwood /'drɪftwʊd/ *n* pezzi *mpl* di legno galleggianti

drill /drɪl/ *n* trapano *m*; *Mil* esercitazione *f* ● *vt* trapanare; *Mil* fare esercitare ● *vi Mil* esercitarsi; ~ **for oil** trivellare in cerca di petrolio

drily /'draɪlɪ/ *adv* seccamente

drink /drɪŋk/ *n* bevanda *f*; (*alcoholic*) bicchierino *m*; **have a** ~ bere qualcosa; **a** ~ **of water** un po' d'acqua ● *vt/i* (*pt* **drank**, *pp* **drunk**) bere

■ **drink to** *vt* (*toast*) brindare a

■ **drink up** *vt* finire ● *vi* finire il bicchiere

drinkable /'drɪŋkəbl/ *a* potabile

drink-driving *n Br* guida *f* in stato di ebbrezza

drinker /'drɪŋkə(r)/ *n* bevitore, -trice *mf*

drinking chocolate /'drɪŋkɪŋ/ *n Br* cioccolata *f* in polvere

drinking water *n* acqua *f* potabile

drink: drink problem *n Br* **he has a** ~ ~ beve. **drinks cupboard** *n Br* mobile *m* bar. **drinks dispenser** *n Br* distributore *m* di bevande. **drinks machine** *n Br* distributore *m* di bevande. **drinks party** *n Br* cocktail *m inv*

drip /drɪp/ *n* gocciolamento *m*; (*drop*) goccia *f*; *Med* flebo *f inv*; (*fam: person*) mollaccione, -a *mf* ● *vi* (*pt/pp* **dripped**) gocciolare

drip-dry *a* che non si stira

drip-feed *n* flebo[clisi] *f inv*

dripping /'drɪpɪŋ/ *n* (*from meat*) grasso *m* d'arrosto ● *a* ~ [**wet**] fradicio

drive /draɪv/ *n* (*in car*) giro *m*; (*entrance*) viale *m*; (*energy*) grinta *f*; *Psych* pulsione *f*; (*organized effort*) operazione *f*; *Techn* motore *m*; *Comput* lettore *m*, unità *f inv* ● *v* (*pt* **drove** *pp* **driven**) ● *vt* portare ⟨*person by car*⟩; guidare ⟨*car*⟩; (*Sport: hit*) mandare; *Techn* far funzionare; ~ **sb mad** far diventare matto qcno ● *vi* guidare

■ **drive at** *vt* **what are you driving at?** dove vuoi arrivare?

■ **drive away** *vt* portare via in macchina; (*chase*) cacciare ● *vi* andare via in macchina

■ **drive in** *vt* piantare ⟨*nail*⟩ ● *vi* arrivare [in macchina]

■ **drive off** *vt* portare via in macchina; (*chase*) cacciare ● *vi* andare via in macchina

■ **drive on** *vi* proseguire; ~ **on!** avanti!

■ **drive up** *vi* arrivare (*in macchina*)

drive-in *a* ~ **cinema** cinema *m inv* drive-in

drivel /'drɪvl/ *n fam* sciocchezze *fpl*

driven /'drɪvn/ *see* **drive**

driver /'draɪvə(r)/ *n* guidatore, -trice *mf*; (*of train*) conducente *mf*

drive-through *n Am* drive-in *m inv*

driveway /'draɪvweɪ/ *n* strada *f* d'accesso

driving /'draɪvɪŋ/ *a* ⟨*rain*⟩ violento; ⟨*force*⟩ motore ● *n* guida *f*

driving: driving force *n* spinta *f*; (*person behind*) forza *f* trainante. **driving instructor** *n* istruttore, -trice *mf* di guida. **driving**

lesson *n* lezione *f* di guida. **driving licence** *n* patente *f* di guida. **driving mirror** *n* (*rearview*) specchietto *m* retrovisore. **driving school** *n* scuola *f* guida. **driving seat** *n* **be in the** ~ ~ essere alla guida. **driving test** *n* esame *m* di guida; **take one's** ~ ~ fare l'esame di guida

drizzle /'drɪzl/ *n* pioggerella *f* ● *vi* piovigginare

droll /drəʊl/ *a* divertente

drone /drəʊn/ *n* (*bee*) fuco *m*; (*sound*) ronzio *m*

■ **drone on** *vi* (*talk boringly*) tirarla per le lunghe

drool /druːl/ *vi* sbavare; ~ **over sth/sb** *fig fam* sbavare per qcsa/qcno

droop /druːp/ *vi* abbassarsi; ⟨*flowers:*⟩ afflosciarsi

drop /drɒp/ *n* (*of liquid*) goccia *f*; (*fall*) caduta *f*; (*in price, temperature*) calo *m* ● *v* (*pt/pp* **dropped**) ● *vt* far cadere; sganciare ⟨*bomb*⟩; (*omit*) omettere; (*give up*) abbandonare; ~ **the subject** cambiare discorso ● *vi* cadere; ⟨*price, temperature, wind:*⟩ calare; ⟨*ground:*⟩ essere in pendenza

■ **drop behind** *vi* rimanere indietro

■ **drop by** *vi* = **drop in**

■ **drop in** *vi* passare

■ **drop off** *vt* depositare ⟨*person*⟩ ● *vi* cadere; (*fall asleep*) assopirsi

■ **drop out** *vi* cadere; (*from race, society*) ritirarsi; ~ **out of school** lasciare la scuola

drop handlebars *npl* manubrio *m* ricurvo

drop-out *n* persona *f* contro il sistema sociale

droppings /'drɒpɪŋz/ *npl* sterco *m*

drop shot *n Sport* drop shot *m inv*, smorzata *f*

drop zone *n* (*for supplies etc*) zona *f* di lancio

drought /draʊt/ *n* siccità *f*

drove /drəʊv/ *see* **drive**

droves /drəʊvz/ *npl* **in** ~ in massa

drown /draʊn/ *vi* annegare ● *vt* annegare; coprire ⟨*noise*⟩; **he was** ~**ed** è annegato

drowse /draʊz/ *vi* sonnecchiare; (*be very sleepy*) essere sonnolento

drowsiness /'draʊzɪnɪs/ *n* sonnolenza *f*

drowsy /'draʊzɪ/ *a* sonnolento

drudgery /'drʌdʒərɪ/ *n* lavoro *m* pesante e noioso

drug /drʌg/ *n* droga *f*; *Med* farmaco *m*; **take** ~**s** drogarsi ● *vt* (*pt/pp* **drugged**) drogare

drug: drug abuse *n* abuso *m* di stupefacenti. **drug addict** *n* tossicomane, -a *mf*. **drug addiction** *n* tossicodipendenza *f*. **drug dealer** *n* spacciatore, -trice *mf* [di droga]

druggist /'drʌgɪst/ *n Am* farmacista *mf*

drug: Drug Squad *n Br* [squadra *f*] narcotici *f*. **drugs raid** *n* operazione *f* antidroga. **drugs ring** *n* rete *f* di narcotrafficanti. **drugstore** /'drʌgstɔː(r)/ *n Am* negozio *m* di generi vari, inclusi medicinali, che funge anche da bar; (*dispensing*) farmacia *f*. **drug-taking** *n* consumo *m* di stupefacenti; *Sport* doping *m inv*.

drug test *n Sport* antidoping *m inv.* **drug user** *n* tossicomane -a *mf*

drum /drʌm/ *n* tamburo *m*; (*for oil*) bidone *m*; ~**s** *pl* (*in pop group*) batteria *f* ● *v* (*pt/pp* **drummed**) ● *vi* suonare il tamburo; (*in pop group*) suonare la batteria ● *vt* ~ **sth into sb** *fam* ripetere qcsa a qcno cento volte; ~ **one's fingers on the table** taburellare con le dita sul tavolo

drum kit *n* batteria *f*

drummer /'drʌmə(r)/ *n* percussionista *mf*; (*in pop group*) batterista *mf*

drumstick /'drʌmstɪk/ *n* bacchetta *f*; (*of chicken, turkey*) coscia *f*

drunk /drʌŋk/ *see* **drink** ● *a* ubriaco; **get** ~ ubriacarsi ● *n* ubriaco, -a *mf*

drunkard /'drʌŋkəd/ *n* ubriacone, -a *mf*

drunken /'drʌŋkən/ *a* ubriaco

drunken driving *n* guida *f* in stato di ebbrezza

dry /draɪ/ *a* (**drier, driest**) asciutto; ‹climate, country› secco ● *vt/i* asciugare; ~ **one's eyes** asciugarsi le lacrime

■ **dry out** *vi* ‹clothes:› asciugarsi; ‹alcoholic:› disintossicarsi

■ **dry up** *vi* seccarsi; ‹fig: source:› prosciugarsi; (*fam: be quiet*) stare zitto; (*do dishes*) asciugare i piatti

dry: dry cell *n* cella *f* a secco. **dry-clean** *vt* pulire a secco. **dry-cleaner's** *n* (*shop*) tintoria *f*

dryer /'draɪə/ *n* = **drier**

dry ice *n* ghiaccio *m* secco

drying-up /draɪɪŋ-'/ *n Br* **do the** ~ asciugare i piatti

dryness /'draɪnɪs/ *n* secchezza *f*

dry rot *n* carie *f* del legno

DSS *n Br abbr* (**Department of Social Security**) (*local office*) ≈ Ufficio *m* della Previdenza Sociale; (*ministry*) ≈ Istituto *m* Nazionale della Previdenza Sociale

DTI *n Br abbr* (**Department of Trade and Industry**) ≈ Ministero *m* del Commercio e dell'Industria

DTP *n abbr* (**desktop publishing**) desktop publishing *m inv*

dual /'dju:əl/ *a* doppio

dual carriageway *n* strada *f* a due carreggiate

dual-purpose *a* a doppio uso

dub /dʌb/ *vt* (*pt/pp* **dubbed**) doppiare ‹film›; (*name*) soprannominare

dubbing /'dʌbɪŋ/ *n* doppiaggio *m*

dubious /'dju:bɪəs/ *a* dubbio; **be** ~ **about** avere dei dubbi riguardo

dubiously /'dju:bɪəslɪ/ *adv* ‹look at› con aria dubbiosa; ‹say› con esitazione

Dublin /'dʌblɪn/ *n* Dublino *f*

duchess /'dʌtʃɪs/ *n* duchessa *f*

duck /dʌk/ *n* anatra *f* ● *vt* (*in water*) immergere; ~ **one's head** abbassare la testa ● *vi* abbassarsi

■ **duck out of** *vt* sottrarsi a ‹task›

duckling /'dʌklɪŋ/ *n* anatroccolo *m*

duct /dʌkt/ *n* condotto *m*; *Anat* dotto *m*

dud /dʌd/ *a Mil fam* disattivato; ‹coin› falso; ‹cheque› a vuoto ● *n fam* (*banknote*) banconota *f* falsa; (*Mil: shell*) granata *f* disattivata

due /dju:/ *a* dovuto; **be** ~ ‹train:› essere previsto; **the baby is** ~ **next week** il bambino dovrebbe nascere la settimana prossima; ~ **to** (*owing to*) a causa di; **be** ~ **to** (*causally*) essere dovuto a; **I'm** ~ **to...** dovrei...; **in** ~ **course** a tempo debito ● *adv* ~ **north** direttamente a nord

duel /'dju:əl/ *n* duello *m*

dues /dju:z/ *npl* quota *f* [di iscrizione]

duet /dju:'et/ *n* duetto *m*

duffle coat /'dʌf(ə)l/ *n* montgomery *m inv*

dug /dʌg/ *see* **dig**

duke /dju:k/ *n* duca *m*

dull /dʌl/ *a* (*overcast, not bright*) cupo; (*not shiny*) opaco; ‹sound› soffocato; (*boring*) monotono; (*stupid*) ottuso ● *vt* intorpidire ‹mind›; attenuare ‹pain›

dullness /'dʌlnɪs/ *n* (*of life*) monotonia *f*; (*of company, conversation*) noia *f*; (*no shine*) opacità *f*

dully /'dʌllɪ/ *adv* ‹say, repeat› monotonamente

duly /'dju:lɪ/ *adv* debitamente

dumb /dʌm/ *a* muto; (*fam: stupid*) ottuso

dumbfounded /dʌm'faʊndɪd/ *a* sbigottito

dummy /'dʌmɪ/ *n* (*tailor's*) manichino *m*; (*for baby*) succhiotto *m*; (*model*) riproduzione *f*

dummy run *n* (*trial*) prova *f*

dump /dʌmp/ *n* (*for refuse*) scarico *m*; (*fam: town*) mortorio *m*; **be down in the** ~**s** *fam* essere depresso ● *vt* scaricare; (*fam: put down*) lasciare; (*fam: get rid of*) liberarsi di

dumping /'dʌmpɪŋ/ *n Fin* dumping *m inv*, esportazione *f* sottocosto; **no** ~ divieto *m* di scarico

dumpling /'dʌmplɪŋ/ *n* gnocco *m*

dumpy /'dʌmpɪ/ *a* (*plump*) tracagnotto

dunce /dʌns/ *n* zuccone, -a *mf*

dune /dju:n/ *n* duna *f*

dung /dʌŋ/ *n* sterco *m*

dungarees /dʌŋgə'ri:z/ *npl* tuta *f sg*

dungeon /'dʌndʒən/ *n* prigione *f* sotterranea

dunk /dʌŋk/ *vt* inzuppare

dunno /də'nəʊ/ *fam* (*I don't know*) boh

duo /'dju:əʊ/ *n* duo *m inv*; *Mus* duetto *m*

dupe /dju:p/ *n* zimbello *m* ● *vt* gabbare

duplicate¹ /'dju:plɪkət/ *a* doppio ● *n* duplicato *m*; (*document*) copia *f*; **in** ~ in duplicato

duplicate² /'dju:plɪkeɪt/ *vt* fare un duplicato di; ‹research:› essere una ripetizione di ‹work›

duplicator /'dju:plɪkeɪtə(r)/ *n* duplicatore *m*

duplicity /dju'plɪsətɪ/ *n* duplicità *f*, doppiezza *f*

durable /'djʊərəbl/ *a* resistente; durevole ‹basis, institution›

duration /djʊə'reɪʃn/ *n* durata *f*

duress /djʊə'res/ *n* costrizione *f*; **under** ~ sotto minaccia

during /'djʊərɪŋ/ *prep* durante

dusk /dʌsk/ n crepuscolo m
dusky /'dʌskɪ/ a ⟨complexion⟩ scuro
dust /dʌst/ n polvere f ●vt spolverare;
⟨sprinkle⟩ cospargere ⟨cake⟩ (**with** di) ●vi
spolverare
dust: dustbin n pattumiera f. **dustbin man**
n Br netturbino m. **dust-cart** n camion m della nettezza urbana. **dust cover** n (on book)
sopraccoperta f; (on furniture) telo m di protezione
duster /'dʌstə(r)/ n strofinaccio m
dust: dust-jacket n sopraccoperta f.
dustman n spazzino m. **dustpan** n paletta f
per la spazzatura. **dust sheet** n (on
furniture) telo m di protezione
dusty /'dʌstɪ/ a (**-ier, -iest**) polveroso
Dutch /dʌtʃ/ a olandese; **go** ~ fam fare alla
romana ●n ⟨language⟩ olandese m; **the** ~ pl
gli olandesi
Dutch courage n spavalderia f ispirata
dall'alcool
Dutchman /'dʌtʃmən/ n olandese m
dutiable /'djuːtɪəbl/ a soggetto a imposta
dutiful /'djuːtɪfl/ a rispettoso
dutifully /'djuːtɪfʊlɪ/ adv a dovere
duty /'djuːtɪ/ n dovere m; (task) compito m;
(tax) dogana f; **be on** ~ essere di servizio
duty: duty chemist n farmacia f di turno.
duty-free a esente da dogana ●n duty-free m
inv. **duty-free allowance** n limite m d'acquisto di merci esenti da dogana. **duty roster,
duty rota** n tabella f dei turni

duvet /'duːveɪ/ n piumone m
duvet cover n Br copripiumone m
dwarf /dwɔːf/ n (pl **-s** or **dwarves**) nano, -a
mf ●vt rimpicciolire
dwell /dwel/ vi (pt/pp **dwelt**) liter dimorare
■ **dwell on** vt fig soffermarsi su
dweller /'dwelə(r)/ n **city/town** ~ cittadino, -a mf
dwelling /'dwelɪŋ/ n abitazione f
dwindle /'dwɪndl/ vi diminuire
dwindling /'dwɪndlɪŋ/ a ⟨strength, health⟩
in calo; ⟨resources, audience, interest⟩ in diminuzione
dye /daɪ/ n tintura f ●vt (pres p **dyeing**) tingere
dyed-in-the-wool /daɪdɪnðə'wʊl/ a inveterato
dying /'daɪɪŋ/ see **die²**
dyke /daɪk/ n (to prevent flooding) diga f;
(beside ditch) argine m; (Br: ditch) canale m di
scolo
dynamic /daɪ'næmɪk/ a dinamico
dynamics /daɪ'næmɪks/ n dinamica fsg
dynamism /'daɪnə'mɪzm/ n dinamismo m
dynamite /'daɪnəmaɪt/ n dinamite f
dynamo /'daɪnəməʊ/ n dinamo f inv
dynasty /'dɪnəstɪ/ n dinastia f
dysentery /'dɪsntrɪ/ n dissenteria f
dyslexia /dɪs'leksɪə/ n dislessia f
dyslexic /dɪs'leksɪk/ a dislessico

Ee

e, E /iː/ n (letter) e, E f inv; Mus mi m
E abbr (**east**) E
each /iːtʃ/ a ogni ●pron ognuno; **£1** ~ una
sterlina ciascuno; **they love/hate** ~ **other** si
amano/odiano; **we lend** ~ **other money** ci
prestiamo i soldi; **bet on a horse** ~ **way**
puntare su un cavallo piazzato e vincente
eager /'iːgə(r)/ a ansioso (**to do** di fare);
⟨pupil⟩ avido di sapere
eager beaver n fam **be an** ~ ~ essere pieno di zelo
eagerly /'iːgəlɪ/ adv ⟨wait⟩ ansiosamente;
⟨offer⟩ premurosamente
eagerness /'iːgənɪs/ n premura f
eagle /'iːgl/ n aquila f
eagle-eyed /-'aɪd/ a (sharp-eyed) che ha un
occhio di falco
ear /ɪə(r)/ n orecchio m; (of corn) spiga f
earache /'ɪəreɪk/ n mal m d'orecchi
eardrum /'ɪədrʌm/ n timpano m
earl /ɜːl/ n conte m
ear lobe n lobo m dell'orecchio
early /'ɜːlɪ/ a (**-ier, -iest**) (before expected
time) in anticipo; ⟨spring⟩ prematuro; ⟨reply⟩
pronto; ⟨works, writings⟩ primo; **be here** ~!
sii puntuale!; **you're** ~! sei in anticipo!; ~
morning walk passeggiata f mattutina; **in
the** ~ **morning** la mattina presto; **in the** ~
spring all'inizio della primavera; ~
retirement prepensionamento m ●adv presto; (ahead of time) in anticipo; ~ **in the**
morning la mattina presto
early warning n **come as an** ~ ~ **of sth**
essere il segno premonitore di qcsa
early warning system n Mil sistema m
d'allarme avanzato
earmark /'ɪəmɑːk/ vt riservare (**for** a)
earmuffs /'ɪəmʌfs/ npl paraorecchie m inv
earn /ɜːn/ vt guadagnare; (deserve) meritare
earned income /ɜːnd/ n reddito m da lavoro
earner /'ɜːnə(r)/ n (person) persona f che
guadagna; **the main [revenue]** ~ la principale fonte di sostentamento; **a nice little** ~
fam un'ottima fonte di guadagno
earnest /'ɜːnɪst/ a serio ●n **in** ~ sul serio

earnestly /'ɜ:nɪstlɪ/ *adv* con aria seria

earning power /'ɜ:nɪŋ/ *n* (*of person*) capacità *f* di guadagno; (*of company*) redditività *f* *inv*

earnings /'ɜ:nɪŋz/ *npl* guadagni *mpl*; (*salary*) stipendio *m*

ear nose and throat department *n* reparto *m* otorinolaringoiatrico

ear: earphones *npl* cuffia *fsg*. **earplug** *n* (*for noise*) tappo *m* per le orecchie. **ear-ring** *n* orecchino *m*. **earshot** *n* **within ~** a portata d'orecchio; **he is out of ~** non può sentire. **ear-splitting** /'ɪəsplɪtɪŋ/ *a* (*scream, shout*) lacerante

earth /ɜ:θ/ *n* terra *f*; (*of fox*) tana *f*; **where/ what on ~?** dove/che diavolo? ● *vt Electr* mettere a terra

earthenware /'ɜ:θnweə/ *n* terraglia *f*

earthly /'ɜ:θlɪ/ *a* terrestre; **be no ~ use** *fam* essere perfettamente inutile

earth: earthquake *n* terremoto *m*. **earth sciences** *npl* scienze *fpl* della terra. **earthshaking** *a fam* (*news*) sconvolgente; (*experience*) travolgente. **earth tremor** *n* scossa *f* sismica. **earthwork** *n* (*embankment*) terrapieno *m*; (*excavation work*) lavori *mpl* di scavo. **earthworm** *n* lombrico *m*

earthy /'ɜ:θɪ/ *a* terroso; (*coarse*) grossolano

earwax /'ɪəwæks/ *n* cerume *m*

earwig /'ɪəwɪg/ *n* forbicina *f*

ease /i:z/ *n* **at ~** a proprio agio; **at ~!** *Mil* riposo!; **ill at ~** a disagio; **with ~** con facilità ● *vt* calmare (*pain*); alleviare (*tension, shortage*); (*slow down*) rallentare; (*loosen*) allentare ● *vi* (*pain, situation, wind:*) calmarsi

■ **ease off** *vi* (*pain, pressure, tension:*) attenuarsi ● *vt* (*remove gently*) togliere con delicatezza

■ **ease up** *vi* = **ease off**

easel /'i:zl/ *n* cavalletto *m*

easily /'i:zɪlɪ/ *adv* con facilità; **~ the best** certamente il meglio

east /i:st/ *n* est *m*; **to the ~ of** a est di ● *a* dell'est ● *adv* verso est

east: East Africa *n* Africa *f* orientale. **East Berlin** *n* Berlino *f* Est. **eastbound** *a* (*carriageway, traffic*) diretto a est. **East End** *n quartiere m nella zona est di Londra*

Easter /'i:stə(r)/ *n* Pasqua *f*

Easter: Easter egg *n* uovo *m* di Pasqua; **Easter Monday** *n* lunedì *m* dell'Angelo, Pasquetta *f*. **Easter Sunday** *n* [domenica *f* di] Pasqua *f*

easterly /'i:stəlɪ/ *a* da levante

eastern /'i:stən/ *a* orientale

Eastern block *n* paesi *mpl* dell'est

east: East German *n Pol* tedesco, -a *mf* dell'est. **East Germany** *n Pol* Germania *f* est. **East Indies** *npl* Indie *fpl* orientali

eastward[s] /'i:stwəd[z]/ *adv* verso est

easy /'i:zɪ/ *a* (**-ier, -iest**) facile; **take it** *or* **things ~** prendersela con calma; **take it ~!** (*don't get excited*) calma!; **go ~ with** andarci piano con

easy: easy-care *a* facilmente lavabile. **easy**

chair *n* poltrona *f*. **easy-going** *a* conciliante; **too ~** troppo accomodante. **easy money** *n* facili guadagni *mpl*. **easy terms** *npl* facilitazioni *fpl* di pagamento

eat /i:t/ *vt/i* (*pt* **ate**, *pp* **eaten**) mangiare

■ **eat into** *vt* intaccare

■ **eat out** *vi* mangiar fuori

■ **eat up** *vt* mangiare tutto (*food*); *fig* inghiottire (*profits*)

eatable /'i:təbl/ *a* mangiabile

eater /'i:tə(r)/ *n* (*apple*) mela *f* da tavola; **be a big ~** (*person:*) essere una buona forchetta; **he's a fast ~** mangia sempre in fretta

eatery /'i:tərɪ/ *n fam* tavola *f* calda

eating /'i:tɪŋ/: **eating apple** *n* mela *f* non da cuocere. **eating disorder** *n* disoressia *f*. **eating habits** *npl* abitudini *fpl* alimentari

eau-de-Cologne /əʊdəkə'ləʊn/ *n* acqua *f* di Colonia

eaves /i:vz/ *npl* cornicione *msg*

eavesdrop /'i:vzdrɒp/ *vi* (*pt/pp* **~dropped**) origliare; **~ on** ascoltare di nascosto

ebb /eb/ *n* (*tide*) riflusso *m*; **at a low ~** *fig* a terra ● *vi* rifluire; *fig* declinare

ebony /'ebənɪ/ *n* ebano *m*

EBRD *n abbr* (**European Bank for Reconstruction and Development**) BERS *f*

ebullient /ɪ'bʌlɪənt/ *a* esuberante

EC *n abbr* (**European Community**) CE *f*

eccentric /ek'sentrɪk/ *a & n* eccentrico, -a *mf*

eccentricity /eksen'trɪsətɪ/ *n* eccentricità *f* *inv*

ecclesiastical /ɪkli:zɪ'æstɪkl/ *a* ecclesiastico

ECG *n abbr* (**electrocardiogram; electrocardiograph**) ECG

echo /'ekəʊ/ *n* (*pl* **-es**) eco *f or m* ● *v* (*pt/pp* **echoed**, *pres p* **echoing**) ● *vt* echeggiare; ripetere (*words*) ● *vi* risuonare (**with** di)

eclectic /ɪ'klektɪk/ *n* eclettico

eclipse /ɪ'klɪps/ *n Astr* eclissi *f inv* ● *vt fig* eclissare

eco+ /'i:kəʊ/ *pref* eco+

eco-friendly *a* che rispetta l'ambiente

ecological /i:kə'lɒdʒɪkl/ *a* ecologico

ecologist /ɪ'kɒlədʒɪst/ *n* ecologo, -a *mf* ● *a* ecologico

ecology /ɪ'kɒlədʒɪ/ *n* ecologia *f*

economic /i:kə'nɒmɪk/ *a* economico

economical /i:kə'nɒmɪkl/ *a* economico

economically /i:kə'nɒmɪklɪ/ *adv* economicamente; (*thriftily*) in economia; **~ priced** *a* prezzo economico

economic analyst *n* analista *mf* economico,-a

economics /i:kə'nɒmɪks/ *n* economia *f*

economist /ɪ'kɒnəmɪst/ *n* economista *mf*

economize /ɪ'kɒnəmaɪz/ *vi* economizzare (**on** su)

economy /ɪ'kɒnəmɪ/ *n* economia *f*

economy: economy class *n Aeron* classe *f* turistica. **economy drive** *n* campagna *f* di risparmio. **economy pack, economy size** *n* confezione *f* economica *inv*

ecosystem /ˈiːkəʊsɪstəm/ n ecosistema m
ecstasy /ˈekstəsɪ/ n estasi f inv; (drug) ecstasy f
ecstatic /ɪkˈstætɪk/ a estatico
ecstatically /ɪkˈstætɪklɪ/ adv estaticamente
ectopic pregnancy /ekˈtɒpɪk/ n gravidanza f extrauterina
ecu /ˈeɪkjuː/ n ecu m inv
Ecuador /ˈekwədɔː(r)/ n Ecuador m
ecumenical /iːkjʊˈmenɪkl/ a ecumenico
eczema /ˈeksɪmə/ n eczema m
eddy /ˈedɪ/ n vortice m
Eden /ˈiːd(ə)n/ n eden m, paradiso m terrestre
edge /edʒ/ n bordo m; (of knife) filo m; (of road) ciglio m; **on ~** con i nervi tesi; **have the ~ on** fam avere un vantaggio su ● vt bordare
■ **edge forward** vi avanzare lentamente
edgeways /ˈedʒweɪz/ adv di fianco; **I couldn't get a word in ~** non ho potuto infilare neanche mezza parola nel discorso
edging /ˈedʒɪŋ/ n bordo m
edgy /ˈedʒɪ/ a nervoso
edible /ˈedəbl/ a commestibile; **this pizza's not ~** questa pizza è immangiabile
edict /ˈiːdɪkt/ n editto m
edifice /ˈedɪfɪs/ n edificio m
edify /ˈedɪfaɪ/ vt (pt/pp -ied) edificare
edifying /ˈedɪfaɪɪŋ/ a edificante
Edinburgh /ˈedɪmb(ə)rə/ n Edimburgo f
edit /ˈedɪt/ vt (pt/pp edited) far la revisione di (text); curare l'edizione di (anthology, dictionary); dirigere (newspaper); montare (film); editare (tape); **~ed by** (book) a cura di
■ **edit out** vt tagliare
edition /ɪˈdɪʃn/ n edizione f
editor /ˈedɪtə(r)/ n (of anthology, dictionary) curatore, -trice mf; (of newspaper) redattore, -trice mf; (of film) responsabile mf del montaggio
editorial /edɪˈtɔːrɪəl/ a redazionale ● n Journ editoriale m
educate /ˈedjʊkeɪt/ vt istruire; educare (public, mind); **be ~d at Eton** essere educato a Eton
educated /ˈedjʊkeɪtɪd/ a istruito
education /edjʊˈkeɪʃn/ n istruzione f; (culture) cultura f, educazione f
educational /edjʊˈkeɪʃnəl/ a istruttivo; (visit) educativo; (publishing) didattico
educationalist /edjʊˈkeɪʃnəlɪst/ n studioso, -a mf di pedagogia
educationally /edjʊˈkeɪʃnəlɪ/ adv (disadvantaged, privileged) dal punto di vista degli studi; (useless, useful) dal punto di vista didattico
educational: **educational psychology** n psicopedagogia f, psicologia f dell'educazione. **educational television** n televisione f scolastica
education: **education authority** n Br autorità f pl scolastiche. **education committee** n Br consiglio m scolastico. **education de-**

partment n Br ministero m della pubblica istruzione; (in local government) provveditorato m agli studi; (in university) istituto m di pedagogia
educative /ˈedjʊkətɪv/ a educativo, istruttivo
educator /ˈedjʊkeɪtə(r)/ n educatore, -trice mf
Edwardian /edˈwɔːdɪən/ n del regno di Edoardo VII
EEC n abbr (**European Economic Community**) CEE f ● attrib (policy, directive) della CEE
eel /iːl/ n anguilla f
eerie /ˈɪərɪ/ a (-ier, -iest) inquietante
efface /ɪˈfeɪs/ vt cancellare
effect /ɪˈfekt/ n effetto m; **in ~** in effetti; **take ~** (law:) entrare in vigore; (medicine:) fare effetto ● vt effettuare
effective /ɪˈfektɪv/ a efficace; (striking) che colpisce; (actual) di fatto; **~ from** in vigore a partire da
effectively /ɪˈfektɪvlɪ/ adv efficacemente; (actually) di fatto
effectiveness /ɪˈfektɪvnɪs/ n efficacia f
effeminate /ɪˈfemɪnət/ a effeminato
effervescent /efəˈvesnt/ a effervescente
effete /ɪˈfiːt/ a (a person) senza nerbo; (civilization) che ha fatto il suo tempo
efficacious /efɪˈkeɪʃəs/ a efficace
efficacy /ˈefɪkəsɪ/ n efficacia f
efficiency /ɪˈfɪʃənsɪ/ n efficienza f; (of machine) rendimento m
efficient /ɪˈfɪʃənt/ a efficiente
efficiently /ɪˈfɪʃəntlɪ/ adv efficientemente
effigy /ˈefɪdʒɪ/ n effigie f
effluent /ˈefluənt/ n (waste) refluo m; (river) emissario m ● attrib (treatment, management) dei reflui
effort /ˈefət/ n sforzo m; **make an ~** sforzarsi
effortless /ˈefətlɪs/ a facile
effortlessly /ˈefətlɪslɪ/ adv con facilità
effrontery /ɪˈfrʌntərɪ/ n sfrontatezza f
effusion /ɪˈfjuːʒn/ n (emotional) effusione f
effusive /ɪˈfjuːsɪv/ a espansivo; (speech) caloroso
EFL n abbr (**English as a Foreign Language**) EFL m ● attrib (teacher, course) di inglese come lingua straniera
EFT n abbr **electronic funds transfer**
EFTA /ˈeftə/ n abbr (**European Free Trade Association**) EFTA f
e.g. abbr (**exempli gratia**) per es.
egalitarian /ɪɡælɪˈteərɪən/ a egalitario
egg /eg/ n uovo m
■ **egg on** vt fam incitare
egg: **egg box** n cartone m di uova. **eggcup** n portauovo m inv. **egg custard** n crema f pasticciera. **eggplant** n pej fam intellettuale mf. **eggplant** n Am melanzana f. **egg-shaped** /ˈegʃeɪpt/ a ovale. **eggshell** n guscio m d'uovo. **egg-timer** n clessidra f per misurare il tempo di cottura delle uova. **egg whisk** n

frusta *f*. **egg white** *n* albume *m*, bianco *m* d'uovo. **egg yolk** *n* tuorlo *m*, rosso *m* d'uovo

ego /ˈiːgəʊ/ *n* ego *m*

egocentric /iːgəʊˈsentrɪk/ *a* egocentrico

egoism /ˈegəʊɪzm/ *n* egoismo *m*

egoist /ˈegəʊɪst/ *n* egoista *mf*

egotism /ˈegəʊtɪzm/ *n* egotismo *m*

egotist /ˈegəʊtɪst/ *n* egotista *mf*

Egypt /ˈiːdʒɪpt/ *n* Egitto *m*

Egyptian /ɪˈdʒɪpʃn/ *a & n* egiziano, -a *mf*

eiderdown /ˈaɪdədaʊn/ *n* ⟨quilt⟩ piumino *m*

eight /eɪt/ *a & n* otto *m*

eighteen /eɪˈtiːn/ *a & n* diciotto *m*

eighteenth /eɪˈtiːnθ/ *a & n* diciottesimo, -a *mf*

eighth /eɪtθ/ *a & n* ottavo, -a *mf*

eightieth /ˈeɪtɪɪθ/ *a & n* ottantesimo, -a *mf*

eighty /ˈeɪtɪ/ *a & n* ottanta *m*

Eire /ˈeərə/ *n* Repubblica *f* d'Irlanda

either /ˈaɪðə(r)/ *a & pron* ~ [of them] l'uno o l'altro; **I don't like** ~ [of them] non mi piace né l'uno né l'altro; **on** ~ **side** da tutte e due le parti ● *adv* **I don't** ~ nemmeno io; **I don't like John or his brother** ~ non mi piace John e nemmeno suo fratello ● *conj* ~ **John or his brother will be there** ci saranno o John o suo fratello; **I don't like** ~ **John or his brother** non mi piacciono né John né suo fratello; ~ **you go to bed or** [else]**...** o vai a letto o [altrimenti]...

ejaculate /ɪˈdʒækjʊleɪt/ *vi* eiaculare ● *vt* ⟨exclaim⟩ prorompere

ejaculation /ɪˌdʒækjʊleɪʃn/ *n* eiaculazione *f*; ⟨exclamation⟩ esclamazione *f*

eject /ɪˈdʒekt/ *vt* eiettare ⟨pilot⟩; espellere ⟨tape, drunk⟩

ejection /ɪˈdʒekʃn/ *n* ⟨of gases, waste, troublemaker⟩ espulsione *f*; ⟨of lava⟩ emissione *f*; *Aeron* eiezione *f*

eke /iːk/ *vt* ~ **out** far bastare; ⟨increase⟩ arrotondare; ~ **out a living** arrangiarsi

elaborate[1] /ɪˈlæbərət/ *a* elaborato

elaborate[2] /ɪˈlæbəreɪt/ *vi* entrare nei particolari ⟨on di⟩

elaborately /ɪˈlæbərətlɪ/ *adv* in modo elaborato

elaboration /ɪˌlæbəˈreɪʃn/ *n* ⟨of plan, theory⟩ elaborazione *f*

elapse /ɪˈlæps/ *vi* trascorrere

elastic /ɪˈlæstɪk/ *a* elastico ● *n* elastico *m*

elasticated /ɪˈlæstɪkeɪtɪd/ *a* ⟨waistband, bandage⟩ elastico; ⟨material⟩ elasticizzato

elastic band *n* elastico *m*

elasticity /ɪlæsˈtɪsətɪ/ *n* elasticità *f*

elated /ɪˈleɪtɪd/ *a* esultante

elation /ɪˈleɪʃn/ *n* euforia *f*

elbow /ˈelbəʊ/ *n* gomito *m*

elbow grease *n fam* olio *m* di gomito

elbow room *n* ⟨room to move⟩ spazio *m* vitale; **there isn't much** ~~ **in this kitchen** si è un po' allo stretto in questa cucina

elder[1] /ˈeldə(r)/ *n* ⟨tree⟩ sambuco *m*

elder[2] *a* maggiore ● *n* **the** ~ il/la maggiore

elderberry /ˈeldəbərɪ/ *n* baca *f* di sambuco

elderly /ˈeldəlɪ/ *a* anziano

elder statesman *n* decano *m* della politica

eldest /ˈeldɪst/ *a* maggiore ● *n* **the** ~ il/la maggiore

elect /ɪˈlekt/ *a* **the president** ~ il futuro presidente ● *vt* eleggere; ~ **to do sth** decidere di fare qcsa

election /ɪˈlekʃn/ *n* elezione *f*

electioneering /ɪˌlekʃəniərɪŋ/ *n* ⟨campaigning⟩ propaganda *f* elettorale; *pej* elettoralismo *m*

elective /ɪˈlektɪv/ *a* ⟨office, official⟩ elettivo, eletto; ⟨empowered to elect⟩ elettorale; *Sch, Univ* facoltativo; ~ **surgery** interventi *mpl* chirurgici facoltativi

elector /ɪˈlektə(r)/ *n* elettore, -trice *mf*

electoral /ɪˈlektərəl/ *a* elettorale

electoral roll *n* liste *fpl* elettorali

electorate /ɪˈlektərət/ *n* elettorato *m*

electric /ɪˈlektrɪk/ *a* elettrico

electrical /ɪˈlektrɪkl/ *a* elettrico

electrical engineer *n* elettrotecnico *m*

electrical engineering *n* elettrotecnica *f*

electrically /ɪˈlektrɪk(ə)lɪ/ *adv* ~ **driven** [a motore] elettrico

electric blanket *n* termocoperta *f*

electric fire *n* stufa *f* elettrica

electrician /ɪlekˈtrɪʃn/ *n* elettricista *m*

electricity /ɪlekˈtrɪsətɪ/ *n* elettricità *f*

electricity board *n Br* azienda *f* elettrica

electricity supply *n* alimentazione *f* elettrica

electric shock *n* get an ~ ~ prendere la scossa

electric storm *n* temporale *m*

electrify /ɪˈlektrɪfaɪ/ *vt* ⟨pt/pp -**ied**⟩ elettrificare; *fig* elettrizzare

electrifying /ɪˈlektrɪfaɪɪŋ/ *a fig* elettrizzante

electrocute /ɪˈlektrəkjuːt/ *vt* fulminare; ⟨execute⟩ giustiziare sulla sedia elettrica

electrocution /ɪlektrəˈkjuːʃn/ *n* elettrocuzione *f*

electrode /ɪˈlektrəʊd/ *n* elettrodo *m*

electrolysis /ɪlekˈtrɒlɪsɪs/ *n Chem* elettrolisi *f*; ⟨hair removal⟩ depilazione *f* diatermica

electron /ɪˈlektrɒn/ *n* elettrone *m*

electronic /ɪlekˈtrɒnɪk/ *a* elettronico

electronic: electronic banking *n* servizi *mpl* bancari telematici. **electronic engineer** *n* tecnico *m* elettronico; ⟨with diploma⟩ perito *m* elettronico; ⟨with degree⟩ ingegnere *m* elettronico. **electronic engineering** *n* ingegneria *f* elettronica. **electronic eye** *n* cellula *f* fotoelettrica. **electronic funds transfer** *n* sistemi *mpl* telematici di trasferimento fondi. **electronic mail** *n* posta *f* elettronica

electronics /ɪlekˈtrɒnɪks/ *n* elettronica *f*

electro-shock therapy, electro-shock treatment /ɪˈlektrəʊ-/ *n* terapia *f* elettroshock

elegance /ˈelɪɡəns/ *n* eleganza *f*

elegant /ˈelɪɡənt/ *a* elegante

elegantly /ˈelɪɡəntlɪ/ *adv* elegantemente

elegy /ˈelɪdʒɪ/ *n* elegia *f*

element /'elɪmənt/ n elemento m
elementary /elɪ'mentərɪ/ a elementare
elephant /'elɪfənt/ n elefante m
elephantine /elɪ'fæntaɪn/ a ⟨person⟩ mastodontico
elevate /'elɪveɪt/ vt elevare
elevation /elɪ'veɪʃn/ n elevazione f; ⟨height⟩ altitudine f; ⟨angle⟩ alzo m
elevator /'elɪveɪtə(r)/ n Am ascensore m
eleven /ɪ'levn/ a & n undici m
eleven plus n ⟨formerly⟩ esame m di ammissione alla scuola secondaria inglese
elevenses /ɪ'levənzɪz/ n Br fam pausa f per il caffè (a metà mattina)
eleventh /ɪ'levənθ/ a & n undicesimo, -a mf; **at the ~ hour** fam all'ultimo momento
elf /elf/ n (pl elves) elfo m
elicit /ɪ'lɪsɪt/ vt ottenere
eligible /'elɪdʒəbl/ a eleggibile; **~ young man** buon partito; **be ~ for** aver diritto a
eliminate /ɪ'lɪmɪneɪt/ vt eliminare
elimination /ɪlɪmɪ'neɪʃn/ n eliminazione f; **by a process of ~** procedendo per eliminazione
élite /eɪ'liːt/ n fior fiore m
élitist /eɪ'liːtɪst/ a elitista
ellipse /ɪ'lɪps/ n ellisse f
elliptical /ɪ'lɪptɪk(ə)l/ a also fig ellittico
elm /elm/ n olmo m
elocution /elə'kjuːʃn/ n elocuzione f
elongate /'iːlɒŋgeɪt/ vt allungare
elope /ɪ'ləʊp/ vi fuggire [per sposarsi]
elopement /ɪ'ləʊpmənt/ n fuga f romantica
eloquence /'eləkwəns/ n eloquenza f
eloquent /'eləkwənt/ a eloquente
eloquently /'eləkwəntlɪ/ adv con eloquenza
El Salvador /el'sælvədɔː(r)/ n El Salvador m; **in ~ ~** nel Salvador
else /els/ adv altro; **who ~?** e chi altro?; **he did of course, who ~?** l'ha fatto lui e chi, se no?; **nothing ~** nient'altro; **or ~** altrimenti; **someone ~** qualcun altro; **somewhere ~** da qualche altra parte; **anyone ~** chiunque altro; ⟨as question⟩ nessun'altro?; **anything ~** qualunque altra cosa; ⟨as question⟩ altro?
elsewhere /els'weə(r)/ adv altrove
elucidate /ɪ'luːsɪdeɪt/ vt delucidare
elude /ɪ'luːd/ vt eludere; ⟨avoid⟩ evitare; **the name ~s me** il nome mi sfugge
elusive /ɪ'luːsɪv/ a elusivo
emaciated /ɪ'meɪsɪeɪtɪd/ a emaciato
e-mail n e-mail f, posta f elettronica ● vt spedire per e-mail
e-mail address n indirizzo m di posta elettronica
emanate /'eməneɪt/ vi emanare
emancipated /ɪ'mænsɪpeɪtɪd/ a emancipato
emancipation /ɪmænsɪ'peɪʃn/ n emancipazione f; ⟨of slaves⟩ liberazione f
emasculate /ɪ'mæskjʊleɪt/ vt evirare; fig svigorire
embalm /ɪm'bɑːm/ vt imbalsamare
embankment /ɪm'bæŋkmənt/ n argine m; Rail massicciata f
embargo /em'bɑːgəʊ/ n (pl -es) embargo m

embark /ɪm'bɑːk/ vi imbarcarsi; **~ on** intraprendere
embarkation /embɑː'keɪʃn/ n imbarco m
embarrass /em'bærəs/ vt imbarazzare
embarrassed /em'bærəst/ a imbarazzato
embarrassing /em'bærəsɪŋ/ a imbarazzante
embarrassment /em'bærəsmənt/ n imbarazzo m
embassy /'embəsɪ/ n ambasciata f
embed /ɪm'bedɪd/ vt Comput integrare ⟨command⟩; **~ded in** ⟨gem⟩ incastonato in; ⟨plant⟩ piantato in; ⟨sharp object⟩ conficcato in; ⟨rock⟩ incluso in; **~ded** ⟨traditions, feelings⟩ radicato; **be ~ded in** fig radicarsi in
embellish /ɪm'belɪʃ/ vt abbellire
embers /'embəz/ npl braci fpl
embezzle /ɪm'bezl/ vt appropriarsi indebitamente di
embezzlement /ɪm'bez(ə)lmənt/ n appropriazione f indebita
embitter /ɪm'bɪtə(r)/ vt amareggiare
emblem /'embləm/ n emblema m
emblematic /emblə'mætɪk/ a emblematico
embodiment /ɪm'bɒdɪmənt/ n incarnazione f
embody /ɪm'bɒdɪ/ vt (pt/pp -ied) incorporare; **~ what is best in...** rappresentare quanto c'è di meglio in...
embolism /'embəlɪzm/ n Med embolia f
emboss /ɪm'bɒs/ vt sbalzare ⟨metal⟩; stampare in rilievo ⟨paper⟩
embossed /ɪm'bɒst/ a in rilievo
embrace /ɪm'breɪs/ n abbraccio m ● vt abbracciare ● vi abbracciarsi
embroider /ɪm'brɔɪdə(r)/ vt ricamare ⟨design⟩; fig abbellire
embroidery /ɪm'brɔɪdərɪ/ n ricamo m
embroil /ɪm'brɔɪl/ vt become **~ed in sth** rimanere invischiato in qcsa
embryo /'embrɪəʊ/ n embrione m
embryonic /embrɪ'ɒnɪk/ a Biol, fig embrionale
emend /ɪ'mend/ vt emendare
emerald /'emərəld/ n smeraldo m
emerge /ɪ'mɜːdʒ/ vi emergere; ⟨come into being: nation⟩ nascere; ⟨sun, flowers⟩ spuntare fuori
emergence /ɪ'mɜːdʒəns/ n emergere m; ⟨of new country⟩ nascita f
emergency /ɪ'mɜːdʒənsɪ/ n emergenza f; **in an ~** in caso di emergenza
emergency: emergency ambulance service n pronto soccorso m autoambulanze. **emergency case** n Med caso m di emergenza. **emergency centre** n ⟨for refugees etc⟩ centro m di accoglienza; Med centro m di soccorso mobile. **emergency exit** n uscita f di sicurezza. **emergency landing** n Aeron atterraggio m di fortuna. **emergency laws** npl Pol leggi fpl straordinarie. **emergency number** n numero m di emergenza. **emergency powers** npl Pol poteri mpl straordinari. **emergency rations** npl viveri

mpl di sopravvivenza. **emergency service** *n Med* servizio *m* di pronto soccorso. **emergency services** *npl* servizi *mpl* di pronto intervento. **emergency surgery** *n* **undergo ~ ~** essere operato d'urgenza. **emergency ward** *n* [reparto *m* di] pronto soccorso *m*. **emergency worker** *n* addetto *m* a operazioni di soccorso

emergent /ɪ'mɜːdʒənt/ *a* ⟨industry, nation⟩ emergente

emery board/'eməri/*n* limetta *f* per le unghie (*di carta*)

emery paper *n* carta *f* vetrata

emigrant /'emɪgrənt/ *n* emigrante *mf*

emigrate /'emɪgreɪt/ *vi* emigrare

emigration /emɪ'greɪʃn/ *n* emigrazione *f*

eminence /'emɪnəns/ *n* (*fame*) eminenza *f*, gloria *f*; (*honour*) distinzione *f*; (*hill*) altura *f*

eminent /'emɪnənt/ *a* eminente

eminently /'emɪnəntlɪ/ *adv* eminentemente

emirate /'emɪrət/ *n* emirato *m*

emissary /'emɪsərɪ/ *n* emissario *m* (**to** di)

emission /ɪ'mɪʃn/ *n* emissione *f*; (*of fumes*) esalazione *f*

emit /ɪ'mɪt/ *vt* (*pt/pp* **emitted**) emettere; esalare ⟨fumes⟩

Emmy /'emɪ/ *n* Emmy *m* Oscar *m inv* televisivo americano

emotion /ɪ'məʊʃn/ *n* emozione *f*

emotional /ɪ'məʊʃənəl/ *a* denso di emozione; ⟨person, reaction⟩ emotivo; **become ~** avere una reazione emotiva; **don't get so ~** non lasciarti prendere dalle emozioni

emotionless /ɪ'məʊʃənlɪs/ *a* impassibile

emotive /ɪ'məʊtɪv/ *a* emotivo

empathize /'empəθaɪz/ *vi* **~ with sb** immedesimarsi nei problemi di qcno

empathy /'empəθɪ/ *n* comprensione *f*

emperor /'empərə(r)/ *n* imperatore *m*

emphasis /'emfəsɪs/ *n* enfasi *f*; **put the ~ on sth** accentuare qcsa

emphasize /'emfəsaɪz/ *vt* accentuare ⟨word, syllable⟩; sottolineare ⟨need⟩

emphatic /ɪm'fætɪk/ *a* categorico

emphatically /ɪm'fætɪklɪ/ *adv* categoricamente

empire /'empaɪə(r)/ *n* impero *m*

empirical /em'pɪrɪkl/ *a* empirico

empiricism /em'pɪrɪsɪzm/ *n* empirismo *m*

employ /em'plɔɪ/ *vt* impiegare; *fig* usare ⟨tact⟩

employable /em'plɔɪəbl/ *a* ⟨person⟩ che ha i requisiti per svolgere un lavoro

employee /emplɔɪ'iː/ *n* impiegato, -a *mf*

employee buyout *n* rilevamento *m* dipendenti

employer /em'plɔɪə(r)/ *n* datore *m* di lavoro

employment /em'plɔɪmənt/ *n* occupazione *f*; (*work*) lavoro *m*

employment: employment agency *n* ufficio *m* di collocamento. **employment contract** *n* contratto *m* di lavoro. **employment exchange** *n* agenzia *f* di collocamento. **employment figures** *npl* dati *mpl* su l'occupazione. **Employment Minister, Em-**

ployment Secretary *n* ministro *m* del lavoro

emporium /em'pɔːrɪəm/ *n hum* emporio *m*

empower /ɪm'paʊə(r)/ *vt* autorizzare; (*enable*) mettere in grado

empress /'emprɪs/ *n* imperatrice *f*

empties /'emptɪz/ *npl* vuoti *mpl*

emptiness /'emptɪnɪs/ *n* vuoto *m*

empty /'emptɪ/ *a* vuoto; ⟨promise, threat⟩ vano ● *v* (*pt/pp* **-ied**) ● *vt* vuotare ⟨container⟩ ● *vi* vuotarsi
 ■ **empty out** *vt/i* = **empty**

empty-handed /-'hændɪd/ *a* ⟨arrive, leave⟩ a mani vuote

empty-headed /-'hedɪd/ *a* scriteriato

EMS *n abbr* (**European Monetary System**) SME *m*

emulate /'emjʊleɪt/ *vt* emulare

emulsify /ɪ'mʌlsɪfaɪ/ *v* (*pt/pp* **-ied**) ● *vt* emulsionare ● *vi* emulsionarsi

emulsion /ɪ'mʌlʃn/ *n* emulsione *f*

enable /ɪ'neɪbl/ *vt* **~ sb to** mettere qcno in grado di

enact /ɪ'nækt/ *vt Theat* rappresentare; decretare ⟨law⟩

enamel /ɪ'næml/ *n* smalto *m* ● *vt* (*pt/pp* **enamelled**) smaltare

enamelling /ɪ'næməlɪŋ/ *n* (*process*) smaltatura *f*; (*art*) decorazione *f* a smalto

enamoured /ɪ'næməd/ *a* **be ~ of** essere innamorato di

enc. *abbr* (**enclosures**) alleg.

encampment /ɪn'kæmpmənt/ *n* accampamento *m*

encapsulate /en'kæpsjʊleɪt/ *vt* (*include*) incapsulare; (*summarize*) sintetizzare

encase /en'keɪs/ *vt* rivestire (**in** di)

encash /en'kæʃ/ *vt Br* incassare

encephalogram /en'kefələgræm/ *n* encefalogramma *m*

enchant /ɪn'tʃɑːnt/ *vt* incantare

enchanting /ɪn'tʃɑːntɪŋ/ *a* incantevole

enchantment /ɪn'tʃɑːntmənt/ *n* incanto *m*

encircle /ɪn'sɜːkl/ *vt* circondare

encl *abbr* (**enclosed; enclosure**) all.

enclave /'enkleɪv/ *n* enclave *f inv*; *fig* territorio *m*

enclose /ɪn'kləʊz/ *vt* circondare ⟨land⟩; (*in letter*) allegare (**with** a)

enclosed /ɪn'kləʊzd/ *a* ⟨space⟩ chiuso; (*in letter*) allegato

enclosure /ɪn'kləʊʒə(r)/ *n* (*at zoo*) recinto *m*; (*in letter*) allegato *m*

encode /ɪn'kəʊd/ *vt* codificare

encoder /ɪn'kəʊdə(r)/ *n* codificatore, -trice *mf*

encompass /ɪn'kʌmpəs/ *vt* (*include*) comprendere

encore /'ɒŋkɔː(r)/ *n & int* bis *m inv*

encounter /ɪn'kaʊntə(r)/ *n* incontro *m*; (*battle*) scontro *m* ● *vt* incontrare

encourage /ɪn'kʌrɪdʒ/ *vt* incoraggiare; promuovere ⟨the arts, independence⟩

encouragement /ɪn'kʌrɪdʒmənt/ *n* incoraggiamento *m*; (*of the arts*) promozione *f*

encouraging /ɪnˈkʌrɪdʒɪŋ/ a incoraggiante; ⟨smile⟩ di incoraggiamento

encroach /ɪnˈkrəʊtʃ/ vt ~ **on** invadere ⟨land, privacy⟩; abusare di ⟨time⟩; interferire con ⟨rights⟩

encrust /enˈkrʌst/ vt **be ~ed with** ⟨ice⟩ essere incrostato di; ⟨jewels⟩ essere tempestato di

encumber /ɪnˈkʌmbə(r)/ vt ~**ed with** essere carico di ⟨children, suitcases⟩; ingombro di ⟨furniture⟩

encumbrance /ɪnˈkʌmbrəns/ n peso m

encyclop[a]edia /ɪnsaɪkləˈpiːdɪə/ n enciclopedia f

encyclop[a]edic /ɪnsaɪkləˈpiːdɪk/ a enciclopedico

end /end/ n fine f; ⟨of box, table, piece of string⟩ estremità f; ⟨of town, room⟩ parte f; ⟨purpose⟩ fine m; **in the ~** alla fine; **at the ~ of May** alla fine di maggio; **at the ~ of the street/garden** in fondo alla strada/al giardino; **on ~** ⟨upright⟩ in piedi; **for days on ~** per giorni e giorni; **for six days on ~** per sei giorni di fila; **put an ~ to sth** mettere fine a qcsa; **make ~s meet** fam sbarcare il lunario; **no ~ of** fam un sacco di ● vt/i finire
■ **end in** vt ⟨word:⟩ terminare in; finire in ⟨failure, argument⟩
■ **end off** vt concludere ⟨meal, speech⟩
■ **end up** vi finire; ~ **up doing sth** finire col fare qcsa

endanger /ɪnˈdeɪndʒə(r)/ vt rischiare ⟨one's life⟩; mettere a repentaglio ⟨sb else, success of sth⟩

endear /ɪnˈdɪə(r)/ vt ~ **oneself to sb** conquistarsi la simpatia di qcno; ~ **sb to** conquistare a qcno la simpatia di

endearing /ɪnˈdɪərɪŋ/ a accattivante

endearingly /ɪnˈɪərɪŋlɪ/ adv ⟨smile⟩ in modo accattivante; ~ **honest** di un'onestà disarmante

endearment /ɪnˈdɪəmənt/ n **term of ~** vezzeggiativo m

endeavour /ɪnˈdevə(r)/ n tentativo m ● vi sforzarsi (**to** di)

endemic /enˈdemɪk/ a endemico ● n ⟨situation⟩ endemia f

ending /ˈendɪŋ/ n fine f; Gram desinenza f

endive /ˈendaɪv/ n indivia f

endless /ˈendlɪs/ a interminabile; ⟨patience⟩ infinito

endlessly /ˈendlɪslɪ/ adv continuamente; ⟨patient⟩ infinitamente

endocrinology /endəʊkrɪˈnɒlədʒɪ/ n endocrinologia f

endorse /enˈdɔːs/ vt girare ⟨cheque⟩; ⟨sports personality:⟩ fare pubblicità a ⟨product⟩; approvare ⟨plan⟩

endorsement /enˈdɔːsmənt/ n ⟨of cheque⟩ girata f; ⟨of plan⟩ conferma f; ⟨on driving licence⟩ registrazione f su patente di un'infrazione

endow /ɪnˈdaʊ/ vt dotare

endowment insurance /ɪnˈdaʊmənt/ n assicurazione f sulla vita che fornisce un reddito in caso di sopravvivenza

end: **endpaper** n risguardo m. **end product** n prodotto m finito. **end result** n risultato m finale

endurable /ɪnˈdjʊərəbl/ a sopportabile

endurance /ɪnˈdjʊərəns/ n resistenza f; **it is beyond ~** è insopportabile

endurance test n prova f di resistenza

endure /ɪnˈdjʊə(r)/ vt sopportare ● vi durare

enduring /ɪnˈdjʊərɪŋ/ a duraturo

end user n utente m finale

enema /ˈenɪmə/ n Med clistere m

enemy /ˈenəmɪ/ n nemico, -a mf ● attrib nemico

energetic /enəˈdʒetɪk/ a energico

energetically /enəˈdʒetɪklɪ/ adv ⟨speak, promote, publicize⟩ vigorosamente; ⟨work, exercise⟩ con energia; ⟨deny⟩ risolutamente

energize /ˈenədʒaɪz/ vt stimolare; Electr alimentare [elettricamente]

energizing /ˈenədʒaɪzɪŋ/ a ⟨influence⟩ stimolante

energy /ˈenədʒɪ/ n energia f

energy: **energy efficiency** n razionalizzazione f del consumo energetico. **energy resources** npl risorse fpl energetiche. **energy saving** n risparmio m energetico ● a **energy-saving** ⟨device⟩ che fa risparmiare energia; ⟨measure⟩ per risparmiare energia

enervate /ˈenəveɪt/ vt snervare

enfold /enˈfəʊld/ vt avvolgere

enforce /ɪnˈfɔːs/ vt far rispettare ⟨law⟩

enforced /ɪnˈfɔːst/ a forzato

enforcement /ɪnˈfɔːsmənt/ n applicazione f; ⟨of discipline⟩ imposizione f

engage /ɪnˈgeɪdʒ/ vt assumere ⟨staff⟩; Theat ingaggiare; Auto ingranare ⟨gear⟩; ~ **sb in conversation** fare conversazione con qcno ● vi Techn ingranare; ~ **in** impegnarsi in

engaged /ɪnˈgeɪdʒd/ a ⟨in use, busy⟩ occupato; ⟨person⟩ impegnato; ⟨to be married⟩ fidanzato; **get ~** fidanzarsi (**to** con)

engaged tone n Br segnale m di occupato

engagement /ɪnˈgeɪdʒmənt/ n fidanzamento m; ⟨appointment⟩ appuntamento m; Mil combattimento m

engagement ring n anello m di fidanzamento

engagements book n agenda f

engaging /ɪnˈgeɪdʒɪŋ/ a attraente

engender /ɪnˈdʒendə(r)/ vt fig generare

engine /ˈendʒɪn/ n motore m; Rail locomotrice f

engine driver n macchinista m

engineer /endʒɪˈnɪə(r)/ n ingegnere m; ⟨service, installation⟩ tecnico m; Naut, Am Rail macchinista m ● vt fig architettare

engineering /endʒɪˈnɪərɪŋ/ n ingegneria f

engine: **engine failure** n guasto m [al motore]; ⟨in jet⟩ avaria f. **engine oil** n olio m [del] motore. **engine room** n sala f macchine. **engine shed** n Rail deposito m

England /ˈɪŋglənd/ n Inghilterra f

English /ˈɪŋglɪʃ/ a inglese; **the ~ Channel**

la Manica ● *n* (*language*) inglese *m*; **the ~** *pl* gli inglesi

English: English as a Foreign Language *n* inglese *m* come lingua straniera. **English as a Second Language** *n* inglese *m* come seconda lingua. **Englishman** *n* inglese *m*. **English rose** *n* donna *f* dalla bellezza tipicamente inglese. **English speaker** *n* anglofono, -a *mf*. **English-speaking** *a* anglofono. **Englishwoman** *n* inglese *f*

engrave /ɪn'ɡreɪv/ *vt* incidere

engraving /ɪn'ɡreɪvɪn/ *n* incisione *f*

engross /ɪn'ɡrəʊs/ *vt* **~ed in** assorto in

engrossing /ɪn'ɡrəʊsɪn/ *a* avvincente

engulf /ɪn'ɡʌlf/ *vt* (*fire, waves:*) inghiottire

enhance /ɪn'hɑːns/ *vt* accrescere (*beauty, reputation*); migliorare (*performance*)

enigma /ɪ'nɪɡmə/ *n* enigma *m*

enigmatic /enɪɡ'mætɪk/ *a* enigmatico

enjoy /ɪn'dʒɔɪ/ *vt* godere di (*good health*); **~ oneself** divertirsi; **I ~ cooking/painting** mi piace cucinare/dipingere; **I ~ed the meal/film** mi è piaciuto il pranzo/il film; **~ your meal** buon appetito

enjoyable /ɪn'dʒɔɪəbl/ *a* piacevole

enjoyment /ɪn'dʒɔɪmənt/ *n* piacere *m*

enlarge /ɪn'lɑːdʒ/ *vt* ingrandire ● *vi* **~ upon** dilungarsi su

enlargement /ɪn'lɑːdʒmənt/ *n* ingrandimento *m*

enlarger /ɪn'lɑːdʒə(r)/ *n Phot* ingranditore *m*

enlighten /ɪn'laɪtn/ *vt* illuminare

enlightened /ɪn'laɪtənd/ *a* progressista

enlightenment /ɪn'laɪtənmənt/ *n* **The E~** l'Illuminismo *m*

enlist /ɪn'lɪst/ *vt Mil* reclutare; **~ sb's help** farsi aiutare da qcno ● *vi Mil* arruolarsi

enliven /ɪn'laɪvn/ *vt* animare

enmesh /en'meʃ/ *vt* **become ~ed in** *fig* impegolarsi in

enmity /'enmətɪ/ *n* inimicizia *f*

ennoble /en'nəʊbl/ *vt* nobilitare

enormity /ɪ'nɔːmətɪ/ *n* enormità *f*

enormous /ɪ'nɔːməs/ *a* enorme

enormously /ɪ'nɔːməslɪ/ *adv* estremamente; (*grateful*) infinitamente

enough /ɪ'nʌf/ *a & n* abbastanza; **I didn't bring ~ clothes** non ho portato abbastanza vestiti; **have you had ~?** (*to eat/drink*) hai mangiato/bevuto abbastanza?; **I've had ~!** *fam* ne ho abbastanza!; **is that ~?** basta?; **that's ~!** basta così!; **£50 isn't ~** 50 sterline non sono sufficienti ● *adv* abbastanza; **you're not working fast ~** non lavori abbastanza in fretta; **funnily ~** stranamente

enquire /ɪn'kwaɪə(r)/ *vi* domandare; **~ about** chiedere informazioni su

enquiry /ɪn'kwaɪərɪ/ *n* domanda *f*; (*investigation*) inchiesta *f*

enrage /ɪn'reɪdʒ/ *vt* fare arrabbiare

enrich /ɪn'rɪtʃ/ *vt* arricchire; (*improve*) migliorare (*vocabulary*)

enrol /ɪn'rəʊl/ *vi* (*pt/pp* **-rolled**) (*for exam, in club*) iscriversi (**for, in** a)

enrolment /ɪn'rəʊlmənt/ *n* iscrizione *f*

ensconced /ɪn'skɒnst/ *a* comodamente sistemato (**in** in)

ensemble /ɒn'sɒmbl/ *n* (*clothing & Mus*) complesso *m*

ensign /'ensaɪn/ *n* insegna *f*

enslave /ɪn'sleɪv/ *vt* render schiavo

ensue /ɪn'sjuː/ *vi* seguire; **~ from** sorgere da; **the ensuing discussion** la discussione che ne è seguita

en suite /ɒ̃'swiːt/ *n* (*bathroom*) camera *f* con bagno annesso ● *a* (*bathroom*) annesso; (*room*) con bagno

ensure /ɪn'ʃʊə(r)/ *vt* assicurare; **~ that** (*person:*) assicurarsi che; (*measure:*) garantire che

ENT *n abbr* (**Ear Nose and Throat**) otorino *m*

entail /ɪn'teɪl/ *vt* comportare; **what does it ~?** in che cosa consiste?

entangle /ɪn'tæŋgl/ *vt* **get ~d in** rimanere impigliato in; *fig* rimanere coinvolto in

entanglement /ɪn'tæŋg(ə)lmənt/ *n* (*emotional*) legame *m* sentimentale; (*complicated situation*) pasticcio *m*

enter /'entə(r)/ *vt* entrare in; iscrivere (*horse, runner in race*); cominciare (*university*); partecipare a (*competition*); *Comput* immettere (*data*); (*write down*) scrivere ● *vi* entrare; *Theat* entrare in scena; (*register as competitor*) iscriversi; (*take part*) partecipare (**in** a) ● *n Comput* invio *m*

■ **enter into** *vt* (*begin*) intavolare (*negotiations, an argument*)

enteritis /entə'raɪtɪs/ *n* enterite *f*

enterprise /'entəpraɪz/ *n* impresa *f*; (*quality*) iniziativa *f*

enterprising /'entəpraɪzɪn/ *a* intraprendente

entertain /entə'teɪn/ *vt* intrattenere; (*invite*) ricevere; nutrire (*ideas, hopes*); prendere in considerazione (*possibility*) ● *vi* intrattenersi; (*have guests*) ricevere

entertainer /entə'teɪnə(r)/ *n* artista *mf*

entertaining /entə'teɪnɪn/ *a* (*person*) di gradevole compagnia; (*evening, film, play*) divertente

entertainment /entə'teɪnmənt/ *n* (*amusement*) intrattenimento *m*

enthral /ɪn'θrɔːl/ *vt* (*pt/pp* **enthralled**) **be ~led** essere affascinato (**by** da)

enthralling /ɪn'θrɔːlɪn/ *a* (*novel, performance*) affascinante

enthuse /ɪn'θjuːz/ *vi* **~ over** entusiasmarsi per

enthusiasm /ɪn'θjuːzɪæzm/ *n* entusiasmo *m*

enthusiast /ɪn'θjuːzɪæst/ *n* entusiasta *mf*

enthusiastic /ɪnθjuːzɪ'æstɪk/ *a* entusiastico

enthusiastically /ɪnθjuːzɪ'æstɪklɪ/ *adv* entusiasticamente

entice /ɪn'taɪs/ *vt* attirare

enticement /ɪn'taɪsmənt/ *n* (*incentive*) incentivo *m*

enticing /ɪn'taɪsɪn/ *a* (*prospect, offer*) allettante; ⟨person⟩ seducente; ⟨food, smell⟩ invitante

entire /ɪn'taɪə(r)/ a intero

entirely /ɪn'taɪəlɪ/ adv del tutto; **I'm not ~ satisfied** non sono completamente soddisfatto

entirety /ɪn'taɪərətɪ/ n **in its ~** nell'insieme

entitled /ɪn'taɪtld/ a ⟨book⟩ intitolato; **be ~ to sth** aver diritto a qcsa

entitlement /ɪn'taɪtlmənt/ n diritto m

entity /'entətɪ/ n entità f

entomology /entə'mɒlədʒɪ/ n entomologia f

entourage /'ɒntʊrɑ:ʒ/ n entourage m inv

entrails /'entreɪlz/ npl intestini mpl

entrance¹ /'entrəns/ n entrata f; Theat entrata f in scena; (right to enter) ammissione f; **'no ~'** 'ingresso vietato'

entrance² /ɪn'trɑ:ns/ vt estasiare

entrance: entrance examination n esame m di ammissione. **entrance fee** n **how much is the ~ ~?** quanto costa il biglietto di ingresso? **entrance hall** n (in house) ingresso m. **entrance requirements** npl requisiti mpl di ammissione. **entrance ticket** n biglietto m d'ingresso

entrancing /ɪn'trɑ:nsɪŋ/ a incantevole

entrant /'entrənt/ n concorrente mf

entreat /ɪn'tri:t/ vt supplicare

entreatingly /ɪn'tri:tɪŋlɪ/ adv ⟨beg, ask⟩ in tono implorante

entreaty /ɪn'tri:tɪ/ n supplica f

entrée /'ɒtreɪ/ n Br (starter) primo m; (Am: main course) secondo m; **her wealth gave her an ~ into high society** il denaro le ha aperto le porte dell'alta società

entrenched /ɪn'trentʃt/ a ⟨ideas, views⟩ radicato

entrepreneur /ɒntrəprə'nɜ:(r)/ n imprenditore, -trice mf

entrepreneurial /ɒntrəprə'nɜ:rɪəl/ a imprenditoriale; **have ~ skills** avere il senso degli affari

entrust /ɪn'trʌst/ vt **~ sb with sth, ~ sth to sb** affidare qcsa a qcno

entry /'entrɪ/ n ingresso m; (way in) entrata f; (in directory etc) voce f; (in appointment diary) appuntamento m; **no ~** ingresso vietato; Auto accesso vietato

entry: entry fee n quota f di iscrizione. **entry form** n modulo m di ammissione. **entry permit** n visto m di entrata. **entryphone** n citofono m. **entry requirements** npl requisiti mpl di ammissione. **entry visa** n visto m di ingresso

entwine /ɪn'twaɪn/ vt also fig intrecciare

E-number n Br sigla f degli additivi

enumerate /ɪ'nju:məreɪt/ vt enumerare

enumeration /ɪnju:mə'reɪʃn/ n (list) enumerazione f; (counting) conto m

enunciate /ɪ'nʌnsɪeɪt/ vt enunciare

enunciation /ɪnʌnsɪ'eɪʃn/ n (of principle, facts) enunciazione f; (of word) articolazione f

envelop /ɪn'veləp/ vt (pt/pp enveloped) avviluppare

envelope /'envələʊp/ n busta f

enviable /'envɪəbl/ a invidiabile

envious /'envɪəs/ a invidioso

enviously /'envɪəslɪ/ adv con invidia

environment /ɪn'vaɪrənmənt/ n ambiente m

environmental /ɪnvaɪrən'mentl/ a ambientale

environmental health n salute f pubblica

environmentalist /ɪnvaɪrən'mentəlɪst/ n ambientalista mf

environmentally /ɪnvaɪrən'mentəlɪ/ adv **~ friendly** che rispetta l'ambiente

environmental scientist n studioso, -a mf di ecologia applicata

Environmental Studies npl Br Sch ecogeografia f e ecobiologia f

envisage /ɪn'vɪzɪdʒ/ vt prevedere

envoy /'envɔɪ/ n inviato, -a mf

envy /'envɪ/ n invidia f ● vt (pt/pp -ied) **~ sb sth** invidiare qcno per qcsa

enzyme /'enzaɪm/ n enzima m

ephemeral /ɪ'femərəl/ a effimero

epic /'epɪk/ a epico ● n epopea f

epicentre /'epɪsentə(r)/ n epicentro m

epidemic /epɪ'demɪk/ n epidemia f

epidermis /epɪ'dɜ:mɪs/ n epidermide f

epidural /epɪ'djʊərəl/ n Med anestesia f epidurale

epigram /'epɪɡræm/ n epigramma m

epilepsy /'epɪlepsɪ/ n epilessia f

epileptic /epɪ'leptɪk/ a & n epilettico, -a mf

epilogue /'epɪlɒɡ/ n epilogo m

Epiphany /ɪ'pɪfənɪ/ n Epifania f

episode /'epɪsəʊd/ n episodio m

episodic /epɪ'sɒdɪk/ a episodico

epistle /ɪ'pɪsl/ n liter epistola f

epitaph /'epɪtɑ:f/ n epitaffio m

epithet /'epɪθet/ n epiteto m

epitome /ɪ'pɪtəmɪ/ n epitome f

epitomize /ɪ'pɪtəmaɪz/ vt essere il classico esempio di

epoch /'i:pɒk/ n epoca f

epoch-making a che fa epoca

eponymous /ɪ'pɒnɪməs/ a eponimo

equable /'ekwəbl/ a ⟨climate⟩ temperato; ⟨temperament⟩ equilibrato

equably /'ekwəblɪ/ adv con serenità

equal /'i:kwl/ a ⟨parts, amounts⟩ uguale; **of ~ height** della stessa altezza; **be ~ to the task** essere a l'altezza del compito ● n pari m inv; **treat sb as an ~** trattare qcno da pari a pari ● vt (pt/pp **equalled**) (be same in quantity as) essere pari a; (rival) uguagliare; **5 plus 5 ~s 10** 5 più 5 [è] uguale a 10

equality /ɪ'kwɒlətɪ/ n uguaglianza f

equalize /'i:kwəlaɪz/ vi Sport pareggiare

equalizer /'i:kwəlaɪzə(r)/ n Sport pareggio m; **get the ~** pareggiare

equally /'i:kwəlɪ/ adv ⟨divide⟩ in parti uguali; **~ intelligent** della stessa intelligenza; **~,...** allo stesso tempo...

equal: equal opportunities npl uguaglianza f dei diritti. **Equal Opportunities Commission** n Br commissione f per l'ugua-

glianza dei diritti nei rapporti di lavoro.
equal opportunity *attrib* ⟨*legislation*⟩ per
l'uguaglianza dei diritti nei rapporti di lavoro; ⟨*employer*⟩ che applica l'uguaglianza dei
diritti. **equal rights** *npl* parità *f* dei diritti.
equals sign *n* segno *m* uguale
equanimity /ekwə'nɪmətɪ/ *n* equanimità *f*
equate /ɪ'kweɪt/ *vt* ~ sth with sth equipa-
rare qcsa a qcsa
equation /ɪ'kweɪʒn/ *n Math* equazione *f*
equator /ɪ'kweɪtə(r)/ *n* equatore *m*
equatorial /ekwə'tɔ:rɪəl/ *a* equatoriale
equestrian /ɪ'kwestrɪən/ *a* equestre
equidistant /i:kwɪ'dɪstənt/ *a* equidistante
equilateral /i:kwɪ'lætərəl/ *a* equilatero
equilibrium /i:kwɪ'lɪbrɪəm/ *n* equilibrio *m*
equine /'ekwaɪn/ *a* ⟨*disease, species*⟩ equino;
⟨*features*⟩ cavallino
equinox /'i:kwɪnɒks/ *n* equinozio *m*
equip /ɪ'kwɪp/ *vt* (*pt/pp* **equipped**) equipaggiare; attrezzare ⟨*kitchen, office*⟩
equipment /ɪ'kwɪpmənt/ *n* attrezzatura *f*
equitable /'ekwɪtəbl/ *a* giusto
equity /'ekwətɪ/ *n* ⟨*justness*⟩ equità *f*; *Comm*
azioni *fpl*
equity: equity capital *n Fin* capitale *m*
azionario. **equity financing** *n Fin* finanziamento *m* attraverso l'emissione di azioni.
equity market *n Fin* mercato *m* azionario
equivalent /ɪ'kwɪvələnt/ *a* equivalente; be
~ **to** equivalere a ● *n* equivalente *m*
equivocal /ɪ'kwɪvəkl/ *a* equivoco
equivocate /ɪ'kwɪvəkeɪt/ *vi* parlare in modo
equivoco, giocare sull'equivoco
equivocation /ɪkwɪvə'keɪʃn/ *n* affermazione *f* equivoca; **too much** ~ troppi equivoci
era /'ɪərə/ *n* età *f*; (*geological*) era *f*
eradicate /ɪ'rædɪkeɪt/ *vt* eradicare
erase /ɪ'reɪz/ *vt* cancellare
erase head *n Comput* testina *f* di cancellazione
eraser /ɪ'reɪzə(r)/ *n* gomma *f* [da cancellare];
(*for blackboard*) cancellino *m*
erasure /ɪ'reɪʒə(r)/ *n* (*act*) cancellazione *f*;
(*on paper*) cancellatura *f*
erect /ɪ'rekt/ *a* eretto ● *vt* erigere
erection /ɪ'rekʃn/ *n* erezione *f*
ergonomic /ɜ:gə'nɒmɪk/ *a* ergonomico;
⟨*seat*⟩ anatomico
ergonomics /ɜ:gə'nɒmɪks/ *n* ergonomia
Erie /'ɪərɪ/ *n* **Lake** ~ il lago Erie
ERM *n abbr* **Exchange Rate Mechanism**
ermine /'ɜ:mɪn/ *n* ermellino *m*
erode /ɪ'rəʊd/ *vt* ⟨*water:*⟩ erodere; ⟨*acid:*⟩ corrodere
erogenous /ɪ'rɒdʒɪnəs/ *a* erogeno
erosion /ɪ'rəʊʒn/ *n* erosione *f*; (*by acid*) corrosione *f*
erotic /ɪ'rɒtɪk/ *a* erotico
erotica /ɪ'rɒtɪkə/ *npl* (*art*) arte *f* erotica;
(*literature*) letteratura *f* erotica; *Cinema* film
mpl erotici
eroticism /ɪ'rɒtɪsɪzm/ *n* erotismo *m*
err /ɜ:(r)/ *vi* errare; (*sin*) peccare
errand /'erənd/ *n* commissione *f*

errant /'erənt/ *a* ⟨*husband, wife*⟩ infedele
erratic /ɪ'rætɪk/ *a* irregolare; ⟨*person,
moods*⟩ imprevedibile; ⟨*exchange rate*⟩ incostante
erroneous /ɪ'rəʊnɪəs/ *a* erroneo
erroneously /ɪ'rəʊnɪəslɪ/ *adv* erroneamente
error /'erə(r)/ *n* errore *m*; **in** ~ per errore
error message *n Comput* messaggio *m* di
errore
ersatz /'ɜ:sæts/ *n* surrogato *m*; ~ **tobacco**
surrogato del tabacco
erudite /'erʊdaɪt/ *a* erudito
erudition /erʊ'dɪʃn/ *n* erudizione *f*
erupt /ɪ'rʌpt/ *vi* eruttare; ⟨*spots:*⟩ spuntare;
(*fig: in anger*) dare in escandescenze
eruption /ɪ'rʌpʃn/ *n* eruzione *f*; *fig* scoppio *m*
escalate /'eskəleɪt/ *vi* intensificarsi ● *vt* intensificare
escalation /eskə'leɪʃn/ *n* escalation *f inv*
escalator /'eskəleɪtə(r)/ *n* scala *f* mobile
escapade /'eskəpeɪd/ *n* scappatella *f*
escape /ɪ'skeɪp/ *n* fuga *f*; (*from prison*) evasione *f*; **have a narrow** ~ cavarsela per un
pelo ● *vi* ⟨*prisoner:*⟩ evadere (**from** da); sfuggire (**from sb** alla sorveglianza di qcno);
⟨*animal:*⟩ scappare; ⟨*gas:*⟩ fuoriuscire ● *vt* ~
notice passare inosservato; **the name** ~**s**
me mi sfugge il nome
escape chute *n Aeron* scivolo *m*
escape clause *n* clausola *f* di recesso
escapee /ɪskeɪ'pi:/ *n* evaso *m*
escape hatch *n Naut* portello *m* di sicurezza
escape route *n* (*for fugitives*) itinerario *m*
di fuga; (*in case of fire etc*) percorso *m* di emergenza
escapism /ɪ'skeɪpɪzm/ *n* evasione *f* dalla realtà
escapologist /eskə'pɒlədʒɪst/ *n illusionista mf capace di liberarsi dalle catene*
escarpment /es'kɑ:pmənt/ *n* scarpata *f*
eschew /ɪs'tʃu:/ *vt* evitare ⟨*discussion*⟩; rifuggire ⟨*temptation*⟩; rifuggire da ⟨*violence
ecc*⟩
escort[1] /'eskɔ:t/ *n* (*of person*) accompagnatore, -trice *mf*; *Mil etc* scorta *f*
escort[2] /ɪ'skɔ:t/ *vt* accompagnare; *Mil etc*
scortare
Eskimo /'eskɪməʊ/ *n* esquimese *mf*
esophagus /ɪ'sɒfəgəs/ *n Am* esofago *m*
esoteric /esə'terɪk/ *a* esoterico
ESP *n abbr* (**extrasensory perception**)
ESP *f*; *n abbr* **English for Special Purposes**
esp *abbr* **especially**
especial /ɪ'speʃl/ *a* speciale
especially /ɪ'speʃəlɪ/ *adv* specialmente;
⟨*kind*⟩ particolarmente
espionage /'espɪənɑ:ʒ/ *n* spionaggio *m*
espouse /ɪ'spaʊz/ *vt* abbracciare ⟨*cause*⟩
espresso /e'spresəʊ/ *n* (*coffee*) espresso *m*
Esq *Br abbr* (**esquire**) **James McBride,** ~
Egr. Sig. James McBride
essay /'eseɪ/ *n* saggio *m*; *Sch* tema *f*

essence /'esns/ n essenza f; **in ~** in sostanza
essential /ɪ'senʃl/ a essenziale ● n **the ~s** pl l'essenziale m
essentially /ɪ'senʃəlɪ/ adv essenzialmente
est abbr (**established**) fondato nel
establish /ɪ'stæblɪʃ/ vt stabilire ‹contact, lead›; fondare ‹firm›; ‹prove› accertare; **~ oneself as** affermarsi come
established /ɪ'stæblɪʃt/ a ‹way of doing sth, view› generalmente accettato; ‹company› affidabile; ‹brand› riconosciuto; **a well ~ fact** un dato di fatto; **the ~ church** la religione di Stato
establishment /ɪ'stæblɪʃmənt/ n ‹firm› azienda f; **the E~** l'establishment m
estate /ɪ'steɪt/ n tenuta f; ‹possessions› patrimonio m; ‹housing› quartiere m residenziale
estate: estate agent n agente m immobiliare. **estate car** n giardiniera f. **estate duty** n Br imposta f di successione
esteem /ɪ'stiːm/ n stima f ● vt stimare; ‹consider› giudicare
ester /'estə(r)/ n estere m
estimate¹ /'estɪmət/ n valutazione f; Comm preventivo m; **at a rough ~** a occhio e croce
estimate² /'estɪmeɪt/ vt stimare
estimated time of arrival /'estɪmeɪtɪd/ n ora f prevista di arrivo
estimation /estɪ'meɪʃn/ n ‹esteem› stima f; **in my ~** ‹judgement› a mio giudizio
Estonia /ɪ'stəʊnɪə/ n Estonia f
estrange /ɪ'streɪndʒ/ vt estraniare; **~d from sb** separato da qcno; **her ~d husband** il marito da cui è separata
estrangement /ɪ'streɪndʒmənt/ n disamoramento m
estuary /'estjʊərɪ/ n estuario m
ETA n abbr **estimated time of arrival**
et al /et'æl/ abbr (**et alii**) e altri
etc /et'setərə/ abbr (**et cetera**) ecc
et cetera, etcetera /et'setərə/ adv eccetera
etch /etʃ/ vt incidere all'acquaforte; **~ed on her memory** fig impresso nella sua memoria
etching /'etʃɪŋ/ n acquaforte f
eternal /ɪ'tɜːnl/ a eterno
eternal life n vita f eterna
eternally /ɪ'tɜːnəlɪ/ adv eternamente
eternal triangle n eterno triangolo m
eternity /ɪ'tɜːnətɪ/ n eternità f
ether /'iːθə(r)/ n etere m
ethereal /ɪ'θɪərɪəl/ a etereo
ethic /'eθɪk/ n etica f
ethical /'eθɪkl/ a etico
ethics /'eθɪks/ n etica f
Ethiopia /iːθɪ'əʊpɪə/ n Etiopia f
ethnic /'eθnɪk/ a etnico
ethnically /'eθnɪklɪ/ adv etnicamente
ethnic cleansing n epurazione f etnica
ethnology /eθ'nɒlədʒɪ/ n etnologia f
ethos /'iːθɒs/ n **company ~** filosofia f dell'azienda
etiquette /'etɪket/ n etichetta f
etymology /etɪ'mɒlədʒɪ/ n etimologia f
EU n abbr (**European Union**) UE f

eucalyptus /juːkə'lɪptəs/ n eucalipto m
eugenics /juː'dʒenɪks/ n eugenetica f
eulogize /'juːlədʒaɪz/ vt fare il panegirico di
● vi **~ over sth** tessere le lodi di qcsa
eulogy /'juːlədʒɪ/ n elogio m
eunuch /'juːnək/ n eunuco m
euphemism /'juːfəmɪzm/ n eufemismo m
euphemistic /juːfə'mɪstɪk/ a eufemistico
euphemistically /juːfə'mɪstɪklɪ/ adv eufemisticamente
euphoria /juː'fɔːrɪə/ n euforia f
euphoric /juː'fɒrɪk/ a euforico
Eurasian /jʊ'reɪʒ(ə)n/ a ‹people, region› eurasiatico
EURATOM /jʊr'ætəm/ n abbr (**European Atomic Energy Community**) EURATOM f
eurhythmics /jʊ'rɪðmɪks/ n ginnastica f ritmica
Euro- /'jʊərəʊ-/: **eurobond** n eurobbligazione f. **Eurocheque** n eurochèque m inv. **eurocurrency** n eurovaluta f. **Eurodollar** n eurodollaro m. **euromarket** n euromercato m. **Euro-MP** n eurodeputato, -a mf
Europe /'jʊərəp/ n Europa f
European /jʊərə'pɪən/ a & n europeo, -a mf
European: European Bank for Reconstruction and Development n Banca f Europea per la Ricostruzione e lo Sviluppo. **European Commission** n Commissione f Europea. **European Community** n Comunità f Europea. **European Court of Human Rights** n Corte f europea per i diritti dell'uomo. **European Court of Justice** n Corte f europea di giustizia. **European Economic Community** n Comunità f Economica Europea. **European Free Trade Association** n Associazione f Europea di Libero Scambio. **European Monetary System** n Sistema m Monetario Europeo. **European Monetary Union** n Unione f Monetaria Europea. **European Parliament** n Parlamento m Europeo. **European Union** n Unione f Europea
Euro-sceptic n Br euroscettico, -a mf
euthanasia /juːθə'neɪzɪə/ n eutanasia f
evacuate /ɪ'vækjʊeɪt/ vt evacuare ‹building, area›
evacuation /ɪvækjʊ'eɪʃn/ n evacuazione f
evacuee /ɪvækjʊ'iː/ n sfollato m
evade /ɪ'veɪd/ vt evadere ‹taxes›; evitare ‹the enemy, authorities›; **~ the issue** evitare l'argomento
evaluate /ɪ'væljʊeɪt/ vt valutare
evaluation /ɪvæljʊ'eɪʃn/ n valutazione f, stima f
evangelical /iːvæn'dʒelɪkl/ a evangelico
evangelist /ɪ'vændʒəlɪst/ n evangelista m
evaporate /ɪ'væpəreɪt/ vi evaporare; fig svanire
evaporation /ɪvæpə'reɪʃn/ n evaporazione f
evasion /ɪ'veɪʒn/ n evasione f
evasive /ɪ'veɪsɪv/ a evasivo
evasively /ɪ'veɪsɪvlɪ/ adv in modo evasivo
eve /iːv/ n liter vigilia f
even /'iːvn/ a ‹level› piatto; ‹same, equal› uguale; ‹regular› regolare; ‹number› pari;

get ~ with vendicarsi di; **now we're ~** adesso siamo pari ● *adv* anche, ancora; **~ if** anche se; **~ so** con tutto ciò; **not ~** nemmeno; **~ bigger/hotter** ancora più grande/caldo ● *vt* **~ the score** *Sport* pareggiare

■ **even out** *vi* livellarsi

■ **even up** *vt* livellare

even-handed /-'hændɪd/ *a* imparziale

evening /'i:vnɪŋ/ *n* sera *f*; (*whole evening*) serata *f*; **this ~** stasera; **in the ~** la sera

evening: evening class *n* corso *m* serale. **evening dress** *n* (*man's*) abito *m* scuro; (*woman's*) abito *m* da sera. **evening performance** *n* spettacolo *m* serale. **evening primrose** *n* enotera *f*. **evening star** *n* Venere *f*

evenly /'i:vnlɪ/ *adv* ⟨*distributed*⟩ uniformemente; ⟨*breathe*⟩ regolarmente; ⟨*divided*⟩ in uguali parti

event /ɪ'vent/ *n* avvenimento *m*; (*function*) manifestazione *f*; *Sport* gara *f*; **in the ~ of** nell'eventualità di; **in the ~** alla fine

even-tempered /-'tempəd/ *a* pacato

eventful /ɪ'ventfʊl/ *a* movimentato

eventing /ɪ'ventɪŋ/ *n Br* concorso *m* ippico completo

eventual /ɪ'ventjʊəl/ *a* **the ~ winner was...** alla fine il vincitore è stato...

eventuality /ɪventjʊ'ælətɪ/ *n* eventualità *f*

eventually /ɪ'ventjʊəlɪ/ *adv* alla fine; **~!** finalmente!

ever /'evə(r)/ *adv* mai; **I haven't ~...** non ho mai...; **for ~** per sempre; **hardly ~** quasi mai; **~ since** da quando; (*since that time*) da allora; **~ so** *fam* veramente

evergreen /'evəgri:n/ *n* sempreverde *m*

everlasting /evə'læstɪŋ/ *a* eterno

every /'evrɪ/ *a* ogni; **~ one** ciascuno; **~ other day** un giorno si un giorno no

everybody /'evrɪbɒdɪ/ *pron* tutti *pl*

everyday /'evrɪdeɪ/ *a* quotidiano, di ogni giorno

everyone /'evrɪwʌn/ *pron* tutti *pl*; **~ else** tutti gli altri

everyplace /'evrɪpleɪs/ *adv Am fam* = **everywhere**

everything /'evrɪθɪŋ/ *pron* tutto; **~ else** tutto il resto

everywhere /'evrɪweə(r)/ *adv* dappertutto; (*wherever*) dovunque

evict /ɪ'vɪkt/ *vt* sfrattare

eviction /ɪ'vɪkʃn/ *n* sfratto *m*

evidence /'evɪdəns/ *n* evidenza *f*; *Jur* testimonianza *f*; **give ~** testimoniare

evident /'evɪdənt/ *a* evidente

evidently /'evɪdəntlɪ/ *adv* evidentemente

evil /'i:vl/ *a* cattivo ● *n* male *m*

evil-smelling /-'smelɪŋ/ *a* puzzolente

evocative /ɪ'vɒkətɪv/ *a* evocativo; **be ~ of** evocare

evoke /ɪ'vəʊk/ *vt* evocare

evolution /i:və'lu:ʃn/ *n* evoluzione *f*

evolutionary /i:və'lu:ʃ(ə)rɪ/ *a* evolutivo

evolve /ɪ'vɒlv/ *vt* evolvere ● *vi* evolversi

ewe /ju:/ *n* pecora *f*

ex /eks/ *n* (*fam: former partner*) ex *mf*

ex+ *pref* ex+

exacerbate /ɪg'sæsəbeɪt/ *vt* esacerbare ⟨*situation*⟩

exact /ɪg'zækt/ *a* esatto ● *vt* esigere

exacting /ɪg'zæktɪŋ/ *a* esigente

exactitude /ɪg'zæktɪtju:d/ *n* esattezza *f*

exactly /ɪg'zæktlɪ/ *adv* esattamente; **not ~** non proprio

exactness /ɪg'zæktnɪs/ *n* precisione *f*

exaggerate /ɪg'zædʒəreɪt/ *vt/i* esagerare

exaggerated /ɪg'zædʒəreɪtɪd/ *a* esagerato; **he has an ~ sense of his own importance** si crede chissà chi

exaggeration /ɪgzædʒə'reɪʃn/ *n* esagerazione *f*

exalt /ɪg'zɔ:lt/ *vt* elevare; (*praise*) vantare

exam /ɪg'zæm/ *n* esame *m*

examination /ɪgzæmɪ'neɪʃn/ *n* esame *m*; (*of patient*) visita *f*; (*of wreckage*) ispezione *f*

examination paper *n* testo *m* d'esame

examine /ɪg'zæmɪn/ *vt* esaminare; visitare ⟨*patient*⟩

examinee /ɪgzæmɪ'ni:/ *n* esaminando *m*

examiner /ɪg'zæmɪnə(r)/ *n Sch* esaminatore, -trice *mf*

example /ɪg'zɑ:mpl/ *n* esempio *m*; **for ~** per esempio; **make an ~ of sb** punire qcno per dare un esempio; **be an ~ to sb** dare il buon esempio a qcno

exasperate /ɪg'zæspəreɪt/ *vt* esasperare

exasperation /ɪgzæspə'reɪʃn/ *n* esasperazione *f*

excavate /'ekskəveɪt/ *vt* scavare; *Archaeol* fare gli scavi di

excavation /ekskə'veɪʃn/ *n* scavo *m*

excavator /'ekskəveɪtə(r)/ *n* (*machine*) escavatrice *f*, escavatore *m*

exceed /ɪk'si:d/ *vt* eccedere

exceedingly /ɪk'si:dɪŋlɪ/ *adv* estremamente

excel /ɪk'sel/ *v* (*pt/pp* **excelled**) ● *vi* eccellere ● *vt* **~ oneself** superare se stessi

excellence /'eksələns/ *n* eccellenza *f*

Excellency /'eksələnsɪ/ *n* (*title*) Eccellenza *f*

excellent /'eksələnt/ *a* eccellente

excellently /'eksələntlɪ/ *adv* in modo eccellente

except /ɪk'sept/ *prep* eccetto, tranne; **~ for** eccetto, tranne; **~ that...** eccetto che... ● *vt* eccettuare

excepting /ɪk'septɪŋ/ *prep* eccetto, tranne

exception /ɪk'sepʃn/ *n* eccezione *f*; **take ~ to** fare obiezioni a

exceptional /ɪk'sepʃənəl/ *a* eccezionale

exceptionally /ɪk'sepʃənəlɪ/ *adv* eccezionalmente

excerpt /'eksɜ:pt/ *n* estratto *m*

excess /ɪk'ses/ *n* eccesso *m*; **in ~ of** oltre

excess baggage *n* bagaglio *m* eccedente

excess fare *n* supplemento *m*

excessive /ɪk'sesɪv/ *a* eccessivo

excessively /ɪk'sesɪvlɪ/ *adv* eccessivamente

excess postage *n* soprattassa *f* postale

excess profits *npl* sovraprofitto *m*

exchange /ɪks'tʃeɪndʒ/ n scambio m; Teleph centrale f; Comm cambio m; [**stock**] ~ borsa f valori; **in** ~ in cambio (**for** di) ● vt scambiare (**for** con); cambiare ⟨money⟩; ~ **views** scambiarsi i punti di vista; ~ **contracts** fare il rogito

exchange: exchange control n controllo m dei cambi. **exchange controls** npl misure fpl di controllo dei cambi. **exchange rate** n tasso m di cambio. **Exchange Rate Mechanism** n meccanismo m di cambio dello Sme.

exchequer /ɪks'tʃekə(r)/ n Pol tesoro m
excise¹ /'eksaɪz/ n dazio m
excise² /ek'saɪz/ vt recidere
excise duty n dazio m
excitable /ɪk'saɪtəbl/ a eccitabile
excite /ɪk'saɪt/ vt eccitare
excited /ɪk'saɪtɪd/ a eccitato; **get** ~ eccitarsi
excitedly /ɪk'saɪtɪdlɪ/ adv tutto eccitato
excitement /ɪk'saɪtmənt/ n eccitazione f
exciting /ɪk'saɪtɪŋ/ a eccitante; ⟨story, film⟩ appassionante; ⟨holiday⟩ entusiasmante
excl abbr **excluding**
exclaim /ɪk'skleɪm/ vt/i esclamare
exclamation /eksklə'meɪʃn/ n esclamazione f
exclamation mark n, Am **exclamation point** n punto m esclamativo
exclude /ɪk'sklu:d/ vt escludere
excluding /ɪk'sklu:dɪŋ/ pron escluso
exclusion /ɪk'sklu:ʒn/ n esclusione f
exclusion zone n zona f proibita
exclusive /ɪk'sklu:sɪv/ a ⟨rights, club⟩ esclusivo; ⟨interview⟩ in esclusiva; ~ **of...** ...escluso
exclusively /ɪk'sklu:sɪvlɪ/ adv esclusivamente
excommunicate /ekskə'mju:nɪkeɪt/ vt scomunicare
excrement /'ekskrɪmənt/ n escremento m
excreta /ɪk'skri:tə/ npl escrementi mpl
excrete /ɪk'skri:t/ vt espellere; secernere ⟨liquid⟩
excretion /ɪk'skri:ʃn/ n (of animal, human) escremento m
excruciating /ɪk'skru:ʃieɪtɪŋ/ a atroce ⟨pain⟩; (fam: very bad) spaventoso
excursion /ɪk'skɜ:ʃn/ n escursione f
excusable /ɪk'skju:zəbl/ a perdonabile
excuse¹ /ɪk'skju:s/ n scusa f
excuse² /ɪk'skju:z/ vt scusare; ~ **from** esonerare da; ~ **me!** (to get attention) scusi!; (to get past) permesso!, scusi!; (indignant) come ha detto?
ex-directory a be ~ non figurare sull'elenco telefonico
exec /ɪg'zek/ n Am abbr fam **executive**
execrable /'eksɪkrəbl/ a esecrabile
executable file /'eksɪkju:təbl/ n Comput eseguibile m
execute /'eksɪkju:t/ vt eseguire; (put to death) giustiziare; attuare ⟨plan⟩
execution /eksɪ'kju:ʃn/ n esecuzione f; (of plan) attuazione f

executioner /eksɪ'kju:ʃənə(r)/ n boia m inv
executive /ɪg'zekjʊtɪv/ a esecutivo ● n dirigente mf; Pol esecutivo m
executive: executive committee n comitato m esecutivo. **executive director** n direttore, -trice mf [esecutivo, -a]. **executive jet** n jet m inv privato. **executive producer** n Cinema direttore, -trice mf di produzione. **executive secretary** n segretario, -a mf di direzione
executor /ɪg'zekjʊtə(r)/ n Jur esecutore, -trice mf
exemplary /ɪg'zemplərɪ/ a esemplare
exemplify /ɪg'zemplɪfaɪ/ vt (pt/pp -ied) esemplificare
exempt /ɪg'zempt/ a esente ● vt esentare (**from** da)
exemption /ɪg'zempʃn/ n esenzione f
exercise /'eksəsaɪz/ n esercizio m; Mil esercitazione f; **physical** ~**s** ginnastica f; **take** ~ fare del moto; **you need more** ~ devi muoverti di più ● vt esercitare ⟨muscles, horse⟩; portare a spasso ⟨dog⟩; usare ⟨patience⟩; mettere in pratica ⟨skills⟩ ● vi esercitarsi; ~ **more** fare più moto
exercise bike n cyclette[R] f inv
exercise book n quaderno m
exert /ɪg'zɜ:t/ vt esercitare; ~ **oneself** sforzarsi
exertion /ɪg'zɜ:ʃn/ n sforzo m
ex gratia /eks'greɪʃə/ a ⟨award, payment⟩ a titolo di favore
exhale /eks'heɪl/ vt/i esalare
exhaust /ɪg'zɔ:st/ n Auto scappamento m; (pipe) tubo m di scappamento
exhausted /ɪg'zɔ:stɪd/ a esausto
exhaust fumes npl fumi mpl di scarico m ● vt esaurire
exhausting /ɪg'zɔ:stɪŋ/ a estenuante; ⟨climate, person⟩ sfibrante
exhaustion /ɪg'zɔ:stʃn/ n esaurimento m
exhaustive /ɪg'zɔ:stɪv/ a fig esauriente
exhibit /ɪg'zɪbɪt/ n oggetto m esposto; Jur reperto m ● vt esporre; fig dimostrare
exhibition /eksɪ'bɪʃn/ n mostra f; (of strength, skill) dimostrazione f
exhibition centre n palazzo m delle esposizioni
exhibitionist /eksɪ'bɪʃənɪst/ n esibizionista mf
exhibitor /ɪg'zɪbɪtə(r)/ n espositore, -trice mf
exhilarated /ɪg'zɪləreɪtɪd/ a rallegrato
exhilarating /ɪg'zɪləreɪtɪŋ/ a stimolante; ⟨mountain air⟩ tonificante
exhilaration /ɪgzɪlə'reɪʃn/ n allegria f
exhort /ɪg'zɔ:t/ vt esortare
exhume /ɪg'zju:m/ vt esumare
exile /'eksaɪl/ n esilio m; (person) esule mf ● vt esiliare
exist /ɪg'zɪst/ vi esistere
existence /ɪg'zɪstəns/ n esistenza f; **in** ~ esistente; **be in** ~ esistere
existential /egzɪ'stenʃ(ə)l/ a esistenziale
existentialism /egzɪ'stenʃəlɪzm/ n esistenzialismo m

existing /ɪg'zɪstɪŋ/ *a* ⟨*policy, management, leadership*⟩ attuale; ⟨*laws, order*⟩ vigente

exit /'eksɪt/ *n* uscita *f*; *Theat* uscita *f* di scena ● *vi Theat* uscire di scena; *Comput* uscire (**from** da)

exit sign *n* cartello *m* di uscita

exodus /'eksədəs/ *n* esodo *m*

ex officio /eksə'fɪʃɪəʊ/ *a* ⟨*member*⟩ di diritto

exonerate /ɪg'zɒnəreɪt/ *vt* esonerare

exorbitant /ɪg'zɔːbɪtənt/ *a* esorbitante

exorcism /'eksɔːsɪzm/ *n* esorcismo *m*

exorcist /'eksɔːsɪst/ *n* esorcista *mf*

exorcize /'eksɔːsaɪz/ *vt* esorcizzare

exotic /ɪg'zɒtɪk/ *a* esotico

exotica /ɪg'zɒtɪkə/ *npl* oggetti *mpl* esotici

expand /ɪk'spænd/ *vt* espandere; sviluppare ⟨*economy*⟩ ● *vi* espandersi; *Comm* svilupparsi; ⟨*metal:*⟩ dilatarsi

■ **expand on** *vt* (*explain better*) approfondire

expandable /ɪk'spændəbl/ *a* ⟨*Comput: memory*⟩ espandibile

expanding /ɪk'spændɪŋ/ *a* ⟨*file*⟩ a soffietto *inv*; ⟨*population, sector*⟩ in espansione; ⟨*bracelet*⟩ allungabile

expanse /ɪk'spæns/ *n* estensione *f*

expansion /ɪk'spænʃn/ *n* espansione *f*; *Comm* sviluppo *m*; (*of metal*) dilatazione *f*

expansion board, expansion card *n* *Comput* scheda *f* di espansione

expansionist /ɪk'spænʃənɪst/ *n & a* espansionista *mf*

expansion slot *n* *Comput* fessura *f* [per la scheda] di espansione, slot *m* di espansione

expansive /ɪk'spænsɪv/ *a* espansivo

expatriate /eks'pætrɪət/ *n* espatriato, -a *mf*

expect /ɪk'spekt/ *vt* aspettare ⟨*letter, baby*⟩; (*suppose*) pensare; (*demand*) esigere; **I ~ so** penso di sì; **we ~ to arrive on Monday** contiamo di arrivare lunedì; **I didn't ~ that** questo non me lo aspettavo; **she ~s too much from him** pretende troppo da lui; **be ~ing** essere in stato interessante

expectancy /ɪk'spektənsɪ/ *n* aspettativa *f*

expectant /ɪk'spektənt/ *a* in attesa; **~ mother** donna *f* incinta

expectantly /ɪk'spektəntlɪ/ *adv* con impazienza

expectation /ekspek'teɪʃn/ *n* aspettativa *f*, speranza *f*

expediency /ɪk'spiːdɪənsɪ/ *n* (*appropriateness*) opportunità *f*; (*self-interest*) opportunismo *m*

expedient /ɪk'spiːdɪənt/ *a* conveniente ● *n* espediente *m*

expedite /'ekspɪdaɪt/ *vt fml* accelerare

expedition /ekspɪ'dɪʃn/ *n* spedizione *f*

expeditionary /ekspɪ'dɪʃənərɪ/ *a* *Mil* di spedizione

expeditionary force *n* corpo *m* di spedizione

expel /ɪk'spel/ *vt* (*pt/pp* **expelled**) espellere

expend /ɪk'spend/ *vt* consumare

expendable /ɪk'spendəbl/ *a* sacrificabile

expenditure /ɪk'spendɪtʃə(r)/ *n* spesa *f*

expense /ɪk'spens/ *n* spesa *f*; **business ~s** *pl* spese *fpl*; **at my ~** a mie spese; **at the ~ of** *fig* a spese di

expense account *n* conto *m* spese

expensive /ɪk'spensɪv/ *a* caro, costoso

expensively /ɪk'spensɪvlɪ/ *adv* costosamente

experience /ɪk'spɪərɪəns/ *n* esperienza *f* ● *vt* provare ⟨*sensation*⟩; avere ⟨*problem*⟩

experienced /ɪk'spɪərɪənst/ *a* esperto

experiment /ɪk'sperɪmənt/ *n* esperimento *m* ● /ɪk'sperɪment/ *vi* sperimentare

experimental /ɪksperɪ'mentl/ *a* sperimentale

experimentation /ɪksperɪmen'teɪʃn/ *n* sperimentazione *f*; **~ with drugs** esperienza *f* della droga

expert /'ekspɜːt/ *n* & *n* esperto, -a *mf*

expertise /ekspɜː'tiːz/ *n* competenza *f*

expertly /'ekspɜːtlɪ/ *adv* abilmente

expiate /'ekspɪeɪt/ *vt* espiare ⟨*crime, sin*⟩; fare ammenda per ⟨*guilt*⟩

expiration /ekspɪ'reɪʃn/ *n* (*end, exhalation*) espirazione *f*

expire /ɪk'spaɪə(r)/ *vi* scadere

expiry /ɪk'spaɪərɪ/ *n* scadenza *f*

expiry date *n* data *f* di scadenza

explain /ɪk'spleɪn/ *vt* spiegare

■ **explain away** *vt* (*give reasons for*) trovare delle giustificazioni per

explanation /eksplə'neɪʃn/ *n* spiegazione *f*

explanatory /ɪk'splænətərɪ/ *a* esplicativo

expletive /ɪk'spliːtɪv/ *n* imprecazione *f*

explicit /ɪk'splɪsɪt/ *a* esplicito

explicitly /ɪk'splɪsɪtlɪ/ *adv* esplicitamente

explode /ɪk'spləʊd/ *vi* esplodere ● *vt* fare esplodere

exploit¹ /'eksplɔɪt/ *n* impresa *f*

exploit² /ɪk'splɔɪt/ *vt* sfruttare

exploitation /eksplɔɪ'teɪʃn/ *n* sfruttamento *m*

exploitative /ɪk'splɔɪtətɪv/ *a* inteso a sfruttare gli individui; ⟨*attitude, system*⟩ a carattere di sfruttamento

exploration /eksplə'reɪʃn/ *n* esplorazione *f*

exploratory /ɪk'splɒrətərɪ/ *a* esplorativo

explore /ɪk'splɔː(r)/ *vt* esplorare; *fig* studiare ⟨*implications*⟩

explorer /ɪk'splɔːrə(r)/ *n* esploratore, -trice *mf*

explosion /ɪk'spləʊʒn/ *n* esplosione *f*

explosive /ɪk'spləʊsɪv/ *a & n* esplosivo *m*

exponent /ɪk'spəʊnənt/ *n* esponente *mf*

exponential /ekspə'nenʃəl/ *a* esponenziale

export¹ /'ekspɔːt/ *n* esportazione *f*

export² /ek'spɔːt/ *vt* esportare

export: **export agent** *n* esportatore, -trice *mf*. **export control** *n* controllo *m* delle esportazioni. **export credit** *n* credito *m* all'esportazione. **export drive** *n* campagna *f* di esportazione. **export duty** *n* tassa *f* di esportazione. **export earnings** *npl* ricavato *m* delle esportazioni

exporter /ek'spɔ:tə(r)/ *n* esportatore, -trice *mf*

export: export finance *n* finanziamento *m* delle esportazioni. **export-import company** *n* azienda di import-export. **export licence** *n* licenza *f* di esportazione. **export market** *n* mercato *m* delle esportazioni. **export trade** *n* commercio *m* di esportazione

expose /ɪk'spəʊz/ *vt* esporre; (*reveal*) svelare; smascherare ‹*traitor etc*›

exposée /ɪk'spəʊzeɪ/ *n* (*of scandal*) rivelazioni *fpl*

exposition /ekspə'zɪʃn/ *n* (*of facts*) esposizione *f*

exposure /ɪk'spəʊʒə(r)/ *n* esposizione *f*; *Med* espozione *f* prolungata al freddo/caldo; (*of crimes*) smascheramento *m*; **24 ~s** *Phot* 24 pose

exposure meter *n Phot* esposimetro *m*

exposure time *n Phot* tempo *m* di esposizione

expound /ɪk'spaʊnd/ *vt* esporre

express /ɪk'spres/ *a* espresso ● *adv* ‹*send*› per espresso ● *n* (*train*) espresso *m* ● *vt* esprimere; **~ oneself** esprimersi

expression /ɪk'spreʃn/ *n* espressione *f*

expressionless /ɪk'spreʃənlɪs/ *a* ‹*tone, voice*› distaccato; ‹*playing*› piatto; ‹*eyes, face*› inespressivo

expressive /ɪk'spresɪv/ *a* espressivo

expressively /ɪk'spresɪvlɪ/ *adv* espressamente

expulsion /ɪk'spʌlʃn/ *n* espulsione *f*

expurgate /'ekspəgeɪt/ *vt* espurgare

exquisite /ek'skwɪzɪt/ *a* squisito

exquisitely /ek'skwɪzɪtlɪ/ *adv* ‹*dressed, written*› in modo elegante e raffinato; **~ beautiful** di una bellezza fine

ex-serviceman /'sɜ:vɪsmən/ *n* ex-combattente *m*

ex-servicewoman /'sɜ:vɪswʊmən/ *n* ex-combattente *f*

extant /ɪk'stænt/ *a* ancora esistente

extempore /ɪk'stempərɪ/ *adv* ‹*speak*› senza preparazione

extend /ɪk'stend/ *vt* prolungare ‹*visit, road*›; prorogare ‹*visa, contract*›; ampliare ‹*building, knowledge*›; (*stretch out*) allungare; tendere ‹*hand*› ● *vi* ‹*garden, knowledge:*› estendersi

extendable /ɪk'stendəbl/ *a* ‹*cable*› allungabile; ‹*contract*› prorogabile

extension /ɪk'stenʃn/ *n*) prolungamento *m*; (*of visa, contract*) proroga *f*; (*of treaty*) ampliamento *m*; (*part of building*) annesso *m*; (*length of cable*) prolunga *f*; *Teleph* interno *m*; **~ 226** interno 226

extension ladder *n* scala *f* allungabile

extension lead *n Electr* prolunga *f*

extensive /ɪk'stensɪv/ *a* ampio, vasto

extensively /ɪk'stensɪvlɪ/ *adv* ampiamente

extent /ɪk'stent/ *n* (*scope*) portata *f*; **to a certain ~** fino a un certo punto; **to such an ~ that...** fino al punto che...

extenuating /ɪk'stenjʊeɪtɪŋ/ *a* **~ circumstances** attenuanti *fpl*

exterior /ɪk'stɪərɪə(r)/ *a* & *n* esterno *m*

exterminate /ɪk'stɜ:mɪneɪt/ *vt* sterminare

extermination /ɪkstɜ:mɪ'neɪʃn/ *n* sterminio *m*

external /ɪk'stɜ:nl/ *a* esterno *m*; **for ~ use only** *Med* per uso esterno

externalize /ɪk'stɜ:nəlaɪz/ *vt* esteriorizzare

externally /ɪk'stɜ:nəlɪ/ *adv* esternamente

externals /ɪk'stɜ:n(ə)lz/ *npl* apparenze *fpl*

extinct /ɪk'stɪŋkt/ *a* estinto

extinction /ɪk'stɪŋkʃn/ *n* estinzione *f*

extinguish /ɪk'stɪŋgwɪʃ/ *vt* estinguere

extinguisher /ɪk'stɪŋgwɪʃə(r)/ *n* estintore *m*

extol /ɪk'stəʊl/ *vt* (*pt/pp* **extolled**) lodare

extort /ɪk'stɔ:t/ *vt* estorcere

extortion /ɪk'stɔ:ʃn/ *n* estorsione *f*

extortionate /ɪk'stɔ:ʃənət/ *a* esorbitante

extra /'ekstrə/ *a* in più; ‹*train*› straordinario; **an ~ £10** 10 sterline extra, 10 sterline in più ● *adv* in più; (*especially*) più; **pay ~** pagare in più, pagare extra; **~ strong/busy** fortissimo/occupatissimo ● *n Theat* comparsa *f*; **~s** *pl* extra *mpl*

extra charge *n* supplemento *m*; **at no ~ ~** senza ulteriori spese

extract¹ /'ekstrækt/ *n* estratto *m*

extract² /ɪk'strækt/ *vt* estrarre ‹*tooth, oil*›; strappare ‹*secret*›; ricavare ‹*truth*›

extraction /ɪk'strækʃn/ *n* (*process*) estrazione *f*; **of French ~** di origine francese

extractor [fan] /ɪk'stræktə(r)/ *n* aspiratore *m*

extra-curricular /-kə'rɪkjʊlə(r)/ *a* extrascolastico

extradite /'ekstrədaɪt/ *vt Jur* estradare

extradition /ekstrə'dɪʃn/ *n* estradizione *f*

extra-dry *a* ‹*sherry, wine*› extra dry *inv*

extra-fast *a* ultrarapido

extra-large *a* ‹*pullover, shirt*› extra large *inv*

extramarital /ekstrə'mærɪtəl/ *a* extraconiugale

extramural /ekstrə'mjʊərəl/ *a Br Univ* ‹*course, lecture*› organizzato dall'università e aperto a tutti

extraneous /ɪk'streɪnɪəs/ *a* (*not essential*) inessenziale; ‹*issue, detail*› superfluo

extraordinarily /ɪk'strɔ:dɪnərɪlɪ/ *adv* straordinariamente

extraordinary /ɪk'strɔ:dɪnərɪ/ *a* straordinario

extrapolate /ɪk'stræpəleɪt/ *vt* arguire; *Math* estrapolare

extrasensory perception /ekstrə-'sensərɪ/ *n* percezione *f* extrasensoriale

extra-special *a* eccezionale

extra-strong *a* ‹*thread*› robustissimo; ‹*coffee*› fortissimo; ‹*disinfectant, weed killer*› potentissimo; ‹*paper*› ultraresistente *inv*

extraterrestrial /ekstrətɪ'restrɪəl/ *n* & *a* extraterrestre *mf*

extra time n tempo m supplementare; **play ~ ~** giocare i tempi supplementari

extravagance /ɪk'strævəgəns/ n (with money) prodigalità f; (of behaviour) stravaganza f

extravagant /ɪk'strævəgənt/ a spendaccione; (bizarre) stravagante; ‹claim› esagerato

extravagantly /ɪk'strævəgəntlɪ/ adv dispendiosamente

extravaganza /ɪkstrævə'gænzə/ n rappresentazione f spettacolare

extreme /ɪk'stri:m/ a estremo ● n estremo m; **in the ~** al massimo

extremely /ɪk'stri:mlɪ/ adv estremamente

extremism /ɪk'stri:mɪzm/ n estremismo m

extremist /ɪk'stri:mɪst/ n estremista mf

extremity /ɪk'stremətɪ/ n (end) estremità f inv

extricate /'ekstrɪkeɪt/ vt districare

extrovert /'ekstrəvɜ:t/ n estroverso, -a mf

exuberance /ɪg'zju:bərəns/ n esuberanza f

exuberant /ɪg'zju:bərənt/ a esuberante

exude /ɪg'zju:d/ vt also fig trasudare

exult /ɪg'zʌlt/ vi esultare

exultant /ɪg'zʌltənt/ a esultante; ‹cry› di esultanza

exultantly /ɪg'zʌltəntlɪ/ adv con esultanza

ex-works a ‹price, value› franco fabbrica

eye /aɪ/ n occhio m; (of needle) cruna f; **keep an ~ on** tener d'occhio; **see ~ to ~** aver le stesse idee ● vt (pt/pp eyed, pres p ey[e]ing) guardare

■ **eye up** vt adocchiare ‹sb›

eye: eyeball n bulbo m oculare. **eyebath** n bagno m oculare. **eyebrow** n sopracciglio m (pl sopracciglia f). **eyebrow pencil** n matita f per le sopracciglia. **eye-catching** /'aɪkætʃɪŋ/ a che attira l'attenzione. **eye contact** n avoid ~ ~ with sb evitare di incrociare lo sguardo di qcno; **try to make ~ ~ with sb** tentare di incrociare lo sguardo di qcno. **eyedrops** npl collirio m

eyeful /'aɪfʊl/ n get an ~ (of sth) avere gli occhi pieni (di qcsa); (fam: good look) lustrarsi la vista

eye: eyeglass n (monocle) monocolo m. **eyeglasses** npl Am occhiali mpl [da vista]. **eyelash** n ciglio m (pl ciglia f).

eyelet /'aɪlɪt/ n occhiello m

eye: eye-level a ‹grill, shelf› all'altezza degli occhi. **eyelid** n palpebra f. **eye make-up** n trucco m per gli occhi. **eye-opener** n rivelazione f. **eyepatch** n benda f per gli occhi. **eye-shade** n visiera f. **eyeshadow** n ombretto m. **eyesight** n vista f. **eyesore** n fam pugno m nell'occhio. **eye strain** n affaticamento m degli occhi. **eye test** n esame m della vista. **eyewash** n bagno m oculare; (fig: nonsense) fumo m negli occhi. **eyewitness** n testimone mf oculare

eyrie /'ɪərɪ/ n nido m d'aquila

....

Ff

....

f, F /ef/ n (letter) f, F f inv; Mus fa m inv

FA n Br abbr (Football Association) associazione f calcistica britannica, ≈ FIGC f

fable /'feɪbl/ n favola f

fabric /'fæbrɪk/ n also fig tessuto m

fabricate /'fæbrɪkeɪt/ vt fabbricare; inventare ‹story›

fabrication /fæbrɪ'keɪʃn/ n invenzione f; (manufacture) fabbricazione f

fabric softener /sɒfnə(r)/ n ammorbidente m

fabulous /'fæbjʊləs/ a fam favoloso

façade /fə'sɑ:d/ n (of building, person) facciata f

face /feɪs/ n faccia f, viso m; (grimace) smorfia f; (surface) faccia f; (of clock) quadrante m; **pull ~s** far boccacce; **in the ~ of** di fronte a; **on the ~ of it** in apparenza ● vt essere di fronta a; (confront) affrontare; **~ north** ‹house:› dare a nord; **~ the fact that** arrendersi al fatto che

■ **face up to** vt accettare ‹facts›; affrontare ‹person›

face flannel n ≈ guanto m di spugna

faceless /'feɪslɪs/ a anonimo

facelift /'feɪslɪft/ n plastica f facciale

face powder n cipria f

facet /'fæsɪt/ n sfaccettatura f; fig aspetto m

facetious /fə'si:ʃəs/ a spiritoso. **~ remarks** spiritosaggini mpl

face: face pack n maschera f di bellezza. **face saving** a ‹plan, solution› per salvare la faccia. **face to face** a ‹meeting› a quattr'occhi ● adv ‹be seated› faccia a faccia; **meet sb ~ to ~** avere un incontro a quattr'occhi con qcno; **come ~ to ~ with** trovarsi di fronte a. **face value** n (of money) valore m nominale; **take sb/sth at ~ ~** fermarsi alle apparenze

facial /'feɪʃl/ a facciale ● n trattamento m di bellezza al viso

facile /'fæsaɪl/ a semplicistico

facilitate /fə'sɪlɪteɪt/ vt rendere possibile; (make easier) facilitare

facility /fə'sɪlətɪ/ n facilità f; **facilities** pl (of area, in hotel etc) attrezzature fpl; **credit facilities** pl facilitazioni fpl di pagamento

facing /'feɪsɪŋ/ prep ~ **the sea** ‹house› che

125

dà sul mare; **the person ~ me** la persona di fronte a me

facsimile /fæk'sɪməlɪ/ n facsimile m

fact /fækt/ n fatto m; **in ~** infatti

fact finding a ⟨mission, tour, trip⟩ di inchiesta

faction /'fækʃn/ n fazione f

factional /'fækʃnəl/ a ⟨leader, activity⟩ di una fazione; ⟨fighting, arguments⟩ tra fazioni

factor /'fæktə(r)/ n fattore m

factory /'fæktərɪ/ n fabbrica f

factory: factory farming n allevamento m su scala industriale. **factory floor** n (place) reparto m produzione; (workers) operai mpl. **factory inspector** n verificatore, -trice mf. **factory made** a prodotto in fabbrica. **factory unit** n unità f inv di produzione. **factory worker** n operaio, -a mf

fact sheet n (one issue) prospetto m illustrativo; (periodical) bollettino m d'informazione

factual /'fæktʃʊəl/ a **be ~** attenersi ai fatti

factually /'fæktʃʊəlɪ/ adv ⟨inaccurate⟩ dal punto di vista dei fatti

faculty /'fækəltɪ/ n facoltà f inv

fad /fæd/ n capriccio m

faddish /'fædɪʃ/ a ⟨person⟩ sempre in preda a una nuova mania

fade /feɪd/ vi sbiadire; ⟨sound, light:⟩ affievolirsi; ⟨flower:⟩ appassire

■ **fade in** vt cominciare in dissolvenza ⟨picture⟩

■ **fade out** vt finire in dissolvenza ⟨picture⟩

faded /'feɪdɪd/ a ⟨clothing, carpet, colour⟩ sbiadito; ⟨flower, beauty⟩ appassito; ⟨glory⟩ svanito

faeces /'fi:si:z/ npl feci fpl

fag /fæg/ n (chore) fatica f; (fam: cigarette) sigaretta f; (Am sl: homosexual) frocio m

fag end n fam mozzicone m di sigaretta, cicca f; (of day, decade, conversation) fine f; (of material) scampolo m

fagged /fægd/ a **~ out** fam stanco morto

faggot /'fægət/ n (meatball) polpetta f di carne; (firewood) fascina f

Fahrenheit /'færənhaɪt/ a Fahrenheit

fail /feɪl/ n **without ~** senz'altro ● vi ⟨attempt:⟩ fallire; ⟨eyesight, memory:⟩ indebolirsi; ⟨engine, machine:⟩ guastarsi; ⟨marriage:⟩ andare a rotoli; (in exam) essere bocciato; **~ to do sth** non fare qcsa; **I tried but I ~ed** ho provato ma non ci sono riuscito; **a ~ed politician** un politico fallito ● vt non superare ⟨exam⟩; bocciare ⟨candidate⟩; (disappoint) deludere; **words ~ me** mi mancano le parole; **unless my memory ~s me** se la memoria non mi tradisce

failing /'feɪlɪŋ/ n difetto m ● prep **~ that** altrimenti

fail-safe a ⟨device, system⟩ di sicurezza

failure /'feɪljə(r)/ n fallimento m; (mechanical) guasto m; (person) incapace mf

faint /feɪnt/ a leggero; ⟨memory⟩ vago; **feel ~** sentirsi mancare ● n svenimento m ● vi svenire

faint-hearted /-'hɑːtɪd/ a timido

fainting fit /'feɪntɪŋ/ n svenimento m

faintly /'feɪntlɪ/ adv ⟨slightly⟩ leggermente

faintness /'feɪntnɪs/ n (physical) debolezza f

fair¹ /feə(r)/ n fiera f

fair² a ⟨hair, person⟩ biondo; ⟨skin⟩ chiaro; ⟨weather⟩ bello; (just) giusto; (quite good) discreto; Sch abbastanza bene; **a ~ amount** abbastanza ● adv **play ~** fare un gioco pulito

fair copy n bella copia f

fairground /'feəgraʊnd/ n luna park m inv

fairly /'feəlɪ/ adv con giustizia; (rather) discretamente, abbastanza

fair-minded /feə'maɪndɪd/ a equo

fairness /'feənɪs/ n giustizia f

fair: fair play n fair play m inv. **fair skinned** /-'skɪnd/ a di carnagione chiara. **fairway** n Naut via f d'acqua navigabile; (in golf) fairway m inv. **fair weather friend** n pej amico m finché tutto va bene

fairy /'feərɪ/ n fata f; **good ~** fata [buona]; **wicked ~** strega f

fairy: fairy godmother n fata f buona. **fairy lights** npl Br lampadine fpl colorate. **fairy story, fairy-tale** n fiaba f

faith /feɪθ/ n fede f; (trust) fiducia f; **in good/bad ~** in buona/mala fede

faithful /'feɪθfl/ a fedele

faithfully /'feɪθfʊlɪ/ adv fedelmente; **yours ~** distinti saluti

faithfulness /'feɪθfʊlnɪs/ n fedeltà f

faith-healer /hi:lə(r)/ n guaritore, -trice mf

faithless /'feɪθlɪs/ a ⟨friend, servant⟩ sleale; ⟨husband⟩ infedele

fake /feɪk/ a falso ● n falsificazione f; (person) impostore m ● vt falsificare; (pretend) fingere

falcon /'fɔːlkən/ n falcone m

Falklands /'fɔːlkləndz/ npl le isole Falkland, le isole Malvine

fall /fɔːl/ n caduta f; (in prices) ribasso m; (Am: autumn) autunno m; **have a ~** fare una caduta ● vi (pt fell, pp fallen) cadere; ⟨night:⟩ scendere; **~ in love** innamorarsi

■ **fall about** vi (with laughter) morire dal ridere

■ **fall back on** vt ritornare su

■ **fall down** vi cadere; ⟨building:⟩ crollare

■ **fall for** vt fam innamorarsi di ⟨person⟩; cascarci ⟨sth, trick⟩

■ **fall in** vi caderci dentro; (collapse) crollare; Mil mettersi in riga; **~ in with** concordare con ⟨suggestion, plan⟩

■ **fall off** vi cadere; (diminish) diminuire

■ **fall out** vi (quarrel) litigare; **his hair is ~ing out** perde i capelli

■ **fall over** vi cadere

■ **fall through** vi ⟨plan:⟩ andare a monte

fallacious /fə'leɪʃəs/ a fallace

fallacy /'fæləsɪ/ n errore m

fallible /'fæləbl/ a fallibile

Fallopian tube /fə'ləʊpɪən/ n tromba f di Falloppio

fallout /'fɔːlaʊt/ n pioggia f radioattiva

fallout shelter n rifugio m antiatomico

fallow /'fæləʊ/ *a* lie ~ essere a maggese

false /fɔːls/ *a* falso

false bottom *n* doppio fondo *m*

falsehood /'fɔːlshʊd/ *n* menzogna *f*

falsely /'fɔːlslɪ/ *adv* falsamente

falseness /'fɔːlsnɪs/ *n* falsità *f*

false: false pretences *npl* **under ~ ~** sotto false spoglie; *Jur* con la frode. **false start** *n Sport* falsa partenza *f*. **false teeth** *npl* dentiera *f*

falsetto /fɔːl'setəʊ/ *n* (*voice*) falsetto *m inv* ● *a* in falsetto

falsification /fɔːlsɪfɪ'keɪʃn/ *n* (*of document, figures*) falsificazione *f*; (*of truth, facts*) deformazione *f*

falsify /'fɔːlsɪfaɪ/ *vt* (*pt/pp* **-ied**) falsificare

falsity /'fɔːlsətɪ/ *n* falsità *f*

falter /'fɔːltə(r)/ *vi* vacillare; (*making speech*) esitare

fame /feɪm/ *n* fama *f*

famed /feɪmd/ *a* rinomato

familiar /fə'mɪljə(r)/ *a* familiare; **be ~ with** (*know*) conoscere; **become too ~** prendersi troppo confidenze

familiarity /fəmɪlɪ'ærətɪ/ *n* familiarità *f*

familiarize /fə'mɪliəraɪz/ *vt* familiarizzare; **~ oneself with sth** familiarizzarsi con qcsa

family /'fæməlɪ/ *n* famiglia *f*

family: family allowance *n* assegni *mpl* familiari. **family circle** *n* (*group*) cerchia *f* familiare; *Am Theat* seconda galleria *f*. **family doctor** *n* medico *m* di famiglia. **family life** *n* vita *f* familiare. **family name** *n* cognome *m*. **family planning** *n* pianificazione *f* familiare. **family tree** *n* albero *m* genealogico

famine /'fæmɪn/ *n* carestia *f*

famished /'fæmɪʃt/ *a* **be ~** *fam* avere una fame da lupo

famous /'feɪməs/ *a* famoso

fan[1] /fæn/ *n* ventilatore *m*; (*handheld*) ventaglio *m* ● *v* (*pt/pp* **fanned**) ● *vt* far vento a; **~ oneself** sventagliarsi; *fig* **~ the flames** soffiare sul fuoco

■ **fan out** *vi* spiegarsi a ventaglio

fan[2] *n* (*admirer*) ammiratore, -trice *mf*, fan *mf*; *Sport* tifoso *m*; (*of Verdi etc*) appassionato, -a *mf*

fanatic /fə'nætɪk/ *n* fanatico, -a *mf*

fanatical /fə'nætɪkl/ *a* fanatico

fanatically /fə'æntɪklɪ/ *adv* con fanatismo

fanaticism /fə'nætɪsɪzm/ *n* fanatismo *m*

fan belt *n* cinghia *f* per ventilatore

fanciful /'fænsɪfl/ *a* fantasioso

fancy /'fænsɪ/ *n* fantasia *f*; **I've taken a real ~ to him** mi è molto simpatico; **as the ~ takes you** come ti pare ● *a* fantasia *inv* ● *vt* (*believe*) credere; (*fam: want*) aver voglia di; **he fancies you** *fam* gli piaci; **~ that!** ma guarda un po'!

fancy dress *n* costume *m*

fanfare /'fænfeə(r)/ *n* fanfara *f*

fang /fæŋ/ *n* zanna *f*; (*of snake*) dente *m*

fan: fan heater *n* termoventilatore *m*.

fanlight *n* lunetta *f*. **fan mail** *n* posta *f* dei fans

fantasize /'fæntəsaɪz/ *vi* fantasticare

fantastic /fæn'tæstɪk/ *a* fantastico

fantasy /'fæntəsɪ/ *n* fantasia *f*

far /fɑː(r)/ *adv* lontano; (*much*) molto; **by ~** di gran lunga; **~ away** lontano; **as ~ as the church** fino alla chiesa; **how ~ is it from here?** quanto dista da qui? **as ~ as I know** per quanto io sappia ● *a* ⟨*end, side*⟩ altro; **the F~ East** l'Estremo Oriente *m*; **in the ~ distance** in lontananza

farce /fɑːs/ *n* farsa *f*

farcical /'fɑːsɪkl/ *a* ridicolo

fare /feə(r)/ *n* tariffa *f*; (*food*) vitto *m*

fare-dodger /-dɒdʒə(r)/ *n* passeggero, -a *mf* senza biglietto

farewell /feə'wel/ *int liter* addio! ● *n* addio *m*; **~ dinner** cena *f* d'addio

far-fetched /-'fetʃt/ *a* improbabile

far flung /-'flʌŋ/ *a* (*remote*) remoto; (*widely distributed*) sparpagliato; ⟨*network*⟩ esteso

farm /fɑːm/ *n* fattoria *f* ● *vi* fare l'agricoltore ● *vt* coltivare ⟨*land*⟩

farmer /'fɑːmə(r)/ *n* agricoltore *m*

farmhand /'fɑːmhænd/ *n* bracciante *m*

farmhouse /'fɑːmhaʊs/ *n* casa *f* colonica

farming /'fɑːmɪŋ/ *n* agricoltura *f*

farm produce *n* prodotto *m* agricolo

farmyard /'fɑːmjɑːd/ *n* aia *f*

far-reaching /-'riːtʃɪŋ/ *a* ⟨*programme, plan, proposal*⟩ di larga portata; ⟨*effect, implication, change*⟩ notevole

far-sighted /-'saɪtɪd/ *a* ⟨*policy*⟩ lungimirante; (*Am: long-sighted*) presbite

fart /fɑːt/ *fam n* scoreggia *f* ● *vi* scoreggiare

farther /'fɑːðə(r)/ *adv* più lontano ● *a* **at the ~ end of** all'altra estremità di

fascia /'feɪʃə/ *n Br* (*dashboard*) cruscotto *m*

fascinate /'fæsɪneɪt/ *vt* affascinare

fascinating /'fæsɪneɪtɪŋ/ *a* affascinante

fascination /fæsɪ'neɪʃn/ *n* fascino *m*

fascism /'fæʃɪzm/ *n* fascismo *m*

fascist /'fæʃɪst/ *a* & *n* fascista *mf*

fashion /'fæʃn/ *n* moda *f*; (*manner*) maniera *f*; **in ~** di moda; **out of ~** non più di moda ● *vt* modellare

fashionable /'fæʃ(ə)nəbl/ *a* di moda; **be ~** essere alla moda

fashionably /'fæʃ(ə)nəblɪ/ *adv* alla moda

fashion: fashion designer *n* stilista *mf*. **fashion house** *n* casa *f* di moda. **fashion model** *n* indossatore, -trice *mf*, modello, -a *mf*

fast[1] /fɑːst/ *a* veloce; ⟨*colour*⟩ indelebile; **be ~** ⟨*clock:*⟩ andare avanti ● *adv* velocemente; (*firmly*) saldamente; **~er!** più in fretta!; **be ~ asleep** dormire profondamente

fast[2] *n* digiuno *m* ● *vi* digiunare

fasten /'fɑːsn/ *vt* allacciare; chiudere ⟨*window*⟩; (*stop flapping*) mettere un fermo a ● *vi* allacciarsi

fastener /'fɑːsnə(r)/ *n*, **fastening** /'fɑːsnɪŋ/ *n* chiusura *f*

fast: fast food *n* fast food *m inv* ● *attrib* ⟨*chain*⟩ di fast food; **~ ~ restaurant** *n* fast food *m inv.* **fast forward** *n* avanzamento *m* veloce ● *vt* far avanzare velocemente ⟨*tape*⟩ ● *attrib* ⟨*key, button*⟩ di avanzamento veloce. **fast growing** *a* in rapida espansione.

fastidious /fə'stɪdɪəs/ *a* esigente

fast: fast lane *n Auto* corsia *f* di sorpasso; **life in the ~ ~** *fig* vita *f* frenetica. **fast-talking** *a* ⟨*salesperson*⟩ che raggira con la sua parlantina

fat /fæt/ *a* (**fatter, fattest**) ⟨*person, cheque*⟩ grasso; *fam* **that's a ~ lot of use** non serve a un accidente ● *n* grasso *m*

fatal /'feɪtl/ *a* mortale; ⟨*error*⟩ fatale

fatalism /'feɪtəlɪzm/ *n* fatalismo *m*

fatalist /'feɪtəlɪst/ *n* fatalista *mf*

fatality /fə'tælətɪ/ *n* morte *f*

fatally /'feɪtəlɪ/ *adv* mortalmente

fate /feɪt/ *n* destino *m*

fated /'feɪtɪd/ *a* destinato; **it was ~** era destino

fateful /'feɪtfʊl/ *a* fatidico

fat free *a* magro

fat-head *n fam* zuccone, -a *mf*

father /'fɑːðə(r)/ *n* padre *m* ● *vt* generare ⟨*child*⟩

father: Father Christmas Babbo *m* Natale. **father confessor** *n Relig* confessore *m.* **father figure** *n* figura *f* paterna. **fatherhood** *n* paternità *f.* **father-in-law** *n* (*pl* ~**s-in-law**) suocero *m.* **fatherland** *n* patria *f*

fatherly /'fɑːðəlɪ/ *a* paterno

Father's Day /'fɑːðəz/ *n* la festa del papà

fathom /'fæðəm/ *n Naut* braccio *m* ● *vt* ~ [**out**] comprendere

fatigue /fə'tiːg/ *n* fatica *f* ● *vt* affaticare

fatness /'fætnɪs/ *n* grassezza *f*

fatten /'fætn/ *vt* ingrassare ⟨*animal*⟩

fattening /'fætnɪŋ/ *a* **cream is ~** la panna fa ingrassare

fatty /'fætɪ/ *a* grasso ● *n fam* ciccione, -a *mf*

fatuous /'fætjʊəs/ *a* fatuo

faucet /'fɔːsɪt/ *n Am* rubinetto *m*

fault /fɔːlt/ *n* difetto *m; Geol* faglia *f; Tennis* fallo *m;* **be at ~** avere torto; **find ~ with** trovare da ridire su; **it's your ~** è colpa tua ● *vt* criticare

fault-finding /'fɔːltfaɪndɪŋ/ *n* ⟨*of person*⟩ atteggiamento *m* ipercritico; *Techn* localizzazione *f* del guasto ● *a* ⟨*attitude*⟩ da criticone; ⟨*person*⟩ ipercritico

faultless /'fɔːltlɪs/ *a* impeccabile

faultlessly /'fɔːltlɪslɪ/ *adv* impeccabilmente

faulty /'fɔːltɪ/ *a* difettoso

fauna /'fɔːnə/ *n* fauna *f*

faux pas /fəʊ'pɑː/ *n* gaffe *f inv*

favour /'feɪvə(r)/ *n* favore *m;* **be in ~ of** sth essere a favore di qcsa; **do sb a ~** fare un piacere a qcno ● *vt* (*prefer*) preferire

favourable /'feɪv(ə)rəbl/ *a* favorevole

favourably /'feɪv(ə)rəblɪ/ *adv* favorevolmente

favourite /'feɪv(ə)rɪt/ *a* preferito ● *n* preferito, -a *mf; Sport* favorito, -a *mf*

favouritism /'feɪv(ə)rɪtɪzm/ *n* favoritismo *m*

fawn /fɔːn/ *a* fulvo ● *n* ⟨*animal*⟩ cerbiatto *m*

fax /fæks/ *n* (*document, machine*) fax *m inv;* **by ~** per fax ● *vt* faxare

fax machine *n* fax *m inv*

fax-modem *n* fax-modem *m inv*

faze /feɪz/ *vt fam* scompaginare

fear /fɪə(r)/ *n* paura *f;* **no ~!** *fam* vai tranquillo! ● *vt* temere ● *vi* ~ **for sth** temere per qcsa

fearful /'fɪəfl/ *a* pauroso; (*awful*) terribile

fearless /'fɪəlɪs/ *a* impavido

fearlessly /'fɪəlɪslɪ/ *adv* senza paura

fearsome /'fɪəsəm/ *a* spaventoso

feasibility /fiːzɪ'bɪlətɪ/ *n* praticabilità *f*

feasible /'fiːzəbl/ *a* fattibile; (*possible*) probabile

feast /fiːst/ *n* festa *f;* (*banquet*) banchetto *m* ● *vi* banchettare

■ **feast on** *vt* godersi

feat /fiːt/ *n* impresa *f*

feather /'feðə(r)/ *n* piuma *f;* **you could have knocked me down with a ~** sono rimasto di sasso

feather: feather-brained /-breɪnd/ *a* che non ha un briciolo di cervello. **feather duster** *n* piumino *m* (*per spolverare*). **featherweight** *n* peso *m* piuma *inv*

feature /'fiːtʃə(r)/ *n* (*quality*) caratteristica *f; Journ* articolo *m;* ~**s** *pl* (*of face*) lineamenti *mpl* ● *vt* ⟨*film:*⟩ avere come protagonista ● *vi* (*on a list etc*) comparire

feature film *n* lungometraggio *m*

feature length film *n* lungometraggio *m*

February /'februərɪ/ *n* febbraio *m*

feces /'fiːsiːz/ *npl* feci *fpl*

feckless /'feklɪs/ *a* inetto

fecund /'fekənd/ *a* fecondo

fed /fed/ *see* **feed** ● *a* **be ~ up** *fam* essere stufo (**with** di)

federal /'fed(ə)rəl/ *a* federale

federalist /'fed(ə)rəlɪst/ *n & a* federalista *mf*

Federal Republic of Germany *n* Repubblica *f* Federale Tedesca

federate /'fed(ə)rət/ *a* federato

federation /fedə'reɪʃn/ *n* federazione *f*

fee /fiː/ *n* tariffa *f;* (*lawyer's, doctor's*) onorario *m;* (*for membership, school*) quota *f*

feeble /'fiːbl/ *a* debole; ⟨*excuse*⟩ fiacco

feeble minded /-'maɪndɪd/ *a* deficiente

feebleness /'fiːblnɪs/ *n* debolezza *f*

feed /fiːd/ *n* mangiare *m;* (*for baby*) pappa *f;* **five ~s a day** cinque pasti al giorno ● *v* (*pt/pp* **fed**) ● *vt* dar da mangiare a ⟨*animal*⟩; (*support*) nutrire; ~ **sth into sth** inserire qcsa in qcsa; ~ **paper into the printer** alimentare la stampante con fogli ● *vi* mangiare

■ **feed up** *vt* ingrassare ⟨*sb*⟩

feedback /'fiːdbæk/ *n* controreazione *f;* (*of information*) reazione *f,* feedback *m*

feeder /'fiːdə(r)/ *n* (*for printer, photocopier*) mettifoglio *m inv;* (*Br: bib*) bavaglino *m;* (*road*) raccordo *m*

feeding bottle /'fiːdɪŋ/ *n Br* biberon *m inv*

feeding time *n* (*in zoo*) l'ora *f* del pasto degli animali

feel /fiːl/ *v* (*pt/pp* **felt**) ● *vt* sentire; (*experience*) provare; (*think*) pensare; (*touch:*

searching) tastare; (*touch: for texture*) toccare
● *vi* ~ **soft/hard** essere duro/morbido al tatto; ~ **hot/hungry** aver caldo/fame; ~ **ill** sentirsi male; **I don't** ~ **like it** non ne ho voglia; **how do you** ~ **about it?** (*opinion*) che te ne pare?; **it doesn't** ~ **right** non mi sembra giusto
■ **feel for** *vt* (*feel sympathy for*) dispiacersi per
■ **feel up to** *vt* ~ **up to doing sth** sentirsi in grado di fare qcsa; **I don't** ~ **up to it** non me la sento
feeler /ˈfiːlə(r)/ *n* (*of animal*) antenna *f*; **put out** ~**s** *fig* tastare il terreno
feel-good factor *n* sensazione *f* di benessere
feeling /ˈfiːlɪŋ/ *n* sentimento *m*; (*awareness*) sensazione *f*
fee paying *a* ⟨*school*⟩ a pagamento, privato; ⟨*parent, pupil*⟩ che paga l'iscrizione (*a una scuola privata*)
feet /fiːt/ *see* **foot**
feign /feɪn/ *vt* simulare
feint /feɪnt/ *n* finta *f*
feisty /ˈfaɪstɪ/ *a Am* (*quarrelsome*) stizzoso; (*fam: lively*) esuberante
felicitous /fəˈlɪsɪtəs/ *a* felice
feline /ˈfiːlaɪn/ *a* felino
fell[1] /fel/ *vt* (*knock down*) abbattere
fell[2] *see* **fall**
fellow /ˈfeləʊ/ *n* (*of society*) socio *m*; (*fam: man*) tipo *m*
fellow: fellow citizen *n* concittadino, -a *mf*. **fellow countryman** *n* compatriota *m*. **fellow men** *npl* prossimi *mpl*
fellowship /ˈfeləʊʃɪp/ *n* cameratismo *m*; (*group*) associazione *f*; *Univ* incarico *m* di ricercatore, -trice *mf*
fellow traveller *n* compagno, -a *mf* di viaggio; *Pol, fig* compagno, -a *mf* di strada
felon /ˈfelən/ *n Jur* criminale *mf*
felony /ˈfelənɪ/ *n* delitto *m*
felt[1] /felt/ *see* **feel**
felt[2] *n* feltro *m*. ~**[-tipped] pen** /-tɪptˈpen/ *n* pennarello *m*
female /ˈfiːmeɪl/ *a* femminile; **the** ~ **antelope** l'antilope femmina ● *n* femmina *f*
feminine /ˈfemɪnɪn/ *a* femminile ● *n Gram* femminile *m*
femininity /femɪˈnɪnətɪ/ *n* femminilità *f*
feminist /ˈfemɪnɪst/ *a & n* femminista *mf*
fen /fen/ *n* zona *f* paludosa
fence /fens/ *n* recinto *m*; (*fam: person*) ricettatore *m* ● *vi Sport* tirar di scherma
■ **fence in** *vt* chiudere in un recinto
fencer /ˈfensə(r)/ *n* schermidore *m*
fencing /ˈfensɪŋ/ *n* steccato *m*; *Sport* scherma *f*
fend /fend/ *vi* ~ **for oneself** badare a se stesso
■ **fend off** *vt* parare; difendersi da ⟨*criticisms*⟩
fender /ˈfendə(r)/ *n* parafuoco *m inv*; *Naut* parabordo *m*; (*Am: on car*) parafango *m*
fennel /ˈfenl/ *n* finocchio *m*

ferment[1] /ˈfɜːment/ *n* fermento *m*
ferment[2] /fəˈment/ *vi* fermentare ● *vt* far fermentare
fermentation /fɜːmenˈteɪʃn/ *n* fermentazione *f*
fern /fɜːn/ *n* felce *f*
ferocious /fəˈrəʊʃəs/ *a* feroce
ferocity /fəˈrɒsətɪ/ *n* ferocia *f*
ferret /ˈferɪt/ *n* furetto *m*
■ **ferret out** *vt* scovare
ferrous /ˈferəs/ *a* ferroso
ferry /ˈferɪ/ *n* traghetto *m* ● *vt* (*pt/pp* **-ied**) traghettare
ferryman /ˈferɪmən/ *n* traghettatore *m*
fertile /ˈfɜːtaɪl/ *a* fertile
fertility /fɜːˈtɪlətɪ/ *n* fertilità *f*
fertility drug *n* farmaco *m* contro la sterilità
fertilize /ˈfɜːtɪlaɪz/ *vt* fertilizzare ⟨*land, ovum*⟩
fertilizer /ˈfɜːtɪlaɪzə(r)/ *n* fertilizzante *m*
fervent /ˈfɜːvənt/ *a* fervente
fervour /ˈfɜːvə(r)/ *n* fervore *m*
fester /ˈfestə(r)/ *vi* suppurare
festival /ˈfestɪvl/ *n Mus, Theat* festival *m*; *Relig* festa *f*
festive /ˈfestɪv/ *a* festivo; ~ **season** periodo *m* delle feste natalizie
festivities /feˈstɪvətɪz/ *npl* festeggiamenti *mpl*
festoon /feˈstuːn/ *vt* ~ **with** ornare di
fetch /fetʃ/ *vt* andare/venire a prendere; (*be sold for*) raggiungere [il prezzo di]
fetching /ˈfetʃɪŋ/ *a* attraente
fête /feɪt/ *n* festa *f* ● *vt* festeggiare
fetid /ˈfetɪd/ *a* fetido
fetish /ˈfetɪʃ/ *n* feticcio *m*
fetter /ˈfetə(r)/ *vt* incatenare
fettle /ˈfetl/ *n* **in fine** ~ in buona forma
fetus /ˈfiːtəs/ *n* (*pl* **-tuses**) feto *m*
feud /fjuːd/ *n* faida *f*
feudal /ˈfjuːdl/ *a* feudale
fever /ˈfiːvə(r)/ *n* febbre *f*
fevered /ˈfiːvəd/ *a* ⟨*brow*⟩ febbricitante; ⟨*imagination*⟩ febbrile
feverish /ˈfiːvərɪʃ/ *a* febbricitante; *fig* febbrile
fever pitch *n* **bring a crowd to** ~ ~ esaltare la folla
few /fjuː/ *a* pochi; **every** ~ **days** ogni due o tre giorni; **a** ~ **people** alcuni; ~ **people know that** poche persone lo sanno; ~**er reservations** meno prenotazioni; **the** ~**est number** il numero più basso ● *pron* pochi; ~ **of us** pochi di noi; **a** ~ alcuni; **quite a** ~ parecchi; ~**er than last year** meno dell'anno scorso
fez /fez/ *n* fez *m inv*
fiancé /fɪˈɒnseɪ/ *n* fidanzato *m*
fiancée /fɪˈɒnseɪ/ *n* fidanzata *f*
fiasco /fɪˈæskəʊ/ *n* fiasco *m*
fib /fɪb/ *n* storia *f*; **tell a** ~ raccontare una storia
fibber /ˈfɪbə(r)/ *n fam* contaballe *mf inv*
fibre /ˈfaɪbə(r)/ *n* fibra *f*

fibre: fibreglass *n* fibra *f* di vetro ● *attrib* in fibra di vetro. **fibre optic** *a* ⟨*cable*⟩ a fibre ottiche. **fibre optics** *npl* fibra *f* ottica

fibroid /ˈfaɪbrɔɪd/ *n* fibroma *m* ● *a* fibroso

fibula /ˈfɪbjʊlə/ *n* Anat perone *m*

fiche /fiːʃ/ *n* microscheda *f*

fickle /ˈfɪkl/ *a* incostante

fiction /ˈfɪkʃn/ *n* [**works of**] ~ narrativa *f*; (*fabrication*) finzione *f*

fictional /ˈfɪkʃənəl/ *a* immaginario

fictitious /fɪkˈtɪʃəs/ *a* fittizio

fiddle /ˈfɪdl/ *n fam* violino *m*; (*cheating*) imbroglio *m* ● *vi* gingillarsi (**with** con) ● *vt fam* truccare ⟨*accounts*⟩

fiddly /ˈfɪdlɪ/ *a* intricato

fidelity /fɪˈdelətɪ/ *n* fedeltà *f*

fidget /ˈfɪdʒɪt/ *vi* agitarsi

fidgety /ˈfɪdʒətɪ/ *a* agitato

field /fiːld/ *n* campo *m*

field day *n* **have a** ~ ~ ⟨*press, critics:*⟩ godersela; (*make money*) fare affari d'oro

fielder /ˈfiːldə(r)/ *n* Sport esterno *m*

field: field events *npl* atletica *fsg* leggera. **field glasses** *npl* binocolo *msg.* **Field Marshal** *n* feldmaresciallo *m.* **field mouse** *n* topo *m* campagnolo. **fieldwork** *n* ricerche *fpl* sul terreno

fiend /fiːnd/ *n* demonio *m*

fiendish /ˈfiːndɪʃ/ *a* diabolico

fierce /fɪəs/ *a* feroce

fiercely /ˈfɪəslɪ/ *adv* ferocemente

fierceness /ˈfɪəsnɪs/ *n* ferocia *f*

fiery /ˈfaɪərɪ/ *a* (**-ier, -iest**) focoso

fiesta /fɪˈestə/ *n* sagra *f*

fife /faɪf/ *n* piffero *m*

fifteen /fɪfˈtiːn/ *a & n* quindici *m*

fifteenth /fɪfˈtiːnθ/ *a & n* quindicesimo, -a *mf*

fifth /fɪfθ/ *a & n* quinto, -a *mf*

fiftieth /ˈfɪftɪɪθ/ *a & n* cinquantesimo, -a *mf*

fifty /ˈfɪftɪ/ *a & n* cinquanta *m*

fifty-fifty *a* **have a** ~ **chance** avere una probabilità su due ● *adv* **go** ~ fare [a] metà e metà; **split sth** ~ dividersi qcsa a metà

fig /fɪg/ *n* fico *m*

fight /faɪt/ *n* lotta *f*; (*brawl*) zuffa *f*; (*argument*) litigio *m*; (*boxing*) incontro *m* ● *v* (*pt/pp* **fought**) ● *vt also fig* combattere ● *vi* combattere; (*brawl*) azzuffarsi; (*argue*) litigare

■ **fight back** *vi* reagire ● *vt* frenare ⟨*tears*⟩

■ **fight for** *vt* lottare per ⟨*freedom, independence*⟩

■ **fight off** *vt* combattere ⟨*cold*⟩

fighter /ˈfaɪtə(r)/ *n* combattente *mf*; Aeron caccia *m inv*; **he's a** ~ ha uno spirito combattivo

fighter-bomber *n* cacciabombardiere *m*

fighter pilot *n* pilota *m* di cacciabombardiere

fighting /ˈfaɪtɪŋ/ *n* combattimento *m*

fighting chance *n* **have a** ~ ~ avere buone probabilità

fighting fit *a* in piena forma

figment /ˈfɪgmənt/ *n* **it's a** ~ **of your**

imagination questo è tutta una tua invenzione

fig tree *n* fico *m*

figurative /ˈfɪgərətɪv/ *a* ⟨*sense*⟩ figurato; ⟨*art*⟩ figurativo

figuratively /ˈfɪgərətɪvlɪ/ *adv* ⟨*use*⟩ in senso figurato

figure /ˈfɪgə(r)/ *n* (*digit*) cifra *f*; (*carving, sculpture, illustration, form*) figura *f*; (*body shape*) linea *f*; ~ **of speech** modo *m* di dire ● *vi* (*appear*) figurare ● *vt* (Am: *think*) pensare

■ **figure out** *vt* dedurre; capire ⟨*person*⟩

figure: figurehead *n* figura *f* simbolica. **figure of speech** *n* modo *m* di dire; (*literary device*) figura *f* retorica. **figure skating** *n* pattinaggio *m* artistico

figurine /ˈfɪgəriːn/ *n* statuetta *f*

filament /ˈfɪləmənt/ *n* filamento *m*

filch /fɪltʃ/ *vt fam* rubacchiare

file[1] /faɪl/ *n* scheda *f*; (*set of documents*) incartamento *m*; (*folder*) cartellina *f*; Comput file *m inv* ● *vt* archiviare ⟨*documents*⟩

file[2] *n* (*line*) fila *f*; **in single** ~ in fila

file[3] *n* Techn lima *f* ● *vt* limare

file manager *n* Comput file manager *m inv*

filial /ˈfɪlɪəl/ *a* filiale

filibuster /ˈfɪlɪbʌstə(r)/ *n* ostruzionismo *m* parlamentare

filigree /ˈfɪlɪgriː/ *n* filigrana *f*

filing /ˈfaɪlɪŋ/ *n* archiviazione *f*

filing: filing cabinet *n* schedario *m*, classificatore *m.* **filing card** *n* scheda *f.* **filing clerk** *n* archivista *mf*

filings /ˈfaɪlɪŋz/ *npl* limatura *fsg*

filing system *n* sistema *m* di classificazione, sistema *m* di archivio

fill /fɪl/ *n* **eat one's** ~ mangiare a sazietà ● *vt* riempire; otturare ⟨*tooth*⟩ ● *vi* riempirsi

■ **fill in** *vt* compilare ⟨*form*⟩

■ **fill in for** *vt* rimpiazzare ⟨*sb*⟩

■ **fill in on** *vt* ~ **sb in on sth** mettere qcno al corrente di qcsa

■ **fill out** *vt* compilare ⟨*form*⟩

■ **fill up** *vi* ⟨*room, tank:*⟩ riempirsi; Auto far il pieno ● *vt* riempire

fillet /ˈfɪlɪt/ *n* filetto *m* ● *vt* (*pt/pp* **filleted**) disossare

fillet steak *n* bistecca *f* di filetto

fill in *n* (*fam: replacement*) rimpiazzo *m*

filling /ˈfɪlɪŋ/ *n* Culin ripieno *m*; (*of tooth*) piombatura *f*

filling station *n* stazione *f* di rifornimento

filly /ˈfɪlɪ/ *n* puledra *f*

film /fɪlm/ *n* Cinema film *m inv*; Phot pellicola *f*; [**cling**] ~ pellicola *f* per alimenti ● *vt/i* filmare

film: film-goer /ˈfɪlmgəʊə(r)/ *n* frequentatore, -trice *mf* di cinema. **film industry** *n* industria *f* cinematografica. **filmset** *n* allestimento *m* scenico. **film star** *n* star *f inv*, divo, -a *mf*

filmy /ˈfɪlmɪ/ *a* (*thin: fabric, screen*) trasparente; (*thin*) sottilissimo

filter /ˈfɪltə(r)/ *n* filtro *m* ● *vt* filtrare

■ **filter through** *vi* ⟨*news:*⟩ trapelare

filter: filter cigarette *n* sigaretta *f* con filtro. **filter coffee** *n* (*ground coffee*) caffè *m* macinato per filtro; (*cup of coffee*) caffè *m inv* fatto con il filtro. **filter-paper** *n* carta *f* da filtro. **filter tip** *n* filtro *m*; (*cigarette*) sigaretta *f* col filtro

filth /fɪlθ/ *n* sudiciume *m*

filthy /'fɪlθɪ/ *a* (**-ier, -iest**) sudicio; (*language*) sconcio

filthy rich *a fam* ricco sfondato

fin /fɪn/ *n* pinna *f*

final /'faɪnl/ *a* finale; (*conclusive*) decisivo ● *n Sport* finale *f*; **~s** *pl Univ* esami *mpl* finali

finale /fɪ'nɑːlɪ/ *n* finale *m*

finalist /'faɪnəlɪst/ *n* finalista *mf*

finality /faɪ'nælətɪ/ *n* finalità *f*

finalize /'faɪnəlaɪz/ *vt* mettere a punto (*text*); definire (*agreement*)

finally /'faɪnəlɪ/ *adv* (*at last*) finalmente; (*at the end*) alla fine; (*to conclude*) per finire

finance /'faɪnæns/ *n* finanza *f* ● *vt* finanziare

finance director *n* direttore, -trice *mf* finanziario, -a

finance company, finance house *n* società *f* finanziaria

financial /faɪ'nænʃl/ *a* finanziario

financially /faɪ'nænʃəlɪ/ *adv* finanziariamente

financial year *n Br* esercizio *m* [finanziario]

finch /fɪntʃ/ *n* fringuello *m*

find /faɪnd/ *n* scoperta *f* ● *vt* (*pt/pp* **found**) trovare; (*establish*) scoprire; **~ sb guilty** *Jur* dichiarare qcno colpevole

■ **find out** *vt* scoprire ● *vi* (*enquire*) informarsi

findings /'faɪndɪŋz/ *npl* conclusioni *fpl*

fine¹ /faɪn/ *n* (*penalty*) multa *f* ● *vt* multare

fine² *a* bello; (*slender*) fine; **he's ~** (*in health*) sta bene ● *adv* bene; **that's cutting it ~** non ci lascia molto tempo. ● *int* [va] bene

fine arts *npl* belle arti *fpl*

finely /'faɪnlɪ/ *adv* (*cut*) finemente

finery /'faɪnərɪ/ *n* splendore *m*

finesse /fɪ'nes/ *n* finezza *f*

fine-tooth[ed] comb /-tuː'θ[t]/ *n* **go over sth with a ~ ~** passare qcsa al setaccio

fine-tune *vt* mettere a punto

fine tuning *n* messa *f* a punto

finger /'fɪŋgə(r)/ *n* dito *m* (*pl* dita *f*) ● *vt* tastare

finger: finger bowl *n* lavadita *m inv*. **finger hole** *n Mus* foro *m*. **fingermark** *n* ditata *f*. **fingernail** *n* unghia *f*. **finger-paint** *vi* dipingere con le dita. **fingerprint** *n* impronta *f* digitale. **fingertip** *n* punta *f* del dito; **have sth at one's ~s** sapere qcsa a menadito; (*close at hand*) avere qcsa a portata di mano

finicky /'fɪnɪkɪ/ *a* (*person*) pignolo; (*task*) intricato

finish /'fɪnɪʃ/ *n* fine *f*; (*finishing line*) traguardo *m*; (*of product*) finitura *f*; **have a good ~** (*runner:*) avere un buon finale ● *vt* finire; **~ reading** finire di leggere ● *vi* finire

■ **finish off** *vt* finire (*sth*); (*fam: exhaust*) sfinire

■ **finish with** *vt* (*no longer be using*) finire (*di adoperare*); (*end relationship with*) lasciare

■ **finish up** *vt* finire (*drink, meal*)

finishing line /'fɪnɪʃɪŋlaɪn/ *n* traguardo *m*

finishing touches /'tʌtʃɪz/ *npl* ritocchi *mpl*

finite /'faɪnaɪt/ *a* limitato

Finland /'fɪnlənd/ *n* Finlandia *f*

Finn /fɪn/ *n* finlandese *mf*

Finnish /'fɪnɪʃ/ *a* finlandese ● *n* (*language*) finnico *m*

fiord /fjɔːd/ *n* fiordo *m*

fir /fɜː(r)/ *n* abete *m*

fir cone *n* pigna *f* (*di abete*)

fire /'faɪə(r)/ *n* fuoco *m*; (*forest, house*) incendio *m*; **be on ~** bruciare; **catch ~** prendere fuoco; **set ~ to** dar fuoco a; **under ~** sotto il fuoco ● *vt* cuocere (*pottery*); sparare (*shot*); tirare (*gun*); (*fam: dismiss*) buttar fuori ● *vi* sparare (**at** a)

fire: fire alarm *n* allarme *m* antincendio *inv*. **firearm** *n* arma *f* da fuoco. **fire brigade** *n* vigili *mpl* del fuoco. **fire door** *n* porta *f* antincendio. **fire drill** *n* esercitazione *f* per l'evacuazione in caso di incendio. **fire engine** *n* autopompa *f*. **fire escape** *n* uscita *f* di sicurezza. **fire extinguisher** *n* estintore *m*. **fireman** *n* pompiere *m*, vigile *m* del fuoco. **fireplace** *n* caminetto *m*. **fireside** *n* **by** *or* **at the ~** accanto al fuoco. **fire station** *n* caserma *f* dei pompieri. **firewood** *n* legna *f* (*da ardere*). **firework** *n* fuoco *m* d'artificio; **~s** *pl* (*display*) fuochi *mpl* d'artificio

firing squad /'faɪərɪŋ/ *n* plotone *m* d'esecuzione

firm¹ /fɜːm/ *n* ditta *f*, azienda *f*

firm² *a* fermo; (*soil*) compatto; (*stable, properly fixed*) solido; (*resolute*) risoluto

firmly /'fɜːmlɪ/ *adv* (*hold*) stretto; (*say*) con fermezza

first /fɜːst/ *a & n* primo, -a *mf*; **at ~** all'inizio; **who's ~?** chi è il primo?; **from the ~** [fɪn] dall'inizio ● *adv* (*arrive, leave*) per primo; (*beforehand*) prima; (*in listing*) prima di tutto, innanzitutto

first: first aid *n* pronto soccorso *m*. **first-aid kit** *n* cassetta *f* di pronto soccorso. **first-class** *a* di prim'ordine; *Rail* di prima classe ● *adv* (*travel*) in prima classe. **first edition** *n* prima edizione *f*. **first floor** *n* primo piano *m*; (*Am: ground floor*) pianterreno *m*

firstly /'fɜːstlɪ/ *adv* in primo luogo

first: first name *n* nome *m* di battesimo. **first night** *n Theat* prima *f*. **first-rate** *a* ottimo. **first time buyer** *n* acquirente *mf* della prima casa

firth /fɜːθ/ *n* foce *f*

fiscal /'fɪskəl/ *a* fiscale

fiscal year *n Am* esercizio *m* finanziario

fish /fɪʃ/ *n* pesce *m* ● *vt/i* pescare

■ **fish out** *vt* tirar fuori

fishbone /'fɪʃbəʊn/ *n* lisca *f*

fishmonger /'fɪʃmʌŋgə(r)/ *n* pescivendo-lo *m*

fisherman /'fɪʃəmən/ *n* pescatore *m*

fish farm *n* vivaio *m*

fish finger *n* bastoncino *m* di pesce

fishing /'fɪʃɪŋ/ *n* pesca *f*

fishing boat *n* peschereccio *m*

fishing rod *n* canna *f* da pesca

fishnet /'fɪʃnet/ *a* ‹stockings› a rete

fish slice *n* paletta *f* per fritti

fishy /'fɪʃɪ/ *a* (*fam: suspicious*) sospetto

fission /'fɪʃn/ *n Phys* fissione *f*

fist /fɪst/ *n* pugno *m*

fistful /'fɪstfʊl/ *n* manciata *f*, pugno *m*

fit¹ /fɪt/ *n* (*attack*) attacco *m*; (*of rage*) accesso *m*; (*of generosity*) slancio *m*

fit² *a* (**fitter**, **fittest**) (*suitable*) adatto; (*healthy*) in buona salute; *Sport* in forma; **be ~ to do sth** essere in grado di fare qcsa; **~ to eat** buono da mangiare; **keep ~** tenersi in forma; **do as you see ~** fai come ritieni meglio

fit³ *n* (*of clothes*) taglio *m*; **it's a good ~** ‹coat etc:› ti/le sta bene ● *v* (*pt/pp* **fitted**) ● *vi* (*be the right size*) andare bene; **it won't ~** (*no room*) non ci sta ● *vt* (*fix*) applicare (**to** a); (*install*) installare; **it doesn't ~ me** ‹coat etc:› non mi va bene; **~ with** fornire di

■ **fit in** *vi* ‹person:› adattarsi; **it won't ~ in** (*no room*) non ci sta ● *vt* (*in schedule, vehicle*) trovare un buco per

fitful /'fɪtfl/ *a* irregolare

fitfully /'fɪtfʊlɪ/ *adv* ‹sleep› a sprazzi

fitment /'fɪtmənt/ *n* **~s** (*in house*) impianti *mpl* fissi

fitness /'fɪtnɪs/ *n* (*suitability*) capacità *f*; [**physical**] ~ forma *f*, fitness *m*

fitted: fitted carpet *n* moquette *f inv.* **fitted cupboard** *n* armadio *m* a muro; (*smaller*) armadietto *m* a muro. **fitted kitchen** *n* cucina *f* componibile. **fitted sheet** *n* lenzuolo *m* con angoli

fitter /'fɪtə(r)/ *n* installatore, -trice *mf*

fitting /'fɪtɪŋ/ *a* appropriato ● *n* (*of clothes*) prova *f*; *Techn* montaggio *m*; **~s** *pl* accessori *mpl*

fitting room *n* camerino *m*

five /faɪv/ *a* & *n* cinque *m*

five-a-side *n Br* (*football*) partita *f* di calcio con cinque giocatori per squadra

fiver /'faɪvə(r)/ *n fam* biglietto *m* da cinque sterline

fix /fɪks/ *n* (*sl: drugs*) pera *f*; **be in a ~** *fam* essere nei guai ● *vt* fissare; (*repair*) aggiustare; preparare ‹meal›

■ **fix up** *vt* fissare ‹meeting›

fixation /fɪk'seɪʃn/ *n* fissazione *f*

fixative /'fɪksətɪv/ *n* fissativo *m*

fixed /'fɪkst/ *a* fisso

fixed assets *npl* attività *fpl* fisse, immobilizzazioni *fpl*

fixed price *n* prezzo *m* a forfait

fixer /'fɪksə(r)/ *n Phot* fissatore *m*; (*fam: person*) trafficone, -a *mf*

fixture /'fɪkstʃə(r)/ *n Sport* incontro *m*; **~s and fittings** impianti *mpl* fissi

fizz /fɪz/ *vi* frizzare

fizzle /'fɪzl/ *vi* **~ out** finire in nulla

fizzy /'fɪzɪ/ *a* gassoso

fizzy drink *n* bibita *f* gassata

fjord /fjɔːd/ *n* fiordo *m*

flab /flæb/ *n fam* ciccia *f* cascante

flabbergasted /'flæbəgɑːstɪd/ *a* **be ~** rimanere a bocca aperta

flabby /'flæbɪ/ *a* floscio

flag¹ /flæg/ *n* bandiera *f*

flag² *vi* (*pt/pp* **flagged**) cedere

■ **flag down** *vt* (*pt/pp* **flagged**) far segno di fermarsi a ‹taxi›

flagellation /flædʒə'leɪʃn/ *n* flagellazione *f*

flagon /'flægən/ *n* bottiglione *m*

flagpole /'flægpəʊl/ *n* asta *f* della bandiera

flagrant /'fleɪgrənt/ *a* flagrante

flagship /'flægʃɪp/ *n Naut* nave *f* ammiraglia; *fig* fiore *m* all'occhiello

flagstone /'flægstəʊn/ *n* pietra *f* da lastricare

flail /fleɪl/ *n* (*for threshing corn etc*) correggiato *m* ● *vt* battere ‹corn›

■ **flail about, flail around** *vi* ‹arms, legs:› agitare

flair /fleə(r)/ *n* (*skill*) talento *m*; (*style*) stile *m*

flak /flæk/ *n Mil* artiglieria *f* antiaerea; (*fig fam: criticism*) valanga *f* di critiche; **take a lot of ~** subire molte critiche

flake /fleɪk/ *n* fiocco *m* ● *vi* **~** [**off**] cadere in fiocchi

flaky /'fleɪkɪ/ *a* a scaglie

flaky pastry *n* pasta *f* sfoglia

flamboyant /flæm'bɔɪənt/ *a* ‹personality› brillante; ‹tie› sgargiante

flame /fleɪm/ *n* fiamma *f*

flamenco /flə'meŋkəʊ/ *n* flamenco *m*

flame retardant /rɪtɑːdənt/ *a* ‹substance, chemical› ignifugo; ‹furniture, fabric› ignifugato

flame-thrower /-θrəʊə(r)/ *n Mil* lanciafiamme *m inv*

flamingo /flə'mɪŋgəʊ/ *n* fenicottero *m*

flammable /'flæməbl/ *a* infiammabile

flan /flæn/ *n* [**fruit**] **~** crostata *f*

flange /flændʒ/ *n* (*on pipe etc*) flangia *f*

flank /flæŋk/ *n* fianco *m* ● *vt* fiancheggiare

flannel /'flæn(ə)l/ *n* flanella *f*; (*for washing*) ≈ guanto *m* di spugna

flannelette /flænə'let/ *n* flanella *f* di cotone

flannels /'flæn(ə)lz/ *npl* (*trousers*) pantaloni *mpl* di flanella

flap /flæp/ *n* (*of pocket, envelope*) risvolto *m*; (*of table*) ribalta *f*; **in a ~** *fam* in grande agitazione ● *v* (*pt/pp* **flapped**) ● *vi* sbattere; *fam* agitarsi ● *vt* **~ its wings** battere le ali

flapjack /'flæpdʒæk/ *n Br* dolcetto *m* di fiocchi d'avena; *Am* frittella *f*

flare /fleə(r)/ *n* fiammata *f*; (*device*) razzo *m*

■ **flare up** *vi* ‹rash:› venire fuori; ‹fire:› fare una fiammata; ‹person, situation:› esplodere

flared /fleəd/ *a* ‹garment› svasato

flash /flæʃ/ *n* lampo *m*; **in a ~** *fam* in un attimo ● *vi* lampeggiare; ~ **past** passare come un bolide ● *vt* lanciare ⟨*smile*⟩; ~ **one's headlights** lampeggiare; ~ **a torch at** puntare una torcia su

flash: flashback *n* scena *f* retrospettiva. **flashbulb** *n Phot* flash *m inv*. **flashcard** *n Sch* scheda *f* didattica

flasher /ˈflæʃə(r)/ *n Auto* lampeggiatore *m*

flash: flash flood *n* alluvione *f* improvvisa. **flashgun** *n Phot* flash *m inv*. **flashlight** *n Phot* flash *m inv*; (*Am: torch*) torcia *f* [elettrica]. **flashpoint** *n* (*trouble spot*) punto *m* caldo; *Chem* punto *m* di infiammabilità

flashy /ˈflæʃɪ/ *a* vistoso

flask /flɑːsk/ *n* fiasco *m*; (*vacuum* ~) termos *m inv*

flat /flæt/ *a* (**flatter, flattest**) piatto; ⟨*refusal*⟩ reciso; ⟨*beer*⟩ sgassato; ⟨*battery*⟩ scarico; ⟨*tyre*⟩ a terra; **A ~** *Mus* la bemolle ● *n* appartamento *m*; *Mus* bemolle *m*; (*puncture*) gomma *f* a terra

flat: flat broke *a fam* completamente al verde. **flat feet** *npl* piedi *mpl* piatti. **flatfish** *n* pesce *m* piatto. **flat-footed** /a* **be ~ ~** avere i piedi piatti. **flat hunting** *n Br* **go ~ ~** andare in cerca di un appartamento

flatly /ˈflætlɪ/ *adv* ⟨*refuse*⟩ categoricamente

flat: flatmate *n Br persona f con cui si divide un appartamento*. **flat out** *adv* ⟨*drive, work*⟩ a tutto gas; **it only does 120 kph ~ ~** arriva a 120 km all'ora andando a tutta manetta; **go ~ ~ for sth** mettercela tutta per fare qcsa. **flat racing** *n* corse *fpl* piane. **flat rate** *n* forfait *m inv*; (*unitary rate*) tariffa *f* unica ● *attrib* ⟨*fee, tax*⟩ forfettario. **flat spin** *n Aeron* virata *f* piatta; **be in a ~ ~** *fam* essere in fibrillazione

flatten /ˈflætn/ *vt* appiattire

flatter /ˈflætə(r)/ *vt* adulare

flattering /ˈflætərɪŋ/ *a* ⟨*comments*⟩ lusinghiero; ⟨*colour, dress*⟩ che fa sembrare più bello

flattery /ˈflætərɪ/ *n* adulazione *f*

flat tyre *n* gomma *f* a terra

flatulence /ˈflætjʊləns/ *n* flatulenza *f*

flaunt /flɔːnt/ *vt* ostentare

flautist /ˈflɔːtɪst/ *n* flautista *mf*

flavour /ˈfleɪvə(r)/ *n* sapore *m* ● *vt* condire; **chocolate ~ed** al sapore di cioccolato

flavour-enhancer /-ɪnhɑːˈnsə(r)/ *n* esaltatore *m* dell'aroma

flavouring /ˈfleɪvərɪŋ/ *n* condimento *m*

flavourless /ˈfleɪvəlɪs/ *a* insipido

flaw /flɔː/ *n* difetto *m*

flawless /ˈflɔːlɪs/ *a* perfetto

flax /flæks/ *n* lino *m*

flaxen /ˈflæksən/ *a* ⟨*hair*⟩ biondo platino

flea /fliː/ *n* pulce *f*

flea: flea-bitten /ˈfliːbɪtən/ *a* infestato dalle pulci; *fig* pidocchioso. **flea market** *n* mercato *m* delle pulci. **fleapit** *n Br fam pej* pidocchietto *m*

fleck /flek/ *n* macchiolina *f*

fled /fled/ *see* **flee**

fledg[e]ling /ˈfledʒlɪŋ/ *n* uccellino *m* (*che ha*

appena messo le ali) ● *attrib fig* ⟨*democracy, enterprise*⟩ giovane; ⟨*party, group*⟩ alle prime armi

flee /fliː/ *vt/i* (*pt/pp* **fled**) fuggire (**from** da)

fleece /fliːs/ *n* pelliccia *f* ● *vt fam* spennare

fleecy /ˈfliːsɪ/ *a* ⟨*lining*⟩ felpato

fleet /fliːt/ *n* flotta *f*; (*of cars*) parco *m*

fleeting /ˈfliːtɪŋ/ *a* **catch a ~ glance of sth** intravedere qcsa; **for a ~ moment** per un attimo

Flemish /ˈflemɪʃ/ *a* fiammingo

flesh /fleʃ/ *n* carne *f*; **in the ~** in persona; **one's own ~ and blood** il proprio sangue

■ **flesh out** *vt* dare più consistenza a ⟨*essay etc*⟩

flesh eating /-iːtɪŋ/ *a* carnivoro

flesh wound *n* ferita *f* superficiale

fleshy /ˈfleʃɪ/ *a* carnoso

flew /fluː/ *see* **fly²**

flex¹ /fleks/ *vt* flettere ⟨*muscle*⟩

flex² *n Electr* filo *m*

flexibility /fleksəˈbɪlətɪ/ *n* flessibilità *f*

flexible /ˈfleksəbl/ *a* flessibile

flexitime /ˈfleksɪtaɪm/ *n* orario *m* flessibile

flick /flɪk/ *vt* dare un buffetto a; ~ **sth off sth** togliere qcsa da qcsa con un colpetto

■ **flick through** *vt* sfogliare

flicker /ˈflɪkə(r)/ *vi* tremolare

flick knife *n Br* coltello *m* a scatto

flier /ˈflaɪə(r)/ *n* = **flyer**

flight¹ /flaɪt/ *n* (*fleeing*) fuga *f*; **take ~** darsi alla fuga

flight² *n* (*flying*) volo *m*; ~ **of stairs** rampa *f*

flight: flight attendant *n* assistente *mf* di volo. **flight bag** *n* bagaglio *m* a mano. **flight deck** *n Aeron* cabina *f* di pilotaggio; *Naut* ponte *m* di volo. **flight engineer** *n* motorista *mf* di bordo. **flight lieutenant** *n Mil* capitano *m*. **flight path** *n* traiettoria *f* di volo. **flight recorder** *n* registratore *m* di volo

flighty /ˈflaɪtɪ/ *a* (**-ier, -iest**) frivolo

flimsy /ˈflɪmzɪ/ *a* (**-ier, -iest**) ⟨*material*⟩ leggero; ⟨*shelves*⟩ poco robusto; ⟨*excuse*⟩ debole

flinch /flɪntʃ/ *vi* (*wince*) sussultare; (*draw back*) ritirarsi; ~ **from a task** *fig* sottrarsi a un compito

fling /flɪŋ/ *n* **have a ~** (*fam: affair*) aver un'avventura ● *vt* (*pt/pp* **flung**) gettare

flint /flɪnt/ *n* pietra *f* focaia; (*for lighter*) pietrina *f*

flip /flɪp/ *v* (*pt/pp* **flipped**) *vt* dare un colpetto a; buttare in aria ⟨*coin*⟩. ● *vi fam* uscire dai gangheri; (*go mad*) impazzire

■ **flip through** *vt* sfogliare

flip chart *n* lavagna *f* a fogli mobili

flip-flop *n* (*sandal*) infradito *m inv*; (*Comput: device*) flip-flop *m inv*, multivibratore *m* bistabile; (*Am: about face*) voltafaccia *m inv*

flippant /ˈflɪpənt/ *a* irriverente

flipper /ˈflɪpə(r)/ *n* pinna *f*

flipping /ˈflɪpɪŋ/ *Br fam a* maledetto ● *adv* ⟨*stupid, painful, cold*⟩ maledettamente

flip side *n* (*of record*) retro *m*; (*fig: other side*) rovescio *m*

flirt /flɜːt/ *n* civetta *f* ● *vi* flirtare

flirtation /flɜːˈteɪʃn/ *n* flirt *m inv*

flirtatious /flɜːˈteɪʃəs/ *a* civettuolo

flit /flɪt/ *vi* (*pt/pp* **flitted**) volteggiare

float /fləʊt/ *n* galleggiante *m*; (*in procession*) carro *m*; (*money*) riserva *f* di cassa ● *vi* galleggiare; *Fin* fluttuare

floating rate interest /ˈfləʊtɪŋ/ *n Fin* interesse *m* a tasso variabile

floating voter *n Pol* elettore, -trice *mf* indeciso,-a

flock /flɒk/ *n* gregge *m*; (*of birds*) stormo *m* ● *vi* affollarsi

floe /fləʊ/ *n* banchisa *f*

flog /flɒg/ *vt* (*pt/pp* **flogged**) bastonare; (*fam: sell*) vendere

flood /flʌd/ *n* alluvione *f*; (*of river*) straripamento *m*; (*fig: of replies, letters, tears*) diluvio *m*; **be in ~** ⟨*river:*⟩ essere straripato ● *vt* allagare ● *vi* ⟨*river:*⟩ straripare

flood: flood control *n* prevenzione *f* delle inondazioni. **flood damage** *n* danno *m* provocato da un'inondazione. **floodgate** *n* chiusa *f*; **open the ~s** *fig* spalancare le porte. **floodlight** *n* riflettore *m* ● *vt* (*pt/pp* **floodlit**) illuminare con riflettori. **floodplain** *n* pianura *f* alluvionale. **flood tide** *n* marea *f* montante. **flood waters** *npl* acque *fpl* alluvionali

floor /flɔː(r)/ *n* pavimento *m*; (*storey*) piano *m*; (*for dancing*) pista *f* ● *vt* (*baffle*) confondere; (*knock down*) stendere ⟨*person*⟩

floor: floorboard *n* asse *f* del pavimento. **floorcloth** *n* straccio *m* per lavare il pavimento. **floor exercises** *npl* esercizi *mpl* a terra. **floor manager** *n TV* direttore, -trice *mf* di studio; *Comm* gerente *mf* di un negozio. **floor polish** *n* cera *f* per il pavimento. **floor show** *n* spettacolo *m* di varietà. **floor space** *n* superficie *f*; **we don't have the ~ ~** non abbiamo lo spazio

flop /flɒp/ *n fam* (*failure*) tonfo *m*; *Theat* fiasco *m* ● *vi* (*pt/pp* **flopped**) (*fam: fail*) far fiasco

■ **flop down** *vi* accasciarsi

floppy /ˈflɒpɪ/ *a* floscio

floppy disk *n* floppy disk *m inv*

floppy [disk] drive *n* lettore *m* di floppy

flora /ˈflɔːrə/ *n* flora *f*

floral /ˈflɔːrəl/ *a* floreale

Florence /ˈflɒrəns/ *n* Firenze *f*

Florentine /ˈflɒrəntaɪn/ *a* fiorentino

florid /ˈflɒrɪd/ *a* ⟨*complexion*⟩ florido; ⟨*style*⟩ troppo ricercato

florist /ˈflɒrɪst/ *n* fioriao, -a *mf*

flotsam /ˈflɒtsəm/ *n* relitti *mpl* alla deriva

flounce /flaʊns/ *n* balza *f* ● *vi* **~ out** uscire con aria melodrammatica

flounder¹ /ˈflaʊndə(r)/ *vi* dibattersi; ⟨*speaker:*⟩ impappinarsi

flounder² *n* (*fish*) passera *f* di mare

flour /ˈflaʊə(r)/ *n* farina *f*

flourish /ˈflʌrɪʃ/ *n* gesto *m* drammatico; (*scroll*) ghirigoro *m* ● *vi* prosperare ● *vt* brandire

floury /ˈflaʊərɪ/ *a* farinoso

flout /flaʊt/ *vt* fregarsene di ⟨*rules*⟩

flow /fləʊ/ *n* flusso *m* ● *vi* scorrere; (*hang loosely*) ricadere

flow chart *n* diagramma *m* di flusso

flower /ˈflaʊə(r)/ *n* fiore *m* ● *vi* fiorire

flower arrangement *n* composizione *f* floreale

flower bed *n* aiuola *f*

flowered /ˈflaʊəd/ *a* a fiori

flower garden *n* giardino *m* fiorito

flowering /ˈflaʊərɪŋ/ *n Bot* fioritura *f*; (*fig: development*) espansione *f* ● *a* ⟨*shrub, tree*⟩ in fiore; **early/late ~** a fioritura precoce/tardiva

flower: flowerpot *n* vaso *m* [per i fiori]. **flower shop** *n* fiorista *m*. **flower show** *n* mostra *f* floreale

flowery /ˈflaʊərɪ/ *a* fiorito

flown /fləʊn/ *see* **fly²**

fl oz *abbr* **fluid ounces**

flu /fluː/ *n* influenza *f*

fluctuate /ˈflʌktjʊeɪt/ *vi* fluttuare

fluctuation /flʌktjʊˈeɪʃn/ *n* fluttuazione *f*

flue /fluː/ *n* (*of chimney, stove*) canna *f* fumaria

fluent /ˈfluːənt/ *a* spedito; **speak ~ Italian** parlare correntemente l'italiano

fluently /ˈfluːəntlɪ/ *adv* speditamente

fluff /flʌf/ *n* peluria *f*

fluffy /ˈflʌfɪ/ *a* (**-ier, -iest**) vaporoso; ⟨*toy*⟩ di peluche

fluid /ˈfluːɪd/ *a* fluido ● *n* fluido *m*

fluid ounce *n* oncia *f* fluida

fluke /fluːk/ *n* colpo *m* di fortuna

flummox /ˈflʌməks/ *vt fam* sbalestrare

flung /flʌŋ/ *see* **fling**

flunk /flʌŋk/ *vt Am fam* essere bocciato in

fluorescent /flʊəˈresnt/ *a* fluorescente

fluorescent lighting *n* luce *f* fluorescente

fluoride /ˈflʊəraɪd/ *n* fluoruro *m*

flurry /ˈflʌrɪ/ *n* (*snow*) raffica *f*; *fig* agitazione *f*

flush /flʌʃ/ *n* (*blush*) [vampata *f* di] rossore *m* ● *vi* arrossire ● *vt* lavare con un getto d'acqua; **~ the toilet** tirare l'acqua ● *a* a livello (**with** di); (*fam: affluent*) a soldi

flushed /flʌʃt/ *a* ⟨*cheeks*⟩ rosso; **~ with** eccitato da (*success*); raggiante di (*pride*)

flustered /ˈflʌstəd/ *a* in agitazione; **get ~** mettersi in agitazione

flute /fluːt/ *n* flauto *m*

flutter /ˈflʌstə(r)/ *n* battito *m* ● *vi* svolazzare

flux /flʌks/ *n* **in a state of ~** in uno stato di flusso

fly¹ /flaɪ/ *n* (*pl* **flies**) mosca *f*

fly² *v* (*pt* **flew**, *pp* **flown**) ● *vi* volare; (*go by plane*) andare in aereo; ⟨*flag:*⟩ sventolare; (*rush*) precipitarsi; **~ open** spalancarsi ● *vt* pilotare ⟨*plane*⟩; trasportare [in aereo] ⟨*troops, supplies*⟩; volare con ⟨*Alitalia etc*⟩

fly³ *n* & **flies** *pl* (*on trousers*) patta *f*

flyaway /ˈflaɪəweɪ/ *a* ⟨*hair*⟩ che non stanno a posto

fly: fly-by-night *a* ⟨*person*⟩ irresponsabile; ⟨*company*⟩ non affidabile. **flycatcher**

/'flaɪkætʃə(r)/ n pigliamosche m inv. **fly-drive** a con la formula aereo più auto

flyer /'flaɪə(r)/ n aviatore m; (leaflet) volantino m

fly-fishing n pesca f con la mosca

flying /'flaɪɪŋ/ n aviazione f

flying: flying buttress n arco m rampante. **flying colours: with ~ ~** a pieni voti. **flying saucer** n disco m volante. **flying start** n ottima partenza f; **get off to a ~ ~** partire benissimo. **flying visit** n visita f lampo inv

fly: flyleaf n risguardo m. **fly on the wall** a ⟨documentary⟩ con telecamera nascosta. **flyover** n cavalcavia m inv. **fly-past** n Br Aeron parata f aerea. **flysheet** n (handbill) volantino m; (of tent) soprattenda m inv

foal /fəʊl/ n puledro m

foam /fəʊm/ n schiuma f; (synthetic) gommapiumaᴿ f ● vi spumare; **~ at the mouth** far la bava alla bocca

foam rubber n gommapiumaᴿ f

fob /fɒb/ vt (pt/pp **fobbed**) **~ sth off** affibbiare qcsa (**on sb** a qcno); **~ sb off** liquidare qcno

focal /'fəʊkl/ a focale

focal point n (of village, building) centro m di attrazione; (main concern) punto m centrale; (in optics) fuoco m; **the room lacks a ~ ~** nella stanza manca un punto che focalizzi l'attenzione

focus /'fəʊkəs/ n fuoco m; **in ~** a fuoco; **out of ~** sfocato ● v (pt/pp **focused** or **focussed**) ● vt fig concentrare (**on** su) ● vi **~ on sth** Phot mettere a fuoco qcsa; fig concentrarsi su qcsa

fodder /'fɒdə(r)/ n foraggio m

foe /fəʊ/ n nemico, -a mf

foetal /'fiːtl/ a fetale

foetid /'fetɪd/ a fetido

foetus /'fiːtəs/ n (pl **-tuses**) feto m

fog /fɒg/ n nebbia f

fog bank n banco m di nebbia

fogey /'fəʊgɪ/ n **old ~** persona f antiquata

foggy /'fɒgɪ/ a (**foggier, foggiest**) nebbioso; **it's ~** c'è nebbia; **I haven't got the foggiest** [idea] fam hon ne ho la più pallida idea

foghorn /'fɒghɔːn/ n sirena f da nebbia

fog lamp, foglight /'fɒglaɪt/ n Auto [faro m] antinebbia m inv

foible /'fɔɪbl/ n punto m debole

foil¹ /fɔɪl/ n lamina f di metallo

foil² vt (thwart) frustrare

foil³ n (sword) fioretto m

foist /fɔɪst/ vt appioppare (**on sb** a qcno)

fold¹ /fəʊld/ n (for sheep) ovile m

fold² n piega f ● vt piegare; **~ one's arms** incrociare le braccia ● vi piegarsi; (fail) crollare

■ **fold up** vt ripiegare ⟨chair⟩ ● vi essere pieghevole; ⟨fam: business:⟩ collassare

foldaway /'fəʊldəweɪ/ a ⟨bed⟩ pieghevole; ⟨table⟩ estraibile

folder /'fəʊldə(r)/ n cartella f

folding /'fəʊldɪŋ/ a pieghevole

folding seat n strapuntino m, sedile m pieghevole

folding stool n sgabello m pieghevole

fold-out n (in magazine) pieghevole m

foliage /'fəʊlɪɪdʒ/ n fogliame m

folk /fəʊk/ npl gente f; **my ~s** (family) i miei; **hello there ~s** ciao a tutti

folk: folk dance n danza f popolare. **folklore** n folclore m. **folk medicine** n rimedio m della nonna. **folk memory** n memoria f collettiva. **folk music** n musica f folk. **folk song** n canto m popolare. **folk wisdom** n saggezza f popolare

follow /'fɒləʊ/ vt/i seguire; **it doesn't ~** non è necessariamente così; **~ suit** fig fare lo stesso; **as ~s** come segue

■ **follow up** vt fare seguito a ⟨letter⟩

follower /'fɒləʊə(r)/ n seguace mf

following /'fɒləʊɪŋ/ a seguente ● n seguito m; (supporters) seguaci mpl ● prep in seguito a

follow-on n seguito m

follow-up n (of socialwork case) controllo m; (of patient, ex inmate) visita f di controllo; (film, record, single, programme) seguito m ● attrib ⟨survey, work, interview⟩ successivo; **~ letter** lettera f che fa seguito

folly /'fɒlɪ/ n follia f

foment /fə'ment/ vt fig fomentare

fond /fɒnd/ a affezionato; ⟨hope⟩ vivo; **be ~ of** essere appassionato di ⟨music⟩; **I'm ~ of...** ⟨food, person⟩ mi piace moltissimo...

fondle /'fɒndl/ vt coccolare

fondly /'fɒndlɪ/ adv ⟨hope⟩ ingenuamente

fondness /'fɒndnɪs/ n affetto m; (for things) amore m

font /fɒnt/ n fonte f battesimale; Typ carattere m di stampa

food /fuːd/ n cibo m; (for animals, groceries) mangiare m; **let's buy some ~** compriamo qualcosa da mangiare

food: food mixer n frullatore m. **food poisoning** n intossicazione f alimentare. **food processor** n tritatutto m inv elettrico. **foodstuffs** npl generi mpl alimentari

fool¹ /fuːl/ n sciocco, -a mf; **she's no ~** non è una stupida; **make a ~ of oneself** rendersi ridicolo ● vt prendere in giro ● vi **~ around** giocare; ⟨husband, wife:⟩ avere l'amante

fool² n Culin crema f

foolhardy /'fuːlhɑːdɪ/ a temerario

foolish /'fuːlɪʃ/ a stolto

foolishly /'fuːlɪʃlɪ/ adv scioccamente

foolishness /'fuːlɪʃnɪs/ n sciocchezza f

foolproof /'fuːlpruːf/ a facilissimo

foolscap /'fuːlskæp/ n (Br: paper) carta f protocollo

foot /fʊt/ n (pl **feet**) piede m; (of animal) zampa f; (measure) piede (=30,48 cm); **on ~** a piedi; **on one's feet** in piedi; **put one's ~ in it** fam fare una gaffe

footage /'fʊtɪdʒ/ n (piece of film) spezzone m; **news ~** servizio m [filmato]

foot: foot-and-mouth disease n afta f

epizootica. **football** *n* calcio *m*; (*ball*) pallone *m*. **footballer** *n* giocatore *m* di calcio. **football pools** *npl* totocalcio *m*. **footbrake** *n* freno *m* a pedale. **footbridge** *n* passerella *f*. **foothills** *npl* colline *fpl* pedemontane. **foothold** *n* punto *m* d'appoggio. **footing** *n* **lose one's ~** perdere l'appiglio; **on an equal ~** in condizioni di parità. **footlights** *npl* luci *npl* della ribalta. **footloose and fancy-free** *a* libero come l'aria. **footman** *n* valletto *m*. **footnote** *n* nota *f* a piè di pagina. **footpath** *n* sentiero *m*. **footprint** *n* orma *f*; (*of machine*) ingombro *m*. **footrest** *n* poggiapiedi *m inv*. **footsore** *a* **be ~** avere male ai piedi. **footstep** *n* passo *m*; **follow in sb's ~s** *fig* seguire l'esempio di qcno. **footstool** *n* sgabellino *m*. **footwear** *n* calzature *fpl*

for /fə(r)/, *accentato* /fɔː(r)/ *prep* per; **~ this reason** per questa ragione; **I have lived here ~ ten years** vivo qui da dieci anni; **~ supper** per cena; **~ all that** nonostante questo; **what ~?** a che scopo?; **send ~ a doctor** chiamare un dottore; **fight ~ a cause** lottare per una causa; **go ~ a walk** andare a fare una passeggiata; **there's no need ~ you to go** non c'è bisogno che tu vada; **it's not ~ me to say** no sta a me dirlo; **now you're ~ it** ora sei nei pasticci ● *conj* poiché, perché

forage /ˈfɒrɪdʒ/ *n* foraggio *m* ● *vi* **~ for** cercare

foray /ˈfɒreɪ/ *n* *Mil* incursione *f*; **make a ~ into** (*politics, acting*) tentare la strada di

forbade /fəˈbæd/ *see* **forbid**

forbearance /fɔːˈbeərəns/ *n* pazienza *f*

forbearing /fɔːˈbeərɪŋ/ *a* tollerante

forbid /fəˈbɪd/ *vt* (*pt* **forbade**, *pp* **forbidden**) proibire

forbidding /fəˈbɪdɪŋ/ *a* (*prospect*) che spaventa; (*stern*) severo

force /fɔːs/ *n* forza *f*; **in ~** in vigore; (*in large numbers*) in massa; **come into ~** entrare in vigore; **the** [armed] **~s** *pl* le forze armate ● *vt* forzare; **~ sth on sb** (*decision*) imporre qcsa a qcno; (*drink*) costringere qcno a fare qcsa

■ **force back** *vt* trattenere (*tears*)

■ **force down** *vt* buttar giù (*controvoglia*) (*food, drink*)

forced /fɔːst/ *a* forzato

forced landing *n* atterraggio *m* forzato

force-feed *vt* (*pt/pp* **-fed**) nutrire a forza

forceful /ˈfɔːsfʊl/ *a* energico

forcefully /ˈfɔːsfʊlɪ/ *adv* (*say, argue*) con forza

forceps /ˈfɔːseps/ *npl* forcipe *m*

forcible /ˈfɔːsəbl/ *a* forzato

forcibly /ˈfɔːsəblɪ/ *adv* forzatamente

ford /fɔːd/ *n* guado *m* ● *vt* guadare

fore /fɔː(r)/ *n* **to the ~** in vista; **come to the ~** salire alla ribalta

forearm /ˈfɔːrɑːm/ *n* avambraccio *m*

forebears /ˈfɔːbeəz/ *npl* antenati *mpl*

foreboding /fɔːˈbəʊdɪŋ/ *n* presentimento *m*

forecast /ˈfɔːkɑːst/ *n* previsione *f* ● *vt* (*pt/pp* **forecast**) prevedere

forecaster /ˈfɔːkɑːstə(r)/ *n* pronosticatore, -trice *mf*; (*economic*) analista *mf* della congiuntura; (*of weather*) meteorologo, -a *mf*

fore: forecourt *n* (*of garage*) spiazzo *m* [antistante]. **forefathers** *npl* antenati *mpl*. **forefinger** *n* [dito *m*] indice *m*. **forefront** *n* **be in the ~** essere all'avanguardia. **foregone** *a* **be a ~ conclusion** essere una cosa scontata. **foreground** *n* primo piano *m*. **forehand** *n* *Tennis* diritto *m*

forehead /ˈfɔːhed, ˈfɒrɪd/ *n* fronte *f*

foreign /ˈfɒrən/ *a* straniero; (*trade*) estero; (*not belonging*) estraneo; **he is ~** è uno straniero

foreign currency *n* valuta *f* estera

foreigner /ˈfɒrənə(r)/ *n* straniero, -a *mf*

foreign: foreign exchange *n* (*currency*) valuta *f* estera. **foreign language** *n* lingua *f* straniera. **Foreign Office** *n* ministero *m* degli [affari] Esteri. **Foreign Secretary** *n* Ministro *m* degli Esteri

foreleg /ˈfɔːleg/ *n* zampa *f* anteriore

foreman /ˈfɔːmən/ *n* caporeparto *m*

foremost /ˈfɔːməʊst/ *a* principale ● *adv* **first and ~** in primo luogo

forename /ˈfɔːneɪm/ *n* nome *m* di battesimo

forensic /fəˈrensɪk/ *a* **~ medicine** medicina legale

forensic scientist *n* medico *m* legale

forerunner /ˈfɔːrʌnə(r)/ *n* precursore *m*

foresee /fɔːˈsiː/ *vt* (*pt* **-saw**, *pp* **-seen**) prevedere

foresight /ˈfɔːsaɪt/ *n* previdenza *f*

foreskin /ˈfɔːskɪn/ *n* *Anat* prepuzio *m*

forest /ˈfɒrɪst/ *n* foresta *f*

forestall /fɔːˈstɔːl/ *vt* prevenire

forester /ˈfɒrɪstə(r)/ *n* guardia *f* forestale

forest fire *n* incendio *m* del bosco

forest ranger /ˈreɪndʒə(r)/ *n* *Am* guardia *f* forestale

forestry /ˈfɒrɪstrɪ/ *n* silvicoltura *f*

foretaste /ˈfɔːteɪst/ *n* pregustazione *f*

foretell /fɔːˈtel/ *vt* (*pt/pp* **-told**) predire

forethought /ˈfɔːθɔːt/ *n* accortezza *f*, previdenza *f*

forever /fəˈrevə(r)/ *adv* per sempre; **he's ~ complaining** si lamenta sempre

forewarn /fɔːˈwɔːn/ *vt* avvertire

foreword /ˈfɔːwɜːd/ *n* prefazione *f*

forfeit /ˈfɔːfɪt/ *n* (*in game*) pegno *m*; *Jur* penalità *f* ● *vt* perdere

forfeiture /ˈfɔːfɪtʃə(r)/ *n* (*of right*) perdita *f*; (*of property*) confisca *f*

forgave /fəˈgeɪv/ *see* **forgive**

forge¹ /fɔːdʒ/ *vi* **~ ahead** (*runner:*) lasciarsi indietro gli altri; *fig* farsi strada

forge² *n* fucina *f* ● *vt* fucinare; (*counterfeit*) contraffare

forger /ˈfɔːdʒə(r)/ *n* contraffattore *m*

forgery /ˈfɔːdʒərɪ/ *n* contraffazione *f*

forget /fəˈget/ *vt/i* (*pt* **-got**, *pp* **-gotten**) dimenticare; dimenticarsi di (*language, skill*); **~ oneself** perdere la padronanza di sé

forgetful /fə'getfʊl/ *a* smemorato

forgetfulness /fə'getfʊlnɪs/ *n* smemoratez-za *f*

forget-me-not *n* non-ti-scordar-di-mé *m inv*

forgettable /fə'getəbl/ *a* ⟨*day, fact, film*⟩ da dimenticare

forgive /fə'gɪv/ *vt* (*pt* **-gave**, *pp* **-given**) **~ sb for sth** perdonare qcno per qcsa

forgiveness /fə'gɪvnɪs/ *n* perdono *m*

forgiving /fə'gɪvɪŋ/ *a* ⟨*person*⟩ indulgente

forgo /fɔː'gəʊ/ *vt* (*pt* **-went**, *pp* **-gone**) rinunciare a

forgot(ten) /fə'gɒt(n)/ *see* **forget**

fork /fɔːk/ *n* forchetta *f*; (*for digging*) forca *f*; (*in road*) bivio *m* ● *vi* ⟨*road:*⟩ biforcarsi; **~ right** prendere a destra

■ **fork out** *vt fam* sborsare ● *vi* sborsare soldi

forked lightning /fɔːkt/ *n* fulmine *m* ramificato

fork-lift truck *n* elevatore *m*

forlorn /fə'lɔːn/ *a* ⟨*look*⟩ perduto; ⟨*place*⟩ derelitto; **~ hope** speranza *f* vana

form /fɔːm/ *n* forma *f*; (*document*) modulo *m*; *Sch* classe *f* ● *vt* formare; formulare ⟨*opinion*⟩ ● *vi* formarsi

formal /'fɔːml/ *a* formale

formalin /'fɔːməlɪn/ *n* formalina *f*

formality /fɔː'mælətɪ/ *n* formalità *f inv*

formally /'fɔːməlɪ/ *adv* in modo formale; (*officially*) ufficialmente

format /'fɔːmæt/ *n* formato *m* ● *vt* formattare ⟨*disk, page*⟩

formation /fɔː'meɪʃn/ *n* formazione *f*

formative /'fɔːmətɪv/ *a* **~ years** anni formativi

former /'fɔːmə(r)/ *a* precedente; ⟨*PM, colleague*⟩ ex; **the ~, the latter** il primo, l'ultimo

formerly /'fɔːməlɪ/ *adv* precedentemente; (*in olden times*) in altri tempi

formidable /'fɔːmɪdəbl/ *a* formidabile

formless /'fɔːmlɪs/ *a* ⟨*mass*⟩ informe; ⟨*novel*⟩ che manca di struttura

form teacher *n Br Sch* ≈ coordinatore, -trice *mf* del consiglio di classe

formula /'fɔːmjʊlə/ *n* (*pl* **-ae** /'fɔːmjʊliː/ *or* **-s**) formula *f*

formulate /'fɔːmjʊleɪt/ *vt* formulare

formulation /fɔːmjʊ'leɪʃn/ *n* formulazione *f*

fornication /fɔːnɪ'keɪʃn/ *n* fornicazione *f*

forsake /fə'seɪk/ *vt* (*pt* **-sook** /fə'sʊk/, *pp* **-saken**) abbandonare

forseeable /fə'siːəbl/ *a* **in the ~ future** in futuro per quanto si possa prevedere

forswear /fɔː'sweə(r)/ *vt* ⟨*renounce*⟩ abiurare

fort /fɔːt/ *n Mil* forte *m*

forte /'fɔːteɪ/ *n* [pezzo *m*] forte *m*

forth /fɔːθ/ *adv* **back and ~** avanti e indietro; **and so ~** e così via

forthcoming /fɔːθ'kʌmɪŋ/ *a* prossimo; (*communicative*) communicativo; **no re-**

sponse was ~ non arrivava nessuna risposta

forthright /'fɔːθraɪt/ *a* schietto

forthwith /fɔː'θwɪð/ *adv* immediatamente

fortieth /'fɔːtɪɪθ/ *a & n* quarantesimo, -a *mf*

fortification /fɔːtɪfɪ'keɪʃn/ *n* fortificazione *f*

fortify /'fɔːtɪfaɪ/ *vt* (*pt/pp* **-ied**) fortificare; *fig* rendere forte

fortitude /'fɔːtɪtjuːd/ *n* coraggio *m*

fortnight /'fɔːtnaɪt/ *n Br* quindicina *f*

fortnightly /'fɔːtnaɪtlɪ/ *a* bimensile ● *adv* ogni due settimane

fortress /'fɔːtrɪs/ *n* fortezza *f*

fortuitous /fɔː'tjuːɪtəs/ *a* fortuito

fortunate /'fɔːtʃənət/ *a* fortunato; **that's ~!** meno male!

fortunately /'fɔːtʃənətlɪ/ *adv* fortunatamente

fortune /'fɔːtʃuːn/ *n* fortuna *f*

fortune cookie *n Am* biscottino *m* che racchiude un foglietto con una predizione

fortune-teller *n* indovino, -a *mf*

forty /'fɔːtɪ/ *a & n* quaranta *m*; **have ~ winks** *fam* fare un pisolino

forum /'fɔːrəm/ *n* foro *m*

forward /'fɔːwəd/ *adv* avanti; (*towards the front*) in avanti; **move ~** andare avanti ● *a* in avanti; (*presumptuous*) sfacciato ● *n Sport* attaccante *m* ● *vt* inoltrare ⟨*letter*⟩; spedire ⟨*goods*⟩

forward buying *n Fin* acquisto *m* a termine

forwarding address *n* indirizzo *m* a cui inoltrare la corrispondenza

forward planning *n* pianificazione *f* a lungo termine

forwards /'fɔːwədz/ *adv* avanti

fossil /'fɒs(ə)l/ *n* fossile *m*

fossil fuel *n* combustibile *m* fossile

fossilized /'fɒsɪlaɪzd/ *a* fossile; ⟨*ideas*⟩ fossilizzato

foster /'fɒstə(r)/ *vt* allevare ⟨*child*⟩

foster child *n* figlio, -a *mf* inaffidamento

foster mother *n* madre *f* affidataria

fought /fɔːt/ *see* **fight**

foul /faʊl/ *a* ⟨*smell, taste*⟩ cattivo; ⟨*air*⟩ viziato; ⟨*language*⟩ osceno; ⟨*mood, weather*⟩ orrendo ● *vt* inquinare ⟨*water*⟩; *Sport* commettere un fallo contro; ⟨*nets, rope:*⟩ impigliarsi in

■ **foul up** *vt* (*fam: spoil*) mandare in malora

foul-mouthed /-'maʊðd/ *a* sboccato

foul play *n Jur* delitto *m* ● *n Sport* fallo *m*

foul-smelling /-'smelɪŋ/ *a* puzzo. **foul up** *n fam* intoppo *m*

found¹ /faʊnd/ *see* **find**

found² *vt* fondare

foundation /faʊn'deɪʃn/ *n* (*basis*) fondamento *m*; (*charitable*) fondazione *f*; **~s** *pl* (*of building*) fondamenta *fpl*; **lay the ~-stone** porre la prima pietra

foundation course *n Br Univ* corso *m* propedeutico

founder¹ /'faʊndə(r)/ *n* fondatore, -trice *mf*

founder² *vi* ⟨*ship:*⟩ affondare

foundry /'faʊndrɪ/ n fonderia f
fount /faʊnt/ n Typ carattere m [stampa]
fountain /'faʊntɪn/ n fontana f
fountain pen n penna f stilografica
four /fɔː(r)/ a & n quattro m
four: four four time n Mus quattro quarti.
  four-letter word n parolaccia f. **four-poster**
  [**bed**] n letto m a baldacchino
foursome /'fɔːsəm/ n quartetto m
four-stroke a ‹engine› a quattro tempi
fourteen /fɔː'tiːn/ a & n quattordici m
fourteenth /fɔː'tiːnθ/ a & n quattordicesi-
  mo, -a mf
fourth /fɔːθ/ a & n quarto, -a mf
fourthly /'fɔːθlɪ/ adv in quarto luogo
fourth rate a ‹job, hotel, film› di terz'ordine
four-wheel drive [**vehicle**] n quattro per
  quattro m inv
fowl /faʊl/ n pollame m
fox /fɒks/ n volpe f ● vt (puzzle) ingannare
fox: fox cub n volpacchiotto m. **fox fur** n
  pelliccia f di volpe. **foxglove** n digitale f.
  foxhound n foxhound m inv. **fox-hunt** n caccia f alla volpe. **fox terrier** n fox-terrier m inv.
  foxtrot n fox-trot m inv
foxy /'fɒksɪ/ a (-ier, -iest) (fam: sexy) sexy
  inv; (crafty) scaltro
foyer /'fɔɪeɪ/ n Theat ridotto m; (in hotel) salone m d'ingresso
fracas /'frækɑː/ n baruffa f
fraction /'frækʃn/ n frazione f
fractionally /'frækʃənəlɪ/ adv (slightly) leggermente
fracture /'fræktʃə(r)/ n frattura f ● vt
  fratturare ● vi fratturarsi
fragile /'frædʒaɪl/ a fragile
fragment /'frægmənt/ n frammento m
fragmentary /'frægm(ə)ntərɪ/ a frammentario
fragrance /'freɪgrəns/ n fragranza f
fragrant /'freɪgrənt/ a fragrante
frail /freɪl/ a gracile
frailty /'freɪltɪ/ n (imperfection) debolezza f;
  (of person: moral) fragilità f inv; (of person:
  physical) gracilità f; (of health, state)
  precarietà f inv
frame /freɪm/ n (of picture, door, window) cornice f; (of spectacles) montatura f; Anat ossatura f; (structure, of bike) telaio m; ~ **of mind**
  stato m d'animo ● vt incorniciare ‹picture›;
  fig formulare; (sl: incriminate) montare
framework /'freɪmwɜːk/ n struttura f;
  within the ~ of the law nell'ambito della
  legge
franc /fræŋk/ n franco m
France /frɑːns/ n Francia f
franchise /'fræntʃaɪz/ n Pol diritto m di
  voto; Comm franchigia f
Franciscan /fræn'sɪskən/ n francescano m
frank¹ /fræŋk/ vt affrancare ‹letter›
frank² a franco
Frankfurt /'fræŋkfɜːt/ n Francoforte f
frankfurter /'fræŋkfɜːtə(r)/ n würstel m inv
frankincense /'fræŋkɪnsens/ n incenso m

franking machine /'fræŋkɪŋ/ n affranca-
  trice f
frankly /'fræŋklɪ/ adv francamente
frantic /'fræntɪk/ a frenetico; **be ~ with**
  worry essere agitatissimo
frantically /'fræntɪklɪ/ adv freneticamente
fraternal /frə'tɜːnl/ a fraterno
fraternity /frə'tɜːnətɪ/ n (club) associazione
  f; (spirit, brotherhood) fratellanza f
fraud /frɔːd/ n frode f; (person) impostore m
fraudulent /'frɔːdjʊlənt/ a fraudolento
fraught /frɔːt/ a ~ **with** pieno di
fray¹ /freɪ/ n mischia f
fray² vi sfilacciarsi
frayed /freɪd/ a ‹cuffs› sfilacciato; ‹nerves› a
  pezzi
frazzle /'fræz(ə)l/ n **be worn to a ~** essere
  ridotto uno straccio; **burn sth to a ~**
  carbonizzare qcsa
freak /friːk/ n fenomeno m; (person) scherzo
  m di natura; (fam: weird person) tipo m
  strambo ● a anormale
■ **freak out** vi (fam: lose control, go crazy)
  andar fuori di testa
freakish /'friːkɪʃ/ a strambo
freckle /'frekl/ n lentiggine f
freckled /'frekld/ a lentigginoso
free /friː/ a (**freer, freest**) libero; ‹ticket,
  copy› gratuito; (lavish) generoso; ~ **of**
  charge gratuito; **set ~** liberare; ~ **with...**
  Comm in omaggio per... ● vt (pt/pp **freed**) liberare
free agent n persona f libera di agire come
  vuole
free and easy a disinvolto
freebee, freebie /'friːbɪ/ n fam (free gift)
  omaggio m; (trip) viaggio m gratuito;
  (newspaper) giornale m gratuito
freedom /'friːdəm/ n libertà f
free: free enterprise n liberalismo m economico. **free fall** n caduta f libera. **free-for-
  all** n (disorganized situation, fight) baraonda
  f. **freehand** adv a mano libera. **freehold** n
  proprietà f [fondiaria] assoluta. **free house** n
  Br pub m inv che non è legato a nessun produttore di birra. **free-kick** n calcio m di punizione. **freelance** a & adv indipendente.
  freeloader n fam scroccone m
freely /'friːlɪ/ adv liberamente; (generously)
  generosamente; **I ~ admit that...** devo ammettere che...
free: Freemason n massone m. **Freemasonry** n massoneria f. **freephone**
  number n numero m verde. **free-range egg**
  n uovo m di gallina ruspante. **free sample** n
  campione m gratuito. **free spirit** n persona f
  che ama la sua indipendenza. **free-standing**
  a ‹heater› non incassato; ‹statue› a tutto tondo; ‹lamp› a stelo. **freestyle** n stile m libero.
  free trade n libero scambio m. **free trial**
  period n periodo m di prova gratuito.
  freeway n Am autostrada f. **freewheel** vi
  ‹car:› (in neutral) andare in folle; (with engine
  switched off) andare a motore spento;
  ‹bicycle:› andare a ruota libera

freeze /fri:z/ vt (pt **froze**, pp **frozen**) gelare; bloccare ⟨wages⟩ vi ⟨water:⟩ gelare; **it's freezing** si gela; **my hands are freezing** ho le mani congelate

freeze-dried a liofilizzato

freeze-frame n (video) fermo m immagine

freezer /'fri:zə(r)/ n freezer m inv, congelatore m

freezing /'fri:zɪŋ/ a gelido ● n **below** ~ sotto zero

freezing fog n nebbia f ghiacciata

freezing point n punto m di congelamento

freight /freɪt/ n carico m

freight charges npl costi mpl di spedizione

freighter /'freɪtə(r)/ n nave f da carico

freight forwarder n spedizioniere m

freight train n Am treno m merci

French /frentʃ/ a francese ● n (language) francese m; **the** ~ pl i francesi

French: French beans npl fagiolini mpl [verdi]. **French bread** n filone m (di pane). **French Canadian** n canadese mf francofono, -a ● a del Canada francofono. **French doors** npl porta-finestra f inv. **French dressing** n Br vinaigrette f inv. **French fries** npl patate fpl fritte. **French horn** n corno m da caccia. **French kiss** n bacio m profondo. **French knickers** npl culottes fpl. **Frenchman** n francese m. **French polish** n vernice f a olio e gommalacca. **French toast** n pane m immerso nell'uovo sbattuto e fritto. **French window** n porta-finestra f. **Frenchwoman** n francese f

frenetic /frə'netɪk/ a ⟨activity⟩ frenetico

frenzied /'frenzɪd/ a frenetico

frenzy /'frenzɪ/ n frenesia f

frequency /'fri:kwənsɪ/ n frequenza f

frequent[1] /'fri:kwənt/ a frequente

frequent[2] /frɪ'kwent/ vt frequentare

frequently /'fri:kwəntlɪ/ adv frequentemente

fresco /'freskəʊ/ n affresco m

fresh /freʃ/ a fresco; (new) nuovo; (Am: cheeky) sfacciato

freshen /'freʃn/ vi ⟨wind:⟩ rinfrescare

■ **freshen up** vt dare una rinfrescata a ● vi rinfrescarsi

fresh-faced /-'feɪst/ a dalla faccia giovanile

freshly /'freʃlɪ/ adv di recente

freshman /'freʃmən/ n Am matricola f; (fig: in congress, in firm) nuovo arrivato m

freshness /'freʃnɪs/ n freschezza f

freshwater /'freʃwɔ:tə(r)/ a di acqua dolce

fret /fret/ vi (pt/pp **fretted**) inquietarsi

fretful /'fretfʊl/ a irritabile

fretsaw /'fretsɔ:/ n seghetto m da traforo

fretwork /'fretwɜ:k/ n [lavoro m di] traforo m

Freudian slip /'frɔɪdɪən/ n lapsus m inv freudiano

friar /'fraɪə(r)/ n frate m

friction /'frɪkʃn/ n frizione f

Friday /'fraɪdeɪ/ n venerdì m inv

fridge /frɪdʒ/ n frigo m

fried /fraɪd/ see **fry** ● a fritto; ~ **egg** uovo m fritto

friend /frend/ n amico, -a mf

friendly /'frendlɪ/ a (-ier, -iest) ⟨relations, meeting, match⟩ amichevole; ⟨neighbourhood, smile⟩ piacevole; ⟨software⟩ di facile uso; **be** ~ **with** essere amico di

friendship /'frendʃɪp/ n amicizia f

frieze /fri:z/ n fregio m

frigate /'frɪgət/ n fregata f

fright /fraɪt/ n paura f; **take** ~ spaventarsi

frighten /'fraɪt(ə)n/ vt spaventare

■ **frighten away** vt far scappare ⟨bird, intruder⟩

frightened /'fraɪtənd/ a spaventato; **be** ~ aver paura (**of** di)

frightening /'fraɪt(ə)nɪŋ/ a spaventoso

frightful /'fraɪtfl/ a terribile

frightfully /'fraɪtfʊlɪ/ adv terribilmente

frigid /'frɪdʒɪd/ a frigido

frigidity /frɪ'dʒɪdətɪ/ n freddezza f; Psych frigidità f

frill /frɪl/ n volant m inv

frilly /'frɪlɪ/ a ⟨dress⟩ con tanti volant

fringe /frɪndʒ/ n frangia f; (of hair) frangetta f; (fig: edge) margine m

fringe benefits npl benefici mpl supplementari

frisk /frɪsk/ vt (search) perquisire

frisky /'frɪskɪ/ a (-ier, -iest) vispo

fritter /'frɪtə(r)/ n frittella f

■ **fritter away** vt sprecare

frivolity /frɪ'vɒlətɪ/ n frivolezza f

frivolous /'frɪvələs/ a frivolo

frizzy /'frɪzɪ/ a (-ier, -iest) crespo

fro /frəʊ/ see **to**

frock /frɒk/ n abito m

frog /frɒg/ n rana f

frog: frogman n uomo m rana inv. **frogmarch** vt Br portare via a forza. **frogs' legs** npl cosce fpl di rana. **frogspawn** n uova fpl di rana

frolic /'frɒlɪk/ vi (pt/pp **frolicked**) ⟨lambs:⟩ sgambettare; ⟨fam: people⟩ folleggiare

from /frɒm/ prep da; ~ **Monday** da lunedì; ~ **that day** da quel giorno; **he's** ~ **London** è di Londra; **this is a letter** ~ **my brother** questa è una lettera di mio fratello; **documents** ~ **the 16th century** documenti del XVI secolo; **made** ~ fatto con; **she felt ill** ~ **fatigue** si sentiva male dalla stanchezza; ~ **now on** d'ora in poi

front /frʌnt/ n parte f anteriore; (fig: organization etc) facciata f; (of garment) davanti m; (sea~) lungomare m; Mil, Pol, Meteorol fronte m; **in** ~ **of** davanti a; **in** ~ **at the** ~ davanti; **to the** ~ avanti ● a davanti; ⟨page, row, wheel⟩ anteriore

frontage /'frʌntɪdʒ/ n (of house) facciata f; **with ocean/river** ~ (access) prospiciente l'oceano/il fiume

frontal /'frʌntl/ a frontale

front: front bench n Br Pol parlamentari mpl di maggiore importanza. **front door** n porta f d'entrata. **front garden** n giardino m d'avanti

frontier /'frʌntɪə(r)/ n frontiera f

front: **front line** n Mil prima linea f; **be in the ~ ~** fig essere in prima linea. **front of house** n Br Theat foyer m inv. **front runner** n Sport concorrente mf in testa; (favourite) favorito, -a mf. **front-wheel drive** n trazione f anteriore

frost /frɒst/ n gelo m; (hoar~) brina f

frostbite /'frɒs(t)baɪt/ n congelamento m

frostbitten /'frɒs(t)bɪtən/ a congelato

frosted /'frɒstɪd/ a **~ glass** vetro m smerigliato

frostily /'frɒstɪlɪ/ adv gelidamente

frosting /'frɒstɪŋ/ n Am Culin glassa f

frosty /'frɒstɪ/ a (-ier, iest) also fig gelido

froth /frɒθ/ n schiuma f ● vi far schiuma

frothy /'frɒθɪ/ a (-ier, iest) schiumoso

frown /fraʊn/ n cipiglio m ● vi aggrottare le sopraciglia

■ **frown on** vt disapprovare

froze /frəʊz/ see **freeze**

frozen /'frəʊzn/ see **freeze** ● a (corpse, hand) congelato; (wastes) gelido; Culin surgelato; **I'm ~** sono gelato

frozen food n surgelati mpl

frugal /'fru:gl/ a frugale

frugally /'fru:gəlɪ/ adv frugalmente

fruit /fru:t/ n frutto m; (collectively) frutta f; **eat more ~** mangia più frutta

fruit: **fruit bowl** n fruttiera f. **fruit cake** n dolce m con frutta candita. **fruit cocktail** n macedonia f [di frutta]. **fruit drop** n drop m inv alla frutta

fruiterer /'fru:tərə(r)/ n fruttivendolo, -a mf

fruit farmer n frutticoltore m

fruit fly n moscerino m della frutta

fruitful /'fru:tfʊl/ a fig fruttuoso

fruit gum n caramella f alla frutta

fruition /fru:'ɪʃn/ n **come to ~** dare dei frutti

fruit juice n succo m di frutta

fruitless /'fru:tlɪs/ a infruttuoso

fruitlessly /'fru:tlɪslɪ/ adv senza risultato

fruit machine n macchinetta f mangiasoldi

fruit salad n macedonia f [di frutta]

fruity /'fru:tɪ/ a (wine) fruttato

frump /frʌmp/ n donna f scialba

frumpy /'frʌmpɪ/ a scialbo

frustrate /frʌ'streɪt/ vt frustrare; rovinare (plans)

frustrating /frʌ'streɪtɪŋ/ a frustrante

frustration /frʌ'streɪʃn/ n frustrazione f

fry[1] /fraɪ/ n inv **small ~** fig pesce m piccolo

fry[2] vt/i (pt/pp **fried**) friggere

frying pan n padella f

fuchsia /'fju:ʃə/ n fucsia f

fuck /fʌk/ vulg vt/i scopare ● n **I don't give a ~** me ne sbatto; **what the ~ are you doing?** ch e cazzo fai? ● int cazzo!

■ **fuck off** vi (vulg) **~ off!** vaffanculo!

■ **fuck up** vt (vulg: ruin) mandare a puttane

fucking /'fʌkɪŋ/ a vulg del cazzo

fuddled /'fʌd(ə)ld/ a (confused) confuso; (slightly drunk) brillo

fuddy-duddy /'fʌdɪdʌdɪ/ n fam matusa mf inv

fudge /fʌdʒ/ n caramella f a base di zucchero, burro e latte

fuel /'fju:əl/ n carburante m; fig nutrimento m ● vt fig alimentare

fuel: **fuel consumption** n consumo m di carburante. **fuel efficient** a economico. **fuel injection** n iniezione f. **fuel injection engine** n motore m a iniezione. **fuel oil** n nafta f. **fuel pump** n pompa f della benzina. **fuel tank** n serbatoio m

fuggy /'fʌgɪ/ a (Br: smoky) fumoso

fugitive /'fju:dʒɪtɪv/ n fuggiasco, -a mf

fugue /fju:g/ n Mus fuga f

fulcrum /'fʊlkrəm/ n fulcro m

fulfil /fʊl'fɪl/ vt (pt/pp **-filled**) soddisfare (conditions, need); adempiere a (promise); realizzare (dream, desire); **~ oneself** realizzarsi

fulfilling /fʊl'fɪlɪŋ/ a soddisfacente

fulfilment /fʊl'fɪlmənt/ n **sense of ~** senso m di appagamento

full /fʊl/ a pieno (**of** di); (detailed) esauriente; (bus, hotel) completo; (skirt) ampio; **at ~ speed** a tutta velocità; **in ~ swing** in pieno fervore ● adv in pieno; **you know ~ well that** sai benissimo che ● n **in ~** per intero

full: **full-back** n difensore m. **full beam** n Auto [fari mpl] abbaglianti mpl. **full-blown** /-'bləʊn/ a (epidemic) vero a e proprio; (disease) conclamato. **full board** n pensione f completa. **full-bodied** /-'bɒdɪd/ a (wine) corposo. **full-frontal** a (photograph) di nudo frontale. **full house** n Theat tutto esaurito m inv; (in poker) full m inv. **full-length** a (dress) lungo; (curtain) lungo fino a terra; (portrait) intero; **~ film** lungometraggio m. **full moon** n luna f piena. **full-scale** a (model) in scala reale; (alert) di massima gravità. **full stop** n punto m. **full-time** a & adv a tempo pieno

fully /'fʊlɪ/ adv completamente; (in detail) dettagliatamente; **~ booked** (hotel, restaurant) tutto prenotato

fully fledged /-'fledʒd/ a (bird) che ha messo tutte le penne; (lawyer) con tutte le qualifiche; (member) a tutti gli effetti

fulsome /'fʊlsəm/ a esagerato

fumble /'fʌmbl/ vi **~ in** rovistare in; **~ with** armeggiare con; **~ for one's keys** rovistare alla ricerca delle chiavi

fume /fju:m/ vi (be angry) essere furioso

fumes /fju:mz/ npl fumi mpl; (from car) gas mpl di scarico

fumigate /'fju:mɪgeɪt/ vt suffumicare

fun /fʌn/ n divertimento m; **for ~** per ridere; **make ~ of** prendere in giro; **have ~** divertirsi

function /'fʌŋkʃn/ n funzione f; (event) cerimonia f ● vi funzionare; **~ as** (serve as) funzionare da

functional /'fʌŋkʃ(ə)nəl/ a funzionale

function key n Comput tasto m [di] funzioni

function room n sala f di ricevimento

fund /fʌnd/ n fondo m; fig pozzo m; ~s pl fondi mpl ● vt finanziare

fundamental /fʌndə'mentl/ a fondamentale

fundamentalist /fʌndə'mentəlɪst/ n fondamentalista mf

funding /'fʌndɪŋ/ n (financial aid) finanziamento m; (of debt) consolidamento m

fund-raiser /-reɪzə(r)/ n (person) promotore, -trice mf di raccolte di fondi; (event) manifestazione f per la raccolta di fondi

fund-raising /-reɪzɪŋ/ n raccolta f di fondi

funeral /'fju:nərəl/ n funerale m

funeral: funeral directors n impresa f di pompe funebri. **funeral home, funeral parlour** Am n camera f ardente. **funeral march** n marcia f funebre. **funeral service** n rito m funebre

funereal /fju:'nɪərɪəl/ a lugubre

funfair /'fʌnfeə(r)/ n luna park m inv

fungal /'fʌŋgəl/ a (infection) micotico

fungus /'fʌŋgəs/ n (pl -gi /'fʌŋgaɪ/) fungo m

funicular /fju:'nɪkjʊlə(r)/ n funicolare f

fun loving /'fʌnlʌvɪŋ/ a (person) amante del divertimento

funnel /'fʌnl/ n imbuto m; (on ship) ciminiera f

funnily /'fʌnɪlɪ/ adv comicamente; (oddly) stranamente; ~ **enough** strano a dirsi

funny /'fʌnɪ/ a (-ier, -iest) buffo; (odd) strano

funny bone n osso m del gomito

funny business n fam affare m losco

fur /fɜ:(r)/ n pelo m; (for clothing) pelliccia f; (in kettle) deposito m

fur coat n pelliccia f

furious /'fjʊərɪəs/ a furioso

furiously /'fjʊərɪəslɪ/ adv furiosamente

furl /fɜ:l/ vt serrare (sail)

furnace /'fɜ:nɪs/ n fornace f

furnish /'fɜ:nɪʃ/ vt ammobiliare (flat); fornire (supplies)

furnished /'fɜ:nɪʃt/ a ~ **room** stanza f ammobiliata

furnishings /'fɜ:nɪʃɪŋz/ npl mobili mpl

furniture /'fɜ:nɪtʃə(r)/ n mobili mpl

furniture remover /rɪmu:və(r)/ n Br impresa f di traslochi

furniture van n furgone m per i traslochi

furore /fjʊ'rɔ:rɪ/ n (outrage, criticism) scalpore m; (acclaim) entusiasmo m

furred /fɜ:d/ a (tongue) impastato

furrow /'fʌrəʊ/ n solco m

furry /'fɜ:rɪ/ a (animal) peloso; (toy) di peluche

further /'fɜ:ðə(r)/ a (additional) ulteriore; **at the ~ end** all'altra estremità; **until ~ notice** fino a nuovo avviso ● adv più lontano; **~,...** inoltre,...; **~ off** più lontano ● vt promuovere

further education n istruzione f parauniversitaria

furthermore /fɜ:ðə'mɔ:(r)/ adv per di più

furthest /'fɜ:ðɪst/ a più lontano ● adv più lontano; **the ~ advanced of the students** lo studente più avanti

furtive /'fɜ:tɪv/ a furtivo

furtively /'fɜ:tɪvlɪ/ adv furtivamente

fury /'fjʊərɪ/ n furore m

fuse[1] /fju:z/ n (of bomb) detonatore m; (cord) miccia f

fuse[2] n Electr fusibile m ● vt fondere; Electr far saltare ● vi fondersi; Electr saltare; **the lights have ~d** sono saltate le luci

fuse box n scatola f dei fusibili

fuselage /'fju:zəlɑ:ʒ/ n Aeron fusoliera f

fuse wire n [filo m di] fusibile m

fusillade /fju:zɪl'ɑ:d/ n Mil scarica f; fig raffica f

fusion /'fju:ʒn/ n fusione f

fuss /fʌs/ n storie fpl; **make a ~** fare storie; **make a ~ of** colmare di attenzioni ● vi fare storie

fussy /'fʌsɪ/ a (-ier, -iest) (person) difficile da accontentare; (clothes etc) pieno di fronzoli

fusty /'fʌstɪ/ a che odora di stantio; (smell) di stantio

futile /'fju:taɪl/ a inutile

futility /fju:'tɪlətɪ/ n futilità f

future /'fju:tʃə(r)/ a & n futuro; **in ~** in futuro

future perfect n futuro m anteriore

futures npl Fin contratti mpl a termine

futuristic /fju:tʃə'rɪstɪk/ a futuristico

fuzz /fʌz/ n the ~ (sl: police) la pula

fuzzy /'fʌzɪ/ a (-ier, -iest) (hair) crespo; (photo) sfuocato

Gg

g, G /dʒiː/ *n* (*letter*) g, G *f inv*; *Mus* sol *m inv*
g *abbr* (**gram(s)**) g
gab /gæb/ *n fam* **have the gift of the ~** avere la parlantina
gabardine /ˈgæbəˈdiːn/ *n* gabardine *f*
gabble /ˈgæb(ə)l/ *vi* parlare troppo in fretta
gable /ˈgeɪb(ə)l/ *n* frontone *m*
gad /gæd/ *vi* (*pt/pp* **gadded**) **~ about** andarsene in giro
gadget /ˈgædʒɪt/ *n* aggeggio *m*
Gaelic /ˈgeɪlɪk/ *a & n* gaelico *m*
gaff /gæf/ *n Br fam* **blow the ~** spifferare un segreto; **blow the ~ on sth** svelare la verità su qcsa
gaffe /gæf/ *n* gaffe *f inv*
gaffer /ˈgæfə(r)/ *n* (*Br: foreman*) caposquadra *m*; (*Br: boss*) capo *m*; *Cinema, TV* tecnico *m* delle luci
gag /gæg/ *n* bavaglio *m*; (*joke*) battuta *f* ● *vt* (*pt/pp* **gagged**) imbavagliare
gaga /ˈgɑːɡɑː/ *a fam* rimbambito
gage /geɪdʒ/ *n & vt Am* = **gauge**
gaiety /ˈgeɪətɪ/ *n* allegria *f*
gaily /ˈgeɪlɪ/ *adv* allegramente
gain /geɪn/ *n* guadagno *m*; (*increase*) aumento *m* ● *vt* acquisire; **~ weight** aumentare di peso; **~ access** accedere ● *vi* ⟨*clock:*⟩ andare avanti
gainful /ˈgeɪnful/ *a* **~ employment** lavoro *m* remunerativo
gainsay /geɪnˈseɪ/ *vt* contraddire ⟨*person*⟩; contestare ⟨*argument*⟩
gait /geɪt/ *n* andatura *f*
gala /ˈgɑːlə/ *n* gala *f*; **swimming ~** manifestazione *f* di nuoto ● *attrib* di gala
galaxy /ˈgæləksɪ/ *n* galassia *f*
gale /geɪl/ *n* bufera *f*
gale warning *n* avvertimento *m* di imminente bufera
gall /ɡɔːl/ *n* (*impudence*) impudenza *f*
gallant /ˈgælənt/ *a* coraggioso; (*chivalrous*) galante
gallantly /ˈgæləntlɪ/ *adv* galantemente
gallantry /ˈgæləntrɪ/ *n* coraggio *m*
gall bladder *n* cistifellea *f*
gallery /ˈgælərɪ/ *n* galleria *f*
galley /ˈgælɪ/ *n* (*ship's kitchen*) cambusa *f*
galley [**proof**] *n* bozza *f* in colonna
Gallic /ˈgælɪk/ *a* francese
gallivant /ˈgælɪvænt/ *vi fam* andare in giro
gallon /ˈgælən/ *n* gallone *m* (= *4,5 l*; *Am* = *3,7 l*)
gallop /ˈgæləp/ *n* galoppo *m* ● *vi* galoppare
gallows /ˈgæləʊz/ *n* forca *f*
gallstone /ˈɡɔːlstəʊn/ *n* calcolo *m* biliare
galore /ɡəˈlɔː(r)/ *adv* a bizzeffe

galvanize /ˈgælvənaɪz/ *vt Techn* galvanizzare; *fig* stimolare (**into** a)
Gambia /ˈgæmbɪə/ *n* Gambia *f*
gambit /ˈgæmbɪt/ *n* prima mossa *f*
gamble /ˈgæmbl/ *n* (*risk*) azzardo *m* ● *vi* giocare; (*on Stock Exchange*) speculare; **~ on** (*rely*) contare su
gambler /ˈgæmblə(r)/ *n* giocatore, -trice *mf* [d'azzardo]
gambling /ˈgæmblɪŋ/ *n* gioco *m* [d'azzardo]
gambol /ˈgæmb(ə)l/ *vi* saltellare
game /geɪm/ *n* gioco *m*; (*match*) partita *f*; (*animals, birds*) selvaggina *f*; **~s** *pl Sch* ≈ ginnastica *f* ● *a* (*brave*) coraggioso; **are you ~?** ti va?; **be ~ for** essere pronto per
game: game bird *n* uccello *m* da cacciagione. **gamekeeper** *n* guardacaccia *m inv*. **game park** *n* = **game reserve. game point** *n Tennis* game point *m inv*. **game reserve** *n* (*for hunting*) riserva *f* di caccia; (*for preservation*) parco *m* naturale [faunistico]. **game show** *n* ≈ quiz *m inv* televisivo
gamesmanship /ˈgeɪmzmənʃɪp/ *n* stratagemmi *mpl*
game warden *n* guardacaccia *m inv*
gaming laws /ˈgeɪmɪŋ/ *npl* leggi *fpl* che regolano il gioco d'azzardo
gaming machine *n* slot machine *f inv*
gammon /ˈgæmən/ *n* coscia *f* di maiale affumicata
gamut /ˈgæmət/ *n fig* gamma *f*
gander /ˈgændə(r)/ *n* oca *f* maschio; **take a ~ at sth** *fam* dare un'occhiata a qcsa
gang /gæŋ/ *n* banda *f*; (*of workmen*) squadra *f* ■ **gang up** *vi* far comunella (**on** contro)
gangland /ˈgæŋlænd/ *n* malavita *f*
gangleader /ˈgæŋliːdə(r)/ *n* capobanda *mf inv*
gangling /ˈgæŋglɪŋ/ *a* spilungone
gangplank /ˈgæŋplæŋk/ *n* passerella *f*
gang rape *n* stupro *m* collettivo
gangrene /ˈgæŋgriːn/ *n* cancrena *f*
gangrenous /ˈgæŋgrɪnəs/ *a* cancrenoso
gangster /ˈgæŋstə(r)/ *n* gangster *m inv*
gangway /ˈgæŋweɪ/ *n* passaggio *m*; *Naut, Aeron* passerella *f*
gaol /dʒeɪl/ *n* carcere *m* ● *vt* incarcerare
gaoler /ˈdʒeɪlə(r)/ *n* carceriere *m*
gap /gæp/ *n* spazio *m*; (*in ages, between teeth*) scarto *m*; (*in memory*) vuoto *m*; (*in story*) punto *m* oscuro
gape /geɪp/ *vi* stare a bocca aperta; (*be wide open*) spalancarsi; **~ at** guardare a bocca aperta
gaping /ˈgeɪpɪŋ/ *a* aperto
garage /ˈgærɑːʒ/ *n* garage *m inv*; (*for*

repairs) meccanico *m*; (*for petrol*) stazione *f* di servizio

garage mechanic *n* meccanico *m*

garage sale *n vendita f di articoli usati a casa propria*

garb /gɑ:b/ *n* tenuta *f*

garbage /'gɑ:bɪdʒ/ *n* immondizia *f*; (*nonsense*) idiozie *fpl*

garbage can *n Am* bidone *m* dell'immondizia

garbled /'gɑ:bld/ *a* confuso

garden /'gɑ:dn/ *n* giardino *m*; [**public**] ~**s** *pl* giardini *mpl* pubblici ● *vi* fare giardinaggio

garden centre *n Br* vivaio *m* (*che vende anche articoli da giardinaggio*)

garden city *n città f inv* giardino

gardener /'gɑ:dnə(r)/ *n* giardiniere, -a *mf*

garden flat *n appartamento m al pianterreno o seminterrato che dà sul giardino*

gardening /'gɑ:dnɪŋ/ *n* giardinaggio *m*

garden: garden shears *npl* cesoie *fpl.* **garden suburb** *n* periferia *f* verde. **garden-variety** *a* ⟨*Am: writer, book*⟩ insignificante

gargle /'gɑ:gl/ *n* gargarismo *m* ● *vi* fare gargarismi

gargoyle /'gɑ:gɔɪl/ *n* gargouille *f inv*

garish /'geərɪʃ/ *a* sgargiante

garland /'gɑ:lənd/ *n* ghirlanda *f*

garlic /'gɑ:lɪk/ *n* aglio *m*

garlic bread *n* pane *m* condito con aglio

garlic press *n* spremiaglio *m inv*

garment /'gɑ:mənt/ *n* indumento *m*

garnet /'gɑ:nɪt/ *n* granato *m*

garnish /'gɑ:nɪʃ/ *n* guarnizione *f* ● *vt* guarnire

garret /'gærɪt/ *n* soffitta *f*

garrison /'gærɪsn/ *n* guarnigione *f*

garrotte /gə'rɒt/ *n Br* garrotta *f* ● *vt* (*strangle*) strangolare

garrulous /'gærʊləs/ *a* chiacchierone

garter /'gɑ:tə(r)/ *n* giarrettiera *f*; (*Am: for man's socks*) reggicalze *m inv* da uomo

gas /gæs/ *n* gas *m inv*; (*Am fam: petrol*) benzina *f* ● *v* (*pt/pp* **gassed**) ● *vt* asfissiare ● *vi fam* blaterare

gas: gas burner *n* becco *m* a gas. **gas chamber** *n* camera *f* a gas. **gas cooker** *n* cucina *f* a gas

gaseous /'gæsɪəs/ *a* gassoso

gas fire *n* stufa *f* a gas

gas-fired /-faɪəd/ *a* ⟨*boiler, water heater*⟩ a gas

gash /gæʃ/ *n* taglio *m* ● *vt* tagliare; ~ **one's arm** farsi un taglio nel braccio

gasket /'gæskɪt/ *n Techn* guarnizione *f*

gas: gas main *n* conduttura *f* del gas. **gas mask** *n* maschera *f* antigas. **gas meter** *n* contatore *m* del gas

gasoline /'gæsəli:n/ *n Am* benzina *f*

gasp /gɑ:sp/ *vi* avere il fiato mozzato

gas ring *n Br* (*fixed*) bruciatore *m*; (*portable*) fornelletto *m* [portatile]

gas station *n Am* distributore *m* di benzina

gassy /'gæsɪ/ *a* ⟨*drink*⟩ gassato

gastric /'gæstrɪk/ *a* gastrico

gastric flu *n* influenza *f* gastro-intestinale

gastric ulcer *n* ulcera *f* gastrica

gastritis /gæ'straɪtɪs/ *n* gastrite *f*

gastroenteritis /gæstrəʊentə'raɪtɪs/ *n* gastroenterite *f*

gastronomy /gæ'strɒnəmɪ/ *n* gastronomia *f*

gate /geɪt/ *n* cancello *m*; (*at airport*) uscita *f*

gâteau /'gætəʊ/ *n* torta *f*

gate: gatecrash *vt* entrare senza invito a ● *vi* entrare senza invito. **gatecrasher** *n* intruso, -a *mf*. **gatehouse** *n* (*to castle*) corpo *m* di guardia; (*to park*) casa *f* del custode. **gatekeeper** *n* custode *mf*. **gatepost** *n* palo *m* del cancello. **gateway** *n* ingresso *m*

gather /'gæðə(r)/ *vt* raccogliere; (*conclude*) dedurre; (*in sewing*) arricciare; ~ **speed** acquistare velocità; ~ **together** radunare ⟨*people, belongings*⟩; (*obtain gradually*) acquistare ● *vi* ⟨*people:*⟩ radunarsi; **a storm is** ~**ing** si sta preparando un acquazzone

gathering /'gæðərɪŋ/ *n* **family** ~ ritrovo *m* di famiglia

gauche /gəʊʃ/ *a* ⟨*person, attitude*⟩ impacciato; ⟨*remark*⟩ inopportuno

gaudy /'gɔ:dɪ/ *a* (**-ier, -iest**) pacchiano

gauge /geɪdʒ/ *n* calibro *m*; *Rail* scartamento *m*; (*device*) indicatore *m* ● *vt* misurare; *fig* stimare

gaunt /gɔ:nt/ *a* (*thin*) smunto

gauntlet /'gɔ:ntlɪt/ *n* **throw down the** ~ lanciare il guanto della sfida

gauze /gɔ:z/ *n* garza *f*

gave /geɪv/ *see* **give**

gawky /'gɔ:kɪ/ *a* (**-ier, -iest**) sgraziato

gawp /gɔ:p/ *vi* ~ (**at**) *fam* guardare con aria da ebete

gay /geɪ/ *a* gaio; (*homosexual*) omosessuale; ⟨*bar, club*⟩ gay

gaze /geɪz/ *n* sguardo *m* fisso ● *vi* guardare; ~ **at** fissare; ~ **into space** avere lo sguardo perso nel vuoto

gazelle /gə'zel/ *n* gazzella *f*

gazette /gə'zet/ *n* (*official journal*) bollettino *m* ufficiale; (*newspaper title*) gazzetta *f*

gazetteer /gæzɪ'tɪə(r)/ *n* (*book*) dizionario *m* geografico; (*part of book*) indice *m* dei nomi geografici

gazump /gə'zʌmp/ *vt Comm sl* **we've been** ~**ed** il proprietario della casa ha optato per un'offerta migliore dopo avere accettato la nostra

GB *abbr* (**Great Britain**) GB

GBH *n abbr* (**grievous bodily harm**) lesioni *fpl* personali grave

GCSE *n Br abbr* (**General Certificate of Secondary Education**) *esami mpl conclusivi della scuola dell'obbligo*

GDP *n abbr* (**gross domestic product**) PIL *m*

gear /gɪə(r)/ *n* equipaggiamento *m*; *Techn* ingranaggio *m*; *Auto* marcia *f*; **in** ~ con la marcia innestata; **change** ~ cambiare marcia ● *vt* finalizzare (**to** a) ● *vi* ~ **up for** prepararsi per ⟨*election*⟩

gearbox /'gɪəbʊks/ *n Auto* scatola *f* del cambio

gear lever, *Am* **gear shift** *n* leva *f* del cambio

geese /giːs/ *see* **goose**

geezer /'giːzə(r)/ *n sl* tipo *m*

gel /dʒel/ *n* gel *m inv*

gelatine /'dʒelətɪn/ *n* gelatina *f*

gelatinous /dʒɪ'lætɪnəs/ *a* gelatinoso

gelding /'geldɪŋ/ *n* (*horse*) castrone *m*; (*castration*) castrazione *f*

gelignite /'dʒelɪɡnaɪt/ *n* gelatina *f* esplosiva

gem /dʒem/ *n* gemma *f*

Gemini /'dʒemɪnaɪ/ *n Astr* Gemelli *mpl*

gen /dʒen/ *n Br fam* informazioni *fpl*; **what's the ~ on this?** cosa c'è da sapere su questo?

gender /'dʒendə(r)/ *n Gram* genere *m*

gene /dʒiːn/ *n* gene *m*

genealogy /dʒiːnɪ'ælədʒɪ/ *n* genealogia *f*

gene pool *n* pool *m* genetico

general /'dʒenrəl/ *a* generale ● *n* generale *m*; **in ~** in generale

general election *n* elezioni *fpl* politiche

generalization /dʒenrəlaɪ'zeɪʃn/ *n* generalizzazione *f*

generalize /'dʒenrəlaɪz/ *vi* generalizzare

general knowledge *n* cultura *f* generale

generally /'dʒenrəlɪ/ *adv* generalmente

general: general practitioner *n* medico *m* generico. **general public** *n* [grande] pubblico *m*. **general-purpose** *a* multiuso *inv*

generate /'dʒenəreɪt/ *vt* generare

generation /dʒenə'reɪʃn/ *n* generazione *f*

generation gap *n* gap *m inv* generazionale

generator /'dʒenəreɪtə(r)/ *n* generatore *m*

generic /dʒɪ'nerɪk/ *a* **~ term** termine *m* generico

generosity /dʒenə'rɒsətɪ/ *n* generosità *f*

generous /'dʒenərəs/ *a* generoso

generously /'dʒenərəslɪ/ *adv* generosamente

genesis /'dʒenəsɪs/ *n fig* genesi *f inv*

genetic /dʒɪ'netɪk/ *a* genetico

genetic engineering *n* ingegneria *f* genetica

genetic fingerprinting /'fɪŋɡəprɪntɪŋ/ *n* impronte *fpl* genetiche

geneticist /dʒɪ'netɪsɪst/ *n* genetista *mf*

genetics /dʒɪ'netɪks/ *n* genetica *f*

Geneva /dʒɪ'niːvə/ *n* Ginevra *f*

genial /'dʒiːnɪəl/ *a* gioviale

genially /'dʒiːnɪəlɪ/ *adv* con giovialità

genie /'dʒiːnɪ/ *n* genio *m*

genitals /'dʒenɪtlz/ *npl* genitali *mpl*

genitive /'dʒenɪtɪv/ *a & n* **~** [**case**] genitivo *m*

genius /'dʒiːnɪəs/ *n* (*pl* **-uses**) genio *m*

Genoa /'dʒenəʊə/ *n* Genova *f*

genocide /'dʒenəsaɪd/ *n* genocidio *m*

genre /'ʒɒrə/ *n* genere *m* [letterario]

gent /dʒent/ *n fam* signore *m*; **the ~s** *sg* il bagno per uomini

genteel /dʒen'tiːl/ *a* raffinato

gentle /'dʒentl/ *a* delicato; (*breeze, tap, slope*) leggero

gentleman /'dʒentlmən/ *n* signore *m*; (*well-mannered*) gentiluomo *m*

gentleness /'dʒentlnɪs/ *n* delicatezza *f*

gently /'dʒentlɪ/ *adv* delicatamente

gentry /'dʒentrɪ/ *n* alta borghesia *f*

genuine /'dʒenjʊɪn/ *a* genuino

genuinely /'dʒenjʊmlɪ/ *adv* (*sorry*) sinceramente

genus /'dʒiːnəs/ *n Biol* genere *m*

geographer /dʒɪ'ɒɡrəfə(r)/ *n* geografo *m*

geographical /dʒɪə'ɡræfɪkl/ *a* geografico

geographically /dʒɪə'ɡræfɪklɪ/ *adv* geographicamente

geography /dʒɪ'ɒɡrəfɪ/ *n* geografia *f*

geological /dʒɪə'lɒdʒɪkl/ *a* geologico

geologist /dʒɪ'ɒlədʒɪst/ *n* geologo, -a *mf*

geology /dʒɪ'ɒlədʒɪ/ *n* geologia *f*

geometric[al] /dʒɪə'metrɪk[l]/ *a* geometrico

geometry /dʒɪ'ɒmətrɪ/ *n* geometria *f*

geophysics /dʒɪəʊ'fɪzɪks/ *n* geofisica *f*

geopolitical /dʒɪː:əʊpə'lɪtɪkl/ *a* geopolitico

Georgian /'dʒɔːdʒən/ *n & a* georgiano, -a *mf*; (*language*) georgiano *m*

geranium /dʒə'reɪnɪəm/ *n* geranio *m*

gerbil /'dʒɜː:bəl/ *n* gerbillo *m*

geriatric /dʒerɪ'ætrɪk/ *a* geriatrico

geriatrics /dʒerɪ'ætrɪks/ *n* geriatria *f*

geriatric ward *n* reparto *m* geriatria

germ /dʒɜːm/ *n* germe *m*; **~s** *pl* microbi *mpl*

German /'dʒɜːmən/ *n & a* tedesco, -a *mf*; (*language*) tedesco *m*

germane /dʒə'meɪn/ *a* (*point, remark*) pertinente

Germanic /dʒə'mænɪk/ *a* germanico

German measles *n* rosolia *f*

German shepherd *n* pastore *m* tedesco

Germany /'dʒɜːmənɪ/ *n* Germania *f*

germinate /'dʒɜːmɪneɪt/ *vi* germogliare

germ warfare *n* guerra *f* batteriologica

gerrymandering /'dʒerɪmænd(ə)rɪŋ/ *n* manipolazione *f* dei confini di una circoscrizione elettorale

gerund /'dʒerənd/ *n* gerundio *m*

gestate /dʒe'steɪt/ *vi Biol* essere incinta; *fig* maturare

gestation /dʒe'steɪʃən/ *n* gestazione *f*

gesticulate /dʒe'stɪkjʊleɪt/ *vi* gesticolare

gesture /'dʒestʃə(r)/ *n* gesto *m*

get /get/ *v* (*pt/pp* **got**, *pp Am also* **gotten**, *pres p* **getting**) ● *vt* (*receive*) ricevere; (*obtain*) ottenere; trovare (*job*); (*buy, catch, fetch*) prendere; (*transport, deliver to airport etc*) portare; (*reach on telephone*) trovare; (*fam: understand*) comprendere; preparare (*meal*); **~ sb to do sth** far fare qcsa a qcno ● *vi* (*become*) **~ tired/bored/angry** stancarsi/annoiarsi/arrabbiarsi; **I'm ~ting hungry** mi sta venendo fame; **~ real!** fatti furbo!; **~ dressed/married** vestirsi/sposarsi; **~ sth ready** preparare qcsa; **~ nowhere** non concludere nulla; **this is ~ting us nowhere** questo non ci è di nessun aiuto; **~ to** (*reach*) arrivare a

■ **get about** vi ⟨person:⟩ muoversi; ⟨rumour:⟩ circolare

■ **get along** vi = **get on**

■ **get along with** vt andare d'accordo con ⟨sb⟩

■ **get around** vi = **get about**

■ **get at** vi (criticize) criticare; **I see what you're ~ting at** ho capito cosa vuoi dire; **what are you ~ting at?** dove vuoi andare a parare?

■ **get away** vi (leave) andarsene; (escape) scappare

■ **get back** vi tornare; **I'll ~ back to you** ci faccio sapere ● vt (recover) riavere; **~ one's own back** rifarsi

■ **get behind with** vt rimanere indietro con

■ **get by** vi passare; (manage) cavarsela

■ **get down** vi scendere; **~ down to work** mettersi al lavoro ● vt (depress) buttare giù

■ **get in** vi entrare ● vt mettere dentro ⟨washing⟩; far venire ⟨plumber⟩

■ **get off** vi scendere; (from work) andarsene; Jur essere assolto; **~ off the bus/one's bike** scendere dal pullman/dalla bici ● vt (remove) togliere

■ **get on** vi salire; (be on good terms) andare d'accordo; (make progress) andare avanti; (in life) riuscire; **~ on the bus/one's bike** salire sul pullman/sulla bici; **how are you ~ting on?** come va?

■ **get out** vi uscire; (of car) scendere; **~ out!** fuori! ● vt togliere ⟨cork, stain⟩

■ **get out of** vt (avoid doing) evitare

■ **get over** vi andare al di là ● vt fig riprendersi da ⟨illness⟩

■ **get round** vt aggirare ⟨rule⟩; rigirare ⟨person⟩ ● vi **I never ~ round to it** non mi sono mai deciso a farlo

■ **get through** vi (on telephone) prendere la linea

■ **get up** vi alzarsi; (climb) salire; **~ up a hill** salire su una collina

get: getaway n fuga f. **get-together** n incontro m fra amici. **get-up** n tenuta f. **get-up-and-go** n dinamismo m

geyser /ˈgiːzə(r)/ n scaldabagno m; Geol geyser m inv

G-force n forza f di gravità

ghastly /ˈgɑːstlɪ/ a (-ier, -iest) terribile; **feel ~** sentirsi da cani

gherkin /ˈgɜːkɪn/ n cetriolino m

ghetto /ˈgetəʊ/ n ghetto m

ghetto blaster /blɑːstə(r)/ n fam radioregistratore m stereo portatile

ghost /gəʊst/ n fantasma m

ghostly /ˈgəʊstlɪ/ a spettrale

ghost town n città f inv fantasma

ghost writer n negro m

ghoulish /ˈguːlɪʃ/ a macabro

giant /ˈdʒaɪənt/ n gigante m ● a gigante

gibberish /ˈdʒɪbərɪʃ/ n stupidaggini fpl

gibe /dʒaɪb/ n malignità f inv ● vi beffarsi (**at** di)

giblets /ˈdʒɪblɪts/ npl frattaglie fpl

giddiness /ˈgɪdɪnɪs/ n vertigini fpl

giddy /ˈgɪdɪ/ a (-ier, -iest) vertiginoso; **feel ~** avere le vertigini

giddy spell n giramento m di testa

gift /gɪft/ n dono m; (made to charity) donazione f

gifted /ˈgɪftɪd/ a dotato

gift: gift token n Br buono m acquisto. **gift voucher** n Br buono m acquisto. **gift-wrap** vt impacchettare in carta da regalo

gig /gɪg/ n Mus fam concerto m

gigantic /dʒaɪˈgæntɪk/ a gigantesco

giggle /ˈgɪg(ə)l/ n risatina f ● vi ridacchiare

giggly /ˈgɪglɪ/ a ⟨person⟩ che ha la ridarella

gild /gɪld/ vt dorare

gilding /ˈgɪldɪŋ/ n doratura f

gill /dʒɪl/ n (measure) quarto m di pinta

gills /gɪlz/ npl branchia fsg

gilt /gɪlt/ a dorato ● n doratura f

gilt-edged stock /-edʒd/ n Fin investimento m sicuro

gimlet /ˈgɪmlɪt/ n succhiello m

gimmick /ˈgɪmɪk/ n trovata f

gimmicky /ˈgɪmɪkɪ/ a ⟨production⟩ pieno di trovate a effetto

gin /dʒɪn/ n gin m inv

ginger /ˈdʒɪndʒə(r)/ a rosso fuoco inv; ⟨cat⟩ rosso ● n zenzero m

ginger: ginger ale n bibita f gassata allo zenzero. **ginger beer** n bibita f allo zenzero. **gingerbread** n panpepato m. **ginger-haired** /-ˈheəd/ a con i capelli rossi

gingerly /ˈdʒɪndʒəlɪ/ adv con precauzione

ginger nut, ginger snap n biscotto m allo zenzero

gingham /ˈgɪŋəm/ n tessuto m vichy

gin rummy n variante f del gioco del ramino

gipsy /ˈdʒɪpsɪ/ n = **gypsy**

giraffe /dʒɪˈrɑːf/ n giraffa f

girder /ˈgɜːdə(r)/ n Techn trave f

girdle /ˈgɜːdl/ n cintura f; (corset) busto m

girl /gɜːl/ n ragazza f; (female child) femmina f

girl: girl Friday n segretaria f tuttofare inv. **girlfriend** n amica f; (of boy) ragazza f. **girl guide** n Br giovane esploratrice f

girlish /ˈgɜːlɪʃ/ a da ragazza

giro /ˈdʒaɪərəʊ/ n bancogiro m; (cheque) sussidio m di disoccupazione

girth /gɜːθ/ n circonferenza f

gist /dʒɪst/ n **the ~** la sostanza

give /gɪv/ n elasticità f ● v (pt gave, pp given) ● vt dare; (as present) regalare (**to** a); fare ⟨lecture, present, shriek⟩; donare ⟨blood⟩; **~ birth** partorire ● vi (to charity) fare delle donazioni; (yield) cedere

■ **give away** vt dar via; (betray) tradire; (distribute) assegnare; **~ away the bride** portare la sposa all'altare

■ **give back** vt restituire

■ **give in** vt consegnare ● vi (yield) arrendersi

■ **give off** vt emanare

■ **give out** vi ⟨supplies, patience:⟩ esaurirsi;

⟨*engine, heart*:⟩ fermarsi ● *vt* (*distribute*) distribuire; diffondere ⟨*heat*⟩
■ **give over** *vi* ~ **over!** piantala!
■ **give up** *vt* rinunciare a; ~ **oneself up** arrendersi ● *vi* rinunciare
■ **give way** *vi* cedere; *Auto* dare la precedenza; (*collapse*) crollare
give-and-take *n* concessioni *fpl* reciproche
given /'gɪvn/ *see* **give** ● *a* ~ **name** nome *m* di battesimo
glacier /'glæsɪə(r)/ *n* ghiacciaio *m*
glad /glæd/ *a* contento (**of** di)
gladden /'glædn/ *vt* rallegrare
glade /gleɪd/ *n* radura *f*
gladiator /'glædɪeɪtə(r)/ *n* gladiatore *m*
gladiolus /glædɪ'əʊləs/ *n* gladiolo *m*
gladly /'glædlɪ/ *adv* volentieri
glamorize /'glæməraɪz/ *vt* rendere affascinante
glamorous /'glæmərəs/ *a* affascinante
glamour /'glæmə(r)/ *n* fascino *m*
glance /glɑːns/ *n* sguardo *m* ● *vi* ~ **at** dare un'occhiata a
■ **glance up** *vi* alzare gli occhi
gland /glænd/ *n* glandola *f*
glandular /'glændjʊlə(r)/ *a* ghiandolare
glandular fever *n* mononucleosi *f*
glare /gleə(r)/ *n* bagliore *m*; (*look*) occhiataccia *f* ● *vi* ~ **at** dare un'occhiataccia a
glaring /'gleərɪŋ/ *a* sfolgorante; ⟨*mistake*⟩ madornale
glass /glɑːs/ *n* vetro *m*; (*for drinking*) bicchiere *m*
glasses /'glɑːsɪz/ *npl* (*spectacles*) occhiali *mpl*
glasshouse /'glɑːshaʊs/ *n* serra *f*
glassy /'glɑːsɪ/ *a* vitreo
glassy-eyed /-'aɪd/ *a* (*from drink, illness*) che ha gli occhi vitrei
glaucoma /glɔː'kəʊmə/ *n* glaucoma *m*
glaze /gleɪz/ *n* smalto *m* ● *vt* mettere i vetri a ⟨*door, window*⟩; smaltare ⟨*pottery*⟩; *Culin* spennellare
glazed /gleɪzd/ *a* ⟨*eyes*⟩ vitreo
glazier /'gleɪzɪə(r)/ *n* vetraio *m*
gleam /gliːm/ *n* luccichio *m* ● *vi* luccicare
glean /gliːn/ *vt* racimolare ⟨*information*⟩
glee /gliː/ *n* gioia *f*
gleeful /'gliːfʊl/ *a* gioioso
gleefully /'gliːfʊlɪ/ *adv* giosamente
glen /glen/ *n* vallone *m*
glib /glɪb/ *a pej* insincero
glibly /'glɪblɪ/ *adv pej* senza sincerità
glide /glaɪd/ *vi* scorrere; (*through the air*) planare
glider /'glaɪdə(r)/ *n* aliante *m*
gliding /'glaɪdɪŋ/ *n* volo *m* a vela
glimmer /'glɪmə(r)/ *n* barlume *m* ● *vi* emettere un barlume
glimpse /glɪmps/ *n* occhiata *f*; **catch a** ~ **of** intravedere ● *vt* intravedere
glint /glɪnt/ *n* luccichio *m* ● *vi* luccicare
glisten /'glɪsn/ *vi* luccicare
glitch /glɪtʃ/ *n Comput* problema *m* tecnico

glitter /'glɪtə(r)/ *vi* brillare
gloat /gləʊt/ *vi* gongolare (**over** su)
global /'gləʊbl/ *a* mondiale
global warming *n* riscaldamento *m* dell'atmosfera terrestre
globe /gləʊb/ *n* globo *m*; (*as a map*) mappamondo *m*
globe-trotting /-trɒtɪŋ/ *n* viaggi *mpl* intorno al mondo ● *a* ⟨*life*⟩ da giramondo; ⟨*person*⟩ giramondo
globule /'glɒbjuːl/ *n* globulo *m*
gloom /gluːm/ *n* oscurità *f*; (*sadness*) tristezza *f*
gloomily /'gluːmɪlɪ/ *adv* (*sadly*) con aria cupa
gloomy /'gluːmɪ/ *a* (**-ier, -iest**) cupo
glorify /'glɔːrɪfaɪ/ *vt* (*pt/pp* **-ied**) glorificare; **a glorified waitress** niente più che una cameriera
glorious /'glɔːrɪəs/ *a* splendido; ⟨*deed, hero*⟩ glorioso
glory /'glɔːrɪ/ *n* gloria *f*; (*splendour*) splendore *m*; (*cause for pride*) vanto *m* ● *vi* ~ **in** vantarsi di
glory-hole *n fam* ripostiglio *m*
gloss /glɒs/ *n* lucentezza *f*
■ **gloss over** *vt* sorvolare su
glossary /'glɒsərɪ/ *n* glossario *m*
gloss paint *n* vernice *f* lucida
glossy /'glɒsɪ/ *a* (**-ier, -iest**) lucido; ⟨*paper*⟩ patinato; ~ [**magazine**] rivista *f* femminile
glottal stop /'glɒt(ə)l/ *n* occlusiva *f* glottale
glove /glʌv/ *n* guanto *m*
glove compartment *n Auto* cruscotto *m*
glove puppet *n* burattino *m*
glow /gləʊ/ *n* splendore *m*; (*in cheeks*) rossore *m*; (*of candle*) luce *f* soffusa ● *vi* risplendere; ⟨*candle*:⟩ brillare; ⟨*person*:⟩ avvampare
glower /'glaʊə(r)/ *vi* ~ (**at**) guardare in cagnesco
glowing /'gləʊɪŋ/ *a* ardente; ⟨*account*⟩ entusiastico
glow-worm *n* lucciola *f*
glucose /'gluːkəʊs/ *n* glucosio *m*
glue /gluː/ *n* colla *f* ● *vt* (*pres p* **gluing**) incollare
glue-sniffing /-snɪfɪŋ/ *n* sniffare *m* la colla
glum /glʌm/ *a* (**glummer, glummest**) tetro
glumly /'glʌmlɪ/ *adv* con aria tetra
glut /glʌt/ *n* eccesso *m*
glutinous /'gluːtɪnəs/ *a* colloso
glutton /'glʌtən/ *n* ghiottone, -a *mf*
gluttonous /'glʌtənəs/ *a* ghiotto
gluttony /'glʌtənɪ/ *n* ghiottoneria *f*
glycerine /'glɪsəriːn/ *n* glicerina *f*
gm *abbr* (**gram**) g
gnarled /nɑːld/ *a* nodoso
gnash /næʃ/ *vt* ~ **one's teeth** digrignare i denti
gnat /næt/ *n* moscerino *m*
gnaw /nɔː/ *vt* rosicchiare
gnome /nəʊm/ *n* gnomo *m*
GNP *n abbr* (**gross national product**) PNL *m*
go /gəʊ/ *n* (*pl* **goes**) energia *f*; (*attempt*) tenta-

tivo *m*; **on the go** in movimento; **at one go** in una sola volta; **it's your go** tocca a te; **make a go of it** riuscire ● *vi* (*pt* **went**, *pp* **gone**) andare; (*leave*) andar via; (*vanish*) sparire; (*become*) diventare; (*be sold*) vendersi; **go and see** andare a vedere; **go swimming/ shopping** andare a nuotare/fare spese; **where's the time gone?** come ha fatto il tempo a volare così?; **it's all gone** è finito; **be going to do** stare per fare; **I'm not going to** non ne ho nessuna intenzione; **to go** ⟨*Am: hamburgers etc*⟩ da asporto; **a coffee to go** un caffè da portar via

■ **go about** *vi* andare in giro
■ **go about** *vt* affrontare ⟨*task*⟩
■ **go after** *vt* (*chase, pursue*) correr dietro a
■ **go ahead** *vi* (*event*) aver luogo; **go ahead with** mandare avanti ⟨*plans, wedding*⟩
■ **go away** *vi* andarsene
■ **go back** *vi* ritornare
■ **go by** *vi* passare
■ **go down** *vi* scendere; ⟨*sun:*⟩ tramontare; ⟨*ship:*⟩ affondare; ⟨*swelling:*⟩ diminuire
■ **go for** *vt* andare a prendere; andare a cercare ⟨*doctor*⟩; (*choose*) optare per; (*fam: attack*) aggredire; **he's not the kind I go for** non è il genere che mi attira
■ **go in** *vi* entrare
■ **go in for** *vt* partecipare a ⟨*competition*⟩; darsi a ⟨*tennis*⟩
■ **go off** *vi* andarsene; ⟨*alarm:*⟩ scattare; ⟨*gun, bomb:*⟩ esplodere; ⟨*food, milk:*⟩ andare a male; **go off well** riuscire
■ **go on** *vi* andare avanti; **what's going on?** cosa succede?
■ **go on at** *vt fam* scocciare
■ **go on with** *vt* (*continue*) andare avanti con
■ **go out** *vi* uscire; ⟨*light, fire:*⟩ spegnersi
■ **go out with** *vt* uscire con ⟨*sb*⟩
■ **go over** *vi* andare ● *vt* (*check*) controllare
■ **go round** *vi* andare in giro; (*visit*) andare; (*turn*) girare; **is there enough to go round?** ce n'è abbastanza per tutti?
■ **go through** *vi* ⟨*bill, proposal:*⟩ passare ● *vt* (*suffer*) subire; (*check*) controllare; (*read*) leggere
■ **go under** *vi* passare sotto; ⟨*ship, swimmer:*⟩ andare sott'acqua; (*fail*) fallire
■ **go up** *vi* salire; ⟨*Theat: curtain:*⟩ aprirsi
■ **go with** *vt* accompagnare
■ **go without** *vt* fare a meno di ⟨*supper, sleep*⟩ ● *vi* fare senza

goad /gəʊd/ *vt* spingere (**into** a); (*taunt*) spronare

go-ahead *a* ⟨*person, company*⟩ intraprendente ● *n* okay *m*

goal /gəʊl/ *n* porta *f*; (*point scored*) gol *m inv*; (*in life*) obiettivo *m*; **score a** ~ segnare

goalie /'gəʊlɪ/ *fam*, **goalkeeper** /'gəʊlki:pə(r)/ *n* portiere *m*

goalpost /'gəʊlpəʊst/ *n* palo *m*

goat /gəʊt/ *n* capra *f*

goatee /gəʊ'ti:/ *n* pizzo *m*

■ **gobble up** /'gɒbl/ *vt* tranguiare

gobbledygook /'gɒb(ə)ldɪguːk/ *n* ostrogoto *m*

go-between *n* intermediario, -a *mf*

goblet /'gɒblɪt/ *n* calice *m*

goblin /'gɒblɪn/ *n* folletto *m*

gobsmacked /'gɒbsmækt/ *a Br fam* **I was** ~ sono rimasto a bocca aperta

God, god /gɒd/ *n* Dio *m*, dio *m*

god: godchild *n* figlioccio, -a *mf*. **goddamn** *a* maledetto. **god-daughter** *n* figlioccia *f*

goddess /'gɒdes/ *n* dea *f*

god: godfather *n* padrino *m*. **god-fearing** /-fɪərɪŋ/ *a* timorato di Dio. **god-forsaken** /-fəseɪkən/ *a* dimenticato da Dio

godless /'gɒdlɪs/ *a* empio

godlike /'gɒdlaɪk/ *a* divino

godly /'gɒdlɪ/ *a* (**-ier, iest**) pio

god: godmother *n* madrina *f*. **godparents** *npl* padrino *m* e madrina *f*. **godsend** *n* manna *f*. **godson** *n* figlioccio *m*

goer /'gəʊə(r)/ *n Br* **be a** ~ ⟨*car:*⟩ essere una bomba

go-getter *n* ambizioso, -a *mf*

go-getter /'gəʊgetə(r)/ *n* persona *f* intraprendente

go-getting /-getɪŋ/ *a* intraprendente

goggle /'gɒgl/ *vi fam* ~ **at** fissare con gli occhi sgranati ·

goggles *npl* occhiali *mpl*; (*of swimmer*) occhialini *mpl* [da piscina]; (*of worker*) occhiali *mpl* protettivi

going /'gəʊɪŋ/ *a* ⟨*price, rate*⟩ corrente; ~ **concern** azienda *f* florida ● *n* **it's hard** ~ è una faticaccia; **while the** ~ **is good** finché si può

going-over *n* (*cleaning*) pulizia *f* da cima a fondo; (*examination*) revisione *f*; **the doctor gave me a thorough** ~ il dottore mi ha fatto una visita completa; **give sb a** ~ (*beat up*) dare una manica di botte a qcno

goings-on *npl* avvenimenti *mpl*

go-kart /-kɑːt/ *n* go-kart *m inv*

go-karting /-kɑːtɪŋ/ *n* kartismo *m*; **go** ~ fare del kartismo

gold /gəʊld/ *n* oro *m* ● *a* d'oro

gold-digger *n fig* cacciatore, -trice *mf* di dote

gold dust *n* polvere *f* d'oro; *fig* cosa *f* rara

golden /'gəʊldn/ *a* dorato

golden handshake *n Br* buonuscita *f* (*al termine di un rapporto di lavoro*)

golden wedding *n* nozze *fpl* d'oro

gold: goldfish *n inv* pesce *m* rosso. **gold mine** *n* miniera *f* d'oro. **gold-plated** /'pleɪtɪd/ *a* placcato d'oro. **goldsmith** *n* orefice *m*

golf /gɒlf/ *n* golf *m*

golf club *n* circolo *m* di golf; (*implement*) mazza *f* da golf

golf course *n* campo *m* di golf

golfer /'gɒlfə(r)/ *n* giocatore, -trice *mf* di golf

golliwog /'gɒlɪwɒg/ *n* bambolotto *m* negro

gondola /'gɒndələ/ *n* gondola *f*

gondolier /gɒndə'lɪə(r)/ *n* gondoliere *m*

gone /gɒn/ *see* **go**

goner /'gɒnə(r)/ *n fam* **be a ~** essere spacciato

gong /gɒŋ/ *n* gong *m inv*

gonorrh[o]ea /gɒnə'rɪə/ *n* gonorrea *f*

good /gʊd/ *a* (**better, best**) buono; ⟨*child, footballer, singer*⟩ bravo; ⟨*holiday, film*⟩ bello; **~ at** bravo in; **a ~ deal of anger** molta rabbia; **as ~ as** ⟨*almost*⟩ quasi; **~ morning, ~ afternoon** buon giorno; **~ evening** buona sera; **~ night** buonanotte; **have a ~ time** divertirsi ● *n* bene *m*; **for ~** per sempre; **do ~** far del bene; **do sb ~** far bene a qcno; **it's no ~** è inutile; **be up to no ~** combinare qualcosa

goodbye /gʊd'baɪ/ *int* arrivederci

good: good-for-nothing *n* buono, -a *mf* a nulla ● *a* **her ~ son** quel buono a nulla di suo figlio. **Good Friday** *n* Venerdì *m* Santo. **good-humoured** /-'hju:məd/ *a* amichevole; ⟨*remark, smile*⟩ bonario

goodies /'gʊdɪz/ *npl* ⟨*fam: to eat*⟩ bontà *fpl*

good-looking /-'lʊkɪŋ/ *a* bello

good-natured /-'neɪtʃəd/ *a* **be ~** avere un buon carattere

goodness /'gʊdnɪs/ *n* bontà *f*; **my ~!** santo cielo!; **thank ~!** grazie al cielo!

goods /gʊdz/ *npl* prodotti *mpl*

goods train *n* treno *m* merci

good-time girl *n* ⟨*fun-loving*⟩ ragazza *f* allegra; ⟨*euph: prostitute*⟩ donnina *f* allegra

goodwill /gʊd'wɪl/ *n* buona *f* volontà; *Comm* avviamento *m*

goody /'gʊdɪ/ *n* ⟨*fam: person*⟩ buono *m*

goody-goody *n* santarellino, -a *mf*

gooey /'gu:ɪ/ *a fam* appiccicaticcio; *fig* sdolcinato

goof /gu:f/ *vi fam* cannare

goofy /'gu:fɪ/ *a fam* sciocco

goon /gu:n/ *n* ⟨*clown*⟩ svitato *m*; ⟨*thug*⟩ picchiatore *m*

goose /gu:s/ *n* (*pl* **geese**) oca *f*

goose: gooseberry /'gʊzbərɪ/ *n* uva *f* spina. **goose-flesh** *n*, **goose-pimples** *npl* pelle *fsg* d'oca. **goose-step** *n* passo *m* dell'oca

gore[1] /gɔ:(r)/ *n* sangue *m*

gore[2] *vt* incornare

gorge /gɔ:dʒ/ *n Geog* gola *f* ● *vt* **~ oneself** ingozzarsi

gorgeous /'gɔ:dʒəs/ *a* stupendo

gorilla /gə'rɪlə/ *n* gorilla *m inv*

gormless /'gɔ:mlɪs/ *a fam* stupido

gorse /gɔ:s/ *n* ginestrone *m*

gory /'gɔ:rɪ/ *a* (**-ier, -iest**) cruento

gosh /gɒʃ/ *int fam* caspita

gosling /'gɒzlɪŋ/ *n* ochetta *f*

go-slow *n* forma *f* di protesta che consiste in un rallentamento del ritmo di lavoro

gospel /'gɒspl/ *n* vangelo *m*

gospel truth *n* sacrosanta verità *f*

gossamer /'gɒsəmə(r)/ *n* ⟨*fabric*⟩ mussola *f*; ⟨*cobweb*⟩ fili *mpl* di ragnatela

gossip /'gɒsɪp/ *n* pettegolezzi *mpl*; ⟨*person*⟩ pettegolo, -a *mf* ● *vi* pettegolare

gossip column *n* cronaca *f* mondana

gossipy /'gɒsɪpɪ/ *a* pettegolo

got /gɒt/ *see* **get**; **have ~** avere; **have ~ to do sth** dover fare qcsa

Gothic /'gɒθɪk/ *a* gotico

gotten /'gɒtn/ *Am see* **get**

gouge /gaʊdʒ/ *vt* **~ out** cavare

goulash /'gu:læʃ/ *n* gulash *m inv*

gourd /gʊəd/ *n* ⟨*fruit*⟩ zucca *f*

gourmet /'gʊəmeɪ/ *n* buongustaio, -a *mf*

gout /gaʊt/ *n* gotta *f*

govern /'gʌv(ə)n/ *vt/i* governare; ⟨*determine*⟩ determinare

governess /'gʌvənɪs/ *n* istitutrice *f*

government /'gʌvnmənt/ *n* governo *m*

governmental /gʌvn'mentl/ *a* governativo

government stocks *npl* titoli *mpl* di stato

governor /'gʌvənə(r)/ *n* governatore *m*; ⟨*of school*⟩ amministratore, -trice *mf*; ⟨*of prison*⟩ direttore, -trice *mf*; ⟨*fam: boss*⟩ capo *m*

gown /gaʊn/ *n* vestito *m*; *Univ, Jur* toga *f*

GP *abbr* **general practitioner**

grab /græb/ *vt* ⟨*pt/pp* **grabbed**⟩ **~ [hold of]** afferrare

Grace *n* **his/your ~** ⟨*duke*⟩ il signor duca; ⟨*archbishop*⟩ Sua Eccellenza; **her/your ~** ⟨*duchess*⟩ la signora duchessa

grace /greɪs/ *n* grazia *f*; ⟨*before meal*⟩ benedicite *m inv*; **with good ~** volentieri; **say ~** dire il benedicite; **three days' ~** tre giorni di proroga

graceful /'greɪsfʊl/ *a* aggraziato

gracefully /'greɪsfʊlɪ/ *adv* con grazia

gracious /'greɪʃəs/ *a* cortese; ⟨*elegant*⟩ lussuoso

gradation /grə'deɪʃn/ *n* gradazione *f*

grade /greɪd/ *n* livello *m*; *Comm* qualità *f*; *Sch* voto *m*; ⟨*Am Sch: class*⟩ classe *f*; *Am* = **gradient** ● *vt Comm* classificare; *Sch* dare il voto a

grade crossing *n Am* passaggio *m* a livello

gradient /'greɪdɪənt/ *n* pendenza *f*

gradual /'grædʒʊəl/ *a* graduale

gradually /'grædʒʊəlɪ/ *adv* gradualmente

graduate[1] /'grædʒʊət/ *n* laureato, -a *mf*

graduate[2] /'grædʒʊeɪt/ *vi Univ* laurearsi

graduated /'grædʒʊeɪtɪd/ *a* ⟨*container*⟩ graduato

graduation /grædʒʊ'eɪʃn/ *n* laurea *f*; ⟨*calibration*⟩ graduazione *f*

graduation ceremony *n* cerimonia *f* di consegna dei diplomi di laurea

graffiti /grə'fi:tɪ/ *npl* graffiti *mpl*

graffiti artist *n* pittore, -trice *mf* di graffiti

graft /grɑ:ft/ *n Bot, Med* innesto *m*; ⟨*Med: organ*⟩ trapianto *m*; ⟨*fam: hard work*⟩ duro lavoro *m*; ⟨*fam: corruption*⟩ corruzione *f* ● *vt* innestare; trapiantare ⟨*organ*⟩

grain /greɪn/ *n* ⟨*of sand, salt*⟩ granello *m*; ⟨*of rice*⟩ chicco *m*; ⟨*cereals*⟩ cereali *mpl*; ⟨*in wood*⟩ venatura *f*; **it goes against the ~** *fig* è contro la mia/sua natura

grainy /'greɪnɪ/ *a* ⟨*photograph*⟩ sgranato; ⟨*paintwork*⟩ granulato

gram /græm/ *n* grammo *m*

grammar /'græmə(r)/ *n* grammatica *f*

grammarian /grə'meərɪən/ n grammatico, -a mf

grammar school n ≈ liceo m

grammatical /grə'mætɪkl/ a grammaticale

grammatically /grə'mætɪklɪ/ adv grammaticalmente

gran /græn/ n fam nonna f

granary /'grænərɪ/ n granaio m

grand /grænd/ a grandioso; fam eccellente

grand: grandad /'grændæd/ n fam nonno m. **grandchild** n nipote mf. **granddaughter** n nipote f

grandeur /'grændʒə(r)/ n grandiosità f

grand: grandfather n nonno m. **grandfather clock** n pendolo m (che poggia a terra)

grandiose /'grændɪəʊs/ a grandioso

grand: grandmother n nonna f. **grandparents** npl nonni mpl. **grand piano** n pianoforte m a coda. **grand slam** n vittoria f di tutte le fasi di una gara. **grandson** n nipote m. **grandstand** n tribuna f

granite /'grænɪt/ n granito m

granny /'grænɪ/ n fam nonna f

granny flat n Br appartamentino m indipendente per genitori anziani annesso all'abitazione principale

grant /grɑːnt/ n (money) sussidio m; Univ borsa f di studio ● vt accordare; (admit) ammettere; **take sth for ~ed** dare per scontato qcsa; **take sb for ~ed** considerare quello che qcno fa come dovuto

granular /'grænjʊlə(r)/ a granulare

granulated /'grænjʊleɪtɪd/ a ~ **sugar** zucchero m semolato

granule /'grænjuːl/ n granello m

grape /greɪp/ n acino m; ~s pl uva fsg

grapefruit /'greɪpfruːt/ n inv pompelmo m

grapevine /'greɪpvaɪn/ n vite f; **hear sth on the ~** sentir dire in giro qcsa

graph /grɑːf/ n grafico m

graphic /'græfɪk/ a grafico; (vivid) vivido

graphically /'græfɪklɪ/ adv graficamente; (vividly) vividamente

graphic design n grafica f

graphic designer n grafico, -a mf

graphics /'græfɪks/ n grafica f

graphics card n Comput scheda f grafica

graphite /'græfaɪt/ n grafite f

graphologist /græ'fɒlədʒɪst/ n grafologo, -a mf

graph paper n carta f millimetrata

grapple /'græpl/ vi ~ **with** also fig essere alle prese con

grasp /grɑːsp/ n stretta f; (understanding) comprensione f ● vt afferrare

grasping /'grɑːspɪŋ/ a avido

grass /grɑːs/ n erba f;

grass: grasshopper n cavalletta f. **grassland** n prateria f. **grassroots** npl base f; **at the ~** alla base. **grass snake** n biscia f

grassy /'grɑːsɪ/ a erboso

grate¹ /greɪt/ n grata f

grate² vt Culin grattugiare; ~ **one's teeth** far stridere i denti ● vi stridere

grateful /'greɪtfl/ a grato

gratefully /'greɪtfʊlɪ/ adv con gratitudine

grater /'greɪtə(r)/ n Culin grattugia f

gratification /grætɪfɪ'keɪʃn/ n soddisfazione f

gratified /'grætɪfaɪd/ a appagato

gratify /'grætɪfaɪ/ vt (pt/pp -ied) appagare

gratifying /'grætɪfaɪɪŋ/ a appagante

grating /'greɪtɪŋ/ n grata f

gratis /'grɑːtɪs/ adv gratis

gratitude /'grætɪtjuːd/ n gratitudine f

gratuitous /grə'tjuːɪtəs/ a gratuito

gratuity /grə'tjuːətɪ/ n gratifica f

grave¹ /greɪv/ a grave

grave² n tomba f

gravedigger /'greɪvdɪgə(r)/ n becchino m

gravel /'grævl/ n ghiaia f

gravelly /'grævəlɪ/ a (voice) rauco

gravely /'greɪvlɪ/ adv gravemente

graven image /'greɪvən/ n idolo m

gravestone /'greɪvstəʊn/ n lapide f

graveyard /'greɪvjɑːd/ n cimitero m

gravitate /'grævɪteɪt/ vi gravitare

gravity /'grævɒtɪ/ n gravità f

gravy /'greɪvɪ/ n sugo m della carne

gray /greɪ/ a Am = **grey**

graze¹ /greɪz/ vi (animal:) pascolare

graze² n escoriazione f ● vt (touch lightly) sfiorare; (scrape) escoriare; sbucciarsi (knee)

grease /griːs/ n grasso m ● vt ungere

greasepaint /'griːspeɪnt/ n cerone m

greaseproof paper /griːspruːf'peɪpə(r)/ n carta f oleata

greaser /'griːsə(r)/ n (motorcyclist) componente m di una banda giovanile di motociclisti

greasy /'griːsɪ/ a (-ier, -iest) untuoso; (hair, skin) grasso

great /greɪt/ a grande; (fam: marvellous) eccezionale

great: great-aunt n prozia f. **Great Britain** n Gran Bretagna f. **Great Dane** n danese m. **great-grandchildren** npl pronipoti mpl. **great-grandfather** n bisnonno m. **great-grandmother** n bisnonna f

greatly /'greɪtlɪ/ adv enormemente

greatness /'greɪtnɪs/ n grandezza f

great-uncle n prozio m

Grecian /'griːʃ(ə)n/ a greco

Greece /griːs/ n Grecia f

greed /griːd/ n avidità f; (for food) ingordigia f

greedily /'griːdɪlɪ/ adv avidamente; (eat) con ingordigia

greedy /'griːdɪ/ a (-ier, -iest) avido; (for food) ingordo

Greek /griːk/ a & n greco, -a mf; (language) greco m

green /griːn/ a verde; (fig: inexperienced) immaturo ● n verde m; (grass) prato m; (in golf) green m inv; ~s pl verdura f; **the G~s** pl Pol i verdi

green: green beans n fagiolini mpl. **green belt** n zona f verde intorno a una città. **green card** n carta f verde; Am permesso m di soggiorno

greenery /'gri:nərɪ/ n verde m
green: green-eyed monster /-aɪd-'mɒnstə(r)/ n gelosia f. **greenfinch** n verdone m. **green fingers** npl **have ~ ~** avere il police verde. **greenfly** n afide m. **greengage** n susina f verde. **greengrocer** n fruttivendolo, -a mf. **greenhorn** n (new) novellino m; (gullible) pivello m. **greenhouse** n serra f. **greenhouse effect** n effetto m serra. **Greenland** n Groenlandia f. **green light** n fam verde m. **green salad** n insalata f verde
greet /gri:t/ vt salutare; (welcome) accogliere
greeting /'gri:tɪŋ/ n saluto m; (welcome) accoglienza f
greetings card /'gri:tɪŋz/ n biglietto m d'auguri
gregarious /grɪ'geərɪəs/ a gregario; (person) socievole
gremlin /'gremlɪn/ n hum spirito m maligno
grenade /grɪ'neɪd/ n granata f
grenadier /grenə'dɪə(r)/ n Mil guardia f reale inglese
grew /gru:/ see **grow**
grey /greɪ/ a grigio; (hair) bianco ● n grigio m ● vi diventare bianco
grey: greyhound n levriero m. **grey matter** n (brain) materia f grigia. **grey squirrel** n scoiattolo m grigio
grid /grɪd/ n griglia f; (on map) reticolato m; Electr rete f
griddle /'grɪd(ə)l/ n (for meat) piastra f
grid: gridiron n griglia f; Am campo m di football americano. **gridlock** n (fig: deadlock) situazione f di stallo; (in traffic) imbottigliamento m. **grid reference** n coordinate fpl
grief /gri:f/ n dolore m; **come to ~** (plans:) naufragare
grief-stricken /-strɪkən/ a affranto dal dolore
grievance /'gri:vəns/ n lamentela f
grieve /gri:v/ vt addolorare ● vi essere addolorato
grievous /'gri:vəs/ a doloroso
grievously /'gri:vəslɪ/ adv tristemente
grill /grɪl/ n graticola f; (for grilling) griglia f; **mixed ~** grigliata f mista ● vt/i cuocere alla griglia; (interrogate) sottoporre al terzo grado
grille /grɪl/ n grata f
grim /grɪm/ a (**grimmer, grimmest**) arcigno; (determination) accanito
grimace /'grɪməs/ n smorfia f ● vi fare una smorfia
grime /graɪm/ n sudiciume m
grimly /'grɪmlɪ/ adv accanitamente
Grim Reaper n Morte f
grimy /'graɪmɪ/ a (**-ier, -iest**) sudicio
grin /grɪn/ n sorriso m ● vi (pt/pp **grinned**) fare un gran sorriso
grind /graɪnd/ n (fam: hard work) sfacchinata f ● vt (pt/pp **ground**) macinare; affilare (knife); (Am: mince) tritare; **~ one's teeth** digrignare i denti
grindstone /'graɪndstəʊn/ n mola f; **keep**

one's nose to the ~ lavorare indefessamente
grip /grɪp/ n presa f; fig controllo m; (bag) borsone m; **be in the ~ of** essere in preda a; **get a ~ of oneself** controllarsi ● vt (pt/pp **gripped**) afferrare; (tyres:) far presa su; tenere avvinto (attention)
gripe /graɪp/ vi (fam: grumble) lagnarsi
gripping /'grɪpɪŋ/ a avvincente
grisly /'grɪzlɪ/ a (**-ier, -iest**) raccapricciante
gristle /'grɪsl/ n cartilagine f
grit /grɪt/ n graniglia f; (for roads) sabbia f; (courage) coraggio m ● vt (pt/pp **gritted**) spargere sabbia su (road); **~ one's teeth** serrare i denti
gritter /'grɪtə(r)/ n Br Aut spandighiaia m inv
gritty /'grɪtɪ/ a (sandy) pieno di terra; (gravelly) ghiaioso; (hard, determined) grintoso; (novel, film) crudo
grizzle /'grɪzl/ vi piagnucolare
grizzly /'grɪzlɪ/ n (bear) grizzly m inv
groan /grəʊn/ n gemito m ● vi gemere
grocer /'grəʊsə(r)/ n droghiere, -a mf
groceries /'grəʊsərɪz/ npl generi mpl alimentari
grocer's [shop] n drogheria f
groggy /'grɒgɪ/ a (**-ier, -iest**) stordito; (unsteady) barcollante
groin /grɔɪn/ n Anat inguine m
groom /gru:m/ n sposo m; (for horse) stalliere m ● vt strigliare (horse); fig preparare; **well-~ed** ben curato
groove /gru:v/ n scanalatura f
grope /grəʊp/ vi brancolare; **~ for** cercare a tastoni
gross /grəʊs/ a obeso; (coarse) volgare; (glaring) grossolano; (salary, weight) lordo ● n inv grossa f
gross domestic product n prodotto m interno lordo
gross indecency n Jur oltraggio m al pudore
grossly /'grəʊslɪ/ adv (very) enormemente
gross national product n prodotto m nazionale lordo
grotesque /grəʊ'tesk/ a grottesco
grotesquely /grəʊ'tesklɪ/ adv in modo grottesco
grotto /'grɒtəʊ/ n (pl **-es**) grotta f
grotty /'grɒtɪ/ a (**-ier, -iest**) (fam: flat, street) squallido
grouch /graʊtʃ/ vi brontolare (about contro)
grouchy /'graʊtʃɪ/ a brontolone
ground[1] /graʊnd/ see **grind**
ground[2] n terra f; Sport terreno m; (reason) ragione f; **~s** pl (park) giardini mpl; (of coffee) fondi mpl ● vi (ship:) arenarsi ● vt bloccare a terra (aircraft); Am Electr mettere a terra
ground: ground control n base f di controllo. **ground crew** n personale m di terra. **ground floor** n pianterreno m
grounding /'graʊndɪŋ/ n base f

groundless /'graʊndlɪs/ a infondato
ground: **ground rules** npl principi mpl fondamentali. **groundsheet** n telone m impermeabile. **groundwork** n lavoro m di preparazione
group /gruːp/ n gruppo m ● vt raggruppare ● vi raggrupparsi
groupage /'gruːpɪdʒ/ n Comm raggruppamento m
group leader n capogruppo m
grouse[1] /graʊs/ n inv gallo m cedrone
grouse[2] vi fam brontolare
grove /grəʊv/ n boschetto m
grovel /'grɒvl/ vi (pt/pp **grovelled**) strisciare
grovelling /'grɒv(ə)lɪŋ/ a leccapiedi inv
grow /grəʊ/ v (pt **grew**, pp **grown**) ● vi crescere; (become) diventare; (unemployment, fear:) aumentare; (town:) ingrandirsi ● vt coltivare; ~ **one's hair** farsi crescere i capelli
■ **grow on** vt (fam: become pleasing to) **it'll ~ on you** finirà a per piacerti
■ **grow out of** vt **he's ~n out of his jumper** il golf gli è diventato troppo piccolo
■ **grow up** vi crescere; (town:) svilupparsi
growbag /'grəʊbæg/ n sacco m di terriccio entro cui si coltivano piante
grower /'grəʊə(r)/ n coltivatore, -trice mf
growing pains /'grəʊɪŋ/ npl (of child) dolori mpl della crescita; (fig: of firm, project) difficoltà fpl iniziali nello sviluppo
growl /graʊl/ n grugnito m ● vi ringhiare
grown /grəʊn/ see **grow** ● a adulto
grown-up a & n adulto, -a mf
growth /grəʊθ/ n crescita f; (increase) aumento m; Med tumore m
growth rate n tasso m di crescita
groyne /grɔɪn/ n Br pennello m (per difendere le spiagge dall'erosione)
grub /grʌb/ n larva f; (fam: food) mangiare m
grubby /'grʌbɪ/ a (-ier, -iest) sporco
grudge /grʌdʒ/ n rancore m; **bear sb a ~** portare rancore a qcno ● vt dare a malincuore
grudging /'grʌdʒɪŋ/ a reluttante
grudgingly /'grʌdʒɪŋlɪ/ adv a malincuore
gruelling /'gruːəlɪŋ/ a estenuante
gruesome /'gruːsəm/ a macabro
gruff /grʌf/ a burbero
gruffly /'grʌflɪ/ adv in modo burbero
grumble /'grʌmbl/ vi brontolare (**at** contro)
grumpy /'grʌmpɪ/ a (-ier, -iest) scorbutico
grunge /grʌndʒ/ n (dirt) lerciume m; (style) grunge m inv
grunt /grʌnt/ n grugnito m ● vi fare un grugnito
G-string n (garment) tanga m inv
guarantee /gærən'tiː/ n garanzia f ● vt garantire
guarantor /gærən'tɔː(r)/ n garante mf
guard /gɑːd/ n guardia f; (security) guardiano m; (on train) capotreno m; Techn schermo m protettivo; **be on the ~** essere di guardia; **on one's ~** in guardia ● vt sorvegliare; (protect) proteggere
■ **guard against** vt guardarsi da

guard-dog n cane m da guardia
guarded /'gɑːdɪd/ a guardingo
guardian /'gɑːdɪən/ n (of minor) tutore, -trice mf
guardian angel n also fig angelo m custode
guard: **guard of honour** n guardia f d'onore. **guardroom** n corpo m di guardia. **guard's van** n Br Rail carrozza f bagagliaio
guava /'gwɑːvə/ n (fruit) guava f; (tree) albero m di guava
guerrilla /gə'rɪlə/ n guerrigliero, -a mf
guerrilla warfare n guerriglia f
guess /ges/ n supposizione f ● vt indovinare ● vi indovinare; (Am: suppose) supporre
guesstimate /'gestɪmət/ n calcolo m approssimativo
guesswork /'geswɜːk/ n supposizione f
guest /gest/ n ospite mf; (in hotel) cliente mf
guest: **guest house** n pensione f. **guest room** n camera f degli ospiti. **guest worker** n lavoratore m immigrato; lavoratrice f immigrata
guff /gʌf/ n (nonsense) stupidaggini fpl
guffaw /gʌ'fɔː/ n sghignazzata f ● vi sghignazzare
guidance /'gaɪdəns/ n guida f; (advice) consigli mpl
guide /gaɪd/ n guida f; [Girl] **G~** giovane esploratrice f ● vt guidare
guidebook /'gaɪdbʊk/ n guida f turistica
guided missile /'gaɪdɪd/ n missile m teleguidato
guide dog n cane m per ciechi
guided tour n giro m guidato
guidelines /'gaɪdlaɪnz/ npl direttive fpl
guiding principle /gaɪdɪŋ'prɪnsɪp(ə)l/ n direttrice f
guild /gɪld/ n corporazione f
guile /gaɪl/ n astuzia f
guileless /'gaɪlɪs/ a senza malizia
guillotine /'gɪləti:n/ n ghigliottina f; (for paper) taglierina f
guilt /gɪlt/ n colpa f
guiltily /'gɪltɪlɪ/ adv con aria colpevole
guilty /'gɪltɪ/ a (-ier, -iest) colpevole; **have a ~ conscience** avere la coscienza sporca
guinea /'gɪnɪ/ n ghinea f
guinea fowl faraona f
guinea pig n porcellino m d'India; (in experiments) cavia f
guise /gaɪz/ n **in the ~ of** sotto le spoglie di
guitar /gɪ'tɑː(r)/ n chitarra f
guitarist /gɪ'tɑːrɪst/ n chitarrista mf
Gulag /'guːlæg/ n gulag m inv
gulf /gʌlf/ n Geog golfo m; fig abisso m
gull /gʌl/ n gabbiano m
gullet /'gʌlɪt/ n esofago m; (throat) gola f
gullible /'gʌləbl/ a credulone
gully /'gʌlɪ/ n burrone m; (drain) canale m di scolo
gulp /gʌlp/ n azione f di deglutire; (of food) boccone m; (of liquid) sorso m ● vi deglutire
■ **gulp down** vt tranguiare (food); scolarsi (liquid)

gum¹ /gʌm/ n *Anat* gengiva f
gum² n gomma f; (*chewing-gum*) gomma f da masticare, chewing-gum m inv ● vt (*pt/pp* **gummed**) ingommare (**to** a)
gumboot /'gʌmbuːt/ n stivale m di gomma
gummed /gʌmd/ see **gum²** ● a ⟨label⟩ adesivo
gumption /'gʌmpʃn/ n fam buon senso m
gumshoe /'gʌmʃuː/ n (*fam: private investigator*) investigatore m privato
gum tree n fam **be up a ~** essere in difficoltà
gun /gʌn/ n pistola f; (*rifle*) fucile m; (*cannon*) cannone m; **he had a ~** era armato
■ **gun down** vt (*pt/pp* **gunned**) freddare
gun: gun barrel n canna f di fucile. **gunboat** n cannoniera f. **gun dog** n cane m da caccia. **gunfire** n spari mpl; (*of cannon*) colpi mpl [di cannone]
gunge /gʌndʒ/ n Br poltiglia f [disgustosa]
gung-ho /gʌŋ'həʊ/ a hum (*eager for war*) guerrafondaio; (*overzealous*) esaltato
gunman /'gʌnmən/ n uomo m armato
gunner /'gʌnə(r)/ n artigliere m
gun: gunpoint n **hold sb up at ~** assalire qcno a mano armata. **gunpowder** n polvere f da sparo. **gunshot** n colpo m [di pistola]. **gunslinger** n pistolero m
gurgle /'gɜːgl/ vi gorgogliare; ⟨baby:⟩ fare degli urletti
guru /'guːruː/ n guru m inv
gush /gʌʃ/ vi sgorgare; (*enthuse*) parlare con troppo entusiasmo (**over** di)
■ **gush out** vi sgorgare
gushing /'gʌʃɪŋ/ a eccessivamente entusiastico
gusset /'gʌsɪt/ n gherone m
gust /gʌst/ n (*of wind*) raffica f
gusto /'gʌstəʊ/ n **with ~** con trasporto
gusty /'gʌstɪ/ a ventoso

gut /gʌt/ n intestino m; **~s** pl pancia f; (*fam: courage*) fegato m ● vt (*pt/pp* **gutted**) *Culin* svuotare delle interiora; **~ted by fire** sventrato da un incendio
gutsy /'gʌtsɪ/ a (*brave*) coraggioso; (*spirited*) gagliardo
gutter /'gʌtə(r)/ n canale m di scolo; (*on roof*) grondaia f; fig bassifondi mpl
guttering /'gʌtərɪŋ/ n grondaie fpl
gutter press n stampa f scandalistica
guttersnipe /'gʌtəsnaɪp/ n ragazzo, -a mf di strada
guttural /'gʌtərəl/ a gutturale
guv, guvnor /gʌv, 'gʌvnə(r)/ n (Br fam: boss) capo m
guy /gaɪ/ n fam tipo m, tizio m
Guy Fawkes Day /fɔːks/ n Br anniversario m del fallimento della Congiura delle Polveri (5 novembre)
guzzle /'gʌzl/ vt ingozzarsi con ⟨food⟩; **he's ~d the lot** si è sbafato tutto
gym /dʒɪm/ n fam palestra f; (*gymnastics*) ginnastica f
gymkhana /dʒɪm'kɑːnə/ n manifestazione f equestre
gymnasium /dʒɪm'neɪzɪəm/ n palestra f
gymnast /'dʒɪmnæst/ n ginnasta mf
gymnastics /dʒɪm'næstɪks/ n ginnastica f
gym shoes npl scarpe fpl da ginnastica
gym-slip n Sch ≈ grembiule m (da bambina)
gynaecologist /gaɪnɪ'kɒlədʒɪst/ n ginecologo, -a mf
gynaecology /gaɪnɪ'kɒlədʒɪ/ n ginecologia f
gyp /dʒɪp/ n Br **my back is giving me ~** ho un terribile mal di schiena
gypsum /'dʒɪpsəm/ n gesso m
gypsy /'dʒɪpsɪ/ n zingaro, -a mf
gyrate /dʒaɪ'reɪt/ vi roteare

Hh

h, H /eɪtʃ/ n h, H f inv
haberdashery /hæbə'dæʃərɪ/ n merceria f; Am negozio m d'abbigliamento da uomo
habit /'hæbɪt/ n abitudine f; (*Relig: costume*) tonaca f; **be in the ~ of doing sth** avere l'abitudine di fare qcsa
habitable /'hæbɪtəbl/ a abitabile
habitat /'hæbɪtæt/ n habitat m inv
habitation /hæbɪ'teɪʃn/ n **unfit for human ~** inagibile
habit-forming /-fɔːmɪŋ/ a **be ~** creare assuefazione
habitual /hə'bɪtjʊəl/ a abituale; ⟨smoker, liar⟩ inveterato
habitually /hə'bɪtjʊəlɪ/ adv regolarmente

hack¹ /hæk/ n (*writer*) scribacchino, -a mf
hack² vt tagliare; **~ to pieces** tagliare a pezzi
hacker /'hækə(r)/ n Comput pirata m informatico
hacking /'hækɪŋ/ n Comput pirateria f informatica
hacking cough n brutta tosse f
hackles /'hæk(ə)lz/ npl (*on animal*) pelo m del collo; (*on bird*) piumaggio m del collo; **make sb's ~ rise** fig far imbestialire qcno
hackney cab /'hæknɪ/ n fml taxi m inv
hackneyed /'hæknɪd/ a trito [e ritrito]
hacksaw /'hæksɔː/ n seghetto m
had /hæd/ see **have**

haddock /'hædək/ n inv eglefino m

haematoma /hi:mə'təumə/ n ematoma f

haemoglobin /hi:mə'gləubın/ n emoglobina f

haemophilia /hi:mə'fılıə/ n emofilia f

haemophiliac /hi:mə'fılıæk/ n emofiliaco, -a mf

haemorrhage /'hemərıdʒ/ n emorragia f

haemorrhoids /'hemərɔıdz/ npl emorroidi fpl

hag /hæg/ n old ~ vecchia befana f

haggard /'hægəd/ a sfatto

haggis /'hægıs/ n piatto m scozzese a base di frattaglie di pecora e avena

haggle /'hægl/ vi contrattare (**over** per)

ha! ha! /ha:'ha:/ int ah! ah!

hail[1] /heıl/ vt salutare; far segno a ⟨taxi⟩ ● vi ~ **from** provenire da

hail[2] n grandine f ● vi grandinare

hailstone /'heılstəun/ n chicco m di grandine

hailstorm /'heılstɔ:m/ n grandinata f

hair /heə(r)/ n capelli mpl; ⟨on body, of animal⟩ pelo m; **wash one's** ~ lavarsi i capelli

hair: hairband n ⟨rigid⟩ cerchietto m; ⟨elastic⟩ fascia f [per capelli]. **hairbrush** n spazzola f per capelli. **hair curler** n arricciacapelli m inv. **haircut** n taglio m di capelli; **have a** ~ farsi tagliare i capelli. **hairdo** n fam pettinatura f. **hairdresser** n parrucchiere, -a mf. **hairdryer** n fon m inv; ⟨with hood⟩ casco m [asciugacapelli]. **hair gel** n gel m inv [per capelli]. **hairgrip** n molletta f [per capelli]

hairless /'heəlıs/ a ⟨animal⟩ senza peli; ⟨body, chin⟩ glabro

hair: hairline n ⟨on head⟩ attaccatura f dei capelli. **hairline crack** n incrinatura f sottilissima. **hairline fracture** n Med frattura f capillare. **hairnet** n retina f per capelli. **hairpiece** n toupet m inv. **hairpin** n forcina f. **hairpin bend** n tornante m, curva f a gomito. **hair-raising** /'heəreızıŋ/ a terrificante. **hair remover** n crema f depilatoria. **hairslide** n Br fermacapelli m inv. **hair-splitting** /'heəsplıtıŋ/ n pedanteria f. **hairspray** n lacca f [per capelli]. **hairstyle** n acconciatura f. **hairstylist** n parrucchiere, -a mf. **hair transplant** n trapianto m di capelli

hairy /'heərı/ a (**-ier, -iest**) peloso; ⟨fam: frightening⟩ spaventoso

Haiti /'heıtı/ n Haiti m

Haitian /'heıʃ(ə)n/ n & a haitiano, -a mf; ⟨language⟩ haitiano m

hake /heık/ n inv nasello m

halcyon days /'hælsıən/ npl bei tempi mpl andati

hale /heıl/ a ~ **and hearty** in piena forma

half /ha:f/ n (pl **halves**) metà f inv; **cut in** ~ tagliare a metà; **one and a** ~ uno e mezzo; ~ **a dozen** mezza dozzina; ~ **an hour** mezz'ora ● a mezzo; [at] ~ **price** [a] metà prezzo ● adv a metà; ~ **past two** le due e mezza

half: half-and-half a mezzo e mezzo ● adv a metà; **go** ~ fare a metà. **half-back** n mediano

m. **half-baked** a fam che non sta in piedi. **half board** n mezza pensione f. **half-breed** n & a mezzosangue mf inv. **half-brother** n fratellastro m. **half-caste** n meticcio, -a mf. **half-century** n mezzo secolo m. **half cock** n **go off at** ~ ~ partire col piede sbagliato. **half-conscious** a semicosciente. **halfcrown, half a crown** n Br mezza corona f. **half-cut** a ⟨fam: drunk⟩ ciucco. **half day** n mezza giornata f. **half-dead** a also fig mezzo morto. **half-dozen** n mezza dozzina f. **half fare** n metà tariffa f. **half-hearted** /-'ha:tıd/ a esitante. **half hour** n mezz'ora f. **half-hourly** a & adv ogni mezz'ora. **half-length** a ⟨portrait⟩ a mezzo busto. **half-light** n penombra f. **half mast** n at ~ ~ a mezz'asta. **half measures** npl mezze misure fpl. **half-moon** n mezzaluna f; ⟨of fingernail⟩ lunula f ● attrib ⟨spectacles⟩ a mezzaluna. **half pay** n metà stipendio m. **halfpenny** /'heıpnı/ n Br mezzo penny m inv. **half-pint** n mezza pinta f (Br = 0, 28 l, Am = 0, 24 l); ⟨beer⟩ piccola f; fig mezza calzetta f. **half price** a a metà prezzo ● adv [a] metà prezzo. **half size** n ⟨of shoe⟩ mezzo numero m ● a ⟨copy⟩ ridotto della metà. **half smile** n mezzo sorriso m. **half-starved** a mezzo morto di fame. **half-term** n vacanza f di metà trimestre. **half-time** n Sport intervallo m. **half-truth** n mezza verità f inv. **halfway** a the ~ **mark/stage** il livello intermedio ● adv a metà strada; **get** ~ fig arrivare a metà. **halfway house** n ⟨compromise⟩ via f di mezzo; ⟨rehabilitation centre⟩ centro m di riabilitazione per ex detenuti. **halfway line** n Sport linea f mediana. **halfwit** n idiota mf. **half-year** n Fin, Comm semestre m ● attrib ⟨profit, results⟩ semestrale. **half-yearly** a ⟨meeting, payment⟩ semestrale

halibut /'hælıbət/ n inv ippoglosso m

halitosis /hælı'təusıs/ n alitosi f inv

hall /hɔ:l/ n ⟨entrance⟩ ingresso m; ⟨room⟩ sala f; ⟨mansion⟩ residenza f di campagna; ~ **of residence** Univ casa f dello studente

hallelujah /(h)ælı'lu:jə/ int alleluia!

hallmark /'hɔ:lma:k/ n marchio m di garanzia; fig marchio m

hallo /hə'ləu/ int ciao!; ⟨on telephone⟩ pronto!; **say** ~ **to** salutare

hall of residence n residenza f universitaria

hallowed /'hæləud/ a ⟨ground⟩ consacrato; ⟨tradition⟩ sacro

Halloween /hæləu'i:n/ n vigilia f d'Ognissanti e notte delle streghe, celebrata soprattutto dai bambini

hallucinate /hə'lu:sıneıt/ vi avere le allucinazioni

hallucination /həlu:sı'neıʃn/ n allucinazione f

hallucinatory /hə'lu:sınət(ə)rı/ a ⟨drug⟩ allucinogeno

hallucinogen /hə'lu:sınədʒən/ n sostanza f allucinante

hallucinogenic /həlu:sınə'dʒenık/ a allucinogeno

hallway /'hɔːlweɪ/ n ingresso m

halo /'heɪləʊ/ n (pl -es) aureola f; Astr alone m

halogen /'hælədʒən/ n alogeno m

halt /hɔːlt/ n alt m inv; **come to a ~** fermarsi; ⟨traffic:⟩ bloccarsi ● vi fermarsi; **~!** alt! ● vt fermare

halter /'hɔːltə(r)/ n (for horse) cavezza f

halter-neck n modello m con allacciatura dietro il collo che lascia la schiena scoperta

halting /'hɔːltɪŋ/ a esitante

haltingly /'hɔːltɪŋlɪ/ adv con esitazione

halve /hɑːv/ vt dividere a metà; (reduce) dimezzare

ham /hæm/ n prosciutto m; Theat attore, -trice mf da strapazzo

hamburger /'hæmbɜːgə(r)/ n hamburger m inv

ham-fisted /-'fɪstɪd/ a Br fam maldestro

hamlet /'hæmlɪt/ n paesino m

hammer /'hæmə(r)/ n martello m ● vt martellare ● vi **~ at/on** picchiare a

■ **hammer in** vt piantare ⟨nail⟩

hammer and sickle n falce f e martello m

hammock /'hæmək/ n amaca f

hamper[1] /'hæmpə(r)/ n cesto m; **[gift] ~** cestino m

hamper[2] vt ostacolare

hamster /'hæmstə(r)/ n criceto m

hamstring /'hæmstrɪŋ/ n (of horse) tendine m del garretto; (of human) tendine m del ginocchio ● vt fig rendere impotente

hand /hænd/ n mano f; (of clock) lancetta f; (writing) scrittura f; (worker) manovale m; **all ~s** Naut l'equipaggio al completo; **at ~, to ~** a portata di mano; **by ~** a mano; **on the one ~** da un lato; **on the other ~** d'altra parte; **out of ~** incontrollabile; (summarily) su due piedi; **in ~** in corso; (situation) sotto controllo; (available) disponibile; **give sb a ~** dare una mano a qcno; **~ in ~** ⟨run, walk⟩ mano nella mano; **go ~ in ~** fig andare di pari passo (**with** con) ● vt porgere

■ **hand back** vt restituire ⟨sth⟩

■ **hand down** vt tramandare

■ **hand in** vt consegnare

■ **hand on** vt passare

■ **hand out** vt distribuire

■ **hand over** vt passare; (to police) consegnare

hand: handbag n borsa f (da signora). **hand baggage** n bagaglio m a mano. **handball** n pallamano f; (fault in football) fallo m di mano; **~!** mano! **handbasin** n lavandino m. **handbook** n manuale m. **handbrake** n freno m a mano. **handcart** n carretto m. **hand cream** n crema f per le mani. **handcuffs** npl manette fpl. **hand-dryer, hand-drier** n asciugamani m inv ad aria

handful /'hændfʊl/ n manciata f; **be [quite] a ~** fam essere difficile da tenere a freno

hand: hand grenade n bomba f a mano. **handgun** n pistola f. **hand-held** a a mano

handicap /'hændɪkæp/ n handicap m inv

handicapped /'hændɪkæpt/ a **mentally/physically ~** mentalmente/fisicamente handicappato

handicraft /'hændɪkrɑːft/ n artigianato m

handiwork /'hændɪwɜːk/ n opera f

handkerchief /'hæŋkətʃɪf/ n (pl **~s & -chieves**) fazzoletto m

handle /'hændl/ n manico m; (of door) maniglia f; **fly off the ~** fam perdere le staffe ● vt maneggiare; occuparsi di ⟨problem, customer⟩; prendere ⟨difficult person⟩; trattare ⟨subject⟩; **be good at handling sb** saperci fare con qcno

handlebar moustache /hændlbɑːmə-'stɑːʃ/ n baffi mpl a manubrio

handlebars /'hændlbɑːz/ npl manubrio m

handler /'hændlə(r)/ n (of dog) addestratore, -trice mf

hand: hand lotion n lozione f per le mani. **hand-luggage** n bagaglio m a mano. **handmade** a fatto a mano. **handout** n (at lecture) foglio m informativo; (fam: money) elemosina f. **handover** n (of prisoner, ransom) consegna f; (of property, territory) cessione f; **~ of power** passaggio m delle consegne. **hand-pick** vt scegliere ⟨produce⟩; selezionare con cura ⟨staff⟩. **handrail** n corrimano m. **hand-reared** /-'rɪəd/ a ⟨animal⟩ allattato con il biberon. **handset** n Teleph ricevitore m. **handshake** n stretta f di mano. **hand signal** n Auto segnalazione f con la mano. **hands-off** a ⟨policy⟩ di non intervento; ⟨manager⟩ che delega le responsabilità

handsome /'hænsəm/ a bello; (fig: generous) generoso; ⟨salary⟩ considerevole

hand: hands-on a ⟨experience⟩ pratico; ⟨approach⟩ pragmatico; ⟨control⟩ diretto; ⟨manager⟩ che segue direttamente le varie attività. **handspring** n salto m sulle mani. **handstand** n verticale f. **hand-to-hand** a & adv ⟨fight⟩ corpo a corpo. **hand-to-mouth** a ⟨existence⟩ precario. **hand towel** n asciugamano m. **hand-woven** /-'wəʊvən/ a tessuto a mano. **handwriting** n calligrafia f. **handwritten** a scritto a mano

handy /'hændɪ/ a (**-ier, -iest**) pratico; ⟨person⟩ abile; **have/keep ~** avere/tenere a portata di mano

handyman /'hændɪmæn/ n tuttofare m inv

hang /hæŋ/ vt (pt/pp **hung**) appendere ⟨picture⟩; (pt/pp **hanged**) impiccare ⟨criminal⟩; **~ oneself** impiccarsi; **~ wallpaper** tappezzare ● vi (pt/pp **hung**) pendere; ⟨hair:⟩ scendere ● n **get the ~ of it** fam afferrare

■ **hang about** vi gironzolare

■ **hang on** vi tenersi stretto; (fam: wait) aspettare; Teleph restare in linea

■ **hang on to** vt tenersi stretto a; (keep) tenere

■ **hang out** vi spuntare; **where does he usually ~ out?** fam dove bazzica di solito? ● vt stendere ⟨washing⟩

■ **hang up** vt appendere; Teleph riattaccare ● vi essere appeso; Teleph riattaccare

hangar /'hæŋə(r)/ n hangar m inv

hanger /'hæŋə(r)/ n gruccia f

hanger-on n leccapiedi mf inv

hang-glider n deltaplano m

hang-gliding n deltaplano m

hang: hangman n boia m. **hangover** n postumi mpl della sbornia. **hang-up** n fam complesso m

hank /hæŋk/ n (of hair) ciocca f; (of wool etc) matassa f

hanker /'hæŋkə(r)/ vi ~ **after sth** smaniare per qcsa

hanky /'hæŋkɪ/ n fam fazzoletto m

hanky-panky /hæŋkɪ'pæŋkɪ/ n fam qualcosa m di losco

ha'penny /'heɪpnɪ/ n Br abbr (**halfpenny**) mezzo penny m inv

haphazard /hæp'hæzəd/ a a casaccio; **in a ~ fashion** a casaccio

haphazardly /hæp'hæzədlɪ/ adv a casaccio

hapless /'hæplɪs/ a sventurato

happen /'hæpn/ vi capitare, succedere; **as it ~s** per caso; **I ~ed to meet him** mi è capitato di incontrarlo; **what has ~ed to him?** cosa gli è capitato?; (become of) che fine ha fatto?

happening /'hæp(ə)nɪŋ/ n avvenimento m

happily /'hæpɪlɪ/ adv felicemente; (fortunately) fortunatamente

happiness /'hæpɪnɪs/ n felicità f

happy /'hæpɪ/ a (-ier, -iest) contento, felice

happy: happy-go-lucky a spensierato. **happy hour** n ora f in cui nei pub le bevande vengono vendute a prezzi scontati. **happy medium** n giusto mezzo m

harangue /hə'ræŋ/ vt (morally) fare un sermone a; (politically) arringare

harass /'hærəs/ vt perseguitare

harassed /'hærəst/ a stressato

harassment /'hærəsmənt/ n persecuzione f; **sexual ~** molestie fpl sessuali

harbinger /'ha:bɪndʒə(r)/ n liter segnale m; (person) precursore m; precorritrice f

harbour /'ha:bə(r)/ n porto m ● vt dare asilo a; nutrire (grudge)

hard /ha:d/ a duro; (question, problem) difficile; **~ of hearing** duro d'orecchi; **be ~ on sb** (person:) essere duro con qcno ● adv (work) duramente; (pull, hit, rain, snow) forte; **~ hit by unemployment** duramente colpito dalla disoccupazione; **take sth ~** non accettare qcsa; **think ~!** pensaci bene!; **try ~** mettercela tutta; **try ~er** metterci più impegno; **~ done by** fam trattato ingiustamente

hard: hard and fast a (rule, distinction) preciso. **hardback** n edizione f rilegata. **hardboard** n truciolato m. **hard-boiled** /-'bɔɪld/ a (egg) sodo. **hard cash** n contante m. **hard copy** n copia f stampata. **hard core** n (in construction) massicciata f; (of group, demonstrators) zoccolo m duro ● a (pornography, video) hard-core; (supporter, opponent) irriducibile. **hard disk** n hard disk m inv, disco m rigido. **hard drug** n droga f pesante. **hard-earned** /-'ɜnd/ a (cash) sudato

harden /'ha:dn/ vi indurirsi

hard: hard-faced /-'feɪst/ a (person) dai trat-

ti duri. **hard-fought** a (battle) accanito. **hard hat** n casco m. **hard-headed** /-'hedɪd/ a pratico; (businessman) dal sangue freddo. **hard-hearted** /-'ha:tɪd/ a dal cuore duro. **hard labour** n Br lavori mpl forzati. **hard lens** n lente f a contatto rigida. **hardline** a (policy, regime) duro ● n linea f dura; **~ lines!** che sfortuna!. **hardliner** n Pol fautore, -trice mf della linea dura. **hard luck** n sfortuna f. **hard-luck story** n **give sb a ~ ~** raccontare a qcno le proprie disgrazie

hardly /'ha:dlɪ/ adv appena; **~ ever** quasi mai

hardness /'ha:dnɪs/ n durezza f

hard: hard-nosed /-'nəʊzd/ a (attitude, businessman, government) duro. **hard-on** n fam erezione f. **hard porn** n pornografia f hard-core. **hard-pressed** /-'prest/ a in difficoltà; (for time) a corto di tempo. **hard rock** n Mus hard rock m. **hard sell** n tecnica f di vendita aggressiva

hardship /'ha:dʃɪp/ n avversità f inv

hard: hard shoulder n Auto corsia f d'emergenza. **hard up** a fam a corto di soldi; **~ up for sth** a corto di qcsa. **hardware** n ferramenta fpl; Comput hardware m inv. **hard-wearing** /-'weərɪŋ/ a resistente. **hard-wood** n legno m duro. **hard-working** /-'wɜ:kɪŋ/ a **be ~** essere un gran lavoratore

hardy /'ha:dɪ/ a (-ier, -iest) dal fisico resistente; (plant) che sopporta il gelo

hare /heə(r)/ n lepre f

hare-brained /'heəbreɪnd/ a (scheme) da scervellati; (person) scervellato

harelip /heə'lɪp/ n labbro m leporino

harem /ha:ri:m/ n serraglio m

■ **hark back** /ha:k/ vt fig ~ ~ **to** ritornare su

harm /ha:m/ n male m; (damage) danni mpl; **out of ~'s way** in un posto sicuro; **it won't do any ~** non farà certo male ● vt far male a; (damage) danneggiare

harmful /'ha:mfʊl/ a dannoso

harmless /'ha:mlɪs/ a innocuo

harmonica /ha:'mɒnɪkə/ n armonica f [a bocca]

harmonious /ha:'məʊnɪəs/ a armonioso

harmoniously /ha:'məʊnɪəslɪ/ adv in armonia

harmonize /'ha:mənaɪz/ vi fig armonizzare

harmony /'ha:mənɪ/ n armonia f

harness /'ha:nɪs/ n finimenti mpl; (of parachute) imbracatura f ● vt bardare (horse); sfruttare (resources)

harp /ha:p/ n arpa f

■ **harp on** vi fam insistere (**about** su)

harpist /'ha:pɪst/ n arpista mf

harpoon /ha:'pu:n/ n arpione m

harpsichord /'ha:psɪkɔ:d/ n clavicembalo m

harrow /'hærəʊ/ n erpice m

harrowing /'hærəʊɪŋ/ a straziante

harry /'hærɪ/ vt (pursue, harass) assillare

harsh /ha:ʃ/ a duro; (light) abbagliante

harshly /'ha:ʃlɪ/ adv duramente

harshness /'hɑːʃnɪs/ n durezza f

harvest /'hɑːvɪst/ n raccolta f; (of grapes) vendemmia f; (crop) raccolto m ● vt raccogliere

harvester /'hɑːvɪstə(r)/ n (person) mietitore, -trice mf; (machine) mietritrice f

harvest festival n festa f del raccolto

has /hæz/ see have

has-been /-biːn/ n fam (person) persona f che ha fatto il suo tempo; (thing) anticaglia f

hash /hæʃ/ n **make a ~ of** fam fare un casino con

hashish /'hæʃɪʃ/ n hascish m

hassle /'hæsl/ n fam rottura f ● vt rompere le scatole a

hassock /'hæsək/ n cuscino m di inginocchiatoio

haste /heɪst/ n fretta f; **make ~** affrettarsi

hasten /'heɪsn/ vi affrettarsi ● vt affrettare

hastily /'heɪstɪlɪ/ adv frettolosamente

hasty /'heɪstɪ/ a (-ier, -iest) frettoloso; ⟨decision⟩ affrettato

hat /hæt/ n cappello m

hatbox /'hætbɒks/ n cappelliera f

hatch¹ /hætʃ/ n (for food) sportello m passavivande inv; Naut boccaporto m

hatch² vi ~ [out] rompere il guscio; ⟨egg:⟩ schiudersi ● vt covare; tramare ⟨plot⟩

■ **hatch up** vt tramare ⟨plot⟩

hatchback /'hætʃbæk/ n Auto tre/cinque porte m inv; (door) porta f del bagagliaio

hatchet /'hætʃɪt/ n ascia f

hate /heɪt/ n odio m ● vt odiare

hateful /'heɪtfʊl/ a odioso

hate mail n lettere fpl offensive o minatorie

hatpin /'hætpɪn/ n spillone m

hatred /'heɪtrɪd/ n odio m

hat-trick n tripletta f

haughtily /'hɔːtɪlɪ/ adv altezzosamente

haughty /'hɔːtɪ/ a (-ier, -iest) altezzoso

haul /hɔːl/ n (fish) pescata f; (loot) bottino m; (pull) tirata f ● vt tirare; trasportare ⟨goods⟩ ● vi ~ **on** tirare

haulage /'hɔːlɪdʒ/ n trasporto m

haulier /'hɔːlɪə(r)/ n autotrasportatore m

haunch /hɔːntʃ/ n anca f

haunt /hɔːnt/ n ritrovo m ● vt frequentare; (linger in the mind) perseguitare; **this house is ~ed** questa casa è abitata da fantasmi

have /hæv/ vt (3 sg pres tense **has**; pt/pp **had**) avere; fare ⟨breakfast, bath, walk etc⟩; ~ **a drink** bere qualcosa; ~ **lunch/dinner** pranzare/cenare; ; ~ **a rest** riposarsi; **I had my hair cut** mi sono tagliata i capelli; **we had the flat painted** abbiamo fatto tinteggiare la casa; **I had it made** l'ho fatto fare; ~ **to do sth** dover fare qcsa; ~ **him telephone me tomorrow** digli di telefonarmi domani; **he has** or **he's got two houses** ha due case; **you've got the money, ~n't you?** hai i soldi, no? ● v aux avere; (with verbs of motion & some others) essere; **I ~ seen him** l'ho visto; **he has never been there** non ci è mai stato ● npl **the ~s and the ~-nots** i ricchi e i poveri

■ **have in** vt avere in casa/ufficio etc ⟨builders etc⟩

■ **have off** vt fam **he's having it off with his secretary** si fa la segretaria

■ **have on** vt (be wearing) portare; (dupe) prendere in giro; **I've got something on tonight** ho un impegno stasera; **you're having me on!** tu mi stai prendendo in giro!

■ **have out** vt ~ **it out with sb** chiarire le cose con qcno; ~ **a tooth out** farsi togliere un dente

haven /'heɪvn/ n fig rifugio m

haver /'heɪvə(r)/ vi (dither) titubare

haversack /'hævəsæk/ n zaino m

havoc /'hævək/ n strage f; **play ~ with** fig scombussolare

haw /hɔː/ see hum

Hawaii /hə'waɪɪ/ n le Hawaii

Hawaiian /hə'waɪən/ n & a hawaiano, -a mf; (language) hawaiano m

hawk¹ /hɔːk/ n falco m

hawk² vt vendere in giro

hawker /'hɔːkə(r)/ n venditore, -trice mf ambulante

hawkish /'hɔːkɪʃ/ a Pol intransigente

hawthorn /'hɔːθɔːn/ n biancospino m

hay /heɪ/ n fieno m

hay: hay fever n raffreddore m da fieno. **hayloft** n fienile m. **haymaking** n fienagione f. **haystack** n pagliaio m. **haywire** a fam **go ~** dare i numeri; ⟨plans:⟩ andare all'aria

hazard /'hæzəd/ n (risk) rischio m ● vt rischiare; ~ **a guess** azzardare un'ipotesi

hazardous /'hæzədəs/ a rischioso

hazard [warning] lights npl Auto luci fpl d'emergenza

haze /heɪz/ n foschia f

hazel /'heɪz(ə)l/ n nocciolo m; (colour) [color m] nocciola m

hazelnut /'heɪz(ə)lnʌt/ n nocciola f

hazy /'heɪzɪ/ a (-ier, -iest) nebbioso; ⟨fig: person⟩ confuso; ⟨memories⟩ vago

he /hiː/ pron lui; **he's tired** è stanco; **I'm going but he's not** io vengo, ma lui no

head /hed/ n testa f; (of firm) capo m; (of primary school) direttore, -trice mf; (of secondary school) preside mf; (on beer) schiuma f; **use your ~!** usa la testa!; **be off one's ~** essere fuori di testa; **have a good ~ for business** avere il senso degli affari; **have a good ~ for heights** non soffrire di vertigini; **10 pounds a ~** 10 sterline a testa; **20 ~ of cattle** 20 capi di bestiame; ~ **first** a capofitto; ~ **over heels in love** innamorato pazzo; ~**s or tails?** testa o croce? ● vt essere a capo di; essere in testa a ⟨list⟩; colpire di testa ⟨ball⟩ ● vi ~ **for** dirigersi verso

head: headache n mal m di testa. **headband** n fascia f per capelli. **head boy** n Br Sch alunno m che rappresenta la scuola nelle manifestazioni ufficiali e che ha responsabilità speciali. **head-butt** vt dare una testata a. **head case** n fam **be a ~ ~** essere matto da legare. **head cold** n raffreddore m di testa. **headcount** n **do a ~** contare i presenti.

head of department n capo mf reparto.
headdress n acconciatura f
header /'hedə(r)/ n colpo m di testa; (dive) tuffo m di testa; (on document) intestazione f
head: headgear n copricapo m. **head girl** n Br Sch alunna f che rappresenta la scuola nelle manifestazioni ufficiali e che ha responsabilità speciali. **headhunter** n also Comm cacciatore, -trice mf di teste. **headhunting** n Comm ricerca f ad hoc di personale. **heading** n (in list etc) titolo m. **headlamp** n Auto fanale m. **headland** n promontorio m. **headlight** n Auto fanale m. **headline** n titolo m. **headlong** a & adv a capofitto. **head louse** n pidocchio m. **headmaster** n (of primary school) direttore m; (of secondary school) preside m. **headmistress** n (of primary school) direttrice f; (of secondary school) preside f. **head office** n sede f centrale. **head-on** a ⟨collision⟩ frontale ●adv frontalmente. **headphones** npl cuffie fpl. **headquarters** npl sede fsg; Mil quartier msg generale. **headrest** n poggiatesta m inv. **headroom** n sottotetto m; (of bridge) altezza f libera di passaggio. **headscarf** n foulard m inv, fazzoletto m. **headstand** n do a ~ fare la verticale. **head start** n have a ~ ~ partire avvantaggiato. **headstone** n (of grave) lapide f. **headstrong** a testardo. **head teacher** n (of primary school) direttore, -trice mf; (of secondary school) preside mf. **head-to-head** n confronto m diretto ●a diretto. **head waiter** n capocameriere m. **headway** n progresso m. **headwind** n vento m di prua
heady /'hedɪ/ a che dà alla testa
heal /hiːl/ vt/i guarire
healer /'hiːlə(r)/ n guaritore, -trice mf; **time is a great ~** il tempo guarisce tutti i mali
health /helθ/ n salute f
health: health care n assistenza f sanitaria. **health centre** n Br ambulatorio m. **health check** n controllo m medico. **health club** n club m ginnico. **health farm** n centro m di rimessa in forma. **health foods** npl alimenti mpl macrobiotici. **health-food shop** n negozio m di macrobiotica. **health hazard** n pericolo m per la salute
healthily /'helθɪlɪ/ adv in modo sano
health: health insurance n assicurazione f contro malattie. **health officer** n ufficiale m sanitario. **health resort** n (in mountains, by sea) stazione f climatica; (spa town) stazione f termale. **health visitor** n Br infermiere, -a mf che fa visite a domicilio. **health warning** n avviso m del ministero della sanità
healthy /'helθɪ/ a (-ier, -iest) sano
heap /hiːp/ n mucchio m; **~s of** fam un sacco di ●vt ~ [up] ammucchiare; **~ed teaspoon** un cucchiaino abbondante
hear /hɪə(r)/ vt/i (pt/pp **heard**) sentire; **~, ~!** bravo!
■ **hear about** vt (learn of) sentir parlare di
■ **hear from** vi aver notizie di
■ **hear of** vi sentir parlare di; **he would not ~ of it** non ne ha voluto sentir parlare

hearing /'hɪərɪŋ/ n udito m; Jur udienza f
hearing aid n apparecchio m acustico
hearing-impaired /-ɪm'peəd/ a audioleso
hearsay /'hɪəseɪ/ n **from ~** per sentito dire
hearse /hɜːs/ n carro m funebre
heart /hɑːt/ n cuore m; **~s** pl (Cards) cuori mpl; **at ~** di natura; **by ~** a memoria
heart: heartache n pena f. **heart attack** n infarto m. **heartbeat** n battito m cardiaco. **heartbreak** n afflizione f. **heartbreaking** a straziante. **heart-broken** a **be ~** avere il cuore spezzato. **heartburn** n mal m di stomaco. **heart disease** n malattia f cardiaca
hearten /'hɑːt(ə)n/ vt rincuorare
heart failure n arresto m cardiaco
heartfelt /'hɑːtfelt/ a di cuore
hearth /hɑːθ/ n focolare m
hearthrug /'hɑːθrʌg/ n tappeto m davanti al camino
heartily /'hɑːtɪlɪ/ adv di cuore; ⟨eat⟩ con appetito; **be ~ sick of sth** non poterne più di qcsa
heartland /'hɑːtlænd/ n (industrial, rural) cuore m; Pol roccaforte f
heartless /'hɑːtlɪs/ a spietato
heartlessly /'hɑːtlɪslɪ/ adv in modo spietato
heart: heart-lung machine n polmone m artificiale. **heart rate** n battito m cardiaco. **heart-rending** /-rendɪŋ/ a ⟨sigh, story⟩ straziante. **heart-searching** n esame m di coscienza. **heart surgeon** n cardiochirurgo, mf. **heartthrob** n fam rubacuori m inv. **heart-to-heart** n conversazione f a cuore aperto ●a a cuore aperto. **heart transplant** n trapianto m di cuore. **heart-warming** a toccante
hearty /'hɑːtɪ/ a caloroso; ⟨meal⟩ copioso; ⟨person⟩ gioviale
heat /hiːt/ n calore m; Sport prova f eliminatoria ●vt scaldare ●vi scaldarsi
■ **heat up** vt scaldare ⟨food, drink⟩; riscaldare ⟨room⟩
heated /'hiːtɪd/ a ⟨swimming pool⟩ riscaldato; ⟨discussion⟩ animato
heater /'hiːtə(r)/ n (for room) stufa f; (for water) boiler m inv; Auto riscaldamento m
heath /hiːθ/ n brughiera f
heat haze n foschia f (dovuta all'afa)
heathen /'hiːðn/ a & n pagano, -a mf
heather /'heðə(r)/ n erica f
heating /'hiːtɪŋ/ n riscaldamento m
heat: heat loss n perdita f di calore. **heat-resistant** a resistente al calore. **heat sink** n dissipatore m termico. **heatstroke** n colpo m di sole. **heat treatment** n Med termoterapia f. **heatwave** n ondata f di calore
heave /hiːv/ vt tirare; (lift) tirare su; (fam: throw) gettare; emettere ⟨sigh⟩ ●vi tirare; **my stomach ~d** avevo la nausea
heaven /'hev(ə)n/ n paradiso m; **~ help you if...** Dio ti scampi se...; **raise one's eyes to ~** alzare gli occhi al cielo; **H~s!** santo cielo!
heavenly /'hev(ə)nlɪ/ a celeste; fam delizioso

heaven-sent /-'sent/ *a* ⟨*opportunity*⟩ provvidenziale

heavily /'hevɪlɪ/ *adv* pesantemente; ⟨*smoke, drink etc*⟩ molto

heaviness /'hevɪnɪs/ *n* pesantezza *f*

heavy /'hevɪ/ *a* (**-ier, -iest**) pesante; ⟨*traffic*⟩ intenso; ⟨*rain, cold*⟩ forte; **be a ~ smoker/ drinker** essere un gran fumatore/bevitore

heavy: heavy-duty *a* ⟨*equipment, shoes*⟩ molto resistente. **heavy goods vehicle** *n* veicolo *m* pesante da trasporto. **heavy-handed** /-'hændɪd/ *a* ⟨*severe*⟩ severo; ⟨*clumsy*⟩ maldestro. **heavy industry** *n* industria *f* pesante. **heavy metal** *n* *Mus* heavy metal *m*. **heavyweight** *n* peso *m* massimo

Hebrew /'hi:bru:/ *a* & *nm* ebreo

heck /hek/ *fam int* cavolo ● *n* **a ~ of a lot of** un sacco di; **what the ~ !** chi se ne frega!; **what the ~ is going on?** che cavolo succede?

heckle /'hekl/ *vt* interrompere di continuo

heckler /'heklə(r)/ *n* disturbatore, -trice *mf*

hectare /'hekteə(r)/ *n* ettaro *m*

hectic /'hektɪk/ *a* frenetico

hectoring /'hektərɪŋ/ *a* prepotente

hedge /hedʒ/ *n* siepe *f* ● *vi fig* essere evasivo

hedge: hedge-clippers *npl* cesoie *fpl*. **hedgehog** *n* riccio *m*. **hedgerow** *n* siepe *f*

hedonism /'hi:dənɪzm/ *n* edonismo *m*

hedonistic /hi:də'nɪstɪk/ *a* edonistico

heebie-jeebies /hi:bɪ'dʒi:bɪz/ *npl fam* **give sb the ~** far venire i brividi a qcno

heed /hi:d/ *n* **pay ~ to** prestare ascolto a ● *vt* prestare ascolto a

heedless /'hi:dlɪs/ *a* noncurante

heel[1] /hi:l/ *n* tallone *m*; (*of shoe*) tacco *m*; **down at ~** *fig* trasandato; **take to one's ~s** *fam* darsela a gambe

heel[2] *vi* **~ over** *Naut* inclinarsi

heel bar *n* calzolaio *m*

hefty /'heftɪ/ *a* (**-ier, -iest**) massiccio

heifer /'hefə(r)/ *n* giovenca *f*

height /haɪt/ *n* altezza *f*; (*of plane*) altitudine *f*; (*of season, fame*) culmine *m*

heighten /'haɪt(ə)n/ *vt fig* accrescere

heinous /'hi:nəs/ *a* abominevole

heir /eə(r)/ *n* erede *mf*

heiress /eə'res/ *n* ereditiera *f*

heirloom /'eəlu:m/ *n* cimelio *m* di famiglia

heist /haɪst/ *n* *Am fam* furto *m*; (*armed*) rapina *f*

held /held/ *see* **hold**[2]

helicopter /'helɪkɒptə(r)/ *n* elicottero *m*

heliport /'helɪpɔ:t/ *n* eliporto *m*

helium /'hi:lɪəm/ *n* elio *m*

helix /'hi:lɪks/ *n* elica *f*

hell /hel/ *n* inferno *m*; **go to ~!** *sl* va' al diavolo!; **make sb's life ~** rendere la vita infernale a qcno ● *int* porca miseria!

hell-bent *a* **~ on doing sth** deciso a tutti i costi a fare qcsa

Hellenic /hr'lenɪk/ *a* ellenico

hellfire /'helfaɪə(r)/ *n* pene *fpl* dell'inferno

hell-for-leather *adv fam* **go ~** andare a spron battuto

hello /hə'ləʊ/ *int* & *n* = **hallo**

Hell's angel *n* Hell's angel *m inv*

helm /helm/ *n* timone *m*; **at the ~** *fig* al timone

helmet /'helmɪt/ *n* casco *m*

help /help/ *n* aiuto *m*; (*employee*) aiuto *m* domestico; **that's no ~** non è d'aiuto ● *vt* aiutare; **~ oneself to sth** servirsi di qcsa; **~ yourself** (*at table*) serviti pure; **I could not ~ laughing** non ho potuto trattenermi dal ridere; **it cannot be ~ed** non c'è niente da fare; **I can't ~ it** non ci posso far niente ● *vi* aiutare

■ **help out** *vt* dare una mano a ● *vi* dare una mano

helper /'helpə(r)/ *n* aiutante *mf*

helpful /'helpfʊl/ *a* ⟨*person*⟩ di aiuto; ⟨*advice*⟩ utile

helping /'helpɪŋ/ *n* porzione *f*

helping hand *n* **give sb a ~ ~** dare una mano a qcno

helpless /'helplɪs/ *a* (*unable to manage*) incapace; (*powerless*) impotente

helplessly /'helplɪslɪ/ *adv* con impotenza; ⟨*laugh*⟩ incontrollatamente

help window *n* *Comput* finestrella *f* di aiuto

helter-skelter /heltə'skeltə(r)/ *adv* in fretta e furia ● *n* scivolo *m* a spirale nei luna park

hem /hem/ *n* orlo *m* ● *vt* (*pt/pp* **hemmed**) orlare

■ **hem in** *vt* intrappolare

hemisphere /'hemɪsfɪə(r)/ *n* emisfero *m*

hemline /'hemlaɪn/ *n* orlo *m*

hemlock /'hemlɒk/ *n* cicuta *f*

hemp /hemp/ *n* canapa *f*

hen /hen/ *n* gallina *f*; (*any female bird*) femmina *f*

hence /hens/ *adv* (*for this reason*) quindi; (*from now on*) a partire da ora; (*from here*) da qui

henceforth /hens'fɔ:θ/ *adv fml* (*from that time on*) da allora in poi; (*from now on*) d'ora in poi

henchman /'hentʃmən/ *n* *pej* tirapiedi *m inv*

hen-coop *n* stia *f*

hen house *n* pollaio *m*

henna /'henə/ *n* henné *m*

hen-party *n* *fam* festa *f* di addio al celibato per sole donne

henpecked /'henpekt/ *a* tiranneggiato dalla moglie

hepatitis /hepə'taɪtɪs/ *n* epatite *f*

her /hɜ:(r)/ *poss a* suo *m*, sua *f*, suoi *mpl*, sue *fpl*; **~ job/house** il suo lavoro/la sua casa; **her mother/father** sua madre/suo padre ● *pers pron* (*direct object*) la; (*indirect object*) le; (*after prep*) lei; **I know ~** la conosco; **give ~ the money** dalle i soldi; **give it to ~** daglielo; **I came with ~** sono venuto con lei; **it's ~** è lei; **I've seen ~** l'ho vista; **I've seen ~, but not him** ho visto lei, ma non lui

herald /'herəld/ *vt* annunciare

heraldic /he'rældɪk/ *a* araldico

heraldry /'herəldrɪ/ n araldica f

herb /hɜːb/ n erba f

herbaceous /hɜː'beɪʃəs/ a erbaceo; **~ border** aiuola f

herbal /'hɜːb(ə)l/ a alle erbe

herbalist /'hɜːbəlɪst/ n erborista mf

herbal tea n tisana f

herb garden n aromatario m

herbs /hɜːbz/ npl (for cooking) aromi mpl [da cucina]; (medicinal) erbe fpl

herb tea n tisana f

herculean /hɜːkjʊ'liːən/ a ⟨task⟩ erculeo

herd /hɜːd/ n gregge m ● vt (tend) sorvegliare; (drive) far muovere; fig ammassare

■ **herd together** vi raggrupparsi ● vt raggruppare

here /hɪə(r)/ adv qui, qua; **in ~** qui dentro; **come/bring ~** vieni/porta qui; **~ is..., ~ are...** ecco...; **~ you are!** ecco qua!

here: hereabouts /hɪərə'baʊts/ adv Br da queste parti. **hereafter** adv in futuro. **here and now** adv seduta stante ● n **the ~ ~ ~** il presente. **hereby** adv con la presente

hereditary /hɪ'redɪtərɪ/ a ereditario

heredity /hɪ'redɪtɪ/ n ereditarietà f

heresy /'herəsɪ/ n eresia f

heretic /'herətɪk/ n eretico, -a mf

herewith /hɪə'wɪð/ adv Comm con la presente

heritage /'herɪtɪdʒ/ n eredità f

hermetic /hɜː'metɪk/ a ermetico

hermetically /hɜː'metɪklɪ/ adv ermeticamente

hermit /'hɜːmɪt/ n eremita mf

hernia /'hɜːnɪə/ n ernia f

hero /'hɪərəʊ/ n (pl -es) eroe m

heroic /hɪ'rəʊɪk/ a eroico

heroically /hɪ'rəʊɪklɪ/ adv eroicamente

heroin /'herəʊɪn/ n eroina f (droga)

heroine /'herəʊɪn/ n eroina f

heroism /'herəʊɪzm/ n eroismo m

heron /'herən/ n airone m

hero-worship n culto m degli eroi ● vt venerare

herpes /'hɜːpiːz/ n herpes m

herring /'herɪŋ/ n aringa f

herringbone /'herɪŋbəʊn/ a ⟨pattern⟩ spigato

hers /hɜːz/ poss pron il suo m, la sua f, i suoi mpl, le sue fpl; **a friend of ~** un suo amico; **friends of ~** dei suoi amici; **that is ~** quello è suo; (as opposed to mine) quello è il suo

herself /hə'self/ pers pron (reflexive) si; (emphatic) lei stessa; (after prep) sé, se stessa; **she poured ~ a drink** si è versata da bere; **she told me so ~** me lo ha detto lei stessa; **she's proud of ~** è fiera di sé; **by ~** da sola

hesitant /'hezɪtənt/ a esitante

hesitantly /'hezɪtəntlɪ/ adv con esitazione

hesitate /'hezɪteɪt/ vi esitare

hesitation /hezɪ'teɪʃn/ n esitazione f

hessian /'hesɪən/ n tela f di iuta

heterogeneous /hetərə'dʒiːnɪəs/ a eterogeneo

heterosexual /hetərəʊ'sekʃʊəl/ a eterosessuale

het up /het/ a fam agitato

hew /hjuː/ vt (pt hewed, pp hewed or hewn) spaccare

hexagon /'heksəgən/ n esagono m

hexagonal /hek'sægənl/ a esagonale

hey /heɪ/ int ehi!

heyday /'heɪdeɪ/ n tempi mpl d'oro

hey presto /heɪ'prestəʊ/ int (magic) e voilà!

HGV abbr heavy goods vehicle

hi /haɪ/ int ciao!

hiatus /haɪ'eɪtəs/ n (pl -tuses) iato m

hibernate /'haɪbəneɪt/ vi andare in letargo

hibernation /haɪbə'neɪʃn/ n letargo m

hiccup /'hɪkʌp/ n singhiozzo m; (fam: hitch) intoppo m; **have the ~s** avere il singhiozzo ● vi fare un singhiozzo

hick /hɪk/ n Am fam buzzurro, -a mf

hick town n Am fam città f inv provinciale

hid /hɪd/, **hidden** /'hɪdn/ see **hide²**

hide¹ /haɪd/ n (leather) pelle f (di animale)

hide² vt (pt hid, pp hidden) nascondere ● vi nascondersi

hide-and-seek n play **~** giocare a nascondino

hideaway /'haɪdəweɪ/ n (secluded place) rifugio m; (hiding place) nascondiglio m

hidebound /'haɪdbaʊnd/ a (conventional) limitato

hideous /'hɪdɪəs/ a orribile

hideously /'hɪdɪəslɪ/ adv orribilmente

hideout /'haɪdaʊt/ n nascondiglio m

hiding¹ /'haɪdɪŋ/ n (fam: beating) bastonata; (defeat) batosta f

hiding² n **go into ~** sparire dalla circolazione

hierarchic[al] /haɪə'rɑːkɪk[l]/ a gerarchico

hierarchy /'haɪərɑːkɪ/ n gerarchia f

hieroglyphics /haɪərə'glɪfɪks/ npl geroglifici mpl

hi-fi /'haɪfaɪ/ n abbr (high fidelity) hi-fi m inv; (set of equipment) impianto m hi-fi, stereo m inv

higgledy-piggledy /hɪgldɪ'pɪgldɪ/ adv alla rinfusa

high /haɪ/ a alto; ⟨meat⟩ che comincia ad andare a male; ⟨wind⟩ forte; (on drugs) fatto; **it's ~ time we did something about it** è ora di fare qualcosa in proposito ● adv in alto; **~ and low** in lungo e in largo ● n massimo m; (temperature) massima f; **from on ~** dall'alto; **be on a ~** fam essere fatto

high: high and dry a fig **leave sb ~ ~ ~** piantare in asso qcno. **high beam** n Am abbagliante m. **high-born** a nobile. **highbrow** a & n intellettuale mf. **high chair** n seggiolone m. **high-class** a ⟨hotel, shop, car⟩ d'alta classe; (prostitute) di alto bordo. **high command** n stato m maggiore. **High Commission** n alto commissariato m. **High Commissioner** n alto commissario m. **High Court** n ≈ Corte f Suprema. **high-definition** a ad alta definizione. **high diving** n tuffo m

higher education /haɪəredjuˈkeɪʃn/ n istruzione f universitaria

higher mathematics n matematica f avanzata

high: highfaluting /haɪfəˈluːtɪŋ/ a fam ‹ideas› pretenzioso; ‹language› pomposo. **high fashion** n alta moda f. **high-fibre** a ‹diet› ricco di fibre. **high-fidelity** n alta fedeltà f ● a ad alta fedeltà. **high finance** n alta finanza f. **high-flier** n (person) persona f che mira alto. **high-flown** a ‹phrases› ampolloso. **high-flying** a ‹aircraft› da alta quota; ‹career› ambizioso; ‹person› che mira alto. **high-frequency** a alta frequenza f. **High German** n alto tedesco m. **high-grade** a ‹oil, mineral, product› di prima qualità. **high ground** n collina f; **take the moral ~ ~** assumere un atteggiamento moralistico. **high-handed** /-ˈhændɪd/ a dispotico. **high-handedly** /-ˈhændɪdlɪ/ adv dispoticamente. **high-heeled** /-hiːld/ a coi tacchi alti. **high heels** npl tacchi mpl alti. **high jinks** /dʒɪŋks/ npl baldoria f. **high jump** n salto m in alto

Highland games /haɪlənd/ n manifestazione f tradizionale scozzese con gare sportive e musicali

Highlands /ˈhaɪləndz/ npl Highlands fpl (regione della Scozia del nord)

high-level a ‹talks› ad alto livello; ‹official› di alto livello

high life n bella vita f

highlight /ˈhaɪlaɪt/ vt (emphasize, with pen) evidenziare ● n (in art) riflesso m, colpo m di sole; (in hair) riflesso m, colpo m di sole; (of exhibition) parte f saliente; (of week, year) avvenimento m saliente; (of match, show) momento m clou

highlighter /ˈhaɪlaɪtə(r)/ n (marker) evidenziatore m

highly /ˈhaɪlɪ/ adv molto; **speak ~ of** lodare; **think ~ of** avere un'alta opinione di

highly-paid /-ˈpeɪd/ a ben pagato

highlystrung /-ˈstrʌŋ/ a nervoso

high: High Mass n messa f solenne. **high-minded** /-ˈmaɪndɪd/ a ‹person› di animo nobile. **high-necked** /-ˈnekt/ a a collo alto. **Highness** /ˈhaɪnɪs/ n altezza f; **Your ~** Sua Altezza

high: high noon n mezzogiorno m in punto. **high-performance** a ad alta prestazione. **high-pitched** /-ˈpɪtʃt/ a ‹voice, sound› acuto. **high point** n momento m culminante. **high-powered** a ‹car, engine› molto potente; ‹job› di alta responsabilità; ‹person› dinamico. **high pressure** n Meteorol alta pressione f ● attrib Techn ad alta pressione; ‹job› stressante. **high priest** n Relig gran sacerdote m; fig guru m inv. **high priestess** n Relig, fig gran sacerdotessa f. **high-principled** a ‹person› di alti principi. **high-profile** a ‹politician, group› di spicco; ‹visit› di grande risonanza. **high-ranking** a di alto rango. **high-rise** a ‹building› molto alto ● n edificio m molto alto. **high road** n strada f principale. **high school** n Am ≈ scuola f superiore; Br ≈ scuola f media e superiore. **high sea** n on

the ~ ~s in alto mare. **high season** n alta stagione f. **high society** n alta società f. **high-sounding** /-ˈsaʊndɪŋ/ a ‹title› altisonante. **high-speed** a ‹train, film› rapido. **high-spirited** a pieno di brio. **high spirits** npl brio m. **high spot** n momento m culminante. **high street** n strada f principale. **high-street shop** n negozio m popolare. **high tea** n pasto m pomeridiano servito insieme al tè. **high tech** /ˈtek/ n high tech f. **high tide** n alta marea f. **high treason** n alto tradimento m. **high voltage** n alta tensione f

highway /ˈhaɪweɪ/ n public ~ strada f pubblica

highway: Highway Code n Br Codice m stradale. **highwayman** n brigante m. **highway robbery** n brigantaggio m

high wire n filo m (per acrobati)

hijack /ˈhaɪdʒæk/ vt dirottare ● n dirottamento m

hijacker /ˈhaɪdʒækə(r)/ n dirottatore, -trice mf

hijacking /ˈhaɪdʒækɪŋ/ n dirottamento m

hike /haɪk/ n escursione f a piedi; (in price) aumento m ● vi fare un'escursione a piedi

hiker /ˈhaɪkə(r)/ n escursionista mf

hilarious /hrˈleərɪəs/ a da morir dal ridere

hilarity /hrˈlærətɪ/ n ilarità f

hill /hɪl/ n collina f; (mound) collinetta f; (slope) altura f

hill-billy /-bɪlɪ/ n Am montanaro m degli Stati Uniti sudorientali

hillock /ˈhɪlək/ n poggio m

hillside /ˈhɪlsaɪd/ n pendio m

hilltop /ˈhɪltɒp/ n sommità f inv di una collina

hilly /ˈhɪlɪ/ a collinoso

hilt /hɪlt/ n impugnatura f; **to the ~** ‹fam: support› fino in fondo; ‹mortgaged› fino al collo

him /hɪm/ pers pron (direct object) lo; (indirect object) gli; (with prep) lui; **I know ~** lo conosco; **give ~ the money** dagli i soldi; **give it to ~** daglielo; **I spoke to ~** gli ho parlato; **it's ~** è lui; **she loves ~** lo ama; **a she loves ~, not you** ama lui, non te

Himalayas /hɪmə'leɪəz/ npl Himalaia msg

himself /hɪm'self/ pers pron (reflexive) si; (emphatic) lui stesso; (after prep) sé, se stesso; **he poured ~ out a drink** si è versato da bere; **he told me so ~** me lo ha detto lui stesso; **he's proud of ~** è fiero di sé; **by ~** da solo

hind /haɪnd/ a posteriore

hinder /ˈhɪndə(r)/ vt intralciare

hindquarters /ˈhaɪn(d)kwɔːtəz/ npl didietro m

hindrance /ˈhɪndrəns/ n intralcio m

hindsight /ˈhaɪndsaɪt/ n with ~ con il senno del poi

Hindu /ˈhɪnduː/ a & n indù mf inv

Hinduism /ˈhɪnduɪzm/ n induismo m

hinge /hɪndʒ/ n cardine m ● vi ~ **on** fig dipendere da

hint /hɪnt/ n (clue) accenno m; (advice) sugge-

rimento *m*; (*indirect suggestion*) allusione *f*; (*trace*) tocco *m* ● *vt* ~ **that...** far capire che...
● *vi* ~ **at** alludere a
hinterland /'hɪntələænd/ *n* entroterra *m inv*, hinterland *m inv*
hip /hɪp/ *n* fianco *m*
hip bone *n* ileo *m*
hip flask *n* fiaschetta *f*
hippie /'hɪpɪ/ *n* hippy *mf inv*
hippo /'hɪpəʊ/ *n fam* ippopotamo *m*
hip pocket *n* tasca *f* posteriore
Hippocratic oath /hɪpə'krætɪk/ *a* giuramento *m* d'Ippocrate
hippopotamus /hɪpə'pɒtəməs/ *n* (*pl* -muses *or* -mi /hɪpə'pɒtəmaɪ/) ippopotamo *m*
hip replacement *n* protesi *f inv* all'anca
hire /'haɪə(r)/ *vt* affittare; assumere ⟨*person*⟩; ~ [**out**] affittare ● *n* noleggio *m*; '**for ~**' 'affittasi'
hire car *n* macchina *f* a noleggio
hire purchase *n Br* acquisto *m* rateale; **on ~ ~** a rate
his /hɪz/ *poss a* suo *m*, sua *f*, suoi *mpl*, sue *fpl*; ~ **job/house** il suo lavoro/la sua casa; ~ **mother/father** sua madre/suo padre ● *poss pron* il suo *m*, la sua *f*, i suoi *mpl*, le sue *fpl*; **a friend of** ~ un suo amico; **friends of** ~ dei suoi amici; **that is** ~ questo è suo; (*as opposed to mine*) questo è il suo
Hispanic /hɪ'spænɪk/ *a* ispanico
hiss /hɪs/ *n* sibilo *m*; (*of disapproval*) fischio *m* ● *vt* fischiare ● *vi* sibilare; (*in disapproval*) fischiare
historian /hɪ'stɔːrɪən/ *n* storico, -a *mf*
historic /hɪ'stɒrɪk/ *a* storico
historical /hɪ'stɒrɪkl/ *a* storico
historically /hɪ'stɒrɪklɪ/ *adv* storicamente
history /'hɪstərɪ/ *n* storia *f*; **make ~** passare alla storia
histrionic /hɪstrɪ'ɒnɪk/ *a* istrionico
histrionics /hɪstrɪ'ɒnɪks/ *npl* scene *fpl*
hit /hɪt/ *n* (*blow*) colpo *m*; (*fam: success*) successo *m*; **score a direct** ~ ⟨*missile:*⟩ colpire in pieno ● *vt/i* (*pt/pp* **hit**, *pres p* **hitting**) colpire; ~ **one's head on the table** battere la testa contro il tavolo; **the car** ~ **the wall** la macchina ha sbattuto contro il muro; ~ **the target** colpire il bersaglio; ~ **the nail on the head** fare centro; ~ **the roof** *fam* perdere le staffe
■ **hit back** *vi* (*retaliate*) ribattere
■ **hit off** *vt* ~ **it off** andare d'accordo
■ **hit on** *vt fig* trovare
hit: hit-and-miss *a* ⟨*affair, undertaking*⟩ imprevedibile; ⟨*method*⟩ a casaccio. **hit-and-run** *a* ⟨*raid, attack*⟩ lampo *inv*; ⟨*accident*⟩ causato da un pirata della strada. **hit-and-run driver** *a* pirata *m* della strada
hitch /hɪtʃ/ *n* intoppo *m*; **technical** ~ problema *m* tecnico ● *vt* attaccare; ~ **a lift** chiedere un passaggio
■ **hitch up** *vt* tirarsi su ⟨*trousers*⟩
hitch: hitch-hike *vi* fare l'autostop. **hitchhiker** *n* autostoppista *mf*. **hitch-hiking** *n* autostop *m*

hi-tech *a see* **high tech**
hither /'hɪðə(r)/ *adv* ~ **and thither** di qua e di là
hitherto /hɪðə'tuː/ *adv* finora
hit: hit list *n* lista *f* degli obiettivi. **hit man** *n* sicario *m*. **hit-or-miss** *a* **on a very** ~ **basis** all'improvvisata. **hit parade** *n* hit parade *f inv*, classifica *f*
HIV *n abbr* (**human immunodeficiency virus**) HIV *m*
hive /haɪv/ *n* alveare *m*; ~ **of industry** fucina *f* di lavoro
■ **hive off** *vt Comm* separare
HIV positive *a* sieropositivo
HMS *abbr* **His/Her Majesty's Ship**
hoard /hɔːd/ *n* provvista *f*; (*of money*) gruzzolo *m* ● *vt* accumulare
hoarding /'hɔːdɪŋ/ *n* palizzata *f*; (*with advertisements*) tabellone *m* per manifesti pubblicitari
hoar frost /'hɔː(r)/ *n* brina *f*
hoarse /hɔːs/ *a* rauco
hoarsely /'hɔːslɪ/ *adv* con voce rauca
hoarseness /'hɔːsnɪs/ *n* raucedine *f*
hoary /'hɔːrɪ/ *a* ⟨*person*⟩ con i capelli bianchi; ~ **old joke** barzelletta *f* vecchia
hoax /həʊks/ *n* scherzo *m*; (*false alarm*) falso allarme *m*
hoaxer /'həʊksə(r)/ *n* burlone, -a *mf*
hob /hɒb/ *n* piano *m* di cottura
hobble /'hɒbl/ *vi* zoppicare
hobby /'hɒbɪ/ *n* hobby *m inv*
hobby horse *n fig* fissazione *f*
hobnailed /'hɒbneɪld/ *a* ~ **boots** *pl* scarponi *mpl* chiodati
■ **hobnob with** /'hɒbnɒb/ *vt* (*pt/pp* **hobnobbed**) frequentare
hobo /'həʊbəʊ/ *n Am* vagabondo, -a *mf*
hock /hɒk/ *n* vino *m* bianco del Reno
hockey /'hɒkɪ/ *n* hockey *m*
hocus-pocus /həʊkəs'pəʊkəs/ *n* (*trickery*) trucco *m*
hod /hɒd/ *n* (*for coal*) secchio *m* del carbone; (*for bricks*) cassetta *f* (*per trasportare mattoni*)
hoe /həʊ/ *n* zappa *f* ● *vt* (*pres p* **hoeing**) zappare
hog /hɒg/ *n* maiale *m* ● *vt* (*pt/pp* **hogged**) *fam* monopolizzare
hog-tie /'hɒgtaɪ/ *vt* legare le quattro zampe di ⟨*pig, cow*⟩; *Am fig* ostacolare ⟨*person*⟩
hogwash /'hɒgwɒʃ/ *n fam* cretinate *fpl*
hoi polloi /hɔɪpɒ'lɔɪ/ *npl* plebaglia *fsg*
hoist /hɔɪst/ *n* montacarichi *m inv*; (*fam: push*) spinta *f* in su ● *vt* sollevare; innalzare ⟨*flag*⟩; levare ⟨*anchor*⟩
hoity-toity /hɔɪtɪ'tɔɪtɪ/ *a fam* altezzoso
hokum /'həʊkəm/ *n Am fam* (*sentimentality*) polpettone *m* sentimentale; (*nonsense*) cretinate *fpl*
hold[1] /həʊld/ *n Naut, Aeron* stiva *f*
hold[2] *n* presa *f*; (*fig: influence*) ascendente *m*; **get** ~ **of** trovare; procurarsi ⟨*information*⟩ ● *v* (*pt/pp* **held**) ● *vt* tenere; ⟨*container:*⟩ contenere; essere titolare di ⟨*licence, passport*⟩;

trattenere ⟨*breath, suspect*⟩; mantenere vivo ⟨*interest*⟩; ⟨*civil servant etc:*⟩ occupare ⟨*position*⟩; (*retain*) mantenere; **~ sb's hand** tenere qcno per mano; **~ one's tongue** tenere la bocca chiusa; **~ sb responsible** considerare qcno responsabile; **~ that** (*believe*) ritenere che ● *vi* tenere; ⟨*weather, luck:*⟩ durare; ⟨*offer:*⟩ essere valido; *Teleph* restare in linea; **I don't ~ with the idea that...** *fam* non sono d'accordo sul fatto che...

▪ **hold against** *vt* **~ sth against sb** avercela con qcno per qcsa

▪ **hold back** *vt* rallentare ● *vi* esitare

▪ **hold down** *vt* tenere a bada ⟨*sb*⟩

▪ **hold on** *vi* (*wait*) attendere; *Teleph* restare in linea

▪ **hold on to** *vt* aggrapparsi a; (*keep*) tenersi

▪ **hold out** *vt* porgere ⟨*hand*⟩; *fig* offrire ⟨*possibility*⟩ ● *vi* (*resist*) resistere

▪ **hold up** *vt* tenere su; (*delay*) rallentare; (*rob*) assalire; **~ one's head up** *fig* tenere la testa alta

holdall /'həʊldɔ:l/ *n* borsone *m*

holder /'həʊldə(r)/ *n* titolare *mf*; (*of record*) detentore, -trice *mf*; (*container*) astuccio *m*

holding /'həʊldɪŋ/ *n* (*land*) terreno *m* in affitto; *Comm* azioni *fpl*

holding company *n* società *f inv* finanziaria

hold-up *n* ritardo *m*; (*attack*) rapina *f* a mano armata

hole /həʊl/ *n* buco *m*

holiday /'hɒlɪdeɪ/ *n* vacanza *f*; (*public*) giorno *m* festivo; (*day off*) giorno *m* di ferie; **go on ~** andare in vacanza ● *vi* andare in vacanza

holiday: holiday home *n* casa *f* per le vacanze. **holiday job** *n* (*Br: in summer*) lavoretto *m* estivo. **holiday-maker** *n* vacanziere *mf*. **holiday resort** *n* luogo *m* di villeggiatura

holier-than-thou /həʊlɪəðən'ðaʊ/ *a* ⟨*attitude*⟩ da santerellino

holiness /'həʊlɪnɪs/ *n* santità *f*; **Your H~** Sua Santità

Holland /'hɒlənd/ *n* Olanda *f*

holler /'hɒlə(r)/ *vi* urlare (**at** contro)

hollow /'hɒləʊ/ *a* cavo; ⟨*promise*⟩ a vuoto; ⟨*voice*⟩ assente; ⟨*cheeks*⟩ infossato ● *n* cavità *f inv*; (*in ground*) affossamento *m*

▪ **hollow out** *vt* scavare

holly /'hɒlɪ/ *n* agrifoglio *m*

hollyhock /'hɒlɪhɒk/ *n* malvone *m*

holocaust /'hɒləkɔ:st/ *n* olocausto *m*

hologram /'hɒləgræm/ *n* ologramma *m*

holograph /'hɒləgrɑ:f/ *n* documento *m* olografo

hols /hɒlz/ *n Br fam abbr* (**holidays**) vacanze *fpl*

holster /'həʊlstə(r)/ *n* fondina *f*

holy /'həʊlɪ/ *a* (**-ier, -est**) santo; ⟨*water*⟩ benedetto

holy: Holy Ghost *or* **Spirit** *n* Spirito *m* Santo. **Holy Scriptures** sacre scritture *fpl*. **Holy Week** *n* settimana *f* santa

homage /'hɒmɪdʒ/ *n* omaggio *m*; **pay ~ to** rendere omaggio a

homburg /'hɒmbɜ:g/ *n* cappello *m* di feltro

home /həʊm/ *n* casa *f*; (*for children*) istituto *m*; (*for old people*) casa *f* di riposo; (*native land*) patria *f* ● *adv* **at ~** a casa; (*football*) in casa; **feel at ~** sentirsi a casa propria; **come/go ~** venire/andare a casa; **drive a nail ~** piantare un chiodo a fondo. ● *a* domestico; ⟨*movie, video*⟩ casalingo; ⟨*team*⟩ ospitante; *Pol* nazionale

home: home address *n* indirizzo *m* di casa. **home brew** *n* (*beer*) birra *f* fatta in casa. **homecoming** *n* (*return home*) ritorno *m* a casa. **home computer** *n* computer *m inv* da casa. **Home Counties** *npl* contee *fpl* intorno a Londra. **home economics** *n Sch* economia *f* domestica. **home front** *n* (*during war*) fronte *m* interno; (*in politics*) politica *f* interna. **home game** *n* gioco *m* in casa. **home ground** *n* play on one's **~ ~** giocare in casa. **home-grown** /-'grəʊn/ *a* ⟨*produce*⟩ del proprio orto; *fig* nostrano. **home help** *n* aiuto *m* domestico (*per persone non autosufficienti*). **homeland** *n* patria *f*

homeless /'həʊmlɪs/ *a* senza tetto

home loan *n* mutuo *m* per la casa

homeloving /'həʊmlʌvɪŋ/ *a* casalingo

homely /'həʊmlɪ/ *a* (**-ier, -iest**) *a* semplice; ⟨*atmosphere*⟩ familiare; (*Am: ugly*) bruttino

home-made *a* fatto in casa

home market *n* mercato *m* interno

Home Office *n Br* ministero *m* degli interni

homeopathic /həʊmɪə'pæθɪk/ *a* omeopatico

homeopathy /həʊmɪ'ɒpəθɪ/ *n* omeopatia *f*

home: Home Secretary *n Br* ≈ ministro *m* degli interni. **homesick** *a* be **~** avere nostalgia (**for**) di). **homesickness** *n* nostalgia *f* di casa. **homestead** *n* fattoria *f*. **home town** *n* città *f inv* natia. **home truth** *n* tell sb a few **~ ~s** dirne quattro a qcno. **home video** *n* filmato *m* di videoamatore

homeward /'həʊmwəd/ *a* di ritorno ● *adv* **~[s]** verso casa; **~ bound** sulla strada del ritorno; **travel ~[s]** tornare a casa

homework /'həʊmwɜ:k/ *n Sch* compiti *mpl*

homey /'həʊmɪ/ *a* (*home-loving*) casalingo; (*cosy*) accogliente

homicide /'hɒmɪsaɪd/ *n* (*crime*) omicidio *m*

homily /'hɒmɪlɪ/ *n* omelia *f*

homing /'həʊmɪŋ/ *a* ⟨*missile, device*⟩ autoguidato

homing pigeon piccione *f* homing

homoeopathic /həʊmɪə'pæθɪk/ *a* omeopatico

homoeopathy /həʊmɪ'ɒpəθɪ/ *n* omeopatia *f*

homogeneous /hɒmə'dʒi:nɪəs/ *a* omogeneo

homogenize /hə'mɒdʒənaɪz/ *vt* omogeneizzare

homogenous /hə'mɒdʒənəs/ *a* omogeneo

homograph /'hɒməgrɑ:f/ *n* omografo *m*

homonym /'hɒmənɪm/ *n* omonimo *m*

homophobia /həʊmə'fəʊbɪə/ n omofobia f
homosexual /həʊmə'sekʃʊəl/ a & n omo-sessuale mf
hone /həʊn/ vt (sharpen) affilare; (perfect) affinare
honest /'ɒnɪst/ a onesto; (frank) sincero
honestly /'ɒnɪstlɪ/ adv onestamente; (frankly) sinceramente; ~! ma insomma!
honesty /'ɒnɪstɪ/ n onestà f; (frankness) sincerità f
honey /'hʌnɪ/ n miele m; (fam: darling) tesoro m
honeycomb /'hʌnɪkəʊm/ n favo m
honeydew melon /'hʌnɪdjuː/ n melone m (dalla buccia gialla)
honeymoon /'hʌnɪmuːn/ n luna f di miele
honeysuckle /'hʌnɪsʌkl/ n caprifoglio m
Hong Kong /hɒŋ'kɒŋ/ n Hong Kong f
honk /hɒŋk/ vi Aut clacsonare
honky-tonk /'hɒŋkɪtɒŋk/ a (piano) honky-tonky inv
honorary /'ɒnərərɪ/ a onorario
honorific /ɒnə'rɪfɪk/ a onorifico
honour /'ɒnə(r)/ n onore m ● vt onorare
honourable /'ɒnərəbl/ a onorevole
honourably /'ɒnərəblɪ/ adv con onore
honours degree /'ɒnəz/ n ≈ diploma m di laurea
hood /hʊd/ n cappuccio m; (of pram) tettuccio m; (over cooker) cappa f; Am Auto cofano m
hoodlum /'huːdləm/ n teppista m
hoodwink /'hʊdwɪŋk/ vt fam infinocchiare
hoof /huːf/ n (pl ~s or hooves) zoccolo m
hoo-ha /'huːhɑː/ n fam cause a ~ fare scalpore
hook /hʊk/ n gancio m; (for crochet) uncinetto m; (for fishing) amo m; off the ~ Teleph staccato; fig fuori pericolo; by ~ or by crook in un modo o nell'altro ● vt agganciare ● vi agganciarsi
hookah /'hʊkə/ n narghilè m inv
hook and eye n gancino m
hooked /hʊkt/ a (nose) adunco; ~ on (fam: drugs) dedito a; be ~ on skiing essere un fanatico dello sci
hooker /'hʊkə(r)/ n Am sl battona f
hookey /'hʊkɪ/ n play ~ Am fam marinare la scuola
hooligan /'huːlɪgən/ n teppista f
hooliganism /'huːlɪgənɪzm/ n teppismo m
hoop /huːp/ n cerchio m
hoopla /'huːplɑː/ n (Br: at fair) lancio m degli anelli (nei luna park); (Am: fuss) trambusto m
hooray /hʊ'reɪ/ int & n = **hurrah**
hoot /huːt/ n colpo m di clacson; (of siren) ululato m; (of owl) grido m; ~s of laughter risate fpl ● vi (owl:) gridare; (car:) clacsonare; (siren:) ululare; (jeer) fischiare
hooter /'huːtə(r)/ n (siren) sirena f; Auto clacson m inv; (Br fam: nose) nasone m
hoover® /'huːvə(r)/ n aspirapolvere m inv ● vt passare l'aspirapolvere su (carpet); pas-

sare l'aspirapolvere in (room) ● vi passare l'aspirapolvere
hop¹ /hɒp/ n luppolo m
hop² n saltello m; catch sb on the ~ fam prendere qcno alla sprovvista ● vi (pt/pp hopped) saltellare; ~! fam tela!
■ **hop in** vi fam saltar su
■ **hop out** vi fam saltar giù; ~ ~ to the shops fare un salto ai negozi
hope /həʊp/ n speranza f; there's no ~ of that happening non c'è nessuna speranza che succeda ● vi sperare (for in); I ~ so/not spero di sì/no ● vt ~ that sperare che
hopeful /'həʊpfʊl/ a pieno di speranza; (promising) promettente; be ~ that avere buone speranze che
hopefully /'həʊpfʊlɪ/ adv con speranza; (it is hoped) se tutto va bene
hopeless /'həʊplɪs/ a senza speranze; (useless) impossibile; (incompetent) incapace
hopelessly /'həʊplɪslɪ/ adv disperatamente; (inefficient, lost) completamente
hopelessness /'həʊplɪsnɪs/ n disperazione f
hopscotch /'hɒpskɒtʃ/ n campana f (gioco)
horde /hɔːd/ n orda f
horizon /hə'raɪzn/ n orizzonte m; on the ~ all'orizzonte
horizontal /hɒrɪ'zɒntl/ a orizzontale
horizontal bar n sbarra f orizzontale
horizontally /hɒrɪ'zɒntəlɪ/ adv orizzontalmente
hormonal /hɔː'məʊnəl/ a ormonale
hormone /'hɔːməʊn/ n ormone m
hormone replacement therapy n terapia f ormonale sostitutiva
horn /hɔːn/ n corno m; Auto clacson m inv
hornet /'hɔːnɪt/ n calabrone m
horn-rimmed /-rɪmd/ a (spectacles) con la montatura di tartaruga
horny /'hɔːnɪ/ a calloso; (fam: sexually) arrapato
horoscope /'hɒrəskəʊp/ n oroscopo m
horrendous /hə'rendəs/ a spaventoso
horrible /'hɒrəbl/ a orribile
horribly /'hɒrəblɪ/ adv orribilmente
horrid /'hɒrɪd/ a orrendo
horrific /hə'rɪfɪk/ a raccapricciante; (fam: accident, prices, story) terrificante
horrify /'hɒrɪfaɪ/ vt (pt/pp -ied) far inorridire; I was horrified ero inorridito
horrifying /'hɒrɪfaɪɪŋ/ a terrificante
horror /'hɒrə(r)/ n orrore m
horror film n film m inv dell'orrore
hors-d'œuvre /ɔː'dɜːvr/ n antipasto m
horse /hɔːs/ n cavallo m
horse: horseback n on ~ a cavallo. **horsebox** n furgone m per il trasporto dei cavalli. **horse chestnut** n ippocastano m. **horsefly** n tafano m. **horsehair** n crine m di cavallo. **horseman** n cavaliere m. **horse manure** n concime m. **horseplay** n gioco m pesante. **horsepower** n cavallo m [vapore]. **horse racing** n corse fpl di cavalli.

horseradish *n* rafano *m*. **horseshoe** *n* ferro *m* di cavallo

hors[e]y /'hɔːsɪ/ *a* ‹person› che adora i cavalli; ‹face› cavallino

horticultural /hɔːtɪ'kʌltʃʊrəl/ *a* di orticoltura

horticulture /'hɔːtɪkʌltʃə(r)/ *n* orticoltura *f*

hose /həʊz/ *n* (pipe) manichetta *f*

■ **hose down** *vt* lavare con la manichetta

hosepipe /'həʊzpaɪp/ *n* manichetta *f*

hosiery /'həʊʒərɪ/ *n* maglieria *f*

hospice /'hɒspɪs/ *n* (for the terminally ill) ospedale *m* per i malati in fase terminale

hospitable /hɒ'spɪtəbl/ *a* ospitale

hospitably /hɒ'spɪtəblɪ/ *adv* con ospitalità

hospital /'hɒspɪtl/ *n* ospedale *m*

hospitality /hɒspɪ'tælətɪ/ *n* ospitalità *f*

hospitalize /'hɒspɪtəlaɪz/ *vt* ricoverare [in ospedale]

host¹ /həʊst/ *n* **a ~ of** una moltitudine di

host² *n* ospite *m*

host³ *n* Relig ostia *f*

hostage /'hɒstɪdʒ/ *n* ostaggio *m*; **hold sb ~** tenere qcno in ostaggio

hostel /'hɒstl/ *n* ostello *m*

hostess /'həʊstɪs/ *n* padrona *f* di casa; Aeron hostess *f inv*

hostile /'hɒstaɪl/ *a* ostile

hostility /hɒ'stɪlətɪ/ *n* ostilità *f*; **hostilities** *pl* ostilità *fpl*

hot /hɒt/ *a* (**hotter, hottest**) caldo; (spicy) piccante; **I am** *or* **feel ~** ho caldo; **it is ~** fa caldo; **in ~ water** *fig* nei guai

hot: hot-air balloon *n* mongolfiera *f*. **hotbed** *n* *fig* focolaio *m*. **hot-blooded** /-'blʌdɪd/ *a* ‹person› focoso; ‹reaction› passionale. **hot cake** *n* **sell like ~ ~s** andare a ruba

hotchpotch /'hɒtʃpɒtʃ/ *n* miscuglio *m*

hot: hot cross bun *n* panino *m* dolce con spezie e uvette, tipicamente pasquale. **hot dog** *n* hot dog *m inv*. **hotdogging** *n* sci *m* acrobatico

hotel /həʊ'tel/ *n* hotel *m inv*, albergo *m*

hotelier /həʊ'telɪə(r)/ *n* albergatore, -trice *mf*

hot: hotfoot *adv hum* ‹go› di gran carriera. **hothead** *n* persona *f* impetuosa. **hot-headed** /-'hedɪd/ *a* impetuoso. **hothouse** *n* serra *f*. **hotline** *n* linea *f* diretta; Mil, Pol telefono *m* rosso

hotly /'hɒtlɪ/ *adv fig* accanitamente

hot: hotplate *n* piastra *f* riscaldante. **hotshot** *n fam* persona *f* di successo; *pej* carrierista *mf*. **hot tap** *n* rubinetto *m* dell'acqua calda. **hot-tempered** /-'tempəd/ *a* irascibile. **hot-water bottle** *n* borsa *f* dell'acqua calda

hound /haʊnd/ *n* cane da caccia *m* ● *vt fig* perseguire

hour /'aʊə(r)/ *n* ora *f*

hourglass /'aʊəglɑːs/ *n* clessidra *f*

hourly /'aʊəlɪ/ *a* ad ogni ora; ‹pay, rate› a ora. ● *adv* ogni ora

house¹ /haʊs/ *n* casa *f*; Pol Camera *f*; Theat sala *f*; **at my ~** a casa mia, da me

house² /haʊz/ *vt* alloggiare ‹person›; incastrare ‹machine›

house: houseboat *n* casa *f* galleggiante. **housebreaking** *n* furto *m* con scasso. **household** *n* casa *f*, famiglia *f*. **householder** *n* capo *m* di famiglia. **housekeeper** *n* governante *f* di casa. **housekeeping** *n* governo *m* della casa; (money) soldi *mpl* per le spese di casa. **house plant** *n* pianta *f* da appartamento. **house-proud** *a* orgoglioso della propria casa. **house-trained** /-treɪnd/ *a* che non sporca in casa. **house-warming [party]** *n* festa *f* di inaugurazione della nuova casa. **housewife** *n* casalinga *f*. **housework** *n* lavori *mpl* domestici

housing /'haʊzɪŋ/ *n* alloggio *m*; Techn alloggiamento *m*

housing estate *n* zona *f* residenziale

hovel /'hɒvl/ *n* tugurio *m*

hover /'hɒvə(r)/ *vi* librarsi; (linger) indugiare; **~ on the brink of doing sth** essere sul punto di fare qcsa

hovercraft /'hɒvəkrɑːft/ *n* hovercraft *m inv*

how /haʊ/ *adv* come; **~ are you?** come stai?; **~ about a coffee/going on holiday?** che ne diresti di un caffè/di andare in vacanza?; **~ do you do?** molto lieto!; **~ old are you?** quanti anni hai?; **~ long** quanto tempo; **~ many** quanti; **~ much** quanto; **~ often** ogni quanto; **and ~!** eccome!; **~ odd!** che strano!

however /haʊ'evə(r)/ *adv* (nevertheless) comunque; **~ small** per quanto piccolo

howl /haʊl/ *n* ululato *m* ● *vi* ululare; (cry with laughter) singhiozzare

howler /'haʊlə(r)/ *n fam* strafalcione *m*

HP *abbr* **hire purchase**; *abbr* (**horse power**) C.V.

HQ *n Mil abbr* (**headquarters**) Q.G.

HRT *n abbr* (**hormone replacement therapy**) terapia *f* ormonale sostitutiva

hub /hʌb/ *n* mozzo *m*; *fig* centro *m*

hubbub /'hʌbʌb/ *n* baccano *m*

hubcap /'hʌbkæp/ *n* coprimozzo *m*

huckleberry /'hʌklbərɪ/ *n Am* mirtillo *m* americano

huddle /'hʌdl/ *vi* **~ together** rannicchiarsi l'uno contro l'altro

hue¹ /hjuː/ *n* colore *m*

hue² *n* **~ and cry** clamore *m*

huff /hʌf/ *n* **be in a/go into a ~** fare il broncio

hug /hʌg/ *n* abbraccio *m*; **give sb a ~** abbracciare qcno ● *vt* (*pt/pp* **hugged**) abbracciare; (keep close to) tenersi vicino a; aggrapparsi a ‹wall›

huge /hjuːdʒ/ *a* enorme

hugely /'hjuːdʒlɪ/ *adv* enormemente

huh /hʌ/ *int* (inquiry) eh?; (in surprise) oh!

hulk /hʌlk/ *n* (of ship, tank etc) carcassa *f*

hulking /'hʌlkɪŋ/ *a fam* grosso

hull /hʌl/ *n Naut* scafo *m*

hullabaloo /hʌləbə'luː/ *n fam* (noise) trambusto *m*; (outcry) fracasso *m*

hullo /həˈləʊ/ *int* = **hallo**

hum /hʌm/ *n* ronzio *m* ● *vt* (*pt/pp* **hummed**) canticchiare ● *vi* ⟨*motor:*⟩ ronzare; *fig* fervere di attività; **~ and haw** esitare

human /ˈhjuːmən/ *a* umano ● *n* essere *m* umano

human being *n* essere *m* umano

human resources *npl* risorse *fpl* umane

humane /hjuːˈmeɪn/ *a* umano

humanely /hjuːˈmeɪnlɪ/ *adv* umanamente

humanitarian /hjuːmænɪˈteərɪən/ *a & n* umanitario, -a *mf*

humanities /hjuːˈmænɪtɪz/ *pl Univ* dottrine *fpl* umanistiche

humanity /hjuːˈmænətɪ/ *n* umanità *f*

humble /ˈhʌmbl/ *a* umile ● *vt* umiliare

humbly /ˈhʌmblɪ/ *adv* umilmente

humbug /ˈhʌmbʌɡ/ *n* ⟨*nonsense*⟩ sciocchezze *fpl*; ⟨*dishonesty*⟩ falsità *f*; (*Br: sweet*) caramella *f* alla menta

humdrum /ˈhʌmdrʌm/ *a* noioso

humid /ˈhjuːmɪd/ *a* umido

humidifier /hjuːˈmɪdɪfaɪə(r)/ *n* umidificatore *m*

humidity /hjuːˈmɪdətɪ/ *n* umidità *f*

humiliate /hjuːˈmɪlɪeɪt/ *vt* umiliare

humiliating /hjuːˈmɪlɪeɪtɪŋ/ *a* avvilente

humiliation /hjuːmɪlɪˈeɪʃn/ *n* umiliazione *f*

humility /hjuːˈmɪlətɪ/ *n* umiltà *f*

hummingbird /ˈhʌmɪŋbɜːd/ *n* colibrì *m inv*

hummock /ˈhʌmək/ *n* ⟨*of earth*⟩ poggio *m*

humorist /ˈhjuːmərɪst/ *n* umorista *mf*

humorous /ˈhjuːmərəs/ *a* umoristico

humorously /ˈhjuːmərəslɪ/ *adv* con spirito

humour /ˈhjuːmə(r)/ *n* umorismo *m*; (*mood*) umore *m*; **have a sense of ~** avere il senso dell'umorismo ● *vt* compiacere

hump /hʌmp/ *n* protuberanza *f*; (*of camel, hunchback*) gobba *f*; **he's got the ~** *sl* è di malumore

humpback[ed] bridge /ˈhʌm(p)bæk[t]/ *n* ponte *m* a schiena d'asino

humus /ˈhjuːməs/ *n* humus *m*

hunch /hʌntʃ/ *n* (*idea*) intuizione *f*

hunchback /ˈhʌntʃbæk/ *n* gobbo, -a *mf*

hunched /hʌntʃt/ *a* **~ up** incurvato

hundred /ˈhʌndrəd/ *a* **one/a ~** cento ● *n* cento *m inv*; **~s of** centinaia di

hundredfold /ˈhʌndrədfəʊld/ *adv* **increase a ~** centuplicare

hundredth /ˈhʌndrədθ/ *a & n* centesimo *m*

hundredweight /ˈhʌndrədweɪt/ *n* cinquanta chili *m*

hung /hʌŋ/ *see* **hang**

Hungarian /hʌŋˈɡeərɪən/ *n & a* ungherese *mf*; (*language*) ungherese *m*

Hungary /ˈhʌŋɡərɪ/ *n* Ungheria *f*

hunger /ˈhʌŋɡə(r)/ *n* fame *f*

■ **hunger for** *vt* aver fame di

hunger strike *n* sciopero *m* della fame

hung-over *a* **be ~** avere i postumi della sbornia

hungrily /ˈhʌŋɡrɪlɪ/ *adv* con appetito

hungry /ˈhʌŋɡrɪ/ *a* (**-ier, -iest**) affamato; **be ~** aver fame

hung-up *a fam* (*tense*) complessato; **be ~ on sb/sth** (*obsessed*) essere fissato con qcsa

hunk /hʌŋk/ *n* grosso pezzo *m*; (*fam: man*) figo *m*

hunky-dory /hʌŋkɪˈdɔːrɪ/ *a fam* perfetto

hunt /hʌnt/ *n* caccia *f* ● *vt* andare a caccia di ⟨*animal*⟩; dare la caccia a ⟨*criminal*⟩ ● *vi* andare a caccia; **~ for** cercare

hunter /ˈhʌntə(r)/ *n* cacciatore *m*

hunting /ˈhʌntɪŋ/ *n* caccia *f*

hunt saboteur *n Br* sabotatore, -trice *mf* della caccia

huntsman /ˈhʌntsmən/ *n* (*hunter*) cacciatore *m*; (*fox-hunter*) cacciatore *m* di volpe

hurdle /ˈhɜːdl/ *n Sport & fig* ostacolo *m*

hurdler /ˈhɜːdlə(r)/ *n* ostacolista *mf*

hurdy-gurdy /hɜːdɪˈɡɜːdɪ/ *n* organino *m*

hurl /hɜːl/ *vt* scagliare

hurly-burly /hɜːlɪˈbɜːlɪ/ *n* chiasso *m*

hurrah /hʊˈrɑː/, **hurray** /hʊˈreɪ/ *int* urrà! ● *n* urrà *m*

hurricane /ˈhʌrɪkən/ *n* uragano *m*

hurried /ˈhʌrɪd/ *a* affrettato; ⟨*job*⟩ fatto in fretta

hurriedly /ˈhʌrɪdlɪ/ *adv* in fretta

hurry /ˈhʌrɪ/ *n* fretta *f*; **be in a ~** aver fretta ● *vi* (*pt/pp* **-ied**) affrettarsi

■ **hurry up** *vi* sbrigarsi ● *vt* mettere fretta a ⟨*person*⟩; accelerare ⟨*things*⟩

hurt /hɜːt/ *n* male *m* ● *v* (*pt/pp* **hurt**) ● *vt* far male a; (*offend*) ferire ● *vi* far male; **my leg ~s** mi fa male la gamba

hurtful /ˈhɜːtfʊl/ *a fig* offensivo

hurtle /ˈhɜːtl/ *vi* **~ along** andare a tutta velocità

husband /ˈhʌzbənd/ *n* marito *m*

hush /hʌʃ/ *n* silenzio *m*

■ **hush up** *vt* mettere a tacere

hushed /hʌʃt/ *a* ⟨*voice*⟩ sommesso

hush-hush *a fam* segretissimo

husky /ˈhʌskɪ/ *a* (**-ier, -iest**) ⟨*voice*⟩ rauco

hussar /hʊˈzɑː(r)/ *n* ussaro *m*

hustings /ˈhʌstɪŋz/ *n* **on the ~** in campagna elettorale

hustle /ˈhʌsl/ *vt* affrettare ● *n* attività *f* incessante; **~ and bustle** trambusto *m*

hut /hʌt/ *n* capanna *f*

hutch /hʌtʃ/ *n* congliera *f*

hyacinth /ˈhaɪəsɪnθ/ *n* giacinto *m*

hybrid /ˈhaɪbrɪd/ *a* ibrido ● *n* ibrido *m*

hydrangea /haɪˈdreɪndʒə/ *n* ortensia *f*

hydrant /ˈhaɪdrənt/ *n* [**fire**] **~** idrante *m*

hydraulic /haɪˈdrɔːlɪk/ *a* idraulico

hydrocarbon /haɪdrəʊˈkɑːbən/ *n* idrocarburo *m*

hydrochloric /haɪdrəˈklɔːrɪk/ *a* **~ acid** acido *m* cloridrico

hydroelectric /haɪdrəʊɪˈlektrɪk/ *a* idroelettrico

hydroelectric power station *n* centrale *f* idroelettrica

hydrofoil /ˈhaɪdrəfɔɪl/ *n* aliscafo *m*

hydrogen /ˈhaɪdrədʒən/ *n* idrogeno *m*

hydrolysis /haɪˈdrɒləsɪs/ *n* idrolisi *f*

hydrophobia /haɪdrəˈfəʊbɪə/ *n* idrofobia *f*

hydroplane /'haɪdrəpleɪn/ n (boat) aliscafo m; (Am: seaplane) idrovolante m
hydrotherapy /haɪdrəʊ'θerəpɪ/ n idroterapia f
hyena /haɪ'i:nə/ n iena f
hygiene /'haɪdʒi:n/ n igiene m
hygienic /haɪ'dʒi:nɪk/ a igienico
hygienically /haɪ'dʒi:nɪklɪ/ adv igienicamente
hymn /hɪm/ n inno m
hymn book n libro m dei canti
hype /haɪp/ n fam grande pubblicità f; **media ~** battage m pubblicitario
■ **hype up** vt fam fare grande pubblicità a ⟨film, star, book⟩; (exaggerate) gonfiare
hyper /'haɪpə(r)/ a fam eccitato
hyperactive /haɪpər'æktɪv/ a iperattivo
hyperactivity /haɪpəræk'tɪvɪtɪ/ n iperattività f
hyperbole /haɪ'pɜ:bəlɪ/ n iperbole f
hypercritical /haɪpə'krɪtɪkl/ a ipercritico
hypermarket /'haɪpəma:kɪt/ n ipermercato m
hypersensitive /haɪpə'sensɪtɪv/ a pej permaloso; (physically) ipersensibile
hypertension /haɪpə'tenʃn/ n ipertensione f
hypertext /'haɪpətekst/ n Comput ipertesto m
hyperventilate /haɪpə'ventɪleɪt/ vi iperventilare
hyphen /'haɪfn/ n trattino m
hyphenate /'haɪfəneɪt/ vt unire con trattino
hypnosis /hɪp'nəʊsɪs/ n ipnosi f

hypnotherapy /hɪpnəʊ'θerəpɪ/ n ipnoterapia f
hypnotic /hɪp'nɒtɪk/ a ipnotico
hypnotism /'hɪpnətɪzm/ n ipnotismo m
hypnotist /'hɪpnətɪst/ n ipnotizzatore, -trice mf
hypnotize /'hɪpnətaɪz/ vt ipnotizzare
hypoallergenic /haɪpəʊælə'dʒenɪk/ a anallergico
hypochondria /haɪpə'kɒndrɪə/ n ipocondria f
hypochondriac /haɪpə'kɒndrɪæk/ a & n ipocondriaco, -a mf
hypocrisy /hɪ'pɒkrəsɪ/ n ipocrisia f
hypocrite /'hɪpəkrɪt/ n ipocrita mf
hypocritical /hɪpə'krɪtɪkl/ a ipocrita
hypocritically /hɪpə'krɪtɪklɪ/ adv ipocriticamente
hypodermic /haɪpə'dɜ:mɪk/ a & n ~ [syringe] siringa f ipodermica
hypotenuse /haɪ'pɒtənju:z/ n ipotenusa f
hypothermia /haɪpəʊ'θɜ:mɪə/ n ipotermia f
hypothesis /haɪ'pɒθəsɪs/ n ipotesi f inv
hypothetical /haɪpə'θetɪkl/ a ipotetico
hypothetically /haɪpə'θetɪklɪ/ adv in teoria; ⟨speak⟩ per ipotesi
hysterectomy /hɪstə'rektəmɪ/ n isterectomia f
hysteria /hɪ'stɪərɪə/ n isterismo m
hysterical /hɪ'sterɪkl/ a isterico
hysterically /hɪ'sterɪklɪ/ adv istericamente; ~ **funny** da morir dal ridere
hysterics /hɪ'sterɪks/ npl attacco m isterico

. . . .

Ii

. . . .

i, I /aɪ/ n (letter)i, I f inv
I /aɪ/ pron io; **I'm tired** sono stanco; **he's going, but I'm not** lui va, ma io no
ibex /'aɪbeks/ n stambecco m
ice /aɪs/ n ghiaccio m ● vt glassare ⟨cake⟩
■ **ice over, ice up** vi ghiacciarsi
ice: ice age n era f glaciale. **ice axe** n piccozza f per il ghiaccio. **iceberg** n iceberg m inv. **icebox** n Am frigorifero m. **ice-breaker** n Naut rompighiaccio m inv. **ice bucket** n secchiello m del ghiaccio. **ice cap** n calotta f glaciale. **ice-cold** a ghiacciato. **ice cream** n gelato m. **ice-cream parlour** n gelateria f. **ice-cream sundae** n coppa f [di] gelato guarnita. **ice cube** n cubetto m di ghiaccio. **ice dancer** n ballerino, -a mf sul ghiaccio. **ice floe** n banco m di ghiaccio. **ice hockey** hockey m su ghiaccio.
Iceland /'aɪslənd/ n Islanda f
Icelander /'aɪsləndə(r)/ n islandese mf
Icelandic /aɪs'lændɪk/ a & n islandese m

ice: ice lolly n ghiacciolo m. **ice pack** n impacco m di ghiaccio. **ice pick** n piccone m da ghiaccio. **ice rink** n pista f di pattinaggio. **ice-skate** n pattino m da ghiaccio. **ice-skater** pattinatore, -trice mf sul ghiaccio. **ice-skating** pattinaggio m sul ghiaccio. **ice-tray** n vaschetta f per il ghiaccio
icicle /'aɪsɪkl/ n ghiacciolo m
icily /'aɪsɪlɪ/ adv gelidamente
icing /'aɪsɪŋ/ n glassa f
icing sugar n zucchero m a velo
icon /'aɪkɒn/ n icona f
icy /'aɪsɪ/ a (-ier, -iest) ghiacciato; fig gelido
id /ɪd/ n the ~ l'Es m
ID n abbr (identification, identity) documento m d'identità; **ID card** n carta f d'identità
idea /aɪ'dɪə/ n idea f; **I've no ~!** non ne ho idea!
ideal /aɪ'dɪəl/ a ideale ● n ideale m
idealism /aɪ'dɪəlɪzm/ n idealismo m

idealist /aɪˈdɪəlɪst/ n idealista mf
idealistic /aɪdɪəˈlɪstɪk/ a idealistico
idealize /aɪˈdɪəlaɪz/ vt idealizzare
ideally /aɪˈdɪəlɪ/ adv idealmente
identical /aɪˈdentɪkl/ a identico
identifiable /aɪdentɪˈfaɪəbl/ a identificabile
identification /aɪdentɪfɪˈkeɪʃn/ n identificazione f; (proof of identity) documento m di riconoscimento
identify /aɪˈdentɪfaɪ/ vt (pt/pp -ied) identificare ● vi ~ with identificarsi con
identikit® /aɪˈdentɪkɪt/ n identikit m inv
identikit® picture n identikit m inv
identity /aɪˈdentətɪ/ n identità f inv
identity card n carta f d'identità
identity parade n confronto m all'americana
ideological /aɪdɪəˈlɒdʒɪkl/ a ideologico
ideology /aɪdɪˈɒlədʒɪ/ n ideologia f
idiocy /ˈɪdɪəsɪ/ n idiozia f
idiom /ˈɪdɪəm/ n idioma f
idiomatic /ɪdɪəˈmætɪk/ a idiomatico
idiomatically /ɪdɪəˈmætɪklɪ/ adv in modo idiomatico
idiosyncrasy /ɪdɪəˈsɪŋkrəsɪ/ n idiosincrasia f
idiot /ˈɪdɪət/ n idiota mf
idiotic /ɪdɪˈɒtɪk/ a idiota
idle /ˈaɪd(ə)l/ a (lazy) pigro, ozioso; (empty) vano; (machine) fermo ● vi oziare; (engine:) girare a vuoto
idleness /ˈaɪd(ə)lnɪs/ n ozio m
idly /ˈaɪdlɪ/ adv oziosamente
idol /ˈaɪd(ə)l/ n idolo m
idolize /ˈaɪdəlaɪz/ vt idolatrare
idyll /ˈɪdɪl/ n idillio m
idyllic /ɪˈdɪlɪk/ a idillico
i.e. abbr (id est) cioè
if /ɪf/ conj se; **as if** come se
iffy /ˈɪfɪ/ a incerto
igloo /ˈɪɡluː/ n igloo m inv
ignite /ɪɡˈnaɪt/ vt dar fuoco a ● vi prender fuoco
ignition /ɪɡˈnɪʃn/ n Auto accensione f
ignition key n chiave f d'accensione
ignoramus /ɪɡnəˈreɪməs/ n ignorante mf
ignorance /ˈɪɡnərəns/ n ignoranza f
ignorant /ˈɪɡnərənt/ a (lacking knowledge) ignaro; (rude) ignorante
ignore /ɪɡˈnɔː(r)/ vt ignorare
ill /ɪl/ a ammalato; **feel ~ at ease** sentirsi a disagio ● adv male ● n male m
ill: ill-advised /-ədˈvaɪzd/ a avventato. **ill-bred** /-ˈbred/ a maleducato. **ill-considered** /-kənˈsɪdəd/ a (measure, remark) avventato. **ill effect** n effetto m negativo
illegal /ɪˈliːɡl/ a illegale
illegality /ɪlɪˈɡælətɪ/ n illegalità f
illegally /ɪˈliːɡəlɪ/ adv illegalmente
illegible /ɪˈledʒəbl/ a illeggibile
illegibly /ɪˈledʒəblɪ/ adv in modo illeggibile
illegitimacy /ɪlɪˈdʒɪtɪməsɪ/ n illegittimità f
illegitimate /ɪlɪˈdʒɪtɪmət/ a illegittimo
ill: ill-equipped /-ɪˈkwɪpt/ a non equipaggiato. **ill-fated** /-ˈfeɪtɪd/ a sfortunato. **ill feeling**

n rancore m. **ill-fitting** a (garment, shoe) che non va bene. **ill-founded** /-ˈfaʊndɪd/ a (argument, gossip) infondato. **ill-gotten gains** /ɪlɡɒ(t)nˈɡeɪnz/ a guadagni mpl illeciti.
ill health n problemi mpl di salute
illicit /ɪˈlɪsɪt/ a illecito
illicitly /ɪˈlɪsɪtlɪ/ adv illecitamente
ill-informed /-ɪnˈfɔːmd/ a (person) male informato
illiteracy /ɪˈlɪtərəsɪ/ n analfabetismo m
illiterate /ɪˈlɪtərət/ a & n analfabeta mf
ill-mannered /-ˈmænəd/ a maleducato
illness /ˈɪlnɪs/ n malattia f
illogical /ɪˈlɒdʒɪkl/ a illogico
illogically /ɪˈlɒdʒɪklɪ/ adv illogicamente
ill: ill-prepared /-prɪˈpeəd/ a impreparato. **ill-timed** /-ˈtaɪmd/ a (arrival) inopportuno; (campaign) fatto al momento sbagliato. **ill-treat** vt maltrattare. **ill-treatment** n maltrattamento m
illuminate /ɪˈluːmɪneɪt/ vt illuminare
illuminating /ɪˈluːmɪneɪtɪŋ/ a chiarificatore
illumination /ɪluːmɪˈneɪʃn/ n illuminazione f
illusion /ɪˈluːʒn/ n illusione f; **be under the ~ that** avere l'illusione che
illusory /ɪˈluːsərɪ/ a illusorio
illustrate /ˈɪləstreɪt/ vt illustrare
illustration /ɪləˈstreɪʃn/ n illustrazione f
illustrative /ˈɪləstrətɪv/ a illustrativo
illustrator /ˈɪləstreɪtə(r)/ n illustratore, -trice mf
illustrious /ɪˈlʌstrɪəs/ a illustre
ill will n malanimo m
image /ˈɪmɪdʒ/ n immagine f; (exact likeness) ritratto m
image-conscious a attento all'immagine
imagery /ˈɪmɪdʒərɪ/ n immagini fpl
imaginable /ɪˈmædʒɪnəbl/ a immaginabile
imaginary /ɪˈmædʒɪnərɪ/ a immaginario
imagination /ɪmædʒɪˈneɪʃn/ n immaginazione f, fantasia f; **it's your ~** è solo una tua idea
imaginative /ɪˈmædʒɪnətɪv/ a fantasioso
imaginatively /ɪˈmædʒɪnətɪvlɪ/ adv con fantasia or immaginazione
imagine /ɪˈmædʒɪn/ vt immaginare; (wrongly) inventare
imbalance /ɪmˈbæləns/ n squilibrio m
imbecile /ˈɪmbəsiːl/ n imbecille mf
imbibe /ɪmˈbaɪb/ vt ingerire; fig assorbire ● vi hum bere
imbue /ɪmˈbjuː/ vt ~d with impregnato di
imitate /ˈɪmɪteɪt/ vt imitare
imitation /ɪmɪˈteɪʃn/ n imitazione f
imitative /ˈɪmɪtətɪv/ a imitativo
imitator /ˈɪmɪteɪtə(r)/ n imitatore, -trice mf
immaculate /ɪˈmækjʊlət/ a immacolato
immaculately /ɪˈmækjʊlətlɪ/ adv immacolatamente
immaterial /ɪməˈtɪərɪəl/ a (unimportant) irrilevante
immature /ɪməˈtʃʊə(r)/ a immaturo
immeasurable /ɪˈmeʒərəbl/ a incommensurabile

immediacy /ɪ'miːdɪəsɪ/ n immediatezza f
immediate /ɪ'miːdɪət/ a immediato; ‹relative› stretto; **in the ~ vicinity** nelle immediate vicinanze
immediately /ɪ'miːdɪətlɪ/ adv immediatamente; **~ next to** subito accanto a ● conj [non] appena
immemorial /ɪmɪ'mɔːrɪəl/ a **from time ~** da tempo immemorabile
immense /ɪ'mens/ a immenso
immensely /ɪ'menslɪ/ adv immensamente
immensity /ɪ'mensətɪ/ n immensità f
immerse /ɪ'mɜːs/ vt immergere; **be ~d in** fig essere immerso in
immersion /ɪ'mɜːʃn/ n immersione f
immersion heater n scaldabagno m inv elettrico
immigrant /'ɪmɪgrənt/ n immigrante mf
immigrate /'ɪmɪgreɪt/ vi immigrare
immigration /ɪmɪ'greɪʃn/ n immigrazione f
imminence /'ɪmɪnəns/ n imminenza f
imminent /'ɪmɪnənt/ a imminente
immobile /ɪ'məʊbaɪl/ a immobile
immobilize /ɪ'məʊbɪlaɪz/ vt immobilizzare
immoderate /ɪ'mɒdərət/ a smodato
immodest /ɪ'mɒdɪst/ a immodesto
immoral /ɪ'mɒrəl/ a immorale
immorality /ɪmə'rælətɪ/ n immoralità f
immortal /ɪ'mɔːtl/ a immortale
immortality /ɪmɔː'tælətɪ/ n immortalità f
immortalize /ɪ'mɔːtəlaɪz/ vt immortalare
immovable /ɪ'muːvəbl/ a fig irremovibile
immune /ɪ'mjuːn/ a immune (**to/from** da)
immune system n sistema m immunitario
immunity /ɪ'mjuːnətɪ/ n immunità f
immunization /ɪmjʊnaɪ'zeɪʃn/ n immunizzazione f
immunize /'ɪmjʊnaɪz/ vt immunizzare
immunodeficiency /ɪmjʊnəʊdɪ'fɪʃənsɪ/ n immunodeficienza f
immunology /ɪmjʊ'nɒlədʒɪ/ n immunologia f
immutable /ɪ'mjuːtəbl/ a immutabile
imp /ɪmp/ n diavoletto m
impact /'ɪmpækt/ n impatto m
impacted /ɪm'pæktɪd/ a ‹tooth› incluso; ‹fracture› incuneato
impair /ɪm'peə(r)/ vt danneggiare
impale /ɪm'peɪl/ vt impalare
impalpable /ɪm'pælpəbl/ a (intangible) impalpabile
impart /ɪm'pɑːt/ vt impartire
impartial /ɪm'pɑːʃəl/ a imparziale
impartiality /ɪmpɑːʃɪ'ælətɪ/ n imparzialità f
impassable /ɪm'pɑːsəbl/ a impraticabile
impasse /æm'pɑːs/ n fig impasse f inv
impassioned /ɪm'pæʃnd/ a appassionato
impassive /ɪm'pæsɪv/ a impassibile
impassively /ɪm'pæsɪvlɪ/ adv impassibilmente
impatience /ɪm'peɪʃns/ n impazienza f
impatient /ɪm'peɪʃnt/ a impaziente
impatiently /ɪm'peɪʃntlɪ/ adv impazientemente
impeach /ɪm'piːtʃ/ vt accusare

impeccable /ɪm'pekəbl/ a impeccabile
impeccably /ɪm'pekəblɪ/ adv in modo impeccabile
impede /ɪm'piːd/ vt impedire
impediment /ɪm'pedɪmənt/ n impedimento m; (in speech) difetto m
impel /ɪm'pel/ vt (pt/pp **impelled**) costringere; **feel ~led to** sentire l'obbligo di
impending /ɪm'pendɪŋ/ a imminente
impenetrable /ɪm'penɪtrəbl/ a impenetrabile
imperative /ɪm'perətɪv/ a imperativo; ● n Gram imperativo m
imperceptible /ɪmpə'septəbl/ a impercettibile
imperfect /ɪm'pɜːfɪkt/ a imperfetto; (faulty) difettoso ● n Gram imperfetto m
imperfection /ɪmpə'fekʃn/ n imperfezione f
imperial /ɪm'pɪərɪəl/ a imperiale
imperialism /ɪm'pɪərɪəlɪzm/ n imperialismo m
imperialist /ɪm'pɪərɪəlɪst/ n imperialista mf
imperil /ɪm'perəl/ vt (pt/pp **imperilled**) mettere in pericolo
imperious /ɪm'pɪərɪəs/ a imperioso
imperiously /ɪm'pɪərɪəslɪ/ adv di modo imperioso
impermeable /ɪm'pɜːmɪəbl/ a impermeabile
impersonal /ɪm'pɜːsənəl/ a impersonale
impersonate /ɪm'pɜːsəneɪt/ vt impersonare
impersonation /ɪmpɜːsə'neɪʃn/ n imitazione f
impersonator /ɪm'pɜːsəneɪtə(r)/ n imitatore, -trice mf
impertinence /ɪm'pɜːtɪnəns/ n impertinenza f
impertinent /ɪm'pɜːtɪnənt/ a impertinente
imperturbable /ɪmpə'tɜːbəbl/ a imperturbabile
impervious /ɪm'pɜːvɪəs/ a **~ to** fig indifferente a
impetuous /ɪm'petjʊəs/ a impetuoso
impetuously /ɪm'petjʊəslɪ/ adv impetuosamente
impetus /'ɪmpɪtəs/ n impeto m
impiety /ɪm'paɪətɪ/ n Relig empietà f
■ **impinge on** /ɪm'pɪndʒ/ vt (affect) influire su; (restrict) condizionare
impious /'ɪmpɪəs/ a Relig empio
impish /'ɪmpɪʃ/ a birichino
implacable /ɪm'plækəbl/ a implacabile
implant¹ /ɪm'plɑːnt/ vt trapiantare; fig inculcare
implant² /'ɪmplɑːnt/ n trapianto m
implausible /ɪm'plɔːzəbl/ a poco plausibile
implement¹ /'ɪmplɪmənt/ n attrezzo m
implement² /'ɪmplɪment/ vt mettere in atto
implicate /'ɪmplɪkeɪt/ vt implicare
implication /ɪmplɪ'keɪʃn/ n implicazione f; **by ~** implicitamente
implicit /ɪm'plɪsɪt/ a implicito; (absolute) assoluto

implicitly /ɪm'plɪsɪtlɪ/ *adv* implicitamente; (*absolutely*) completamente

implied /ɪm'plaɪd/ *a* implicito, sottinteso

implore /ɪm'plɔ:(r)/ *vt* implorare

imploring /ɪm'plɔ:rɪŋ/ *a* implorante

implosion /ɪm'pləʊʒn/ *n* implosione *f*

imply /ɪm'plaɪ/ *vt* (*pt/pp* **-ied**) implicare; **what are you ~ing?** che cosa vorresti insinuare?

impolite /ɪmpə'laɪt/ *a* sgarbato

impolitely /ɪmpə'laɪtlɪ/ *adv* sgarbatamente

import¹ /'ɪmpɔ:t/ *n Comm* importazione *f*; (*importance*) importanza *f*; (*meaning*) rilevanza *f*

import² /ɪm'pɔ:t/ *vt* importare

importance /ɪm'pɔ:təns/ *n* importanza *f*

important /ɪm'pɔ:tənt/ *a* importante

importation /ɪmpɔ:'teɪʃn/ *n Comm* importazione *f*

import duty /'ɪmpɔ:t/ *n* dazio *m* d'importazione

importer /ɪm'pɔ:tə(r)/ *n* importatore, -trice *mf*

import-export /'ɪmpɔ:t'ekspɔ:t/ *n* import-export *m*

importing country /ɪm'pɔ:tɪŋ/ *n* paese *m* di importazione

impose /ɪm'pəʊz/ *vt* imporre (**on** a) ● *vi* imporsi; **~ on** abusare di

imposing /ɪm'pəʊzɪŋ/ *a* imponente

imposition /ɪmpə'zɪʃn/ *n* imposizione *f*

impossibility /ɪm'pɒsɪbɪlətɪ/ *n* impossibilità *f*

impossible /ɪm'pɒsəbl/ *a* impossibile

impossibly /ɪm'pɒsəblɪ/ *adv* impossibilmente

impostor /ɪm'pɒstə(r)/ *n* impostore, -trice *mf*

impotence /'ɪmpətəns/ *n* impotenza *f*

impotent /'ɪmpətənt/ *a* impotente

impound /ɪm'paʊnd/ *vt* confiscare

impoverished /ɪm'pɒvərɪʃt/ *a* impoverito

impracticable /ɪm'præktɪkəbl/ *a* impraticabile

impractical /ɪm'præktɪkl/ *a* non pratico

imprecise /ɪmprɪ'saɪs/ *a* impreciso

impregnable /ɪm'pregnəbl/ *a* imprendibile

impregnate /'ɪmpregneɪt/ *vt* impregnare (**with** di); *Biol* fecondare

impresario /ɪmprɪ'sɑ:rɪəʊ/ *n* (*pl* **-os**) impresario *m* (*di spettacoli*)

impress /ɪm'pres/ *vt* imprimere; *fig* colpire (*positivamente*); **~ sth [up]on sb** fare capire qcsa a qcno

impression /ɪm'preʃn/ *n* impressione *f*; (*imitation*) imitazione *f*

impressionable /ɪm'preʃənəbl/ *a* ‹child, mind› influenzabile

impressionism /ɪm'preʃənɪzm/ *n* impressionismo *m*

impressionist /ɪm'preʃənɪst/ *n* imitatore, -trice *mf*; (*artist*) impressionista *mf*

impressionistic /ɪmpreʃə'nɪstɪk/ *a* impressionista; ‹account› approssimativo

impressive /ɪm'presɪv/ *a* imponente

imprint¹ /'ɪmprɪnt/ *n* impressione *f*

imprint² /ɪm'prɪnt/ *vt* imprimere; **~ed on my mind** impresso nella mia memoria

imprison /ɪm'prɪzən/ *vt* incarcerare

imprisonment /ɪm'prɪzənmənt/ *n* reclusione *f*

improbable /ɪm'prɒbəbl/ *a* improbabile

impromptu /ɪm'prɒmptju:/ *a* improvvisato ● *adv* in modo improvvisato

improper /ɪm'prɒpə(r)/ *a* ‹use› improprio; ‹behaviour› scorretto

improperly /ɪm'prɒpəlɪ/ *adv* scorrettamente

impropriety /ɪmprə'praɪətɪ/ *n* scorrettezza *f*

improve /ɪm'pru:v/ *vt/i* migliorare

■ **improve [up]on** *vt* perfezionare

improvement /ɪm'pru:vmənt/ *n* miglioramento *m*

improvident /ɪm'prɒvɪdənt/ *a* (*heedless of the future*) imprevidente

improvisation /ɪmprəvaɪ'zeɪʃn/ *n* improvvisazione *f*

improvise /'ɪmprəvaɪz/ *vt/i* improvvisare

imprudent /ɪm'pru:dənt/ *a* imprudente

impudence /'ɪmpjʊdəns/ *n* sfrontatezza *f*

impudent /'ɪmpjʊdənt/ *a* sfrontato

impudently /'ɪmpjʊdəntlɪ/ *adv* sfrontatamente

impulse /'ɪmpʌls/ *n* impulso *m*; **on [an] ~** impulsivamente

impulse buying *n* acquisti *mpl* fatti d'impulso

impulsive /ɪm'pʌlsɪv/ *a* impulsivo

impulsively /ɪm'pʌlsɪvlɪ/ *adv* impulsivamente

impunity /ɪm'pju:nətɪ/ *n* **with ~** impunemente

impure /ɪm'pjʊə(r)/ *a* impuro

impurity /ɪm'pjʊərətɪ/ *n* impurità *f inv*; **impurities** *pl* impurità *fpl*

impute /ɪm'pju:t/ *vt* imputare (**to** a)

in /ɪn/ *prep* in; (*with names of towns*) a; **in the garden** in giardino; **in the street** in *or* per strada; **in bed/hospital** a letto/all'ospedale; **in the world** nel mondo; **in the rain** sotto la pioggia; **in the sun** al sole; **in this heat** con questo caldo; **in summer/winter** in estate/inverno; **in 1995** nel 1995; **in the evening** la sera; **he's arriving in two hours' time** arriva fra due ore; **deaf in one ear** sordo da un orecchio; **in the army** nell'esercito; **in English/Italian** in inglese/italiano; **in ink/pencil** a penna/matita; **in red** ‹dressed, circled› di rosso; **the man in the raincoat** l'uomo con l'impermeabile; **in a soft/loud voice** a voce bassa/alta; **one in ten people** una persona su dieci; **in doing this, he...** nel far questo,...; **in itself** in sé; **in that** in quanto ● *adv* (*at home*) a casa; (*indoors*) dentro; **he's not in yet** non è ancora arrivato; **in there/here** lì/qui dentro; **ten in all** dieci in tutto; **day in, day out** giorno dopo giorno; **have it in for sb** *fam* avercela con qcno; **send him in** fallo entrare; **come in** entrare; **bring in the washing** portare dentro i panni ● *a* (*fam: in* *fashion*) di moda ● *n* **the ins and outs** i dettagli

inability /ɪnəˈbɪlətɪ/ *n* incapacità *f*
inaccessible /ɪnækˈsesəbl/ *a* inaccessibile
inaccuracy /ɪnˈækjʊrəsɪ/ *n* inesattezza *f*
inaccurate /ɪnˈækjʊrət/ *a* inesatto
inaccurately /ɪnˈækjʊrətlɪ/ *adv* in modo inesatto
inaction /ɪnˈækʃn/ *n* (*not being active*) inazione *f*; (*failure to act*) inerzia *f*
inactive /ɪnˈæktɪv/ *a* inattivo
inactivity /ɪnækˈtɪvətɪ/ *n* inattività *f*
inadequacy /ɪnˈædɪkwəsɪ/ *n* inadeguatezza *f*
inadequate /ɪnˈædɪkwət/ *a* inadeguato
inadequately /ɪnˈædɪkwətlɪ/ *adv* inadeguatamente
inadmissible /ɪnædˈmɪsəbl/ *a* inammissibile
inadvertent /ɪnədˈvɜːtənt/ *a* involontario
inadvertently /ɪnədˈvɜːtəntlɪ/ *adv* inavvertitamente
inadvisable /ɪnædˈvaɪzəbl/ *a* sconsigliabile
inalienable /ɪnˈeɪlɪənəbl/ *a* inalienabile
inane /ɪˈneɪn/ *a* futile
inanely /ɪˈneɪnlɪ/ *adv* in modo vacuo
inanimate /ɪnˈænɪmət/ *a* esanime
inanity /ɪˈnænətɪ/ *n* stupidità *f inv*
inapplicable /məˈplɪkəbl/ *a* inapplicabile
inappropriate /ɪnəˈprəʊprɪət/ *a* inadatto
inapt /ɪnˈæpt/ *a* (*inappropriate*) inappropriato
inarticulate /ɪnɑːˈtɪkjʊlət/ *a* inarticolato
inasmuch /ɪnəzˈmʌtʃ/ *conj* ~ **as** (*insofar as*) in quanto; (*seeing that*) poiché
inattention /ɪnəˈtenʃn/ *n* disattenzione *f*
inattentive /ɪnəˈtentɪv/ *a* disattento
inaudible /ɪnˈɔːdəbl/ *a* impercettibile
inaudibly /ɪnˈɔːdəblɪ/ *adv* in modo impercettibile
inaugural /ɪnˈɔːgjʊrəl/ *a* inaugurale
inaugurate /ɪnˈɔːgjʊreɪt/ *vt* inaugurare
inauguration /ɪnɔːgjʊˈreɪʃn/ *n* inaugurazione *f*
inauspicious /ɪnɔːˈspɪʃəs/ *a* infausto
in-between *a* intermedio
inborn /ˈɪnbɔːn/ *a* innato
inbred /ɪnˈbred/ *a* congenito
inbreeding /ɪnˈbriːdɪŋ/ *n* (*in animals*) inbreeding *m*; (*in humans*) unioni *mpl* fra consanguinei
inbuilt /ɪnˈbɪlt/ *a* 〈*feeling*〉 innato
incalculable /ɪnˈkælkjʊləbl/ *a* incalcolabile
incandescence /ɪnkænˈdesəns/ *n liter* incandescenza *f*
incandescent /ɪnkænˈdesənt/ *a liter* incandescente
incapable /ɪnˈkeɪpəbl/ *a* incapace
incapacitate /ɪnkəˈpæsɪteɪt/ *vt* rendere incapace
incapacity /ɪnkəˈpæsətɪ/ *n also Jur* incapacità *f*
incarcerate /ɪnˈkɑːsəreɪt/ *vt* incarcerare

incarnate /ɪnˈkɑːnət/ *a* **the devil** ~ il diavolo in carne e ossa
incarnation /ɪnkɑːˈneɪʃn/ *n* incarnazione *f*
incendiary /ɪnˈsendɪərɪ/ *a* incendiario ● *n* ~ [**bomb**] bomba *f* incendiaria
incendiary device *n* ordigno *m* incendiario
incense[1] /ˈɪnsens/ *n* incenso *m*
incense[2] /ɪnˈsens/ *vt* esasperare
incentive /ɪnˈsentɪv/ *n* incentivo *m*
inception /ɪnˈsepʃn/ *n* inizio *m*
incessant /ɪnˈsesənt/ *a* incessante
incessantly /ɪnˈsesəntlɪ/ *adv* incessantemente
incest /ˈɪnsest/ *n* incesto *m*
incestuous /ɪnˈsestjʊəs/ *a* incestuoso
inch /ɪntʃ/ *n* pollice *m* (= *2.54 cm*) ● *vi* ~ **forward** avanzare gradatamente
incidence /ˈɪnsɪdəns/ *n* incidenza *f*
incident /ˈɪnsɪdənt/ *n* incidente *m*
incidental /ɪnsɪˈdentl/ *a* incidentale; ~ **expenses** spese *fpl* accessorie
incidentally /ɪnsɪˈdent(ə)lɪ/ *adv* incidentalmente; (*by the way*) a proposito
incident room *n* (*for criminal investigation*) centrale *f* operativa
incinerate /ɪnˈsɪnəreɪt/ *vt* incenerire
incinerator /ɪnˈsɪnəreɪtə(r)/ *n* inceneritore *m*
incipient /ɪnˈsɪpɪənt/ *a* incipiente
incision /ɪnˈsɪʒn/ *n* incisione *f*
incisive /ɪnˈsaɪsɪv/ *a* incisivo
incisor /ɪnˈsaɪzə(r)/ *n* incisivo *m*
incite /ɪnˈsaɪt/ *vt* incitare
incitement /ɪnˈsaɪtmənt/ *n* incitamento *m*
incivility /ɪnsɪˈvɪlətɪ/ *n* scortesia *f*
incl *abbr* **inclusive**; *abbr* **including**
inclement /ɪnˈklemənt/ *a* inclemente
inclination /ɪnklɪˈneɪʃn/ *n* inclinazione *f*
incline[1] /ɪnˈklaɪn/ *vt* inclinare; **be ~d to do sth** essere propenso a fare qcsa ● *vi* inclinarsi
incline[2] /ˈɪnklaɪn/ *n* pendio *m*
include /ɪnˈkluːd/ *vt* includere
including /ɪnˈkluːdɪŋ/ *prep* incluso
inclusion /ɪnˈkluːʒn/ *n* inclusione *f*
inclusive /ɪnˈkluːsɪv/ *a* incluso; ~ **of** comprendente; **be ~ of** comprendere. ● *adv* incluso
incognito /ɪnkɒgˈniːtəʊ/ *adv* incognito
incoherent /ɪnkəˈhɪərənt/ *a* incoerente; (*because drunk etc*) incomprensibile
incoherently /ɪnkəˈhɪərəntlɪ/ *adv* incoerentemente; (*because drunk etc*) incomprensibilmente
income /ˈɪnkəm/ *n* reddito *m*
income bracket *n* fascia *f* di reddito
income tax *n* imposta *f* sul reddito
income tax return *n* dichiarazione *f* dei redditi
incoming /ˈɪnkʌmɪŋ/ *a* in arrivo; ~ **tide** marea *f* montante
incommunicado /ɪnkəmjuːnɪˈkɑːdəʊ/ *a* (*involuntarily*) segregato; **he's ~** (*in meeting*) non vuole essere disturbato

incomparable /ɪnˈkɒmp(ə)rəbl/ *a* incomparabile

incompatibility /ɪnkəmpætɪˈbɪlətɪ/ *n* incompatibilità *f*

incompatible /ɪnkəmˈpætəbl/ *a* incompatibile

incompetence /ɪnˈkɒmpɪtəns/ *n* incompetenza *f*

incompetent /ɪnˈkɒmpɪtənt/ *a* incompetente

incomplete /ɪnkəmˈpliːt/ *a* incompleto

incomprehensible /ɪnkɒmprɪˈhensəbl/ *a* incomprensibile

inconceivable /ɪnkənˈsiːvəbl/ *a* inconcepibile

inconclusive /ɪnkənˈkluːsɪv/ *a* inconcludente

incongruity /ɪnkɒŋˈgruːətɪ/ *n* (*of appearance*) contrasto *m*; (*of situation*) assurdità *f inv*

incongruous /ɪnˈkɒŋgrʊəs/ *a* contrastante

inconsequential /ɪnkɒnsɪˈkwenʃl/ *a* senza importanza

inconsiderate /ɪnkənˈsɪdərət/ *a* trascurabile

inconsistency /ɪnkənˈsɪstənsɪ/ *n* incoerenza *f*

inconsistent /ɪnkənˈsɪstənt/ *a* incoerente; **be ~ with** non essere coerente con

inconsistently /ɪnkənˈsɪstəntlɪ/ *adv* in modo incoerente

inconsolable /ɪnkənˈsəʊləbl/ *a* inconsolabile

inconspicuous /ɪnkənˈspɪkjʊəs/ *a* non appariscente

inconspicuously /ɪnkənˈspɪkjʊəslɪ/ *adv* modestamente

inconstancy /ɪnˈkɒnstənsɪ/ *n* incostanza *f*

inconstant /ɪnˈkɒnstənt/ *a* (*conditions*) variabile; (*lover*) volubile

incontestable /ɪnkənˈtestəbl/ *a* incontestabile

incontinence /ɪnˈkɒntɪnəns/ *n* incontinenza *f*

incontinent /ɪnˈkɒntɪnənt/ *a* incontinente

inconvenience /ɪnkənˈviːnɪəns/ *n* scomodità *f*; (*drawback*) inconveniente *m*; **put sb to ~** dare disturbo a qcno

inconvenient /ɪnkənˈviːnɪənt/ *a* scomodo; (*time, place*) inopportuno

inconveniently /ɪnkənˈviːnɪəntlɪ/ *adv* in modo inopportuno

incorporate /ɪnˈkɔːpəreɪt/ *vt* incorporare; (*contain*) comprendere

incorrect /ɪnkəˈrekt/ *a* incorretto

incorrectly /ɪnkəˈrektlɪ/ *adv* scorrettamente

incorrigible /ɪnˈkɒrɪdʒəbl/ *a* incorreggibile

incorruptible /ɪnkəˈrʌptəbl/ *a* incorruttibile

increase¹ /ˈɪnkriːs/ *n* aumento *m*; **on the ~** in aumento

increase² /ɪnˈkriːs/ *vt/i* aumentare

increasing /ɪnˈkriːsɪŋ/ *a* (*impatience etc*) crescente; (*numbers*) in aumento

increasingly /ɪnˈkriːsɪŋlɪ/ *adv* sempre più

incredible /ɪnˈkredəbl/ *a* incredibile

incredibly /ɪnˈkredəblɪ/ *adv* incredibilmente

incredulity /ɪnkrəˈdjuːlətɪ/ *n* incredulità *f*

incredulous /ɪnˈkredjʊləs/ *a* incredulo

increment /ˈɪnkrɪmənt/ *n* incremento *m*

incremental /ɪnkrɪˈmentəl/ *a* *Comput, Math* incrementale; (*effect, measures*) progressivo

incriminate /ɪnˈkrɪmɪneɪt/ *vt Jur* incriminare

in-crowd *n* **be in with the ~** frequentare gente alla moda

incubate /ˈɪnkjʊbeɪt/ *vt* incubare

incubation /ɪnkjʊˈbeɪʃn/ *n* incubazione *f*

incubation period *n Med* periodo *m* di incubazione

incubator /ˈɪnkjʊbeɪtə(r)/ *n* (*for baby*) incubatrice *f*

inculcate /ˈɪnkʌlkeɪt/ *vt* inculcare

incumbent /ɪnˈkʌmbənt/ *a* **be ~ on sb** incombere a qcno

incur /ɪnˈkɜː(r)/ *vt* (*pt/pp* **incurred**) incorrere; contrarre (*debts*)

incurable /ɪnˈkjʊərəbl/ *a* incurabile

incurably /ɪnˈkjʊərəblɪ/ *adv* incurabilmente

incursion /ɪnˈkɜːʃn/ *n* incursione *f*

indebted /ɪnˈdetɪd/ *a* obbligato (**to** verso)

indecency /ɪnˈdiːsənsɪ/ *n* oscenità *f*; (*offence*) atti *mpl* osceni; **gross ~** atti *mpl* osceni

indecent /ɪnˈdiːsənt/ *a* indecente

indecent assault *n* atti *mpl* di libidine violenta

indecent exposure *n* esibizionismo *m* (*dei genitali*)

indecipherable /ɪndɪˈsaɪfərəbl/ *a* indecifrabile

indecision /ɪndɪˈsɪʒn/ *n* indecisione *f*

indecisive /ɪndɪˈsaɪsɪv/ *a* indeciso

indecisiveness /ɪndɪˈsaɪsɪvnɪs/ *n* indecisione *f*

indeed /ɪnˈdiːd/ *adv* (*in fact*) difatti; **yes ~!** sì, certamente!; **~ I am/do** veramente!; **very much ~** moltissimo; **thank you very much ~** grazie infinite; **~?** davvero?

indefatigable /ɪndɪˈfætɪgəbl/ *a* instancabile

indefensible /ɪndɪˈfensəbl/ *a Mil* indifendibile; (*morally*) ingiustificabile; (*logically*) insostenibile

indefinable /ɪndɪˈfaɪnəbl/ *a* indefinibile

indefinite /ɪnˈdefɪnɪt/ *a* indefinito

indefinitely /ɪnˈdefɪnɪtlɪ/ *adv* indefinitamente; (*postpone*) a tempo indeterminato

indelible /ɪnˈdeləbl/ *a* indelebile

indelibly /ɪnˈdeləblɪ/ *adv* in modo indelebile

indelicacy /ɪnˈdelɪkəsɪ/ *n* (*tactlessness*) mancanza *f* di tatto; (*coarseness*) rozzezza *f*

indelicate /ɪnˈdelɪkət/ *a* (*tactless*) privo di tatto; (*coarse*) rozzo

indemnity /ɪnˈdemnətɪ/ *n* indennità *f inv*

indent¹ /ˈɪndent/ *n Typ* rientranza *f* dal margine

indent² /ɪn'dent/ vt Typ fare rientrare dal margine

indentation /ɪnden'teɪʃn/ n (notch) intaccatura f

independence /ɪndɪ'pendəns/ n indipendenza f

Independence Day n Am = anniversario m dell'Indipendenza degli USA (4 luglio)

independent /ɪndɪ'pendənt/ a indipendente

independently /ɪndɪ'pendəntlɪ/ adv indipendentemente

in-depth a ⟨analysis, study, knowledge⟩ approfondito

indescribable /ɪndɪ'skraɪbəbl/ a indescrivibile

indescribably /ɪndɪ'skraɪbəblɪ/ adv indescrivibilmente

indestructible /ɪndɪ'strʌktəbl/ a indistruttibile

indeterminate /ɪndɪ'tɜ:mɪnət/ a indeterminato

index /'ɪndeks/ n indice m

indexation /ɪndek'seɪʃn/ n indicizzazione f

index: index card n scheda f. **index finger** n dito m indice. **index-linked** a ⟨pension⟩ legato al costo della vita

India /'ɪndɪə/ n India f

Indian /'ɪndɪən/ a indiano; (American) indiano [d'America] ● n indiano, -a mf; (American) indiano [d'America], pellerossa mf inv

Indian: Indian elephant n elefante m indiano. **Indian ink** n inchiostro m di China. **Indian Ocean** n oceano m Indiano. **Indian summer** n estate f di San Martino

indicate /'ɪndɪkeɪt/ vt indicare; (register) segnare ● vi Auto mettere la freccia; ~ **left** mettere la freccia a sinistra

indication /ɪndɪ'keɪʃn/ n indicazione f

indicative /ɪn'dɪkətɪv/ a **be ~ of** essere indicativo di ● n Gram indicativo m

indicator /'ɪndɪkeɪtə(r)/ n Auto freccia f

indict /ɪn'daɪt/ vt accusare

indictment /ɪn'daɪtmənt/ n Jur imputazione f

indie /'ɪndɪ/ a fam Cinema, Mus indipendente; ● n (band) complesso m musicale legato a un'etichetta indipendente; (film) film m prodotto da una casa di produzione indipendente

indifference /ɪn'dɪf(ə)rəns/ n indifferenza f

indifferent /ɪn'dɪf(ə)rənt/ a indifferente; (not good) mediocre

indifferently /ɪn'dɪf(ə)rəntlɪ/ adv in modo indifferente; (not well) in modo mediocre

indigenous /ɪn'dɪdʒɪnəs/ a indigeno

indigestible /ɪndɪ'dʒestəbl/ a indigesto

indigestion /ɪndɪ'dʒestʃn/ n indigestione f

indignant /ɪn'dɪgnənt/ a indignato

indignantly /ɪn'dɪgnəntlɪ/ adv con indignazione

indignation /ɪndɪg'neɪʃn/ n indignazione f

indignity /ɪn'dɪgnətɪ/ n umiliazione f

indigo /'ɪndɪgəʊ/ n indaco m

indirect /ɪndaɪ'rekt/ a indiretto

indirectly /ɪndaɪ'rektlɪ/ adv indirettamente

indiscernible /ɪndɪ'sɜ:nəbl/ a indistinguibile

indiscreet /ɪndɪ'skri:t/ a indiscreto

indiscretion /ɪndɪ'skreʃn/ n indiscrezione f

indiscriminate /ɪndɪ'skrɪmɪnət/ a indiscriminato

indiscriminately /ɪndɪ'skrɪmɪnətlɪ/ adv senza distinzione

indispensable /ɪndɪ'spensəbl/ a indispensabile

indisposed /ɪndɪ'spəʊzd/ a indisposto

indisputable /ɪndɪ'spju:təbl/ a indisputabile

indisputably /ɪndɪ'spju:təblɪ/ adv indisputabilmente

indistinct /ɪndɪ'stɪŋkt/ a indistinto

indistinctly /ɪndɪ'stɪŋktlɪ/ adv indistintamente

indistinguishable /ɪndɪ'stɪŋgwɪʃəbl/ a indistinguibile

individual /ɪndɪ'vɪdjʊəl/ a individuale ● n individuo m

individualist /ɪndɪ'vɪdjʊəlɪst/ n individualista mf

individualistic /ɪndɪvɪdjʊə'lɪstɪk/ a individualistico

individuality /ɪndɪvɪdjʊ'ælətɪ/ n individualità f

individually /ɪndɪ'vɪdjʊəlɪ/ adv individualmente

indivisible /ɪndɪ'vɪzəbl/ a indivisibile

Indochina /ɪndəʊ'tʃaɪnə/ n Indocina f

indoctrinate /ɪn'dɒktrɪneɪt/ vt indottrinare

Indo-European /ɪndəʊ-jʊərə'pɪən/ a indoeuropeo

indolence /'ɪndələns/ n indolenza

indolent /'ɪndələnt/ a indolente

indomitable /ɪn'dɒmɪtəbl/ a indomito

Indonesia /ɪndə'ni:zjə/ n Indonesia f

Indonesian /ɪndə'ni:zjən/ a & n (person) indonesiano, -a mf; (language) indonesiano m

indoor /'ɪndɔ:(r)/ a interno; (shoes) per casa; (plant) da appartamento; (swimming pool etc) coperto

indoors /ɪn'dɔ:z/ adv dentro; **go ~** andare dentro

indubitable /ɪn'dju:bɪtəbl/ a indubitabile

indubitably /ɪn'dju:bɪtəblɪ/ adv indubitabilmente

induce /ɪn'dju:s/ vt indurre (**to** a); (produce) causare

inducement /ɪn'dju:smənt/ n (incentive) incentivo m

induction /ɪn'dʌkʃn/ n (inauguration) introduzione f; (of labour) parto m indotto; Electr induzione f

induction ceremony n cerimonia f inaugurale

induction course n corso m introduttivo

indulge /ɪn'dʌldʒ/ vt soddisfare; viziare (child) ● vi ~ **in** concedersi

indulgence /ɪn'dʌldʒəns/ n lusso m; (leniency) indulgenza f

indulgent /ɪn'dʌldʒənt/ a indulgente

industrial /ɪn'dʌstrɪəl/ a industriale; **take ~ action** scioperare

industrial: industrial accident n infortunio m sul lavoro. **industrial dispute** n vertenza f sindacale. **industrial espionage** n spionaggio m industriale. **industrial estate** n zona f industriale. **industrial tribunal** n tribunale m del lavoro

industrialist /ɪn'dʌstrɪəlɪst/ n industriale mf

industrialized /ɪn'dʌstrɪəlaɪzd/ a industrializzato

industrial tribunal n tribunale m competente per i conflitti di lavoro

industrial waste n rifiuti mpl industriali

industrious /ɪn'dʌstrɪəs/ a industrioso

industriously /ɪn'dʌstrɪəslɪ/ adv in modo industrioso

industry /'ɪndəstrɪ/ n industria f; (zeal) operosità f

inebriated /ɪ'niːbrɪeɪtɪd/ a ebbro

inedible /ɪn'edəbl/ a immangiabile

ineffective /ɪnɪ'fektɪv/ a inefficace

ineffectively /ɪnɪ'fektɪvlɪ/ adv inutilmente, invano

ineffectual /ɪnɪ'fektʃʊəl/ a inutile; (person) inconcludente

inefficiency /ɪnɪ'fɪʃənsɪ/ n inefficienza f

inefficient /ɪnɪ'fɪʃnt/ a inefficiente

ineligible /ɪn'elɪdʒəbl/ a inadatto

inept /ɪ'nept/ a inetto

ineptitude /ɪ'neptɪtjuːd/ n inettitudine f

inequality /ɪnɪ'kwɒlətɪ/ n ineguaglianza f

inert /ɪ'nɜːt/ a inerte

inertia /ɪ'nɜːʃə/ n inerzia f

inescapable /ɪnɪ'skeɪpəbl/ a inevitabile

inestimable /ɪn'estɪməbl/ a inestimabile

inevitable /ɪn'evɪtəbl/ a inevitabile

inevitably /ɪn'evɪtəblɪ/ adv inevitabilmente

inexact /ɪnɪg'zækt/ a inesatto

inexcusable /ɪnɪk'skjuːzəbl/ a imperdonabile

inexhaustible /ɪnɪg'zɔːstəbl/ a inesauribile

inexorable /ɪn'eksərəbl/ a inesorabile

inexorably /ɪn'egzərəblɪ/ adv inesorabilmente

inexpensive /ɪnɪk'spensɪv/ a poco costoso

inexpensively /ɪnɪk'spensɪvlɪ/ adv a buon mercato

inexperience /ɪnɪk'spɪərɪəns/ n inesperienza f

inexperienced /ɪnɪk'spɪərɪənst/ a inesperto

inexplicable /ɪnɪk'splɪkəbl/ a inesplicabile

inexplicably /ɪnɪk'splɪkəblɪ/ adv inesplicabilmente, inspiegabilmente

inextricable /ɪnɪk'strɪkəbl/ a inestricabile

inextricably /ɪnɪk'strɪkəblɪ/ adv inestricabilmente

infallibility /ɪnfælɪr'bɪlətɪ/ n infallibilità f

infallible /ɪn'fæləbl/ a infallibile

infamous /'ɪnfəməs/ a infame; (person) famigerato

infamy /'ɪnfəmɪ/ n infamia f

infancy /'ɪnfənsɪ/ n infanzia f; **in its ~** fig agli inizi

infant /'ɪnfənt/ n bambino, -a mf piccolo, -a

infanticide /ɪn'fæntɪsaɪd/ n infanticidio m

infantile /'ɪnfəntaɪl/ a infantile

infantry /'ɪnfəntrɪ/ n fanteria f

infant school n scuola f elementare per bambini dai 5 ai 7 anni

infatuated /ɪn'fætʃʊeɪtɪd/ a infatuato (**with** di)

infatuation /ɪnfætʃʊ'eɪʃn/ n infatuazione f

infect /ɪn'fekt/ vt infettare; **become ~ed** (wound:) infettarsi

infection /ɪn'fekʃn/ n infezione f

infectious /ɪn'fekʃəs/ a infettivo

infer /ɪn'fɜː(r)/ vt (pt/pp **inferred**) dedurre (**from** da); (imply) implicare

inference /'ɪnfərəns/ n deduzione f

inferior /ɪn'fɪərɪə(r)/ a inferiore; (goods) scadente; (in rank) subalterno ● n inferiore mf; (in rank) subalterno, -a mf

inferiority /ɪnfɪərɪ'ɒrətɪ/ n inferiorità f

inferiority complex n complesso m di inferiorità

infernal /ɪn'fɜːnl/ a infernale

inferno /ɪn'fɜːnəʊ/ n inferno m

infertile /ɪn'fɜːtaɪl/ a sterile

infertility /ɪnfə'tɪlətɪ/ n sterilità f

infest /ɪn'fest/ vt **be ~ed with** essere infestato di

infestation /ɪnfe'steɪʃn/ n infestazione f

infidelity /ɪnfɪ'delətɪ/ n infedeltà f inv

infighting /'ɪnfaɪtɪŋ/ n fig lotta f per il potere

infiltrate /'ɪnfɪltreɪt/ vt infiltrare; Pol infiltrarsi in

infiltration /ɪnfɪl'treɪʃn/ n infiltrazione f

infinite /'ɪnfɪnɪt/ a infinito

infinitely /'ɪnfɪnɪtlɪ/ adv infinitamente

infinitesimal /ɪnfɪnɪ'tesɪml/ a infinitesimo

infinitive /ɪn'fɪnətɪv/ n Gram infinito m

infinity /ɪn'fɪnətɪ/ n infinità f

infirm /ɪn'fɜːm/ a debole

infirmary /ɪn'fɜːm(ə)rɪ/ n infermeria f

infirmity /ɪn'fɜːmətɪ/ n debolezza f

in flagrante delicto /ɪnfləgræntɪdɪ'lɪktəʊ/ adv in flagrante

inflame /ɪn'fleɪm/ vt infiammare

inflamed /ɪn'fleɪmd/ a infiammato; **become ~** infiammarsi

inflammable /ɪn'flæməbl/ a infiammabile

inflammation /ɪnflə'meɪʃn/ n infiammazione f

inflammatory /ɪn'flæmətrɪ/ a incendiario

inflatable /ɪn'fleɪtəbl/ a gonfiabile

inflate /ɪn'fleɪt/ vt gonfiare

inflated /ɪn'fleɪtɪd/ a (price, fee, claim) eccessivo; (style) ampolloso; (tyre) gonfio; **an ~ ego** un'alta opinione di sé

inflation /ɪn'fleɪʃn/ n inflazione f

inflationary /ɪn'fleɪʃənərɪ/ a inflazionario

inflect /ɪn'flekt/ vt flettere (noun, adjective); modulare (voice)

inflected /ɪn'flektɪd/ a (language) flessivo; (form) flesso

inflection /ɪnˈflekʃn/ *n* (*of voice*) modulazione *f*

inflexible /ɪnˈfleksəbl/ *a* inflessibile

inflexion /ɪnˈflekʃn/ *n* inflessione *f*

inflict /ɪnˈflɪkt/ *vt* infliggere (**on** a)

in-flight *a* a bordo

influence /ˈɪnflʊəns/ *n* influenza *f*; **use one's ~** esercitare la propria influenza ● *vt* influenzare

influential /ɪnflʊˈenʃl/ *a* influente

influenza /ɪnflʊˈenzə/ *n* influenza *f*

influx /ˈɪnflʌks/ *n* affluenza *f*

info /ˈɪnfəʊ/ *n fam* informazione *f*

inform /ɪnˈfɔːm/ *vt* informare; **keep sb ~ed** tenere qcno al corrente ● *vi* **~ against** denunziare

informal /ɪnˈfɔːməl/ *a* informale; (*agreement*) ufficioso

informality /ɪnfəˈmælətɪ/ *n* informalità *f inv*

informally /ɪnˈfɔːməlɪ/ *adv* in modo informale

informant /ɪnˈfɔːmənt/ *n* informatore, -trice *mf*

information /ɪnfəˈmeɪʃn/ *n* informazioni *fpl*; **a piece of ~** un'informazione

information: information desk *n* banco *m* informazioni. **information highway** *n* autostrada *f* telematica. **information officer** *n* addetto, -a *mf* stampa. **information processing** *n* elaborazione *f* dati. **information system** *n* sistema *m* informativo. **information technology** *n* informatica *f*

informative /ɪnˈfɔːmətɪv/ *a* informativo; (*film, book*) istruttivo

informer /ɪnˈfɔːmə(r)/ *n* informatore, -trice *mf*; *Pol* delatore, -trice *mf*

infra-red /ɪnfrəˈred/ *a* infrarosso

infrastructure /ˈɪnfrəstrʌktʃə(r)/ *n* infrastruttura *f*

infrequent /ɪnˈfriːkwənt/ *a* infrequente

infrequently /ɪnˈfriːkwəntlɪ/ *adv* raramente

infringe /ɪnˈfrɪndʒ/ *vt* **~ on** usurpare

infringement /ɪnˈfrɪndʒmənt/ *n* violazione *f*

infuriate /ɪnˈfjʊərɪeɪt/ *vt* infuriare

infuriating /ɪnˈfjʊərɪeɪtɪŋ/ *a* esasperante

infuse /ɪnˈfjuːz/ *vi* (*tea:*) restare in infusione

infusion /ɪnˈfjuːʒn/ *n* (*drink*) infusione *f*; (*of capital, new blood*) afflusso *m*

ingenious /ɪnˈdʒiːnɪəs/ *a* ingegnoso

ingenuity /ɪndʒɪˈnjuːətɪ/ *n* ingegnosità *f*

ingenuous /ɪnˈdʒenjʊəs/ *a* ingenuo

ingest /ɪnˈdʒest/ *vt* ingerire (*food*); assimilare (*fact*)

ingot /ˈɪŋgət/ *n* lingotto *m*

ingrained /ɪnˈgreɪnd/ *a* (*in person*) radicato; (*dirt*) incrostato

ingratiate /ɪnˈgreɪʃɪeɪt/ *vt* **~ oneself with sb** ingraziarsi qcno

ingratitude /ɪnˈgrætɪtjuːd/ *n* ingratitudine *f*

ingredient /ɪnˈgriːdɪənt/ *n* ingrediente *m*

ingrowing /ˈɪngrəʊɪŋ/ *a* (*nail*) incarnito

inhabit /ɪnˈhæbɪt/ *vt* abitare

inhabitable /ɪnˈhæbɪtəbl/ *a* abitabile

inhabitant /ɪnˈhæbɪtənt/ *n* abitante *mf*

inhale /ɪnˈheɪl/ *vt* aspirare; *Med* inalare ● *vi* inspirare; (*when smoking*) aspirare

inhaler /ɪnˈheɪlə(r)/ *n* (*device*) inalatore *m*

inherent /ɪnˈhɪərənt/ *a* inerente

inherit /ɪnˈherɪt/ *vt* ereditare

inheritance /ɪnˈherɪtəns/ *n* eredità *f inv*

inhibit /ɪnˈhɪbɪt/ *vt* inibire

inhibited /ɪnˈhɪbɪtɪd/ *a* inibito

inhibition /ɪnhɪˈbɪʃn/ *n* inibizione *f*

inhospitable /ɪnhɒˈspɪtəbl/ *a* inospitale

in-house *a* (*training*) interno all'azienda; (*magazine*) aziendale

inhuman /ɪnˈhjuːmən/ *a* disumano

inimitable /ɪˈnɪmɪtəbl/ *a* inimitabile

iniquitous /ɪˈnɪkwɪtəs/ *a* iniquo

initial /ɪˈnɪʃl/ *a* iniziale ● *n* iniziale *f* ● *vt* (*pt/pp* **initialled**) siglare

initially /ɪˈnɪʃəlɪ/ *adv* all'inizio

initiate /ɪˈnɪʃɪeɪt/ *vt* iniziare

initiation /ɪnɪʃɪˈeɪʃn/ *n* iniziazione *f*

initiative /ɪˈnɪʃətɪv/ *n* iniziativa *f*; **take the ~** prendere l'iniziativa

inject /ɪnˈdʒekt/ *vt* iniettare

injection /ɪnˈdʒekʃn/ *n* iniezione *f*

in-joke *n* **it's an ~** è una battuta tra di noi/loro

injunction /ɪnˈdʒʌŋkʃn/ *n* ingiunzione *f*

injure /ˈɪndʒə(r)/ *vt* ferire; (*wrong*) nuocere; **the ~d party** la parte lesa

injury /ˈɪndʒərɪ/ *n* ferita *f*; (*wrong*) torto *m*

injury time *n Sport* recupero *m*

injustice /ɪnˈdʒʌstɪs/ *n* ingiustizia *f*; **do sb an ~** giudicare qcno in modo sbagliato

ink /ɪŋk/ *n* inchiostro *m*

ink-jet printer *n* stampante *f* a getto d'inchiostro

inkling /ˈɪŋklɪŋ/ *n* sentore *m*

inky /ˈɪŋkɪ/ *a* macchiato d'inchiostro

inlaid /ɪnˈleɪd/ *a* intarsiato

inland /ˈɪnlənd/ *a* interno ● *adv* all'interno

Inland Revenue *n* fisco *m*

in-laws /ˈɪnlɔːz/ *npl fam* parenti *mpl* acquisiti

inlay /ˈɪnleɪ/ *n* intarsio *m*

inlet /ˈɪnlet/ *n* insenatura *f*; *Techn* entrata *f*

inmate /ˈɪnmeɪt/ *n* (*of hospital*) degente *mf*; (*of prison*) carcerato, -a *mf*

inn /ɪn/ *n* locanda *f*

innards /ˈɪnədz/ *npl fam* frattaglie *fpl*

innate /ɪˈneɪt/ *a* innato

inner /ˈɪnə(r)/ *a* interno

inner city *n* quartieri *mpl* nel centro di una città caratterizzati da problemi sociali ● *attrib* (*problems*) dell'area urbana con problemi sociali

inner ear *n* orecchio *m* interno

innermost /ˈɪnəməʊst/ *a* il più profondo

inner tube *n* camera *f* d'aria

innings /ˈɪnɪŋz/ *nsg* (*in cricket*) turno *m* di battuta; **have had a good ~** (*Br fig: when leaving job etc*) aver avuto una carriera lunga e gratificante; (*when dead*) aver avuto una vita lunga e piena di soddisfazioni

innkeeper /'ɪnki:pə(r)/ *n* locandiere, -a *mf*

innocence /'ɪnəsəns/ *n* innocenza *f*

innocent /'ɪnəsənt/ *a* innocente

innocently /'ɪnəsəntlɪ/ *adv* innocentemente

innocuous /ɪ'nɒkjʊəs/ *a* innocuo

innovate /'ɪnəveɪt/ *vi* innovare

innovation /ɪnə'veɪʃn/ *n* innovazione *f*

innovative /'ɪnəvətɪv/ *a* innovativo

innovator /'ɪnəveɪtə(r)/ *n* innovatore, -trice *mf*

innuendo /ɪnjʊ'endəʊ/ *n* (*pl* **-es**) insinuazione *f*

innumerable /ɪ'nju:mərəbl/ *a* innumerevole

inoculate /ɪ'nɒkjʊleɪt/ *vt* vaccinare

inoculation /ɪnɒkjʊ'leɪʃn/ *n* vaccinazione *f*

inoffensive /ɪnə'fensɪv/ *a* inoffensivo

inoperable /ɪn'ɒpərəbl/ *a* inoperabile

inopportune /ɪn'ɒpətju:n/ *a* inopportuno

inordinate /ɪ'nɔ:dɪnət/ *a* smodato

inordinately /ɪ'nɔ:dɪnətlɪ/ *adv* smodatamente

inorganic /ɪnɔ:'gænɪk/ *a* inorganico

in-patient *n* degente *mf*

input /'ɪnpʊt/ *n* input *m inv*, ingresso *m*

inquest /'ɪnkwest/ *n* inchiesta *f*

inquire /ɪn'kwaɪə(r)/ *vi* informarsi (**about** su); ~ **into** far indagini su ● *vt* domandare

inquiring /ɪn'kwaɪərɪŋ/ *a* ⟨*mind*⟩ curioso; ⟨*look, voice*⟩ interrogativo

inquiry /ɪn'kwaɪərɪ/ *n* domanda *f*; (*investigation*) inchiesta *f*

inquisitive /ɪn'kwɪzətɪv/ *a* curioso

inquisitively /ɪn'kwɪzɪtɪvlɪ/ *adv* con molta curiosità

inroad /'ɪnrəʊd/ *n* **make ~s into** intaccare ⟨*savings*⟩; cominciare a risolvere ⟨*problem*⟩

insalubrious /ɪnsə'lu:brɪəs/ *a* (*dirty*) insalubre; (*sleazy*) sordido

insane /ɪn'seɪn/ *a* pazzo; *fig* insensato

insanitary /ɪn'sænɪt(ə)rɪ/ *a* malsano

insanity /ɪn'sænətɪ/ *n* pazzia *f*

insatiable /ɪn'seɪʃəbl/ *a* insaziabile

inscribe /ɪn'skraɪb/ *vt* iscrivere

inscription /ɪn'skrɪpʃn/ *n* iscrizione *f*

inscrutable /ɪn'skru:təbl/ *a* impenetrabile

insect /'ɪnsekt/ *n* insetto *m*

insecticide /ɪn'sektɪsaɪd/ *n* insetticida *m*

insect repellent *n* insettifugo *m*

insecure /ɪnsɪ'kjʊə(r)/ *a* malsicuro; ⟨*fig: person*⟩ insicuro

insecurity /ɪnsɪ'kjʊərətɪ/ *n* mancanza *f* di sicurezza

insemination /ɪnsemɪ'neɪʃn/ *n* inseminazione *f*

insensitive /ɪn'sensɪtɪv/ *a* insensibile

inseparable /ɪn'sep(ə)rəbl/ *a* inseparabile

insert[1] /'ɪnsз:t/ *n* inserto *m*

insert[2] /ɪn'sз:t/ *vt* inserire

insertion /ɪn'sз:ʃn/ *n* inserzione *f*

inset /'ɪnset/ *n* (*map, photo*) dettaglio *m* ● *a* ~ **with** ⟨*necklace*⟩ incastonato di; ⟨*table*⟩ intarsiato di

inshore /ɪn'ʃɔ:(r)/ *a* ⟨*current*⟩ diretta a riva;

⟨*fishing, waters, current*⟩ costiero; ⟨*wind*⟩ dal mare ● *adv* ⟨*fish*⟩ sotto costa

inside /ɪn'saɪd/ *n* interno *m*; ~**s** *pl fam* pancia *f* ● *adv* dentro; ~ **out** a rovescio; (*thoroughly*) a fondo ● *prep* dentro; (*of time*) entro

inside lane *n* Auto corsia *f* interna

inside leg *n* interno *m* della gamba

insider /ɪn'saɪdə(r)/ *n* persona *f* all'interno

insider dealer, insider trader *n* Fin persona *f* che pratica l'insider trading

insider dealing, insider trading /'di:lɪŋ, 'treɪdɪŋ/ *n* Fin insider trading *m*

insidious /ɪn'sɪdɪəs/ *a* insidioso

insidiously /ɪn'sɪdɪəslɪ/ *adv* insidiosamente

insight /'ɪnsaɪt/ *n* intuito *m* (**into** per); **an ~ into** un quadro di

insignia /ɪn'sɪgnɪə/ *npl* insegne *fpl*

insignificant /ɪnsɪg'nɪfɪkənt/ *a* insignificante

insincere /ɪnsɪn'sɪə(r)/ *a* poco sincero

insincerity /ɪnsɪn'serətɪ/ *n* mancanza *f* di sincerità

insinuate /ɪn'sɪnjʊeɪt/ *vt* insinuare

insinuation /ɪnsɪnjʊ'eɪʃn/ *n* insinuazione *f*

insipid /ɪn'sɪpɪd/ *a* insipido

insist /ɪn'sɪst/ *vi* insistere (**on** per) ● *vt* ~ **that** insistere che

insistence /ɪn'sɪstəns/ *n* insistenza *f*

insistent /ɪn'sɪstənt/ *a* insistente

insistently /ɪn'sɪstəntlɪ/ *adv* insistentemente

insofar /ɪnsə'fɑ:(r)/ *conj* ~ **as** (*to the extent that*) nella misura in cui; (*seeing that*) in quanto; ~ **as I know** per quanto ne sappia

insole /'ɪnsəʊl/ *n* soletta *f*

insolence /'ɪnsələns/ *n* insolenza *f*

insolent /'ɪnsələnt/ *a* insolente

insolently /'ɪnsələntlɪ/ *adv* con insolenza

insoluble /ɪn'sɒljʊbl/ *a* insolubile

insolvency /ɪn'sɒlvənsɪ/ *n* insolvenza *f*

insolvent /ɪn'sɒlvənt/ *a* insolvente

insomnia /ɪn'sɒmnɪə/ *n* insonnia *f*

insomniac /ɪn'sɒmɪæk/ *n* persona *f* che soffre di insonnia

insomuch /ɪnsə'mʌtʃ/ *conj* ~ **as** (*to the extent that*) nella misura in cui; (*seeing that*) in quanto

inspect /ɪn'spekt/ *vt* ispezionare; controllare ⟨*ticket*⟩

inspection /ɪn'spekʃn/ *n* ispezione *f*; (*of ticket*) controllo *m*

inspector /ɪn'spektə(r)/ *n* ispettore, -trice *mf*; (*of tickets*) controllore *m*

inspiration /ɪnspə'reɪʃn/ *n* ispirazione *f*

inspire /ɪn'spaɪə(r)/ *vt* ispirare

inspired /ɪn'spaɪəd/ *a* ⟨*person, performance*⟩ ispirato; ⟨*idea*⟩ luminosa

instability /ɪnstə'bɪlətɪ/ *n* instabilità *f*

install /ɪn'stɔ:l/ *vt* installare; insediare ⟨*person*⟩

installation /ɪnstə'leɪʃn/ *n* installazione *f*

instalment /ɪn'stɔ:lmənt/ *n* Comm rata *f*; (*of serial*) puntata *f*; (*of publication*) fascicolo *m*

instance /'ɪnstəns/ *n* (*case*) caso *m*;

(*example*) esempio *m*; **in the first ~** in primo luogo; **for ~** per esempio

instant /'ɪnstənt/ *a* immediato; *Culin* espresso ● *n* istante *m*

instantaneous /ɪnstən'teɪnɪəs/ *a* istantaneo

instant coffee *n* caffè *m inv* solubile

instantly /'ɪnstəntlɪ/ *adv* immediatamente

instant replay *n Sport* replay *m inv*

instead /ɪn'sted/ *adv* invece; **~ of doing** anziché fare; **~ of me** al mio posto; **~ of going** invece di andare

instep /'ɪnstep/ *n* collo *m* del piede

instigate /'ɪnstɪgeɪt/ *vt* istigare

instigation /ɪnstɪ'geɪʃn/ *n* istigazione *f*; **at his ~** dietro suo suggerimento

instigator /'ɪnstɪgeɪtə(r)/ *n* istigatore, -trice *mf*

instil /ɪn'stɪl/ *vt* (*pt/pp* **instilled**) inculcare (**into** in)

instinct /'ɪnstɪŋkt/ *n* istinto *m*

instinctive /ɪn'stɪŋktɪv/ *a* istintivo

instinctively /ɪn'stɪŋktɪvlɪ/ *adv* istintivamente

institute /'ɪnstɪtjuːt/ *n* istituto *m* ● *vt* istituire ⟨*scheme*⟩; iniziare ⟨*search*⟩; intentare ⟨*legal action*⟩

institution /ɪnstɪ'tjuːʃn/ *n* istituzione *f*; (*home for elderly*) istituto *m* per anziani; (*for mentally ill*) istituto *m* per malati di mente

institutionalize /ɪnstɪ'tjuːʃənəlaɪz/ *vt* istituzionalizzare

institutionalized /ɪnstɪ'tjuːʃənəlaɪzd/ *a* ⟨*racism, violence*⟩ istituzionalizzato; **become ~** (*officially established*) essere istituzionalizzato; **be ~d** ⟨*person:*⟩ non essere autonomo a causa di un lungo soggiorno in ospedale psichiatrico

instruct /ɪn'strʌkt/ *vt* istruire; (*order*) ordinare

instruction /ɪn'strʌkʃn/ *n* istruzione *f*; **~s** *pl* (*orders*) ordini *mpl*

instructive /ɪn'strʌktɪv/ *a* istruttivo

instructor /ɪn'strʌktə(r)/ *n* istruttore, -trice *mf*

instrument /'ɪnstrʊmənt/ *n* strumento *m*

instrumental /ɪnstrʊ'ment(ə)l/ *a* strumentale; **be ~ in** contribuire a

instrumentalist /ɪnstrʊ'mentəlɪst/ *n* strumentista *mf*

insubordinate /ɪnsə'bɔːdɪnət/ *a* insubordinato

insubordination /ɪnsəbɔːdɪ'neɪʃn/ *n* insubordinazione *f*

insubstantial /ɪnsəb'stænʃəl/ *a* (*unreal*) irreale; ⟨*evidence*⟩ inconsistente; ⟨*flimsy, building*⟩ poco solido; ⟨*meal*⟩ poco sostanzioso

insufferable /ɪn'sʌf(ə)rəbl/ *a* insopportabile

insufficient /ɪnsə'fɪʃənt/ *a* insufficiente

insufficiently /ɪnsə'fɪʃəntlɪ/ *adv* insufficientemente

insular /'ɪnsjʊlə(r)/ *a fig* gretto

insulate /'ɪnsjʊleɪt/ *vt* isolare

insulating tape /'ɪnsjʊleɪtɪŋ/ *n* nastro *m* isolante

insulation /ɪnsjʊ'leɪʃn/ *n* isolamento *m*

insulator /'ɪnsjʊleɪtə(r)/ *n* isolante *m*

insulin /'ɪnsjʊlɪn/ *n* insulina *f*

insult¹ /'ɪnsʌlt/ *n* insulto *m*

insult² /ɪn'sʌlt/ *vt* insultare

insuperable /ɪn'suːpərəbl/ *a* insuperabile

insurable value /ɪn'ʃʊərəbl/ *n* valore *m* assicurabile

insurance /ɪn'ʃʊərəns/ *n* assicurazione *f*

insurance: insurance broker *n* broker *mf inv* d'assicurazioni. **insurance claim** *n* richiesta *f* di indennizzo (*ad assicurazione*). **insurance policy** *n* polizza *f* d'assicurazione. **insurance premium** *n* premio *m* assicurativo

insure /ɪn'ʃʊə(r)/ *vt* assicurare

insurgent /ɪn'sɜːdʒənt/ *n* rivoltoso, -a *mf*

insurmountable /ɪnsə'maʊntəbl/ *a* insormontabile

insurrection /ɪnsə'rekʃn/ *n* insurrezione *f*

intact /ɪn'tækt/ *a* intatto

intake /'ɪnteɪk/ *n* immissione *f*; (*of food*) consumo *m*

intangible /ɪn'tændʒəbl/ *a* intangibile

integral /'ɪntɪgrəl/ *a* integrale

integrate /'ɪntɪgreɪt/ *vt* integrare ● *vi* integrarsi

integration /ɪntɪ'greɪʃn/ *n* integrazione *f*

integrity /ɪn'tegrətɪ/ *n* integrità *f*

intellect /'ɪntəlekt/ *n* intelletto *m*

intellectual /ɪntə'lektjʊəl/ *a & n* intellettuale *mf*

intelligence /ɪn'telɪdʒəns/ *n* intelligenza *f*; *Mil* informazioni *fpl*

intelligent /ɪn'telɪdʒənt/ *a* intelligente

intelligently /ɪn'telɪdʒəntlɪ/ *adv* intelligentemente

intelligentsia /ɪntelɪ'dʒentsɪə/ *n* intellighenzia *f*

intelligible /ɪn'telɪdʒəbl/ *a* intelligibile

intemperate /ɪn'temp(ə)rət/ *a* ⟨*language, person*⟩ intemperante; ⟨*weather*⟩ rigido; ⟨*attack*⟩ violento

intend /ɪn'tend/ *vt* destinare; (*have in mind*) aver intenzione di; **be ~ed for** essere destinato a

intended /ɪn'tendɪd/ *a* ⟨*visit, purchase*⟩ programmato; ⟨*result*⟩ voluto, desiderato ● *n* **her ~** *hum* il suo fidanzato; **his ~** *hum* la sua fidanzata

intense /ɪn'tens/ *a* intenso; ⟨*person*⟩ dai sentimenti intensi

intensely /ɪn'tenslɪ/ *adv* intensamente; (*very*) estremamente

intensification /ɪntensɪfɪ'keɪʃn/ *n* intensificazione *f*

intensify /ɪn'tensɪfaɪ/ *v* (*pt/pp* **-ied**) ● *vt* intensificare ● *vi* intensificarsi

intensity /ɪn'tensətɪ/ *n* intensità *f*

intensive /ɪn'tensɪv/ *a* intensivo; **~ care** [**unit**] terapia *f* intensiva; (*for people in coma*) rianimazione *f*

intensive care [unit] *n* [reparto *m*] rianimazione *f*

intensively /ɪn'tensɪvlɪ/ *adv* intensivamente

intent /ɪn'tent/ *a* intento; **~ on** (*absorbed in*) preso da; **be ~ on doing sth** essere intento a fare qcsa ● *n* intenzione *f*; **to all ~s and purposes** a tutti gli effetti

intention /ɪn'tenʃn/ *n* intenzione *f*

intentional /ɪn'tenʃənəl/ *a* intenzionale

intentionally /ɪn'tenʃənəlɪ/ *adv* intenzionalmente

intently /ɪn'tentlɪ/ *adv* attentamente

inter /ɪn'tɜː(r)/ *vt* (*pt/pp* **interred**) *fml* interrare

interaction /ɪntər'ækʃn/ *n* cooperazione *f*

interactive /ɪntər'æktɪv/ *a* interattivo

interactive video *n* video *m* interattivo

interbreed /ɪntə'briːd/ *vt* ibridare ● *vi* incrociarsi

interbreeding /ɪntə'briːdɪŋ/ *n* ibridazione *f*

intercede /ɪntə'siːd/ *vi* intercedere (**on behalf of** a favore di)

intercept /ɪntə'sept/ *vt* intercettare

interchange /'ɪntətʃeɪndʒ/ *n* scambio *m*; *Auto* raccordo *m* [autostradale]

interchangeable /ɪntə'tʃeɪndʒəbl/ *a* interscambiabile

intercity /ɪntə'sɪtɪ/ *n* (*Br: train*) intercity *m inv* ● *a* intercity

intercom /'ɪntəkɒm/ *n* citofono *m*

interconnecting /ɪntəkə'nektɪŋ/ *a* ⟨*rooms*⟩ comunicante

intercontinental /ɪntəkɒntɪ'nentəl/ *a* intercontinentale

intercourse /'ɪntəkɔːs/ *n* (*sexual*) rapporti *mpl* [sessuali]

interdepartmental /ɪntədiːpɑːt'ment(ə)l/ *a Univ, Comm* interdipartimentale; *Pol* interministeriale

interdependent /ɪntədɪ'pendənt/ *a* interdipendente

interdisciplinary /ɪntədɪsɪ'plɪnərɪ/ *a* interdisciplinare

interest /'ɪntrəst/ *n* interesse *m*; **have an ~ in** *Comm* essere cointeressato in; **be of ~** essere interessante ● *vt* interessare ● *a* interessato

interest-bearing *a* fruttifero

interest-free loan *n* prestito *m* senza interessi

interesting /'ɪnt(ə)rəstɪŋ/ *a* interessante

interest rate *n* tasso *m* di interesse

interface /'ɪntəfeɪs/ *n Comput, fig* interfaccia *f* ● *vi* interfacciarsi ● *vt* interfacciare

interfere /ɪntə'fɪə(r)/ *vi* interferire; **~ with** interferire con

interference /ɪntə'fɪərəns/ *n* interferenza *f*

interim /'ɪntərɪm/ *a* temporaneo; **~ payment** acconto *m* ● *n* **in the ~** nel frattempo

interior /ɪn'tɪərɪə(r)/ *a* interiore ● *n* interno *m*

interior decorator *n* arredatore, -trice *mf*

interior designer *n* (*of colours, fabrics etc*) arredatore, -trice *mf*; (*of walls, space*) architetto *m* d'interni

interject /ɪntə'dʒekt/ *vt* intervenire

interjection /ɪntə'dʒekʃn/ *n Gram* interiezione *f*; (*remark*) intervento *m*

interlink /ɪntə'lɪŋk/ *vt* connettere; **be ~ed with** essere connesso con

interlocking /'ɪntəlɒkɪŋ/ *a* a incastro

interloper /'ɪntələupə(r)/ *n* intruso, -a *mf*

interlude /'ɪntəluːd/ *n* intervallo *m*

intermarry /ɪntə'mærɪ/ *vi* sposarsi tra parenti; ⟨*different groups:*⟩ contrarre matrimoni misti

intermediary /ɪntə'miːdɪərɪ/ *n* intermediario, -a *mf*

intermediate /ɪntə'miːdɪət/ *a* intermedio

interminable /ɪn'tɜːmɪnəbl/ *a* interminabile

intermission /ɪntə'mɪʃn/ *n* intervallo *m*

intermittent /ɪntə'mɪtənt/ *a* intermittente

intermittently /ɪntə'mɪtəntlɪ/ *adv* a intermittenza

intern /ɪn'tɜːn/ *vt* internare

internal /ɪn'tɜːnl/ *a* interno

internal combustion engine *n* motore *m* a scoppio

internally /ɪn'tɜːnəlɪ/ *adv* internamente; ⟨*deal with*⟩ all'interno

international /ɪntə'næʃ(ə)nəl/ *a* internazionale ● *n* (*game*) incontro *m* internazionale; (*player*) competitore, -trice *mf* in gare internazionali

internationally /ɪntə'næʃ(ə)nəlɪ/ *adv* internazionalmente; **it applies ~** ha validità internazionale

international: international money order *n* vaglia *m inv* postale internazionale. **International Phonetic Alphabet** *n* Alfabeto *m* Fonetico Internazionale. **international reply coupon** *n* tagliando *m* di risposta internazionale

Internet /'ɪntənet/ *n* Internet *m*

internist /ɪn'tɜːnɪst/ *n Am* internista *mf*

internment /ɪn'tɜːnmənt/ *n* internamento *m*

interplay /'ɪntəpleɪ/ *n* azione *f* reciproca

interpolate /ɪn'tɜːpəleɪt/ *vt* interpolare

interpose /ɪntə'pəuz/ *vt* (*insert*) frapporre; interrompere con ⟨*comment, remark*⟩

interpret /ɪn'tɜːprɪt/ *vt* interpretare ● *vi* fare l'interprete.

interpretation /ɪntɜːprɪ'teɪʃn/ *n* interpretazione *f*

interpreter /ɪn'tɜːprɪtə(r)/ *n* interprete *mf*

interpreting /ɪn'tɜːprɪtɪŋ/ *n* interpretariato *m*

interrelated /ɪntərɪ'leɪtɪd/ *a* ⟨*facts*⟩ in correlazione

interrogate /ɪn'terəgeɪt/ *vt* interrogare

interrogation /ɪnterə'geɪʃn/ *n* interrogazione *f*; (*by police*) interrogatorio *m*

interrogative /ɪntə'rɒgətɪv/ *a & n* **~ [pronoun]** interrogativo *m*

interrupt /ɪntə'rʌpt/ *vt/i* interrompere

interruption /ɪntə'rʌpʃn/ *n* interruzione *f*

intersect /ɪntə'sekt/ *vi* intersecarsi ● *vt* intersecare

intersection /ɪntə'sekʃn/ *n* intersezione *f*; (*of street*) incrocio *m*

interspersed /ɪntə'spɜ:st/ *a* ~ **with** inframmezzato di

interstate /'ɪntəsteɪt/ *Am n* superstrada *f* fra stati ● *a* ⟨*commerce, links*⟩ fra stati

intertwine /ɪntə'twaɪn/ *vi* attorcigliarsi

interval /'ɪntəvl/ *n* intervallo *m*; **bright ~s** *pl* schiarite *fpl*

intervene /ɪntə'vi:n/ *vi* intervenire

intervention /ɪntə'venʃn/ *n* intervento *m*

interview /'ɪntəvju:/ *n Journ* intervista *f*; (*for job*) colloquio *m* [di lavoro] ● *vt* intervistare

interviewee /ɪntəvju:'i:/ *n* (*on TV, radio, in survey*) intervistato, -a *mf*; (*for job*) persona *f* sottoposta a un colloquio di lavoro

interviewer /'ɪntəvju:ə(r)/ *n* intervistatore, -trice *mf*

interweave /ɪntə'wi:v/ *vt* intrecciare ⟨*themes, threads*⟩; mischiare ⟨*rhythms*⟩

intestinal /ɪnte'staɪnəl/ *a* intestinale

intestine /ɪn'testɪn/ *n* intestino *m*

intimacy /'ɪntɪməsɪ/ *n* intimità *f*

intimate[1] /'ɪntɪmət/ *a* intimo; **be ~ with** (*sexually*) avere relazioni intime con

intimate[2] /'ɪntɪmeɪt/ *vt* far capire; (*imply*) suggerire

intimately /'ɪntɪmətlɪ/ *adv* intimamente

intimidate /ɪn'tɪmɪdeɪt/ *vt* intimidire

intimidation /ɪntɪmɪ'deɪʃn/ *n* intimidazione *f*

into /'ɪntə/, *di fronte a una vocale* /'ɪntʊ/ *prep* dentro, in; **go ~ the house** andare dentro [casa] *o* in casa; **be ~** (*fam: like*) essere appassionato di; **I'm not ~ that** questo non mi piace; **7 ~ 21 goes 3** il 7 nel 21 ci sta 3 volte; **translate ~ French** tradurre in francese; **get ~ trouble** mettersi nei guai

intolerable /ɪn'tɒlərəbl/ *a* intollerabile

intolerance /ɪn'tɒlərəns/ *n* intolleranza *f*

intolerant /ɪn'tɒlərənt/ *a* intollerante

intonation /ɪntə'neɪʃn/ *n* intonazione *f*

intone /ɪn'təʊn/ *vt* recitare ⟨*prayer*⟩

intoxicated /ɪn'tɒksɪkeɪtɪd/ *a* inebriato

intoxication /ɪntɒksɪ'keɪʃn/ *n* ebbrezza *f*

intractable /ɪn'træktəbl/ *a* intrattabile; ⟨*problem*⟩ insolubile

intramural /ɪntrə'mjʊərəl/ *a* ⟨*studies*⟩ tenuto in sede

intransigence /ɪn'trænzɪdʒəns/ *n* intransigenza *f*

intransigent /ɪn'trænzɪdʒənt/ *a* intransigente

intransitive /ɪn'trænzɪtɪv/ *a* intransitivo

intransitively /ɪn'trænzɪtɪvlɪ/ *adv* intransitivamente

intrauterine device /ɪntrəju:təramdɪ-'vaɪs/ *n Med* spirale *f*, dispositivo *m* anticoncezionale intrauterino

intravenous /ɪntrə'vi:nəs/ *a* endovenoso

intravenous drip *n* flebo[clisi] *f inv*

intravenously /ɪntrə'vi:nəslɪ/ *adv* per via endovenosa

in-tray *n* vassoio *m* per pratiche e corrispondenza da evadere

intrepid /ɪn'trepɪd/ *a* intrepido

intricacy /'ɪntrɪkəsɪ/ *n* complessità *f*

intricate /'ɪntrɪkət/ *a* complesso

intrigue /ɪn'tri:g/ *n* intrigo *m* ● *vt* intrigare ● *vi* tramare

intriguing /ɪn'tri:gɪŋ/ *a* intrigante

intrinsic /ɪn'trɪnsɪk/ *a* intrinseco

introduce /ɪntrə'dju:s/ *vt* presentare; (*bring in, insert*) introdurre

introduction /ɪntrə'dʌkʃn/ *n* introduzione *f*; (*to person*) presentazione *f*; (*to book*) prefazione *f*

introductory /ɪntrə'dʌktərɪ/ *a* introduttivo

introspective /ɪntrə'spektɪv/ *a* introspettivo

introvert /'ɪntrəvɜ:t/ *n* introverso, -a *mf*

introverted /'ɪntrəvɜ:tɪd/ *a* introverso

intrude /ɪn'tru:d/ *vi* intromettersi

intruder /ɪn'tru:də(r)/ *n* intruso, -a *mf*

intrusion /ɪn'tru:ʒn/ *n* intrusione *f*

intuition /ɪntjʊ'ɪʃn/ *n* intuito *m*

intuitive /ɪn'tju:ɪtɪv/ *a* intuitivo

intuitively /ɪn'tju:ɪtɪvlɪ/ *adv* intuitivamente

inundate /'ɪnəndeɪt/ *vt fig* inondare (**with** di)

inure /ɪn'jʊə(r)/ *vt* **become ~d to sth** assuefarsi a qcsa

invade /ɪn'veɪd/ *vt* invadere

invader /ɪn'veɪdə(r)/ *n* invasore *m*.

invalid[1] /'ɪnvəlɪd/ *n* invalido, -a *mf*

invalid[2] /ɪn'vælɪd/ *a* non valido

invalidate /ɪn'vælɪdeɪt/ *vt* invalidare

invaluable /ɪn'væljʊ(ə)bl/ *a* prezioso; (*priceless*) inestimabile

invariable /ɪn'veərɪəbl/ *a* invariabile

invariably /ɪn'veərɪəblɪ/ *adv* invariabilmente

invasion /ɪn'veɪʒn/ *n* invasione *f*

invective /ɪn'vektɪv/ *n* invettiva *f*

invent /ɪn'vent/ *vt* inventare

invention /ɪn'venʃn/ *n* invenzione *f*

inventive /ɪn'ventɪv/ *a* inventivo

inventor /ɪn'ventə(r)/ *n* inventore, -trice *mf*

inventory /'ɪnvəntrɪ/ *n* inventario *m*

inverse /ɪn'vɜ:s/ *a* inverso ● *n* inverso *m*

inversely /ɪn'vɜ:slɪ/ *adv* inversamente

invert /ɪn'vɜ:t/ *vt* invertire; **in ~ed commas** tra virgolette

invertebrate /ɪn'vɜ:tɪbrət/ *a & n* invertebrato *m*

invest /ɪn'vest/ *vt* investire ● *vi* fare investimenti; **~ in** (*fam: buy*) comprarsi

investigate /ɪn'vestɪgeɪt/ *vt* investigare

investigation /ɪnvestɪ'geɪʃn/ *n* investigazione *f*

investigative journalism /ɪn'vestɪgətɪv/ *n* dietrologia *f*

investiture /ɪn'vestɪtjə(r)/ *n* investitura *f*

investment /ɪn'vestmənt/ *n* investimento *m*

investment: investment capital *n* capitale *m* di investimento. **investment income** *n* reddito *m* da investimenti. **investment trust** *n* fondo *m* comune di investimento

investor /ɪn'vestə(r)/ *n* investitore, -trice *mf*

inveterate /ɪn'vetərət/ *a* inveterato

invidious /ɪn'vɪdɪəs/ *a* ingiusto; ⟨position⟩ antipatico

invigilate /ɪn'vɪdʒɪleɪt/ *vi Sch* sorvegliare lo svolgimento di un esame

invigilator /ɪn'vɪdʒɪleɪtə(r)/ *n persona f che sorveglia lo svolgimento di un esame*

invigorate /ɪn'vɪgəreɪt/ *vt* rinvigorire

invigorating /ɪn'vɪgəreɪtɪŋ/ *a* tonificante

invincible /ɪn'vɪnsəbl/ *a* invincibile

inviolable /ɪn'vaɪələbl/ *a* inviolabile

invisible /ɪn'vɪzəbl/ *a* invisibile

invisible ink *n* inchiostro *m* simpatico

invitation /ɪnvɪ'teɪʃn/ *n* invito *m*

invite /ɪn'vaɪt/ *vt* invitare; ⟨attract⟩ attirare

■ **invite in** *vt* invitare a entrare

■ **invite round** *vt* invitare a casa

inviting /ɪn'vaɪtɪŋ/ *a* invitante

in vitro fertilization /ɪnviːtrəʊfɜːtɪlaɪ'zeɪʃn/ *n* fecondazione *f* in vitro

invoice /'ɪnvɔɪs/ *n* fattura *f* ● *vt* ~ **sb** emettere una fattura a qcno

invoke /ɪn'vəʊk/ *vt* invocare

involuntarily /ɪn'vɒlʌntərɪlɪ/ *adv* involontariamente

involuntary /ɪn'vɒləntrɪ/ *a* involontario

involve /ɪn'vɒlv/ *vt* comportare; ⟨affect, include⟩ coinvolgere; ⟨entail⟩ implicare; **get ~d with sb** legarsi a qcno; ⟨romantically⟩ legarsi sentimentalmente a qcno

involved /ɪn'vɒlvd/ *a* complesso

involvement /ɪn'vɒlvmənt/ *n* coinvolgimento *m*

invulnerable /ɪn'vʌln(ə)rəbl/ *a* invulnerabile; ⟨position⟩ inattaccabile

inward /'ɪnwəd/ *a* interno; ⟨thoughts etc⟩ interiore

inward investment *n Comm* investimento *m* di capitali stranieri

inward-looking /'ɪnwədlʊkɪŋ/ *a* ⟨person⟩ egocentrico; ⟨society, policy⟩ chiuso

inwardly /'ɪnwədlɪ/ *adv* interiormente

inward[s] /'ɪnwəd[z]/ *adv* verso l'interno

iodine /'aɪədiːn/ *n* iodio *m*

Ionian Sea /aɪəʊnɪən/ *n* mar *m* Ionio

iota /aɪ'əʊtə/ *n* briciolo *m*

IOU *abbr* (**I owe you**) pagherò *m inv*

IPA *n abbr* (**International Phonetic Alphabet**) AFI *m*

IQ *abbr* (**intelligence quotient**) Q.I. *m*

IRA *abbr* (**Irish Republican Army**) I.R.A. *f*

Iran /ɪ'rɑːn/ *n* Iran *m*

Iranian /ɪ'reɪnɪən/ *a & n* iraniano, -a *mf*

Iraq /ɪ'rɑːk/ *n* Iraq *m*

Iraqi /ɪ'rɑːkɪ/ *a & n* iracheno, -a *mf*

irascible /ɪ'ræsəbl/ *a* irascibile

irate /aɪ'reɪt/ *a* adirato

Ireland /'aɪələnd/ *n* Irlanda *f*

iris /'aɪrɪs/ *n Anat* iride *f*; *Bot* iris *f inv*

Irish /'aɪrɪʃ/ *a* irlandese ● *n* **the ~** *pl* gli irlandesi

Irishman /'aɪrɪʃmən/ *n* irlandese *m*

Irishwoman /'aɪrɪʃwʊmən/ *n* irlandese *f*

irk /ɜːk/ *vt* infastidire

irksome /'ɜːksəm/ *a* fastidioso

iron /'aɪən/ *a* di ferro ● *n* ferro *m*; ⟨appliance⟩ ferro *m* [da stiro] ● *vt/i* stirare

■ **iron out** *vt* eliminare stirando; *fig* appianare

Iron Curtain *n* cortina *f* di ferro

iron fist *n fig* pugno *m* di ferro

ironic[al] /aɪ'rɒnɪk[l]/ *a* ironico

ironing /'aɪənɪŋ/ *n* stirare *m*; ⟨articles⟩ roba *f* da stirare; **do the ~** stirare

ironing board *n* asse *f* da stiro

iron lung *n* polmone *m* d'acciaio

ironmonger /'aɪənmʌŋgə(r)/ *n* **~'s** [**shop**] negozio *m* di ferramenta

irony /'aɪərənɪ/ *n* ironia *f*

irradiate /ɪ'reɪdɪeɪt/ *vt* irradiare

irrational /ɪ'ræʃənl/ *a* irrazionale

irreconcilable /ɪ'rekənsaɪləbl/ *a* irreconciliabile

irrecoverable /ɪrɪ'kʌv(ə)rəbl/ *a* ⟨debt, object⟩ irrecuperabile; ⟨loss⟩ irreparabile

irredeemable /ɪrɪ'diːməbl/ *a* ⟨Fin: shares, loan⟩ irredimibile; ⟨loss⟩ irreparabile; ⟨Relig: sinner⟩ che non è redimibile

irrefutable /ɪrɪ'fjuːtəbl/ *a* irrefutabile

irregular /ɪ'regjʊlə(r)/ *a* irregolare

irregularity /ɪregjʊ'lærətɪ/ *n* irregolarità *f inv*

irregularly /ɪ'regjʊləlɪ/ *adv* in modo irregolare

irrelevant /ɪ'reləvənt/ *a* non pertinente

irreparable /ɪ'repərəbl/ *a* irreparabile

irreparably /ɪ'rep(ə)rəblɪ/ *adv* irreparabilmente

irreplaceable /ɪrɪ'pleɪsəbl/ *a* insostituibile

irrepressible /ɪrɪ'presəbl/ *a* irrefrenabile; ⟨person⟩ incontenibile

irreproachable /ɪrɪ'prəʊtʃəbl/ *a* irreprensibile

irresistible /ɪrɪ'zɪstəbl/ *a* irresistibile

irresolute /ɪ'rezəluːt/ *a* irresoluto

irrespective /ɪrɪ'spektɪv/ *a* **~ of** senza riguardo per

irresponsible /ɪrɪ'spɒnsəbl/ *a* irresponsabile

irresponsibly /ɪrɪ'spɒnsəblɪ/ *adv* irresponsabilmente

irretrievable /ɪrɪ'triːvəbl/ *a* ⟨loss, harm⟩ irreparabile

irreverence /ɪ'revərəns/ *n* irriverenza *f*

irreverent /ɪ'revərənt/ *a* irriverente

irreverently /ɪ'revərəntlɪ/ *adv* in modo irreverente

irreversible /ɪrɪ'vɜːsəbl/ *a* irreversibile

irreversibly /ɪrɪ'vɜːsɪblɪ/ *adv* irreversibilmente

irrevocable /ɪ'revəkəbl/ *a* irrevocabile

irrevocably /ɪ'revəkəblɪ/ *adv* irrevocabilmente

irrigate /'ɪrɪgeɪt/ *vt* irrigare

irrigation /ɪrɪ'geɪʃn/ *n* irrigazione *f*

irritability /ɪrɪtə'bɪlətɪ/ *n* irritabilità *f*

irritable /'ɪrɪtəbl/ *a* irritabile

irritant /'ɪrɪtənt/ n sostanza f irritante; (*fig: person*) persona f irritante

irritate /'ɪrɪteɪt/ vt irritare

irritated /'ɪrɪteɪtɪd/ a irritato, stizzito

irritating /'ɪrɪteɪtɪŋ/ a irritante

irritation /ɪrɪ'teɪʃn/ n irritazione f

is /ɪz/ see **be**

Islam /'ɪzlɑːm/ n Islam m

Islamic /ɪz'læmɪk/ a islamico

island /'aɪlənd/ n isola f; (*in road*) isola f spartitraffico

islander /'aɪləndə(r)/ n isolano, -a mf

island hopping /'aɪləndhɒpɪŋ/ n **go ~ ~** andare di isola in isola

isle /aɪl/ n *liter* isola f

isms /'ɪz(ə)mz/ npl pej ismi mpl

isobar /'aɪsəbɑː(r)/ n isobara f

isolate /'aɪsəleɪt/ vt isolare

isolated /'aɪsəleɪtɪd/ a isolato

isolation /aɪsə'leɪʃn/ n isolamento m

isosceles /aɪ'sɒsəliːz/ a isoscele

Israel /'ɪzreɪl/ n Israele m

Israeli /ɪz'reɪlɪ/ a & n israeliano, -a mf

issue /'ɪʃuː/ n (*outcome*) risultato m; (*of magazine*) numero m; (*of stamps etc*) emissione f; (*offspring*) figli mpl; (*matter, question*) questione f; **at ~** in questione; **take ~ with sb** prendere posizione contro qcno ● vt distribuire ‹*supplies*›; rilasciare ‹*passport*›; emettere ‹*stamps, order*›; pubblicare ‹*book*›; **be ~d with sth** ricevere qcsa ● vi **~ from** uscire da

isthmus /'ɪsməs/ n (*pl* **-muses**) istmo m

it /ɪt/ pron (*direct object*) lo m, la f; (*indirect object*) gli m, le f; **it's broken** è rotto/rotta; **will it be enough?** basterà?; **it's hot** fa caldo; **it's raining** piove; **it's me** sono io; **who is it?** chi è?; **it's two o'clock** sono le due; **I doubt it** ne dubito; **take it with you** prendilo con te; **give it a wipe** dagli una pulita

IT n abbr (**information technology**) informatica f

Italian /ɪ'tæljən/ a & n italiano, -a mf; (*language*) italiano m

italic /ɪ'tælɪk/ a in corsivo

italics /ɪ'tælɪks/ npl corsivo msg; **in ~** in corsivo

Italy /'ɪtəlɪ/ n Italia f

itch /ɪtʃ/ n prurito m ● vi avere prurito, prudere; **be ~ing to** fam avere una voglia matta di

itching powder /'ɪtʃɪŋ/ n polverina f che dà prurito

itchy /'ɪtʃɪ/ a che prude; **my foot is ~** ho prurito al piede; **have ~ feet** fig avere la terra che scotta sotto i piedi

item /'aɪtəm/ n articolo m; (*on agenda, programme*) punto m; (*on invoice*) voce f; **~ [of news]** notizia f

itemize /'aɪtəmaɪz/ vt dettagliare ‹*bill*›

itinerant /aɪ'tɪnərənt/ a itinerante

itinerary /aɪ'tɪnərərɪ/ n itinerario m

its /ɪts/ poss pron suo m, sua f, suoi mpl, sue fpl; **~ mother/cage** sua madre/la sua gabbia

it's = **it is, it has**

itself /ɪt'self/ pron (*reflexive*) si; (*emphatic*) essa stessa; **the baby looked at ~ in the mirror** il bambino si è guardato nello specchio; **by ~** da solo; **the machine in ~ is simple** la macchina di per sé è semplice

ITV abbr (**Independent Television**) stazione f televisiva privata

IUD n abbr (**intrauterine device**) spirale f

IVF n abbr **in vitro fertilization**

ivory /'aɪvərɪ/ n avorio m ● attrib d'avorio

Ivory Coast n Costa f d'Avorio

ivory tower n fig torre f d'avorio

ivy /'aɪvɪ/ n edera f

Jj

j, J /dʒeɪ/ n (*letter*)j, J f inv

jab /dʒæb/ n colpo m secco; (*fam: injection*) puntura f ● vt (*pt/pp* **jabbed**) punzecchiare

jabber /'dʒæbə(r)/ vi borbottare

jack /dʒæk/ n Auto cric m inv; Teleph jack m inv; (*in cards*) fante m, jack m inv

▪ **jack in** vt sl piantare ‹*job*›

▪ **jack up** vt Auto sollevare [con il cric]; fam aumentare di molto ‹*salary etc*›

jackal /'dʒæk(ə)l/ n sciacallo m

jackboot /'dʒækbuːt/ n stivale m militare

jackdaw /'dʒækdɔː/ n taccola f

jacket /'dʒækɪt/ n giacca f; (*of book*) sopraccoperta f

jacket potato n patata f cotta al forno con la buccia

jack-in-the-box n scatola f a sorpresa contenente un pupazzo a molla

jackknife /'dʒæknaɪf/ n coltello m a serramanico ● vi sbandare finendo di traverso rispetto al rimorchio

jackpot /'dʒækpɒt/ n premio m (*di una lotteria*); **win the ~** vincere alla lotteria; **hit the ~** fig fare un colpo grosso

jackrabbit /'dʒækræbɪt/ n lepre f americana

jade /dʒeɪd/ n giada f ● attrib di giada

jaded /'dʒeɪdɪd/ a spossato

jagged /'dʒægɪd/ a dentellato

jail /dʒeɪl/ = **gaol**
jail: jailbird n avanzo m di galera. **jailbreak** n evasione f. **jail sentence** n condanna f al carcere
jalopy /dʒəˈlɒpɪ/ n fam vecchia carretta f
jam[1] /dʒæm/ n marmellata f
jam[2] n Auto ingorgo m; ⟨fam: difficulty⟩ guaio m ● v ⟨pt/pp **jammed**⟩ ● vt ⟨cram⟩ pigiare; disturbare ⟨broadcast⟩; inceppare ⟨mechanism, drawer etc⟩; be **~med** ⟨roads:⟩ essere congestionato ● vi ⟨mechanism:⟩ incepparsi; ⟨window, drawer:⟩ incastrarsi
■ **jam on** vt **~ on the brakes** inchiodare
Jamaica /dʒəˈmeɪkə/ n Giamaica f
Jamaican /dʒəˈmeɪkən/ a & n giamaicano, -a mf
jam: jam jar n barattolo m per la marmellata. **jam-packed** a fam pieno zeppo. **jampot** n vasetto m per la marmellata
jangle /ˈdʒæŋgl/ vt far squillare ● vi squillare
janitor /ˈdʒænɪtə(r)/ n ⟨caretaker⟩ custode m; (in school) bidello, -a mf
January /ˈdʒænjʊərɪ/ n gennaio m
Japan /dʒəˈpæn/ n Giappone m
Japanese /dʒæpəˈniːz/ a & n giapponese mf; (language) giapponese m
jar[1] /dʒɑː(r)/ n (glass) barattolo m
jar[2] vi ⟨pt/pp **jarred**⟩ ⟨sound:⟩ stridere
jargon /ˈdʒɑːgən/ n gergo m
jarring /ˈdʒɑːrɪŋ/ a stridente
jasmine /ˈdʒæsmɪn/ n gelsomino m
jaundice /ˈdʒɔːndɪs/ n itterizia f
jaundiced /ˈdʒɔːndɪst/ a fig inacidito
jaunt /dʒɔːnt/ n gita f
jaunty /ˈdʒɔːntɪ/ a (-ier, -iest) sbarazzino
javelin /ˈdʒævlɪn/ n giavellotto m
jaw /dʒɔː/ n mascella f; (bone) mandibola f ● vi fam ciarlare
jawbone /ˈdʒɔːbəʊn/ n Anat osso m mascellare
jaywalker /ˈdʒeɪwɔːkə(r)/ n pedone m indisciplinato
jazz /dʒæz/ n jazz m
■ **jazz up** vt ravvivare
jazz band n complesso m di jazz
jazzy /ˈdʒæzɪ/ a vistoso
jealous /ˈdʒeləs/ a geloso
jealously /ˈdʒeləslɪ/ adv gelosamente
jealousy /ˈdʒeləsɪ/ n gelosia f
jeans /dʒiːnz/ npl [blue] jeans mpl
jeep /dʒiːp/ n jeep f inv
jeer /dʒɪə(r)/ n scherno m ● vi schernire; **~ at** prendersi gioco di ● vt (boo) fischiare
jell /dʒel/ vi concretarsi
jellied /ˈdʒelɪd/ a ⟨eels⟩ in gelatina
jelly /ˈdʒelɪ/ n gelatina f
jelly: jelly baby n caramella f gommosa a forma di pupazzetto. **jelly bean** n caramella f di gelatina di frutta. **jellyfish** n medusa f
jemmy /ˈdʒemɪ/ n piede m di porco
jeopardize /ˈdʒepədaɪz/ vt mettere in pericolo
jeopardy /ˈdʒepədɪ/ n **in ~** in pericolo
jerk /dʒɜːk/ n scatto m, scossa f ● vt scattare

● vi sobbalzare; ⟨limb, muscle:⟩ muoversi a scatti
jerkily /ˈdʒɜːkɪlɪ/ adv a scatti
jerkin /ˈdʒɜːkɪn/ n gilè m inv
jerky /ˈdʒɜːkɪ/ a traballante
jerry-built /ˈdʒerɪbɪlt/ a pej costruito alla bell'e meglio
jersey /ˈdʒɜːzɪ/ n maglia f; Sport maglietta f; (fabric) jersey m
Jerusalem /dʒəˈruːsələm/ n Gerusalemme f
jest /dʒest/ n scherzo m; **in ~** per scherzo ● vi scherzare
jester /ˈdʒestə(r)/ n buffone m
Jesuit /ˈdʒezjʊɪt/ n gesuita m ● a gesuitico
Jesus /ˈdʒiːzəs/ n Gesù m
jet[1] /dʒet/ n (stone) giaietto m
jet[2] n (of water) getto m; (nozzle) becco m; (plane) aviogetto m, jet m inv
jet: jet-black a nero ebano. **jet engine** n motore m a reazione. **jet fighter** n caccia m inv a reazione. **jetfoil** n aliscafo m. **jet lag** n scombussolamento m da fuso orario. **jet-propelled** /-prəˈpeld/ a a reazione. **jet propulsion** n propulsione f a getto
jettison /ˈdʒetɪsn/ vt gettare a mare; fig abbandonare
jetty /ˈdʒetɪ/ n molo m
Jew /dʒuː/ n ebreo m
jewel /ˈdʒuːəl/ n gioiello m
jewelled /ˈdʒuːəld/ a ornato di pietre preziose
jeweller /ˈdʒuːələ(r)/ n gioielliere m; **~'s** [**shop**] gioielleria f
jewellery /ˈdʒuːəlrɪ/ n gioielli mpl
Jewess /ˈdʒuːɪs/ n ebrea f
Jewish /ˈdʒuːɪʃ/ a ebreo
Jew's harp n Mus scacciapensieri m inv
jib /dʒɪb/ vi ⟨pt/pp **jibbed**⟩ fig mostrarsi riluttante (**at** a)
jibe /dʒaɪb/ n see **gibe**
jiffy /ˈdʒɪfɪ/ n fam **in a ~** in un batter d'occhio
Jiffy bag® n busta f imbottita
jig /dʒɪg/ n Mus giga f (danza popolare)
jiggle /ˈdʒɪg(ə)l/ vt scuotere
jigsaw /ˈdʒɪgsɔː/ n **~** [**puzzle**] puzzle m inv
jilt /dʒɪlt/ vt piantare
jingle /ˈdʒɪŋgl/ n (rhyme) canzoncina f pubblicitaria ● vi tintinnare ● vt far tintinnare
jingoist /ˈdʒɪŋgəʊɪst/ n Pol sciovinista mf
jingoistic /dʒɪŋgəʊˈɪstɪk/ a Pol sciovinistico
jinx /dʒɪŋks/ n fam (person) iettatore, -trice mf; **it's got a ~ on it** è iellato
jinxed /dʒɪŋkst/ a **be ~** essere iellato
jitters /ˈdʒɪtəz/ npl fam **have the ~** aver una gran fifa
jittery /ˈdʒɪtərɪ/ a fam in preda alla fifa
jive /dʒaɪv/ n (Am fam: talk) storie fpl
Jnr abbr **junior**
job /dʒɒb/ n lavoro m; **this is going to be quite a ~** fam [questa] non sarà un'impresa facile; **it's a good ~ that ...** meno male che...
job: jobcentre n ufficio m statale di collocamento. **job description** n mansionario m. **job-hunting** n ricerca f impiego
jobless /ˈdʒɒblɪs/ a senza lavoro

181

job: job lot *n* (*at auction*) *insieme m di oggetti disparati.* **job satisfaction** *n* soddisfazione *f* nel lavoro. **job security** *n* sicurezza *f* di impiego. **job-share** *n* (*position*) posto *m* condiviso ● *attrib* ‹*scheme*› di condivisione del posto di lavoro. **job-sharing** /-'ʃeərɪŋ/ *n* job sharing *m inv*

jockey /'dʒɒkɪ/ *n* fantino *m*

jocular /'dʒɒkjʊlə(r)/ *a* scherzoso

jocularly /'dʒɒkjʊləlɪ/ *adv* scherzosamente

jodhpurs /'dʒɒdpəz/ *npl* calzoni *mpl* alla cavallerizza

Joe Bloggs /dʒəʊ'blɒgz/ *n* l'uomo qualunque

jog /'dʒɒg/ *n* colpetto *m*; **at a ~** in un balzo; *Sport* **go for a ~** andare a fare jogging ● *v* (*pt/pp* **jogged**) ● *vt* (*hit*) urtare; **~ sb's memory** farlo ritornare in mente a qcno ● *vi* *Sport* fare jogging

■ **jog along** *vi fig* tirare avanti

jogging /'dʒɒgɪŋ/ *n* jogging *m*

john /dʒɒn/ *n* (*Am fam: toilet*) gabinetto *m*

John Bull *n* il tipico inglese

John Doe *n Am* uomo *m* non identificato

join /dʒɔɪn/ *n* giuntura *f* ● *vt* raggiungere, unire; raggiungere ‹*person*›; (*become member of*) iscriversi a; entrare in ‹*firm*› ● *vi* ‹*roads:*› congiungersi

■ **join in** *vi* partecipare

■ **join up** *vi Mil* arruolarsi ● *vt* unire

■ **join up with** *vt* (*meet*) raggiungere ‹*friends*›; congiungersi a ‹*road, river*›

joiner /'dʒɔɪnə(r)/ *n* falegname *m*

joint /dʒɔɪnt/ *a* comune ● *n* articolazione *f*; (*in wood, brickwork*) giuntura *f*; *Culin* arrosto *m*; (*fam: bar*) bettola *f*; (*sl: drug*) spinello *m*

joint account *n* conto *m* [corrente] comune

joint agreement *n* accordo *m* collettivo

jointed /'dʒɔɪntɪd/ *a* ‹*Culin, chicken*› tagliato a pezzi; ‹*doll, puppet*› snodabile; ‹*rod, pole*› smontabile

joint effort *n* collaborazione *f*

joint honours *npl Br Univ* laurea *f* in due discipline

jointly /'dʒɔɪntlɪ/ *adv* unitamente

joint owner *n* comproprietario, -a *mf*

joint venture *n* joint venture *f inv*

joist /dʒɔɪst/ *n* travetto *m*

joke /dʒəʊk/ *n* (*trick*) scherzo *m*; (*funny story*) barzelletta *f* ● *vi* scherzare

joker /'dʒəʊkə(r)/ *n* burlone, -a *mf*; (*in cards*) jolly *m inv*

joking /'dʒəʊkɪŋ/ *n* **~ apart** scherzi a parte

jokingly /'dʒəʊkɪŋlɪ/ *adv* per scherzo

jollity /'dʒɒlətɪ/ *n* allegria *f*

jolly /'dʒɒlɪ/ *a* (**-ier, -iest**) allegro ● *adv fam* molto

Jolly Roger /'rɒdʒə(r)/ *n* bandiera *f* dei pirati

jolt /dʒəʊlt/ *n* scossa *f*, sobbalzo *m* ● *vt* far sobbalzare ● *vi* sobbalzare

Jordan /'dʒɔːdn/ *n* Giordania *f*; (*river*) Giordano *m*

Jordanian /dʒɔː'deɪnɪən/ *a & n* giordano, -a *mf*

joss stick /'dʒɒs/ *n* bastoncino *m* d'incenso

jostle /'dʒɒsl/ *vt* spingere

jot /dʒɒt/ *n* nulla *f*

■ **jot down** *vt* (*pt/pp* **jotted**) annotare

jotter /'dʒɒtə(r)/ *n* taccuino *m*; (*with a spine*) quaderno *m*

jottings /'dʒɒtɪŋz/ *npl* annotazioni *fpl*

journal /'dʒɜːnl/ *n* giornale *m*; (*diary*) diario *m*

journalese /dʒɜːnə'liːz/ *n* gergo *m* giornalistico

journalism /'dʒɜːnəlɪzm/ *n* giornalismo *m*

journalist /'dʒɜːnəlɪst/ *n* giornalista *mf*

journey /'dʒɜːnɪ/ *n* viaggio *m* ● *vi* viaggiare

jovial /'dʒəʊvɪəl/ *a* gioviale

jowl /dʒaʊl/ *n* (*jaw*) mascella *f*; (*fleshy fold*) guancia *f*; **cheek by ~ with sb** fianco a fianco con qcno

joy /dʒɔɪ/ *n* gioia *f*

joyful /'dʒɔɪfʊl/ *a* gioioso

joyfully /'dʒɔɪfʊlɪ/ *adv* con gioia

joyless /'dʒɔɪlɪs/ *a* ‹*occasion*› triste; ‹*marriage*› infelice

joy: joyride *n fam* giro *m* con una macchina rubata. **joyrider** *n fam* persona *f* che ruba una macchina per andare a fare un giro. **joystick** *n Comput* joystick *m inv*

Jr *abbr* **junior**

jubilant /'dʒuːbɪlənt/ *a* giubilante

jubilation /dʒuːbɪ'leɪʃn/ *n* giubilo *m*

jubilee /'dʒuːbɪliː/ *n* giubileo *m*

Judaism /'dʒuːdeɪɪzm/ *n* giudaismo *m*

judder /'dʒʌdə(r)/ *vi* vibrare violentemente

judge /dʒʌdʒ/ *n* giudice *m* ● *vt* giudicare; (*estimate*) valutare; (*consider*) ritenere ● *vi* giudicare (**by** da)

judgement /'dʒʌdʒmənt/ *n* giudizio *m*; *Jur* sentenza *f*

judicial /dʒuː'dɪʃl/ *a* giudiziario

judiciary /dʒuː'dɪʃərɪ/ *n* magistratura *f*

judicious /dʒuː'dɪʃəs/ *a* giudizioso

judo /'dʒuːdəʊ/ *n* judo *m*

jug /dʒʌg/ *n* brocca *f*; (*small*) bricco *m*

juggernaut /'dʒʌgənɔːt/ *n fam* grosso autotreno *m*

juggle /'dʒʌgl/ *vi* fare giochi di destrezza

juggler /'dʒʌglə(r)/ *n* giocoliere, -a *mf*

jugular /'dʒʌgjʊlə(r)/ *n* giugulare *f*; **go straight for the ~** *fig* colpire nel punto debole

juice /dʒuːs/ *n* succo *m*; **~ extractor** *n* spremiagrumi *m inv* elettrico

juicy /'dʒuːsɪ/ *a* (**-ier, -iest**) succoso; ‹*fam: story*› piccante

jukebox /'dʒuːkbɒks/ *n* juke-box *m inv*

July /dʒʊ'laɪ/ *n* luglio *m*

jumble /'dʒʌmbl/ *n* accozzaglia *f* ● *vt* **~ [up]** mischiare

jumble sale *n* vendita *f* di beneficenza

jumbo /'dʒʌmbəʊ/ *n* **~ [jet]** jumbo jet *m inv*

jump /dʒʌmp/ *n* salto *m*; (*in prices*) balzo *m*; (*in horse racing*) ostacolo *m* ● *vi* saltare; (*with fright*) sussultare; ‹*prices:*› salire rapidamen-

te; **~ to conclusions** saltare alle conclusioni
● *vt* saltare; **~ the gun** *fig* precipitarsi; **~ the queue** non rispettare la fila
■ **jump at** *vt fig* accettare con entusiasmo
⟨*offer*⟩
■ **jump down** *vt* **~ down sb's throat** saltare addosso a qcno
■ **jump in** *vi* (*to vehicle*) saltar su
■ **jump up** *vi* rizzarsi in piedi
jumped-up /dʒʌmpt'ʌp/ *a* montato
jumper /'dʒʌmpə(r)/ *n* (*sweater*) golf *m inv*
jump: jump jet *n* aeroplano *m* a decollo e atterraggio verticali. **jump leads** *npl* cavi *mpl* per batteria. **jump-start** *vt far partire con i cavi da batteria*. **jumpsuit** *n* tuta *f*
jumpy /'dʒʌmpɪ/ *a* nervoso
junction /'dʒʌŋkʃn/ *n* (*of roads*) incrocio *m*; *Rail* nodo *m* ferroviario
juncture /'dʒʌŋktʃə(r)/ *n* **at this ~** a questo punto
June /dʒuːn/ *n* giugno *m*
Jungian /'jʊŋɪən/ *a* junghiano
jungle /'dʒʌŋgl/ *n* giungla *f*
junior /'dʒuːnɪə(r)/ *a* giovane; (*in rank*) subalterno; *Sport* junior *inv* ● *n* **the ~s** *pl Sch* i più giovani
junior doctor *n* assistente *mf* ospedaliero, -a
junior school *n* scuola *f* elementare
juniper /'dʒuːnɪpə(r)/ *n* ginepro *m*
junk /dʒʌŋk/ *n* cianfrusaglie *fpl*
junk food *n fam* cibo *m* poco sano, porcherie *fpl*
junkie /'dʒʌŋkɪ/ *n sl* tossico, -a *mf*
junk: junk mail *n* posta *f* spazzatura. **junk shop** *n* negozio *m* di rigattiere. **junkyard** *n* (*for scrap*) rottamaio *m*; (*for old cars*) cimitero *m* delle macchine
junta /'dʒʌntə/ *n* giunta *f* militare
jurisdiction /dʒʊərɪs'dɪkʃn/ *n* giurisdizione *f*

jurisprudence /dʒʊrɪs'pruːdəns/ *n* giurisprudenza *f*
jurist /'dʒʊərɪst/ *n* giurista *mf*
juror /'dʒʊərə(r)/ *n* giurato, -a *mf*
jury /'dʒʊərɪ/ *n* giuria *f*
jury box *n* banco *m* dei giurati
jury service *n* **do ~ ~** far parte di una giuria popolare
just /dʒʌst/ *a* giusto ● *adv* (*barely*) appena; (*simply*) solo; (*exactly*) esattamente; **~ as tall** altrettanto alto; **~ as I was leaving** proprio quando stavo andando via; **I've ~ seen her** l'ho appena vista; **it's ~ as well** meno male; **~ at that moment** proprio in quel momento; **~ listen!** almeno ascolta!; **I'm ~ going** sto andando proprio ora
justice /'dʒʌstɪs/ *n* giustizia *f*; **do ~ to** rendere giustizia a; **J~ of the Peace** giudice *m* conciliatore
justifiable /dʒʌstɪ'faɪəbl/ *a* giustificabile
justifiably /dʒʌstɪ'faɪəblɪ/ *adv* in modo giustificato
justification /dʒʌstɪfɪ'keɪʃn/ *n* giustificazione *f*
justified /'dʒʌstɪfaɪd/ *a* ⟨*action*⟩ motivato
justify /'dʒʌstɪfaɪ/ *vt* (*pt/pp* **-ied**) giustificare
justly /'dʒʌstlɪ/ *adv* giustamente
justness /'dʒʌstnɪs/ *n* (*of decision*) giustezza *f*; (*of claim, request*) legittimità *f*
jut /dʒʌt/ *vi* (*pt/pp* jutted) **~ out** sporgere
jute /dʒuːt/ *n* iuta *f*
juvenile /'dʒuːvənaɪl/ *a* giovanile; (*childish*) infantile; (*for the young*) per i giovani ● *n* giovane *mf*
juvenile: juvenile crime *n* criminalità *f* presso i giovani . **juvenile delinquency** *n* delinquenza *f* giovanile. **juvenile delinquent** *n* delinquente *mf* minorile. **juvenile offender** *n Jur* imputato, -a *mf* minorenne
juxtapose /dʒʌkstə'pəʊz/ *vt* giustapporre

Kk

k, K /keɪ/ *n* (*letter*) k, K *f inv*
K *abbr* (**kilo**) k; *abbr* (**kilobyte**) KB, Kbyte *m inv*; *abbr* **thousand pounds**; **he earns £50 K** guadagna 50 mila sterline
kaleidoscope /kə'laɪdəskəʊp/ *n* caleidoscopio *m*
kangaroo /kæŋgə'ruː/ *n* canguro *m*
kaput /kə'pʊt/ *a fam* kaputt *inv*
karaoke /kærɪ'əʊkɪ/ *n* karaoke *m inv*
karate /kə'rɑːtɪ/ *n* karatè *m*
kart /kɑːt/ *n* kart *m inv*
Kashmir /kæʃ'mɪə(r)/ *n* Kashmir *m*
Kashmiri /kæʃ'mɪərɪ/ *a* del Kashmir ● *n* nativo, -a *mf* del Kashmir

kayak /'kaɪæk/ *n* kayak *m inv*
KB *n abbr* (**kilobyte**) KB, Kbyte *m inv*
kebab /kɪ'bæb/ *n Culin* spiedino *m* di carne
kedgeree /'kedʒəriː/ *n Br* piatto *m* indiano a base di pesce, riso e uova
keel /kiːl/ *n* chiglia *f*
■ **keel over** *vi* capovolgersi
keen /kiːn/ *a* (*intense*) acuto; ⟨*interest*⟩ vivo; (*eager*) entusiastico; ⟨*competition*⟩ feroce; ⟨*wind, knife*⟩ tagliente; **~ on** entusiasta di; **she's ~ on him** le piace molto; **be ~ to do sth** avere voglia di fare qcsa
keenly /'kiːnlɪ/ *adv* intensamente
keenness /'kiːnnɪs/ *n* entusiasmo *m*

keep /kiːp/ n (*maintenance*) mantenimento m; (*of castle*) maschio m; **for ~s** per sempre ● v (*pt/pp* **kept**) ● vt tenere; (*not throw away*) conservare; (*detain*) trattenere; mantenere ⟨*family, promise*⟩; tenere ⟨*shop*⟩; allevare ⟨*animals*⟩; rispettare ⟨*law, rules*⟩; **~ sth hot** tenere qcsa in caldo; **~ sb waiting** far aspettare qcno; **~ sth to oneself** tenere qcsa per sé; ● vi (*remain*) rimanere; (*food:*) conservarsi; **~ calm** rimanere calmo; **~ left/right** tenere la sinistra/la destra; **~ [on] doing sth** continuare a fare qcsa

■ **keep at** vt (*persevere with*) **~ at it!** non mollare!

■ **keep away** vi non avvicinarsi, stare alla larga ● vt tenere lontano

■ **keep away from** vt non avvicinarsi a ⟨*fire*⟩; stare alla larga da ⟨*sb*⟩; **~ sb away from sth** tener qcno lontano da qcsa

■ **keep back** vt trattenere ⟨*person*⟩; **~ sth back from sb** tenere nascosto qcsa a qcno ● vi tenersi indietro

■ **keep down** vi star giù ● vt mandar giù ⟨*food*⟩; mantenere basso ⟨*prices, inflation etc*⟩; **~ one's voice down** non alzare la voce

■ **keep from** vt **~ sb from doing sth** prevenire qcno dal fare qcsa; **~ sb from** impedire a qcno di ⟨*falling*⟩; **~ sb from their work** distogliere qcno dal lavoro; **~ sth from sb** tenere nascosto qcsa a qcno; **~ the truth from sb** nascondere la verità a qcno

■ **keep in** vt (*in school*) trattenere oltre l'orario per punizione; reprimere ⟨*indignation, anger etc*⟩

■ **keep in with** vt mantenersi in buoni rapporti con

■ **keep off** vt (*avoid*) astenersi da ⟨*cigarettes, chocolate etc*⟩; evitare ⟨*delicate subject*⟩

■ **keep on** vi (*continue one's journey*) proseguire; *fam* assillare (**at sb** qcno) ● vt non togliersi ⟨*coat, hat*⟩; tenere ⟨*employee*⟩

■ **keep out of** vt (*person:*) non entrare in ⟨*place*⟩; tenersi fuori da ⟨*argument*⟩; **~ sb out of** tenere qcno alla larga da ⟨*place*⟩; **~ me out of this!** lasciamene fuori!

■ **keep to** vt non deviare da ⟨*path, subject*⟩; **~ sth to oneself** tenere qcsa per sè

■ **keep up** vi (*remain level*) stare al passo; ⟨*rain, good weather:*⟩ mantenersi ● vt (*continue*) continuare; (*prevent from going to bed*) tenere alzato; mantenere alto ⟨*prices*⟩; tener su ⟨*trousers*⟩

keeper /'kiːpə(r)/ n custode mf

keep-fit n ginnastica f

keeping /'kiːpɪŋ/ n custodia f; **be in ~ with** essere in armonia con

keepsake /'kiːpseɪk/ n ricordo m

keg /keg/ n barilotto m

kelp /kelp/ n laminaria f, fuco m

kennel /'kenl/ n canile m; **~s** pl (*boarding*) canile m; (*breeding*) allevamento m di cani

Kenya /'kenjə/ n Kenia m

Kenyan /'kenjən/ a & n keniota mf

kept /kept/ *see* **keep**

kerb /kɜːb/ n bordo m del marciapiede

kernel /'kɜːnl/ n nocciolo m

kerosene /'kerəsiːn/ n Am cherosene m

kestrel /'kestrəl/ n gheppio m

ketchup /'ketʃʌp/ n ketchup m

kettle /'ket(ə)l/ n bollitore m; **put the ~ on** mettere l'acqua a bollire

kettledrum /'ket(ə)ldrʌm/ n timpano m

key /kiː/ n also Mus chiave f; (*of piano, typewriter*) tasto m ● vt **~ [in]** digitare ⟨*character*⟩; **could you ~ this?** puoi battere questo?

key: keyboard n Comput, Mus tastiera f. **keyboarder** n tastierista mf. **keyboard player** n tastierista mf

keyed-up /kiːd'ʌp/ a (*excited*) teso; (*anxious*) estremamente agitato; (*ready to act*) psicologicamente preparato

key: keyhole n buco m della serratura. **key money** n (*for apartment*) somma f richiesta ad un affittuario quando si trasferisce nell'abitazione. **keynote** n Mus tonica f; (*main theme*) tema m principale. **keynote speech** n discorso m programmatico. **keypad** n Comput tastiera f numerica. **keyring** n portachiavi m inv. **key signature** n Mus armatura f di chiave. **keystroke** n Comput keystroke m inv. **keyword** n parola f chiave

kg abbr (**kilogram**) kg

khaki /'kɑːkɪ/ a cachi inv ● n cachi m

kibbutz /kɪ'bʊts/ n (*pl* **-es** *or* **-im**) kibbutz m inv

kibosh /'kaɪbɒʃ/ n fam **put the ~ on sth** mandare all'aria qcsa

kick /kɪk/ n calcio m; (*fam: thrill*) piacere m; **for ~s** fam per spasso; **get a ~ out of sth** trovare un piacere incredibile in qcsa ● vt dar calci a; **~ the bucket** fam crepare ● vi ⟨*animal:*⟩ scalciare; ⟨*person:*⟩ dare calci

■ **kick around** vi fam essere in giro ● vt buttar giù ⟨*idea*⟩

■ **kick in** vt sfondare a calci ⟨*door*⟩

■ **kick off** vi Sport dare il calcio d'inizio; *fam* iniziare

■ **kick out** vt (*fam: of school, club etc*) sbatter fuori

■ **kick up** vt **~ up a row** fare una scenata

kickback /'kɪkbæk/ n fam tangente f

kick-off n Sport calcio m d'inizio; **for a ~** fam tanto per cominciare

kid /kɪd/ n capretto m; (*fam: child*) ragazzino, -a mf ● v (*pt/pp* **kidded**) ● vt fam prendere in giro. ● vi fam scherzare

kid gloves npl guanti mpl di capretto; **handle sb with ~ ~** trattare qcno con i guanti

kidnap /'kɪdnæp/ vt (*pt/pp* **-napped**) rapire, sequestrare

kidnapper /'kɪdnæpə(r)/ n sequestratore, -trice mf, rapitore, -trice mf

kidnapping /'kɪdnæpɪŋ/ n rapimento m, sequestro m [di persona]

kidney /'kɪdnɪ/ n rene m; Culin rognone m

kidney: kidney bean n fagiolo m comune. **kidney dialysis** n dialisi f. **kidney failure** n collasso m renale. **kidney machine** n rene m artificiale. **kidney-shaped** /'kɪdnɪʃeɪpt/ *a* a forma di fagiolo. **kidney stone** *n* calcolo *m* renale

kill /kɪl/ *vt* uccidere; *fig* metter fine a; ammazzare ‹*time*›

■ **kill off** *vt* eliminare ‹*people*›; distruggere ‹*plants, insects*›

killer /'kɪlə(r)/ *n* assassino, -a *mf*; **it was a real ~** *fig* è stato micidiale

killer instinct *n* istinto *m* di uccidere; *fig* spietatezza *f*

killer whale *n* orca *f*

killing /'kɪlɪŋ/ *n* uccisione *f*; ‹*murder*› omicidio *m*

killjoy /'kɪldʒɔɪ/ *n* guastafeste *mf inv*

kiln /kɪln/ *n* fornace *f*

kilo /'kiːləʊ/ *n* chilo *m*

kilo /'kɪlə/: **~byte** kilobyte *m inv*. **kilogram** *n* chilogrammo *m*. **kilohertz** /'kɪləhɜːts/ *n* chilohertz *m inv*. **kilometre** *n* chilometro *m*. **kilowatt** *n* chilowatt *m inv*

kilt /kɪlt/ *n* kilt *m inv* ‹*gonnellino degli scozzesi*›

kimono /kɪ'məʊnəʊ/ *n* kimono *m inv*, chimono *m inv*

kin /kɪn/ *n* congiunti *mpl*; **next of ~** parente *m* stretto

kind¹ /kaɪnd/ *n* genere *m*, specie *f*; ‹*brand, type*› tipo *m*; **what ~ of car?** che tipo di macchina?; **~ of** *fam* alquanto; **two of a ~** due della stessa specie

kind² *a* gentile, buono; **~ to animals** amante degli animali; **~ regards** cordiali saluti

kindergarten /'kɪndəgɑːtn/ *n* asilo *m* infantile

kind-hearted /-'hɑːtɪd/ *a* ‹*person*› di [buon] cuore

kindle /'kɪndl/ *vt* accendere

kindly /'kaɪndlɪ/ *a* (**-ier, -iest**) benevolo ● *adv* gentilmente; (*if you please*) per favore

kindness /'kaɪndnɪs/ *n* gentilezza *f*

kindred /'kɪndrɪd/ *a* **she's a ~ spirit** è la mia/sua/tua anima gemella

kinetic /kɪ'netɪk/ *a* cinetico

king /kɪŋ/ *n* re *m inv*

kingdom /'kɪŋdəm/ *n* regno *m*

kingfisher /'kɪŋfɪʃə(r)/ *n* martin *m inv* pescatore

kingly /'kɪŋlɪ/ *a also fig* regale

king-sized /'kɪŋsaɪzd/ *a* ‹*cigarette*› king-size *inv*, lungo; ‹*bed*› matrimoniale grande

kink /kɪŋk/ *n* attorcigliamento *m*

kinky /'kɪŋkɪ/ *a fam* bizzarro

kinship /'kɪnʃɪp/ *n* (*blood relationship*) parentela *f*; (*empathy*) affinità *f*

kiosk /'kiːɒsk/ *n* chiosco *m*; *Teleph* cabina *f* telefonica

kip /kɪp/ *n fam* pisolino *m*; **have a ~** schiacciare un pisolino ● *vi* (*pt/pp* **kipped**) *fam* dormire

kipper /'kɪpə(r)/ *n* aringa *f* affumicata

kirk /kɜːk/ *n* ‹*Scottish*› chiesa *f*

kiss /kɪs/ *n* bacio *m* ● *vt* baciare ● *vi* baciarsi

kiss of death *n* colpo *m* di grazia

kiss of life *n* respirazione *f* bocca a bocca;

give sb the ~ ~ ~ fare la respirazione bocca a bocca a qcno

kissogram /'kɪsəgræm/ *n* servizio *m* commerciale in cui un messaggio di auguri viene scherzosamente recapitato con un bacio da una ragazza in abiti succinti

kit /kɪt/ *n* equipaggiamento *m*, kit *m inv*; (*tools*) attrezzi *mpl*; (*construction ~*) pezzi *mpl* da montare, kit *m inv* ● *vt* (*pt/pp* **kitted**) **~ out** equipaggiare

kitbag /'kɪtbæg/ *n* sacco *m* a spalla

kitchen /'kɪtʃɪn/ *n* cucina *f* ● *attrib* di cucina

kitchenette /kɪtʃɪ'net/ *n* cucinino *m*

kitchen: kitchen foil *n* carta *f* di alluminio. **kitchen garden** *n* orto *m*. **kitchen paper** *n* carta *f* da cucina. **kitchen roll** *n* Scottex® *m inv*. **kitchen scales** *npl* bilancia *f* da cucina. **kitchensink** *n* lavello *m*; **everything bar the ~** *fig* proprio tutto quanto. **kitchen-sink drama** *n* teatro *m* neorealista. **kitchen towel** *n* Scottex® *m inv*. **kitchen unit** *n* elemento *m* componibile da cucina. **kitchenware** *n* (*crockery*) stoviglie *fpl*; (*implements*) utensili *mpl* da cucina

kite /kaɪt/ *n* aquilone *m*

kitemark /'kaɪtmɑːk/ *n* *Br* marchio *m* di conformità alle norme britanniche

kith /kɪθ/ *n* **~ and kin** amici e parenti *mpl*

kitsch /kɪtʃ/ *n* kitsch *m inv*

kitten /'kɪtn/ *n* gattino *m*

kitty /'kɪtɪ/ *n* (*money*) cassa *f* comune

kiwi /'kiːwiː/ *n* *Zool* kiwi *m inv*

kiwi fruit *n* kiwi *m inv*

kleptomania /kleptə'meɪnɪə/ *n* cleptomania *f*

kleptomaniac /kleptə'meɪnɪæk/ *n* cleptomane *mf*

km *abbr* (**kilometre**) km

kmh *abbr* (**kilometres per hour**) km/h

knack /næk/ *n* tecnica *f*; **have the ~ for doing sth** avere la capacità di fare qcsa

knapsack /'næpsæk/ *n* sacco *m* da montagna

knave /neɪv/ *m* (*in cards*) fante *m*; (*rogue*) furfante *m*

knead /niːd/ *vt* impastare

knee /niː/ *n* ginocchio *m*; **go down on one's ~s to sb** inginocchiarsi davanti a qcno

kneecap /'niːkæp/ *n* rotula *f*

kneel /niːl/ *vi* (*pt/pp* **knelt**) **~ [down]** inginocchiarsi; **be ~ing** essere inginocchiato

knee-length *a* ‹*boots*› alto; ‹*skirt*› al ginocchio; ‹*socks*› lungo

knee-pad *n* ginocchiera *f*

knees-up /'niːzʌp/ *n* *Br fam* festa *f*

knell /nel/ *n* campana *f* a morto; **sound the death ~ for sth** segnare la fine di qcsa

knelt /nelt/ *see* **kneel**

knew /njuː/ *see* **know**

knickerbocker glory /nɪkəbɒkə'glɔːrɪ/ *n* coppa *f* [gelato] gigante

knickers /'nɪkəz/ *npl* mutandine *fpl*

knick-knacks /'nɪknæks/ *npl* ninnoli *mpl*

knife /naɪf/ *n* (*pl* **knives**) coltello *m* ● *vt fam* accoltellare

knife: knife-edge *n* **be on a ~** ⟨*person:*⟩ trovarsi sul filo del rasoio; ⟨*negotiations:*⟩ essere appeso a un filo. **knifepoint** *n* **at ~** sotto la minaccia di un coltello. **knife sharpener** *n* affilacoltelli *m inv*

knight /naɪt/ *n* cavaliere *m*; (*in chess*) cavallo *m* ● *vt* nominare cavaliere

knighthood /'naɪthʊd/ *n* **receive a ~** ricevere il titolo di cavaliere

knit /nɪt/ *vt/i* (*pt/pp* **knitted**) lavorare a maglia; **~ one, purl one** un diritto, un rovescio; **~ one's brow** aggrottare le sopracciglia

knitted /'nɪtɪd/ *a* lavorato a maglia

knitting /'nɪtɪŋ/ *n* lavorare *m* a maglia; (*product*) lavoro *m* a maglia

knitting needle *n* ferro *m* da calza

knitwear /'nɪtweə(r)/ *n* maglieria *f*

knives /naɪvz/ *npl see* **knife**

knob /nɒb/ *n* pomello *m*; (*of stick*) pomo *m*; (*of butter*) noce *f*

knobbly /'nɒblɪ/ *a* nodoso; (*bony*) spigoloso

knock /nɒk/ *n* colpo *m;* **there was a ~ at the door** hanno bussato alla porta ● *vt* bussare a ⟨*door*⟩; (*fam: criticize*) denigrare; **~ a hole in sth** fare un buco in qcsa; **~ one's head** battere la testa (**on** contro) ● *vi* (*at door*) bussare

■ **knock about** *vt* malmenare ● *vi fam* girovagare

■ **knock back** *vt* (*fam: drink quickly*) buttar giù tutto d'un fiato

■ **knock down** *vt* far cadere; (*with fist*) stendere con un pugno; (*in car*) investire; (*demolish*) abbattere; (*fam: reduce*) ribassare ⟨*price*⟩

■ **knock off** *vt* (*fam: steal*) fregare; (*fam: complete quickly*) fare alla bell'e meglio ● *vi* (*fam: cease work*) staccare

■ **knock out** *vt* eliminare; (*make unconscious*) mettere K.O.; (*fam: anaesthetize*) addormentare

■ **knock over** *vt* rovesciare; (*in car*) investire

■ **knock up** *vt fam* (*prepare quickly*) buttare giù; (*sl: make pregnant*) mettere incinta

knock: knockabout *n Sport* **have a ~** palleggiare. **knock-down furniture** *n* mobili *mpl* componibili. **knock-down price** *n* prezzo *m* stracciato

knocker /'nɒkə(r)/ *n* battente *m*; (*critic*) denigratore, -trice *mf*

knocking-off time /nɒkɪŋ'ɒf/ *n* **~ ~ is five o'clock** si stacca alle cinque

knock: knock-kneed /-'ni:d/ *a* con gambe storte. **knock-on effect** *n* implicazioni *fpl*. **knock-out** *n* knock-out *m inv*; **be a ~** *fig* essere uno schianto

knoll /nəʊl/ *n* collinetta *f*

knot /nɒt/ *n* nodo *m*; **to tie the ~** *fam* convolare a giuste nozze ● *vt* (*pt/pp* **knotted**) annodare; *Br fam* **get ~ted!** vai a farti friggere!

knotty /'nɒtɪ/ *a* (**-ier, -iest**) *fam* spinoso

know /nəʊ/ *v* (*pt* **knew**, *pp* **known**) ● *vt* sapere; conoscere ⟨*person, place*⟩; (*recognize*) riconoscere; **get to ~ sb** conoscere qcno; **~ how to swim** sapere nuotare; **~ right from wrong** saper distinguere il bene dal male ● *vi* sapere; **did you ~ about this?** lo sapevi? ● *n* **in the ~** *fam* al corrente

■ **know of** *vt* conoscere; **not that I ~ of** non che io sappia

know-all *n fam* sapientone, -a *mf*

know-how *n* abilità *f*

knowing /'nəʊɪŋ/ *a* d'intesa

knowingly /'nəʊɪŋlɪ/ *adv* (*intentionally*) consapevolmente; ⟨*smile etc*⟩ con un aria d'intesa

knowledgable /'nɒlɪdʒəbl/ *a* ben informato

knowledge /'nɒlɪdʒ/ *n* conoscenza *f*

known /nəʊn/ *a* noto

knuckle /'nʌkl/ *n* nocca *f*

■ **knuckle down** *vi* darci sotto (**to** con)

■ **knuckle under** *vi* sottomettersi

koala [**bear**] /kəʊ'ɑ:lə/ *n* koala *m inv*

Koran /kə'rɑ:n/ *n* Corano *m*

Korea /kə'rɪə/ *n* Corea *f*

Korean /kə'rɪən/ *a* & *n* coreano, -a *mf*; (*language*) coreano *m*

Korean // *a* & *n* coreano, -a *mf*

kosher /'kəʊʃə(r)/ *a* kasher *inv*

kowtow /kaʊ'taʊ/ *vi* piegarsi

kph *abbr* (**kilometres per hour**) km/h

kudos /'kju:dɒs/ *n fam* gloria *f*

Kurd /'kɜ:d/ *n* curdo,-a *mf* ● *a* curdo

Kurdish /'kɜ:dɪʃ/ *a* & *n* (*language*) curdo *m*

Kurdistan /kɜ:dɪ'stɑ:n/ *n* Kurdistan *m*

Kuwait /kʊ'weɪt/ *n* Kuwait *m*

Kuwaiti /kʊ'weɪtɪ/ *a* & *n* kuwaitiano, -a *mf*

kW *abbr* (**kilowatt**) kW

kWh *abbr* (**kilowatt-hour**) kWh

I, L /eɪ/ n (letter) l, L f inv
L abbr (**lake**) L; abbr (**large**) L; abbr (**learner**) P; abbr (**left**) sinistra f; abbr (**line**) v; abbr (**litre(s)**) l
lab /læb/ n fam laboratorio m
lab assistant n assistente mf di laboratorio
lab coat n camice m
label /ˈleɪbl/ n etichetta f ● vt (pt/pp **labelled**) mettere un'etichetta a; fig etichettare ⟨person⟩
labelling /ˈleɪbəlɪŋ/ n (act) etichettatura f
laboratory /ləˈbɒrətrɪ/ n laboratorio m
laborious /ləˈbɔːrɪəs/ a laborioso
laboriously /ləˈbɔːrɪəslɪ/ adv in modo laborioso
labor union /ˈleɪbə/ n Am sindacato m
labour /ˈleɪbə(r)/ n lavoro m; (workers) manodopera f; Med doglie fpl; **be in ~** avere le doglie; **L~** Pol partito m laburista ● attrib Pol laburista ● vi lavorare ● vt **~ the point** fig ribadire il concetto
labour camp n campo m di lavoro
laboured /ˈleɪbəd/ a ⟨breathing⟩ affannato
labourer /ˈleɪbərə(r)/ n manovale m
labour exchange n old ufficio m di collocamento
labour force n manodopera f
labouring /ˈleɪbərɪŋ/ n lavoro m manuale
labour: labour-intensive a ad uso intensivo di lavoro; **be ~** richiedere molta manodopera. **labour market** n mercato m del lavoro. **Labour Party** n Partito m laburista. **labour relations** npl relazioni fpl industriali. **labour-saving** /ˈleɪbəseɪvɪŋ/ a che fa risparmiare lavoro e fatica. **labour ward** n reparto m maternità
labrador /ˈlæbrədɔː(r)/ n (dog) labrador m inv
lab technician n technico, -a mf di laboratorio
laburnum /ləˈbɜːnəm/ n maggiociondolo m
labyrinth /ˈlæbərɪnθ/ n labirinto m
lace /leɪs/ n pizzo m; (of shoe) laccio m ● attrib di pizzo ● vt allacciare ⟨shoes⟩; correggere ⟨drink⟩
lacerate /ˈlæsəreɪt/ vt lacerare
laceration /læsəˈreɪʃn/ n lacerazione f
lace-up [shoe] n scarpa f stringata
lack /læk/ n mancanza f; **~ of interest** disinteressamento m; **~ of evidence** insufficienza f di prove ● vt **the programme ~s originality** il programma manca di originalità; **I ~ the time** mi manca il tempo ● vi **be ~ing** mancare; **be ~ing in sth** mancare di qcsa
lackadaisical /lækəˈdeɪzɪkl/ a senza entusiasmo

lackey /ˈlækɪ/ n lacchè m inv
lacklustre /ˈlæklʌstə(r)/ a scialbo
laconic /ləˈkɒnɪk/ a laconico
laconically /ləˈkɒnɪklɪ/ adv laconicamente
lacquer /ˈlækə(r)/ n lacca f
lactate /lækˈteɪt/ vi produrre latte
lactation /lækˈteɪʃn/ n lattazione f
lacy /ˈleɪsɪ/ a di pizzo
lad /læd/ n ragazzo m
ladder /ˈlædə(r)/ n scala f; (in tights) sfilatura f ● vi sfilarsi
ladderproof /ˈlædəpruːf/ a ⟨stockings⟩ indemagliabile
laddish /ˈlædɪʃ/ a fam da ragazzacci
laden /ˈleɪdn/ a carico (**with** di)
la-di-da /lɑːdɪˈdɑː/ a affettato
ladle /ˈleɪdl/ n mestolo m ● vt **~ [out]** versare (col mestolo)
lady /ˈleɪdɪ/ n signora f; (title) Lady f; **ladies [room]** n bagno m per donne
lady: ladybird n, Am **ladybug** n coccinella f. **lady-in-waiting** /-ˈweɪtɪŋ/ n dama f di corte. **ladykiller** n fam dongiovanni m inv. **ladylike** /ˈleɪdɪlaɪk/ a signorile
lady: lady mayoress n moglie f del Lord Mayor. **Ladyship** n her/your **~** (to aristocrat) ≈ Signora Contessa. **lady's maid** n cameriera f personale
lag[1] /læg/ vi (pt/pp **lagged**) **~ behind** restare indietro
lag[2] vt (pt/pp **lagged**) isolare ⟨pipes⟩
lager /ˈlɑːgə(r)/ n birra f chiara
lager lout n Br pej giovinastro m ubriaco
lagging /ˈlægɪŋ/ n (for pipes) materiale m isolante
lagoon /ləˈguːn/ n laguna f
laid /leɪd/ see **lay**[3]; sl **get ~** scopare
laid-back a fam rilassato
lain /leɪn/ see **lie**[2]
lair /leə(r)/ n tana f
laird /leəd/ n (in Scotland) proprietario m terriero
laity /ˈleɪətɪ/ n laicato m
lake /leɪk/ n lago m. **~ Garda** lago di Garda
lakeside /ˈleɪksaɪd/ n riva f del lago ● attrib ⟨café, scenery⟩ della/sulla riva del lago
lama /ˈlɑːmə/ n lama m inv
lamb /læm/ n agnello m
lambast[e] /læmˈbeɪst/ vt biasimare ⟨person, organization⟩
lamb: lamb chop n cotoletta f d'agnello. **lambskin** n pelle f d'agnello. **lambswool** n lana f d'agnello, lambswool m inv
lame /leɪm/ a zoppo; fig ⟨argument⟩ zoppicante; ⟨excuse⟩ traballante

lamé /'lɑːmeɪ/ *n* lamé *m*

lame duck *n* (*person*) inetto, -a *mf*; (*firm*) azienda *f* in cattive acque

lament /lə'ment/ *n* lamento *m* ● *vt* lamentare ● *vi* lamentarsi

lamentable /'læməntəbl/ *a* deplorevole

laminated /'læmɪneɪtɪd/ *a* laminato

lamp /læmp/ *n* lampada *f*; (*in street*) lampione *m*

lampoon /læm'puːn/ *n* satira *f* ● *vt* fare oggetto di satira

lamp-post *n* lampione *m*

lampshade /'læmpʃeɪd/ *n* paralume *m*

lance /lɑːns/ *n* lancia *f* ● *vt* Med incidere

lance corporal *n* appuntato *m*

lancet /'lɑːnsɪt/ *n* Med bisturi *m inv*

land /lænd/ *n* terreno *m*; (*country*) paese *m*; (*as opposed to sea*) terra *f*; **plot of** ~ pezzo *m* di terreno ● *vt* Naut sbarcare; ⟨*fam: obtain*⟩ assicurarsi; **be** ~**ed with sth** *fam* ritrovarsi fra capo e collo qcsa ● *vi* Aeron atterrare; (*fall*) cadere; ~ **on one's feet** *fig* cadere in piedi

■ **land up** *vi fam* finire

land: land agent *n* (*on estate*) fattore *m*. **land army** *n gruppo m di lavoratrici agricole durante la seconda guerra mondiale*. **landfall** *n Naut* approdo *m*; **make** ~ (*reach*) approdare; (*sight*) avvistare terra. **landfill site** *n discarica f in cui i rifiuti vengono interrati*

landing /'lændɪŋ/ *n Naut* sbarco *m*; *Aeron* atterraggio *m*; (*top of stairs*) pianerottolo *m*

landing: landing card *n Aeron, Naut* carta *f* di sbarco. **landing craft** *n* mezzo *m* da sbarco. **landing gear** *n Aeron* carrello *m* d'atterraggio. **landing lights** *npl* luci *fpl* d'atterraggio. **landing party** *n Mil* reparto *m* da sbarco. **landing-stage** *n* pontile *m* da sbarco. **landing strip** *n* pista *f* d'atterraggio

land: landlady *n* proprietaria *f*; (*of flat*) padrona *f* di casa. **landlocked** *a* privo di sbocco sul mare. **landlord** *n* proprietario *m*; (*of flat*) padrone *m* di casa. **landlubber** *n* marinaio *m* d'acqua dolce. **landmark** *n* punto *m* di riferimento; *fig* pietra *f* miliare. **land mass** *n* continente *m*. **landmine** *n Mil* mina *f* terrestre. **landowner** *n* proprietario, -a *mf* terriero, -a. **landscape** *n* paesaggio *m*. **landscape architect** *n* paesaggista *mf*. **landscape gardener** *n* paesaggista *mf*. **landslide** *n* frana *f*; *Pol* valanga *f* di voti. **landslip** *n* smottamento *m*

lane /leɪn/ *n* sentiero *m*; *Auto, Sport* corsia *f*

lane closure *n* (*on motorway*) chiusura *f* di corsia

lane markings *n* (*on road*) [strisce *fpl* di] mezzeria *f*

langoustine /'lɒŋɡʊstiːn/ *n* scampo *m*

language /'læŋɡwɪdʒ/ *n* lingua *f*; (*speech, style, Comput*) linguaggio *m*

language barrier *n* barriera *f* linguistica

language laboratory *n* laboratorio *m* linguistico

languid /'læŋɡwɪd/ *a* languido

languidly /'læŋɡwɪdlɪ/ *adv* languidamente

languish /'læŋɡwɪʃ/ *vi* languire

languor /'læŋɡə(r)/ *n* languore *m*

lank /læŋk/ *a* ⟨*hair*⟩ liscio

lanky /'læŋkɪ/ *a* (**-ier, -iest**) allampanato

lanolin /'lænəlɪn/ *n* lanolina *f*

lantern /'læntən/ *n* lanterna *f*

lanyard /'lænjəd/ *n* (*Naut: rope*) cima *f*

lap[1] /læp/ *n* grembo *m*

lap[2] *n* (*Sport, of journey*) tappa *f*; ~ **of honour** giro *m* d'onore ● *v* (*pt/pp* **lapped**) ● *vi* ⟨*water:*⟩ ~ **against** lambire ● *vt* Sport doppiare

lap[3] *vt* (*pt/pp* **lapped**) ~ **up** bere avidamente; bersi completamente ⟨*lies*⟩; credere ciecamente a ⟨*praise*⟩

lap and shoulder belt *n* Auto, Aeron cintura *f* di sicurezza

laparoscope /'læpərəʃkəʊp/ *n* laparoscopio *m*

laparoscopy /læpə'rɒskəpɪ/ *n* laparoscopia *f*

lap belt *n* Auto, Aeron cintura *f* di sicurezza addominale

lapdog /'læpdɒɡ/ *n* cane *m* da salotto; **he's her** ~ è il suo cagnolino

lapel /lə'pel/ *n* bavero *m*

Lapland /'læplænd/ *n* Lapponia *f*

lapse /læps/ *n* sbaglio *m*; (*moral*) sbandamento *m* [morale]; (*of time*) intervallo *m* ● *vi* (*expire*) scadere; (*morally*) scivolare; ~ **into** cadere in

laptop /'læptɒp/ *n* ~ [**computer**] computer *m inv* portabile, laptop *m inv*

larceny /'lɑːsənɪ/ *n* furto *m*

larch /lɑːtʃ/ *n* larice *m*

lard /lɑːd/ *n* strutto *m*

larder /'lɑːdə(r)/ *n* dispensa *f*

large /lɑːdʒ/ *a & adv* grande; ⟨*number, amount*⟩ grande, grosso; **by and** ~ in complesso; **at** ~ in libertà; (*in general*) ampiamente

large intestine *n* intestino *m* crasso

largely /'lɑːdʒlɪ/ *adv* ~ **because of** in gran parte a causa di

largeness /'lɑːdʒnɪs/ *n* grandezza *f*

large-scale *a* ⟨*map*⟩ a grande scala; ⟨*operation*⟩ su larga scala

largesse /lɑː'ʒes/ *n* generosità *f*

lark[1] /lɑːk/ *n* (*bird*) allodola *f*

lark[2] *n* (*joke*) burla *f*

■ **lark about** *vi* giocherellare

larva /'lɑːvə/ *n* (*pl* **-vae** /'lɑːviː/) larva *f*

laryngitis /lærɪn'dʒaɪtɪs/ *n* laringite *f*

larynx /'lærɪŋks/ *n* laringe *f*

lasagne /lə'zænjə/ *n* lasagne *fpl*

lascivious /lə'sɪvɪəs/ *a* lascivo

laser /'leɪzə(r)/ *n* laser *m inv*

laser disc *n* disco *m* laser

laser printer *n* stampante *f* laser

lash /læʃ/ *n* frustata *f*; (*eyelash*) ciglio *m* ● *vt* (*whip*) frustare; (*tie*) legare fermamente

■ **lash out** *vi* attaccare; (*spend*) sperperare (**on** in)

lashings /'læʃɪŋz/ *npl* ~ **of** *fam* una marea di

lass /læs/ n ragazzina f

lasso /lə'su:/ n lazo m

last /lɑ:st/ a ⟨final⟩ ultimo; ⟨recent⟩ scorso; ~ **year** l'anno scorso; ~ **night** ieri sera; **at** ~ alla fine; **at** ~**!** finalmente!; **that's the** ~ **straw** fam questa è l'ultima goccia ● n ultimo, -a mf; **the** ~ **but one** il penultimo ● adv per ultimo; ⟨last time⟩ l'ultima volta; ~ **but not least** per ultimo ma non il meno importante ● vi durare

lasting /'lɑ:stɪŋ/ a durevole

lastly /'lɑ:stlɪ/ adv infine

last: last name n ⟨surname⟩ cognome m. **last rites** npl Relig estrema unzione f. **Last Supper** n Ultima Cena f

latch /lætʃ/ n chiavistello m; ⟨on gate⟩ saliscendi m inv; **leave the door on the** ~ chiudere la porta senza far scattare la serratura

■ **latch on to** vt fissarsi con ⟨person, idea⟩

latchkey /'lætʃki:/ n chiave f di casa

latchkey child n bambino m che ha le chiavi di casa in quanto i genitori lavorano

late /leɪt/ a ⟨delayed⟩ in ritardo; ⟨at a late hour⟩ tardo; ⟨deceased⟩ defunto; **it's** ~ ⟨at night⟩ è tardi; **in** ~ **November** alla fine di Novembre; **of** ~ recentemente; **be a** ~ **developer** ⟨child:⟩ essere lento nell'apprendimento ● adv tardi; **stay up** ~ stare alzati fino a tardi

latecomer /'leɪtkʌmə(r)/ n ritardatario, -a mf; ⟨to political party etc⟩ nuovo, -a arrivato, -a mf

lately /'leɪtlɪ/ adv recentemente

lateness /'leɪtnɪs/ n ora f tarda; ⟨delay⟩ ritardo m

latent /'leɪtnt/ a latente

later /'leɪtə(r)/ a ⟨train⟩ che parte più tardi; ⟨edition⟩ più recente ● adv più tardi; ~ **on** più tardi, dopo

lateral /'lætərəl/ a laterale

late riser /'raɪzə(r)/ n dormiglione, -a mf

latest /'leɪtɪst/ a ultimo; ⟨most recent⟩ più recente; **the** ~ **[news]** le ultime notizie ● n **six o'clock at the** ~ alle sei al più tardi

latex /'leɪteks/ n la[t]tice m

lath /læθ/ n assicella f

lathe /leɪð/ n tornio m

lather /'lɑ:ðə(r)/ n schiuma f ● vt insaponare ● vi far schiuma

Latin /'lætɪn/ a latino ● n latino m

Latin America n America f Latina

Latin American n & a latino-americano mf

Latino /lə'ti:nəʊ/ n Am latino-americano, -a mf

latitude /'lætɪtjuːd/ n Geog latitudine f; fig libertà f d'azione

latrine /lə'tri:n/ n latrina f

latter /'lætə(r)/ a ultimo ● n **the** ~ quest'ultimo

latter-day a moderno

latterly /'lætəlɪ/ adv ultimamente

lattice /'lætɪs/ n traliccio m

lattice window n finestra f con vetri a losanghe

lattice-work n intelaiatura f a traliccio

Latvia /'lætvɪə/ n Lettonia f

Latvian /'lætvɪən/ a & n lettone mf; ⟨language⟩ lettone m

laudable /'lɔːdəbl/ a lodevole

laudatory /'lɔːdətrɪ/ a elogiativo

laugh /lɑːf/ n risata f ● vi ridere ⟨**at/about** di⟩; ~ **at sb** ⟨mock⟩ prendere in giro qcno

laughable /'lɑːfəbl/ a ridicolo

laughing gas /'lɑːfɪŋ/ n gas m inv esilarante

laughing stock n zimbello m

laughter /'lɑːftə(r)/ n risata f

launch[1] /lɔːntʃ/ n ⟨boat⟩ lancia f

launch[2] n lancio m; ⟨of ship⟩ varo m ● vt lanciare ⟨rocket, product⟩; varare ⟨ship⟩; sferrare ⟨attack⟩

■ **launch into** vt intraprendere ⟨career⟩; imbarcarsi in ⟨speech⟩

launcher /'lɔːntʃə(r)/ n lanciamissili m inv

launch[ing] pad /'lɔːntʃ[ɪŋ]/ n piattaforma f di lancio; fig trampolino m di lancio

launder /'lɔːndə(r)/ vt lavare e stirare; ~ **money** fig riciclare denaro sporco

launderette /lɔːndə'ret/ n lavanderia f automatica

laundry /'lɔːndrɪ/ n lavanderia f; ⟨clothes⟩ bucato m

laureate /'lɒrɪət/ a **poet** ~ poeta m di corte; **Nobel** ~ vincitore, -trice mf del Nobel

laurel /'lɒrəl/ n lauro m; **rest on one's** ~**s** fig dormire sugli allori

lav /læv/ n Br fam gabinetto m

lava /'lɑːvə/ n lava f

lavatorial /lævə'tɔːrɪəl/ a ⟨humour⟩ scatologico

lavatory /'lævətrɪ/ n gabinetto m

lavender /'lævəndə(r)/ n lavanda f

lavender blue a color lavanda

lavish /'lævɪʃ/ a copioso; ⟨wasteful⟩ prodigo; **on a** ~ **scale** su vasta scala ● vt ~ **sth on sb** ricoprire qcno di qcsa

lavishly /'lævɪʃlɪ/ adv copiosamente

law /lɔː/ n legge f; **study** ~ studiare giurisprudenza, studiare legge; ~ **and order** ordine m pubblico; **take the** ~ **into one's own hands** farsi giustizia da sé; ~ **of the jungle** legge della giungla

law-abiding /'lɔːəbaɪdɪŋ/ a che rispetta la legge

lawbreaker /'lɔːbreɪkə(r)/ n persona f che infrange la legge

law court n tribunale m

lawful /'lɔːfʊl/ a legittimo

lawfully /'lɔːfʊlɪ/ adv legittimamente

lawfulness /'lɔːfʊlnɪs/ n legalità f

lawless /'lɔːlɪs/ a senza legge

lawmaker /'lɔːmeɪkə(r)/ n legislatore m

lawn /lɔːn/ n prato m [all'inglese]

lawnmower /'lɔːnməʊə(r)/ n tosaerba m inv

law school n facoltà f di giurisprudenza

lawsuit /'lɔːsuːt/ n causa f

lawyer /'lɔːjə(r)/ n avvocato m

lax /læks/ a negligente; ⟨morals etc⟩ lassista

laxative /'læksətɪv/ n lassativo m

laxity /'læksətɪ/ *n* lassismo *m*

lay[1] /leɪ/ *a* laico; *fig* profano

lay[2] *see* **lie**[2]

lay[3] *vt* (*pt/pp* **laid**) porre, mettere; apparecchiare ‹*table*› ● *vi* ‹*hen:*› fare le uova

■ **lay aside** *vt* mettere da parte

■ **lay down** *vt* posare; stabilire ‹*rules, conditions*›

■ **lay in** *vt* farsi una scorta di ‹*coal, supplies etc*›

■ **lay into** *vt sl* picchiare

■ **lay off** *vt* licenziare ‹*workers*› ● *vi·* (*fam: stop*) ~ **off!** smettila!

■ **lay on** *vt* (*organize*) organizzare

■ **lay out** *vt* (*display, set forth*) esporre; (*plan*) pianificare ‹*garden*›; (*spend*) sborsare; *Typ* impaginare

■ **lay up** *vt* **I was laid up in bed for a week** sono stato costretto a letto per una settimana

layabout /'leɪəbaʊt/ *n* fannullone, -a *mf*

lay-by *n* piazzola *f* di sosta

layer /'leɪə(r)/ *n* strato *m*

layette /ler'et/ *n* corredino *m*

layman /'leɪmən/ *n* profano *m*

layout /'leɪaʊt/ *n* disposizione *f*; *Typ* impaginazione *f*, layout *m inv*

lay preacher *n* predicatore *m* laico

laze /leɪz/ *vi* ~ [**about**] oziare

lazily /'leɪzɪlɪ/ *adv* ‹*move, wander etc*› pigramente

laziness /'leɪzɪnɪs/ *n* pigrizia *f*

lazy /'leɪzɪ/ *a* (**-ier, -iest**) pigro

lazybones /'leɪzɪbəʊnz/ *n* poltrone, -a *mf*

lazy eye *n* ambliopia *f*

lb *abbr* (**pound**) libbra

LCD *n abbr* (**liquid crystal display**) LCD *m*

lead[1] /led/ *n* piombo *m*; (*of pencil*) mina *f*

lead[2] /li:d/ *n* guida *f*; (*leash*) guinzaglio *m*; (*flex*) filo *m*; (*clue*) indizio *m*; *Theat* parte *f* principale; (*distance ahead*) distanza *f* (over su); **in the** ~ in testa; **follow sb's** ~ seguire l'esempio di qcno ● *vt* (*pt/pp* **led**) condurre; dirigere ‹*expedition, party etc*›; (*induce*) indurre; ~ **the way** mettersi in testa; ~ **into temptation** indurre in tentazione ● *vi* (*be in front*) condurre; (*in race, competition*) essere in testa

■ **lead astray** *vt* sviare

■ **lead away** *vt* portar via

■ **lead on** *vt* ingannare

■ **lead off** *vi* (*begin*) cominciare ● *vt* (*take away*) portare via

■ **lead to** *vt* portare a

■ **lead up to** *vt* precludere; **the period ~ing up to the election** il periodo precedente le elezioni; **what's this ~ing up to?** dove porta questo?

leaded /'ledɪd/ *a* con piombo

leaden /'ledən/ *a* di piombo

leader /'li:də(r)/ *n* capo *m*; (*of orchestra*) primo violino *m*; (*in newspaper*) articolo *m* di fondo

leadership /'li:dəʃɪp/ *n* direzione *f*, leadership *f inv*; **show** ~ mostrare capacità di comando

lead-free /'ledfri:/ *a* senza piombo

lead-in /'li:dɪn/ *n* presentazione *f*

leading[1] /'li:dɪŋ/ *a* principale

leading[2] /'ledɪŋ/ *n* *Typ* interlinea *m*

leading /'li:dɪŋ/: **leading article** *n* articolo *m* di fondo. **leading edge** *n* *Aeron* bordo *m* d'attacco; **at the** ~ ~ **of** (*technology*) all'avanguardia in. **leading lady** attrice *f* principale. **leading light** *n* personaggio *m* di spicco. **leading man** attore *m* principale. **leading question** *n* domanda *f* che influenza la risposta

lead poisoning *n* saturnismo *m*

leaf /li:f/ *n* (*pl* **leaves**) foglia *f*; (*of table*) asse *f*; *fig* **take a** ~ **out of sb's book** imparare la lezione di qcno; **turn over a new** ~ voltare pagina

■ **leaf through** *vt* sfogliare

leaflet /'li:flɪt/ *n* dépliant *m inv*; (*advertising*) dépliant *m inv* pubblicitario; (*political*) manifestino *m*

leafy /'li:fɪ/ *a* ‹*tree*› ricco di foglie; ‹*wood*› molto verde; ‹*suburb, area*› ricco di verde

league /li:g/ *n* lega *f*; *Sport* campionato *m*; **be in** ~ **with** essere in combutta con

league table *n* classifica *f* del campionato

leak /li:k/ *n* (*hole*) fessura *f*; *Naut* falla *f*; (*of gas & fig*) fuga *f* ● *vi* colare; ‹*ship:*› fare acqua; ‹*liquid, gas:*› fuoriuscire ● *vt* ~ **sth to sb** *fig* far trapelare qcsa a qcno

leakage /'li:kɪdʒ/ *n* perdita *f*; (*of gas & fig*) fuga *f*

leaky /'li:kɪ/ *a* che perde; *Naut* che fa acqua

lean[1] /li:n/ *a* magro

lean[2] *v* (*pt/pp* **leaned** *or* **leant** /lent/) ● *vt* appoggiare (**against/on** contro/su); ~ **one's elbows on the table** appoggiare i gomiti sul tavolo ● *vi* appoggiarsi (**against/on** contro/su); (*not be straight*) pendere; **be ~ing against** essere appoggiato contro; ~ **on sb** (*depend on*) appoggiarsi a qcno; (*fam: exert pressure on*) stare col calcagne di qcno

■ **lean back** *vi* sporgersi indietro

■ **lean forward** *vi* piegarsi in avanti

■ **lean out** *vi* sporgersi

■ **lean over** *vi* piegarsi

■ **lean towards** *vt* (*favour*) propendere per

leaning /'li:nɪŋ/ *a* pendente; **the L~ Tower of Pisa** la torre di Pisa, la torre pendente ● *n* tendenza *f*

leanness /'li:nnɪs/ *n* magrezza *f*

lean-to *n* garage *m inv* adiacente alla casa

leap /li:p/ *n* salto *m* ● *vi* (*pt/pp* **leapt** /lept/ *or* **leaped**) saltare; **he leapt at it** *fam* l'ha preso al volo

leapfrog /'li:pfrɒg/ *n* cavallina *f*

leap year *n* anno *m* bisestile

learn /lɜːn/ *v* (*pt/pp* **learnt** *or* **learned**) ● *vt* imparare; ~ **to swim** imparare a nuotare; **I have ~ed that...** (*heard*) sono venuto a sapere che...; *fig* **he's ~t his lesson** ha imparato la lezione ● *vi* imparare; **as I've ~t to my cost** come ho imparato a mie spese

learned /'lɜːnɪd/ *a* colto

learner /'lɜːnə(r)/ n also Auto principiante mf

learning /'lɜːnɪŋ/ n cultura f

learning: learning curve n curva f di apprendimento. **learning difficulties** npl (of schoolchildren) difficoltà fpl d'apprendimento. **learning disability** n difficoltà fpl d'apprendimento

lease /liːs/ n contratto m d'affitto; (rental) affitto m; **the job has given him a new ~ of life** grazie al lavoro ha ripreso gusto alla vita ● vt affittare

leasehold /'liːshəʊld/ n proprietà f in affitto

leaseholder /'liːshəʊldə(r)/ n titolare mf di un contratto d'affitto

leash /liːʃ/ n guinzaglio m

least /liːst/ a più piccolo; (smallest amount) meno; **you've got ~ luggage** hai meno bagagli di tutti ● n **the ~** il meno; **that's the ~ of my worries** questa è la cosa che mi preoccupa di meno; **at ~** almeno; **not in the ~** niente affatto ● adv meno; **the ~ expensive wine** il vino meno caro

leather /'leðə(r)/ n pelle f; (of soles) cuoio m ● attrib di pelle/cuoio; **~ jacket** giubbotto m di pelle

leathery /'leðərɪ/ a (meat, skin) duro

leave /liːv/ n (holiday) congedo m; Mil licenza f; **on ~** in congedo/licenza; **take one's ~ of absence** aspettativa f ● v (pt/pp **left**) ● vt lasciare; uscire da (house, office); (forget) dimenticare; **there is nothing left** non è rimasto niente; **~ sb in peace** lasciare in pace qcno ● vi andare via; (train, bus:) partire

■ **leave aside** vt (disregard) lasciare da parte

■ **leave behind** vt lasciare; (forget) dimenticare

■ **leave out** vt omettere; (not put away) lasciare fuori

leaves /liːvz/ see **leaf**

Lebanese /lebə'niːz/ a & n libanese mf

Lebanon /'lebənən/ n Libano m

lecher /'letʃə(r)/ n libertino m

lecherous /'letʃərəs/ a lascivo

lechery /'letʃərɪ/ n lascivia f

lectern /'lektɜːn/ n leggio m, scannello m

lecture /'lektʃə(r)/ n conferenza f; Univ lezione f; (reproof) ramanzina f ● vi fare una conferenza (**on** su); Univ insegnare (**on sth** qcsa) ● vt ~ **sb** rimproverare qcno

lecturer /'lektʃərə(r)/ n conferenziere, -a mf; Univ docente mf universitaria, -a

lecture room n Br Univ aula f magna

lectureship /'lektʃəʃɪp/ n Br Univ docenza f universitaria

lecture theatre n Br Univ aula f magna

LED n abbr (**light-emitting diode**) LED m inv

led /led/ see **lead²**

ledge /ledʒ/ n cornice f; (of window) davanzale m

ledger /'ledʒə(r)/ n libro m mastro

leech /liːtʃ/ n sanguisuga f

leek /liːk/ n porro m

leer /lɪə(r)/ n sguardo m libidinoso ● vi ~ (**at**) guardare in modo libidinoso

lees /liːz/ npl (wine sediment) fondi mpl

leeway /'liːweɪ/ n fig libertà f di azione

left¹ /left/ see **leave**

left² a sinistro ● adv a sinistra ● n also Pol sinistra f; **on the ~** a sinistra

left-hand drive a (car) con la guida a sinistra

left-handed /-'hændɪd/ a mancino; (scissors etc) per mancini

leftie /'leftɪ/ n sinistrorso, -a mf

leftist /'leftɪst/ a & n sinistrorso, -a mf

left: left luggage [office] n deposito m bagagli. **leftovers** npl rimasugli mpl. **left wing** n Pol sinistra f; Sport ala f sinistra. **left-wing** a Pol di sinistra. **left-winger** n Pol persona f di sinistra; Sport ala f sinistra

leg /leg/ n gamba f; (of animal) zampa f; (of journey) tappa f; Culin (of chicken) coscia f; (of lamb) cosciotto m; **be on one's last ~s** (machine:) funzionare per miracolo; **not have a ~ to stand on** non avere una ragione che regga ● vi ~ **it** fam darsela a gambe

legacy /'legəsɪ/ n lascito m

legal /'liːgl/ a legale; **take ~ action** intentare un'azione legale

legal: legal adviser n consulente mf legale. **legal aid** n gratuito patrocinio m. **legal eagle** n hum principe m del foro

legality /lɪ'gælətɪ/ n legalità f

legalization /liːgəlaɪ'zeɪʃn/ n legalizzazione f

legalize /'liːgəlaɪz/ vt legalizzare

legally /'liːgəlɪ/ adv legalmente

legal tender n valuta f a corso legale

legend /'ledʒənd/ n leggenda f

legendary /'ledʒəndərɪ/ a leggendario

leggings /'legɪŋz/ npl (for baby) ghette fpl; (for woman) pantacollant mpl; (for man) gambali mpl

leggy /'legɪ/ a (person) con le gambe lunghe

Leghorn /'leghɔːn/ n Livorno f

legibility /ledʒə'brlətɪ/ n leggibilità f

legible /'ledʒəbl/ a leggibile

legibly /'ledʒəblɪ/ adv in modo leggibile

legion /'liːdʒn/ n legione f

legionnaire /liːdʒə'neə(r)/ n Mil legionario m

legionnaire's disease n legionellosi f

legislate /'ledʒɪsleɪt/ vi legiferare

legislation /ledʒɪs'leɪʃn/ n legislazione f

legislative /'ledʒɪslətɪv/ a legislativo

legislator /'ledʒɪsleɪtə(r)/ n legislatore m

legislature /'ledʒɪsleɪtʃə(r)/ n legislatura f

legitimacy /lɪ'dʒɪtɪməsɪ/ n (lawfulness) legittimità f; (of argument) validità f

legitimate /lɪ'dʒɪtɪmət/ a legittimo; (excuse) valido

legitimately /lɪ'dʒɪtɪmətlɪ/ adv legittimamente

legitimize /lɪdʒɪtɪ'maɪz/ vt rendere legittimo

legless /'leglɪs/ a senza gambe; (Br: drunk) ubriaco fradicio

leg: leg-pulling *n* presa *f* in giro. **legroom** *n* spazio *m* per le gambe. **leg warmer** *n* scaldamuscoli *m inv*. **legwork** *n* fatica *f*; **do the ~** fare da galoppino

leisure /'leʒə(r)/ *n* tempo *m* libero; **at your ~** con comodo

leisure centre *n* centro *m* sportivo e ricreativo

leisurely /'leʒəlɪ/ *a* senza fretta

leisure time *n* tempo *m* libero

leisurewear /'leʒəweə(r)/ *n* abbigliamento *m* per il tempo libero

lemming /'lemɪŋ/ *n* lemming *m inv*

lemon /'lemən/ *n* limone *m*

lemonade /lemə'neɪd/ *n* limonata *f*

lemon: lemon curd *n* crema *f* al limone. **lemon juice** *n* (*drink*) succo *m* di limone. **lemon sole** *n* sogliola *f* limanda. **lemon squash** *n* sciroppo *m* di limone. **lemon tea** *n* tè *m inv* al limone. **lemon yellow** *n* giallo *m* limone ● *a* giallo limone

lend /lend/ *vt* (*pt/pp* **lent**) prestare; **~ a hand** *fig* dare una mano; **~ an ear** prestare ascolto; **~ itself to** prestarsi a

lender /'lendə(r)/ *n* prestatore, -trice *mf*

lending library /'lendɪŋ/ *n* biblioteca *f* per il prestito

length /leŋθ/ *n* lunghezza *f*; (*piece*) pezzo *m*; (*of wallpaper*) parte *f*; (*of visit*) durata *f*; **at ~** a lungo; (*at last*) alla fine

lengthen /'leŋθən/ *vt* allungare ● *vi* allungarsi

lengthways /'leŋθweɪz/ *adv* per lungo

lengthwise /'leŋθwaɪz/ *adv* longitudinale

lengthy /'leŋθɪ/ *a* (**-ier, -iest**) lungo

lenience /'liːnɪəns/ *n* indulgenza *f*

lenient /'liːnɪənt/ *a* indulgente

leniently /'liːnɪəntlɪ/ *adv* con indulgenza

lens /lenz/ *n* lente *f*; *Phot* obiettivo *m*; (*of eye*) cristallino *m*

Lent /lent/ *n* Quaresima *f*

lent *see* **lend**

lentil /'lentl/ *n Bot* lenticchia *f*

Leo /'liːəʊ/ *n Astr* Leone *m*

leopard /'lepəd/ *n* leopardo *m*

leopardskin /'lepədskɪn/ *n* pelle *f* di leopardo ● *attrib* di [pelle di] leopardo

leotard /'liːətɑːd/ *n* body *m inv*

leper /'lepə(r)/ *n* lebbroso, -a *mf*; *fig* appestato, -a *mf*

leprosy /'leprəsɪ/ *n* lebbra *f*

lesbian /'lezbɪən/ *a* lesbico ● *n* lesbica *f*

lesbianism /'lezbɪənɪzm/ *n* lesbismo *m*

lesion /'liːʒn/ *n* lesione *f*

less /les/ *a* meno di; **~ and ~** sempre meno; ● *adv & prep* meno ● *n* meno *m*

lessee /le'siː/ *n Jur* affittuario, -a *mf*

lessen /'lesn/ *vt/i* diminuire

lesser /'lesə(r)/ *a* minore; **the ~ of two evils** il minore fra i due mali

lesson /'lesn/ *n* lezione *f*; **teach sb a ~** *fig* dare una lezione a qcno

lessor /le'sɔː/ *n Jur* locatore, -trice *mf*

lest /lest/ *conj liter* per timore che

let /let/ *vt* (*pt/pp* **let**, *pres p* **letting**) lasciare,

permettere; (*rent*) affittare; **~ alone** (*not to mention*) tanto meno; **'to ~'** 'affittasi'; **~ us go** andiamo; **~ sb do sth** lasciare fare qcsa a qcno, permettere a qcno di fare qcsa; **~ me know** fammi sapere; **just ~ him try!** che ci provi solamente!; **~ oneself go** lasciarsi andare; **~ oneself in for sth** *fam* impelagarsi in qcsa ● *n* Tennis colpo *m* nullo; (*Br*: lease) contratto *m* d'affitto ● *vi* **~ fly at sb** aggredire qcno

■ **let down** *vt* sciogliersi ⟨*hair*⟩; abbassare ⟨*blinds*⟩; (*lengthen*) allungare; (*disappoint*) deludere; **don't ~ me down** conto su di te

■ **let in** *vt* far entrare

■ **let off** *vt* far partire; (*not punish*) perdonare; **~ sb off doing sth** abbonare qcsa a qcno; **~ off steam** *fig* scaricarsi

■ **let on** *vi sl* **don't ~ on** non spifferare niente

■ **let out** *vt* far uscire; (*make larger*) allargare; emettere ⟨*scream, groan*⟩

■ **let through** *vt* far passare

■ **let up** *vi fam* diminuire

let-down *n* delusione *f*

lethal /'liːθl/ *a* letale; **~ dose** *n* dose *f* letale

lethargic /lɪ'θɑːdʒɪk/ *a* apatico

lethargy /'leθədʒɪ/ *n* apatia *f*

let-out *n fam* via *f* d'uscita

letter /'letə(r)/ *n* lettera *f*

letter: letter of apology *n* lettera *f* di scuse. **letter bomb** *n* lettera *f* esplosiva. **letter box** *n* buca *f* per le lettere. **letter of credit** *n Comm* lettera *f* di credito. **letterhead** *n* (*heading*) intestazione *f*; (*paper*) carta *f* intestata

lettering /'letərɪŋ/ *n* caratteri *mpl*

letter of introduction *n* lettera *f* di presentazione

lettuce /'letɪs/ *n* lattuga *f*

let-up *n fam* pausa *f*

leukaemia /luː'kiːmɪə/ *n* leucemia *f*

level /'levl/ *a* piano; (*in height, competition*) allo stesso livello; ⟨*spoonful*⟩ raso; **draw ~ with sb** affiancare qcno; **do one's ~ best** fare del proprio meglio ● *n* livello *m*; **on the ~** *fam* giusto ● *vt* (*pt/pp* **levelled**) livellare; (*aim*) puntare (**at** su)

■ **level off** *vi* ⟨*inflation, unemployment:*⟩ stabilizzarsi

■ **level out** *vi* ⟨*surface:*⟩ diventare pianeggiante; ⟨*aircraft:*⟩ mettersi in orizzontale

■ **level with** *vt* (*fam*: be honest with) essere franco con

level: level crossing *n* passaggio *m* a livello. **level-headed** /-'hedɪd/ *a* posato. **level pegging** *n* **it's ~ ~ so far** finora sono alla pari

lever /'liːvə(r)/ *n* leva *f*

■ **lever off, lever up** *vt* sollevare (*con una leva*)

leverage /'liːvərɪdʒ/ *n* azione *f* di una leva; *fig* influenza *f*

leveret /'levərət/ *n* leprotto *m*

levitate /'levɪteɪt/ *vi* levitare

levity /'levətɪ/ *n* leggerezza *f*

levy /'levi/ vt (pt/pp **levied**) imporre ⟨tax⟩

lewd /lju:d/ a osceno

lexical /'leksɪkəl/ a lessicale

lexicographer /leksɪ'kɒgrəfə(r)/ n lessicografo, -a mf

lexicographic /leksɪkə'græfɪk/ a lessicografico

lexicography /leksɪ'kɒgrəfɪ/ n lessicografia f

lexicon /'leksɪkən/ n lessico m

liability /laɪə'bɪlətɪ/ n responsabilità f; (fam: burden) peso m; **liabilities** pl passività fpl

liable /'laɪəbl/ a responsabile (**for** di); **be ~ to** ⟨rain, break etc⟩ rischiare di; (tend to) tendere a

liaise /lɪ'eɪz/ vi fam essere in contatto

liaison /lɪ'eɪzɒn/ n contatti mpl; Mil collegamento m; (affair) relazione f

liar /'laɪə(r)/ n bugiardo, -a mf

Lib Dem /lɪb'dem/ Br Pol abbr **Liberal Democrat**

libel /'laɪbl/ n diffamazione f ● vt (pt/pp **libelled**) diffamare

libellous /'laɪbələs/ a diffamatorio

liberal /'lɪb(ə)rəl/ a (tolerant) di larghe vedute; (generous) generoso. **L~** a Pol liberale ● n liberale mf

Liberal Democrat n Br Pol liberaldemocratico, -a mf

liberalization /lɪbərəlaɪ'zeɪʃn/ n (of trade) liberalizzazione f

liberalize /'lɪbərəlaɪz/ vt liberalizzare

liberally /'lɪbrəlɪ/ adv liberalmente

liberate /'lɪbəreɪt/ vt liberare

liberated /'lɪbəreɪtɪd/ a ⟨woman⟩ emancipata

liberating /'lɪbəreɪtɪŋ/ a liberatorio

liberation /lɪbə'reɪʃn/ n liberazione f; (of women) emancipazione f

liberator /'lɪbəreɪtə(r)/ n liberatore, -trice mf

libertarian /lɪbə'teərɪən/ a & n liberale nmf

libertarianism /lɪbə'teərɪənɪzm/ n liberalismo m

liberty /'lɪbətɪ/ n libertà f; **take the ~ of doing sth** prendersi la libertà di fare qcsa; **take liberties** prendersi delle libertà; **be at ~ to do sth** essere libero di fare qcsa

libido /lɪ'biːdəʊ/ n libido f inv

Libra /'liːbrə/ n Astr Bilancia f

librarian /laɪ'breərɪən/ n bibliotecario, -a mf

library /'laɪbrərɪ/ n biblioteca f

libretto /lɪ'bretəʊ/ n (pl **-tti** or **-ttos**) libretto m di opera

Libya /'lɪbɪə/ n Libia f

Libyan /'lɪbɪən/ a & n libico, -a mf

lice /laɪs/ see **louse**

licence /'laɪsns/ n licenza f; (for TV) canone m televisivo; (for driving) patente f; (freedom) sregolatezza f

licence number n numero m di targa

licence plate n targa f

license /'laɪsns/ vt autorizzare; **be ~d** ⟨car:⟩ avere il bollo; ⟨restaurant:⟩ essere autorizzato alla vendita di alcolici

licensee /laɪsən'siː/ n titolare mf di licenza (per la vendita di alcolici)

licensing hours /'laɪsənsɪŋ/ npl Br orario m in cui è permessa la vendita di alcolici

licentious /laɪ'senʃəs/ a licenzioso

licentiousness /laɪ'senʃəsnɪs/ n licenziosità f

lichen /'laɪkən/ n Bot lichene m

lick /lɪk/ n leccata f; **a ~ of paint** una passata leggera di pittura ● vt leccare; (fam: defeat) battere; leccarsi ⟨lips⟩; fam **~ sb into shape** rendere qcno efficiente

lid /lɪd/ n coperchio m; (of eye) palpebra f; **keep the ~ on sth** fam non lasciare trapelare qcsa

lido /'liːdəʊ/ n (beach) lido m; (Br: pool) piscina f scoperta

lie[1] /laɪ/ n bugia f; **tell a ~** mentire ● vi (pt/pp **lied**, pres p **lying**) mentire

lie[2] vi (pt **lay**, pp **lain**, pres p **lying**) ⟨person:⟩ sdraiarsi; ⟨object:⟩ stare; (remain) rimanere; **leave sth lying about** or **around** lasciare qcsa in giro; **here ~s...** qui giace...; **~ low** tenersi nascosto

■ **lie back** vi (relax) rilassarsi

■ **lie down** vi sdraiarsi

■ **lie in** vi (stay in bed) rimanere a letto

Liechtenstein /'lɪktənstaɪn/ n Liechtenstein m

lie detector n macchina f della verità

lie-down n **have a ~** fare un riposino

lie-in n fam **have a ~** restare a letto fino a tardi

lieu /lju:/ n **in ~ of** in luogo di

lieutenant /lef'tenənt/ n tenente m

life /laɪf/ n (pl **lives**) vita f; **give one's ~ for sb/one's country** dare la vita per qcno/la patria; **give one's ~ to** (devote oneself to) dedicare la propria vita a; **lose one's ~** perdere la vita; **for dear ~** per salvare la pelle; **not on your ~!** fam neanche morto!

life: life-and-death a ⟨struggle⟩ disperato. **lifebelt** n salvagente m. **lifeblood** n fig linfa f vitale. **lifeboat** n lancia f di salvataggio; (on ship) scialuppa f di salvataggio. **lifebuoy** n salvagente m. **life expectancy** n vita f media. **life form** n forma f di vita. **lifeguard** n (on beach etc) bagnino, -a mf. **life-imprisonment** n ergastolo m. **life insurance** n assicurazione f sulla vita. **life jacket** n giubbotto m di salvataggio

lifeless /'laɪflɪs/ a inanimato

life: lifelike a realistico. **lifeline** n sagola f di salvataggio. **lifelong** a di tutta la vita

lifer /'laɪfə(r)/ n fam ergastolano, -a mf

life: life sentence n condanna f all'ergastolo. **life-size[d]** /'laɪfsaɪz[d]/ a in grandezza naturale. **lifespan** n durata f della vita. **life story** n biografia f. **lifestyle** n stile m di vita. **lifetime** n vita f; **the chance of a ~** l'occasione unica; **~ guarantee** garanzia f a vita

lift /lɪft/ n ascensore m; Auto passaggio m; **give sb a ~** dare un passaggio a qcno; **I got a ~** mi hanno dato un passaggio ● vt sollevare;

revocare ⟨restrictions⟩; (fam: steal) rubare ● vi ⟨fog:⟩ alzarsi

■ **lift off** vi ⟨rocket:⟩ partire

■ **lift up** vt sollevare

liftboy n Br lift m inv

lift-off n decollo m (di razzo)

ligament /'lɪgəmənt/ n Anat legamento m

light[1] /laɪt/ a (not dark) luminoso; ~ **green** verde chiaro ● n luce f; (lamp) lampada f; **in the** ~ **of** alla luce di; **have you got a** ~? ha da accendere?; **come to** ~ essere rivelato ● vt (pt/pp **lit** or **lighted**) accendere; (illuminate) illuminare

■ **light up** vt accendere ⟨pipe, cigarette⟩; illuminare ⟨face⟩; rischiarare ⟨sky⟩ ● vi ⟨face:⟩ illuminarsi

light[2] a (not heavy) leggero; **make** ~ **of** non dare peso a ● adv travel ~ viaggiare con poco bagaglio

light bulb n lampadina f

lighten[1] /'laɪtn/ vt illuminare

lighten[2] vt alleggerire ⟨load⟩

light entertainment n varietà m inv

lighter /'laɪtə(r)/ n accendino m

lighter fuel n (liquid) gas m inv da accendino

light: light-fingered /-'fɪŋgəd/ a svelto di mano. **light-headed** /-'hedɪd/ a sventato. **light-hearted** /-'hɑ:tɪd/ a spensierato. **lighthouse** n faro m. **light industry** n industria f leggera

lighting /'laɪtɪŋ/ n illuminazione f

lightly /'laɪtlɪ/ adv leggermente; ⟨accuse⟩ con leggerezza; ⟨take sth⟩ alla leggera; (without concern) senza dare importanza alla cosa; **get off** ~ cavarsela a buon mercato

lightness /'laɪtnɪs/ n leggerezza f

lightning /'laɪtnɪŋ/ n lampo m, fulmine m

lightning conductor n parafulmine m

lightning strike n sciopero m a sorpresa

light: light-pen n (for computer screen) penna f ottica. **lightweight** a leggero ● n (in boxing) peso m leggero. **light year** n anno m luce; **it was** ~ ~**s ago** è stato secoli fa

like[1] /laɪk/ a simile ● prep come; ~ **this/that** così; **what's he** ~? com'è? ● conj (fam: as) come; (Am: as if) come se

like[2] vt piacere, gradire; **I should** or **would** ~ vorrei, gradirei; **I** ~ **him** mi piace; **I** ~ **this car** mi piace questa macchina; **I** ~ **dancing** mi piace ballare; **I** ~ **that!** fam questa mi è piaciuta!; ~ **it** or **lump it!** abbozzala! ● n ~**s and dislikes** pl gusti mpl

likeable /'laɪkəbl/ a simpatico

likelihood /'laɪklɪhʊd/ n probabilità f

likely /'laɪklɪ/ a (-ier, -iest) probabile ● adv probabilmente; **not** ~! fam neanche per sogno!

like-minded /laɪk'maɪndɪd/ a con gusti affini

liken /'laɪkən/ vt paragonare (to a)

likeness /'laɪknɪs/ n somiglianza f

likewise /'laɪkwaɪz/ adv lo stesso

liking /'laɪkɪŋ/ n gusto m; **is it to your** ~? è di suo gusto?; **take a** ~ **to sb** prendere qcno in simpatia

lilac /'laɪlək/ n lillà m ● a color lillà

Lilo® /'laɪləʊ/ n materassino m gonfiabile

lilting /'lɪltɪŋ/ a cadenzato

lily /'lɪlɪ/ n giglio m

lily of the valley n mughetto m

lily pond n stagno m con ninfee

limb /lɪm/ n arto m

limber /'lɪmbə(r)/ vi ~ **up** sciogliersi i muscoli

limbo /'lɪmbəʊ/ n (Relig, fig, dance) limbo m; **be in** ~ ⟨person:⟩ essere nel limbo del dubbio; ⟨future of sth:⟩ essere in sospeso

lime[1] /laɪm/ n (fruit) cedro m; (tree) tiglio m

lime[2] n calce f

lime: lime-green a & n verde m limone.

limelight /'laɪmlaɪt/ n **be in the** ~ essere molto in vista. **limestone** /'laɪmstəʊn/ n calcare m

limit /'lɪmɪt/ n limite m; **be the** ~! fam questo è troppo! ● vt limitare (**to** a)

limitation /lɪmɪ'teɪʃn/ n limite m

limited /'lɪmɪtɪd/ a ristretto

limited: limited company n società f inv a responsabilità limitata. **limited edition** n (book, lithograph) edizione f limitata. **limited liability** n responsabilità f limitata

limitless /'lɪmɪtlɪs/ a infinito

limousine /'lɪməzi:n/ n limousine f inv

limp[1] /lɪmp/ n andatura f zoppicante; **have a** ~ zoppicare ● vi zoppicare

limp[2] a floscio

limpet /'lɪmpɪt/ n **be like a** ~ fig essere attaccaticcio

limpid /'lɪmpɪd/ a limpido

limp-wristed /-'rɪstɪd/ a pej effeminato

linchpin /'lɪntʃpɪn/ n (fig: essential element) perno m

line[1] /laɪn/ n linea f; (length of rope, cord) filo m; (of writing) riga f; (of poem) verso m; (row) fila f; (wrinkle) ruga f; (of business) settore m; (Am: queue) coda f; **in** ~ **with** in conformità con; **bring into** ~ mettere al passo ⟨structure, law⟩; **in the** ~ **of duty** (of policeman) nell'esercizio delle proprie funzioni; ~ **of fire** linea f di tiro; **stand in** ~ (Am: queue) fare la coda; **in** ~ **for** ⟨promotion etc⟩ in lista per; **on the** ~ ⟨job, career⟩ in serio pericolo; **read between the** ~**s** fig leggere tra le righe ● vt segnare; fiancheggiare ⟨street⟩; foderare ⟨garment⟩

■ **line up** vi allinearsi ● vt allineare

lineage /'lɪnɪdʒ/ n lignaggio m

linear /'lɪnɪə(r)/ a lineare

lined[1] /laɪnd/ a ⟨face⟩ rugoso; ⟨paper⟩ a righe

lined[2] a ⟨garment⟩ foderato

line manager n line manager m inv

linen /'lɪnɪn/ n lino m; (articles) biancheria f ● attrib di lino

linen basket n cesto m della biancheria

liner /'laɪnə(r)/ n nave f di linea

linesman /'laɪnzmən/ n Sport guardalinee m inv

line-up n (personnel, Sport) formazione f; (identification) confronto m all'americana

linger /'lɪŋgə(r)/ *vi* indugiare
lingerie /'lɒʒərɪ/ *n* biancheria *f* intima (*da donna*)
lingering /'lɪŋgərɪŋ/ *a* ‹*illness*› lento; ‹*look*› prolungato; ‹*doubt*› persistente
linguist /'lɪŋgwɪst/ *n* linguista *mf*
linguistic /lɪŋ'gwɪstɪk/ *a* linguistico
linguistically /lɪŋ'gwɪstɪklɪ/ *adv* linguisticamente
linguistics /lɪŋ'gwɪstɪks/ *n* linguistica *fsg*
lining /'laɪnɪŋ/ *n* (*of garment*) fodera *f*; (*of brakes*) guarnizione *f*
link /lɪŋk/ *n* (*of chain*) anello *m*; *fig* legame *m* ● *vt* collegare; ~ **arms** prendersi sotto braccio
■ **link up** *vi* unirsi (**with** a); *TV* collegarsi
linkage /'lɪŋkɪdʒ/ *n* (*connection*) connessione *f*; (*in genetics*) associazione *f*
links /lɪŋks/ *n or npl* campo *msg* da golf
link-up *n* collegamento *m*
lino /'laɪnəʊ/ *n*, **linoleum** /lɪ'nəʊlɪəm/ *n* linoleum *m*
linseed oil /'lɪnsiːdɔɪl/ *n* olio *m* [di semi] di lino
lint /lɪnt/ *n* garza *f*
lintel /'lɪntəl/ *n* architrave *m*
lion /'laɪən/ *n* leone *m*; **get the ~'s share** *fig* prendersi la fetta più grossa
lion cub *n* leoncino *m*
lioness /'laɪənɪs/ *n* leonessa *f*
lip /lɪp/ *n* labbro *m* (*pl* labbra *f*); (*edge*) bordo *m*
lip gloss *n* lucidalabbra *m inv*
liposuction /'laɪpəʊsʌkʃn/ *n* liposuzione *f*
lip: lip-read *vi* leggere le labbra. **lip-reading** *n* lettura *f* delle labbra. **lipsalve** *n* burro *m* [di] cacao. **lip-service** *n* **pay ~ to** approvare soltanto a parole. **lipstick** *n* rossetto *m*
liquefy /'lɪkwɪfaɪ/ *v* (*pt/pp* -**ied**) ● *vt* liquefare ● *vi* liquefarsi
liqueur /lɪ'kjʊə(r)/ *n* liquore *m*
liquid /'lɪkwɪd/ *n* liquido *m* ● *a* liquido
liquidate /'lɪkwɪdeɪt/ *vt* liquidare
liquidation /lɪkwɪ'deɪʃn/ *n* liquidazione *f*; **go into ~** *Comm* andare in liquidazione
liquidator /'lɪkwɪdeɪtə(r)/ *n* liquidatore, -trice *mf*
liquid crystal display *n* visualizzatore *m* a cristalli liquidi
liquidize /'lɪkwɪdaɪz/ *vt* rendere liquido
liquidizer /'lɪkwɪdaɪzə(r)/ *n Culin* frullatore *m*
liquor /'lɪkə(r)/ *n* bevanda *f* alcoolica
liquorice /'lɪkərɪs/ *n* liquirizia *f*
liquor store *n Am* negozio *m* di alcolici
lira /'lɪərə/ *n* lira *f*; **50,000 lire** 50.000 lire
lisp /lɪsp/ *n* pronuncia *f* con la lisca; **have a ~** parlare con la lisca ● *vi* parlare con la lisca
list¹ /lɪst/ *n* lista *f* ● *vt* elencare
list² *vi* ‹*ship:*› inclinarsi
listen /'lɪsn/ *vi* ascoltare; ~ **to** ascoltare
listener /'lɪs(ə)nə(r)/ *n* ascoltatore, -trice *mf*
listeria /lɪ'stɪərɪə/ *n* (*illness*) listeriosi *f*; (*bacteria*) listeria *f*
listings /'lɪstɪŋz/ *npl TV* programma *m* tv
listless /'lɪstlɪs/ *a* svogliato
listlessly /'lɪstlɪslɪ/ *adv* in modo svogliato

lit /lɪt/ *see* **light¹**
litany /'lɪtənɪ/ *n* litania *f*
literacy /'lɪtərəsɪ/ *n* alfabetizzazione *f*
literal /'lɪtərəl/ *a* letterale
literally /'lɪt(ə)rəlɪ/ *adv* letteralmente
literary /'lɪtərərɪ/ *a* letterario
literary critic *n* critico, -a *mf* letterario, -a
literate /'lɪtərət/ *a* **be ~** saper leggere e scrivere
literati /lɪtə'rɑːtiː/ *npl* letterati *mpl*
literature /'lɪtrətʃə(r)/ *n* letteratura *f*
lithe /laɪð/ *a* flessuoso
lithographer /lɪ'θɒgrəfə(r)/ *n* litografo, -a *mf*
lithography /lɪ'θɒgrəfɪ/ *n* litografia *f*
Lithuania /lɪθjʊ'eɪnɪə/ *n* Lituania *f*
Lithuanian /lɪθjʊ'eɪnɪən/ *a & n* lituano, -a *mf*; (*language*) lituano *m*
litigation /lɪtɪ'geɪʃn/ *n* causa *f* [giudiziaria]
litmus paper /'lɪtməs/ *n* cartina *f* di tornasole
litmus test *n Chem* test *m inv* con cartina di tornasole; *fig* prova *f* del nove
litre /'liːtə(r)/ *n* litro *m*
litter /'lɪtə(r)/ *n* immondizie *fpl*; *Zool* figliata *f* ● *vt* **be ~ed with sth** essere ingombrato di qcsa
litter-bin *n* bidone *m* della spazzatura
litterbug /'lɪtəbʌg/ *n persona f che butta per terra cartacce e rifiuti*
little /'lɪtl/ *a* piccolo; (*not much*) poco ● *adv* & *n* poco *m*; **a ~** un po'; **a ~ water** un po' d'acqua; **a ~ better** un po' meglio; ~ **by ~** a poco a poco
little finger *n* mignolo *m* (*della mano*)
little-known *a* poco noto
liturgical /lɪ'tɜːdʒɪkl/ *a* liturgico
liturgy /'lɪtədʒɪ/ *n* liturgia *f*
live¹ /laɪv/ *a* vivo; ‹*ammunition*› carico; ~ **broadcast** trasmissione *f* in diretta; **be ~** *Electr* essere sotto tensione; ~ **wire** *n fig* persona *f* dinamica ● *adv* ‹*broadcast*› in diretta
live² /lɪv/ *vi* vivere; (*reside*) abitare; ~ **with** convivere con
■ **live down** *vt* far dimenticare
■ **live for** *vt* vivere solo per ‹*one's work, family*›
■ **live off** *vt* vivere alle spalle di
■ **live on** *vt* vivere di ● *vi* sopravvivere
■ **live through** *vt* vivere
■ **live together** *vi* ‹*friends:*› vivere insieme; ‹*lovers:*› convivere
■ **live up** *vt* ~ **it up** far la bella vita
■ **live up to** *vt* essere all'altezza di
■ **live with** *vt* convivere con ‹*lover, situation*›; vivere con ‹*mother etc*›
lived-in /'lɪvdɪn/ *a* **have that ~ look** ‹*room, flat:*› avere un'aria vissuta
live-in *a* ‹*maid, nanny*› che vive in casa
livelihood /'laɪvlɪhʊd/ *n* mezzi *mpl* di sostentamento
liveliness /'laɪvlɪnɪs/ *n* vivacità *f*
lively /'laɪvlɪ/ *a* (-**ier**, -**iest**) vivace
■ **liven up** /'laɪvn/ *vt* vivacizzare ● *vi* vivacizzarsi

liver /'lɪvə(r)/ n fegato m
liver pâté n pâté m inv di fegato
Liverpudlian /lɪvə'pʌdlɪən/ n (born there) originario, -a mf di Liverpool; (living there) abitante mf di Liverpool
lives /laɪvz/ see **life**
livestock /'laɪvstɒk/ n bestiame m
livid /'lɪvɪd/ a fam livido
living /'lɪvɪŋ/ a vivo ● n **earn one's ~** guadagnarsi da vivere; **the ~** pl i vivi
living room n soggiorno m
lizard /'lɪzəd/ n lucertola f
load /ləʊd/ n carico m; **~s of** fam un sacco di; **that's a ~ off my mind** mi sono tolto un peso [dallo stomaco] ● vt ~ **[up]** caricare
loaded /'ləʊdɪd/ a carico; (fam: rich) ricchissimo; **~ question** domanda f esplosiva f
loading bay /'ləʊdɪŋ/ n piazzola f di carico e scarico
loaf[1] /ləʊf/ n (pl **loaves**) pane m; (round) pagnotta f; **use one's ~** (fam) pensare con il proprio cervello
loaf[2] vi oziare
loafer /'ləʊfə(r)/ n (idler) scansafatiche mf inv; (shoe) mocassino m
loan /ləʊn/ n prestito m; **on ~** in prestito ● vt prestare
loan shark n fam strozzino, -a mf
loath /ləʊθ/ a **be ~ to do sth** essere restio a fare qcsa
loathe /ləʊð/ vt detestare
loathing /'ləʊðɪŋ/ n disgusto m
loathsome /'ləʊðsəm/ a disgustoso
loaves /ləʊvz/ see **loaf**
lob /lɒb/ vt (pres p etc **-bb-**) lanciare in alto; Sport respingere a pallonetto ● n Sport pallonetto m
lobby /'lɒbɪ/ n atrio m; Pol gruppo m di pressione, lobby m inv
lobbyist /'lɒbɪɪst/ n lobbista mf
lobe /ləʊb/ n (of ear) lobo m
lobelia /lə'bi:lɪə/ n lobelia f
lobster /'lɒbstə(r)/ n aragosta f
lobster pot n nassa f per aragoste
local /'ləʊkl/ a locale; **under ~ anaesthetic** sotto anestesia locale; **I'm not ~** non sono del posto ● n abitante mf del luogo; (fam: public house) pub m inv locale
local: **local authority** n autorità f locale. **local bus** n bus m locale. **local call** n Teleph telefonata f urbana. **local government** n autorità f inv locale. **local network** n Comput rete f locale
locality /ləʊ'kælətɪ/ n zona f
localized /'ləʊkəlaɪzd/ a localizzato
locally /'ləʊkəlɪ/ adv localmente; ⟨live, work⟩ nei paraggi
locate /ləʊ'keɪt/ vt situare; trovare ⟨person⟩; **be ~d** essere situato
location /ləʊ'keɪʃn/ n posizione f; **filmed on ~** girato in esterni
loch /lɒx/ n lago m
lock[1] /lɒk/ n (of hair) ciocca f
lock[2] n (on door) serratura f; (on canal) chiu-

sa f ● vt chiudere a chiave; bloccare ⟨wheels⟩ ● vi chiudersi
■ **lock in** vt chiudere dentro
■ **lock out** vt chiudere fuori
■ **lock up** vt (in prison) mettere dentro ● vi chiudere
locker /'lɒkə(r)/ n armadietto m
locket /'lɒkɪt/ n medaglione m
lock: **lockout** n serrata f. **locksmith** n fabbro m. **lock-up** n (prison) guardina f
loco /'ləʊkəʊ/ a (Br: crazy) toccato
locomotion /ləʊkə'məʊʃn/ n locomozione f
locomotive /ləʊkə'məʊtɪv/ n locomotiva f
locum /'ləʊkəm/ n sostituto, -a mf
locust /'ləʊkəst/ n locusta f
lodge /lɒdʒ/ n (porter's) portineria f; (masonic) loggia f ● vt presentare ⟨claim, complaint⟩; (with bank, solicitor) depositare; **be ~d** essersi conficcato ● vi essere a pensione (**with** da); (become fixed) conficcarsi
lodger /'lɒdʒə(r)/ n inquilino, -a mf
lodgings /'lɒdʒɪŋ/ npl camere fpl in affitto
loft /lɒft/ n soffitta f
lofty /'lɒftɪ/ a (**-ier**, **-iest**) alto; (haughty) altezzoso
log /lɒg/ n ceppo m; Auto libretto m di circolazione; Naut giornale m di bordo; **sleep like a ~** fam dormire come un ghiro ● vt (pt/pp **logged**) registrare
■ **log in** vi aprire una sessione
■ **log off** vi disconnettersi
■ **log on** vi connettersi (**to** a)
■ **log out** vi chiudere una sessione
logarithm /'lɒgərɪðm/ n logaritmo m
logbook /'lɒgbʊk/ n Naut giornale m di bordo; Auto libretto m di circolazione
logger /'lɒgə(r)/ n boscaiolo m
loggerheads /'lɒgəhedz/ npl **be at ~** fam essere in totale disaccordo
logic /'lɒdʒɪk/ n logica f
logical /'lɒdʒɪkl/ a logico
logically /'lɒdʒɪklɪ/ adv logicamente
logistics /lə'dʒɪstɪks/ npl logistica f
logo /'ləʊgəʊ/ n logo m inv
loin /lɔɪn/ n Culin lombata f
loin chop n lombatina f
loincloth /'lɔɪnklɒθ/ n perizoma m
loiter /'lɔɪtə(r)/ vi gironzolare
loll /lɒl/ vi **~ about** (posture) stravaccarsi; (do nothing) starsene in panciolle
lollipop /'lɒlɪpɒp/ n lecca-lecca m inv
lollop /'lɒləp/ vi ⟨rabbit, person:⟩ avanzare a balzi
lolly /'lɒlɪ/ n lecca-lecca m inv; (fam: money) quattrini mpl
Lombardy /'lɒmbədɪ/ n Lombardia f
London /'lʌndən/ n Londra f ● attrib londinese, di Londra
Londoner /'lʌndənə(r)/ n londinese mf
lone /ləʊn/ a solitario
loneliness /'ləʊnlɪnɪs/ n solitudine f
lonely /'ləʊnlɪ/ a (**-ier**, **-iest**) solitario; ⟨person⟩ solo
loner /'ləʊnə(r)/ n persona f solitaria
lonesome /'ləʊnsəm/ a solo

long¹ /lɒŋ/ *a* (**-er** /'lɒŋgə(r)/, **-est** /'lɒŋgɪst/) lungo; **a ~ time** molto tempo; **a ~ way** distante; **in the ~ run** a lungo andare; (*in the end*) alla fin fine ● *adv* a lungo, lungamente; **how ~ is it?** quanto è lungo?; (*in time*) quanto dura?; **all day ~** tutto il giorno; **not ~ ago** non molto tempo fa; **before ~** fra breve; **he's no ~er here** non è più qui; **as** *or* **so ~ as** finché; (*provided that*) purché; **so ~!** *fam* ciao!; **will you be ~?** ti ci vuole molto?

long² *vi* **~ for** desiderare ardentemente

long: long-awaited *a* tanto atteso. **long-distance** *a* a grande distanza; *Sport* di fondo; (*call*) interurbano. **long division** *n* divisione *f*

longevity /lɒn'dʒevəti/ *n* longevità *f*

long: long face *n* muso *m* lungo. **longhand** /'lɒŋhænd/ *n* **in ~** in scrittura ordinaria. **long-haul** *attrib* su lunga distanza; (*plane*) per lunghi tragitti

longing /'lɒŋɪŋ/ *a* desideroso ● *n* brama *f*

longingly /'lɒŋɪŋlɪ/ *adv* con desiderio

longitude /'lɒŋgɪtjuːd/ *n Geog* longitudine *f*

long: long-life milk *n* latte *m* a lunga conservazione. **long-lived** /-'lɪvd/ *a* longevo. **long jump** *n* salto *m* in lungo. **long-playing record** *n* 33 giri *m inv*. **long-range** *a Mil, Aeron* a lunga portata; (*forecast*) a lungo termine. **long-sighted** /-'saɪtɪd/ *a* presbite. **long-sleeved** /-'sliːvd/ *a* a maniche lunghe. **long-standing** *a* di vecchia data. **long-suffering** *a* infinitamente paziente. **long-term** *a* a lunga scadenza. **long wave** *n* onde *fpl* lunghe. **long-winded** /-'wɪndɪd/ *a* prolisso

loo /luː/ *n fam* gabinetto *m*

look /lʊk/ *n* occhiata *f*; (*appearance*) aspetto *m*; [**good**] **~s** *pl* bellezza *f*; **have a ~ at** dare un'occhiata a ● *vi* guardare; (*seem*) sembrare; **~ here!** mi ascolti bene!; **~ at** guardare; **~ for** cercare; **~ sb in the eye** guardare negli occhi qcno; **~ sb up and down** guardare qcno dall'alto in basso; **~ a fool** fare la figura del cretino; **~ young/old for one's age** portarsi bene/male gli anni; **~ like** (*resemble*) assomigliare a; **it ~s as if it's going to rain** sembra che stia per piovere; **~ sharp** (*fam: hurry up*) darsi una mossa

■ **look after** *vt* badare a

■ **look ahead** *vi* (*think of the future*) guardare al futuro

■ **look back** *vi* girarsi; (*think of the past*) guardare indietro

■ **look down** *vi* guardare in basso; **~ down on sb** *fig* guardare dall'alto in basso qcno

■ **look forward to** *vt* essere impaziente di

■ **look in on** *vt* passare da

■ **look into** *vt* (*examine*) esaminare

■ **look on** *vi* (*watch*) guardare ● *vt* **~ sb/sth as** (*consider to be*) considerare qcno/qcsa come

■ **look on to** *vt* (*room:*) dare su

■ **look out** *vi* guardare fuori; (*take care*) fare attenzione; **~ out!** attento! ● *vt* cercare (*sth for sb*)

■ **look out for** *vt* cercare

■ **look over** *vt* riguardare (*notes*); ispezionare (*house*)

■ **look round** *vi* girarsi; (*in shop, town etc*) dare un'occhiata

■ **look through** *vt* dare un'occhiata a (*script, notes*)

■ **look to** *vt* (*rely on*) contare su

■ **look up** *vi* guardare in alto ● *vt* cercare [nel dizionario] (*word*); (*visit*) andare a trovare

■ **look up to** *vt fig* rispettare

look-alike *n* sosia *mf inv*

looker-on /lʊkər'ɒn/ *n* (*pl* **lookers-on**) spettatore, -trice *mf*

look-in *n Br fam* **give sb a ~** dare una chance a qcno; **get a ~** avere una chance

lookout /'lʊkaʊt/ *n* guardia *f*; (*prospect*) prospettiva *f*; **be on the ~ for** tenere gli occhi aperti per

loom¹ /luːm/ *n* telaio *m*

loom² *vi* apparire; *fig* profilarsi

loony /'luːnɪ/ *a & n fam* matto, -a *mf*; **~ bin** manicomio *m*

loop /luːp/ *n* cappio *m*; (*on garment*) passante *m*

loophole /'luːphəʊl/ *n* (*in the law*) scappatoia *f*

loopy /'luːpɪ/ *a fam* matto

loose /luːs/ *a* libero; (*knot*) allentato; (*page*) staccato; (*clothes*) largo; (*morals*) dissoluto; (*inexact*) vago; **be at a ~ end** non sapere cosa fare; **come ~** (*knot:*) sciogliersi; **set ~** liberare

loose: loose change *n* spiccioli *mpl*. **loose chippings** *npl* ghiaino *m*. **loose-leaf notebook** *n* raccoglitore *m* di fogli

loosely /'luːslɪ/ *adv* scorrevolmente; (*defined*) vagamente

loosen /'luːsn/ *vt* sciogliere

■ **loosen up** *vt* sciogliere (*muscles*) ● *vi* (*fam: relax*) rilassarsi

loot /luːt/ *n* bottino *m* ● *vt/i* depredare

looter /'luːtə(r)/ *n* predatore, -trice *mf*

looting /'luːtɪŋ/ *n* saccheggio *m*

■ **lop off** /lɒp/ *vt* (*pt/pp* **lopped**) potare

lop-eared /'lɒpɪəd/ *a* con le orecchie [a] penzoloni

■ **lope off** /ləʊp'ɒf/ *vi* andarsene a passi lunghi

lopsided /lɒp'saɪdɪd/ *a* sbilenco

loquacious /lə'kweɪʃəs/ *a* loquace

lord /lɔːd/ *n* signore *m*; (*title*) Lord *m*; **House of L~s** Camera *f* dei Lords; **the L~'s Prayer** il Padrenostro; **good L~!** Dio mio!

Lordship /'lɔːdʃɪp/ *n* **your/his ~** (*of noble*) Sua Signoria; **your ~** (*to judge*) Signor Giudice

lore /lɔː(r)/ *n* tradizioni *fpl*

lorry /'lɒrɪ/ *n* camion *m inv*

lorry driver *n* camionista *mf*

lose /luːz/ *v* (*pt/pp* **lost**) ● *vt* perdere; **~ heart** perdersi d'animo; **~ one's inhibitions** disinibirsi; **~ one's nerve** farsi prendere dalla paura; **~ sight of** perdere di vista, perdere d'occhio; **~ touch with** perdere di vista; **~ track of time** perdere la nozione del tempo; **~ weight** calare di peso ● *vi* perdere; ⟨*clock:*⟩ essere indietro

■ **lose out** *vi* rimetterci

loser /'luːzə(r)/ *n* perdente *mf*

losing battle /'luːzɪŋ/ *n* battaglia *f* persa

loss /lɒs/ *n* perdita *f*; **~es** *pl* Comm perdite *fpl*; **be at a ~** essere perplesso; **be at a ~ for words** non trovare le parole; **make a ~** Comm subire una perdita

loss: **loss adjuster** /'lɒsədʒˌʌstə(r)/ *n* Comm perito *m* di assicurazione. **loss-leader** *n* articolo *m* civetta. **loss-making** /'lɒsmeɪkɪŋ/ *a* ⟨*company*⟩ in passivo; ⟨*product*⟩ che non vende

lost /lɒst/ *see* **lose** ● *a* perduto; **get ~** perdersi; **get ~!** *fam* va a quel paese!

lost and found *n Am* oggetti *mpl* smarriti

lost property office *n* ufficio *m* oggetti smarriti

lot[1] /lɒt/ ⟨*at auction*⟩ lotto *m*; ⟨*piece of land*⟩ lotto *m*; **draw ~s** tirare a sorte

lot[2] *n* **the ~** il tutto; **a ~ of**, **~s of** molti; **the ~ of you** tutti voi; **it has changed a ~** è cambiato molto

lotion /'ləʊʃn/ *n* lozione *f*

lottery /'lɒtərɪ/ *n* lotteria *f*

lottery ticket *n* biglietto *m* della lotteria

loud /laʊd/ *a* sonoro, alto; ⟨*colours*⟩ sgargiante ● *adv* forte; **out ~** ad alta voce

loud hailer /'heɪlə(r)/ *n* megafono *m*

loudly /'laʊdlɪ/ *adv* forte

loudspeaker /laʊd'spiːkə(r)/ *n* altoparlante *m*

lounge /laʊndʒ/ *n* salotto *m*; ⟨*in hotel*⟩ salone *m* ● *vi* poltrire

■ **lounge about** *vi* stare in panciolle

lounge suit *n* vestito *m* da uomo ⟨*formale*⟩

louse /laʊs/ *n* ⟨*pl* **lice**⟩ pidocchio *m*

■ **louse up** *vt* ⟨*fam: ruin*⟩ guastare

lousy /'laʊzɪ/ *a* (**-ier, -iest**) *fam* schifoso

lout /laʊt/ *n* zoticone *m*

loutish /'laʊtɪʃ/ *a* rozzo

louvred /'luːvəd/ *a* ⟨*door, blinds*⟩ con le gelosie

lovable /'lʌvəbl/ *a* adorabile

love /lʌv/ *n* amore *m*; ⟨*Tennis*⟩ zero *m*; **in ~** innamorato (**with** di) ● *vt* amare ⟨*person, country*⟩; **I ~ watching tennis** mi piace molto guardare il tennis

love: **love affair** *n* relazione *f* [sentimentale]. **lovebite** *n* succhiotto *m*. **love letter** *n* lettera *f* d'amore. **love life** *n* vita *f* sentimentale. **lovemaking** *n* il fare l'amore

lovely /'lʌvlɪ/ *a* (**-ier, -iest**) bello; ⟨*in looks*⟩ bello, attraente; ⟨*in character*⟩ piacevole; ⟨*meal*⟩ delizioso; **have a ~ time** divertirsi molto

lover /'lʌvə(r)/ *n* amante *mf*

love song *n* canzone *f* d'amore

love story *n* storia *f* d'amore

lovey-dovey /lʌvɪ'dʌvɪ/ *a Br fam* **get all ~** fare i piccioncini

loving /'lʌvɪŋ/ *a* affettuoso

lovingly /'lʌvɪŋlɪ/ *adv* affettuosamente

low /ləʊ/ *a* basso; ⟨*depressed*⟩ giù *inv* ● *adv*

basso; **feel ~** sentirsi giù ● *n* minimo *m*; *Meteorol* depressione *f*; **at an all-time ~** ⟨*prices etc*⟩ al livello minimo

low: **lowbrow** /'ləʊbraʊ/ *a* di scarsa cultura. **low-calorie** *a* ipocalorico. **low-cut** *a* ⟨*dress*⟩ scollato. **low gear** *n Auto* marcia *f* bassa

lower /'ləʊə(r)/ *a & adv see* **low** ● *vt* abbassare; **~ oneself** abbassarsi

lowest common denominator /'ləʊɪst ...dɪ'nɒmɪneɪtə(r)/ *n* minimo denominatore *m* comune

low: **low-fat** *a* ⟨*diet*⟩ a basso contenuto di grassi; ⟨*cheese, milk*⟩ magro. **low-grade** *a* di qualità inferiore. **low-key** *a* fig moderato. **lowlands** *npl* pianure *fpl*

lowly /'ləʊlɪ/ *a* (**-ier, -iest**) umile

low tide *n* bassa marea *f*

loyal /'lɔɪəl/ *a* leale

loyally /'lɔɪəlɪ/ *adv* lealmente

loyalty /'lɔɪəltɪ/ *n* lealtà *f*

lozenge /'lɒzɪndʒ/ *n* losanga *f*; ⟨*tablet*⟩ pastiglia

LP *n abbr* (**long-playing record**) LP *m inv*

L-plate *n Br Auto* cartello *m* che indica che il conducente non ha ancora preso la patente

LSD *n* LSD *m*

Ltd *abbr* (**Limited**) s.r.l.

lubricant /'luːbrɪkənt/ *n* lubrificante *m*

lubricate /'luːbrɪkeɪt/ *vt* lubrificare

lubrication /luːbrɪ'keɪʃn/ *n* lubrificazione *f*

lucid /'luːsɪd/ *a* ⟨*explanation*⟩ chiaro; ⟨*sane*⟩ lucido

lucidity /luː'sɪdətɪ/ *n* lucidità *f*; ⟨*of explanation*⟩ chiarezza *f*

luck /lʌk/ *n* fortuna *f*; **bad ~** sfortuna *f*; **good ~!** buona fortuna!

luckily /'lʌkɪlɪ/ *adv* fortunatamente

lucky /'lʌkɪ/ *a* (**-ier, -iest**) fortunato; **be ~** essere fortunato; ⟨*thing:*⟩ portare fortuna

lucky charm *n* portafortuna *m inv*

lucky dip *n* pesca *f* di beneficenza

lucrative /'luːkrətɪv/ *a* lucrativo

lucre /'luːkə(r)/ *n* ⟨*fam: money*⟩ soldi *mpl*

ludicrous /'luːdɪkrəs/ *a* ridicolo

ludicrously /'luːdɪkrəslɪ/ *adv* ⟨*expensive, complex*⟩ eccessivamente

ludo /'luːdəʊ/ *n Br* gioco *m* da tavola

lug /lʌg/ *vt* (*pt/pp* **lugged**) *fam* trascinare

luggage /'lʌgɪdʒ/ *n* bagaglio *m*

luggage: **luggage-rack** *n* portabagagli *m inv*. **luggage trolley** *n* carrello *m* portabagagli. **luggage van** *n* bagagliaio *m*

lughole /'lʌghəʊl/ *n* ⟨*Br fam: ear*⟩ orecchio *m*

lugubrious /lʊ'guːbrɪəs/ *a* lugubre

lukewarm /'luːkwɔːm/ *a* tiepido; fig poco entusiasta

lull /lʌl/ *n* pausa *f* ● *vt* **~ to sleep** cullare

lullaby /'lʌləbaɪ/ *n* ninnananna *f*

lumbago /lʌm'beɪgəʊ/ *n* lombaggine *f*

lumbar /'lʌmbə(r)/ *a* lombare

lumber /'lʌmbə(r)/ *n* cianfrusaglie *fpl*; ⟨*Am: timber*⟩ legname *m* ● *vt fam* **~ sb with sth** affibbiare qcsa a qcno

lumberjack /'lʌmbədʒæk/ *n* tagliaboschi *m inv*

luminary /'lu:mɪnərɪ/ n (fig: person) lumina-re mf

luminous /'lu:mɪnəs/ a luminoso

lump¹ /lʌmp/ n (of sugar) zolletta f; (swelling) gonfiore m; (in breast) nodulo m; (in sauce) grumo m; **a ~ in one's throat** un groppo alla gola ● vt ~ **together** ammucchiare

lump² vt ~ **it** fam **you'll just have to ~ it** che ti piaccia o no è così

lump sugar n zucchero m in zollette

lump sum n somma f globale

lumpy /'lʌmpɪ/ a (-ier, -iest) grumoso

lunacy /'lu:nəsɪ/ n follia f

lunar /'lu:nə(r)/ a lunare

lunatic /'lu:nətɪk/ n pazzo, -a mf

lunch /lʌntʃ/ n pranzo m; **she's gone to ~** è andata a pranzo; **let's have ~ together sometime** pranziamo qualche volta insieme ● vi pranzare

lunch box n cestino m del pranzo

luncheon /'lʌntʃn/ n (formal) pranzo m

luncheon meat n carne f in scatola

luncheon voucher n buono m pasto

lunch hour n intervallo m per il pranzo

lunchtime /'lʌntʃtaɪm/ n ora f di pranzo

lung /lʌŋ/ n polmone m

lung cancer n cancro m al polmone

lunge /lʌndʒ/ vi lanciarsi (**at** su)

lurch¹ /lɜ:tʃ/ n **leave in the ~** fam lasciare nei guai

lurch² vi barcollare

lure /lʊə(r)/ n esca f; fig lusinga f ● vt adescare

lurid /'lʊərɪd/ a (gaudy) sgargiante; (sensational) sensazionalistico

lurk /lɜ:k/ vi appostarsi

luscious /'lʌʃəs/ a saporito; fig sexy inv

lush /lʌʃ/ a lussureggiante

lust /lʌst/ n lussuria f ● vi ~ **after** desiderare [fortemente]

lustful /'lʌstfʊl/ a lussurioso

lustre /'lʌstə(r)/ n lustro m

lusty /'lʌstɪ/ a (-ier, -iest) vigoroso

lute /lu:t/ n liuto m

Luxembourg /'lʌksəmbɜ:g/ n (city) Lus-semburgo f; (state) Lussemburgo m

luxuriant /lʌg'ʒʊərɪənt/ a lussureggiante, ri-goglioso

luxuriantly /lʌg'ʒʊərɪəntlɪ/ adv rigogliosa-mente

luxurious /lʌg'ʒʊərɪəs/ a lussuoso

luxuriously /lʌg'ʒʊərɪəslɪ/ adv lussuosa-mente

luxury /'lʌkʃərɪ/ n lusso m; **live in ~** vivere nel lusso ● attrib di lusso

LV abbr **luncheon voucher**

LW abbr (**long wave**) OL

lychee /'laɪtʃi:/ n litchi m inv

lych-gate /'lɪtʃ-/ n entrata f coperta di un ci-mitero

lycra® /'laɪkrə/ n lycra f

lying /'laɪɪŋ/ see **lie¹**, **lie²** ● n mentire m

lymph gland /'lɪmf/ n linfoghiandola f

lymph node n linfonodo m

lynch /lɪntʃ/ vt linciare

lynchpin /'lɪntʃpɪn/ n fig pilastro m

lynx /lɪŋks/ n lince f

lyric /'lɪrɪk/ a lirico

lyrical /'lɪrɪkl/ a lirico; (fam: enthusiastic) entusiasta. **~ poetry** n poesia f lirica

lyricism /'lɪrɪsɪzm/ n lirismo m

lyrics /'lɪrɪks/ npl parole fpl

Mm

m, M /em/ n (letter) m, M f inv

m abbr (**metre(s)**) m; abbr (**million**) milione m; abbr (**mile(s)**) miglio

MA n abbr (**Master of Arts**) (diploma) lau-rea f in lettere; (person) laureato, -a mf in let-tere; Am abbr **Massachusetts**

ma'am /mɑ:m/ int signora; (to queen) Sua Al-tezza

mac /mæk/ n fam impermeabile m

macabre /mə'kɑ:br/ a macabro

macaroni /mækə'rəʊnɪ/ n maccheroni mpl

macaroni cheese n maccheroni mpl gratinati al formaggio

macaroon /mækə'ru:n/ n ≈ amaretto m

mace¹ /meɪs/ n (staff) mazza f

mace² n (spice) macis mf

Macedonia /mæsə'dəʊnɪə/ n Macedonia f

machete /mə'ʃetɪ/ n machete m inv

Machiavellian /mækɪə'velɪən/ a machia-vellico

machinations /mækɪ'neɪʃnz/ macchina-zioni fpl

machine /mə'ʃi:n/ n macchina f ● vt (sew) cucire a macchina; Techn lavorare a macchi-na

machine: machine-gun n mitragliatrice f. **machine operator** n addetto, -a mf alle mac-chine. **machine-readable** a ‹data, text› leg-gibile dalla macchina

machinery /mə'ʃi:nərɪ/ n macchinario m; fig meccanismo m

machine: machine-stitch vt cucire a mac-china. **machine tool** n macchina f utensile. **machine translation** n traduzione f elettro-nica

machinist /mə'ʃi:nɪst/ n macchinista mf;

(*on sewing machine*) lavorante *mf* adetto, -a alla macchina da cucire

machismo /məˈkɪzməʊ/ *n* machismo *m*

macho /ˈmætʃəʊ/ *a* macho *inv*

mackerel /ˈmækr(ə)l/ *n inv* sgombro *m*

mackintosh /ˈmækɪntɒʃ/ *n* impermeabile *m*

macro /ˈmækrəʊ/ *n Comput* macro *f inv*

macrocosm /ˈmækrəʊkɒzm/ *n* macrocosmo *m*

mad /mæd/ *a* (**madder, maddest**) pazzo, matto; (*fam: angry*) furioso (**at** con); **like ~** *fam* come un pazzo; **be ~ about sb/sth** (*fam: keen on*) andare matto per qcno/qcsa

Madagascar /mædəˈgæskə(r)/ *n* Madagascar *m*

madam /ˈmædəm/ *n* signora *f*

mad cow disease *n* morbo *m* della mucca pazza

madden /ˈmædən/ *vt* (*make angry*) far diventare matto

maddening /ˈmæd(ə)nɪŋ/ *a* (*delay, person*) esasperante

made /meɪd/ *see* **make**

Madeira cake /məˈdɪərə/ *n* pan *m* di Spagna

made to measure *a* [fatto] su misura

made-up *a* (*wearing make-up*) truccato; (*road*) asfaltata; (*story*) inventato

madhouse /ˈmædhaʊs/ *n fam* manicomio *m*; **it's like a ~ in here!** sembra di essere in un manicomio

madly /ˈmædlɪ/ *adv fam* follemente; **~ in love** innamorato follemente

madman /ˈmædmən/ *n* pazzo *m*

madness /ˈmædnɪs/ *n* pazzia *f*

madonna /məˈdɒnə/ *n* madonna *f*

madwoman /ˈmædwʊmən/ *n* pazza *f*

mafia /ˈmæfɪə/ *n also fig* mafia *f*

mag /mæg/ *n abbr* **magazine**

magazine /mægəˈziːn/ *n* rivista *f; Mil, Phot* magazzino *m*

maggot /ˈmægət/ *n* verme *m*

maggoty /ˈmægətɪ/ *a* coi vermi

Magi /ˈmeɪdʒaɪ/ *npl* **the ~** i Re Magi

magic /ˈmædʒɪk/ *n* magia *f*; (*tricks*) giochi *mpl* di prestigio ● *a* magico; (*trick*) di prestigio

magical /ˈmædʒɪkl/ *a* magico

magic carpet *n* tappeto *m* volante

magician /məˈdʒɪʃn/ *n* mago, -a *mf*; (*entertainer*) prestigiatore, -trice *mf*

magistrate /ˈmædʒɪstreɪt/ *n* magistrato *m*

magistrate's court *n* ≈ pretura *f*

magnanimity /mægnəˈnɪmətɪ/ *n* magnanimità *f*

magnanimous /mægˈnænɪməs/ *a* magnanimo

magnesia /mægˈniːʃə/ *n* magnesia *f*

magnet /ˈmægnɪt/ *n* magnete *m*, calamita *f*

magnetic /mægˈnetɪk/ *a* magnetico

magnetic tape *n* nastro *m* magnetico

magnetism /ˈmægnətɪzm/ *n* magnetismo *m*

magnetize /ˈmægnətaɪz/ *vt* magnetizzare

magnification /mægnɪfɪˈkeɪʃn/ *n* ingrandimento *m*

magnificence /mægˈnɪfɪsəns/ *n* magnificenza *f*

magnificent /mægˈnɪfɪsənt/ *a* magnifico

magnificently /mægˈnɪfɪsəntlɪ/ *adv* magnificamente

magnify /ˈmægnɪfaɪ/ *vt* (*pt/pp* **-ied**) ingrandire; (*exaggerate*) ingigantire

magnifying glass /ˈmægnɪfaɪɪŋ/ *n* lente *f* d'ingrandimento

magnitude /ˈmægnɪtjuːd/ *n* grandezza *f*; (*importance*) importanza *f*; **a project of this ~** un progetto di tale portata

magnum opus /mægnəmˈɒpəs/ *n* opera *f* principale

magpie /ˈmægpaɪ/ *n* gazza *f*

mahogany /məˈhɒgənɪ/ *n* mogano *m* ● *attrib* di mogano

maid /meɪd/ *n* cameriera *f*; **old ~** *pej* zitella *f*

maiden /ˈmeɪdn/ *n liter* fanciulla *f* ● *a* (*speech, voyage*) inaugurale

maiden aunt *n* zia *f* zitella

maiden name *n* nome *m* da ragazza

mail /meɪl/ *n* posta *f* ● *vt* impostare

mail: mailbag *n* sacco *m* postale. **mail bomb** *n* pacco *m* esplosivo (*arrivato per posta*). **mailbox** *n Am* cassetta *f* delle lettere; (*e-mail*) casella *f* postale. **mail coach** *n Rail* vagone *m* postale. **mail delivery** *n* consegna *f* della posta

mailing address /ˈmeɪlɪŋ/ *n* recapito *m* postale

mailing list *n* elenco *m* d'indirizzi per un mailing

mail: mailman /ˈmeɪlmən/ *n Am* postino *m*. **mail order** *n* vendita *f* per corrispondenza ● *attrib* (*business*) di vendita per corrispondenza; (*goods*) comprati per corrispondenza. **mail-order catalogue** catalogo *m* di vendita per corrispondenza. **mail-order firm** *n* ditta *f* di vendita per corrispondenza. **mail room** *n* reparto *m* spedizioni. **mailshot** *n* mailing *m inv.* **mail train** *n* treno *m* postale. **mail van** *n* (*delivery vehicle*) furgone *m* postale; (*in train*) vagone *m* postale

maim /meɪm/ *vt* menomare

main[1] /meɪn/ *n* (*water, gas, electricity*) conduttura *f* principale

main[2] *a* principale; **the ~ thing is to...** la cosa essenziale è di... ● *n* **in the ~** in complesso

main: main course *n* secondo *m*. **main deck** *n* ponte *m* di coperta. **mainframe** *n Comput* mainframe *m inv.* **mainland** *n* continente *m*. **main line** *n Rail* linea *f* principale ● *attrib* (*station, terminus, train*) della linea principale

mainly /ˈmeɪnlɪ/ *adv* principalmente

main: main memory *n Comput* memoria *f* principale. **main office** *n* (*of company*) sede *f* centrale. **main road** *n* strada *f* principale. **mainsail** *n* randa *f*, vela *f* di taglio. **mainstay** *n fig* pilastro *m*. **main street** *n* via *f* principale

maintain /meɪnˈteɪn/ *vt* mantenere; (*keep in repair*) curare la manutenzione di; (*claim*) sostenere

maintenance /ˈmeɪntənəns/ n mantenimento m; (care) manutenzione f; (allowance) alimenti mpl

maintenance grant n (for student) presalario m

maintenance order n Br obbligo m degli alimenti

maisonette /meɪzəˈnet/ n appartamento m a due piani

maize /meɪz/ n granoturco m

Maj abbr (**Major**) Mag

majestic /məˈdʒestɪk/ a maestoso

majestically /məˈdʒestɪklɪ/ adv maestosamente

majesty /ˈmædʒəstɪ/ n maestà f inv; **His/Her M~** Sua Maestà

major /ˈmeɪdʒə(r)/ a maggiore; ~ **road** strada f con diritto di precedenza ● n Mil, Mus maggiore m ● vi Am ~ **in** specializzarsi in

Majorca /məˈjɔːkə/ n Maiorca f

major general n generale m di divisione

majority /məˈdʒɒrətɪ/ n maggioranza f; **be in the** ~ avere la maggioranza

make /meɪk/ n (brand) marca f ● v (pt/pp made) ● vt fare; (earn) guadagnare; rendere ⟨happy, clear⟩; prendere ⟨decision⟩; ~ **sb laugh** far ridere qcno; ~ **sb do sth** far fare qcsa a qcno; ~ **it** (to party, top of hill etc) farcela; **what time do you** ~ **it?** che ore fai? ● vi ~ **as if to** fare per

■ **make after** vt (chase) inseguire

■ **make do** vi arrangiarsi

■ **make for** vt dirigersi verso

■ **make good** vi riuscire ● vt compensare ⟨loss⟩; risarcire ⟨damage⟩

■ **make off** vi fuggire

■ **make off with** vt (steal) sgraffignare

■ **make out** vt (distinguish) distinguere; (write out) rilasciare ⟨cheque⟩; compilare ⟨list⟩; (claim) far credere

■ **make over** vt cedere

■ **make up** vt (constitute) comporre; (complete) completare; (invent) inventare; (apply cosmetics to) truccare; fare ⟨parcel⟩; ~ **up one's mind** decidersi; ~ **it up** (after quarrel) riconciliarsi ● vi (after quarrel) fare la pace

■ **make up for** vt compensare; ~ **up for lost time** recuperare il tempo perso

■ **make up to** vt arruffianarsi

make: make-believe a finto ● n finzione f. **make-do-and-mend** vi arrangiarsi col poco che si ha. **make-over** n trasformazione f

maker /ˈmeɪkə(r)/ n fabbricante mf; **M~** Relig Creatore m; **send sb to meet his/her** ~ spedire qcno all'altro mondo

make: makeshift /ˈ/ a di fortuna ● n espediente m. **make-up** n trucco m; (character) natura f. **make-up artist** n truccatore, -trice mf. **make-up bag** n astuccio m per il trucco. **make-up remover** n struccante m

making /ˈmeɪkɪŋ/ n (manufacture) fabbricazione f; **be the** ~ **of** essere la causa del successo di; **have the** ~**s of** aver la stoffa di; **in the** ~ in formazione

maladjusted /mæləˈdʒʌstɪd/ a disadattato

maladjustment /mæləˈdʒʌstmənt/ n disadattamento m

Malagasy /mæləˈgæzɪ/ n (native of Madagascar) malgascio, -a mf; (language) malgascio m

malaise /məˈleɪz/ n fig malessere m

malaria /məˈleərɪə/ n malaria f

Malaysia /məˈleɪzɪə/ n Malesia f

Malaysian /məˈleɪzən/ n & a malese mf

male /meɪl/ a maschile ● n maschio m

male: male chauvinist [**pig**] n [sporco m] maschilista m. **male menopause** n andropausa f. **male model** n indossatore m. **male nurse** n infermiere m. **male voice choir** n coro m maschile

malevolence /məˈlevələns/ n malevolenza f

malevolent /məˈlevələnt/ a malevolo

malformation /mælfɔːˈmeɪʃn/ n malformazione f

malformed /mælˈfɔːmd/ a malformato

malfunction /mælˈfʌŋkʃn/ n funzionamento m imperfetto ● vi funzionare male

Mali /ˈmɑːlɪ/ n Mali m

malice /ˈmælɪs/ n malignità f; **bear sb** ~ voler del male a qcno

malicious /məˈlɪʃəs/ a maligno

maliciously /məˈlɪʃəslɪ/ adv con malignità

malign /məˈlaɪn/ vt malignare su

malignancy /məˈlɪgnənsɪ/ n malignità f

malignant /məˈlɪgnənt/ a maligno

malinger /məˈlɪŋgə(r)/ vi fingersi malato

malingerer /məˈlɪŋgərə(r)/ n scansafatiche mf inv

mall /mæl/ n (shopping arcade, in suburb) centro m commerciale; (Am: street) strada f pedonale

mallard /ˈmælɑːd/ n germano m reale

malleable /ˈmælɪəbl/ a malleabile

mallet /ˈmælɪt/ n martello m di legno

malnourished /mælˈnʌrɪʃt/ a malnutrito

malnutrition /mælnjuˈtrɪʃn/ n malnutrizione f

malpractice /mælˈpræktɪs/ n negligenza f

malt /mɔːlt/ n malto m

Malta /ˈmɔːltə/ n Malta f

Maltese /mɔːlˈtiːz/ a & n maltese mf

maltreat /mælˈtriːt/ vt maltrattare

maltreatment /mælˈtriːtmənt/ n maltrattamento m

malt whisky n whisky m inv di malto

mammal /ˈmæml/ n mammifero m

mammary /ˈmæmərɪ/ a mammario

mammograph /ˈmæməgrɑːf/ n mammografia f

mammoth /ˈmæməθ/ a mastodontico ● n mammut m inv

man /mæn/ n (pl men) uomo m; (chess, draughts) pedina f; **the** ~ **in the street** l'uomo della strada; ~ **to** ~ da uomo a uomo ● vt (pt/pp manned) equipaggiare; far funzionare ⟨pump⟩; essere di servizio a ⟨counter, telephones⟩

manacle /ˈmænəkl/ vt ammanettare

manage /ˈmænɪdʒ/ vt dirigere; gestire ⟨shop, affairs⟩; (cope with) farcela; ~ **to do sth** riuscire a fare qcsa ● *vi* riuscire; (*cope*) farcela (**on** con)

manageable /'mænɪdʒəbl/ *a* ‹*hair*› docile; ‹*size*› maneggevole

management /'mænɪdʒmənt/ *n* gestione *f*; **the ~** la direzione

management: management accounting *n* contabilità *f* di gestione. **management buyout** *n* buyout *m inv* da parte dei manager, rilevamento *m* dirigenti. **management consultancy** *n* (*firm*) consulente *m* aziendale; (*activity*) consulenza *f* aziendale. **management consultant** *n* consulente *mf* aziendale

manager /'mænɪdʒə(r)/ *n* direttore *m*; (*of shop, bar*) gestore *m*; *Sport* manager *m inv*

manageress /mænɪdʒə'res/ *n* direttrice *f*

managerial /mænɪ'dʒɪərɪəl/ *a* ~ **staff** personale *m* direttivo

managing /'mænɪdʒɪŋ/ *a* ~ **director** direttore, -trice *mf* generale

mandarin /'mændərɪn/ *n* ~ **[orange]** mandarino *m*

mandate /'mændeɪt/ *n* mandato *m*

mandatory /'mændətrɪ/ *a* obbligatorio

mandolin /'mændəlɪn/ *n* mandolino *m*

mandrake /'mændreɪk/ *n* mandragola *f*

mane /meɪn/ *n* criniera *f*

manful /'mænfl/ *a* coraggioso

manfully /'mænfʊlɪ/ *adv* coraggiosamente

mangle /'mæŋgl/ *vt* (*damage*) maciullare

mango /'mæŋgəʊ/ *n* (*pl* -**es**) mango *m*

mangrove /'mæŋgrəʊv/ *n* mangrovia *f*

mangy /'meɪndʒɪ/ *a* ‹*dog*› rognoso

manhandle /'mænhændl/ *vt* malmenare

manhole /'mænhəʊl/ *n* botola *f*

manhole cover *n* tombino *m*

manhood /'mænhʊd/ *n* età *f* adulta; (*quality*) virilità *f*

man-hour *n* ora *f* lavorativa

manhunt /'mænhʌnt/ *n* caccia *f* all'uomo

mania /'meɪnɪə/ *n* mania *f*

maniac /'meɪnɪæk/ *n* maniaco, -a *mf*

manic /'mænɪk/ *a* (*obsessive*) maniacale; (*frenetic*) frenetico

manic depression *n* psicosi *f inv* maniaco-depressiva

manic-depressive *a* maniaco-depressivo

manicure /'mænɪkjʊə(r)/ *n* manicure *f inv* ● *vt* fare la manicure a

manicurist /'mænɪkjʊərɪst/ *n* manicure *f inv*

manifest /'mænɪfest/ *a* manifesto ● *n Comm* manifesto *m* ● *vt* manifestare; ~ **itself** manifestarsi

manifestation /mænɪfe'steɪʃn/ *n* manifestazione *f*

manifestly /'mænɪfestlɪ/ *adv* palesemente

manifesto /mænɪ'festəʊ/ *n* manifesto *m*

manifold /'mænɪfəʊld/ *a* molteplice

manipulate /mə'nɪpjʊleɪt/ *vt* manipolare

manipulation /mənɪpjʊ'leɪʃn/ *n* manipolazione *f*

mankind /mæn'kaɪnd/ *n* genere *m* umano

manly /'mænlɪ/ *a* virile

man-made *a* artificiale; ~ **fibre** *n* fibra *f* sintetica

manna /'mænə/ *n* manna *f*; ~ **from heaven** *fig* manna *f* dal cielo

mannequin /'mænɪkɪn/ *n* manichino *m*

manner /'mænə(r)/ *n* maniera *f*; **in this ~** in questo modo; **have no ~s** avere dei pessimi modi; **good/bad ~s** buone/cattive maniere

mannered /'mænəd/ *pej* manierato

mannerism /'mænərɪzm/ *n* affettazione *f*

mannish /'mænɪʃ/ *a* mascolino

manoeuvrable /mə'nu:vrəbl/ *a* manovrabile

manoeuvre /mə'nu:və(r)/ *n* manovra *f* ● *vt* fare manovra con ‹*vehicle*›; manovrare ‹*person*›

manor /'mænə(r)/ *n* maniero *m*

manpower /'mænpaʊə(r)/ *n* manodopera *f*

manse /mæns/ *n* canonica *f*

mansion /'mænʃn/ *n* palazzo *m*

manslaughter /'mænslɔ:tə(r)/ *n* omicidio *m* colposo

mantelpiece /'mæntlpi:s/ *n* mensola *f* di caminetto

mantis /'mæntɪs/ *n* mantide *f*

Mantua /'mæntjʊə/ *n* Mantova *f*

manual /'mænjʊəl/ *a* manuale ● *n* manuale *m*

manufacture /mænjʊ'fæktʃə(r)/ *vt* fabbricare ● *n* manifattura *f*

manufacturer /mænjʊ'fæktʃərə(r)/ *n* fabbricante *m*

manure /mə'njʊə(r)/ *n* concime *m*

manuscript /'mænjʊskrɪpt/ *n* manoscritto *m*

Manx /mæŋks/ *n* (*language*) lingua *f* parlata nell'isola di Man; **the ~** *pl* (*people*) gli abitanti dell'isola di Man

many /'menɪ/ *a & pron* molti; **there are as ~ boys as girls** ci sono tanti ragazzi quante ragazze; **as ~ as 500** ben 500; **as ~ as that** così tanti; **as ~** altrettanti; **very ~**, **a good/great ~** moltissimi; ~ **a time** molte volte

many-sided /-'saɪdɪd/ *a* ‹*personality, phenomenon*› sfaccettato

map /mæp/ *n* carta *f* geografica; (*of town*) mappa *f*

■ **map out** *vt* (*pt/pp* **mapped**) *fig* programmare

maple /'meɪpl/ *n* acero *m*

mar /mɑ:(r)/ *vt* (*pt/pp* **marred**) rovinare

marathon /'mærəθən/ *n* maratona *f*

marauder /mə'rɔ:də(r)/ *n* predone *m*

marble /'mɑ:bl/ *n* marmo *m*; (*for game*) pallina *f* ● *attrib* di marmo

March /mɑ:tʃ/ *n* marzo *m*

march /mɑ:tʃ/ *n* marcia *f*; (*protest*) dimostrazione *f* ● *vi* marciare ● *vt* far marciare; ~ **sb off** scortare qcno fuori

marcher /'mɑ:tʃə(r)/ *n* (*in procession, band*) persona *f* che marcia in una processione, in un corteo ecc; (*in demonstration*) dimostrante *mf*

marchioness /mɑ:ʃə'nes/ *n* marchesa *f*

march past *n* sfilata *f*

mare /'meə(r)/ *n* giumenta *f*

margarine /mɑːdʒəˈriːn/ n margarina f
marge /mɑːdʒ/ n (Br fam: margarine) margarina f
margin /ˈmɑːdʒɪn/ n margine m
marginal /ˈmɑːdʒɪnəl/ a marginale
marginally /ˈmɑːdʒɪnəlɪ/ adv marginalmente
marigold /ˈmærɪɡəʊld/ n calendula f
marijuana /mærʊˈwɑːnə/ n marijuana f
marina /məˈriːnə/ n porticciolo m
marinade /mærɪˈneɪd/ n marinata f ● vt marinare
marine /məˈriːn/ a marino ● n (sailor) soldato m di fanteria marina
Marine Corps n i Marine
marine engineer n ingegnere m navale; (works in engine room) macchinista m
marionette /mærɪəˈnet/ n marionetta f
marital /ˈmærɪtl/ a coniugale; ~ **status** stato m civile
maritime /ˈmærɪtaɪm/ a marittimo
marjoram /ˈmɑːdʒərəm/ n maggiorana f
mark¹ /mɑːk/ n (currency) marco m
mark² n (stain) macchia f; (sign, indication) segno m; Sch voto m; **be the ~ of** designare ● vt segnare; (stain) macchiare; Sch correggere; Sport marcare; ~ **time** Mil segnare il passo; fig non far progressi; ~ **my words** ricordati quello che dico
■ **mark down** vt (reduce the price of) ribassare
■ **mark out** vt delimitare; fig designare
■ **mark up** vt (increase the price of) aumentare
marked /mɑːkt/ a marcato
markedly /ˈmɑːkɪdlɪ/ adv notevolmente
marker /ˈmɑːkə(r)/ n (for highlighting) evidenziatore m; Sport marcatore m; (of exam) esaminatore, -trice mf
marker pen n evidenziatore m
market /ˈmɑːkɪt/ n mercato m ● vt vendere al mercato; (launch) commercializzare; **on the ~** sul mercato
market: market analyst n analista mf di mercato. **market day** n giorno m di mercato. **market economy** n economia f di mercato. **market forces** npl forze fpl di mercato. **market garden** n orto m. **market gardener** n ortofrutticoltore, -trice mf
marketing /ˈmɑːkɪtɪŋ/ n marketing m
marketing: marketing campaign n campagna f promozionale or pubblicitaria. **marketing department** n ufficio m marketing. **marketing man** n addetto, -a mf al marketing. **marketing mix** n mix m inv del marketing. **marketing strategy** n strategia f di marketing
market: market leader n (company, product) leader m inv del mercato. **market place** n (square, Fin) mercato m. **market price** n prezzo m di mercato. **market research** n ricerca f di mercato. **market square** n piazza f del mercato. **market stall** n banco m del mercato. **market survey** n indagine f di mercato. **market town** n cittadi-

na f dove si tiene il mercato. **market trader** n venditore, -trice mf al mercato. **market value** n valore m di mercato
markings /ˈmɑːkɪŋz/ npl (on animal) colori mpl
marksman /ˈmɑːksmən/ n tiratore m scelto
marksmanship /ˈmɑːksmənʃɪp/ n abilità f nel tiro
mark-up n (margin) margine m di vendita; (price increase) aumento m
marmalade /ˈmɑːməleɪd/ n marmellata f d'arance
maroon /məˈruːn/ a marrone rossastro
marooned /məˈruːnd/ a abbandonato
marquee /mɑːˈkiː/ n tendone m; (Am: awning) pensilina f con pubblicità
marquess /ˈmɑːkwɪs/ n marchese m
marquetry /ˈmɑːkɪtrɪ/ n intarsio m
marquis /ˈmɑːkwɪs/ n marchese m
marriage /ˈmærɪdʒ/ n matrimonio m
marriage: marriage ceremony n cerimonia f nuziale. **marriage certificate** n certificato m di matrimonio. **marriage guidance counsellor** n consulente mf matrimoniale. **marriage of convenience** n matrimonio m di convenienza
married /ˈmærɪd/ a sposato; ⟨life⟩ coniugale
marrow /ˈmærəʊ/ n Anat midollo m; (vegetable) zucca f
marrowbone /ˈmærəʊbəʊn/ n midollo m osseo
marry /ˈmærɪ/ vt (pt/pp -ied) sposare; **get married** sposarsi ● vi sposarsi
marsh /mɑːʃ/ n palude f
marshal /ˈmɑːʃl/ n (steward) cerimoniere m ● vt (pt/pp **marshalled**) fig organizzare ⟨arguments⟩
marshmallow /mɑːʃˈmæləʊ/ n caramella f gommosa e pastosa
marshy /ˈmɑːʃɪ/ a paludoso
marsupial /mɑːˈsuːpɪəl/ n marsupiale m
marten /ˈmɑːtɪn/ n martora f
martial /ˈmɑːʃl/ a marziale
Martian /ˈmɑːʃn/ a & n marziano, -a mf
martinet /mɑːtɪˈnet/ n fanatico, -a mf della disciplina
martyr /ˈmɑːtə(r)/ n martire mf ● vt martirizzare
martyrdom /ˈmɑːtədəm/ n martirio m
martyred /ˈmɑːtəd/ a fam da martire
marvel /ˈmɑːvl/ n meraviglia f ● vi (pt/pp **marvelled**) meravigliarsi (**at** di)
marvellous /ˈmɑːvələs/ a meraviglioso
marvellously /ˈmɑːvələslɪ/ adv meravigliosamente
Marxism /ˈmɑːksɪzm/ n marxismo m
Marxist /ˈmɑːksɪst/ a & n marxista mf
marzipan /ˈmɑːzɪpæn/ n marzapane m
mascara /mæˈskɑːrə/ n mascara m inv
mascot /ˈmæskət/ n mascotte f inv
masculine /ˈmæskjʊlɪn/ a maschile ● n Gram maschile m
masculinity /mæskjʊˈlɪnətɪ/ n mascolinità f
mash /mæʃ/ n Culin fam purè m inv ● vt impastare

mashed potatoes /mæʃt/ *npl* purè *m inv* di patate

mask /mɑːsk/ *n* maschera *f* ● *vt* mascherare

masked ball /mɑːskt'bɔːl/ *n* ballo *m* in maschera

masking tape /'mɑːskɪŋ/ *n* nastro *m* di carta adesiva

masochism /'mæsəkɪzm/ *n* masochismo *m*

masochist /'mæsəkɪst/ *n* masochista *mf*

Mason /'meɪsn/ *n* massone *m*

mason *n* muratore *m*

Masonic /mə'sɒnɪk/ *a* massonico

masonry /'meɪsnrɪ/ *n* muratura *f*; **two tons of** ~ due tonnellate di pietre

masquerade /mæskə'reɪd/ *n fig* mascherata *f* ● *vi* ~ **as** (*pose*) farsi passare per

mass[1] /mæs/ *n Relig* messa *f*

mass[2] *n* massa *f*; ~**es of** *fam* un sacco di ● *vi* ammassarsi

massacre /'mæsəkə(r)/ *n* massacro *m* ● *vt* massacrare

massage /'mæsɑːʒ/ *n* massaggio *m* ● *vt* massaggiare; *fig* manipolare ‹*statistics*›

masseur /mæ'sɜː(r)/ *n* massaggiatore *m*

masseuse /mæ'sɜːz/ *n* massaggiatrice *f*

mass grave *n* fossa *f* comune

mass hysteria *n* isterismo *m* di massa

massive /'mæsɪv/ *a* enorme

massively /'mæsɪvlɪ/ *adv* estremamente

mass: mass market *n* mercato *m* di massa ● *attrib* del mercato di massa. **mass media** *npl* mezzi *mpl* di comunicazione di massa, mass media *mpl*. **mass murder** *n* omicidio *m* di massa. **mass murderer** *n* omicida *mf* di massa. **mass-produce** *vt* produrre in serie. **mass production** *n* produzione *f* in serie. **mass screening** *n Med* controllo *m* su larga scala

mast /mɑːst/ *n Naut* albero *m*; (*for radio*) antenna *f*

master /'mɑːstə(r)/ *n* maestro *m*, padrone *m*; (*teacher*) professore *m*; (*of ship*) capitano *m*; **M~** (*boy*) signorino *m* ● *vt* imparare perfettamente; avere padronanza di ‹*language*›

master: master bedroom *n* camera *f* da letto principale. **master builder** *n* capomastro *m*. **master copy** *n* originale *m*. **master disk** *n Comput* disco *m* master. **master key** *n* passe-partout *m inv*

masterly /'mɑːstəlɪ/ *a* magistrale

master: mastermind *n* cervello *m* ● *vt* ideare e dirigere. **Master of Arts** *n* (*diploma*) laurea *f* in lettere; (*person*) laureato, -a *mf* in lettere. **master of ceremonies** *n* (*presenting entertainment*) presentatore *m*; (*of formal occasion*) maestro *m* delle cerimonie. **Master of Science** *n* (*diploma*) laurea *f* in discipline scientifiche; (*person*) laureato, -a *mf* in discipline scientifiche. **masterpiece** *n* capolavoro *m*. **master plan** *n* piano *m* generale. **master race** *n* razza *f* superiore. **master stroke** *n* colpo *m* da maestro. **master tape** *n* nastro *m* matrice

mastery /'mæstərɪ/ *n* (*of subject*) padronanza *f*

masticate /'mæstɪkeɪt/ *vi* masticare

masturbate /'mæstəbeɪt/ *vi* masturbarsi

masturbation /mæstə'beɪʃn/ *n* masturbazione *f*

mat /mæt/ *n* stuoia *f*; (*on table*) sottopiatto *m*

match[1] /mætʃ/ *n Sport* partita *f*; (*equal*) uguale *mf*; (*marriage*) matrimonio *m*; (*person to marry*) partito *m*; **be a good** ~ ‹*colours:*› intonarsi bene; **be no** ~ **for** non essere dello stesso livello di ● *vt* (*equal*) uguagliare; (*be like*) andare bene con ● *vi* intonarsi

match[2] *n* fiammifero *m*

matchbox /'mætʃbɒks/ *n* scatola *f* di fiammiferi

matching /'mætʃɪŋ/ *a* intonato

match: matchmaker *n* **he's a successful** ~ (*for couples*) è stato l'artefice di molti matrimoni. **match point** *n Tennis* match point *m inv*. **matchstick** *n* fiammifero *m*

mate[1] /meɪt/ *n* compagno, -a *mf*; (*assistant*) aiuto *m*; *Naut* secondo *m*; (*fam: friend*) amico, -a *mf* ● *vi* accoppiarsi ● *vt* accoppiare

mate[2] *n* (*in chess*) scacco *m* matto

material /mə'tɪərɪəl/ *n* materiale *m*; (*fabric*) stoffa *f*; **raw** ~**s** *pl* materie *fpl* prime ● *a* materiale

materialism /mə'tɪərɪəlɪzm/ *n* materialismo *m*

materialistic /mətɪərɪə'lɪstɪk/ *a* materialistico

materialize /mə'tɪərɪəlaɪz/ *vi* materializzarsi

maternal /mə'tɜːnl/ *a* materno

maternity /mə'tɜːnətɪ/ *n* maternità *f*

maternity: maternity clothes *npl* abiti *mpl* pre-maman. **maternity department** *n* (*in store*) reparto *m* pre-maman. **maternity hospital** *n* maternità *f inv*. **maternity leave** *n* congedo *m* per maternità. **maternity unit** *n* reparto *m* maternità. **maternity ward** *n* maternità *f inv*

matey /'meɪtɪ/ *a fam* amichevole

math /mæθ/ *n Am* matematica *f*

mathematical /mæθə'mætɪkl/ *a* matematico

mathematically /mæθə'mætɪklɪ/ *adv* matematicamente

mathematician /mæθəmə'tɪʃn/ *n* matematico, -a *mf*

mathematics /mæθ'mætɪks/ *n* matematica *fsg*

maths /mæθs/ *n fam* matematica *fsg*

matinée /'mætɪneɪ/ *n Theat* matinée *f inv*

mating /'meɪtɪŋ/ *n* accoppiamento *m*

mating call *n* richiamo *m* [per l'accoppiamento]

mating season *n* stagione *f* degli amori

matriarchal /meɪtrɪ'ɑːkl/ *a* matriarcale

matriarchy /'meɪtrɪɑːkɪ/ *n* matriarchia *f*

matrices /'meɪtrɪsiːz/ *see* **matrix**

matriculate /mə'trɪkjʊleɪt/ *vi* immatricolarsi

matriculation /mətrɪkjʊ'leɪʃn/ *n* immatricolazione *f*

matrimonial /mætrɪ'məʊnɪəl/ *a* matrimoniale

matrimony /'mætrɪmənɪ/ *n* matrimonio *m*
matrix /'meɪtrɪks/ *n* (*pl* **matrices** /'meɪtrɪsiːz/) matrice *f*
matron /'meɪtrən/ *n* (*of hospital*) capo-infermiera *f*; (*of school*) governante *f*
matronly /'meɪtrənlɪ/ *a* matronale
matron of honour *n Br* damigella *f* d'onore (*sposata*)
matt /mæt/ *a* opaco
matted /'mætɪd/ *a* ~ **hair** capelli *mpl* tutti appiccicati tra loro
matter /'mætə(r)/ *n* (*affair*) faccenda *f*; (*question*) questione *f*; (*pus*) pus *m*; (*Phys: substance*) materia *f*; **money ~s** questioni *fpl* di soldi; **as a ~ of fact** a dire la verità; **what is the ~?** che cosa c'è? ● *vi* importare; ~ **to sb** essere importante per qcno; **it doesn't ~** non importa
matter-of-fact *a* pratico
matting /'mætɪŋ/ *n* materiale *m* per stuoie
mattress /'mætrɪs/ *n* materasso *m*
maturation /mætʃʊ'reɪʃn/ *n* (*of tree, body*) sviluppo *m*; (*of whisky, wine*) invecchiamento *m*; (*of cheese*) stagionatura *f*
mature /mə'tʃʊə(r)/ *a* maturo; *Comm* in scadenza ● *vi* maturare ● *vt* far maturare
mature student *n Br* persona *f* che riprende gli studi universitari dopo i 25 anni
maturity /mə'tʃʊərətɪ/ *n* maturità *f*; *Comm* maturazione *f*
maudlin /'mɔːdlɪn/ *a* ⟨*song*⟩ sdolcinato; ⟨*person*⟩ piagnucoloso
maul /mɔːl/ *vt* malmenare
Maundy /'mɔːndɪ/ *n* ~ **Thursday** giovedì *m* santo
Mauritius /mə'rɪʃəs/ *n* [isola *f* di] Maurizio *f*
mausoleum /mɔːsə'lɪəm/ *n* mausoleo *m*
mauve /məʊv/ *a* malva
maverick /'mævərɪk/ *n, a* anticonformista *mf*
mawkish /'mɔːkɪʃ/ *a* sdolcinato
maxi /'mæksɪ/ *n* (*dress*) vestito *m* alla caviglia; (*skirt*) gonna *f* alla caviglia
maxim /'mæksɪm/ *n* massima *f*
maximization /mæksɪmaɪ'zeɪʃn/ *n* massimizzazione *f*
maximum /'mæksɪməm/ *a* massimo; **ten minutes** ~ dieci minuti al massimo ● *n* (*pl* -**ima**) massimo *m*
maximum security prison *n* carcere *m* di massima sicurezza
May /meɪ/ *n* maggio *m*
may *v aux* (*solo al presente*) potere; ~ **I come in?** posso entrare?; **if I** ~ **say so** se mi posso permettere; ~ **you both are very happy** siate felici; **I** ~ **as well stay** potrei anche rimanere; **it** ~ **be true** potrebbe esser vero; **she** ~ **be old, but...** sarà anche vecchia, ma...
maybe /'meɪbɪ/ *adv* forse, può darsi
may: May-bug *n* maggiolino *m*. **Mayday** *n Radio* mayday *m inv*. **May Day** *n* il primo maggio
mayhem /'meɪhem/ *n* **create** ~ creare scompiglio
mayonnaise /meɪə'neɪz/ *n* maionese *f*

mayor /'meə(r)/ *n* sindaco *m*
mayoress /meə'res/ *n* sindaco *m*; (*wife of mayor*) moglie *f* del sindaco
maypole /'meɪpəʊl/ *n* palo *m* intorno al quale si balla durante la celebrazione del primo maggio
May queen *n* reginetta *f* di calendimaggio
maze /meɪz/ *n* labirinto *m*
Mb *abbr* (**megabyte**) Mb *m inv*
MBA *n abbr* (**Master of Business Administration**) laurea *f inv* in economia e commercio
MBE *n Br abbr* (**Member of the Order of the British Empire**) *onorificenza f britannica*
MBO *n abbr* **management buyout**
MC *n abbr* (**Master of Ceremonies**) (*in cabaret*) presentatore *m*; (*at banquet*) maestro *m* delle cerimonie; *Am abbr* (**Member of Congress**) membro *m* del Congresso
McCoy /mə'kɔɪ/ *n* **this whisky is the real** ~ questo è un vero whisky
MD *abbr* (**Managing Director**) direttore, -trice *mf* generale; *abbr* (**Doctor of Medicine**) dottore *m* in medicina; *Am abbr* **Maryland**
ME *n abbr* (**myalgic encephalomyelitis**) encefalomelite *f* mialgica; *Am abbr* **Maine**
me /miː/ *pers pron* (*object*) mi; (*with preposition*) me; **he knows me** mi conosce; **she called me, not you** ha chiamato me, non te; **give me the money** dammi i soldi; **give it to me** dammelo; **he explained it to me** me lo ha spiegato; **it's me** sono io
mead /miːd/ *n* idromele *m*
meadow /'medəʊ/ *n* prato *m*
meagre /'miːgə(r)/ *a* scarso
meal¹ /miːl/ *n* pasto *m*; **did you enjoy your** ~? ha mangiato bene?
meal² *n* (*grain*) farina *f*
meal ticket *n* (*fig: quality, qualification*) fonte *f* di guadagno; **he's only a** ~ ~ **to her** le interessano solo i suoi soldi
mealy-mouthed /miːlɪ'maʊð/ *a* ambiguo
mean¹ /miːn/ *a* avaro; (*unkind*) meschino; (*low in rank*) basso; (*accommodation*) misero
mean² *a* medio ● *n* (*average*) media *f*; **Greenwich** ~ **time** ora *f* media di Greenwich
mean³ *vt* (*pt/pp* **meant**) voler dire; (*signify*) significare; (*intend*) intendere; **I** ~ **it** lo dico seriamente; ~ **well** avere buone intenzioni; **be** ~**t for** ⟨*present:*⟩ essere destinato a; ⟨*remark:*⟩ essere riferito a
meander /mɪ'ændə(r)/ *vi* vagare
meaning /'miːnɪŋ/ *n* significato *m*
meaningful /'miːnɪŋfʊl/ *a* significativo
meaningless /'miːnɪŋlɪs/ *a* senza senso
meanness /'miːnnɪs/ *n* (*with money*) avarizia *f*; (*unkindness*) meschinità *f*
means /miːnz/ *n* mezzo *m*; ~ **of transport** mezzo *m* di trasporto; **by** ~ **of** per mezzo di; **by all** ~! certamente!; **by no** ~ niente affatto ● *npl* (*resources*) mezzi *mpl*; ~ **test** *n* accertamento *m* patrimoniale

meant /ment/ *see* **mean³**

meantime /'mi:ntaɪm/ *n* **in the ~** nel frattempo ● *adv* intanto

meanwhile /'mi:nwaɪl/ *adv* intanto

measles /'mi:zlz/ *nsg* morbillo *m*

measly /'mi:zlɪ/ *a fam* misero

measurable /'meʒərəbl/ *a* misurabile

measure /'meʒə(r)/ *n* misura *f* ● *vt/i* misurare

■ **measure out** *vt* dosare ⟨*amount*⟩

■ **measure up to** *vt fig* essere all'altezza di

measured /'meʒəd/ *a* misurato

measurement /'meʒəmənt/ *n* misura *f*

measuring jug /'meʒərɪŋ/ *n* dosatore *m*

measuring spoon *n* misurino *m*

meat /mi:t/ *n* carne *f*

meat: meatball *n Culin* polpetta *f* di carne. **meat-eater** *n* ⟨*animal*⟩ carnivoro *m*; **I'm not a ~** non mangio carne. **meat hook** *n* gancio *m* da macellaio. **meat loaf** *n* polpettone *m*. **meat pie** *n* tortino *m* di carne

meaty /'mi:tɪ/ *a* (**-ier, -iest**) di carne; *fig* sostanzioso

Mecca /'mekə/ *n* La Mecca

mechanic /mɪ'kænɪk/ *n* meccanico *m*

mechanical /mɪ'kænɪkl/ *a* meccanico

mechanical engineering *n* ingegneria *f* meccanica

mechanically /mɪ'kænɪklɪ/ *adv* meccanicamente

mechanics /mɪ'kænɪks/ *n* meccanica *f* ● *npl* meccanismo *msg*

mechanism /'mekənɪzm/ *n* meccanismo *m*

mechanize /'mekənaɪz/ *vt* meccanizzare

medal /'medl/ *n* medaglia *f*

medallion /mɪ'dælɪən/ *n* medaglione *m*

medallist /'medəlɪst/ *n* vincitore, -trice *mf* di una medaglia

meddle /'medl/ *vi* immischiarsi (**in** di); ⟨*tinker*⟩ armeggiare (**with** con)

media /'mi:dɪə/ *n see* **medium** ● *npl* **the ~** i mass media

median /'mi:dɪən/ *a* **~ strip** *Am* banchina *f* spartitraffico

media studies *npl* scienze *fpl* delle comunicazioni

mediate /'mi:dɪeɪt/ *vi* fare da mediatore

mediation /mi:dɪ'eɪʃn/ *n* mediazione *f*

mediator /'mi:dɪeɪtə(r)/ *n* mediatore, -trice *mf*

medic /'medɪk/ *n* ⟨*fam: doctor*⟩ medico *m*; ⟨*fam: student*⟩ studente, -essa *mf* di medicina; *Mil fam* infermiere, -a *mf* militare

medical /'medɪkl/ *a* medico ● *n* visita *f* medica

medical: medical care *n* assistenza *f* medica. **medical check-up** *n* controllo *m* medico. **medical history** *n* anamnesi *f inv*. **medical insurance** *n* assicurazione *f* sanitaria

medically /'medɪklɪ/ *adv* **~ qualified** con qualifiche di medico; **~ fit** in buona salute

medical: medical officer *n Mil* ufficiale *m* medico. **medical profession** *n* ⟨*occupation*⟩ professione *f* del medico; ⟨*doctors collectively*⟩

categoria *f* medica. **medical student** *n* studente, -essa *mf* di medicina

medicated /'medɪkeɪtɪd/ *a* medicato

medication /medɪ'keɪʃn/ *n* ⟨*drugs*⟩ medicinali *mpl*; **are you on any ~?** sta prendendo delle medicine?

medicinal /mɪ'dɪsɪnl/ *a* medicinale

medicine /'medsən/ *n* medicina *f*

medicine: medicine ball *n* palla *f* medica. **medicine bottle** *n* flacone *m*. **medicine cabinet** *n* armadietto *m* dei medicinali. **medicine man** *n* stregone *m*

medieval /medɪ'i:vl/ *a* medievale

mediocre /mi:dɪ'əʊkə(r)/ *a* mediocre

mediocrity /mi:dɪ'ɒkrətɪ/ *n* mediocrità *f*

meditate /'medɪteɪt/ *vi* meditare (**on** su)

meditative /'medɪtətɪv/ *a* ⟨*music, person*⟩ meditativo; ⟨*mood, expression*⟩ meditabondo

Mediterranean /medɪtə'reɪnɪən/ *n* **the ~ [Sea]** il [mare] Mediterraneo ● *a* mediterraneo

medium /'mi:dɪəm/ *a* medio; *Culin* di media cottura ● *n* (*pl* **media**) mezzo *m*; (*pl* **-s**) ⟨*person*⟩ medium *mf inv*

medium: medium dry *a* ⟨*drink*⟩ semisecco. **medium-length** *a* ⟨*book, film, hair*⟩ di media lunghezza. **medium-range** *a* ⟨*missile*⟩ di media portata. **medium-rare** *a* ⟨*meat*⟩ appena al sangue. **medium-sized** /'mi:dɪəmsaɪzd/ *a* di taglia media. **medium wave** *n* onde *fpl* medie

medley /'medlɪ/ *n* miscuglio *m*; *Mus* miscellanea *f*

meek /mi:k/ *a* mite, mansueto

meekly /'mi:klɪ/ *adv* docilmente

meet /mi:t/ *v* (*pt/pp* **met**) ● *vt* incontrare; ⟨*at station, airport*⟩ andare incontro a; ⟨*for first time*⟩ far la conoscenza di; pagare ⟨*bill*⟩; soddisfare ⟨*requirements*⟩ ● *vi* incontrarsi; ⟨*committee:*⟩ riunirsi; **~ with** incontrare ⟨*problem*⟩; incontrarsi con ⟨*person*⟩ ● *n* raduno *m* [sportivo]

■ **meet up** *vi* ⟨*people:*⟩ incontrarsi; **~ up with sb** incontrare qcno

meeting /'mi:tɪŋ/ *n* riunione *f*, meeting *m inv*; ⟨*large*⟩ assemblea *f*; ⟨*by chance*⟩ incontro *m*; **be in a ~** essere in riunione

meeting-place *n* luogo *m* d'incontro

meeting-point *n* punto *m* d'incontro

mega+ /'megə/ *pref* mega+

megabyte /'megəbaɪt/ *n Comput* megabyte *m inv*

megalith /'megəlɪθ/ *n* megalite *m*

megalomania /megələ'meɪnɪə/ *n* megalomania *f*

megaphone /'megəfəʊn/ *n* megafono *m*

melancholy /'melənkəlɪ/ *a* malinconico ● *n* malinconia *f*

mellow /'meləʊ/ *a* ⟨*wine*⟩ generoso; ⟨*sound, colour*⟩ caldo; ⟨*person*⟩ dolce ● *vi* ⟨*person:*⟩ addolcirsi

melodic /mɪ'lɒdɪk/ *a* melodico

melodious /mɪ'ləʊdɪəs/ *a* melodioso

melodrama /'melədrɑ:mə/ *n* melodramma *m*

melodramatic /melədrə'mætɪk/ a melodrammatico

melodramatically /melədrə'mætɪklɪ/ adv in modo melodrammatico

melody /'melədɪ/ n melodia f

melon /'melən/ n melone m

melt /melt/ vt sciogliere ● vi sciogliersi

■ **melt away** vi ‹snow:› sciogliersi; ‹crowd:› disperdersi; ‹support:› venir meno

■ **melt down** vt fondere

meltdown /'meltdaʊn/ n (in nuclear reactor) fusione f del nocciolo

melting point /'meltɪŋ/ n punto m di fusione

melting pot n fig crogiuolo m

member /'membə(r)/ n membro m; **be a ~ of the family** far parte della famiglia

member: member countries paesi mpl membri. **Member of Parliament** deputato, -a mf. **Member of the European Parliament** n eurodeputato, -a mf

membership /'membəʃɪp/ n iscrizione f; (members) soci mpl

membrane /'membreɪn/ n membrana f

memento /mɪ'mentəʊ/ n ricordo m

memo /'meməʊ/ n promemoria m inv

memoirs /'memwa:z/ npl ricordi mpl

memo pad n blocchetto m

memorabilia /memərə'bɪlɪə/ npl cimeli mpl

memorable /'memərəbl/ a memorabile

memorandum /memə'rændəm/ n promemoria m inv

memorial /mɪ'mɔ:rɪəl/ n monumento m

memorial service n funzione f commemorativa

memorize /'meməraɪz/ vt memorizzare

memory /'memərɪ/ n also Comput memoria f; (thing remembered) ricordo m; **from ~** a memoria; **in ~ of** in ricordo di

men /men/ see **man**

menace /'menəs/ n minaccia f; (nuisance) piaga f ● vt minacciare

menacing /'menəsɪŋ/ a minaccioso

menacingly /'menəsɪŋlɪ/ adv minacciosamente

mend /mend/ vt riparare; (darn) rammendare ● n **on the ~** in via di guarigione

menfolk /'menfəʊk/ n uomini mpl

menial /'mi:nɪəl/ a umile

meningitis /menɪn'dʒaɪtɪs/ n meningite f

menopause /'menəpɔ:z/ n menopausa f

Menorca /mɪ'nɔ:kə/ n Minorca f

men's room n toilette f inv degli uomini

menstruate /'menstrʊeɪt/ vi mestruare

menstruation /menstrʊ'eɪʃn/ n mestruazione f

menswear /'menzweə(r)/ n abbigliamento m per uomo

mental /'mentl/ a mentale; (fam: mad) pazzo

mental: mental arithmetic n calcolo m mentale. **mental block** n blocco m psicologico. **mental health** n (of person) salute f mentale. **mental health care** n assistenza f psi-

chiatrica. **mental home** n clinica f psichiatrica. **mental illness** n malattia f mentale

mentality /men'tælətɪ/ n mentalità f inv

mentally /'mentəlɪ/ adv mentalmente; **~ ill** malato di mente

mentholated /'menθəleɪtɪd/ a al mentolo

mention /'menʃn/ n menzione f ● vt menzionare; **don't ~ it** non c'è di che

mentor /'mentɔ:(r)/ n mentore m

menu /'menju:/ n menu m inv

MEP n abbr (**Member of the European Parliament**) eurodeputato, -a mf

mercantile /'mɜ:kəntaɪl/ a mercantile

mercenary /'mɜ:sɪnərɪ/ a mercenario ● n mercenario m

merchandise /'mɜ:tʃəndaɪz/ n merce f

merchant /'mɜ:tʃənt/ n commerciante mf

merchant: merchant bank n Br banca f d'affari. **merchant banker** n (owner) proprietario, -a mf di una banca d'affari; (executive) dirigente mf di banca d'affari. **merchant navy** n marina f mercantile

merciful /'mɜ:sɪfl/ a misericordioso

mercifully /'mɜ:sɪfʊlɪ/ adv fam grazie a Dio

merciless /'mɜ:sɪlɪs/ a spietato

mercilessly /'mɜ:sɪlɪslɪ/ adv senza pietà

mercurial /mɜ:'kjʊərɪəl/ a fig volubile

mercury /'mɜ:kjʊrɪ/ n mercurio m

mercy /'mɜ:sɪ/ n misericordia f; **be at sb's ~** essere alla mercé o in balia di qcno

mercy killing n eutanasia f

mere /mɪə(r)/ a solo

merely /'mɪəlɪ/ adv solamente

merest /'mɪərɪst/ a minimo

merge /mɜ:dʒ/ vi fondersi ● vt Comm fondere

merger /'mɜ:dʒə(r)/ n fusione f

meridian /mə'rɪdɪən/ n meridiano m

meringue /mə'ræŋ/ n meringa f

merit /'merɪt/ n merito m; (advantage) qualità f inv ● vt meritare

mermaid /'mɜ:meɪd/ n sirena f

merrily /'merɪlɪ/ adv allegramente

merriment /'merɪmənt/ n baldoria f

merry /'merɪ/ a (-ier, -iest) allegro; **~ Christmas!** Buon Natale!; **make ~** far festa

merry-go-round n giostra f

merry-making /'merɪmeɪkɪŋ/ n festa f

mesh /meʃ/ n maglia f

mesmerize /'mezməraɪz/ vt ipnotizzare

mesmerized /'mezməraɪzd/ a fig ipnotizzato

mess /mes/ n disordine m, casino m fam; (trouble) guaio m; (something spilt) sporco m; Mil mensa f; **make a ~ of** (botch) fare un pasticcio di

■ **mess about** vi perder tempo; **~ about with** armeggiare con ● vt prendere in giro ‹person›

■ **mess up** vt mettere in disordine, incasinare fam; (botch) mandare all'aria

■ **mess with** vt (fam: interfere with) trafficare con ‹computer, radio etc›; contrariare ‹person›

message /'mesɪdʒ/ n messaggio m

mess dress n Mil uniforme f di gala

messenger /'mesɪndʒə(r)/ n messaggero m

messenger boy n fattorino m

Messiah /mɪ'saɪə/ n Messia m

Messrs /'mesəz/ npl (on letter) ~ **Smith** Spett. ditta Smith

messy /'mesɪ/ a (**-ier, -iest**) disordinato; (in dress) sciatto

met /met/ see **meet**

metabolism /mɪ'tæbəlɪzm/ n metabolismo m

metal /'metl/ n metallo m ● a di metallo

metal detector n metal detector m inv

metal fatigue n fatica f del metallo

metallic /mɪ'tælɪk/ a metallico

metallurgy /mɪ'tælədʒɪ/ n metallurgia f

metal polish n lucido m per metalli

metalwork /'metlwɜːk/ n lavorazione f del metallo

metamorphose /metə'mɔːfəʊz/ vt trasformare ● vi trasformarsi (**into** in)

metamorphosis /metə'mɔːfəsɪs/ n (pl **-phoses** /metə'mɔːfəsiːz/) metamorfosi f inv

metaphor /'metəfə(r)/ n metafora f

metaphorical /metə'fɒrɪkl/ a metaforico

metaphorically /metə'fɒrɪklɪ/ adv metaforicamente

metaphysical /metə'fɪzɪkl/ a metafisico; (abstract) astruso

meteor /'miːtɪə(r)/ n meteora f

meteoric /miːtɪ'ɒrɪk/ a fig fulmineo

meteorite /'miːtɪəraɪt/ n meteorite m

meteorological /miːtɪərə'lɒdʒɪkl/ a meteorologico

Meteorological Office n Ufficio m meteorologico

meteorologist /miːtɪə'rɒlədʒɪst/ n meteorologo, -a mf

meteorology /miːtɪə'rɒlədʒɪ/ n meteorologia f

meter[1] /'miːtə(r)/ n contatore m

meter[2] n Am = **metre**

meter reader n persona f incaricata di leggere il contatore (di gas, elettricità)

methane /'miːθeɪn/ n metano m

method /'meθəd/ n metodo m

method acting n metodo m dell'Actors' Studio

method actor n attore m che segue il metodo dell'Actors' Studio

methodical /mɪ'θɒdɪkl/ a metodico

methodically /mɪ'θɒdɪklɪ/ adv metodicamente

Methodist /'meθədɪst/ n metodista mf

methodology /meθə'dɒlədʒɪ/ n metodologia f

meths /meθs/ n fam alcol m denaturato

methyl /'miːθaɪl/ n metile m

methylated /'meθɪleɪtɪd/ a ~ **spirit[s]** alcol m denaturato

meticulous /mɪ'tɪkjʊləs/ a meticoloso

meticulously /mɪ'tɪkjʊləslɪ/ adv meticolosamente

metre /'miːtə(r)/ n metro m

metric /'metrɪk/ a metrico

metrication /metrɪ'keɪʃn/ n conversione f al sistema metrico

metronome /'metrənəʊm/ n metronomo m

metropolis /mɪ'trɒpəlɪs/ n metropoli f inv

metropolitan /metrə'pɒlɪtən/ a metropolitano

metropolitan district n Br circoscrizione f amministrativa urbana

Metropolitan police n Br polizia f di Londra

mew /mjuː/ n miao m ● vi miagolare

mews /mjuːz/ n Br (stables) scuderie fpl; (street) stradina f; (yard) cortile m

mews flat n Br piccolo appartamento m ricavato da vecchie scuderie

Mexican /'meksɪkən/ a & n messicano, -a mf

Mexican wave n ola f inv

Mexico /'meksɪkəʊ/ n Messico m

mezzanine /'metsəniːn/ n mezzanino m

miaow /mɪ'aʊ/ n miao m ● vi miagolare

mice /maɪs/ see **mouse**

Michaelmas /'mɪkəlməs/ n festa f di San Michele (29 settembre)

Michaelmas daisy n Br margherita f settembrina

Michaelmas Term n Br Univ primo trimestre m

mickey /'mɪkɪ/ n **take the** ~ **out of** prendere in giro

Mickey Mouse n Topolino m

microbe /'maɪkrəʊb/ n microbo m

microchip /'maɪkrəʊtʃɪp/ n microchip m inv

microcomputer /'maɪkrəʊkəmpjuːtə(r)/ n microcomputer m inv

microcosm /'maɪkrəkɒzm/ n microcosmo m

micro: microfilm /'maɪkrəfɪlm/ n microfilm m inv. **micromesh tights** npl collant mpl velati. **microphone** microfono m. **microphysics** n microfisica f. **microprocessor** n microprocessore m. **microscope** n microscopio m. **microscopic** a microscopico. **microsurgery** n microchirurgia f. **microwave** n microonda f; (oven) forno m a microonde

mid /mɪd/ a ~ **May** metà maggio; **in** ~ **air** a mezz'aria

midday /mɪd'deɪ/ n mezzogiorno m

middle /'mɪdl/ a di centro; **the M**~ **Ages** il medioevo; **the** ~ **class[es]** la classe media; **the M**~ **East** il Medio Oriente ● n mezzo m; **in the** ~ **of** (room, floor etc) in mezzo a; **in the** ~ **of the night** nel pieno della notte, a notte piena

middle: middle-aged /-'eɪdʒd/ a di mezza età. **middle-age spread** n pancetta f di mezza età. **Middle America** n (social group) ceto m medio americano a tendenza conservatrice. **middlebrow** a (book) per il lettore medio; (person) con interessi culturali convenzionali. **middle-class** a borghese. **middle distance** n Phot, Cinema secondo piano m; **gaze into the** ~ ~ avere lo sguardo perso nel vuoto. **Middle English** n medio inglese m. **middle finger** n dito m medio. **middle ground** m Pol centro m; **occupy the** ~ ~

adottare una posizione intermedia. **middle-income** *a* ⟨*person, family, country*⟩ dal reddito medio

middleman /'mɪdlmæn/ *n Comm* intermediario *m*

middle: middle manager *n* quadro *m* intermedio. **middle-of-the-road** *a* (*ordinary*) ordinario; ⟨*policy*⟩ moderato. **middle-size[d]** /-saɪz[d]/ *a* di misura media. **middleweight** *n* peso *m* medio

middling /'mɪdlɪŋ/ *a* discreto

midfield /mɪd'fiːld/ *n* centrocampo *m*

midfield player *n* centrocampista *m*

midge /mɪdʒ/ *n* moscerino *m*

midget /'mɪdʒɪt/ *n* nano, -a *mf*

Midlands /'mɪdləndz/ *npl* **the ~** l'Inghilterra *fsg* centrale

mid-life *n* mezza età *f*

mid-life crisis *n* crisi *f inv* di mezza età

midnight /'mɪdnaɪt/ *n* mezzanotte *f*

mid-range *attrib* ⟨*car*⟩ (*in price*) di prezzo medio; (*in power*) di media cilindrata; ⟨*hotel*⟩ intermedio; **be in the ~** ⟨*product, hotel:*⟩ essere nella media

midriff /'mɪdrɪf/ *n* diaframma *m*

mid-season *a* di metà stagione

midshipman /'mɪdʃɪpmən/ *n Br* cadetto *m* di marina; *Am* allievo *m* dell'Accademia Navale

midst /mɪdst/ *n* **in the ~ of** in mezzo a; **in our ~** fra di noi, in mezzo a noi

midstream /mɪd'striːm/ *adv* **in ~** (*in river*) nel mezzo della corrente; (*fig: in speech*) nel mezzo del discorso

midsummer /'mɪdsʌmə(r)/ *n* mezza estate *f*

Midsummer's Day *n* festa *f* di San Giovanni (*24 giugno*)

mid-term *attrib Sch* di metà trimestre; *Pol* a metà del mandato del governo

midway /'mɪdweɪ/ *adv* a metà strada

midweek /mɪd'wiːk/ *a* di metà settimana ● *adv* a metà settimana

midwife /'mɪdwaɪf/ *n* ostetrica *f*

midwifery /'mɪdwɪfrɪ/ *n* ostetricia *f*

midwinter /mɪd'wɪntə(r)/ *n* pieno inverno *m*

miffed /mɪft/ *a fam* seccato

might¹ /maɪt/ *v aux* **I ~** potrei; **will you come? – I ~** vieni? – può darsi; **it ~ be true** potrebbe essere vero; **I ~ as well stay** potrei anche restare; **he asked if he ~ go** ha chiesto se poteva andare; **you ~ have drowned** avresti potuto affogare; **you ~ have said so!** avresti potuto dirlo!

might² *n* potere *m*

mighty /'maɪtɪ/ *a* (**-ier, -iest**) potente ● *adv fam* molto

migraine /'miːgreɪn/ *n* emicrania *f*

migrant /'maɪgrənt/ *a* migratore ● *n* (*bird*) migratore, -trice *mf*; (*person: for work*) emigrante *mf*

migrate /maɪ'greɪt/ *vi* migrare

migration /maɪ'greɪʃn/ *n* migrazione *f*

migratory /maɪ'greɪtərɪ/ *a* ⟨*animal*⟩ migratore

mike /maɪk/ *n fam* microfono *f*

Milan /mɪ'læn/ *n* Milano *f*

Milanese /mɪlə'niːz/ *a* milanese

mild /maɪld/ *a* ⟨*weather*⟩ mite; (*person*) dolce; ⟨*flavour*⟩ delicato; (*illness*) leggero

mildew /'mɪldjuː/ *n* muffa *f*

mildly /'maɪldlɪ/ *adv* moderatamente; ⟨*say*⟩ dolcemente; **to put it ~** a dir poco, senza esagerazione

mildness /'maɪldnɪs/ *n* (*of person, words*) dolcezza *f*; (*of weather*) mitezza *f*

mile /maɪl/ *n* miglio *m* (= *1,6 km*); **~s nicer** *fam* molto più bello; **~s too big** *fam* eccessivamente grande

mileage /'maɪlɪdʒ/ *n* chilometraggio *m*

mileage allowance *n* indennità *f inv* di trasferta per chilometro

milestone /'maɪlstəʊn/ *n* pietra *f* miliare

milieu /mɪ'ljɜː/ *n* ambiente *m*

militant /'mɪlɪtənt/ *a & n* militante *mf*

militarism /'mɪlɪtərɪzm/ *n* militarismo *m*

militarize /'mɪlɪtəraɪz/ *vt* militarizzare

military /'mɪlɪtrɪ/ *a* militare

military: military academy *n* accademia *f* militare. **military policeman** *n* agente *m* di polizia militare. **military service** *n* servizio *m* militare

militate /'mɪlɪteɪt/ *vi* **~ against** opporsi a

militia /mɪ'lɪʃə/ *n* milizia *f*

milk /mɪlk/ *n* latte *m* ● *vt* mungere

milk: milk chocolate *n* cioccolato *m* al latte. **milk float** *n Br* furgone *m* del lattaio. **milk jug** *n* bricco *m* del latte. **milkman** *n* lattaio *m*. **milk pudding** *n* budino *m* a base di latte. **milk shake** *n* frappé *m inv*. **milk train** *n* primo treno *m* del mattino

milky /'mɪlkɪ/ *a* (**-ier, -iest**) latteo; ⟨*tea etc*⟩ con molto latte. **Milky Way** *n Astr* Via *f* Lattea

mill /mɪl/ *n* mulino *m*; (*factory*) fabbrica *f*; (*for coffee etc*) macinino *m* ● *vt* macinare ⟨*grain*⟩

■ **mill about, mill around** *vi* brulicare

millennium /mɪ'lenɪəm/ *n* millennio *m*

miller /'mɪlə(r)/ *n* mugnaio *m*

millet /'mɪlɪt/ *n* miglio *m*

milligram /'mɪlɪgræm/ *n* milligrammo *m*

millimetre /'mɪlɪmiːtə(r)/ *n* millimetro *m*

million /'mɪljən/ *a & n* milione *m*; **a ~ pounds** un milione di sterline

millionaire /mɪljə'neə(r)/ *n* miliardario, -a *mf*

millipede /'mɪlɪpiːd/ *n* millepiedi *m inv*

mill: millpond *n* **like a ~** calmo come una tavola. **millstone** *n* **a ~ round one's neck** *fig* un peso; **mill-wheel** *n* ruota *f* di mulino

milometer /maɪ'lɒmɪtə(r)/ *n Br* ≈ contachilometri *m inv*

mime /maɪm/ *n* mimo *m* ● *vt* mimare

mime artist *n* mimo, -a *mf*

mimic /'mɪmɪk/ *n* imitatore, -trice *mf* ● *vt* (*pt/pp* **mimicked**) imitare

mimicry /'mɪmɪkrɪ/ *n* mimetismo *m*

mimosa /mɪ'məʊzə/ *n* mimosa *f*

minaret /mɪnə'ret/ *n* minareto *m*

mince /mɪns/ *n* carne *f* tritata ● *vt Culin* tritare; **not ~ words** parlare senza mezzi termini

mincemeat /'mɪnsmi:t/ n miscuglio m di frutta secca; **make ~ of** fig demolire

mince pie n pasticcino m a base di frutta secca

mincer /'mɪnsə(r)/ n tritacarne m inv

mind /maɪnd/ n mente f; (sanity) ragione f; **to my ~** a mio parere; **give sb a piece of one's ~** dire chiaro e tondo a qcno quello che si pensa; **make up one's ~** decidersi; **have sth in ~** avere qcsa in mente; **bear sth in ~** tenere presente qcsa; **have something on one's ~** essere preoccupato; **have a good ~ to** avere una grande voglia di; **I have changed my ~** ho cambiato idea; **be out of one's ~** essere fuori di sé ● vt (look after) occuparsi di; **I don't ~ the noise** il rumore non mi dà fastidio; **I don't ~ what we do** non mi importa quello che facciamo; **~ the step!** attenzione al gradino! ● vi **I don't ~** non mi importa; **never ~!** non importa!; **do you ~ if...?** ti dispiace se...?

■ **mind out** vi **~ out!** [fai] attenzione!

mind: **mind-bending** /-bendɪŋ/ a ‹problem› complicatissimo; **~ drugs** psicofarmaci mpl. **mind-blowing** /-bləʊɪŋ/ a fam sconvolgente. **mind-boggling** /-bɒglɪŋ/ a fam incredibile

minded /'maɪndɪd/ a **if you're so ~** se vuole

minder /'maɪndə(r)/ n (Br: bodyguard) gorilla m inv; (for child) baby-sitter mf inv

mindful /'maɪndfʊl/ a **~ of** attento a

mindless /'maɪndlɪs/ a noncurante

mind-reader n persona f che legge nel pensiero; **I'm not a ~** non leggo nel pensiero

mine[1] /maɪn/ poss pron il mio m, la mia f, i miei mpl, le mie fpl; **a friend of ~** un mio amico; **friends of ~** dei miei amici; **that is ~** questo è mio; (as opposed to yours) questo è il mio

mine[2] n miniera f; (explosive) mina f ● vt estrarre; Mil minare

mine-detector n rivelatore m di mine

minefield /'maɪnfi:ld/ n also fig campo m minato

miner /'maɪnə(r)/ n minatore m

mineral /'mɪnərəl/ n minerale m ● a minerale

mineral: **mineral oil** n (Am: paraffin) olio m minerale. **mineral rights** npl concessioni fpl minerarie. **mineral water** n acqua f minerale

minesweeper /'maɪnswi:pə(r)/ n dragamine m inv

mingle /'mɪŋgl/ vi **~ with** mescolarsi a

mini /'mɪnɪ/ n see **miniskirt**

mini+ pref mini+

miniature /'mɪnɪtʃə(r)/ a in miniatura ● n miniatura f

miniature golf n minigolf m inv

miniature railway n trenino m

mini: **mini-budget** n Br Pol budget m inv provvisorio. **minibus** n minibus m inv, pulmino m. **minicab** n taxi m inv

minim /'mɪnɪm/ n Mus minima f

minimal /'mɪnɪməl/ a minimo

minimally /'mɪnɪməlɪ/ adv (very slightly) minimamente

minimarket /'mɪnɪmɑ:kɪt/ n minimarket m inv

minimize /'mɪnɪmaɪz/ vt minimizzare

minimum /'mɪnɪməm/ n (pl **-ima**) minimo m ● a minimo; **ten minutes ~** minimo dieci minuti

mining /'maɪnɪŋ/ n estrazione f ● attrib estrattivo

mining engineer n ingegnere m minerario

miniskirt /'mɪnɪskɜ:t/ n minigonna f

minister /'mɪnɪstə(r)/ n ministro m; Relig pastore m

ministerial /mɪnɪ'stɪərɪəl/ a ministeriale

minister of state n Br Pol titolo m di un parlamentare con competenze specifiche in seno a un ministero

ministry /'mɪnɪstrɪ/ n Pol ministero m; **the ~** Relig il ministero sacerdotale

mink /mɪŋk/ n visone m

minnow /'mɪnəʊ/ n (fish) pesciolino m d'acqua dolce

minor /'maɪnə(r)/ a minore ● n minorenne mf

Minorca /mɪ'nɔ:kə/ n Minorca f

minority /maɪ'nɒrətɪ/ n minoranza f; (age) minore età f

minority leader n Am Pol leader mf inv dell'opposizione

minority rule n governo m di minoranza

minor offence n Br reato m minore

minor road n strada f secondaria

minster /'mɪnstə(r)/ n (cathedral) cattedrale f

mint[1] /mɪnt/ n zecca f; fam patrimonio m ● a **in ~ condition** in condizione perfetta ● vt coniare

mint[2] n (herb) menta f

mint-flavoured /-fleɪvəd/ a al gusto di menta

minuet /mɪnjʊ'et/ n minuetto m

minus /'maɪnəs/ prep meno; (fam: without) senza ● n **~ [sign]** meno m

minute[1] /'mɪnɪt/ n minuto m; **in a ~** (shortly) in un minuto; **~s** pl (of meeting) verbale msg

minute[2] /maɪ'nju:t/ a minuto; (precise) minuzioso

minute hand /'mɪnɪt/ n lancetta f dei minuti

minutely /maɪ'nju:tlɪ/ adv ‹vary, differ› di poco; ‹describe, examine› minuziosamente

minutiae /maɪ'nju:ʃɪaɪ/ npl minuzie fpl

miracle /'mɪrəkl/ n miracolo m

miraculous /mɪ'rækjʊləs/ a miracoloso

mirage /'mɪrɑ:ʒ/ n miraggio m

mire /'maɪə(r)/ n pantano m

mirror /'mɪrə(r)/ n specchio m ● vt rispecchiare

mirror image n (exact replica) copia f esatta; (inverse) immagine f speculare

mirth /mɜ:θ/ n ilarità f

misadventure /mɪsæd'ventʃə(r)/ n disavventura f

misanthropist /mɪˈzænθrəpɪst/ n misantropo, -a mf

misapprehension /mɪsæprɪˈhenʃn/ n malinteso m; **be under a ~** avere frainteso

misappropriate /mɪsəˈprəʊprɪeɪt/ vt appropriarsi indebitamente di ⟨funds⟩

misbehave /mɪsbɪˈheɪv/ vi comportarsi male

misbehaviour /mɪsbɪˈheɪvjə(r)/ n comportamento m scorretto

miscalculate /mɪsˈkælkjʊleɪt/ vt/i calcolare male

miscalculation /mɪskælkjʊˈleɪʃn/ n calcolo m sbagliato

miscarriage /ˈmɪskærɪdʒ/ n aborto m spontaneo; **~ of justice** errore m giudiziario

miscarry /mɪsˈkærɪ/ vi abortire

miscellaneous /mɪsəˈleɪnɪəs/ a assortito

miscellany /mɪˈselənɪ/ n ⟨of people, things⟩ misto m; ⟨anthology⟩ miscellanea f

mischief /ˈmɪstʃɪf/ n malefatta f; ⟨harm⟩ danno m

mischievous /ˈmɪstʃɪvəs/ a ⟨naughty⟩ birichino; ⟨malicious⟩ dannoso

mischievously /ˈmɪstʃɪvəslɪ/ adv in modo birichino

misconceived /mɪskənˈsiːvd/ a ⟨argument, project⟩ sbagliato

misconception /mɪskənˈsepʃn/ n concetto m erroneo

misconduct /mɪsˈkɒndʌkt/ n cattiva condotta f

misconstrue /mɪskənˈstruː/ vt fraintendere

miscount /mɪsˈkaʊnt/ vt/i contare male

misdeed /mɪsˈdiːd/ n misfatto m

misdemeanour /mɪsdɪˈmiːnə(r)/ n reato m

misdirect /mɪsdaɪˈrekt/ vt mettere l'indirizzo sbagliato su ⟨letter, parcel⟩; dare istruzioni sbagliate a ⟨jury⟩; **the letter was ~ed to our old address** la lettera ci è stata erroneamente spedita al vecchio indirizzo

miser /ˈmaɪzə(r)/ n avaro m

miserable /ˈmɪzrəbl/ a ⟨unhappy⟩ infelice; ⟨wretched⟩ miserabile; ⟨fig: weather⟩ deprimente

miserably /ˈmɪzrəblɪ/ adv ⟨live, fail⟩ miseramente; ⟨say⟩ tristemente

miserly /ˈmaɪzəlɪ/ a avaro; ⟨amount⟩ ridicolo

misery /ˈmɪzərɪ/ n miseria f; ⟨fam: person⟩ piagnone, -a mf

misfire /mɪsˈfaɪə(r)/ vi ⟨gun:⟩ far cilecca; ⟨plan etc:⟩ non riuscire

misfit /ˈmɪsfɪt/ n disadattato, -a mf

misfortune /mɪsˈfɔːtʃuːn/ n sfortuna f

misgivings /mɪsˈɡɪvɪŋz/ npl dubbi mpl

misguided /mɪsˈɡaɪdɪd/ a fuorviato

mishandle /mɪsˈhændl/ vt gestire male ⟨operation, meeting⟩; non prendere per il verso giusto ⟨person⟩; ⟨roughly⟩ maneggiare senza precauzioni ⟨object⟩; maltrattare ⟨person, animal⟩

mishap /ˈmɪshæp/ n disavventura f

mishear /mɪsˈhɪə(r)/ vt sentire male

mishmash /ˈmɪʃmæʃ/ n fam guazzabuglio m

misinform /mɪsɪnˈfɔːm/ vt informar male

misinformation /mɪsɪnfəˈmeɪʃn/ n informazioni fpl sbagliate

misinterpret /mɪsɪnˈtɜːprɪt/ vt fraintendere

misinterpretation /mɪsɪntɜːprɪˈteɪʃn/ n interpretazione f sbagliata

misjudge /mɪsˈdʒʌdʒ/ vt giudicar male; ⟨estimate wrongly⟩ valutare male

mislay /mɪsˈleɪ/ vt ⟨pt/pp -laid⟩ smarrire

mislead /mɪsˈliːd/ vt ⟨pt/pp -led⟩ fuorviare

misleading /mɪsˈliːdɪŋ/ a fuorviante

mismanage /mɪsˈmænɪdʒ/ vt amministrare male

mismanagement /mɪsˈmænɪdʒmənt/ n cattiva amministrazione f

mismatch /ˈmɪsmætʃ/ n discordanza f

misname /mɪsˈneɪm/ vt dare il nome sbagliato a

misnomer /mɪsˈnəʊmə(r)/ n termine m improprio

misogynist /mɪsˈɒdʒənɪst/ n misogino m

misplace /mɪsˈpleɪs/ vt mettere in un posto sbagliato; **~ one's trust** riporre male la propria fiducia

misprint /ˈmɪsprɪnt/ n errore m di stampa

mispronounce /mɪsprəˈnaʊns/ vt pronunciare male

mispronunciation /mɪsprənʌnsɪˈeɪʃn/ n ⟨act⟩ pronuncia f sbagliata; ⟨instance⟩ errore m di pronuncia

misquote /mɪsˈkwəʊt/ vt citare erroneamente

misread /mɪsˈriːd/ vt leggere male ⟨sentence, meter⟩; ⟨misinterpret⟩ fraintendere ⟨actions⟩

misrepresent /mɪsreprɪˈzent/ vt rappresentare male

misrepresentation /mɪsreprɪzenˈteɪʃn/ n ⟨of facts, opinions⟩ travisamento m

Miss /mɪs/ n ⟨pl -es⟩ signorina f

miss n colpo m mancato ● vt ⟨fail to hit or find⟩ mancare; perdere ⟨train, bus, class⟩; ⟨feel the loss of⟩ sentire la mancanza di; **I ~ed that part** ⟨failed to notice⟩ mi è sfuggita quella parte; **~ the point** non afferrare il punto ● vi but **he ~ed** ⟨failed to hit⟩ ma l'ha mancato

■ **miss out** vt saltare, omettere

misshapen /mɪsˈʃeɪpən/ a malformato

missile /ˈmɪsaɪl/ n missile m

missing /ˈmɪsɪŋ/ a mancante; ⟨person⟩ scomparso; Mil disperso; **be ~** essere introvabile; **~ in action** Mil disperso

mission /ˈmɪʃn/ n missione f

missionary /ˈmɪʃənrɪ/ n missionario, -a mf

missive /ˈmɪsɪv/ n missiva f

misspell /mɪsˈspel/ vt ⟨pt/pp -spelt, -spelled⟩ sbagliare l'ortografia di

misspent /mɪsˈspent/ a **a ~ youth** una gioventù sprecata

mist /mɪst/ n ⟨fog⟩ foschia f; **because of the ~ on the windows** a causa dei vetri appannati

■ **mist up** vi appannarsi, annebbiarsi

mistake /mɪˈsteɪk/ n sbaglio m; **by ~** per sbaglio ● vt ⟨pt mistook, pp mistaken⟩ sbagliare ⟨*road, house*⟩; fraintendere ⟨*meaning, words*⟩; ~ **for** prendere per

mistaken /mɪ'steɪkən/ *a* sbagliato; **be ~** sbagliarsi; ~ **identity** errore *m* di persona

mistakenly /mɪ'steɪkənlɪ/ *adv* erroneamente

mister /'mɪstə(r)/ *n* signore *m*

mistletoe /'mɪsltəʊ/ *n* vischio *m*

mistranslate /mɪstrænz'leɪt/ *vt* tradurre in modo sbagliato

mistranslation /mɪstrænz'leɪʃn/ *n* traduzione *f* sbagliata

mistreat /mɪs'triːt/ maltrattare

mistreatment /mɪs'triːtmənt/ *n* maltrattamento *m*

mistress /'mɪstrɪs/ *n* padrona *f*; (*teacher*) maestra *f*; (*lover*) amante *f*

mistrust /mɪs'trʌst/ *n* sfiducia *f* ● *vt* non aver fiducia in

misty /'mɪstɪ/ *a* (**-ier, -iest**) nebbioso; *fig* indistinto

misty-eyed /-'aɪd/ *a* ⟨*look*⟩ commosso; **he goes all ~ about it** a parlarne si commuove

misunderstand /mɪsʌndə'stænd/ *vt* (*pt/pp* **-stood**) fraintendere

misunderstanding /mɪsʌndə'stændɪŋ/ *n* malinteso *m*

misuse[1] /mɪs'juːz/ *vt* usare male

misuse[2] /mɪs'juːs/ *n* cattivo uso *m*

mite /maɪt/ *n Zool* acaro *m*; (*child*) piccino, -a *mf*

mitigate /'mɪtɪgeɪt/ *vt* attenuare

mitigating /'mɪtɪgeɪtɪŋ/ *a* attenuante

mitt /mɪt/ *n* (*no separate fingers*) muffola *f*; (*cut-off fingers*) mezzo guanto *m*; (*in baseball*) guantone *m*; (*fam: hand*) mano *f*

mitten /'mɪtn/ *n* manopola *f*, muffola *f*

mix /mɪks/ *n* (*combination*) mescolanza *f*; *Culin* miscuglio *m*; (*ready-made*) preparato *m* ● *vt* mischiare ● *vi* mischiarsi; ⟨*person:*⟩ inserirsi; ~ **with** (*associate with*) frequentare

■ **mix in** *vt* incorporare ⟨*eggs, flour etc*⟩

■ **mix up** *vt* mescolare ⟨*papers*⟩; (*confuse, mistake for*) confondere

mixed /mɪkst/ *a* misto; ~ **up** ⟨*person*⟩ confuso

mixed: mixed ability *a* ⟨*class, teaching*⟩ per alunni di capacità diverse. **mixed bag: it was a very ~ ~** *n fig* c'era un po' di tutto. **mixed blessing: be a ~ ~** *n* avere vantaggi e svantaggi. **mixed doubles** *npl Tennis* doppio *m* misto. **mixed economy** *n* economia *f* mista. **mixed grill** *n* grigliata *f* di carne mista. **mixed marriage** *n* matrimonio *m* misto. **mixed-media** *a* multimediale. **mixed metaphor** *n* abbinamento *m* di parte di due o più metafore diverse con effetto comico

mixed-up *a* ⟨*person, emotions*⟩ confuso

mixed vegetables *npl* verdure *fpl* miste

mixer /'mɪksə(r)/ *n Culin* frullatore *m*, mixer *m inv*; **he's a good ~** è un tipo socievole

mixing /'mɪksɪŋ/ *n* (*of people, objects, ingredients*) mescolamento *m*; *Mus* mixaggio *m*

mixture /'mɪkstʃə(r)/ *n* mescolanza *f*; (*medicine*) sciroppo *m*; *Culin* miscela *f*

mix-up *n* (*confusion*) confusione *f*; (*mistake*) pasticcio *m*

mm *abbr* (**millimetre(s)**) mm

MO *abbr* (**medical officer**) ufficiale *m* medico; *abbr* (**money order**) vaglia *m inv* postale; *Am abbr* **Missouri**

moan /məʊn/ *n* lamento *m* ● *vi* lamentarsi; (*complain*) lagnarsi

moat /məʊt/ *n* fossato *m*

mob /mɒb/ *n* folla *f*; (*rabble*) gentaglia *f*; (*fam: gang*) banda *f* ● *vt* (*pt/pp* **mobbed**) assalire

mobile /'məʊbaɪl/ *a* mobile ● *n* composizione *f* mobile; (*phone*) [telefono *m*] cellulare *m*

mobile: mobile home *n* casa *f* roulotte. **mobile library** *n Br* biblioteca *f* itinerante. **mobile phone** *n* [telefono *m*] cellulare *m*. **mobile shop** *n* furgone *m* attrezzato per la vendita

mobility /mə'bɪlətɪ/ *n* mobilità *f*

mobility allowance *n Br* indennità *f inv* di accompagnamento

mobilization /məʊbɪlaɪ'zeɪʃn/ *n* mobilitazione *f*

mobilize /'məʊbɪlaɪz/ *vt* mobilitare

mocha /'mɒkə/ *n* moca *m inv*

mock /mɒk/ *a* finto ● *vt* canzonare

mockery /'mɒkərɪ/ *n* derisione *f*; **a ~ of** una parodia di

mock-up *n* modello *m* in scala

MoD *n Br abbr* (**Ministry of Defence**) Ministero *m* della Difesa

modal /'məʊdl/ *a* ~ **auxiliary** verbo *m* modale

mod con /mɒd'kɒn/ *Br abbr* (**modern convenience**) **all ~s** tutti i confort

mode /məʊd/ *n* modo *m*; *Comput* modalità *f*

model /'mɒdl/ *n* modello *m*; [*fashion*] ~ indossatore, -trice *mf*, modello, -a *mf* ● *a* ⟨*yacht, plane*⟩ in miniatura; ⟨*pupil, husband*⟩ esemplare, modello ● *v* (*pt/pp* **modelled**) ● *vt* indossare ⟨*clothes*⟩ ● *vi* fare l'indossatore, -trice *mf*; (*for artist*) posare

modelling /'mɒd(ə)lɪŋ/ *n* (*with clay etc*) modellare *m* con la creta; (*of clothes*) professione *f* di indossatore; **do some ~** (*for artist*) fare il modello

modelling clay *n* creta *f* per modellare

modem /'məʊdem/ *n* modem *m inv* ● *vt* mandare per modem

moderate[1] /'mɒdəreɪt/ *vt* moderare ● *vi* moderarsi

moderate[2] /'mɒdərət/ *a* moderato ● *n Pol* moderato, -a *mf*

moderately /'mɒdərətlɪ/ *adv* ⟨*drink, speak etc*⟩ moderatamente; ⟨*good, bad etc*⟩ relativamente

moderation /mɒdə'reɪʃn/ *n* moderazione *f*; **in ~** con moderazione

modern /'mɒdn/ *a* moderno

modern-day *a* attuale

modernism /'mɒdənɪzm/ *n* modernismo *m*

modernity /mə'dɜːnətɪ/ *n* modernità *f*

modernization /mɒdənaɪ'zeɪʃn/ *n* modernizzazione *f*

modernize /'mɒdənaɪz/ *vt* modernizzare

modern languages *npl* lingue *fpl* moderne

modest /'mɒdɪst/ *a* modesto

modesty /'mɒdɪstɪ/ *n* modestia *f*

modicum /'mɒdɪkəm/ *n* **a ~ of** un po' di

modification /mɒdɪfɪ'keɪʃn/ *n* modificazione *f*

modifier /'mɒdɪfaɪə(r)/ *n* (*in linguistics*) modificatore *m*

modify /'mɒdɪfaɪ/ *vt* (*pt/pp* **-fied**) modificare

modular /'mɒdjʊlə(r)/ *a* ‹course› a moduli; ‹construction, furniture› modulare

modulate /'mɒdjʊleɪt/ *vt/i* modulare

module /'mɒdjuːl/ *n* modulo *m*

modus operandi /məʊdəsɒpə'rændi:/ *n* modus operandi *m inv*

mohican /məʊ'hiːkən/ *n* (*hairstyle*) taglio *m* [di capelli] alla moicana

moist /mɔɪst/ *a* umido

moisten /'mɔɪsn/ *vt* inumidire

moisture /'mɔɪstʃə(r)/ *n* umidità *f*

moisturizer /'mɔɪstʃəraɪzə(r)/ *n* [crema *f*] idratante *m*

molar /'məʊlə(r)/ *n* molare *m*

molasses /mə'læsɪz/ *n Am* melassa *f*

mole[1] /məʊl/ *n* (*on face etc*) neo *m*

mole[2] *n Zool* talpa *f*

mole[3] *n* (*breakwater*) molo *m*

molecular /mə'lekjʊlə(r)/ *a* molecolare

molecule /'mɒlɪkjuːl/ *n* molecola *f*

molehill /'məʊlhɪl/ *n* monticello *m*

moleskin /'məʊlskɪn/ *n* (*fur*) pelliccia *f* di talpa

molest /mə'lest/ *vt* molestare

mollify /'mɒlɪfaɪ/ *vt* (*pt/pp* **-ied**) placare

mollusc /'mɒləsk/ *n* mollusco *m*

mollycoddle /'mɒlɪkɒdl/ *vt* tenere nella bambagia

molten /'məʊltən/ *a* fuso

mom /mɒm/ *n Am fam* mamma *f*

moment /'məʊmənt/ *n* momento *m*; **at the ~** in questo momento

momentarily /məʊmən'terɪlɪ/ *adv* (*for an instant*) per un momento; (*Am: at any moment*) da un momento all'altro; (*Am: very soon*) tra un momento

momentary /'məʊməntrɪ/ *a* momentaneo

momentous /mə'mentəs/ *a* molto importante

momentum /mə'mentəm/ *n* impeto *m*

monarch /'mɒnək/ *n* monarca *m*

monarchist /'mɒnəkɪst/ *n* monarchico, -a *mf*

monarchy /'mɒnəkɪ/ *n* monarchia *f*

monastery /'mɒnəstrɪ/ *n* monastero *m*

monastic /mə'næstɪk/ *a* monastico

Monday /'mʌndeɪ/ *n* lunedì *m inv*

monetary /'mʌnɪtrɪ/ *a* monetario

money /'mʌnɪ/ *n* denaro *m*

money: money box *n* salvadanaio *m*. **moneylender** *n* usuraio *m*. **money order** *n* vaglia *m inv* postale

mongrel /'mʌŋgrəl/ *n* bastardo *m*

monitor /'mɒnɪtə(r)/ *n Techn* monitor *m inv* ● *vt* controllare

monk /mʌŋk/ *n* monaco *m*

monkey /'mʌŋkɪ/ *n* scimmia *f*

■ **monkey about with** *vt* (*fam: interfere with*) armeggiare con

monkey: monkey business *n fam* (*fooling*) scherzi *mpl*; (*cheating*) imbrogli *mpl*. **monkey-nut** *n* nocciolina *f* americana. **monkey wrench** *n* chiave *f* inglese a rullino

monkfish /'mʌŋkfɪʃ/ *n* bottatrice *f*

mono /'mɒnəʊ/ *n* mono *m*

monochrome /'mɒnəkrəʊm/ *a* monocromatico; *Cinema, TV* in bianco e nero

monocle /'mɒnəkl/ *n* monocolo *m*

monogamy /mə'nɒgəmɪ/ *n* monogamia *f*

monogram /'mɒnəgræm/ *n* monogramma *m*

monograph /'mɒnəgrɑːf/ *n* monografia *f*

monolith /'mɒnəlɪθ/ *n* monolito *m*

monologue /'mɒnəlɒg/ *n* monologo *m*

monomania /mɒnə'meɪnɪə/ *n* monomania *f*

monoplane /'mɒnəpleɪn/ *n* monoplano *m*

monopolize /mə'nɒpəlaɪz/ *vt* monopolizzare

monopoly /mə'nɒpəlɪ/ *n* monopolio *m*

monoski /'mɒnəʊskiː/ *n* monosci *m inv* ● *vi* praticare il monosci

monosodium glutamate /mɒnəsəʊdɪəm'gluːtəmeɪt/ *n* glutammato *m* di sodio

monosyllabic /mɒnəsɪ'læbɪk/ *a* monosillabico

monosyllable /'mɒnəsɪləbl/ *n* monosillabo *m*

monotone /'mɒnətəʊn/ *n* **speak in a ~** parlare con tono monotono

monotonous /mə'nɒtənəs/ *a* monotono

monotonously /mə'nɒtənəslɪ/ *adv* di modo monotono

monotony /mə'nɒtənɪ/ *n* monotonia *f*

monsoon /mɒn'suːn/ *n* monsone *m*

monster /'mɒnstə(r)/ *n* mostro *m*

monstrosity /mɒn'strɒsətɪ/ *n* mostruosità *f*

monstrous /'mɒnstrəs/ *a* mostruoso

montage /mɒn'tɑːʒ/ *n* montaggio *m*

Mont Blanc /mɒn'blɒ̃/ *n* Monte *m* Bianco

month /mʌnθ/ *n* mese *m*

monthly /'mʌnθlɪ/ *a* mensile ● *adv* mensilmente ● *n* (*periodical*) mensile *m*

monument /'mɒnjʊmənt/ *n* monumento *m*

monumental /mɒnjʊ'mentl/ *a fig* monumentale

monumentally /mɒnjʊ'mentəlɪ/ *adv* ‹boring, ignorant› enormemente

moo /muː/ *n* muggito *m* ● *vi* (*pt/pp* **mooed**) muggire

mooch /muːtʃ/ *vi* **~ about** *fam* gironzolare; **~ about the house** gironzolare per casa

mood /muːd/ *n* umore *m*; **be in a good/bad ~** essere di buon/cattivo umore; **be in the ~ for** essere in vena di

moody /'muːdɪ/ *a* (**-ier, -iest**) (*variable*) lunatico; (*bad-tempered*) di malumore

moon /muːn/ *n* luna *f*; **over the ~** *fam* al settimo cielo

■ **moon about, moon around** *vi* (*fam: wander aimlessly*) gironzolare

■ **moon over** *vt fam* sospirare d'amore per ⟨*sb*⟩

moon: moonbeam *n* raggio *m* di luna. **moon buggy** *n* veicolo *m* lunare. **moonlight** *n* chiaro *m* di luna ● *vi fam* lavorare in nero. **moonlighting** *n fam* lavoro *m* in nero. **moonlit** *a* illuminato dalla luna. **moonshine** *n* (*nonsense*) fantasie *fpl*; (*Am: liquor*) liquore *m* di contrabbando

moor¹ /mʊə(r)/ *n* brughiera *f*

moor² *vt Naut* ormeggiare

moorhen /'mʊəhen/ *n* gallinella *f* d'acqua

mooring /'mʊərɪŋ/ *n* (*place*) ormeggio *m*; **~s** *pl* (*chains*) ormeggi *mpl*

Moorish /'mʊərɪʃ/ *a* moresco

moorland /'mʊələnd/ *n* brughiera *f*

moose /muːs/ *n* (*pl* **moose**) alce *m*

moot /muːt/ *a* **it's a ~ point** è un punto controverso

mop /mɒp/ *m* mocio^R *m inv*; **~ of hair** zazzera *f* ● *vt* (*pt/pp* **mopped**) lavare con il mocio

■ **mop up** *vt* (*dry*) asciugare con il mocio^R; (*clean*) pulire con il mocio

mope /məʊp/ *vi* essere depresso

■ **mope about, mope around** *vi* trascinarsi

moped /'məʊped/ *n* ciclomotore *m*

moral /'mɒrəl/ *a* morale ● *n* morale *f*

morale /mə'rɑːl/ *n* morale *m*; **be a ~-booster** tirare su di morale

moral fibre *n* forza *f* morale

moralistic /mɒrə'lɪstɪk/ *a* moralistico

morality /mə'rælətɪ/ *n* moralità *f*

moralize /'mɒrəlaɪz/ *vi* moraleggiare

morally /'mɒrəlɪ/ *adv* moralmente

morals /'mɒrəlz/ *npl* moralità *f*

moratorium /mɒrə'tɔːrɪəm/ *n* moratoria *f*

morbid /'mɔːbɪd/ *a* morboso

more /mɔː(r)/ *a* più; **a few ~ books** un po' più di libri; **some ~ tea?** ancora un po' di tè?; **there's no ~ bread** non c'è più pane; **there are no ~ apples** non ci sono più mele; **one ~ word and...** ancora una parola e... ● *pron* di più; **would you like some ~?** ne vuoi ancora?; **no ~, thank you** non ne voglio più, grazie ● *adv* più; **~ interesting** più interessante; **~ (and ~) quickly** (sempre) più veloce; **~ than** più di; **I don't love him any ~** no lo amo più; **once ~** ancora una volta; **~ or less** più o meno; **the ~ I see him, the ~ I like him** più lo vedo, più mi piace

moreish /'mɔːrɪʃ/ *a fam* **be ~** tirare per la gola

moreover /mɔː'rəʊvə(r)/ *adv* inoltre

morgue /mɔːg/ *n* obitorio *m*

MORI /'mɔːrɪ/ *n abbr* (**Market Opinion Research Institute**) *istituto m di sondaggio e ricerche di mercato*

moribund /'mɒrɪbʌnd/ *a* moribondo

morning /'mɔːnɪŋ/ *n* mattino *m*, mattina *f*; **spend the ~ doing sth** passare la mattinata facendo qcsa; **in the ~** del mattino; (*tomorrow*) domani mattina

morning: morning-after pill *n* pillola *f* del giorno dopo. **morning coffee** *n* caffè *m inv* del mattino. **morning dress** *n* tight *m inv*. **morning sickness** *n* nausea *f* mattutina

Moroccan /mə'rɒk(ə)n/ *a & n* marocchino, -a *mf*

Morocco /mə'rɒkəʊ/ *n* Marocco *m*

morocco leather *n* marocchino *m*

moron /'mɔːrɒn/ *n fam* deficiente *mf*

morose /mə'rəʊs/ *a* scontroso

morosely /mə'rəʊslɪ/ *adv* in modo scontroso

morphine /'mɔːfiːn/ *n* morfina *f*

morris dance /'mɒrɪs/ *n* danza *f* tradizionale inglese

Morse /mɔːs/ *n* **~ [code]** [codice *m*] Morse *m*

morsel /'mɔːsl/ *n* (*food*) boccone *m*

mortal /'mɔːtl/ *a & n* mortale *mf*

mortal combat *n* duello *m* mortale

mortality /mɔː'tælətɪ/ *n* mortalità *f*

mortally /'mɔːtəlɪ/ *adv* ⟨*wounded, offended*⟩ a morte; ⟨*afraid*⟩ da morire

mortar /'mɔːtə(r)/ *n* mortaio *m*

mortgage /'mɔːgɪdʒ/ *n* mutuo *m*; (*money raised on collateral of property*) ipoteca *f* ● *vt* ipotecare

mortgage: mortgage rate *n* tasso *m* d'interesse sui mutui. **mortgage relief** *n* sgravio *m* fiscale sui mutui. **mortgage repayment** *n* rata *f* del mutuo

mortician /mɔː'tɪʃn/ *n Am* impresario, -a *mf* di pompe funebri

mortification /mɔːtɪfɪ'keɪʃn/ *n* (*of the flesh, embarrassment*) mortificazione *f*

mortify /'mɔːtɪfaɪ/ *vt* (*pt/pp* **-ied**) mortificare

mortuary /'mɔːtjʊərɪ/ *n* camera *f* mortuaria

mosaic /məʊ'zeɪɪk/ *n* mosaico *m*

Moscow /'mɒskəʊ/ *n* Mosca *f*

Moselle /məʊ'zel/ *n* (*wine*) vino *m* della Mosella

Moses /'məʊzɪz/ *n* Mosè

Moslem /'mʊzlɪm/ *a & n* musulmano, -a *mf*

mosque /mɒsk/ *n* moschea *f*

mosquito /mɒs'kiːtəʊ/ *n* (*pl* **-es**) zanzara *f*

mosquito: mosquito bite *n* puntura *m* di zanzara. **mosquito net** *n* zanzariera *f*. **mosquito repellent** *n* antizanzare *m inv*

moss /mɒs/ *n* muschio *m*

mossy /'mɒsɪ/ *a* muschioso

most /məʊst/ *a* (*majority*) la maggior parte di; **for the ~ part** per lo più ● *adv* più, maggiormente; (*very*) estremamente, molto; **the ~ interesting day** la giornata più interessante; **a ~ interesting day** una giornata estremamente interessante; **the ~ beautiful woman in the world** la donna più bella del mondo; **~ unlikely** veramente improbabile ● *pron* **~ of them** la maggior parte di loro; **at [the] ~** al massimo; **make the ~ of** sfruttare al massimo; **~ of the time** la maggior parte del tempo

mostly /'məʊs(t)lɪ/ *adv* per lo più

MOT *n Br* revisione *f* obbligatoria di autoveicoli

motel /məʊ'tel/ *n* motel *m inv*

moth /mɒθ/ *n* falena *f*; **[clothes-]~** tarma *f*

mothball /'mɒθbɔːl/ *n* pallina *f* di naftalina

moth-eaten /-iːtən/ *a* tarmato
mother /'mʌðə(r)/ *n* madre *f*; **Mother's Day** la festa della mamma ● *vt* fare da madre a
motherboard /'mʌðəbɔːd/ *n* scheda *f* madre
motherhood /'mʌðəhʊd/ *n* maternità *f*
Mothering Sunday /mʌðərɪŋ'sʌndeɪ/ *n* la festa della mamma
mother-in-law *n* (*pl* **mothers-in-law**) suocera *f*
motherland /'mʌðəlænd/ *n* patria *f*
motherless /'mʌðəlɪs/ *a* orfano, -a *mf* di madre
motherly /'mʌðəlɪ/ *a* materno
mother: mother-of-pearl *n* madreperla *f*. **mother's boy** *n* mammone *m*. **Mother's Day** *n* la festa della mamma. **mother's help** *n Br* aiuto *m* domestico. **mother-to-be** *n* futura mamma *f*. **mother tongue** *n* madrelingua *f*
mothproof /'mɒθpruːf/ *a* antitarmico
motif /məʊ'tiːf/ *n* motivo *m*
motion /'məʊʃn/ *n* moto *m*; (*proposal*) mozione *f*; (*gesture*) gesto *m* ● *vt/i* ~ [**to**] **sb to come in** fare segno a qcno di entrare
motionless /'məʊʃ(ə)nlɪs/ *a* immobile
motionlessly /'məʊʃənlɪslɪ/ *adv* senza alcun movimento
motion picture *n* film *m inv* [per il cinema] ● *attrib* (*industry*) cinematografico
motivate /'məʊtɪveɪt/ *vt* motivare
motivation /məʊtɪ'veɪʃn/ *n* motivazione *f*
motive /'məʊtɪv/ *n* motivo *m*
motley /'mɒtlɪ/ *a* disparato
motor /'məʊtə(r)/ *n* motore *m*; (*car*) macchina *f* ● *a* a motore; *Anat* motore ● *vi* andare in macchina
Motorail /'məʊtəreɪl/ *n* treno *m* per trasporto auto
motorbike /'məʊtəbaɪk/ *n fam* moto *f inv*
motor boat *n* motoscafo *m*
motorcade /'məʊtəkeɪd/ *n Am* corteo *m* di auto
motor: motor car *n* automobile *f*. **motorcycle** *n* motocicletta *f*. **motorcycle escort** *n* scorta *f* di motociclette. **motorcycle messenger** *n* corriere *m* in moto. **motorcyclist** *n* motociclista *mf*. **motorhome** *n* camper *m inv*; (*towed*) roulotte *f inv*
motoring /'məʊtərɪŋ/ *n* automobilismo *m*
motorist /'məʊtərɪst/ *n* automobilista *mf*
motor: motor launch *n* motolancia *f*. **motor mechanic** *n* meccanico *m*. **motormouth** *n fam* chiacchierone, -a *mf*. **motor oil** *n* olio *m* lubrificante. **motor racing** *n* corse *fpl* automobilistiche. **motor scooter** *n* vespa *f*. **motor vehicle** *n* autoveicolo *m*. **motorway** *n* autostrada *f*
mottled /'mɒtld/ *a* chiazzato
motto /'mɒtəʊ/ *n* (*pl* **-es**) motto *m*
mould[1] /'məʊld/ *n* (*fungus*) muffa *f*
mould[2] *n* stampo *m* ● *vt* foggiare; *fig* formare
moulder /'məʊldə(r)/ *vi* (*corpse, refuse:*) andare in decomposizione
moulding /'məʊldɪŋ/ *n Archit* cornice *f*
mouldy /'məʊldɪ/ *a* ammuffito; (*fam: worthless*) ridicolo

moult /məʊlt/ *vi* (*bird:*) fare la muta; (*animal:*) perdere il pelo
mound /maʊnd/ *n* mucchio *m*; (*hill*) collinetta *f*
mount /maʊnt/ *n* (*horse*) cavalcatura *f*; (*of jewel, photo, picture*) montatura *f* ● *vt* montare a (*horse*); salire su (*bicycle*); incastonare (*jewel*); incorniciare (*photo, picture*) ● *vi* aumentare
■ **mount up** *vi* aumentare
mountain /'maʊntɪn/ *n* montagna *f*; **make a ~ out of a molehill** fare di una mosca un elefante
mountain bike *n* mountain bike *f inv*
mountain climbing *n* alpinismo *m*
mountaineer /maʊntɪ'nɪə(r)/ *n* alpinista *mf*
mountaineering /maʊntɪ'nɪərɪŋ/ *n* alpinismo *m*
mountainous /'maʊntɪnəs/ *a* montagnoso
mountain range *n* catena *f* montuosa
mountain top *n* cima *f* di montagna
mounted police /maʊntɪdpə'liːs/ *n* polizia *f* a cavallo
mourn /mɔːn/ *vt* lamentare ● *vi* ~ **for** piangere la morte di
mourner /'mɔːnə(r)/ *n* persona *f* che participa a un funerale
mournful /'mɔːnfʊl/ *a* triste
mournfully /'mɔːnfʊlɪ/ *adv* tristemente
mourning /'mɔːnɪŋ/ *n* **in ~** in lutto
mouse /maʊs/ *n* (*pl* **mice**) topo *m*; *Comput* mouse *m inv*
mouse: mousehole *n* tana *f* di topi/di un topo. **mouse mat** *n Comput* tappetino *m*. **mousetrap** *f* trappola *f* [per topi]
mousse /muːs/ *n Culin* mousse *f inv*
moustache /mə'stɑːʃ/ *n* baffi *mpl*
mousy /'maʊsɪ/ *a* (*colour*) grigio topo
mouth[1] /maʊð/ *vt* ~ **sth** dire qcsa silenziosamente muovendo solamente le labbra
mouth[2] /maʊθ/ *n* bocca *f*; (*of river*) foce *f*
mouthful /'maʊθfʊl/ *n* boccone *m*
mouth: mouth organ *n* armonica *f* [a bocca]. **mouthpiece** *n* imboccatura *f*; (*fig: person*) portavoce *m inv*. **mouth-to-mouth resuscitation** *n* respirazione *f* bocca-bocca. **mouthwash** *n* acqua *f* dentifricia. **mouth-watering** /-wɔːtərɪŋ/ *a* che fa venire l'acquolina in bocca
movable /'muːvəbl/ *a* movibile
move /muːv/ *n* mossa *f*; (*moving house*) trasloco *m*; **on the ~** in movimento; **get a ~ on** *fam* darsi una mossa ● *vt* muovere; (*emotionally*) commuovere; spostare (*car, furniture*); (*transfer*) trasferire; (*propose*) proporre; ~ **house** traslocare ● *vi* muoversi; (*move house*) traslocare; **don't ~!** non muoverti!
■ **move about, move around** *vi* (*in house*) muoversi; (*in country*) spostarsi
■ **move along** *vi* andare avanti ● *vt* muovere in avanti
■ **move away** *vi* allontanarsi; (*move house*) trasferirsi ● *vt* allontanare

■ **move forward** *vi* avanzare ● *vt* spostare avanti

■ **move in** *vi* (*to a house*) trasferirsi

■ **move off** *vi* ⟨*vehicle:*⟩ muoversi

■ **move on** *vi* (*move to another place*) muoversi ● *vt* ⟨*police:*⟩ far circolare

■ **move on to** *vt* passare a ⟨*new topic, next question*⟩

■ **move out** *vi* (*of house*) andare via

■ **move over** *vi* spostarsi ● *vt* spostare

■ **move up** *vi* muoversi; (*advance, increase*) avanzare

movement /'muːvmənt/ *n* movimento *m*; (*of clock*) meccanismo *m*

movie /'muːvɪ/ *n* film *m inv*; **go to the ~s** andare al cinema

movie: movie camera *n* cinepresa *f*. **movie director** *n* regista *mf* cinematografico, -a. **movie-goer** *n* persona *f* che va al cinema. **movie star** *n* stella *f* del cinema, star *f inv* del cinema

moving /'muːvɪŋ/ *a* mobile; (*touching*) commovente

mow /məʊ/ *vt* (*pt* **mowed**, *pp* **mown** or **mowed**) tagliare ⟨*lawn*⟩

■ **mow down** *vt* (*destroy*) sterminare

mower /'məʊə(r)/ *n* tosaerba *m inv*

MP *abbr* (**Member of Parliament**) deputato, -a *mf*

mpg *abbr* (**miles per gallon**) miglia al gallone

mph *abbr* (**miles per hour**) miglia all'ora

Mr /'mɪstə(r)/ *n* (*pl* **Messrs**) Signor *m*

Mrs /'mɪsɪz/ *n* Signora *f*

Ms /mɪz/ *n* Signora *f* (*modo m formale di rivolgersi ad una donna quando non si vuole connotarla come sposata o nubile*)

MS *n abbr* (**multiple sclerosis**) sclerosi *f* a placche *or* multipla; *abbr* (**manuscript**) ms; *Am abbr* **Mississippi**

MSc *n abbr* (**Master of Science**) (*diploma*) laurea *f* in discipline scientifiche; (*person*) laureato, -a *mf* in discipline scientifiche

much /mʌtʃ/ *a, adv & pron* molto; **~ as** per quanto; **I love you just as ~ as before/him** ti amo quanto prima/lui; **as ~ as £5 million** ben cinque milioni di sterline; **as ~ as that** così tanto; **very ~** tantissimo, moltissimo; **~ the same** quasi uguale

muck /mʌk/ *n* (*dirt*) sporcizia *f*; (*farming*) letame *m*; (*fam: filth*) porcheria *f*

■ **muck about** *vi fam* perder tempo; **~ about with** trafficare con

■ **muck in** *vi fam* dare una mano

■ **muck up** *vt fam* rovinare; (*make dirty*) sporcare

muckraking /'mʌkreɪkɪŋ/ *n* scandalismo *m*

mucky /'mʌkɪ/ *a* (**-ier, -iest**) sudicio

mucus /'mjuːkəs/ *n* muco *m*

mud /mʌd/ *n* fango *m*

muddle /'mʌdl/ *n* disordine *m*; (*mix-up*) confusione *f* ● *vt* **~ [up]** confondere ⟨*dates*⟩

■ **muddle through** *vi* farcela alla bell'e meglio

muddle-headed /-'hedɪd/ *a* ⟨*plan*⟩ confuso; ⟨*person*⟩ confusionario

muddy /'mʌdɪ/ *a* (**-ier, -iest**) ⟨*path*⟩ fangoso; ⟨*shoes*⟩ infangato

mud: mudflat *n* distesa *f* di fango. **mudguard** *n* parafango *m*. **mud hut** *n* capanna *f* di fango. **mudpack** *n* (*for beauty treatment*) maschera *f* di fango. **mud pie** *n* formina *f* di fango. **mudslide** *n* colata *f* di fango. **mud-slinging** /-slɪŋɪŋ/ *n* diffamazione *f*

muesli /'mjuːzlɪ/ *n* muesli *m inv*

muffle /'mʌfl/ *vt* smorzare ⟨*sound*⟩

■ **muffle up** *vi* (*for warmth*) imbacuccarsi

muffler /'mʌflə(r)/ *n* sciarpa *f*; *Am Auto* marmitta *f*

mug[1] /mʌg/ *n* tazza *f*; (*for beer*) boccale *m*; (*fam: face*) muso *m*; (*fam: simpleton*) pollo *m*

mug[2] *vt* (*pt/pp* **mugged**) aggredire e derubare

■ **mug up** *vt* (*fam: learn*) imparare alla bell'e meglio

mugger /'mʌgə(r)/ *n* assalitore, -trice *mf*

mugging /'mʌgɪŋ/ *n* aggressione *f* per furto

muggy /'mʌgɪ/ *a* (**-ier, -iest**) afoso

mulatto /mjuː'lætəʊ/ *a & n Am* mulatto, -a *mf*

mulberry /'mʌlb(ə)rɪ/ *n Am* (*fruit*) mora *f* di gelso; (*tree*) gelso *m*

mule[1] /mjuːl/ *n* mulo *m*

mule[2] *n* (*slipper*) ciabatta *f*

mulish /'mjuːlɪʃ/ *a* testardo

mull /mʌl/ *vt* **~ over** rimuginare su

mulled /mʌld/ *a* **~ wine** vin brûlé *m inv*

multi+ /'mʌltɪ/ *pref* multi+

multi-access *n Comput* accesso *m* multiplo

multichannel /mʌltɪ'tʃænəl/ *a* ⟨*television*⟩ con molti canali

multicoloured /'mʌltɪkʌləd/ *a* variopinto

multicultural /mʌltɪ'kʌltʃərəl/ *a* multiculturale

multidisciplinary /mʌltɪdɪsɪ'plɪnərɪ/ *a* *Sch, Univ* pluridisciplinare

multifaceted /mʌltɪ'fæsɪtɪd/ *a* ⟨*gemstone*⟩ sfaccettato; ⟨*career*⟩ variegato; ⟨*personality*⟩ sfaccettato

multifunction /mʌltɪ'fʌŋkʃn/ *a* multifunzionale

multigym /'mʌltɪdʒɪm/ *n* attrezzo *m* multiuso

multilateral /mʌltɪ'læt(ə)rəl/ *a Pol* multilaterale

multilevel /'mʌltɪlevəl/ *a* ⟨*parking, access*⟩ a più piani; ⟨*analysis*⟩ a più livelli

multilingual /mʌltɪ'lɪŋgwəl/ *a* multilingue *inv*

multimedia /mʌltɪ'miːdɪə/ *n* multimedia *mpl* ● *a* multimediale

multinational /mʌltɪ'næʃnəl/ *a* multinazionale ● *n* multinazionale *f*

multi-party /'mʌltɪpɑːtɪ/ *a* ⟨*government, system*⟩ pluripartitico

multiple /'mʌltɪpl/ *a & n* multiplo *m*

multiple: multiple choice question *n Sch* test *m inv* a scelta multipla. **multiple**

ownership n comproprietà f. **multiple pile-up** n tamponamento m a catena. **multiple sclerosis** n sclerosi f a placche or multipla. **multiple store** n Br negozio m appartenente a una catena

multiplex /'mʌltɪpleks/ n Teleph multiplex m inv; Cinema cinema m inv multisale ● a Teleph in multiplex

multiplication /mʌltɪplɪ'keɪʃn/ n moltiplicazione f

multiply /'mʌltɪplaɪ/ v (pt/pp -ied) ● vt moltiplicare (**by** per) ● vi moltiplicarsi

multi-purpose a ⟨tool, gadget⟩ multiuso inv; ⟨organization⟩ con più scopi

multi-storey a ~ **car park** parcheggio m a più piani

multi-track a ⟨sound system⟩ a più piste

multitude /'mʌltɪtjuːd/ n moltitudine f; **hide a ~ of sins** ⟨rug etc.⟩ nascondere un sacco di magagne

multi-user a ⟨system, installation⟩ multiutente

mum[1] /mʌm/ a **keep ~** fam non aprire bocca

mum[2] n fam mamma f

mumble /'mʌmbl/ vt/i borbottare

mumbo-jumbo /mʌmbəʊ'dʒʌmbəʊ/ n (fam: speech, writing) paroloni mpl

mummy[1] /'mʌmɪ/ n fam mamma f

mummy[2] n Archaeol mummia f

mummy's boy n Br pej mammone m

mumps /mʌmps/ n orecchioni mpl

munch /mʌntʃ/ vt/i sgranocchiare

mundane /mʌn'deɪn/ a ⟨everyday⟩ banale

municipal /mjʊ'nɪsɪpl/ a municipale

munitions /mjʊ'nɪʃnz/ npl munizioni fpl

mural /'mjʊərəl/ n dipinto m murale

murder /'mɜːdə(r)/ n assassinio m ● vt assassinare; (fam: ruin) massacrare

murder case n caso m di omicidio

murder charge n imputazione f di omicidio

murderer /'mɜːdərə(r)/ n assassino, -a mf

murderous /'mɜːdərəs/ a omicida

murky /'mɜːkɪ/ a (-ier, -iest) oscuro

murmur /'mɜːmə(r)/ n mormorio m ● vt/i mormorare

murmuring /'mɜːmərɪŋ/ n mormorio m; **~s** pl (of discontent) segnali mpl di malcontento

muscle /'mʌsl/ n muscolo m

■ **muscle in** vi sl intromettersi (**to** in)

muscle strain n strappo m muscolare

muscular /'mʌskjʊlə(r)/ a muscolare; (strong) muscoloso

muscular dystrophy /'dɪstrəfɪ/ n distrofia f muscolare

muse /mjuːz/ vi meditare (**on** su)

museum /mjuː'zɪəm/ n museo m

mushroom /'mʌʃrʊm/ n fungo m ● vi fig spuntare come funghi

mushroom cloud n fungo m atomico

mushy /'mʌʃɪ/ a fig sdolcinato

music /'mjuːzɪk/ n musica f; (written) spartito m; **set to ~** musicare

musical /'mjuːzɪkl/ a musicale; ⟨person⟩ do-

tato di senso musicale ● n commedia f musicale

musical box n carillon m inv

musical instrument n strumento m musicale

music: music box n carillon m inv. **music centre** n impianto m stereo. **music hall** n teatro m di varietà

musician /mjuː'zɪʃn/ n musicista mf

music lover n amante mf della musica

musicology /mjuːzɪ'kɒlədʒɪ/ n musicologia f

music: music stand n leggio m. **music stool** n sgabello m per pianoforte. **music video** n video clip m inv

musings /'mjuːzɪŋz/ npl riflessioni fpl

musket /'mʌskɪt/ n moschetto m

musketeer /mʌskə'tɪə(r)/ n moschettiere m

musky /'mʌskɪ/ a muschiato

Muslim /'mʊzlɪm/ a & n musulmano, -a mf

mussel /'mʌsl/ n cozza f

must /mʌst/ v aux (solo al presente) dovere; **you ~ not be late** non devi essere in ritardo; **she ~ have finished by now** (probability) deve aver finito ormai ● n a ~ fam una cosa da non perdere

mustard /'mʌstəd/ n senape f

muster /'mʌstə(r)/ vt radunare ⟨troops⟩; fare appello a ⟨strength⟩

musty /'mʌstɪ/ a (-ier, -iest) stantio

mutant /'mjuːtənt/ n & a mutante mf

mutate /mjuː'teɪt/ vi ⟨cell, organism⟩ subire una mutazione; **~ into** ⟨alien, monster⟩ trasformarsi in ● vt far subire una mutazione

mutation /mjuː'teɪʃn/ n Biol mutazione f

mute /mjuːt/ a muto

muted /'mjuːtɪd/ a smorzato

mutilate /'mjuːtɪleɪt/ vt mutilare

mutilation /mjuːtɪ'leɪʃn/ n mutilazione f

mutinous /'mjuːtɪnəs/ a ammutinato

mutiny /'mjuːtɪnɪ/ n ammutinamento m ● vi (pt/pp -ied) ammutinarsi

mutter /'mʌtə(r)/ n borbottio m ● vt/i borbottare

mutton /'mʌtn/ n carne f di montone

mutual /'mjuːtjʊəl/ a reciproco; (fam: common) comune

mutually /'mjuːtjʊəlɪ/ adv reciprocamente

Muzak® /'mjuːzæk/ n musica f di sottofondo

muzzle /'mʌzl/ n (of animal) muso m; (of firearm) bocca f; (for dog) museruola f ● vt fig mettere il bavaglio a

MW abbr (**medium wave**) OM

my /maɪ/ poss a mio m, mia f, miei mpl, mie fpl; **my job/house** il mio lavoro/la mia casa; **my mother/father** mia madre/mio padre

myalgic encephalomyelitis /maɪ-ældʒɪkensefələʊmaɪ'laɪtɪs/ n encefalomielite f mialgica

myopic /maɪ'ɒpɪk/ a miope

myself /maɪ'self/ pers pron (reflexive) mi; (emphatic) me stesso; (after prep) me; **I've seen it ~** l'ho visto io stesso; **by ~** da solo; **I thought to ~** ho pensato tra me e me; **I'm proud of ~** sono fiero di me

mysterious /mɪ'stɪərɪəs/ a misterioso

mysteriously /mɪ'stɪərɪəslɪ/ *adv* misteriosamente

mystery /'mɪstərɪ/ *n* mistero *m*; ~ [**story**] racconto *m* del mistero

mystery play *n* mistero *m* (*teatrale*)

mystery tour *n* viaggio *m* con destinazione a sorpresa

mystic[al] /'mɪstɪk[l]/ *a* mistico

mysticism /'mɪstɪsɪzm/ *n* misticismo *m*

mystification /ˌmɪstɪfɪ'keɪʃn/ *n* disorientamento *m*

mystified /'mɪstɪfaɪd/ *a* disorientato

mystify /'mɪstɪfaɪ/ *vt* disorientare

mystique /mɪ'stiːk/ *n* mistica *f*

myth /mɪθ/ *n* mito *m*

mythical /'mɪθɪkl/ *a* mitico

mythological /mɪθə'lɒdʒɪkl/ *a* mitologico

mythology /mɪ'θɒlədʒɪ/ *n* mitologia *f*

Nn

n, N /en/ *n* (*letter*) n, N *f inv*

N *abbr* (**north**) N

n/a, N/A *abbr* (**not applicable**) non pertinente

nab /næb/ *vt* (*pt/pp* **nabbed**) *fam* beccare

nadir /'neɪdɪə/ *n* nadir *m*; *fig* punto *m* più basso, fondo *m*

naff /næf/ *a Br fam* banale

nag[1] /næg/ *n* (*horse*) ronzino *m*

nag[2] *v* (*pt/pp* **nagged**) ● *vt* assillare ● *vi* essere insistente ● *n* (*person*) brontolone, -a *mf*

nagging /'nægɪŋ/ *a* (*pain*) persistente

nail /neɪl/ *n* chiodo *m*; (*of finger, toe*) unghia *f*; **on the ~** *fam* sull'unghia

■ **nail down** *vt* inchiodare; ~ **sb down to a time/price** far fissare a qcno un'ora/un prezzo

nail: nail-biting /-baɪtɪŋ/ *n* abitudine *f* di mangiarsi le unghie ● *a* (*match, finish*) mozzafiato *inv*; (*wait*) esasperante. **nail brush** *n* spazzolino *m* da unghie. **nail clippers** *npl* tronchesina *m*. **nail file** *n* limetta *f* da unghie. **nail polish** *n* smalto *m* [per unghie]. **nail polish remover** *n* acetone *m*, solvente *m* per unghie. **nail scissors** *npl* forbicine *fpl* da unghie. **nail varnish** *n* smalto *m* [per unghie]

naïve /naɪ'iːv/ *a* ingenuo

naïvely /naɪ'iːvlɪ/ *adv* ingenuamente

naïvety /naɪ'iːvətɪ/ *n* ingenuità *f*

naked /'neɪkɪd/ *a* nudo; **with the ~ eye** a occhio nudo

nakedness /'neɪkɪdnɪs/ *n* nudità *f*

name /neɪm/ *n* nome *m*; **what's your ~?** come ti chiami?; **my ~ is Matthew** mi chiamo Matthew; **I know her by ~** la conosco di nome; **by the ~ of Bates** di nome Bates; **make a ~ for oneself** farsi un nome; **call sb ~s** *fam* insultare qcno ● *vt* (*to position*) nominare; chiamare (*baby*); (*identify*) citare; **be ~d after** essere chiamato col nome di

name day *n Relig* onomastico *m*

name-drop *vi* **he's always ~ping** si vanta sempre di conoscere persone famose

nameless /'neɪmlɪs/ *a* senza nome

namely /'neɪmlɪ/ *adv* cioè

name: nameplate *n* targhetta *f*. **namesake** *n* omonimo, -a *mf*. **name tag** *n* targhetta *f* attaccata a un oggetto con il nome del proprietario. **name tape** *n* fettuccia *f* attaccata a un oggetto con il nome del proprietario

Namibia /nə'mɪbɪə/ *n* Namibia *f*

nanny /'nænɪ/ *n* bambinaia *f*

nanny goat *n* capra *f*

nap /næp/ *n* pisolino *m*; **have a ~** fare un pisolino ● *vi* **catch sb ~ping** cogliere qcno alla sprovvista

napalm /'neɪpɑːm/ *n* napalm *m*

nape /neɪp/ *n* ~ [**of the neck**] nuca *f*

napkin /'næpkɪn/ *n* tovagliolo *m*

Naples /'neɪp(ə)lz/ *n* Napoli *f*

nappy /'næpɪ/ *n* pannolino *m*

nappy liner *n* filtrante *m*

nappy rash *n Br* eritema *m* da pannolini

narcotic /nɑː'kɒtɪk/ *a & n* narcotico *m*

narcotics agent *n Am* agente *m* della squadra antidroga

narked /nɑːkt/ *a fam* scocciato

narrate /nə'reɪt/ *vt* narrare

narration /nə'reɪʃn/ *n* narrazione *f*

narrative /'nærətɪv/ *a* narrativo ● *n* narrazione *f*

narrator /nə'reɪtə(r)/ *n* narratore, -trice *mf*

narrow /'nærəʊ/ *a* stretto; (*fig: views*) ristretto; (*margin, majority*) scarso; **have a ~ escape** scamparla per un pelo ● *vi* restringersi

■ **narrow down** *vt* (*reduce*) restringere

narrowly /'nærəʊlɪ/ *adv* ~ **escape death** evitare la morte per un pelo

narrow-minded /-'maɪndɪd/ *a* di idee ristrette

nasal /'neɪzl/ *a* nasale

nasal spray *n* spray *m inv* nasale

nastily /'nɑːstɪlɪ/ *adv* (*spitefully*) con cattiveria

nasty /'nɑːstɪ/ *a* (**-ier, -iest**) (*smell, person, remark*) cattivo; (*injury, situation, weather*) brutto; **turn ~** (*person:*) diventare cattivo; (*situation:*) mettersi male; (*weather:*) volgere al brutto

nation /'neɪʃn/ *n* nazione *f*

national /'næʃən(ə)l/ a nazionale ● n cittadino, -a mf

national: national anthem n inno m nazionale. **National Curriculum** n Br programma m scolastico ministeriale per il Galles e l'Inghilterra. **national debt** n debito m pubblico. **National Front** n Br partito m britannico di estrema destra. **national grid** n Electr rete f elettrica nazionale. **National Health** n Br servizio m nazionale di assistenza sanitaria. **National Health Service** n servizio m sanitario britannico. **National Insurance** n ≈ Previdenza f sociale. **National Insurance number** n numero m di Previdenza sociale

nationalism /'næʃənəlɪzm/ n nazionalismo m

nationality /næʃə'nælətɪ/ n nazionalità f inv

nationalization /næʃənəlaɪ'zeɪʃn/ n nazionalizzazione

nationalize /'næʃənəlaɪz/ vt nazionalizzare

nationally /'næʃənəlɪ/ adv a livello nazionale

national: national monument n monumento m nazionale. **National Savings Bank** n Br Cassa f di risparmio. **national service** n Br servizio m militare. **National Trust** n Br associazione f per la tutela del patrimonio culturale e ambientale in Gran Bretagna

nation state n stato-nazione m

nationwide /'neɪʃnwaɪd/ a su scala nazionale

native /'neɪtɪv/ a nativo; (innate) innato ● n nativo, -a mf; (local inhabitant) abitante mf del posto; (outside Europe) indigeno, -a mf; **she's a ~ of Venice** è originaria di Venezia

native: Native American a & n amerindio, -a mf. **native land** n paese m nativo. **native language** n lingua f madre. **native speaker** n persona f di madrelingua; **Italian ~ ~s** Italiani madrelingua

Nativity /nə'tɪvətɪ/ n **the ~** la Natività

Nativity play n rappresentazione f sulla nascita di Gesù

Nato, NATO /'neɪtəʊ/ n abbr (North Atlantic Treaty Organization) NATO f

natter /'nætə(r)/ n **have a ~** fam fare quattro chiacchiere ● vi fam chiacchierare

natty /'nætɪ/ a fam (smart) chic inv; (clever) geniale

natural /'nætʃ(ə)rəl/ a naturale

natural: natural childbirth n parto m indolore. **natural gas** n metano m. **natural history** n storia f naturale

naturalist /'nætʃ(ə)rəlɪst/ n naturalista mf

naturalization /nætʃ(ə)rəlaɪ'zeɪʃn/ n naturalizzazione f

naturalize /'nætʃ(ə)rəlaɪz/ vt naturalizzare

naturally /'nætʃ(ə)rəlɪ/ adv (of course) naturalmente; (by nature) per natura

nature /'neɪtʃə(r)/ n natura f; **by ~** per natura

nature: nature conservancy n protezione f della natura. **nature reserve** n riserva f naturale. **nature trail** n percorso m ecologico

naturism /'neɪtʃərɪzm/ n nudismo m

naturist /'neɪtʃərɪst/ n naturista mf ● a naturistico

naught /nɔːt/ n = **nought**

naughtily /'nɔːtɪlɪ/ adv male

naughtiness /'nɔːtɪnɪs/ n (of child, pet) birbanteria f; (of joke, suggestion) maliziosità f inv

naughty /'nɔːtɪ/ a (-ier, -iest) monello; (slightly indecent) spinto

nausea /'nɔːzɪə/ n nausea f

nauseate /'nɔːzɪeɪt/ vt nauseare

nauseating /'nɔːzɪeɪtɪŋ/ a nauseante

nauseatingly /'nɔːzɪeɪtɪŋlɪ/ adv (rich, sweet) disgustosamente

nauseous /'nɔːzɪəs/ a **I feel ~** ho la nausea

nautical /'nɔːtɪkl/ a nautico

nautical mile n miglio m marino

naval /'neɪvl/ a navale

naval: naval base n base f navale. **naval dockyard** n cantiere m navale militare. **naval officer** n ufficiale m di marina. **naval station** n base f navale. **naval stores** npl (depot) magazzini mpl della marina militare

nave /neɪv/ n navata f centrale

navel /'neɪvl/ n ombelico m

navigable /'nævɪgəbl/ a navigabile

navigate /'nævɪgeɪt/ vi navigare; Auto fare da navigatore ● vt navigare su (river)

navigation /nævɪ'geɪʃn/ n navigazione f

navigational /nævɪ'geɪʃənəl/ a (instruments) di navigazione; (science) della navigazione

navigator /'nævɪgeɪtə(r)/ n navigatore m

navvy /'nævɪ/ n manovale m

navy /'neɪvɪ/ n marina f ● ~ **[blue]** a blu scuro inv ● n blu m inv scuro

nay /neɪ/ adv anzi ● n (negative vote) no m

Nazi /'nɑːtsɪ/ n & a nazista mf

NBC n abbr (**National Broadcasting Company**) NBC f (rete nazionale televisiva statunitense)

NC Am abbr **North Carolina**

NCO n abbr (**non-commissioned officer**) sottufficiale m

ND Am abbr **North Dakota**

NE abbr (**north-east**) NE

Ne Am abbr **Nebraska**

Neapolitan /nɪə'pɒlɪtən/ a & n napoletano, -a mf

near /nɪə(r)/ a vicino; (future) prossimo; **the ~est bank** la banca più vicina ● adv vicino; **draw ~** avvicinarsi; **~ at hand** a portata di mano ● prep vicino a; **he was ~ to tears** aveva le lacrime agli occhi ● vt avvicinarsi a

nearby /nɪə'baɪ/ a & adv vicino

Near East n Medio Oriente m

nearly /'nɪəlɪ/ adv quasi; **it's not ~ enough** non è per niente sufficiente

near miss n **have a ~ ~** (planes, cars:) evitare per poco uno scontro

nearness /'nɪənɪs/ n vicinanza f

near: nearside n Auto (in Britain) lato m sinistro; (in America, rest of Europe) lato m de-

stro. **near-sighted** /-'saɪtɪd/ a Am miope.
near-sightedness n miopia f

neat /niːt/ a (tidy) ordinato; (clever) efficace; (undiluted) liscio

neaten /'niːtən/ vt riordinare ‹pile of paper›; dare un'aggiustatina a ‹tie, skirt›

neatly /'niːtlɪ/ adv ordinatamente; (cleverly) efficacemente

neatness /'niːtnɪs/ n (tidiness) ordine m

necessarily /nesə'serɪlɪ/ adv necessariamente

necessary /'nesəsərɪ/ a necessario

necessitate /nɪ'sesɪteɪt/ vt rendere necessario

necessity /nɪ'sesətɪ/ n necessità f inv

neck /nek/ n collo m; (of dress) colletto m; ~ **and** ~ testa a testa

necking /'nekɪŋ/ n fam pomiciate fpl

neck: necklace /'neklɪs/ n collana f.
neckline n scollatura f. **necktie** n cravatta f

nectar /'nektə(r)/ n nettare m

neé /neɪ/ a ~ **Brett** nata Brett

need /niːd/ n bisogno m; **be in** ~ essere bisognoso; **be in** ~ **of** avere bisogno di; **if** ~ **be** se ce ne fosse bisogno; **there is a** ~ **for** c'è bisogno di; **there is no** ~ **for that** non ce n'è bisogno; **there is no** ~ **for you to go** non c'è bisogno che tu vada ● vt aver bisogno di; **I** ~ **to know** devo saperlo; **it** ~**s to be done** bisogna farlo ● v aux **you** ~ **not go** non c'è bisogno che tu vada; ~ **I come?** devo venire?

needful /'niːdfʊl/ a necessario ● n **do the** ~ fare il necessario

needle /'niːdl/ n ago m; (for knitting) uncinetto m; (of record player) puntina f ● vt (fam: annoy) punzecchiare

needless /'niːdlɪs/ a inutile

needlessly /'niːdlɪslɪ/ adv inutilmente

needlework /'niːdlwɜːk/ n cucito m

needs /niːdz/ adv ~ **must** il dovere chiama

need-to-know a we have a ~ policy la nostra politica consiste nel tenere informati solo i diretti interessati

needy /'niːdɪ/ a (-ier, -iest) bisognoso

negate /nɪ'geɪt/ vt (cancel out) annullare; mettere in forma negativa ‹sentence›; (contradict) contraddire; (deny) negare

negation /nɪ'geɪʃn/ n negazione f

negative /'negətɪv/ a negativo ● n negazione f; Phot negativo m; **in the** ~ Gram alla forma negativa

neglect /nɪ'glekt/ n trascuratezza f; **state of** ~ stato di abbandono ● vt trascurare; **he** ~**ed to write** non si è curato di scrivere

neglected /nɪ'glektɪd/ a trascurato

neglectful /nɪ'glektfʊl/ a negligente; **be** ~ **of** trascurare

negligée /'neglɪʒeɪ/ n négligé m inv

negligence /'neglɪdʒəns/ n negligenza f

negligent /'neglɪdʒənt/ a negligente

negligently /'neglɪdʒəntlɪ/ adv con negligenza

negligible /'neglɪdʒəbl/ a trascurabile

negotiable /nɪ'gəʊʃəbl/ a ‹road› transitabi-

le; Comm negoziabile; **not** ~ ‹cheque› non trasferibile

negotiate /nɪ'gəʊʃɪeɪt/ vt negoziare; Auto prendere ‹bend› ● vi negoziare

negotiating /nɪ'gəʊʃɪeɪtɪŋ/ a ‹rights› al negoziato; ‹team, committee› che conduce le trattative; ‹ploy, position› di negoziato; **the** ~ **table** il tavolo delle trattative

negotiation /nɪgəʊʃɪ'eɪʃn/ n negoziato m

negotiator /nɪ'gəʊʃɪeɪtə(r)/ n negoziatore, -trice mf

Negro /'niːgrəʊ/ a & n (pl -es) negro, -a mf

neigh /neɪ/ vi nitrire

neighbour /'neɪbə(r)/ n vicino, -a mf

neighbourhood /'neɪbəhʊd/ n vicinato m; **in the** ~ **of** nei dintorni di; fig circa

neighbourhood watch scheme n vigilanza f da parte della gente del quartiere

neighbouring /'neɪbərɪŋ/ a vicino

neighbourly /'neɪbəlɪ/ a amichevole

neither /'naɪðə(r)/ a & pron nessuno dei due, né l'uno né l'altro ● adv ~... **nor** né... né ● conj nemmeno, neanche; ~ **do/did I** nemmeno io

neo+ /'niːəʊ/ pref neo+

neologism /nɪ'ɒlədʒɪzm/ n neologismo m

neon /'niːɒn/ n neon m

neon light n luce f al neon

nephew /'nevjuː/ n nipote m

nephritis /nɪ'fraɪtəs/ n nefrite f

nepotism /'nepətɪzm/ n nepotismo m

nerve /nɜːv/ n nervo m; (fam: courage) coraggio m; (fam: impudence) faccia f tosta!; **lose one's** ~ perdersi d'animo; **you've got a** ~! hai una bella faccia tosta!; **live on one's** ~**s** vivere con i nervi a fior di pelle; **be a bag of** ~**s** avere i nervi a fior di pelle

nerve-racking /'nɜːvrækɪŋ/ a logorante

nerviness /'nɜːvɪnɪs/ n Br nervosismo m; Am grinta f

nervous /'nɜːvəs/ a nervoso; **he makes me** ~ mi mette in agitazione

nervous breakdown n esaurimento m nervoso

nervous energy n energia f in eccesso

nervously /'nɜːvəslɪ/ adv nervosamente

nervousness /'nɜːvəsnɪs/ n nervosismo m; (before important event) tensione f

nervous system n sistema m nervoso

nervous wreck n fascio m di nervi

nervy /'nɜːvɪ/ a (-ier, -iest) nervoso; (Am: impudent) sfacciato

nest /nest/ n nido m ● vi fare il nido

nested /'nestɪd/ a Comput nidificato

nest egg n gruzzolo m

nesting /'nestɪŋ/ n Zool nidificazione f; Comput nesting m inv, nidificazione f ● attrib ‹habit› di nidificare; ‹place› per nidificare; ‹season› della nidificazione

nestle /'nesl/ vi accoccolarsi
■ **nestle up to** vt accoccolarsi accanto a ‹sb›

nestling /'neslɪŋ/ n nidiace m

net¹ /net/ n rete f ● vt (pt/pp netted) (catch) prendere (con la rete)

net² *a* netto; **~ of VAT** al netto dell'IVA ● *vt* (*pt/pp* **netted**) incassare un utile netto di

netball /'netbɔ:l/ *n sport m inv femminile, simile a pallacanestro*

net cord *n* corda *f* di rete; *Tennis* (*shot*) net *m inv*

Netherlands /'neðələndz/ *npl* **the ~** i Paesi Bassi

netting /'netɪŋ/ *n* [**wire**] ~ reticolato *m*

nettle /'netl/ *n* ortica *f*

net ton *n Am* tonnellata *f* corta americana

network /'netwɜ:k/ *n* rete *f*

network card *n Comput* scheda *f* di rete

networked /'netwɜ:kt/ *a Comput* collegato in rete

networking /'netwɜ:kɪŋ/ *n* (*establishing contacts*) stabilimento *m* di una rete di contatti; *Comput* collegamento *m* in rete

neuralgia /njʊə'rældʒə/ *n* nevralgia *f*

neuritis /njʊə'raɪtɪs/ *n* nevrite *f*

neurologist /njʊə'rɒlədʒɪst/ *n* neurologo, -a *mf*

neurology /njʊə'rɒlədʒɪ/ *n* neurologia *f*

neurosis /njʊə'rəʊsɪs/ *n* (*pl* **-oses** /njʊə-'rəʊsi:z/) nevrosi *f inv*

neurosurgeon /'njʊərəsɜ:dʒən/ *n* neurochirurgo *m*

neurotic /njʊə'rɒtɪk/ *a* nevrotico

neurotically /njʊə'rɒtɪklɪ/ *adv* in modo ossessivo

neuter /'nju:tə(r)/ *a Gram* neutro ● *n Gram* neutro *m* ● *vt* sterilizzare

neutral /'nju:trəl/ *a* neutro; (*country, person*) neutrale ● *n* **in ~** *Auto* in folle

neutrality /nju:'træləti/ *n* neutralità *f*

neutralize /'nju:trəlaɪz/ *vt* neutralizzare

never /'nevə(r)/ *adv* [non...] mai; (*fam: expressing disbelief*) ma va; **~ again** mai più; **well I ~!** chi l'avrebbe detto!

never-ending *a* interminabile

nevermore /nevə'mɔ:(r)/ *adv* mai più

never-never *n fam* **buy sth on the ~** comprare qcsa a rate

never-never land *n* mondo *m* dei sogni

nevertheless /nevəðə'les/ *adv* tuttavia

new /nju:/ *a* nuovo

new: New Age *n* New Age *f inv* ● *attrib* (*music, ideas, sect*) New Age *inv.* **new blood** *n* nuove leve *fpl.* **newborn** *a* neonato. **New Caledonia** *n* Nuova Caledonia *f.* **newcomer** *n* nuovo, -a arrivato, -a *mf.* **newfangled** *a pej* modernizzante. **newfound** *a* nuovo

Newfoundland /'nju:fən(d)lənd/ *n* Terranova *f*

New Guinea *n* Nuova Guinea *f*

newish /'nju:ɪʃ/ *a* abbastanza nuovo

new: new-laid /'nju:leɪd/ *a* fresco. **new look** *a* (*car, team*) nuovo; (*edition, show*) rinnovato; (*product*) dall'aspetto nuovo ● *n* **they have given the shop a completely ~ ~** hanno completamente rinnovato il negozio

newly /'nju:lɪ/ *adv* (*recently*) di recente

newly-built *a* costruito di recente

newly-weds /'nju:lɪwedz/ *npl* sposini *mpl*

new moon *n* luna *f* nuova

newness /'nju:nɪs/ *n* novità *f*

news /nju:z/ *n* notizie *fpl*; *TV* telegiornale *m*; *Radio* giornale *m* radio; **piece of ~** notizia *f*

news: news agency *n* agenzia *f* di stampa. **newsagent's** *n Br* giornalaio *m* (*che vende anche tabacchi, caramelle ecc*). **news bulletin** *n* notiziario *m*. **newscast** *n Am* notiziario *m*. **newscaster** *n* giornalista *mf* televisivo, -a/radiofonico, -a. **news conference** *n* conferenza *f* stampa *inv*. **newsdealer** *n Am* giornalaio, -a *mf*. **news desk** *n* (*at newspaper*) redazione *f*. **news editor** *n* caporedattore, -trice *mf* di servizi di cronaca. **newsflash** *n* notizia *f* flash. **news headlines** *npl TV* titoli *mpl* delle principali notizie. **news item** *n* notizia *f* di attualità. **newsletter** *n* bollettino *m* d'informazione

newspaper /'nju:zpeɪpə(r)/ *n* giornale *m*; (*material*) carta *f* di giornale

newspaper: newspaperman *n* giornalista *m*. **newspaper office** *n* ufficio *m* della redazione. **newspaperwoman** *n* giornalista *f*

newspeak /'nju:spi:k/ *n Am* politichese *m*

news: newsprint *n* (*paper*) carta *f* da giornale; (*ink*) inchiostro *m* di stampa. **newsreader** *n* giornalista *mf* televisivo, -a/ radiofonico, -a. **newsroom** *n* redazione *f*. **news sheet** *n* bollettino *m*. **newsstand** *n* edicola *f*. **news value** *n* interesse *m* mediatico. **newsworthy** *a* che merita di essere pubblicato

newsy /'nju:zɪ/ *a* (*letter*) pieno di notizie

newt /nju:t/ *n* tritone *m*

new: new technology *n* nuova technologia *f*. **New Testament** *n* Nuovo Testamento *m*. **new wave** *n* & *a* new wave *f inv*. **New Year** *n* (*January 1st*) capodanno *m*; (*next year*) l'anno *m* nuovo; **Happy ~ ~!** buon anno!; **closed for ~ ~** chiuso per le feste di capodanno; **see in the ~ ~** festeggiare il capodanno. **New Year Honours list** *n Br* lista *f* delle persone che ricevono decorazioni il 1 gennaio. **New Year's Day** *n* Capodanno *m*. **New Year's Eve** *n* vigilia *f* di Capodanno. **New Year's resolution** *n* proposito *m* per l'anno nuovo. **New Zealand** *n* Nuova Zelanda *f*. **New Zealander** *n* neozelandese *mf*

next /nekst/ *a* prossimo; (*adjoining*) vicino; **who's ~?** a chi tocca?; **the ~ best thing would be to** alternativamente la cosa migliore sarebbe di; **~ door** accanto; **~ to nothing** quasi niente; **the ~ day** il giorno dopo; **~ week** la settimana prossima; **the week after ~** fra due settimane; **the ~ thing I knew** la sola cosa che ho saputo dopo ● *adv* dopo; **when will you see him ~?** quando lo rivedi la prossima volta?; **~ to** accanto a ● *n* seguente *mf*; **~ of kin** parente *m* prossimo

next door *a* (*dog, bell*) dei vicini; (*office*) accanto *inv*; **the girl ~** *also fig* la ragazza della porta accanto ● *adv* (*live, move in*) nella casa accanto

next-door neighbour *n* vicino *m* di casa

nexus /'neksəs/ *n* (*network*) rete *f*

NF *n Br Pol abbr* **National Front**

NH *Am abbr* **New Hampshire**

NHS *n abbr* **National Health Service**

NI *n Br abbr* **(National Insurance)** previdenza *f* sociale; *abbr* **(Northern Ireland)** Irlanda *f* del Nord

nib /nɪb/ *n* pennino *m*

nibble /'nɪbl/ *vt/i* mordicchiare

■ **nibble at, nibble on** *vt* = **nibble**

Nicaragua /nɪkə'ræɡjʊə/ *n* Nicaragua *m*

nice /naɪs/ *a* ⟨*day, weather, holiday*⟩ bello; ⟨*person*⟩ gentile, simpatico; ⟨*food*⟩ buono; **it was ~ meeting you** è stato un piacere conoscerla

nicely /'naɪslɪ/ *adv* gentilmente; (*well*) bene

niceties /'naɪsətɪz/ *npl* finezze *fpl*

niche /niːʃ/ *n* nicchia *f*

niche market *n* mercato *m* specializzato

nick /nɪk/ *n* tacca *f*; (*on chin etc*) taglietto *m*; (*fam: prison*) galera *f*; (*fam: police station*) centrale *f* [di polizia]; **in the ~ of time** *fam* appena in tempo; **in good ~** *fam* in buono stato ● *vt* intaccare; (*fam: steal*) fregare; (*fam: arrest*) beccare; **~ one's chin** farsi un taglietto nel mento

nickel /'nɪkl/ *n* nichel *m*; *Am* moneta *f* da cinque centesimi

nickel-and-dime *a Am fam* da quattro soldi

nickelodeon /nɪkəl'əʊdɪən/ *n* (*Am: juke box*) juke box *m inv*

nickname /'nɪkneɪm/ *n* soprannome *m* ● *vt* soprannominare

nicotine /'nɪkətiːn/ *n* nicotina *f*

niece /niːs/ *n* nipote *f*

nifty /'nɪftɪ/ *a fam* (*skilful*) geniale; (*attractive*) sfizioso

Nigeria /naɪ'dʒɪərɪə/ *n* Nigeria *f*

Nigerian /naɪ'dʒɪərɪən/ *a & n* nigeriano, -a *mf*

niggardly /'nɪɡədlɪ/ *a* ⟨*person*⟩ tirchio; ⟨*salary*⟩ misero

niggle /'nɪɡl/ *fam n* (*complaint*) cosetta *f* da ridire ● *vi* (*complain*) lamentarsi in continuazione ● *vt* (*irritate*) dar fastidio a

niggling /'nɪɡlɪŋ/ *a* ⟨*detail*⟩ insignificante; ⟨*pain*⟩ fastidioso; ⟨*doubt*⟩ persistente

night /naɪt/ *n* notte *f*; (*evening*) sera *f*; **at ~** la notte, di notte; (*in the evening*) la sera, di sera; **Monday ~** lunedì notte/sera; **work ~s** lavorare la notte ● *a* di notte

night: nightcap *n* papalina *f*; (*drink*) bicchierino *m* bevuto prima di andare a letto. **nightclub** *n* locale *m* notturno, night[-club] *m inv*. **nightclubbing** *n* **go ~** andare nei night [club]. **nightdress** *n* camicia *f* da notte. **nightfall** *n* crepuscolo *m*. **nightgown,** *fam* **nightie** *n* camicia *f* da notte. **nightlife** *n* vita *f* notturna. **night light** *n* lumino *m* da notte

nightly /'naɪtlɪ/ *a* di notte, di sera ● *adv* ogni notte, ogni sera

nightmare /'naɪtmeə(r)/ *n* also fig incubo *m*

nightmarish /'naɪtmeərɪʃ/ *a* da incubo

night: night owl nottambulo, -a *mf*. **night porter** *n* portiere *m* di notte. **night school** scuola *f* serale. **nightshade** *n* Bot **deadly ~**

belladonna *f*. **night shelter** *n* dormitorio *m* pubblico. **nightshift** *n* (*workers*) turno *m* di notte; **be on the ~** fare il turno di notte. **nightshirt** *n* camicia *f* da notte (*da uomo*). **nightspot** *n* night club *m inv*. **nightstand** *n Am* comodino *m*. **nightstick** *n* (*Am: truncheon*) manganello *m*. **night-time** *n* **at ~** di notte, la notte. **night vision** *n* visione *f* notturna. **nightwatchman** *n* guardiano *m* notturno. **nightwear** *n* indumenti *mpl* da notte

nil /nɪl/ *n* nulla *m*; *Sport* zero *m*

Nile /naɪl/ *n* Nilo *m*

nimble /'nɪmbl/ *a* agile

nimbly /'nɪmblɪ/ *adv* agilmente

nincompoop /'nɪŋkəmpuːp/ *n fam* scemo *m*

nine /naɪn/ *a & n* nove *m*

ninepin /'naɪnpɪn/ *n* birillo *m*; **be falling like ~s** ⟨*troops, guards, candidates:*⟩ cadere come le mosche

nineteen /naɪn'tiːn/ *a & n* diciannove *m*

nineteenth /naɪn'tiːnθ/ *a & n* diciannovesimo, -a *mf*

ninetieth /'naɪntɪθ/ *a & n* novantesimo, -a *mf*

nine-to-five *a* ⟨*job*⟩ in un ufficio; ⟨*routine*⟩ dell'ufficio ● *adv* ⟨*work*⟩ dalle nove alle cinque

ninety /'naɪntɪ/ *a & n* novanta *m*

ninth /naɪnθ/ *a & n* nono, -a *mf*

nip /nɪp/ *n* pizzicotto *m*; (*bite*) morso *m* ● *vt* pizzicare; (*bite*) mordere; **~ in the bud** *fig* stroncare sul nascere ● *vi* (*fam: run*) fare un salto

nipper /'nɪpə(r)/ *n fam* ragazzino, -a *mf*

nipple /'nɪpl/ *n* capezzolo *m*; (*Am: on bottle*) tettarella *f*

nippy /'nɪpɪ/ *a* (**-ier, -iest**) *fam* (*cold*) pungente; (*quick*) svelto

nit /nɪt/ *n* (*egg*) lendine *m*; (*larva*) larva *f* di pidocchio

nit-pick *vi* cercare il pelo nell'uovo

nitrate /'naɪtreɪt/ *n* nitrato *m*

nitric /'naɪtrɪk/ *a* nitrico

nitrogen /'naɪtrədʒn/ *n* azoto *m*

nitty-gritty /nɪtɪ'ɡrɪtɪ/ *n fam* **the ~** il nocciolo [della questione]; **get down to the ~** arrivare al dunque

nitwit /'nɪtwɪt/ *n fam* imbecille *mf*

NJ *Am abbr* **New Jersey**

NM *Am abbr* **New Mexico**

no /nəʊ/ *adv* no ● *n* (*pl* **noes**) no *m invar* ● *a* nessuno; **I have no time** non ho tempo; **in no time** in un baleno; **'no parking'** 'sosta vietata'; **'no smoking'** 'vietato fumare'; **it's no go** è inutile; **no one** = **nobody**

no., No. *abbr* (**number**) No.

Noah /'nəʊə/ *n* Noè *m*; **~'s Ark** l'arca *f* di Noè

nobility /nəʊ'bɪlətɪ/ *n* nobiltà *f*

noble /'nəʊbl/ *a* nobile

nobleman /'nəʊblmən/ *n* nobile *m*

noble-minded /-'maɪndɪd/ *a* di animo nobile

noble savage *n* buon selvaggio *m*

nobly /'nəʊblɪ/ *adv* (*selflessly*) generosamente; **~ born** di nobili natali

nobody /'nəʊbədɪ/ *pron* nessuno; **he knows ~** non conosce nessuno; **he's ~ important** non è nessuno d'importante ● *n* **he's a ~** non è nessuno

no claims bonus *n* abbuono *m* in assenza di sinistri

nocturnal /nɒk'tɜ:nl/ *a* notturno

nod /nɒd/ *n* cenno *m* del capo; **give a ~** fare un cenno col capo ● *v* (*pt*/*pp* **nodded**) ● *vi* fare un cenno col capo; (*in agreement*) fare di sì col capo ● *vt* **~ one's head** fare di sì col capo

■ **nod off** *vi* assopirsi

node /nəʊd/ *n* nodo *m*

nodule /'nɒdju:l/ *n* nodulo *m*

no-go *a fam* **it's ~** non è possibile

no-go area *n* quartiere *m* caldo in cui la polizia può accedere solo con la forza

no-hoper /nəʊ'həʊpə(r)/ *n* persona *f* senza prospettive

noise /nɔɪz/ *n* rumore *m*; (*loud*) rumore *m*, chiasso *m*

noiseless /'nɔɪzlɪs/ *a* silenzioso

noiselessly /'nɔɪzlɪslɪ/ *adv* silenziosamente

noise level *n* intensità *f inv* del rumore

noise pollution *n* inquinamento *m* da rumore

noisily /'nɔɪzɪlɪ/ *adv* rumorosamente

noisy /'nɔɪzɪ/ *a* (**-ier, -iest**) rumoroso

nomad /'nəʊmæd/ *n* nomade *mf*

nomadic /nəʊ'mædɪk/ *a* nomade

nominal /'nɒmɪnl/ *a* nominale

nominally /'nɒmɪnəlɪ/ *adv* nominalmente

nominate /'nɒmɪneɪt/ *vt* proporre come candidato; (*appoint*) designare

nomination /nɒmɪ'neɪʃn/ *n* nomina *f*; (*person nominated*) candidato, -a *mf*

nominative /'nɒmɪnətɪv/ *a* & *n* *Gram* **~** [**case**] nominativo *m*

nominee /nɒmɪ'ni:/ *n* persona *f* nominata

non+ /nɒn/ *pref* non+, in+

non-academic *a* (*course*) pratico; (*staff*) non insegnante

non-addictive *a* che non dà assuefazione

non-alcoholic *a* analcolico

non-attendance *n* mancata presenza *f*

non-believer *n* non credente *mf*

nonchalant /'nɒnʃələnt/ *a* disinvolto

nonchalantly /'nɒnʃələntlɪ/ *adv* in modo disinvolto

non-classified *a* (*information*) non confidenziale

non-combustible *a* incombustibile

non-commercial *a* (*event, activity*) senza fini di lucro

non-commissioned /-kə'mɪʃnd/ *a* **~ officer** sottufficiale *m*

non-committal /-kə'mɪtəl/ *a* che non si sbilancia

non-compliance *n* (*with standards*) non conformità *f* (**with** a); (*with orders*) inadempienza *f* (**with** a)

nonconformist /nɒnkən'fɔ:mɪst/ *a* & *n* anticonformista *mf*

non-cooperation *n* non cooperazione *f*

non-denominational /-dɪnɒmɪ'neɪʃənəl/ *a* (*church*) ecumenico; (*school*) laico

nondescript /'nɒndɪskrɪpt/ *a* qualunque

none /nʌn/ *pron* (*person*) nessuno; (*thing*) niente; **~ of us** nessuno di noi; **~ of this** niente di questo; **there's ~ left** non ce n'è più ● *adv* **she's ~ too pleased** non è per niente soddisfatta; **I'm ~ the wiser** non ne so più di prima

non-EC *a* (*national*) extracomunitario; (*country*) che non appartiene alla Comunità Europea

nonentity /nɒ'nentətɪ/ *n* nullità *f inv*

non-essentials /-ɪ'senʃlz/ *npl* (*details*) dettagli *mpl*; (*objects*) cose *fpl* accessorie

nonetheless /nʌnðə'les/ *adv* = **nevertheless**

non-event *n* delusione *f*

non-existent *a* inesistente

non-family *a* al di fuori della famiglia

non-fat *a* magro; (*diet*) senza grassi

non-fiction *n* saggistica *f*

non-flammable *a* non infiammabile

non-fulfilment *n* (*of* contract, obligation) inadempienza *f* (**of** a); (*of* desire) inappagamento *m*

non-infectious *a* non infettivo

non-iron *a* che non si stira

non-judgmental *a* imparziale

non-league *a* *Sport* fuori campionato

no-no *n fam* cosa *f* proibita; **that's a ~** è un argomento tabù

no-nonsense *a* (*manner, attitude*) diretto; (*tone*) spiccio; (*look, policy*) pratico; (*person*) franco

non-partisan *a* imparziale

non-party *a* (*issue, decision*) apartitico; (*person*) indipendente

non-person *n* (*insignificant person*) nullità *f inv*; **officially, he is a ~** *Pol* ufficialmente non è mai esistito

nonplussed /nɒn'plʌst/ *a* perplesso

non-professional *a* dilettante

non-profit-making /-'prɒfɪtmeɪkɪŋ/ *a* (*organization*) senza fini di lucro

non-redeemable *a* *Fin* vincolato

non-refillable *a* (*lighter, pen*) non ricaricabile; (*can, bottle*) non riutilizzabile

non-religious *a* laico

non-resident *a* (*job, course*) non residenziale; *Comput* che non risiede in permanenza nella memoria centrale ● *n* non residente *mf*

non-residential *a* (*guest*) di passaggio; (*student, visitor*) non residente; (*caretaker*) che non alloggia sul posto; (*area*) non residenziale

non-returnable *a* (*bottle*) a perdere

non-segregated *a* (*area*) non segregato; (*society*) non segregazionista

nonsense /'nɒnsəns/ *n* sciocchezze *fpl*

nonsensical /nɒn'sensɪkl/ *a* assurdo

non sequitur /nɒn'sekwɪtə(r)/ *n* affermazione *f* senza legame con quanto detto prima

non-skid *a* antiscivolo *inv*

non-smoker *n* non fumatore, -trice *mf*;

(compartment) scompartimento *m* non fumatori

non-specialized *a* non specializzato

non-starter *n* **be a ~** *(person:)* non avere nessuna probabilità di riuscita; *(plan, idea:)* essere destinato al fallimento

non-stick *a* antiaderente

non-stop *a* *(talk, work, pressure, noise)* continuo; *(train)* diretto; *(journey)* senza fermate; *(flight)* senza scalo ● *adv* *(work, talk)* senza sosta; *(travel, fly)* senza scalo

non-swimmer *n* persona *f* che non sa nuotare

non-taxable *a* non imponibile

non-union *a* *(person)* non iscritto a un sindacato; *(company)* non sindacalizzato

non-violent *a* non violento

non-white, non-White *n* persona *f* di colore

noodles /'nu:dlz/ *npl* taglierini *mpl*

nook /nʊk/ *n* cantuccio *m*

noon /nu:n/ *n* mezzogiorno *m*; **at ~** a mezzogiorno

no one *pron* nessuno

noose /nu:s/ *n* nodo *m* scorsoio

nor /nɔ:(r)/ *adv & conj* né; **~ do I** neppure io

Nordic /'nɔ:dɪk/ *a* nordico

norm /nɔ:m/ *n* norma *f*

normal /'nɔ:ml/ *a* normale

normality /nɔ:'mælətɪ/ *n* normalità *f*

normally /'nɔ:məlɪ/ *adv* *(usually)* normalmente

Norman /'nɔ:mən/ *a* normanno; *(landscape, village)* della Normandia ● *n* normanno *m*

Norse /nɔ:s/ *a* *(mythology, saga)* norreno

north /nɔ:θ/ *n* nord *m*; **to the ~ of** a nord di ● *a* del nord, settentrionale ● *adv* a nord

North Africa *n* Africa *f* del Nord

North African *a & n* nordafricano, -a *mf*

North America *n* America *f* del Nord

North American *a & n* nordamericano, -a *mf*

Northants /nɔ:'θænts/ *Br abbr* **Northamptonshire**

northbound /'nɔ:θbaʊnd/ *a* *(traffic, carriageway)* in direzione nord

Northd *Br abbr* **Northumberland**

north: north-east *a* di nord-est, nord-orientale ● *n* nord-est *m* ● *adv* a nord-est; *(travel)* verso nord-est. **north-easterly** *a* *(point)* a nord-est; *(wind)* di nord-est ● *n* vento *m* di nord-est. **northeastern** /nɔ:θ'i:stən/ *a* nordorientale

northerly /'nɔ:ðəlɪ/ *a* *(direction)* nord; *(wind)* del nord

northern /'nɔ:ðən/ *a* del nord, settentrionale

Northern Ireland *n* Irlanda *f* del Nord

Northern Lights *npl* aurora *f* boreale

north: North Pole *n* polo *m* nord. **North Sea** *n* Mare *m* del Nord. **North Star** *n* stella *f* polare

northward[s] /'nɔ:θwəd[z]/ *adv* verso nord

north: north-west *a* di nord-ovest, nordoccidentale ● *n* nord-ovest *m* ● *adv* a nord-ovest; *(travel)* verso nord-ovest. **north-**

westerly *a* *(point)* a nord-ovest; *(wind)* di nord-ovest ● *n* vento *m* di nord-ovest. **northwestern** *a* nordoccidentale

Norway /'nɔ:weɪ/ *n* Norvegia *f*

Norwegian /nɔ:'wi:dʒn/ *a & n* norvegese *mf*

nose /nəʊz/ *n* naso *m*

■ **nose about** *vi* curiosare

nosebleed /'nəʊzbli:d/ *n* emorragia *f* nasale

nosedive /'nəʊzdaɪv/ *n* Aeron picchiata *f*; **take a ~** *(fig: prices:)* scendere vertiginosamente

nosey /'nəʊzɪ/ *a* = **nosy**

no-show *n* persona *f* che non si è presentata

nosily /'nəʊzɪlɪ/ *adv* in modo indiscreto

nostalgia /nɒ'stældʒɪə/ *n* nostalgia *f*

nostalgic /nɒ'stældʒɪk/ *a* nostalgico

nostril /'nɒstrəl/ *n* narice *f*

nosy /'nəʊzɪ/ *a* (**-ier, -iest**) *fam* ficcanaso *inv*

not /nɒt/ *adv* non; **he is ~ Italian** non è italiano; **I hope ~** spero di no; **~ all of us have been invited** non siamo stati tutti invitati; **if ~** se no; **~ at all** niente affatto; **~ a bit** per niente; **~ even** neanche; **~ yet** non ancora; **in the ~ too distant future** in un futuro non troppo lontano; **~ only... but also...** non solo... ma anche...

notable /'nəʊtəbl/ *a* *(remarkable)* notevole

notably /'nəʊtəblɪ/ *adv* *(in particular)* in particolare

notary /'nəʊtərɪ/ *n* notaio *m*; **~ public** notaio *m*

notation /nəʊ'teɪʃn/ *n* notazione *f*

notch /nɒtʃ/ *n* tacca *f*

■ **notch up** *vt* *(score)* segnare

note /nəʊt/ *n* nota *f*; *(short letter, banknote)* biglietto *m*; *(memo, written comment etc)* appunto *m*; **of ~** *(person)* di spicco; *(comments, event)* degno di nota; **make a ~ of** prendere nota di; **take ~ of** *(notice)* prendere nota di ● *vt* *(notice)* notare; *(write)* annotare

■ **note down** *vt* annotare

notebook /'nəʊtbʊk/ *n* taccuino *m*; Comput notebook *m inv*

noted /'nəʊtɪd/ *a* noto, celebre (**for** per)

note: notepad *n* blocco *m* per appunti. **notepaper** *n* carta *f* da lettere. **noteworthy** *a* degno di nota

nothing /'nʌθɪŋ/ *pron* niente, nulla ● *adv* niente affatto; **for ~** *(free, in vain)* per niente; *(with no reason)* senza motivo; **~ but** nient'altro che; **~ much** poco o nulla; **~ interesting** niente di interessante; **it's ~ to do with you** non ti riguarda

notice /'nəʊtɪs/ *n* *(on board)* avviso *m*; *(review)* recensione *f*; *(termination of employment)* licenziamento *m*; [**advance**] **~** preavviso *m*; **two months' ~** due mesi di preavviso; **at short ~** con breve preavviso; **until further ~** fino nuovo avviso; **give** [**in one's**] **~** *(employee:)* dare le dimissioni; **give an employee ~** dare il preavviso a un impiegato; **take no ~** non fare caso a; **take no ~!** non farci caso! ● *vt* notare

noticeable /'nəʊtɪsəbl/ *a* evidente

noticeably /'nəʊtɪsəblɪ/ *adv* sensibilmente

noticeboard /'nəʊtɪsbɔːd/ n bacheca f
notification /nəʊtɪfɪ'keɪʃn/ n notifica f
notify /'nəʊtɪfaɪ/ vt (pt/pp -ied) notificare
notion /'nəʊʃn/ n idea f, nozione f; **he hasn't the slightest ~ of time** gli manca completamente la nozione del tempo; **~s** pl (Am: haberdashery) merceria f
notoriety /nəʊtə'raɪətɪ/ n notorietà f
notorious /nəʊ'tɔːrɪəs/ a famigerato; **be ~ for** essere tristemente famoso per
notoriously /nəʊ'tɔːrɪəslɪ/ adv **they're ~ unreliable** tutti sanno che su di loro non si può mai fare affidamento
Notts /nɒts/ Br abbr **Nottinghamshire**
notwithstanding /nɒtwɪð'stændɪŋ/ prep malgrado ● adv ciononostante
nougat /'nuːgət/ n torrone m
nought /nɔːt/ n zero m
noughts and crosses n tris m
noun /naʊn/ n nome m, sostantivo m
nourish /'nʌrɪʃ/ vt nutrire
nourishing /'nʌrɪʃɪŋ/ a nutriente
nourishment /'nʌrɪʃmənt/ n nutrimento m
novel /'nɒvl/ a insolito ● n romanzo m
novelette /nɒvə'let/ n (oversentimental) romanzetto m rosa
novelist /'nɒvəlɪst/ n romanziere, -a mf
novelty /'nɒvltɪ/ n novità f; **novelties** pl (objects) oggettini mpl
November /nəʊ'vembə(r)/ n novembre m
novice /'nɒvɪs/ n novizio, -a mf
now /naʊ/ adv ora, adesso; **by ~** ormai; **just ~** proprio ora; **right ~** subito; **~ and again**, **~ and then** ogni tanto; **~, ~!** su! ● conj **~ [that]** ora che, adesso che
nowadays /'naʊədeɪz/ adv oggigiorno
nowhere /'nəʊweə(r)/ adv in nessun posto, da nessuna parte
noxious /'nɒkʃəs/ a nocivo
nozzle /'nɒzl/ n bocchetta f
nr abbr **near**
NSPCC n Br abbr (**National Society for the Prevention of Cruelty to Children**) Società f nazionale per la protezione dell'infanzia
NT abbr **New Testament**
nth /enθ/ a Math, fig **to the ~ power/ degree** all'ennesima potenza; **for the ~ time** per l'ennesima volta
nuance /'njuːɒs/ n sfumatura f
nub /nʌb/ n **the ~ of the matter** il nocciolo della questione
nubile /'njuːbaɪl/ a (attractive) desiderabile
nuclear /'njuːklɪə(r)/ a nucleare
nuclear: nuclear bomb n bomba f atomica. **nuclear deterrent** n deterrente m nucleare. **nuclear energy** n energia f nucleare. **nuclear-free zone** n Br zona f denuclearizzata. **nuclear physics** n fisica f nucleare. **nuclear power** n (energy) energia f nucleare; (country) potenza f nucleare. **nuclear power station** n centrale f nucleare. **nuclear shelter** n rifugio m antiatomico
nucleus /'njuːklɪəs/ n (pl **-lei** /'njuːklɪaɪ/) nucleo m

nude /njuːd/ a nudo ● n nudo m; **in the ~** nudo
nudge /nʌdʒ/ n colpetto m di gomito ● vt dare un colpetto col gomito a
nudism /'njuːdɪzm/ n nudismo m
nudist /'njuːdɪst/ n nudista mf
nudity /'njuːdətɪ/ n nudità f
nugget /'nʌgɪt/ n pepita f
nuisance /'njuːsns/ n seccatura f; (person) piaga f; **what a ~!** che seccatura!
nuisance call n Teleph telefonata f anonima
null /nʌl/ a **~ and void** nullo
nullify /'nʌlɪfaɪ/ vt (pt/pp -ied) annullare
numb /nʌm/ a intorpidito; **~ with cold** intirizzito dal freddo ● vt intorpidire
number /'nʌmbə(r)/ n numero m; **a ~ of people** un certo numero di persone ● vt numerare; (include) annoverare
numbering /'nʌmbərɪŋ/ n numerazione f
number one n (most important) numero uno m; **look after ~ ~** (oneself) pensare prima di tutto a se stessi
number plate n targa f
numeracy /'njuːmərəsɪ/ n **improve standards of ~** migliorare il livello nel calcolo
numeral /'njuːmərəl/ n numero m, cifra f
numerate /'njuːmərət/ a **be ~** saper fare i calcoli
numerical /njuː'merɪkl/ a numerico; **in ~ order** in ordine numerico
numerically /njuː'merɪklɪ/ adv numericamente
numeric keypad /njuː'merɪk/ n Comput tastierino m numerico
numerous /'njuːmərəs/ a numeroso
nun /nʌn/ n suora f
nuptial /'nʌpʃl/ a nuziale ● **~s** npl nozze fpl
nurse /nɜːs/ n infermiere, -a mf; **children's ~** bambinaia f ● vt curare
nursery /'nɜːsərɪ/ n stanza f dei bambini; (for plants) vivaio m; **[day] ~** asilo m
nursery: nursery rhyme n filastrocca f. **nursery school** n scuola f materna. **nursery slope** n Br pista f per principianti
nurse's aid n Am aiuto infermiere, -a mf
nursing /'nɜːsɪŋ/ n professione f d'infermiere
nursing auxiliary n Br aiuto infermiere, -a mf
nursing home n casa f di cura per anziani
nurture /'nɜːtʃə(r)/ vt allevare; fig coltivare
nut /nʌt/ n noce f; Techn dado m; (fam: head) zucca f
nutcrackers /'nʌtkrækəz/ npl schiaccianoci m inv
nutmeg /'nʌtmeg/ n noce f moscata
nutrient /'njuːtrɪənt/ n sostanza f nutritiva
nutrition /njuː'trɪʃn/ n nutrizione f
nutritionist /njuː'trɪʃənɪst/ n nutrizionista mf
nutritious /njuː'trɪʃəs/ a nutriente
nuts /nʌts/ npl frutta f secca; **be ~** fam essere svitato

nutshell /'nʌtʃel/ *n* guscio *m* di noce; **in a ~** *fig* in parole povere

nuzzle /'nʌzl/ *vt* ⟨*horse, dog:*⟩ strofinare il muso contro

NV *Am abbr* **Nevada**

NW *abbr* (**north-west**) NO

NY *Am abbr* **New York**

NYC *Am abbr* **New York City**

nylon /'naɪlɒn/ *n* nailon *m*; **~s** *pl* calze *fpl* di nailon ● *attrib* di nailon

nymph /nɪmf/ *n* ninfa *f*

nymphomaniac /nɪmfə'meɪnɪæk/ *n* ninfomane *f* ● *a* da ninfomane

NZ *abbr* **New Zealand**

....

Oo

....

o, O /əʊ/ *n* (*letter*) o, O *f inv*

O /əʊ/ *n Teleph* zero *m*

oaf /əʊf/ *n* (*pl* **oafs**) zoticone, -a *mf*

oak /əʊk/ *n* quercia *f* ● *attrib* di quercia

OAP *abbr* (**old-age pensioner**) pensionato, -a *mf*

oar /ɔ:(r)/ *n* remo *m*

oarsman /'ɔ:zmən/ *n* vogatore *m*

oasis /əʊ'eɪsɪs/ *n* (*pl* **oases** /əʊ'eɪsi:z/) oasi *f inv*

oatcake /'əʊtkeɪk/ *n* galletta *f* di avena

oath /əʊθ/ *n* giuramento *m*; (*swear-word*) bestemmia *f*

oatmeal /'əʊtmi:l/ *n* farina *f* d'avena

oats /əʊts/ *npl* avena *fsg*; *Culin* [**rolled**] **~** fiocchi *mpl* di avena

obdurate /'ɒbdjʊərət/ *a* (*stubborn*) irremovibile; (*hardhearted*) insensibile

OBE *n Br abbr* (**Officer of the** (**Order of the**) **British Empire**) *onorificenza f britannica*

obedience /ə'bi:dɪəns/ *n* ubbidienza *f*

obedient /ə'bi:dɪənt/ *a* ubbidiente

obediently /ə'bi:dɪəntlɪ/ *adv* ubbidientemente

obelisk /'ɒbəlɪsk/ *n* obelisco *m*

obese /ə'bi:s/ *a* obeso

obesity /ə'bi:sətɪ/ *n* obesità *f*

obey /ə'beɪ/ *vt* ubbidire a; osservare ⟨*instructions, rules*⟩ ● *vi* ubbidire

obituary /ə'bɪtjʊərɪ/ *n* necrologio *m*

object[1] /'ɒbdʒɪkt/ *n* oggetto *m*; *Gram* complemento *m* oggetto; **money is no ~** i soldi non sono un problema

object[2] /əb'dʒekt/ *vi* (*be against*) opporsi (**to** a); **~ that…** obiettare che…

objection /əb'dʒekʃn/ *n* obiezione *f*; **have no ~** non avere niente in contrario

objectionable /əb'dʒekʃ(ə)nəbl/ *a* discutibile; ⟨*person*⟩ sgradevole

objective /əb'dʒektɪv/ *a* oggettivo ● *n* obiettivo *m*

objectively /əb'dʒektɪvlɪ/ *adv* obiettivamente

objectivity /ɒbdʒek'tɪvətɪ/ *n* oggettività *f*

objector /əb'dʒektə(r)/ *n* oppositore, -trice *mf*

obligation /ɒblɪ'geɪʃn/ *n* obbligo *m*; **be**

under an ~ avere un obbligo; **without ~** senza impegno

obligatory /ə'blɪgətrɪ/ *a* obbligatorio

oblige /ə'blaɪdʒ/ *vt* (*compel*) obbligare; (*do a small service for*) fare una cortesia a; **much ~d** grazie mille

obliging /ə'blaɪdʒɪŋ/ *a* disponibile

oblique /ə'bli:k/ *a* obliquo; *fig* indiretto. **~ [stroke]** *n* barra *f*

obliterate /ə'blɪtəreɪt/ *vt* obliterare

obliteration /əblɪtə'reɪʃn/ *n* (*of mark, memory*) rimozione *f*; (*of city*) annientamento *m*

oblivion /ə'blɪvɪən/ *n* oblio *m*

oblivious /ə'blɪvɪəs/ *a* **be ~** essere dimentico (**of, to** di)

oblong /'ɒblɒŋ/ *a* oblungo ● *n* rettangolo *m*

obnoxious /əb'nɒkʃəs/ *a* detestabile

oboe /'əʊbəʊ/ *n* oboe *m inv*

obscene /əb'si:n/ *a* osceno; ⟨*profits, wealth*⟩ vergognoso

obscenity /əb'senətɪ/ *n* oscenità *f inv*

obscure /əb'skjʊə(r)/ *a* oscuro ● *vt* oscurare; (*confuse*) mettere in ombra

obscurity /əb'skjʊərətɪ/ *n* oscurità *f*

obsequious /əb'si:kwɪəs/ *a* ossequioso

observable /əb'zɜ:vəbl/ *a* (*discernible*) percettibile

observance /əb'zɜ:vəns/ *n* (*of custom*) osservanza *f*

observant /əb'zɜ:vənt/ *a* attento

observation /ɒbzə'veɪʃn/ *n* osservazione *f*

observation car *n* carrozza *f* belvedere

observation tower *n* torre *f* di osservazione

observatory /əb'zɜ:vətrɪ/ *n* osservatorio *m*

observe /əb'zɜ:v/ *vt* osservare; (*notice*) notare; (*keep, celebrate*) celebrare

observer /əb'zɜ:və(r)/ *n* osservatore, -trice *mf*

obsess /əb'ses/ *vt* **be ~ed by** essere fissato con

obsession /əb'seʃn/ *n* fissazione *f*

obsessive /əb'sesɪv/ *a* ossessivo

obsessively /əb'sesɪvlɪ/ *adv* ossessivamente

obsolescence /ɒbsə'lesəns/ *n* obsolescenza *f*; **built-in ~** obsolescenza *f* programmata

obsolete /'ɒbsəli:t/ *a* obsoleto; ⟨*word*⟩ desueto; ⟨*idea*⟩ sorpassato

obstacle /'ɒbstəkl/ n ostacolo m

obstacle course n Mil, fig percorso m a ostacoli

obstacle race n corsa f a ostacoli

obstetrician /ɒbstə'trɪʃn/ n ostetrico, -a mf

obstetrics /əb'stetrɪks/ n ostetricia f

obstinacy /'ɒbstɪnəsɪ/ n ostinazione f

obstinate /'ɒbstɪnət/ a ostinato

obstinately /'ɒbstɪnətlɪ/ adv ostinatamente

obstreperous /əb'strepərəs/ a turbolento

obstruct /əb'strʌkt/ vt ostruire; (hinder) ostacolare

obstruction /əb'strʌkʃn/ n ostruzione f; (obstacle) ostacolo m

obstructive /əb'strʌktɪv/ a be ~ ⟨person:⟩ creare dei problemi

obtain /əb'teɪn/ vt ottenere ● vi prevalere

obtainable /əb'teɪnəbl/ a ottenibile

obtrusive /əb'truːsɪv/ a ⟨object⟩ stonato

obtuse /əb'tjuːs/ a ottuso

obverse /'ɒbvɜːs/ a the ~ side/face (of coin) l'altra faccia f

obviate /'ɒbvɪeɪt/ vt fml ovviare a

obvious /'ɒbvɪəs/ a ovvio

obviously /'ɒbvɪəslɪ/ adv ovviamente

occasion /ə'keɪʒn/ n occasione f; (event) evento m; on ~ talvolta; on the ~ of in occasione di ● vt cagionare

occasional /ə'keɪʒənl/ a saltuario; he has the ~ glass of wine ogni tanto beve un bicchiere di vino

occasionally /ə'keɪʒənəlɪ/ adv ogni tanto

occult /ɒ'kʌlt/ a occulto

occupancy /'ɒkjʊpənsɪ/ n available for immediate ~ libero immediatamente; change of ~ cambio m di inquilino

occupant /'ɒkjʊpənt/ n occupante mf; (of vehicle) persona f a bordo

occupation /ɒkjʊ'peɪʃn/ n occupazione f; (job) professione f

occupational /ɒkjʊ'peɪʃənl/ a professionale

occupational: occupational hazard n rischio m professionale. **occupational health** n medicina f del lavoro. **occupational pension** n Br pensione f di lavoro. **occupational psychologist** n psicologo, -a mf del lavoro. **occupational therapist** n ergoterapista mf. **occupational therapy** n ergoterapia f

occupier /'ɒkjʊpaɪə(r)/ n residente mf

occupy /'ɒkjʊpaɪ/ vt (pt/pp occupied) occupare; (keep busy) tenere occupato

occur /ə'kɜː(r)/ vi (pt/pp occurred) accadere; (exist) trovarsi; it ~red to me that mi è venuto in mente che

occurrence /ə'kʌrəns/ n (event) fatto m

ocean /'əʊʃn/ n oceano m

ocean-going /'əʊʃəngəʊɪŋ/ a ⟨ship⟩ d'alto mare

ochre /'əʊkə(r)/ n & a (colour) ocra f

o'clock /ə'klɒk/ adv it's 7 ~ sono le sette; at 7 ~ alle sette

octagon /'ɒktəgən/ n ottagono m

octagonal /ɒk'tægənl/ a ottagonale

octave /'ɒktɪv/ n Mus ottava f

octet /ɒk'tet/ n Mus ottetto m

October /ɒk'təʊbə(r)/ n ottobre m

octogenarian /ɒktədʒɪ'neərɪən/ n & a ottantenne mf

octopus /'ɒktəpəs/ n (pl -puses) polpo m

oculist /'ɒkjʊlɪst/ oculista mf

OD n abbr (overdose) overdose f inv

odd /ɒd/ a ⟨number⟩ dispari; (not of set) scompagnato; (strange) strano; **forty ~** quaranta e rotti; **~ jobs** lavoretti mpl; **the ~ one out** l'eccezione f; **at ~ moments** a tempo perso; **have the ~ glass of wine** avere un bicchiere di vino ogni tanto

oddball /'ɒdbɔːl/ n fam eccentrico, -a mf

odd bod /'ɒdbɒd/ n Br fam tipo, -a mf strano, -a

oddity /'ɒdətɪ/ n stranezza f

odd-job man n tuttofare m inv

oddly /'ɒdlɪ/ adv stranamente; **~ enough** stranamente

oddment /'ɒdmənt/ n (of fabric) scampolo m

odds /ɒdz/ npl (chances) probabilità fpl; **at ~** in disaccordo; **~ and ends** cianfrusaglie fpl; **it makes no ~** non fa alcuna differenza

odds-on a be the ~ favourite (in betting) essere il gran favorito; **she has an ~ chance of...** ha molte probabilità di...; **it is ~ that** è molto probabile che

ode /əʊd/ n ode f

odious /'əʊdɪəs/ a odioso

odium /'əʊdɪəm/ n odio m

odometer /əʊ'dɒmɪtə(r)/ n Am contachilometri m inv, odometro m

odour /'əʊdə(r)/ n odore m

odourless /'əʊdəlɪs/ a inodore

odyssey /'ɒdɪsɪ/ n odissea f

OECD n abbr (Organization for Economic Cooperation and Development) OCSE f

oedema /ɪ'diːmə/ n edema m

oesophagus /ɪ'sɒfəgəs/ n esofago m

oestrogen /'iːstrədʒən/ n estrogeno m

of /ɒv/ prep di; **a cup of tea/coffee** una tazza di tè/caffè; **the hem of my skirt** l'orlo della mia gonna; **the summer of 1989** l'estate del 1989; **the two of us** noi due; **made of** di; **that's very kind of you** è molto gentile da parte tua; **a friend of mine** un mio amico; **a child of three** un bambino di tre anni; **the fourth of January** il quattro gennaio; **within a year of their divorce** a circa un anno dal loro divorzio; **half of it** la metà; **the whole of the room** tutta la stanza

off /ɒf/ prep da; (distant from) lontano da; **take £10 ~ the price** ridurre il prezzo di 10 sterline; **~ the coast** presso la costa; **a street ~ the main road** una traversa della via principale; (near) una strada vicina alla via principale; **get ~ the ladder** scendere dalla scala; **get ~ the bus** uscire dall'autobus; **leave the lid ~ the saucepan** lasciare la pentola senza il coperchio ● adv ⟨button, handle⟩ staccato; ⟨light, machine⟩ spento; ⟨brake⟩ tolto; ⟨tap⟩ chiuso; **'off'** (on appliance) 'off'; **2 kilometres ~** a due chilometri di distanza; **a long way** ~ molto distante; (*time*) lontano; ~ **and on** di tanto in tanto; **with his hat/coat** ~ senza il cappotto/ cappello; **with the light** ~ a luce spenta; **20%** ~ 20% di sconto; **be** ~ (*leave*) andar via; *Sport* essere partito; (*food:*) essere andato a male; (*all gone*) essere finito; (*wedding, engagement:*) essere cancellato; **I'm** ~ **drugs/ alcohol** ho smesso di drogarmi/bere; **be** ~ **one's food** non avere appetito; **she's** ~ **today** (*on holiday*) è in ferie oggi; (*ill*) è malata oggi; **I'm** ~ **home** vado a casa; **you'd be better** ~ **doing...** faresti meglio a fare...; **have a day** ~ avere un giorno di vacanza; **drive/sail** ~ andare via

offal /'ɒfl/ *n Culin* frattaglie *fpl*

offbeat /'ɒfbiːt/ *a* insolito

off-centre *a Br* fuori centro

off chance *n* there's an ~ ~ that c'è una remota possibilità che; **just on the** ~ ~ that nella remota possibilità che

off colour *a* (*not well*) giù di forma; (*joke, story*) sporco

offence /ə'fens/ *n* (*illegal act*) reato *m*; **give** ~ offendere; **take** ~ offendersi (**at** per)

offend /ə'fend/ *vt* offendere

offender /ə'fendə(r)/ *n Jur* colpevole *mf*

offensive /ə'fensɪv/ *a* offensivo● *n* offensiva *f*; **go on the** ~ passare all'offensiva

offer /'ɒfə(r)/ *n* offerta *f*; **on special** ~ in offerta speciale ● *vt* offrire; opporre (*resistance*); ~ **sb sth** offrire qcsa a qcno; ~ **to do sth** offrirsi di fare qcsa

offering /'ɒfərɪŋ/ *n* offerta *f*

offer price *n Comm* prezzo *m* d'offerta

offertory /'ɒfətrɪ/ *n Relig* offertorio *m*

offhand /ɒf'hænd/ *a* (*casual*) spiccio ● *adv* su due piedi

office /'ɒfɪs/ *n* ufficio *m*; (*post, job*) carica *f*

office: office automation *n* burotica *f*. **office block** *n Br* complesso *m* di uffici. **office building** *n Br* complesso *m* di uffici. **office hours** *npl* orario *m* di ufficio. **office junior** *n* fattorino, -a *mf*. **office politics** *n* intrighi *mpl* di ufficio

officer /'ɒfɪsə(r)/ *n* ufficiale *m*; (*police*) agente *m* [di polizia]

office worker *n* impiegato, -a *mf*

official /ə'fɪʃl/ *a* ufficiale ● *n* funzionario, -a *mf*; *Sport* dirigente *m*

officialdom /ə'fɪʃəldəm/ *n* burocrazia *f*

officially /ə'fɪʃəlɪ/ *adv* ufficialmente

officiate /ə'fɪʃɪeɪt/ *vi* officiare

officious /ə'fɪʃəs/ *a* autoritario

officiously /ə'fɪʃəslɪ/ *adv* in modo autoritario

offing /'ɒfɪŋ/ *n* **in the** ~ in vista

off-key *a Mus* stonato

off-licence *n* negozio *m* per la vendita di alcolici

off-limits *a* off-limits *inv*

off-line *a Comput* fuori linea *inv*, off-line *inv*

offload /ɒf'ləʊd/ *vt* scaricare

off-peak *a* (*travel*) fuori dagli orari di punta; (*electricity*) a tariffa notturna ridotta; ~ **call** *Teleph* telefonata *f* a tariffa ridotta

offprint /'ɒfprɪnt/ *n* estratto *m*

off-putting /-pʊtɪŋ/ *a fam* scoraggiante

off-screen *a* (*voice, action*) fuoricampo *inv*; (*relationship*) nella vita privata ● *adv* nella vita privata

off-season *a* (*losses*) di bassa stagione; (*cruise*) in bassa stagione

offset /'ɒfset/ *vt* (*pt/pp* **-set**, *pres p* **-setting**) controbilanciare

offset printing *n* offset *m inv*

offshoot /'ɒfʃuːt/ *n* ramo *m*; *fig* diramazione *f*

offshore /'ɒfʃɔː(r)/ *a* (*wind*) di terra; (*company, investment*) offshore *inv*

offside /ɒf'saɪd/ *a Sport* [in] fuori gioco; (*wheel etc*) (*left*) sinistro; (*right*) destro

offspring /'ɒfsprɪŋ/ *n* prole *m*

off-stage *adv* dietro le quinte

off-the-cuff *a* (*remark*) spontaneo; (*speech*) improvvisato

off-the-peg *a* (*garment*) prêt-à-porter *inv*, confezionato

off-the-shelf *a Comm* standard *inv*

off-the-shoulder *a* (*dress*) senza bretelle

off-the-wall *a* (*fam: sense of humour*) strano

off-white *a* bianco sporco

often /'ɒfn/ *adv* spesso; **how** ~ ogni quanto; **every so** ~ una volta ogni tanto

ogle /'əʊgl/ *vt* mangiarsi con gli occhi

ogre /'əʊgə(r)/ *n* orco *m*

oh /əʊ/ *int* oh!; **oh dear** oh Dio!

OHMS *Br abbr* (**On Her/His Majesty's Service**) *abbreviazione f apposta su corrispondenza ufficiale del governo*

oil /ɔɪl/ *n* olio *m*; (*petroleum*) petrolio *m*; (*for heating*) nafta *f* ● *vt* oliare

oil: oil-burning *a* (*stove, boiler*) a nafta. **oil can** *n* (*applicator*) oliatore *m*. **oil change** *n* cambio *m* dell'olio. **oilcloth** *n* tela *f* cerata. **oilfield** *n* giacimento *m* di petrolio. **oil filter** *n* filtro *m* dell'olio. **oil-fired** /-faɪəd/ *a* (*furnace, heating*) a nafta. **oil gauge** *n* indicatore *m* [del livello] dell'olio. **oil heater** *n* stufa *f* a nafta. **oil lamp** *n* lampada *f* a olio. **oil paint** *n* colore *m* a olio. **oil painting** *n* pittura *f* a olio. **oil pipeline** *n* oleodotto *m*. **oil pressure** *n* pressione *f* dell'olio. **oil-producing** /-prədjuːsɪŋ/ *a* (*country*) produttore di petrolio. **oil refinery** *n* raffineria *f* di petrolio. **oil rig** *n* piattaforma *f* petrolifera, offshore *m inv*. **oilskins** *npl* vestiti *mpl* di tela cerata. **oil slick** *n* chiazza *f* di petrolio. **oil spill** *n* fuoriuscita *f* di petrolio. **oil stove** *n* stufa *f* a nafta. **oil tank** *n* (*domestic*) serbatoio *m* della nafta; (*industrial*) cisterna *f* della nafta. **oil tanker** *n* petroliera *f*. **oil well** *n* pozzo *m* petrolifero

oily /'ɔɪlɪ/ *a* (**-ier, -iest**) unto; *fig* untuoso

ointment /'ɔɪntmənt/ *n* pomata *f*

OK /əʊ'keɪ/ *int* va bene, o.k. ● *a* **if that's OK with you** se ti va bene; **she's OK** (*well*) sta bene; **is the milk still OK?** il latte è ancora buono? ● adv (well) bene ● vt (anche **okay**) (pt/pp **OK'd, okayed**) dare l'o.k. a

old /əʊld/ a vecchio; ⟨girlfriend⟩ ex; **how ~ is she?** quanti anni ha?; **she is ten years ~** ha dieci anni

old: old age n vecchiaia f. **old-age pension** n Br pensione f di vecchiaia. **old-age pensioner** n pensionato, -a mf. **old boy** n Sch ex-allievo m. **old country** n paese m d'origine

olden /'əʊldən/ a **the ~ days** i tempi andati

old-established /-ɪ'stæblɪʃt/ a di lunga data

olde-worlde /əʊldɪ'wɜːldɪ/ a hum dall'aria falsamente antica

old: old-fashioned /-'fæʃ(ə)nd/ a antiquato. **old favourite** n ⟨book, play⟩ classico m; ⟨song, film⟩ vecchio successo m. **old flame** n fam vecchia fiamma f. **old girl** n ex-allieva f. **Old Glory** n bandiera f statunitense. **old hand** n **be an ~ ~ at sth/at doing sth** saperci fare con qcsa/a fare qcsa. **old hat** a fam **be ~ ~** essere roba vecchia

oldie /'əʊldɪ/ n ⟨person⟩ vecchio, -a mf; ⟨film, song⟩ vecchio successo m

old: old lady n ⟨elderly woman⟩ signora f anziana; **my ~ ~** ⟨mother⟩ la mia vecchia; ⟨wife⟩ la mia signora. **old maid** n zitella f. **old man** n ⟨elderly man⟩ uomo m anziano; ⟨old: dear chap⟩ vecchio m mio; **my ~ ~** ⟨father⟩ il mio vecchio; ⟨husband⟩ mio marito m; **the ~ ~** ⟨boss⟩ il capo. **old master** n ⟨work⟩ dipinto m antico (specialmente di un pittore europeo del XIII-XVII secolo). **old people's home** n casa f di riposo. **old soldier** n ⟨former soldier⟩ veterano m. **Old Testament** n Antico Testamento m. **old-time** a di un tempo; **~ dancing** ballo m liscio. **old-timer** n veterano, -a mf. **old wives' tale** n superstizione f. **old woman** n ⟨elderly lady⟩ donna f anziana; **my ~ ~** ⟨mother⟩ mia madre f; ⟨wife⟩ la mia signora; **be an ~ ~** ⟨pej: man:⟩ essere una donnicciola

olive /'ɒlɪv/ n ⟨fruit, colour⟩ oliva f; ⟨tree⟩ olivo m ● a d'oliva; ⟨colour⟩ olivastro

olive: olive branch n fig ramoscello m d'olivo. **olive grove** n oliveto m. **olive oil** n olio m di oliva. **olive-skinned** /-'skɪnd/ a olivastro

Olympic /ə'lɪmpɪk/ a olimpico

Olympic Games, Olympics npl Olimpiadi fpl

ombudsman /'ɒmbʊdzmən/ n difensore m civico

omelette /'ɒmlɪt/ n omelette f inv

omen /'əʊmən/ n presagio m

ominous /'ɒmɪnəs/ a sinistro

omission /ə'mɪʃn/ n omissione f

omit /ə'mɪt/ vt (pt/pp **omitted**) omettere; **~ to do sth** tralasciare di fare qcsa

omnibus /'ɒmnɪbəs/ n ⟨bus⟩ omnibus m inv

omnibus edition n Br TV replica f delle puntate precedenti

omnipotent /ɒm'nɪpətənt/ a onnipotente

on /ɒn/ prep su; ⟨on horizontal surface⟩ su, sopra; **on Monday** lunedì; **on Mondays** di lu-

nedì; **on the first of May** il primo di maggio; **on arriving** all'arrivo; **on one's finger** nel dito; **on foot** a piedi; **on the right/left** a destra/sinistra; **on the Rhine/Thames** sul Reno/Tamigi; **on the radio/television** alla radio/televisione; **on the bus/train** in autobus/treno; **go on the bus/train** andare in autobus/treno; **get on the bus/train** salire sull'autobus/sul treno; **on me** ⟨with me⟩ con me; **it's on me** fam tocca a me ● adv ⟨further on⟩ dopo; ⟨switched on⟩ acceso; ⟨brake⟩ inserito; ⟨in operation⟩ in funzione; **'on'** ⟨on machine⟩ 'on'; **he had his hat/coat on** portava il cappello/cappotto; **without his hat/coat on** senza cappello/capotto; **with/without the lid on** con/senza coperchio; **be on** ⟨film, programme, event:⟩ esserci; **it's not on** fam non è giusto; **be on at** fam tormentare (**to** per); **on and on** senza sosta; **on and off** a intervalli; **and so on** e così via; go on continuare; **stick on** attaccare; **sew on** cucire

once /wʌns/ adv una volta; ⟨formerly⟩ un tempo; **~ upon a time there was** c'era una volta; **at ~** subito; ⟨at the same time⟩ contemporaneamente; **~ and for all** una volta per tutte ● conj ⟨non⟩ appena

once-over n fam **give sb/sth the ~** ⟨look, check⟩ dare un'occhiata veloce a qcno/ qcsa

oncoming /'ɒnkʌmɪŋ/ a che si avvicina dalla direzione opposta

one /wʌn/ a uno, una; **not ~ person** nemmeno una persona ● n uno m ● pron uno; ⟨impersonal⟩ si; **~** another l'un l'altro; **~ by ~** [a] uno a uno; **~ never knows** non si sa mai

one-armed bandit /wʌnɑːmd'bændɪt/ n slot-machine f inv

one-dimensional /-daɪ'menʃənəl/ a unidimensionale; **be ~** ⟨fig: character:⟩ mancare di spessore

one-eyed /-'aɪd/ a con un occhio solo

one-for-one a = **one-to-one**

one-handed /-'hændɪd/ adv ⟨catch, hold⟩ con una sola mano

one-horse town n fam cittadina f di provincia

one-legged /-'legɪd/ a con una sola gamba

one-liner n battuta f d'effetto

one-man a ⟨bobsled⟩ monoposto inv; ⟨for one person⟩ per una sola persona; **she's a ~ woman** è una donna fedele; **it's a ~ outfit/ operation** manda avanti tutto da solo

one-man band n musicista m che suona più strumenti contemporaneamente; **be a ~ ~** fig mandare avanti tutto da solo

one-off a Br ⟨experiment, order, deal⟩ unico e irripetibile; ⟨event, decision, offer, payment⟩ eccezionale; ⟨example, design⟩ unico; ⟨issue, magazine⟩ speciale

one-parent family n famiglia f con un solo genitore

one-room flat, one-room apartment n monolocale m

one's /wʌnz/ poss a **one has to look after**

~ health ci si deve preoccupare della propria salute

oneself /wʌn'self/ *pron* (*reflexive*) si; (*emphatic*) sé, se stesso; **by ~** da solo; **be proud of ~** essere fieri di sé

one-shot *a Am* = **one-off**

one-sided /-'saɪdɪd/ *a* unilaterale

one-time *a* ex *inv*

one-to-one *a* (*personal relationship*) tra due persone; (*private lesson*) individuale; (*correspondence*) di uno a uno

one-upmanship /-'ʌpmənʃɪp/ *n* arte *f* di primeggiare

one-way *a* (*street*) a senso unico; (*ticket*) di sola andata

one-woman *a* it's a **~ outfit** manda avanti tutto da sola; **he's a ~ man** è un uomo fedele

ongoing /'ɒngəʊɪŋ/ *a* (*process*) continuo; (*battle, saga*) in corso

onion /'ʌnjən/ *n* cipolla *f*

on-line *a Comput* in linea, on-line *inv*; **go ~ to...** connettersi a...; **~ time** durata *f* del collegamento

onlooker /'ɒnlʊkə(r)/ *n* spettatore, -trice *mf*

only /'əʊnlɪ/ *a* solo; **~ child** figlio, -a *mf* unico, -a ● *adv & conj* solo, solamente; **~ just** appena

o.n.o. *Br abbr* (**or nearest offer**) trattabile

on-off *a* (*button, control*) di accensione

onrush /'ɒnrʌʃ/ *n* (*of people, water*) ondata *f*

on-screen *a* sullo schermo

onset /'ɒnset/ *n* (*beginning*) inizio *m*

onshore /'ɒnʃɔː(r)/ *a* (*wind*) di mare; (*work*) a terra

onside /ɒn'saɪd/ *a & adv Sport* non in fuorigioco

on-site *a* sul posto

onslaught /'ɒnslɔːt/ *n* attacco *m*

on-stage *a & adv* in scena

on-the-job *a* (*training*) in sede

on-the-spot *a* (*advice, quotation*) immediato

onto /'ɒntu:/ *prep* (*also* **on to**) su

onus /'əʊnəs/ *n* **the ~ is on me** spetta a me la responsabilità (**to** di)

onward[s] /'ɒnwəd[z]/ *adv* in avanti; **from then ~** da allora [in poi]

oodles /'u:dlz/ *n fam* un sacco

ooh /u:/ *int* oh!

oomph /u:mf/ *n fam* verve *f inv*

oops /u:ps/ *int* ops!

ooze /u:z/ *vi* fluire

op /ɒp/ *n* = **operation**

opal /'əʊpl/ *n* opale *f*

opaque /əʊ'peɪk/ *a* opaco

Opec, OPEC /'əʊpek/ *n abbr* (**Organization of Petroleum Exporting Countries**) OPEC *f*

open /'əʊpən/ *a* aperto; (*free to all*) pubblico; (*job*) vacante; **in the ~ air** all'aperto ● *n* **in the ~** all'aperto; *fig* alla luce del sole ● *vt* aprire ● *vi* aprirsi; (*shop:*) aprire; (*flower:*) sbocciare

■ **open onto** *vt* (*door, window:*) dare su

■ **open out** *vi* (*road:*) allargarsi; (*flower:*) aprirsi ● *vt* aprire (*map, newspaper*)

■ **open up** *vt* aprire ● *vi* aprirsi

■ **open with** *vi* (*start with*) iniziare con

open: open-air *a* (*pool, market, stage*) all'aperto. **opencast mining** *n Br* miniera *f* a cielo aperto. **open competition** *n* concorso *m*. **open day** *n* giorno *m* di apertura al pubblico. **open-ended** /-'endɪd/ *a* (*relationship, question, contract*) aperto; (*stay*) a tempo indeterminato; (*period*) indeterminato; (*strategy*) flessibile

opener /'əʊpənə(r)/ *n* (*for tins*) apriscatole *m inv*; (*for bottles*) apribottiglie *m inv*

open: open government *n* politica *f* di trasparenza. **open-handed** /-'hændɪd/ *a* generoso. **open-heart surgery** *n* intervento *m* a cuore aperto. **open house** *n* (*Am: open day*) giornata *f* di apertura al pubblico; **it's always ~ ~ at the Batemans'** i Bateman sono sempre molto ospitali

opening /'əʊpənɪŋ/ *n* apertura *f*; (*beginning*) inizio *m*; (*job*) posto *m* libero

opening: opening balance *n Fin* saldo *m* iniziale. **opening ceremony** *n* cerimonia *f* inaugurale. **opening hours** *npl* orario *m* d'apertura

openly /'əʊpənlɪ/ *adv* apertamente

open: open market *n Econ* mercato *m* aperto. **open-minded** /-'maɪndɪd/ *a* aperto; (*broad-minded*) di vedute larghe. **open-mouthed** /-'maʊðd/ *a* a bocca aperta. **open-necked** /-'nekt/ *a* (*shirt*) col colletto sbottonato

openness /'əʊpənnɪs/ *n* (*of government, atmosphere*) trasparenza *f*; (*candour*) franchezza *f*; (*receptiveness*) apertura *f* mentale

open: open-plan *a* a pianta aperta. **open sandwich** *n* tartina *f*. **open scholarship** *n Univ* borsa *f* di studio assegnata per concorso. **open season** *n* (*in hunting*) stagione *f* della caccia. **open secret** *n* segreto *m* di Pulcinella. **open ticket** *n* biglietto *m* aperto. **Open University** *n Br Univ* corsi *mpl* universitari per corrispondenza. **open verdict** *n Jur* verdetto *m* che dichiara non accertabili le cause della morte

opera /'ɒpərə/ *n* opera *f*

operable /'ɒpərəbl/ *a* operabile

opera: opera glasses *npl* binocolo *msg* da teatro. **opera house** *n* teatro *m* lirico. **opera-singer** *n* cantante *mf* lirico, -a

operate /'ɒpəreɪt/ *vt* far funzionare (*machine, lift*); azionare (*lever, brake*); mandare avanti (*business*) ● *vi Techn* funzionare; (*be in action*) essere in funzione; *Mil, fig* operare

■ **operate on** *vt Med* operare

operatic /ɒpə'rætɪk/ *a* lirico, operistico

operating /'ɒpəreɪtɪŋ/: **operating costs** *npl* spese *fpl* di esercizio. **operating instructions** *npl* istruzioni *fpl* per l'uso. **operating room** *n Am* sala *f* operatoria. **operating system** *n Comput* sistema *m* operativo. **operating table** *n Med* tavolo *m* operatorio. **operating theatre** *n Br* sala *f* operatoria

operation /ɒpə'reɪʃn/ n operazione f; Tech funzionamento m; **in ~** Techn in funzione; **come into ~** fig entrare in funzione; ⟨law:⟩ entrare in vigore; **have an ~** Med subire un'operazione

operational /ɒpə'reɪʃənəl/ a operativo; ⟨law etc⟩ in vigore

operations room n Mil centro m operativo; ⟨police⟩ centrale f operativa

operative /'ɒpərətɪv/ a operativo

operator /'ɒpəreɪtə(r)/ n ⟨user⟩ operatore, -trice mf; Teleph centralinista mf

operetta /ɒpə'retə/ n operetta f

ophthalmic /ɒf'θælmɪk/ a oftalmico

opinion /ə'pɪnjən/ n opinione f; **in my ~** secondo me

opinionated /ə'pɪnɪəneɪtɪd/ a dogmatico

opinion poll n sondaggio m di opinione

opium /'əʊpɪəm/ n oppio m

opponent /ə'pəʊnənt/ n avversario, -a mf

opportune /'ɒpətjuːn/ a opportuno

opportunist /ɒpə'tjuːnɪst/ n opportunista mf

opportunistic /ɒpətjʊ'nɪstɪk/ a opportunistico

opportunity /ɒpə'tjuːnəti/ n opportunità f inv

oppose /ə'pəʊz/ vt opporsi a; **be ~d to sth** esssere contrario a qcsa; **as ~d to** al contrario di

opposing /ə'pəʊzɪŋ/ a avversario; ⟨opposite⟩ opposto

opposite /'ɒpəzɪt/ a opposto; ⟨house⟩ di fronte; **~ number** fig controparte f; **the ~ sex** l'altro sesso ● n contrario m ● adv di fronte ● prep di fronte a

opposition /ɒpə'zɪʃn/ n opposizione f

oppress /ə'pres/ vt opprimere

oppression /ə'preʃn/ n oppressione f

oppressive /ə'presɪv/ a oppressivo; ⟨heat⟩ opprimente

oppressor /ə'presə(r)/ n oppressore m

■ **opt for** /ɒpt/ vt optare per

■ **opt out** vi dissociarsi (**of** da)

optic /'ɒptɪk/ a ⟨nerve, disc, fibre⟩ ottico

optical /'ɒptɪkl/ a ottico; **~ illusion** illusione f ottica

optician /ɒp'tɪʃn/ n ottico, -a mf

optics /'ɒptɪks/ n ottica f

optimism /'ɒptɪmɪzm/ n ottimismo m

optimist /'ɒptɪmɪst/ n ottimista mf

optimistic /ɒptɪ'mɪstɪk/ a ottimistico

optimistically /ɒptɪ'mɪstɪklɪ/ adv ottimisticamente

optimize /'ɒptɪmaɪz/ vt ottimizzare

optimum /'ɒptɪməm/ a ottimale ● n (pl -ima) optimum m

option /'ɒpʃn/ n scelta f; Comm opzione f

optional /'ɒpʃənəl/ a facoltativo; **~ extras** optional m inv

opulence /'ɒpjʊləns/ n opulenza f

opulent /'ɒpjʊlənt/ a opulento

opus /'əʊpəs/ n (pl opuses or opera) opera f

or /ɔː(r)/ conj o, oppure; ⟨after negative⟩ né; **or**

[else] se no; **in a year or two** fra un anno o due

oracle /'ɒrəkl/ n oracolo m

oral /'ɔːrəl/ a orale ● n fam esame m orale

orally /'ɔːrəli/ adv oralmente

orange /'ɒrɪndʒ/ n arancia f; (colour) arancione m ● a arancione

orangeade /ɒrɪndʒ'eɪd/ n aranciata f

orange: orange blossom n fiori mpl d'arancio. **orange juice** n succo m d'arancia. **orange peel** n scorza f d'arancia. **orange squash** n Br succo m d'arancia (diluito in acqua). **orange tree** n arancio m

oration /ə'reɪʃn/ n orazione f

orator /'ɒrətə(r)/ n oratore, -trice mf

oratorio /ɒrə'tɔːrɪəʊ/ n oratorio m

oratory /'ɒrətrɪ/ n oratorio m

orbit /'ɔːbɪt/ n orbita f ● vt orbitare

orbital /'ɔːbɪtl/ a **~ road** tangenziale f

orchard /'ɔːtʃəd/ n frutteto m

orchestra /'ɔːkɪstrə/ n orchestra f

orchestral /ɔː'kestrəl/ a orchestrale

orchestra pit n [fossa f dell']orchestra f

orchestrate /'ɔːkɪstreɪt/ vt orchestrare

orchid /'ɔːkɪd/ n orchidea f

ordain /ɔː'deɪn/ vt decretare; Relig ordinare

ordeal /ɔː'diːl/ n fig terribile esperienza f

order /'ɔːdə(r)/ n ordine m; Comm ordinazione f; **out of ~** ⟨machine⟩ fuori servizio; **in ~ that** affinché; **in ~ to** per; **take holy ~s** prendere i voti ● vt ordinare

■ **order about, order around** vt ⟨give orders to⟩ impartire ordini a

order book n registro m degli ordini

order form n modulo m di ordinazione

orderly /'ɔːdəlɪ/ a ordinato ● n Mil attendente m; Med inserviente m

orderly officer n Mil attendente m

order number n numero m d'ordine

ordinal /'ɔːdɪnəl/ n & a ordinale m

ordinarily /ɔːdɪ'nerɪlɪ/ adv ⟨normally⟩ normalmente

ordinary /'ɔːdɪnərɪ/ a ordinario

ordination /ɔːdɪ'neɪʃn/ n Relig ordinazione f

ordnance /'ɔːdnəns/ n Mil materiale m militare

Ordnance Survey n Br istituto m cartografico; **Ordnance Survey Map** carta f topografica dell'istituto cartografico

ore /ɔː(r)/ n minerale m grezzo

oregano /ɒrɪ'gɑːnəʊ/ n origano m

organ /'ɔːgən/ n Anat, Mus organo m

organ donor n Med donatore, -trice mf di organi

organic /ɔː'gænɪk/ a organico; (without chemicals) biologico

organically /ɔː'gænɪklɪ/ adv organicamente; **~ grown** coltivato biologicamente

organic: organic chemistry n chimica f organica. **organic farm** n azienda f agricola specializzata in prodotti biologici. **organic farming** n agricoltura f biologica

organism /'ɔːgənɪzm/ n organismo m

organist /'ɔːgənɪst/ n organista mf

organization /ɔːgənaɪˈzeɪʃn/ n organizzazione f

organizational /ɔːgənaɪˈzeɪʃənl/ a ⟨ability, role⟩ organizzativo

organize /ˈɔːgənaɪz/ vt organizzare

organized crime /ɔːgənaɪzdˈkraɪm/ n criminalità f organizzata

organized labour n manodopera f organizzata

organizer /ˈɔːgənaɪzə(r)/ n organizzatore, -trice mf

organ transplant n Med trapianto m di organi

orgasm /ˈɔːgæzm/ n orgasmo m

orgy /ˈɔːdʒɪ/ n orgia f

Orient /ˈɔːrɪənt/ n Oriente m

oriental /ɔːrɪˈentl/ a orientale; **~ carpet** tappeto m persiano ● n orientale mf

orientate /ˈɔːrɪenteɪt/ vt **~ oneself** orientarsi

orientation /ɔːrɪənˈteɪʃn/ n orientamento m

orienteering /ɔːrɪenˈtɪərɪŋ/ n orientamento m

orifice /ˈɒrɪfɪs/ n orifizio m

origin /ˈɒrɪdʒɪn/ n origine f

original /əˈrɪdʒɪnl/ a originario; (not copied, new) originale; ● n originale m; **in the ~** in versione originale

originality /ərɪdʒɪˈnælətɪ/ n originalità f

originally /əˈrɪdʒɪnəlɪ/ adv originariamente

originate /əˈrɪdʒɪneɪt/ vi **~ in** avere origine in

originator /əˈrɪdʒɪneɪtə(r)/ n ideatore, -trice mf

Orkney /ˈɔːknɪ/ n (also **Orkney Islands**) Orcadi fpl

ornament /ˈɔːnəmənt/ n ornamento m; (on mantelpiece etc) soprammobile m

ornamental /ɔːnəˈmentl/ a ornamentale

ornamentation /ɔːnəmenˈteɪʃn/ n decorazione f

ornate /ɔːˈneɪt/ a ornato

ornithologist /ɔːnɪˈθɒlədʒɪst/ n ornitologo, -a mf

ornithology /ɔːnɪˈθɒlədʒɪ/ n ornitologia f

orphan /ˈɔːfn/ n orfano, -a mf ● vt rendere orfano; **be ~ed** rimanere orfano; **be ~ed by...** essere reso orfano da...

orphanage /ˈɔːfənɪdʒ/ n orfanotrofio m

orphaned /ˈɔːfənd/ a reso orfano

orthodox /ˈɔːθədɒks/ a ortodosso

orthopaedic /ɔːθəˈpiːdɪk/ a ortopedico

orthopaedics /ɔːθəˈpiːdɪks/ n ortopedia f

OS abbr (**outsize**) per taglie forti

oscillate /ˈɒsɪleɪt/ vi oscillare

osmosis /ɒzˈməʊsɪs/ n osmosi f inv; **by ~** per osmosi

ostensible /ɒˈstensəbl/ a apparente

ostensibly /ɒˈstensəblɪ/ adv apparentemente

ostentation /ɒstenˈteɪʃn/ n ostentazione f

ostentatious /ɒstenˈteɪʃəs/ a ostentato

ostentatiously /ɒstenˈteɪʃəslɪ/ adv ostentatamente

osteopath /ˈɒstɪəpæθ/ n osteopata mf

osteoporosis /ɒstɪəʊpəˈrəʊsɪs/ n osteoporosi f

ostracism /ˈɒstrəsɪzm/ n ostracismo m

ostracize /ˈɒstrəsaɪz/ vt ostracizzare

ostrich /ˈɒstrɪtʃ/ n struzzo m

other /ˈʌðə(r)/ a, pron & n altro, -a mf; **the ~ [one]** l'altro, -a mf; **the ~ two** gli altri due; **two ~s** altri due; **~ people** gli altri; **any ~ questions?** altre domande?; **every ~ day** (alternate days) a giorni alterni; **the ~ day** l'altro giorno; **the ~ evening** l'altra sera; **someone/something or ~** qualcuno/qualcosa ● adv **~ than him** tranne lui; **somehow or ~** in qualche modo; **somewhere or ~** da qualche parte

otherwise /ˈʌðəwaɪz/ adv altrimenti; (differently) diversamente

other-worldly /ʌðəˈwɜːldlɪ/ a disinteressato alle cose materiali

OTT abbr fam (**over-the-top**) esagerato

otter /ˈɒtə(r)/ n lontra f

OU n Br abbr (**Open University**) corsi mpl universitari per corrispondenza

ouch /aʊtʃ/ int ahi!

ought /ɔːt/ v aux I/we **~ to stay** dovrei/dovremmo rimanere; **he ~ not to have done it** non avrebbe dovuto farlo; **that ~ to be enough** questo dovrebbe bastare

ounce /aʊns/ n oncia f (= 28,35 g)

our /ˈaʊə(r)/ poss a il nostro m, la nostra f, i nostri mpl, le nostre fpl; **~ mother/father** nostra madre/nostro padre

ours /ˈaʊəz/ poss pron il nostro m, la nostra f, i nostri mpl, le nostre fpl; **a friend of ~** un nostro amico; **friends of ~** dei nostri amici; **that is ~** quello è nostro; (as opposed to yours) quello è il nostro

ourselves /aʊəˈselvz/ pers pron (reflexive) ci; (emphatic) noi, noi stessi; **we poured ~ a drink** ci siamo versati da bere; **we heard it ~** l'abbiamo sentito noi stessi; **we are proud of ~** siamo fieri di noi; **by ~** da soli

oust /aʊst/ vt rimuovere

out /aʊt/ adv fuori; (not alight) spento; **be ~** ⟨flower:⟩ essere sbocciato; ⟨workers:⟩ essere in sciopero; ⟨calculation:⟩ essere sbagliato; Sport essere fuori; (unconscious) aver perso i sensi; (fig: not feasible) fuori questione; **the sun is ~** è uscito il sole; **~ and about** in piedi; **get ~!** fam fuori!; **you should get ~ more** dovresti uscire più spesso; **~ with it!** fam sputa il rospo!; **be ~ to** avere l'intenzione di; ● prep **~ of** fuori da; **~ of date** non aggiornato; ⟨passaporto⟩ scaduto; **~ of order** guasto; **~ of print/stock** esaurito; **~ of sorts** indisposto; **~ of tune** (singer) stonato; (instrument) scordato; **be ~ of bed/ the room** fuori dal letto/dalla stanza; **~ of breath** senza fiato; **~ of danger** fuori pericolo; **~ of work** disoccupato; **nine ~ of ten** nove su dieci; **be ~ of sugar/bread** rimanere senza zucchero/pane; **go ~ of the room** uscire dalla stanza

out-and-out a ⟨success, failure⟩ totale; ⟨villain, liar⟩ vero e proprio

outback /'aʊtbæk/ n entroterra m inv australiano

outbid /aʊt'bɪd/ vt (pt/pp -bid, pres p -bidding) ~ sb rilanciare l'offerta di qcno

outboard /'aʊtbɔːd/ a ~ motor fuoribordo m inv

outbreak /'aʊtbreɪk/ n (of war) scoppio m; (of disease) insorgenza f

outbuilding /'aʊtbɪldɪŋ/ n costruzione f annessa

outburst /'aʊtbɜːst/ n esplosione f

outcast /'aʊtkɑːst/ n esule mf; (social) escluso m

outclass /aʊt'klɑːs/ vt surclassare

outcome /'aʊtkʌm/ n risultato m

outcrop /'aʊtkrɒp/ n affioramento m

outcry /'aʊtkraɪ/ n protesta f

outdated /aʊt'deɪtɪd/ a sorpassato

outdo /aʊt'duː/ vt (pt -did, pp -done) superare

outdoor /'aʊtdɔː(r)/ a (life, sports) all'aperto; ~ swimming pool piscina f scoperta

outdoors /aʊt'dɔːz/ adv all'aria aperta; go ~ uscire all'aria aperta

outer /'aʊtə(r)/ a esterno

outer space n spazio m cosmico

outfit /'aʊtfɪt/ n equipaggiamento m; (clothes) completo m; (fam: organization) organizzazione f

outfitter /'aʊtfɪtə(r)/ n men's ~'s negozio m di abbigliamento maschile

outflow /'aʊtfləʊ/ n (of money) uscite fpl

outgoing /'aʊtgəʊɪŋ/ a (president) uscente; (mail) in partenza; (sociable) estroverso ● npl ~s uscite fpl

outgrow /aʊt'grəʊ/ vi (pt -grew, pp -grown) diventare troppo grande per

outhouse /'aʊthaʊs/ n costruzione f annessa

outing /'aʊtɪŋ/ n gita f

outlandish /aʊt'lændɪʃ/ a stravagante

outlast /aʊt'lɑːst/ vt durare più a lungo di

outlaw /'aʊtlɔː/ n fuorilegge mf inv ● vt dichiarare illegale

outlay /'aʊtleɪ/ n spesa f

outlet /'aʊtlet/ n sbocco m; fig sfogo m; Comm punto m [di] vendita

outline /'aʊtlaɪn/ n contorno m; (summary) sommario m ● vt tracciare il contorno di; (describe) descrivere

outline agreement n abbozzo m di accordo

outlive /aʊt'lɪv/ vt sopravvivere a

outlook /'aʊtlʊk/ n vista f; (future prospect) prospettiva f; (attitude) visione f

outlying /'aʊtlaɪɪŋ/ a ~ areas zone fpl periferiche

outmanoeuvre /aʊtmə'nuːvə(r)/ vt ~ sb passare in vantaggio su qcno con un'abile manovra

outmoded /aʊt'məʊdɪd/ a fuori moda

outnumber /aʊt'nʌmbə(r)/ vt superare in numero

out of bounds a & adv (area) vietato all'accesso

out-of-date a (theory, concept) sorpassato; (ticket, passport) scaduto

out-of-pocket a be out of pocket essere in perdita; ~ expenses spese fpl extra

out-of-the-way a (places) fuori mano

outpatient /'aʊtpeɪʃnt/ n paziente mf esterno, -a; ~s' department ambulatorio m

outpost /'aʊtpəʊst/ n avamposto m

output /'aʊtpʊt/ n produzione f

outrage /'aʊtreɪdʒ/ n oltraggio m ● vt oltraggiare

outrageous /aʊt'reɪdʒəs/ a oltraggioso; (price) scandaloso

outrider /'aʊtraɪdə(r)/ n battistrada m inv

outright¹ /'aʊtraɪt/ a completo; (refusal) netto

outright² /aʊt'raɪt/ adv completamente; (at once) immediatamente; (frankly) francamente

outrun /aʊt'rʌn/ vt superare

outsell /aʊt'sel/ vt vendere meglio di (product)

outset /'aʊtset/ n inizio m; from the ~ fin dall'inizio

outside¹ /'aʊtsaɪd/ a esterno ● n esterno m; from the ~ dall'esterno; at the ~ al massimo

outside² /aʊt'saɪd/ adv all'esterno, fuori; (out of doors) fuori; go ~ andare fuori ● prep fuori da; (in front of) davanti a

outsider /aʊt'saɪdə(r)/ n estraneo, -a mf

outsize /'aʊtsaɪz/ a smisurato; (clothes) per taglie forti

outskirts /'aʊtskɜːts/ npl sobborghi mpl

outsmart /aʊt'smɑːt/ vt essere più furbo di

outspoken /aʊt'spəʊkn/ a schietto

outspread /'aʊtspred/ a (wings) spiegato; (arms, fingers) disteso

outstanding /aʊt'stændɪŋ/ a eccezionale; (landmark) prominente; (not settled) in sospeso

outstandingly /aʊt'stændɪŋlɪ/ adv eccezionalmente; ~ good eccezionale

outstay /aʊt'steɪ/ vt ~ one's welcome abusare dell'ospitalità di qcno

outstretched /'aʊtstretʃt/ a allungato

outstrip /aʊt'strɪp/ vt (pt/pp -stripped) superare

out-tray n vassoio m per corrispondenza e pratiche evase

outvote /aʊt'vəʊt/ vt mettere in minoranza

outward /'aʊtwəd/ a esterno; (journey) di andata ● adv verso l'esterno

outwardly /'aʊtwədlɪ/ adv esternamente

outwards /'aʊtwədz/ adv verso l'esterno

outweigh /aʊt'weɪ/ vt aver maggior peso di

outwit /aʊt'wɪt/ vt (pt/pp -witted) battere in astuzia

outworker /'aʊtwɜːkə(r)/ n Br lavoratore, -trice mf a domicilio

outworn /aʊt'wɔːn/ a (outmoded) sorpassato

oval /'əʊvl/ a ovale ● n ovale m

ovary /'əʊvərɪ/ n Anat ovaia f

ovation /əʊ'veɪʃn/ n ovazione f

oven /'ʌvn/ n forno m

oven: oven cleaner *n* detergente *m* per il forno. **oven glove** *n* guanto *m* da forno. **ovenproof** *a* da forno. **oven-ready** *a* pronto da mettere in forno

over /'əʊvə(r)/ *prep* sopra; *(across)* al di là di; *(during)* durante; *(more than)* più di; **~ the phone** al telefono; **~ the page** alla pagina seguente; **all ~ Italy** in tutta [l']Italia; *‹travel›* per l'Italia ● *adv Math* col resto di; *(ended)* finito; **~ again** un'altra volta; **~ and ~** più volte; **~ and above** oltre a; **~ here/ there** qui/là; **all ~** *(everywhere)* dappertutto; **it's all ~** è tutto finito; **I ache all ~** ho male dappertutto; **come/bring ~** venire/portare; **turn ~** girare

over+ *pref (too)* troppo

overact /əʊvər'ækt/ *vi* strafare

overactive /əʊvər'æktɪv/ *a* ‹*imagination*› sbrigliato

overall¹ /'əʊvərɔːl/ *n* grembiule *m*

overall² /əʊvər'ɔːl/ *a* complessivo; *(general)* generale ● *adv* complessivamente

overalls /'əʊvərɔːlz/ *npl* tuta *fsg* [da lavoro]

overarm /'əʊvərɑːm/ *a & adv* ‹*throw*› col braccio al di sopra della spalla

overawe /əʊvər'ɔː/ *vt fig* intimidire

overbalance /əʊvə'bæləns/ *vi* perdere l'equilibrio

overbearing /əʊvə'beərɪŋ/ *a* prepotente

overblown /əʊvə'bləʊn/ *a* ‹*style*› ampolloso

overboard /'əʊvəbɔːd/ *adv Naut* in mare

overbook /əʊvə'bʊk/ *vt* accettare un numero di prenotazioni superiore ai posti disponibili

overburden /əʊvə'bɜːdən/ *vt* sovraccaricare (**with** di)

overcapacity /əʊvəkə'pæsəti/ *n* eccesso *m* di capacità produttiva

overcast /'əʊvəkɑːst/ *a* coperto

overcharge /əʊvə'tʃɑːdʒ/ *vt* **~ sb** far pagare più del dovuto a ● *vi* far pagare più del dovuto

overcoat /'əʊvəkəʊt/ *n* cappotto *m*

overcome /əʊvə'kʌm/ *vt* (*pt* **-came**, *pp* **-come**) vincere; **be ~ by** essere sopraffatto da

overcompensate /əʊvə'kɒmpənseɪt/ *vi* compensare eccessivamente

overconfident /əʊvə'kɒnfɪdənt/ *a* troppo sicuro di sé

overcook /əʊvə'kʊk/ *vt* cuocere troppo

overcrowded /əʊvə'kraʊdɪd/ *a* sovraffollato

overcrowding /əʊvə'kraʊdɪŋ/ *n* (*in transport*) calca *f*; (*in city, institution*) sovraffollamento *m*

overdo /əʊvə'duː/ *vt* (*pt* **-did**, *pp* **-done**) esagerare; (*cook too long*) stracuocere; **~ it** (*fam: do too much*) strafare

overdose /'əʊvədəʊs/ *n* overdose *f inv*

overdraft /'əʊvədrɑːft/ *n* scoperto *m*; **have an ~** avere il conto scoperto

overdraw /əʊvə'drɔː/ *vt* (*pt* **-drew**, *pp* **-drawn**) **~ one's account** andare allo scoperto; **be ~n by...** ‹*account:*› essere scoperto di...

overdressed /əʊvə'drest/ *a* troppo elegante

overdrive /'əʊvədraɪv/ *n Auto* overdrive *m inv*

overdue /əʊvə'djuː/ *a* in ritardo

overeat /əʊvər'iːt/ *vi* mangiare troppo

overemphasize /əʊvər'emfəsaɪz/ *vt* esagerare ‹*importance*›; dare troppo rilievo a ‹*aspect, fact*›

overenthusiastic /əʊvərɪnθjuːzɪ'æstɪk/ *a* troppo entusiasta

overestimate /əʊvər'estɪmeɪt/ *vt* sopravvalutare

overexcited /əʊvərɪk'saɪtɪd/ *a* sovreccitato; **get ~** sovreccitarsi

overexert /əʊvərɪg'zɜːt/ *vt* **~ oneself** sovraffaticarsi

overexposure /əʊvərek'spəʊʒə(r)/ *n Phot* sovresposizione *f*; (*in the media*) attenzione *f* eccessiva da parte dei media

overfeed /əʊvə'fiːd/ *vt* sovralimentare ‹*child, pet*›; concimare troppo ‹*plant*›

overflow¹ /'əʊvəfləʊ/ *n* (*water*) acqua *f* che deborda; (*people*) pubblico *m* in eccesso; (*outlet*) scarico *m*

overflow² /əʊvə'fləʊ/ *vi* debordare

overgenerous /əʊvə'dʒenərəs/ *a* ‹*amount*› troppo generoso

overgrown /əʊvə'grəʊn/ *a* ‹*garden*› coperto di erbacce

overhang¹ /'əʊvəhæŋ/ *n* sporgenza *f*

overhang² /əʊvə'hæŋ/ *v* (*pt/pp* **-hung**) ● *vi* sporgere ● *vt* sovrastare

overhanging /əʊvə'hæŋɪŋ/ *a* ‹*ledge, cliff*› sporgente

overhaul¹ /'əʊvəhɔːl/ *n* revisione *f*

overhaul² /əʊvə'hɔːl/ *vt Techn* revisionare

overhead¹ /əʊvə'hed/ *adv* in alto

overhead² /'əʊvəhed/ *a* aereo; ‹*railway*› sopraelevato; ‹*lights*› da soffitto ● *npl* **~s** spese *fpl* generali

overhead: overhead light *n* lampada *f* da soffitto. **overhead locker** *n Aeron* armadietto *m* [per il bagaglio a mano]. **overhead projector** *n* lavagna *f* luminosa

overhear /əʊvə'hɪə(r)/ *vt* (*pt/pp* **-heard**) sentire per caso ‹*conversation*›; **I ~d him saying it** l'ho sentito per caso mentre lo diceva

overheat /əʊvə'hiːt/ *vi Auto* surriscaldarsi ● *vt* surriscaldare

over-indulge *vi* eccedere ● *vt* viziare ‹*child*›

over-indulgence *n* (*excess*) eccesso *m*; (*laxity towards*) indulgenza *f* eccessiva

overjoyed /əʊvə'dʒɔɪd/ *a* felicissimo

overkill /'əʊvəkɪl/ *n* (*exaggerated treatment*) esagerazione *f*

overland /'əʊvəlænd/ *a & adv* via terra; **~ route** via *f* terrestre

overlap /əʊvə'læp/ *v* (*pt/pp* **-lapped**) ● *vi* sovrapporsi ● *vt* sovrapporre

overlay /əʊvə'leɪ/ *vt* ricoprire

overleaf /əʊvə'liːf/ *adv* sul retro

overload¹ /əʊvə'ləʊd/ *vt* sovraccaricare

overload² /'əʊvələʊd/ *n Electr* sovratensioni *pl*

overlook /əʊvə'lʊk/ vt dominare; (fail to see, ignore) lasciarsi sfuggire

overly /'əʊvəlɪ/ adv eccessivamente

overmanned /əʊvə'mænd/ a con un'eccedenza di personale

overmanning /əʊvə'mænɪŋ/ n eccesso m di personale

overmuch /əʊvə'mʌtʃ/ adv troppo

overnight[1] /əʊvə'naɪt/ adv per la notte; **stay ~** fermarsi a dormire

overnight[2] /əʊvə'naɪt/ a notturno

overnight bag n piccola borsa f da viaggio

overnight stay n sosta f per la notte

overpass /'əʊvəpɑːs/ n cavalcavia m inv

overpay /əʊvə'peɪ/ vt (pt/pp **-paid**) strapagare

overplay /əʊvə'pleɪ/ vt (exaggerate) esagerare

overpopulated /əʊvə'pɒpjʊleɪtɪd/ a sovrappopolato

overpower /əʊvə'paʊə(r)/ vt sopraffare

overpowering /əʊvə'paʊərɪŋ/ a insostenibile

overpriced /əʊvə'praɪst/ a troppo caro

overproduce /əʊvəprə'djuːs/ vt produrre in eccesso

overqualified /əʊvə'kwɒlɪfaɪd/ a troppo qualificato

overrate /əʊvə'reɪt/ vt sopravvalutare

overrated /əʊvə'reɪtɪd/ a sopravvalutato

overreach /əʊvə'riːtʃ/ vt **~ oneself** puntare troppo in alto

overreact /əʊvərɪ'ækt/ vi avere una reazione eccessiva

overreaction /əʊvərɪ'ækʃn/ n reazione f eccessiva

override /əʊvə'raɪd/ vt (pt **-rode**, pp **-ridden**) passare sopra a

overriding /əʊvə'raɪdɪŋ/ a prevalente

overrule /əʊvə'ruːl/ vt annullare (decision); **we were ~d by the chairman** il direttore ha prevalso su di noi

overrun /əʊvə'rʌn/ vt (pt **-ran**, pp **-run**, pres p **-running**) invadere; oltrepassare (time); **be ~ with** essere invaso da

overseas[1] /əʊvə'siːz/ adv oltremare

overseas[2] /'əʊvəsiːz/ a d'oltremare

oversee /əʊvə'siː/ vt (pt **-saw**, pp **-seen**) sorvegliare

oversell /əʊvə'sel/ vt lodare esageratamente (idea, plan)

oversensitive /əʊvə'sensɪtɪv/ a (person) ipersensibile

oversexed /əʊvə'sekst/ a fam **be ~** essere un maniaco/una maniaca del sesso

overshadow /əʊvə'ʃædəʊ/ vt adombrare

overshoot /əʊvə'ʃuːt/ vt (pt/pp **-shot**) oltrepassare

oversight /'əʊvəsaɪt/ n disattenzione f; **an ~** una svista

oversimplification /əʊvəsɪmplɪfɪ'keɪʃn/ n semplificazione f eccessiva

oversimplified /əʊvə'sɪmplɪfaɪd/ a semplicistico

oversimplify /əʊvə'sɪmplɪfaɪ/ vt semplificare eccessivamente

oversize[d] /əʊvə'saɪz[d]/ a più grande del normale

oversleep /əʊvə'sliːp/ vi (pt/pp **-slept**) svegliarsi troppo tardi

overspend /əʊvə'spend/ vi spendere troppo

overspending /əʊvə'spendɪŋ/ n spese fpl eccessive; Fin spese fpl superiori al bilancio di previsione

overspill /'əʊvəspɪl/ n (excess amount) eccedenza f ● attrib **~ housing development** ≈ città f inv satellite; **~ population** popolazione f in eccesso

overstaffed /əʊvə'stɑːft/ a **be ~** avere personale in eccedenza

overstaffing /əʊvə'stɑːfɪŋ/ n eccedenza f di personale

overstate /əʊvə'steɪt/ vt esagerare; **its importance cannot be ~d** la sua importanza non sarà mai sottolineata a sufficienza; **~ the case** esagerare le cose

overstatement /əʊvə'steɪtmənt/ n esagerazione f

overstay /əʊvə'steɪ/ vt **~ one's time** trattenersi troppo a lungo; **~ one's visa** trattenersi oltre la scadenza del visto

overstep /əʊvə'step/ vt (pt/pp **-stepped**) **~ the mark** oltrepassare ogni limite

overstretched /əʊvə'stretʃt/ a (person) sovraccarico [di lavoro]; (budget, resources) sfruttato fino al limite

oversubscribed /əʊvəsəb'skraɪbd/ a (share issue) sottoscritto in eccesso; (offer, tickets) richiesto oltre la disponibilità

overt /əʊ'vɜːt/ a palese

overtake /əʊvə'teɪk/ vt/i (pt **-took**, pp **-taken**) sorpassare

overtaking /əʊvə'teɪkɪŋ/ n sorpasso m; **no ~** divieto di sorpasso

overtax /əʊvə'tæks/ vt fig abusare di

over-the-counter a (medicines) venduto senza ricetta

over-the-top a fam esagerato; **go over the top** esagerare

overthrow[1] /'əʊvəθrəʊ/ n Pol rovesciamento m

overthrow[2] /əʊvə'θrəʊ/ vt (pt **-threw**, pp **-thrown**) Pol rovesciare

overtime /'əʊvətaɪm/ n lavoro straordinario m ● adv **work ~** fare lo straordinario

overtired /əʊvə'taɪəd/ a sovraffaticato

overtly /əʊ'vɜːtlɪ/ adv apertamente

overtone /'əʊvətəʊn/ n fig sfumatura f

overture /'əʊvətjʊə(r)/ n Mus preludio m; **~s** pl fig approccio msg; **make ~s to** mostrare un atteggiamento di apertura verso

overturn /əʊvə'tɜːn/ vt ribaltare ● vi ribaltarsi

overvalue /əʊvə'væljuː/ vt sopravvalutare (currency, property)

overview /'əʊvəvjuː/ n visione f d'insieme

overweight /əʊvə'weɪt/ a sovrappeso

overwhelm /əʊvə'welm/ vt sommergere (**with** di); (with emotion) confondere

overwhelming /əʊvə'welmɪŋ/ a travolgente; ⟨victory, majority⟩ schiacciante

overwhelmingly /əʊvə'welmɪŋlɪ/ adv ⟨vote, accept, reject⟩ con una maggioranza schiacciante; ⟨generous⟩ straordinariamente

overwork /əʊvə'wɜːk/ n lavoro m eccessivo ● vt far lavorare eccessivamente ● vi lavorare eccessivamente

overwrite /əʊvə'raɪt/ vt Comput registare sopra a

overwrought /əʊvə'rɔːt/ a in stato di agitazione

ovulation /ɒvjʊ'leɪʃn/ n ovulazione f

ow /aʊ/ int ahi!

owe /əʊ/ vt also fig dovere ([to] sb a qcno); ~ sb sth dovere qcsa a qcno

owing /'əʊɪŋ/ a be ~ ⟨money:⟩ essere da pagare ● prep ~ to a causa di

owl /aʊl/ n gufo m

own¹ /əʊn/ a proprio ● pron a car of my ~ una macchina per conto mio; **on one's ~** da solo; **hold one's ~ with** tener testa a; **get one's ~ back** fam prendersi una rivincita

own² vt possedere; (confess) ammettere; I don't ~ it non mi appartiene
■ **own up** vi confessare (**to sth** qcsa)

owner /'əʊnə(r)/ n proprietario, -a mf

owner: owner-driver n persona f che guida un'auto di sua proprietà. **owner-occupied** /-'ɒkjʊpaɪd/ a abitato dal proprietario. **owner-occupier** n persona f chi abita in una casa di sua proprietà

ownership /'əʊnəʃɪp/ n proprietà f

ox /ɒks/ n (pl oxen) bue m (pl buoi)

Oxbridge /'ɒksbrɪdʒ/ n le università di Oxford e Cambridge

oxide /'ɒksaɪd/ n ossido m

oxidize /'ɒksɪdaɪz/ vt ossidare ● vi ossidarsi

oxygen /'ɒksɪdʒən/ n ossigeno m

oxygen mask n maschera f a ossigeno

oyster /'ɔɪstə(r)/ n ostrica f

oz abbr (**ounce(s)**) oncia f

ozone /'əʊzəʊn/ n ozono m

ozone: ozone depletion n distruzione f dell'ozonosfera. **ozone-friendly** a che non danneggia l'ozono. **ozone layer** n fascia f d'ozono

Pp

p, P /piː/ n (letter) p, P f inv; Br abbr **penny, pence**

PA abbr (**personal assistant**) segretario, -a mf personale; Am abbr (**Pennsylvania**) Pennsylvania f

p.a. abbr (**per annum**) all'anno

pace /peɪs/ n passo m; (speed) ritmo m; keep ~ **with** camminare di pari passo con ● vi ~ **up and down** camminare avanti e indietro

pacemaker /'peɪsmeɪkə(r)/ n Med pacemaker m inv; (runner) battistrada m inv

pace-setter n (athlete) battistrada m inv

Pacific /pə'sɪfɪk/ a & n the ~ [Ocean] l'oceano m Pacifico, il Pacifico

pacifier /'pæsɪfaɪə(r)/ n Am ciuccio m, succhiotto m

pacifism /'pæsɪfɪzm/ n pacifismo m

pacifist /'pæsɪfɪst/ n pacifista mf

pacify /'pæsɪfaɪ/ vt (pt/pp -ied) placare ⟨person⟩; pacificare ⟨country⟩

pack /pæk/ n (of cards) mazzo m; (of hounds) muta f; (of wolves, thieves) branco m; (of cigarettes etc) pacchetto m; **a ~ of lies** un mucchio di bugie ● vt impacchettare ⟨article⟩; fare ⟨suitcase⟩; mettere in valigia ⟨swimsuit etc⟩; (press down) comprimere; **~ed** (crowded) strapieno, pieno zeppo ● vi fare i bagagli; **send sb ~ing** fam mandare qcno a quel paese
■ **pack in** vt fam mollare ⟨job⟩; ~ **it in!** (stop it) piantala!

■ **pack off** vt (send) spedire
■ **pack out** vt be ~ed out ⟨cinema, shops:⟩ essere strapieno, essere pieno zeppo
■ **pack up** vt impacchettare ● vi fam ⟨machine:⟩ guastarsi

package /'pækɪdʒ/ n pacco m ● vt impacchettare

package: package deal n offerta f tutto compreso. **package holiday** n vacanza f organizzata. **package tour** n viaggio m organizzato

packaging /'pækɪdʒɪŋ/ n (materials) confezione f; (promotion: of product) presentazione f pubblicitaria

packed lunch /pækt/ n pranzo m al sacco

packer /'pækə(r)/ n (in factory) imballatore, -trice mf

packet /'pækɪt/ n pacchetto m; **cost a ~** fam costare un sacco

pack ice n banchisa f

packing /'pækɪŋ/ n imballaggio m

pact /pækt/ n patto m

pad¹ /pæd/ n imbottitura f; (for writing) blocnotes m inv, taccuino m; (fam: home) casa f ● vt (pt/pp **padded**) imbottire

pad² vi (pt/pp **padded**) camminare con passo felpato
■ **pad out** vt gonfiare

padded /'pædɪd/: **padded bra** n reggiseno m imbottito. **padded cell** n cella f con le pareti imbottite. **padded envelope** n busta f

padding /'pædɪŋ/ n imbottitura f; (in written work) fronzoli mpl

paddle /'pædl/ n pagaia f; **go for a ~** sguazzare ● vt (row) spingere remando ● vi (wade) sguazzare

paddling pool n (public) piscina f per bambini; (inflatable) piscina f gonfiabile

paddock /'pædək/ n recinto m

padlock /'pædlɒk/ n lucchetto m ● vt chiudere con lucchetto

padre /'pɑːdreɪ/ n padre m

Padua /'pædjʊə/ n Padova f

paediatric /piːdɪ'ætrɪk/ a pediatrico

paediatrician /piːdɪə'trɪʃn/ n pediatra mf

paediatrics /piːdɪ'ætrɪks/ n pediatria f

paedophile /'piːdəʊfaɪl/ n pedofilo, -a mf

paedophilia /piːdəʊ'fɪlɪə/ n pedofilia f

pagan /'peɪgən/ a & n pagano, -a mf

paganism /'peɪgənɪzm/ n paganesimo m

page[1] /peɪdʒ/ n pagina f

page[2] n (boy) paggetto m; (in hotel) fattorino m ● vt far chiamare (person)

pageant /'pædʒənt/ n parata f

pageantry /'pædʒəntrɪ/ n cerimoniale m

page proof n bozza f definitiva

pager /'peɪdʒə(r)/ n cercapersone m inv

page three n Br terza pagina f di quotidiano scandalistico inglese con una pin-up

page three girl n Br pin-up f inv

paid /peɪd/ see **pay** ● a ~ **employment** lavoro m remunerato; **put ~ to** mettere fine a

paid-up a Br (member) che ha pagato la sua quota; (instalment) versato

pail /peɪl/ n secchio m

pain /peɪn/ n dolore m; **be in ~** soffrire; **take ~s to do sth** fare il possibile per fare qcsa; **~ in the neck** fam rottura f di scatole; (person) rompiscatole mf inv ● vt fig addolorare

pained /peɪnd/ a addolorato

painful /'peɪnfʊl/ a doloroso; (laborious) penoso

painfully /'peɪnfʊlɪ/ adv ~ **shy** incredibilmente timido

painkiller /'peɪnkɪlə(r)/ n calmante m

painkilling /'peɪnkɪlɪŋ/ a antinevralgico

painless /'peɪnlɪs/ a indolore

painlessly /'peɪnlɪslɪ/ adv in modo indolore

painstaking /'peɪnzteɪkɪŋ/ a minuzioso

paint /peɪnt/ n pittura f; **~s** pl colori mpl ● vt/i pitturare; (artist:) dipingere; **~ the town red** folleggiare

■ **paint over** vt (cover with paint) coprire di vernice

paintbox /'peɪntbɒks/ n scatola f di colori

paintbrush /'peɪntbrʌʃ/ n pennello m

painter /'peɪntə(r)/ n pittore, -trice mf; (decorator) imbianchino m

pain threshold n soglia f del dolore

painting /'peɪntɪŋ/ n pittura f; (picture) dipinto m

paint: paintpot n latta f di pittura. **paint remover** n sverniciante m. **paint roller** n rullo m. **paint spray** n pistola f a spruzzo.

paint stripper n (tool) macchina f sverniciante; (chemical) sverniciante m. **paintwork** n pittura f

pair /peə(r)/ n paio m; (of people) coppia f; **a ~ of trousers/scissors** un paio di pantaloni/forbici

■ **pair off** vi mettersi in coppia

pajamas /pə'dʒɑːməz/ npl Am pigiama msg

Pakistan /pɑːkɪ'stɑːn/ n Pakistan m

Pakistani /pɑːkɪ'stɑːnɪ/ a & n pakistano, -a mf

pal /pæl/ n fam amico, -a mf

■ **pal up** vi (fam: become friends) fare amicizia (with con)

palace /'pælɪs/ n palazzo m

palaeontologist /pælɪən'tɒlədʒɪst/ n paleontologo, -a mf

palaentology /pælɪən'tɒlədʒɪ/ n paleontologia f

palatable /'pælətəbl/ a gradevole al gusto

palate /'pælət/ n palato m

palatial /pə'leɪʃl/ a sontuoso

palaver /pə'lɑːvə(r)/ n (fam: fuss) storie fpl

pale[1] /peɪl/ n (stake) palo m; **beyond the ~** fig inaccettabile

pale[2] a pallido ● vi impallidire; **~ into insignificance** diventare insignificante

paleness /'peɪlnɪs/ n pallore m

Palestine /'pælɪstaɪn/ n Palestina f

Palestinian /pælə'stɪnɪən/ a & n palestinese mf

palette /'pælɪt/ n tavolozza f

palette knife n spatola f

paling /'peɪlɪŋ/ n (stake) palo m; (fence) palizzata f

palisade /pælɪ'seɪd/ n (fence) palizzata f

pall /pɔːl/ n drappo m funebre; fig velo m di tristezza; (of smoke) cappa f ● vi stufare

pallet /'pælɪt/ n pallet m inv

palliative /'pælɪətɪv/ n palliativo m

pallid /'pælɪd/ a pallido

pallor /'pælə(r)/ n pallore m

palm /pɑːm/ n palmo m; (tree) palma f

■ **palm off** vt ~ **sth off on sb** rifilare qcsa a qcno

palmist /'pɑːmɪst/ n chiromante mf

palmistry /'pɑːmɪstrɪ/ n chiromanzia f

Palm Sunday n domenica f delle palme

palpable /'pælpəbl/ a palpabile; (perceptible) tangibile

palpate /pæl'peɪt/ vi palpare

palpitate /'pælpɪteɪt/ vi palpitare

palpitations /pælpɪ'teɪʃnz/ npl palpitazioni fpl

paltry /'pɔːltrɪ/ a (-ier, -iest) insignificante

pampas /'pæmpəs/ n pampas fpl

pamper /'pæmpə(r)/ vt viziare

pamphlet /'pæmflɪt/ n opuscolo m

pan /pæn/ n tegame m, pentola f; (for frying) padella f; (of scales) piatto m ● vt (pt/pp **panned**) (fam: criticize) stroncare

■ **pan out** vi (fam: develop) mettersi

panacea /pænə'sɪə/ n panacea f

panache /pə'næʃ/ n stile m

pancake /'pænkeɪk/ n crêpe f inv, frittella f

Pancake Day n martedì m inv grasso

pancreas /'pæŋkrıəs/ n pancreas m inv

panda /'pændə/ n panda m inv

panda car n macchina f della polizia

pandemonium /pændı'məunıəm/ n pandemonio m

pander /'pændə(r)/ vi ~ **to sb** compiacere qcno

p & p n abbr (**postage and packing**) spese fpl di spedizione

pane /peın/ n ~ **[of glass]** vetro m

panel /'pænl/ n pannello m; (group of people) giuria f; ~ **of experts** gruppo m di esperti; ~ **of judges** giuria f

panelling /'pænəlıŋ/ n pannelli mpl

panellist /'pænəlıst/ n Radio, TV partecipante mf

pan-fry vt friggere

pang /pæŋ/ n ~**s of hunger** morsi mpl della fame; ~**s of conscience** rimorsi mpl di coscienza

panic /'pænık/ n panico m ● vi (pt/pp **panicked**) lasciarsi prendere dal panico

panic: panic button n fam hit the ~ ~ farsi prendere dal panico. **panic buying** n accaparramento m. **panic-stricken** /'pænıkstrıkən/ a in preda al panico

panicky /'pænıkı/ a che si lascia prendere dal panico facilmente

pannier /'pænıə(r)/ n (on bike) borsa f; (on mule) bisaccia f

panorama /pænə'rɑ:mə/ n panorama m

panoramic /pænə'ræmık/ a panoramico

pan scourer n paglietta f

pansy /'pænzı/ n viola f del pensiero; (fam: effeminate man) finocchio m

pant /pænt/ vi ansimare

pantechnicon /pæn'teknıkən/ n furgone m per traslochi

panther /'pænθə(r)/ n pantera f

panties /'pæntız/ npl mutandine fpl

panting /'pæntıŋ/ a ansante

pantomime /'pæntəmaım/ n pantomima f

pantry /'pæntrı/ n dispensa f

pants /pænts/ npl (underwear) mutande fpl; (woman's) mutandine fpl; (trousers) pantaloni mpl

panty /'pæntı/: **panty girdle** n guaina f. **pantyhose** n Am collant m inv. **panty-liner** n salvaslip m inv

paparazzi /pæpə'rætzı/ npl paparazzi mpl

papal /'peıpl/ a papale

paper /'peıpə(r)/ n carta f; (wallpaper) carta f da parati; (newspaper) giornale m; (exam) esame m scritto; (treatise) saggio m; ~**s** pl (documents) documenti mpl; (for identification) documento msg [d'identità]; **on** ~ in teoria; **put down on** ~ mettere per iscritto ● attrib di carta; (version) su carta ● vt tappezzare

■ **paper over** vt ~ **over the cracks** dissimulare le divergenze

paper: paperback n edizione f economica. **paper bank** n cassonetto m per la raccolta della carta. **paper boy** n ragazzo m che reca-

pita i giornali a domicilio. **paper chain** n festone m di carta. **paper chase** n corsa f campestre in cui i partecipanti seguono una scia di pezzetti di carta. **paper clip** n graffetta f. **paper currency** n banconote fpl. **paper feed tray** n Comput vassoio m della carta. **paperknife** n tagliacarte m inv. **paper mill** n cartiera f. **paper money** n cartamoneta f. **paper napkin** n tovagliolo m di carta. **paper round** n **he does a** ~ ~ recapita i giornali a domicilio. **paper shredder** n distruttore m di documenti. **paper-thin** a sottilissimo. **paper towel** n (toilet) asciugamano m di carta; (kitchen) carta f asciugatutto. **paperweight** n fermacarte m inv. **paperwork** n lavoro m d'ufficio

papery /'peıpərı/ a ⟨texture, leaves⟩ cartaceo

paprika /pə'pri:kə/ n paprica f

par /pɑ:(r)/ n (in golf) par m inv; **on a ~ with** alla pari con; **feel below** ~ essere una po' giù di tono

para¹ /'pærə/ n (paragraph) paragrafo m

para² n Br Mil parà m inv

parable /'pærəbl/ n parabola f

parachute /'pærəʃu:t/ n paracadute m inv ● vi lanciarsi col paracadute

parachutist /'pærəʃu:tıst/ n paracadutista mf

parade /pə'reıd/ n (military) parata f militare; (display) sfoggio m ● vi sfilare ● vt (show off) far sfoggio di

parade ground n piazza f d'armi

paradigm /'pærədaım/ n paradigma m

paradise /'pærədaıs/ n paradiso m

paradox /'pærədɒks/ n paradosso m

paradoxical /pærə'dɒksıkl/ a paradossale

paradoxically /pærə'dɒksıklı/ adv paradossalmente

paraffin /'pærəfın/ n paraffina f; (oil) cherosene m

paragliding /'pærəglaıdıŋ/ n parapendio m

paragon /'pærəgən/ n ~ **of virtue** modello m di virtù

paragraph /'pærəgrɑ:f/ n paragrafo m

parallel /'pærəlel/ a & adv parallelo ● n Geog, fig parallelo m; (line) parallela f ● vt essere paragonabile a

parallel bars npl parallele fpl

parallelogram /pærə'leləugræm/ n Math parallelogramma m

parallel port n Comput porta f parallela

paralyse /'pærəlaız/ vt paralizzare

paralysis /pə'ræləsıs/ n (pl -ses) /pə-'ræləsi:z/ paralisi f inv

paralytic /pærə'lıtık/ a ⟨person⟩ paralitico; ⟨arm, leg⟩ paralizzato; (Br fam: drunk) ubriaco fradicio

paramedic /pærə'medık/ n paramedico m

parameter /pə'ræmıtə(r)/ n parametro m

paramilitary /pærə'mılıtrı/ n appartenente mf a un gruppo paramilitare ● a paramilitare

paramount /'pærəmaunt/ a supremo; **be** ~ essere essenziale

paranoia /pærə'nɔıə/ n paranoia f

paranoid /'pærənɔıd/ a paranoico

paranormal /ˌpærə'nɔːməl/ a & n paranormale m

parapet /'pærəpɪt/ n parapetto m

paraphernalia /ˌpærəfə'neɪlɪə/ n armamentario m

paraphrase /'pærəfreɪz/ n parafrasi f inv ● vt parafrasare

paraplegic /ˌpærə'pliːdʒɪk/ a & n paraplegico, -a mf

parascending /'pærəsendɪŋ/ n Br paracadutismo m ascensionale

parasite /'pærəsaɪt/ n parassita mf

parasitic /ˌpærə'sɪtɪk/ a parassitario

parasol /'pærəsɒl/ n parasole m

paratrooper /'pærətruːpə(r)/ n paracadutista m

parboil /'pɑːbɔɪl/ vt scottare

parcel /'pɑːsl/ n pacco m

■ **parcel up** vt impacchettare ‹clothes etc›

parch /pɑːtʃ/ vt disseccare; **be ~ed** ‹person:› morire dalla sete

parchment /'pɑːtʃmənt/ n pergamena f

pardon /'pɑːdn/ n perdono m; Jur grazia f; ~? prego?; **I beg your ~?** fml chiedo scusa?; **I do beg your ~** (sorry) chiedo scusa! ● vt perdonare; Jur graziare

pare /peə(r)/ vt (peel) pelare

parent /'peərənt/ n genitore m

parentage /'peərəntɪdʒ/ n natali mpl

parental /pə'rentl/ a dei genitori

parent company n casa f madre

parenthesis /pə'renθəsɪs/ n (pl -ses /pə-'renθəsiːz/) parentesi f inv

parer /'peərə(r)/ n sbucciatore m

pariah /pə'raɪə/ n paria m

parings /'peərɪŋz/ npl (of fruit) bucce fpl; (of nails) ritagli mpl di unghie

Paris /'pærɪs/ n Parigi f

parish /'pærɪʃ/ n parrocchia f

parishioner /pə'rɪʃənə(r)/ n parrocchiano, -a mf

parish priest n (Catholic) parroco m; (Protestant) pastore m

Parisian /pə'rɪzɪən/ a & n parigino, -a mf

parity /'pærətɪ/ n parità f

park /pɑːk/ n parco m ● vt Auto posteggiare, parcheggiare; ~ **oneself** fam installarsi ● vi posteggiare, parcheggiare

parka /'pɑːkə/ n parka m inv

park-and-ride n parcheggio m collegato al centro di una città da mezzi pubblici

parking /'pɑːkɪŋ/ n parcheggio m, posteggio m; **'no ~'** 'divieto di sosta'

parking: parking attendant n parcheggiatore, -trice mf, posteggiatore, -trice mf. **parking lot** n Am posteggio m, parcheggio m. **parking meter** n parchimetro m. **parking space** n posteggio m, parcheggio m

park: parkland n parco m. **park ranger, park warden** n guardaparco m inv

parliament /'pɑːləmənt/ n parlamento m

parliamentary /ˌpɑːlə'mentərɪ/ a parlamentare

parlour /'pɑːlə(r)/ n salotto m

parochial /pə'rəʊkɪəl/ a parrocchiale; fig ristretto

parochialism /pə'rəʊkɪəlɪzm/ n campanilismo m

parody /'pærədɪ/ n parodia f ● vt (pt/pp -ied) parodiare

parole /pə'rəʊl/ n **on ~** sulla parola; **eligible for ~** suscettibile di essere liberato sulla parola ● vt mettere in libertà sulla parola

paroxysm /'pærəksɪzm/ n accesso m

parquet floor /'pɑːkeɪ/ n parquet m

parquet flooring /'flɔːrɪŋ/ n parquet m inv

parrot /'pærət/ n pappagallo m

parry /'pærɪ/ vt (pt/pp -ied) parare ‹blow›; (in fencing) eludere

parse /pɑːz/ vt fare l'analisi grammaticale di ‹sentence›; Comput analizzare la sintassi di

parsimonious /ˌpɑːsɪ'məʊnɪəs/ a parsimonioso

parsing /'pɑːzɪŋ/ n analisi f grammaticale; Comput analisi f sintattica

parsley /'pɑːslɪ/ n prezzemolo m

parsnip /'pɑːsnɪp/ n pastinaca f

parson /'pɑːsn/ n pastore m

part /pɑːt/ n parte f; (of machine) pezzo m; **for my ~** per quanto mi riguarda; **on the ~ of** da parte di; **take sb's ~** prendere le parti di qcno; **take ~ in** prendere parte a ● adv in parte ● vt ~ **one's hair** farsi la riga ● vi ‹people:› separarsi; ~ **with** separarsi da

part exchange n **take in ~ ~** prendere indietro come pagamento parziale

partial /'pɑːʃl/ a parziale; **be ~ to** aver un debole per

partiality /ˌpɑːʃɪ'ælətɪ/ n (liking) predilezione f

partially /'pɑːʃəlɪ/ adv parzialmente; ~ **sighted** parzialmente cieco

participant /pɑː'tɪsɪpənt/ n partecipante mf

participate /pɑː'tɪsɪpeɪt/ vi partecipare (in a)

participation /pɑːˌtɪsɪ'peɪʃn/ n partecipazione f

participatory /pɑːtɪsɪ'peɪtərɪ/ a partecipativo

participle /'pɑːtɪsɪpl/ n participio m; **present/past ~** participio presente/passato

particle /'pɑːtɪkl/ n Phys, Gram particella f

particular /pə'tɪkjʊlə(r)/ a particolare; (precise) meticoloso; pej difficile; **in ~** in particolare

particularly /pə'tɪkjʊləlɪ/ adv particolarmente

particulars /pə'tɪkjʊləz/ npl particolari mpl

parting /'pɑːtɪŋ/ n separazione f; (in hair) scriminatura f ● attrib di commiato

partisan /pɑːtɪ'zæn/ n partigiano, -a mf

partition /pɑː'tɪʃn/ n (wall) parete f divisoria; Pol divisione f ● vt dividere

■ **partition off** vt separare

partly /'pɑːtlɪ/ adv in parte

partner /'pɑːtnə(r)/ n Comm socio, -a mf; (sport, in relationship) compagno, -a mf

partnership /'pɑ:tnəʃɪp/ *n Comm* società *f inv*

part: part of speech *n* categoria *f* grammaticale. **part owner** *n* comproprietario, -a *mf*. **part payment** *n* acconto *m*

partridge /'pɑ:trɪdʒ/ *n* pernice *f*

part-time *a & adv* part time; **be** *or* **work ~** lavorare part time

part-way *adv* **~ through the evening** a metà serata

party /'pɑ:tɪ/ *n* ricevimento *m*, festa *f*; (*group*) gruppo *m*; *Pol* partito *m*; *Jur* parte *f*; **be ~ to** essere parte attiva in

party: party dress *n* abito *m* da sera. **party-goer** *n* festaiolo, -a *mf*. **party hat** *n* cappellino *m* di carta. **party leader** *n* dirigente *m* di partito. **party line** *n Teleph* duplex *m inv*; *Pol* linea *f* del partito. **party piece** *n* pezzo *m* forte; **do one's ~ ~** esibirsi nel proprio pezzo forte. **party political broadcast** *n* comunicato *m* di partito (*trasmesso per radio o per televisione*). **party politics** *n* politica *f* di partito. **party wall** *n* muro *m* divisorio

pass /pɑ:s/ *n* lasciapassare *m inv*; (*in mountains*) passo *m*; *Sport* passaggio *m*; (*Sch: mark*) [voto *m*] sufficiente *m*; **get a ~** *Sch* ottenere la sufficienza; **make a ~ at** *fam* fare delle avances a ● *vt* passare; (*overtake*) sorpassare; (*approve*) far passare; (*exceed*) oltrepassare; fare ‹*remark*›; esprimere ‹*judgement*›; *Jur* pronunciare ‹*sentence*›; **~ water** orinare; **~ the time** passare il tempo ● *vi* passare; (*in exam*) essere promosso; **let sth ~** *fig* lasciar correre qcsa; **~!** (*in game*) passo!

■ **pass as** *vt* = **pass for**

■ **pass away** *vi* mancare

■ **pass by** *vi* (*go past*) passare

■ **pass down** *vt* passare; *fig* trasmettere

■ **pass for** *vt* (*be accepted as*) passare per

■ **pass off** *vi* (*disappear*) passare; (*take place*) svolgersi ● *vt* **~ sb/sth off as** far passare qcno/qcsa per

■ **pass on** *vt* passare ‹*message, information*›

■ **pass on to** *vt* passare a ‹*new subject, next question*›

■ **pass out** *vi fam* svenire

■ **pass over** *vt* (*not mention*) passare sopra a; **~ sb over for promotion** non prendere in considerazione qcno per una promozione ● *vi* (*die*) spirare

■ **pass round** *vt* far passare

■ **pass through** *vt* attraversare

■ **pass up** *vt* passare; (*fam: miss*) lasciarsi scappare

passable /'pɑ:səbl/ *a* ‹*road*› praticabile; (*satisfactory*) passabile

passage /'pæsɪdʒ/ *n* passaggio *m*; (*corridor*) corridoio *m*; (*voyage*) traversata *f*

pass book *n Fin* libretto *m* di risparmio

passé /pæ'seɪ/ *a pej* sorpassato

passenger /'pæsɪndʒə(r)/ *n* passeggero, -a *mf*

passenger: passenger compartment *n Br Auto* abitacolo *m*. **passenger ferry** *n* tra-

ghetto *m*. **passenger plane** *n* aereo *m* passeggeri. **passenger seat** *n* posto *m* accanto al guidatore. **passenger train** *n* treno *m* passeggeri

passepartout /pæspɑ:'tu:/ *n* (*key, frame*) passe-partout *m inv*

passer-by /pɑ:sə'baɪ/ *n* (*pl* **-s-by**) passante *mf*

passing place /'pɑ:sɪŋ/ *n* piazzola *f* di sosta per consentire il transito dei veicoli nei due sensi

passing shot *n Tennis* passante *m*

passion /'pæʃn/ *n* passione *f*

passionate /'pæʃənət/ *a* appassionato

passionately /'pæʃənətlɪ/ *adv* appassionatamente

passion fruit *n* frutto *m* della passione

passive /'pæsɪv/ *a & n* passivo *m*

passively /'pæsɪvlɪ/ *adv* passivamente

passiveness /'pæsɪvnɪs/ *n* passività *f*

passive resistance *n* resistenza *f* passiva

passive smoking *n* fumo *m* passivo

pass: pass-key (*master-key*) passe-partout *m inv*; (*for access*) chiave *f*. **pass-mark** *n Sch* [voto *m*] sufficiente *m*. **Passover** *n* Pasqua *f* ebraica. **passport** *n* passaporto *m*. **password** *n* parola *f* d'ordine

past /pɑ:st/ *a* passato; (*former*) ex; **that's all ~** tutto questo è passato; **in the ~ few days** nei giorni scorsi; **the ~ week** la settimana scorsa ● *n* passato *m* ● *prep* oltre; **at ten ~ two** alle due e dieci ● *adv* oltre; **go/come ~** passare

pasta /'pæstə/ *n* pasta[sciutta] *f*

paste /peɪst/ *n* pasta *f*; (*dough*) impasto *m*; (*adhesive*) colla *f* ● *vt* incollare

■ **paste down** *vt* incollare

■ **paste in** *vt* incollare

■ **paste up** *vt* affiggere ‹*notice, poster*›

paste jewellery *n* bigiotteria *f*

pastel /'pæstl/ *n* pastello *m* ● *attrib* pastello

pasteurization /pɑ:stʃəraɪ'zeɪʃn/ *n* pastorizzazione *f*

pasteurize /'pɑ:stʃəraɪz/ *vt* pastorizzare

pasteurized /'pɑ:stʃəraɪzd/ *a* pastorizzato

pastille /'pæstɪl/ *n* pastiglia *f*

pastime /'pɑ:staɪm/ *n* passatempo *m*

pasting /'peɪstɪŋ/ *n* (*fam: defeat, criticism*) batosta *f*

past master *n* esperto, -a *mf*

pastor /'pɑ:stə(r)/ *n* pastore *m*

pastoral /'pɑ:stərəl/ *a* pastorale

past participle *n* participio *m* passato

pastrami /pæ'strɑ:mɪ/ *n* carne *f* di manzo affumicata

pastry /'peɪstrɪ/ *n* pasta *f*; **pastries** *pl* pasticcini *mpl*

past tense *n* passato *m*

pasture /'pɑ:stʃə(r)/ *n* pascolo *m*

pasty[1] /'pæstɪ/ *n* ≈ pasticcio *m*

pasty[2] /'peɪstɪ/ *a* smorto

pat /pæt/ *n* buffetto *m*; (*of butter*) pezzetto *m* ● *adv* **have sth off ~** conoscere qcsa a menadito ● *vt* (*pt/pp* **patted**) dare un buffetto a; **~ sb on the back** *fig* congratularsi con qcno

patch /pætʃ/ n toppa f; (spot) chiazza f; (period) periodo m; **not a ~ on** fam molto inferiore a ● vt mettere una toppa su
■ **patch up** vt riparare alla bell'e meglio; appianare ⟨quarrel⟩

patchwork /'pætʃwɜ:k/ n patchwork m inv; fig mosaico m

patchy /'pætʃɪ/ a incostante

pâté /'pæteɪ/ n pâté m inv

patent /'peɪtnt/ a palese ● n brevetto m ● vt brevettare

patent leather n vernice m

patently /'peɪtəntlɪ/ adv in modo palese

paternal /pə'tɜ:nl/ a paterno

paternalism /pə'tɜ:nəlɪzm/ n paternalismo m

paternalistic /pətɜ:nə'lɪstɪk/ a paternalistico

paternity /pə'tɜ:nətɪ/ n paternità f

paternity leave n congedo m di paternità

paternity suit n causa f per il riconoscimento di paternità

path /pɑ:θ/ n (pl ~s /pɑ:ðz/) sentiero m; (orbit) traiettoria f; fig strada f

pathetic /pə'θetɪk/ a patetico; (fam: very bad) penoso

pathological /pæθə'lɒdʒɪkl/ a patologico

pathologist /pə'θɒlədʒɪst/ n patologo, -a mf

pathology /pə'θɒlədʒɪ/ n patologia f

pathos /'peɪθɒs/ n pathos m

patience /'peɪʃns/ n pazienza f; (game) solitario m

patient /'peɪʃnt/ a & n paziente mf

patiently /'peɪʃntlɪ/ adv pazientemente

patio /'pætɪəʊ/ n terrazza f

patio doors npl portafinestra f

patio garden n cortile m

patriarch /'peɪtrɪɑ:k/ n patriarca m

patriarchal /peɪtrɪ'ɑ:kəl/ a patriarcale

patriarchy /'peɪtrɪɑ:kɪ/ n patriarcato m

patriot /'pætrɪət/ n patriota mf

patriotic /pætrɪ'ɒtɪk/ a patriottico

patriotism /'pætrɪətɪzm/ n patriottismo m

patrol /pə'trəʊl/ n pattuglia f ● vt/i pattugliare

patrol car n autopattuglia f

patron /'peɪtrən/ n patrono m; (of charity) benefattore, -trice mf; (of the arts) mecenate mf; (customer) cliente mf

patronage /'pætrənɪdʒ/ n patrocinio m; (of shop etc) frequentazione f

patronize /'pætrənaɪz/ vt frequentare abitualmente; fig trattare con condiscendenza

patronizing /'pætrənaɪzɪŋ/ a condiscendente

patronizingly /'pætrənaɪzɪŋlɪ/ adv con condiscendenza

patron saint n [santo, -a mf] patrono, -a mf

patter[1] /'pætə(r)/ n picchiettio m ● vi picchiettare

patter[2] n (of salesman) chiacchiere fpl

pattern /'pætn/ n motivo m; (for knitting, sewing, in behaviour) modello m

patterned /'pætənd/ a ⟨material⟩ fantasia

paunch /pɔ:ntʃ/ n pancia f

pauper /'pɔ:pə(r)/ n povero, -a mf

pause /pɔ:z/ n pausa f ● vi fare una pausa

pave /peɪv/ vt pavimentare; **~ the way** preparare la strada (**for** a)

pavement /'peɪvmənt/ n marciapiede m

pavilion /pə'vɪljən/ n padiglione m; (Cricket) costruzione f annessa al campo da gioco con gli spogliatoi

paving /'peɪvɪŋ/ n lastricato m

paving slab, paving stone n lastra f di pietra

paw /pɔ:/ n zampa f ● vt fam mettere le zampe addosso a

pawn[1] /pɔ:n/ n (in chess) pedone m; fig pedina f

pawn[2] vt impegnare ● n **in ~** in pegno

pawnbroker /'pɔ:nbrəʊkə(r)/ n prestatore, -trice mf su pegno

pawnshop /'pɔ:nʃɒp/ n monte m di pietà

pawpaw /'pɔ:pɔ:/ n papaia f

pay /peɪ/ n paga f; **in the ~ of** al soldo di ● v (pt/pp **paid**) ● vt pagare; prestare ⟨attention⟩; fare ⟨compliment, visit⟩; **~ cash** pagare in contanti ● vi pagare; (be profitable) rendere; **it doesn't ~ to...** fig è fatica sprecata...; **~ in instalments** pagare a rate; **~ through the nose** fam pagare profumatamente

■ **pay back** vt ripagare

■ **pay for** vt pagare per

■ **pay in** vt versare

■ **pay off** vt saldare ⟨debt⟩ ● vi fig dare dei frutti

■ **pay out** vt (spend) pagare

■ **pay up** vi pagare

payable /'peɪəbl/ a pagabile; **make ~ to** intestare a

PAYE Br abbr (**pay-as-you-earn**) trattenute fpl fiscali alla fonte

payee /peɪ'i:/ n beneficiario m

payer /'peɪə(r)/ n pagante mf

paying-in slip /peɪɪŋ'ɪn/ n distinta f di versamento

payload /'peɪləʊd/ n (of bomb) carica f esplosiva; (of aircraft, ship) carico m utile

payment /'peɪmənt/ n pagamento m; **~ by instalments** pagamento m rateale

pay: pay packet n busta f paga. **payphone** n telefono m pubblico. **payroll** n (list) libro m paga; (sum of money) paga f del personale; (employees collectively) personale m. **payslip** n busta f paga inv

PC abbr (**personal computer**) PC m inv; abbr (**police constable**) agente m di polizia

pc abbr (**per cent**) per cento; abbr (**politically correct**) politicamente corretto; abbr (**postcard**) cartolina f postale

pd Am abbr (**police department**) reparto m di polizia

PE n abbr (**physical education**) educazione f fisica

pea /pi:/ n pisello m

peace /pi:s/ n pace f; **~ of mind** tranquillità f

peaceable /'pi:səbl/ a pacifico

peace envoy n mediatore, -trice mf

peaceful /'pi:sfʊl/ a calmo, sereno

peacefully /'pi:sfʊlɪ/ *adv* in pace
peace: peacekeeping *n Mil, Pol* mantenimento *m* della pace ● *attrib* ⟨*force, troops*⟩ di mantenimento della pace. **peacemaker** *n* mediatore, -trice *mf*. **peacetime** *n* tempo *m* di pace ● *attrib* ⟨*planning, government*⟩ del tempo di pace; ⟨*army, alliance, training*⟩ in tempo di pace. **peace treaty** *n* trattato *m* di pace
peach /pi:tʃ/ *n* pesca *f*; (*tree*) pesco *m*
peacock /'pi:kɒk/ *n* pavone *m*
pea green *a* verde pisello
peak /pi:k/ *n* picco *m*; *fig* culmine *m*
peaked cap /pi:kt/ *n* berretto *m* a punta
peak hours *npl* ore *fpl* di punta
peak season *n* alta stagione *f*
peaky /'pi:kɪ/ *a* malaticcio
peal /pi:l/ *n* (*of bells*) scampanio *m*; **~s of laughter** fragore *msg* di risate
peanut /'pi:nʌt/ *n* nocciolina *f* [americana]; **~s** *pl fam* miseria *fsg*
peanut butter *n* burro *m* di arachidi
pear /peə(r)/ *n* pera *f*; (*tree*) pero *m*
pearl /pɜ:l/ *n* perla *f*
pearl: pearl barley *n* orzo *m* perlato. **pearl-diver** *n* pescatore, -trice *mf* di perle. **pearl grey** *n* grigio *m* perla *inv* ● *a* grigio perla *inv*
Pearly Gates /'pɜ:lɪ/ *npl hum* porte *fpl* del paradiso
peasant /'peznt/ *n* contadino, -a *mf*
peat /pi:t/ *n* torba *f*
pebble /'pebl/ *n* ciottolo *m*
pebble-dash *n* intonaco *m* a pinocchino
pecan /'pi:kən/ *n* (*tree*) pecan *m inv*; (*nut*) noce *f* pecan *inv*
peck /pek/ *n* beccata *f*; (*kiss*) bacetto *m* ● *vt* beccare; (*kiss*) dare un bacetto a
■ **peck at** *vi* beccare
pecking order /'pekɪŋ/ *n* gerarchia *f*
peckish /'pekɪʃ/ *a* **be ~** *fam* avere un languorino allo stomaco
pectoral /'pektərəl/ *a & n* pettorale *m*
peculiar /pɪ'kju:lɪə(r)/ *a* strano; (*special*) particolare; **~ to** tipico di
peculiarity /pɪˌkju:lɪ'ærətɪ/ *n* stranezza *f*; (*feature*) particolarità *f inv*
peculiarly /pɪ'kju:lɪəlɪ/ *adv* singolarmente
pecuniary /pə'kju:nɪərɪ/ *a* pecuniario
pedagogical /pedə'ɡɒdʒɪkl/ *a* pedagogico
pedagogy /'pedəɡɒdʒɪ/ *n* pedagogia *f*
pedal /'pedl/ *n* pedale *m* ● *vi* pedalare
pedal bin *n* pattumiera *f* a pedale
pedant /'pedənt/ *n* pedante *m*
pedantic /pɪ'dæntɪk/ *a* pedante
pedantically /pɪ'dæntɪklɪ/ *adv* in modo pedante
pedantry /'pedəntrɪ/ *n* pedanteria *f*
peddle /'pedl/ *vt* vendere porta a porta
pedestal /'pedɪstl/ *n* piedistallo *m*
pedestrian /pɪ'destrɪən/ *n* pedone *m* ● *a fig* scadente
pedestrian crossing *n* passaggio *m* pedonale
pedestrian precinct *n* zona *f* pedonale
pedicure /'pedɪkjʊə(r)/ *n* pedicure *f inv*

pedigree /'pedɪɡri:/ *n* pedigree *m inv*; (*of person*) lignaggio *m* ● *attrib* ⟨*animal*⟩ di razza, con pedigree
pedlar /'pedlə(r)/ *n* venditore, -trice *mf* ambulante
pee /pi:/ *fam vi* (*pt/pp* peed) fare la pipì ● *n* **go for a ~** andare a fare la pipì
peek /pi:k/ *fam vi* sbirciare ● *n* **take a ~ at sth** dare una sbirciata a qcsa
peekaboo /pi:kə'bu:/ *int* cucù
peel /pi:l/ *n* buccia *f* ● *vt* sbucciare ● *vi* ⟨*nose etc.*⟩ spellarsi; ⟨*paint.*⟩ staccarsi
■ **peel off** *vt* togliersi ⟨*item of clothing*⟩ ● *vi* ⟨*wallpaper.*⟩ staccarsi; ⟨*skin.*⟩ squamarsi
peeler /'pi:lə(r)/ *n* sbucciatore *m*
peelings /'pi:lɪŋz/ *npl* bucce *fpl*
peep /pi:p/ *n* sbirciata *f* ● *vi* sbirciare
peephole /'pi:phəʊl/ *n* spioncino *m*
Peeping Tom /'pi:pɪŋ/ *n fam* guardone *m*
peer¹ /pɪə(r)/ *vi* **~ at** scrutare
peer² *n* nobile *m*; **his ~s** *pl* (*in rank*) i suoi pari; (*in age*) i suoi coetanei
peerage /'pɪərɪdʒ/ *n Br Pol* nobiltà *f*; (*book*) almanacco *m* nobiliare; **be given a ~** essere elevato al rango di pari
peer group *n* (*of same status*) pari *mpl*; (*of same age*) coetanei *mpl*; **~ ~ pressure** pressione *f* esercitata dal gruppo cui si appartiene
peerless /'pɪəlɪs/ *a* impareggiabile
peeved /pi:vd/ *a fam* irritato
peevish /'pi:vɪʃ/ *a fam* irritabile
peg /peɡ/ *n* (*hook*) piolo *m*; (*for tent*) picchetto *m*; (*for clothes*) molletta *f*; **off the ~** *fam* prêt-à-porter ● *vt* (*pt/pp* pegged) fissare ⟨*prices*⟩; stendere con le mollette ⟨*washing*⟩
pegboard /'peɡbɔ:d/ *n* segnapunti *m inv*
pejorative /pɪ'dʒɒrətɪv/ *a* peggiorativo
pejoratively /pɪ'dʒɒrətɪvlɪ/ *adv* in modo peggiorativo
Peke /pi:k/ *n fam* (*dog*) pechinese *m*
Peking /pi:'kɪŋ/ *n* Pechino *f*
Pekin[g]ese /pi:kɪ'ni:z/ *n* pechinese *m*
pelican /'pelɪkən/ *n* pellicano *m*
pelican crossing *n* passaggio *m* pedonale con semaforo
pellet /'pelɪt/ *n* pallottola *f*
pell-mell /pel'mel/ *adv* alla rinfusa
pelmet /'pelmɪt/ *n* mantovana *f*
pelt¹ /pelt/ *n* (*skin*) pelliccia *f*
pelt² *vt* bombardare ● *vi* (*fam: run fast*) catapultarsi; (*rain heavily*) venir giù a fiotti
■ **pelt along** *vi* (*move quickly*) precipitarsi lungo
■ **pelt down** *vi* ⟨*rain.*⟩ venir giù a fiotti
pelvis /'pelvɪs/ *n Anat* bacino *m*
pen¹ /pen/ *n* (*for animals*) recinto *m*
pen² *n* penna *f*; (*ball-point*) penna *f* a sfera
penal /'pi:nl/ *a* penale
penal code *n* codice *m* penale
penalize /'pi:nəlaɪz/ *vt* penalizzare
penalty /'penltɪ/ *n* sanzione *f*; (*fine*) multa *f*; (*in football*) [calcio *m* di] rigore *m*
penalty: penalty area, penalty box *n* area *f* di rigore. **penalty clause** *n Comm, Jur*

clausola f penale. **penalty kick** n [calcio m di] rigore m. **penalty shootout** n rigori mpl

penance /'penəns/ n penitenza f

pence /pens/ see **penny**

penchant /'pɒ̃ʃɒ̃/ n debole m

pencil /'pensl/ n matita f ● vt (pt/pp **pencilled**) segnare a matita

■ **pencil in** vt annotare provvisoriamente ‹date›

pencil case n [astuccio m] portamatite m inv

pencil sharpener n temperamatite m inv

pendant /'pendənt/ n ciondolo m

pending /'pendɪŋ/ a in sospeso ● prep in attesa di

pendulum /'pendjʊləm/ n pendolo m

penetrate /'penɪtreɪt/ vt/i penetrare

penetrating /'penɪtreɪtɪŋ/ a ‹sound, stare› penetrante; ‹remark› acuto

penetration /penɪ'treɪʃn/ n penetrazione f

penfriend /'penfrend/ n amico, -a mf di penna

penguin /'peŋgwɪn/ n pinguino m

penicillin /penɪ'sɪlɪn/ n penicillina f

peninsula /pɪ'nɪnsjʊlə/ n penisola f

penis /'piːnɪs/ n pene m

penitence /'penɪtəns/ n penitenza f

penitent /'penɪtənt/ a & n penitente mf

penitentiary /penɪ'tenʃərɪ/ n Am penitenziario m

penknife /'pennaɪf/ n temperino m

pen-name n pseudonimo m

pennant /'penənt/ n bandiera f

penniless /'penɪlɪs/ a senza un soldo

penny /'penɪ/ n (pl **pence**; single coins **pennies**) penny m; Am centesimo m; **spend a ~** fam andare in bagno; **the ~'s dropped!** fam ci è arrivato!

penny: penny-farthing n velocipede m. **penny-pinching** /'penɪpɪntʃɪŋ/ a taccagno ● n taccagneria f. **penny whistle** n zufolo m

pen-pusher n fam scribaccino, -a mf

pension /'penʃn/ n pensione f

■ **pension off** vt (force to retire) mandare in pensione

pensioner /'penʃənə(r)/ n pensionato, -a mf

pension fund n fondo m pensioni; (of an individual) fondo m pensione

pension scheme n piano m di pensionamento

pensive /'pensɪv/ a pensoso

pentagon /'pentəgən/ n pentagono m; Am Pol **the P~** il Pentagono

pentagonal /pen'tægənəl/ a pentagonale

pentathlete /pen'tæθliːt/ n pentatleta mf

pentathlon /pen'tæθlɒn/ n pentathlon m inv

Pentecost /'pentɪkɒst/ n Pentecoste f

pent-up /'pentʌp/ a represso

penultimate /pɪ'nʌltɪmət/ a penultimo

penury /'penjʊrɪ/ n miseria f

peony /'pɪənɪ/ n peonia f

people /'piːpl/ npl persone fpl, gente fsg; (citizens) popolo msg; **a lot of ~** una marea di gente; **the ~** la gente; **English ~** gli inglesi;

~ say si dice; **for four ~** per quattro ● vt popolare

PEP /pep/ Br abbr (**personal equity plan**) piano m di investimento azionario personale

■ **pep up** vt vivacizzare ‹party, conversation›; tirare su ‹person›

pepper /'pepə(r)/ n pepe m; (vegetable) peperone m ● vt (season) pepare

pepper: peppercorn n grano m di pepe. **peppercorn rent** affitto m nominale. **pepper mill** n macinapepe m inv. **peppermint** n menta f peperita; (sweet) caramella f alla menta. **pepper pot** n pepiera f

pep pill /'peppɪl/ n fam stimolante m

pep talk n discorso m d'incoraggiamento

peptic /'peptɪk/ a peptico

peptic ulcer n ulcera f peptica

per /pɜː(r)/ prep per

per annum /pər'ænəm/ adv all'anno

per capita /pə'kæpɪtə/ a & adv pro capite

perceive /pə'siːv/ vt percepire; (interpret) interpretare

per cent adv percento

percentage /pə'sentɪdʒ/ n percentuale f

perceptible /pə'septəbl/ a percettibile; fig sensibile

perceptibly /pə'septɪblɪ/ adv percettibilmente; fig sensibilmente

perception /pə'sepʃn/ n percezione f

perceptive /pə'septɪv/ a perspicace

perch¹ /pɜːtʃ/ n pertica f ● vi ‹bird:› appollaiarsi

perch² n inv (fish) pesce m persico

percolate /'pɜːkəleɪt/ vi infiltrarsi; ‹coffee:› passare

percolator /'pɜːkəleɪtə(r)/ n caffettiera f a filtro

percussion /pə'kʌʃn/ n percussione f

percussion instrument n strumento m a percussione

percussionist /pə'kʌʃ(ə)nɪst/ n percussionista mf

peremptory /pə'remptərɪ/ a perentorio

perennial /pə'renɪəl/ a perenne ● n pianta f perenne

perfect¹ /'pɜːfɪkt/ a perfetto ● n Gram passato m prossimo

perfect² /pə'fekt/ vt perfezionare

perfection /pə'fekʃn/ n perfezione f; **to ~** alla perfezione

perfectionism /pə'fekʃənɪzm/ n perfezionismo m

perfectionist /pə'fekʃ(ə)nɪst/ a & n perfezionista mf

perfectly /'pɜːfɪktlɪ/ adv perfettamente

perfidious /pə'fɪdɪəs/ a perfido

perforate /'pɜːfəreɪt/ vt perforare

perforated /'pɜːfəreɪtɪd/ a perforato; ‹ulcer› perforante

perforation /pɜːfə'reɪʃn/ n perforazione f

perform /pə'fɔːm/ vt compiere, fare; eseguire ‹operation, sonata›; recitare ‹role›; mettere in scena ‹play› ● vi Theat recitare; Techn funzionare

performance /pə'fɔːməns/ n esecuzione f;

(*at theatre, cinema*) rappresentazione *f*; *Techn* rendimento *m*

performance bonus *n* premio *m* di produttività

performance-related *a* commensurato alla produttività

performer /pəˈfɔːmə(r)/ *n* artista *mf*

performing arts /pəˈfɔːmɪŋ/ *npl* arti *fpl* dello spettacolo

perfume /ˈpɜːfjuːm/ *n* profumo *m*

perfumed /ˈpɜːfjuːmd/ *a* profumato

perfunctory /pəˈfʌŋktərɪ/ *a* superficiale

perhaps /pəˈhæps/ *adv* forse

peril /ˈperɪl/ *n* pericolo *m*

perilous /ˈperɪləs/ *a* pericoloso

perilously /ˈperɪləslɪ/ *adv* pericolosamente

perimeter /pəˈrɪmɪtə(r)/ *n* perimetro *m*

period /ˈpɪərɪəd/ *n* periodo *m*; (*menstruation*) mestruazioni *fpl*; *Sch* ora *f* di lezione; (*full stop*) punto *m* fermo ● *attrib* ⟨*costume*⟩ d'epoca; ⟨*furniture*⟩ in stile

periodic /pɪərɪˈɒdɪk/ *a* periodico

periodical /pɪərɪˈɒdɪkl/ *n* periodico *m*, rivista *f*

periodically /pɪərɪˈɒdɪklɪ/ *adv* periodicamente

period of notice *n* periodo *m* di preavviso

peripheral /pəˈrɪfərəl/ *a* periferico ● *n* *Comput* periferica *f*

periphery /pəˈrɪfərɪ/ *n* periferia *f*

periscope /ˈperɪskəʊp/ *n* periscopio *m*

perish /ˈperɪʃ/ *vi* (*rot*) deteriorarsi; (*die*) perire

perishable /ˈperɪʃəbl/ *a* deteriorabile ● *~s* *npl* merce *f* deperibile

perished /ˈperɪʃt/ *a* (*fam: freezing cold*) **be ~** essere intirizzito

perishing /ˈperɪʃɪŋ/ *a fam* **it's ~** fa freddo da morire

peritonitis /perɪtəˈnaɪtɪs/ *n* peritonite *f*

perjure /ˈpɜːdʒə(r)/ *vt* **~ oneself** spergiurare

perjury /ˈpɜːdʒərɪ/ *n* spergiuro *m*

perk¹ /pɜːk/ *n fam* vantaggio *m*

perk² *vi Am* ⟨*coffee:*⟩ passare

■ **perk up** *vt* tirare su ● *vi* tirarsi su

perky /ˈpɜːkɪ/ *a* allegro

perm /pɜːm/ *n* permanente *f* ● *vt* **~ sb's hair** fare la permanente a qno

permanent /ˈpɜːmənənt/ *a* permanente; ⟨*job, address*⟩ stabile

permanently /ˈpɜːmənəntlɪ/ *adv* stabilmente

permeable /ˈpɜːmɪəbl/ *a* permeabile

permeate /ˈpɜːmɪeɪt/ *vt* impregnare

permissible /pəˈmɪsəbl/ *a* ammissibile

permission /pəˈmɪʃn/ *n* permesso *m*

permissive /pəˈmɪsɪv/ *a* permissivo

permit¹ /pəˈmɪt/ *vt* (*pt/pp* **-mitted**) permettere; **~ sb to do sth** permettere a qcno di fare qcsa

permit² /ˈpɜːmɪt/ *n* autorizzazione *f*

pernicious /pəˈnɪʃəs/ *a* pernicioso

pernickety /pəˈnɪkətɪ/ *a Br fam* puntiglioso, pignolo; (*about food*) difficile

peroxide blonde /pəˈrɒksaɪd/ *n* bionda *f* ossigenata

perpendicular /pɜːpənˈdɪkjʊlə(r)/ *a & n* perpendicolare *f*

perpetrate /ˈpɜːpɪtreɪt/ *vt* perpetrare

perpetrator /ˈpɜːpɪtreɪtə(r)/ *n* autore, -trice *mf*

perpetual /pəˈpetjʊəl/ *a* perenne

perpetually /pəˈpetjʊəlɪ/ *adv* perennemente

perpetuate /pəˈpetjʊeɪt/ *vt* perpetuare

perplex /pəˈpleks/ *vt* lasciare perplesso

perplexed /pəˈplekst/ *a* perplesso

perplexity /pəˈpleksətɪ/ *n* perplessità *f inv*

perquisite /ˈpɜːkwɪzɪt/ *n* fringe benefit *m inv*, beneficio *m* accessorio

per se /pɜːˈseɪ/ *adv* in sé

persecute /ˈpɜːsɪkjuːt/ *vt* perseguitare

persecution /pɜːsɪˈkjuːʃn/ *n* persecuzione *f*

persecutor /ˈpɜːsɪkjuːtə(r)/ *n* persecutore, -trice *mf*

perseverance /pɜːsɪˈvɪərəns/ *n* perseveranza *f*

persevere /pɜːsɪˈvɪə(r)/ *vi* perseverare

persevering /pɜːsɪˈvɪərɪŋ/ *a* assiduo

Persian /ˈpɜːʃn/ *a* persiano

persist /pəˈsɪst/ *vi* persistere; **~ in doing sth** persistere nel fare qcsa

persistence /pəˈsɪstəns/ *n* persistenza *f*

persistent /pəˈsɪstənt/ *a* persistente

persistently /pəˈsɪstəntlɪ/ *adv* persistentemente

person /ˈpɜːsn/ *n* persona *f*; **in ~** di persona

persona /pəˈsəʊnə/ *n Psych* individuo *m*; *Theat* personaggio *m*

personable /ˈpɜːsənəbl/ *a* di bella presenza

personage /ˈpɜːsənɪdʒ/ *n* personaggio *m*

personal /ˈpɜːsənl/ *a* personale

personal: personal allowance *n* (*in taxation*) quota *f* non imponibile. **personal assistant** *n* segretario, -a *mf* personale. **personal belongings** *npl* effetti *mpl* personali. **personal computer** *n* personal computer *m inv*. **personal hygiene** *n* igiene *f* personale

personality /pɜːsəˈnælətɪ/ *n* personalità *f inv*; (*on TV*) personaggio *m*

personalize /ˈpɜːsənəlaɪz/ *vt* personalizzare ⟨*stationery, clothing*⟩; mettere sul piano personale ⟨*issue, dispute*⟩

personal loan *n* prestito *m* a privato

personally /ˈpɜːsənəlɪ/ *adv* personalmente

personal organizer *n Comput* agenda *f* elettronica

personal stereo *n* walkman ᴷ *m inv*

personification /pəsɒnɪfɪˈkeɪʃn/ *n* **the ~ of** la personificazione di

personify /pəˈsɒnɪfaɪ/ *vt* (*pt/pp* **-ied**) personificare

personnel /pɜːsəˈnel/ *n* personale *m*

personnel director *n* direttore, -trice *mf* del personale

personnel management *n* gestione *f* del personale

perspective /pəˈspektɪv/ *n* prospettiva *f*

perspex® /ˈpɜːspeks/ *n* plexiglas ᴷ *m*

perspicacious /pɜːspɪˈkeɪʃəs/ a perspicace
perspiration /pɜːspɪˈreɪʃn/ n sudore m
perspire /pəˈspaɪə(r)/ vi sudare
persuade /pəˈsweɪd/ vt persuadere
persuasion /pəˈsweɪʒn/ n persuasione f; (belief) convinzione f
persuasive /pəˈsweɪsɪv/ a persuasivo
persuasively /pəˈsweɪsɪvlɪ/ adv in modo persuasivo
pert /pɜːt/ a (lively) esuberante
pertinent /ˈpɜːtɪnənt/ a pertinente (**to** a)
perturb /pəˈtɜːb/ vt perturbare
perturbing /pəˈtɜːbɪŋ/ a conturbante
Peru /pəˈruː/ n Perù m
peruse /pəˈruːz/ vt leggere
Peruvian /pəˈruːvɪən/ a & n peruviano, -a mf
pervade /pəˈveɪd/ vt pervadere
pervasive /pəˈveɪsɪv/ a pervasivo
perverse /pəˈvɜːs/ a perverso; (illogical) irragionevole
perversely /pəˈvɜːslɪ/ adv in modo perverso
perversion /pəˈvɜːʃn/ n perversione f
perversity /pəˈvɜːsɪtɪ/ n perversità f
pervert[1] /pəˈvɜːt/ vt deviare (course of justice)
pervert[2] /ˈpɜːvɜːt/ n pervertito, -a mf
perverted /pəˈvɜːtɪd/ a perverso
pessary /ˈpesərɪ/ n candeletta f
pessimism /ˈpesɪmɪzm/ n pessimismo m
pessimist /ˈpesɪmɪst/ n pessimista mf
pessimistic /pesɪˈmɪstɪk/ a pessimistico
pessimistically /pesɪˈmɪstɪklɪ/ adv in modo pessimistico
pest /pest/ n piaga f; (fam: person) peste f
pester /ˈpestə(r)/ vt molestare
pesticide /ˈpestɪsaɪd/ n pesticida m
pestilential /pestɪˈlenʃəl/ a (hum: annoying) fastidiosissimo
pestle /ˈpesl/ n pestello m
pet /pet/ n animale m domestico; (favourite) cocco, -a mf ● a (favourite) prediletto ● v (pt/pp **petted**) ● vt coccolare ● vi (couple:) praticare il petting
petal /ˈpetl/ n petalo m
peter /ˈpiːtə(r)/ vi ~ **out** finire
petite /pəˈtiːt/ a minuto
petition /pəˈtɪʃn/ n petizione f
pet name n vezzeggiativo m
petrified /ˈpetrɪfaɪd/ a (frightened) pietrificato
petrify /ˈpetrɪfaɪ/ vt (pt/pp -**ied**) pietrificare
petrochemical /petrəʊˈkemɪkl/ n petrol-chimico m
petrodollar /ˈpetrəʊdɒlə(r)/ n petroldollaro m
petrol /ˈpetrəl/ n Br benzina f
petrol bomb n Br [bomba f] molotov f inv
petroleum /pɪˈtrəʊlɪəm/ n petrolio m
petroleum jelly n vaselina f
petrol: petrol-pump n Br pompa f di benzina. **petrol station** n Br stazione f di servizio. **petrol tank** n Br serbatoio m della benzina
pet shop n negozio m di animali
petticoat /ˈpetɪkəʊt/ n sottoveste f
pettifogging /ˈpetɪfɒgɪŋ/ a pej cavilloso

petty /ˈpetɪ/ a (-**ier**, -**iest**) insignificante; (mean) meschino
petty cash n cassa f per piccole spese
petty-minded /-ˈmaɪndɪd/ a meschino
petulance /ˈpetjʊləns/ n petulanza f
petulant /ˈpetjʊlənt/ a petulante
pew /pjuː/ n banco m (di chiesa)
pewter /ˈpjuːtə(r)/ n peltro m
phallic /ˈfælɪk/ a fallico
phallic symbol n simbolo m fallico
phallus /ˈfæləs/ n fallo m
phantom /ˈfæntəm/ n fantasma m
Pharaoh /ˈfeərəʊ/ n faraone m
pharmaceutical /fɑːməˈsjuːtɪkl/ a farmaceutico
pharmacist /ˈfɑːməsɪst/ n farmacista mf
pharmacy /ˈfɑːməsɪ/ n farmacia f
phase /feɪz/ n fase f ● vt **phase in/out** introdurre/eliminare gradualmente
Ph.D. abbr (**Doctor of Philosophy**) ≈ dottorato m di ricerca
pheasant /ˈfeznt/ n fagiano m
phenomenal /fɪˈnɒmɪnl/ a fenomenale; (incredible) incredibile
phenomenally /fɪˈnɒmɪnəlɪ/ adv incredibilmente
phenomenon /fɪˈnɒmɪnən/ n (pl -**na**) fenomeno m
phew /fjuː/ int (when too hot, in relief) uff!; (in surprise) oh!
philanderer /fɪˈlændərə(r)/ n donnaiolo m
philanthropic /fɪlənˈθrɒpɪk/ a filantropico
philanthropist /fɪˈlænθrəpɪst/ n filantropo, -a mf
philatelist /fɪˈlætəlɪst/ n filatelico, -a mf
philately /fɪˈlætəlɪ/ n filatelia f
philharmonic /fɪlhɑːˈmɒnɪk/ n (orchestra) orchestra f filarmonica ● a filarmonico
Philippines /ˈfɪlɪpiːnz/ npl Filippine fpl
philistine /ˈfɪlɪstaɪn/ a & n filisteo, -a mf
philology /fɪˈlɒlədʒɪ/ n filologia f
philosopher /fɪˈlɒsəfə(r)/ n filosofo, -a mf
philosophical /fɪləˈsɒfɪkl/ a filosofico
philosophically /fɪləˈsɒfɪklɪ/ adv con filosofia
philosophy /fɪˈlɒsəfɪ/ n filosofia f
phlebitis /flɪˈbaɪtɪs/ n flebite f
phlegm /flem/ n Med flemma f
phlegmatic /fleɡˈmætɪk/ a flemmatico
phobia /ˈfəʊbɪə/ n fobia f
phobic /ˈfəʊbɪk/ a fobico
phoenix /ˈfiːnɪks/ n fenice f
phone /fəʊn/ n telefono m; **be on the** ~ avere il telefono m; (be phoning) essere al telefono ● vt telefonare a ● vi telefonare
■ **phone back** vt/i richiamare
■ **phone in** vi telefonare al lavoro; **he** ~**d in sick** ha telefonato [al lavoro] per dire che è ammalato
■ **phone up** vi telefonare ● vt dare un colpo di telefono a
phone: phone book n guida f del telefono. **phone box** n cabina f telefonica. **phone call** telefonata f. **phonecard** n scheda f telefonica.

phone-in *n* trasmissione *f* con chiamate in diretta

phoneme /'fəʊni:m/ *n* fonema *m*

phone number *n* numero *m* telefonico

phonetic /fə'netɪk/ *a* fonetico

phonetics /fə'netɪks/ *n* fonetica *f*

phoney /'fəʊnɪ/ *a* (**-ier, -iest**) fasullo ● *n* ciarlatano, -a *mf*

phonology /fə'nɒlədʒɪ/ *n* fonologia *f*

phosphate /'fɒsfeɪt/ *n* fosfato *m*

phosphorus /'fɒsfərəs/ *n* fosforo *m*

photo /'fəʊtəʊ/ *n* foto *f*

photo: photo album *n* album *m* inv di fotografie. **photocell** *n* fotocellula *f*. **photocopier** *n* fotocopiatrice *f*. **photocopy** *n* fotocopia *f* ● *vt* fotocopiare. **photoengraving** *n* fotoincisione *f*. **photo finish** *n* fotofinish *m*. **Photofit®** *n Br* photofit *m* inv

photogenic /fəʊtəʊ'dʒenɪk/ *a* fotogenico

photograph /'fəʊtəgra:f/ *n* fotografia *f* ● *vt* fotografare

photographer /fə'tɒgrəfə(r)/ *n* fotografo, -a *mf*

photographic /fəʊtə'græfɪk/ *a* fotografico

photography /fə'tɒgrəfɪ/ *n* fotografia *f*

photo: photojournalism *n* fotoreportage *m*. **photojournalist** *n* fotogiornalista *mf*. **photomontage** /fəʊtəʊmɒn'ta:ʒ/ *n* fotomontaggio *m*. **photosynthesis** *n* fotosintesi *f*

phrase /freɪz/ *n* espressione *f* ● *vt* esprimere

phrase book *n* libro *m* di fraseologia

phut /fʌt/ *adv* fam **go ~** ⟨car, washing machine etc.⟩ scassarsi; ⟨plan:⟩ andare in fumo

physical /'fɪzɪkl/ *a* fisico

physical education *n* educazione *f* fisica

physically /'fɪzɪklɪ/ *adv* fisicamente

physician /fɪ'zɪʃn/ *n* medico *m*

physicist /'fɪzɪsɪst/ *n* fisico, -a *mf*

physics /'fɪzɪks/ *n* fisica *f*

physio /'fɪzɪəʊ/ *n Br fam* (*physiotherapist*) fisioterapista *mf*; (*physiotherapy*) fisioterapia *f*

physiology /fɪzɪ'ɒlədʒɪ/ *n* fisiologia *f*

physiotherapist /fɪzɪəʊ'θerəpɪst/ *n* fisioterapista *mf*

physiotherapy /fɪzɪəʊ'θerəpɪ/ *n* fisioterapia *f*

physique /fɪ'zi:k/ *n* fisico *m*

pianist /'pɪənɪst/ *n* pianista *mf*

piano /pɪ'ænəʊ/ *n* piano *m*

pianola® /pɪə'nəʊlə/ *n* pianola® *f*

piazza /pɪ'ætsə/ *n* (*public square*) piazza *f*; (*Am: veranda*) veranda *f*

pick¹ /pɪk/ *n* (*tool*) piccone *m*

pick² *n* scelta *f*; **take your ~** prendi quello che vuoi ● *vt* (*select*) scegliere; cogliere ⟨flowers⟩; scassinare ⟨lock⟩; borseggiare ⟨pockets⟩; **~ one's nose** mettersi le dita nel naso; **~ a quarrel** attaccar briga; **~ holes in sth** (*fam: criticize*) criticare qcsa ● *vi* **~ and choose** fare il difficile; **~ at one's food** spilluzzicare

■ **pick off** *vt* (*remove*) togliere

■ **pick on** *vt* (*fam: nag*) assillare; **he always ~s on me** ce l'ha con me

■ **pick out** *vt* (*identify*) individuare

■ **pick up** *vt* sollevare; raccogliere ⟨fallen object, information⟩; prendere in braccio ⟨baby⟩; prendere ⟨passengers, habit⟩; ⟨police:⟩ arrestare ⟨criminal⟩; *fam* rimorchiare ⟨girl⟩; prendersi ⟨illness⟩; captare ⟨signal⟩; (*buy*) comprare; (*learn*) imparare; (*collect*) andare/venire a prendere; **~ oneself up** riprendersi ● *vi* (*improve*) recuperare; ⟨weather:⟩ rimettersi

pickaxe /'pɪkæks/ *n* piccone *m*

picker /'pɪkə(r)/ *n* raccoglitore, -trice *mf*

picket /'pɪkɪt/ *n* picchettista *mf* ● *vt* picchettare

picket line *n* picchetto *m*

pickle /'pɪkl/ *n* **~s** *pl* sottaceti *mpl*; **in a ~** *fig* nei pasticci ● *vt* mettere sottaceto

pick-me-up *n* (*alcohol*) cicchetto *m*; (*medicine*) tonico *m*

pickpocket /'pɪkpɒkɪt/ *n* borsaiolo *m*

pick-up *n* (*truck*) furgone *m*; (*on record-player*) pickup *m* inv

picky /'pɪkɪ/ *a* (*fam: choosy, fussy*) difficile

picnic /'pɪknɪk/ *n* picnic *m* ● *vi* (*pt/pp* **-nicked**) fare un picnic

pictogram /'pɪktəgræm/ *n* (*symbol*) pittogramma *m*; (*chart*) tabella *f*

pictorial /pɪk'tɔ:rɪəl/ *a* illustrato

picture /'pɪktʃə(r)/ *n* (*painting*) quadro *m*; (*photo*) fotografia *f*; (*drawing*) disegno *m*; (*film*) film *m* inv; **as pretty as a ~** ⟨girl⟩ bella come una Madonna; **put sb in the ~** *fig* mettere qcno al corrente; **the ~s** *Br fam* il cinema ● *vt* (*imagine*) immaginare

picturesque /pɪktʃə'resk/ *a* pittoresco

piddle /'pɪdl/ *vi fam* fare pipì

pie /paɪ/ *n* torta *f*

piece /pi:s/ *n* pezzo *m*; (*in game*) pedina *f*; **a ~ of bread /paper** un pezzo di pane /carta; **a ~ of news /advice/junk** una notizia /un consiglio/una patacca; **take to ~s** smontare

■ **piece together** *vt* montare; *fig* ricostruire

piecemeal /'pi:smi:l/ *adv* un po' alla volta

piecework /'pi:swɜ:k/ *n* lavoro *m* a cottimo

pie chart *n* grafico *f* a torta

Piedmont /'pi:dmɒnt/ *n* Piemonte *m*

pier /pɪə(r)/ *n* molo *m*; (*pillar*) pilastro *m*

pierce /pɪəs/ *vt* perforare; **~ a hole in sth** fare un buco in qcsa

piercing /'pɪəsɪŋ/ *a* penetrante

pig /pɪg/ *n* maiale *m*

pigeon /'pɪdʒɪn/ *n* piccione *m*

pigeon-hole *n* casella *f* ● *vt* incasellare

pigeon-toed /-təʊd/ *a* **be ~** camminare con i piedi in dentro

piggery /'pɪgərɪ/ *n* (*pigsty*) porcile *m*; (*fam: overeating*) ingordigia *f*

piggyback /'pɪgɪbæk/ *n* **give sb a ~** portare qcno sulle spalle

piggy bank /'pɪgɪ/ *n* salvadanaio *m*

pig-headed /-'hedɪd/ *a fam* cocciuto

piglet /'pɪglət/ n maialino m, porcellino m
pigment /'pɪgmənt/ n pigmento m
pigmentation /pɪgmən'teɪʃn/ n pigmentazione f
pigskin /'pɪgskɪn/ n pelle f di cinghiale
pigtail /'pɪgteɪl/ n (plait) treccina f
pike /paɪk/ n inv (fish) luccio m
pilchard /'pɪltʃəd/ n sardina f
pile /paɪl/ n (heap) pila f ● vt ~ **sth on to sth** appilare qcsa su qcsa
■ **pile in** vi (enter, get on) entrare disordinatamente
■ **pile up** vt accatastare ● vi ammucchiarsi
piles /paɪlz/ npl emorroidi fpl
pile-up n tamponamento m a catena
pilfering /'pɪlfərɪŋ/ n piccoli furti mpl
pilgrim /'pɪlgrɪm/ n pellegrino, -a mf
pilgrimage /'pɪlgrɪmɪdʒ/ n pellegrinaggio m
pill /pɪl/ n pillola f
pillage /'pɪlɪdʒ/ vt saccheggiare
pillar /'pɪlə(r)/ n pilastro m
pillar box n buca f delle lettere
pillion /'pɪljən/ n sellino m posteriore; **ride ~** viaggiare dietro
pillory /'pɪlərɪ/ vt (pt/pp -ied) fig mettere alla berlina
pillow /'pɪləʊ/ n guanciale m
pillowcase /'pɪləʊkeɪs/ n federa f
pilot /'paɪlət/ n pilota mf ● vt pilotare
pilot light n fiamma f di sicurezza
pimp /pɪmp/ n protettore m
pimple /'pɪmpl/ n foruncolo m
PIN /pɪn/ n abbr (**personal identification number**) [numero m di] codice m segreto
pin /pɪn/ n spillo m; Electr spinotto m; Med chiodo m; **I have ~s and needles in my leg** fam mi formicola una gamba ● vt (pt/pp **pinned**) appuntare (**to/on** su); (sewing) fissare con gli spilli; (hold down) immobilizzare; ~ **sb down to a date** ottenere un appuntamento da qcno; ~ **sth on sb** fam addossare a qcno la colpa di qcsa
■ **pin up** vt appuntare; (on wall) affiggere
pinafore /'pɪnəfɔ:(r)/ n grembiule m
pinafore dress n scamiciato m
pinball /'pɪnbɔ:l/ n flipper m inv
pinball machine n flipper m inv
pincers /'pɪnsəz/ npl tenaglie fpl
pinch /pɪntʃ/ n pizzicotto m; (of salt) presa f; **at a ~** fam in caso di bisogno ● vt pizzicare; (fam: steal) fregare ● vi (shoe:) stringere
pincushion /'pɪnkʊʃən/ n puntaspilli m inv
pine[1] /paɪn/ n (tree) pino m
pine[2] vi **she is pining for you** le manchi molto
■ **pine away** vi deperire
pine: pineapple n ananas m inv. **pine cone** n pigna f. **pine-needle** n ago m di pino. **pine nut** n pinolo m
ping /pɪŋ/ n rumore m metallico
ping-pong n ping-pong m
pinhead /'pɪnhed/ n capocchia f di spillo; fam, pej testa f di rapa
pink /pɪŋk/ a rosa inv

pinking shears, pinking scissors /'pɪŋkɪŋ/ npl forbici fpl a zigzag
pinnacle /'pɪnəkl/ n guglia f
PIN number n codice m segreto
pinpoint /'pɪnpɔɪnt/ vt definire con precisione
pinprick /'pɪnprɪk/ n puntura f di spillo; (fig: of jealousy, remorse) punta f
pinstripe /'pɪnstraɪp/ a gessato
pint /paɪnt/ n pinta f (= 0,571, Am: 0,47 l); **a ~** fam una birra media
pin-up n ragazza f da copertina, pin-up f inv
pioneer /paɪə'nɪə(r)/ n pioniere, -a mf ● vt essere un pioniere di
pious /'paɪəs/ a pio
pip[1] /pɪp/ n (seed) seme m
pip[2] n **the ~s** il segnale orario; (telephone) il segnale telefonico
pip[3] vt (pt/pp **pipped**) **be ~ped at the post** essere battuto all'ultimo minuto
pipe /paɪp/ n tubo m; (for smoking) pipa f; **the ~s** pl Mus la cornamusa ● vt far arrivare con tubature (water, gas etc); Culin mettere
■ **pipe down** vi fam abbassare la voce; (shut up) stare zitto
■ **pipe up** vi ~ **with a suggestion** venir fuori con una proposta
pipe-cleaner n scovolino m
piped music /paɪpt/ n musichetta f di sottofondo
pipe dream n illusione f
pipeline /'paɪplaɪn/ n conduttura f; **in the ~** fam in cantiere
piper /'paɪpə(r)/ n suonatore m di cornamusa
piping /'paɪpɪŋ/ a ~ **hot** bollente
pique /pi:k/ n **in a fit of ~** risentito
piracy /'paɪrəsɪ/ n pirateria f
piranha /pɪ'rɑ:nə/ n piranha m
pirate /'paɪrət/ n pirata m ● vt pirateggiare
pirate copy n copia f pirata
pirated a /'paɪrətɪd/ pirateggiato
pirate radio n radio f pirata
pirouette /pɪru:'et/ n piroetta f ● vi piroettare
Pisces /'paɪsi:z/ n Astr Pesci mpl
piss /pɪs/ sl n piscia f ● vi pisciare
■ **piss about, piss around** sl vi (waste time, play the fool) cazzeggiare ● vt ~ **sb about** rompere le palle a qcno
■ **piss down** vi sl **it's ~ing down** (raining heavily) piove a dirotto
■ **piss off** sl vt fare incacchiare; **that type of behaviour ~es me off** questi comportamenti mi stanno sulle palle ● vi (leave) filarsela; ~ **off!** levati dalle palle!, va' a cagare!
pissed /pɪst/ a sl sbronzo; ~ **as a newt** sbronzo come una cocuzza
pissed off a sl scoglionato
pistachio [nut] /pɪ'stæʃɪəʊ/ n pistacchio m
pistol /'pɪstl/ n pistola f
piston /'pɪstn/ n Techn pistone m
pit /pɪt/ n fossa f; (mine) miniera f; (for orchestra) orchestra f; (of stomach) bocca f ● vt (pt/pp **pitted**) fig opporre (**against** a)
pit-a-pat /'pɪtəpæt/ n **go ~** (heart:) palpitare

pitch¹ /pɪtʃ/ n (tone) tono m; (level) altezza f; (in sport) campo m; (fig: degree) grado m ● vt montare ⟨tent⟩

pitch² n (substance) pece f

■ **pitch in** vi fam mettersi sotto

pitch-black a nero come la pece; ⟨night⟩ buio pesto

pitch-dark a buio pesto

pitcher /'pɪtʃə(r)/ n brocca f

pitchfork /'pɪtʃfɔːk/ n forca f

piteous /'pɪtɪəs/ a pietoso

pitfall /'pɪtfɔːl/ n fig trabocchetto m

pith /pɪθ/ n (of lemon, orange) interno m della buccia; fig essenza f

pithy /'pɪθɪ/ a (-ier, -iest) fig conciso

pitiable /'pɪtɪəbl/ a pietoso

pitiful /'pɪtɪfl/ a pietoso

pitifully /'pɪtɪfʊlɪ/ adv da far pietà

pitiless /'pɪtɪlɪs/ a spietato

pitilessly /'pɪtɪlɪslɪ/ adv senza pietà

pittance /'pɪtns/ n miseria f

pitted /'pɪtɪd/ a ⟨surface⟩ bucherellato; ⟨face, skin⟩ butterato; ⟨olive⟩ snocciolato

pituitary /pɪ'tjuːɪt(ə)rɪ/ a pituitario

pituitary gland n ghiandola f pituitaria, ipofisi f

pity /'pɪtɪ/ n pietà f; [what a] ~! che peccato!; take ~ on avere compassione di ● vt aver pietà di

pivot /'pɪvət/ n perno m; fig fulcro m ● vi imperniarsi (on su)

pivotal /'pɪvətl/ a ⟨role⟩ centrale; ⟨decision⟩ cruciale

pixel /'pɪksəl/ n pixel m inv

pixie /'pɪksɪ/ n folletto m

pizza /'piːtsə/ n pizza f

placard /'plækɑːd/ n cartellone m

placate /plə'keɪt/ vt placare

place /pleɪs/ n posto m (fam: house) casa f; (in book) segno m; **feel out of** ~ sentirsi fuori posto; **take** ~ aver luogo; **all over the** ~ dappertutto ● vt collocare; (remember) identificare; ~ **an order** fare un'ordinazione; be ~**d** (in race) piazzarsi

placebo /plə'siːbəʊ/ n Med placebo m inv; fig contentino m

place mat n sottopiatto m

placement /'pleɪsmənt/ n (act: in accommodation) collocamento m; (Br: job) stage m inv

place name n toponimo m

placenta /plə'sentə/ n placenta f

placid /'plæsɪd/ a placido

plagiarist /'pleɪdɪərɪst/ n plagiario, -a mf

plagiarism /'pleɪdɪərɪzm/ n plagio m

plagiarize /'pleɪdɪəraɪz/ vt plagiare

plague /pleɪg/ n peste f

plaice /pleɪs/ n inv platessa f

plaid /plæd/ n (fabric) plaid m inv; (pattern) motivo m scozzese ● attrib ⟨scarf, shirt⟩ scozzese

plain /pleɪn/ a chiaro; (simple) semplice; (not pretty) scialbo; (not patterned) normale; ⟨chocolate⟩ fondente; **in** ~ **clothes** in borghese ● adv (simply) semplicemente ● n pianura f

plain-clothes a ⟨policeman etc⟩ in borghese

plainly /'pleɪnlɪ/ adv francamente; (simply) semplicemente; (obviously) chiaramente

plain paper fax n fax m inv a carta comune

plain-spoken a franco

plaintiff /'pleɪntɪf/ n Jur parte f lesa

plaintive /'pleɪntɪv/ a lamentoso

plaintively /'pleɪntɪvlɪ/ adv con aria lamentosa

plait /plæt/ n treccia f ● vt intrecciare

plan /plæn/ n progetto m, piano m ● vt (pt/pp **planned**) progettare; (intend) prevedere

plane¹ /pleɪn/ n (tree) platano m

plane² n aeroplano m; (in geometry) piano m

plane³ n (tool) pialla f ● vt piallare

plane crash n incidente m aereo

planet /'plænɪt/ n pianeta m

plank /plæŋk/ n asse f

■ **plank down** vt (fam: put down) mollare

plankton /'plæŋktən/ n plancton m

planning /'plænɪŋ/ n pianificazione f

planning permission n licenza f edilizia

plant /plɑːnt/ n pianta f; (machinery) impianto m; (factory) stabilimento m ● vt piantare; ~ **oneself in front of sb** piantarsi davanti a qcno

plantation /plæn'teɪʃn/ n piantagione f

planter /'plɑːntə(r)/ n (person) piantatore, -trice mf; (machine) piantatrice f

plant life n flora f

plaque /plɑːk/ n placca f

plasma /'plæzmə/ n plasma m

plaster /'plɑːstə(r)/ n intonaco m; Med gesso m; (sticking ~) cerotto m; **in** ~ ingessato ● vt intonacare ⟨wall⟩; (cover) ricoprire

plastered /'plɑːstəd/ a (sl: drunk) sbronzo

plasterer /'plɑːstərə(r)/ n intonacatore m

plaster of Paris n gesso m

plastic /'plæstɪk/ n plastica f ● a plastico

Plasticine® /'plæstɪsiːn/ n Plastilina® f

plastic surgeon n chirurgo m plastico

plastic surgery n chirurgia f plastica

plate /pleɪt/ n piatto m; (flat sheet) placca f; (gold and silverware) argenteria f; (in book) tavola f fuori testo ● vt (cover with metal) placcare

plateau /'plætəʊ/ n (pl ~x /'plætəʊz/) altopiano m ● vi fig livellarsi

platform /'plætfɔːm/ n (stage) palco m; Rail marciapiede m; Pol piattaforma f; ~ **5** binario 5

platform shoes npl scarpe fpl con la zeppa

platinum /'plætɪnəm/ n platino m ● attrib di platino

platitude /'plætɪtjuːd/ n luogo m comune

platonic /plə'tɒnɪk/ a platonico

platoon /plə'tuːn/ n Mil plotone m

platter /'plætə(r)/ n piatto m da portata

platypus /'plætɪpəs/ n ornitorinco m

plausibility /plɔːzɪ'bɪlɪtɪ/ n plausibilità f

plausible /'plɔːzəbl/ a plausibile

play /pleɪ/ n gioco m; Theat, TV dramma m, opera f teatrale; (performance) rappresentazione f; Radio sceneggiato m radiofonico; ~

on words gioco *m* di parole ● *vt* giocare a; (*act*) recitare; suonare ⟨*instrument*⟩; giocare ⟨*card*⟩ ● *vi* giocare; *Mus* suonare; **~ by the rules** stare alle regole; **~ with fire** scherzare con il fuoco; **~ dumb** fare lo gnorri; **~ safe** non prendere rischi

■ **play along** *vi* **~ along with sb** (*fam: cooperate*) fare il gioco di qcno

■ **play around with** *vt* (*meddle with*) cincischiarsi con

■ **play back** *vt* riascoltare ⟨*recording*⟩

■ **play down** *vt* minimizzare

■ **play on** *vi* (*continue to play*) continuare a giocare ● *vt* (*exploit*) giocare su

■ **play up** *vi fam* fare i capricci

play-acting *n* commedia *f*

playboy /'pleɪbɔɪ/ *n* playboy *m inv*

player /'pleɪə(r)/ *n* giocatore, -trice *mf*

playful /'pleɪfʊl/ *a* scherzoso

playfully /'pleɪfʊlɪ/ *adv* in modo scherzoso

playground /'pleɪgraʊnd/ *n Sch* cortile *m* (*per la ricreazione*)

playgroup /'pleɪgru:p/ *n* asilo *m*

playing card /'pleɪɪŋ/ *n* carta *f* da gioco

playing field *n* campo *m* da gioco

play: playmate *n* compagno, -a *mf* di gioco. **playpen** *n* box *m inv*. **playroom** /'pleɪru:m/ *n* ludoteca *f*. **plaything** *n* giocattolo *m*. **playwright** /'pleɪraɪt/ *n* drammaturgo, -a *mf*

plaza /'plɑ:zə/ *n* (*public square*) piazza *f*; (*shopping ~*) centro *m* commerciale; (*Am: services point*) area *f* di servizio; (*Am: toll point*) casello *m*

plc *abbr* (**public limited company**) s.r.l.

plea /pli:/ *n* richiesta *f*; **enter a ~ of not guilty** *Jur* dichiararsi non colpevole; **make a ~ for** fare un appello a

plead /pli:d/ *vi* fare appello (**for** a); **~ guilty** dichiararsi colpevole; **~ with sb** implorare qcno ● *vt Jur* perorare ⟨*case*⟩

pleasant /'pleznt/ *a* piacevole

pleasantly /'plezntlɪ/ *adv* piacevolmente; ⟨*say, smile*⟩ cordialmente

pleasantry /'plezntrɪ/ *n* (*joke*) battuta *f*; **pleasantries** (*pl: polite remarks*) convenevoli *mpl*

please /pli:z/ *adv* per favore; **~ do** prego ● *vt* far contento; **~ oneself** fare il proprio comodo; **~ yourself!** come vuoi!; *pej* fai come ti pare!

pleased /pli:zd/ *a* lieto; **~ with/about** contento di

pleasing /'pli:zɪŋ/ *a* gradevole

pleasurable /'pleʒərəbl/ *a* gradevole

pleasure /'pleʒə(r)/ *n* piacere *m*; **with ~** con piacere, volentieri

pleat /pli:t/ *n* piega *f* ● *vt* pieghettare

pleated /'pli:tɪd/ *a* a pieghe

pleb /pleb/ *n fam* plebeo, -a *mf*

plebby /'plebɪ/ *a fam* plebeo

plebeian /plɪ'bi:ən/ *pej n* plebeo, -a *mf* ● *a* plebeo

plebiscite /'plebɪsɪt/ *n* plebiscito *m*

pledge /pledʒ/ *n* pegno *m*; (*promise*) promes-

sa *f* ● *vt* (*pawn*) impegnare; **~ to do sth** impegnarsi a fare qcsa

plenary /'pli:nərɪ/ *a* ⟨*session*⟩ plenario; ⟨*powers*⟩ pieno; ⟨*authority*⟩ assoluto

plentiful /'plentɪfl/ *a* abbondante

plenty /'plentɪ/ *n* abbondanza *f*; **~ of money** molti soldi; **~ of people** molta gente; **I've got ~** ne ho in abbondanza

pleurisy /'plʊərəsɪ/ *n* pleurite *f*

pliability /plaɪə'bɪlɪtɪ/ *n* flessibilità *f*

pliable /'plaɪəbl/ *a* flessibile

pliers /'plaɪəz/ *npl* pinze *fpl*

plight /plaɪt/ *n* triste condizione *f*

plimsolls /'plɪmsəlz/ *npl* scarpe *fpl* da ginnastica

plinth /plɪnθ/ *n* plinto *m*

plod /plɒd/ *vi* (*pt/pp* **plodded**) trascinarsi; (*work hard*) sgobbare

plodder /'plɒdə(r)/ *n* sgobbone, -a *mf*

plonk[1] /plɒŋk/ *n fam* vino *m*; (*poor wine*) vinaccio *m*

plonk[2] *vt* (*fam: put*) sbattere

plop /plɒp/ *n* plop *m inv* ● *vi* (*pt/pp* **plopped**) fare plop

plot /plɒt/ *n* complotto *m*; (*of novel*) trama *f*; **~ of land** appezzamento *m* [di terreno] ● *vt/i* (*pt/pp* **plotted**) complottare

plotter /'plɒtə(r)/ *n* (*schemer*) cospiratore, -trice *mf*; *Comput* plotter *m inv*, tracciatore *m*

plough /plaʊ/ *n* aratro *m* ● *vt/i* arare

■ **plough back** *vt Comm* reinvestire

■ **plough into** *vt* (*crash into*) schiantarsi contro

■ **plough through** *vt* procedere a fatica in

ploughman /'plaʊmən/ *n* aratore *m*

ploughman's lunch *n Br* piatto *m* freddo a base di pane formaggio e sottaceti

plow /plaʊ/ *Am n* aratro *m* ● *vt/i* arare

ploy /plɔɪ/ *n fam* manovra *f*

pluck /plʌk/ *n* fegato *m* ● *vt* strappare; depilare ⟨*eyebrows*⟩; spennare ⟨*bird*⟩; cogliere ⟨*flower*⟩

■ **pluck up** *vt* **~ up courage** farsi coraggio

plucky /'plʌkɪ/ *a* (**-ier, -iest**) coraggioso

plug /plʌg/ *n* tappo *m*; *Electr* spina *f*; *Auto* candela *f*; (*fam: advertisement*) pubblicità *f inv* ● *vt* (*pt/pp* **plugged**) tappare; (*fam: advertise*) pubblicizzare

■ **plug away** *vi* (*work hard*) lavorare sodo

■ **plug in** *vt Electr* inserire la spina di

plughole /'plʌghəʊl/ *n Br* scarico *m*

plug-in *a* con la spina

plum /plʌm/ *n* prugna *f*; (*tree*) prugno *m*

plumage /'plu:mɪdʒ/ *n* piumaggio *m*

plumb /plʌm/ *a* verticale ● *adv* esattamente

■ **plumb in** *vt* collegare

plumber /'plʌmə(r)/ *n* idraulico *m*

plumbing /'plʌmɪŋ/ *n* impianto *m* idraulico

plumb line *n* filo *m* a piombo

plume /plu:m/ *n* piuma *f*

plummet /'plʌmɪt/ *vi* precipitare; ⟨*prices:*⟩ crollare

plump /plʌmp/ *a* paffuto

■ **plump down** *vt* (*put down*) lasciare cadere

■ **plump for** *vt* scegliere

plumpness /ˈplʌmpnɪs/ *n* rotondità *f*

plunder /ˈplʌndə(r)/ *n* (*booty*) bottino *m* ● *vt* saccheggiare

plunge /plʌndʒ/ *n* tuffo *m*; **take the ~** *fam* buttarsi ● *vt* tuffare; *fig* sprofondare; **~ sb into despair** piombare qcno nella disperazione ● *vi* tuffarsi

plunger /ˈplʌndʒə(r)/ *n* (*tool*) sturalavandini *m inv*; (*handle*) stantuffo *m*

plunging /ˈplʌndʒɪŋ/ *a* **~ neckline** scollatura *f* profonda

pluperfect /pluːˈpɜːfɪkt/ *n* trapassato *m* prossimo

plural /ˈplʊərəl/ *a* & *n* plurale *m*

plus /plʌs/ *prep* più ● *a* in più; **500 ~** più di 500 ● *n* più *m*; (*advantage*) extra *m inv*

plush /plʌʃ/ *a* ⟨*hotel etc*⟩ lussuoso

plutonium /pluːˈtəʊnɪəm/ *n* plutonio *m*

ply /plaɪ/ *vt* (*pt/pp* **plied**) esercitare ⟨*trade*⟩; **~ sb with drink** continuare a offrire da bere a qcno

plywood /ˈplaɪwʊd/ *n* compensato *m*

PM *abbr* **Prime Minister**

p.m. *abbr* (**post meridiem**) del pomeriggio

PMS *n abbr* (**premenstrual syndrome**) sindrome *f* premestruale

PMT *n abbr* (**premenstrual tension**) tensione *f* premestruale

pneumatic /njuːˈmætɪk/ *a* pneumatico

pneumatic drill *n* martello *m* pneumatico

pneumonia /njuːˈməʊnɪə/ *n* polmonite *f*

PO *abbr* (**Post Office**) ≈ P.T.; *abbr* (**postal order**) vaglia *m inv* postale

poach /pəʊtʃ/ *vt Culin* bollire; cacciare di frodo ⟨*deer*⟩; pescare di frodo ⟨*salmon*⟩; **~ed egg** uovo *m* in camicia

poacher /ˈpəʊtʃə(r)/ *n* bracconiere *m*

PO Box *n abbr* (**Post Office Box**) C.P. *f*

pocket /ˈpɒkɪt/ *n* tasca *f*; **~ of resistance** sacca *f* di resistenza; **be out of ~** rimetterci ● *vt* intascare

pocket-book *n* taccuino *m*; (*wallet*) portafoglio *m*

pocket-money *n* denaro *m* per le piccole spese

pock-marked /ˈpɒkmɑːkt/ *a* butterato

pod /pɒd/ *n* baccello *m*

podgy /ˈpɒdʒɪ/ *a* (**-ier, -iest**) grassoccio

podiatrist /pəˈdaɪətrɪst/ *n Am* pedicure *mf inv*

podium /ˈpəʊdɪəm/ *n* podio *m*

poem /ˈpəʊɪm/ *n* poesia *f*

poet /ˈpəʊɪt/ *n* poeta *m*

poetic /pəʊˈetɪk/ *a* poetico

poetic licence *n* licenza *f* poetica

Poet Laureate /ˈlɔːrɪət/ *n* poeta *m* laureato

poetry /ˈpəʊɪtrɪ/ *n* poesia *f*

po-faced /pəʊˈfeɪst/ *a Br fam* **look/be ~** avere un'aria di disapprovazione

poignancy /ˈpɔɪnjənsɪ/ *n* pregnanza *f*

poignant /ˈpɔɪnjənt/ *a* pregnante

point /pɔɪnt/ *n* punto *m*; (*sharp end*) punta *f*; (*meaning, purpose*) senso *m*; *Electr* presa *f*; **what is the ~?** a che scopo?; **the ~ is** il fatto

è; **I don't see the ~** non vedo il senso; **up to a ~** fino a un certo punto; **be on the ~ of doing sth** essere sul punto di fare qcsa; **~s** *pl Rail* scambio *m*; **good/bad ~s** aspetti *mpl* positivi/negativi ● *vt* puntare (**at** verso) ● *vi* (*with finger*) puntare il dito; **~ at/to** ⟨*person:*⟩ mostrare col dito; ⟨*indicator:*⟩ indicare; **~ and click** *Comput* punta e clicca

■ **point out** *vt* far notare ⟨*fact*⟩; **~ sth out to sb** far notare qcsa a qcno

point-blank *a* a bruciapelo

pointed /ˈpɔɪntɪd/ *a* appuntito; ⟨*question*⟩ diretto

pointer /ˈpɔɪntə(r)/ *n* (*piece of advice*) consiglio *m*

pointillism /ˈpwæntɪlɪzm/ *n* divisionismo *m*

pointillist /ˈpwæntɪlɪst/ *n* divisionista *mf*

pointing /ˈpɔɪntɪŋ/ *n Constr* rifinitura *f* con la malta

pointing device *n Comput* dispositivo *m* di puntamento

pointless /ˈpɔɪntlɪs/ *a* inutile

point: point of order *n* mozione *f* d'ordine. **point of sale** *n* (*place*) punto *m* di vendita; (*promotional material*) materiale *m* pubblicitario. **point-of-sale promotion** *n* promozione *f* punto vendita. **point of view** *n* punto *m* di vista

poise /pɔɪz/ *n* padronanza *f*

poised /pɔɪzd/ *a* in equilibrio; (*composed*) padrone di sé; **~ to** sul punto di

poison /ˈpɔɪzn/ *n* veleno *m* ● *vt* avvelenare

poisoned /ˈpɔɪz(ə)nd/ *a* avvelenato

poisoner /ˈpɔɪzənə(r)/ *n* avvelenatore, -trice *mf*

poisonous /ˈpɔɪzənəs/ *a* velenoso

poison-pen letter *n* lettera *f* anonima diffamatoria

poke /pəʊk/ *n* spintarella *f* ● *vt* spingere; ⟨*fire*⟩ attizzare; (*put*) ficcare; **~ fun at** prendere in giro

■ **poke about** *vi* frugare

■ **poke out** *vi* (*protrude*) spuntare

poker[1] /ˈpəʊkə(r)/ *n* attizzatoio *m*

poker[2] *n* (*Cards*) poker *m*

poker-faced /ˈfeɪst/ *a* ⟨*person*⟩ impassibile

poky /ˈpəʊkɪ/ *a* (**-ier, -iest**) angusto

Poland /ˈpəʊlənd/ *n* Polonia *f*

polar /ˈpəʊlə(r)/ *a* polare

polar bear *n* orso *m* bianco

polarity /pəˈlærətɪ/ *n Electr, Phys, fig* polarità *f inv*

polarize /ˈpəʊləraɪz/ *vt* polarizzare

polarized *a* polarizzato

Pole /pəʊl/ *n* polacco, -a *mf*

pole[1] *n* palo *m*

pole[2] *n Geog, Electr* polo *m*

polemic /pəˈlemɪk/ *n* polemica *f*

polemical /pəˈlemɪkl/ *a* polemico

pole star *n* stella *f* polare

pole vault *n* salto *m* con l'asta

police /pəˈliːs/ *n* polizia *f* ● *vt* pattugliare ⟨*area*⟩; sorvegliare ⟨*behaviour*⟩

police: police car *n* gazzella *f*. **policeman** *n* poliziotto *m*. **police state** *n* stato *m* militarista. **police station** n commissariato m. **policewoman** n donna f poliziotto

policy¹ /'pɒlɪsɪ/ n politica f

policy² n (insurance) polizza f

polio /'pəʊlɪəʊ/ n polio f

Polish /'pəʊlɪʃ/ a & n polacco m

polish /'pɒlɪʃ/ n (shine) lucentezza f; (substance) lucido m; (for nails) smalto m; fig raffinatezza f ● vt lucidare; fig smussare

■ **polish off** vt fam finire; far fuori (food)

■ **polish up** vt rispolverare (Italian)

polished /'pɒlɪʃt/ a (manner) raffinato; (performance) senza sbavature

polisher /'pɒlɪʃə(r)/ n (machine) lucidatrice f

polite /pə'laɪt/ a cortese

politely /pə'laɪtlɪ/ adv cortesemente

politeness /pə'laɪtnɪs/ n cortesia f

politic /'pɒlɪtɪk/ a prudente

political /pə'lɪtɪkl/ a politico

politically /pə'lɪtɪklɪ/ adv dal punto di vista politico; **~ correct** politicamente corretto

politician /pɒlɪ'tɪʃn/ n politico m

politicize /pə'lɪtɪsaɪz/ vt politicizzare

politics /'pɒlɪtɪks/ n politica f

polka /'pɒlkə/ n polka f

polka dot n pois nm inv, pallino m ● attrib a pois

poll /pəʊl/ n votazione f; (election) elezioni fpl; [opinion] **~** sondaggio m d'opinione; **go to the ~s** andare alle urne ● vt ottenere (votes)

pollen /'pɒlən/ n polline m

polling booth /'pəʊlɪŋ/ n cabina f elettorale

polling station n seggio m elettorale

pollster /'pəʊlstə(r)/ n (person) persona f che esegue un sondaggio d'opinione

poll tax n imposta f locale sulle persone fisiche

pollutant /pə'lu:tənt/ n sostanza f inquinante

pollute /pə'lu:t/ vt inquinare

polluted /pə'lu:tɪd/ a inquinato

polluter /pə'lu:tə(r)/ n inquinatore, -trice mf

pollution /pə'lu:ʃn/ n inquinamento m

polo /'pəʊləʊ/ n polo m

polo neck n collo m alto

polo shirt n dolcevita f

poly /'pɒlɪ/ n (Br fam: polytechnic) politecnico m

poly bag n sacchetto m di plastica

polyester /pɒlɪ'estə(r)/ n poliestere m

polygamous /pə'lɪgəməs/ a poligamico

polygamy /pə'lɪgəmɪ/ n poligamia f

polymath /'pɒlɪmæθ/ n erudito, -a mf

polymer /'pɒlɪmə(r)/ n polimero m

polystyrene® /pɒlɪ'staɪri:n/ n polistirolo m

polytechnic /pɒlɪ'teknɪk/ n politecnico m

polythene /'pɒlɪθi:n/ n politene m

polythene bag n sacchetto m di plastica

polyunsaturates /pɒlɪʌn'sætjʊreɪts/ npl grassi mpl polinsaturi

pomade /pə'meɪd/ n pomata f

pomegranate /'pɒmɪgrænɪt/ n melagrana f

pomp /pɒmp/ n pompa f

pompon /'pɒmpɒn/ n pompon m

pomposity /pɒm'pɒsətɪ/ n pomposità f

pompous /'pɒmpəs/ a pomposo

pompously /'pɒmpəslɪ/ adv pomposamente

poncy /'pɒnsɪ/ a fam da finocchio; (person) finocchio

pond /pɒnd/ n stagno m

ponder /'pɒndə(r)/ vt/i ponderare

ponderous /'pɒndərəs/ a ponderoso; fig pesante

pong /pɒŋ/ n fam puzza f ● vi puzzare

pontiff /'pɒntɪf/ n pontefice m

pontificate /pɒn'tɪfɪkeɪt/ vi pontificare

pontoon /pɒn'tu:n/ n (float) galleggiante m; (pier) pontile m; (Br: game) ventuno m

pony /'pəʊnɪ/ n pony m inv

ponytail /'pəʊnɪteɪl/ n coda f di cavallo

pony-trekking /'pəʊnɪtrekɪŋ/ n escursioni fpl col pony

pooch /pu:tʃ/ n (fam: dog) cagnetto m

poodle /'pu:dl/ n barboncino m

poof /pʊf/, **poofter** /'pʊftə(r)/ n (Br fam: homosexual) finocchio m

pooh /pu:/ int (scorn, disgust) puah! ● n (Br: baby talk) popò f inv

pooh-pooh /pu:'pu:/ vt fam ridere di (suggestion)

pool¹ /pu:l/ n (of water, blood) pozza f; [swimming] **~** piscina f

pool² n (common fund) cassa f comune; (in cards) piatto m; (game) biliardo m a buca; **~s** pl ≈ totocalcio msg ● vt mettere insieme

pooped /pu:pt/ a fam **be ~** [out] essere stanco morto

poor /pʊə(r)/ a povero; (not good) scadente; **in ~ health** in cattiva salute ● npl **the ~** i poveri

poorly /'pʊəlɪ/ a **be ~** non stare bene ● adv male

pop¹ /pɒp/ n botto m; (drink) bibita f gasata ● v (pt/pp popped) ● vt (fam: put) mettere; (burst) far scoppiare ● vi (burst) scoppiare

■ **pop in** vi fam fare un salto

■ **pop out** vi fam fare un salto fuori; **~ out to the shop** fare un salto al negozio

■ **pop up** vi (fam: appear unexpectedly) saltare fuori

pop² n fam musica f pop ● attrib pop inv

popcorn /'pɒpkɔ:n/ n popcorn m inv

pope /pəʊp/ n papa m

poplar /'pɒplə(r)/ n pioppo m

poppy /'pɒpɪ/ n papavero m

pop sock n gambaletto m

populace /'pɒpjʊləs/ n popolo m

popular /'pɒpjʊlə(r)/ a popolare; (belief) diffuso

popularity /pɒpjʊ'lærətɪ/ n popolarità f

popularize /'pɒpjʊləraɪz/ vt divulgare

populate /'pɒpjʊleɪt/ vt popolare

population /pɒpjʊ'leɪʃn/ n popolazione f

populist /'pɒpjʊlɪst/ a & n populista mf

populous /'pɒpjʊləs/ a popoloso

pop-up book n libro m con immagini tridimensionali

pop-up toaster n tostapane m inv a espulsione automatica

porcelain /'pɔːsəlɪn/ n porcellana f
porch /pɔːtʃ/ n portico m; Am veranda f
porcupine /'pɔːkjʊpaɪn/ n porcospino m
pore[1] /pɔː(r)/ n poro m
pore[2] vi ~ **over** immergersi in
pork /pɔːk/ n carne f di maiale
porn /pɔːn/ n fam porno m
porno /'pɔːnəʊ/ a fam porno inv
pornographic /pɔːnə'græfɪk/ a pornografi-co
pornography /pɔː'nɒgrəfɪ/ n pornografia f
porous /'pɔːrəs/ a poroso
porpoise /'pɔːpəs/ n focena f
porridge /'pɒrɪdʒ/ n farinata f di fiocchi d'avena
port[1] /pɔːt/ n porto m
port[2] n (Naut: side) babordo m
port[3] n (wine) porto m
portable /'pɔːtəbl/ a & n portatile m
Portakabin® /'pɔːtəkæbɪn/ n baracca f pre-fabbricata
portcullis /pɔːt'kʌlɪs/ n saracinesca f
portentous /pɔː'tentəs/ a (significant) so-lenne; (ominous) infausto
porter /'pɔːtə(r)/ n portiere m; (for luggage) facchino m
portfolio /pɔːt'fəʊlɪəʊ/ n cartella f; Comm portafoglio m
porthole /'pɔːthəʊl/ n oblò m inv
portion /'pɔːʃn/ n parte f; (of food) porzione f
portly /'pɔːtlɪ/ a (-ier, -iest) corpulento
portrait /'pɔːtrɪt/ n ritratto m
portrait painter n ritrattista mf
portray /pɔː'treɪ/ vt ritrarre; (represent) de-scrivere; (actor:) impersonare
portrayal /pɔː'treɪəl/ n ritratto m; (by actor) impersonazione f
Portugal /'pɔːtjʊgl/ n Portogallo m
Portuguese /pɔːtjʊ'giːz/ a & n portoghese mf; (language) portoghese m
pose /pəʊz/ n posa f ● vt porre (problem, question) ● vi (for painter) posare; ~ **as** atteg-giarsi a
poser /'pəʊzə(r)/ n fam (puzzle) rompicapo m inv; (person) montato, -a mf
posh /pɒʃ/ a fam lussuoso; (people) danaroso
position /pə'zɪʃn/ n posizione f; (job) posto m; (status) ceto m [sociale] ● vt posizionare
positive /'pɒzɪtɪv/ a positivo; (certain) sicu-ro; (progress) concreto ● n positivo m
positively /'pɒzɪtɪvlɪ/ adv positivamente; (decidedly) decisamente
posse /'pɒsɪ/ n gruppo m di volontari armati
possess /pə'zes/ vt possedere
possession /pə'zeʃn/ n possesso m; ~**s** pl beni mpl
possessive /pə'zesɪv/ a possessivo
possessiveness /pə'zesɪvnɪs/ n carattere m possessivo
possessor /pə'zesə(r)/ n possessore, -ditrice mf
possibility /pɒsə'bɪlətɪ/ n possibilità f inv
possible /'pɒsəbl/ a possibile
possibly /'pɒsəblɪ/ adv possibilmente; **I couldn't ~ accept** non mi è possibile accet-

tare; **he can't ~ be right** non è possibile che abbia ragione; **could you ~...?** potrebbe per favore...?
possum /'pɒsəm/ n fam opossum m inv; **play ~** far finta di dormire; (pretend to be dead) fare il morto
post[1] /pəʊst/ n (pole) palo m ● vt affiggere (notice)
post[2] n (place of duty) posto m ● vt appostare; (transfer) assegnare
post[3] n (mail) posta f; **by ~** per posta ● vt spedire; (put in letter box) imbucare; (as opposed to fax) mandare per posta; **keep sb ~ed** tenere qcno al corrente
post+ pref post+
postage /'pəʊstɪdʒ/ n affrancatura f; **~ and packaging** spese fpl di posta
postage stamp n francobollo m
postal /'pəʊstl/ a postale
postal order n vaglia m inv postale
post: postbox n cassetta f delle lettere. **postcard** n cartolina f. **postcode** n codice m postale. **post-date** vt postdatare
poster /'pəʊstə(r)/ n poster m inv; (advertising, election) cartellone m
posterior /pɒ'stɪərɪə(r)/ n fam posteriore m
posterity /pɒ'sterətɪ/ n posterità f
postgraduate /pəʊs(t)'grædjʊət/ n laurea-to, -a mf che continua gli studi ● a successivo alla laurea
posthumous /'pɒstjʊməs/ a postumo
posthumously /'pɒstjʊməslɪ/ adv dopo la morte
posting /'pəʊstɪŋ/ n (job) incarico m; (Br: in mail) spedizione f
postman /'pəʊstmən/ n postino m
postmark /'pəʊstmɑːk/ n timbro m postale
post-mortem /-'mɔːtəm/ n autopsia f
post-natal /-'neɪtl/ a post-partum
post office n ufficio m postale
post office box n casella f postale
postpone /pəʊs(t)'pəʊn/ vt rimandare
postponement /pəʊs(t)'pəʊnmənt/ n rin-vio m
postscript /'pəʊs(t)skrɪpt/ n poscritto m
posture /'pɒstʃə(r)/ n posizione f
post-war a del dopoguerra
pot /pɒt/ n vaso m; (for tea) teiera f; (for coffee) caffettiera f; (for cooking) pentola f; (sl: marijuana) erba f; **~s of money** fam un sac-co di soldi; **go to ~** fam andare in malora
potash /'pɒtæʃ/ n potassa f
potassium /pə'tæsɪəm/ n potassio m
potato /pə'teɪtəʊ/ n (pl **-es**) patata f
potato-peeler /-'piːlə(r)/ n tagliapatate m inv
pot-bellied /'pɒtbelɪd/ a panciuto
pot-belly /'pɒtbelɪ/ n fam pancione m
potent /'pəʊtənt/ a potente
potentate /'pəʊtənteɪt/ n potentato m
potential /pə'tenʃl/ a potenziale ● n poten-ziale m
potentially /pə'tenʃəlɪ/ adv potenzialmente
pot: pothole n cavità f inv; (in road) buca f. **potholer** n speleologo, -a mf. **pot-luck** n take

~ affidarsi alla sorte. **pot plant** *n* pianta *f* da appartamento. **pot-shot** *n* **take a ~ at** sparare a casaccio a

potted /'pɒtɪd/ *a* conservato; (*shortened*) condensato

potted plant *n* pianta *f* da appartamento

potter¹ /'pɒtə(r)/ *vi* ~ **[about]** gingillarsi

potter² *n* vasaio, -a *mf*

pottery /'pɒtərɪ/ *n* lavorazione *f* della ceramica; (*articles*) ceramiche *fpl*; (*workshop*) laboratorio *m* di ceramiche

potting compost /'pɒtɪŋ/ *n* terriccio *m*

potty /'pɒtɪ/ *a* (**-ier, -iest**) *fam* matto ● *n* vasino *m*

pouch /paʊtʃ/ *n* marsupio *m*

pouffe /puːf/ *n* pouf *m inv*

poultry /'pəʊltrɪ/ *n* pollame *m*

pounce /paʊns/ *vi* balzare; ~ **on** saltare su

pound¹ /paʊnd/ *n* libbra *f* (= *0,454 kg*); (*money*) sterlina *f*

pound² *vt* battere ● *vi* ⟨*heart:*⟩ battere forte; (*run heavily*) correre pesantemente

pound³ *n* (*for cars*) deposito *m* auto

pounding /'paʊndɪŋ/ *n* martellio *m* ● *a* martellante

pour /pɔː(r)/ *vt* versare ● *vi* riversarsi; (*with rain*) piovere a dirotto

■ **pour out** *vi* riversarsi fuori ● *vt* versare ⟨*drink*⟩; sfogare ⟨*troubles*⟩

pout /paʊt/ *vi* fare il broncio ● *n* broncio

poverty /'pɒvətɪ/ *n* povertà *f*

POW *n abbr* (**prisoner of war**) prigioniero, -a *mf* di guerra

powder /'paʊdə(r)/ *n* polvere *f*; (*cosmetic*) cipria *f* ● *vt* polverizzare; (*face*) incipriare

powder room *n euph* toilette *f inv* per signore

powdery /'paʊdərɪ/ *a* polveroso

power /'paʊə(r)/ *n* potere *m*; *Electr* corrente *f* [elettrica]; *Math* potenza *f*

power cut *n* interruzione *f* di corrente

powered /'paʊəd/ *a* ~ **by electricity** alimentato da corrente elettrica

powerful /'paʊəfʊl/ *a* potente

powerhouse /'paʊəhaʊs/ *n* (*fig: person*) persona *f* dinamica e energica; **a ~ of ideas** un vulcano di idee

powerless /'paʊəlɪs/ *a* impotente

power: power-on light *n* spia *f* di accensione. **power station** *n* centrale *f* elettrica. **power steering** *n Auto* servosterzo *m*. **power switch** *n* pulsante *m* di alimentazione. **power unit** *n* (*of computer etc*) alimentatore *m*

pow-wow /'paʊwaʊ/ *n* (*of American Indians*) raduno *m* tribale; (*fam: discussion*) discussione *f*

pp *abbr* (**pages**) pp.; *abbr* (**per procurationem**) pp.

PR *n abbr* (**proportional representation**) proporzionale *f*; *abbr* (**public relations**) pubbliche relazioni *fpl*

practicable /'præktɪkəbl/ *a* praticabile

practical /'præktɪkl/ *a* pratico

practicality /præktɪ'kælɪtɪ/ *n* praticità *f*

practical joke *n* scherzo *m* pratico

practically /'præktɪklɪ/ *adv* praticamente

practice /'præktɪs/ *n* pratica *f*; (*custom*) usanza *f*; (*habit*) abitudine *f*; (*exercise*) esercizio *m*; *Sport* allenamento *m*; **in ~** (*in reality*) in pratica; **out of ~** fuori esercizio; **put into ~** mettere in pratica

practise /'præktɪs/ *vt* fare pratica in; (*carry out*) mettere in pratica; esercitare ⟨*profession*⟩ ● *vi* esercitarsi; ⟨*doctor:*⟩ praticare

practised /'præktɪst/ *a* esperto

pragmatic /præg'mætɪk/ *a* pragmatico

pragmatism /'prægmətɪzm/ *n* pragmatismo *m*

pragmatist /'prægmətɪst/ *n* pragmatico, -a *mf*

praise /preɪz/ *n* lode *f* ● *vt* lodare

praiseworthy /'preɪzwɜːðɪ/ *a* lodevole

pram /præm/ *n* carrozzella *f*

prance /prɑːns/ *vi* saltellare

prank /præŋk/ *n* tiro *m*

prattle /'prætl/ *vi* parlottare

prawn /prɔːn/ *n* gambero *m*

prawn cocktail *n* cocktail *m inv* di gamberetti

pray /preɪ/ *vi* pregare

prayer /preə(r)/ *n* preghiera *f*

preach /priːtʃ/ *vt/i* predicare

preacher /'priːtʃə(r)/ *n* predicatore, -trice *mf*

preamble /priː'æmbl/ *n* preambolo *m*

pre-arrange /priː-/ *vt* predisporre

precarious /prɪ'keərɪəs/ *a* precario

precariously /prɪ'keərɪəslɪ/ *adv* in modo precario

precast /'priːkɑːst/ *a* ⟨*concrete*⟩ prefabbricato

precaution /prɪ'kɔːʃn/ *n* precauzione *f*; **as a ~** per precauzione

precautionary /prɪ'kɔːʃnərɪ/ *a* preventivo

precede /prɪ'siːd/ *vt* precedere

precedence /'presɪdəns/ *n* precedenza *f*

precedent /'presɪdənt/ *n* precedente *m*

preceding /prɪ'siːdɪŋ/ *a* precedente

preceptor /prɪ'septə(r)/ *n Am Univ* precettore *m*

precinct /'priːsɪŋkt/ *n* (*traffic-free*) zona *f* pedonale; (*Am: district*) circoscrizione *f*

precious /'preʃəs/ *a* prezioso; ⟨*style*⟩ ricercato ● *adv fam* ~ **little** ben poco

precipice /'presɪpɪs/ *n* precipizio *m*

precipitate¹ /prɪ'sɪpɪtət/ *a* precipitoso

precipitate² /prɪ'sɪpɪteɪt/ *vt* precipitare

precipitation /prɪsɪpɪ'teɪʃn/ *n* precipitazione *f*

précis /'preɪsiː/ *n* (*pl* **précis** /'preɪsiːz/) sunto *m*

precise /prɪ'saɪs/ *a* preciso

precisely /prɪ'saɪslɪ/ *adv* precisamente

precision /prɪ'sɪʒn/ *n* precisione *f*

preclude /prɪ'kluːd/ *vt* precludere

precocious /prɪ'kəʊʃəs/ *a* precoce

precociousness /prɪ'kəʊʃəsnɪs/ *n* precocità *f*

preconceived /pri:kən'si:vd/ a preconcetto

preconception /pri:kən'sepʃn/ n preconcetto m

precondition /pri:kən'dıʃn/ n presupposto m ● vt Psych condizionare

precook /pri:'kʊk/ vt cuocere in anticipo

precursor /pri:'kɜ:sə(r)/ n precursore m

predator /'predətə(r)/ n predatore, -trice mf

predatory /'predət(ə)rı/ a rapace

predecessor /'pri:dısesə(r)/ n predecessore, -a mf

predetermine /pri:dı'tɜ:mın/ vt predeterminare

predicament /prı'dıkəmənt/ n situazione f difficile

predicate /'predıkət/ n Gram predicato m

predicative /prı'dıkətıv/ a predicativo

predict /prı'dıkt/ vt predire

predictable /prı'dıktəbl/ a prevedibile

prediction /prı'dıkʃn/ n previsione f

predigested /pri:daı'dʒestıd/ a predigerito

predisposition /pri:dıspə'zıʃn/ n predisposizione f

predominant /prı'dɒmınənt/ a predominante

predominate /prı'dɒmıneıt/ vi predominare

pre-eminent /pri:'emınənt/ a preminente

pre-empt /pri:'empt/ vt (prevent) prevenire

pre-emptive /pri:'emptıv/ a preventivo

preen /pri:n/ vt lisciarsi; ~ **oneself** fig farsi bello

prefab /'pri:fæb/ n fam casa f prefabbricata

prefabricated /pri:'fæbrıkeıtıd/ a prefabbricato

preface /'prefıs/ n prefazione f

prefatory /'prefət(ə)rı/ a ⟨comments⟩ preliminare; ⟨pages, notes⟩ introduttivo

prefect /'pri:fekt/ n Sch studente, -tessa mf della scuola superiore con responsabilità disciplinari ecc

prefer /prı'fɜ:(r)/ vt (pt/pp **preferred**) preferire; **I ~ to walk** preferisco camminare

preferable /'prefərəbl/ a preferibile (**to** a)

preferably /'prefərəblı/ adv preferibilmente

preference /'prefərəns/ n preferenza f

preferential /prefə'renʃl/ a preferenziale

prefix /'pri:fıks/ n prefisso m

pregnancy /'pregnənsı/ n gravidanza f

pregnant /'pregnənt/ a incinta

preheat /pri:'hi:t/ vt preriscaldare ⟨oven⟩

prehensile /pri:'hensaıl/ a prensile

prehistoric /pri:hıs'tɒrık/ a preistorico

pre-ignition /pri:ıg'nıʃn/ n preaccensione f

pre-installed /pri:ın'stɔ:ld/ a preinstallato

prejudge /pri:'dʒʌdʒ/ vt giudicare prematuramente ⟨issue⟩

prejudice /'predʒʊdıs/ n pregiudizio m ● vt influenzare (**against** contro); (harm) danneggiare

prejudiced /'predʒʊdıst/ a prevenuto

preliminary /prı'lımınərı/ a preliminare

preloaded /pri:'ləʊdıd/ a precaricato

prelude /'prelju:d/ n preludio m

premarital /pri:'mærıtl/ a prematrimoniale

premarital sex n rapporti mpl prematrimoniali

premature /'premətjʊə(r)/ a prematuro

premature birth n parto m prematuro

prematurely /'premətjʊəlı/ adv prematuramente

premeditated /pri:'medıteıtıd/ a premeditato

premenstrual syndrome /pri:'menstrʊəl/ n sindrome f premestruale

premenstrual tension n tensione f premestruale

premier /'premıə(r)/ a primario ● n Pol primo ministro m, premier m inv

première /'premıeə(r)/ n prima f

premiership /'premıəʃıp/ n Pol carica f di primo ministro nel Regno Unito; ≈ presidenza f del consiglio

premises /'premısız/ npl locali mpl; **on the ~** sul posto

premium /'pri:mıəm/ n premio m; **be at a ~** essere una cosa rara

premonition /premə'nıʃn/ n presentimento m

prenatal /pri:'neıtl/ a esp Am prenatale

preoccupied /pri:'ɒkjupaıd/ a preoccupato

preoperative /pri:'ɒp(ə)rətıv/ a preoperatorio

preordained /pri:ɔ:'deınd/ a prestabilito; ⟨outcome⟩ predestinato

prep /prep/ n Sch compiti mpl

pre-packed /pri:'pækt/ a preconfezionato

prepaid /pri:'peıd/ a pagato in anticipo; ⟨envelope⟩ già affrancato

preparation /prepə'reıʃn/ n preparazione f; **~s** pl preparativi mpl

preparatory /prı'pærətrı/ a preparatorio; **~ to** come preparazione per

prepare /prı'peə(r)/ vt preparare ● vi prepararsi (**for** per); **~d to** disposto a

prepay /pri:'peı/ vt (pt/pp **-paid**) pagare in anticipo

preponderance /prı'pɒndərəns/ n preponderanza f

preponderantly /prı'pɒndərəntlı/ adv in modo preponderante

preponderate /prı'pɒndəreıt/ vi predominare

preposition /prepə'zıʃn/ n preposizione f

prepossessing /pri:pə'zesıŋ/ a attraente

preposterous /prı'pɒstərəs/ a assurdo

pre-programmed /pri:'prəʊɡræmd/ a programmato; Comput preprogrammato

prep school n scuola f elementare privata

pre-recorded /-rı'kɔ:dıd/ a in differita

prerequisite /pri:'rekwızıt/ n condizione f sine qua non

prerogative /prı'rɒɡətıv/ n prerogativa f

Presbyterian /prezbı'tıərıən/ a & n presbiteriano, -a mf

pre-school /'pri:sku:l/ n Am scuola f materna, asilo m ● a ⟨child⟩ in età prescolastica; ⟨years⟩ prescolastico

prescribe /prɪ'skraɪb/ *vt* prescrivere

prescription /prɪ'skrɪpʃn/ *n Med* ricetta *f*

prescriptive /prɪ'skrɪptɪv/ *a* normativo

presence /'prezns/ *n* presenza *f*; ~ **of mind** presenza *f* di spirito

present[1] /'preznt/ *a* presente ● *n* presente *m*; **at** ~ attualmente

present[2] *n* (*gift*) regalo *m*; **give sb sth as a** ~ regalare qcsa a qcno

present[3] /prɪ'zent/ *vt* presentare; ~ **sb with an award** consegnare un premio a qcno

presentable /prɪ'zentəbl/ *a* **be** ~ essere presentabile

presentation /prezn'teɪʃn/ *n* presentazione *f*

present-day *a* attuale

presenter /prɪ'zentə(r)/ *n TV, Radio* presentatore, -trice *mf*

presently /'prezntlɪ/ *adv* fra poco; (*Am: now*) attualmente

preservation /prezə'veɪʃn/ *n* conservazione *f*

preservative /prɪ'zɜ:vətɪv/ *n* conservante *m*

preserve /prɪ'zɜ:v/ *vt* preservare; (*maintain, Culin*) conservare ● *n* (*in hunting & fig*) riserva *f*; (*jam*) marmellata *f*

pre-set /pri:'set/ *vt* programmare

pre-shrunk /pri:'ʃrʌŋk/ *a* 〈*fabric*〉 irrestringibile

preside /prɪ'zaɪd/ *vi* presiedere (**over** a)

presidency /'prezɪdənsɪ/ *n* presidenza *f*

president /'prezɪdənt/ *n* presidente *m*

presidential /prezɪ'denʃl/ *a* presidenziale

pre-soak /pri:'səʊk/ *vt* mettere in ammollo

press /pres/ *n* (*machine*) pressa *f*; (*newspapers*) stampa *f* ● *vt* premere; pressare 〈*flower*〉; (*iron*) stirare; (*squeeze*) stringere ● *vi* (*urge*) incalzare

■ **press ahead** *vi* (*continue*) proseguire

■ **press for** *vi* fare pressione per; **be** ~**ed for** (*short of*) essere a corto di

■ **press on** *vi* andare avanti

press: press conference *n* conferenza *f* stampa. **press cutting** *n* ritaglio *m* di giornale. **press-gang** *vt* forzare

pressing /'presɪŋ/ *a* urgente

press: press release *n* comunicato *m* stampa. **press stud** *n* [bottone *m*] automatico *m*. **press-up** *n* flessione *f*

pressure /'preʃə(r)/ *n* pressione *f* ● *vt* = **pressurize**

pressure-cooker *n* pentola *f* a pressione

pressure group *n* gruppo *m* di pressione

pressurize /'preʃəraɪz/ *vt* far pressione su

pressurized /'preʃəraɪzd/ *a* 〈*cabin*〉 pressurizzato

prestige /pre'sti:ʒ/ *n* prestigio *m*

prestigious /pre'stɪdʒəs/ *a* prestigioso

presumably /prɪ'zju:məblɪ/ *adv* presumibilmente

presume /prɪ'zju:m/ *vt* presumere; ~ **to do sth** permettersi di fare qcsa ● *vi* ~ **on** approfittare di

presumption /prɪ'zʌmpʃn/ *n* presunzione *f*; (*boldness*) impertinenza *f*

presumptuous /prɪ'zʌmptjʊəs/ *a* impertinente

presuppose /pri:sə'pəʊz/ *vt* presupporre

presupposition /pri:sʌpə'zɪʃn/ *n* presupposizione *f*

pre-tax /'pri:tæks/ *a* al lordo d'imposta

pretence /prɪ'tens/ *n* finzione *f*; (*pretext*) pretesto *m*; **it's all** ~ è tutta una scena

pretend /prɪ'tend/ *vt* fingere; (*claim*) pretendere ● *vi* fare finta

pretender /prɪ'tendə(r)/ *n* pretendente *mf*

pretentious /prɪ'tenʃəs/ *a* pretenzioso

preterite /'pretərɪt/ *n* preterito *m*

pretext /'pri:tekst/ *n* pretesto *m*

pretty /'prɪtɪ/ *a* (**-ier, -iest**) carino ● *adv* (*fam: fairly*) abbastanza

prevail /prɪ'veɪl/ *vi* prevalere; ~ **on sb to do sth** convincere qcno a fare qc

prevailing /prɪ'veɪlɪŋ/ *a* prevalente

prevalence /'prevələns/ *n* diffusione *f*

prevalent /'prevələnt/ *a* diffuso

prevaricate /prɪ'værɪkeɪt/ *vi* tergiversare

prevent /prɪ'vent/ *vt* impedire; ~ **sb [from] doing sth** impedire a qcno di fare qcsa

preventable /prɪ'ventəbl/ *a* evitabile

prevention /prɪ'venʃn/ *n* prevenzione *f*

preventive /prɪ'ventɪv/ *a* preventivo

preview /'pri:vju:/ *n* anteprima *f*

previous /'pri:vɪəs/ *a* precedente

previously /'pri:vɪəslɪ/ *adv* precedentemente

pre-war /pri:'wɔ:/ *a* anteguerra

pre-wash /'pri:wɒʃ/ *n* prelavaggio *m*

prey /preɪ/ *n* preda *f*; **bird of** ~ uccello *m* rapace ● *vi* ~ **on** far preda di; ~ **on sb's mind** attanagliare qcno

price /praɪs/ *n* prezzo *m* ● *vt Comm* fissare il prezzo di

price: price-conscious *adj* consapevole dell'andamento dei prezzi. **price cutting** *n* taglio *m* dei prezzi. **price increase** *n* aumento *m* di prezzo

priceless /'praɪslɪs/ *a* inestimabile; (*fam: amusing*) spassosissimo

price: price list *n* listino *m* prezzi. **price/performance ratio** *n* rapporto *m* prezzo/prestazioni. **price range** *n* gamma *f* di prezzi. **price tag** *n* talloncino *m* del prezzo. **price war** *n* guerra *f* dei prezzi

pricey /'praɪsɪ/ *a fam* caro

pricing policy /'praɪsɪŋ/ *n* politica *f* di determinazione dei prezzi

prick /prɪk/ *n* puntura *f*; *vulg* (*penis*) cazzo *m*; (*person*) stronzo *m* ● *vt* pungere

■ **prick up** *vt* ~ **up one's ears** rizzare le orecchie

prickle /'prɪkl/ *n* spina *f*; (*sensation*) formicolio *m*

prickly /'prɪklɪ/ *a* pungente; 〈*person*〉 irritabile

pride /praɪd/ *n* orgoglio *m*; (*of lions*) branco *m*; ~ **of place** posizione *f* d'onore ● *vt* ~ **oneself on** vantarsi di

priest /pri:st/ *n* prete *m*

priesthood /'pri:sthʊd/ *n* (*clergy*) clero *m*;

(calling) sacerdozio *m*; **enter the ~** farsi prete

prig /prɪg/ *n* presuntuoso *m*

priggish /ˈprɪgɪʃ/ *a* presuntuoso

prim /prɪm/ *a* (**primmer, primmest**) perbenino

primacy /ˈpraɪməsɪ/ *n* primato *m*; *(of party, power)* supremazia *f*; *Relig* carica *f* di primate

prima facie /praɪməˈfeɪʃiː/ *adv* *(at first)* a prima vista ● *a* a prima vista legittimo

primal /ˈpraɪməl/ *a* *(quality, myth, feeling)* primitivo

primarily /ˈpraɪmərɪlɪ/ *adv* in primo luogo

primary /ˈpraɪmərɪ/ *a* primario; *(chief)* principale

primary school *n* scuola *f* elementare

primate /ˈpraɪmeɪt/ *n* *Zool, Relig* primate *m*

prime[1] /praɪm/ *a* principale, primo; *(first-rate)* eccellente ● *n* **be in one's ~** essere nel fiore degli anni

prime[2] *vt* preparare *(surface, person)*

Prime Minister *n* Primo Ministro *m*

primer /ˈpraɪmə(r)/ *n* *(paint)* base *f*; *(for detonating)* innesco *m*

prime time *n* prime time *m inv*, fascia *f* di massimo ascolto ● *attrib* *(advertising, programme)* nella fascia di massimo ascolto

primeval /praɪˈmiːvl/ *a* primitivo

primitive /ˈprɪmɪtɪv/ *a* primitivo

primordial /praɪˈmɔːdɪəl/ *a* primordiale

primrose /ˈprɪmrəʊz/ *n* primula *f*

prince /prɪns/ *n* principe *m*

princely /ˈprɪnslɪ/ *a* *(life, rôle)* da principe; *(amount, style)* principesco

princess /prɪnˈses/ *n* principessa *f*

principal /ˈprɪnsəpl/ *a* principale ● *n* *Sch* preside *m*

principality /prɪnsɪˈpælətɪ/ *n* principato *m*

principally /ˈprɪnsəplɪ/ *adv* principalmente

principle /ˈprɪnsəpl/ *n* principio *m*; **in ~** in teoria; **on ~** per principio; **~s** *pl* *(fundamentals)* fondamenti *mpl*

print /prɪnt/ *n* *(mark, trace)* impronta *f*; *Phot* copia *f*; *(letters)* stampatello *m*; *(picture)* stampa *f*; **in ~** *(printed out)* stampato; *(book)* in commercio; **out of ~** esaurito ● *vt/i* stampare; *(write in capitals)* scrivere in stampatello ■ **print out** *vt/i Comput* stampare

printed matter /ˈprɪntɪd/ *n* stampe *fpl*

printer /ˈprɪntə(r)/ *n* stampante *f*; *(person)* tipografo, -a *mf*

printer port *n* porta *f* per la stampante

printing /ˈprɪntɪŋ/ *n* tipografia *f*

printout /ˈprɪntaʊt/ *n* *Comput* stampa *f*

print speed *n* velocità *f* di stampa

prior /ˈpraɪə(r)/ *a* precedente ● *prep* **~ to** prima di

priority /praɪˈɒrətɪ/ *n* precedenza *f*; *(matter)* priorità *f inv*

prise /praɪz/ *vt* **~ open/up** forzare

prism /ˈprɪzm/ *n* prisma *m*

prison /ˈprɪzn/ *n* prigione *f*

prisoner /ˈprɪz(ə)nə(r)/ *n* prigioniero, -a *mf*

prison sentence *n* pena *f* detentiva

prissy /ˈprɪsɪ/ *a* *(person)* perbenista

pristine /ˈprɪstiːn/ *a* originario; *(unspoilt)* intatto

privacy /ˈprɪvəsɪ/ *n* privacy *f*

private /ˈpraɪvət/ *a* privato; *(car, secretary, letter)* personale ● *n Mil* soldato *m* semplice; **in ~** in privato

private enterprise *n* iniziativa *f* privata

private property *n* proprietà *f* privata

privately /ˈpraɪvətlɪ/ *adv* *(funded, educated etc)* privatamente; *(in secret)* in segreto; *(confidentially)* in privato; *(inwardly)* interiormente

privation /praɪˈveɪʃn/ *n* privazione *f*; **~s** *pl* stenti *mpl*

privatization /praɪvətaɪˈzeɪʃn/ *n* privatizzazione *f*

privatize /ˈpraɪvətaɪz/ *vt* privatizzare

privilege /ˈprɪvɪlɪdʒ/ *n* privilegio *m*

privileged /ˈprɪvɪlɪdʒd/ *a* privilegiato

privy /ˈprɪvɪ/ *a* **be ~ to** essere al corrente di

prize /praɪz/ *n* premio *m* ● *a* *(idiot etc)* perfetto ● *vt* apprezzare

prize: prize-giving /ˈpraɪzgɪvɪŋ/ *n* premiazione *f*. **prizewinner** *n* vincitore, -trice *mf*. **prize-winning** *a* vincente

pro /prəʊ/ *n* *(fam: professional)* professionista *mf*; **the ~s and cons** il pro e il contro

probability /prɒbəˈbɪlətɪ/ *n* probabilità *f inv*

probable /ˈprɒbəbl/ *a* probabile

probably /ˈprɒbəblɪ/ *adv* probabilmente

probate /ˈprəʊbeɪt/ *n* *Jur* omologazione *f*

probation /prəˈbeɪʃn/ *n* prova *f*; *Jur* libertà *f* vigilata

probationary /prəˈbeɪʃnərɪ/ *a* in prova; **~ period** periodo *m* di prova

probationer /prəˈbeɪʃnə(r)/ *n* *(employee on trial)* impiegato, -a *mf* in prova; *(trainee)* apprendista *mf*

probe /prəʊb/ *n* sonda *f*; *(fig: investigation)* indagine *f* ● *vt* sondare; *(investigate)* esaminare a fondo

probing /ˈprəʊbɪŋ/ *a* *(question)* penetrante

problem /ˈprɒbləm/ *n* problema *m* ● *attrib* difficile

problematic /prɒbləˈmætɪk/ *a* problematico

problem page *n* posta *f* del cuore

procedural /prəˈsiːdʒərəl/ *a* *(detail, error)* procedurale

procedure /prəˈsiːdʒə(r)/ *n* procedimento *m*

proceed /prəˈsiːd/ *vi* procedere ● *vt* **~ to do sth** proseguire facendo qcsa

proceedings /prəˈsiːdɪŋz/ *npl* *(report)* atti *mpl*; *Jur* azione *fsg* legale

proceeds /ˈprəʊsiːdz/ *npl* ricavato *msg*

process /ˈprəʊses/ *n* processo *m*; *(procedure)* procedimento *m*; **in the ~** nel far ciò ● *vt* trattare; *Admin* occuparsi di; *Phot* sviluppare

procession /prəˈseʃn/ *n* processione *f*

processor /ˈprəʊsesə(r)/ *n* *Comput* processore *m*; *(for food)* tritatutto *m inv*

pro-choice /prəʊˈtʃɔɪs/ *a* abortista

proclaim /prəˈkleɪm/ *vt* proclamare

proclamation /prɒkləˈmeɪʃn/ *n* proclamazione *f*

proclivity /prə'klɪvətɪ/ n tendenza f

procrastinate /prə'kræstɪneɪt/ vi procrastinare

procrastination /prəkræstɪ'neɪʃn/ n procrastinazione f

procreate /'prəʊkrɪeɪt/ vi procreare

procreation /prəʊkrɪ'eɪʃn/ n procreazione f

procure /prə'kjʊə(r)/ vt ottenere

prod /prɒd/ n colpetto m ● vt (pt/pp **prodded**) punzecchiare; fig incitare

prodigal /'prɒdɪgl/ a prodigo

prodigal son n figliol m prodigo

prodigious /prə'dɪdʒəs/ a prodigioso

prodigy /'prɒdɪdʒɪ/ n [infant] ~ bambino m prodigio

produce¹ /'prɒdjuːs/ n prodotti mpl; ~ of **Italy** prodotto in Italia

produce² /prə'djuːs/ vt produrre; (bring out) tirar fuori; (cause) causare; (fam: give birth to) fare

producer /prə'djuːsə(r)/ n produttore m

product /'prɒdʌkt/ n prodotto m

product range n gamma f di prodotti

production /prə'dʌkʃn/ n produzione f; Theat spettacolo m

production: production control n controllo m della produzione. **production director** n direttore, -trice mf della produzione. **production line** n catena f di montaggio. **production management** n gestione f della produzione. **production manager** n direttore, -trice mf della produzione

productive /prə'dʌktɪv/ a produttivo

productivity /prɒdʌk'tɪvətɪ/ n produttività f

product range n gamma f di prodotti

profane /prə'feɪn/ a profano; (blasphemous) blasfemo

profanity /prə'fænətɪ/ n (oath) bestemmia f

profess /prə'fes/ vt (claim) dichiarare

professed /prə'fest/ a (claiming to be) sedicente

profession /prə'feʃn/ n professione f

professional /prə'feʃnəl/ a professionale; (not amateur) professionista; (piece of work) da professionista; (man) di professione ● n professionista mf

professionalism /prə'feʃnəlɪzm/ n (of person, organization, work) professionalità f; Sport professionismo m

professionally /prə'feʃnəlɪ/ adv professionalmente

professor /prə'fesə(r)/ n professore m [universitario]

professorial /prɒfə'sɔːrɪəl/ a (duties, post, salary) professorale

proffer /'prɒfə(r)/ vt (hold out) porgere; (fig: offer) offrire

proficiency /prə'fɪʃnsɪ/ n competenza f

proficient /prə'fɪʃnt/ a competente (in in)

profile /'prəʊfaɪl/ n profilo m

profit /'prɒfɪt/ n profitto m ● vi ~ **from** trarre profitto da

profitable /'prɒfɪtəbl/ a proficuo

profitably /'prɒfɪtəblɪ/ adv in modo proficuo

profit and loss account n conto m profitti e perdite

profiteer /prɒfɪ'tɪə(r)/ n profittatore, -trice mf

profiterole /prə'fɪtərəʊl/ n profiterole m inv

profit margin n margine m di profitto

profit-sharing n partecipazione f agli utili

profligate /'prɒflɪgət/ a (extravagant) spendaccione; (dissolute) dissoluto; (spending) eccessivo

pro forma invoice /fɔːmə/ n fattura f proforma

profound /prə'faʊnd/ a profondo

profoundly /prə'faʊndlɪ/ adv profondamente

profuse /prə'fjuːs/ a ~ **apologies** una profusione di scuse

profusely /prə'fjuːslɪ/ adv profusamente

profusion /prə'fjuːʒn/ n profusione f; **in** ~ in abbondanza

progeny /'prɒdʒənɪ/ n progenie f inv

prognosis /prɒg'nəʊsɪs/ n (pl **-oses**) (prediction) previsione f; Med prognosi f inv

prognosticate /prɒg'nɒstɪkeɪt/ vt pronosticare

program /'prəʊgræm/ n Comput programma m ● vt (pt/pp **programmed**) programmare

programme /'prəʊgræm/ n Br programma m

programmer /'prəʊgræmə(r)/ n Comput programmatore, -trice mf

programming /'prəʊgræmɪŋ/ n programmazione f

progress¹ /'prəʊgres/ n progresso m; **in** ~ in corso; **make** ~ fig fare progressi

progress² /prə'gres/ vi progredire; fig fare progressi

progressive /prə'gresɪv/ a progressivo; (reforming) progressista

progressively /prə'gresɪvlɪ/ adv progressivamente

prohibit /prə'hɪbɪt/ vt proibire

prohibition /prəʊhɪ'bɪʃn/ n proibizione; **P~** Am proibizionismo m

prohibitive /prə'hɪbɪtɪv/ a proibitivo

prohibitively /prə'hɪbɪtɪvlɪ/ adv (expensive) in modo proibitivo

project¹ /'prɒdʒekt/ n progetto m; Sch ricerca f

project² /prə'dʒekt/ vt proiettare (film, image) ● vi (jut out) sporgere

projectile /prə'dʒektaɪl/ n proiettile m

projection /prə'dʒekʃn/ n (of figures) proiezione f

projector /prə'dʒektə(r)/ n proiettore m

proletarian /prəʊlə'teərɪən/ a & n proletario, -a mf

proletariat /prəʊlɪ'teərɪət/ n proletariato m

pro-life /prəʊ'laɪf/ a antiabortista

proliferate /prə'lɪfəreɪt/ vi proliferare

proliferation /prəlɪfə'reɪʃn/ n proliferazione f

prolific /prə'lɪfɪk/ a prolifico

prologue /'prəʊlɒg/ n prologo m

prolong /prə'lɒŋ/ vt prolungare

prom /prɒm/ n (*Br fam: at seaside*) lungomare m *inv*; (*Am fam: at high school*) ballo m studentesco

promenade /prɒmə'nɑ:d/ n lungomare m *inv*

prominence /'prɒmɪnəns/ n (*of person, issue*) importanza f; (*of object*) sporgenza f; (*hill*) rilievo m

prominent /'prɒmɪnənt/ a prominente; (*conspicuous*) di rilievo

promiscuity /prɒmɪ'skju:əti/ n promiscuità f

promiscuous /prə'mɪskjʊəs/ a promiscuo

promise /'prɒmɪs/ n promessa f ● vt promettere; ~ **sb that** promettere a qcno che; **I ~d to** l'ho promesso

Promised Land /prɒmɪst'lænd/ n Terra f Promessa

promising /'prɒmɪsɪŋ/ a promettente

promo /'prəʊməʊ/ n (*fam: of product*) campagna f promozionale; (*video*) video m inv promozionale

promontory /'prɒmənt(ə)rɪ/ n promontorio m

promote /prə'məʊt/ vt promuovere; **be ~d** essere promosso

promoter /prə'məʊtə(r)/ n promotore, -trice mf

promotion /prə'məʊʃn/ n promozione f

promotional /prə'məʊʃnəl/ a Comm promozionale

prompt /prɒmpt/ a immediato; (*punctual*) puntuale ● adv in punto ● vt incitare (**to** a); *Theat* suggerire a ● vi suggerire ● n Comput prompt m inv

prompter /'prɒmptə(r)/ n suggeritore, -trice mf

promptly /'prɒmptlɪ/ adv puntualmente

Proms /prɒmz/ npl rassegna f di concerti estivi di musica classica presso l'Albert Hall a Londra

prone /prəʊn/ a prono; **be ~ to do sth** essere incline a fare qcsa

prong /prɒŋ/ n dente m

pronoun /'prəʊnaʊn/ n pronome m

pronounce /prə'naʊns/ vt pronunciare; (*declare*) dichiarare

pronounced /prə'naʊnst/ a (*noticeable*) pronunciato

pronouncement /prə'naʊnsmənt/ n dichiarazione f

pronunciation /prənʌnsɪ'eɪʃn/ n pronuncia f

proof /pru:f/ n prova f; *Typ* bozza f, prova f; **12% ~** 12° ● a ~ **against** a prova di

proof-reader n correttore, -trice mf di bozze

proof-reading n revisione f di bozze

prop[1] /prɒp/ n puntello m ● vt (*pt/pp* **propped**) ~ **open** tenere aperto; ~ **against** (*lean*) appoggiare a

■ **prop up** vt sostenere

prop[2] n Theat, fam accessorio m di scena

propaganda /prɒpə'gændə/ n propaganda f

propagate /'prɒpəgeɪt/ vt propagare

propagator /'prɒpəgeɪtə(r)/ n propagatore m

propane /'prəʊpeɪn/ n propano m

propel /prə'pel/ vt (*pt/pp* **propelled**) spingere

propellant /prə'pelənt/ n (*in aerosol*) gas m inv propellente; (*in rocket*) propellente m

propeller /prə'pelə(r)/ n elica f

propelling pencil /prə'pelɪŋ/ n portamina m inv

propensity /prə'pensətɪ/ n tendenza f

proper /'prɒpə(r)/ a corretto; (*suitable*) adatto; (*fam: real*) vero [e proprio]

properly /'prɒpəlɪ/ adv correttamente

proper name, proper noun n nome m proprio

property /'prɒpətɪ/ n proprietà f inv

property developer n impresa f edile; (*person*) impresario m edile

property market n mercato m immobiliare

prophecy /'prɒfəsɪ/ n profezia f

prophesy /'prɒfɪsaɪ/ vt (*pt/pp* **-ied**) profetizzare

prophet /'prɒfɪt/ n profeta m

prophetic /prə'fetɪk/ a profetico

prophylactic /prɒfɪ'læktɪk/ n (*condom*) profilattico m, preservativo m; (*Med: treatment*) misura f profilattica ● a profilattico

proponent /prə'pəʊnənt/ n fautore, -trice mf

proportion /prə'pɔ:ʃn/ n proporzione f; (*share*) parte f; **be in ~** essere proporzionato (**to** a); **be out of ~** essere sproporzionato; ~**s** pl (*dimensions*) proporzioni fpl

proportional /prə'pɔ:ʃnəl/ a proporzionale

proportionally /prə'pɔ:ʃnəlɪ/ adv in proporzione

proportional representation n rappresentanza f proporzionale

proposal /prə'pəʊzl/ n proposta f; (*of marriage*) proposta f di matrimonio

propose /prə'pəʊz/ vt proporre; (*intend*) proporsi ● vi fare una proposta di matrimonio

proposition /prɒpə'zɪʃn/ n proposta f; (*fam: task*) impresa f

proprietor /prə'praɪətə(r)/ n proprietario, -a mf

propriety /prə'praɪətɪ/ n correttezza f; **the proprieties** pl l'etichetta f

propulsion /prə'pʌlʃn/ n propulsione f

pro rata /'rɑːtə/ a **on a ~ ~ basis** in proporzione

prosaic /prə'zeɪɪk/ a prosaico

proscribe vt (*exile*) esiliare; (*ban*) bandire

prose /prəʊz/ n prosa f

prosecute /'prɒsɪkjuːt/ vt intentare azione contro

prosecution /prɒsɪ'kjuːʃn/ n azione f giudiziaria; **the ~** l'accusa f

prosecutor /'prɒsɪkjuːtə(r)/ n [**Public**] **P~** Pubblico Ministero m

prospect[1] /'prɒspekt/ n (*expectation*) prospettiva f; (*view*) vista f

prospect[2] /prə'spekt/ vi ~ **for** cercare

prospective /prə'spektɪv/ a (*future*) futuro; (*possible*) potenziale

prospector /prə'spektə(r)/ n cercatore m

prospectus /prə'spektəs/ n prospetto m

prosper /'prɒspə(r)/ vi prosperare; ⟨person:⟩ stare bene finanziariamente

prosperity /prɒ'sperəti/ n prosperità f

prosperous /'prɒspərəs/ a prospero

prostate /'prɒsteit/ n prostata f

prosthesis /prɒs'θi:sɪs/ n protesi f

prostitute /'prɒstɪtju:t/ n prostituta f ● vt fig prostituire

prostitution /prɒstɪ'tju:ʃn/ n prostituzione f

prostrate /'prɒstreit/ a prostrato; ~ **with grief** fig prostrato dal dolore

protagonist /prə'tægənɪst/ n protagonista mf

protect /prə'tekt/ vt proteggere (**from** da)

protection /prə'tekʃn/ n protezione f

protective /prə'tektɪv/ a protettivo

protector /prə'tektə(r)/ n protettore, -trice mf

protégé /'prɒtɪʒeɪ/ n protetto m

protein /'prəʊti:n/ n proteina f

protest¹ /'prəʊtest/ n protesta f

protest² /prə'test/ vt/i protestare

Protestant /'prɒtɪstənt/ a & n protestante mf

Protestantism /'prɒtɪstəntɪzm/ n protestantesimo m

protestation /prɒtɪ'steiʃn/ n protesta f

protester /prə'testə(r)/ n contestatore, -trice mf; (at demonstration) dimostrante mf

protocol /'prəʊtəkɒl/ n protocollo m

prototype /'prəʊtətaip/ n prototipo m

protract /prə'trækt/ vt protrarre

protracted /prə'træktɪd/ a prolungato

protractor /prə'træktə(r)/ n goniometro m

protrude /prə'tru:d/ vi sporgere

protuberance /prə'tu:bərəns/ n protuberanza f

proud /praʊd/ a fiero (**of** di)

proudly /'praʊdli/ adv fieramente

prove /pru:v/ vt provare ● vi ~ **to be a lie** rivelarsi una bugia

proven /'pru:vən/ a dimostrato

proverb /'prɒvɜ:b/ n proverbio m

proverbial /prə'vɜ:bɪəl/ a proverbiale

provide /prə'vaid/ vt fornire; ~ **sb with sth** fornire qcsa a qcno ● vi ~ **for** (allow for) tenere conto di; ⟨law:⟩ prevedere

provided /prə'vaidɪd/ conj ~ [**that**] purché

providence /'prɒvɪdəns/ n provvidenza f

provident /'prɒvɪdənt/ a previdenziale

providential /prɒvɪ'denʃl/ a provvidenziale

provider /prə'vaidə(r)/ n (in family) persona f che mantiene la famiglia

providing /prə'vaidɪŋ/ conj = **provided**

province /'prɒvɪns/ n provincia f; fig campo m

provincial /prə'vɪnʃl/ a provinciale

provincialism /prə'vɪnʃəlɪzm/ n provincialismo m

provision /prə'vɪʒn/ n (of food, water) approvvigionamento m (**of** di); (of law) disposizione f; **make ~ for** ⟨law:⟩ prevedere; **~s** pl provviste fpl

provisional /prə'vɪʒ(ə)nəl/ a provvisorio

provisionally /prə'vɪʒ(ə)nəli/ adv provvisoriamente

proviso /prə'vaizəʊ/ n condizione f

provocation /prɒvə'keiʃn/ n provocazione f

provocative /prə'vɒkətɪv/ a provocatorio; (sexually) provocante

provocatively /prə'vɒkətɪvli/ adv in modo provocatorio; (smile, be dressed) in modo provocante

provoke /prə'vəʊk/ vt provocare

provost /'prɒvəst/ n Am Univ decano m; Br Univ, Sch rettore m; (in Scotland) sindaco m

prow /praʊ/ n prua f

prowess /'praʊɪs/ n abilità f inv

prowl /praʊl/ vi aggirarsi ● n **on the ~** in cerca di preda

prowler /'praʊlə(r)/ n tipo m sospetto

proximity /prɒk'sɪməti/ n prossimità f

proxy /'prɒksi/ n procura f; (person) persona f che agisce per procura

prude /pru:d/ n **be a ~** essere eccessivamente pudico

prudence /'pru:dəns/ n prudenza f

prudent /'pru:dənt/ a prudente; (wise) oculatezza f

prudently /'pru:dəntli/ adv con prudenza

prudish /'pru:dɪʃ/ a eccessivamente pudico

prudishness /'pru:dɪʃnɪs/ n eccessivo pudore m

prune¹ /pru:n/ n prugna f secca

prune² vt potare

pry /praɪ/ vi (pt/pp **pried**) ficcare il naso

prying /'praɪɪŋ/ a curioso

PS n abbr (**postscriptum**) PS m inv

psalm /sɑ:m/ n salmo m

pseud /sju:d/ n fam intellettualoide mf

pseudonym /'sju:dənɪm/ n pseudonimo m

■ **psych out** /saik/ vt (fam: unnerve) snervare

■ **psych up** vt (fam: prepare mentally) preparare psicologicamente

psychedelic /saikə'delik/ a psichedelico

psychiatric /saiki'ætrik/ a psichiatrico

psychiatrist /sai'kaiətrist/ n psichiatra mf

psychic /'saikik/ n sensitivo, -a mf ● a psichico; **I'm not ~** non sono un indovino

psychoanalyse /saikəʊ'ænəlaiz/ vt psicanalizzare

psychoanalysis /saikəʊə'næləsis/ n psicanalisi f

psychoanalyst /saikəʊ'ænəlist/ n psicanalista mf

psychological /saikə'lɒdʒikl/ a psicologico

psychologically /saikə'lɒdʒikli/ adv psicologicamente

psychologist /sai'kɒlədʒist/ n psicologo, -a mf

psychology /sai'kɒlədʒi/ n psicologia f

psychopath /'saikəpæθ/ n psicopatico, -a mf

psychopathic /saikə'pæθik/ a psicopatico

psychosis /sai'kəʊsis/ n psicosi f inv

psychosomatic /saikəʊsə'mætik/ a psicosomatico

psychotherapist /saɪkəʊ'θerəpɪst/ *n* psicoterapista *mf*, psicoterapeuta *mf*

psychotic /saɪ'kɒtɪk/ *a* & *n* psicotico, -a *mf*

PT *n abbr* (**physical training**) educazione *f* fisica

PTA *n abbr* (**Parent-Teacher Association**) ≈ consiglio *m* d'istituto

PTO *abbr* (**please turn over**) vedi retro

pub /pʌb/ *n fam* pub *m inv*

puberty /'pju:bətɪ/ *n* pubertà *f*

pubic hair /'pju:bɪk/ *n* peli *mpl* del pube

public /'pʌblɪk/ *a* pubblico; **make ~** rendere pubblico ● **in the ~** il pubblico; **in ~** in pubblico

public address system *n* impianto *m* di amplificazione

publican /'pʌblɪkən/ *n* gestore, -trice *mf*/proprietario, -a *mf* di un pub

publication /pʌblɪ'keɪʃn/ *n* pubblicazione *f*

public: public convenience *n* gabinetti *mpl* pubblici. **public holiday** *n* festa *f* nazionale. **public house** *n* pub *m inv*

publicist /'pʌblɪsɪst/ *n* (*press agent*) pressagent *mf inv*, addetto, -a *mf* stampa

publicity /pʌb'lɪsətɪ/ *n* pubblicità *f*

publicity department *n* settore *m* pubblicità

publicity director *n* direttore, -trice *mf* della pubblicità

publicize /'pʌblɪsaɪz/ *vt* pubblicizzare

public library *n* biblioteca *f* pubblica

public limited company /'lɪmɪtɪd/ *n* società *f inv* per azioni

publicly /'pʌblɪklɪ/ *adv* pubblicamente

public: public opinion *n* opinione *f* pubblica. **public relations** *npl* pubbliche relazioni *fpl*. **public relations department** *n* ufficio *m* pubbliche relazioni. **public relations officer** *n* addetto, -a *mf* alle pubbliche relazioni. **public school** *n* scuola *f* privata; *Am* scuola *f* pubblica. **public sector** *n* settore *m* pubblico. **public-spirited** *a* **be ~** essere dotato di senso civico. **public transport** *n* mezzi *mpl* pubblici

publish /'pʌblɪʃ/ *vt* pubblicare

publisher /'pʌblɪʃə(r)/ *n* editore *m*; (*firm*) editore *m*, casa *f* editrice

publishing /'pʌblɪʃɪŋ/ *n* editoria *f*

puce /pju:s/ *a* color bruno rossastro

puck /pʌk/ *n* (*in ice-hockey*) disco *m*; (*sprite*) folletto *m*

pucker /'pʌkə(r)/ *vi* ⟨*material:*⟩ arricciarsi

pudding /'pʊdɪŋ/ *n* dolce *m* cotto al vapore; (*course*) dolce *m*

puddle /'pʌdl/ *n* pozzanghera *f*

pudgy /'pʌdʒɪ/ *a* (**-ier, -iest**) grassoccio

puerile /'pjʊəraɪl/ *a* puerile

puff /pʌf/ *n* (*of wind*) soffio *m*; (*of smoke*) tirata *f*; (*for powder*) piumino *m* ● *vt* sbuffare

■ **puff at** *vt* tirare boccate da ⟨*pipe*⟩

■ **puff out** *vt* lasciare senza fiato ⟨*person*⟩; spegnere ⟨*candle*⟩

puffed /pʌft/ *a* (*out of breath*) senza fiato

puff pastry *n* pasta *f* sfoglia

puff sleeve *n* manica *f* a palloncino

puffy /'pʌfɪ/ *a* gonfio

pug /pʌg/ *n* (*dog*) carlino *m*

pugnacious /pʌg'neɪʃəs/ *a* aggressivo

pull /pʊl/ *n* trazione *f*; (*fig: attraction*) attrazione *f*; (*fam: influence*) influenza *f* ● *vt* tirare; estrarre ⟨*tooth*⟩; stirarsi ⟨*muscle*⟩; **~ a fast one** *fam* giocare un brutto tiro; **~ faces** far boccacce; **~ oneself together** ricomporsi; **~ one's weight** mettercela tutta; **~ sb's leg** *fam* prendere in giro qcno

■ **pull ahead** *vi* (*move in front*) passare davanti

■ **pull away** *vi* (*increase one's lead*) distanziarsi

■ **pull down** *vt* (*demolish*) demolire

■ **pull in** *vi Auto* accostare

■ **pull off** *vt* togliere; *fam* azzeccare

■ **pull out** *vt* tirar fuori ● *vi Auto* spostarsi; (*of competition*) ritirarsi

■ **pull over** *vi Aut* accostare

■ **pull through** *vi* (*recover*) farcela

■ **pull together** *vi* (*co-operate*) sommare le forze

■ **pull up** *vt* sradicare ⟨*plant*⟩; (*reprimand*) rimproverare ● *vi Auto* fermarsi

pull-down menu *n Comput* menu *m inv* a discesa

pulley /'pʊlɪ/ *n Techn* puleggia *f*

pull-in *n Br* (*lay-by*) piazzuola *f* di sosta; (*café*) bar *m inv* sul bordo della strada

pullover /'pʊləʊvə(r)/ *n* pullover *m inv*

pulmonary /'pʌlmənərɪ/ *a* polmonare

pulp /pʌlp/ *n* poltiglia *f*; (*of fruit*) polpa *f*; (*for paper*) pasta *f*

pulpit /'pʊlpɪt/ *n* pulpito *m*

pulsar /'pʌlsɑ:(r)/ *n* pulsar *m inv*

pulsate /pʌl'seɪt/ *vi* pulsare

pulse /pʌls/ *n* polso *m*

pulses /'pʌlsɪz/ *npl* legumi *mpl* secchi

pulverize /'pʌlvəraɪz/ *vt* polverizzare

puma /'pju:mə/ *n* puma *m inv*

pumice /'pʌmɪs/ *n* pomice *f*

pummel /'pʌml/ *vt* (*pt/pp* **pummelled**) prendere a pugni

pump /pʌmp/ *n* pompa *f* ● *vt* pompare; *fam* cercare di estorcere informazioni da

■ **pump up** *vt* (*inflate*) gonfiare

pumpkin /'pʌmpkɪn/ *n* zucca *f*

pun /pʌn/ *n* gioco *m* di parole

punch¹ /pʌntʃ/ *n* pugno *m*; (*device*) pinza *f* per forare ● *vt* dare un pugno a; forare ⟨*ticket*⟩; perforare ⟨*hole*⟩

punch² *n* (*drink*) punch *m inv*

punch: Punch-and-Judy show *n* spettacolo *m* di burattini. **punch-drunk** *a* (*in boxing*) groggy *inv*; *fig* stordito. **punchline** *n* battuta *f* finale. **punch-up** *n* rissa *f*

punctual /'pʌŋktjʊəl/ *a* puntuale

punctuality /pʌŋktjʊ'ælətɪ/ *n* puntualità *f*

punctually /'pʌŋktjʊəlɪ/ *adv* puntualmente

punctuate /'pʌŋktjʊeɪt/ *vt* punteggiare

punctuation /pʌŋktjʊ'eɪʃn/ *n* punteggiatura *f*

punctuation mark *n* segno *m* di interpunzione

puncture /'pʌŋktʃə(r)/ n foro m; (tyre) foratura f ● vt forare

pundit /'pʌndɪt/ n esperto m

pungency /'pʌndʒənsɪ/ n asprezza f

pungent /'pʌndʒənt/ a acre

punish /'pʌnɪʃ/ vt punire

punishable /'pʌnɪʃəbl/ a punibile

punishment /'pʌnɪʃmənt/ n punizione f

punitive /'pju:nɪtɪv/ a punitivo

punk /pʌŋk/ n punk m inv

punk rock n punk rock m inv

punk rocker /'rɒkə(r)/ n punk mf inv

punnet /'pʌnɪt/ n cestello m

punt /pʌnt/ n (boat) barchino m

punter /'pʌntə(r)/ n (gambler) scommettitore, -trice mf; (fam: client) consumatore, -trice mf

puny /'pju:nɪ/ a (-ier, -iest) striminzito

pup /pʌp/ n = **puppy**

pupil /'pju:pl/ n alluno, -a mf; (of eye) pupilla f

puppet /'pʌpɪt/ n marionetta f; (glove ~, fig) burattino m

puppy /'pʌpɪ/ n cucciolo m

purchase /'pɜ:tʃəs/ n acquisto m; (leverage) presa f ● vt acquistare

purchase: purchase invoice n fattura f di acquisto. **purchase ledger** n libro m mastro degli acquisti. **purchase order** n ordine m di acquisto. **purchase price** n prezzo m di acquisto

purchaser /'pɜ:tʃəsə(r)/ n acquirente mf

purchasing [department] /'pɜ:tʃəsɪŋ/ n ufficio m acquisti

purdah /'pɜ:də/ n reclusione f delle donne in alcune società musulmane e indù

pure /pjʊə(r)/ a puro

pure-bred /-bred/ n (horse) purosangue m inv ● a purosangue inv

purée /'pjʊəreɪ/ n purè m inv ● vt passare

purely /'pjʊəlɪ/ adv puramente

purgatory /'pɜ:gətrɪ/ n purgatorio m

purge /pɜ:dʒ/ Pol n epurazione f ● vt epurare

purification /pjʊərɪfɪ'keɪʃn/ n purificazione f

purify /'pjʊərɪfaɪ/ vt (pt/pp -ied) purificare

purist /'pjʊərɪst/ a & n purista mf

puritan /'pjʊərɪtən/ n puritano, -a mf ● a fig puritano

puritanical /pjʊərɪ'tænɪkl/ a puritano

purity /'pjʊərɪtɪ/ n purità f

purl /pɜ:l/ n (Knitting) maglia f rovescia ● vt/i lavorare a rovescio

purple /'pɜ:pl/ a viola inv

purport /pə'pɔ:t/ vt ~ **to be** farsi passare per

purpose /'pɜ:pəs/ n scopo m; (determination) fermezza f; **on** ~ apposta

purpose-built /-'bɪlt/ a costruito ad hoc

purposeful /'pɜ:pəsfʊl/ a deciso

purposefully /'pɜ:pəsfʊlɪ/ adv con decisione

purposely /'pɜ:pəslɪ/ adv apposta

purpose-made a Br fatto appositamente

purr /pɜ:(r)/ vi (cat:) fare le fusa

purse /pɜ:s/ n borsellino m; (Am: handbag) borsa f ● vt increspare (lips)

purser /'pɜ:sə(r)/ n commissario m di bordo

pursue /pə'sju:/ vt inseguire; fig proseguire

pursuer /pə'sju:ə(r)/ n inseguitore, -trice mf

pursuit /pə'sju:t/ n inseguimento m; (fig: of happiness) ricerca f; (pastime) attività f inv; **in** ~ all'inseguimento

pus /pʌs/ n pus m

push /pʊʃ/ n spinta f; (fig: effort) sforzo m; (drive) iniziativa f; **at a** ~ in caso di bisogno; **get the** ~ fam essere licenziato ● vt spingere; premere (button); (pressurize) far pressione su; **be** ~**ed for time** fam non avere tempo ● vi spingere

■ **push around** vt (bully) fare il prepotente con

■ **push aside** vt scostare

■ **push back** vt respingere

■ **push for** vt fare pressione per ottenere (reform)

■ **push off** vt togliere ● vi (fam: leave) levarsi dai piedi

■ **push on** vi (continue) continuare

■ **push over** vt (cause to fall) far cadere

■ **push through** vt (have accepted quickly) fare accettare

■ **push up** vt alzare (price)

push-button n pulsante m

pushchair /'pʊʃtʃeə(r)/ n passeggino m

pusher /'pʊʃə(r)/ n (fam: of drugs) spacciatore, -trice mf [di droga]

push: pushover n fam bazzecola f. **push-start** vt spingere (per far partire) (vehicle) ● n **give sth a** ~ dare una spinta a qcsa. **push-up** n flessione f

pushy /'pʊʃɪ/ a fam troppo intraprendente

puss /pʊs/ n, **pussy** /'pʊsɪ/ n micio m

■ **pussyfoot around** /'pʊsɪfʊt/ vi fam tergiversare

pussyfooting /'pʊsɪfʊtɪŋ/ n fam tentennamento m ● a (fam: attitude, behaviour) tergiversante

put /pʊt/ vt (pt/pp put, pres p **putting**) mettere; ~ **the cost of sth at £50** valutare il costo di qcsa 50 sterline; ~ **an end to** porre fine o termine a; ~ **in writing** mettere per iscritto; ~ **into effect** mettere in opera ● vi ~ **to sea** salpare ● a **stay** ~! rimani lì!

■ **put about** vt mettere in giro (rumour)

■ **put across** vt raccontare (joke); esprimere (message)

■ **put aside** vt mettere da parte

■ **put away** vt mettere via

■ **put back** vt rimettere; mettere indietro (clock)

■ **put by** vt mettere da parte

■ **put down** vt mettere giù; (suppress) reprimere; (kill) sopprimere; (write) annotare; (criticize unfairly) sminuire; ~ **one's foot down** fam essere fermo; Auto dare un'accelerata; ~ **down to** (attribute) attribuire

■ **put forward** vt avanzare; mettere avanti (clock)

■ **put in** vt (insert) introdurre; (submit) presentare ● vi ~ **in for** far domanda di

■ **put off** vt spegnere (light); (postpone) rimandare; **~ sb off** tenere a bada qcno; (*deter*) smontare qcno; (*disconcert*) distrarre qcno; **~ sb off sth** (*disgust*) disgustare qcno di qcsa ∎ **put on** *vt* mettersi ‹*clothes*›; mettere ‹*brake*›; *Culin* mettere su; accendere ‹*light*›; mettere in scena ‹*play*›; prendere ‹*accent*›; **~ on weight** mettere su qualche chilo; **he's just ~ting it on** è solo una messa in scena ∎ **put on to** *vt* (*help find*) indicare ‹*doctor, restaurant etc*› ∎ **put out** *vt* spegnere ‹*fire, light*›; tendere ‹*hand*›; (*inconvenience*) creare degli inconvenienti a ∎ **put through** *vt* far passare; *Teleph* **I'll ~ you through to him** glielo passo ∎ **put to** *vt* **~ sb to trouble** scomodare qcno; **I ~ it to you that…** ritengo che… ∎ **put together** *vt* montare ‹*machine*›; fare ‹*model, jigsaw*› ∎ **put up** *vt* alzare; erigere ‹*building*›; montare ‹*tent*›; aprire ‹*umbrella*›; affiggere ‹*notice*›; aumentare ‹*price*›; ospitare ‹*guest*›; **~ sb up to sth** mettere qcsa in testa a qcno ∎ *vi* (*at hotel*) stare; **~ up with** sopportare

putrefaction /pjuːtrɪˈfækʃn/ *n* putrefazione *f*
putrefy /ˈpjuːtrɪfaɪ/ *vi* (*pt/pp* **-ied**) putrefarsi
putrid /ˈpjuːtrɪd/ *a* putrido
putt /pʌt/ *n* putt *m inv* ∎ *vi* colpire leggermente
putty /ˈpʌtɪ/ *n* mastice *m*
put-up job *n fam* truffa *f*
puzzle /ˈpʌzl/ *n* enigma *m*; (*jigsaw*) puzzle *m inv* ∎ *vt* lasciare perplesso ∎ *vi* **~ over** scervellarsi su
∎ **puzzle out** *vt* trovare ‹*solution*›
puzzling /ˈpʌzlɪŋ/ *a* inspiegabile
pvc *n* PVC *m* ∎ *attrib* di PVC
pygmy /ˈpɪgmɪ/ *n* pigmeo, -a *mf*
pyjamas /pəˈdʒɑːməz/ *npl* pigiama *msg*
pylon /ˈpaɪlən/ *n* pilone *m*
pyramid /ˈpɪrəmɪd/ *n* piramide *f*
pyre /paɪə(r)/ *n* pira *f*
pyrex® /ˈpaɪreks/ *n* Pyrex *m*
pyromaniac /paɪrəˈmeɪnɪæk/ *n* piromane *mf*
pyrotechnics /paɪrəˈtekniks/ *n* (*display*) fuochi *mpl* pirotecnici
python /ˈpaɪθn/ *n* pitone *m*

Qq

q, Q /kjuː/ *n* (*letter*) q, Q *f inv*
QC *n Br Jur* avvocato *m* di rango superiore
QED *abbr* (**quod erat demonstrandum**) qed
quack[1] /kwæk/ *n* qua qua *m inv* ∎ *vi* fare qua qua
quack[2] *n* (*doctor*) ciarlatano *m*
quad /kwɒd/ *n* (*fam: court*) = **quadrangle**; **~s** *pl fam* = **quadruplets**
quadrangle /ˈkwɒdræŋgl/ *n* quadrangolo *m*; (*court*) cortile *m* quadrangolare
quadratic equation /kwɒˈdrætɪk/ *n* equazione *f* di secondo grado
quadriplegic /kwɒdrɪˈpliːdʒɪk/ *a* quadriplegico
quadruped /ˈkwɒdruped/ *n* quadrupede *m*
quadruple /ˈkwɒdrupl/ *a* quadruplo ∎ *vt* quadruplicare ∎ *vi* quadruplicarsi
quadruplets /kwɒdˈruːplɪts/ *npl* quattro gemelli *mpl*
quadruplicate /kwɒdˈruːplɪkət/ *n* **in ~** quattro copie
quagmire /ˈkwɒgmaɪə(r)/ *n* pantano *m*
quail /kweɪl/ *vi* farsi prendere dalla paura
quaint /kweɪnt/ *a* pittoresco; (*odd*) bizzarro
quake /kweɪk/ *n fam* terremoto *m* ∎ *vi* tremare
Quaker /ˈkweɪkə(r)/ *n* quacchero, -a *mf*
qualification /kwɒlɪfɪˈkeɪʃn/ *n* qualifica *f*; (*reservation*) riserva *f*

qualified /ˈkwɒlɪfaɪd/ *a* qualificato; (*limited*) con riserva
qualifier /ˈkwɒlɪfaɪə(r)/ *n Sport* concorrente *mf* qualificato, -a
qualify /ˈkwɒlɪfaɪ/ *v* (*pt/pp* **-ied**) ∎ *vt* ‹*course:*› dare la qualifica a (**as** di); (*entitle*) dare diritto a; (*limit*) precisare ∎ *vi* ottenere la qualifica; *Sport* qualificarsi
qualitative /ˈkwɒlɪtətɪv/ *a* qualitativo
quality /ˈkwɒlətɪ/ *n* qualità *f inv*
quality: quality assurance *n* verifica *f* qualità. **quality control** *n* controllo *m* [di] qualità. **quality controller** *n* addetto, -a *mf* al controllo di qualità
qualm /kwɑːm/ *n* scrupolo *m*
quandary /ˈkwɒndərɪ/ *n* dilemma *m*
quango /ˈkwæŋgəʊ/ *n Br* organismo *m* autonomo, ma finanziato dal governo
quantifiable /ˈkwɒntɪfaɪəbl/ *a* quantificabile
quantitative /ˈkwɒntɪtətɪv/ *a* quantitativo
quantity /ˈkwɒntətɪ/ *n* quantità *f inv*; **in ~** in grande quantità
quantity surveyor *n* geometra *mf* che calcola quantità e costo di materiali da costruzione
quantum leap /kwɒntəmˈliːp/ *n fig* balzo *m* in avanti
quantum mechanics *n* meccanica *f* quantistica
quarantine /ˈkwɒrəntiːn/ *n* quarantena *f*

quarrel /'kwɒrəl/ n lite f ● vi (pt/pp **quarrelled**) litigare

quarrelsome /'kwɒrəlsəm/ a litigioso

quarry¹ /'kwɒrɪ/ n (prey) preda f

quarry² n cava f

quart /kwɔ:t/ n = 1.14 litro

quarter /'kwɔ:tə(r)/ n quarto m; (of year) trimestre m; Am 25 centesimi mpl; **~s** pl Mil quartiere msg; **at [a] ~ to six** alle sei meno un quarto; **from all ~s** da tutti i lati ● vt dividere in quattro

quarterdeck /'kwɔ:tədek/ n Naut cassero m

quarter-final n quarto m di finale

quarterly /'kwɔ:təlɪ/ a trimestrale ● adv trimestralmente

quartermaster /'kwɔ:təmɑ:stə(r)/ n (in navy) timoniere m; (in army) furiere m

quartet /kwɔ:'tet/ n quartetto m

quartz /kwɔ:ts/ n quarzo m; **~ watch** orologio m al quarzo

quash /kwɒʃ/ vt annullare; soffocare ‹rebellion›

quasi+ /'kweɪzaɪ/ pref semi+

quaver /'kweɪvə(r)/ n Mus croma f ● vi tremolare

quay /ki:/ n banchina f

queasiness /'kwi:zɪnɪs/ n nausea f

queasy /'kwi:zɪ/ a **I feel ~** ho la nausea

Quebec /kwɪ'bek/ n (province) Quebec m; (town) Quebec f

queen /kwi:n/ n regina f

queen bee n ape f regina; **she thinks she's the ~** ~ fig si crede chissà chi

queenly /'kwi:nlɪ/ a da regina

queen mother n regina f madre

Queen: Queen's Counsel n Br Jur avvocato m di rango superiore. **Queen's English** n Br **speak the ~** ~ parlare un inglese corretto e senza accento. **Queen's evidence** n Br Jur **turn ~** ~ deporre contro i propri complici. **Queen's Regulations** npl Br Mil codice m militare

queer /kwɪə(r)/ a strano; (dubious) sospetto; (fam: homosexual) finocchio ● n fam finocchio m

quell /kwel/ vt reprimere

quench /kwentʃ/ vt **~ one's thirst** dissetarsi

query /'kwɪərɪ/ n domanda f; (question mark) punto m interrogativo ● vt (pt/pp -**ied**) interrogare; (doubt) mettere in dubbio

quest /kwest/ n ricerca f (**for** di)

question /'kwestʃən/ n domanda f; (for discussion) questione f; **out of the ~** fuori discussione; **without ~** senza dubbio; **in ~** in questione ● vt interrogare; (doubt) mettere in dubbio

questionable /'kwestʃ(ə)nəbl/ a discutibile

questioner /'kwestʃ(ə)nə(r)/ n interrogante mf

questioning /'kwestʃ(ə)nɪŋ/ n (of person) interrogatorio m; (of criteria) messa f in discussione ● a ‹look, tone› inquisitorio

question mark n punto m interrogativo

question master n presentatore, -trice mf di quiz

questionnaire /kwestʃə'neə(r)/ n questionario m

question tag n domanda f di conferma

queue /kju:/ n coda f, fila f ● vi ~ [**up**] mettersi in coda (**for** per)

queue-jump vi Br passare davanti alle altre persone in coda

quibble /'kwɪbl/ vi cavillare

quick /kwɪk/ a veloce; **be ~!** sbrigati!; **have a ~ meal** fare uno spuntino ● adv in fretta ● n **be cut to the ~** fig essere punto sul vivo

quick: quick-assembly a facile da montare. **quick-fire** a ‹questions› a mitraglia. **quick-freeze** vt surgelare

quickie /'kwɪkɪ/ n fam (question) domanda f rapida; (drink) bicchierino m rapido; (film) cortometraggio m

quicklime /'kwɪklaɪm/ n calce f viva

quickly /'kwɪklɪ/ adv in fretta

quick: quicksand n sabbie fpl mobili. **quick-setting** /-'setɪŋ/ a a presa rapida. **quicksilver** n Chem argento m vivo, mercurio m. **quick-tempered** /-'tempəd/ a collerico. **quick-witted** /-'wɪtɪd/ a ‹reaction› pronto; ‹person› sveglio

quid /kwɪd/ n inv fam sterlina f

quid pro quo /kwɪdprəʊ'kwəʊ/ n contraccambio m

quiet /'kwaɪət/ a (calm) tranquillo; (silent) silenzioso; (voice, music) basso; **keep ~ about** fam non raccontare a nessuno ● n quiete f; **on the ~** di nascosto

quieten /'kwaɪətn/ vt calmare

■ **quieten down** vt calmare ● vi calmarsi

quietly /'kwaɪətlɪ/ adv (peacefully) tranquillamente; ‹say› a bassa voce

quietness /'kwaɪətnɪs/ n quiete f

quiff /kwɪf/ n (Br: hair) ciocca f

quill /kwɪl/ n penna f d'uccello; (spine) spina f

quilt /kwɪlt/ n piumino m

quilted /'kwɪltɪd/ a trapuntato

quilting /'kwɪltɪŋ/ n (fabric) matelassé m inv

quince /kwɪns/ n cotogna f; (tree) melo m cotogno

quinine /'kwɪni:n/ n chinino m

quins /kwɪnz/ npl fam = **quintuplets**

quintessential /kwɪntɪ'senʃl/ a ‹quality› fondamentale

quintet /kwɪn'tet/ n quintetto m

quintuple /'kwɪntjʊpl/ vt quintuplicare ● a quintuplo

quintuplets /'kwɪntjʊplɪts/ npl cinque gemelli mpl

quip /kwɪp/ n battuta f ● vt (pt/pp **quipped**) dire scherzando

quirk /kwɜ:k/ n stranezza f

quisling /'kwɪzlɪŋ/ n pej collaborazionista mf

quit /kwɪt/ v (pt/pp **quitted** or **quit**) ● vt lasciare; (give up) smettere (**doing** di fare); Comput uscire da ● vi (fam: resign) andarsene; *Comput* uscire; **give sb notice to** ~ dare a qcno preavviso di sfratto

quite /kwaɪt/ *adv* (*fairly*) abbastanza; (*completely*) completamente; (*really*) veramente; ~ **[so]!** proprio così!; ~ **a few** parecchi

quits /kwɪts/ *a* pari

quiver /'kwɪvə(r)/ *vi* tremare

quiz /kwɪz/ *n* (*game*) quiz *m inv* ● *vt* (*pt/pp* **quizzed**) interrogare

quiz game, quiz show *n* quiz *m inv*

quizzical /'kwɪzɪkl/ *a* sardonico

quoit /kwɔɪt/ *n* anello *m* (*del gioco*)

quoits *n* (*game*) gioco *m* degli anelli

quorum /'kwɔːrəm/ *n* quorum *m inv*; **have a** ~ avere il quorum

quota /'kwəʊtə/ *n* quota *f*

quotation /kwəʊ'teɪʃn/ *n* citazione *f*; (*price*) preventivo *m*; (*of shares*) quota *f*

quotation marks *npl* virgolette *fpl*

quote /kwəʊt/ *n fam* = **quotation; in** ~**s** tra virgolette ● *vt* citare; quotare (*price*); ~**d on the Stock Exchange** quotato in Borsa

---

Rr

---

r, R /ɑ:(r)/ *n a* (*letter*) r, R *f inv*; **the three Rs** leggere, scrivere e contare

R *n Br abbr* (**regina**) regina *f*

rabbi /'ræbaɪ/ *n* rabbino *m*; (*title*) rabbi

rabbit /'ræbɪt/ *n* coniglio *m*

■ **rabbit on** *vi fam* **what's he** ~**ting on about now?** cosa sta blaterando?

rabbit hutch *n* conigliera *f*

rabble /'ræbl/ *n* **the** ~ la plebaglia

rabble rouser /raʊʒə(r)/ *n* agitatore, -trice *nmf*

rabble rousing *n* incitazione *f* alla violenza

rabid /'ræbɪd/ *a fig* rabbioso

rabies /'reɪbiːz/ *n* rabbia *f*

raccoon /rə'kuːn/ *n* procione *m*, orsetto *m* lavatore

race[1] /reɪs/ *n* (*people*) razza *f*

race[2] *n* corsa *f* ● *vi* correre ● *vt* gareggiare con; fare correre ⟨*horse*⟩

racecourse /'reɪskɔːs/ *n* ippodromo *m*

racehorse /'reɪshɔːs/ *n* cavallo *m* da corsa

racer /'reɪsə(r)/ *n* (*bike*) bicicletta *f* da corsa; (*motorbike*) motocicletta *f* da corsa; (*car*) automobile *f* da corsa; (*runner, cyclist etc*) corridore, -trice *mf*

race relations *npl* rapporti *mpl* tra le razze

race riots *npl* scontri *mpl* razziali

racetrack /'reɪstræk/ *n* pista *f*

racial /'reɪʃl/ *a* razziale

racialism /'reɪʃəlɪzm/ *n* razzismo *m*

racially /'reɪʃ(ə)lɪ/ *adv* razzialmente

racing /'reɪsɪŋ/ *n* corse *fpl*; (*horse-*~) corse *fpl* dei cavalli

racing car *n* macchina *f* da corsa

racing driver *n* corridore *m* automobilistico

racism /'reɪsɪzm/ *n* razzismo *m*

racist /'reɪsɪst/ *a & n* razzista *mf*

rack[1] /ræk/ *n* (*for bikes*) rastrelliera *f*; (*for luggage*) portabagagli *m inv*; (*for plates*)

scolapiatti *m inv* ● *vt* ~ **one's brains** scervellarsi

rack[2] *n* **go to** ~ **and ruin** andare in rovina

racket[1] /'rækɪt/ *n Sport* racchetta *f*

racket[2] *n* (*din*) chiasso *m*; (*swindle*) truffa *f*; (*crime*) racket *m inv*, giro *m*

racketeer /rækɪ'tɪə(r)/ *n* trafficante *m*

racketeering /rækɪ'tɪərɪŋ/ *n* traffici *mpl* illeciti

racking /'rækɪŋ/ *a* ⟨*pain*⟩ atroce

raconteur /'rækɪt/ *n* bravo narratore *m*, brava narratrice *f*

racy /'reɪsɪ/ *a* (**-ier, -iest**) vivace; (*risqué*) osé *inv*, spinto

radar /'reɪdɑ:(r)/ *n* radar *m*

radar trap *n Auto* tratto *m* di strada sul quale la polizia controlla la velocità dei veicoli

radial /'reɪdɪəl/ *n* (*tyre*) [pneumatico *m*] radiale *m* ● *a* ⟨*lines, roads*⟩ radiale

radiance /'reɪdɪəns/ *n* radiosità *f*

radiant /'reɪdɪənt/ *a* raggiante

radiate /'reɪdɪeɪt/ *vt* irradiare ● *vi* ⟨*heat:*⟩ irradiarsi; ⟨*roads:*⟩ partire

radiation /reɪdɪ'eɪʃn/ *n* radiazione *f*

radiator /'reɪdɪeɪtə(r)/ *n* radiatore *m*

radical /'rædɪkl/ *a & n* radicale *mf*

radicalism /'rædɪkəlɪzm/ *n* radicalismo *m*

radically /'rædɪklɪ/ *adv* radicalmente

radio /'reɪdɪəʊ/ *n* radio *f inv* ● *vt* mandare via radio ⟨*message*⟩

radioactive /reɪdɪəʊ'æktɪv/ *a* radioattivo

radioactive waste *n* scorie *fpl* radioattive

radioactivity /reɪdɪəʊæk'tɪvətɪ/ *n* radioattività *f*

radio cassette player *n* radioregistratore *m*

radio-controlled *a* radiocomandato

radiographer /reɪdɪ'ɒgrəfə(r)/ *n* radiologo, -a *mf*

radiography /reɪdɪ'ɒgrəfɪ/ *n* radiografia *f*

radio ham *n* radioamatore, -trice *mf*

radiologist /ˌreɪdɪˈɒlədʒɪst/ *n* radiologo, -a *mf*

radiotherapy /ˌreɪdɪəʊˈθerəpɪ/ *n* radioterapia *f*

radish /ˈrædɪʃ/ *n* ravanello *m*

radius /ˈreɪdɪəs/ *n* (*pl* **-dii** /ˈreɪdɪaɪ/) raggio *m*

raffle /ˈræfl/ *n* lotteria *f* ● *vt* mettere in palio

raft /rɑːft/ *n* zattera *f*

rafter /ˈrɑːftə(r)/ *n* trave *f*

rag¹ /ræg/ *n* straccio *m*; (*pej: newspaper*) giornalaccio *m*; **in ~s** stracciato

rag² *vt* (*pt/pp* **ragged**) *fam* fare scherzi a ● *n Univ festa f di beneficenza organizzata da studenti universitari*

ragamuffin /ˈrægəmʌfɪn/ *n* monellaccio *m*

rag-and-bone man *n Br* rigattiere *m*, straccivendolo *m*

ragbag /ˈrægbæg/ *n fig* accozzaglia *f*

rage /reɪdʒ/ *n* rabbia *f*; **all the ~** *fam* all'ultima moda ● *vi* infuriarsi; ‹*storm:*› infuriare; ‹*epidemic:*› imperversare

ragged /ˈrægɪd/ *a* logoro; ‹*edge*› frastagliato

raging /ˈreɪdʒɪŋ/ *a* ‹*blizzard, sea*› furioso; ‹*thirst, pain*› atroce; ‹*passion, argument*› acceso

raglan /ˈræglən/ *a* raglan *inv* ● *n* manica *f* raglan

rag trade *n fam* settore *m* dell'abbigliamento

rag week *n Br Univ settimana f di manifestazioni a scopo benefico organizzate dagli studenti*

raid /reɪd/ *n* (*by thieves*) rapina *f*; *Mil* incursione *f*, raid *m inv*; (*by police*) irruzione *f* ● *vt Mil* fare un'incursione in; ‹*police, thieves:*› fare irruzione in

raider /ˈreɪdə(r)/ *n* (*of bank*) rapinatore, -trice *mf*

rail¹ /reɪl/ *n* ringhiera *f*; *Rail* rotaia *f*; *Naut* parapetto *m*; **by ~** per ferrovia

rail² *vi* **~ against** *or* **at** inveire contro

railcard /ˈreɪlkɑːd/ *n* tessera *f* di riduzione ferroviaria

railings /ˈreɪlɪŋz/ *npl* ringhiera *f*

railroad /ˈreɪlrəʊd/ *n Am* = **railway** ● *vt* **~ sb into doing sth** spingere qcno a fare qcsa

railroad schedule *n Am* orario *m* ferroviario

rail traffic *n* traffico *m* ferroviario

railway /ˈreɪlweɪ/ *n* ferrovia *f*

railwayman /ˈreɪlweɪmən/ *n* ferroviere *m*

railway station *n* stazione *f* ferroviaria

rain /reɪn/ *n* pioggia *f* ● *vi* piovere; **~ down on sb** *fig* piovere addosso a qcno ● *vt* **~ blows on sb** tempestare qcno di colpi

■ **rain off** *vt* **be ~ed off** essere annullato a causa della pioggia

rain: rainbow *n* arcobaleno *m*. **raincheck** *n Am* **can I take a ~?** facciamo un'altra volta. **raincoat** *n* impermeabile *m*. **raindrop** *n* goccia *f* di pioggia. **rainfall** *n* precipitazione *f* [atmosferica]. **rainforest** *n* foresta *f* pluviale, foresta *f* equatoriale. **rainstorm** *n* temporale *m*. **rain water** *n* acqua *f* piovana

rainy /ˈreɪnɪ/ *a* (**-ier, -iest**) piovoso

rainy day *n* **save sth for a ~** *fig* mettere qcsa in serbo per i tempi di magra

raise /reɪz/ *n Am* aumento *m* ● *vt* alzare; levarsi ‹*hat*›; allevare ‹*children, animals*›; sollevare ‹*question*›; ottenere ‹*money*›; **~ hell** indiavolarsi; **~ a laugh** ‹*joke, remark:*› far ridere; **~ the stakes** rilanciare; **~ one's voice** alzare la voce

raisin /ˈreɪzn/ *n* uvetta *f*; **~s** *pl* uvetta *f*, uva *f* passa

Raj /rɑːʒ/ *n* governo *m* britannico in India

rake /reɪk/ *n* rastrello *m* ● *vt* rastrellare

■ **rake in** *vt fam* farsi ‹*profits, money*›; **he's raking it in** sta facendo un sacco di soldi

■ **rake together** *vt fig* racimolare ‹*money*›

■ **rake up** *vt* raccogliere col rastrello; *fam* rivangare

rake-off *n fam* parte *f*

rakish /ˈreɪkɪʃ/ *a* (*dissolute*) dissoluto; (*jaunty*) disinvolto

rally /ˈrælɪ/ *n* raduno *m*; *Auto* rally *m inv*; (*Tennis*) scambio *m*; (*recovery*) ripresa *f* ● *v* (*pt/pp* **-ied**) ● *vt* radunare ● *vi* radunarsi; (*recover strength*) riprendersi

RAM /ræm/ *n* memoria *f* RAM

ram /ræm/ *n* montone *m*; *Astr* Ariete *m* ● *vt* (*pt/pp* **rammed**) cozzare contro

ramble /ˈræmbl/ *n* escursione *f* ● *vi* gironzolare; (*in speech*) divagare

■ **ramble on** *vi fam* parlare/scrivere a ruota libera

rambler /ˈræmblə(r)/ *n* escursionista *mf*; (*rose*) rosa *f* rampicante

rambling /ˈræmblɪŋ/ *a* (*in speech*) sconnesso; ‹*club*› escursionistico

ramification /ˌræmɪfɪˈkeɪʃən/ *n* ramificazione *f*

ramify /ˈræmɪfaɪ/ *vi* (*pt/pp* **-ied**) ramificarsi

ramp /ræmp/ *n* rampa *f*; *Auto* dosso *m*

rampage /ˈræmpeɪdʒ/ *n* **be/go on the ~** scatenarsi ● *vi* **~ through the streets** scatenarsi per le strade

rampant /ˈræmpənt/ *a* dilagante; (*in heraldry*) rampante

rampart /ˈræmpɑːt/ *n* bastione *f*

ramshackle /ˈræmʃækl/ *a* sgangherato

ran /ræn/ *see* **run**

ranch /rɑːntʃ/ *n* ranch *m inv*

rancher /ˈrɑːntʃə(r)/ *n* (*worker*) cow-boy *m inv*; (*owner*) proprietario *m* di ranch

rancid /ˈrænsɪd/ *a* rancido

rancour /ˈræŋkə(r)/ *n* rancore *m*

R&B *n* rhythm and blues *m*

R&D *n* ricerca *f* e sviluppo *m*

random /ˈrændəm/ *a* casuale; **~ sample** campione *m* a caso ● *n* **at ~** a casaccio

random-access *a* ad accesso casuale

random-access memory *n* memoria *f* viva

randy /ˈrændɪ/ *a* (**-ier, -iest**) *fam* eccitato

rang /ræŋ/ *see* **ring²**

range /reɪndʒ/ *n* serie *f*; *Comm, Mus* gamma *f*; (*of mountains*) catena *f*; (*distance*) raggio *m*;

(*for shooting*) portata *f*; (*stove*) cucina *f* economica; **at a ~ of** a una distanza di ● *vi* estendersi; **~ from... to...** andare da... la...

ranger /'reɪndʒə(r)/ *n* guardia *f* forestale

rank¹ /ræŋk/ *n* (*row*) riga *f*; *Mil* grado *m*; (*social position*) rango *m*; **the ~ and file** la base; **the ~s** *pl Mil* i soldati *mpl* semplici ● *vt* (*place*) annoverare (**among** tra) ● *vi* (*be placed*) collocarsi

rank² *a* ⟨*smell*⟩ puzzolente; ⟨*plants*⟩ rigoglioso; *fig* vero e proprio

rankle /'ræŋkl/ *vi fig* bruciare; **it still ~s with him** gli brucia ancora

ransack /'rænsæk/ *vt* rovistare; (*pillage*) saccheggiare

ransom /'rænsəm/ *n* riscatto *m*; **hold sb to ~** tenere qcno in ostaggio per il riscatto

rant /rænt/ *vi* **~** [**and rave**] inveire; **what's he ~ing on about?** cosa sta blaterando?

rap /ræp/ *n* colpo *m* secco; *Mus* rap *m* ● *v* (*pt/ pp* **rapped**) ● *vt* dare colpetti a; **~ sb over the knuckles** *fig* dare una tirata d'orecchie a qcno ● *vi* **~ at** bussare a

rape¹ /reɪp/ *n Bot* colza *f*

rape² *n* (*sexual*) stupro *m* ● *vt* violentare, stuprare

rape[seed] oil /'reɪp[si:d]/ *n* olio *m* [di semi] di colza

rapid /'ræpɪd/ *a* rapido

rapidity /rə'pɪdətɪ/ *n* rapidità *f*

rapidly /'ræpɪdlɪ/ *adv* rapidamente

rapids /'ræpɪdz/ *npl* rapida *fsg*

rapist /'reɪpɪst/ *n* violentatore *m*

rapper /'ræpə(r)/ *n* (*Br: door-knocker*) battiporta *m inv*; *Mus* rapper *mf inv*

rapport /ræ'pɔ:(r)/ *n* rapporto *m* di intesa

rapt /ræpt/ *a* ⟨*look*⟩ rapito; **~ in** assorto in

rapturous /'ræptʃərəs/ *a* entusiastico

rapturously /'ræptʃərəslɪ/ *adv* entusiasticamente

rapture /'ræptʃə(r)/ *n* estasi *f*

rare¹ /reə(r)/ *a* raro

rare² *a Culin* al sangue

rarefied /'reərɪfaɪd/ *a* rarefatto

rarely /'reəlɪ/ *adv* raramente

raring /'reərɪŋ/ *a fam* **be ~ to** non vedere l'ora di

rarity /'reərətɪ/ *n* rarità *f inv*

rascal /'rɑ:skl/ *n* mascalzone *m*

rash¹ /ræʃ/ *n Med* eruzione *f*

rash² *a* avventato

rasher /'ræʃə(r)/ *n* fetta *f* di pancetta

rashly /'ræʃlɪ/ *adv* avventatamente

rashness /'ræʃnɪs/ *n* avventatezza *f*

rasp /rɑ:sp/ *n* (*noise*) stridio *m*

raspberry /'rɑ:zbərɪ/ *n* lampone *m*

rasping /'rɑ:spɪŋ/ *a* stridente

rat /ræt/ *n* topo *m*; (*fam: person*) carogna *f*; **smell a ~** *fam* sentire puzzo di bruciato ● *vi* (*pt/pp* **ratted**) *fam* **~ on** far la spia a

rat-a-tat-tat /rætətæ(t)'tæt/ *n* toc toc *m inv*

rat-catcher *n* addetto, -a *mf* alla derattizzazione

ratchet /'rætʃɪt/ *n* (*toothed rack*) cremagliera *f*

rate /reɪt/ *n* (*speed*) velocità *f inv*; (*of payment*) tariffa *f*; (*of exchange*) tasso *m*; **~s** *pl* (*taxes*) imposte *fpl* comunali sui beni immobili; **at any ~** in ogni caso; **at this ~** di questo passo ● *vt* stimare; **~ among** annoverare tra ● *vi* **~ as** essere considerato

ratepayer /'reɪtpeɪə(r)/ *n* contribuente *mf*

rather /'rɑ:ðə(r)/ *adv* piuttosto; **~!** eccome!; **~ too...** un po' troppo...

ratification /rætɪfɪ'keɪʃn/ *n* ratifica *f*

ratify /'rætɪfaɪ/ *vt* (*pt/pp* **-ied**) ratificare

rating /'reɪtɪŋ/ *n* valutazione *f*; (*class*) livello *m*; (*sailor*) marinaio *m* semplice; **~s** *pl Radio, TV* indice *m* d'ascolto, audience *f inv*

ratio /'reɪʃɪəʊ/ *n* rapporto *m*; **in a ~ of two to one** in [un] rapporto di due a uno

ration /'ræʃn/ *n* razione *f* ● *vt* razionare

rational /'ræʃənl/ *a* razionale

rationale /ræʃə'nɑ:l/ *n* (*logic*) base *f* logica; (*reasons*) ragioni *fpl*

rationalize /'ræʃ(ə)nəlaɪz/ *vt/i* razionalizzare

rationally /'ræʃ(ə)nəlɪ/ *adv* razionalmente

rationing /'ræʃ(ə)nɪŋ/ *n* razionamento *m*

rat race *n fam* corsa *f* al successo

rattan /rə'tæn/ *n* (*tree, material*) malacca *f*

rattle /'rætl/ *n* tintinnio *m*; (*toy*) sonaglio *m* ● *vi* tintinnare ● *vt* (*shake*) scuotere; *fam* innervosire

■ **rattle off** *vt fam* sciorinare

■ **rattle on** *vi* (*talk at length*) parlare ininterrottamente

■ **rattle through** *vt* (*say quickly*) dire velocemente; (*do quickly*) fare velocemente

rattlesnake /'rætlsneɪk/ *n* serpente *m* a sonagli

ratty /'rætɪ/ *a* (*Br fam: grumpy*) irascibile; ⟨*Am: hair*⟩ sudicio

raucous /'rɔ:kəs/ *a* rauco

raunchy /'rɔ:ntʃɪ/ *a fam* ⟨*performer, voice, song*⟩ sexy *inv*; (*bawdy*) spinto

ravage /'rævɪdʒ/ *vt* devastare

ravages /'rævɪdʒɪz/ *npl* danni *mpl*

rave /reɪv/ *vi* vaneggiare; **~ about** andare in estasi per

raven /'reɪvn/ *n* corvo *m* imperiale

ravenous /'rævənəs/ *a* ⟨*person*⟩ affamato

rave-up *n Br fam* festa *f* animata

ravine /rə'vi:n/ *n* gola *f*

raving /'reɪvɪŋ/ *a* **~ mad** *fam* matto da legare

ravings /'reɪvɪŋz/ *npl* vaneggiamenti *mpl*

ravioli /rævɪ'əʊlɪ/ *n* ravioli *mpl*

ravishing /'rævɪʃɪŋ/ *a* incantevole

raw /rɔ:/ *a* crudo; (*not processed*) grezzo; ⟨*weather*⟩ gelido; (*inexperienced*) inesperto

raw deal *n* **get a ~ ~** *fam* farsi fregare

rawhide *n* (*leather*) cuoio *m* grezzo

Rawlplug® /'rɔ:lplʌg/ *n* tassello *m*

raw materials *npl* materie *fpl* prime

ray /reɪ/ *n* raggio *m*; **~ of hope** barlume *m* di speranza

rayon® /'reɪɒn/ *n* raion® *m*

raze /reɪz/ *vt* **~ to the ground** radere al suolo

razor /'reɪzə(r)/ *n* rasoio *m*

razor blade *n* lametta *f* da barba
razor-sharp *a* affilatissimo
razzle /'ræzl/ *n Br fam* **go on the ~** andare a fare baldoria
razzle-dazzle *n fam* baldoria *f*
razzmatazz /ræzmə'tæz/ *n fam* clamore *m*
RC *n* (**Roman Catholic**) cattolico, -a *mf* ● *a* cattolico
re /ri:/ *prep* con riferimento a
reach /ri:tʃ/ *n* portata *f*; (*of river*) tratto *m*; **within ~** a portata di mano; **out of ~ of** fuori dalla portata di; **within easy ~** facilmente raggiungibile ● *vt* arrivare a ‹*place, decision*›; (*contact*) contattare; (*pass*) passare; **I can't ~ it** non ci arrivo ● *vi* arrivare (**to** a); **I can't ~** non ci arrivo; **~ for** allungare la mano per prendere
react /rɪ'ækt/ *vi* reagire
reaction /rɪ'ækʃn/ *n* reazione *f*
reactionary /rɪ'ækʃ(ə)nərɪ/ *a & n* reazionario, -a *mf*
reactor /rɪ'æktə(r)/ *n* reattore *m*
read /ri:d/ *vt* (*pt/pp* read /red/) leggere; *Univ* studiare ● *vi* leggere; ‹*instrument:*› indicare
■ **read back** *vt* (*say aloud*) rileggere
■ **read on** *vi* (*continue reading*) continuare a leggere
■ **read out** *vt* leggere ad alta voce
■ **read up on** *vt* studiare a fondo
readable /'ri:dəbl/ *a* piacevole a leggersi; (*legible*) leggibile
reader /'ri:də(r)/ *n* lettore, -trice *mf*; (*book*) antologia *f*
readership /'ri:dəʃɪp/ *n* numero *m* di lettori
read head *n Comput* testina *f* di lettura
readily /'redɪlɪ/ *adv* volentieri; (*easily*) facilmente
readiness /'redɪnɪs/ *n* disponibilità *f*; **in ~** pronto
reading /'ri:dɪŋ/ *n* lettura *f*
readjust /ri:ə'dʒʌst/ *vt* regolare di nuovo ● *vi* riabituarsi (**to** a)
readjustment /ri:ə'dʒʌstmənt/ *n* riadattamento *m*
read-only memory *n Comput* memoria *f* di sola lettura
ready /'redɪ/ *a* (**-ier, -iest**) pronto; (*quick*) veloce; **get ~** prepararsi
ready: ready-made *a* confezionato. **ready-mixed** *a* già miscelato. **ready money** *n* contanti *mpl*. **ready-to-wear** *a* prêt-à-porter
reaffirm /ri:ə'fɜ:m/ *vt* riaffermare
reafforestation /ri:əfɒrɪ'steɪʃn/ *n* rimboschimento *m*
real /ri:l/ *a* vero; ‹*increase*› reale ● *adv Am fam* veramente
real estate *n* beni *mpl* immobili
realign /ri:ə'laɪn/ *vt* riallineare ● *vi fig* formare nuove alleanze
realignment /ri:ə'laɪnmənt/ *n Pol* formazione *f* di nuove alleanze; *Fin* riallineamento *m*
realism /'rɪəlɪzm/ *n* realismo *m*
realist /'rɪəlɪst/ *n* realista *mf*

realistic /rɪə'lɪstɪk/ *a* realistico
realistically /rɪə'lɪstɪklɪ/ *adv* realisticamente
reality /rɪ'ælətɪ/ *n* realtà *f inv*
realization /rɪəlaɪ'zeɪʃn/ *n* realizzazione *f*
realize /'rɪəlaɪz/ *vt* realizzare
real life *n* realtà *f*; **in ~ life** nella realtà
real-life *attrib* autentico
reallocate /ri:'æləkeɪt/ *vt* riassegnare
reallocation /ri:ælə'keɪʃn/ *n* riassegnazione *f*
really /'rɪəlɪ/ *adv* davvero
realm /relm/ *n* regno *m*
real time *n* tempo *m* reale; **in ~ ~** in tempo reale ● *a* in tempo reale
realtor /'rɪəltə(r)/ *n Am* agente *mf* immobiliare
realty /'rɪəltɪ/ *n Am* beni *mpl* immobili
reanimate /ri:'ænɪmeɪt/ *vt* rianimare
reap /ri:p/ *vt* mietere
reappear /ri:ə'pɪə(r)/ *vi* riapparire
reappearance /ri:ə'pɪərəns/ *n* ricomparsa *f*
reapply /ri:ə'plaɪ/ *vi* (*pt/pp* **-ied**) ripresentare domanda
reappoint /ri:ə'pɔɪnt/ *vt* riconfermare
reappraisal /ri:ə'preɪzl/ *n* riconsiderazione *f*
reappraise /ri:ə'preɪz/ *vt* riesaminare ‹*question, policy*›; rivalutare ‹*writer, work*›
rear¹ /rɪə(r)/ *a* posteriore; *Auto* di dietro
rear² *vt* allevare ● *vi* ~ [**up**] ‹*horse:*› impennarsi ● *n* **the ~** (*of building*) il retro; (*of bus, plane*) la parte posteriore; **from the ~** da dietro
rear end *n fam* didietro *m*
rearguard /'rɪəgɑ:d/ *n Mil, fig* retroguardia *f*
rear light *n* luce *f* posteriore
rearm /ri:'ɑ:m/ *vt* riarmare ● *vi* riarmarsi
rearmament /ri:'ɑ:məmənt/ *n* riarmo *m*
rearmost /'rɪəməʊst/ *a* ultimo; ‹*carriage*› di coda
rearrange /ri:ə'reɪndʒ/ *vt* cambiare la disposizione di
rear-view mirror *n Auto* specchietto *m* retrovisore
reason /'ri:zn/ *n* ragione *f*; **within ~** nei limiti del ragionevole; **listen to ~** ascoltare la ragione ● *vi* ragionare; **~ with** cercare di far ragionare
reasonable /'ri:znəbl/ *a* ragionevole
reasonably /'ri:znəblɪ/ *adv* (*in reasonable way, fairly*) ragionevolmente
reasoning /'ri:znɪŋ/ *n* ragionamento *m*
reassemble /ri:ə'semb(ə)l/ *vt* riassemblare
reassembly /ri:ə'semblɪ/ *n* riassemblaggio *m*
reassess /ri:ə'ses/ *vt* riesaminare ‹*problem, situation*›; riaccertare ‹*tax liability*›
reassessment /ri:ə'sesmənt/ *n* (*of situation*) riesame *m*; (*of tax*) nuovo accertamento *m*
reassurance /ri:ə'ʃʊərəns/ *n* rassicurazione *f*

reassure /riːəˈʃʊə(r)/ *vt* rassicurare; **~ sb of sth** rassicurare qcno su qcsa

reassuring /riːəˈʃʊərɪŋ/ *a* rassicurante

reawaken /riːəˈweɪkn/ *vt fig* risvegliare ⟨*interest*⟩

rebate /ˈriːbeɪt/ *n* rimborso *m*; (*discount*) deduzione *f*

rebel[1] /ˈrebl/ *n* ribelle *mf*

rebel[2] /rɪˈbel/ *vi* (*pt/pp* **rebelled**) ribellarsi

rebellion /rɪˈbeljən/ *n* ribellione *f*

rebellious /rɪˈbeljəs/ *a* ribelle

rebelliousness /rɪˈbeliːəsnɪs/ *n* spirito *m* di ribellione

rebirth /riːˈbɜːθ/ *n* rinascita *f*

reboot /riːˈbuːt/ *vt Comput* reinizializzare

reborn /riːˈbɔːn/ *a Relig* **be ~** rinascere; **be ~ as sth** rinascere come qcsa

rebound[1] /rɪˈbaʊnd/ *vi* rimbalzare; *fig* ricadere

rebound[2] /ˈriːbaʊnd/ *n* rimbalzo *m*

rebuff /rɪˈbʌf/ *n* rifiuto *m* ● *vt* respingere

rebuild /riːˈbɪld/ *vt* (*pt/pp* **-built**) ricostruire

rebuke /rɪˈbjuːk/ *n* rimprovero *m* ● *vt* rimproverare

rebut /rɪˈbʌt/ *vt* confutare

rebuttal /rɪˈbʌtl/ *n* rifiuto *m*

recalcitrant /rɪˈkælsɪtrənt/ *a fml* ricalcitrante

recalculate /riːˈkælkjʊleɪt/ *vt* ricalcolare

recall /rɪˈkɔːl/ *n* richiamo *m*; **beyond ~** irrevocabile ● *vt* richiamare; riconvocare ⟨*diplomat, parliament*⟩; (*remember*) rievocare

recant /rɪˈkænt/ *vi* abiurare

recap /ˈriːkæp/ *vt/i fam* = **recapitulate** ● *n* ricapitolazione *f*

recapitulate /riːkəˈpɪtjʊleɪt/ *vt/i* ricapitolare

recapture /riːˈkæptʃə(r)/ *vt* riconquistare; ricatturare ⟨*person, animal*⟩

recast /riːˈkɑːst/ *vt* rimaneggiare ⟨*text, plan*⟩; riformulare ⟨*sentence*⟩

recede /rɪˈsiːd/ *vi* allontanarsi

receding /rɪˈsiːdɪŋ/ *a* ⟨*forehead, chin*⟩ sfuggente; **have ~ hair** essere stempiato

receipt /rɪˈsiːt/ *n* ricevuta *f*; (*receiving*) ricezione *f*; **~s** *pl Comm* entrate *fpl*

receive /rɪˈsiːv/ *vt* ricevere

receiver /rɪˈsiːvə(r)/ *n Teleph* ricevitore *m*; *Radio, TV* apparecchio *m* ricevente; (*of stolen goods*) ricettatore, -trice *mf*

receivership /rɪˈsiːvəʃɪp/ *n Br* **go into ~** essere sottomesso all'amministrazione controllata

receiving end /rɪˈsiːvɪŋ/ *n* **be on the ~** essere dall'altro lato della barricata

recent /ˈriːsnt/ *a* recente

recently /ˈriːsəntlɪ/ *adv* recentemente

receptacle /rɪˈseptəkl/ *n* recipiente *m*

reception /rɪˈsepʃn/ *n* ricevimento *m*; (*welcome*) accoglienza *f*; *Radio* ricezione *f*; **~ [desk]** (*in hotel*) reception *f inv*

receptionist /rɪˈsepʃənɪst/ *n* persona *f* alla reception

receptive /rɪˈseptɪv/ *a* ricettivo

recess /rɪˈses/ *n* rientranza *f*; (*holiday*) vacanza *f*; *Am Sch* intervallo *m*

recession /rɪˈseʃn/ *n* recessione *f*

recharge /riːˈtʃɑːdʒ/ *vt* ricaricare

recidivism /rɪˈsɪdɪvɪzm/ *n* recidività *f*

recidivist /rɪˈsɪdɪvɪst/ *n* recidivo, -a *mf*

recipe /ˈresəpɪ/ *n* ricetta *f*

recipe book *n* libro *m* di ricette

recipient /rɪˈsɪpɪənt/ *n* (*of letter, parcel*) destinatario, -a *mf*; (*of money*) beneficiario, -a *mf*

reciprocal /rɪˈsɪprəkl/ *a* reciproco

reciprocate /rɪˈsɪprəkeɪt/ *vt* ricambiare

recital /rɪˈsaɪtl/ *n* recital *m inv*

recitation /resɪˈteɪʃn/ *n* recitazione *f*

recite /rɪˈsaɪt/ *vt* recitare; (*list*) elencare

reckless /ˈreklɪs/ *a* ⟨*action, decision*⟩ sconsiderato; **be a ~ driver** guidare in modo spericolato

recklessly /ˈreklɪslɪ/ *adv* in modo sconsiderato

recklessness /ˈreklɪsnɪs/ *n* sconsideratezza *f*

reckon /ˈrekən/ *vt* calcolare; (*consider*) pensare; **be ~ed** essere considerato

■ **reckon on, reckon with** *vt* fare i conti con

■ **reckon without** *vt* fare i conti senza

reclaim /rɪˈkleɪm/ *vt* reclamare; bonificare ⟨*land*⟩

recline /rɪˈklaɪn/ *vi* sdraiarsi

reclining /rɪˈklaɪnɪŋ/ *a* ⟨*seat*⟩ reclinabile

recluse /rɪˈkluːs/ *n* recluso, -a *mf*

reclusive /rɪˈkluːsɪv/ *a* solitario

recognition /rekəgˈnɪʃn/ *n* riconoscimento *m*; **in ~** come riconoscimento (**of** per); **beyond ~** irriconoscibile

recognize /ˈrekəgnaɪz/ *vt* riconoscere

recoil[1] /ˈriːkɔɪl/ *n* (*of gun*) rinculo *m*

recoil[2] /rɪˈkɔɪl/ *vi* (*in fear*) indietreggiare

recollect /rekəˈlekt/ *vt* ricordare

recollection /rekəˈlekʃn/ *n* ricordo *m*

recommence /riːkəˈmens/ *vt/i* ricominciare

recommend /rekəˈmend/ *vt* raccomandare

recommendation /rekəmenˈdeɪʃn/ *n* raccomandazione *f*

recommended retail price /rekəˈmendɪd/ *n Comm* prezzo *m* di vendita raccomandato

recompense /ˈrekəmpens/ *n* ricompensa *f* ● *vt* ricompensare

reconcile /ˈrekənsaɪl/ *vt* riconciliare; conciliare ⟨*facts*⟩; far quadrare ⟨*bank statement*⟩; **~ oneself to** rassegnarsi a

reconciliation /rekənsɪlɪˈeɪʃn/ *n* riconciliazione *f*

recondition /riːkənˈdɪʃn/ *vt* ripristinare; **~ed engine** motore *m* che ha subito riparazioni

reconnaissance /rɪˈkɒnɪsns/ *n Mil* ricognizione *f*; **on ~** in ricognizione

reconnoitre /rekəˈnɔɪtə(r)/ *vi* (*pres p* **-tring**) fare una ricognizione ● *vt* fare una ricognizione di

reconsider /ri:kən'sɪdə(r)/ *vt* riconsiderare

reconstruct /ri:kən'strʌkt/ *vt* ricostruire

reconstruction /ri:kən'strʌkʃn/ *n* ricostruzione *f*

reconvene /ri:kən'vi:n/ *vi* riunirsi nuovamente

record¹ /rɪ'kɔ:d/ *vt* registrare; (*make a note of*) annotare

record² /'rekɔ:d/ *n* (*file*) documentazione *f*; *Mus* disco *m*; *Sport* record *m inv*; **~s** *pl* (*files*) schedario *msg*; **keep a ~ of** tener nota di; **off the ~** in via ufficiosa; **have a [criminal] ~** avere la fedina penale sporca

record-breaker /'rekɔ:dbreɪkə(r)/ *n* **be a ~** battere un record

recorded delivery /rɪ'kɔ:dɪd/ *n* raccomandata *f*

recorder /rɪ'kɔ:də(r)/ *n Mus* flauto *m* dolce

recording /rɪ'kɔ:dɪŋ/ *n* registrazione *f*

recording studio *n* sala *f* di registrazione

record player *n* giradischi *m inv*

recount /rɪ'kaʊnt/ *vt* raccontare

re-count¹ /rɪ'kaʊnt/ *vt* ricontare

re-count² /'ri:kaʊnt/ *n Pol* nuovo conteggio *m*

recoup /rɪ'ku:p/ *vt* rifarsi di (*losses*)

recourse /rɪ'kɔ:s/ *n* **have ~ to** ricorrere a

recover /rɪ'kʌvə(r)/ *vt/i* recuperare

re-cover /ri:'kʌvə(r)/ *vt* rifoderare

recovery /rɪ'kʌvərɪ/ *n* recupero *m*; (*of health*) guarigione *f*

recreation /rekrɪ'eɪʃn/ *n* ricreazione *f*

recreational /rekrɪ'eɪʃənəl/ *a* ricreativo

recrimination /rɪkrɪmɪ'neɪʃn/ *n* recriminazione *f*

recruit /rɪ'kru:t/ *n Mil* recluta *f*; **new ~** (*member*) nuovo, -a adepto, -a *mf*; (*worker*) neoassunto, -a *mf* ● *vt* assumere (*staff*)

recruitment /rɪ'kru:tmənt/ *n* assunzione *f*

rectangle /'rektæŋgl/ *n* rettangolo *m*

rectangular /rek'tæŋgjʊlə(r)/ *a* rettangolare

rectify /'rektɪfaɪ/ *vt* (*pt/pp* **-ied**) rettificare

rector /'rektə(r)/ *n Univ* rettore *m*

rectory /'rektərɪ/ *n* presbiterio *m*

rectum /'rektəm/ *n* retto *m*

recuperate /rɪ'kju:pəreɪt/ *vi* ristabilirsi

recur /rɪ'kɜ:(r)/ *vi* (*pt/pp* **recurred**) ricorrere; (*illness:*) ripresentarsi

recurrence /rɪ'kʌrəns/ *n* ricorrenza *f*; (*of illness*) ricomparsa *f*

recurrent /rɪ'kʌrənt/ *a* ricorrente

recyclable /ri:'saɪkləbl/ *a* riciclabile

recycle /ri:'saɪkl/ *vt* riciclare; **~d paper** carta *f* riciclata

recycling /ri:'saɪklɪŋ/ *n* riciclaggio *m*

red /red/ *a* (**redder, reddest**) rosso ● *n* rosso *m*; **be in the ~** (*account:*) essere scoperto; (*person:*) avere il conto scoperto

red: **redbrick** *a Univ* di recente fondazione. **Red Cross** *n* Croce *f* rossa. **redcurrant** *n* ribes *m* rosso

redden /'redn/ *vt* arrossare ● *vi* arrossire

reddish /'redɪʃ/ *a* rossastro

redecorate /ri:'dekəreɪt/ *vt* (*paint*) ridipingere; (*wallpaper*) ritappezzare

redeem /rɪ'di:m/ *vt* (*Relig, from pawnshop*) riscattare; **~ing quality** unico aspetto *m* positivo

redefine /ri:dɪ'faɪn/ *vt* ridefinire

redemption /rɪ'dempʃn/ *n* riscatto *m*

redeploy /ri:dɪ'plɔɪ/ *vt* ridistribuire

red: **red-faced** *a also fig* paonazzo. **red-haired** /-'heəd/ *a* con i capelli rossi. **red-handed** /-'hændɪd/ *a* **catch sb ~** cogliere qcno con le mani nel sacco. **red herring** *n* diversione *f*. **red-hot** *a* rovente

redial /ri:'daɪəl/ *Teleph vt* ricomporre ● *vi* ricomporre il numero

redirect /ri:daɪ'rekt/ *vt* mandare al nuovo indirizzo (*letter*)

rediscover /ri:dɪ'skʌvə(r)/ *vt* riscoprire

redistribute /ri:dɪs'trɪbju:t/ *vt* ridistribuire

redistribution /ri:dɪstrɪ'bju:ʃn/ *n* ridistribuzione *f*

red-letter day *n* giorno *m* memorabile. **red light** *n Auto* semaforo *m* rosso; **go through a ~ ~** passare col rosso. **red light district** *n* quartiere *m* a luci rosse. **red meat** *n* carne *f* rossa

redness /'rednɪs/ *n* rossore *m*

redo /ri:'du:/ *vt* (*pt* **-did**, *pp* **-done**) rifare

redolent /'redələnt/ *a* profumato (**of** di)

redouble /ri:'dʌbl/ *vt* raddoppiare

redraft /ri:'drɑ:ft/ *vt* stendere nuovamente

redress /rɪ'dres/ *n* riparazione *f* ● *vt* ristabilire (*balance*)

red tape *n fam* burocrazia *f*

reduce /rɪ'dju:s/ *vt* ridurre; *Culin* far consumare

reductio ad absurdum /rɪdʌktɪəʊædæb-'sɜ:dəm/ *n* ragionamento *m* per assurdo

reduction /rɪ'dʌkʃn/ *n* riduzione *f*

redundancy /rɪ'dʌndənsɪ/ *n* licenziamento *m*; (*payment*) cassa *f* integrazione

redundant /rɪ'dʌndənt/ *a* superfluo; **make ~** licenziare; **be made ~** essere licenziato

reed /ri:d/ *n Bot* canna *f*

reedy /'ri:dɪ/ *a* (*voice, tone*) acuto

reef /ri:f/ *n* scogliera *f*

reefer /'ri:fə(r)/ *n* (*jacket*) giubbotto *m* a doppio petto; (*fam: dope*) spinello *m*

reef knot *n* nodo *m* piano

reek /ri:k/ *vi* puzzare (**of** di)

reel /ri:l/ *n* bobina *f* ● *vi* (*stagger*) vacillare

■ **reel off** *vt fig* snocciolare

re-elect *vt* rieleggere

re-election *n* rielezione *f*

re-emerge *vi* riemergere

re-emergence *n* ricomparsa *f*

re-enact /ri:ɪ'nækt/ *vt* ricostruire (*crime*); *Jur* rimettere in vigore; recitare nuovamente (*role*)

re-enter /ri:'entə(r)/ *vt* rientrare in

re-entry *n* (*of spacecraft*) rientro *m*

re-establish *vt* ristabilire, ripristinare

re-establishment *n* ripristino *m*

re-examination *n* riesame *m*

re-examine *vt* riesaminare

refectory /rɪ'fektərɪ/ *n* refettorio *m*; *Univ* mensa *f* universitaria

refer /rɪˈfɜː(r)/ v (pt/pp **referred**) ● vt rinviare ‹matter›; indirizzare ‹person› ● vi ~ **to** fare allusione a; ‹consult› rivolgersi a ‹book›; **are you ~ring to me?** alludi a me?

referee /refəˈriː/ n arbitro m; (for job) garante mf ● vt/i (pt/pp **refereed**) arbitrare

reference /ˈref(ə)rəns/ n riferimento m; (in book) nota f bibliografica; (for job) referenza f; Comm **'your ~'** 'riferimento'; **with ~ to** con riferimento a; **make [a] ~ to** fare riferimento a

reference: reference book n libro m di consultazione. **reference library** n biblioteca f per la consultazione. **reference number** n numero m di riferimento

referendum /refəˈrendəm/ n referendum m inv

referral /rɪˈfɜːrəl/ n (of matter, problem) deferimento m; Med (act) invio m di un paziente a un altro medico; ‹person› paziente mf mandato da un medico a un altro

refill¹ /riːˈfɪl/ vt riempire di nuovo; ricaricare ‹pen, lighter›

refill² /ˈriːfɪl/ n (for pen) ricambio m

refine /rɪˈfaɪn/ vt raffinare

refined /rɪˈfaɪnd/ a raffinato

refinement /rɪˈfaɪnmənt/ n raffinatezza f

refinery /rɪˈfaɪnərɪ/ n raffineria f

refining /rɪˈfaɪnɪŋ/ n Techn raffinazione f

refit¹ /ˈriːfɪt/ n Naut raddobbo m; (of shop, factory etc) rinnovo m

refit² /riːˈfɪt/ vt raddobbare ‹ship›; rinnovare ‹shop, factory etc›

reflate /riːˈfleɪt/ vt reflazionare ‹economy›

reflect /rɪˈflekt/ vt riflettere; **be ~ed in** essere riflesso in ● vi (think) riflettere (**on** su); ~ **badly on sb** fig mettere in cattiva luce qcno

reflection /rɪˈflekʃn/ n riflessione f; (image) riflesso m; **on ~** dopo riflessione

reflective /rɪˈflektɪv/ a riflessivo

reflectively /rɪˈflektɪvlɪ/ adv in modo riflessivo

reflector /rɪˈflektə(r)/ n riflettore m

reflex /ˈriːfleks/ n riflesso m ● attrib di riflesso

reflexive /rɪˈfleksɪv/ a riflessivo

refloat /riːˈfləʊt/ vt Naut, Comm rimettere a galla

reforestation /riːforɪˈsteɪʃn/ n rimboschimento m

reform /rɪˈfɔːm/ n riforma f ● vt riformare ● vi correggersi.

reformat /riːˈfɔːmæt/ vt riformattare

Reformation /refəˈmeɪʃn/ n Relig Riforma f

reformer /rɪˈfɔːmə(r)/ n riformatore, -trice mf

refrain¹ /rɪˈfreɪn/ n ritornello m

refrain² vi astenersi (**from** da)

refresh /rɪˈfreʃ/ vt rinfrescare

refresher course /rɪˈfreʃə(r)/ n corso m d'aggiornamento

refreshing /rɪˈfreʃɪŋ/ a rinfrescante

refreshments /rɪˈfreʃmənts/ npl rinfreschi mpl

refrigerate /rɪˈfrɪdʒəreɪt/ vt conservare in frigo; Ind refrigerare

refrigerated lorry /rɪˈfrɪdʒəreɪtɪd/ n camion m inv frigorifero

refrigeration /rɪfrɪdʒəˈreɪʃn/ n Ind refrigerazione f

refrigerator /rɪˈfrɪdʒəreɪtə(r)/ n frigorifero m

refuel /riːˈfjuːəl/ v (pt/pp **-fuelled**) ● vt rifornire di carburante ● vi fare rifornimento

refuge /ˈrefjuːdʒ/ n rifugio m; **take ~** rifugiarsi

refugee /refjʊˈdʒiː/ n rifugiato, -a mf

refund¹ /ˈriːfʌnd/ n rimborso m

refund² /rɪˈfʌnd/ vt rimborsare

refurbish /riːˈfɜːbɪʃ/ vt rimettere a nuovo

refurbishment /riːˈfɜːbɪʃmənt/ n rinnovo m

refusal /rɪˈfjuːzl/ n rifiuto m

refuse¹ /rɪˈfjuːz/ vt/i rifiutare; ~ **to do sth** rifiutare di fare qcsa

refuse² /ˈrefjuːs/ n rifiuti mpl

refuse collection n raccolta f dei rifiuti

refute /rɪˈfjuːt/ vt confutare

regain /rɪˈɡeɪn/ vt riconquistare

regal /ˈriːɡl/ a regale

regalia /rɪˈɡeɪlɪə/ npl insegne fpl reali

regard /rɪˈɡɑːd/ n (heed) riguardo m; (respect) considerazione f; ~**s** pl saluti mpl; **send/give my ~s to your brother** salutami tuo fratello; **with ~ to** riguardo a ● vt (consider) considerare (**as** come); **as ~s** riguardo a

regarding /rɪˈɡɑːdɪŋ/ prep riguardo a

regardless /rɪˈɡɑːdlɪs/ adv lo stesso; ~ **of** senza badare a

regatta /rɪˈɡætə/ n regata f

regency /ˈriːdʒənsɪ/ n reggenza f

regenerate /rɪˈdʒenəreɪt/ vt rigenerare ● vi rigenerarsi

regent /ˈriːdʒənt/ n reggente mf

reggae /ˈreɡeɪ/ n reggae m

regime /reɪˈʒiːm/ n regime m

regiment¹ /ˈredʒɪmənt/ n reggimento m

regiment² /ˈredʒɪment/ vt irreggimentare

regimental /redʒɪˈmentl/ a reggimentale

regimentation /redʒɪmənˈteɪʃn/ n irreggimentazione f

regimented /ˈredʒɪmentɪd/ a irreggimentato

region /ˈriːdʒən/ n regione f; **in the ~ of** fig approssimativamente

regional /ˈriːdʒənl/ a regionale

register /ˈredʒɪstə(r)/ n registro m ● vt registrare; mandare tramite assicurata ‹letter, package›; assicurare ‹luggage›; immatricolare ‹motor vehicle›; mostrare ‹feeling› ● vi ‹instrument:› funzionare; ‹student:› iscriversi (**for** a); **it didn't ~ with me** fig non ci ho fatto attenzione; ~ **with** iscriversi nella lista di ‹doctor›

registered letter /ˈredʒɪstəd/ n lettera f assicurata

registered trademark n marchio m depositato

registrar /redʒɪˈstrɑː(r)/ n ufficiale m di stato civile

registration /redʒɪ'streɪʃn/ n (of vehicle) immatricolazione f; (of letter, luggage) assicurazione f; (for course) iscrizione f

registration fee n tassa f d'iscrizione

registration number n Auto [numero m di] targa f

registry office /'redʒɪstrɪ/ n anagrafe f

regress /rɪ'gres/ vi Biol, Psych, fig regredire

regression /rɪ'greʃən/ n regressione f

regressive /rɪ'gresɪv/ a Biol, Psych regressivo

regret /rɪ'gret/ n rammarico m ● vt (pt/pp **regretted**) rimpiangere; **I ~ that** mi rincresce che

regretfully /rɪ'gretfʊlɪ/ adv con rammarico

regrettable /rɪ'gretəbl/ a spiacevole

regrettably /rɪ'gretəblɪ/ adv spiacevolmente; (before adjective) deplorevolmente

regroup /ri:'gru:p/ vi riorganizzarsi

regular /'regjʊlə(r)/ a regolare; (usual) abituale ● n cliente mf abituale

regularity /regjʊ'lærətɪ/ n regolarità f

regularly /'regjʊləlɪ/ adv regolarmente

regulate /'regʊleɪt/ vt regolare

regulation /regjʊ'leɪʃn/ n (rule) regolamento m

regulator /'regjʊleɪtə(r)/ n (person) regolatore, -trice mf; (device) regolatore m

regurgitate /rɪ'gɜːdʒɪteɪt/ vt rigurgitare; fig pej ripetere meccanicamente

rehabilitate /ri:hə'bɪlɪteɪt/ vt riabilitare

rehabilitation /ri:həbɪlɪ'teɪʃn/ n riabilitazione f

rehash¹ /ri:'hæʃ/ vt rimaneggiare

rehash² /'ri:hæʃ/ n rimaneggiamento m

rehearsal /rɪ'hɜːsl/ n Theat prova f

rehearse /rɪ'hɜːs/ vt/i provare

reheat /ri:'hi:t/ vt scaldare di nuovo

rehouse /ri:'haʊz/ vt rialloggiare

reign /reɪn/ n regno m ● vi regnare

reimburse /ri:ɪm'bɜːs/ vt ~ **sb for sth** rimborsare qcsa a qcno

reimbursement /ri:ɪm'bɜːsmənt/ n rimborso m

rein /reɪn/ n redine f

reincarnate /ri:ɪn'kɑːneɪt/ vt **be ~d** reincarnarsi

reincarnation /ri:ɪnkɑː'neɪʃn/ n reincarnazione f

reindeer /'reɪndɪə(r)/ n inv renna f

reinforce /ri:ɪn'fɔːs/ vt rinforzare

reinforced concrete n cemento m armato

reinforcement /ri:ɪn'fɔːsmənt/ n rinforzo m; ~**s** pl Mil rinforzi mpl

reinstate /ri:ɪn'steɪt/ vt reintegrare

reinstatement /ri:ɪn'steɪtmənt/ n reintegrazione f

reinterpret /ri:ɪn'tɜːprɪt/ vt reinterpretare

reinterpretation /ri:ɪntɜːprɪ'teɪʃn/ n reinterpretazione f

reintroduce /ri:ɪntrə'dju:s/ vt reintrodurre

reintroduction /ri:ɪntrə'dʌkʃn/ n reintroduzione f

reiterate /ri:'ɪtəreɪt/ vt reiterare

reiteration /ri:ɪtə'reɪʃn/ n reiterazione f

reject /rɪ'dʒekt/ vt rifiutare

rejection /rɪ'dʒekʃn/ n rifiuto m; Med rigetto m

rejects /'ri:dʒekts/ npl Comm scarti mpl

rejig /ri:'dʒɪg/ vt (pt/pp **rejigged**) Br riorganizzare

rejoice /rɪ'dʒɔɪs/ vi liter rallegrarsi

rejoicing /rɪ'dʒɔɪsɪŋ/ n gioia f

rejoin /rɪ'dʒɔɪn/ vt riassociarsi a ⟨club, party⟩; Mil reintegrarsi in ⟨regiment⟩; (answer) replicare

rejuvenate /rɪ'dʒuːvəneɪt/ vt rinnovare; ringiovanire ⟨person⟩

rejuvenation /rɪdʒuːvə'neɪʃn/ n rinnovamento m; (of person) ringiovanimento m

rekindle /ri:'kɪndl/ vt riattizzare

relapse /rɪ'læps/ n ricaduta f ● vi ricadere

relate /rɪ'leɪt/ vt (tell) riportare; (connect) collegare

■ **relate to** vt riferirsi a; identificarsi con ⟨person⟩

related /rɪ'leɪtɪd/ a imparentato (**to** a); ⟨ideas etc⟩ affine

relation /rɪ'leɪʃn/ n rapporto m; (person) parente mf

relationship /rɪ'leɪʃnʃɪp/ n rapporto m; (blood tie) parentela f; (affair) relazione f

relative /'relətɪv/ n parente mf ● a relativo

relatively /'relətɪvlɪ/ adv relativamente

relativity /relə'tɪvətɪ/ n relatività f

relativity theory n Phys teoria f della relatività

relaunch¹ /'ri:lɔːntʃ/ n rilancio m

relaunch² /ri:'lɔːntʃ/ vt rilanciare

relax /rɪ'læks/ vt rilassare; allentare ⟨pace, grip⟩ ● vi rilassarsi

relaxation /ri:læk'seɪʃn/ n rilassamento m, relax m; (recreation) svago m

relaxed /rɪ'lækst/ a rilassato

relaxing /rɪ'læksɪŋ/ a rilassante

relay¹ /ri:'leɪ/ vt (pt/pp **-layed**) trasmettere

relay² /'ri:leɪ/ n Electr relais m inv; **work in ~s** fare i turni

relay [race] /'ri:leɪ/ n [corsa f a] staffetta f

release /rɪ'li:s/ n rilascio m; (of film) distribuzione f ● vt liberare; lasciare ⟨hand⟩; togliere ⟨brake⟩; distribuire ⟨film⟩; rilasciare ⟨information etc⟩

relegate /'relɪgeɪt/ vt relegare; **be ~d** Br Sport essere retrocesso

relegation /relɪ'geɪʃn/ n relegazione f; Br Sport retrocessione f

relent /rɪ'lent/ vi cedere

relentless /rɪ'lentlɪs/ a inflessibile; (unceasing) incessante

relentlessly /rɪ'lentlɪslɪ/ adv incessantemente

relevance /'reləvəns/ n pertinenza f

relevant /'reləvənt/ a pertinente (**to** a)

reliability /rɪlaɪə'bɪlətɪ/ n affidabilità f

reliable /rɪ'laɪəbl/ a affidabile

reliably /rɪ'laɪəblɪ/ adv in modo affidabile; **be ~ informed** sapere da fonte certa

reliance /rɪ'laɪəns/ n fiducia f (**on** in)

reliant /rɪ'laɪənt/ a fiducioso (**on** in)

relic /'relɪk/ n Relig reliquia f; **~s** pl resti mpl

relief /rɪ'li:f/ n sollievo m; (assistance) soccorso m; (distraction) diversivo m; (replacement) cambio m; (in art) rilievo m; **in ~** in rilievo

relief map n carta f in rilievo

relief train n treno m supplementare

relieve /rɪ'li:v/ vt alleviare; (take over from) dare il cambio a; **~ of** liberare da ⟨burden⟩

religion /rɪ'lɪdʒən/ n religione f

religious /rɪ'lɪdʒəs/ a religioso

religiously /rɪ'lɪdʒəslɪ/ adv (conscientiously) scrupolosamente

relinquish /rɪ'lɪŋkwɪʃ/ vt abbandonare; **~ sth to sb** rinunciare a qcsa in favore di qcno

relish /'relɪʃ/ n gusto m; Culin salsa f ● vt fig apprezzare

relive /ri:'lɪv/ vt rivivere

reload /ri:'ləʊd/ vt ricaricare

relocate /ri:lə'keɪt/ vt trasferire ● vi trasferirsi

relocation /ri:lə'keɪʃn/ n (of employee, company) trasferimento m

relocation allowance n indennità f inv di trasferimento

reluctance /rɪ'lʌktəns/ n riluttanza f

reluctant /rɪ'lʌktənt/ a riluttante

reluctantly /rɪ'lʌktəntlɪ/ adv con riluttanza, a malincuore

rely /rɪ'laɪ/ vi (pt/pp -ied) **~ on** dipendere da; (trust) contare su

remain /rɪ'meɪn/ vi restare

remainder /rɪ'meɪndə(r)/ n resto m; Comm rimanenza f ● vt Comm svendere

remaining /rɪ'meɪnɪŋ/ a restante

remains /rɪ'meɪnz/ npl resti mpl; (dead body) spoglie fpl

remake /'ri:meɪk/ n (of film, recording) remake m inv

remand /rɪ'mɑ:nd/ n **on ~** in custodia cautelare ● vt **~ in custody** rinviare con detenzione provvisoria

remark /rɪ'mɑ:k/ n osservazione f ● vt osservare

remarkable /rɪ'mɑ:kəbl/ a notevole

remarkably /rɪ'mɑ:kəblɪ/ adv notevolmente

remarry /ri:'mærɪ/ vi (pt/pp -ied) risposarsi

remaster /ri:'mɑ:stə(r)/ vt incidere di nuovo ⟨recording⟩

rematch /'ri:mætʃ/ n Sport partita f di ritorno; (in boxing) secondo incontro m

remedial /rɪ'mi:dɪəl/ a correttivo; Med curativo

remedy /'remədɪ/ n rimedio m (**for** contro) ● vt (pt/pp -ied) rimediare a

remember /rɪ'membə(r)/ vt ricordare, ricordarsi; **~ to do sth** ricordarsi di fare qcsa; **~ me to him** salutamelo ● vi ricordarsi

Remembrance Day /rɪ'membrəns/ n commemorazione f dei caduti (11 novembre)

remind /rɪ'maɪnd/ vt **~ sb of sth** ricordare qcsa a qcno

reminder /rɪ'maɪndə(r)/ n ricordo m; (memo)

promemoria m inv; (letter) lettera f di sollecito; (to pay) sollecitazione f di pagamento

reminisce /remɪ'nɪs/ vi rievocare il passato

reminiscences /remɪ'nɪsənsɪz/ npl reminiscenze fpl

reminiscent /remɪ'nɪsənt/ a **be ~ of** richiamare alla memoria

remiss /rɪ'mɪs/ a negligente

remission /rɪ'mɪʃn/ n remissione f; (of sentence) condono m

remit /rɪ'mɪt/ vt (pt/pp **remitted**) rimettere ⟨money⟩

remittance /rɪ'mɪtəns/ n rimessa f

remix[1] /ri:'mɪks/ vt Mus rimixare

remix[2] /'ri:mɪks/ n Mus rimixaggio m

remnant /'remnənt/ n resto m; (of material) scampolo m; (trace) traccia f

remonstrate /'remənstreɪt/ vi fare rimostranze (**with sb** a qcno)

remorse /rɪ'mɔ:s/ n rimorso m

remorseful /rɪ'mɔ:sfʊl/ a pieno di rimorso

remorsefully /rɪ'mɔ:sfʊlɪ/ adv con rimorso

remorseless /rɪ'mɔ:slɪs/ a spietato

remorselessly /rɪ'mɔ:slɪslɪ/ adv senza pietà

remote /rɪ'məʊt/ a remoto; (slight) minimo

remote: remote access n Comput accesso m remoto. **remote control** n telecomando m. **remote-controlled** a telecomandato

remotely /rɪ'məʊtlɪ/ adv lontanamente; **be not ~...** non essere lontanamente...

remoteness /rɪ'məʊtnɪs/ n lontananza f

remould /'ri:məʊld/ n pneumatico m ricostruito

remount /ri:'maʊnt/ vt rimontare in sella a ⟨bike, horse⟩

remov[e]able /rɪ'mu:vəbl/ a rimovibile

removal /rɪ'mu:vl/ n rimozione f; (from house) trasloco m

removal man n addetto m ai traslochi

removal van n camion m inv da trasloco

remove /rɪ'mu:v/ vt togliere; togliersi ⟨clothes⟩; eliminare ⟨stain, doubts⟩

remuneration /rɪmju:nə'reɪʃn/ n rimunerazione f

remunerative /rɪ'mju:nərətɪv/ a rimunerativo

renaissance /rə'neɪsõs/ n rinascita f; **R~** Rinascimento m

renal /'ri:nəl/ a renale

render /'rendə(r)/ vt rendere ⟨service⟩

rendering /'rend(ə)rɪŋ/ n Mus interpretazione f

rendezvous /'rɒndeɪvu:/ vi esp Mil incontrarsi

rendition /ren'dɪʃn/ n interpretazione f

renegade /'renɪgeɪd/ n rinnegato, -a mf

renege /rɪ'neɪg/ vi venire meno (**on** a)

renegotiate /ri:nɪ'gəʊʃɪeɪt/ vt rinegoziare

renegotiation /ri:nɪgəʊʃɪ'eɪʃn/ n rinegoziato m

renew /rɪ'nju:/ vt rinnovare ⟨contract⟩

renewable /rɪ'nju:əbl/ a rinnovabile

renewal /rɪ'nju:əl/ n rinnovo m

renounce /rɪ'naʊns/ vt rinunciare a

renovate /'renəveɪt/ *vt* rinnovare
renovation /renə'veɪʃn/ *n* rinnovo *m*
renown /rɪ'naʊn/ *n* fama *f*
renowned /rɪ'naʊnd/ *a* rinomato
rent /rent/ *n* affitto *m* ● *vt* affittare; **~ [out]** dare in affitto
rental /'rentl/ *n* affitto *m*
rent boy *n* ragazzo *m* di vita
rent-free *a* ⟨*accommodation*⟩ gratuito ● *adv* ⟨*live, use*⟩ senza pagare l'affitto
renunciation /rɪnʌnsɪ'eɪʃn/ *n* rinuncia *f*
reopen /riː'əʊpən/ *vt/i* riaprire
reorganization /riːɔːɡənaɪ'zeɪʃn/ *n* riorganizzazione *f*
reorganize /riː'ɔːɡənaɪz/ *vt* riorganizzare
rep /rep/ *n* *Comm fam* rappresentante *mf*; *Theat* ≈ teatro *m* stabile
repackage /riː'pækɪdʒ/ *vt* *Comm* cambiare la confezione di; (*fig: change public image of*) cambiare l'immagine pubblica di; cambiare i termini di ⟨*proposal*⟩
repaint /riː'peɪnt/ *vt* ridipingere
repair /rɪ'peə(r)/ *n* riparazione *f*; **in good/ bad ~** in buone/cattive condizioni ● *vt* riparare
reparation /repə'reɪʃn/ *n* **make ~s for sth** risarcire qcsa
repartee /repɑː'tiː/ *n* botta e risposta *m inv*; **piece of ~** risposta *f* pronta
repatriate /riː'pætrɪeɪt/ *vt* rimpatriare
repatriation /riː'pætrɪ'eɪʃn/ *n* rimpatrio *m*
repay /riː'peɪ/ *vt* (*pt/pp* **-paid**) ripagare
repayment /riː'peɪmənt/ *n* rimborso *m*
repeal /rɪ'piːl/ *n* abrogazione *f* ● *vt* abrogare
repeat /rɪ'piːt/ *n* *TV* replica *f* ● *vt/i* ripetere; **~ oneself** ripetersi
repeated /rɪ'piːtɪd/ *a* ripetuto
repeatedly /rɪ'piːtɪdlɪ/ *adv* ripetutamente
repel /rɪ'pel/ *vt* (*pt/pp* **repelled**) respingere; *fig* ripugnare
repellent /rɪ'pelənt/ *a* ripulsivo
repent /rɪ'pent/ *vi* pentirsi
repentance /rɪ'pentəns/ *n* pentimento *m*
repentant /rɪ'pentənt/ *a* pentito
repercussions /riːpə'kʌʃnz/ *npl* ripercussioni *fpl*
repertoire /'repətwɑː(r)/ *n* repertorio *m*
repertory /'repətrɪ/ *n* ≈ teatro *m* stabile
repertory company *n* compagnia *f* di un teatro stabile
repetition /repɪ'tɪʃn/ *n* ripetizione *f*
repetitious /repɪ'tɪʃəs/, **repetitive** /rɪ'petɪtɪv/ *a* ripetitivo
replace /rɪ'pleɪs/ *vt* (*put back*) rimettere a posto; (*take the place of*) sostituire; **~ sth with sth** sostituire qcsa con qcsa
replacement /rɪ'pleɪsmənt/ *n* sostituzione *f*; (*person*) sostituto, -a *mf*
replacement part *n* pezzo *m* di ricambio
replant /riː'plɑːnt/ *vt* ripiantare
replay /'riːpleɪ/ *n* *Sport* partita *f* ripetuta; [action] **~** replay *m inv*
replenish /rɪ'plenɪʃ/ *vt* rifornire ⟨*stocks*⟩; (*refill*) riempire di nuovo
replete /rɪ'pliːt/ *a* **~ with** riempito di

replica /'replɪkə/ *n* copia *f*
replicate /'replɪkeɪt/ *vt* ripetere ⟨*experiment*⟩
reply /rɪ'plaɪ/ *n* risposta *f* (**to** a) ● *vt/i* (*pt/pp* **replied**) rispondere
reply-paid envelope *n* busta *f* affrancata per rispondere
report /rɪ'pɔːt/ *n* rapporto *m*; *TV, Radio* servizio *m*; *Journ* cronaca *f*; *Sch* pagella *f*; (*rumour*) diceria *f* ● *vt* riportare; **~ sb to the police** denunciare qcno alla polizia ● *vi* riportare; (*present oneself*) presentarsi (**to** a)
reportedly /rɪ'pɔːtɪdlɪ/ *adv* secondo quanto si dice
reporter /rɪ'pɔːtə(r)/ *n* cronista *mf*, reporter *mf inv*
repose /rɪ'pəʊz/ *n* riposo *m*
repository /rɪ'pɒzɪt(ə)rɪ/ *n* (*place*) deposito *m*; (*of secret, authority*) depositario, -a *mf*
repossess /riːpə'zes/ *vt* riprendere possesso di
repossession /riːpə'zeʃn/ *n* esproprio *m*
repot /riː'pɒt/ *vt* rinvasare ⟨*plant*⟩
reprehensible /reprɪ'hensəbl/ *a* riprovevole
represent /reprɪ'zent/ *vt* rappresentare
representation /reprɪzen'teɪʃn/ *n* rappresentazione *f*; **make ~s to** fare delle rimostranze a
representative /reprɪ'zentətɪv/ *a* rappresentativo ● *n* rappresentante *mf*
repress /rɪ'pres/ *vt* reprimere
repression /rɪ'preʃn/ *n* repressione *f*
repressive /rɪ'presɪv/ *a* repressivo
reprieve /rɪ'priːv/ *n* commutazione *f* della pena capitale; (*postponement*) sospensione *f* della pena capitale; *fig* tregua *f* ● *vt* sospendere la sentenza a; *fig* risparmiare
reprimand /'reprɪmɑːnd/ *n* rimprovero *m* ● *vt* rimproverare
reprint¹ /'riːprɪnt/ *n* ristampa *f*
reprint² /riː'prɪnt/ *vt* ristampare
reprisal /rɪ'praɪzl/ *n* rappresaglia *f*; **in ~ for** per rappresaglia contro
reproach /rɪ'prəʊtʃ/ *n* rimprovero *m* ● *vt* rimproverare a (**for doing sth** di fare qcsa)
reproachful /rɪ'prəʊtʃfʊl/ *a* riprovevole
reproachfully /rɪ'prəʊtʃfʊlɪ/ *adv* con aria di rimprovero
reprocess /riː'prəʊses/ *vt* trattare di nuovo
reproduce /riːprə'djuːs/ *vt* riprodurre ● *vi* riprodursi
reproduction /riːprə'dʌkʃn/ *n* riproduzione *f*
reproduction furniture *n* riproduzioni *fpl* di mobili antichi
reproductive /riːprə'dʌktɪv/ *a* riproduttivo
reproof /rɪ'pruːf/ *n* rimprovero *m*
reprove /rɪ'pruːv/ *vt* rimproverare
reptile /'reptaɪl/ *n* rettile *m*
republic /rɪ'pʌblɪk/ *n* repubblica *f*
republican /rɪ'pʌblɪkn/ *a & n* repubblicano, -a *mf*
republish /riː'pʌblɪʃ/ *vt* ripubblicare

repudiate /rɪ'pju:dɪeɪt/ *vt* ripudiare; respingere ⟨*view, suggestion*⟩

repugnance /rɪ'pʌgnəns/ *n* ripugnanza *f*

repugnant /rɪ'pʌgnənt/ *a* ripugnante

repulse /rɪ'pʌls/ *vt fml* respingere ⟨*attack*⟩; rifiutare ⟨*assistance*⟩

repulsion /rɪ'pʌlʃn/ *n* repulsione *f*

repulsive /rɪ'pʌlsɪv/ *a* ripugnante

reputable /'repjʊtəbl/ *a* affidabile

reputation /repjʊ'teɪʃn/ *n* reputazione *f*

repute /rɪ'pju:t/ *n* reputazione *f*

reputed /rɪ'pju:tɪd/ *a* presunto; **he is ~ to be** si presume che sia

reputedly /rɪ'pju:tɪdlɪ/ *adv* presumibilmente

request /rɪ'kwest/ *n* richiesta *f* ● *vt* richiedere

request stop *n* fermata *f* a richiesta

requiem /'rekwɪəm/ *n* requiem *m inv*

require /rɪ'kwaɪə(r)/ *vt* (*need*) necessitare di; (*demand*) esigere

required /rɪ'kwaɪəd/ *a* richiesto

requirement /rɪ'kwaɪəmənt/ *n* esigenza *f*; (*condition*) requisito *m*

requisite /'rekwɪzɪt/ *a* necessario ● *n* **toilet/travel ~s** *pl* articoli *mpl* da toilette/ viaggio

requisition /rekwɪ'zɪʃn/ *n* ~ **[order]** [domanda *f* di] requisizione *f* ● *vt* requisire

reread /ri:'ri:d/ *vt* rileggere

re-release /ri:rɪ'li:s/ *n* (*of film*) nuova distribuzione *f* ● *vt* ridistribuire ⟨*film*⟩

reroof /ri:'ru:f/ *vt* rifare il tetto di ⟨*building*⟩

reroute /ri:'ru:t/ *vt* dirottare ⟨*flight, traffic*⟩

rerun /'ri:rʌn/ *n* (*of film, play*) replica *f*; (*fig: repeat*) ripetizione *f*

resale /ri:'seɪl/ *n* rivendita *f*

reschedule /ri:'ʃedju:l/ *vt* (*change date of*) cambiare la data di; (*change time of*) cambiare l'orario di; rinegoziare ⟨*debt*⟩

rescind /rɪ'sɪnd/ *vt* rescindere

rescue /'reskju:/ *n* salvataggio *m* ● *vt* salvare

rescuer /'reskjʊə(r)/ *n* salvatore, -trice *mf*

research /rɪ'sɜ:tʃ/ *n* ricerca *f* ● *vt* fare ricerche su; *Journ* fare un'inchiesta su ● *vi* ~ **into** fare ricerche su

research and development *n* ricerca *f* e sviluppo *m*

researcher /rɪ'sɜ:tʃə(r)/ *n* ricercatore, -trice *mf*

research fellow *n Br Univ* ricercatore, -trice *mf*

resell /ri:'sel/ *vt* (*pt/pp* **resold**) rivendere

resemblance /rɪ'zembləns/ *n* rassomiglianza *f*

resemble /rɪ'zembl/ *vt* rassomigliare a

resent /rɪ'zent/ *vt* risentirsi per

resentful /rɪ'zentfʊl/ *a* pieno di risentimento

resentfully /rɪ'zentfʊlɪ/ *adv* con risentimento

resentment /rɪ'zentmənt/ *n* risentimento *m*

reservation /rezə'veɪʃn/ *n* (*booking*) prenotazione *f*; (*doubt, enclosure*) riserva *f*

reserve /rɪ'zɜ:v/ *n* riserva *f*; (*shyness*) riserbo *m* ● *vt* riservare; riservarsi ⟨*right*⟩

reserved /rɪ'zɜ:vd/ *a* riservato

reservoir /'rezəvwɑ:(r)/ *n* bacino *m* idrico

reset /ri:'set/ *vt* riprogrammare ⟨*clock*⟩; (*zero*) azzerare

reshape /ri:'ʃeɪp/ *vt* ristrutturare

reshuffle /ri:'ʃʌfl/ *Pol n* rimpasto *m* ● *vt* rimpastare

reside /rɪ'zaɪd/ *vi* risiedere

residence /'rezɪdəns/ *n* residenza *f*; (*stay*) soggiorno *m*

residence permit *n* permesso *m* di soggiorno

resident /'rezɪdənt/ *a* & *n* residente *mf*

residential /rezɪ'denʃl/ *a* residenziale

residential area *n* quartiere *m* residenziale

residual /rɪ'zɪdjʊəl/ *a* residuo

residue /'rezɪdju:/ *n* residuo *m*

resign /rɪ'zaɪn/ *vt* dimettersi da; ~ **oneself to** rassegnarsi a ● *vi* dare le dimissioni

resignation /rezɪg'neɪʃn/ *n* rassegnazione *f*; (*from job*) dimissioni *fpl*

resigned /rɪ'zaɪnd/ *a* rassegnato

resignedly /rɪ'zaɪnɪdlɪ/ *adv* con rassegnazione

resilient /rɪ'zɪlɪənt/ *a* elastico; *fig* con buone capacità di ripresa

resin /'rezɪn/ *n* resina *f*

resist /rɪ'zɪst/ *vt* resistere a ● *vi* resistere

resistance /rɪ'zɪstəns/ *n* resistenza *f*

resistant /rɪ'zɪstənt/ *a* resistente

resit /ri:'sɪt/ *Br vt* (*pt/pp* **resat**) ridare ⟨*exam*⟩ ● *n* esame *m* di recupero

resize /ri:'saɪz/ *vt* ridimensionare

resolute /'rezəlu:t/ *a* risoluto

resolutely /'rezəlu:tlɪ/ *adv* con risolutezza

resolution /rezə'lu:ʃn/ *n* risolutezza *f*

resolve /rɪ'zɒlv/ *n* risolutezza *f*; (*decision*) risoluzione *f* ● *vt* (*solve*) risolvere; ~ **to do** decidere di fare

resolved /rɪ'zɒlvd/ *a* risoluto

resonance /'rezənəns/ *n* risonanza *f*

resonant /'rezənənt/ *a* risonante

resonate /'rezəneɪt/ *vi* risuonare

resort /rɪ'zɔ:t/ *n* (*place*) luogo *m* di villeggiatura; **as a last ~** come ultima risorsa ● *vi* ~ **to** ricorrere a

resound /rɪ'zaʊnd/ *vi* risonare (**with** di)

resounding /rɪ'zaʊndɪŋ/ *a* ⟨*success*⟩ risonante

resoundingly /rɪ'zaʊndɪŋlɪ/ *adv* in modo risonante

resource /rɪ'zɔ:s/ *n* ~**s** *pl* risorse *fpl*

resourceful /rɪ'zɔ:sfʊl/ *a* pieno di risorse; ⟨*solution*⟩ ingegnoso

resourcefulness /rɪ'zɔ:sfʊlnɪs/ *n* ingegnosità *f*

respect /rɪ'spekt/ *n* rispetto *m*; (*aspect*) aspetto *m*; **with ~ to** per quanto riguarda ● *vt* rispettare

respectability /rɪspektə'bɪlətɪ/ *n* rispettabilità *f*

respectable /rɪ'spektəbl/ *a* rispettabile

respectably /rɪˈspektəblɪ/ adv rispettabil-
mente

respectful /rɪˈspektfʊl/ a rispettoso

respectfully /rɪˈspektfʊlɪ/ adv rispettosamente

respective /rɪˈspektɪv/ a rispettivo

respectively /rɪˈspektɪvlɪ/ adv rispettiva-
mente

respiration /respɪˈreɪʃn/ n respirazione f

respirator /ˈrespɪreɪtə(r)/ n (apparatus) respiratore m

respite /ˈrespaɪt/ n respiro m

resplendent /rɪˈsplendənt/ a risplendente

respond /rɪˈspɒnd/ vi rispondere; (react) reagire (**to** a); ⟨patient:⟩ rispondere (**to** a)

respondent /rɪˈspɒndənt/ n Jur convenuto,
-a mf; (to questionnaire) interrogato, -a mf

response /rɪˈspɒns/ n risposta f; (react)
reazione f

responsibility /rɪspɒnsɪˈbɪlətɪ/ n responsabilità f inv

responsible /rɪˈspɒnsəbl/ a responsabile;
(trustworthy) responsabile; ⟨job⟩ impegnativo

responsibly /rɪˈspɒnsəblɪ/ adv in modo responsabile

responsive /rɪˈspɒnsɪv/ a **be ~** ⟨audience
etc:⟩ reagire; ⟨brakes:⟩ essere sensibile; **she
wasn't very ~** non era molto cooperativa

respray[1] /riːˈspreɪ/ vt riverniciare ⟨vehicle⟩

respray[2] /ˈriːspreɪ/ n riverniciatura f; **it's
had a ~** è stato riverniciato

rest[1] /rest/ n riposo m; Mus pausa f; **have a
~** riposarsi ● vt riposare; (lean, place) appoggiare (**on** su) ● vi riposarsi; ⟨elbows:⟩ appoggiarsi; ⟨hopes:⟩ riposare; **it ~s with you** sta a
te

■ **rest up** vi riposars

rest[2] n **the ~** il resto; (people) gli altri

restart /riːˈstɑːt/ vt rimettere in moto
⟨engine⟩; riprendere ⟨talks⟩

restate /riːˈsteɪt/ vt (say differently)
riformulare; (say again) ribadire

restaurant /ˈrestərɒnt/ n ristorante m

restaurant car n vagone m ristorante

restful /ˈrestfl/ a riposante

rest home n casa f di riposo

restitution /restɪˈtjuːʃn/ n restituzione f

restive /ˈrestɪv/ a irrequieto

restless /ˈrestlɪs/ a nervoso

restlessly /ˈrestlɪslɪ/ adv nervosamente

restlessness /ˈrestlɪsnɪs/ agitazione f

restock /riːˈstɒk/ vt rifornire ⟨shelf, shop⟩
● vi rifornirsi

restoration /restəˈreɪʃn/ n ristabilimento
m; (of building) restauro m; (of stolen property
etc) restituzione f

restore /rɪˈstɔː(r)/ vt ristabilire; restaurare
⟨building⟩; (give back) restituire

restorer /rɪˈstɔːrə(r)/ n (person) restaurato-
re, -trice mf

restrain /rɪˈstreɪn/ vt trattenere; **~ oneself**
controllarsi

restrained /rɪˈstreɪnd/ a controllato

restraint /rɪˈstreɪnt/ n restrizione f;
(moderation) ritegno m

restrict /rɪˈstrɪkt/ vt limitare (**to** a)

restriction /rɪˈstrɪkʃn/ n limite m;
(restraint) restrizione f

restrictive /rɪˈstrɪktɪv/ a limitativo

restring /riːˈstrɪŋ/ vt rinfilare ⟨necklace,
beads⟩; sostituire le corde di ⟨instrument, rac-
ket⟩

restroom /ˈrestruːm/ n Am toilette f inv

restructure /riːˈstrʌktʃə(r)/ vt ristrutturare

restructuring /riːˈstrʌktʃərɪŋ/ n ristrutturazione f

resubmit /riːsʌbˈmɪt/ vt ripresentare

restyle /riːˈstaɪl/ vt cambiare il taglio di
⟨hair⟩; cambiare la linea di ⟨car⟩; rimodernare ⟨shop⟩

result /rɪˈzʌlt/ n risultato m; **as a ~** di conseguenza; **as a ~ of** a causa di ● vi **~ from** risultare da; **~ in** portare a

resume /rɪˈzjuːm/ vt/i riprendere

résumé /ˈrezjʊmeɪ/ n riassunto m; Am
curriculum m inv vitae

resumption /rɪˈzʌmpʃn/ n ripresa f

resurface /riːˈsɜːfɪs/ vi ⟨sub, person,
rumour:⟩ riemergere ● vt rifare la copertura
di ⟨road⟩

resurgence /rɪˈsɜːdʒəns/ n rinascita f

resurrect /rezəˈrekt/ vt fig risuscitare

resurrection /rezəˈrekʃn/ n **the R~** Relig
la Risurrezione

resuscitate /rɪˈsʌsɪteɪt/ vt rianimare

resuscitation /rɪsʌsɪˈteɪʃn/ n rianimazione f

retail /ˈriːteɪl/ n vendita f al minuto o al dettaglio ● a & adv al minuto ● vt vendere al minuto ● vi **~ at** essere venduto al pubblico al
prezzo di

retailer /ˈriːteɪlə(r)/ n dettagliante mf

retail price n prezzo m al minuto

retain /rɪˈteɪn/ vt conservare; (hold back)
trattenere

retainer /rɪˈteɪnə(r)/ n (fee) anticipo m; (old:
servant) servitore, -trice mf

retake[1] /riːˈteɪk/ vt Cinema girare di nuovo;
Sch, Univ ridare; Mil riconquistare

retake[2] /ˈriːteɪk/ n Cinema ulteriore ripresa f

retaliate /rɪˈtælɪeɪt/ vi vendicarsi

retaliation /rɪtælɪˈeɪʃn/ n rappresaglia f; **in
~ for** per rappresaglia contro

retarded /rɪˈtɑːdɪd/ a ritardato

retch /retʃ/ vi avere conati di vomito

retention /rɪˈtenʃn/ n conservazione f; (of
information) memorizzazione f; (of fluid)
ritenzione f

retentive /rɪˈtentɪv/ a ⟨memory⟩ buono

retentiveness /rɪˈtentɪvnɪs/ n capacità f di
memorizzazione

rethink /riːˈθɪŋk/ vt (pt/pp **rethought**) riconsiderare ● n **have a ~** riconsiderare la
cosa

reticence /ˈretɪsəns/ n reticenza f

reticent /ˈretɪsənt/ a reticente

retina /ˈretɪnə/ n retina f

retinue /ˈretɪnjuː/ n seguito m

retire /rɪˈtaɪə(r)/ vi andare in pensione;

(*withdraw*) ritirarsi ● *vt* mandare in pensione ⟨*employee*⟩

retired /rɪˈtaɪəd/ *a* in pensione

retirement /rɪˈtaɪəmənt/ *n* pensione *f*; **since my ~** da quando sono andato in pensione

retirement age *n* età *f* della pensione

retiring /rɪˈtaɪərɪŋ/ *a* riservato

retort /rɪˈtɔːt/ *n* replica *f*; *Chem* storta *f* ● *vt* ribattere

retouch /riːˈtʌtʃ/ *vt Phot* ritoccare

retouching /riːˈtʌtʃɪŋ/ *n Phot* ritocco *m*

retrace /rɪˈtreɪs/ *vt* ripercorrere; **~ one's steps** ritornare sui propri passi

retract /rɪˈtrækt/ *vt* ritirare; ritrattare ⟨*statement, accusation*⟩ ● *vi* ritrarsi

retractable /rɪˈtræktəbl/ *a* ⟨*landing gear*⟩ retrattile; ⟨*pen*⟩ con la punta retrattile

retraction /rɪˈtrækʃn/ *n* ritiro *m*; (*of statement, accusation*) ritrattazione *f*

retrain /riːˈtreɪn/ *vt* riqualificare ● *vi* riqualificarsi

retread /ˈriːtred/ *n* pneumatico *m* ricostruito

retreat /rɪˈtriːt/ *n* ritirata *f*; (*place*) ritiro *m* ● *vi* ritirarsi; *Mil* battere in ritirata

retrench /rɪˈtrentʃ/ *vi* ridurre le spese

retrenchment /rɪˈtrentʃmənt/ *n* riduzione *f* delle spese

retrial /riːˈtraɪəl/ *n* nuovo processo *m*

retribution /retrɪˈbjuːʃn/ *n* castigo *m*

retrievable /rɪˈtriːvəbl/ *a* recuperabile

retrieval /rɪˈtriːvəl/ *n* recupero *m*

retrieve /rɪˈtriːv/ *vt* recuperare

retroactive /retrəʊˈæktɪv/ *a* retroattivo

retroactively /retrəʊˈæktɪvlɪ/ *adv* retroattivamente

retrograde /ˈretrəgreɪd/ *a* retrogrado

retrospect /ˈretrəspekt/ *n* **in ~** guardando indietro

retrospective /retrəˈspektɪv/ *a* ⟨*exhibit*⟩ retrospettivo; ⟨*legislation*⟩ retroattivo ● *n* retrospettiva *f*

retrospectively /retrəˈspektɪvlɪ/ *adv* retrospettivamente

retrovirus /ˈretrəʊvaɪrəs/ *n* retrovirus *m* inv

retry /riːˈtraɪ/ *vt Jur* riprocessare; *Comput* riprovare

return /rɪˈtɜːn/ *n* ritorno *m*; (*giving back*) restituzione *f*; *Comm* profitto *m*; (*ticket*) biglietto *m* di andata e ritorno; **by ~ [of post]** a stretto giro di posta; **in ~** in cambio (**for** di); **many happy ~s!** cento di questi giorni!; **~ on investment** utile *m* sul capitale investito ● *vi* ritornare ● *vt* (*give back*) restituire; ricambiare ⟨*affection, invitation*⟩; (*put back*) rimettere; (*send back*) mandare indietro; (*elect*) eleggere

returnable /rɪˈtɜːnəbl/ *a* restituibile

return: return flight *n* volo *m* di andata e ritorno. **return match** *n* rivincita *f*. **return ticket** *n* biglietto *m* di andata e ritorno

reunification /riːjuːnɪfɪˈkeɪʃn/ *n* riunificazione *f*

reunify /riːˈjuːnɪfaɪ/ *vt* riunificare

reunion /riːˈjuːnjən/ *n* riunione *f*

reunite /riːjʊˈnaɪt/ *vt* riunire

reusable /riːˈjuːzəbl/ *a* riutilizzabile

reuse /riːˈjuːz/ *vt* riutilizzare

rev /rev/ *n Auto* giro; **~s per minute** regime *m* di giri ● *vt* **~ [up]** far andare su di giri ● *vi* andare su di giri

revaluation /riːvæljʊˈeɪʃn/ *n* rivalutazione *f*

revalue /riːˈvæljuː/ *vt Comm* rivalutare

revamp /riːˈvæmp/ *vt* riorganizzare ⟨*company*⟩; rimodernare ⟨*building, clothing*⟩

rev counter *n* contagiri *m*

Rev[d] *abbr* (**Reverend**) Reverendo

reveal /rɪˈviːl/ *vt* rivelare; ⟨*dress:*⟩ scoprire

revealing /rɪˈviːlɪŋ/ *a* rivelatore; ⟨*dress*⟩ osé inv

revel /ˈrevl/ *vi* (*pt/pp* **revelled**) **~ in sth** godere di qcsa

revelation /revəˈleɪʃn/ *n* rivelazione *f*

reveller /ˈrevələ(r)/ *n* festaiolo, -a *mf*

revelry /ˈrevəlrɪ/ *n* baldoria *f*

revenge /rɪˈvendʒ/ *n* vendetta *f*; *Sport* rivincita *f*; **take ~** vendicarsi (**on sb for sth** di qcno per qcsa) ● *vt* vendicare

revenue /ˈrevənjuː/ *n* reddito *m*

reverberate /rɪˈvɜːbəreɪt/ *vi* riverberare

reverberations /rɪvɜːbəˈreɪʃnz/ *npl fig* ripercussione *f*

revere /rɪˈvɪə(r)/ *vt* riverire

reverence /ˈrevərəns/ *n* riverenza *f*

Reverend /ˈrevərənd/ *a* reverendo

reverent /ˈrevərənt/ *a* riverente

reverential /revəˈrenʃ(ə)l/ *a* riverente

reverently /ˈrevərəntlɪ/ *adv* rispettosamente

reverie /ˈrevərɪ/ *n* sogno *m* ad occhi aperti

reversal /rɪˈvɜːsl/ *n* inversione *f*

reverse /rɪˈvɜːs/ *a* opposto; **in ~ order** in ordine inverso ● *n* contrario *m*; (*back*) rovescio *m*; *Auto* marcia *m* indietro ● *vt* invertire; **~ the car into the garage** entrare in garage a marcia indietro; **~ the charges** *Teleph* fare una telefonata a carico del destinatario ● *vi* *Auto* fare marcia indietro

reverse charge [phone-]call *n* telefonata *f* a carico del destinatario

reversing lights /rɪˈvɜːsɪŋ/ *npl* luci *fpl* di retromarcia

revert /rɪˈvɜːt/ *vi* **~ to** tornare a

review /rɪˈvjuː/ *n* (*survey*) rassegna *f*; (*re-examination*) riconsiderazione *f*; *Mil* rivista *f*; (*of book, play*) recensione *f* ● *vt* riesaminare ⟨*situation*⟩; *Mil* passare in rivista; recensire ⟨*book, play*⟩

reviewer /rɪˈvjuːə(r)/ *n* critico, -a *mf*

revile /rɪˈvaɪl/ *vt* ingiuriare

revise /rɪˈvaɪz/ *vt* rivedere; (*for exam*) ripassare

revision /rɪˈvɪʒn/ *n* revisione *f*; (*for exam*) ripasso *m*

revisionism /rɪˈvɪʒənɪzm/ *n* revisionismo *m*

revisionist /rɪˈvɪʒənɪst/ *a & n* revisionista *mf*

revisit /riːˈvɪzɪt/ *vt* rivisitare ⟨*person, museum etc*⟩
revitalization /riːvaɪtəlaɪˈzeɪʃn/ *n* rivitalizzazione *f*
revitalize /riːˈvaɪtəlaɪz/ *vt* rivitalizzare
revival /rɪˈvaɪvl/ *n* ritorno *m*; (*of patient*) recupero *m*; (*from coma*) risveglio *m*
revivalist /rɪˈvaɪvəlɪst/ *a* Relig revivalista
revive /rɪˈvaɪv/ *vt* resuscitare; rianimare ⟨*person*⟩ ● *vi* riprendersi; ⟨*person:*⟩ rianimarsi
revocation /revəˈkeɪʃn/ *n* (*of decision, order*) revoca *f*; (*of law*) abrogazione *f*; (*of will*) annullamento *m*
revoke /rɪˈvəʊk/ *vt* revocare ⟨*decision, order*⟩; abrogare ⟨*law*⟩; annullare ⟨*will*⟩
revolt /rɪˈvəʊlt/ *n* rivolta *f* ● *vi* ribellarsi ● *vt* rivoltare
revolting /rɪˈvəʊltɪŋ/ *a* rivoltante
revolution /revəˈluːʃn/ *n* rivoluzione *f*; **~s per minute** Auto giri *mpl* al minuto
revolutionary /revəˈluːʃənərɪ/ *a* & *n* rivoluzionario, -a *mf*
revolutionize /revəˈluːʃənaɪz/ *vt* rivoluzionare
revolve /rɪˈvɒlv/ *vi* ruotare; **~ around** girare intorno a
revolver /rɪˈvɒlvə(r)/ *n* rivoltella *f*, revolver *m inv*
revolving /rɪˈvɒlvɪŋ/ *a* ruotante
revolving doors *npl* porta *f* girevole
revue /rɪˈvjuː/ *n* rivista *f*
revulsion /rɪˈvʌlʃn/ *n* ripulsione *f*
reward /rɪˈwɔːd/ *n* ricompensa *f* ● *vt* ricompensare
rewarding /rɪˈwɔːdɪŋ/ *a* gratificante
rewind /riːˈwaɪnd/ *vt* riavvolgere ⟨*tape, film*⟩
rewind button /ˈriːwaɪnd/ *n* tasto *m* di riavvolgimento
rewire /riːˈwaɪə(r)/ *vt* rifare l'impianto elettrico di
reword /riːˈwɜːd/ *vt* esprimere con parole diverse
rework /riːˈwɜːk/ *vt* modificare
rewrite /riːˈraɪt/ *vt* (*pt* **rewrote**, *pp* **rewritten**) riscrivere
rhapsody /ˈræpsədɪ/ *n* rapsodia *f*
rhesus /ˈriːsəs/ *n* reso *m*
rhesus-negative *a* Rh-negativo
rhesus-positive *a* Rh-positivo
rhetoric /ˈretərɪk/ *n* retorica *f*
rhetorical /rɪˈtɒrɪkl/ *a* retorico
rhetorically /rɪˈtɒrɪklɪ/ *adv* retoricamente
rhetorical question *n* domanda *f* retorica
rheumatic /rʊˈmætɪk/ *a* reumatico
rheumatism /ˈruːmətɪzm/ *n* reumatismo *m*
rheumatoid arthritis /ˈruːmətɔɪd/ *n* periartrite *f*
Rhine /raɪn/ *n* Reno *m*
rhino /ˈraɪnəʊ/ *n fam* rinoceronte *m*
rhinoceros /raɪˈnɒsərəs/ *n* rinoceronte *m*
rhombus /ˈrɒmbəs/ *n* rombo *m*
rhubarb /ˈruːbɑːb/ *n* rabarbaro *m*
rhyme /raɪm/ *n* rima *f*; (*poem*) filastrocca *f* ● *vi* rimare; **~ with sth** far rima con qcsa

rhythm /ˈrɪðm/ *n* ritmo *m*
rhythmic[al] /ˈrɪðmɪk[l]/ *a* ritmico
rhythmically /ˈrɪðmɪklɪ/ *adv* con ritmo
rhythm method *n* (*of contraception*) metodo *m* Ogino-Knauss
rib /rɪb/ *n* costola *f*; **~s** *pl* Culin costata *f* ● *vt* (*pt/pp* **ribbed**) *fam* punzecchiare
ribald /ˈrɪbld/ *a* spinto
ribbon /ˈrɪbən/ *n* nastro *m*; **in ~s** a brandelli
ribcage /ˈrɪbkeɪdʒ/ *n* gabbia *f* toracica, cassa *f* toracica
rice /raɪs/ *n* riso *m*
ricefield /ˈraɪsfiːld/ *n* risaia *f*
rice-paper *n* Culin carta *f* di riso
rich /rɪtʃ/ *a* ricco; ⟨*food*⟩ pesante ● *n* **the ~** *pl* i ricchi; **~es** *pl* ricchezze *fpl*
richly /ˈrɪtʃlɪ/ *adv* riccamente; ⟨*deserve*⟩ largamente
Richter scale /ˈrɪktə(r)/ *n* scala *f* Richter
rick /rɪk/ *vt Br* **~ one's ankle** prendere una storta alla caviglia
rickets /ˈrɪkɪts/ *n* rachitismo *m*
rickety /ˈrɪkətɪ/ *a* malfermo
rickshaw /ˈrɪkʃɔː/ *n* risciò *m inv*
ricochet /ˈrɪkəʃeɪ/ *vi* rimbalzare ● *n* rimbalzo *m*
rid /rɪd/ *vt* (*pt/pp* **rid**, *pres p* **ridding**) sbarazzare ⟨**of** di⟩; **get ~ of** sbarazzarsi di
riddance /ˈrɪdns/ *n* **good ~!** che liberazione!
ridden /ˈrɪdn/ *see* **ride**
riddle /ˈrɪdl/ *n* enigma *m*
riddled /ˈrɪdld/ *a* **~ with** crivellato di
ride /raɪd/ *n* (*on horse*) cavalcata *f*; (*in vehicle*) giro *m*; (*journey*) viaggio *m*; **take sb for a ~** *fam* prendere qcno in giro ● *v* (*pt* **rode**, *pp* **ridden**) ● *vt* montare ⟨*horse*⟩; andare su ⟨*bicycle*⟩ ● *vi* andare a cavallo; ⟨*jockey, showjumper:*⟩ cavalcare; ⟨*cyclist:*⟩ andare in bicicletta; (*in vehicle*) viaggiare
rider /ˈraɪdə(r)/ *n* cavallerizzo, -a *mf*; (*in race*) fantino *m*; (*on bicycle*) ciclista *mf*; (*in document*) postilla *f*
ridge /rɪdʒ/ *n* spigolo *m*; (*on roof*) punta *f*; (*of mountain*) cresta *f*; (*of high pressure*) zona *f* a alta pressione [atmosferica]
ridicule /ˈrɪdɪkjuːl/ *n* ridicolo *m* ● *vt* mettere in ridicolo
ridiculous /rɪˈdɪkjʊləs/ *a* ridicolo
ridiculously /rɪˈdɪkjʊləslɪ/ *adv* in modo ridicolo; **~ expensive/easy** carissimo/facilissimo
riding /ˈraɪdɪŋ/ *n* equitazione *f* ● *attrib* d'equitazione
rife /raɪf/ *a* **be ~** essere diffuso; **~ with** pieno di
riff-raff /ˈrɪfræf/ *n* marmaglia *f*
rifle /ˈraɪfl/ *n* fucile *m* ● *vt* **~ [through]** mettere a soqquadro
rifle-range *n* tiro *m* al bersaglio
rift /rɪft/ *n* fessura *f*; *fig* frattura *f*
rig[1] /rɪg/ *n* equipaggiamento *m*; (*at sea*) piattaforma *f* per trivellazioni subacquee
rig[2] *vt* (*pt/pp* **rigged**) manovrare ⟨*election*⟩
■ **rig out** *vt* equipaggiare; (*with clothes*) parare

■ **rig up** *vt* allestire

rigging /'rɪgɪŋ/ *n Naut* sartiame *m*; *(of election, competition)* broglio *m*

right /raɪt/ *a* giusto; *(not left)* destro; **be ~** ‹*person:*› aver ragione; ‹*clock:*› essere giusto; **put ~** mettere all'ora ‹*clock*›; correggere ‹*person*›; rimediare a ‹*situation*›; **that's ~!** proprio così!; **do you have the ~ time?** ha l'ora esatta? ● *adv (correctly)* bene; *(not left)* a destra; *(directly)* proprio; *(completely)* completamente; **~ away** immediatamente; **too ~!** altroché! ● *n* giusto *m*; *(not left)* destra *f*; *(what is due)* diritto *m*; **the R~** *Pol* la destra; **on/to the ~** a destra; **be in the ~** essere nel giusto; **by ~s** secondo giustizia; **be within one's ~s** avere tutti i diritti (**in doing sth** di fare qcsa) ● *vt* raddrizzare; **~ a wrong** *fig* riparare a un torto

right angle *n* angolo *m* retto

righteous /'raɪtʃəs/ *a* virtuoso; *(cause)* giusto

rightful /'raɪtfl/ *a* legittimo

rightfully /'raɪtfʊlɪ/ *adv* legittimamente

right-handed /-'hændɪd/ *a* che usa la mano destra

right-hand man *n fig* braccio *m* destro

rightly /'raɪtlɪ/ *adv* giustamente

right-minded /-'maɪndɪd/ *a* sensato

right of way *n* diritto *m* di transito; *(path)* passaggio *m*; *Auto* precedenza *f*

right-on *int fam* bene! ● *a fam* **they're very ~** sono molto impegnati

rights issue *n* emissione *f* riservata agli azionisti

right: right-thinking *a* sensato. **right turn** *n* svolta *f* a destra. **right wing** *n Pol* destra; *Sport* ala *f* destra. **right-wing** *a Pol* di destra. **right-winger** *n Pol* persona *f* di destra; *Sport* ala *f* destra

rigid /'rɪdʒɪd/ *a* rigido

rigidity /rɪ'dʒɪdətɪ/ *n* rigidità f

rigmarole /'rɪgmərəʊl/ *n* trafila *f*; *(story)* tiritera *f*

rigor mortis /rɪgə'mɔːtɪs/ *n* rigidità *f* cadaverica

rigorous /'rɪgərəs/ *a* rigoroso

rigorously /'rɪgərəslɪ/ *adv* rigorosamente

rigour /'rɪgə(r)/ *n* rigore *m*

rig-out *n (fam: clothes)* tenuta *f*

rile /raɪl/ *vt fam* irritare

rim /rɪm/ *n* bordo *m*; *(of wheel)* cerchione *m*

rind /raɪnd/ *n (on cheese)* crosta *f*; *(on bacon)* cotenna *f*

ring[1] /rɪŋ/ *n (circle)* cerchio *m*; *(on finger)* anello *m*; *(boxing)* ring *m inv*; *(for circus)* pista *f*; **stand in a ~** essere in cerchio ● *vt* accerchiare; **~ in red** fare un cerchio rosso intorno a

ring[2] *n* suono *m*; **give sb a ~** *Teleph* dare un colpo di telefono a qcno ● *v (pt* **rang***, pp* **rung)** ● *vt* suonare; *Teleph* telefonare a; **it ~s a bell** *fig* mi dice qualcosa; **~ the changes** *fig* cambiare ● *vi* suonare; *Teleph* telefonare; **~ true** aver l'aria di essere vero

■ **ring back** *vt/i Teleph* richiamare

■ **ring off** *vi Teleph* riattaccare

■ **ring out** *vi (voice, shot etc:)* risuonare chiaramente

■ **ring round** *vi Teleph* fare un giro di telefonate

■ **ring up** *Teleph vt* telefonare a ● *vi* telefonare

ring-binder /'rɪŋbaɪndə(r)/ *n* raccoglitore *m* ad anelli

ring finger *n* anulare *m*

ringing /'rɪŋɪŋ/ *n (noise of bell, alarm)* suono *m*; *(in ears)* fischio *m*

ringleader /'rɪŋliːdə(r)/ *n* capobanda *m*

ringlet /'rɪŋlɪt/ *n* boccolo *m*

ring: ringmaster *n* direttore *m* di circo. **ring-pull** *n* linguetta *f*. **ring-pull can** *n* lattina *f* con linguetta. **ring road** *n* circonvallazione *f*. **ringside** *n* **at the ~** in prima fila; **have a ~ seat** *fig* essere in prima fila

rink /rɪŋk/ *n* pista *f* di pattinaggio

rinse /rɪns/ *n* risciacquo *m*; *(hair colour)* cachet *m inv* ● *vt* sciacquare

■ **rinse off** *vt* sciacquare via

■ **rinse out** *vt* sciacquare ‹*cup, glass*›; sciacquare via ‹*shampoo, soap*›

riot /'raɪət/ *n* rissa *f*; *(of colour)* accozzaglia *f*; **~s** *pl* disordini *mpl*; **run ~** impazzare ● *vi* creare disordini

riot act *n* **read the ~ ~ to sb** *fig* dare una lavata di capo a qcno

rioter /'raɪətə(r)/ *n* dimostrante *mf*

riot gear *n* tenuta *f* antisommossa

riotous /'raɪətəs/ *a* sfrenato

riotously /'raɪətəslɪ/ *adv* **~ funny** divertente da morire

riot police *n* DIGOS *f*, Divisione *f* Investigazioni Generali e Operazioni Speciali

RIP *abbr* **(rest in peace)** R.I.P.

rip /rɪp/ *n* strappo *m* ● *v (pt/pp* **ripped)** ● *vt* strappare; **~ open** aprire con uno strappo ● *vi* strapparsi; **let ~** scatenarsi

■ **rip off** *vt (remove)* togliere; *(fam: cheat)* fregare

■ **rip up** *vt* stracciare ‹*letter*›

ripcord /'rɪpkɔːd/ *n* cavo *m* di spiegamento

ripe /raɪp/ *a* maturo; ‹*cheese*› stagionato

ripen /'raɪpn/ *vi* maturare; ‹*cheese:*› stagionarsi ● *vt* far maturare; stagionare ‹*cheese*›

ripeness /'raɪpnɪs/ *n* maturazione f

rip-off *n fam* frode *f*; **these prices are a ~!** questi prezzi sono un furto!

riposte /rɪ'pɒst/ *n* replica *f*

ripple /'rɪpl/ *n* increspatura *f*; *(sound)* mormorio *m* ● *vt* increspare ● *vi* incresparsi

rip-roaring /'rɪprɔːrɪŋ/ *a (fam: success)* travolgente

rise /raɪz/ *n (of sun)* levata *f*; *(fig: to fame, power)* ascesa *f*; *(increase)* aumento *m*; **give ~ to** dare adito a ● *vi (pt* **rose***, pp* **risen)** alzarsi; ‹*sun:*› sorgere; ‹*dough:*› lievitare; ‹*prices, water level:*› aumentare; *(to power, position)* arrivare **(to** a); *(rebel)* sollevarsi; ‹*Parliament, court:*› aggiornare la seduta; *(for holidays)* sospendere i lavori

■ **rise above** *vt* superare ‹*difficulty*›

riser /'raɪzə(r)/ *n* early ~ persona *f* mattiniera

rising /'raɪzɪŋ/ *a* ⟨*sun*⟩ levante; ~ **generation** nuova generazione *f* ● *n* ⟨*revolt*⟩ sollevazione *f*

risk /rɪsk/ *n* rischio *m*; **run the ~ of** correre il rischio di; **at ~** in pericolo; **at one's own ~** a proprio rischio e pericolo; **at the ~ of doing sth** a costo di fare qcsa ● *vt* rischiare

risky /'rɪskɪ/ *a* (**-ier, -iest**) rischioso

risotto /rɪ'zɒtəʊ/ *n* risotto *m*

risqué /'rɪskeɪ/ *a* spinto

rissole /'rɪsəʊl/ *n* crocchetta *f*

rite /raɪt/ *n* rito *m*; **last ~s** *pl* estrema unzione *fsg*

ritual /'rɪtjʊəl/ *a & n* rituale *m*

ritzy /'rɪtsɪ/ *a* ⟨*fam: hotel, style, decoration*⟩ lussuoso

rival /'raɪvl/ *a* rivale ● *n* rivale *mf*; ~**s** *pl* *Comm* concorrenti *mpl* ● *vt* (*pt/pp* **rivalled**) rivaleggiare con

rivalry /'raɪv(ə)lrɪ/ *n* rivalità *f* *inv*; *Comm* concorrenza *f*

river /'rɪvə(r)/ *n* fiume *m*

river: riverbank *n* riva *f* di fiume. **river-bed** *n* letto *m* del fiume. **riverside** *n* lungofiume *m* ● *attrib* sul fiume

rivet /'rɪvɪt/ *n* rivetto *m* ● *vt* rivettare; **be ~ed by** *fig* essere avvinto da

riveting /'rɪvɪtɪŋ/ *a fig* avvincente

Riviera /rɪvɪ'eərə/ *n* **the French ~** la Costa Azzurra; **the Italian ~** la riviera ligure

roach /rəʊtʃ/ *n* ⟨*fish*⟩ lasca *f*; ⟨*Am fam: insect*⟩ scarafaggio *m*

road /rəʊd/ *n* strada *f*, via *f*; **be on the ~** viaggiare

road: roadblock *n* blocco *m* stradale. **road haulage** *n* trasporto *m* su strada. **road hog** *n* *fam* pirata *m* della strada

roadie /'rəʊdɪ/ *n* roadie *m inv*

road: road map *n* carta *f* stradale. **road safety** *n* sicurezza *f* sulle strade. **road sense** *n* prudenza *f* (*per strada*). **roadshow** *n* ⟨*play, show*⟩ spettacolo *m* di tournée; ⟨*publicity tour*⟩ giro *m* promozionale. **roadside** *n* bordo *m* della strada. **road sign** cartello *m* stradale. **road surface** *n* fondo *m* stradale. **road sweeper** *n* ⟨*person*⟩ spazzino, -a *nmf*; ⟨*machine*⟩ autospazzatrice *f*. **road tax** *n* tassa *f* di circolazione. **roadway** *n* carreggiata *f*, corsia *f*. **roadworks** *npl* lavori *mpl* stradali. **roadworthy** *a* sicuro

roam /rəʊm/ *vi* girovagare

roar /rɔː(r)/ *n* ruggito *m*; ~**s of laughter** scroscio *msg* di risa ● *vi* ruggire; ⟨*lorry, thunder:*⟩ rombare; ~ **with laughter** ridere fragorosamente

■ **roar out** *vt* gridare

■ **roar past** *vi* ⟨*move noisily*⟩ passare rombando

roaring /'rɔːrɪŋ/ *a* **do a ~ trade** *fam* fare affari d'oro ● *adv* ~ **drunk** *fam* ubriaco fradicio

roast /rəʊst/ *a* arrosto; ~ **pork** arrosto *m* di maiale ● *n* arrosto *m* ● *vt* arrostire ⟨*meat*⟩ ● *vi* arrostirsi

roasting [**hot**] /'rəʊstɪŋ/ *a fam* caldissimo

roasting pan *n* teglia *f* per arrosti

rob /rɒb/ *vt* (*pt/pp* **robbed**) derubare (**of** di); svaligiare ⟨*bank*⟩

robber /'rɒbə(r)/ *n* rapinatore *m*

robbery /'rɒbərɪ/ *n* rapina *f*

robe /rəʊb/ *n* tunica *f*; ⟨*Am: bathrobe*⟩ accappatoio *m*

robin /'rɒbɪn/ *n* pettirosso *m*

robot /'rəʊbɒt/ *n* robot *m inv*

robotic /rəʊ'bɒtɪk/ *a* ⟨*movement, voice*⟩ robotico; ⟨*tool, device, machine*⟩ robotizzato

robotics *n* robotica *f*

robust /rəʊ'bʌst/ *a* robusto

rock[1] /rɒk/ *n* roccia *f*; ⟨*in sea*⟩ scoglio *m*; ⟨*sweet*⟩ zucchero *m* candito; **on the ~s** ⟨*ship*⟩ incagliato; ⟨*marriage*⟩ finito; ⟨*drink*⟩ con ghiaccio

rock[2] *vt* cullare ⟨*baby*⟩; ⟨*shake*⟩ far traballare; ⟨*shock*⟩ scuotere ● *vi* dondolarsi

rock[3] *n Mus* rock *m*

rock: rock and roll *n* rock and roll *m*. **rock-bottom** *a* bassissimo ● *n* livello *m* più basso; **hit ~** toccare il fondo. **rock-climber** *n* scalatore, -trice *nmf*. **rock-climbing** *n* roccia *f*

rockery /'rɒkərɪ/ *n* giardino *m* roccioso

rocket /'rɒkɪt/ *n* razzo *m*; **give sb a ~** *fam* fare un cicchetto a qcno ● *vi* salire alle stelle

rocket launcher /'lɔːntʃə(r)/ *n* lanciarazzi *m inv*

rock face *n* parete *f* rocciosa

rocking chair /'rɒkɪŋ/ *n* sedia *f* a dondolo

rocking horse *n* cavallo *m* a dondolo

rocky /'rɒkɪ/ *a* (**-ier, -iest**) roccioso; *fig* traballante

rod /rɒd/ *n* bacchetta *f*; ⟨*for fishing*⟩ canna *f*

rode /rəʊd/ *see* ride

rodent /'rəʊdnt/ *n* roditore *m*

roe[1] /rəʊ/ *n* uova *fpl* di pesce; ⟨*soft*⟩ latte *m* di pesce

roe[2] *n* (*pl* roe *or* roes) ~[**-deer**] capriolo *m*

roebuck /'rəʊbʌk/ *n* capriolo *m* maschio

roger /'rɒdʒə(r)/ *int Teleph* ricevuto

rogue /rəʊg/ *n* farabutto *m*

role /rəʊl/ *n* ruolo *m*

role model *n Psych* modello *m* comportamentale

role-play, role-playing /'rəʊlpleɪŋ/ *n Psych* role playing *m inv*

roll /rəʊl/ *n* rotolo *m*; ⟨*bread*⟩ panino *m*; ⟨*list*⟩ lista *f*; ⟨*of ship, drum*⟩ rullio *m* ● *vi* rotolare; **be ~ing in money** *fam* nuotare nell'oro ● *vt* spianare ⟨*lawn, pastry*⟩; ~**ed into one** allo stesso tempo

■ **roll back** *vt* ridurre ⟨*prices*⟩

■ **roll by** *vi* ⟨*time:*⟩ passare

■ **roll in** *vi* ⟨*fam: arrive in large quantities*⟩ arrivare a valanghe; ⟨*arrive*⟩ arrivare

■ **roll on** *vi* ~ **on Friday!** non vedo l'ora che sia venerdì!

■ **roll over** *vi* rigirarsi; ⟨*fam: capitulate*⟩ arrendersi

■ **roll up** *vt* arrotolare; rimboccarsi ⟨*sleeves*⟩ ● *vi fam* arrivare

roll-call *n* appello *m*

roller /'rəʊlə(r)/ n rullo m; (for hair) bigodino m

roller: rollerblade n pattino m a rotelle in linea ● vi pattinare (con pattini in linea). **roller blind** n tapparella f. **roller coaster** n montagne fpl russe. **roller skate** n pattino m a rotelle

rollicking /'rɒlɪkɪŋ/ a **have a ~ time** divertirsi da pazzi

rolling /'rəʊlɪŋ/ n **rolling pin** n mattarello m. **rolling stock** n materiale m rotabile. **rolling stone** n fig vagabondo, -a mf

roll: rollneck n collo m alto; (whole sweater) dolcevita f. **roll-on** n ⟨deodorant⟩ deodorante m a sfera. **roll-on roll-off ferry** n traghetto m roll-on roll-off

ROM /rɒm/ n Comput ROM f inv

Roman /'rəʊmən/ a (also print) romano ● n romano, -a mf

Roman Catholic a & n cattolico, -a mf

romance /rəʊ'mæns/ n (love-affair) storia f d'amore; (book) romanzo m rosa

Romania /rəʊ'meɪnɪə/ n Romania f

Romanian /rəʊ'meɪnɪən/ a & n rumeno, -a mf; (language) rumeno m

roman numeral n numero m romano

romantic /rəʊ'mæntɪk/ a romantico

romantically /rəʊ'mæntɪklɪ/ adv romanticamente

romanticism /rəʊ'mæntɪsɪzm/ n romanticismo m

romanticize /rəʊ'mæntɪsaɪz/ vt romanticizzare

romanticized /rəʊ'mæntɪsaɪzd/ a romanzato

Rome /rəʊm/ n Roma f

Romeo /'rəʊmɪəʊ/ n (fam: ladykiller) dongiovanni m inv

romp /rɒmp/ n gioco m rumoroso ● vi giocare rumorosamente

■ **romp home** vi (win easily) vincere senza difficoltà

■ **romp through** vt fam passare senza difficoltà ⟨exam⟩ ● vi riuscire senza difficoltà

rompers /'rɒmpəz/ npl pagliaccetto msg

roof /ru:f/ n tetto m; (of mouth) palato m; **live under one ~** vivere sotto lo stesso tetto; **go through the ~** (fam: increase) andare alle stelle; (be very angry) andare su tutte le furie ● vt mettere un tetto su

roof-rack n portabagagli m inv

rooftop /'ru:ftɒp/ n tetto m; **shout it from the ~s** fig gridarlo ai quattro venti

rook /rʊk/ n corvo m; (in chess) torre f ● vt (fam: swindle) fregare

rookie /'rʊkɪ/ n Am fam novellino, -a mf

room /ru:m/ n stanza f; (bedroom) camera f; (for functions) sala f; (space) spazio m

room: room-mate n (Am: flatmate) compagno, -a mf di appartamento; (in same room) compagno, -a mf di stanza. **room service** n servizio m in camera. **room temperature** n temperatura f ambiente

roomy /'ru:mɪ/ a spazioso; ⟨clothes⟩ ampio

roost /ru:st/ n posatoio m ● vi appollaiarsi

rooster /'ru:stə(r)/ n gallo m

root¹ /ru:t/ n radice f; **take ~** metter radici; **put down ~s** fig metter radici ● vi metter radici

root² vi **~ about** grufolare; **~ for sb** Am fam fare il tifo per qcno

■ **root out** vt fig scovare

rope /rəʊp/ n corda f; **know the ~s** fam conoscere i trucchi del mestiere

■ **rope in** vt fam coinvolgere

rope ladder n scala f di corda

ropey /'rəʊpɪ/ a Br fam scadente; **feel ~** sentirsi poco bene

rosary /'rəʊzərɪ/ n rosario m

rose¹ /rəʊz/ n rosa f; (of watering-can) bocchetta f

rose² see **rise**

rosé /'rəʊzeɪ/ n [vino m] rosé m inv

rosebud /'rəʊzbʌd/ n bocciolo m di rosa

rosehip /'rəʊzhɪp/ n frutto m della rosa canina

rosemary /'rəʊzmərɪ/ n rosmarino m

rose-tinted spectacles /'rəʊztɪntɪd/ npl **wear ~** vedere tutto rosa

rosette /rəʊ'zet/ n coccarda f

roster /'rɒstə(r)/ n tabella f dei turni

rostrum /'rɒstrəm/ n podio m

rosy /'rəʊzɪ/ a (-ier, -iest) roseo

rot /rɒt/ n marciume m; (fam: nonsense) sciocchezze fpl ● vi (pt/pp rotted) marcire

rota /'rəʊtə/ n tabella f dei turni

rotary /'rəʊtərɪ/ a rotante

rotate /rəʊ'teɪt/ vt far ruotare; avvicendare ⟨crops⟩ ● vi ruotare

rotation /rəʊ'teɪʃn/ n rotazione f; **in ~** a turno

rote /rəʊt/ n **by ~** meccanicamente

rotten /'rɒtn/ a marcio; fam schifoso; ⟨person⟩ penoso

rotund /rəʊ'tʌnd/ a paffuto

rotunda /rəʊ'tʌndə/ n rotonda f

rouble /'ru:bl/ n rublo m

rough /rʌf/ a (not smooth) ruvido; ⟨ground⟩ accidentato; ⟨behaviour⟩ rozzo; ⟨sport⟩ violento; ⟨area⟩ malfamato; ⟨crossing, time⟩ brutto; ⟨estimate⟩ approssimativo ● adv ⟨play⟩ grossolanamente; **sleep ~** dormire sotto i ponti ● n **do sth in ~** far qcsa alla bell'e meglio ● vt ~ **it** vivere senza confort

■ **rough out** vt abbozzare

■ **rough up** vt fam malmenare ⟨person⟩

roughage /'rʌfɪdʒ/ n fibre fpl

rough: rough-and-ready a ⟨person, manner⟩ sbrigativo; ⟨conditions, method⟩ rudimentale. **rough-and-tumble** n (rough play) zuffa f. **rough copy** n brutta copia f. **rough draft** n abbozzo m

roughen /'rʌfən/ vt rendere ruvido ⟨surface⟩

roughly /'rʌflɪ/ adv rozzamente; (more or less) pressappoco

roughness /'rʌfnɪs/ n ruvidità f; (of behaviour) rozzezza f

rough paper n carta f da brutta

roughshod /'rʌfʃɒd/ adv **ride ~ over** infischiarsi di ⟨*person, objection*⟩; calpestare ⟨*feelings*⟩

roulette /ruːˈlet/ *n* roulette f

round /raʊnd/ *a* rotondo ● *n* tondo *m*; (*slice*) fetta *f*; (*of visits, drinks*) giro *m*; (*of competition*) partita *f*; (*boxing*) ripresa *f*, round *m inv*; **do one's ~s** ⟨*doctor:*⟩ fare il giro delle visite ● *prep* intorno a; **open ~ the clock** aperto ventiquattr'ore ● *adv* **all ~** tut-t'intorno; **ask sb ~** invitare qcno; **go/come ~ to** (*a friend etc*) andare da; **turn/look ~** gi-rarsi; **~ about** (*approximately*) intorno a ● *vt* arrotondare; girare ⟨*corner*⟩

■ **round down** *vt* arrotondare (*per difetto*)

■ **round off** *vt* (*end*) terminare

■ **round on** *vt* aggredire

■ **round up** *vt* radunare; arrotondare ⟨*prices*⟩

roundabout /ˈraʊndəbaʊt/ *a* indiretto ● *n* giostra *f*; (*for traffic*) rotonda *f*

round: round bracket *n* parentesi *f* tonda. **round figure** *n* cifra *f* tonda. **round robin** *n* petizione *f*

rounders /ˈraʊndəz/ *n* Br Sport gioco *m* si-mile al baseball

round: round-shouldered /-ˈʃəʊldəd/ *a* con le spalle curve. **round table** *n* tavola *f* rotonda. **round the clock** *adv* 24 ore su 24. **round-the-clock** *a* ⟨Br: care, surveillance⟩ ventiquattr'ore su ventiquattro. **round trip** *n* viaggio *m* di an-data e ritorno. **round-up** *n* (*of suspects*) retata *f*; (*of cattle*) raduno *m*; (*summary*) riepilogo *m*

rouse /raʊz/ *vt* svegliare; risvegliare ⟨*suspicion, interest*⟩

rousing /ˈraʊzɪŋ/ *a* ⟨*speech*⟩ che solleva il morale; ⟨*music*⟩ trionfale

rout /raʊt/ *vt Mil, fig* sbaragliare ● *n* disfatta *f*

route /ruːt/ *n* itinerario *m*; Naut, Aeron rotta *f*; (*of bus*) percorso *m*

routine /ruːˈtiːn/ *a* di routine ● *n* routine *f* inv; Theat numero *m*

routinely /ruːˈtiːnlɪ/ *adv* d'ufficio

rove /rəʊv/ *vi* girovagare

roving /ˈrəʊvɪŋ/ *a* ⟨*reporter, ambassador*⟩ itinerante

roving eye *n* **have a ~** essere sempre in cerca di avventure amorose

row[1] /rəʊ/ *n* (*line*) fila *f*; **three years in a ~** tre anni di fila

row[2] *vi* (*in boat*) remare ● *vt* **~ a boat** remare

row[3] /raʊ/ *n fam* (*quarrel*) litigata *f*; (*noise*) baccano *m*; **we've had a ~** abbiamo litigato ● *vi fam* litigare

rowboat /ˈrəʊbəʊt/ *n Am* barca *f* a remi

rowdy /ˈraʊdɪ/ *a* (**-ier, -iest**) chiassoso ● *n* attaccabrighe *m inv*

rower /ˈrəʊə(r)/ *n* rematore, -trice *mf*

rowing boat /ˈrəʊɪŋ/ *n* barca *f* a remi

rowing machine *n* vogatore *m*

rowlock /ˈrɒlək/ *n Br* scalmo *m*

royal /ˈrɔɪəl/ *a* reale ● *n* membro *m* della fa-miglia reale

royally /ˈrɔɪəlɪ/ *adv* regalmente

royalties /ˈrɔɪəltɪz/ *npl* (*payments*) diritti *mpl* d'autore

royalty /ˈrɔɪəltɪ/ *n* appartenenza *f* alla fami-glia reale; (*persons*) i membri della famiglia reale

rpm *abbr* (**revolutions per minute**) giri *mpl* al minuto

rub /rʌb/ *n* sfregata *f* ● *vt* (*pt/pp* **rubbed**) sfre-gare; **~ one's hands** fregarsi le mani

■ **rub along** *vi* sopportarsi [a vicenda]

■ **rub down** *vt* frizionare ⟨*person, body*⟩; le-vigare ⟨*wood*⟩

■ **rub in** *vt* far assorbire (massaggiando) ⟨*cream*⟩; **don't ~ it in** *fam* non rigirare il col-tello nella piaga

■ **rub off** *vt* mandar via sfregando ⟨*stain*⟩; (*from blackboard*) cancellare ● *vi* andar via; **~ off on** essere trasmesso a

■ **rub out** *vt* cancellare

■ **rub up** *vt* **~ sb up the wrong way** pren-dere qcno per il verso sbagliato

rubber /ˈrʌbə(r)/ *n* gomma *f*; (*eraser*) gomma *f* [da cancellare]

rubber: rubber band *n* elastico *m*. **rubber bullet** *n* proiettile *m* di gomma. **rubberneck** *n fam* (*onlooker*) curioso, -a *mf*; (*tourist*) turi-sta *mf*. **rubber plant** *n* ficus *m inv*. **rubber-stamp** *vt fig* approvare senza discutere

rubbery /ˈrʌbərɪ/ *a* gommoso

rubbish /ˈrʌbɪʃ/ *n* immondizie *fpl*; (*fam: nonsense*) idiozie *fpl*; (*fam: junk*) robaccia *f* ● *vt fam* fare a pezzi

rubbish bin *n* pattumiera *f*

rubbish dump *n* discarica *f*; (*official*) di-scarica *f* comunale

rubbishy /ˈrʌbɪʃɪ/ *a fam* schifoso

rubble /ˈrʌbl/ *n* macerie *fpl*

rub-down *n* strofinata *f*

rubella /ruˈbelə/ *n* rosolia *f*

rubric /ˈruːbrɪk/ *n* rubrica *f*

ruby /ˈruːbɪ/ *n* rubino *m* ● *attrib* di rubini; ⟨*lips*⟩ scarlatta

rucksack /ˈrʌksæk/ *n* zaino *m*

ructions /ˈrʌkʃ(ə)nz/ *npl fam* finimondo *msg*; **there'll be ~ if he finds out** se lo sco-pre, succede il finimondo

rudder /ˈrʌdə(r)/ *n* timone *m*

ruddy /ˈrʌdɪ/ *a* (**-ier, -iest**) rubicondo; *fam* maledetto

rude /ruːd/ *a* scortese; (*improper*) spinto

rudely /ˈruːdlɪ/ *adv* scortesemente

rudeness /ˈruːdnɪs/ *n* scortesia *f*

rudimentary /ruːdɪˈmentərɪ/ *a* rudimentale

rudiments /ˈruːdɪmənts/ *npl* rudimenti *mpl*

rue[1] /ruː/ *vt* pentirsi di ⟨*decision*⟩; **~ the day** maledire il giorno

rue[2] *n Bot* ruta *f*

rueful /ˈruːfl/ *a* rassegnato

ruefully /ˈruːfʊlɪ/ *adv* con rassegnazione

ruffian /ˈrʌfɪən/ *n* farabutto *m*

ruffle /ˈrʌfl/ *n* gala *f* ● *vt* scompigliare ⟨*hair*⟩

rug /rʌg/ *n* tappeto *m*; (*blanket*) coperta *f*

rugby /ˈrʌgbɪ/ *n* **~ [football]** rugby *m*

rugby league *n* rugby *m* a tredici

rugby union *n* rugby *m* a quindici

rugged /ˈrʌgɪd/ *a* ⟨*coastline*⟩ roccioso; ⟨*face, personality*⟩ duro

ruin /'ruːɪn/ *n* rovina *f*; **in ~s** in rovina ● *vt* rovinare

ruined /'ruːɪnd/ *a* ⟨*building, clothes*⟩ rovinato

ruinous /'ruːɪnəs/ *a* estremamente costoso

rule /ruːl/ *n* regola *f*; ⟨*control*⟩ ordinamento *m*; ⟨*for measuring*⟩ metro *m*; **~s** *pl* regolamento *msg*; **as a ~** generalmente; **make it a ~ to do sth** fare qcsa sistematicamente ● *vt* governare; dominare ⟨*colony, behaviour*⟩; **~ that** stabilire che ● *vi* governare

■ **rule out** *vt* escludere

ruled /ruːld/ *a* ⟨*paper*⟩ a righe

rule of thumb *n* principio *m* empirico

ruler /'ruːlə(r)/ *n* capo *m* di Stato; ⟨*sovereign*⟩ sovrano, -a *mf*; ⟨*measure*⟩ righello *m*, regolo *m*

ruling /'ruːlɪŋ/ *a* ⟨*class*⟩ dirigente; ⟨*party*⟩ di governo ● *n* decisione *f*

rum[1] /rʌm/ *n* rum *m inv*

rum[2] *a* ⟨*fam: peculiar*⟩ curioso

rumble /'rʌmbl/ *n* rombo *m*; ⟨*of stomach*⟩ brontolio *m* ● *vi* rombare; ⟨*stomach:*⟩ brontolare

rumble strip *n* banda *f* rumorosa

rumbustious /rʌm'bʌstʃəs/ *a* ⟨*noisy, very lively*⟩ chiassoso

ruminant /'ruːmɪnənt/ *n* ruminante *m*

ruminate /'ruːmɪneɪt/ *vi* ⟨*animals:*⟩ ruminare; ⟨*think*⟩ rimuginare

rummage /'rʌmɪdʒ/ *vi* rovistare (**in/ through** in)

rummy /'rʌmɪ/ *n* ramino *m*

rumour /'ruːmə(r)/ *n* diceria *f* ● *vt* **it is ~ed that** si dice che

rumour-monger /'ruːməmʌŋgə(r)/ *n* persona *f* che sparge pettegolezzi

rump /rʌmp/ *n* natiche *fpl*

rumple /'rʌmpl/ *vt* sgualcire ⟨*clothes, sheets, papers*⟩; scompigliare ⟨*hair*⟩

rump steak *n* bistecca *f* di girello

rumpus /'rʌmpəs/ *n fam* baccano *m*

run /rʌn/ *n* ⟨*on foot*⟩ corsa *f*; ⟨*distance to be covered*⟩ tragitto *m*; ⟨*outing*⟩ giro *m*; *Theat* rappresentazioni *fpl*; ⟨*in skiing*⟩ pista *f*; ⟨*Am: ladder*⟩ smagliatura *f* ⟨*in calze*⟩; **at a ~** di corsa; **~ of bad luck** periodo *m* sfortunato; **on the ~** in fuga; **have the ~ of** avere a disposizione; **in the long ~** a lungo termine ● *v* (*pt* **ran**, *pp* **run**, *pres p* **running**) ● *vi* correre; ⟨*river:*⟩ scorrere; ⟨*nose, makeup:*⟩ colare; ⟨*bus:*⟩ fare servizio; ⟨*play:*⟩ essere in cartellone; ⟨*colours:*⟩ sbiadire; ⟨*in election*⟩ presentarsi [come candidato]; ⟨*software:*⟩ girare; **~ aground** insabbiarsi; **~ low on, ~ short of** essere a corto di ● *vt* ⟨*manage*⟩ dirigere; tenere ⟨*house*⟩; ⟨*drive*⟩ dare un passaggio a; correre ⟨*risk*⟩; *Comput* lanciare; *Journ* pubblicare ⟨*article*⟩; ⟨*pass*⟩ far scorrere ⟨*eyes, hand*⟩; **~ a temperature** avere la febbre; **~ a bath** far scorrere l'acqua per il bagno

■ **run about** *vi* ⟨*children:*⟩ correre di qua e di là; ⟨*be busy*⟩ correre

■ **run across** *vt* imbattersi in

■ **run after** *vt* ⟨*chase*⟩ rincorrere; ⟨*romantically*⟩ andare dietro a

■ **run along** *vi* ⟨*go away*⟩ andare via

■ **run away** *vi* scappare [via], andare via di corsa; ⟨*from home*⟩ scappare di casa

■ **run away with** *vt* scappare con ⟨*lover, money*⟩; **she let her enthusiasm ~ away with her** si è lasciata trasportare dall'entusiasmo

■ **run back** *vi* correre indietro ● *vt* ⟨*transport by car*⟩ riaccompagnare

■ **run back over** *vt* ⟨*review*⟩ rivedere

■ **run down** *vi* ⟨*clock:*⟩ scaricarsi; ⟨*stocks:*⟩ esaurirsi ● *vt* *Auto* investire; ⟨*reduce*⟩ esaurire; ⟨*fam: criticize*⟩ denigrare

■ **run in** *vi* entrare di corsa

■ **run into** *vi* ⟨*meet*⟩ imbattersi in; ⟨*knock against*⟩ urtare

■ **run off** *vi* scappare [via], andare via di corsa; ⟨*from home*⟩ scappare di casa ● *vt* stampare ⟨*copies*⟩

■ **run off with** *vt* = **run away with**

■ **run on** *vi* ⟨*meeting:*⟩ protrarsi; ⟨*person:*⟩ chiacchierare senza sosta

■ **run out** *vi* uscire di corsa; ⟨*supplies, money:*⟩ esaurirsi; **~ out of** rimanere senza

■ **run over** *vi* correre; ⟨*overflow*⟩ traboccare ● *vt* ⟨*review*⟩ dare una scorsa a; *Auto* investire

■ **run through** *vt* ⟨*use up*⟩ fare fuori; ⟨*be present in*⟩ pervadere; ⟨*review*⟩ dare una scorsa a

■ **run to** *vt* ⟨*be enough for*⟩ essere sufficiente per; ⟨*have enough money for*⟩ potersi permettere

■ **run up** *vi* salire di corsa; ⟨*towards*⟩ arrivare di corsa ● *vt* accumulare ⟨*debts, bill*⟩; ⟨*sew*⟩ cucire

■ **run up against** *vt* incontrare ⟨*difficulties*⟩

run: **runabout** *n* ⟨*vehicle*⟩ utilitaria *f*. **run-around** *n* **he's giving me/her the ~** mi/la sta menando per il naso. **runaway** *n* fuggitivo, -a *mf*, fuggiasco, -a *mf*; ⟨*child*⟩ ragazzo, -a *mf* scappato, -a di casa ● *a* ⟨*person*⟩ in fuga; ⟨*child*⟩ scappato di casa; ⟨*inflation*⟩ galoppante; ⟨*success*⟩ eclatante. **run-down** *a* ⟨*area*⟩ in abbandono; ⟨*person*⟩ esaurito ● *n* analisi *f*

rung[1] /rʌŋ/ *n* ⟨*of ladder*⟩ piolo *m*

rung[2] *see* **ring**[2]

run-in *n* ⟨*fam: argument*⟩ lite *f*

runner /'rʌnə(r)/ *n* podista *mf*; ⟨*in race*⟩ corridore, -trice *mf*; ⟨*on sledge*⟩ pattino *f*; ⟨*carpet*⟩ guida *f*

runner bean *n* fagiolino *m*

runner-up *n* secondo, -a classificato, -a *mf*

running /'rʌnɪŋ/ *a* in corsa; ⟨*water*⟩ corrente; **four times ~** quattro volte di seguito ● *n* corsa *f*; ⟨*management*⟩ direzione *f*; **be in the ~** essere in lizza

running commentary *n* cronaca *f*

runny /'rʌnɪ/ *a* semiliquido; **~ nose** naso *m* che cola

run-of-the-mill *a* ordinario

runs /rʌnz/ *npl* **the ~** ⟨*fam: diarrhoea*⟩ la sciolta

runt /rʌnt/ *n* ⟨*of litter*⟩ animale *m* più piccolo

e debole di una figliata; *(pej: weakling)* mezza cartuccia *f*
run-through *n* prova *f* generale
run-up *n Sport* rincorsa *f*; **the ~ to** il periodo precedente
runway /'rʌnweɪ/ *n* pista *f*
rupee /ru:'pi:/ *n* rupia *f*
rupture /'rʌptʃə(r)/ *n* rottura *f*; *Med* ernia *f* ● *vt* rompere; **~ oneself** farsi venire l'ernia ● *vi* rompersi
rural /'rʊərəl/ *a* rurale
ruse /ru:z/ *n* astuzia *f*
rush¹ /rʌʃ/ *n Bot* giunco *m*
rush² *n* fretta *f*; **in a ~** di fretta ● *vi* precipitarsi ● *vt* far premura a; **~ sb to hospital** trasportare qcno di corsa all'ospedale
■ **rush away, rush off** *vi* andar via in fretta
rush hour *n* ora *f* di punta ● *attrib* delle ore di punta
rusk /rʌsk/ *n* biscotto *m*

Russia /'rʌʃə/ *n* Russia *f*
Russian /'rʌʃən/ *a* & *n* russo, -a *mf*; *(language)* russo *m*
Russian roulette *n* roulette *f* russa
rust /rʌst/ *n* ruggine *f* ● *vi* arrugginirsi ● *vt* arruginire
rustic /'rʌstɪk/ *a* rustico
rustle /'rʌsl/ *vi* frusciare ● *vt* far frusciare; *Am* rubare *(cattle)*
■ **rustle up** *vt fam* fare *(meal, cup of coffee)*
rustler /'rʌslə(r)/ *n* ladro *m* di bestiame
rustproof /'rʌstpru:f/ *a* a prova di ruggine
rusty /'rʌstɪ/ *a* **(-ier, -iest)** arrugginito
rut /rʌt/ *n* solco *m*; **in a ~** *fam* nella routine
ruthless /'ru:θlɪs/ *a* spietato
ruthlessly /'ru:θlɪslɪ/ *adv* spietatamente
ruthlessness /'ru:θlɪsnɪs/ *n* spietatezza *f*
rutting /'rʌtɪŋ/ *n* accoppiamento *m*
rutting season *n* stagione *f* degli amori
rye /raɪ/ *n* segale *f*

Ss

s, S /es/ *n (letter)* s, S *f inv*
S *abbr* **small**; *abbr* **(south)** S
sabbath /'sæbəθ/ *n* domenica *f*; *(Jewish)* sabato *m*
sabbatical /sə'bætɪkl/ *n Univ* anno *m* sabbatico
sable /'seɪbl/ *n (animal, fur)* zibellino *m*
sabotage /'sæbətɑːʒ/ *n* sabotaggio *m* ● *vt* sabotare
saboteur /sæbə'tɜː(r)/ *n* sabotatore, -trice *mf*
sabre /'seɪbə(r)/ *n* sciabola *f*
sac /sæk/ *n Anat, Zool* sacco *m*; *Bot* sacca *f*; **honey ~** cestella *f*
saccharin /'sækərɪn/ *n* saccarina *f*
sachet /'sæʃeɪ/ *n* bustina *f*; *(scented)* sacchetto *m* profumato
sack¹ /sæk/ *vt (plunder)* saccheggiare
sack² *n* sacco *m*; **get the ~** *fam* essere licenziato; **give sb the ~** licenziare qcno ● *vt fam* licenziare
sackcloth /'sækklɒθ/ *n* tela *f* di sacco; **wear ~ and ashes** cospargersi il capo di cenere
sackful /'sækfʊl/ *n* sacco *m (contenuto)*
sacking /'sækɪŋ/ *n* tela *f* per sacchi; *(fam: dismissal)* licenziamento *m*
sackload /'sækləʊd/ *n* sacco *m (contenuto)*
sacrament /'sækrəmənt/ *n* sacramento *m*
sacred /'seɪkrɪd/ *a* sacro
sacred cow /kaʊ/ *n (institution)* istituzione *f* intoccabile; *(principle)* principio *m* inderogabile; *(person)* mostro *m* sacro
sacrifice /'sækrɪfaɪs/ *n* sacrificio *m* ● *vt* sacrificare; **~ oneself** immolarsi
sacrificial /sækrɪ'fɪʃəl/ *a (victim)* sacrificale

sacrilege /'sækrɪlɪdʒ/ *n* sacrilegio *m*
sacrilegious /sækrɪ'lɪdʒəs/ *a* sacrilego
sacristy /'sækrɪstɪ/ *n* sagrestia *f*
sacrosanct /'sækrəʊsæŋkt/ *a* sacrosanto
sacrum /'sækrʌm/ *n Anat* osso *m* sacro
sad /sæd/ *a* **(sadder, saddest)** triste
sadden /'sædn/ *vt* rattristare
saddle /'sædl/ *n* sella *f*; **be in the ~** *fig* tenere le redini ● *vt* sellare; **I've been ~d with...** *fig* mi hanno affibbiato...
sadism /'seɪdɪzm/ *n* sadismo *m*
sadist /'seɪdɪst/ *n* sadico, -a *mf*
sadistic /sə'dɪstɪk/ *a* sadico
sadistically /sə'dɪstɪklɪ/ *adv* sadicamente
sadly /'sædlɪ/ *adv* tristemente; *(unfortunately)* sfortunatamente
sadness /'sædnɪs/ *n* tristezza *f*
sadomasochism /seɪdəʊ'mæsəkɪzm/ *n* sadomasochismo *m*
sadomasochist /seɪdəʊ'mæsəkɪst/ *n* sadomasochismo *m*
sadomasochistic /seɪdəʊ'mæsəkɪstɪk/ *a* sadomasochistico
sae *abbr* **stamped addressed envelope**
safari /sə'fɑːrɪ/ *n* safari *m inv*
safari park *n* zoosafari *m inv*
safe /seɪf/ *a* sicuro; *(out of danger)* salvo; *(object)* al sicuro; **~ and sound** sano e salvo ● *n* cassaforte *f*
safe: safe-breaker *n* scassinatore, -trice *mf*. **safeguard** *n* protezione *f* ● *vt* proteggere. **safe keeping** *n* custodia *f*; **for ~** in custodia
safely /'seɪflɪ/ *adv* in modo sicuro; *(arrive)* senza incidenti; *(assume)* con certezza

safe sex *n* sesso *m* sicuro

safety /'seɪftɪ/ *n* sicurezza *f*

safety: safety belt *n* cintura *f* di sicurezza.
safety catch *n* sicura *f*. **safety curtain** *n*
tagliafuoco *m*. **safety-deposit box** *n* cassetta *f* di sicurezza. **safety glass** *n* vetro *m* di
sicurezza. **safety net** *n* (*for acrobat*) rete *f* di
protezione; *fig* protezione. **safety pin** *n* spilla
f di sicurezza *o* da balia. **safety razor** *n* rasoio *m* di sicurezza. **safety valve** *n* valvola *f* di
sicurezza; *fig* valvola *f* di sfogo

saffron /'sæfrən/ *n* zafferano *m*

sag /sæg/ *vi* (*pt/pp* **sagged**) abbassarsi

saga /'sɑːɡə/ *n* saga *f*

sagacity /sə'ɡæsətɪ/ *n* sagacia *f*

sage[1] /seɪdʒ/ *n* (*herb*) salvia *f*

sage[2] *a* & *n* saggio, -a *mf*

sagely /'seɪdʒlɪ/ *adv* (*reply, nod*) saggiamente

Sagittarius /sædʒɪ'teərɪəs/ *n* Sagittario *m*

sago /'seɪɡəʊ/ *n* sagù *m*

Sahara /sə'hɑːrə/ *n* Sahara *m*

said /sed/ *see* **say**

sail /seɪl/ *n* vela *f*; (*trip*) giro *m* in barca a vela
● *vi* navigare; *Sport* praticare la vela; (*leave*)
salpare ● *vt* pilotare

■ **sail through** *vt* superare senza problemi
(*exam*)

sailboard /'seɪlbɔːd/ *n* tavola *f* del windsurf

sailboarding /'seɪlbɔːdɪŋ/ *n* windsurf *m inv*

sailboat /'seɪlbəʊt/ *n* Am barca *f* a vela

sailing /'seɪlɪŋ/ *n* vela *f*

sailing boat *n* barca *f* a vela

sailing ship *n* veliero *m*

sailor /'seɪlə(r)/ *n* marinaio *m*

saint /seɪnt/ *n* santo, -a *mf*

sainthood /'seɪnthʊd/ *n* santità *f*

saintly /'seɪntlɪ/ *a* da santo

sake /seɪk/ *n* **for the ~ of** (*person*) per il
bene di; (*peace*) per amor di; **for the ~ of it**
per il gusto di farlo

salacious /sə'leɪʃəs/ *a* (*joke*) salace; (*book*)
licenzioso; (*look*) lascivo

salad /'sæləd/ *n* insalata *f*

salad: salad bar *n* tavola *f* fredda. **salad
bowl** *n* insalatiera *f*. **salad cream** *n* salsa *f*
per condire l'insalata. **salad days** *npl* anni
mpl verdi. **salad dressing** *n* condimento *m*
per insalata

salami /sə'lɑːmɪ/ *n* salame *m*

salaried /'sælərɪd/ *a* stipendiato

salary /'sælərɪ/ *n* stipendio *m*

salary review *n* revisione *f* dello stipendio

salary scale *n* tabella *f* retributiva

sale /seɪl/ *n* vendita *f*; (*at reduced prices*)
svendita *f*; **for/on ~** in vendita; **'for ~'**
'vendesi'

sales: sales and marketing *n* vendite *fpl* e
marketing. **sales and marketing department** *n* ufficio *m* vendite e marketing. **sales
assistant** *n* commesso, -a *mf*. **sales director** *n* capo *mf* dell'ufficio vendite. **sales engineer** *n* tecnico *m* commerciale. **sales figures** *npl* volumi *mpl* d'affari. **sales force** *n*
rappresentanti *mpl*. **sales invoice** *n* fattura *f*
di vendita. **sales ledger** *n* partitario *m*

vendite. salesman *n* venditore *m*; (*traveller*)
rappresentante *m*. **salesroom** *n* (*for auc-
tions*) sala *f* d'aste. **sales team** *n* team *m inv*
vendite. **saleswoman** *n* venditrice *f*

salient /'seɪlɪənt/ *a* saliente

saline /'seɪlaɪn/ *a* salino

saliva /sə'laɪvə/ *n* saliva *f*

salivary glands /sə'laɪvərɪ/ *npl* ghiandole
fpl salivari

salivate /'sælɪveɪt/ *vi* salivare; **the smell of
chicken roasting makes me ~** l'odore di
pollo arrosto mi fa venire l'acquolina in bocca

sallow /'sæləʊ/ *a* giallastro

sally /'sælɪ/ *n* (*witty remark*) battuta *f*; *Mil*
sortita *f* ● *vi* saltar fuori

salmon /'sæmən/ *n* salmone *m*

salmonella /sælmə'nelə/ *n* salmonella *f*

salmon-pink *a* [rosa *inv*] salmone *inv*

salmon trout *n* trota *f* salmonata

salon /'sælɒn/ *n* salone *m*

saloon /sə'luːn/ *n* Auto berlina *f*; (*Am: bar*)
bar *m*

salsa /'sælsə/ *n* salsa *f*

salt /sɔːlt/ *n* sale *m* ● *a* salato; (*fish, meat*)
sotto sale ● *vt* salare; (*cure*) mettere sotto
sale

salt cellar *n* saliera *f*

saltiness /'sɔːltɪnɪs/ *n* salinità *f*

salt water *n* acqua *f* di mare

salt-water fish *n* pesce *m* d'acqua salata

salty /'sɔːltɪ/ *a* salato

salubrious /sə'luːbrɪəs/ *a* (*neighbourhood*)
raccomandabile; **it's not a very ~ area** è
una zona poco raccomandabile

salutary /'sæljʊtərɪ/ *a* salutare

salute /sə'luːt/ *Mil n* saluto *m* ● *vt* salutare
● *vi* fare il saluto

salvage /'sælvɪdʒ/ *n* Naut recupero *m* ● *vt*
recuperare

salvation /sæl'veɪʃn/ *n* salvezza *f*

Salvation Army *n* Esercito *m* della Salvezza

salve /sælv/ *vt* **~ one's conscience** mettersi la coscienza a posto

salver /'sælvə(r)/ *n* vassoio *m* (*di metallo*)

salvo /'sælvəʊ/ *n* salva *f*

samba /'sæmbə/ *n* samba *f*

same /seɪm/ *a* stesso (**as** di) ● *pron* **the ~** lo
stesso; **be all the ~** essere tutti uguali ● *adv*
the ~ nello stesso modo; **all the ~** (*however*)
lo stesso; **the ~ to you** altrettanto

same-day delivery *n* consegna *f* in giornata

sample /'sɑːmpl/ *n* campione *m* ● *vt* testare

sanatorium /sænə'tɔːrɪəm/ *n* casa *f* di cura

sanctify /'sæŋktɪfaɪ/ *vt* (*pt/pp* **-fied**) santifi-
care

sanctimonious /sæŋktɪ'məʊnɪəs/ *a* mora-
leggiante

sanction /'sæŋkʃn/ *n* (*approval*) autorizzazione *f*; (*penalty*) sanzione *f* ● *vt* autorizzare

sanctity /'sæŋktətɪ/ *n* santità *f*

sanctuary /'sæŋktjʊərɪ/ *n* Relig santuario
m; (*refuge*) asilo *m*; (*for wildlife*) riserva *f*

sanctum /'sæŋktəm/ *n* (*holy place*) santuario *m*; (*private place*) rifugio *m*; **the inner ~** Relig il Sancta Sanctorum

sand /sænd/ *n* sabbia *f* ● *vt* ~ **[down]** carteggiare

sandal /'sændl/ *n* sandalo *m*

sand: sandbag *n* sacchetto *m* di sabbia. **sandbank** *n* banco *m* di sabbia. **sand dune** *n* duna *f*. **sandblast** *vt* sabbiare. **sandblasting** *n* sabbiatura *f*. **sandcastle** *n* castello *m* di sabbia

sander /'sændə(r)/ *n* (*machine*) levigatrice *f*

Sandinista /sændɪ'niːstə/ *a* & *n* sandinista

sand: sandpaper *n* carta *f* vetrata ● *vt* cartavetrare. **sandpit** *n* recinto *m* contenente *sabbia dove giocano i bambini*. **sandstone** *n* arenaria *f*. **sandstorm** *n* tempesta *f* di sabbia

sandwich /'sænwɪdʒ/ *n* tramezzino *m* ● *vt* ~**ed between** schiacciato tra

sandwich course *n* corso *m* che comprende dei periodi di tirocinio

sandwich-man *n* uomo *m* sandwich

sandy /'sændɪ/ *a* (**-ier, -iest**) (*beach, soil*) sabbioso; (*hair*) biondiccio

sane /seɪn/ *a* (*not mad*) sano di mente; (*sensible*) sensato

sang /sæŋ/ *see* **sing**

sangria /sæŋ'griə/ *n* sangria *f*

sanguine /'sæŋgwɪn/ *a* ottimistico

sanitary /'sænɪtərɪ/ *a* igienico; (*system*) sanitario

sanitary napkin *n Am*, **sanitary towel** *n* assorbente *m* igienico

sanitation /sænɪ'teɪʃn/ *n* impianti *mpl* igienici

sanity /'sænətɪ/ *n* sanità *f* di mente; (*sensibleness*) buon senso *m*

sank /sæŋk/ *see* **sink**

Santa [Claus] /'sæntə[klɔːz]/ *n* Babbo *m* Natale

sap /sæp/ *n* Bot linfa *f* ● *vt* (*pt/pp* **sapped**) indebolire

sapling /'sæplɪŋ/ *n* alberello *m*

sapper /'sæpə(r)/ *n Br Mil* geniere *m*

sapphire /'sæfaɪə(r)/ *n* zaffiro *m* ● *attrib* blu zaffiro *inv*

sarcasm /'sɑːkæzm/ *n* sarcasmo *m*

sarcastic /sɑː'kæstɪk/ *a* sarcastico

sarcastically /sɑː'kæstɪklɪ/ *adv* sarcasticamente

sarcophagus /sɑː'kɒfəgəs/ *n* sarcofago *m*

sardine /sɑː'diːn/ *n* sardina *f*

Sardinia /sɑː'dɪnɪə/ *n* Sardegna *f*

Sardinian /sɑː'dɪnɪən/ *a* & *n* sardo, -a *mf*

sardonic /sɑː'dɒnɪk/ *a* sardonico

sardonically /sɑː'dɒnɪklɪ/ *adv* sardonicamente

sari /'sɑːrɪ/ *n* sari *m inv*

sarong /sə'rɒŋ/ *n* pareo *m*

SAS *n Br abbr* (**Special Air Service**) *commando mpl britannici per operazioni speciali*

sash /sæʃ/ *n* fascia *f*; (*for dress*) fusciacca *f*

sashay /'sæʃeɪ/ *vi fam* (*casually*) camminare in modo disinvolto; (*seductively*) camminare in modo provocante

sassy /'sæsɪ/ *a Am fam* (*cheeky*) sfacciato; (*smart*) chic *inv*

sat /sæt/ *see* **sit**

Satan /'seɪtən/ *n* Satana *m*

satanic /sə'tænɪk/ *a* satanico

satchel /'sætʃl/ *n* cartella *f*

sated /'seɪtɪd/ *a* (*person*) sazio; (*desire*) appagato; (*appetite*) soddisfatto

satellite /'sætəlaɪt/ *n* satellite *m*

satellite dish *n* antenna *f* parabolica

satellite television *n* televisione *f* via satellite

satiate /'seɪʃɪeɪt/ *vt* saziare (*person*); appagare (*desire*); soddisfare (*appetite*)

satin /'sætɪn/ *n* raso *m* ● *attrib* di raso

satire /'sætaɪə(r)/ *n* satira *f*

satirical /sə'tɪrɪkl/ *a* satirico

satirically /sə'tɪrɪklɪ/ *adv* satiricamente

satirist /'sætərɪst/ *n* scrittore, -trice *mf* satirico, -a; (*comedian*) comico, -a *mf* satirico, -a

satirize /'sætɪraɪz/ *vt* satireggiare

satisfaction /sætɪs'fækʃn/ *n* soddisfazione *f*; **be to sb's ~** soddisfare qcno

satisfactorily /sætɪs'fækt(ə)rɪlɪ/ *adv* in modo soddisfacente

satisfactory /sætɪs'fæktərɪ/ *a* soddisfacente

satisfy /'sætɪsfaɪ/ *vt* (*pp/pp* **-ied**) soddisfare; (*convince*) convincere; **be satisfied** essere soddisfatto

satisfying /'sætɪsfaɪɪŋ/ *a* soddisfacente

saturate /'sætʃəreɪt/ *vt* inzuppare (**with** di); Chem, fig saturare (**with** di)

saturated /'sætʃəreɪtɪd/ *a* saturo

saturation /sætʃə'reɪʃn/ *n* **reach ~ point** raggiungere il punto di saturazione

Saturday /'sætədeɪ/ *n* sabato *m*

Saturn /'sætən/ *n* Saturno *m*

sauce /sɔːs/ *n* salsa *f*; (*cheek*) impertinenza *f*

saucepan /'sɔːspən/ *n* pentola *f*

saucer /'sɔːsə(r)/ *n* piattino *m*

saucy /'sɔːsɪ/ *a* (**-ier, -iest**) impertinente

Saudi /'saʊdɪ/ *a* saudita ● *n* (*person*) saudita *mf*; (*country*) Arabia *f* Saudita

Saudi Arabia /ə'reɪbɪə/ *n* Arabia *f* Saudita

Saudi Arabian *a* & *n* saudita *mf*

sauerkraut /'saʊəkraʊt/ *n* crauti *mpl*

sauna /'sɔːnə/ *n* sauna *f*

saunter /'sɔːntə(r)/ *vi* andare a spasso

sausage /'sɒsɪdʒ/ *n* salsiccia *f*; (*dried*) salame *m*

sausage dog /'sɒsɪdʒdɒg/ *n fam* bassotto *m*

sausage roll *n* involtino *m* di pasta sfoglia con salsiccia

sauté /'səʊteɪ/ *vt* rosolare ● *a* rosolato

savage /'sævɪdʒ/ *a* feroce; (*tribe, custom*) selvaggio ● *n* selvaggio, -a *mf* ● *vt* fare a pezzi

savagely /'sævɪdʒlɪ/ *adv* (*attack*) selvaggiamente; (*criticize*) ferocemente

savagery /'sævɪdʒrɪ/ *n* ferocia *f*

save /seɪv/ *n* Sport parata *f* ● *vt* salvare (**from** da); (*keep, collect*) tenere; risparmiare (*time, money*); (*avoid*) evitare; Sport parare (*goal*); Comput salvare, memorizzare; **~ face** salvar la faccia ● *vi* ~ **[up]** risparmiare ● *prep* salvo

saver /'seɪvə(r)/ *n* risparmiatore, -trice *mf*

saving grace /'seɪvɪŋ'greɪs/ *n* **that's his one ~** ~ si salva grazie a questo

savings /'seɪvɪŋz/ *npl* (*money*) risparmi *mpl*

savings: savings account *n* libretto *m* di risparmio. **savings and loan association** *n Am* associazione *f* mutua di risparmi e prestiti. **savings bank** *n* cassa *f* di risparmio

saviour /'seɪvjə(r)/ *n* salvatore *m*

savoir faire /sævwɑː'feə(r)/ *n* (*social*) savoir-faire *m*

savory /'seɪvərɪ/ *n Bot* santoreggia *f*

savour /'seɪvə(r)/ *n* sapore *m* ● *vt* assaporare

savoury /'seɪvərɪ/ *a* salato; *fig* rispettabile

saw[1] /sɔː/ *see* **see**[1]

saw[2] *n* sega *f* ● *vt* (*pt* **sawed**, *pp* **sawn** *or* **sawed**) segare

sawdust /'sɔːdʌst/ *n* segatura *f*

sawmill /'sɔːmɪl/ *n* segheria *f*

Saxon /'sæksən/ *a & n* sassone *mf*; (*language*) sassone *m*

saxophone /'sæksəfəʊn/ *n* sassofono *m*

saxophonist /sæk'sʊfənɪst/ *n* sassofonista *mf*

say /seɪ/ *n* **have one's ~** dire la propria; **have a ~** avere voce in capitolo ● *vt/i* (*pt/pp* **said**) dire; **that is to ~** cioè; **that goes without ~ing** questo è ovvio; **when all is said and done** alla fine dei conti; **~ yes/no** dire di sì/no; **just ~ the word and I'll come** tu chiama e io vengo. **what more can I ~?** che altro dire?. **some time next week ~?** la prossima settimana, diciamo?; **the clock ~s ten to six** la sveglia fa le sei meno dieci; **you can ~ that again!** puoi dirlo forte!; **the tree is said to be very old** a quanto pare l'albero è vecchissimo; **he said you were to bring the car** ha detto che dovevi portare la macchina; **it ~s a lot for him that...** il fatto che...la dice lunga sul suo conto; **what have you got to ~ for yourself?** che scusa hai?; **to ~ nothing of...** per non parlare di...; **what would you ~ to a new car?** cosa ne diresti di una macchina nuova?

saying /'seɪɪŋ/ *n* proverbio *m*

scab /skæb/ *n* crosta *f*; *pej* crumiro *m*

scabby /'skæbɪ/ *a* (*plant*) coperto di galle; (*skin*) coperto di croste; (*animal*) rognoso; (*fam: nasty*) schifoso

scaffold /'skæfəld/ *n* patibolo *m*

scaffolding /'skæfəldɪŋ/ *n* impalcatura *f*

scalar /'skeɪlə(r)/ *a* scalare

scald /skɔːld/ *vt* scottare; (*milk*) scaldare ● *n* scottatura *f*

scalding /'skɔːldɪŋ/ *a* bollente

scale[1] /skeɪl/ *n* (*of fish*) scaglia *f*

scale[2] *n* scala *f*; **on a grand ~** su vasta scale; **to ~** in scala; **~ of values** scala *f* di valori ● *vt* (*climb*) scalare

■ scale down *vt* diminuire

scale model *n* modello *m* in scala

scales /skeɪlz/ *npl* (*for weighing*) bilancia *fsg*

scallop /'skɒləp/ *n* (*in sewing*) smerlo *m*, festone *m*; *Zool* pettine *m*; *Culin* cappasanta *f*

● *vt* (*in sewing*) smerlare; **~ed potatoes** patate *fpl* gratinate

scalp /skælp/ *n* cuoio *m* capelluto ● *vt* scalpare

scalpel /'skælpl/ *n* bisturi *m inv*

scaly /'skeɪlɪ/ *a* (*wing, fish*) squamoso; (*plaster, wall*) scrostato

scam /skæm/ *n fam* fregatura *f*

scamper /'skæmpə(r)/ *vi* **~ away** sgattaiolare via

scampi /'skæmpɪ/ *npl* scampi *mpl*

scan /skæn/ *n Med* scanning *m inv*, scansioscintigrafia *f* ● *v* (*pt/pp* **scanned**) ● *vt* scrutare; (*quickly*) dare una scorsa a; *Med* fare uno scanning di; *Comput* scannerizzare ● *vi* (*poetry:*) scandire

scandal /'skændl/ *n* scandalo *m*; (*gossip*) pettegolezzi *mpl*

scandalize /'skændəlaɪz/ *vt* scandalizzare

scandalmonger /'skænd(ə)lmʌŋgə(r)/ *n* malalingua *f*

scandalous /'skændələs/ *a* scandaloso

Scandinavia /skændɪ'neɪvɪə/ *n* Scandinavia *f*

Scandinavian /skændɪ'neɪvɪən/ *a & n* scandinavo, -a *mf*

scanner /'skænə(r)/ *n Med, Comput* scanner *m inv*; (*radar*) antenna *f* radar; (*for bar codes*) lettore *m* di codice a barre

scanning /'skænɪŋ/ *n Comput* scannerizzazione *f*

scant /skænt/ *a* scarso

scantily /'skæntɪlɪ/ *adv* scarsamente; (*clothed*) succintamente

scanty /'skæntɪ/ *a* (**-ier**, **-iest**) scarso; (*clothing*) succinto

scapegoat /'skeɪpgəʊt/ *n* capro *m* espiatorio

scar /skɑː(r)/ *n* cicatrice *f* ● *vt* (*pt/pp* **scarred**) lasciare una cicatrice a

scar tissue *n* tessuto *m* di cicatrizzazione

scarce /skeəs/ *a* scarso; *fig* raro; **make oneself ~** *fam* svignarsela

scarcely /'skeəslɪ/ *adv* appena; **~ anything** quasi niente

scarcity /'skeəsətɪ/ *n* scarsezza *f*

scare /skeə(r)/ *n* spavento *m*; (*panic*) panico *m* ● *vt* spaventare; **be ~d** aver paura (**of** di)

■ scare away *vt* far scappare

scarecrow /'skeəkrəʊ/ *n* spaventapasseri *m inv*

scaremonger /'skeəmʌŋgə(r)/ *n* allarmista *mf*

scaremongering /'skeəmʌŋgərɪŋ/ *n* allarmismo *m*

scarf /skɑːf/ *n* (*pl* **scarves**) sciarpa *f*; (*square*) foulard *m inv*

scarlet /'skɑːlət/ *a* scarlatto

scarlet fever *n* scarlattina *f*

scarper /'skɑːpə(r)/ *vi Br fam* squagliarsela

scary /'skeərɪ/ *a* **be ~** far paura

scathing /'skeɪðɪŋ/ *a* mordace

scatter /'skætə(r)/ *vt* spargere; (*disperse*) disperdere ● *vi* disperdersi

scatterbrained /'skætəbreɪnd/ *a fam* scervellato

scattered /'skætəd/ *a* sparso

scatty /'skætɪ/ *a* (**-ier, -iest**) *fam* svitato

scavenge /'skævɪndʒ/ *vi* frugare nella spazzatura

scavenger /'skævɪndʒə(r)/ *n persona f che fruga nella spazzatura*

scenario /sɪ'nɑːrɪəʊ/ *n* scenario *m*

scene /siːn/ *n* scena *f*; (*quarrel*) scenata *f*; **behind the ~s** dietro le quinte

scenery /'siːnərɪ/ *n* scenario *m*

scenic /'siːnɪk/ *a* panoramico

scent /sent/ *n* odore *m*; (*trail*) scia *f*; (*perfume*) profumo *m*

scented /'sentɪd/ *a* profumato (**with** di)

sceptic /'skeptɪk/ *n* scettico, -a *mf*

sceptical /'skeptɪkl/ *a* scettico

sceptically /'skeptɪklɪ/ *adv* in modo scettico

scepticism /'skeptɪsɪzm/ *n* scetticismo *m*

schedule /'ʃedjuːl/ *n* piano *m*, programma *m*; (*of work*) programma *m*; (*Am: timetable*) orario *m*; **behind ~** indietro; **on ~** nei tempi previsti; **according to ~** secondo i tempi previsti ● *vt* prevedere

scheduled flight /ʃedjuːld'flaɪt/ *n* volo *m* di linea

schematic /skɪ'mætɪk/ *a* schematico

scheme /skiːm/ *n* (*plan*) piano *m*; (*plot*) macchinazione *f* ● *vi pej* macchinare

scheming /'skiːmɪŋ/ *n pej* macchinazioni *fpl*, intrighi *mpl* ● *a* ⟨*person*⟩ intrigante

schism /'skɪzm/ *n* scisma *m*

schizophrenia /skɪtsə'friːnɪə/ *n* schizofrenia *f*

schizoprenic /skɪtsə'frenɪk/ *a* schizofrenico

schmaltzy /'ʃmɒltsɪ/ *a* sdolcinato

scholar /'skɒlə(r)/ *n* studioso, -a *mf*

scholarly /'skɒləlɪ/ *a* erudito

scholarship /'skɒləʃɪp/ *n* erudizione *f*; (*grant*) borsa *f* di studio

scholastic /skə'læstɪk/ *a* scolastico

school /skuːl/ *n* scuola *f*; (*in university*) facoltà *f*; (*of fish*) branco *m* ● *vt* addestrare ⟨*animal*⟩

school: school age *n* **of ~ ~** in età scolare. **schoolboy** *n* scolaro *m*. **schoolchild** *n* scolaro, -a *mf*. **schooldays** *npl* tempi *mpl* della scuola. **schoolgirl** *n* scolara *f*. **school leaver** *n* ≈ neo-diplomato, -a *mf*. **school-leaving age** *n* età *f* della scuola dell'obbligo

schooling /'skuːlɪŋ/ *n* istruzione *f*

school: schoolmaster *n* maestro *m*; (*secondary*) insegnante *m*. **schoolmistress** *n* maestra *f*; (*secondary*) insegnante *f*. **schoolteacher** *n* insegnante *mf*

schooner /'skuːnə(r)/ *n* (*Am: glass*) boccale *m* da birra; (*Br: glass*) grande bicchiere *m* da sherry; (*boat*) goletta *f*

sciatica /saɪ'ætɪkə/ *n* sciatica *f*

science /'saɪəns/ *n* scienza *f*

science fiction *n* fantascienza *f*

scientific /saɪən'tɪfɪk/ *a* scientifico

scientifically /saɪən'tɪfɪklɪ/ *adv* scientificamente

scientist /'saɪəntɪst/ *n* scienziato, -a *mf*

sci-fi /'saɪfaɪ/ *n fam* fantascienza *f*

scintillate /'sɪntɪleɪt/ *vi fig* brillare

scintillating /'sɪntɪleɪtɪŋ/ *a* brillante

scissors /'sɪzəz/ *npl* forbici *fpl*

scoff[1] /skɒf/ *vi* **~ at** schernire

scoff[2] *vt fam* divorare

scold /skəʊld/ *vt* sgridare

scolding /'skəʊldɪŋ/ *n* sgridata *f*

scollop /'skɒləp/ **= scallop**

scone /skɒn/ *n pasticcino m da tè*

scoop /skuːp/ *n* paletta *f*; *Journ* scoop *m inv*
■ **scoop out** *vt* svuotare
■ **scoop up** *vt* tirar su

scoot /skuːt/ *vi fam* filare

scooter /'skuːtə(r)/ *n* motoretta *f*

scope /skəʊp/ *n* portata *f*; (*opportunity*) opportunità *f inv*

scorch /skɔːtʃ/ *vt* bruciare

scorcher /'skɔːtʃə(r)/ *n fam* giornata *f* torrida

scorching /'skɔːtʃɪŋ/ *a* caldissimo

score /skɔː(r)/ *n* punteggio *m*; *Mus* partitura *f*; (*for film, play*) musica *f*; **a ~** [**of**] (*twenty*) una ventina [di]; **keep [the] ~** tenere il punteggio; **on that ~** a questo proposito ● *vt* segnare ⟨*goal*⟩; (*cut*) incidere ● *vi* far punti; (*in football etc*) segnare; (*keep score*) tenere il punteggio
■ **score out** *vt* cancellare

scoreboard *n* /'skɔːbɔːd/ tabellone *m* segnapunti

scorer /'skɔːrə(r)/ *n* segnapunti *m inv*; (*of goals*) giocatore, -trice *mf* che segna; **top ~** cannoniere *m*

scorn /skɔːn/ *n* disprezzo *m* ● *vt* disprezzare

scornful /'skɔːnfʊl/ *a* sprezzante

scornfully /'skɔːnfʊlɪ/ *adv* sdegnosamente

Scorpio /'skɔːpɪəʊ/ *n Astr* Scorpione *m*

scorpion /'skɔːpɪən/ *n* scorpione *m*

Scot /skɒt/ *n* scozzese *mf*

Scotch *a* scozzese ● *n* (*whisky*) whisky *m* [scozzese]

scotch /skɒtʃ/ *vt* far cessare

Scotch egg *n Br* polpetta *f* di salsiccia che racchiude un uovo sodo

scot-free *a* **get off ~** cavarsela impunemente

Scotland /'skɒtlənd/ *n* Scozia *f*

Scots, Scottish /skɒts, 'skɒtɪʃ/ *a* scozzese

scoundrel /'skaʊndrəl/ *n* mascalzone *m*

scour[1] /'skaʊə(r)/ *vt* (*search*) perlustrare

scour[2] *vt* (*clean*) strofinare

scourer /'skaʊərə(r)/ *n* (*pad*) paglietta *f*

scouring pad /'skaʊərɪŋ/ *n* paglietta *f* in lana d'acciaio

scourge /skɜːdʒ/ *n* flagello *m*

Scout *n* [**Boy**] **~** [boy]scout *m inv*

scout /skaʊt/ *n Mil* esploratore *m* ● *vi* **~ for** andare in cerca di

scowl /skaʊl/ *n* sguardo *m* torvo ● *vi* guardare [di] storto

Scrabble® /'skræbl/ *n* Scarabeo* *m*

■ **scrabble around** vi (search) cercare a tastoni

scraggy /'skrægɪ/ a (-ier, -iest) pej scarno

scram /skræm/ vi fam levarsi dai piedi

scramble /'skræmbl/ n (climb) arrampicata f ● vi (clamber) arrampicarsi; ~ **for** azzuffarsi per ● vt Teleph creare delle interferenze in; (eggs) strapazzare

scrambled eggs /'skræmbəld/ npl uova fpl strapazzate

scrambler /'skræmblə(r)/ n (Br: motorcyclist) [moto]crossista mf

scrap[1] /skræp/ n (fam: fight) litigio m

scrap[2] n pezzetto m; (metal) ferraglia f; ~**s** pl (of food) avanzi mpl ● vt (pt/pp **scrapped**) buttare via

scrapbook /'skræpbʊk/ n album m inv

scrape /skreɪp/ vt raschiare; (damage) graffiare

■ **scrape through** vi passare per un pelo

■ **scrape together** vt racimolare

scraper /'skreɪpə(r)/ n raschietto m

scrap: scrap heap n **be on the** ~ ~ fig essere inutile. **scrap iron** n ferraglia f. **scrap merchant** n ferrovecchio m. **scrap paper** n carta f qualsiasi

scrappy /'skræpɪ/ a frammentario

scrapyard /'skræpjɑːd/ n deposito m di ferraglia; (for cars) cimitero m delle macchine

scratch /skrætʃ/ n graffio m; (to relieve itch) grattata f; **start from** ~ partire da zero; **up to** ~ (work) all'altezza ● vt graffiare; (to relieve itch) grattare ● vi grattarsi

scratchy /'skrætʃɪ/ a (recording) pieno di fruscii

scrawl /skrɔːl/ n scarabocchio m ● vt/i scarabocchiare

scrawny /'skrɔːnɪ/ a (-ier, -iest) pej magro

scream /skriːm/ n strillo m; **be a** ~ (fam: situation, film, person:) essere uno spasso ● vt/i strillare

scree /skriː/ n ghiaione m

screech /skriːtʃ/ n stridore m; ~ **of tyres** sgommata f ● vi stridere ● vt strillare

screen /skriːn/ n paravento m; Cinema, TV, Comput schermo m ● vt proteggere; (conceal) riparare; proiettare (film); (candidates) passare al setaccio; Med sottoporre a visita medica

screening /'skriːnɪŋ/ n Med visita f medica; (of film) proiezione f

screen: screenplay n sceneggiatura f. **screen saver** n Comput salvaschermo m. **screen test** n Cinema provino m. **screenwriter** n Cinema sceneggiatore, -trice mf

screw /skruː/ n vite f ● vt avvitare; vulg trombare; ~ **sth to sth** avvitare qcsa a qcsa

■ **screw up** vt (crumple) accartocciare; strizzare (eyes); storcere (face); (sl: bungle) mandare all'aria; ~ **up one's courage** prendere il coraggio a due mani

screwdriver /'skruːdraɪvə(r)/ n cacciavite m inv

screwed up /skruːd/ a fam incasinato

screw top n tappo m a vite

screwy /'skruːɪ/ a (-ier, -iest) fam svitato

scribble /'skrɪbl/ n scarabocchio m ● vt/i scarabocchiare

scrimmage /'skrɪmɪdʒ/ n (struggle) zuffa f; (Am: in football) mischia f

scrimp /skrɪmp/ vi risparmiare; ~ **and save** risparmiare fino all'osso; ~ **on sth** risparmiare su qcsa

script /skrɪpt/ n scrittura f; (of film etc) sceneggiatura f

Scriptures /'skrɪptʃəz/ npl Sacre Scritture fpl

scriptwriter /'skrɪptraɪtə(r)/ n sceneggiatore, -trice mf

scroll /skrəʊl/ n rotolo m (di pergamena); (decoration) voluta f ● vi Comput far scorrere

Scrooge /skruːdʒ/ n fam tirchio, -a mf

scrotum /'skrəʊtəm/ n scroto m

scrounge /skraʊndʒ/ vt/i scroccare

scrounger /'skraʊndʒə(r)/ n scroccone, -a mf

scrub[1] /skrʌb/ n (land) boscaglia f

scrub[2] vt/i (pt/pp **scrubbed**) strofinare; (fam: cancel) cancellare (plan)

scrubbing brush /'skrʌbɪŋ/ n spazzolone m

scruff /skrʌf/ n **by the** ~ **of the neck** per la collottola

scruffy /'skrʌfɪ/ a (-ier, -iest) trasandato

scrum /skrʌm/ n (in rugby) mischia f

scrum half n mediano m di mischia

scrunch /skrʌntʃ/ vi (footsteps in snow, tyres:) scricchiolare ● n scricchiolio m

■ **scrunch up** vt accartocciare

scruple /'skruːpl/ n scrupolo m; **have no** ~**s** essere senza scrupoli

scrupulous /'skruːpjʊləs/ a scrupoloso

scrupulously /'skruːpjʊləslɪ/ adv scrupolosamente

scrutinize /'skruːtɪnaɪz/ vt scrutinare

scrutiny /'skruːtɪnɪ/ n (look) esame m minuzioso

scuba diver /'skuːbə/ n sommozzatore, -trice mf

scuba diving n immersione f subacquea

scud /skʌd/ vi (pt/pp **scudded**) (clouds:) muoversi velocemente

scuff /skʌf/ vt strascicare (one's feet)

scuffle /'skʌfl/ n tafferuglio m

scull /skʌl/ vi (with two oars) vogare di coppia; (with one oar) vogare a bratto ● n (boat) imbarcazione f da regata con un vogatore

scullery /'skʌlərɪ/ n retrocucina f

sculpt /skʌlpt/ vt/i scolpire

sculptor /'skʌlptə(r)/ n scultore m

sculpture /'skʌlptʃə(r)/ n scultura f

scum /skʌm/ n schiuma f; (people) feccia f

scurrilous /'skʌrɪləs/ a scurrile

scurry /'skʌrɪ/ vi (pt/pp **-ied**) affrettare il passo

scuttle[1] /'skʌtl/ n secchio m per il carbone

scuttle[2] vt affondare (ship)

scuttle[3] vi (hurry) ~ **away** correre via

scythe /saɪð/ n falce f

SE *abbr* (**south-east**) SE

sea /si:/ *n* mare *m*; **at ~** in mare; *fig* confuso; **by ~** via mare; **by the ~** sul mare

sea: seabed *n* fondale *m* marino. **seabird** *n* uccello *m* marino. **seaboard** *n* costiera *f*. **seafaring** *a* ⟨*nation*⟩ marinaro. **seafood** *n* frutti *mpl* di mare. **seagull** *n* gabbiano *m*.

sea horse *n* cavalluccio *m* marino

seal¹ /si:l/ *n* *Zool* foca *f*

seal² *n* sigillo *m*; *Techn* chiusura *f* ermetica ● *vt* sigillare; *Techn* chiudere ermeticamente ■ **seal off** *vt* bloccare ⟨*area*⟩

sea level *n* livello *m* del mare; **above ~ ~** sopra il livello del mare

sealing wax /'si:lɪŋ/ *n* ceralacca *f*

sea lion *n* leone *m* marino

seam /si:m/ *n* cucitura *f*; (*of coal*) strato *m*

seaman /'si:mən/ *n* marinaio *m*

seamless /'si:mlɪs/ *a* senza cucitura

seamy /'si:mɪ/ *a* ⟨*scandal*⟩ sordido; ⟨*area*⟩ malfamato

seance /'seɪɑːns/ *n* seduta *f* spiritica

seaplane /'si:pleɪn/ *n* idrovolante *m*

seaport /'si:pɔːt/ *n* porto *m* di mare

sear /sɪə(r)/ *vt* cauterizzare ⟨*wound*⟩; rosolare [a fuoco vivo] ⟨*meat*⟩; ⟨*scorch*⟩ disseccare

search /sɜːtʃ/ *n* ricerca *f*; (*official*) perquisizione *f*; **in ~ of** alla ricerca di ● *vt* frugare (**for** alla ricerca di); perlustrare ⟨*area*⟩; (*officially*) perquisire ● *vi* **~ for** cercare

search and replace *n* *Comput* ricerca *f* e sostituzione

searching /'sɜːtʃɪŋ/ *a* penetrante

search: searchlight *n* riflettore *m*. **search party** *n* squadra *f* di ricerca. **search warrant** *n* mandato *m* di perquisizione

searing /'sɪərɪŋ/ *a* bruciante; ⟨*pace*⟩ travolgente; ⟨*pain*⟩ lancinante

sea: seascape *n* paesaggio *m* marino. **seasick** *a* **be/get ~** avere il mal di mare. **seaside** *n* **at/to the ~** al mare. **seaside resort** *n* stazione *f* balneare. **seaside town** *n* città *f* di mare

season /'si:zn/ *n* stagione *f* ● *vt* (*flavour*) condire; **in ~** ⟨*fruit*⟩ di stagione; ⟨*animal*⟩ in calore

seasonal /'si:zənəl/ *a* stagionale

seasoned /'si:znd/ *a* ⟨*Culin: dish*⟩ condito; ⟨*timber*⟩ stagionato; ⟨*actor, politician*⟩ consumato; ⟨*leader*⟩ di provata capacità; **~ traveller** persona *f* che ha viaggiato molto; **~ soldier** veterano *m*

seasoning /'si:z(ə)nɪŋ/ *n* condimento *m*

season ticket *n* abbonamento *m*

seat /si:t/ *n* (*chair*) sedia *f*; (*in car*) sedile *m*; (*place to sit*) posto *m* [a sedere]; (*bottom*) didietro *m*; (*of government*) sede *f*; **take a ~** sedersi ● *vt* mettere a sedere; (*have seats for*) aver posti [a sedere] per; **remain ~ed** mantenere il proprio posto

seat belt *n* cintura *f* di sicurezza; **fasten one's ~ ~** allacciare la cintura di sicurezza

seating /'si:tɪŋ/ *n* (*places*) posti *mpl* a sedere; (*arrangement*) disposizione *f* dei posti a sedere

seating capacity *n* numero *m* dei posti a sedere

sea: sea urchin *n* riccio *m* di mare. **seaweed** *n* alga *f* marina. **seaworthy** *a* in stato di navigare

sec /sek/ *n* (*fam: short instant*) attimo *m*, secondo *m*; *abbr* (**second**) s

secateurs /sekə'tɜːz/ *npl* cesoie *fpl*

secede /sɪ'si:d/ *vi* staccarsi

secession /sɪ'seʃn/ *n* secessione *f*

secluded /sɪ'klu:dɪd/ *a* appartato

seclusion /sɪ'klu:ʒn/ *n* isolamento *m*

second¹ /sɪ'kɒnd/ *vt* (*transfer*) distaccare

second² /'sekənd/ *a* secondo; **in ~ gear** *Auto* in seconda; **on ~ thoughts** ripensandoci meglio; **be having ~ thoughts** ripensarci; ● *n* secondo *m*; **~s** *pl* (*goods*) merce *fsg* di seconda scelta; **have ~s** (*at meal*) fare il bis; **John the S~** Giovanni Secondo ● *adv* (*in race*) al secondo posto ● *vt* assistere; appoggiare ⟨*proposal*⟩

secondary /'sekəndrɪ/ *a* secondario

secondary school *n* ≈ scuola *f* media (*inferiore e superiore*)

second: second-best *a* secondo dopo il migliore; **be ~** *pej* essere un ripiego. **second-class** *a* di seconda classe. **second class** *adv* ⟨*travel, send*⟩ in seconda classe

seconder /'sekəndə(r)/ *n* (*of motion*) persona *f* che appoggia una mozione

second-guess *vt* anticipare

second hand *n* (*on watch, clock*) lancetta *f* dei secondi

second-hand *a* ⟨*car, goods, news, information*⟩ di seconda mano; ⟨*clothes*⟩ usato; ⟨*market*⟩ dell'usato; ⟨*opinion*⟩ preso a prestito ● *adv* ⟨*sell*⟩ di seconda mano

second in command *n* vice *mf inv*; *Mil* vicecomandante *m*

secondly /'sekəndlɪ/ *adv* in secondo luogo

secondment /sɪ'kɒndmənt/ *n* **on ~** in trasferta

second-rate *a* di second'ordine

secrecy /'si:krəsɪ/ *n* segretezza *f*; **in ~** in segreto

secret /'si:krɪt/ *a* segreto ● *n* segreto *m*; **make no ~ of sth** non fare mistero di qcsa

secret agent *n* agente *m* segreto

secretarial /sekrə'teərɪəl/ *a* ⟨*work, staff*⟩ di segreteria

secretariat /sekrə'teərɪət/ *n* segretariato *m*

secretary /'sekrətərɪ/ *n* segretario, -a *mf*

Secretary of State *n* Segretario *m* di Stato; *Am Pol* ministro *m* degli Esteri

secret ballot *n* scrutinio *m* segreto, votazione *f* a scrutinio segreto

secrete /sɪ'kri:t/ *vt* secernere ⟨*poison*⟩

secretion /sɪ'kri:ʃn/ *n* secrezione *f*

secretive /'si:krətɪv/ *a* riservato

secretly /'si:krɪtlɪ/ *adv* segretamente

secretness /'si:krɪtnɪs/ *n* riserbo *m*

secret: secret police *n* polizia *f* segreta. **secret service** *n* servizi *mpl* segreti. **secret society** *n* società *f* segreta

sect /sekt/ *n* setta *f*

sectarian /sek'teəriən/ n & a settario, -a mf
section /'sekʃn/ n sezione f
sector /'sektə(r)/ n settore m
secular /'sekjʊlə(r)/ a secolare; ⟨education⟩ laico
secure /sɪ'kjʊə(r)/ a sicuro ● vt proteggere; chiudere bene ⟨door⟩; rendere stabile ⟨ladder⟩; ⟨obtain⟩ assicurarsi
securely /sɪ'kjʊəlɪ/ adv saldamente
security /sɪ'kjʊərətɪ/ n sicurezza f; (for loan) garanzia f; **securities** pl titoli mpl
security: Security Council n (of the UN) Consiglio m di Sicurezza. **security guard** n guardia f giurata. **security risk** n be a ~ ~ costituire un pericolo per la sicurezza
sedan /sɪ'dæn/ n Am berlina f
sedate¹ /sɪ'deɪt/ a posato
sedate² vt somministrare sedativi a
sedately /sɪ'deɪtlɪ/ adv in modo posato
sedation /sɪ'deɪʃn/ n somministrazione f di sedativi; **be under** ~ essere sotto l'effetto di sedativi
sedative /'sedətɪv/ a sedativo ● n sedativo m
sedentary /'sedəntərɪ/ a sedentario
sediment /'sedɪmənt/ n sedimento m
seduce /sɪ'dju:s/ vt sedurre
seduction /sɪ'dʌkʃn/ n seduzione f
seductive /sɪ'dʌktɪv/ a seducente
seductively /sɪ'dʌktɪvlɪ/ adv con aria seducente
see¹ /si:/ v (pt **saw**, pp **seen**) ● vt vedere; (understand) capire; (escort) accompagnare; **go and** ~ andare a vedere; (visit) andare a trovare; ~ **you!** ci vediamo!; ~ **you later!** a più tardi!; ~**ing that** visto che; ~ **sb out**, ~ **sb to the door** accompagnare qcno alla porta; **I can't** ~ **myself doing this forever** non mi ci vedo a farlo per sempre; **I can't think what she** ~**s in him** non capisco cosa trovi in lui; ~ **reason** ragionare; **you're** ~**ing things** hai le traveggole ● vi vedere; (understand) capire; ~ **that** (make sure) assicurarsi che; **let me** ~ (think) fammi pensare; **I** ~ (understand) ho capito
■ **see about** vt occuparsi di
■ **see off** vt veder partire; (chase away) mandar via
■ **see through** vi vedere attraverso; fig non farsi ingannare da ● vt portare a buon fine
■ **see to** vi occuparsi di
see² n Relig diocesi f inv
seed /si:d/ n seme m; Tennis testa f di serie; **go to** ~ fare seme; fig lasciarsi andare
seeded player /'si:dɪd/ n Tennis testa f di serie
seedless /'si:dlɪs/ a senza semi
seedling /'si:dlɪŋ/ n pianticella f
seedy /'si:dɪ/ a (-ier, -iest) squallido; **feel** ~ fam sentirsi poco bene
seek /si:k/ vt (pt/pp **sought**) cercare
■ **seek out** vt scovare
seeker /'si:kə(r)/ n ~ **after** or **for sth** persona f che è alla ricerca di qcsa; **gold** ~ cercatore, -trice mf d'oro
seem /si:m/ vi sembrare

seeming /'si:mɪŋ/ a apparente
seemingly /'si:mɪŋlɪ/ adv apparentemente
seemly /'si:mlɪ/ a decoroso
seen /si:n/ see **see¹**
seep /si:p/ vi filtrare
seepage /'si:pɪdʒ/ n (leak: from container) perdita f; Geol trasudamento m superficiale; (trickle) lenta fuoriuscita f; (into structure, soil) infiltrazione f
see-saw /'si:sɔ:/ n altalena f
seethe /si:ð/ vi ~ **with anger** ribollire di rabbia
see-through a trasparente
segment /'segmənt/ n segmento m; (of orange) spicchio m
segregate /'segrɪgeɪt/ vt segregare
segregation /segrɪ'geɪʃn/ n segregazione f
seismic /'saɪzmɪk/ a sismico
seismograph /'saɪzməgrɑ:f/ n sismografo m
seismology /saɪz'mɒlədʒɪ/ n sismologia f
seize /si:z/ vt afferrare; Jur confiscare; ~ **the opportunity** prendere la palla al balzo
■ **seize up** vi Techn bloccarsi
seizure /'si:ʒə(r)/ n Jur confisca f; Med colpo m [apoplettico]
seldom /'seldəm/ adv raramente
select /sɪ'lekt/ a scelto; (exclusive) esclusivo ● vt scegliere; selezionare ⟨team⟩
selection /sɪ'lekʃn/ n selezione f
selective /sɪ'lektɪv/ a selettivo
selectively /sɪ'lektɪvlɪ/ adv con criterio
selector /sɪ'lektə(r)/ n Sport selezionatore, -trice mf
self /self/ n io m
self: self-addressed a con il proprio indirizzo. **self-addressed envelope** n busta f affrancata con il proprio indirizzo. **self-adhesive** a autoadesivo. **self-analysis** n autoanalisi f. **self-assembly** a da montare. **self-assurance** n sicurezza f di sé. **self-assured** a sicuro di sé. **self-catering** a in appartamento attrezzato di cucina. **self-centred** a egocentrico. **self-cleaning** a ⟨oven⟩ autopulente. **self-confessed** a dichiarato. **self-confidence** n fiducia f in se stesso. **self-confident** a sicuro di sé. **self-conscious** a impacciato. **self-contained** a ⟨flat⟩ con ingresso indipendente. **self-control** n autocontrollo m. **self-defence** n autodifesa f; Jur legittima difesa f. **self-denial** n abnegazione f. **self-destruct** vi ⟨missile, spacecraft:⟩ autodistruggersi. **self-destruction** n autodistruzione f; fig autolesionismo m. **self-determination** n autodeterminazione f. **self-discipline** n autodisciplina f. **self-employed** a che lavora in proprio; **the** ~ i lavoratori autonomi. **self-esteem** n stima f di sé. **self-evident** a ovvio. **self-explanatory** a **be** ~ parlare da sé. **self-financing** /-faɪ'nænsɪŋ/ n autofinanziamento m. **self-governing** /-'gʌvənɪŋ/ a autonomo. **self-government** n autogoverno m. **self-help** n iniziativa f personale. **self-important** a borioso. **self-imposed** /-ɪm'pəʊzd/ a autoimposto. **self-improvement** n crescita f

personale. **self-indulgent** *a* indulgente con se stesso. **self-inflicted** *a* **Anna's problems are** ~ sono problemi che Anna si è creata da sé; ~ **wound** autolesione *f*. **self-interest** *n* interesse *m* personale

selfish /'selfɪʃ/ *a* egoista

selfishly /'selfɪʃlɪ/ *adv* egoisticamente

selfishness /'selfɪʃnɪs/ *n* egoismo *m*

selfless /'selflɪs/ *a* disinteressato

selflessly /'selflɪslɪ/ *adv* disinteressatamente

selflessness /'selflɪsnɪs/ *n* disinteresse *m*

self: **self-locking** /-'lɒkɪŋ/ *a* ⟨*door*⟩ a chiusura automatica. **self-made** *a* che si è fatto da sé. **self-pity** *n* autocommiserazione *f*. **self-portrait** *n* autoritratto *m*. **self-possessed** /-pə'zest/ *a* padrone di sé. **self-preservation** *n* istinto *m* di conservazione. **self-raising flour** *Br*, **self-rising flour** *Am* /-'reɪzɪŋ, -'raɪzɪŋ/ *n* farina *f* contenente lievito. **self-respect** *n* amor *m* proprio. **self-righteous** *a* presuntuoso. **self-sacrifice** *n* abnegazione *f*. **selfsame** *a* stesso. **self-satisfied** *a* compiaciuto di sé. **self-service** *n* self-service *m inv* ● *attrib* self-service. **self-styled** *a* sedicente. **self-sufficiency** *n* autosufficienza *f*. **self-sufficient** *a* autosufficiente. **self-supporting** *a* ⟨*person*⟩ indipendente (*economicamente*). **self-tan** *n* autoabbronzante *m*. **self-tanning** /-'tænɪŋ/ *a* autoabbronzante. **self-taught** /-'tɔːt/ *a* ⟨*person*⟩ autodidatta. **self-willed** /-'wɪld/ *a* ostinato

sell /sel/ *v* (*pt/pp* **sold**) ● *vt* vendere; **be sold out** essere esaurito; ~ **sb on the idea of...** *fam* convincere qcno di... ● *vi* vendersi

■ **sell off** *vt* liquidare

■ **sell up** *vi* liquidare i propri beni

sell-by date *n* data *f* di scadenza per la vendita

seller /'selə(r)/ *n* venditore, -trice *mf*

sellers' market /'seləzmɑːkɪt/ *n* mercato *m* al rialzo

selling price /'selɪŋ/ *n* prezzo *m* di vendita

Sellotape® /'seləʊteɪp/ *n* nastro *m* adesivo, scotch* *m*

sell-out *n* (*fam: betrayal*) tradimento *m*; **be a** ~ ⟨*concert:*⟩ fare il tutto esaurito

selvage, selvedge /'selvɪdʒ/ *n* cimosa *f*

selves /selvz/ *pl of* **self**

semantic /sɪ'mæntɪk/ *a* semantico

semantics /sɪ'mæntɪks/ *n* (*subject*) semantica *f*; **that's just** ~ sono solo sfumature di significato

semblance /'sembləns/ *n* parvenza *f*

semen /'siːmən/ *n Anat* liquido *m* seminale

semester /sɪ'mestə(r)/ *n Am* semestre *m*

semi /'semɪ/ *n* (*Br: house*) villetta *f* bifamiliare; *Am Auto* autoarticolato *m*

semi+ *pref* semi+

semi: **semi-automatic** *a* semiautomatico. **semibreve** *n Mus* semibreve *f*. **semicircle** *n* semicerchio *m*. **semicircular** *a* semicircolare. **semicolon** *n* punto e virgola *m*. **semi-darkness** *n* semioscurità *f*. **semi-**

detached *a* gemella ● *n* casa *f* gemella.

semi-final *n* semifinale *f*

seminal /'semɪnəl/ *a* (*major*) determinante

seminar /'semɪnɑː(r)/ *n* seminario *m*

seminary /'semɪnərɪ/ *n* seminario *m*

semi: **semi-precious** *a* semiprezioso; ~ **stone** pietra *f* dura. **semi-skilled** /-'skɪld/ *a* qualificato. **semi-skimmed** /-'skɪmd/ *a* parzialmente scremato. **semitone** *n Mus* semitono *m*

semolina /semə'liːnə/ *n* semolino *m*

senate /'senət/ *n* senato *m*

senator /'senətə(r)/ *n* senatore *m*

send /send/ *vt/i* (*pt/pp* **sent**) mandare; (*by mail*) spedire

■ **send away for** *vt* farsi spedire ⟨*information etc*⟩

■ **send down** *vt* (*send to prison*) mandare in galera

■ **send for** *vt* mandare a chiamare ⟨*person*⟩; far venire ⟨*thing*⟩

■ **send in** *vt* presentare ⟨*application*⟩; far entrare ⟨*person*⟩

■ **send off** *vt* spedire ⟨*letter, parcel*⟩; espellere ⟨*footballer*⟩

■ **send up** *vt fam* parodiare

sender /'sendə(r)/ *n* mittente *mf*; **return to** ~ (*on letter*) rispedire al mittente

send-off *n* commiato *m*

senile /'siːnaɪl/ *a* arteriosclerotico

senile dementia /dɪ'menʃə/ *n* demenza *f* senile

senility /sɪ'nɪlətɪ/ *n* senilismo *m*

senior /'siːnɪə(r)/ *a* più vecchio; (*in rank*) superiore ● *n* (*in rank*) superiore *mf*; (*in sport*) senior *mf*; **she's two years my** ~ è più vecchia di me di due anni

senior citizen *n* anziano, -a *mf*

seniority /siːnɪ'brətɪ/ *n* anzianità *f* di servizio

senior management *n* alta dirigenza *f*

sensation /sen'seɪʃn/ *n* sensazione *f*; **cause a** ~ fare scalpore

sensational /sen'seɪʃənəl/ *a* sensazionale

sensationalize /sen'seɪʃənəlaɪz/ *vt pej* dare un tono scandalistico a

sensationally /sen'seɪʃənəlɪ/ *adv* in modo sensazionale

sense /sens/ *n* senso *m*; (*common ~*) buon senso *m*; **in a** ~ in un certo senso; **make** ~ aver senso ● *vt* sentire

senseless /'senslɪs/ *a* insensato; (*unconscious*) privo di sensi

senselessly /'senslɪslɪ/ *adv* insensatamente

sensible /'sensəbl/ *a* sensato; (*suitable*) appropriato

sensibly /'sensəblɪ/ *adv* in modo appropriato

sensitive /'sensətɪv/ *a* sensibile; (*touchy*) suscettibile

sensitively /'sensətɪvlɪ/ *adv* con sensibilità

sensitivity /sensə'tɪvətɪ/ *n* sensibilità *f inv*

sensitize /'sensɪtaɪz/ *vt* **become ~d to** (*allergic to*) diventare ipersensibile a

sensor /'sensə(r)/ *n* sensore *m*
sensory /'sensərɪ/ *a* sensoriale
sensual /'sensjʊəl/ *a* sensuale
sensuality /sensjʊ'ælətɪ/ *n* sensualità *f inv*
sensuous /'sensjʊəs/ *a* voluttuoso
sent /sent/ *see* **send**
sentence /'sentəns/ *n* frase *f*; *Jur* sentenza *f*; (*punishment*) condanna *f* ● *vt* ~ **to** condannare a
sentiment /'sentɪmənt/ *n* sentimento *m*; (*opinion*) opinione *f*; (*sentimentality*) sentimentalismo *m*
sentimental /sentɪ'mentl/ *a* sentimentale; *pej* sentimentalista
sentimentality /sentɪmen'tælətɪ/ *n* sentimentalità *f inv*
sentinel /'sentɪnəl/ *n* sentinella *f*
sentry /'sentrɪ/ *n* sentinella *f*
separable /'sepərəbl/ *a* separabile
separate[1] /'sepərət/ *a* separato
separate[2] /'sepəreɪt/ *vt* separare ● *vi* separarsi
separately /'sepərətlɪ/ *adv* separatamente
separates /'sepərəts/ *npl* [indumenti *npl*] coordinati *npl*
separation /sepə'reɪʃn/ *n* separazione *f*
separatist /'sepərətɪst/ *n & a* separatista *mf*
sepia /'si:pɪə/ *n* (*colour*) seppia *m*
September /sep'tembə(r)/ *n* settembre *m*
septic /'septɪk/ *a* settico; **go** ~ infettarsi
septicaemia /septɪ'si:mɪə/ *n* setticemia *f*
septic tank *n* fossa *f* biologica
sequel /'si:kwəl/ *n* seguito *m*
sequence /'si:kwəns/ *n* sequenza *f*; **in** ~ nell'ordine giusto
sequential /sɪ'kwenʃəl/ *a* sequenziale
sequin /'si:kwɪn/ *n* lustrino *m*, paillette *f inv*
Serb /sɜ:b/ *a & n* serbo, -a *mf*
Serbia /'sɜ:bɪə/ *n* Serbia *f*
Serbian /'sɜ:bɪən/ *n* serba, -a *mf*; (*language*) serbo *m* ● *a* serbo
Serbo-Croat[ian] /sɜ:bəʊ'krəʊæt, sɜ:bəʊkrəʊ'eɪʃən/ *n* (*language*) serbo-croato *m* ● *a* serbo-croato
serenade /serə'neɪd/ *n* serenata *f* ● *vt* fare una serenata a
serene /sɪ'ri:n/ *a* sereno
serenely /sɪ'ri:nlɪ/ *adv* serenamente
serenity /sɪ'renətɪ/ *n* serenità *f inv*
sergeant /'sɑ:dʒənt/ *n* sergente *m*
sergeant major *n* sergente *m* maggiore
serial /'sɪərɪəl/ *n* racconto *m* a puntate; *TV* sceneggiato *m* a puntate; *Radio* commedia *f* radiofonica a puntate ● *a* Comput seriale
serialize /'sɪərɪəlaɪz/ *vt* pubblicare a puntate; *Radio, TV* trasmettere a puntate
serial killer *n* serial killer *mf inv*
serial number *n* numero *m* di serie
serial port *n* Comput porta *f* seriale
series /'sɪəri:z/ *n* serie *f inv*
serious /'sɪərɪəs/ *a* serio; (*illness, error*) grave
seriously /'sɪərɪəslɪ/ *adv* seriamente; (*ill*) gravemente; **take** ~ prendere sul serio

seriousness /'sɪərɪəsnɪs/ *n* serietà *f*; (*of situation*) gravità *f*
sermon /'sɜ:mən/ *n* predica *f*
seropositive /sɪərəʊ'pɒzɪtɪv/ *a* sieropositivo
serpent /'sɜ:pənt/ *n* serpente *m*
serrated /se'reɪtɪd/ *a* dentellato
serum /'sɪərəm/ *n* siero *m*
servant /'sɜ:vənt/ *n* domestico, -a *mf*
serve /sɜ:v/ *n* Tennis servizio *m* ● *vt* servire; *Jur* notificare (*writ*) (**on sb** a qcno); scontare (*sentence*); ~ **its purpose** servire al proprio scopo; **it** ~**s you right!** ben ti sta!; ~**s two** per due persone ● *vi* prestare servizio; *Tennis* servire; ~ **as** servire da
server /'sɜ:və(r)/ *n* (*piece of cutlery*) posata *f* di portata; (*plate*) piatto *m* di portata; (*tray*) vassoio *m* di portata; *Sport* giocatore, -trice *mf* che effettua il servizio; *Comput* server *m inv*, servitore *m*
service /'sɜ:vɪs/ *n* servizio *m*; *Relig* funzione *f*; (*maintenance*) revisione *f*; ~**s** *pl* forze *fpl* armate; (*on motorway*) area *f* di servizio; **in the** ~**s** sotto le armi; **of** ~ **to** utile a; **out of** ~ (*machine:*) guasto ● *vt* Techn revisionare
serviceable /'sɜ:vɪsəbl/ *a* utilizzabile; (*hard-wearing*) resistente; (*practical*) pratico
service: service area *n* area *f* di servizio. **service charge** *n* servizio *m*. **service company** *n* compagnia *f* del settore terziario. **service industry** *n* industria *f* terziaria. **serviceman** *n* militare *m*. **service provider** *n* fornitore *m* di servizi. **service road** *n* strada *f* d'accesso. **service station** *n* stazione *f* di servizio
serviette /sɜ:vɪ'et/ *n* tovagliolo *m*
servile /'sɜ:vaɪl/ *a* servile
servility /sə'vɪlɪtɪ/ *n* servilismo *m*
serving /'sɜ:vɪŋ/ *a* (*officer*) di carriera ● *n* (*helping*) porzione *f*
session /'seʃn/ *n* seduta *f*; *Jur* sessione *f*; *Univ* anno *m* accademico
set /set/ *n* serie *f inv*, set *m inv*; (*of crockery, cutlery*) servizio *m*; *TV, Radio* apparecchio *m*; *Math* insieme *m*; *Theat* scenario *m*; *Cinema, Tennis* set *m inv*; (*of people*) circolo *m*; (*of hair*) messa *f* in piega ● *a* (*ready*) pronto; (*rigid*) fisso; (*book*) in programma; **be** ~ **on doing sth** essere risoluto a fare qcsa; **be** ~ **in one's ways** essere abitudinario ● *v* (*pt/pp* **set**, *pres p* **setting**) ● *vt* mettere, porre; mettere (*alarm clock*); assegnare (*task, homework*); fissare (*date, limit*); chiedere (*questions*); montare (*gem*); assestare (*bone*); apparecchiare (*table*); *Typ* comporre; ~ **fire to** dare fuoco a; ~ **free** liberare; ~ **a good example** dare il buon esempio; ~ **sail for** far vela per; ~ **in motion** dare inizio a; ~ **to music** musicare; **the film is** ~ **in Rome**/**the 18th century** il film è ambientato a Roma/nel XVIII secolo; ~ **to music** musicare; ~ **about doing sth** mettersi a fare qcsa ● *vi* (*sun:*) tramontare; (*jelly, concrete:*) solidificarsi; ~ **to work** (**on sth**) mettersi al lavoro (su qcsa)

■ **set back** *vt* mettere indietro; (*hold up*) ritardare; (*fam: cost*) costare a

■ **set off** *vi* partire ● *vt* avviare; mettere ⟨*alarm*⟩; fare esplodere ⟨*bomb*⟩

■ **set out** *vi* partire; ~ **out to do sth** proporsi di fare qcsa ● *vt* disporre; (*state*) esporre

■ **set to** *vi* mettersi all'opera

■ **set up** *vt* fondare ⟨*company*⟩; istituire ⟨*committee*⟩

setback /'setbæk/ *n* (*hitch*) contrattempo *m*; *Mil* sconfitta *f*, scacco *m*; *Fin* tracollo *m*; (*in health*) ricaduta *f*

set design *n* scenografia *f*

set designer *n* scenografo, -a *mf*

set meal *n* menù *m inv* fisso

settee /se'ti:/ *n* divano *m*

setter /'setə(r)/ *n* (*dog*) setter *m inv*

setting /'setɪŋ/ *n* scenario *m*; (*position*) posizione *f*; (*of sun*) tramonto *m*; (*of jewel*) montatura *f*

settle /'setl/ *vt* (*decide*) definire; risolvere ⟨*argument*⟩; fissare ⟨*date*⟩; calmare ⟨*nerves*⟩; saldare ⟨*bill*⟩; **that's ~d then** allora è deciso ● *vi* (*live*) stabilirsi; ⟨*snow, dust, bird:*⟩ posarsi; (*subside*) assestarsi; ⟨*sediment:*⟩ depositarsi

■ **settle down** *vi* sistemarsi; (*stop making noise*) calmarsi

■ **settle for** *vt* accontentarsi di

■ **settle up** *vi* regolare i conti

settlement /'setlmənt/ *n* (*agreement*) accordo *m*; (*of bill*) saldo *m*; *Comm* liquidazione *f*; (*colony*) insediamento *m*

settler /'setlə(r)/ *n* colonizzatore, -trice *mf*

set-to *n fam* zuffa *f*; (*verbal*) battibecco *m*

set-up *n* situazione *f*

seven /'sevn/ *a & n* sette *m*

seventeen /sevn'ti:n/ *a & n* diciassette *m*

seventeenth /sevn'ti:nθ/ *a & n* diciassettesimo, -a *mf*

seventh /sevnθ/ *a & n* settimo, -a *mf*

seventieth /'sevntɪɪθ/ *a & n* settantesimo, -a *mf*

seventy /'sevntɪ/ *a & n* settanta *m*

seven-year itch *n fam* crisi *f inv* del settimo anno

sever /'sevə(r)/ *vt* troncare ⟨*relations*⟩

several /'sevrəl/ *a & pron* parecchi

severance /'sev(ə)rəns/ *n* ~ **pay** trattamento *m* di fine rapporto

severe /sɪ'vɪə(r)/ *a* severo; ⟨*pain*⟩ violento; ⟨*illness*⟩ grave; ⟨*winter*⟩ rigido

severely /sɪ'vɪəlɪ/ *adv* severamente; ⟨*ill*⟩ gravemente

severity /sɪ'verətɪ/ *n* severità *f*; (*of pain*) violenza *f*; (*of illness*) gravità *f*; (*of winter*) rigore *m*

sew /səʊ/ *vt/i* (*pt* **sewed**, *pp* **sewn** or **sewed**) cucire

■ **sew up** *vt* ricucire

sewage /'su:ɪdʒ/ *n* acque *fpl* di scolo

sewer /'su:ə(r)/ *n* fogna *f*

sewing /'səʊɪŋ/ *n* cucito *m*; (*work*) lavoro *m* di cucito

sewing machine *n* macchina *f* da cucire

sewn /səʊn/ *see* **sew**

sex /seks/ *n* sesso *m*; **have ~** avere rapporti sessuali, fare l'amore

sex appeal *n* sex appeal *m*

sex change operation *n* intervento *m* per il cambiamento di sesso

sexism /'seksɪzm/ *n* sessismo *m*

sexist /'seksɪst/ *a* sessista *mf*

sex: sex life *n* vita *f* sessuale. **sex maniac** *n* maniaco *m* sessuale. **sex offender** *n* colpevole *mf* di delitti a sfondo sessuale

sextet /seks'tet/ *n* sestetto *m*

sex tourism *n* turismo *m* a scopo sessuale

sexual /'seksjʊəl/ *a* sessuale

sexual: sexual assault *n* atti *mpl* di libidine violenta. **sexual equality** *n* parità *f* dei sessi. **sexual harassment** *n* molestie *fpl* sessuali. **sexual intercourse** *n* rapporti *mpl* sessuali

sexuality /seksjʊ'ælətɪ/ *n* sessualità *f*

sexually /'seksjʊəlɪ/ *adv* sessualmente; **be ~ assaulted** subire atti di libidine violenta

sexually transmitted disease /trænz'mɪtɪd/ *n* malattia *f* trasmissibile per via sessuale

sexy /'seksɪ/ *a* (**-ier, -iest**) sexy *inv*

sh /ʃ/ *int* silenzio!, sst!

shabbily /'ʃæbɪlɪ/ *adv* in modo scialbo; ⟨*treat*⟩ in modo meschino

shabbiness /'ʃæbɪnɪs/ *n* trasandatezza *f*; (*of treatment*) meschinità *f*

shabby /'ʃæbɪ/ *a* (**-ier, -iest**) scialbo; ⟨*treatment*⟩ meschino

shack /ʃæk/ *n* catapecchia *f*

shackles /'ʃæklz/ *npl* catene *fpl*

shade /ʃeɪd/ *n* ombra *f*; (*of colour*) sfumatura *f*; (*for lamp*) paralume *m*; (*Am: for window*) tapparella *f*; **a ~ better** un tantino meglio ● *vt* riparare dalla luce; (*draw lines on*) ombreggiare

shades /ʃeɪdz/ *npl fam* occhiali *mpl* da sole

shading /'ʃeɪdɪŋ/ *n* (*slight variation in colour*) tonalità *f inv*; (*to give effect of darkness*) ombreggiature *fpl*

shadow /'ʃædəʊ/ *n* ombra *f* ● *vt* (*follow*) pedinare

shadow boxing *n* allenamento *m* di boxe con l'ombra

Shadow Cabinet *n* governo *m* ombra

shadowy /'ʃædəʊɪ/ *a* (*indistinct*) confuso

shady /'ʃeɪdɪ/ *a* (**-ier, -iest**) ombroso; (*fam: disreputable*) losco

shaft /ʃɑːft/ *n Techn* albero *m*; (*of light*) raggio *m*; (*of lift, mine*) pozzo *m*; **~s** *pl* (*of cart*) stanghe *fpl*

shaggy /'ʃægɪ/ *a* (**-ier, -iest**) irsuto; ⟨*animal*⟩ dal pelo arruffato

shaggy dog story *n fam* barzelletta *f* interminabile dal finale deludente

shake /ʃeɪk/ *n* scrollata *f* ● *v* (*pt* **shook**, *pp* **shaken**) ● *vt* scuotere; agitare ⟨*bottle*⟩; far tremare ⟨*building*⟩; **~ hands with** stringere la mano a; **~ one's head** scuotere la testa ● *vi* tremare

■ **shake off** *vt* scrollarsi di dosso

shaken [up] /'ʃeɪkən/ a (after accident etc) scosso

shaker /'ʃeɪkə(r)/ n (for salad) centrifuga f [asciugaverdure]; (for dice) bicchiere m; (for cocktails) shaker m inv; (for pepper) pepaiola f; (for salt) saliera f

shake-up n Pol rimpasto m; Comm ristrutturazione f

shakily /'ʃeɪkɪlɪ/ adv ⟨say sth⟩ con voce tremante; ⟨walk⟩ con passo esitante

shaky /'ʃeɪkɪ/ a (-ier, -iest) tremante; ⟨table etc⟩ traballante; (unreliable) vacillante

shall /ʃæl/ v aux I ~ go andrò; **we ~ see** vedremo; **what ~ I do?** cosa faccio?; **I'll come too, ~ I?** vengo anch'io, no?; **thou shalt not kill** liter non uccidere; **passengers ~ remain seated** i passeggeri devono rimanere seduti

shallot /ʃə'lɒt/ n scalogno m

shallow /'ʃæləʊ/ a basso, poco profondo; ⟨dish⟩ poco profondo; fig superficiale

sham /ʃæm/ a falso ● n finzione f; (person) spaccone, -a mf ● vt (pt/pp **shammed**) simulare

shambles /'ʃæmblz/ n baraonda fsg

shame /ʃeɪm/ n vergogna f; **it's a ~ that** è un peccato che; **what a ~!** che peccato!; **~ on you!** vergognati!; **put sb/sth to ~** far sfigurare qcno/qcsa

shamefaced /ʃeɪm'feɪst/ a vergognoso

shameful /'ʃeɪmfl/ a vergognoso

shamefully /'ʃeɪmfʊlɪ/ adv vergognosamente

shameless /'ʃeɪmlɪs/ a spudorato

shamelessly /'ʃeɪmlɪslɪ/ adv spudoratamente

shampoo /ʃæm'pu:/ n shampoo m inv; **~ and set** shampoo m inv e messa in piega ● vt fare uno shampoo a ⟨carpet, person's hair etc⟩

shamrock /'ʃæmrɒk/ n trifoglio m (simbolo dell'Irlanda)

shandy /'ʃændɪ/ n bevanda f a base di birra e gassosa

shank /ʃæŋk/ n garretto m; (of knife) manico m; (of golf club) impugnatura f; (of screw) gambo m; (of anchor) fuso m; (of person) gamba f (dal ginocchio in giù)

shan't /ʃɑ:nt/ = **shall not**

shanty /'ʃæntɪ/ n (hut) baracca f; (song) marinaro

shanty town /'ʃæntɪtaʊn/ n bidonville f inv, baraccopoli f inv

shape /ʃeɪp/ n forma f; (figure) ombra f; **take ~** prendere forma; **get back in ~** ritornare in forma; **be out of ~** non essere in forma ● vt dare forma a (into di) ● vi ~ **[up]** mettere la testa a posto; **~ up nicely** mettersi bene

shapeless /'ʃeɪplɪs/ a informe

shapely /'ʃeɪplɪ/ a (-ier, -iest) ben fatto

shard /ʃɑ:d/ n frammento m; (of clay) coccio m

share /ʃeə(r)/ n porzione f; Comm azione f ● vt dividere; condividere ⟨views⟩ ● vi dividere; **~ in** partecipare a

■ **share out** vt spartire; (including oneself) spartirsi

share: share capital n capitale m azionario. **share dealing** n contrattazione f di azioni. **shareholder** n azionista mf. **shareholding** n titoli mpl azionari. **share index** n indice m azionario

shark /ʃɑ:k/ n squalo m, pescecane m; fig truffatore, -trice mf

sharp /ʃɑ:p/ a ⟨knife etc⟩ tagliente; ⟨pencil⟩ appuntito; ⟨drop⟩ a picco; ⟨reprimand⟩ severo; ⟨outline⟩ marcato; ⟨alert⟩ acuto; (unscrupulous) senza scrupoli; **~ pain** fitta f ● adv **at three o'clock ~** alle tre in punto; **look ~!** sbrigati! ● n Mus diesis m inv

sharpen /'ʃɑ:pn/ vt affilare ⟨knife⟩; appuntire ⟨pencil⟩

sharpener /'ʃɑ:pnə(r)/ n (for pencils) temperamatite m inv; (for knife) affilacoltelli m inv

shatter /'ʃætə(r)/ vt frantumare; fig mandare in frantumi

shattered /'ʃætəd/ a (fam: exhausted) a pezzi ● vi frantumarsi

shave /ʃeɪv/ n rasatura f; **have a ~** farsi la barba ● vt radere ● vi radersi

shaver /'ʃeɪvə(r)/ n rasoio m elettrico

shaving /'ʃeɪvɪŋ/: **shaving-brush** n pennello m da barba. **shaving foam** n schiuma f da barba. **shaving soap** n sapone m da barba

shawl /ʃɔ:l/ n scialle m

she /ʃi:/ pers pron lei; **~ is tired** è stanca; **I'm going, but ~ is not** io vado, ma lei no

sheaf /ʃi:f/ n (pl **sheaves**) fascio m

shear /ʃɪə(r)/ vt (pt **sheared**, pp **shorn** or **sheared**) tosare

shears /ʃɪəz/ npl (for hedge) cesoie fpl

sheath /ʃi:θ/ n (pl **~s** /ʃi:ðz/) guaina f

sheathe /ʃi:ð/ vt rinfoderare; rivestire ⟨cable⟩

sheaves /ʃi:vz/ see **sheaf**

shed[1] /ʃed/ n baracca f; (for cattle) stalla f

shed[2] vt (pt/pp **shed**, pres p **shedding**) perdere; versare ⟨blood, tears⟩; **~ light on** far luce su

sheen /ʃi:n/ n lucentezza f

sheep /ʃi:p/ n inv pecora f

sheepdog /'ʃi:pdɒg/ n cane m da pastore

sheepish /'ʃi:pɪʃ/ a imbarazzato

sheepishly /'ʃi:pɪʃlɪ/ adv con aria imbarazzata

sheepskin /'ʃi:pskɪn/ n (pelle f di) montone m

sheer /ʃɪə(r)/ a puro; (steep) a picco; (transparent) trasparente ● adv a picco

sheet /ʃi:t/ n lenzuolo m; (of paper) foglio m; (of glass, metal) lastra f

sheet lightning n bagliore m diffuso dei lampi; (without a storm) lampi mpl di calore

sheet music n spartiti mpl

sheikh /ʃeɪk/ n sceicco m

shelf /ʃelf/ n (pl **shelves**) ripiano m; (set of shelves) scaffale m

shelf-life n (of product) durata f di conservazione; (fig: of technology, pop music) durata f di vita; (*fig: of politician, star*) periodo *m* di gloria

shell /ʃel/ *n* conchiglia *f*; (*of egg, snail, tortoise*) guscio *m*; (*of crab*) corazza *f*; (*of unfinished building*) ossatura *f*; Mil granata *f* ● *vt* sgusciare ⟨*peas*⟩; Mil bombardare

■ **shell out** *vi fam* sborsare

shell: shellfish *n inv* mollusco *m*; Culin frutti *mpl* di mare. **shell-shocked** /ʃelʃɒkt/ *a* ⟨*soldier*⟩ traumatizzato da un bombardamento; *fig* in stato di shock. **shell suit** *n* tuta *f* di acetato

shelter /ʃeltə(r)/ *n* rifugio *m*; (*air raid ~*) rifugio *m* antiaereo; **take ~** rifugiarsi ● *vt* riparare (**from** da); *fig* mettere al riparo; (*give lodging to*) dare asilo a ● *vi* rifugiarsi

sheltered /ʃeltəd/ *a* ⟨*spot*⟩ riparato; ⟨*life*⟩ ritirato

shelve /ʃelv/ *vt* accantonare ⟨*project*⟩ ● *vi* ⟨*slope:*⟩ scendere

shelves /ʃelvz/ *see* **shelf**

shelving /ʃelvɪŋ/ *n* ⟨*shelves*⟩ ripiani *mpl*

shepherd /ʃepəd/ *n* pastore *m* ● *vt* guidare

shepherdess /ʃepədes/ *n* pastora *f*

shepherd's pie /ʃepədzˈpaɪ/ *n* pasticcio *m* di carne tritata e patate

sherbet /ʃɜːbət/ *n* (*Br: powder*) polverina *f* effervescente al gusto di frutta; (*Am: sorbet*) sorbetto *m*

sheriff /ʃerɪf/ *n* sceriffo *m*

Sherpa /ʃɜːpə/ *n* scerpa *m*

sherry /ʃerɪ/ *n* sherry *m inv*

shield /ʃiːld/ *n* scudo *m*; (*for eyes*) maschera *f*; Techn schermo *m* ● *vt* proteggere (**from** da)

shift /ʃɪft/ *n* cambiamento *m*; (*in position*) spostamento *m*; (*at work*) turno *m* ● *vt* spostare; (*take away*) togliere; riversare ⟨*blame*⟩ ● *vi* spostarsi; ⟨*wind:*⟩ cambiare; (*fam: move quickly*) darsi una mossa

shift key *n* tasto *m* delle maiuscole

shiftless /ʃɪftlɪs/ *a* privo di risorse

shift work *n* turni *mpl*

shift worker *n* turnista *mf*

shifty /ʃɪftɪ/ *a* (**-ier, -iest**) *pej* losco; ⟨*eyes*⟩ sfuggente

Shiite /ʃiːaɪt/ *a & n* sciita *mf*

shilling /ʃɪlɪŋ/ *n* scellino *m*

shilly-shally /ʃɪlɪʃælɪ/ *vi* titubare

shimmer /ʃɪmə(r)/ *n* luccichio *m* ● *vi* luccicare

shin /ʃɪn/ *n* stinco *m* ● *vi* **~ up/down sth** ⟨*climb*⟩ arrampicarsi su/scendere giù da qcsa

shin-guard *n* parastinchi *m inv*

shindig /ʃɪndɪg/ *n fam* (*party*) baldoria *f*; (*disturbance*) pandemonio *m*

shindy /ʃɪndɪ/ *n fam* (*disturbance*) pandemonio *m*; (*party*) baldoria *f*

shine /ʃaɪn/ *n* lucentezza *f*; **give sth a ~** dare una lucidata a qcsa ● *v* (*pt/pp* **shone**) ● *vi* splendere; (*reflect light*) brillare; ⟨*hair, shoes:*⟩ essere lucido ● *vt* **~ a light on** puntare una luce su

shingle /ʃɪŋgl/ *n* (*pebbles*) ghiaia *f*

shingles /ʃɪŋglz/ *n* Med fuochi *mpl* di Sant'Antonio

shiny /ʃaɪnɪ/ *a* (**-ier, -iest**) lucido

ship /ʃɪp/ *n* nave *f* ● *vt* (*pt/pp* **shipped**) spedire; (*by sea*) spedire via mare

shipbuilder /ʃɪpbɪldə(r)/ *n* costruttore *m* navale

shipbuilding /ʃɪpbɪldɪŋ/ *n* costruzione *f* di navi

shipment /ʃɪpmənt/ *n* spedizione *f*; (*consignment*) carico *m*

shipowner /ʃɪpəʊnə(r)/ *n* armatore *m*

shipper /ʃɪpə(r)/ *n* spedizioniere *m*

shipping /ʃɪpɪŋ/ *n* trasporto *m*; (*traffic*) imbarcazioni *fpl*

shipping agent *n* spedizioniere *m*

shipping company *n* compagnia *f* di spedizione

ship: shipshape *a & adv* in perfetto ordine. **shipwreck** *n* naufragio *m*. **shipwrecked** *a* naufragato. **shipyard** *n* cantiere *m* navale

shire /ʃaɪə(r)/ *n* Br contea *f*

shire-horse *n* cavallo *m* da tiro

shirk /ʃɜːk/ *vt* scansare

shirker /ʃɜːkə(r)/ *n* scansafatiche *mf inv*

shirt /ʃɜːt/ *n* camicia *f*; **in ~-sleeves** in maniche di camicia

shirty /ʃɜːtɪ/ *a* Br fam incavolato; **get ~ with sb** incavolarsi con qcno

shish kebab /ʃɪʃkɪˈbæb/ *n* spiedino *m* di carne e verdure

shit /ʃɪt/ *vulg n & int* merda *f* ● *vi* (*pt/pp* **shit**) cagare

shit-scared *a vulg* **be ~** farsela sotto

shiver /ʃɪvə(r)/ *n* brivido *m* ● *vi* rabbrividire

shoal /ʃəʊl/ *n* (*of fish*) banco *m*

shock /ʃɒk/ *n* (*impact*) urto *m*; Electr scossa *f* [elettrica]; *fig* colpo *m*, shock *m inv*; Med shock *m inv*; **get a ~** Electr prendere la scossa; **in ~** Med in stato di shock ● *vt* scioccare

shock absorber *n* Auto ammortizzatore *m*

shocking /ʃɒkɪŋ/ *a* scioccante; ⟨*fam: weather, handwriting etc*⟩ tremendo

shockingly /ʃɒkɪŋlɪ/ *adv* ⟨*behave*⟩ in modo pessimo; ⟨*expensive*⟩ eccessivamente

shocking pink *n* rosa *m* shocking

shock: shockproof *a* antiurto. **shock treatment** *n* terapia *f* d'urto. **shock wave** *n* onda *f* d'urto

shod /ʃɒd/ *see* **shoe**

shoddily /ʃɒdɪlɪ/ *adv* in modo scadente

shoddy /ʃɒdɪ/ *a* (**-ier, -iest**) scadente

shoe /ʃuː/ *n* scarpa *f*; (*of horse*) ferro *m* ● *vt* (*pt/pp* **shod**, *pres p* **shoeing**) ferrare ⟨*horse*⟩

shoe: shoehorn *n* calzante *m*. **shoelace** *n* laccio *m* da scarpa. **shoemaker** *n* calzolaio *m*. **shoe rack** *n* scarpiera *f*. **shoe-shop** *n* calzoleria *f*. **shoestring** *n* **on a ~** *fam* con una miseria. **shoe-tree** *n* forma *f* da scarpa

shone /ʃɒn/ *see* **shine**

shoo /ʃuː/ *vt* **~ away** cacciar via ● *int* sciò!

shook /ʃʊk/ *see* **shake**

shoot /ʃuːt/ *n* Bot germoglio *m*; (*hunt*) battuta *f* di caccia ● *v* (*pt/pp* **shot**) ● *vt* sparare; girare ⟨*film*⟩; **~ oneself in the foot** *fig* darsi la zappa sui piedi ● *vi* ⟨*hunt*⟩ andare a caccia

■ **shoot down** *vt* abbattere

■ **shoot out** *vi* (*rush*) precipitarsi fuori

■ **shoot up** *vi* (*grow*) crescere in fretta; ⟨*prices:*⟩ salire di colpo

shooting /'ʃuːtɪŋ/ *n* (*pastime*) caccia *f*; (*killing*) uccisione *f* ● *a* ⟨*pain*⟩ lancinante

shooting range *n* poligono *m* di tiro

shoot-out *n fam* sparatoria *f*

shop /ʃɒp/ *n* negozio *m*; (*workshop*) officina *f*; **talk ~** *fam* parlare di lavoro ● *vi* (*pt/pp* **shopped**, *pres p* **shopping**) far compere; **go ~ping** andare a fare compere

■ **shop around** *vi* confrontare i prezzi

shop: shop assistant *n* commesso, -a *mf*. **shop floor** *n* problemi on the **~ ~** problemi tra gli operai. **shopkeeper** *n* negoziante *mf*. **shoplifter** *n* taccheggiatore, -trice *mf*. **shoplifting** *n* taccheggio *m*

shopper /'ʃɒpə(r)/ *n* compratore, -trice *mf*

shopping /'ʃɒpɪŋ/ *n* compere *fpl*; (*articles*) acquisti *mpl*; **do the ~** fare la spesa

shopping: shopping bag *n* borsa *f* per la spesa. **shopping centre** *n* centro *m* commerciale. **shopping list** *n* lista *f* della spesa. **shopping mall** *n* centro *m* commerciale. **shopping trolley** *n* carrello *m*

shop steward *n* rappresentante *mf* sindacale

shop window *n* vetrina *f*

shore /ʃɔː(r)/ *n* riva *f*

■ **shore up** *vt* puntellare ⟨*building, wall*⟩

shorn /ʃɔːn/ *see* **shear**

short /ʃɔːt/ *a* corto; (*not lasting*) breve; ⟨*person*⟩ basso; (*curt*) brusco; **a ~ time ago** poco tempo fa; **be ~ of** essere a corto di; **be in ~ supply** essere scarso; *fig* essere raro; **Mick is ~ for Michael** Mick è il diminutivo di Michael; **cut ~** interrompere ⟨*holiday*⟩; **to cut a long story ~...** per farla breve...; **in the ~ term** nell'immediato futuro, a breve termine ● *adv* bruscamente; **in ~** in breve; **~ of doing** a meno di fare; **go ~** essere privato (**of** di); **stop ~ of doing sth** non arrivare fino a fare qcsa; **you're 10p ~** mancano 10 pence ● *n* (*Cinema*) cortometraggio *m*

shortage /'ʃɔːtɪdʒ/ *n* scarsità *f inv*

short: shortbread *n* biscotto *m* di pasta frolla. **short-change** *vt* dare meno resto del dovuto a; (*deliberately*) imbrogliare sul resto; *fig* imbrogliare. **short circuit** *n* corto *m* circuito ● *vt* mandare in cortocircuito ● *vi* causare un cortocircuito. **shortcoming** *n* difetto *m*. **shortcrust pastry** *n* pasta *f* frolla. **short cut** *n* scorciatoia *f*

shorten /'ʃɔːtn/ *vt* abbreviare; accorciare ⟨*garment*⟩

short: shortfall *n* (*in budget, accounts*) deficit *m inv*. **shorthand** *n* stenografia *f*. **shorthanded** /-'hændɪd/ *a* a corto di personale. **shorthand typist** *n* stenodattilografo, -a *mf*. **short list** *n* lista *f* dei candidati selezionati per un lavoro. **short-lived** /-'lɪvd/ *a* di breve durata

shortly /'ʃɔːtlɪ/ *adv* presto; **~ before/after** poco prima/dopo

shortness /'ʃɔːtnɪs/ *n* brevità *f inv*; (*of person*) bassa statura *f*

short notice *n* **at ~ ~** con poco preavviso

short-range *a* di breve portata

shorts /ʃɔːts/ *npl* calzoncini *mpl* corti

short: short-sighted /-'saɪtɪd/ *a* miope. **short-sleeved** /-'sliːvd/ *a* a maniche corte. **short-staffed** /-'stɑːft/ *a* a corto di personale. **short story** *n* racconto *m*, novella *f*. **short-tempered** /-'tempəd/ *a* irascibile. **short-term** *a* a breve termine. **short time** *n* **be on ~ ~** ⟨*worker:*⟩ fare orario ridotto. **short wave** *n* onde *fpl* corte. **short wave radio** *n* radio *f inv* a onde corte

shot /ʃɒt/ *see* **shoot** ● *n* colpo *m*; (*pellets*) piombini *mpl*; (*person*) tiratore *m*; *Phot* foto *f inv*; (*injection*) puntura *f*; (*fam: attempt*) prova *f*; **like a ~** *fam* come un razzo

shot: shotgun *n* fucile *m* da caccia. **shotputter** *n* pesista *mf*. **shot-putting** *n* *Sport* lancio *m* del peso

should /ʃʊd/ *v aux* **I ~ go** dovrei andare; **I ~ have seen him** avrei dovuto vederlo; **you ~n't have said that** non avresti dovuto dire questo; **I ~ like** mi piacerebbe; **this ~ be enough** questo dovrebbe bastare; **if he ~ come** se dovesse venire, se venisse

shoulder /'ʃəʊldə(r)/ *n* spalla *f*; **~ to ~** gomito a gomito ● *vt* mettersi in spalla; *fig* accollarsi

shoulder: shoulder bag *n* borsa *f* a tracolla. **shoulder blade** *n* scapola *f*. **shoulder pad** *n* spallina *f*. **shoulder strap** *n* spallina *f*; (*of bag*) tracolla *f*

shout /ʃaʊt/ *n* grido *m* ● *vt/i* gridare

■ **shout at** *vi* alzar la voce con

■ **shout down** *vt* azzittire gridando

shouting /'ʃaʊtɪŋ/ *n* grida *fpl*

shove /ʃʌv/ *n* spintone *m* ● *vt* spingere; (*fam: put*) ficcare ● *vi* spingere

■ **shove off** *vi fam* togliersi di torno

shovel /'ʃʌvl/ *n* pala *f* ● *vt* (*pt/pp* **shovelled**) spalare

show /ʃəʊ/ *n* (*display*) manifestazione *f*; (*exhibition*) mostra *f*; (*ostentation*) ostentazione *f*; *Theat, TV* spettacolo *m*; (*programme*) programma *m*; **on ~** esposto ● *v* (*pt* **showed**, *pp* **shown**) ● *vt* mostrare; (*put on display*) esporre; proiettare ⟨*film*⟩; **~ sb to the door** accompagnare qcno alla porta; **~ sb the door** mettere alla porta qcno ● *vi* ⟨*film:*⟩ essere proiettato; **your slip is ~ing** ti si vede la sottoveste

■ **show in** *vt* fare accomodare

■ **show off** *vi fam* mettersi in mostra ● *vt* mettere in mostra

■ **show out** *vt* **~ sb out** fare uscire qcno

■ **show up** *vi* risaltare; (*fam: arrive*) farsi vedere ● *vt* (*fam: embarrass*) far fare una brutta figura a

show: showbiz /'ʃəʊbɪz/ *n fam* mondo *m* dello spettacolo. **show business** *n* mondo *m* dello spettacolo. **showcase** *n also fig* vetrina *f* ● *attrib* ⟨*village, prison*⟩ modello. **showdown** *n* regolamento *m* dei conti

shower /ˈʃaʊə(r)/ n doccia f; (of rain) acquaz- zone m; **have a ~** fare la doccia ● vt **~ with** coprire di ● vi fare la doccia

shower: shower-cap n cuffia f da doccia. **shower-curtain** tenda f della doccia. **shower-head** n bocchetta f. **showerproof** a impermeabile

showery /ˈʃaʊərɪ/ a **it was ~** ci sono stati diversi acquazzoni

showjumper /ˈʃəʊdʒʌmpə(r)/ n cavaliere m/cavallerizza f di salto ad ostacoli

showjumping /ˈʃəʊdʒʌmpɪŋ/ n concorso m ippico

shown /ʃəʊn/ see show

show: show-off n esibizionista mf. **showpiece** n pezzo m forte. **showplace** n attrazione f. **showroom** n salone m [per] esposizioni

showy /ˈʃəʊɪ/ a appariscente

shrank /ʃræŋk/ see shrink

shrapnel /ˈʃræpnl/ n schegge fpl di granata, shrapnel m

shred /ʃred/ n brandello m; fig briciolo m ● vt (pt/pp **shredded**) fare a brandelli; Culin tagliuzzare

shredder /ˈʃredə(r)/ n distruttore m di docu- menti

shrew /ʃru:/ n Zool toporagno m; (pej: woman) bisbetica f

shrewd /ʃru:d/ a accorto

shrewdly /ˈʃru:dlɪ/ adv con accortezza

shrewdness /ˈʃru:dnɪs/ n accortezza f

shriek /ʃri:k/ n strillo m ● vt/i strillare

shrift /ʃrɪft/ n **give sb short ~** liquidare qcno rapidamente

shrill /ʃrɪl/ a penetrante

shrillness /ˈʃrɪlnɪs/ n acutezza f

shrilly /ˈʃrɪlɪ/ adv in modo penetrante

shrimp /ʃrɪmp/ n gamberetto m

shrine /ʃraɪn/ n (place) santuario m

shrink /ʃrɪŋk/ vi (pt **shrank**, pp **shrunk**) re- stringersi; (draw back) ritrarsi (**from** da) ● n fam strizzacervelli mf inv

shrinkage /ˈʃrɪŋkɪdʒ/ n (of fabric) restrin- gimento m; (of area, company) rimpiccio- limento m; (in a shop) perdite fpl; (of resources) diminuzione f

shrinking violet /ʃrɪŋkɪŋˈvaɪələt/ n hum mammoletta f

shrink: shrink-proof a irrestringibile. **shrink-resistant** a irrestringibile. **shrink- wrap** vt avvolgere nella pellicola trasparente ● n pellicola f trasparente

shrivel /ˈʃrɪvl/ vi (pt/pp **shrivelled**) raggrin- zare

shroud /ʃraʊd/ n sudario m; fig manto m; **~ed in** fig avvolto in

Shrove /ʃrəʊv/ n **~ Tuesday** martedì m grasso

shrub /ʃrʌb/ n arbusto m

shrubbery /ˈʃrʌbərɪ/ n (in garden) zona f piantata ad arbusti

shrug /ʃrʌg/ n scrollata f di spalle ● vt/i (pt/ pp **shrugged**) ~ [one's shoulders] scrolla- re le spalle

■ **shrug off** vt ignorare

shrunk /ʃrʌŋk/ see shrink. **~en** . a rimpicciolito

shudder /ˈʃʌdə(r)/ n fremito m ● vi fremere

shuffle /ˈʃʌfl/ vi strascicare i piedi ● vt me- scolare ⟨cards⟩ ● n strascicamento m; (at cards) mescolata f

shufty /ˈʃʊftɪ/ n Br fam **have a ~ at sth** dare un'occhiata a qcsa

shun /ʃʌn/ vt (pt/pp **shunned**) rifuggire

shunt /ʃʌnt/ vt smistare

shush /ʃʊʃ/ int zitto!

shut /ʃʌt/ v (pt/pp **shut**, pres p **shutting**) ● vt chiudere ● vi chiudersi; ⟨shop:⟩ chiudere

■ **shut down** vt/i chiudere

■ **shut off** vt chiudere ⟨water, gas⟩

■ **shut out** vt bloccare ⟨light⟩; impedire ⟨view⟩; scacciare ⟨memory⟩

■ **shut up** vt chiudere; fam far tacere ● vi fam stare zitto; **~ up!** stai zitto!

shutdown /ˈʃʌtdaʊn/ n chiusura f

shut-eye n (fam: short sleep) **get some ~** fare un pisolino

shutter /ˈʃʌtə(r)/ n serranda f; Phot otturato- re m

shuttle /ˈʃʌtl/ n navetta f ● vi far la spola

shuttlecock /ˈʃʌtlkɒk/ n volano m

shuttle service n servizio m pendolare

shy /ʃaɪ/ a (timid) timido ● vi (pt/pp **shied**) ⟨horse:⟩ fare uno scarto

■ **shy away from** vt rifuggire da

shyly /ˈʃaɪlɪ/ adv timidamente

shyness /ˈʃaɪnɪs/ n timidezza f

sibylline /ˈsɪbɪlaɪn/ a sibillino

Siamese /saɪəˈmi:z/ a siamese

Siamese twins npl fratelli mpl/sorelle fpl siamesi

sibling /ˈsɪblɪŋ/ n (brother) fratello m; (sister) sorella f; **~s** pl fratelli mpl

sibling rivalry n rivalità f tra fratelli

Sicilian /sɪˈsɪlɪən/ a & n siciliano, -a mf

Sicily /ˈsɪsɪlɪ/ n Sicilia f

sick /sɪk/ a ammalato; ⟨humour⟩ macabro; **be ~** (vomit) vomitare; **be ~ of sth** fam essere stufo di qcsa; **feel ~** aver la nausea

sicken /ˈsɪkn/ vt disgustare ● vi **be ~ing for something** covare qualche malanno

sickening /ˈsɪkənɪŋ/ a disgustoso

sick leave n congedo m per malattia

sickly /ˈsɪklɪ/ a (-ier, -iest) malaticcio

sickness /ˈsɪknɪs/ n malattia f; (vomiting) nausea f

sickness benefit n sussidio m di malattia

sickroom /ˈsɪkru:m/ n camera f dell'amma- lato

side /saɪd/ n lato m; (of person, mountain) fianco m; (of road) bordo m; **on the ~** (as sideline) come attività secondaria; **~ by ~** fianco a fianco; **take ~s** immischiarsi; **take sb's ~** prendere le parti di qcno; **be on the safe ~** andare sul sicuro ● attrib laterale ● vi **~ with** parteggiare per

side: sideboard n credenza f. **sideburns** npl

basette *fpl*. **side effect** *n* effetto *m* collaterale. **sidekick** *n fam* (*companion*) compare *mf*; (*assistant*) braccio *m* destro. **sidelights** *npl* luci *fpl* di posizione. **sideline** *n* attività *f inv* complementare. **sidelong** *a* ~ **glance** sguincio *m*. **side road** *n* strada *f* secondaria. **side-saddle** *adv* all'amazzone. **sideshow** *n* attrazione *f*. **sidestep** *vt* schivare. **side street** *n* strada *f* laterale. **sidetrack** *vt* sviare. **sidewalk** *n Am* marciapiede *m*. **sideways** *adv* obliquamente

siding /ˈsaɪdɪŋ/ *n* binario *m* di raccordo

sidle /ˈsaɪdl/ *vi* camminare furtivamente (**up to** verso)

siege /siːdʒ/ *n* assedio *m*

Sierra Leone /sɪeərəlɪˈəʊn/ *n* Sierra Leone *f*

siesta /sɪˈestə/ *n* siesta *f*; **take a** ~ fare una siesta

sieve /sɪv/ *n* setaccio *m* ● *vt* setacciare

sift /sɪft/ *vt* setacciare; ~ [**through**] *fig* passare al setaccio

sigh /saɪ/ *n* sospiro *m*; **give a** ~ sospirare ● *vi* sospirare

sight /saɪt/ *n* vista *f*; (*on gun*) mirino *m*; **the** ~**s** *pl* le cose da vedere; **at first** ~ a prima vista; **be within/out of** ~ essere/non essere in vista; **within** ~ **of** vicino a; **lose** ~ **of** perdere di vista; **know by** ~ conoscere di vista; **have bad** ~ vederci male ● *vt* avvistare

sightseeing /ˈsaɪtsiːɪŋ/ *n* **go** ~ andare a visitare posti

sightseer /ˈsaɪtsiːə(r)/ *n* turista *mf*

sign /saɪn/ *n* segno *m*; (*notice*) insegna *f* ● *vt/i* firmare

■ **sign for** *vt* firmare la ricevuta di (*letter, parcel*); firmare un contratto con (*football club*)

■ **sign in** *vi* (*hotel guest:*) firmare il registro

■ **sign on** *vi* (*as unemployed*) presentarsi all'ufficio di collocamento; *Mil* arruolarsi

■ **sign up** *vi Mil* arruolarsi; ~ **up for a course** iscriversi a un corso

signal /ˈsɪɡnl/ *n* segnale *m* ● *v* (*pt/pp* **signalled**) ● *vt* segnalare ● *vi* fare segnali; ~ **to sb** far segno a qcno (**to** di)

signal box *n* cabina *f* di segnalazione

signalman /ˈsɪɡnlmən/ *n* casellante *m*

signatory /ˈsɪɡnət(ə)rɪ/ *n* firmatario, -a *mf*

signature /ˈsɪɡnətʃə(r)/ *n* firma *f*

signature tune *n* sigla *f* [musicale]

signet ring /ˈsɪɡnɪt/ *n* anello *m* con sigillo

significance /sɪɡˈnɪfɪkəns/ *n* significato *m*

significant /sɪɡˈnɪfɪkənt/ *a* significativo

significantly /sɪɡˈnɪfɪkəntlɪ/ *adv* in modo significativo

signify /ˈsɪɡnɪfaɪ/ *vt* (*pt/pp* **-ied**) indicare

signing /ˈsaɪnɪŋ/ *n* (*of treaty*) firma *f*; (*of footballer*) ingaggio *m*; (*footballer*) nuovo acquisto *m*; (*sign language*) linguaggio *m* dei segni

sign language *n* linguaggio *m* dei segni

signpost /ˈsaɪnpəʊst/ *n* segnalazione *f* stradale

Sikh /siːk/ *n* sikh *mf inv* ● *a* sikh *inv*

silage /ˈsaɪlɪdʒ/ *n* foraggio *m* conservato in silo

silence /ˈsaɪləns/ *n* silenzio *m*; **in** ~ in silenzio ● *vt* far tacere

silencer /ˈsaɪlənsə(r)/ *n* (*on gun*) silenziatore *m*; *Auto* marmitta *f*

silent /ˈsaɪlənt/ *a* silenzioso; (*film*) muto; **remain** ~ rimanere in silenzio; **the** ~ **majority** la maggioranza silenziosa

silently /ˈsaɪləntlɪ/ *adv* silenziosamente

silhouette /sɪluˈet/ *n* sagoma *f*, silhouette *f inv* ● *vt* **be** ~**d** profilarsi

silica gel /ˈsɪlɪkə/ *n* gel *m inv* di silice

silicon /ˈsɪlɪkən/ *n* silicio *m*

silicon chip *n Comput* chip *m inv* di silicio, piastrina *f* di silicio

silicone /ˈsɪlɪkəʊn/ *n Chem* silicone *m*

silicone varnish *n* vernice *f* siliconica

silk /sɪlk/ *n* seta *f* ● *attrib* di seta

silkworm /ˈsɪlkwɜːm/ *n* baco *m* da seta

silky /ˈsɪlkɪ/ *a* (**-ier, -iest**) come la seta

sill /ʃɪl/ *n* davanzale *m*

silly /ˈʃɪlɪ/ *a* (**-ier, -iest**) sciocco

silo /ˈsaɪləʊ/ *n* silo *m*

silt /sɪlt/ *n* melma *f*

silver /ˈsɪlvə(r)/ *a* d'argento; (*paper*) argentato ● *n* argento *m*; (*silverware*) argenteria *f*

silver: silver-plated *a* placcato d'argento. **silver service** *n* servizio *m* a tavola in cui il cameriere fa il giro dei commensali. **silversmith** *n* argentiere *m*. **silverware** *n* argenteria *f*. **silver wedding** *n* nozze *fpl* d'argento

silvery /ˈsɪlvərɪ/ *a* argentino

similar /ˈsɪmɪlə(r)/ *a* simile

similarity /sɪmɪˈlærətɪ/ *n* somiglianza *f*

similarly /ˈsɪmɪləlɪ/ *adv* in modo simile

simile /ˈsɪmɪlɪ/ *n* similitudine *f*

simmer /ˈsɪmə(r)/ *vi* bollire lentamente ● *vt* far bollire lentamente

■ **simmer down** *vi* calmarsi

simper /ˈsɪmpə(r)/ *vi* ostentare un sorriso

simpering /ˈsɪmp(ə)rɪŋ/ *a* (*smile*) affettato; (*person*) smanceroso

simple /ˈsɪmpl/ *a* semplice; (*person*) sempliciotto

simple-minded /-ˈmaɪndɪd/ *a* sempliciotto

simpleton /ˈsɪmpltən/ *n* sempliciotto, -a *mf*

simplicity /sɪmˈplɪsətɪ/ *n* semplicità *f*

simplification /sɪmplɪfɪˈkeɪʃn/ *n* semplificazione *f*

simplify /ˈsɪmplɪfaɪ/ *vt* (*pt/pp* **-ied**) semplificare

simplistic /sɪmˈplɪstɪk/ *a* semplicistico

simply /ˈsɪmplɪ/ *adv* semplicemente

simulate /ˈsɪmjʊleɪt/ *vt* simulare

simulation /sɪmjʊˈleɪʃn/ *n* simulazione *f*

simulcast /ˈsɪməlkɑːst/ *vt* teleradiotrasmettere

simultaneous /sɪmlˈteɪnɪəs/ *a* simultaneo

simultaneously /sɪməlˈteɪnɪəslɪ/ *adv* simultaneamente

sin /sɪn/ *n* peccato *m* ● *vi* (*pt/pp* **sinned**) peccare

since /sɪns/ *prep* da; ~ **when?** da quando in qua? ● *adv* da allora ● *conj* da quando; (*because*) siccome

sincere /sɪn'sɪə(r)/ *a* sincero

sincerely /sɪn'sɪəlɪ/ *adv* sinceramente; **Yours ~** Distinti saluti

sincerity /sɪn'serətɪ/ *n* sincerità *f*

sine /saɪn/ *n Math* seno *m*

sinew /'sɪnjuː/ *n* tendine *m*

sinful /'sɪnfl/ *a* peccaminoso

sing /sɪŋ/ *vt/i* (*pt* **sang**, *pp* **sung**) cantare

singalong /'sɪŋəlɒŋ/ *n* **have a ~** cantare [tutti] insieme

singe /sɪndʒ/ *vt* (*pres p* **singeing**) bruciacchiare

singer /'sɪŋə(r)/ *n* cantante *mf*

singer-songwriter /-'sɒŋraɪtə(r)/ *n* cantautore, -trice *mf*

singing /'sɪŋɪŋ/ *n* canto *m*

single /'sɪŋgl/ *a* solo; (*not double*) semplice; (*unmarried*) celibe; ⟨*woman*⟩ nubile; ⟨*room*⟩ singolo; ⟨*bed*⟩ a una piazza; **I haven't spoken to a ~ person** non ho parlato con nessuno ● *n* (*ticket*) biglietto *m* di sola andata; (*record*) singolo *m*

■ **single out** *vt* scegliere; (*distinguish*) distinguere

single: single-breasted /-'brestɪd/ *a* a un petto. **single cream** *n* panna *f* da cucina fluida. **single currency** *n* (*in Europe*) moneta *f* unica. **single-decker** /-'dekə(r)/ *n* autobus *m inv* (*a un piano solo*). **single file** *adv* in fila indiana. **single-handed** /-'hændɪd/ *a & adv* da solo. **single-handedly** /-'hændɪdlɪ/ *adv* da solo. **single market** *n* mercato *m* unico. **single-minded** /-'maɪndɪd/ *a* risoluto. **single parent** *n* genitore *m* che alleva il figlio da solo

singles /'sɪŋglz/ *npl Tennis* singolo *m*; (*people*) single *mpl*; **the women's ~** il singolo femminile

singles bar *n* bar ritrovo *m inv* per single

single-sex *a* (*for boys*) maschile; (*for girls*) femminile

single-storey *a* ⟨*house*⟩ a un piano

singly /'sɪŋglɪ/ *adv* singolarmente

sing-song *Br a* ⟨*voice, dialect*⟩ che ha una sua particolare cadenza ● *n* **have a ~** cantare [tutti] insieme

singular /'sɪŋgjʊlə(r)/ *a Gram* singolare; (*uncommon*) eccezionale ● *n* singolare *m*

singularly /'sɪŋgjʊləlɪ/ *adv* singolarmente

sinister /'sɪnɪstə(r)/ *a* sinistro

sink /sɪŋk/ *n* lavandino *m* ● *v* (*pt* **sank**, *pp* **sunk**) ● *vi* affondare ● *vt* affondare ⟨*ship*⟩; scavare ⟨*shaft*⟩; investire ⟨*money*⟩

■ **sink in** *vi* penetrare; **it took a while to ~ in** (*fam: be understood*) c'è voluto un po' a capirlo

sinker /'sɪŋkə(r)/ *n* (*in fishing*) piombo *m*; *Am Culin* ≈ bombolone *m*

sinking /'sɪŋkɪŋ/ *n* affondamento *m*

sink unit *n* mobile *m* di cucina comprendente il lavandino

sinner /'sɪnə(r)/ *n* peccatore, -trice *mf*

sinuous /'sɪnjʊəs/ *a* sinuoso

sinus /'saɪnəs/ *n* seno *m* paranasale

sinusitis /saɪnə'saɪtɪs/ *n* sinusite *f*

sip /sɪp/ *n* sorso *m* ● *vt* (*pt/pp* **sipped**) sorseggiare

siphon /'saɪfn/ *n* (*bottle*) sifone *m*

■ **siphon off** *vt* travasare (*con sifone*)

sir /sɜː(r)/ *n* signore *m*; **S~** (*title*) Sir *m*; **Dear S~** Egregio Signore; **Dear S~s** Spettabile ditta

sire /saɪə(r)/ *vt* generare

siren /'saɪrən/ *n* sirena *f*

sirloin /'sɜːlɔɪn/ *n* (*of beef*) controfiletto *m*

sirloin steak *n* bistecca *f* di controfiletto

sissy /'sɪsɪ/ *n* feminuccia *f*

sister /'sɪstə(r)/ *n* sorella *f*; (*nurse*) [infermiera *f*] caposala *f*

sisterhood /'sɪstəhʊd/ *n Relig* congregazione *f* religiosa femminile; (*in feminism*) solidarietà *f inv* femminile

sister-in-law *n* (*pl* ~**s-in-law**) cognata *f*

sisterly /'sɪstəlɪ/ *a* da sorella

Sistine Chapel /'sɪstiːn/ *n* Cappella *f* Sistina

sit /sɪt/ *v* (*pt/pp* **sat**, *pres p* **sitting**) ● *vi* essere seduto; (*sit down*) sedersi; ⟨*committee:*⟩ riunirsi ● *vt* sostenere ⟨*exam*⟩

■ **sit back** *vi fig* starsene con le mani in mano

■ **sit by** *vi* starsene a guardare

■ **sit down** *vi* mettersi a sedere; **please ~ down** si accomodi; **~ down!** siediti!

■ **sit for** *vi* posare per ⟨*portrait*⟩

■ **sit on** *vt* far parte di ⟨*committee*⟩

■ **sit up** *vi* mettersi seduto; (*not slouch*) star seduto diritto; (*stay up*) stare alzato

sitcom /'sɪtkɒm/ *n fam* situation comedy *f inv*

sit-down *n Br* **have a ~** sedersi un momento

site /saɪt/ *n* posto *m*; *Archaeol* sito *m*; (*building* ~) cantiere *m* ● *vt* collocare

sit-in /'sɪtɪn/ *n* occupazione *f* (*di fabbrica ecc*); sit-in *m inv*

sitter /'sɪtə(r)/ *n* (*babysitter*) baby-sitter *mf inv*; (*for artist*) modello *m*

sitting /'sɪtɪŋ/ *n* seduta *f*; (*for meals*) turno *m*

sitting: sitting duck *n fam* facile bersaglio *m*. **sitting room** *n* salotto *m*. **sitting tenant** *n* locatario *m* residente

situate /'sɪtjʊeɪt/ *vt* situare

situated /'sɪtjʊeɪtɪd/ *a* situato

situation /sɪtjʊ'eɪʃn/ *n* situazione *f*; (*location*) posizione *f*; (*job*) posto *m*; **'~s vacant'** 'offerte di lavoro'

situation report *n* quadro *m* della situazione

sit-ups *npl* addominali *mpl*

six /sɪks/ *a & n* sei *m*

six-pack *n* confezione *f* da sei (*di bottiglie o lattine*)

sixteen /sɪks'tiːn/ *a & n* sedici *m*

sixteenth /sɪks'tiːnθ/ *a & n* sedicesimo, -a *mf*

sixteenth-century *a* cinquecentesco

sixth /sɪksθ/ *a & n* sesto, -a *mf*

sixth form N Sch ultimo biennio m facoltativo della scuola superiore

sixth sense n sesto senso m

sixtieth /'sɪkstɪɪθ/ a & n sessantesimo, -a mf

sixty /'sɪkstɪ/ a & n sessanta m

size /saɪz/ n dimensioni fpl; (of clothes) taglia f, misura f; (of shoes) numero m; **what ~ is the room?** che dimensioni ha la stanza?

■ **size up** vt fam valutare

sizeable /'saɪzəbl/ a piuttosto grande

sizzle /'sɪzl/ vi sfrigolare

skate¹ /skeɪt/ n inv (fish) razza f

skate² n pattino m ● vi pattinare

■ **skate over** vt fig glissare su

skateboard /'skeɪtbɔːd/ n skate-board m inv

skateboarder /'skeɪtbɔːdə(r)/ n persona f che va in skate-board

skateboarding /'skeɪtbɔːdɪŋ/ n skate-board m

skater /skeɪt/ n pattinatore, -trice mf

skating /'skeɪtɪŋ/ n pattinaggio m

skating rink n pista f di pattinaggio

skeletal /'skelɪtl/ a also fig scheletrico; ⟨disease⟩ dello scheletro

skeleton /'skelɪtn/ n scheletro m

skeleton key n passe-partout m inv

skeleton staff n personale m ridotto

sketch /sketʃ/ n schizzo m; Theat sketch m inv ● vt fare uno schizzo di

■ **sketch out** vt delineare

sketchbook /'sketʃbʊk/ n (for sketching) album m inv per schizzi; (book of sketches) album m inv di schizzi

sketchily /'sketʃɪlɪ/ adv in modo abbozzato

sketchpad /'sketʃpæd/ n blocco m per schizzi

sketchy /'sketʃɪ/ a (-ier, -iest) abbozzato

skew /skju:/ vt alterare ⟨figures⟩

skewer /'skjʊə(r)/ n spiedo m

ski /ski:/ n sci m inv ● vi (pt/pp skied, pres p skiing) sciare; **go ~ing** andare a sciare

skid /skɪd/ n slittata f; **go into a ~** slittare ● vi (pt/pp skidded) slittare

skid mark n segno m di frenata

skier /'ski:ə(r)/ n sciatore, -trice mf

skiing /'ski:ɪŋ/ n sci m

ski instructor n maestro, -a mf di sci

ski jump n (competition) salto m con gli sci; (slope) trampolino m

skilful /'skɪlfl/ a abile

skilfully /'skɪlfʊlɪ/ adv abilmente

ski lift n impianto m di risalita

skill /skɪl/ n abilità f inv

skilled /skɪld/ a dotato; ⟨worker⟩ specializzato

skillet /'skɪlət/ n Am padella f

skim /skɪm/ vt (pt/pp skimmed) schiumare; scremare ⟨milk⟩

■ **skim off** vt togliere

■ **skim over** vt sfiorare ⟨surface, subject⟩

■ **skim through** vt scorrere

skimmed milk /skɪmd/ n latte m scremato

skimp /skɪmp/ vi **~ on** lesinare su

skimpy /'skɪmpɪ/ a (-ier, -iest) succinto

skin /skɪn/ n pelle f; (on fruit) buccia f;

soaked to the ~ fradicio fino all'osso ● vt (pt/pp skinned) spellare

skin: skin cancer n cancro m alla pelle. **skincare** n cura f della pella. **skin cream** n crema f per la pelle. **skin-deep** a superficiale. **skin diver** n sub mf inv. **skin diving** n nuoto m subacqueo

skinflint /'skɪnflɪnt/ n miserabile mf

skin graft n innesto m epidermico

skinhead /'skɪnhed/ n skinhead m

skinny /'skɪnɪ/ a (-ier, -iest) molto magro

skint /skɪnt/ a fam al verde

skintight /skɪn'taɪt/ a aderente

skip¹ /skɪp/ n (container) benna f

skip² n salto m ● v (pt/pp skipped) ● vi saltellare; (with rope) saltare la corda ● vt omettere

ski: ski pants npl pantaloni mpl da sci. **ski pass** n ski-pass m inv. **ski pole** n racchetta f da sci

skipper /'skɪpə(r)/ n skipper m inv

skipping /'skɪpɪŋ/ n salto m della corda

skipping rope n corda f per saltare

ski rack n portasci m inv

ski resort n stazione f sciistica

skirmish /'skɜːmɪʃ/ n scaramuccia f

skirt /skɜːt/ n gonna f ● vt costeggiare

skirting board /'skɜːtɪŋ/ n battiscopa m inv, zoccolo m

ski: ski run n pista f da sci. **ski slope** n pista f da sci. **ski stick** n racchetta f da sci

skit /skɪt/ n bozzetto m comico

skittish /'skɪtɪʃ/ a (difficult to handle) ombroso; (playful) giocherellone

skittle /'skɪtl/ n birillo m

skive /skaɪv/ vi fam fare lo scansafatiche

skivvy /'skɪvɪ/ n Br fam sguattera f

ski wax n sciolina f

skulduggery /skʌl'dʌgərɪ/ n fam imbrogli mpl

skulk /skʌlk/ vi aggirarsi furtivamente

skull /skʌl/ n cranio m

skunk /skʌŋk/ n moffetta f; (person) farabutto m

sky /skaɪ/ n cielo m

sky: skydiving n paracadutismo m in caduta libera. **sky-high** a ⟨prices⟩ alle stelle; ⟨rates⟩ esorbitante ● adv rise **~** salire alle stelle. **skylight** n lucernario m. **skyline** n (of city) profilo m. **skyrocket** vi ⟨prices:⟩ andare alle stelle. **skyscraper** n grattacielo m

slab /slæb/ n lastra f; (slice) fetta f; (of chocolate) tavoletta f

slack /slæk/ a lento; ⟨person⟩ fiacco ● vi fare lo scansafatiche

■ **slack off** vi rilassarsi

slacken /'slækn/ vi allentare; **~ [off]** ⟨trade:⟩ rallentare; ⟨speed, rain:⟩ diminuire ● vt allentare; diminuire ⟨speed⟩

slacker /'slækə(r)/ n lazzarone m

slacks /slæks/ npl pantaloni mpl sportivi

slag /slæg/ n scorie fpl

■ **slag off** vt (pt/pp slagged) Br fam sparlare di

slain /sleɪn/ see **slay**

slalom /'slɑ:ləm/ n slalom m inv

slam /slæm/ v (pt/pp **slammed**) ● vt sbattere; (fam: criticize) stroncare ● vi sbattere

slammer /'slæmə(r)/ n (fam: prison) galera f

slander /'slɑ:ndə(r)/ n diffamazione f ● vt diffamare

slanderer /'slɑ:ndərə(r)/ n diffamatore, -trice mf

slanderous /'slɑ:nd(ə)rəs/ a diffamatorio

slang /slæŋ/ n gergo m

slangy /'slæŋɪ/ a gergale

slant /slɑ:nt/ n pendenza f; (point of view) angolazione f; **on the ~** in pendenza ● vt pendere; fig distorcere ⟨report⟩ ● vi pendere

slanted /'slæntɪd/ a ⟨fig: report⟩ tendenzioso

slap /slæp/ n schiaffo m ● vt (pt/pp **slapped**) schiaffeggiare; (put) schiaffare ● adv in pieno

slap: slap bang adv fam **he went ~ ~ into the wall** è andato a sbattere in pieno contro il muro. **slapdash** a fam frettoloso. **slapstick** n farsa f da torte in faccia. **slap-up** a fam di prim'ordine

slash /slæʃ/ n taglio m; Typ barra f obliqua ● vt tagliare; ridurre drasticamente ⟨prices⟩; **~ one's wrists** svenarsi

slat /slæt/ n stecca f

slate /sleɪt/ n ardesia f ● vt fam fare a pezzi

slater /'sleɪtə(r)/ n (roofer) addetto m alla ricopertura dei tetti con tegole di ardesia; Zool onisco m

slatted /'slætɪd/ a ⟨shutter⟩ a stecche

slaughter /'slɔ:tə(r)/ n macello m; (of people) massacro m ● vt macellare; massacrare ⟨people⟩

slaughterhouse /'slɔ:təhaʊs/ n macello m

Slav /slɑ:v/ a slavo ● n slavo, -a mf

slave /sleɪv/ n schiavo, -a mf ● vi ~ [**away**] lavorare come un negro

slave-driver n schiavista mf

slavery /'sleɪvərɪ/ n schiavitù f

Slavic /'slɑ:vɪk/ a slavo

slavish /'sleɪvɪʃ/ a servile

slavishly /'sleɪvɪʃlɪ/ adv in modo servile

Slavonic /slə'vɒnɪk/ a slavo

slay /sleɪ/ vt (pt **slew**, pp **slain**) ammazzare

sleaze /sli:z/ n fam (pornography) pornografia f; (corruption) corruzione f

sleazy /'sli:zɪ/ a (-ier, -iest) sordido

sled /sled/ n slitta f ● vi andare in slitta

sledge /sledʒ/ n slitta f

sledgehammer /'sledʒhæmə(r)/ n martello m

sleek /sli:k/ a liscio, lucente; (well-fed) pasciuto

sleep /sli:p/ n sonno m; **go to ~** addormentarsi; **put to ~** far addormentare; **in my ~** nel sonno; **a good night's ~** una bella dormita ● v (pt/pp **slept**) ● vi dormire; **~ like a log** dormire come un ghiro; **~ on it** dormirci sopra; **~ with sb** andare a letto con qcno ● vt **~s six** ha sei posti letto

■ **sleep around** vi andare a letto con tutti

■ **sleep in** vi dormire più a lungo

sleeper /'sli:pə(r)/ n Rail treno m con vagoni

letto; (compartment) vagone m letto; (on track) traversina f; **be a light/heavy ~** avere il sonno leggero/pesante

sleepily /'sli:pɪlɪ/ adv con aria assonnata

sleeping /'sli:pɪŋ/: **sleeping bag** n sacco m a pelo. **sleeping car** n vagone m letto. **sleeping partner** n Br Comm socio m accomodante. **sleeping pill** n sonnifero m. **sleeping policeman** n dosso m di rallentamento

sleepless /'sli:plɪs/ a insonne; **have a ~ night** passare una notte insonne

sleeplessness /'sli:plɪsnɪs/ n insonnia f

sleep: sleepsuit n tutina f. **sleepwalk** vi essere sonnambulo. **sleepwalker** n sonnambulo, -a mf. **sleepwalking** n sonnambulismo m

sleepy /'sli:pɪ/ a (-ier, -iest) assonnato; **be ~** aver sonno

sleet /sli:t/ n nevischio m ● vi **it is ~ing** nevischia

sleeve /sli:v/ n manica f; (for record) copertina f

sleeveless /'sli:vlɪs/ a senza maniche

sleigh /sleɪ/ n slitta f

sleight /slaɪt/ n **~ of hand** gioco m di prestigio

slender /'slendə(r)/ a snello; ⟨fingers, stem⟩ affusolato; fig scarso; ⟨chance⟩ magro

slept /slept/ see **sleep**

sleuth /slu:θ/ n investigatore m, detective m inv

slew¹ /slu:/ vi girare

slew² see **slay**

slice /slaɪs/ n fetta f ● vt affettare; **~d bread** pane m a cassetta

slick /slɪk/ a liscio; (cunning) astuto ● n (of oil) chiazza f di petrolio

slide /slaɪd/ n scivolata f; (in playground) scivolo m; (for hair) fermaglio m [per capelli]; Phot diapositiva f ● v (pt/pp **slid**) ● vi scivolare ● vt far scivolare

slide rule n regolo m calcolatore

sliding /'slaɪdɪŋ/ a ⟨door, seat⟩ scorrevole

sliding scale n scala f mobile

slight /slaɪt/ a leggero; ⟨importance⟩ poco; (slender) esile; **~est** minimo; **not in the ~est** niente affatto ● vt offendere ● n offesa f

slightly /'slaɪtlɪ/ adv leggermente

slim /slɪm/ a (**slimmer, slimmest**) snello; fig scarso; ⟨chance⟩ magro ● vi dimagrire

slime /slaɪm/ n melma f

slimy /'slaɪmɪ/ a melmoso; fig viscido

sling /slɪŋ/ n Med benda f al collo ● vt (pt/pp **slung**) fam lanciare

sling-back n sandalo m (chiuso davanti)

slingshot /'slɪŋʃɒt/ n fionda f

■ **slink in** /slɪŋk/ vi (pt/pp **slunk**) entrare furtivamente

slinky /'slɪŋkɪ/ a ⟨fam: dress⟩ sexy inv, attillato

slip /slɪp/ n scivolata f; (mistake) lieve errore m; (petticoat) sottoveste f; (for pillow) federa f; (paper) scontrino m; **give sb the ~** fam sbarazzarsi di qcno; **~ of the tongue** lapsus *m inv* ● *v* (*pt/pp* **slipped**) ● *vi* scivolare; (*go quickly*) sgattaiolare; (*decline*) retrocedere; **let sth ~** (*reveal*) lasciarsi sfuggire qcsa ● *vt* **he ~ped it into his pocket** se l'è infilato in tasca; **~ sb's mind** sfuggire di mente a qcno

■ **slip away** *vi* sguisciar via; ⟨*time:*⟩ sfuggire

■ **slip into** *vi* infilarsi ⟨*clothes*⟩

■ **slip on** *vt* infilarsi ⟨*jacket etc*⟩

■ **slip up** *vi fam* sbagliare

slip-knot *n* nodo *m* scorsoio

slip-on [shoe] *n* mocassino *m*

slipped disc /slɪpt'dɪsk/ *n Med* ernia *f* del disco

slipper /'slɪpə(r)/ *n* pantofola *f*

slippery /'slɪpərɪ/ *a* scivoloso

slip road *n* bretella *f*

slipshod /'slɪpʃɒd/ *a* trascurato

slip-up *n fam* sbaglio *m*

slit /slɪt/ *n* spacco *m*; (*tear*) strappo *m*; (*hole*) fessura *f* ● *vt* (*pt/pp* **slit**) tagliare

slither /'slɪðə(r)/ *vi* scivolare

sliver /'slɪvə(r)/ *n* scheggia *f*

slob /slɒb/ *n fam* (*messy*) maiale *m*; (*lazy*) pelandrone *m*

slobber /'slɒbə(r)/ *vi* sbavare

sloe /sləʊ/ *n* (*fruit*) prugnola *f*; (*bush*) prugnolo *m*

slog /slɒg/ *n* [*hard*] **~** sgobbata *f* ● *vi* (*pt/pp* **slogged**) (*work*) sgobbare

slogan /'sləʊgən/ *n* slogan *m inv*

slop /slɒp/ *vt* (*pt/pp* **slopped**) versare

■ **slop over** *vi* versarsi

slope /sləʊp/ *n* pendenza *f*; (*ski ~*) pista *f* ● *vi* essere inclinato, inclinarsi

■ **slope off** *vi* scantonare

sloping /'sləʊpɪŋ/ *a* in pendenza

sloppiness /'slɒpmɪs/ *n* (*of work*) sciatteria *f*

sloppy /'slɒpɪ/ *a* (**-ier, -iest**) ⟨*work*⟩ trascurato; ⟨*worker*⟩ negligente; (*in dress*) sciatto; (*sentimental*) sdolcinato

slosh /slɒʃ/ *vi fam* ⟨*person, feet:*⟩ sguazzare; ⟨*water:*⟩ scrosciare ● *vt* (*fam: hit*) colpire

sloshed /slɒʃt/ *a fam* sbronzo

slot /slɒt/ *n* fessura *f*; (*time-~*) spazio *m* ● *vt* (*pt/pp* **slotted**) infilare

■ **slot in** *vi* incastrarsi

sloth /sləʊθ/ *n* accidia *f*

slot machine *n* distributore *m* automatico; (*for gambling*) slot-machine *f inv*

slouch /slaʊtʃ/ *vi* (*in chair*) stare scomposto

Slovak /'sləʊvæk/ *a* & *n* slovacco, -a *mf*

Slovakia /sləʊ'vækɪə/ *n* Slovacchia *f*

Slovene /'sləʊviːn/ *a* & *n* sloveno, -a *mf*

Slovenia /sləʊə'viːnɪə/ *n* Slovenia *f*

slovenliness /'slʌvənlɪnɪs/ *n* sciatteria *f*

slovenly /'slʌvnlɪ/ *a* sciatto

slow /sləʊ/ *a* lento; **be ~** ⟨*clock:*⟩ essere indietro; **in ~ motion** al rallentatore ● *adv* lentamente

■ **slow down** *vt/i* rallentare

■ **slow up** *vt/i* rallentare

slowcoach /'sləʊkəʊtʃ/ *n fam* tartaruga *f*

slowly /'sləʊlɪ/ *adv* lentamente

slowness /'sləʊnɪs/ *n* lentezza *f*

slow puncture *n* foratura *f*

sludge /slʌdʒ/ *n* fanghiglia *f*

slug /slʌg/ *n* lumacone *m*; (*bullet*) pallottola *f*

sluggish /'slʌgɪʃ/ *a* lento

sluggishly /'slʌgɪʃnɪs/ *adv* lentamente

sluice /sluːs/ *n* chiusa *f*

sluice gate *n* saracinesca *f* (*di chiusa*)

slum /slʌm/ *n* (*house*) tugurio *m*; **~s** *pl* bassifondi *mpl*

slumber /'slʌmbə(r)/ *n* sonno *m* ● *vi* dormire

slump /slʌmp/ *n* crollo *m*; (*economic*) depressione *f* ● *vi* crollare

slung /slʌŋ/ *see* **sling**

slunk /slʌŋk/ *see* **slink**

slur /slɜː(r)/ *n* (*discredit*) calunnia *f* ● *vt* (*pt/pp* **slurred**) biascicare

slurp /slɜːp/ *vt/i* bere rumorosamente

slurry /'slʌrɪ/ *n* (*waste from animals*) liquame *m*; (*waste from factory*) fanghiglia *f* semiliquida; (*of cement*) impasto *m* semiliquido

slush /slʌʃ/ *n* pantano *m* nevoso; *fig* sdolcinatezza *f*

slush fund *n* fondi *mpl* neri

slushy /'slʌʃɪ/ *a* fangoso; (*sentimental*) sdolcinato

slut /slʌt/ *n* sgualdrina *f*

sly /slaɪ/ *a* (**-er, -est**) scaltro ● *n* **on the ~** di nascosto

slyly /'slaɪlɪ/ *adv* scaltramente

SM *n abbr* **sadomasochism**

smacker /'smækə(r)/ *n* (*fam: kiss*) bacio *m*; **500 ~s** (£*500*) 500 sterline

smack[1] /smæk/ *n* (*on face*) schiaffo *m*; (*on bottom*) sculaccione *m* ● *vt* (*on face*) schiaffeggiare; (*on bottom*) sculacciare; **~ one's lips** far schioccare le labbra ● *adv fam* in pieno

smack[2] *vi* **~ of** *fig* sapere di

small /smɔːl/ *a* piccolo; **be out/work until the ~ hours** fare le ore piccole ● *adv* **chop up ~** fare a pezzettini ● *n* **the ~ of the back** le reni

small: small ads *npl* annunci *mpl* [commerciali]. **small business** *n* piccola impresa *f*. **small change** *n* spiccioli *mpl*. **smallholding** *n* piccola tenuta *f*. **small hours** *npl* ore *fpl* piccole. **small letter** *n* lettera *f* minuscola. **small-minded** /-'maɪndɪd/ *a* meschino. **smallpox** *n* vaiolo *m*. **small print** *n* caratteri *mpl* piccoli; **read the ~ ~** *fig* leggere tutto fin nei minimi particolari. **small talk** *n* chiacchiere *fpl*; **make ~** fare conversazione

smarmy /'smɑːmɪ/ *a* (**-ier, -iest**) *fam* untuoso

smart /smɑːt/ *a* elegante; (*clever*) intelligente; (*brisk*) svelto; **be ~** (*fam: cheeky*) fare il furbo ● *vi* (*hurt*) bruciare

smart alec[k] /'smɑːtælɪk/ *n fam* sapientone *m*

smart card *n* carta *f* intelligente

smarten /'smɑːt(ə)n/ *vt* **~ oneself up** farsi bello

smartly /'smɑːtlɪ/   *adv*   elegantemente;

(cleverly) intelligentemente; *(briskly)* velocemente; *(cheekily)* sfacciatamente

smart money *n fam* **the ~ ~ was on Desert Orchid** gli esperti hanno puntato su Desert Orchid

smash /smæʃ/ *n* fragore *m*; *(collision)* scontro *m*; *Tennis* schiacciata *f* ● *vt* spaccare; *Tennis* schiacciare ● *vi* spaccarsi; *(crash)* schiantarsi (**into** contro)

■ **smash up** *vt* distruggere *‹car, bar›*

smash-and-grab *n Br* rapina *f* a un negozio *(con sfascio di vetrina)*

smashed /smæʃt/ *a ‹window›* in frantumi; *‹vehicle›* sfasciato; *‹limb›* fracassato; *(fam: on drugs)* fatto; *(fam: on alcohol)* ubriaco fradicio

smash [hit] *n* successo *m*

smashing /'smæʃɪŋ/ *a fam* fantastico

smattering /'smætərɪŋ/ *n* infarinatura *f*

smear /smɪə(r)/ *n* macchia *f*; *Med* striscio *m* ● *vt* imbrattare; *(coat)* spalmare (**with** di); *fig* calunniare ● *vi* sbavare

smear campaign *n* campagna *f* diffamatoria

smear test *n Med* striscio *m*, Pap test *m inv*

smell /smel/ *n* odore *m*; *(sense)* odorato *m* ● *v* *(pt/pp* **smelt** *or* **smelled)** ● *vt* odorare; *(sniff)* annusare ● *vi* odorare (**of** di); **that ~s good** ha un buon odore

smelling salts /'smelɪŋ/ *npl Med* sali *mpl*

smelly /'smelɪ/ *a* (**-ier, -iest**) puzzolente

smelt¹ /smelt/ *see* **smell**

smelt² *vt* fondere

smidgeon /'smɪdʒɪn/ *n (of something to eat)* pizzico *m*; *(of something to drink)* goccio *m*

smile /smaɪl/ *n* sorriso *m* ● *vi* sorridere; **~ at** sorridere a *‹sb›*; sorridere di *‹sth›*

smirk /smɜːk/ *n* sorriso *m* compiaciuto ● *vi* sorridere con aria compiaciuta

smithereens /smɪðə'riːnz/ *npl* **to/in ~** in mille pezzi

smithy /'smɪðɪ/ *n* fucina *f*

smitten /'smɪtn/ *a* **~ with** tutto preso da

smock /smɒk/ *n* grembiule *m*

smog /smɒg/ *n* smog *m inv*

smoke /sməʊk/ *n* fumo *m* ● *vt/i* fumare

smoked /sməʊkt/ *a* affumicato

smoke-free zone *n* zona *f* non-fumatori; **'~'** 'vietato fumare'

smokeless /'sməʊklɪs/ *a* senza fumo; *‹fuel›* che non fa fumo

smoker /'sməʊkə(r)/ *n* fumatore, -trice *mf*; *Rail* vagone *m* fumatori

smokescreen /'sməʊkskriːn/ *n also fig* cortina *f* di fumo

smoking /'sməʊkɪŋ/ *n* fumo *m*; **'no ~'** 'vietato fumare'; **'~ or non-~?'** 'fumatori o non fumatori?'

smoky /'sməʊkɪ/ *a* (**-ier, -iest**) fumoso; *‹taste›* di fumo

smooch /smuːtʃ/ *vi fam* pomiciare

smooth /smuːð/ *a* liscio; *‹movement›* scorrevole; *‹sea›* calmo; *‹manners›* mellifluo ● *vt* lisciare; **~ things over** sistemare le cose

■ **smooth out** *vt* lisciare

smoothly /'smuːðlɪ/ *adv* in modo scorrevole; **go ~** andare liscio

smooth-tongued /-'tʌŋd/ *a pej* mellifluo

smother /'smʌðə(r)/ *vt* soffocare

smoulder /'sməʊldə(r)/ *vi* fumare; *(with rage)* consumarsi

smudge /smʌdʒ/ *n* macchia *f* ● *vt/i* imbrattare

smug /smʌg/ *a* (**smugger, smuggest**) compiaciuto

smuggle /'smʌgl/ *vt* contrabbandare

smuggler /'smʌglə(r)/ *n* contrabbandiere, -a *mf*

smuggling /'smʌglɪŋ/ *n* contrabbando *m*

smugly /'smʌglɪ/ *adv* con aria compiaciuta

smugness /'smʌgnɪs/ *n* compiacimento *m*

smut /smʌt/ *n* macchia *f* di fuliggine; *fig* sconcezza *f*

smutty /'smʌtɪ/ *a* (**-ier, -iest**) fuligginoso; *fig* sconcio

snack /snæk/ *n* spuntino *m*

snack-bar *n* snack bar *m inv*

snag¹ /snæg/ *n (problem)* intoppo *m*

snag² *vt* smagliarsi *‹tights›* (**on** con)

snail /sneɪl/ *n* lumaca *f*; **at a ~'s pace** a passo di lumaca

snake /sneɪk/ *n* serpente *m*

snake: snakebite *n* morso *m* di serpente. **snake charmer** *n* incantatore, -trice *mf* di serpenti. **snakes and ladders** *n Br* gioco *m* dell'oca

snap /snæp/ *n* colpo *m* secco; *(photo)* istantanea *f* ● *attrib ‹decision›* istantaneo ● *v (pt/pp* **snapped)** ● *vi (break)* spezzarsi ● *vt (break)* spezzare; *(say)* dire seccamente; *Phot* fare un'istantanea di; schioccare *‹fingers›*

■ **snap at** *‹dog:›* cercare di azzannare; *‹person:›* parlare seccamente a

■ **snap off** *vt* **~ sb's head off** *fam* aggredire qcno

■ **snap out** *vi* **~ out of it** venirne fuori

■ **snap up** *vt* afferrare

snappy /'snæpɪ/ *a* (**-ier, -iest**) scorbutico; *(smart)* elegante; **make it ~!** sbrigati!

snapshot /'snæpʃɒt/ *n* istantanea *f*

snare /sneə(r)/ *n* trappola *f*

snarl /snɑːl/ *n* ringhio *m* ● *vi* ringhiare

snarled-up /snɑːld'ʌp/ *a ‹traffic›* bloccato

snarl-up *n (in traffic, network)* ingorgo *m*

snatch /snætʃ/ *n* strappo *m*; *(fragment)* brano *m*; *(theft)* scippo *m*; **make a ~ at sth** cercare di afferrare qcsa ● *vt* strappare [di mano] (**from** a); *(steal)* scippare; rapire *‹child›*

snazzy /'snæzɪ/ *a fam* sciccoso

sneak /sniːk/ *n (fam: devious person)* tipo, -a *mf* subdolo, -a; *(Br fam: telltale)* spia *f* ● *vt (fam: steal)* fregare; rubare *‹kiss›*; **~ a glance at** dare una sbirciatina a ● *vi (Br fam: tell tales)* fare la spia ● *attrib ‹visit›* furtivo; **have a ~ preview of sth** vedere qcsa in anteprima

■ **sneak away** *vi* sgattaiolare via

■ **sneak in** *vi* sgattaiolare dentro

■ **sneak out** *vi* sgattaiolare fuori

sneakers /'sni:kəz/ *npl Am* scarpe *fpl* da ginnastica

sneaking /'sni:kɪŋ/ *a* furtivo; ⟨suspicion⟩ vago

sneaky /'sni:kɪ/ *a* sornione

sneer /snɪə(r)/ *n* ghigno *m* ● *vi* sogghignare; ~ **at** ⟨mock⟩ ridere di

sneeze /sni:z/ *n* starnuto *m* ● *vi* starnutire; **it's not to be ~d at** non ci sputerei sopra

snide /snaɪd/ *a fam* insinuante

sniff /snɪf/ *n* ⟨of dog⟩ annusata *f*; **give a ~** ⟨person.⟩ tirare su col naso ● *vi* tirare su col naso ● *vt* odorare ⟨flower⟩; sniffare ⟨glue⟩; ⟨dog:⟩ annusare

sniffer dog /'snɪfə/ *n* cane *m* poliziotto (antidroga, antiterrorismo)

sniffle /'snɪfl/ *n* **have a ~** or **the ~s** (slight cold) avere un po' di raffreddore; **give a ~** tirar su col naso ● *vi* tirar su col naso

sniffy /'snɪfɪ/ *a* (fam: haughty) con la puzza sotto il naso

snigger /'snɪɡə(r)/ *n* risatina *f* soffocata ● *vi* ridacchiare

snip /snɪp/ *n* taglio *m*; (fam: bargain) affare *m* ● *vt/i* ~ **[at]** tagliare

snipe /snaɪp/ *vi* ~ **at** tirare su; *fig* sparare a zero su

sniper /'snaɪpə(r)/ *n* cecchino *m*

snippet /'snɪpɪt/ *n* **a ~ of information/ news** una breve notizia/informazione

snivel /'snɪvl/ *vi* (pt/pp **snivelled**) piagnucolare

snivelling /'snɪv(ə)lɪŋ/ *a* piagnucoloso

snob /snɒb/ *n* snob *mf inv*

snobbery /'snɒbərɪ/ *n* snobismo *m*

snobbish /'snɒbɪʃ/ *a* da snob; **be ~** ⟨person:⟩ essere uno/una snob; ⟨club etc:⟩ essere molto snob

snobbishness /'snɒbɪʃnɪs/ *n* snobismo *m*

snog /snɒg/ *vi Br sl* pomiciare

snooker /'snu:kə(r)/ *n* (game) snooker *m*; (shot) impallatura *f* ● *vt Sport* impallare; *fig* mettere in difficoltà

snoop /snu:p/ *n* spia *f* ● *vi fam* curiosare

snooper /'snu:pə(r)/ *n* ficcanaso *mf*

snooty /'snu:tɪ/ *a fam* sdegnoso

snooze /snu:z/ *n* sonnellino *m* ● *vi* fare un sonnellino

snore /snɔ:(r)/ *vi* russare

snoring /'snɔ:rɪŋ/ *n* il russare

snorkel /'snɔ:kl/ *n* respiratore *m*

snort /snɔ:t/ *n* sbuffo *n* ● *vi* sbuffare ● *vt* fiutare ⟨cocaine⟩

snot /snɒt/ *n* (fam: mucus) moccolo *m*

snotty /'snɒtɪ/ *a fam* ⟨nose⟩ moccicoso; (disagreeable) sgradevole

snotty-nosed kid /-nəʊzd/ *n* moccioso, -a *mf*

snout /snaʊt/ *n* grugno *m*

snow /snəʊ/ *n* neve *f* ● *vi* nevicare; **~ed under with** *fig* sommerso di

snow: snowball *n* palla *f* di neve ● *vi fig* fare a palle di neve. **snowdrift** *n* cumulo *m* di neve. **snowdrop** *n* bucaneve *m inv*. **snowfall**

n nevicata *f*. **snowflake** *n* fiocco *m* di neve. **snowman** *n* pupazzo *m* di neve. **snowmobile** /'snəʊməbi:l/ *n* gatto *m* delle nevi. **snowplough** *n* spazzaneve *m inv*. **snowstorm** *n* tormenta *f*. **snow tyres** *npl* pneumatici *mpl* chiodati

snowy /'snəʊɪ/ *a* nevoso

Snr *abbr* **Senior**

snub /snʌb/ *n* sgarbo *m* ● *vt* (pt/pp **snubbed**) snobbare

snub-nosed /'snʌbnəʊzd/ *a* dal naso all'insù

snuff[1] /snʌf/ *n* tabacco *m* da fiuto

snuff[2] *vt* ~ **[out]** spegnere ⟨candle⟩; ~ **it** *fam* tirare le cuoia

snug /snʌg/ *a* (**snugger, snuggest**) comodo; (tight) aderente

snuggle /'snʌgl/ *vi* rannicchiarsi (**up to** accanto a)

so /səʊ/ *adv* così; **so far** finora; **so am I** anch'io; **so I see** così pare; **you've left the door open – so I have!** hai lasciato la porta aperta – è vero!; **that is so** è così; **so much** così tanto; **so much the better** tanto meglio; **so it is** proprio così; **if so** se è così; **so as to** in modo da; **so long!** *fam* a presto! ● *pron* **I hope/think/am afraid so** spero/penso/temo di sì; **I told you so** te l'ho detto; **because I say so** perché lo dico io; **I did so!** l'ho fatto!; **so saying/doing,...** così dicendo/facendo,...; **or so** circa; **very much so** sì, molto; **and so forth** *or* **on** e così via ● *conj* (therefore) perciò; (in order that) così; **so that** affinché; **so there!** ecco!; **so what?** e allora?; **so where have you been?** allora, dove sei stato?

soak /səʊk/ *vt* mettere a bagno ● *vi* stare a bagno

■ **soak in** *vi* penetrare

■ **soak into** *vt* ⟨liquid:⟩ penetrare

■ **soak up** *vt* assorbire

soaked /səʊkt/ *a* fradicio; ~ **in sth** impregnato di qcsa

soaking /'səʊkɪŋ/ *n* ammollo *m* ● *a & adv* ~ **[wet]** *fam* inzuppato

so-and-so *n* Tal dei Tali *mf*; (euphemism) specie *f* di imbecille

soap /səʊp/ *n* sapone *m*

soap opera *n* telenovella *f*, soap opera *f inv*

soap powder *n* detersivo *m* in polvere

soapy /'səʊpɪ/ *a* (**-ier, -iest**) insaponato

soar /sɔ:(r)/ *vi* elevarsi; ⟨prices:⟩ salire alle stelle

S.O.B. *n Am abbr* **son of a bitch**

sob /sɒb/ *n* singhiozzo *m* ● *vi* (pt/pp **sobbed**) singhiozzare

sobbing /'sɒbɪŋ/ *n* singhiozzi *mpl*

sober /'səʊbə(r)/ *a* sobrio; (serious) serio

■ **sober up** *vi* ritornare sobrio

soberly /'səʊbəlɪ/ *adv* sobriamente; (seriously) con aria seria

sobriety /sə'braɪətɪ/ *n* (not drinking) sobrietà *f*; (seriousness) serietà *f*

sob story *n* storia *f* lacrimevole

so-called /'səʊkɔ:ld/ *a* cosiddetto

soccer /'sɒkə(r)/ *n* calcio *m*

soccer pitch n campo m di calcio

soccer player n giocatore m di calcio

sociable /'səʊʃəbl/ a socievole

social /'səʊʃl/ a sociale; (sociable) socievole

social climber n arrampicatore, -trice mf sociale

social climbing n arrivismo m sociale

socialism /'səʊʃəlɪzm/ n socialismo m

socialist /'səʊʃəlɪst/ a socialista ● n socialista mf

socialite /'səʊʃəlaɪt/ n persona f che fa vita mondana

socialize /'səʊʃəlaɪz/ vi socializzare

socially /'səʊʃəlɪ/ adv socialmente; **know sb ~** frequentare qcno

social: **social security** n previdenza f sociale. **social services** npl servizi mpl sociali. **social work** n assistenza f sociale. **social worker** n assistente mf sociale

society /sə'saɪətɪ/ n società f inv

socio-economic /səʊsɪəʊiːkə'nɒmɪk/ a socioeconomico

sociological /səʊsɪə'lɒdʒɪkl/ a sociologico

sociologist /səʊsɪ'ɒlədʒɪst/ n sociologo, -a mf

sociology /səʊsɪ'ɒlədʒɪ/ n sociologia f

sock[1] /sɒk/ n calzino m; (kneelength) calza f

sock[2] fam n pugno m ● vt dare un pugno a

socket /'sɒkɪt/ n (of eye) orbita f; (wall plug) presa f [di corrente]; (for bulb) portalampada m inv

sod /sɒd/ n fam stronzo m; **you lucky ~!** che fortuna sfacciata!

■ **sod off** vi fam togliersi dai piedi

soda /'səʊdə/ n soda f; Am gazzosa f

soda water n seltz m inv

sodden /'sɒdn/ a inzuppato

sodium /'səʊdɪəm/ n sodio m

sodium bicarbonate n bicarbonato m di sodio

Sod's Law /sɒdz/ n fam hum regola f per cui, se qualcosa può andare storto, va storto

sofa /'səʊfə/ n divano m

sofa bed n divano m letto

soft /sɒft/ a morbido, soffice; (voice) sommesso; (light, colour) tenue; (not strict) indulgente; (fam: silly) stupido

soft: **soft-boiled** /-'bɔɪld/ a (egg) bazzotto. **soft contact lenses** npl lenti fpl a contatto morbide. **soft drink** n bibita f analcolica. **soft drug** n droga f leggera

soften /'sɒfn/ vt ammorbidire; fig attenuare ● vi ammorbidirsi

softener /'sɒf(ə)nə(r)/ n (for water) dolcificatore m; (substance) anti-calcare m inv; (for fabrics) ammorbidente m

soft: **soft furnishings** npl tappeti mpl e tessuti mpl da arredamento. **soft-hearted** a dal cuore tenero. **soft ice-cream** n mantecato m

softie /'sɒftɪ/ n fam = **softy**

softly /'sɒftlɪ/ adv (say) sottovoce; (treat) con indulgenza; (play music) in sottofondo

soft: **soft-pedal** vt fig minimizzare. **soft porn** n fam pornografia f soft[-core]. **soft sell** n metodo m di vendita basato sulla per-

suasione. **soft soap** n fig lusinghe fpl. **soft-soap** vt fig lusingare. **soft-spoken** a dalla voce dolce. **soft spot** n **have a ~ ~ for sb** avere un debole per qcno. **soft-top** n Auto decappottabile f. **soft touch** n **be a ~ ~** lasciarsi spremere. **soft toy** n pupazzo m di peluche

software /'sɒftweə(r)/ n software m

software: **software engineer** n softwarista mf. **software house** n software house f. **software package** n pacchetto m software. **software writer** n scrittore, -trice mf di programmi

softy /'sɒftɪ/ n fam (weak person) pappamolle mf inv; (indulgent person) bonaccione, -a mf

soggy /'sɒgɪ/ a (-ier, -iest) zuppo

soil[1] /sɔɪl/ n suolo m

soil[2] vt sporcare

solace /'sɒləs/ n sollievo m

solar /'səʊlə(r)/ a solare

solar: **solar energy** n energia f solare. **solar panel** n pannello m solare. **solar power** n energia f solare. **solar system** n sistema m solare

sold /səʊld/ see **sell**

solder /'səʊldə(r)/ n lega f da saldatura ● vt saldare

soldier /'səʊldʒə(r)/ n soldato m

■ **soldier on** vi perseverare

sole[1] /səʊl/ n (of foot) pianta f; (of shoe) suola f

sole[2] n (fish) sogliola f

sole[3] a unico, solo

sole agency n rappresentanza f esclusiva

solecism /'sɒlɪsɪzm/ n (social) scorrettezza f; (linguistic) solecismo m

solely /'səʊllɪ/ adv unicamente

solemn /'sɒləm/ a solenne

solemnity /sə'lemnətɪ/ n solennità f inv

solemnly /'sɒləmlɪ/ adv solennemente

sol-fa /'sɒlfɑː/ n solfeggio m

solicit /sə'lɪsɪt/ vt sollecitare ● vi (prostitute:) adescare

soliciting /sə'lɪsɪtɪŋ/ n Jur adescamento m

solicitor /sə'lɪsɪtə(r)/ n avvocato m

solicitous /sə'lɪsɪtəs/ a premuroso

solicitously /sə'lɪsɪtəslɪ/ adv premurosamente

solid /'sɒlɪd/ a solido; (oak, gold) massiccio; **it took a ~ hour** ci è voluta ben un'ora ● n (figure) solido m; **~s** pl (food) cibi mpl solidi

solidarity /sɒlɪ'dærətɪ/ n solidarietà f inv

solidify /sə'lɪdɪfaɪ/ vi (pt/pp -ied) solidificarsi

soliloquy /sə'lɪləkwɪ/ n soliloquio m

solitaire /sɒlɪ'teə(r)/ n solitario m

solitary /'sɒlɪtərɪ/ a solitario; (sole) solo

solitary confinement n cella f di isolamento

solitude /'sɒlɪtjuːd/ n solitudine f

solo /'səʊləʊ/ n Mus assolo m ● a (flight) in solitario ● adv in solitario

soloist /'səʊləʊɪst/ n solista mf

solstice /'sɒlstɪs/ n solstizio m

soluble /'sɒljʊbl/ a solubile

solution /sə'lu:ʃn/ *n* soluzione *f*

solvable /'sɒlvəbl/ *a* risolvibile

solve /sɒlv/ *vt* risolvere

solvency /'sɒlvənsɪ/ *n Fin* solvibilità *f*

solvent /'sɒlvənt/ *a & n* solvente *m*

solvent abuse *n* uso *m* di solventi come stupefacenti

Somali /səʊ'mɑːlɪ/ *a & n* somalo, -a *mf*

Somalia /səʊ'mɑːlɪə/ *n* Somalia *f*

sombre /'sɒmbə(r)/ *a* tetro; ⟨clothes⟩ scuro

some /sʌm/ *a* (*a certain amount of*) del; (*a certain number of*) alcuni, dei; ~ **bread/water** del pane/dell'acqua; ~ **books/oranges** dei libri/delle arance; **I need ~ money/books** ho bisogno di soldi/libri; **do ~ shopping** fare qualche acquisto; ~ **day** un giorno o l'altro ● *pron* (*a certain amount*) un po'; (*a certain number*) alcuni; **I want ~** ne voglio; **would you like ~?** ne vuoi?; ~ **of the butter** una parte del burro; ~ **of the apples/women** alcune delle mele/donne

somebody /'sʌmbədɪ/ *pron* qualcuno *m*; ~ **else will bring it** la porterà un altro ● *n* **he thinks he's** ~ si crede chissà chi

somehow /'sʌmhaʊ/ *adv* in qualche modo; ~ **or other** in un modo o nell'altro

someone /'sʌmwʌn/ *pron & n* = **somebody**

somersault /'sʌməsɔːlt/ *n* capriola *f*; **turn a** ~ fare una capriola ● *vi* fare una capriola

something /'sʌmθɪŋ/ *pron* qualche cosa, qualcosa; ~ **different** qualcosa di diverso; ~ **like** un po' come; (*approximately*) qualcosa come; **see** ~ **of sb** vedere qcno ogni tanto; **she is** ~ **of an expert** è un'esperta

sometime /'sʌmtaɪm/ *adv* un giorno o l'altro; ~ **last summer** durante l'estate scorsa ● *a* ex

sometimes /'sʌmtaɪmz/ *adv* qualche volta

somewhat /'sʌmwɒt/ *adv* piuttosto

somewhere /'sʌmweə(r)/ *adv* da qualche parte ● *pron* ~ **to eat** un posto in cui mangiare

son /sʌn/ *n* figlio *m*

sonar /'səʊnɑ:(r)/ *n* sonar *m*

sonata /sə'nɑːtə/ *n* sonata *f*

song /sɒŋ/ *n* canzone *f*

song: song and dance *n* **make a** ~ ~ ~ **about sth** (*fuss*) far tante storie per qcsa. **songbird** *n* uccello *m* canoro. **songwriter** *n* compositore, -trice *mf* di canzoni

sonic /'sɒnɪk/ *a* sonico

sonic boom *n* bang *m inv* sonico

son-in-law *n* (*pl* ~**s-in-law**) genero *m*

sonnet /'sɒnɪt/ *n* sonetto *m*

son of a bitch *n fam* figlio *m* di un cane

sonorous /'sɒnərəs/ *a* sonoro; ⟨name⟩ altisonante

soon /su:n/ *adv* presto; (*in a short time*) tra poco; **as** ~ **as** [non] appena; **as** ~ **as possible** il più presto possibile; ~**er or later** prima o poi; **the** ~**er the better** prima è, meglio è; **no** ~**er had I arrived than...** ero appena arrivato quando...; **I would** ~**er go** preferirei andare; ~ **after** subito dopo

soot /sʊt/ *n* fuliggine *f*

soothe /su:ð/ *vt* calmare

soothing /'su:ðɪŋ/ *a* calmante

sooty /'sʊtɪ/ *a* fuligginoso

sop /sɒp/ *n* **throw a** ~ **to** dare un contentino a

sophisticated /sə'fɪstɪkeɪtɪd/ *a* sofisticato; (*complex*) complesso

sophistication /səfɪstɪ'keɪʃn/ *n* (*elegance*) sofisticatezza *f*, raffinatezza *f*; (*complexity*) complessità *f*

soporific /sɒpə'rɪfɪk/ *a* soporifero

soppiness /'sɒpɪnɪs/ *n fam* svenevolezza *f*

sopping /'sɒpɪŋ/ *a & adv* **be** ~ **[wet]** essere bagnato fradicio

soppy /'sɒpɪ/ *a* (**-ier, -iest**) *fam* svenevole

soprano /sə'prɑːnəʊ/ *n* soprano *m*

sorcerer /'sɔːsərə(r)/ *n* stregone *m*

sorceress /'sɔːsərɪs/ *n* strega *f*, maga *f*

sorcery /'sɔːsərɪ/ *n* (*witchcraft*) stregoneria *f*

sordid /'sɔːdɪd/ *a* sordido

sordidness /'sɔːdɪdnɪs/ *n* sordidezza *f*

sore /sɔː(r)/ *a* dolorante; (*Am: vexed*) arrabbiato; **it's** ~ fa male; **have a** ~ **throat** avere mal di gola; **it's a** ~ **point with her** è un punto delicato per lei ● *n* piaga *f*

sorely /'sɔːlɪ/ *adv* (*tempted*) seriamente

soreness /'sɔːnɪs/ *n* dolore *m*

sorrel /'sɒrəl/ *n Bot* acetosa *f*

sorrow /'sɒrəʊ/ *n* tristezza *f*

sorrowful /'sɒrəʊfʊl/ *a* triste

sorrowfully /'sɒrəʊfʊlɪ/ *adv* tristemente

sorry /'sɒrɪ/ *a* (**-ier, -iest**) (*sad*) spiacente; (*wretched*) pietoso; **you'll be** ~! te ne pentirai!; **I am** ~ mi dispiace; **be** *or* **feel** ~ **for** provare compassione per; ~! scusa!; (*more polite*) scusi!

sort /sɔːt/ *n* tipo *m*; **it's a** ~ **of fish** è un tipo di pesce; **be out of** ~**s** (*fam: unwell*) stare poco bene ● *vt* classificare; *fam* sistemare ⟨problem, person⟩

■ **sort out** *vt* selezionare ⟨papers⟩; *fig* risolvere ⟨problem⟩; occuparsi di ⟨person⟩

sort code *n Fin* coordinate *fpl* bancarie

sorter /'sɔːtə(r)/ *n* (*on photocopier*) fascicolatrice *f*, fascicolatore *m*

SOS *n* SOS *m*; *fig* segnale *m* di soccorso

so-so *a & adv* così così

sotto voce /sɒtəʊ'vəʊtʃeɪ/ *adv* ⟨say, add⟩ sottovoce

soufflé /'su:fleɪ/ *n* sufflè *m*

sought /sɔːt/ *see* **seek**

sought-after *a* ⟨job, brand, person⟩ richiesto

soul /səʊl/ *n* anima *f*; **poor** ~ poveretto; **there was not a** ~ **in sight** non c'era anima viva

soul-destroying /-dɪstrɔɪŋ/ *a* ⟨job⟩ che abbrutisce

soulful /'səʊlfʊl/ *a* sentimentale

soul: soulmate *n* anima *f* gemella. **soul-searching** /-sɜːtʃɪŋ/ *n* esame *m* di coscienza. **soul-stirring** /-stɜːrɪŋ/ *a* molto commovente

sound[1] /saʊnd/ *a* sano; (*sensible*) saggio;

(*secure*) solido; ⟨*thrashing*⟩ clamoroso ● *adv*
~ asleep profondamente addormentato
sound² *n* suono *m*; (*noise*) rumore *m*; **I don't
like the ~ of it** *fam* non mi suona bene ● *vi*
suonare; (*seem*) aver l'aria; **it ~s to me as
if...** mi sa che... ● *vt* (*pronounce*) pronunciare;
Med auscoltare ⟨*chest*⟩
■ **sound off** *vi* fare grandi discorsi
■ **sound out** *vt fig* sondare
sound: sound barrier *n* muro *m* del suono.
sound bite *n* breve frase *f* dal forte impatto
mediatico. **sound card** *n Comput* scheda *f* sonora. **sound effect** *n* effetto *m* sonoro.
sound engineer *n* tecnico *m* del suono
soundless /'saʊndlɪs/ *a* silenzioso
soundlessly /'saʊndlɪslɪ/ *adv* silenziosamente
soundly /'saʊndlɪ/ *adv* ⟨*sleep*⟩ profondamente; ⟨*defeat*⟩ clamorosamente
sound: soundproof *a* impenetrabile al suono ● *vt* insonorizzare. **sound system** *n* (*hifi*)
stereo *m*; (*for disco etc*) impianto *m* audio.
soundtrack *n* colonna *f* sonora
soup /su:p/ *n* minestra *f*; **in the ~** *fam* nei
pasticci
souped-up /su:pt'ʌp/ *a fam* ⟨*engine*⟩ truccato
soup: soup kitchen *n* mensa *f* dei poveri.
soup plate *n* piatto *m* fondo. **soup spoon** *n*
cucchiaio *m* da minestra
sour /'saʊə(r)/ *a* agro; (*not fresh & fig*) acido
source /sɔ:s/ *n* fonte *f*; **at ~** ⟨*deducted*⟩ alla
fonte
sour: sour cream *n* panna *f* acida. **sour-
faced** /saʊə'feɪst/ *a* ⟨*person*⟩ dall'espressione
dura. **sour grapes** *npl fam* **it's just ~ ~** [**on
his part**] fa come la volpe con l'uva
south /saʊθ/ *n* sud *m*; **to the ~ of** a sud di
● *a* del sud, meridionale ● *adv* a sud
south: South Africa *n* Sudafrica *f*. **South
African** *a* & *n* sudafricano, -a *mf*. **South
America** *n* America *f* del Sud. **South
American** *a* & *n* sud-americano, -a *mf*.
southbound *a* ⟨*traffic*⟩ diretto a sud;
⟨*carriageway*⟩ sud. **south-east** *n* sud-est *m*
southerly /'sʌðəlɪ/ *a* del sud
southern /'sʌðən/ *a* del sud, meridionale; **~
Italy** il Mezzogiorno
southerner /'sʌðənə(r)/ *n* meridionale *mf*
southpaw /'saʊθpɔ:/ *n* (*in boxing*) pugile *m*
mancino
South Pole *n* polo *m* Sud
southward[s] /'saʊθwəd[z]/ *adv* verso sud
south-west /saʊθ'west/ *n* sud-ovest *m*
south-western /saʊθ'westən/ *a* sudocci-
dentale
souvenir /su:və'nɪə(r)/ *n* ricordo *m*,
souvenir *m inv*
sovereign /'sɒvrɪn/ *a* & *n* sovrano, -a *mf*
sovereignty /'sɒvrɪntɪ/ *n* sovranità *f inv*
Soviet /'səʊvɪət/ *a* sovietico
Soviet Union *n* Unione *f* Sovietica
sow¹ /saʊ/ *n* scrofa *f*
sow² /səʊ/ *vt* (*pt* **sowed**, *pp* **sown** *or* **sowed**)
seminare

soya bean /'sɔɪə/ *n* soia *f*
soy sauce /sɔɪ/ *n* salsa *f* di soia
sozzled /'sɒzld/ *a fam* sbronzo
spa /spɑ:/ *n* stazione *f* termale
space /speɪs/ *n* spazio *m* ● *a* ⟨*research etc*⟩
spaziale ● *vt* **~** [**out**] distanziare
space: space age *n* era *f* spaziale ● *attrib*
dell'era spaziale. **space bar** *n* barra *f* spazio.
spacecraft *n* navetta *f* spaziale. **space
cadet** *n fig fam* allucinato, -a *mf*. **space capsule** *n* capsula *f* spaziale. **spaced out**
/speɪst'aʊt/ *a fam* **he's completely ~ ~** è
completamente fuori di testa. **space-saving**
a poco ingombrante. **spaceship** *n* astronave
f. **space shuttle** *n* shuttle *m*. **space travel** *n*
viaggi *mpl* nello spazio. **space walk** *n* passeggiata *f* nello spazio
spacing /'speɪsɪŋ/ *n* distanziamento *m*;
single/double ~ interlinea *m* semplice/dop-
pio
spacious /'speɪʃəs/ *a* spazioso
spade /speɪd/ *n* vanga *f*; (*for child*) paletta *f*;
~s *pl* (*Cards*) picche *fpl*; **call a ~ a ~** dire
pane al pane e vino al vino
spadework /'speɪdwɜ:k/ *n fig* lavoro *m* preparatorio
spaghetti /spə'getɪ/ *n* spaghetti *mpl*
spaghetti bolognese /bʊlə'neɪz/ *n* spaghetti *mpl* al ragù
spaghetti junction *n fam* intricato raccordo *m* autostradale
Spain /speɪn/ *n* Spagna *f*
span¹ /spæn/ *n* spanna *f*; (*of arch*) luce *f*; (*of
time*) arco *m*; (*of wings*) apertura *f* ● *vt* (*pt/pp*
spanned) estendersi su
span² *see* **spick**
Spaniard /'spænjəd/ *n* Spagnolo, -a *mf*
spaniel /'spænjəl/ *n* spaniel *m inv*
Spanish /'spænɪʃ/ *a* spagnolo ● *n* (*language*)
spagnolo *m*; **the ~** *pl* gli Spagnoli
spank /spæŋk/ *vt* sculacciare
spanking /'spæŋkɪŋ/ *n* sculacciata *f* ● *a fam*
at a ~ pace con passo spedito ● *adv fam* **a ~
new car** una macchina nuova di zecca
spanner /'spænə(r)/ *n* chiave *f* inglese
spar /spɑ:(r)/ *vi* (*pt/pp* **sparred**) (*boxing*) allenarsi; (*argue*) litigare
spare /speə(r)/ *a* (*surplus*) in più;
(*additional*) di riserva; **go ~** (*fam: be very
angry*) andare su tutte le furie ● *n* (*part*) ricambio *m* ● *vt* risparmiare; (*do without*)
fare a meno di; **can you ~ five minutes?**
avresti cinque minuti?; **no expense was
~d** non si è badato a spese; **to ~** (*surplus*)
in eccedenza
spare: spare part *n* pezzo *m* di ricambio.
spare ribs *npl* costine *fpl*. **spare room** *n*
stanza *f* degli ospiti. **spare time** *n* tempo *m*
libero. **spare tyre** *n Br Auto* gomma *f* di scorta; (*fam: fat*) trippa *f*. **spare wheel** *n* ruota *f*
di scorta
sparing /'speərɪŋ/ *a* parco (**with** di)
sparingly /'speərɪŋlɪ/ *adv* con parsimonia
spark /spɑ:k/ *n* scintilla *f*
■ **spark off** *vt* far scoppiare

sparkle /'spɑːkl/ n scintillio m ● vi scintillare

sparkling /'spɑːklɪŋ/ a frizzante; ⟨wine⟩ spumante

spark-plug n Auto candela f

sparrow /'spærəʊ/ n passero m

sparse /spɑːs/ a rado

sparsely /'spɑːslɪ/ adv scarsamente; ~ **populated** ⟨area⟩ a bassa densità di popolazione

sparseness /'spɑːsnɪs/ n (of vegetation) radezza f

spartan /'spɑːtn/ a spartano

spasm /'spæzm/ n spasmo m

spasmodic /spæz'mɒdɪk/ a spasmodico

spasmodically /spæz'mɒdɪklɪ/ adv spasmodicamente

spastic /'spæstɪk/ a spastico ● n spastico, -a mf

spat /spæt/ see spit¹

spate /speɪt/ n (series) successione f; **be in full** ~ essere in piena

spatial /'speɪʃl/ a spaziale

spatio-temporal /speɪʃɪəʊ'tempərəl/ a spazio-temporale

spatter /'spætə(r)/ vt/i schizzare

spatula /'spætjʊlə/ n spatola f

spawn /spɔːn/ n uova fpl (di pesci, rane ecc) ● vi deporre le uova ● vt fig generare

spay /speɪ/ vt sterilizzare

speak /spiːk/ v (pt spoke, pp spoken) ● vi parlare (**to** a); **~ing!** Teleph sono io! ● vt dire; **~ one's mind** dire quello che si pensa

■ **speak for** vt parlare a nome di; **~ for yourself!** parla per te!

■ **speak of** vt **~ well/ill of sb** parlare bene/male di qcno; **nothing to ~ of** niente di speciale; (quantity) non un granché; **~ing of holidays...** a proposito di vacanze...

■ **speak out** vi (protest) parlare

■ **speak up** vi parlare più forte; **~ up for oneself** farsi valere

speaker /'spiːkə(r)/ n parlante mf; (in public) oratore, -trice mf; (of stereo) cassa f

speaking terms /'spiːkɪŋ/ npl **we are not on ~** ~ non ci parliamo

spear /'spɪə(r)/ n lancia f ● vt trafiggere

spearhead /'spɪəhed/ vt fig essere l'iniziatore di

spearmint /'spɪəmɪnt/ n menta f verde

spec /spek/ n **on ~** fam (take, use) in prova; ⟨go somewhere⟩ per ispezione

special /'speʃl/ a speciale

special: special correspondent n inviato, -a mf speciale. **special delivery** n espresso m. **special effect** n Cinema, TV effetto m speciale ● attrib ~ ~s ⟨specialist, team⟩ degli effetti speciali. **special envoy** n inviato, -a mf speciale

specialist /'speʃəlɪst/ n specialista mf

speciality /speʃɪ'ælətɪ/ n specialità f inv

specialize /'speʃəlaɪz/ vi specializzarsi

specially /'speʃəlɪ/ adv specialmente; (particularly) particolarmente

special offer n vendita f promozionale

special treatment n trattamento m di riguardo

species /'spiːʃiːz/ n specie f inv

specific /spə'sɪfɪk/ a specifico

specifically /spə'sɪfɪklɪ/ adv in modo specifico

specifications /spesɪfɪ'keɪʃnz/ npl descrizione f

specify /'spesɪfaɪ/ vt (pt/pp -ied) specificare

specimen /'spesɪmən/ n campione m

specious /'spiːʃəs/ a ⟨argument, reasoning⟩ specioso

speck /spek/ n macchiolina f; (particle) granello m

speckled /'spekld/ a picchiettato

specs /speks/ npl fam occhiali mpl

spectacle /'spektəkl/ n (show) spettacolo m

spectacles /'spektəklz/ npl occhiali mpl

spectacular /spek'tækjʊlə(r)/ a spettacolare

spectacularly /spek'tækjʊləlɪ/ adv in modo spettacolare

spectator /spek'teɪtə(r)/ n spettatore, -trice mf

spectator sport n sport m inv di intrattenimento

spectre /'spektə(r)/ n spettro m

spectrum /'spektrəm/ n (pl -tra) spettro m; fig gamma f

speculate /'spekjʊleɪt/ vi speculare

speculation /spekjʊ'leɪʃn/ n speculazione f

speculative /'spekjʊlətɪv/ a speculativo

speculator /'spekjʊleɪtə(r)/ n speculatore, -trice mf

sped /sped/ see speed

speech /spiːtʃ/ n linguaggio m; (address) discorso m; **make a ~, give a ~** fare un discorso

speech day n Sch giorno m della premiazione

speechless /'spiːtʃlɪs/ a senza parole

speech: speech therapist n logoterapista mf. **speech therapy** n logoterapia f. **speech-writer** n persona f che scrive i discorsi di personaggi pubblici

speed /spiːd/ n velocità f inv; (gear) marcia f; **at ~** a tutta velocità ● vi (pt/pp sped) andare veloce ● (pt/pp speeded) (go too fast) andare a velocità eccessiva

■ **speed up** (pt/pp speeded up) vt/i accelerare

speed: speedboat n motoscafo m. **speed bump** n rallentatore m. **speed camera** n autovelox® m inv

speedily /'spiːdɪlɪ/ adv rapidamente

speeding /'spiːdɪŋ/ n eccesso m di velocità

speeding fine n multa f per eccesso di velocità

speed limit n limite m di velocità

speed merchant n fam fanatico, -a mf della velocità

speedometer /spiː'dɒmɪtə(r)/ n tachimetro m

speed skating n pattinaggio m di velocità

speed trap n Auto tratto m di strada sul

*quale la polizia controlla la velocità dei veico-
li*

speedy /'spi:dɪ/ *a* (**-ier, -iest**) rapido
speleologist /spi:lɪ'ɒlədʒɪst/ *n* speleologo,
-a *mf*
speleology /spi:lɪ'ɒlədʒɪ/ *n* speleologia *f*
spell[1] /spel/ *n* (*turn*) turno *m*; (*of weather*) periodo *m*
spell[2] *v* (*pt/pp* **spelled** *or* **spelt**) ● *vt* **how do
you ~...?** come si scrive...?; **could you ~
that for me?** me lo può compitare?; **~
disaster** *fig* essere disastroso ● *vi* **he can't
~** fa molti errori d'ortografia
spell[3] *n* (*magic*) incantesimo *m*
■ **spell out** *vt* compitare; *fig* spiegare
spellbound /'spelbaʊnd/ *a* affascinato
spellchecker /'speltʃekə(r)/ *n* Comput correttore *m* ortografico
spelling /'spelɪŋ/ *n* ortografia *f*
spelt /spelt/ *see* **spell**[2]
spend /spend/ *vt/i* (*pt/pp* **spent**) spendere;
passare ⟨*time*⟩
spending money /'spendɪŋ/ *n* soldi *mpl*
per le piccole spese
spendthrift /'spendθrɪft/ *a* spendaccione;
⟨*habit, policy*⟩ dispendioso ● *n* spendaccione,
-a *mf*
spent /spent/ *see* **spend**
sperm /spɜ:m/ *n* spermatozoo *m*; (*semen*)
sperma *m*
sperm bank *n* banca *f* dello sperma
sperm count *n* conteggio *m* di spermatozoi
spermicidal /spɜ:mɪ'saɪdl/ *a* spermicida
inv
spermicide /'spɜ:mɪsaɪd/ *n* spermicida *m*
spew /spju:/ *vt/i* vomitare
sphere /sfɪə(r)/ *n* sfera *f*
sphere of influence *n* sfera *f* di influenza
spherical /'sferɪkl/ *a* sferico
spice /spaɪs/ *n* spezia *f*; *fig* pepe *m*
spick /spɪk/ *a* **~ and span** lindo
spicy /'spaɪsɪ/ *a* piccante
spider /'spaɪdə(r)/ *n* ragno *m*
spiel /ʃpɪəl/ *n fam* (*sales pitch*) imbonimento
m; (*long repetitive speech*) tiritera *f*; **he gave
me some ~ about...** mi ha raccontato un
sacco di storie su...
spike /spaɪk/ *n* punta *f*; Bot, Zool spina *f*; (*on
shoe*) chiodo *m*
spikes *npl* (*shoes*) scarpe *fpl* chiodate
spiky /'spaɪkɪ/ *a* ⟨*plant*⟩ spinoso
spill /spɪl/ *v* (*pt/pp* **spilt** *or* **spilled**) ● *vt* versare ⟨*blood*⟩; **~ the beans** *fam* vuotare il sac-
co ● *vi* rovesciarsi
spillage /'spɪlɪdʒ/ *n* (*of oil, chemical*) perdita *f*
spin /spɪn/ *v* (*pt/pp* **spun**, *pres p* **spinning**)
● *vt* far girare; filare ⟨*wool*⟩; centrifugare
⟨*washing*⟩ ● *vi* girare; ⟨*washing machine:*⟩
centrifugare ● *n* rotazione *f*; (*short drive*)
giretto *m*
■ **spin out** *vt* far durare
spinach /'spɪnɪdʒ/ *n* spinaci *mpl*
spinal /'spaɪnl/ *a* spinale
spinal column *n* colonna *f* vertebrale

spinal cord *n* midollo *m* spinale
spindle /'spɪndl/ *n* fuso *m*
spindly /'spɪndlɪ/ *a* affusolato
spin doctor *n* persona *f* incaricata di presentare le scelte di un partito politico sotto una
luce favorevole
spin-drier *n* centrifuga *f*
spine /spaɪn/ *n* spina *f* dorsale; (*of book*) dorso *m*; Bot, Zool spina *f*
spineless /'spaɪnlɪs/ *a fig* smidollato
spinning /'spɪnɪŋ/ *n* filatura *f*
spinning wheel *n* filatoio *m*
spin-off *n* ricaduta *f*
spinster /'spɪnstə(r)/ *n* donna *f* nubile; (*old
maid, fam*) zitella *f*
spiny /'spaɪnɪ/ *a* ⟨*plant, animal*⟩ spinoso
spiral /'spaɪrəl/ *a* a spirale ● *n* spirale *f* ● *vi*
(*pt/pp* **spiralled**) formare una spirale
spiral staircase *n* scala *f* a chiocciola
spire /'spaɪə(r)/ *n* guglia *f*
spirit /'spɪrɪt/ *n* spirito *m*; (*courage*) ardore *m*;
~s *pl* (*alcohol*) liquori *mpl*; **in good ~s** di
buon umore; **in low ~s** abbattuto
■ **spirit away** *vt* far sparire
spirited /'spɪrɪtɪd/ *a* vivace; (*courageous*) pieno d'ardore
spirit level *n* livella *f* a bolla d'aria
spirit stove *n* fornellino *m* [da campeggio]
spiritual /'spɪrɪtjʊəl/ *a* spirituale ● *n*
spiritual *m*
spiritualism /'spɪrɪtjʊəlɪzm/ *n* spiritismo *m*
spiritualist /'spɪrɪtjʊəlɪst/ *n* spiritista *mf*
spit[1] /spɪt/ *n* (*for roasting*) spiedo *m*
spit[2] *n* sputo *m* ● *vt/i* (*pt/pp* **spat**, *pres p*
spitting) sputare; ⟨*cat:*⟩ soffiare; ⟨*fat:*⟩
sfrigolare; **it's ~ting [with rain]** pioviggi-
na; **the ~ting image of** il ritratto
spiccicato di
■ **spit out** *vt* sputare ⟨*food*⟩; **~ it out!** *fam* sputa l'osso!
spite /spaɪt/ *n* dispetto *m*; **in ~ of** malgrado
● *vt* far dispetto a
spiteful /'spaɪtfʊl/ *a* indispettito
spitefully /'spaɪtfʊlɪ/ *adv* con aria indispet-
tita
spittle /'spɪtl/ *n* saliva *f*
splash /splæʃ/ *n* schizzo *m*; (*of colour*) macchia *f*; (*fam: drop*) goccio *m* ● *vt* schizzare; **~
sb with sth** schizzare qcno di qcsa ● *vi* schizzare
■ **splash about** *vi* schizzarsi
■ **splash down** *vi* ⟨*spacecraft:*⟩ ammarare
■ **splash out** *vi* (*spend freely*) darsi alle spese folli
splashdown /'splæʃdaʊn/ *n* ammaraggio *m*
splatter /'splætə(r)/ *vt* schizzare; **~ sb/sth
with sth** schizzare qcno/qcsa di qcsa ● *vi* **~
onto/over sth** ⟨*ink, paint:*⟩ schizzare su qcsa
splay /spleɪ/ *vt* divaricare ⟨*legs, feet, fingers*⟩;
svasare ⟨*end of pipe etc*⟩; strombare ⟨*side of
window, door*⟩; **~ed** ⟨*feet, fingers, legs*⟩ scar-
tato
spleen /spli:n/ *n* Anat milza *f*
splendid /'splendɪd/ *a* splendido

splendidly /'splendɪdlɪ/ *adv* splendidamente

splendour /'splendə(r)/ *n* splendore *m*

splint /splɪnt/ *n Med* stecca *f*

splinter /'splɪntə(r)/ *n* scheggia *f* ● *vi* scheggiarsi

splinter group *n* gruppo *m* scissionista

split /splɪt/ *n* fessura *f*; ⟨*quarrel*⟩ rottura *f*; ⟨*division*⟩ scissione *f*; ⟨*tear*⟩ strappo *m* ● *v* ⟨*pt/pp* **split**, *pres p* **splitting**⟩ ● *vt* spaccare; ⟨*share, divide*⟩ dividere; ⟨*tear*⟩ strappare; **~ hairs** spaccare il capello in quattro; **~ one's sides** sbellicarsi dalle risa ● *vi* spaccarsi; ⟨*tear*⟩ strapparsi; ⟨*divide*⟩ dividersi; **~ on sb** *fam* denunciare qcno ● *a* **a ~ second** una frazione di secondo

■ **split up** *vt* dividersi ● *vi* ⟨*couple:*⟩ separarsi

split: split ends *npl* ⟨*in hair*⟩ doppie punte *fpl.* **split personality** *n* sdoppiamento *m* della personalità. **split screen** *n* schermo *m* diviso

splitting /'splɪtɪŋ/ *a* **have a ~ headache** avere un tremendo mal di testa

splutter /'splʌtə(r)/ *vi* farfugliare

spoil /spɔɪl/ *n* **~s** *pl* bottino *msg* ● *v* ⟨*pt/pp* **spoilt** *or* **spoiled**⟩ ● *vt* rovinare; viziare ⟨*person*⟩ ● *vi* andare a male

spoiler /'spɔɪlə(r)/ *n Auto, Aeron* spoiler *m inv*

spoilsport /'spɔɪlspɔːt/ *n* guastafeste *mf inv*

spoilt /spɔɪlt/ *a* ⟨*child*⟩ viziato; **be ~ for choice** non avere che l'imbarazzo della scelta

spoke[1] /spəʊk/ *n* raggio *m*

spoke[2] *see* **speak**

spoken /'spəʊkən/ *see* **speak** ● *a* ⟨*language*⟩ parlato; **be ~ for** essere messo da parte per qualcuno

spokesman /'spəʊksmən/ *n* portavoce *m inv*

spokesperson /'spəʊkspɜːsn/ *n* portavoce *mf*

spokeswoman /'spəʊkswʊmən/ *n* portavoce *f*

sponge /spʌndʒ/ *n* spugna *f* ● *vt* pulire con la spugna ● *vi* **~ on** *fam* scroccare da

sponge bag *n* nécessaire *m inv*

sponge cake *n* pan *m* di Spagna

sponger /'spʌndʒə(r)/ *n* scroccone, -a *mf*

spongy /'spʌndʒɪ/ *a* spugnoso

sponsor /'spɒnsə(r)/ *n* garante *mf*; *Radio, TV* sponsor *m inv*; ⟨*god-parent*⟩ padrino *m*, madrina *f*; ⟨*for membership*⟩ socio, -a *mf* garante ● *vt* sponsorizzare

sponsorship /'spɒnsəʃɪp/ *n* sponsorizzazione *f*

sponsorship deal *n* accordo *m* con uno sponsor

spontaneity /spɒntə'neɪɪtɪ/ *n* spontaneità *f*

spontaneous /spɒn'teɪnɪəs/ *a* spontaneo

spontaneously /spɒn'teɪnɪəslɪ/ *adv* spontaneamente

spoof /spuːf/ *n fam* parodia *f*

spook /spuːk/ *fam vt* ⟨*haunt*⟩ perseguitare; ⟨*frighten*⟩ spaventare ● *n* ⟨*ghost*⟩ fantasma *m*; ⟨*Am: spy*⟩ spia *f*

spooky /'spuːkɪ/ *a* ⟨**-ier, -iest**⟩ *fam* sinistro

spool /spuːl/ *n* bobina *f*

spooling /'spuːlɪŋ/ *n Comput* spooling *m*

spoon /spuːn/ *n* cucchiaio *m* ● *vt* mettere col cucchiaio

spoonerism /'spuːnərɪzm/ *n scambio m delle iniziali di due parole con effetto umoristico*

spoon-feed *vt* ⟨*pt/pp* **-fed**⟩ *fig* imboccare

spoonful /'spuːnfʊl/ *n* cucchiaiata *f*

sporadic /spə'rædɪk/ *a* sporadico

sporadically /spə'rædɪklɪ/ *adv* sporadicamente

spore /spɔː(r)/ *n* spora *f*

sporran /'spɒrən/ *n borsa f di cuoio o pelo portata alla cintura dagli scozzesi insieme al kilt*

sport /spɔːt/ *n* sport *m inv*; **be a [good] ~!** sii sportivo! ● *vt* sfoggiare

sporting /'spɔːtɪŋ/ *a* sportivo

sporting calendar *n* calendario *m* sportivo

sporting chance *n* possibilità *f inv*

sports: sports car *n* automobile *f* sportiva. **sports coat** *n*, **sports jacket** *n* giacca *f* sportiva. **sportsman** *n* sportivo *m.* **sportswoman** *n* sportiva *f.* **sports writer** *n* giornalista *mf* sportivo, -a

sporty /'spɔːtɪ/ *a* ⟨**-ier, -iest**⟩ sportivo

spot /spɒt/ *n* macchia *f*; ⟨*pimple*⟩ brufolo *m*; ⟨*place*⟩ posto *m*; ⟨*in pattern*⟩ pois *m inv*; ⟨*of rain*⟩ goccia *f*; ⟨*of water*⟩ goccio *m*; **~s** *pl* ⟨*rash*⟩ sfogo *msg*; **a ~ of** *fam* un po' di; **a ~ of bother** qualche problema; **on the ~** sul luogo; ⟨*immediately*⟩ immediatamente; **in a [tight] ~** *fam* in difficoltà ● *vt* ⟨*pt/pp* **spotted**⟩ macchiare; ⟨*fam: notice*⟩ individuare

spot check *n* ⟨*without warning*⟩ controllo *m* a sorpresa; **do a ~ ~ on sth** dare una controllata a qcsa

spotless /'spɒtlɪs/ *a* immacolato

spot: spotlight *n* riflettore *m*; *fig* riflettori *mpl.* **spot-on** *a Br* esatto. **spot rate** *n Fin* tasso *m* di cambio a vista

spotted /'spɒtɪd/ *a* ⟨*material*⟩ a pois

spotty /'spɒtɪ/ *a* ⟨**-ier, -iest**⟩ ⟨*pimply*⟩ brufoloso

spot-weld *vt* saldare a punti

spouse /spaʊz/ *n* consorte *mf*

spout /spaʊt/ *n* becco *m*; **up the ~** ⟨*fam: ruined*⟩ all'aria ● *vi* zampillare ⟨**from** da⟩

sprain /spreɪn/ *n* slogatura *f* ● *vt* slogare; **~ one's ankle** slogarsi la caviglia

sprang /spræŋ/ *see* **spring**[2]

sprat /spræt/ *n* spratto *m*

sprawl /sprɔːl/ *vi* ⟨*in chair*⟩ stravaccarsi; ⟨*city etc:*⟩ estendersi; **go ~ing** ⟨*fall*⟩ cadere disteso

sprawling /'sprɔːlɪŋ/ *a* ⟨*suburb, city*⟩ che si propaga disordinatamente; ⟨*handwriting*⟩ che occupa tutta la pagina

spray[1] /spreɪ/ *n* ⟨*of flowers*⟩ rametto *m*; ⟨*bouquet*⟩ mazzolino *m*

spray[2] *n* spruzzo *m*; ⟨*from sea*⟩ spruzzo *m*; ⟨*preparation*⟩ spray *m inv*; ⟨*container*⟩ spruzzatore *m* ● *vt* spruzzare

spray-gun *n* pistola *f* a spruzzo
spray-on *a* ⟨*conditioner, glitter*⟩ spray *inv*
spread /spred/ *n* estensione *f*; (*of disease*) diffusione *f*; (*paste*) crema *f*; (*fam: feast*) banchetto *m* ● *v* (*pt/pp* **spread**) ● *vt* spargere; spalmare ⟨*butter, jam*⟩; stendere ⟨*cloth, arms*⟩; diffondere ⟨*news, disease*⟩; dilazionare ⟨*payments*⟩; **~ sth with** spalmare qcsa di ● *vi* spargersi; ⟨*butter:*⟩ spalmarsi; ⟨*disease:*⟩ diffondersi
■ **spread out** *vt* sparpagliare ● *vi* sparpagliarsi
spread-eagled /-'i:gld/ *a* a gambe e braccia aperte
spreadsheet /'spredʃi:t/ *n* Comput foglio *m* elettronico
spree /spri:/ *n fam* **go on a ~** far baldoria; **go on a shopping ~** fare spese folli
sprig /sprɪg/ *n* rametto *m*
sprightly /'spraɪtlɪ/ *a* (**-ier, -iest**) vivace
spring[1] /sprɪŋ/ *n* primavera *f*; **in ~, in the ~** in primavera ● *attrib* primaverile
spring[2] *n* (*jump*) balzo *m*; (*water*) sorgente *f*; (*device*) molla *f*; (*elasticity*) elasticità *f* ● *v* (*pt* **sprang**, *pp* **sprung**) ● *vi* balzare; (*arise*) provenire (**from** da); **~ to mind** saltare in mente ● *vt* **he just sprang it on me** me l'ha detto a cose fatte compiuto
■ **spring up** *vi* balzare; *fig* spuntare
spring: springboard *n* trampolino *m*. **spring chicken** *n Culin* pollastrello *m*, pollastrella *f*; **she's no ~ ~** *fam* non è una giovincella. **spring-clean** *vt* pulire a fondo. **spring-cleaning** *n* pulizie *fpl* di Pasqua. **spring onion** *n* cipollina *f*. **springtime** *n* primavera *f*
sprinkle /'sprɪŋkl/ *vt* (*scatter*) spruzzare ⟨*liquid*⟩; spargere ⟨*flour, cocoa*⟩; **~ sth with** spruzzare qcsa di ⟨*liquid*⟩; cospargere qcsa di ⟨*flour, cocoa*⟩
sprinkler /'sprɪŋklə(r)/ *n* sprinkler *m inv*; (*for garden*) irrigatore *m*
sprinkling /'sprɪŋklɪŋ/ *n* (*of liquid*) spruzzatina *f*; (*of pepper, salt*) pizzico *m*; (*of flour, sugar*) spolveratina *f*; (*of knowledge*) infarinatura *f*; (*of people*) pugno *m*
sprint /sprɪnt/ *n* sprint *m inv* ● *vi* fare uno sprint; *Sport* sprintare
sprinter /'sprɪntə(r)/ *n* sprinter *mf inv*
sprite /spraɪt/ *n* folletto *m*
spritzer /'sprɪtsə(r)/ *n* spriz *m inv*, spritzer *m inv*
sprout /spraʊt/ *n* germoglio *m*; [**Brussels**] **~s** *pl* cavolini *mpl* di Bruxelles ● *vi* germogliare
spruce /spru:s/ *a* elegante ● *n* abete *m*
■ **spruce up** *vt* dare una ripulita a
sprung /sprʌŋ/ *see* **spring**[2] ● *a* molleggiato
spry /spraɪ/ *a* (**-er, -est**) arzillo
spud /spʌd/ *n fam* patata *f*
spun /spʌn/ *see* **spin**
spur /spɜ:(r)/ *n* sperone *m*; (*stimulus*) stimolo *m*; (*road*) svincolo *m*; **on the ~ of the moment** su due piedi ● *vt* (*pt/pp* **spurred**) **~ [on]** *fig* spronare

spurious /'spjʊərɪəs/ *a* falso
spuriously /'spjʊərɪəslɪ/ *adv* falsamente
spurn /spɜ:n/ *vt* sdegnare
spurt /spɜ:t/ *n* getto *m*; *Sport* scatto *m*; **put on a ~** fare uno scatto ● *vi* sprizzare; (*increase speed*) scattare
sputter /'spʌtə(r)/ *vi* ⟨*engine:*⟩ scoppiettare ● *n* colpi *mpl* irregolari del motore
spy /spaɪ/ *n* spia *f* ● *vi* spiare ● *vt* (*fam: see*) spiare
■ **spy on** *vt* spiare
■ **spy out** *vt* esplorare
spying /'spaɪɪŋ/ *n* spionaggio *m*
squabble /'skwɒbl/ *n* bisticcio *m* ● *vi* bisticciare
squabbling /'skwɒblɪŋ/ *n* bisticci *mpl*
squad /skwɒd/ *n* squadra *f*
squaddie /'skwɒdɪ/ *n Br fam* soldato *m* semplice
squadron /'skwɒdrən/ *n Mil* squadrone *m*; *Aeron, Naut* squadriglia *f*
squalid /'skwɒlɪd/ *a* squallido
squalidly /'skwɒlɪdlɪ/ *adv* squallidamente
squall /skwɔ:l/ *n* (*howl*) strillo *m*; (*storm*) bufera *f* ● *vi* strillare
squally /'skwɔ:lɪ/ *a* burrascoso
squalor /'skwɒlə(r)/ *n* squallore *m*
squander /'skwɒndə(r)/ *vt* sprecare
square /skweə(r)/ *a* quadrato; ⟨*meal*⟩ sostanzioso; (*fam: old-fashioned*) vecchio stampo; **all ~** *fam* pari ● *n* quadrato *m*; (*in city*) piazza *f*; (*on chessboard*) riquadro *m*; **be back to one** riessere al punto di partenza ● *vt* (*settle*) far quadrare; *Math* elevare al quadrato ● *vi* (*agree*) armonizzare
■ **square up** *vi* (*settle accounts*) saldare
■ **square up to** *vt* affrontare
square dance *n* quadriglia *f*
squarely /'skweəlɪ/ *adv* direttamente
square root *n* radice *f* quadrata
squash /skwɒʃ/ *n* calca *f*; (*drink*) spremuta *f*; (*sport*) squash *m*; (*vegetable*) zucca *f* ● *vt* schiacciare; soffocare ⟨*rebellion*⟩
squashy /'skwɒʃɪ/ *a* floscio
squat /skwɒt/ *a* tarchiato ● *n fam* edificio *m* occupato abusivamente ● *vi* (*pt/pp* **squatted**) accovacciarsi; **~ in** occupare abusivamente
squatter /'skwɒtə(r)/ *n* occupante *mf* abusivo, -a
squaw /skwɔ:/ *n* squaw *f inv*
squawk /skwɔ:k/ *n* gracchio *m* ● *vi* gracchiare
squeak /skwi:k/ *n* squittio *m*; (*of hinge, brakes*) cigolio *m* ● *vi* squittire; ⟨*hinge, brakes:*⟩ cigolare
squeaking /'skwi:kɪŋ/ *n* (*of door, hinge*) cigolio *m*
squeaky /'skwi:kɪ/ *a* ⟨*door, hinge*⟩ cigolante
squeaky-clean *a fam* ⟨*glass, hair*⟩ lucente; ⟨*floor*⟩ tirato a specchio; *fig* ⟨*person*⟩ senza vizi; ⟨*company*⟩ al di sopra di ogni sospetto
squeal /skwi:l/ *n* strillo *m*; (*of brakes*) cigolio *m* ● *vi* strillare; *sl* spifferare

squeamish /'skwi:mɪʃ/ *a* dallo stomaco delicato; (*scrupulous*) troppo scrupoloso

squeegee /'skwi:dʒi:/ *n Phot* rullo *m* asciugatore; (*for glasses*) lavavetri *m inv*

squeeze /skwi:z/ *n* stretta *f*; (*crush*) pigia pigia *m inv*; **give sb's hand a ~** dare a qcno una stretta di mano ● *vt* premere; (*to get juice*) spremere; stringere (*hand*); (*force*) spingere a forza; (*fam: extort*) estorcere (**out of** da)

■ **squeeze in/out** *vi* sgusciare dentro/fuori

■ **squeeze up** *vi* stringersi

squelch /skweltʃ/ *vi* sguazzare

squib /skwɪb/ *n* petardo *m*

squid /skwɪd/ *n* calamaro *m*

squidgy /'skwɪdʒɪ/ *a* (*Br fam: squashy*) molliccio

squiggle /'skwɪgl/ *n* scarabocchio *m*

squint /skwɪnt/ *n* strabismo *m* ● *vi* essere strabico

squire /'skwaɪə(r)/ *n* signorotto *m* di campagna

squirm /skwɜ:m/ *vi* contorcersi; (*feel embarrassed*) sentirsi imbarazzato

squirrel /'skwɪrəl/ *n* scoiattolo *m*

squirt /skwɜ:t/ *n* spruzzo *m*; (*fam: person*) presuntuoso *m* ● *vt/i* spruzzare

St *abbr* (**Saint**) S; *abbr* **Street**

stab /stæb/ *n* pugnalata *f*; coltellata *f*; (*sensation*) fitta *f*; (*fam: attempt*) tentativo *m* ● *vt* (*pt/pp* **stabbed**) pugnalare, accoltellare

stability /stə'bɪlətɪ/ *n* stabilità *f inv*

stabilization /steɪbɪlaɪ'zeɪʃn/ *n* stabilizzazione *f*

stabilize /'steɪbɪlaɪz/ *vt* stabilizzare ● *vi* stabilizzarsi

stabilizer /'steɪbɪlaɪzə(r)/ *n* stabilizzatore *m*; (*on bike*) rotella *f*; (*in food*) stabilizzante *m*

stable¹ /'steɪbl/ *a* stabile

stable² *n* stalla *f*; (*establishment*) scuderia *f*

staccato /stə'kɑ:təʊ/ *a Mus* staccato; (*gasps, shots*) intermittente ● *adv* (*play*) staccatamente

stack /stæk/ *n* catasta *f*; (*of chimney*) comignolo *m*; (*chimney*) ciminiera *f*; (*fam: large quantity*) montagna *f*; **~s of** (*money, time, work*) un sacco di ● *vt* accatastare

stadium /'steɪdɪəm/ *n* stadio *m*

staff /stɑ:f/ *n* (*stick*) bastone *m*; (*employees*) personale *m*; (*teachers*) corpo *m* insegnante; *Mil* Stato *m* Maggiore ● *vt* fornire di personale

staffroom /'stɑ:fru:m/ *n Sch* sala *f* insegnanti

stag /stæg/ *n* cervo *m*

stage /steɪdʒ/ *n* palcoscenico *m*; (*profession*) teatro *m*; (*in journey*) tappa *f*; (*in process*) stadio *m*; **go on the ~** darsi al teatro; **by** *or* **in ~s** a tappe ● *vt* mettere in scena; (*arrange*) organizzare

stage: stagecoach *n* diligenza *f*. **stage door** *n* ingresso *m* degli artisti. **stage fright** *n* panico *m* da palcoscenico. **stage-manage** *vt fig* orchestrare. **stage manager** *n* diretto-

re, -trice *mf* di scena. **stage-struck** /-strʌk/ *a* appassionatissimo di teatro

stagger /'stægə(r)/ *vi* barcollare ● *vt* sbalordire; scaglionare (*holidays, payments etc*); **I was ~ed** sono rimasto sbalordito ● *n* vacillamento *m*

staggering /'stægərɪŋ/ *a* sbalorditivo

stagnant /'stægnənt/ *a* stagnante

stagnate /stæg'neɪt/ *vi fig* [ri]stagnare

stagnation /stæg'neɪʃn/ *n fig* inattività *f*

stag night, stag party *n* addio *m* al celibato

staid /steɪd/ *a* posato

stain /steɪn/ *n* macchia *f*; (*for wood*) mordente *m* ● *vt* macchiare; (*wood*) dare il mordente a

stained glass /steɪnd'glɑ:s/ *n* vetro *m* colorato

stained-glass window *n* vetrata *f* colorata

stainless /'steɪnlɪs/ *a* senza macchia

stainless steel *n* acciaio *m* inossidabile

stain remover *n* smacchiatore *m*

stair /steə(r)/ *n* gradino *m*; **~s** *pl* scale *fpl*

staircase /'steəkeɪs/ *n* scale *fpl*

stake /steɪk/ *n* palo *m*; (*wager*) posta *f*; *Comm* partecipazione *f*; **at ~** in gioco ● *vt* puntellare; (*wager*) scommettere; **~ a claim to sth** rivendicare qcsa

stake-out *n fam* sorveglianza *f*

stalactite /'stæləktaɪt/ *n* stalattite *f*

stalagmite /'stæləgmaɪt/ *n* stalagmite *f*

stale /steɪl/ *a* stantio; (*air*) viziato; (*uninteresting*) trito [e ritrito]

stalemate /'steɪlmeɪt/ *n* (*in chess*) stallo *m*; (*deadlock*) situazione *f* di stallo

stalk¹ /stɔ:k/ *n* gambo *m*

stalk² *vt* inseguire ● *vi* camminare impettito

stalker /'stɔ:kə(r)/ *n* (*of person*) persona *f* che perseguita qcno per cui ha una fissazione maniacale

stalking /'stɔ:kɪŋ/ *n* (*of person*) persecuzione *f* di una persona per cui si ha una fissazione maniacale

stall /stɔ:l/ *n* box *m inv*; (*in market*) bancarella *f*; **~s** *pl Theat* platea *f* ● *vi* (*engine:*) spegnersi; *fig* temporeggiare ● *vt* far spegnere (*engine*); tenere a bada (*person*)

stallholder /'stɔ:lhəʊldə(r)/ *n* bancarellista *mf*

stallion /'stæljən/ *n* stallone *m*

stalwart /'stɔ:lwət/ *a* fedele ● *n* sostenitore *m* fedele

stamina /'stæmɪnə/ *n* [capacità *f* di] resistenza *f*

stammer /'stæmə(r)/ *n* balbettio *m* ● *vt/i* balbettare

stamp /stæmp/ *n* (*postage ~*) francobollo *m*; (*instrument*) timbro *m*; *fig* impronta *f* ● *vt* affrancare (*letter*); timbrare (*bill*); battere (*feet*)

■ **stamp out** *vt* spegnere; *fig* soffocare

stamp collecting *n* filatelia *f*

stamp collector *n* collezionista *mf* di francobolli

stamped addressed envelope busta *f* affrancata per la risposta

stampede /stæm'piːd/ *n* fuga *f* precipitosa; *fam* fuggifuggi *m inv* ● *vi* fuggire precipitosamente

stance /stɑːns/ *n* posizione *f*

stand /stænd/ *n* (*for bikes*) rastrelliera *f*; (*at exhibition*) stand *m inv*; (*in market*) bancarella *f*; (*in stadium*) gradinata *f*; *fig* posizione *f* ● *v* (*pt/pp* **stood**) ● *vi* stare in piedi; (*rise*) alzarsi [in piedi]; (*be*) trovarsi; (*be candidate*) essere candidato (**for** a); (*stay valid*) rimanere valido; **I don't know where I ~** non so qual'è la mia posizione; **~ still** non muoversi; **~ firm** *fig* tener duro; **~ on ceremony** formalizzarsi; **~ together** essere solidali; **~ to lose/gain** rischiare di perdere/vincere; **~ to reason** essere logico ● *vt* (*withstand*) resistere a; (*endure*) sopportare; (*place*) mettere; **~ a chance** avere una possibilità; **~ one's ground** tener duro; **~ the test of time** superare la prova del tempo; **~ sb a beer** offrire una birra a qcno

■ **stand back** *vi* (*withdraw*) farsi da parte

■ **stand by** *vi* stare a guardare; (*be ready*) essere pronto ● *vt* (*support*) appoggiare

■ **stand down** *vi* (*retire*) ritirarsi

■ **stand for** *vt* (*mean*) significare; (*tolerate*) tollerare

■ **stand in for** *vt* sostituire

■ **stand out** *vi* spiccare

■ **stand up** *vi* alzarsi [in piedi]

■ **stand up for** *vt* prendere le difese di; **~ up for oneself** farsi valere

■ **stand up to** *vt* affrontare

stand-alone *a Comput* indipendente

standard /'stændəd/ *a* standard; **be ~ practice** essere pratica corrente ● *n* standard *m inv*; *Techn* norma *f*; (*level*) livello *m*; (*quality*) qualità *f inv*; (*flag*) stendardo *m*; **~s** *pl* (*morals*) valori *mpl*

standardization /stændədaɪ'zeɪʃn/ *n* standardizzazione *f*

standardize /'stændədaɪz/ *vt* standardizzare

standard lamp *n* lampada *f* a stelo

standard of living *n* tenore *m* di vita

standby /'stændbaɪ/ *n* (*person*) riserva *f* ● *attrib* (*circuit, battery*) di emergenza; (*passenger*) in lista di attesa; (*ticket*) stand-by *inv* ● *adv* (*fly*) col biglietto stand-by

stand-in *n* controfigura *f*

standing /'stændɪŋ/ *a* (*erect*) in piedi; (*permanent*) permanente ● *n* posizione *f*; (*duration*) durata *f*

standing: standing order *n* ordine *m* permanente. **standing ovation** *n* give sb a **~ ~** alzarsi per applaudire qcno. **standing room** *n* posti *mpl* in piedi

stand-offish /stænd'ɒfɪʃ/ *a* scostante

stand: standpoint *n* punto *m* di vista. **standstill** *n* **come to a ~** fermarsi; **at a ~** in un periodo di stasi. **stand-up** *a* (*buffet*) in piedi; (*argument*) accanito ● *n* (*comedy*) recital *m inv* di un comico. **stand-up comedian**

---

stank /stæŋk/ *see* **stink**

stanza /'stænzə/ *n* strofa *f*

staple¹ /'steɪpl/ *n* (*product*) prodotto *m* principale

staple² *n* graffa *f*, pinzatrice *f* ● *vt* pinzare

staple diet *n* a **~ ~ of** una dieta basata principalmente su

staple gun *n* pistola *f* sparachiodi

stapler /'steɪplə(r)/ *n* pinzatrice *f*, cucitrice *f*

staple remover *n* levapunti *m inv*

star /stɑː(r)/ *n* stella *f*; (*asterisk*) asterisco *m*; *Theat, Cinema, Sport* divo, -a *mf*, stella *f* ● *vi* (*pt/pp* **starred**) essere l'interprete principale (**in** di)

starboard /'stɑːbəd/ *n* tribordo *m*

starch /stɑːtʃ/ *n* amido *m* ● *vt* inamidare

starchy /'stɑːtʃɪ/ *a* ricco di amido; *fig* compito

stardom /'stɑːdəm/ *n* celebrità *f*

stare /steə(r)/ *n* sguardo *m* fisso ● *vi* **it's rude to ~** è da maleducati fissare la gente; **~ at** fissare; **~ into space** guardare nel vuoto

starfish /'stɑːfɪʃ/ *n* stella *f* di mare

stark /stɑːk/ *a* austero; (*contrast*) forte ● *adv* completamente; **~ naked** completamente nudo

starlet /'stɑːlɪt/ *n* stellina *f*

starling /'stɑːlɪŋ/ *n* storno *m*

starlit /'stɑːlɪt/ *a* stellato

starry /'stɑːrɪ/ *a* stellato

starry-eyed /-'aɪd/ *a fam* ingenuo

star-struck /-strʌk/ *a* ossessionato dalle celebrità

star-studded /-stʌdɪd/ *a* (*cast, line-up*) con molti interpreti famosi; (*sky*) stellato

start /stɑːt/ *n* inizio *m*; (*departure*) partenza *f*; (*jump*) sobbalzo *m*; **from the ~** [fin] dall'inizio; **for a ~** tanto per cominciare; **give sb a ~** *Sport* dare un vantaggio a qcno ● *vi* [in]cominciare; (*set out*) avviarsi; (*engine, car:*) partire; (*jump*) trasalire; **to ~ with,...** tanto per cominciare,... ● *vt* [in]cominciare; (*cause*) dare inizio a; (*found*) mettere su; mettere in moto (*car*); mettere in giro (*rumour*)

■ **start off** *vi* (*begin*) cominciare

■ **start on** *vt fam* (*attack*) criticare; (*nag*) punzecchiare

■ **start out** *vi* (*on journey*) partire

■ **start up** *vt* mettere in funzione (*engine*); intentare (*business*)

starter /'stɑːtə(r)/ *n Culin* primo *m* [piatto *m*]; (*in race: giving signal*) starter *m inv*; (*participant*) concorrente *mf*; *Auto* motorino *m* d'avviamento

starting point /'stɑːtɪŋ/ *n* punto *m* di partenza

starting salary *n* stipendio *m* iniziale

startle /'stɑːtl/ *vt* far trasalire; (*news:*) sconvolgere

startling /'stɑːtlɪŋ/ *a* sconvolgente

start-up capital *n* capitale *m* di avviamento

starvation /stɑː'veɪʃn/ *n* fame *f*

starve /stɑ:v/ vi morire di fame ● vt far morire di fame

stash /stæʃ/ vt fam ~ [**away**] nascondere

state /steɪt/ n stato m; Pol Stato m; (grand style) pompa f; ; **be in a** ~ ⟨person:⟩ essere agitato; **lie in** ~ essere esposto ● attrib di Stato; Sch pubblico; (with ceremony) di gala ● vt dichiarare; (specify) precisare

state-aided /-'eɪdɪd/ a sovvenzionato dallo Stato

State Department n Am Pol ministero m degli [affari] esteri

stateless /'steɪtlɪs/ a apolide

stately /'steɪtlɪ/ a (**-ier, -iest**) maestoso

stately home n dimora f signorile

statement /'steɪtmənt/ n dichiarazione f; Jur deposizione f; (from bank) estratto m conto; (account) rapporto m

state: state of the art a ⟨technology⟩ il più avanzato. **state of emergency** n stato m di emergenza. **state of play** punteggio m

stateside /'steɪtsaɪd/ a degli Stati Uniti ● adv negli Stati Uniti

statesman /'steɪtsmən/ n statista m

static /'stætɪk/ a statico

static electricity n elettricità f statica

station /'steɪʃn/ n stazione f; (police) commissariato m ● vt appostare ⟨guard⟩; **be ~ed in Germany** essere di stanza in Germania

stationary /'steɪʃənərɪ/ a immobile

stationer /'steɪʃənə(r)/ n ~'s [**shop**] cartoleria f

stationery /'steɪʃənərɪ/ n cartoleria f

station wagon n Am familiare f

statistical /stə'tɪstɪkl/ a statistico

statistically /stə'tɪstɪklɪ/ adv statisticamente

statistician /stætɪs'tɪʃn/ n esperto m di statistica

statistics /stə'tɪstɪks/ n (subject) statistica f; (pl: figures) statistiche fpl

statue /'stætju:/ n statua f

statuesque /stætjʊ'esk/ a statuario

stature /'stætʃə(r)/ n statura f

status /'steɪtəs/ n condizione f; (high rank) alto rango m

status bar n Comput barra f di stato

status symbol n status symbol m inv

statute /'stætju:t/ n statuto m

statutory /'stætjʊtərɪ/ a statutario

staunch /stɔ:ntʃ/ a fedele

staunchly /'stɔ:ntʃlɪ/ adv fedelmente

stave /steɪv/ vt ~ **off** tenere lontano

stay /steɪ/ n soggiorno m ● vi restare, rimanere; (reside) alloggiare; ~ **the night** passare la notte; ~ **put** non muoversi ● vt ~ **the course** resistere fino alla fine

■ **stay away** vi stare lontano

■ **stay behind** vi non andare con gli altri

■ **stay in** vi (at home) stare in casa; Sch restare a scuola dopo le lezioni

■ **stay on** vi (remain) rimanere; ~ **on at school** continuare gli studi

■ **stay up** vi stare su; ⟨person:⟩ stare alzato

staying power /'steɪɪŋ/ n capacità f di resistenza

STD abbr **sexually transmitted disease**

STD [area] code n Br prefisso m [di teleselezione]

stead /sted/ n **in his** ~ in sua vece; **stand sb in good** ~ tornare utile a qcno

steadfast /'stedfɑ:st/ a fedele; ⟨refusal⟩ fermo

steadily /'stedɪlɪ/ adv (continually) continuamente

steady /'stedɪ/ a (**-ier, -iest**) saldo, fermo; ⟨breathing⟩ regolare; ⟨job, boyfriend⟩ fisso; (dependable) serio ● adv **be going** ~ ⟨couple:⟩ fare coppia fissa

steak /steɪk/ n (for stew) spezzatino m; (for grilling, frying) bistecca f

steal /sti:l/ vt (pt **stole**, pp **stolen**) rubare (from da); ~ **the show** essere al centro d'attenzione

■ **steal in/out** vi entrare/uscire furtivamente

stealth /stelθ/ n **by** ~ di nascosto

stealthily /'stelθɪlɪ/ adv furtivamente

stealthy /'stelθɪ/ a furtivo

steam /sti:m/ n vapore m; **under one's own** ~ fam da solo; **let off** ~ fig sfogarsi ● vt Culin cucinare a vapore ● vi fumare

■ **steam up** vi ⟨window:⟩ appannarsi

steamed up /sti:md'ʌp/ a ⟨get ~ up⟩ (angry) andare su tutte le furie

steam engine n locomotiva f

steam iron n ferro m [da stiro] a vapore

steamer /'sti:mə(r)/ n piroscafo m; (saucepan) pentola f a vapore

steamroller /'sti:mrəʊlə(r)/ n rullo m compressore

steamy /'sti:mɪ/ a appannato; ⟨fig: scene⟩ spinto

steel /sti:l/ n acciaio m ● vt ~ **oneself** temprarsi

steel wool n lana f d'acciaio

steely /'sti:lɪ/ a d'acciaio

steep[1] /sti:p/ vt (soak) lasciare a bagno; ~**ed in** fig immerso in

steep[2] a ripido; ⟨fam: price⟩ esorbitante

steeple /'sti:pl/ n campanile m

steeplechase /'sti:pltʃeɪs/ n corsa f ippica a ostacoli

steeplejack /'sti:pldʒæk/ n persona f che ripara campanili e ciminiere

steeply /'sti:plɪ/ adv ripidamente

steer /stɪə(r)/ vt/i guidare; ~ **clear of** stare alla larga da

steering /'stɪərɪŋ/ n Auto sterzo m

steering: steering column n Auto piantone m dello sterzo. **steering committee** n comitato m direttivo. **steering lock** n Auto bloccasterzo m; (turning circle) angolo m di massima sterzata. **steering wheel** n volante m

stem[1] /stem/ n stelo m; (of glass) gambo m; (of word) radice f ● vi (pt/pp **stemmed**) ~ **from** derivare da

stem[2] vt (pt/pp **stemmed**) contenere

stem ginger n zenzero m sciroppato

stench /stentʃ/ n fetore m

stencil /'stensl/ n stampino m; (decoration) stampo m ● vt (pt/pp **stencilled**) stampinare

stenographer /stɪ'nɒɡrəfə(r)/ n stenografo, -a mf

stenography /stɪ'nɒɡrəfɪ/ n stenografia f

step /step/ n gradino m; (stair) gradino m; ~s pl (ladder) scaleo m; **in ~** al passo; **be out of ~** non stare al passo; **~ by ~** un passo alla volta ● vi (pt/pp **stepped**) **~ into** entrare in; **~ into sb's shoes** succedere a qcno; **~ out of** uscire da; **~ out of line** sgarrare

■ **step down** vi fig dimettersi

■ **step forward** vi farsi avanti

■ **step in** vi fig intervenire

■ **step up** vt (increase) aumentare

step: stepbrother n fratellastro m. **stepchild** n figliastro, -a mf. **stepdaughter** n figliastra f. **stepfather** n patrigno m. **stepladder** n scaleo m. **stepmother** n matrigna f

stepping stone /'stepɪŋ/ n pietra f per guadare; fig trampolino m

stepsister /'stepsɪstə(r)/ n sorellastra f

stepson /'stepsʌn/ n figliastro m

stereo /'sterɪəʊ/ n stereo m; **in ~** in stereofonia

stereophonic /sterɪəʊ'fɒnɪk/ a stereofonico

stereoscopic /sterɪəʊ'skɒpɪk/ a stereoscopico

stereotype /'sterɪətaɪp/ n stereotipo m

stereotyped /'sterɪətaɪpt/ a stereotipato

sterile /'steraɪl/ a sterile

sterility /stə'rɪlətɪ/ n sterilità f

sterilization /sterəlaɪ'zeɪʃn/ n sterilizzazione f

sterilize /'sterɪlaɪz/ vt sterilizzare

sterling /'stɜːlɪŋ/ a fig apprezzabile ● n sterlina f

sterling silver n argento m pregiato

stern¹ /stɜːn/ a severo

stern² n (of boat) poppa f

sternly /'stɜːnlɪ/ adv severamente

steroid /'sterɔɪd/ n steroide m

stet /stet/ (in proofreading) vive

stethoscope /'steθəskəʊp/ n stetoscopio m

stetson /'stetsən/ n cappello m da cow boy

stew /stjuː/ n stufato m; **in a ~** fam agitato ● vt/i cuocere in umido; **~ed fruit** frutta f cotta

steward /'stjuːəd/ n (at meeting) organizzatore, -trice mf; (on ship, aicraft) steward m inv

stewardess /stjuː'ə'des/ n hostess f inv

stick¹ /stɪk/ n bastone m; (of celery, rhubarb) gambo m; Sport mazza f

stick² v (pt/pp **stuck**) ● vt (stab) conficcare; (glue) attaccare; (fam: put) mettere; (fam: endure) sopportare; **be stuck** ⟨vehicle, person:⟩ essere bloccato; ⟨drawer:⟩ essere incastrato; **stuck in a traffic jam** bloccato nel traffico; **be stuck for an answer** non saper cosa rispondere; **stuck on** fam attratto da; **be stuck with sth** fam farsi incastrare con qcsa ● vi (adhere) attaccarsi (**to** a); (jam) bloccarsi

■ **stick around** vi (fam: stay) rimanere

■ **stick at** vt ~ **at it** fam tener duro; ~ **at nothing** fam non fermarsi di fronte a niente

■ **stick by** vt (be faithful to) rimanere al fianco di ⟨sb⟩

■ **stick down** vt incollare ⟨flap⟩; (fam: write down, put down) mettere

■ **stick out** vi (project) sporgere; (fam: catch the eye) risaltare ● vt fam fare ⟨tongue⟩; ~ **it out** (endure) tener duro; ~ **one's neck out** sbilanciarsi

■ **stick to** vt (keep to) attenersi a ⟨rules, facts⟩; mantenere ⟨story⟩; perseverare in ⟨task⟩; **I'll ~ to beer** continuo con la birra

■ **stick up** vi (project) sporgere

■ **stick up for** vt fam difendere

■ **stick with** vt (remain with) rimanere con ⟨sb⟩

sticker /'stɪkə(r)/ n autoadesivo m

sticking plaster /'stɪkɪŋ/ n cerotto m

stick insect n stecco m

stick-in-the-mud n retrogrado m

stickler /'stɪklə(r)/ n **be a ~ for** tenere molto a

stick-up n fam rapina f a mano armata

sticky /'stɪkɪ/ a (**-ier, -iest**) appiccicoso; (adhesive) adesivo; (fig: difficult) difficile

stiff /stɪf/ a rigido; ⟨brush, task⟩ duro; ⟨person⟩ controllato; ⟨drink⟩ forte; ⟨penalty⟩ severo; ⟨price⟩ alto; **bored ~** fam annoiato a morte; **~ neck** torcicollo m

stiffen /'stɪfn/ vt irrigidire ● vi irrigidirsi

stiffly /'stɪflɪ/ adv rigidamente; ⟨smile, answer⟩ in modo controllato

stiffness /'stɪfnɪs/ n rigidità f

stifle /'staɪfl/ vt soffocare

stifling /'staɪflɪŋ/ a soffocante

stigma /'stɪɡmə/ n marchio m

stile /staɪl/ n scaletta f

stiletto /stɪ'letəʊ/ n stiletto m; ~ **heels** tacchi mpl a spillo; ~**s** (pl: shoes) scarpe fpl coi tacchi a spillo

still¹ /stɪl/ n distilleria f

still² a fermo; ⟨drink⟩ non gasato; **keep/stand ~** stare fermo ● n quiete f; (photo) posa f ● adv ancora; (nevertheless) nondimeno, comunque; **I'm ~ not sure** non sono ancora sicuro

stillborn /'stɪlbɔːn/ a nato morto

still life n natura f morta

stilted /'stɪltɪd/ a artificioso

stilts /stɪlts/ npl trampoli mpl

stimulant /'stɪmjʊlənt/ n eccitante m

stimulate /'stɪmjʊleɪt/ vt stimolare

stimulating /'stɪmjʊleɪtɪŋ/ a stimolante

stimulation /stɪmjʊ'leɪʃn/ n stimolo m

stimulus /'stɪmjʊləs/ n (pl **-li** /'stɪmjʊlaɪ/) stimolo m

sting /stɪŋ/ n puntura f; (organ) pungiglione m ● v (pt/pp **stung**) ● vt pungere; ⟨jellyfish:⟩ pizzicare ● vi ⟨insect:⟩ pungere

stinging nettle /'stɪŋɪŋ/ n ortica f

stingy /'stɪndʒɪ/ a (**-ier, -iest**) tirchio

stink /stɪŋk/ n puzza f ● vi (pt **stank**, pp **stunk**) puzzare

stink bomb n fialetta f puzzolente

stinker /'stɪŋkə(r)/ n (fam: difficult problem etc) rompicapo m

stinking /'stɪŋkɪŋ/ adv be ~ **rich** fam essere ricco sfondato

stint /stɪnt/ n lavoro m; **do one's** ~ fare la propria parte ● vt ~ **on** lesinare su

stipend /'staɪpend/ n congrua f

stipulate /'stɪpjʊleɪt/ vt porre come condizione

stipulation /stɪpjʊ'leɪʃn/ n condizione f

stir /stɜː(r)/ n mescolata f; (commotion) trambusto m ● v (pt/pp **stirred**) ● vt muovere; (mix) mescolare ● vi muoversi

■ **stir up** vt fomentare ⟨hatred⟩

stir-fry vt saltare in padella ● n pietanza f saltata in padella

stirrup /'stɪrəp/ n staffa f

stitch /stɪtʃ/ n punto m; (Knitting) maglia f; (pain) fitta f; **have sb in** ~**es** fam far ridere qcno a crepapelle ● vt cucire

■ **stitch up** vt ricucire ⟨wound⟩; **the deal's** ~**ed up** l'affare è concluso

stoat /stəʊt/ n ermellino m

stock /stɒk/ n (for use or selling) scorta f, stock m inv; (livestock) bestiame m; (lineage) stirpe f; Fin titoli mpl; Culin brodo m; **in** ~ disponibile; **out of** ~ esaurito; **take** ~ fig fare il punto ● a solito ● vt ⟨shop:⟩ vendere; approvvigionare ⟨shelves⟩

■ **stock up** vi far scorta (**with** di)

stock: stockbroker n agente m di cambio. **stock car** n (for racing) stock-car m inv. **stock-car racing** n corsa f di stock-car. **stock cube** n dado m [da brodo]. **Stock Exchange** n Borsa f Valori

stocking /'stɒkɪŋ/ n calza f

stockist /'stɒkɪst/ n rivenditore m

stock: stockmarket n mercato m azionario. **stockpile** vt fare scorta di ● n riserva f. **stock-still** a immobile. **stocktaking** n Comm inventario m

stocky /'stɒkɪ/ a (-**ier**, -**iest**) tarchiato

stodge /stɒdʒ/ n (Br fam: food) ammazzafame m inv

stodgy /'stɒdʒɪ/ a indigesto

stoic /'stəʊɪk/ n stoico, -a mf

stoical /'stəʊɪkl/ a stoico

stoically /'stəʊɪklɪ/ adv stoicamente

stoicism /'stəʊɪsɪzm/ n stoicismo m

stoke /stəʊk/ vt alimentare

stole[1] /stəʊl/ n stola f

stole[2], **stolen** /'stəʊln/ see **steal**

stolid /'stɒlɪd/ a apatico

stolidly /'stɒlɪdlɪ/ adv apaticamente

stomach /'stʌmək/ n pancia f; Anat stomaco m ● vt fam reggere

stomach-ache n mal m di pancia

stomp /stɒmp/ vi (walk heavily) camminare con passo pesante

stone /stəʊn/ n pietra f; (in fruit) nocciolo m; Med calcolo m; (weight) 6,348 kg; **within a**

~**'s throw of** a un tiro di schioppo da ● a di pietra ● vt snocciolare ⟨fruit⟩

Stone Age n età f della pietra

stone-cold a gelido

stone-cold sober a perfettamente sobrio

stoned /stəʊnd/ a (fam: on drugs, drink) fatto

stone: stone-deaf a fam sordo come una campana. **stonemason** n scalpellino m. **stonework** n lavoro m in muratura

stony /'stəʊnɪ/ a pietroso; ⟨glare⟩ glaciale

stony-broke a Br fam al verde

stood /stʊd/ see **stand**

stooge /stuːdʒ/ n Theat spalla f; (underling) tirapiedi mf inv

stool /stuːl/ n sgabello m

stool-pigeon n fam informatore, -trice mf

stoop /stuːp/ n curvatura f; **walk with a** ~ camminare con la schiena curva ● vi stare curvo; (bend down) chinarsi; fig abbassarsi

stop /stɒp/ n (break) sosta f; (for bus, train) fermata f; Gram punto m; **come to a** ~ fermarsi; **put a** ~ **to sth** mettere fine a qcsa ● v (pt/pp **stopped**) ● vt fermare; arrestare ⟨machine⟩; (prevent) impedire; ~ **sb doing sth** impedire a qcno di fare qcsa; ~ **doing sth** smettere di fare qcsa; ~ **that!** smettila!; ~ **a cheque** bloccare un assegno ● vi fermarsi; ⟨rain:⟩ smettere ● int fermo!

■ **stop by** vi (make a brief visit) passare

■ **stop off** vi fare una sosta

■ **stop up** vt otturare ⟨sink⟩; tappare ⟨hole⟩

■ **stop with** vi (fam: stay with) fermarsi da

stop: stopcock n rubinetto m di arresto. **stopgap** n palliativo m; (person) tappabuchi m inv. **stop lights** npl luci fpl di arresto. **stopover** n sosta f; Aeron scalo m

stoppage /'stɒpɪdʒ/ n ostruzione f; (strike) interruzione f; (deduction) trattenute fpl

stopper /'stɒpə(r)/ n tappo m

stop press n ultimissime fpl

stopwatch /'stɒpwɒtʃ/ n cronometro m

storage /'stɔːrɪdʒ/ n deposito m; (in warehouse) immagazzinaggio m; Comput memoria f

store /stɔː(r)/ n (stock) riserva f; (shop) grande magazzino m; (depot) deposito m; **in** ~ in deposito; **there's trouble in** ~ **for him** ci sono guai in vista per lui; **what the future has in** ~ **for me** cosa mi riserva il futuro; **set great** ~ **by** tenere in gran conto ● vt tenere; (in warehouse, Comput) immagazzinare

■ **store up** vt (accumulate) far scorte di

store card n carta f di credito di grandi magazzini

storeroom /'stɔːruːm/ n magazzino m

storey /'stɔːrɪ/ n piano m

stork /stɔːk/ n cicogna f

storm /stɔːm/ n temporale m; (with thunder) tempesta f ● vt prendere d'assalto

stormy /'stɔːmɪ/ a tempestoso

story /'stɔːrɪ/ n storia f; (in newspaper) articolo m

storybook /'stɔːrɪbʊk/ n libro m di racconti

storyteller /ˈstɔːrɪtelə(r)/ n (writer) narratore, -trice mf; (liar) contaballe mf inv

stout /staʊt/ a (shoes) resistente; (fat) robusto; (defence) strenuo ● n birra f scura

stoutly /ˈstaʊtlɪ/ adv strenuamente

stove /stəʊv/ n cucina f [economica]; (for heating) stufa f

stow /stəʊ/ vt metter via

■ **stow away** vi Naut imbarcarsi clandestinamente

stowaway /ˈstəʊəweɪ/ n passeggero, -a mf clandestino, -a

straddle /ˈstrædl/ vt stare a cavalcioni su; (standing) essere a cavallo su

strafe /streɪf/ vt mitragliare da bassa quota

straggle /ˈstrægl/ vi crescere disordinatamente; (dawdle) rimanere indietro

straggler /ˈstræglə(r)/ n persona f che rimane indietro

straggly /ˈstræglɪ/ a **have ~ hair** avere pochi capelli sottili

straight /streɪt/ a diritto, dritto; (answer, question, person) diretto; (tidy) in ordine; (drink, hair) liscio; **three ~ wins** tre vittorie di seguito ● adv diritto, dritto; (directly) direttamente; **~ away** immediatamente; **~ on** or **ahead** diritto; **~ out** fig apertamente; **go ~** fam rigare diritto; **put sth ~** mettere qcsa in ordine; **sit/stand up ~** stare diritto; **let's get something ~** mettiamo una cosa in chiaro

straighten /ˈstreɪtn/ vt raddrizzare ● vi raddrizzarsi; **~ [up]** (person:) mettersi diritto

■ **straighten out** vt fig chiarire (situation)

straight: straight face n **keep a ~ ~** restare serio. **straight-faced** /-ˈfeɪst/ a con l'aria seria. **straightforward** a franco; (simple) semplice. **straight man** n Theat spalla f

strain¹ /streɪn/ n (streak) vena f; Bot varietà f inv; (of virus) forma f

strain² n tensione f; (injury) stiramento m; **~s** pl (of music) note fpl; **put a ~ on** fig introdurre delle tensioni in; **under a lot of ~** estremamente sotto pressione ● vt tirare; sforzare (eyes, voice); stirarsi (muscle); Culin scolare ● vi sforzarsi

strained /streɪnd/ a (relations) teso

strainer /ˈstreɪnə(r)/ n colino m

strait /streɪt/ n stretto m; **in dire ~s** in serie difficoltà

straitjacket /ˈstreɪtdʒækɪt/ n camicia f di forza

strait-laced /-ˈleɪst/ a puritano

strand¹ /strænd/ n (of thread) gugliata f; (of beads) filo m; (of hair) capello m

strand² vt **be ~ed** rimanere bloccato

strange /streɪndʒ/ a strano; (not known) sconosciuto; (unaccustomed) estraneo

strangely /ˈstreɪndʒlɪ/ adv stranamente; **~ enough** curiosamente

strangeness /ˈstreɪndʒnɪs/ n stranezza f

stranger /ˈstreɪndʒə(r)/ n estraneo, -a mf

strangle /ˈstræŋgl/ vt strangolare; fig reprimere

stranglehold /ˈstræŋglhəʊld/ n (physical grip) presa f alla gola; (fig: powerful control) stretta f mortale; **have a ~ on sth** fig avere in pugno qcsa

strangulation /stræŋgjʊˈleɪʃn/ n strangolamento m

strap /stræp/ n cinghia f; (to grasp in vehicle) maniglia f; (of watch) cinturino m; (shoulder ~) bretella f, spallina f ● vt (pt/pp **strapped**) legare; **~ in/down** assicurare

strapless /ˈstræplɪs/ a (bra, dress) senza spalline

strapped /stræpt/ a fam **be ~ for** essere a corto di

strapping /ˈstræpɪŋ/ a robusto

strata /ˈstrɑːtə/ see **stratum**

stratagem /ˈstrætədʒəm/ n stratagemma m

strategic /strəˈtiːdʒɪk/ a strategico

strategically /strəˈtiːdʒɪklɪ/ adv strategicamente

strategist /ˈstrætədʒɪst/ n stratega mf

strategy /ˈstrætədʒɪ/ n strategia f

stratosphere /ˈstrɑːtəsfɪə(r)/ n stratosfera f

stratum /ˈstrɑːtəm/ n (pl **strata**) strato m

straw /strɔː/ n paglia f; (single piece) fuscello m; (for drinking) cannuccia f; **the last ~** l'ultima goccia

strawberry /ˈstrɔːbərɪ/ n fragola f

straw poll n Pol sondaggio m d'opinione non ufficiale

stray /streɪ/ a (animal) randagio ● n randagio m ● vi andarsene per conto proprio; (deviate) deviare (**from** da)

streak /striːk/ n striatura f; (fig: trait) vena f; **~s** (pl: in hair) mèches fpl ● vi (move fast) sfrecciare

streaky /ˈstriːkɪ/ a striato; (bacon) grasso

stream /striːm/ n ruscello m; (current) corrente f; (of blood, people) flusso m; Sch classe f; **come on ~** (start operating) entrare in attività; (oil:) cominciare a scorrere ● vi scorrere

■ **stream in** vi entrare a fiotti

■ **stream out** vi uscire a fiotti

streamer /ˈstriːmə(r)/ n (paper) stella f filante; (flag) pennone m

streamline /ˈstriːmlaɪn/ vt rendere aerodinamico; (simplify) snellire

streamlined /ˈstriːmlaɪnd/ a aerodinamico; (simplified) snellito

street /striːt/ n strada f

street: streetcar n Am tram m inv. **street cred** n fam immagine f pubblica. **street lamp** n lampione m. **streetwalker** n passeggiatrice f. **streetwise** a (fam: person) che conosce tutti i trucchi per sopravvivere in una metropoli

strength /streŋθ/ n forza f; (of wall, bridge etc) solidità f; **~s** pl punti mpl forti; **on the ~ of** grazie a

strengthen /ˈstreŋθən/ vt rinforzare

strenuous /ˈstrenjʊəs/ a faticoso; (attempt, denial) energico

strenuously /'strenjʊəslı/ *adv* energicamente

stress /stres/ *n* (*emphasis*) insistenza *f*; *Gram* accento *m* tonico; (*mental*) stress *m inv*; *Mech* spinta *f* ● *vt* (*emphasize*) insistere su; *Gram* mettere l'accento [tonico] su

stressed /strest/ *a* (*mentally*) ~ [**out**] stressato

stressful /'stresfʊl/ *a* stressante

stretch /stretʃ/ *n* stiramento *m*; (*period*) periodo *m* di tempo; (*of road*) tratto *m*; (*elasticity*) elasticità *f*; **at a** ~ di fila; **have a** ~ stirarsi ● *vt* tirare; allargare ⟨*shoes, sweater, etc*⟩; ~ **one's legs** stendere le gambe; ~ **a point** fare uno strappo alla regola ● *vi* (*become wider*) allargarsi; (*extend*) estendersi; ⟨*person:*⟩ stirarsi

■ **stretch out** *vt* allungare ⟨*one's hand, legs*⟩; allargare ⟨*arms*⟩ ● *vi* ⟨*person:*⟩ sdraiarsi; (*land:*) estendersi

stretcher /'stretʃə(r)/ *n* barella *f*

stretchy /'stretʃı/ *a* elastico

strew /stru:/ *vt* (*pt/pp* **strewn** *or* **strewed**) sparpagliare; ~**n with** coperto di

stricken /'strıkn/ *a* prostrato; ~ **with** affetto da ⟨*illness*⟩

strict /strıkt/ *a* severo; (*precise*) preciso

strictly /'strıktlı/ *adv* severamente; ~ **speaking** in senso stretto

strictness /'strıktnıs/ *n* severità *f*

stricture /'strıktʃə(r)/ *n* critica *f*; (*constriction*) restringimento *m*

stride /straɪd/ *n* [lungo] passo *m*; **make great** ~**s** *fig* fare passi da gigante; **take sth in one's** ~ accettare qcsa con facilità ● *vi* (*pt* **strode**, *pp* **stridden**) andare a gran passi

strident /'straɪdənt/ *a* stridente; ⟨*colour*⟩ vistoso

stridently /'straɪdəntlı/ *adv* con voce stridente

strife /straɪf/ *n* conflitto *m*

strike /straɪk/ *n* sciopero *m*; *Mil* attacco *m*; **on** ~ in sciopero ● *v* (*pt/pp* **struck**) ● *vt* colpire; accendere ⟨*match*⟩; trovare ⟨*oil, gold*⟩; (*delete*) depennare; (*occur to*) venire in mente a; *Mil* attaccare; ~ **sb a blow** colpire qcno ● *vi* ⟨*lightning:*⟩ cadere; ⟨*clock:*⟩ suonare; *Mil* attaccare; ⟨*workers:*⟩ scioperare; ~ **lucky** azzeccarla

■ **strike back** *vi* fare rappresaglia; (*at critics*) reagire

■ **strike off** *vt* eliminare; **be struck off** [**the register**] ⟨*doctor:*⟩ essere radiato [dall'albo]

■ **strike out** *vt* eliminare

■ **strike up** *vt* fare ⟨*friendship*⟩; attaccare ⟨*conversation*⟩

strike-breaker *n* persona *f* che non aderisce a uno sciopero

striker /'straɪkə(r)/ *n* scioperante *mf*

striking /'straɪkıŋ/ *a* impressionante; (*attractive*) affascinante

string /strıŋ/ *n* spago *m*; (*of musical instrument, racket*) corda *f*; (*of pearls*) filo *m*; (*of lies*) serie *f*; **the** ~**s** *pl Mus* gli archi; **pull**

~**s** *fam* usare le proprie conoscenze ● *vt* (*pt/ pp* **strung**) (*thread*) infilare ⟨*beads*⟩

■ **string along** *vt* (*fam: deceive*) prendere in giro ● *vi* **I'll** ~ **along** (*come too*) vengo anch'io; ~ **along with sb** andare/venire con qcno

■ **string out** *vi* (*spread out*) allinearsi ● *vt* disporre in fila; **be strung out** (*sl: on drugs*) essere fatto

■ **string together** *vt* mettere insieme ⟨*words, remarks*⟩

string bean *n* fagiolino *m*

stringed /strıŋd/ *a* ⟨*instrument*⟩ a corda

stringent /'strındʒnt/ *a* rigido

stringy /'strıŋı/ *a* ⟨*person, build*⟩ asciutto; ⟨*hair*⟩ come spaghetti; *Culin* filaccioso

strip /strıp/ *n* striscia *f* ● *v* (*pt/pp* **stripped**) ● *vt* spogliare; togliere le lenzuola da ⟨*bed*⟩; scrostare ⟨*wood, furniture*⟩; smontare ⟨*machine*⟩; (*deprive*) privare (**of** di) ● *vi* (*undress*) spogliarsi

■ **strip down** *vt* smontare ⟨*engine*⟩

strip cartoon *n* striscia *f*

strip club *n* locale *m* di strip-tease

stripe /straɪp/ *n* striscia *f*; *Mil* gallone *m*

striped /straɪpt/ *a* a strisce

stripey /'straɪpı/ *a* a strisce, a righe

strip light *n* tubo *m* al neon

stripper /'strıpə(r)/ *n* spogliarellista *mf*; (*solvent*) sverniciatore *m*

strip-search *n* perquisizione *f* (*facendo spogliare qcno*) ● *vt* perquisire (*facendo spogliare*)

striptease /'strıpti:z/ *n* spogliarello *m*, strip-tease *m inv*

strive /straɪv/ *vi* (*pt* **strove**, *pp* **striven**) sforzarsi (**to** di); ~ **for** sforzarsi di ottenere

strobe /strəʊb/ *n* luce *f* stroboscopica

strode /strəʊd/ *see* **stride**

stroke[1] /strəʊk/ *n* colpo *m*; (*of pen*) tratto *m*; (*in swimming*) bracciata *f*; *Med* ictus *m inv*; ~ **of luck** colpo *m* di fortuna; **put sb off his** ~ far perdere il filo a qcno

stroke[2] ● *vt* accarezzare ● *n* carezza *f*

stroll /strəʊl/ *n* passeggiata *f*; **go for a** ~ andare a far due passi ● *vi* passeggiare

stroller /'strəʊlə(r)/ *n* (*Am: push-chair*) passeggino *m*

strong /strɒŋ/ *a* (-**er** /'strɒŋgə(r)/, -**est** /'strɒŋgıst/) forte; ⟨*argument*⟩ valido

strong: strongbox /'strɒŋbɒks/ *n* cassaforte *f*. **stronghold** /'strɒŋhəʊld/ *n* roccaforte *f*. **strong language** *n* (*forceful terms*) linguaggio *m* incisivo; (*swearing*) linguaggio *m* offensivo

strongly /'strɒŋlı/ *adv* fortemente; **feel** ~ **about sth** avere molto a cuore qcsa

strong: strong-minded /-'maındıd/ *a* risoluto. **strong point** *n* punto *m* di forza. **strongroom** *n* camera *f* blindata. **strong stomach** *n* stomaco *m* di ferro

stroppiness /'strɒpınıs/ *n* scontrosità *f*

stroppy /'strɒpı/ *a fam* scorbutico, scontroso

strove /strəʊv/ *see* **strive**

struck /strʌk/ *see* **strike**; ~ **on** *a fam* entusiasta di

structural /'strʌktʃərəl/ *a* strutturale

structurally /'strʌktʃərəlɪ/ *adv* strutturalmente

structure /'strʌktʃə(r)/ *n* struttura *f* ● *vt* strutturare

struggle /'strʌgl/ *n* lotta *f*; **with a** ~ con difficoltà ● *vi* lottare; ~ **for breath** respirare con fatica; ~ **to do sth** fare fatica a fare qcsa; ~ **to one's feet** alzarsi con fatica

strum /strʌm/ *vt/i* (*pt/pp* **strummed**) strimpellare

strung /strʌŋ/ *see* **string**

strut[1] /strʌt/ *n* (*component*) puntello *m*

strut[2] *vi* (*pt/pp* **strutted**) camminare impettito

stub /stʌb/ *n* mozzicone *m*; (*counterfoil*) matrice *f* ● *vt* (*pt/pp* **stubbed**) ~ **one's toe** sbattere il dito del piede (**on** contro)

■ **stub out** *vt* spegnere ⟨*cigarette*⟩

stubble /'stʌbl/ *n* (*on face*) barba *f* ispida

stubbly /'stʌblɪ/ *a* ispido

stubborn /'stʌbən/ *a* testardo; ⟨*refusal*⟩ ostinato

stubbornly /'stʌbənlɪ/ *adv* testardamente; ⟨*refuse*⟩ ostinatamente

stubbornness /'stʌbənnɪs/ *n* (*of person*) testardaggine *f*

stubby /'stʌbɪ/ *a* (**-ier, -iest**) tozzo

stucco /'stʌkəʊ/ *n* stucco *m*

stuck /stʌk/ *see* **stick**[2]

stuck-up *a fam* snob *inv*

stud[1] /stʌd/ *n* (*on boot*) tacchetto *m*; (*on jacket*) borchia *f*; (*for ear*) orecchino *m* [a bottone]

stud[2] *n* (*of horses*) scuderia *f*

studded with /'stʌdɪd/ *a fig* tempestato di

student /'stju:dənt/ *n* studente *m*, studentessa *f*; (*school child*) scolaro, -a *mf*

student nurse *n* studente, -tessa *mf* infermiere, -a

stud-horse *n* stallone *m* [da monta]

studied /'stʌdɪd/ *a* intenzionale; ⟨*politeness*⟩ studiato

studio /'stju:dɪəʊ/ *n* studio *m*

studio apartment *n Am* monolocale *m*

studio flat *n* monolocale *m*

studious /'stju:dɪəs/ *a* studioso; ⟨*attention*⟩ studiato

studiously /'stju:dɪəslɪ/ *adv* studiosamente; (*carefully*) attentamente

stud mare *n* giumenta *f* fattrice

study /'stʌdɪ/ *n* studio *m* ● *vt/i* (*pt/pp* **-ied**) studiare; ~ **for an exam** preparare un esame

stuff /stʌf/ *n* materiale *m*; (*fam: things*) roba *f* ● *vt* riempire; (*with padding*) imbottire; *Culin* farcire; ~ **sth into a drawer/one's pocket** ficcare qcsa alla rinfusa in un cassetto/in tasca; ~ **oneself** ingozzarsi (**with** di); **get** ~**ed!** *fam* va' a quel paese!

stuffing /'stʌfɪŋ/ *n* (*padding*) imbottitura *f*; *Culin* ripieno *m*

stuffy /'stʌfɪ/ *a* (**-ier, -iest**) che sa di chiuso; (*old-fashioned*) antiquato

stultifying /'stʌltɪfaɪɪŋ/ *a* che abbrutisce

stumble /'stʌmbl/ *vi* inciampare; ~ **across** *or* **on** imbattersi in

stumbling block /'stʌmblɪŋ/ *n* ostacolo *m*

stump /stʌmp/ *n* ceppo *m*; (*of limb*) moncone *m*

■ **stump up** *vt/i fam* sganciare

stumped /stʌmpt/ *a fam* perplesso

stumpy /'stʌmpɪ/ *a* (**-ier, -iest**) ⟨*person, legs*⟩ tozzo

stun /stʌn/ *vt* (*pt/pp* **stunned**) stordire; (*astonish*) sbalordire

stung /stʌŋ/ *see* **sting**

stunk /stʌŋk/ *see* **stink**

stunned /stʌnd/ *a* (⟨*expression*⟩) sbalordito

stunning /'stʌnɪŋ/ *a fam* favoloso; ⟨*blow, victory*⟩ sbalorditivo

stunt[1] /stʌnt/ *n fam* trovata *f* pubblicitaria

stunt[2] *vt* arrestare lo sviluppo di

stunted /'stʌntɪd/ *a* stentato

stuntman /'stʌntmən/ *n* stuntman *m inv*, cascatore *m*

stuntwoman /'stʌntwʊmən/ *n* stuntwoman *f inv*

stupefaction /stju:pɪ'fækʃn/ *n* stupore *m*

stupefy /'stju:pɪfaɪ/ *vt* (*pt/pp* **-ied**) (*astonish*) stupire

stupefying /'stju:pɪfaɪɪŋ/ *a* stupefacente

stupendous /stju:'pendəs/ *a* stupendo

stupendously /stju:'pendəslɪ/ *adv* stupendamente

stupid /'stju:pɪd/ *a* stupido

stupidity /stju:'pɪdətɪ/ *n* stupidità *f*

stupidly /'stju:pɪdlɪ/ *adv* stupidamente

stupor /'stju:pə(r)/ *n* torpore *m*

sturdy /'stɜ:dɪ/ *a* (**-ier, -iest**) robusto; ⟨*furniture*⟩ solido

stutter /'stʌtə(r)/ *n* balbuzie *f*; **have a** ~ balbettare ● *vt/i* balbettare

sty[1] /staɪ/ *n* (*pl* **sties**) porcile *m*

sty[2], **stye** *n* (*pl* **styes**) *Med* orzaiolo *m*

style /staɪl/ *n* stile *m*; (*fashion*) moda *f*; (*sort*) tipo *m*; (*hair* ~) pettinatura *f*; **in** ~ in grande stile

stylish /'staɪlɪʃ/ *a* elegante

stylishly /'staɪlɪʃlɪ/ *adv* con eleganza

stylist /'staɪlɪst/ *n* stilista *mf*; (*hair-* ~) *n* parrucchiere, -a *mf*

stylistic /staɪ'lɪstɪk/ *a* stilistico

stylistically /staɪ'lɪstɪklɪ/ *adv* stilisticamente

stylized /'staɪlaɪzd/ *a* stilizzato

stylus /'staɪləs/ *n* (*on record player*) puntina *f*

styptic pencil /'stɪptɪk/ *n* matita *f* emostatica

suave /swɑ:v/ *a* dai modi garbati

sub-aqua /sʌb'ækwə/ *a* ⟨*club*⟩ di sport subacquei

subcommittee /'sʌbkəmɪtɪ/ *n* sottocommissione *f*

subconscious /sʌb'kɒnʃəs/ *a* subcosciente ● *n* subcosciente *m*

subconsciously /sʌb'kɒnʃəslɪ/ *adv* in modo inconscio

subcontinent /sʌb'kɒntɪnənt/ n sub-continente m

subcontract /sʌbkən'trækt/ vt sub-appaltare (**to** a)

subcontractor /'sʌbkəntræktə(r)/ n sub-appaltatore, -trice mf

subdirectory /sʌbdaɪrektərɪ/ n Comput sottodirectory f inv

subdivide /sʌbdɪ'vaɪd/ vt suddividere

subdivision /'sʌbdɪvɪʒn/ n suddivisione f

subdue /səb'dju:/ vt sottomettere; (make quieter) attenuare

subdued /səb'dju:d/ a ‹light› attenuato; ‹person, voice› pacato

subhuman /sʌb'hju:mən/ a (cruel, not fit for humans) disumano; ‹fam: appearance› da paleolitico

subject[1] /'sʌbdʒɪkt/ a ~ **to** soggetto a; (depending on) subordinato a; ~ **to availability** nei limiti della disponibilità ● n soggetto m; (of ruler) suddito, -a mf; Sch materia f; **change the** ~ parlare di qualcos'altro

subject[2] /səb'dʒekt/ vt (to attack, abuse) sottoporre; assoggettare ‹country›

subjective /səb'dʒektɪv/ a soggettivo

subjectively /səb'dʒektɪvlɪ/ adv soggettivamente

subjectiveness /səb'dʒektɪvnɪs/ n soggetività f

subjugate /'sʌbdʒʊgeɪt/ vt soggiogare, sottomettere

subjugation /sʌbdʒə'geɪʃn/ n sottomissione f

subjunctive /səb'dʒʌŋktɪv/ a & n congiuntivo m

sub-let /sʌb'let/ vt (pt/pp -**let**, pres p -**letting**) subaffittare

sublime /sə'blaɪm/ a sublime

sublimely /sə'blaɪmlɪ/ adv sublimamente

subliminal /sə'blɪmɪnl/ a subliminale

sub-machine gun n mitraglietta f

submarine /'sʌbməri:n/ n sommergibile m

submerge /səb'mɜ:dʒ/ vt immergere; **be** ~**d** essere sommerso ● vi immergersi

submission /səb'mɪʃn/ n sottomissione f

submissive /səb'mɪsɪv/ a sottomesso

submissively /səb'mɪsɪvlɪ/ adv remissivamente

submissiveness /səb'mɪsɪvnɪs/ n remissività f

submit /səb'mɪt/ v (pt/pp -**mitted**, pres p -**mitting**) ● vt sottoporre ● vi sottomettersi

subnormal /sʌb'nɔ:ml/ a ‹temperature› al di sotto della norma; ‹person› subnormale

subordinate[1] /sə'bɔ:dɪnət/ a & n subordinato, -a mf

subordinate[2] /sə'bɔ:dɪneɪt/ vt subordinare (**to** a)

subpoena /səb'pi:nə/ n mandato m di comparizione ● vt citare

subroutine /'sʌbru:ti:n/ n Comput subroutine f

subscribe /səb'skraɪb/ vi contribuire; ~ **to** abbonarsi a ‹newspaper›; sottoscrivere ‹fund›; fig aderire a ‹theory›

subscriber /səb'skraɪbə(r)/ n abbonato, -a mf

subscription /səb'skrɪpʃn/ n (to club) sottoscrizione f; (to newspaper) abbonamento m

subsequent /'sʌbsɪkwənt/ a susseguente

subsequently /'sʌbsɪkwəntlɪ/ adv in seguito

subservience /səb'sɜ:vɪəns/ n asservimento m

subservient /səb'sɜ:vɪənt/ a subordinato; (servile) servile

subserviently /səb'sɜ:vɪəntlɪ/ adv servilmente

subset /'sʌbset/ n Math sottoinsieme m

subside /səb'saɪd/ vi sprofondare; ‹ground:› avvallarsi; ‹storm:› placarsi

subsidence /'sʌbsɪdəns/ n (of land) cedimento m

subsidiary /səb'sɪdɪərɪ/ a secondario ● n ~ [**company**] filiale f

subsidize /'sʌbsɪdaɪz/ vt sovvenzionare

subsidy /'sʌbsɪdɪ/ n sovvenzione f

subsist /səb'sɪst/ vi vivere (**on** di)

subsistence /səb'sɪstəns/ n sussistenza f

substance /'sʌbstəns/ n sostanza f

sub-standard /sʌb'stændəd/ a di qualità inferiore

substantial /səb'stænʃl/ a sostanziale; ‹meal› sostanzioso; (strong) solido

substantially /səb'stænʃəlɪ/ adv sostanzialmente; (built) solidamente

substantiate /səb'stænʃɪeɪt/ vt comprovare

substitute /'sʌbstɪtju:t/ n sostituto m ● vt ~ **A for B** sostituire B con A ● vi ~ **for sb** sostituire qcno

substitution /sʌbstɪ'tju:ʃn/ n sostituzione f

subterfuge /'sʌbtəfju:dʒ/ n sotterfugio m

subterranean /sʌbtə'reɪnɪən/ a sotterraneo

subtext /'sʌbtekst/ n storia f secondaria; fig messaggio m implicito

subtitle /'sʌbtaɪtl/ n sottotitolo m ● vt sottotitolare

subtle /'sʌtl/ a sottile; ‹taste, perfume› delicato

subtlety /'sʌtltɪ/ n sottigliezza f

subtly /'sʌtlɪ/ adv sottilmente

subtotal /'sʌbtəutl/ n totale m parziale

subtract /səb'trækt/ vt sottrarre

subtraction /səb'trækʃn/ n sottrazione f

suburb /'sʌbɜ:b/ n sobborgo m; **in the** ~**s** in periferia

suburban /sə'bɜ:bən/ a suburbano

suburbia /sə'bɜ:bɪə/ n sobborghi mpl

subversive /səb'vɜ:sɪv/ a sovversivo

subway /'sʌbweɪ/ n sottopassaggio m; (Am: railway) metropolitana f, metrò m inv

sub-zero /sʌb'zɪərəu/ a sottozero inv

succeed /sək'si:d/ vi riuscire (**in doing sth** a fare qcsa); (follow) succedere (**to** a) ● vt succedere a ‹king›

succeeding /sək'si:dɪŋ/ a successivo

success /sək'ses/ n successo m; **be a** ~ (in life) aver successo

successful /sək'sesfʊl/ *a* riuscito; ‹*businessman, artist etc*› di successo

successfully /sək'sesfʊlɪ/ *adv* con successo

succession /sək'seʃn/ *n* successione *f*; **in ~** di seguito

successive /sək'sesɪv/ *a* successivo

successively /sə'sesɪvlɪ/ *adv* successivamente

successor /sək'sesə(r)/ *n* successore *m*

succinct /sək'sɪŋkt/ *a* succinto

succinctly /sək'sɪŋktlɪ/ *adv* succintamente

succour /'sʌkə(r)/ *vt* soccorrere ● *n* soccorso *m*

succulence /'sʌkjʊləns/ *n* succulenza *f*

succulent /'ʃʌkjʊlənt/ *a* succulento

succumb /sə'kʌm/ *vi* soccombere (**to** a)

such /sʌtʃ/ *a* tale; **~ a book** un libro così; **~ a thing** una cosa del genere; **~ a long time ago** talmente tanto tempo fa; **there is no ~ thing/person** non c'è una cosa/persona così ● *pron* **as ~** in quanto tale; **~ as** come; **and ~** e simili; **~ as it is** per quel che vale; **if ~ is the case** se questo è il caso

suchlike /'sʌtʃlaɪk/ *pron fam* di tal genere

suck /ʃʌk/ *vt* succhiare

■ **suck up** *vt* assorbire

■ **suck up to** *vt fam* fare il lecchino con

sucker /'ʃʌkə(r)/ *n Bot* pollone *m*; (*fam: person*) credulone, -a *mf*

suckle /'ʃʌkl/ *vt* allattare

suction /'sʌkʃn/ *n* aspirazione f

Sudan /sʊ'dæn/ *n* Sudan *m*

Sudanese /sʊdən'i:z/ *a & n* sudanese *mf*

sudden /'sʌdn/ *a* improvviso ● *n* **all of a ~** all'improvviso

suddenly /'sʌdənlɪ/ *adv* improvvisamente

suds /sʌdz/ *npl* (*foam*) schiuma *f*; (*soapy water*) acqua *f* saponata

sue /su:/ *v* (*pres p* **suing**) ● *vt* fare causa a (**for** per) ● *vi* fare causa

suede /sweɪd/ *n* pelle *f* scamosciata

suet /'su:ɪt/ *n* grasso *m* di rognone

suffer /'sʌfə(r)/ *vi* soffrire (**from** per) ● *vt* soffrire di ‹*pain*›; subire ‹*loss etc*›

sufferance /'sʌf(ə)rəns/ *n* **you're here on ~** qui tu sei appena tollerato

suffering /'sʌf(ə)rɪŋ/ *n* sofferenza *f*

suffice /sə'faɪs/ *vi* bastare

sufficient /sə'fɪʃənt/ *a* sufficiente

sufficiently /sə'fɪʃəntlɪ/ *adv* sufficientemente

suffix /'sʌfɪks/ *n* suffisso *m*

suffocate /'sʌfəkeɪt/ *vt/i* soffocare

suffocation /sʌfə'keɪʃn/ *n* soffocamento *m*

suffrage /'sʌfrɪdʒ/ *n* (*right*) diritto *m* di voto; (*system*) suffragio *m*

suffragette /sʌfrə'dʒet/ *n* suffragetta *f*

sugar /'ʃʊgə(r)/ *n* zucchero *m* ● *vt* zuccherare; **~ the pill** *fig* addolcire la pillola

sugar: sugar basin, sugar bowl *n* zuccheriera *f*. **sugar-coated** /-'kəʊtɪd/ *a* ricoperto di zucchero. **sugar cube** *n* zolletta *f*. **sugar daddy** *n fam* vecchio amante *m* danaroso. **sugar lump** *n* zolletta *f*

sugary /'ʃʊgərɪ/ *a* zuccheroso; *fig* sdolcinato

suggest /sə'dʒest/ *vt* suggerire; (*indicate, insinuate*) fare pensare a

suggestible /sə'dʒestəbl/ *a* suggestionabile

suggestion /sə'dʒestʃən/ *n* suggerimento *m*; (*trace*) traccia *f*

suggestive /sə'dʒestɪv/ *a* allusivo; **be ~ of** fare pensare a

suggestively /sə'dʒestɪvlɪ/ *adv* in modo allusivo

suicidal /su:ɪ'saɪdl/ *a* suicida

suicide /'su:ɪsaɪd/ *n* suicidio *m*; (*person*) suicida *mf*; **commit ~** suicidarsi

suicide attempt *n* tentato suicidio *m*

suicide pact *n* patto *m* suicida

suit /su:t/ *n* vestito *m*; (*woman's*) tailleur *m* inv; (*Cards*) seme *m*; *Jur* causa *f*; **follow ~** *fig* fare lo stesso ● *vt* andar bene a; (*adapt*) adattare (**to** a); (*be convenient for*) andare bene per; **be ~ed to** *or* **for** essere adatto a; **~ yourself!** fa' come vuoi!

suitability /su:tə'bɪlɪtɪ/ *n* adeguatezza *f*

suitable /'su:təbl/ *a* adatto

suitably /'su:təblɪ/ *adv* convenientemente

suitcase /'su:tkeɪs/ *n* valigia *f*

suite /swi:t/ *n* suite *f* inv; (*of furniture*) divano *m* e poltrone *fpl* assortiti

sulk /sʌlk/ *vi* fare il broncio

sulkily /'sʌlkɪlɪ/ *adv* con aria imbronciata

sulky /'sʌlkɪ/ *a* imbronciato

sullen /'sʌlən/ *a* svogliato

sullenly /'sʌlənlɪ/ *adv* svogliatamente

sulphur /'sʌlfə(r)/ *n* zolfo *m*

sulphur dioxide /daɪ'ɒksaɪd/ *n* anidride *f* solforosa

sulphuric acid /sʌl'fjʊərɪk/ *n* acido *m* solforico

sultana /sʌl'tɑ:nə/ *n* uva *f* sultanina

sultry /'sʌltrɪ/ *a* (**-ier, -iest**) ‹*weather*› afoso; *fig* sensuale

sum /sʌm/ *n* somma *f*; *Sch* addizione *f*

■ **sum up** *v* (*pt/pp* **summed**) ● *vi* riassumere ● *vt* valutare

summarily /sʌ'merɪlɪ/ *adv* sommariamente; ‹*dismissed*› sbrigativamente

summarize /'sʌməraɪz/ *vt* riassumere

summary /'sʌmərɪ/ *n* sommario *m* ● *a* sommario; ‹*dismissal*› sbrigativo

summer /'sʌmə(r)/ *n* estate *f*; **in ~**, **in the ~** in estate

summer: summer house *n* padiglione *m*. **summertime** *n* (*season*) estate *f*. **summer time** *n* (*clock change*) ora *f* legale

summery /'sʌmərɪ/ *a* estivo

summing-up /sʌmɪŋ'ʌp/ *n* riepilogo *m*; *Jur* ricapitolazione *f* del processo

summit /'sʌmɪt/ *n* cima *f*

summit conference *n* vertice *m*

summon /'sʌmən/ *vt* convocare; *Jur* citare

■ **summon up** *vt* raccogliere ‹*strength*›; rievocare ‹*memory*›

summons /'sʌmənz/ *n Jur* citazione *f* ● *vt* citare in giudizio

sump /sʌmp/ *n Auto* coppa *f* dell'olio

sumptuous /'sʌmptjʊəs/ *a* sontuoso

sumptuously /'sʌmptjʊəslɪ/ *adv* sontuosamente

sum total *n* totale *m*

sun /sʌn/ *n* sole *m* ● *vt* (*pt/pp* **sunned**) ~ **oneself** prendere il sole

sun: sunbathe *vi* prendere il sole. **sunbed** *n* lettino *m* solare. **sunblock** *n* prodotto *m* solare a protezione totale. **sunburn** *n* scottatura *f* (*solare*). **sunburnt** *a* scottato (*dal sole*). **sun cream** *n* crema *f* solare

sundae /'sʌndeɪ/ *n* gelato *m* guarnito

Sunday /'sʌndeɪ/ *n* domenica *f*

sundial /'sʌndaɪəl/ *n* meridiana *f*

sun-dried tomatoes /'sʌndraɪd/ *npl* pomodori *mpl* secchi

sundry /'sʌndrɪ/ *a* svariati; **all and** ~ tutti quanti

sunflower /'sʌnflaʊə(r)/ *n* girasole *m*

sung /sʌŋ/ *see* **sing**

sunglasses /'sʌnglɑːsɪz/ *npl* occhiali *mpl* da sole

sunk /sʌŋk/ *see* **sink**

sunken /'sʌŋkn/ *a* incavato

sunlamp /'sʌnlæmp/ *n* lampada *f* abbronzante

sunlight /'sʌnlaɪt/ *n* [luce *f* del] sole *m*

sunny /'sʌnɪ/ *a* (**-ier, -iest**) assolato

sun: sunrise *n* alba *f*. **sunroof** *n* Auto tettuccio *m* apribile. **sunscreen** *n* (*to prevent sunburn*) crema *f* solare protettiva. **sunset** *n* tramonto *m*. **sunshade** *n* parasole *m*. **sunshine** *n* [luce *f* del] sole *m*. **sunshine roof** *n* tettuccio *m* apribile. **sunstroke** *n* insolazione *f*. **suntan** *n* abbronzatura *f*. **suntan lotion** *n* antisolare *m*. **sun-tanned** *a* abbronzato. **suntan oil** *n* olio *m* solare

super /'suːpə(r)/ *a fam* fantastico

superannuated /suːpər'ænjʊeɪtɪd/ *a fig* che ha fatto il suo tempo

superannuation /suːpərænjʊ'eɪʃn/ *n* (*contributions*) contributi *mpl* pensionistici; (*pension*) pensione *f*

superannuation fund *n* fondo *m* pensione

superb /sʊ'pɜːb/ *a* splendido

superbly /sʊ'pɜːblɪ/ *adv* splendidamente

supercilious /suːpə'sɪlɪəs/ *a* altezzoso

superciliously /suːpə'sɪlɪəslɪ/ *adv* in modo altezzoso

superficial /suːpə'fɪʃl/ *a* superficiale

superficiality /suːpəfɪʃɪ'ælɪtɪ/ *n* superficialità *f*

superficially /suːpə'fɪʃəlɪ/ *adv* superficialmente

superfluous /sʊ'pɜːflʊəs/ *a* superfluo

superhighway /'suːpəhaɪweɪ/ *n* [**information**] ~ *Comput* autostrada *f* telematica

superhuman /suːpə'hjuːmən/ *a* sovrumano

superimpose /suːpərɪm'pəʊz/ *vt* sovrapporre (*picture, soundtrack*) (**on** a); ~**d title** titolo *m* in sovrimpressione

superintendent /suːpərɪn'tendənt/ *n* (*of police*) commissario *m* di polizia

superior /suː'pɪərɪə(r)/ *a & n* superiore, -a *mf*

superiority /suːpɪərɪ'ɒrətɪ/ *n* superiorità *f*

superlative /suː'pɜːlətɪv/ *a* eccellente ● *n* superlativo *m*

superlatively /suː'pɜːlətɪvlɪ/ *adv* (*perform*) in modo eccezionale; (*good*) estremamente

superman /'suːpəmæn/ *n* superuomo *m*

supermarket /'suːpəmɑːkɪt/ *n* supermercato *m*

supermodel /'suːpəmɒdl/ *n* top model *f*, supermodella *f*

supernatural /suːpə'nætʃrəl/ *a* soprannaturale

superpower /'suːpəpaʊə(r)/ *n* superpotenza *f*

superscript /'suːpəskrɪpt/ *a* (*number, letter*) all'esponente

supersede /suːpə'siːd/ *vt* rimpiazzare

supersonic /suːpə'sɒnɪk/ *a* supersonico

superstition /suːpə'stɪʃn/ *n* superstizione *f*

superstitious /suːpə'stɪʃəs/ *a* superstizioso

superstitiously /suːpə'stɪʃəslɪ/ *adv* in modo superstizioso

superstore /'suːpəstɔː(r)/ *n* ipermercato *m*

superstructure /'suːpəstrʌktʃə(r)/ *n* sovrastruttura *f*

supertax /'suːpətæks/ *n* Fin soprattassa *f*

supervise /'suːpəvaɪz/ *vt* supervisionare

supervision /suːpə'vɪʒn/ *n* supervisione *f*

supervisor /'suːpəvaɪzə(r)/ *n* supervisore *m*

supervisory /suːpə'vaɪzərɪ/ *a* di supervisione

superwoman /'suːpəwʊmən/ *n* superdonna *f*

supper /'sʌpə(r)/ *n* cena *f*; **have** ~ cenare

supple /'sʌpl/ *a* slogato

supplement /'sʌplɪmənt/ *n* supplemento *m* ● *vt* integrare

supplementary /sʌplɪ'mentərɪ/ *a* supplementare

supplier /sə'plaɪə(r)/ *n* fornitore, -trice *mf*

supply /sə'plaɪ/ *n* fornitura *f*; Econ offerta *f*; **be in short** ~ scarseggiare; ~ **and demand** domanda *f* e offerta *f*; **supplies** *pl* Mil approvvigionamenti *mpl* ● *vt* (*pt/pp* **-ied**) fornire; ~ **sb with sth** fornire qcsa a qcno

supply teacher *n* supplente *mf*

support /sə'pɔːt/ *n* sostegno *m*; (*base*) supporto *m*; (*keep*) sostentamento *m* ● *vt* sostenere; mantenere (*family*); (*give money to*) mantenere finanziariamente; Sport fare il tifo per; Comput supportare

supporter /sə'pɔːtə(r)/ *n* sostenitore, -trice *mf*; Sport tifoso, -a *mf*

supporting actor /sə'pɔːtɪŋ/ *n* attore *m* non protagonista

supporting actress *n* attrice *f* non protagonista

supportive /sə'pɔːtɪv/ *a* incoraggiante; **be** ~ **of sb** dare tutto il proprio appoggio a qcno

support stockings *npl* calze *fpl* elastiche

suppose /sə'pəʊz/ *vt* (*presume*) supporre; (*imagine*) pensare; **be** ~**d to do** dover fare; **not be** ~**d to** non avere il permesso di; **I** ~ **so** suppongo di sì

supposedly /sə'pəʊzɪdlɪ/ *adv* presumibilmente

supposition /sʌpə'zɪʃn/ *n* supposizione *f*

suppository /sʌ'pɒzɪtrɪ/ *n* supposta *f*

suppress /sə'pres/ *vt* sopprimere

suppressant /sə'presənt/ *n Med* inibitore *m*

suppression /sə'preʃn/ *n* soppressione *f*

suppurate /'sʌpjʊreɪt/ *vi* suppurare

supremacy /su:'preməsɪ/ *n* supremazia *f*

supreme /su:'pri:m/ *a* supremo

supremo /su:'pri:məʊ/ *n* massima autorità *f inv*

surcharge /'sɜ:tʃɑ:dʒ/ *n* supplemento *m*

sure /ʃʊə(r)/ *a* sicuro, certo; **make ~** accertarsi; **be ~ to do it** accertati di farlo ● *adv Am fam* certamente; **~ enough** infatti

sure-fire *a fam* garantito

sure-footed /-'fʊtɪd/ *a* agile

surely /'ʃʊəlɪ/ *adv* certamente; (*Am: gladly*) volentieri

surety /'ʃʊərətɪ/ *n* garanzia *f*; **stand ~ for sb/sth** fare da garante a qcno/per qcsa

surf /'sɜ:f/ *n* schiuma *f* ● *vt* **~ the Net** surfare in Internet

surface /'sɜ:fɪs/ *n* superficie *f*; **on the ~** *fig* in apparenza ● *vi* (*emerge*) emergere

surface mail *n* **by ~ ~** per posta ordinaria

surface-to-air missile *n* missile *m* terra-aria

surfboard /'sɜ:fbɔ:d/ *n* tavola *f* da surf

surfeit /'sɜ:fɪt/ *n* eccesso *m*

surfer /'sɜ:fə(r)/ *n* surfista *mf*

surfing /'sɜ:fɪŋ/ *n* surf *m*

surge /sɜ:dʒ/ *n* (*of sea*) ondata *f*; (*of interest*) aumento *m*; (*in demand*) impennata *f*; (*of anger, pity*) impeto *m* ● *vi* riversarsi; **~ forward** buttarsi in avanti

surgeon /'sɜ:dʒən/ *n* chirurgo *m*

surgery /'sɜ:dʒərɪ/ *n* chirurgia *f*; (*place, consulting room*) ambulatorio *m*; (*hours*) *fpl* di visita; **have ~** subire un'intervento [chirurgico]

surgical /'sɜ:dʒɪkl/ *a* chirurgico

surgically /'sɜ:dʒɪklɪ/ *adv* chirurgicamente

surliness /'sɜ:lɪnɪs/ *n* scontrosità *f*

surly /'sɜ:lɪ/ *a* (**-ier, -iest**) scontroso

surmise /sə'maɪz/ *vt* supporre

surmount /sə'maʊnt/ *vt* sormontare

surname /'sɜ:neɪm/ *n* cognome *m*

surpass /sə'pɑ:s/ *vt* superare

surplus /'sɜ:pləs/ *a* d'avanzo; **be ~ to requirements** essere in eccedenza rispetto alle necessità ● *n* sovrappiù *m*

surprise /sə'praɪz/ *n* sorpresa *f* ● *vt* sorprendere; **be ~d** essere sorpreso (**at** da)

surprising /sə'praɪzɪŋ/ *a* sorprendente

surprisingly /sə'praɪzɪŋlɪ/ *adv* sorprendentemente; **~ enough** stranamente

surreal /sə'rɪəl/ *a* surreale

surrealism /sə'rɪəlɪzm/ *n* surrealismo *m*

surrealist /sə'rɪəlɪst/ *n* surrealista *mf* ● *a* surrealistico

surrender /sə'rendə(r)/ *n* resa *f* ● *vi* arrendersi ● *vt* cedere

surreptitious /sʌrəp'tɪʃəs/ *a* furtivo

surreptitiously /sʌrəp'tɪʃəslɪ/ *adv* furtivamente

surrogate /'sʌrəgət/ *n* surrogato *m*

surrogate mother *n* madre *f* surrogata *o* in prestito

surround /sə'raʊnd/ *vt* circondare; **~ed by** circondato da

surrounding /sə'raʊndɪŋ/ *a* circostante

surroundings /sə'raʊndɪŋz/ *npl* dintorni *mpl*

surtax /'sɜ:tæks/ *n* soprattassa *f*; (*on income*) imposta *f* supplementare

surveillance /sə'veɪləns/ *n* sorveglianza *f*; **under ~** sotto sorveglianza

survey[1] /'sɜ:veɪ/ *n* sguardo *m*; (*poll*) sondaggio *m*; (*investigation*) indagine *f*; (*of land*) rilevamento *m*; (*of house*) perizia *f*

survey[2] /sə'veɪ/ *vt* esaminare; fare un rilevamento di ⟨*land*⟩; fare una perizia di ⟨*building*⟩

surveyor /sə'veɪə(r)/ *n* perito *m*; (*of land*) topografo, -a *mf*

survival /sə'vaɪvl/ *n* sopravvivenza *f*; (*relic*) resto *m*

survive /sə'vaɪv/ *vt* sopravvivere a ● *vi* sopravvivere

survivor /sə'vaɪvə(r)/ *n* superstite *mf*; **be a ~** *fam* riuscire sempre a cavarsela

susceptible /sə'septəbl/ *a* influenzabile; **~ to** sensibile a

suspect[1] /sə'spekt/ *vt* sospettare; (*assume*) supporre

suspect[2] /'sʌspekt/ *a & n* sospetto, -a *mf*

suspend /sə'spend/ *vt* appendere; (*stop, from duty*) sospendere

suspender belt /sə'spendə/ *n* reggicalze *m inv*

suspenders /sə'spendəz/ *npl* giarretiere *fpl*; (*Am: braces*) bretelle *fpl*

suspense /sə'spens/ *n* tensione *f*; (*in book etc*) suspense *f*

suspension /sə'spenʃn/ *n Auto* sospensione *f*

suspension bridge *n* ponte *m* sospeso

suspicion /sə'spɪʃn/ *n* sospetto *m*; (*trace*) pizzico *m*; **under ~** sospettato

suspicious /səs'pɪʃəs/ *a* sospettoso; (*arousing suspicion*) sospetto

suspiciously /sə'spɪʃəslɪ/ *adv* sospettosamente; (*arousing suspicion*) in modo sospetto

■ **suss out** /sʌs/ *vt Br fam* intuire ⟨*person*⟩; capire ⟨*software, technique*⟩; **I've got you ~ed** [**out**] ho scoperto il tuo piano

sustain /sə'steɪn/ *vt* sostenere; mantenere ⟨*life*⟩; subire ⟨*injury*⟩

sustained /sə'steɪnd/ *a* ⟨*effort*⟩ prolungato

sustenance /'sʌstɪnəns/ *n* nutrimento *m*

suture *n* /'su:tʃə(r)/ sutura *f*

SW *abbr* (**south-west**) SO

swab /swɒb/ *n Med* tampone *m*

swagger /'swægə(r)/ *vi* pavoneggiarsi

swallow[1] /'swɒləʊ/ *vt/i* inghiottire

■ **swallow up** *vt* divorare; ⟨*earth, crowd*⟩ inghiottire

swallow[2] *n* (*bird*) rondine *f*

swam /swæm/ *see* **swim**

swamp /swɒmp/ *n* palude *f* ● *vt fig* sommergere

swampy /'swɒmpɪ/ *a* paludoso

swan /swɒn/ *n* cigno *m*

swank /swæŋk/ *vi fam* darsi delle arie

swanky /'swæŋkɪ/ *a* ⟨*fam: posh*⟩ snob *inv*

swap /swɒp/ *n fam* scambio *m* ● *vt* (*pt/pp* **swapped**) *fam* scambiare (**for** con) ● *vi* fare cambio

swarm /swɔːm/ *n* sciame *m* ● *vi* sciamare; **be ~ing with** *fig* brulicare di

swarthy /'swɔːðɪ/ *a* (**-ier, -iest**) di carnagione scura

swashbuckling /'swɒʃbʌklɪŋ/ *a* ⟨*hero, appearance*⟩ spericolato; ⟨*adventure, tale*⟩ di cappa e spada

swastika /'swɒstɪkə/ *n* svastica *f*

swat /swɒt/ *vt* (*pt/pp* **swatted**) schiacciare

swathe /sweɪð/ *n* ⟨*of grass, corn*⟩ falciata *f*; ⟨*land*⟩ larga striscia *f* ● *vt* (*in bandages, silk*) avvolgere

sway /sweɪ/ *n fig* influenza *f* ● *vi* oscillare; ⟨*person:*⟩ ondeggiare ● *vt* ⟨*influence*⟩ influenzare

swear /sweə(r)/ *v* (*pt* **swore**, *pp* **sworn**) ● *vt* giurare; **I could have sworn that ...** avrei giurato che ... ● *vi* giurare; ⟨*curse*⟩ dire parolacce; **I'd ~ to it!** ci potrei giurare!; **~ at sb** imprecare contro qcno; **~ by** ⟨*believe in*⟩ credere ciecamente in
■ **swear off** *vt* ⟨*fam: give up*⟩ smettere di

swear word *n* parolaccia *f*

sweat /swet/ *n* sudore *m* ● *vi* sudare ● *vt* **~ blood** sudare sangue
■ **sweat out** *vt* **~ it out** (*endure to the end*) tener duro fino alla fine

sweatband /'swetbænd/ *n* fascia *f* per il sudore; ⟨*for wrist*⟩ polsino *m*

sweater /'swetə(r)/ *n* golf *m inv*

sweatshirt /'swetʃɜːt/ *n* felpa *f*

sweaty /'swetɪ/ *a* sudato

Swede /swiːd/ *n* svedese *mf*

swede *n* rapa *f* svedese

Sweden /'swiːdn/ *n* Svezia *f*

Swedish /'swiːdɪʃ/ *a* & *n* svedese *m*

sweep /swiːp/ *n* scopata *f*, spazzata *f*; ⟨*curve*⟩ curva *f*; ⟨*movement*⟩ movimento *m* ampio; **make a clean ~** *fig* fare piazza pulita ● *v* (*pt/pp* **swept**) ● *vt* scopare, spazzare; ⟨*wind:*⟩ spazzare; **~ the board** fare piazza pulita ● *vi* ⟨*go swiftly*⟩ andare rapidamente; ⟨*wind:*⟩ soffiare
■ **sweep away** *vt fig* spazzare via
■ **sweep up** *vt* spazzare

sweeper /'swiːpə(r)/ *n* ⟨*machine*⟩ spazzatrice *f*; ⟨*person*⟩ spazzino *m*; ⟨*in football*⟩ libero *m*

sweeping /'swiːpɪŋ/ *a* ⟨*gesture*⟩ ampio; ⟨*statement*⟩ generico; ⟨*changes*⟩ radicale

sweet /swiːt/ *a* dolce; **have a ~ tooth** essere goloso ● *n* caramella *f*; ⟨*dessert*⟩ dolce *m*

sweet: sweet and sour *a* agrodolce. **sweetbread** *n* ⟨*veal*⟩ animella *f* di vitello; ⟨*lamb*⟩ animella di agnello. **sweetcorn** *n* mais *m*, granturco *m*

sweeten /'swiːtn/ *vt* addolcire

sweetener /'swiːtnə(r)/ *n* dolcificante *m*; ⟨*fam: incentive*⟩ incentivo *m*; ⟨*fam: bribe*⟩ bustarella *f*

sweetheart /'swiːthɑːt/ *n* innamorato, -a *mf*; **hi, ~** ciao, tesoro

sweetly /'swiːtlɪ/ *adv* dolcemente

sweetness /'swiːtnɪs/ *n* dolcezza *f*

sweet: sweet pea *n* pisello *m* odoroso. **sweetshop** *n* negozio *m* di dolciumi. **sweet-talk** *vt* **~ sb into doing sth** convincere qcno a fare qcsa con tante belle parole

swell /swel/ *n* ⟨*of sea*⟩ mare *m* lungo ● *v* (*pt* **swelled**, *pp* **swollen** or **swelled**) ● *vi* gonfiarsi; ⟨*increase*⟩ aumentare ● *vt* gonfiare; ⟨*increase*⟩ far salire ● *a fam* eccellente

swelling /'swelɪŋ/ *n* gonfiore *m*

swelter /'sweltə(r)/ *vi* soffocare [dal caldo]

sweltering [**hot**] /'sweltərɪŋ/ *a* ⟨*day*⟩ afoso

swept /swept/ *see* **sweep**

swerve /swɜːv/ *vi* deviare bruscamente

swift /swɪft/ *a* rapido

swiftly /'swɪftlɪ/ *adv* rapidamente

swiftness /'swɪftnɪs/ *n* rapidità *f*

swig /swɪg/ *fam n* sorso *m* ● *vt* (*pt/pp* **swigged**) scolarsi

swill /swɪl/ *n* ⟨*for pigs*⟩ brodaglia *f* ● *vt* **~ [out]** risciacquare

swim /swɪm/ *n* **have a ~** fare una nuotata ● *vi* (*pt* **swam**, *pp* **swum**) nuotare; ⟨*room:*⟩ girare; **go ~ming** andare a nuotare; **my head is ~ming** mi gira la testa ● *vt* percorrere a nuoto ⟨*distance*⟩

swimmer /'swɪmə(r)/ *n* nuotatore, -trice *mf*

swimming /'swɪmɪŋ/ *n* nuoto *m*

swimming baths *npl* piscina *fsg*

swimming costume *n* costume *m* da bagno

swimmingly /'swɪmɪŋlɪ/ *adv* **go ~** andar liscio

swimming pool *n* piscina *f*

swimming trunks *npl* calzoncini *mpl* da bagno

swimsuit /'swɪmsuːt/ *n* costume *m* da bagno

swindle /'swɪndl/ *n* truffa *f* ● *vt* truffare

swindler /'swɪndlə(r)/ *n* truffatore, -trice *mf*

swine /swaɪn/ *n fam* porco *m*

swing /swɪŋ/ *n* oscillazione *f*; ⟨*shift*⟩ cambiamento *m*; ⟨*seat*⟩ altalena *f*; *Mus* swing *m*; **in full ~** in piena attività ● (*pt/pp* **swung**) ● *vi* oscillare; ⟨*on swing, sway*⟩ dondolare; ⟨*dangle*⟩ penzolare; ⟨*turn*⟩ girare ● *vt* oscillare; far deviare ⟨*vote*⟩

swing-door *n* porta *f* a vento

swingeing /'swɪndʒɪŋ/ *a* ⟨*increase*⟩ drastico

swingometer /swɪŋ'ɒmɪtə(r)/ *n* strumento *m* che permette di seguire l'andamento delle votazioni

swipe /swaɪp/ *n fam* botta *f* ● *vt fam* colpire; ⟨*fam: steal*⟩ rubare; far passare nella macchinetta ⟨*credit card*⟩

swirl /swɜːl/ *n* ⟨*of smoke, dust*⟩ turbine *m* ● *vt* far girare ● *vi* ⟨*water:*⟩ fare mulinello

swish[1] /swɪʃ/ *a fam* chic

swish[2] *vi* schioccare

Swiss /swɪs/ *a & n* svizzero, -a *mf*; **the ~** *pl* gli svizzeri

Swiss roll *n* rotolo *m* di pan di Spagna ripieno di marmellata

switch /swɪtʃ/ *n* interruttore *m*; (*change*) mutamento *m* ● *vt* cambiare; (*exchange*) scambiare ● *vi* cambiare; **~ to** passare a

■ **switch off** *vt* spegnere

■ **switch on** *vt* accendere

■ **switch over** *vi TV* cambiare [canale]; **~ over to** passare a

■ **switch round** *vt* (*change one for the other*) scambiare

switch: switchback *n* montagne *fpl* russe. **switchblade** *n* coltello *m* a scatto. **switchboard** *n* centralino *m*

switched line /swɪtʃt/ *n Teleph* linea *f* commutata

swither /ˈswɪðə(r)/ *vi* (*fam: hesitate*) tentennare

Switzerland /ˈswɪtsələnd/ *n* Svizzera *f*

swivel /ˈswɪvl/ *v* (*pt/pp* **swivelled**) ● *vt* girare ● *vi* girarsi

swizz /swɪz/ *n* (*fam: swindle*) fregatura *f*

swollen /ˈswəʊlən/ *see* **swell** ● *a* gonfio

swollen-headed /-ˈhedɪd/ *a* presuntuoso

swoon /swuːn/ *vi* svenire

swoop /swuːp/ *n* (*by police*) incursione *f* ● *vi* **~ [down]** ⟨*bird:*⟩ piombare; *fig* fare un'incursione

sword /sɔːd/ *n* spada *f*

swordfish /ˈsɔːdfɪʃ/ *n* pesce *m* spada *inv*

swore /swɔː(r)/ *see* **swear**

sworn /swɔːn/ *see* **swear**

sworn enemy *n* nemico *m* giurato

swot /swɒt/ *n fam* sgobbone, -a *mf* ● *vt* (*pt/pp* **swotted**) *fam* sgobbare (**for an exam** per un esame

swum /swʌm/ *see* **swim**

swung /swʌŋ/ *see* **swing**

sycamore /ˈsɪkəmɔː(r)/ *n* sicomoro *m*

sycophant /ˈsɪkəfænt/ *n* adulatore, -trice *mf*

sycophantic /sɪkəˈfæntɪk/ *a* adulatorio

syllable /ˈsɪləbl/ *n* sillaba *f*

syllabus /ˈsɪləbəs/ *n* programma *m* [dei corsi]

syllogism /ˈsɪlədʒɪzm/ *n* sillogismo *m*

sylph /sɪlf/ *n* silfide *f*

symbiosis /sɪmbaɪˈəʊsɪs/ *n* simbiosi *f* *inv*

symbiotic /sɪmbaɪˈɒtɪk/ *a* simbiotico

symbol /ˈsɪmbl/ *n* simbolo *m* (**of** di)

symbolic /sɪmˈbɒlɪk/ *a* simbolico

symbolically /sɪmˈbɒlɪklɪ/ *adv* simbolicamente

symbolism /ˈsɪmbəlɪzm/ *n* simbolismo *m*

symbolist /ˈsɪmbəlɪst/ *n* simbolista *mf*

symbolize /ˈsɪmbəlaɪz/ *vt* simboleggiare

symmetrical /sɪˈmetrɪkl/ *a* simmetrico

symmetrically /sɪˈmetrɪklɪ/ *adv* simmetricamente

symmetry /ˈsɪmətrɪ/ *n* simmetria *f*

sympathetic /sɪmpəˈθetɪk/ *a* (*understanding*) comprensivo; (*showing pity*) compassionevole

sympathetically /sɪmpəˈθetɪklɪ/ *adv* con comprensione/compassione

sympathize /ˈsɪmpəθaɪz/ *vi* capire; (*in grief*) solidarizzare; **~ with sb** capire qcno/ solidarizzare con qcno

sympathizer /ˈsɪmpəθaɪzə(r)/ *n Pol* simpatizzante *mf*

sympathy /ˈsɪmpəθɪ/ *n* comprensione *f*; (*pity*) compassione *f*; (*condolences*) condoglianze *fpl*; **in ~ with** ⟨*strike*⟩ per solidarietà con

symphonic /sɪmˈfɒnɪk/ *a* sinfonico

symphony /ˈsɪmfənɪ/ *n* sinfonia *f*

symptom /ˈsɪmptəm/ *n* sintomo *m*

symptomatic /sɪmptəˈmætɪk/ *a* sintomatico (**of** di)

synagogue /ˈsɪnəgɒg/ *n* sinagoga *f*

sync[h] /sɪŋk/ *n* sincronia *f*; **be out of ~** essere sfasato; **be in ~** essere in sincronia; **be in ~ with/out of ~ with** essere sincronizzato/sfasato rispetto a

synchronize /ˈsɪŋkrənaɪz/ *vt* sincronizzare

synchronous /ˈsɪŋkrənəs/ *a* sincrono

syndicate /ˈsɪndɪkət/ *n* gruppo *m*

syndrome /ˈsɪndrəʊm/ *n* sindrome *f*

synonym /ˈsɪnənɪm/ *n* sinonimo *m*

synonymous /sɪˈnɒnɪməs/ *a* sinonimo

synopsis /sɪˈnɒpsɪs/ *n* (*pl* **-opses** /sɪnˈɒpsiːz/) (*of opera, ballet*) trama *f*; (*of book*) riassunto *m*

syntactic[al] /sɪnˈtæktɪk[l]/ *a* sintattico

syntax /ˈsɪntæks/ *n* sintassi *f* *inv*

synthesis /ˈsɪnθəsɪs/ *n* (*pl* **-theses** /ˈsɪnθəsiːz/) sintesi *f* *inv*

synthesize /ˈsɪnθəsaɪz/ *vt* sintetizzare

synthesizer /ˈsɪnθəsaɪzə(r)/ *n Mus* sintetizzatore *m*

synthetic /sɪnˈθetɪk/ *a* sintetico ● *n* fibra *f* sintetica

syphilis /ˈsɪfɪlɪs/ *n* sifilide *f*

Syria /ˈsɪrɪə/ *n* Siria *f*

Syrian /ˈsɪrɪən/ *a & n* siriano, -a *mf*

syringe /sɪˈrɪndʒ/ *n* siringa *f* ● *vt* siringare

syrup /ˈsɪrəp/ *n* sciroppo *m*; *Br* tipo *m* di melassa

syrupy /ˈsɪrəpɪ/ *a* sciropposo

system /ˈsɪstəm/ *n* sistema *m*

systematic /sɪstəˈmætɪk/ *a* sistematico

systematically /sɪstəˈmætɪklɪ/ *adv* sistematicamente

systems: systems analysis *n* analisi *f* dei sistemi. **systems analyst** *n* analista *mf* programmatore, -trice *mf*. **systems design** *n* progettazione *f* di sistemi. **systems engineer** *n* sistemista *mf*

Tt

t, T /ti:/ n (letter) t, T f inv
tab /tæb/ n linguetta f; (with name) etichetta
f; **keep ~s on** fam sorvegliare; **pick up the
~** fam pagare il conto
tabby /'tæbɪ/ n gatto m tigrato
tab key n tasto m tabulatore
table /'teɪbl/ n tavolo m; (list) tavola f; **at
[the] ~** a tavola
table: ~ of contents tavola f delle materie
● vt proporre. **table-cloth** n tovaglia f. **table
lamp** n lampada f da tavolo. **table salt** n sale
m fine. **tablespoon** n cucchiaio m da tavola.
tablespoonful n cucchiaiata f
tablet /'tæblɪt/ n pastiglia f; (slab) lastra f; **~
of soap** saponetta f
table tennis n tennis m da tavolo; (everyday
level) ping pong m
tabloid /'tæblɔɪd/ n tabloid m inv; pej giornale m scandalistico
taboo /tə'bu:/ a tabù inv ● n tabù m inv
tabulate /'tæbjʊleɪt/ vt tabulare
tabulation /tæbjʊ'leɪʃn/ n (of data, results)
tabulazione f
tabulator /'tæbjʊleɪtə(r)/ n tabulatore m
tachometer /tæ'kɒmɪtə(r)/ n tachimetro m
tachograph /'tækəgrɑ:f/ n tachigrafo m
tacit /'tæsɪt/ a tacito
tacitly /'tæsɪtlɪ/ adv tacitamente
taciturn /'tæsɪtɜ:n/ a taciturno
tack /tæk/ n (nail) chiodino m; (stitch) imba-
stitura f; Naut virata f; fig linea f di condotta
● vt inchiodare; (sew) imbastire ● vi Naut virare
tackle /'tækl/ n (equipment) attrezzatura f;
(football etc) contrasto m, tackle m inv ● vt affrontare
tacky /'tækɪ/ a (paint) non ancora asciutto;
(glue) appiccicoso; fig pacchiano
tact /tækt/ n tatto m
tactful /'tæktfʊl/ a pieno di tatto; (remark)
delicato
tactfully /'tæktfʊlɪ/ adv con tatto
tactical /'tæktɪkl/ a tattico
tactically /'tæktɪklɪ/ adv tatticamente
tactician /tæk'tɪʃn/ n stratega mf
tactics /'tæktɪks/ npl tattica fsg
tactile /'tæktaɪl/ a tattile
tactless /'tæktlɪs/ a privo di tatto
tactlessly /'tæktlɪslɪ/ adv senza tatto
tactlessness /'tæktlɪsnɪs/ n mancanza f di
tatto; (of remark) indelicatezza f
tadpole /'tædpəʊl/ n girino m
taffeta /'tæfɪtə/ n taffettà m
tag[1] /tæg/ n (label) etichetta f ● vt (pt/pp
tagged) attaccare l'etichetta a

tag[2] n (game) acchiapparello m
■ **tag along** vi seguire passo passo
■ **tag on** vt (attach) aggiungere
tail /teɪl/ n coda f; **~s** pl (tailcoat) frac m inv
● vt (fam: follow) pedinare
■ **tail off** vi diminuire
tail: tailback n coda f. **tail-end** n parte f finale; (of train) coda f. **tail light** n fanalino m di
coda
tailor /'teɪlə(r)/ n sarto m ● vt **~ sth to sb's
needs** adattare qcsa alle esigenze di qcno
tailor-made a fatto su misura
tailspin /'teɪlspɪn/ n Aeron vite f di coda
tailwind /'teɪlwɪnd/ n vento m di coda
taint /teɪnt/ vt contaminare
take /teɪk/ n (Cinema) ripresa f ● v (pt took,
pp taken) ● vt prendere; (to a place) portare
⟨person, object⟩; (contain) contenere
⟨passengers etc⟩; (endure) sopportare;
(require) occorrere; (teach) insegnare; (study)
studiare ⟨subject⟩; fare ⟨exam, holiday,
photograph, walk, bath⟩; sentire ⟨pulse⟩; misurare ⟨sb's temperature⟩; **~ sth to the
cleaner's** portare qcsa in lavanderia; **~ sb
home** (by car) portare qcno a casa; **~ sb
prisoner** fare prigioniero qcno; **be ~n ill** am-
malarsi; **~ sth calmly** prendere con calma
qcsa; **~ the dog for a walk** portare a spasso
il cane; **~ one's time doing sth** fare qcsa
con calma; **this will only ~ a minute** ci vuole solo un minuto; **I ~ it that...** (assume) pre-
sumo che...; **~ it from me!** (believe me) dai
retta a me! ● vi ⟨plant:⟩ attecchire
■ **take aback** vt (surprise) cogliere di sorpresa
■ **take after** vt assomigliare a
■ **take against** vt (turn against) prendere
in antipatia
■ **take apart** vt (dismantle) smontare
■ **take away** vt (with one) portare via;
(remove) togliere; (subtract) sottrarre; **'to ~
away'** 'da asporto'
■ **take back** vt riprendere; ritirare
⟨statement⟩; (return) riportare [indietro]; **she
took him back** (as husband, boyfriend) lo ha
perdonato
■ **take down** vt prendere giù; (remove) tirare
giù; (write down) prendere nota di
■ **take in** vt (bring indoors) portare dentro;
(to one's home) ospitare; (understand) capire;
(deceive) ingannare; (garment); (make smaller)
(include) includere; vedere ⟨film etc⟩
■ **take off** vt togliersi ⟨clothes⟩; (deduct) togliere; (mimic) imitare; **~ time off** prendere
delle vacanze; **~ oneself off** andarsene ● vi

Aeron decollare; *(fam: leave)* andarsene; *(become successful)* decollare

■ **take on** *vt* farsi carico di; assumere ⟨*employee*⟩; *(as opponent)* prendersela con; ~ **it on oneself to do sth** arrogarsi il diritto di fare qcsa

■ **take out** *vt* portare fuori; togliere ⟨*word, stain*⟩; *(withdraw)* ritirare ⟨*money, books*⟩; ~ **out a subscription to sth** abbonarsi a qcsa; **she took a pen out of her pocket** ha preso una penna dalla tasca; **I'm taking my wife out tonight** esco con mia moglie stasera; ~ **sb out to dinner** portare a cena fuori qcno; **it'll ~ you out of yourself** *(take your mind off things)* servirà a distrarti; ~ **it out on sb** *fam* prendersela con qcno

■ **take over** *vt* assumere il controllo di ⟨*firm*⟩ ● *vi* ~ **over from sb** sostituire qcno; *(permanently)* succedere a qcno

■ **take to** *vt (as a habit)* darsi a; **I took to her** *(liked)* mi è piaciuta

■ **take up** *vt* portare su; accettare ⟨*offer*⟩; intraprendere ⟨*profession*⟩; dedicarsi a ⟨*hobby*⟩; prendere ⟨*time*⟩; occupare ⟨*space*⟩; tirare su ⟨*floor-boards*⟩; accorciare ⟨*dress*⟩; ~ **sth up with sb** discutere qcsa con qcno; ~ **sb up on sth** *(question further)* chiedere ulteriori chiarimenti a qcno su qcsa; **I'll ~ you up on your offer** *(accept)* accetto la tua offerta ● *vi* ~ **up with sb** legarsi a qcno

takeaway /'teɪkəweɪ/ *n (meal)* piatto *m* da asporto; *(restaurant)* ristorante *m che prepara piatti da asporto*

take-home pay *n* stipendio *m* netto

taken /'teɪkən/ *a* ⟨*room etc*⟩ occupato; **be very ~ with sb/sth** essere conquistato da qcno/qcsa

take: take-off *n Aeron* decollo *m.* **takeover** *n* rilevamento *m.* **takeover bid** *n* offerta *f* pubblica di acquisto

takings /'teɪkɪŋz/ *npl* incassi *mpl*

talcum /'tælkəm/ *n* ~ **[powder]** talco *m*

tale /teɪl/ *n* storia *f*; *pej* fandonia *f*; **tell ~s** fare la spia

talent /'tælənt/ *n* talento *m*

talent scout *n* talent scout *mf inv*

talented /'tæləntɪd/ *a* [ricco] di talento

talisman /'tælɪzmən/ *n* talismano *m*

talk /tɔːk/ *n* conversazione *f*; *(lecture)* conferenza *f*; *(gossip)* chiacchere *fpl*; **make small ~** parlare del più e del meno ● *vi* parlare ● *vt* parlare di ⟨*politics etc*⟩; ~ **sb into sth** convincere qcno di qcsa

■ **talk about** *vt* parlare di; ~ **about bad luck!** e quando si dice la sfortuna!

■ **talk back** *vi (reply defiantly)* rispondere

■ **talk down to** *vt (patronize)* parlare con condiscendenza a

■ **talk of** *vt* parlare di; ~**ing of food…** a proposito di mangiare…

■ **talk over** *vt* discutere

■ **talk to** *vt* parlare con; *(reprimand)* fare un discorsetto a; ~ **to oneself** parlare da solo

talkative /'tɔːkətɪv/ *a* loquace

talking head /'tɔːkɪŋ/ *n* mezzobusto *m*

talking-to *n* sgridata *f*

talk show *n* talk show *m inv*

tall /tɔːl/ *a* alto; **how ~ are you?** quanto sei alto?

tall: tallboy *n* cassettone *m.* ~ **order** *n* impresa *f* difficile. **tall story** *n* frottola *f*

tally /'tælɪ/ *n* conteggio *m*; **keep a ~ of** tenere il conto di ● *vi* coincidere

talon /'tælən/ *n* artiglio *m*

tambourine /tæmbə'riːn/ *n* tamburello *m*

tame /teɪm/ *a* ⟨*animal*⟩ domestico; *(dull)* insulso ● *vt* domare

tamely /'teɪmlɪ/ *adv* docilmente

tamer /'teɪmə(r)/ *n* domatore, -trice *mf*

tamper /'tæmpə(r)/ *vi* ~ **with** manomettere

tampon /'tæmpɒn/ *n* tampone *m*

tan /tæn/ *a* marrone rossiccio *inv* ● *n* marrone *m* rossiccio; *(from sun)* abbronzatura *f* ● *v* *(pt/pp* **tanned***)* ● *vt* conciare ⟨*hide*⟩ ● *vi* abbronzarsi

tandem /'tændəm/ *n* tandem *m inv*; **in ~** in tandem

tang /tæŋ/ *n* sapore *m* forte; *(smell)* odore *m* penetrante

tanga /'tæŋgə/ *n* tanga *m inv*

tangent /'tændʒənt/ *n* tangente *f*; **go off at a ~** *fam* partire per la tangente

tangerine /tændʒə'riːn/ *n (fruit)* tipo *m* di mandarino; *(colour)* arancione *m* ● *a* arancione

tangible /'tændʒəbl/ *a* tangibile

tangibly /'tændʒəblɪ/ *adv* tangibilmente

tangle /'tæŋgl/ *n* groviglio *m*; *(in hair)* nodo *m* ● *vt* ~ **[up]** aggrovigliare ● *vi* aggrovigliarsi

tango /'tæŋgəʊ/ *n* tango *m*

tangy /'tæŋɪ/ *a* forte; ⟨*smell*⟩ penetrante

tank /tæŋk/ *n* contenitore *m*; *(for petrol)* serbatoio *m*; *(fish ~)* acquario *m*; *Mil* carro *m* armato

tankard /'tæŋkəd/ *n* boccale *m*

tanker /'tæŋkə(r)/ *n* nave *f* cisterna; *(lorry)* autobotte *f*

tank top *n* canottiera *f*

tanned /tænd/ *a* abbronzato

tannin /'tænɪn/ *n* tannino *m*

Tannoy® /'tænɔɪ/ *n Br* sistema *m* di altoparlanti

tantalize /'tæntəlaɪz/ *vt* tormentare

tantalizing /'tæntəlaɪzɪŋ/ *a* allettante; ⟨*smell*⟩ stuzzicante

tantamount /'tæntəmaʊnt/ *a* ~ **to** equivalente a

tantrum /'tæntrəm/ *n* scoppio *m* d'ira; **throw a ~** fare i capricci

tap /tæp/ *n* rubinetto *m*; *(knock)* colpo *m*; **on ~** a disposizione ● *v (pt/pp* **tapped***)* ● *vt* dare un colpetto a; sfruttare ⟨*resources*⟩; mettere sotto controllo ⟨*telephone*⟩ ● *vi* picchiettare

tap-dance *n* tip tap *m* ● *vi* ballare il tip tap

tap-dancer *n* ballerino, -a *mf* di tip tap

tape /teɪp/ *n* nastro *m*; *(recording)* cassetta *f* ● *vt* legare con nastro; *(record)* registrare

tape: tape backup drive *n Comput* unità *f*

tape deck | team up

di backup a nastro. **tape deck** n piastra f.
tape-measure n metro m [a nastro]
taper /'teɪpə(r)/ n candela f sottile ● vi assottigliarsi
■ **taper off** vi assottigliarsi
tapered /'teɪpəd/ a ‹trousers› affusolato
tape-record vt registrare su nastro.
tape recorder n registratore m. **tape
recording** n registrazione f. **tape streamer**
n Comput unità f a nastro magnetico
tapestry /'tæpɪstrɪ/ n arazzo m
tapeworm /'teɪpwɜːm/ n verme m solitario,
tenia f
tapping /'tæpɪŋ/ n ‹noise› picchiettio m
tap water n acqua f del rubinetto
tar /tɑː(r)/ n catrame m ● vt ‹pt/pp tarred› in-
catramare
tardy /'tɑːdɪ/ a ‹-ier, -iest› tardivo
target /'tɑːgɪt/ n bersaglio m; fig obiettivo m
● vt stabilire come obiettivo ‹market›
target market n mercato m obiettivo
target practice n tiro m al bersaglio
tariff /'tærɪf/ n ‹price› tariffa f; ‹duty› dazio m
● a tariffario
Tarmac® /'tɑːmæk/ n macadam m al catrame
tarmac n asfalto m; ‹Br: of airfield› pista f
● attrib ‹road, footpath› asfaltato ● vt
asfaltare
tarnish /'tɑːnɪʃ/ vi ossidarsi ● vt ossidare;
fig macchiare
tarpaulin /tɑːˈpɔːlɪn/ n telone m impermeabile
tarragon /'tærəgən/ n dragoncello m
tart¹ /tɑːt/ a aspro; fig acido
tart² n crostata f; ‹individual› crostatina f;
‹sl: prostitute› donnaccia f
■ **tart up** vt fam ~ **oneself up** agghindarsi
tartan /'tɑːtn/ n tessuto m scozzese, tartan m
inv ● attrib di tessuto scozzese
tartar /'tɑːtə(r)/ n ‹on teeth› tartaro m
tartar sauce n salsa f tartara
task /tɑːsk/ n compito m; **take sb to ~** riprendere qcno
task force n Pol commissione f; Mil task-
force f inv
tassel /'tæsl/ n nappa f
taste /teɪst/ n gusto m; ‹sample› assaggio m;
get a ~ of sth fig assaporare il gusto di qcsa;
in good/bad ~ di buongusto/di cattivo gusto
● vt sentire il sapore di; ‹sample› assaggiare
● vi sapere ‹of di›; **it ~s lovely** è ottimo; ~
like sth sapere di qcsa
taste buds npl papille f pl gustative
tasteful /'teɪs(t)fʊl/ a di ‹buon› gusto
tastefully /'teɪs(t)fʊlɪ/ adv con gusto
tasteless /'teɪs(t)lɪs/ a senza gusto
tastelessly /'teɪs(t)lɪslɪ/ adv con cattivo gusto
taster /'teɪstə(r)/ n ‹foretaste› assaggio m;
‹person› assaggiatore, -trice mf
tasty /'teɪstɪ/ a ‹-ier, -iest› saporito
tat /tæt/ see **tit²**
tattered /'tætəd/ a cencioso; ‹pages› stracciato

tatters /'tætəz/ npl **in ~** a brandelli
tattle /'tætl/ vi spettegolare ● n pettegolezzo m
tattoo¹ /tæ'tuː/ n tatuaggio m ● vt tatuare
tattoo² n Mil parata f militare
tatty /'tætɪ/ a ‹-ier, -iest› ‹clothes, person›
trasandato; ‹book› malandato
taught /tɔːt/ see **teach**
taunt /tɔːnt/ n scherno m ● vt schernire
Taurus /'tɔːrəs/ n Astr Toro m
taut /tɔːt/ a teso
tauten /'tɔːtən/ vt tendere ● vi tendersi
tautology /tɔːˈtɒlədʒɪ/ n tautologia f
tavern /'tævən/ n liter taverna f
tawdry /'tɔːdrɪ/ a ‹-ier, -iest› pacchiano
tawny /'tɔːnɪ/ a fulvo
tax /tæks/ n tassa f; ‹on income› imposte f pl;
before ~ ‹price› tasse escluse; ‹salary› lordo
● vt tassare; fig mettere alla prova; ~ **with**
accusare di
taxable /'tæksəbl/ a tassabile; ~ **income**
reddito m imponibile
taxation /tæk'seɪʃn/ n tasse f pl; ~ **at
source** ritenuta f alla fonte
tax: tax allowance n detrazione f di imposta. **tax avoidance** n elusione f fiscale. **tax
bracket** n scaglione m d'imposta. **tax break**
n agevolazione f fiscale. **tax burden** n
aggravio m fiscale. **tax code** n codice m fiscale. **tax consultant** n fiscalista m. **tax-
deductible** a detraibile. **tax disc** n Auto bollo m. **tax evader** n evasore m fiscale. **tax
evasion** n evasione f fiscale. **tax-free** a esen-
tasse. **tax haven** n paradiso m fiscale. **tax
incentive** n incentivo m fiscale
taxi /'tæksɪ/ n taxi m inv ● vi ‹pt/pp taxied,
pres p taxiing› ‹aircraft:› rullare
taxi driver n tassista m f
taxing /'tæksɪŋ/ a ‹exhausting› sfiancante
taxi rank n posteggio m per taxi
taxman /'tæksmæn/ n **the ~** il fisco
tax: taxpayer n contribuente m f. **tax
rebate** n rimborso m d'imposta. **tax return**
n dichiarazione f dei redditi. **tax shelter** n
paradiso m fiscale. **tax system** n regime m
fiscale
TB n abbr ‹tuberculosis› TBC f
tbsp abbr ‹tablespoon›
tea /tiː/ n tè m inv
tea-bag n bustina f di tè
tea-break n intervallo m per il tè
teach /tiːtʃ/ vt/i ‹pt/pp taught› insegnare; ~
sb sth insegnare qcsa a qcno; ~ **sb a lesson**
fig dare una lezione a qcno
teacher /'tiːtʃə(r)/ n insegnante m f;
‹primary› maestro, -a m f
teaching /'tiːtʃɪŋ/ n insegnamento m
tea: teacloth n ‹for drying› asciugapiatti m
inv. **tea cosy** n copriteiera f. **teacup** n tazza f
da tè
teak /tiːk/ n tek m
tea leaves npl tè m inv sfuso; ‹when
infused› fondi mpl di tè
team /tiːm/ n squadra f; fig équipe f inv
■ **team up** vi unirsi

team: team captain n caposquadra mf.
team manager n direttore m sportivo.
team-mate n compagno m di squadra. **team
spirit** n spirito m di squadra. **teamwork** n
lavoro m di squadra; fig lavoro m d'équipe
teapot /'ti:pɒt/ n teiera f
tear[1] /teə(r)/ n strappo m ● v (pt **tore**, pp
torn) ● vt strappare; ~ **to pieces** or **shreds**
fare a pezzi; stroncare ⟨book, film⟩ ● vi strappare; ⟨material:⟩ strapparsi; (run) precipitarsi
  ■ **tear apart** vt (fig: criticize) fare a pezzi;
  (separate) dividere
  ■ **tear away** vt ~ **oneself away from** staccarsi da ⟨television⟩; abbandonare a malincuore ⟨party⟩
  ■ **tear into** vt fam (reprimand) attaccare duramente; (make a vigorous start on) dare dentro a
  ■ **tear open** vt aprire strappando
  ■ **tear out** vt staccare; ~ **one's hair out**
  mettersi le mani nei capelli
  ■ **tear up** vt strappare; rompere ⟨agreement⟩
tear[2] /tɪə(r)/ n lacrima f
tearaway /'teərəweɪ/ n giovane teppista mf
tearful /'tɪəfʊl/ a ⟨person⟩ in lacrime;
⟨farewell⟩ lacrimevole
tearfully /'tɪəfʊlɪ/ adv in lacrime
tear gas /'tɪə/ n gas m lacrimogeno
tearing /'teərɪŋ/ a **be in a ~ hurry** avere
una gran fretta
tear-jerker /'tɪədʒɜːkə(r)/ n fam **this film is
a real ~** è davvero un film strappalacrime
tease /ti:z/ vt prendere in giro ⟨person⟩; tormentare ⟨animal⟩
teasel /'ti:zl/ n Bot cardo m
teaset /'ti:set/ n servizio m da tè
tea shop n sala f da tè
teasing /'ti:zɪŋ/ a canzonatorio
tea: teaspoon n cucchiaino m [da tè].
teaspoon[ful] n cucchiaino m. **tea-strainer**
n colino m per il tè
teat /ti:t/ n capezzolo m; (on bottle) tettarella f
tea towel n strofinaccio m [per i piatti]
technical /'teknɪkl/ a tecnico
technicality /teknɪ'kælətɪ/ n tecnicismo m;
Jur cavillo m giuridico
technically /'teknɪklɪ/ adv tecnicamente;
(strictly) strettamente
technician /tek'nɪʃn/ n tecnico, -a mf
technique /tek'ni:k/ n tecnica f
technocrat /'teknəkræt/ n tecnocrate m
technological /teknə'lɒdʒɪkl/ a tecnologi-
co
technologically /teknə'lɒdʒɪklɪ/ adv tec-
nologicamente
technology /tek'nɒlədʒɪ/ n tecnologia f
teddy /'tedɪ/ n ~ **[bear]** orsacchiotto m
tedious /'ti:dɪəs/ a noioso
tedium /'ti:dɪəm/ n tedio m
tee /ti:/ n (Golf) tee m inv
teem /ti:m/ vi (rain) piovere a dirotto; **be
~ing with** (full of) pullulare di
teen /ti:n/ a ⟨fashion, idol⟩ degli adolescenti

teenage /'ti:neɪdʒ/ a per ragazzi; ~ **boy/girl**
adolescente mf
teenager /'ti:neɪdʒə(r)/ n adolescente mf
teens /ti:nz/ npl **the ~** l'adolescenza fsg; **be
in one's ~** essere adolescente
teeny /'ti:nɪ/ a fam (-ier, -iest) piccolissimo
teeny-weeny /'ti:nɪ'wi:nɪ/ a fam minuscolo
tee-shirt n T-shirt f inv, maglietta f [a maniche corte]
teeter /'ti:tə(r)/ vi barcollare
teeth /ti:θ/ see **tooth**
teethe /ti:ð/ vi mettere i primi dent
teething troubles /'ti:ðɪŋ/ npl fig difficoltà fpl iniziali
teetotal /ti:'təʊtl/ a astemio
teetotaller /ti:'təʊt(ə)lə(r)/ n astemio, -a mf
TEFL /'tefl/ n insegnamento m dell'inglese
come lingua straniera
telebanking /'telɪbæŋkɪŋ/ n servizi mpl
bancari telematici
telecast /'telɪkɑːst/ n trasmissione f televisiva ● vt far vedere in televisione
telecomms /'telɪkɒmz/ npl telecomunicazioni fpl
telecommunications /telɪkəmju:nɪ'keɪ-
ʃnz/ npl telecomunicazioni fpl
telecommuter /telɪkə'mju:tə(r)/ n persona
f che lavora da casa su computer
telecommuting /telɪkə'mju:tɪŋ/ n lavoro
m su computer da casa
teleconference /'telɪkɒnf(ə)r(ə)ns/ n videoconferenza f
telegenic /telɪ'dʒenɪk/ a telegenico
telegram /'telɪɡræm/ n telegramma m
telegraph /'telɪɡrɑːf/ n telegrafo m
telegraphic /telɪ'ɡræfɪk/ a telegrafico
telegraph pole n palo m del telegrafo
telematics /telɪ'mætɪks/ n telematica f
telemessage /'telɪmesɪdʒ/ n Br telegramma m
telepathic /telɪ'pæθɪk/ a telepatico
telepathy /tɪ'lepəθɪ/ n telepatia f; **by ~** per
telepatia
telephone /'telɪfəʊn/ n telefono m; **be on
the ~** avere il telefono; (be telephoning) essere al telefono ● vt telefonare a ● vi telefonare
**telephone: telephone answering ser-
vice** n segreteria f telefonica. **telephone
book** n elenco m telefonico. **telephone
booking** n prenotazione f telefonica.
telephone booth n, **telephone box** n cabina f telefonica. **telephone call** n telefonata f.
telephone conversation n conversazione f
telefonica. **telephone directory** n elenco m
telefonico. **telephone helpline** n servizio m
telefonico. **telephone message** n messaggio m telefonico. **telephone number** n numero m di telefono. **telephone tapping** n in-
tercettazione f telefonica
telephonist /tɪ'lefənɪst/ n telefonista mf
telephoto /telɪ'fəʊtəʊ/ a ~ **lens** tele-
obiettivo m
teleprinter /'telɪprɪntə(r)/ n telescrivente f

telerecording /'telɪkrɪkɔːdɪŋ/ n programma m [televisivo] registrato

telesales /'telɪseɪlz/ n vendita f per telefono

telescope /'telɪskəʊp/ n telescopio m

telescopic /telɪ'skɒpɪk/ a telescopico

teleshopping /'telɪʃɒpɪŋ/ n acquisti mpl per telefono

teletext /'telɪtekst/ n televideo m

telethon /'telɪθɒn/ n telethon m inv

televise /'telɪvaɪz/ vt trasmettere per televisione

television /'telɪvɪʒn/ n televisione f; **watch ~** guardare la televisione; **on ~** alla televisione

television: television channel n rete f televisiva. **television licence** n abbonamento m alla televisione. **television licence fee** n costo m dell'abbonamento alla televisione. **television programme** n programma m televisivo. **television screen** n teleschermo m. **television serial** n sceneggiato m. **television set** n televisore m

televisual /telɪ'vɪʒʊəl/ a televisivo

telex /'teleks/ n telex m inv ● vt mandare via telex ⟨message⟩; mandare un telex a ⟨person⟩

tell /tel/ vt (pt/pp told) dire; raccontare ⟨story⟩; (distinguish) distinguere (**from** da); **~ sb sth** dire qcsa a qcno; **~ sb to do sth** dire a qcno di fare qcsa; **~ the time** dire l'ora; **I couldn't ~ why...** non sapevo perché...; **you're ~ing me!** a chi lo dici! ● vi (produce an effect) avere effetto; **time will ~** il tempo ce lo dirà; **his age is beginning to ~** l'età comincia a farsi sentire [per lui]; **don't ~ me** non dirmelo; **you mustn't ~** non devi dire niente

■ **tell apart** vt distinguere

■ **tell off** vt sgridare

■ **tell on** vt (Sch: inform against) fare la spia a

teller /'telə(r)/ n (in bank) cassiere, -a mf

telling /'telɪŋ/ a significativo; ⟨argument⟩ efficace

telling-off n cicchetto m

tell-tale n spione, -a mf ● a rivelatore

telly /'telɪ/ n fam tv f inv, tele f inv

temerity /tɪ'merətɪ/ n audacia f

temp /temp/ fam n impiegato, -a mf temporaneo, -a ● vi lavorare come impiegato, -a temporaneo, -a

temper /'tempə(r)/ n (disposition) carattere m; (mood) umore m; (anger) collera f; **lose one's ~** arrabbiarsi; **be in a ~** essere arrabbiato; **keep one's ~** mantenere la calma ● vt fig temperare

temperament /'temprəmənt/ n temperamento m

temperamental /temprə'mentl/ a (moody) capriccioso

temperamentally /temprə'mentəlɪ/ adv **they are ~ unsuited** tra loro c'è incompatibilità di carattere

temperance /'tempərəns/ n (abstinence) astinenza f dal bere

temperate /'tempərət/ a ⟨climate⟩ temperato

temperature /'temprətʃə(r)/ n temperatura f; **have** or **run a ~** avere la febbre

tempest /'tempɪst/ n tempesta f

tempestuous /tem'pestjʊəs/ a tempestoso

template /'templɪt/ n sagoma f

temple¹ /'templ/ n tempio m

temple² n Anat tempia f

tempo /'tempəʊ/ n ritmo m; Mus tempo m

temporal /'tempər(ə)l/ a temporale

temporarily /tempə'rerɪlɪ/ adv temporaneamente; ⟨introduced, erected⟩ provvisoriamente

temporary /'tempərərɪ/ a temporaneo; ⟨measure, building⟩ provvisorio

tempt /tempt/ vt tentare; sfidare ⟨fate⟩; **~ sb to** indurre qcno a; **be ~ed** essere tentato (**to** di); **I am ~ed by the offer** l'offerta mi tenta

temptation /temp'teɪʃn/ n tentazione f

tempting /'temptɪŋ/ a allettante; ⟨food, drink⟩ invitante

temptress /'temptrɪs/ n seduttrice f

ten /ten/ a & n dieci m; **the T~ Commandments** i Dieci Comandamenti

tenable /'tenəbl/ a fig sostenibile

tenacious /tɪ'neɪʃəs/ a tenace

tenacity /tɪ'næsətɪ/ n tenacia f

tenant /'tenənt/ n inquilino, -a mf; Comm locatario, -a mf

tend¹ /tend/ vt (look after) prendersi cura di

tend² vi **~ to do sth** tendere a far qcsa

tendency /'tendənsɪ/ n tendenza f

tendentious /ten'denʃəs/ a tendenzioso

tender¹ /'tendə(r)/ n Comm offerta f; **put out to ~** dare in appalto; **be legal ~** avere corso legale ● vt offrire; presentare ⟨resignation⟩

tender² a tenero; (painful) dolorante

tender-hearted /-hɑːtɪd/ a dal cuore tenero

tenderize /'tendəraɪz/ vt rendere tenero ⟨meat⟩

tenderly /'tendəlɪ/ adv teneramente

tenderness /'tendənɪs/ n tenerezza f; (painfulness) dolore m

tendon /'tendən/ n tendine m

tendril /'tendrɪl/ n (of plant) viticcio m

tenement /'tenəmənt/ n casamento m

tenet /'tenɪt/ n principio m

tenner /'tenə(r)/ n fam biglietto m da dieci sterline

tennis /'tenɪs/ n tennis m

tennis: tennis ball n palla f da tennis. **tennis-court** n campo m da tennis. **tennis match** n partita f di tennis. **tennis player** n tennista mf. **tennis racket** n racchetta f da tennis. **tennis shoes** npl scarpe fpl da tennis

tenor /'tenə(r)/ n tenore m

tense¹ /tens/ n Gram tempo m

tense² a teso ● vt tendere ⟨muscle⟩

■ **tense up** vi tendersi

tension /'tenʃn/ n tensione f

tent /tent/ n tenda f

tentacle /'tentəkl/ n tentacolo m

tentative /'tentətɪv/ *a* provvisorio; ⟨smile, gesture⟩ esitante

tentatively /'tentətɪvlɪ/ *adv* timidamente; ⟨accept⟩ provvisoriamente

tent city *n* tendopoli *f inv*

tenterhooks /'tentəhʊks/ *npl* **be on ~** essere sulle spine

tenth /tenθ/ *a & n* decimo, -a *mf*

tenuous /'tenjʊəs/ *a fig* debole

tenure /'tenjə/ *n* ⟨period of office⟩ permanenza *f* in carica; ⟨Univ: job security⟩ ruolo *m*; ⟨of land, property⟩ possesso *m*; **security of ~** ⟨of land, property⟩ diritto *m* di possesso

tepid /'tepɪd/ *a* tiepido

tercentenary /tɜ:sen'ti:nərɪ/ *n* terzo centenario *m*

term /tɜ:m/ *n* periodo *m*; *Sch Univ* trimestre *m*; ⟨in Italy⟩ *Sch* quadrimestre *m*; *Univ* semestre *m*; ⟨expression⟩ termine *m*; **~s** *pl* ⟨conditions⟩ condizioni *fpl*; **~ of office** carica *f*; **in the short/long ~** a breve/lungo termine; **be on good/bad ~s** essere in buoni/cattivi rapporti; **come to ~s with** accettare ⟨past, fact⟩; **easy ~s** facilità *fpl* di pagamento; **~s of reference** *pl* ⟨of committee⟩ competenze *fpl*

terminal /'tɜ:mɪnl/ *a* finale; *Med* terminale ● *n Aeron* terminal *m inv*; *Rail* stazione *f* di testa; ⟨of bus⟩ capolinea *m*; ⟨on battery⟩ morsetto *m*; *Comput* terminale *m*

terminally /'tɜ:mɪnəlɪ/ *adv* **be ~ ill** essere in fase terminale

terminate /'tɜ:mɪneɪt/ *vt* terminare; rescindere ⟨contract⟩; interrompere ⟨pregnancy⟩ ● *vi* terminare; **~ in** finire in

termination /tɜ:mɪ'neɪʃn/ *n* termine *m*; *Med* interruzione *f* di gravidanza

terminologist /tɜ:mɪ'nɒlədʒɪst/ *n* linguista *mf* specializzato, -a in terminologia

terminology /tɜ:mɪ'nɒlədʒɪ/ *n* terminologia *f*

terminus /'tɜ:mɪnəs/ *n* (*pl* **-ni** /'tɜ:mɪnaɪ/) ⟨for bus⟩ capolinea *m*; ⟨for train⟩ stazione *f* di testa

term-time *n* **during ~** durante il trimestre

terrace /'terəs/ *n* terrazza *f*; ⟨houses⟩ fila *f* di case a schiera; **the ~s** *pl Sport* le gradinate

terraced house /'terəsd/ *n* casa *f* a schiera

terracotta /terə'kɒtə/ *n* ⟨earthenware⟩ terracotta *f*; ⟨colour⟩ color *m* terracotta

terrain /te'reɪn/ *n* terreno *m*

terrestrial /tɪ'restrɪəl/ *n* terrestre *mf* ● *a* terrestre; **~ television** televisione *f* terrestre

terrible /'terəbl/ *a* terribile

terribly /'terəblɪ/ *adv* terribilmente; **I'm ~ sorry** sono infinitamente spiacente

terrier /'terɪə(r)/ *n* terrier *m inv*

terrific /tə'rɪfɪk/ *a fam* ⟨excellent⟩ fantastico; ⟨huge⟩ enorme

terrifically /tə'rɪfɪklɪ/ *adv fam* terribilmente

terrify /'terɪfaɪ/ *vt* (*pt/pp* **-ied**) atterrire; **be terrified** essere terrorizzato

terrifying /'terɪfaɪɪŋ/ *a* terrificante

territorial /terɪ'tɔ:rɪəl/ *a* territoriale

territorial waters /wɔ:təz/ *npl* acque *fpl* territoriali

territory /'terɪtərɪ/ *n* territorio *m*

terror /'terə(r)/ *n* terrore *m*

terrorism /'terərɪzm/ *n* terrorismo *m*

terrorist /'terərɪst/ *n* terrorista *mf*

terrorize /'terəraɪz/ *vt* terrorizzare

terror-stricken *a* terrorizzato

terry towelling /terɪ'taʊəlɪŋ/ *n* tessuto *m* di spugna

terse /tɜ:s/ *a* conciso

tersely /'tɜ:slɪ/ *adv* concisamente

tertiary /'tɜ:ʃ(ə)rɪ/ *a* ⟨era, industry, sector⟩ terziario; ⟨education, college⟩ superiore

Terylene® /'terɪli:n/ *n* terilene® *m*

test /test/ *n* esame *m*; ⟨in laboratory⟩ esperimento *m*; ⟨of friendship, machine⟩ prova *f*; ⟨of intelligence, aptitude⟩ test *m inv*; **put to the ~** mettere alla prova; **pass one's ~** *Auto* passare l'esame di guida ● *vt* esaminare; provare ⟨machine⟩

testament /'testəmənt/ *n* testamento *m*; **Old/New T~** Antico/Nuovo Testamento *m*

test-drive *vt* ⟨manufacturer:⟩ collaudare; ⟨buyer:⟩ provare ● *n* collaudo *m*; prova *f*

tester /'testə(r)/ *n* ⟨person⟩ collaudatore, -trice *mf*; ⟨device⟩ tester *m inv*; ⟨sample: of make-up, perfume⟩ campione *m*

testicle /'testɪkl/ *n* testicolo *m*

testify /'testɪfaɪ/ *vt/i* (*pt/pp* **-ied**) testimoniare

testily /'testɪlɪ/ *adv* ⟨say, reply⟩ in modo scontroso

testimonial /testɪ'məʊnɪəl/ *n* lettera *f* di referenze

testimony /'testɪmənɪ/ *n* testimonianza *f*

test market *n* mercato *m* di prova

test match *n* partita *f* internazionale

testosterone /tes'tɒstərəʊn/ *n* testosterone *m*

test: test pilot *n* pilota *mf* collaudatore, -trice. **test tube** *n* provetta *f*. **test tube baby** *n fam* bambino, -a *mf* in provetta

testy /'testɪ/ *a* irascibile

tetanus /'tetənəs/ *n* tetano *m*

tetanus injection *n* antitetanica *f*

tetchy /'tetʃɪ/ *a* facilmente irritabile

tether /'teðə(r)/ *n* **be at the end of one's ~** non poterne più ● *vt* legare

Teutonic /tju:'tɒnɪk/ *a* teutonico

text /tekst/ *n* testo *m*

textbook /'tekstbʊk/ *n* manuale *m*

textile /'tekstaɪl/ *a* tessile ● *n* stoffa *f*

textual /'tekstjʊəl/ *a* testuale

texture /'tekstʃə(r)/ *n* ⟨of skin⟩ grana *f*; ⟨of food⟩ consistenza *f*; **of a smooth ~** ⟨to the touch⟩ soffice al tatto

Thai /taɪ/ *a & n* tailandese *mf*; ⟨language⟩ tailandese *m*

Thailand /'taɪlænd/ *n* Tailandia *f*

Thames /temz/ *n* Tamigi *m*

than /ðən/ *accentato* /ðæn/ *conj* che; ⟨with numbers, names⟩ di; **older ~ me** più vecchio di me

thank /θæŋk/ *vt* ringraziare; **~ you [very much]** grazie [mille]

thankful /'θæŋkfʊl/ a grato
thankfully /'θæŋkfʊlɪ/ adv con gratitudine; (happily) fortunatamente
thankless /'θæŋklɪs/ a ingrato
thanks /θæŋks/ npl ringraziamenti mpl; ~! fam grazie!; ~ to grazie a; no ~ to you! non certo grazie a te!
thank-you letter n lettera f di ringraziamento
that /ðæt/ a & pron (pl those) quel, quei pl; (before s + consonant, gn, ps, z) quello, quegli pl; (before vowel) quell' mf, quegli mpl, quelle fpl; ~ **shop** quel negozio; **those shops** quei negozi; ~ **mirror** quello specchio; ~ **man/woman** quell'uomo/quella donna; **those men/women** quegli uomini/quelle donne; ~ **one** quello; **I don't like those** quelli non mi piacciono; ~ **is** cioè; **is** ~ **you?** sei tu?; **who is** ~? chi è?; **what did you do after** ~? cosa hai fatto dopo?; **like** ~ in questo modo, così; **a man like** ~ un uomo così; ~ **is why** ecco perché; ~ **is the reason she gave me** questa è la ragione che mi ha dato; ~ **is the easiest thing to do** è la cosa più facile da fare; ~**'s it!** (you've understood) ecco!; (I've finished) ecco fatto!; (I've had enough) basta così!; (there's nothing more) tutto qui!; ~**'s** ~! (with job) ecco fatto!; (with relationship) è tutto finito!; **and** ~**'s** ~! punto e basta! ● adv così; **it wasn't** ~ **good** non era poi così buono ● rel pron che; **the man** ~ **I spoke to** l'uomo con cui ho parlato; **the day** ~ **I saw him** il giorno in cui l'ho visto; **all** ~ **I know** tutto quello che so ● conj che; **I think** ~... penso che...
thatch /θætʃ/ n tetto m di paglia
thatched /θætʃt/ a coperto di paglia
thaw /θɔː/ n disgelo m ● vt fare scongelare ⟨food⟩ ● vi ⟨food:⟩ scongelarsi; **it's** ~**ing** sta sgelando
the /ðə/ di fronte a una vocale /ðiː/ def art il m, la f; i mpl, le fpl; (before s + consonant, gn, ps, z) lo m, gli mpl; (before vowel) l'mf, gli mpl, le fpl; **at** ~ **cinema/station** al cinema/alla stazione; **from** ~ **cinema/station** dal cinema/dalla stazione ● adv ~ **more** ~ **better** più ce n'è meglio è; (with reference to pl) più ce ne sono, meglio è; **all** ~ **better** tanto meglio
theatre /'θɪətə(r)/ n teatro m; Med sala f operatoria
theatregoer /'θiːətəgəʊə(r)/ n persona f che va a teatro
theatregoing /'θiːətəgəʊɪŋ/ n l'andare m a teatro
theatrical /θɪ'ætrɪkl/ a teatrale; (showy) melodrammatico
theft /θeft/ n furto m
theft-proof a antiscippo
their /ðeə/ poss a il loro m, la loro f, i loro mpl, le loro fpl; ~ **mother/father** la loro madre/il loro padre
theirs /ðeəz/ poss pron il loro m, la loro f, i loro mpl, le loro fpl; **a friend of** ~ un loro amico; **friends of** ~ dei loro amici; **those are** ~ quelli sono loro; (as opposed to ours) quelli sono i loro

them /ðem/ pers pron (direct object) li m, le f; (indirect object) gli, loro fml; (after prep: with people) loro; (after preposition: with things) essi; **we haven't seen** ~ non li/le abbiamo visti/viste; **give** ~ **the money** dai loro or dagli i soldi; **give it to** ~ daglielo; **I've spoken to** ~ ho parlato con loro; **it's** ~ sono loro
theme /θiːm/ n tema m
theme: **theme park** n parco m a tema.
theme song n motivo m conduttore
themselves /ðem'selvz/ pron (reflexive) sì; (emphatic) se stessi; **they poured** ~ **a drink** si sono versati da bere; **they said so** ~ lo hanno detto loro stessi; **they kept it to** ~ se lo sono tenuti per sé; **by** ~ da soli
then /ðen/ adv allora; (next) poi; **by** ~ (in the past) ormai; (in the future) per allora; **since** ~ sin da allora; **before** ~ prima di allora; **from** ~ **on** da allora in poi; **now and** ~ ogni tanto; **there and** ~ all'istante ● a di allora
thence /ðens/ adv (from there) di là; (therefore) perciò
theologian /θɪə'ləʊdʒɪən/ n teologo, -a mf
theological /θɪə'lɒdʒɪkl/ a teologico
theology /θɪ'ɒlədʒɪ/ n teologia f
theorem /'θɪərəm/ n teorema m
theoretical /θɪə'retɪkl/ a teorico
theoretically /θɪə'retɪklɪ/ adv teoricamente
theorist /'θɪərɪst/ n teorico m
theorize /'θɪəraɪz/ vi teorizzare
theory /'θɪərɪ/ n teoria f; **in** ~ in teoria
therapeutic /θerə'pjuːtɪk/ a terapeutico
therapist /'θerəpɪst/ n terapista mf
therapy /'θerəpɪ/ n terapia f
there /ðeə(r)/ adv là, lì; **down/up** ~ laggiù/lassù; ~ **is/are** c'è/ci sono; ~ **he/she is** eccolo/eccola ● int ~, ~! dai, su!
there: **thereabouts** adv [or] ~**abouts** (roughly) all'incirca. **thereafter** adv dopo di che. **thereby** adv in tal modo. **therefore** /'ðeəfɔː(r)/ adv perciò. **therein** adv ~ **lies...** in ciò risiede...; **contained** ~ (Jur: in contract) contenuto nello stesso
thermal /'θɜːml/ a termico; ⟨treatment⟩ termale
thermal: **thermal paper** n carta f termica. **thermal printer** n stampante f termica. **thermal underwear** n biancheria f che mantiene la temperatura corporea
thermometer /θə'mɒmɪtə(r)/ n termometro m
Thermos® /'θɜːməs/ n ~ [**flask**] termos m inv
thermostat /'θɜːməstæt/ n termostato m
thesaurus /θɪ'sɔːrəs/ n (of particular field) dizionario m specialistico; (of synonyms) dizionario m dei sinonimi
these /ðiːz/ see **this**
thesis /'θiːsɪs/ n (pl -ses /-siːz/) tesi f inv
they /ðeɪ/ pers pron loro; ~ **are tired** sono stanchi; **we're going, but** ~ **are not** noi andiamo, ma loro no; ~ **say** (generalizing) si dice; ~ **are building a new road** stanno costruendo una nuova strada
thick /θɪk/ a spesso; ⟨forest⟩ fitto; ⟨liquid⟩

denso; ‹*hair*› folto; (*fam: stupid*) ottuso; (*fam: close*) molto unito; **be 5 mm ~** essere 5 mm di spessore; **give sb a ~ ear** *fam* dare uno schiaffone a qcno ● *adv* densamente ● *n* **in the ~ of** nel mezzo di

thicken /'θɪkn/ *vt* ispessire ‹*sauce*› ● *vi* ispessirsi; ‹*fog*:› infittirsi

thicket /'θɪkɪt/ *n* boscaglia *f*

thickhead /'θɪkhed/ *n fam* zuccone *mf*

thickie /'θɪkɪ/ *n fam* zucca *f* vuota

thickly /'θɪklɪ/ *adv* densamente; ‹*cut*› a fette spesse

thickness /'θɪknɪs/ *n* spessore *m*

thicko /'θɪkəʊ/ *n fam* zucca *f* vuota

thickset /'θɪkset/ *a* tozzo

thick-skinned /-'skɪnd/ *a fam* insensibile

thief /θi:f/ *n* (*pl* **thieves**) ladro, -a *mf*

thieving /'θi:vɪŋ/ *a* ladro ● *n* furti *mpl*

thigh /θaɪ/ *n* coscia *f*

thimble /'θɪmbl/ *n* ditale *m*

thimbleful /'θɪmbəlfʊl/ *n* (*of wine etc*) goccino *m*

thin /θɪn/ *a* (**thinner, thinnest**) sottile; ‹*shoes, sweater*› leggero; ‹*liquid*› liquido; ‹*person*› magro; ‹*fig: excuse, plot*› inconsistente; **be [going] ~ on top** (*be going bald*) perdere i capelli; **vanish into ~ air** volatilizzarsi ● *adv* = **thinly** ● *v* (*pt/pp* **thinned**) ● *vt* diluire ‹*liquid*› ● *vi* diradarsi

■ **thin down** *vt* diluire ‹*paint etc*› ● *vi* (*become slimmer*) dimagrire

■ **thin out** *vi* diradarsi

thing /θɪŋ/ *n* cosa *f*; **~s** *pl* (*belongings*) roba *fsg*; **for one ~** in primo luogo; **the right ~** la cosa giusta; **just the ~!** proprio quel che ci vuole!; **how are ~s?** come vanno le cose?; **the latest ~** *fam* l'ultima cosa; **the best ~ would be** la cosa migliore sarebbe; **poor ~!** poveretto!; **have a ~ about** (*be frightened of*) aver la fobia di; (*be attracted to*) avere un debole per

thingumabob /'θɪŋəməbɒb/ *n fam* coso *m*

thingumajig /'θɪŋəmədʒɪg/ *n fam* coso *m*

think /θɪŋk/ *vt/i* (*pt/pp* **thought**) pensare; (*believe*) credere; **I ~ so** credo di sì; **what do you ~?** (*what is your opinion?*) cosa ne pensi?; **~ of/about** pensare a; **what do you ~ of it?** cosa ne pensi di questo?; **~ of doing sth** pensare di fare qcsa; **~ better of it** ripensarci; **~ for oneself** pensare con la propria testa

■ **think again** *vi* pensarci su; **you can ~ again!** sei matto!

■ **think ahead** *vi* pensare al futuro; **~ ahead to sth** pensare in anticipo a qcsa

■ **think back** *vi* **~ back to sth** ripensare a qcsa

■ **think out** *vt* mettere a punto ‹*strategy*›

■ **think over** *vt* riflettere su

■ **think through** *vt* riflettere bene su ‹*problem*›

■ **think up** *vt* escogitare; trovare ‹*name*›

thinker /'θɪŋkə(r)/ *n* pensatore, -trice *mf*

thinking /'θɪŋkɪŋ/ *n* (*opinion*) opinione *f*

think-tank *n* gruppo *m* d'esperti

thinly /'θɪnlɪ/ *adv* ‹*populated*› scarsamente; ‹*disguised*› leggermente; ‹*cut*› a fette sottili

thinness /'θɪnnɪs/ *n* (*of person*) magrezza *f*; (*of material*) finezza *f*

thin-skinned /-'skɪnd/ *a* (*sensitive*) permaloso

third /θɜ:d/ *a & n* terzo, -a *mf*

third degree *n* **give sb the ~ ~** fare il terzo grado a qcno

third-degree burns *npl* ustioni *fpl* di terzo grado

thirdly /'θɜ:dlɪ/ *adv* terzo

third: **third party** *n* (*in insurance, law*) terzi *mpl*. **third-party insurance** *n* assicurazione *f* contro terzi. **third person** *n* terzo *m*. **third-rate** *a* scadente. **Third World** *n* Terzo Mondo *m*

thirst /θɜ:st/ *n* sete *f*

thirstily /'θɜ:stɪlɪ/ *adv* con sete

thirsty /'θɜ:stɪ/ *a* assetato; **be ~** aver sete

thirteen /θɜ:'ti:n/ *a & n* tredici *m*

thirteenth /θɜ:'ti:nθ/ *a & n* tredicesimo, -a *mf*

thirtieth /'θɜ:tɪɪθ/ *a & n* trentesimo, -a *mf*

thirty /'θɜ:tɪ/ *a & n* trenta *m*

this /ðɪs/ *a* (*pl* **these**) questo; **~ man/woman** quest'uomo/questa donna; **these men/women** questi uomini/queste donne; **~ one** questo; **~ evening/morning** stamattina/stasera ● *pron* (*pl* **these**) questo; **we talked about ~ and that** abbiamo parlato del più e del meno; **like ~** così; **~ is Peter** questo è Peter; *Teleph* sono Peter; **who is ~?** chi è?; *Teleph* chi parla?; **~ is the happiest day of my life** è il giorno più felice della mia vita ● *adv* così; **~ big** così grande

thistle /'θɪsl/ *n* cardo *m*

thong /θɒŋ/ *n* (*on whip*) cinghia *f*; (*on shoe, garment*) laccetto *m*; (*underwear*) cache-sexe *m inv*; **~s** (*pl: sandals*) infradito *mpl* or *fpl*

thorn /θɔ:n/ *n* spina *f*

thorny /'θɔ:nɪ/ *a* spinoso

thorough /'θʌrə/ *a* completo; ‹*knowledge*› profondo; ‹*clean, search, training*› a fondo; ‹*person*› scrupoloso

thorough: **thoroughbred** *n* purosangue *m inv*. **thoroughfare** *n* via *f* principale; **'no ~'** 'strada non transitabile '

thoroughly /'θʌrəlɪ/ *adv* ‹*clean, search, know sth*› a fondo; (*extremely*) estremamente

thoroughness /'θʌrənɪs/ *n* completezza *f*

those /ðəʊz/ *see* **that**

though /ðəʊ/ *conj* sebbene; **as ~** come se ● *adv fam* tuttavia

thought /θɔ:t/ *see* **think** ● *n* pensiero *m*; (*idea*) idea *f*; **I've given this some ~** ci ho pensato su

thoughtful /'θɔ:tfʊl/ *a* pensieroso; (*considerate*) premuroso

thoughtfully /'θɔ:tfʊlɪ/ *adv* pensierosamente; (*considerately*) premurosamente

thoughtfulness /'θɔ:tfʊlnɪs/ *n* (*kindness*) considerazione *f*

thoughtless /'θɔ:tlɪs/ *a* (*inconsiderate*) sconsiderato

thoughtlessness /'θɔ:tlısnıs/ *n* sconsideratezza *f*

thoughtlessly /'θɔ:tlıslı/ *adv* con noncuranza

thought-provoking *a* ‹*book, film etc*› che fa riflettere

thousand /'θaʊznd/ *a* one/a ~ mille *m inv* ● *n* mille *m inv*; ~s of migliaia *fpl* di

thousandth /'θaʊzndθ/ *a & n* millesimo

thrash /θræʃ/ *vt* picchiare; (*defeat*) sconfiggere

■ **thrash about** *vi* dibattersi

■ **thrash out** *vt* mettere a punto

thrashing /'θræʃıŋ/ *n* (*defeat*) sconfitta *f*; **give sb a** ~ (*beating*) picchiare qcno

thread /θred/ *n* filo *m*; (*of screw*) filetto *m* ● *vt* infilare ‹*beads*›; ~ one's way through farsi strada fra

threadbare /'θredbeə/ *a* logoro

threat /θret/ *n* minaccia *f*

threaten /'θretn/ *vt* minacciare (**to do** di fare)● *vi fig* incalzare

threatening /'θretnıŋ/ *a* minaccioso; ‹*sky, atmosphere*› sinistro

threateningly /'θretnıŋlı/ *adv* minacciosamente

three /θri:/ *a & n* tre *m*

three-dimensional /-daı'menʃ(ə)nəl/ *a* tridimensionale

threefold /'θri:fəʊld/ *a & adv* triplo

three: three-legged /-'legıd/ *a* con tre gambe. **three-piece suit** *n* vestito *m* da uomo con panciotto. **three-piece suite** *n* insieme *m* di divano e due poltrone coordinati. **three-quarter length** *a* ‹*portrait*› di tre quarti; ‹*sleeve*› a tre quarti. **three-quarters** *adv* ‹*empty, full, done*› per tre quarti

threesome /'θri:səm/ *n* trio *m*

three-wheeler /-'wi:lə(r)/ *n* (*car*) auto *f inv* a tre ruote

thresh /θreʃ/ *vt* trebbiare

threshold /'θreʃəʊld/ *n* soglia *f*

threw /θru:/ *see* **throw**

thrift /θrıft/ *n* economia *f*

thrifty /'θrıftı/ *a* parsimonioso

thrill /θrıl/ *n* emozione *f*; (*of fear*) brivido *m* ● *vt* entusiasmare; **be ~ed with** essere entusiasta di

thriller /'θrılə(r)/ *n* (*book*) [romanzo *m*] giallo *m*; (*film*) [film *m inv*] giallo *m*

thrilling /'θrılıŋ/ *a* eccitante

thrive /θraıv/ *vi* (*pt* thrived *or* throve, *pp* thrived) ‹*business:*› prosperare; ‹*child, plant:*› crescere bene; **I ~ on pressure** mi piace essere sotto tensione

thriving /'θraıvıŋ/ *a* fiorente

throat /θrəʊt/ *n* gola *f*; **sore** ~ mal *m* di gola

throaty /'θrəʊtı/ *a* (*husky*) roco; (*fam: with sore throat*) rauco

throb /θrɒb/ *n* pulsazione *f*; (*of heart*) battito *m* ● *vi* (*pt/pp* throbbed) (*vibrate*) pulsare; ‹*heart:*› battere

throes /θrəʊz/ *npl* **in the** ~ **of** *fig* alle prese con

thrombosis /θrɒm'bəʊsıs/ *n* trombosi *f*

throne /θrəʊn/ *n* trono *m*

throng /θrɒŋ/ *n* calca *f*

throttle /'θrɒtl/ *n* (*on motorbike*) manopola *f* di accelerazione ● *vt* strozzare

through /θru:/ *prep* attraverso; (*during*) durante; (*by means of*) tramite; (*thanks to*) grazie a; **Saturday** ~ **Tuesday** *Am* da sabato a martedì incluso ● *adv* attraverso; ~ **and** ~ fino in fondo; **wet** ~ completamente bagnato; **read sth** ~ dare una lettura a qcsa; **let** ~ lasciar passare ‹*sb*› ● *a* ‹*train*› diretto; **be** ~ (*finished*) aver finito; *Teleph* avere la comunicazione

throughout /θru:'aʊt/ *prep* per tutto ● *adv* completamente; (*time*) per tutto il tempo

throve /θrəʊv/ *see* **thrive**

throw /θrəʊ/ *n* tiro *m* ● *vt* (*pt* threw, *pp* thrown) lanciare; (*throw away*) gettare; azionare ‹*switch*›; disarcionare ‹*rider*›; (*fam: disconcert*) disorientare; *fam* dare ‹*party*›

■ **throw about** *vt* spargere; ~ one's money about sbandierare i propri soldi

■ **throw away** *vt* gettare via

■ **throw in** *vt* (*include at no extra cost*) aggiungere [gratuitamente]; (*in football*) rimettere in gioco; ~ **the towel** *or* **the sponge** *fig* abbandonare il campo

■ **throw off** *vt* seminare ‹*pursuers*›; liberarsi di ‹*cold, infection etc*›

■ **throw together** *vt* (*assemble hastily*) mettere insieme; improvvisare ‹*meal*›; (*bring into contact*) fare incontrare

■ **throw out** *vt* gettare via; rigettare ‹*plan*›; buttare fuori ‹*person*›

■ **throw up** *vt* alzare ● *vi* (*vomit*) vomitare

throw: throwaway *a* ‹*remark*› buttato lì; ‹*paper cup*› usa e getta *inv*. **throwback** *n Biol* atavismo *m*; *fig* regressione *f*. **throw-in** *n Sport* rimessa *f* laterale

thrush /θrʌʃ/ *n* tordo *m*; *Med* mughetto *m*; (*in woman*) candida *f*

thrust /θrʌst/ *n* spinta *f*● *vt* (*pt/pp* thrust) (*push*) spingere; (*insert*) conficcare; ~ [up]on imporre a

thud /θʌd/ *n* tonfo *m*

thug /θʌg/ *n* deliquente *m*

thuggish /'θʌgıʃ/ *a* violento

thumb /θʌm/ *n* pollice *m*; **as a rule of** ~ come regola generale; **under sb's** ~ succube di qcno ● *vt* ~ **a lift** fare l'autostop

■ **thumb through** *vt* sfogliare

thumb: thumb-index *n* indice *m* a rubrica. **thumbnail sketch** *n* breve descrizione *f*. **thumbs down** *n fam* **get the** ~ non ottenere l'okay; **give sb/sth the** ~ ~ non dare l'okay a qcno/qcsa. **thumbs up** *n fam* **get the** ~ ~ ricevere l'okay; **give sb/sth the** ~ ~ dare l'okay a qcno/qcsa. **thumbtack** *n Am* cimice *f*, puntina *f* [da disegno]

thump /θʌmp/ *n* colpo *m*; (*noise*) tonfo *m* ● *vt* battere su ‹*table, door*›; battere ‹*fist*›; colpire ‹*person*› ● *vi* battere (**on** su); ‹*heart:*› battere forte

■ **thump about** *vi* camminare pesantemente

thumping /'θʌmpɪŋ/ a (fam: very large) enorme; **a ~ headache** un mal di testa martellante

thunder /'θʌndə(r)/ n tuono m; (loud noise) rimbombo m ● vi tuonare; (make loud noise) rimbombare

thunderbolt /'θʌndəbəʊlt/ n folgore f

thunderclap /'θʌndəklæp/ n rombo m di tuono

thundering /'θʌndərɪŋ/ a (fam: very big or great) tremendo

thunderous /'θʌndərəs/ a (applause) scrosciante

thunderstorm /'θʌndəstɔ:m/ n temporale m

thunderstruck /'θʌndəstrʌk/ a sbigottito

thundery /'θʌndərɪ/ a temporalesco

Thursday /'θɜ:zdeɪ/ n giovedì m inv

thus /ðʌs/ adv così

thwack /θwæk/ vt colpire ● n colpo m

thwart /θwɔ:t/ vt ostacolare

thyme /taɪm/ n timo m

thyroid /'θaɪrɔɪd/ n tiroide f

tiara /tɪ'ɑ:rə/ n diadema m

Tiber /'taɪbə(r)/ n Tevere m

tick¹ /tɪk/ **n on ~** fam a credito

tick² n (sound) ticchettio m; (mark) segno m; (fam: instant) attimo m ● vi ticchettare

■ **tick off** vt spuntare; fam sgridare

■ **tick over** vi (engine:) andare al minimo

ticket /'tɪkɪt/ n biglietto m; (for item deposited, library) tagliando m; (label) cartellino m; (fine) multa f

ticket: ticket-collector n controllore m. **ticket-holder** n persona f munita di biglietto. **ticket-office** n biglietteria f. **ticket tout** n Br bagarino m

tickle /'tɪkl/ n solletico m ● vt fare il solletico a; (amuse) divertire ● vi fare prurito

ticklish /'tɪklɪʃ/ a che soffre il solletico; (problem) delicato

tidal /'taɪdl/ a (river, harbour) di marea

tidal wave n onda f di marea

tiddly /'tɪdlɪ/ a (Br fam: drunk) brillo

tiddlywinks /'tɪdlɪwɪŋks/ n gioco m delle pulci

tide /taɪd/ n marea f; (of events) corso m; **the ~ is in/out** c'è alta/bassa marea

■ **tide over** vt ~ **sb over** aiutare qcno a andare avanti

tidemark /'taɪdmɑ:k/ n linea f di marea; (Br fig: line of dirt) tracce fpl di sporco (nella vasca da bagno)

tidily /'taɪdɪlɪ/ adv in modo ordinato

tidiness /'taɪdɪnɪs/ n ordine m

tidy /'taɪdɪ/ a (-ier, -iest) ordinato; (fam: amount) bello ● vt ordinare

■ **tidy away** vt mettere a posto (toys, books)

■ **tidy out** vt mettere in ordine (drawer, cupboard)

■ **tidy up** vt ordinare; ~ **oneself up** mettersi in ordine

tie /taɪ/ n cravatta f; (cord) legaccio m; (fig: bond) legame m; (restriction) impedimento m;

Sport pareggio m ● v (pres p **tying**) ● vt legare; fare (knot); **be ~d** (in competition) essere in parità ● vi pareggiare

■ **tie down** vt anche fig legare

■ **tie in with** vi corrispondere a

■ **tie on** vt attaccare

■ **tie up** vt legare; vincolare (capital); **be ~d up** (busy) essere occupato

tie: tie-break[er] n Tennis tie-break m inv; (in quiz) spareggio m. **tie-dye** vt tingere annodando. **tie-on** a (label) volante. **tiepin** n fermacravatta m

tier /tɪə(r)/ n fila f; (of cake) piano m; (in stadium) gradinata f

tiff /tɪf/ n battibecco m

tiger /'taɪgə(r)/ n tigre f

tiger's-eye /'taɪgəz/ n occhio m di tigre

tight /taɪt/ a stretto; (taut) teso; (fam: drunk) sbronzo; (fam: mean) spilorcio; ~ **corner** fam brutta situazione f ● adv strettamente; (hold) forte; (closed) bene

tighten /'taɪtn/ vt stringere; avvitare (screw); intensificare (control); ~ **one's belt** fig tirare la cinghia ● vi stringersi

■ **tighten up** vt stringere (screw); rendere più severo (security) ● vi (become stricter) diventare più severo

tight: tight-fisted /-'fɪstɪd/ a tirchio. **tight-fitting** /-'fɪtɪŋ/ a attillato. **tight-knit** a (fig: community, group) unito. **tight-lipped** /-'lɪpt/ a **they are remaining ~ about events** mantengono il riserbo riguardo all'accaduto

tightly /'taɪtlɪ/ adv strettamente; (hold) forte; (closed) bene

tightrope /'taɪtrəʊp/ n fune f (da funamboli)

tights /taɪts/ npl collant m inv

tigress /'taɪgrɪs/ n tigre f femmina

tile /taɪl/ n mattonella f; (on roof) tegola f ● vt rivestire di mattonelle (wall); coprire con tegole (roof)

till¹ /tɪl/ prep & conj = **until**

till² n cassa f

tiller /'tɪlə(r)/ n barra f del timone

tilt /tɪlt/ n inclinazione f; **at full ~** a tutta velocità ● vt inclinare ● vi inclinarsi

timber /'tɪmbə(r)/ n legname m

time /taɪm/ n tempo m; (occasion) volta f; (by clock) ora f; **two ~s four** due volte quattro; **at any ~** in qualsiasi momento; **this ~** questa volta; **at ~s, from ~ to ~** ogni tanto; ~ **and again** cento volte; **two at a ~** due alla volta; **on ~** in orario; **in ~** in tempo; (eventually) col tempo; **in no ~ at all** velocemente; **in a year's ~** fra un anno; **behind ~** in ritardo; **behind the ~s** antiquato; **for the ~ being** per il momento; **what is the ~?** che ora è?; **by the ~ we arrive** quando arriviamo; **do you have the ~?** (what ~ is it?) hai l'ora?; **did you have a nice ~?** ti sei divertito?; **have a good ~!** divertiti! ● vt scegliere il momento per; cronometrare (race); **be well ~d** essere ben calcolato

time: time bomb n bomba f a orologeria. **time-consuming** a che porta via molto tempo. **time-honoured** /-ʊnəd/ a venerando.

timekeeper *n Sport* cronometrista *mf*; **be a good ~** (*be punctual*) essere sempre puntuale. **time lag** *n* intervallo *m* [di tempo]

timeless /'taɪmlɪs/ *a* eterno

time limit *n* limite *m* di tempo

timely /'taɪmlɪ/ *a* opportuno

time off *n* (*leave*) permesso *m*; **take some ~ ~** prendere delle ferie

time-out *n* (*break*) pausa *f*; *Sport* time out *m inv*

timer /'taɪmə(r)/ *n* timer *m inv*

time: **timescale** *n* periodo *m*. **timeshare** *n* (*apartment*) appartamento *m* in multiproprietà; (*house*) casa *f* in multiproprietà. **time sheet** *n* foglio *m* di presenza. **time signal** *n* segnale *m* orario. **time span** *n* arco *m* di tempo. **time switch** *n* interruttore *m* a tempo. **timetable** *n* orario *m*. **time zone** *n* fuso *m* orario

timid /'tɪmɪd/ *a* (*shy*) timido; (*fearful*) timoroso

timidly /'tɪmɪdlɪ/ *adv* timidamente

timidness /'tɪmɪdnɪs/ *n* (*shyness*) timidezza *f*; (*fear*) paura *f*

timing /'taɪmɪŋ/ *n Sport, Techn* cronometraggio *m*; **the ~ of the election** il momento scelto per le elezioni; **have no sense of ~** non saper scegliere il momento opportuno

timorous /'tɪm(ə)rəs/ *a* timoroso

timpani /'tɪmpənɪ/ *npl* timpani *mpl*

tin /tɪn/ *n* stagno *m*; (*container*) barattolo *m* ● *vt* (*pt/pp* **tinned**) inscatolare

tin foil *n* [carta *f*] stagnola *f*

tinge /tɪndʒ/ *n* sfumatura *f* ● *vt* **~d with** *fig* misto a

tingle /'tɪŋgl/ *vi* pizzicare

tinker /'tɪŋkə(r)/ *vi* armeggiare

tinkle /'tɪŋkl/ *n* tintinnio *m*; (*fam: phone call*) colpo *m* di telefono ● *vi* tintinnare

tinned /tɪnd/ *a* in scatola

tinnitus /'tɪnɪtəs/ *n Med* ronzio *m* auricolare

tinny /'tɪnɪ/ *a* ‹*sound, music*› metallico; (*badly made*) che sembra fatta di latta

tin-opener /-əʊpnə(r)/ *n* apriscatole *m inv*

tinpot /'tɪnpɒt/ *a pej* ‹*firm*› da due soldi

tinsel /'tɪnsl/ *n* filo *m* d'argento

tint /tɪnt/ *n* tinta *f* ● *vt* tingersi ‹*hair*›; **~ed glasses** occhiali *mpl* colorati

tiny /'taɪnɪ/ *a* (**-ier, -iest**) minuscolo

tip¹ /tɪp/ *n* (*point, top*) punta *f*

tip² *n* (*money*) mancia *f*; (*advice*) consiglio *m*; (*for rubbish*) discarica *f* ● *v* (*pt/pp* **tipped**) ● *vt* (*tilt*) inclinare; (*overturn*) capovolgere; (*pour*) versare; (*reward*) dare una mancia a ● *vi* inclinarsi; (*overturn*) capovolgersi

■ **tip off** *vt* **~ sb off** (*inform*) fare una soffiata a qcno

■ **tip out** *vt* rovesciare

■ **tip over** *vt* capovolgere ● *vi* capovolgersi

■ **tip up** *vt* sollevare ‹*seat*›; (*overturn*) rovesciare

tip-off *n* soffiata *f*

tipped /tɪpt/ *a* ‹*cigarette*› col filtro

tipple /'tɪpl/ *vi* bere [alcool] ● *n* **have a ~**

prendere un bicchierino; **my favourite ~** il mio liquore preferito

tipster /'tɪpstə(r)/ *n esperto m che dà suggerimenti su cavalli da corsa, azioni ecc*

tipsy /'tɪpsɪ/ *a fam* brillo

tiptoe /'tɪptəʊ/ *n* **on ~** in punta di piedi

tip-top *a fam* in condizioni perfette

tirade /taɪ'reɪd/ *n* filippica *f*

tire /'taɪə(r)/ *vt* stancare ● *vi* stancarsi

tired /'taɪəd/ *a* stanco; **~ of** stanco di; **~ out** stanco morto

tiredness /'taɪədnɪs/ *n* stanchezza *f*

tireless /'taɪəlɪs/ *a* instancabile

tirelessly /'taɪəlɪslɪ/ *adv* instancabilmente

tiresome /'taɪəsəm/ *a* fastidioso

tiring /'taɪərɪŋ/ *a* stancante

tissue /'tɪʃuː/ *n* tessuto *m*; (*handkerchief*) fazzolettino *m* di carta

tissue-paper *n* carta *f* velina

tit¹ /tɪt/ *n* (*bird*) cincia *f*

tit² *n* **~ for tat** pan per focaccia

tit³ *n fam* (*breast*) tetta *f*; (*fool*) stupido *m*

titbit /'tɪtbɪt/ *n* ghiottoneria *f*; (*fig: of news*) notizia *f* appetitosa

titillate /'tɪtɪleɪt/ *vt* titillare

titivate /'tɪtɪveɪt/ *vt* agghindare; **~ oneself** agghindarsi

title /'taɪtl/ *n* titolo *m*

title: **title deed** *n* atto *m* di proprietà. **title-holder** *n* detentore, -trice *mf* del titolo. **title-page** *n* frontespizio *m*. **title role** *n* ruolo *m* principale

titter /'tɪtə(r)/ *vi* ridere nervosamente ● *n* risatina *f* nervosa

tittle-tattle /'tɪtltætl/ *n* pettegolezzi *mpl*

titular /'tɪtjʊlə(r)/ *a* nominale

tizzy /'tɪzɪ/ *n fam* **in a ~** in grande agitazione

to /tuː/, *atono* /tə/ *prep* a; (*to countries*) in; (*towards*) verso; (*up to, until*) fino a; **I'm going to John's/the butcher's** vado da John/dal macellaio; **come/go to sb** venire/andare da qcno; **to Italy/Switzerland** in Italia/Svizzera; **I've never been to Rome** non sono mai stato a Roma; **go to the market** andare al mercato; **to the toilet/my room** in bagno/camera mia; **to an exhibition** a una mostra; **to university** all'università; **twenty/quarter to eight** le otto meno venti/un quarto; **5 to 6 kilos** da 5 a 6 chili; **to the end** alla fine; **to this day** fino a oggi; **to the best of my recollection** per quanto mi possa ricordare; **give/say sth to sb** dare/dire qcsa a qcno; **give it to me** dammelo; **there's nothing to it** è una cosa da niente ● *verbal constructions* **to go** andare; **learn to swim** imparare a nuotare; **I want to/have to go** voglio/devo andare; **it's easy to forget** è facile da dimenticare; **too ill/tired to go** troppo malato/stanco per andare; **you have to** devi; **I don't want to** non voglio; **he wants to be a teacher** vuole diventare un insegnante; **live to be 90** vivere fino a 90 anni; **he was the last to arrive** è stato l'ultimo ad arrivare; **to be honest,...** per essere sincero,... ● *adv* **pull to** chiudere; **to and fro** avanti e indietro

toad /təʊd/ n rospo m

toadstool /'təʊdstu:l/ n fungo m velenoso

■ **toady to** /'təʊdɪ/ vi fare da leccapiedi a

toast /təʊst/ n pane m tostato; (drink) brindisi m inv ●vt tostare ⟨bread⟩; (drink a ~ to) brindare a

toaster /'təʊstə(r)/ n tostapane m inv

toastrack /'təʊstræk/ n portatoast m inv

tobacco /tə'bækəʊ/ n tabacco m

tobacconist's [**shop**] /tə'bækənɪsts [ʃɒp]/ n tabaccheria f

toboggan /tə'bɒgən/ n toboga m inv ●vi andare in toboga

today /tə'deɪ/ a & adv oggi m; **a week ~** una settimana a oggi; **~'s paper** il giornale di oggi

toddle /'tɒdl/ vi ⟨child:⟩ cominciare a camminare; **~ into town** fam fare una passeggiata in centro; **I must be toddling** fam devo scappare

toddler /'tɒdlə(r)/ n bambino, -a mf piccolo, -a

toddy /'tɒdɪ/ n grog m inv

to-do /tə'du:/ n fam baccano m

toe /təʊ/ n dito m del piede; (of footwear) punta f; **on one's ~s** fig pronto ad agire; **big ~** alluce m; **little ~** mignolo m [del piede] ●vt **~ the line** rigar diritto

toe-hold n punto m d'appoggio

toenail /'təʊneɪl/ n unghia f del piede

toff /tɒf/ n fam elegantone, -a mf

toffee /'tɒfɪ/ n caramella f al mou

toffee apple n mela f caramellata

toffee-nosed a Br fam con la puzza sotto il naso

together /tə'geðə(r)/ adv insieme; (at the same time) allo stesso tempo; **~ with** insieme a

toggle /'tɒgl/ n (fastening) olivetta f

toil /tɔɪl/ n duro lavoro m ●vi lavorare duramente

toilet /'tɔɪlɪt/ n (lavatory) gabinetto m

toilet bag n nécessaire m inv

toilet paper n carta f igienica

toiletries /'tɔɪlɪtrɪz/ npl articoli mpl da toilette

toilet: toilet roll n rotolo m di carta igienica. **toilet soap** n sapone m. **toilet tissue** n carta f igienica. **toilet-train** vt **~ a child** insegnare a un bambino a usare il vasino. **toilet water** n acqua f di colonia

token /'təʊkən/ n segno m; (counter) gettone m; (voucher) buono m ●attrib simbolico

told /təʊld/ see **tell** ● a **all ~** in tutto

tolerable /'tɒl(ə)rəbl/ a tollerabile; (not bad) discreto

tolerably /'tɒl(ə)rəblɪ/ adv discretamente

tolerance /'tɒl(ə)r(ə)ns/ n tolleranza f

tolerant /'tɒl(ə)r(ə)nt/ a tollerante

tolerantly /'tɒl(ə)r(ə)ntlɪ/ adv con tolleranza

tolerate /'tɒləreɪt/ vt tollerare

toll¹ /təʊl/ n pedaggio m; **death ~** numero m di morti; **take a heavy ~** costare gravi perdite

toll² vi suonare a morto

toll-booth n casello m

toll-free number n Am Teleph numero m verde

tom /tɒm/ n (cat) gatto m maschio

tomato /tə'mɑ:təʊ/ n (pl -es) pomodoro m

tomato: tomato ketchup n ketchup m. **tomato purée** n concentrato m di pomodoro. **tomato sauce** n salsa f di pomodoro

tomb /tu:m/ n tomba f

tomboy /'tɒmbɔɪ/ n maschiaccio m

tombstone /'tu:mstəʊn/ n pietra f tombale

tom-cat n gatto m maschio

tome /təʊm/ n tomo m

tomfoolery /tɒm'fu:lərɪ/ n stupidaggini fpl

tomorrow /tə'mɒrəʊ/ a & adv domani; **~ morning** domani mattina; **the day after ~** dopodomani; **see you ~!** a domani!

tom-tom n tamtam m inv

ton /tʌn/ n tonnellata f (= 1,016 kg); **~s of** fam un sacco di

tonal /'təʊnl/ a tonale

tonality /təʊ'nælətɪ/ n tonalità f inv

tone /təʊn/ n tono m; (colour) tonalità f inv

■ **tone down** vt attenuare

■ **tone in** vi intonarsi

■ **tone up** vt tonificare ⟨muscles⟩

tone-deaf a be **~** non avere orecchio

toneless /'təʊnlɪs/ a (unmusical) piatto

toner /'təʊnə(r)/ n toner m

tongs /tɒŋz/ npl pinze fpl

tongue /tʌŋ/ n lingua f; **~ in cheek** ⟨fam: say⟩ ironicamente

tongue: tongue-lashing n (severe reprimand) strigliata f. **tongue-tied** a senza parole. **tongue-twister** n scioglilingua m inv

tonic /'tɒnɪk/ n tonico m; (for hair) lozione f per i capelli; fig toccasana m inv; **~ [water]** acqua f tonica

tonight /tə'naɪt/ adv stanotte; (evening) stasera ●n questa notte f; (evening) questa sera f

tonnage /'tʌnɪdʒ/ n stazza f

tonne /tʌn/ n tonnellata f metrica

tonsil /'tɒnsl/ n Anat tonsilla f; **have one's ~s out** operarsi di tonsille

tonsillitis /tɒnsə'laɪtɪs/ n tonsillite f; **have ~** avere la tonsillite

too /tu:/ adv troppo; (also) anche; **~ many** troppi; **~ much** troppo; **~ little** troppo poco

took /tʊk/ see **take**

tool /tu:l/ n attrezzo m

tool: tool-bag n borsa f degli attrezzi. **tool bar** n Comput barra f strumenti. **toolbox** n cassetta f degli attrezzi. **tool kit** n astuccio m di attrezzi

toot /tu:t/ n suono m di clacson ●vi Auto clacsonare

tooth /tu:θ/ n (pl **teeth**) dente m

tooth ache /'tu:θeɪk/ n mal m di denti; **have ~** avere mal di denti

toothbrush /'tu:θbrʌʃ/ n spazzolino m da denti

toothless /'tu:θlɪs/ a sdentato

toothpaste /'tu:θpeɪst/ n dentifricio m

toothpick /'tu:θpɪk/ n stuzzicadenti m inv

toothy /'tu:θɪ/ *a* **give a ~ grin** fare un sorriso a trentadue denti

top[1] /tɒp/ *n* (*toy*) trottola *f*

top[2] *n* cima *f*; *Sch* primo, -a *mf*; (*upper part or half*) parte *f* superiore; (*of page, list, street*) inizio *m*; (*upper surface*) superficie *f*; (*lid*) coperchio *m*; (*of bottle*) tappo *m*; (*garment*) maglia *f*; (*blouse*) camicia *f*; *Auto* marcia *f* più alta; **at the ~** *fig* al vertice; **at the ~ of one's voice** a squarciagola; **on ~/on ~ of** sopra; **on ~ of that** (*besides*) per di più; **from ~ to bottom** da cima a fondo; **blow one's ~** *fam* perdere le staffe; **over the ~** (*fam: exaggerated, too much*) eccessivo ● *a* in alto; (*official, floor of building*) superiore; (*pupil, musician etc*) migliore; (*speed*) massimo ● *vt* (*pt/pp* **topped**) essere in testa a (*list*); (*exceed*) sorpassare; **~ped with ice-cream** ricoperto di gelato; **~ oneself** *sl* suicidarsi
■ **top up** *vt* riempire

topaz /'təʊpæz/ *n* topazio *m*

top: top brass *n fam* pezzi *mpl* grossi. **topcoat** *n* (*of paint*) strato *m* finale. **top floor** *n* ultimo piano *m*. **top gear** *n Auto* marcia *f* più alta. **top hat** *n* cilindro *m*. **top-heavy** *a* con la parte superiore sovraccarica

topic /'tɒpɪk/ *n* soggetto *m*; (*of conversation*) argomento *m*

topical /'tɒpɪkl/ *a* d'attualità; **very ~** di grande attualità

topless /'tɒplɪs/ *a & adv* topless

top-level *a* ad alto livello

topmost /'tɒpməʊst/ *a* più alto

top: top-notch *a fam* eccellente. **top-of-the-range** *a* (*model*) della fascia più alta

topping /'tɒpɪŋ/ *n* **with a chocolate ~** ricoperto di cioccolato; **pizza with a ham and mushroom ~** pizza al prosciutto e funghi

topple /'tɒpl/ *vt* rovesciare ● *vi* rovesciarsi
■ **topple off** *vi* cadere

top: top-ranking *a* (*official*) di massimo grado. **top secret** *a* segretissimo, top secret *inv*. **top security** *a* di massima sicurezza. **topsoil** *n* strato *m* superficiale del terreno. **topspin** *n* topspin *m inv*

topsy-turvy /tɒpsɪ'tɜ:vɪ/ *a & adv* sottosopra

top ten *npl* primi dieci *mpl* in classifica

top-up *n* **would you like a ~?** ti riempio il bicchiere/la tazza?

torch /tɔ:tʃ/ *n* torcia *f* [elettrica]; (*flaming*) fiaccola *f*

torchlight procession /'tɔ:tʃlaɪt/ *n* fiaccolata *f*

tore /tɔ:(r)/ *see* **tear**[1]

torment[1] /'tɔ:ment/ *n* tormento *m*

torment[2] /tɔ:'ment/ *vt* tormentare

tormentor /tɔ:'mentə(r)/ *n* tormentatore, -trice *mf*

torn /tɔ:n/ *see* **tear**[1] ● *a* bucato

tornado /tɔ:'neɪdəʊ/ *n* (*pl* -**es**) tornado *m inv*

torpedo /tɔ:'pi:dəʊ/ *n* (*pl* -**es**) siluro *m* ● *vt* silurare

torpid /'tɔ:pɪd/ *a* intorpidito

torrent /'tɒrənt/ *n* torrente *m*

torrential /tə'renʃl/ *a* (*rain*) torrenziale

torrid /'tɒrɪd/ *a* torrido

torso /'tɔ:səʊ/ *n* torso *m*; (*in art*) busto *m*

tortoise /'tɔ:təs/ *n* tartaruga *f*

tortoiseshell /'tɔ:təsʃel/ *n* tartaruga *f*

tortuous /'tɔ:tʃʊəs/ *a* tortuoso

tortuously /'tɔ:tʃʊəslɪ/ *adv* tortuosamente

torture /'tɔ:tʃə(r)/ *n* tortura *f* ● *vt* torturare

Tory /'tɔ:rɪ/ *Br n* conservatore, -trice *mf* (*appartenente al partito britannico dei conservatori*) ● *a* del partito conservatore

toss /tɒs/ *vt* gettare; (*into the air*) lanciare in aria; (*shake*) scrollare; (*horse:*) disarcionare; mescolare (*salad*); rivoltare facendo saltare in aria (*pancake*); **~ a coin** fare testa o croce ● *vi* **~ and turn** (*in bed*) rigirarsi; **let's ~ for it** facciamo testa o croce

toss-up *n fam* **let's have a ~ to decide** facciamo testa o croce

tot[1] /tɒt/ *n* bimbetto, -a *mf*; (*fam: of liquor*) goccio *m*

tot[2] *vt* (*pt/pp* **totted**) **~ up** *fam* fare la somma di

total /'təʊtl/ *a* totale ● *n* totale *m* ● *vt* (*pt/pp* **totalled**) ammontare a; (*add up*) sommare

totalitarian /təʊtælɪ'teərɪən/ *a* totalitario

totally /'təʊtəlɪ/ *adv* totalmente

tote bag /təʊt/ *n* sporta *f*

totem pole /'təʊtəm/ *n* totem *m inv*

totter /'tɒtə(r)/ *vi* barcollare; (*government:*) vacillare

touch /tʌtʃ/ *n* tocco *m*; (*sense*) tatto *m*; (*contact*) contatto *m*; (*trace*) traccia *f*; (*of irony, humour*) tocco *m*; **get/be in ~** mettersi/essere in contatto ● *vt* toccare; (*lightly*) sfiorare; (*equal*) eguagliare; (*fig: move*) commuovere ● *vi* toccarsi
■ **touch down** *vi Aeron* atterrare
■ **touch off** *vi fig* scatenare
■ **touch on** *vt fig* accennare a
■ **touch up** *vt* ritoccare (*painting*); **~ sb up** (*sexually*) allungare le mani su qcno

touch-and-go *a* incerto

touchdown /'tʌtʃdaʊn/ *n Aeron* atterraggio *m*; *Sport* meta *f*

touché /tu:'ʃeɪ/ *int fig* touché!

touched /tʌtʃt/ *a* (*crazy*) toccato

touching /'tʌtʃɪŋ/ *a* commovente

touchingly /'tʌtʃɪŋlɪ/ *adv* in modo commovente

touch: touchline *n* (*in football*) linea *f* laterale; (*in rugby*) touche *nf inv*. **touch[-sensitive] screen** *n Comput* schermo *m* a sfioramento. **touch-type** *vi* dattilografare a tastiera cieca. **touch-typing** *n* dattilografia *f* a tastiera cieca. **touch-up** *n* (*of paintwork*) ritocco *m*

touchy /'tʌtʃɪ/ *a* permaloso; (*subject*) delicato

tough /tʌf/ *a* duro; (*severe, harsh*) severo; (*durable*) resistente; (*resilient*) forte; **~!** (*fam: too bad*) peggio per te/lui!

toughen /'tʌfn/ *vt* rinforzare
■ **toughen up** *vt* rendere più forte (*person*)

toupee /'tu:peɪ/ *n* toupet *m inv*

tour /tʊə(r)/ *n* giro *m*; (*of building, town*) visita *f*; *Theat, Sport* tournée *f inv*; *(of duty)* servizio *m* ● *vt* visitare ● *vi* fare un giro turistico; *Theat* essere in tournée

tour guide *n* guida *f* turistica

tourism /'tʊərɪzm/ *n* turismo *m*

tourist /'tʊərɪst/ *n* turista *mf* ● *attrib* turistico

tourist: tourist class *n* classe *f* turistica. **tourist office** *n* ufficio *m* turistico. **tourist resort** *n* località *f* turistica. **tourist route** *n* itinerario *m* turistico. **tourist trap** *n locale o località per turisti dove i prezzi sono molto alti*

touristy /'tʊərɪstɪ/ *a fam pej* da turisti; **it's too ~ here** è troppo turistico qui

tournament /'tʊənəmənt/ *n* torneo *m*

tourniquet /'tʊənɪkeɪ/ *n* laccio *m* emostatico

tour operator *n* tour operator *mf inv*, operatore, -trice *mf* turistico, -a

tousle /'taʊzl/ *vt* spettinare

tout /taʊt/ *n (ticket ~)* bagarino *m*; *(horse-racing)* informatore *m* ● *vi* **~ for** sollecitare

tow /təʊ/ *n* rimorchio *m*; **'on ~'** 'a rimorchio'; **in ~** *fam* al seguito ● *vt* rimorchiare

■ **tow away** *vt* portare via col carro attrezzi

toward[s] /tə'wɔːd(z)/ *prep* verso *(with respect to)* nei riguardi di

tow bar *n* barra *f* di rimorchio

towel /'taʊəl/ *n* asciugamano *m*

■ **towel down** *vt* asciugare

towelling /'taʊəlɪŋ/ *n* spugna *f*

towelling robe *n* accappatoio *m*

towel rail *n* portasciugamano *m*

tower /'taʊə(r)/ *n* torre *f*; **be a ~ of strength to sb** essere di grande conforto per qcno ● *vi* **~ above** dominare

tower block *n* palazzone *m*

towering /'taʊərɪŋ/ *a* torreggiante; ⟨*rage*⟩ violento

tow line *n* cavo *m* da rimorchio

town /taʊn/ *n* città *f inv*; **in ~** nel centro

town: town centre *n* centro *m* della città. **town council** *n* municipalità *f*. **town hall** *n* municipio *m*. **town planner** *n* urbanista *mf*. **town planning** *n* urbanistica *f*

towpath /'təʊpɑːθ/ *n* strada *f* alzaia

tow rope *n* cavo *m* da rimorchio

toxic /'tɒksɪk/ *a* tossico

toxicity /tɒk'sɪsɪtɪ/ *n* tossicità *f*

toxic waste *n* rifiuti *mpl* tossici

toxicologist /tɒksɪ'kɒlədʒɪst/ *n* tossicologo, -a *mf*

toxicology /tɒksɪ'kɒlədʒɪ/ *n* tossicologia *f*

toxin /'tɒksɪn/ *n* tossina *f*

toy /tɔɪ/ *n* giocattolo *m*

■ **toy with** *vt* giocherellare con

toyboy /'tɔɪbɔɪ/ *n Br fam* uomo-oggetto *m*

toyshop /'tɔɪʃɒp/ *n* negozio *m* di giocattoli

trace /treɪs/ *n* traccia *f* ● *vt* seguire le tracce di; *(find)* rintracciare; *(draw)* tracciare; *(with tracing-paper)* ricalcare

■ **trace back** *vt* trovare tracce di ⟨*family*⟩

■ **trace out** *vt* tracciare

tracer /'treɪsə(r)/ *n Mil* proiettile *m* tracciante

tracing /'treɪsɪŋ/ *n* ricalco *m*

tracing-paper *n* carta *f* da ricalco

track /træk/ *n* traccia *f*; *(path, Sport)* pista *f*; *Rail* binario *m*; **keep ~ of** tenere d'occhio ● *vt* seguire le tracce di

■ **track down** *vt* scovare

trackball /'trækbɔːl/ *n Comput* trackball *f inv*

tracker /'trækə(r)/ *n (dog)* segugio *m*

track record *n fig* background *m inv*

tracksuit /'træksuːt/ *n* tuta *f* da ginnastica

tract /trækt/ *n (pamphlet)* opuscolo *m*

tractable /'træktəbl/ *a* trattabile; *(docile)* maneggevole

traction /'trækʃn/ *n (of wheel)* trazione *f*

traction engine *n* trattore *m*

tractor /'træktə(r)/ *n* trattore *m*

trade /treɪd/ *n* commercio *m*; *(line of business)* settore *m*; *(craft)* mestiere *m*; **by ~** di mestiere ● *vt* commerciare; **~ sth for sth** scambiare qcsa per qcsa ● *vi* commerciare

■ **trade in** *vt (give in part exchange)* dare in pagamento parziale

■ **trade off** *vt* scambiare

■ **trade on** *vt* approfittarsi di

trade: trade deficit *n* bilancio *m* commerciale in deficit. **trade discount** *n* sconto *m* commerciale. **trade fair** *n* fiera *f* commerciale. **trade-in** *n* permuta *f* come pagamento parziale. **trade mark** *n* marchio *m* di fabbrica. **trade-name** *n* nome *m* depositato. **trade-off** *n* compromesso *m*. **trade price** *n* prezzo *m* all'ingrosso

trader /'treɪdə(r)/ *n* commerciante *mf*

trade secret *n* segreto *m* commerciale

tradesman /'treɪdzmən/ *n (joiner etc)* operaio *m*

trade: trade union *n* sindacato *m*. **trade unionist** *n* sindacalista *mf*. **trade union representative** *n* rappresentante *mf* sindacale

trading /'treɪdɪŋ/ *n* commercio *m*

trading: trading estate *n* zona *f* industriale. **trading floor** *n Fin* sala *f* delle contrattazioni. **trading stamp** *n* bollino *m* premio

tradition /trə'dɪʃn/ *n* tradizione *f*

traditional /trə'dɪʃnl/ *a* tradizionale

traditionalist /trə'dɪʃ(ə)lɪst/ *n* tradizionalista *mf*

traditionally /trə'dɪʃ(ə)lɪ/ *adv* tradizionalmente

traffic /'træfɪk/ *n* traffico *m* ● *vi* trafficare

traffic: traffic calming measures *npl* misure *fpl* per rallentare il traffico in città. **traffic circle** *n Am* isola *f* rotatoria. **traffic island** *n* isola *f* spartitraffico. **traffic jam** *n* ingorgo *m*. **traffic lights** *npl* semaforo *msg*. **traffic offence** *n* infrazione *f* al codice della strada. **traffic warden** *n* vigile *m* [urbano]; *(woman)* vigilessa *f*

tragedy /'trædʒədɪ/ *n* tragedia *f*

tragic /'trædʒɪk/ *a* tragico

tragically /'trædʒɪklɪ/ *adv* tragicamente

trail /treɪl/ n traccia f; (path) sentiero m ● vi strisciare; ⟨plant:⟩ arrampicarsi; ~ **[behind]** rimanere indietro; (in competition) essere in svantaggio ● vt trascinare

trail bike n moto f fuoristrada

trailblazer /'treɪlbleɪzə(r)/ n pioniere, -a mf

trailblazing /'treɪlbleɪzɪŋ/ a innovatore

trailer /'treɪlə(r)/ n Auto rimorchio m; (Am: caravan) roulotte f inv; (film) presentazione f (di un film)

train /treɪn/ n treno m; (of dress) strascico m; **by ~** in treno; **~ of thought** filo m dei pensieri ● vt formare professionalmente; Sport allenare; (aim) puntare; educare ⟨child⟩; addestrare ⟨animal, soldier⟩; far crescere ⟨plant⟩ ● vi fare il tirocinio; Sport allenarsi

trained /treɪnd/ a ⟨animal⟩ addestrato (**to do** a fare)

trainee /treɪ'ni:/ n apprendista mf

trainer /'treɪnə(r)/ n Sport allenatore, -trice mf; (in circus) domatore, -trice mf; (of dog, race-horse) addestratore, -trice mf; **~s** (pl: shoes) scarpe fpl da ginnastica

training /'treɪnɪŋ/ n tirocinio m; Sport allenamento m; (of animal, soldier) addestramento m

training college n istituto m professionale

train set n trenino m

traipse /treɪps/ vi ~ **around** fam andare in giro

trait /treɪt/ n caratteristica f

traitor /'treɪtə(r)/ n traditore, -trice mf

trajectory /trə'dʒekt(ə)rɪ/ n traiettoria f

tram /træm/ n tram m inv

tram-lines npl rotaie fpl del tram

tramp /træmp/ n (hike) camminata f; (vagrant) barbone, -a mf; (of feet) calpestio m ● vi camminare con passo pesante; (hike) percorrere a piedi

■ **trample on** /'træmpl/ vt calpestare

trampoline /'træmpəli:n/ n trampolino m

trance /trɑːns/ n trance f inv

tranquil /'træŋkwɪl/ a tranquillo

tranquillity /træŋ'kwɪlətɪ/ n tranquillità f

tranquillizer /'træŋkwɪlaɪzə(r)/ n tranquillante m

transact /træn'zækt/ vt trattare

transaction /træn'zækʃn/ n transazione f

transatlantic /trænzət'læntɪk/ a ⟨crossing, flight⟩ transatlantico; ⟨attitude, accent⟩ americano

transceiver /træn'si:və(r)/ n ricetrasmittente f

transcend /træn'send/ vt trascendere

transcontinental /trænzkɒntɪ'nent(ə)l/ a transcontinentale

transcribe /træn'skraɪb/ vt trascrivere

transcript /'trænskrɪpt/ n trascrizione f

transcription /træn'skrɪpʃn/ n trascrizione f

transept /'trænsept/ n transetto m

transfer¹ /'trænsfɜ:(r)/ n trasferimento m; Sport cessione f; (design) decalcomania f

transfer² /træns'fɜ:(r)/ v (pt/pp trans-ferred) ● vt trasferire; Sport cedere ● vi trasferirsi; (when travelling) cambiare

transfer fee n (for footballer) prezzo m d'acquisto

transfer list n (in football) lista f di giocatori da cedere

transferable /træns'fɜ:rəbl/ a trasferibile

transfigure /træns'fɪgə/ vt trasfigurare

transfix /træns'fɪks/ vt trafiggere; fig immobilizzare

transfixed /træns'fɪkst/ a (with fascination) folgorato; (with horror) paralizzato

transform /træns'fɔ:m/ vt trasformare

transformation /trænsfə'meɪʃn/ n trasformazione f

transformer /træns'fɔ:mə(r)/ n trasformatore m

transfusion /træns'fju:ʒn/ n trasfusione f

transgression /træns'greʃn/ n Jur trasgressione f; Relig peccato m

transient /'trænzɪənt/ a passeggero

transistor /træn'zɪstə(r)/ n transistor m inv; (radio) radiolina f a transistor

transit /'trænzɪt/ n transito m; **in ~** ⟨goods⟩ in transito

transition /træn'zɪʃn/ n transizione f

transitional /træn'zɪʃənl/ a di transizione

transitive /'trænzɪtɪv/ a transitivo

transitively /'trænzɪtɪvlɪ/ adv transitivamente

transit lounge n sala f d'attesa transiti

transitory /'trænzɪtərɪ/ a transitorio

transit passenger n passeggero m in transito

translate /trænz'leɪt/ vt tradurre

translation /trænz'leɪʃn/ n traduzione f

translation agency n agenzia f di traduzioni

translator /trænz'leɪtə(r)/ n traduttore, -trice mf

translucent /trænz'lu:snt/ a liter traslucido

transmissible /trænz'mɪsəbl/ a trasmissibile

transmission /trænz'mɪʃn/ n trasmissione f

transmit /trænz'mɪt/ vt (pt/pp trans-mitted) trasmettere

transmitter /trænz'mɪtə(r)/ n trasmettitore m

transparency /træn'spærənsɪ/ n Phot diapositiva f

transparent /træn'spærənt/ a trasparente

transpire /træn'spaɪə(r)/ vi emergere; (fam: happen) accadere

transplant¹ /'trænsplɑːnt/ n trapianto m

transplant² /træns'plɑːnt/ vt trapiantare

transport¹ /'trænspɔːt/ n trasporto m; **do you have ~?** hai un mezzo di trasporto?

transport² /træn'spɔːt/ vt trasportare

transportation /trænspɔː'teɪʃn/ n trasporto m

transpose /træns'pəʊz/ vt trasporre

transsexual /trænz'seksʃʊəl/ n transessuale mf ● a transessuale

trans-shipment /trænzˈʃɪpmənt/ n trasbordo m

transverse /trænzˈvɜːs/ a trasversale

transvestite /trænzˈvestaɪt/ n travestito, -a mf

trap /træp/ n trappola f; (fam: mouth) boccaccia f; (carriage) calesse m ● vt (pt/pp **trapped**) intrappolare; schiacciare ⟨finger in door⟩; **be ~ped** essere intrappolato

trapdoor /ˈtræpdɔː(r)/ n botola f

trapeze /trəˈpiːz/ n trapezio m

trappings /ˈtræpɪŋz/ npl (dress) ornamenti mpl; **the ~ of wealth/success** i segni esteriori della ricchezza/del successo

trash /træʃ/ n robaccia f; (rubbish) spazzatura f; (nonsense) schiocchezze fpl

trashcan /ˈtræʃkæn/ n Am pattumiera f, secchio m della spazzatura

trashy /ˈtræʃɪ/ a scadente

trauma /ˈtrɔːmə/ n trauma m

traumatic /trɔːˈmætɪk/ a traumatico

traumatize /ˈtrɔːmətaɪz/ vt traumatizzare

travel /ˈtrævl/ n viaggi mpl ● v (pt/pp **travelled**) ● vi viaggiare; (to work) andare ● vt percorrere ⟨distance⟩

travel: travel agency n agenzia f di viaggi. **travel agent** n agente mf di viaggio. **travel expenses** npl spese fpl di viaggio

traveller /ˈtrævələ(r)/ n viaggiatore, -trice mf; Comm commesso m viaggiatore; **~s** pl (gypsies) zingari mpl

traveller's cheque n traveller's cheque m inv

travelling salesman /ˈtrævəlɪŋ/ n commesso m viaggiatore

travelogue /ˈtrævəlɒg/ n (film) documentario m di viaggio; (talk) conferenza f su un viaggio

travel-sick a **be/get ~** (on plane) soffrire il mal d'aria; (in car) soffrire il mal d'auto; (on boat) soffrire il mal di mare

travel-sickness n (on plane) mal m d'aria; (in car) mal m d'auto; (on boat) mal m di mare ● attrib ⟨pills⟩ per il mal d'aria/d'auto/di mare

traverse /trəˈvɜːs/ vt traversare

travesty /ˈtrævɪstɪ/ n (fig: farce) farsa f; **a ~ of justice** una presa in giro della giustizia

trawler /ˈtrɔːlə(r)/ n peschereccio m

tray /treɪ/ n vassoio m; (for baking) teglia f; (for documents) vaschetta f; (of printer, photocopier) vassoio m, cassetto m

treacherous /ˈtretʃərəs/ a traditore; ⟨weather, currents⟩ pericoloso

treachery /ˈtretʃ(ə)rɪ/ n tradimento m

treacle /ˈtriːkl/ n melassa f

tread /tred/ n andatura f; (step) gradino m; (of tyre) battistrada m inv ● vi (pt **trod**, pp **trodden**) (walk) camminare

■ **tread on** vt calpestare ⟨grass⟩; pestare ⟨foot⟩

treadmill /ˈtredmɪl/ n fig solito tran tran m

treason /ˈtriːzn/ n tradimento m

treasonable /ˈtriːz(ə)nəbl/ a proditorio

treasure /ˈtreʒə(r)/ n tesoro m ● vt tenere in gran conto

treasurer /ˈtreʒərə(r)/ n tesoriere, -a mf

treasury /ˈtreʒərɪ/ n **the T~** il Ministero del Tesoro

treat /triːt/ n piacere m; (present) regalo m; **give sb a ~** fare una sorpresa a qcno ● vt trattare; Med curare; **~ sb to sth** offrire qcsa a qcno; **~ sb for sth** Med sottoporre qcno ad una cura per qcsa

treatise /ˈtriːtɪz/ n trattato m

treatment /ˈtriːtmənt/ n trattamento m; Med cura f

treaty /ˈtriːtɪ/ n trattato m

treble /ˈtrebl/ a triplo; **~ the amount** il triplo ● n Mus (voice) voce f bianca ● vt triplicare ● vi triplicarsi

treble clef n chiave f di violino

tree /triː/ n albero m

tree: tree house n capanna f su un albero. **treetop** n cima f di un albero. **tree trunk** n tronco m d'albero

trek /trek/ n scarpinata f; (as holiday) trekking m inv ● vi (pt/pp **trekked**) farsi una scarpinata; (on holiday) fare trekking

trekking /ˈtrekɪŋ/ n trekking m

trellis /ˈtrelɪs/ n graticolato m

tremble /ˈtrembl/ vi tremare (**with** di)

trembling /ˈtremblɪŋ/ a tremante

tremendous /trɪˈmendəs/ a (huge) enorme; (fam: excellent) formidabile

tremendously /trɪˈmendəslɪ/ adv (very) straordinariamente; (a lot) enormemente

tremor /ˈtremə(r)/ n tremito m; **[earth] ~** scossa f [sismica]

tremulous /ˈtremjʊləs/ a tremulo

trench /trentʃ/ n fosso m; Mil trincea f

trenchant /ˈtrentʃənt/ a ⟨comment, criticism⟩ mordace

trench coat n trench m inv

trend /trend/ n tendenza f; (fashion) moda f

trend-setter n persona f che detta la moda

trend-setting a che detta la moda

trendy /ˈtrendɪ/ a (-ier, -iest) fam di or alla moda

trepidation /trepɪˈdeɪʃn/ n trepidazione f

trespass /ˈtrespəs/ vi **~ on** introdursi abusivamente in; fig abusare di

trespasser /ˈtrespəsə(r)/ n intruso, -a mf

trestle /ˈtresl/ n cavalletto m

trestle table n tavolo m a cavalletto

trial /ˈtraɪəl/ n Jur processo m; (test, ordeal) prova f; **on ~** in prova; Jur in giudizio; **by ~ and error** per tentativi

trial period n periodo m di prova

trial run n (preliminary test) prova f

triangle /ˈtraɪæŋgl/ n triangolo m

triangular /traɪˈæŋgjʊlə(r)/ a triangolare

tribal /ˈtraɪbl/ a tribale

tribe /traɪb/ n tribù f inv

tribulation /trɪbjuˈleɪʃn/ n tribolazione f

tribunal /traɪˈbjuːnl/ n tribunale m

tributary /ˈtrɪbjʊtərɪ/ n affluente m

tribute /ˈtrɪbjuːt/ n tributo m; **pay ~** rendere omaggio

trice /traɪs/ *n* **in a ~** in un attimo

tricentenary /traɪsen'tiːnərɪ/ *n* terzo centenario *m* ● *a* del terzo centenario

trick /trɪk/ *n* trucco *m*; (*joke*) scherzo *m*; (*Cards*) presa *f*; **do the ~** *fam* funzionare; **play a ~ on** fare uno scherzo a ● *vt* imbrogliare; **~ of the trade** trucco *m* del mestiere
■ **trick into** *vt* **~** sb into doing sth convincere qcno a fare qcsa con l'inganno
■ **trick out** *vt* **~** sb out of sth fregare qcno a qcsa

trick cyclist *n* (*sl: psychiatrist*) psichiatra *mf*

trickle /'trɪkl/ *vi* colare
■ **trickle in** *vi fig* entrare poco per volta
■ **trickle out** *vi fig* uscire poco per volta

trickster /'trɪkstə(r)/ *n* imbroglione, -a *mf*

tricky /'trɪkɪ/ *a* (**-ier, -iest**) *a* ⟨*operation*⟩ complesso; ⟨*situation*⟩ delicato

tricolour /'trɪkələ(r)/ *n* tricolore *m*

tricycle /'traɪsɪkl/ *n* triciclo *m*

tried /traɪd/ *see* **try**

tried and tested *a* ⟨*method*⟩ sperimentato

trifle /'traɪfl/ *n* inezia *f*; *Culin* zuppa *f* inglese

trifling /'traɪflɪŋ/ *a* insignificante

trig /trɪg/ *n* (*fam: trigonometry*) trigonometria *f*

trigger /'trɪgə(r)/ *n* grilletto *m*; *fig* causa *f* ● *vt* **~** [**off**] scatenare

trigger-happy *a fam* dalla pistola facile; *fig* impulsivo

trigonometry /trɪgə'nɒmɪtrɪ/ *n* trigonometria *f*

trilateral /traɪ'lætərəl/ *a* trilaterale

trilby /'trɪlbɪ/ *n* cappello *m* di feltro

trill /trɪl/ *n Mus* trillo *m*

trilogy /'trɪlədʒɪ/ *n* trilogia *f*

trim /trɪm/ *a* (**trimmer, trimmest**) curato; ⟨*figure*⟩ snello ● *n* (*of hair, hedge*) spuntata *f*; (*decoration*) rifinitura *f*; **in good ~** in buono stato; ⟨*person*⟩ in forma ● *vt* (*pt/pp* **trimmed**) spuntare ⟨*hair etc*⟩; (*decorate*) ornare; *Naut* orientare
■ **trim off** *vt* tagliare via

trimming /'trɪmɪŋ/ *n* bordo *m*; **~s** *pl* (*of pastry*) ritagli *mpl*; (*decorations*) guarnizioni *fpl*; **with all the ~s** *Culin* guarnito

Trinity /'trɪnətɪ/ *n* **the** [**Holy**] **~** la [Santissima] Trinità

trinket /'trɪŋkɪt/ *n* ninnolo *m*

trio /'triːəʊ/ *n* trio *m*

trip /trɪp/ *n* (*excursion*) gita *f*; (*journey*) viaggio *m*; (*stumble*) passo *m* falso ● *v* (*pt/pp* **tripped**) ● *vt* far inciampare ● *vi* inciampare (**on/over** in)
■ **trip up** *vt* far inciampare

tripartite /traɪ'pɑːtaɪt/ *a* tripartito

tripe /traɪp/ *n* trippa *f*; (*sl: nonsense*) fesserie *fpl*

triple /'trɪpl/ *a* triplo ● *vt* triplicare ● *vi* triplicarsi

triplets /'trɪplɪts/ *npl* tre gemelli *mpl*

triplicate /'trɪplɪkət/ *n* **in ~** in triplice copia

tripod /'traɪpɒd/ *n* treppiede *m inv*

tripper /'trɪpə(r)/ *n* gitante *mf*

trite /traɪt/ *a* banale

triteness /'traɪtnɪs/ *n* banalità *f*

triumph /'traɪʌmf/ *n* trionfo *m* ● *vi* trionfare (**over** su)

triumphant /traɪ'ʌmf(ə)nt/ *a* trionfante

triumphantly /traɪ'ʌmf(ə)ntlɪ/ *adv* ⟨*exclaim*⟩ con tono trionfante

triumvirate /traɪ'ʌmvɪrət/ *n* triumvirato *m*

trivia /'trɪvɪə/ *npl* cose *fpl* secondarie

trivial /'trɪvɪəl/ *a* insignificante

triviality /trɪvɪ'ælətɪ/ *n* banalità *f inv*

trivialize /'trɪvɪəlaɪz/ *vt* sminuire

trod, trodden /trɒd, 'trɒdn/ *see* **tread**

trolley /'trɒlɪ/ *n* carrello *m*; (*Am: tram*) tram *m inv*

trolley bus *n* filobus *m inv*

trombone /trɒm'bəʊn/ *n* trombone *m*

trombonist /trɒm'bəʊnɪst/ *n* trombonista *mf*

troop /truːp/ *n* gruppo *m*; **~s** *pl* truppe *fpl* ● *vi* **~ in/out** entrare/uscire in gruppo

trooper /'truːpə(r)/ *n Mil* soldato *m* di cavalleria; (*Am: policeman*) poliziotto *m*

trophy /'trəʊfɪ/ *n* trofeo *m*

tropic /'trɒpɪk/ *n* tropico *m*; **~s** *pl* tropici *mpl*

tropical /'trɒpɪkl/ *a* tropicale

tropical fruit *n* frutta *f inv* esotica

trot /trɒt/ *n* trotto *m* ● *vi* (*pt/pp* **trotted**) trottare
■ **trot out** *vt* (*fam: produce*) tirar fuori

trotter /'trɒtə(r)/ *n Culin* piedino *m* di maiale

trouble /'trʌbl/ *n* guaio *m*; (*difficulties*) problemi *mpl*; (*inconvenience, Med*) disturbo *m*; (*conflict*) conflitto *m*; **be in ~** essere nei guai; ⟨*swimmer, climber:*⟩ essere in difficoltà; **get into ~** finire nei guai; **get sb into ~** mettere qcno nei guai; **take the ~ to do sth** darsi la pena di far qcsa; **it's no ~** nessun disturbo; **the ~ with you is...** il tuo problema è... ● *vt* (*worry*) preoccupare; (*inconvenience*) disturbare; ⟨*conscience, old wound:*⟩ tormentare ● *vi* **don't ~!** non ti disturbare!

troubled /'trʌbld/ *a* ⟨*mind*⟩ inquieto; ⟨*person, expression*⟩ preoccupato; ⟨*times, area*⟩ difficile; ⟨*waters, sleep*⟩ agitato

troublemaker /'trʌblmeɪkə(r)/ *n* **be a ~** seminare zizzania

troublesome /'trʌblsəm/ *a* fastidioso

trouble spot *n* zona *f* calda

trough /trɒf/ *n* trogolo *m*; (*atmospheric*) depressione *f*

trounce /traʊns/ *vt* (*in competition*) schiacciare

troupe /truːp/ *n* troupe *f inv*

trouser press *n* stiracalzoni *m inv*

trousers /'traʊzəz/ *npl* pantaloni *mpl*

trouser suit *n* tailleur *m inv* pantalone

trousseau /'truːsəʊ/ *n* corredo *m*

trout /traʊt/ *n inv* trota *f inv*

trowel /'traʊəl/ *n* (*for gardening*) paletta *f*; (*for builder*) cazzuola *f*

truant /'truːənt/ *n* **play ~** marinare la scuola

truce /truːs/ *n* tregua *f*

truck /trʌk/ n (lorry) camion m inv

trucker /'trʌkə(r)/ n (fam: lorry driver) camionista mf

truck farmer n Am ortofrutticoltore m, ortolano m

truculent /'trʌkjʊlənt/ a aggressivo

truculently /'trʌkjʊləntlɪ/ adv aggressivamente

trudge /trʌdʒ/ n camminata f faticosa ● vi arrancare

true /truː/ a vero; **come ~** avverarsi

true-life a ⟨adventure, story⟩ vero

truffle /'trʌfl/ n tartufo m

truism /'truːɪzm/ n truismo m

truly /'truːlɪ/ adv veramente; **Yours ~** Distinti saluti

trump /trʌmp/ n ⟨Cards⟩ atout m inv ● vt prendere con l'atout

■ **trump up** vt fam inventare

trump card n fig asso m nella manica

trumpet /'trʌmpɪt/ n tromba f

trumpeter /'trʌmpɪtə(r)/ n trombettista mf

truncate /trʌŋkeɪt/ vt tagliare ⟨text⟩; interrompere ⟨process, journey, event⟩

truncheon /'trʌntʃn/ n manganello m

trundle /'trʌndl/ vt far rotolare ● vi rotolare

trunk /trʌŋk/ n (of tree, body) tronco m; (of elephant) proboscide f; (for travelling, storage) baule m; (Am: of car) bagagliaio m, portabagagli m inv

trunk road n statale f

trunks /trʌŋks/ npl calzoncini mpl da bagno

truss /trʌs/ n Med cinto m erniario

■ **truss up** vt legare

trust /trʌst/ n fiducia f; (group of companies) trust m inv; (organization) associazione f; **on ~** sulla parola ● vt fidarsi di; (hope) augurarsi ● vi **~ in** credere in; **~ to** affidarsi a

trusted /'trʌstɪd/ a fidato

trustee /trʌs'tiː/ n amministratore, -trice mf fiduciario, -a

trustful /'trʌstfʊl/ a fiducioso

trustfully /'trʌstfʊlɪ/ adv fiduciosamente

trust fund n fondo m fiduciario

trusting /'trʌstɪŋ/ a fiducioso

trustworthiness /'trʌstwɜːðɪnɪs/ n (of person) affidabilità f; (of source) attendibilità f

trustworthy /'trʌstwɜːðɪ/ a fidato

trusty /'trʌstɪ/ a fam fidato

truth /truːθ/ n (pl -s /truːðz/) verità f inv

truthful /'truːθfʊl/ a ⟨person⟩ sincero; ⟨statement⟩ veritiero

truthfully /'truːθfʊlɪ/ adv sinceramente

truthfulness /'truːθfʊlnɪs/ n (of person) sincerità f; (of account) veridicità f

try /traɪ/ n tentativo m, prova f; (in rugby) meta f; **I'll give it a ~** faccio un tentativo ● v (pt/pp tried) ● vt provare; (be a strain on) mettere a dura prova; Jur processare ⟨person⟩; discutere ⟨case⟩; **~ to do sth** provare a fare qcsa ● vi provare

■ **try for** vi cercare di ottenere

■ **try on** vt provarsi ⟨garment⟩

■ **try out** vt provare

trying /'traɪɪŋ/ a duro; ⟨person⟩ irritante

try-out n **give sb a ~** mettere alla prova qcno

tsar /zɑː/ n zar m inv

tsarina /tsɑːˈriːnə/ n zarina f

tsarist /'tsɑːrɪst/ a zarista

T-shirt n maglietta f

tsp abbr **teaspoonful**

tub /tʌb/ n tinozza f; (carton) vaschetta f; (bath) vasca f da bagno

tuba /'tjuːbə/ n Mus tuba f

tubby /'tʌbɪ/ a (-ier, -iest) tozzo

tube /tjuːb/ n tubo m; (of toothpaste) tubetto m; Br Rail metro f

tuber /'tjuːbə(r)/ n tubero m

tuberculosis /tjuːbɜːkjʊ'ləʊsɪs/ n tubercolosi f

tubing /'tjuːbɪŋ/ n tubi mpl

tubular /'tjuːbjʊlə(r)/ a tubolare

tuck /tʌk/ n piega f ● vt (put) infilare

■ **tuck away** vt (put in a safe place) mettere al sicuro; (eat) spolverare

■ **tuck in** vt rimboccare; **~ sb in** rimboccare le coperte a qcno ● vi (fam: eat) mangiare con appetito

■ **tuck into** vt mangiare di gusto ⟨meal⟩; **~ sth into one's pocket** infilarsi in tasca qcsa; **~ sb into bed** rimboccare le coperte a qcno

■ **tuck up** vt rimboccarsi ⟨sleeves⟩; (in bed) rimboccare le coperte a

Tuesday /'tjuːzdeɪ/ n martedì m inv

tuft /tʌft/ n ciuffo m

tug /tʌg/ n strattone m; Naut rimorchiatore m ● v (pt/pp tugged) ● vt tirare ● vi dare uno strattone

tug of war n tiro m alla fune

tuition /tjuː'ɪʃn/ n lezioni fpl

tulip /'tjuːlɪp/ n tulipano m

tumble /'tʌmbl/ n ruzzolone m ● vi ruzzolare; **~ to sth** (fam: realize) afferrare qcsa

tumbledown /'tʌmbldaʊn/ a cadente

tumble-drier n asciugabiancheria f

tumbler /'tʌmblə(r)/ n bicchiere m (senza stelo)

tummy /'tʌmɪ/ n fam pancia f

tummy button n fam ombelico m

tumour /'tjuːmə(r)/ n tumore m

tumult /'tjuːmʌlt/ n tumulto m

tumultuous /tjuː'mʌltjʊəs/ a tumultuoso

tuna /'tjuːnə/ n tonno m

tune /tjuːn/ n motivo m; **out of/in ~** ⟨instrument⟩ scordato/accordato; ⟨person⟩ stonato/intonato; **to the ~ of** fam per la modesta somma di ● vt accordare ⟨instrument⟩; sintonizzare ⟨radio, TV⟩; mettere a punto ⟨engine⟩

■ **tune in** vt sintonizzare ● vi sintonizzarsi (**to** su)

■ **tune up** vi ⟨orchestra:⟩ accordare gli strumenti

tuneful /'tjuːnfl/ a melodioso

tuner /'tjuːnə(r)/ n accordatore, -trice mf; Radio, TV sintonizzatore m

tune-up n (of engine) messa f a punto

tungsten /'tʌŋstən/ n tungsteno m
tunic /'tjuːnɪk/ n tunica f; Mil giacca f; Sch ≈ grembiule m
tuning-fork /'tuːnɪŋ/ n diapason m inv
Tunisia /tjuː'nɪzɪə/ n Tunisia f
Tunisian /tjuː'nɪzɪən/ a & n tunisino, -a mf
tunnel /'tʌnl/ n tunnel m inv ● vi (pt/pp **tunnelled**) scavare un tunnel
tuppence /'tʌpəns/ n due penny
turban /'tɜːbən/ n turbante m
turbine /'tɜːbaɪn/ n turbina f
turbo /'tɜːbəʊ/ n turbo m inv
turbocharged /'tɜːbəʊtʃɑːdʒd/ a con motore turbo
turbocharger /'tɜːbəʊtʃɑːdʒə(r)/ n turbocompressore m
turbot /'tɜːbət/ n rombo m gigante
turbulence /'tɜːbjʊləns/ n turbolenza f
turbulent /'tɜːbjʊlənt/ a turbolento
turd /tɜːd/ n sl (excrement) stronzo m; (pej: person) stronzo, -a mf
tureen /tjʊ'riːn/ n zuppiera f
turf /tɜːf/ n erba f; (segment) zolla f erbosa
■ **turf out** vt fam buttar fuori
turf accountant n allibratore m
turgid /'tɜːdʒɪd/ a (style, water) turgido
Turin /tjʊ'rɪn/ n Torino m
Turk /tɜːk/ n turco, -a mf
Turkey /'tɜːkɪ/ n Turchia f
turkey n tacchino m
Turkish /'tɜːkɪʃ/ a turco
Turkish bath n bagno m turco
Turkish delight n cubetti mpl di gelatina ricoperti di zucchero a velo
turmeric /'tɜːmərɪk/ n (spice) curcumina f; (plant) curcuma f
turmoil /'tɜːmɔɪl/ n tumulto m
turn /tɜːn/ n (rotation, short walk) giro m; (in road) svolta f, curva f; (development) svolta f; Theat numero m; (fam: attack) crisi f; **a ~ for the better/worse** un miglioramento/peggioramento m; **do sb a good ~** rendere un servizio a qcno; **take ~s** fare a turno; **in ~** a turno; **out of ~** (speak) a sproposito; **it's your ~** tocca a te ● vt girare voltare (back, eyes); dirigere (gun, attention) ● vi girare; (person:) girarsi; (leaves:) ingiallire; (become) diventare; **~ right/left** girare a destra/sinistra; **~ sour** inacidirsi; **~ to sb** girarsi verso qcno; fig rivolgersi a qcno
■ **turn against** vi diventare ostile a ● vt mettere contro
■ **turn around** vi (person:) girarsi; (car:) girare ● vt girare (object); risollevare (company)
■ **turn away** vt mandare via (people); girare dall'altra parte (head) ● vi girarsi dall'altra parte
■ **turn back** vi tornare indietro ● vt mandare indietro (people); ripiegare (covers, sheet etc)
■ **turn down** vt piegare (collar); abbassare (heat, gas, sound); respingere (person, proposal)
■ **turn in** vt ripiegare in dentro (edges); con-

segnare (lost object) ● vi (fam: go to bed) andare a letto; **~ in to the drive** entrare nel viale
■ **turn into** vt (become) diventare
■ **turn off** vt spegnere; chiudere (tap, water); **~ sb off** (fam: disgust) fare schifo a qcno ● vi (car:) girare
■ **turn on** vt accendere; aprire (tap, water); (fam: attract) eccitare ● vi (attack) attaccare
■ **turn out** vt (expel) mandar via; spegnere (light, gas); (produce) produrre; (empty) svuotare (room, cupboard) ● vi (transpire) risultare; (to see, do sth) venire; **~ out well/badly** (cake, dress:) riuscire bene/male; (situation:) andare bene/male
■ **turn over** vt girare; **~ sb over to the police** consegnare qcno alla polizia; **he ~ed the business over to her** le ha ceduto l'azienda ● vi girarsi; **please ~ over** vedi retro
■ **turn round** vi girarsi; (car:) girare
■ **turn up** vt tirare su (collar); alzare (heat, gas, sound, radio) ● vi farsi vedere
turn: turn-about n (fig: change of direction) cambiamento m. **turnaround** n (in attitude) dietrofront m inv; (of fortune) capovolgimento m; (for the better) ripresa f. **turncoat** n voltagabbana mf inv
turning /'tɜːnɪŋ/ n svolta f
turning-point n svolta f decisiva
turnip /'tɜːnɪp/ n rapa f
turn: turn-off n strada f laterale; **it's a real ~** fam ti fa davvero passar la voglia. **turn-on** n fam **be a real ~** essere veramente eccitante. **turnout** n (of people) affluenza f. **turnover** n Comm giro m d'affari, fatturato m; (of staff) ricambio m. **turnpike** n Am autostrada f. **turnround** n (in policy etc) cambiamento m. **turnstile** n cancelletto m girevole. **turntable** n piattaforma f girevole; (on record-player) piatto m. **turn-up** n (of trousers) risvolto m
turpentine /'tɜːpəntaɪn/ n trementina f
turquoise /'tɜːkwɔɪz/ a (colour) turchese ● n turchese m
turret /'tʌrɪt/ n torretta f
turtle /'tɜːtl/ n tartaruga f acquatica
turtle-dove n tortora f
turtleneck /'tɜːtlnek/ n collo m a lupetto; (sweater) maglia f a lupetto
Tuscan /'tʌskən/ a toscano
Tuscany /'tʌskənɪ/ n Toscana f
tusk /tʌsk/ n zanna f
tussle /'tʌsl/ n zuffa f ● vi azzuffarsi
tussock /'tʌsək/ n ciuffo m d'erba
tut /tʌt/ vi fare un'esclamazione di disapprovazione ● int ts!
tutor /'tjuːtə(r)/ n insegnante mf privato, -a; Univ insegnante mf universitario, -a che segue individualmente un ristretto numero di studenti
tutorial /tjuː'tɔːrɪəl/ n discussione f col tutor
tutorial package n Comput software m di autoapprendimento
tuxedo /tʌk'siːdəʊ/ n Am smoking m inv
TV abbr (**television**) tv f inv, tivù f inv

twaddle /'twɒdl/ *n* scemenze *fpl*

twain /twein/ *npl* **the ~** i due; **and never the ~ shall meet** e mai i due si incontreranno

twang /twæŋ/ *n* (*in voice*) suono *m* nasale ● *vt* far vibrare

tweak /twi:k/ *vt* tirare ⟨*ear, nose*⟩; (*adjust*) apportare delle modifiche a ● *n* (*adjustment*) modifica *f*; **give sb's ears a ~** dare una tirata d'orecchie a qcno

twee /twi:/ *a Br fam* ⟨*manner*⟩ affettato

tweed /twi:d/ *n* tweed *m inv*

tweezers /'twi:zəz/ *npl* pinzette *f*

twelfth /twelfθ/ *a & n* dodicesimo, -a *mf*

twelve /twelv/ *a & n* dodici *m*

twentieth /'twentiiθ/ *a & n* ventesimo, -a *mf*

twenty /'twenti/ *a & n* venti *m*

twerp /twɜ:p/ *n fam* stupido, -a *mf*

twice /twais/ *adv* due volte; **she's done ~ as much as you** ha fatto il doppio di quanto hai fatto tu

twiddle /'twidl/ *vt* giocherellare con; **~ one's thumbs** *fig* girarsi i pollici

twig[1] /twig/ *n* ramoscello *m*

twig[2] *vt/i* (*pt/pp* **twigged**) *fam* intuire

twilight /'twailait/ *n* crepuscolo *m*

twill /twil/ *n* spigato *m*

twin /twin/ *n* gemello, -a *mf* ● *attrib* gemello

twin beds *npl* letti *mpl* gemelli

twine /twain/ *n* spago *m* ● *vi* intrecciarsi; ⟨*plant:*⟩ attorcigliarsi ● *vt* intrecciare

twinge /twindʒ/ *n* fitta *f*; **~ of conscience** rimorso *m* di coscienza

twinkle /'twiŋkl/ *n* scintillio *m* ● *vi* scintillare

twinning /'twiniŋ/ *n* (*of companies*) gemellaggio *m*

twin town *n* città *f inv* gemellata

twirl /twɜ:l/ *vt* far roteare ● *vi* volteggiare ● *n* piroetta *f*

twist /twist/ *n* torsione *f*; (*curve*) curva *f*; (*in rope*) attorcigliata *f*; (*in book, plot*) colpo *m* di scena; **round the ~** (*fam: crazy*) ammattito ● *vt* attorcigliare ⟨*rope*⟩; torcere ⟨*metal*⟩; girare ⟨*knob, cap*⟩; (*distort*) distorcere; **~ one's ankle** storcersi la caviglia ● *vi* attorcigliarsi; ⟨*road:*⟩ essere pieno di curve

twister /'twistə(r)/ *n fam* imbroglione, -a *mf*; (*tornado*) tornado *m inv*

twit /twit/ *n fam* cretino, -a *mf*

twitch /twitʃ/ *n* tic *m inv*; (*jerk*) strattone *m* ● *vi* contrarsi

twitchy /'twitʃi/ *a* (*fam: nervous*) nervosetto

twitter /'twitə(r)/ *n* cinguettio *m*; **in a ~** *fam* agitato ● *vi* cinguettare; ⟨*person:*⟩ cianciare

■ **twitter on about** *vt* parlare incessantemente di

two /tu:/ *a & n* due *m*; **put ~ and ~ together** fare due più due

two: two-faced /-'feist/ *a* falso. **two-piece** *a* (*swimsuit*) due pezzi *m inv*; (*suit*) completo *m*. **two-seater** /-si:tə(r)/ *n* biposto *m inv*. **twosome** /'tu:səm/ *n* coppia *f*. **two-time** *vt fam* fare le corna a. **two-tone** *a* (*in colour*) bicolore; (*in sound*) bitonale. **two-way** *a* ⟨*traffic*⟩ a doppio senso di marcia

tycoon /tai'ku:n/ *n* magnate *m*

tying /'taiiŋ/ *see* **tie**

type /taip/ *n* tipo *m*; (*printing*) carattere *m* [tipografico] ● *vt/i* scrivere a macchina

type: typecast *vt Theat, fig* far fare sempre la stessa parte a ⟨*person*⟩ ● *a* a ruolo fisso. **typeface** *n* carattere *m* tipografico. **typeset** *vt* comporre. **typesetter** *n* compositore *m*. **typewriter** *n* macchina *f* da scrivere. **typewritten** *a* dattiloscritto

typhoid /'taifɔid/ *n* febbre *f* tifoidea

typhoon /tai'fu:n/ *n* tifone *m*

typical /'tipikl/ *a* tipico

typically /'tipikli/ *adv* tipicamente; (*as usual*) come al solito

typify /'tipifai/ *vt* (*pt/pp* **-ied**) essere tipico di

typing /'taipiŋ/ *n* dattilografia *f*

typist /'taipist/ *n* dattilografo, -a *mf*

typo /'taipəʊ/ *n* errore *m* di stampa; (*keying error*) errore *m* di battitura

typography /tai'pɒgrəfi/ *n* tipografia *f*

tyrannical /ti'rænikl/ *a* tirannico

tyrannize /'tirənaiz/ *vt* tiranneggiare

tyranny /'tirəni/ *n* tirannia *f*

tyrant /'tairənt/ *n* tiranno, -a *mf*

tyre /'taiə(r)/ *n* gomma *f*, pneumatico *m*

tyre pressure *n* pressione *f* delle gomme

Tyrrhenian Sea /ti'ri:niən/ *n* mar *m* Tirreno

tzar /za:/ *n* zar *m*

tzarina /tsɑ:'ri:nə/ *n* zarina *f*

Uu

u, U /juː/ *n* (*letter*) u, U *f inv*
u *abbr* Cinema (**universal**) per tutti
U-bend *n* (*in pipe*) gomito *m*; (*in road*) curva *f* a gomito
ubiquitous /juːˈbɪkwɪtəs/ *a* onnipresente
udder /ˈʌdə(r)/ *n* mammella *f* (*di vacca, capra etc*)
UFO *abbr* (**unidentified flying object**) ufo *m inv*
Uganda /juːˈɡændə/ *n* Uganda *f*
Ugandan /juːˈɡændən/ *a & n* ugandese *mf*
ugliness /ˈʌɡlɪnɪs/ *n* bruttezza *f*
ugly /ˈʌɡlɪ/ *a* (**-ier, -iest**) brutto
UK *abbr* **United Kingdom**
Ukraine /juːˈkreɪn/ *n* Ucraina *f*
Ukrainian /juːˈkreɪnɪən/ *a & n* ucraino, -a *mf*; (*language*) ucraino *m*
ulcer /ˈʌlsə(r)/ *n* ulcera *f*
ulterior /ʌlˈtɪərɪə(r)/ *a* ~ **motive** secondo fine *m*
ultimate /ˈʌltɪmət/ *a* definitivo; (*final*) finale; (*fundamental*) fondamentale
ultimately /ˈʌltɪmətlɪ/ *adv* alla fine
ultimatum /ʌltɪˈmeɪtəm/ *n* ultimatum *m inv*
ultramarine /ʌltrəməˈriːn/ *a* oltremarino ● *n* azzurro *m* oltremarino
ultrasound /ˈʌltrəsaʊnd/ *n* Med ecografia *f*
ultrasound scan *n* ecografia *m*
ultrasound scanner *n* scanner *m inv* per ecografia
ultraviolet /ʌltrəˈvaɪələt/ *a* ultravioletto
umbilical /ʌmˈbɪlɪkl/ *a* ~ **cord** cordone *m* ombelicale
umbrage /ˈʌmbrɪdʒ/ *n* take ~ offendersi
umbrella /ʌmˈbrelə/ *n* ombrello *m*
umbrella stand *n* portaombrelli *m inv*
umpire /ˈʌmpaɪə(r)/ *n* arbitro *m* ● *vt/i* arbitrare
umpteen /ʌmpˈtiːn/ *a fam* innumerevole
umpteenth /ʌmpˈtiːnθ/ *a fam* ennesimo; **for the ~ time** per l'ennesima volta
UN *abbr* (**United Nations**) ONU *f*
unabashed /ʌnəˈbæʃt/ *a* spudorato
unabated /ʌnəˈbeɪtɪd/ *a* (*enthusiasm*) inalterato; **continue ~** (*gales:*) continuare con la stessa intensità
unable /ʌnˈeɪbl/ *a* **be ~ to do sth** non potere fare qcsa; (*not know how*) non sapere fare qcsa
unabridged /ʌnəˈbrɪdʒd/ *a* integrale
unacceptable /ʌnəkˈseptəbl/ *a* (*proposal, suggestion*) inaccettabile
unaccompanied /ʌnəˈkʌmpnɪd/ *a* non accompagnato; (*luggage*) incustodito

unaccountable /ʌnəˈkaʊntəbl/ *a* inspiegabile
unaccountably /ʌnəˈkaʊntəblɪ/ *adv* inspiegabilmente
unaccounted /ʌnəˈkaʊntɪd/ *a* **be ~ for** (*not explained*) non avere spiegazione; (*not found*) mancare
unaccustomed /ʌnəˈkʌstəmd/ *a* insolito; **be ~ to** non essere abituato a
unadorned /ʌnəˈdɔːnd/ *a* (*walls*) disadorno
unadulterated /ʌnəˈdʌltəreɪtɪd/ *a* (*water*) puro; (*wine*) non sofisticato; *fig* assoluto
unadventurous /ʌnədˈventʃ(ə)rəs/ *a* (*person, production*) poco avventuroso; (*meal*) poco fantasioso
unaided /ʌnˈeɪdɪd/ *a* senza aiuto
unalloyed /ʌnəˈlɔɪd/ *a fig* puro
unanimity /juːnəˈnɪmətɪ/ *n* unanimità *f*
unanimous /juːˈnænɪməs/ *a* unanime
unanimously /juːˈnænɪməslɪ/ *adv* all'unanimità
unannounced /ʌnəˈnaʊnst/ *a* inaspettato
unanswerable /ʌnˈɑːns(ə)rəbl/ *a* (*remark, case*) irrefutabile; (*question*) senza risposta
unappealing /ʌnəˈpiːlɪŋ/ *a* poco attraente
unappetizing /ʌnˈæpetaɪzɪŋ/ *a* poco appetitoso
unappreciated /ʌnəˈpriːʃɪeɪtɪd/ *a* (*work of art*) incompreso
unappreciative /ʌnəˈpriːʃ(ɪ)ətɪv/ *a* (*audience*) indifferente; (*person*) ingrato
unapproachable /ʌnəˈprəʊtʃəbl/ *a* (*person*) inavvicinabile
unarmed /ʌnˈɑːmd/ *a* disarmato
unarmed combat *n* lotta *f* senza armi
unashamedly /ʌnəˈʃeɪmd/ *adv* sfacciatamente
unasked /ʌnˈɑːskt/ *adv* **he came ~** è venuto senza che nessuno glielo chiedesse
unassuming /ʌnəˈsjuːmɪŋ/ *a* senza pretese
unattached /ʌnəˈtætʃd/ *a* staccato; (*person*) senza legami
unattainable /ʌnəˈteɪnəbl/ *a* irraggiungibile
unattended /ʌnəˈtendɪd/ *a* incustodito
unattractive /ʌnəˈtræktɪv/ *a* (*person*) poco attraente; (*proposition*) poco allettante; (*characteristic*) sgradevole; (*building, furniture*) brutto
unauthorized /ʌnˈɔːθəraɪzd/ *a* non autorizzato
unavailable /ʌnəˈveɪləbl/ *a* non disponibile
unavoidable /ʌnəˈvɔɪdəbl/ *a* inevitabile
unavoidably /ʌnəˈvɔɪdəblɪ/ *adv* inevitabil-

mente; **I was ~ detained** sono stato tratte-nuto da cause di forza maggiore

unaware /ʌnəˈweə/ a **be ~ of sth** non rendersi conto di qcsa

unawares /ʌnəˈweəz/ adv **catch sb ~** prendere qcno alla sprovvista

unbalanced /ʌnˈbælənst/ a non equilibrato; (*mentally*) squilibrato

unbearable /ʌnˈbeərəbl/ a insopportabile

unbearably /ʌnˈbeərəblɪ/ adv insopportabilmente

unbeatable /ʌnˈbiːtəbl/ a imbattibile

unbeaten /ʌnˈbiːtən/ a imbattuto

unbecoming /ʌnbɪˈkʌmɪŋ/ a ⟨garment⟩ che non dona

unbeknown /ʌnbɪˈnəʊn/ a *fam* **~ to me** a mia insaputa

unbelievable /ʌnbɪˈliːvəbl/ a incredibile

unbend /ʌnˈbend/ vi (pt/pp **-bent**) (*relax*) distendersi

unbiased /ʌnˈbaɪəst/ a obiettivo

unblock /ʌnˈblɒk/ vt sbloccare

unbolt /ʌnˈbəʊlt/ vt togliere il chiavistello di

unborn /ʌnˈbɔːn/ a non ancora nato

unbreakable /ʌnˈbreɪkəbl/ a infrangibile

unbridled /ʌnˈbraɪdld/ a sfrenato

unbuckle /ʌnˈbʌkl/ vt slacciare ⟨belt⟩

unburden /ʌnˈbɜːdən/ vt **~ oneself** *fig* sfogarsi (**to** con)

unbutton /ʌnˈbʌtən/ vt sbottonare

uncalled-for /ʌnˈkɔːldfɔː(r)/ a fuori luogo

uncannily /ʌnˈkænɪlɪ/ adv incredibilmente

uncanny /ʌnˈkænɪ/ a sorprendente; ⟨silence, feeling⟩ inquietante

uncared-for /ʌnˈkeədfɔː(r)/ a ⟨house, pet⟩ trascurato

uncaring /ʌnˈkeərɪŋ/ a ⟨world⟩ indifferente

unceasing /ʌnˈsiːsɪŋ/ a incessante

uncensored /ʌnˈsensəd/ a ⟨film, book⟩ non censurato

unceremonious /ʌnserɪˈməʊnɪəs/ a (abrupt) brusco

unceremoniously /ʌnserɪˈməʊnɪəslɪ/ adv senza tante cerimonie

uncertain /ʌnˈsɜːtən/ a incerto; ⟨weather⟩ instabile; **in no ~ terms** senza mezzi termini

uncertainty /ʌnˈsɜːtəntɪ/ n incertezza f

unchallenged /ʌnˈtʃælɪndʒd/ a ⟨statement, decision⟩ incontestato; **I can't let that go ~** non posso non contestarlo

unchanged /ʌnˈtʃeɪndʒd/ a invariato

uncharacteristic /ʌnkærəktəˈrɪstɪk/ a ⟨generosity⟩ insolito

uncharitable /ʌnˈtʃærɪtəbl/ a duro

uncivilized /ʌnˈsɪvɪlaɪzd/ a ⟨people, nation⟩ non civilizzato; ⟨treatment, conditions⟩ incivile

unclassified /ʌnˈklæsɪfaɪd/ a ⟨document, information⟩ non riservato; ⟨road⟩ non classificato

uncle /ˈʌŋkl/ n zio m

unclear /ʌnˈkliːr/ a ⟨instructions, reason, voice, writing⟩ non chiaro; ⟨future⟩ incerto;

be ~ about sth ⟨person:⟩ non aver ben chiaro qcsa

unclog /ʌnˈklɒg/ vt sturare ⟨pipe⟩

uncoil /ʌnˈkɔɪl/ vt srotolare

uncomfortable /ʌnˈkʌmftəbl/ a scomodo; imbarazzante ⟨silence, situation⟩; **feel ~** *fig* sentirsi a disagio

uncomfortably /ʌnˈkʌmftəblɪ/ adv ⟨sit⟩ scomodamente; (*causing alarm etc*) spaventosamente

uncommon /ʌnˈkɒmən/ a insolito

uncommunicative /ʌnkəˈmjuːnɪkətɪv/ a poco comunicativo

uncompromising /ʌnˈkɒmprəmaɪzɪŋ/ a intransigente

unconditional /ʌnkənˈdɪʃənl/ a incondizionato

unconditionally /ʌnkənˈdɪʃnəlɪ/ adv incondizionatamente

unconscious /ʌnˈkɒnʃəs/ a privo di sensi; (*unaware*) inconsapevole; **be ~ of sth** non rendersi conto di qcsa

unconsciously /ʌnˈkɒnʃəslɪ/ adv inconsapevolmente

uncontested /ʌnkənˈtestɪd/ a ⟨Pol: seat⟩ non disputato

uncontrollable /ʌnkənˈtrəʊləbl/ a incontrollabile; ⟨sobbing⟩ irrefrenabile

uncontrollably /ʌnkənˈtrəʊləblɪ/ adv ⟨increase⟩ incontrollatamente; ⟨laugh, sob⟩ senza potersi controllare

unconventional /ʌnkənˈvenʃnəl/ a poco convenzionale

unconvincing /ʌnkənˈvɪnsɪŋ/ a poco convincente

uncooked /ʌnˈkʊkt/ a crudo

uncooperative /ʌnkəʊˈɒpr(ə)tɪv/ a poco cooperativo

uncork /ʌnˈkɔːk/ vt sturare

uncorroborated /ʌnkəˈrɒbəreɪtɪd/ a non convalidato

uncouth /ʌnˈkuːθ/ a zotico

uncover /ʌnˈkʌvə(r)/ vt scoprire; portare alla luce ⟨buried object⟩

uncross /ʌnˈkrɒs/ vt disincrociare ⟨legs, arms⟩

unctuous /ˈʌŋktjʊəs/ a untuoso

uncultivated /ʌnˈkʌltɪveɪtɪd/ a incolto

undamaged /ʌnˈdæmɪdʒd/ a intatto

undaunted /ʌnˈdɔːntɪd/ a imperterrito; **~ by sth** per nulla intimidito da qcsa

undecided /ʌndɪˈsaɪdɪd/ a indeciso; (*not settled*) incerto

undefined /ʌndɪˈfaɪnd/ a ⟨objective, nature⟩ indeterminato

undelivered /ʌndɪˈlɪvəd/ a ⟨mail⟩ non recapitato

undeniable /ʌndɪˈnaɪəbl/ a innegabile

undeniably /ʌndɪˈnaɪəblɪ/ adv innegabilmente

under /ˈʌndə(r)/ prep sotto; (*less than*) al di sotto di; **~ there** lì sotto; **~ repair/construction** in riparazione/costruzione; **~ way** *fig* in corso; ● adv (~ *water*) sott'acqua; (*unconscious*) sotto anestesia

underachieve /ˌʌndərə'tʃiːv/ *vi Sch* restare al di sotto delle proprie possibilità

underarm /'ʌndərɑːm/ *a ⟨deodorant⟩* per le ascelle; *⟨hair⟩* sotto le ascelle; *⟨service, throw⟩* dal basso verso l'alto

undercarriage /'ʌndəkærɪdʒ/ *n Aeron* carrello *m*

undercharge /ˌʌndə'tʃɑːdʒ/ *vt* far pagare meno del dovuto a

underclothes /'ʌndəkləʊðz/ *npl* biancheria *fsg* intima

undercoat /'ʌndəkəʊt/ *n* prima mano *f*

undercook /ˌʌndə'kʊk/ *vt* non cuocere abbastanza

undercover /ˌʌndə'kʌvə(r)/ *a* clandestino

undercurrent /'ʌndəkʌrənt/ *n* corrente *f* sottomarina; *fig* sottofondo *m*

undercut /ˌʌndə'kʌt/ *vt (pt/pp* **-cut**) *Comm* vendere a minor prezzo di

underdeveloped /ˌʌndədɪ'veləpt/ *a ⟨country⟩* sottosviluppato; *Phot* non completamente sviluppato

underdog /'ʌndədɒg/ *n* perdente *m*

underdone /ˌʌndə'dʌn/ *a ⟨meat⟩* al sangue

underemployed /ˌʌndərɪm'plɔɪd/ *a ⟨person⟩* sottoccupato; *⟨resources, equipment etc⟩* non sfruttato completamente

underequipped /ˌʌndərɪ'kwɪpt/ *a ⟨army, person⟩* insufficientemente equipaggiato; *⟨schools, gym⟩* insufficientemente attrezzato

underestimate /ˌʌndər'estɪmeɪt/ *vt* sottovalutare

underexpose /ˌʌndərɪks'pəʊz/ *vt Phot* sottoesporre

underfed /ˌʌndə'fed/ *a* denutrito

underfloor /'ʌndəflɔː(r)/ *a ⟨pipes, wiring⟩* sotto il pavimento

underfoot /ˌʌndə'fʊt/ *adv* sotto i piedi; **trample ~** calpestare

underfunded /ˌʌndə'fʌndɪd/ *a* insufficientemente finanziato

underfunding /ˌʌndə'fʌndɪŋ/ *n* finanziamento *m* insufficiente

undergo /ˌʌndə'gəʊ/ *vt (pt* **-went**, *pp* **-gone**) subire *⟨operation, treatment⟩*; **~ repair** essere in riparazione

undergraduate /ˌʌndə'grædʒʊət/ *n* studente, -tessa *mf* universitario, -a

underground[1] /ˌʌndə'graʊnd/ *adv* sottoterra

underground[2] /'ʌndəgraʊnd/ *a* sotterraneo; *(secret)* clandestino ● *n (railway)* metropolitana *f*

underground car park *n* parcheggio *m* sotterraneo

undergrowth /'ʌndəgrəʊθ/ *n* sottobosco *m*

underhand /'ʌndəhænd/ *a* subdolo

underlay /'ʌndəleɪ/ *n* strato *m* di gomma o feltro posto sotto la moquette

underlie /ˌʌndə'laɪ/ *vt (pt* **-lay**, *pp* **-lain**, *pres p* **-lying**) *fig* essere alla base di

underline /ˌʌndə'laɪn/ *vt* sottolineare

underling /'ʌndəlɪŋ/ *n pej* subalterno, -a *mf*

underlying /ˌʌndə'laɪɪŋ/ *a fig* fondamentale

undermanned /ˌʌndə'mænd/ *a ⟨factory⟩* a corto di mano d'opera

undermentioned /ˌʌndə'menʃnd/ *a* sottoindicato

undermine /ˌʌndə'maɪn/ *vt fig* minare

underneath /ˌʌndə'niːθ/ *prep* sotto; **~ it** sotto ● *adv* sotto

undernourished /ˌʌndə'nʌrɪʃt/ *a* denutrito

underpaid /ˌʌndə'peɪd/ *a* mal pagato

underpants /'ʌndəpænts/ *npl* mutande *fpl*

underpass /'ʌndəpɑːs/ *n* sottopassaggio *m*

underpay /ˌʌndə'peɪ/ *vt* sottopagare *⟨employee⟩*

underpin /ˌʌndə'pɪn/ *vt* puntellare *⟨wall⟩*; rafforzare *⟨currency, power, theory⟩*; essere alla base di *⟨religion, society⟩*

underpopulated /ˌʌndə'pɒpjʊleɪtɪd/ *a* sottopopolato

underprivileged /ˌʌndə'prɪvɪlɪdʒd/ *a* non abbiente

underrate /ˌʌndə'reɪt/ *vt* sottovalutare

underseal /'ʌndəsiːl/ *n Auto* antiruggine *m inv*

under-secretary /ˌʌndə'sekrət(ə)rɪ/ *n Br Pol* sottosegretario *m*

undersell /ˌʌndə'sel/ *vt* vendere a prezzo inferiore rispetto a *⟨competitor⟩*; pubblicizzare poco *⟨product⟩*

undersexed /ˌʌndə'sekst/ *a* con scarsa libido

undershirt /'ʌndəʃɜːt/ *n Am* maglia *f* della pelle

undersigned /ˌʌndə'saɪnd/ *a* sottoscritto

undersized /ˌʌndə'saɪzd/ *a ⟨portion⟩* scarso; *⟨animal⟩* troppo piccolo; *⟨person⟩* di statura inferiore alla media

understaffed /ˌʌndə'stɑːft/ *a* a corto di personale

understand /ˌʌndə'stænd/ *vt (pt/pp* **-stood**) capire; **I ~ that...** *(have heard)* mi risulta che... ● *vi* capire

understandable /ˌʌndə'stændəbl/ *a* comprensibile

understandably /ˌʌndə'stændəblɪ/ *adv* comprensibilmente

understanding /ˌʌndə'stændɪŋ/ *a* comprensivo ● *n* comprensione *f*; *(agreement)* accordo *m*; **reach an ~** trovare un accordo; **on the ~ that** a condizione che

understatement /'ʌndəsteɪtmənt/ *n* **that's an ~** non è dire abbastanza

understudy /'ʌndəstʌdɪ/ *n Theat* sostituto, -a *mf*

undertake /ˌʌndə'teɪk/ *vt (pt* **-took**, *pp* **-taken**) intraprendere; **~ to do sth** impegnarsi a fare qcsa

undertaker /'ʌndəteɪkə(r)/ *n* impresario *m* di pompe funebri; **[firm of] ~s** *n* impresa *f* di pompe funebri

undertaking /ˌʌndə'teɪkɪŋ/ *n* impresa *f*; *(promise)* promessa *f*

under-the-counter *a ⟨goods, supply, trade⟩* comprato/venduto sottobanco

undertone /'ʌndətəʊn/ *n fig* sottofondo *m*; **in an ~** sottovoce

undervalue /ʌndə'vælju:/ vt sottovalutare; **the shares are ~d** le azioni si sono svalutate

underwater¹ /'ʌndəwɔ:tə(r)/ a subacqueo

underwater² /ʌndə'wɔ:tə(r)/ adv sott'acqua

under way a **be ~ ~** ⟨vehicle:⟩ essere in corsa; ⟨filming, talks:⟩ essere in corso; **get ~ ~** ⟨vehicle:⟩ mettersi in viaggio; ⟨preparations, season:⟩ avere inizio

underwear /'ʌndəweə(r)/ n biancheria f intima

underweight /ʌndə'weɪt/ a sotto peso

underworld /'ʌndəwɜ:ld/ n ⟨criminals⟩ malavita f

underwriter /'ʌndəraɪtə(r)/ n assicuratore m

undeserved /ʌndɪ'zɜ:vd/ a ⟨praise, reward, win⟩ immeritato; ⟨blame, punish⟩ ingiusto

undeservedly /ʌndɪ'zɜ:vɪdlɪ/ adv ⟨praise, reward, win⟩ immeritatamente; ⟨blame, punish⟩ ingiustamente

undesirable /ʌndɪ'zaɪərəbl/ a indesiderato; ⟨person⟩ poco raccomandabile

undetected /ʌndɪ'tektɪd/ a ⟨crime, cancer⟩ non scoperto; ⟨flaw, movement, intruder⟩ non visto; **go ~** ⟨cancer, crime:⟩ non essere scoperto; ⟨person:⟩ passare inosservato ● adv ⟨break in, listen⟩ senza essere scoperto

undeveloped /ʌndɪ'veləpt/ a non sviluppato; ⟨land⟩ non sfruttato

undies /'ʌndɪz/ npl fam biancheria f intima (da donna)

undignified /ʌn'dɪgnɪfaɪd/ a poco dignitoso

undisciplined /ʌn'dɪsɪplɪnd/ a indisciplinato

undiscovered /ʌndɪs'kʌvəd/ a ⟨secret⟩ non svelato; ⟨crime, document⟩ non scoperto; ⟨land⟩ inesplorato; ⟨species⟩ sconosciuto; ⟨talent⟩ non ancora scoperto

undiscriminating /ʌndɪs'krɪmɪneɪtɪŋ/ a che non sa fare distinzioni

undisputed /ʌndɪ'spju:tɪd/ a indiscusso

undisturbed /ʌndɪ'stɜ:bd/ a ⟨sleep, night⟩ indisturbato

undivided /ʌndɪ'vaɪdɪd/ a ⟨loyalty, attention⟩ assoluto

undo /ʌn'du:/ vt (pt **-did**, pp **-done**) disfare; slacciare ⟨dress, shoes⟩; sbottonare ⟨shirt⟩; fig, Comput annullare

undone /ʌn'dʌn/ a ⟨shirt, button⟩ sbottonato; ⟨shoes, dress⟩ slacciato; (not accomplished) non fatto; **leave ~** ⟨job⟩ tralasciare

undoubted /ʌn'daʊtɪd/ a indubbio

undoubtedly /ʌn'daʊtɪdlɪ/ adv senza dubbio

undress /ʌn'dres/ vt spogliare; **get ~ed** spogliarsi ● vi spogliarsi

undrinkable /ʌn'drɪŋkəbl/ a (unpleasant) imbevibile; (dangerous) non potabile

undue /ʌn'dju:/ a eccessivo

undulating /'ʌndjʊleɪtɪŋ/ a ondulato; ⟨country⟩ collinoso

unduly /ʌn'dju:lɪ/ adv eccessivamente

undying /ʌn'daɪɪŋ/ a eterno

unearned /ʌn'ɜ:nd/ a immeritato; **~ income** rendita f

unearth /ʌn'ɜ:θ/ vt dissotterrare; fig scovare; scoprire ⟨secret⟩

unearthly /ʌn'ɜ:θlɪ/ a soprannaturale; **at an ~ hour** fam a un'ora impossibile

unease /ʌn'i:z/ n disagio m

uneasy /ʌn'i:zɪ/ a a disagio; ⟨person⟩ inquieto; ⟨feeling⟩ inquietante; ⟨truce⟩ precario

uneatable /ʌn'i:təbl/ a immangiabile

uneconomic /ʌni:kə'nɒmɪk/ a poco remunerativo

uneconomical /ʌni:kə'nɒmɪkl/ a poco economico

uneducated /ʌn'edjʊkeɪtɪd/ a ⟨person⟩ non istruito; ⟨tastes⟩ non raffinato; ⟨accent, speech⟩ da persona non istruita

unemployed /ʌnem'plɔɪd/ a disoccupato ● npl **the ~** i disoccupati

unemployment /ʌnem'plɔɪmənt/ n disoccupazione f

unemployment benefit n sussidio m di disoccupazione

unending /ʌn'endɪŋ/ a senza fine

unenthusiastic /ʌnɪmθju:zɪ'æstɪk/ a poco entusiasta

unequal /ʌn'i:kwəl/ a disuguale; ⟨struggle⟩ impari; **be ~ to a task** non essere all'altezza di un compito

unequalled /ʌn'i:kwəld/ a ⟨achievement, quality, record⟩ ineguagliato

unequally /ʌn'i:kwəlɪ/ adv in modo disuguale

unequivocal /ʌnɪ'kwɪvəkl/ a inequivocabile; ⟨person⟩ esplicito

unequivocally /ʌnɪ'kwɪvəklɪ/ adv inequivocabilmente

unerring /ʌn'ɜ:rɪŋ/ a infallibile

unethical /ʌn'eθɪkl/ a immorale

uneven /ʌn'i:vən/ a irregolare; ⟨distribution⟩ ineguale; ⟨number⟩ dispari

unevenly /ʌn'i:vənlɪ/ adv irregolarmente; ⟨distributed⟩ inegualmente

uneventful /ʌnɪ'ventfʊl/ a senza avvenimenti di rilievo

unexciting /ʌnɪk'saɪtɪŋ/ a poco entusiasmante

unexpected /ʌnɪk'spektɪd/ a inaspettato

unexpectedly /ʌnɪk'spektɪdlɪ/ adv inaspettatamente

unexplored /ʌnɪk'splɔ:d/ a inesplorato

unfailing /ʌn'feɪlɪŋ/ a infallibile

unfair /ʌn'feə/ a ingiusto

unfair dismissal n licenziamento m ingiustificato

unfairly /ʌn'feəlɪ/ adv ingiustamente

unfairness /ʌn'feənɪs/ n ingiustizia f

unfaithful /ʌn'feɪθfʊl/ a infedele

unfamiliar /ʌnfə'mɪljə(r)/ a sconosciuto; **be ~ with** non conoscere

unfashionable /ʌn'fæʃnəbl/ a fuori moda

unfasten /ʌn'fɑ:sn/ vt slacciare; (detach) staccare

unfathomable /ʌnˈfæð(ə)məbl/ a imperscrutabile

unfavourable /ʌnˈfeɪv(ə)rəbl/ a sfavorevole; ⟨impression⟩ negativo

unfeeling /ʌnˈfiːlɪŋ/ a insensibile

unfinished /ʌnˈfɪnɪʃt/ a da finire; ⟨business⟩ in sospeso

unfit /ʌnˈfɪt/ a inadatto; (morally) indegno; Sport fuori forma; **~ for work** non in grado di lavorare; **~ for human consumption** non commestibile

unflappable /ʌnˈflæpəbl/ a fam calmo

unflattering /ʌnˈflæt(ə)rɪŋ/ a ⟨clothes, hairstyle⟩ che non dona; ⟨portrait, description⟩ poco lusinghiero

unflinching /ʌnˈflɪntʃɪŋ/ a risoluto

unfold /ʌnˈfəʊld/ vt spiegare; (spread out) aprire; fig rivelare ● vi ⟨view:⟩ spiegarsi

unforeseeable /ʌnfɔːˈsiːəbl/ a imprevedibile

unforeseen /ʌnfɔːˈsiːn/ a imprevisto

unforgettable /ʌnfəˈgetəbl/ a indimenticabile

unforgivable /ʌnfəˈgɪvəbl/ a imperdonabile

unforgiving /ʌnfəˈgɪvɪŋ/ a che non perdona

unfortunate /ʌnˈfɔːtʃənət/ a sfortunato; (regrettable) spiacevole; ⟨remark, choice⟩ infelice

unfortunately /ʌnˈfɔːtʃənətlɪ/ adv purtroppo

unfounded /ʌnˈfaʊndɪd/ a infondato

unfriendly /ʌnˈfrendlɪ/ a ⟨person, remark⟩ scortese, poco amichevole; ⟨place, climate, reception⟩ ostile; ⟨software⟩ difficile da usare

unfulfilled /ʌnfʊlˈfɪld/ a ⟨prophecy⟩ non avverato; ⟨promise⟩ non mantenuto; ⟨ambition⟩ non realizzato; ⟨desire, need⟩ non soddisfatto; ⟨condition⟩ non rispettato; **feel ~** essere insoddisfatto

unfurl /ʌnˈfɜːl/ vt spiegare ● vi spiegarsi

unfurnished /ʌnˈfɜːnɪʃt/ a non ammobiliato

ungainly /ʌnˈgeɪnlɪ/ a sgraziato

ungentlemanly /ʌnˈdʒentlmənlɪ/ a non da gentiluomo

ungodly /ʌnˈgɒdlɪ/ a empio; **~ hour** fam ora f impossibile

ungracious /ʌnˈgreɪʃəs/ a sgarbato

ungrateful /ʌnˈgreɪtfʊl/ a ingrato

ungratefully /ʌnˈgreɪtfʊlɪ/ adv senza riconoscenza

unhappily /ʌnˈhæpɪlɪ/ adv infelicemente; (unfortunately) purtroppo

unhappiness /ʌnˈhæpɪnɪs/ n infelicità f

unhappy /ʌnˈhæpɪ/ a infelice; (not content) insoddisfatto (**with** di)

unharmed /ʌnˈhɑːmd/ a incolume

unhealthy /ʌnˈhelθɪ/ a poco sano; (insanitary) malsano

unheard-of /ʌnˈhɜːdəv/ a ⟨actor, brand⟩ mai sentito; ⟨levels, price⟩ incredibile

unheated /ʌnˈhiːtɪd/ a senza riscaldamento

unheeded /ʌnˈhiːdɪd/ a ignorato; **go ~** ⟨warning, plea:⟩ venir ignorato

unhelpful /ʌnˈhelpfʊl/ a ⟨person, attitude⟩

poco disponibile; ⟨witness⟩ che non collabora; ⟨remark⟩ di poco aiuto

unholy /ʌnˈhəʊlɪ/ a ⟨alliance, pact⟩ paradossale; ⟨fam: mess, hour⟩ indecente

unhook /ʌnˈhʊk/ vt sganciare; staccare ⟨picture⟩

unhurt /ʌnˈhɜːt/ a illeso

unhygienic /ʌnhaɪˈdʒiːnɪk/ a non igienico

unicorn /ˈjuːnɪkɔːn/ n unicorno m

unidentified /ʌnaɪˈdentɪfaɪd/ a non identificato

unification /juːnɪfɪˈkeɪʃn/ n unificazione f

uniform /ˈjuːnɪfɔːm/ a uniforme ● n uniforme f

uniformly /ˈjuːnɪfɔːmlɪ/ adv uniformemente

unify /ˈjuːnɪfaɪ/ vt (pt/pp -ied) unificare

unilateral /juːnɪˈlæt(ə)rəl/ a unilaterale

unilaterally /juːnɪˈlæt(ə)rəlɪ/ adv unilateralmente

unimaginable /ʌnɪˈmædʒɪnəbl/ a inimmaginabile

unimaginative /ʌnɪˈmædʒɪnətɪv/ a privo di fantasia

unimportant /ʌnɪmˈpɔːtənt/ a irrilevante

uninformed /ʌnɪnˈfɔːmd/ a ⟨person⟩ disinformato

uninhabited /ʌnɪnˈhæbɪtɪd/ a disabitato

uninhibited /ʌnɪnˈhɪbɪtɪd/ a ⟨person, attitude⟩ disinibito; ⟨performance, remarks⟩ disinvolto; **be ~ about doing sth** non avere problemi a fare qcsa

uninitiated /ʌnɪˈnɪʃɪeɪtɪd/ a ⟨person⟩ non iniziato ● npl **the ~** i profani

uninspired /ʌnɪnˈspaɪəd/ a privo di immaginazione; ⟨performance⟩ piatto; ⟨times⟩ banale

unintentional /ʌnɪnˈtenʃənl/ a involontario

unintentionally /ʌnɪnˈtenʃənəlɪ/ adv involontariamente

uninvited /ʌnɪnˈvaɪtɪd/ a ⟨attentions⟩ non richiesto; **~ guest** ospite mf senza invito

union /ˈjuːnɪən/ n unione f; (trade ~) sindacato m

Union Jack n bandiera f del Regno Unito

unique /juːˈniːk/ a unico

uniquely /juːˈniːklɪ/ adv unicamente

unisex /ˈjuːnɪseks/ a unisex inv

unison /ˈjuːnɪsn/ n **in ~** all'unisono

unit /ˈjuːnɪt/ n unità f inv; (department) reparto m; (of furniture) elemento m

unit cost n costo m unitario

unite /juːˈnaɪt/ vt unire ● vi unirsi

united /juːˈnaɪtɪd/ a unito

united: United Kingdom n Regno m Unito. **United Nations** n [Organizzazione f delle] Nazioni Unite fpl. **United States [of America]** n Stati mpl Uniti [d'America]

unit trust n Fin fondo m comune di investimento aperto

unity /ˈjuːnətɪ/ n unità f; (agreement) accordo m

universal /juːnɪˈvɜːsl/ a universale

universally /juːnɪˈvɜːsəlɪ/ *adv* universalmente

universe /ˈjuːnɪvɜːs/ *n* universo *m*

university /juːnɪˈvɜːsətɪ/ *n* università *f inv* ● *attrib* universitario

unjust /ʌnˈdʒʌst/ *a* ingiusto

unjustifiable /ʌnˈdʒʌstɪfaɪəbl/ *a* ingiustificato

unjustifiably /ʌnˈdʒʌstɪfaɪəblɪ/ *adv* ⟨*act*⟩ senza giustificazione

unjustified /ʌnˈdʒʌstɪfaɪd/ *a* ⟨*suspicion*⟩ ingiustificato

unjustly /ʌnˈdʒʌstlɪ/ *adv* ingiustamente

unkempt /ʌnˈkempt/ *a* trasandato; ⟨*hair*⟩ arruffato

unkind /ʌnˈkaɪnd/ *a* scortese

unkindly /ʌnˈkaɪndlɪ/ *adv* in modo scortese

unkindness /ʌnˈkaɪndnɪs/ *n* mancanza *f* di gentilezza

unknown /ʌnˈnəʊn/ *a* sconosciuto

unlawful /ʌnˈlɔːfʊl/ *a* illecito, illegale

unlawfully /ʌnˈlɔːfʊlɪ/ *adv* illegalmente

unleaded /ʌnˈledɪd/ *a* senza piombo

unleash /ʌnˈliːʃ/ *vt fig* scatenare

unless /ənˈles/ *conj* a meno che; ~ **I am mistaken** se non mi sbaglio

unlicensed /ʌnˈlaɪsnst/ *a* ⟨*transmitter, activity*⟩ abusivo; ⟨*vehicle*⟩ senza bollo; ⟨*restaurant*⟩ non autorizzato a vendere alcolici

unlike /ʌnˈlaɪk/ *a* (*not the same*) diversi ● *prep* diverso da; **that's ~ him** non è da lui; ~ **me, he...** diversamente da me, lui...

unlikely /ʌnˈlaɪklɪ/ *a* improbabile

unlimited /ʌnˈlɪmɪtɪd/ *a* illimitato

unlined /ʌnˈlaɪnd/ *a* ⟨*face*⟩ senza rughe; ⟨*paper*⟩ senza righe; ⟨*garment, curtain*⟩ senza fodera

unlit /ʌnˈlɪt/ *a* ⟨*cigarette, fire*⟩ spento; ⟨*room, street*⟩ non illuminato

unload /ʌnˈləʊd/ *vt* scaricare

unlock /ʌnˈlɒk/ *vt* aprire (*con chiave*)

unloved /ʌnˈlʌvd/ *a* **feel ~** ⟨*person:*⟩ non sentirsi amato

unlucky /ʌnˈlʌkɪ/ *a* sfortunato; **it's ~ to...** porta sfortuna...

unmade /ʌnˈmeɪd/ *a* ⟨*bed*⟩ sfatto

unmade-up *a* ⟨*road*⟩ non asfaltato

unmanageable /ʌnˈmænɪdʒəbl/ *a* ⟨*number, company*⟩ difficile da gestire; ⟨*hair, child, animal*⟩ ribelle; ⟨*size*⟩ ingombrante

unmanly /ʌnˈmænlɪ/ *a* poco virile

unmanned /ʌnˈmænd/ *a* senza equipaggio

unmarked /ʌnˈmɑːkt/ *a* Sport smarcato; ⟨*skin*⟩ senza segni; ⟨*container*⟩ non contrassegnato; ~ **police car** [auto *f inv*] civetta *f*

unmarried /ʌnˈmærɪd/ *a* non sposato

unmarried mother *n* ragazza *f* madre

unmask /ʌnˈmɑːsk/ *vt fig* smascherare

unmentionable /ʌnˈmenʃnəbl/ *a* innominabile

unmistakable /ʌnmɪˈsteɪkəbl/ *a* inconfondibile

unmistakably /ʌnmɪˈsteɪkəblɪ/ *adv* chiaramente

unmitigated /ʌnˈmɪtɪɡeɪtɪd/ *a* assoluto

unmoved /ʌnˈmuːvd/ *a fig* impassibile

unnamed /ʌnˈneɪmd/ *a* (*not having a name*) senza nome; (*name not divulged*) di cui non si conosce il nome; **the as yet ~ winner...** il vincitore di cui ancora non si conosce il nome...

unnatural /ʌnˈnætʃər(ə)l/ *a* innaturale; *pej* anormale

unnaturally /ʌnˈnætʃər(ə)lɪ/ *adv* in modo innaturale; *pej* in modo anormale

unnecessarily /ʌnˈnesəs(ə)rɪlɪ/ *adv* inutilmente

unnecessary /ʌnˈnesəs(ə)rɪ/ *a* inutile

unnerving /ʌnˈnɜːvɪŋ/ *a* inquietante

unnoticed /ʌnˈnəʊtɪst/ *a* inosservato

unobservant /ʌnəbˈzɜːvənt/ *a* senza spirito d'osservazione

unobserved /ʌnəbˈzɜːvd/ *a* inosservato; **go ~** passare inosservato

unobtainable /ʌnəbˈteɪnəbl/ *a* ⟨*product*⟩ introvabile; ⟨*phone number*⟩ non ottenibile

unobtrusive /ʌnəbˈtruːsɪf/ *a* discreto

unobtrusively /ʌnəbˈtruːsɪvlɪ/ *adv* in modo discreto

unoccupied /ʌnˈɒkjuːpaɪd/ *a* ⟨*house, block, shop*⟩ vuoto; ⟨*table, seat*⟩ libero

unofficial /ʌnəˈfɪʃl/ *a* non ufficiale

unofficially /ʌnəˈfɪʃ(ə)lɪ/ *adv* ufficiosamente

unopened /ʌnˈəʊpənd/ *a* ⟨*bottle, packet*⟩ chiuso; ⟨*package*⟩ ancora incartato

unorthodox /ʌnˈɔːθədɒks/ *a* poco ortodosso

unpack /ʌnˈpæk/ *vi* disfare le valigie ● *vt* svuotare ⟨*parcel*⟩; spacchettare ⟨*books*⟩; ~ **one's case** disfare la valigia

unpaid /ʌnˈpeɪd/ *a* da pagare; ⟨*work*⟩ non retribuito

unpalatable /ʌnˈpælətəbl/ *a* sgradevole

unparalleled /ʌnˈpærəleld/ *a* senza pari

unpasteurized /ʌnˈpɑːstʃəraɪzd/ *a* non pastorizzato

unperturbed /ʌnpəˈtɜːbd/ *a* imperturbato

unpick /ʌnˈpɪk/ *vt* disfare

unplanned /ʌnˈplænd/ *a* ⟨*stoppage, increase*⟩ imprevisto

unpleasant /ʌnˈplezənt/ *a* sgradevole; ⟨*person*⟩ maleducato

unpleasantly /ʌnˈplezəntlɪ/ *adv* sgradevolmente; ⟨*behave*⟩ maleducatamente

unpleasantness /ʌnˈplezəntnɪs/ *n* (*bad feeling*) tensioni *fpl*

unplug /ʌnˈplʌɡ/ *vt* (*pt/pp* **-plugged**) staccare

unpolluted /ʌnpəˈluːtɪd/ *a* ⟨*water*⟩ non inquinato; ⟨*mind*⟩ incontaminato

unpopular /ʌnˈpɒpjʊlə(r)/ *a* impopolare

unprecedented /ʌnˈpresɪdentɪd/ *a* senza precedenti

unpredictable /ʌnprɪˈdɪktəbl/ *a* imprevedibile

unprejudiced /ʌnˈpredʒʊdɪst/ *a* ⟨*person*⟩ senza pregiudizi; ⟨*opinion, judgement*⟩ imparziale

unpremeditated /ʌnpriːˈmedɪteɪtɪd/ *a* involontario

unprepared /ʌnprɪˈpeəd/ a impreparato

unprepossessing /ʌnpriːpəˈzesɪŋ/ a poco attraente

unpretentious /ʌnprɪˈtenʃəs/ a senza pretese

unprincipled /ʌnˈprɪnsɪpəld/ a senza principi; ⟨behaviour⟩ scorretto

unprofessional /ʌnprəˈfeʃnl/ a non professionale; **it's ~** è una mancanza di professionalità

unprofitable /ʌnˈprɒfɪtəbl/ a non redditizio

unprompted /ʌnˈprɒm(p)tɪd/ a ⟨offer⟩ spontaneo; ⟨answer⟩ non suggerito

unpronounceable /ʌnprəˈnaʊnsəbl/ a impronunciabile

unprovoked /ʌnprəˈvəʊkt/ a ⟨attack, aggression⟩ non provocato; **the attack was ~** l'attacco è avvenuto senza provocazione

unqualified /ʌnˈkwɒlɪfaɪd/ a non qualificato; ⟨fig: absolute⟩ assoluto

unquestionable /ʌnˈkwestʃənəbl/ a incontestabile

unquote /ʌnˈkwəʊt/ vi chiudere le virgolette

unravel /ʌnˈrævl/ vt ⟨pt/pp **-ravelled**⟩ districare; ⟨in knitting⟩ disfare

unreal /ʌnˈrɪəl/ a irreale; fam inverosimile

unrealistic /ʌnrɪəˈlɪstɪk/ a ⟨character, presentation⟩ poco realistico; ⟨expectation, aim⟩ irrealistico; ⟨person⟩ poco realista

unreasonable /ʌnˈriːz(ə)nəbl/ a irragionevole

unrecognizable /ʌnˈrekəgnaɪzəbl/ a irriconoscibile

unrecorded /ʌnrɪˈkɔːdɪd/ a non documentato; **go ~** non essere documentato

unrefined /ʌnrɪˈfaɪnd/ a ⟨person, manners, style⟩ rozzo; ⟨oil⟩ greggio; ⟨flour, sugar⟩ non raffinato

unrehearsed /ʌnrɪˈhɜːst/ a ⟨response, action⟩ imprevisto; ⟨speech⟩ improvvisato

unrelated /ʌnrɪˈleɪtɪd/ a ⟨facts⟩ senza rapporto (**to** con); ⟨person⟩ non imparentato (**to** con)

unrelenting /ʌnrɪˈlentɪŋ/ a ⟨person⟩ ostinato; ⟨stare⟩ insistente; ⟨pursuit⟩ continuo; ⟨heat, zeal⟩ costante

unreliable /ʌnrɪˈlaɪəbl/ a inattendibile; ⟨person⟩ inaffidabile, che non dà affidamento

unremitting /ʌnrɪˈmɪtɪŋ/ a costante; ⟨struggle⟩ continuo

unrepeatable /ʌnrɪˈpiːtəbl/ a ⟨offer, bargain⟩ unico; **his comment was ~** il commento che ha fatto è irripetibile

unrepentant /ʌnrɪˈpentənt/ a irriducibile; ⟨sinner⟩ impenitente

unrequited /ʌnrɪˈkwaɪtɪd/ a non corrisposto

unreservedly /ʌnrɪˈzɜːvɪdlɪ/ adv senza riserve; ⟨frankly⟩ francamente

unresolved /ʌnrɪˈzɒlvd/ a irrisolto

unrest /ʌnˈrest/ n fermenti mpl

unripe /ʌnˈraɪp/ a ⟨fruit⟩ acerbo; ⟨wheat⟩ non maturo

unrivalled /ʌnˈraɪvəld/ a ineguagliato

unroll /ʌnˈrəʊl/ vt srotolare ● vi srotolarsi

unruffled /ʌnˈrʌfld/ a ⟨person⟩ imperturbato; ⟨hair⟩ a posto; ⟨water⟩ non mosso; **be ~** ⟨person:⟩ rimanere imperturbato; ⟨person, hair:⟩ essere a posto

unruly /ʌnˈruːlɪ/ a indisciplinato

unsafe /ʌnˈseɪf/ a pericoloso

unsaid /ʌnˈsed/ a inespresso

unsalaried /ʌnˈsælərɪd/ a ⟨post⟩ non stipendiato

unsalted /ʌnˈsɔːltɪd/ a non salato

unsatisfactory /ʌnsætɪsˈfækt(ə)rɪ/ a poco soddisfacente

unsavoury /ʌnˈseɪvərɪ/ a equivoco

unscathed /ʌnˈskeɪðd/ a illeso

unscheduled /ʌnˈʃedjuːld/ a ⟨flight⟩ supplementare; ⟨appearance, speech⟩ fuori programma; ⟨stop⟩ non programmato

unscramble /ʌnˈskræmbl/ vt decifrare ⟨code, words⟩; sbrogliare ⟨ideas, thoughts⟩

unscrew /ʌnˈskruː/ vt svitare

unscrupulous /ʌnˈskruːpjʊləs/ a senza scrupoli

unseasoned /ʌnˈsiːznd/ a ⟨wood⟩ non stagionato; ⟨food⟩ scondito

unseemly /ʌnˈsiːmlɪ/ a indecoroso

unselfish /ʌnˈselfɪʃ/ a disinteressato

unsettled /ʌnˈsetld/ a in agitazione; ⟨weather⟩ variabile; ⟨bill⟩ non saldato

unshakeable /ʌnˈʃeɪkəbl/ a categorico

unshaven /ʌnˈʃeɪvn/ a non rasato

unsightly /ʌnˈsaɪtlɪ/ a brutto

unsinkable /ʌnˈsɪŋkəbl/ a ⟨ship, object⟩ inaffondabile; ⟨hum: personality⟩ che non si deprime

unskilled /ʌnˈskɪld/ a non specializzato

unskilled worker n manovale m

unsmiling /ʌnˈsmaɪlɪŋ/ a ⟨person⟩ serioso

unsociable /ʌnˈsəʊʃəbl/ a scontroso

unsolicited /ʌnsəˈlɪsɪtɪd/ a ⟨help, advice⟩ non richiesto; ⟨job application⟩ spontaneo

unsophisticated /ʌnsəˈfɪstɪkeɪtɪd/ a semplice

unsound /ʌnˈsaʊnd/ a ⟨building, reasoning⟩ poco solido; ⟨advice⟩ poco sensato; **of ~ mind** malato di mente

unspeakable /ʌnˈspiːkəbl/ a indicibile

unspoiled /ʌnˈspɔɪld/ a ⟨town⟩ non deturpato; ⟨landscape⟩ intatto; **she was ~ by fame** la fama non l'ha cambiata

unstable /ʌnˈsteɪbl/ a instabile; (mentally) squilibrato

unsteadily /ʌnˈstedɪlɪ/ adv ⟨walk, speak⟩ in modo malsicuro

unsteady /ʌnˈstedɪ/ a malsicuro

unstoppable /ʌnˈstɒpəbl/ a ⟨force, momentum⟩ inarrestabile

unstressed /ʌnˈstrest/ a ⟨vowel, word⟩ atono

unstuck /ʌnˈstʌk/ a **come ~** staccarsi; ⟨fam: project⟩ andare a monte

unsuccessful /ʌnsəkˈsesfʊl/ a fallimentare; **be ~** ⟨in attempt⟩ non aver successo

unsuccessfully /ʌnsək'sesfʊlɪ/ *adv* senza successo

unsuitable /ʌn'su:təbl/ *a* ⟨*inappropriate*⟩ inadatto; ⟨*inconvenient*⟩ inopportuno

unsupervised /ʌn'su:pəvaɪzd/ *a* ⟨*activity*⟩ non controllato

unsuspecting /ʌnsə'spektɪŋ/ *a* fiducioso

unsweetened /ʌn'swi:tənd/ *a* senza zucchero

unsympathetic /ʌnsɪmpə'θetɪk/ *a* ⟨*person, attitude, manner, tone*⟩ poco comprensivo; ⟨*person, character*⟩ antipatico; **she is ~ to the cause** non appoggia la causa

untamed /ʌn'teɪmd/ *a* ⟨*lion*⟩ non addomesticato; ⟨*passion, person*⟩ indomito

untangle /ʌn'tæŋgl/ *vt* sbrogliare ⟨*threads*⟩; risolvere ⟨*difficulties, mystery*⟩

unthinkable /ʌn'θɪŋkəbl/ *a* impensabile

unthought-of /ʌn'θɔ:təv/ *a* impensato; **hitherto ~** finora impensato

untidily /ʌn'taɪdɪlɪ/ *adv* disordinatamente

untidiness /ʌn'taɪdmɪs/ *n* disordine *m*

untidy /ʌn'taɪdɪ/ *a* disordinato

untie /ʌn'taɪ/ *vt* slegare

until /ən'tɪl/ *prep* fino a; **not ~** non prima di; **~ the evening** fino alla sera; **~ his arrival** fino al suo arrivo ● *conj* finché, fino a quando; **not ~ you've seen it** non prima che tu l'abbia visto

untimely /ʌn'taɪmlɪ/ *a* inopportuno; ⟨*premature*⟩ prematuro

untiring /ʌn'taɪərɪŋ/ *a* instancabile

untold /ʌn'təʊld/ *a* ⟨*wealth*⟩ incalcolabile; ⟨*suffering*⟩ indescrivibile; ⟨*story*⟩ inedito

untouched /ʌn'tʌtʃt/ *a* ⟨*unchanged, undisturbed*⟩ intatto; ⟨*unscathed*⟩ incolume; ⟨*unaffected*⟩ non toccato; **leave one's dinner/a meal ~** non toccare cibo

untoward /ʌntə'wɔ:d/ *a* **if nothing ~ happens** se non capita un imprevisto

untrained /ʌn'treɪnd/ *a* ⟨*voice*⟩ non impostato; ⟨*eye, artist, actor*⟩ inesperto; **be ~** ⟨*worker:*⟩ non avere una formazione professionale

untranslatable /ʌntrænz'leɪtəbl/ *a* intraducibile

untreated /ʌn'tri:tɪd/ *a* ⟨*sewage, water*⟩ non depurato; ⟨*illness*⟩ non curato

untrue /ʌn'tru:/ *a* falso; **that's ~** non è vero

unused[1] /ʌn'ju:zd/ *a* non usato

unused[2] /ʌn'ju:st/ *a* **be ~ to** non essere abituato a

unusual /ʌn'ju:ʒʊəl/ *a* insolito

unusually /ʌn'ju:ʒʊəlɪ/ *adv* insolitamente

unveil /ʌn'veɪl/ *vt* scoprire

unversed /ʌn'vɜ:st/ *a* inesperto (**in** di)

unwanted /ʌn'wɒntɪd/ *a* ⟨*child, pet, visitor*⟩ indesiderato; ⟨*goods, produce*⟩ che non serve; **feel ~** sentirsi respinto

unwarranted /ʌn'wɒrəntɪd/ *a* ingiustificato

unwelcome /ʌn'welkəm/ *a* sgradito

unwell /ʌn'wel/ *a* indisposto

unwieldy /ʌn'wi:ldɪ/ *a* ingombrante

unwilling /ʌn'wɪlɪŋ/ *a* riluttante

unwillingly /ʌn'wɪlɪŋlɪ/ *adv* malvolentieri

unwind /ʌn'waɪnd/ *v* (*pt/pp* **unwound**) ● *vt* svolgere, srotolare ● *vi* svolgersi, srotolarsi; ⟨*fam: relax*⟩ rilassarsi

unwise /ʌn'waɪz/ *a* imprudente

unwisely /ʌn'waɪzlɪ/ *adv* imprudentemente

unwitting /ʌn'wɪtɪŋ/ *a* involontario; ⟨*victim*⟩ inconsapevole

unwittingly /ʌn'wɪtɪŋlɪ/ *adv* involontariamente

unworldly /ʌn'wɜ:ldlɪ/ *a* ⟨*not materialistic*⟩ poco materialista; ⟨*naive*⟩ ingenuo; ⟨*spiritual*⟩ non materialista

unworthy /ʌn'wɜ:ðɪ/ *a* non degno

unwrap /ʌn'ræp/ *vt* (*pt/pp* **-wrapped**) scartare ⟨*present, parcel*⟩

unwritten /ʌn'rɪtn/ *a* tacito

unyielding /ʌn'ji:ldɪŋ/ *a* rigido

unzip /ʌn'zɪp/ *vt* aprire [la cerniera di] ⟨*garment, bag*⟩

up /ʌp/ *adv* su; ⟨*not in bed*⟩ alzato; ⟨*road*⟩ smantellato; ⟨*theatre curtain, blinds*⟩ alzato; ⟨*shelves, tent*⟩ montato; ⟨*notice*⟩ affisso; ⟨*building*⟩ costruito; **prices are up** i prezzi sono aumentati; **be up for sale** essere in vendita; **up here/there** quassù/lassù; **time's up** tempo scaduto; **what's up?** *fam* cosa è successo?; **up to** ⟨*as far as*⟩ fino a; **be up to** essere all'altezza di ⟨*task*⟩; **what's he up to?** *fam* cosa sta facendo?; ⟨*plotting*⟩ cosa sta combinando?; **I'm up to page 100** sono arrivato a pagina 100; **feel up to it** sentirsela; **be one up on sb** *fam* essere in vantaggio su qcno; **go up** salire; **lift up** alzare; **up against** *fig* alle prese con ● *prep* su; **the cat ran/is up the tree** il gatto è salito di corsa/è sull'albero; **further up this road** più avanti su questa strada; **row up the river** risalire il fiume; **go up the stairs** salire su per le scale; **be up the pub** *fam* essere al pub; **be up on** *or* **in sth** essere bene informato su qcsa ● *npl* **ups and downs** alti *mpl* e bassi

up-and-coming *a* promettente

upbeat /'ʌpbi:t/ *a* ottimistico

upbringing /'ʌpbrɪŋɪŋ/ *n* educazione *f*

update /ʌp'deɪt/ *vt* aggiornare

upfront /ʌp'frʌnt/ *a* *fam* ⟨*frank*⟩ aperto; ⟨*money*⟩ anticipato ● *adv* ⟨*pay*⟩ in anticipo

upgrade /ʌp'greɪd/ *vt* promuovere ⟨*person*⟩; modernizzare ⟨*equipment*⟩ ● *n* aggiornamento *m*

upheaval /ʌp'hi:vl/ *n* scompiglio *m*

uphill /ʌp'hɪl/ *a* in salita; *fig* arduo ● *adv* in salita

uphold /ʌp'həʊld/ *vt* (*pt/pp* **upheld**) sostenere ⟨*principle*⟩; confermare ⟨*verdict*⟩

upholster /ʌp'həʊlstə(r)/ *vt* tappezzare

upholsterer /ʌp'həʊlstərə(r)/ *n* tappezziere, -a *mf*

upholstery /ʌp'həʊlstərɪ/ *n* tappezzeria *f*

upkeep /'ʌpki:p/ *n* mantenimento *m*

uplifting /ʌp'lɪftɪŋ/ *a* ⟨*morally*⟩ edificante

up-market *a* di qualità

upon /ə'pɒn/ *prep* su; **~ arriving home** una volta arrivato a casa

upper /'ʌpə(r)/ a superiore ● n (of shoe) to-
maia f

upper: upper-case a maiuscolo. **upper
circle** n seconda galleria f. **upper class** n
alta borghesia f. **upper crust** a hum aristocratico. **upper hand** n **have the ~ ~** avere il
sopravvento. **upper middle class** n ceto m
medio-alto

uppermost /'ʌpəməʊst/ a più alto; **that's ~
in my mind** è la mia preoccupazione principale

upright /'ʌpraɪt/ a dritto; ⟨piano⟩ verticale;
⟨honest⟩ retto ● n montante m

upright freezer n freezer m inv verticale

uprising /'ʌpraɪzɪŋ/ n rivolta f

upriver /ʌp'rɪvə/ adv ⟨lie⟩ a monte; ⟨sail⟩
controcorrente

uproar /'ʌprɔː(r)/ n tumulto m; **be in an ~**
essere in trambusto

uproot /ʌp'ruːt/ vt sradicare

upset[1] /ʌp'set/ vt (pt/pp **upset**, pres p
upsetting) rovesciare; sconvolgere ⟨plan⟩;
⟨distress⟩ turbare; **get ~ about sth** prendersela per qcsa; **be very ~** essere sconvolto;
have an ~ stomach avere l'intestino disturbato

upset[2] /'ʌpset/ n scombussolamento m

upshot /'ʌpʃɒt/ n risultato m

upside down adv sottosopra; **turn ~ ~** capovolgere

upstage /ʌp'steɪdʒ/ vt Theat, fig distogliere
l'attenzione del pubblico da ● adv Theat
⟨stand⟩ al fondo del palcoscenico; ⟨move⟩ verso il fondo del palcoscenico

upstairs[1] /ʌp'steəz/ adv [al piano] di sopra

upstairs[2] /'ʌpsteəz/ a del piano superiore

upstart /'ʌpstɑːt/ n arrivato, -a mf

upstream /ʌp'striːm/ adv controcorrente

upsurge /'ʌpsɜːdʒ/ n (in sales) aumento m
improvviso; (of enthusiasm, crime) ondata f

uptake /'ʌpteɪk/ n **be slow on the ~** essere
lento nel capire; **be quick on the ~** capire le
cose al volo

uptight /ʌp'taɪt/ a teso

up-to-date a moderno; ⟨news⟩ ultimo;
⟨person, information, records⟩ aggiornato

up-to-the-minute a ⟨information⟩ dell'ultimo minuto

uptown /'ʌptaʊn/ a ⟨Am: smart⟩ dei quartieri alti

upturn /'ʌptɜːn/ n ripresa f

upward /'ʌpwəd/ a verso l'alto, in su; **~
slope** salita f ● adv **~[s]** verso l'alto; **~s of**
oltre

upwardly mobile /ʌpwədlɪ'məʊbaɪl/ a che
sale nella scala sociale

uranium /jʊ'reɪnɪəm/ n uranio m

urban /'ɜːbən/ a urbano

urban blight, urban decay n degrado m
urbano

urbane /ɜː'beɪn/ a cortese

urban planning n urbanistica f

urge /ɜːdʒ/ n forte desiderio m ● vt esortare
(**to** a)

■ **urge on** vt spronare

urgency /'ɜːdʒənsɪ/ n urgenza f

urgent /'ɜːdʒənt/ a urgente

urgently /'ɜːdʒəntlɪ/ adv urgentemente

urinal /jʊ'raɪml/ n ⟨fixture⟩ orinale m; ⟨place⟩
vespasiano m

urinate /'jʊərɪneɪt/ vi urinare

urine /'jʊərɪn/ n urina f

urn /ɜːn/ n urna f; ⟨for tea⟩ contenitore m mu-
nito di cannella che si trova nei self-service,
mense ecc

US n abbr (**United States**) U.S.A. mpl

us /ʌs/ pers pron ci; ⟨after prep⟩ noi; **they
know us** ci conoscono; **give us the money**
dateci i soldi; **give it to us** datecelo; **they
showed it to us** ce l'hanno fatto vedere;
they meant us, not you intendevano noi,
non voi; **it's us** siamo noi; **she hates us** ci
odia

USA n abbr (**United States of America**)
U.S.A. mpl

usable /'juːzəbl/ a usabile

usage /'juːsɪdʒ/ n uso m

use[1] /juːs/ n uso m; **be of ~** essere utile; **be
of no ~** essere inutile; **make ~ of** usare;
⟨exploit⟩ sfruttare; **it is no ~** è inutile;
what's the ~? a che scopo?

use[2] /juːz/ vt usare

■ **use up** vt consumare

used[1] /juːzd/ a usato

used[2] /juːst/ pt **be ~ to sth** essere abituato a
qcsa; **get ~ to** abituarsi a; **he ~ to say** diceva; **he ~ to live here** viveva qui

useful /'juːsfl/ a utile

usefulness /'juːsflnɪs/ n utilità f

useless /'juːslɪs/ a inutile; ⟨fam: person⟩ incapace; **you're ~!** sei un idiota!

user /'juːzə(r)/ n utente mf

user: user-friendliness n facilità f d'uso.
user-friendly a facile da usare. **user
manual** n manuale m d'uso

usher /'ʌʃə(r)/ n Theat maschera f; Jur uscie-
re m; ⟨at wedding⟩ persona f che accompagna
gli invitati a un matrimonio ai loro posti in
chiesa

■ **usher in** vt fare entrare ⟨person⟩; inaugurare ⟨new age⟩

usherette /ʌʃə'ret/ n maschera f

USSR n URSS f

usual /'juːʒʊəl/ a usuale; **as ~** come al solito

usually /'juːʒʊəlɪ/ adv di solito

usurp /jʊ'zɜːp/ vt usurpare

usurper /jʊ'zɜːpə(r)/ n usurpatore, -trice
mf

utensil /juː'tensl/ n utensile m

uterus /'juːtərəs/ n utero m

utilitarian /juːtɪlɪ'teərɪən/ a funzionale

utility /juː'tɪlətɪ/ n utilità f; ⟨public⟩ servizio m

utility: utility company n servizio m pubblico. **utility program** n Comput [program-
ma m di] utilità f. **utility room** n stanza f in
casa privata per il lavaggio, la stiratura dei
panni ecc

utilize /'juːtɪlaɪz/ vt utilizzare

utmost /'ʌtməʊst/ a estremo ● n one's ~
tutto il possibile

Utopia /juːˈtəʊpɪə/ n utopia f
Utopian /juːˈtəʊpɪən/ n utopista mf ● a utopistico
utter[1] /ˈʌtə(r)/ a totale
utter[2] vt emettere ⟨sigh, sound⟩; proferire ⟨word⟩

utterance /ˈʌtərəns/ n dichiarazione f
utterly /ˈʌtəlɪ/ adv completamente
U-turn n Auto inversione f a U; fig marcia f in dietro
UV abbr (ultraviolet) UVA mpl
Uzbekistan /ʌzbekɪˈstɑːn/ n Uzbekistan m

....

Vv

....

v, V /viː/ n (letter) v, V f inv
v abbr (versus) contro; abbr (volt) V m
vac /væk/ n Br abbr (vacation) vacanze fpl
vacancy /ˈveɪk(ə)nsɪ/ n (job) posto m vacante; (room) stanza f disponibile
vacant /ˈveɪknt/ a libero; ⟨position⟩ vacante; ⟨look⟩ assente
vacant possession n Br Jur bene m immobile libero
vacate /vəˈkeɪt/ vt lasciare libero
vacation /vəˈkeɪʃn/ n Univ & Am vacanza f
vaccinate /ˈvæksɪneɪt/ vt vaccinare
vaccination /væksɪˈneɪʃn/ n vaccinazione f
vaccine /ˈvæksiːn/ n vaccino m
vacillate /ˈvæsɪleɪt/ vi tentennare
vacuous /ˈvækjʊəs/ a ⟨person, look, expression⟩ vacuo; ⟨person⟩ superficiale
vacuum /ˈvækjʊəm/ n vuoto m ● vt passare l'aspirapolvere in/su
vacuum: vacuum cleaner n aspirapolvere m inv. **vacuum flask** n thermos® m inv. **vacuum-packed** a confezionato sottovuoto
vagabond /ˈvæɡəbɒnd/ n vagabondo, -a mf
vagaries /ˈveɪɡərɪz/ npl capricci mpl
vagina /vəˈdʒaɪnə/ n Anat vagina f
vagrancy /ˈveɪɡrənsɪ/ n Jur vagabondaggio m
vagrant /ˈveɪɡrənt/ n vagabondo, -a mf
vague /veɪɡ/ a vago; ⟨outline⟩ impreciso; (absent-minded) distratto; **I'm still ~ about it** non ho ancora le idee chiare in proposito
vaguely /ˈveɪɡlɪ/ adv vagamente
vagueness /ˈveɪɡnɪs/ n (imprecision) vaghezza f; (of wording, proposals) indeterminatezza f; (of image) nebulosità f; (of thinking) imprecisione f
vain /veɪn/ a vanitoso; ⟨hope, attempt⟩ vano; **in ~** invano
vainly /ˈveɪnlɪ/ adv vanamente
valance /ˈvæləns/ n (above curtains) mantovana f; (on bed base) balza f
vale /veɪl/ n liter valle f
valentine /ˈvæləntaɪn/ n (card) biglietto m di San Valentino
Valentine's Day n giorno m di San Valentino
valet /ˈvæleɪ/ n servitore m personale
valiant /ˈvælɪənt/ a valoroso
valiantly /ˈvælɪəntlɪ/ adv coraggiosamente
valid /ˈvælɪd/ a valido

validate /ˈvælɪdeɪt/ vt (confirm) convalidare
validity /vəˈlɪdətɪ/ n validità f
valley /ˈvælɪ/ n valle f
valour /ˈvælə(r)/ n valore m
valuable /ˈvæljʊəbl/ a di valore; fig prezioso
valuables /ˈvæljʊəblz/ npl oggetti mpl di valore
valuation /væljʊˈeɪʃn/ n valutazione f
value /ˈvæljuː/ n valore m; (usefulness) utilità f ● vt valutare; (cherish) apprezzare
value added tax /ˈædɪd/ n imposta f sul valore aggiunto
valued /ˈvæljuːd/ a (appreciated) apprezzato
valuer /ˈvæljʊə(r)/ n stimatore, -trice mf
valve /vælv/ n valvola f
vamp /væmp/ n vamp f inv
vampire /ˈvæmpaɪə(r)/ n vampiro m
van /væn/ n furgone m
vandal /ˈvændl/ n vandalo, -a mf
vandalism /ˈvænd(ə)lɪzm/ n vandalismo m
vandalize /ˈvænd(ə)laɪz/ vt vandalizzare
vane /veɪn/ n banderuola f
vanguard /ˈvænɡɑːd/ n avanguardia f; **in the ~** all'avanguardia
vanilla /vəˈnɪlə/ n vaniglia f
vanish /ˈvænɪʃ/ vi svanire
vanishing: vanishing cream n crema f base per il trucco. **vanishing point** n punto m di fuga. **vanishing trick** n trucco m da illusionista per far sparire un oggetto; **he's done his ~ ~ again** fam è sparito come al solito
vanity /ˈvænətɪ/ n vanità f inv
vanity bag, vanity case n beauty-case m inv
vanity mirror n Auto specchietto m di cortesia
vanquish /ˈvæŋkwɪʃ/ vt sconfiggere ⟨enemy⟩
vantage point /ˈvɑːntɪdʒ/ n punto m d'osservazione; fig punto m di vista
vaporize /ˈveɪpəraɪz/ vt vaporizzare ⟨liquid⟩
vapour /ˈveɪpə(r)/ n vapore m
vapour trail n scia f
variable /ˈveərɪəbl/ a variabile; (adjustable) regolabile
variance /ˈveərɪəns/ n **be at ~** essere in disaccordo
variant /ˈveərɪənt/ n variante f
variation /veərɪˈeɪʃn/ n variazione f

varicose /'værɪkəʊs/ *a* ~ **veins** vene *fpl* varicose

varied /'veərɪd/ *a* vario; ⟨*diet*⟩ diversificato; ⟨*life*⟩ movimentato

variegated /'veərɪəgeɪtɪd/ *a* variegato

variety /və'raɪətɪ/ *n* varietà *f inv*

various /'veərɪəs/ *a* vario

variously /'veərɪəslɪ/ *adv* variamente

varnish /'vɑːnɪʃ/ *n* vernice *f*; (*for nails*) smalto *m* ● *vt* verniciare; ~ **one's nails** mettersi lo smalto

vary /'veərɪ/ *vt/i* (*pt/pp* **-ied**) variare

varying /'veərɪŋ/ *a* variabile; (*different*) diverso

vascular /'væskjʊlə/ *a* Anat, Bot vascolare

vase /vɑːz/ *n* vaso *m*

vasectomy /və'sektəmɪ/ *n* vasectomia *f*

vast /vɑːst/ *a* vasto; ⟨*difference, amusement*⟩ enorme

vastly /'vɑːstlɪ/ *adv* ⟨*superior*⟩ di gran lunga; ⟨*different, amused*⟩ enormemente

VAT /viːeɪ'tiː:, væt/ *abbr* (**value added tax**) I.V.A. *f*

vat /væt/ *n* tino *m*

vaudeville /'vɔːdəvɪl/ *n* Theat varietà *m*

vault[1] /vɔːlt/ *n* (*roof*) volta *f*; (*in bank*) caveau *m inv*; (*tomb*) cripta *f*

vault[2] *n* salto *m* ● *vt/i* ~ [**over**] saltare

VCR *n abbr* (**video cassette recorder**) VCR *m*

VD *abbr* (**venereal disease**) malattia *f* venerea

VDU *abbr* (**visual display unit**) VDU *m*

veal /viːl/ *n* carne *f* di vitello ● *attrib* di vitello

vector /'vektə(r)/ *n* Biol, Math vettore *m*; Aeron rotta *f*

veer /vɪə(r)/ *vi* cambiare direzione; Naut, Auto virare

vegan /'viːgn/ *n* vegetaliano, -a *mf* ● *a* vegetaliano

vegetable /'vedʒtəbl/ *n* (*food*) verdura *f*; (*when growing*) ortaggio *m* ● *attrib* ⟨*oil, fat*⟩ vegetale

vegetarian /vedʒɪ'teərɪən/ *a & n* vegetariano, -a *mf*

vegetate /'vedʒɪteɪt/ *vi* vegetare

vegetation /vedʒɪ'teɪʃn/ *n* vegetazione *f*

vehemence /'viːəməns/ *n* veemenza *f*

vehement /'viːəmənt/ *a* veemente

vehemently /'viːəməntlɪ/ *adv* con veemenza

vehicle /'viːɪkl/ *n* veicolo *m*; (*fig: medium*) mezzo *m*

vehicular /vɪ'hɪkjʊlə/ *a* **no** ~ **access**, **no** ~ **traffic** circolazione vietata

veil /veɪl/ *n* velo *m* ● *vt* velare

vein /veɪn/ *n* vena *f*; (*mood*) umore *m*; (*manner*) tenore *m*

veined /veɪnd/ *a* venato

Velcro® /'velkrəʊ/ *n* ~ **fastening** chiusura *f* con velcro

vellum /'veləm/ *n* pergamena *f*

velocity /vɪ'lɒsətɪ/ *n* velocità *f inv*

velvet /'velvɪt/ *n* velluto *m*

velvety /'velvətɪ/ *a* vellutato

venal /'viːnl/ *a* venale

vendetta /ven'detə/ *n* vendetta *f*

vending machine /'vendɪŋ/ *n* distributore *m* automatico

vendor /'vendə(r)/ *n* venditore, -trice *mf*

veneer /və'nɪə(r)/ *n* impiallacciatura *f*; *fig* vernice *f*

veneered /və'nɪəd/ *a* impiallacciato

venerable /'venərəbl/ *a* venerabile

veneration /venə'reɪʃn/ *n* venerazione *f*

venereal /vɪ'nɪərɪəl/ *a* ~ **disease** malattia *f* venerea

Venetian /və'niːʃn/ *a & n* veneziano, -a *mf*

Venetian blind *n* persiana *f* alla veneziana

Venezuela /venɪz'weɪlə/ *n* Venezuela *m*

Venezuelan /venɪz'weɪlən/ *a & n* venezuelano, -a *mf*

vengeance /'vendʒəns/ *n* vendetta *f*; **with a** ~ *fam* a più non posso

Venice /'venɪs/ *n* Venezia *f*

venison /'venɪsn/ *n* Culin carne *f* di cervo

venom /'venəm/ *n* veleno *m*

venomous /'venəməs/ *a* velenoso

vent[1] /vent/ *n* presa *f* d'aria; **give** ~ **to** *fig* dar libero sfogo a ● *vt fig* sfogare ⟨*anger*⟩

vent[2] *n* (*in jacket*) spacco *m*

ventilate /'ventɪleɪt/ *vt* ventilare

ventilation /ventɪ'leɪʃn/ *n* ventilazione *f*; (*installation*) sistema *m* di ventilazione

ventilator /'ventɪleɪtə(r)/ *n* ventilatore *m*

ventriloquist /ven'trɪləkwɪst/ *n* ventriloquo, -a *mf*

venture /'ventʃə(r)/ *n* impresa *f* ● *vt* azzardare ● *vi* avventurarsi

venture capital *n* capitale *m* a rischio

venue /'venjuː/ *n* luogo *m* (*di convegno, concerto ecc*)

veracity /və'ræsətɪ/ *n* veridicità *f*

veranda /və'rændə/ *n* veranda *f*

verb /vɜːb/ *n* verbo *m*

verbal /'vɜːbl/ *a* verbale

verbally /'vɜːb(ə)lɪ/ *adv* verbalmente

verbatim /vɜː'beɪtɪm/ *a* letterale ● *adv* parola per parola

verbose /vɜː'bəʊs/ *a* prolisso

verdict /'vɜːdɪkt/ *n* verdetto *m*; (*opinion*) parere *m*

verdigris /'vɜːdɪgriː/ *n* verderame *m*

verge /vɜːdʒ/ *n* orlo *m*; **be on the** ~ **of doing sth** essere sul punto di fare qcsa

■ **verge on** *vt fig* rasentare

verger /'vɜːdʒə(r)/ *n* sagrestano *m*

verification /verɪfɪ'keɪʃn/ *n* verifica *f*

verify /'verɪfaɪ/ *vt* (*pt/pp* **-ied**) verificare; (*confirm*) confermare

veritable /'verɪtəbl/ *a* vero

vermicelli /vɜːmɪ'tʃelɪ/ *n* (*pasta*) capelli *mpl* d'angelo; (*chocolate*) pezzettini *mpl* di cioccolato per decorazione

vermilion /və'mɪljən/ *n* rosso *m* vermiglio ● *a* vermiglio

vermin /'vɜːmɪn/ *n* animali *mpl* nocivi

vermouth /'vɜːməθ/ *n* vermut *m inv*

vernacular /və'nækjʊlə(r)/ *n* vernacolo *m*

verruca /vəˈruːkə/ n verruca f

versatile /ˈvɜːsətaɪl/ a versatile

versatility /vɜːsəˈtɪlətɪ/ n versatilità f

verse /vɜːs/ n verso m; (of Bible) versetto m; (poetry) versi mpl

versed /vɜːst/ a ~ **in** versato in

versifier /ˈvɜːsɪfaɪə(r)/ n pej versificatore, -trice mf

version /ˈvɜːʃn/ n versione f; (translation) traduzione f

versus /ˈvɜːsəs/ prep contro

vertebra /ˈvɜːtɪbrə/ n (pl -**brae** /-briː/) Anat vertebra f

vertebrate /ˈvɜːtɪbrət/ n vertebrato m ● a vertebrato

vertex /ˈvɜːteks/ n Anat sommità f inv del capo; Math vertice m

vertical /ˈvɜːtɪkl/ a & n verticale m

vertically /ˈvɜːtɪklɪ/ adv verticalmente

vertigo /ˈvɜːtɪɡəʊ/ n Med vertigine f

verve /vɜːv/ n verve f

very /ˈverɪ/ adv molto; ~ **much** molto; ~ **little** pochissimo; ~ **many** moltissimi; ~ **few** pochissimi; ~ **probably** molto probabilmente; ~ **well** benissimo; **at the ~ most** tutt'al più; **at the ~ latest** al più tardi ● a **the ~ first** il primissimo; **the ~ thing** proprio ciò che ci vuole; **at the ~ end/beginning** proprio alla fine/all'inizio; **that ~ day** proprio quel giorno; **the ~ thought** la sola idea; **only a ~ little** solo un pochino

vespers /ˈvespəz/ npl vespri mpl

vessel /ˈvesl/ n nave f; (receptacle) recipiente m; Anat vaso m

vest /vest/ n maglia f della pelle; (Am: waistcoat) gilè m inv ● vt ~ **sth in sb** investire qcno di qcsa

vested interest /vestɪdˈɪntrəst/ n interesse m personale

vestige /ˈvestɪdʒ/ n (of past) vestigio m

vestment /ˈvestmənt/ n Relig paramento m

vestry /ˈvestrɪ/ n sagrestia f

vet /vet/ n veterinario, -a mf ● vt (pt/pp **vetted**) controllare minuziosamente

veteran /ˈvetərən/ n veterano, -a mf

veteran car n auto f inv d'epoca (costruita prima del 1916)

veterinary /ˈvetərɪnərɪ/ a veterinario

veterinary surgeon n medico m veterinario

veto /ˈviːtəʊ/ n (pl -**es**) veto m ● vt proibire

vetting /ˈvetɪŋ/ n verifica f del passato di un individuo

vex /veks/ vt irritare

vexation /vekˈseɪʃn/ n irritazione f

vexatious /vekˈseɪʃəs/ a (person) fastidioso; (situation) spiacevole

vexed /vekst/ a irritato; ~ **question** questione f controversa

vexing /ˈveksɪŋ/ a irritante

VHF abbr (very high frequency) VHF

via /ˈvaɪə/ prep via; (by means of) attraverso

viability /vaɪəˈbɪlətɪ/ n probabilità f di sopravvivenza; (of proposition) attuabilità f

viable /ˈvaɪəbl/ a (life form, relationship, company) in grado di sopravvivere; (proposition) attuabile

viaduct /ˈvaɪədʌkt/ n viadotto m

vibes /vaɪbz/ npl fam **I'm getting good/bad** ~ provo una sensazione gradevole/sgradevole

vibrant /ˈvaɪbrənt/ a fig che sprizza vitalità

vibrate /vaɪˈbreɪt/ vi vibrare

vibration /vaɪˈbreɪʃn/ n vibrazione f

vicar /ˈvɪkə(r)/ n parroco m (protestante)

vicarage /ˈvɪkərɪdʒ/ n casa f parrocchiale

vicarious /vɪˈkeərɪəs/ a indiretto

vice¹ /vaɪs/ n vizio m

vice² n Techn morsa f

vice: **vice-captain** n Sport vicecapitano m. **vice-chairman** n vicepresidente mf. **vice-chancellor** n Br Univ vicerettore m; Am Jur vicecancelliere m. **vice-president** n vicepresidente mf. **vice-principal** n (of senior school) vicepreside mf; (of junior school, college) vicedirettore, -trice mf

vice squad n buoncostume f

vice versa /vaɪsəˈvɜːsə/ adv viceversa

vicinity /vɪˈsɪnətɪ/ n vicinanza f; **in the ~ of** nelle vicinanze di

vicious /ˈvɪʃəs/ a cattivo; (attack) brutale; (animal) pericoloso

vicious circle n circolo m vizioso

viciously /ˈvɪʃəslɪ/ adv (attack) brutalmente

victim /ˈvɪktɪm/ n vittima f

victimization /vɪktɪmaɪˈzeɪʃn/ n vittimizzazione f

victimize /ˈvɪktɪmaɪz/ vt vittimizzare

victor /ˈvɪktə(r)/ n vincitore m

Victorian /vɪkˈtɔːrɪən/ n persona f vissuta in epoca vittoriana ● a (writer, poverty, age) vittoriano

victorious /vɪkˈtɔːrɪəs/ a vittorioso

victory /ˈvɪktərɪ/ n vittoria f

video /ˈvɪdɪəʊ/ n video m inv; (cassette) videocassetta f; (recorder) videoregistratore m ● attrib video ● vt registrare

video: **video camera** n videocamera f, telecamera f. **video card** n scheda f video. **video cassette** n videocassetta f. **video clip** n videoclip m inv. **videoconference** n videoconferenza f. **video game** n videogioco m. **video library** n videoteca f. **video nasty** n film m inv con scene violente o pornografiche. **video recorder** n videoregistratore m. **video shop** n negozio m che affitta o vende videocassette. **video surveillance** n videosorveglianza f. **videotape** n videocassetta f

vie /vaɪ/ vi (pres p **vying**) rivaleggiare

Vienna /vɪˈenə/ n Vienna f

Viennese /vɪəˈniːz/ a viennese

Vietnam /vɪetˈnæm/ n Vietnam m

Vietnamese /vɪetnæˈmiːz/ a & n vietnamita mf; (language) vietnamita m

view /vjuː/ n vista f; (photographed, painted) veduta f; (opinion) visione f; **look at the ~** guardare il panorama; **in my ~** secondo me; **in ~ of** in considerazione di; **on ~** esposto; **with a ~ to** con l'intenzione di ● vt visitare

⟨*house*⟩; (*consider*) considerare ● *vi TV* guardare

viewer /'vju:ə(r)/ *n TV* telespettatore, -trice *mf*; *Phot* visore *m*

viewfinder /'vju:faɪndə(r)/ *n Phot* mirino *m*

viewing /'vju:ɪŋ/ *n TV* programmi *mpl* della televisione; (*of film*) proiezione *f*; (*of new range*) presentazione *f*; (*of exhibition, house*) visita *f*; **it makes good ~** *TV* vale la pena di vederlo; **what's tonight's ~?** cosa danno alla tv stasera? ● *attrib* ⟨*habits, preferences*⟩ dei telespettatori; **the ~ public** i telespettatori

view phone *n* videotelefono *m*

viewpoint /'vju:pɔɪnt/ *n* punto *m* di vista

vigil /'vɪdʒɪl/ *n* veglia *f*

vigilance /'vɪdʒɪləns/ *n* vigilanza *f*

vigilant /'vɪdʒɪlənt/ *a* vigile

vigilante /vɪdʒɪ'lænti/ *n membro m di un'organizzazione privata per la prevenzione della criminalità*

vigorous /'vɪg(ə)rəs/ *a* vigoroso

vigorously /'vɪg(ə)rəslɪ/ *adv* vigorosamente

vigour /'vɪgə(r)/ *n* vigore *m*

vile /vaɪl/ *a* disgustoso; ⟨*weather*⟩ orribile; ⟨*temper, mood*⟩ pessimo

vilification /vɪlɪfɪ'keɪʃn/ *n* denigrazione *f*

villa /'vɪlə/ *n* (*for holidays*) casa *f* di villeggiatura

village /'vɪlɪdʒ/ *n* paese *m*

village green *n giardino m pubblico nel centro di un paese*

village hall *n sala f utilizzata per feste e altre attività*

villager /'vɪlɪdʒə(r)/ *n* paesano, -a *mf*

villain /'vɪlən/ *n* furfante *m*; (*in story*) cattivo *m*

villainous /'vɪlənəs/ *a* infame

vim /vɪm/ *n fam* energia *f*

vindicate /'vɪndɪkeɪt/ *vt* (*from guilt*) discolpare; **you are ~d** ti sei dimostrato nel giusto

vindictive /vɪn'dɪktɪv/ *a* vendicativo

vine /vaɪn/ *n* vite *f*

vinegar /'vɪnɪgə(r)/ *n* aceto *m*

vinegary /'vɪnɪg(ə)rɪ/ *a* agro

vineyard /'vɪnjɑ:d/ *n* vigneto *m*

vintage /'vɪntɪdʒ/ *a* ⟨*wine*⟩ d'annata ● *n* (*year*) annata *f*

vintage car *n* auto *f inv* d'epoca (*costruita tra il 1917 e il 1930*)

vintage year *n also fig* anno *m* memorabile

vinyl /'vaɪnɪl/ *n* vinile *m* ● *attrib* ⟨*paint*⟩ vinilico

viola /vɪ'əʊlə/ *n Mus* viola *f*

violate /'vaɪəleɪt/ *vt* violare

violation /vaɪə'leɪʃn/ *n* violazione *f*

violence /'vaɪələns/ *n* violenza *f*

violent /'vaɪələnt/ *a* violento

violently /'vaɪələntlɪ/ *adv* violentemente

violet /'vaɪələt/ *a* violetto ● *n* (*flower*) violetta *f*; (*colour*) violetto *m*

violin /vaɪə'lɪn/ *n* violino *m*

violinist /vaɪə'lɪnɪst/ *n* violinista *mf*

VIP *n abbr* (**very important person**) vip *mf*

viper /'vaɪpə(r)/ *n* vipera *f*

virgin /'vɜ:dʒɪn/ *a* vergine ● *n* vergine *f*

virginal /'vɜ:dʒɪn(ə)l/ *a* verginale

virginals /'vɜ:dʒɪn(ə)lz/ *npl Mus* spinetta *f*

Virginia creeper /vədʒɪnɪə'kri:pə(r)/ *n* vite *f* del Canada

virginity /və'dʒɪnətɪ/ *n* verginità *f*

Virgo /'vɜ:gəʊ/ *n Astr* Vergine *f*

virile /'vɪraɪl/ *a* virile

virility /vɪ'rɪlətɪ/ *n* virilità *f*

virologist /vaɪ'rɒlədʒɪst/ *n* virologo *m*

virtual /'vɜ:tjʊəl/ *a* effettivo

virtually /'vɜ:tjʊəlɪ/ *adv* praticamente

virtual reality *n* realtà *f* virtuale

virtue /'vɜ:tju:/ *n* virtù *f inv*; (*advantage*) vantaggio *m*; **by** *or* **in ~ of** a causa di

virtuoso /vɜ:tʊ'əʊzəʊ/ *n* (*pl* **-si** /-zi:/) virtuoso *m*

virtuous /'vɜ:tjʊəs/ *a* virtuoso

virulent /'vɪrʊlənt/ *a* virulento

virus /'vaɪərəs/ *n* virus *m inv*

visa /'vi:zə/ *n* visto *m*

vis-à-vis /vi:zɑ:'vi:/ *prep* rispetto a

visceral /'vɪs(ə)rəl/ *a* ⟨*power, performance*⟩ viscerale

viscount /'vaɪkaʊnt/ *n* visconte *m*

viscous /'vɪskəs/ *a* vischioso

visibility /vɪzə'bɪlətɪ/ *n* visibilità *f*

visible /'vɪzəbl/ *a* visibile

visibly /'vɪzəblɪ/ *adv* visibilmente

vision /'vɪʒn/ *n* visione *f*; (*sight*) vista *f*

visionary /'vɪʒ(ə)rɪ/ *a & n* visionario, -a *mf*

vision mixer *n* (*person*) tecnico *m* del mixaggio video; (*equipment*) mixaggio *m* video

visit /'vɪzɪt/ *n* visita *f* ● *vt* andare a trovare ⟨*person*⟩; andare da ⟨*doctor etc*⟩; visitare ⟨*town, building*⟩

visiting /'vɪzɪtɪŋ/: **visiting card** *n* biglietto *m* da visita. **visiting hours** *npl* orario *m* delle visite. **visiting lecturer** *n* conferenziere, -a *mf*. **visiting team** *n* squadra *f* ospite. **visiting time** *n* orario *m* delle visite

visitor /'vɪzɪtə(r)/ *n* ospite *mf*; (*of town, museum*) visitatore, -trice *mf*; (*in hotel*) cliente *mf*

visitor centre *n centro m di accoglienza e di informazione per i visitatori*

visitors' book *n* (*in exhibition*) albo *m* dei visitatori; (*in hotel*) registro *m* dei clienti

visor /'vaɪzə(r)/ *n* visiera *f*; *Auto* parasole *m*

vista /'vɪstə/ *n* (*view*) panorama *m*

visual /'vɪzjʊəl/ *a* visivo

visual: visual aids *npl* supporto *m* visivo. **visual arts** *npl* arti *fpl* visive. **visual display unit** *n* visualizzatore *m*

visualize /'vɪzjʊəlaɪz/ *vt* visualizzare

visually /'vɪzjʊəlɪ/ *adv* visualmente; **~ handicapped** non vedente

vital /'vaɪtl/ *a* vitale

vitality /vaɪ'tælətɪ/ *n* vitalità *f*

vitally /'vaɪtəlɪ/ *adv* estremamente

vital statistics *npl fam* misure *fpl*

vitamin /'vɪtəmɪn/ *n* vitamina *f*

vitreous /'vɪtrɪəs/ *a* vetroso; ⟨*enamel*⟩ vetrificato

vitriolic /vɪtrɪ'ɒlɪk/ a Chem di vetriolo; fig al vetriolo

vituperative /vɪ'tju:p(ə)rətɪv/ a ingiurioso

viva /'vaɪvə/ n Br Univ [esame m] orale m

vivacious /vɪ'veɪʃəs/ a vivace

vivaciously /vɪ'veɪʃəslɪ/ adv vivacemente

vivacity /vɪ'væsətɪ/ n vivacità f

vivid /'vɪvɪd/ a vivido

vividly /'vɪvɪdlɪ/ adv in modo vivido

vivisect /'vɪvɪsekt/ vt vivisezionare

vivisection /vɪvɪ'sekʃn/ n vivisezione f

vixen /'vɪksn/ n volpe f femmina

viz /vɪz/ adv cioè

vocabulary /və'kæbjʊlərɪ/ n vocabolario m; (list) glossario m

vocal /'vəʊkl/ a vocale; (vociferous) eloquente

vocal cords npl corde fpl vocali

vocalist /'vəʊkəlɪst/ n vocalista mf

vocalize /'vəʊkəlaɪz/ vt (fig: express) esprimere a parole; articolare ‹sound›

vocation /və'keɪʃn/ n vocazione f

vocational /və'keɪʃ(ə)nl/ a di orientamento professionale

vociferous /və'sɪfərəs/ a vociante

vodka /'vɒdkə/ n vodka f inv

vogue /vəʊg/ n moda f; **in** ~ in voga

voice /vɔɪs/ n voce f ● vt esprimere

voice box n Anat laringe f

voiceless /'vɔɪslɪs/ a ‹minority› silenzioso; ‹group› privo del diritto di parola

voicemail /'vɔɪsmeɪl/ n posta f elettronica vocale

voice-over n voce f fuori campo

void /vɔɪd/ a (not valid) nullo; ~ **of** privo di ● n vuoto m

vol /vɒl/ abbr (**volume**) vol.

volatile /'vɒlətaɪl/ a volatile; ‹person› volubile

volcanic /vɒl'kænɪk/ a vulcanico

volcano /vɒl'keɪnəʊ/ n vulcano m

volition /və'lɪʃn/ n **of his own** ~ di sua spontanea volontà

volley /'vɒlɪ/ n (of gunfire) raffica f; (Tennis) volée f inv

volleyball /'vɒlɪbɔ:l/ n pallavolo f

volt /vəʊlt/ n volt m inv

voltage /'vəʊltɪdʒ/ n Electr voltaggio m

voluble /'vɒljʊbl/ a loquace

volume /'vɒlju:m/ n volume m; (of work, traffic) quantità f inv

volume control n volume m

voluntarily /'vɒləntərɪlɪ/ adv volontariamente

voluntary /'vɒləntərɪ/ a volontario

voluntary redundancy n Br dimissioni fpl volontarie

voluntary work n volontariato m

volunteer /vɒlən'tɪə(r)/ n volontario, -a mf
● vt offrire volontariamente ‹information›
● vi offrirsi volontario; Mil arruolarsi come volontario

voluptuous /və'lʌptjʊəs/ a voluttuoso

vomit /'vɒmɪt/ n vomito m ● vt/i vomitare

voodoo /'vu:du:/ n vudu m inv

voracious /və'reɪʃəs/ a vorace

vortex /'vɔ:teks/ n vortice m; fig turbine m

vote /vəʊt/ n voto m; (ballot) votazione f; (right) diritto m di voto; **take a** ~ **on** votare su ● vi votare ● vt ~ **sb president** eleggere qcno presidente

■ **vote down** vt (reject by vote) bocciare ai voti

■ **vote in** vt (elect) eleggere

vote of confidence n Pol, fig voto m di fiducia

vote of thanks n discorso m di ringraziamento

voter /'vəʊtə(r)/ n elettore, -trice mf

voting /'vəʊtɪŋ/ n votazione f

voting age n età f inv per votare

voting booth n cabina f elettorale

vouch /vaʊtʃ/ vi ~ **for** garantire per

voucher /'vaʊtʃə(r)/ n buono m

vow /vaʊ/ n voto m ● vt giurare

vowel /'vaʊəl/ n vocale f

vox pop /vɒks'pɒp/ n TV, Radio opinione f pubblica

voyage /'vɔɪɪdʒ/ n viaggio m [marittimo]; (in space) viaggio m [nello spazio]

V-sign n (offensive gesture) gestaccio m; (victory sign) segno m di vittoria

VSO abbr (**Voluntary Service Overseas**) servizio m civile volontario nei paesi in via di sviluppo

vulgar /'vʌlgə(r)/ a volgare

vulgar fraction n Math frazione f ordinaria

vulgarity /vʌl'gærətɪ/ n volgarità f inv

vulnerable /'vʌlnərəbl/ a vulnerabile

vulture /'vʌltʃə(r)/ n avvoltoio m

vying /'vaɪɪŋ/ see **vie**

Ww

w, W /'dʌblju:/ n (letter) w, W f inv
W abbr (**West**) O; abbr Electr (**watt**) w
wad /wɒd/ n batuffolo m; (bundle) rotolo m
wadding /'wɒdɪŋ/ n ovatta f
waddle /'wɒdl/ vi camminare ondeggiando
wade /weɪd/ vi guadare
■ **wade in** vi (fam: start working) mettersi al lavoro; (take part) prendere parte
■ **wade into** vt (attack) scagliarsi contro
■ **wade through** vt fam procedere faticosamente in ⟨book⟩
wader /'weɪdə(r)/ n Zool trampoliere m; **~s** (pl: boots) stivaloni mpl di gomma
wafer /'weɪfə(r)/ n cialda f, wafer m inv; Relig ostia f
wafer-thin a sottilissimo
waffle[1] /'wɒfl/ vi fam blaterare
waffle[2] n Culin cialda f
waft /wɒft/ vt trasportare ● vi diffondersi
wag /wæg/ v (pt/pp **wagged**) ● vt agitare ● vi agitarsi
wage[1] /weɪdʒ/ vt dichiarare ⟨war⟩; lanciare ⟨campaign⟩
wage[2] n & **~s** pl salario msg
wage earner n salariato, -a mf
wage packet n busta f paga
wager /'weɪdʒə(r)/ n scommessa f
waggle /'wægl/ vt dimenare ● vi dimenarsi
wagon /'wægən/ n carro m; Rail vagone m merci; **be on the ~** fam astenersi dall'alcol
waif /weɪf/ n trovatello, -a mf
wail /weɪl/ n piagnucolio m; (of wind) lamento m; (of baby) vagito m ● vi piagnucolare; ⟨wind:⟩ lamentarsi; ⟨baby:⟩ vagire
Wailing Wall /'weɪlɪŋ/ n Muro m del pianto
waist /weɪst/ n vita f
waist: waistband n cintura f. **waistcoat** n gilè m inv; (of man's suit) panciotto m. **waistline** n vita f. **waist measurement** n giro m vita
wait /weɪt/ n attesa f; **lie in ~ for** appostarsi per sorprendere ● vi aspettare; **~ at table** servire i tavoli; **~ for** aspettare ● vt **~ one's turn** aspettare il proprio turno
■ **wait about, wait around** vi aspettare
■ **wait behind** vi trattenersi
■ **wait in** vi rimanere a casa ad aspettare
■ **wait on** vt servire
■ **wait up** vi rimanere alzato ad aspettare; **don't ~ up for me** non mi aspettate alzato
waiter /'weɪtə(r)/ n cameriere m
waiter service n servizio m al tavolo
waiting /'weɪtɪŋ/: **waiting game** n **play a ~** ~ n temporeggiare. **waiting list** n lista f d'attesa. **waiting room** n sala f d'aspetto
waitress /'weɪtrɪs/ n cameriera f

waive /weɪv/ vt rinunciare a ⟨claim⟩; non tener conto di ⟨rule⟩
waiver /'weɪvə(r)/ n Jur rinuncia f
wake[1] /weɪk/ n veglia f funebre ● v (pt **woke**, pp **woken**) **~** [**up**] ● vt svegliare ● vi svegliarsi
■ **wake up to** vt **~ up to the fact that...** (realize) aprire gli occhi di fronte al fatto che...
wake[2] n Naut scia f; **in the ~ of** fig nella scia di
wakeful /'weɪkfʊl/ a ⟨night⟩ insonne
waken /'weɪkn/ vt svegliare ● vi svegliarsi
wake-up call n sveglia f telefonica
Wales /weɪlz/ n Galles m
walk /wɔːk/ n passeggiata f; (gait) andatura f; (path) sentiero m; **go for a ~** andare a fare una passeggiata; **~ of life** livello m sociale ● vi camminare; (as opposed to drive etc) andare a piedi; (ramble) passeggiare; '**~**' Am (at crossing) 'avanti' ● vt portare a spasso ⟨dog⟩; percorrere ⟨streets⟩
■ **walk into** vt entrare in ⟨room⟩; andare a sbattere contro ⟨door, lamp post⟩; cadere in ⟨trap⟩; trovare facilmente ⟨job⟩
■ **walk off** vi (leave) andarsene
■ **walk off with** vt (win easily) riportare senza difficoltà; (take, steal) portarsi via
■ **walk out** vi ⟨husband, employee:⟩ andarsene; ⟨workers:⟩ scioperare
■ **walk out of** vt uscire da ⟨room⟩; abbandonare ⟨meeting⟩
■ **walk out on** vt lasciare
■ **walk over** vt **~ all over sb** (defeat) stracciare qcno; (treat badly) trattare qcno come una pezza da piedi
■ **walk through** vt superare senza difficoltà ⟨exam, interview⟩
■ **walk up** vi (as opposed to taking the lift) salire a piedi; (approach) avvicinarsi
walkabout /'wɔːkəbaʊt/ n escursione f periodica degli aborigeni australiani nell'entroterra; (by royalty) incontro m con la folla; **go ~** ⟨queen, politician:⟩ camminare tra la folla
walker /'wɔːkə(r)/ n camminatore, -trice mf; (rambler) escursionista mf
walkie-talkie /wɔːkɪ'tɔːkɪ/ n walkie-talkie m inv
walk-in a **~ closet** stanzino m
walking /'wɔːkɪŋ/ n camminare m; (rambling) fare m delle escursioni
walking: walking boots npl scarponi mpl [da trekking]. **walking distance** n **it's within ~** ~ ci si arriva a piedi. **walking**

frame *n Med* deambulatore *m.* **walking pace** *n* passo *m.* **walking shoes** *npl* scarpe *fpl* da passeggio. **walking-stick** *n* bastone *m* da passeggio. **walking wounded** *npl feriti mpl in grado di camminare*

walk: Walkman® *n* Walkman *m inv.* **walk-on** *n Theat* comparsa *f* ● *a ⟨role⟩* piccolo. **walkout** *n* sciopero *m.* **walkover** *n fig* vittoria *f* facile. **walkway** *n* passaggio *m* pedonale

wall /wɔːl/ *n* muro *m*; **go to the ~** *fam* andare a rotoli; **drive sb up the ~** *fam* far diventare matto qcno

■ **wall up** *vt* murare

wallchart /'wɔːltʃɑːt/ *n* tabellone *m*

walled /wɔːld/ *a ⟨city⟩* fortificato

wallet /'wɒlɪt/ *n* portafoglio *m*

wallflower /'wɔːlflaʊə(r)/ *n* violaciocca *f*

wall hanging *n* decorazione *f* murale

wallop /'wɒləp/ *n fam* colpo *m* ● *vt* (*pt/pp* **walloped**) *fam* colpire

walloping /'wɒləpɪŋ/ *fam a* enorme ● *adv* **~ great** (*very big*) enorme ● *n* **give sb a ~** suonarle a qcno

wallow /'wɒləʊ/ *vi* sguazzare; (*in self-pity, grief*) crogiolarsi

wallpaper /'wɔːlpeɪpə(r)/ *n* tappezzeria *f* ● *vt* tappezzare

wall-to-wall *a* che copre tutto il pavimento

walnut /'wɔːlnʌt/ *n* noce *f*

waltz /wɔːlts/ *n* valzer *m inv* ● *vi* ballare il valzer; **he came ~ing up and said** *fam* è arrivato e ha detto con nonchalance

■ **waltz off with** *vt* (*fam: take, win*) portarsi via

■ **waltz through** *vt* superare facilmente ⟨*exam*⟩

wan /wɒn/ *a* esangue

wand /wɒnd/ *n* (*magic ~*) bacchetta *f* [magica]

wander /'wɒndə(r)/ *vi* girovagare; (*fig: digress*) divagare

■ **wander about** *vi* andare a spasso

■ **wander away** *vi* allontanarsi

■ **wander off** *vi* allontanarsi; **I'd better be ~ing off** *fam* è meglio che vada

wanderer /'wɒndərə(r)/ *n* vagabondo, -a *mf*

wanderlust /'wɒndəlʌst/ *n* smania *f* dei viaggi

wane /weɪn/ *n* **be on the ~** essere in fase calante ● *vi* calare

wangle /'wæŋgl/ *vt fam* rimediare ⟨*invitation, holiday*⟩

waning /'weɪnɪŋ/ *n* (*of moon*) calare *m*; (*weakening*) declino *m* ● *a ⟨moon⟩* calante; ⟨*popularity*⟩ in declino

wannabee /'wɒnəbiː/ *n fam* persona *f* che sogna di diventare famosa

want /wɒnt/ *n* (*hardship*) bisogno *m*; (*lack*) mancanza *f* ● *vt* volere; (*need*) aver bisogno di; **~ [to have] sth** volere qcsa; **~ to do sth** voler fare qcsa; **we ~ to stay** vogliamo rimanere; **I ~ you to go** voglio che tu vada; **it ~s painting** ha bisogno di essere dipinto; **you ~ to learn to swim** bisogna che impari a nuotare ● *vi* **~ for** mancare di

wanted /'wɒntɪd/ *a* ricercato

wanted list *n* lista *f* dei ricercati

wanting /'wɒntɪŋ/ *a* **be ~** mancare; **be ~ in** mancare di

wanton /'wɒntən/ *a ⟨cruelty, neglect⟩* gratuito; (*morally*) debosciato

war /wɔː(r)/ *n* guerra *f*; *fig* lotta *f* (**on** contro); **at ~** in guerra

warble /'wɔːbl/ *vt/i* trillare; ⟨*singer:*⟩ gorgheggiare

war cabinet *n* consiglio *m* di guerra

war cry *n* grido *m* di guerra

ward /wɔːd/ *n* (*in hospital*) reparto *m*; (*child*) minore *m* sotto tutela

■ **ward off** *vt* evitare; parare ⟨*blow*⟩

warden /'wɔːdn/ *n* guardiano, -a *mf*

warder /'wɔːdə(r)/ *n* guardia *f* carceraria

wardrobe /'wɔːdrəʊb/ *n* guardaroba *m*

wardrobe assistant *n* costumista *mf*

ward round *n Med* giro *m* delle corsie

ward sister *n Br Med* caposala *f inv*

warehouse /'weəhaʊs/ *n* magazzino *m*

wares /weəz/ *npl* merci *mpl*

warfare /'wɔːfeə/ *n* guerra *f*

war: war game *n Mil* simulazione *f* di scontro militare. **warhead** *n* testata *f.* **warhorse** *n* cavallo *m* da battaglia; (*fig: campaigner*) veterano *m*

warily /'weərɪlɪ/ *adv* cautamente

warlike /'wɔːlaɪk/ *a* bellicoso

warm /wɔːm/ *a* caldo; ⟨*welcome*⟩ caloroso; **be ~** ⟨*person:*⟩ aver caldo; **it is ~** ⟨*weather*⟩ fa caldo ● *vt* scaldare

■ **warm up** *vt* scaldare ● *vi* scaldarsi; *fig* animarsi

warm-blooded /-'blʌdɪd/ *a Zool* con temperatura corporea costante

war memorial *n* monumento *m* ai caduti

warm-hearted /-'hɑːtɪd/ *a* espansivo

warmly /'wɔːmlɪ/ *adv* ⟨*greet*⟩ calorosamente; ⟨*dress*⟩ in modo pesante

warmongering /'wɔːmʌŋgərɪŋ/ *n* bellicismo *m* ● *a ⟨article⟩* bellicistico; ⟨*person*⟩ guerrafondaio

warmth /wɔːmθ/ *n* calore *m*

warm-up *n Sport* riscaldamento *m*; (*of musicians*) prove *fpl*

warn /wɔːn/ *vt* avvertire

■ **warn off** *vt* dare un avvertimento a

warning /'wɔːnɪŋ/ *n* avvertimento *m*; (*advance notice*) preavviso *m*

warp /wɔːp/ *vt* deformare; *fig* distorcere ● *vi* deformarsi

warpaint /'wɔːpeɪnt/ *n Mil* pitture *fpl* di guerra

warpath /'wɔːpɑːθ/ *n* **on the ~** sul sentiero di guerra

warped /wɔːpt/ *a* deformato; ⟨*personality*⟩ contorto; ⟨*sexuality*⟩ deviato; ⟨*view*⟩ distorto

warplane /'wɔːpleɪn/ *n* aereo *m* da guerra

warrant /'wɒrənt/ *n* (*for arrest, search*) mandato *m* ● *vt* (*justify*) giustificare; (*guarantee*) garantire

warranty /'wɒrəntɪ/ *n* garanzia *f*

warren /'wɒr(ə)n/ *n* (*of rabbits*) area *f* piena

di tane di conigli; (*building, maze of streets*) labirinto *m*

warring /'wɔːrɪŋ/ *a* in guerra

warrior /'wɒrɪə(r)/ *n* guerriero, -a *mf*

Warsaw /'wɔːsɔː/ *n* Varsavia *f*

warship /'wɔːʃɪp/ *n* nave *f* da guerra

wart /wɔːt/ *n* porro *m*

wartime /'wɔːtaɪm/ *n* tempo *m* di guerra

war-torn /'wɔːtɔːn/ *a* logorato dalla guerra

wary /'weərɪ/ *a* (**-ier, -iest**) (*careful*) cauto; (*suspicious*) diffidente

was /wɒz/ *see* **be**

wash /wɒʃ/ *n* lavata *f*; (*clothes*) bucato *m*; (*in washing machine*) lavaggio *m*; **have a ~** darsi una lavata ● *vt* lavare; ⟨*sea:*⟩ bagnare; **~ one's hands** lavarsi le mani ● *vi* lavarsi

■ **wash away** *vt* ⟨*rain:*⟩ portare via; ⟨*sea, floodwaters:*⟩ spazzare via

■ **wash off** *vt* lavar via ⟨*stain, mud*⟩ ● *vi* andar via

■ **wash out** *vt* sciacquare ⟨*soap*⟩; sciacquarsi ⟨*mouth*⟩

■ **wash up** *vt* lavare ● *vi* lavare i piatti; *Am* lavarsi

washable /'wɒʃəbl/ *a* lavabile

wash: wash-and-wear *a* che non si stira. **washbasin** *n* lavandino *m*. **wash cloth** *n Am* ≈ guanto *m* da bagno

washed out /wɒʃt'aʊt/ *a* (*faded*) scolorito; (*tired*) spossato

washed up *a fam* (*finished*) finito; (*tired*) distrutto

washer /'wɒʃə(r)/ *n Techn* guarnizione *f*; (*machine*) lavatrice *f*

washer-dryer /-'draɪə(r)/ *n* asciugabiancheria *m inv*

washing /'wɒʃɪŋ/ *n* bucato *m*

washing: washing machine *n* lavatrice *f*. **washing powder** *n* detersivo *m*. **washing soda** *n* soda *f* da bucato. **washing-up** *n* **do the ~** lavare i piatti. **washing-up bowl** *n* bacinella *f* (*per i piatti*). **washing-up liquid** *n* detersivo *m* per i piatti. **washing-up water** *n* rigovernatura *f*

wash: wash load *n* carico *m* di lavatrice. **wash-out** *n* disastro *m*. **washroom** *n* bagno *m*

wasp /wɒsp/ *n* vespa *f*

waspish /'wɒspɪʃ/ *a* pungente

wastage /'weɪstɪdʒ/ *n* perdita *f*

waste /weɪst/ *n* spreco *m*; (*rubbish*) rifiuto *m*; **~s** *pl* distesa *fsg* desolata; **~ of time** perdita *f* di tempo ● *a* ⟨*product*⟩ di scarto; ⟨*land*⟩ desolato; **lay ~** devastare ● *vt* sprecare

■ **waste away** *vi* deperire

waste: wastebasket *n* cestino *m* della carta straccia. **waste bin** *n* (*for paper*) cestino *m* della carta straccia; (*for rubbish*) secchio *m* della spazzatura. **waste disposal unit** *n* eliminatore *m* di rifiuti

wasteful /'weɪstfʊl/ *a* dispendioso

waste: waste paper *n* carta *f* straccia. **waste-paper basket** *n* cestino *m* per la carta [straccia]. **waste pipe** *n* tubo *m* di scarico

watch /wɒtʃ/ *n* guardia *f*; (*period of duty*) turno *m* di guardia; (*timepiece*) orologio *m*; **be on the ~** stare all'erta ● *vt* guardare ⟨*film, match, television*⟩; (*be careful of, look after*) stare attento a ● *vi* guardare

■ **watch out** *vi* (*be careful*) stare attento (**for** a)

■ **watch out for** *vt* (*look for*) fare attenzione all'arrivo di ⟨*person*⟩

watchdog /'wɒtʃdɒg/ *n* cane *m* da guardia

watchful /'wɒtʃfʊl/ *a* attento

watchfully /'wɒtʃfʊlɪ/ *adv* attentamente

watch: watchmaker *n* orologiaio, -a *mf*. **watchman** *n* guardiano *m*. **watch strap** *n* cinturino *m* dell'orologio. **watchtower** *n* torre *f* di guardia. **watchword** *n* motto *m*

water /'wɔːtə(r)/ *n* acqua *f*; **~s** *pl* acque *fpl* ● *vt* annaffiare ⟨*garden, plant*⟩; (*dilute*) annacquare; dare da bere a ⟨*horse etc*⟩ ● *vi* ⟨*eyes:*⟩ lacrimare; **my mouth was ~ing** avevo l'acquolina in bocca

■ **water down** *vt* diluire; *fig* attenuare

water: water authority *n* ente *m* dell'acqua. **waterbird** *n* uccello *m* acquatico. **water bottle** *n* borraccia *f*. **watercolour** *n* acquerello *m*. **water company** *n* società *f inv* dell'acqua. **watercress** *n* crescione *m*. **water-divining** *n* rabdomanzia *f*. **waterfall** *n* cascata *f*. **waterfront** *n* (*by lakeside, riverside*) riva *f*; (*on harbour*) zona *f* portuale. **waterhole** *n* pozza *f* d'acqua

watering can /'wɔːtərɪŋ/ *n* annaffiatoio *m*

water: water lily *n* ninfea *f*. **waterline** *n* linea *f* di galleggiamento. **waterlogged** *a* inzuppato. **water main** *n* conduttura *f* dell'acqua. **watermark** *n* filigrana *f*. **watermeadow** *n* marcita *f*. **watermelon** *n* cocomero *m*. **watermill** *n* mulino *m* ad acqua. **water polo** *n* pallanuoto *f*. **water-power** *n* energia *f* idraulica. **waterproof** *a* ⟨*coat*⟩ impermeabile; ⟨*make-up*⟩ water-proof *inv* ● *n* impermeabile *m*. **waterproofs** *npl* sovrapantaloni *mpl* e giacca impermeabili. **water rates** *mpl Br* tariffe *fpl* dell'acqua. **water-resistant** *a* ⟨*sun cream*⟩ resistente all'acqua; ⟨*garment, watch*⟩ impermeabile. **watershed** *n* spartiacque *m inv*; *fig* svolta *f*. **waterside** *n* riva *f* ● *attrib* ⟨*cafe, hotel*⟩ sulla riva. **water-skiing** *n* sci *m* nautico. **water softener** *n* (*equipment*) addolcitore *m*; (*substance*) anticalcare *m inv*. **water-soluble** *a* idrosolubile. **water sport** *n* sport *m inv* acquatico. **water-table** *n Geog* superficie *f* freatica. **watertight** *a* stagno; *fig* irrefutabile. **water tower** *n* serbatoio *m* idrico a torre. **waterway** *n* canale *m* navigabile. **waterwheel** *n* ruota *f* idraulica. **water wings** *npl* braccioli *mpl*. **waterworks** *n* impianto *m* idrico; **turn on the ~** *fam* mettersi a piangere come una fontana

watery /'wɔːtərɪ/ *a* acquoso; ⟨*eyes*⟩ lacrimoso

watt /wɒt/ *n* watt *m inv*

wattage /'wɒtɪdʒ/ *n* wattaggio *m*

wave /weɪv/ *n* onda *f*; (*gesture*) cenno *m*; *fig* ondata *f* ● *vt* agitare; **~ one's hand** agitare la mano ● *vi* far segno; ⟨*flag:*⟩ sventolare

■ **wave aside** *vt* respingere ⟨*criticism*⟩

■ **wave down** *vt* far segno di fermarsi a ⟨*vehicle*⟩

waveband /'weɪvbænd/ *n* gamma *f* d'onda

wavelength /'weɪvleŋθ/ *n* lunghezza *f* d'onda; **be on the same ~** *fig* essere sulla stessa lunghezza d'onda

waver /'weɪvə(r)/ *vi* vacillare; ⟨*hesitate*⟩ esitare

wavy /'weɪvɪ/ *a* ondulato

wax¹ /wæks/ *vi* ⟨*moon:*⟩ crescere; ⟨*fig: become*⟩ diventare

wax² *n* cera *f*; ⟨*in ear*⟩ cerume *m* ● *vt* dare la cera a

waxworks /'wækswɜːks/ *n* museo *m* delle cere

waxy /'wæksɪ/ *a* ⟨*skin, texture*⟩ cereo

way /weɪ/ *n* percorso *m*; ⟨*direction*⟩ direzione *f*; ⟨*manner, method*⟩ modo *m*; **~s** *pl* ⟨*customs*⟩ abitudini *fpl*; **be in the ~** essere in mezzo; **on the ~ to Rome** andando a Roma; **I'll do it on the ~** lo faccio mentre vado; **it's on my ~** è sul mio percorso; **a long ~ off** lontano; **this ~** da questa parte; ⟨*like this*⟩ così; **by the ~** a proposito; **by ~ of** come; ⟨*via*⟩ via; **either ~** ⟨*whatever we do*⟩ in un modo o nell'altro; **in some ~s** sotto certi aspetti; **in a ~** in un certo senso; **in a bad ~** ⟨*person*⟩ molto grave; **out of the ~** fuori mano; **under ~** in corso; **lead the ~** far strada; *fig* aprire la strada; **make ~** far posto (**for** a); **give ~** *Auto* dare la precedenza; **go out of one's ~** *fig* scomodarsi (**to** per); **get one's [own] ~** averla vinta ● *adv* **~ behind** molto indietro

way in *n* entrata *f*

waylay /weɪ'leɪ/ *vt* ⟨*pt/pp* **-laid**⟩ aspettare al varco ⟨*person*⟩; intercettare ⟨*letter*⟩

way-out *a fam* eccentrico

way out *n* uscita *f*; *fig* via *f* d'uscita

wayside /'weɪsaɪd/ *n* bordo *m*; **fall by the ~** ⟨*morally*⟩ smarrire la retta via; ⟨*fail*⟩ fallire

wayward /'weɪwəd/ *a* capriccioso

WC *abbr* WC; **the WC** il gabinetto

we /wiː/ *pers pron* noi; **we're the last** siamo gli ultimi; **they're going, but we're not** loro vanno, ma noi no

weak /wiːk/ *a* debole; ⟨*liquid*⟩ leggero; **go ~ at the knees** *fam* sentirsi piegare le ginocchia

weaken /'wiːkn/ *vt* indebolire ● *vi* indebolirsi

weakling /'wiːklɪŋ/ *n* smidollato, -a *mf*

weakly /'wiːklɪ/ *adv* debolmente

weak-minded /-'maɪndɪd/ *a* ⟨*indecisive*⟩ debole; ⟨*simple*⟩ poco intelligente

weakness /'wiːknɪs/ *n* debolezza *f*, ⟨*liking*⟩ debole *m*

weak-willed /-'wɪld/ *a* debole

weal /wiːl/ *n* piaga *f*

wealth /welθ/ *n* ricchezza *f*; *fig* gran quantità *f*

wealthy /'welθɪ/ *a* (**-ier, -iest**) ricco

wean /wiːn/ *vt* svezzare

weapon /'wepən/ *n* arma *f*

wear /weə(r)/ *n* ⟨*clothing*⟩ abbigliamento *m*; **for everyday ~** da portare tutti i giorni; **~ [and tear]** usura *f* ● *v* (*pt* **wore**, *pp* **worn**) ● *vt* portare; ⟨*damage*⟩ consumare; **~ a hole in sth** logorare qcsa fino a fare un buco; **what shall I ~?** cosa mi metto? ● *vi* consumarsi; ⟨*last*⟩ durare

■ **wear away** *vt* consumare ● *vi* consumarsi

■ **wear down** *vt* estenuare ⟨*opposition etc*⟩

■ **wear off** *vi* scomparire; ⟨*effect:*⟩ finire

■ **wear out** *vt* consumare [fino in fondo]; ⟨*exhaust*⟩ estenuare ● *vi* estenuarsi

wearable /'weərəbl/ *a* portabile

wearily /'wɪərɪlɪ/ *adv* stancamente

weariness /'wɪərɪnɪs/ *n* stanchezza *f*

weary /'wɪərɪ/ *a* (**-ier, -iest**) sfinito ● *v* (*pt/pp* **wearied**) ● *vt* sfinire ● *vi* **~ of** stancarsi di

weasel /'wiːzl/ *n* donnola *f*

weather /'weðə(r)/ *n* tempo *m*; **in this ~** con questo tempo; **under the ~** *fam* giù di corda ● *vt* sopravvivere a ⟨*storm*⟩

weather: weather balloon *n* pallone *m* sonda. **weather-beaten** /-biːtn/ *a* ⟨*face*⟩ segnato dalle intemperie. **weathercock** *n* gallo *m* segnavento. **weather forecast** *n* previsioni *fpl* del tempo. **weatherman** *n* TV meteorologo *m*. **weatherproof** *a* ⟨*garment, shoe*⟩ impermeabile; ⟨*shelter, door*⟩ resistente alle intemperie. **weather-vane** *n* banderuola *f*

weave¹ /wiːv/ *vi* (*pt/pp* **weaved**) ⟨*move*⟩ zigzagare

weave² *n* ⟨*Tex*⟩ tessuto *m* ● *vt* (*pt* **wove**, *pp* **woven**) tessere; intrecciare ⟨*flowers etc*⟩; intrecciare le fila di ⟨*story etc*⟩

weaver /'wiːvə(r)/ *n* tessitore, -trice *mf*

web /web/ *n* rete *f*; ⟨*of spider*⟩ ragnatela *f*

webbed feet /webd'fiːt/ *npl* piedi *mpl* palmati

web page *n* Comput pagina *f* web

web site *n* Comput sito *m* web

wed /wed/ *vt* (*pt/pp* **wedded**) sposare ● *vi* sposarsi

wedding /'wedɪŋ/ *n* matrimonio *m*

wedding: wedding bells *npl fig* marcia *f* nuziale. **wedding breakfast** *n* rinfresco *m* di nozze. **wedding cake** *n* torta *f* nuziale. **wedding day** *n* giorno *m* del matrimonio. **wedding dress** *n* vestito *m* da sposa. **wedding march** *n* marcia *f* nuziale. **wedding night** *n* prima notte *f* di nozze. **wedding reception** *n* ricevimento *m* di nozze. **wedding ring** *n* fede *f*. **wedding vows** *npl* voti *mpl* nuziali

wedge /wedʒ/ *n* zeppa *f*; ⟨*for splitting wood*⟩ cuneo *m*; ⟨*of cheese*⟩ fetta *f* ● *vt* ⟨*fix*⟩ fissare

wedlock /'wedlɒk/ *n* **born out of ~** nato fuori dal matrimonio

Wednesday /'wenzdeɪ/ *n* mercoledì *m inv*

wee¹ /wiː/ *a fam* piccolo

wee² *n fam* **do a ~** fare la pipì ● *vi fam* fare la pipì

weed /wiːd/ *n* erbaccia *f*; ⟨*fam: person*⟩ mollusco *m* ● *vt* estirpare le erbacce da ● *vi* estirpare le erbacce

■ **weed out** *vt fig* eliminare
weedkiller /'wi:dkɪlə(r)/ *n* erbicida *m*
weedy /'wi:dɪ/ *a fam* mingherlino
week /wi:k/ *n* settimana *f*
weekday /'wi:keɪ/ *n* giorno *m* feriale
weekend /'wi:kend/ *n* fine *m* settimana
weekly /'wi:klɪ/ *a* settimanale ● *n* settimanale *m* ● *adv* settimanalmente
weep /wi:p/ *vi* (*pt/pp* **wept**) piangere
weeping willow /wi:pɪŋ'wɪləʊ/ *n* salice *m* piangente
weepy /'wi:pɪ/ *a* ⟨*film*⟩ strappalacrime *inv*
weigh /weɪ/ *vt/i* pesare; **~ anchor** levare l'ancora
■ **weigh down** *vt fig* piegare
■ **weigh in** *vi* (*fam: join in discussion*) intromettersi
■ **weigh out** *vt* pesare ⟨*amount of flour etc*⟩
■ **weigh up** *vt fig* soppesare; valutare ⟨*person*⟩
weighing machine /'weɪɪŋ/ *n* bilancia *f*
weight /weɪt/ *n* peso *m*; **put on/lose ~** ingrassare/dimagrire
weighting /'weɪtɪŋ/ *n* (*allowance*) indennità *f inv*
weightlessness /'weɪtlɪsnɪs/ *n* assenza *f* di gravità
weight: weightlifter *n* sollevatore *m* di pesi. **weightlifting** *n* sollevamento *m* pesi. **weight training** *n* **do ~ ~** allenarsi con i pesi. **weight-watcher** *n* (*in group*) persona *f* che segue una dieta dimagrante
weighty /'weɪtɪ/ *a* (**-ier**, **-iest**) pesante; (*important*) di un certo peso
weir /wɪə(r)/ *n* chiusa *f*
weird /wɪəd/ *a* misterioso; (*bizarre*) bizzarro
welcome /'welkəm/ *a* benvenuto; **you're ~!** prego!; **you're ~ to have it/to come** prendilo/vieni pure ● *n* accoglienza *f* ● *vt* accogliere; (*appreciate*) gradire
welcoming /'welkəmɪŋ/ *a* ⟨*ceremony*⟩ di benvenuto; ⟨*committee, smile*⟩ di accoglienza; ⟨*house*⟩ accogliente
weld /weld/ *vt* saldare
welder /'weldə(r)/ *n* saldatore *m*
welfare /'welfeə(r)/ *n* benessere *m*; (*aid*) assistenza *f*; *Am* previdenza *f* sociale
welfare: welfare services *n* servizi *mpl* sociali. **Welfare State** *n* Stato *m* assistenziale. **welfare work** *n* assistenza *m* sociale
well¹ /wel/ *n* pozzo *m*; (*oil ~*) pozzo *m*; (*of staircase*) tromba *f*
well² *adv* (**better, best**) bene; **as ~** anche; **as ~ as** (*in addition*) oltre a; **~ done!** bravo!; **very ~** benissimo ● *a* **he is not ~** non sta bene; **get ~ soon!** guarisci presto! ● *int* beh!; **~ I never!** ma va!
well: well-attended /-ə'tendɪd/ *a* ben frequentato. **well-behaved** /-bɪ'heɪvd/ *a* educato. **well-being** /'welbi:ɪŋ/ *n* benessere *m*. **well-bred** /wel'bred/ *a* beneducato. **well-defined** /-dɪ'faɪnd/ *a* ⟨*role, boundary*⟩ ben definito; ⟨*outline, image*⟩ netto. **well-disposed** /-dɪ'spəʊzd/ *a* benevolo; **be ~ towards** essere bendisposto verso ⟨*person*⟩; essere favorevole

a ⟨*idea*⟩. **well done** /dʌn/ *a* ⟨*task*⟩ ben fatto; *Culin* ben cotto. **well-educated** *a* istruito; (*cultured*) colto. **well-founded** /-'faʊndɪd/ *a* fondato. **well-heeled** /-'hi:ld/ *a fam* danaroso. **well-informed** /-ɪn'fɔ:md/ *a* beninformato
wellingtons /'welɪŋtənz/ *npl* stivali *mpl* di gomma
well: well-judged /-'dʒʌdʒd/ *a* ⟨*performance*⟩ molto intelligente; ⟨*shot*⟩ ben assestato; ⟨*statement, phrase*⟩ ben ponderato. **well-kept** /-'kept/ *a* ⟨*garden*⟩ curato; ⟨*secret*⟩ ben custodito. **well-known** /-'nəʊn/ *a* famoso. **well-liked** /-'laɪkt/ *a* popolare. **well-made** /-'meɪd/ *a* benfatto. **well-mannered** /-'mænəd/ *a* educato. **well-meaning** *a* con buone intenzioni. **well-meant** /-'ment/ *a* con le migliori intenzioni. **well-nigh** /'welnaɪ/ *adv* quasi. **well-off** *a* benestante. **well-read** /-'red/ *a* colto. **well-spoken** /-'spəʊkən/ *a* ⟨*person*⟩ che parla bene. **well-thought-of** *a* stimato. **well-to-do** *a* ricco. **well-trodden** /-'trɒdn/ *a* also *fig* battuto. **well-wisher** /'welwɪʃə(r)/ *n* simpatizzante *mf*. **well-worn** /-'wɔ:n/ *a* ⟨*steps, floorboards*⟩ consunto; ⟨*carpet, garment*⟩ logoro; ⟨*fig: argument*⟩ trito e ritrito
Welsh /welʃ/ *a & n* gallese *mf*; (*language*) gallese *m*; **the ~** *pl* i gallesi
Welshman /'welʃmən/ *n* gallese *m*
Welsh rabbit *n* toast *m inv* al formaggio
welt /welt/ *n* (*on shoe*) rinforzo *m*; (*on skin*) segno *m* di frustata
went /went/ *see* **go**
wept /wept/ *see* **weep**
were /wɜ:(r)/ *see* **be**
west /west/ *n* ovest *m*; **to the ~ of** a ovest di; **the W~** l'Occidente *m* ● *a* occidentale ● *adv* verso occidente; **go ~** *fam* andare in malora
west: West Bank *n* Cisgiordania *f*. **West Country** *n* sud-ovest *m* dell'Inghilterra. **West End** *n* zona *f* di Londra con un'alta concentrazione di teatri e negozi di lusso
westerly /'westəlɪ/ *a* verso ovest; occidentale ⟨*wind*⟩
western /'westən/ *a* occidentale ● *n* western *m inv*
Westerner /'westənə(r)/ *n* occidentale *mf*
West Germany *n* Germania *f* Occidentale
West Indian *a & n* antillese *mf*
West Indies /'ɪndɪz/ *npl* Antille *fpl*
westward[s] /'westwəd[z]/ *adv* verso ovest
wet /wet/ *a* (**wetter, wettest**) bagnato; fresco ⟨*paint*⟩; (*rainy*) piovoso; ⟨*fam: person*⟩ smidollato; **get ~** bagnarsi ● *vt* (*pt/pp* **wet, wetted**) bagnare
wet: wet blanket *n* guastafeste *mf inv*. **wet fish** *n Br* pesce *m* fresco. **wet-look** *a* ⟨*plastic, leather*⟩ lucido. **wet-nurse** *n* balia *f*. **wetsuit** *n* muta *f*
whack /wæk/ *n fam* colpo *m* ● *vt fam* dare un colpo a
whacked /wækt/ *a fam* stanco morto
whacking /'wækɪŋ/ *a* (*Br fam: enormous*) enorme ● *n fam* sculacciata *f*

whacky /'wækɪ/ a ⟨fam: joke, person etc⟩ demenziale

whale /weɪl/ n balena f; **have a ~ of a time** fam divertirsi un sacco

wham /wæm/ int bum!

wharf /wɔːf/ n banchina f

what /wɒt/ pron che, [che] cosa; **~ for?** perché?; **~ is that for?** a che cosa serve?; **~ is it?** (what do you want) cosa c'è?; **~ is it like?** com'è?; **~ is your name?** come ti chiami?; **~ is the weather like?** com'è il tempo?; **~ is the film about?** di cosa parla il film?; **~ is he talking about?** di cosa sta parlando?; **he asked me ~ she had said** mi ha chiesto cosa ha detto; **~ about going to the cinema?** e se andassimo al cinema?; **~ about the children?** (what will they do) e i bambini?; **~ if it rains?** e se piove? ● a quale, che; **take ~ books you want** prendi tutti i libri che vuoi; **~ kind of a** che tipo di; **at ~ time?** a che ora? ● adv che; **~ a lovely day!** che bella giornata! ● int **~!** [che] cosa!; **~?** [che] cosa?

whatever /wɒt'evə(r)/ a qualunque ● pron qualsiasi cosa; **~ is it?** cos'è?; **~ he does** qualsiasi cosa faccia; **~ happens** qualunque cosa succeda; **nothing ~** proprio niente

whatnot /'wɒtnɒt/ n coso m; (stand) scaffaletto m; **and ~** (and so on) e così via

what's-his-name /'wɒtsɪzneɪm/ n fam coso m

whatsit /'wɒtsɪt/ n fam aggeggio m, coso m

what's-its-name n fam coso, -a mf

whatsoever /wɒtsəʊ'evə(r)/ a & pron = **whatever**

wheat /wiːt/ n grano m, frumento m

wheatgerm /'wiːtdʒɜːm/ n germoglio m di grano

wheatmeal /'wiːtmiːl/ n farina f di frumento

wheedle /'wiːdl/ vt **~ sth out of sb** ottenere qcsa da qualcuno con le lusinghe

wheel /wiːl/ n ruota f; (steering ~) volante m; **at the ~** al volante ● vt (push) spingere ● vi (circle) ruotare; **~ round** ruotare

wheel: wheelbarrow n carriola f. **wheelchair** n sedia f a rotelle. **wheel clamp** n ceppo m bloccaruote

wheeler-dealer /wiːlə'diːlə(r)/ n trafficone, -a mf

wheeze /wiːz/ vi ansimare

wheezy /'wiːzɪ/ a ⟨voice, cough⟩ dal respiro affannato

when /wen/ adv & conj quando; **the day ~** il giorno in cui; **~ swimming/reading** nuotando/leggendo

whence /wens/ adv liter donde

whenever /wen'evə(r)/ adv & conj in qualsiasi momento; (every time that) ogni volta che; **~ did it happen?** quando è successo?

where /weə(r)/ adv & conj dove; **the street ~ I live** la via in cui abito; **~ do you come from?** da dove vieni?

whereabouts[1] /weərə'baʊts/ adv dove

whereabouts[2] /'weərəbaʊts/ n **nobody knows his ~** nessuno sa dove si trova

whereas /weər'æz/ conj dal momento che; (in contrast) mentre

whereby /weə'baɪ/ adv attraverso il quale

whereupon /weərə'pɒn/ adv dopo di che

wherever /weər'evə(r)/ adv & conj dovunque; **~ is he?** dov'è mai?; **~ possible** dovunque sia possibile

wherewithal /'weəwɪðɔːl/ n mezzi mpl

whet /wet/ vt (pt/pp **whetted**) aguzzare ⟨appetite⟩

whether /'weðə(r)/ conj se; **~ you like it or not** che ti piaccia o no

which /wɪtʃ/ a & pron quale; **~ one?** quale?; **~ one of you?** chi di voi?; **~ way?** (direction) in che direzione? ● rel pron (object) che; **~ he does frequently** cosa che fa spesso; **after ~** dopo di che; **on/in ~** su/in cui

whichever /wɪtʃ'evə(r)/ a & pron qualunque; **~ it is** qualunque sia; **~ one of you** chiunque tra voi

whiff /wɪf/ n zaffata f; **have a ~ of sth** odorare qcsa

while /waɪl/ n **a long ~** un bel po'; **a little ~** un po' ● conj mentre; (as long as) finché; (although) sebbene; **he met her ~ in exile** l'ha incontrata mentre era in esilio

■ **while away** vt passare ⟨time⟩

whilst /waɪlst/ conj = **while**

whim /wɪm/ n capriccio m

whimper /'wɪmpə(r)/ vi piagnucolare; ⟨dog:⟩ mugolare

whimsical /'wɪmzɪkl/ a capriccioso; ⟨story⟩ fantasioso

whine /waɪn/ n lamento m; (of dog) guaito m ● vi lamentarsi; ⟨dog:⟩ guaire

whinny /'wɪnɪ/ n nitrito m ● vi ⟨horse:⟩ nitrire

whip /wɪp/ n frusta f; (Pol: person) parlamentare mf incaricato, -a di assicurarsi della presenza dei membri del suo partito alle votazioni ● vt (pt/pp **whipped**) frustare; Culin sbattere; (snatch) afferrare; (fam: steal) fregare

■ **whip up** vt (incite) stimolare; fam improvvisare ⟨meal⟩

whiplash injury /'wɪplæʃ/ n Med colpo m di frusta

whipped cream /wɪpt'kriːm/ n panna f montata

whipping boy /'wɪpɪŋ/ n capro m espiatorio

whip-round n fam colletta f; **have a ~** fare una colletta

whirl /wɜːl/ n (movement) rotazione f; **my mind's in a ~** ho le idee confuse ● vi girare rapidamente ● vt far girare rapidamente

whirlpool /'wɜːlpuːl/ n vortice m

whirlwind /'wɜːlwɪnd/ n turbine m

whirr /wɜː(r)/ vi ronzare

whisk /wɪsk/ n Culin frullino m ● vt Culin frullare

■ **whisk away** vt portare via

whisker /'wɪskə(r)/ n **~s** pl (of cat) baffi mpl; (on man's cheek) basette fpl; **by a ~** per un pelo

whisky /'wɪskɪ/ n whisky m inv

whisper /'wɪspə(r)/ n sussurro m; (rumour) diceria f ● vt/i sussurrare

whispering gallery /'wɪspərɪŋ/ n galleria f acustica

whistle /'wɪsl/ n fischio m; (instrument) fischietto m ● vt fischiettare ● vi fischiettare; ⟨referee⟩ fischiare

whistle-stop tour n Pol giro m elettorale

white /waɪt/ a bianco; **go ~** (pale) sbiancare ● n bianco; (of egg) albume m; (person) bianco, -a mf

white: whitebait n bianchetti npl. **whiteboard** n lavagna f bianca. **white coffee** n caffè m inv macchiato. **white-collar worker** n colletto m bianco. **white elephant** n (public project) progetto m dispendioso e di scarsa efficacia; (building) cattedrale f nel deserto; (item, knicknack) oggetto m inutile. **white goods** n (linen) biancheria f per la casa; (appliances) elettrodomestici mpl. **Whitehall** n strada f di Londra, sede degli uffici del governo britannico; fig amministrazione f britannica. **white horses** npl cavalloni mpl. **white-hot** a ⟨metal⟩ arroventato. **white knight** n Fin white knight m inv. **white lie** n bugia f pietosa

whiten /'waɪtn/ vt imbiancare ● vi sbiancare

whitener /'waɪt(ə)nə(r)/ n (for shoes) bianchetto m; (for clothes) sbiancante m; (for coffee, tea) surrogato m del latte

whiteness /'waɪtnɪs/ n bianchezza f

white: white tie n (tie) cravattino m bianco; (formal dress) frac m inv. **whitewash** n intonaco m; fig copertura f ● vt dare una mano d'intonaco a; fig coprire. **white water** n rapide fpl. **white wedding** n matrimonio m in bianco

whither /'wɪðə(r)/ adv liter dove

whiting /'waɪtɪŋ/ n (fish) merlano m

Whitsun /'wɪtsn/ n Pentecoste f

■ **whittle away** /'wɪtl/ vt intaccare ⟨savings⟩; ridurre ⟨lead in race⟩

■ **whittle down** vt ridurre

whiz[z] /wɪz/ vi (pt/pp **whizzed**) sibilare

whiz[z]-kid n fam giovane m prodigio

who /hu:/ inter pron chi ● rel pron che; **the children, ~ were all tired, ...** i bambini, che erano tutti stanchi,...

whodunnit /hu:'dʌnɪt/ n fam [romanzo m] giallo m

whoever /hu:'evə(r)/ pron chiunque; **~ he is** chiunque sia; **~ can that be?** chi può mai essere?

whole /həʊl/ a tutto; (not broken) intatto; **the ~ truth** tutta la verità; **the ~ world** il mondo intero; **the ~ lot** (everything) tutto; (pl) tutti; **the ~ lot of you** tutti voi ● n tutto m; **as a ~** nell'insieme; **on the ~** tutto considerato; **the ~ of Italy** tutta l'Italia

whole: wholefood n cibo m macrobiotico. **wholehearted** /'həʊlhɑːtɪd/ a di tutto cuore. **wholemeal** a integrale. **whole milk** n latte m intero. **whole number** n numero m intero

wholesale /'həʊlseɪl/ a & adv all'ingrosso; fig in massa

wholesaler /'həʊlseɪlə(r)/ n grossista mf

wholesome /'həʊlsəm/ a sano

wholly /'həʊlɪ/ adv completamente

wholly-owned subsidiary n consociata f interamente controllata

whom /hu:m/ rel pron che; **the man ~ I saw** l'uomo che ho visto; **to/with ~** a/con cui ● inter pron chi; **to ~ did you speak?** con chi hai parlato?

whoop /wu:p/ n (shout) grido m ● vi gridare

whoopee /'wʊpɪ/ int evviva! ● n hum **make ~** (have fun) fare baldoria; (make love) fare l'amore

whooping cough /'hu:pɪŋ/ n pertosse f

whoosh /wʊʃ/ int vuum!

whopper /'wɒpə(r)/ n fam (lie) balla f; **what a ~!** è veramente gigantesco!

whopping /'wɒpɪŋ/ a fam enorme

whore /hɔ:(r)/ n puttana f vulg

whorl /wɔ:l/ n (of cream, chocolate etc) ghirigoro m; (of fingerprint) spirale f

whose /hu:z/ rel pron il cui; **people ~ name begins with D** le persone i cui nomi cominciano con la D ● inter pron di chi; **~ is that?** di chi è quello? ● a ~ **car did you use?** di chi è la macchina che hai usato?

Who's Who n pubblicazione f annuale con l'elenco delle personalità di spicco

why /waɪ/ adv (inter) perché; **the reason ~** la ragione per cui; **that's ~** per questo ● int diamine!

WI abbr (**Women's Institute**); Am abbr **Wisconsin**

wick /wɪk/ n stoppino m

wicked /'wɪkɪd/ a cattivo; (mischievous) malizioso

wicker /'wɪkə(r)/ n vimini mpl ● attrib di vimini

wicket /'wɪkɪt/ n (field gate) cancelletto m; Sport porta f; (Am: of ticket office etc) sportello m; **be on a sticky ~** fam essere in una situazione difficile

wide /waɪd/ a largo; ⟨experience, knowledge⟩ vasto; ⟨difference⟩ profondo; (far from target) lontano; **10 cm ~** largo 10 cm; **how ~ is it?** quanto è largo? ● adv (off target) lontano dal bersaglio; **~ awake** del tutto sveglio; **~ open** spalancato; **open ~!** apri bene!; **far and ~** in lungo e in largo

wide-angle lens n grandangolo m

wide-eyed /-'aɪd/ a ⟨person, innocence⟩ ingenuo; (with fear, surprise) con gli occhi sbarrati

widely /'waɪdlɪ/ adv largamente; ⟨known, accepted⟩ generalmente; ⟨different⟩ profondamente

widen /'waɪdn/ vt allargare; **~ the gap** fig accentuare il contrasto ● vi allargarsi

wide open a ⟨door, window, eyes⟩ spalancato

wide screen n Cinema schermo m panoramico

widespread /'waɪdspred/ a diffuso

widow /'wɪdəʊ/ n vedova f

widowed /'wɪdəʊd/ a vedovo

widower /'wɪdəʊə(r)/ n vedovo m

width /wɪdθ/ n larghezza f; (of material) altezza f

widthways /'wɪdθweɪz/ adv trasversalmente

wield /wiːld/ vt maneggiare; esercitare ⟨power⟩

wife /waɪf/ n (pl **wives**) moglie f

wife battering /'waɪfbæt(ə)rɪŋ/ n maltrattamento m della coniuge

wig /wɪg/ n parrucca f

wiggle /'wɪgl/ vi dimenarsi ● vt dimenare

wild /waɪld/ a selvaggio; ⟨animal, flower⟩ selvatico; (furious) furibondo; ⟨applause⟩ fragoroso; (idea) folle; (with joy) pazzo; (guess) azzardato; **be ~ about** (keen on) andare pazzo per ● adv **run ~** crescere senza controllo ● n **in the ~** allo stato naturale; **the ~s** pl le zone sperdute

wild: wild card n jolly m inv; Comput carattere m jolly. **wildcat strike** n sciopero m selvaggio. **wild dog** n cane m randagio

wilderness /'wɪldənɪs/ n deserto m; (fig: garden) giungla f

wild-eyed /-'aɪd/ a (distressed) dall'aria angosciata; (angry) dallo sguardo minaccioso. **wildfire** n **spread like ~** allargarsi a macchia d'olio. **wild flower** n fiore m di campo. **wildfowl** n (bird) uccello m selvatico; (birds collectively) uccelli mpl selvatici; (game) selvaggina f di penna. **wild-goose chase** n ricerca f inutile. **wildlife** n animali mpl selvatici. **wildlife park** n parco m naturale. **wildlife reserve** n riserva f naturale. **wildlife sanctuary** n riserva f naturale

wildly /'waɪldlɪ/ adv fig ⟨exaggerated⟩ estremamente; ⟨speak⟩ senza riflettere; ⟨applaud⟩ fragorosamente; ⟨hit out⟩ all'impazzata

Wild West n far west m

wiles /waɪlz/ npl astuzie fpl

wilful /'wɪlfʊl/ a intenzionale; ⟨person, refusal⟩ ostinato

wilfully /'wɪlfʊlɪ/ adv intenzionalmente; ⟨refuse⟩ ostinatamente

will[1] /wɪl/ v aux **he ~ arrive tomorrow** arriverà domani; **I won't tell him** non glielo dirò; **you ~ be back soon, won't you?** tornerai presto, no?; **he ~ be there, won't he?** sarà là, no?; **she ~ be there by now** sarà là ormai; **~ you go?** (do you intend to go) pensi di andare?; **~ you go to the baker's and buy...?** puoi andare dal panettiere a comprare...?; **~ you be quiet!** vuoi stare calmo!; **~ you have some wine?** vuoi del vino?; **the engine won't start** la macchina non parte

will[2] n volontà f inv; (document) testamento m

willing /'wɪlɪŋ/ a disposto; (eager) volonteroso

willingly /'wɪlɪŋlɪ/ adv volentieri

willingness /'wɪlɪŋnɪs/ n buona volontà f

willow /'wɪləʊ/ n salice m

willowy /'wɪləʊɪ/ a ⟨person, figure⟩ slanciato

will-power n forza f di volontà

willy-nilly /wɪlɪ'nɪlɪ/ adv (at random) a casaccio; (wanting to or not) volente o nolente

wilt /wɪlt/ vi appassire

wily /'waɪlɪ/ a (-ier, -iest) astuto

wimp /wɪmp/ n rammollito, -a mf

wimpish /'wɪmpɪʃ/ a ⟨fam: behaviour⟩ da rammollito

wimpy /'wɪmpɪ/ a ⟨fam: person⟩ rammollito

win /wɪn/ n vittoria f; **have a ~** riportare una vittoria ● v (pt/pp won; pres p winning) ● vt vincere; conquistare ⟨fame⟩ ● vi vincere

■ **win back** vt recuperare

■ **win over** vt convincere

■ **win through** vi (fam: be successful) uscire vittorioso

wince /wɪns/ vi contrarre il viso

winch /wɪntʃ/ n argano m

■ **winch up** vt tirare con l'argano

wind[1] /wɪnd/ n vento m; (breath) fiato m; ⟨fam: flatulence⟩ aria f; **get/have the ~ up** fam aver fifa; **get ~ of** aver sentore di; **in the ~** nell'aria ● vt **~ sb** lasciare qcno senza fiato; **~ a baby** far fare il ruttino a un neonato

wind[2] /waɪnd/ v (pt/pp wound) ● vt (wrap) avvolgere; (move by turning) far girare; ⟨clock⟩ caricare ● vi ⟨road:⟩ serpeggiare

■ **wind down** vi (relax) rilassarsi; (gradually come to an end) diminuire ● vt (gradually bring to an end) metter fine in modo graduale a

■ **wind up** /waɪnd/ vt caricare ⟨clock⟩; concludere ⟨proceedings⟩; fam sfottere ⟨sb⟩ ● vi (end up) **~ up doing sth** finire per fare qcsa

wind /wɪnd/: **windbreak** n frangivento m. **windcheater** n Br giacca f a vento. **windchill factor** n fattore m di raffreddamento da vento. **wind energy** n forza f del vento. **windfall** n fig fortuna f inaspettata; **~s** pl (fruit) frutta f abbattuta dal vento

winder /'waɪndə(r)/ n (for car window) manovella f alzacristalli; (for watch) bottone m di carica

winding /'waɪndɪŋ/ a tortuoso

wind instrument /'wɪnd/ n strumento m a fiato

windmill /'wɪn(d)mɪl/ n mulino m a vento

window /'wɪndəʊ/ n finestra f; (of car) finestrino m; (of shop) vetrina f

window: window box n cassetta f per i fiori. **window cleaner** n (person) lavavetri mf inv. **window display** n Comm esposizione f in vetrina. **window dresser** n vetrinista mf. **window dressing** n vetrinistica f; fig fumo m negli occhi. **window envelope** n busta f a finestra. **window frame** n telaio m di finestra. **window ledge** n davanzale m. **window pane** n vetro m. **window-shopping** n **go ~** andare in giro a vedere le vetrine. **window sill** n davanzale m

wind /wɪnd/: **windpipe** n trachea f. **windscreen** n, Am **windshield** n parabrezza m inv. **windscreen washer** n getto m d'acqua. **windscreen-wiper** n tergicristallo m. **wind-sleeve** n manica f a vento. **wind-sock** n manica f a vento. **wind surfing** n windsurf m inv. **windswept** a esposto al vento; ⟨person⟩ scompigliato

windy /'wɪndɪ/ a (-ier, -iest) ventoso

wine /waɪn/ n vino m

wine: wine bar n ≈ enoteca f. **wine box** n contenitore m di vino con rubinetto. **wine cooler** n (ice bucket) secchiello m del ghiaccio; (Am: drink) bibita f leggermente alcolica. **wineglass** n bicchiere m da vino. **wine list** n carta f dei vini. **wine merchant** n commerciante mf di vini. **wine producer** n produttore, -trice mf di vini. **wine rack** n portabottiglie m inv

winery /'waɪnərɪ/ n Am vigneto m

wine tasting /'waɪnteɪstɪŋ/ n degustazione f di vini

wing /wɪŋ/ n ala f; Auto parafango m; **~s** pl Theat quinte fpl; **under sb's ~** sotto l'ala [protettiva] di qcno

wing: wing chair n poltrona f con ampio schienale. **wing collar** n colletto m rigido. **wing commander** n tenente m colonnello delle forze aeree

winger /'wɪŋə(r)/ n Sport ala f

wing: wing-half n (in soccer) mediano m. **wing mirror** n Br specchietto m laterale. **wing nut** n dado m ad alette. **wingspan** n apertura f alare

wink /wɪŋk/ n strizzata f d'occhio; **not sleep a ~** non chiudere occhio ● vi strizzare l'occhio; ⟨light:⟩ lampeggiare

winner /'wɪnə(r)/ n vincitore, -trice mf

winning /'wɪnɪŋ/ a vincente; ⟨smile⟩ accattivante

winning post n linea f d'arrivo

winnings /'wɪnɪŋz/ npl vincite fpl

winning streak n periodo m fortunato; **be on a ~** essere in un periodo fortunato

winsome /'wɪnsəm/ a accattivante

winter /'wɪntə(r)/ n inverno m

winter sports npl sport mpl invernali

wintertime /'wɪntətaɪm/ n inverno m

wintry /'wɪntrɪ/ a invernale

wipe /waɪp/ n passata f; (to dry) asciugata f ● vt strofinare; (dry) asciugare

■ **wipe off** vt asciugare; (erase) cancellare

■ **wipe out** vt annientare; eliminare ⟨village⟩; estinguere ⟨debt⟩

■ **wipe up** vt asciugare ⟨dishes⟩

wiper blade /'waɪpə/ n Auto bordo f gommato del tergicristallo

wire /'waɪə(r)/ n fil m di ferro; (electrical) filo m elettrico

wire: wire brush n spazzola f metallica. **wire-cutters** n tronchese msg. **wire-haired** /-'heəd/ a dal pelo ispido

wireless /'waɪəlɪs/ n radio f inv

wire: wire mesh n rete f metallica. **wire netting** n rete f metallica. **wire wool** n lana f d'acciaio

wiring /'waɪərɪŋ/ n impianto m elettrico

wiry /'waɪərɪ/ a (-ier, -iest) ⟨person⟩ dal fisico asciutto; ⟨hair⟩ ispido

wisdom /'wɪzdəm/ n saggezza f; (of action) sensatezza f

wisdom tooth n dente m del giudizio

wise /waɪz/ a saggio; (prudent) sensato

■ **wise up** fam vi (become more aware) aprire gli occhi ● vt aprire gli occhi a (**to** su)

wisecrack /'waɪzkræk/ fam n battuta f salace ● vi far battute salaci

wise guy n fam sapientone m

wisely /'waɪzlɪ/ adv saggiamente; ⟨act⟩ sensatamente

Wise Men npl Re Magi mpl

wish /wɪʃ/ n desiderio m; **make a ~** esprimere un desiderio; **with best ~es** con i migliori auguri ● vt desiderare; **~ sb well** fare tanti auguri a qcno; **I ~ you every success** ti auguro buona fortuna; **I ~ you could stay** vorrei che tu potessi rimanere; **~ sth on sb** fam sbolognare qcsa a qcno ● vi **~ for sth** desiderare qcsa

wishbone /'wɪʃbəʊn/ n forcella f (di pollo o tacchino)

wishful /'wɪʃfʊl/ a **~ thinking** illusione f

wishy-washy /'wɪʃɪwɒʃɪ/ a ⟨colour⟩ spento; ⟨personality⟩ insignificante

wisp /wɪsp/ n (of hair) ciocca f; (of smoke) filo m; (of grass) ciuffo m

wisteria /wɪs'tɪərɪə/ n glicine m

wistful /'wɪstfʊl/ a malinconico

wistfully /'wɪstfʊlɪ/ adv malinconicamente

wit /wɪt/ n spirito m; (person) persona f di spirito; **be at one's ~s' end** non saper che pesci pigliare; **scared out of one's ~s** spaventato a morte

witch /wɪtʃ/ n strega f

witch: witchcraft n magia f. **witch doctor** n stregone m. **witch-hunt** n caccia f alle streghe

with /wɪð/ prep con; (fear, cold, jealousy etc) di; **I'm not ~ you** fam non ti seguo; **can I leave it ~ you?** (task) puoi occupartene tu?; **~ no regrets/money** senza rimpianti/soldi; **be ~ it** fam essere al passo coi tempi; (alert) essere concentrato

withdraw /wɪð'drɔː/ v (pt -drew, pp -drawn) ● vt ritirare; prelevare ⟨money⟩ ● vi ritirarsi

withdrawal /wɪð'drɔː(ə)l/ n ritiro m; (of money) prelevamento m; (from drugs) crisi f inv di astinenza; Psych chiusura f in se stessi

withdrawal symptoms npl sintomi mpl da crisi di astinenza

withdrawn /wɪð'drɔːn/ see **withdraw** ● a ⟨person⟩ chiuso in se stesso

wither /'wɪðə(r)/ vi ⟨flower:⟩ appassire

withering /'wɪðərɪŋ/ a ⟨look⟩ fulminante

withhold /wɪð'həʊld/ vt (pt/pp -**held**) rifiutare ⟨consent⟩ (**from** a); nascondere ⟨information⟩ (**from** a); trattenere ⟨smile⟩

within /wɪð'ɪn/ prep in; (before the end of) entro; **~ the law** legale ● adv all'interno

without /wɪð'aʊt/ prep senza; **~ stopping** senza fermarsi; **how could it have happened ~ you noticing it?** come è potuto succedere senza che tu lo notassi?

withstand /wɪð'stænd/ vt (pt/pp -**stood**) resistere a

witness /'wɪtnɪs/ n testimone mf; **bear ~** portare testimonianza ● vt ≈ autenticare ⟨signature⟩; essere testimone di ⟨accident⟩

witness box, *Am* **witness-stand** *n* banco *m* dei testimoni

witticism /'wɪtɪsɪzm/ *n* spiritosaggine *f*

wittingly /'wɪtɪŋlɪ/ *adv* consapevolmente

witty /'wɪtɪ/ *a* (**-ier, -iest**) spiritoso

wives /waɪvz/ *see* **wife**

wizard /'wɪzəd/ *n* mago *m*

wizardry /'wɪzədrɪ/ *n* stregoneria *f*

wizened /'wɪznd/ *a* raggrinzito

wk *abbr* **week**

wobble /'wɒbl/ *vi* traballare

wobbly /'wɒblɪ/ *a* traballante

wodge /wɒdʒ/ *n fam* mucchio *m*

woe /wəʊ/ *n* afflizione *f*; ~ **is me!** me meschino!

woeful /'wəʊfʊl/ *a* ‹story, sight› triste; ‹lack› vergognoso

woke, woken /wəʊk, 'wəʊkn/ *see* **wake¹**

wolf /wʊlf/ *n* (*pl* **wolves** /wʊlvz/) lupo *m*; (*fam: womanizer*) donnaiolo *m* ● *vt* ~ [**down**] divorare

wolf: wolf cub *n* cucciolo *m* di lupo. **wolfhound** *n Br* cane *m* lupo. **wolf whistle** *n* fischio *m* ● *vi* ~**-whistle at sb** fischiare dietro a qcno

woman /'wʊmən/ *n* (*pl* **women**) donna *f*

womanizer /'wʊmənaɪzə(r)/ *n* donnaiolo *m*

womanly /'wʊmənlɪ/ *a* femmineo

womb /wuːm/ *n* utero *m*

women /'wɪmɪn/ *see* **woman**

women's: Women's Institute *n* associazione *f che si occupa dei problemi delle donne.* **Women's Libber** /wɪmɪnz'lɪbə(r)/ *n* femminista *f*. **Women's Liberation** *n* movimento *m* femminista. **women's movement** *n* movimento *m* per l'emancipazione della donna. **women's studies** *npl storia f dell'emancipazione femminile*

won /wʌn/ *see* **win**

wonder /'wʌndə(r)/ *n* meraviglia *f*; (*surprise*) stupore *m*; **no** ~! non c'è da stupirsi!; **it's a** ~ **that...** è incredibile che... ● *vi* restare in ammirazione; (*be surprised*) essere sorpreso; **I** ~ è quello che mi chiedo; **I** ~ **whether she is ill** mi chiedo se è malata?

wonderful /'wʌndəfʊl/ *a* meraviglioso

wonderfully /'wʌndəfʊlɪ/ *adv* meravigliosamente

wonderland /'wʌndəlænd/ *n* paese *m* delle meraviglie

wonky /'wɒŋkɪ/ *a Br fam* (*faulty*) difettoso; ‹furniture› traballante; (*crooked*) storto

wont /wəʊnt/ *n* **as was his** ~ come suo solito ● *a* **he was** ~ **to fall asleep** era solito addormentarsi

won't /wəʊnt/ = **will not**

woo /wuː/ *vt* corteggiare; *fig* cercare di accattivarsi ‹voters›; cercare di ottenere ‹fame, fortune›

wood /wʊd/ *n* legno *m*; (*for burning*) legna *f*; (*forest*) bosco *m*; **out of the** ~ *fig* fuori pericolo; **touch** ~! tocca ferro!

woodcarving /'wʊdkɑːvɪŋ/ *n* scultura *f* di legno

wooded /'wʊdɪd/ *a* boscoso

wooden /'wʊdn/ *a* di legno; *fig* legnoso

wooden horse *n* cavallo *m* di Troia

wooden spoon *n* mestolo *m* di legno; *fig* premio *m* di consolazione

wood: woodlouse *n* onisco *m*. **woodpecker** *n* picchio *m*. **wood pigeon** *n* colombaccio *m*. **wood shavings** *npl* trucioli *mpl*. **woodshed** *n* legnaia *f*. **wood stove** *n* stufa *f* a legna. **woodwind** *n* strumenti *mpl* a fiato. **woodwork** *n* (*wooden parts*) parti *fpl* in legno; (*craft*) falegnameria *f*. **woodworm** *n* tarlo *m*

woody /'wʊdɪ/ *a* legnoso; ‹hill› boscoso

wool /wʊl/ *n* lana *f*; **pull the** ~ **over sb's eyes** gettar fumo negli occhi a qcno ● *attrib* di lana

woollen /'wʊlən/ *a* di lana

woollens /'wʊlənz/ *npl* capi *mpl* di lana

woolly /'wʊlɪ/ *a* (**-ier, -iest**) ‹sweater› di lana; *fig* confuso

woozy /'wuːzɪ/ *a* intontito

word /wɜːd/ *n* parola *f*; (*news*) notizia *f*; **by** ~ **of mouth** a viva voce; **have a** ~ **with** dire due parole a; **have** ~**s** bisticciare; **in other** ~**s** in altre parole; **go back on one's** ~ rimangiarsi la parola

word-for-word *a* ‹translation› letterale ● *adv* parola per parola

wording /'wɜːdɪŋ/ *n* parole *fpl*

word: word-perfect *a* che sa a memoria. **word processing** *n Comput* word processing *m*, elaborazione *f* testi. **word processor** *n* sistema *m* di videoscrittura, word processor *m inv*

wordy /'wɜːdɪ/ *a* prolisso

wore /wɔː(r)/ *see* **wear**

work /wɜːk/ *n* lavoro *m*; (*of art*) opera *f*; ~**s** *pl* (*factory*) fabbrica *fsg*; (*mechanism*) meccanismo *msg*; **at** ~ al lavoro; **out of** ~ disoccupato ● *vi* lavorare; ‹machine, ruse:› funzionare; (*study*) studiare ● *vt* far funzionare ‹machine›; far lavorare ‹employee›; far studiare ‹student›; ~ **one's way through sth** (*read*) leggere attentamente

■ **work off** *vt* sfogare ‹anger›; lavorare per estinguere ‹debt›; fare sport per smaltire ‹weight›

■ **work out** *vt* elaborare ‹plan›; risolvere ‹problem›; calcolare ‹bill›; **I** ~**ed out how he did it** ho capito come l'ha fatto ● *vi* evolvere

■ **work up** *vt* **I've** ~**ed up an appetite** mi è venuto appetito; **don't get** ~**ed up** (*anxious*) non farti prendere dal panico; (*angry*) non arrabbiarti

workable /'wɜːkəbl/ *a* (*feasible*) fattibile

workaday /'wɜːkədeɪ/ *a* ‹clothes, life› ordinario

workaholic /wɜːkə'hɒlɪk/ *n* staccanovista *mf*

work: workbench *n* banco *m* da lavoro. **workbook** *n* (*blank*) quaderno *m*; (*with exercises*) libro *m* di esercizi. **workday** *n* giorno *m* lavorativo

worker /'wɜːkə(r)/ n lavoratore, -trice mf; (manual) operaio, -a mf

work: work experience n esperienza f professionale; (part of training programme) stage m inv. **workforce** n forza f lavoro. **workhorse** n fig lavoratore, -trice mf indefesso, -a

working /'wɜːkɪŋ/ a (clothes etc) da lavoro; (day) feriale; **in ~ order** funzionante

working: working capital n capitale m netto di esercizio. **working-class** a operaio; **be ~** appartenere alla classe operaia ● **working class** n classe f operaia. **working week** n settimana f lavorativa.

work: workload n carico m di lavoro. **workman** n operaio m. **workmanlike** a fatto con competenza. **workmanship** n lavorazione f. **workmate** n collega mf. **work of art** n opera f d'arte. **workout** n allenamento m. **work permit** n permesso m di lavoro. **workplace** n posto m di lavoro. **work-sharing** n divisione f di un posto di lavoro tra più persone. **workshop** n officina f; (discussion) dibattito m. **work-shy** a pigro. **workstation** n stazione f di lavoro. **work surface** n piano m di lavoro. **worktop** n piano m di lavoro. **work-to-rule** n sciopero m bianco

world /wɜːld/ n mondo m; **a ~ of difference** una differenza abissale; **out of this ~** favoloso; **think the ~ of sb** andare matto per qcno

world: world-class a di livello internazionale. **World Cup** n (in football) Coppa f del Mondo. **world-famous** a di fama mondiale

worldly /'wɜːldlɪ/ a materiale; (person) materialista

worldly-wise a vissuto

world war n guerra f mondiale

worldwide /'wɜːldwaɪd/ a mondiale ● adv mondialmente

worm /wɜːm/ n verme m ● vt ~ **one's way into sb's confidence** conquistarsi la fiducia di qcno in modo subdolo

■ **worm out** vt ~ **sth out of sb** carpire qcsa a qcno

worm-eaten /'wɜːmiːtən/ a (wood) tarlato; (fruit) bacato

wormhole /'wɜːmhəʊl/ n (in wood) buco m di tarlo; (in fruit, plant) buco m del verme

worn /wɔːn/ see **wear** ● a sciupato

worn-out a consumato; (person) sfinito

worried /'wʌrɪd/ a preoccupato

worrier /'wʌrɪə(r)/ n ansioso, -a mf; **he's a terrible ~** è ansioso da morire

worry /'wʌrɪ/ n preoccupazione f ● v (pt/pp worried) ● vt preoccupare; (bother) disturbare ● vi preoccuparsi

worrying /'wʌrɪɪŋ/ a preoccupante

worse /wɜːs/ a peggiore ● adv peggio ● n peggio m

worsen /'wɜːsn/ vt/i peggiorare

worse off a **be ~ ~ than** stare peggio di; **be £100 ~ ~** avere 100 sterline in meno

worship /'wɜːʃɪp/ n culto m; (service) funzione f; **Your/His W~** (to judge) signor giudice/il

giudice ● v (pt/pp **-shipped**) ● vt venerare ● vi andare a messa

worst /wɜːst/ a peggiore ● adv peggio ● n **the ~** il peggio; **get the ~ of it** avere la peggio; **if the ~ comes to the ~** nella peggiore delle ipotesi

worsted /'wʊstɪd/ n lana f pettinata

worth /wɜːθ/ n valore m; **£10 ~ of petrol** 10 sterline di benzina ● a be ~ valere; **be ~ it** fig valerne la pena; **it is ~ trying** vale la pena di provare; **it's ~ my while** mi conviene; **I'll make it ~ your while** te ne ricompenserò

worthless /'wɜːθlɪs/ a senza valore

worthwhile /wɜːθ'waɪl/ a che vale la pena; (cause) lodevole

worthy /'wɜːðɪ/ a degno; (cause, motive) lodevole

would /wʊd/ v aux I ~ **do it** lo farei; ~ **you go?** andresti?; ~ **you mind if I opened the window?** ti dispiace se apro la finestra?; **he ~ come if he could** verrebbe se potesse; **he said he ~n't** ha detto di no; **he said he ~n't have** ha detto che non lo avrebbe fatto; ~ **you like a drink?** vuoi qualcosa da bere?; **what ~ you like to drink?** cosa prendi da bere?; **you ~n't, ~ you?** non lo faresti, vero?

would-be a (pej: actor, singer etc) sedicente; (investor, buyer) aspirante

wound[1] /wuːnd/ n ferita f ● vt ferire

wound[2] /waʊnd/ see **wind**[2]

wove, woven /wəʊv, 'wəʊvn/ see **weave**[2]

wow /waʊ/ n (fam: success) successone m; (in sound system) wow m ● vt fam entusiasmare (person) ● int caspita!

WP abbr (**word processing**) elaborazione f testi

wpm abbr (**words per minute**) parole fpl al minuto

wrangle /'ræŋgl/ n litigio m ● vi litigare

wrap /ræp/ n (shawl) scialle m ● vt (pt/pp wrapped) ~ [up] avvolgere; (present) incartare; **be ~ped up in** fig essere completamente preso da ● vi ~ **up warmly** coprirsi bene

wraparound /'ræpəraʊnd/ a (skirt) a pareo; (window, windscreen) panoramico

wrapper /'ræpə(r)/ n (for sweet) carta f [di caramella]

wrapping /'ræpɪŋ/ n materiale m da imballaggio

wrapping paper n carta f da pacchi; (for gift) carta f da regalo

wrath /rɒθ/ n ira f

wreak /riːk/ vt ~ **havoc with sth** scombussolare qcsa

wreath /riːθ/ n (pl ~s /riːðz/) corona f

wreathed /riːðd/ a ~ **in** avvolto in (mists); **her face was ~ in smiles** era raggiante

wreck /rek/ n (of ship) relitto m; (of car) carcassa f; (person) rottame m ● vt far naufragare; demolire (car)

wreckage /'rekɪdʒ/ n rottami mpl; fig brandelli mpl

wrecked /rekt/ a (ship, car) distrutto;

⟨*building*⟩ demolito; (*fig: exhausted*) distrutto

wren /ren/ *n* scricciolo *m*

wrench /rentʃ/ *n* (*injury*) slogatura *f*; (*tool*) chiave *f* inglese; (*pull*) strattone *m*; **it was a ~ leaving home** *fig* è stato un passo difficile andarsene da casa ● *vt* (*pull*) strappare; slogarsi ⟨*wrist, ankle etc*⟩

wrest /rest/ *vt* strappare (**from** a)

wrestle /'resl/ *vi* lottare corpo a corpo; *fig* lottare

wrestler /'reslə(r)/ *n* lottatore, -trice *mf*

wrestling /'reslɪŋ/ *n* lotta *f* libera; (*all-in*) catch *m*

wretch /retʃ/ *n* disgraziato, -a *mf*

wretched /'retʃɪd/ *a* odioso; ⟨*weather*⟩ orribile; **feel ~** (*unhappy*) essere triste; (*ill*) sentirsi malissimo

wriggle /'rɪgl/ *n* contorsione *f* ● *vi* contorcersi; (*move forward*) strisciare; **~ out of sth** *fam* sottrarsi a qcsa

wriggly /'rɪglɪ/ *a* ⟨*person*⟩ che si dimena; ⟨*snake, worm*⟩ che si contorce

wring /rɪŋ/ *vt* (*pt*/*pp* **wrung**) torcere ⟨*sb's neck*⟩; strizzare ⟨*clothes*⟩; **~ one's hands** torcersi le mani; **~ sth out of sb** *fig* estorcere qcsa a qcno; **~ing wet** inzuppato

wrinkle /'rɪŋkl/ *n* grinza *f*; (*on skin*) ruga *f* ● *vt/i* raggrinzire

wrinkled /'rɪŋkld/ *a* ⟨*skin, face*⟩ rugoso; ⟨*clothes*⟩ raggrinzito

wrist /rɪst/ *n* polso *m*

wristband /'rɪs(t)bænd/ *n* polsino *m*; (*on watch*) cinturino *m*

wristwatch /'rɪstwɒtʃ/ *n* orologio *m* da polso

writ /rɪt/ *n* *Jur* mandato *m*

write /raɪt/ *vt/i* (*pt* **wrote**, *pp* **written**, *pres p* **writing**) scrivere

■ **write away for** *vt* richiedere per posta ⟨*information*⟩

■ **write back** *vi* rispondere

■ **write down** *vt* annotare

■ **write in** *vi* scrivere

■ **write off** *vt* cancellare ⟨*debt*⟩; distruggere ⟨*car*⟩

■ **write out** *vt* fare ⟨*cheque, prescription*⟩; (*copy*) ricopiare

■ **write up** *vt* redigere; aggiornare ⟨*diary*⟩; elaborare ⟨*notes*⟩

write-off *n* (*car*) rottame *m*

writer /'raɪtə(r)/ *n* autore, -trice *mf*; **she's a ~** è una scrittrice

writer's block *n* blocco *m* dello scrittore

write-up *n* (*review*) recensione *f*

writhe /raɪð/ *vi* contorcersi; **~ with embarrassment** vergognarsi a morte

writing /'raɪtɪŋ/ *n* (*occupation*) scrivere *m*; (*words*) scritte *fpl*; (*handwriting*) scrittura *f*; **~s** *pl* scritti *mpl*; **in ~** per iscritto

writing: writing desk *n* scrivania *f*. **writing pad** *n* (*for notes*) bloc-notes *m inv*; (*for letters*) blocco *m* di carta da lettere. **writing paper** *n* carta *f* da lettera

written /'rɪtn/ *see* **write**

wrong /rɒŋ/ *a* sbagliato; **be ~** ⟨*person:*⟩ sbagliare; **what's ~?** cosa c'è che non va? ● *adv* ⟨*spelt*⟩ in modo sbagliato; **go ~** ⟨*person:*⟩ sbagliare; ⟨*machine:*⟩ funzionare male; ⟨*plan:*⟩ andar male; **don't get me ~** non fraintendermi ● *n* ingiustizia *f*; **in the ~** dalla parte del torto; **know right from ~** distinguere il bene dal male ● *vt* fare torto a

wrong-foot *vt* *Sport, fig* prendere in contropiede

wrongful /'rɒŋfʊl/ *a* ingiusto

wrongfully /'rɒŋfʊlɪ/ *adv* ⟨*accuse*⟩ ingiustamente

wrongly /'rɒŋlɪ/ *adv* in modo sbagliato; ⟨*accuse, imagine*⟩ a torto; ⟨*informed*⟩ male

wrote /rəʊt/ *see* **write**

wrought iron /rɔːt'aɪən/ *n* ferro *m* battuto ● *attrib* di ferro battuto

wrung /rʌŋ/ *see* **wring**

wry /raɪ/ *a* (**-er, -est**) ⟨*humour, smile*⟩ beffardo

WYSIWYG /'wɪzɪwɪg/ *abbr* *Comput* (**what you see is what you get**) ciò che vedi è ciò che ottieni

Xx

x, X /eks/ *n* (*letter*) x, X *f inv*; (*anonymous person, place etc*) X
x *n Math* x *f inv*
X certificate *a Br* vietato ai minori di 18 anni
xenophobia /zenəˈfəʊbɪə/ *n* xenofobia *f*
xerox® /ˈzɪərɒks/ *vt* xerocopiare ● *n* (*machine*) xerocopiatrice *f*; (*document*) xerocopia *f*

Xmas /ˈkrɪsməs/ *n fam* Natale *m*
X-ray *n* (*picture*) radiografia *f*; **have an ~** farsi fare una radiografia ● *vt* passare ai raggi X
X-ray machine *n* apparecchio *m* radiografico
xxx *n* (*at end of letter*) baci *mpl*

Yy

y, Y /waɪ/ *n* (*letter*) y, Y *f inv*
yacht /jɒt/ *n* yacht *m inv*; (*for racing*) barca *f* a vela
yachting /ˈjɒtɪŋ/ *n* vela *f*
yak /jæk/ *n Zool* yak *m inv*
Yale® /jeɪl/ *n* (*lock*) serratura *f* di sicurezza
yam /jæm/ *n* (*tropical*) igname *m*; (*Am: sweet potato*) patata *f* dolce
Yank /jæŋk/ *n fam* americano, -a *mf*
yank *vt fam* tirare
Yankee /ˈjæŋkɪ/ *n* (*pej: American*) yankee *m inv*; (*soldier*) nordista *m*; (*Am: of Northern USA*) abitante *mf* degli USA settentrionali; (*Am: inhabitant of New England*) abitante *mf* della Nuova Inghilterra
yap /jæp/ *vi* (*pt/pp* **yapped**) ⟨*dog:*⟩ guaire
yapping /ˈjæpɪŋ/ *n* (*of dogs*) guaiti *mpl*; (*fam: of people*) ciance *fpl*
yard¹ /jɑːd/ *n* cortile *m*; (*for storage*) deposito *m*; **the Y~** *fam* Scotland Yard *f* (*polizia londinese*)
yard² *n* iarda *f* (= *91,44 cm*)
yardstick /ˈjɑːdstɪk/ *n fig* pietra *f* di paragone
yarn /jɑːn/ *n* filo *m*; (*fam: tale*) storia *f*
yashmak /ˈjæʃmæk/ *n* velo *m* (*delle donne musulmane*)
yawn /jɔːn/ *n* sbadiglio *m* ● *vi* sbadigliare
yawning /ˈjɔːnɪŋ/ *a* **~ gap** sbadiglio *m*
yd *abbr* **yard**
yeah /je/ *adv fam* sì; **oh ~ ?** ma davvero?
year /jɪə(r)/ *n* anno *m*; (*of wine*) annata *f*; **for ~s** *fam* da secoli
yearbook /ˈjɪəbʊk/ *n* annuario *m*
yearly /ˈjɪəlɪ/ *a* annuale ● *adv* annualmente
yearn /jɜːn/ *vi* struggersi
yearning /ˈjɜːnɪŋ/ *n* desiderio *m* struggente
year-round *a* ⟨*supply, source*⟩ permanente

yeast /jiːst/ *n* lievito *m*
yell /jel/ *n* urlo *m* ● *vi* urlare
yelling /ˈjelɪŋ/ *n* urla *fpl*
yellow /ˈjeləʊ/ *a & n* giallo *m*
yellow-belly *n fam* fifone *m*
yellow card *n Sport* cartellino *m* giallo
yellowish /ˈjeləʊɪʃ/ *a* giallastro
yellow pages *npl* pagine *fpl* gialle
yellowy /ˈjeləʊɪ/ *a* giallastro
yelp /jelp/ *n* (*of dog*) guaito *m* ● *vi* ⟨*dog:*⟩ guaire
Yemen /ˈjemən/ *n* Yemen *m*
Yemeni /ˈjemənɪ/ *a & n* yemenita *mf*
yen /jen/ *n* forte desiderio *m* (**for** di)
yeoman /ˈjəʊmən/ *n Br* piccolo proprietario *m* terriero; **Y~ of the Guard** guardiano *m* della Torre di Londra
yep /jep/ *adv fam* sì
yes /jes/ *adv* sì ● *n* sì *m inv*
yes-man *n fam* tirapiedi *m inv*
yesterday /ˈjestədeɪ/ *n & adv* ieri *m inv*; **~'s paper** il giornale di ieri; **the day before ~** l'altroieri; **~ afternoon** ieri pomeriggio; **~ evening** ieri sera; **~ morning** ieri mattina
yet /jet/ *adv* ancora; **as ~** fino ad ora; **not ~** non ancora; **the best ~** il migliore finora ● *conj* eppure
yew /juː/ *n* tasso *m* (*albero*)
Y-fronts *npl Br* slip *m inv* da uomo con apertura
YHA *Br abbr* (**Youth Hostels Association**) associazione *f* degli ostelli della gioventù
Yiddish /ˈjɪdɪʃ/ *n* yiddish *m*
yield /jiːld/ *n* produzione *f*; ⟨*profit*⟩ reddito *m* ● *vt* produrre; fruttare ⟨*profit*⟩ ● *vi* cedere; *Am Auto* dare la precedenza
yielding /ˈjiːldɪŋ/ *a* (*submissive*) arrendevole; ⟨*ground*⟩ cedevole; ⟨*person*⟩ flessibile

YMCA *abbr* (**Young Men's Christian Association**) Associazione *f* Cristiana dei Giovani

yodel /'jəʊdl/ *vi* (*pt/pp* **yodelled**) cantare jodel

yoga /'jəʊgə/ *n* yoga *m*

yoghurt /'jɒgət/ *n* yogurt *m inv*

yoke /jəʊk/ *n* giogo *m*; (*of garment*) carré *m inv*

yokel /'jəʊkl/ *n* zotico, -a *mf*

yolk /jəʊk/ *n* tuorlo *m*

yonder /'jɒndə(r)/ *adv liter* laggiù

yonks /jɒŋks/ *npl fam* **I haven't seen him for ~** è un secolo che non lo vedo

yore /jɔ:(r)/ *n* **in days of ~** un tempo

you /ju:/ *pers pron* (*subject*) tu, voi *pl*; (*formal*) lei, voi *pl*; (*direct/indirect object*) ti, vi *pl*; (*formal: direct object*) la; (*formal: indirect object*) le; (*after prep*) te, voi *pl*; (*formal: after prep*) lei; **~ are very kind** (*sg*) sei molto gentile; (*formal*) è molto gentile; (*pl & formal pl*) siete molto gentili; **~ can stay, but he has to go** (*sg*) tu puoi rimanere, ma lui deve andarsene; (*pl*) voi potete rimanere, ma lui deve andarsene; **all of ~** tutti voi; **I'll give ~ the money** (*sg*) ti darò i soldi; (*pl*) vi darò i soldi; **I'll give it to ~** (*sg*) te/(*pl*) ve lo darò; **it does ~ good** (*sg*) ti/(*pl*) vi fa bene; **it was ~!** (*sg*) eri tu!; (*pl*) eravate voi!; **~ has to be careful these days** si deve fare attenzione di questi tempi; **~ can't tell the difference** non puoi vedere la differenza

you'd /ju:d/ *abbr* **you would**; **you had**

you-know-what *pron fam* sai cosa

you-know-who *pron fam* sai chi

you'll /ju:l/ *abbr* **you will**

you're /jʊə(r)/ *abbr* **you are**

you've /ju:v/ *abbr* **you have**

young /jʌŋ/ *a* giovane; **~ lady** signorina *f*; **~ man** giovanotto *m*; **her ~ man** (*boyfriend*) il suo ragazzo ● *npl* (*animals*) piccoli *mpl*; **the ~** (*people*) i giovani

young blood *n* nuove leve *fpl*

youngish /'jʌŋɪʃ/ *a* abbastanza giovane

young-looking *a* dall'aria giovanile

young offender *n* delinquente *mf* minorenne

youngster /'jʌŋstə(r)/ *n* ragazzo, -a *mf*; (*child*) bambino, -a *mf*

your /jɔ:(r)/ *poss a* tuo *m*, tua *f*, tuoi *mpl*, tue *fpl*; (*formal*) suo *m*, sua *f*, suoi *mpl*, sue *fpl*; (*pl & formal pl*) vostro *m*, vostra *f*, vostri *mpl*, vostre *fpl*; **~ task/house** il tuo compito/la tua casa; (*formal*) il suo compito/la sua casa; (*pl & formal pl*) il vostro compito/la vostra casa; **~ mother/father** tua madre/tuo padre; (*formal*) sua madre/suo padre; (*pl & formal pl*) vostra madre/vostro padre

yours /jɔ:z/ *poss pron* il tuo *m*, la tua *f*, i tuoi *mpl*, le tue *fpl*; (*formal*) il suo *m*, la sua *f*, i suoi *mpl*, le sue *fpl*; (*pl & formal pl*) il vostro *m*, la vostra *f*, i vostri *mpl*, le vostre *fpl*; **a friend of ~** un tuo/suo/vostro amico; **friends of ~** dei tuoi/vostri/suoi amici; **that is ~** quello è tuo/vostro/suo; (*as opposed to mine*) quello è il tuo/il vostro/il suo

yourself /jɔ:'self/ *pers pron* (*reflexive*) ti; (*formal*) si; (*emphatic*) te stesso; (*formal*) sé, se stesso; **do pour ~ a drink** versati da bere; (*formal*) si versi da bere; **you said so ~** lo hai detto tu stesso; (*formal*) lo ha detto lei stesso; **you can be proud of ~** puoi essere fiero di te/di sé; **by ~** da solo

yourselves /jɔ:'selvz/ *pers pron* (*reflexive*) vi; (*emphatic*) voi stessi; **do pour ~ a drink** versatevi da bere; **you said so ~** lo avete detto voi stessi; **you can be proud of ~** potete essere fieri di voi; **by ~** da soli

youth /ju:θ/ *n* (*pl* **youths** /ju:ð:z/) gioventù *f inv*; (*boy*) giovanetto *m*; **the ~** (*young people*) i giovani

youthful /'ju:θfʊl/ *a* giovanile

youth: youth hostel *n* ostello *m* [della gioventù]; **youth hostelling** *n viaggiare m pernottando in ostelli della gioventù*. **youth work** *n* lavoro *m* di educatore. **youth worker** *n* educatore, -trice *mf*

yo-yo® /'jəʊjəʊ/ *n* yo-yo *m inv* ● *vi* (*prices, inflation:*) andare su e giù

yr *abbr* **year**

Yugoslav /'ju:gəslɑ:v/ *a & n* jugoslavo, -a *mf*

Yugoslavia /ju:gə'slɑ:vɪə/ *n* Jugoslavia *f*

Yule log /ju:l/ *n* tronchetto *m* natalizio

yup /jʌp/ *adv fam* sì

yuppie /'jʌpɪ/ *n* yuppie *mf inv*

yuppie flu *n* sindrome *f* da affaticamento cronico

YWCA *abbr* (**Young Women's Christian Association**) Associazione *f* Cristiana delle Giovani

Zz

z, Z /zed/ *n (letter)* z, Z *f inv*
zany /'zeɪnɪ/ *a* (**-ier, -iest**) demenziale
zap /zæp/ *n (fam: energy)* energia *f* ● *vt (pt/pp*
  zapped) *fam (destroy)* distruggere ‹*town*›; far
  fuori ‹*person, animal*›; *(fire at)* fulminare;
  (Comput: delete) cancellare
zapper /'zæpə(r)/ *n (fam: for TV)* telecomando *m*
zeal /ziːl/ *n* zelo *m*
zealot /'zelət/ *n fig* fanatico *m*
zealous /'zeləs/ *a* zelante
zealously /'zeləslɪ/ *adv* con zelo
zebra /'zebrə/ *n* zebra *f*
zebra crossing *n* passaggio *m* pedonale,
  zebre *fpl*
zenith /'zenɪθ/ *n* zenit *m inv; fig* apogeo *m*
zero /'zɪərəʊ/ *n* zero *m*
zero: zero gravity *n* assenza *f* di gravità.
  zero hour *n Mil, fig* ora *f* zero. **zero-rated**
  /-'reɪtɪd/ *a Br* esente [da] IVA
zest /zest/ *n* gusto *m*; *(peel)* scorza *f (di agrumi)*
zigzag /'zɪgzæg/ *n* zigzag *m inv* ● *vi (pt/pp*
  -zagged) zigzagare
zilch /zɪltʃ/ *n fam* un tubo; **I understood ~**
  non ho capito un tubo
Zimbabwe /zɪm'bæbweɪ/ *n* Zimbabwe *m*
Zimmer® /'zɪmə(r)/ *n Br* deambulatore *m*

zinc /zɪŋk/ *n* zinco *m*
zinc oxide *n* ossido *m* di zinco
zing /zɪŋ/ *n fam (energy)* brio *m*; *(sound)* sibilo *m* ● *vt (Am: criticize)* stroncare
Zionism /'zaɪənɪzm/ *n* sionismo *m*
zip /zɪp/ *n* ~ [**fastener**] cerniera *f* [lampo]
  ● *vt (pt/pp* **zipped**) ~ [**up**] chiudere con la
  cerniera [lampo]
■ **zip along** *vi (move quickly)* procedere velocemente
zip code *n Am* codice *m* [di avviamento] postale, C.A.P.
zipper /'zɪpə(r)/ *n Am* cerniera *f* [lampo]
zippy /'zɪpɪ/ *a (fam: vehicle)* scattante
zither /'zɪðə(r)/ *n* cetra *f*
zodiac /'zəʊdɪæk/ *n* zodiaco *m*
zombie /'zɒmbɪ/ *n fam* zombi *mf inv*
zone /zəʊn/ *n* zona *f*
zoning /'zəʊnɪŋ/ *n* zonazione *f*
zonked /zɒŋkt/ *a (fam: on drugs, drunk,
  tired)* fatto
zoo /zuː/ *n* zoo *m inv*
zoological /zəʊə'lɒdʒɪkl/ *a* zoologico
zoologist /zəʊ'ɒlədʒɪst/ *n* zoologo, -a *mf*
zoology /zəʊ'ɒlədʒɪ/ *n* zoologia *f*
zoom /zuːm/ *vi* sfrecciare
zoom lens *n* zoom *m inv*
zucchini /zʊ'kiːnɪ/ *n* zucchino *m*, zucchina *f*

ITALIAN VERB TABLES

REGULAR VERBS:

1. in **-are** (*eg* **compr|are**)

> **Present** ~o, ~i, ~a, ~iamo, ~ate, ~ano
> **Imperfect** ~avo, ~avi, ~ava, ~avamo, ~avate, ~avano
> **Past historic** ~ai, ~asti, ~ò, ~ammo, ~aste, ~arono
> **Future** ~erò, ~erai, ~erà, ~eremo, ~erete, ~eranno
> **Present subjunctive** ~i, ~i, ~i, ~iamo, ~iate, ~ino
> **Past subjunctive** ~assi, ~assi, ~asse, ~assimo, ~aste, ~assero
> **Present participle** ~ando
> **Past participle** ~ato
> **Imperative** ~a (*fml* ~i), ~iamo, ~ate
> **Conditional** ~erei, ~eresti, ~erebbe, ~eremmo, ~ereste, ~erebbero

2. in **-ere** (*eg* **vend|ere**)

> **Pres** ~o, ~i, ~e, ~iamo, ~ete, ~ono
> **Impf** ~evo, ~evi, ~eva, ~evamo, ~evate, ~evano
> **Past hist** ~ei *or* ~etti, ~esti, ~è *or* ~ette, ~emmo, ~este, ~erono *or* ~ettero
> **Fut** ~erò, ~erai, ~erà, ~eremo, ~erete, ~eranno
> **Pres sub** ~a, ~a, ~a, ~iamo, ~iate, ~ano
> **Past sub** ~essi, ~essi, ~esse, ~essimo, ~este, ~essero
> **Pres part** ~endo
> **Past part** ~uto
> **Imp** ~i (*fml* ~a), ~iamo, ~ete
> **Cond** ~erei, ~eresti, ~erebbe, ~eremmo, ~ereste, ~erebbero

3. in **-ire** (*eg* **dorm|ire**)

> **Pres** ~o, ~i, ~e, ~iamo, ~ite, ~ono
> **Impf** ~ivo, ~ivi, ~iva, ~ivamo, ~ivate, ~ivano
> **Past hist** ~ii, ~isti, ~ì, ~immo, ~iste, ~irono
> **Fut** ~irò, ~irai, ~irà, ~iremo, ~irete, ~iranno
> **Pres sub** ~a, ~a, ~a, ~iamo, ~iate, ~ano
> **Past sub** ~issi, ~issi, ~isse, ~issimo, ~iste, ~issero
> **Pres part** ~endo
> **Past part** ~ito
> **Imp** ~i (*fml* ~a), ~iamo, ~ite
> **Cond** ~irei, ~iresti, ~irebbe, ~iremmo, ~ireste, ~irebbero

Notes

- Many verbs in the third conjugation take *isc* between the stem and the ending in the first, second, and third person singular and in the third person plural of the present, the present subjunctive, and the imperative: fin|ire **Pres** ~isco, ~isci, ~isce, ~iscono. **Pres sub** ~isca, ~iscano **Imp** ~isci.

- The three forms of the imperative are the same as the corresponding forms of the present for the second and third conjugation. In the first conjugation the forms are also the same except for the second person singular: present *compri*, imperative *compra*. The negative form of the second person singular is formed by putting *non* before the infinitive for all conjugations: *non comprare*. In polite forms the third person of the present subjunctive is used instead for all conjugations: *compri*.

IRREGULAR VERBS:

Certain forms of all irregular verbs are regular (except for *essere*). These are: the second person plural of the present, the past subjunctive, and the present participle. All forms not listed below are regular and can be derived from the parts given. Only those irregular verbs considered to be the most useful are shown in the tables.

accadere   *as* **cadere**

accendere   • **Past hist** accesi, accendesti • **Past part** acceso

affliggere   • **Past hist** afflissi, affliggesti • **Past part** afflitto

ammettere   *as* **mettere**

andare   • **Pres** vado, vai, va, andiamo, andate, vanno • **Fut** andrò *etc* • **Pres sub** vada, vadano • **Imp** va', vada, vadano

apparire   • **Pres** appaio *or* apparisco, appari *or* apparisci, appare *or* apparisce, appaiono *or* appariscono • **Past hist** apparvi *or* apparsi, apparisti, apparve *or* apparì *or* apparse, apparvero *or* apparirono *or* apparsero • **Pres sub** appaia *or* apparisca

aprire   • **Pres** apro • **Past hist** aprii, apristi • **Pres sub** apra • **Past part** aperto

avere   • **Pres** ho, hai, ha, abbiamo, hanno • **Past hist** ebbi, avesti, ebbe, avemmo, aveste, ebbero • **Fut** avrò *etc* • **Pres sub** abbia *etc* • **Imp** abbi, abbia, abbiate, abbiano

bere   • **Pres** bevo *etc* • **Impf** bevevo *etc* • **Past hist** bevvi *or* bevetti, bevesti • **Fut** berrò *etc* • **Pres sub** beva *etc* • **Past sub** bevessi *etc* • **Pres part** bevendo • **Cond** berrei *etc*

cadere   • **Past hist** caddi, cadesti • **Fut** cadrò *etc*

chiedere   • **Past hist** chiesi, chiedesti • **Pres sub** chieda *etc* • **Past part** chiesto *etc*

chiudere   • **Past hist** chiusi, chiudesti • **Past part** chiuso

cogliere   • **Pres** colgo, colgono • **Past hist** colsi, cogliesti • **Pres sub** colga • **Past part** colto

correre   • **Past hist** corsi, corresti • **Past part** corso

crescere   • **Past hist** crebbi • **Past part** cresciuto

cuocere   • **Pres** cuocio, cuociamo, cuociono • **Past hist** cossi, cocesti • **Past part** cotto

dare   • **Pres** do, dai, da, diamo, danno • **Past hist** diedi *or* detti, desti • **Fut** darò *etc* • **Pres sub** dia *etc* • **Past sub** dessi *etc* • **Imp** da' (*fml* dia)

dire	• **Pres** dico, dici, dice, diciamo, dicono • **Impf** dicevo *etc* • **Past hist** dissi, dicesti • **Fut** dirò *etc* • **Pres sub** dica, diciamo, diciate, dicano • **Past sub** dicessi *etc* • *Pres part* dicendo • **Past part** detto • **Imp** di' (*fml* dica)
dovere	• **Pres** devo *or* debbo, devi, deve, dobbiamo, devono *or* debbono • **Fut** dovrò *etc* • **Pres sub** deva *or* debba, dobbiamo, dobbiate, devano *or* debbano • **Cond** dovrei *etc*
essere	• **Pres** sono, sei, è, siamo, siete, sono • **Impf** ero, eri, era, eravamo, eravate, erano • **Past hist** fui, fosti, fu, fummo, foste, furono • **Fut** sarò *etc* • **Pres sub** sia *etc* • **Past sub** fossi, fossi, fosse, fossimo, foste, fossero • **Past part** stato • **Imp** sii (*fml* sia), siate • **Cond** sarei *etc*
fare	• **Pres** faccio, fai, fa, facciamo, fanno • **Impf** facevo *etc* • **Past hist** feci, facesti • **Fut** farò *etc* • **Pres sub** faccia *etc* • **Past sub** facessi *etc* • **Pres part** facendo • **Past part** fatto • **Imp** fa' (*fml* faccia) • **Cond** farei *etc*
fingere	• **Past hist** finsi, fingesti, finsero • **Past part** finto
giungere	• **Past hist** giunsi, giungesti, giunsero • **Past part** giunto
leggere	• **Past hist** lessi, leggesti • **Past part** letto
mettere	• **Past hist** misi, mettesti • **Past part** messo
morire	• **Pres** muoio, muori, muore, muoiono • **Fut** morirò *or* morrò *etc* • **Pres sub** muoia • **Past part** morto
muovere	• **Past hist** mossi, movesti • **Past part** mosso
nascere	• **Past hist** nacqui, nascesti • **Past part** nato
offrire	• **Past hist** offersi *or* offrii, offristi • **Pres sub** offra • **Past part** offerto
parere	• **Pres** paio, pari, pare, pariamo, paiono • **Past hist** parvi *or* parsi, paresti • **Fut** parrò *etc* • **Pres sub** paia, paiamo *or* pariamo, pariate, paiano • **Past part** parso
piacere	• **Pres** piaccio, piaci, piace, piacciamo, piacciono • **Past hist** piacqui, piacesti, piacque, piacemmo, piaceste, piacquero • **Pres sub** piaccia *etc* • **Past part** piaciuto
porre	• **Pres** pongo, poni, pone, poniamo, ponete, pongono • **Impf** ponevo *etc* • **Past hist** posi, ponesti • **Fut** porrò *etc* • **Pres sub** ponga, poniamo, poniate, pongano • **Past sub** ponessi *etc*
potere	• **Pres** posso, puoi, può, possiamo, possono • **Fut** potrò *etc* • **Pres sub** possa, possiamo, possiate, possano • **Cond** potrei *etc*
prendere	• **Past hist** presi, prendesti • **Past part** preso
ridere	• **Past hist** risi, ridesti • **Past part** riso

rimanere • **Pres** rimango, rimani, rimane, rimaniamo, rimangono • **Past hist** rimasi, rimanesti • **Fut** rimarrò *etc* • **Pres sub** rimanga • **Past part** rimasto • **Cond** rimarrei

salire • **Pres** salgo, sali, sale, saliamo, salgono • **Pres sub** salga, saliate, salgano

sapere • **Pres** so, sai, sa, sappiamo, sanno • **Past hist** seppi, sapesti • **Fut** saprò *etc* • **Pres sub** sappia *etc* • **Imp** sappi (*fml* sappia), sappiate • **Cond** saprei *etc*

scegliere • **Pres** scelgo, scegli, sceglie, scegliamo, scelgono • **Past hist** scelsi, scegliesti *etc* • **Past part** scelto

scrivere • **Past hist** scrissi, scrivesti *etc* • **Past part** scritto

sedere • **Pres** siedo *or* seggo, siedi, siede, siedono • **Pres sub** sieda *or* segga

spegnere • **Pres** spengo, spengono • **Past hist** spensi, spegnesti • **Past part** spento

stare • **Pres** sto, stai, sta, stiamo, stanno • **Past hist** stetti, stesti • **Fut** starò *etc* • **Pres sub** stia *etc* • **Past sub** stessi *etc* • **Past part** stato • **Imp** sta' (*fml* stia)

tacere • **Pres** taccio, tacciono • **Past hist** tacqui, tacque, tacquero • **Pres sub** taccia

tendere • **Past hist** tesi • **Past part** teso

tenere • **Pres** tengo, tieni, tiene, tengono • **Past hist** tenni, tenesti • **Fut** terrò *etc* • **Pres sub** tenga

togliere • **Pres** tolgo, tolgono • **Past hist** tolsi, tolse, tolsero • **Pres sub** tolga, tolgano • **Past part** tolto • *Imp fml* tolga

trarre • **Pres** traggo, trai, trae, traiamo, traete, traggono • **Past hist** trassi, traesti • **Fut** trarrò *etc* • **Pres sub** tragga • **Past sub** traessi *etc* • **Past part** tratto

uscire • **Pres** esco, esci, esce, escono • **Pres sub** esca • **Imp** esci (*fml* esca)

valere • **Pres** valgo, valgono • **Past hist** valsi, valesti • **Fut** varrò *etc* • **Pres sub** valga, valgano • **Past part** valso • **Cond** varrei *etc*

vedere • **Past hist** vidi, vedesti • **Fut** vedrò *etc* • **Past part** visto *or* veduto • **Cond** vedrei *etc*

venire • **Pres** vengo, vieni, viene, vengono • **Past hist** venni, venisti • **Fut** verrò *etc*

vivere • **Past hist** vissi, vivesti • **Fut** vivrò *etc* • **Past part** vissuto • **Cond** vivrei *etc*

volere • **Pres** voglio, vuoi, vuole, vogliamo, volete, vogliono • **Past hist** volli, volesti • **Fut** vorrò *etc* • **Pres sub** voglia *etc* • **Imp** vogliate • **Cond** vorrei *etc*

379

English irregular verbs

Infinitive	Past Tense	Past Participle	Infinitive	Past Tense	Past Participle
Infinito	*Passato*	*Participio passato*	*Infinito*	*Passato*	*Participio passato*
arise	arose	arisen	**feed**	fed	fed
awake	awoke	awoken	**feel**	felt	felt
be	was	been	**fight**	fought	fought
bear	bore	borne	**find**	found	found
beat	beat	beaten	**flee**	fled	fled
become	became	become	**fling**	flung	flung
begin	began	begun	**fly**	flew	flown
behold	beheld	beheld	**forbid**	forbade	forbidden
bend	bent	bent	**forget**	forgot	forgotten
beseech	beseeched besought	beseeched besought	**forgive**	forgave	forgiven
			forsake	forsook	forsaken
bet	bet, betted	bet, betted	**freeze**	froze	frozen
bid	bade, bid	bidden, bid	**get**	got	got, gotten *Am*
bind	bound	bound	**give**	gave	given
bite	bit	bitten	**go**	went	gone
bleed	bled	bled	**grind**	ground	ground
blow	blew	blown	**grow**	grew	grown
break	broke	broken	**hang**	hung, hanged (*vt*)	hung, hanged
breed	bred	bred	**have**	had	had
bring	brought	brought	**hear**	heard	heard
build	built	built	**hew**	hewed	hewed, hewn
burn	burnt, burned	burnt, burned	**hide**	hid	hidden
burst	burst	burst	**hit**	hit	hit
bust	busted, bust	busted, bust	**hold**	held	held
buy	bought	bought	**hurt**	hurt	hurt
cast	cast	cast	**keep**	kept	kept
catch	caught	caught	**kneel**	knelt	knelt
choose	chose	chosen	**know**	knew	known
cling	clung	clung	**lay**	laid	laid
come	came	come	**lead**	led	led
cost	cost, costed (*vt*)	cost, costed	**lean**	leaned, leant	leaned, leant
creep	crept	crept	**leap**	leapt, leaped	leapt, leaped
cut	cut	cut	**learn**	learnt, learned	learnt, learned
deal	dealt	dealt			
dig	dug	dug	**leave**	left	left
do	did	done	**lend**	lent	lent
draw	drew	drawn	**let**	let	let
dream	dreamt, dreamed	dreamt, dreamed	**lie**	lay	lain
			light	lit, lighted	lit, lighted
drink	drank	drunk			
drive	drove	driven	**lose**	lost	lost
dwell	dwelt	dwelt	**make**	made	made
eat	ate	eaten	**mean**	meant	meant
fall	fell	fallen	**meet**	met	met

Infinitive	Past Tense	Past Participle	Infinitive	Past Tense	Past Participle
Infinito	*Passato*	*Participio passato*	*Infinito*	*Passato*	*Participio passato*
mow	mowed	mown, mowed	spend	spent	spent
overhang	overhung	overhung	spill	spilt, spilled	spilt, spilled
pay	paid	paid	spin	spun	spun
put	put	put	spit	spat	spat
quit	quitted, quit	quitted, quit	split	split	split
read	read /red/	read /red/	spoil	spoilt, spoiled	spoilt, spoiled
rid	rid	rid	spread	spread	spread
ride	rode	ridden	spring	sprang	sprung
ring	rang	rung	stand	stood	stood
rise	rose	risen	steal	stole	stolen
run	ran	run	stick	stuck	stuck
saw	sawed	sawn, sawed	sting	stung	stung
say	said	said	stink	stank	stunk
see	saw	seen	strew	strewed	strewn, strewed
seek	sought	sought	stride	strode	stridden
sell	sold	sold	strike	struck	struck
send	sent	sent	string	strung	strung
set	set	set	strive	strove	striven
sew	sewed	sewn, sewed	swear	swore	sworn
shake	shook	shaken	sweep	swept	swept
shear	sheared	shorn, sheared	swell	swelled	swollen, swelled
shed	shed	shed	swim	swam	swum
shine	shone	shone	swing	swung	swung
shit	shit	shit	take	took	taken
shoe	shod	shod	teach	taught	taught
shoot	shot	shot	tear	tore	torn
show	showed	shown	tell	told	told
shrink	shrank	shrunk	think	thought	thought
shut	shut	shut	thrive	thrived, throve	thrived, thriven
sing	sang	sung	throw	threw	thrown
sink	sank	sunk	thrust	thrust	thrust
sit	sat	sat	tread	trod	trodden
slay	slew	slain	understand	understood	understood
sleep	slept	slept	undo	undid	undone
slide	slid	slid	wake	woke	woken
sling	slung	slung	wear	wore	worn
slit	slit	slit	weave	wove	woven
smell	smelt, smelled	smelt, smelled	weep	wept	wept
sow	sowed	sown, sowed	wet	wet, wetted	wet, wetted
speak	spoke	spoken	win	won	won
speed	sped, speeded	sped, speeded	wind	wound	wound
spell	spelled, spelt	spelled, spelt	wring	wrung	wrung
			write	wrote	written